TAFSIR
AL-JALALAYN

تفسير الجلالين

JALALU'D-DIN AL-MAHALLI
AND JALALU'D-DIN AS-SUYUTI

"Glory belongs to God who has sent down upon his servant the Book and has not assigned unto it any crookedness." (18:1)

بسم الله الرحمن الرحيم

In the Name Of Allah,
the Most Merciful, the Most Beneficent

Dar Al Taqwa Ltd. 2007

ISBN 1-870582-61-6

Translation: Aisha Bewley

Editor: Abdalhaqq Bewley and Muhammad Isa Waley

Production: Bookwork, Norwich

Published by:
Dar Al Taqwa Ltd.
7A Melcombe Street
Baker Street
London NW1 6AE

Printed and bound in Germany by Bercker

Foreword

In the Name of Allah, the Most Merciful, the All-Compassionate

The Qur'an describes itself as "that Book, without any doubt, containing guidance for those who have *taqwā*" (*al-Baqara,* 1). *Taqwā* is the quality which characterises the actions of those who have fearful awareness of Allah and fully realise that after death each one of us will end up either in Paradise or in Hell-Fire, for ever. To benefit from this Divine Guidance fully and with certainty requires a thorough knowledge of the Arabic language. One must also know which *ayas* ('verses'; literally 'signs') have been abrogated, and which abrogated them. It is also essential to be acquainted with *asbāb al-nuzūl*, meaning the circumstances in which a given *āya*, series of *āyas*, or *sūra* was revealed; and to know what the Prophet Muḥammad, may Allah bless him and grant him peace, taught his Companions, may Allah be pleased with all of them, concerning the meaning of any given *aya* or *āyas*. All this is vital in order to avoid the danger of misreading the Signs and ascribing to them meanings which are inaccurate or inappropriate.

In order to gain access to this precious knowledge and to the wisdom it engenders, it is necessary to refer to a *tafsīr* or commentary that is based on authoritative transmitted knowledge and is free from the subjective speculation that characterises certain more recent commentaries. There are a number of standard classical *tafsīrs* that have stood the test of time, such as those by aṭ-Ṭabarī, al-Qurtubī, Ibn Juzayy, Ibn Kathīr, and Qāḍī Abū Bakr ibn al-'Arabī. Some fill several volumes and require prolonged study, while others are shorter and more concentrated. Among the briefest and most easily accessible is *Tafsīr al-Jalālayn*, which ever since its completion more than half a millennium ago has been considered the essential first text in the study of the meanings of the Qur'an by teachers and students throughout the Islamic world.

Those who are well-versed in classical Arabic can refer to any of the standard *tafsīrs* they may find. But what of the Muslim whose mother tongue is not Arabic? How can he or she begin to approach the meanings of the Qur'an without being daunted at the outset? How can the seeker's hunger for knowledge be both satisfied and further stimulated without risk of either an overdose or indigestion? The answer is to refer to a reliable translation of the text, and also to a reliable translation of at least one authoritative commentary. Such a resource is now available at last in the form of a full translation of *Tafsiī al-Jalālayn*, a work renowned for its clarity, for its simplicity, for its concision while including all the essential elements, and for its clear explanations of points of Arabic grammar.

With the needs of the English-speaking seeker particularly in mind, the present work has been undertaken by Hajj Abdalhaqq and Hajja Aisha Bewley, whose many translations of Arabic classical works are widely known and appreciated for their clarity, accuracy and immediacy – and for their avoidance of arid, mind-bound obfuscation. The Bewleys' translation of the Qur'an – which has been guided, as they humbly acknowledge in their Preface, by what has been transmitted by "the great*mufassirun* of the past who spent so much time and energy in unearthing, preserving and passing on the meaning of Allah's Book and in protecting it from unacceptable interpretation and deviation" – has already become established as one of the leading contemporary English renderings.

It is therefore with pride, and with joy, that Dar Al-Taqwa presents Hajj Abdalhaqq and Hajja Aisha Bewley's translation of *Tafsīr al-Jalālayn*, a work designed to help make the meanings of the Qur'an accessible, to prepare the seeker for approaching the more complex commentaries – and now at hand to assist English-speaking Muslims in understanding the classical Arabic in which the Qur'an was revealed and in which most of the authoritative *tafsīr*s were written. Inshā'llāh, whenever they recite the Qur'an in the original Arabic or listen to it being recited, its true meanings will flow swiftly and uninterruptedly into their hearts, illuminating their intellects, adorning their lives, and preparing them for and guiding them towards the Garden in the Next World which awaits all those who had *taqwā* in this world, "remaining in it timelessly, for ever, as reward for what they did." (*Qur'an*: 46.13).

And all praise is for Allah, Lord of the Universe.

Hajj Ahmad Thomson
London

Table of Contents

Preface

The publication of this translation of the *Tafsīr al-Jalālayn* is something of a landmark in the history of classical Islamic literature in the English language. There have been partial translations of several of the great classical *tafsīr*s but complete access to the enormous and enlightening scholarship of the great commentators of the past has up until now not been available to the English speaker who is not able to read these seminal works in the original Arabic. This has meant that for the great majority of English-speaking Muslims an amplified understanding of the Quranic *āyat*s was dependant on people possessing a high level of Arabic or limited to those modern commentaries which do exist in English but which lack the authority of the great works of the classical commentators. We are, therefore, very pleased to be able to present this work to the English speaking Muslim world and hope that it will prove the means to an expanded understanding of Allah's Book for many people.

The *Tafsīr al-Jalālayn* has, since its publication more than half a millennium ago, been considered the essential first text in the study of the meaning of the Qur'an by teachers and students of the Qur'anic text throughout the entire Islamic world from West Africa to Indonesia. Although it is among the shortest and simplest of the complete commentaries of the Qur'an, it is surprisingly comprehensive and profound. It has always been held in the highest esteem by all the scholars of Islam and there is no doubt at all that anyone who applies themselves to the conscientious study of it will emerge as a better-educated Muslim.

The name *"al-Jalālayn"* (the two Jalāls) was given to it because it is the work of two people with the name Jalālu'd-Dīn. It was started by Jalālu'd-Dīn Muḥammad ibn Aḥmad al-Maḥallī (1389-1459), who was said to have "such an acute intelligence that it could pierce a diamond". He began halfway through the Qur'an with *Sūrat al-Kahf* and ended with *Sūrat an-Nās* and the *Fātiha*. He died before he could start the other half and the work was then taken over by his student, the prolific Jalālu'd-Dīn as-Suyūṭī, who then, aged twenty-two at the time, succeeded in completing the work in the matter of a few months. As-

Suyūṭī was to go on to be one of the most prolific, if indeed not the most prolific, author in the annals of Islamic history. Seven hundred and twenty-three works are attributed to his pen, covering every aspect of the Islamic sciences.

'Abdu'r-Raḥmān as-Suyūṭī was born in 849 /1445 in Mamluk Egypt, in Asyut , from which he derives his name. His father was Persian and his mother Turkish. His father, who had been the qāḍī there, died when he was still young, but left his son financially independent and hence able to pursue his studies, and he devoted himself to them assiduously. His training was taken in hand by a Sufi friend of his father. He first became a *ḥāfiẓ* of the Qur'an at the age of eight, and then went on to study all the Islamic sciences, studying with more than 150 scholars. He also travelled extensively in quest of knowledge – to Damascus, the Hijaz, Yemen, India, Morocco, the lands south of Morocco, as well as places in Egypt.

In Cairo he became a professor in one subject after another and eventually became the head professor of the madrasa where he taught. In 1501 his opponents attempted to implicate him in the misappropriation of funds and he withdrew to the island of Rawda in the Nile, where he devoted himself to writing books and died four years later at the age of sixty-two, on Thurday 18th Jumādā al-Ūlā 911 A.H. (17th October 1505 C.E.)

The present translation has followed the original by embedding the commentary on each *āyat* within the Qur'anic text. The actual text of the Qur'an is in bold italic characters while the commentary is in plain text. The English rendering of the Qur'anic text used in this translation is that of *The Noble Quran* by A. and A. Bewley published by Bookwork, slightly adapted to meet the specific needs of the *Jalālayn* text. The Arabic text of the Qur'an has been placed on pages opposite the *Jalālayn* translation, which continues until the commentary on the *āyat*s in that portion of the Arabic text has been covered. Then the next page of Arabic is inserted until it in turn has been covered by the *tafsīr* and that continues until the end of the each *sūra*. So if a reader wishes to refer back to the original Arabic they simply have to look at the number at the beginning of the *āyat* they are reading and then look back to the preceding passage of Arabic and locate the the same number which, in the Arabic text, comes at the end of the *āyat* concerned.

Many comments of a grammatical nature have not been included in this translation because a reasonably advanced level of Arabic is needed to appreciate them and so they are really only useful for people who would be better off studying them in the original language anyway. On the other hand, the different Quranic readings noted by the authors have nearly all been incorporated, for two reasons. Firstly, they often involve a slight change of meaning which is reflected in the English version. Secondly, this aspect of the Qur'an is all too frequently neglected by English speakers who are often restricted to a single reading and are therefore unaware of the different possibilities which add such richness to the Quranic text.

Finally we ask Allah, *tabāraka wa ta'ālā*, to accept this from us, to forgive us for any shortcomings in our work and to make it a means for greater understanding of His Book and for a wider propagation of His *dīn*.

Abdalhaqq Bewley

1
Al-Fātiḥa

بِسْمِ ٱللَّهِ ٱلرَّحْمَٰنِ ٱلرَّحِيمِ ﴿١﴾

ٱلْحَمْدُ لِلَّهِ رَبِّ ٱلْعَٰلَمِينَ ﴿٢﴾

ٱلرَّحْمَٰنِ ٱلرَّحِيمِ ﴿٣﴾ مَٰلِكِ يَوْمِ ٱلدِّينِ ﴿٤﴾

إِيَّاكَ نَعْبُدُ وَإِيَّاكَ نَسْتَعِينُ ﴿٥﴾ ٱهْدِنَا

ٱلصِّرَٰطَ ٱلْمُسْتَقِيمَ ﴿٦﴾ صِرَٰطَ ٱلَّذِينَ أَنْعَمْتَ

عَلَيْهِمْ غَيْرِ ٱلْمَغْضُوبِ عَلَيْهِمْ

وَلَا ٱلضَّآلِّينَ ﴿٧﴾

In the name of Allah, All Merciful, Most Merciful

Praise be to Allah, the Lord of all the worlds,
the All-Merciful, the Most Merciful
the King of the Day of Repayment.
You alone we worship
You alone we ask for help.
Guide us on the Straight Path,
the Path of those You have blessed,
not of those with anger on them,
nor of the misguided.

Sūrat al-Fātiḥa is Makkan and contains seven *āyat*s. If the *basmala* is counted as an *āyat*, then the seventh begins with the words "*the Path of those You have blessed*"; if it is not counted then the seventh begins with the words "*not of those with anger on them*". It is said that the command *"Say:"* is implied at the beginning in order to make the words "*You only*" appropriate, since that is what is said by Allah's slaves.

2. *Praise be to Allah* is an enunciatory sentence by which praise of Allah is intended. It implies that Allah alone is the Possessor of all praise from creation, or that He alone merits their praise. ***The Lord of all the worlds*** means that He is the King of all creatures, men, jinn, angels, animals and other things. Each of these is called a "world", so there is the world of men, the world of jinn, and so forth. He governs all of them in the plural, *"'ālamīn"* which indicates all of them. The word is derived from *'alāma* (sign) because each constitutes a sign which indicates the One who brought it into existence.

3. *The All-Merciful, Most Merciful* means that He is the One who possesses all mercy, and to have mercy means to desire good for the object of mercy.

4. *The King of the Day of Repayment (*dīn*),* i.e. "requital". It is a reference to the Day of Rising. This is singled out to be mentioned because it is clear that on that Day no one will have sovereignty except Allah Almighty, as indicated by His words: *"To whom does sovereignty belong today? To Allah."* (40:16) Some read it as "*mālik*" with a long "a" which means "the Owner of the entire affair on the Day of Rising," or the One who always bears that description as in *"the Forgiver of wrong action."* (40:3) It is valid for this grammatical form to denote an adjective or a definite noun.

5. *You alone we worship. To You alone we turn for help.* This means "We single You out for adoration in respect of *tawḥīd* and other things. We seek Your help in respect of worship and other things."

6. *Guide us on the Straight Path:* means "Direct us to it." It is followed by its appositive:

7. *... the Path of those You have blessed* with guidance, ***not of those with anger on them,*** who are the Jews, ***nor of the misguided,*** who are the Christians. The grammatical structure here shows that those who are guided are not the Jews or the Christians. Allah Almighty knows best what is correct, and to Him is the return and the homecoming. May Allah bless our Master Muḥammad and His family and Companions and grant them abundant peace always and forever. Allah is enough for us and the best Protector. There is no strength nor power except by Allah, the High, the Immense.

2. *Sūrat al-Baqara*
The Cow

بِسْمِ ٱللَّهِ ٱلرَّحْمَٰنِ ٱلرَّحِيمِ

الٓمٓ ﴿١﴾ ذَٰلِكَ ٱلْكِتَٰبُ لَا رَيْبَۛ فِيهِۛ هُدًى
لِّلْمُتَّقِينَ ﴿٢﴾ ٱلَّذِينَ يُؤْمِنُونَ بِٱلْغَيْبِ وَيُقِيمُونَ ٱلصَّلَوٰةَ
وَمِمَّا رَزَقْنَٰهُمْ يُنفِقُونَ ﴿٣﴾ وَٱلَّذِينَ يُؤْمِنُونَ بِمَآ أُنزِلَ
إِلَيْكَ وَمَآ أُنزِلَ مِن قَبْلِكَ وَبِٱلْءَاخِرَةِ هُمْ يُوقِنُونَ ﴿٤﴾
أُوْلَٰٓئِكَ عَلَىٰ هُدًى مِّن رَّبِّهِمْۖ وَأُوْلَٰٓئِكَ
هُمُ ٱلْمُفْلِحُونَ ﴿٥﴾

Sūrat al-Baqara is Madinan and contains 286 *āyat*s.

1. ***ALIF. LAM. MIM.*** Allah knows best what is meant by this.

2. ***That,*** meaning this ***is the Book*** which Muḥammad recites***, without any doubt,*** or uncertainty about the fact that it is from Allah. The use of the word "that" indicates great esteem. ***It contains guidance,*** in that the Book itself guides, ***for the godfearing*** (*muttaqūn*)***.*** They are those who have *taqwā,* meaning that they obey the commands of Allah and avoid His prohibitions in order to save themselves from the Fire.

3. ***Those who believe in the Unseen***, affirming things they cannot see, such as the Resurrection, the Garden and the Fire, ***and establish the prayer,*** performing it with all its requirements, ***and spend from what We have provided for them,*** spending what they have been given in ways commensurate with obedience to Allah.

4. ***Those who believe in what has been sent down to you*** (the Qur'ān) ***and what was sent down before you*** (the Torah, Gospel and

إِنَّ ٱلَّذِينَ كَفَرُوا۟ سَوَآءٌ عَلَيْهِمْ ءَأَنذَرْتَهُمْ أَمْ لَمْ تُنذِرْهُمْ
لَا يُؤْمِنُونَ ﴿٦﴾ خَتَمَ ٱللَّهُ عَلَىٰ قُلُوبِهِمْ وَعَلَىٰ سَمْعِهِمْ ۖ وَعَلَىٰٓ
أَبْصَٰرِهِمْ غِشَٰوَةٌ ۖ وَلَهُمْ عَذَابٌ عَظِيمٌ ﴿٧﴾ وَمِنَ ٱلنَّاسِ
مَن يَقُولُ ءَامَنَّا بِٱللَّهِ وَبِٱلْيَوْمِ ٱلْءَاخِرِ وَمَا هُم بِمُؤْمِنِينَ ﴿٨﴾
يُخَٰدِعُونَ ٱللَّهَ وَٱلَّذِينَ ءَامَنُوا۟ وَمَا يَخْدَعُونَ إِلَّآ أَنفُسَهُمْ
وَمَا يَشْعُرُونَ ﴿٩﴾ فِى قُلُوبِهِم مَّرَضٌ فَزَادَهُمُ ٱللَّهُ مَرَضًا ۖ
وَلَهُمْ عَذَابٌ أَلِيمٌۢ بِمَا كَانُوا۟ يَكْذِبُونَ ﴿١٠﴾ وَإِذَا قِيلَ لَهُمْ
لَا تُفْسِدُوا۟ فِى ٱلْأَرْضِ قَالُوٓا۟ إِنَّمَا نَحْنُ مُصْلِحُونَ ﴿١١﴾
أَلَآ إِنَّهُمْ هُمُ ٱلْمُفْسِدُونَ وَلَٰكِن لَّا يَشْعُرُونَ ﴿١٢﴾ وَإِذَا قِيلَ
لَهُمْ ءَامِنُوا۟ كَمَآ ءَامَنَ ٱلنَّاسُ قَالُوٓا۟ أَنُؤْمِنُ كَمَآ ءَامَنَ ٱلسُّفَهَآءُ ۗ
أَلَآ إِنَّهُمْ هُمُ ٱلسُّفَهَآءُ وَلَٰكِن لَّا يَعْلَمُونَ ﴿١٣﴾ وَإِذَا لَقُوا۟
ٱلَّذِينَ ءَامَنُوا۟ قَالُوٓا۟ ءَامَنَّا وَإِذَا خَلَوْا۟ إِلَىٰ شَيَٰطِينِهِمْ قَالُوٓا۟ إِنَّا
مَعَكُمْ إِنَّمَا نَحْنُ مُسْتَهْزِءُونَ ﴿١٤﴾ ٱللَّهُ يَسْتَهْزِئُ بِهِمْ وَيَمُدُّهُمْ
فِى طُغْيَٰنِهِمْ يَعْمَهُونَ ﴿١٥﴾ أُو۟لَٰٓئِكَ ٱلَّذِينَ ٱشْتَرَوُا۟ ٱلضَّلَٰلَةَ
بِٱلْهُدَىٰ فَمَا رَبِحَت تِّجَٰرَتُهُمْ وَمَا كَانُوا۟ مُهْتَدِينَ ﴿١٦﴾
مَثَلُهُمْ كَمَثَلِ ٱلَّذِى ٱسْتَوْقَدَ نَارًا فَلَمَّآ أَضَآءَتْ مَا حَوْلَهُۥ
ذَهَبَ ٱللَّهُ بِنُورِهِمْ وَتَرَكَهُمْ فِى ظُلُمَٰتٍ لَّا يُبْصِرُونَ ﴿١٧﴾ صُمٌّۢ
بُكْمٌ عُمْىٌ فَهُمْ لَا يَرْجِعُونَ ﴿١٨﴾ أَوْ كَصَيِّبٍ مِّنَ ٱلسَّمَآءِ فِيهِ
ظُلُمَٰتٌ وَرَعْدٌ وَبَرْقٌ يَجْعَلُونَ أَصَٰبِعَهُمْ فِىٓ ءَاذَانِهِم مِّنَ ٱلصَّوَٰعِقِ
حَذَرَ ٱلْمَوْتِ ۚ وَٱللَّهُ مُحِيطٌۢ بِٱلْكَٰفِرِينَ ﴿١٩﴾ يَكَادُ ٱلْبَرْقُ يَخْطَفُ

other Revelations), ***and are certain about the Next World,*** meaning they know definitively that it exists.

5. ***They*** (those We have described above) ***are the people guided by their Lord. They are the ones who have success,*** meaning they will gain the Garden and be far from the Fire.

6. ***As for those who disbelieve,*** such as Abū Jahl, Abū Lahab and their like, ***it makes no difference to them whether you warn them or do not warn them, they will not believe.*** Allah knows that about them so it is no good desiring them to believe. Warning someone means telling them about something while trying to give them fear of it to avert them from it.

7. ***Allah has sealed up their hearts,*** by stamping a coating on them and making them solid so that no good is able to penetrate them, ***and hearing,*** precluding them from benefiting from what they hear of the Truth, ***and over their eyes is a blindfold,*** a covering preventing them from seeing the Truth. ***They will have a terrible punishment*** which will be severe and everlasting.

8. This was revealed about the hypocrites. ***Among the people there are some who say, "We believe in Allah and the Last Day,"*** meaning the Day of Rising because it is the last of all days, ***when they do not believe.***

9. ***They think they deceive Allah and those who believe*** by outwardly displaying something different from their concealed unbelief so as to avert worldly judgements from themselves. ***They deceive*** (read as *yukhādi'ūna* and *yakhda'ūna*) ***no one but themselves*** because the evil effects of their deceit come back on them and they are disgraced in this world since Allah has acquainted His Prophet, may Allah bless him and grant him peace, with what they are concealing; and they will also be punished in the Next World. ***But they are not aware of it.*** They do not know that they are deceiving themselves. Here the attempt at "deceit" (*mukhāda'a*) comes from one side, although the verbal noun can imply reciprocity.

10. ***There is a sickness in their hearts*** taking the form of doubt and hypocrisy. It is an illness of the heart because it weakens it. ***And Allah has increased their sickness*** through the Qur'ān revealing their unbelief. ***They will have a painful punishment on account of***

their denial (read as *yukadhdhibūna* and *yakdhibūna*). The former means denial and refers to their denial of the Prophet, may Allah bless him and grant him peace; the latter means lying and refers to their lying when they said, "We believed".

11. ***When they*** (these people) ***are told, "Do not cause corruption on the earth,"*** by unbelief and twisting away from belief, ***they say, "We are only putting things right."*** They only reply that they were not causing corruption. Therefore Allah refutes them in the next *āyat*.

12 ***No indeed!*** This is a notification of the truth of the matter. ***They are the corrupters, but they are not aware*** of that.

13. ***When they are told, "Believe in the way that the people*** (the Companions of the Prophet, may Allah bless him and grant him peace) ***believe," they say, "What! Are we to believe in the way that fools*** (the ignorant) ***believe?"*** So what they are saying is: "Do not do as they do." The Almighty refutes them and tells us about them: ***No indeed! They are the fools, but they do not know*** that.

14. ***When they meet those who believe, they say, "We believe." But then when they go apart*** and return ***to their* shayṭāns*,*** who are their leaders, ***they say, "We are really with you*** in your religion. ***We were only mocking*** them by making a display of belief."

15. ***But Allah is mocking them*** to repay them for their mocking, ***and drawing them on*** by granting them a respite, ***as they wander blindly in their excessive insolence.*** They wander, bewildered, going to and fro in their overstepping of the proper bounds through their rejection and unbelief.

16. ***Those are the people who have sold guidance for misguidance,*** exchanging one for the other. ***Their trade has brought no profit***, rather they have suffered a loss by going to the Fire for ever. ***They are not guided*** in what they have done.

17. ***Their likeness*** in their hypocrisy ***is that of people who light a fire*** in the darkness, ***and then when it has lit up all around them,*** so they are able to see and can warm themselves and temporarily escape their fear, ***Allah removes*** (extinguishes) ***their light and leaves them in darkness, unable to see*** what is around them. They are fearful and bewildered, not knowing which way to turn. This is

أَبْصَٰرَهُمْ ۚ كُلَّمَآ أَضَآءَ لَهُم مَّشَوْا۟ فِيهِ وَإِذَآ أَظْلَمَ عَلَيْهِمْ قَامُوا۟ ۚ
وَلَوْ شَآءَ ٱللَّهُ لَذَهَبَ بِسَمْعِهِمْ وَأَبْصَٰرِهِمْ ۚ إِنَّ ٱللَّهَ عَلَىٰ كُلِّ
شَىْءٍ قَدِيرٌ ﴿٢٠﴾ يَٰٓأَيُّهَا ٱلنَّاسُ ٱعْبُدُوا۟ رَبَّكُمُ ٱلَّذِى خَلَقَكُمْ
وَٱلَّذِينَ مِن قَبْلِكُمْ لَعَلَّكُمْ تَتَّقُونَ ﴿٢١﴾ ٱلَّذِى جَعَلَ لَكُمُ
ٱلْأَرْضَ فِرَٰشًا وَٱلسَّمَآءَ بِنَآءً وَأَنزَلَ مِنَ ٱلسَّمَآءِ مَآءً فَأَخْرَجَ
بِهِۦ مِنَ ٱلثَّمَرَٰتِ رِزْقًا لَّكُمْ ۖ فَلَا تَجْعَلُوا۟ لِلَّهِ أَندَادًا وَأَنتُمْ
تَعْلَمُونَ ﴿٢٢﴾ وَإِن كُنتُمْ فِى رَيْبٍ مِّمَّا نَزَّلْنَا عَلَىٰ عَبْدِنَا
فَأْتُوا۟ بِسُورَةٍ مِّن مِّثْلِهِۦ وَٱدْعُوا۟ شُهَدَآءَكُم مِّن دُونِ ٱللَّهِ
إِن كُنتُمْ صَٰدِقِينَ ﴿٢٣﴾ فَإِن لَّمْ تَفْعَلُوا۟ وَلَن تَفْعَلُوا۟ فَٱتَّقُوا۟
ٱلنَّارَ ٱلَّتِى وَقُودُهَا ٱلنَّاسُ وَٱلْحِجَارَةُ ۖ أُعِدَّتْ لِلْكَٰفِرِينَ ﴿٢٤﴾
وَبَشِّرِ ٱلَّذِينَ ءَامَنُوا۟ وَعَمِلُوا۟ ٱلصَّٰلِحَٰتِ أَنَّ لَهُمْ جَنَّٰتٍ
تَجْرِى مِن تَحْتِهَا ٱلْأَنْهَٰرُ ۖ كُلَّمَا رُزِقُوا۟ مِنْهَا مِن ثَمَرَةٍ
رِّزْقًا ۙ قَالُوا۟ هَٰذَا ٱلَّذِى رُزِقْنَا مِن قَبْلُ ۖ وَأُتُوا۟ بِهِۦ مُتَشَٰبِهًا ۖ
وَلَهُمْ فِيهَآ أَزْوَٰجٌ مُّطَهَّرَةٌ ۖ وَهُمْ فِيهَا خَٰلِدُونَ ﴿٢٥﴾
۞ إِنَّ ٱللَّهَ لَا يَسْتَحْىِۦٓ أَن يَضْرِبَ مَثَلًا مَّا بَعُوضَةً فَمَا
فَوْقَهَا ۚ فَأَمَّا ٱلَّذِينَ ءَامَنُوا۟ فَيَعْلَمُونَ أَنَّهُ ٱلْحَقُّ مِن
رَّبِّهِمْ ۖ وَأَمَّا ٱلَّذِينَ كَفَرُوا۟ فَيَقُولُونَ مَاذَآ أَرَادَ ٱللَّهُ
بِهَٰذَا مَثَلًا ۘ يُضِلُّ بِهِۦ كَثِيرًا وَيَهْدِى بِهِۦ كَثِيرًا ۚ
وَمَا يُضِلُّ بِهِۦٓ إِلَّا ٱلْفَٰسِقِينَ ﴿٢٦﴾ ٱلَّذِينَ يَنقُضُونَ عَهْدَ
ٱللَّهِ مِنۢ بَعْدِ مِيثَٰقِهِۦ وَيَقْطَعُونَ مَآ أَمَرَ ٱللَّهُ بِهِۦٓ أَن يُوصَلَ

the case with those who make a false show of belief in this world. When they die, they will experience fear and punishment.

18. ***Deaf*** to the truth so they are unable to accept it; ***dumb*** to uttering good; ***blind*** to the Path of guidance so they unable to see it. ***They will not return*** from misguidance.

19. Now comes another metaphor for the hypocrites likening them to people in a thunderstorm. ***Or that of a storm-cloud*** (*ṣayyib* from the verb *ṣāba, yaṣūbu,* meaning to come down, meaning a dense black cloud which comes down out of the sky) ***in the sky, full of*** layers of ***darkness, thunder,*** which is the angel in charge of it or is also said to be the sound it makes, ***and lightning*** which reinforces the sound of thunder, by which they are rebuked. ***They put*** the tips of ***their fingers in their ears*** trying to protect them ***against the*** ear-splitting ***thunderclaps*** so that they do not hear them, ***fearful of death.*** They fear death when they hear them. This is a metaphor for what happened with some people when the Qur'an was revealed. Their unbelief is likened to the darkness of the cloud, the Qur'anic threat to thunder, and the vivid clarity of its arguments to lightning. They block their ears so as not to hear it, out of fear that it might make them incline to belief and abandon their religion. They consider that to be tantamount to death. ***Allah encompasses the unbelievers*** with His knowledge and power and they cannot escape Him.

20. ***The lightning all but takes away their sight*** when it flashes on them suddenly. ***Whenever they have light*** from its flash, ***they walk in it, but whenever darkness covers them, they halt*** when it goes dark again. This is a metaphor of how what is in the Qur'ān alarms their hearts. They affirm things they like in it but stop at what they dislike. ***If Allah wished, He could take away their hearing and their sight,*** both outward and inward. ***Allah has power over all things*** and can do whatever He wills, including removing what was mentioned.

21. ***Mankind*** (here implying "People of Makka")! ***Worship your Lord,*** meaning affirm His unity, ***who created you,*** originating you out of nothing, ***and*** created ***those before you, so that hopefully you will be godfearing*** and by your worship of Him protect yourselves from His punishment. The word *la'alla* (hopefully, perhaps) basically implies hope and expectation but when used by the Almighty it becomes definite.

22. ***It is He who made*** (created) ***the earth a couch for you,*** meaning something which is spread out and laid down (the earth is neither too hard nor too soft, either of which would make it impossible to live on), ***and the sky a dome*** like a roof. ***He sends down water from the sky and by it brings forth*** various ***fruits for your provision. Do not, then, knowingly make others equal to Allah*** by assigning partners to Allah in your worship when you know that He is the Creator and that they create nothing and that only the One who creates can truly be given the name of God.

23. ***If you have doubts about what We have sent down to Our slave,*** what has been revealed of the Qur'ān by Allah to the Prophet Muḥammad, ***produce another sūra like it,*** and bring its equal in respect of eloquence and structure and reporting about the Unseen. The minimum amount required for a *sūra* would be three *āyats*. ***And call your witnesses*** (the gods you worship) ***besides Allah*** to help you, ***if you are telling the truth*** about Muḥammad making this up by himself. Do the same thing yourselves: you are eloquent speakers of Arabic like him. Since they were unable to do so, Allah addresses them in the following *āyat*.

24. ***If you do not do that***, emphasising their incapacity – ***and you will not do it,*** their incapacity will be perpetual – ***then fear,*** by believing in Allah and that that this is not the speech of a mortal, ***the Fire whose fuel is people*** (unbelievers) ***and stones*** such as idols which, because its heat is so great, burn in it like firewood burns the fires of this world, ***made ready for the unbelievers*** who will be punished in it.

25. ***Give the good news*** (information) ***to those who believe*** in Allah ***and do right actions*** in the form of obligatory duties and voluntary good deeds ***that they will have Gardens*** with trees and dwelling places in them and there will be ***rivers flowing under them.*** They will flow under the trees and palaces there. A river (*nahr*) is a place where water flows because the water excavates (*nahara*) a channel. ***When they are given fruit there as provision,*** in other words eat the fruit of that Garden, ***they will say, "This is what we were given before,"*** meaning that it resembles what they have had before in the

Garden. ***But they were only given a simulation of it*** because the fruits are the same in colour and yet different in taste. ***They will have there spouses*** among the houris and others ***of perfect purity,*** meaning that they will be free of menstruation or any other kind of impurity, ***and will remain there timelessly, for ever,*** never leaving it or passing away.

26. This *āyat* was revealed to refute the Jews, who had said, when Allah made an example of a fly in His words, *"And if a fly steals something away from them"* (22:73) and a spider, in His words, *"that of the spider"* (29:41), "What does Allah mean by mentioning these insignificant things?" Allah replies to them by saying: ***Allah is not ashamed to make an example of a gnat or of an even smaller thing.*** ("Smaller" can also mean "bigger", the point being that Allah does not fail to make clear what can be learned from something, no matter what its size.) ***As for those who believe, they know*** that the analogy ***is the truth from their Lord*** and describes what actually occurs. ***But as for those who disbelieve, they say, "What does Allah mean by this example?"*** The question asked by the unbelievers is in reality a denial, meaning "There is in fact no purpose in it." ***He misguides*** from the truth ***many by*** this example since they reject it ***and guides many*** of the believers ***by it*** through their affirmation of it. ***But He only misguides the deviators*** who have abandoned obedience to Allah.

27. ***Those who break Allah's contract,*** going back on what has been agreed in the Books about believing in Muḥammad, may Allah bless him and grant him peace, ***after it has been agreed*** and firmly covenanted, ***and sever what Allah has commanded to be joined*** in respect of believing in the Prophet, maintaining ties of kinship and other such things, ***and cause corruption on the earth*** by perpetrating acts of disobedience and turning away from belief. ***It is those*** who warrant this description ***who are the lost*** since they will go to the Fire forever.

28. ***How,*** people of Makka, ***can you disbelieve in Allah when you were dead*** as lifeless sperm in your fathers' loins ***and then He gave you life*** in the womb and in this world by breathing the spirit into you? The use of a question here is to show amazement at their unbelief when the evidence is so clear; or it might also be a question

وَيُفْسِدُونَ فِي ٱلْأَرْضِ أُوْلَٰٓئِكَ هُمُ ٱلْخَٰسِرُونَ ﴿٢٧﴾
كَيْفَ تَكْفُرُونَ بِٱللَّهِ وَكُنتُمْ أَمْوَٰتًا فَأَحْيَٰكُمْ
ثُمَّ يُمِيتُكُمْ ثُمَّ يُحْيِيكُمْ ثُمَّ إِلَيْهِ تُرْجَعُونَ ﴿٢٨﴾ هُوَ
ٱلَّذِي خَلَقَ لَكُم مَّا فِي ٱلْأَرْضِ جَمِيعًا ثُمَّ ٱسْتَوَىٰٓ إِلَى
ٱلسَّمَآءِ فَسَوَّىٰهُنَّ سَبْعَ سَمَٰوَٰتٍ وَهُوَ بِكُلِّ شَيْءٍ عَلِيمٌ ﴿٢٩﴾
وَإِذْ قَالَ رَبُّكَ لِلْمَلَٰٓئِكَةِ إِنِّي جَاعِلٌ فِي ٱلْأَرْضِ خَلِيفَةً
قَالُوٓاْ أَتَجْعَلُ فِيهَا مَن يُفْسِدُ فِيهَا وَيَسْفِكُ ٱلدِّمَآءَ وَنَحْنُ
نُسَبِّحُ بِحَمْدِكَ وَنُقَدِّسُ لَكَ قَالَ إِنِّيٓ أَعْلَمُ مَا لَا تَعْلَمُونَ
﴿٣٠﴾ وَعَلَّمَ ءَادَمَ ٱلْأَسْمَآءَ كُلَّهَا ثُمَّ عَرَضَهُمْ عَلَى ٱلْمَلَٰٓئِكَةِ
فَقَالَ أَنۢبِـُٔونِي بِأَسْمَآءِ هَٰٓؤُلَآءِ إِن كُنتُمْ صَٰدِقِينَ ﴿٣١﴾ قَالُواْ
سُبْحَٰنَكَ لَا عِلْمَ لَنَآ إِلَّا مَا عَلَّمْتَنَآ إِنَّكَ أَنتَ ٱلْعَلِيمُ ٱلْحَكِيمُ
﴿٣٢﴾ قَالَ يَٰٓـَٔادَمُ أَنۢبِئْهُم بِأَسْمَآئِهِمْ فَلَمَّآ أَنۢبَأَهُم بِأَسْمَآئِهِمْ قَالَ
أَلَمْ أَقُل لَّكُمْ إِنِّيٓ أَعْلَمُ غَيْبَ ٱلسَّمَٰوَٰتِ وَٱلْأَرْضِ وَأَعْلَمُ مَا
تُبْدُونَ وَمَا كُنتُمْ تَكْتُمُونَ ﴿٣٣﴾ وَإِذْ قُلْنَا لِلْمَلَٰٓئِكَةِ ٱسْجُدُواْ
لِأَدَمَ فَسَجَدُوٓاْ إِلَّآ إِبْلِيسَ أَبَىٰ وَٱسْتَكْبَرَ وَكَانَ مِنَ ٱلْكَٰفِرِينَ
﴿٣٤﴾ وَقُلْنَا يَٰٓـَٔادَمُ ٱسْكُنْ أَنتَ وَزَوْجُكَ ٱلْجَنَّةَ وَكُلَا مِنْهَا رَغَدًا
حَيْثُ شِئْتُمَا وَلَا تَقْرَبَا هَٰذِهِ ٱلشَّجَرَةَ فَتَكُونَا مِنَ ٱلظَّٰلِمِينَ ﴿٣٥﴾
فَأَزَلَّهُمَا ٱلشَّيْطَٰنُ عَنْهَا فَأَخْرَجَهُمَا مِمَّا كَانَا فِيهِ وَقُلْنَا ٱهْبِطُواْ
بَعْضُكُمْ لِبَعْضٍ عَدُوٌّ وَلَكُمْ فِي ٱلْأَرْضِ مُسْتَقَرٌّ وَمَتَٰعٌ إِلَىٰ حِينٍ ﴿٣٦﴾
فَتَلَقَّىٰٓ ءَادَمُ مِن رَّبِّهِۦ كَلِمَٰتٍ فَتَابَ عَلَيْهِ إِنَّهُۥ هُوَ ٱلتَّوَّابُ ٱلرَّحِيمُ ﴿٣٧﴾

intended as a rebuke. ***Then He will make you die*** at the end of your allotted life-spans ***and then give you life again*** at the resurrection, ***and then you will be returned to Him*** after the resurrection for the reckoning of your actions. Allah is alluding to the fact of resurrection which the unbelievers deny.

29. ***It is He who created everything on the earth for you,*** for your benefit and for you to reflect on, ***and then,*** after creating the earth, ***directed His attention up to heaven and arranged it into seven regular heavens*** which is another sign. ***He has knowledge of all things*** in general and in detail. Do you not realise that the One who is able to create all that from nothing – and it is far greater than you – is able to bring you back to life again?

30. Remember, O Muḥammad ***when your Lord said to the angels, "I am putting a regent*** (Ādam) ***on the earth*** to carry out My judgements in it." ***They said, "Why put on it one who will cause corruption on it*** by acts of disobedience ***and shed blood*** in it by killing as the jinn had done, (they had been in the earth before man and when they caused corruption, Allah sent the angels against them who drove them to the islands and mountains) ***when we glorify You with praise,*** saying 'Glory be to You and by Your praise,' ***and proclaim Your purity,*** exonerating You absolutely from anything at all which is not fitting for You?" The angels were saying that they were more entitled to be regents than mankind. ***He said, "I know what You do not know."*** Allah informs them that He knows why it is correct to appoint Ādam and his descendants as regents even though among them are those who will obey and those who will rebel. For that reason justice will be manifested between them. They had said, "Our Lord will not create any creature nobler in His sight than us, nor any with more knowledge, since we existed before any such creature existed and have seen what he has not seen." So Allah Almighty created Ādam from the surface (*adīm*) of the earth by taking from every type of soil and He mixed it with different kinds of water and fashioned man and breathed the spirit into him so that he became alive and sentient after having been an inanimate substance.

31. ***He taught Ādam the names of all things*** by putting that knowledge into his heart. ***Then He arrayed them*** (the masculine plural (*hum*) is used for these things rather than the feminine singular ending (*hā*) normally used for things in the plural because they include intelligent beings) ***before the angels and said*** to rebuke them, ***"Tell me the names of these if you are telling the truth,*** since you say that I have not created any with more knowledge than you and that you are more entitled to be regents."

32. ***They said, "Glory be to You!*** indicating "We do not oppose you! ***We have no knowledge except what You have taught us. You are indeed the All-Knowing, the All-Wise."*** Nothing is outside of Allah's knowledge and wisdom.

33. ***He*** (Allah) ***said, "Ādam, tell them*** (the angels) ***their names,*** the names of all things." So he told them their proper names and the wisdom behind their creation. ***When he had told them their names, He*** (Allah) ***said*** to rebuke them, ***"Did I not tell you that I know the Unseen of the heavens and the earth*** and what is hidden in them, ***and I know what you make known,*** referring to the angels' words, "Why put on it...?", ***and what you hide?"*** referring to their statement that Allah would not create any being with more honour and knowledge than them.

34. Remember when ***We said to the angels, "Prostrate to Ādam!"*** This prostration is a prostration of greeting by bowing. ***And they prostrated, with the exception of Iblīs.*** Iblīs, the progenitor of the jinn, was with the angels. ***He refused*** to prostrate ***and was arrogant,*** too proud to do prostrate to him, saying, "I am better than him," ***and was one of the unbelievers*** in the absolute knowledge of Allah.

35. ***We said, "Ādam, live in the Garden, you*** (the grammatical form of the expression "live" *"askun anta"* repeats the pronoun *"anta"* "you" in order to stress it. It is normally merely implicit in the imperative.) ***and your wife,*** (Ḥawwā', who was created from his left rib) ***and eat freely*** (over a vast area without any restriction) ***from it wherever you will. But do not approach this tree*** by eating from it ***and so become wrongdoers*** (people of disobedience)." The tree was either wheat or grapes or something else.

36. ***But Shayṭān*** (Iblīs) ***made them slip up*** (read as *fa-azal - lahumā* and *fa-azālahumā*) ***by means of it*** and removed them from the Garden by saying to them, "Shall I direct you the Tree of Immortality?" and, by swearing by Allah to them that he was giving

قُلْنَا ٱهْبِطُوا۟ مِنْهَا جَمِيعًا ۖ فَإِمَّا يَأْتِيَنَّكُم مِّنِّى هُدًى فَمَن تَبِعَ
هُدَاىَ فَلَا خَوْفٌ عَلَيْهِمْ وَلَا هُمْ يَحْزَنُونَ ﴿٣٨﴾ وَٱلَّذِينَ كَفَرُوا۟
وَكَذَّبُوا۟ بِـَٔايَٰتِنَآ أُو۟لَٰٓئِكَ أَصْحَٰبُ ٱلنَّارِ ۖ هُمْ فِيهَا خَٰلِدُونَ ﴿٣٩﴾
يَٰبَنِىٓ إِسْرَٰٓءِيلَ ٱذْكُرُوا۟ نِعْمَتِىَ ٱلَّتِىٓ أَنْعَمْتُ عَلَيْكُمْ وَأَوْفُوا۟ بِعَهْدِىٓ
أُوفِ بِعَهْدِكُمْ وَإِيَّٰىَ فَٱرْهَبُونِ ﴿٤٠﴾ وَءَامِنُوا۟ بِمَآ أَنزَلْتُ
مُصَدِّقًا لِّمَا مَعَكُمْ وَلَا تَكُونُوٓا۟ أَوَّلَ كَافِرٍۭ بِهِۦ ۖ وَلَا تَشْتَرُوا۟ بِـَٔايَٰتِى
ثَمَنًا قَلِيلًا وَإِيَّٰىَ فَٱتَّقُونِ ﴿٤١﴾ وَلَا تَلْبِسُوا۟ ٱلْحَقَّ بِٱلْبَٰطِلِ
وَتَكْتُمُوا۟ ٱلْحَقَّ وَأَنتُمْ تَعْلَمُونَ ﴿٤٢﴾ وَأَقِيمُوا۟ ٱلصَّلَوٰةَ وَءَاتُوا۟
ٱلزَّكَوٰةَ وَٱرْكَعُوا۟ مَعَ ٱلرَّٰكِعِينَ ﴿٤٣﴾ ۞ أَتَأْمُرُونَ ٱلنَّاسَ بِٱلْبِرِّ
وَتَنسَوْنَ أَنفُسَكُمْ وَأَنتُمْ تَتْلُونَ ٱلْكِتَٰبَ ۚ أَفَلَا تَعْقِلُونَ ﴿٤٤﴾
وَٱسْتَعِينُوا۟ بِٱلصَّبْرِ وَٱلصَّلَوٰةِ ۚ وَإِنَّهَا لَكَبِيرَةٌ إِلَّا عَلَى ٱلْخَٰشِعِينَ
﴿٤٥﴾ ٱلَّذِينَ يَظُنُّونَ أَنَّهُم مُّلَٰقُوا۟ رَبِّهِمْ وَأَنَّهُمْ إِلَيْهِ رَٰجِعُونَ ﴿٤٦﴾
يَٰبَنِىٓ إِسْرَٰٓءِيلَ ٱذْكُرُوا۟ نِعْمَتِىَ ٱلَّتِىٓ أَنْعَمْتُ عَلَيْكُمْ وَأَنِّى فَضَّلْتُكُمْ
عَلَى ٱلْعَٰلَمِينَ ﴿٤٧﴾ وَٱتَّقُوا۟ يَوْمًا لَّا تَجْزِى نَفْسٌ عَن نَّفْسٍ شَيْـًٔا وَلَا
يُقْبَلُ مِنْهَا شَفَٰعَةٌ وَلَا يُؤْخَذُ مِنْهَا عَدْلٌ وَلَا هُمْ يُنصَرُونَ ﴿٤٨﴾
وَإِذْ نَجَّيْنَٰكُم مِّنْ ءَالِ فِرْعَوْنَ يَسُومُونَكُمْ سُوٓءَ ٱلْعَذَابِ
يُذَبِّحُونَ أَبْنَآءَكُمْ وَيَسْتَحْيُونَ نِسَآءَكُمْ ۚ وَفِى ذَٰلِكُم بَلَآءٌ
مِّن رَّبِّكُمْ عَظِيمٌ ﴿٤٩﴾ وَإِذْ فَرَقْنَا بِكُمُ ٱلْبَحْرَ فَأَنجَيْنَٰكُمْ
وَأَغْرَقْنَآ ءَالَ فِرْعَوْنَ وَأَنتُمْ تَنظُرُونَ ﴿٥٠﴾ وَإِذْ وَٰعَدْنَا مُوسَىٰٓ
أَرْبَعِينَ لَيْلَةً ثُمَّ ٱتَّخَذْتُمُ ٱلْعِجْلَ مِنۢ بَعْدِهِۦ وَأَنتُمْ ظَٰلِمُونَ

them good counsel, persuaded them to eat some of it, ***expelling them from where they were*** living in bliss. ***We said, "Descend*** to earth, you and your descendants, ***as enemies to each other*** where your descendants will wrong one another. ***You will have residence*** (a place to live) ***on the earth and enjoyment*** of its fruits ***for a time*** (until you die).*"*

37. ***Then Ādam received some words from his Lord,*** (one reading has the name of Ādam in the accusative, *Ādama,* and "words" in the nominative, *kalimātun*, so that the meaning becomes "words came to Ādam") He inspired Ādam with the words: *"Our Lord, we have wronged ourselves and if You do not forgive us and show mercy to us, we will be among the lost."*(7:23) and Ādam made supplication using them ***and He turned towards him*** and Allah accepted his repentance. ***He is the Ever-Returning,*** always turning to His slaves, ***the Most Merciful,*** always showing mercy towards them.

38. ***We said, "Go down from it*** (the Garden), ***every one of you!*** *"Every one of you"* is added to include the rest of mankind with Ādam. ***Then when guidance*** in the form of a Book or a Messenger ***comes to you from Me, those who follow My guidance*** and believe in Me and obey Me ***will feel no fear and will know no sorrow*** in the Next World because they will enter the Garden.

39. ***But those who disbelieve and deny Our Signs*** (Books) ***are the Companions of the Fire, remaining in it timelessly, for ever.*** They will stay there never emerging from it.

40. ***Tribe of Israel*** (descendants of Ya'qūb)***! remember the blessing I conferred on you,*** meaning your ancestors, by rescuing you from Pharaoh, parting the sea, and sending the manna and quail and other things for which you should show gratitude by obeying Allah. ***Honour My contract*** which I made with you to believe in Muḥammad ***and I will honour your contract*** which I made with you to reward you for that by admitting you into the Garden. ***Have dread of Me alone,*** meaning fear not fulfilling your contract with Me by preferring something else to it.

41. ***Believe in what I have sent down*** (the Qur'ān), ***confirming what is with you*** (the Torah and what it says regarding *tawḥīd* and prophethood). ***Do not be the first*** of the People of the Book ***to disbelieve in it*** because you will bear the sin of those who follow you.

And do not sell and exchange ***My Signs*** in your Book containing the description of Muḥammad ***for a paltry price,*** for the sake of gaining a few goods of this world, meaning do not conceal it fearing you will lose what you lent the Muslims. ***Have fear of Me alone.*** Fear only Me regarding that and do not fear anything or anyone other than Me.

42. ***Do not mix up truth*** which has been revealed to you ***with false - hood*** which you fabricate ***and knowingly hide the truth*** about Muḥammad when you know it to be the truth.

43. ***Establish the prayer and pay zakāt and bow with those who bow*** (Muḥammad and his Companions). This was revealed about the Jewish scholars. They used to say to their Muslim relatives, "Remain firm in the *dīn* of Muḥammad. It is the truth."

44. ***Do you order people to devoutness,*** to believe in Muḥammad, ***and forget yourselves*** by failing to do so yourselves, in which case you should not command it, ***when you recite the Book,*** the Torah which contains the threat about people whose words are different from their deeds***? Will you not use your intellect*** and understand that what you do is evil and so turn back from it***?***

45. ***Seek help*** in your affairs ***in steadfastness,*** which entails forcing the self to do what it dislikes, ***and the prayer,*** which is mentioned in the singular to exalt it. In *ḥadīth* we find: "The company of the Prophet, may Allah bless him and grant him peace, were commanded to hasten to *the prayer.*" It is said that this *āyat* is addressed to the Jews because they deviated from belief through avarice and love of leadership. Commanding steadfastness may mean fasting because fasting breaks the appetite, and the prayer is prescribed because it brings about humility and nullifies pride. ***But that,*** the prayer, ***is a very hard thing, except for the humble,*** those who submit to obedience:

46. ***...those who are aware*** (certain) ***that they will meet their Lord*** after their resurrection ***and that they will return to Him*** and be made to account for their actions in the Next World.

47. ***Tribe of Israel! Remember the blessing I conferred on you*** by being thankful and obeying Me, ***and that I preferred you***, meaning your ancestors, ***over all other beings*** in their time.

﴿٥١﴾ ثُمَّ عَفَوْنَا عَنكُم مِّنۢ بَعْدِ ذَٰلِكَ لَعَلَّكُمْ تَشْكُرُونَ ﴿٥٢﴾
وَإِذْ ءَاتَيْنَا مُوسَى ٱلْكِتَٰبَ وَٱلْفُرْقَانَ لَعَلَّكُمْ تَهْتَدُونَ ﴿٥٣﴾
وَإِذْ قَالَ مُوسَىٰ لِقَوْمِهِۦ يَٰقَوْمِ إِنَّكُمْ ظَلَمْتُمْ أَنفُسَكُم
بِٱتِّخَاذِكُمُ ٱلْعِجْلَ فَتُوبُوٓا۟ إِلَىٰ بَارِئِكُمْ فَٱقْتُلُوٓا۟ أَنفُسَكُمْ ذَٰلِكُمْ
خَيْرٌ لَّكُمْ عِندَ بَارِئِكُمْ فَتَابَ عَلَيْكُمْ ۚ إِنَّهُۥ هُوَ ٱلتَّوَّابُ ٱلرَّحِيمُ
﴿٥٤﴾ وَإِذْ قُلْتُمْ يَٰمُوسَىٰ لَن نُّؤْمِنَ لَكَ حَتَّىٰ نَرَى ٱللَّهَ جَهْرَةً
فَأَخَذَتْكُمُ ٱلصَّٰعِقَةُ وَأَنتُمْ تَنظُرُونَ ﴿٥٥﴾ ثُمَّ بَعَثْنَٰكُم مِّنۢ
بَعْدِ مَوْتِكُمْ لَعَلَّكُمْ تَشْكُرُونَ ﴿٥٦﴾ وَظَلَّلْنَا عَلَيْكُمُ
ٱلْغَمَامَ وَأَنزَلْنَا عَلَيْكُمُ ٱلْمَنَّ وَٱلسَّلْوَىٰ ۖ كُلُوا۟ مِن طَيِّبَٰتِ مَا
رَزَقْنَٰكُمْ ۖ وَمَا ظَلَمُونَا وَلَٰكِن كَانُوٓا۟ أَنفُسَهُمْ يَظْلِمُونَ ﴿٥٧﴾
وَإِذْ قُلْنَا ٱدْخُلُوا۟ هَٰذِهِ ٱلْقَرْيَةَ فَكُلُوا۟ مِنْهَا حَيْثُ شِئْتُمْ رَغَدًا
وَٱدْخُلُوا۟ ٱلْبَابَ سُجَّدًا وَقُولُوا۟ حِطَّةٌ نَّغْفِرْ لَكُمْ خَطَٰيَٰكُمْ ۚ
وَسَنَزِيدُ ٱلْمُحْسِنِينَ ﴿٥٨﴾ فَبَدَّلَ ٱلَّذِينَ ظَلَمُوا۟ قَوْلًا
غَيْرَ ٱلَّذِى قِيلَ لَهُمْ فَأَنزَلْنَا عَلَى ٱلَّذِينَ ظَلَمُوا۟ رِجْزًا مِّنَ
ٱلسَّمَآءِ بِمَا كَانُوا۟ يَفْسُقُونَ ﴿٥٩﴾ ۞ وَإِذِ ٱسْتَسْقَىٰ مُوسَىٰ
لِقَوْمِهِۦ فَقُلْنَا ٱضْرِب بِّعَصَاكَ ٱلْحَجَرَ ۖ فَٱنفَجَرَتْ مِنْهُ
ٱثْنَتَا عَشْرَةَ عَيْنًا ۖ قَدْ عَلِمَ كُلُّ أُنَاسٍ مَّشْرَبَهُمْ ۖ كُلُوا۟
وَٱشْرَبُوا۟ مِن رِّزْقِ ٱللَّهِ وَلَا تَعْثَوْا۟ فِى ٱلْأَرْضِ مُفْسِدِينَ ﴿٦٠﴾
وَإِذْ قُلْتُمْ يَٰمُوسَىٰ لَن نَّصْبِرَ عَلَىٰ طَعَامٍ وَٰحِدٍ فَٱدْعُ لَنَا رَبَّكَ
يُخْرِجْ لَنَا مِمَّا تُنۢبِتُ ٱلْأَرْضُ مِنۢ بَقْلِهَا وَقِثَّآئِهَا وَفُومِهَا

48. ***Have fear of a Day*** (the Day of Rising) ***when no self will be able to compensate for another in any way, no intercession be accepted*** (read as *yuqbalu* and *taqbalu)* ***from it*** so you will have no intercessors, ***no ransom*** (*'adl,* which usually means justice but here means ransom) ***taken from it, and none will be helped*** against the punishment.

49. Remember ***when We rescued you,*** meaning your ancestors, although this *āyat* and what follows it is addressed to those Jews who existed at the time of our Prophet, may Allah bless him and grant him peace, ***from the people of Pharaoh.*** This recalls what happened to their ancestors in order to remind them of Allah's blessing to them so that they would believe. ***They were inflicting an evil punishment*** (the worst kind of punishment) ***on you – slaughtering your sons and letting your women live.*** The reason for the killing of their sons was that Pharoah's priests said that a boy would be born among the tribe of Israel who would be the cause of the loss of his kingdom. ***In that there was an immense trial from your Lord.*** "That" may refer either to the punishment or the rescue and so the "trial" either may be either an affliction or a blessing.

50. ***And*** remember ***when We parted the sea for you*** so that you could cross through it when you were fleeing from your enemies ***and rescued you*** from drowning***, and drowned the people of Pharaoh*** along with him ***while you watched*** the sea cover them.

51. ***And when We allotted*** (read as *wā'adnā* and *wa'adnā)* ***forty nights to Mūsā.*** At the end of the forty nights the Torah was revealed to Mūsā so that the Jews could act on it. ***Then you adopted the Calf*** which the Sāmirī manufactured as a god ***when he*** (Mūsā) ***had gone*** to his appointment ***and you were wrongdoers*** by devoting your worship to what was not appropriate for it.

52. ***Then We pardoned you after that*** by wiping away your sins after that incident ***so that perhaps you would show thanks*** for Our blessing.

53. ***Remember when We gave Mūsā the Book*** (the Torah) ***and the Discrimination*** between truth and falsehood, the lawful and unlawful, ***so that perhaps you would be guided*** away from misguidance.

54. ***And when Mūsā said to his people*** who were worshipping the Calf, ***"My people! You wronged yourselves by adopting the Calf*** as a god, ***so turn towards your Maker*** who created you to worship Him ***and kill yourselves.*** This means to let those who are innocent kill the evildoers among you. ***That*** (killing) ***is the best thing for you in your Maker's sight."*** He made them prepare to carry that out, and then sent a black cloud over them so that they would not see one another and be moved by mercy until about seventy thousand had been killed. ***And He turned towards you*** and accepted your repentance. ***He is the Ever-Returning, the Most Merciful.***

55. ***And when*** you went with Mūsā to apologise to Allah for worshipping the Calf and you heard what he said, then ***you said, "Mūsā, we will not believe in you until we see Allah with our own eyes." So the thunder-bolt*** (the Divine Blast which caused them to die) ***struck you dead while you were looking*** at what happened to them.

56. ***Then We brought you back to life after your death, so that perhaps you would show thanks*** for Our blessing to you.

57. ***And We shaded you with clouds,*** causing thin clouds to give you shade and protect you from the heat of the sun in the desert, ***and sent down*** in it ***manna and quails*** which are truffles and small birds, ***to you*** and We said: ***"Eat of the good things We have provided for you*** and do not hoard them up and be ungrateful for the blessing you have been given." However, they did hoard them up and so their provision stopped coming. ***They did not wrong Us*** by that; ***rather it was themselves they were wronging,*** bringing ill fortune on themselves by what they did.

58. Remember ***when We said*** to them after they left the desert, ***"Go into this town*** (Jerusalem or Jericho) ***and eat from it wheresoever you like, freely*** (without restriction). ***Enter the gate*** of the city ***prostrating*** (bowing) ***and say, 'Relieve us of our burdens!'*** This expression, *ḥiṭṭa* in Arabic, means "remove our sins from us". ***Your mistakes will be forgiven.*** There are three readings for the word "forgiven": "We will forgive" with *nūn* (*naghfir*), "they (the mistakes) will be forgiven" with *tā'* (*tughfar*), and "He will forgive" with *yā'* (*yaghfir*). ***We will grant increase to all good-doers*** as a reward for their obedience."

59. ***But those*** among them ***who did wrong substituted words other than those they had been given.*** It is related that they said, "A grain (*ḥibba*) of barley!" and entered the city on their buttocks. The grammatical form emphasises the ugliness of what they did. ***So We sent down a plague,*** *rijz* meaning plague and a punishment, ***from heaven on those who did wrong because they were deviators.*** This was sent down because of their deviation (*fisq*), meaning their failure to show obedience, and as a result of it something like seventy thousand of them perished within a very short period of time.

60. ***And*** remember ***when Mūsā was looking for water for his people*** after they became thirsty in the desert. ***We said, "Strike the rock with your staff."*** The rock referred to is the same rock which had run off with Mūsā's clothes when they accused him of having a deformity because he did not undress in front of them. It was square like a man's head, made of marble or alabaster. He struck it and ***then twelve fountains gushed out from it***, the same as the number of the tribes, ***and all the people knew their drinking place.*** Each tribe had their own drinking place which no one else shared. We said to them, ***"Eat and drink of Allah's provision and do not go about the earth corrupting it."*** This is repeated for emphasis.

61. ***And when you said, "Mūsā, we will not put up with just one kind of food*** (manna and quail)***, so ask your Lord to supply to us some of what the earth produces – its green vegetables, cucumbers, grains, lentils and onions," he*** (Mūsā) ***said*** to them, ***"Do you want to replace what is better with what is inferior?*** Mūsā asked them if they wanted what was inferior and the question implies disapproval. When they refused to retract, he prayed to Allah Almighty who said, ***Go back to Egypt,*** meaning go back down to one of the cities and ***then*** in it ***you will have what*** plants ***you are asking for." Abasement*** (humiliation) ***and destitution were stamped upon them.*** Destitution was the effect of the poverty resulting from their abasement and disgrace, which continues to attach itself to them, even if they are rich, just as the minted dirham is stamped by its die. ***They brought down*** (returned with) ***anger*** and that stamp ***from Allah upon themselves. That was because they rejected Allah's Signs and killed the Prophets*** (such as Zakariyyā and Yaḥyā) ***without any right to do so*** and so it was arrant wrongdoing. ***That was because they rebelled***

وَعَدَسِهَا وَبَصَلِهَا ۖ قَالَ أَتَسْتَبْدِلُونَ ٱلَّذِى هُوَ أَدْنَىٰ
بِٱلَّذِى هُوَ خَيْرٌ ۚ ٱهْبِطُوا۟ مِصْرًا فَإِنَّ لَكُم مَّا سَأَلْتُمْ ۗ
وَضُرِبَتْ عَلَيْهِمُ ٱلذِّلَّةُ وَٱلْمَسْكَنَةُ وَبَآءُو بِغَضَبٍ مِّنَ
ٱللَّهِ ۗ ذَٰلِكَ بِأَنَّهُمْ كَانُوا۟ يَكْفُرُونَ بِـَٔايَٰتِ ٱللَّهِ وَيَقْتُلُونَ
ٱلنَّبِيِّـۧنَ بِغَيْرِ ٱلْحَقِّ ۗ ذَٰلِكَ بِمَا عَصَوا۟ وَّكَانُوا۟ يَعْتَدُونَ ﴿٦١﴾
إِنَّ ٱلَّذِينَ ءَامَنُوا۟ وَٱلَّذِينَ هَادُوا۟ وَٱلنَّصَٰرَىٰ وَٱلصَّٰبِـِٔينَ
مَنْ ءَامَنَ بِٱللَّهِ وَٱلْيَوْمِ ٱلْءَاخِرِ وَعَمِلَ صَٰلِحًا فَلَهُمْ أَجْرُهُمْ
عِندَ رَبِّهِمْ وَلَا خَوْفٌ عَلَيْهِمْ وَلَا هُمْ يَحْزَنُونَ ﴿٦٢﴾ وَإِذْ
أَخَذْنَا مِيثَٰقَكُمْ وَرَفَعْنَا فَوْقَكُمُ ٱلطُّورَ خُذُوا۟ مَآ ءَاتَيْنَٰكُم
بِقُوَّةٍ وَٱذْكُرُوا۟ مَا فِيهِ لَعَلَّكُمْ تَتَّقُونَ ﴿٦٣﴾ ثُمَّ تَوَلَّيْتُم مِّنۢ
بَعْدِ ذَٰلِكَ ۖ فَلَوْلَا فَضْلُ ٱللَّهِ عَلَيْكُمْ وَرَحْمَتُهُۥ لَكُنتُم مِّنَ
ٱلْخَٰسِرِينَ ﴿٦٤﴾ وَلَقَدْ عَلِمْتُمُ ٱلَّذِينَ ٱعْتَدَوا۟ مِنكُمْ فِى ٱلسَّبْتِ
فَقُلْنَا لَهُمْ كُونُوا۟ قِرَدَةً خَٰسِـِٔينَ ﴿٦٥﴾ فَجَعَلْنَٰهَا نَكَٰلًا لِّمَا
بَيْنَ يَدَيْهَا وَمَا خَلْفَهَا وَمَوْعِظَةً لِّلْمُتَّقِينَ ﴿٦٦﴾ وَإِذْ قَالَ
مُوسَىٰ لِقَوْمِهِۦٓ إِنَّ ٱللَّهَ يَأْمُرُكُمْ أَن تَذْبَحُوا۟ بَقَرَةً ۖ قَالُوٓا۟ أَتَتَّخِذُنَا
هُزُوًا ۖ قَالَ أَعُوذُ بِٱللَّهِ أَنْ أَكُونَ مِنَ ٱلْجَٰهِلِينَ ﴿٦٧﴾ قَالُوا۟
ٱدْعُ لَنَا رَبَّكَ يُبَيِّن لَّنَا مَا هِىَ ۚ قَالَ إِنَّهُۥ يَقُولُ إِنَّهَا بَقَرَةٌ لَّا فَارِضٌ
وَلَا بِكْرٌ عَوَانٌۢ بَيْنَ ذَٰلِكَ ۖ فَٱفْعَلُوا۟ مَا تُؤْمَرُونَ ﴿٦٨﴾
قَالُوا۟ ٱدْعُ لَنَا رَبَّكَ يُبَيِّن لَّنَا مَا لَوْنُهَا ۚ قَالَ إِنَّهُۥ يَقُولُ
إِنَّهَا بَقَرَةٌ صَفْرَآءُ فَاقِعٌ لَّوْنُهَا تَسُرُّ ٱلنَّٰظِرِينَ ﴿٦٩﴾

and went beyond the limits in disobedience to Allah. The repetition in the last sentence is used for stress.

62. ***Those who believe*** in the previous Prophets, ***those who are Jews, and the Christians and Sabaeans*** (a group of Jews or Christians), ***all*** of them ***who believe in Allah and the Last Day*** in the time of our Prophet ***and act rightly*** according to his *Sharī'a*, ***will have their reward*** for their actions ***with their Lord. They will feel no fear and they will know no sorrow.*** This reverts back to the third person plural pronoun, as used in the beginning of the *āyat* in *"those who believe."*

63. Remember ***when We made the covenant with you*** to act according to what is in the Torah ***and lifted up the Mount above your heads:*** Mount Sinai was uprooted and held over their heads when they refused to accept. We said, ***"Take hold vigorously*** (with seriousness and effort) ***of what We have given you and pay heed to what is in it*** by acting on it, ***so that perhaps you will be godfearing*** and so avoid the Fire or disobedience."

64. ***Then after that*** covenant and promise to obey ***you turned away, and were it not for Allah's favour to you and His mercy*** demonstrated by turning to you or delaying the punishment, ***you would have been among the lost*** (destroyed).

65. ***You are well aware of*** (know) ***those of you who broke*** the limits and ***the Sabbath*** by fishing on the Sabbath which Allah had forbidden them to do. They were people of the town of Ayla. ***We said to them, "Be apes, despised, cast out."*** They were cast out and died after three days.

66. ***We made it*** (that punishment) ***an exemplary punishment for those there then and those coming afterwards*** to deter others, both their contemporaries and those after them, from doing the same kind of thing, ***and a warning to the godfearing.*** Those who fear Allah are specified because they benefit from being warned whereas others do not.

67. ***And*** remember ***when Mūsā said to his people*** when one of them had been murdered and it was not known who had done it and they asked Mūsā to pray to Allah for them to solve it and he did so. He said, ***"Allah commands you to sacrifice a cow," they said, "What!***

قَالُوا۟ ٱدْعُ لَنَا رَبَّكَ يُبَيِّن لَّنَا مَا هِىَ إِنَّ ٱلْبَقَرَ تَشَٰبَهَ عَلَيْنَا وَإِنَّآ
إِن شَآءَ ٱللَّهُ لَمُهْتَدُونَ ﴿٧٠﴾ قَالَ إِنَّهُۥ يَقُولُ إِنَّهَا بَقَرَةٌ لَّا ذَلُولٌ
تُثِيرُ ٱلْأَرْضَ وَلَا تَسْقِى ٱلْحَرْثَ مُسَلَّمَةٌ لَّا شِيَةَ فِيهَا ۚ قَالُوا۟
ٱلْـَٰٔنَ جِئْتَ بِٱلْحَقِّ ۚ فَذَبَحُوهَا وَمَا كَادُوا۟ يَفْعَلُونَ ﴿٧١﴾ وَإِذْ
قَتَلْتُمْ نَفْسًا فَٱدَّٰرَْٰٔتُمْ فِيهَا ۖ وَٱللَّهُ مُخْرِجٌ مَّا كُنتُمْ تَكْتُمُونَ ﴿٧٢﴾
فَقُلْنَا ٱضْرِبُوهُ بِبَعْضِهَا ۚ كَذَٰلِكَ يُحْىِ ٱللَّهُ ٱلْمَوْتَىٰ وَيُرِيكُمْ
ءَايَٰتِهِۦ لَعَلَّكُمْ تَعْقِلُونَ ﴿٧٣﴾ ثُمَّ قَسَتْ قُلُوبُكُم مِّنۢ بَعْدِ ذَٰلِكَ
فَهِىَ كَٱلْحِجَارَةِ أَوْ أَشَدُّ قَسْوَةً ۚ وَإِنَّ مِنَ ٱلْحِجَارَةِ لَمَا يَتَفَجَّرُ
مِنْهُ ٱلْأَنْهَٰرُ ۚ وَإِنَّ مِنْهَا لَمَا يَشَّقَّقُ فَيَخْرُجُ مِنْهُ ٱلْمَآءُ ۚ وَإِنَّ
مِنْهَا لَمَا يَهْبِطُ مِنْ خَشْيَةِ ٱللَّهِ ۗ وَمَا ٱللَّهُ بِغَٰفِلٍ عَمَّا تَعْمَلُونَ
﴿٧٤﴾ ۞ أَفَتَطْمَعُونَ أَن يُؤْمِنُوا۟ لَكُمْ وَقَدْ كَانَ فَرِيقٌ مِّنْهُمْ
يَسْمَعُونَ كَلَٰمَ ٱللَّهِ ثُمَّ يُحَرِّفُونَهُۥ مِنۢ بَعْدِ مَا عَقَلُوهُ
وَهُمْ يَعْلَمُونَ ﴿٧٥﴾ وَإِذَا لَقُوا۟ ٱلَّذِينَ ءَامَنُوا۟ قَالُوٓا۟ ءَامَنَّا
وَإِذَا خَلَا بَعْضُهُمْ إِلَىٰ بَعْضٍ قَالُوٓا۟ أَتُحَدِّثُونَهُم بِمَا فَتَحَ
ٱللَّهُ عَلَيْكُمْ لِيُحَآجُّوكُم بِهِۦ عِندَ رَبِّكُمْ ۚ أَفَلَا تَعْقِلُونَ ﴿٧٦﴾
أَوَلَا يَعْلَمُونَ أَنَّ ٱللَّهَ يَعْلَمُ مَا يُسِرُّونَ وَمَا يُعْلِنُونَ ﴿٧٧﴾
وَمِنْهُمْ أُمِّيُّونَ لَا يَعْلَمُونَ ٱلْكِتَٰبَ إِلَّآ أَمَانِىَّ وَإِنْ هُمْ
إِلَّا يَظُنُّونَ ﴿٧٨﴾ فَوَيْلٌ لِّلَّذِينَ يَكْتُبُونَ ٱلْكِتَٰبَ بِأَيْدِيهِمْ
ثُمَّ يَقُولُونَ هَٰذَا مِنْ عِندِ ٱللَّهِ لِيَشْتَرُوا۟ بِهِۦ ثَمَنًا قَلِيلًا ۖ
فَوَيْلٌ لَّهُم مِّمَّا كَتَبَتْ أَيْدِيهِمْ وَوَيْلٌ لَّهُم مِّمَّا يَكْسِبُونَ

Are you making a mockery of us by giving such an answer***?" He said, "I seek refuge with Allah from being one of the ignorant*** who mock***!"***

68. When they knew that he was serious, ***they said, "Ask your Lord to make it clear to us what it should be like*** by a detailed description of it***." He said, "He says that she should be a cow, not old or virgin*** (young)***, but somewhere between the two*** ages. ***So do as you have been told,"*** meaning "Slaughter it as you have been ordered to."

69. ***They said, "Ask your Lord to make it clear to us what colour it should be." He said, "He says that she should be a red cow, the colour of sorrel, a pleasure to all who look."*** The colour should be very vivid and very pleasing to the eye.

70. ***They said, "Ask your Lord to make it clear to us what it should be like,*** whether it should be a grazing or working cow. ***Cows are all much the same to us.*** The genus of cows are similar to us and, because there are many different sorts, we are not sure which one is meant. ***Then if Allah wills, we will be guided."*** According to a *ḥadīth*, "If they had not said 'if Allah wills' it would never have been clear to them."

71. ***He said, "He says that it should be a cow not been trained to plough or irrigate the fields*** – it should not be a working animal and "not being trained" is part of the prohibition – ***completely sound*** with no defects or marks from work, ***without a blemish,*** a trace of any other colour, ***on it." They said, "Now you have brought the truth."*** ("Now you have made it completely clear.") So they looked for such an animal and found it with a pious youth and his mother and they bought it in exchange for filling the house with gold. ***So they sacrificed it – but they almost did not do it.*** They almost did not do it because it was so expensive. In *ḥadīth*, "If they had sacrificed any cow, it would have been enough for them, but they made things difficult for themselves by their questions and so Allah made it difficult for them."

72. Remember ***when you killed someone and violently accused each other of it*** (argued about it) ***and Allah brought out what you were hiding*** regarding the matter.

73. ***We said, "Hit him,*** the murdered man, ***with part of it!"*** He was hit with the cow's tongue or tail and then he came back to life and said, "So-and-so and so-and-so killed me," naming his cousins, and died again. So the two murderers were denied inheritance and were executed. Then Allah says, ***"In that way*** (bringing back the murdered man to life) ***Allah gives life to the dead, and He shows you His Signs*** (indications of His power) ***so that hopefully you will understand:*** in order that you may reflect and realise that the One who has the power to bring one soul back to life can also bring many souls back to life and so you should have faith.

74. ***Then your hearts,*** Jews, ***became hardened*** against the Truth ***after that,*** (this instance of bringing the dead to life and the signs before it) ***so they were like rocks*** in hardness ***or even harder still*** than stones. ***There are some rocks from which rivers gush forth, and others which split open and water comes out, and others which crash down*** from high to low ***out of fear of Allah,*** but you are not affected, nor softened nor do you fear. ***Allah is not unaware of what you do*** (read as *ta'lamūna,* "you do" and *ya'lamūna* "they do"); Allah defers you to your appointed time.

75. ***Do you*** (believers) ***really hope they*** (the Jews) ***will follow you in belief when a group of them*** (a group of their rabbis) ***heard Allah's Word*** in the Torah ***and then, after grasping*** and understanding ***it, knowingly distorted*** and altered ***it?*** They forged lies, so do not hold out any hope for them; they have already disbelieved. The question implies disapproval of what they did.

76. ***When they*** (the hypocritical Jews) ***meet those who believe, they say, "We believe*** that Muḥammad is a Prophet and the good news about him is in our Book.***" But when they*** return and ***go apart with one another, they*** (their leaders who did not behave hypocritically) ***say*** to the hypocrites, ***"Why do you speak to them*** (the believers) ***about what Allah has disclosed to you,*** about what the Torah says of the description of Muḥammad, ***so that they can use it as an argument against you before your Lord*** in the Next World, saying that you did not follow Muḥammad although you knew that he spoke the truth? ***Will you not use your intellect?"*** "Why do you not show more sense when you speak to them, and stop telling them this?"

﴿٧٩﴾ وَقَالُوا۟ لَن تَمَسَّنَا ٱلنَّارُ إِلَّآ أَيَّامًا مَّعْدُودَةً ۚ قُلْ
أَتَّخَذْتُمْ عِندَ ٱللَّهِ عَهْدًا فَلَن يُخْلِفَ ٱللَّهُ عَهْدَهُۥٓ ۖ أَمْ تَقُولُونَ
عَلَى ٱللَّهِ مَا لَا تَعْلَمُونَ ﴿٨٠﴾ بَلَىٰ مَن كَسَبَ سَيِّئَةً
وَأَحَٰطَتْ بِهِۦ خَطِيٓـَٔتُهُۥ فَأُو۟لَٰٓئِكَ أَصْحَٰبُ ٱلنَّارِ ۖ هُمْ
فِيهَا خَٰلِدُونَ ﴿٨١﴾ وَٱلَّذِينَ ءَامَنُوا۟ وَعَمِلُوا۟ ٱلصَّٰلِحَٰتِ
أُو۟لَٰٓئِكَ أَصْحَٰبُ ٱلْجَنَّةِ ۖ هُمْ فِيهَا خَٰلِدُونَ ﴿٨٢﴾ وَإِذْ
أَخَذْنَا مِيثَٰقَ بَنِىٓ إِسْرَٰٓءِيلَ لَا تَعْبُدُونَ إِلَّا ٱللَّهَ وَبِٱلْوَٰلِدَيْنِ
إِحْسَانًا وَذِى ٱلْقُرْبَىٰ وَٱلْيَتَٰمَىٰ وَٱلْمَسَٰكِينِ وَقُولُوا۟
لِلنَّاسِ حُسْنًا وَأَقِيمُوا۟ ٱلصَّلَوٰةَ وَءَاتُوا۟ ٱلزَّكَوٰةَ ثُمَّ
تَوَلَّيْتُمْ إِلَّا قَلِيلًا مِّنكُمْ وَأَنتُم مُّعْرِضُونَ ﴿٨٣﴾
وَإِذْ أَخَذْنَا مِيثَٰقَكُمْ لَا تَسْفِكُونَ دِمَآءَكُمْ وَلَا تُخْرِجُونَ
أَنفُسَكُم مِّن دِيَٰرِكُمْ ثُمَّ أَقْرَرْتُمْ وَأَنتُمْ تَشْهَدُونَ ﴿٨٤﴾
ثُمَّ أَنتُمْ هَٰٓؤُلَآءِ تَقْتُلُونَ أَنفُسَكُمْ وَتُخْرِجُونَ فَرِيقًا
مِّنكُم مِّن دِيَٰرِهِمْ تَظَٰهَرُونَ عَلَيْهِم بِٱلْإِثْمِ وَٱلْعُدْوَٰنِ
وَإِن يَأْتُوكُمْ أُسَٰرَىٰ تُفَٰدُوهُمْ وَهُوَ مُحَرَّمٌ عَلَيْكُمْ
إِخْرَاجُهُمْ ۚ أَفَتُؤْمِنُونَ بِبَعْضِ ٱلْكِتَٰبِ وَتَكْفُرُونَ
بِبَعْضٍ ۚ فَمَا جَزَآءُ مَن يَفْعَلُ ذَٰلِكَ مِنكُمْ إِلَّا خِزْىٌ
فِى ٱلْحَيَوٰةِ ٱلدُّنْيَا ۖ وَيَوْمَ ٱلْقِيَٰمَةِ يُرَدُّونَ إِلَىٰٓ أَشَدِّ ٱلْعَذَابِ ۗ
وَمَا ٱللَّهُ بِغَٰفِلٍ عَمَّا تَعْمَلُونَ ﴿٨٥﴾ أُو۟لَٰٓئِكَ ٱلَّذِينَ ٱشْتَرَوُا۟
ٱلْحَيَوٰةَ ٱلدُّنْيَا بِٱلْءَاخِرَةِ ۖ فَلَا يُخَفَّفُ عَنْهُمُ ٱلْعَذَابُ وَلَا هُمْ

77. Allah Almighty says, "***Do they not know that Allah knows what they keep secret and what they make public?*** This is a question meant for confirmation and means: "Is the realisation of this not enough to make them cease doing it?"

78. ***Some of them*** (Jews) ***are illiterate, knowing nothing of the Book*** (the Torah) ***but wishful thinking,*** the lies they have learned from their leaders and have then believed. In their denial of the prophethood of the Prophet and other things about which they disagree ***they only speculate.*** They have no real knowledge.

79. ***Woe*** (a terrible punishment) ***to those who write the Book with their own hands*** differently from what is in their possession ***and then say, "This is from Allah," to sell it for a paltry price*** in this world. They are the Jews who removed the description of the Prophet, may Allah bless him and grant him peace, which was in the Torah and the verse of stoning and other things which they wrote differently from how they were originally revealed! ***Woe to them for what their hands have written*** and forged! ***Woe to them for what they earn*** by the bribes they have received!

80. ***They say*** when they are threatened with the Fire, ***"The Fire will only touch us for a number of days."*** claiming that it will only burn them for forty days, which was the period during which their ancestors worshipped the Calf. Then the revelation came, ***Say*** to them, Muḥammad, ***"Have you made a contract*** and covenant ***with Allah – then Allah will not break His contract*** regarding that – ***or are you rather saying about Allah what you do not know?"*** You are indeed saying what you do not know.

81. ***No indeed! Those who persist*** and continue to ***accumulate bad actions*** by *shirk* ***and are surrounded*** on every side and overcome ***by their mistakes*** (read in both the singular, *khaṭī'atuhu*, and the plural, *khaṭī'ātuhu*) so that they die as idolaters, ***such people are the Companions of the Fire, remaining in it timelessly, for ever.***

82. ***Whereas those who believe and do right actions, such people are the Companions of the Garden, remaining in it timelessly, for ever.***

83. Remember ***when We made a covenant with the tribe of Israel*** in the Torah: We said, ***"Worship*** (read as both *ta'budūna* in the second person and *ya'budūna* in the third person) ***none but Allah*** (although this is grammatically a report, it is actually a prohibition) ***and be good to your parents*** by being dutiful ***and to relatives*** as well as parents ***and to orphans and the very poor. And speak good*** (read as *ḥusn* as well as *ḥasan*) ***words to people***, meaning command what is known to be right and forbid what is recognised as wrong and be truthful about Muḥammad, and to be gentle with people. ***And establish the prayer and pay zakāt." But then you turned away*** (Allah is telling them that although they had accepted to do all that, they nevertheless did not fulfil it. The *āyat* changes from the third person to the second person, from "them" to "you", but it is still their forefathers who are intended) – ***except a few of you. You turned aside*** just as your forefathers did.

84. ***And when We made a covenant with you*** and We told you ***not to shed your blood*** by killing one another ***and not to expel one another from your homes,*** evicting someone from his own home, ***you agreed*** and accepted that covenant ***and were all witnesses*** to one another.

85. ***Then you are the people who are killing one another and expelling a group among you from their homes, ganging up*** (read as *taẓāharūna* and *taẓẓāharūna*) ***against them in wrongdoing*** (disobedience) ***and enmity*** (injustice). ***Yet if they are brought to you as captives*** (read as *usārā* and *usrā*), ***you ransom them*** (read as *tufādūhum* and *tafdūhum*) from captivity with money and other things ***when it was forbidden for you to expel them in the first place!*** The expression, "when it was forbidden for you to expel them" refers back to the words to "expelling a group", and what is said between the two expressions is in parenthesis. It means: In the same way that it is unlawful for you not to ransom them, so it was unlawful to expel them at all. The Jewish clan of Qurayẓa had an alliance with Aws and that of Naḍīr with Khazraj, and each party fought with their allies and destroyed the other's homes and expelled them from them. But when they were captured they ransomed them. When they were asked, 'Why do you fight them and then ransom them?" they replied, "We are commanded to ransom." When they were asked, "But why did you fight them?" They replied, "To avoid embarrassment if our allies were defeated." Allah then asks, "***Do***

يُنصَرُونَ ﴿٨٦﴾ وَلَقَدْ ءَاتَيْنَا مُوسَى ٱلْكِتَٰبَ وَقَفَّيْنَا مِنۢ
بَعْدِهِۦ بِٱلرُّسُلِ ۖ وَءَاتَيْنَا عِيسَى ٱبْنَ مَرْيَمَ ٱلْبَيِّنَٰتِ وَأَيَّدْنَٰهُ
بِرُوحِ ٱلْقُدُسِ ۗ أَفَكُلَّمَا جَآءَكُمْ رَسُولٌۢ بِمَا لَا تَهْوَىٰٓ أَنفُسُكُمُ
ٱسْتَكْبَرْتُمْ فَفَرِيقًا كَذَّبْتُمْ وَفَرِيقًا تَقْتُلُونَ ﴿٨٧﴾ وَقَالُوا۟
قُلُوبُنَا غُلْفٌۢ ۚ بَل لَّعَنَهُمُ ٱللَّهُ بِكُفْرِهِمْ فَقَلِيلًا مَّا يُؤْمِنُونَ ﴿٨٨﴾
وَلَمَّا جَآءَهُمْ كِتَٰبٌ مِّنْ عِندِ ٱللَّهِ مُصَدِّقٌ لِّمَا مَعَهُمْ وَكَانُوا۟
مِن قَبْلُ يَسْتَفْتِحُونَ عَلَى ٱلَّذِينَ كَفَرُوا۟ فَلَمَّا جَآءَهُم
مَّا عَرَفُوا۟ كَفَرُوا۟ بِهِۦ ۚ فَلَعْنَةُ ٱللَّهِ عَلَى ٱلْكَٰفِرِينَ ﴿٨٩﴾
بِئْسَمَا ٱشْتَرَوْا۟ بِهِۦٓ أَنفُسَهُمْ أَن يَكْفُرُوا۟ بِمَآ أَنزَلَ
ٱللَّهُ بَغْيًا أَن يُنَزِّلَ ٱللَّهُ مِن فَضْلِهِۦ عَلَىٰ مَن يَشَآءُ مِنْ عِبَادِهِۦ ۖ
فَبَآءُو بِغَضَبٍ عَلَىٰ غَضَبٍ ۚ وَلِلْكَٰفِرِينَ عَذَابٌ مُّهِينٌ
﴿٩٠﴾ وَإِذَا قِيلَ لَهُمْ ءَامِنُوا۟ بِمَآ أَنزَلَ ٱللَّهُ قَالُوا۟ نُؤْمِنُ بِمَآ
أُنزِلَ عَلَيْنَا وَيَكْفُرُونَ بِمَا وَرَآءَهُۥ وَهُوَ ٱلْحَقُّ مُصَدِّقًا
لِّمَا مَعَهُمْ ۗ قُلْ فَلِمَ تَقْتُلُونَ أَنۢبِيَآءَ ٱللَّهِ مِن قَبْلُ إِن كُنتُم
مُّؤْمِنِينَ ﴿٩١﴾ ۞ وَلَقَدْ جَآءَكُم مُّوسَىٰ بِٱلْبَيِّنَٰتِ
ثُمَّ ٱتَّخَذْتُمُ ٱلْعِجْلَ مِنۢ بَعْدِهِۦ وَأَنتُمْ ظَٰلِمُونَ ﴿٩٢﴾
وَإِذْ أَخَذْنَا مِيثَٰقَكُمْ وَرَفَعْنَا فَوْقَكُمُ ٱلطُّورَ خُذُوا۟
مَآ ءَاتَيْنَٰكُم بِقُوَّةٍ وَٱسْمَعُوا۟ ۖ قَالُوا۟ سَمِعْنَا وَعَصَيْنَا
وَأُشْرِبُوا۟ فِى قُلُوبِهِمُ ٱلْعِجْلَ بِكُفْرِهِمْ ۚ قُلْ
بِئْسَمَا يَأْمُرُكُم بِهِۦٓ إِيمَٰنُكُمْ إِن كُنتُم مُّؤْمِنِينَ ﴿٩٣﴾

you, then, believe in one part of the Book (the command to ransom) ***and reject another*** (the command not to fight and not to expel and gang up)***? What repayment will there be for any of you who do that except disgrace*** by humiliation and abasement ***in this world?*** Their disgrace was realised through the killing of Qurayẓa and expulsion of Naḍīr and the imposition of the *jizya*. ***And on the Day of Rising, they will be returned to the harshest of punishments. Allah is not unaware of what you do*** (read as *ta'malūna* "what you do" and *ya'malūna* "what they do").

86. ***Those are the people who trade the Next World for this world*** by preferring this world to the Next World. ***The punishment will not be lightened for them. They will not be helped.*** They will not be protected from the punishment.

87. ***We gave Mūsā the Book*** (the Torah) ***and sent a succession of Messengers after him,*** meaning one Messenger after another. ***We gave 'Īsā, son of Maryam, the Clear Signs,*** referring to his miracles such as bringing the dead to life and healing the blind and lepers, ***and reinforced him*** (strengthened him) ***with the Purest Rūḥ*** (Jibrīl). Jibrīl is called the "Purest *Rūḥ*" because of his complete purity. He accompanied 'Īsā wherever he went. ***Why then, whenever a Messenger came to you with something*** of the truth ***your lower selves did not desire*** or want, ***did you*** not go straight but ***grow*** too ***arrogant*** to follow the truth when it came to you, ***and deny some of them*** such as 'Īsā ***and murder others*** such as Zakariyyā and Yaḥyā? This is a question by which rebuke is intended. In "murder" the imperfect tense rather than the past tense is used because it describes a past state which continued over time.

88. ***They said*** to the Prophet in mockery, ***"Our hearts are uncircumcised."*** This means that they did not pay attention to what the Almighty says. *Ghulf* is the plural of *aghlaf* and the meaning is that there is something covering their hearts, so they do not understand what you say. Allah Almighty says, "***Rather,*** counteracting what they said, ***Allah has cursed them for their unbelief.*** He has removed them far from His mercy and disappointed their hopes of acceptance – on account of their unbelief, not because of any defect in their hearts. ***What little faith they have!*** The paucity of their belief is stressed by the extra *mā*.

89. ***When a Book*** (the Qur'ān) ***does come to them from Allah, confirming what is with them*** (the Torah) – ***even though before that***, before it came, ***they were praying for victory over those who disbelieve*** saying, "O Allah, help us against them with the Prophet who will be sent at the end of time!" – ***yet when what they recognise*** of the truth ***does come to them*** (a reference to the sending of the Prophet), ***they disbelieve it*** out of envy and fear of losing their position of leadership. ***Allah's curse is on the unbelievers.***

90. ***What an evil thing they have sold themselves for*** (the loss of their portion of the reward), ***by disbelieving in*** (rejecting) ***what Allah has sent down*** (the Qur'ān), ***outraged*** out of intense envy ***that Allah should send down*** (read as *yunzila* and *yunazzila*) ***His favour***, referring to Revelation, ***down on whichever of His slaves He wills*** and desires to make a Messenger. ***They have brought down anger*** from Allah for their rejection of what was revealed ***upon anger on themselves.*** "Anger" is indefinite to stress its terrible nature. They deserved it for squandering the Torah and rejecting 'Īsā. ***Those who disbelieve will have a humiliating punishment.***

91. ***When they are told, "Believe in what Allah has sent down*** (the Qur'ān and other revealed Books)," ***they say, "We believe in what was sent down to us*** (the Torah)," Allah says, ***and they disbelieve anything beyond that***, other than it or after it, referring to the Qur'ān, ***even though it is the truth, confirming what they have. Say*** to them, ***"Why then, if you are believers*** in the Torah, ***did you previously kill the Prophets of Allah*** when the Torah forbade you to kill them?" This is addressed to the Jews present in the time of our Prophet but refers to what their forefathers did because they were happy with what their ancestors did.

92. ***Mūsā brought you the Clear Signs*** (his miracles such as the staff turning into a snake, his hand turning white and splitting the sea); ***then, after he left*** and went to keep his appointment with his Lord, ***you adopted the Calf*** as a god ***and were wrongdoers*** by doing that.

93. Remember ***when We made a covenant with you*** to act by the Torah ***and lifted up the Mount*** Sinai ***above your heads*** when you refused to do that, so that it was about to fall on them, and then We said: ***"Take hold vigorously*** (with seriousness and effort) ***of what***

قُلْ إِن كَانَتْ لَكُمُ ٱلدَّارُ ٱلْءَاخِرَةُ عِندَ ٱللَّهِ خَالِصَةً مِّن
دُونِ ٱلنَّاسِ فَتَمَنَّوُا۟ ٱلْمَوْتَ إِن كُنتُمْ صَـٰدِقِينَ ﴿٩٤﴾
وَلَن يَتَمَنَّوْهُ أَبَدًۢا بِمَا قَدَّمَتْ أَيْدِيهِمْ ۗ وَٱللَّهُ عَلِيمٌۢ بِٱلظَّـٰلِمِينَ
﴿٩٥﴾ وَلَتَجِدَنَّهُمْ أَحْرَصَ ٱلنَّاسِ عَلَىٰ حَيَوٰةٍ وَمِنَ ٱلَّذِينَ
أَشْرَكُوا۟ ۚ يَوَدُّ أَحَدُهُمْ لَوْ يُعَمَّرُ أَلْفَ سَنَةٍ وَمَا هُوَ بِمُزَحْزِحِهِۦ
مِنَ ٱلْعَذَابِ أَن يُعَمَّرَ ۗ وَٱللَّهُ بَصِيرٌۢ بِمَا يَعْمَلُونَ ﴿٩٦﴾ قُلْ
مَن كَانَ عَدُوًّا لِّجِبْرِيلَ فَإِنَّهُۥ نَزَّلَهُۥ عَلَىٰ قَلْبِكَ بِإِذْنِ ٱللَّهِ
مُصَدِّقًا لِّمَا بَيْنَ يَدَيْهِ وَهُدًى وَبُشْرَىٰ لِلْمُؤْمِنِينَ
﴿٩٧﴾ مَن كَانَ عَدُوًّا لِّلَّهِ وَمَلَـٰٓئِكَتِهِۦ وَرُسُلِهِۦ وَجِبْرِيلَ
وَمِيكَىٰلَ فَإِنَّ ٱللَّهَ عَدُوٌّ لِّلْكَـٰفِرِينَ ﴿٩٨﴾ وَلَقَدْ أَنزَلْنَآ
إِلَيْكَ ءَايَـٰتٍۭ بَيِّنَـٰتٍ ۖ وَمَا يَكْفُرُ بِهَآ إِلَّا ٱلْفَـٰسِقُونَ ﴿٩٩﴾
أَوَكُلَّمَا عَـٰهَدُوا۟ عَهْدًا نَّبَذَهُۥ فَرِيقٌ مِّنْهُم ۚ بَلْ أَكْثَرُهُمْ
لَا يُؤْمِنُونَ ﴿١٠٠﴾ وَلَمَّا جَآءَهُمْ رَسُولٌ مِّنْ عِندِ ٱللَّهِ
مُصَدِّقٌ لِّمَا مَعَهُمْ نَبَذَ فَرِيقٌ مِّنَ ٱلَّذِينَ أُوتُوا۟ ٱلْكِتَـٰبَ
كِتَـٰبَ ٱللَّهِ وَرَآءَ ظُهُورِهِمْ كَأَنَّهُمْ لَا يَعْلَمُونَ ﴿١٠١﴾
وَٱتَّبَعُوا۟ مَا تَتْلُوا۟ ٱلشَّيَـٰطِينُ عَلَىٰ مُلْكِ سُلَيْمَـٰنَ ۖ وَمَا كَفَرَ
سُلَيْمَـٰنُ وَلَـٰكِنَّ ٱلشَّيَـٰطِينَ كَفَرُوا۟ يُعَلِّمُونَ ٱلنَّاسَ
ٱلسِّحْرَ وَمَآ أُنزِلَ عَلَى ٱلْمَلَكَيْنِ بِبَابِلَ هَـٰرُوتَ وَمَـٰرُوتَ ۚ
وَمَا يُعَلِّمَانِ مِنْ أَحَدٍ حَتَّىٰ يَقُولَآ إِنَّمَا نَحْنُ فِتْنَةٌ فَلَا تَكْفُرْ ۖ
فَيَتَعَلَّمُونَ مِنْهُمَا مَا يُفَرِّقُونَ بِهِۦ بَيْنَ ٱلْمَرْءِ وَزَوْجِهِۦ ۚ

We have given you and listen and accept what you have been commanded to do.*"* ***They said, "We hear*** what you say ***and disobey*** your command.*"* ***They were made to drink the Calf into their hearts,*** so that love for it became intermingled with their hearts in the same way that a drink permeates through the body, ***for their unbelief. Say*** to them, ***"If you are believers*** in the Torah as you claim, ***what an evil thing*** in the form of worshipping the Calf ***your belief has made you do!"*** This means that they are not really believers because true belief would never direct them to worship the Calf. Although it is their forefathers who are being directly referred to, they are included with them because they too do not believe in the Torah and have denied Muḥammad. True belief in the Torah would in fact make them accept him.

94. ***Say*** to them, ***"If the Abode of the Next World*** (the Garden) ***with Allah is for you alone*** and exclusively, ***to the exclusion of all others*** as you claim, ***then long for death if you are telling the truth."*** Allah challenges this wishful thinking, making it subject to two conditions: truthfulness in their claim and yearning for death.

95. ***But they will never ever long for it because of what they have done,*** referring to their rejection of the Prophet, may Allah bless him and grant him peace. ***Allah knows the wrongdoers,*** those who disbelieve, and will repay them appropriately.

96. Allah begins this *āyat* with the letter *lām* of the oath and says: ***Rather you will find them the people greediest*** and most eager ***for life, along with those who attribute partners to Allah*** (those who deny the Resurrection). In fact the Jews are even greedier for life than the idolaters, because they know that they will end up in the Fire, whereas the idolaters deny it altogether. ***Any of them would love*** (wish) ***to be allowed to live a thousand years. But being allowed to live would not save him*** or put him far away ***from the punishment*** (the Fire). ***Allah sees everything they do.*** (read as *y̲a'malūna* "they do" and *t̲a'malūna* "you do"). Allah will give them their just deserts.

97. ***Say*** to them, ***"Anyone who is an enemy to Jibrīl*** let him die in his rage and he ***should know that it was he who brought it*** (the Qur'ān) ***down upon your heart, by Allah's authority*** (command), ***confirming what came before*** of the revealed Books, ***and as guid -***

ance from misguidance ***and good news*** of the Garden ***for the believers.*** Ibn Ṣūriyā, a Jew, asked the Prophet or 'Umar which angel brought the revelation. "Jibrīl," was the reply. He said, "He is our enemy. He brings the punishment. If it had been Mīkā'īl, we would have believed. He brings fruitfulness and peace." Then this *āyat* was revealed and the Prophet was instructed to tell them this.

98. ***"Anyone who is an enemy of Allah and of His angels, and of His Messengers and of Jibrīl*** (also read as *Jabrīl*) ***and Mīkā'īl*** (also read as *Mīkāl*)***, should know that Allah is an enemy to the unbelievers."*** Adding the names of Jibrīl and Mīkā'īl after the angels as a whole have been mentioned is an example of "adding the specific to the general".

99. ***We have sent down Clear Signs to you***, Muḥammad, ***and no one disbelieves them except the deviators*** who reject them. They are clear and evident Signs which refute the words of Ibn Ṣūriyā to the Prophet, may Allah bless him and grant him peace,"You have brought us nothing."

100. ***Why is it that whenever they make a contract*** with Allah to believe in the Prophet if he appears and not to help the unbelievers against him, ***a group of them disdainfully tosses it aside*** and break it? It is a question implying denial. ***No indeed! Most of them do not believe.***

101. ***When a Messenger*** (Muḥammad, may Allah bless him and grant him peace) ***comes to them from Allah confirming what is with them, a group of those who have been given the Book*** (the Torah) ***disdainfully toss the Book of Allah behind their backs*** by not acting according to its orders regarding belief in the Messenger and other things, ***as if they did not know*** what was in it about him being a true Prophet or that it was the Book of Allah.

102. As well as tossing it aside, ***they follow what*** (the magic) ***the shayṭāns recited in the reign of Sulaymān.*** The *shayṭāns* buried the magic under Sulaymān's throne when his kingdom was wrested away. It is also said that they used to listen and add lies to what they had heard and convey that to the priests who recorded it. When word spread that the jinn knew the Unseen, Sulaymān collected the books and buried them. When he died, the *shayṭāns* directed people to the spot and they dug them up and found magic in them. So they gained

وَمَا هُم بِضَآرِّينَ بِهِۦ مِنْ أَحَدٍ إِلَّا بِإِذْنِ ٱللَّهِ ۚ وَيَتَعَلَّمُونَ
مَا يَضُرُّهُمْ وَلَا يَنفَعُهُمْ ۚ وَلَقَدْ عَلِمُوا۟ لَمَنِ ٱشْتَرَىٰهُ
مَا لَهُۥ فِى ٱلْءَاخِرَةِ مِنْ خَلَٰقٍ ۚ وَلَبِئْسَ مَا شَرَوْا۟ بِهِۦٓ
أَنفُسَهُمْ ۚ لَوْ كَانُوا۟ يَعْلَمُونَ ﴿١٠٢﴾ وَلَوْ أَنَّهُمْ ءَامَنُوا۟
وَٱتَّقَوْا۟ لَمَثُوبَةٌ مِّنْ عِندِ ٱللَّهِ خَيْرٌ ۖ لَّوْ كَانُوا۟ يَعْلَمُونَ
﴿١٠٣﴾ يَٰٓأَيُّهَا ٱلَّذِينَ ءَامَنُوا۟ لَا تَقُولُوا۟ رَٰعِنَا وَقُولُوا۟
ٱنظُرْنَا وَٱسْمَعُوا۟ ۗ وَلِلْكَٰفِرِينَ عَذَابٌ أَلِيمٌ ﴿١٠٤﴾
مَّا يَوَدُّ ٱلَّذِينَ كَفَرُوا۟ مِنْ أَهْلِ ٱلْكِتَٰبِ وَلَا ٱلْمُشْرِكِينَ
أَن يُنَزَّلَ عَلَيْكُم مِّنْ خَيْرٍ مِّن رَّبِّكُمْ ۗ وَٱللَّهُ يَخْتَصُّ
بِرَحْمَتِهِۦ مَن يَشَآءُ ۚ وَٱللَّهُ ذُو ٱلْفَضْلِ ٱلْعَظِيمِ ﴿١٠٥﴾
۞ مَا نَنسَخْ مِنْ ءَايَةٍ أَوْ نُنسِهَا نَأْتِ بِخَيْرٍ مِّنْهَآ أَوْ مِثْلِهَآ ۗ
أَلَمْ تَعْلَمْ أَنَّ ٱللَّهَ عَلَىٰ كُلِّ شَىْءٍ قَدِيرٌ ﴿١٠٦﴾ أَلَمْ تَعْلَمْ أَنَّ ٱللَّهَ لَهُۥ
مُلْكُ ٱلسَّمَٰوَٰتِ وَٱلْأَرْضِ ۗ وَمَا لَكُم مِّن دُونِ ٱللَّهِ مِن
وَلِىٍّ وَلَا نَصِيرٍ ﴿١٠٧﴾ أَمْ تُرِيدُونَ أَن تَسْـَٔلُوا۟ رَسُولَكُمْ
كَمَا سُئِلَ مُوسَىٰ مِن قَبْلُ ۗ وَمَن يَتَبَدَّلِ ٱلْكُفْرَ بِٱلْإِيمَٰنِ
فَقَدْ ضَلَّ سَوَآءَ ٱلسَّبِيلِ ﴿١٠٨﴾ وَدَّ كَثِيرٌ مِّنْ أَهْلِ
ٱلْكِتَٰبِ لَوْ يَرُدُّونَكُم مِّنۢ بَعْدِ إِيمَٰنِكُمْ كُفَّارًا حَسَدًا
مِّنْ عِندِ أَنفُسِهِم مِّنۢ بَعْدِ مَا تَبَيَّنَ لَهُمُ ٱلْحَقُّ ۖ فَٱعْفُوا۟
وَٱصْفَحُوا۟ حَتَّىٰ يَأْتِىَ ٱللَّهُ بِأَمْرِهِۦٓ ۗ إِنَّ ٱللَّهَ عَلَىٰ كُلِّ شَىْءٍ قَدِيرٌ
﴿١٠٩﴾ وَأَقِيمُوا۟ ٱلصَّلَوٰةَ وَءَاتُوا۟ ٱلزَّكَوٰةَ ۚ وَمَا تُقَدِّمُوا۟ لِأَنفُسِكُم

power through the magic and rejected the books of their Prophets. Allah declared Sulaymān innocent of their claims and refuted the claim of the Jews who said, "Look at Muḥammad mentioning Sulaymān among the Prophets when he was only a sorcerer!" ***Sulaymān did not disbelieve*** and so could not have practised magic because it constitutes unbelief, ***but the shayṭāns did, teaching people sorcery and*** teaching them ***what had been sent down,*** by inspiring them with magic, ***to Hārūt and Mārūt, the two angels*** (read as *malakayn,* "two angels" and also *malikayn,* "two kings") ***in Babylon*** (a town in Iraq), ***who taught no one without first saying to him,*** giving him good advice, ***"We are merely a trial and temptation*** from Allah to people to test them by teaching it to them, so that whoever learns it is an unbeliever and whoever abandons it is a believer, ***so do not disbelieve*** by learning it." According to Ibn 'Abbās, they were two sorcerers who taught magic. It is said that they are two angels sent down to test people. If someone refused to do anything but learn magic, then they taught it to him. ***People learned from them how to separate a man and his wife*** by making them hate one another, ***but they,*** the magicians, ***cannot harm anyone by it,*** magic, ***except with Allah's permission*** and by His will. ***They have learned what will harm them*** in the Next World ***and will not benefit them.*** Such is magic. ***They*** (the Jews) ***know that any who deal in it,*** by choosing it or taking it in exchange for the Book of Allah, ***will have no share*** of the Garden ***in the Next World. What an evil thing they have sold themselves for,*** bartering away their portion of the Garden when they learn magic so the Fire becomes mandatory for them, ***if they only knew*** the truth of the punishment for what they do they would certainly not do it***!***

103. ***If only they*** (the Jews) ***had believed*** in the Prophet, may Allah bless him and grant him peace, and the Qur'ān ***and been godfearing*** and shown fear of the punishment of Allah by abandoning their acts of disobedience such as sorcery, then they would have been rewarded. ***A reward from Allah is better*** for them than the evil they did, ***if they only knew.*** If they had realised that that was better, they would certainly have chosen it.

104. ***O you who believe, do not say*** to the Prophet, ***"Rā'inā"; say*** instead, ***"Undhurnā," and listen well*** to what you are told and accept it. ***The unbelievers will have a painful punishment*** in the Fire. This command came because the word "*rā'inā*", although it means "Look towards us," in Arabic, was a curse in Hebrew derived from *ru'una* which had the meaning of flippancy; so the Jews were happy to use it when addressing the Prophet, may Allah bless him and grant him peace. The believers were forbidden to use it and were instructed to use another unambiguous expression meaning the same thing.

105. ***Those of the People of the Book who disbelieve and the idolaters*** among the Arabs ***do not like anything good,*** such as Revelation, ***to be sent down to you from your Lord*** out of envy towards you. ***But Allah selects for His mercy***, here meaning Prophethood, ***whomever He wills. Allah's favour is truly vast.*** "Idolaters" are added to the People of the Book for clarification.

106. When the unbelievers attacked the possibility of abrogation and said, "Muḥammad commands his companions to do something one day and forbids them it the next," this was revealed. ***Whenever We abrogate*** (read as *nansakh* and *nunsikh*) ***an āyat*** by changing the judgement it contains, in expression or in recitation ***or cause it to be forgotten,*** meaning that We hold it back and do not send down its decrees and remove its recitation, or keep it in the Preserved Tablet, ***We bring one better than it*** and more beneficial for people in that it is easier or has a greater reward ***or equal to it*** in respect of obligation and reward. ***Do you not know that Allah has power over all things,*** meaning that He can alter, change or affirm as He likes*?*

107. ***Do you not know that Allah is He to Whom the sovereignty of the heavens and the earth belongs*** and Who does whatever He wills, ***and that, besides Allah, you have no protector and no helper?*** There is no one who is able to protect the unbelievers or to avert His punishment from them. This was in response to a request from the people of Makka to be made wealthy and for Ṣafā to be turned into gold.

108. ***Or do you want to question your Messenger as Mūsā was questioned*** by his people ***before?*** This was when they asked if he could show them Allah openly and other things. ***Anyone who exchanges belief for unbelief*** by not considering the Clear Signs but proposing something else instead, ***has definitely gone astray from***

مِّنْ خَيْرٍ تَجِدُوهُ عِندَ ٱللَّهِ ۗ إِنَّ ٱللَّهَ بِمَا تَعْمَلُونَ بَصِيرٌ
١١٠ وَقَالُوا۟ لَن يَدْخُلَ ٱلْجَنَّةَ إِلَّا مَن كَانَ هُودًا أَوْ نَصَٰرَىٰ ۗ
تِلْكَ أَمَانِيُّهُمْ ۗ قُلْ هَاتُوا۟ بُرْهَٰنَكُمْ إِن كُنتُمْ
صَٰدِقِينَ ١١١ بَلَىٰ مَنْ أَسْلَمَ وَجْهَهُۥ لِلَّهِ وَهُوَ مُحْسِنٌ
فَلَهُۥٓ أَجْرُهُۥ عِندَ رَبِّهِۦ وَلَا خَوْفٌ عَلَيْهِمْ وَلَا هُمْ يَحْزَنُونَ ١١٢
وَقَالَتِ ٱلْيَهُودُ لَيْسَتِ ٱلنَّصَٰرَىٰ عَلَىٰ شَىْءٍ وَقَالَتِ ٱلنَّصَٰرَىٰ
لَيْسَتِ ٱلْيَهُودُ عَلَىٰ شَىْءٍ وَهُمْ يَتْلُونَ ٱلْكِتَٰبَ ۗ كَذَٰلِكَ قَالَ
ٱلَّذِينَ لَا يَعْلَمُونَ مِثْلَ قَوْلِهِمْ ۚ فَٱللَّهُ يَحْكُمُ بَيْنَهُمْ يَوْمَ ٱلْقِيَٰمَةِ
فِيمَا كَانُوا۟ فِيهِ يَخْتَلِفُونَ ١١٣ وَمَنْ أَظْلَمُ مِمَّن مَّنَعَ مَسَٰجِدَ
ٱللَّهِ أَن يُذْكَرَ فِيهَا ٱسْمُهُۥ وَسَعَىٰ فِى خَرَابِهَآ ۚ أُو۟لَٰٓئِكَ مَا كَانَ
لَهُمْ أَن يَدْخُلُوهَآ إِلَّا خَآئِفِينَ ۚ لَهُمْ فِى ٱلدُّنْيَا خِزْىٌ
وَلَهُمْ فِى ٱلْءَاخِرَةِ عَذَابٌ عَظِيمٌ ١١٤ وَلِلَّهِ ٱلْمَشْرِقُ وَٱلْمَغْرِبُ ۚ
فَأَيْنَمَا تُوَلُّوا۟ فَثَمَّ وَجْهُ ٱللَّهِ ۚ إِنَّ ٱللَّهَ وَٰسِعٌ عَلِيمٌ ١١٥
وَقَالُوا۟ ٱتَّخَذَ ٱللَّهُ وَلَدًا ۗ سُبْحَٰنَهُۥ ۖ بَل لَّهُۥ مَا فِى ٱلسَّمَٰوَٰتِ
وَٱلْأَرْضِ ۖ كُلٌّ لَّهُۥ قَٰنِتُونَ ١١٦ بَدِيعُ ٱلسَّمَٰوَٰتِ وَٱلْأَرْضِ ۖ
وَإِذَا قَضَىٰٓ أَمْرًا فَإِنَّمَا يَقُولُ لَهُۥ كُن فَيَكُونُ ١١٧ وَقَالَ ٱلَّذِينَ
لَا يَعْلَمُونَ لَوْلَا يُكَلِّمُنَا ٱللَّهُ أَوْ تَأْتِينَآ ءَايَةٌ ۗ كَذَٰلِكَ
قَالَ ٱلَّذِينَ مِن قَبْلِهِم مِّثْلَ قَوْلِهِمْ ۘ تَشَٰبَهَتْ قُلُوبُهُمْ ۗ
قَدْ بَيَّنَّا ٱلْءَايَٰتِ لِقَوْمٍ يُوقِنُونَ ١١٨ إِنَّآ أَرْسَلْنَٰكَ
بِٱلْحَقِّ بَشِيرًا وَنَذِيرًا ۖ وَلَا تُسْـَٔلُ عَنْ أَصْحَٰبِ ٱلْجَحِيمِ ١١٩

the level way. Such a person has strayed from the Path of the Truth and the Straight Path.

109. ***Many of the People of the Book would love it if they could make you revert to being unbelievers after you have believed, showing their innate envy,*** meaning that their corrupted selves have prompted them to act in this way, ***now that the truth is clear to them*** in the Torah about the Prophet, may Allah bless him and grant him peace. ***But you should pardon*** them and leave them alone ***and overlook*** by turning away and not paying them attention ***until Allah gives His command*** to fight them. ***Truly Allah has power over all things.***

110. ***Establish the prayer and pay zakāt. Any good you forward for yourselves,*** such as maintaining ties of kin and *ṣadaqa*, ***you will find*** its reward ***with Allah. Certainly Allah sees everything you do*** and will repay you for it.

111. ***They say, "No one will enter the Garden except for Jews*** (*hūd*, the plural of *hā'id*) ***and Christians."*** This *āyat* refers to an argument between the Jews of Madina and the Christians of Najrān in the presence of the Prophet, may Allah bless him and grant him peace. The Jews said that only the Jews would enter Paradise and the Christians said that only the Christians would enter it. ***Such*** statements are examples of the delusions which they hold and ***is their vain hope. Say*** to them, ***"Produce your evidence*** of that ***if you are telling the truth*** about it."

112. ***Not so*** because the truth is that others besides these two groups will enter the Garden! ***All who submit themselves completely to Allah*** (literally: "to the face of Allah" and the word "face" is mentioned here because it is the noblest part of the body and all the rest of the body follows it) ***and are good-doers*** by affirming the unity of Allah, ***will find their reward with their Lord***, the reward for their actions in the Garden. ***They will feel no fear and will know no sorrow*** in the Next World.

113. ***The Jews say, "The Christians have nothing to stand on,"*** and reject 'Īsā, ***and the Christians say, "The Jews have nothing to stand on,"*** and reject Mūsā, ***and yet they both recite the Book.*** Both groups recite revealed Books and the Book of the Jews affirms 'Īsā and the Book of the Christians affirms Mūsā. ***Those who do not***

know (the idolaters among the Arabs and others) ***say the same as they say,*** that any one who has any religion other than theirs has nothing. ***Allah will judge between them on the Day of Rising regarding the things about which they differ*** in respect of the *dīn* and then those who affirm the truth will enter the Garden and those who affirm falsehood will enter the Fire.

114. ***Who could do greater wrong,*** meaning no one does greater wrong, ***than someone who bars access to the mosques of Allah, preventing His name from being remembered in them*** in prayer and glorification, ***and goes about destroying them*** by actual destruction or putting them out of use? This was revealed about the Romans who destroyed Jerusalem or the idolaters who prevented the Prophet, may Allah bless him and grant him peace, from going to the House of Allah in the year of Ḥudaybiyya (6 AH). ***Such people will never be able to enter them – except in fear.*** This is a report which conveys the meaning of a command, meaning "Make them fearful through *jihād* so that none of them enters it feeling safe." ***They will have dis-grace in this world*** through being killed, captured and made to pay *jizya* ***and in the Next World they will have a terrible punishment*** in the Fire.

115. This *āyat* was revealed when the Jews attacked the changing of the *qibla* from Jerusalem to Makka, or it may refer to doing supererogatory prayers while mounted on a journey, facing whichever direction the animal is going. ***Both East and West,*** meaning the entire earth, ***belong to Allah, so wherever you turn*** your faces in the prayer at His command, ***the Face of Allah is there*** in His *qibla* with which He is pleased. ***Allah is All-Encompassing,*** encompassing everything His bounty, ***All-Knowing*** about how to manage His creation.

116. This verse can be read with or without *wa,* "and", at the beginning. ***They*** (the Jews and Christians and those who say that the angels are the daughters of Allah.) ***say, "Allah has a son."*** Allah Almighty says, ***Glory be to Him!,*** disassociating Him from all of that. ***No, everything in the heavens and the earth belongs to Him*** as His kingdom, creation and slaves. Absolute authority is not compatible with having children. It is not logical. ***Everything is obedient to***

Him in every way He desires of it to be. The masculine plural is used because of the dominance of rational beings in the group.

117. ***The Originator of the heavens and the earth*** who brings things into existence without any prior model. ***When He decides on something*** and wants to bring it into existence, ***He just says to it, "Be!" and it is,*** comes into existence.

118. ***Those who do not know*** (the unbelievers of Makka) ***say*** to the Prophet, may Allah bless him and grant him peace, ***"If only Allah would speak to us*** and tell us that you are His Messenger, ***or some sign come to us*** which will give us clear evidence that you are telling the truth," ***just like those before them*** among the unbelievers of past nations ***who said*** to their Prophets ***the same as they say*** by way being stubborn and demanding miracles. ***Their hearts are much the same*** in respect of disbelief and stubbornness. This is meant to console the Prophet. ***We have made the Signs clear to people who have certainty,*** those who know that the Qur'anic signs (*āyāt*) truly are Signs and believe in them.

119. ***We have sent you***, Muḥammad, ***with the Truth*** (Divine Guidance), ***bringing good news*** of the Garden to those who respond ***and giving warning*** about the Fire for those who do not respond. ***You will not be asked*** (read as *lā tus'alū* "you will not be asked" and *lā tas'al,* "do not ask") ***about the inhabitants of the Blazing Fire,*** meaning the unbelievers who do not believe. You only have to convey the Message.

120. ***The Jews and the Christians will never be pleased with you until you follow their religion. Say, "Allah's guidance*** (Islam) ***is the true guidance*** and anything other than that is misguidance." ***If,*** theoretically, ***you were to follow their whims and desires*** which they invite you to follow, ***after the knowledge that has come to you,*** which is Revelation from Allah, ***you would find no protector or helper*** to protect and defend you ***against Allah.***

121. ***Those to whom We have given the Book, who recite it in the way it should be recited,*** in the way it was revealed, ***such people believe in it.*** This was revealed about a group of Abyssinians who came and became Muslim. ***As for those who reject it,*** who reject the

وَلَن تَرۡضَىٰ عَنكَ ٱلۡيَهُودُ وَلَا ٱلنَّصَٰرَىٰ حَتَّىٰ تَتَّبِعَ مِلَّتَهُمۡۗ قُلۡ إِنَّ
هُدَى ٱللَّهِ هُوَ ٱلۡهُدَىٰۗ وَلَئِنِ ٱتَّبَعۡتَ أَهۡوَآءَهُم بَعۡدَ ٱلَّذِي جَآءَكَ
مِنَ ٱلۡعِلۡمِۙ مَا لَكَ مِنَ ٱللَّهِ مِن وَلِيّٖ وَلَا نَصِيرٍ ١٢٠ ٱلَّذِينَ ءَاتَيۡنَٰهُمُ
ٱلۡكِتَٰبَ يَتۡلُونَهُۥ حَقَّ تِلَاوَتِهِۦٓ أُوْلَٰٓئِكَ يُؤۡمِنُونَ بِهِۦۗ وَمَن يَكۡفُرۡ بِهِۦ
فَأُوْلَٰٓئِكَ هُمُ ٱلۡخَٰسِرُونَ ١٢١ يَٰبَنِيٓ إِسۡرَٰٓءِيلَ ٱذۡكُرُواْ نِعۡمَتِيَ ٱلَّتِيٓ
أَنۡعَمۡتُ عَلَيۡكُمۡ وَأَنِّي فَضَّلۡتُكُمۡ عَلَى ٱلۡعَٰلَمِينَ ١٢٢ وَٱتَّقُواْ يَوۡمٗا
لَّا تَجۡزِي نَفۡسٌ عَن نَّفۡسٖ شَيۡـٔٗا وَلَا يُقۡبَلُ مِنۡهَا عَدۡلٞ وَلَا تَنفَعُهَا
شَفَٰعَةٞ وَلَا هُمۡ يُنصَرُونَ ١٢٣ ۞ وَإِذِ ٱبۡتَلَىٰٓ إِبۡرَٰهِـۧمَ رَبُّهُۥ بِكَلِمَٰتٖ
فَأَتَمَّهُنَّۖ قَالَ إِنِّي جَاعِلُكَ لِلنَّاسِ إِمَامٗاۖ قَالَ وَمِن ذُرِّيَّتِيۖ قَالَ لَا
يَنَالُ عَهۡدِي ٱلظَّٰلِمِينَ ١٢٤ وَإِذۡ جَعَلۡنَا ٱلۡبَيۡتَ مَثَابَةٗ لِّلنَّاسِ
وَأَمۡنٗا وَٱتَّخِذُواْ مِن مَّقَامِ إِبۡرَٰهِـۧمَ مُصَلّٗىۖ وَعَهِدۡنَآ إِلَىٰٓ إِبۡرَٰهِـۧمَ
وَإِسۡمَٰعِيلَ أَن طَهِّرَا بَيۡتِيَ لِلطَّآئِفِينَ وَٱلۡعَٰكِفِينَ وَٱلرُّكَّعِ
ٱلسُّجُودِ ١٢٥ وَإِذۡ قَالَ إِبۡرَٰهِـۧمُ رَبِّ ٱجۡعَلۡ هَٰذَا بَلَدًا ءَامِنٗا وَٱرۡزُقۡ
أَهۡلَهُۥ مِنَ ٱلثَّمَرَٰتِ مَنۡ ءَامَنَ مِنۡهُم بِٱللَّهِ وَٱلۡيَوۡمِ ٱلۡأٓخِرِۖ قَالَ وَمَن كَفَرَ
فَأُمَتِّعُهُۥ قَلِيلٗا ثُمَّ أَضۡطَرُّهُۥٓ إِلَىٰ عَذَابِ ٱلنَّارِۖ وَبِئۡسَ ٱلۡمَصِيرُ ١٢٦
وَإِذۡ يَرۡفَعُ إِبۡرَٰهِـۧمُ ٱلۡقَوَاعِدَ مِنَ ٱلۡبَيۡتِ وَإِسۡمَٰعِيلُ رَبَّنَا تَقَبَّلۡ
مِنَّآۖ إِنَّكَ أَنتَ ٱلسَّمِيعُ ٱلۡعَلِيمُ ١٢٧ رَبَّنَا وَٱجۡعَلۡنَا مُسۡلِمَيۡنِ
لَكَ وَمِن ذُرِّيَّتِنَآ أُمَّةٗ مُّسۡلِمَةٗ لَّكَ وَأَرِنَا مَنَاسِكَنَا وَتُبۡ عَلَيۡنَآۖ
إِنَّكَ أَنتَ ٱلتَّوَّابُ ٱلرَّحِيمُ ١٢٨ رَبَّنَا وَٱبۡعَثۡ فِيهِمۡ رَسُولٗا
مِّنۡهُمۡ يَتۡلُواْ عَلَيۡهِمۡ ءَايَٰتِكَ وَيُعَلِّمُهُمُ ٱلۡكِتَٰبَ وَٱلۡحِكۡمَةَ

Book by twisting its meaning, ***they are the losers*** because they will end up in the Fire.

122. ***Tribe of Israel! Remember the blessing I conferred on you, and that I preferred you over all other beings.*** This was already explained in the commentary on 2:40.

123. ***Have fear of a Day when no self will be able to compensate for another in any way, and no ransom be accepted from it, and no intercession benefit it, and they will not be helped*** or defended against the punishment of Allah or ransomed from it.

124. Remember ***when Ibrāhīm*** (also read as *Ibrāhām*) ***was tested*** and tried ***by his Lord with certain words*** which are certain commands and intentions which he discharged, ***which he carried out completely.*** It is said that they were the *ḥajj* rites, and it is also said that it refers to the ten attributes of the natural form (*al-fiṭra*) which are rinsing the mouth, snuffing water up the nose, using the toothpick, clipping the moustache, letting the beard grow, cutting the nails, plucking the hair of the armpits, shaving the pubes, circumcision, and cleansing oneself with water (in the lavatory). He carried them out in full. ***He*** (Allah) ***said*** to him, ***"I will make you a model*** (*imām*), meaning a model in the *dīn*, ***for mankind." He asked, "And what of my descendants?"*** meaning "Will my progeny be imāms too?" ***He said, "My contract*** for the imamate ***does not include the wrongdoers***, those of them who disbelieve." This indicates that those who are not wrongdoers will deserve it.

125. ***And when We made the House*** (the Ka'ba) ***a place of return*** for people to resort to from every direction, ***a sanctuary for mankind,*** making it secure from injustice and raids which happen elsewhere, so that even if a man meets his father's killer there, he may not attack him. "O mankind, ***take*** (read as *attakhadhū* and *attakhidhū*) ***the Maqām of Ibrāhīm***, the place where he stood when overseeing the building the House, ***as a place of prayer,*** as a place to pray two *rak'ats* after *ṭawāf*." ***We contracted with Ibrāhīm and Ismā'īl*** and commanded them: ***"Purify My House*** of idols ***for those who circle it, and those who stay there, and those who bow and who prostrate,*** those who pray (*rukka'* is the plural of *rāki'*)."

126. ***And when Ibrāhīm said, "My Lord, make this a place of safety,*** and Allah granted his request and made it a sanctuary in which blood may not be shed, no one may be wronged, game may not be hunted, and whose plants may not be uprooted, ***and provide its inhabitants with fruits,*** the fruits being provided by the Ta'if caravan from Syria since Makka was barren, devoid of plants or water – ***all of them who believe in Allah and the Last Day."*** They are singled as the beneficiaries of the supplication to accordance with Allah's words above, *"My contract does not reach the wrongdoers."* ***He*** (Allah) ***said, "I will let him who disbelieves enjoy himself*** (*umti'uhu* and *umatti'uhu*) ***a little*** with provision in this world during his lifetime ***and then I will drive him to the punishment of the Fire*** in the Next World from which there is no escape. ***What an evil destination*** to return to!"

127. ***And*** remember ***when Ibrāhīm built the foundations*** or the walls ***of the House with Ismā'īl:*** They said, ***"Our Lord, accept this*** building ***from us! You are the All-Hearing*** of words, ***the All-Knowing*** of actions.

128. ***Our Lord, make us both Muslims submitted to You***, who obey you, ***and*** make ***our descendants a Muslim community submitted to You.*** The preposition *min* here is partitive in this instance because Allah's contract does not extend to the wrongdoers. ***Show us*** and teach us ***our rites of worship*** (our laws of worship or the *ḥajj*) ***and turn towards Us. You are the Ever-Relenting, the Most Merciful.*** They voiced repentance, in spite of their Prophetic protection from wrongdoing, out of humility and in order to teach their offspring to do the same.

129. ***Our Lord, raise up among them*** (the people of the House) ***a Messenger from them,*** from among themselves; and Allah answered their supplication with Muḥammad, may Allah bless him and grant him peace, ***to recite Your Signs*** (the Qur'ān) ***to them and teach them the Book*** (the Qur'ān) ***and Wisdom*** (the judgements it contains) ***and purify them*** from *shirk*. ***You are the Almighty,*** the Overcomer, ***the All-Wise*** in what You produce."

130. ***Who would deliberately renounce the religion of Ibrāhīm*** and abandon it ***except someone who reveals himself to be a fool,*** someone who is ignorant that his self is created by Allah and must worship Him

وَيُزَكِّيهِمْۚ إِنَّكَ أَنتَ ٱلْعَزِيزُ ٱلْحَكِيمُ ١٢٩ وَمَن يَرْغَبُ عَن
مِّلَّةِ إِبْرَٰهِـۧمَ إِلَّا مَن سَفِهَ نَفْسَهُۥۚ وَلَقَدِ ٱصْطَفَيْنَٰهُ فِى ٱلدُّنْيَاۖ
وَإِنَّهُۥ فِى ٱلْـَٔاخِرَةِ لَمِنَ ٱلصَّٰلِحِينَ ١٣٠ إِذْ قَالَ لَهُۥ رَبُّهُۥٓ أَسْلِمْۖ
قَالَ أَسْلَمْتُ لِرَبِّ ٱلْعَٰلَمِينَ ١٣١ وَوَصَّىٰ بِهَآ إِبْرَٰهِـۧمُ بَنِيهِ
وَيَعْقُوبُ يَٰبَنِىَّ إِنَّ ٱللَّهَ ٱصْطَفَىٰ لَكُمُ ٱلدِّينَ فَلَا تَمُوتُنَّ إِلَّا
وَأَنتُم مُّسْلِمُونَ ١٣٢ أَمْ كُنتُمْ شُهَدَآءَ إِذْ حَضَرَ يَعْقُوبَ
ٱلْمَوْتُ إِذْ قَالَ لِبَنِيهِ مَا تَعْبُدُونَ مِنۢ بَعْدِى قَالُوا۟ نَعْبُدُ
إِلَٰهَكَ وَإِلَٰهَ ءَابَآئِكَ إِبْرَٰهِـۧمَ وَإِسْمَٰعِيلَ وَإِسْحَٰقَ إِلَٰهًا
وَٰحِدًا وَنَحْنُ لَهُۥ مُسْلِمُونَ ١٣٣ تِلْكَ أُمَّةٌ قَدْ خَلَتْۖ لَهَا
مَا كَسَبَتْ وَلَكُم مَّا كَسَبْتُمْۖ وَلَا تُسْـَٔلُونَ عَمَّا كَانُوا۟ يَعْمَلُونَ ١٣٤
وَقَالُوا۟ كُونُوا۟ هُودًا أَوْ نَصَٰرَىٰ تَهْتَدُوا۟ۗ قُلْ بَلْ مِلَّةَ إِبْرَٰهِـۧمَ
حَنِيفًاۖ وَمَا كَانَ مِنَ ٱلْمُشْرِكِينَ ١٣٥ قُولُوٓا۟ ءَامَنَّا بِٱللَّهِ وَمَآ
أُنزِلَ إِلَيْنَا وَمَآ أُنزِلَ إِلَىٰٓ إِبْرَٰهِـۧمَ وَإِسْمَٰعِيلَ وَإِسْحَٰقَ وَيَعْقُوبَ
وَٱلْأَسْبَاطِ وَمَآ أُوتِىَ مُوسَىٰ وَعِيسَىٰ وَمَآ أُوتِىَ ٱلنَّبِيُّونَ
مِن رَّبِّهِمْ لَا نُفَرِّقُ بَيْنَ أَحَدٍ مِّنْهُمْ وَنَحْنُ لَهُۥ مُسْلِمُونَ ١٣٦
فَإِنْ ءَامَنُوا۟ بِمِثْلِ مَآ ءَامَنتُم بِهِۦ فَقَدِ ٱهْتَدَوا۟ۖ وَّإِن تَوَلَّوْا۟ فَإِنَّمَا
هُمْ فِى شِقَاقٍۖ فَسَيَكْفِيكَهُمُ ٱللَّهُۚ وَهُوَ ٱلسَّمِيعُ ٱلْعَلِيمُ
١٣٧ صِبْغَةَ ٱللَّهِۖ وَمَنْ أَحْسَنُ مِنَ ٱللَّهِ صِبْغَةًۖ وَنَحْنُ لَهُۥ
عَٰبِدُونَ ١٣٨ قُلْ أَتُحَآجُّونَنَا فِى ٱللَّهِ وَهُوَ رَبُّنَا وَرَبُّكُمْ
وَلَنَآ أَعْمَٰلُنَا وَلَكُمْ أَعْمَٰلُكُمْ وَنَحْنُ لَهُۥ مُخْلِصُونَ ١٣٩ أَمْ

– or someone who makes light of it and demeans it? ***We chose him*** (Ibrāhīm) ***in this world*** for the Message and the close friendship of Allah ***and in the Next World he will be one of the righteous*** and he will have a very high rank.

131. Remember ***when his Lord said to him, "Become a Muslim*** and obey Allah and make the *dīn* sincerely His!" ***he said, "I am a Muslim who has submitted to the Lord of all the worlds."***

132. ***Ibrāhīm directed*** (read as *waṣā* and *awṣā*) ***his sons to this*** religion, ***as did Ya'qūb*** his sons: He said, ***"My sons! Allah has chosen this* dīn** (Islam) ***for you, so do not die except as Muslims."*** They are commanded not to abandon Islam and to remain firm as Muslims until they die.

133. When the Jews said, "Do you not know that when he died, Ya'qūb commanded his sons to follow Judaism?", this *āyat* was revealed which begins with *am*, which makes it a question. ***Or were you present when death came to Ya'qūb and he said to his sons, "What will you worship when I have gone*** (after my death)***?" They said, "We will worship your God, the God of your forefathers, Ibrāhīm and Ismā'īl*** (Ismā'īl is counted as a forefather because the uncle is counted with the father) ***and Isḥāq – one God*** (an appositive for "your God"). ***We are Muslims submitted to Him."*** This is what actually happened. Those Jews were not present and they have ascribed to him something which he did not say.

134. ***That***, referring to Ibrāhīm and Ya'qūb and their sons, ***was a community which has long since passed away.*** It is past and gone. ***It has what it earned*** by their actions, meaning the repayment for that. ***You***, O Jews, ***have what you have earned. You will not be questioned about what they did,*** as they will not be questioned about what you did. This sentence stresses what was said before it.

135. ***They say, "Be Jews or Christians and you will be guided."*** *"Or"* marks the distinction between two separate statements. The first statement was made by the Jews of Madina and the second by the Christians of Najrān. ***Say*** to them, ***"Rather adopt*** and follow ***the religion of Ibrāhīm, a man of natural pure belief.*** A man of natural pure belief (*ḥanīf*) is one who naturally inclines from all other religions to the Straight *Dīn*. ***He was not one of the idolaters."***

136. ***Say*** (addressed to the believers), ***"We believe in Allah and what has been sent down to us*** of the Qur'ān ***and what was sent down to Ibrāhīm*** of the Ten Scrolls ***and Ismā'īl and Isḥāq and Ya'qūb and the Tribes,*** his sons, ***and what Mūsā and 'Īsā were given,*** the Torah and the Gospel respectively, ***and what all the Prophets were given by their Lord*** by way of Books and Signs. ***We do not differentiate between any of them,*** making us believe in some and reject some as the Jews and Christians do. ***We are Muslims submitted to Him."***

137. ***If their belief*** (that of the Jews and Christians) ***is the same as yours then they are guided. But if they turn away*** from believing in it, ***they are entrenched in hostility*** and clear opposition to you. ***Allah will be enough for you***, O Muḥammad, ***against them*** and will deal with their hostility. ***He is the All-Hearing,*** hearing their words, ***the All-Knowing***, knowing their states. That actually happened through the killing of Qurayẓa and the expulsion of Naḍīr and the imposition of the *jizya* on all the People of the Book.

138. ***The colouring*** (a verbal noun reinforcing "we believe" in 2:136 above which implies: "Allah has coloured us.") ***of Allah – and what colouring could be better than Allah's?*** (i.e. none is better.) What is meant is the *dīn* on which He naturally formed people so that its effect appears on the person who adopts it, as the dye shows in a garment. There is nothing better than it. ***It is Him we worship.***

139. The Jews said to the Muslims, "We are the people of the first Book and our *qibla* is older, and there were no Prophets among the Arabs. If Muḥammad were a Prophet, he would have been one of us," and then this *āyat* was revealed. ***Say*** to them, ***"Do you argue with us about Allah*** who has chosen a Prophet from among the Arabs ***when He is our Lord and your Lord*** and so He can choose anyone He wills? ***We have our actions*** for which we will be repaid ***and you have your actions*** for which you will be repaid. It is not impossible that our actions may entitle us to ennoblement. ***We act for Him alone."*** We are sincerely devoted to Allah in our actions and the *dīn* as you are not. So we are more entitled to be chosen. The question implies disapproval. The three sentences describe different states.

تَقُولُونَ إِنَّ إِبْرَٰهِـۧمَ وَإِسْمَٰعِيلَ وَإِسْحَٰقَ وَيَعْقُوبَ
وَٱلْأَسْبَاطَ كَانُوا۟ هُودًا أَوْ نَصَٰرَىٰ ۗ قُلْ ءَأَنتُمْ أَعْلَمُ أَمِ ٱللَّهُ ۗ
وَمَنْ أَظْلَمُ مِمَّن كَتَمَ شَهَٰدَةً عِندَهُۥ مِنَ ٱللَّهِ ۗ وَمَا ٱللَّهُ
بِغَٰفِلٍ عَمَّا تَعْمَلُونَ ﴿١٤٠﴾ تِلْكَ أُمَّةٌ قَدْ خَلَتْ ۖ لَهَا مَا كَسَبَتْ
وَلَكُم مَّا كَسَبْتُمْ ۖ وَلَا تُسْـَٔلُونَ عَمَّا كَانُوا۟ يَعْمَلُونَ ﴿١٤١﴾
۞ سَيَقُولُ ٱلسُّفَهَآءُ مِنَ ٱلنَّاسِ مَا وَلَّىٰهُمْ عَن قِبْلَتِهِمُ ٱلَّتِى كَانُوا۟
عَلَيْهَا ۚ قُل لِّلَّهِ ٱلْمَشْرِقُ وَٱلْمَغْرِبُ ۚ يَهْدِى مَن يَشَآءُ إِلَىٰ صِرَٰطٍ
مُّسْتَقِيمٍ ﴿١٤٢﴾ وَكَذَٰلِكَ جَعَلْنَٰكُمْ أُمَّةً وَسَطًا لِّتَكُونُوا۟
شُهَدَآءَ عَلَى ٱلنَّاسِ وَيَكُونَ ٱلرَّسُولُ عَلَيْكُمْ شَهِيدًا ۗ وَمَا
جَعَلْنَا ٱلْقِبْلَةَ ٱلَّتِى كُنتَ عَلَيْهَآ إِلَّا لِنَعْلَمَ مَن يَتَّبِعُ ٱلرَّسُولَ
مِمَّن يَنقَلِبُ عَلَىٰ عَقِبَيْهِ ۚ وَإِن كَانَتْ لَكَبِيرَةً إِلَّا عَلَى ٱلَّذِينَ
هَدَى ٱللَّهُ ۗ وَمَا كَانَ ٱللَّهُ لِيُضِيعَ إِيمَٰنَكُمْ ۚ إِنَّ ٱللَّهَ بِٱلنَّاسِ
لَرَءُوفٌ رَّحِيمٌ ﴿١٤٣﴾ قَدْ نَرَىٰ تَقَلُّبَ وَجْهِكَ فِى ٱلسَّمَآءِ ۖ
فَلَنُوَلِّيَنَّكَ قِبْلَةً تَرْضَىٰهَا ۚ فَوَلِّ وَجْهَكَ شَطْرَ ٱلْمَسْجِدِ
ٱلْحَرَامِ ۚ وَحَيْثُ مَا كُنتُمْ فَوَلُّوا۟ وُجُوهَكُمْ شَطْرَهُۥ ۗ وَإِنَّ ٱلَّذِينَ
أُوتُوا۟ ٱلْكِتَٰبَ لَيَعْلَمُونَ أَنَّهُ ٱلْحَقُّ مِن رَّبِّهِمْ ۗ وَمَا ٱللَّهُ بِغَٰفِلٍ
عَمَّا يَعْمَلُونَ ﴿١٤٤﴾ وَلَئِنْ أَتَيْتَ ٱلَّذِينَ أُوتُوا۟ ٱلْكِتَٰبَ بِكُلِّ
ءَايَةٍ مَّا تَبِعُوا۟ قِبْلَتَكَ ۚ وَمَآ أَنتَ بِتَابِعٍ قِبْلَتَهُمْ ۚ وَمَا بَعْضُهُم
بِتَابِعٍ قِبْلَةَ بَعْضٍ ۚ وَلَئِنِ ٱتَّبَعْتَ أَهْوَآءَهُم مِّنۢ بَعْدِ
مَا جَآءَكَ مِنَ ٱلْعِلْمِ ۙ إِنَّكَ إِذًا لَّمِنَ ٱلظَّٰلِمِينَ ﴿١٤٥﴾

140. ***Or do you say*** (read as *taqūlūn* "you say" and *yaqūlūn* "they say") ***that Ibrāhīm and Ismā'īl and Isḥāq and Ya'qūb and the Tribes were Jews or Christians? Say*** to them, ***"Do you know better or Allah?"*** This means, of course, that Allah knows better. Allah disassociated Ibrāhīm from them in saying, *"Ibrāhīm was neither a Jew nor a Christian."* (3:67) Those mentioned with him followed him. ***Who could do greater wrong than someone who hides*** from people ***the evidence he has been given by Allah?*** This means that no one does greater wrong than someone who conceals the evidence they have, and refers to those Jews who concealed the testimony of Allah in the Torah about Ibrāhīm following the *Ḥanafiyya* (natural *dīn*). ***Allah is not unaware of what you do.*** This is a threat.

141. ***That was a community which has long since passed away. It has what it earned. You have what you have earned. You will not be questioned about what they did.*** This has already been covered in the commentary on *āyat* 134 above.

142. ***The fools*** (the ignorant) ***among the people*** (the Jews and idolaters) ***will ask, "What has made them*** (the Prophet and believers) ***turn around from the direction they used to face*** when the *qibla* changed from Jerusalem to Makka?" The fact that the future particle is used in "will ask" indicates that it is a report from the Unseen about something which had not yet occurred. ***Say, "Both East and West belong to Allah.*** All directions belong to Allah and He can command any direction He likes and cannot be opposed. ***He guides whoever He wills to a straight path*** (the *dīn* of Islam)." Some people are guided to that.

143. ***In this way***, by guiding you to it, ***We have made you***, community of Muḥammad, ***a middlemost nation,*** good and just, ***so that you may act as witnesses against mankind*** on the Day of Rising that the Messengers conveyed the Message ***and the Messenger as a witness against you*** that he conveyed it. ***We only appointed the direction you used to face,*** which was the Ka'ba towards which the Prophet had first prayed; when he emigrated, he was commanded to face Jerusalem as the Jews did, and he did so for sixteen or seventeen months, after which the *qibla* changed back, ***in order to distinguish*** manifestly ***those who follow the Messenger*** and confirm him ***from those who turn round on their heels*** and revert to unbelief, doubting the *dīn* and thinking that the Prophet, may Allah bless him and grant him peace, was confused about that matter. One group reverted. ***Though in truth it*** (turning towards it) ***is a very hard thing*** and difficult for people – ***except for those*** among them ***Allah has guided. Allah would never let your belief go to waste.*** Allah would not allow your prayers towards Jerusalem to be wasted. He will reward you for them. The reason for the revelation of this sentence was a question which was asked regarding those who had died before the change. ***Allah is All-Gentle, Most Merciful to mankind*** to the believers, in not letting their actions go to waste. Gentleness (*ra'fa*) means intense compassion.

144. ***We have*** certainly ***seen you looking up into heaven, turning this way and that,*** hoping for Revelation and yearning for the command to face the Ka'ba, desiring that because the Ka'ba was the *qibla* of Ibrāhīm and because the Prophet was calling on the Arabs to become Muslim, ***so We will turn*** and change ***you towards a direction which will please you*** and which you like. ***Turn your face*** in the prayer, ***therefore, towards the Sacred Mosque,*** the Ka'ba. ***Wherever you are,*** O community, ***turn your faces towards it*** in the prayer. ***Those given the Book know it*** (facing the Ka'ba) ***is the*** firm ***truth from their Lord*** because of what their Books say regarding the description of the Prophet and that he would turn towards it. ***Allah is not unaware of what they do*** (read as *y̲a'malun*, "what they do", and *t̲a'malun*, "what you do"). The former implies that Allah is not unaware of what the Jews do, who know the truth about the *qibla* and the latter that He is not unaware of the believers and what they do in respect of obeying the command to change the *qibla.*

145. ***If you were to bring every Sign*** confirming your truthfulness regarding the matter of the *qibla* ***to those given the Book, they still would not follow your direction*** out of stubbornness. ***You do not follow their direction.*** This stops any desire of his for them to become Muslim because they desire him to revert to their position. ***They do not follow each other's direction.*** The Jews do not follow the direction of the Christians and vice versa. ***If,*** theoretically, ***you followed their whims and desires*** to which they call you, ***after the knowledge*** of Revelation ***that has come to you, you would then be one of the wrongdoers.***

ٱلَّذِينَ ءَاتَيۡنَٰهُمُ ٱلۡكِتَٰبَ يَعۡرِفُونَهُۥ كَمَا يَعۡرِفُونَ أَبۡنَآءَهُمۡۖ وَإِنَّ
فَرِيقٗا مِّنۡهُمۡ لَيَكۡتُمُونَ ٱلۡحَقَّ وَهُمۡ يَعۡلَمُونَ ١٤٦ ٱلۡحَقُّ مِن
رَّبِّكَۖ فَلَا تَكُونَنَّ مِنَ ٱلۡمُمۡتَرِينَ ١٤٧ وَلِكُلّٖ وِجۡهَةٌ هُوَ مُوَلِّيهَاۖ
فَٱسۡتَبِقُواْ ٱلۡخَيۡرَٰتِۚ أَيۡنَ مَا تَكُونُواْ يَأۡتِ بِكُمُ ٱللَّهُ جَمِيعًاۚ
إِنَّ ٱللَّهَ عَلَىٰ كُلِّ شَيۡءٖ قَدِيرٞ ١٤٨ وَمِنۡ حَيۡثُ خَرَجۡتَ فَوَلِّ
وَجۡهَكَ شَطۡرَ ٱلۡمَسۡجِدِ ٱلۡحَرَامِۖ وَإِنَّهُۥ لَلۡحَقُّ مِن رَّبِّكَۗ وَمَا
ٱللَّهُ بِغَٰفِلٍ عَمَّا تَعۡمَلُونَ ١٤٩ وَمِنۡ حَيۡثُ خَرَجۡتَ فَوَلِّ وَجۡهَكَ
شَطۡرَ ٱلۡمَسۡجِدِ ٱلۡحَرَامِۚ وَحَيۡثُ مَا كُنتُمۡ فَوَلُّواْ وُجُوهَكُمۡ
شَطۡرَهُۥ لِئَلَّا يَكُونَ لِلنَّاسِ عَلَيۡكُمۡ حُجَّةٌ إِلَّا ٱلَّذِينَ ظَلَمُواْ
مِنۡهُمۡ فَلَا تَخۡشَوۡهُمۡ وَٱخۡشَوۡنِي وَلِأُتِمَّ نِعۡمَتِي عَلَيۡكُمۡ وَلَعَلَّكُمۡ
تَهۡتَدُونَ ١٥٠ كَمَآ أَرۡسَلۡنَا فِيكُمۡ رَسُولٗا مِّنكُمۡ
يَتۡلُواْ عَلَيۡكُمۡ ءَايَٰتِنَا وَيُزَكِّيكُمۡ وَيُعَلِّمُكُمُ ٱلۡكِتَٰبَ
وَٱلۡحِكۡمَةَ وَيُعَلِّمُكُم مَّا لَمۡ تَكُونُواْ تَعۡلَمُونَ ١٥١ فَٱذۡكُرُونِيٓ
أَذۡكُرۡكُمۡ وَٱشۡكُرُواْ لِي وَلَا تَكۡفُرُونِ ١٥٢ يَٰٓأَيُّهَا ٱلَّذِينَ
ءَامَنُواْ ٱسۡتَعِينُواْ بِٱلصَّبۡرِ وَٱلصَّلَوٰةِۚ إِنَّ ٱللَّهَ مَعَ ٱلصَّٰبِرِينَ ١٥٣
وَلَا تَقُولُواْ لِمَن يُقۡتَلُ فِي سَبِيلِ ٱللَّهِ أَمۡوَٰتُۢۚ بَلۡ أَحۡيَآءٞ وَلَٰكِن
لَّا تَشۡعُرُونَ ١٥٤ وَلَنَبۡلُوَنَّكُم بِشَيۡءٖ مِّنَ ٱلۡخَوۡفِ وَٱلۡجُوعِ
وَنَقۡصٖ مِّنَ ٱلۡأَمۡوَٰلِ وَٱلۡأَنفُسِ وَٱلثَّمَرَٰتِۗ وَبَشِّرِ ٱلصَّٰبِرِينَ
١٥٥ ٱلَّذِينَ إِذَآ أَصَٰبَتۡهُم مُّصِيبَةٞ قَالُوٓاْ إِنَّا لِلَّهِ وَإِنَّآ إِلَيۡهِ رَٰجِعُونَ
١٥٦ أُوْلَٰٓئِكَ عَلَيۡهِمۡ صَلَوَٰتٞ مِّن رَّبِّهِمۡ وَرَحۡمَةٞۖ وَأُوْلَٰٓئِكَ

146. ***Those We have given the Book recognise him*** (Muḥammad) ***as they recognise their own sons*** because they have his description in their books. Ibn Salām said, "When I saw him, I recognised him as I recognise my son." Indeed the recognition of Muḥammad is even more immediate. ***Yet a group of them knowingly conceal the truth*** of his description despite their full knowledge of it.

147. ***The truth is from your Lord, so on no account be among the doubters.*** Do not be among those who doubt it in any manner. This is more intensive than just "Do not doubt."

148. ***Each*** (community) ***person faces a particular direction*** (*qibla*) to which they turn in their prayer and remembrance of their Lord, ***so race each other to the good*** by hastening to acts of obedience and hoping for their acceptance. ***Wherever you are, Allah will bring you all together*** on the Day of Rising and repay you for your deeds. ***Truly Allah has power over all things.***

149. ***Wherever you come from*** when you have been on a journey, ***turn your face to the Sacred Mosque. This is certainly the truth from your Lord. Allah is not unaware of what you do*** (read as *ta'malun,*"what you do", and *ya'malun,* "what they do"). The instruction to face the Sacred Mosque is reiterated to clarify that the ruling to do this applies when travelling and in all other situations.

150. ***Wherever you come from, turn your face to the Sacred Mosque. Wherever you are, turn your faces towards it,*** a further repetition for stress, ***so that people*** (the Jews and the idolaters) ***will have no argument against you,*** no grounds for arguing with you about turning to another *qibla.* This is said to negate the position which had been taken by the Jews and idolaters regarding the *qibla.* The Jews had been saying, "He denies our *dīn*, but follows our *qibla.*" And the idolaters had been saying, "He claims to follow the religion of Ibrāhīm but faces a different *qibla* to it." ***except for those among them who do wrong*** by their obdurate stubbornness. They then said that the Prophet, may Allah bless him and grant him peace, only chose Makka because he inclined to the *dīn* of his ancestors. The sentence means. "No one will speak against you except those people." ***And then you should not fear them*** regarding their quarrelling about your change of *qibla* ***but rather fear Me*** by obeying My command – ***and so that I may complete My blessing upon you***

by guiding you to the salient points of your *dīn*, ***so that hopefully you will be guided*** to the Truth.

151. ***For this,*** to complete it, ***We sent a Messenger to you from among you,*** Muḥammad, may Allah bless him and grant him peace, ***to recite Our Signs*** (the Qur'ān) ***to you and purify you*** from *shirk,* ***and teach you the Book*** (the Qur'ān) ***and Wisdom*** (the judgements it contains) ***and teach you things you did not know before.***

152. ***Remember Me*** by the prayer and glorification and other such things – ***I will remember you.*** It is said that this means "I will requite you." In a *ḥadīth qudsī* we find: "Whoever remembers Me in himself, I remember him in Myself. Whoever remembers Me in an assembly, I remember him in a better assembly than it." ***Show thanks to Me*** by obeying Me ***and do not be ungrateful*** by disobeying Me.

153. ***O you who believe, seek help*** for the Next World ***in steadfastness*** in obedience and in the face of misfortune ***and the prayer.*** The prayer is mentioned because it is done repeatedly and has great stature. ***Allah is with the steadfast*** by helping them.

154. ***Do not say that those who are killed in the Way of Allah are dead. On the contrary, they are alive*** (According to a *ḥadīth* their spirits are in the beaks of green birds going wherever they wish in the Garden) ***but you are not aware of it.*** You have no knowledge of that.

155. ***We will test you with a certain amount of fear*** of the enemy ***and hunger*** through drought ***and loss of wealth*** by destruction ***and life*** through fighting, old age and illness ***and fruits*** through pests. This is to test you to see if you will be steadfast. ***But give good news to the steadfast*** that they will have the Garden in return for the affliction they have suffered with patience*:*

156. ***Those who, when disaster strikes them, say, "We belong to Allah and to Him we will return."*** Meaning: "We are the property and slaves of Allah and He can do what He wills with us. We return to Him in the Next World where He will requite us." In the *ḥadīth*, "If anyone says this in affliction, Allah will repay him and give him a better replacement." It is reported that the Prophet's lamp went out

هُمُ ٱلْمُهْتَدُونَ ﴿١٥٧﴾ ۞ إِنَّ ٱلصَّفَا وَٱلْمَرْوَةَ مِن شَعَآئِرِ ٱللَّهِ ۖ
فَمَنْ حَجَّ ٱلْبَيْتَ أَوِ ٱعْتَمَرَ فَلَا جُنَاحَ عَلَيْهِ أَن يَطَّوَّفَ
بِهِمَا ۚ وَمَن تَطَوَّعَ خَيْرًا فَإِنَّ ٱللَّهَ شَاكِرٌ عَلِيمٌ ﴿١٥٨﴾ إِنَّ ٱلَّذِينَ
يَكْتُمُونَ مَآ أَنزَلْنَا مِنَ ٱلْبَيِّنَٰتِ وَٱلْهُدَىٰ مِنۢ بَعْدِ مَا بَيَّنَّٰهُ
لِلنَّاسِ فِى ٱلْكِتَٰبِ ۙ أُو۟لَٰٓئِكَ يَلْعَنُهُمُ ٱللَّهُ وَيَلْعَنُهُمُ ٱللَّٰعِنُونَ
﴿١٥٩﴾ إِلَّا ٱلَّذِينَ تَابُوا۟ وَأَصْلَحُوا۟ وَبَيَّنُوا۟ فَأُو۟لَٰٓئِكَ أَتُوبُ
عَلَيْهِمْ ۚ وَأَنَا ٱلتَّوَّابُ ٱلرَّحِيمُ ﴿١٦٠﴾ إِنَّ ٱلَّذِينَ كَفَرُوا۟ وَمَاتُوا۟ وَهُمْ
كُفَّارٌ أُو۟لَٰٓئِكَ عَلَيْهِمْ لَعْنَةُ ٱللَّهِ وَٱلْمَلَٰٓئِكَةِ وَٱلنَّاسِ أَجْمَعِينَ
﴿١٦١﴾ خَٰلِدِينَ فِيهَا ۖ لَا يُخَفَّفُ عَنْهُمُ ٱلْعَذَابُ وَلَا هُمْ يُنظَرُونَ
﴿١٦٢﴾ وَإِلَٰهُكُمْ إِلَٰهٌ وَٰحِدٌ ۖ لَّآ إِلَٰهَ إِلَّا هُوَ ٱلرَّحْمَٰنُ ٱلرَّحِيمُ ﴿١٦٣﴾
إِنَّ فِى خَلْقِ ٱلسَّمَٰوَٰتِ وَٱلْأَرْضِ وَٱخْتِلَٰفِ ٱلَّيْلِ وَٱلنَّهَارِ
وَٱلْفُلْكِ ٱلَّتِى تَجْرِى فِى ٱلْبَحْرِ بِمَا يَنفَعُ ٱلنَّاسَ وَمَآ أَنزَلَ ٱللَّهُ
مِنَ ٱلسَّمَآءِ مِن مَّآءٍ فَأَحْيَا بِهِ ٱلْأَرْضَ بَعْدَ مَوْتِهَا وَبَثَّ فِيهَا
مِن كُلِّ دَآبَّةٍ وَتَصْرِيفِ ٱلرِّيَٰحِ وَٱلسَّحَابِ ٱلْمُسَخَّرِ
بَيْنَ ٱلسَّمَآءِ وَٱلْأَرْضِ لَءَايَٰتٍ لِّقَوْمٍ يَعْقِلُونَ ﴿١٦٤﴾ وَمِنَ
ٱلنَّاسِ مَن يَتَّخِذُ مِن دُونِ ٱللَّهِ أَندَادًا يُحِبُّونَهُمْ كَحُبِّ ٱللَّهِ ۖ
وَٱلَّذِينَ ءَامَنُوٓا۟ أَشَدُّ حُبًّا لِّلَّهِ ۗ وَلَوْ يَرَى ٱلَّذِينَ ظَلَمُوٓا۟ إِذْ يَرَوْنَ
ٱلْعَذَابَ أَنَّ ٱلْقُوَّةَ لِلَّهِ جَمِيعًا وَأَنَّ ٱللَّهَ شَدِيدُ ٱلْعَذَابِ ﴿١٦٥﴾
إِذْ تَبَرَّأَ ٱلَّذِينَ ٱتُّبِعُوا۟ مِنَ ٱلَّذِينَ ٱتَّبَعُوا۟ وَرَأَوُا۟ ٱلْعَذَابَ
وَتَقَطَّعَتْ بِهِمُ ٱلْأَسْبَابُ ﴿١٦٦﴾ وَقَالَ ٱلَّذِينَ ٱتَّبَعُوا۟ لَوْ أَنَّ

and he said this. 'Ā'isha said, "It is only a lamp." He said, "Everything that annoys a believer is affliction." (Abū Dāwūd)

157. ***Those are the ones who will have blessings*** of forgiveness ***and mercy*** and comfort ***from their Lord; they are the ones who are the guided*** to what is right.

158. ***Ṣafā and Marwa*** (two rocky outcrops in Makka) ***are among the Sacred Landmarks of Allah*** (the signs of the *Dīn* of Allah, *sha'ā'ir* is the plural of *sha'īra*), ***so anyone who goes on ḥajj to the House or does 'umra incurs no wrong*** (sin) ***in going back and forth*** (*sa'y*) ***between them.*** The root meaning of "going on *ḥajj*" is to aim for and doing *'umra* means visiting. You go between them seven times. This was revealed when the Muslims disliked doing that because the people of the *Jāhiliyya* used to do it and there were idols on them which they used to touch. Ibn 'Abbās said that *sa'y* is not an obligation since removal of sin implies choice. Ash-Shāfi'ī and others said that it is a pillar and the Prophet, may Allah bless him and grant him peace, made it clear that it is obligatory when he said, "Allah has prescribed *sa'y* for you" (al-Bayhaqī). He said, "Begin with what Allah began with," meaning start at Ṣafā. (Muslim) ***If anyone spontaneously does good*** (read as *taṭawwa'* or *yaṭṭawwa'*), meaning any good he does which is not imposed on him, such as *ṭawāf* or anything else, ***Allah is All-Thankful*** and will show gratitude for his action by rewarding him for it, ***All-Knowing*** of what he does.

159. This *āyat* was revealed about the Jews. ***Those*** people ***who hide the Clear Signs and Guidance We have sent down***, such as the *āyat* of stoning and the description of Muḥammad, ***after We have made it clear to people in the Book*** (the Torah), ***Allah curses them*** by putting them far from His mercy, ***and the cursers curse them*** – The cursers are the angels and the believers, or everything which calls down the curse on them.

160. ***...except for those who repent*** and turn away from that ***and put things right*** by acting righteously ***and make things*** they had concealed ***clear. I turn towards them*** and accept their repentance. ***I am the Ever-Relenting, the Most Merciful*** to the believers.

161. ***But as for those who disbelieve, and die while still unbelievers, the curse of Allah is upon them and that of the angels and all mankind.*** They deserve that both in this world and the Next. The curse is said to be universal or that of believers.

162. ***They will be under it*** (the curse and the Fire) ***forever. The punishment will not be lightened for them*** for even the blink of an eye. ***They will be granted no reprieve,*** enabling them to repent or offer excuses.

163. This *āyat* was revealed when they said, "Describe your Lord to us." ***Your God*** who deserves to be worshipped by you ***is One God*** since there is none like Him in His Essence or His attributes. ***There is no god but Him.*** He is ***the All-Merciful, the Most Merciful.*** They asked the Prophet for evidence and the next *āyat* was revealed.

164. ***In the creation of the heavens and the earth*** and all the wonders they contain, ***and the alternation of the night and day,*** their coming and going, shortening and lengthening, ***and the*** heavy ***ships which sail*** and do not sink in ***the seas to people's benefit*** with regard to commerce and transport, ***and the water*** (rain) ***which Allah sends down from the sky – by which He brings the earth to life*** with plants ***when it was dead*** and dry ***and scatters about in it creatures of every kind*** which grow by eating the plants – ***and the varying direction of the winds,*** which change and veer to north and south, and are both hot and cold, ***and the clouds subservient between heaven and earth*** driven by the command of Allah wherever He wishes, ***there are Signs*** which indicate His Oneness ***for people who use their intellect*** and reflect.

165. ***Some people set up equals*** (idols) ***to Allah*** other than Him, ***loving*** and esteeming ***them*** and humbling themselves to them ***as they should love Allah. But those who believe have more love for Allah*** than the others have for their idols because they do not turn from Him at all in any state, whereas when the unbelievers are suffering hardship, then they turn to Allah. ***If only,*** Muḥammad, ***you could see*** (know) ***those who do wrong*** by making others equal to Allah ***at the time when they see the punishment,*** then you would see something truly terrible, ***and that*** is because ***truly all strength*** (all power and sovereignty) ***belongs to Allah, and that Allah is severe in punishment.*** If only they knew in this world about the punishment of Allah

لَنَا كَرَّةً فَنَتَبَرَّأَ مِنْهُمْ كَمَا تَبَرَّءُوا۟ مِنَّا ۗ كَذَٰلِكَ يُرِيهِمُ ٱللَّهُ
أَعْمَٰلَهُمْ حَسَرَٰتٍ عَلَيْهِمْ ۖ وَمَا هُم بِخَٰرِجِينَ مِنَ ٱلنَّارِ ﴿١٦٧﴾
يَٰٓأَيُّهَا ٱلنَّاسُ كُلُوا۟ مِمَّا فِى ٱلْأَرْضِ حَلَٰلًا طَيِّبًا وَلَا تَتَّبِعُوا۟
خُطُوَٰتِ ٱلشَّيْطَٰنِ ۚ إِنَّهُۥ لَكُمْ عَدُوٌّ مُّبِينٌ ﴿١٦٨﴾ إِنَّمَا يَأْمُرُكُم
بِٱلسُّوٓءِ وَٱلْفَحْشَآءِ وَأَن تَقُولُوا۟ عَلَى ٱللَّهِ مَا لَا تَعْلَمُونَ ﴿١٦٩﴾
وَإِذَا قِيلَ لَهُمُ ٱتَّبِعُوا۟ مَآ أَنزَلَ ٱللَّهُ قَالُوا۟ بَلْ نَتَّبِعُ مَآ أَلْفَيْنَا عَلَيْهِ
ءَابَآءَنَآ ۗ أَوَلَوْ كَانَ ءَابَآؤُهُمْ لَا يَعْقِلُونَ شَيْـًٔا وَلَا
يَهْتَدُونَ ﴿١٧٠﴾ وَمَثَلُ ٱلَّذِينَ كَفَرُوا۟ كَمَثَلِ ٱلَّذِى يَنْعِقُ
بِمَا لَا يَسْمَعُ إِلَّا دُعَآءً وَنِدَآءً ۚ صُمٌّۢ بُكْمٌ عُمْىٌ فَهُمْ لَا يَعْقِلُونَ
﴿١٧١﴾ يَٰٓأَيُّهَا ٱلَّذِينَ ءَامَنُوا۟ كُلُوا۟ مِن طَيِّبَٰتِ مَا رَزَقْنَٰكُمْ
وَٱشْكُرُوا۟ لِلَّهِ إِن كُنتُمْ إِيَّاهُ تَعْبُدُونَ ﴿١٧٢﴾ إِنَّمَا حَرَّمَ
عَلَيْكُمُ ٱلْمَيْتَةَ وَٱلدَّمَ وَلَحْمَ ٱلْخِنزِيرِ وَمَآ أُهِلَّ بِهِۦ
لِغَيْرِ ٱللَّهِ ۖ فَمَنِ ٱضْطُرَّ غَيْرَ بَاغٍ وَلَا عَادٍ فَلَآ إِثْمَ عَلَيْهِ ۚ إِنَّ ٱللَّهَ
غَفُورٌ رَّحِيمٌ ﴿١٧٣﴾ إِنَّ ٱلَّذِينَ يَكْتُمُونَ مَآ أَنزَلَ ٱللَّهُ مِنَ
ٱلْكِتَٰبِ وَيَشْتَرُونَ بِهِۦ ثَمَنًا قَلِيلًا ۙ أُو۟لَٰٓئِكَ مَا يَأْكُلُونَ
فِى بُطُونِهِمْ إِلَّا ٱلنَّارَ وَلَا يُكَلِّمُهُمُ ٱللَّهُ يَوْمَ ٱلْقِيَٰمَةِ
وَلَا يُزَكِّيهِمْ وَلَهُمْ عَذَابٌ أَلِيمٌ ﴿١٧٤﴾ أُو۟لَٰٓئِكَ ٱلَّذِينَ
ٱشْتَرَوُا۟ ٱلضَّلَٰلَةَ بِٱلْهُدَىٰ وَٱلْعَذَابَ بِٱلْمَغْفِرَةِ ۚ فَمَآ
أَصْبَرَهُمْ عَلَى ٱلنَّارِ ﴿١٧٥﴾ ذَٰلِكَ بِأَنَّ ٱللَّهَ نَزَّلَ ٱلْكِتَٰبَ
بِٱلْحَقِّ ۗ وَإِنَّ ٱلَّذِينَ ٱخْتَلَفُوا۟ فِى ٱلْكِتَٰبِ لَفِى شِقَاقٍ بَعِيدٍ ﴿١٧٦﴾

and that power belongs to Allah alone – but that will only be seen on the Day of Rising – they would never have made anything else equal to Allah in their sight.

166. ***When those who were followed*** (the leaders) ***disown those who followed them*** and deny that they misguided them, ***and they see the punishment, and the connection between them is cut,*** the connection of kinship and love between them in this world being what is severed,

167. ***...those who followed will say, "If only we could have another chance*** to return to this world, ***we would disown them*** (those they followed) ***just as they have disowned us*** today.***" In that way Allah will show them their*** evil ***actions,*** when they see the severity of His punishment and disown one another, ***as a cause of anguish and remorse*** and regret ***for them. They will never emerge from the Fire*** once they have entered it.

168. This *āyat* was revealed about those who forbade eating certain grazing animals. ***Mankind! eat what is good and lawful***, stressing its enjoyability ***on the earth. And do not follow in the footsteps of Shayṭān:*** his way. ***He truly is an outright enemy to you.*** He is a clear enemy.

169. ***He only commands you to do evil*** (sin) ***and indecent acts*** which are considered ugly in terms of the Sharī'a ***and to say about Allah what you do not know.*** *Shayṭān* causes you to make unlawful what is not unlawful and other such things.

170. ***When they*** (the unbelievers) ***are told, "Follow what Allah has sent down to you*** regarding *tawḥīd* and considering wholesome things lawful," ***They say, "We are following what we found our fathers doing*** with regard to worshipping idols and making certain animals unlawful." The Almighty says, ***What,*** do they follow them ***even though their fathers did not understand a thing*** about the *dīn* ***and were not guided*** to the truth? The question indicates the objection.

171. ***The likeness of those who are unbelievers*** in respect of the one who calls them to guidance ***is that of someone who yells out to something which cannot hear – it is nothing but a cry and a call,*** a noise whose meaning is not understood. When they hear the warning they do not take any notice of it, like sheep who hear the voice of their shepherd and do not understand what he says. They are ***deaf – dumb – blind. They do not use their intellect*** to understand the warning.

172. ***You who believe! Eat of the good*** (lawful) ***things We have provided for you and give thanks to Allah*** for what He has made lawful for you ***if you worship Him alone.***

173. ***He has only forbidden you*** to eat ***carrion,*** spilled ***blood,*** as from cattle, ***and pork*** (lit. meat of pigs, which is specifically mentioned because it is the main thing and the rest follows it) ***and what has been consecrated to other than Allah***, what is sacrificed in the name of anything else. Consecration refers to the words which are voiced to idols during sacrifice. It is eating these things which is forbidden, carrying on from the subject matter of the previous *āyat.* Then there are those animals which have not been slaughtered correctly. This is a general rule and the *Sunna* makes clear the specific rulings about fish and locusts. ***But anyone who is forced*** and compelled by necessity ***to eat it*** (one of these things) – ***without desiring it*** to rebel against the Muslims ***or going to excess in it*** with no intention of opposing them, as when he is involved in highway robbery – ***commits no crime*** and incurs no sin in eating. ***Allah is Ever-Forgiving, Most Merciful.*** Allah forgives His friends, and is merciful to people who obey Him in granting them this dispensation. It does not apply to rebels and aggressors, or to anyone on a journey whose aim is to go against the *Sharī'a*, or to runaway slaves and collectors of illegal taxes. It is not lawful for them to eat any of these things as long as they have not repented, as ash-Shāfi'ī says.

174. ***Those***, meaning the Jews, ***who conceal what Allah has sent down of the Book*** which includes the mention of the Prophet, may Allah bless him and grant him peace, ***and sell it cheap*** in exchange for the things of this world and out of fear of being surpassed, instead of disclosing it, ***take nothing into their bellies but the Fire*** because that will be where they end up. ***On the Day of Rising Allah will not speak to them*** because of His anger at them ***or purify them*** of the filth of their sins. ***They will have a painful punishment*** which is the Fire.

175. ***Those are the ones who have sold guidance for misguidance,*** taking what is in this world in exchange for it, ***and*** the ***forgiveness*** prepared for them in the Next World if they had not done what they did ***for*** the ***punishment*** they will now receive. ***How steadfastly they will endure the Fire!*** How strong their endurance must be! This expresses the amazement of the believers at their committing things that make the punishment inevitable with no apparent concern.

176. ***That*** (which was mentioned about their taking Fire into their bellies and what is mentioned after that) ***is because Allah has sent down the Book with truth*** and then they differed with it, believing in some of it and disbelieving in some which they conceal, ***and those who differ with the Book*** in that way ***are entrenched in hostility*** and opposition and are far from the Truth. This is generally taken as referring to the Jews but it is also said to refer to the idolaters inasmuch as they claimed that some of it was poetry, some sorcery and some soothsaying.

177. ***Goodness does not lie in turning your faces*** in the prayer ***to the East or to the West.*** This was revealed to refute the Jews and Christians in their claim. ***Rather, those with true goodness*** (read as *birr* and *barr*) ***are those who believe in Allah and the Last Day, the Angels, the Book*** (meaning Scripture generically) ***and the Prophets, and who, despite their love for it, give away their wealth to their relatives and to orphans and the very poor, and to travellers and beggars and to set slaves free*** (those with a *kitāba* contract and captives), ***and who establish the prayer and pay*** the obligatory ***zakāt*** and voluntary almsgiving; ***those who honour their contracts***, both with Allah and with people, ***when they make them, and are steadfast in poverty and in illness and in battle,*** times of hardship in general and fighting in the Way of Allah in particular. ***Those*** with this description ***are the people who are true*** in their belief or truly deserve to be called good. ***They are the people who are truly godfearing*** and fear Allah.

178. ***O you who believe!*** equal ***Retaliation is prescribed*** and obliged in description and action ***for you in the case of people killed: free man*** is killed ***for free man*** and not killed for a slave, ***slave for slave, female for female.*** The *Sunna* makes it clear that a man may be killed in retaliation for a woman. They are considered on a par in the

۞ لَّيْسَ ٱلْبِرَّ أَن تُوَلُّوا۟ وُجُوهَكُمْ قِبَلَ ٱلْمَشْرِقِ وَٱلْمَغْرِبِ وَلَـٰكِنَّ
ٱلْبِرَّ مَنْ ءَامَنَ بِٱللَّهِ وَٱلْيَوْمِ ٱلْـَٔاخِرِ وَٱلْمَلَـٰٓئِكَةِ وَٱلْكِتَـٰبِ
وَٱلنَّبِيِّـۧنَ وَءَاتَى ٱلْمَالَ عَلَىٰ حُبِّهِۦ ذَوِى ٱلْقُرْبَىٰ وَٱلْيَتَـٰمَىٰ
وَٱلْمَسَـٰكِينَ وَٱبْنَ ٱلسَّبِيلِ وَٱلسَّآئِلِينَ وَفِى ٱلرِّقَابِ وَأَقَامَ
ٱلصَّلَوٰةَ وَءَاتَى ٱلزَّكَوٰةَ وَٱلْمُوفُونَ بِعَهْدِهِمْ إِذَا عَـٰهَدُوا۟ ۖ
وَٱلصَّـٰبِرِينَ فِى ٱلْبَأْسَآءِ وَٱلضَّرَّآءِ وَحِينَ ٱلْبَأْسِ ۗ أُو۟لَـٰٓئِكَ ٱلَّذِينَ
صَدَقُوا۟ ۖ وَأُو۟لَـٰٓئِكَ هُمُ ٱلْمُتَّقُونَ ﴿١٧٧﴾ يَـٰٓأَيُّهَا ٱلَّذِينَ ءَامَنُوا۟ كُتِبَ
عَلَيْكُمُ ٱلْقِصَاصُ فِى ٱلْقَتْلَى ۖ ٱلْحُرُّ بِٱلْحُرِّ وَٱلْعَبْدُ بِٱلْعَبْدِ وَٱلْأُنثَىٰ
بِٱلْأُنثَىٰ ۚ فَمَنْ عُفِىَ لَهُۥ مِنْ أَخِيهِ شَىْءٌ فَٱتِّبَاعٌۢ بِٱلْمَعْرُوفِ وَأَدَآءٌ
إِلَيْهِ بِإِحْسَـٰنٍ ۗ ذَٰلِكَ تَخْفِيفٌ مِّن رَّبِّكُمْ وَرَحْمَةٌ ۗ فَمَنِ ٱعْتَدَىٰ
بَعْدَ ذَٰلِكَ فَلَهُۥ عَذَابٌ أَلِيمٌ ﴿١٧٨﴾ وَلَكُمْ فِى ٱلْقِصَاصِ حَيَوٰةٌ
يَـٰٓأُو۟لِى ٱلْأَلْبَـٰبِ لَعَلَّكُمْ تَتَّقُونَ ﴿١٧٩﴾ كُتِبَ عَلَيْكُمْ
إِذَا حَضَرَ أَحَدَكُمُ ٱلْمَوْتُ إِن تَرَكَ خَيْرًا ٱلْوَصِيَّةُ لِلْوَٰلِدَيْنِ
وَٱلْأَقْرَبِينَ بِٱلْمَعْرُوفِ ۖ حَقًّا عَلَى ٱلْمُتَّقِينَ ﴿١٨٠﴾ فَمَنۢ بَدَّلَهُۥ
بَعْدَمَا سَمِعَهُۥ فَإِنَّمَآ إِثْمُهُۥ عَلَى ٱلَّذِينَ يُبَدِّلُونَهُۥٓ ۚ إِنَّ ٱللَّهَ سَمِيعٌ عَلِيمٌ ﴿١٨١﴾
فَمَنْ خَافَ مِن مُّوصٍ جَنَفًا أَوْ إِثْمًا فَأَصْلَحَ بَيْنَهُمْ فَلَآ إِثْمَ
عَلَيْهِ ۚ إِنَّ ٱللَّهَ غَفُورٌ رَّحِيمٌ ﴿١٨٢﴾ يَـٰٓأَيُّهَا ٱلَّذِينَ ءَامَنُوا۟ كُتِبَ
عَلَيْكُمُ ٱلصِّيَامُ كَمَا كُتِبَ عَلَى ٱلَّذِينَ مِن قَبْلِكُمْ
لَعَلَّكُمْ تَتَّقُونَ ﴿١٨٣﴾ أَيَّامًا مَّعْدُودَٰتٍ ۚ فَمَن كَانَ مِنكُم
مَّرِيضًا أَوْ عَلَىٰ سَفَرٍ فَعِدَّةٌ مِّنْ أَيَّامٍ أُخَرَ ۚ وَعَلَى ٱلَّذِينَ

dīn. A Muslim, even a slave, cannot be killed in retaliation for a free unbeliever. ***But if someone is absolved by his brother,*** for instance when a killer is forgiven by the brother of the dead person who thereby forgoes retaliation, ***blood-money*** (the fact that this is indefinite may imply forgoing some of it or that one or some of the relatives pardon the perpetrator) ***should be claimed*** by the dead person's relative from the killer ***with correctness,*** without any harshness in asking for the blood money ***and*** it should be ***paid*** by the killer to the relative of the deceased ***with good will***, without delay or diminution. Allah uses the term "brother" in order to encourage forgiveness and also to showing that even killing does not rupture the brotherhood of faith. The fact that "correctness" follows "absolving" means that either one or the other of them is obligatory. That is one of the positions of ash-Shāfi'ī. The second is that if the parents do not specify either, there is nothing. In that case the killer must pay the money to the dead person's heir without delay or reduction. ***That*** judgement of retaliation and pardoning the killer in return for blood money ***is an easement and a mercy*** to you ***from your Lord*** since He gave you scope in that and neither of them is imposed on you in the way that retaliation is imposed on the Jews and blood money on the Christians. ***Anyone who goes beyond the limits*** – if the relative kills the murderer – ***after this*** (pardoning him) ***will receive a painful punishment*** in the Next World with the Fire, or in this world by being killed.

179. ***There is life*** and great deterrence ***for you in retaliation, people of intelligence,*** people with intellects, because if someone knows that he will be killed then he be will deterred from killing and preserve his own life as well as that of the person he wants to kill, and it was prescribed ***so that perhaps you will be godfearing*** and so that killing may be avoided out of fear of retaliation.

180. ***It is prescribed*** (obligatory for you) ***for you, when death approaches one of you*** for any reason ***and if he has some goods to leave, to make a will in favour of his parents and relatives, correctly and fairly*** with justice by not leaving away in excess of a third of your estate and not giving preference to the rich: ***a*** stressed ***duty for all who are godfearing*** and fear Allah. This was abrogated by the

Āyat of Inheritance (4:11) and the *ḥadīth* in at-Tirmidhī, "There can be no bequest for an heir."

181. ***Then if anyone*** (any witness or executor) ***alters it*** (the will) ***after hearing it*** and knowing what is in it, ***the crime*** for any alteration in what was dictated ***is on the part of those who alter it. Allah is All-Hearing,*** hearing the words, ***All-Knowing,*** knowing what was done and will repay the person for his actions.

182. ***But if anyone fears bias,*** inclining from what is right inadvertently, ***or wrongdoing,*** by deliberately exceeding the third he is allowed to leave apart from the prescribed shares or singling out someone wealthy, ***on the part of the person making the will*** (read as *muwaṣṣin* or *mawṣin*), ***and puts things right between the people involved*** by commanding what is just, ***in that case he has not committed any crime*** in doing that. ***Allah is Ever-Forgiving, Most Merciful.***

183. ***You who believe! Fasting is prescribed*** and made mandatory ***for you, as it was prescribed for those*** nations ***before you – so that hopefully you will be godfearing*** by avoiding acts of disobedience, because fasting subdues the appetites which are the beginning of such acts –

184. ***... for a specified number of days,*** of a determined number which is known: in other words, Ramaḍān, as will be mentioned. They are few in number in order to make it easy for those who are required to fast. ***But any of you who are ill*** when the time comes ***or on a journey,*** during which the prayer may be shortened and during which fasting is difficult for the traveller, he can break the fast and then he ***should fast a number of other days*** to make up those he missed. ***For those who are*** not ***able to fast*** on account of old age or an incurable illness, ***their fidya is to feed the poor,*** which involves feeding a poor person the amount normally eaten in a day, and that is considered to be a *mudd* of the staple food of the land for each day. At the beginning of Islam, people could choose between fasting and *fidya*, but then fasting became incumbent through His words, *"Whoever of you is present in the month of Ramaḍān should fast it."* Ibn 'Abbās said, "except for pregnant and nursing women" when they break the fast out of fear for their child. The *āyat* stands and is not abrogated in respect of them. ***And if someone does good of his***

يُطِيقُونَهُۥ فِدْيَةٌ طَعَامُ مِسْكِينٍ ۖ فَمَن تَطَوَّعَ خَيْرًا فَهُوَ خَيْرٌ
لَّهُۥ ۚ وَأَن تَصُومُوا۟ خَيْرٌ لَّكُمْ ۖ إِن كُنتُمْ تَعْلَمُونَ ﴿١٨٤﴾ شَهْرُ
رَمَضَانَ ٱلَّذِىٓ أُنزِلَ فِيهِ ٱلْقُرْءَانُ هُدًى لِّلنَّاسِ
وَبَيِّنَٰتٍ مِّنَ ٱلْهُدَىٰ وَٱلْفُرْقَانِ ۚ فَمَن شَهِدَ مِنكُمُ ٱلشَّهْرَ
فَلْيَصُمْهُ ۖ وَمَن كَانَ مَرِيضًا أَوْ عَلَىٰ سَفَرٍ فَعِدَّةٌ مِّنْ
أَيَّامٍ أُخَرَ ۗ يُرِيدُ ٱللَّهُ بِكُمُ ٱلْيُسْرَ وَلَا يُرِيدُ بِكُمُ
ٱلْعُسْرَ وَلِتُكْمِلُوا۟ ٱلْعِدَّةَ وَلِتُكَبِّرُوا۟ ٱللَّهَ عَلَىٰ مَا
هَدَىٰكُمْ وَلَعَلَّكُمْ تَشْكُرُونَ ﴿١٨٥﴾ وَإِذَا سَأَلَكَ
عِبَادِى عَنِّى فَإِنِّى قَرِيبٌ ۖ أُجِيبُ دَعْوَةَ ٱلدَّاعِ إِذَا دَعَانِ ۖ
فَلْيَسْتَجِيبُوا۟ لِى وَلْيُؤْمِنُوا۟ بِى لَعَلَّهُمْ يَرْشُدُونَ ﴿١٨٦﴾
أُحِلَّ لَكُمْ لَيْلَةَ ٱلصِّيَامِ ٱلرَّفَثُ إِلَىٰ نِسَآئِكُمْ ۚ هُنَّ لِبَاسٌ
لَّكُمْ وَأَنتُمْ لِبَاسٌ لَّهُنَّ ۗ عَلِمَ ٱللَّهُ أَنَّكُمْ كُنتُمْ تَخْتَانُونَ
أَنفُسَكُمْ فَتَابَ عَلَيْكُمْ وَعَفَا عَنكُمْ ۖ فَٱلْـَٰٔنَ بَٰشِرُوهُنَّ
وَٱبْتَغُوا۟ مَا كَتَبَ ٱللَّهُ لَكُمْ ۚ وَكُلُوا۟ وَٱشْرَبُوا۟ حَتَّىٰ يَتَبَيَّنَ لَكُمُ
ٱلْخَيْطُ ٱلْأَبْيَضُ مِنَ ٱلْخَيْطِ ٱلْأَسْوَدِ مِنَ ٱلْفَجْرِ ۖ ثُمَّ أَتِمُّوا۟ ٱلصِّيَامَ
إِلَى ٱلَّيْلِ ۚ وَلَا تُبَٰشِرُوهُنَّ وَأَنتُمْ عَٰكِفُونَ فِى ٱلْمَسَٰجِدِ ۗ
تِلْكَ حُدُودُ ٱللَّهِ فَلَا تَقْرَبُوهَا ۗ كَذَٰلِكَ يُبَيِّنُ ٱللَّهُ ءَايَٰتِهِۦ
لِلنَّاسِ لَعَلَّهُمْ يَتَّقُونَ ﴿١٨٧﴾ وَلَا تَأْكُلُوٓا۟ أَمْوَٰلَكُم بَيْنَكُم
بِٱلْبَٰطِلِ وَتُدْلُوا۟ بِهَآ إِلَى ٱلْحُكَّامِ لِتَأْكُلُوا۟ فَرِيقًا مِّنْ
أَمْوَٰلِ ٱلنَّاسِ بِٱلْإِثْمِ وَأَنتُمْ تَعْلَمُونَ ﴿١٨٨﴾ ۞ يَسْـَٔلُونَكَ

own accord by paying a larger amount of *fidya,* ***it is better for him. But that you should fast is better for you*** than breaking the fast and feeding, ***if you only knew*** how much good you gain by those days.

185. Those days are ***the month of Ramaḍān*** which ***is the one in which the Qur'an was sent down*** from the Preserved Tablet to the lowest heaven on the Night of Power ***as guidance*** away from misguidance ***for mankind, with Clear Signs containing guidance*** which guide to the Truth about judgements ***and discrimination*** between truth and falsehood. ***Any of you who are resident for the month should fast it. But any of you who are ill or on a journey should fast a number of other days*** as mentioned before, and it is repeated so that no one should imagine that it is abrogated by the generality of the expression "is present". ***Allah desires ease for you; He does not desire difficulty for you.*** That is why Allah allows you to break the fast on account of illness and travelling which is like an illness. You are commanded to fast and ***you should complete*** (read as *tukammilū* and *tukmilū*) ***the number of days*** of the fast of Ramaḍān ***and proclaim Allah's Greatness*** when you have finished fasting ***for the guidance He has given you*** to the pillars of his *dīn* ***so that hopefully you will be thankful*** to Allah for that.

186. When a group asked the Prophet, may Allah bless him and grant him peace, "Is our Lord near so that we may speak with Him?" this was revealed: ***If My slaves ask you about Me, I am near*** to them through My knowledge. So inform them that ***I answer the call of the caller when he calls on Me*** by giving him what he asks for. ***They should therefore respond to Me*** when I call on them to obey Me ***and believe in Me*** and continue to believe in Me, ***so that hopefully they will be rightly guided.***

187. ***On the night of the fast it is lawful for you to have sexual relations with your wives.*** This was revealed to abrogate the prohibition at the beginning of Islam when it was forbidden to eat or drink after the *'Ishā'* prayer. ***They are clothing for you and you for them.*** The clothing metaphor alludes to their mutual embrace and the need of each of them for the other. ***Allah knows that you have been betraying yourselves*** by having intercourse during the night of fasting and other things. They apologised to the Prophet, may Allah bless him and grant him peace, ***and He has turned towards you and***

excused you and accepted their repentance. ***Now*** it is lawful for you and ***you may have sexual intercourse with them and seek what Allah has written for you,*** meaning what Allah has allowed you of sexual intercourse or decreed for you of children. ***Eat and drink*** during the entire night ***until you can clearly discern the white thread from the black thread of the*** true ***dawn,*** referring to the black of night and the whiteness of dawn, ***then fulfil the fast*** from the first light of dawn ***until the night appears*** at the setting of the sun which marks the beginning of the night. ***But do not have sexual intercourse with them*** (women) ***while you are in retreat*** (doing *i'tikāf*) ***in the mosques.*** No one in retreat is permitted to leave the mosque to have intercourse with his wife, and then return. ***These*** decrees ***are Allah's limits*** which He has defined for fasting, ***so do not go near them.*** The words "do not go near them" are stronger than the words "do not exceed them" which we find in another *āyat* (2:227). ***In this way does Allah make His Signs clear to people so that hopefully they will be godfearing*** and avoid the things He has prohibited.

188. ***Do not devour one another's property by false means*** by consuming one another's property by *ḥarām* means, such as stealing and usurpation, ***nor offer it to the judges as a bribe,*** bribing them to give judgement in your favour, ***trying through crime to knowingly usurp a portion of other people's property,*** taking it while knowing the claim to be false.

189. ***They will ask you***, Muḥammad, ***about the crescent moons*** (*ahilla,* is the plural of *hilāl*). The crescent moon is the moon when it first appears and then begins to increase in size, since the moon does not remain in one state as the sun does. ***Say*** to them, ***"They are set times*** (*mawāqīt* is the plural of *mīqāt*) ***for mankind and for the ḥajj."*** By them people know the time for their crops and trade, and women count their periods by them, and fasting and breaking the fast is done by them. The time of *ḥajj* is also known by them. If the moon was always in the same state, these things would not have been known. ***It is not devoutness for you to enter houses by the back*** in *iḥrām*. The Makkan custom before Islam was to make an entrance by which they entered and left from the backs of their houses without using the door. They did that claiming it was devoutness to do so. ***Rather devoutness is possessed by those who are godfear -***

عَنِ ٱلْأَهِلَّةِ ۖ قُلْ هِىَ مَوَٰقِيتُ لِلنَّاسِ وَٱلْحَجِّ ۗ وَلَيْسَ ٱلْبِرُّ
بِأَن تَأْتُوا۟ ٱلْبُيُوتَ مِن ظُهُورِهَا وَلَٰكِنَّ ٱلْبِرَّ مَنِ ٱتَّقَىٰ ۗ
وَأْتُوا۟ ٱلْبُيُوتَ مِنْ أَبْوَٰبِهَا ۚ وَٱتَّقُوا۟ ٱللَّهَ لَعَلَّكُمْ
تُفْلِحُونَ ﴿١٨٩﴾ وَقَٰتِلُوا۟ فِى سَبِيلِ ٱللَّهِ ٱلَّذِينَ يُقَٰتِلُونَكُمْ
وَلَا تَعْتَدُوٓا۟ ۚ إِنَّ ٱللَّهَ لَا يُحِبُّ ٱلْمُعْتَدِينَ ﴿١٩٠﴾
وَٱقْتُلُوهُمْ حَيْثُ ثَقِفْتُمُوهُمْ وَأَخْرِجُوهُم مِّنْ حَيْثُ أَخْرَجُوكُمْ ۚ وَٱلْفِتْنَةُ
أَشَدُّ مِنَ ٱلْقَتْلِ ۚ وَلَا تُقَٰتِلُوهُمْ عِندَ ٱلْمَسْجِدِ ٱلْحَرَامِ حَتَّىٰ يُقَٰتِلُوكُمْ
فِيهِ ۖ فَإِن قَٰتَلُوكُمْ فَٱقْتُلُوهُمْ ۗ كَذَٰلِكَ جَزَآءُ ٱلْكَٰفِرِينَ ﴿١٩١﴾ فَإِنِ ٱنتَهَوْا۟
فَإِنَّ ٱللَّهَ غَفُورٌ رَّحِيمٌ ﴿١٩٢﴾ وَقَٰتِلُوهُمْ حَتَّىٰ لَا تَكُونَ فِتْنَةٌ وَيَكُونَ
ٱلدِّينُ لِلَّهِ ۖ فَإِنِ ٱنتَهَوْا۟ فَلَا عُدْوَٰنَ إِلَّا عَلَى ٱلظَّٰلِمِينَ ﴿١٩٣﴾ ٱلشَّهْرُ ٱلْحَرَامُ
بِٱلشَّهْرِ ٱلْحَرَامِ وَٱلْحُرُمَٰتُ قِصَاصٌ ۚ فَمَنِ ٱعْتَدَىٰ عَلَيْكُمْ فَٱعْتَدُوا۟
عَلَيْهِ بِمِثْلِ مَا ٱعْتَدَىٰ عَلَيْكُمْ ۚ وَٱتَّقُوا۟ ٱللَّهَ وَٱعْلَمُوٓا۟ أَنَّ ٱللَّهَ مَعَ
ٱلْمُتَّقِينَ ﴿١٩٤﴾ وَأَنفِقُوا۟ فِى سَبِيلِ ٱللَّهِ وَلَا تُلْقُوا۟ بِأَيْدِيكُمْ إِلَى ٱلتَّهْلُكَةِ ۛ
وَأَحْسِنُوٓا۟ ۛ إِنَّ ٱللَّهَ يُحِبُّ ٱلْمُحْسِنِينَ ﴿١٩٥﴾ وَأَتِمُّوا۟ ٱلْحَجَّ وَٱلْعُمْرَةَ لِلَّهِ ۚ
فَإِنْ أُحْصِرْتُمْ فَمَا ٱسْتَيْسَرَ مِنَ ٱلْهَدْىِ ۖ وَلَا تَحْلِقُوا۟ رُءُوسَكُمْ حَتَّىٰ يَبْلُغَ
ٱلْهَدْىُ مَحِلَّهُۥ ۚ فَمَن كَانَ مِنكُم مَّرِيضًا أَوْ بِهِۦٓ أَذًى مِّن رَّأْسِهِۦ فَفِدْيَةٌ
مِّن صِيَامٍ أَوْ صَدَقَةٍ أَوْ نُسُكٍ ۚ فَإِذَآ أَمِنتُمْ فَمَن تَمَتَّعَ بِٱلْعُمْرَةِ إِلَى ٱلْحَجِّ
فَمَا ٱسْتَيْسَرَ مِنَ ٱلْهَدْىِ ۚ فَمَن لَّمْ يَجِدْ فَصِيَامُ ثَلَٰثَةِ أَيَّامٍ فِى ٱلْحَجِّ وَسَبْعَةٍ
إِذَا رَجَعْتُمْ ۗ تِلْكَ عَشَرَةٌ كَامِلَةٌ ۗ ذَٰلِكَ لِمَن لَّمْ يَكُنْ أَهْلُهُۥ حَاضِرِى
ٱلْمَسْجِدِ ٱلْحَرَامِ ۚ وَٱتَّقُوا۟ ٱللَّهَ وَٱعْلَمُوٓا۟ أَنَّ ٱللَّهَ شَدِيدُ ٱلْعِقَابِ ﴿١٩٦﴾

ing. (Or the truly devout person is the one who shows fear of Allah by not opposing Him.) ***So come to houses by their doors*** when in *iḥrām* ***and be fearful of Allah, so that hopefully you will be suc - cessful.***

190. When the Prophet was barred from the Sacred Mosque in the year of Ḥudaybiyya, he made peace with the unbelievers on the basis that he would return the coming year during which they would leave Makka for three days. So when, the next year, he prepared for the promised *'umra,* there was a fear that Quraysh would not abide by the agreement and would fight them. The Muslims disliked the idea of fighting the idolaters in the *Ḥaram* or while they were in *iḥrām* or in the sacred month and so the following *āyats* were revealed: ***Fight in the Way of Allah*** to elevate Allah's *dīn* ***against those who fight you*** (the unbelievers), ***but do not go beyond the limits*** by initiating the fighting. ***Allah does not love those who go beyond the limits.*** Allah does not love those who exceed what is prescribed for them. This was abrogated by *Sūrat at-Tawba* or by Allah's words in the following *āyat*.

191. ***Kill them wherever you come across them and expel them from where they expelled you*** (Makka). That happened in the Year of the Conquest of Makka. ***Fitna*** (*shirk* on their part) ***is worse than killing*** them in the Ḥaram or in *iḥrām* which they thought dreadful. ***Do not fight them in the Sacred Mosque,*** meaning in the Ḥaram of Makka, ***until they fight you there. But if they do fight you*** in it, ***then kill them*** in it. ***That is how*** (by killing and expelling them) ***the unbelievers should be repaid.*** The word *qātalū,* "fight' in this *āyat* is also read as *qatalū* in some readings, in which case it means "kill".

192. ***But if they cease*** disbelieving and become Muslim, ***Allah is Ever-Forgiving*** towards them, ***Most Merciful*** towards them.

193. ***Fight them until there is no more fitna*** (*shirk*) in existence ***and the dīn*** (worship) ***belongs to Allah alone*** and none but Him is worshipped. ***If they cease*** committing *shirk* ***there should be no enmity*** by killing or in any other way ***towards any but wrongdoers.*** If someone is not a wrongdoer, there must be no aggression against him.

194. ***Sacred month in return for sacred month*** (if they fight you in a sacred month, retaliate by fighting them in the same way. This is to counteract those Muslims who thought it terrible to do so.) – ***sacred things are subject to retaliation.*** Sacred things entail retaliation when they are violated. ***So if anyone oversteps the limits against you*** by fighting in the Ḥaram, *iḥrām* or sacred months, ***overstep against him the same as he did to you.*** This is called equivalence since it should take a similar form. ***But be fearful of Allah*** by helping and not transgressing. ***Know that Allah is with those who are godfearing.*** Allah will provide help and assistance to the godfearing.

195. ***Spend in the Way of Allah*** in obedience to Him on *jihād* and other things. ***Do not cast yourselves into destruction.*** The destruction referred to is brought about by refusing to spend in *jihād* or abandoning it because that will make the enemy stronger against you. ***And do good*** by spending and other things***: Allah loves good-doers.*** Allah will reward those who do that.

196. ***Perform the ḥajj and 'umra for Allah,*** meaning carry out their duties. ***If you are forcibly prevented*** by the enemy from completing them, ***make whatever sacrifice is feasible*** for you, which means a sheep. ***But do not shave your heads*** and come out of *iḥrām* ***until the sacrificial animal*** mentioned ***has reached the place of sacrifice*** where it is lawful to sacrifice them. Ash-Shāfi'ī considers that to refer to the place where someone is prevented from continuing and so he slaughters there. He comes out of *iḥrām* and distributes the meat to the poor and shaves his head. ***If any of you are ill or have a head injury*** such as head lice or a head wound, so that he has to shave while in *iḥrām*, ***the expiation*** for doing that ***is fasting*** for three days ***or ṣadaqa*** in the form of three *ṣā's* of the staple food of the land to six people ***or sacrifice*** by slaughtering a sheep, or it may mean that there is a choice, ***when you are safe*** from the enemy when he goes away or is not there ***and well again.*** Shaving without excuse, however, entails full *kaffāra.* The same ruling applies to people who have a valid excuse for breaking the conditions of *iḥrām* in other ways, such as by wearing perfume, clothes or hair oil. ***Anyone who comes out of iḥrām between 'umra and ḥajj,*** meaning someone who does a *tamattu' ḥajj,* ***should make whatever sacrifice is feasible.*** It is called *tamattu'* because he enjoys (*tamatta'*) doing

ٱلْحَجُّ أَشْهُرٌ مَّعْلُومَٰتٌ ۚ فَمَن فَرَضَ فِيهِنَّ ٱلْحَجَّ فَلَا رَفَثَ
وَلَا فُسُوقَ وَلَا جِدَالَ فِى ٱلْحَجِّ ۗ وَمَا تَفْعَلُوا۟ مِنْ خَيْرٍ
يَعْلَمْهُ ٱللَّهُ ۗ وَتَزَوَّدُوا۟ فَإِنَّ خَيْرَ ٱلزَّادِ ٱلتَّقْوَىٰ ۚ وَٱتَّقُونِ
يَٰٓأُو۟لِى ٱلْأَلْبَٰبِ ﴿١٩٧﴾ لَيْسَ عَلَيْكُمْ جُنَاحٌ أَن
تَبْتَغُوا۟ فَضْلًا مِّن رَّبِّكُمْ ۚ فَإِذَآ أَفَضْتُم مِّنْ
عَرَفَٰتٍ فَٱذْكُرُوا۟ ٱللَّهَ عِندَ ٱلْمَشْعَرِ ٱلْحَرَامِ ۖ
وَٱذْكُرُوهُ كَمَا هَدَىٰكُمْ وَإِن كُنتُم مِّن قَبْلِهِۦ
لَمِنَ ٱلضَّآلِّينَ ﴿١٩٨﴾ ثُمَّ أَفِيضُوا۟ مِنْ حَيْثُ أَفَاضَ
ٱلنَّاسُ وَٱسْتَغْفِرُوا۟ ٱللَّهَ ۚ إِنَّ ٱللَّهَ غَفُورٌ رَّحِيمٌ ﴿١٩٩﴾
فَإِذَا قَضَيْتُم مَّنَٰسِكَكُمْ فَٱذْكُرُوا۟ ٱللَّهَ كَذِكْرِكُمْ
ءَابَآءَكُمْ أَوْ أَشَدَّ ذِكْرًا ۗ فَمِنَ ٱلنَّاسِ مَن
يَقُولُ رَبَّنَآ ءَاتِنَا فِى ٱلدُّنْيَا وَمَا لَهُۥ فِى ٱلْءَاخِرَةِ مِنْ
خَلَٰقٍ ﴿٢٠٠﴾ وَمِنْهُم مَّن يَقُولُ رَبَّنَآ ءَاتِنَا فِى ٱلدُّنْيَا
حَسَنَةً وَفِى ٱلْءَاخِرَةِ حَسَنَةً وَقِنَا عَذَابَ ٱلنَّارِ ﴿٢٠١﴾
أُو۟لَٰٓئِكَ لَهُمْ نَصِيبٌ مِّمَّا كَسَبُوا۟ ۚ وَٱللَّهُ سَرِيعُ ٱلْحِسَابِ ﴿٢٠٢﴾
۞ وَٱذْكُرُوا۟ ٱللَّهَ فِىٓ أَيَّامٍ مَّعْدُودَٰتٍ ۚ فَمَن تَعَجَّلَ فِى
يَوْمَيْنِ فَلَآ إِثْمَ عَلَيْهِ وَمَن تَأَخَّرَ فَلَآ إِثْمَ عَلَيْهِ ۚ لِمَنِ ٱتَّقَىٰ ۗ
وَٱتَّقُوا۟ ٱللَّهَ وَٱعْلَمُوٓا۟ أَنَّكُمْ إِلَيْهِ تُحْشَرُونَ ﴿٢٠٣﴾ وَمِنَ
ٱلنَّاسِ مَن يُعْجِبُكَ قَوْلُهُۥ فِى ٱلْحَيَوٰةِ ٱلدُّنْيَا وَيُشْهِدُ ٱللَّهَ
عَلَىٰ مَا فِى قَلْبِهِۦ وَهُوَ أَلَدُّ ٱلْخِصَامِ ﴿٢٠٤﴾ وَإِذَا تَوَلَّىٰ سَعَىٰ

things normally forbidden during the *ḥajj* by coming out of *iḥrām* after completing *'umra* and then re-adopting it for the *ḥajj* itself. The sacrifice to be offered for doing this is a sheep after coming out of *iḥrām*. It is best done on the Day of Sacrifice. ***For anyone who cannot*** find a sacrifice because there is none available or he does not have the necessary money, ***there are three days' fast*** which he should do ***on ḥajj***, while in *iḥrām* (So the person doing this must go into *iḥrām* before the 7th Dhū'l-Ḥijja and it is best to do so before the 6th because it is disliked to fast the Day of 'Arafa while on *ḥajj*. Nor is it permitted to fast during the days of *tashrīq* according to the soundest of two positions of ash-Shāfi'ī) ***and seven*** more ***on your return*** when one returns home from Makka after finishing the *ḥajj* – ***that is ten*** days of fasting ***in all.*** There is a change in the text from third to second person. ***That*** (the ruling mentioned about the obligation to sacrifice or fast for a *tamattu' ḥajj*) ***is for anyone whose family does not live near the Sacred Mosque,*** those who live a distance of more than two stages away from the Ḥaram. According to ash-Shāfi'ī, those who live nearer than that owe neither sacrifice nor fast if they do *tamattu'*. The mention of "family" indicates the precondition of residence. If someone arrives before the months of *ḥajj* and is not resident and does *tamattu'* he must follow the ruling, according to one of two views of ash-Shāfi'ī; the second view is that he does not have to. "Family" alludes to the person on *ḥajj*. Alongside the *tamattu' ḥajj* is what is mentioned in the *Sunna* about the *qirān ḥajj*, which is to go into *iḥrām* for both *ḥajj* and *'umra* together. ***Be fearful of Allah*** in respect of what He has commanded and what He has forbidden ***and know that Allah is severe in retribution*** against those who oppose Him.

197. ***The*** time of the ***ḥajj takes place during well-known months*** – Shawwāl, Dhū'l-Qa'da and the first ten days of Dhū'l-Ḥijja or the whole of it. ***If anyone undertakes the obligation of hajj in them*** by going into *iḥrām*, ***there must be no sexual intercourse, no wrongdoing*** or acts of rebellion, ***nor any quarrelling during ḥajj.*** This is a firm prohibition. ***Whatever good you do*** such as giving *ṣadaqa*, ***Allah knows it*** and will reward you for it. And the following was revealed about the people of Yemen who used to make *ḥajj* without taking any provision and so relied on other people for their entire maintenance. ***Take provision*** for your journey, ***but the best provision is fearfulness of Allah*** which protects one from asking people and other things. ***So be fearful of Me, people of intelligence!***

198. ***There is nothing wrong in seeking bounty*** (provision) ***from your Lord*** by trading during the *ḥajj*. This was revealed to refute those who disliked doing that. ***When you pour down from Arafat*** after the Standing there, ***remember Allah,*** after the night at Muzdalifa, with *talbiya*, by saying "*lā ilaha illā'llāh*" and making supplication ***at the Sacred Landmark.*** The "Sacred Landmark" is the other mountain at Muzdalifa called Qaziḥ. According to a *ḥadīth* the Prophet, may Allah bless him and grant him peace, stood there invoking Allah and supplicating to Him until the sun was quite yellow. (Muslim) ***Remember Him because He has guided you*** to the pillars of His *dīn* and the practices of His *ḥajj,* ***even though before this*** (received this guidance) ***you were astray.***

199. ***Then press on,*** Quraysh, ***from where the people press on,*** meaning go on from 'Arafat to Muzdalifa and stand there together with the rest of the people, ***and ask Allah's forgiveness*** for your sins. Quraysh used to stand at Muzdalifa above the place where the others stood. ***Allah is Ever-Forgiving*** to the believers, ***Most Merciful*** towards them.

200. ***When you have completed the rites,*** the acts of worship of your *ḥajj* by stoning the *Jamra al-'Aqaba*, performing *ṭawāf* and staying at Minā, ***remember Allah*** with *takbīr* and praise, ***as you used to remember your forefathers*** because you used to boast and brag about your forefathers at the end of *ḥajj* before the coming of Islam – ***or even more*** than you used to remember them. ***There are some people who say, "Our Lord, give us*** a portion of ***good in this world."*** They may be given it but ***they will have no share in the Next World.***

201. ***And there are others who say, "Our Lord, give us good*** (blessings) ***in this world, and good in the Next World*** (the Garden)***, and safeguard us from the punishment of the Fire*** by our not entering it." These two *āyats* illustrate the difference between the idolaters, who think only of this world, and the believers, who are aiming for the Next World as well, and encourage the quest for good in both abodes as a reward in both is promised.

202. ***They will have a good share*** (a reward) ***from what they have earned*** through their actions in the *ḥajj* and the supplication they have made. ***Allah is swift at reckoning.*** The reckoning of Allah over all of His creation will take, according to a *ḥadīth*, about half a day going by the length of days in this world.
203. ***Remember Allah*** by calling out the *takbīr* when stoning the *jamras* ***on the designated days,*** the three days of *Tashrīq*. ***Those who hurry on*** from Minā ***in two days*** (those who leave on the second of the days of *tashrīq* after stoning the *jamras*), ***have done no wrong*** by hurrying on, ***and those who stay another day,*** remaining for the third day and stoning the *jamras*, ***have done no wrong*** by doing that – people can choose regarding that matter. There is no sin for ***those of them who are godfearing,*** who fear Allah on the *ḥajj* because only those who do are true *ḥājjīs*. ***So be fearful of Allah. And know that you will be gathered back to Him*** in the Next World and He will repay you for your actions.

204. ***Among the people there is a man whose words about the life of this world excite your admiration,*** but you will not admire him in the Next World because of the difference in his belief, ***and he calls Allah to witness what is in his heart,*** that it is in harmony with what he says, ***while he is in fact the most hostile of adversaries.*** He is the strongest adversary to you and your followers because he is hostile to you. This *āyat* refers to al-Akhnas ibn Sharīq, who was a hypocrite but sweet in his words to the Prophet, may Allah bless him and grant him peace, swearing that he believed him and loved him. The Prophet brought him near but then Allah exposed him. Then he passed by some fields and donkeys belonging to the Muslims and burned the crops and killed the animals in the night, as is reported in the next *āyat*.

205. ***When he leaves you, he goes about the earth corrupting it, destroying crops and animals,*** which constitutes great corruption. ***Allah does not love corruption*** and is not pleased with it.

206. ***When he is told to be fearful of Allah*** in what he does, ***he is seized by pride*** and arrogance and compulsion to behave sinfully overcome him, ***which drives him to wrongdoing*** which he has been commanded to avoid. ***Hell will be enough for him! What an evil resting-place!***

فِى ٱلْأَرْضِ لِيُفْسِدَ فِيهَا وَيُهْلِكَ ٱلْحَرْثَ وَٱلنَّسْلَ ۗ وَٱللَّهُ
لَا يُحِبُّ ٱلْفَسَادَ ﴿٢٠٥﴾ وَإِذَا قِيلَ لَهُ ٱتَّقِ ٱللَّهَ أَخَذَتْهُ ٱلْعِزَّةُ
بِٱلْإِثْمِ ۚ فَحَسْبُهُۥ جَهَنَّمُ ۚ وَلَبِئْسَ ٱلْمِهَادُ ﴿٢٠٦﴾ وَمِنَ
ٱلنَّاسِ مَن يَشْرِى نَفْسَهُ ٱبْتِغَآءَ مَرْضَاتِ ٱللَّهِ ۗ وَٱللَّهُ
رَءُوفٌۢ بِٱلْعِبَادِ ﴿٢٠٧﴾ يَٰٓأَيُّهَا ٱلَّذِينَ ءَامَنُوا۟ ٱدْخُلُوا۟
فِى ٱلسِّلْمِ كَآفَّةً وَلَا تَتَّبِعُوا۟ خُطُوَٰتِ ٱلشَّيْطَٰنِ ۚ
إِنَّهُۥ لَكُمْ عَدُوٌّ مُّبِينٌ ﴿٢٠٨﴾ فَإِن زَلَلْتُم مِّنۢ بَعْدِ
مَا جَآءَتْكُمُ ٱلْبَيِّنَٰتُ فَٱعْلَمُوٓا۟ أَنَّ ٱللَّهَ عَزِيزٌ حَكِيمٌ
﴿٢٠٩﴾ هَلْ يَنظُرُونَ إِلَّآ أَن يَأْتِيَهُمُ ٱللَّهُ فِى ظُلَلٍ مِّنَ ٱلْغَمَامِ
وَٱلْمَلَٰٓئِكَةُ وَقُضِىَ ٱلْأَمْرُ ۚ وَإِلَى ٱللَّهِ تُرْجَعُ ٱلْأُمُورُ ﴿٢١٠﴾
سَلْ بَنِىٓ إِسْرَٰٓءِيلَ كَمْ ءَاتَيْنَٰهُم مِّنْ ءَايَةٍۭ بَيِّنَةٍ ۗ وَمَن يُبَدِّلْ نِعْمَةَ
ٱللَّهِ مِنۢ بَعْدِ مَا جَآءَتْهُ فَإِنَّ ٱللَّهَ شَدِيدُ ٱلْعِقَابِ ﴿٢١١﴾ زُيِّنَ لِلَّذِينَ
كَفَرُوا۟ ٱلْحَيَوٰةُ ٱلدُّنْيَا وَيَسْخَرُونَ مِنَ ٱلَّذِينَ ءَامَنُوا۟ ۘ وَٱلَّذِينَ
ٱتَّقَوْا۟ فَوْقَهُمْ يَوْمَ ٱلْقِيَٰمَةِ ۗ وَٱللَّهُ يَرْزُقُ مَن يَشَآءُ بِغَيْرِ حِسَابٍ
﴿٢١٢﴾ كَانَ ٱلنَّاسُ أُمَّةً وَٰحِدَةً فَبَعَثَ ٱللَّهُ ٱلنَّبِيِّۦنَ مُبَشِّرِينَ
وَمُنذِرِينَ وَأَنزَلَ مَعَهُمُ ٱلْكِتَٰبَ بِٱلْحَقِّ لِيَحْكُمَ بَيْنَ ٱلنَّاسِ
فِيمَا ٱخْتَلَفُوا۟ فِيهِ ۚ وَمَا ٱخْتَلَفَ فِيهِ إِلَّا ٱلَّذِينَ أُوتُوهُ مِنۢ بَعْدِ
مَا جَآءَتْهُمُ ٱلْبَيِّنَٰتُ بَغْيًۢا بَيْنَهُمْ ۖ فَهَدَى ٱللَّهُ ٱلَّذِينَ ءَامَنُوا۟
لِمَا ٱخْتَلَفُوا۟ فِيهِ مِنَ ٱلْحَقِّ بِإِذْنِهِۦ ۗ وَٱللَّهُ يَهْدِى مَن يَشَآءُ إِلَىٰ
صِرَٰطٍ مُّسْتَقِيمٍ ﴿٢١٣﴾ أَمْ حَسِبْتُمْ أَن تَدْخُلُوا۟ ٱلْجَنَّةَ وَلَمَّا

207. ***And among the people are some who give up*** and sell ***every - thing,*** expending themselves in obedience to Allah, ***desiring the good pleasure of Allah.*** This refers particularly to Ṣuhayb, may Allah be pleased with him. When the idolaters started to persecute him, he emigrated to Madina and left his property to them. ***Allah is All-Gentle with His slaves*** by guiding them to that which contains His pleasure.

208. This was revealed about 'Abdullāh ibn Salām and his companions when they continued to venerate Saturday as the sabbath and disliked eating camels after becoming Muslim. ***O you who believe! enter Islam*** (read as *salm* and *silm*) ***totally,*** meaning "follow all its laws". ***Do not follow in the footsteps*** and paths ***of Shayṭān*** which he has made seem attractive in order to divide you. ***He is an outright*** (clear) ***enemy to you.***

209. ***If you backslide,*** inclining away from taking on all of Islam, ***after the Clear Signs*** and manifest evidence that it is the truth ***have come to you, know that Allah is Almighty*** in taking revenge against you, ***All-Wise*** in what He does.

210. ***What are they*** (those who do not enter Islam) ***waiting for but for*** the command of ***Allah to come to them,*** in a form such as the arrival of His punishment, ***in the shadows of the clouds, together with the angels, in which case the matter will have been settled*** and their destruction commanded? ***All matters return to Allah*** in the Next World and He will repay everyone for their actions.

211. ***Ask,*** Muḥammad, ***the Tribe of Israel*** as a rebuke ***how many Clear Signs We gave to them,*** such as the dividing of the sea and the descent of manna and quail, and yet they exchanged them for disbelief. ***If anyone alters Allah's blessing after it has come to him*** and changes the signs which are a means to guidance out of disbelief, ***Allah is severe in retribution*** towards him.

212. ***To those who disbelieve*** among the people of Makka, ***the life of this world is*** misrepresented by being ***painted in glowing colours*** so that they love it, ***and they laugh at those who believe*** because of their proverty, like Bilāl, 'Ammār and Ṣuhayb; in other words, they mock the believers and vaunt themselves over them because of their wealth. ***But on the Day of Rising those who fear Allah*** and avoided *shirk* ***will be over them. Allah provides for whomever He wills***

يَأۡتِكُم مَّثَلُ ٱلَّذِينَ خَلَوۡاْ مِن قَبۡلِكُمۖ مَّسَّتۡهُمُ ٱلۡبَأۡسَآءُ وَٱلضَّرَّآءُ
وَزُلۡزِلُواْ حَتَّىٰ يَقُولَ ٱلرَّسُولُ وَٱلَّذِينَ ءَامَنُواْ مَعَهُۥ مَتَىٰ نَصۡرُ ٱللَّهِۗ
أَلَآ إِنَّ نَصۡرَ ٱللَّهِ قَرِيبٞ ٢١٤ يَسۡـَٔلُونَكَ مَاذَا يُنفِقُونَۖ قُلۡ
مَآ أَنفَقۡتُم مِّنۡ خَيۡرٖ فَلِلۡوَٰلِدَيۡنِ وَٱلۡأَقۡرَبِينَ وَٱلۡيَتَٰمَىٰ وَٱلۡمَسَٰكِينِ
وَٱبۡنِ ٱلسَّبِيلِۗ وَمَا تَفۡعَلُواْ مِنۡ خَيۡرٖ فَإِنَّ ٱللَّهَ بِهِۦ عَلِيمٞ ٢١٥
كُتِبَ عَلَيۡكُمُ ٱلۡقِتَالُ وَهُوَ كُرۡهٞ لَّكُمۡۖ وَعَسَىٰٓ أَن تَكۡرَهُواْ
شَيۡـٔٗا وَهُوَ خَيۡرٞ لَّكُمۡۖ وَعَسَىٰٓ أَن تُحِبُّواْ شَيۡـٔٗا وَهُوَ شَرّٞ لَّكُمۡۗ
وَٱللَّهُ يَعۡلَمُ وَأَنتُمۡ لَا تَعۡلَمُونَ ٢١٦ يَسۡـَٔلُونَكَ عَنِ ٱلشَّهۡرِ
ٱلۡحَرَامِ قِتَالٖ فِيهِۖ قُلۡ قِتَالٞ فِيهِ كَبِيرٞۖ وَصَدٌّ عَن سَبِيلِ ٱللَّهِ
وَكُفۡرُۢ بِهِۦ وَٱلۡمَسۡجِدِ ٱلۡحَرَامِ وَإِخۡرَاجُ أَهۡلِهِۦ مِنۡهُ أَكۡبَرُ
عِندَ ٱللَّهِۚ وَٱلۡفِتۡنَةُ أَكۡبَرُ مِنَ ٱلۡقَتۡلِۗ وَلَا يَزَالُونَ يُقَٰتِلُونَكُمۡ
حَتَّىٰ يَرُدُّوكُمۡ عَن دِينِكُمۡ إِنِ ٱسۡتَطَٰعُواْۚ وَمَن يَرۡتَدِدۡ
مِنكُمۡ عَن دِينِهِۦ فَيَمُتۡ وَهُوَ كَافِرٞ فَأُوْلَٰٓئِكَ حَبِطَتۡ
أَعۡمَٰلُهُمۡ فِي ٱلدُّنۡيَا وَٱلۡأٓخِرَةِۖ وَأُوْلَٰٓئِكَ أَصۡحَٰبُ ٱلنَّارِۖ
هُمۡ فِيهَا خَٰلِدُونَ ٢١٧ إِنَّ ٱلَّذِينَ ءَامَنُواْ وَٱلَّذِينَ
هَاجَرُواْ وَجَٰهَدُواْ فِي سَبِيلِ ٱللَّهِ أُوْلَٰٓئِكَ يَرۡجُونَ رَحۡمَتَ
ٱللَّهِۚ وَٱللَّهُ غَفُورٞ رَّحِيمٞ ٢١٨ ۞ يَسۡـَٔلُونَكَ عَنِ ٱلۡخَمۡرِ
وَٱلۡمَيۡسِرِۖ قُلۡ فِيهِمَآ إِثۡمٞ كَبِيرٞ وَمَنَٰفِعُ لِلنَّاسِ وَإِثۡمُهُمَآ
أَكۡبَرُ مِن نَّفۡعِهِمَاۗ وَيَسۡـَٔلُونَكَ مَاذَا يُنفِقُونَ قُلِ ٱلۡعَفۡوَۗ
كَذَٰلِكَ يُبَيِّنُ ٱللَّهُ لَكُمُ ٱلۡأٓيَٰتِ لَعَلَّكُمۡ تَتَفَكَّرُونَ ٢١٩

without any reckoning. They will have vast provision in the Next World or this world when those who were mocked come to own the property and persons of the mockers.

213. ***Mankind was a single nation*** in respect of their belief and then they differed from one another so that some believed and some disbelieved. ***Then Allah sent out Prophets*** to them ***bringing good news*** about the Garden for those who believe ***and giving warning*** to those who disbelieve about the Fire, ***and with them He sent down the Book*** (all the Divine Revelations) ***with truth, to decide*** by it ***between people regarding their differences*** in respect of the *dīn*. ***Only those who were given it*** (the Book) ***differed about it*** so that some believed and some disbelieved, ***after the Clear Signs*** and manifest evidence of *tawḥīd* ***had come to them, envying one another*** (meaning the unbelievers). ***Then, by His permission*** (by His will), ***Allah guided those who believed to the truth of that about which they had differed. Allah guides whomever He wills to a straight path,*** the Path of Truth.

214. This was revealed about afflictions which beset the Muslims. ***Or did you suppose that you would enter the Garden without facing the same*** afflictions ***as*** were faced by ***those*** believers ***who came before you?*** So you should be patient as they were patient. Extreme ***poverty and illness afflicted them and they were shaken*** and alarmed with various type of affliction, ***to the point that the Messenger and those who believed with him*** felt that help was slow in coming to end their hardship and ***said, "When is Allah's help coming*** which we were promised?" Allah answered them: ***Be assured that Allah's help is very near*** and will definitely come.

215. ***They will ask you***, Muḥammad, ***what they should give away,*** meaning what they should spend. The enquirer was 'Amr ibn al-Jamūḥ. He was an old man with wealth and asked the Prophet, may Allah bless him and grant him peace, what he should spend, and on whom. ***Say*** to them, ***"Any wealth you give away,*** whether a little or a lot, ***should go to your parents and relatives and to orphans and the very poor and travellers."*** This makes it clear who the recipients should be. ***Whatever good you do,*** in spending or anything else, ***Allah knows it*** and will reward you for it.

216. ***Fighting*** against the unbelievers ***is prescribed*** and hereby made obligatory ***for you even if it is hateful to you*** and it is disliked because it entails hardship. ***It may be that you hate a thing when it is good for you and it may be that you love a thing when it is bad for you.*** This is because the self seld is naturally inclined to lower appetites which will bring about its destruction, and is averse to duties which make happiness mandatory for it. So you may dislike fighting, but it is good for you: either through winning victory and booty or by gaining martyrdom and its reward. There is evil in avoiding it because that entails abasement, poverty and loss of r eward. ***Allah knows*** what is good for you ***and you do not know*** that. So hasten to what He commands you.

217. The Prophet, may Allah bless him and grant him peace, sent the first of his expeditions, which was led by 'Abdullāh ibn Jahsḥ; they fought the idolaters and killed Ibn al-Ḥadramī on the last day of Jumādā al-Ākhira and went on into the sacred month of Rajab. So the unbelievers blamed them for allowing fighting in a sacred month and then this was revealed. ***They will ask you about the Sacred Month and fighting in it. Say*** to them, ***"Fighting in it is a serious matter*** and a sin***; but barring access to the Way of Allah*** (His *dīn*) ***and rejecting Him and barring access to the Sacred Mosque*** in Makka ***and expelling its people,*** meaning the Prophet, peace be upon him, and the believers, ***from it are far more serious*** and a worse sin ***in the sight of Allah*** than fighting in it. ***The oppression of idolatry*** (*fitna* on your part) ***is worse than killing*** you in it." ***They*** (the unbelievers) ***will not stop fighting you*** (the believers) ***until they make you revert*** to unbelief ***from your* dīn*, if they are able. As for any of you who revert from their* dīn *and die unbelievers, their*** righteous ***actions will come to nothing in this world and the Next.*** There is nothing sent ahead by them and no reward for them. The fact that death is mentioned here as a limitation means that if he were to revert to Islam his actions would not be invalid and he would be rewarded for them and would not have to repeat them: such as having to repeat *ḥajj*, for instance. That is the position of ash-Shāfi'ī. ***They are the Companions of the Fire, remaining in it timelessly, forever.***

فِي ٱلدُّنۡيَا وَٱلۡأٓخِرَةِۗ وَيَسۡـَٔلُونَكَ عَنِ ٱلۡيَتَٰمَىٰۖ قُلۡ إِصۡلَاحٞ لَّهُمۡ
خَيۡرٞۖ وَإِن تُخَالِطُوهُمۡ فَإِخۡوَٰنُكُمۡۚ وَٱللَّهُ يَعۡلَمُ ٱلۡمُفۡسِدَ مِنَ
ٱلۡمُصۡلِحِۚ وَلَوۡ شَآءَ ٱللَّهُ لَأَعۡنَتَكُمۡۚ إِنَّ ٱللَّهَ عَزِيزٌ حَكِيمٞ ﴿٢٢٠﴾
وَلَا تَنكِحُواْ ٱلۡمُشۡرِكَٰتِ حَتَّىٰ يُؤۡمِنَّۚ وَلَأَمَةٞ مُّؤۡمِنَةٌ خَيۡرٞ
مِّن مُّشۡرِكَةٖ وَلَوۡ أَعۡجَبَتۡكُمۡۗ وَلَا تُنكِحُواْ ٱلۡمُشۡرِكِينَ حَتَّىٰ
يُؤۡمِنُواْۚ وَلَعَبۡدٞ مُّؤۡمِنٌ خَيۡرٞ مِّن مُّشۡرِكٖ وَلَوۡ أَعۡجَبَكُمۡۗ أُوْلَٰٓئِكَ
يَدۡعُونَ إِلَى ٱلنَّارِۖ وَٱللَّهُ يَدۡعُوٓاْ إِلَى ٱلۡجَنَّةِ وَٱلۡمَغۡفِرَةِ بِإِذۡنِهِۦۖ
وَيُبَيِّنُ ءَايَٰتِهِۦ لِلنَّاسِ لَعَلَّهُمۡ يَتَذَكَّرُونَ ﴿٢٢١﴾ وَيَسۡـَٔلُونَكَ
عَنِ ٱلۡمَحِيضِۖ قُلۡ هُوَ أَذٗى فَٱعۡتَزِلُواْ ٱلنِّسَآءَ فِي ٱلۡمَحِيضِ
وَلَا تَقۡرَبُوهُنَّ حَتَّىٰ يَطۡهُرۡنَۖ فَإِذَا تَطَهَّرۡنَ فَأۡتُوهُنَّ مِنۡ حَيۡثُ
أَمَرَكُمُ ٱللَّهُۚ إِنَّ ٱللَّهَ يُحِبُّ ٱلتَّوَّٰبِينَ وَيُحِبُّ ٱلۡمُتَطَهِّرِينَ ﴿٢٢٢﴾
نِسَآؤُكُمۡ حَرۡثٞ لَّكُمۡ فَأۡتُواْ حَرۡثَكُمۡ أَنَّىٰ شِئۡتُمۡۖ وَقَدِّمُواْ لِأَنفُسِكُمۡۚ
وَٱتَّقُواْ ٱللَّهَ وَٱعۡلَمُوٓاْ أَنَّكُم مُّلَٰقُوهُۗ وَبَشِّرِ ٱلۡمُؤۡمِنِينَ
﴿٢٢٣﴾ وَلَا تَجۡعَلُواْ ٱللَّهَ عُرۡضَةٗ لِّأَيۡمَٰنِكُمۡ أَن تَبَرُّواْ
وَتَتَّقُواْ وَتُصۡلِحُواْ بَيۡنَ ٱلنَّاسِۗ وَٱللَّهُ سَمِيعٌ عَلِيمٞ ﴿٢٢٤﴾
لَّا يُؤَاخِذُكُمُ ٱللَّهُ بِٱللَّغۡوِ فِيٓ أَيۡمَٰنِكُمۡ وَلَٰكِن يُؤَاخِذُكُم بِمَا كَسَبَتۡ
قُلُوبُكُمۡۗ وَٱللَّهُ غَفُورٌ حَلِيمٞ ﴿٢٢٥﴾ لِّلَّذِينَ يُؤۡلُونَ مِن نِّسَآئِهِمۡ تَرَبُّصُ
أَرۡبَعَةِ أَشۡهُرٖۖ فَإِن فَآءُو فَإِنَّ ٱللَّهَ غَفُورٞ رَّحِيمٞ ﴿٢٢٦﴾ وَإِنۡ عَزَمُواْ
ٱلطَّلَٰقَ فَإِنَّ ٱللَّهَ سَمِيعٌ عَلِيمٞ ﴿٢٢٧﴾ وَٱلۡمُطَلَّقَٰتُ يَتَرَبَّصۡنَ
بِأَنفُسِهِنَّ ثَلَٰثَةَ قُرُوٓءٖۚ وَلَا يَحِلُّ لَهُنَّ أَن يَكۡتُمۡنَ مَا خَلَقَ ٱللَّهُ فِيٓ

218. When the expedition thought that even if they were free of wrong actions, they still would not obtain a reward, the following was revealed. ***Those who believe and emigrate*** and leave their homeland ***and do* jihād *in the Way of Allah,*** striving to elevate the *dīn,* ***can expect Allah's mercy*** and reward. ***Allah is Ever-Forgiving*** to the believers, ***Most Merciful*** towards them.

219. ***They will ask you about*** the judgement regarding ***intoxicants and gambling. Say*** to them, ***"There is great*** (read as *kabīr* "great" and in one reading *kathīr* "much") ***wrong in*** using ***both of them*** since they cause quarrels, mutual abuse and foul language ***and also certain benefits for mankind,*** including pleasure and joy in wine and getting money without effort in gambling. ***But the wrong*** and corruption ***in them is greater than the benefit."*** The harm which originates from them is far worse than any benefit which accrues. When this was revealed, some people continued to drink while others abstained until the *āyat* of *Sūrat al-Mā'ida* forbade it absolutely. ***They will ask you what*** and how much ***they should give away. Say,*** "Spend ***whatever is surplus to your needs."*** Do not spend what you need and harm yourselves by doing that. ***In this way*** as was explained to you, ***Allah makes the Signs clear to you, so that hopefully you will reflect...***

220. ***... on*** the business of ***this world and the Next*** and take what is the best for you regarding it. ***They will ask you about the property of orphans*** and difficulties they face in looking after it because if they consume it they commit wrong, but if they separate their own property from that of the orphans and prepare food for them alone from it, that results in hardship. ***Say, "Managing it in their best interests is best."*** Managing their property is for the sake of its growth and shared profit is better than leaving it untouched and unproductive. ***If you mix your property with theirs***, mixing your outlay with theirs, ***they are your brothers*** in the *dīn.* Part of the business of a brother is to share with his brother, meaning that you may do so. ***Allah knows a squanderer*** who wastes their property through mixing with their own ***from a good manager*** who improves it for them. Both of them will be repaid. ***If Allah had wanted, He could have been hard on you,*** constricting you by forbidding the mixing of property. ***Allah is Almighty*** and has control of His command, ***All-Wise*** in what He does.

221. ***Do not***, Muslims, ***marry idolatrous*** (unbelieving) ***women until they believe. A believing slavegirl is better for you than an idolatress*** who is free, ***even though she may attract you*** by her beauty and wealth. The reason for the revelation of this *āyat* was the shame attached to marrying a slave and the desire to marry a free idolatress. This refers non-*Kitābī* women, by the *āyat, "chaste women of the People of the Book.* (5)" ***And do not give*** Muslim ***women in marriage to idolatrous men until they believe. A believing slave is better for you than an idolater, even though he may attract you*** by handsomeness and wealth. ***Such people*** (idolaters) ***call you to the Fire*** by inviting you to actions which result in the Fire and so it is not proper to marry them, ***whereas Allah calls you*** on the tongue of His Prophets, ***with His permission,*** (by His will) ***to*** actions which result in ***the Garden and forgiveness.*** So you must respond by marrying His friends. ***He makes His Signs clear to people so that hopefully they will pay heed*** and be warned.

222. ***They will ask you about menstruation*** or about its status and what women should do during it. ***Say, "It is an impurity,*** or its status is that it is an impurity, ***so keep apart from women during menstruation and do not approach them*** (do not have sexual intercourse during menstruation or any sexual activity involving the place where it occurs) ***until they have purified themselves*** (read as *yaṭahharna* and *yaṭhurna*) by having a *ghusl* after it has ended. ***But once they have purified themselves, then go to*** (have sexual intercourse with) ***them in the way that Allah has enjoined on you"*** which you avoided during menstruation, confining yourselves to kissing them instead and not exceeding that. ***Allah loves*** and He will reward and honour ***those who turn back from wrongdoing*** and repent of wrong actions ***and He loves those who purify themselves*** from impurity.

223. ***Your women are fertile fields for you,*** meaning the place of producing offspring, ***so come to your fertile fields***, meaning the site for procreation, which is the vagina, ***however you like,*** standing, sitting or lying down, from the front or the back, to refute the statement of the Jews that if someone come to his wife from behind she will have a squint-eyed child. ***Send good ahead for yourselves*** by righteous actions like saying the *basmala* in intercourse ***and be fearful of Allah*** regarding His commands and prohibitions. ***Know that you are going to meet Him*** at the Resurrection and He will repay you for your actions. ***And give good news to the believers*** who fear that they will meet Allah.

224. ***Do not, by your oaths*** made using the Name of Allah, ***make Allah a pretext*** and barrier by swearing a lot of oaths by Allah ***to avoid good action and being fearful of Allah and putting things right between people.*** It is disliked to make such an oath and it is a *sunna* to break it. It is expiated by going against it and doing good, and so breaking it is in fact an act of obedience. Do not prevent yourselves from performing acts of piety and the like by swearing not to do them. Such people should do *kaffāra* because the reason for the revelation of this *āyat* was to prevent barring people from doing good. ***Allah is All-Hearing*** of what You say, ***All-Knowing*** of your states.

225. ***Allah will not take you to task for inadvertent statements in your oaths,*** meaning things which the tongue says without any aim of swearing like, "No, by Allah" and "Yes, by Allah" for which there is no *kaffāra*, ***but He will take you to task for the intention your hearts have made*** in respect of oaths you truly intend to make. ***Allah is Ever-Forgiving*** of what is inadvertent, ***All-Forbearing*** because He does not punish many who deserves it.

226. ***Those who swear to abstain from sexual relations with their wives,*** vowing not to have sexual intercourse with them, ***may wait for a period of up to four months*** in which they can retract the oath and have sexual intercourse with them. ***If they then retract their oath*** in that time and have sexual intercourse, ***Allah is Ever-Forgiving*** of the harm they did to the woman through the oath, ***Most Merciful*** towards them by deferring the punishment of those who deserve it.

227. ***If they are determined to divorce*** and do not retract, divorce occurs. ***Allah is All-Hearing*** of what they say, ***All-Knowing*** of their resolve. This means that after the waiting period mentioned, they only have the option of retraction or divorce.

228. ***Divorced women should wait by themselves*** and not marry anyone else ***for three menstrual cycles*** from the moment of the divorce;

أَرْحَامِهِنَّ إِن كُنَّ يُؤْمِنَّ بِٱللَّهِ وَٱلْيَوْمِ ٱلْـَٔاخِرِ ۚ وَبُعُولَتُهُنَّ أَحَقُّ بِرَدِّهِنَّ
فِى ذَٰلِكَ إِنْ أَرَادُوٓا۟ إِصْلَٰحًا ۚ وَلَهُنَّ مِثْلُ ٱلَّذِى عَلَيْهِنَّ بِٱلْمَعْرُوفِ ۚ
وَلِلرِّجَالِ عَلَيْهِنَّ دَرَجَةٌ ۗ وَٱللَّهُ عَزِيزٌ حَكِيمٌ ﴿٢٢٨﴾ ٱلطَّلَٰقُ مَرَّتَانِ ۖ
فَإِمْسَاكٌۢ بِمَعْرُوفٍ أَوْ تَسْرِيحٌۢ بِإِحْسَٰنٍ ۗ وَلَا يَحِلُّ لَكُمْ أَن
تَأْخُذُوا۟ مِمَّآ ءَاتَيْتُمُوهُنَّ شَيْـًٔا إِلَّآ أَن يَخَافَآ أَلَّا يُقِيمَا حُدُودَ
ٱللَّهِ ۖ فَإِنْ خِفْتُمْ أَلَّا يُقِيمَا حُدُودَ ٱللَّهِ فَلَا جُنَاحَ عَلَيْهِمَا فِيمَا ٱفْتَدَتْ
بِهِۦ ۗ تِلْكَ حُدُودُ ٱللَّهِ فَلَا تَعْتَدُوهَا ۚ وَمَن يَتَعَدَّ حُدُودَ ٱللَّهِ فَأُو۟لَٰٓئِكَ
هُمُ ٱلظَّٰلِمُونَ ﴿٢٢٩﴾ فَإِن طَلَّقَهَا فَلَا تَحِلُّ لَهُۥ مِنۢ بَعْدُ حَتَّىٰ تَنكِحَ
زَوْجًا غَيْرَهُۥ ۗ فَإِن طَلَّقَهَا فَلَا جُنَاحَ عَلَيْهِمَآ أَن يَتَرَاجَعَآ إِن ظَنَّآ أَن
يُقِيمَا حُدُودَ ٱللَّهِ ۗ وَتِلْكَ حُدُودُ ٱللَّهِ يُبَيِّنُهَا لِقَوْمٍ يَعْلَمُونَ ﴿٢٣٠﴾
وَإِذَا طَلَّقْتُمُ ٱلنِّسَآءَ فَبَلَغْنَ أَجَلَهُنَّ فَأَمْسِكُوهُنَّ بِمَعْرُوفٍ أَوْ
سَرِّحُوهُنَّ بِمَعْرُوفٍ ۚ وَلَا تُمْسِكُوهُنَّ ضِرَارًا لِّتَعْتَدُوا۟ ۚ وَمَن يَفْعَلْ
ذَٰلِكَ فَقَدْ ظَلَمَ نَفْسَهُۥ ۚ وَلَا تَتَّخِذُوٓا۟ ءَايَٰتِ ٱللَّهِ هُزُوًا ۚ وَٱذْكُرُوا۟
نِعْمَتَ ٱللَّهِ عَلَيْكُمْ وَمَآ أَنزَلَ عَلَيْكُم مِّنَ ٱلْكِتَٰبِ وَٱلْحِكْمَةِ
يَعِظُكُم بِهِۦ ۚ وَٱتَّقُوا۟ ٱللَّهَ وَٱعْلَمُوٓا۟ أَنَّ ٱللَّهَ بِكُلِّ شَىْءٍ عَلِيمٌ ﴿٢٣١﴾
وَإِذَا طَلَّقْتُمُ ٱلنِّسَآءَ فَبَلَغْنَ أَجَلَهُنَّ فَلَا تَعْضُلُوهُنَّ أَن يَنكِحْنَ
أَزْوَٰجَهُنَّ إِذَا تَرَٰضَوْا۟ بَيْنَهُم بِٱلْمَعْرُوفِ ۗ ذَٰلِكَ يُوعَظُ بِهِۦ مَن كَانَ
مِنكُمْ يُؤْمِنُ بِٱللَّهِ وَٱلْيَوْمِ ٱلْـَٔاخِرِ ۗ ذَٰلِكُمْ أَزْكَىٰ لَكُمْ وَأَطْهَرُ ۗ وَٱللَّهُ
يَعْلَمُ وَأَنتُمْ لَا تَعْلَمُونَ ﴿٢٣٢﴾ ۞ وَٱلْوَٰلِدَٰتُ يُرْضِعْنَ أَوْلَٰدَهُنَّ
حَوْلَيْنِ كَامِلَيْنِ ۖ لِمَنْ أَرَادَ أَن يُتِمَّ ٱلرَّضَاعَةَ ۚ وَعَلَى ٱلْمَوْلُودِ لَهُۥ رِزْقُهُنَّ

qurū', "menstrual cycles" is the plural of *qar'*, which can refer either to the period of purity between periods of menstruation or or to the period of menstruation itself. This applies to women whose marriage has been consummated. If the marriage has not been consummated there is no *'idda* to observe, as shown by Allah's words: *"There is no 'idda for you to calculate for them"* (33:49) in another *āyat*. The *'idda* of a child is three months and that of a pregnant women ends when she gives birth, as is stated in *Sūrat at-Ṭalāq* 65:4. The *'idda* of a slave is two menstrual cycles ***and it is not lawful for them*** (divorced women) ***to conceal what Allah has created in their wombs*** (menstruation or pregnancy) ***if they believe in Allah and the Last Day. Their husbands have the right to take them back within that*** waiting ***time, if they*** both ***desire to be reconciled,*** avoiding any harm to the wife. This is to encourage a good intention, not a precondition for the husband taking his wife back, since he clearly has the right to do so. This is the revocable divorce. No one else has any right to marry them while they are in their *'idda*. ***Women possess rights*** from their husbands ***similar to those*** rights ***held over them*** by their husbands ***to be honoured with fairness*** as prescribed in the Sharī'a: good treatment, lack of injury and other such things; ***but men have a degree above them.*** Men have a degree of excellence since they pay the *mahr* and support women financially. ***Allah is Almighty*** in His kingdom, ***All-Wise*** in how He manages His creation.

229. ***Divorce can be pronounced twice;*** this concerns the revocable divorce, ***in which case wives may be retained with correctness and courtesy***, without inflicting any harm, ***or released*** (let go) ***with good will. It is not lawful,*** husbands, ***for you to keep anything you have given them*** of any dowry if you divorce them ***unless a couple fear that they will not remain within Allah's limits***, meaning that they will not perform the duties prescribed for them. ***If you fear that they will not remain within Allah's limits, there is nothing wrong in a wife ransoming herself with some of what she has received.*** A wife can pay to be divorced and in such a case there is no harm in the husband taking it or the wife in paying it. ***These*** rulings which were mentioned ***are Allah's limits, so do not overstep them.***

230. ***But if a man divorces his wife a third time, she is not lawful for him after that,*** after the third divorce, ***until she has married another husband*** and consummates the marriage with him, as it says in the *ḥadīth* in the two *Ṣaḥīḥ* collections. ***Then if he*** (the second husband) ***divorces her, there is nothing wrong in the original couple getting back together*** after the end of the *'idda* ***provided they think they will remain within Allah's limits. These are Allah's limits which He has made clear to people who know*** and reflect.

231. ***When you divorce women and they are near the end of their 'idda, then either retain them with correctness and courtesy,*** without harming them, ***or release them with correctness and courtesy,*** letting them go without inflicting any harm on them at the end of their *'idda*. ***Do not retain them by force, thus overstepping the limits*** by forcing them to ransom themselves and trying to drag things out. ***Anyone who does that has wronged himself*** and exposed himself to Allah's punishment. ***Do not make a mockery of Allah's Signs*** by opposing them. ***Remember Allah's blessing*** (Islam) ***upon you and the Book*** (the Qur'an) ***and Wisdom*** (the rulings in it) ***He has sent down to you to admonish you***, by showing gratitude to Him through acting on it. ***Be fearful of Allah and know that Allah has knowledge of all things*** so that nothing is hidden from Him.

232. ***When you divorce women and they are near the end of their 'idda, do not prevent them*** (this is addressed to the guardians of the women) ***from marrying their first husbands*** who have divorced them ***if they*** (the husbands and the wives) ***have mutually agreed to it with correctness and courtesy*** according to the Sharī'a. The reason for the revelation of this *āyat* was that the sister of Ma'qil ibn Yasār was divorced by her husband and then he wanted to take her back but Ma'qil prevented him from doing so, as al-Ḥākim related. ***This*** prohibition of preventing them from remarrying ***is an admonition for those of you who believe in Allah and the Last Day*** because you are the ones who will benefit from it. ***That*** (not preventing them) ***is better and purer for you*** because of the uncertainty which is feared for the couple because of the connection between them. ***Allah knows*** where your best interests lie ***and you do not know*** that. That is why you must follow His command.

وَكِسْوَتُهُنَّ بِٱلْمَعْرُوفِ لَا تُكَلَّفُ نَفْسٌ إِلَّا وُسْعَهَا لَا تُضَآرَّ
وَٰلِدَةٌۢ بِوَلَدِهَا وَلَا مَوْلُودٌ لَّهُۥ بِوَلَدِهِۦ وَعَلَى ٱلْوَارِثِ مِثْلُ ذَٰلِكَ
فَإِنْ أَرَادَا فِصَالًا عَن تَرَاضٍ مِّنْهُمَا وَتَشَاوُرٍ فَلَا جُنَاحَ عَلَيْهِمَا وَإِنْ
أَرَدتُّمْ أَن تَسْتَرْضِعُوٓا۟ أَوْلَٰدَكُمْ فَلَا جُنَاحَ عَلَيْكُمْ إِذَا سَلَّمْتُم مَّآ
ءَاتَيْتُم بِٱلْمَعْرُوفِ وَٱتَّقُوا۟ ٱللَّهَ وَٱعْلَمُوٓا۟ أَنَّ ٱللَّهَ بِمَا تَعْمَلُونَ بَصِيرٌ ٢٣٣
وَٱلَّذِينَ يُتَوَفَّوْنَ مِنكُمْ وَيَذَرُونَ أَزْوَٰجًا يَتَرَبَّصْنَ بِأَنفُسِهِنَّ
أَرْبَعَةَ أَشْهُرٍ وَعَشْرًا فَإِذَا بَلَغْنَ أَجَلَهُنَّ فَلَا جُنَاحَ عَلَيْكُمْ
فِيمَا فَعَلْنَ فِىٓ أَنفُسِهِنَّ بِٱلْمَعْرُوفِ وَٱللَّهُ بِمَا تَعْمَلُونَ خَبِيرٌ
٢٣٤ وَلَا جُنَاحَ عَلَيْكُمْ فِيمَا عَرَّضْتُم بِهِۦ مِنْ خِطْبَةِ ٱلنِّسَآءِ
أَوْ أَكْنَنتُمْ فِىٓ أَنفُسِكُمْ عَلِمَ ٱللَّهُ أَنَّكُمْ سَتَذْكُرُونَهُنَّ
وَلَٰكِن لَّا تُوَاعِدُوهُنَّ سِرًّا إِلَّآ أَن تَقُولُوا۟ قَوْلًا مَّعْرُوفًا
وَلَا تَعْزِمُوا۟ عُقْدَةَ ٱلنِّكَاحِ حَتَّىٰ يَبْلُغَ ٱلْكِتَٰبُ أَجَلَهُۥ
وَٱعْلَمُوٓا۟ أَنَّ ٱللَّهَ يَعْلَمُ مَا فِىٓ أَنفُسِكُمْ فَٱحْذَرُوهُ وَٱعْلَمُوٓا۟
أَنَّ ٱللَّهَ غَفُورٌ حَلِيمٌ ٢٣٥ لَّا جُنَاحَ عَلَيْكُمْ إِن طَلَّقْتُمُ ٱلنِّسَآءَ
مَا لَمْ تَمَسُّوهُنَّ أَوْ تَفْرِضُوا۟ لَهُنَّ فَرِيضَةً وَمَتِّعُوهُنَّ عَلَى ٱلْمُوسِعِ
قَدَرُهُۥ وَعَلَى ٱلْمُقْتِرِ قَدَرُهُۥ مَتَٰعًۢا بِٱلْمَعْرُوفِ حَقًّا عَلَى ٱلْمُحْسِنِينَ
٢٣٦ وَإِن طَلَّقْتُمُوهُنَّ مِن قَبْلِ أَن تَمَسُّوهُنَّ وَقَدْ فَرَضْتُمْ
لَهُنَّ فَرِيضَةً فَنِصْفُ مَا فَرَضْتُمْ إِلَّآ أَن يَعْفُونَ أَوْ يَعْفُوَا۟
ٱلَّذِى بِيَدِهِۦ عُقْدَةُ ٱلنِّكَاحِ وَأَن تَعْفُوٓا۟ أَقْرَبُ لِلتَّقْوَىٰ
وَلَا تَنسَوُا۟ ٱلْفَضْلَ بَيْنَكُمْ إِنَّ ٱللَّهَ بِمَا تَعْمَلُونَ بَصِيرٌ ٢٣٧

233. ***Mothers should nurse their children for two full*** ("full" is for stress) ***years – for those who wish to complete the full term of nursing*** which is not more than that. ***It is the duty of the fathers*** (of the children) ***to feed and clothe them*** (the mothers while they are nursing) ***with correctness and courtesy*** according to ability – ***no self is charged beyond what it can bear. No mother should be put under pressure in respect of her child*** by forcing her to nurse when she refuses ***nor any father in respect of his child*** by making him spend more than he is able to. The child is ascribed to both parents because the affections of the child extend to both of them. ***The same duty is incumbent on the heir*** of the father, who is the child. The heir has a right to the money of his guardian. He has a similar entitlement to provision and clothing to the mother's. ***If the couple*** (the parents) ***both wish weaning to take place*** before the two years are up ***after mutual agreement and consultation*** between them in respect of the best interests of the child, ***there is nothing wrong in their doing so*** and that is acceptable. The following is addressed to the fathers: ***If you wish to find wet-nurses*** other than their mothers ***for your children, there is nothing wrong in your doing so provided you hand over to them what you have agreed to give*** in payment to them ***with correctness and courtesy,*** cheerfully and correctly. ***Be fearful of Allah and know that Allah sees what you do,*** nothing being hidden from Him.

234. ***Those of you who die leaving wives behind: they should wait by themselves*** as an *'idda* after marriage ***for four months and ten nights.*** The end of the *'idda* of a pregnant woman, however, is whenever she gives birth, as stated in the *Āyat* of Divorce (65:4). The *'idda* of a slavegirl is half that according to the *Sunna.* ***When their*** **'idda** ***comes to an end, you*** guardians ***are not to blame for anything they do with themselves*** by way of adorning themselves and showing that they are ready for new marriage proposals ***with correctness and courtesy*** which is correct in the *Sharī'a.* ***Allah is aware of what you do,*** knowing your inward as well as the outward.

235. ***Nor is there anything wrong in any allusion to marriage you make to a woman,*** who is widowed and in *'idda,* as when a man says, "You are beautiful," or "Who could find anyone like you?" or "By the Lord, I desire you", ***nor for any you keep to yourself*** by concealing your intention to marry them. ***Allah knows that you will say things to them*** by proposals you make and what you allude to and that is permitted. ***But do not make secret arrangements with them*** to marry them, ***rather only speak with correctness and cour - tesy,*** in a manner which is correct in the *Sharī'a*. ***Do not finally decide on the marriage contract until the prescribed period*** (*'idda*) ***has come to its end. Know that Allah knows what is in your selves*** of resolve and other things, ***so beware of Him*** and His punishment if you resolve on marriage! ***And know that Allah is Ever-Forgiving*** of the one He warns, ***Ever-Forbearing***, deferring the punishment from the one who deserves it.

236. ***There is nothing wrong in your divorcing women before you have touched them*** (read as *tamassū*, "you have touched" and *tumāssū*, "you have had intercourse with") ***them or allotted a dowry to them. But give them a gift*** which they will enjoy – ***he who is wealthy according to his means and he who is less well off accord - ing to his means*** – and in this case the social rank of the wife is not considered – ***a gift to be given with correctness and courtesy*** in accordance with the *Shari'a:* ***a duty for all good-doers,*** those who obey Allah.

237. ***If you divorce them before you have touched them but have already allotted them a dowry, they should have half the amount you allotted*** and you can take half back, ***unless they forgo it,*** unless the wife forgoes it, ***or the one in charge of the marriage contract forgoes it,*** in other words the husband allows her to take the entire amount. Ibn 'Abbās said that this means the guardian should do this if the girl is secluded. ***To forgo it is closer to being godfearing. Do not forget to show generosity to one another*** and be kind to one another. ***Allah sees what you do*** and will repay you for it.

238. ***Safeguard the*** five ***prayers*** by performing them at their proper times – ***especially the middle prayer.*** The middle prayer may be *'Aṣr*, *Ṣubḥ*, *Ẓuhr* or another. It is singled out for mention because of its excellence. ***Stand in*** the prayer out of ***obedience to Allah*** since the Prophet, may Allah bless him and grant him peace, said, "Every *qanūt* in the Qur'ān means obedience." (Aḥmad and others) It is said that it means silence, based on the *ḥadīth* of Zayd ibn Arqam, "We used to speak in the prayer until this was revealed and we were com-

حَٰفِظُواْ عَلَى ٱلصَّلَوَٰتِ وَٱلصَّلَوٰةِ ٱلۡوُسۡطَىٰ وَقُومُواْ لِلَّهِ
قَٰنِتِينَ ﴿٢٣٨﴾ فَإِنۡ خِفۡتُمۡ فَرِجَالًا أَوۡ رُكۡبَانٗاۖ فَإِذَآ أَمِنتُمۡ
فَٱذۡكُرُواْ ٱللَّهَ كَمَا عَلَّمَكُم مَّا لَمۡ تَكُونُواْ تَعۡلَمُونَ
﴿٢٣٩﴾ وَٱلَّذِينَ يُتَوَفَّوۡنَ مِنكُمۡ وَيَذَرُونَ أَزۡوَٰجٗا وَصِيَّةٗ
لِّأَزۡوَٰجِهِم مَّتَٰعًا إِلَى ٱلۡحَوۡلِ غَيۡرَ إِخۡرَاجٖۚ فَإِنۡ خَرَجۡنَ
فَلَا جُنَاحَ عَلَيۡكُمۡ فِي مَا فَعَلۡنَ فِيٓ أَنفُسِهِنَّ مِن
مَّعۡرُوفٖۗ وَٱللَّهُ عَزِيزٌ حَكِيمٞ ﴿٢٤٠﴾ وَلِلۡمُطَلَّقَٰتِ مَتَٰعُۢ
بِٱلۡمَعۡرُوفِۖ حَقًّا عَلَى ٱلۡمُتَّقِينَ ﴿٢٤١﴾ كَذَٰلِكَ يُبَيِّنُ
ٱللَّهُ لَكُمۡ ءَايَٰتِهِۦ لَعَلَّكُمۡ تَعۡقِلُونَ ﴿٢٤٢﴾ ۞ أَلَمۡ تَرَ
إِلَى ٱلَّذِينَ خَرَجُواْ مِن دِيَٰرِهِمۡ وَهُمۡ أُلُوفٌ حَذَرَ ٱلۡمَوۡتِ
فَقَالَ لَهُمُ ٱللَّهُ مُوتُواْ ثُمَّ أَحۡيَٰهُمۡۚ إِنَّ ٱللَّهَ لَذُو فَضۡلٍ عَلَى
ٱلنَّاسِ وَلَٰكِنَّ أَكۡثَرَ ٱلنَّاسِ لَا يَشۡكُرُونَ ﴿٢٤٣﴾
وَقَٰتِلُواْ فِي سَبِيلِ ٱللَّهِ وَٱعۡلَمُوٓاْ أَنَّ ٱللَّهَ سَمِيعٌ عَلِيمٞ ﴿٢٤٤﴾
مَّن ذَا ٱلَّذِي يُقۡرِضُ ٱللَّهَ قَرۡضًا حَسَنٗا فَيُضَٰعِفَهُۥ لَهُۥٓ أَضۡعَافٗا
كَثِيرَةٗۚ وَٱللَّهُ يَقۡبِضُ وَيَبۡصُۜطُ وَإِلَيۡهِ تُرۡجَعُونَ ﴿٢٤٥﴾
أَلَمۡ تَرَ إِلَى ٱلۡمَلَإِ مِنۢ بَنِيٓ إِسۡرَٰٓءِيلَ مِنۢ بَعۡدِ مُوسَىٰٓ إِذۡ قَالُواْ
لِنَبِيّٖ لَّهُمُ ٱبۡعَثۡ لَنَا مَلِكٗا نُّقَٰتِلۡ فِي سَبِيلِ ٱللَّهِۖ قَالَ
هَلۡ عَسَيۡتُمۡ إِن كُتِبَ عَلَيۡكُمُ ٱلۡقِتَالُ أَلَّا تُقَٰتِلُواْۖ
قَالُواْ وَمَا لَنَآ أَلَّا نُقَٰتِلَ فِي سَبِيلِ ٱللَّهِ وَقَدۡ أُخۡرِجۡنَا
مِن دِيَٰرِنَا وَأَبۡنَآئِنَاۖ فَلَمَّا كُتِبَ عَلَيۡهِمُ ٱلۡقِتَالُ تَوَلَّوۡاْ

manded to be silent and forbidden to speak." (al-Bukhārī and Muslim).

239. ***If you are afraid*** of the enemy, flood or wild beasts, ***then pray on foot or mounted.*** Pray however you can, facing the *qibla* or not and indicating *rukū'* and prostration. ***But when you are safe*** and free from fear, ***remember Allah*** in the prayer ***in the way He taught you when previously you did not know*** with all its obligatory elements and duties which you did not know before He taught you.

240. ***Those of you who die leaving wives behind should make a bequest of maintenance*** and clothing ***to their wives for a*** full ***year*** from their death and they are obliged to wait ***without having to leave their homes. But if they do then leave you***, executor of the dead person, ***are not to blame for anything they do with themselves with correctness and courtesy,*** such as adorning themselves or abandoning mourning, or thereby putting an end to their maintenance. ***Allah is Almighty*** in His kingdom, ***All-Wise*** in what He does. This bequest was abrogated by the *Āyat* of Inheritance when waiting for a year was changed to four months and ten days which was revealed later. The widow's right to a dwelling is confirmed by ash-Shāfi'ī.

241. ***Divorced women should*** be given and ***receive maintenance given with correctness and courtesy*** according to one's ability***: a duty for all godfearing people*** who fear Allah. Allah repeats "godfearing" to make it general since the previous *āyat* was specific.

242. ***In this way Allah makes His Signs clear to you,*** making clear these mentioned rulings, ***so that hopefully you will use your intellect*** and reflect.

243. The following question is one of wonder and desire to hear the response. ***What do you think about those who left their homes in thousands***, variously said to have been four, eight, thirty, forty or seventy thousand, ***in fear of death?*** They were people from the tribe of Israel who fled when there was a plague in their land. Then ***Allah said to them, "Die!"*** and they died ***and then brought them back to life*** eight or more days later, after the supplication of their Prophet Ezekiel. They lived for some time after being brought back from death wearing things which resembled shrouds, remaining in their tribes. ***Allah shows great favour for mankind,*** part of which was bringing those people to life, ***but most people are not grateful.*** They

إِلَّا قَلِيلًا مِّنْهُمْ ۗ وَٱللَّهُ عَلِيمٌۢ بِٱلظَّٰلِمِينَ ﴿٢٤٦﴾ وَقَالَ
لَهُمْ نَبِيُّهُمْ إِنَّ ٱللَّهَ قَدْ بَعَثَ لَكُمْ طَالُوتَ مَلِكًا ۚ
قَالُوٓا۟ أَنَّىٰ يَكُونُ لَهُ ٱلْمُلْكُ عَلَيْنَا وَنَحْنُ أَحَقُّ بِٱلْمُلْكِ
مِنْهُ وَلَمْ يُؤْتَ سَعَةً مِّنَ ٱلْمَالِ ۚ قَالَ إِنَّ ٱللَّهَ ٱصْطَفَىٰهُ
عَلَيْكُمْ وَزَادَهُۥ بَسْطَةً فِى ٱلْعِلْمِ وَٱلْجِسْمِ ۖ وَٱللَّهُ
يُؤْتِى مُلْكَهُۥ مَن يَشَآءُ ۚ وَٱللَّهُ وَٰسِعٌ عَلِيمٌ ﴿٢٤٧﴾
وَقَالَ لَهُمْ نَبِيُّهُمْ إِنَّ ءَايَةَ مُلْكِهِۦٓ أَن يَأْتِيَكُمُ
ٱلتَّابُوتُ فِيهِ سَكِينَةٌ مِّن رَّبِّكُمْ وَبَقِيَّةٌ مِّمَّا
تَرَكَ ءَالُ مُوسَىٰ وَءَالُ هَٰرُونَ تَحْمِلُهُ ٱلْمَلَٰٓئِكَةُ ۚ
إِنَّ فِى ذَٰلِكَ لَءَايَةً لَّكُمْ إِن كُنتُم مُّؤْمِنِينَ ﴿٢٤٨﴾
فَلَمَّا فَصَلَ طَالُوتُ بِٱلْجُنُودِ قَالَ إِنَّ ٱللَّهَ مُبْتَلِيكُم
بِنَهَرٍ فَمَن شَرِبَ مِنْهُ فَلَيْسَ مِنِّى وَمَن لَّمْ يَطْعَمْهُ فَإِنَّهُۥ
مِنِّىٓ إِلَّا مَنِ ٱغْتَرَفَ غُرْفَةًۢ بِيَدِهِۦ ۚ فَشَرِبُوا۟ مِنْهُ إِلَّا قَلِيلًا
مِّنْهُمْ ۚ فَلَمَّا جَاوَزَهُۥ هُوَ وَٱلَّذِينَ ءَامَنُوا۟ مَعَهُۥ قَالُوا۟
لَا طَاقَةَ لَنَا ٱلْيَوْمَ بِجَالُوتَ وَجُنُودِهِۦ ۚ قَالَ ٱلَّذِينَ
يَظُنُّونَ أَنَّهُم مُّلَٰقُوا۟ ٱللَّهِ كَم مِّن فِئَةٍ قَلِيلَةٍ
غَلَبَتْ فِئَةً كَثِيرَةًۢ بِإِذْنِ ٱللَّهِ ۗ وَٱللَّهُ مَعَ ٱلصَّٰبِرِينَ ﴿٢٤٩﴾
وَلَمَّا بَرَزُوا۟ لِجَالُوتَ وَجُنُودِهِۦ قَالُوا۟ رَبَّنَآ أَفْرِغْ
عَلَيْنَا صَبْرًا وَثَبِّتْ أَقْدَامَنَا وَٱنصُرْنَا عَلَى ٱلْقَوْمِ
ٱلْكَٰفِرِينَ ﴿٢٥٠﴾ فَهَزَمُوهُم بِإِذْنِ ٱللَّهِ وَقَتَلَ

do not thank Allah. This meant to encourage the believers to fight, which is why the next *āyat* continues with the instruction to do so.

244. ***Fight in the Way of Allah*** to elevate His *dīn*. ***Know that Allah is All-Hearing,*** hearing your words, ***All-Knowing***, knowing your states and He will repay you.

245. ***Is there anyone who will make Allah a generous loan*** by spending his wealth in the Way of Allah with a cheerful heart ***so that He can multiply*** (*yuḍā'ifahu* and *yuḍa''ifahu*) ***it for him many times over,*** from ten to more than seven hundred times***? Allah both restricts*** and withholds provision from anyone He wishes as a test for him ***and expands*** the provsion of anyone He wishes as a test for them. ***And you will be returned to Him*** in the Next World at the Resurrection, when He will repay you for your actions.

246. ***What do you think about*** the story and news of ***the nobles*** and the community ***of the tribe of Israel after Mūsā's time*** (after his death)***, when they said to one of their Prophets*** (Samuel)***, "Give us a king*** and establish him for us, ***and we will fight*** together with him ***in the way of Allah!"?*** He will organise us and we will support him. ***He*** (this Prophet) ***said*** to them***, "Is it not possible*** (read as *'asaytum* and *'asītum*) ***that if fighting were prescribed for you, you would not fight?"*** This is a question that confirms and records, because that is what actually occurred. ***They said, "How could we not fight in the way of Allah when we have been driven from our homes and children*** who have been captured and killed***?"*** That was done by the people of Goliath. In other words, they said that there was nothing to impede them doing that if it became necessary. Allah Almighty continues: ***But then when fighting was prescribed for them, they turned their backs*** and were cowardly – ***except for a few of them*** who crossed the river with Saul as will be mentioned. ***Allah knows the wrongdoers*** and will repay them. The Prophet asked his Lord to send them a king and Allah responded to them by giving them Ṭālūt (Saul).

247. ***Their Prophet said to them, "Allah has appointed Saul to be your king." They said, "How can he have kingship over us when we have much more right to kingship than he does?*** They asked this because he was not one of the scions of nobility or prophethood. He was a tanner or a shepherd. ***He has not even much wealth*** to help him to establish the kingdom!" ***He*** (the Prophet) ***said*** to them, ***"Allah has chosen him*** to be king ***over you and favoured him greatly in*** expansion in ***knowledge and physical strength.*** At that time, he was the most knowledgeable of the Israelites and the handsomest and the one with the best physique. ***Allah gives kingship to anyone He wills*** and none can oppose it. ***Allah is All-Encompassing,*** vast in bounty, ***All-Knowing,*** knowing who is worthy to be king."

248. ***Their Prophet said to them*** when they asked him for a sign of kingship, ***"The sign of his kingship is that the Ark will come to you,*** which contained images of the Prophets. Allah sent it down to Ādam. When the Amlekites conquered the Jews they captured the Ark. The Israelites used to open it against their enemy and bring it to the front in fighting and it gave them tranquillity as Allah says: ***containing serenity,*** peace of mind for your hearts, ***from your Lord and certain relics left by the families of Mūsā and Hārūn.*** The relics referred to were the sandals and staff of Mūsā, the turban of Hārūn, a piece of the manna which came down, and pieces of the tablets Mūsā received from Allah. ***It will be borne by angels. There is a sign*** of his kingship ***for you in that if you are believers."*** The angels carried it between heaven and earth while they were looking at it until it was placed with Saul. Then they affirmed his kingship and hastened to fight and he chose seventy thousand young men.

249. ***When Saul marched out with the army*** from Jerusalem when it was hot and they asked him for water, ***he said, "Allah will test you with a river*** to show who among you is obedient and who is disobedient. It was between Jordan and Palestine. ***Anyone who drinks from it is not with me,*** in other words not one of my followers. ***But anyone who does not taste it is with me – except for him who merely scoops up a little*** (read as *ghurfa* and *gharfa*) ***in his hand*** and is content with that without taking any more. Such are my followers." ***But*** when they reached it, ***they,*** (most of them) ***drank from it – except for a few of them*** who were content with handfuls. It is related that it was enough for both them and their animals. They numbered around three hundred and ten. ***Then when he and those who had faith with him*** (those who confined themselves to a handful), ***had crossed it, they*** (those who had drunk from it) ***said, "We do not***

دَاوُۥدُ جَالُوتَ وَءَاتَىٰهُ ٱللَّهُ ٱلْمُلْكَ وَٱلْحِكْمَةَ
وَعَلَّمَهُۥ مِمَّا يَشَآءُ ۗ وَلَوْلَا دَفْعُ ٱللَّهِ ٱلنَّاسَ بَعْضَهُم
بِبَعْضٍ لَّفَسَدَتِ ٱلْأَرْضُ وَلَٰكِنَّ ٱللَّهَ ذُو
فَضْلٍ عَلَى ٱلْعَٰلَمِينَ ﴿٢٥١﴾ تِلْكَ ءَايَٰتُ ٱللَّهِ
نَتْلُوهَا عَلَيْكَ بِٱلْحَقِّ ۚ وَإِنَّكَ لَمِنَ ٱلْمُرْسَلِينَ ﴿٢٥٢﴾
۞ تِلْكَ ٱلرُّسُلُ فَضَّلْنَا بَعْضَهُمْ عَلَىٰ بَعْضٍ ۘ مِّنْهُم مَّن كَلَّمَ ٱللَّهُ ۖ
وَرَفَعَ بَعْضَهُمْ دَرَجَٰتٍ ۚ وَءَاتَيْنَا عِيسَى ٱبْنَ مَرْيَمَ ٱلْبَيِّنَٰتِ
وَأَيَّدْنَٰهُ بِرُوحِ ٱلْقُدُسِ ۗ وَلَوْ شَآءَ ٱللَّهُ مَا ٱقْتَتَلَ ٱلَّذِينَ
مِنۢ بَعْدِهِم مِّنۢ بَعْدِ مَا جَآءَتْهُمُ ٱلْبَيِّنَٰتُ وَلَٰكِنِ ٱخْتَلَفُوا۟
فَمِنْهُم مَّنْ ءَامَنَ وَمِنْهُم مَّن كَفَرَ ۚ وَلَوْ شَآءَ ٱللَّهُ مَا ٱقْتَتَلُوا۟
وَلَٰكِنَّ ٱللَّهَ يَفْعَلُ مَا يُرِيدُ ﴿٢٥٣﴾ يَٰٓأَيُّهَا ٱلَّذِينَ ءَامَنُوٓا۟ أَنفِقُوا۟
مِمَّا رَزَقْنَٰكُم مِّن قَبْلِ أَن يَأْتِىَ يَوْمٌ لَّا بَيْعٌ فِيهِ وَلَا خُلَّةٌ وَلَا
شَفَٰعَةٌ ۗ وَٱلْكَٰفِرُونَ هُمُ ٱلظَّٰلِمُونَ ﴿٢٥٤﴾ ٱللَّهُ لَآ إِلَٰهَ إِلَّا هُوَ
ٱلْحَىُّ ٱلْقَيُّومُ ۚ لَا تَأْخُذُهُۥ سِنَةٌ وَلَا نَوْمٌ ۚ لَّهُۥ مَا فِى ٱلسَّمَٰوَٰتِ وَمَا
فِى ٱلْأَرْضِ ۗ مَن ذَا ٱلَّذِى يَشْفَعُ عِندَهُۥٓ إِلَّا بِإِذْنِهِۦ ۚ يَعْلَمُ مَا بَيْنَ
أَيْدِيهِمْ وَمَا خَلْفَهُمْ ۖ وَلَا يُحِيطُونَ بِشَىْءٍ مِّنْ عِلْمِهِۦٓ إِلَّا بِمَا
شَآءَ ۚ وَسِعَ كُرْسِيُّهُ ٱلسَّمَٰوَٰتِ وَٱلْأَرْضَ ۖ وَلَا يَـُٔودُهُۥ حِفْظُهُمَا ۚ
وَهُوَ ٱلْعَلِىُّ ٱلْعَظِيمُ ﴿٢٥٥﴾ لَآ إِكْرَاهَ فِى ٱلدِّينِ ۖ قَد تَّبَيَّنَ ٱلرُّشْدُ
مِنَ ٱلْغَىِّ ۚ فَمَن يَكْفُرْ بِٱلطَّٰغُوتِ وَيُؤْمِنۢ بِٱللَّهِ فَقَدِ
ٱسْتَمْسَكَ بِٱلْعُرْوَةِ ٱلْوُثْقَىٰ لَا ٱنفِصَامَ لَهَا ۗ وَٱللَّهُ سَمِيعٌ عَلِيمٌ ﴿٢٥٦﴾

have the strength to face Goliath and his troops today and fight him." They were cowardly and would not cross it. ***But those who were sure that they were going to meet Allah*** at the Resurrection and had crossed it ***said, "How many a small force has triumphed over a much greater one with Allah's permission*** (His will). ***Allah is with the steadfast***, giving them help and victory."

250. ***When they came out against Goliath and his troops*** and they formed ranks to fight, ***they said, "Our Lord, pour down steadfastness upon us, make our feet firm*** by making our hearts strong in *jihād*, ***and help us against the people of the unbelievers."***

251. ***And with Allah's permission*** (by His will) ***they routed them. Dāwūd***, who was in Saul's army, ***killed Goliath and Allah gave him kingship*** in the tribe of Israel ***and wisdom,*** meaning Prophethood, after the death of Samuel and Saul and no one had had both of them before him, ***and taught him whatever He willed,*** such as making armour and the speech of birds. ***If it were not for Allah's driving some people back by means of others, the earth would have been corrupted*** because the idolaters would have dominated and killed the Muslims and destroyed their mosques. ***But Allah possesses favour for all the worlds*** by driving them back by one another.

252. ***These*** Signs ***are Allah's Signs which We recite to you,*** Muḥammad, ***with truth. You are indeed one of the Messengers.*** This is stressed to refute the position of the unbelievers that he was not a Messenger.

253. ***These Messengers*** (or "These are Messengers"): ***We favoured some of them over others*** with a special trait which none of the others had. ***Allah spoke directly to some of them*** like Mūsā ***and raised up some of them in rank*** like Muḥammad, may Allah bless him and grant him peace, with universal supplication, the seal of prophethood, and selecting his Community over all communities, miracles and many special qualities. ***We gave Clear Signs to 'Īsā, son of Maryam, and reinforced him with the Spirit of Purity,*** Jibrīl, going with him wherever he went. ***If Allah had willed,*** He could have guided all people and then ***those who came after them***, meaning the nations of the Prophets, ***would not have fought each other after the clear Signs came to them, but they differed*** and misled one another by Allah's will. ***Among them there are those who believe*** — remain firm in their faith — ***and among them there are those who disbelieve***, like the Christians after 'Īsā. ***If Allah had willed, they would not have fought each other.*** The repetition is for stress. ***But Allah does whatever He desires.*** He gives success to whomever He wishes and leaves in the lurch whomever He wishes.

254. ***You who believe! Give away some of what We have provided for you*** as *zakāt* ***before a Day arrives on which there is no trading,*** meaning ransom, ***no close friendship*** which benefits ***and no intercession*** without His permission. That means the Day of Rising. ***It is the rejectors*** of Allah or those who reject what He has imposed on them ***who are the wrongdoers*** by putting the command of Allah elsewhere than its proper place.

255. ***Allah. There is no god but Him,*** there is nothing but Him truly worshipped in existence, ***the Living,*** Constantly Abiding, ***the Self-Sustaining,*** the One who undertakes to manage His creation. ***He is not subject to drowsiness or sleep. Everything in the heavens and the earth belongs to Him.*** Kingdom, creation and slaves all belong to Him absolutely. ***Who can intercede,*** in other words none can, ***with Him except by His permission*** to do so? ***He knows what is before them*** (creation) ***and what is behind them*** (the business of this world and the Next World). ***And they cannot grasp any of His knowledge*** and do not know any known things ***save what He wills.*** They only know what He informs them of through His Messengers. ***His Footstool encompasses the heavens and the earth...*** It is said that this means that His knowledge encompasses the heavens and the earth. It is also said that the Footstool (*Kursi*) itself encompasses them in its immensity, according to the *ḥadīth*, "The seven heavens are only like seven dirhams thrown into the desert." ***... and their preservation*** (that of the Heavens and the earth) ***does not tire Him*** (wear Him out). ***He is the Most High*** above His creation by His overwhelming power, ***the Magnificent*** and Immense.

256. ***There is no compulsion where the dīn is concerned*** to compel people to enter it. ***Right guidance has become clearly distinct from error.*** Guidance is clear by the evident signs that belief is right guidance and unbelief is error. This was revealed about some of the Anṣār who had children and wanted to force them into Islam. ***Anyone who rejects false gods*** (*ṭāghūt* which means *Shayṭān* or

ٱللَّهُ وَلِيُّ ٱلَّذِينَ ءَامَنُواْ يُخۡرِجُهُم مِّنَ ٱلظُّلُمَٰتِ إِلَى ٱلنُّورِۖ
وَٱلَّذِينَ كَفَرُوٓاْ أَوۡلِيَآؤُهُمُ ٱلطَّٰغُوتُ يُخۡرِجُونَهُم مِّنَ
ٱلنُّورِ إِلَى ٱلظُّلُمَٰتِۗ أُوْلَٰٓئِكَ أَصۡحَٰبُ ٱلنَّارِۖ هُمۡ فِيهَا
خَٰلِدُونَ ﴿٢٥٧﴾ أَلَمۡ تَرَ إِلَى ٱلَّذِي حَآجَّ إِبۡرَٰهِـۧمَ فِي رَبِّهِۦٓ
أَنۡ ءَاتَىٰهُ ٱللَّهُ ٱلۡمُلۡكَ إِذۡ قَالَ إِبۡرَٰهِـۧمُ رَبِّيَ ٱلَّذِي يُحۡيِۦ
وَيُمِيتُ قَالَ أَنَا۠ أُحۡيِۦ وَأُمِيتُۖ قَالَ إِبۡرَٰهِـۧمُ فَإِنَّ ٱللَّهَ يَأۡتِي
بِٱلشَّمۡسِ مِنَ ٱلۡمَشۡرِقِ فَأۡتِ بِهَا مِنَ ٱلۡمَغۡرِبِ فَبُهِتَ ٱلَّذِي
كَفَرَۗ وَٱللَّهُ لَا يَهۡدِي ٱلۡقَوۡمَ ٱلظَّٰلِمِينَ ﴿٢٥٨﴾ أَوۡ كَٱلَّذِي مَرَّ
عَلَىٰ قَرۡيَةٖ وَهِيَ خَاوِيَةٌ عَلَىٰ عُرُوشِهَا قَالَ أَنَّىٰ يُحۡيِۦ هَٰذِهِ ٱللَّهُ
بَعۡدَ مَوۡتِهَاۖ فَأَمَاتَهُ ٱللَّهُ مِاْئَةَ عَامٖ ثُمَّ بَعَثَهُۥۖ قَالَ كَمۡ لَبِثۡتَۖ
قَالَ لَبِثۡتُ يَوۡمًا أَوۡ بَعۡضَ يَوۡمٖۖ قَالَ بَل لَّبِثۡتَ مِاْئَةَ عَامٖ
فَٱنظُرۡ إِلَىٰ طَعَامِكَ وَشَرَابِكَ لَمۡ يَتَسَنَّهۡۖ وَٱنظُرۡ إِلَىٰ
حِمَارِكَ وَلِنَجۡعَلَكَ ءَايَةٗ لِّلنَّاسِۖ وَٱنظُرۡ إِلَى
ٱلۡعِظَامِ كَيۡفَ نُنشِزُهَا ثُمَّ نَكۡسُوهَا لَحۡمٗاۚ فَلَمَّا
تَبَيَّنَ لَهُۥ قَالَ أَعۡلَمُ أَنَّ ٱللَّهَ عَلَىٰ كُلِّ شَيۡءٖ قَدِيرٞ ﴿٢٥٩﴾
وَإِذۡ قَالَ إِبۡرَٰهِـۧمُ رَبِّ أَرِنِي كَيۡفَ تُحۡيِ ٱلۡمَوۡتَىٰۖ قَالَ أَوَلَمۡ
تُؤۡمِنۖ قَالَ بَلَىٰ وَلَٰكِن لِّيَطۡمَئِنَّ قَلۡبِيۖ قَالَ فَخُذۡ أَرۡبَعَةٗ مِّنَ
ٱلطَّيۡرِ فَصُرۡهُنَّ إِلَيۡكَ ثُمَّ ٱجۡعَلۡ عَلَىٰ كُلِّ جَبَلٖ مِّنۡهُنَّ جُزۡءٗا
ثُمَّ ٱدۡعُهُنَّ يَأۡتِينَكَ سَعۡيٗاۚ وَٱعۡلَمۡ أَنَّ ٱللَّهَ عَزِيزٌ حَكِيمٞ ﴿٢٦٠﴾
مَّثَلُ ٱلَّذِينَ يُنفِقُونَ أَمۡوَٰلَهُمۡ فِي سَبِيلِ ٱللَّهِ كَمَثَلِ حَبَّةٍ

idols and can be singular or plural) ***and believes in Allah has grasped the Firmest Handhold which will never give way. Allah is All-Hearing*** of what is said, ***All-Knowing,*** of what is done.

257. ***Allah is the Protector*** and Helper ***of those who believe. He brings them out of the darkness*** of unbelief ***to the light*** of belief. ***But those who disbelieve have false gods as protectors. They take them from the light into the darkness.*** The mention of removal is either to mirror the preceding words or about those among the Jews who believed in the Prophet before his mission and then rejected him afterwards. ***Those are the Companions of the Fire remaining in it timelessly, forever.***

258. ***What about him who argued with Ibrāhīm about his Lord, on the basis that Allah had given him sovereignty?*** This is a reference to Nimrod who was moved to do this by his pride in the blessings which Allah had given him. He asked Ibrāhīm, "Who is your Lord to whom you call?" and ***Ibrāhīm said, "My Lord is He who gives life and causes to die."*** He creates life and death in physical bodies. ***He said, "I too give life and cause to die*** by killing or pardoning people at will." He called for two men and killed one and let the other live. When he saw that the king was stupid, ***Ibrāhīm*** moved on to even clearer evidence and ***said, "Allah makes the sun come from the East. Make it come from the West." And the one who disbelieved was dumbfounded*** and confused. ***Allah does not guide wrongdoing people*** who disbelieve to conclusive evidence in the argument.

259. ***Or*** what about ***the one who passed by a town*** (Jerusalem) ***which had fallen into ruin?*** This was 'Uzayr who was riding on a donkey and had with him a basket of figs and a cup of juice. The town was in ruins because of what Nebuchadnezzar had done to it. ***He asked, "How can Allah restore this to life when it has died?"*** He asked this question exalting the power of Allah, not out of doubt. ***Allah caused him to die a hundred years*** and ***then brought him back to life*** to demonstrate to him the answer to his question. ***Then He*** (Allah) ***asked*** him, ***"How long have you been here?" He replied, "I have been here a day or part of a day."*** He said this because he went to sleep and died at the beginning of the day and was brought to life at sunset and so he thought that it was the same day. ***He said, "Not so! You have been here a hundred years. Look***

at your food (figs) ***and drink*** (juice) – ***it has not gone bad*** (read as *yatasanna* and *yatasanna*) or altered through time – ***and look at your donkey*** and how it is – and he saw that it was dead and its bones bleached. We did that so that you would know and ***so We can make you a Sign*** of the resurrection ***for all mankind. Look at the bones*** of your donkey – ***how We raise them up*** (read as *nunshizuhā*, *nanshizuhā*, and *nunshiruhā*) ***and clothe them in flesh."*** He looked at it and the bones came together and had flesh and the spirit was breathed into it and the donkey brayed. ***When it had become clear to him*** by this witnessing, ***he said, "Now I know*** (read as *a'lamu* "I know" and *a'lam*, in which case the meaning becomes "Know that…") ***that Allah has power over everything."***

260. Remember ***when Ibrāhīm said, "My Lord, show me how You bring the dead to life." He*** (Allah) ***asked, "Do you not then believe*** that it is in My power to bring to life?" Allah asked this question, knowing that Ibrāhīm believed, in order to answer what he asked and inform listeners of what he meant. ***He*** (Ibrāhīm) ***replied, "Indeed I do*** believe***! But*** I asked this ***so that my heart may be at peace*** through the actual eye-witnessing of proof." ***He said, "Take four birds and train them to yourself*** (read as *ṣirhum,* meaning "make them incline to you", and *surhum*, meaning "cut them up and mix up their flesh and feathers") ***Then put a part of them on each mountain*** of your land ***and call them*** to come to you. ***They will come*** swiftly ***rushing to you. Know that Allah is Mighty,*** His power is unlimited, ***Wise*** in what He does." So Ibrāhīm took a peacock, eagle, crow and cock and did to them what he was told, and took their heads with him and called them; and their parts flew to one another until they were complete and then rejoined their heads.

261. ***The likeness*** of the expenditure ***of those who spend their wealth in the Way of Allah*** in obedience to Him ***is that of a grain which produces seven ears, in every ear there is a hundred grains.*** That is how their spending is multiplied seven hundred times. ***Allah gives such multiplied increase***, and even more than that, ***to whomever He wills. Allah is All-Encompassing*** in His bounty, ***All-Knowing*** of what multiplication is merited.

262. ***Those who spend their wealth in the Way of Allah, and then do not follow what they have spent*** on someone ***by demands for***

أَنۢبَتَتۡ سَبۡعَ سَنَابِلَ فِي كُلِّ سُنۢبُلَةٖ مِّاْئَةُ حَبَّةٖۗ وَٱللَّهُ يُضَٰعِفُ
لِمَن يَشَآءُۚ وَٱللَّهُ وَٰسِعٌ عَلِيمٌ ٢٦١ ٱلَّذِينَ يُنفِقُونَ أَمۡوَٰلَهُمۡ
فِي سَبِيلِ ٱللَّهِ ثُمَّ لَا يُتۡبِعُونَ مَآ أَنفَقُواْ مَنّٗا وَلَآ أَذٗى لَّهُمۡ
أَجۡرُهُمۡ عِندَ رَبِّهِمۡ وَلَا خَوۡفٌ عَلَيۡهِمۡ وَلَا هُمۡ يَحۡزَنُونَ
٢٦٢ ۞ قَوۡلٞ مَّعۡرُوفٞ وَمَغۡفِرَةٌ خَيۡرٞ مِّن صَدَقَةٖ يَتۡبَعُهَآ
أَذٗىۗ وَٱللَّهُ غَنِيٌّ حَلِيمٞ ٢٦٣ يَٰٓأَيُّهَا ٱلَّذِينَ ءَامَنُواْ لَا تُبۡطِلُواْ
صَدَقَٰتِكُم بِٱلۡمَنِّ وَٱلۡأَذَىٰ كَٱلَّذِي يُنفِقُ مَالَهُۥ رِئَآءَ ٱلنَّاسِ
وَلَا يُؤۡمِنُ بِٱللَّهِ وَٱلۡيَوۡمِ ٱلۡأٓخِرِۖ فَمَثَلُهُۥ كَمَثَلِ صَفۡوَانٍ عَلَيۡهِ
تُرَابٞ فَأَصَابَهُۥ وَابِلٞ فَتَرَكَهُۥ صَلۡدٗاۖ لَّا يَقۡدِرُونَ عَلَىٰ
شَيۡءٖ مِّمَّا كَسَبُواْۗ وَٱللَّهُ لَا يَهۡدِي ٱلۡقَوۡمَ ٱلۡكَٰفِرِينَ ٢٦٤
وَمَثَلُ ٱلَّذِينَ يُنفِقُونَ أَمۡوَٰلَهُمُ ٱبۡتِغَآءَ مَرۡضَاتِ ٱللَّهِ
وَتَثۡبِيتٗا مِّنۡ أَنفُسِهِمۡ كَمَثَلِ جَنَّةِۭ بِرَبۡوَةٍ أَصَابَهَا وَابِلٞ
فَـَٔاتَتۡ أُكُلَهَا ضِعۡفَيۡنِ فَإِن لَّمۡ يُصِبۡهَا وَابِلٞ فَطَلّٞۗ
وَٱللَّهُ بِمَا تَعۡمَلُونَ بَصِيرٌ ٢٦٥ أَيَوَدُّ أَحَدُكُمۡ أَن تَكُونَ
لَهُۥ جَنَّةٞ مِّن نَّخِيلٖ وَأَعۡنَابٖ تَجۡرِي مِن تَحۡتِهَا ٱلۡأَنۡهَٰرُ لَهُۥ
فِيهَا مِن كُلِّ ٱلثَّمَرَٰتِ وَأَصَابَهُ ٱلۡكِبَرُ وَلَهُۥ ذُرِّيَّةٞ ضُعَفَآءُ
فَأَصَابَهَآ إِعۡصَارٞ فِيهِ نَارٞ فَٱحۡتَرَقَتۡۗ كَذَٰلِكَ يُبَيِّنُ ٱللَّهُ
لَكُمُ ٱلۡأٓيَٰتِ لَعَلَّكُمۡ تَتَفَكَّرُونَ ٢٦٦ يَٰٓأَيُّهَا ٱلَّذِينَ
ءَامَنُوٓاْ أَنفِقُواْ مِن طَيِّبَٰتِ مَا كَسَبۡتُمۡ وَمِمَّآ أَخۡرَجۡنَا
لَكُم مِّنَ ٱلۡأَرۡضِۖ وَلَا تَيَمَّمُواْ ٱلۡخَبِيثَ مِنۡهُ تُنفِقُونَ وَلَسۡتُم

gratitude by saying things like, "I was good to you," ***or insulting words,*** by mentioning it, for instance, to someone who does not like it to be mentioned, ***will have their reward,*** for spending, ***with their Lord. They will feel no fear and know no sorrow*** in the Next World.

263. ***Correct and courteous words,*** good words when answering someone who asks for something, ***together with forgiveness*** when someone is hard-pressed ***are better than*** **ṣadaqa** ***followed by insulting words*** by demanding gratitude and criticising his asking. ***Allah is Rich beyond need*** of *ṣadaqa,* ***All-Forbearing*** in that He defers the punishment of those who harm and insult others.

264. ***O you who believe! Do not nullify*** the reward for ***your ṣadaqa by demands for gratitude or insulting words, like*** (in the way that it is nullified by) ***him who spends his wealth, showing off to people and not believing in Allah and the Last Day*** – in other words, a hypocrite. ***His likeness is that of a smooth rock coated with soil, which, when heavy rain falls on it, is left stripped bare***, with nothing left on it. ***They have no power over anything they have earned.*** This example of a hypocrite illustrates those who spend to show off to people and the plural pronoun is used to show that it applies to all who do this. They act but will find no reward for their actions in the Next World, just as no earth is firmly attached to the stone and so the rain washes it off. ***Allah does not guide the people of the unbelievers.***

265. ***The likeness of*** the spending of ***those who spend their wealth, desiring the pleasure of Allah and firmness for themselves,*** seeking to realise the reward for it as opposed to the hypocrites who do not hope for that since they deny it, ***is that of a garden on a hillside*** (read as *rabwa* and *rubwa*), ***which, when heavy rain falls on it, doubles its produce*** (read as *aklahā* and *ukulahā*). ***And if heavy rain does not fall then there is drizzle.*** Drizzle is light rain which is enough because the garden is raised. So it gives fruit, whether there is a lot of rain or a little. It is like that with spending: it grows with Allah and He will repay them whether it is a little or a lot. ***Allah sees everything you do*** and will repay you for it.

266. ***Would any of you like to have a garden of dates and grapes, with rivers flowing underneath, containing all kinds of fruits, then to be stricken with old age*** so that you become too weak to earn

بِـَٔاخِذِيهِ إِلَّآ أَن تُغۡمِضُواْ فِيهِۚ وَٱعۡلَمُوٓاْ أَنَّ ٱللَّهَ غَنِيٌّ حَمِيدٌ
٢٦٧ ٱلشَّيۡطَٰنُ يَعِدُكُمُ ٱلۡفَقۡرَ وَيَأۡمُرُكُم بِٱلۡفَحۡشَآءِۖ
وَٱللَّهُ يَعِدُكُم مَّغۡفِرَةٗ مِّنۡهُ وَفَضۡلٗاۗ وَٱللَّهُ وَٰسِعٌ عَلِيمٞ ٢٦٨
يُؤۡتِي ٱلۡحِكۡمَةَ مَن يَشَآءُۚ وَمَن يُؤۡتَ ٱلۡحِكۡمَةَ فَقَدۡ
أُوتِيَ خَيۡرٗا كَثِيرٗاۗ وَمَا يَذَّكَّرُ إِلَّآ أُوْلُواْ ٱلۡأَلۡبَٰبِ ٢٦٩
وَمَآ أَنفَقۡتُم مِّن نَّفَقَةٍ أَوۡ نَذَرۡتُم مِّن نَّذۡرٖ فَإِنَّ ٱللَّهَ
يَعۡلَمُهُۥۗ وَمَا لِلظَّٰلِمِينَ مِنۡ أَنصَارٍ ٢٧٠ إِن تُبۡدُواْ
ٱلصَّدَقَٰتِ فَنِعِمَّا هِيَۖ وَإِن تُخۡفُوهَا وَتُؤۡتُوهَا ٱلۡفُقَرَآءَ
فَهُوَ خَيۡرٞ لَّكُمۡۚ وَيُكَفِّرُ عَنكُم مِّن سَيِّـَٔاتِكُمۡۗ
وَٱللَّهُ بِمَا تَعۡمَلُونَ خَبِيرٞ ٢٧١ ۞ لَّيۡسَ عَلَيۡكَ هُدَىٰهُمۡ
وَلَٰكِنَّ ٱللَّهَ يَهۡدِي مَن يَشَآءُۗ وَمَا تُنفِقُواْ مِنۡ خَيۡرٖ
فَلِأَنفُسِكُمۡۚ وَمَا تُنفِقُونَ إِلَّا ٱبۡتِغَآءَ وَجۡهِ ٱللَّهِۚ
وَمَا تُنفِقُواْ مِنۡ خَيۡرٖ يُوَفَّ إِلَيۡكُمۡ وَأَنتُمۡ لَا تُظۡلَمُونَ
٢٧٢ لِلۡفُقَرَآءِ ٱلَّذِينَ أُحۡصِرُواْ فِي سَبِيلِ ٱللَّهِ
لَا يَسۡتَطِيعُونَ ضَرۡبٗا فِي ٱلۡأَرۡضِ يَحۡسَبُهُمُ
ٱلۡجَاهِلُ أَغۡنِيَآءَ مِنَ ٱلتَّعَفُّفِ تَعۡرِفُهُم بِسِيمَٰهُمۡ
لَا يَسۡـَٔلُونَ ٱلنَّاسَ إِلۡحَافٗاۗ وَمَا تُنفِقُواْ مِنۡ خَيۡرٖ
فَإِنَّ ٱللَّهَ بِهِۦ عَلِيمٌ ٢٧٣ ٱلَّذِينَ يُنفِقُونَ أَمۡوَٰلَهُم
بِٱلَّيۡلِ وَٱلنَّهَارِ سِرّٗا وَعَلَانِيَةٗ فَلَهُمۡ أَجۡرُهُمۡ عِندَ
رَبِّهِمۡ وَلَا خَوۡفٌ عَلَيۡهِمۡ وَلَا هُمۡ يَحۡزَنُونَ ٢٧٤

because of that ***and have children who are weak,*** who are young and cannot earn, ***and then for a fierce whirlwind containing fire to come and strike it so that it goes up in flames?*** That leaves such a person more needy than he was and he is left with weak bewildered children who can do nothing. This is a metaphor for someone who shows off and seeks to molest people. He does not benefit here and is in even greater need in the Next World. The question implies a negative reply. Ibn 'Abbās reported that it is about a man who performed good deeds and then Shayṭān sent for him and he did rebellious acts until his good actions were burned up. ***Thus***, by what was mentioned, ***does Allah make His Signs clear to you, so that perhaps you will reflect*** and take note.

267. ***You who believe! Give away some of the good things you have earned*** by paying *zakāt* ***and some of what*** (good fruits and grains) ***the earth produces for you. Do not have recourse to bad things when you give*** *zakāt*, ***things you would only take with your eyes tight shut*** if you were given them. They are such that you would not take them, so how can you pay the right of Allah with them? ***Know that Allah is Rich beyond need*** of your spending, ***Praiseworthy*** in every instance.

268. ***Shayṭān promises you poverty*** and makes you fear it if you give *ṣadaqa* in order to make you refuse to do so, ***and commands you to avarice.*** He wants you to be stingy and refuse to pay *zakāt*. ***Allah promises you forgiveness from Him*** in exchange for spending ***and abundance***, provision which will replace what you have spent. ***Allah is All-Encompassing*** in His bounty, ***All-Knowing,*** knowing who spends.

269. ***He gives wisdom,*** useful knowledge which leads to action, ***to whoever He wills and he who has been given wisdom has been given great good.*** Such a person receives a lot of good because he will have eternal happiness. ***But no one pays heed but people of intelligence.***

270. ***Whatever amount you spend*** of *zakāt* or *ṣadaqa* ***or vow you make*** and fulfil, ***Allah knows it*** and will repay it. ***The wrongdoers***, who do not pay *zakāt* or who spend incorrectly in disobedience to Allah, ***have no helpers*** to protect them from Allah's punishment.

271. ***If you make your*** voluntary **ṣadaqa** ***public, that is good. But if you conceal it and give it to the poor, that is better for you and it will erase*** (read as *yukaffiru,* "it will erase" and *nukaffiru,* "We will erase") ***some of your bad actions from you.*** Concealing voluntary giving is better than making it public it or giving it to the rich whereas in the case of the obligatory *zakāt*, it is better to make it public so that it will be taken as an example, so that there is no suspicion and so that it will be given to the specified classes of needy. ***Allah is aware of everything you do,*** knowing the inward as well as the outward, nothing being hidden from Him.

272. When the Messenger of Allah, may Allah bless him and grant him peace, refused to give *ṣadaqa* to the idolaters to encourage them to repent, this *āyat* was revealed. ***You are not responsible for their guidance,*** meaning you are not responsible for making people enter Islam, only for conveying the Message, ***but Allah guides whomever He wills*** to enter Islam. ***Whatever good*** (wealth) ***you give away is to your own benefit*** because there is a reward for it, ***when you give desiring only the Face of Allah***, your giving being only for the sake of His reward and not prompted by the desires of this world. This is a report which in fact entails a prohibition. ***Whatever good you give away will be repaid to you in full.*** You will receive full compensation without lacking anything. ***You will not be wronged.*** The last two sentences reinforce the first.

273. ***It*** (*ṣadaqa*) ***is for the poor who are held back*** by *jihād* ***in the Way of Allah, unable to travel in the land*** to travel for trade and livelihood because they were distracted from it by *jihād*. This was revealed about the people of the Ṣuffa. They were four hundred Muhājirūn (Emigrants from Makka) who wanted to learn the Qur'ān and go out on expeditions. Because of their state ***the ignorant consider them rich because of their reticence*** to beg which they refrain from doing. ***You will know them by their mark.*** Their sign is humility and signs of striving. ***They do not ask people*** for something and swear ***insistently.*** They do not ask at all, let alone insistently. ***Whatever good you give away, Allah knows it*** and will reward you for what you give away.

ٱلَّذِينَ يَأْكُلُونَ ٱلرِّبَوٰاْ لَا يَقُومُونَ إِلَّا كَمَا يَقُومُ ٱلَّذِى
يَتَخَبَّطُهُ ٱلشَّيْطَٰنُ مِنَ ٱلْمَسِّ ذَٰلِكَ بِأَنَّهُمْ قَالُوٓاْ إِنَّمَا ٱلْبَيْعُ
مِثْلُ ٱلرِّبَوٰاْ وَأَحَلَّ ٱللَّهُ ٱلْبَيْعَ وَحَرَّمَ ٱلرِّبَوٰاْ فَمَن جَآءَهُۥ مَوْعِظَةٌ
مِّن رَّبِّهِۦ فَٱنتَهَىٰ فَلَهُۥ مَا سَلَفَ وَأَمْرُهُۥٓ إِلَى ٱللَّهِ وَمَنْ عَادَ
فَأُوْلَٰٓئِكَ أَصْحَٰبُ ٱلنَّارِ هُمْ فِيهَا خَٰلِدُونَ ﴿٢٧٥﴾ يَمْحَقُ
ٱللَّهُ ٱلرِّبَوٰاْ وَيُرْبِى ٱلصَّدَقَٰتِ وَٱللَّهُ لَا يُحِبُّ كُلَّ كَفَّارٍ أَثِيمٍ ﴿٢٧٦﴾
إِنَّ ٱلَّذِينَ ءَامَنُواْ وَعَمِلُواْ ٱلصَّٰلِحَٰتِ وَأَقَامُواْ ٱلصَّلَوٰةَ
وَءَاتَوُاْ ٱلزَّكَوٰةَ لَهُمْ أَجْرُهُمْ عِندَ رَبِّهِمْ وَلَا خَوْفٌ عَلَيْهِمْ
وَلَا هُمْ يَحْزَنُونَ ﴿٢٧٧﴾ يَٰٓأَيُّهَا ٱلَّذِينَ ءَامَنُواْ ٱتَّقُواْ ٱللَّهَ
وَذَرُواْ مَا بَقِىَ مِنَ ٱلرِّبَوٰٓاْ إِن كُنتُم مُّؤْمِنِينَ ﴿٢٧٨﴾ فَإِن لَّمْ تَفْعَلُواْ
فَأْذَنُواْ بِحَرْبٍ مِّنَ ٱللَّهِ وَرَسُولِهِۦ وَإِن تُبْتُمْ فَلَكُمْ رُءُوسُ
أَمْوَٰلِكُمْ لَا تَظْلِمُونَ وَلَا تُظْلَمُونَ ﴿٢٧٩﴾ وَإِن كَانَ
ذُو عُسْرَةٍ فَنَظِرَةٌ إِلَىٰ مَيْسَرَةٍ وَأَن تَصَدَّقُواْ خَيْرٌ لَّكُمْ
إِن كُنتُمْ تَعْلَمُونَ ﴿٢٨٠﴾ وَٱتَّقُواْ يَوْمًا تُرْجَعُونَ فِيهِ إِلَى
ٱللَّهِ ثُمَّ تُوَفَّىٰ كُلُّ نَفْسٍ مَّا كَسَبَتْ وَهُمْ لَا يُظْلَمُونَ ﴿٢٨١﴾
يَٰٓأَيُّهَا ٱلَّذِينَ ءَامَنُوٓاْ إِذَا تَدَايَنتُم بِدَيْنٍ إِلَىٰٓ أَجَلٍ مُّسَمًّى
فَٱكْتُبُوهُ وَلْيَكْتُب بَّيْنَكُمْ كَاتِبٌۢ بِٱلْعَدْلِ وَلَا يَأْبَ
كَاتِبٌ أَن يَكْتُبَ كَمَا عَلَّمَهُ ٱللَّهُ فَلْيَكْتُبْ وَلْيُمْلِلِ
ٱلَّذِى عَلَيْهِ ٱلْحَقُّ وَلْيَتَّقِ ٱللَّهَ رَبَّهُۥ وَلَا يَبْخَسْ مِنْهُ شَيْـًٔا
فَإِن كَانَ ٱلَّذِى عَلَيْهِ ٱلْحَقُّ سَفِيهًا أَوْ ضَعِيفًا أَوْ لَا يَسْتَطِيعُ

274. ***Those who give away their wealth by night and by day, secretly and openly, will have their reward with their Lord. They will feel no fear and know no sorrow.***

275. ***Those who practise usury,*** those who take it (it constitutes any unjustified increase in any transaction in the form of money or goods in either amount or the length of the term) ***will not rise from the grave except as someone driven mad by Shayṭān's touch. That***, the reason for the revelation of this *āyat*, ***is because they say, "Trade is the same as usury*** in respect of its permissibility.***"*** Allah then refutes what they said: ***But Allah has permitted trade and He has forbidden usury. Any who receive a warning from their Lord and then desist*** from consuming it, ***may keep what they received in the past*** before the prohibition, and do not have to return it, ***and their affair is up to Allah,*** whether such a person will be forgiven or not. ***But any who return to it*** and consume usury by making it comparable to lawful sales ***will be the Companions of the Fire, remaining in it timelessly, forever.***

276. ***Allah obliterates usury,*** reducing it and removing its blessing, ***but makes ṣadaqa grow in value,*** increasing it and makes its reward increase***! Allah does not love any persistently ungrateful wrongdoer*** who makes usury lawful and is a deviant by consuming it, in other words He will punish him.

277. ***Those who believe and do right actions and establish the prayer and pay zakāt will have their reward with their Lord. They will feel no fear and know no sorrow.***

278. ***You who believe! Show fear of Allah and forgo any remaining usury if you are believers.*** This was revealed when one of the Companions asked after the prohibition about usury he had received before it.

279. ***If you do not*** do what you are commanded, ***know that it means war from Allah and His Messenger*** against you. This is an immense threat. When it was revealed, they said, "War with Him is inevitable." ***But if you turn in repentance you may have your capital, without wronging*** by increase ***and without being wronged*** by decrease.

280. ***If someone*** (a debtor) ***is in difficult circumstances,*** he should be granted a delay and ***there should be a deferral until things are***

أَن يُمِلَّ هُوَ فَلْيُمْلِلْ وَلِيُّهُۥ بِٱلْعَدْلِ ۚ وَٱسْتَشْهِدُوا۟ شَهِيدَيْنِ
مِن رِّجَالِكُمْ ۖ فَإِن لَّمْ يَكُونَا رَجُلَيْنِ فَرَجُلٌ وَٱمْرَأَتَانِ
مِمَّن تَرْضَوْنَ مِنَ ٱلشُّهَدَآءِ أَن تَضِلَّ إِحْدَىٰهُمَا فَتُذَكِّرَ
إِحْدَىٰهُمَا ٱلْأُخْرَىٰ ۚ وَلَا يَأْبَ ٱلشُّهَدَآءُ إِذَا مَا دُعُوا۟ ۚ وَلَا تَسْـَٔمُوٓا۟
أَن تَكْتُبُوهُ صَغِيرًا أَوْ كَبِيرًا إِلَىٰٓ أَجَلِهِۦ ۚ ذَٰلِكُمْ أَقْسَطُ
عِندَ ٱللَّهِ وَأَقْوَمُ لِلشَّهَـٰدَةِ وَأَدْنَىٰٓ أَلَّا تَرْتَابُوٓا۟ ۖ إِلَّآ أَن تَكُونَ
تِجَـٰرَةً حَاضِرَةً تُدِيرُونَهَا بَيْنَكُمْ فَلَيْسَ عَلَيْكُمْ جُنَاحٌ
أَلَّا تَكْتُبُوهَا ۗ وَأَشْهِدُوٓا۟ إِذَا تَبَايَعْتُمْ ۚ وَلَا يُضَآرَّ كَاتِبٌ
وَلَا شَهِيدٌ ۚ وَإِن تَفْعَلُوا۟ فَإِنَّهُۥ فُسُوقٌۢ بِكُمْ ۗ وَٱتَّقُوا۟
ٱللَّهَ ۖ وَيُعَلِّمُكُمُ ٱللَّهُ ۗ وَٱللَّهُ بِكُلِّ شَىْءٍ عَلِيمٌ ﴿٢٨٢﴾
۞ وَإِن كُنتُمْ عَلَىٰ سَفَرٍ وَلَمْ تَجِدُوا۟ كَاتِبًا فَرِهَـٰنٌ مَّقْبُوضَةٌ ۖ
فَإِنْ أَمِنَ بَعْضُكُم بَعْضًا فَلْيُؤَدِّ ٱلَّذِى ٱؤْتُمِنَ أَمَـٰنَتَهُۥ وَلْيَتَّقِ
ٱللَّهَ رَبَّهُۥ ۗ وَلَا تَكْتُمُوا۟ ٱلشَّهَـٰدَةَ ۚ وَمَن يَكْتُمْهَا فَإِنَّهُۥٓ
ءَاثِمٌ قَلْبُهُۥ ۗ وَٱللَّهُ بِمَا تَعْمَلُونَ عَلِيمٌ ﴿٢٨٣﴾ لِّلَّهِ مَا فِى ٱلسَّمَـٰوَٰتِ
وَمَا فِى ٱلْأَرْضِ ۗ وَإِن تُبْدُوا۟ مَا فِىٓ أَنفُسِكُمْ أَوْ تُخْفُوهُ
يُحَاسِبْكُم بِهِ ٱللَّهُ ۖ فَيَغْفِرُ لِمَن يَشَآءُ وَيُعَذِّبُ مَن يَشَآءُ ۗ
وَٱللَّهُ عَلَىٰ كُلِّ شَىْءٍ قَدِيرٌ ﴿٢٨٤﴾ ءَامَنَ ٱلرَّسُولُ بِمَآ أُنزِلَ
إِلَيْهِ مِن رَّبِّهِۦ وَٱلْمُؤْمِنُونَ ۚ كُلٌّ ءَامَنَ بِٱللَّهِ وَمَلَـٰٓئِكَتِهِۦ وَكُتُبِهِۦ
وَرُسُلِهِۦ لَا نُفَرِّقُ بَيْنَ أَحَدٍ مِّن رُّسُلِهِۦ ۚ وَقَالُوا۟ سَمِعْنَا
وَأَطَعْنَا ۖ غُفْرَانَكَ رَبَّنَا وَإِلَيْكَ ٱلْمَصِيرُ ﴿٢٨٥﴾ لَا يُكَلِّفُ

easier (read as *maysara* and *maysura*). ***But making a free gift of it*** (read as *taṣṣaddaqū* and *taṣaddaqū*) and freeing the debtor ***would be better for you if you only knew,*** so do it. We read in a *ḥadīth*, "Whoever grants a delay to one in difficulty or reduces it for him, Allah will shade him on a day in which there is no shade but His shade." (Muslim)

281. ***Show fear of a Day*** (the Day of Rising) ***when you will be returned to Allah. Then*** on that Day ***every self will be paid in full for what it earned*** whether its actions were good or evil. ***They will not be wronged.*** Their good deeds will not be decreased nor their bad deeds increased.

282. ***You who believe! When you take on a debt for a specified period,*** like a credit sale or loan, ***write it down*** to avoid any dispute. ***A writer should write it*** (the debt) ***down between you justly.*** Write it down correctly and do not add to the amount or term, nor decrease it. ***No writer should refuse to write*** when he is asked to do so***; as Allah has taught him*** by being generous to him so that he can write, he should not be miserly with his ability to do so and ***so he should write.*** It is stressed that ***the one incurring the debt should dictate*** because he is the one against whom there is testimony and so he confirms and knows what he owes, ***and should fear Allah his Lord and not reduce it*** (what he owes) ***in any way. If the person incurring the debt is incompetent*** or a wastrel ***or*** too ***weak*** to dictate because he is very young or old ***or unable to dictate*** because he is dumb or ignorant of the language or something similar, ***then his guardian,*** executor, translator or custodian ***should dictate for him justly. Two*** free, adult Muslim ***men among you should act as witnesses*** to the debt. ***But if there are not two men, then a man and two women*** should act as witnesses ***with whom you are satisfied as witnesses*** because of their *dīn* and integrity***; then*** the reason that women are doubled is so that ***if one of them*** (the women) ***forgets*** the testimony owing to lack of intelligence or confusion, ***the other can remind*** (read as *tudhakkira* and *tudhkira*) ***her.*** She can remind her if the other is misguided or turning in that direction. ***Witnesses should not refuse when they are called upon*** to act as witnesses. ***Do not think it too trivial*** or be too lazy ***to write down*** the right to which you testify because that happens frequently, ***whether small or large, with the***

date that it falls due, the time when it must be repaid. ***Doing that*** (writing it down) ***is more just in Allah's sight and more helpful when bearing witness***, and more likely to establish justice, because it reminds people, ***and more likely to eliminate any doubt*** about the amount and the period it is due – ***unless it*** (the transaction) ***is an immediate transaction hand to hand, taken and given without delay. There is nothing wrong in your not writing that*** transaction ***down. Call witnesses when you trade*** to remove disagreement. This and what is before it is recommended. ***Neither writer nor witness should be put under pressure*** by the one who owes the debt or the one to whom it is owed to alter or attempt to prevent testimony or writing, or to harm them by forcing them to write or testimony to what is not correct. ***If you do that*** which you are forbidden***, it is degeneracy*** (abandonment of obedience to Allah) ***on your part. Be fearful of Allah*** regarding His commands and prohibition ***and Allah will give you knowledge*** of your best interests. ***Allah has knowledge of everything.***

283. ***If you are on a journey*** when you contract a debt ***and cannot find a writer, something can be left,*** with which all parties are satisfied, ***as a security*** (read as *rihān* and *ruhun*, the plural of *rahn*). It is clear that the *Sunna* permits leaving a pledge while at home even when there is a scribe available. The qualification mentioned here is because leaving a pledge when on a journey is a stronger priority. ***If you leave things on trust with one another*** as when a debtor leaves something with his creditor as a security for what he owes, the creditor may not pawn it and ***the one who is trusted must deliver up his trust and be fearful of Allah his Lord*** regarding returning it. ***Do not conceal testimony*** when you are asked to give it. ***If someone does conceal it, his heart commits a crime.*** The heart is singled out for mention, because when it sins, the other parts of a person follow it and will receive the punishment due to wrongdoers. ***Allah knows everything you do,*** nothing being hidden from Him.

284. ***Everything in the heavens and everything in the earth belongs to Allah. Whether you divulge what is in yourselves*** of evil and resolve on it ***or keep it hidden, Allah will still*** inform you of it and ***call you to account for it*** on the Day of Rising. ***He forgives***

whomever He wills and He punishes whomever He wills. Allah has power over everything in respect of repayment and reward.

285. ***The Messenger*** Muḥammad, may Allah bless him and grant him peace, ***believes in what has been sent down to him*** of the Qur'an ***from his Lord, and so do the believers. Each one believes in Allah and His angels and His Books*** (read as *kutubihi*, plural and *kitābihi*, singular) ***and His Messengers.*** They say: ***We do not differ - entiate between any of His Messengers,*** not believing in some and rejecting some as the Jews and Christians do. ***They say, "We hear*** what you have commanded us and accept it ***and we obey.*** We ask you to ***forgive us, our Lord! The final destination is to You."*** The final destination refers to the Resurrection. When the *āyat* before it was revealed, the believers complained about the inner whispering they were subject to, and the thought of having to account for it was very difficult for them. So the following was revealed

286. ***Allah does not charge any self beyond what it can bear,*** only burdening it with what it is capable of fulfilling. ***For it is*** the reward of the good it did and ***what it has earned; against it is what it has warranted*** of the evil it did: in other words, the burden of that. No one will be punished for the sin of another, or for anything his *nafs* whispered to him but which he did not do. Say: ***Our Lord, do not take us to task*** by punishing us ***if we forget or make a mistake!*** Do not punish us if we inadvertently or deliberately abandon what is correct as You did those before us. Allah removed that from this community as in the *ḥadīth* and so the request is an acknowledgement of the blessing of Allah. ***Our Lord, do not load us with such a burden*** which is too heavy for us to bear ***as You loaded onto those before us***, meaning the tribe of Israel, such as a person having to kill themselves in repentance or having to pay a quarter of one's property in *zakāt* or cutting away anything with impurity on it. ***Our Lord, do not load us with that*** (with obligations or afflictions) ***which we have not the strength to bear! And pardon us*** for our wrong actions; ***and forgive us; and have mercy on us.*** Mercy is added to forgiveness. ***You are our Master*** and in charge of us, ***so help us against the people of the unbelievers***. Establish the proof against the unbelievers and enable us to overcome them in fighting. The duty of the Master is to help those He protects against their enemies. We read in a *ḥadīth*, "When this *āyat* was revealed, the Prophet, may Allah bless him and grant him peace, recited it, and after every sentence the words, 'I have done it,' were heard."

ٱللَّهُ نَفۡسًا إِلَّا وُسۡعَهَاۚ لَهَا مَا كَسَبَتۡ وَعَلَيۡهَا مَا ٱكۡتَسَبَتۡۗ
رَبَّنَا لَا تُؤَاخِذۡنَآ إِن نَّسِينَآ أَوۡ أَخۡطَأۡنَاۚ رَبَّنَا وَلَا تَحۡمِلۡ
عَلَيۡنَآ إِصۡرٗا كَمَا حَمَلۡتَهُۥ عَلَى ٱلَّذِينَ مِن قَبۡلِنَاۚ رَبَّنَا وَلَا
تُحَمِّلۡنَا مَا لَا طَاقَةَ لَنَا بِهِۦۖ وَٱعۡفُ عَنَّا وَٱغۡفِرۡ لَنَا وَٱرۡحَمۡنَآۚ
أَنتَ مَوۡلَىٰنَا فَٱنصُرۡنَا عَلَى ٱلۡقَوۡمِ ٱلۡكَٰفِرِينَ ٢٨٦

سُورَةُ آلِ عِمۡرَانَ

بِسۡمِ ٱللَّهِ ٱلرَّحۡمَٰنِ ٱلرَّحِيمِ

الٓمٓ ﴿١﴾ ٱللَّهُ لَآ إِلَٰهَ إِلَّا هُوَ ٱلۡحَيُّ ٱلۡقَيُّومُ ﴿٢﴾ نَزَّلَ عَلَيۡكَ ٱلۡكِتَٰبَ
بِٱلۡحَقِّ مُصَدِّقٗا لِّمَا بَيۡنَ يَدَيۡهِ وَأَنزَلَ ٱلتَّوۡرَىٰةَ وَٱلۡإِنجِيلَ ﴿٣﴾ مِن
قَبۡلُ هُدٗى لِّلنَّاسِ وَأَنزَلَ ٱلۡفُرۡقَانَۗ إِنَّ ٱلَّذِينَ كَفَرُواْ بِـَٔايَٰتِ ٱللَّهِ لَهُمۡ
عَذَابٞ شَدِيدٞۗ وَٱللَّهُ عَزِيزٞ ذُو ٱنتِقَامٍ ﴿٤﴾ إِنَّ ٱللَّهَ لَا يَخۡفَىٰ عَلَيۡهِ
شَيۡءٞ فِي ٱلۡأَرۡضِ وَلَا فِي ٱلسَّمَآءِ ﴿٥﴾ هُوَ ٱلَّذِي يُصَوِّرُكُمۡ
فِي ٱلۡأَرۡحَامِ كَيۡفَ يَشَآءُۚ لَآ إِلَٰهَ إِلَّا هُوَ ٱلۡعَزِيزُ ٱلۡحَكِيمُ ﴿٦﴾ هُوَ
ٱلَّذِيٓ أَنزَلَ عَلَيۡكَ ٱلۡكِتَٰبَ مِنۡهُ ءَايَٰتٞ مُّحۡكَمَٰتٌ هُنَّ أُمُّ ٱلۡكِتَٰبِ
وَأُخَرُ مُتَشَٰبِهَٰتٞۖ فَأَمَّا ٱلَّذِينَ فِي قُلُوبِهِمۡ زَيۡغٞ فَيَتَّبِعُونَ مَا تَشَٰبَهَ
مِنۡهُ ٱبۡتِغَآءَ ٱلۡفِتۡنَةِ وَٱبۡتِغَآءَ تَأۡوِيلِهِۦۗ وَمَا يَعۡلَمُ تَأۡوِيلَهُۥٓ إِلَّا ٱللَّهُۗ
وَٱلرَّٰسِخُونَ فِي ٱلۡعِلۡمِ يَقُولُونَ ءَامَنَّا بِهِۦ كُلّٞ مِّنۡ عِندِ رَبِّنَاۗ وَمَا يَذَّكَّرُ
إِلَّآ أُوْلُواْ ٱلۡأَلۡبَٰبِ ﴿٧﴾ رَبَّنَا لَا تُزِغۡ قُلُوبَنَا بَعۡدَ إِذۡ هَدَيۡتَنَا وَهَبۡ
لَنَا مِن لَّدُنكَ رَحۡمَةًۚ إِنَّكَ أَنتَ ٱلۡوَهَّابُ ﴿٨﴾ رَبَّنَآ إِنَّكَ جَامِعُ
ٱلنَّاسِ لِيَوۡمٖ لَّا رَيۡبَ فِيهِۚ إِنَّ ٱللَّهَ لَا يُخۡلِفُ ٱلۡمِيعَادَ ﴿٩﴾
إِنَّ ٱلَّذِينَ كَفَرُواْ لَن تُغۡنِيَ عَنۡهُمۡ أَمۡوَٰلُهُمۡ وَلَآ أَوۡلَٰدُهُم
مِّنَ ٱللَّهِ شَيۡـٔٗاۖ وَأُوْلَٰٓئِكَ هُمۡ وَقُودُ ٱلنَّارِ ﴿١٠﴾ كَدَأۡبِ ءَالِ
فِرۡعَوۡنَ وَٱلَّذِينَ مِن قَبۡلِهِمۡۚ كَذَّبُواْ بِـَٔايَٰتِنَا فَأَخَذَهُمُ ٱللَّهُ بِذُنُوبِهِمۡۗ
وَٱللَّهُ شَدِيدُ ٱلۡعِقَابِ ﴿١١﴾ قُل لِّلَّذِينَ كَفَرُواْ سَتُغۡلَبُونَ

3. *Sūrat Al 'Imran*
The Family of 'Imrān

It is Madinan, with 199 or 200 *āyats*; revealed after *Sūrat al-Anfāl*.

1. ***Alif Lam Mim***. Only Allah knows what these letters mean.

2. ***Allah. There is no god but Him, the Living, the Self-Sustaining.***

3. ***He has sent down to you***, Muḥammad, ***the Book*** (the Qur'an) ***with truth,*** which articulates the truth in its reports, ***confirming what was there*** of the Books ***before it. And He sent down the Torah and the Gospel, previously,*** before the Qur'ān, ***as guidance*** away from misguidance ***for mankind*** who follow them, ***and He has sent down*** ("sent down" is repeated a third time because both the Torah and the Gospel were sent down each at one go, which was not the case with other Divine Revelations) ***the Discrimination*** (the Divine Books which distinguish the true from the false). It is mentioned after the three named Books in order to include others.

4. ***Those who reject Allah's Signs*** (the Qur'ān or any other Divine signs) ***will have a terrible punishment. Allah is Almighty*** in His command and nothing can prevent Allah carrying out His threat and promise, ***Exactor of Revenge.*** He possesses severe punishment, beyond anything anyone else is capable of, for all those who rebel against Him.

5. ***Allah is He from Whom nothing is hidden, either in the earth or in heaven.*** He knows everything that occurs throughout all existence, both in general and in detail, but He mentions heaven and earth in particular because human perception does not extend beyond them.

6. ***It is He who forms you in the womb however He wills*** as male or female, white or black and all the other variations. ***There is no god but Him, the Almighty*** in His kingdom, ***the All-Wise*** in what He does.

7. ***It is He who sent down the Book to you from Him: āyats which are clearly explicit*** so that their judgements are clear – ***they are the Mother of the Book,*** the basis which is relied on when making judgement – ***and others are open to interpretation,*** those whose meanings are not immediately obvious, as is the case with the letters at the beginnings of *sūras*. All are perfect in accordance with Allah's words, *"A Book whose verses are perfectly constructed"* (11:1) meaning that there is no fault in them. They are open to interpretation according to His words, *"a Book consistent"* (39:23), meaning it resembles itself in respect of excellence and truthfulness. ***Those with deviation in their hearts*** who incline away from the Truth seek and ***follow what is open to interpretation in it, desiring conflict*** by falling into doubtful and unclear things through their ignorance, and ***seeking its inner meaning. No one knows its inner meaning but Allah*** alone. ***Those firmly rooted in knowledge say, "We believe in it.*** We believe in all those unclear things whose meaning is only known by Allah and we do not know its meaning. ***All of it***, the clearly explicit and that which is open to interpretation, ***is from our Lord." But only people of intelligence pay heed.*** The next *āyat* gives the words of the intelligent when they see those who deviate in this way.

8. ***"Our Lord, do not make our hearts deviate*** and incline away from the truth by seeking an interpretation in a way which is not appropriate for us, as the hearts of those deviants do, ***after You have guided us*** to the truth. ***And give us mercy from You*** by making us firm. ***You are the Ever-Giving.***

9. ***"Our Lord, You are the Gatherer of mankind to a Day about which there is no doubt,*** referring to the Day of Rising on which Allah will repay people for their actions as He has promised. In this *āyat* there is a change of case from the second to third person: ***Allah will not break His promise*** about the Resurrection." These two *āyats* are a supplication which clarifies that the concern of these people is the Next World. That is why they ask to be made firm in respect of guidance so that they may obtain the reward based on what Muslim and al-Bukhārī transmitted from 'Ā'isha when she said that the Messenger of Allah, may Allah bless him and grant him peace, recited the above verse and said, "When you see people who follow what is open to interpretation, know that those are the ones whom Allah has named, so beware of them." Aṭ-Ṭabarānī related in *al-Kabīr* from Abū Mūsā al-Ash'arī that the Prophet, may Allah bless him and grant him peace, said, "I only fear three qualities for my community," and one of them he mentioned was that the Book would be opened to them and believers would take it to seek its interpretation although its interpretation is only known by Allah and those firmly rooted in knowledge who say, *"We believe in it. All of it is from our Lord. But only people of intelligence pay heed."*

10. ***As for those who disbelieve, their wealth and children will not help them*** or defend them ***against*** the punishment of ***Allah in any way. They are fuel for the Fire.***

11. ***As was the case*** and custom ***with the people of Pharaoh and those before them*** such as those of 'Ād and Thamūd. ***They denied Our Signs so Allah seized them*** and destroyed them ***for their wrong actions.*** This sentence explains the one before it. ***Allah is Fierce in Retribution.*** This was revealed when the Prophet, may Allah bless him and grant him peace, commanded the Jews to become Muslim after he returned from Badr. They said, "Do not be deluded by the fact that you killed a group of Quraysh who do not know how to fight."

12. ***Say,*** Muḥammad, ***to those*** of the Jews ***who disbelieve, "You will be overwhelmed*** (read as *sa-ṯughlabūna* "you will be overwhelmed" and in one reading *sa-y̱ughlabūna* "they will be overwhelmed") in this world by being killed, being captured and paying *jizya* (which is what happened), ***and crowded*** in any case ***into Hell*** in the Next World and you will enter it. ***What an evil resting-place!"***

13. ***There was a sign*** (lesson) ***for you*** (the verb "was" (*kāna*) is used here to make a clear separation between this *āyat* and the preceding one) ***in the two parties which met together*** at the Battle of Badr, ***one party fighting in the Way of Allah*** (obeying Him), meaning the Prophet and his Companions – three hundred and thirteen men with two horses, six sets of armour, and eighty swords. Most were on foot, ***and the other unbelievers. They saw them*** (read as *yarawnahum,* "they saw them" and *tarawnahum,* "you saw them") ***as twice their number with their own eyes,*** with clear sight. The unbelievers saw the Muslims as twice their number and they were

وَتُحْشَرُونَ إِلَىٰ جَهَنَّمَ ۚ وَبِئْسَ ٱلْمِهَادُ ﴿١٢﴾ قَدْ كَانَ
لَكُمْ ءَايَةٌ فِى فِئَتَيْنِ ٱلْتَقَتَا ۖ فِئَةٌ تُقَٰتِلُ فِى سَبِيلِ ٱللَّهِ
وَأُخْرَىٰ كَافِرَةٌ يَرَوْنَهُم مِّثْلَيْهِمْ رَأْىَ ٱلْعَيْنِ ۚ وَٱللَّهُ
يُؤَيِّدُ بِنَصْرِهِۦ مَن يَشَآءُ ۗ إِنَّ فِى ذَٰلِكَ لَعِبْرَةً لِّأُو۟لِى
ٱلْأَبْصَٰرِ ﴿١٣﴾ زُيِّنَ لِلنَّاسِ حُبُّ ٱلشَّهَوَٰتِ مِنَ ٱلنِّسَآءِ
وَٱلْبَنِينَ وَٱلْقَنَٰطِيرِ ٱلْمُقَنطَرَةِ مِنَ ٱلذَّهَبِ وَٱلْفِضَّةِ
وَٱلْخَيْلِ ٱلْمُسَوَّمَةِ وَٱلْأَنْعَٰمِ وَٱلْحَرْثِ ۗ ذَٰلِكَ مَتَٰعُ
ٱلْحَيَوٰةِ ٱلدُّنْيَا ۖ وَٱللَّهُ عِندَهُۥ حُسْنُ ٱلْمَـَٔابِ ﴿١٤﴾ ۞ قُلْ
أَؤُنَبِّئُكُم بِخَيْرٍ مِّن ذَٰلِكُمْ ۚ لِلَّذِينَ ٱتَّقَوْا۟ عِندَ رَبِّهِمْ جَنَّٰتٌ
تَجْرِى مِن تَحْتِهَا ٱلْأَنْهَٰرُ خَٰلِدِينَ فِيهَا وَأَزْوَٰجٌ مُّطَهَّرَةٌ
وَرِضْوَٰنٌ مِّنَ ٱللَّهِ ۗ وَٱللَّهُ بَصِيرٌۢ بِٱلْعِبَادِ ﴿١٥﴾
ٱلَّذِينَ يَقُولُونَ رَبَّنَآ إِنَّنَآ ءَامَنَّا فَٱغْفِرْ لَنَا ذُنُوبَنَا وَقِنَا
عَذَابَ ٱلنَّارِ ﴿١٦﴾ ٱلصَّٰبِرِينَ وَٱلصَّٰدِقِينَ وَٱلْقَٰنِتِينَ
وَٱلْمُنفِقِينَ وَٱلْمُسْتَغْفِرِينَ بِٱلْأَسْحَارِ ﴿١٧﴾ شَهِدَ
ٱللَّهُ أَنَّهُۥ لَآ إِلَٰهَ إِلَّا هُوَ وَٱلْمَلَٰٓئِكَةُ وَأُو۟لُوا۟ ٱلْعِلْمِ قَآئِمًۢا بِٱلْقِسْطِ ۚ
لَآ إِلَٰهَ إِلَّا هُوَ ٱلْعَزِيزُ ٱلْحَكِيمُ ﴿١٨﴾ إِنَّ ٱلدِّينَ عِندَ
ٱللَّهِ ٱلْإِسْلَٰمُ ۗ وَمَا ٱخْتَلَفَ ٱلَّذِينَ أُوتُوا۟ ٱلْكِتَٰبَ إِلَّا مِنۢ
بَعْدِ مَا جَآءَهُمُ ٱلْعِلْمُ بَغْيًۢا بَيْنَهُمْ ۗ وَمَن يَكْفُرْ بِـَٔايَٰتِ
ٱللَّهِ فَإِنَّ ٱللَّهَ سَرِيعُ ٱلْحِسَابِ ﴿١٩﴾ فَإِنْ حَآجُّوكَ فَقُلْ أَسْلَمْتُ
وَجْهِىَ لِلَّهِ وَمَنِ ٱتَّبَعَنِ ۗ وَقُل لِّلَّذِينَ أُوتُوا۟ ٱلْكِتَٰبَ وَٱلْأُمِّيِّـۧنَ
ءَأَسْلَمْتُمْ ۚ فَإِنْ أَسْلَمُوا۟ فَقَدِ ٱهْتَدَوا۟ ۖ وَّإِن تَوَلَّوْا۟ فَإِنَّمَا

about a thousand. ***Allah reinforces with His help whomever He wills.*** Allah helped them and Allah strengthens whomever He wishes. ***There is instruction in that*** which was mentioned ***for people of insight*** who reflect on it and have faith.

14. ***To mankind the love of worldly appetites*** (the things which the human self desires and calls for and which Allah makes attractive as an affliction or Shayṭān does so) ***is painted in glowing colours: women and children, and heaped-up mounds of gold and silver, and horses with fine markings,*** thoroughbred horses, ***and livestock,*** camels, cattle and sheep or goats, ***and fertile farmland. All that*** which has been mentioned ***is merely the enjoyment of the life of this world.*** These things are enjoyed in this world and then will vanish. ***The best destination is in the presence of Allah.*** The best destination refers to the Garden, and that is what should be desired.

15. ***Say,*** Muḥammad, to your people, ***"Shall I tell you of something better than that*** (those appetites mentioned)***?"*** It is a question which implies an affirmative answer. ***Those who are godfearing*** and avoid *shirk* ***will have Gardens with their Lord, with rivers flowing under them, remaining in them timelessly, forever, and*** when they enter them they will have ***purified wives,*** purified of menstruation and all other impurities, ***and the Pleasure*** (read as *riḍwān* and *ruḍwān*, meaning great contentment) ***of Allah. Allah sees*** and knows ***His slaves,*** and will repay them all for their actions.

16. ***... those who say, "Our Lord, we believe*** and affirm Allah and His Messenger, ***so forgive us our wrong actions and safeguard us from the punishment of the Fire."***

17. ***The steadfast*** in obedience who avoid disobedience, ***the truthful*** in belief, ***the obedient*** to Allah, ***the givers*** who give *ṣadaqa,* ***and those who seek forgiveness*** of Allah ***before dawn***, saying "O Allah, forgive us" at the end of the night which is the special time for *dhikr* because, for most people, it is a time of heedlessness and sleep.

18. ***Allah bears witness*** and makes it clear to His creation by evidence and signs ***that there is no god but Him,*** and nothing in existence can be truly worshipped but Him, ***as do the angels*** also bear witness by affirmation ***and the people of knowledge*** among the Prophets and the believers by belief and word, ***upholding justice*** by

عَلَيۡكَ ٱلۡبَلَٰغُۗ وَٱللَّهُ بَصِيرُۢ بِٱلۡعِبَادِ ﴿٢٠﴾ إِنَّ ٱلَّذِينَ يَكۡفُرُونَ
بِـَٔايَٰتِ ٱللَّهِ وَيَقۡتُلُونَ ٱلنَّبِيِّـۧنَ بِغَيۡرِ حَقّٖ وَيَقۡتُلُونَ
ٱلَّذِينَ يَأۡمُرُونَ بِٱلۡقِسۡطِ مِنَ ٱلنَّاسِ فَبَشِّرۡهُم
بِعَذَابٍ أَلِيمٍ ﴿٢١﴾ أُوْلَـٰٓئِكَ ٱلَّذِينَ حَبِطَتۡ أَعۡمَٰلُهُمۡ
فِي ٱلدُّنۡيَا وَٱلۡأٓخِرَةِ وَمَا لَهُم مِّن نَّـٰصِرِينَ ﴿٢٢﴾
أَلَمۡ تَرَ إِلَى ٱلَّذِينَ أُوتُواْ نَصِيبٗا مِّنَ ٱلۡكِتَٰبِ يُدۡعَوۡنَ إِلَىٰ كِتَٰبِ
ٱللَّهِ لِيَحۡكُمَ بَيۡنَهُمۡ ثُمَّ يَتَوَلَّىٰ فَرِيقٞ مِّنۡهُمۡ وَهُم مُّعۡرِضُونَ ﴿٢٣﴾
ذَٰلِكَ بِأَنَّهُمۡ قَالُواْ لَن تَمَسَّنَا ٱلنَّارُ إِلَّآ أَيَّامٗا مَّعۡدُودَٰتٖۖ وَغَرَّهُمۡ
فِي دِينِهِم مَّا كَانُواْ يَفۡتَرُونَ ﴿٢٤﴾ فَكَيۡفَ إِذَا جَمَعۡنَٰهُمۡ
لِيَوۡمٖ لَّا رَيۡبَ فِيهِ وَوُفِّيَتۡ كُلُّ نَفۡسٖ مَّا كَسَبَتۡ وَهُمۡ
لَا يُظۡلَمُونَ ﴿٢٥﴾ قُلِ ٱللَّهُمَّ مَٰلِكَ ٱلۡمُلۡكِ تُؤۡتِي ٱلۡمُلۡكَ
مَن تَشَآءُ وَتَنزِعُ ٱلۡمُلۡكَ مِمَّن تَشَآءُ وَتُعِزُّ مَن تَشَآءُ وَتُذِلُّ
مَن تَشَآءُۖ بِيَدِكَ ٱلۡخَيۡرُۖ إِنَّكَ عَلَىٰ كُلِّ شَيۡءٖ قَدِيرٞ ﴿٢٦﴾ تُولِجُ ٱلَّيۡلَ
فِي ٱلنَّهَارِ وَتُولِجُ ٱلنَّهَارَ فِي ٱلَّيۡلِۖ وَتُخۡرِجُ ٱلۡحَيَّ مِنَ ٱلۡمَيِّتِ
وَتُخۡرِجُ ٱلۡمَيِّتَ مِنَ ٱلۡحَيِّۖ وَتَرۡزُقُ مَن تَشَآءُ بِغَيۡرِ حِسَابٖ ﴿٢٧﴾
لَّا يَتَّخِذِ ٱلۡمُؤۡمِنُونَ ٱلۡكَٰفِرِينَ أَوۡلِيَآءَ مِن دُونِ ٱلۡمُؤۡمِنِينَۖ وَمَن
يَفۡعَلۡ ذَٰلِكَ فَلَيۡسَ مِنَ ٱللَّهِ فِي شَيۡءٍ إِلَّآ أَن تَتَّقُواْ مِنۡهُمۡ
تُقَىٰةٗۗ وَيُحَذِّرُكُمُ ٱللَّهُ نَفۡسَهُۥۗ وَإِلَى ٱللَّهِ ٱلۡمَصِيرُ ﴿٢٨﴾ قُلۡ
إِن تُخۡفُواْ مَا فِي صُدُورِكُمۡ أَوۡ تُبۡدُوهُ يَعۡلَمۡهُ ٱللَّهُۗ وَيَعۡلَمُ مَا فِي
ٱلسَّمَٰوَٰتِ وَمَا فِي ٱلۡأَرۡضِۗ وَٱللَّهُ عَلَىٰ كُلِّ شَيۡءٖ قَدِيرٞ ﴿٢٩﴾

managing His creation in a just way. ***There is no god but Him,*** repeated for stress, ***the Almighty*** in His sovereignty, ***the All-Wise*** in what He does.

19. ***The only*** acceptable ***dīn in the sight of Allah is Islam,*** the *Sharī'a* brought by all the Messengers which is based on *tawḥīd.* ***Those given the Book*** (the Jews and Christians) ***only differed*** about the *dīn*, in that some of them declared Allah's unity and some disbelieved, ***after knowledge*** of *tawḥīd* ***had come to them, envying one another. As for those who reject Allah's Signs, Allah is Swift at Reckoning*** and in repaying people for what they have done.

20. ***If they*** (the unbelievers) ***argue*** regarding the *dīn* ***with you,*** Muḥammad, ***say*** to them, ***"I have submitted my face completely to Allah*** and obey Him, ***as have all who follow me."*** The word "face" is mentioned because it is the noblest part of the body and the rest follows it. ***Say to those given the Book*** (the Jews and Christians) ***and those who have no Book*** (the Arab idolaters), ***"Have you become Muslim?" If they become Muslim, they have been guided*** away from misguidance. ***If they turn away*** from Islam, ***you are only responsible for conveying the message. Allah sees His slaves*** and will repay people for their actions. This was before the command to fight came.

21. ***As for those who reject Allah's Signs, and kill*** (or "fight" in one reading) ***the Prophets without any legal right, and kill those who command justice, give them good news of a painful punishment.*** Those referred to here are the Jews. It is reported that they killed forty-three Prophets; one hundred and seventy of their worshippers forbade them to do so, and they killed them on the same day. Allah mentions "good news" to mock them.

22. ***They are the ones whose actions come to nothing in this world and the Next World.*** Whatever good they have done, such as giving *ṣadaqa* and maintaining ties of kinship, is of no value. ***They will have no helpers*** to help them in the face of Allah's punishment.

23. ***Do you not see those who have been given a portion of the Book*** (the Torah) ***being called upon to let Allah's Book judge between them? But then a group of them turn away in aversion.*** They refuse to accept its rulings. Two of the Jews committed adultery and went for judgement to the Prophet, may Allah bless him and grant him peace, and he judged that they should be stoned. They refused to accept this and then the Torah was brought and the judgement was found in it and so they were stoned. This made the Jews angry.

24. ***That*** turning away ***is because they say, "The Fire will only touch us for a number of days."*** They said that the Fire would only touch them for the number of days that their ancestors had worshipped the Calf, which was forty days. ***Their fabrications*** regarding this and other things ***have deluded them in their*** **dīn.**

25 ***But how will it be*** (what will their state be) ***when We gather them all together for a Day about which there is no doubt*** (the Day of Rising)**?** ***Every self*** (the People of the Book and others) ***will be paid in full for what it earned*** of actions, good or bad. ***They*** (people in general) ***will not be wronged*** by the slightest depreciation of a good action or exaggeration of an evil one.

26. This was revealed when the Messenger of Allah, may Allah bless him and grant him peace, promised his Community sovereignty over Persia and Byzantium and the hypocrites said, "How unlikely!" ***Say, "O Allah! Master of the Kingdom! You give sovereignty to whomever*** of your creatures ***You will. You take sovereignty from whomever You will. You exalt whomever You will. You abase whomever You will*** by taking sovereignty from him. ***All good*** and evil ***is in Your hands*** (subject to Your power). ***You have power over everything.***

27. ***You merge the night into the day. You merge the day into the night*** by increasing or decreasing the one or the other. ***You bring out the living from the dead***, as human beings come from drops of sperm or birds from eggs. ***You bring out the dead from the living*** such as the sperm and eggs from their living hosts. ***You provide for whom You will without any reckoning***, meaning give them unlimited provision."

28. ***The believers should not take unbelievers as friends*** and protectors ***rather than believers. Anyone who does that*** and befriends unbelievers ***has nothing whatsoever to do with*** the *dīn* of ***Allah – unless it is because you are afraid of them***, unless it is dissimula-

يَوۡمَ تَجِدُ كُلُّ نَفۡسٖ مَّا عَمِلَتۡ مِنۡ خَيۡرٖ مُّحۡضَرٗا وَمَا عَمِلَتۡ
مِن سُوٓءٖ تَوَدُّ لَوۡ أَنَّ بَيۡنَهَا وَبَيۡنَهُۥٓ أَمَدَۢا بَعِيدٗاۗ وَيُحَذِّرُكُمُ
ٱللَّهُ نَفۡسَهُۥۗ وَٱللَّهُ رَءُوفُۢ بِٱلۡعِبَادِ ٣٠ قُلۡ إِن كُنتُمۡ تُحِبُّونَ ٱللَّهَ
فَٱتَّبِعُونِي يُحۡبِبۡكُمُ ٱللَّهُ وَيَغۡفِرۡ لَكُمۡ ذُنُوبَكُمۡۚ وَٱللَّهُ غَفُورٞ رَّحِيمٞ
٣١ قُلۡ أَطِيعُواْ ٱللَّهَ وَٱلرَّسُولَۖ فَإِن تَوَلَّوۡاْ فَإِنَّ ٱللَّهَ لَا يُحِبُّ
ٱلۡكَٰفِرِينَ ٣٢ ۞ إِنَّ ٱللَّهَ ٱصۡطَفَىٰٓ ءَادَمَ وَنُوحٗا وَءَالَ إِبۡرَٰهِيمَ
وَءَالَ عِمۡرَٰنَ عَلَى ٱلۡعَٰلَمِينَ ٣٣ ذُرِّيَّةَۢ بَعۡضُهَا مِنۢ بَعۡضٖۗ وَٱللَّهُ
سَمِيعٌ عَلِيمٌ ٣٤ إِذۡ قَالَتِ ٱمۡرَأَتُ عِمۡرَٰنَ رَبِّ إِنِّي نَذَرۡتُ لَكَ
مَا فِي بَطۡنِي مُحَرَّرٗا فَتَقَبَّلۡ مِنِّيٓۖ إِنَّكَ أَنتَ ٱلسَّمِيعُ ٱلۡعَلِيمُ ٣٥ فَلَمَّا
وَضَعَتۡهَا قَالَتۡ رَبِّ إِنِّي وَضَعۡتُهَآ أُنثَىٰ وَٱللَّهُ أَعۡلَمُ بِمَا وَضَعَتۡ
وَلَيۡسَ ٱلذَّكَرُ كَٱلۡأُنثَىٰۖ وَإِنِّي سَمَّيۡتُهَا مَرۡيَمَ وَإِنِّيٓ أُعِيذُهَا بِكَ
وَذُرِّيَّتَهَا مِنَ ٱلشَّيۡطَٰنِ ٱلرَّجِيمِ ٣٦ فَتَقَبَّلَهَا رَبُّهَا بِقَبُولٍ
حَسَنٖ وَأَنۢبَتَهَا نَبَاتًا حَسَنٗا وَكَفَّلَهَا زَكَرِيَّاۖ كُلَّمَا دَخَلَ عَلَيۡهَا
زَكَرِيَّا ٱلۡمِحۡرَابَ وَجَدَ عِندَهَا رِزۡقٗاۖ قَالَ يَٰمَرۡيَمُ أَنَّىٰ لَكِ هَٰذَاۖ
قَالَتۡ هُوَ مِنۡ عِندِ ٱللَّهِۖ إِنَّ ٱللَّهَ يَرۡزُقُ مَن يَشَآءُ بِغَيۡرِ حِسَابٍ ٣٧
هُنَالِكَ دَعَا زَكَرِيَّا رَبَّهُۥۖ قَالَ رَبِّ هَبۡ لِي مِن لَّدُنكَ ذُرِّيَّةٗ
طَيِّبَةًۖ إِنَّكَ سَمِيعُ ٱلدُّعَآءِ ٣٨ فَنَادَتۡهُ ٱلۡمَلَٰٓئِكَةُ وَهُوَ قَآئِمٞ
يُصَلِّي فِي ٱلۡمِحۡرَابِ أَنَّ ٱللَّهَ يُبَشِّرُكَ بِيَحۡيَىٰ مُصَدِّقَۢا بِكَلِمَةٖ مِّنَ
ٱللَّهِ وَسَيِّدٗا وَحَصُورٗا وَنَبِيّٗا مِّنَ ٱلصَّٰلِحِينَ ٣٩ قَالَ رَبِّ
أَنَّىٰ يَكُونُ لِي غُلَٰمٞ وَقَدۡ بَلَغَنِيَ ٱلۡكِبَرُ وَٱمۡرَأَتِي عَاقِرٞۖ قَالَ

tion out of fear of them so that the befriending takes place with the tongue alone and not the heart. This was before Islam became mighty, when Islam had no power in the land. ***Allah advises*** and warns ***you to beware of Him*** and have fear of Him because He will become angry with you if you make friends with them. ***The final destination is to Allah*** and when you return to Him He will repay you for what you have done.

29. ***Say*** to them, ***"Whether you conceal what is in your*** hearts in your ***breasts*** of loyalty to them ***or make it known, Allah knows it. He knows everything in the heavens and everything in the earth. Allah has power over everything"*** and has the power to punish them for their attachment to unbelievers.

30. Remember ***the Day that each self finds the good it did and the evil it did present there in front of it, it will wish there were a great distance between it and them*** so that it would not reach him. ***Allah advises you to beware of Him.*** This is repeated here for added emphasis. ***Allah is All-Gentle with His slaves.***

31. This was revealed when the idolaters said, "We only worship idols out of love of Allah so that they may bring us near to Him." ***Say*** to them, O Muḥammad, ***"If you love Allah, then follow me and Allah will love you*** and reward you ***and forgive you for your wrong actions. Allah is Ever-Forgiving,*** forgiving those who follow the Prophet for anything they did before that, ***Most Merciful."***

32. ***Say*** to them, ***"Obey Allah and the Messenger*** regarding the *tawḥīd* He commands you to implement." ***Then if they turn away*** from obedience, ***Allah does not love*** (will punish) ***the unbelievers.*** The final sentence uses the noun "unbelievers" rather than the pronoun "them" to make it absolutely clear what such people are.

33. ***Allah chose Ādam and Nūḥ and the family of Ibrāhīm and the family of 'Imrān over all other beings,*** placing Prophethood among their descendants –

34. ***... descendants one of the other. Allah is All-Hearing, All-Knowing.***

35. Remember ***when the wife of 'Imrān*** (Ḥanna) was old and wanted a child and prayed to Allah and, when she found that she was pregnant, ***said, "My Lord, I have pledged*** (consecrated) ***what is in***

my womb to You, devoting it completely ***to Your service,*** sincere and chaste, and free from the concerns of the world, to serve Your holy Temple. ***Please accept my prayer. You are the All-Hearing*** of people's supplications, ***the All-Knowing*** of their intentions." 'Imrān died during the period of her pregnancy.

36. ***When she gave birth*** to a girl while hoping for a boy since only boys could be consecrated in that way, ***she said*** to excuse herself, ***"My Lord! I have given birth to a girl" – and Allah knew very well what she had given birth to*** (read as *waḍa'at,* "she had given birth to" and *waḍa'tu,* "I have given birth to"), generally understood to be a Divine interpolation, ***for male*** which she had asked for ***is not like female*** which she was given. That is because she intended to devote her child to service which was not appropriate for a girl because females are weak and must be secluded and are subject to menstruation and the like. – ***"and I have named her Maryam and placed her and her children in Your safekeeping from the Accursed Shayṭān."*** It is related in *ḥadīth* that Shayṭān pricks every child who is born on the day he is born and so it cries out – except for Maryam and her son. (al-Bukhārī and Muslim)

37. ***Her Lord accepted her with approval,*** Allah accepted Maryam from her mother, ***and made her grow in health and beauty.*** It is said that she grew in one day the amount a normal child grows in a year and her mother took her to the rabbis who were the temple custodians in Jerusalem and she said, "This vowed one is for you to care for," and they argued about her because she was the daughter of their High Priest. Zakariyyā said, "I am more entitled to be her guardian because I am married to her maternal aunt." They said, "Not until we draw lots." Twenty-nine of them would go to the river Jordan and throw their pens in and the one whose pen stayed put and rose to the surface would be entitled to care for her. It was the pen of Zakariyyā which rose. So he took her and built a room for her in the temple with a stairway which only he used. He used to come and give her food and water and oil. He would find summer fruits with her in winter and winter fruits in summer. As Allah says, ***Zakariyyā became her guardian*** (read as *kafalahā* or *kaffalahā)* and she was entrusted to him. ***Every time Zakariyyā visited her in the Upper Room*** (the noblest place in the temple) ***he found food with her. He***

said, "Maryam, how did you get this?" She, who was a child, ***said, "It is from Allah.*** He brought it to me from the Garden. ***Allah provides for whomever He wills without any reckoning,*** giving them unlimited provision without them doing anything to entitle them to it."

38 When Zakariyyā saw that, he realised that the One who has the power to bring fruit outside its time also had the power to give him a child in his old age. The people of his family had died out, so ***then and there Zakariyyā called on his Lord*** when he entered the Upper Room to pray for a child in the night ***and said, "O Lord, grant me from Your favour an upright descendant. You are the Hearer of Prayer*** and answer it."

39. *The angels* (Jibrīl) ***called out to him while he was standing in prayer in the Upper Room*** in the temple: ***"Allah gives you the good news*** (read as *yubashshiruka* and *yabshuruka*) ***of Yaḥyā, who will come to confirm a Word from Allah,*** 'Īsā, who is the Spirit of Allah and is called a "Word" because he was created by the Divine Word "Be", ***and will be a*** followed ***leader and a celibate, a Prophet and one of the righteous."*** It is related that Yaḥyā did not commit a wrong action nor was he ever suspected of doing so.

40. *He said, "O Lord, how can I possibly have a son when I have reached old age and my wife is barren?"* He was one hundred and twenty and his wife was ninety-eight. ***He said, "It*** (the command) ***will be so*** and Allah will create a son from the two of you. ***Allah does whatever He wills."*** Nothing is beyond His power. It was the demonstration of this immense power which inspired his request so that it could be answered. When his soul yearned for swift good news, he said what is reported in the next *āyat*.

41. *He said, "My Lord, appoint a Sign* of my wife's pregnancy ***for me." He said, "Your Sign*** of it ***is that you will not speak to people for three days*** and nights, ***except by gesture.*** He was prevented from speaking to them, but not from invoking Allah. ***Remember your Lord frequently and glorify Him*** (pray to Him) ***in the evening and the early morning*** (at the beginning and end of the day)."

كَذَٰلِكَ ٱللَّهُ يَفْعَلُ مَا يَشَآءُ ﴿٤٠﴾ قَالَ رَبِّ ٱجْعَل لِّيٓ ءَايَةً ۖ
قَالَ ءَايَتُكَ أَلَّا تُكَلِّمَ ٱلنَّاسَ ثَلَٰثَةَ أَيَّامٍ إِلَّا رَمْزًا ۗ وَٱذْكُر
رَّبَّكَ كَثِيرًا وَسَبِّحْ بِٱلْعَشِيِّ وَٱلْإِبْكَٰرِ ﴿٤١﴾ وَإِذْ قَالَتِ
ٱلْمَلَٰٓئِكَةُ يَٰمَرْيَمُ إِنَّ ٱللَّهَ ٱصْطَفَىٰكِ وَطَهَّرَكِ وَٱصْطَفَىٰكِ
عَلَىٰ نِسَآءِ ٱلْعَٰلَمِينَ ﴿٤٢﴾ يَٰمَرْيَمُ ٱقْنُتِى لِرَبِّكِ وَٱسْجُدِى
وَٱرْكَعِى مَعَ ٱلرَّٰكِعِينَ ﴿٤٣﴾ ذَٰلِكَ مِنْ أَنۢبَآءِ ٱلْغَيْبِ نُوحِيهِ
إِلَيْكَ ۚ وَمَا كُنتَ لَدَيْهِمْ إِذْ يُلْقُونَ أَقْلَٰمَهُمْ أَيُّهُمْ يَكْفُلُ
مَرْيَمَ وَمَا كُنتَ لَدَيْهِمْ إِذْ يَخْتَصِمُونَ ﴿٤٤﴾ إِذْ قَالَتِ
ٱلْمَلَٰٓئِكَةُ يَٰمَرْيَمُ إِنَّ ٱللَّهَ يُبَشِّرُكِ بِكَلِمَةٍ مِّنْهُ ٱسْمُهُ ٱلْمَسِيحُ
عِيسَى ٱبْنُ مَرْيَمَ وَجِيهًا فِى ٱلدُّنْيَا وَٱلْءَاخِرَةِ وَمِنَ ٱلْمُقَرَّبِينَ ﴿٤٥﴾
وَيُكَلِّمُ ٱلنَّاسَ فِى ٱلْمَهْدِ وَكَهْلًا وَمِنَ ٱلصَّٰلِحِينَ ﴿٤٦﴾
قَالَتْ رَبِّ أَنَّىٰ يَكُونُ لِى وَلَدٌ وَلَمْ يَمْسَسْنِى بَشَرٌ ۖ قَالَ كَذَٰلِكِ
ٱللَّهُ يَخْلُقُ مَا يَشَآءُ ۚ إِذَا قَضَىٰٓ أَمْرًا فَإِنَّمَا يَقُولُ لَهُۥ كُن فَيَكُونُ ﴿٤٧﴾
وَيُعَلِّمُهُ ٱلْكِتَٰبَ وَٱلْحِكْمَةَ وَٱلتَّوْرَىٰةَ وَٱلْإِنجِيلَ ﴿٤٨﴾
وَرَسُولًا إِلَىٰ بَنِىٓ إِسْرَٰٓءِيلَ أَنِّى قَدْ جِئْتُكُم بِـَٔايَةٍ مِّن رَّبِّكُمْ ۖ
أَنِّىٓ أَخْلُقُ لَكُم مِّنَ ٱلطِّينِ كَهَيْـَٔةِ ٱلطَّيْرِ فَأَنفُخُ فِيهِ
فَيَكُونُ طَيْرًۢا بِإِذْنِ ٱللَّهِ ۖ وَأُبْرِئُ ٱلْأَكْمَهَ وَٱلْأَبْرَصَ
وَأُحْىِ ٱلْمَوْتَىٰ بِإِذْنِ ٱللَّهِ ۖ وَأُنَبِّئُكُم بِمَا تَأْكُلُونَ وَمَا تَدَّخِرُونَ
فِى بُيُوتِكُمْ ۚ إِنَّ فِى ذَٰلِكَ لَءَايَةً لَّكُمْ إِن كُنتُم مُّؤْمِنِينَ ﴿٤٩﴾
وَمُصَدِّقًا لِّمَا بَيْنَ يَدَىَّ مِنَ ٱلتَّوْرَىٰةِ وَلِأُحِلَّ لَكُم
بَعْضَ ٱلَّذِى حُرِّمَ عَلَيْكُمْ ۚ وَجِئْتُكُم بِـَٔايَةٍ مِّن رَّبِّكُمْ

42. Remember ***when the angels*** (Jibrīl) ***said, "Maryam, Allah has chosen you and purified you*** of the touch of men ***and has chosen you over all other women*** of your time.

43. ***Maryam, obey your Lord and prostrate and bow with those who bow*** (pray with those who pray)."

44. ***This*** (what We have mentioned about Zakariyyā and Maryam) ***is news from the Unseen,*** of things which you did not see, Muḥammad, ***which We reveal to you. You were not with them when they cast their reeds*** into the water to draw lots ***to see which of them should be the guardian of Maryam*** and have custody of her. ***You were not with them when they quarrelled*** about it. This news is Revelation.

45. Remember ***when the angels*** (Jibrīl) ***said, "Maryam, Allah gives you the good news of a Word*** (a child) ***from Him. His name is the Messiah, 'Īsā, son of Maryam,*** addressing her to inform her that her child had no father since the custom is to ascribe male children to their father, ***of high esteem in this world,*** by reason of his Prophethood, ***and the Next World,*** by reason of his intercession and high degree, ***and one of those brought near*** to Allah.

46. ***He will speak to people in the cradle,*** as an infant before the age of speech, ***and also when fully grown, and will be one of the righteous."***

47. ***She said, "My Lord! How can I have a son when no man has ever touched me,*** either within marriage or at any other time?" ***He said, "It*** (the matter) ***shall be so."*** Allah is well able to create a child without a father. ***Allah creates whatever He wills. When He decides on*** creating ***something, He simply says to it, "Be!" and it is*** and then it comes into existence.

48. ***"He will teach*** (read as *yu'allimu*, "He will teach" and *nu'allimu*, "We will teach") ***him the Book*** (writing) ***and Wisdom, and the Torah and the Gospel,***

49. ***as a Messenger to the Tribe of Israel,*** while still a child and after also puberty. Jibrīl breathed into the collar of Maryam's shift and she became pregnant. More about this is mentioned in *Sūrat Maryam.* When Allah sent 'Īsā to the tribe of Israel he said, 'I am the Messenger of Allah to you. ***I have brought you a Sign*** of my truth-

فَاتَّقُوا اللَّهَ وَأَطِيعُونِ ﴿٥٠﴾ إِنَّ اللَّهَ رَبِّي وَرَبُّكُمْ فَاعْبُدُوهُ ۗ
هَٰذَا صِرَاطٌ مُّسْتَقِيمٌ ﴿٥١﴾ ۞ فَلَمَّا أَحَسَّ عِيسَىٰ مِنْهُمُ
الْكُفْرَ قَالَ مَنْ أَنصَارِي إِلَى اللَّهِ ۖ قَالَ الْحَوَارِيُّونَ نَحْنُ
أَنصَارُ اللَّهِ آمَنَّا بِاللَّهِ وَاشْهَدْ بِأَنَّا مُسْلِمُونَ ﴿٥٢﴾
رَبَّنَا آمَنَّا بِمَا أَنزَلْتَ وَاتَّبَعْنَا الرَّسُولَ فَاكْتُبْنَا مَعَ
الشَّاهِدِينَ ﴿٥٣﴾ وَمَكَرُوا وَمَكَرَ اللَّهُ ۖ وَاللَّهُ خَيْرُ
الْمَاكِرِينَ ﴿٥٤﴾ إِذْ قَالَ اللَّهُ يَا عِيسَىٰ إِنِّي مُتَوَفِّيكَ وَرَافِعُكَ
إِلَيَّ وَمُطَهِّرُكَ مِنَ الَّذِينَ كَفَرُوا وَجَاعِلُ الَّذِينَ اتَّبَعُوكَ
فَوْقَ الَّذِينَ كَفَرُوا إِلَىٰ يَوْمِ الْقِيَامَةِ ۖ ثُمَّ إِلَيَّ مَرْجِعُكُمْ
فَأَحْكُمُ بَيْنَكُمْ فِيمَا كُنتُمْ فِيهِ تَخْتَلِفُونَ ﴿٥٥﴾ فَأَمَّا الَّذِينَ
كَفَرُوا فَأُعَذِّبُهُمْ عَذَابًا شَدِيدًا فِي الدُّنْيَا وَالْآخِرَةِ وَمَا
لَهُم مِّن نَّاصِرِينَ ﴿٥٦﴾ وَأَمَّا الَّذِينَ آمَنُوا وَعَمِلُوا
الصَّالِحَاتِ فَيُوَفِّيهِمْ أُجُورَهُمْ ۗ وَاللَّهُ لَا يُحِبُّ الظَّالِمِينَ ﴿٥٧﴾
ذَٰلِكَ نَتْلُوهُ عَلَيْكَ مِنَ الْآيَاتِ وَالذِّكْرِ الْحَكِيمِ ﴿٥٨﴾ إِنَّ
مَثَلَ عِيسَىٰ عِندَ اللَّهِ كَمَثَلِ آدَمَ ۖ خَلَقَهُ مِن تُرَابٍ ثُمَّ قَالَ
لَهُ كُن فَيَكُونُ ﴿٥٩﴾ الْحَقُّ مِن رَّبِّكَ فَلَا تَكُن مِّنَ الْمُمْتَرِينَ ﴿٦٠﴾
فَمَنْ حَاجَّكَ فِيهِ مِن بَعْدِ مَا جَاءَكَ مِنَ الْعِلْمِ فَقُلْ تَعَالَوْا نَدْعُ
أَبْنَاءَنَا وَأَبْنَاءَكُمْ وَنِسَاءَنَا وَنِسَاءَكُمْ وَأَنفُسَنَا وَأَنفُسَكُمْ
ثُمَّ نَبْتَهِلْ فَنَجْعَل لَّعْنَتَ اللَّهِ عَلَى الْكَاذِبِينَ ﴿٦١﴾
إِنَّ هَٰذَا لَهُوَ الْقَصَصُ الْحَقُّ ۚ وَمَا مِنْ إِلَٰهٍ إِلَّا اللَّهُ ۚ وَإِنَّ اللَّهَ لَهُوَ

fulness ***from your Lord. I will create*** and mould something like ***the form of a bird out of clay for you and then breathe into it and it will be a bird*** (read as *ṭayran* and *ṭā'iran*) ***by Allah's permission*** (by Allah's will). So he created a bat for them, for it is like a bird, and it flew while they were looking, vanished from their sight and fell down dead so that the action of the creature would be clearly distinguished from the action of the Creator, who is Allah, and so that it would be known that perfection belongs to Allah alone. ***I will heal the blind,*** people who are born blind, ***and lepers*** (the blind and lepers are mentioned because they had a defect, and 'Īsā was sent at a time when medicine was very important; he would heal fifty thousand people in a day by supplication provided that they were already believers), ***I will bring the dead to life, by Allah's permission*** ("Allah's permission" is repeated to negate any assumption of divinity. 'Īsā brought to life a friend of his, the son of an old woman who was the daughter of a tax-collector, and Sām, the son of Nūḥ, who died again immediately afterwards), ***I will tell you what you eat and what you store up in your homes*** which I have not seen. Thus he would tell a person what he had eaten and was going to eat. ***There is a Sign for you in that*** which has been mentioned ***if you are believers.***

50. ***I come confirming the Torah I find already there, and to make lawful for you some of what was previously forbidden to you.*** What he made lawful were fish and birds which have no talons and the fat of cattle and sheep. It is also said that "some" means "all". ***I have brought you a Sign from your Lord.*** This is repeated for stress. ***So be fearful of Allah and obey me*** in respect of what I command regarding the implementation of Allah's unity and obedience to Him.

51. ***Allah is my Lord and your Lord so worship Him. That*** which I command you ***is a straight path.'"*** They denied him and did not believe in him.

52. ***When 'Īsā sensed*** (was aware of) ***unbelief on their part*** and the fact that they wanted to kill him, ***he said, "Who will be my helpers*** on the journey ***to*** help the *dīn* of ***Allah?" The disciples said, "We are Allah's helpers,*** in other words: "We will help Allah's *dīn*." They were the close friends of 'Īsā, the first to believe in him and numbered twelve men. The word for "disciples", *ḥawwāriyyūn*, comes from *ḥawar* which means pure whiteness. It is said that they were fullers who bleached clothes, in other words made them white. They continued: ***"We believe in Allah. Bear witness***, 'Īsā, ***that we are Muslims.***

53. ***"Our Lord, we believe in what You have sent down*** of the Gospel ***and have followed the Messenger*** ('Īsā) ***so write us down among the witnesses,*** those who testify to Your oneness and sincerely follow Your Messenger."

54. Allah Almighty says: ***They plotted and Allah plotted.*** The unbelievers of the Israelites plotted against 'Īsā when they surrendered him to those who wanted kill to him. Allah plotted by substituting a likeness of 'Īsā in his place so that those who wanted to kill him killed the likeness while 'Īsā himself was raised to heaven. ***But Allah is the best of plotters*** and has better knowledge of the plotters.

55. Remember ***when Allah said, "'Īsā, I will take you back and raise you up to Me*** from this world without your dying ***and purify you of*** and distance you from ***the people who disbelieve. And I will place the people who follow you*** and affirm your Prophethood among the Muslims and Christians ***above,*** both in terms of physical force and conclusive argument, ***those*** (the Jews) ***who disbelieve*** in you ***until the Day of Rising. Then you will all return to Me, and I will judge between you regarding the things about which you differed*** in respect of matters of the *dīn*.

56. ***As for those who disbelieve, I will punish them with a harsh punishment in this world*** by their being killed, being captured and paying the *jizya*, ***and the Next World*** by the Fire. ***They will have no helpers*** to defend them against it."

57. ***As for those who believe and do right actions, He will pay them*** (read as *yuwaffīhim*, "He will pay them" and *nuwaffīhim*, "We will pay them") ***their wages in full. Allah does not love wrongdoers***, meaning He will punish them. It is related that Allah sent a cloud and raised 'Īsā up and carried him to his mother. She wept and he said to her, "The Resurrection will reunite us." That happened on the Night of Power in Jerusalem when he was thirty-three years old. His mother lived for six years after him. Al-Bukhārī and Muslim relate a *ḥadīth* to the effect that he will descend near the House (the Ka'ba) and give judgements according to the Sharī'a of our Prophet, kill the Dajjāl and pigs, and break the crosses and impose *jizya*. In a *ḥadīth* reported by Muslim it says that he will remain on earth for seven years. A *ḥadīth* from Abū Dāwūd aṭ-Ṭayālisī reports forty years. Then he will die and the funeral prayer will be said over him. It is possible that what is meant by the forty years is the total time he will remain on earth both before and after his being raised up to heaven.

58. ***That*** which has been mentioned about 'Īsā ***is what We recite*** and recount ***to you***, Muḥammad, ***of the Signs and the wise Reminder*** (the Qur'an).

59. ***The likeness of 'Īsā*** with respect to its great rarity ***in Allah's sight is the same as Ādam*** in that 'Īsā was created without a father. The unusual is compared to the more unusual to reinforce the argument and to give it more weight. ***He created him from earth and then He said to him, "Be*** a human being!***" and he was.*** That is like the creation of 'Īsā in that Allah said, "Be" and he was.

60. ***It***, what happened to 'Īsā, ***is the truth from your Lord, so do not be among the doubters*** and doubt it.

61. ***If anyone*** of the Christians ***argues with you about him after the knowledge*** of the matter ***that has come to you, say*** to them, ***"Come then! Let us summon our sons and your sons, and our women and your women, and ourselves and yourselves*** and gather them together. ***Then let us make earnest supplication and call down the curse of Allah upon the liars,"*** saying, "O Allah, curse the one who lies about the matter of 'Īsā." The Prophet, may Allah bless him and grant him peace, invited the delegation of Christians from Najrān who had argued with him and they said, "We will think about it and then come back to you." Those of influence among them said to them, "You have acknowledged his Prophethood. Anyone cursed by a Prophet is destroyed." They came to him and he went out with al-Ḥasan, al-Ḥusayn, Fāṭima and 'Alī and said to them, "When I have made supplication, say 'Amen'." The Christians refused to perform the mutual curse and made peace based on paying the *jizya*. Abū Nu'aym related it and Ibn 'Abbās said, "If those people had come out to make the supplication, they would have returned and found

ٱلۡعَزِيزُ ٱلۡحَكِيمُ ﴿٦٢﴾ فَإِن تَوَلَّوۡاْ فَإِنَّ ٱللَّهَ عَلِيمُۢ بِٱلۡمُفۡسِدِينَ ﴿٦٣﴾
قُلۡ يَٰٓأَهۡلَ ٱلۡكِتَٰبِ تَعَالَوۡاْ إِلَىٰ كَلِمَةٖ سَوَآءِۭ بَيۡنَنَا وَبَيۡنَكُمۡ
أَلَّا نَعۡبُدَ إِلَّا ٱللَّهَ وَلَا نُشۡرِكَ بِهِۦ شَيۡـٔٗا وَلَا يَتَّخِذَ بَعۡضُنَا
بَعۡضًا أَرۡبَابٗا مِّن دُونِ ٱللَّهِۚ فَإِن تَوَلَّوۡاْ فَقُولُواْ ٱشۡهَدُواْ بِأَنَّا
مُسۡلِمُونَ ﴿٦٤﴾ يَٰٓأَهۡلَ ٱلۡكِتَٰبِ لِمَ تُحَآجُّونَ فِيٓ
إِبۡرَٰهِيمَ وَمَآ أُنزِلَتِ ٱلتَّوۡرَىٰةُ وَٱلۡإِنجِيلُ إِلَّا مِنۢ بَعۡدِهِۦٓۚ أَفَلَا
تَعۡقِلُونَ ﴿٦٥﴾ هَٰٓأَنتُمۡ هَٰٓؤُلَآءِ حَٰجَجۡتُمۡ فِيمَا لَكُم بِهِۦ
عِلۡمٞ فَلِمَ تُحَآجُّونَ فِيمَا لَيۡسَ لَكُم بِهِۦ عِلۡمٞۚ وَٱللَّهُ يَعۡلَمُ وَأَنتُمۡ
لَا تَعۡلَمُونَ ﴿٦٦﴾ مَا كَانَ إِبۡرَٰهِيمُ يَهُودِيّٗا وَلَا نَصۡرَانِيّٗا وَلَٰكِن كَانَ
حَنِيفٗا مُّسۡلِمٗا وَمَا كَانَ مِنَ ٱلۡمُشۡرِكِينَ ﴿٦٧﴾ إِنَّ أَوۡلَى ٱلنَّاسِ
بِإِبۡرَٰهِيمَ لَلَّذِينَ ٱتَّبَعُوهُ وَهَٰذَا ٱلنَّبِيُّ وَٱلَّذِينَ ءَامَنُواْۗ وَٱللَّهُ وَلِيُّ
ٱلۡمُؤۡمِنِينَ ﴿٦٨﴾ وَدَّت طَّآئِفَةٞ مِّنۡ أَهۡلِ ٱلۡكِتَٰبِ لَوۡ يُضِلُّونَكُمۡ
وَمَا يُضِلُّونَ إِلَّآ أَنفُسَهُمۡ وَمَا يَشۡعُرُونَ ﴿٦٩﴾ يَٰٓأَهۡلَ
ٱلۡكِتَٰبِ لِمَ تَكۡفُرُونَ بِـَٔايَٰتِ ٱللَّهِ وَأَنتُمۡ تَشۡهَدُونَ ﴿٧٠﴾
يَٰٓأَهۡلَ ٱلۡكِتَٰبِ لِمَ تَلۡبِسُونَ ٱلۡحَقَّ بِٱلۡبَٰطِلِ وَتَكۡتُمُونَ ٱلۡحَقَّ
وَأَنتُمۡ تَعۡلَمُونَ ﴿٧١﴾ وَقَالَت طَّآئِفَةٞ مِّنۡ أَهۡلِ ٱلۡكِتَٰبِ ءَامِنُواْ
بِٱلَّذِيٓ أُنزِلَ عَلَى ٱلَّذِينَ ءَامَنُواْ وَجۡهَ ٱلنَّهَارِ وَٱكۡفُرُوٓاْ ءَاخِرَهُۥ
لَعَلَّهُمۡ يَرۡجِعُونَ ﴿٧٢﴾ وَلَا تُؤۡمِنُوٓاْ إِلَّا لِمَن تَبِعَ دِينَكُمۡ قُلۡ إِنَّ
ٱلۡهُدَىٰ هُدَى ٱللَّهِ أَن يُؤۡتَىٰٓ أَحَدٞ مِّثۡلَ مَآ أُوتِيتُمۡ أَوۡ يُحَآجُّوكُمۡ
عِندَ رَبِّكُمۡۗ قُلۡ إِنَّ ٱلۡفَضۡلَ بِيَدِ ٱللَّهِ يُؤۡتِيهِ مَن يَشَآءُۗ وَٱللَّهُ وَٰسِعٌ
عَلِيمٞ ﴿٧٣﴾ يَخۡتَصُّ بِرَحۡمَتِهِۦ مَن يَشَآءُۗ وَٱللَّهُ ذُو ٱلۡفَضۡلِ

neither money nor family." It is said, "If they had gone out they would have been burned up."

62. ***This*** which has been mentioned ***is the true account*** about which there is no doubt. ***There is no god besides Allah. Allah – He is the Almighty*** in His Kingdom, ***the All-Wise*** in what He does.

63. ***And if they turn away*** from belief, ***Allah knows the corrupters*** and will repay them.

64. ***Say, "O People of the Book*** (the Jews and Christians)***! Come to a proposition which is the same for us and you*** – it is ***that we should worship none but Allah and not attribute any partners to Him and not take one another as lords besides Allah,"*** as they have done with their rabbis and monks. ***If they turn away*** from *tawḥīd*, ***say*** to them, ***"Bear witness that we are Muslims***, declaring the oneness of Allah."

65. When the Jews said that Ibrāhīm was a Jew and that they were following his *dīn* and the Christians said the same thing, this was revealed. ***O People of the Book! Why do you argue concerning Ibrāhīm*** and claim that he followed your religion ***when the Torah and Gospel were only sent down*** a long time ***after him*** and Judaism and Christianity only developed after their revelation***? Why do you not use your intellect*** and see that what you say is false?

66. ***You are people arguing about something you have no knowledge of,*** when you argue about Mūsā and 'Īsā and claim that you are following their *dīn*. ***Why do you argue about something you have no knowledge of*** regarding Ibrāhīm***? Allah knows*** about the matter. ***You do not know.*** Allah then clears Ibrāhīm of what they say.

67. ***Ibrāhīm was neither a Jew nor a Christian, but a man of pure natural belief,*** a *ḥanīf* who inclines from all other religions to the Straight *Dīn:* ***a Muslim*** and affirmer of the Divine Unity. ***He was no idolater.***

68. ***The people with the strongest claim to Ibrāhīm are those who followed him*** in his time ***and this Prophet,*** Muḥammad, since he agrees with him in most of his Sharī'a, ***and those*** of his Community ***who believe.*** So they are more entitled to say that they are following the *dīn* of Ibrāhīm than others are. ***Allah is the Protector of the believers,*** helping and protecting them.

69. This was revealed when the Jews invited Mu'ādh, Ḥudhayfa and 'Ammār to their *dīn*. ***A group of the People of the Book would love to misguide you. They only misguide themselves*** because they incur the sin of their misguidance and the believers do not obey them, ***but they are not aware of it.***

70. ***People of the Book! Why do you reject Allah's Signs,*** meaning the Qur'an which includes the description of Muḥammad, ***when you yourselves are there as witnesses*** that it is the truth*?*

71. ***People of the Book! Why do you mix up truth with falsehood*** by twisting and lying and concealing the description of the Prophet ***and knowingly conceal the truth*** when you know it is true*?*

72. ***A group of the People of the Book*** (some of the Jews) ***say*** to others of them, ***"At the beginning of the day believe in what was sent down to those who believe,*** meaning the Qur'ān, ***and then at the end of the day reject it, so that perhaps they*** (the believers) ***will revert*** from their *dīn,* since they will say, 'Why did these people revert after entering it? They possess knowledge. They must have done that because they know it to be false.'"

73. They also said: ***"Do not believe anyone except for those who follow your own* dīn** and agree with it." Allah says: ***Say*** to them, ***"Allah's guidance is true guidance.*** It is Islam and anything else constitutes misguidance. Then an interpolation follows: ***But you think it is impossible for anyone to be given the same as you were given,*** referring to the Book, wisdom, and excellence of character, ***or to argue with you before your Lord."*** The Jews are warning people not to go near anyone of that description or they might follow their *dīn*. It implies that the believers will defeat them on the Day of Rising because their *dīn* is sounder. Allah says: ***Say, "All favour is in Allah's Hand and He gives it to whomever He wills.*** How can they say that no one will be given the same as they had been given? ***Allah is All-Encompassing*** with His bounty, ***All-Knowing*** of the people who merit it.

74. ***"He selects for His mercy whoever He wills. Allah's favour is indeed immense."***

75. ***Among the People of the Book there are some who, if you entrust them with a pile of gold*** (a great deal of wealth), ***will return***

ٱلۡعَظِيمِ ﴿٧٤﴾ ۞ وَمِنۡ أَهۡلِ ٱلۡكِتَٰبِ مَنۡ إِن تَأۡمَنۡهُ بِقِنطَارٖ
يُؤَدِّهِۦٓ إِلَيۡكَ وَمِنۡهُم مَّنۡ إِن تَأۡمَنۡهُ بِدِينَارٖ لَّا يُؤَدِّهِۦٓ إِلَيۡكَ إِلَّا
مَا دُمۡتَ عَلَيۡهِ قَآئِمٗاۗ ذَٰلِكَ بِأَنَّهُمۡ قَالُواْ لَيۡسَ عَلَيۡنَا فِي ٱلۡأُمِّيِّـۧنَ
سَبِيلٞ وَيَقُولُونَ عَلَى ٱللَّهِ ٱلۡكَذِبَ وَهُمۡ يَعۡلَمُونَ ﴿٧٥﴾
بَلَىٰۚ مَنۡ أَوۡفَىٰ بِعَهۡدِهِۦ وَٱتَّقَىٰ فَإِنَّ ٱللَّهَ يُحِبُّ ٱلۡمُتَّقِينَ ﴿٧٦﴾ إِنَّ
ٱلَّذِينَ يَشۡتَرُونَ بِعَهۡدِ ٱللَّهِ وَأَيۡمَٰنِهِمۡ ثَمَنٗا قَلِيلًا أُوْلَٰٓئِكَ لَا
خَلَٰقَ لَهُمۡ فِي ٱلۡأٓخِرَةِ وَلَا يُكَلِّمُهُمُ ٱللَّهُ وَلَا يَنظُرُ إِلَيۡهِمۡ
يَوۡمَ ٱلۡقِيَٰمَةِ وَلَا يُزَكِّيهِمۡ وَلَهُمۡ عَذَابٌ أَلِيمٞ ﴿٧٧﴾
وَإِنَّ مِنۡهُمۡ لَفَرِيقٗا يَلۡوُۥنَ أَلۡسِنَتَهُم بِٱلۡكِتَٰبِ لِتَحۡسَبُوهُ
مِنَ ٱلۡكِتَٰبِ وَمَا هُوَ مِنَ ٱلۡكِتَٰبِ وَيَقُولُونَ هُوَ
مِنۡ عِندِ ٱللَّهِ وَمَا هُوَ مِنۡ عِندِ ٱللَّهِ وَيَقُولُونَ عَلَى ٱللَّهِ ٱلۡكَذِبَ
وَهُمۡ يَعۡلَمُونَ ﴿٧٨﴾ مَا كَانَ لِبَشَرٍ أَن يُؤۡتِيَهُ ٱللَّهُ ٱلۡكِتَٰبَ
وَٱلۡحُكۡمَ وَٱلنُّبُوَّةَ ثُمَّ يَقُولَ لِلنَّاسِ كُونُواْ عِبَادٗا لِّي مِن
دُونِ ٱللَّهِ وَلَٰكِن كُونُواْ رَبَّٰنِيِّـۧنَ بِمَا كُنتُمۡ تُعَلِّمُونَ ٱلۡكِتَٰبَ
وَبِمَا كُنتُمۡ تَدۡرُسُونَ ﴿٧٩﴾ وَلَا يَأۡمُرَكُمۡ أَن تَتَّخِذُواْ ٱلۡمَلَٰٓئِكَةَ
وَٱلنَّبِيِّـۧنَ أَرۡبَابًاۗ أَيَأۡمُرُكُم بِٱلۡكُفۡرِ بَعۡدَ إِذۡ أَنتُم مُّسۡلِمُونَ ﴿٨٠﴾
وَإِذۡ أَخَذَ ٱللَّهُ مِيثَٰقَ ٱلنَّبِيِّـۧنَ لَمَآ ءَاتَيۡتُكُم مِّن كِتَٰبٖ
وَحِكۡمَةٖ ثُمَّ جَآءَكُمۡ رَسُولٞ مُّصَدِّقٞ لِّمَا مَعَكُمۡ لَتُؤۡمِنُنَّ
بِهِۦ وَلَتَنصُرُنَّهُۥۚ قَالَ ءَأَقۡرَرۡتُمۡ وَأَخَذۡتُمۡ عَلَىٰ ذَٰلِكُمۡ إِصۡرِيۖ
قَالُوٓاْ أَقۡرَرۡنَاۚ قَالَ فَٱشۡهَدُواْ وَأَنَا۠ مَعَكُم مِّنَ ٱلشَّٰهِدِينَ ﴿٨١﴾

it to you, such as 'Abdullāh ibn Salām who kept twelve hundred *uqiyyas* of gold for a Qurayshī man and returned it to him. ***But there are others among them who, if you entrust them with a single dinar, will not return it to you*** because of their double-dealing, ***unless you stay standing over them*** and do not leave them. If you leave them, they deny any liability, as Ka'b ibn al-Ashraf did. A Qurayshī entrusted a dinar to him and he denied it. ***That*** (not returning trusts) ***is because they say, "We are under no obligation where the Gentiles*** (the Arabs) ***are concerned."*** The sin is that they say that they are allowed to be unjust to those who differ from their religion and attribute that to Allah. Allah says: ***They tell a lie against Allah*** when they ascribe that to Him ***and they know it.***

76. The opposite is true. ***No, the truth is, if people honour their contracts*** for or against themselves by conveying trusts and other things, ***and show fear of Him*** by abandoning acts of disobedience and performing acts of obedience, ***Allah loves all godfearing people*** and will reward them.

77. This was revealed about the Jews who altered the description of the Prophet, may Allah bless him and grant him peace, and Allah's contract with them in the Torah and about those of them who swore false oaths regarding their claims or when selling goods. ***Those who sell*** and exchange ***Allah's contract*** with them to believe in the Prophet and fulfil their trusts ***and their own oaths,*** which they falsely swear by Allah, ***for a paltry price*** from this world, ***such people will have no portion in the Next World and on the Day of Rising Allah***, out of anger, ***will not speak to them or look at them*** with mercy ***or purify them. They will have a painful punishment.***

78. ***Among them is a group*** among the People of the Book, such as Ka'b ibn al-Ashraf, ***who distort the Book with their tongues*** by altering its recitation from what was actually revealed to their distortion of the description of the Prophet contained in it and other things ***so that you think it*** (the distortion) ***is from the Book*** which Allah revealed ***when it is not from the Book. They say, "It is from Allah," but it is not from Allah. They tell a lie against Allah and they know it*** (know that they are lying).

79. This was revealed when the Christians of Najrān said that 'Īsā had commanded them to take him as a Lord or, possibly, when one of the Muslims wanted to prostrate to the Prophet, may Allah bless him and grant him peace. ***It is not right for any human being that Allah should give him the Book and Judgement,*** meaning understanding of the *Sharī'a, **and Prophethood, and then that he should say to people, "Be slaves to me rather than Allah." Rather he will say, "Be people of the Lord because of your knowledge of the Book*** (literally "by what you know", *ta'lamūna*, which is also read as *tu'allimūna,* "what you teach") ***and because you study."*** The benefit of knowledge lies in acting by it.

80. *He* (Allah) ***would never command you to take the angels and Prophets as Lords.*** This is an addition to the previous *āyat* on account of the fact that the Sabaeans deified the angels, the Jews 'Uzayr and the Christians 'Īsā. ***Would He command you to disbelieve after being Muslim?*** He would never do that.

81 Remember ***when Allah made a covenant with the Prophets: "Now that I have given you*** (read as *ātaytukum*, "I have given you" and *ātaynākum*, "We have given you") ***a share of the Book and Wisdom and then a Messenger***, meaning Muḥammad, may Allah bless him and grant him peace, ***comes to you confirming what is with you*** of the Book and Wisdom, ***you must believe in him and help him."*** The covenant is that when they and their nations meet him, they must follow him. ***He*** (Allah) ***asked*** them, ***"Do you agree*** to that ***and undertake*** and accept ***My charge*** and covenant ***on that condition?" They replied, "We agree!" He said, "Bear witness*** against yourselves and your followers! ***I am with you as one of the witnesses*** against you and them."

82. *Any who turn away after that* undertaking, ***they are the degenerate.***

83. *Is it other than the* dīn *of Allah that they desire* (read as *yabghūna*, "they desire" or *tabghūna,* "you desire") ***when everything in the heavens and earth, willingly or unwillingly, submits to Him and they will be returned*** (read as *yurja'ūna*, "they will be returned" or *turja'ūna,* "you will be returned") ***to Him?*** The interrogative *hamza* at the beginning of the sentence implies a negative response.

فَمَن تَوَلَّىٰ بَعۡدَ ذَٰلِكَ فَأُوْلَٰٓئِكَ هُمُ ٱلۡفَٰسِقُونَ ٨٢
أَفَغَيۡرَ دِينِ ٱللَّهِ يَبۡغُونَ وَلَهُۥٓ أَسۡلَمَ مَن فِي ٱلسَّمَٰوَٰتِ
وَٱلۡأَرۡضِ طَوۡعٗا وَكَرۡهٗا وَإِلَيۡهِ يُرۡجَعُونَ ٨٣
قُلۡ ءَامَنَّا بِٱللَّهِ وَمَآ أُنزِلَ عَلَيۡنَا وَمَآ أُنزِلَ عَلَىٰٓ إِبۡرَٰهِيمَ
وَإِسۡمَٰعِيلَ وَإِسۡحَٰقَ وَيَعۡقُوبَ وَٱلۡأَسۡبَاطِ وَمَآ أُوتِيَ
مُوسَىٰ وَعِيسَىٰ وَٱلنَّبِيُّونَ مِن رَّبِّهِمۡ لَا نُفَرِّقُ بَيۡنَ أَحَدٖ
مِّنۡهُمۡ وَنَحۡنُ لَهُۥ مُسۡلِمُونَ ٨٤ وَمَن يَبۡتَغِ غَيۡرَ ٱلۡإِسۡلَٰمِ
دِينٗا فَلَن يُقۡبَلَ مِنۡهُ وَهُوَ فِي ٱلۡأٓخِرَةِ مِنَ ٱلۡخَٰسِرِينَ ٨٥
كَيۡفَ يَهۡدِي ٱللَّهُ قَوۡمٗا كَفَرُواْ بَعۡدَ إِيمَٰنِهِمۡ وَشَهِدُوٓاْ
أَنَّ ٱلرَّسُولَ حَقّٞ وَجَآءَهُمُ ٱلۡبَيِّنَٰتُۚ وَٱللَّهُ لَا يَهۡدِي ٱلۡقَوۡمَ
ٱلظَّٰلِمِينَ ٨٦ أُوْلَٰٓئِكَ جَزَآؤُهُمۡ أَنَّ عَلَيۡهِمۡ لَعۡنَةَ ٱللَّهِ
وَٱلۡمَلَٰٓئِكَةِ وَٱلنَّاسِ أَجۡمَعِينَ ٨٧ خَٰلِدِينَ فِيهَا لَا يُخَفَّفُ
عَنۡهُمُ ٱلۡعَذَابُ وَلَا هُمۡ يُنظَرُونَ ٨٨ إِلَّا ٱلَّذِينَ تَابُواْ مِنۢ
بَعۡدِ ذَٰلِكَ وَأَصۡلَحُواْ فَإِنَّ ٱللَّهَ غَفُورٞ رَّحِيمٌ ٨٩ إِنَّ ٱلَّذِينَ
كَفَرُواْ بَعۡدَ إِيمَٰنِهِمۡ ثُمَّ ٱزۡدَادُواْ كُفۡرٗا لَّن تُقۡبَلَ تَوۡبَتُهُمۡ
وَأُوْلَٰٓئِكَ هُمُ ٱلضَّآلُّونَ ٩٠ إِنَّ ٱلَّذِينَ كَفَرُواْ وَمَاتُواْ وَهُمۡ
كُفَّارٞ فَلَن يُقۡبَلَ مِنۡ أَحَدِهِم مِّلۡءُ ٱلۡأَرۡضِ ذَهَبٗا وَلَوِ
ٱفۡتَدَىٰ بِهِۦٓۗ أُوْلَٰٓئِكَ لَهُمۡ عَذَابٌ أَلِيمٞ وَمَا لَهُم مِّن نَّٰصِرِينَ ٩١
لَن تَنَالُواْ ٱلۡبِرَّ حَتَّىٰ تُنفِقُواْ مِمَّا تُحِبُّونَۚ وَمَا تُنفِقُواْ مِن شَيۡءٖ
فَإِنَّ ٱللَّهَ بِهِۦ عَلِيمٞ ٩٢ ۞ كُلُّ ٱلطَّعَامِ كَانَ حِلّٗا لِّبَنِيٓ

84. ***Say*** to them, Muḥammad, ***"We believe in Allah and what has been sent down to us and what was sent down to Ibrāhīm, Ismā'īl, Isḥāq, and Ya'qūb and the Tribes, and what Mūsā and 'Īsā and all the Prophets were given by their Lord. We do not differentiate between any of them*** by confirming some and denying others. ***We are Muslims submitting to Him."*** We are sincere in our worship.

85. This was revealed about some people who apostatised and joined the unbelievers. ***If anyone desires anything other than Islam as a*** **dīn,** ***it will not be accepted from him, and in the Next World he will be among the losers*** because he will go to the Fire and remain in it forever.

86. ***How can Allah guide a people who have disbelieved after having had belief?*** This means that Allah will not guide them. ***They bore witness that the Messenger was true and that the Clear Signs*** which are the outward evidence of the truthfulness of the Prophet ***had come to them. Allah does not guide wrongdoing people.*** The wrongdoers are the unbelievers.

87. ***The repayment of such people is that Allah's curse is on them, and that of the angels and of all mankind.***

88. ***They will be under it,*** either the curse or the Fire, ***forever. Their punishment will not be lightened. They will be granted no reprieve,***

89. ***Except for those who turn in repentance after that and put things right*** by acting righteously. ***Truly Allah is Ever-Forgiving*** to them, ***Most Merciful*** to them.

90. This was revealed about the Jews. ***Those who disbelieve*** in 'Īsā ***after having had belief*** in Mūsā, ***and then increase in their unbelief*** in Muḥammad, ***their repentance will not be accepted*** when they die unbelievers. ***They are the misguided.***

91. ***As for those who disbelieve and die while still unbelievers,*** the amount of ***the whole earth filled with gold would not be accepted from any of them if they were to offer it as a ransom.*** The consequential conjunction *fa-* introduces the second clause because the unacceptability of any ransom is a consequence of dying as an unbeliever. ***They will have a painful punishment. They will have no helpers*** and no one to avert the punishment from them.

إِسۡرَٰٓءِيلَ إِلَّا مَا حَرَّمَ إِسۡرَٰٓءِيلُ عَلَىٰ نَفۡسِهِۦ مِن قَبۡلِ أَن تُنَزَّلَ
ٱلتَّوۡرَىٰةُۚ قُلۡ فَأۡتُواْ بِٱلتَّوۡرَىٰةِ فَٱتۡلُوهَآ إِن كُنتُمۡ صَٰدِقِينَ
٩٣ فَمَنِ ٱفۡتَرَىٰ عَلَى ٱللَّهِ ٱلۡكَذِبَ مِنۢ بَعۡدِ ذَٰلِكَ فَأُوْلَٰٓئِكَ
هُمُ ٱلظَّٰلِمُونَ ٩٤ قُلۡ صَدَقَ ٱللَّهُۗ فَٱتَّبِعُواْ مِلَّةَ إِبۡرَٰهِيمَ حَنِيفٗا
وَمَا كَانَ مِنَ ٱلۡمُشۡرِكِينَ ٩٥ إِنَّ أَوَّلَ بَيۡتٖ وُضِعَ لِلنَّاسِ لَلَّذِي
بِبَكَّةَ مُبَارَكٗا وَهُدٗى لِّلۡعَٰلَمِينَ ٩٦ فِيهِ ءَايَٰتُۢ بَيِّنَٰتٞ مَّقَامُ
إِبۡرَٰهِيمَۖ وَمَن دَخَلَهُۥ كَانَ ءَامِنٗاۗ وَلِلَّهِ عَلَى ٱلنَّاسِ حِجُّ ٱلۡبَيۡتِ
مَنِ ٱسۡتَطَاعَ إِلَيۡهِ سَبِيلٗاۚ وَمَن كَفَرَ فَإِنَّ ٱللَّهَ غَنِيٌّ عَنِ ٱلۡعَٰلَمِينَ
٩٧ قُلۡ يَٰٓأَهۡلَ ٱلۡكِتَٰبِ لِمَ تَكۡفُرُونَ بِـَٔايَٰتِ ٱللَّهِ وَٱللَّهُ شَهِيدٌ
عَلَىٰ مَا تَعۡمَلُونَ ٩٨ قُلۡ يَٰٓأَهۡلَ ٱلۡكِتَٰبِ لِمَ تَصُدُّونَ عَن
سَبِيلِ ٱللَّهِ مَنۡ ءَامَنَ تَبۡغُونَهَا عِوَجٗا وَأَنتُمۡ شُهَدَآءُۗ وَمَا ٱللَّهُ
بِغَٰفِلٍ عَمَّا تَعۡمَلُونَ ٩٩ يَٰٓأَيُّهَا ٱلَّذِينَ ءَامَنُوٓاْ إِن تُطِيعُواْ
فَرِيقٗا مِّنَ ٱلَّذِينَ أُوتُواْ ٱلۡكِتَٰبَ يَرُدُّوكُم بَعۡدَ إِيمَٰنِكُمۡ كَٰفِرِينَ ١٠٠
وَكَيۡفَ تَكۡفُرُونَ وَأَنتُمۡ تُتۡلَىٰ عَلَيۡكُمۡ ءَايَٰتُ ٱللَّهِ وَفِيكُمۡ
رَسُولُهُۥۗ وَمَن يَعۡتَصِم بِٱللَّهِ فَقَدۡ هُدِيَ إِلَىٰ صِرَٰطٖ مُّسۡتَقِيمٖ ١٠١
يَٰٓأَيُّهَا ٱلَّذِينَ ءَامَنُواْ ٱتَّقُواْ ٱللَّهَ حَقَّ تُقَاتِهِۦ وَلَا تَمُوتُنَّ إِلَّا وَأَنتُم
مُّسۡلِمُونَ ١٠٢ وَٱعۡتَصِمُواْ بِحَبۡلِ ٱللَّهِ جَمِيعٗا وَلَا تَفَرَّقُواْۚ
وَٱذۡكُرُواْ نِعۡمَتَ ٱللَّهِ عَلَيۡكُمۡ إِذۡ كُنتُمۡ أَعۡدَآءٗ فَأَلَّفَ بَيۡنَ قُلُوبِكُمۡ
فَأَصۡبَحۡتُم بِنِعۡمَتِهِۦٓ إِخۡوَٰنٗا وَكُنتُمۡ عَلَىٰ شَفَا حُفۡرَةٖ مِّنَ ٱلنَّارِ
فَأَنقَذَكُم مِّنۡهَاۗ كَذَٰلِكَ يُبَيِّنُ ٱللَّهُ لَكُمۡ ءَايَٰتِهِۦ لَعَلَّكُمۡ تَهۡتَدُونَ

92. ***You will not attain true goodness,*** meaning its reward, which is the Garden, ***until you give of what you love*** of your property. ***Whatever you give away, Allah knows it*** and will repay you for it.

93. The following *āyat* revealed when the Jews said, "You claim that you are following the religion of Ibrāhīm, but he did not eat camel meat or drink camel milk." ***All food was lawful for the Tribe of Israel except what Israel*** (Ya'qūb) ***made unlawful for himself before the Torah was sent down.*** He prohibited camel meat for himself because of an illness he was suffering from. He vowed that if he was healed he would not eat it and so he made it unlawful for himself. This was after Ibrāhīm, and so it had not been unlawful for Ibrāhīm in his time as they claimed. ***Say*** to them, ***"Bring the Torah and read it out*** to prove the truth of what they say ***if you speak the truth."*** They were dumbfounded and did not do so. Then Allah makes the statement in the following *āyat*:

94. ***So any who, after this,*** after the production of the evidence that the prohibition came from Ya'qūb, not in the time of Ibrāhīm, ***invent a lie against Allah are indeed wrongdoers*** by transgressing against the truth in favour of falsehood.

95. ***Say,*** Muḥammad, ***"Allah speaks the truth*** in this as in all reports, ***so follow the religion of Ibrāhīm,*** which I am following, ***a man of pure natural belief*** (a *ḥanīf,* someone who inclines from all other religions to the *dīn* of Islam). ***He was no idolater."***

96. The following *āyat* was revealed when the Jews said, "Our *qibla* existed before your *qibla*." ***The first House established for*** worship for ***mankind was that at Bakka, a place of blessing and a guidance for all beings*** (the *qibla* for everyone). The use of Bakka rather than Makka reflects a Makkan dialect; it is called that because it bears down (*bakka*) on the necks of tyrants. The angels built it before the creation of Ādam whereas al-Aqṣā in Jerusalem was built after that. There were forty years between them, as is reported in the two *Ṣaḥīḥ* collections.

97. ***In it are Clear Signs*** – one of them is ***the Station of Ibrāhīm,*** which is the stone on which he stood when building the House. On it is the mark of his feet which can still be seen. Other signs are the multiplication of good deeds there and the fact that birds do not fly over it. ***All who enter it are safe*** from being killed, injustice, and other things. **Ḥajj** (read *as ḥijj* and *ḥajj*) ***to the House is a duty owed to Allah by all mankind – those who can find a way to do it.*** The Prophet, may Allah bless him and grant him peace, explained that "can find a way" refers to provision and a mount (as in al-Ḥākim and others). ***But if anyone disbelieves*** in Allah and the obligation of *ḥajj*, ***Allah is Rich beyond need of any being*** and has no need of jinn, men and angels worshipping Him.

98. ***Say, "People of the Book! Why do you reject Allah's Signs*** (the Qur'an) ***when Allah is Witness of everything you do*** and will repay you?"

99. ***Say, "People of the Book! Why do you debar*** and divert ***those who believe from the Way of Allah*** (His *dīn*), by your denying the Prophet and concealing his blessing, ***desiring to make it crooked,*** attempting to make it deviate from the Truth, ***when you yourselves are witnesses to it*** and know that the straight *dīn* is the *dīn* of Islam as is clear in your own Books? ***Allah is not heedless of anything you do*** in terms of disbelief and denial." He is deferring them to the time when He will repay them.

100. This *āyat* was revealed when a Jew passed by Aws and Khazraj and envied their cohesion. He mentioned the past differences they used to have in the time of the *Jāhiliyya* and they began to quarrel and almost fight. ***O you who believe! If you obey a group of those given the Book, they will make you revert to being unbelievers after you have believed.***

101. ***How can you disbelieve, when Allah's Signs are recited to you and the Messenger is there among you?*** This is a question of wonder and rebuke. ***Whoever holds fast to Allah has been guided to a straight path.***

102. ***You who believe! Be fearful of Allah with the fear that is His due***, by obeying Him: so do not disobey, but be thankful; do not show ingratitude, but remember and do not forget ***and do not die except as Muslims*** declaring Allah's oneness.

103. ***Hold fast to the rope of Allah*** (His *dīn*) ***all together, and do not separate*** after having entered Islam. ***Remember Allah's blessing upon you,*** Aws and Khazraj, ***when you were enemies*** before Islam

﴿١٠٣﴾ وَلۡتَكُن مِّنكُمۡ أُمَّةٞ يَدۡعُونَ إِلَى ٱلۡخَيۡرِ وَيَأۡمُرُونَ بِٱلۡمَعۡرُوفِ
وَيَنۡهَوۡنَ عَنِ ٱلۡمُنكَرِۚ وَأُوْلَٰٓئِكَ هُمُ ٱلۡمُفۡلِحُونَ ﴿١٠٤﴾ وَلَا
تَكُونُواْ كَٱلَّذِينَ تَفَرَّقُواْ وَٱخۡتَلَفُواْ مِنۢ بَعۡدِ مَا جَآءَهُمُ ٱلۡبَيِّنَٰتُۚ
وَأُوْلَٰٓئِكَ لَهُمۡ عَذَابٌ عَظِيمٞ ﴿١٠٥﴾ يَوۡمَ تَبۡيَضُّ وُجُوهٞ وَتَسۡوَدُّ
وُجُوهٞۚ فَأَمَّا ٱلَّذِينَ ٱسۡوَدَّتۡ وُجُوهُهُمۡ أَكَفَرۡتُم بَعۡدَ إِيمَٰنِكُمۡ
فَذُوقُواْ ٱلۡعَذَابَ بِمَا كُنتُمۡ تَكۡفُرُونَ ﴿١٠٦﴾ وَأَمَّا ٱلَّذِينَ ٱبۡيَضَّتۡ
وُجُوهُهُمۡ فَفِي رَحۡمَةِ ٱللَّهِۖ هُمۡ فِيهَا خَٰلِدُونَ ﴿١٠٧﴾ تِلۡكَ ءَايَٰتُ
ٱللَّهِ نَتۡلُوهَا عَلَيۡكَ بِٱلۡحَقِّۗ وَمَا ٱللَّهُ يُرِيدُ ظُلۡمٗا لِّلۡعَٰلَمِينَ ﴿١٠٨﴾
وَلِلَّهِ مَا فِي ٱلسَّمَٰوَٰتِ وَمَا فِي ٱلۡأَرۡضِۚ وَإِلَى ٱللَّهِ تُرۡجَعُ ٱلۡأُمُورُ
﴿١٠٩﴾ كُنتُمۡ خَيۡرَ أُمَّةٍ أُخۡرِجَتۡ لِلنَّاسِ تَأۡمُرُونَ بِٱلۡمَعۡرُوفِ
وَتَنۡهَوۡنَ عَنِ ٱلۡمُنكَرِ وَتُؤۡمِنُونَ بِٱللَّهِۗ وَلَوۡ ءَامَنَ
أَهۡلُ ٱلۡكِتَٰبِ لَكَانَ خَيۡرٗا لَّهُمۚ مِّنۡهُمُ ٱلۡمُؤۡمِنُونَ
وَأَكۡثَرُهُمُ ٱلۡفَٰسِقُونَ ﴿١١٠﴾ لَن يَضُرُّوكُمۡ إِلَّآ أَذٗىۖ
وَإِن يُقَٰتِلُوكُمۡ يُوَلُّوكُمُ ٱلۡأَدۡبَارَ ثُمَّ لَا يُنصَرُونَ ﴿١١١﴾ ضُرِبَتۡ
عَلَيۡهِمُ ٱلذِّلَّةُ أَيۡنَ مَا ثُقِفُوٓاْ إِلَّا بِحَبۡلٖ مِّنَ ٱللَّهِ وَحَبۡلٖ مِّنَ ٱلنَّاسِ
وَبَآءُو بِغَضَبٖ مِّنَ ٱللَّهِ وَضُرِبَتۡ عَلَيۡهِمُ ٱلۡمَسۡكَنَةُۚ ذَٰلِكَ
بِأَنَّهُمۡ كَانُواْ يَكۡفُرُونَ بِـَٔايَٰتِ ٱللَّهِ وَيَقۡتُلُونَ ٱلۡأَنۢبِيَآءَ بِغَيۡرِ
حَقّٖۚ ذَٰلِكَ بِمَا عَصَواْ وَّكَانُواْ يَعۡتَدُونَ ﴿١١٢﴾ ۞ لَيۡسُواْ سَوَآءٗۗ
مِّنۡ أَهۡلِ ٱلۡكِتَٰبِ أُمَّةٞ قَآئِمَةٞ يَتۡلُونَ ءَايَٰتِ ٱللَّهِ ءَانَآءَ ٱلَّيۡلِ
وَهُمۡ يَسۡجُدُونَ ﴿١١٣﴾ يُؤۡمِنُونَ بِٱللَّهِ وَٱلۡيَوۡمِ ٱلۡأٓخِرِ

and He joined your hearts together through Islam ***so that you became brothers by His blessing*** in the *dīn* and by political unity. ***You were on the very brink of a pit of the Fire*** and there was nothing to stop you falling into it and dying as disbelievers ***and He saved you from it*** by faith. ***Thus does Allah make His Signs clear to you,*** as in the case of this *āyat,* ***so that perhaps you will be guided.***

104. ***Let there be a community among you who call people to the good,*** meaning Islam, ***and enjoin what is recognised as right, and forbid what is known to be wrong:*** those who do these this, ***they are the successful.*** This is partitive because what is mentioned is a *farḍ kifāya*. Not everyone is obliged to do it. The ignorant, for instance, are absolved from it.

105. ***Do not be like those who split up*** from their *dīn* ***and differed*** about it ***after the Clear Signs came to them.*** This is a reference to the Jews and Christians. ***They will have a terrible punishment...***

106. ***...on the Day*** (the Day of Rising) ***when faces are whitened and faces are blackened. As for those whose faces are blackened,*** meaning the disbelievers who will be cast into the Fire and this is said to them by way of rebuke, ***"What! Did you reject after having belief*** when you accepted Allah's covenant? ***Taste the punishment because you disbelieved!"***

107. ***As for those whose faces are whitened*** (the believers), ***they are in the mercy of Allah*** (His Garden), ***remaining in it timelessly, for - ever.***

108. ***These*** Signs ***are Allah's Signs which We recite to you***, Muḥammad, ***with truth. Allah does not desire wrong for any being*** and would never punish anyone who had done no wrong.

109. ***Everything in the heavens and everything in the earth belongs to Allah.*** All that exists is His property, His creation and His slaves. ***All matters return to Allah.***

110. ***You***, nation of Muḥammad, ***are the best nation*** in the knowledge of Allah ***ever to be produced*** (to have appeared) ***before mankind. You enjoin what is recognised as right, and forbid what is known to be wrong, and believe in Allah. If the People of the Book believed*** as 'Abdullāh ibn Salām and his companions did, ***it***

وَيَأۡمُرُونَ بِٱلۡمَعۡرُوفِ وَيَنۡهَوۡنَ عَنِ ٱلۡمُنكَرِ وَيُسَٰرِعُونَ
فِي ٱلۡخَيۡرَٰتِۖ وَأُوْلَٰٓئِكَ مِنَ ٱلصَّٰلِحِينَ ﴿١١٤﴾ وَمَا يَفۡعَلُواْ
مِنۡ خَيۡرٖ فَلَن يُكۡفَرُوهُۗ وَٱللَّهُ عَلِيمُۢ بِٱلۡمُتَّقِينَ ﴿١١٥﴾
إِنَّ ٱلَّذِينَ كَفَرُواْ لَن تُغۡنِيَ عَنۡهُمۡ أَمۡوَٰلُهُمۡ وَلَآ أَوۡلَٰدُهُم
مِّنَ ٱللَّهِ شَيۡـٔٗاۖ وَأُوْلَٰٓئِكَ أَصۡحَٰبُ ٱلنَّارِۚ هُمۡ فِيهَا خَٰلِدُونَ ﴿١١٦﴾
مَثَلُ مَا يُنفِقُونَ فِي هَٰذِهِ ٱلۡحَيَوٰةِ ٱلدُّنۡيَا كَمَثَلِ رِيحٖ فِيهَا
صِرٌّ أَصَابَتۡ حَرۡثَ قَوۡمٖ ظَلَمُوٓاْ أَنفُسَهُمۡ فَأَهۡلَكَتۡهُۚ وَمَا
ظَلَمَهُمُ ٱللَّهُ وَلَٰكِنۡ أَنفُسَهُمۡ يَظۡلِمُونَ ﴿١١٧﴾ يَٰٓأَيُّهَا ٱلَّذِينَ
ءَامَنُواْ لَا تَتَّخِذُواْ بِطَانَةٗ مِّن دُونِكُمۡ لَا يَأۡلُونَكُمۡ خَبَالٗا
وَدُّواْ مَا عَنِتُّمۡ قَدۡ بَدَتِ ٱلۡبَغۡضَآءُ مِنۡ أَفۡوَٰهِهِمۡ وَمَا تُخۡفِي
صُدُورُهُمۡ أَكۡبَرُۚ قَدۡ بَيَّنَّا لَكُمُ ٱلۡأٓيَٰتِۖ إِن كُنتُمۡ تَعۡقِلُونَ ﴿١١٨﴾
هَٰٓأَنتُمۡ أُوْلَآءِ تُحِبُّونَهُمۡ وَلَا يُحِبُّونَكُمۡ وَتُؤۡمِنُونَ بِٱلۡكِتَٰبِ كُلِّهِۦ
وَإِذَا لَقُوكُمۡ قَالُوٓاْ ءَامَنَّا وَإِذَا خَلَوۡاْ عَضُّواْ عَلَيۡكُمُ ٱلۡأَنَامِلَ
مِنَ ٱلۡغَيۡظِۚ قُلۡ مُوتُواْ بِغَيۡظِكُمۡۗ إِنَّ ٱللَّهَ عَلِيمُۢ بِذَاتِ ٱلصُّدُورِ ﴿١١٩﴾
إِن تَمۡسَسۡكُمۡ حَسَنَةٞ تَسُؤۡهُمۡ وَإِن تُصِبۡكُمۡ سَيِّئَةٞ يَفۡرَحُواْ
بِهَاۖ وَإِن تَصۡبِرُواْ وَتَتَّقُواْ لَا يَضُرُّكُمۡ كَيۡدُهُمۡ شَيۡـًٔاۗ
إِنَّ ٱللَّهَ بِمَا يَعۡمَلُونَ مُحِيطٞ ﴿١٢٠﴾ وَإِذۡ غَدَوۡتَ مِنۡ أَهۡلِكَ
تُبَوِّئُ ٱلۡمُؤۡمِنِينَ مَقَٰعِدَ لِلۡقِتَالِۗ وَٱللَّهُ سَمِيعٌ عَلِيمٌ ﴿١٢١﴾
إِذۡ هَمَّت طَّآئِفَتَانِ مِنكُمۡ أَن تَفۡشَلَا وَٱللَّهُ وَلِيُّهُمَاۗ وَعَلَى
ٱللَّهِ فَلۡيَتَوَكَّلِ ٱلۡمُؤۡمِنُونَ ﴿١٢٢﴾ وَلَقَدۡ نَصَرَكُمُ ٱللَّهُ بِبَدۡرٖ وَأَنتُمۡ

(belief) ***would be better for them. Some of them are believers but most of them are degenerate*** and unbelievers.

111. ***They*** (the Jews) ***will not harm you***, Muslims, ***except with abusive words*** (curses and threats). ***If they fight you, they will turn their backs on you*** in flight. ***Then they will not be helped*** against you, but you will have victory over them.

112. ***They will be plunged into abasement wherever they are found,*** and nowhere will they have any power or stability, ***unless they have a treaty with Allah and with the people*** (the believers). That means a treaty with the believers for security in exchange for paying the *jizya*. That is their only protection. ***They have brought down*** and returned with ***anger from Allah upon themselves, and they have been plunged into destitution. That was because they rejected Allah's Signs and killed the Prophets without any legal right. That was because they disobeyed*** the command of Allah ***and went beyond the limits*** (beyond the lawful into the unlawful).

113. ***They*** (all the People of the Book) ***are not all the same. There is a community among the People of the Book who are upright*** (straight and holding firmly to the truth, such as 'Abdullāh ibn Salām and his companions). ***They recite Allah's Signs throughout the*** hours of the ***night and they prostrate*** in prayer.

114. ***They believe in Allah and the Last Day, and enjoin the right and forbid the wrong, and compete in doing good***; Those who are like that, ***they are among the righteous.*** Some of them are not like that and are not among the righteous.

115. ***They will not be denied*** (read as *yukfarū*, "they will not be denied" and *tukfarū*, "you will not be denied") ***the reward for any good thing they do*** (read as *yaf'alū,* "they do" and *taf'alū*, "you do"). With the *tā'* (you), it is directed at the Muslim Community, and with the *yā'* (they), it refers to the "upright Community". In both cases the meaning is that far from not receiving a reward, you certainly will be rewarded for it. ***Allah knows the godfearing.***

116. ***As for those who disbelieve, their wealth and children will not help them*** or protect them ***against*** the punishment of ***Allah in any way.*** The masculine pronoun is used because men tend to protect themselves through their wealth and by seeking the help of their children. ***They will be the Companions of the Fire, remaining in it timelessly, forever.***

117. ***The likeness of what they*** (the unbelievers) ***spend in their life in this world*** in enmity to the Prophet, may Allah bless him and grant him peace, whether it be charity or anything else, ***is that of a wind with an icy bite to it,*** a violent wind which might be hot or freezing, ***which strikes the crops of a people who have wronged themselves*** by their unbelief and disobedience to Allah ***and destroys them.*** So their giving does not benefit them and what they spent will be gone and will not help them. ***Allah did not wrong them*** by the loss of what they spent; ***rather it was themselves they wronged*** by the unbelief which brought that about.

118. ***You who believe! Do not take any outside yourselves as intimates*** (close friends who are acquainted with your secrets). ***They*** (others among the Jews, Christians and hypocrites) ***will do anything to damage you.*** They will not confine themselves to corrupting you. ***They love*** and hope for ***what causes you distress*** and is very harmful to you. ***Hatred*** and enmity towards you ***has appeared out of their mouths*** when they attack you and acquaint the idolaters with your secrets, ***but what*** (the enmity) ***their breasts hide is far worse. We have made the Signs*** of their enmity ***clear to you if you use your intellect,*** so do not befriend them.

119. ***There you***, believers, ***are loving them*** because they are kin and friends ***when they do not love you*** because they differ from you in their *dīn*, ***even though you believe in all the Books***, because they do not believe in your Book. ***When they meet you, they say, "We believe." But when they go away they bite*** the ends of ***their fingers out of rage against you.*** They experience intense anger at what they see of your cohesion. "Biting fingers" metaphorically illustrates the strength of their anger. ***Say, "Die in your rage."*** This means "Remain in it until your death. What you want to see will never happen." ***Allah knows what the hearts*** of those people ***contain.***

120. ***If a good thing happens to you*** such as a victory or the acquisition of booty, ***it galls*** and upsets ***them. If a bad thing strikes you*** such as a defeat and or drought ***they rejoice at it.*** The gist of the *āyat* is that such people are hostile so one should not take them as friends; rather avoid them. ***But if you are steadfast*** in the face of the harm

أَذِلَّةٞۖ فَٱتَّقُواْ ٱللَّهَ لَعَلَّكُمۡ تَشۡكُرُونَ ١٢٣ إِذۡ تَقُولُ لِلۡمُؤۡمِنِينَ
أَلَن يَكۡفِيَكُمۡ أَن يُمِدَّكُمۡ رَبُّكُم بِثَلَٰثَةِ ءَالَٰفٖ مِّنَ ٱلۡمَلَٰٓئِكَةِ
مُنزَلِينَ ١٢٤ بَلَىٰٓۚ إِن تَصۡبِرُواْ وَتَتَّقُواْ وَيَأۡتُوكُم مِّن فَوۡرِهِمۡ
هَٰذَا يُمۡدِدۡكُمۡ رَبُّكُم بِخَمۡسَةِ ءَالَٰفٖ مِّنَ ٱلۡمَلَٰٓئِكَةِ مُسَوِّمِينَ
١٢٥ وَمَا جَعَلَهُ ٱللَّهُ إِلَّا بُشۡرَىٰ لَكُمۡ وَلِتَطۡمَئِنَّ قُلُوبُكُم بِهِۦۗ وَمَا
ٱلنَّصۡرُ إِلَّا مِنۡ عِندِ ٱللَّهِ ٱلۡعَزِيزِ ٱلۡحَكِيمِ ١٢٦ لِيَقۡطَعَ طَرَفٗا
مِّنَ ٱلَّذِينَ كَفَرُوٓاْ أَوۡ يَكۡبِتَهُمۡ فَيَنقَلِبُواْ خَآئِبِينَ ١٢٧ لَيۡسَ لَكَ
مِنَ ٱلۡأَمۡرِ شَيۡءٌ أَوۡ يَتُوبَ عَلَيۡهِمۡ أَوۡ يُعَذِّبَهُمۡ فَإِنَّهُمۡ ظَٰلِمُونَ
١٢٨ وَلِلَّهِ مَا فِي ٱلسَّمَٰوَٰتِ وَمَا فِي ٱلۡأَرۡضِۚ يَغۡفِرُ لِمَن يَشَآءُ
وَيُعَذِّبُ مَن يَشَآءُۚ وَٱللَّهُ غَفُورٞ رَّحِيمٞ ١٢٩ يَٰٓأَيُّهَا ٱلَّذِينَ
ءَامَنُواْ لَا تَأۡكُلُواْ ٱلرِّبَوٰٓاْ أَضۡعَٰفٗا مُّضَٰعَفَةٗۖ وَٱتَّقُواْ ٱللَّهَ
لَعَلَّكُمۡ تُفۡلِحُونَ ١٣٠ وَٱتَّقُواْ ٱلنَّارَ ٱلَّتِيٓ أُعِدَّتۡ لِلۡكَٰفِرِينَ
١٣١ وَأَطِيعُواْ ٱللَّهَ وَٱلرَّسُولَ لَعَلَّكُمۡ تُرۡحَمُونَ ١٣٢
۞ وَسَارِعُوٓاْ إِلَىٰ مَغۡفِرَةٖ مِّن رَّبِّكُمۡ وَجَنَّةٍ عَرۡضُهَا
ٱلسَّمَٰوَٰتُ وَٱلۡأَرۡضُ أُعِدَّتۡ لِلۡمُتَّقِينَ ١٣٣ ٱلَّذِينَ يُنفِقُونَ
فِي ٱلسَّرَّآءِ وَٱلضَّرَّآءِ وَٱلۡكَٰظِمِينَ ٱلۡغَيۡظَ وَٱلۡعَافِينَ
عَنِ ٱلنَّاسِۗ وَٱللَّهُ يُحِبُّ ٱلۡمُحۡسِنِينَ ١٣٤ وَٱلَّذِينَ إِذَا
فَعَلُواْ فَٰحِشَةً أَوۡ ظَلَمُوٓاْ أَنفُسَهُمۡ ذَكَرُواْ ٱللَّهَ فَٱسۡتَغۡفَرُواْ
لِذُنُوبِهِمۡ وَمَن يَغۡفِرُ ٱلذُّنُوبَ إِلَّا ٱللَّهُ وَلَمۡ يُصِرُّواْ عَلَىٰ
مَا فَعَلُواْ وَهُمۡ يَعۡلَمُونَ ١٣٥ أُوْلَٰٓئِكَ جَزَآؤُهُم مَّغۡفِرَةٞ

they wish you ***and godfearing,*** fearing Allah regarding taking them as friends and other things, ***their scheming will not harm you*** (read as *yaḍirkum* and *yaḍurrukum)* ***in any way. Allah encompasses everything they do*** (read as *y̲a'malūn*, "they do" and *t̲a'malūn*, "you do"), and Allah will repay them for what they do.

121. Remember, Muḥammad, ***when you left your family*** in Madina ***early in the day to settle the believers in their battle stations. Allah is All-Hearing*** of your words, ***All-Knowing*** of your states. This is about the Battle of Uḥud when the Prophet, peace be upon him, set out with nine hundred and fifty men while the unbelievers numbered three thousand. He camped by a ravine on Saturday 7th Shawwāl 3 AH with his back and his army to the mountain of Uḥud. He arranged the ranks and put a group of archers under the command of 'Abdullāh ibn Jubayr on the top of the mountain. He said, "Defend us with arrows and do not let any come at us from behind; do not leave your position, whether we are winning or losing."

122. ***And when two of your clans*** (the Banū Salama and Banū Ḥāritha) who remained on the flanks of the army, ***were on the point of losing heart,*** lacking the courage to fight and wanting to return when 'Abdullāh ibn Ubayy the hypocrite and his companions retreated. He said, "We will fight for the sake of our lives and children." He said to Abū Jābir as-Salamī, "I swear by Allah in reference to your Prophet and your selves, that if there were to be fighting we would go with you." But Allah made them firm and they did not leave. ***Allah was their Protector*** and Helper. ***Let the believers put their trust in Allah*** and no one else.

123. This *āyat* was revealed when they were defeated, to remind them of Allah's blessing upon them. ***Allah helped you at Badr***, a place between Makka and Madina ***when you were weak*** through having few weapons and small numbers, ***so be fearful of Allah, so that perhaps you will be thankful*** for Allah's blessings upon you.

124. ***And***, in victory, ***when you said to the believers,*** to promise them and encourage them, ***"Is it not enough for you that your Lord reinforced you with three thousand angels, sent down*** (read as "*munzalīn*" and "*munazzalīn*")***?"***

125. ***Yes indeed,*** Allah will be enough for you! In *Sūrat al-Anfāl*, there were a thousand angels because Allah helped them first with them; and then it became three thousand, then five thousand. ***But if you are steadfast*** in meeting the enemy, ***and godfearing,*** fearing to oppose Allah, ***and they*** (the idolaters) ***come upon you suddenly, your Lord will reinforce you with five thousand angels, clearly identified*** (read as *musawwimīna* and *musawwamīna*). They were steadfast, and Allah fulfilled His promise: angels fought alongside them on horseback wearing yellow or white turbans whose ends hung between their shoulders.

126. ***Allah only did this*** (reinforced you) ***for it to be good news*** of victory ***for you and so that your hearts might be stilled by it*** and not be alarmed by the large number of the enemy and the smallness of your numbers – ***help comes from no one but Allah, the Almighty, the All-Wise*** who gives help to whomever He wishes and victory is not dictated by the size of the army.

127. ***...and so that He might cut off*** and destroy ***a group of those who disbelieve*** by killing or capture ***or crush them*** in defeat, ***and they might be turned back disappointed*** by not obtaining what they desired.

128. The following was revealed when the Prophet's tooth, may Allah bless him and grant him peace, was broken and his face injured during the Battle of Uḥud. He said, "How can a people be successful when they have stained the face of their Prophet with blood?" ***You have no part in the affair.*** The command belongs to Allah, so be steadfast. ***Either He will turn to them*** with Islam ***or He will punish them, for they are the wrongdoers*** by disbelieving.

129. ***Everything in the heavens and everything in the earth belongs to Allah.*** All things are His domain, His creation and His slaves. ***He forgives whomever He wills and punishes whomever He wills. Allah is Ever-Forgiving*** to His friends, ***Most Merciful*** to the people who obey Him.

130. ***You who believe! Do not feed on usury, multiplied and then remultiplied*** by a thousand or less, since the money owed increases at the end of the term if repayment is delayed. ***Be fearful of Allah*** by abandoning usury ***so that perhaps you will be successful.***

131. ***Be fearful of the Fire which has been prepared for*** the punishment of ***those who disbelieve.***

132. ***Obey Allah and the Messenger so that perhaps you will gain mercy.***

133. ***Race each other*** (read with a preceding *wa,* "and" and without it) ***to forgiveness from your Lord and a Garden whose width is the heavens and the earth,*** as wide as them if they were put together, ***prepared for the godfearing:*** Allah prepares it as the reward for performing acts of obedience and abandoning acts of disobedience.

134. ***...those who give*** in obedience to Allah ***in times of both ease and hardship, those who control their rage*** and do not act on it when they might do so ***and pardon other people*** who have wronged them and do not punish them. ***Allah loves good-doers:*** by those actions and will reward them.

135. ***...those who, when they act indecently*** and commit an ugly sin like fornication, ***or wrong themselves*** by something less than that, like a kiss, ***remember Allah*** and His threat ***and ask forgiveness for their bad actions – who can forgive bad actions except Allah? – and do not knowingly persist***, knowing it to be disobedience, ***in what they were doing***, but cease doing it.

136. ***Their recompense is forgiveness from their Lord, and Gardens with rivers flowing under them, remaining in them timelessly, forever.*** This means that it is decreed that they will be in it forever when they enter it. ***How excellent is the reward of those who act*** and obey Allah. This is their wage.

137. This was revealed after the setback at Uḥud. ***Whole societies have passed away before your time, so travel the earth and see the end result of the deniers.*** "Whole societies" (*sunan*) means the ways of the unbelievers. It means that their punishment will be deferred and then they will be seized. Believers, travel and see the end of those who denied the Messengers: the end of their business was destruction. Therefore do not be grieved by their temporary victory. They are being left until to their time.

138. ***This*** Qur'an ***is a clear explanation for all mankind, and guidance*** from misguidance ***and admonition for the godfearing*** among them.

مِّن رَّبِّهِمۡ وَجَنَّٰتٞ تَجۡرِي مِن تَحۡتِهَا ٱلۡأَنۡهَٰرُ خَٰلِدِينَ
فِيهَاۚ وَنِعۡمَ أَجۡرُ ٱلۡعَٰمِلِينَ ١٣٦ قَدۡ خَلَتۡ مِن قَبۡلِكُمۡ سُنَنٞ
فَسِيرُواْ فِي ٱلۡأَرۡضِ فَٱنظُرُواْ كَيۡفَ كَانَ عَٰقِبَةُ ٱلۡمُكَذِّبِينَ
١٣٧ هَٰذَا بَيَانٞ لِّلنَّاسِ وَهُدٗى وَمَوۡعِظَةٞ لِّلۡمُتَّقِينَ ١٣٨
وَلَا تَهِنُواْ وَلَا تَحۡزَنُواْ وَأَنتُمُ ٱلۡأَعۡلَوۡنَ إِن كُنتُم مُّؤۡمِنِينَ
١٣٩ إِن يَمۡسَسۡكُمۡ قَرۡحٞ فَقَدۡ مَسَّ ٱلۡقَوۡمَ قَرۡحٞ مِّثۡلُهُۥۚ
وَتِلۡكَ ٱلۡأَيَّامُ نُدَاوِلُهَا بَيۡنَ ٱلنَّاسِ وَلِيَعۡلَمَ ٱللَّهُ ٱلَّذِينَ
ءَامَنُواْ وَيَتَّخِذَ مِنكُمۡ شُهَدَآءَۗ وَٱللَّهُ لَا يُحِبُّ ٱلظَّٰلِمِينَ ١٤٠
وَلِيُمَحِّصَ ٱللَّهُ ٱلَّذِينَ ءَامَنُواْ وَيَمۡحَقَ ٱلۡكَٰفِرِينَ ١٤١ أَمۡ
حَسِبۡتُمۡ أَن تَدۡخُلُواْ ٱلۡجَنَّةَ وَلَمَّا يَعۡلَمِ ٱللَّهُ ٱلَّذِينَ جَٰهَدُواْ
مِنكُمۡ وَيَعۡلَمَ ٱلصَّٰبِرِينَ ١٤٢ وَلَقَدۡ كُنتُمۡ تَمَنَّوۡنَ ٱلۡمَوۡتَ مِن
قَبۡلِ أَن تَلۡقَوۡهُ فَقَدۡ رَأَيۡتُمُوهُ وَأَنتُمۡ تَنظُرُونَ ١٤٣ وَمَا مُحَمَّدٌ
إِلَّا رَسُولٞ قَدۡ خَلَتۡ مِن قَبۡلِهِ ٱلرُّسُلُۚ أَفَإِيْن مَّاتَ أَوۡ قُتِلَ
ٱنقَلَبۡتُمۡ عَلَىٰٓ أَعۡقَٰبِكُمۡۚ وَمَن يَنقَلِبۡ عَلَىٰ عَقِبَيۡهِ فَلَن يَضُرَّ
ٱللَّهَ شَيۡـٔٗاۗ وَسَيَجۡزِي ٱللَّهُ ٱلشَّٰكِرِينَ ١٤٤ وَمَا كَانَ
لِنَفۡسٍ أَن تَمُوتَ إِلَّا بِإِذۡنِ ٱللَّهِ كِتَٰبٗا مُّؤَجَّلٗاۗ وَمَن يُرِدۡ
ثَوَابَ ٱلدُّنۡيَا نُؤۡتِهِۦ مِنۡهَا وَمَن يُرِدۡ ثَوَابَ ٱلۡأٓخِرَةِ نُؤۡتِهِۦ
مِنۡهَاۚ وَسَنَجۡزِي ٱلشَّٰكِرِينَ ١٤٥ وَكَأَيِّن مِّن نَّبِيّٖ قَٰتَلَ مَعَهُۥ
رِبِّيُّونَ كَثِيرٞ فَمَا وَهَنُواْ لِمَآ أَصَابَهُمۡ فِي سَبِيلِ ٱللَّهِ وَمَا ضَعُفُواْ
وَمَا ٱسۡتَكَانُواْۗ وَٱللَّهُ يُحِبُّ ٱلصَّٰبِرِينَ ١٤٦ وَمَا كَانَ قَوۡلَهُمۡ
إِلَّآ أَن قَالُواْ رَبَّنَا ٱغۡفِرۡ لَنَا ذُنُوبَنَا وَإِسۡرَافَنَا فِيٓ أَمۡرِنَا وَثَبِّتۡ

139. ***Do not give up*** and flag when fighting the unbelievers ***and do not be downhearted*** and sorrowful for what befell you at Uḥud**.** ***You shall be uppermost*** by defeating them ***if you are*** truly ***believers.***

140. ***If you have received a wound*** (read as *qarḥ* and *qurḥ*) at Uḥud, ***they*** (the unbelievers) ***have already received a similar wound*** at Badr**.** ***We send such days to people in rotation,*** one day for one group and one for another so that they might be warned, ***so that Allah may know*** with outward knowledge ***those who believe*** and are sincere in their belief from others who do not, ***and may gather*** those who have been granted the honour of being ***martyrs from among you. Allah does not love wrongdoers***, here meaning the unbelievers, and will punish them. Whatever blessings they enjoy in this world are simply to draw them on.

141. ***...and so that Allah can purge*** and purify ***those who believe*** from sins through affliction ***and wipe out*** and destroy ***the unbelievers.***

142. ***Or did you imagine that you were going to enter the Garden without Allah knowing*** by outward manifest knowledge ***those among you who had struggled and knowing the steadfast*** in the face of affliction***?***

143. ***You were longing for death before you met it.*** You said, "Would that we could have a day like that of Badr so that we might obtain what the martyrs obtained then!" ***Now you have seen it*** (the fighting) ***with your own eyes.*** So why were you defeated? This was revealed about the Muslims' defeat when word spread that the Prophet, may Allah bless him and grant him peace, had been killed. The hypocrites said, "If he has been killed, then revert to your old religion."

144. ***Muḥammad is only a Messenger before whom other Messengers have passed away. If he were to die or be killed*** like others, ***would you turn on your heels*** and revert to unbelief***?*** This sentence is a question that implies a negative answer. It means that he is not an object of worship so that you should revert if he dies. ***Those who turn on their heels do not harm Allah in any way***, but only harms themselves. ***Allah will recompense the thankful*** for His blessings by their standing firm.

أَقۡدَامَنَا وَٱنصُرۡنَا عَلَى ٱلۡقَوۡمِ ٱلۡكَٰفِرِينَ ١٤٧ فَـَٔاتَىٰهُمُ ٱللَّهُ
ثَوَابَ ٱلدُّنۡيَا وَحُسۡنَ ثَوَابِ ٱلۡأٓخِرَةِۗ وَٱللَّهُ يُحِبُّ ٱلۡمُحۡسِنِينَ ١٤٨
يَٰٓأَيُّهَا ٱلَّذِينَ ءَامَنُوٓاْ إِن تُطِيعُواْ ٱلَّذِينَ كَفَرُواْ
يَرُدُّوكُمۡ عَلَىٰٓ أَعۡقَٰبِكُمۡ فَتَنقَلِبُواْ خَٰسِرِينَ ١٤٩
بَلِ ٱللَّهُ مَوۡلَىٰكُمۡۖ وَهُوَ خَيۡرُ ٱلنَّٰصِرِينَ ١٥٠ سَنُلۡقِي
فِي قُلُوبِ ٱلَّذِينَ كَفَرُواْ ٱلرُّعۡبَ بِمَآ أَشۡرَكُواْ بِٱللَّهِ
مَا لَمۡ يُنَزِّلۡ بِهِۦ سُلۡطَٰنٗاۖ وَمَأۡوَىٰهُمُ ٱلنَّارُۚ وَبِئۡسَ
مَثۡوَى ٱلظَّٰلِمِينَ ١٥١ وَلَقَدۡ صَدَقَكُمُ ٱللَّهُ
وَعۡدَهُۥٓ إِذۡ تَحُسُّونَهُم بِإِذۡنِهِۦۖ حَتَّىٰٓ إِذَا فَشِلۡتُمۡ
وَتَنَٰزَعۡتُمۡ فِي ٱلۡأَمۡرِ وَعَصَيۡتُم مِّنۢ بَعۡدِ مَآ أَرَىٰكُم
مَّا تُحِبُّونَۚ مِنكُم مَّن يُرِيدُ ٱلدُّنۡيَا وَمِنكُم
مَّن يُرِيدُ ٱلۡأٓخِرَةَۚ ثُمَّ صَرَفَكُمۡ عَنۡهُمۡ لِيَبۡتَلِيَكُمۡۖ
وَلَقَدۡ عَفَا عَنكُمۡۗ وَٱللَّهُ ذُو فَضۡلٍ عَلَى ٱلۡمُؤۡمِنِينَ
١٥٢ ۞ إِذۡ تُصۡعِدُونَ وَلَا تَلۡوُۥنَ عَلَىٰٓ أَحَدٖ
وَٱلرَّسُولُ يَدۡعُوكُمۡ فِيٓ أُخۡرَىٰكُمۡ فَأَثَٰبَكُمۡ
غَمَّۢا بِغَمّٖ لِّكَيۡلَا تَحۡزَنُواْ عَلَىٰ مَا فَاتَكُمۡ
وَلَا مَآ أَصَٰبَكُمۡۗ وَٱللَّهُ خَبِيرُۢ بِمَا تَعۡمَلُونَ ١٥٣
ثُمَّ أَنزَلَ عَلَيۡكُم مِّنۢ بَعۡدِ ٱلۡغَمِّ أَمَنَةٗ نُّعَاسٗا يَغۡشَىٰ طَآئِفَةٗ
مِّنكُمۡۖ وَطَآئِفَةٞ قَدۡ أَهَمَّتۡهُمۡ أَنفُسُهُمۡ يَظُنُّونَ بِٱللَّهِ غَيۡرَ
ٱلۡحَقِّ ظَنَّ ٱلۡجَٰهِلِيَّةِۖ يَقُولُونَ هَل لَّنَا مِنَ ٱلۡأَمۡرِ مِن شَيۡءٖۗ

145. ***No self can die except with Allah's permission, at a predetermined time*** which is decreed. Everyone has a lifespan that cannot be decreased or lengthened. Defeat does not avert death and standing firm does not end life. ***If anyone desires reward in this world*** through his actions, ***We will give him some of it,*** some of this world as a reward but nothing of the Next. ***If anyone desires the reward of the Next World, We will give him some of it*** as reward. ***We will recompense the thankful.***

146. ***How many a Prophet has fought*** (read as *qātala*, "has fought" and *qutila,* "has been killed") ***when there were many thousands with him. They did not*** become cowardly and ***give up in the face of what assailed them*** (wounds or the killing of their Prophets and companions) ***in the Way of Allah, nor did they weaken*** in their *jihād*, ***nor did they yield*** to the enemy as you did when it was said that the Prophet was killed. ***Allah loves the steadfast*** in affliction and will reward them.

147. ***All they said,*** when their Prophet was killed and they remained firm and steadfast, ***was, "Our Lord, forgive us our wrong actions and any excesses we have gone to*** by exceeding the limits ***in what we have done*** by way of causing harm because of the afflictions and oppression which have come to us ***and make our feet firm*** with strength in *jihād* ***and help us against the people who disbelieve."***

148. ***So Allah gave them the reward of this world*** through victory and booty, ***and the best reward of the Next World,*** the Garden whose good is greater than anything that can be deserved. ***Allah loves good-doers.***

149. ***You who believe! If you obey those who disbelieve*** in respect of what they command you to do, ***they will turn you on your heels*** and make you revert to disbelief ***and you will be transformed into losers.***

150. ***No, Allah is your Protector*** and Helper, ***and He is the best of helpers***; so obey Him, not them.

151. ***We will cast terror*** (read as *ru'b* and *ru'ub*) ***into the hearts of those who disbelieve*** when they resolved to return and eradicate the Muslims after Uḥud but then became terrified and did not, ***because of their attributing partners to Allah*** and associating idols with

قُلْ إِنَّ ٱلْأَمْرَ كُلَّهُۥ لِلَّهِ ۗ يُخْفُونَ فِىٓ أَنفُسِهِم مَّا لَا يُبْدُونَ لَكَ ۖ
يَقُولُونَ لَوْ كَانَ لَنَا مِنَ ٱلْأَمْرِ شَىْءٌ مَّا قُتِلْنَا هَـٰهُنَا ۗ قُل لَّوْ كُنتُمْ
فِى بُيُوتِكُمْ لَبَرَزَ ٱلَّذِينَ كُتِبَ عَلَيْهِمُ ٱلْقَتْلُ إِلَىٰ مَضَاجِعِهِمْ ۖ
وَلِيَبْتَلِىَ ٱللَّهُ مَا فِى صُدُورِكُمْ وَلِيُمَحِّصَ مَا فِى قُلُوبِكُمْ ۗ
وَٱللَّهُ عَلِيمٌۢ بِذَاتِ ٱلصُّدُورِ ﴿١٥٤﴾ إِنَّ ٱلَّذِينَ تَوَلَّوْا۟ مِنكُمْ
يَوْمَ ٱلْتَقَى ٱلْجَمْعَانِ إِنَّمَا ٱسْتَزَلَّهُمُ ٱلشَّيْطَـٰنُ بِبَعْضِ مَا
كَسَبُوا۟ ۖ وَلَقَدْ عَفَا ٱللَّهُ عَنْهُمْ ۗ إِنَّ ٱللَّهَ غَفُورٌ حَلِيمٌ ﴿١٥٥﴾ يَـٰٓأَيُّهَا
ٱلَّذِينَ ءَامَنُوا۟ لَا تَكُونُوا۟ كَٱلَّذِينَ كَفَرُوا۟ وَقَالُوا۟ لِإِخْوَٰنِهِمْ إِذَا
ضَرَبُوا۟ فِى ٱلْأَرْضِ أَوْ كَانُوا۟ غُزًّى لَّوْ كَانُوا۟ عِندَنَا مَا مَاتُوا۟ وَمَا
قُتِلُوا۟ لِيَجْعَلَ ٱللَّهُ ذَٰلِكَ حَسْرَةً فِى قُلُوبِهِمْ ۗ وَٱللَّهُ يُحْىِۦ وَيُمِيتُ ۗ
وَٱللَّهُ بِمَا تَعْمَلُونَ بَصِيرٌ ﴿١٥٦﴾ وَلَئِن قُتِلْتُمْ فِى سَبِيلِ ٱللَّهِ
أَوْ مُتُّمْ لَمَغْفِرَةٌ مِّنَ ٱللَّهِ وَرَحْمَةٌ خَيْرٌ مِّمَّا يَجْمَعُونَ ﴿١٥٧﴾
وَلَئِن مُّتُّمْ أَوْ قُتِلْتُمْ لَإِلَى ٱللَّهِ تُحْشَرُونَ ﴿١٥٨﴾ فَبِمَا رَحْمَةٍ مِّنَ
ٱللَّهِ لِنتَ لَهُمْ ۖ وَلَوْ كُنتَ فَظًّا غَلِيظَ ٱلْقَلْبِ لَٱنفَضُّوا۟ مِنْ حَوْلِكَ ۖ
فَٱعْفُ عَنْهُمْ وَٱسْتَغْفِرْ لَهُمْ وَشَاوِرْهُمْ فِى ٱلْأَمْرِ ۖ فَإِذَا عَزَمْتَ
فَتَوَكَّلْ عَلَى ٱللَّهِ ۚ إِنَّ ٱللَّهَ يُحِبُّ ٱلْمُتَوَكِّلِينَ ﴿١٥٩﴾ إِن يَنصُرْكُمُ ٱللَّهُ
فَلَا غَالِبَ لَكُمْ ۖ وَإِن يَخْذُلْكُمْ فَمَن ذَا ٱلَّذِى يَنصُرُكُم مِّنۢ
بَعْدِهِۦ ۗ وَعَلَى ٱللَّهِ فَلْيَتَوَكَّلِ ٱلْمُؤْمِنُونَ ﴿١٦٠﴾ وَمَا كَانَ لِنَبِىٍّ أَن
يَغُلَّ ۚ وَمَن يَغْلُلْ يَأْتِ بِمَا غَلَّ يَوْمَ ٱلْقِيَـٰمَةِ ۚ ثُمَّ تُوَفَّىٰ كُلُّ
نَفْسٍ مَّا كَسَبَتْ وَهُمْ لَا يُظْلَمُونَ ﴿١٦١﴾ أَفَمَنِ ٱتَّبَعَ رِضْوَٰنَ

Allah in their worship *for which He has not sent down any authority* or proof for worshipping them. ***Their shelter will be the Fire. How evil is the abode of the wrongdoers*** (the unbelievers).

152. ***Allah fulfilled His promise*** of victory ***to you when you were slaughtering them by His permission*** (by His will). ***But then you faltered*** when some were too cowardly to fight, ***disputing the command, and disobeyed*** the command of the Prophet to stay in place on the top of the mountain to shoot, ***after He*** (Allah) ***showed you what you love,*** meaning victory. Some of them said, "We will go. Our comrades are victorious." Some did not disobey the order but others left their position to seek booty after Allah had made them think victory had been gained. ***Among you are those who want this world*** and left the position to seek booty ***and among you are those who want the Next World*** and stood firm until they were killed, such as 'Abdullāh ibn Jubayr and his companions. ***Then*** when defeat was decreed, ***He turned you from them*** (the unbelievers) ***in order to test you*** to see who would be sincere among you – ***but He has pardoned you*** for what you did. ***Allah possesses favour*** and pardon ***for the believers.***

153. Remember ***when you were scrambling up the slope,*** trying to flee from the enemy, ***refusing to turn back for anyone, and the Messenger was calling to you from the rear***, saying, "To me, slaves of Allah!" ***Allah rewarded you*** in requital for that ***with one distress*** (defeat) ***in return for another*** (your causing sorrow to the Messenger by disobeying his command) ***so you would not feel grief for what escaped you*** of booty ***and what assailed you*** of defeat. ***Allah is aware of everything you do.***

154. ***Then He sent down to you, after the distress, security, restful sleep overcoming*** (read as *yaghshā* and *taghshā*) ***a group of you,*** (the believers) who grew drowsy and dropped their swords. ***Whereas another group became prey to anxious thoughts,*** being consumed by fear and only able to think of saving their own skins rather than of the safety of the Prophet and his Companions as a whole. They could not sleep. They were hypocrites, subject to ***thinking other than the truth about Allah*** – such ***thoughts belonging to the days of ignorance*** before Islam because they believed that the Prophet had been killed or would not be victorious as he had been promised – ***saying,***

"Do we have any say in the affair at all, meaning the victory which we have been promised?" ***Say*** to them, ***"The affair belongs entirely to Allah."*** This is stressed. The Decree belongs to Allah and He does whatever He wills. ***They are concealing within themselves things which they do not disclose to you, saying, "If we had only had a say in the affair, none of us would have been killed here in this place."*** By this they meant, "If we had had the choice, we would not have gone out to be killed, but we went out unwillingly." ***Say*** to them, ***"Even if you had been inside your homes*** and among you were those whose death Allah had decreed, ***those people*** among you ***for whom being killed was decreed would have gone out to their place of death,*** to where they would fall and would be killed." Staying at home would not have helped them because Allah's decree must come to pass. Allah did what He did at Uḥud ***so that Allah might test what is in your breasts,*** whether it is sincerity or hypocrisy, ***and purge*** and distinguish ***what is in your hearts. Allah knows all the hearts contain.*** Nothing in the heart is hidden from Him, but He puts people to the test so that their true state may become apparent to others.

155. ***Those of you who turned their backs*** fleeing from the fighting ***on the day the two armies clashed*** when the Muslims fought the unbelievers at Uḥud and only twelve men of the Muslims stood firm ***– it was Shayṭān who made them slip,*** by his whispering, ***for what they had done***, for their sins, one of which was disobeying the command of the Messenger of Allah, may Allah bless him and grant him peace. ***But Allah has pardoned them. Allah is Ever-Forgiving*** to the believers, ***All-Forbearing*** by not rushing to the punishment of those who disobey.

156. ***You who believe! Do not be like those who disbelieve*** (meaning the hypocrites here) ***and say of their brothers when they are going on journeys*** and die ***or military expeditions*** during which they are killed, ***"If they had only been with us, they would not have died or been killed."*** Do not say the same as they say. That is ***so that*** in the end of their affair ***Allah may make that anguish for them in their hearts. It is Allah Who gives life and causes to die***, so remaining behind will not prevent death. ***Allah sees everything you do*** (read as ta'lamūna, "you do" and ya'lamūna, "they do") and will repay you for it.

157. ***If you are killed in the Way of Allah*** in *jihād* ***or if you die*** (read as *muttum* or *mittum*) while on the journey, ***forgiveness*** for your wrong actions ***and mercy from Allah*** for you ***are better than anything which they can amass*** (read as *yajma'ūna*, "they can amass" and *tajma'ūna*, "you can amass").

158. ***If you die or you are killed*** through *jihād* or any other cause, ***it is*** only ***to Allah that you will be gathered*** in the Next World, and He will repay you.

159. ***It is a mercy from Allah that you,*** Muḥammad, ***were gentle with them*** and it is part of your character to make things easy when people disagree with you. ***If you had been rough*** and shown bad character ***or hard of heart*** and harsh with them, ***they would have scattered from around you. So pardon them*** for what they did ***and ask forgiveness for them*** for their sins until I forgive them, ***and consult with them*** for their opinions ***in the affair*** regarding matters concerning them, such as war and other things, in order to win over their hearts and so that doing that becomes an established *sunna* – the Prophet, may Allah bless him and grant him peace, often consulted his Companions. ***Then when you have reached a firm decision*** and have resolved to carry out what you want to do after consultation, ***put your trust in Allah. Allah loves those who put their trust in Him.***

160. ***If Allah helps you*** as He did against your enemies, as at the Battle of Badr, ***no one can vanquish you. If He forsakes you*** and fails to help you as at Uḥud, ***who can help you after that*** (His abandonment of you)***? So the believers should put their trust in Allah.***

161. When a red saddle-cloth from the booty went missing at Uḥud, some people said, "Perhaps the Prophet has taken it." ***No Prophet would ever be guilty of misappropriation.*** It is not fitting for a Prophet to cheat in respect of the booty, so do not suspect him of doing so. ***Those who misappropriate, will arrive on the Day of Rising with what they have misappropriated***, carrying it on their shoulders. ***Then every self will be paid in full for what it earned*** (did). ***They will not be wronged.***

ٱللَّهِ كَمَنۢ بَآءَ بِسَخَطٖ مِّنَ ٱللَّهِ وَمَأۡوَىٰهُ جَهَنَّمُۚ وَبِئۡسَ ٱلۡمَصِيرُ
١٦٢ هُمۡ دَرَجَٰتٌ عِندَ ٱللَّهِۗ وَٱللَّهُ بَصِيرُۢ بِمَا يَعۡمَلُونَ ١٦٣
لَقَدۡ مَنَّ ٱللَّهُ عَلَى ٱلۡمُؤۡمِنِينَ إِذۡ بَعَثَ فِيهِمۡ رَسُولٗا مِّنۡ أَنفُسِهِمۡ
يَتۡلُواْ عَلَيۡهِمۡ ءَايَٰتِهِۦ وَيُزَكِّيهِمۡ وَيُعَلِّمُهُمُ ٱلۡكِتَٰبَ
وَٱلۡحِكۡمَةَ وَإِن كَانُواْ مِن قَبۡلُ لَفِي ضَلَٰلٖ مُّبِينٍ ١٦٤
أَوَلَمَّآ أَصَٰبَتۡكُم مُّصِيبَةٞ قَدۡ أَصَبۡتُم مِّثۡلَيۡهَا قُلۡتُمۡ أَنَّىٰ هَٰذَاۖ
قُلۡ هُوَ مِنۡ عِندِ أَنفُسِكُمۡۗ إِنَّ ٱللَّهَ عَلَىٰ كُلِّ شَيۡءٖ قَدِيرٞ ١٦٥
وَمَآ أَصَٰبَكُمۡ يَوۡمَ ٱلۡتَقَى ٱلۡجَمۡعَانِ فَبِإِذۡنِ ٱللَّهِ وَلِيَعۡلَمَ ٱلۡمُؤۡمِنِينَ
١٦٦ وَلِيَعۡلَمَ ٱلَّذِينَ نَافَقُواْۚ وَقِيلَ لَهُمۡ تَعَالَوۡاْ قَٰتِلُواْ فِي سَبِيلِ ٱللَّهِ
أَوِ ٱدۡفَعُواْۖ قَالُواْ لَوۡ نَعۡلَمُ قِتَالٗا لَّٱتَّبَعۡنَٰكُمۡۗ هُمۡ لِلۡكُفۡرِ
يَوۡمَئِذٍ أَقۡرَبُ مِنۡهُمۡ لِلۡإِيمَٰنِۚ يَقُولُونَ بِأَفۡوَٰهِهِم مَّا لَيۡسَ
فِي قُلُوبِهِمۡۗ وَٱللَّهُ أَعۡلَمُ بِمَا يَكۡتُمُونَ ١٦٧ ٱلَّذِينَ قَالُواْ لِإِخۡوَٰنِهِمۡ
وَقَعَدُواْ لَوۡ أَطَاعُونَا مَا قُتِلُواْۗ قُلۡ فَٱدۡرَءُواْ عَنۡ أَنفُسِكُمُ
ٱلۡمَوۡتَ إِن كُنتُمۡ صَٰدِقِينَ ١٦٨ وَلَا تَحۡسَبَنَّ ٱلَّذِينَ قُتِلُواْ فِي
سَبِيلِ ٱللَّهِ أَمۡوَٰتَۢاۚ بَلۡ أَحۡيَآءٌ عِندَ رَبِّهِمۡ يُرۡزَقُونَ ١٦٩ فَرِحِينَ
بِمَآ ءَاتَىٰهُمُ ٱللَّهُ مِن فَضۡلِهِۦ وَيَسۡتَبۡشِرُونَ بِٱلَّذِينَ لَمۡ يَلۡحَقُواْ
بِهِم مِّنۡ خَلۡفِهِمۡ أَلَّا خَوۡفٌ عَلَيۡهِمۡ وَلَا هُمۡ يَحۡزَنُونَ ١٧٠
۞ يَسۡتَبۡشِرُونَ بِنِعۡمَةٖ مِّنَ ٱللَّهِ وَفَضۡلٖ وَأَنَّ ٱللَّهَ لَا يُضِيعُ أَجۡرَ
ٱلۡمُؤۡمِنِينَ ١٧١ ٱلَّذِينَ ٱسۡتَجَابُواْ لِلَّهِ وَٱلرَّسُولِ مِنۢ بَعۡدِ مَآ
أَصَابَهُمُ ٱلۡقَرۡحُۚ لِلَّذِينَ أَحۡسَنُواْ مِنۡهُمۡ وَٱتَّقَوۡاْ أَجۡرٌ عَظِيمٌ ١٧٢

162. ***Is one who pursues the pleasure of Allah,*** obeying him and not misappropriating, ***the same as one who incurs displeasure from Allah*** by disobeying Him and misappropriating ***and whose refuge is Hell? What an evil destination!***

163. ***They have different ranks*** and stations ***with Allah.*** Anyone who follows the pleasure of Allah will gain the reward and those who bring down anger on themselves will be punished. ***Allah sees everything they do*** and will repay them.

164. ***Allah showed great kindness to the believers when He sent a Messenger to them from among themselves,*** an Arab like them, to enable them to understand and to honour them, not a angel or a non-Arab, ***to recite His Signs*** (the Qur'an) ***to them and purify them*** of sins ***and teach them the Book*** (the Qur'an) ***and Wisdom*** (the *Sunna*), ***even though before that,*** before he was sent, ***they were clearly misguided.***

165. ***Why is it that when a calamity happens to you,*** as at Uḥud when seventy of you were killed, ***when you have already inflicted twice as much,*** since at Badr you killed seventy and captured seventy, ***you say*** in amazement, ***"How could this*** failure ***possibly happen*** when we are Muslims and the Messenger of Allah is among us?" ***Say*** to them in response to their question, ***"It has come from yourselves*** because you left your positions and that was the reason for your failure." ***Allah has power over everything.*** Allah has power to give or deny victory and He repaid you for your disobedience to the command you were given.

166. ***What assailed you on the day the two armies met*** at Uḥud ***was by Allah's permission*** (His will) ***so that He would know the*** true ***believers*** with clear and manifest knowledge...

167. ***...and so that He would know the hypocrites. They*** ('Abdullāh ibn Ubayy and his companions) ***were told*** when they left the fighting, ***"Come and fight*** Allah's enemies ***in the Way of Allah or at least help defend us*** by reinforcing us with your numbers even if you do not fight." ***They said, "If we knew how to fight*** (were good at it), ***we would certainly follow you."*** But Allah refutes them: ***They were closer to unbelief that day than to belief,*** by showing their true colours and letting down the believers, when before that they had been closer to belief by their outward statements, ***saying with their mouths what was not in their hearts.*** If they had known any fighting would be involved, they would certainly not have followed you. ***And Allah knows best what*** (the hypocrisy) ***they are hiding.***

168. ***Those who said of their brothers*** in the *dīn,* ***when they themselves had stayed behind*** from *jihād,* ***"If they had only obeyed us,*** meaning the martyrs of Uḥud, or their brothers, and stayed behind, ***they would not have been killed." Say*** to them, ***"Ward off death then from yourselves if you are telling the truth."*** So they are told to keep death away from themselves by staying at home if they can.

169. This was revealed about the martyrs. ***Do not suppose that those killed*** (read as *qutilū,* "killed" and *quttilū* "slaughtered") ***in the Way of Allah,*** meaning for the sake of His *dīn,* ***are dead. No indeed! They are alive and well provided for in the very presence of their Lord…*** Their spirits are carried in the crops of green birds flying in the Garden wherever they wish, as the *ḥadīth* states. They eat of the fruits of the Garden and delight in them.

170. ***… delighting in the favour Allah has bestowed on them, rejoicing over those they left behind*** (their brother believers), ***who have not yet joined them, feeling no fear***, about those who have not joined them, ***and knowing no sorrow…*** in the Next World because they rejoice in their absolute security from all harm.

171. ***… rejoicing in blessings,*** His reward, ***and favour from Allah, and that Allah does not let the wage of the believers go to waste.***

172. ***Those who did good*** by obeying him ***and were godfearing*** and feared to oppose Allah ***among those who responded to Allah and the Messenger***, when the Prophet, may Allah bless him and grant him peace, called on Khazraj to go out to fight when Abū Sufyān and his companions wanted to return and meet with the Prophet at the market of Badr the year after Uḥud, ***after the wound had been inflicted on them will have an immense reward***, which is the Garden*:*

173. ***… those,*** an appositive continuing on from the previous *āyat,* meaning Nu'aym ibn Mas'ūd al-Ashjā'ī, ***to whom people,*** meaning Abū Sufyān and his companions, ***said, "The people have gathered*** their forces ***against you*** to eradicate you, ***so fear them*** and do not go

ٱلَّذِينَ قَالَ لَهُمُ ٱلنَّاسُ إِنَّ ٱلنَّاسَ قَدْ جَمَعُوا۟ لَكُمْ فَٱخْشَوْهُمْ
فَزَادَهُمْ إِيمَٰنًا وَقَالُوا۟ حَسْبُنَا ٱللَّهُ وَنِعْمَ ٱلْوَكِيلُ ﴿١٧٣﴾
فَٱنقَلَبُوا۟ بِنِعْمَةٍ مِّنَ ٱللَّهِ وَفَضْلٍ لَّمْ يَمْسَسْهُمْ سُوٓءٌ وَٱتَّبَعُوا۟
رِضْوَٰنَ ٱللَّهِ ۗ وَٱللَّهُ ذُو فَضْلٍ عَظِيمٍ ﴿١٧٤﴾ إِنَّمَا ذَٰلِكُمُ ٱلشَّيْطَٰنُ
يُخَوِّفُ أَوْلِيَآءَهُۥ فَلَا تَخَافُوهُمْ وَخَافُونِ إِن كُنتُم مُّؤْمِنِينَ ﴿١٧٥﴾
وَلَا يَحْزُنكَ ٱلَّذِينَ يُسَٰرِعُونَ فِى ٱلْكُفْرِ ۚ إِنَّهُمْ لَن يَضُرُّوا۟ ٱللَّهَ
شَيْـًٔا ۗ يُرِيدُ ٱللَّهُ أَلَّا يَجْعَلَ لَهُمْ حَظًّا فِى ٱلْءَاخِرَةِ ۖ وَلَهُمْ عَذَابٌ
عَظِيمٌ ﴿١٧٦﴾ إِنَّ ٱلَّذِينَ ٱشْتَرَوُا۟ ٱلْكُفْرَ بِٱلْإِيمَٰنِ لَن يَضُرُّوا۟
ٱللَّهَ شَيْـًٔا وَلَهُمْ عَذَابٌ أَلِيمٌ ﴿١٧٧﴾ وَلَا يَحْسَبَنَّ ٱلَّذِينَ كَفَرُوٓا۟
أَنَّمَا نُمْلِى لَهُمْ خَيْرٌ لِّأَنفُسِهِمْ ۚ إِنَّمَا نُمْلِى لَهُمْ لِيَزْدَادُوٓا۟ إِثْمًا ۚ
وَلَهُمْ عَذَابٌ مُّهِينٌ ﴿١٧٨﴾ مَّا كَانَ ٱللَّهُ لِيَذَرَ ٱلْمُؤْمِنِينَ عَلَىٰ مَآ
أَنتُمْ عَلَيْهِ حَتَّىٰ يَمِيزَ ٱلْخَبِيثَ مِنَ ٱلطَّيِّبِ ۗ وَمَا كَانَ ٱللَّهُ لِيُطْلِعَكُمْ
عَلَى ٱلْغَيْبِ وَلَٰكِنَّ ٱللَّهَ يَجْتَبِى مِن رُّسُلِهِۦ مَن يَشَآءُ ۖ فَـَٔامِنُوا۟ بِٱللَّهِ
وَرُسُلِهِۦ ۚ وَإِن تُؤْمِنُوا۟ وَتَتَّقُوا۟ فَلَكُمْ أَجْرٌ عَظِيمٌ ﴿١٧٩﴾ وَلَا
يَحْسَبَنَّ ٱلَّذِينَ يَبْخَلُونَ بِمَآ ءَاتَىٰهُمُ ٱللَّهُ مِن فَضْلِهِۦ هُوَ خَيْرًا
لَّهُم ۖ بَلْ هُوَ شَرٌّ لَّهُمْ ۖ سَيُطَوَّقُونَ مَا بَخِلُوا۟ بِهِۦ يَوْمَ ٱلْقِيَٰمَةِ ۗ
وَلِلَّهِ مِيرَٰثُ ٱلسَّمَٰوَٰتِ وَٱلْأَرْضِ ۗ وَٱللَّهُ بِمَا تَعْمَلُونَ خَبِيرٌ ﴿١٨٠﴾
لَّقَدْ سَمِعَ ٱللَّهُ قَوْلَ ٱلَّذِينَ قَالُوٓا۟ إِنَّ ٱللَّهَ فَقِيرٌ وَنَحْنُ أَغْنِيَآءُ ۘ
سَنَكْتُبُ مَا قَالُوا۟ وَقَتْلَهُمُ ٱلْأَنۢبِيَآءَ بِغَيْرِ حَقٍّ وَنَقُولُ
ذُوقُوا۟ عَذَابَ ٱلْحَرِيقِ ﴿١٨١﴾ ذَٰلِكَ بِمَا قَدَّمَتْ أَيْدِيكُمْ

out against them." ***But that*** statement ***merely increased them in belief*** and certainty ***and they said, "Allah is enough for us and the best of guardians*** and the One to Whom we entrust our affair." They went out with the Prophet, may Allah bless him and grant him peace, to the market of Badr and Allah cast terror into the heart of Abū Sufyān and his companions so that they did not keep their appointment. The Companions had goods with them which they sold, realising a profit. Thereupon Allah said:

174. ***So they returned*** from Badr ***with blessings and bounty from Allah,*** with peace and profit, ***and no evil*** by way of killing or wounding ***touched them. They pursued the pleasure of Allah*** by obeying Allah and His Messenger in going out. ***Allah's favour is indeed immense*** towards those who obey Him.

175. He who actually said that to you ***was only Shayṭān frightening you through his friends*** (the unbelievers). ***But do not fear them – fear Me*** and do not abandon My command ***if you are believers.***

176. ***Do not let those who rush headlong into unbelief*** by resorting quickly to supporting the unbelievers, namely the people of Makka or the hypocrites, ***sadden you*** (read as *yaḥzunuka* and *yuḥzinuka*). Do not be worried by their unbelief. ***They do not harm Allah in any way*** by what they do. They only harm themselves. ***Allah desires to assign no portion*** of the Garden ***to them in the Next World.*** That is how Allah will disappoint them. ***They will have a terrible punishment*** in the Fire forever.

177. ***Those who sell belief for unbelief*** (exchanging one for the other) ***do not harm Allah in any way*** by their unbelief. ***They will have a painful punishment.***

178. ***Those who disbelieve should not imagine that the extra time***, the delay, ***We grant to them*** by giving them longer to live in this world ***is good for them.*** "They should not imagine" (*yaḥsabanna*) is also read as "you should not imagine" (*taḥsabanna*) in which case the meaning becomes: "You should not imagine that the extra time We grant to those who disbelieve..." ***We only allow them more time so they will increase in evil-doing*** by disobeying Allah. ***They will have a humiliating punishment*** in the Next World.

179. ***Allah will only leave the believers in the position you***, people, ***now are in***, where the sincere are mixed with others, ***so that He can sift out*** (read as *yamīza* and *yumayyiza*) and distinguish ***the rotten*** hypocrite ***from the good*** believer by clear and difficult obligations which will make that distinction clear, as He did on the Day of Uḥud. ***Allah has not given you access to the Unseen*** enabling you to recognise the hypocrites from others before the sifting. ***But Allah chooses from His Messengers whomever He wills*** to acquaint with His Unseen, as He acquainted the Prophet, may Allah bless him and grant him peace, with the state of the hypocrites. ***So believe in Allah and His Messengers. If you believe and are godfearing*** and fear hypocrisy ***you will have an immense reward.***

180. ***Those who are stingy with the bounty Allah has given them***, by being miserly about giving the *zakāt* due on it, ***should not suppose that that*** (their miserliness) ***is better for them. No indeed, it*** (their miserliness) ***is worse for them! What they were stingy with*** (the *zakāt* due on their property) ***will be hung around their necks on the Day of Rising***, as a snake biting them, as we find in the *ḥadīth*. ***Allah is the Inheritor of the heavens and the earth*** when the world ends, ***and Allah is aware of everything you do*** (read as *ta'malūna*, "what you do" and *ya'malūna*, "what they do") and will repay you for that.

181. ***Allah has heard the words of those who say, "Allah is poor and we are rich."*** It was the Jews who said this when the *āyat "Who will lend Allah a good loan?"* (2:245) was revealed. They said, "If He were rich, He would not ask for a loan." ***We will write down*** (read as *sa-naktubu*, "We will write", and *sa-yuktabu*, "it will be written") meaning command it to be written, ***what they said*** in the books of their actions so that they can be repaid for it ***and their killing of the Prophets without a legal right; and We will say, "Taste the punishment of the Burning"*** by entering it. Allah will speak to them in the Next World on the tongues of the angels.

182. When they are thrown into the Fire, this will be said to them: ***That*** (punishment) ***is on account of what you did*** (lit. "what your hands advanced"). "Hands" are designated because most actions are done using them. ***Allah does not wrong His slaves*** by punishing them for anything other than their own wrong actions.

وَأَنَّ ٱللَّهَ لَيۡسَ بِظَلَّٰمٖ لِّلۡعَبِيدِ ١٨٢ ٱلَّذِينَ قَالُوٓاْ إِنَّ
ٱللَّهَ عَهِدَ إِلَيۡنَآ أَلَّا نُؤۡمِنَ لِرَسُولٍ حَتَّىٰ يَأۡتِيَنَا بِقُرۡبَانٖ
تَأۡكُلُهُ ٱلنَّارُۗ قُلۡ قَدۡ جَآءَكُمۡ رُسُلٞ مِّن قَبۡلِي بِٱلۡبَيِّنَٰتِ
وَبِٱلَّذِي قُلۡتُمۡ فَلِمَ قَتَلۡتُمُوهُمۡ إِن كُنتُمۡ صَٰدِقِينَ ١٨٣
فَإِن كَذَّبُوكَ فَقَدۡ كُذِّبَ رُسُلٞ مِّن قَبۡلِكَ جَآءُو بِٱلۡبَيِّنَٰتِ
وَٱلزُّبُرِ وَٱلۡكِتَٰبِ ٱلۡمُنِيرِ ١٨٤ كُلُّ نَفۡسٖ ذَآئِقَةُ ٱلۡمَوۡتِۗ
وَإِنَّمَا تُوَفَّوۡنَ أُجُورَكُمۡ يَوۡمَ ٱلۡقِيَٰمَةِۖ فَمَن زُحۡزِحَ
عَنِ ٱلنَّارِ وَأُدۡخِلَ ٱلۡجَنَّةَ فَقَدۡ فَازَۗ وَمَا ٱلۡحَيَوٰةُ ٱلدُّنۡيَآ
إِلَّا مَتَٰعُ ٱلۡغُرُورِ ١٨٥ ۞ لَتُبۡلَوُنَّ فِيٓ أَمۡوَٰلِكُمۡ
وَأَنفُسِكُمۡ وَلَتَسۡمَعُنَّ مِنَ ٱلَّذِينَ أُوتُواْ ٱلۡكِتَٰبَ
مِن قَبۡلِكُمۡ وَمِنَ ٱلَّذِينَ أَشۡرَكُوٓاْ أَذٗى كَثِيرٗاۚ
وَإِن تَصۡبِرُواْ وَتَتَّقُواْ فَإِنَّ ذَٰلِكَ مِنۡ عَزۡمِ ٱلۡأُمُورِ ١٨٦
وَإِذۡ أَخَذَ ٱللَّهُ مِيثَٰقَ ٱلَّذِينَ أُوتُواْ ٱلۡكِتَٰبَ لَتُبَيِّنُنَّهُۥ لِلنَّاسِ
وَلَا تَكۡتُمُونَهُۥ فَنَبَذُوهُ وَرَآءَ ظُهُورِهِمۡ وَٱشۡتَرَوۡاْ بِهِۦ ثَمَنٗا
قَلِيلٗاۖ فَبِئۡسَ مَا يَشۡتَرُونَ ١٨٧ لَا تَحۡسَبَنَّ ٱلَّذِينَ يَفۡرَحُونَ
بِمَآ أَتَواْ وَّيُحِبُّونَ أَن يُحۡمَدُواْ بِمَا لَمۡ يَفۡعَلُواْ فَلَا تَحۡسَبَنَّهُم
بِمَفَازَةٖ مِّنَ ٱلۡعَذَابِۖ وَلَهُمۡ عَذَابٌ أَلِيمٞ ١٨٨ وَلِلَّهِ مُلۡكُ
ٱلسَّمَٰوَٰتِ وَٱلۡأَرۡضِۗ وَٱللَّهُ عَلَىٰ كُلِّ شَيۡءٖ قَدِيرٌ ١٨٩ إِنَّ فِي
خَلۡقِ ٱلسَّمَٰوَٰتِ وَٱلۡأَرۡضِ وَٱخۡتِلَٰفِ ٱلَّيۡلِ وَٱلنَّهَارِ لَأٓيَٰتٖ
لِّأُوْلِي ٱلۡأَلۡبَٰبِ ١٩٠ ٱلَّذِينَ يَذۡكُرُونَ ٱللَّهَ قِيَٰمٗا وَقُعُودٗا
وَعَلَىٰ جُنُوبِهِمۡ وَيَتَفَكَّرُونَ فِي خَلۡقِ ٱلسَّمَٰوَٰتِ وَٱلۡأَرۡضِ

183. ***Those***, meaning those described above, ***who say*** to Muḥammad, ***"Allah has made a contract with us*** in the Torah ***that we should not believe in any Messenger until he brings us a sacrifice consumed by fire."*** This refers to sacrifices which they used to make to Allah. The sign that the sacrifice was accepted was that a white fire would come down heaven and consume it while leaving the place untouched. That was a tradition in the tribe of Israel but not in the case of the Messiah and Muḥammad. ***Say*** to them to rebuke them, ***"Messengers came to you before me with the Clear Signs*** (miracles) ***and with what you say,*** such as Zakariyyā and Yaḥyā, whom you killed." This is addressed to those in the time of the Prophet, even though these things happened before their time, because they are happy with what happened then. ***"So why did you kill them if you are telling the truth*** when you say that you will believe when this happens?"

184. ***If they deny you, Messengers before you were also denied, who brought the Clear Signs*** and miracles ***and written texts*** such as the Pages of Ibrāhīm, ***and the Illuminating Book***, Revelations like the Torah and Gospel. So be patient as they were patient.

185. ***Every self will taste death. You will be paid your wages*** for your actions ***in full on the Day of Rising. Anyone who is distanced from the Fire and admitted to the Garden has triumphed*** and obtained his greatest desire. Living ***the life of this world is only the enjoyment of*** false ***delusion*** and fleeting pleasure which will soon pass.

186. ***You will be tested in your wealth*** by obligatory expenses and losses of wealth ***and in your selves*** through the imposition of acts of worship and afflictions ***and you will hear many abusive words***, cursing, attacking and insulting your women, ***from those given the Book*** (the Jews and Christians) ***before you and from those*** Arab idolaters ***who worship idols. But if you are steadfast*** in the face of that ***and godfearing*** with respect to your obligations, ***that is the most resolute course to take.*** That is one of the things which should be resolved on.

187. Remember ***when Allah made a covenant with those given the Book***, referring to His covenant with the Jews in the Torah: ***"You must make it*** (the Book), ***clear to people and not conceal it*** (the

Book)." ***But they toss it*** (the covenant) ***in disdain behind their backs*** and do not act by it ***and sell it for a paltry price*** of this world, by selling their position of leadership in knowledge. They concealed the truth, fearing to miss out on this world. ***What an evil sale they make!*** This is a poor transaction.

188. ***Do not suppose*** (read as *taḥsabanna*, "do not suppose" and *yaḥsabanna*, "they should not suppose" in two places) ***that those who exult in what they have done*** in misguiding others ***and love to be praised for what they have not done*** in holding to the truth when they are in fact misguided, ***do not suppose them to have escaped*** to a place where they are safe from ***the punishment*** of the Next World. They will be in the place where they will be punished: Jahannam. ***They will have a painful punishment.***

189. ***The kingdom of the heavens and the earth belongs to Allah.*** Allah possesses the treasures of rain, provision, plants and all other things. ***Allah has power over everything.*** He has power to punish the unbelievers and save the believers.

190. ***In the creation of the heavens and the earth*** and all the wonders which they contain, ***and the alternation of night and day,*** their coming and going and their shortening and lengthening, ***there are Signs*** which indicate the power of Allah ***for people of intelligence:***

191. ***those who remember Allah standing, sitting and lying on their sides***, in other words in every state, (According to Ibn 'Abbās, it refers to praying in those positions when no other is possible) ***and reflect on the creation of the heavens and the earth*** which leads them to see the evidence of the power of their Creator throughout existence and so they say: ***"Our Lord, You did not create this*** creation which we see ***for nothing*** (to no purpose). Rather it indicates Your power, ***Glory be to You***, exalted above fruitless action! ***Safeguard us from the punishment of the Fire.***

192. ***Our Lord, those You cast into the Fire*** for eternity, ***You have indeed disgraced*** and humiliated. ***The wrongdoers*** (the unbelievers) ***will have no helpers.*** This is an example of the use of the explicit rather than the implicit – saying 'wrongdoers' rather than simply saying 'They' – and indicates that their disgrace will be personal. They will have no one to protect them from the punishment of Allah.

رَبَّنَا مَا خَلَقْتَ هَٰذَا بَٰطِلًا سُبْحَٰنَكَ فَقِنَا عَذَابَ ٱلنَّارِ ١٩١
رَبَّنَآ إِنَّكَ مَن تُدْخِلِ ٱلنَّارَ فَقَدْ أَخْزَيْتَهُۥ ۖ وَمَا لِلظَّٰلِمِينَ مِنْ
أَنصَارٍ ١٩٢ رَّبَّنَآ إِنَّنَا سَمِعْنَا مُنَادِيًا يُنَادِى لِلْإِيمَٰنِ أَنْ
ءَامِنُوا۟ بِرَبِّكُمْ فَـَٔامَنَّا ۚ رَبَّنَا فَٱغْفِرْ لَنَا ذُنُوبَنَا وَكَفِّرْ عَنَّا
سَيِّـَٔاتِنَا وَتَوَفَّنَا مَعَ ٱلْأَبْرَارِ ١٩٣ رَبَّنَا وَءَاتِنَا مَا وَعَدتَّنَا
عَلَىٰ رُسُلِكَ وَلَا تُخْزِنَا يَوْمَ ٱلْقِيَٰمَةِ ۗ إِنَّكَ لَا تُخْلِفُ ٱلْمِيعَادَ ١٩٤
فَٱسْتَجَابَ لَهُمْ رَبُّهُمْ أَنِّى لَآ أُضِيعُ عَمَلَ عَٰمِلٍ مِّنكُم مِّن
ذَكَرٍ أَوْ أُنثَىٰ ۖ بَعْضُكُم مِّنۢ بَعْضٍ ۖ فَٱلَّذِينَ هَاجَرُوا۟ وَأُخْرِجُوا۟
مِن دِيَٰرِهِمْ وَأُوذُوا۟ فِى سَبِيلِى وَقَٰتَلُوا۟ وَقُتِلُوا۟ لَأُكَفِّرَنَّ
عَنْهُمْ سَيِّـَٔاتِهِمْ وَلَأُدْخِلَنَّهُمْ جَنَّٰتٍ تَجْرِى مِن تَحْتِهَا
ٱلْأَنْهَٰرُ ثَوَابًا مِّنْ عِندِ ٱللَّهِ ۗ وَٱللَّهُ عِندَهُۥ حُسْنُ ٱلثَّوَابِ ١٩٥
لَا يَغُرَّنَّكَ تَقَلُّبُ ٱلَّذِينَ كَفَرُوا۟ فِى ٱلْبِلَٰدِ ١٩٦ مَتَٰعٌ قَلِيلٌ
ثُمَّ مَأْوَىٰهُمْ جَهَنَّمُ ۚ وَبِئْسَ ٱلْمِهَادُ ١٩٧ لَٰكِنِ ٱلَّذِينَ ٱتَّقَوْا۟
رَبَّهُمْ لَهُمْ جَنَّٰتٌ تَجْرِى مِن تَحْتِهَا ٱلْأَنْهَٰرُ خَٰلِدِينَ فِيهَا
نُزُلًا مِّنْ عِندِ ٱللَّهِ ۗ وَمَا عِندَ ٱللَّهِ خَيْرٌ لِّلْأَبْرَارِ ١٩٨ وَإِنَّ مِنْ
أَهْلِ ٱلْكِتَٰبِ لَمَن يُؤْمِنُ بِٱللَّهِ وَمَآ أُنزِلَ إِلَيْكُمْ وَمَآ
أُنزِلَ إِلَيْهِمْ خَٰشِعِينَ لِلَّهِ لَا يَشْتَرُونَ بِـَٔايَٰتِ ٱللَّهِ ثَمَنًا
قَلِيلًا ۗ أُو۟لَٰٓئِكَ لَهُمْ أَجْرُهُمْ عِندَ رَبِّهِمْ ۗ إِنَّ ٱللَّهَ
سَرِيعُ ٱلْحِسَابِ ١٩٩ يَٰٓأَيُّهَا ٱلَّذِينَ ءَامَنُوا۟ ٱصْبِرُوا۟
وَصَابِرُوا۟ وَرَابِطُوا۟ وَٱتَّقُوا۟ ٱللَّهَ لَعَلَّكُمْ تُفْلِحُونَ ٢٠٠

193. ***Our Lord, we have heard a caller*** (either Muḥammad or the Qur'an) ***calling*** people ***to belief: 'Believe in your Lord!' and we have believed*** him. ***Our Lord, forgive us our wrong actions, erase our bad actions from us*** and do not punish us for them, ***and take us*** (our souls) ***back to You with the truly good*** (the righteous Prophets).

194. ***Our Lord, give us what You promised us through*** (on the tongues of) ***Your Messengers*** by way of mercy and bounty and the Messengers asking Allah for that for their followers. His promise will not fail even those who ask to be among them despite their uncertainty of being entitled to it. "Our Lord" is repeated to stress the entreaty. ***And do not disgrace us on the Day of Rising. You will not break Your promise*** of resurrection and repayment."

195. ***Their Lord responds to them*** (to their supplication)***: "I will not let the deeds of any doer among you go to waste, male or female – you are both the same in that respect.*** Women and men are equal in rewards, blessings and actions. This was revealed when Umm Salama said, "Messenger of Allah, I do not hear women mentioned at all in respect of the Hijra." ***Those who emigrated*** from Makka to Madina ***and were driven from their homes and suffered harm in My Way***, for the sake of My *dīn,* ***and fought*** the unbelievers ***and were killed, I will erase their bad actions from them*** by covering them with My forgiveness ***and admit them into Gardens with rivers flowing under them, as a reward from Allah. The best of all rewards*** and repayment ***is with Allah."***

196. This *āyat* was sent down when the Muslims said, "We see that the enemies of Allah are having a good time whereas we are in great difficulty. They move about the land trading and making money." ***Do not be deceived by the fact that the people who disbelieve move freely about the earth*** trading and earning.

197. ***A brief enjoyment*** in this world which will then vanish***; then their shelter will be Hell. What an evil resting-place!***

198. ***But those who fear their Lord will have Gardens with rivers flowing under them, remaining in them timelessly, forever: hospitality from Allah.*** Hospitality is what is prepared for the guest. It is accusative to make it adverbial. ***What is with Allah is better for the truly good*** than the enjoyment of this world.

199. ***Among the people of the Book there are some,*** such as 'Abdullāh ibn Salām and his companions and the Negus, ***who believe in Allah and what has been sent down to you*** (the Qur'an) ***and what was sent down to them*** (the Torah and Gospel) ***and who are humble before Allah. They do not sell Allah's Signs*** which they have in the Torah and the Gospel about the Prophet, may Allah bless him and grant him peace, being sent ***for a paltry price*** (a little of this world), seeking to conceal it out of fear of loss of leadership as other Jews did. ***Such people will have their reward*** for their actions ***with their Lord*** twice over, as is stated in *Sūrat al-Qaṣaṣ* (28:54). ***And Allah is Swift at the Reckoning,*** which He will accomplish in less than half a day of this world.

200. ***O you who believe! Be steadfast*** in acts of obedience, hardship and not disobeying. ***Be supreme in steadfastness*** against the unbelievers so that they do not have more steadfastness than you. ***Be firm on the battlefield*** in *jihād*. ***And show fear of Allah*** in all your states ***– so that perhaps you will be successful*** and win the Garden and be safe from the Fire.

سورة النساء

بِسۡمِ ٱللَّهِ ٱلرَّحۡمَٰنِ ٱلرَّحِيمِ

يَٰٓأَيُّهَا ٱلنَّاسُ ٱتَّقُواْ رَبَّكُمُ ٱلَّذِي خَلَقَكُم مِّن نَّفۡسٖ وَٰحِدَةٖ وَخَلَقَ مِنۡهَا
زَوۡجَهَا وَبَثَّ مِنۡهُمَا رِجَالٗا كَثِيرٗا وَنِسَآءٗۚ وَٱتَّقُواْ ٱللَّهَ ٱلَّذِي تَسَآءَلُونَ
بِهِۦ وَٱلۡأَرۡحَامَۚ إِنَّ ٱللَّهَ كَانَ عَلَيۡكُمۡ رَقِيبٗا ﴿١﴾ وَءَاتُواْ ٱلۡيَتَٰمَىٰٓ أَمۡوَٰلَهُمۡۖ
وَلَا تَتَبَدَّلُواْ ٱلۡخَبِيثَ بِٱلطَّيِّبِۖ وَلَا تَأۡكُلُوٓاْ أَمۡوَٰلَهُمۡ إِلَىٰٓ أَمۡوَٰلِكُمۡۚ إِنَّهُۥ
كَانَ حُوبٗا كَبِيرٗا ﴿٢﴾ وَإِنۡ خِفۡتُمۡ أَلَّا تُقۡسِطُواْ فِي ٱلۡيَتَٰمَىٰ فَٱنكِحُواْ
مَا طَابَ لَكُم مِّنَ ٱلنِّسَآءِ مَثۡنَىٰ وَثُلَٰثَ وَرُبَٰعَۖ فَإِنۡ خِفۡتُمۡ أَلَّا تَعۡدِلُواْ
فَوَٰحِدَةً أَوۡ مَا مَلَكَتۡ أَيۡمَٰنُكُمۡۚ ذَٰلِكَ أَدۡنَىٰٓ أَلَّا تَعُولُواْ ﴿٣﴾ وَءَاتُواْ
ٱلنِّسَآءَ صَدُقَٰتِهِنَّ نِحۡلَةٗۚ فَإِن طِبۡنَ لَكُمۡ عَن شَيۡءٖ مِّنۡهُ نَفۡسٗا فَكُلُوهُ
هَنِيٓـٔٗا مَّرِيٓـٔٗا ﴿٤﴾ وَلَا تُؤۡتُواْ ٱلسُّفَهَآءَ أَمۡوَٰلَكُمُ ٱلَّتِي جَعَلَ ٱللَّهُ لَكُمۡ
قِيَٰمٗا وَٱرۡزُقُوهُمۡ فِيهَا وَٱكۡسُوهُمۡ وَقُولُواْ لَهُمۡ قَوۡلٗا مَّعۡرُوفٗا ﴿٥﴾ وَٱبۡتَلُواْ
ٱلۡيَتَٰمَىٰ حَتَّىٰٓ إِذَا بَلَغُواْ ٱلنِّكَاحَ فَإِنۡ ءَانَسۡتُم مِّنۡهُمۡ رُشۡدٗا فَٱدۡفَعُوٓاْ
إِلَيۡهِمۡ أَمۡوَٰلَهُمۡۖ وَلَا تَأۡكُلُوهَآ إِسۡرَافٗا وَبِدَارًا أَن يَكۡبَرُواْۚ وَمَن كَانَ
غَنِيّٗا فَلۡيَسۡتَعۡفِفۡۖ وَمَن كَانَ فَقِيرٗا فَلۡيَأۡكُلۡ بِٱلۡمَعۡرُوفِۚ فَإِذَا
دَفَعۡتُمۡ إِلَيۡهِمۡ أَمۡوَٰلَهُمۡ فَأَشۡهِدُواْ عَلَيۡهِمۡۚ وَكَفَىٰ بِٱللَّهِ حَسِيبٗا ﴿٦﴾
لِّلرِّجَالِ نَصِيبٞ مِّمَّا تَرَكَ ٱلۡوَٰلِدَانِ وَٱلۡأَقۡرَبُونَ وَلِلنِّسَآءِ نَصِيبٞ
مِّمَّا تَرَكَ ٱلۡوَٰلِدَانِ وَٱلۡأَقۡرَبُونَ مِمَّا قَلَّ مِنۡهُ أَوۡ كَثُرَۚ نَصِيبٗا
مَّفۡرُوضٗا ﴿٧﴾ وَإِذَا حَضَرَ ٱلۡقِسۡمَةَ أُوْلُواْ ٱلۡقُرۡبَىٰ وَٱلۡيَتَٰمَىٰ
وَٱلۡمَسَٰكِينُ فَٱرۡزُقُوهُم مِّنۡهُ وَقُولُواْ لَهُمۡ قَوۡلٗا مَّعۡرُوفٗا

4. *Sūrat an-Nisā'*
Women

This *sūra* is Madinan with 175 or 176 verses. Revealed after *Sūrat al-Mumtahana* (60).

1. ***Mankind*** (people of Makka)***! Be fearful of your Lord*** and His punishment by obeying Him ***who created you from a single self*** (Ādam) ***and created its mate*** (Ḥawwā') ***from it***, from one of his left ribs, ***and then disseminated*** and spread out ***many men and women from the two of them*** (Ādam and Ḥawwā')***. Be fearful of Allah, in whose name you make demands on one another*** (read as *tasā'alūna* and *tassā'alūna),* asking one another for things saying, "I ask you by Allah", ***and also be fearful of Him in respect of your families*** (your relatives): in other words, fear becoming alienated from them. The Arabs used to swear by their lineages. ***Allah watches over you continually.*** Allah observes your actions and will repay you for them; and He always does so.

2. This was revealed about an orphan who asked for his property from his guardian, who refused to give it to him. ***Give orphans*** (young children with no father) ***their property*** when they come of age, ***and do not substitute bad*** (unlawful) ***things for good*** (lawful), as people used to do by taking good property and then replacing it with something inferior. ***Do not assimilate their property into your own*** by consuming it. ***To do that is a serious crime*** (an immense sin). When this was revealed, people stopped taking on the guardianship of orphans. Some of them had eight or ten wives and were not fair between them, and so the following *āyat* was revealed:

3. ***If you are afraid of not behaving justly towards orphans*** and seek not to be constricted in respect of their affairs and also fear that you will not be fair between your wives, ***then marry other permissible women, two, three or four.*** Do not marry more than four. ***But if you are afraid of not treating them equally*** in respect of maintenance and division, ***then*** marry ***only one, or*** confine yourself to ***those you own as slaves*** who do not have the rights that wives have.

That (marrying no more than four or marrying just one) ***makes it more likely that you will not be unfair.***

4. ***Give women their dowry as an outright gift*** cheerfully and without reservation. ***But if they are happy to give you some of it*** (the dowry) and give it to you, ***make use of it with pleasure and good-will*** to a praiseworthy end. There is no harm for you in the Next World in doing this. This was revealed to refute those who disapproved of doing so.

5. ***Do not,*** guardians, ***hand over to the simple-minded*** (spendthrift men, women or children) ***any property of theirs*** in your possession ***for which Allah has made you responsible*** (read as *qiyāman* and *qiyaman)* which you manage on their behalf knowing that they will waste it; ***but provide for them*** and feed ***and clothe them out of it, and speak to them correctly and courteously*** and give them their property when they are capable of dealing with it sensibly.

6. ***Keep a close check on orphans*** and test them before they reach adulthood and the age of responsibility in terms of their *dīn* and the disposal of their worldly affairs ***until they reach a marriageable age*** and reach puberty or the age of marriage, which is fifteen according to ash-Shāfi'ī; ***then if you perceive that they have sound judgement*** with regard to their *dīn* and ability to manage property, ***hand over their property to them. Do not,*** guardians, ***consume it extravagantly***, illicitly ***and precipitately, before they come of age***, hurrying to spend it out of the fear that they will grow up and you will have to hand it over. ***Those*** guardians ***who are wealthy should abstain from it altogether*** and should not spend any of it. ***Those who are poor should use it sensibly and correctly***, taking some in payment for their guardianship. ***When you hand over their property to them*** (the orphans), ***ensure that there are witnesses on their behalf*** when you return their property to the orphans in your charge and are free of it so that there should not be any dispute and there will be evidence to it. This is guidance. ***Allah is enough as a Reckoner.*** He will call His creation to account and He knows their actions.

7. This was revealed to refute the custom in pre-Islamic times whereby women and children did not inherit. ***Men*** (sons and relatives) ***receive a share of what their*** deceased ***parents and relatives leave***

and women receive a share of what their parents and relatives leave – a fixed share, whether it be a little or a lot. They receive a defined share to relieve them of anxiety.

8. ***If other relatives*** who do not inherit ***or orphans or poor people attend the sharing-out*** of the inheritance, ***provide for them from it*** (give them something) ***and speak to them correctly and courteously***, making the excuse to them that you do not own the property and that it is mainly for the children of the deceased. It is said that the judgement in this *āyat* has been abrogated and it is also said that it has not. But people are remiss if they fail to act on it. It is generally said to be recommended, although Ibn 'Abbās says that it is mandatory.

9. ***People should show concern*** for orphans ***in the same way that they would fear for*** their own ***small children if they were to die leaving them behind***, fearing destitution for them. ***They should be fearful of Allah*** regarding orphans and treat them as they would like their own descendants to be treated after them, ***and say words that are appropriate.*** Those present with someone who is dying should speak correctly to him by counselling him to give *ṣadaqa* of less than one third of his wealth and to leave the rest for his heirs so that they are not destitute.

10. ***People who consume the property of orphans wrongfully*** (without legal right) ***consume nothing in their bellies except fire***, because that will lead them to it. ***They will roast in a Searing Blaze,*** a fierce fire in which they will burn.

11. ***Allah instructs*** and commands ***you regarding your children*** as was mentioned: ***a male*** among them ***gets the same as the share of two females.*** When they are together the male has half and the females share half between them. If there is one daughter, she has a third and the son has two-thirds. If he is the only child he gets the lot. ***If there are more than two daughters they get two-thirds of what you leave.*** If there are only daughters, even if there are only two, they receive two-thirds in accordance with the *āyat, "If there are two sisters they receive two-thirds of what he leaves"* (4:176) and also because a daughter is entitled to a third when she has one brother and so it is more fitting for to her receive the same when she has one sister. ***If she is one on her own she gets a half. Each of your parents get a sixth of what you leave if you have children***, male or

﴿٨﴾ وَلْيَخْشَ ٱلَّذِينَ لَوْ تَرَكُوا۟ مِنْ خَلْفِهِمْ ذُرِّيَّةً ضِعَٰفًا
خَافُوا۟ عَلَيْهِمْ فَلْيَتَّقُوا۟ ٱللَّهَ وَلْيَقُولُوا۟ قَوْلًا سَدِيدًا ﴿٩﴾
إِنَّ ٱلَّذِينَ يَأْكُلُونَ أَمْوَٰلَ ٱلْيَتَٰمَىٰ ظُلْمًا إِنَّمَا يَأْكُلُونَ فِى
بُطُونِهِمْ نَارًا ۖ وَسَيَصْلَوْنَ سَعِيرًا ﴿١٠﴾ يُوصِيكُمُ ٱللَّهُ
فِىٓ أَوْلَٰدِكُمْ ۖ لِلذَّكَرِ مِثْلُ حَظِّ ٱلْأُنثَيَيْنِ ۚ فَإِن كُنَّ نِسَآءً
فَوْقَ ٱثْنَتَيْنِ فَلَهُنَّ ثُلُثَا مَا تَرَكَ ۖ وَإِن كَانَتْ وَٰحِدَةً فَلَهَا
ٱلنِّصْفُ ۚ وَلِأَبَوَيْهِ لِكُلِّ وَٰحِدٍ مِّنْهُمَا ٱلسُّدُسُ مِمَّا تَرَكَ إِن
كَانَ لَهُۥ وَلَدٌ ۚ فَإِن لَّمْ يَكُن لَّهُۥ وَلَدٌ وَوَرِثَهُۥٓ أَبَوَاهُ فَلِأُمِّهِ ٱلثُّلُثُ ۚ
فَإِن كَانَ لَهُۥٓ إِخْوَةٌ فَلِأُمِّهِ ٱلسُّدُسُ ۚ مِنۢ بَعْدِ وَصِيَّةٍ يُوصِى
بِهَآ أَوْ دَيْنٍ ۗ ءَابَآؤُكُمْ وَأَبْنَآؤُكُمْ لَا تَدْرُونَ أَيُّهُمْ أَقْرَبُ لَكُمْ
نَفْعًا ۚ فَرِيضَةً مِّنَ ٱللَّهِ ۗ إِنَّ ٱللَّهَ كَانَ عَلِيمًا حَكِيمًا ﴿١١﴾
۞ وَلَكُمْ نِصْفُ مَا تَرَكَ أَزْوَٰجُكُمْ إِن لَّمْ يَكُن
لَّهُنَّ وَلَدٌ ۚ فَإِن كَانَ لَهُنَّ وَلَدٌ فَلَكُمُ ٱلرُّبُعُ مِمَّا
تَرَكْنَ ۚ مِنۢ بَعْدِ وَصِيَّةٍ يُوصِينَ بِهَآ أَوْ دَيْنٍ ۚ
وَلَهُنَّ ٱلرُّبُعُ مِمَّا تَرَكْتُمْ إِن لَّمْ يَكُن لَّكُمْ وَلَدٌ ۚ
فَإِن كَانَ لَكُمْ وَلَدٌ فَلَهُنَّ ٱلثُّمُنُ مِمَّا تَرَكْتُم ۚ
مِّنۢ بَعْدِ وَصِيَّةٍ تُوصُونَ بِهَآ أَوْ دَيْنٍ ۗ وَإِن كَانَ
رَجُلٌ يُورَثُ كَلَٰلَةً أَوِ ٱمْرَأَةٌ وَلَهُۥٓ أَخٌ أَوْ أُخْتٌ فَلِكُلِّ
وَٰحِدٍ مِّنْهُمَا ٱلسُّدُسُ ۚ فَإِن كَانُوٓا۟ أَكْثَرَ مِن ذَٰلِكَ
فَهُمْ شُرَكَآءُ فِى ٱلثُّلُثِ ۚ مِنۢ بَعْدِ وَصِيَّةٍ يُوصَىٰ بِهَآ

female. The term "parents" refers to both mothers and fathers, each of whom receives one sixth. Grandsons are equated with children and grandparents with parents. ***If you are childless*** and on your own or with a spouse, ***and your heirs are your parents, your mother gets a third*** after the spouses have taken their share and then the residue goes to the father. ***If you have brothers or sisters,*** more than one, male or female, ***your mother gets a sixth,*** and the father gets the rest, the siblings of the deceased receiving nothing, ***after*** paying ***any bequest you make or*** settling ***any debts.*** Bequests are paid before debts even if the debt was incurred after the bequest was made. ***With regard to your fathers and your sons, you do not know which of them is going to benefit you more*** in this world and the Next. It may be that a person thinks that their son is more beneficial and gives him the inheritance but then the father proves to be more beneficial, or vice versa. Allah is the One who knows that, and so allot them their due inheritance. ***These are obligatory shares from Allah. Allah is All-Knowing*** about His creation, ***All-Wise*** in managing it for them.

12. ***You get half of what your wives leave if they are childless,*** whether by you or other husbands. ***If they have children you get a quarter of what they leave after any bequest they make or any debts.*** There is consensus that this extends to the grandchildren. ***They*** (wives) ***get a quarter of what you leave if you are childless. If you have children,*** whether by them or other women, ***they get one eighth of what you leave after any bequest you make or any debts.*** There is consensus that this extends to the grandchildren. ***If a man or woman has no direct heirs***, either parent or child, ***but has a brother or sister*** by the same mother (*min umm,* "from the mother" was actually read by Ibn Mas'ūd and others), ***each of them gets one sixth*** of the estate. ***If there are more*** (siblings by the mother) ***than that*** (one) ***they share in one third,*** brothers and sisters taking equal amounts, ***after any bequest you make or any debts, making sure that no one's*** (none of the heirs') ***rights are prejudiced*** by a bequest of more than a third. ***This is an instruction from Allah*** which He commands you. ***Allah is All-Knowing*** of how to manage His creation in shares of inheritance, ***All-Forbearing*** by deferring punishment from those who oppose Him. The *Sunna* specifies that inheri-

أَوْ دَيْنٍ غَيْرَ مُضَآرٍّۚ وَصِيَّةً مِّنَ ٱللَّهِۗ وَٱللَّهُ عَلِيمٌ حَلِيمٌ
﴿١٢﴾ تِلْكَ حُدُودُ ٱللَّهِۚ وَمَن يُطِعِ ٱللَّهَ وَرَسُولَهُۥ
يُدْخِلْهُ جَنَّٰتٍ تَجْرِى مِن تَحْتِهَا ٱلْأَنْهَٰرُ
خَٰلِدِينَ فِيهَاۚ وَذَٰلِكَ ٱلْفَوْزُ ٱلْعَظِيمُ ﴿١٣﴾
وَمَن يَعْصِ ٱللَّهَ وَرَسُولَهُۥ وَيَتَعَدَّ حُدُودَهُۥ يُدْخِلْهُ
نَارًا خَٰلِدًا فِيهَا وَلَهُۥ عَذَابٌ مُّهِينٌ ﴿١٤﴾
وَٱلَّٰتِى يَأْتِينَ ٱلْفَٰحِشَةَ مِن نِّسَآئِكُمْ فَٱسْتَشْهِدُوا۟
عَلَيْهِنَّ أَرْبَعَةً مِّنكُمْۖ فَإِن شَهِدُوا۟ فَأَمْسِكُوهُنَّ فِى
ٱلْبُيُوتِ حَتَّىٰ يَتَوَفَّىٰهُنَّ ٱلْمَوْتُ أَوْ يَجْعَلَ ٱللَّهُ لَهُنَّ سَبِيلًا
﴿١٥﴾ وَٱلَّذَانِ يَأْتِيَٰنِهَا مِنكُمْ فَـَٔاذُوهُمَاۖ فَإِن تَابَا
وَأَصْلَحَا فَأَعْرِضُوا۟ عَنْهُمَآۗ إِنَّ ٱللَّهَ كَانَ تَوَّابًا رَّحِيمًا
﴿١٦﴾ إِنَّمَا ٱلتَّوْبَةُ عَلَى ٱللَّهِ لِلَّذِينَ يَعْمَلُونَ ٱلسُّوٓءَ بِجَهَٰلَةٍ
ثُمَّ يَتُوبُونَ مِن قَرِيبٍ فَأُو۟لَٰٓئِكَ يَتُوبُ ٱللَّهُ عَلَيْهِمْۗ وَكَانَ
ٱللَّهُ عَلِيمًا حَكِيمًا ﴿١٧﴾ وَلَيْسَتِ ٱلتَّوْبَةُ لِلَّذِينَ
يَعْمَلُونَ ٱلسَّيِّـَٔاتِ حَتَّىٰٓ إِذَا حَضَرَ أَحَدَهُمُ ٱلْمَوْتُ
قَالَ إِنِّى تُبْتُ ٱلْـَٰٔنَ وَلَا ٱلَّذِينَ يَمُوتُونَ وَهُمْ كُفَّارٌۚ
أُو۟لَٰٓئِكَ أَعْتَدْنَا لَهُمْ عَذَابًا أَلِيمًا ﴿١٨﴾ يَٰٓأَيُّهَا ٱلَّذِينَ
ءَامَنُوا۟ لَا يَحِلُّ لَكُمْ أَن تَرِثُوا۟ ٱلنِّسَآءَ كَرْهًاۖ وَلَا تَعْضُلُوهُنَّ
لِتَذْهَبُوا۟ بِبَعْضِ مَآ ءَاتَيْتُمُوهُنَّ إِلَّآ أَن يَأْتِينَ بِفَٰحِشَةٍ
مُّبَيِّنَةٍۚ وَعَاشِرُوهُنَّ بِٱلْمَعْرُوفِۚ فَإِن كَرِهْتُمُوهُنَّ فَعَسَىٰٓ

tance is withheld in the event of homicide, difference of religion or slavery.

13. ***These*** (judgements mentioned about orphans and inheritance) ***are Allah's limits,*** the laws of Allah which He has defined for His slaves so that they should act by them and not overstep them. ***As for him who obeys Allah and His Messenger*** in His decrees, ***He will admit him*** (read as *yudkhilhu*, "He will admit him" and *nukhilhu*, "We will admit him") ***into Gardens with rivers flowing under them, remaining in them timelessly, forever. That is the Great Victory.***

14. ***As for him who disobeys Allah and His Messenger and over-steps His limits, He will admit*** (again read as *yudkhilhu*, "He will admit him" and *nukhilhu*, "We will admit him") ***him into a Fire, to remain in it timelessly, forever. He will have a humiliating punish-ment.***

15. ***If any of your women commit fornication, four of you*** (Muslim men) ***must be witnesses against them*** that they have committed it. ***If they bear witness, detain them in their homes*** and keep them from socialising with people ***until death releases them*** when the angels take their souls ***or Allah ordains another procedure for their case,*** some other way to emerge from their imprisonment. The Muslims were commanded to do that at the beginning of Islam and then Allah ordained flogging with one hundred lashes for virgins who fornicate and exiling them for a year, and for married women He prescribed stoning. A *ḥadīth* clarified the penalty when the Prophet, may Allah bless him and grant him peace, said, "Take it from me. Allah has ordained another procedure for them." (Muslim)

16. ***If two men*** (read as *alladhāni* and *alladhānni*) ***commit a like abomination*** (fornication or sodomy), ***punish them*** by cursing them and beating them with sandals, ***and if they repent*** of it ***and reform*** their behaviour, ***leave them alone*** and do not harm them. ***Allah is Ever-returning*** towards those who repent, ***Most Merciful*** to them. This *āyat* was abrogated by the *ḥadd* punishment for fornication. That also applies to sodomy, according to ash-Shāfi'ī, but one who is guilty of it is not to be stoned, in his view, even if he has been married. He is to be flogged and exiled. The meaning here is more likely to be sodomy because of the grammatical use of the dual; but fornication is not excluded. They are alike in harm, and in the need for repentance and turning away. Men in particular are mentioned, because imprisonment for women was mentioned in the previous *āyat*.

17. ***Allah*** has prescribed for Himself that by His bounty He ***only accepts the repentance of those who do evil*** (an act of disobedience) ***in ignorance*** when they did not know that what they were doing was disobedience ***and then quickly repent of doing it*** before they die. ***Allah turns towards such people*** and accepts their repentance. ***Allah is All-Knowing*** of His creation, ***All-Wise*** in what He does to them.

18. ***There is no repentance for people who persist in doing evil*** (wrong actions) ***until death appears to them*** and they are on the point of death, ***and who then say*** when they see that they are dying, ***"Now I repent,"*** which is of no use and is not accepted, ***nor for people who die as unbelievers*** and who repent in the Next World when they see the punishment. That will certainly not be accepted from them. ***We have prepared for them a painful punishment.***

19. ***You who believe! It is not lawful for you to inherit women by force*** (read as *karhan* and *kurhan*) if the women concerned object to it. In the time of *Jāhiliyya* people inherited their relatives' wives. If they wished, they married them without dowry or married them and took their dowry and let them ransom themselves with what they inherited, or they would inherit from them when they died. They were now forbidden to do that. ***Nor may you treat them harshly*** by preventing such women from marrying others by keeping hold of them or having any desire to cause harm to them, ***so that you can make off with part of what you have given them*** by taking their dower – ***unless they commit an act of flagrant*** (read as *mubayyina* and *mubayyana*) ***indecency,*** unless they clearly commit adultery or disobey you, in order to force them to ransom themselves through a *khul'* divorce. ***Live together with them correctly and courteously,*** with good words and giving them their maintenance and a place to live. ***If you dislike them,*** be patient, ***it may well be that you dislike something when Allah has placed a lot of good in it.*** Perhaps it is through them that you will have the blessing of a righteous child.

20. ***If you desire to exchange one wife for another*** through divorce, ***and have given your original wife a large amount*** in dowry, ***do not take any of it. Would you take it by means of slander*** (injustice)

أَن تَكْرَهُواْ شَيْـًٔا وَيَجْعَلَ ٱللَّهُ فِيهِ خَيْرًا كَثِيرًا ﴿١٩﴾
وَإِنْ أَرَدتُّمُ ٱسْتِبْدَالَ زَوْجٍ مَّكَانَ زَوْجٍ وَءَاتَيْتُمْ
إِحْدَىٰهُنَّ قِنطَارًا فَلَا تَأْخُذُواْ مِنْهُ شَيْـًٔاۚ أَتَأْخُذُونَهُۥ
بُهْتَٰنًا وَإِثْمًا مُّبِينًا ﴿٢٠﴾ وَكَيْفَ تَأْخُذُونَهُۥ وَقَدْ أَفْضَىٰ
بَعْضُكُمْ إِلَىٰ بَعْضٍ وَأَخَذْنَ مِنكُم مِّيثَٰقًا
غَلِيظًا ﴿٢١﴾ وَلَا تَنكِحُواْ مَا نَكَحَ ءَابَآؤُكُم مِّنَ
ٱلنِّسَآءِ إِلَّا مَا قَدْ سَلَفَۚ إِنَّهُۥ كَانَ فَٰحِشَةً وَمَقْتًا
وَسَآءَ سَبِيلًا ﴿٢٢﴾ حُرِّمَتْ عَلَيْكُمْ أُمَّهَٰتُكُمْ
وَبَنَاتُكُمْ وَأَخَوَٰتُكُمْ وَعَمَّٰتُكُمْ وَخَٰلَٰتُكُمْ وَبَنَاتُ
ٱلْأَخِ وَبَنَاتُ ٱلْأُخْتِ وَأُمَّهَٰتُكُمُ ٱلَّٰتِيٓ أَرْضَعْنَكُمْ
وَأَخَوَٰتُكُم مِّنَ ٱلرَّضَٰعَةِ وَأُمَّهَٰتُ نِسَآئِكُمْ
وَرَبَٰٓئِبُكُمُ ٱلَّٰتِي فِي حُجُورِكُم مِّن نِّسَآئِكُمُ
ٱلَّٰتِي دَخَلْتُم بِهِنَّ فَإِن لَّمْ تَكُونُواْ دَخَلْتُم بِهِنَّ
فَلَا جُنَاحَ عَلَيْكُمْ وَحَلَٰٓئِلُ أَبْنَآئِكُمُ ٱلَّذِينَ
مِنْ أَصْلَٰبِكُمْ وَأَن تَجْمَعُواْ بَيْنَ ٱلْأُخْتَيْنِ
إِلَّا مَا قَدْ سَلَفَۗ إِنَّ ٱللَّهَ كَانَ غَفُورًا رَّحِيمًا ﴿٢٣﴾
۞ وَٱلْمُحْصَنَٰتُ مِنَ ٱلنِّسَآءِ إِلَّا مَا مَلَكَتْ أَيْمَٰنُكُمْۖ
كِتَٰبَ ٱللَّهِ عَلَيْكُمْۚ وَأُحِلَّ لَكُم مَّا وَرَآءَ ذَٰلِكُمْ أَن تَبْتَغُواْ
بِأَمْوَٰلِكُم مُّحْصِنِينَ غَيْرَ مُسَٰفِحِينَۚ فَمَا ٱسْتَمْتَعْتُم بِهِۦ
مِنْهُنَّ فَـَٔاتُوهُنَّ أُجُورَهُنَّ فَرِيضَةًۚ وَلَا جُنَاحَ عَلَيْكُمْ

and downright crime (clear and evident wrongdoing)*?* The question in the following *āyat* is by way of rebuke and objection.

21. ***How could you take it*** in any way ***when you have been intimate with each other*** through sexual intercourse, which obliges payment of the dowry, ***and they have made a binding contract with you?*** The "contract" here refers to what Allah has commanded about keeping them correctly or letting them go with kindness.

22. ***Do not marry any women your fathers have already married – except for what took place in the past***, which is overlooked**.** ***That*** (marrying them) ***is an indecent act, a loathsome thing and an evil way*** which incurs Allah's anger and is evil behaviour**.**

23. ***Unlawful for you*** to marry ***are: your mothers,*** (and grandmothers on either side) ***your daughters*** (and granddaughters) ***and your sisters*** through either parent; ***your maternal aunts,*** the sisters of your mothers and grandmothers, ***and paternal aunts,*** the sisters of your fathers and grandfathers, ***your brothers' daughters and your sisters' daughters,*** including their children, ***your foster mothers who have suckled you,*** referring to suckling before the child is two years old at least five times, as the *ḥadīth* states, ***your foster sisters by suckling,*** and the *Sunna* adds their daughters, and aunts and nieces according to the *ḥadīth*, "Suckling makes unlawful what marriage makes unlawful" (al-Bukhārī and Muslim), ***your wives' mothers, your stepdaughters***, daughters of your wife by a previous husband, ***who are under your protection*** and whom you are bringing up*;* ***the daughters of your wives you have had sexual relations with – though if you have not had sexual relations with them there is nothing blameworthy for you in it then*** in marrying their daughters if you have divorced them; ***the wives of your sons whom you have fathered,*** not those you have adopted and cared for whose ex-wives you can marry, ***and marrying two sisters at the same time*** whether they are by blood or nursing, and the *Sunna* adds to this, marriage with a woman and her aunt although it is permitted to marry one on divorcing the other and to own two sisters as slaves provided you only have relations with one ***– except for what took place in the past*** before Islam, and you incur no sin in respect of that. ***Allah is Ever-Forgiving*** of what took place before the prohibition**,** ***Most Merciful*** to you in that respect**.**

فِيمَا تَرَٰضَيْتُم بِهِۦ مِنۢ بَعْدِ ٱلْفَرِيضَةِۚ إِنَّ ٱللَّهَ كَانَ عَلِيمًا
حَكِيمًا ﴿٢٤﴾ وَمَن لَّمْ يَسْتَطِعْ مِنكُمْ طَوْلًا أَن يَنكِحَ
ٱلْمُحْصَنَٰتِ ٱلْمُؤْمِنَٰتِ فَمِن مَّا مَلَكَتْ أَيْمَٰنُكُم مِّن
فَتَيَٰتِكُمُ ٱلْمُؤْمِنَٰتِۚ وَٱللَّهُ أَعْلَمُ بِإِيمَٰنِكُم بَعْضُكُم مِّنۢ
بَعْضٍۚ فَٱنكِحُوهُنَّ بِإِذْنِ أَهْلِهِنَّ وَءَاتُوهُنَّ أُجُورَهُنَّ
بِٱلْمَعْرُوفِ مُحْصَنَٰتٍ غَيْرَ مُسَٰفِحَٰتٍ وَلَا مُتَّخِذَٰتِ
أَخْدَانٍۚ فَإِذَآ أُحْصِنَّ فَإِنْ أَتَيْنَ بِفَٰحِشَةٍ فَعَلَيْهِنَّ نِصْفُ
مَا عَلَى ٱلْمُحْصَنَٰتِ مِنَ ٱلْعَذَابِۚ ذَٰلِكَ لِمَنْ خَشِىَ
ٱلْعَنَتَ مِنكُمْۚ وَأَن تَصْبِرُوا۟ خَيْرٌ لَّكُمْۗ وَٱللَّهُ غَفُورٌ رَّحِيمٌ
﴿٢٥﴾ يُرِيدُ ٱللَّهُ لِيُبَيِّنَ لَكُمْ وَيَهْدِيَكُمْ سُنَنَ ٱلَّذِينَ
مِن قَبْلِكُمْ وَيَتُوبَ عَلَيْكُمْۗ وَٱللَّهُ عَلِيمٌ حَكِيمٌ ﴿٢٦﴾
وَٱللَّهُ يُرِيدُ أَن يَتُوبَ عَلَيْكُمْ وَيُرِيدُ ٱلَّذِينَ يَتَّبِعُونَ
ٱلشَّهَوَٰتِ أَن تَمِيلُوا۟ مَيْلًا عَظِيمًا ﴿٢٧﴾ يُرِيدُ ٱللَّهُ أَن يُخَفِّفَ
عَنكُمْۚ وَخُلِقَ ٱلْإِنسَٰنُ ضَعِيفًا ﴿٢٨﴾ يَٰٓأَيُّهَا ٱلَّذِينَ
ءَامَنُوا۟ لَا تَأْكُلُوٓا۟ أَمْوَٰلَكُم بَيْنَكُم بِٱلْبَٰطِلِ إِلَّآ أَن
تَكُونَ تِجَٰرَةً عَن تَرَاضٍ مِّنكُمْۚ وَلَا تَقْتُلُوٓا۟ أَنفُسَكُمْۚ
إِنَّ ٱللَّهَ كَانَ بِكُمْ رَحِيمًا ﴿٢٩﴾ وَمَن يَفْعَلْ ذَٰلِكَ عُدْوَٰنًا
وَظُلْمًا فَسَوْفَ نُصْلِيهِ نَارًاۚ وَكَانَ ذَٰلِكَ عَلَى ٱللَّهِ
يَسِيرًا ﴿٣٠﴾ إِن تَجْتَنِبُوا۟ كَبَآئِرَ مَا تُنْهَوْنَ عَنْهُ نُكَفِّرْ
عَنكُمْ سَيِّـَٔاتِكُمْ وَنُدْخِلْكُم مُّدْخَلًا كَرِيمًا ﴿٣١﴾

24. ***And also*** forbidden to you are ***married women*** before their husbands have divorced them, free Muslims or not, except for slaves – ***except those you have taken in war as slaves.*** You may have relations with them if they have husbands in the Abode of War after *istibrā'* (the waiting period to ascertain whether they are pregnant). ***This is what Allah has prescribed for you. Apart from that He has made all other women lawful for you provided you seek them with your wealth*** through a dowry or ownership, ***in marriage and not in fornication. When you consummate your marriage with them, give them their prescribed dowry. There is nothing wrong in any further agreement you might come to*** with them ***after the dowry has been given*** which may involve lowering or increasing the amount of dowry agreed upon. ***Allah is All-Knowing*** of His creation, ***All-Wise*** in how He manages them.

25. ***If any of you do not have the means***, in other words does not have sufficient money, ***to marry believing free women, you may marry believing slavegirls. Allah knows best about your belief.*** It is enough in this context that belief consist of outward affirmation. Inward convictions are left to Allah, who alone knows what they are. This is to give consolation for having to marry slavegirls. ***You are all the same in that respect*** (in respect of the *dīn*). You are equal in the *dīn* so do not be too proud to marry them. ***Marry them with their owners' permission and give them their dowries correctly and courteously,*** without delay or decrease, ***as*** chaste ***married women, not in*** open ***fornication or taking them as*** secret ***lovers*** in fornication. ***When they are married*** (read as *uḥṣinna* and *aḥṣanna*), ***if they commit fornication they should receive half the punishment of free women.*** Slaves, male and female, receive half the punishment, so they receive fifty lashes and are exiled for six months. They are not to be stoned. ***This*** (marrying slavegirls when lacking wealth) ***is for those of you who are afraid of committing fornication*** (*'anat*). The root of *'anat* means "hardship" and fornication is so called that because it is the reason for the *ḥadd* and punishment in the Next World. The words *"those of you"* excludes those free men who do not fear fornication, and so it is not lawful for those who do not fear committing it to marry slaves, or for those with enough wealth to marry a free woman. That is the position of ash-Shāfi'ī. "Believing slavegirls" excludes disbelieving women, whom it is not lawful to marry even if one lacks the financial means to marry and fears fornication. ***But being patient is better for you*** than marrying slavegirls so that your child is not born as a slave. ***Allah is Ever-Forgiving, Most Merciful*** in granting you scope in that.

26. ***Allah desires to make things*** (the laws of your *dīn* and what is in your best interests) ***clear to you and to guide you to the practices of those*** Prophets ***before you*** who made things lawful and unlawful and so that you follow them as well, ***and to turn towards you*** to bring you back from disobedience to obedience. ***Allah is All-Knowing*** of you, ***All-Wise*** in what He manages for you.

27. ***Allah desires to turn towards you, but those who pursue their lower appetites*** among the Jews, Christians, Magians or fornicators ***desire to make you deviate completely*** and turn from the truth and commit what is forbidden to you, so that you will be the same as them.

28. ***Allah desires to make things lighter for you.*** He desires to lighten the decrees of the *Sharī'a* for you. ***Man was created*** too ***weak*** to refrain from women or the indulgence of his lower appetites.

29. ***You who believe! Do not consume one another's property by false means,*** in other words in a way that is *ḥarām* in the Sharī'a such as usury and misappropriation, ***but only by means of*** goods exchanged in ***mutually agreed trade. And do not kill yourselves*** by committing what will lead to your destruction in this world or the Next. ***Allah is Most Merciful to you*** in forbidding you to do that.

30. ***As for anyone who does that*** (the prohibited transactions referred to above) ***in enmity*** (purposefully transgressing the lawful) ***and wrongdoing*** out of injustice, ***We will roast him in a Fire*** which We will make him enter so that he burns in it. ***That is an easy matter for Allah.***

31. ***If you avoid the serious wrong actions you have been forbidden to do,*** those which are reported with a threat, such as killing, fornication and theft and Ibn 'Abbās said, "They are closer to seven hundred", ***We will erase your bad actions*** (minor wrong actions) ***from you*** through your obedience, ***and admit*** (read as *madkhalan* or *mud -*

وَلَا تَتَمَنَّوْاْ مَا فَضَّلَ ٱللَّهُ بِهِۦ بَعْضَكُمْ عَلَىٰ بَعْضٍۚ لِّلرِّجَالِ
نَصِيبٌ مِّمَّا ٱكْتَسَبُواْۖ وَلِلنِّسَآءِ نَصِيبٌ مِّمَّا ٱكْتَسَبْنَۚ
وَسْـَٔلُواْ ٱللَّهَ مِن فَضْلِهِۦٓۗ إِنَّ ٱللَّهَ كَانَ بِكُلِّ شَيْءٍ
عَلِيمًا ٣٢ وَلِكُلٍّ جَعَلْنَا مَوَٰلِيَ مِمَّا تَرَكَ ٱلْوَٰلِدَانِ
وَٱلْأَقْرَبُونَۚ وَٱلَّذِينَ عَقَدَتْ أَيْمَٰنُكُمْ فَـَٔاتُوهُمْ
نَصِيبَهُمْۚ إِنَّ ٱللَّهَ كَانَ عَلَىٰ كُلِّ شَيْءٍ شَهِيدًا ٣٣
ٱلرِّجَالُ قَوَّٰمُونَ عَلَى ٱلنِّسَآءِ بِمَا فَضَّلَ ٱللَّهُ بَعْضَهُمْ
عَلَىٰ بَعْضٍ وَبِمَآ أَنفَقُواْ مِنْ أَمْوَٰلِهِمْۚ فَٱلصَّٰلِحَٰتُ
قَٰنِتَٰتٌ حَٰفِظَٰتٌ لِّلْغَيْبِ بِمَا حَفِظَ ٱللَّهُۚ وَٱلَّٰتِي تَخَافُونَ
نُشُوزَهُنَّ فَعِظُوهُنَّ وَٱهْجُرُوهُنَّ فِي ٱلْمَضَاجِعِ
وَٱضْرِبُوهُنَّۖ فَإِنْ أَطَعْنَكُمْ فَلَا تَبْغُواْ عَلَيْهِنَّ سَبِيلًاۗ
إِنَّ ٱللَّهَ كَانَ عَلِيًّا كَبِيرًا ٣٤ وَإِنْ خِفْتُمْ شِقَاقَ
بَيْنِهِمَا فَٱبْعَثُواْ حَكَمًا مِّنْ أَهْلِهِۦ وَحَكَمًا مِّنْ أَهْلِهَآ إِن
يُرِيدَآ إِصْلَٰحًا يُوَفِّقِ ٱللَّهُ بَيْنَهُمَآۗ إِنَّ ٱللَّهَ كَانَ عَلِيمًا خَبِيرًا
٣٥ ۞ وَٱعْبُدُواْ ٱللَّهَ وَلَا تُشْرِكُواْ بِهِۦ شَيْـًٔاۖ وَبِٱلْوَٰلِدَيْنِ
إِحْسَٰنًا وَبِذِي ٱلْقُرْبَىٰ وَٱلْيَتَٰمَىٰ وَٱلْمَسَٰكِينِ وَٱلْجَارِ
ذِي ٱلْقُرْبَىٰ وَٱلْجَارِ ٱلْجُنُبِ وَٱلصَّاحِبِ بِٱلْجَنۢبِ
وَٱبْنِ ٱلسَّبِيلِ وَمَا مَلَكَتْ أَيْمَٰنُكُمْۗ إِنَّ ٱللَّهَ لَا يُحِبُّ مَن
كَانَ مُخْتَالًا فَخُورًا ٣٦ ٱلَّذِينَ يَبْخَلُونَ وَيَأْمُرُونَ
ٱلنَّاسَ بِٱلْبُخْلِ وَيَكْتُمُونَ مَآ ءَاتَىٰهُمُ ٱللَّهُ

khalan, meaning the action of admitting you or the place to which you are admitted, which is Paradise) ***you by a Gate of Honour.***

32. ***Do not covet what Allah has given to some of you in preference to others*** in either this world or the *dīn*, so as not to allow that to lead to mutual envy and hatred – ***men have a portion of what they acquire*** by *jihād* and other things ***and women have a portion of what they acquire,*** as a reward for obeying their husbands and guarding their private parts. This was revealed when Umm Salama said, "We wish we had been men so we could perform *jihād* and have a reward like that of men." ***But ask Allah for His bounty*** which you need. ***Allah has knowledge of everything,*** including where to bestow bounty and what you ask for.

33. ***We have appointed heirs for everything that parents and relatives leave.*** *'Aṣaba* are paternal kin and they inherit what is left over of the estate. ***If you have a bond*** (read as *'aqadat* and *'āqadat*) ***with people, give them their share.*** "A bond" refers to an alliance formed with people in pre-Islamic times for help and inheritance. Their share is a sixth. ***Allah is Witness of everything.*** He is aware of you and your states. This ruling was abrogated by Allah's later words about inheritance.

34. ***Men have charge of women*** by teaching and taking charge ***because Allah has preferred the one above the other*** in terms of knowledge, intelligence and custody, ***and because they*** (men) ***spend their wealth on them*** (women) in maintenance. ***Right-acting women are obedient*** to their husbands, ***safeguarding their husbands' interests*** and their private parts ***in their absence as Allah has guarded them*** through their husbands when they are there. ***If there are women whose disobedience you fear, you may admonish them*** and make them fear Allah, ***refuse to sleep with them*** and go to another bed, ***and then beat them***, but not hard if the other courses of action do not work. ***But if they obey you do not look for a way to punish them*** (beating them unjustly). ***Allah is All-High, Most Great.*** Beware lest Allah punish you for behaving unjustly towards them.

35. ***If you fear*** or know of ***a breach between a couple, send*** with their consent ***an arbiter*** who is fair ***from his people*** (his relatives) ***and an arbiter from her people.*** The husband delegates to his arbiter authority to carry out the divorce or to accept compensation, and the wife delegates to her arbiter authority to carry out *khul'*. The arbiters argue it out and command the one in the wrong to desist, or else they disagree. Allah says: ***If the two of them*** (the arbiters) ***desire to put things right, Allah will bring about a reconciliation between them,*** (the couple) in other words enable them to obey by putting things right or separating. ***Allah is All-Knowing, All-Aware*** of the inward and outward of people.

36. ***Worship Allah*** and affirm His oneness ***and do not attribute partners to Him. Be good*** and dutiful and gentle ***to your parents and relatives and to orphans and the very poor, and to neighbours who are related to you*** or close to you, ***and neighbours who are not related to you*** or are far from you, ***and to companions***, friends on a journey or at work or a wife, ***and travellers and your slaves. Allah does not love anyone vain or boastful*** to others about what they have been given.

37. ***As for those who are stingy*** in respect of what they are obliged to give ***and command other people to be stingy, and hide the bounty Allah has given them*** of knowledge and wealth (the Jews), ***We have prepared a humiliating punishment for those who disbelieve...*** It is a strong threat against them.

38. ***...and also for those who spend their wealth to show off to people, not believing in Allah and the Last Day,*** such as the hypocrites and the people of Makka. ***Anyone who has Shayṭān as his comrade*** and acts by his command like these people, ***what an evil comrade he is!***

39. ***What harm would it have done them to believe in Allah and the Last Day and give of what Allah has provided for them?*** The question implies a negative answer, meaning that there would, of course, be no harm. ***Allah knows everything about them*** and will repay them for what they do.

40. ***Allah does not wrong anyone by so much as*** the weight of ***the smallest mote*** (the smallest ant), meaning that their good actions will not be decreased in the slightest or their evil actions increased. ***And if there is a good deed,*** even the size of a mote, done by a believer, ***Allah will multiply it*** (read as *yuḍā'ifhā* and *yuḍa''ifhā*) between ten

مِن فَضۡلِهِۦۗ وَأَعۡتَدۡنَا لِلۡكَٰفِرِينَ عَذَابٗا مُّهِينٗا ٣٧
وَٱلَّذِينَ يُنفِقُونَ أَمۡوَٰلَهُمۡ رِئَآءَ ٱلنَّاسِ وَلَا يُؤۡمِنُونَ
بِٱللَّهِ وَلَا بِٱلۡيَوۡمِ ٱلۡأٓخِرِۗ وَمَن يَكُنِ ٱلشَّيۡطَٰنُ لَهُۥ قَرِينٗا فَسَآءَ
قَرِينٗا ٣٨ وَمَاذَا عَلَيۡهِمۡ لَوۡ ءَامَنُواْ بِٱللَّهِ وَٱلۡيَوۡمِ ٱلۡأٓخِرِ وَأَنفَقُواْ
مِمَّا رَزَقَهُمُ ٱللَّهُۚ وَكَانَ ٱللَّهُ بِهِمۡ عَلِيمًا ٣٩ إِنَّ ٱللَّهَ لَا يَظۡلِمُ
مِثۡقَالَ ذَرَّةٖۖ وَإِن تَكُ حَسَنَةٗ يُضَٰعِفۡهَا وَيُؤۡتِ مِن لَّدُنۡهُ
أَجۡرًا عَظِيمٗا ٤٠ فَكَيۡفَ إِذَا جِئۡنَا مِن كُلِّ أُمَّةِۭ بِشَهِيدٖ
وَجِئۡنَا بِكَ عَلَىٰ هَٰٓؤُلَآءِ شَهِيدٗا ٤١ يَوۡمَئِذٖ يَوَدُّ ٱلَّذِينَ
كَفَرُواْ وَعَصَوُاْ ٱلرَّسُولَ لَوۡ تُسَوَّىٰ بِهِمُ ٱلۡأَرۡضُ وَلَا يَكۡتُمُونَ
ٱللَّهَ حَدِيثٗا ٤٢ يَٰٓأَيُّهَا ٱلَّذِينَ ءَامَنُواْ لَا تَقۡرَبُواْ ٱلصَّلَوٰةَ
وَأَنتُمۡ سُكَٰرَىٰ حَتَّىٰ تَعۡلَمُواْ مَا تَقُولُونَ وَلَا جُنُبًا إِلَّا عَابِرِي
سَبِيلٍ حَتَّىٰ تَغۡتَسِلُواْۚ وَإِن كُنتُم مَّرۡضَىٰٓ أَوۡ عَلَىٰ سَفَرٍ أَوۡ جَآءَ
أَحَدٞ مِّنكُم مِّنَ ٱلۡغَآئِطِ أَوۡ لَٰمَسۡتُمُ ٱلنِّسَآءَ فَلَمۡ تَجِدُواْ مَآءٗ
فَتَيَمَّمُواْ صَعِيدٗا طَيِّبٗا فَٱمۡسَحُواْ بِوُجُوهِكُمۡ وَأَيۡدِيكُمۡۗ إِنَّ
ٱللَّهَ كَانَ عَفُوًّا غَفُورًا ٤٣ أَلَمۡ تَرَ إِلَى ٱلَّذِينَ أُوتُواْ نَصِيبٗا مِّنَ
ٱلۡكِتَٰبِ يَشۡتَرُونَ ٱلضَّلَٰلَةَ وَيُرِيدُونَ أَن تَضِلُّواْ ٱلسَّبِيلَ ٤٤
وَٱللَّهُ أَعۡلَمُ بِأَعۡدَآئِكُمۡۚ وَكَفَىٰ بِٱللَّهِ وَلِيّٗا وَكَفَىٰ بِٱللَّهِ نَصِيرٗا ٤٥
مِّنَ ٱلَّذِينَ هَادُواْ يُحَرِّفُونَ ٱلۡكَلِمَ عَن مَّوَاضِعِهِۦ وَيَقُولُونَ
سَمِعۡنَا وَعَصَيۡنَا وَٱسۡمَعۡ غَيۡرَ مُسۡمَعٖ وَرَٰعِنَا لَيَّۢا بِأَلۡسِنَتِهِمۡ
وَطَعۡنٗا فِي ٱلدِّينِۚ وَلَوۡ أَنَّهُمۡ قَالُواْ سَمِعۡنَا وَأَطَعۡنَا وَٱسۡمَعۡ وَٱنظُرۡنَا

and seven hundred times ***and*** as well as that will ***pay out an immense reward directly from Him*** which no one can calculate.

41. ***How will it be when We bring a witness from every nation and bring you***, Muḥammad, ***as a witness against them?*** What will the state of the unbelievers be when We bring a Prophet from their community who will testify against them?

42. ***On that day*** when it arrives, ***those who disbelieved and disobeyed the Messenger will wish that they were one with the level earth.*** They will wish that they were dust like the earth because of the terrible terror, as we read in another *āyat*, *"And the unbeliever will say, "Oh, if only I were dust!"* (78:40). ***They will not be able to hide any occurrence from Allah.*** Then they will not be able to conceal anything they did even though they may have done so from others when they first did it.

43. ***O you who believe! Do not approach the prayer***, in other words do not pray, ***when you are drunk so that you know what you are saying*** (until you are sober) ... The reason this *āyat* was revealed was that some people would join the group prayer while drunk. ***...or in a state of major impurity*** due to sexual intercourse or ejaculation ***– unless you are travelling*** on a journey ***– until you have washed yourselves completely.*** Then you can pray. An exception is made for travellers because they have a different ruling, which will be mentioned. It is also said that what is meant is entering places of worship, such as mosques, in that state, except while travelling or passing through without staying. ***If you are ill*** in such a way that using water will be harmful to you ***or on a journey*** and you are in *janāba* or have broken *wuḍū'*, ***or any of you have come from the lavatory or touched*** (read as *lāmastum* and *lamastum*) ***women,*** and both words mean touching with the hand, as Ibn 'Umar said and ash-Shāfi'ī believes, and that extends to the rest of the skin. Ibn 'Abbās says that it means sexual intercourse, ***and you cannot find any water*** with which to purify yourself for the prayer after having looked for it and searched thoroughly (except in the case of the person who is ill), ***then do* tayammum *with pure earth*** when the time for prayer has arrived, ***wiping your faces and your hands*** to the elbows. ***Allah is Ever-Pardoning, Ever-Forgiving.***

لَكَانَ خَيْرًا لَّهُمْ وَأَقْوَمَ وَلَٰكِن لَّعَنَهُمُ ٱللَّهُ بِكُفْرِهِمْ فَلَا يُؤْمِنُونَ
إِلَّا قَلِيلًا ﴿٤٦﴾ يَٰٓأَيُّهَا ٱلَّذِينَ أُوتُوا۟ ٱلْكِتَٰبَ ءَامِنُوا۟ بِمَا نَزَّلْنَا
مُصَدِّقًا لِّمَا مَعَكُم مِّن قَبْلِ أَن نَّطْمِسَ وُجُوهًا فَنَرُدَّهَا
عَلَىٰٓ أَدْبَارِهَآ أَوْ نَلْعَنَهُمْ كَمَا لَعَنَّآ أَصْحَٰبَ ٱلسَّبْتِ ۚ وَكَانَ أَمْرُ
ٱللَّهِ مَفْعُولًا ﴿٤٧﴾ إِنَّ ٱللَّهَ لَا يَغْفِرُ أَن يُشْرَكَ بِهِۦ وَيَغْفِرُ مَا دُونَ
ذَٰلِكَ لِمَن يَشَآءُ ۚ وَمَن يُشْرِكْ بِٱللَّهِ فَقَدِ ٱفْتَرَىٰٓ إِثْمًا عَظِيمًا
﴿٤٨﴾ أَلَمْ تَرَ إِلَى ٱلَّذِينَ يُزَكُّونَ أَنفُسَهُم ۚ بَلِ ٱللَّهُ يُزَكِّى مَن يَشَآءُ
وَلَا يُظْلَمُونَ فَتِيلًا ﴿٤٩﴾ ٱنظُرْ كَيْفَ يَفْتَرُونَ عَلَى ٱللَّهِ ٱلْكَذِبَ ۖ
وَكَفَىٰ بِهِۦٓ إِثْمًا مُّبِينًا ﴿٥٠﴾ أَلَمْ تَرَ إِلَى ٱلَّذِينَ أُوتُوا۟ نَصِيبًا
مِّنَ ٱلْكِتَٰبِ يُؤْمِنُونَ بِٱلْجِبْتِ وَٱلطَّٰغُوتِ وَيَقُولُونَ
لِلَّذِينَ كَفَرُوا۟ هَٰٓؤُلَآءِ أَهْدَىٰ مِنَ ٱلَّذِينَ ءَامَنُوا۟ سَبِيلًا ﴿٥١﴾
أُو۟لَٰٓئِكَ ٱلَّذِينَ لَعَنَهُمُ ٱللَّهُ ۖ وَمَن يَلْعَنِ ٱللَّهُ فَلَن تَجِدَ لَهُۥ نَصِيرًا ﴿٥٢﴾
أَمْ لَهُمْ نَصِيبٌ مِّنَ ٱلْمُلْكِ فَإِذًا لَّا يُؤْتُونَ ٱلنَّاسَ نَقِيرًا ﴿٥٣﴾ أَمْ
يَحْسُدُونَ ٱلنَّاسَ عَلَىٰ مَآ ءَاتَىٰهُمُ ٱللَّهُ مِن فَضْلِهِۦ ۖ فَقَدْ ءَاتَيْنَآ
ءَالَ إِبْرَٰهِيمَ ٱلْكِتَٰبَ وَٱلْحِكْمَةَ وَءَاتَيْنَٰهُم مُّلْكًا عَظِيمًا ﴿٥٤﴾
فَمِنْهُم مَّنْ ءَامَنَ بِهِۦ وَمِنْهُم مَّن صَدَّ عَنْهُ ۚ وَكَفَىٰ بِجَهَنَّمَ سَعِيرًا
﴿٥٥﴾ إِنَّ ٱلَّذِينَ كَفَرُوا۟ بِـَٔايَٰتِنَا سَوْفَ نُصْلِيهِمْ نَارًا كُلَّمَا نَضِجَتْ
جُلُودُهُم بَدَّلْنَٰهُمْ جُلُودًا غَيْرَهَا لِيَذُوقُوا۟ ٱلْعَذَابَ ۗ إِنَّ ٱللَّهَ
كَانَ عَزِيزًا حَكِيمًا ﴿٥٦﴾ وَٱلَّذِينَ ءَامَنُوا۟ وَعَمِلُوا۟ ٱلصَّٰلِحَٰتِ
سَنُدْخِلُهُمْ جَنَّٰتٍ تَجْرِى مِن تَحْتِهَا ٱلْأَنْهَٰرُ خَٰلِدِينَ فِيهَآ أَبَدًا ۖ

44. ***Do you not see those who were given a portion of the Book*** (the Jews) ***trading in misguidance*** (exchanging guidance for it) ***and wanting you to be misguided from the way*** so that you would be like them***?***

45. ***Allah knows best who your enemies are.*** He informs you of them so that you can avoid them. ***Allah is enough*** for you ***as Protector*** against them. ***Allah is enough as Helper*** to defend you against their devices.

46. ***Some of the Jews distort*** and change ***the true meaning of words*** which Allah revealed in the Torah about the description of the Prophet, may Allah bless him and grant him peace, ***saying*** to the Prophet, may Allah bless him and grant him peace, when he commands them to do something, ***"We hear*** what you say ***and disobey*** your order," ***and "Listen without listening,"*** in other words "I have not heard," ***and*** they say to him, "**Rā'inā!**" an expression which they were forbidden to use to address him since it was a curse in their language, ***twisting them with their tongues, disparaging*** and attacking ***the* dīn** of Islam. ***If they had said, "We hear and we obey,"*** instead of "disobey" ***and*** only ***"Listen," and, "*Undhurna!*"** instead of *"Rā'inā!"*, ***that would have been better for them*** than what they said ***and more upright*** and just. ***But Allah has cursed them*** and put them far from His mercy ***for their unbelief. Very few of them,*** such as 'Abdullah ibn Salām and his companions, ***are believers.***

47. ***You who have been given the Book! Believe in what We have sent down*** (the Qur'an) ***confirming what is with you*** (the Torah), ***before We obliterate faces,*** eyes, nose and eyebrows, ***turning them inside out*** and make the face like a blank sheet, ***or We curse you*** by transforming you into monkeys ***as We cursed the Companions of the Sabbath*** by so transforming them. ***Allah's command is always carried out.*** When this was revealed 'Abdullah ibn Salām became Muslim. It is said that it is a conditional threat and that when some of them became Muslim that threat was removed. It is said that the obliteration and transmogrification it refers to will take place at the end of time.

48. ***Allah does not forgive partners being attributed to Him; but He forgives whomever He wills*** to be be forgiven ***for anything*** (wrong actions) ***apart from that***, so that he enters the Garden without punishment, and He will punish any of the believers He wishes for their sins and then admit them to the Garden after that. ***Anyone who attributes partners to Allah has committed a terrible crime.***

49. ***Do you not see those who claim to be purified?*** This refers to the Jews who say, *"We are the sons of Allah and His loved ones."* (5:18), signifying that they do not need to be purified. ***No, Allah purifies whomever He wills*** through true belief. ***They will not be wronged by so much as the smallest mote.*** They will not be wronged in any way at all.

50. ***Look*** in amazement at ***how they invent lies against Allah*** by doing that. ***That is enough as an outright*** and clear ***felony.***

51. This was revealed about Ka'b ibn al-Ashraf and other Jewish scholars when they went to Makka and were made aware of those killed at Badr, and they encouraged the idolaters to take revenge and fight the Prophet, may Allah bless him and grant him peace. ***Do you not see those who were given a portion of the Book believing in idols and false gods***, the idols of Quraysh, ***and saying of those who disbelieve,*** referring to Abū Sufyān and his people when they said to them, "Who is more guided: us, when we are the guardians of the House and give water to pilgrims, hospitality to guests and ransom captives, or Muḥammad, who opposes the *dīn* of his fathers and cuts himself off from his own kin?" ***"These people*** (you) ***are better guided*** and straighter ***on their path than the believers?"***

52. ***Those are the ones Allah has cursed. And if someone is cursed by Allah you will not find any helper for him*** against the punishment of Allah when it comes.

53. ***Or do they indeed really own a portion of the Kingdom?*** They possess none of the kingdom at all. ***In that case they do not give so much as a scrap to other people*** because of their extreme miserliness*!* "A scrap" (*naqīr*) is something insignificant. The word means the spot on the back of a date-stone and is used to designate the smallest of things.

54. ***Or do they in fact envy other people*** (the Prophet, may Allah bless him and grant him peace) ***for the bounty Allah has granted them?*** This means Prophethood and having many wives, meaning that they wanted to remove Prophethood from him and say, "If he was really a Prophet, he would not be occupied with women." ***We gave the family of Ibrāhīm***, such as Mūsā, Dāwūd and Sulaymān, ***the Book and Wisdom*** and Prophethood, ***and We gave them an immense kingdom.*** Dāwūd had ninety-nine wives and Sulaymān had a hundred.

55. ***Some of them believe in him*** (Muḥammad, may Allah bless him and grant him peace) ***and some bar access to him,*** turning away and refusing to believe in him. ***Hell will be enough as a Searing Blaze,*** the punishment for those who do not believe.

56. ***As for those who reject Our Signs, We will roast them in a Fire*** and put them into it, where they will burn. ***Every time their skins are burned off, We will replace them with new skins,*** making them revert to their unburned state, ***so that they can taste the punishment*** and so that it will be even severer for them. ***Allah is Almighty*** and has the power to do anything, ***All-Wise*** in His creation.

57. ***But as for those who believe and do right actions, We will admit them into Gardens with rivers flowing under them, remaining in them timelessly, forever without end. In them they will have spouses of perfect purity,*** purified of menstruation and every other kind of impurity, ***and We will admit them into cool, refreshing shade.*** The shade of the Garden is constant and not changed by the sun; it lasts forever.

58. ***Allah commands you to return to their owners the things you hold on trust,*** the rights which one has been entrusted with. This *āyat* was revealed when 'Alī seized the key of the Ka'ba from 'Uthmān ibn Ṭalḥa, its keeper, when the Prophet, may Allah bless him and grant him peace, conquered Makka at the Conquest and he refused to give it to him. 'Uthmān said, "If I had recognised him as the Messenger of Allah, I would not have refused to give it to him." The Messenger of Allah, may Allah bless him and grant him peace, ordered 'Alī to return it to him and said, "That prerogative is yours forever." 'Uthmān liked that and then the Prophet recited this *āyat* to him and he became Muslim. When he died, he gave the key to his brother Shayba and it remained with his descendants. Although there was a particular reason for the revelation of this *āyat*, its meaning is made general by the use of the plural. ***And, when you judge***

لَهُمْ فِيهَآ أَزْوَٰجٌ مُّطَهَّرَةٌ ۖ وَنُدْخِلُهُمْ ظِلًّا ظَلِيلًا ﴿٥٧﴾ ۞ إِنَّ
ٱللَّهَ يَأْمُرُكُمْ أَن تُؤَدُّوا۟ ٱلْأَمَٰنَٰتِ إِلَىٰٓ أَهْلِهَا وَإِذَا حَكَمْتُم بَيْنَ
ٱلنَّاسِ أَن تَحْكُمُوا۟ بِٱلْعَدْلِ ۚ إِنَّ ٱللَّهَ نِعِمَّا يَعِظُكُم بِهِۦٓ ۗ إِنَّ ٱللَّهَ كَانَ سَمِيعًۢا
بَصِيرًا ﴿٥٨﴾ يَٰٓأَيُّهَا ٱلَّذِينَ ءَامَنُوٓا۟ أَطِيعُوا۟ ٱللَّهَ وَأَطِيعُوا۟ ٱلرَّسُولَ وَأُو۟لِى
ٱلْأَمْرِ مِنكُمْ ۖ فَإِن تَنَٰزَعْتُمْ فِى شَىْءٍ فَرُدُّوهُ إِلَى ٱللَّهِ وَٱلرَّسُولِ إِن كُنتُمْ
تُؤْمِنُونَ بِٱللَّهِ وَٱلْيَوْمِ ٱلْءَاخِرِ ۚ ذَٰلِكَ خَيْرٌ وَأَحْسَنُ تَأْوِيلًا ﴿٥٩﴾
أَلَمْ تَرَ إِلَى ٱلَّذِينَ يَزْعُمُونَ أَنَّهُمْ ءَامَنُوا۟ بِمَآ أُنزِلَ إِلَيْكَ
وَمَآ أُنزِلَ مِن قَبْلِكَ يُرِيدُونَ أَن يَتَحَاكَمُوٓا۟ إِلَى ٱلطَّٰغُوتِ
وَقَدْ أُمِرُوٓا۟ أَن يَكْفُرُوا۟ بِهِۦ وَيُرِيدُ ٱلشَّيْطَٰنُ أَن يُضِلَّهُمْ
ضَلَٰلًۢا بَعِيدًا ﴿٦٠﴾ وَإِذَا قِيلَ لَهُمْ تَعَالَوْا۟ إِلَىٰ مَآ أَنزَلَ
ٱللَّهُ وَإِلَى ٱلرَّسُولِ رَأَيْتَ ٱلْمُنَٰفِقِينَ يَصُدُّونَ عَنكَ
صُدُودًا ﴿٦١﴾ فَكَيْفَ إِذَآ أَصَٰبَتْهُم مُّصِيبَةٌۢ بِمَا
قَدَّمَتْ أَيْدِيهِمْ ثُمَّ جَآءُوكَ يَحْلِفُونَ بِٱللَّهِ إِنْ أَرَدْنَآ إِلَّآ
إِحْسَٰنًا وَتَوْفِيقًا ﴿٦٢﴾ أُو۟لَٰٓئِكَ ٱلَّذِينَ يَعْلَمُ ٱللَّهُ مَا
فِى قُلُوبِهِمْ فَأَعْرِضْ عَنْهُمْ وَعِظْهُمْ وَقُل لَّهُمْ فِىٓ
أَنفُسِهِمْ قَوْلًۢا بَلِيغًا ﴿٦٣﴾ وَمَآ أَرْسَلْنَا مِن رَّسُولٍ إِلَّا
لِيُطَاعَ بِإِذْنِ ٱللَّهِ ۚ وَلَوْ أَنَّهُمْ إِذ ظَّلَمُوٓا۟ أَنفُسَهُمْ
جَآءُوكَ فَٱسْتَغْفَرُوا۟ ٱللَّهَ وَٱسْتَغْفَرَ لَهُمُ ٱلرَّسُولُ
لَوَجَدُوا۟ ٱللَّهَ تَوَّابًا رَّحِيمًا ﴿٦٤﴾ فَلَا وَرَبِّكَ لَا يُؤْمِنُونَ
حَتَّىٰ يُحَكِّمُوكَ فِيمَا شَجَرَ بَيْنَهُمْ ثُمَّ لَا يَجِدُوا۟

between people, to judge with justice. He commands you to judge. ***How excellent is what Allah exhorts you to do!*** Allah's command regarding handing over trusts and judging with justice is excellent. ***Allah is All-Hearing*** of what is said, ***All-Seeing*** of what is done.

59. ***You who believe! Obey Allah and obey the Messenger and those in command among you*** (rulers when they command you to obey Allah and His Messenger). ***If you have a dispute*** and disagree ***about something, refer it back to*** the Book of ***Allah and the Messenger*** himself, while he was alive, and then to his *Sunna,* in order to search out the right answer, ***if you believe in Allah and the Last Day. That*** (referring to the Book and *Sunna*) ***is the best thing to do and has the best result.*** That is better than dispute and speaking from mere opinion.

60. This *āyat* was revealed when a Jew and hypocrite quarrelled and the hypocrite called for Ka'b ibn al-Ashraf to judge between them and the Jew called on the Prophet. They came to him and he judged for the Jew, but the hypocrite was not satisfied. They went to 'Umar with the same question and the Jew mentioned the Prophet's judgement to him. He asked the hypocrite, "Is that true?" "Yes," he replied, and so 'Umar killed him. ***Do you not see those who claim that they believe in what has been sent down to you and what was sent down before you, still desiring to turn to a satanic source for judgement***, with great transgression, namely to Ka'b ibn al-Ashraf, ***in spite of being ordered to reject it*** and not to follow it? ***Shaytan wants to misguide them far away*** from the truth.

61 ***When they are told, "Come to what Allah has sent down***, of the judgement of the Qur'an, ***and to the Messenger*** to judge between you," ***you see the hypocrites turning away from you completely*** and turning to others.

62. ***How will it be*** and what will they do ***when a disaster*** and punishment ***strikes them because of what they have done*** by way of disbelief and disobedience: will they then be able to turn away and flee from it? No. They turn away ***and then they come to you swearing by Allah,*** "By taking judgement to someone else, ***we desired nothing but good and reconciliation*** between two opponents by making the judgement easy rather than burdensome."

فِىٓ أَنفُسِهِمْ حَرَجًا مِّمَّا قَضَيْتَ وَيُسَلِّمُوا۟ تَسْلِيمًا ﴿٦٥﴾
وَلَوْ أَنَّا كَتَبْنَا عَلَيْهِمْ أَنِ ٱقْتُلُوٓا۟ أَنفُسَكُمْ أَوِ ٱخْرُجُوا۟ مِن
دِيَٰرِكُم مَّا فَعَلُوهُ إِلَّا قَلِيلٌ مِّنْهُمْ ۖ وَلَوْ أَنَّهُمْ فَعَلُوا۟ مَا يُوعَظُونَ
بِهِۦ لَكَانَ خَيْرًا لَّهُمْ وَأَشَدَّ تَثْبِيتًا ﴿٦٦﴾ وَإِذًا لَّءَاتَيْنَٰهُم مِّن
لَّدُنَّآ أَجْرًا عَظِيمًا ﴿٦٧﴾ وَلَهَدَيْنَٰهُمْ صِرَٰطًا مُّسْتَقِيمًا ﴿٦٨﴾
وَمَن يُطِعِ ٱللَّهَ وَٱلرَّسُولَ فَأُو۟لَٰٓئِكَ مَعَ ٱلَّذِينَ أَنْعَمَ ٱللَّهُ عَلَيْهِم
مِّنَ ٱلنَّبِيِّـۧنَ وَٱلصِّدِّيقِينَ وَٱلشُّهَدَآءِ وَٱلصَّٰلِحِينَ ۚ وَحَسُنَ
أُو۟لَٰٓئِكَ رَفِيقًا ﴿٦٩﴾ ذَٰلِكَ ٱلْفَضْلُ مِنَ ٱللَّهِ ۚ وَكَفَىٰ
بِٱللَّهِ عَلِيمًا ﴿٧٠﴾ يَٰٓأَيُّهَا ٱلَّذِينَ ءَامَنُوا۟ خُذُوا۟ حِذْرَكُمْ
فَٱنفِرُوا۟ ثُبَاتٍ أَوِ ٱنفِرُوا۟ جَمِيعًا ﴿٧١﴾ وَإِنَّ مِنكُمْ لَمَن لَّيُبَطِّئَنَّ
فَإِنْ أَصَٰبَتْكُم مُّصِيبَةٌ قَالَ قَدْ أَنْعَمَ ٱللَّهُ عَلَىَّ إِذْ لَمْ أَكُن مَّعَهُمْ
شَهِيدًا ﴿٧٢﴾ وَلَئِنْ أَصَٰبَكُمْ فَضْلٌ مِّنَ ٱللَّهِ لَيَقُولَنَّ كَأَن
لَّمْ تَكُنۢ بَيْنَكُمْ وَبَيْنَهُۥ مَوَدَّةٌ يَٰلَيْتَنِى كُنتُ مَعَهُمْ فَأَفُوزَ
فَوْزًا عَظِيمًا ﴿٧٣﴾ ۞ فَلْيُقَٰتِلْ فِى سَبِيلِ ٱللَّهِ ٱلَّذِينَ
يَشْرُونَ ٱلْحَيَوٰةَ ٱلدُّنْيَا بِٱلْءَاخِرَةِ ۚ وَمَن يُقَٰتِلْ فِى
سَبِيلِ ٱللَّهِ فَيُقْتَلْ أَوْ يَغْلِبْ فَسَوْفَ نُؤْتِيهِ أَجْرًا عَظِيمًا ﴿٧٤﴾
وَمَا لَكُمْ لَا تُقَٰتِلُونَ فِى سَبِيلِ ٱللَّهِ وَٱلْمُسْتَضْعَفِينَ مِنَ ٱلرِّجَالِ
وَٱلنِّسَآءِ وَٱلْوِلْدَٰنِ ٱلَّذِينَ يَقُولُونَ رَبَّنَآ أَخْرِجْنَا مِنْ هَٰذِهِ ٱلْقَرْيَةِ
ٱلظَّالِمِ أَهْلُهَا وَٱجْعَل لَّنَا مِن لَّدُنكَ وَلِيًّا وَٱجْعَل لَّنَا مِن لَّدُنكَ
نَصِيرًا ﴿٧٥﴾ ٱلَّذِينَ ءَامَنُوا۟ يُقَٰتِلُونَ فِى سَبِيلِ ٱللَّهِ ۖ وَٱلَّذِينَ كَفَرُوا۟

63. ***Allah knows what is in such people's hearts*** of hypocrisy and lies in their excuses, ***so turn away from them*** and overlook ***and warn them*** and make them fear Allah, ***and speak to them with words that have an effect*** on them so as to make them revert from their unbelief.

64. ***We sent no Messenger except to be obeyed*** in his commands and decrees ***by Allah's permission*** and His command. So he should not be disobeyed or opposed. ***If only when they wronged themselves*** by going to a satanic source for judgement (see 4:60 above), ***they had come to you*** in repentance ***and asked Allah's forgiveness and the Messenger had asked forgiveness for them, they would have found Allah Ever-returning*** to them, ***Most Merciful*** towards them.

65. ***No, by your Lord, they are not believers until they make you their judge in the disputes that break out between them, and then find no resistance***, nor any doubt or constriction, ***within themselves to what you decide but submit themselves completely*** and will obey your judgements without objection.

66. ***If We had prescribed for them to kill themselves or leave their homes,*** as We had prescribed for the tribe of Israel, ***they would not have done so*** (what was prescribed for them) ***except for a very few. But if they had done what they were urged to do*** (obey the Messenger), ***it would have been better for them and far more strengthening*** for their faith.

67. ***In that case*** (if they had been firm), ***We would have paid them an immense reward from Us*** (the Garden).

68. ***And We would have guided them on a straight path.*** Some of the Companions asked the Prophet, may Allah bless him and grant him peace, "How will we see you in the Garden when you are in the high degrees and we are in the lower?" Then the following *āyat* was revealed.

69. ***Whoever obeys Allah and the Messenger*** in what he commands ***will be with those whom Allah has blessed: the Prophets, the men of truth,*** who are the best Companions of the Prophets because of their great truthfulness and sincerity, ***the martyrs*** killed in the Way of Allah, ***and the righteous*** not in the above categories. ***What excellent company such people are!*** They are companions in the Garden because in it they will enjoy seeing them and visiting them and being together with them. They abide in higher degrees than those who visit them there.

70. ***That*** (being with those companions) ***is favour from Allah*** bestowed on them because of their obedience to Him. ***Allah is enough as a Knower*** of the reward of the Next World, so trust in what He tells you about it. None can inform as well as someone who is fully aware.

71. ***You who believe! Take all necessary precautions*** against the enemy, meaning beware of them and be always on the alert regarding them, ***then go out to fight in separate groups*** one after another ***or go out*** together ***as one body.***

72. ***Among you are people who hang back*** from fighting, such as 'Abdullāh ibn Ubayy the Hypocrite and his companions, ***and if you encounter a setback*** such as loss of life or defeat, ***they then say, "Allah has blessed me in that I was not there with them*** and was not wounded."

73. ***But if you encounter favour from Allah*** such as a victory or booty, ***they say*** in regret, ***as if there were*** (read as *takun* and *yakun*) ***no friendship***, recognition and friendship, ***between you and them,*** referring back to "Allah has blessed me…" This is an interjection. ***"Oh! If only I had been with them so that I too might have won a great victory*** and received a large share of booty."

74. ***So let those who sell the life of this world for the Next World fight in the Way of Allah*** to make the *dīn* of Allah victorious. ***If someone fights in the Way of Allah, whether he is killed*** and martyred ***or is victorious*** over the enemy, ***We will pay him an immense reward.***

75. This is an example of a question which is reality a rebuke, meaning there is nothing that could justifiably keep you from fighting. ***What reason could you have for not fighting in the Way of Allah, and for*** the sake of delivering ***those men, women and children who are oppressed*** and are kept by the unbelievers from emigrating and Ibn 'Abbās said, "I and my mother were among them," ***and say*** in supplication, ***"Our Lord, remove us from this city*** (Makka) ***whose inhabitants are wrongdoers*** by their disbelief! ***Give us a protector***

يُقَٰتِلُونَ فِي سَبِيلِ ٱلطَّٰغُوتِ فَقَٰتِلُوٓاْ أَوۡلِيَآءَ ٱلشَّيۡطَٰنِۖ إِنَّ كَيۡدَ
ٱلشَّيۡطَٰنِ كَانَ ضَعِيفًا ٧٦ أَلَمۡ تَرَ إِلَى ٱلَّذِينَ قِيلَ لَهُمۡ كُفُّوٓاْ أَيۡدِيَكُمۡ
وَأَقِيمُواْ ٱلصَّلَوٰةَ وَءَاتُواْ ٱلزَّكَوٰةَ فَلَمَّا كُتِبَ عَلَيۡهِمُ ٱلۡقِتَالُ إِذَا فَرِيقٞ
مِّنۡهُمۡ يَخۡشَوۡنَ ٱلنَّاسَ كَخَشۡيَةِ ٱللَّهِ أَوۡ أَشَدَّ خَشۡيَةٗۚ وَقَالُواْ رَبَّنَا لِمَ
كَتَبۡتَ عَلَيۡنَا ٱلۡقِتَالَ لَوۡلَآ أَخَّرۡتَنَآ إِلَىٰٓ أَجَلٖ قَرِيبٖۗ قُلۡ مَتَٰعُ ٱلدُّنۡيَا
قَلِيلٞ وَٱلۡأٓخِرَةُ خَيۡرٞ لِّمَنِ ٱتَّقَىٰ وَلَا تُظۡلَمُونَ فَتِيلًا ٧٧ أَيۡنَمَا
تَكُونُواْ يُدۡرِككُّمُ ٱلۡمَوۡتُ وَلَوۡ كُنتُمۡ فِي بُرُوجٖ مُّشَيَّدَةٖۗ وَإِن تُصِبۡهُمۡ
حَسَنَةٞ يَقُولُواْ هَٰذِهِۦ مِنۡ عِندِ ٱللَّهِۖ وَإِن تُصِبۡهُمۡ سَيِّئَةٞ يَقُولُواْ
هَٰذِهِۦ مِنۡ عِندِكَۚ قُلۡ كُلّٞ مِّنۡ عِندِ ٱللَّهِۖ فَمَالِ هَٰٓؤُلَآءِ ٱلۡقَوۡمِ لَا يَكَادُونَ
يَفۡقَهُونَ حَدِيثٗا ٧٨ مَّآ أَصَابَكَ مِنۡ حَسَنَةٖ فَمِنَ ٱللَّهِۖ وَمَآ أَصَابَكَ مِن
سَيِّئَةٖ فَمِن نَّفۡسِكَۚ وَأَرۡسَلۡنَٰكَ لِلنَّاسِ رَسُولٗاۚ وَكَفَىٰ بِٱللَّهِ شَهِيدٗا ٧٩
مَّن يُطِعِ ٱلرَّسُولَ فَقَدۡ أَطَاعَ ٱللَّهَۖ وَمَن تَوَلَّىٰ فَمَآ أَرۡسَلۡنَٰكَ
عَلَيۡهِمۡ حَفِيظٗا ٨٠ وَيَقُولُونَ طَاعَةٞ فَإِذَا بَرَزُواْ مِنۡ
عِندِكَ بَيَّتَ طَآئِفَةٞ مِّنۡهُمۡ غَيۡرَ ٱلَّذِي تَقُولُۖ وَٱللَّهُ يَكۡتُبُ
مَا يُبَيِّتُونَۖ فَأَعۡرِضۡ عَنۡهُمۡ وَتَوَكَّلۡ عَلَى ٱللَّهِۚ وَكَفَىٰ بِٱللَّهِ وَكِيلًا
٨١ أَفَلَا يَتَدَبَّرُونَ ٱلۡقُرۡءَانَۚ وَلَوۡ كَانَ مِنۡ عِندِ غَيۡرِ ٱللَّهِ لَوَجَدُواْ
فِيهِ ٱخۡتِلَٰفٗا كَثِيرٗا ٨٢ وَإِذَا جَآءَهُمۡ أَمۡرٞ مِّنَ ٱلۡأَمۡنِ
أَوِ ٱلۡخَوۡفِ أَذَاعُواْ بِهِۦۖ وَلَوۡ رَدُّوهُ إِلَى ٱلرَّسُولِ وَإِلَىٰٓ أُوْلِي
ٱلۡأَمۡرِ مِنۡهُمۡ لَعَلِمَهُ ٱلَّذِينَ يَسۡتَنۢبِطُونَهُۥ مِنۡهُمۡۗ وَلَوۡلَا فَضۡلُ
ٱللَّهِ عَلَيۡكُمۡ وَرَحۡمَتُهُۥ لَٱتَّبَعۡتُمُ ٱلشَّيۡطَٰنَ إِلَّا قَلِيلٗا ٨٣

from You to take care of us***! Give us a helper from You*** to defend us against our oppressors***!"*** Allah answered their supplication and made it easy for some of them to leave; the rest remained until Makka was conquered. The Prophet, may Allah bless him and grant him peace, appointed 'Attāb ibn Usayb to redress the injustices they had suffered.

76. ***Those who believe fight in the Way of Allah. Those who disbelieve fight in the way of false gods*** (Shayṭan)**.** ***So fight the friends of Shaytan*** and be helpers of Allah's *dīn* so that you can overcome them, since your strength is by Allah**.** ***Shaytan's scheming*** against the believers ***is always feeble,*** weak in the face of Allah's scheming against the unbelievers.

77. ***Do you not see those who were told: "Hold back from fighting*** the disbelievers," when a group of Companions asked the Prophet in Makka to give them permission to injure the disbelievers which was not granted, ***"but establish the prayer and pay*** **zakāt*"? Then when fighting is prescribed for them, a group of them fear people***'s punishment (that the unbelievers would kill them) ***as*** the punishment of ***Allah should be feared, or even more than that. They say*** in fear of death, ***"Our Lord, why have you prescribed fighting for us? If only You would give us just a little more time!" Say*** to them, ***"The enjoyment of this world*** (referring to things enjoyed in it or to the enjoyment itself) ***is very brief*** and soon vanishes**.** ***The Next World,*** meaning the Garden, ***is better for those who are godfearing*** and fear the punishment of Allah, abandoning disobedience**.** ***You will not be wronged*** (read as *tuẓlamūna,* "You will not be wronged" and *yuẓlamūna*, "they will not be wronged) ***by so much as the smallest mote."*** The reward for your actions will not be decreased in the least, so strive your hardest.

78. ***Wherever you are, death will catch up with you, even if you are in impregnable fortresses.*** So do not fear fighting for fear that you might be killed. ***If a good thing happens to them*** (the Jews), such as a good harvest and wealth, ***they say, "This has come from Allah." If a bad thing happens to them,*** such as drought and poverty, which happened when the Prophet, may Allah bless him and grant him peace, came to Madina, ***they say, "This has come from you***, Muḥammad, because you bring bad luck.***" Say*** to them,

"Everything, both good and bad, ***comes from Allah." What is the matter with these people that they scarcely understand a single word?*** Why do these people almost not understand anything said to them? This question demonstrates astonishment at their excessive ignorance.

79. ***Any good thing that happens to you***, O human being, ***comes from Allah*** as a favour to you. ***Any bad thing***, any affliction, ***that happens to you comes from yourself*** because of your wrong actions which have brought it on you. ***We have sent you***, Muḥammad, ***to mankind as a Messenger. Allah is enough as a Witness*** to your Message.

80. ***Whoever obeys the Messenger has obeyed Allah. If anyone turns away*** from obeying you, do not be concerned with him, ***We did not send you to them as their keeper*** over their actions. You are a warner, what happens to them is up to Us, and We will repay them. This applied before the command came to fight.

81. When Allah's command comes to them, ***they*** (the hypocrites) ***have the words "Obedience*** to you!" ***on their tongues, but when they leave your presence, a group of them spend the night plotting to do something other than what you say.*** [Or it could mean, what they (the group) say in your presence.] ***Allah is recording*** (commanding that it be recorded) ***their nocturnal plotting*** in their pages so that they can be repaid. ***So let them be*** and excuse them ***and put your trust in Allah. Allah is enough as a Guardian*** so entrust your affairs to Him.

82. ***Will they not reflect on the Qur'an*** and consider the wondrous meanings it contains? ***If it had been from someone other than Allah, they would have found many inconsistencies in it*** regarding its meanings and multi-faceted order.

83. ***When news of any matter*** about the expeditions of the Prophet, may Allah bless him and grant him peace, ***reaches them they spread it about*** and make it known, ***whether it is of a reassuring*** (a victory) ***or disquieting nature*** (a defeat). This was revealed about a group of hypocrites or weak believers who used to blurt things out when they heard them, to weaken the hearts of the believers and injure the Prophet. ***If they had only referred it*** (the news) ***to the Messenger and those in command among them,*** those with influence among

فَقَٰتِلۡ فِي سَبِيلِ ٱللَّهِ لَا تُكَلَّفُ إِلَّا نَفۡسَكَۚ وَحَرِّضِ ٱلۡمُؤۡمِنِينَۖ
عَسَى ٱللَّهُ أَن يَكُفَّ بَأۡسَ ٱلَّذِينَ كَفَرُواْۚ وَٱللَّهُ أَشَدُّ بَأۡسٗا
وَأَشَدُّ تَنكِيلٗا ٨٤ مَّن يَشۡفَعۡ شَفَٰعَةً حَسَنَةٗ يَكُن لَّهُۥ
نَصِيبٞ مِّنۡهَاۖ وَمَن يَشۡفَعۡ شَفَٰعَةٗ سَيِّئَةٗ يَكُن لَّهُۥ كِفۡلٞ مِّنۡهَاۗ
وَكَانَ ٱللَّهُ عَلَىٰ كُلِّ شَيۡءٖ مُّقِيتٗا ٨٥ وَإِذَا حُيِّيتُم بِتَحِيَّةٖ فَحَيُّواْ
بِأَحۡسَنَ مِنۡهَآ أَوۡ رُدُّوهَآۗ إِنَّ ٱللَّهَ كَانَ عَلَىٰ كُلِّ شَيۡءٍ حَسِيبًا ٨٦
ٱللَّهُ لَآ إِلَٰهَ إِلَّا هُوَۚ لَيَجۡمَعَنَّكُمۡ إِلَىٰ يَوۡمِ ٱلۡقِيَٰمَةِ لَا رَيۡبَ فِيهِۗ
وَمَنۡ أَصۡدَقُ مِنَ ٱللَّهِ حَدِيثٗا ٨٧ ۞ فَمَا لَكُمۡ فِي ٱلۡمُنَٰفِقِينَ
فِئَتَيۡنِ وَٱللَّهُ أَرۡكَسَهُم بِمَا كَسَبُوٓاْۚ أَتُرِيدُونَ أَن تَهۡدُواْ مَنۡ
أَضَلَّ ٱللَّهُۖ وَمَن يُضۡلِلِ ٱللَّهُ فَلَن تَجِدَ لَهُۥ سَبِيلٗا ٨٨ وَدُّواْ لَوۡ
تَكۡفُرُونَ كَمَا كَفَرُواْ فَتَكُونُونَ سَوَآءٗۖ فَلَا تَتَّخِذُواْ مِنۡهُمۡ أَوۡلِيَآءَ
حَتَّىٰ يُهَاجِرُواْ فِي سَبِيلِ ٱللَّهِۚ فَإِن تَوَلَّوۡاْ فَخُذُوهُمۡ وَٱقۡتُلُوهُمۡ
حَيۡثُ وَجَدتُّمُوهُمۡۖ وَلَا تَتَّخِذُواْ مِنۡهُمۡ وَلِيّٗا وَلَا نَصِيرًا ٨٩
إِلَّا ٱلَّذِينَ يَصِلُونَ إِلَىٰ قَوۡمِۭ بَيۡنَكُمۡ وَبَيۡنَهُم مِّيثَٰقٌ أَوۡ جَآءُوكُمۡ
حَصِرَتۡ صُدُورُهُمۡ أَن يُقَٰتِلُوكُمۡ أَوۡ يُقَٰتِلُواْ قَوۡمَهُمۡۚ وَلَوۡ شَآءَ
ٱللَّهُ لَسَلَّطَهُمۡ عَلَيۡكُمۡ فَلَقَٰتَلُوكُمۡۚ فَإِنِ ٱعۡتَزَلُوكُمۡ فَلَمۡ يُقَٰتِلُوكُمۡ
وَأَلۡقَوۡاْ إِلَيۡكُمُ ٱلسَّلَمَ فَمَا جَعَلَ ٱللَّهُ لَكُمۡ عَلَيۡهِمۡ سَبِيلٗا ٩٠
سَتَجِدُونَ ءَاخَرِينَ يُرِيدُونَ أَن يَأۡمَنُوكُمۡ وَيَأۡمَنُواْ قَوۡمَهُمۡ كُلَّ
مَا رُدُّوٓاْ إِلَى ٱلۡفِتۡنَةِ أُرۡكِسُواْ فِيهَاۚ فَإِن لَّمۡ يَعۡتَزِلُوكُمۡ وَيُلۡقُوٓاْ إِلَيۡكُمُ
ٱلسَّلَمَ وَيَكُفُّوٓاْ أَيۡدِيَهُمۡ فَخُذُوهُمۡ وَٱقۡتُلُوهُمۡ حَيۡثُ

the great Companions, remaining silent until they had been told about it, ***those among them able to discern the truth about it,*** meaning the Messenger and those in command, ***would have had proper knowledge of it. If it were not for Allah's favour to you*** through Islam ***and His mercy*** through the Qur'an***, all but a very few of you would have followed Shaytan*** in the foul actions he commands.

84. ***So fight,*** Muḥammad, ***in the way of Allah. You are only answerable for yourself.*** Do not be concerned if they stay behind you. The meaning is: "Fight, even if you have to do it on your own. You are promised victory." ***And spur on the believers to fight*** and encourage them to do it. ***It may well be that Allah will curb the force*** (warring) against you ***of those who disbelieve. Allah has greater force*** than them ***and greater power to punish*** them. The Messenger of Allah, may Allah bless him and grant him peace, said, "By the One who has my life in His hand, I will go out, even alone." So seventy riders went to Lesser Badr and Allah lessened the danger from the unbelievers by casting fear into their hearts so that Abū Sufyān refused to go out, as was mentioned in *Sūrat Āl 'Imrān.*

85. ***Those*** people ***who join forces for the good*** which is in accordance with the Sharī'a ***will receive a reward for it. Those who join forces for the bad will be answerable for it*** and have a portion of the burden. ***Allah gives everything what it deserves***, and repays everyone for what they did.

86. ***When you are greeted with a greeting,*** as when someone says "Peace be upon you" to you, ***greet*** the one who greeted you ***with one better than it or return it***, by saying, "Peace be upon you and the mercy and blessings of Allah," or you can simply reply the same, but the more ample greeting is better. ***Allah takes account of everything*** and repays it; and that includes returning greetings. The *sunna* specifies that you should not return the greeting of an unbeliever, innovator, deviant, or someone who greets you while you are answering a call of nature; and those in the bath or eating are also absolved from replying. It is said that replying is disliked in other than the last case. One says to the unbeliever, "And on you."

87. ***Allah – there is no god but Him. He will gather you*** from your graves ***to the Day of Rising about which there is no doubt. And***

whose speech could be truer than Allah's? No one's speech is more truthful.

88. When the people returned from Uḥud, they differed about the hypocrites. Some said that they should be killed and others said no. Then this *āyat* was revealed. ***Why is it that you have become two parties regarding the hypocrites, when Allah has returned them to unbelief for what they did*** of unbelief and disobedience? ***Do you desire to guide people Allah has misguided,*** meaning to consider them among the guided? Both questions in this *āyat* imply a negative reply. ***When Allah misguides someone, you will not find a way*** to guidance ***for him.***

89. ***They would like*** and wish ***you to disbelieve as they have disbelieved so that you*** and them ***would all be the same*** in respect of unbelief. ***Do not take any of them as friends*** even if they display belief ***until they have emigrated in the Way of Allah*** with a genuine emigration which verifies their faith. ***But if they run away*** and stay as they are, ***then seize them*** as captives ***and kill them wherever you find them. Do not take any of them either as a friend or as a helper*** to help you against your enemy.

90. ***Except for those who seek shelter with people with whom you have a treaty*** which gives security to them and those who seek refuge with them; which is the kind of treaty the Prophet, may Allah bless him and grant him peace, made with Hilāl ibn 'Umaymir al-Aslamī, ***or who come to you with their breasts constricted at the thought of fighting either you*** with their people ***or their own people*** with you, and so they do not fight you. Do not turn towards them with the intention of capture or killing. The next part of the verse was abrogated by the *Āyat* of the Sword. ***If Allah had willed, He could have given them the upper hand over you*** by making their hearts strong ***and then they would have fought you,*** but He did not and instead cast fear into their hearts. ***If they keep away from you and do not fight you,*** offering a truce, ***and submit to you, Allah has not given you any way against such people*** to seize and kill them.

91. ***You will find others who desire to be safe from you*** by making a display of belief among you ***and safe from their own people*** by claiming to be unbelievers when they return to them. The people referred to here were Asad and Ghaṭafān. ***Each time they are***

ثَقِفْتُمُوهُمْ ۚ وَأُو۟لَٰٓئِكُمْ جَعَلْنَا لَكُمْ عَلَيْهِمْ سُلْطَٰنًا مُّبِينًا ﴿٩١﴾

وَمَا كَانَ لِمُؤْمِنٍ أَن يَقْتُلَ مُؤْمِنًا إِلَّا خَطَـًٔا ۚ وَمَن قَتَلَ

مُؤْمِنًا خَطَـًٔا فَتَحْرِيرُ رَقَبَةٍ مُّؤْمِنَةٍ وَدِيَةٌ مُّسَلَّمَةٌ إِلَىٰٓ

أَهْلِهِۦٓ إِلَّآ أَن يَصَّدَّقُوا۟ ۚ فَإِن كَانَ مِن قَوْمٍ عَدُوٍّ لَّكُمْ

وَهُوَ مُؤْمِنٌ فَتَحْرِيرُ رَقَبَةٍ مُّؤْمِنَةٍ ۖ وَإِن كَانَ

مِن قَوْمٍۭ بَيْنَكُمْ وَبَيْنَهُم مِّيثَٰقٌ فَدِيَةٌ مُّسَلَّمَةٌ

إِلَىٰٓ أَهْلِهِۦ وَتَحْرِيرُ رَقَبَةٍ مُّؤْمِنَةٍ ۖ فَمَن لَّمْ يَجِدْ

فَصِيَامُ شَهْرَيْنِ مُتَتَابِعَيْنِ تَوْبَةً مِّنَ ٱللَّهِ ۗ وَكَانَ

ٱللَّهُ عَلِيمًا حَكِيمًا ﴿٩٢﴾ وَمَن يَقْتُلْ مُؤْمِنًا

مُّتَعَمِّدًا فَجَزَآؤُهُۥ جَهَنَّمُ خَٰلِدًا فِيهَا وَغَضِبَ

ٱللَّهُ عَلَيْهِ وَلَعَنَهُۥ وَأَعَدَّ لَهُۥ عَذَابًا عَظِيمًا ﴿٩٣﴾ يَٰٓأَيُّهَا

ٱلَّذِينَ ءَامَنُوٓا۟ إِذَا ضَرَبْتُمْ فِى سَبِيلِ ٱللَّهِ فَتَبَيَّنُوا۟ وَلَا تَقُولُوا۟

لِمَنْ أَلْقَىٰٓ إِلَيْكُمُ ٱلسَّلَٰمَ لَسْتَ مُؤْمِنًا تَبْتَغُونَ

عَرَضَ ٱلْحَيَوٰةِ ٱلدُّنْيَا فَعِندَ ٱللَّهِ مَغَانِمُ كَثِيرَةٌ ۚ

كَذَٰلِكَ كُنتُم مِّن قَبْلُ فَمَنَّ ٱللَّهُ عَلَيْكُمْ

فَتَبَيَّنُوٓا۟ ۚ إِنَّ ٱللَّهَ كَانَ بِمَا تَعْمَلُونَ خَبِيرًا ﴿٩٤﴾

لَّا يَسْتَوِى ٱلْقَٰعِدُونَ مِنَ ٱلْمُؤْمِنِينَ غَيْرُ أُو۟لِى ٱلضَّرَرِ وَٱلْمُجَٰهِدُونَ

فِى سَبِيلِ ٱللَّهِ بِأَمْوَٰلِهِمْ وَأَنفُسِهِمْ ۚ فَضَّلَ ٱللَّهُ ٱلْمُجَٰهِدِينَ بِأَمْوَٰلِهِمْ

وَأَنفُسِهِمْ عَلَى ٱلْقَٰعِدِينَ دَرَجَةً ۚ وَكُلًّا وَعَدَ ٱللَّهُ ٱلْحُسْنَىٰ ۚ وَفَضَّلَ ٱللَّهُ

ٱلْمُجَٰهِدِينَ عَلَى ٱلْقَٰعِدِينَ أَجْرًا عَظِيمًا ﴿٩٥﴾ دَرَجَٰتٍ مِّنْهُ وَمَغْفِرَةً

returned to idolatry (*fitna*, meaning *shirk*) ***they are overwhelmed by it*** and are in a worse position. ***If they do not keep away from you*** by not fighting you ***or submit to you or refrain from fighting*** you, ***seize them*** by taking them into captivity ***and kill them wherever you find them. Over such people We have given you clear authority***, clear evidence to kill them because of their treachery.

92. ***A believer should never kill another believer unless it is by mistake.*** Homicide of a believer must only take place unintentionally, such as might happen when hunting or by hitting someone with what would normally be a non-fatal blow. In that case, ***anyone who kills a believer by mistake should free a believing slave and pay blood-money to his family***, the heirs of the victim, ***unless they forgo it as* ṣadaqa** and pardon the killer. It is clear that the Sunnīs consider the amount of blood money to be one hundred camels: twenty two year old camels, twenty three year old females, twenty three year old males, twenty four year olds, and twenty five year olds. They are paid by the tribe (*'āqila*) of the killer, who are his male relatives (*'aṣaba*), and are distributed over three years. The wealthy pay half a dinar and the moderately wealthy a quarter every year. If that is impossible, then the wrongdoer must pay it. ***If he is from a people who are your enemies and is a believer, you should free a believing slave.*** The killer then owes *kaffāra* rather than blood money paid to the family since they are enemies. ***If he*** (the victim) ***is from a people with whom you have a treaty***, as with the people of the *dhimma*, then ***blood money should be paid to his family***, and the blood money is one third of that of a believer if the victim is a Jew or Christian, and three tenths if it is a Magian, ***and you*** (the killer) ***should free a believing slave.*** If one cannot free a slave, then ***anyone who cannot find the means should fast for two consecutive months*** as *kaffāra* for it. Allah did not mention moving on to feeding as in the *ẓihār* divorce. Ash-Shāfi'ī takes that in the sounder of two positions. ***This is a concession from Allah. Allah is All-Knowing*** of His creation, ***All-Wise*** in how He manages them.

93. ***As for anyone who kills a believer deliberately,*** with the intention of doing so and knowing that he is a believer, ***his repayment is Hell, remaining in it timelessly, forever. Allah is angry with him and has cursed him,*** and has put him far from His mercy by His curse, ***and has prepared for him a terrible punishment*** in the Fire. This is interpreted as applying to anyone who desired it or as being his repayment if he is repaid. There is no contradiction here of Allah's words: *"He forgives what is less than that for whomever He wishes."* (4:48) Ibn 'Abbās said that this threat should be taken literally but that it is mitigated by other *āyats* of forgiveness. The *āyats* of *Sūrat al-Baqara* about murder (2:178-9) make it clear that a deliberate murderer should be killed in retaliation for his crime but that blood money is acceptable if he is pardoned. The amount is clear. The *Sunna* clarifies what happens if the homicide is quasi-deliberate or by mistake, which is when someone is killed in a way which would not normally prove fatal, in which case there is no retaliation and blood money is paid.

94. This is a reference to an occasion when some Companions stopped a man of the Banū Sulaym who was driving some sheep. He greeted them, but they said, "You have only said you are Muslim out of fear," and killed him and drove off his sheep. ***O you who believe! When you go out to fight*** in *jihād* ***in the Way of Allah verify things carefully*** (read as *tabayyanū* and in one case *tathabbatū*)***. Do not say, "You are not a believer"***, accusing him of declaring himself a Muslim merely to protect his life and property, ***to someone who greets you as a Muslim*** (lit. gives you the *salām* or *salam*)***, simply out of desire for the goods of this world***, killing him out of desire for booty. The Muslim greeting, or saying the *shahāda*, are sufficient evidence that a person is Muslim. ***In Allah's keeping there is booty in abundance.*** Allah's abundant generosity will dispense with your having to kill people like that for their property. ***That is the way you were before,*** protecting your lives and property by simply saying the *shahāda*, ***but Allah has been kind to you*** by making belief and righteousness the norm. ***So verify things carefully.*** Take stock of the situation before acting, in case you kill a believer and act towards someone who has entered Islam as you used to do in the days before Islam. ***Allah is aware of what you do*** and will reward you.

95. ***Those believers who stay behind*** from *jihād* – ***other than those forced by necessity*** due to chronic illness, blindness and the like – ***are not the same as those who do* jihād *in the way of Allah, sacrificing their wealth and themselves. Allah has given those who do***

وَرَحۡمَةٗۚ وَكَانَ ٱللَّهُ غَفُورٗا رَّحِيمًا ٩٦ إِنَّ ٱلَّذِينَ تَوَفَّىٰهُمُ ٱلۡمَلَٰٓئِكَةُ
ظَالِمِيٓ أَنفُسِهِمۡ قَالُواْ فِيمَ كُنتُمۡۖ قَالُواْ كُنَّا مُسۡتَضۡعَفِينَ فِي ٱلۡأَرۡضِۚ
قَالُوٓاْ أَلَمۡ تَكُنۡ أَرۡضُ ٱللَّهِ وَٰسِعَةٗ فَتُهَاجِرُواْ فِيهَاۚ فَأُوْلَٰٓئِكَ مَأۡوَىٰهُمۡ
جَهَنَّمُۖ وَسَآءَتۡ مَصِيرًا ٩٧ إِلَّا ٱلۡمُسۡتَضۡعَفِينَ مِنَ ٱلرِّجَالِ
وَٱلنِّسَآءِ وَٱلۡوِلۡدَٰنِ لَا يَسۡتَطِيعُونَ حِيلَةٗ وَلَا يَهۡتَدُونَ سَبِيلٗا ٩٨
فَأُوْلَٰٓئِكَ عَسَى ٱللَّهُ أَن يَعۡفُوَ عَنۡهُمۡۚ وَكَانَ ٱللَّهُ عَفُوًّا غَفُورٗا ٩٩
۞ وَمَن يُهَاجِرۡ فِي سَبِيلِ ٱللَّهِ يَجِدۡ فِي ٱلۡأَرۡضِ مُرَٰغَمٗا كَثِيرٗا وَسَعَةٗۚ
وَمَن يَخۡرُجۡ مِنۢ بَيۡتِهِۦ مُهَاجِرًا إِلَى ٱللَّهِ وَرَسُولِهِۦ ثُمَّ يُدۡرِكۡهُ ٱلۡمَوۡتُ
فَقَدۡ وَقَعَ أَجۡرُهُۥ عَلَى ٱللَّهِۗ وَكَانَ ٱللَّهُ غَفُورٗا رَّحِيمٗا ١٠٠ وَإِذَا ضَرَبۡتُمۡ
فِي ٱلۡأَرۡضِ فَلَيۡسَ عَلَيۡكُمۡ جُنَاحٌ أَن تَقۡصُرُواْ مِنَ ٱلصَّلَوٰةِ إِنۡ خِفۡتُمۡ
أَن يَفۡتِنَكُمُ ٱلَّذِينَ كَفَرُوٓاْۚ إِنَّ ٱلۡكَٰفِرِينَ كَانُواْ لَكُمۡ عَدُوّٗا مُّبِينٗا ١٠١
وَإِذَا كُنتَ فِيهِمۡ فَأَقَمۡتَ لَهُمُ ٱلصَّلَوٰةَ فَلۡتَقُمۡ طَآئِفَةٞ
مِّنۡهُم مَّعَكَ وَلۡيَأۡخُذُوٓاْ أَسۡلِحَتَهُمۡۖ فَإِذَا سَجَدُواْ فَلۡيَكُونُواْ
مِن وَرَآئِكُمۡ وَلۡتَأۡتِ طَآئِفَةٌ أُخۡرَىٰ لَمۡ يُصَلُّواْ
فَلۡيُصَلُّواْ مَعَكَ وَلۡيَأۡخُذُواْ حِذۡرَهُمۡ وَأَسۡلِحَتَهُمۡۗ وَدَّ ٱلَّذِينَ
كَفَرُواْ لَوۡ تَغۡفُلُونَ عَنۡ أَسۡلِحَتِكُمۡ وَأَمۡتِعَتِكُمۡ فَيَمِيلُونَ
عَلَيۡكُم مَّيۡلَةٗ وَٰحِدَةٗۚ وَلَا جُنَاحَ عَلَيۡكُمۡ إِن كَانَ بِكُمۡ
أَذٗى مِّن مَّطَرٍ أَوۡ كُنتُم مَّرۡضَىٰٓ أَن تَضَعُوٓاْ أَسۡلِحَتَكُمۡۖ
وَخُذُواْ حِذۡرَكُمۡۗ إِنَّ ٱللَّهَ أَعَدَّ لِلۡكَٰفِرِينَ عَذَابٗا مُّهِينٗا ١٠٢
فَإِذَا قَضَيۡتُمُ ٱلصَّلَوٰةَ فَٱذۡكُرُواْ ٱللَّهَ قِيَٰمٗا وَقُعُودٗا وَعَلَىٰ

jihād ***with their wealth and themselves a higher rank than those who stay behind*** except for those who do so out of necessity, since they are equal in the intention with those who go out. ***Allah has promised the Best*** (the Garden) ***to both*** groups, ***but Allah has preferred those who do*** **jihād** ***over those who stay behind*** without necessity ***by an immense reward:***

96. ***... high ranks***, one above the other, ***conferred by Him as well as forgiveness and mercy. Allah is Ever-Forgiving*** to His friends, ***Most Merciful*** to those who obey Him.

97. This was revealed about a group who became Muslim and did not emigrate and then were killed at Badr with the unbelievers. ***The angels ask*** in rebuke ***those they take while they are wronging themselves*** by staying among unbelievers and not making *hijra*, ***"What were your circumstances?"*** "What were you doing about your *dīn*?" ***They reply*** to excuse themselves, ***"We were oppressed on earth***, unable to establish the *dīn* in Makka." ***They*** (the angels) ***say*** to censure them, ***"Was Allah's earth not wide enough for you to have emigrated elsewhere in it***, to have left the land of the unbelievers for another land as others did?" Allah Almighty says: ***The shelter of such people will be Hell. What an evil journey's end!***

98. ***Except for those men, women and children who really are oppressed and do not have any other possibility***, such as the physical capacity to emigrate or sufficient funds, ***and are not guided to any way*** to emigrate.

99. ***It may well be that Allah will pardon them. Allah is Ever-Pardoning, Ever-Forgiving.***

100. ***Those who emigrate in the Way of Allah will find many places of refuge in the earth*** to which to emigrate ***and ample sustenance*** and provision. ***If anyone leaves his home, emigrating to Allah and His Messenger, and death catches up with him*** on the way, as it did with al-Jundu' ibn Ḍamra al-Laythī, ***it is Allah who will reward him. Allah is Ever-Forgiving, Most Merciful.***

101. ***When you are travelling in the land, there is nothing wrong in your shortening the prayer***, by turning four *rak'ats* into two, ***if you fear that those who disbelieve might harass you***, that an enemy will harm you. ***The unbelievers are your manifest enemies.*** The

جُنُوبِكُمۡۚ فَإِذَا ٱطۡمَأۡنَنتُمۡ فَأَقِيمُواْ ٱلصَّلَوٰةَۚ إِنَّ ٱلصَّلَوٰةَ
كَانَتۡ عَلَى ٱلۡمُؤۡمِنِينَ كِتَٰبٗا مَّوۡقُوتٗا ﴿١٠٣﴾ وَلَا تَهِنُواْ
فِي ٱبۡتِغَآءِ ٱلۡقَوۡمِۖ إِن تَكُونُواْ تَأۡلَمُونَ فَإِنَّهُمۡ يَأۡلَمُونَ كَمَا
تَأۡلَمُونَۖ وَتَرۡجُونَ مِنَ ٱللَّهِ مَا لَا يَرۡجُونَۗ وَكَانَ ٱللَّهُ عَلِيمًا
حَكِيمًا ﴿١٠٤﴾ إِنَّآ أَنزَلۡنَآ إِلَيۡكَ ٱلۡكِتَٰبَ بِٱلۡحَقِّ لِتَحۡكُمَ بَيۡنَ
ٱلنَّاسِ بِمَآ أَرَىٰكَ ٱللَّهُۚ وَلَا تَكُن لِّلۡخَآئِنِينَ خَصِيمٗا ﴿١٠٥﴾
وَٱسۡتَغۡفِرِ ٱللَّهَۖ إِنَّ ٱللَّهَ كَانَ غَفُورٗا رَّحِيمٗا ﴿١٠٦﴾ وَلَا تُجَٰدِلۡ
عَنِ ٱلَّذِينَ يَخۡتَانُونَ أَنفُسَهُمۡۚ إِنَّ ٱللَّهَ لَا يُحِبُّ مَن كَانَ
خَوَّانًا أَثِيمٗا ﴿١٠٧﴾ يَسۡتَخۡفُونَ مِنَ ٱلنَّاسِ وَلَا يَسۡتَخۡفُونَ
مِنَ ٱللَّهِ وَهُوَ مَعَهُمۡ إِذۡ يُبَيِّتُونَ مَا لَا يَرۡضَىٰ مِنَ ٱلۡقَوۡلِۚ وَكَانَ
ٱللَّهُ بِمَا يَعۡمَلُونَ مُحِيطًا ﴿١٠٨﴾ هَٰٓأَنتُمۡ هَٰٓؤُلَآءِ جَٰدَلۡتُمۡ
عَنۡهُمۡ فِي ٱلۡحَيَوٰةِ ٱلدُّنۡيَا فَمَن يُجَٰدِلُ ٱللَّهَ عَنۡهُمۡ يَوۡمَ
ٱلۡقِيَٰمَةِ أَم مَّن يَكُونُ عَلَيۡهِمۡ وَكِيلٗا ﴿١٠٩﴾ وَمَن يَعۡمَلۡ
سُوٓءًا أَوۡ يَظۡلِمۡ نَفۡسَهُۥ ثُمَّ يَسۡتَغۡفِرِ ٱللَّهَ يَجِدِ ٱللَّهَ غَفُورٗا
رَّحِيمٗا ﴿١١٠﴾ وَمَن يَكۡسِبۡ إِثۡمٗا فَإِنَّمَا يَكۡسِبُهُۥ عَلَىٰ نَفۡسِهِۦۚ
وَكَانَ ٱللَّهُ عَلِيمًا حَكِيمٗا ﴿١١١﴾ وَمَن يَكۡسِبۡ خَطِيٓـَٔةً أَوۡ إِثۡمٗا
ثُمَّ يَرۡمِ بِهِۦ بَرِيٓـٔٗا فَقَدِ ٱحۡتَمَلَ بُهۡتَٰنٗا وَإِثۡمٗا مُّبِينٗا ﴿١١٢﴾ وَلَوۡلَا
فَضۡلُ ٱللَّهِ عَلَيۡكَ وَرَحۡمَتُهُۥ لَهَمَّت طَّآئِفَةٞ مِّنۡهُمۡ أَن
يُضِلُّوكَ وَمَا يُضِلُّونَ إِلَّآ أَنفُسَهُمۡۖ وَمَا يَضُرُّونَكَ مِن
شَيۡءٖۚ وَأَنزَلَ ٱللَّهُ عَلَيۡكَ ٱلۡكِتَٰبَ وَٱلۡحِكۡمَةَ وَعَلَّمَكَ

unbelievers are mentioned to clarify the situation. The *Sunna* makes it clear that this only applies to a journey of forty-eight miles or more, which is two stages. The use of the expression "nothing wrong" means that this is a dispensation (*rukhṣa*), which is the position of ash-Shāfi'ī.

102. ***When you are with them*** and you fear the enemy, ***and*** you ***are leading them in the prayer, a group of them should stand with you*** while the other group stands behind, while those standing with you are ***keeping hold of their weapons. When they prostrate*** in the prayer, ***the others should be behind you*** on guard until this group finish the prayers. Then those who have prayed go to guard, and ***then the other group who have not prayed should come and pray with you. They too should be careful and keep hold of their weapons*** until they finish the prayer. The Prophet, may Allah bless him and grant him peace, prayed like that at Baṭn Nakhl as both Muslim and al-Bukhārī relate. ***Those who disbelieve would like you to be negligent of your arms and equipment*** when you pray ***so that they can swoop down on you*** in attack ***once and for all.*** This is the reason for the command to keep your weapons. ***There is nothing wrong, if you are bothered by rain or you are ill, in laying your weapons down*** and not holding them. This means it is obligatory to keep them by you when there is no excuse. That is one of the two opinions of ash-Shāfi'ī. The second is that it is *sunna*, which has more weight. ***But take every precaution*** against the enemy as much as you can. ***Allah has prepared a humiliating punishment for the unbelievers.***

103. ***When you have finished the prayer remember Allah*** by saying *"lā ilāha illā'llāh"* and glorifying Him ***standing, sitting and lying on your sides***; in other words in every state. ***When you are safe again do the prayer in the normal way. The prayer is prescribed for the believers at set times*** and should not be delayed. It was revealed when the Prophet, may Allah bless him and grant him peace, sent a group to look for Abū Sufyān and his companions when they returned from Uḥud and were suffering from wounds.

104. ***Do not relax*** and weaken ***in pursuit of the enemy***, (the unbelievers) in seeking to fight them. ***If you feel pain*** from wounds, ***they too are feeling it just as you are*** from the wounds they suffered in fighting you, ***but you hope for something from Allah they cannot hope for***: victory and reward. So you have more than they have and should be more eager than they are for the fight. ***Allah is All-Knowing*** of all things, ***All-Wise*** in what He does.

105. Ṭa'ma ibn Abayriq stole some armour and hid it with a Jew. When it was found in his possession, Ṭa'ma accused him of stealing it and swore that he himself had not stolen it. His clan asked the Prophet to argue for him to prove his innocence, and then this was revealed. ***We have sent down the Book*** (the Qur'ān) ***to you with the Truth so that you can judge between people according to what Allah has shown to you*** and taught you. ***But do not be an advocate for the treacherous*** like Ṭa'ma.

106. ***And ask Allah's forgiveness*** for what was intended. ***Allah is Ever-Forgiving, Most Merciful.***

107. ***Do not argue on behalf of those who betray themselves*** by acts of rebellion, the effects of which will rebound on them. ***Allah does not love any evildoing traitors.*** He will punish them.

108. ***They*** (Ṭa'ma and his cronies) ***try to conceal themselves*** out of shame ***from people, but they cannot conceal themselves from Allah. He is with them*** with His knowledge ***when they spend the night saying things which are not pleasing to Him.*** That situation occurred when they resolved to lie about stealing and attribute it to the Jew. ***Allah encompasses everything they do*** in knowledge.

109. ***Here you*** (Ṭa'ma's clan) ***are arguing on their behalf*** (Ṭa'ma and his cronies) ***in this world, but who will argue with Allah on their behalf on the Day of Rising*** when He punishes them***? Who will act as guardian for them then?*** Who will look after them and protect them? No one will be able to.

110. ***Anyone who does evil*** by which he wrongs another, as Ṭa'ma did in accusing the Jew, ***or wrongs himself*** by committing a wrong action which is confined to himself, ***and then*** repents and ***asks Allah's forgiveness*** for it ***will find Allah Ever-Forgiving, Most Merciful*** to him.

111. ***If anyone commits an evil action, the responsibility for it is his alone*** because it rebounds on him and does not harm anyone else. ***Allah is All-Knowing, All-Wise*** in what He does.

مَا لَمْ تَكُن تَعْلَمُ ۚ وَكَانَ فَضْلُ ٱللَّهِ عَلَيْكَ عَظِيمًا ﴿١١٣﴾
۞ لَّا خَيْرَ فِى كَثِيرٍ مِّن نَّجْوَىٰهُمْ إِلَّا مَنْ أَمَرَ بِصَدَقَةٍ
أَوْ مَعْرُوفٍ أَوْ إِصْلَٰحٍۭ بَيْنَ ٱلنَّاسِ ۚ وَمَن يَفْعَلْ ذَٰلِكَ
ٱبْتِغَآءَ مَرْضَاتِ ٱللَّهِ فَسَوْفَ نُؤْتِيهِ أَجْرًا عَظِيمًا ﴿١١٤﴾ وَمَن
يُشَاقِقِ ٱلرَّسُولَ مِنۢ بَعْدِ مَا تَبَيَّنَ لَهُ ٱلْهُدَىٰ وَيَتَّبِعْ غَيْرَ
سَبِيلِ ٱلْمُؤْمِنِينَ نُوَلِّهِۦ مَا تَوَلَّىٰ وَنُصْلِهِۦ جَهَنَّمَ ۖ وَسَآءَتْ
مَصِيرًا ﴿١١٥﴾ إِنَّ ٱللَّهَ لَا يَغْفِرُ أَن يُشْرَكَ بِهِۦ وَيَغْفِرُ مَا دُونَ
ذَٰلِكَ لِمَن يَشَآءُ ۚ وَمَن يُشْرِكْ بِٱللَّهِ فَقَدْ ضَلَّ ضَلَٰلًۢا بَعِيدًا
﴿١١٦﴾ إِن يَدْعُونَ مِن دُونِهِۦٓ إِلَّآ إِنَٰثًا وَإِن يَدْعُونَ
إِلَّا شَيْطَٰنًا مَّرِيدًا ﴿١١٧﴾ لَّعَنَهُ ٱللَّهُ ۘ وَقَالَ لَأَتَّخِذَنَّ
مِنْ عِبَادِكَ نَصِيبًا مَّفْرُوضًا ﴿١١٨﴾ وَلَأُضِلَّنَّهُمْ وَلَأُمَنِّيَنَّهُمْ
وَلَءَامُرَنَّهُمْ فَلَيُبَتِّكُنَّ ءَاذَانَ ٱلْأَنْعَٰمِ وَلَءَامُرَنَّهُمْ
فَلَيُغَيِّرُنَّ خَلْقَ ٱللَّهِ ۚ وَمَن يَتَّخِذِ ٱلشَّيْطَٰنَ وَلِيًّا
مِّن دُونِ ٱللَّهِ فَقَدْ خَسِرَ خُسْرَانًا مُّبِينًا ﴿١١٩﴾
يَعِدُهُمْ وَيُمَنِّيهِمْ ۖ وَمَا يَعِدُهُمُ ٱلشَّيْطَٰنُ إِلَّا غُرُورًا ﴿١٢٠﴾
أُو۟لَٰٓئِكَ مَأْوَىٰهُمْ جَهَنَّمُ وَلَا يَجِدُونَ عَنْهَا مَحِيصًا ﴿١٢١﴾
وَٱلَّذِينَ ءَامَنُوا۟ وَعَمِلُوا۟ ٱلصَّٰلِحَٰتِ سَنُدْخِلُهُمْ
جَنَّٰتٍ تَجْرِى مِن تَحْتِهَا ٱلْأَنْهَٰرُ خَٰلِدِينَ فِيهَآ أَبَدًا ۖ وَعْدَ
ٱللَّهِ حَقًّا ۚ وَمَنْ أَصْدَقُ مِنَ ٱللَّهِ قِيلًا ﴿١٢٢﴾ لَّيْسَ بِأَمَانِيِّكُمْ
وَلَآ أَمَانِىِّ أَهْلِ ٱلْكِتَٰبِ ۗ مَن يَعْمَلْ سُوٓءًا يُجْزَ بِهِۦ

112. ***Anyone who commits an error*** (a minor wrong action) ***or an evil action*** (a major wrong action) ***and then ascribes it to someone who is innocent, bears the weight of slander and clear wrongdoing*** for what he did.

113. ***Were it not for Allah's favour to you***, Muḥammad, ***and His mercy,*** meaning protection here, ***a group of them,*** the people with Ṭa'ma, ***would almost have managed to mislead you*** from judging by the truth by confusing you about what happened. ***But they mislead no one but themselves and do not harm you at all*** because the evil effects of their misguidance will rebound back on themselves. ***Allah has sent down the Book*** (the Qur'ān) ***and Wisdom*** (the rulings it contains) ***to you and taught you what you did not know before,*** referring to rulings and matters of the Unseen. ***Allah's favour to you*** by doing that and other things ***is indeed immense.***

114. ***There is no good in much of their secret talk*** – what people gather together to talk about privately – ***except in the case of those who enjoin ṣadaqa, or what is right, or putting things right between people. If anyone does that, seeking the pleasure of Allah*** and none of the rewards of this world, ***We will give him an immense reward*** (read as *nu'tīhi*, "We will give him" and *yu'tīhi*, "He will give him").

115. ***But if anyone opposes the Messenger*** regarding what Allah has revealed of the Truth ***after the guidance*** and Truth ***has become clear to him*** through the witnessing of miracles, ***and,*** by disbelieving, ***follows other than the path of the believers***, which is that of following the *dīn*, ***We will hand him over to whatever he has turned to,*** to his misguidance and leave him to it in this world, ***and We will*** admit him to the Fire in the Next World and ***roast him in Hell. What an evil destination*** to return to!

116. ***Allah does not forgive partners being attributed to Him, but He forgives whomever He wills for anything apart from that. Anyone who attributes partners to Allah has gone far*** from the Truth ***into misguidance.***

117. ***What they call on*** and what the idolaters worship ***apart from Him are female idols*** such as al-Lāt, al-'Uzzā and al-Manāt. ***What***

they call on in their worship ***is an arrogant*** disobedient ***Shaytan*** (Iblīs) whom they follow in his disobedience to Allah ***...***

118. ***...whom Allah has cursed***, putting him far from Allah's mercy. ***He*** (Shayṭān) ***said, "I will take a definite portion of Your slaves*** whom I will call to obey me.

119. ***I will lead them astray*** from the truth by whisperings ***and fill them with false hopes,*** filling their hearts with desire for long life and to be resurrected without reckoning. ***I will command them and they will cut off the ears of cattle*** following the superstition of the *baḥīra* (*see Glossary*). ***I will command them and they will change Allah's creation,*** change Allah's *dīn* by unbelief and by making lawful what Allah has made unlawful and unlawful what is lawful." ***Anyone who takes Shayṭān as his protector*** and obeys Shayṭān ***instead of Allah has clearly lost everything*** and will certainly end up eternally in the Fire.

120. ***He makes promises to them*** of long lives ***and fills them with false hopes*** of this world and that there will no resurrection or reckoning. ***But what Shaytan promises them*** in that way ***is nothing but*** false ***delusion.***

121. ***The shelter of such people will be Hell. They will find no escape route from it.***

122. ***But as for those who believe and do right actions, We will admit them into Gardens with rivers flowing under them, remaining in them timelessly, forever without end. Allah's promise is true.*** Allah's promise is a true promise which will certainly come to pass. ***Whose speech could be truer than Allah's?***

123. This was revealed when the Muslims and People of the Book were boasting against one another. ***It is not a matter of wishful thinking on your part*** and not theoretical, ***or of the wishful thinking of the People of the Book.*** It is by righteous action. ***Anyone who does evil will be repaid for it*** either in the Next World or in this world by affliction through trials, as is reported in *ḥadīth*s. ***He will not find any protector*** to preserve him ***or helper*** to defend him ***besides Allah.***

124. ***Anyone, male or female, who does right actions and is a believer, will enter the Garden. They will not be wronged by as***

وَلَا يَجِدْ لَهُۥ مِن دُونِ ٱللَّهِ وَلِيًّا وَلَا نَصِيرًا ﴿١٢٣﴾ وَمَن
يَعْمَلْ مِنَ ٱلصَّٰلِحَٰتِ مِن ذَكَرٍ أَوْ أُنثَىٰ وَهُوَ مُؤْمِنٌ
فَأُو۟لَٰٓئِكَ يَدْخُلُونَ ٱلْجَنَّةَ وَلَا يُظْلَمُونَ نَقِيرًا ﴿١٢٤﴾ وَمَنْ
أَحْسَنُ دِينًا مِّمَّنْ أَسْلَمَ وَجْهَهُۥ لِلَّهِ وَهُوَ مُحْسِنٌ وَٱتَّبَعَ
مِلَّةَ إِبْرَٰهِيمَ حَنِيفًا ۗ وَٱتَّخَذَ ٱللَّهُ إِبْرَٰهِيمَ خَلِيلًا ﴿١٢٥﴾ وَلِلَّهِ مَا
فِى ٱلسَّمَٰوَٰتِ وَمَا فِى ٱلْأَرْضِ ۚ وَكَانَ ٱللَّهُ بِكُلِّ شَىْءٍ
مُّحِيطًا ﴿١٢٦﴾ وَيَسْتَفْتُونَكَ فِى ٱلنِّسَآءِ ۖ قُلِ ٱللَّهُ يُفْتِيكُمْ
فِيهِنَّ وَمَا يُتْلَىٰ عَلَيْكُمْ فِى ٱلْكِتَٰبِ فِى يَتَٰمَى ٱلنِّسَآءِ
ٱلَّٰتِى لَا تُؤْتُونَهُنَّ مَا كُتِبَ لَهُنَّ وَتَرْغَبُونَ أَن تَنكِحُوهُنَّ
وَٱلْمُسْتَضْعَفِينَ مِنَ ٱلْوِلْدَٰنِ وَأَن تَقُومُوا۟ لِلْيَتَٰمَىٰ
بِٱلْقِسْطِ ۚ وَمَا تَفْعَلُوا۟ مِنْ خَيْرٍ فَإِنَّ ٱللَّهَ كَانَ بِهِۦ عَلِيمًا ﴿١٢٧﴾
وَإِنِ ٱمْرَأَةٌ خَافَتْ مِنۢ بَعْلِهَا نُشُوزًا أَوْ إِعْرَاضًا فَلَا جُنَاحَ
عَلَيْهِمَآ أَن يُصْلِحَا بَيْنَهُمَا صُلْحًا ۚ وَٱلصُّلْحُ خَيْرٌ ۗ وَأُحْضِرَتِ
ٱلْأَنفُسُ ٱلشُّحَّ ۚ وَإِن تُحْسِنُوا۟ وَتَتَّقُوا۟ فَإِنَّ ٱللَّهَ كَانَ
بِمَا تَعْمَلُونَ خَبِيرًا ﴿١٢٨﴾ وَلَن تَسْتَطِيعُوٓا۟ أَن تَعْدِلُوا۟
بَيْنَ ٱلنِّسَآءِ وَلَوْ حَرَصْتُمْ ۖ فَلَا تَمِيلُوا۟ كُلَّ ٱلْمَيْلِ
فَتَذَرُوهَا كَٱلْمُعَلَّقَةِ ۚ وَإِن تُصْلِحُوا۟ وَتَتَّقُوا۟ فَإِنَّ ٱللَّهَ
كَانَ غَفُورًا رَّحِيمًا ﴿١٢٩﴾ وَإِن يَتَفَرَّقَا يُغْنِ ٱللَّهُ كُلًّا
مِّن سَعَتِهِۦ ۚ وَكَانَ ٱللَّهُ وَٰسِعًا حَكِيمًا ﴿١٣٠﴾ وَلِلَّهِ مَا فِى
ٱلسَّمَٰوَٰتِ وَمَا فِى ٱلْأَرْضِ ۗ وَلَقَدْ وَصَّيْنَا ٱلَّذِينَ أُوتُوا۟ ٱلْكِتَٰبَ

much as the tiniest mote. "Tiniest mote" (*naqīr*) refers to the size of the spot on a date stone.

125. ***Who***, here meaning no one, ***has a better* dīn *than someone who submits himself completely to Allah*** and makes his actions sincere ***and is a good-doer*** (someone who affirms the unity of Allah) ***and follows the religion of Ibrāhīm,*** which is in harmony with the *dīn* of Islam, ***a man of pure natural belief***, inclining from all other religions to the true *dīn*. ***Allah took Ibrāhīm as an intimate friend.*** An "intimate friend" is one who is sincere in his love.

126. ***Everything in the heavens and everything in the earth belongs to Allah.*** It is all His property, His creation and His creatures. ***Allah encompasses everything*** in knowledge and power. Such is His constant attribute.

127. ***They will ask you for a definitive ruling***, a *fatwā*, ***about women*** and their inheritance. ***Say*** to them, ***"Allah gives you a definitive ruling about them; and also what is recited to you in the Book*** (the Qur'an) of the *āyats* of inheritance, and He also gives you a ruling ***about orphan girls to whom you do not give the inheritance they are owed*** in the way prescribed for them, ***while at the same time desiring to marry them,*** and you, guardians, do not desire to marry them because they are unattractive but want to prevent them from marrying because you desire their inheritance. He gives you a definite ruling that you should not do that, ***and also about young children who are denied their rights; and*** He also commands ***that you should act justly with respect to orphans*** regarding inheritance and dowries." ***Whatever good you do, Allah knows it*** and will repay you for it.

128. ***If a woman fears cruelty,*** referring to unkindness perpetrated by her husband by not sleeping with her and refusing to give her sufficient maintenance for her needs because he dislikes her and has his eye on someone more beautiful, ***or aversion on her husband's part, there is nothing wrong in the couple becoming reconciled*** (read as *yuṣliḥā* and *yaṣṣālaḥā*) in terms of agreeing to equitable division of time and maintenance, although it is also possible for a woman to forgo something if she agrees to that in exchange for the continued companionship of her husband. Otherwise the husband must give her

مِن قَبۡلِكُمۡ وَإِيَّاكُمۡ أَنِ ٱتَّقُواْ ٱللَّهَۚ وَإِن تَكۡفُرُواْ فَإِنَّ لِلَّهِ
مَا فِي ٱلسَّمَٰوَٰتِ وَمَا فِي ٱلۡأَرۡضِۚ وَكَانَ ٱللَّهُ غَنِيًّا حَمِيدٗا ١٣١
وَلِلَّهِ مَا فِي ٱلسَّمَٰوَٰتِ وَمَا فِي ٱلۡأَرۡضِۚ وَكَفَىٰ بِٱللَّهِ وَكِيلًا ١٣٢
إِن يَشَأۡ يُذۡهِبۡكُمۡ أَيُّهَا ٱلنَّاسُ وَيَأۡتِ بِـَٔاخَرِينَۚ وَكَانَ
ٱللَّهُ عَلَىٰ ذَٰلِكَ قَدِيرٗا ١٣٣ مَّن كَانَ يُرِيدُ ثَوَابَ ٱلدُّنۡيَا فَعِندَ
ٱللَّهِ ثَوَابُ ٱلدُّنۡيَا وَٱلۡأٓخِرَةِۚ وَكَانَ ٱللَّهُ سَمِيعَۢا بَصِيرٗا ١٣٤
۞ يَٰٓأَيُّهَا ٱلَّذِينَ ءَامَنُواْ كُونُواْ قَوَّٰمِينَ بِٱلۡقِسۡطِ شُهَدَآءَ لِلَّهِ
وَلَوۡ عَلَىٰٓ أَنفُسِكُمۡ أَوِ ٱلۡوَٰلِدَيۡنِ وَٱلۡأَقۡرَبِينَۚ إِن يَكُنۡ غَنِيًّا
أَوۡ فَقِيرٗا فَٱللَّهُ أَوۡلَىٰ بِهِمَاۖ فَلَا تَتَّبِعُواْ ٱلۡهَوَىٰٓ أَن تَعۡدِلُواْۚ وَإِن
تَلۡوُۥٓاْ أَوۡ تُعۡرِضُواْ فَإِنَّ ٱللَّهَ كَانَ بِمَا تَعۡمَلُونَ خَبِيرٗا ١٣٥ يَٰٓأَيُّهَا
ٱلَّذِينَ ءَامَنُوٓاْ ءَامِنُواْ بِٱللَّهِ وَرَسُولِهِۦ وَٱلۡكِتَٰبِ ٱلَّذِي نَزَّلَ
عَلَىٰ رَسُولِهِۦ وَٱلۡكِتَٰبِ ٱلَّذِيٓ أَنزَلَ مِن قَبۡلُۚ وَمَن يَكۡفُرۡ
بِٱللَّهِ وَمَلَٰٓئِكَتِهِۦ وَكُتُبِهِۦ وَرُسُلِهِۦ وَٱلۡيَوۡمِ ٱلۡأٓخِرِ فَقَدۡ ضَلَّ
ضَلَٰلَۢا بَعِيدًا ١٣٦ إِنَّ ٱلَّذِينَ ءَامَنُواْ ثُمَّ كَفَرُواْ ثُمَّ ءَامَنُواْ
ثُمَّ كَفَرُواْ ثُمَّ ٱزۡدَادُواْ كُفۡرٗا لَّمۡ يَكُنِ ٱللَّهُ لِيَغۡفِرَ لَهُمۡ وَلَا لِيَهۡدِيَهُمۡ
سَبِيلَۢا ١٣٧ بَشِّرِ ٱلۡمُنَٰفِقِينَ بِأَنَّ لَهُمۡ عَذَابًا أَلِيمًا ١٣٨ ٱلَّذِينَ
يَتَّخِذُونَ ٱلۡكَٰفِرِينَ أَوۡلِيَآءَ مِن دُونِ ٱلۡمُؤۡمِنِينَۚ أَيَبۡتَغُونَ
عِندَهُمُ ٱلۡعِزَّةَ فَإِنَّ ٱلۡعِزَّةَ لِلَّهِ جَمِيعٗا ١٣٩ وَقَدۡ نَزَّلَ عَلَيۡكُمۡ فِي
ٱلۡكِتَٰبِ أَنۡ إِذَا سَمِعۡتُمۡ ءَايَٰتِ ٱللَّهِ يُكۡفَرُ بِهَا وَيُسۡتَهۡزَأُ بِهَا فَلَا
تَقۡعُدُواْ مَعَهُمۡ حَتَّىٰ يَخُوضُواْ فِي حَدِيثٍ غَيۡرِهِۦٓۚ إِنَّكُمۡ إِذٗا مِّثۡلُهُمۡۗ

her full due or divorce her. ***Reconciliation is better*** than separation or aversion. Allah then clarifies the natural tendencies of the human character: ***But people are prone to selfish greed*** (intense miserliness which is intrinsic to human beings). What is being referred to is a kind of quality that is an inseparable part of the human character. It means that it is very difficult for a woman to forgo her portion and very difficult for a man to give it up when he loves another. ***If you do good*** to women ***and are godfearing,*** fearing to be unjust to them, ***Allah is aware of everything you do*** and will repay you for it.

129. ***You will not be able to be completely fair between your wives*** with respect to love, ***however hard you try*** to do so. ***But do not be completely partial*** to the one you love mor regarding division of time and maintenance ***so as to leave a wife, as it were, suspended in midair***, like a widow rather than a married woman. ***And if you make amends*** by being just in the division ***and are godfearing*** by avoiding injustice, ***Allah is Ever-Forgiving*** about the bias which happened before, ***Most Merciful*** to you in that regard.

130. ***If a couple do separate*** by divorce, ***Allah will enrich each of them*** so that he or she has no need of the other ***from His boundless wealth***, providing her with another husband and him with another wife. ***Allah is All-Encompassing*** with vast favour to His creation, ***All-Wise*** in His management.

131. ***Everything in the heavens and everything in the earth belongs to Allah. We have instructed those given the Book*** (generic, meaning Revealed Books) ***before you*** (the Jews and the Christians) ***and you yourselves*** (the people of the Qur'an) ***to be fearful of Allah*** and fear His punishment by obeying Him and We said to them and you: ***but if you disbelieve*** and reject what you have been commanded to do, ***everything in the heavens and everything in the earth belongs to Allah*** as His creation, property and slaves, and so your unbelief will not harm Him. ***Allah is Rich beyond need*** of His creatures' worship, ***Praiseworthy*** in what He does to them.

132. ***Everything in the heavens and everything in the earth belongs to Allah.*** This is repeated to stress the necessity for fear of Allah. ***Allah is enough as a guardian.*** He is a witness over all in the heaven and the earth.

133. ***If He willed, O mankind, He could remove you altogether and produce others instead***, putting them in their place. ***Allah certainly has the power to do that.***

134. ***If anyone desires the reward of this world*** in return for his actions, ***the reward of this world and the Next World is with Allah*** for those who desire them, and is not found to be with anyone else. So no one should limit their seeking to the inferior. Rather they should raise their sights to the highest possibility with sincerity, since all good is with Him alone.

135. ***You who believe! Be upholders of justice, bearing witness for Allah alone*** by acknowledging the truth and not concealing it, ***even against yourselves or your parents and relatives. Whether they***, those against whom you testify, ***are rich or poor, Allah is well able to look after them*** and knows better what is best for them. ***Do not follow your own desires*** in your testimony by trying to please the rich or out of mercy for the poor ***and deviate from the truth. If you twist*** (read as *talwū* and *talū*) the testimony ***or turn away*** by not giving it, ***Allah is aware of everything you do*** and Allah will repay you for it.

136. ***You who believe!*** Continue to ***believe in Allah and His Messenger and the Book*** (the Qur'ān) ***He has sent down*** (read as *nazzala*, "He has sent down" and *nuzzila*, "which has been sent down") ***to His Messenger*** (Muḥammad, may Allah bless him and grant him peace) ***and the Book*** (generic, referring to all previous Revealed Books) ***He sent down*** (read as *anzala*, "He sent down" and *unzila*, "which was sent down") on Messengers ***before. Anyone who disbelieves in Allah, His angels, His Books, His Messengers, and the Last Day has gone far into misguidance*** from the Truth.

137. ***Those who believe*** in Mūsā (the Jews) ***and then disbelieve*** by worshipping the Calf, ***and then believe*** after that ***and then disbelieve*** in 'Īsā, ***and then increase in unbelief*** by then disbelieving in Muḥammad, ***Allah will not forgive them*** for what they did ***or guide them on any path*** to the truth.

138. ***Give news***, Muḥammad, ***to the hypocrites that they will have a painful punishment*** (the Fire).

إِنَّ ٱللَّهَ جَامِعُ ٱلْمُنَٰفِقِينَ وَٱلْكَٰفِرِينَ فِى جَهَنَّمَ جَمِيعًا ﴿١٤٠﴾
ٱلَّذِينَ يَتَرَبَّصُونَ بِكُمْ فَإِن كَانَ لَكُمْ فَتْحٌ مِّنَ ٱللَّهِ قَالُوٓا۟ أَلَمْ
نَكُن مَّعَكُمْ وَإِن كَانَ لِلْكَٰفِرِينَ نَصِيبٌ قَالُوٓا۟ أَلَمْ نَسْتَحْوِذْ
عَلَيْكُمْ وَنَمْنَعْكُم مِّنَ ٱلْمُؤْمِنِينَ ۚ فَٱللَّهُ يَحْكُمُ بَيْنَكُمْ يَوْمَ
ٱلْقِيَٰمَةِ ۗ وَلَن يَجْعَلَ ٱللَّهُ لِلْكَٰفِرِينَ عَلَى ٱلْمُؤْمِنِينَ سَبِيلًا ﴿١٤١﴾
إِنَّ ٱلْمُنَٰفِقِينَ يُخَٰدِعُونَ ٱللَّهَ وَهُوَ خَٰدِعُهُمْ وَإِذَا قَامُوٓا۟ إِلَى
ٱلصَّلَوٰةِ قَامُوا۟ كُسَالَىٰ يُرَآءُونَ ٱلنَّاسَ وَلَا يَذْكُرُونَ ٱللَّهَ إِلَّا
قَلِيلًا ﴿١٤٢﴾ مُّذَبْذَبِينَ بَيْنَ ذَٰلِكَ لَآ إِلَىٰ هَٰٓؤُلَآءِ وَلَآ إِلَىٰ هَٰٓؤُلَآءِ ۚ
وَمَن يُضْلِلِ ٱللَّهُ فَلَن تَجِدَ لَهُۥ سَبِيلًا ﴿١٤٣﴾ يَٰٓأَيُّهَا ٱلَّذِينَ ءَامَنُوا۟
لَا تَتَّخِذُوا۟ ٱلْكَٰفِرِينَ أَوْلِيَآءَ مِن دُونِ ٱلْمُؤْمِنِينَ ۚ أَتُرِيدُونَ
أَن تَجْعَلُوا۟ لِلَّهِ عَلَيْكُمْ سُلْطَٰنًا مُّبِينًا ﴿١٤٤﴾ إِنَّ ٱلْمُنَٰفِقِينَ
فِى ٱلدَّرْكِ ٱلْأَسْفَلِ مِنَ ٱلنَّارِ وَلَن تَجِدَ لَهُمْ نَصِيرًا ﴿١٤٥﴾
إِلَّا ٱلَّذِينَ تَابُوا۟ وَأَصْلَحُوا۟ وَٱعْتَصَمُوا۟ بِٱللَّهِ وَأَخْلَصُوا۟
دِينَهُمْ لِلَّهِ فَأُو۟لَٰٓئِكَ مَعَ ٱلْمُؤْمِنِينَ ۖ وَسَوْفَ يُؤْتِ ٱللَّهُ
ٱلْمُؤْمِنِينَ أَجْرًا عَظِيمًا ﴿١٤٦﴾ مَّا يَفْعَلُ ٱللَّهُ بِعَذَابِكُمْ
إِن شَكَرْتُمْ وَءَامَنتُمْ ۚ وَكَانَ ٱللَّهُ شَاكِرًا عَلِيمًا ﴿١٤٧﴾
۞ لَّا يُحِبُّ ٱللَّهُ ٱلْجَهْرَ بِٱلسُّوٓءِ مِنَ ٱلْقَوْلِ إِلَّا مَن ظُلِمَ ۚ وَكَانَ
ٱللَّهُ سَمِيعًا عَلِيمًا ﴿١٤٨﴾ إِن تُبْدُوا۟ خَيْرًا أَوْ تُخْفُوهُ أَوْ تَعْفُوا۟ عَن
سُوٓءٍ فَإِنَّ ٱللَّهَ كَانَ عَفُوًّا قَدِيرًا ﴿١٤٩﴾ إِنَّ ٱلَّذِينَ يَكْفُرُونَ
بِٱللَّهِ وَرُسُلِهِۦ وَيُرِيدُونَ أَن يُفَرِّقُوا۟ بَيْنَ ٱللَّهِ وَرُسُلِهِۦ

139. ***Do those who take the people who disbelieve*** (the hypocrites) ***as protectors, rather than the believers,*** since they suppose that the unbelievers have power, ***hope to find power and strength with them?*** This is a question which negates their action: in other words, they will not find it with them. ***Power and strength belong entirely to Allah*** in this world and the Next, and only His friends obtain it.

140. ***He has sent down*** (read as *nazzala*, "He has sent down" and *nuzzila*, "It has been sent down") ***to you in the Book*** in the Qur'ān in *Sūrat al-A'nām* (6:68) ***that when you hear Allah's Signs*** (the Qur'ān) ***being disbelieved and mocked at by people, you must not sit with them*** (the unbelievers and mockers) ***until they start to talk of other things; if you did*** sit with them, ***you would be just the same as them*** and share in the sin they commit. ***Allah will gather all the hypocrites and unbelievers into Hell*** as they were gathered together in unbelief and mockery in this world.

141. ***Those who anticipate the worst*** fortune ***for you say, "Were we not with you*** with regard to the *dīn* and *jihād?"* ***whenever you gain a victory*** and booty ***from Allah.*** They say this because they want some of the booty. ***But if the unbelievers have a success*** over you, ***they say*** to them, ***"Did we not have the upper hand over you and yet in spite of that keep the believers away from you?"*** meaning: "We could have captured you and killed you but we kept the believers from attacking and defeating you and seizing you, and we send information about them to you; so you owe us a favour." Allah Almighty says: ***Allah will judge between you*** and them ***on the Day of Rising*** by admitting the believers to the Garden and the unbelievers to the Fire. ***Allah will not give the unbelievers any way against the believers***, to wipe them out.

142. ***The hypocrites think that they deceive Allah*** by outwardly displaying the opposite of the unbelief inside them in order to save themselves from worldly judgements against them, ***but He is deceiving them.*** He will repay them for their deceit and they will be disgraced in this world since Allah will acquaint His Prophet, may Allah bless him and grant him peace, with what is inside them and they will also be punished in the Next World. ***When they get up to pray*** with the believers, ***they get up lazily, showing off*** their prayer ***to people, and only remembering Allah a little***, praying to show off.

143. ***They vacillate between the two***, belief and unbelief – ***not joining these,*** the unbelievers, ***or joining those***, the believers. ***If Allah misguides someone, you will not find any way for him*** to be guided.

144. ***You who believe! Do not take those who disbelieve as friends rather than the believers. Do you want to give Allah clear proof against you*** of your hypocrisy by taking them as friends?

145. ***The hypocrites are in the lowest level of the Fire*** (its deepest depth). ***You will not find any helper for them*** to protect them from the punishment;

146. ***Except those who repent*** of hypocrisy ***and put things right*** by acting righteously ***and hold fast to Allah*** and trust in Him ***and dedicate their* dīn *to Allah alone***, free of showing off. ***They are with the believers*** in what they do and ***Allah will give the believers an immense reward*** in the Next World (the Garden).

147. ***Why should Allah punish you if you are thankful*** for His blessings to you ***and believe*** in Him? The question implies a negative response. ***Allah is All-Thankful*** for the actions of the believers by rewarding them, ***All-Knowing*** of His creation.

148. ***Allah does not like evil words to be voiced out loud*** by anyone and will punish them for it, ***except in the case of someone who has been wronged***, who is not to be blamed for speaking out loud in strong terms about the injustice he has suffered and calling for redress against the perpetrator. ***Allah is All-Hearing*** of what is said, ***All-Knowing*** of His creation.

149. ***If you reveal a good act***, which you have done, ***or keep it hidden, or pardon an evil act*** of injustice, ***Allah is Ever-Pardoning, All-Powerful.***

150. ***Those who disbelieve in Allah and His Messengers and desire to make division between Allah and His Messengers*** by believing in some and disbelieving in others, ***saying, "We believe in some*** Messengers ***and disbelieve in some*** of them," ***wanting to take a pathway*** they can follow ***in between*** (between belief and unbelief),

151. ***...such people are the true unbelievers.*** This confirms what comes before it. ***We have prepared a humiliating punishment*** (the Fire) ***for the unbelievers.***

وَيَقُولُونَ نُؤْمِنُ بِبَعْضٍ وَنَكْفُرُ بِبَعْضٍ وَيُرِيدُونَ
أَن يَتَّخِذُوا۟ بَيْنَ ذَٰلِكَ سَبِيلًا ﴿١٥٠﴾ أُو۟لَٰٓئِكَ هُمُ ٱلْكَٰفِرُونَ
حَقًّا ۚ وَأَعْتَدْنَا لِلْكَٰفِرِينَ عَذَابًا مُّهِينًا ﴿١٥١﴾ وَٱلَّذِينَ ءَامَنُوا۟
بِٱللَّهِ وَرُسُلِهِۦ وَلَمْ يُفَرِّقُوا۟ بَيْنَ أَحَدٍ مِّنْهُمْ أُو۟لَٰٓئِكَ سَوْفَ
يُؤْتِيهِمْ أُجُورَهُمْ ۗ وَكَانَ ٱللَّهُ غَفُورًا رَّحِيمًا ﴿١٥٢﴾ يَسْـَٔلُكَ
أَهْلُ ٱلْكِتَٰبِ أَن تُنَزِّلَ عَلَيْهِمْ كِتَٰبًا مِّنَ ٱلسَّمَآءِ ۚ فَقَدْ سَأَلُوا۟
مُوسَىٰٓ أَكْبَرَ مِن ذَٰلِكَ فَقَالُوٓا۟ أَرِنَا ٱللَّهَ جَهْرَةً فَأَخَذَتْهُمُ
ٱلصَّٰعِقَةُ بِظُلْمِهِمْ ۚ ثُمَّ ٱتَّخَذُوا۟ ٱلْعِجْلَ مِنۢ بَعْدِ مَا جَآءَتْهُمُ
ٱلْبَيِّنَٰتُ فَعَفَوْنَا عَن ذَٰلِكَ ۚ وَءَاتَيْنَا مُوسَىٰ سُلْطَٰنًا مُّبِينًا ﴿١٥٣﴾
وَرَفَعْنَا فَوْقَهُمُ ٱلطُّورَ بِمِيثَٰقِهِمْ وَقُلْنَا لَهُمُ ٱدْخُلُوا۟ ٱلْبَابَ سُجَّدًا
وَقُلْنَا لَهُمْ لَا تَعْدُوا۟ فِى ٱلسَّبْتِ وَأَخَذْنَا مِنْهُم مِّيثَٰقًا غَلِيظًا ﴿١٥٤﴾
فَبِمَا نَقْضِهِم مِّيثَٰقَهُمْ وَكُفْرِهِم بِـَٔايَٰتِ ٱللَّهِ وَقَتْلِهِمُ ٱلْأَنۢبِيَآءَ
بِغَيْرِ حَقٍّ وَقَوْلِهِمْ قُلُوبُنَا غُلْفٌۢ ۚ بَلْ طَبَعَ ٱللَّهُ عَلَيْهَا بِكُفْرِهِمْ
فَلَا يُؤْمِنُونَ إِلَّا قَلِيلًا ﴿١٥٥﴾ وَبِكُفْرِهِمْ وَقَوْلِهِمْ عَلَىٰ مَرْيَمَ
بُهْتَٰنًا عَظِيمًا ﴿١٥٦﴾ وَقَوْلِهِمْ إِنَّا قَتَلْنَا ٱلْمَسِيحَ عِيسَى ٱبْنَ مَرْيَمَ
رَسُولَ ٱللَّهِ وَمَا قَتَلُوهُ وَمَا صَلَبُوهُ وَلَٰكِن شُبِّهَ لَهُمْ ۚ وَإِنَّ ٱلَّذِينَ
ٱخْتَلَفُوا۟ فِيهِ لَفِى شَكٍّ مِّنْهُ ۚ مَا لَهُم بِهِۦ مِنْ عِلْمٍ إِلَّا ٱتِّبَاعَ ٱلظَّنِّ ۚ
وَمَا قَتَلُوهُ يَقِينًۢا ﴿١٥٧﴾ بَل رَّفَعَهُ ٱللَّهُ إِلَيْهِ ۚ وَكَانَ ٱللَّهُ عَزِيزًا حَكِيمًا
﴿١٥٨﴾ وَإِن مِّنْ أَهْلِ ٱلْكِتَٰبِ إِلَّا لَيُؤْمِنَنَّ بِهِۦ قَبْلَ مَوْتِهِۦ ۖ وَيَوْمَ
ٱلْقِيَٰمَةِ يَكُونُ عَلَيْهِمْ شَهِيدًا ﴿١٥٩﴾ فَبِظُلْمٍ مِّنَ ٱلَّذِينَ هَادُوا۟

152. ***Those who believe in Allah and*** all ***His Messengers and do not differentiate between any of them, We will pay them*** (read as *nu'tīhim*, "We will pay them" and *yu'tīhim*, "He will pay them") ***their wages*** as a reward for their actions. ***Allah is Ever-Forgiving*** of His friends, ***Most Merciful*** to the people who obey Him.

153. ***The People of the Book*** (the Jews) ***will ask you,*** O Muḥammad, out of obduracy, ***to bring down a Book from heaven to them*** all at once, as it was sent down to Mūsā. If you think that is terrible, ***they,*** i.e. their ancestors ***asked Mūsā for even more than that. They said, "Let us see Allah with our own eyes." So the lightning-bolt struck them down*** and killed them as a punishment ***for their wrongdoing*** because they were exigent in their asking. ***Then they adopted the Calf*** as a god ***after the Clear Signs***, the miracles which proved Allah's Oneness, ***had come to them; but We pardoned them for that*** and did not eradicate them ***and gave Mūsā clear authority*** over them, as is shown by the fact that he commanded them to kill themselves and they obeyed him.

154. ***We lifted up the Mount above their heads in accordance with the covenant they had made,*** to force them to take on the covenant which they had accepted out of fear, ***and We said to them, "Enter the gate*** of the city ***prostrating,*** bowing,***" and We said to them, "Do not break*** (read as *ta'dū* and *ta''adū*) ***the Sabbath,"*** by fishing, ***and We made a binding covenant with them*** but they broke it.

155. (There is clearly something elided here so that the meaning is something like "Allah cursed them because...") ***Because of the fact that they broke their covenant, and rejected Allah's Signs, and killed the Prophets without any right and said,*** to the Prophet, may Allah bless him and grant him peace, ***"Our hearts are uncircum - cised*** and do not understand what you say,***" Allah has stamped them*** and sealed them ***with unbelief*** and so they do not pay any attention to warnings. ***So they do not believe, except for a few*** of them like 'Abdullāh ibn Salām and his companions.

156. ***And for their*** second ***unbelief*** in 'Īsā, ***and their utterance of a monstrous slander against Maryam***, accusing her of fornication,

157. ***...and their*** boastfully ***saying, "We killed the Messiah, 'Īsā, son of Maryam, Messenger of Allah"*** as they claim. They are punished for affirming that, although Allah then denies that they killed him: ***They did not kill him and they did not crucify him but it was made to seem so to them.*** The person killed and crucified was a companion of 'Īsā who was made to look like him so that they thought that it was him. ***Those who argue about him*** ('Īsā) ***are in doubt about it***, about killing him, as one of them said when he saw the body of the person who had been killed, "It is the face of 'Īsā but not his body. It is not him." Others said, "It is him." ***They have no real knowledge of it*** (his killing), ***just conjecture.*** They follow the supposition which they imagine to be the case. ***But they certainly did not kill him.*** This stresses its negation.

158. ***Allah raised him up to Himself. Allah is Almighty*** in His kingdom, ***All-Wise*** in what He does.

159. ***There is not one of the People of the Book who will not believe in him before he*** (the Person of the Book or possibly 'Īsā) ***dies*** at the time they see the angels of death and then their belief will not help them, or, possibly, before the death of 'Īsā after he descends shortly before the Final Hour as reported in the *ḥadīth; **and on the Day of Rising, he*** (i.e. 'Īsā) ***will be a witness against them*** about what they did when he was sent to them.

160. ***Because of wrongdoing on the part of the Jews, We made unlawful for them some good things which had previously been lawful for them*** which is clarified in Allah's words, *"We made unlawful for the Jews every animal with an undivided hoof..."* (6:146)***; and because of their obstructing many people from the way of Allah*** (from the true *dīn*).

161. ***...and because of their practising usury when they were forbidden to do it*** in the Torah, ***and because of their consuming people's wealth by wrongful means,*** employing bribery to obtain favourable judgement, ***We have prepared a painful punishment for those among them who disbelieve.***

162. ***But those of them who are firmly rooted in knowledge*** (such as 'Abdullāh ibn Salām) ***and the believers*** (the Muhājirūn and Anṣār) ***believe in what has been sent down to you and what was sent down before you*** by way of Divine Books***: those who perform the prayer and pay* zakāt, *and believe in Allah and the Last Day – We will pay*** (read as *nu'tīhim*, "We will pay them" and *yu'tīhim*, "He will pay them") ***such people a huge wage*** (the Garden).

حَرَّمۡنَا عَلَيۡهِمۡ طَيِّبَٰتٍ أُحِلَّتۡ لَهُمۡ وَبِصَدِّهِمۡ عَن سَبِيلِ ٱللَّهِ
كَثِيرٗا ١٦٠ وَأَخۡذِهِمُ ٱلرِّبَوٰاْ وَقَدۡ نُهُواْ عَنۡهُ وَأَكۡلِهِمۡ أَمۡوَٰلَ ٱلنَّاسِ
بِٱلۡبَٰطِلِۚ وَأَعۡتَدۡنَا لِلۡكَٰفِرِينَ مِنۡهُمۡ عَذَابًا أَلِيمٗا ١٦١ لَّٰكِنِ
ٱلرَّٰسِخُونَ فِي ٱلۡعِلۡمِ مِنۡهُمۡ وَٱلۡمُؤۡمِنُونَ يُؤۡمِنُونَ بِمَآ أُنزِلَ إِلَيۡكَ وَمَآ
أُنزِلَ مِن قَبۡلِكَۚ وَٱلۡمُقِيمِينَ ٱلصَّلَوٰةَۚ وَٱلۡمُؤۡتُونَ ٱلزَّكَوٰةَ
وَٱلۡمُؤۡمِنُونَ بِٱللَّهِ وَٱلۡيَوۡمِ ٱلۡأٓخِرِ أُوْلَٰٓئِكَ سَنُؤۡتِيهِمۡ أَجۡرًا عَظِيمًا ١٦٢
۞ إِنَّآ أَوۡحَيۡنَآ إِلَيۡكَ كَمَآ أَوۡحَيۡنَآ إِلَىٰ نُوحٖ وَٱلنَّبِيِّـۧنَ مِنۢ بَعۡدِهِۦۚ
وَأَوۡحَيۡنَآ إِلَىٰٓ إِبۡرَٰهِيمَ وَإِسۡمَٰعِيلَ وَإِسۡحَٰقَ وَيَعۡقُوبَ
وَٱلۡأَسۡبَاطِ وَعِيسَىٰ وَأَيُّوبَ وَيُونُسَ وَهَٰرُونَ وَسُلَيۡمَٰنَۚ
وَءَاتَيۡنَا دَاوُۥدَ زَبُورٗا ١٦٣ وَرُسُلٗا قَدۡ قَصَصۡنَٰهُمۡ عَلَيۡكَ
مِن قَبۡلُ وَرُسُلٗا لَّمۡ نَقۡصُصۡهُمۡ عَلَيۡكَۚ وَكَلَّمَ ٱللَّهُ مُوسَىٰ
تَكۡلِيمٗا ١٦٤ رُّسُلٗا مُّبَشِّرِينَ وَمُنذِرِينَ لِئَلَّا يَكُونَ
لِلنَّاسِ عَلَى ٱللَّهِ حُجَّةُۢ بَعۡدَ ٱلرُّسُلِۚ وَكَانَ ٱللَّهُ عَزِيزًا حَكِيمٗا
١٦٥ لَّٰكِنِ ٱللَّهُ يَشۡهَدُ بِمَآ أَنزَلَ إِلَيۡكَۖ أَنزَلَهُۥ بِعِلۡمِهِۦۖ
وَٱلۡمَلَٰٓئِكَةُ يَشۡهَدُونَۚ وَكَفَىٰ بِٱللَّهِ شَهِيدًا ١٦٦ إِنَّ ٱلَّذِينَ
كَفَرُواْ وَصَدُّواْ عَن سَبِيلِ ٱللَّهِ قَدۡ ضَلُّواْ ضَلَٰلَۢا بَعِيدًا
١٦٧ إِنَّ ٱلَّذِينَ كَفَرُواْ وَظَلَمُواْ لَمۡ يَكُنِ ٱللَّهُ لِيَغۡفِرَ لَهُمۡ وَلَا
لِيَهۡدِيَهُمۡ طَرِيقًا ١٦٨ إِلَّا طَرِيقَ جَهَنَّمَ خَٰلِدِينَ فِيهَآ أَبَدٗاۚ
وَكَانَ ذَٰلِكَ عَلَى ٱللَّهِ يَسِيرٗا ١٦٩ يَٰٓأَيُّهَا ٱلنَّاسُ قَدۡ جَآءَكُمُ
ٱلرَّسُولُ بِٱلۡحَقِّ مِن رَّبِّكُمۡ فَـَٔامِنُواْ خَيۡرٗا لَّكُمۡۚ وَإِن تَكۡفُرُواْ

163. ***We have revealed to you as We revealed to Nūḥ and the Prophets who came after him. And We revealed to Ibrāhīm and*** his sons, ***Ismā'īl and Isḥāq, and Ya'qub and the Tribes, and 'Īsā and Ayyūb and Yūnus and Hārūn and Sulaymān. And We gave Dāwūd the* Zabūr.** The *Zabūr* was the book given to Dāwūd. It is also read as the verbal noun *zubūr*, which means "written".

164. We have sent ***Messengers We have already told you about and Messengers We have not told you about.*** It is related that Allah sent eight thousand Prophets: four thousand from the tribe of Israel and four thousand from other peoples. This will be further mentioned in the commentary on *Sūrat Ghāfir* (40). ***And Allah spoke directly to Mūsā*** without any intermediary.

165. ***Messengers bringing good news*** of the reward for belief ***and giving warning*** of the punishment for those who disbelieve – We sent them ***so that people would have no argument against Allah after the coming of the Messengers***, so that they would not be able to say, "Our Lord, if only You had sent us a Messenger we would have been believers." We sent them so that they would have no excuse. ***Allah is Almighty*** in His kingdom, ***All-Wise*** in what He does.

166. This was revealed when the Jews asked about the Prophethood of Muḥammad, may Allah bless him and grant him peace, and then denied it. ***But Allah bears witness*** (and makes his Prophethood clear) ***to what He has sent down to you*** of the Inimitable Qur'ān. ***He has sent it down with His knowledge.*** He knows it or what is in it. ***The angels bear witness as well. And Allah is enough as a witness*** to that.

167. ***Those who disbelieve*** in Allah ***and bar access to*** people to ***the way of Allah***, the *dīn* of Islam, by concealing the description of Muḥammad, meaning the Jews, ***have gone far into misguidance*** from the Truth.

168. ***Allah will not forgive those who disbelieve*** in Allah ***and do wrong*** to His Prophet by concealing his description, ***or guide them on any path…***

169. ***…except the path of Hell,*** the path which leads to it, ***remaining in it timelessly***, once they enter it, ***forever without end. That is easy for Allah.***

فَإِنَّ لِلَّهِ مَا فِي ٱلسَّمَٰوَٰتِ وَٱلۡأَرۡضِۚ وَكَانَ ٱللَّهُ عَلِيمًا حَكِيمٗا ١٧٠
يَٰٓأَهۡلَ ٱلۡكِتَٰبِ لَا تَغۡلُواْ فِي دِينِكُمۡ وَلَا تَقُولُواْ
عَلَى ٱللَّهِ إِلَّا ٱلۡحَقَّۚ إِنَّمَا ٱلۡمَسِيحُ عِيسَى ٱبۡنُ مَرۡيَمَ رَسُولُ
ٱللَّهِ وَكَلِمَتُهُۥٓ أَلۡقَىٰهَآ إِلَىٰ مَرۡيَمَ وَرُوحٞ مِّنۡهُۖ فَـَٔامِنُواْ بِٱللَّهِ
وَرُسُلِهِۦۖ وَلَا تَقُولُواْ ثَلَٰثَةٌۚ ٱنتَهُواْ خَيۡرٗا لَّكُمۡۚ إِنَّمَا ٱللَّهُ إِلَٰهٞ
وَٰحِدٞۖ سُبۡحَٰنَهُۥٓ أَن يَكُونَ لَهُۥ وَلَدٞۘ لَّهُۥ مَا فِي ٱلسَّمَٰوَٰتِ
وَمَا فِي ٱلۡأَرۡضِۗ وَكَفَىٰ بِٱللَّهِ وَكِيلٗا ١٧١ لَّن يَسۡتَنكِفَ
ٱلۡمَسِيحُ أَن يَكُونَ عَبۡدٗا لِّلَّهِ وَلَا ٱلۡمَلَٰٓئِكَةُ ٱلۡمُقَرَّبُونَۚ
وَمَن يَسۡتَنكِفۡ عَنۡ عِبَادَتِهِۦ وَيَسۡتَكۡبِرۡ فَسَيَحۡشُرُهُمۡ
إِلَيۡهِ جَمِيعٗا ١٧٢ فَأَمَّا ٱلَّذِينَ ءَامَنُواْ وَعَمِلُواْ ٱلصَّٰلِحَٰتِ
فَيُوَفِّيهِمۡ أُجُورَهُمۡ وَيَزِيدُهُم مِّن فَضۡلِهِۦۖ وَأَمَّا ٱلَّذِينَ
ٱسۡتَنكَفُواْ وَٱسۡتَكۡبَرُواْ فَيُعَذِّبُهُمۡ عَذَابًا أَلِيمٗا وَلَا
يَجِدُونَ لَهُم مِّن دُونِ ٱللَّهِ وَلِيّٗا وَلَا نَصِيرٗا ١٧٣ يَٰٓأَيُّهَا ٱلنَّاسُ
قَدۡ جَآءَكُم بُرۡهَٰنٞ مِّن رَّبِّكُمۡ وَأَنزَلۡنَآ إِلَيۡكُمۡ نُورٗا مُّبِينٗا ١٧٤
فَأَمَّا ٱلَّذِينَ ءَامَنُواْ بِٱللَّهِ وَٱعۡتَصَمُواْ بِهِۦ فَسَيُدۡخِلُهُمۡ
فِي رَحۡمَةٖ مِّنۡهُ وَفَضۡلٖ وَيَهۡدِيهِمۡ إِلَيۡهِ صِرَٰطٗا مُّسۡتَقِيمٗا ١٧٥
يَسۡتَفۡتُونَكَ قُلِ ٱللَّهُ يُفۡتِيكُمۡ فِي ٱلۡكَلَٰلَةِۚ إِنِ ٱمۡرُؤٌاْ هَلَكَ
لَيۡسَ لَهُۥ وَلَدٞ وَلَهُۥٓ أُخۡتٞ فَلَهَا نِصۡفُ مَا تَرَكَۚ وَهُوَ يَرِثُهَآ
إِن لَّمۡ يَكُن لَّهَا وَلَدٞۚ فَإِن كَانَتَا ٱثۡنَتَيۡنِ فَلَهُمَا ٱلثُّلُثَانِ مِمَّا تَرَكَۚ
وَإِن كَانُوٓاْ إِخۡوَةٗ رِّجَالٗا وَنِسَآءٗ فَلِلذَّكَرِ مِثۡلُ حَظِّ ٱلۡأُنثَيَيۡنِۗ
يُبَيِّنُ ٱللَّهُ لَكُمۡ أَن تَضِلُّواْۗ وَٱللَّهُ بِكُلِّ شَيۡءٍ عَلِيمُۢ ١٧٦

170. ***O Mankind!*** (people of Makka) ***The Messenger*** Muḥammad, may Allah bless him and grant him peace, ***has brought you the truth from your Lord, so it is better for you*** than what you do now ***to believe*** in it. ***But if you disbelieve*** in it, ***everything in the heavens and the earth belongs to Allah.*** All are His property, His creation and His creatures and so your unbelief will not harm Him. ***Allah is All-Knowing*** about His creation, ***All-Wise*** in what He does to them.

171. ***O People of the Book!*** (here meaning Christians) ***Do not go to excess concerning your*** **dīn** and exceed the limits. ***Say nothing but the truth about Allah***, placing Allah far beyond having a partner or child. ***The Messiah, 'Īsā son of Maryam, was only the Messenger of Allah and His Word, which He cast into Maryam, and a Spirit*** (someone possessing a spirit) ***from Him***. The Spirit is ascribed to Allah to honour 'Īsā. The fact that he is called Spirit does not, as they claim, make him the son of God or a god together with Him or one of a divine trinity. Allah is free of any such combination or ascription of that to Him. ***So believe in Allah and His Messengers. Do not say, "Three*** gods: Allah, 'Īsā and his mother.***" It is better that you stop*** saying these things. Affirming the Divine Unity better. ***Allah is only One God. He is too Glorious to have a son! Everything in the heavens and everything in the earth belongs to Him.*** All are His creation, kingdom and slaves. ***Allah is enough as a Guardian*** and witness to that.

172. ***The Messiah*** whom you claim as a god ***would never disdain*** (be too arrogant or proud) ***to be a slave to Allah, nor would the angels near to Him*** be too arrogant to be slave s. This is part of a slight digression in which Allah refutes those who claim that 'Īsā was a god and that the angels are daughters of Allah. This addressed to the Christians who made that claim. ***If any do disdain to worship Him and grow arrogant, He will in any case gather them all to Him*** in the Next World.

173. ***As for those who believe and do right actions, He will pay them their wages in full*** (the reward for their actions) ***and will give them increase from His favour***: which is as the *hadith* says: "what the eye has not seen nor the ear heard and has not occurred to the heart of man." ***As for those who show disdain and grow*** too ***arro - gant*** to worship Him, ***He will punish them with a painful punish -***

ment (the Fire). ***They will not find any protector*** to defend them ***or*** any ***helper for themselves besides Allah.***

174. ***O Mankind! A clear proof has come to you from your Lord*** that Muḥammad, may Allah bless him and grant him peace, is the Prophet of Allah. ***We have sent down a Clear Light to you*** (the Qur'an).

175. ***As for those who believe in Allah and hold fast to Him, He will admit them into mercy and favour from Him, and will guide them to Him on a Straight Path*** (the *dīn* of Islam).

176. ***They will ask you for a definitive ruling*** about someone who dies without a direct heir, which means with neither children nor parents. ***Say: "Allah gives you a definitive ruling about people who die without direct heirs: if a man dies childless but has a sister,*** meaning both a full sister by both parents and also just by the father, ***she gets half of what he*** (her brother) ***leaves, and he is her heir if she dies childless.*** Her brother inherits all she leaves. If she has a male child, he gets nothing. If she has a daughter, he gets what is left after her share. If there is a brother or sister by the mother, the share is a sixth, as mentioned at the beginning of the *sūra*. ***If there are two sisters*** or more, ***they get two-thirds of what he*** (the brother) ***leaves*** (this was revealed about Jābir, who died leaving sisters). ***If there are brothers and sisters*** as heirs, ***the males get the share of two females. Allah makes things clear to you*** and clarifies the laws of His *dīn* ***so you may not go astray. Allah has knowledge of everything.*** Part of that is inheritance. The two *Ṣaḥīḥ* collections report from al-Barā' that this was the last *āyat* to be revealed concerning the shares of inheritance.

سُورَةُ المَائِدَة

بِسْمِ ٱللَّهِ ٱلرَّحْمَٰنِ ٱلرَّحِيمِ

يَٰٓأَيُّهَا ٱلَّذِينَ ءَامَنُوٓا۟ أَوْفُوا۟ بِٱلْعُقُودِ ۚ أُحِلَّتْ لَكُم بَهِيمَةُ
ٱلْأَنْعَٰمِ إِلَّا مَا يُتْلَىٰ عَلَيْكُمْ غَيْرَ مُحِلِّى ٱلصَّيْدِ وَأَنتُمْ حُرُمٌ ۗ إِنَّ ٱللَّهَ
يَحْكُمُ مَا يُرِيدُ ١ يَٰٓأَيُّهَا ٱلَّذِينَ ءَامَنُوا۟ لَا تُحِلُّوا۟ شَعَٰٓئِرَ ٱللَّهِ
وَلَا ٱلشَّهْرَ ٱلْحَرَامَ وَلَا ٱلْهَدْىَ وَلَا ٱلْقَلَٰٓئِدَ وَلَآ ءَآمِّينَ ٱلْبَيْتَ
ٱلْحَرَامَ يَبْتَغُونَ فَضْلًا مِّن رَّبِّهِمْ وَرِضْوَٰنًا ۚ وَإِذَا حَلَلْتُمْ فَٱصْطَادُوا۟ ۚ
وَلَا يَجْرِمَنَّكُمْ شَنَـَٔانُ قَوْمٍ أَن صَدُّوكُمْ عَنِ ٱلْمَسْجِدِ
ٱلْحَرَامِ أَن تَعْتَدُوا۟ ۘ وَتَعَاوَنُوا۟ عَلَى ٱلْبِرِّ وَٱلتَّقْوَىٰ ۖ وَلَا تَعَاوَنُوا۟
عَلَى ٱلْإِثْمِ وَٱلْعُدْوَٰنِ ۚ وَٱتَّقُوا۟ ٱللَّهَ ۖ إِنَّ ٱللَّهَ شَدِيدُ ٱلْعِقَابِ ٢
حُرِّمَتْ عَلَيْكُمُ ٱلْمَيْتَةُ وَٱلدَّمُ وَلَحْمُ ٱلْخِنزِيرِ وَمَآ أُهِلَّ لِغَيْرِ ٱللَّهِ
بِهِۦ وَٱلْمُنْخَنِقَةُ وَٱلْمَوْقُوذَةُ وَٱلْمُتَرَدِّيَةُ وَٱلنَّطِيحَةُ وَمَآ أَكَلَ
ٱلسَّبُعُ إِلَّا مَا ذَكَّيْتُمْ وَمَا ذُبِحَ عَلَى ٱلنُّصُبِ وَأَن تَسْتَقْسِمُوا۟
بِٱلْأَزْلَٰمِ ۚ ذَٰلِكُمْ فِسْقٌ ۗ ٱلْيَوْمَ يَئِسَ ٱلَّذِينَ كَفَرُوا۟ مِن دِينِكُمْ
فَلَا تَخْشَوْهُمْ وَٱخْشَوْنِ ۚ ٱلْيَوْمَ أَكْمَلْتُ لَكُمْ دِينَكُمْ وَأَتْمَمْتُ
عَلَيْكُمْ نِعْمَتِى وَرَضِيتُ لَكُمُ ٱلْإِسْلَٰمَ دِينًا ۚ فَمَنِ ٱضْطُرَّ فِى
مَخْمَصَةٍ غَيْرَ مُتَجَانِفٍ لِّإِثْمٍ ۙ فَإِنَّ ٱللَّهَ غَفُورٌ رَّحِيمٌ ٣
يَسْـَٔلُونَكَ مَاذَآ أُحِلَّ لَهُمْ ۖ قُلْ أُحِلَّ لَكُمُ ٱلطَّيِّبَٰتُ ۙ وَمَا عَلَّمْتُم
مِّنَ ٱلْجَوَارِحِ مُكَلِّبِينَ تُعَلِّمُونَهُنَّ مِمَّا عَلَّمَكُمُ ٱللَّهُ ۖ فَكُلُوا۟ مِمَّآ أَمْسَكْنَ
عَلَيْكُمْ وَٱذْكُرُوا۟ ٱسْمَ ٱللَّهِ عَلَيْهِ ۖ وَٱتَّقُوا۟ ٱللَّهَ ۚ إِنَّ ٱللَّهَ سَرِيعُ ٱلْحِسَابِ

5. *Sūrat al-Mā'ida*
The Table

Madinan with 120 *āyat*s and revealed after *Sūrat al-Fatḥ* (48).

1. ***O you who believe! Fulfil your contracts!*** Those between people and Allah and those with other people. ***All livestock animals*** (camels, cattle, and sheep) ***are lawful for you*** to eat after proper slaughter, ***except those that are recited to you now*** – which are forbidden in the coming *āyat "Forbidden for you are..."* (5:3), and this is a general statement which is then followed by the absolute exceptions to it – ***but it is still not lawful to hunt while you are in* ihrām.** ***Allah makes whatever judgements He wills*** about lawfulness and other things and there is no opposing that.

2. ***You who believe! Do not***, on the basis of false claims, ***profane the sacred rites of Allah*** – the hallmarks of the *dīn*. Do not profane them by hunting in the state of *iḥrām* – ***or the sacred months*** – by fighting in them – ***or the sacrificial animals*** – animals which are earmarked for the Ḥaram – ***or the ritual garlands*** – referring to animals which are garlanded from the bushes of the Ḥaram so that they are protected: do not attack them or their owners – ***or those heading for the Sacred House*** – by fighting them – ***desiring profit*** from good trade ***and good pleasure from their Lord*** by their intention. With reference to non-Muslims this was abrogated by *Sūrat at-Tawba*. ***When you have come out of* iḥrām, *then hunt for game*** – so hunting becomes permitted. ***Do not let hatred for a people who debar you from the Sacred Mosque incite you into going beyond the limits*** by killing such people or others. ***Help each other to goodness*** by doing what Allah has commanded ***and fear of Allah*** by avoiding what He has forbidden. ***Do not help each other to wrongdoing*** (acts of disobedience) ***and enmity*** – by transgressing the bounds of Allah. ***Be fearful of Allah*** – showing your fear of His punishment by obeying Him. ***Allah is Severe in Retribution*** towards those who oppose Him.

3. ***Forbidden for you*** to eat ***are carrion,*** spilled ***blood*** – when taken from slaughtered livestock – ***and pork, and what has been consecrated to other than Allah*** – by being slaughtered in other than His

Name – ***and animals which have been strangled, and animals which have been killed by a blow, and animals which have fallen to their death*** from a high to a low place, ***and animals which have been gored*** and killed by the goring, ***and animals which wild beasts have eaten – except those*** in these categories ***you are able to slaughter properly*** by managing to slaughter them while they are still alive – ***and animals which have been sacrificed*** to idols ***on altars, and deciding things by means of divining arrows*** – eating these categories is forbidden. "Divining arrows" are small featherless arrows without points. There were seven of them and they were in the keeping of the Custodian of the Ka'ba. There were marks on them and they were used for making judgements; those who utilised them did what they commanded and avoided what they forbade – ***that is degeneracy*** (abandonment of obedience). The following was revealed on the Day of 'Arafat during the Farewell Ḥajj. ***Today the unbelievers have despaired of overcoming your*** **dīn** – by making you leave it when they desired you to do so, because of the strength they see in it. ***So do not be afraid of them but be afraid of Me. Today I have perfected your*** **dīn** ***for you*** – by finalising its rulings and obligations and indeed after this there was no further revelation about the *ḥalāl* and *ḥarām* – ***and completed My blessing upon you*** – by perfecting it or by the safe entry of the Muslims into Makka – ***and am pleased with Islam as a*** **dīn** and have chosen it ***for you. But if anyone is forced by hunger*** to eat anything which has been forbidden him, ***not intending any wrongdoing*** – in other words, without inclining to disobedience – ***Allah is Ever-Forgiving*** for what he eats, ***Most Merciful*** to him in allowing him to do something which is not allowed to someone who intends to do wrong like, for instance, a highway robber or rebel, to whom this dispensation does not apply and who is not allowed to eat that.

4. ***They will ask you***, Muḥammad, ***what*** food ***is lawful for them. Say: "All good*** (wholesome) ***things are lawful for you, and also what is caught for you by hunting animals*** – such as dogs, birds of prey and other hunting animals – ***which you have trained*** to hunt ***as Allah has taught you*** and released after the game. The animals caught by them are lawful provided they kill them and do not eat from them, whereas if the animals are untrained, what they catch is

﴿٤﴾ ٱلْيَوْمَ أُحِلَّ لَكُمُ ٱلطَّيِّبَٰتُ ۖ وَطَعَامُ ٱلَّذِينَ أُوتُوا۟ ٱلْكِتَٰبَ حِلٌّ
لَّكُمْ وَطَعَامُكُمْ حِلٌّ لَّهُمْ ۖ وَٱلْمُحْصَنَٰتُ مِنَ ٱلْمُؤْمِنَٰتِ وَٱلْمُحْصَنَٰتُ
مِنَ ٱلَّذِينَ أُوتُوا۟ ٱلْكِتَٰبَ مِن قَبْلِكُمْ إِذَآ ءَاتَيْتُمُوهُنَّ أُجُورَهُنَّ
مُحْصِنِينَ غَيْرَ مُسَٰفِحِينَ وَلَا مُتَّخِذِىٓ أَخْدَانٍ ۗ وَمَن يَكْفُرْ
بِٱلْإِيمَٰنِ فَقَدْ حَبِطَ عَمَلُهُۥ وَهُوَ فِى ٱلْءَاخِرَةِ مِنَ ٱلْخَٰسِرِينَ ﴿٥﴾
يَٰٓأَيُّهَا ٱلَّذِينَ ءَامَنُوٓا۟ إِذَا قُمْتُمْ إِلَى ٱلصَّلَوٰةِ فَٱغْسِلُوا۟
وُجُوهَكُمْ وَأَيْدِيَكُمْ إِلَى ٱلْمَرَافِقِ وَٱمْسَحُوا۟ بِرُءُوسِكُمْ
وَأَرْجُلَكُمْ إِلَى ٱلْكَعْبَيْنِ ۚ وَإِن كُنتُمْ جُنُبًا فَٱطَّهَّرُوا۟ ۚ
وَإِن كُنتُم مَّرْضَىٰٓ أَوْ عَلَىٰ سَفَرٍ أَوْ جَآءَ أَحَدٌ مِّنكُم مِّنَ ٱلْغَآئِطِ
أَوْ لَٰمَسْتُمُ ٱلنِّسَآءَ فَلَمْ تَجِدُوا۟ مَآءً فَتَيَمَّمُوا۟ صَعِيدًا طَيِّبًا
فَٱمْسَحُوا۟ بِوُجُوهِكُمْ وَأَيْدِيكُم مِّنْهُ ۚ مَا يُرِيدُ ٱللَّهُ
لِيَجْعَلَ عَلَيْكُم مِّنْ حَرَجٍ وَلَٰكِن يُرِيدُ لِيُطَهِّرَكُمْ
وَلِيُتِمَّ نِعْمَتَهُۥ عَلَيْكُمْ لَعَلَّكُمْ تَشْكُرُونَ ﴿٦﴾
وَٱذْكُرُوا۟ نِعْمَةَ ٱللَّهِ عَلَيْكُمْ وَمِيثَٰقَهُ ٱلَّذِى وَاثَقَكُم
بِهِۦٓ إِذْ قُلْتُمْ سَمِعْنَا وَأَطَعْنَا ۖ وَٱتَّقُوا۟ ٱللَّهَ ۚ إِنَّ ٱللَّهَ عَلِيمٌۢ بِذَاتِ
ٱلصُّدُورِ ﴿٧﴾ يَٰٓأَيُّهَا ٱلَّذِينَ ءَامَنُوا۟ كُونُوا۟ قَوَّٰمِينَ لِلَّهِ
شُهَدَآءَ بِٱلْقِسْطِ ۖ وَلَا يَجْرِمَنَّكُمْ شَنَـَٔانُ قَوْمٍ عَلَىٰٓ
أَلَّا تَعْدِلُوا۟ ۚ ٱعْدِلُوا۟ هُوَ أَقْرَبُ لِلتَّقْوَىٰ ۖ وَٱتَّقُوا۟ ٱللَّهَ ۚ إِنَّ
ٱللَّهَ خَبِيرٌۢ بِمَا تَعْمَلُونَ ﴿٨﴾ وَعَدَ ٱللَّهُ ٱلَّذِينَ ءَامَنُوا۟
وَعَمِلُوا۟ ٱلصَّٰلِحَٰتِ ۙ لَهُم مَّغْفِرَةٌ وَأَجْرٌ عَظِيمٌ ﴿٩﴾
وَٱلَّذِينَ كَفَرُوا۟ وَكَذَّبُوا۟ بِـَٔايَٰتِنَآ أُو۟لَٰٓئِكَ أَصْحَٰبُ
ٱلْجَحِيمِ ﴿١٠﴾ يَٰٓأَيُّهَا ٱلَّذِينَ ءَامَنُوا۟ ٱذْكُرُوا۟ نِعْمَتَ

not lawful. The difference between trained and untrained animals is that the former go when released and stop when told to stop, and hold the game without eating it. An animal cannot be considered to be trained until it has done that three times. If the animal eats from game it has caught, that game cannot be considered part of what it has caught for its owner and so it is not lawful to eat it as reported in the two *Ṣaḥīḥ* collections. Game killed by an arrow when it has been released after the Name of Allah has been mentioned is the same as game caught by trained animals. ***Eat what they catch for you, mentioning Allah's name over it*** when you release the animal after the game. ***And be fearful of Allah. Allah is Swift at Reckoning."***

5. ***Today all good things have been made lawful for you. And the food of those given the Book*** – animals ritually slaughtered by Jews and Christians – ***is also lawful for you and your food is lawful for them. So are chaste women from among the believers and chaste*** (free) ***women of those given the Book before you*** lawful to marry, ***once you have given them their dowries in marriage, not in*** open ***fornication*** with them ***or taking them as lovers*** by secret fornication. ***But as for anyone who rejects belief*** and apostatises, ***his*** prior righteous ***actions come to nothing*** and will not be considered and he will not be rewarded for them, ***and in the Next World he will be among the losers*** if he dies in that state.

6. ***You who believe! When you*** want to ***get up to do the prayer*** and are in a state of minor impurity, ***wash your faces and your hands and your arms to the elbows*** – as the *Sunna* makes clear – ***and wipe over your heads,*** (the *bā'* here is a connective particle and, according to ash-Shāfi'ī, indicates that the minimum of what is named, i.e.. the head, is adequate, so that in his opinion it is only necessary to wipe over part of the head) ***and your feet to the ankles*** – including the ankle joints, as the *Sunna* makes clear. "Your feet" is in the accusative which shows that it continues on from "arms and elbows", meaning that they must be washed as well, not merely wiped. So the hands and feet are washed while the head is wiped. This *āyat* also defines the obligatory order for the purification of these limbs, in the opinion of ash-Shafi'ī. Another aspect of the *Sunna* is that it is mandatory to have an intention for this act of purification as is the case for other acts of worship. ***If you are in a state of major impuri -***

ty, then purify yourselves by doing *ghusl* and washing your whole body. ***But if you are ill*** and would be harmed by water, ***or on a journey, or have come from the lavatory*** and are, therefore, in a state of minor impurity, ***or have touched women,*** as was covered earlier in *Sūrat an-Nisā'* (4:43), ***and cannot find any water*** after looking for it, ***then do* tayammum *with pure earth, and wipe your faces and your hands*** and arms to the elbows with two blows to the ground. The *Sunna* clarifies that what is meant is to fully wipe over the parts indicated. ***Allah does not want to make things difficult for you*** by imposing on you the obligations of *wuḍū'*, *ghusl* and *tayammum*, ***but He does want to purify you*** of impurities and sins ***and to perfect His blessing*** (Islam) ***upon you*** by clarifying the laws of the *dīn* ***so that perhaps you may show thanks*** for His blessings.

7. ***Remember Allah's blessing upon you*** – by guiding you to Islam – ***and the covenant He made with you when you said*** to the Prophet, may Allah bless him and grant him peace, in pledging allegiance to him, ***"We hear and we obey*** in respect of all you command and forbid whether we love or dislike it." ***Be fearful of Allah*** regarding breaking your covenant with Him. ***Allah knows what the hearts contain***, not to mention other things far less hidden.

8. ***You who believe! Show integrity for the sake of Allah*** – carrying out the rights due to Him fairly – ***bearing witness with justice. Do not let hatred for a people*** (the unbelievers) ***incite you into not being just*** so that you incur the brunt of their hostility. ***Be just*** to both enemy and friend. ***That*** (justice) ***is closer to fear of Allah. Be fearful of Allah; Allah is aware of what you do*** and will repay you for it.

9. ***Allah has promised those who believe and do right actions forgiveness and an immense reward*** (the Garden).

10. ***But those who disbelieve and deny Our Signs, are the Companions of the Blazing Fire.***

11. ***You who believe! Remember Allah's blessing upon you when certain people*** (the Quraysh) ***were on the verge of raising their hands against you*** to kill you ***and He held their hands back from you*** and protected you from what they wanted to do to you. ***Be fearful of Allah. Let the believers put their trust in Allah.***

ٱللَّهِ عَلَيۡكُمۡ إِذۡ هَمَّ قَوۡمٌ أَن يَبۡسُطُوٓاْ إِلَيۡكُمۡ أَيۡدِيَهُمۡ
فَكَفَّ أَيۡدِيَهُمۡ عَنكُمۡۖ وَٱتَّقُواْ ٱللَّهَۚ وَعَلَى ٱللَّهِ فَلۡيَتَوَكَّلِ
ٱلۡمُؤۡمِنُونَ ١١ ۞ وَلَقَدۡ أَخَذَ ٱللَّهُ مِيثَٰقَ بَنِيٓ
إِسۡرَٰٓءِيلَ وَبَعَثۡنَا مِنۡهُمُ ٱثۡنَيۡ عَشَرَ نَقِيبٗاۖ وَقَالَ ٱللَّهُ
إِنِّي مَعَكُمۡۖ لَئِنۡ أَقَمۡتُمُ ٱلصَّلَوٰةَ وَءَاتَيۡتُمُ ٱلزَّكَوٰةَ
وَءَامَنتُم بِرُسُلِي وَعَزَّرۡتُمُوهُمۡ وَأَقۡرَضۡتُمُ ٱللَّهَ قَرۡضًا
حَسَنٗا لَّأُكَفِّرَنَّ عَنكُمۡ سَيِّـَٔاتِكُمۡ وَلَأُدۡخِلَنَّكُمۡ
جَنَّٰتٖ تَجۡرِي مِن تَحۡتِهَا ٱلۡأَنۡهَٰرُۚ فَمَن كَفَرَ بَعۡدَ
ذَٰلِكَ مِنكُمۡ فَقَدۡ ضَلَّ سَوَآءَ ٱلسَّبِيلِ ١٢ فَبِمَا
نَقۡضِهِم مِّيثَٰقَهُمۡ لَعَنَّٰهُمۡ وَجَعَلۡنَا قُلُوبَهُمۡ قَٰسِيَةٗۖ
يُحَرِّفُونَ ٱلۡكَلِمَ عَن مَّوَاضِعِهِۦ وَنَسُواْ حَظّٗا مِّمَّا
ذُكِّرُواْ بِهِۦۚ وَلَا تَزَالُ تَطَّلِعُ عَلَىٰ خَآئِنَةٖ مِّنۡهُمۡ إِلَّا قَلِيلٗا مِّنۡهُمۡۖ
فَٱعۡفُ عَنۡهُمۡ وَٱصۡفَحۡۚ إِنَّ ٱللَّهَ يُحِبُّ ٱلۡمُحۡسِنِينَ ١٣
وَمِنَ ٱلَّذِينَ قَالُوٓاْ إِنَّا نَصَٰرَىٰٓ أَخَذۡنَا مِيثَٰقَهُمۡ
فَنَسُواْ حَظّٗا مِّمَّا ذُكِّرُواْ بِهِۦ فَأَغۡرَيۡنَا بَيۡنَهُمُ ٱلۡعَدَاوَةَ
وَٱلۡبَغۡضَآءَ إِلَىٰ يَوۡمِ ٱلۡقِيَٰمَةِۚ وَسَوۡفَ يُنَبِّئُهُمُ ٱللَّهُ
بِمَا كَانُواْ يَصۡنَعُونَ ١٤ يَٰٓأَهۡلَ ٱلۡكِتَٰبِ
قَدۡ جَآءَكُمۡ رَسُولُنَا يُبَيِّنُ لَكُمۡ كَثِيرٗا مِّمَّا
كُنتُمۡ تُخۡفُونَ مِنَ ٱلۡكِتَٰبِ وَيَعۡفُواْ عَن
كَثِيرٖۚ قَدۡ جَآءَكُم مِّنَ ٱللَّهِ نُورٞ وَكِتَٰبٞ
مُّبِينٞ ١٥ يَهۡدِي بِهِ ٱللَّهُ مَنِ ٱتَّبَعَ رِضۡوَٰنَهُۥ
سُبُلَ ٱلسَّلَٰمِ وَيُخۡرِجُهُم مِّنَ ٱلظُّلُمَٰتِ إِلَى

12. ***Allah made a covenant with the Tribe of Israel and We raised up twelve leaders from among them*** – a chief from each of the tribes who was responsible for his people fulfilling the covenant. ***Allah said, "I am with you*** with help and victory. ***If you establish the prayer and pay the* zakāt, *and believe in My Messengers and respect and support them*** and help them, ***and lend a generous loan to Allah*** – by spending in the Way of Allah – ***I will erase your wrong actions from you and admit you into Gardens with rivers flowing under them. Any of you who disbelieve after that*** covenant ***have gone astray from the right way."*** They have erred regarding the path of the Truth. The root of going straight means being in the middle. Then they broke the covenant, and so Allah says:

13. ***But because of their breaking of their covenant, We have cursed them and*** put them far from Our mercy and ***made their hearts hard*** – not soft to accept faith. ***They distort the true meaning of words*** – in the Torah which contain the description of Muḥammad and other things, moving them from the places where Allah put them by changing them, ***and have forgotten*** and abandoned ***a good portion of what they were reminded of*** and were commanded to do in the Torah in respect of following Muḥammad when he came. ***You***, O Prophet, ***will never cease to come upon some act of treachery on their part*** – in respect of breaking their covenant and others things – ***except for a few of them*** who become Muslim. ***Yet pardon them, and overlook. Allah loves good-doers.*** This was abrogated by the *Āyat* of the Sword.

14. ***We also made a covenant with those who say, "We are Christians,"*** – as Allah had done previously with the Jewish Tribe of Israel – ***and they too forgot a good portion of what they were reminded of*** regarding belief and other things in the Gospel, and they too broke their covenant. ***So We stirred up enmity and hatred between them until the Day of Rising*** – by dividing them into their different in such a way that each sect denies the other – ***when Allah will inform them*** in the Next World ***about what they did*** and will repay them for it.

15. ***People of the Book*** – referring to both the Jews and Christians! ***Our Messenger*** Muḥammad ***has come to you, making clear to you much of the Book*** (the Torah and Gospel) ***that you have kept con -***

ٱلنُّورِ بِإِذْنِهِۦ وَيَهْدِيهِمْ إِلَىٰ صِرَٰطٍ مُّسْتَقِيمٍ
١٦ لَّقَدْ كَفَرَ ٱلَّذِينَ قَالُوٓا۟ إِنَّ ٱللَّهَ هُوَ ٱلْمَسِيحُ
ٱبْنُ مَرْيَمَ ۚ قُلْ فَمَن يَمْلِكُ مِنَ ٱللَّهِ شَيْـًٔا إِنْ أَرَادَ
أَن يُهْلِكَ ٱلْمَسِيحَ ٱبْنَ مَرْيَمَ وَأُمَّهُۥ وَمَن فِى
ٱلْأَرْضِ جَمِيعًا ۗ وَلِلَّهِ مُلْكُ ٱلسَّمَٰوَٰتِ وَٱلْأَرْضِ
وَمَا بَيْنَهُمَا ۚ يَخْلُقُ مَا يَشَآءُ ۚ وَٱللَّهُ عَلَىٰ كُلِّ شَىْءٍ قَدِيرٌ ١٧
وَقَالَتِ ٱلْيَهُودُ وَٱلنَّصَٰرَىٰ نَحْنُ أَبْنَٰٓؤُا۟ ٱللَّهِ وَأَحِبَّٰٓؤُهُۥ ۚ قُلْ
فَلِمَ يُعَذِّبُكُم بِذُنُوبِكُم ۖ بَلْ أَنتُم بَشَرٌ مِّمَّنْ خَلَقَ ۚ يَغْفِرُ لِمَن
يَشَآءُ وَيُعَذِّبُ مَن يَشَآءُ ۚ وَلِلَّهِ مُلْكُ ٱلسَّمَٰوَٰتِ وَٱلْأَرْضِ
وَمَا بَيْنَهُمَا ۖ وَإِلَيْهِ ٱلْمَصِيرُ ١٨ يَٰٓأَهْلَ ٱلْكِتَٰبِ قَدْ جَآءَكُمْ
رَسُولُنَا يُبَيِّنُ لَكُمْ عَلَىٰ فَتْرَةٍ مِّنَ ٱلرُّسُلِ أَن تَقُولُوا۟ مَا جَآءَنَا
مِنۢ بَشِيرٍ وَلَا نَذِيرٍ ۖ فَقَدْ جَآءَكُم بَشِيرٌ وَنَذِيرٌ ۗ وَٱللَّهُ عَلَىٰ كُلِّ
شَىْءٍ قَدِيرٌ ١٩ وَإِذْ قَالَ مُوسَىٰ لِقَوْمِهِۦ يَٰقَوْمِ ٱذْكُرُوا۟
نِعْمَةَ ٱللَّهِ عَلَيْكُمْ إِذْ جَعَلَ فِيكُمْ أَنۢبِيَآءَ وَجَعَلَكُم مُّلُوكًا
وَءَاتَىٰكُم مَّا لَمْ يُؤْتِ أَحَدًا مِّنَ ٱلْعَٰلَمِينَ ٢٠ يَٰقَوْمِ ٱدْخُلُوا۟
ٱلْأَرْضَ ٱلْمُقَدَّسَةَ ٱلَّتِى كَتَبَ ٱللَّهُ لَكُمْ وَلَا تَرْتَدُّوا۟ عَلَىٰٓ أَدْبَارِكُمْ
فَتَنقَلِبُوا۟ خَٰسِرِينَ ٢١ قَالُوا۟ يَٰمُوسَىٰٓ إِنَّ فِيهَا قَوْمًا جَبَّارِينَ
وَإِنَّا لَن نَّدْخُلَهَا حَتَّىٰ يَخْرُجُوا۟ مِنْهَا فَإِن يَخْرُجُوا۟ مِنْهَا
فَإِنَّا دَٰخِلُونَ ٢٢ قَالَ رَجُلَانِ مِنَ ٱلَّذِينَ يَخَافُونَ
أَنْعَمَ ٱللَّهُ عَلَيْهِمَا ٱدْخُلُوا۟ عَلَيْهِمُ ٱلْبَابَ فَإِذَا دَخَلْتُمُوهُ
فَإِنَّكُمْ غَٰلِبُونَ ۚ وَعَلَى ٱللَّهِ فَتَوَكَّلُوٓا۟ إِن كُنتُم مُّؤْمِنِينَ ٢٣

cealed – such as the *Āyat* of Stoning and his description – ***and passing over a lot*** – without making it clear since there is no benefit except in clear explanation. ***A Light*** (the Prophet, may Allah bless him and grant him peace) ***has come to you from Allah, and a Clear Book*** (the Qur'an).

16. ***Allah guides by it*** (the Book) ***to the ways of Peace those who follow what pleases Him*** by making them believers. ***He will bring them from the darkness*** of unbelief ***to the light*** of belief ***by His permission*** (His will) ***and guide them to a Straight Path*** (the *Dīn* of Islam).

17. ***Those who say, "Allah is the Messiah, son of Maryam," have disbelieved*** – by making him a god. This means the Jacobites, a group of Christians. ***Say: "Who possesses any power at all over Allah*** to avert His punishment ***if He desires to destroy the Messiah, son of Maryam, and his mother, and everyone else on earth?"*** No one has the power to do that, let alone to turn the Messiah into a god. ***The sovereignty of the heavens and the earth and everything between them belongs to Allah. He creates whatever He wills. Allah has power over everything.***

18. ***The Jews and the Christians*** both ***say, "We are*** like ***Allah's children*** – in the position of sons with their father in respect of Allah's mercy and compassion – ***and His loved ones." Say*** to them, Muḥammad***: "Why, then, does He torment you for your wrong actions*** if you are speaking the truth regarding that when it is clear that fathers do not torment their sons nor lovers those they love, whereas Allah has punished you and so it is clear that you are liars***? No, you are merely human beings among those He has created.*** You have what they have and owe what they owe. ***He forgives whomever He wills and He punishes whoever He wills*** and no one can prevent Him doing that. ***The sovereignty of the heavens and the earth and everything between them belongs to Allah. The final destination is to Him."***

19. ***People of the Book! Our Messenger*** (Muḥammad) ***has come to you, making things*** (the laws of the *dīn*) ***clear to you, after a period with no Messengers*** – the gap between Messengers referred to is that between the Prophet, may Allah bless him and grant him peace, and 'Īsā, peace be on him: a period of five hundred and sixty-nine years – ***lest you should say*** when you are punished, ***"No bringer of good news or warner came to us." A bringer of good news and a warner has come to you.*** Now you have no excuse. ***Allah has power over everything,*** one aspect of which is the power to punish them if they do not follow the Prophet.

20. Remember ***when Mūsā said to his people, "My people! Remember Allah's blessing upon you when He appointed Prophets among you and appointed kings for you*** with courts and entourages ***and gave you what He had not given to anyone else in all the worlds*** – such as manna and quail, the parting of the Sea, and other Divine gifts.

21. ***"My people! Enter the Holy Land which Allah has ordained for you*** and commanded you to enter. This was greater Syria (*Shām*). ***Do not turn back in your tracks*** and be defeated by fear of the enemy ***and so be transformed into losers*** in respect of your efforts."

22. ***They said, "Mūsā! There are tyrants in it.*** They were remnants of the people of 'Ād and were very tall and strong. ***We will not enter it until they leave. If they leave it, then we will go in."***

23. ***Two men among those who were afraid*** – fearing to oppose the command of Allah, Yusha' and Kālib who were among the notables whom Mūsā sent to spy out the circumstances of the tyrants – ***but whom Allah had blessed*** – by preserving them from wrong action so that they concealed what they had learned except from Mūsā, which was not the case with the others who were cowardly and spread the information about – ***said*** to them, ***"Enter the gate*** of the city ***against them!*** Do not fear them. They are merely bodies without hearts. ***Once you have entered it, you will be victorious*** – meaning that out of certainty in the victory of Allah and that He would carry out the promise of victory He had given them. ***Put your trust in Allah if you are believers."***

24. ***They said, "Mūsā! We will never enter it so long as they are there. So you and your Lord go and fight*** them. ***We will stay sitting here*** and not fighting."

25. ***He*** (Mūsā) then ***said, "My Lord, I have no power over anyone*** – to compel them to obey – ***but myself and my brother, so make a clear distinction between us and this degenerate people."***

قَالُواْ يَٰمُوسَىٰٓ إِنَّا لَن نَّدۡخُلَهَآ أَبَدٗا مَّا دَامُواْ فِيهَاۖ فَٱذۡهَبۡ
أَنتَ وَرَبُّكَ فَقَٰتِلَآ إِنَّا هَٰهُنَا قَٰعِدُونَ ٢٤ قَالَ رَبِّ
إِنِّي لَآ أَمۡلِكُ إِلَّا نَفۡسِي وَأَخِيۖ فَٱفۡرُقۡ بَيۡنَنَا وَبَيۡنَ ٱلۡقَوۡمِ
ٱلۡفَٰسِقِينَ ٢٥ قَالَ فَإِنَّهَا مُحَرَّمَةٌ عَلَيۡهِمۡۛ أَرۡبَعِينَ سَنَةٗۛ
يَتِيهُونَ فِي ٱلۡأَرۡضِۚ فَلَا تَأۡسَ عَلَى ٱلۡقَوۡمِ ٱلۡفَٰسِقِينَ
٢٦ ۞ وَٱتۡلُ عَلَيۡهِمۡ نَبَأَ ٱبۡنَيۡ ءَادَمَ بِٱلۡحَقِّ إِذۡ قَرَّبَا قُرۡبَانٗا
فَتُقُبِّلَ مِنۡ أَحَدِهِمَا وَلَمۡ يُتَقَبَّلۡ مِنَ ٱلۡأٓخَرِ قَالَ لَأَقۡتُلَنَّكَۖ
قَالَ إِنَّمَا يَتَقَبَّلُ ٱللَّهُ مِنَ ٱلۡمُتَّقِينَ ٢٧ لَئِنۢ بَسَطتَ إِلَيَّ يَدَكَ
لِتَقۡتُلَنِي مَآ أَنَا۠ بِبَاسِطٖ يَدِيَ إِلَيۡكَ لِأَقۡتُلَكَۖ إِنِّيٓ أَخَافُ ٱللَّهَ
رَبَّ ٱلۡعَٰلَمِينَ ٢٨ إِنِّيٓ أُرِيدُ أَن تَبُوٓأَ بِإِثۡمِي وَإِثۡمِكَ فَتَكُونَ
مِنۡ أَصۡحَٰبِ ٱلنَّارِۚ وَذَٰلِكَ جَزَٰٓؤُاْ ٱلظَّٰلِمِينَ ٢٩ فَطَوَّعَتۡ
لَهُۥ نَفۡسُهُۥ قَتۡلَ أَخِيهِ فَقَتَلَهُۥ فَأَصۡبَحَ مِنَ ٱلۡخَٰسِرِينَ ٣٠
فَبَعَثَ ٱللَّهُ غُرَابٗا يَبۡحَثُ فِي ٱلۡأَرۡضِ لِيُرِيَهُۥ كَيۡفَ يُوَٰرِي
سَوۡءَةَ أَخِيهِۚ قَالَ يَٰوَيۡلَتَىٰٓ أَعَجَزۡتُ أَنۡ أَكُونَ مِثۡلَ هَٰذَا
ٱلۡغُرَابِ فَأُوَٰرِيَ سَوۡءَةَ أَخِيۖ فَأَصۡبَحَ مِنَ ٱلنَّٰدِمِينَ ٣١
مِنۡ أَجۡلِ ذَٰلِكَ كَتَبۡنَا عَلَىٰ بَنِيٓ إِسۡرَٰٓءِيلَ أَنَّهُۥ مَن قَتَلَ
نَفۡسَۢا بِغَيۡرِ نَفۡسٍ أَوۡ فَسَادٖ فِي ٱلۡأَرۡضِ فَكَأَنَّمَا قَتَلَ
ٱلنَّاسَ جَمِيعٗا وَمَنۡ أَحۡيَاهَا فَكَأَنَّمَآ أَحۡيَا ٱلنَّاسَ
جَمِيعٗاۚ وَلَقَدۡ جَآءَتۡهُمۡ رُسُلُنَا بِٱلۡبَيِّنَٰتِ ثُمَّ إِنَّ كَثِيرٗا
مِّنۡهُم بَعۡدَ ذَٰلِكَ فِي ٱلۡأَرۡضِ لَمُسۡرِفُونَ ٣٢ إِنَّمَا
جَزَٰٓؤُاْ ٱلَّذِينَ يُحَارِبُونَ ٱللَّهَ وَرَسُولَهُۥ وَيَسۡعَوۡنَ فِي ٱلۡأَرۡضِ

26. ***He*** (Allah) ***said, "The land*** (the Holy Land) ***will be forbidden to them*** to enter ***for forty years during which they will wander aimlessly about the earth*** – in an area of a few square kilometres, as Ibn 'Abbās said. ***Do not waste grief*** and sorrow ***on this degenerate people."*** It is related that they travelled at night and in the morning found themselves back in the place where they started from. They did the same in daytime, until all of them died except those under twenty years old. It is said that there were six hundred thousand of them. Hārūn and Mūsā died in the desert but it was a mercy for them whereas it was a punishment for the others. Mūsā asked his Lord, when he was dying, to put him within a stone's throw of the Holy Land and He did. Yusha' became a Prophet after the age of forty and commanded that the tyrants be fought. Those who were left went with him and fought on a Friday. The sun stopped for an hour until the fighting was over. Aḥmad related in his *Musnad* the *ḥadīth*, "The sun was not halted for anyone except Yusha'."

27. ***Recite***, Muḥammad, ***to them*** (your people) ***the true account of Ādam's two sons*** (Hābīl and Qābīl) ***when they offered a sacrifice*** to Allah – a ram from Hābīl and crops from Qābīl – ***and it was accepted from one of them*** (Hābil) – known by the fact that lightning came down and burned up his offering – ***but not accepted from the other*** (Qābīl) – who became angry and concealed his envy within himself until Ādam went on *ḥajj*. ***The one said*** to the other, ***"I shall kill you."*** – Hābīl asked him why and Qābīl said, "Because your sacrifice was accepted and mine was not." – ***The other said, "Allah only accepts from the godfearing.***

28. ***Even if you do raise your hand against me to kill me, I am not going to raise my hand against you to kill you. Truly I fear Allah, the Lord of all the worlds.***

29. ***I want you to take on my wrongdoing*** – by killing me – ***and your wrongdoing*** – for what you did before – ***and so become one of the Companions of the Fire.*** I do not want to take on your sin if you kill me so that I become one of the People of the Fire." Allah says: ***That is the repayment of the wrongdoers.***

30. ***So his lower self persuaded him*** – and made it appear attractive to him – ***to kill his brother, and he killed him and became one of the lost*** by killing him; and he did not know what to do with him

فَسَادًا أَن يُقَتَّلُوٓاْ أَوۡ يُصَلَّبُوٓاْ أَوۡ تُقَطَّعَ أَيۡدِيهِمۡ
وَأَرۡجُلُهُم مِّنۡ خِلَٰفٍ أَوۡ يُنفَوۡاْ مِنَ ٱلۡأَرۡضِۚ ذَٰلِكَ
لَهُمۡ خِزۡيٞ فِي ٱلدُّنۡيَاۖ وَلَهُمۡ فِي ٱلۡأٓخِرَةِ عَذَابٌ عَظِيمٌ
٣٣ إِلَّا ٱلَّذِينَ تَابُواْ مِن قَبۡلِ أَن تَقۡدِرُواْ عَلَيۡهِمۡۖ فَٱعۡلَمُوٓاْ
أَنَّ ٱللَّهَ غَفُورٞ رَّحِيمٞ ٣٤ يَٰٓأَيُّهَا ٱلَّذِينَ ءَامَنُواْ
ٱتَّقُواْ ٱللَّهَ وَٱبۡتَغُوٓاْ إِلَيۡهِ ٱلۡوَسِيلَةَ وَجَٰهِدُواْ فِي سَبِيلِهِۦ
لَعَلَّكُمۡ تُفۡلِحُونَ ٣٥ إِنَّ ٱلَّذِينَ كَفَرُواْ لَوۡ أَنَّ
لَهُم مَّا فِي ٱلۡأَرۡضِ جَمِيعٗا وَمِثۡلَهُۥ مَعَهُۥ لِيَفۡتَدُواْ بِهِۦ مِنۡ
عَذَابِ يَوۡمِ ٱلۡقِيَٰمَةِ مَا تُقُبِّلَ مِنۡهُمۡۖ وَلَهُمۡ عَذَابٌ أَلِيمٞ ٣٦
يُرِيدُونَ أَن يَخۡرُجُواْ مِنَ ٱلنَّارِ وَمَا هُم بِخَٰرِجِينَ مِنۡهَاۖ
وَلَهُمۡ عَذَابٞ مُّقِيمٞ ٣٧ وَٱلسَّارِقُ وَٱلسَّارِقَةُ فَٱقۡطَعُوٓاْ
أَيۡدِيَهُمَا جَزَآءَۢ بِمَا كَسَبَا نَكَٰلٗا مِّنَ ٱللَّهِۗ وَٱللَّهُ عَزِيزٌ حَكِيمٞ
٣٨ فَمَن تَابَ مِنۢ بَعۡدِ ظُلۡمِهِۦ وَأَصۡلَحَ فَإِنَّ ٱللَّهَ يَتُوبُ
عَلَيۡهِۗ إِنَّ ٱللَّهَ غَفُورٞ رَّحِيمٌ ٣٩ أَلَمۡ تَعۡلَمۡ أَنَّ ٱللَّهَ لَهُۥ مُلۡكُ
ٱلسَّمَٰوَٰتِ وَٱلۡأَرۡضِ يُعَذِّبُ مَن يَشَآءُ وَيَغۡفِرُ لِمَن يَشَآءُۗ
وَٱللَّهُ عَلَىٰ كُلِّ شَيۡءٖ قَدِيرٞ ٤٠ ۞ يَٰٓأَيُّهَا ٱلرَّسُولُ
لَا يَحۡزُنكَ ٱلَّذِينَ يُسَٰرِعُونَ فِي ٱلۡكُفۡرِ مِنَ ٱلَّذِينَ
قَالُوٓاْ ءَامَنَّا بِأَفۡوَٰهِهِمۡ وَلَمۡ تُؤۡمِن قُلُوبُهُمۡۛ وَمِنَ ٱلَّذِينَ
هَادُواْۛ سَمَّٰعُونَ لِلۡكَذِبِ سَمَّٰعُونَ لِقَوۡمٍ
ءَاخَرِينَ لَمۡ يَأۡتُوكَۖ يُحَرِّفُونَ ٱلۡكَلِمَ مِنۢ بَعۡدِ مَوَاضِعِهِۦۖ

because that was the first human corpse on the earth, so he carried him on his back.

31. ***Then Allah sent a crow which scratched at the earth*** – with its beak and feet and piled it on top of another dead crow until it had covered it – ***to show him how to conceal*** and bury ***his brother's corpse. He said, "O woe is me! Am I not even able to be like this crow and conceal my brother's corpse?" And he became one of the bitterly remorseful*** – for what he had done by carrying him and then burying him.

32. ***...on that account*** (Qābīl's murder). ***So We decreed for the Tribe of Israel that if someone kills another person – unless it is in retaliation for*** killing ***someone else or for causing corruption in the earth*** – by such things as unbelief and fornication and highway robbery ***– it is as if he had murdered all mankind. And if anyone gives life to another person*** – by preventing a murder – ***it is as if he had given life to all mankind.*** Ibn 'Abbās said that murdering all mankind occurs when there is violation of the honour and safety of the person. ***Our Messengers came to them*** (the Tribe of Israel) ***with Clear Signs*** (miracles) ***but even after that many of them committed outrages in the earth*** by exceeding the limits in respect of unbelief, killing and other things.

33. The following was revealed about the 'Uranites when they came to Madina and were ill and the Prophet, may Allah bless him and grant him peace, gave them permission to go out to the camels and drink from their urine and milk. When they recovered again, they killed the herdsman of the Prophet and stole the animals. ***The reprisal against those who wage war on Allah and His Messenger*** by fighting the Muslims ***and go about the earth corrupting it*** by committing highway robbery ***is that they should be killed or crucified, or have their opposite hands and feet cut off*** – right hand and left foot – ***or be banished from the land.*** The conjunction "or", which separates the different punishments, indicates that they should be applied in order of severity according to the particular circumstances of the crime. Killing is for someone who only kills. Crucifixion is for someone who kills and steals. Amputation is for someone who steals but does not kill. Exile is for someone who only causes fear. Ibn 'Abbās said this, and ash-Shāfi'ī follows it. The sounder of two positions is that someone crucified should be left up for three days. Connected to exile are punishments of imprisonment and the like. ***That*** punishment ***will be their degradation in this world and in the Next World they will have a terrible punishment*** in the Fire,

34. ***... except for those*** highwaymen and rebels ***who repent before you gain power over them. Know that Allah is Ever Forgiving*** for what they have done**,** ***Most Merciful*** to them, by allowing a penalty less than those prescribed in the previous *āyat***.** So do not inflict the *ḥadd* on them. Repentance can only mitigate the *ḥadd* of Allah but it does not alter the rights of human beings. This is clear to me and I cannot see any possible opposition to it. Allah knows best. If someone kills and takes property, he is subject to execution and amputation but is not to be crucified. This is the sounder of the positions of ash-Shāfi'ī. Repentance is of no use after someone has been captured. That is the sounder of his two views.

35. ***You who believe! Be fearful of Allah*** – showing fear of His punishment by obeying Him – ***and seek the means*** through obedience ***to draw near to Him, and fight hard in*** jihād ***in His Way*** to elevate His *dīn*, ***so that perhaps you may be successful.***

36. ***As for those who disbelieve, if they had everything on the earth, and the same again with it, to ransom themselves from the punishment of the Day of Rising, it would not be accepted from them. They will have a painful punishment.***

37. ***They will want to get out of the Fire but they will not be able to. They will have an everlasting punishment.***

38. ***As for both male thieves and female thieves, cut off their*** right ***hands*** at the wrist ***in reprisal for what they have done:*** – the *Sunna* makes it clear that amputation takes place on account of a quarter of a dinar or more and if someone steals again, their left foot is cut at the ankle, then their left hand, and after that it is subject to discretion – ***an object lesson*** and punishment ***from Allah. Allah is Almighty*** in His command, ***All-Wise*** in His creation**.**

39. ***But if anyone repents after his wrongdoing*** **–** after stealing – ***and puts things right*** – by amending his behaviour – ***Allah will turn towards him. Allah is Ever-Forgiving, Most Merciful.*** The rights of

يَقُولُونَ إِنْ أُوتِيتُمْ هَٰذَا فَخُذُوهُ وَإِن لَّمْ تُؤْتَوْهُ فَٱحْذَرُوا۟ ۚ
وَمَن يُرِدِ ٱللَّهُ فِتْنَتَهُۥ فَلَن تَمْلِكَ لَهُۥ مِنَ ٱللَّهِ شَيْـًٔا ۚ
أُو۟لَٰٓئِكَ ٱلَّذِينَ لَمْ يُرِدِ ٱللَّهُ أَن يُطَهِّرَ قُلُوبَهُمْ ۚ لَهُمْ فِى
ٱلدُّنْيَا خِزْىٌ ۖ وَلَهُمْ فِى ٱلْـَٔاخِرَةِ عَذَابٌ عَظِيمٌ ﴿٤١﴾
سَمَّٰعُونَ لِلْكَذِبِ أَكَّٰلُونَ لِلسُّحْتِ ۚ فَإِن جَآءُوكَ
فَٱحْكُم بَيْنَهُمْ أَوْ أَعْرِضْ عَنْهُمْ ۖ وَإِن تُعْرِضْ عَنْهُمْ فَلَن
يَضُرُّوكَ شَيْـًٔا ۖ وَإِنْ حَكَمْتَ فَٱحْكُم بَيْنَهُم بِٱلْقِسْطِ ۚ
إِنَّ ٱللَّهَ يُحِبُّ ٱلْمُقْسِطِينَ ﴿٤٢﴾ وَكَيْفَ يُحَكِّمُونَكَ وَعِندَهُمُ
ٱلتَّوْرَىٰةُ فِيهَا حُكْمُ ٱللَّهِ ثُمَّ يَتَوَلَّوْنَ مِنۢ بَعْدِ ذَٰلِكَ ۚ
وَمَآ أُو۟لَٰٓئِكَ بِٱلْمُؤْمِنِينَ ﴿٤٣﴾ إِنَّآ أَنزَلْنَا ٱلتَّوْرَىٰةَ فِيهَا
هُدًى وَنُورٌ ۚ يَحْكُمُ بِهَا ٱلنَّبِيُّونَ ٱلَّذِينَ أَسْلَمُوا۟ لِلَّذِينَ
هَادُوا۟ وَٱلرَّبَّٰنِيُّونَ وَٱلْأَحْبَارُ بِمَا ٱسْتُحْفِظُوا۟ مِن كِتَٰبِ
ٱللَّهِ وَكَانُوا۟ عَلَيْهِ شُهَدَآءَ ۚ فَلَا تَخْشَوُا۟ ٱلنَّاسَ
وَٱخْشَوْنِ وَلَا تَشْتَرُوا۟ بِـَٔايَٰتِى ثَمَنًا قَلِيلًا ۚ وَمَن لَّمْ يَحْكُم
بِمَآ أَنزَلَ ٱللَّهُ فَأُو۟لَٰٓئِكَ هُمُ ٱلْكَٰفِرُونَ ﴿٤٤﴾ وَكَتَبْنَا عَلَيْهِمْ
فِيهَآ أَنَّ ٱلنَّفْسَ بِٱلنَّفْسِ وَٱلْعَيْنَ بِٱلْعَيْنِ وَٱلْأَنفَ
بِٱلْأَنفِ وَٱلْأُذُنَ بِٱلْأُذُنِ وَٱلسِّنَّ بِٱلسِّنِّ وَٱلْجُرُوحَ
قِصَاصٌ ۚ فَمَن تَصَدَّقَ بِهِۦ فَهُوَ كَفَّارَةٌ لَّهُۥ ۚ وَمَن
لَّمْ يَحْكُم بِمَآ أَنزَلَ ٱللَّهُ فَأُو۟لَٰٓئِكَ هُمُ ٱلظَّٰلِمُونَ ﴿٤٥﴾
وَقَفَّيْنَا عَلَىٰٓ ءَاثَٰرِهِم بِعِيسَى ٱبْنِ مَرْيَمَ مُصَدِّقًا لِّمَا بَيْنَ يَدَيْهِ مِنَ

another human being are not restored by repentance, so a thief must return any property he has stolen. The *Sunna* makes it clear that if someone repents before the case is presented to the ruler, the *ḥadd* is not carried out. That is the position of ash-Shāfi'ī.

40. ***Do you not know that the sovereignty of the heavens and earth belongs to Allah?*** This question implies an affirmative response. ***He punishes whoever He wills and forgives whoever He wills. Allah has power over everything,*** including the power to punish or forgive.

41. ***Messenger! Do not be grieved by*** what has been done by ***those who rush into unbelief*** – falling into unbelief quickly at the first possible opportunity – ***from among those who say "We believe" with*** only ***their tongues when their hearts do not believe.*** They are the hypocrites. ***And among the Jews are those who listen to lies,*** which their rabbis have forged and which they accept instead of listening to you ***listening to other people*** among the Jews ***who have not come to you*** – referring to the people of Khaybar. When one of them who had been married committed adultery and they did not want to stone him, Qurayẓa sent a delegation to the Prophet, may Allah bless him and grant him peace, to ask for his judgement regarding the couple – ***distorting words*** – which were in the Torah, such as the verse on stoning – ***from their proper meanings*** – as Allah had revealed them, thereby changing them – ***saying*** to those they sent, ***"If you are given this*** – altered judgement, which is flogging, by Muḥammad, may Allah bless him and grant him peace – ***then take it*** and accept it. ***If,*** however, ***you are not given it*** – and are given a different judgement – ***then beware*** of accepting it!" ***If Allah desires misguidance for someone, you cannot help him*** or defend him ***against Allah in any way. Those are the people whose hearts Allah does not want to purify*** from unbelief. If He desires that, it shall be. ***They will have disgrace in this world*** – through degradation and *jizya,* ***and in the Next World they will have a terrible punishment.***

42. ***They are listeners to lies, consumers of ill-gotten gains*** (read as *suḥt* and *suḥut*): unlawful wealth, such as bribes. ***If they come to you*** so that you can judge between them ***you may either judge between them or turn away from them.*** This is abrogated by Allah's words, *"Judge between them..."* (5:49) below. So the Muslims must give judgement between them when they come to us for it. That is the soundest of the positions of ash-Shāfi'ī. If they present themselves accompanied by a Muslim, it becomes absolutely mandatory to give judgement by consensus. ***If you turn away from them, they cannot harm you in any way. But if you do judge*** between them, ***judge between them justly*** and fairly. ***Allah loves the just,*** who are fair in their judgements, and will reward them.

43. ***How can they make you their judge when they have the Torah with them which contains the judgement of Allah*** about stoning***?*** This is a question which invokes wonder, suggesting that they did not intend by so doing to know the truth but hoped for a judgement which would be easier for them. ***Then even after that*** judgement ***they turn their backs*** when they are presented with the judgement of stoning which is in fact in accordance with their Book. ***Such people are certainly not believers.***

44. ***We sent down the Torah containing guidance*** away from misguidance ***and light*** – here meaning clarification of judgements – ***and the Prophets*** of the Tribe of Israel, ***who had submitted themselves*** and obeyed Allah, ***gave judgement by it for the Jews – as did their scholars and their rabbis – by what they had been allowed to preserve of Allah's Book*** without alteration ***and to which they were witnesses*** – that it was the truth. ***Do not be afraid of people***, Jews, regarding divulging what they have of the description of Muḥammad, stoning and other things: ***be afraid of Me*** regarding concealing it. ***And do not sell*** and exchange ***My Signs for a paltry price***: a little of this world, in return for concealing them. ***Those who do not judge by what Allah has sent down, such people are unbelievers.***

45. ***We prescribed in it*** (the Torah) ***for them: a life for a life –*** you should be killed if you kill someone – ***an eye*** (read as *'aynu* and *'ayna*) gouged out ***for an eye, a nose*** (read as *anfu* and *anfa*) mutilated ***for a nose, an ear*** (read as *udhunu* and *udhuna*) cut off ***for an ear, a tooth*** (read as *sinnu* and *sinna*) extracted ***for a tooth, and retaliation for wounds.*** There is retaliation when it is possible, for instance for the loss of a life, a foot, a hand and similar things, but when it is impossible, arbitration should take place. This judgement, even if was prescribed for the Jews, is also confirmed in our *Sharī'a.*

ٱلتَّوۡرَىٰةِۖ وَءَاتَيۡنَٰهُ ٱلۡإِنجِيلَ فِيهِ هُدٗى وَنُورٞ وَمُصَدِّقٗا لِّمَا بَيۡنَ
يَدَيۡهِ مِنَ ٱلتَّوۡرَىٰةِ وَهُدٗى وَمَوۡعِظَةٗ لِّلۡمُتَّقِينَ ٤٦ وَلۡيَحۡكُمۡ
أَهۡلُ ٱلۡإِنجِيلِ بِمَآ أَنزَلَ ٱللَّهُ فِيهِۚ وَمَن لَّمۡ يَحۡكُم بِمَآ أَنزَلَ
ٱللَّهُ فَأُوْلَٰٓئِكَ هُمُ ٱلۡفَٰسِقُونَ ٤٧ وَأَنزَلۡنَآ إِلَيۡكَ ٱلۡكِتَٰبَ
بِٱلۡحَقِّ مُصَدِّقٗا لِّمَا بَيۡنَ يَدَيۡهِ مِنَ ٱلۡكِتَٰبِ وَمُهَيۡمِنًا
عَلَيۡهِۖ فَٱحۡكُم بَيۡنَهُم بِمَآ أَنزَلَ ٱللَّهُۖ وَلَا تَتَّبِعۡ أَهۡوَآءَهُمۡ
عَمَّا جَآءَكَ مِنَ ٱلۡحَقِّۚ لِكُلّٖ جَعَلۡنَا مِنكُمۡ شِرۡعَةٗ وَمِنۡهَاجٗاۚ
وَلَوۡ شَآءَ ٱللَّهُ لَجَعَلَكُمۡ أُمَّةٗ وَٰحِدَةٗ وَلَٰكِن لِّيَبۡلُوَكُمۡ فِي مَآ
ءَاتَىٰكُمۡۖ فَٱسۡتَبِقُواْ ٱلۡخَيۡرَٰتِۚ إِلَى ٱللَّهِ مَرۡجِعُكُمۡ جَمِيعٗا
فَيُنَبِّئُكُم بِمَا كُنتُمۡ فِيهِ تَخۡتَلِفُونَ ٤٨ وَأَنِ ٱحۡكُم بَيۡنَهُم بِمَآ
أَنزَلَ ٱللَّهُ وَلَا تَتَّبِعۡ أَهۡوَآءَهُمۡ وَٱحۡذَرۡهُمۡ أَن يَفۡتِنُوكَ عَنۢ
بَعۡضِ مَآ أَنزَلَ ٱللَّهُ إِلَيۡكَۖ فَإِن تَوَلَّوۡاْ فَٱعۡلَمۡ أَنَّمَا يُرِيدُ ٱللَّهُ أَن يُصِيبَهُم
بِبَعۡضِ ذُنُوبِهِمۡۗ وَإِنَّ كَثِيرٗا مِّنَ ٱلنَّاسِ لَفَٰسِقُونَ ٤٩ أَفَحُكۡمَ
ٱلۡجَٰهِلِيَّةِ يَبۡغُونَۚ وَمَنۡ أَحۡسَنُ مِنَ ٱللَّهِ حُكۡمٗا لِّقَوۡمٖ يُوقِنُونَ ٥٠
۞يَٰٓأَيُّهَا ٱلَّذِينَ ءَامَنُواْ لَا تَتَّخِذُواْ ٱلۡيَهُودَ وَٱلنَّصَٰرَىٰٓ أَوۡلِيَآءَۘ بَعۡضُهُمۡ
أَوۡلِيَآءُ بَعۡضٖۚ وَمَن يَتَوَلَّهُم مِّنكُمۡ فَإِنَّهُۥ مِنۡهُمۡۗ إِنَّ ٱللَّهَ لَا يَهۡدِي ٱلۡقَوۡمَ
ٱلظَّٰلِمِينَ ٥١ فَتَرَى ٱلَّذِينَ فِي قُلُوبِهِم مَّرَضٞ يُسَٰرِعُونَ فِيهِمۡ
يَقُولُونَ نَخۡشَىٰٓ أَن تُصِيبَنَا دَآئِرَةٞۚ فَعَسَى ٱللَّهُ أَن يَأۡتِيَ بِٱلۡفَتۡحِ أَوۡ أَمۡرٖ
مِّنۡ عِندِهِۦ فَيُصۡبِحُواْ عَلَىٰ مَآ أَسَرُّواْ فِيٓ أَنفُسِهِمۡ نَٰدِمِينَ ٥٢
وَيَقُولُ ٱلَّذِينَ ءَامَنُوٓاْ أَهَٰٓؤُلَآءِ ٱلَّذِينَ أَقۡسَمُواْ بِٱللَّهِ جَهۡدَ أَيۡمَٰنِهِمۡ

But if anyone forgoes that (retaliation) – when he is able to exact it, forgoing it – ***as charity, it will act as expiation for him. Those who do not judge by what Allah has sent down*** regarding retaliation and other things, ***such people are wrongdoers.***

46. ***And We sent 'Īsā son of Maryam following in their*** (the Prophets') ***footsteps, confirming the Torah that came before him. We gave him the Gospel containing guidance*** away from misguidance ***and light*** – meaning here clarification of judgements – ***confirming*** the judgements in ***the Torah that came before it, and as guidance and admonition for the godfearing.***

47. ***The people of the Gospel should judge*** (read as *wal-yaḥkum* and *wal-yaḥkuma*) ***by what*** rulings ***Allah sent down in it. Those who do not judge by what Allah has sent down, such people are degenerate.***

48. ***And We have sent down the Book*** (the Qur'ān) ***to you***, Muḥammad, ***with truth, confirming and conserving the previous Books,*** and testifying to them. ***So judge between them*** – the People of the Book when they present a case to you – ***by what Allah has sent down*** to you, ***and do not follow their whims and desires, so deviating from the Truth that has come to you. We have appointed a law*** (*Sharī'a*) ***and a practice*** (a clear path) ***for every one of you*** (different religious communities) – to follow in respect of your *dīn*. ***Had Allah willed, He would have made you a single nation,*** with a single *Shari'a*, ***but He wanted to test you*** and divide you into groups ***regarding what*** (the different laws) ***has come to you*** to see which of you would obey and which disobey. ***So compete against each other in doing good*** and race to that. ***Every one of you will return to Allah*** at the Resurrection ***and He will inform you regarding the things about which you differed*** in respect of the *dīn*, and repay each of them for their actions.

49. ***Judge between them by what Allah has sent down and do not follow their whims and desires. And beware of them lest they lure you away*** and misguide you ***from some of what Allah has sent down to you. If they turn their backs*** from the revealed judgement and desire something else ***then know that Allah wants to afflict them*** – to punish them in this world – ***with some of their wrong actions*** which they commit, including this turning away. He will

إِنَّهُمْ لَمَعَكُمْ حَبِطَتْ أَعْمَالُهُمْ فَأَصْبَحُوا خَاسِرِينَ ﴿٥٣﴾ يَا أَيُّهَا
الَّذِينَ آمَنُوا مَنْ يَرْتَدَّ مِنْكُمْ عَنْ دِينِهِ فَسَوْفَ يَأْتِي اللَّهُ بِقَوْمٍ يُحِبُّهُمْ
وَيُحِبُّونَهُ أَذِلَّةٍ عَلَى الْمُؤْمِنِينَ أَعِزَّةٍ عَلَى الْكَافِرِينَ يُجَاهِدُونَ فِي
سَبِيلِ اللَّهِ وَلَا يَخَافُونَ لَوْمَةَ لَائِمٍ ذَٰلِكَ فَضْلُ اللَّهِ يُؤْتِيهِ مَنْ يَشَاءُ
وَاللَّهُ وَاسِعٌ عَلِيمٌ ﴿٥٤﴾ إِنَّمَا وَلِيُّكُمُ اللَّهُ وَرَسُولُهُ وَالَّذِينَ آمَنُوا الَّذِينَ
يُقِيمُونَ الصَّلَاةَ وَيُؤْتُونَ الزَّكَاةَ وَهُمْ رَاكِعُونَ ﴿٥٥﴾ وَمَنْ يَتَوَلَّ اللَّهَ
وَرَسُولَهُ وَالَّذِينَ آمَنُوا فَإِنَّ حِزْبَ اللَّهِ هُمُ الْغَالِبُونَ ﴿٥٦﴾ يَا أَيُّهَا الَّذِينَ
آمَنُوا لَا تَتَّخِذُوا الَّذِينَ اتَّخَذُوا دِينَكُمْ هُزُوًا وَلَعِبًا مِنَ الَّذِينَ أُوتُوا
الْكِتَابَ مِنْ قَبْلِكُمْ وَالْكُفَّارَ أَوْلِيَاءَ وَاتَّقُوا اللَّهَ إِنْ كُنْتُمْ مُؤْمِنِينَ ﴿٥٧﴾
وَإِذَا نَادَيْتُمْ إِلَى الصَّلَاةِ اتَّخَذُوهَا هُزُوًا وَلَعِبًا ذَٰلِكَ بِأَنَّهُمْ قَوْمٌ
لَا يَعْقِلُونَ ﴿٥٨﴾ قُلْ يَا أَهْلَ الْكِتَابِ هَلْ تَنْقِمُونَ مِنَّا إِلَّا أَنْ آمَنَّا
بِاللَّهِ وَمَا أُنْزِلَ إِلَيْنَا وَمَا أُنْزِلَ مِنْ قَبْلُ وَأَنَّ أَكْثَرَكُمْ فَاسِقُونَ ﴿٥٩﴾ قُلْ
هَلْ أُنَبِّئُكُمْ بِشَرٍّ مِنْ ذَٰلِكَ مَثُوبَةً عِنْدَ اللَّهِ مَنْ لَعَنَهُ اللَّهُ وَغَضِبَ
عَلَيْهِ وَجَعَلَ مِنْهُمُ الْقِرَدَةَ وَالْخَنَازِيرَ وَعَبَدَ الطَّاغُوتَ أُولَٰئِكَ شَرٌّ
مَكَانًا وَأَضَلُّ عَنْ سَوَاءِ السَّبِيلِ ﴿٦٠﴾ وَإِذَا جَاءُوكُمْ قَالُوا آمَنَّا
وَقَدْ دَخَلُوا بِالْكُفْرِ وَهُمْ قَدْ خَرَجُوا بِهِ وَاللَّهُ أَعْلَمُ بِمَا كَانُوا يَكْتُمُونَ
﴿٦١﴾ وَتَرَىٰ كَثِيرًا مِنْهُمْ يُسَارِعُونَ فِي الْإِثْمِ وَالْعُدْوَانِ وَأَكْلِهِمُ
السُّحْتَ لَبِئْسَ مَا كَانُوا يَعْمَلُونَ ﴿٦٢﴾ لَوْلَا يَنْهَاهُمُ الرَّبَّانِيُّونَ
وَالْأَحْبَارُ عَنْ قَوْلِهِمُ الْإِثْمَ وَأَكْلِهِمُ السُّحْتَ لَبِئْسَ مَا كَانُوا
يَصْنَعُونَ ﴿٦٣﴾ وَقَالَتِ الْيَهُودُ يَدُ اللَّهِ مَغْلُولَةٌ غُلَّتْ أَيْدِيهِمْ وَلُعِنُوا

repay them for all of them in the Next World. ***Many of mankind are degenerate.***

50. ***Do they then seek*** (read as *yabghūna* and *tabghūna*, "you seek") ***the judgement of the Time of Ignorance*** out of desire for mutual flattery and prejudice***? Who could be better at giving judgement than Allah, for people with certainty?*** No one, of course, could be better. The people with certainty are mentioned because they are those who reflect on things deeply.

51. ***O you who believe! Do not take the Jews and Christians as your friends*** – in mutual friendship and love***; they are friends of one another.*** Do not join with them in their unbelief. ***Any of you who takes them as friends is one of them. Allah surely does not guide wrongdoing people*** who befriend the unbelievers.

52. ***Yet you see those with sickness*** (weak faith) ***in their hearts*** – as was the case with 'Abdullāh ibn Ubayy, the hypocrite – ***rushing to them*** in friendship, ***saying*** in excuse, ***"We fear the wheel of fate may turn against us"*** – fearing the advent of drought or defeat or that Muḥammad might not be successful. It is so that they do not single them out – The Almighty continues: ***But it may well be that Allah will bring about victory*** – when the *dīn* of the Prophet triumphs – ***or some other contingency from Him***: the exposure and disgrace of the hypocrites. ***Then they will deeply regret their secret thoughts*** of doubt and befriending the unbelievers.

53. ***Those who believe say*** (read as *yaqūlu* and *yaqūla*) – in amazement to one another when the hypocrites are disgraced by disclosure – ***"Are these the people who swore by Allah, with their most earnest oaths, that they were with you*** in the *dīn?*" Allah says: ***Their*** righteous ***actions have come to nothing*** and are nullified ***and they now are losers.*** They have lost this world through their disgrace and the Next World through eternal punishment.

54. ***O you who believe! If any of you renounce your* dīn** – reverting to unbelief: this shows that Allah knew that that would happen and indeed a group did renounce Islam after the death of the Prophet, may Allah bless him and grant him peace – ***Allah will bring forward a people*** to replace them ***whom He loves and who love Him*** – and the Prophet said about this, "They (the replacements) are the people of this one," and he pointed at Abū Mūsā al-Ash'arī (al-Ḥākim) – ***humble*** and kind ***to the believers, fierce*** and harsh ***to the unbelievers, who fight to the utmost in the Way of Allah and do not fear the blame of any blamer*** – in the way that hypocrites fear the criticism of the unbelievers. ***That is the unbounded favour of Allah which He gives to whoever He wills. Allah is Boundless*** in His favour, ***All-Knowing*** of who deserves it. This *āyat* was revealed when Ibn Salām said, "Messenger of Allah, our people are shunning us."

55. ***Your friend is only Allah and His Messenger and those who believe: those who establish the prayer and pay* zakāt, *and bow*** in humility or who pray voluntary prayers.

56. ***And those who make Allah their friend, and His Messenger and those who believe:*** Allah will help them and support them; ***it is the party of Allah who are the victorious*** through His support of them. This makes it clear that they are His party and His followers.

57. ***O you who believe! Do not take as friends any of those given the Book before you or the unbelievers*** (idolaters) ***who make a mockery and a game out of your* dīn. *Show fear of Allah*** – by not taking them as friends – ***if you are believers*** – and are true in your belief.

58. ***When you call to the prayer*** with the *adhān* ***they make a mockery and a game of it*** (the prayer) – by making fun of it and laughing with one another. ***That*** which they do ***is because they are people who do not use their intellect.***

59. The following was revealed when the Jews asked the Prophet, may Allah bless him and grant him peace, "In which Messengers do you believe?" He said, "We believe in Allah and what He has revealed to us." When he mentioned 'Īsā they said, "We do not know a worse *dīn* than yours." ***Say: "O People of the Book, do you resent*** and dislike ***us for any other reason than that we believe in Allah and what was sent down to us, and what was sent down before*** to the Prophets ***and that most of you are degenerate?"*** In other words: "You only dislike us for our belief and your opposition in not accepting it is sheer deviance."

بِمَا قَالُوا۟ ۘ بَلْ يَدَاهُ مَبْسُوطَتَانِ يُنفِقُ كَيْفَ يَشَآءُ ۚ وَلَيَزِيدَنَّ كَثِيرًا
مِّنْهُم مَّآ أُنزِلَ إِلَيْكَ مِن رَّبِّكَ طُغْيَـٰنًا وَكُفْرًا ۚ وَأَلْقَيْنَا بَيْنَهُمُ ٱلْعَدَٰوَةَ
وَٱلْبَغْضَآءَ إِلَىٰ يَوْمِ ٱلْقِيَـٰمَةِ ۚ كُلَّمَآ أَوْقَدُوا۟ نَارًا لِّلْحَرْبِ أَطْفَأَهَا ٱللَّهُ ۚ
وَيَسْعَوْنَ فِى ٱلْأَرْضِ فَسَادًا ۚ وَٱللَّهُ لَا يُحِبُّ ٱلْمُفْسِدِينَ ﴿٦٤﴾
وَلَوْ أَنَّ أَهْلَ ٱلْكِتَـٰبِ ءَامَنُوا۟ وَٱتَّقَوْا۟ لَكَفَّرْنَا عَنْهُمْ
سَيِّـَٔاتِهِمْ وَلَأَدْخَلْنَـٰهُمْ جَنَّـٰتِ ٱلنَّعِيمِ ﴿٦٥﴾ وَلَوْ أَنَّهُمْ أَقَامُوا۟
ٱلتَّوْرَىٰةَ وَٱلْإِنجِيلَ وَمَآ أُنزِلَ إِلَيْهِم مِّن رَّبِّهِمْ لَأَكَلُوا۟ مِن
فَوْقِهِمْ وَمِن تَحْتِ أَرْجُلِهِم ۚ مِّنْهُمْ أُمَّةٌ مُّقْتَصِدَةٌ ۖ وَكَثِيرٌ مِّنْهُمْ
سَآءَ مَا يَعْمَلُونَ ﴿٦٦﴾ ۞ يَـٰٓأَيُّهَا ٱلرَّسُولُ بَلِّغْ مَآ أُنزِلَ إِلَيْكَ
مِن رَّبِّكَ ۖ وَإِن لَّمْ تَفْعَلْ فَمَا بَلَّغْتَ رِسَالَتَهُۥ ۚ وَٱللَّهُ يَعْصِمُكَ
مِنَ ٱلنَّاسِ ۗ إِنَّ ٱللَّهَ لَا يَهْدِى ٱلْقَوْمَ ٱلْكَـٰفِرِينَ ﴿٦٧﴾ قُلْ يَـٰٓأَهْلَ
ٱلْكِتَـٰبِ لَسْتُمْ عَلَىٰ شَىْءٍ حَتَّىٰ تُقِيمُوا۟ ٱلتَّوْرَىٰةَ وَٱلْإِنجِيلَ
وَمَآ أُنزِلَ إِلَيْكُم مِّن رَّبِّكُمْ ۗ وَلَيَزِيدَنَّ كَثِيرًا مِّنْهُم مَّآ أُنزِلَ
إِلَيْكَ مِن رَّبِّكَ طُغْيَـٰنًا وَكُفْرًا ۖ فَلَا تَأْسَ عَلَى ٱلْقَوْمِ ٱلْكَـٰفِرِينَ
﴿٦٨﴾ إِنَّ ٱلَّذِينَ ءَامَنُوا۟ وَٱلَّذِينَ هَادُوا۟ وَٱلصَّـٰبِـُٔونَ وَٱلنَّصَـٰرَىٰ
مَنْ ءَامَنَ بِٱللَّهِ وَٱلْيَوْمِ ٱلْـَٔاخِرِ وَعَمِلَ صَـٰلِحًا فَلَا خَوْفٌ
عَلَيْهِمْ وَلَا هُمْ يَحْزَنُونَ ﴿٦٩﴾ لَقَدْ أَخَذْنَا مِيثَـٰقَ بَنِىٓ
إِسْرَٰٓءِيلَ وَأَرْسَلْنَآ إِلَيْهِمْ رُسُلًا ۖ كُلَّمَا جَآءَهُمْ رَسُولٌۢ بِمَا
لَا تَهْوَىٰٓ أَنفُسُهُمْ فَرِيقًا كَذَّبُوا۟ وَفَرِيقًا يَقْتُلُونَ ﴿٧٠﴾
وَحَسِبُوٓا۟ أَلَّا تَكُونَ فِتْنَةٌ فَعَمُوا۟ وَصَمُّوا۟ ثُمَّ تَابَ ٱللَّهُ

60. ***Say: "Shall I tell you of a reward*** (repayment) ***with Allah far worse than that*** which you resent: ***those Allah whom has cursed*** and put far from His mercy ***and with whom He is angry – turning some of them into monkeys and into pigs*** by transmogrification – ***and who worshipped*** (read as *'abada* and *'abuda*) ***false gods.*** These are the Jews before them. "False gods" (*ṭāghūt*) refers to Shayṭān. They worship him by obeying him. ***Such people are in a worse situation*** – because they will be in the Fire – ***and further from the right way*** (the Path of the Truth)." The root of straight (*sawā'*) means "middle". This is in contradiction of their words, "There is no *dīn* worse than your *dīn*."

61. ***When they*** (the hypocritical Jews) ***come to you, they say, "We believe." But they entered in unbelief and left*** you ***with it.*** They never believed. ***Allah knows best what they were hiding*** of hypocrisy.

62. ***You see many of them*** (the Jews) ***rushing*** headlong in***to wrongdoing*** (lying) ***and enmity*** (injustice) ***and acquiring unlawful wealth*** such as bribes. ***What an evil thing they do*** by doing that.

63. ***Why do the scholars and rabbis*** among them ***not prohibit them from evil speech*** (lies) ***and acquiring ill-gotten gains? What an evil thing they fabricate*** – by ignoring their prohibition.

64. When their circumstances became reduced because of their denial of the Prophet, may Allah bless him and grant him peace, after they had previously been the wealthiest of people, ***the Jews say, "Allah's hand is chained"*** – implying that He is unable to send provision to them and that He is miserly. Allah is far exalted above that. Allah continues by saying: ***Their hands are chained*** – and kept from performing good actions as a supplication against them – ***and they are cursed for what they say! No! Both His hands are open wide*** – an emphatic description of generosity, and the hands are singled out for mention since what the generous give of their property, they give with their hands – ***and He gives however He wills*** – expanding or constricting and no one can object. ***What has been sent down to you from your Lord increases many of them in insolence and rejection*** of it. ***We have cast enmity and hatred between them*** – each group opposing the others – ***until the Day of Rising. Each time they kindle the fire of war*** against the Prophet, may Allah bless him and grant him peace ***Allah extinguishes it.*** When-ever they try to do that, Allah repels them. ***They rush about the earth, corrupting it*** through acts of disobedience. ***Allah does not love corrupters*** and will punish them.

65. ***If only the People of the Book had believed*** in Muḥammad, may Allah bless him and grant him peace, ***and been godfearing,*** fearing unbelief, ***We would have erased their evil deeds from them and admitted them into Gardens of Delight.***

66. ***If only they had implemented the Torah and the Gospel*** by acting on what their Books contain, which includes belief in the Prophet, may Allah bless him and grant him peace, ***and what*** (Revelation) ***was sent down to them from their Lord, they would have eaten from above their heads and beneath their feet,*** as their provision would have been expanded for them and overflowed from every side. ***Among them there is a moderate group*** – who act by it, those who believed in the Prophet, may Allah bless him and grant him peace, in the way that 'Abdullāh ibn Salām and his companions did, ***but what most of them do is evil.***

67. ***Messenger! Deliver*** all of ***what has been sent down to you from your Lord.*** Do not conceal anything out of fear of something being disliked. ***If you do not do it*** – convey all that has been revealed to you – ***you will not have conveyed His Message*** (read as *risāla* and also in the plural as *risālāt*) because concealing some of it is like concealing all of it. ***Allah will protect you from people*** – from them killing you. The Messenger of Allah, may Allah bless him and grant him peace, used to have guards guarding him until this was revealed and then he said, "Leave. Allah has given me protection." (al-Ḥākim) ***Allah does not guide the people of the unbelievers.***

68. ***Say: "People of the Book! You have nothing*** of the *dīn* ***to stand on until you implement the Torah and the Gospel and what has been sent down to you from your Lord*** – by acting by what is in it, part of which is believing in me." ***What has been sent down to you*** (the Qur'an) ***from your Lord increases many of them in insolence and unbelief*** because they reject it. ***So do not waste your grief*** by feeling sorry ***on the people of the unbelievers*** if they not believe in you. Do not worry about them.

عَلَيۡهِمۡ ثُمَّ عَمُواْ وَصَمُّواْ كَثِيرٞ مِّنۡهُمۡۚ وَٱللَّهُ بَصِيرُۢ بِمَا
يَعۡمَلُونَ ٧١ لَقَدۡ كَفَرَ ٱلَّذِينَ قَالُوٓاْ إِنَّ ٱللَّهَ هُوَ
ٱلۡمَسِيحُ ٱبۡنُ مَرۡيَمَۖ وَقَالَ ٱلۡمَسِيحُ يَٰبَنِيٓ إِسۡرَٰٓءِيلَ ٱعۡبُدُواْ
ٱللَّهَ رَبِّي وَرَبَّكُمۡۖ إِنَّهُۥ مَن يُشۡرِكۡ بِٱللَّهِ فَقَدۡ حَرَّمَ ٱللَّهُ عَلَيۡهِ
ٱلۡجَنَّةَ وَمَأۡوَىٰهُ ٱلنَّارُۖ وَمَا لِلظَّٰلِمِينَ مِنۡ أَنصَارٖ ٧٢
لَّقَدۡ كَفَرَ ٱلَّذِينَ قَالُوٓاْ إِنَّ ٱللَّهَ ثَالِثُ ثَلَٰثَةٖۘ وَمَا مِنۡ
إِلَٰهٍ إِلَّآ إِلَٰهٞ وَٰحِدٞۚ وَإِن لَّمۡ يَنتَهُواْ عَمَّا يَقُولُونَ لَيَمَسَّنَّ
ٱلَّذِينَ كَفَرُواْ مِنۡهُمۡ عَذَابٌ أَلِيمٌ ٧٣ أَفَلَا يَتُوبُونَ
إِلَى ٱللَّهِ وَيَسۡتَغۡفِرُونَهُۥۚ وَٱللَّهُ غَفُورٞ رَّحِيمٞ ٧٤
مَّا ٱلۡمَسِيحُ ٱبۡنُ مَرۡيَمَ إِلَّا رَسُولٞ قَدۡ خَلَتۡ مِن قَبۡلِهِ
ٱلرُّسُلُ وَأُمُّهُۥ صِدِّيقَةٞۖ كَانَا يَأۡكُلَانِ ٱلطَّعَامَۗ
ٱنظُرۡ كَيۡفَ نُبَيِّنُ لَهُمُ ٱلۡأٓيَٰتِ ثُمَّ ٱنظُرۡ أَنَّىٰ
يُؤۡفَكُونَ ٧٥ قُلۡ أَتَعۡبُدُونَ مِن دُونِ ٱللَّهِ مَا لَا
يَمۡلِكُ لَكُمۡ ضَرّٗا وَلَا نَفۡعٗاۚ وَٱللَّهُ هُوَ ٱلسَّمِيعُ ٱلۡعَلِيمُ ٧٦
قُلۡ يَٰٓأَهۡلَ ٱلۡكِتَٰبِ لَا تَغۡلُواْ فِي دِينِكُمۡ غَيۡرَ ٱلۡحَقِّ
وَلَا تَتَّبِعُوٓاْ أَهۡوَآءَ قَوۡمٖ قَدۡ ضَلُّواْ مِن قَبۡلُ وَأَضَلُّواْ
كَثِيرٗا وَضَلُّواْ عَن سَوَآءِ ٱلسَّبِيلِ ٧٧ لُعِنَ ٱلَّذِينَ
كَفَرُواْ مِنۢ بَنِيٓ إِسۡرَٰٓءِيلَ عَلَىٰ لِسَانِ دَاوُۥدَ وَعِيسَى
ٱبۡنِ مَرۡيَمَۚ ذَٰلِكَ بِمَا عَصَواْ وَّكَانُواْ يَعۡتَدُونَ ٧٨
كَانُواْ لَا يَتَنَاهَوۡنَ عَن مُّنكَرٖ فَعَلُوهُۚ لَبِئۡسَ

69. ***Those who believe and those who are Jews and the Sabaeans***, a group of them, ***and the Christians, all who believe in Allah and the Last Day and act rightly will feel no fear and know no sorrow*** in the Next World.

70. ***We made a covenant with the Tribe of Israel*** to believe in Allah and all His Messengers ***and We sent Messengers to them. Each time a Messenger*** from them ***came to them with something*** (religious obligations) ***their lower selves did not desire*** – then they rejected him – ***they denied some and they murdered others***, such as Zakariyyā and Yaḥyā.

71. ***They thought that there would be no trouble***, meaning punishment for their denying and killing the Messengers. ***They were blind*** to the truth and did not see it, ***and deaf*** to hearing it. ***Then Allah turned towards them*** when they repented. ***Then many of them went blind and deaf again. Allah sees what they do*** and will repay them for their actions.

72. ***Those who say, "Allah is the Messiah, the son of Maryam," are unbelievers. The Messiah said*** to them, ***"O Tribe of Israel! Worship Allah, my Lord and your Lord"*** meaning, "I am a slave, and not a god." ***If anyone attributes partners to Allah*** by worshipping anything other than Allah, ***Allah has forbidden him*** entry into ***the Garden and his refuge will be the Fire." The wrongdoers will have no helpers*** to protect them from the punishment of Allah.

73. ***Those who say, "Allah is the third of three*** gods," implying that there is a trinity of Allah, 'Īsā and his mother (a sect of Christians) ***are unbelievers. There is no god but One God. If they do not stop saying what they say*** regarding trinitarianism, and start affirming Allah's unity, ***a painful punishment*** (the Fire) ***will afflict those among them who disbelieve*** – and remain adamant in their unbelief.

74. ***Why do they not turn to Allah and ask for His forgiveness*** for what they have said? This is a question which implies a rebuke. ***Allah is Ever Forgiving*** to those who repent, ***Most Merciful*** to them.

75. ***The Messiah, the son of Maryam, was only a Messenger, before whom Messengers came and went.*** In other words, he was like the other Messengers, not a god as the Christians claimed. ***His***

مَا كَانُواْ يَفْعَلُونَ ﴿٧٩﴾ تَرَىٰ كَثِيرًا مِّنْهُمْ
يَتَوَلَّوْنَ ٱلَّذِينَ كَفَرُواْۚ لَبِئْسَ مَا قَدَّمَتْ لَهُمْ أَنفُسُهُمْ
أَن سَخِطَ ٱللَّهُ عَلَيْهِمْ وَفِي ٱلْعَذَابِ هُمْ خَٰلِدُونَ ﴿٨٠﴾
وَلَوْ كَانُواْ يُؤْمِنُونَ بِٱللَّهِ وَٱلنَّبِيِّ وَمَآ أُنزِلَ إِلَيْهِ
مَا ٱتَّخَذُوهُمْ أَوْلِيَآءَ وَلَٰكِنَّ كَثِيرًا مِّنْهُمْ فَٰسِقُونَ
﴿٨١﴾ ۞ لَتَجِدَنَّ أَشَدَّ ٱلنَّاسِ عَدَٰوَةً لِّلَّذِينَ ءَامَنُواْ ٱلْيَهُودَ
وَٱلَّذِينَ أَشْرَكُواْۖ وَلَتَجِدَنَّ أَقْرَبَهُم مَّوَدَّةً لِّلَّذِينَ
ءَامَنُواْ ٱلَّذِينَ قَالُوٓاْ إِنَّا نَصَٰرَىٰۚ ذَٰلِكَ بِأَنَّ مِنْهُمْ
قِسِّيسِينَ وَرُهْبَانًا وَأَنَّهُمْ لَا يَسْتَكْبِرُونَ ﴿٨٢﴾
وَإِذَا سَمِعُواْ مَآ أُنزِلَ إِلَى ٱلرَّسُولِ تَرَىٰٓ أَعْيُنَهُمْ تَفِيضُ مِنَ
ٱلدَّمْعِ مِمَّا عَرَفُواْ مِنَ ٱلْحَقِّۖ يَقُولُونَ رَبَّنَآ ءَامَنَّا فَٱكْتُبْنَا مَعَ
ٱلشَّٰهِدِينَ ﴿٨٣﴾ وَمَا لَنَا لَا نُؤْمِنُ بِٱللَّهِ وَمَا جَآءَنَا مِنَ ٱلْحَقِّ
وَنَطْمَعُ أَن يُدْخِلَنَا رَبُّنَا مَعَ ٱلْقَوْمِ ٱلصَّٰلِحِينَ ﴿٨٤﴾ فَأَثَٰبَهُمُ
ٱللَّهُ بِمَا قَالُواْ جَنَّٰتٍ تَجْرِي مِن تَحْتِهَا ٱلْأَنْهَٰرُ خَٰلِدِينَ فِيهَاۚ
وَذَٰلِكَ جَزَآءُ ٱلْمُحْسِنِينَ ﴿٨٥﴾ وَٱلَّذِينَ كَفَرُواْ وَكَذَّبُواْ
بِـَٔايَٰتِنَآ أُوْلَٰٓئِكَ أَصْحَٰبُ ٱلْجَحِيمِ ﴿٨٦﴾ يَٰٓأَيُّهَا ٱلَّذِينَ ءَامَنُواْ
لَا تُحَرِّمُواْ طَيِّبَٰتِ مَآ أَحَلَّ ٱللَّهُ لَكُمْ وَلَا تَعْتَدُوٓاْۚ إِنَّ ٱللَّهَ
لَا يُحِبُّ ٱلْمُعْتَدِينَ ﴿٨٧﴾ وَكُلُواْ مِمَّا رَزَقَكُمُ ٱللَّهُ حَلَٰلًا طَيِّبًاۚ
وَٱتَّقُواْ ٱللَّهَ ٱلَّذِيٓ أَنتُم بِهِۦ مُؤْمِنُونَ ﴿٨٨﴾ لَا يُؤَاخِذُكُمُ ٱللَّهُ
بِٱللَّغْوِ فِيٓ أَيْمَٰنِكُمْ وَلَٰكِن يُؤَاخِذُكُم بِمَا عَقَّدتُّمُ ٱلْأَيْمَٰنَۖ

mother was a woman of truth. The title "woman of truth" (*ṣiddīqa*) is an adjective derived from the intensive form of *ṣidq* which means sincere or truthful. ***Both of them ate food*** like other people. Since he was like that, he cannot be a god, because of his constitution and weakness and being subject to urine and faeces. ***See*** in wonder ***how we make the Signs*** of Allah's Oneness ***clear to them! Then see how they are perverted*** from the Truth in spite of the evidence.

76. ***Say: "Do you worship, besides Allah, what has no power to harm or help you, when Allah is the All-Hearing,*** hearing your words, ***the All-Knowing***, knowing your states?" The question implies a negative answer.

77. ***Say: "People of the Book*** (Jews and Christians)***! Do not go to extremes in your* dīn*, asserting other than the truth*** – exceeding the limits by giving 'Īsā a status beyond that which is appropriate for him – ***and do not follow the whims and desires of people who were misguided earlier***, your ancestors who went to extremes, ***and have misguided many others, and are far from the right way*** (the Path of the Truth)."

78. ***Those among the tribe of Israel who disbelieved were cursed on the tongue of Dāwūd*** – and were transformed into apes, a reference to the people of Ayla who fished on the Sabbath – ***and that of 'Īsā, son of Maryam*** – who cursed them and they were changed into pigs. They were the people of the Table (discussed in 5:115) – ***That*** curse ***is because they rebelled and overstepped the limits.***

79. ***They would not restrain one another*** – forbid one another to act in that way – ***from any of the wrong things that they did. How evil were the things they used to do!***

80. ***You***, Muḥammad, ***see many of them taking those who disbelieve*** among the people of Makka ***as friends*** out of hatred for you. ***What*** (this action) ***their lower selves have advanced for them*** in the Next World ***is evil indeed,*** as it involves ***bringing Allah's anger down upon them. They will suffer punishment timelessly, forever.***

81. ***If they had believed in Allah and the Prophet*** (Muḥammad) ***and what has been sent down to him, they would not have taken them*** (the unbelievers) ***as friends. But most of them are degenerate*** (outside of belief).

82. ***You***, Muḥammad, ***will find that the most hostile people to those who believe are the Jews and the idolaters*** (the people of Makka) on account of the intensity of their unbelief and ignorance and their preoccupation with following their desires. ***You will find that the most affectionate people to those who believe are those who say, "We are Christians."*** They are nearest in love to the believers. ***That is because some of them are priests*** (scholars) ***and monks*** (worshippers) ***and because they are not arrogant.*** They are not too proud to follow the truth in the way that the Jews and the people of Makka were. The following *āyat* was revealed about the delegation of the Negus who came from Abyssinia. The Prophet recited *Sūrat Yāsīn,* and they wept and became Muslim. They said, "This is the same as what was revealed to 'Īsā." Allah Almighty says:

83. ***When they listen to what has been sent down to the Messenger*** (the Qur'an), ***you see their eyes overflowing with tears because of what they recognise of the truth. They say, "Our Lord, we believe***, and affirm Your Prophet and Your Book. ***So write us down with the witnesses*** who are brought near by affirming them.

84. They said in answer to those of the Jews who criticised them for their affirmation of Islam: ***How could we not believe in Allah, and the truth that has come to us*** (the Qur'an) – nothing can prevent our belief in the face of the incontrovertible evidence which demands it – ***when we long for our Lord to include us among the people of righteousness***: the believers who enter the Garden*?"* Allah then says:

85. ***Allah will reward them for what they say with Gardens with rivers flowing under them, remaining in them timelessly, forever. That is the recompense of all good-doers*** who do good and have faith.

86. ***As for those who disbelieve and deny Our Signs, they are the Companions of the Blazing Fire.***

87. The following was revealed about a group of Companions who dedicated themselves to fasting and prayer, did not approach women or perfume, and did not eat meat or sleep on beds. ***You who believe, do not make unlawful the good things Allah has made lawful for you, and do not overstep the limits*** by going beyond what Allah has commanded. ***Allah does not love people who overstep the limits.***

فَكَفَّـٰرَتُهُۥٓ إِطۡعَامُ عَشَرَةِ مَسَٰكِينَ مِنۡ أَوۡسَطِ مَا تُطۡعِمُونَ
أَهۡلِيكُمۡ أَوۡ كِسۡوَتُهُمۡ أَوۡ تَحۡرِيرُ رَقَبَةٖۖ فَمَن لَّمۡ يَجِدۡ فَصِيَامُ
ثَلَٰثَةِ أَيَّامٖۚ ذَٰلِكَ كَفَّـٰرَةُ أَيۡمَٰنِكُمۡ إِذَا حَلَفۡتُمۡۚ وَٱحۡفَظُوٓاْ
أَيۡمَٰنَكُمۡۚ كَذَٰلِكَ يُبَيِّنُ ٱللَّهُ لَكُمۡ ءَايَٰتِهِۦ لَعَلَّكُمۡ تَشۡكُرُونَ ٨٩
يَـٰٓأَيُّهَا ٱلَّذِينَ ءَامَنُوٓاْ إِنَّمَا ٱلۡخَمۡرُ وَٱلۡمَيۡسِرُ وَٱلۡأَنصَابُ وَٱلۡأَزۡلَٰمُ رِجۡسٞ
مِّنۡ عَمَلِ ٱلشَّيۡطَٰنِ فَٱجۡتَنِبُوهُ لَعَلَّكُمۡ تُفۡلِحُونَ ٩٠ إِنَّمَا يُرِيدُ
ٱلشَّيۡطَٰنُ أَن يُوقِعَ بَيۡنَكُمُ ٱلۡعَدَٰوَةَ وَٱلۡبَغۡضَآءَ فِي ٱلۡخَمۡرِ وَٱلۡمَيۡسِرِ
وَيَصُدَّكُمۡ عَن ذِكۡرِ ٱللَّهِ وَعَنِ ٱلصَّلَوٰةِۖ فَهَلۡ أَنتُم مُّنتَهُونَ ٩١ وَأَطِيعُواْ
ٱللَّهَ وَأَطِيعُواْ ٱلرَّسُولَ وَٱحۡذَرُواْۚ فَإِن تَوَلَّيۡتُمۡ فَٱعۡلَمُوٓاْ أَنَّمَا عَلَىٰ
رَسُولِنَا ٱلۡبَلَٰغُ ٱلۡمُبِينُ ٩٢ لَيۡسَ عَلَى ٱلَّذِينَ ءَامَنُواْ وَعَمِلُواْ
ٱلصَّـٰلِحَٰتِ جُنَاحٞ فِيمَا طَعِمُوٓاْ إِذَا مَا ٱتَّقَواْ وَّءَامَنُواْ وَعَمِلُواْ
ٱلصَّـٰلِحَٰتِ ثُمَّ ٱتَّقَواْ وَّءَامَنُواْ ثُمَّ ٱتَّقَواْ وَّأَحۡسَنُواْۚ وَٱللَّهُ يُحِبُّ ٱلۡمُحۡسِنِينَ
٩٣ يَـٰٓأَيُّهَا ٱلَّذِينَ ءَامَنُواْ لَيَبۡلُوَنَّكُمُ ٱللَّهُ بِشَيۡءٖ مِّنَ ٱلصَّيۡدِ تَنَالُهُۥٓ
أَيۡدِيكُمۡ وَرِمَاحُكُمۡ لِيَعۡلَمَ ٱللَّهُ مَن يَخَافُهُۥ بِٱلۡغَيۡبِۚ فَمَنِ ٱعۡتَدَىٰ بَعۡدَ
ذَٰلِكَ فَلَهُۥ عَذَابٌ أَلِيمٞ ٩٤ يَـٰٓأَيُّهَا ٱلَّذِينَ ءَامَنُواْ لَا تَقۡتُلُواْ ٱلصَّيۡدَ
وَأَنتُمۡ حُرُمٞۚ وَمَن قَتَلَهُۥ مِنكُم مُّتَعَمِّدٗا فَجَزَآءٞ مِّثۡلُ مَا قَتَلَ مِنَ ٱلنَّعَمِ
يَحۡكُمُ بِهِۦ ذَوَا عَدۡلٖ مِّنكُمۡ هَدۡيَۢا بَٰلِغَ ٱلۡكَعۡبَةِ أَوۡ كَفَّـٰرَةٞ طَعَامُ
مَسَٰكِينَ أَوۡ عَدۡلُ ذَٰلِكَ صِيَامٗا لِّيَذُوقَ وَبَالَ أَمۡرِهِۦۗ عَفَا ٱللَّهُ عَمَّا
سَلَفَۚ وَمَنۡ عَادَ فَيَنتَقِمُ ٱللَّهُ مِنۡهُۚ وَٱللَّهُ عَزِيزٞ ذُو ٱنتِقَامٍ ٩٥
أُحِلَّ لَكُمۡ صَيۡدُ ٱلۡبَحۡرِ وَطَعَامُهُۥ مَتَٰعٗا لَّكُمۡ وَلِلسَّيَّارَةِۖ وَحُرِّمَ

88 ***Eat the lawful and good things Allah has provided for you, and be fearful of Allah, Him in Whom you believe.***

89. ***Allah does not take you to task for your inadvertent oaths***: those voiced without a real intention of making an oath, such as when someone says, "Yes, by Allah" or "No, by Allah", ***but He will take you to task for oaths you make intentionally*** (read as *'aqqadt-tum, 'aqadttum* and *'āqadttum*). ***The expiation*** for breaking an oath ***in that case is to feed ten poor people with the average amount*** – a *mudd* for each person of the quality you usually buy – ***you feed your family, or to clothe them*** with what constitutes the normal dress of a shirt, turban and waist-wrapper or their equivalent. According to ash-Shāfi'ī, it is not enough to simply give the money for these things – ***or to free a slave.*** The slave who is freed must be a believer as in the case of other expiations, such as that for killing and *ẓihār* divorce. This is an example of applying the general to the specific. ***Anyone without the means to do so*** – to pay any of these alternative expiations – ***should fast three days*** as *kaffāra.* It appears that it is not a condition for them to be continuous, and that is the view of ash-Shāfi'ī. ***That*** which has been mentioned ***is the expiation for breaking oaths when you have sworn them. Keep to your oaths*** but break those which are not for righteous actions or putting things right between people, as is stated in *Sūrat al-Baqara* (2:224). ***Thus does Allah make His Signs clear to you, so that perhaps you may be thankful*** for that.

90. ***You who believe! Intoxicants*** – anything which muddles the mind – ***gambling, stone altars*** (idols) ***and divining arrows are filth*** and foulness ***from the handiwork of Shayṭān*** which Shayṭān makes seem attractive. ***Avoid them***, the filth represented by these things, ***completely so that perhaps you may be successful.***

91. ***Shayṭān wants to stir up enmity and hatred between you by means of intoxicants and gambling*** through the evil and conflict which arise out of these things ***and*** – by your distraction with them – ***to debar you from the remembrance of Allah and from the prayer.*** The prayer is mentioned specifically to exalt it. ***So will you not give them up*** and stop doing them***?***

92. ***Obey Allah and obey the Messenger, and beware*** of acts of disobedience***! If you turn your backs*** on obedience, ***then know that***

عَلَيْكُمْ صَيْدُ ٱلْبَرِّ مَا دُمْتُمْ حُرُمًا ۗ وَٱتَّقُوا۟ ٱللَّهَ ٱلَّذِىٓ إِلَيْهِ
تُحْشَرُونَ ﴿٩٦﴾ ۞ جَعَلَ ٱللَّهُ ٱلْكَعْبَةَ ٱلْبَيْتَ ٱلْحَرَامَ
قِيَٰمًا لِّلنَّاسِ وَٱلشَّهْرَ ٱلْحَرَامَ وَٱلْهَدْىَ وَٱلْقَلَٰٓئِدَ ۚ ذَٰلِكَ لِتَعْلَمُوٓا۟
أَنَّ ٱللَّهَ يَعْلَمُ مَا فِى ٱلسَّمَٰوَٰتِ وَمَا فِى ٱلْأَرْضِ وَأَنَّ ٱللَّهَ بِكُلِّ
شَىْءٍ عَلِيمٌ ﴿٩٧﴾ ٱعْلَمُوٓا۟ أَنَّ ٱللَّهَ شَدِيدُ ٱلْعِقَابِ وَأَنَّ ٱللَّهَ
غَفُورٌ رَّحِيمٌ ﴿٩٨﴾ مَّا عَلَى ٱلرَّسُولِ إِلَّا ٱلْبَلَٰغُ ۗ وَٱللَّهُ يَعْلَمُ مَا
تُبْدُونَ وَمَا تَكْتُمُونَ ﴿٩٩﴾ قُل لَّا يَسْتَوِى ٱلْخَبِيثُ وَٱلطَّيِّبُ
وَلَوْ أَعْجَبَكَ كَثْرَةُ ٱلْخَبِيثِ ۚ فَٱتَّقُوا۟ ٱللَّهَ يَٰٓأُو۟لِى ٱلْأَلْبَٰبِ
لَعَلَّكُمْ تُفْلِحُونَ ﴿١٠٠﴾ يَٰٓأَيُّهَا ٱلَّذِينَ ءَامَنُوا۟ لَا تَسْـَٔلُوا۟
عَنْ أَشْيَآءَ إِن تُبْدَ لَكُمْ تَسُؤْكُمْ وَإِن تَسْـَٔلُوا۟ عَنْهَا حِينَ يُنَزَّلُ
ٱلْقُرْءَانُ تُبْدَ لَكُمْ عَفَا ٱللَّهُ عَنْهَا ۗ وَٱللَّهُ غَفُورٌ حَلِيمٌ ﴿١٠١﴾ قَدْ
سَأَلَهَا قَوْمٌ مِّن قَبْلِكُمْ ثُمَّ أَصْبَحُوا۟ بِهَا كَٰفِرِينَ ﴿١٠٢﴾
مَا جَعَلَ ٱللَّهُ مِنۢ بَحِيرَةٍ وَلَا سَآئِبَةٍ وَلَا وَصِيلَةٍ وَلَا حَامٍ ۙ وَلَٰكِنَّ
ٱلَّذِينَ كَفَرُوا۟ يَفْتَرُونَ عَلَى ٱللَّهِ ٱلْكَذِبَ ۖ وَأَكْثَرُهُمْ لَا يَعْقِلُونَ ﴿١٠٣﴾
وَإِذَا قِيلَ لَهُمْ تَعَالَوْا۟ إِلَىٰ مَآ أَنزَلَ ٱللَّهُ وَإِلَى ٱلرَّسُولِ قَالُوا۟
حَسْبُنَا مَا وَجَدْنَا عَلَيْهِ ءَابَآءَنَآ ۚ أَوَلَوْ كَانَ ءَابَآؤُهُمْ لَا يَعْلَمُونَ
شَيْـًٔا وَلَا يَهْتَدُونَ ﴿١٠٤﴾ يَٰٓأَيُّهَا ٱلَّذِينَ ءَامَنُوا۟ عَلَيْكُمْ أَنفُسَكُمْ ۖ
لَا يَضُرُّكُم مَّن ضَلَّ إِذَا ٱهْتَدَيْتُمْ ۚ إِلَى ٱللَّهِ مَرْجِعُكُمْ جَمِيعًا
فَيُنَبِّئُكُم بِمَا كُنتُمْ تَعْمَلُونَ ﴿١٠٥﴾ يَٰٓأَيُّهَا ٱلَّذِينَ ءَامَنُوا۟ شَهَٰدَةُ
بَيْنِكُمْ إِذَا حَضَرَ أَحَدَكُمُ ٱلْمَوْتُ حِينَ ٱلْوَصِيَّةِ ٱثْنَانِ ذَوَا

Our Messenger is only responsible for clearly conveying the Message. The Messenger is only responsible for clear transmission. Allah will repay you for what you do.

93. ***Those who believe and do right actions are not to blame for what they have eaten***, meaning any intoxicants they consumed or gambling they did before the prohibition – ***provided they are god-fearing*** – fearing forbidden things, ***and believe and do right actions, and then are godfearing and believe*** – being firm in fear of Allah and belief – ***and then are godfearing and do good. Allah loves all good-doers*** and will reward them.

94. ***You who believe! Allah will test you with*** small ***game animals*** he sends ***which come within the reach of your hands and*** large game within reach of your ***spears*** – this was revealed when the Muslims were in *iḥrām* at Ḥudaybiyya and the wild animals came and birds sat on their saddles – ***so that Allah will know*** with clear and evident knowledge ***those who fear Him in the Unseen***, because even though they do not see Him, they avoid hunting. ***Anyone who oversteps the limits after this*** prohibition and hunts ***will have a painful punishment.***

95. ***You who believe! Do not kill game while you are in* iḥrām** for *ḥajj* or *'umra*. ***If one of you kills any deliberately, the penalty for it is a livestock animal equivalent*** (read as *jazā'un mithlu* or *jazā'u mithli*) ***to what he killed***, an animal similar to the prohibited game killed, ***as judged by two just men among you*** – by those who can distinguish such things. Ibn 'Abbās, 'Umar and 'Alī judged a camel for an ostrich; Ibn 'Abbās and Abu 'Ubayda judged a cow for a wild cow and ass; and Ibn 'Umar and Ibn 'Awf judged a sheep for a gazelle; and Ibn 'Abbās, 'Umar and others judged a sheep for a dove since they are similar in drinking water – ***a sacrifice to reach the Ka'ba*** – this sacrifice should be carried out in the *Ḥaram* and the meat from it then distributed among the poor people there; it is not permitted to slaughter it where the offence occurred; and if it is something not like livestock, like a sparrow or locust, then its value is owed – ***or expiation*** (requital) ***by feeding*** (read as *kaffāratun ṭā'āmun* and *kaffāratu ṭā'āmin*) ***the poor***, which entails feeding the poor with food of the region concerned equal to the value of the animal chosen, each poor person receiving a *mudd* – ***or fasting commensurate to that*** food – a day for each *mudd,* and if a person is able to, he must feed rather than fast – ***so that he may taste the evil consequences of*** – and heavy repayment for – ***what he did. Allah has pardoned what took place in the past*** regarding killing game before it was forbidden***; but if anyone does it again Allah will take revenge on him. Allah is Almighty*** and overcomes all***, Exactor of Revenge*** on those who disobey Him. The penalty is incurred by those who kill game either deliberately or accidentally.

96. ***What you catch in the sea is lawful for you*** – for both people in *iḥrām* and people not in it, and you may eat its catch, which refers to that which lives exclusively in the sea such as fish, but not things which live on the land as well like crabs – ***and all food from it*** – what the sea casts up – ***for your enjoyment*** in terms of eating ***and that of travellers*** who can provide for themselves from it, ***but land game*** – referring to wild animals living on land which can be eaten – ***is unlawful for you*** to hunt ***while you are in* iḥrām.** If someone not in *iḥrām* catches it and feeds it to someone in *iḥrām*, he may eat it, as the *Sunna* makes clear. ***So be fearful of Allah, Him to whom you will be gathered.***

97. ***Allah has made the Ka'ba, the Sacred House, a special institution for mankind*** – appointed for the human race to establish the *dīn* by performing the *ḥajj* there and as a sanctuary in this world where those who visit it are safe and secure from attack, and all sorts of produce are brought to it – ***and also the sacred months***, read as *shahru'l-haram* in the singular, which is here used as a generic and so is in fact plural and refers to the months of Dhū'l-Qa'da, Dhū'l-Ḥijja, Muḥarram and Rajab. People are safe from fighting during them – ***and the sacrificial animals and the ritual garlands***, whose owners are safe from attack. ***That*** appointment which was mentioned ***is so you may know that Allah knows what is in the heavens and what is in the earth and that Allah has knowledge of everything.*** Allah has ordered this to bring about people's best interests and prevent detrimental things before they occur. This is an indication of His knowledge of both what already exists and also everything that is going to exist.

98. ***Know that Allah is Fierce in Retribution*** against His enemies ***and that Allah is Ever Forgiving*** to His friends, ***Most Merciful*** to them.

99. ***The Messenger is only responsible for conveying the Message*** to you. ***Allah knows what*** actions ***you divulge and what*** actions ***you hide***; and He will repay you for them.

100. ***Say: "Bad*** (unlawful) ***things and good*** (lawful) ***things are not the same, even though the abundance of the bad things may appear good to you*** and delight you." ***Be fearful of Allah*** by shunning them, ***people of intelligence, so that perhaps you will be successful.***

101. The following was revealed when many questions were asked of the Messenger of Allah, may Allah bless him and grant him peace. ***You who believe! Do not ask about matters which, if they were made known to you, would make things difficult for you*** because of the hardship they contain. ***If you do ask about them while the Qur'an is being sent down*** – during the life-time of the Prophet, may Allah bless him and grant him peace – ***they will be made known to you***: in other words, they will become apparent and then you will be vexed by them. Do not ask questions about them. ***Allah has ignored them.*** He has pardoned your asking, so do not do it again. ***Allah is Ever Forgiving, Forbearing.***

102. ***People before you asked*** their Prophets ***about them*** (these things) – and they explained the rulings about them, ***and then later came to reject them*** by refusing to act by those rulings.

103. ***Allah did not institute any such thing*** (ruling) ***as*** **baḥīra** ***or*** **sā'iba** ***or*** **waṣīla** ***or*** **ḥāmi** – which the people of the *Jāhiliyya* used to do. Al-Bukhārī reported from Sa'īd ibn al-Musayyab that the *baḥīra* was an animal whose milk was assigned to idols and which was not allowed to be milked. The *sā'iba* was an animal on which no one could put any loads. The *waṣīla* was a virgin she-camel which was one of a pair of twins and was devoted to their idols. The *ḥāmi* was a stallion camel which had fathered a certain number of camels after, which they left it for their idols and did not allow it to carry anything. ***But those who disbelieve invented lies against Allah*** in ascribing these things to Him falsely. ***Most of them do not use their***

عَدْلٍ مِّنكُمْ أَوْ ءَاخَرَانِ مِنْ غَيْرِكُمْ إِنْ أَنتُمْ ضَرَبْتُمْ فِى ٱلْأَرْضِ
فَأَصَٰبَتْكُم مُّصِيبَةُ ٱلْمَوْتِ ۚ تَحْبِسُونَهُمَا مِنۢ بَعْدِ ٱلصَّلَوٰةِ
فَيُقْسِمَانِ بِٱللَّهِ إِنِ ٱرْتَبْتُمْ لَا نَشْتَرِى بِهِۦ ثَمَنًا وَلَوْ كَانَ ذَا قُرْبَىٰ ۙ
وَلَا نَكْتُمُ شَهَٰدَةَ ٱللَّهِ إِنَّآ إِذًا لَّمِنَ ٱلْءَاثِمِينَ ﴿١٠٦﴾ فَإِنْ عُثِرَ عَلَىٰٓ
أَنَّهُمَا ٱسْتَحَقَّآ إِثْمًا فَـَٔاخَرَانِ يَقُومَانِ مَقَامَهُمَا مِنَ ٱلَّذِينَ
ٱسْتَحَقَّ عَلَيْهِمُ ٱلْأَوْلَيَٰنِ فَيُقْسِمَانِ بِٱللَّهِ لَشَهَٰدَتُنَآ أَحَقُّ
مِن شَهَٰدَتِهِمَا وَمَا ٱعْتَدَيْنَآ إِنَّآ إِذًا لَّمِنَ ٱلظَّٰلِمِينَ ﴿١٠٧﴾ ذَٰلِكَ
أَدْنَىٰٓ أَن يَأْتُوا۟ بِٱلشَّهَٰدَةِ عَلَىٰ وَجْهِهَآ أَوْ يَخَافُوٓا۟ أَن تُرَدَّ أَيْمَٰنٌۢ بَعْدَ
أَيْمَٰنِهِمْ ۗ وَٱتَّقُوا۟ ٱللَّهَ وَٱسْمَعُوا۟ ۗ وَٱللَّهُ لَا يَهْدِى ٱلْقَوْمَ ٱلْفَٰسِقِينَ ﴿١٠٨﴾
۞ يَوْمَ يَجْمَعُ ٱللَّهُ ٱلرُّسُلَ فَيَقُولُ مَاذَآ أُجِبْتُمْ ۖ قَالُوا۟ لَا عِلْمَ
لَنَآ ۖ إِنَّكَ أَنتَ عَلَّٰمُ ٱلْغُيُوبِ ﴿١٠٩﴾ إِذْ قَالَ ٱللَّهُ يَٰعِيسَى ٱبْنَ مَرْيَمَ
ٱذْكُرْ نِعْمَتِى عَلَيْكَ وَعَلَىٰ وَٰلِدَتِكَ إِذْ أَيَّدتُّكَ بِرُوحِ
ٱلْقُدُسِ تُكَلِّمُ ٱلنَّاسَ فِى ٱلْمَهْدِ وَكَهْلًا ۖ وَإِذْ عَلَّمْتُكَ
ٱلْكِتَٰبَ وَٱلْحِكْمَةَ وَٱلتَّوْرَىٰةَ وَٱلْإِنجِيلَ ۖ وَإِذْ تَخْلُقُ
مِنَ ٱلطِّينِ كَهَيْـَٔةِ ٱلطَّيْرِ بِإِذْنِى فَتَنفُخُ فِيهَا فَتَكُونُ طَيْرًۢا
بِإِذْنِى ۖ وَتُبْرِئُ ٱلْأَكْمَهَ وَٱلْأَبْرَصَ بِإِذْنِى ۖ وَإِذْ تُخْرِجُ
ٱلْمَوْتَىٰ بِإِذْنِى ۖ وَإِذْ كَفَفْتُ بَنِىٓ إِسْرَٰٓءِيلَ عَنكَ إِذْ
جِئْتَهُم بِٱلْبَيِّنَٰتِ فَقَالَ ٱلَّذِينَ كَفَرُوا۟ مِنْهُمْ إِنْ هَٰذَآ إِلَّا سِحْرٌ
مُّبِينٌ ﴿١١٠﴾ وَإِذْ أَوْحَيْتُ إِلَى ٱلْحَوَارِيِّۦنَ أَنْ ءَامِنُوا۟ بِى
وَبِرَسُولِى قَالُوٓا۟ ءَامَنَّا وَٱشْهَدْ بِأَنَّنَا مُسْلِمُونَ ﴿١١١﴾ إِذْ قَالَ

intellect, and did not recognise that it was merely an invention of their ancestors'.

104. ***When they are told, "Come to what Allah has sent down and to the Messenger,"*** who makes lawful what you have made unlawful, ***they say, "What we found our fathers doing is enough for us*** in respect of our *dīn* and *Sharī'a.*" Allah says: ***What!*** Is that enough? ***Even if their fathers did not know anything and were not guided*** to the truth***!***

105. ***You who believe! You are only responsible for yourselves.*** You can only protect yourselves and put yourselves right. ***The misguided cannot harm you as long as you are guided.*** It is said that what is meant by this is that those of the People of the Book who are misguided will not harm you. It is also said that it means others on the basis of the *ḥadīth* of Abū Tha'laba al-Khashanī: "I asked the Messenger of Allah, may Allah bless him and grant him peace, about this and he said, 'Command the right and forbid the wrong until you see avarice obeyed, passion followed and this world preferred, and every one with an opinion admiring his own opinion: then, take care of yourself.'" (al-Ḥākim) ***All of you will return to Allah and He will inform you about what you did*** and repay you for it.

106. ***You who believe! When one of you is near to death and makes a will, two just men from among you should act as witnesses*** – this is a command meaning that wills should be witnessed to make clear what is covered by them – ***or, if you are travelling when the misfortune of death occurs, two men from other than yourselves*** – from other than your religion. ***You should detain them after the prayer*** (the *'Aṣr* prayer) ***and, if you are doubtful*** about their testimony, ***they should swear by Allah*** and say: "By Allah, ***We will not sell it for any price*** – anything of this world; or make false testimony or a false oath – ***even to a near relative*** (in his favour), ***and we will not conceal the testimony of Allah*** which we were commanded to give. ***If we did*** conceal it, ***we would indeed be among the wrongdoers."***

107. ***If***, after taking an oath, ***it then comes to light that the two of them have merited the allegation of wrongdoing*** and it is discovered that they have been treacherous or lying in their testimony, as when something is found that makes them suspect or they claim that they have bought something from the dead man or that he has left them something – ***two others*** – relatives of the dead – ***who have the most right to do so*** (take the oath) – they have more right to a bequest since they are heirs – ***should take their place and swear by Allah*** that the witnesses have been false, by saying, ***"Our testimony*** (oath) ***is truer than their testimony. We have not committed perjury.*** We have not exceeded the terms of the oath. ***If we had, we would indeed be among the wrongdoers."*** What happens is that the person dying calls two people to witness his will or he tells them to carry out his instructions. If no one of his *dīn* is there, he may call witnesses of a different faith if he is on a journey or in other than where he lives. If the heirs are unsure about them and claim that they are unreliable because they have taken something or given something to someone claiming that it was a bequest of the deceased, others are s worn in as witnesses. If there is something that indicates that the first witnesses were lying, witnesses closer to the heirs are called upon to take an oath that the earlier ones lied. What they claim has to be believed. The ruling about executors is upheld, but is abrogated as regards the two witnesses. Similarly allowing the testimony of non-Muslims is also abrogated. The *'Aṣr* prayer is mentioned because it is a difficult time; and the two relatives are mentioned because of what happened to them.

Here is what al-Bukhārī reported on this subject. A man of the Banū Sahm went out with Tamīm ad-Dārī and 'Adī ibn Baddā' who were Christians. The man died in a place where there were no Muslims. When the two of them brought his goods back, a silver vessel inlaid with gold was missing, and they were brought before the Prophet, may Allah bless him and grant him peace, and the verse was revealed. They swore that they knew nothing about it but then the vessel was found in Makka. The people there said that they had bought it from Tamīm and 'Adī. Then the second *āyat* was revealed and two male relatives of the man rose and swore oaths.

We read in the version of at-Tirmidhī that 'Amr ibn al-'Āṣ and a another man rose and swore, "We were closer to him." In another version, "He fell ill and he made a bequest to them and commanded them to convey what he had left to his family. When he died, they took the goblet and gave his tribe the rest.

108. ***That*** judgement about the heirs taking the oath afterwards ***makes it more likely that they*** (the witnesses or executors) ***will give their evidence properly***, without alteration or treachery, ***or be afraid that their oaths will be refuted by subsequent oaths*** by the heirs who are summoned, who will swear to their treachery and lies and they will be disgraced and liable; and so they will not lie. ***Be fearful of Allah*** by abandoning treachery and lying, ***and listen carefully*** to what you are commanded, and accept it. ***Allah does not guide degenerate people*** who abandon right guidance.

109. ***On the Day*** (the Day of Rising) ***Allah gathers the Messengers together and says*** to them to rebuke their followers, ***"What response did you receive*** when you called people to believe in Allah's Unity (*tawḥīd*)?" ***they will say, "We do not know*** that. ***You are the Knower of unseen things*** – You know what is invisible to people." They have no knowledge because of the intensity of the terror of the Day of Rising and their alarm. Then the Prophets will testify against their communities when they are silent.

110. Remember ***when Allah said, "'Īsā, son of Maryam, Remember My blessing upon you and to your mother*** – and be thankful for it – ***when I reinforced you with the Spirit of Purity*** (Jibrīl) ***so that you could speak to people in the cradle*** as an infant ***and when you were fully grown***: meaning that he will descend before the Final Hour because he was raised up before he was fully grown, as is mentioned in *Sūrat Āl 'Imrān*, ***and when I taught you the Book and Wisdom, and the Torah and the Gospel; and when you created a bird-shape out of clay by My permission*** (My will) ***and then breathed into it and it became a bird by My permission; and healed the blind and the leper by My permission; and when you brought forth the dead*** alive from their graves ***by My permission; and when I held back the Tribe of Israel from you*** when they wanted to kill you, ***when you brought them the Clear Signs*** (miracles) ***and those of them who disbelieved said, "This*** which you have brought – ***is nothing but outright magic*** (read as *siḥr* and also as *sāḥir*, in which case the meaning becomes: 'This is nothing but an outright magician', referring to 'Īsā)."

111. ***When I inspired the Disciples to believe in Me*** – commanding them on the tongue of 'Īsā – ***and in My Messenger*** 'Īsā, ***they said,***

ٱلْحَوَارِيُّونَ يَٰعِيسَى ٱبْنَ مَرْيَمَ هَلْ يَسْتَطِيعُ رَبُّكَ أَن
يُنَزِّلَ عَلَيْنَا مَآئِدَةً مِّنَ ٱلسَّمَآءِ ۖ قَالَ ٱتَّقُوا۟ ٱللَّهَ إِن كُنتُم
مُّؤْمِنِينَ ﴿١١٢﴾ قَالُوا۟ نُرِيدُ أَن نَّأْكُلَ مِنْهَا وَتَطْمَئِنَّ قُلُوبُنَا
وَنَعْلَمَ أَن قَدْ صَدَقْتَنَا وَنَكُونَ عَلَيْهَا مِنَ ٱلشَّٰهِدِينَ ﴿١١٣﴾
قَالَ عِيسَى ٱبْنُ مَرْيَمَ ٱللَّهُمَّ رَبَّنَآ أَنزِلْ عَلَيْنَا مَآئِدَةً مِّنَ ٱلسَّمَآءِ
تَكُونُ لَنَا عِيدًا لِّأَوَّلِنَا وَءَاخِرِنَا وَءَايَةً مِّنكَ ۖ وَٱرْزُقْنَا وَأَنتَ
خَيْرُ ٱلرَّٰزِقِينَ ﴿١١٤﴾ قَالَ ٱللَّهُ إِنِّى مُنَزِّلُهَا عَلَيْكُمْ ۖ فَمَن يَكْفُرْ بَعْدُ
مِنكُمْ فَإِنِّىٓ أُعَذِّبُهُۥ عَذَابًا لَّآ أُعَذِّبُهُۥٓ أَحَدًا مِّنَ ٱلْعَٰلَمِينَ ﴿١١٥﴾
وَإِذْ قَالَ ٱللَّهُ يَٰعِيسَى ٱبْنَ مَرْيَمَ ءَأَنتَ قُلْتَ لِلنَّاسِ ٱتَّخِذُونِى
وَأُمِّىَ إِلَٰهَيْنِ مِن دُونِ ٱللَّهِ ۖ قَالَ سُبْحَٰنَكَ مَا يَكُونُ لِىٓ أَنْ
أَقُولَ مَا لَيْسَ لِى بِحَقٍّ ۚ إِن كُنتُ قُلْتُهُۥ فَقَدْ عَلِمْتَهُۥ ۚ تَعْلَمُ مَا فِى
نَفْسِى وَلَآ أَعْلَمُ مَا فِى نَفْسِكَ ۚ إِنَّكَ أَنتَ عَلَّٰمُ ٱلْغُيُوبِ ﴿١١٦﴾ مَا
قُلْتُ لَهُمْ إِلَّا مَآ أَمَرْتَنِى بِهِۦٓ أَنِ ٱعْبُدُوا۟ ٱللَّهَ رَبِّى وَرَبَّكُمْ ۚ وَكُنتُ
عَلَيْهِمْ شَهِيدًا مَّا دُمْتُ فِيهِمْ ۖ فَلَمَّا تَوَفَّيْتَنِى كُنتَ أَنتَ ٱلرَّقِيبَ
عَلَيْهِمْ ۚ وَأَنتَ عَلَىٰ كُلِّ شَىْءٍ شَهِيدٌ ﴿١١٧﴾ إِن تُعَذِّبْهُمْ فَإِنَّهُمْ عِبَادُكَ ۖ
وَإِن تَغْفِرْ لَهُمْ فَإِنَّكَ أَنتَ ٱلْعَزِيزُ ٱلْحَكِيمُ ﴿١١٨﴾ قَالَ ٱللَّهُ هَٰذَا يَوْمُ
يَنفَعُ ٱلصَّٰدِقِينَ صِدْقُهُمْ ۚ لَهُمْ جَنَّٰتٌ تَجْرِى مِن تَحْتِهَا ٱلْأَنْهَٰرُ
خَٰلِدِينَ فِيهَآ أَبَدًا ۚ رَّضِىَ ٱللَّهُ عَنْهُمْ وَرَضُوا۟ عَنْهُ ۚ ذَٰلِكَ ٱلْفَوْزُ ٱلْعَظِيمُ ﴿١١٩﴾
لِلَّهِ مُلْكُ ٱلسَّمَٰوَٰتِ وَٱلْأَرْضِ وَمَا فِيهِنَّ ۚ وَهُوَ عَلَىٰ كُلِّ شَىْءٍ قَدِيرٌۢ ﴿١٢٠﴾

'We believe – in You and Your Messenger. ***Bear witness that we are Muslims.'"***

112. Remember ***when the Disciples said, "'Īsā son of Maryam! Can*** you ask ***your Lord*** (read as *Rabbuka* and *Rabbaka*) to ***send down a table to us out of heaven?" He*** ('Īsā) ***said*** to them, ***"Be fearful of Allah*** about asking for Signs ***if you are believers!"***

113. ***They said, "We want*** you to ask so that we will be able ***to eat from it and for our hearts to be at peace*** by increased certainty; ***and to know*** with greater knowledge ***that you have told us the truth*** regarding the truth of your Prophethood, ***and to be among those who witness it."***

114. ***'Īsā son of Maryam said, "O Allah, our Lord, send down a table to us from heaven to be a feast for us*** on the day it is sent down, which we will esteem and honour, ***for the first and last of us*** – for those who will come after us – ***and as a Sign from You*** of Your power and 'Īsā's prophethood. ***Provide for us! You are the Best of Providers!"***

115. ***Allah said*** to answer him, ***"I will send it down*** (read as *munazziluhā* and *munziluhā*) ***to you; but if anyone among you afterwards*** – after it has been sent down – ***disbelieves, I will punish him with a punishment the like of which I will not inflict on anyone else in all the worlds!"*** The angels brought it down from heaven and on it were seven loaves and seven fish. They ate from it until they were full, according to Ibn 'Abbās. In a *ḥadīth* we find: "A table was sent down from heaven on which there was bread and meat, and they were commanded not to be faithless and not to store up anything for later. But they were both faithless and stored up, and so they were transformed into monkeys and pigs."

116. ***And*** remember ***when Allah will say*** on the Day of Rising to rebuke his followers: ***"'Īsā son of Maryam! Did you tell people, 'Take me and my mother as two gods besides Allah'?" he*** ('Īsā) ***will*** tremble and ***say, "Glory be to You!"*** declaring Allah free of inappropriate partners and other things. ***"It is not*** proper ***for me to say what I have no right to say! If I did say it, then You would have known it. You know what is*** concealed ***in my self but I do not know***

what is concealed ***in Your Self*** of known things. ***You are the Knower of all unseen things.***

117. ***I told them only what You ordered me to say:*** That was: ***'Worship Allah, my Lord and your Lord.' I was a witness against them*** – a watcher to prevent what they said – ***as long as I remained among them, but when You took me back to You*** by raising me to heaven, ***You were the Watcher over them*** and Recorder of their actions. ***You are Witness of all things***, including what I said and what they said after I left; and You know everything else as well.

118. ***If You punish them*** – those of them who are unbelievers – ***they are Your slaves.*** You have power over them and can do what You wish with them, and none can oppose You. ***If you forgive them*** – those of them who believe – ***You are the Almighty*** in command, ***the All-Wise*** in action."

119. ***Allah will say, "This*** (the Day of Rising) ***is the Day when the truthfulness of the truthful*** in this world, such as 'Īsā, ***will benefit them*** because it is the Day of Repayment. ***They will have Gardens with rivers flowing under them, remaining in them timelessly, forever without end. Allah is pleased with them*** on account of their obedience, ***and they are pleased with Him*** on account of their reward. ***That is the Great Victory."*** Those who lied in this world will not benefit by realising the truth then, as happens when the unbelievers have faith once they see the punishment.

120. ***The sovereignty of the heavens and the earth***, the treasure-houses of the rain, plants, provision and all other non-sentient things, ***and everything in them belongs to Allah. He has power over everything.*** He rewards the truthful and punishes the liars.

سُورَةُ الأَنۡعَامِ

بِسۡمِ ٱللَّهِ ٱلرَّحۡمَٰنِ ٱلرَّحِيمِ

ٱلۡحَمۡدُ لِلَّهِ ٱلَّذِي خَلَقَ ٱلسَّمَٰوَٰتِ وَٱلۡأَرۡضَ وَجَعَلَ ٱلظُّلُمَٰتِ
وَٱلنُّورَۖ ثُمَّ ٱلَّذِينَ كَفَرُواْ بِرَبِّهِمۡ يَعۡدِلُونَ ١ هُوَ ٱلَّذِي
خَلَقَكُم مِّن طِينٖ ثُمَّ قَضَىٰٓ أَجَلٗاۖ وَأَجَلٞ مُّسَمًّى عِندَهُۥۖ ثُمَّ أَنتُمۡ
تَمۡتَرُونَ ٢ وَهُوَ ٱللَّهُ فِي ٱلسَّمَٰوَٰتِ وَفِي ٱلۡأَرۡضِۖ يَعۡلَمُ سِرَّكُمۡ
وَجَهۡرَكُمۡ وَيَعۡلَمُ مَا تَكۡسِبُونَ ٣ وَمَا تَأۡتِيهِم مِّنۡ ءَايَةٖ مِّنۡ
ءَايَٰتِ رَبِّهِمۡ إِلَّا كَانُواْ عَنۡهَا مُعۡرِضِينَ ٤ فَقَدۡ كَذَّبُواْ بِٱلۡحَقِّ
لَمَّا جَآءَهُمۡۖ فَسَوۡفَ يَأۡتِيهِمۡ أَنۢبَٰٓؤُاْ مَا كَانُواْ بِهِۦ يَسۡتَهۡزِءُونَ ٥ أَلَمۡ
يَرَوۡاْ كَمۡ أَهۡلَكۡنَا مِن قَبۡلِهِم مِّن قَرۡنٖ مَّكَّنَّٰهُمۡ فِي ٱلۡأَرۡضِ مَا لَمۡ
نُمَكِّن لَّكُمۡ وَأَرۡسَلۡنَا ٱلسَّمَآءَ عَلَيۡهِم مِّدۡرَارٗا وَجَعَلۡنَا ٱلۡأَنۡهَٰرَ
تَجۡرِي مِن تَحۡتِهِمۡ فَأَهۡلَكۡنَٰهُم بِذُنُوبِهِمۡ وَأَنشَأۡنَا مِنۢ بَعۡدِهِمۡ قَرۡنًا
ءَاخَرِينَ ٦ وَلَوۡ نَزَّلۡنَا عَلَيۡكَ كِتَٰبٗا فِي قِرۡطَاسٖ فَلَمَسُوهُ بِأَيۡدِيهِمۡ
لَقَالَ ٱلَّذِينَ كَفَرُوٓاْ إِنۡ هَٰذَآ إِلَّا سِحۡرٞ مُّبِينٞ ٧ وَقَالُواْ لَوۡلَآ أُنزِلَ
عَلَيۡهِ مَلَكٞۖ وَلَوۡ أَنزَلۡنَا مَلَكٗا لَّقُضِيَ ٱلۡأَمۡرُ ثُمَّ لَا يُنظَرُونَ ٨
وَلَوۡ جَعَلۡنَٰهُ مَلَكٗا لَّجَعَلۡنَٰهُ رَجُلٗا وَلَلَبَسۡنَا عَلَيۡهِم مَّا
يَلۡبِسُونَ ٩ وَلَقَدِ ٱسۡتُهۡزِئَ بِرُسُلٖ مِّن قَبۡلِكَ فَحَاقَ
بِٱلَّذِينَ سَخِرُواْ مِنۡهُم مَّا كَانُواْ بِهِۦ يَسۡتَهۡزِءُونَ ١٠
قُلۡ سِيرُواْ فِي ٱلۡأَرۡضِ ثُمَّ ٱنظُرُواْ كَيۡفَ كَانَ عَٰقِبَةُ
ٱلۡمُكَذِّبِينَ ١١ قُل لِّمَن مَّا فِي ٱلسَّمَٰوَٰتِ وَٱلۡأَرۡضِۖ قُل لِّلَّهِۚ
كَتَبَ عَلَىٰ نَفۡسِهِ ٱلرَّحۡمَةَۚ لَيَجۡمَعَنَّكُمۡ إِلَىٰ يَوۡمِ ٱلۡقِيَٰمَةِ

6. *Sūrat al-An'ām*
Livestock

Makkan, except for *āyat*s 20, 23, 91, 93, 114, 141, 151, 152, and 153 which are Madinan. It has 165 *āyat*s and was revealed after *Sūrat al-Ḥijr*.

1. ***Praise*** – an established quality – ***belongs to Allah***: this is either to express belief in Him or to praise Him, or to do both at the same time, and is also discussed at the beginning of *Sūrat al-Kahf* (18) – ***who created the heavens and the earth*** – mentioned because they are the largest visible aspect of creation for those who look, ***and appointed*** the creation of every ***darkness and light.*** Allah puts darkness in the plural because there are many things which cause it and that is evidence of His oneness. ***Then those who disbelieve make others equal to their Lord!*** Even though the proof is established, the unbelievers give others equal status to Allah in their worship.

2. ***It is He who created you from clay*** by creating your father Ādam from it, ***and then decreed a fixed term*** – a pre-appointed time when you die and your life comes to an end – ***and another fixed term is specified with Him*** for your resurrection. ***And yet still you***, unbelievers, ***have doubts*** about the resurrection when you know that Allah created you in the first place. The One Who has originated something from nothing is well able to bring it back to life again.

3. ***He is Allah*** and deserves to be worshipped ***in the heavens and in the earth. He knows what you keep secret and what you make public*** between you ***and He knows what you earn*** and do of good or evil.

4. ***Not one of their Lord's Signs*** (the Qur'ān) ***comes to them*** (the people of Makka) ***without their turning away from it.***

5. ***They deny the truth*** (the Qur'ān) ***each time it comes to them but news*** (the results) ***of what they were mocking will certainly reach them.***

6. ***Have they not seen*** during their journeys to Syria and elsewhere ***how many generations*** (nation after nation in the past) ***We destroyed before them which We had established on the earth,*** with strength and expansive territories, ***far more firmly than We have established you?*** There is a change of pronoun from "they" to "you". ***We sent down heaven*** (precipitation) ***on them in abundant rain*** (time after time) ***and made rivers flow under them*** – under their homes. ***But We destroyed them for their wrong actions*** (denial of their Prophets) ***and raised up further generations after them.***

7. ***Even if We were to send down a book to you*** written ***on parchment pages*** as they have demanded ***and they were actually to touch it with their own hands*** – making it even harder to doubt than just seeing it – ***those who disbelieve would still say*** out of their obstinacy ***"This is nothing but outright magic."***

8. ***They say, "Why has an angel not been sent down to him*** (Muḥammad, may Allah bless him and grant him peace) to affirm him***?" If We were to send down an angel*** as they asked, they would still not believe and ***that would be the end of the affair and they would not be reprieved.*** They would be destroyed immediately with no chance for repentance or excuse, as was the custom of Allah with people of the past who were destroyed when what they asked for appeared and they failed to have faith.

9. ***And if We had made him*** (the one who descended to them) ***an angel We would still have made him*** in the form of ***a man*** in order to enable them to see him, since human beings do not have the ability to see angels in their natural state; ***and*** if We had sent him down and made him a man, We would have ***further confused for them the very thing they are confused about*** because they would then have said, "This is just a man like us."

10. The following contains solace for the Prophet, may Allah bless him and grant him peace, ***Messengers before you were also mocked, but those who jeered were engulfed by what they mocked.*** It was the punishment they had been mocking that enveloped them.

11. ***Say*** to them***: "Travel in the earth and see the end result of the deniers,"*** – those who denied the Messengers, and their destruction by the punishment they received**.** This is so they can reflect.

12. ***Say: "To whom does everything in the heavens and earth belong?" Say: "To Allah.*** If they do not say this, there is no other answer. ***He has made mercy incumbent on*** and prescribed it for

لَا رَيْبَ فِيهِ ۚ الَّذِينَ خَسِرُوا أَنفُسَهُمْ فَهُمْ لَا يُؤْمِنُونَ
﴿١٢﴾ ۞ وَلَهُ مَا سَكَنَ فِي اللَّيْلِ وَالنَّهَارِ ۚ وَهُوَ السَّمِيعُ الْعَلِيمُ
﴿١٣﴾ قُلْ أَغَيْرَ اللَّهِ أَتَّخِذُ وَلِيًّا فَاطِرِ السَّمَاوَاتِ وَالْأَرْضِ وَهُوَ يُطْعِمُ
وَلَا يُطْعَمُ ۗ قُلْ إِنِّي أُمِرْتُ أَنْ أَكُونَ أَوَّلَ مَنْ أَسْلَمَ ۖ وَلَا
تَكُونَنَّ مِنَ الْمُشْرِكِينَ ﴿١٤﴾ قُلْ إِنِّي أَخَافُ إِنْ عَصَيْتُ
رَبِّي عَذَابَ يَوْمٍ عَظِيمٍ ﴿١٥﴾ مَنْ يُصْرَفْ عَنْهُ يَوْمَئِذٍ فَقَدْ
رَحِمَهُ ۚ وَذَٰلِكَ الْفَوْزُ الْمُبِينُ ﴿١٦﴾ وَإِنْ يَمْسَسْكَ اللَّهُ بِضُرٍّ
فَلَا كَاشِفَ لَهُ إِلَّا هُوَ ۖ وَإِنْ يَمْسَسْكَ بِخَيْرٍ فَهُوَ عَلَىٰ كُلِّ شَيْءٍ
قَدِيرٌ ﴿١٧﴾ وَهُوَ الْقَاهِرُ فَوْقَ عِبَادِهِ ۚ وَهُوَ الْحَكِيمُ الْخَبِيرُ ﴿١٨﴾
قُلْ أَيُّ شَيْءٍ أَكْبَرُ شَهَادَةً ۖ قُلِ اللَّهُ ۖ شَهِيدٌ بَيْنِي وَبَيْنَكُمْ ۚ وَأُوحِيَ إِلَيَّ هَٰذَا
الْقُرْآنُ لِأُنْذِرَكُمْ بِهِ وَمَنْ بَلَغَ ۚ أَئِنَّكُمْ لَتَشْهَدُونَ أَنَّ مَعَ اللَّهِ
آلِهَةً أُخْرَىٰ ۚ قُلْ لَا أَشْهَدُ ۚ قُلْ إِنَّمَا هُوَ إِلَٰهٌ وَاحِدٌ وَإِنَّنِي بَرِيءٌ مِمَّا
تُشْرِكُونَ ﴿١٩﴾ الَّذِينَ آتَيْنَاهُمُ الْكِتَابَ يَعْرِفُونَهُ كَمَا يَعْرِفُونَ
أَبْنَاءَهُمُ ۘ الَّذِينَ خَسِرُوا أَنْفُسَهُمْ فَهُمْ لَا يُؤْمِنُونَ ﴿٢٠﴾ وَمَنْ أَظْلَمُ
مِمَّنِ افْتَرَىٰ عَلَى اللَّهِ كَذِبًا أَوْ كَذَّبَ بِآيَاتِهِ ۗ إِنَّهُ لَا يُفْلِحُ الظَّالِمُونَ
﴿٢١﴾ وَيَوْمَ نَحْشُرُهُمْ جَمِيعًا ثُمَّ نَقُولُ لِلَّذِينَ أَشْرَكُوا أَيْنَ شُرَكَاؤُكُمُ
الَّذِينَ كُنْتُمْ تَزْعُمُونَ ﴿٢٢﴾ ثُمَّ لَمْ تَكُنْ فِتْنَتُهُمْ إِلَّا أَنْ قَالُوا وَاللَّهِ
رَبِّنَا مَا كُنَّا مُشْرِكِينَ ﴿٢٣﴾ انْظُرْ كَيْفَ كَذَبُوا عَلَىٰ أَنْفُسِهِمْ ۚ وَضَلَّ
عَنْهُمْ مَا كَانُوا يَفْتَرُونَ ﴿٢٤﴾ وَمِنْهُمْ مَنْ يَسْتَمِعُ إِلَيْكَ ۖ وَجَعَلْنَا عَلَىٰ
قُلُوبِهِمْ أَكِنَّةً أَنْ يَفْقَهُوهُ وَفِي آذَانِهِمْ وَقْرًا ۚ وَإِنْ يَرَوْا كُلَّ آيَةٍ
لَا يُؤْمِنُوا بِهَا ۚ حَتَّىٰ إِذَا جَاءُوكَ يُجَادِلُونَكَ يَقُولُ الَّذِينَ كَفَرُوا إِنْ هَٰذَا

Himself as a favour from Him and graciousness in calling them to believe. ***He will gather you to the Day of Rising*** – to repay you for your actions – ***of which there is no doubt. As for those who have ruined their own souls*** by exposing themselves to the punishment, ***they do not believe."***

13. ***All that inhabits the night and the day belongs to Him.*** Allah is the Lord, Creator and Master of everything. ***He is the All-Hearing*** of what is said, ***the All-Knowing*** of what is done.

14. ***Say*** to them: ***"Am I to take other than Allah as my protector*** and worship other than Him, ***the Bringer into being*** and Originator ***of the heavens and the earth, He who feeds*** (gives provision) ***and is not fed*** (provided for)***?" Say: "I am commanded to be the first of the Muslims*** of this Community who submit to Allah, ***and*** I have been told, ***'Do not be among the idolaters*** who ascribe partners to Allah.***'"***

15. ***Say: "I fear, were I to disobey my Lord,*** by worshipping other than Him, ***the punishment of a dreadful Day*** (the Day of Rising).***"***

16. ***Anyone from whom punishment is averted*** by Allah ***on that Day has had great mercy shown him by Allah,*** who desires good for Him. ***That is the Clear Victory*** and manifest salvation.

17. ***If Allah touches you with*** any ***harm,*** such as illness or poverty, ***no one can remove it but Him. If He touches you with*** any ***good,*** such as health and wealth, ***He has power over everything.*** One aspect of this power is the ability to inflict harm and bestow good, and when it comes no one can avert it from you or anyone else.

18. ***He is the Absolute Master over His slaves.*** He has power which no one is able to countermand. ***He is the All-Wise*** about His creation, ***the All-Aware,*** knowing their inward and their outward. This was revealed when the unbelievers said to the Prophet, may Allah bless him and grant him peace, "Bring us someone who will attest to your Prophethood. The People of the Book deny you."

19. ***Say*** to them: ***"What thing is greatest as a witness?" Say: "Allah.*** If they do not say this, there is no other answer. ***He is Witness between me and you*** to my truthfulness. ***This Qur'an has been revealed to me so that I may warn you*** and frighten you ***by it,*** people of Makka, ***and anyone else it*** (the Qur'ān) ***reaches*** among

إِلَّآ أَسَٰطِيرُ ٱلْأَوَّلِينَ ﴿٢٥﴾ وَهُمْ يَنْهَوْنَ عَنْهُ وَيَنْـَٔوْنَ عَنْهُ ۖ وَإِن
يُهْلِكُونَ إِلَّآ أَنفُسَهُمْ وَمَا يَشْعُرُونَ ﴿٢٦﴾ وَلَوْ تَرَىٰٓ إِذْ وُقِفُوا۟ عَلَى ٱلنَّارِ
فَقَالُوا۟ يَٰلَيْتَنَا نُرَدُّ وَلَا نُكَذِّبَ بِـَٔايَٰتِ رَبِّنَا وَنَكُونَ مِنَ ٱلْمُؤْمِنِينَ ﴿٢٧﴾
بَلْ بَدَا لَهُم مَّا كَانُوا۟ يُخْفُونَ مِن قَبْلُ ۖ وَلَوْ رُدُّوا۟ لَعَادُوا۟ لِمَا نُهُوا۟ عَنْهُ
وَإِنَّهُمْ لَكَٰذِبُونَ ﴿٢٨﴾ وَقَالُوٓا۟ إِنْ هِىَ إِلَّا حَيَاتُنَا ٱلدُّنْيَا وَمَا نَحْنُ
بِمَبْعُوثِينَ ﴿٢٩﴾ وَلَوْ تَرَىٰٓ إِذْ وُقِفُوا۟ عَلَىٰ رَبِّهِمْ ۚ قَالَ أَلَيْسَ هَٰذَا
بِٱلْحَقِّ ۚ قَالُوا۟ بَلَىٰ وَرَبِّنَا ۚ قَالَ فَذُوقُوا۟ ٱلْعَذَابَ بِمَا كُنتُمْ تَكْفُرُونَ
﴿٣٠﴾ قَدْ خَسِرَ ٱلَّذِينَ كَذَّبُوا۟ بِلِقَآءِ ٱللَّهِ ۖ حَتَّىٰٓ إِذَا جَآءَتْهُمُ ٱلسَّاعَةُ
بَغْتَةً قَالُوا۟ يَٰحَسْرَتَنَا عَلَىٰ مَا فَرَّطْنَا فِيهَا وَهُمْ يَحْمِلُونَ أَوْزَارَهُمْ
عَلَىٰ ظُهُورِهِمْ ۚ أَلَا سَآءَ مَا يَزِرُونَ ﴿٣١﴾ وَمَا ٱلْحَيَوٰةُ ٱلدُّنْيَآ إِلَّا
لَعِبٌ وَلَهْوٌ ۖ وَلَلدَّارُ ٱلْءَاخِرَةُ خَيْرٌ لِّلَّذِينَ يَتَّقُونَ ۗ أَفَلَا تَعْقِلُونَ
﴿٣٢﴾ قَدْ نَعْلَمُ إِنَّهُۥ لَيَحْزُنُكَ ٱلَّذِى يَقُولُونَ ۖ فَإِنَّهُمْ لَا يُكَذِّبُونَكَ
وَلَٰكِنَّ ٱلظَّٰلِمِينَ بِـَٔايَٰتِ ٱللَّهِ يَجْحَدُونَ ﴿٣٣﴾ وَلَقَدْ كُذِّبَتْ
رُسُلٌ مِّن قَبْلِكَ فَصَبَرُوا۟ عَلَىٰ مَا كُذِّبُوا۟ وَأُوذُوا۟ حَتَّىٰٓ أَتَىٰهُمْ نَصْرُنَا ۚ
وَلَا مُبَدِّلَ لِكَلِمَٰتِ ٱللَّهِ ۚ وَلَقَدْ جَآءَكَ مِن نَّبَإِى۟ ٱلْمُرْسَلِينَ
﴿٣٤﴾ وَإِن كَانَ كَبُرَ عَلَيْكَ إِعْرَاضُهُمْ فَإِنِ ٱسْتَطَعْتَ أَن تَبْتَغِىَ
نَفَقًا فِى ٱلْأَرْضِ أَوْ سُلَّمًا فِى ٱلسَّمَآءِ فَتَأْتِيَهُم بِـَٔايَةٍ ۚ وَلَوْ شَآءَ
ٱللَّهُ لَجَمَعَهُمْ عَلَى ٱلْهُدَىٰ ۚ فَلَا تَكُونَنَّ مِنَ ٱلْجَٰهِلِينَ ﴿٣٥﴾
۞ إِنَّمَا يَسْتَجِيبُ ٱلَّذِينَ يَسْمَعُونَ ۘ وَٱلْمَوْتَىٰ يَبْعَثُهُمُ ٱللَّهُ ثُمَّ إِلَيْهِ
يُرْجَعُونَ ﴿٣٦﴾ وَقَالُوا۟ لَوْلَا نُزِّلَ عَلَيْهِ ءَايَةٌ مِّن رَّبِّهِۦ ۚ قُلْ إِنَّ ٱللَّهَ
قَادِرٌ عَلَىٰٓ أَن يُنَزِّلَ ءَايَةً وَلَٰكِنَّ أَكْثَرَهُمْ لَا يَعْلَمُونَ ﴿٣٧﴾ وَمَا

jinn or men. ***Do you then bear witness that there are other gods together with Allah?"*** This question is an objection. ***Say*** to them***: "I do not bear witness*** to that." ***Say: "He is only One God, and I am free of all*** the idols ***you associate with Him."***

20. ***Those We have given the Book recognise it*** – or recognise Muḥammad from his description in their Book – ***as they recognise their own children. As for those*** of them ***who have lost their own selves, they do not believe*** in him.

21. ***Who could do greater wrong*** – no one does greater wrong – ***than someone who invents lies against Allah*** by ascribing a partner to Him, ***or denies His Signs*** (the Qur'an)***? The wrongdoers*** who do that ***are certainly not successful.***

22. Remember that ***on the Day We gather them all together, We will say*** in rebuke ***to those who attributed partners to Allah, "Where are your partner-gods, for whom you made such claims*** about being partners with Allah?"

23. ***Then they will have*** (read as *takun* or *yakun*) ***no other recourse*** or excuse ***than to say, "By Allah our Lord*** (read as *Rabbinā* and *Rabbanā*), ***We were not idolaters."***

24. Allah says: ***See***, Muḥammad, ***how they lie against themselves*** by denying their idolatry ***and how what they invented has forsaken them!*** Their falsely ascribed gods have abandoned them.

25. ***Some of them listen to you*** when you recite, ***but We have placed covers on their hearts, preventing them from understanding it*** (the Qur'an), ***and heaviness*** (deafness) ***in their ears*** so that they do not hear and accept it. ***Though they see every Sign, they still do not believe it. So that when they come to you, disputing with you, those who disbelieve say, "This*** Qur'an ***is nothing but*** lies, like ***the myths of earlier peoples!"***

26. ***They keep others*** (other people) ***from it*** – from following the Prophet, may Allah bless him and grant him peace – ***and avoid it themselves*** by distancing themselves from it so that they do not believe in him. It is said that this was revealed about Abū Ṭālib, whom prevented people harming the Prophet while not believing in him, in which case "it" should be read as "him." – ***They are only destroying themselves*** by being far from it, because that harms them, ***but they are not aware of it.***

27. ***If you,*** Muḥammad, ***could only see when they are standing before the Fire*** – when they are confronted with it – ***and saying, "Oh! If only we could be sent back again*** to this world, ***we would not deny the Signs of our Lord and would be among the believers."***

28. Allah Almighty says: ***No,*** rejecting the desire for belief they were apparently expressing; ***it is simply that what they were concealing before*** by maintaining that Allah was their Lord and that they were not idolaters ***has been shown to them*** when their limbs testify against them, which is when they make this wish; ***and if they were sent back*** to this world ***they would merely return to what*** (the *shirk*) ***they were forbidden to do. Truly they are liars*** regarding their promise to believe.

29. ***They say***, denying the Resurrection, ***"There is nothing but this life and we will not be raised again."***

30. ***If you could only see when they are standing before*** and presented to ***their Lord***, you would see something terrible. ***He will say*** to them on the tongue of the angels to rebuke them, ***"Is this*** Resurrection and Reckoning ***not the Truth?" They will say, "Yes indeed, by our Lord!*** It is the Truth!" ***He will say, "Then taste the punishment because of your unbelief*** in this world."

31. ***Those who*** completely ***deny the meeting with Allah*** (the Resurrection) ***have lost, until, when the Hour*** (the Day of Rising) ***comes upon them suddenly, they will say*** out of intense pain, ***"Alas for what we neglected there*** in this world!" The word "alas" expresses their pain at that time. ***They will bear their burdens on their backs*** – which will come to them on the Day of Rising in the ugliest of forms and with the foulest stink and will be borne by those responsible for them. ***How evil is what they bear!***

32. ***The life of this world*** – occupation with it – ***is nothing but a game and a diversion.*** What is better are acts of obedience and what helps one to do them. ***The Next World*** (the Garden) ***is better for those who are godfearing*** and fear idolatry. ***Will you not then use your intellect*** (read as *ta'qilūna* and also as *ya'qilūna*, in which case the meaning is "Will they not then use their intellect?") and believe***?***

33. ***We know that what they say*** to you in denial ***distresses you. It is not that they are denying you"*** (*yukadhdhibūnaka*) in secret because they know that he is speaking the truth. Another reading is *yukd - hibūka*, which gives the meaning "It is not that they are calling you a liar." ***The wrongdoers are just refuting*** and denying ***Allah's Signs*** (the Qur'ān).

34. The following is also to give solace to the Prophet, may Allah bless him and grant him peace. ***Messengers before you were also denied but they were steadfast in the face of the denial and injury they suffered until Our help arrived*** in the form of the destruction of their hostile peoples. So be patient until victory comes through the destruction of your people. ***There is no changing the Words of Allah*** (His promises). ***And news of other Messengers has come to you*** – which should set your heart at rest.

35. ***If their turning away*** from Islam ***is hard on you*** because you are eager for them to become Muslim ***then if you can, go down a tun - nel deep into the earth, or climb up a ladder into heaven, and bring them a Sign*** which they ask for. The implied meaning is that you will not be able to do that, so be patient until Allah judges. ***If Allah had willed*** for them to be guided – ***He would have gathered them all to guidance***, but He did not and so they did not believe. ***Do not then be among the ignorant*** by behaving like that.

36. ***Only those who can hear*** and understand ***respond*** to the call to believe. ***As for the dead*** – the unbelievers who resemble the dead in that they cannot hear – ***Allah will raise them up*** in the Next World, ***then to Him they will be returned*** and He will repay them for their actions.

37. ***They*** (the unbelievers of Makka) ***say, "Why is no Sign*** such as the she-camel of Ṣāliḥ, the staff of Mūsā, or the Table of 'Īsā ***sent down to him from his Lord?" Say*** to them, ***"Allah has the power to send down*** (read as *yunzila* and *yunazzila*) ***a Sign*** which they ask for." ***But most of them do not know*** that its descent would be a trial for them and would bring their destruction if they denied it.

38. ***There is no creature crawling on the earth or flying creature, flying on its wings, who are not nations just like yourselves*** in

مِن دَآبَّةٖ فِي ٱلۡأَرۡضِ وَلَا طَٰٓئِرٖ يَطِيرُ بِجَنَاحَيۡهِ إِلَّآ أُمَمٌ أَمۡثَالُكُمۚ
مَّا فَرَّطۡنَا فِي ٱلۡكِتَٰبِ مِن شَيۡءٖۚ ثُمَّ إِلَىٰ رَبِّهِمۡ يُحۡشَرُونَ ٣٨
وَٱلَّذِينَ كَذَّبُواْ بِـَٔايَٰتِنَا صُمّٞ وَبُكۡمٞ فِي ٱلظُّلُمَٰتِۗ مَن يَشَإِ ٱللَّهُ
يُضۡلِلۡهُ وَمَن يَشَأۡ يَجۡعَلۡهُ عَلَىٰ صِرَٰطٖ مُّسۡتَقِيمٖ ٣٩ قُلۡ
أَرَءَيۡتَكُمۡ إِنۡ أَتَىٰكُمۡ عَذَابُ ٱللَّهِ أَوۡ أَتَتۡكُمُ ٱلسَّاعَةُ أَغَيۡرَ ٱللَّهِ
تَدۡعُونَ إِن كُنتُمۡ صَٰدِقِينَ ٤٠ بَلۡ إِيَّاهُ تَدۡعُونَ فَيَكۡشِفُ مَا
تَدۡعُونَ إِلَيۡهِ إِن شَآءَ وَتَنسَوۡنَ مَا تُشۡرِكُونَ ٤١ وَلَقَدۡ أَرۡسَلۡنَآ
إِلَىٰٓ أُمَمٖ مِّن قَبۡلِكَ فَأَخَذۡنَٰهُم بِٱلۡبَأۡسَآءِ وَٱلضَّرَّآءِ لَعَلَّهُمۡ يَتَضَرَّعُونَ
٤٢ فَلَوۡلَآ إِذۡ جَآءَهُم بَأۡسُنَا تَضَرَّعُواْ وَلَٰكِن قَسَتۡ قُلُوبُهُمۡ
وَزَيَّنَ لَهُمُ ٱلشَّيۡطَٰنُ مَا كَانُواْ يَعۡمَلُونَ ٤٣ فَلَمَّا
نَسُواْ مَا ذُكِّرُواْ بِهِۦ فَتَحۡنَا عَلَيۡهِمۡ أَبۡوَٰبَ كُلِّ شَيۡءٍ
حَتَّىٰٓ إِذَا فَرِحُواْ بِمَآ أُوتُوٓاْ أَخَذۡنَٰهُم بَغۡتَةٗ فَإِذَا هُم مُّبۡلِسُونَ ٤٤
فَقُطِعَ دَابِرُ ٱلۡقَوۡمِ ٱلَّذِينَ ظَلَمُواْۚ وَٱلۡحَمۡدُ لِلَّهِ رَبِّ ٱلۡعَٰلَمِينَ ٤٥
قُلۡ أَرَءَيۡتُمۡ إِنۡ أَخَذَ ٱللَّهُ سَمۡعَكُمۡ وَأَبۡصَٰرَكُمۡ وَخَتَمَ عَلَىٰ قُلُوبِكُم
مَّنۡ إِلَٰهٌ غَيۡرُ ٱللَّهِ يَأۡتِيكُم بِهِۗ ٱنظُرۡ كَيۡفَ نُصَرِّفُ ٱلۡأٓيَٰتِ
ثُمَّ هُمۡ يَصۡدِفُونَ ٤٦ قُلۡ أَرَءَيۡتَكُمۡ إِنۡ أَتَىٰكُمۡ عَذَابُ ٱللَّهِ
بَغۡتَةً أَوۡ جَهۡرَةً هَلۡ يُهۡلَكُ إِلَّا ٱلۡقَوۡمُ ٱلظَّٰلِمُونَ ٤٧ وَمَا
نُرۡسِلُ ٱلۡمُرۡسَلِينَ إِلَّا مُبَشِّرِينَ وَمُنذِرِينَۖ فَمَنۡ ءَامَنَ وَأَصۡلَحَ
فَلَا خَوۡفٌ عَلَيۡهِمۡ وَلَا هُمۡ يَحۡزَنُونَ ٤٨ وَٱلَّذِينَ كَذَّبُواْ بِـَٔايَٰتِنَا
يَمَسُّهُمُ ٱلۡعَذَابُ بِمَا كَانُواْ يَفۡسُقُونَ ٤٩ قُل لَّآ أَقُولُ لَكُمۡ
عِندِي خَزَآئِنُ ٱللَّهِ وَلَآ أَعۡلَمُ ٱلۡغَيۡبَ وَلَآ أَقُولُ لَكُمۡ إِنِّي مَلَكٌۖ
إِنۡ أَتَّبِعُ إِلَّا مَا يُوحَىٰٓ إِلَيَّۚ قُلۡ هَلۡ يَسۡتَوِي ٱلۡأَعۡمَىٰ وَٱلۡبَصِيرُۚ

respect of the management of their creation, provision and states. ***We have not omitted anything from the Book*** (the Preserved Tablet) but have recorded everything. ***Then they will be gathered to their Lord.*** Their Lord will decide between His animal creatures regarding every point of difference they have; even between the horned and hornless sheep. Then He will tell them to be dust.

39. ***Those who deny Our Signs*** (the Qur'ān) ***are deaf*** to hearing and accepting it ***and dumb*** to speaking the truth ***in utter darkness*** of unbelief. ***Allah misguides whomever He wills, and*** guides and ***puts whomever He wills on a Straight Path*** (the *Dīn* of Islam).

40. ***Say***, Muḥammad, to the people of Makka: "Tell me: ***What would you think if Allah's punishment were to come upon you*** in this world ***or the Hour*** – the Day of Rising which includes the Final Hour, suddenly? ***Would you call on other than Allah if you are being truthful*** about the idols being able to help you? Call on them then." The truth is that you would not.

41. ***It is Him*** alone ***you call on*** in times of hardship ***and, if He wills, He will*** remove harm and difficulties from you and ***deliver you from whatever it was that made you call on Him; and you will forget*** and abandon ***the partners you ascribed to Him***, the idols which you should not call upon.

42. ***We sent Messengers to nations before you*** but they denied them; ***and*** We ***afflicted those nations with hardship*** (intense poverty) ***and distress*** (illness) ***so that perhaps they would humble themselves*** and believe.

43. ***If only they had humbled themselves when Our violent force*** (Our punishment) ***came upon them!*** In other words, they did not do that when that was what was necessary. ***However, their hearts were hard*** – and not softened to belief – ***and Shayṭān made what*** (the acts of disobedience) ***they were doing*** of ***appear good to them*** and so they persisted in them.

44. ***When they forgot*** and abandoned ***what they had been reminded of*** and cautioned about regarding hardship and distress and they did not heed the warning, then ***We opened up*** (read as *fataḥnā* and *fattaḥnā*) ***the doors to everything for them*** – all manner of blessings to draw them on – ***until, when they were*** proud and ***exulting in***

أَفَلَا تَتَفَكَّرُونَ ﴿٥٠﴾ وَأَنذِرْ بِهِ ٱلَّذِينَ يَخَافُونَ أَن يُحْشَرُوٓا۟
إِلَىٰ رَبِّهِمْ ۙ لَيْسَ لَهُم مِّن دُونِهِۦ وَلِىٌّ وَلَا شَفِيعٌ لَّعَلَّهُمْ يَتَّقُونَ
﴿٥١﴾ وَلَا تَطْرُدِ ٱلَّذِينَ يَدْعُونَ رَبَّهُم بِٱلْغَدَوٰةِ وَٱلْعَشِىِّ يُرِيدُونَ
وَجْهَهُۥ ۖ مَا عَلَيْكَ مِنْ حِسَابِهِم مِّن شَىْءٍ وَمَا مِنْ حِسَابِكَ
عَلَيْهِم مِّن شَىْءٍ فَتَطْرُدَهُمْ فَتَكُونَ مِنَ ٱلظَّٰلِمِينَ ﴿٥٢﴾
وَكَذَٰلِكَ فَتَنَّا بَعْضَهُم بِبَعْضٍ لِّيَقُولُوٓا۟ أَهَٰٓؤُلَآءِ مَنَّ ٱللَّهُ
عَلَيْهِم مِّنۢ بَيْنِنَآ ۗ أَلَيْسَ ٱللَّهُ بِأَعْلَمَ بِٱلشَّٰكِرِينَ ﴿٥٣﴾ وَإِذَا
جَآءَكَ ٱلَّذِينَ يُؤْمِنُونَ بِـَٔايَٰتِنَا فَقُلْ سَلَٰمٌ عَلَيْكُمْ ۖ كَتَبَ
رَبُّكُمْ عَلَىٰ نَفْسِهِ ٱلرَّحْمَةَ ۖ أَنَّهُۥ مَنْ عَمِلَ مِنكُمْ سُوٓءًۢا
بِجَهَٰلَةٍ ثُمَّ تَابَ مِنۢ بَعْدِهِۦ وَأَصْلَحَ فَأَنَّهُۥ غَفُورٌ رَّحِيمٌ ﴿٥٤﴾
وَكَذَٰلِكَ نُفَصِّلُ ٱلْءَايَٰتِ وَلِتَسْتَبِينَ سَبِيلُ ٱلْمُجْرِمِينَ ﴿٥٥﴾
قُلْ إِنِّى نُهِيتُ أَنْ أَعْبُدَ ٱلَّذِينَ تَدْعُونَ مِن دُونِ ٱللَّهِ ۚ قُل لَّآ أَتَّبِعُ
أَهْوَآءَكُمْ ۙ قَدْ ضَلَلْتُ إِذًا وَمَآ أَنَا۠ مِنَ ٱلْمُهْتَدِينَ ﴿٥٦﴾
قُلْ إِنِّى عَلَىٰ بَيِّنَةٍ مِّن رَّبِّى وَكَذَّبْتُم بِهِۦ ۚ مَا عِندِى مَا
تَسْتَعْجِلُونَ بِهِۦٓ ۚ إِنِ ٱلْحُكْمُ إِلَّا لِلَّهِ ۖ يَقُصُّ ٱلْحَقَّ ۖ وَهُوَ خَيْرُ
ٱلْفَٰصِلِينَ ﴿٥٧﴾ قُل لَّوْ أَنَّ عِندِى مَا تَسْتَعْجِلُونَ بِهِۦ لَقُضِىَ
ٱلْأَمْرُ بَيْنِى وَبَيْنَكُمْ ۗ وَٱللَّهُ أَعْلَمُ بِٱلظَّٰلِمِينَ ﴿٥٨﴾
۞ وَعِندَهُۥ مَفَاتِحُ ٱلْغَيْبِ لَا يَعْلَمُهَآ إِلَّا هُوَ ۚ وَيَعْلَمُ مَا فِى
ٱلْبَرِّ وَٱلْبَحْرِ ۚ وَمَا تَسْقُطُ مِن وَرَقَةٍ إِلَّا يَعْلَمُهَا وَلَا حَبَّةٍ
فِى ظُلُمَٰتِ ٱلْأَرْضِ وَلَا رَطْبٍ وَلَا يَابِسٍ إِلَّا فِى كِتَٰبٍ مُّبِينٍ ﴿٥٩﴾

what they had been given, We suddenly seized them with the punishment ***and at once they were in despair*** and gave up all hope of any future good.

45. ***So the last remnant of the people who did wrong was cut off*** and eradicated. ***Praise belongs to Allah, the Lord of all the worlds*** for helping the Messengers and destroying the unbelievers*!*

46. ***Say*** to the people of Makka*:* "Tell me: ***what would you think if Allah took away your hearing*** (made you deaf) ***and your sight*** (made you blind) ***and sealed up*** and stamped ***your hearts*** so you cannot recognise anything; ***what god is there, other than Allah, who could give them back to you*** after He has taken them from you, as they claim*?"* ***Look how We vary the Signs*** and make them clear and they are proofs of Our Oneness**.** ***Yet still they turn away*** from it and do not believe**.**

47. ***Say*** to them*:* ***"What would you think if Allah's punishment were to come upon you suddenly by night or openly by day, would any but the wrongdoing people*** (the unbelievers) ***be destroyed?"*** This means that only they would be destroyed.

48. ***We do not send the Messengers except to bring good news*** of the Garden to those who believe, ***and to give warning*** of the Fire to those who disbelieve**.** ***As for those who believe and put things right*** with righteous action***, they will feel no fear and know no sorrow*** in the Next World**.**

49. ***The punishment will fall on those who deny Our Signs because they were degenerate*** and abandoned obedience.

50. ***Say*** to them*:* ***"I do not say to you that I possess the treasuries of Allah*** from which the provision of all creatures come, ***nor do I know the Unseen*** – which is hidden from me and not revealed to me – ***nor do I say to you that I am an angel. I only follow what has been revealed to me." Say: "Are the blind*** (the unbelievers) ***the same as those who see*** (the believers)***? Will you not reflect*** on that and believe*?"*

51. ***Warn*** and alarm ***by it*** (the Qur'an) ***those who fear they will be gathered to their Lord*** – meaning the rebellious believers – ***having no protector*** to help them ***or intercessor*** to intercede for them ***apart***

from Him, so that perhaps they will be godfearing, which will remove them from the state they are in and so they will perform acts of obedience.

52. ***Do not chase away those who call on their Lord morning and evening, seeking His Face*** by their worship, desiring nothing of the goods of this world. They are the poor. The idolaters attacked them and demanded of the Prophet, may Allah bless him and grant him peace, to drive them away so that they could sit with him. He did so, out of the desire for them to become Muslim. ***Their reckoning is in no way your responsibility*** if their inward is not pleasing ***and your reckoning is in no way their responsibility. Indeed if you did chase them away, you would be among the wrongdoers*** for doing that.

53. ***Thus do We try some of them by means of others*** – the noble through the lowly and the rich through the poor, by making the latter believe first, ***until they*** (the nobles and rich) ***will say*** in objection, ***"Are these*** (the poor) ***the people among us to whom Allah has shown His favour*** by guiding them?" "If what they have is really guidance, we would have been granted it first." Allah says: ***Does not Allah know best those who are thankful*** to Him and so guide them? Indeed He does!

54. ***When those who believe in Our Signs come to you, say*** to them, ***"Peace be upon you!" Your Lord has made mercy incumbent on Himself*** and decreed it for Himself. ***If*** (read as *annahu* and *innahu*) ***anyone among you does evil out of ignorance and then afterwards repents and puts things right*** by righteous actions. ***He is Ever-Forgiving*** to him, ***Most Merciful*** to him.

55. ***In that way*** – as We have made clear in what has been mentioned – ***We make the Signs*** (the Qur'an) ***plain*** and clear so that the truth appears and can be acted on, ***so that the path of the evil-doers may be clearly seen.*** (*sabīlu,* "path", is also read as *sabīla*, in which case the meaning is "so that you may see clearly the path of the evil-doers," this being addressed to the Prophet, may Allah bless him and grant him peace.)

56. ***Say: "I am forbidden to worship those you call upon*** and worship ***besides Allah." Say: "I do not follow your whims and desires*** in my worship. ***If I did*** follow them, ***I would go astray and not be among the guided."***

وَهُوَ ٱلَّذِى يَتَوَفَّىٰكُم بِٱلَّيْلِ وَيَعْلَمُ مَا جَرَحْتُم بِٱلنَّهَارِ ثُمَّ
يَبْعَثُكُمْ فِيهِ لِيُقْضَىٰٓ أَجَلٌ مُّسَمًّى ۖ ثُمَّ إِلَيْهِ مَرْجِعُكُمْ
ثُمَّ يُنَبِّئُكُم بِمَا كُنتُمْ تَعْمَلُونَ ٦٠ وَهُوَ ٱلْقَاهِرُ فَوْقَ عِبَادِهِۦ ۖ
وَيُرْسِلُ عَلَيْكُمْ حَفَظَةً حَتَّىٰٓ إِذَا جَآءَ أَحَدَكُمُ ٱلْمَوْتُ تَوَفَّتْهُ
رُسُلُنَا وَهُمْ لَا يُفَرِّطُونَ ٦١ ثُمَّ رُدُّوٓا۟ إِلَى ٱللَّهِ مَوْلَىٰهُمُ ٱلْحَقِّ ۚ
أَلَا لَهُ ٱلْحُكْمُ وَهُوَ أَسْرَعُ ٱلْحَٰسِبِينَ ٦٢ قُلْ مَن يُنَجِّيكُم مِّن
ظُلُمَٰتِ ٱلْبَرِّ وَٱلْبَحْرِ تَدْعُونَهُۥ تَضَرُّعًا وَخُفْيَةً لَّئِنْ أَنجَىٰنَا مِنْ هَٰذِهِۦ
لَنَكُونَنَّ مِنَ ٱلشَّٰكِرِينَ ٦٣ قُلِ ٱللَّهُ يُنَجِّيكُم مِّنْهَا وَمِن كُلِّ كَرْبٍ
ثُمَّ أَنتُمْ تُشْرِكُونَ ٦٤ قُلْ هُوَ ٱلْقَادِرُ عَلَىٰٓ أَن يَبْعَثَ عَلَيْكُمْ عَذَابًا
مِّن فَوْقِكُمْ أَوْ مِن تَحْتِ أَرْجُلِكُمْ أَوْ يَلْبِسَكُمْ شِيَعًا وَيُذِيقَ بَعْضَكُم
بَأْسَ بَعْضٍ ۗ ٱنظُرْ كَيْفَ نُصَرِّفُ ٱلْءَايَٰتِ لَعَلَّهُمْ يَفْقَهُونَ ٦٥
وَكَذَّبَ بِهِۦ قَوْمُكَ وَهُوَ ٱلْحَقُّ ۚ قُل لَّسْتُ عَلَيْكُم بِوَكِيلٍ ٦٦ لِّكُلِّ
نَبَإٍ مُّسْتَقَرٌّ ۚ وَسَوْفَ تَعْلَمُونَ ٦٧ وَإِذَا رَأَيْتَ ٱلَّذِينَ يَخُوضُونَ فِىٓ
ءَايَٰتِنَا فَأَعْرِضْ عَنْهُمْ حَتَّىٰ يَخُوضُوا۟ فِى حَدِيثٍ غَيْرِهِۦ ۚ وَإِمَّا يُنسِيَنَّكَ
ٱلشَّيْطَٰنُ فَلَا تَقْعُدْ بَعْدَ ٱلذِّكْرَىٰ مَعَ ٱلْقَوْمِ ٱلظَّٰلِمِينَ ٦٨
وَمَا عَلَى ٱلَّذِينَ يَتَّقُونَ مِنْ حِسَابِهِم مِّن شَىْءٍ وَلَٰكِن
ذِكْرَىٰ لَعَلَّهُمْ يَتَّقُونَ ٦٩ وَذَرِ ٱلَّذِينَ ٱتَّخَذُوا۟
دِينَهُمْ لَعِبًا وَلَهْوًا وَغَرَّتْهُمُ ٱلْحَيَوٰةُ ٱلدُّنْيَا ۚ وَذَكِّرْ بِهِۦٓ
أَن تُبْسَلَ نَفْسٌۢ بِمَا كَسَبَتْ لَيْسَ لَهَا مِن دُونِ ٱللَّهِ وَلِىٌّ
وَلَا شَفِيعٌ وَإِن تَعْدِلْ كُلَّ عَدْلٍ لَّا يُؤْخَذْ مِنْهَآ ۗ أُو۟لَٰٓئِكَ

57. ***Say: "I stand on a Clear Sign from my Lord and yet you have denied it*** – denied my Lord by associating others with Him. ***I do not have in my possession what you are in such haste to bring about*** – meaning punishment. ***Jurisdiction over it*** and other things ***belongs to Allah alone. He decides*** (read as *yaqḍī* and also *yaquṣṣu*, in which case the meaning is "He tells") ***the truth and He is the best of Deciders*** and Judges."

58. ***Say*** to them***: "If I did have in my possession what you are in such haste to bring about, the affair between me and you would have been decided*** because I would bring it about and then have nothing more to do. But it is up to Allah. ***Allah has best knowledge of the wrongdoers"*** and will punish them.

59. ***The keys to the Unseen*** – His treasures or the paths leading to His knowledge – ***are in His possession. No one knows them but Him.*** There are five such things, as in the *āyat*: *"Allah has knowledge of the Hour"* (31-34) and in the *ḥadīth* reported by al-Bukhārī. ***He knows everything*** that happens ***in the land*** in deserts, ***and sea*** in towns on the coast. ***No leaf falls without His knowing it. There is no seed in the darkness of the earth, and nothing moist or dry which is not in a Clear Book*** (the Preserved Tablet).

60. ***It is He who takes you back to Himself at night***, taking your souls when you sleep, ***while knowing the things you perpetrate by day, and then wakes you up again*** – restoring your souls to life – ***so that a specified term*** of life ***may be fulfilled. Then you will return to Him*** at the Resurrection. ***Then He will inform you about what you did*** and repay you for it.

61. ***He is the Absolute Master*** with total power ***over His slaves. He sends*** recording ***angels to watch over you*** and record people's actions. ***Then when death comes*** (read as *tawaffat-hu* and *tawafāhu*) ***to one of you, Our messengers*** – the angels who are charged with taking the soul – ***take him, and they do not fail in their duty*** but confine themselves to doing what they are commanded.

62. ***Then they*** (the slaves) ***are returned to Allah, their Master, the Real***, who is firm in His justice and will repay them for their actions. ***Jurisdiction*** and judgement which will be carried out on them – ***belongs to Him alone and He is the Swiftest of Reckoners.*** He will reckon all of creation in half a day going by the measure of the days of this world, according to *ḥadīth*.

63. ***Say***, Muḥammad, to the people of Makka***: "Who rescues you from the*** terrors of the ***darkness of the land and sea*** during your journeys***?*** When ***you call on Him humbly*** in public ***and secretly***, saying***: 'If He rescues us*** (read as *anjāna* and *anjaytanā*, "you rescue us") ***from this*** (this darkness and hardship) ***we will truly be among the thankful*** believers***.'"***

64. ***Say*** to them***: "Allah rescues you*** (read as *yunajjīkum* and *yunjīkum)* ***from it, and from every distress*** and sorrow***. Then you associate others with Him."***

65. ***Say: "He possesses the power to send you punishment from above your heads*** out of heaven, as in the case of stones and the Shout, ***or from underneath your feet*** as when the earth collapses under them, ***or to confuse you in sects*** – different groups with different whims – ***and make you taste each other's violence*** by fighting***."*** The Prophet, may Allah bless him and grant him peace, said when this was revealed: "This is easier," and when what was before it was revealed, he said, "I seek refuge with Your face." (al-Bukhārī) Muslim reports the *ḥadīth*: "I asked Allah that my community should not be subject to mutual violence but He refused to grant that." In another *ḥadīth*, "When this was revealed, the Prophet, peace be upon him, said, 'Either they already exist or they have not yet come about.'" ***Look how We vary the Signs*** (evidence of Our power) – and make them clear to them – ***so that perhaps they will understand*** and know that what they have is false.

66. ***Your people deny it*** (the Qur'an) ***and yet it is the Truth. Say*** to them***: "I am not here as your guardian*** in that your punishment is in my hands. I am merely a warner and what happens to you is Allah's business." This was before the command to fight.

67. ***Every tidings has its time*** – a time at which it will occur when He will punish you – ***and you will certainly come to know."*** This is a threat.

68. ***When you see people involved in mockery of Our Signs*** (the Qur'an), ***turn from them*** and do not sit with them ***until they get involved in other talk. And if Shayṭān should ever cause you to for-***

ٱلَّذِينَ أُبۡسِلُواْ بِمَا كَسَبُواْۖ لَهُمۡ شَرَابٞ مِّنۡ حَمِيمٖ وَعَذَابٌ
أَلِيمُۢ بِمَا كَانُواْ يَكۡفُرُونَ ﴿٧٠﴾ قُلۡ أَنَدۡعُواْ مِن دُونِ ٱللَّهِ
مَا لَا يَنفَعُنَا وَلَا يَضُرُّنَا وَنُرَدُّ عَلَىٰٓ أَعۡقَابِنَا بَعۡدَ إِذۡ هَدَىٰنَا ٱللَّهُ
كَٱلَّذِي ٱسۡتَهۡوَتۡهُ ٱلشَّيَٰطِينُ فِي ٱلۡأَرۡضِ حَيۡرَانَ لَهُۥٓ أَصۡحَٰبٞ
يَدۡعُونَهُۥٓ إِلَى ٱلۡهُدَى ٱئۡتِنَاۗ قُلۡ إِنَّ هُدَى ٱللَّهِ هُوَ ٱلۡهُدَىٰۖ
وَأُمِرۡنَا لِنُسۡلِمَ لِرَبِّ ٱلۡعَٰلَمِينَ ﴿٧١﴾ وَأَنۡ أَقِيمُواْ ٱلصَّلَوٰةَ
وَٱتَّقُوهُۚ وَهُوَ ٱلَّذِيٓ إِلَيۡهِ تُحۡشَرُونَ ﴿٧٢﴾ وَهُوَ ٱلَّذِي
خَلَقَ ٱلسَّمَٰوَٰتِ وَٱلۡأَرۡضَ بِٱلۡحَقِّۖ وَيَوۡمَ يَقُولُ كُن
فَيَكُونُۚ قَوۡلُهُ ٱلۡحَقُّۚ وَلَهُ ٱلۡمُلۡكُ يَوۡمَ يُنفَخُ فِي ٱلصُّورِۚ
عَٰلِمُ ٱلۡغَيۡبِ وَٱلشَّهَٰدَةِۚ وَهُوَ ٱلۡحَكِيمُ ٱلۡخَبِيرُ ﴿٧٣﴾
۞ وَإِذۡ قَالَ إِبۡرَٰهِيمُ لِأَبِيهِ ءَازَرَ أَتَتَّخِذُ أَصۡنَامًا ءَالِهَةً إِنِّيٓ
أَرَىٰكَ وَقَوۡمَكَ فِي ضَلَٰلٖ مُّبِينٖ ﴿٧٤﴾ وَكَذَٰلِكَ نُرِيٓ إِبۡرَٰهِيمَ
مَلَكُوتَ ٱلسَّمَٰوَٰتِ وَٱلۡأَرۡضِ وَلِيَكُونَ مِنَ ٱلۡمُوقِنِينَ ﴿٧٥﴾
فَلَمَّا جَنَّ عَلَيۡهِ ٱلَّيۡلُ رَءَا كَوۡكَبٗاۖ قَالَ هَٰذَا رَبِّيۖ فَلَمَّآ أَفَلَ قَالَ
لَآ أُحِبُّ ٱلۡأٓفِلِينَ ﴿٧٦﴾ فَلَمَّا رَءَا ٱلۡقَمَرَ بَازِغٗا قَالَ هَٰذَا
رَبِّيۖ فَلَمَّآ أَفَلَ قَالَ لَئِن لَّمۡ يَهۡدِنِي رَبِّي لَأَكُونَنَّ مِنَ ٱلۡقَوۡمِ
ٱلضَّآلِّينَ ﴿٧٧﴾ فَلَمَّا رَءَا ٱلشَّمۡسَ بَازِغَةٗ قَالَ هَٰذَا رَبِّي هَٰذَآ
أَكۡبَرُۖ فَلَمَّآ أَفَلَتۡ قَالَ يَٰقَوۡمِ إِنِّي بَرِيٓءٞ مِّمَّا تُشۡرِكُونَ ﴿٧٨﴾
إِنِّي وَجَّهۡتُ وَجۡهِيَ لِلَّذِي فَطَرَ ٱلسَّمَٰوَٰتِ وَٱلۡأَرۡضَ
حَنِيفٗاۖ وَمَآ أَنَا۠ مِنَ ٱلۡمُشۡرِكِينَ ﴿٧٩﴾ وَحَآجَّهُۥ قَوۡمُهُۥۚ قَالَ

get (read as *yunsiyannaka* and *yunassinnaka*) and you sit with them, ***once you remember, do not stay sitting with the wrongdoers.*** The Muslims said, "If we get up and go whenever they are talking, we will not be able to sit in the mosque or do *ṭawāf*." Then the following was revealed:

69. ***Their reckoning*** – that of those who get involved with such talk ***– is in no way the responsibility of those who are godfearing*** when they sit with them. ***But*** they must ***remind them*** and admonish them ***so that perhaps they will be godfearing*** and fear becoming involved in that.

70. ***Abandon those who have made their* dīn** for which they are responsible ***into a game and a diversion*** by mocking it, ***and who have been deluded by the life of this world.*** Do not pay any attention to them. This was revealed before the command to fight. ***Remind*** and admonish people ***by it*** (the Qur'ān) ***lest a person be delivered up to destruction for what he has earned*** (his actions) ***with no protector*** or helper ***or intercessor*** to defend him from the punishment ***besides Allah. Were he to offer every kind of compensation*** as ransom, ***it*** (that ransom) ***would not be accepted from him. Such people are delivered up to destruction for what they have earned. They will have scalding water to drink and a painful punishment because they disbelieved*** (on account of their unbelief).

71. ***Say: "Are we to call on*** and worship ***something besides Allah which can neither help*** us through our worship ***nor harm us*** if we do not worship them, meaning idols, ***and to turn on our heels*** and revert to being idolaters ***after Allah has guided us*** to the *dīn* of Islam, ***like someone the* shayṭāns *have*** misguided and ***lured away in the earth, leaving him confused and bewildered*** – not knowing which way to go – ***despite the fact that he has companions calling him to guidance***, trying to guide him to the Path and ***saying, 'Come with us!'?"*** But he does not respond to them and is destroyed by his refusal to do so. The question is an objection. ***Say: "Allah's guidance, that is true guidance*** and anything else is misguidance. ***We are commanded to submit to the Lord of all the worlds…***

72. ***…and to establish the prayer and be fearful of Him. It is He to Whom you will be gathered*** on the Day of Rising for the Reckoning."

73. ***It is He who created the heavens and the earth with truth.*** Remember ***the day He says*** to the thing, ***"Be!" it is.*** That is a reference to the Day of Rising when Allah will say to creation, "Rise!" and they will rise. ***His speech is Truth***, which means that it must be so and must take place. ***The Kingdom will be His the Day the Trumpet is blown.*** This refers to the Second Blast of the Trumpet by Isrāfīl: no one will have any dominion on that Day but Him: *"To whom belongs dominion today? To Allah."* (40:16) ***The Knower of the Unseen and the Visible*** – whatever is hidden and whatever is seen. ***He is the All-Wise*** in His creation, ***the All-Aware*** of the inward as well as the outward of all things.

74. Remember ***when Ibrāhīm said to his father, Āzar*** – his title, his name being Terakh – ***"Do you take idols as gods?*** He censured him for worshipping idols. This question is meant as a rebuke. ***I see that you and your people are clearly misguided"*** by adopting them, they are plainly misguided from the truth.

75. ***Because of that*** – Our demonstration to him of the misguidance of his father and his people – ***We showed Ibrāhīm the realms of the heavens and the earth*** to indicate evidence of Allah's Oneness, ***so that he might be one of the people of certainty*** regarding that. This sentence is an interpolation into the narrative.

76. ***When night covered him*** and it became dark round him ***he saw a star***, said to be Venus, ***and said*** to his people, who were astrologers: ***"This is my Lord*** as you claim***!" Then when it set*** and disappeared, ***he said, "I do not love what sets"*** by taking them as lords, because the true Lord cannot change or pass away, those being qualities belonging to temporal things.

77. ***Then when he saw the moon rise he said*** to them, ***"This is my Lord!" Then when it set he said, "If my Lord does not guide me, I will be one of the misguided people."*** Then he would be exposed to the misguidance of His people and not be successful.

78. ***Then when he saw the sun rise he said, "This is my Lord! This is greater*** than the stars and the moon***!" Then when it set*** – and the proof was sufficiently strong for him even if his people would not recant – ***he said, "O my people! I am free of what you associate***

أَتُحَٰٓجُّوٓنِّي فِي ٱللَّهِ وَقَدۡ هَدَىٰنِۚ وَلَآ أَخَافُ مَا تُشۡرِكُونَ بِهِۦٓ
إِلَّآ أَن يَشَآءَ رَبِّي شَيۡـٔٗاۗ وَسِعَ رَبِّي كُلَّ شَيۡءٍ عِلۡمًاۗ أَفَلَا
تَتَذَكَّرُونَ ﴿٨٠﴾ وَكَيۡفَ أَخَافُ مَآ أَشۡرَكۡتُمۡ وَلَا
تَخَافُونَ أَنَّكُمۡ أَشۡرَكۡتُم بِٱللَّهِ مَا لَمۡ يُنَزِّلۡ بِهِۦ عَلَيۡكُمۡ
سُلۡطَٰنٗاۚ فَأَيُّ ٱلۡفَرِيقَيۡنِ أَحَقُّ بِٱلۡأَمۡنِۖ إِن كُنتُمۡ تَعۡلَمُونَ ﴿٨١﴾
ٱلَّذِينَ ءَامَنُواْ وَلَمۡ يَلۡبِسُوٓاْ إِيمَٰنَهُم بِظُلۡمٍ أُوْلَٰٓئِكَ لَهُمُ ٱلۡأَمۡنُ
وَهُم مُّهۡتَدُونَ ﴿٨٢﴾ وَتِلۡكَ حُجَّتُنَآ ءَاتَيۡنَٰهَآ إِبۡرَٰهِيمَ عَلَىٰ
قَوۡمِهِۦۚ نَرۡفَعُ دَرَجَٰتٖ مَّن نَّشَآءُۗ إِنَّ رَبَّكَ حَكِيمٌ عَلِيمٞ ﴿٨٣﴾
وَوَهَبۡنَا لَهُۥٓ إِسۡحَٰقَ وَيَعۡقُوبَۚ كُلًّا هَدَيۡنَاۚ وَنُوحًا
هَدَيۡنَا مِن قَبۡلُۖ وَمِن ذُرِّيَّتِهِۦ دَاوُۥدَ وَسُلَيۡمَٰنَ وَأَيُّوبَ
وَيُوسُفَ وَمُوسَىٰ وَهَٰرُونَۚ وَكَذَٰلِكَ نَجۡزِي ٱلۡمُحۡسِنِينَ ﴿٨٤﴾
وَزَكَرِيَّا وَيَحۡيَىٰ وَعِيسَىٰ وَإِلۡيَاسَۖ كُلّٞ مِّنَ ٱلصَّٰلِحِينَ ﴿٨٥﴾
وَإِسۡمَٰعِيلَ وَٱلۡيَسَعَ وَيُونُسَ وَلُوطٗاۚ وَكُلّٗا فَضَّلۡنَا عَلَى
ٱلۡعَٰلَمِينَ ﴿٨٦﴾ وَمِنۡ ءَابَآئِهِمۡ وَذُرِّيَّٰتِهِمۡ وَإِخۡوَٰنِهِمۡۖ وَٱجۡتَبَيۡنَٰهُمۡ
وَهَدَيۡنَٰهُمۡ إِلَىٰ صِرَٰطٖ مُّسۡتَقِيمٖ ﴿٨٧﴾ ذَٰلِكَ هُدَى ٱللَّهِ يَهۡدِي
بِهِۦ مَن يَشَآءُ مِنۡ عِبَادِهِۦۚ وَلَوۡ أَشۡرَكُواْ لَحَبِطَ عَنۡهُم مَّا كَانُواْ
يَعۡمَلُونَ ﴿٨٨﴾ أُوْلَٰٓئِكَ ٱلَّذِينَ ءَاتَيۡنَٰهُمُ ٱلۡكِتَٰبَ وَٱلۡحُكۡمَ وَٱلنُّبُوَّةَۚ
فَإِن يَكۡفُرۡ بِهَا هَٰٓؤُلَآءِ فَقَدۡ وَكَّلۡنَا بِهَا قَوۡمٗا لَّيۡسُواْ بِهَا بِكَٰفِرِينَ
﴿٨٩﴾ أُوْلَٰٓئِكَ ٱلَّذِينَ هَدَى ٱللَّهُۖ فَبِهُدَىٰهُمُ ٱقۡتَدِهۡۗ قُل لَّآ
أَسۡـَٔلُكُمۡ عَلَيۡهِ أَجۡرًاۖ إِنۡ هُوَ إِلَّا ذِكۡرَىٰ لِلۡعَٰلَمِينَ ﴿٩٠﴾

with Allah: from all objects of worship subject to time and space, preferring the One who brings them into existence.

79. He said: ***I have turned my face to Him*** (Allah) in my worship, ***who*** created and ***brought the heavens and earth into being a pure natural believer*** – a *ḥanīf* who is someone who naturally inclines to the Straight *Dīn*. ***I am no idolater*** and associate no one else with Him."

80. ***His people argued with him*** about his *dīn* and threatened him by saying that the idols would cause him harm if he abandoned them. ***He said, "Are you arguing*** (read as *tuḥājjūnnī* and *tuḥajjūnī*) ***with me about*** the Oneness of ***Allah when He has guided me*** to it***? I have no fear of any partner*** among the idols ***you ascribe to Him*** causing me any evil since they have no power to do anything ***unless my Lord should will such a*** disliked ***thing to happen*** to me, in which case it must happen. ***My Lord encompasses everything in His knowledge, so why do you not pay heed*** to this and believe***?***

81 ***Why should I fear the partners you have ascribed*** to Allah, which possess no power to either bring benefit or cause harm, ***when you yourselves apparently have no fear of ascribing partners to Allah*** in worship ***for which*** worship ***He has sent down no authority*** (evidence or proof) ***to you?*** He has power over all things. ***Which of the two parties***, we or you, ***is more entitled to feel safe, if you have any knowledge*** – of the one with the greater right***?*** We are, so follow that. Allah continues:

82. ***Those who believe and do not mix their belief with any wrong-doing*** (*shirk*)**,** as explained in a *ḥadīth* in the two *Ṣaḥīḥ* Collections, ***they are the ones who are safe*** from the punishment***; it is they who are guided."***

83. ***This is the argument We gave to Ibrāhīm*** and by which We guided him, and which he used ***against his people*** when he argued in favour of the Oneness of Allah by the setting of the star and the rest of it. ***We raise the rank*** in knowledge and wisdom ***of anyone We will. Your Lord is All-Wise*** in what He does, ***All-Knowing*** of His creation.

84. ***We gave him Isḥāq and Ya'qūb, each of whom We guided. And before him*** (Ibrāhīm) ***We had guided Nūḥ. And among his*** (Nūḥ's)

descendants were Dāwūd and Sulaymān, and Ayyūb, Yūsuf, Mūsā and Hārūn. That is how We recompense good-doers.

85. ***And Zakariyyā,*** his son ***Yaḥyā, 'Īsā*** son of Maryam ***and Ilyās,*** son of Hārūn. ***All of them were among the righteous.***

86 ***And Ismā'īl, al-Yasa', Yūnus and Lūṭ. All of them We favoured over all beings*** with Prophethood.

87. ***And some*** (The partitive word "some" (*min*) is used to qualify the adjective "all" in the previous *āyat* because some of them had no children and some had unbelievers among their children) ***of their forebears, descendants and brothers, We chose them and guided them to a straight path.***

88. ***That*** to which they were guided ***is Allah's guidance. He guides by it those of His slaves He wills. If they*** – theoretically, because they did not – ***had attributed partners to Him, nothing they did would have been of any use.***

89. ***They are the ones to whom We gave the Book,*** used generically to cover all the Divine Books, ***Judgement*** (wisdom) ***and Prophethood. If these people*** (the people of Makka) ***reject it, We have already entrusted it to a people who did not*** (the *Muhājirūn* and the *Anṣār*).

90. ***They are the ones Allah has guided, so be guided*** (read as *iqtadih* and *iqtadi*) ***by their guidance*** because their Path is one of *tawḥīd* and steadfastness. ***Say*** to the people of Makka, ***"I do not ask you for any wage for it*** (the Qur'an). ***It is simply a reminder*** and warning ***to all beings*** (men and jinn)."

91. ***They*** (the Jews) ***do not measure Allah with His true measure*** – do not esteem Him as He should be esteemed or recognise Him as He should be recognised – ***when they say*** to the Prophet, may Allah bless him and grant him peace, when they debated with him about the Qur'an ***"Allah would not send down anything to a mere human being." Say*** to them: ***"Who then sent down the Book which Mūsā brought as a Light and Guidance for the people?" You put*** (read as *taj'alūnahu* and also *yaj'alūnahu,* "they put") ***it down on sheets of paper*** (separate notebooks) ***to display*** (read as *tubdūna* and *yubdūna*) what you want to display of ***it while concealing*** (read as *tukhfūna* and *yakhfūna*) ***much*** of what is in it, like the description of the

وَمَا قَدَرُوا۟ ٱللَّهَ حَقَّ قَدْرِهِۦٓ إِذْ قَالُوا۟ مَآ أَنزَلَ ٱللَّهُ عَلَىٰ بَشَرٍ مِّن شَىْءٍ ۗ
قُلْ مَنْ أَنزَلَ ٱلْكِتَـٰبَ ٱلَّذِى جَآءَ بِهِۦ مُوسَىٰ نُورًا وَهُدًى لِّلنَّاسِ ۖ
تَجْعَلُونَهُۥ قَرَاطِيسَ تُبْدُونَهَا وَتُخْفُونَ كَثِيرًا ۖ وَعُلِّمْتُم مَّا لَمْ تَعْلَمُوٓا۟
أَنتُمْ وَلَآ ءَابَآؤُكُمْ ۖ قُلِ ٱللَّهُ ۖ ثُمَّ ذَرْهُمْ فِى خَوْضِهِمْ يَلْعَبُونَ ﴿٩١﴾
وَهَـٰذَا كِتَـٰبٌ أَنزَلْنَـٰهُ مُبَارَكٌ مُّصَدِّقُ ٱلَّذِى بَيْنَ يَدَيْهِ وَلِتُنذِرَ
أُمَّ ٱلْقُرَىٰ وَمَنْ حَوْلَهَا ۚ وَٱلَّذِينَ يُؤْمِنُونَ بِٱلْـَٔاخِرَةِ يُؤْمِنُونَ بِهِۦ ۖ
وَهُمْ عَلَىٰ صَلَاتِهِمْ يُحَافِظُونَ ﴿٩٢﴾ وَمَنْ أَظْلَمُ مِمَّنِ ٱفْتَرَىٰ عَلَى
ٱللَّهِ كَذِبًا أَوْ قَالَ أُوحِىَ إِلَىَّ وَلَمْ يُوحَ إِلَيْهِ شَىْءٌ وَمَن قَالَ سَأُنزِلُ
مِثْلَ مَآ أَنزَلَ ٱللَّهُ ۗ وَلَوْ تَرَىٰٓ إِذِ ٱلظَّـٰلِمُونَ فِى غَمَرَٰتِ ٱلْمَوْتِ
وَٱلْمَلَـٰٓئِكَةُ بَاسِطُوٓا۟ أَيْدِيهِمْ أَخْرِجُوٓا۟ أَنفُسَكُمُ ۖ ٱلْيَوْمَ
تُجْزَوْنَ عَذَابَ ٱلْهُونِ بِمَا كُنتُمْ تَقُولُونَ عَلَى ٱللَّهِ غَيْرَ ٱلْحَقِّ
وَكُنتُمْ عَنْ ءَايَـٰتِهِۦ تَسْتَكْبِرُونَ ﴿٩٣﴾ وَلَقَدْ جِئْتُمُونَا فُرَٰدَىٰ
كَمَا خَلَقْنَـٰكُمْ أَوَّلَ مَرَّةٍ وَتَرَكْتُم مَّا خَوَّلْنَـٰكُمْ وَرَآءَ ظُهُورِكُمْ ۖ
وَمَا نَرَىٰ مَعَكُمْ شُفَعَآءَكُمُ ٱلَّذِينَ زَعَمْتُمْ أَنَّهُمْ فِيكُمْ شُرَكَـٰٓؤُا۟ ۚ
لَقَد تَّقَطَّعَ بَيْنَكُمْ وَضَلَّ عَنكُم مَّا كُنتُمْ تَزْعُمُونَ ﴿٩٤﴾
۞ إِنَّ ٱللَّهَ فَالِقُ ٱلْحَبِّ وَٱلنَّوَىٰ ۖ يُخْرِجُ ٱلْحَىَّ مِنَ ٱلْمَيِّتِ وَمُخْرِجُ
ٱلْمَيِّتِ مِنَ ٱلْحَىِّ ۚ ذَٰلِكُمُ ٱللَّهُ ۖ فَأَنَّىٰ تُؤْفَكُونَ ﴿٩٥﴾ فَالِقُ ٱلْإِصْبَاحِ
وَجَعَلَ ٱلَّيْلَ سَكَنًا وَٱلشَّمْسَ وَٱلْقَمَرَ حُسْبَانًا ۚ ذَٰلِكَ تَقْدِيرُ
ٱلْعَزِيزِ ٱلْعَلِيمِ ﴿٩٦﴾ وَهُوَ ٱلَّذِى جَعَلَ لَكُمُ ٱلنُّجُومَ لِتَهْتَدُوا۟
بِهَا فِى ظُلُمَـٰتِ ٱلْبَرِّ وَٱلْبَحْرِ ۗ قَدْ فَصَّلْنَا ٱلْـَٔايَـٰتِ لِقَوْمٍ يَعْلَمُونَ

Prophet, may Allah bless him and grant him peace. ***You***, Jews, ***were taught things*** in the Qur'an ***you did not know*** of in the Torah, ***neither you nor your forefathers*** – making clear that which was unclear for you and about which you disagreed. ***Say: "Allah!"*** This was revealed when they did not say it and there is no other answer. ***Then leave them engrossed in playing their*** false ***games.***

92. ***This*** (Qur'an) ***is a Book We have sent down and blessed, confirming what*** (Divine Books) ***came before it, so that you can warn*** (read as *tundhira* and also *yundhira*, in which case the meaning is "it (the Qur'an) can warn) ***the Mother of Cities*** (Makka) ***and the people*** (the rest of mankind) ***around it. Those who believe in the Next World believe in it and safeguard their prayers*** out of fear of the punishment there.

93. ***Who*** (no one) ***could do greater wrong than someone who invents lies against Allah*** by laying claim to Prophethood when he is not a Prophet – ***or who says, "It has been revealed to me," when nothing has been revealed to him*** – and this was revealed about Musaylima; ***or someone who says, "I will send down the same as Allah has sent down"?*** They are the mockers. They said, "If we had wished, we could have said the like of this." ***If you***, Muḥammad, ***could only see the*** (these) ***wrongdoers in the throes of death when the angels are stretching out their hands*** to them with blows and punishment and saying harshly to them: ***"Disgorge your own selves*** – to us so that we can seize them! ***Today you will be repaid with the punishment of humiliation for saying other than the truth about Allah*** by their false claim of Prophethood and Revelation, ***and being arrogant about His Signs*** by being too proud to believe," then you would indeed have seen a terrible sight.

94. When they are resurrected, they will be told, ***"You have come to us all alone*** – without property, family or children – ***just as We created you at first*** – naked, barefoot and uncircumcised – ***leaving behind you everything We bestowed on you*** – in this world without your choice. It will be said to them in rebuke: ***We do not see your intercessors*** (idols) ***accompanying you, those you claimed were partners for you with Allah*** – and entitled to your worship. ***The link between you*** (read as *baynakum* and *baynukum*) ***is severed*** – there is no longer a connection between them. ***Those you made such claims***

﴿٩٧﴾ وَهُوَ ٱلَّذِىٓ أَنشَأَكُم مِّن نَّفْسٍ وَٰحِدَةٍ فَمُسْتَقَرٌّ وَمُسْتَوْدَعٌ ۗ
قَدْ فَصَّلْنَا ٱلْـَٔايَٰتِ لِقَوْمٍ يَفْقَهُونَ ﴿٩٨﴾ وَهُوَ ٱلَّذِىٓ أَنزَلَ
مِنَ ٱلسَّمَآءِ مَآءً فَأَخْرَجْنَا بِهِۦ نَبَاتَ كُلِّ شَىْءٍ فَأَخْرَجْنَا مِنْهُ
خَضِرًا نُّخْرِجُ مِنْهُ حَبًّا مُّتَرَاكِبًا وَمِنَ ٱلنَّخْلِ مِن طَلْعِهَا
قِنْوَانٌ دَانِيَةٌ وَجَنَّٰتٍ مِّنْ أَعْنَابٍ وَٱلزَّيْتُونَ وَٱلرُّمَّانَ مُشْتَبِهًا
وَغَيْرَ مُتَشَٰبِهٍ ۗ ٱنظُرُوٓا۟ إِلَىٰ ثَمَرِهِۦٓ إِذَآ أَثْمَرَ وَيَنْعِهِۦٓ ۚ إِنَّ فِى ذَٰلِكُمْ
لَـَٔايَٰتٍ لِّقَوْمٍ يُؤْمِنُونَ ﴿٩٩﴾ وَجَعَلُوا۟ لِلَّهِ شُرَكَآءَ ٱلْجِنَّ وَخَلَقَهُمْ ۖ
وَخَرَقُوا۟ لَهُۥ بَنِينَ وَبَنَٰتٍۭ بِغَيْرِ عِلْمٍ ۚ سُبْحَٰنَهُۥ وَتَعَٰلَىٰ عَمَّا
يَصِفُونَ ﴿١٠٠﴾ بَدِيعُ ٱلسَّمَٰوَٰتِ وَٱلْأَرْضِ ۖ أَنَّىٰ يَكُونُ لَهُۥ وَلَدٌ
وَلَمْ تَكُن لَّهُۥ صَٰحِبَةٌ ۖ وَخَلَقَ كُلَّ شَىْءٍ ۖ وَهُوَ بِكُلِّ شَىْءٍ عَلِيمٌ ﴿١٠١﴾
ذَٰلِكُمُ ٱللَّهُ رَبُّكُمْ ۖ لَآ إِلَٰهَ إِلَّا هُوَ ۖ خَٰلِقُ كُلِّ شَىْءٍ
فَٱعْبُدُوهُ ۚ وَهُوَ عَلَىٰ كُلِّ شَىْءٍ وَكِيلٌ ﴿١٠٢﴾ لَّا تُدْرِكُهُ
ٱلْأَبْصَٰرُ وَهُوَ يُدْرِكُ ٱلْأَبْصَٰرَ ۖ وَهُوَ ٱللَّطِيفُ ٱلْخَبِيرُ ﴿١٠٣﴾
قَدْ جَآءَكُم بَصَآئِرُ مِن رَّبِّكُمْ ۖ فَمَنْ أَبْصَرَ فَلِنَفْسِهِۦ ۖ وَمَنْ عَمِىَ
فَعَلَيْهَا ۚ وَمَآ أَنَا۠ عَلَيْكُم بِحَفِيظٍ ﴿١٠٤﴾ وَكَذَٰلِكَ نُصَرِّفُ
ٱلْـَٔايَٰتِ وَلِيَقُولُوا۟ دَرَسْتَ وَلِنُبَيِّنَهُۥ لِقَوْمٍ يَعْلَمُونَ ﴿١٠٥﴾
ٱتَّبِعْ مَآ أُوحِىَ إِلَيْكَ مِن رَّبِّكَ ۖ لَآ إِلَٰهَ إِلَّا هُوَ ۖ وَأَعْرِضْ عَنِ
ٱلْمُشْرِكِينَ ﴿١٠٦﴾ وَلَوْ شَآءَ ٱللَّهُ مَآ أَشْرَكُوا۟ ۗ وَمَا جَعَلْنَٰكَ عَلَيْهِمْ
حَفِيظًا ۖ وَمَآ أَنتَ عَلَيْهِم بِوَكِيلٍ ﴿١٠٧﴾ وَلَا تَسُبُّوا۟ ٱلَّذِينَ
يَدْعُونَ مِن دُونِ ٱللَّهِ فَيَسُبُّوا۟ ٱللَّهَ عَدْوًۢا بِغَيْرِ عِلْمٍ ۗ كَذَٰلِكَ زَيَّنَّا

for in this world, when you claimed that they would intercede for you, ***have forsaken you."***

95. ***Allah is the Splitter of the seed*** (of plants) ***and kernel*** (of palms)**.** ***He brings forth the living from the dead*** – like living mammals and birds from dead sperm and eggs – ***and produces the dead out of the living*** – like sperm and eggs from live animals. ***That*** Splitter and Producer ***is Allah, so how are you perverted?*** How can you turn aside from Islam when the proof is established?

96. ***He is the Splitter of the sky at dawn,*** making the light of dawn appear out of the darkness of night, ***the Appointer of the night as a time of stillness,*** a time when creation rests from toil, ***and of the sun and moon as a means of reckoning*** time, as evidenced in *Sūrat ar-Raḥmān "The sun and moon both run with precision..."* (55:5)**.** ***That*** which is mentioned ***is what the Almighty*** in His kingdom***, the All-Knowing*** of His creation ***has ordained.***

97. ***It is He who has appointed the stars for you so you might be guided by them*** on your journeys ***in the darkness of the land and sea. We have made the Signs*** which indicate Our power clear and ***plain for people who know*** and reflect.

98. ***It is He who first*** created and ***produced you from a single self*** (Ādam) ***then in a resting-place*** (read as *mustaqarr* and *mustaqirr*) in the womb ***and a repository*** in the loins. ***We have made the Signs plain for people who understand*** what is said to them.

99. ***It is He who sends down water from the sky from which We*** (a change from third person singular to the first person plural) ***bring forth growth of every kind, and from that*** (the plants) ***We bring forth green shoots and from them*** (the shoots) ***We bring forth close-packed seeds*** piled on top of one another, as in ears of wheat and similar plants, ***and from the spathes*** (the new growth) ***of the date palm, date clusters hanging down*** near to one another ***and*** from water We produce ***gardens of grapes and olives and pomegranates, both similar*** in terms of leaves ***and dissimilar*** in terms of fruits. ***Look***, you who are addressed, ***at their fruits*** (read as *thamar* and *thumur*) ***as they bear fruit and ripen***, and reflect. ***There are Signs in that*** – of the power of Allah to regenerate, and other things – ***for people who believe.*** Believers are singled out for mention because they are the ones who benefit by these signs in faith as opposed to the unbelievers, who do not.

100. ***Yet they make the jinn co-partners with Allah,*** since they obey them by worshipping idols, ***when He created them*** – so how can they be His partners? ***And they attribute*** (read as *kharaqū* and *kharraqū*) ***sons and daughters to Him without any knowledge*** when they say that 'Uzayr and 'Īsā are the sons and that the angels are the daughters of Allah. ***Glory be to Him! He is far beyond what they describe*** Him – as having a child!

101. ***He is the Originator of the heavens and the earth*** without having any prior example. ***How could He have a son when He has no wife? He created everything and He has knowledge of everything.***

102. ***That is Allah, your Lord. There is no god but Him, the Creator of everything. So worship Him*** and affirm His Unity. ***He is Responsible for everything*** – the Protector of everything.

103. ***Eyesight cannot perceive Him*** – eyes are unable to see Allah, and the vision of Him is confined to the believers in the Next World. The *ḥadīth* about this in the two *Ṣaḥīḥ* Collections says: "You will see your Lord as you see the moon on the night of the full moon." It is said that what is meant is that they cannot encompass Him – ***but He perceives eyesight.*** He sees them and they do not see Him. It is not permitted for other than Him to perceive sight or to perceive Him, or for Him to be perceived by knowledge either. ***He is the All-Penetrating*** – kind to His friends – ***the All-Aware*** of them.

104. Say to them, Muḥammad,: ***"Clear insights*** (proofs) ***have come to you from your Lord. Whoever sees*** them ***clearly*** and believes, ***does so to his own benefit*** when he sees, because he will have the reward of his seeing. ***Whoever is blind*** to them and so misguided, ***it*** (the evil effect of his misguidance) ***is to his own detriment. I am not here as your keeper.*** I do not watch over your actions. I am a warner."

105. ***That*** – the clarification which was mentioned – ***is how We vary the Signs*** and make them clear so that they can reflect, ***so that they*** (the unbelievers) ***say*** at the end of the affair, ***"You have been studying*** (read as *darasta* which implies discussing this with the People of the Book, or *dārasta* which implies consulting past Books and

لِكُلِّ أُمَّةٍ عَمَلَهُمْ ثُمَّ إِلَىٰ رَبِّهِم مَّرْجِعُهُمْ فَيُنَبِّئُهُم بِمَا كَانُوا۟
يَعْمَلُونَ ﴿١٠٨﴾ وَأَقْسَمُوا۟ بِٱللَّهِ جَهْدَ أَيْمَٰنِهِمْ لَئِن جَآءَتْهُمْ ءَايَةٌ
لَّيُؤْمِنُنَّ بِهَا ۚ قُلْ إِنَّمَا ٱلْءَايَٰتُ عِندَ ٱللَّهِ ۖ وَمَا يُشْعِرُكُمْ أَنَّهَآ إِذَا
جَآءَتْ لَا يُؤْمِنُونَ ﴿١٠٩﴾ وَنُقَلِّبُ أَفْـِٔدَتَهُمْ وَأَبْصَٰرَهُمْ كَمَا لَمْ
يُؤْمِنُوا۟ بِهِۦٓ أَوَّلَ مَرَّةٍ وَنَذَرُهُمْ فِى طُغْيَٰنِهِمْ يَعْمَهُونَ ﴿١١٠﴾
۞ وَلَوْ أَنَّنَا نَزَّلْنَآ إِلَيْهِمُ ٱلْمَلَٰٓئِكَةَ وَكَلَّمَهُمُ ٱلْمَوْتَىٰ وَحَشَرْنَا
عَلَيْهِمْ كُلَّ شَىْءٍ قُبُلًا مَّا كَانُوا۟ لِيُؤْمِنُوٓا۟ إِلَّآ أَن يَشَآءَ ٱللَّهُ وَلَٰكِنَّ
أَكْثَرَهُمْ يَجْهَلُونَ ﴿١١١﴾ وَكَذَٰلِكَ جَعَلْنَا لِكُلِّ نَبِىٍّ عَدُوًّا
شَيَٰطِينَ ٱلْإِنسِ وَٱلْجِنِّ يُوحِى بَعْضُهُمْ إِلَىٰ بَعْضٍ زُخْرُفَ
ٱلْقَوْلِ غُرُورًا ۚ وَلَوْ شَآءَ رَبُّكَ مَا فَعَلُوهُ ۖ فَذَرْهُمْ وَمَا يَفْتَرُونَ
﴿١١٢﴾ وَلِتَصْغَىٰٓ إِلَيْهِ أَفْـِٔدَةُ ٱلَّذِينَ لَا يُؤْمِنُونَ بِٱلْءَاخِرَةِ
وَلِيَرْضَوْهُ وَلِيَقْتَرِفُوا۟ مَا هُم مُّقْتَرِفُونَ ﴿١١٣﴾ أَفَغَيْرَ ٱللَّهِ
أَبْتَغِى حَكَمًا وَهُوَ ٱلَّذِىٓ أَنزَلَ إِلَيْكُمُ ٱلْكِتَٰبَ مُفَصَّلًا ۚ
وَٱلَّذِينَ ءَاتَيْنَٰهُمُ ٱلْكِتَٰبَ يَعْلَمُونَ أَنَّهُۥ مُنَزَّلٌ مِّن رَّبِّكَ بِٱلْحَقِّ ۖ
فَلَا تَكُونَنَّ مِنَ ٱلْمُمْتَرِينَ ﴿١١٤﴾ وَتَمَّتْ كَلِمَتُ رَبِّكَ صِدْقًا
وَعَدْلًا ۚ لَّا مُبَدِّلَ لِكَلِمَٰتِهِۦ ۚ وَهُوَ ٱلسَّمِيعُ ٱلْعَلِيمُ ﴿١١٥﴾ وَإِن
تُطِعْ أَكْثَرَ مَن فِى ٱلْأَرْضِ يُضِلُّوكَ عَن سَبِيلِ ٱللَّهِ ۚ إِن
يَتَّبِعُونَ إِلَّا ٱلظَّنَّ وَإِنْ هُمْ إِلَّا يَخْرُصُونَ ﴿١١٦﴾ إِنَّ رَبَّكَ هُوَ
أَعْلَمُ مَن يَضِلُّ عَن سَبِيلِهِۦ ۖ وَهُوَ أَعْلَمُ بِٱلْمُهْتَدِينَ ﴿١١٧﴾
فَكُلُوا۟ مِمَّا ذُكِرَ ٱسْمُ ٱللَّهِ عَلَيْهِ إِن كُنتُم بِـَٔايَٰتِهِۦ مُؤْمِنِينَ ﴿١١٨﴾

extracting this from them)," ***and so We can make it clear to people who know.***

106. ***Follow what has been revealed to you from your Lord*** (the Qur'ān) ***– there is no god but Him – and turn away from the idolaters.***

107. ***If Allah had willed, they would not have attributed partners to Him. We did not appoint you over them as their keeper*** to watch over them and repay them for their actions, ***and you are not set over them as their guardian*** so as to compel them to believe. This was revealed before the command to fight.

108. ***Do not curse those they call upon besides Allah*** (their idols) ***in case that makes them curse Allah in animosity*** (through transgression and injustice) ***without knowledge*** (out of ignorance of Allah). ***Thus*** – by making what those people were doing seem good to them – ***do We make the actions of every nation,*** both good and evil, ***appear to be good to them*** and so they do them. ***Then they will return to their Lord*** in the Next World ***and He will inform them about what they did*** and will repay them.

109. ***They*** (the unbelievers of Makka) ***have sworn by Allah with their most earnest oaths that if a Sign*** which they have asked for ***comes to them they will believe in it. Say*** to them: ***"The Signs are in Allah's hands alone.*** He sends them down as He wishes. I am merely a warner." ***What will make you realise*** – even though you will not – ***that even when a Sign does come, they still will not believe*** (read as *yu'minūna* and also *tu'minūna*, "you will not believe" addressed to the unbelievers) – since that is part of My prior knowledge?

110. ***We will overturn their hearts***, preventing them from perceiving the truth so that they do not understand it, – ***and sight*** – so that they do not see it and do not believe – ***just as when they did not believe in it at first*** – referring to the Signs which were sent down – ***and We will abandon them*** and leave them ***to wander blindly in their overweening insolence***; bewildered in confusion and misguidance.

111. ***Even if We sent down angels to them, and the dead spoke to them*** in the way they were asking for ***and We gathered together everything in front of them right before their eyes*** (read as *qubulan* meaning "wave after wave" and *qibalan* meaning directly visible in front of them) to make them testify to your truthfulness, ***they still would not believe*** – because their unbelief is preordained in the knowledge of Allah – ***unless Allah willed*** that they believe, in which case they would believe. ***The truth is that most of them are ignorant*** of that.

112. ***Thus*** – in the same way that We have made these people your enemies – ***We have appointed as enemies to every Prophet*** **shayṭāns** ***from both mankind and from the jinn, who*** whisper and ***inspire each other with delusion by means of specious words*** in order to beguile them. ***If your Lord had willed, they would not have done it*** (the whispering), ***so abandon them*** (the unbelievers) ***and all they fabricate*** in terms of unbelief and other things which are made to seem attractive to them. This was before the command to fight.

113. ***...so that the hearts of those who do not believe in the Next World incline towards them*** in delusion ***and are pleased with them and perpetrate whatever*** wrong actions ***they perpetrate*** for which they will be punished.

114. The following was revealed when the non-Muslims asked the Prophet, may Allah bless him and grant him peace, to give a judgement between him and them. Say: ***"Am I to desire*** and look for ***other than Allah as a judge*** between me and you ***when it is He who has sent down the Book*** (the Qur'ān) ***to you making everything plain***, distinguishing the true from the false?" ***Those We have given the Book*** (the Torah) – such as 'Abdullāh ibn Salām and his companions – ***know it has been sent down*** (read as *munazzil* and *munzil*) ***from your Lord with truth, so on no account be among the doubters***, those who doubt the Book. The purpose of this is to affirm to those who deny it that the Qur'an is true.

115. ***The Words of your Lord are perfect*** in His judgements and admonitions ***in truthfulness and justice. No one can change His Words*** by making them different or decreasing them. ***He is the All-Hearing*** of what is said, ***the All-Knowing*** of what is done.

116. ***If you obeyed most of those on earth*** (the unbelievers) ***they would misguide you from Allah's Way*** (His *dīn*). ***They follow nothing but conjecture*** when they argue with you about carrion and say

وَمَا لَكُمْ أَلَّا تَأْكُلُوا۟ مِمَّا ذُكِرَ ٱسْمُ ٱللَّهِ عَلَيْهِ وَقَدْ فَصَّلَ
لَكُم مَّا حَرَّمَ عَلَيْكُمْ إِلَّا مَا ٱضْطُرِرْتُمْ إِلَيْهِ ۗ وَإِنَّ كَثِيرًا لَّيُضِلُّونَ
بِأَهْوَآئِهِم بِغَيْرِ عِلْمٍ ۗ إِنَّ رَبَّكَ هُوَ أَعْلَمُ بِٱلْمُعْتَدِينَ ١١٩
وَذَرُوا۟ ظَـٰهِرَ ٱلْإِثْمِ وَبَاطِنَهُۥٓ ۚ إِنَّ ٱلَّذِينَ يَكْسِبُونَ ٱلْإِثْمَ
سَيُجْزَوْنَ بِمَا كَانُوا۟ يَقْتَرِفُونَ ١٢٠ وَلَا تَأْكُلُوا۟ مِمَّا لَمْ يُذْكَرِ
ٱسْمُ ٱللَّهِ عَلَيْهِ وَإِنَّهُۥ لَفِسْقٌ ۗ وَإِنَّ ٱلشَّيَـٰطِينَ لَيُوحُونَ إِلَىٰٓ
أَوْلِيَآئِهِمْ لِيُجَـٰدِلُوكُمْ ۖ وَإِنْ أَطَعْتُمُوهُمْ إِنَّكُمْ لَمُشْرِكُونَ ١٢١
أَوَمَن كَانَ مَيْتًا فَأَحْيَيْنَـٰهُ وَجَعَلْنَا لَهُۥ نُورًا يَمْشِى بِهِۦ فِى
ٱلنَّاسِ كَمَن مَّثَلُهُۥ فِى ٱلظُّلُمَـٰتِ لَيْسَ بِخَارِجٍ مِّنْهَا ۚ كَذَٰلِكَ
زُيِّنَ لِلْكَـٰفِرِينَ مَا كَانُوا۟ يَعْمَلُونَ ١٢٢ وَكَذَٰلِكَ جَعَلْنَا
فِى كُلِّ قَرْيَةٍ أَكَـٰبِرَ مُجْرِمِيهَا لِيَمْكُرُوا۟ فِيهَا ۖ وَمَا
يَمْكُرُونَ إِلَّا بِأَنفُسِهِمْ وَمَا يَشْعُرُونَ ١٢٣ وَإِذَا جَآءَتْهُمْ
ءَايَةٌ قَالُوا۟ لَن نُّؤْمِنَ حَتَّىٰ نُؤْتَىٰ مِثْلَ مَآ أُوتِىَ رُسُلُ ٱللَّهِ ۘ ٱللَّهُ
أَعْلَمُ حَيْثُ يَجْعَلُ رِسَالَتَهُۥ ۗ سَيُصِيبُ ٱلَّذِينَ أَجْرَمُوا۟
صَغَارٌ عِندَ ٱللَّهِ وَعَذَابٌ شَدِيدٌۢ بِمَا كَانُوا۟ يَمْكُرُونَ ١٢٤
فَمَن يُرِدِ ٱللَّهُ أَن يَهْدِيَهُۥ يَشْرَحْ صَدْرَهُۥ لِلْإِسْلَـٰمِ ۖ وَمَن يُرِدْ
أَن يُضِلَّهُۥ يَجْعَلْ صَدْرَهُۥ ضَيِّقًا حَرَجًا كَأَنَّمَا يَصَّعَّدُ
فِى ٱلسَّمَآءِ ۚ كَذَٰلِكَ يَجْعَلُ ٱللَّهُ ٱلرِّجْسَ عَلَى ٱلَّذِينَ
لَا يُؤْمِنُونَ ١٢٥ وَهَـٰذَا صِرَٰطُ رَبِّكَ مُسْتَقِيمًا ۗ قَدْ فَصَّلْنَا
ٱلْـَٔايَـٰتِ لِقَوْمٍ يَذَّكَّرُونَ ١٢٦ ۞ لَهُمْ دَارُ ٱلسَّلَـٰمِ عِندَ رَبِّهِمْ ۖ

that what Allah has killed has as much right to be eaten as what you kill. ***They are only guessing*** – and that is tantamount to denial.

117. ***Your Lord: He knows best who is misguided from His Way and He knows best the guided*** and will repay each of them.

118. ***Eat that over which the name of Allah has been mentioned*** – and slaughter it in His Name – ***if you believe in His Signs.***

119. ***What is the matter with you that you do not eat*** properly slaughtered animals, ***that over which the name of Allah has been mentioned, when He has made plain to you what He has forbidden you*** in the *āyat* which prohibits carrion in *Sūrat al-Mā'ida* (5:3) – ***except when you are forced to eat it?*** In that case it is lawful for you. There is nothing to prevent you from eating what has been mentioned. What it is unlawful to eat has been made clear to you. ***Many people misguide*** (read as *yuḍillūna* and *yaḍillūna*) ***others by their whims and desires*** – which their selves have prompted in making carrion and other things lawful – ***without any knowledge*** on which they can rely. ***Your Lord knows best those who overstep the limits***: who go beyond the unlawful to the lawful.

120. ***Abandon wrong action, outward and inward*** (public and secret). ***Those who commit wrong action*** – said to refer here to fornication and is also said to mean any act of disobedience – ***will be repaid*** in the Next World ***for what they perpetrated*** and earned.

121. ***Do not eat anything over which the name of Allah has not been mentioned*** – if it has died by itself or is killed in the name of something other than Allah. However, if a Muslim slaughters an animal and fails to say the name of Allah either deliberately or through forgetfulness, it is lawful. Ibn 'Abbās said that and ash-Shāfi'ī takes the same position. ***To do so*** – to eat from it – ***is sheer degeneracy*** (*fisq*), which here means stepping outside the bounds of the lawful. ***The* shayṭān*s*** whisper and ***inspire their friends*** (the unbelievers) ***to dispute with you*** about making carrion lawful. ***If you obeyed them*** regarding it, ***you would be idolaters.***

122. The following was revealed about Abū Jahl and others. ***Is someone who was dead*** through unbelief ***and whom We brought to life*** through guidance, ***supplying him with a light by which to walk among people*** – enabling him to distinguish the Truth from other than it, thus making him a believer – ***the same as someone who is in utter darkness*** (an unbeliever) ***unable to emerge from it? That*** – in the same way that He has made belief attractive to the believers – ***is how what they were doing***, the unbelief and acts of disobedience, ***is made to appear good to the unbelievers.***

123. ***And likewise*** – by making the great men in Makka wrongdoers – ***in every city We set up its greatest wrongdoers to plot in it. They plot against themselves alone*** by barring others from belief, because its effect comes back on them; ***but they are not aware of it.***

124. ***When a Sign*** indicating the truthfulness of the Prophet, may Allah bless him and grant him peace, ***comes to them*** (the people of Makka) ***they say, "We will not believe*** in him ***until we have been given the same as the Messengers of Allah were given*** – in terms of Message and Revelation, because we are wealthier and older than him." Allah says: ***Allah knows best where to place His Message*** (read in the singular and plural), meaning that Allah knows the proper place to put it and does so and those people are not worthy of it. ***Debasement in the sight of Allah and a severe punishment will strike those who did wrong for the plots that they devised.***

125. ***When Allah desires to guide someone, He expands his breast to Islam*** by putting light into his heart and making it expand for him so that he accepts Islam, as we find in *ḥadīth*. ***When He desires to misguide someone, He makes his breast narrow*** (read as *ḍayyiqan* and *ḍayqan*) so that he does not accept it ***and constricted*** (read as *ḥaraj* and *ḥarij*) ***as if he were climbing*** (read as *yaṣṣa''adu* and *yaṣṣā'adu*) ***up into the sky.*** When someone like that is obliged to believe, it is very difficult for him. ***That is how Allah casts defilement on those who do not believe.*** "Defilement" (*rijs*) means punishment or Shayṭān, meaning that he has control of such people.

126. ***This*** – the path which you are on, Muḥammad – ***is the path of your Lord – straight***, without any deviation. ***We have made the Signs plain for people who remember***: those who are warned and profit from the warning.

127. ***They will have the Abode of Peace*** (the Garden) ***with their Lord. He is their Protector because of what they have done.***

وَهُوَ وَلِيُّهُم بِمَا كَانُواْ يَعۡمَلُونَ ١٢٧ وَيَوۡمَ يَحۡشُرُهُمۡ جَمِيعٗا
يَٰمَعۡشَرَ ٱلۡجِنِّ قَدِ ٱسۡتَكۡثَرۡتُم مِّنَ ٱلۡإِنسِۖ وَقَالَ أَوۡلِيَآؤُهُم
مِّنَ ٱلۡإِنسِ رَبَّنَا ٱسۡتَمۡتَعَ بَعۡضُنَا بِبَعۡضٖ وَبَلَغۡنَآ أَجَلَنَا ٱلَّذِيٓ
أَجَّلۡتَ لَنَاۚ قَالَ ٱلنَّارُ مَثۡوَىٰكُمۡ خَٰلِدِينَ فِيهَآ إِلَّا مَا شَآءَ ٱللَّهُۗ إِنَّ
رَبَّكَ حَكِيمٌ عَلِيمٞ ١٢٨ وَكَذَٰلِكَ نُوَلِّي بَعۡضَ ٱلظَّٰلِمِينَ بَعۡضَۢا
بِمَا كَانُواْ يَكۡسِبُونَ ١٢٩ يَٰمَعۡشَرَ ٱلۡجِنِّ وَٱلۡإِنسِ أَلَمۡ يَأۡتِكُمۡ
رُسُلٞ مِّنكُمۡ يَقُصُّونَ عَلَيۡكُمۡ ءَايَٰتِي وَيُنذِرُونَكُمۡ لِقَآءَ
يَوۡمِكُمۡ هَٰذَاۚ قَالُواْ شَهِدۡنَا عَلَىٰٓ أَنفُسِنَاۖ وَغَرَّتۡهُمُ ٱلۡحَيَوٰةُ ٱلدُّنۡيَا
وَشَهِدُواْ عَلَىٰٓ أَنفُسِهِمۡ أَنَّهُمۡ كَانُواْ كَٰفِرِينَ ١٣٠ ذَٰلِكَ
أَن لَّمۡ يَكُن رَّبُّكَ مُهۡلِكَ ٱلۡقُرَىٰ بِظُلۡمٖ وَأَهۡلُهَا غَٰفِلُونَ ١٣١
وَلِكُلّٖ دَرَجَٰتٞ مِّمَّا عَمِلُواْۚ وَمَا رَبُّكَ بِغَٰفِلٍ عَمَّا
يَعۡمَلُونَ ١٣٢ وَرَبُّكَ ٱلۡغَنِيُّ ذُو ٱلرَّحۡمَةِۚ إِن يَشَأۡ
يُذۡهِبۡكُمۡ وَيَسۡتَخۡلِفۡ مِنۢ بَعۡدِكُم مَّا يَشَآءُ كَمَآ
أَنشَأَكُم مِّن ذُرِّيَّةِ قَوۡمٍ ءَاخَرِينَ ١٣٣ إِنَّ مَا
تُوعَدُونَ لَأٓتٖۖ وَمَآ أَنتُم بِمُعۡجِزِينَ ١٣٤ قُلۡ يَٰقَوۡمِ
ٱعۡمَلُواْ عَلَىٰ مَكَانَتِكُمۡ إِنِّي عَامِلٞۖ فَسَوۡفَ تَعۡلَمُونَ
مَن تَكُونُ لَهُۥ عَٰقِبَةُ ٱلدَّارِۚ إِنَّهُۥ لَا يُفۡلِحُ ٱلظَّٰلِمُونَ
١٣٥ وَجَعَلُواْ لِلَّهِ مِمَّا ذَرَأَ مِنَ ٱلۡحَرۡثِ وَٱلۡأَنۡعَٰمِ
نَصِيبٗا فَقَالُواْ هَٰذَا لِلَّهِ بِزَعۡمِهِمۡ وَهَٰذَا لِشُرَكَآئِنَاۖ
فَمَا كَانَ لِشُرَكَآئِهِمۡ فَلَا يَصِلُ إِلَى ٱللَّهِۖ
وَمَا كَانَ لِلَّهِ فَهُوَ يَصِلُ إِلَىٰ شُرَكَآئِهِمۡۗ

128. ***On the Day*** – implying "Remember the Day" – ***He gathers*** (read as *yaḥshuru* and *naḥshuru*, "We gather") ***them*** (creation) ***all together*** and it will be said to them***: "O company of jinn! You gained many followers among mankind*** by misleading them." ***And their friends among mankind*** who obeyed them ***will say, "Our Lord, we took benefit from each other*** – human beings benefit from the jinn when they make the fulfilment of their appetites seem good to them and the jinn benefit by people obeying them – ***and now we have reached the term*** (the Day of Rising) ***which You determined for us."*** This is an expression of regret by them. ***He*** (Allah) ***will say*** to them on the tongue of the angels, ***"The Fire is your home. You will be in it timelessly, forever, except as Allah wills"*** – except for the times when they emerge from it to drink boiling water which is outside of it, as He says, *"Then their destination will be the Blazing Fire."* (37:68) Ibn 'Abbās said that the exception is for those whom Allah knows to have some belief in their hearts. ***Your Lord is All-Wise*** in what He does, ***All-Knowing*** of His creation."

129. ***In that way*** – by making rebellious men and jinn support one another – ***We make the wrongdoers friends of one another because of what*** (the acts of disobedience) ***they have done.***

130. ***"O company of jinn and men! Did not Messengers come to you from among you*** from among the whole of mankind, meaning that some of you believed other human beings or messengers of the jinn who have listened to the words of the Messengers and conveyed them to their people, ***relating My Signs to you and warning you of the encounter of this Day of yours?" They will say, "We testify against ourselves*** that it was conveyed to us." ***The life of this world deluded them*** so that they did not believe ***and they testify against themselves that they were unbelievers.***

131. ***That*** sending of Messengers ***was because their Lord would never have destroyed the cities unjustly while their people were unwarned.*** Did He not send a Messenger to them to make things clear to them?

132. ***All*** who act ***have ranks*** of repayment ***according to what*** (the good and evil) ***they did. Your Lord is not heedless of anything they do*** (read as *ya'malūna* and also *ta'malūna*, "you do").

سَآءَ مَا يَحۡكُمُونَ ١٣٦ وَكَذَٰلِكَ زَيَّنَ
لِكَثِيرٖ مِّنَ ٱلۡمُشۡرِكِينَ قَتۡلَ أَوۡلَٰدِهِمۡ
شُرَكَآؤُهُمۡ لِيُرۡدُوهُمۡ وَلِيَلۡبِسُواْ عَلَيۡهِمۡ دِينَهُمۡۖ
وَلَوۡ شَآءَ ٱللَّهُ مَا فَعَلُوهُۖ فَذَرۡهُمۡ وَمَا يَفۡتَرُونَ ١٣٧
وَقَالُواْ هَٰذِهِۦٓ أَنۡعَٰمٞ وَحَرۡثٌ حِجۡرٞ لَّا يَطۡعَمُهَآ إِلَّا مَن
نَّشَآءُ بِزَعۡمِهِمۡ وَأَنۡعَٰمٌ حُرِّمَتۡ ظُهُورُهَا وَأَنۡعَٰمٞ لَّا يَذۡكُرُونَ
ٱسۡمَ ٱللَّهِ عَلَيۡهَا ٱفۡتِرَآءً عَلَيۡهِۚ سَيَجۡزِيهِم بِمَا كَانُواْ
يَفۡتَرُونَ ١٣٨ وَقَالُواْ مَا فِي بُطُونِ هَٰذِهِ ٱلۡأَنۡعَٰمِ
خَالِصَةٞ لِّذُكُورِنَا وَمُحَرَّمٌ عَلَىٰٓ أَزۡوَٰجِنَاۖ وَإِن يَكُن
مَّيۡتَةٗ فَهُمۡ فِيهِ شُرَكَآءُۚ سَيَجۡزِيهِمۡ وَصۡفَهُمۡۚ إِنَّهُۥ
حَكِيمٌ عَلِيمٞ ١٣٩ قَدۡ خَسِرَ ٱلَّذِينَ قَتَلُوٓاْ أَوۡلَٰدَهُمۡ
سَفَهَۢا بِغَيۡرِ عِلۡمٖ وَحَرَّمُواْ مَا رَزَقَهُمُ ٱللَّهُ ٱفۡتِرَآءً عَلَى ٱللَّهِۚ
قَدۡ ضَلُّواْ وَمَا كَانُواْ مُهۡتَدِينَ ١٤٠ ۞ وَهُوَ ٱلَّذِيٓ
أَنشَأَ جَنَّٰتٖ مَّعۡرُوشَٰتٖ وَغَيۡرَ مَعۡرُوشَٰتٖ وَٱلنَّخۡلَ وَٱلزَّرۡعَ
مُخۡتَلِفًا أُكُلُهُۥ وَٱلزَّيۡتُونَ وَٱلرُّمَّانَ مُتَشَٰبِهٗا وَغَيۡرَ
مُتَشَٰبِهٖۚ كُلُواْ مِن ثَمَرِهِۦٓ إِذَآ أَثۡمَرَ وَءَاتُواْ حَقَّهُۥ يَوۡمَ
حَصَادِهِۦۖ وَلَا تُسۡرِفُوٓاْۚ إِنَّهُۥ لَا يُحِبُّ ٱلۡمُسۡرِفِينَ ١٤١
وَمِنَ ٱلۡأَنۡعَٰمِ حَمُولَةٗ وَفَرۡشٗاۚ كُلُواْ مِمَّا رَزَقَكُمُ
ٱللَّهُ وَلَا تَتَّبِعُواْ خُطُوَٰتِ ٱلشَّيۡطَٰنِۚ إِنَّهُۥ لَكُمۡ عَدُوّٞ مُّبِينٞ ١٤٢
ثَمَٰنِيَةَ أَزۡوَٰجٖۖ مِّنَ ٱلضَّأۡنِ ٱثۡنَيۡنِ وَمِنَ ٱلۡمَعۡزِ ٱثۡنَيۡنِۗ
قُلۡ ءَآلذَّكَرَيۡنِ حَرَّمَ أَمِ ٱلۡأُنثَيَيۡنِ أَمَّا ٱشۡتَمَلَتۡ عَلَيۡهِ

133. ***Your Lord is the Rich beyond need*** of His creatures or their worship, ***the Possessor of mercy. If He willed, He could remove you,*** people of Makka, by destroying you ***and replace you with any - thing else*** (other creatures) ***He willed, just as He produced you from the descendants of another people*** whom He removed; but He lets you continue out of mercy to you.

134. ***What you are promised*** in terms of the Final Hour and the punishment ***will come about*** and must come about ***and you can do nothing to prevent it*** or escape Our punishment.

135. ***Say*** to them***: "My people! Do as you are doing, just as I am doing. You will certainly come to know who will have the best Home in the end*** – a praiseworthy outcome in the Next World: you or us. ***The wrongdoers*** (unbelievers) ***will certainly not be successful*** or happy."

136. ***They*** (the unbelievers of Makka) ***assign to Allah a share of the crops and livestock He has created*** – diverting other portions to their guests and the poor, and to their idols which they give to their keepers – ***saying, "This is for Allah," as they allege*** (read *za'm* and *zu'm*) ***"and this is for our idols."*** If any of the share of the idols fell to Allah they would take it away; but if any of Allah's share fell to the idols they would leave it with them, saying that Allah has no need of it, as Allah says. ***Their idols' share does not reach Allah whereas Allah's share reaches their idols! What an evil judgement they make*** in this*!*

137. ***In the same way*** as the other things were made to seem attractive, ***their associates*** of the jinn ***have made killing their children*** by burying their baby daughters alive ***appear good*** (read as *zayyana* and *zuyyina*, when the meaning would be, "Killing their children has been made to seem to good to many of them by their associates.") ***to many of the idolaters, in order to destroy them and confuse them in their* dīn. *If Allah had willed, they would not have done it; so abandon them and what they fabricate.***

138. ***They say, "These animals and crops are sacrosanct. No one may eat them except for those*** servants of the idols and others ***we will," – as they allege*** without any evidence ***– and animals on whose backs it is forbidden to ride*** – like the *sā'iba* and the *ḥāmī* –

and animals over which they do not mention Allah's name when they are slaughtered, mentioning instead the names of their idols and ascribing them falsely to Allah, ***inventing falsehood against Him. He will repay them for the inventions they have devised.***

139. ***They say, "What is in the wombs of these animals is*** lawful ***exclusively for our men and forbidden to our wives*** – referring to the *sā'iba* and *baḥira* (see 5:103)**.** ***But if it is stillborn*** (read as *maytatan* and *maytatun*) ***they are partners in it." He*** (Allah) ***will repay them for their false depiction*** in making things lawful and unlawful. ***He is All-Wise*** in what He does, ***All-Knowing*** of His creation.

140. ***Those who kill*** (read as *qatalū* and *qattalū*) ***their children foolishly without knowledge*** – out of ignorance, by burying their daughters alive – ***and make what Allah has provided for them unlawful, inventing lies against Allah, such people are lost. They are misguided. They are not guided.***

141. ***It is He who*** creates and ***produces gardens, both cultivated*** – crops which spread out on the surface of the earth like melons – ***and wild*** – plants which rise on trunks like palm-trees – ***and palm-trees and crops of diverse kinds*** – fruits and seeds of different shapes and tastes – ***and olives and pomegranates, both similar*** in respect of leaves ***and dissimilar*** in respect of taste. ***Eat of their fruits when they bear fruit*** before they are over-ripe, ***and pay their due*** (their *zakāt*) ***on the day of their harvest*** (read as *ḥaṣādihi* or *ḥiṣādihi*) – a tenth or a twentieth according to the type of irrigation used – ***and do not be profligate*** by giving your whole harvest away so that nothing is left for your family. ***He does not love the profligate*** who exceed the limits He has laid down for them.

142. ***And also animals for riding and for haulage*** – those suited to bearing things, such as large camels – ***and animals for slaughtering and for wool*** – those not fit for haulage, such as small camels and sheep; these are called *farsh* because their bodies are fine and close to the *farsh*, the ground. ***Eat what Allah has provided for you and do not follow in the footsteps of Shayṭān*** – his way of making certain things lawful and unlawful. ***He is your clear-cut enemy***: his hostility towards you is evident.

أَرۡحَامُ ٱلۡأُنثَيَيۡنِۖ نَبِّـُٔونِي بِعِلۡمٍ إِن كُنتُمۡ صَٰدِقِينَ ١٤٣
وَمِنَ ٱلۡإِبِلِ ٱثۡنَيۡنِ وَمِنَ ٱلۡبَقَرِ ٱثۡنَيۡنِۗ قُلۡ ءَآلذَّكَرَيۡنِ
حَرَّمَ أَمِ ٱلۡأُنثَيَيۡنِ أَمَّا ٱشۡتَمَلَتۡ عَلَيۡهِ أَرۡحَامُ ٱلۡأُنثَيَيۡنِۖ
أَمۡ كُنتُمۡ شُهَدَآءَ إِذۡ وَصَّىٰكُمُ ٱللَّهُ بِهَٰذَاۚ فَمَنۡ
أَظۡلَمُ مِمَّنِ ٱفۡتَرَىٰ عَلَى ٱللَّهِ كَذِبٗا لِّيُضِلَّ ٱلنَّاسَ بِغَيۡرِ
عِلۡمٍۗ إِنَّ ٱللَّهَ لَا يَهۡدِي ٱلۡقَوۡمَ ٱلظَّٰلِمِينَ ١٤٤ قُل لَّآ أَجِدُ
فِي مَآ أُوحِيَ إِلَيَّ مُحَرَّمًا عَلَىٰ طَاعِمٖ يَطۡعَمُهُۥٓ إِلَّآ أَن يَكُونَ
مَيۡتَةً أَوۡ دَمٗا مَّسۡفُوحًا أَوۡ لَحۡمَ خِنزِيرٖ فَإِنَّهُۥ رِجۡسٌ أَوۡ
فِسۡقًا أُهِلَّ لِغَيۡرِ ٱللَّهِ بِهِۦۚ فَمَنِ ٱضۡطُرَّ غَيۡرَ بَاغٖ وَلَا عَادٖ فَإِنَّ
رَبَّكَ غَفُورٞ رَّحِيمٞ ١٤٥ وَعَلَى ٱلَّذِينَ هَادُواْ حَرَّمۡنَا
كُلَّ ذِي ظُفُرٖۖ وَمِنَ ٱلۡبَقَرِ وَٱلۡغَنَمِ حَرَّمۡنَا عَلَيۡهِمۡ
شُحُومَهُمَآ إِلَّا مَا حَمَلَتۡ ظُهُورُهُمَآ أَوِ ٱلۡحَوَايَآ أَوۡ مَا
ٱخۡتَلَطَ بِعَظۡمٖۚ ذَٰلِكَ جَزَيۡنَٰهُم بِبَغۡيِهِمۡۖ وَإِنَّا لَصَٰدِقُونَ ١٤٦
فَإِن كَذَّبُوكَ فَقُل رَّبُّكُمۡ ذُو رَحۡمَةٖ وَٰسِعَةٖ وَلَا يُرَدُّ
بَأۡسُهُۥ عَنِ ٱلۡقَوۡمِ ٱلۡمُجۡرِمِينَ ١٤٧ سَيَقُولُ ٱلَّذِينَ أَشۡرَكُواْ
لَوۡ شَآءَ ٱللَّهُ مَآ أَشۡرَكۡنَا وَلَآ ءَابَآؤُنَا وَلَا حَرَّمۡنَا مِن شَيۡءٖۚ
كَذَٰلِكَ كَذَّبَ ٱلَّذِينَ مِن قَبۡلِهِمۡ حَتَّىٰ ذَاقُواْ بَأۡسَنَاۗ
قُلۡ هَلۡ عِندَكُم مِّنۡ عِلۡمٖ فَتُخۡرِجُوهُ لَنَآۖ إِن تَتَّبِعُونَ إِلَّا
ٱلظَّنَّ وَإِنۡ أَنتُمۡ إِلَّا تَخۡرُصُونَ ١٤٨ قُلۡ فَلِلَّهِ ٱلۡحُجَّةُ ٱلۡبَٰلِغَةُۖ
فَلَوۡ شَآءَ لَهَدَىٰكُمۡ أَجۡمَعِينَ ١٤٩ قُلۡ هَلُمَّ شُهَدَآءَكُمُ ٱلَّذِينَ

143. ***There are eight*** categories of animals which may be used for haulage and slaughter ***in pairs*** – male and female***: A pair of sheep and a pair of goats*** (read as *ma'z* and *ma'az*). ***Say***, Muḥammad, to those who sometimes make the females unlawful and other times the males, and then ascribe that to Allah***: "Is it the two males*** of sheep and goats ***He has made unlawful*** for you***, or the two females, or what the wombs of the two females contain*** – male or female***? Inform me*** of how that prohibition came about ***with knowledge if you speak the truth."*** Was it on account of the males, so that all males are unlawful, or the females, so that all females and what their wombs contain are unlawful? How was that specified? The question is one which implies rejection.

144. ***And a pair of camels and a pair of cattle – Say: "Is it the two males He has made unlawful, or the two females, or what the wombs of the two females contain? Were you then witnesses*** (present) ***when Allah gave you this instruction*** about this prohibition, so that you rely on it, or are you in fact merely liars***?" Who*** (no one) ***could do greater wrong than someone who invents lies against Allah*** by saying that, ***thus leading people astray without any knowledge? Allah does not guide the people of the wrongdoers.***

145. ***Say: "I do not find, in what has been revealed to me, any food unlawful to be eaten except for carrion, flowing blood*** – discounting what is in the liver or spleen – ***and pork – for that is unclean*** (unlawful) ***– or some deviance consecrated to other than Allah***: sacrificed in other than the name of Allah***. But if anyone is forced to eat it*** – any of the things which have been mentioned – ***without desiring to or going to excess in it, your Lord is Ever-Forgiving*** about what he has eaten***, Most Merciful*** to him***.*** The other things made clear by the *Sunna*, including all wild animals with claws and birds with talons, should be added to the list of what is unlawful.

146. ***We made unlawful for the Jews every animal with an undivided hoof*** such as camels and ostriches. ***And in respect of cattle and sheep, We made their fat unlawful for them*** – meaning the fat round the kidneys – ***except what is attached to their backs or entrails or mixed up with bone. That*** prohibition ***is how We repaid them for their insolence*** for their wrongdoing which was mentioned in *Sūrat*

يَشْهَدُونَ أَنَّ ٱللَّهَ حَرَّمَ هَٰذَا ۖ فَإِن شَهِدُوا۟ فَلَا تَشْهَدْ
مَعَهُمْ ۚ وَلَا تَتَّبِعْ أَهْوَآءَ ٱلَّذِينَ كَذَّبُوا۟ بِـَٔايَٰتِنَا وَٱلَّذِينَ
لَا يُؤْمِنُونَ بِٱلْءَاخِرَةِ وَهُم بِرَبِّهِمْ يَعْدِلُونَ ﴿١٥٠﴾ ۞ قُلْ
تَعَالَوْا۟ أَتْلُ مَا حَرَّمَ رَبُّكُمْ عَلَيْكُمْ ۖ أَلَّا تُشْرِكُوا۟ بِهِۦ
شَيْـًٔا ۖ وَبِٱلْوَٰلِدَيْنِ إِحْسَٰنًا ۖ وَلَا تَقْتُلُوٓا۟ أَوْلَٰدَكُم مِّنْ
إِمْلَٰقٍ ۖ نَّحْنُ نَرْزُقُكُمْ وَإِيَّاهُمْ ۖ وَلَا تَقْرَبُوا۟ ٱلْفَوَٰحِشَ
مَا ظَهَرَ مِنْهَا وَمَا بَطَنَ ۖ وَلَا تَقْتُلُوا۟ ٱلنَّفْسَ ٱلَّتِى
حَرَّمَ ٱللَّهُ إِلَّا بِٱلْحَقِّ ۚ ذَٰلِكُمْ وَصَّىٰكُم بِهِۦ لَعَلَّكُمْ تَعْقِلُونَ ﴿١٥١﴾
وَلَا تَقْرَبُوا۟ مَالَ ٱلْيَتِيمِ إِلَّا بِٱلَّتِى هِىَ أَحْسَنُ حَتَّىٰ يَبْلُغَ أَشُدَّهُۥ ۖ
وَأَوْفُوا۟ ٱلْكَيْلَ وَٱلْمِيزَانَ بِٱلْقِسْطِ ۖ لَا نُكَلِّفُ نَفْسًا إِلَّا
وُسْعَهَا ۖ وَإِذَا قُلْتُمْ فَٱعْدِلُوا۟ وَلَوْ كَانَ ذَا قُرْبَىٰ ۖ وَبِعَهْدِ
ٱللَّهِ أَوْفُوا۟ ۚ ذَٰلِكُمْ وَصَّىٰكُم بِهِۦ لَعَلَّكُمْ تَذَكَّرُونَ ﴿١٥٢﴾
وَأَنَّ هَٰذَا صِرَٰطِى مُسْتَقِيمًا فَٱتَّبِعُوهُ ۖ وَلَا تَتَّبِعُوا۟ ٱلسُّبُلَ
فَتَفَرَّقَ بِكُمْ عَن سَبِيلِهِۦ ۚ ذَٰلِكُمْ وَصَّىٰكُم بِهِۦ لَعَلَّكُمْ
تَتَّقُونَ ﴿١٥٣﴾ ثُمَّ ءَاتَيْنَا مُوسَى ٱلْكِتَٰبَ تَمَامًا عَلَى ٱلَّذِىٓ
أَحْسَنَ وَتَفْصِيلًا لِّكُلِّ شَىْءٍ وَهُدًى وَرَحْمَةً لَّعَلَّهُم بِلِقَآءِ
رَبِّهِمْ يُؤْمِنُونَ ﴿١٥٤﴾ وَهَٰذَا كِتَٰبٌ أَنزَلْنَٰهُ مُبَارَكٌ فَٱتَّبِعُوهُ
وَٱتَّقُوا۟ لَعَلَّكُمْ تُرْحَمُونَ ﴿١٥٥﴾ أَن تَقُولُوٓا۟ إِنَّمَآ أُنزِلَ ٱلْكِتَٰبُ
عَلَىٰ طَآئِفَتَيْنِ مِن قَبْلِنَا وَإِن كُنَّا عَن دِرَاسَتِهِمْ لَغَٰفِلِينَ
﴿١٥٦﴾ أَوْ تَقُولُوا۟ لَوْ أَنَّآ أُنزِلَ عَلَيْنَا ٱلْكِتَٰبُ لَكُنَّآ أَهْدَىٰ مِنْهُمْ ۚ
فَقَدْ جَآءَكُم بَيِّنَةٌ مِّن رَّبِّكُمْ وَهُدًى وَرَحْمَةٌ ۚ فَمَنْ

an-Nisā' (4:160). ***And We certainly speak the truth*** in Our reports and promises.

147. ***If they call you a liar*** regarding what you say, ***say*** to them: ***"Your Lord possesses boundless mercy*** by not hastening their punishment, and His kindness is demonstrated by His calling them to belief, ***but His violent force*** (punishment) ***cannot be averted*** – when it comes – ***from the people of the evil-doers."***

148. ***Those who attribute partners to Allah will say, "If Allah had willed we would not have ascribed partners to Him, nor would our fathers; nor would we have made anything unlawful."*** "Our idolatry and making things unlawful is by Allah's will, and that must mean that He is pleased with that." Allah said: ***In the same way*** that they have denied, ***the people before them denied*** Our Messengers ***until they felt Our violent force*** (punishment). ***Say: "Do you have some knowledge you can produce for us? You are following*** – regarding the claim you have made – ***nothing but conjecture. You are only guessing*** and in fact lying."

149. ***Say:*** "Since you have no argument ***Allah's is the conclusive*** and complete ***argument. If He had willed He could have guided every one of you."***

150. ***Say: "Produce your witnesses to testify*** in respect of what you have made unlawful, ***that Allah made this unlawful." If they do testify, do not testify with them and do not follow the whims and desires of people who deny Our Signs, and who do not believe in the Next World and make others equal to their Lord***, committing *shirk* by doing so.

151. ***Say: "Come and I will*** read and ***recite to you*** and explain ***what your Lord has commanded you: that you do not attribute any partners to Him; that you are good to your parents; that you do not kill your children*** by burying them alive ***because of poverty.*** Do not fear poverty. ***We will provide for you and them; that you do not approach indecency*** – major wrong actions like fornication – ***outward or inward*** – publicly or in secret; ***that you do not kill any person Allah has made inviolate – except by right*** – in other words in retaliation for someone killed or the implementation of the death penalty for apostasy or the stoning of adulterers. ***That*** which has been mentioned ***is what He instructs you to do so that perhaps you will use your intellect*** and reflect.

152. ***That you do not go near the property of an orphan before he reaches maturity*** – becomes an adult – ***except in a good way*** – which means dealing with it in a proper way to make it grow; ***that you give full measure and full weight with justice*** – not cheating or reducing the weight – ***We charge no self beyond what it can bear*** – so if you err accidentally with regard to weights and measures, and Allah knows that your intention was sound, you will not be punished for it as is stated in *ḥadīth*; ***that you are equitable*** and speak the truth ***when you speak*** in a court of justice or elsewhere – ***even if a near relative is concerned***, whether your testimony is for or against him; ***and that you fulfil Allah's contract. That is what He instructs you to do, so that perhaps you will pay heed*** (read as *tadhakkarūna* and *tadhdhakkarūna*).

153. ***This*** instruction to you ***is my Path – straight – so follow it. Do not follow other ways*** which differ from that ***or you will become cut off from His Way*** (His *dīn*). ***That is what He instructs you to do, so that perhaps you will be godfearing.***

154. ***Then We gave Mūsā the Book*** (the Torah) ***complete*** in blessing ***and perfect for him who does good*** and implements it, ***elucidating everything*** needed in the *dīn*, ***and a guidance and a mercy, so that perhaps they*** (the tribe of Israel) ***will believe in the encounter with their Lord*** at the Resurrection.

155. ***And this*** (the Qur'ān) ***is a Book We have sent down and blessed,*** people of Makka, ***so follow it*** by acting on what it contains ***and be godfearing***, fearing unbelief, ***so that perhaps you will receive mercy.***

156. We sent it down ***so you cannot say: "The Book was only sent down to the two groups*** (the Jews and Christians) ***before us and we were ignorant of their studies*** because it is not in our language and could not read it."

157. ***Nor can you say: "If the Book had been sent down to us, We would have been better guided than them*** because we are more intelligent than them." ***For a Clear Sign has come to you from your Lord, and guidance and mercy*** for whoever who follows it. ***Who***

أَظْلَمُ مِمَّن كَذَّبَ بِـَٔايَٰتِ ٱللَّهِ وَصَدَفَ عَنْهَا ۗ سَنَجْزِى ٱلَّذِينَ
يَصْدِفُونَ عَنْ ءَايَٰتِنَا سُوٓءَ ٱلْعَذَابِ بِمَا كَانُوا۟ يَصْدِفُونَ ١٥٧
هَلْ يَنظُرُونَ إِلَّآ أَن تَأْتِيَهُمُ ٱلْمَلَٰٓئِكَةُ أَوْ يَأْتِىَ رَبُّكَ أَوْ يَأْتِىَ
بَعْضُ ءَايَٰتِ رَبِّكَ ۗ يَوْمَ يَأْتِى بَعْضُ ءَايَٰتِ رَبِّكَ لَا يَنفَعُ نَفْسًا إِيمَٰنُهَا
لَمْ تَكُنْ ءَامَنَتْ مِن قَبْلُ أَوْ كَسَبَتْ فِىٓ إِيمَٰنِهَا خَيْرًا ۗ قُلِ ٱنتَظِرُوٓا۟
إِنَّا مُنتَظِرُونَ ١٥٨ إِنَّ ٱلَّذِينَ فَرَّقُوا۟ دِينَهُمْ وَكَانُوا۟ شِيَعًا لَّسْتَ
مِنْهُمْ فِى شَىْءٍ ۚ إِنَّمَآ أَمْرُهُمْ إِلَى ٱللَّهِ ثُمَّ يُنَبِّئُهُم بِمَا كَانُوا۟ يَفْعَلُونَ
١٥٩ مَن جَآءَ بِٱلْحَسَنَةِ فَلَهُۥ عَشْرُ أَمْثَالِهَا ۖ وَمَن جَآءَ بِٱلسَّيِّئَةِ
فَلَا يُجْزَىٰٓ إِلَّا مِثْلَهَا وَهُمْ لَا يُظْلَمُونَ ١٦٠ قُلْ إِنَّنِى هَدَىٰنِى رَبِّىٓ
إِلَىٰ صِرَٰطٍ مُّسْتَقِيمٍ دِينًا قِيَمًا مِّلَّةَ إِبْرَٰهِيمَ حَنِيفًا ۚ وَمَا كَانَ مِنَ
ٱلْمُشْرِكِينَ ١٦١ قُلْ إِنَّ صَلَاتِى وَنُسُكِى وَمَحْيَاىَ وَمَمَاتِى لِلَّهِ
رَبِّ ٱلْعَٰلَمِينَ ١٦٢ لَا شَرِيكَ لَهُۥ ۖ وَبِذَٰلِكَ أُمِرْتُ وَأَنَا۠ أَوَّلُ ٱلْمُسْلِمِينَ
١٦٣ قُلْ أَغَيْرَ ٱللَّهِ أَبْغِى رَبًّا وَهُوَ رَبُّ كُلِّ شَىْءٍ ۚ وَلَا تَكْسِبُ كُلُّ
نَفْسٍ إِلَّا عَلَيْهَا ۚ وَلَا تَزِرُ وَازِرَةٌ وِزْرَ أُخْرَىٰ ۚ ثُمَّ إِلَىٰ رَبِّكُم مَّرْجِعُكُمْ
فَيُنَبِّئُكُم بِمَا كُنتُمْ فِيهِ تَخْتَلِفُونَ ١٦٤ وَهُوَ ٱلَّذِى جَعَلَكُمْ
خَلَٰٓئِفَ ٱلْأَرْضِ وَرَفَعَ بَعْضَكُمْ فَوْقَ بَعْضٍ دَرَجَٰتٍ لِّيَبْلُوَكُمْ
فِى مَآ ءَاتَىٰكُمْ ۗ إِنَّ رَبَّكَ سَرِيعُ ٱلْعِقَابِ وَإِنَّهُۥ لَغَفُورٌ رَّحِيمٌۢ ١٦٥

(no one) ***could do greater wrong than someone who denies Allah's Signs and turns away from them? We will repay those who turn away from Our Signs with the worst kind of punishment because they turned away.***

158. ***What are they*** (the deniers) ***waiting for but for the angels to come*** (read as *ta'tīhim* and *ya'tīhim*) ***to them*** to take their souls ***or for*** the command of ***your Lord*** (the punishment) ***to come, or for one of your Lord's Signs*** – the signs which indicate the Final Hour – ***to come? On the Day that one of your Lord's Signs does come,*** such as the rising of the sun from the West as we find in the two *Ṣaḥīḥ* collections, ***no belief a self professes will be of use to it if it did not believe before or earn good in its belief.*** By that time repentance will be of no use, as is stated in the *ḥadīth*. ***Say: "Wait, then*** for one of these things. ***We too are waiting*** for that."

159. ***As for those who divide their* dīn** because of the disagreements they have ***and form into sects*** (read as *farraqū* and *fāriqū*) – taking some of their *dīn* and leaving some – ***you have nothing whatsoever to do with them*** and should not turn to them. ***Their case will go back to Allah and then He will inform them*** in the Next World ***about what they did*** and repay them for it. This was abrogated by the Sword Verse.

160. ***Those who produce a good action*** such as saying, *"Lā ilaha illā'llāh"*, ***will receive ten like it*** in repayment. ***But those who produce a bad action will only be repaid with its equivalent, and they will not be wronged*** by having their reward decreased in any way.

161. ***Say: "My Lord has guided me to a Straight Path, a correct* dīn*, the religion of Ibrāhīm, a man of pure natural belief. He was no idolater."***

162. ***Say: "My prayer and my rites*** – referring to acts of worship in the *ḥajj* and elsewhere – ***my living*** (my life) ***and my dying*** (my death) ***are for Allah alone, the Lord of all the worlds…***

163. ***...who has no partner*** in that. ***I am commanded to be like that*** in respect of affirming *tawḥīd* ***and I am the first of the Muslims*** of this community."

164. ***Say: "Am I to desire other than Allah as Lord*** and God ***when He is the Lord*** and Master ***of everything?" What each self earns*** in terms of wrong action ***is for itself alone. No*** (soul) ***bearer of any burden can bear that of any other. Then you will return to your Lord, and He will inform you regarding the things about which you differed.***
165. ***It is He who appointed you successors on the earth and raised some of you above others in rank*** in terms of wealth, position and other things ***so He could test you regarding what He has given you*** to see whether you are disobedient or obedient. ***Your Lord is Swift in Retribution*** against those who disobey Him, ***and He is Ever-Forgiving*** to the believers, ***Most Merciful.***

سُورَةُ الأَعۡرَافِ

بِسۡمِ ٱللَّهِ ٱلرَّحۡمَٰنِ ٱلرَّحِيمِ

الٓمٓصٓ ﴿١﴾ كِتَٰبٌ أُنزِلَ إِلَيۡكَ فَلَا يَكُن فِي صَدۡرِكَ حَرَجٞ مِّنۡهُ
لِتُنذِرَ بِهِۦ وَذِكۡرَىٰ لِلۡمُؤۡمِنِينَ ﴿٢﴾ ٱتَّبِعُواْ مَآ أُنزِلَ إِلَيۡكُم
مِّن رَّبِّكُمۡ وَلَا تَتَّبِعُواْ مِن دُونِهِۦٓ أَوۡلِيَآءَۗ قَلِيلٗا مَّا تَذَكَّرُونَ ﴿٣﴾
وَكَم مِّن قَرۡيَةٍ أَهۡلَكۡنَٰهَا فَجَآءَهَا بَأۡسُنَا بَيَٰتًا أَوۡ هُمۡ قَآئِلُونَ
﴿٤﴾ فَمَا كَانَ دَعۡوَىٰهُمۡ إِذۡ جَآءَهُم بَأۡسُنَآ إِلَّآ أَن قَالُوٓاْ إِنَّا كُنَّا
ظَٰلِمِينَ ﴿٥﴾ فَلَنَسۡـَٔلَنَّ ٱلَّذِينَ أُرۡسِلَ إِلَيۡهِمۡ وَلَنَسۡـَٔلَنَّ
ٱلۡمُرۡسَلِينَ ﴿٦﴾ فَلَنَقُصَّنَّ عَلَيۡهِم بِعِلۡمٖۖ وَمَا كُنَّا غَآئِبِينَ ﴿٧﴾
وَٱلۡوَزۡنُ يَوۡمَئِذٍ ٱلۡحَقُّۚ فَمَن ثَقُلَتۡ مَوَٰزِينُهُۥ فَأُوْلَٰٓئِكَ هُمُ
ٱلۡمُفۡلِحُونَ ﴿٨﴾ وَمَنۡ خَفَّتۡ مَوَٰزِينُهُۥ فَأُوْلَٰٓئِكَ ٱلَّذِينَ خَسِرُوٓاْ
أَنفُسَهُم بِمَا كَانُواْ بِـَٔايَٰتِنَا يَظۡلِمُونَ ﴿٩﴾ وَلَقَدۡ مَكَّنَّٰكُمۡ
فِي ٱلۡأَرۡضِ وَجَعَلۡنَا لَكُمۡ فِيهَا مَعَٰيِشَۗ قَلِيلٗا مَّا تَشۡكُرُونَ ﴿١٠﴾
وَلَقَدۡ خَلَقۡنَٰكُمۡ ثُمَّ صَوَّرۡنَٰكُمۡ ثُمَّ قُلۡنَا لِلۡمَلَٰٓئِكَةِ ٱسۡجُدُواْ
لِأٓدَمَ فَسَجَدُوٓاْ إِلَّآ إِبۡلِيسَ لَمۡ يَكُن مِّنَ ٱلسَّٰجِدِينَ ﴿١١﴾
قَالَ مَا مَنَعَكَ أَلَّا تَسۡجُدَ إِذۡ أَمَرۡتُكَۖ قَالَ أَنَا۠ خَيۡرٞ مِّنۡهُ خَلَقۡتَنِي مِن نَّارٖ
وَخَلَقۡتَهُۥ مِن طِينٖ ﴿١٢﴾ قَالَ فَٱهۡبِطۡ مِنۡهَا فَمَا يَكُونُ لَكَ أَن تَتَكَبَّرَ
فِيهَا فَٱخۡرُجۡ إِنَّكَ مِنَ ٱلصَّٰغِرِينَ ﴿١٣﴾ قَالَ أَنظِرۡنِيٓ إِلَىٰ يَوۡمِ يُبۡعَثُونَ
﴿١٤﴾ قَالَ إِنَّكَ مِنَ ٱلۡمُنظَرِينَ ﴿١٥﴾ قَالَ فَبِمَآ أَغۡوَيۡتَنِي لَأَقۡعُدَنَّ لَهُمۡ
صِرَٰطَكَ ٱلۡمُسۡتَقِيمَ ﴿١٦﴾ ثُمَّ لَأٓتِيَنَّهُم مِّنۢ بَيۡنِ أَيۡدِيهِمۡ وَمِنۡ خَلۡفِهِمۡ
وَعَنۡ أَيۡمَٰنِهِمۡ وَعَن شَمَآئِلِهِمۡۖ وَلَا تَجِدُ أَكۡثَرَهُمۡ شَٰكِرِينَ ﴿١٧﴾ قَالَ

7. *Sūrat al-A'rāf*
The Ramparts

It is Makkan except for *āyats* 163 to 170 which are Madinan. It has 205 or 206 *āyats* and was revealed after *Sūrat Ṣad*.

1. ***Alif Lām Mīm Ṣād.*** Allah knows best what these letters mean.

2. ***It*** (this) ***is a Book sent down to you*** – addressed to the Prophet, may Allah bless him and grant him peace, ***so let there be no constriction in your breast because of it*** (when you convey it) out of the fear that it will be denied – ***so that you can give warning by it and as a reminder to the believers.***

3. Say to them: ***Follow what has been sent down to you from your Lord*** (the Qur'ān) ***and do not*** adopt and ***follow any protectors apart from Him,*** obeying them in disobedience to Allah. ***How little you remember*** (read as *tadhakkarūna*, *yatadhakkarūna* and *tadhdhakkarūna*) and take note.

4. ***How many cities*** – meaning their inhabitants – ***We have destroyed!*** When We wanted to destroy them, ***Our violent force*** (punishment) ***came down on them during the night, or while they were asleep during the day***: having a rest in the middle of the day, even if they were not asleep; in other words, it sometimes comes at night and sometimes in the day.

5. ***And their only utterance, when Our violent force came down on them, was the cry: "Truly we have been wrongdoers!"***

6. ***We will question those to whom the Messengers were sent*** – every nation will be asked about how they answered the Messengers and acted on what he conveyed to them – ***and We will question the Messengers*** about whether they conveyed the Message.

7. ***We will tell them about it with knowledge. We are never absent*** from Our Messengers as they convey the Message or from past nations in respect of their actions.

8. ***The weighing*** of actions – or the pages on which they are recorded in the balance which has a pointer and two scales, as is reported in *ḥadīth* – ***that day*** (the Day of Questioning) ***is the truth*** and justice. This takes place on the Day of Rising. ***As for those whose scales are heavy*** with good actions, ***they are the successful.***

9. ***As for those whose scales are light*** through wrong actions, ***they are the ones who have lost their own selves*** and will go to the Fire ***because they wrongfully rejected Our Signs.***

10. ***We have established you,*** children of Ādam, ***firmly on the earth and granted you your livelihood in it. What little thanks you show*** for that.

11. ***We created you*** in the form of your ancestor Ādam ***and then formed you*** while you were still in his loins, ***and then We said to the angels, "Prostrate to Ādam,"*** with the obeisance of greeting, ***and they prostrated – except for Iblīs***, the progenitor of the jinn who was among the angels. ***He was not among the prostrators.***

12. ***He*** (Allah) ***asked, "What prevented you from prostrating when I commanded you to?" He replied, "I am better than him. You created me from fire and You created him from clay."***

13. ***He said, "Descend from Heaven*** – from the Garden or from the heavens. ***It is not for you to be arrogant in it. So get out*** of it***! You are one of the abased."***

14. ***He said, "Grant me a reprieve until the day they*** (mankind) ***are raised up."***

15. ***He said, "You are one of the reprieved."*** Another *āyat* has *"reprieved until the Day whose time is known,"* (15:38) meaning the first blast of the Trumpet by Israfil.

16. ***He said, "By Your misguidance of me*** – because You have misled me – ***I will lie in ambush for them*** (the children of Ādam) ***on your Straight Path***, the Path which leads to You.

17. ***Then I will come at them, from in front of them and behind them, from their right and from their left*** – in other words, from every direction – and I will prevent them from going on the path. Ibn 'Abbās said that Iblīs was prevented from coming at them from above so that nothing could come between Allah's slave and His mercy. ***You will not find most of them*** to be ***thankful*** believers."

18. ***He said, "Get out of it, reviled and driven out*** far from Allah's mercy. ***As for those of them*** (mankind) ***who follow you, I will fill up Hell with every one of you*** – with your descendants and with

ٱخۡرُجۡ مِنۡهَا مَذۡءُومٗا مَّدۡحُورٗاۖ لَّمَن تَبِعَكَ مِنۡهُمۡ لَأَمۡلَأَنَّ جَهَنَّمَ مِنكُمۡ
أَجۡمَعِينَ ﴿١٨﴾ وَيَٰٓـَٔادَمُ ٱسۡكُنۡ أَنتَ وَزَوۡجُكَ ٱلۡجَنَّةَ فَكُلَا مِنۡ حَيۡثُ
شِئۡتُمَا وَلَا تَقۡرَبَا هَٰذِهِ ٱلشَّجَرَةَ فَتَكُونَا مِنَ ٱلظَّٰلِمِينَ ﴿١٩﴾ فَوَسۡوَسَ
لَهُمَا ٱلشَّيۡطَٰنُ لِيُبۡدِيَ لَهُمَا مَا وُۥرِيَ عَنۡهُمَا مِن سَوۡءَٰتِهِمَا وَقَالَ
مَا نَهَىٰكُمَا رَبُّكُمَا عَنۡ هَٰذِهِ ٱلشَّجَرَةِ إِلَّآ أَن تَكُونَا مَلَكَيۡنِ أَوۡ تَكُونَا
مِنَ ٱلۡخَٰلِدِينَ ﴿٢٠﴾ وَقَاسَمَهُمَآ إِنِّي لَكُمَا لَمِنَ ٱلنَّٰصِحِينَ ﴿٢١﴾
فَدَلَّىٰهُمَا بِغُرُورٖۚ فَلَمَّا ذَاقَا ٱلشَّجَرَةَ بَدَتۡ لَهُمَا سَوۡءَٰتُهُمَا وَطَفِقَا
يَخۡصِفَانِ عَلَيۡهِمَا مِن وَرَقِ ٱلۡجَنَّةِۖ وَنَادَىٰهُمَا رَبُّهُمَآ أَلَمۡ أَنۡهَكُمَا
عَن تِلۡكُمَا ٱلشَّجَرَةِ وَأَقُل لَّكُمَآ إِنَّ ٱلشَّيۡطَٰنَ لَكُمَا عَدُوّٞ مُّبِينٞ ﴿٢٢﴾
قَالَا رَبَّنَا ظَلَمۡنَآ أَنفُسَنَا وَإِن لَّمۡ تَغۡفِرۡ لَنَا وَتَرۡحَمۡنَا لَنَكُونَنَّ مِنَ
ٱلۡخَٰسِرِينَ ﴿٢٣﴾ قَالَ ٱهۡبِطُواْ بَعۡضُكُمۡ لِبَعۡضٍ عَدُوّٞۖ وَلَكُمۡ فِي
ٱلۡأَرۡضِ مُسۡتَقَرّٞ وَمَتَٰعٌ إِلَىٰ حِينٖ ﴿٢٤﴾ قَالَ فِيهَا تَحۡيَوۡنَ وَفِيهَا
تَمُوتُونَ وَمِنۡهَا تُخۡرَجُونَ ﴿٢٥﴾ يَٰبَنِيٓ ءَادَمَ قَدۡ أَنزَلۡنَا عَلَيۡكُمۡ لِبَاسٗا
يُوَٰرِي سَوۡءَٰتِكُمۡ وَرِيشٗاۖ وَلِبَاسُ ٱلتَّقۡوَىٰ ذَٰلِكَ خَيۡرٞۚ ذَٰلِكَ مِنۡ
ءَايَٰتِ ٱللَّهِ لَعَلَّهُمۡ يَذَّكَّرُونَ ﴿٢٦﴾ يَٰبَنِيٓ ءَادَمَ لَا يَفۡتِنَنَّكُمُ
ٱلشَّيۡطَٰنُ كَمَآ أَخۡرَجَ أَبَوَيۡكُم مِّنَ ٱلۡجَنَّةِ يَنزِعُ عَنۡهُمَا لِبَاسَهُمَا
لِيُرِيَهُمَا سَوۡءَٰتِهِمَآۚ إِنَّهُۥ يَرَىٰكُمۡ هُوَ وَقَبِيلُهُۥ مِنۡ حَيۡثُ لَا تَرَوۡنَهُمۡۗ
إِنَّا جَعَلۡنَا ٱلشَّيَٰطِينَ أَوۡلِيَآءَ لِلَّذِينَ لَا يُؤۡمِنُونَ ﴿٢٧﴾ وَإِذَا فَعَلُواْ
فَٰحِشَةٗ قَالُواْ وَجَدۡنَا عَلَيۡهَآ ءَابَآءَنَا وَٱللَّهُ أَمَرَنَا بِهَاۗ قُلۡ إِنَّ ٱللَّهَ
لَا يَأۡمُرُ بِٱلۡفَحۡشَآءِۖ أَتَقُولُونَ عَلَى ٱللَّهِ مَا لَا تَعۡلَمُونَ ﴿٢٨﴾ قُلۡ
أَمَرَ رَبِّي بِٱلۡقِسۡطِۖ وَأَقِيمُواْ وُجُوهَكُمۡ عِندَ كُلِّ مَسۡجِدٖ

mankind." There is a change in the person addressed. This sentence shows that this outcome is conditional, that Allah will punish whoever follows Shayṭān.

19. He said, ***"Ādam, live in the Garden, you and your wife*** (Ḥawwā') – the pronoun "you" is stressed here by being repeated – ***and eat of it wheresoever you like. But do not go near this tree*** and eat from it – and it was wheat – ***lest you become wrongdoers."***

20. *Then Shayṭān* (Iblīs) ***whispered to them, disclosing to them their private parts that were concealed from them. He said, "Your Lord has only forbidden you this tree lest*** – because He did not want that – ***you both become angels*** (an alternative reading for *malakayn,* "angels" is *malikayn,* which means "kings") ***or among those who live forever*** – meaning that eating from it would result in immortality for them." Another *āyat* states: *"Shall I show you the way to the Tree of Everlasting Life and to a kingdom which will never fade away?"* (20:120)

21. *He swore to them* by Allah, ***"I am one of those who give you good advice."***

22. *So he enticed them to do it* and brought them down from their high place ***by means of trickery. Then when they tasted the tree*** and ate from it, ***their private parts were disclosed to them*** so that it was clear to each of them that they had genitals. (The private parts are called *saw'āh*, from a root meaning "bad", because uncovering them harms the person who does it) ***and they started stitching together the leaves of the Garden in order to cover themselves*** with the leaves. ***Their Lord called out to them, "Did I not forbid you this tree and tell you, 'Shaytan is your clear-cut enemy'?"*** The enmity of Shayṭān is clear. The question expects an affirmative answer.

23. *They said, "Our Lord, we have wronged ourselves* by our disobedience. ***If You do not forgive us and have mercy on us, we will be among the lost."***

24. *He said, "Descend,* Ādam and Ḥawwā', – including them and all their descendants – ***as enemies*** – referring to their descendants – ***to one another! You will have residence on the earth and enjoyment for a time***: your life span."

وَٱدۡعُوهُ مُخۡلِصِينَ لَهُ ٱلدِّينَۚ كَمَا بَدَأَكُمۡ تَعُودُونَ ﴿٢٩﴾ فَرِيقًا
هَدَىٰ وَفَرِيقًا حَقَّ عَلَيۡهِمُ ٱلضَّلَٰلَةُۚ إِنَّهُمُ ٱتَّخَذُواْ ٱلشَّيَٰطِينَ
أَوۡلِيَآءَ مِن دُونِ ٱللَّهِ وَيَحۡسَبُونَ أَنَّهُم مُّهۡتَدُونَ ﴿٣٠﴾
۞ يَٰبَنِيٓ ءَادَمَ خُذُواْ زِينَتَكُمۡ عِندَ كُلِّ مَسۡجِدٖ وَكُلُواْ وَٱشۡرَبُواْ
وَلَا تُسۡرِفُوٓاْۚ إِنَّهُۥ لَا يُحِبُّ ٱلۡمُسۡرِفِينَ ﴿٣١﴾ قُلۡ مَنۡ حَرَّمَ زِينَةَ ٱللَّهِ
ٱلَّتِيٓ أَخۡرَجَ لِعِبَادِهِۦ وَٱلطَّيِّبَٰتِ مِنَ ٱلرِّزۡقِۚ قُلۡ هِيَ لِلَّذِينَ ءَامَنُواْ
فِي ٱلۡحَيَوٰةِ ٱلدُّنۡيَا خَالِصَةٗ يَوۡمَ ٱلۡقِيَٰمَةِۗ كَذَٰلِكَ نُفَصِّلُ ٱلۡأٓيَٰتِ
لِقَوۡمٖ يَعۡلَمُونَ ﴿٣٢﴾ قُلۡ إِنَّمَا حَرَّمَ رَبِّيَ ٱلۡفَوَٰحِشَ مَا ظَهَرَ مِنۡهَا وَمَا
بَطَنَ وَٱلۡإِثۡمَ وَٱلۡبَغۡيَ بِغَيۡرِ ٱلۡحَقِّ وَأَن تُشۡرِكُواْ بِٱللَّهِ مَا لَمۡ يُنَزِّلۡ بِهِۦ
سُلۡطَٰنٗا وَأَن تَقُولُواْ عَلَى ٱللَّهِ مَا لَا تَعۡلَمُونَ ﴿٣٣﴾ وَلِكُلِّ أُمَّةٍ أَجَلٞۖ
فَإِذَا جَآءَ أَجَلُهُمۡ لَا يَسۡتَأۡخِرُونَ سَاعَةٗ وَلَا يَسۡتَقۡدِمُونَ ﴿٣٤﴾
يَٰبَنِيٓ ءَادَمَ إِمَّا يَأۡتِيَنَّكُمۡ رُسُلٞ مِّنكُمۡ يَقُصُّونَ عَلَيۡكُمۡ ءَايَٰتِي فَمَنِ
ٱتَّقَىٰ وَأَصۡلَحَ فَلَا خَوۡفٌ عَلَيۡهِمۡ وَلَا هُمۡ يَحۡزَنُونَ ﴿٣٥﴾ وَٱلَّذِينَ
كَذَّبُواْ بِـَٔايَٰتِنَا وَٱسۡتَكۡبَرُواْ عَنۡهَآ أُوْلَٰٓئِكَ أَصۡحَٰبُ ٱلنَّارِۖ هُمۡ
فِيهَا خَٰلِدُونَ ﴿٣٦﴾ فَمَنۡ أَظۡلَمُ مِمَّنِ ٱفۡتَرَىٰ عَلَى ٱللَّهِ كَذِبًا أَوۡ كَذَّبَ
بِـَٔايَٰتِهِۦٓۚ أُوْلَٰٓئِكَ يَنَالُهُمۡ نَصِيبُهُم مِّنَ ٱلۡكِتَٰبِۖ حَتَّىٰٓ إِذَا جَآءَتۡهُمۡ
رُسُلُنَا يَتَوَفَّوۡنَهُمۡ قَالُوٓاْ أَيۡنَ مَا كُنتُمۡ تَدۡعُونَ مِن دُونِ ٱللَّهِۖ
قَالُواْ ضَلُّواْ عَنَّا وَشَهِدُواْ عَلَىٰٓ أَنفُسِهِمۡ أَنَّهُمۡ كَانُواْ كَٰفِرِينَ ﴿٣٧﴾
قَالَ ٱدۡخُلُواْ فِيٓ أُمَمٖ قَدۡ خَلَتۡ مِن قَبۡلِكُم مِّنَ ٱلۡجِنِّ وَٱلۡإِنسِ
فِي ٱلنَّارِۖ كُلَّمَا دَخَلَتۡ أُمَّةٞ لَّعَنَتۡ أُخۡتَهَاۖ حَتَّىٰٓ إِذَا ٱدَّارَكُواْ فِيهَا
جَمِيعٗا قَالَتۡ أُخۡرَىٰهُمۡ لِأُولَىٰهُمۡ رَبَّنَا هَٰٓؤُلَآءِ أَضَلُّونَا فَـَٔاتِهِمۡ

25. ***He said, "On it*** (the earth) ***you will live and on it die and from it you will be brought forth*** at the Resurrection.***"***

26. ***Children of Ādam! We have sent down clothing to you*** which We created for you ***to conceal your private parts, and fine apparel,*** beautiful clothes, ***and the garment of godfearing,*** righteous actions and good behaviour ***that is best! That is one of Allah's Signs*** of His power, ***so that perhaps you will pay heed*** and remember.

27. ***Children of Ādam! Do not let Shayṭān*** mislead you and ***tempt you into trouble*** – in other words, do not follow him so that you are tempted – ***as He expelled your parents*** through temptation ***from the Garden, stripping them of their covering and disclosing to them their private parts. He*** (Shayṭān) ***and his tribe*** (his armies) ***see you from where you do not see them*** because their bodies are subtle or because they are transparent. ***We have made the* shayṭāns *friends*** (helpers and comrades) ***of those who do not believe.***

28. ***Whenever they commit an indecent act***, such as worshipping idols and doing *ṭawāf* of the Ka'ba naked, saying, "We do not do *ṭawāf* wearing clothes. We disobey Allah regarding that," and they were forbidden to do that," ***they say, "We found our fathers doing it*** and we are imitating them ***and Allah commanded us to do it too." Say*** to them***: "Allah does not command indecency. Do you say about Allah what you do not know*** that He said***?"*** The question is an objection.

29. ***Say: "My Lord has commanded justice. Stand and face Him in every mosque,*** prostrating sincerely, ***and call on Him*** (worship Him) ***making your* dīn *sincerely His*** and freeing it from any *shirk*. ***As He originated you*** and created you when you were nothing, ***so you will return*** and come back to life in the Resurrection.***"***

30. ***One group*** of you ***He guided; but another group got the misguidance they deserved. They took the* shayṭāns *as friends instead of Allah and thought that they were guided.***

31. ***Children of Ādam! Wear fine clothing*** which will cover your private parts ***in every mosque*** in the prayer and for *ṭawāf* ***and eat and drink*** what you like ***but do not be profligate. He does not love the profligate.***

32. ***Say*** to refute them***: "Who has forbidden the fine clothing provided by Allah and the good*** enjoyable ***kinds of provision He has produced for His slaves?" Say: "On the Day of Rising such things will be exclusively*** an entitlement ***for those who believed during the life of this world." Thus do We mark out the Signs*** and make them clear ***for people who know*** and reflect and thereby benefit from them.

33. ***Say: "My Lord has forbidden indecency*** – major wrong actions like fornication – ***both open and secret, and wrong action*** (disobedience) ***and wrongful tyranny*** towards people, which is injustice***, and associating anything with Allah for which He has sent down no authority*** or evidence, ***and saying about Allah what you do not know*** by making unlawful what is not unlawful and other such things."

34. ***Every nation has an appointed*** period of ***time. When their time comes, they cannot delay it a single hour or bring it forward.***

35. ***Children of Ādam! If Messengers come to you from among you, recounting My Signs to you, those who are godfearing*** and fear *shirk* ***and put things right*** by righteous action ***will feel no fear and know no sorrow*** in the Next World.

36. ***But as for those who reject Our Signs and are arrogant regarding them*** and do not believe in them, ***they are the Companions of the Fire, remaining in it timelessly, forever.***

37. ***Who*** (no one) ***could do greater wrong than someone who invents lies against Allah*** by ascribing a partner and child to Him, ***or denies His Signs*** (the Qur'an)***? Such people's portion of the Book*** – that which is written on the Preserved Tablet concerning their provision, their lifespan and other such things – ***will catch up with them so that when Our messengers*** (the angels) ***come to them to take them in death, saying*** in rebuke, ***"Where are those you called upon*** and worshipped ***besides Allah?" they will say, "They have forsaken us*** and vanished," ***testifying against themselves*** when they die ***that they were unbelievers.***

38. On the Day of Rising ***He*** (Allah) ***will say, "Enter into the Fire together with the nations of jinn and men who have passed away before you." Each time a nation enters*** the Fire, ***it will curse its sis -***

عَذَابًا ضِعْفًا مِّنَ ٱلنَّارِ ۖ قَالَ لِكُلٍّ ضِعْفٌ وَلَـٰكِن لَّا تَعْلَمُونَ ﴿٣٨﴾
وَقَالَتْ أُولَىٰهُمْ لِأُخْرَىٰهُمْ فَمَا كَانَ لَكُمْ عَلَيْنَا مِن فَضْلٍ
فَذُوقُوا۟ ٱلْعَذَابَ بِمَا كُنتُمْ تَكْسِبُونَ ﴿٣٩﴾ إِنَّ ٱلَّذِينَ كَذَّبُوا۟
بِـَٔايَـٰتِنَا وَٱسْتَكْبَرُوا۟ عَنْهَا لَا تُفَتَّحُ لَهُمْ أَبْوَٰبُ ٱلسَّمَآءِ وَلَا يَدْخُلُونَ
ٱلْجَنَّةَ حَتَّىٰ يَلِجَ ٱلْجَمَلُ فِى سَمِّ ٱلْخِيَاطِ ۚ وَكَذَٰلِكَ نَجْزِى
ٱلْمُجْرِمِينَ ﴿٤٠﴾ لَهُم مِّن جَهَنَّمَ مِهَادٌ وَمِن فَوْقِهِمْ غَوَاشٍ ۚ
وَكَذَٰلِكَ نَجْزِى ٱلظَّـٰلِمِينَ ﴿٤١﴾ وَٱلَّذِينَ ءَامَنُوا۟ وَعَمِلُوا۟
ٱلصَّـٰلِحَـٰتِ لَا نُكَلِّفُ نَفْسًا إِلَّا وُسْعَهَآ أُو۟لَـٰٓئِكَ أَصْحَـٰبُ
ٱلْجَنَّةِ ۖ هُمْ فِيهَا خَـٰلِدُونَ ﴿٤٢﴾ وَنَزَعْنَا مَا فِى صُدُورِهِم مِّنْ غِلٍّ
تَجْرِى مِن تَحْتِهِمُ ٱلْأَنْهَـٰرُ ۖ وَقَالُوا۟ ٱلْحَمْدُ لِلَّهِ ٱلَّذِى هَدَىٰنَا لِهَـٰذَا
وَمَا كُنَّا لِنَهْتَدِىَ لَوْلَآ أَنْ هَدَىٰنَا ٱللَّهُ ۖ لَقَدْ جَآءَتْ رُسُلُ رَبِّنَا بِٱلْحَقِّ ۖ
وَنُودُوٓا۟ أَن تِلْكُمُ ٱلْجَنَّةُ أُورِثْتُمُوهَا بِمَا كُنتُمْ تَعْمَلُونَ ﴿٤٣﴾
وَنَادَىٰٓ أَصْحَـٰبُ ٱلْجَنَّةِ أَصْحَـٰبَ ٱلنَّارِ أَن قَدْ وَجَدْنَا مَا وَعَدَنَا رَبُّنَا حَقًّا
فَهَلْ وَجَدتُّم مَّا وَعَدَ رَبُّكُمْ حَقًّا ۖ قَالُوا۟ نَعَمْ ۚ فَأَذَّنَ مُؤَذِّنٌۢ بَيْنَهُمْ أَن
لَّعْنَةُ ٱللَّهِ عَلَى ٱلظَّـٰلِمِينَ ﴿٤٤﴾ ٱلَّذِينَ يَصُدُّونَ عَن سَبِيلِ ٱللَّهِ وَيَبْغُونَهَا
عِوَجًا وَهُم بِٱلْـَٔاخِرَةِ كَـٰفِرُونَ ﴿٤٥﴾ وَبَيْنَهُمَا حِجَابٌ ۚ وَعَلَى ٱلْأَعْرَافِ
رِجَالٌ يَعْرِفُونَ كُلًّۢا بِسِيمَىٰهُمْ ۚ وَنَادَوْا۟ أَصْحَـٰبَ ٱلْجَنَّةِ أَن سَلَـٰمٌ عَلَيْكُمْ ۚ
لَمْ يَدْخُلُوهَا وَهُمْ يَطْمَعُونَ ﴿٤٦﴾ ۞ وَإِذَا صُرِفَتْ أَبْصَـٰرُهُمْ تِلْقَآءَ
أَصْحَـٰبِ ٱلنَّارِ قَالُوا۟ رَبَّنَا لَا تَجْعَلْنَا مَعَ ٱلْقَوْمِ ٱلظَّـٰلِمِينَ ﴿٤٧﴾ وَنَادَىٰٓ أَصْحَـٰبُ
ٱلْأَعْرَافِ رِجَالًا يَعْرِفُونَهُم بِسِيمَىٰهُمْ قَالُوا۟ مَآ أَغْنَىٰ عَنكُمْ جَمْعُكُمْ
وَمَا كُنتُمْ تَسْتَكْبِرُونَ ﴿٤٨﴾ أَهَـٰٓؤُلَآءِ ٱلَّذِينَ أَقْسَمْتُمْ لَا يَنَالُهُمُ
ٱللَّهُ بِرَحْمَةٍ ۚ ٱدْخُلُوا۟ ٱلْجَنَّةَ لَا خَوْفٌ عَلَيْكُمْ وَلَآ أَنتُمْ تَحْزَنُونَ

ter nation before it which had misled it ***until, when they are all gathered together in it*** and meet one another, ***the last of them*** who followed the earlier peoples ***will say to the first of them*** who were followed ***"Our Lord, those are the ones who misguided us, so give them a double punishment in the Fire." He*** (Allah) ***will say, "Each will have double*** punishmen; ***but you do not know*** (read as *ta'lamū - na* and *ya'lamūna*, "they will not know")." Neither group knows.

39. ***The first of them will say to the last of them, "You are in no way superior to us*** because you disbelieved on account of us, so you and us are the same." Allah will say to them: "***So taste the punish - ment for what you earned."***

40. ***As for those who deny Our Signs and are arrogant regarding them*** and do not believe in them, ***the Gates of Heaven will not be opened for them*** when they ascend with their spirits after death and they will fall into Sijjīn, whereas they will be opened for the believers and they will ascend with their spirits to the seventh heaven, as reported in *ḥadīth*; ***and they will not enter the Garden until a camel goes through a needle's eye.*** Since that is not possible, it means that their entering the Garden is equally impossible. ***That is how We repay the evil-doers*** for their unbelief.

41. ***They will have Hell as a resting-place and covering layers*** of fire ***on top of them. That is how We repay the wrongdoers.***

42. ***As for those who believe and do right actions – We charge no self beyond what it can bear***: its capacity in respect of action. This is an interpolation – ***they are the Companions of the Garden, remain - ing in it timelessly, forever.***

43. ***We will strip away all rancour in their breasts*** – all the malice between them in this world. ***Rivers will flow under them*** – under their palaces – ***and they will say*** when they are settled in their dwellings there, ***"Praise be to Allah who has guided us to this*** action which had this reward***! We would not have been guided, had Allah not guided us. The Messengers of our Lord came with the Truth." It will be proclaimed to them: "This is your Garden which you have inherited for what you did."***

44. ***The Companions of the Garden will call out to the Companions of the Fire*** in confirmation or rebuke, ***"We have found what***

(the reward) ***our Lord promised us to be true. Have you found what*** (the punishment) ***your Lord promised you to be true?" They will say, "Yes!" Between them*** (the two groups) ***a herald will proclaim: "May the curse of Allah be on the wrongdoers…***

45. ***…those who bar*** people ***access to the Way of Allah*** (the *dīn*) ***desiring to make it*** (the Path) ***crooked, and reject the Next World."***

46. ***There will be a dividing wall*** – a barrier, said to be the wall of the Ramparts (*al-A'rāf*), after which the *sūra* is named – ***between them*** (the people of the Garden and the Fire), ***and on the ramparts*** (the wall of the Garden) ***there will be men*** whose good actions and evil actions are equally balanced, as mentioned in *ḥadīth*, and ***who recognise everyone*** (the people of the Garden and the Fire) ***by their mark***, which will be the brightness of the faces of the believers and the darkness of those of the unbelievers when they see them from a high place. ***They will call out to the people of the Garden: "Peace be upon you!"*** Allah says: ***They*** (the People on the Ramparts) ***will not enter it*** (the Garden) ***despite their ardent desire*** to do so. Al-Ḥākim related that Ḥudhayfa said, "That is how it will be when your Lord looks on them. He will say, "Get up and enter the Garden. I have forgiven you."

47. ***When they*** (the People on the Ramparts) ***turn their eyes towards the Companions of the Fire, they will say, "Our Lord, do not place us*** in the Fire ***with the people of the wrongdoers!"***

48. ***The Companions of the Ramparts will call out to men they recognise by their mark*** – men who are among the people of the Fire – ***saying, "What you amassed*** of wealth or its abundance ***was of no use to you*** against the Fire, ***nor was your arrogance*** about faith. They will then say to them, pointing at the weak Muslims:

49. ***Are these the people you swore that Allah's mercy would never reach?"*** It will be said to those Muslims, ***"Enter the Garden. You will feel no fear and know no sorrow."***

50. ***The Companions of the Fire will call out to the Companions of the Garden, "Pour down some water to us, or some of what Allah has given you as provision*** to eat." ***They will say, "Allah has forbidden both of them to the unbelievers:***

﴿٤٩﴾ وَنَادَىٰٓ أَصۡحَٰبُ ٱلنَّارِ أَصۡحَٰبَ ٱلۡجَنَّةِ أَنۡ أَفِيضُواْ عَلَيۡنَا
مِنَ ٱلۡمَآءِ أَوۡ مِمَّا رَزَقَكُمُ ٱللَّهُۚ قَالُوٓاْ إِنَّ ٱللَّهَ حَرَّمَهُمَا عَلَى
ٱلۡكَٰفِرِينَ ﴿٥٠﴾ ٱلَّذِينَ ٱتَّخَذُواْ دِينَهُمۡ لَهۡوٗا وَلَعِبٗا
وَغَرَّتۡهُمُ ٱلۡحَيَوٰةُ ٱلدُّنۡيَاۚ فَٱلۡيَوۡمَ نَنسَىٰهُمۡ كَمَا نَسُواْ
لِقَآءَ يَوۡمِهِمۡ هَٰذَا وَمَا كَانُواْ بِـَٔايَٰتِنَا يَجۡحَدُونَ ﴿٥١﴾
وَلَقَدۡ جِئۡنَٰهُم بِكِتَٰبٖ فَصَّلۡنَٰهُ عَلَىٰ عِلۡمٍ هُدٗى وَرَحۡمَةٗ لِّقَوۡمٖ
يُؤۡمِنُونَ ﴿٥٢﴾ هَلۡ يَنظُرُونَ إِلَّا تَأۡوِيلَهُۥۚ يَوۡمَ يَأۡتِي تَأۡوِيلُهُۥ يَقُولُ
ٱلَّذِينَ نَسُوهُ مِن قَبۡلُ قَدۡ جَآءَتۡ رُسُلُ رَبِّنَا بِٱلۡحَقِّ فَهَل لَّنَا
مِن شُفَعَآءَ فَيَشۡفَعُواْ لَنَآ أَوۡ نُرَدُّ فَنَعۡمَلَ غَيۡرَ ٱلَّذِي كُنَّا نَعۡمَلُۚ
قَدۡ خَسِرُوٓاْ أَنفُسَهُمۡ وَضَلَّ عَنۡهُم مَّا كَانُواْ يَفۡتَرُونَ ﴿٥٣﴾
إِنَّ رَبَّكُمُ ٱللَّهُ ٱلَّذِي خَلَقَ ٱلسَّمَٰوَٰتِ وَٱلۡأَرۡضَ فِي سِتَّةِ
أَيَّامٖ ثُمَّ ٱسۡتَوَىٰ عَلَى ٱلۡعَرۡشِ يُغۡشِي ٱلَّيۡلَ ٱلنَّهَارَ يَطۡلُبُهُۥ حَثِيثٗا
وَٱلشَّمۡسَ وَٱلۡقَمَرَ وَٱلنُّجُومَ مُسَخَّرَٰتِۭ بِأَمۡرِهِۦٓۗ أَلَا لَهُ ٱلۡخَلۡقُ
وَٱلۡأَمۡرُۗ تَبَارَكَ ٱللَّهُ رَبُّ ٱلۡعَٰلَمِينَ ﴿٥٤﴾ ٱدۡعُواْ رَبَّكُمۡ تَضَرُّعٗا
وَخُفۡيَةًۚ إِنَّهُۥ لَا يُحِبُّ ٱلۡمُعۡتَدِينَ ﴿٥٥﴾ وَلَا تُفۡسِدُواْ فِي
ٱلۡأَرۡضِ بَعۡدَ إِصۡلَٰحِهَا وَٱدۡعُوهُ خَوۡفٗا وَطَمَعًاۚ إِنَّ رَحۡمَتَ
ٱللَّهِ قَرِيبٞ مِّنَ ٱلۡمُحۡسِنِينَ ﴿٥٦﴾ وَهُوَ ٱلَّذِي يُرۡسِلُ
ٱلرِّيَٰحَ بُشۡرَۢا بَيۡنَ يَدَيۡ رَحۡمَتِهِۦۖ حَتَّىٰٓ إِذَآ أَقَلَّتۡ سَحَابٗا
ثِقَالٗا سُقۡنَٰهُ لِبَلَدٖ مَّيِّتٖ فَأَنزَلۡنَا بِهِ ٱلۡمَآءَ فَأَخۡرَجۡنَا بِهِۦ مِن كُلِّ
ٱلثَّمَرَٰتِۚ كَذَٰلِكَ نُخۡرِجُ ٱلۡمَوۡتَىٰ لَعَلَّكُمۡ تَذَكَّرُونَ ﴿٥٧﴾
وَٱلۡبَلَدُ ٱلطَّيِّبُ يَخۡرُجُ نَبَاتُهُۥ بِإِذۡنِ رَبِّهِۦۖ وَٱلَّذِي خَبُثَ لَا يَخۡرُجُ
إِلَّا نَكِدٗاۚ كَذَٰلِكَ نُصَرِّفُ ٱلۡأٓيَٰتِ لِقَوۡمٖ يَشۡكُرُونَ ﴿٥٨﴾

51. ***those who took their* dīn *as a diversion and a game, and were deluded by the life of this world." Today We will forget them*** and leave them in the Fire ***just as they forgot the encounter of this Day*** by failing to act for it, ***and refuted Our Signs*** and denied them.

52. ***We have brought them*** (the people of Makka) ***a Book*** (the Qur'ān), ***elucidating everything with knowledge*** – making things clear in terms of information, warning and promises – ***as a guidance and a mercy for people who believe*** in it.

53. ***What are they waiting for but its fulfilment*** – the actualisation of what it contains? ***The Day*** (the Day of Rising) ***its fulfilment occurs, those who forgot it before and*** neglected belief ***will say, "The Messengers of our Lord came with the Truth. Are there any intercessors to intercede for us, or can we be sent back*** to the world, ***so that we ma do something other than what we did***, by affirming Allah's unity and abandoning idolatry?" They will be told, "No, you cannot." Allah Almighty says: ***They have lost their own selves*** since they have gone to destruction ***and what they fabricated*** – the partners with Allah they claimed to exist – ***has forsaken them.***

54. ***Your Lord is Allah, Who created the heavens and the earth in six days*** – referring to the length of time involved, because days as we know them did not yet exist. Then Allah created the sun. If Allah had so willed, He could have created everything in a moment; but He did not do that, in order to instruct His creation to do things step by step – ***and then settled Himself firmly on the Throne.*** (Throne (*'arsh*) linguistically means the seat on which a King sits. To "settle on" (*istawa'*) means "to come into contact with:) ***He covers*** (read as *yughshi* and *yughashsha)* ***the day with the night*** – each covering the other – ***each pursuing the other urgently*** – each seeking the other, ***and the sun and moon and stars are subservient to His command*** and power. ***Truly both*** all ***creation and*** the entire ***command belong to Him. Blessed be Allah, the Lord of all the worlds.***

55. ***Call on your Lord humbly and secretly. He does not love those who overstep the limits*** by making supplication with affectation and raising their voices.

56. ***Do not corrupt the earth*** by acts of disobedience and idolatry ***after it has been put right*** after the Messengers have been sent. ***Call***

لَقَدۡ أَرۡسَلۡنَا نُوحًا إِلَىٰ قَوۡمِهِۦ فَقَالَ يَٰقَوۡمِ ٱعۡبُدُواْ ٱللَّهَ مَا لَكُم
مِّنۡ إِلَٰهٍ غَيۡرُهُۥٓ إِنِّيٓ أَخَافُ عَلَيۡكُمۡ عَذَابَ يَوۡمٍ عَظِيمٖ ٥٩
قَالَ ٱلۡمَلَأُ مِن قَوۡمِهِۦٓ إِنَّا لَنَرَىٰكَ فِي ضَلَٰلٖ مُّبِينٖ ٦٠ قَالَ
يَٰقَوۡمِ لَيۡسَ بِي ضَلَٰلَةٞ وَلَٰكِنِّي رَسُولٞ مِّن رَّبِّ ٱلۡعَٰلَمِينَ
٦١ أُبَلِّغُكُمۡ رِسَٰلَٰتِ رَبِّي وَأَنصَحُ لَكُمۡ وَأَعۡلَمُ مِنَ ٱللَّهِ
مَا لَا تَعۡلَمُونَ ٦٢ أَوَعَجِبۡتُمۡ أَن جَآءَكُمۡ ذِكۡرٞ مِّن رَّبِّكُمۡ عَلَىٰ
رَجُلٖ مِّنكُمۡ لِيُنذِرَكُمۡ وَلِتَتَّقُواْ وَلَعَلَّكُمۡ تُرۡحَمُونَ ٦٣ فَكَذَّبُوهُ
فَأَنجَيۡنَٰهُ وَٱلَّذِينَ مَعَهُۥ فِي ٱلۡفُلۡكِ وَأَغۡرَقۡنَا ٱلَّذِينَ كَذَّبُواْ
بِـَٔايَٰتِنَآۚ إِنَّهُمۡ كَانُواْ قَوۡمًا عَمِينَ ٦٤ ۞ وَإِلَىٰ عَادٍ أَخَاهُمۡ
هُودٗاۚ قَالَ يَٰقَوۡمِ ٱعۡبُدُواْ ٱللَّهَ مَا لَكُم مِّنۡ إِلَٰهٍ غَيۡرُهُۥٓۚ أَفَلَا تَتَّقُونَ
٦٥ قَالَ ٱلۡمَلَأُ ٱلَّذِينَ كَفَرُواْ مِن قَوۡمِهِۦٓ إِنَّا لَنَرَىٰكَ فِي
سَفَاهَةٖ وَإِنَّا لَنَظُنُّكَ مِنَ ٱلۡكَٰذِبِينَ ٦٦ قَالَ يَٰقَوۡمِ
لَيۡسَ بِي سَفَاهَةٞ وَلَٰكِنِّي رَسُولٞ مِّن رَّبِّ ٱلۡعَٰلَمِينَ ٦٧
أُبَلِّغُكُمۡ رِسَٰلَٰتِ رَبِّي وَأَنَا۠ لَكُمۡ نَاصِحٌ أَمِينٌ ٦٨ أَوَعَجِبۡتُمۡ
أَن جَآءَكُمۡ ذِكۡرٞ مِّن رَّبِّكُمۡ عَلَىٰ رَجُلٖ مِّنكُمۡ لِيُنذِرَكُمۡۚ
وَٱذۡكُرُوٓاْ إِذۡ جَعَلَكُمۡ خُلَفَآءَ مِنۢ بَعۡدِ قَوۡمِ نُوحٖ وَزَادَكُمۡ
فِي ٱلۡخَلۡقِ بَصۜۡطَةٗۖ فَٱذۡكُرُوٓاْ ءَالَآءَ ٱللَّهِ لَعَلَّكُمۡ تُفۡلِحُونَ
٦٩ قَالُوٓاْ أَجِئۡتَنَا لِنَعۡبُدَ ٱللَّهَ وَحۡدَهُۥ وَنَذَرَ مَا كَانَ
يَعۡبُدُ ءَابَآؤُنَاۖ فَأۡتِنَا بِمَا تَعِدُنَآ إِن كُنتَ مِنَ ٱلصَّٰدِقِينَ
٧٠ قَالَ قَدۡ وَقَعَ عَلَيۡكُم مِّن رَّبِّكُمۡ رِجۡسٞ وَغَضَبٌۖ
أَتُجَٰدِلُونَنِي فِيٓ أَسۡمَآءٖ سَمَّيۡتُمُوهَآ أَنتُمۡ وَءَابَآؤُكُم
مَّا نَزَّلَ ٱللَّهُ بِهَا مِن سُلۡطَٰنٖۚ فَٱنتَظِرُوٓاْ إِنِّي مَعَكُم مِّنَ

on Him fearfully, fearing His punishment, ***and eagerly***, desiring His mercy. ***Allah's mercy is close to the good-doers*** those who obey Him.

57. *It He is who sends out the winds, bringing advance news* (read here as *bushran*. Other readings have *nushran*, *nashran*, and *nushu - ran*, all of which have a meaning of spreading) ***of His mercy,*** separately, ahead of the rain, ***so that when they*** (the winds) ***have lifted up the heavy clouds*** – heavy with rain – ***We dispatch them*** (the clouds) ***to a dead land*** with no plants growing in it, in order to bring it to life, ***and send down water to it*** (the land), ***by means of which*** (water) ***We bring forth all kinds of fruit. In the same way We will bring forth the dead*** from their graves at the Resurrection, ***so that perhaps you may pay heed*** and believe.

58. *Good land* (fertile soil) ***gives forth its*** good ***plants by the per - mission of its Lord*** – a metaphor for a believer who hears the warning and benefits by it – ***but that*** (land) ***which is bad only gives forth*** plants ***meagrely***, with great difficulty: a metaphor for an unbeliever. ***Thus*** – in the same way that We have made this clear – ***do We vary*** and make clear ***the Signs for a people who are thankful*** to Allah and believe.

59. *We sent Nūḥ to his people and he said, 'My people, worship Allah! You have no other god than Him.* If you worship other than Him, ***I fear for you the punishment of a dreadful Day*** (the Day of Rising).***'***

60. *The ruling circle of his people* (the nobles) ***said, 'We see you in flagrant*** clear ***error.'***

61. *He said, 'My people, I am not in error at all* (the word *ḍalāla* is more general than the usual word *ḍalāl*, and so it is an even more emphatic denial) ***but rather am a Messenger from the Lord of all the worlds…***

62. *…transmitting* (read as *uballighukum* and *ublighukum*) ***my Lord's Message to you and giving you good counsel*** – desiring good for you – ***and I know from Allah what you do not know.***

63. *Or* do you deny and ***are you astonished that a reminder*** and admonition ***should come to you from your Lord by way of*** the tongue of ***a man among you, to warn you*** about the punishment if you do not believe ***and make you have*** **taqwā** of Allah, ***so that perhaps you may gain mercy*** by that***?'***

64. ***But they denied him so We rescued him and those with him*** from drowning ***in the Ark. And We drowned the people who denied Our Signs*** by means of the Flood***. They were a blind people*** – blind to the truth.

65. ***And to 'Ād We sent their brother Hūd, who said, 'My people, worship Allah*** and affirm His unity***! You have no other god than Him. So will you not be godfearing*** and believe***?'***

66. ***The ruling circle of those of his people who were unbelievers said, 'We consider you a fool*** and to be ignorant ***and think you are a liar*** in respect of your message***.'***

67. ***He said, 'My people, I am by no means a fool, but rather am a Messenger from the Lord of all the worlds…***

68. ***…transmitting my Lord's Message to you, and I am a faithful counsellor to you***, entrusted with this Message to you.

69. ***Or are you astonished that a reminder should come to you from your Lord by way of*** the tongue of ***a man among you in order to warn you? Remember when He appointed you successors*** in the earth ***to the people of Nūḥ, and increased you greatly in stature*** – in respect of both strength and height. The tallest of them was a hundred cubits and the shortest was sixty cubits. ***Remember Allah's blessings, so that perhaps you will be successful.'***

70. ***They said, 'Have you come to us to make us worship Allah alone and abandon what our fathers used to worship? Then bring us what*** (the punishment) ***you have promised us if you are telling the truth.'***

71. ***He said, 'Punishment and anger*** are inevitable and ***have come down on you from your Lord. Do you argue with me regarding names which you and your forefathers invented*** – a reference to the idols which they worship – ***and for which Allah has sent down no authority*** or evidence***? Wait, then***, for the punishment***; I am waiting with you*** for it because of your denial of me***.'*** So the barren wind was released against them.

72. ***Then We rescued him*** (Hūd) ***and those*** believers ***with him by mercy from Us, and We cut off the last remnant*** of the people ***of***

ٱلْمُنتَظِرِينَ ﴿٧١﴾ فَأَنجَيْنَٰهُ وَٱلَّذِينَ مَعَهُۥ بِرَحْمَةٍ مِّنَّا
وَقَطَعْنَا دَابِرَ ٱلَّذِينَ كَذَّبُوا۟ بِـَٔايَٰتِنَا ۖ وَمَا كَانُوا۟ مُؤْمِنِينَ
﴿٧٢﴾ وَإِلَىٰ ثَمُودَ أَخَاهُمْ صَٰلِحًا ۗ قَالَ يَٰقَوْمِ ٱعْبُدُوا۟ ٱللَّهَ
مَا لَكُم مِّنْ إِلَٰهٍ غَيْرُهُۥ ۖ قَدْ جَآءَتْكُم بَيِّنَةٌ مِّن
رَّبِّكُمْ ۖ هَٰذِهِۦ نَاقَةُ ٱللَّهِ لَكُمْ ءَايَةً ۖ فَذَرُوهَا تَأْكُلْ
فِىٓ أَرْضِ ٱللَّهِ ۖ وَلَا تَمَسُّوهَا بِسُوٓءٍ فَيَأْخُذَكُمْ عَذَابٌ أَلِيمٌ ﴿٧٣﴾
وَٱذْكُرُوٓا۟ إِذْ جَعَلَكُمْ خُلَفَآءَ مِنۢ بَعْدِ عَادٍ وَبَوَّأَكُمْ
فِى ٱلْأَرْضِ تَتَّخِذُونَ مِن سُهُولِهَا قُصُورًا وَتَنْحِتُونَ
ٱلْجِبَالَ بُيُوتًا ۖ فَٱذْكُرُوٓا۟ ءَالَآءَ ٱللَّهِ وَلَا تَعْثَوْا۟ فِى ٱلْأَرْضِ
مُفْسِدِينَ ﴿٧٤﴾ قَالَ ٱلْمَلَأُ ٱلَّذِينَ ٱسْتَكْبَرُوا۟ مِن
قَوْمِهِۦ لِلَّذِينَ ٱسْتُضْعِفُوا۟ لِمَنْ ءَامَنَ مِنْهُمْ أَتَعْلَمُونَ
أَنَّ صَٰلِحًا مُّرْسَلٌ مِّن رَّبِّهِۦ ۚ قَالُوٓا۟ إِنَّا بِمَآ أُرْسِلَ بِهِۦ
مُؤْمِنُونَ ﴿٧٥﴾ قَالَ ٱلَّذِينَ ٱسْتَكْبَرُوٓا۟ إِنَّا بِٱلَّذِىٓ
ءَامَنتُم بِهِۦ كَٰفِرُونَ ﴿٧٦﴾ فَعَقَرُوا۟ ٱلنَّاقَةَ وَعَتَوْا۟ عَنْ
أَمْرِ رَبِّهِمْ وَقَالُوا۟ يَٰصَٰلِحُ ٱئْتِنَا بِمَا تَعِدُنَآ إِن كُنتَ مِنَ
ٱلْمُرْسَلِينَ ﴿٧٧﴾ فَأَخَذَتْهُمُ ٱلرَّجْفَةُ فَأَصْبَحُوا۟ فِى دَارِهِمْ
جَٰثِمِينَ ﴿٧٨﴾ فَتَوَلَّىٰ عَنْهُمْ وَقَالَ يَٰقَوْمِ لَقَدْ أَبْلَغْتُكُمْ
رِسَالَةَ رَبِّى وَنَصَحْتُ لَكُمْ وَلَٰكِن لَّا تُحِبُّونَ ٱلنَّٰصِحِينَ
﴿٧٩﴾ وَلُوطًا إِذْ قَالَ لِقَوْمِهِۦٓ أَتَأْتُونَ ٱلْفَٰحِشَةَ مَا سَبَقَكُم
بِهَا مِنْ أَحَدٍ مِّنَ ٱلْعَٰلَمِينَ ﴿٨٠﴾ إِنَّكُمْ لَتَأْتُونَ ٱلرِّجَالَ
شَهْوَةً مِّن دُونِ ٱلنِّسَآءِ ۚ بَلْ أَنتُمْ قَوْمٌ مُّسْرِفُونَ ﴿٨١﴾
وَمَا كَانَ جَوَابَ قَوْمِهِۦٓ إِلَّآ أَن قَالُوٓا۟ أَخْرِجُوهُم مِّن

those who denied Our Signs and were not believers and We eradicated them.

73. ***And to*** the tribe of ***Thamūd We sent their brother Ṣāliḥ, who said, 'My people, worship Allah! You have no other god than Him. A Clear Sign*** (miracle) ***has come to you from your Lord*** which indicates my truthfulness. ***This is the She-Camel of Allah as a Sign for you***, they asked him to produce a camel out of a rock: which they saw with their own eyes. ***Leave her alone to eat on Allah's earth and do not harm her in any way*** by hamstringing or striking her ***or a painful punishment will afflict you.***

74. ***Remember when He appointed you successors*** in the earth ***to 'Ād and settled you in the land. You built palaces on its plains*** in which you lived in the summer ***and carved out houses from the mountains*** in which you lived in the winter. ***Remember Allah's blessings and do not go about the earth, corrupting it.'***

75. ***The ruling circle of those of his people who were*** too ***arrogant*** to believe ***said to those*** of his people ***who were oppressed – those among them who had believed – 'Do you know that Ṣāliḥ has been sent*** to you ***from his Lord?' They said, 'We believe in what he has been sent with.'***

76. ***Those who were arrogant said, 'We reject Him in whom you believe.'***

77. The She-Camel and they had alternate days at the water. They became fed up with that ***and they hamstrung the She-camel*** – Quddūr killed it at their command by slaughtering it with a sword – ***spurning their Lord's command, and said, 'Ṣāliḥ! Bring us what*** (the punishment for killing it) ***you have promised us if you are one of the Messengers.'***

78. ***So the earthquake*** – the word used, *rajfa,* means a strong earthquake accompanied by a Shout from heaven – ***seized them and morning found them*** dead, ***lying flattened in their homes.***

79. ***He*** (Ṣāliḥ) ***turned away from them and said, 'My people, I transmitted my Lord's message to you and gave you good counsel. Yet you do not like good counsellors!'***

قَرۡيَتِكُمۡۖ إِنَّهُمۡ أُنَاسٞ يَتَطَهَّرُونَ ﴿٨٢﴾ فَأَنجَيۡنَٰهُ وَأَهۡلَهُۥٓ
إِلَّا ٱمۡرَأَتَهُۥ كَانَتۡ مِنَ ٱلۡغَٰبِرِينَ ﴿٨٣﴾ وَأَمۡطَرۡنَا عَلَيۡهِم
مَّطَرٗاۖ فَٱنظُرۡ كَيۡفَ كَانَ عَٰقِبَةُ ٱلۡمُجۡرِمِينَ ﴿٨٤﴾
وَإِلَىٰ مَدۡيَنَ أَخَاهُمۡ شُعَيۡبٗاۗ قَالَ يَٰقَوۡمِ ٱعۡبُدُواْ ٱللَّهَ
مَا لَكُم مِّنۡ إِلَٰهٍ غَيۡرُهُۥۖ قَدۡ جَآءَتۡكُم بَيِّنَةٞ مِّن
رَّبِّكُمۡۖ فَأَوۡفُواْ ٱلۡكَيۡلَ وَٱلۡمِيزَانَ وَلَا تَبۡخَسُواْ
ٱلنَّاسَ أَشۡيَآءَهُمۡ وَلَا تُفۡسِدُواْ فِي ٱلۡأَرۡضِ بَعۡدَ
إِصۡلَٰحِهَاۚ ذَٰلِكُمۡ خَيۡرٞ لَّكُمۡ إِن كُنتُم مُّؤۡمِنِينَ
﴿٨٥﴾ وَلَا تَقۡعُدُواْ بِكُلِّ صِرَٰطٖ تُوعِدُونَ وَتَصُدُّونَ
عَن سَبِيلِ ٱللَّهِ مَنۡ ءَامَنَ بِهِۦ وَتَبۡغُونَهَا عِوَجٗاۚ
وَٱذۡكُرُوٓاْ إِذۡ كُنتُمۡ قَلِيلٗا فَكَثَّرَكُمۡۖ وَٱنظُرُواْ
كَيۡفَ كَانَ عَٰقِبَةُ ٱلۡمُفۡسِدِينَ ﴿٨٦﴾ وَإِن كَانَ طَآئِفَةٞ
مِّنكُمۡ ءَامَنُواْ بِٱلَّذِيٓ أُرۡسِلۡتُ بِهِۦ وَطَآئِفَةٞ لَّمۡ يُؤۡمِنُواْ
فَٱصۡبِرُواْ حَتَّىٰ يَحۡكُمَ ٱللَّهُ بَيۡنَنَاۚ وَهُوَ خَيۡرُ ٱلۡحَٰكِمِينَ ﴿٨٧﴾
۞ قَالَ ٱلۡمَلَأُ ٱلَّذِينَ ٱسۡتَكۡبَرُواْ مِن قَوۡمِهِۦ لَنُخۡرِجَنَّكَ يَٰشُعَيۡبُ
وَٱلَّذِينَ ءَامَنُواْ مَعَكَ مِن قَرۡيَتِنَآ أَوۡ لَتَعُودُنَّ فِي مِلَّتِنَاۚ قَالَ أَوَلَوۡ
كُنَّا كَٰرِهِينَ ﴿٨٨﴾ قَدِ ٱفۡتَرَيۡنَا عَلَى ٱللَّهِ كَذِبًا إِنۡ عُدۡنَا فِي مِلَّتِكُم
بَعۡدَ إِذۡ نَجَّىٰنَا ٱللَّهُ مِنۡهَاۚ وَمَا يَكُونُ لَنَآ أَن نَّعُودَ فِيهَآ إِلَّآ أَن يَشَآءَ
ٱللَّهُ رَبُّنَاۚ وَسِعَ رَبُّنَا كُلَّ شَيۡءٍ عِلۡمًاۚ عَلَى ٱللَّهِ تَوَكَّلۡنَاۚ رَبَّنَا ٱفۡتَحۡ
بَيۡنَنَا وَبَيۡنَ قَوۡمِنَا بِٱلۡحَقِّ وَأَنتَ خَيۡرُ ٱلۡفَٰتِحِينَ ﴿٨٩﴾ وَقَالَ ٱلۡمَلَأُ

80. ***And*** remember ***Lūṭ, when he said to his people, 'Do you commit an obscenity*** (sodomy with men) ***not perpetrated before you by anyone in all the worlds*** – either among jinn or men***?***

81. ***You*** (prefaced by *innakum* in one reading and *a-innakum* in another, the latter turning the statement into a question) ***come with lust to men instead of women. You are indeed a depraved people***, going beyond the lawful into the unlawful.*'*

82. ***The only answer of his people was to say, 'Expel them*** (Lūṭ and his followers) ***from your city! They are people who keep themselves pure*** from the practice of sodomy!'

83. ***So We rescued him and his family – except for his wife. She was one of those who stayed behind*** for the punishment.

84. ***We rained down a rain*** of baked stones ***upon them*** which destroyed them. ***See the final fate of the evildoers!***

85. ***And to Madyan We sent their brother Shu'ayb, who said, 'My people, worship Allah! You have no other god than Him. A Clear Sign*** – a miracle showing his truthfulness – ***has come to you from your Lord. Give full measure and full weight. Do not diminish people's goods. Do not cause corruption in the land*** by disbelief and acts of disobedience ***after it has been put right*** by the sending of the previous Messengers. ***That is better for you, if you are believers***, so become believers immediately.

86. ***Do not lie in wait on every pathway, threatening people*** – terrorising people by stealing their clothing and taxing them – ***barring those who believe from the Way of Allah***, turning people away from the *dīn* by threatening to kill them, ***desiring to make it*** (the Path) ***crooked. Remember when you were few and He increased your number: see the final fate of the corrupters!*** See how the corrupters denied their Messengers, and their final fate was that they were utterly destroyed.

87. ***There is a group of you who believe in what I have been sent with and a group who do not, so be steadfast until Allah judges between us*** by upholding the truth and destroying falsehood. ***He is the best*** and most just ***of judges.'***

88. ***The ruling circle of those of his people who were*** too ***arrogant*** to believe ***said, 'We will drive you out of our city, Shu'ayb, you and***

ٱلَّذِينَ كَفَرُوا۟ مِن قَوْمِهِۦ لَئِنِ ٱتَّبَعْتُمْ شُعَيْبًا إِنَّكُمْ إِذًا لَّخَـٰسِرُونَ
﴿٩٠﴾ فَأَخَذَتْهُمُ ٱلرَّجْفَةُ فَأَصْبَحُوا۟ فِى دَارِهِمْ جَـٰثِمِينَ ﴿٩١﴾
ٱلَّذِينَ كَذَّبُوا۟ شُعَيْبًا كَأَن لَّمْ يَغْنَوْا۟ فِيهَا ۚ ٱلَّذِينَ كَذَّبُوا۟ شُعَيْبًا
كَانُوا۟ هُمُ ٱلْخَـٰسِرِينَ ﴿٩٢﴾ فَتَوَلَّىٰ عَنْهُمْ وَقَالَ يَـٰقَوْمِ لَقَدْ
أَبْلَغْتُكُمْ رِسَـٰلَـٰتِ رَبِّى وَنَصَحْتُ لَكُمْ ۖ فَكَيْفَ ءَاسَىٰ
عَلَىٰ قَوْمٍ كَـٰفِرِينَ ﴿٩٣﴾ وَمَآ أَرْسَلْنَا فِى قَرْيَةٍ مِّن نَّبِىٍّ إِلَّآ
أَخَذْنَآ أَهْلَهَا بِٱلْبَأْسَآءِ وَٱلضَّرَّآءِ لَعَلَّهُمْ يَضَّرَّعُونَ ﴿٩٤﴾ ثُمَّ
بَدَّلْنَا مَكَانَ ٱلسَّيِّئَةِ ٱلْحَسَنَةَ حَتَّىٰ عَفَوا۟ وَّقَالُوا۟ قَدْ مَسَّ
ءَابَآءَنَا ٱلضَّرَّآءُ وَٱلسَّرَّآءُ فَأَخَذْنَـٰهُم بَغْتَةً وَهُمْ لَا يَشْعُرُونَ ﴿٩٥﴾
وَلَوْ أَنَّ أَهْلَ ٱلْقُرَىٰٓ ءَامَنُوا۟ وَٱتَّقَوْا۟ لَفَتَحْنَا عَلَيْهِم بَرَكَـٰتٍ
مِّنَ ٱلسَّمَآءِ وَٱلْأَرْضِ وَلَـٰكِن كَذَّبُوا۟ فَأَخَذْنَـٰهُم بِمَا كَانُوا۟
يَكْسِبُونَ ﴿٩٦﴾ أَفَأَمِنَ أَهْلُ ٱلْقُرَىٰٓ أَن يَأْتِيَهُم بَأْسُنَا بَيَـٰتًا
وَهُمْ نَآئِمُونَ ﴿٩٧﴾ أَوَأَمِنَ أَهْلُ ٱلْقُرَىٰٓ أَن يَأْتِيَهُم بَأْسُنَا
ضُحًى وَهُمْ يَلْعَبُونَ ﴿٩٨﴾ أَفَأَمِنُوا۟ مَكْرَ ٱللَّهِ ۚ فَلَا يَأْمَنُ
مَكْرَ ٱللَّهِ إِلَّا ٱلْقَوْمُ ٱلْخَـٰسِرُونَ ﴿٩٩﴾ أَوَلَمْ يَهْدِ لِلَّذِينَ
يَرِثُونَ ٱلْأَرْضَ مِنۢ بَعْدِ أَهْلِهَآ أَن لَّوْ نَشَآءُ أَصَبْنَـٰهُم
بِذُنُوبِهِمْ ۚ وَنَطْبَعُ عَلَىٰ قُلُوبِهِمْ فَهُمْ لَا يَسْمَعُونَ ﴿١٠٠﴾
تِلْكَ ٱلْقُرَىٰ نَقُصُّ عَلَيْكَ مِنْ أَنۢبَآئِهَا ۚ وَلَقَدْ جَآءَتْهُمْ رُسُلُهُم
بِٱلْبَيِّنَـٰتِ فَمَا كَانُوا۟ لِيُؤْمِنُوا۟ بِمَا كَذَّبُوا۟ مِن قَبْلُ ۚ
كَذَٰلِكَ يَطْبَعُ ٱللَّهُ عَلَىٰ قُلُوبِ ٱلْكَـٰفِرِينَ ﴿١٠١﴾ وَمَا وَجَدْنَا
لِأَكْثَرِهِم مِّنْ عَهْدٍ ۖ وَإِن وَجَدْنَآ أَكْثَرَهُمْ لَفَـٰسِقِينَ

those who believe along with you, unless you return to our religion.' He said, 'What, even though we detest it? His question implies denial.

89. ***We would be inventing lies against Allah if we returned to your religion after Allah has saved us from it. We could never return to it unless Allah our Lord so willed*** to make us fail. ***Our Lord encompasses everything in His knowledge*** – including His state and their state. ***We have put our trust in Allah. Our Lord, judge between us and our people with truth. You are the best of judges.'***

90. ***The ruling circle of those of his people who disbelieved said*** to one another, ***'If you follow Shu'ayb, you will definitely be lost.'***

91. ***So the*** strong ***earthquake seized them and morning found them*** dead, ***lying flattened in their homes.***

92. ***As for those who denied Shu'ayb, it was as if they had never lived there. It was the people who denied Shu'ayb who were the lost.*** The repetition is intended to add emphasis to the statement.

93. ***So he turned away from them and said, 'My people, I transmitted My Lord's message to you and gave you good counsel*** but you did not believe. ***Why should I grieve for a people of unbelievers?'"*** The question implies a negative answer.

94. ***We have never sent a Prophet to any city without seizing*** and punishing ***its people*** – when they then denied him – ***with hardship*** (extreme poverty) ***and distress***, (illness) ***so that perhaps they would be humble*** and believe.

95. ***Then We gave them good in exchange for evil*** (punishment) ***until they increased in number,*** wealth and health, ***and said,*** in ingratitude for blessings they had received, ***'Our forefathers too underwent both hardship and ease*** in the same way as we have done. This is the mere vicissitudes of time and not punishment from Allah, so continue as you are.' Allah said: ***Then We seized them suddenly*** with the punishment ***when they were not expecting it.***

96. ***If only the people of the cities*** who denied ***had believed*** in Allah and His Messenger ***and been godfearing*** and feared unbelief and rebellion against Allah, ***We would have opened up*** (read as *fataḥnā* and *fattaḥnā*) ***to them blessings from heaven***, in the form of rain, ***and earth***, in the form of plants. ***But they denied the truth*** (the

Messengers)*, so We seized them* and punished them *for what they earned.*

97. ***Do the people of the cities*** who deny ***feel secure against Our violent force*** (punishment) ***coming down on them in the night while they are asleep*** and heedless***?***

98. ***Or do the people of the cities feel secure against Our violent force coming down on them in the day while they are playing games?***

99. ***Do they feel secure against Allah's devising***: His drawing them on by granting them blessings and then seizing them suddenly***? No one feels secure against Allah's devising except for those who are lost.***

100. ***Is it not clear to those who have inherited the earth*** to dwell on it ***after these people that, if We wanted to, We could strike them*** with the punishment ***for their wrong actions,*** as We punished those before them, ***sealing up their hearts so that they cannot hear*** the warning and reflect***?***

101. ***These cities*** which We mentioned – ***We have given you***, Muḥammad, ***news of them*** (their inhabitants)***. Their Messengers came to them with Clear Signs*** (evident miracles) ***but*** when they came to them, ***they were never going to believe in what they had previously disbelieved.*** They would remain with their unbelief. ***That is how Allah seals up the hearts of the disbelievers.***

102. ***We did not find many of them*** (mankind) ***worthy of*** fulfilling ***their contract*** which they agreed to on the day the contract with them was made (see below 7:172)***. We found most of them deviators.***

103. ***And then, after them*** (the Messengers mentioned) ***We sent Mūsā with Our*** nine ***Signs to Pharaoh and his ruling circle*** (his nobles) ***but they wrongfully rejected them. See the final fate of the corrupters***, which was utter destruction on account of their unbelief***!***

104. ***Mūsā said, 'Pharaoh! I am truly a Messenger*** to you ***from the Lord of all the worlds*** – but he rejected him, saying, "I am your Lord" –

105. ***...duty bound*** (read as *'alā* and *'alayya*) ***to say nothing about Allah except the truth. I have come to you with a Clear Sign from***

﴿١٠٢﴾ ثُمَّ بَعَثْنَا مِنۢ بَعْدِهِم مُّوسَىٰ بِـَٔايَٰتِنَآ إِلَىٰ فِرْعَوْنَ وَمَلَإِي۟هِۦ
فَظَلَمُوا۟ بِهَا ۖ فَٱنظُرْ كَيْفَ كَانَ عَٰقِبَةُ ٱلْمُفْسِدِينَ ﴿١٠٣﴾
وَقَالَ مُوسَىٰ يَٰفِرْعَوْنُ إِنِّى رَسُولٌ مِّن رَّبِّ ٱلْعَٰلَمِينَ ﴿١٠٤﴾
حَقِيقٌ عَلَىٰٓ أَن لَّآ أَقُولَ عَلَى ٱللَّهِ إِلَّا ٱلْحَقَّ ۚ قَدْ جِئْتُكُم
بِبَيِّنَةٍ مِّن رَّبِّكُمْ فَأَرْسِلْ مَعِىَ بَنِىٓ إِسْرَٰٓءِيلَ ﴿١٠٥﴾ قَالَ إِن كُنتَ
جِئْتَ بِـَٔايَةٍ فَأْتِ بِهَآ إِن كُنتَ مِنَ ٱلصَّٰدِقِينَ ﴿١٠٦﴾ فَأَلْقَىٰ
عَصَاهُ فَإِذَا هِىَ ثُعْبَانٌ مُّبِينٌ ﴿١٠٧﴾ وَنَزَعَ يَدَهُۥ فَإِذَا هِىَ بَيْضَآءُ
لِلنَّٰظِرِينَ ﴿١٠٨﴾ قَالَ ٱلْمَلَأُ مِن قَوْمِ فِرْعَوْنَ إِنَّ هَٰذَا لَسَٰحِرٌ
عَلِيمٌ ﴿١٠٩﴾ يُرِيدُ أَن يُخْرِجَكُم مِّنْ أَرْضِكُمْ ۖ فَمَاذَا تَأْمُرُونَ ﴿١١٠﴾
قَالُوٓا۟ أَرْجِهْ وَأَخَاهُ وَأَرْسِلْ فِى ٱلْمَدَآئِنِ حَٰشِرِينَ ﴿١١١﴾ يَأْتُوكَ
بِكُلِّ سَٰحِرٍ عَلِيمٍ ﴿١١٢﴾ وَجَآءَ ٱلسَّحَرَةُ فِرْعَوْنَ قَالُوٓا۟ إِنَّ
لَنَا لَأَجْرًا إِن كُنَّا نَحْنُ ٱلْغَٰلِبِينَ ﴿١١٣﴾ قَالَ نَعَمْ وَإِنَّكُمْ
لَمِنَ ٱلْمُقَرَّبِينَ ﴿١١٤﴾ قَالُوا۟ يَٰمُوسَىٰٓ إِمَّآ أَن تُلْقِىَ وَإِمَّآ أَن
نَّكُونَ نَحْنُ ٱلْمُلْقِينَ ﴿١١٥﴾ قَالَ أَلْقُوا۟ ۖ فَلَمَّآ أَلْقَوْا۟ سَحَرُوٓا۟
أَعْيُنَ ٱلنَّاسِ وَٱسْتَرْهَبُوهُمْ وَجَآءُو بِسِحْرٍ عَظِيمٍ ﴿١١٦﴾
۞ وَأَوْحَيْنَآ إِلَىٰ مُوسَىٰٓ أَنْ أَلْقِ عَصَاكَ ۖ فَإِذَا هِىَ تَلْقَفُ مَا
يَأْفِكُونَ ﴿١١٧﴾ فَوَقَعَ ٱلْحَقُّ وَبَطَلَ مَا كَانُوا۟ يَعْمَلُونَ ﴿١١٨﴾ فَغُلِبُوا۟
هُنَالِكَ وَٱنقَلَبُوا۟ صَٰغِرِينَ ﴿١١٩﴾ وَأُلْقِىَ ٱلسَّحَرَةُ سَٰجِدِينَ ﴿١٢٠﴾
قَالُوٓا۟ ءَامَنَّا بِرَبِّ ٱلْعَٰلَمِينَ ﴿١٢١﴾ رَبِّ مُوسَىٰ وَهَٰرُونَ ﴿١٢٢﴾ قَالَ
فِرْعَوْنُ ءَامَنتُم بِهِۦ قَبْلَ أَنْ ءَاذَنَ لَكُمْ ۖ إِنَّ هَٰذَا لَمَكْرٌ مَّكَرْتُمُوهُ

your Lord. So send the tribe of Israel away with me to Syria.' Pharaoh had enslaved them.

106. ***He*** (Pharaoh) ***said, 'If you have come with a Clear Sign*** to support your claim, ***produce it if you are telling the truth*** about it.'

107. ***So he threw down his staff and there it was, unmistakably a*** large ***snake.***

108. ***And he drew out his hand*** from his pocket ***and there it was,*** radiant ***pure white*** – differing from his normal dark skin colour – ***to those who looked.***

109. ***The ruling circle of Pharaoh's people said, 'This is certainly a skilled magician***, an expert in magic. In *Sūrat ash-Shu'arā'*, we find Pharaoh saying this himself (26:34). So it is as if he were saying it to those around them for the sake of consultation.

110. ***...who desires to expel you from your land, so what do you recommend?'***

111. ***They said, 'Detain him and his brother*** – give the command for that to be done – ***and send out marshals to the cities...***

112. ***...to bring you all the skilled magicians*** (read as *sāḥir* and *saḥḥār*).' He wanted to summon those magicians with superior skill to that of Mūsā.

113. ***The magicians came to Pharaoh and they asked, 'Will we receive a reward if we are the winners?'***

114. ***He said, 'Yes, and you will be among those brought near.'***

115. ***They said, 'Mūsā, will you throw*** your staff ***first or shall we be the ones to throw*** what we have?'

116. ***He said, 'You throw.'*** Mūsā's command is permission for them to throw first. ***And when they threw*** their ropes and staffs, ***they cast a spell on the people's eyes*** to divert them from the truth of what they saw ***and caused them to feel great fear of them*** which made them imagine that they were crawling snakes. ***They produced an extremely powerful magic.***

117. ***We revealed to Mūsā, 'Throw down your staff.' And it immediately swallowed up what they had forged.***

118. ***So the Truth took place*** and was confirmed and made manifest ***and what*** (the magic) ***they did was shown to be false.***

فِى ٱلْمَدِينَةِ لِتُخْرِجُوا۟ مِنْهَآ أَهْلَهَا ۖ فَسَوْفَ تَعْلَمُونَ ﴿١٢٣﴾ لَأُقَطِّعَنَّ
أَيْدِيَكُمْ وَأَرْجُلَكُم مِّنْ خِلَٰفٍ ثُمَّ لَأُصَلِّبَنَّكُمْ أَجْمَعِينَ ﴿١٢٤﴾
قَالُوٓا۟ إِنَّآ إِلَىٰ رَبِّنَا مُنقَلِبُونَ ﴿١٢٥﴾ وَمَا تَنقِمُ مِنَّآ إِلَّآ أَنْ ءَامَنَّا
بِـَٔايَٰتِ رَبِّنَا لَمَّا جَآءَتْنَا ۚ رَبَّنَآ أَفْرِغْ عَلَيْنَا صَبْرًا وَتَوَفَّنَا مُسْلِمِينَ
﴿١٢٦﴾ وَقَالَ ٱلْمَلَأُ مِن قَوْمِ فِرْعَوْنَ أَتَذَرُ مُوسَىٰ وَقَوْمَهُۥ لِيُفْسِدُوا۟
فِى ٱلْأَرْضِ وَيَذَرَكَ وَءَالِهَتَكَ ۚ قَالَ سَنُقَتِّلُ أَبْنَآءَهُمْ وَنَسْتَحْىِۦ
نِسَآءَهُمْ وَإِنَّا فَوْقَهُمْ قَٰهِرُونَ ﴿١٢٧﴾ قَالَ مُوسَىٰ لِقَوْمِهِ
ٱسْتَعِينُوا۟ بِٱللَّهِ وَٱصْبِرُوٓا۟ ۖ إِنَّ ٱلْأَرْضَ لِلَّهِ يُورِثُهَا مَن
يَشَآءُ مِنْ عِبَادِهِۦ ۖ وَٱلْعَٰقِبَةُ لِلْمُتَّقِينَ ﴿١٢٨﴾ قَالُوٓا۟ أُوذِينَا
مِن قَبْلِ أَن تَأْتِيَنَا وَمِنۢ بَعْدِ مَا جِئْتَنَا ۚ قَالَ عَسَىٰ رَبُّكُمْ
أَن يُهْلِكَ عَدُوَّكُمْ وَيَسْتَخْلِفَكُمْ فِى ٱلْأَرْضِ
فَيَنظُرَ كَيْفَ تَعْمَلُونَ ﴿١٢٩﴾ وَلَقَدْ أَخَذْنَآ ءَالَ فِرْعَوْنَ
بِٱلسِّنِينَ وَنَقْصٍ مِّنَ ٱلثَّمَرَٰتِ لَعَلَّهُمْ يَذَّكَّرُونَ ﴿١٣٠﴾
فَإِذَا جَآءَتْهُمُ ٱلْحَسَنَةُ قَالُوا۟ لَنَا هَٰذِهِۦ ۖ وَإِن تُصِبْهُمْ سَيِّئَةٌ
يَطَّيَّرُوا۟ بِمُوسَىٰ وَمَن مَّعَهُۥٓ ۗ أَلَآ إِنَّمَا طَٰٓئِرُهُمْ عِندَ ٱللَّهِ وَلَٰكِنَّ
أَكْثَرَهُمْ لَا يَعْلَمُونَ ﴿١٣١﴾ وَقَالُوا۟ مَهْمَا تَأْتِنَا بِهِۦ مِنْ ءَايَةٍ
لِّتَسْحَرَنَا بِهَا فَمَا نَحْنُ لَكَ بِمُؤْمِنِينَ ﴿١٣٢﴾ فَأَرْسَلْنَا عَلَيْهِمُ
ٱلطُّوفَانَ وَٱلْجَرَادَ وَٱلْقُمَّلَ وَٱلضَّفَادِعَ وَٱلدَّمَ ءَايَٰتٍ مُّفَصَّلَٰتٍ
فَٱسْتَكْبَرُوا۟ وَكَانُوا۟ قَوْمًا مُّجْرِمِينَ ﴿١٣٣﴾ وَلَمَّا وَقَعَ عَلَيْهِمُ
ٱلرِّجْزُ قَالُوا۟ يَٰمُوسَى ٱدْعُ لَنَا رَبَّكَ بِمَا عَهِدَ عِندَكَ ۖ لَئِن

119. ***They*** (Pharaoh and his people) ***were defeated then and there, transformed into humbled men.***

120. ***The magicians threw themselves down in prostration.***

121. ***They said, 'We believe in the Lord of all the worlds…***

122. ***…the Lord of Mūsā and Hārūn.'*** They said this because they knew that what they had witnessed the staff doing was not brought about by magic.

123. ***Pharaoh said, 'Have you believed in him*** (Mūsā) ***before I authorised you to do so? This*** which you have done ***is just some plot you have concocted in the city to drive its people from it.***

124. ***I will cut off your opposite hands and feet*** – right hand and left foot – ***and then I will crucify every one of you.'***

125. ***They said, 'We are returning to our Lord*** after our death, no matter how it occurs, in the Next World.

126. ***You are only avenging yourself on us*** and hostile towards us ***because we believed in our Lord's Signs when they came to us. Our Lord, pour down steadfastness upon us*** when Pharaoh does what he has threatened to do to us, so that we do not revert to unbelief***; and take us back to You as Muslims.'***

127. ***The ruling circle of Pharaoh's people said*** to him, ***'Are you going to leave Mūsā and his people to cause corruption in the earth*** by calling on people to oppose you ***and abandon you and your gods?'*** They had small idols which they worshipped. Pharaoh said, "I am your god and their (the idols') god," when he said, *"I am your Lord most high."* (79:24) ***He said, 'We shall kill*** (read as *sa-nuqattilu* and *sa-naqtulu*) ***their sons and let their women live*** as we did to them before. ***We have absolute power over them!'*** They did that to them and the tribe of Israel complained.

128. ***Mūsā told his people, 'Seek help in Allah and be steadfast*** in the face of their oppression. ***The earth belongs to Allah. He bequeaths it*** and gives it ***to any of His slaves He wills. The successful outcome is for those who are godfearing*** – who fear Allah.'

129. ***They said, 'We suffered harm before you came to us and after you came to us.' He said, 'It may well be that your Lord is going to destroy your enemy and make you the successors in the land so that He can see how you behave*** in it.'

كَشَفۡتَ عَنَّا ٱلرِّجۡزَ لَنُؤۡمِنَنَّ لَكَ وَلَنُرۡسِلَنَّ مَعَكَ بَنِيٓ
إِسۡرَٰٓءِيلَ ١٣٤ فَلَمَّا كَشَفۡنَا عَنۡهُمُ ٱلرِّجۡزَ إِلَىٰٓ أَجَلٍ
هُم بَٰلِغُوهُ إِذَا هُمۡ يَنكُثُونَ ١٣٥ فَٱنتَقَمۡنَا مِنۡهُمۡ فَأَغۡرَقۡنَٰهُمۡ
فِي ٱلۡيَمِّ بِأَنَّهُمۡ كَذَّبُواْ بِـَٔايَٰتِنَا وَكَانُواْ عَنۡهَا غَٰفِلِينَ ١٣٦
وَأَوۡرَثۡنَا ٱلۡقَوۡمَ ٱلَّذِينَ كَانُواْ يُسۡتَضۡعَفُونَ مَشَٰرِقَ
ٱلۡأَرۡضِ وَمَغَٰرِبَهَا ٱلَّتِي بَٰرَكۡنَا فِيهَاۖ وَتَمَّتۡ كَلِمَتُ رَبِّكَ
ٱلۡحُسۡنَىٰ عَلَىٰ بَنِيٓ إِسۡرَٰٓءِيلَ بِمَا صَبَرُواْۖ وَدَمَّرۡنَا مَا كَانَ
يَصۡنَعُ فِرۡعَوۡنُ وَقَوۡمُهُۥ وَمَا كَانُواْ يَعۡرِشُونَ ١٣٧
وَجَٰوَزۡنَا بِبَنِيٓ إِسۡرَٰٓءِيلَ ٱلۡبَحۡرَ فَأَتَوۡاْ عَلَىٰ قَوۡمٖ يَعۡكُفُونَ عَلَىٰٓ
أَصۡنَامٖ لَّهُمۡۚ قَالُواْ يَٰمُوسَى ٱجۡعَل لَّنَآ إِلَٰهٗا كَمَا لَهُمۡ ءَالِهَةٞۚ
قَالَ إِنَّكُمۡ قَوۡمٞ تَجۡهَلُونَ ١٣٨ إِنَّ هَٰٓؤُلَآءِ مُتَبَّرٞ مَّا هُمۡ فِيهِ وَبَٰطِلٞ
مَّا كَانُواْ يَعۡمَلُونَ ١٣٩ قَالَ أَغَيۡرَ ٱللَّهِ أَبۡغِيكُمۡ إِلَٰهٗا
وَهُوَ فَضَّلَكُمۡ عَلَى ٱلۡعَٰلَمِينَ ١٤٠ وَإِذۡ أَنجَيۡنَٰكُم
مِّنۡ ءَالِ فِرۡعَوۡنَ يَسُومُونَكُمۡ سُوٓءَ ٱلۡعَذَابِۖ يُقَتِّلُونَ
أَبۡنَآءَكُمۡ وَيَسۡتَحۡيُونَ نِسَآءَكُمۡۚ وَفِي ذَٰلِكُم بَلَآءٞ مِّن
رَّبِّكُمۡ عَظِيمٞ ١٤١ ۞ وَوَٰعَدۡنَا مُوسَىٰ ثَلَٰثِينَ لَيۡلَةٗ
وَأَتۡمَمۡنَٰهَا بِعَشۡرٖ فَتَمَّ مِيقَٰتُ رَبِّهِۦٓ أَرۡبَعِينَ لَيۡلَةٗۚ وَقَالَ
مُوسَىٰ لِأَخِيهِ هَٰرُونَ ٱخۡلُفۡنِي فِي قَوۡمِي وَأَصۡلِحۡ وَلَا تَتَّبِعۡ
سَبِيلَ ٱلۡمُفۡسِدِينَ ١٤٢ وَلَمَّا جَآءَ مُوسَىٰ لِمِيقَٰتِنَا وَكَلَّمَهُۥ
رَبُّهُۥ قَالَ رَبِّ أَرِنِيٓ أَنظُرۡ إِلَيۡكَۚ قَالَ لَن تَرَىٰنِي وَلَٰكِنِ ٱنظُرۡ

130. ***We seized Pharaoh's people with years of drought and scarcity of fruits so that hopefully they would pay heed*** – be warned and believe.

131. ***Whenever a good thing*** (fertility or wealth) ***came to them, they said, 'This is our due*** and we are entitled to it,' and they were not thankful for it. ***But if anything bad happened to them*** (drought or affliction) ***they would blame their ill fortune on Mūsā and those with him*** (the believers). ***No indeed! Their ill fortune will be with Allah*** and He will bring it to them. ***But most of them did not know*** that what befalls them comes from Allah alone.

132. ***They said*** to Mūsā, ***'No matter what kind of Sign you bring us to bewitch us, we will not believe in you.'*** So he made supplication against them.

133. ***So We sent down on them floods***, which entered their houses and submerged those sitting down up to the neck for seven days, ***locusts***, which ate up all of their crops and fruits, ***lice*** or woodworms, which followed up on what the locusts had left, ***frogs***, which filled their houses and got into their food, ***and blood*** in the water: ***Signs, clear and distinct. But they proved*** too ***arrogant*** to believe ***and were an evildoing people.***

134. ***Whenever the plague*** (punishment) ***came down on them they said, 'Mūsā, pray to your Lord for us by the contract He has with you*** to remove the punishment from us if we believe. ***If you remove the plague from us, we will definitely believe in you and send the tribe of Israel away with you.'***

135. ***But when We removed the plague from them*** by the supplication of Mūsā – ***for a fixed term which they fulfilled – they broke their word***: they reneged on their covenant and reverted to their previous unbelief.

136. ***Then We took revenge on them and drowned them in the*** salt ***sea because they denied Our Signs and paid no attention to them*** and did not reflect on them.

137. ***And We bequeathed to the people*** (the tribe of Israel) ***who had been oppressed*** by being enslaved ***the easternmost part of the land We had blessed*** with water and tree – which describes the land of greater Syria – ***and its westernmost part as well. The most excellent***

Word of your Lord – said to refer to His words, *"We desired to show kindness to those who were oppressed in the land..."* (28:5) – ***was fulfilled for the tribe of Israel on account of their steadfastness*** by the destruction of their enemies. ***And We utterly destroyed what Pharaoh and his people made*** flourish ***and the buildings they constructed*** (read as *ya'rishūna* and *ya'rushūna*).

138. ***We conveyed the tribe of Israel across the sea and they came upon some people who were devoting themselves*** (read as *ya'kufūna* and *ya'kifūna*) ***to some idols which they had*** which they had set up to worship. ***They said, 'Mūsā, give us a god*** (an idol to worship) ***just as these people have gods.' He said, 'You are indeed an ignorant people*** for countering Allah's blessing to you with these words.

139. ***What these people are doing is destined for destruction. What they are doing is purposeless.'***

140. ***He said, 'Should I seek something other than Allah as a god for you*** to worship ***when He has favoured you over all other beings?'*** – at that time.

141. Remember ***when We rescued you*** (read as *anjaynākum* and *anjākum* "He rescued you") ***from Pharaoh's people who were inflicting an evil punishment on you*** – imposing hardship on you and inflicting the worst of punishments on you – ***killing your sons and letting your women live. In that*** rescue and that punishment ***there was a huge trial*** both in terms of blessing and affliction ***from your Lord.*** So you should be admonished and refrain from what you have been saying.

142. ***We set aside*** (read as *wā'adnā* and *wa'adnā*) ***thirty nights for Mūsā*** – during which he would fast and after which Allah would speak with him. They constituted the month of Dhū'l-Qa'da and he fasted them. When he had completed them, he disliked the smell of his mouth and used the siwāk to eliminate it, so Allah commanded him to fast another ten so that he could speak to him with the smell of fasting in his mouth as He says here – ***and then completed them with ten*** of the month of Dhū'l-Ḥijja ***so the appointed time of his Lord*** when He promised to speak with him ***was forty nights in all. Mūsā said to his brother Hārūn*** when he left for the mountain to speak with Allah, ***'Be my khalif among my people. Keep*** their

إِلَى ٱلۡجَبَلِ فَإِنِ ٱسۡتَقَرَّ مَكَانَهُۥ فَسَوۡفَ تَرَىٰنِيۚ فَلَمَّا تَجَلَّىٰ
رَبُّهُۥ لِلۡجَبَلِ جَعَلَهُۥ دَكّٗا وَخَرَّ مُوسَىٰ صَعِقٗاۚ فَلَمَّآ أَفَاقَ
قَالَ سُبۡحَٰنَكَ تُبۡتُ إِلَيۡكَ وَأَنَا۠ أَوَّلُ ٱلۡمُؤۡمِنِينَ ١٤٣
قَالَ يَٰمُوسَىٰٓ إِنِّي ٱصۡطَفَيۡتُكَ عَلَى ٱلنَّاسِ بِرِسَٰلَٰتِي وَبِكَلَٰمِي
فَخُذۡ مَآ ءَاتَيۡتُكَ وَكُن مِّنَ ٱلشَّٰكِرِينَ ١٤٤ وَكَتَبۡنَا
لَهُۥ فِي ٱلۡأَلۡوَاحِ مِن كُلِّ شَيۡءٖ مَّوۡعِظَةٗ وَتَفۡصِيلٗا لِّكُلِّ
شَيۡءٖ فَخُذۡهَا بِقُوَّةٖ وَأۡمُرۡ قَوۡمَكَ يَأۡخُذُواْ بِأَحۡسَنِهَاۚ سَأُوْرِيكُمۡ
دَارَ ٱلۡفَٰسِقِينَ ١٤٥ سَأَصۡرِفُ عَنۡ ءَايَٰتِيَ ٱلَّذِينَ يَتَكَبَّرُونَ
فِي ٱلۡأَرۡضِ بِغَيۡرِ ٱلۡحَقِّ وَإِن يَرَوۡاْ كُلَّ ءَايَةٖ لَّا يُؤۡمِنُواْ
بِهَا وَإِن يَرَوۡاْ سَبِيلَ ٱلرُّشۡدِ لَا يَتَّخِذُوهُ سَبِيلٗا وَإِن يَرَوۡاْ
سَبِيلَ ٱلۡغَيِّ يَتَّخِذُوهُ سَبِيلٗاۚ ذَٰلِكَ بِأَنَّهُمۡ كَذَّبُواْ بِـَٔايَٰتِنَا
وَكَانُواْ عَنۡهَا غَٰفِلِينَ ١٤٦ وَٱلَّذِينَ كَذَّبُواْ بِـَٔايَٰتِنَا وَلِقَآءِ
ٱلۡأٓخِرَةِ حَبِطَتۡ أَعۡمَٰلُهُمۡۚ هَلۡ يُجۡزَوۡنَ إِلَّا مَا كَانُواْ
يَعۡمَلُونَ ١٤٧ وَٱتَّخَذَ قَوۡمُ مُوسَىٰ مِنۢ بَعۡدِهِۦ مِنۡ حُلِيِّهِمۡ
عِجۡلٗا جَسَدٗا لَّهُۥ خُوَارٌۚ أَلَمۡ يَرَوۡاْ أَنَّهُۥ لَا يُكَلِّمُهُمۡ وَلَا يَهۡدِيهِمۡ
سَبِيلًاۘ ٱتَّخَذُوهُ وَكَانُواْ ظَٰلِمِينَ ١٤٨ وَلَمَّا سُقِطَ
فِيٓ أَيۡدِيهِمۡ وَرَأَوۡاْ أَنَّهُمۡ قَدۡ ضَلُّواْ قَالُواْ لَئِن لَّمۡ يَرۡحَمۡنَا
رَبُّنَا وَيَغۡفِرۡ لَنَا لَنَكُونَنَّ مِنَ ٱلۡخَٰسِرِينَ ١٤٩
وَلَمَّا رَجَعَ مُوسَىٰٓ إِلَىٰ قَوۡمِهِۦ غَضۡبَٰنَ أَسِفٗا قَالَ بِئۡسَمَا خَلَفۡتُمُونِي
مِنۢ بَعۡدِيٓۖ أَعَجِلۡتُمۡ أَمۡرَ رَبِّكُمۡۖ وَأَلۡقَى ٱلۡأَلۡوَاحَ وَأَخَذَ بِرَأۡسِ

affairs in ***order and do not follow the way of the corrupters*** by agreeing with them to commit acts of disobedience.*'*

143. ***When Mūsā came to Our appointed time*** – the time when it was appointed for Allah to speak to him – ***and his Lord spoke to him*** without any intermediary with words that he heard from every direction, ***he said, 'My Lord, show me Yourself so that I may look at You!' He said, 'You will not*** be able to ***see Me*** – the expression conveys the lack of human ability to see Allah Almighty – ***but look at the mountain*** which is physically stronger than you. ***If it remains firm in its place, then you will see Me***: you will be strong enough to see Me. If it does not, it will be clear that you do not have the capacity to do so.*'* ***But when His Lord manifested Himself to the mountain*** – when the amount of half of a little finger of light appeared to the mountain, as we are told in a *ḥadīth* which al-Ḥākim says is *ṣaḥīh* – ***He crushed it flat*** (read as *dakkan* and *dakkā'a*), meaning pulverised and flattened on the earth, ***and Mūsā fell unconscious to the ground*** out of awe at what he had seen. ***When he regained consciousness he said, 'Glory be to You!*** – declaring Allah disconnected from anything else – ***I turn in repentance to You*** for asking for what I was not commanded to do ***and I am the first of the believers*** in my time*!'*

144. ***He*** (Allah) ***said*** to him, ***'Mūsā, I have chosen you over all mankind*** – referring to the people of his time – ***for My Message*** (read as *risālātī* in the plural and *risālatī* in the singular) ***and My Word*** – My speaking directly to you. ***Take*** from My favour ***what I have given you and be among the thankful*** for My blessings.*'*

145. ***We wrote about everything for him on the Tablets*** of the Torah, which were made from the lote trees of the Garden or emerald, and there were seven or ten of them, ***as an admonition and clarifying all things*** which are needed for the *dīn*. ***'Seize hold of it vigorously*** with strength and striving ***and command your people to adopt the best in it. I will show you the home of the deviators*** (Pharaoh and his followers)*!'* Their home was Egypt.

146. ***I will divert from My Signs*** – the evidence of Allah's power seen in created things and other manifestations – ***all those who are arrogant in the earth without any right,*** and will disappoint them. ***Even if they see every Sign, they will not believe in it. If they see***

أَخِيهِ يَجُرُّهُۥٓ إِلَيۡهِۚ قَالَ ٱبۡنَ أُمَّ إِنَّ ٱلۡقَوۡمَ ٱسۡتَضۡعَفُونِي وَكَادُواْ
يَقۡتُلُونَنِي فَلَا تُشۡمِتۡ بِيَ ٱلۡأَعۡدَآءَ وَلَا تَجۡعَلۡنِي مَعَ ٱلۡقَوۡمِ
ٱلظَّٰلِمِينَ ١٥٠ قَالَ رَبِّ ٱغۡفِرۡ لِي وَلِأَخِي وَأَدۡخِلۡنَا فِي
رَحۡمَتِكَۖ وَأَنتَ أَرۡحَمُ ٱلرَّٰحِمِينَ ١٥١ إِنَّ ٱلَّذِينَ ٱتَّخَذُواْ
ٱلۡعِجۡلَ سَيَنَالُهُمۡ غَضَبٞ مِّن رَّبِّهِمۡ وَذِلَّةٞ فِي ٱلۡحَيَوٰةِ ٱلدُّنۡيَاۚ
وَكَذَٰلِكَ نَجۡزِي ٱلۡمُفۡتَرِينَ ١٥٢ وَٱلَّذِينَ عَمِلُواْ ٱلسَّيِّـَٔاتِ ثُمَّ
تَابُواْ مِنۢ بَعۡدِهَا وَءَامَنُوٓاْ إِنَّ رَبَّكَ مِنۢ بَعۡدِهَا لَغَفُورٞ رَّحِيمٞ
١٥٣ وَلَمَّا سَكَتَ عَن مُّوسَى ٱلۡغَضَبُ أَخَذَ ٱلۡأَلۡوَاحَۖ وَفِي
نُسۡخَتِهَا هُدٗى وَرَحۡمَةٞ لِّلَّذِينَ هُمۡ لِرَبِّهِمۡ يَرۡهَبُونَ ١٥٤ وَٱخۡتَارَ
مُوسَىٰ قَوۡمَهُۥ سَبۡعِينَ رَجُلٗا لِّمِيقَٰتِنَاۖ فَلَمَّآ أَخَذَتۡهُمُ ٱلرَّجۡفَةُ
قَالَ رَبِّ لَوۡ شِئۡتَ أَهۡلَكۡتَهُم مِّن قَبۡلُ وَإِيَّٰيَۖ أَتُهۡلِكُنَا بِمَا فَعَلَ
ٱلسُّفَهَآءُ مِنَّآۖ إِنۡ هِيَ إِلَّا فِتۡنَتُكَ تُضِلُّ بِهَا مَن تَشَآءُ وَتَهۡدِي
مَن تَشَآءُۖ أَنتَ وَلِيُّنَا فَٱغۡفِرۡ لَنَا وَٱرۡحَمۡنَاۖ وَأَنتَ خَيۡرُ ٱلۡغَٰفِرِينَ ١٥٥
۞ وَٱكۡتُبۡ لَنَا فِي هَٰذِهِ ٱلدُّنۡيَا حَسَنَةٗ وَفِي ٱلۡأٓخِرَةِ إِنَّا
هُدۡنَآ إِلَيۡكَۚ قَالَ عَذَابِيٓ أُصِيبُ بِهِۦ مَنۡ أَشَآءُۖ وَرَحۡمَتِي
وَسِعَتۡ كُلَّ شَيۡءٖۚ فَسَأَكۡتُبُهَا لِلَّذِينَ يَتَّقُونَ وَيُؤۡتُونَ
ٱلزَّكَوٰةَ وَٱلَّذِينَ هُم بِـَٔايَٰتِنَا يُؤۡمِنُونَ ١٥٦ ٱلَّذِينَ يَتَّبِعُونَ
ٱلرَّسُولَ ٱلنَّبِيَّ ٱلۡأُمِّيَّ ٱلَّذِي يَجِدُونَهُۥ مَكۡتُوبًا عِندَهُمۡ
فِي ٱلتَّوۡرَىٰةِ وَٱلۡإِنجِيلِ يَأۡمُرُهُم بِٱلۡمَعۡرُوفِ وَيَنۡهَىٰهُمۡ
عَنِ ٱلۡمُنكَرِ وَيُحِلُّ لَهُمُ ٱلطَّيِّبَٰتِ وَيُحَرِّمُ عَلَيۡهِمُ

the way of right guidance – guidance which comes from Allah – ***they will not take it as a way*** and follow it. ***But if they see the way of error*** and misguidance, ***they will take that as a way. That is because they denied Our Signs and paid no attention to them.***

147. ***As for those who denied Our Signs and the encounter of the Next World*** (the Resurrection and other things) ***their actions will come to nothing***: the good actions they did in this world, like maintaining ties of kinship and almsgiving, will be void and so they will have no reward for them because they lack the necessary precondition of true belief in Allah. ***Will they be repaid except for what they did*** (their denial and acts of disobedience)***?***

148. ***After he left*** – after Mūsā went to talk with his Lord – ***Mūsā's people adopted a calf made from their ornaments*** – the jewellery which they had borrowed from the people of Pharaoh for a wedding and kept – ***a form*** of flesh and blood made by the Sāmirī for them ***which made a lowing sound.*** The Sāmirī had taken some dust from the hoof-prints of the horse of Jibrīl and placed it in the mouth of the calf. It brought it to life when it was placed there. ***Did they not see that it could not speak to them or guide them to any way? They adopted it*** as a god ***and so they were wrongdoers*** by doing so.

149. ***When they took full stock of what they had done,*** they regretted worshipping it ***and saw*** and knew that ***they had been misled*** by it; and when Mūsā returned ***they said, 'If our Lord does not have mercy on us and forgive us*** (read as *yaghfir* and *taghfir*), ***we will certainly be among the lost.'***

150. ***When Mūsā returned to his people in anger*** towards them ***and great sorrow, he said*** to them, ***'What an evil thing you did in my absence after I left*** by engaging in idolatry***! Did you want to hasten your Lord's command?' He threw down the Tablets*** of the Torah in anger for the sake of his Lord, and they broke, ***and seized hold of his brother's head*** – grabbing the hair of his brother's head with his right hand and his beard with his left – ***dragging him towards him*** in anger. ***Hārūn said, 'Son of my mother*** – Hārūn mentioned his mother to soften Mūsā's anger, ***the people oppressed me and almost killed me. Do not give my enemies cause to gloat over me*** by your humiliating me. ***Do not include me with the wrongdoing people*** in punishment for worshipping the Calf.'

151. ***He said, 'My Lord, forgive me*** for what I have done to my brother ***and my brother*** – including his brother in the supplication to please him and avert the gloating of enemies from him – ***and admit us into Your mercy. You are the Most Merciful of the merciful.'*** Allah continues:

152. ***As for those who adopted the Calf*** as a god, ***anger*** and punishment ***from their Lord will overtake them together with abasement in the life of this world.*** They were punished by the command to kill themselves and were abased in the life of this world until the Day of Rising. ***That is how We repay the purveyors of falsehood***, those who associated others with Allah and did other evil things.

153. ***But as for those who do evil actions and then subsequently repent and believe*** in Allah, ***in that case*** after that ***your Lord is Ever-Forgiving*** to them, ***Most Merciful*** to them.

154. ***When Mūsā's anger abated he picked up the Tablets*** which he had thrown down, ***and in their inscription*** – what was written on them – ***was guidance*** from misguidance ***and mercy for all of them who feared their Lord.***

155. ***Mūsā chose seventy men from his people*** who had not worshipped the Calf, by Allah's command ***for Our appointed time*** – the time when He had told him to bring them so that they could apologise for what their companions had done in worshipping the Calf and he went out with them – ***and when the*** strong ***earthquake seized them*** – according to Ibn 'Abbās, Allah seized them with the earthquake since they had remained with their people when they worshipped the Calf, and that they were not the ones who had asked to see Him – ***he*** (Mūsā) ***said, 'My Lord, if You had willed, You could have destroyed them previously*** – before he left Egypt with them, so that the tribe of Israel would have seen that there was a reason for their destruction and not suspect him – ***and me as well. Would You destroy us for what the foolish among us did?*** His question implies, "Do not punish us for the sins of others." ***It was only a trial*** – into which the foolish fell – ***from You by which You misguided those You willed and guided those You willed. You are our Protector*** in all our affairs ***so forgive us and have mercy on us. You are the Best of Forgivers.***

ٱلۡخَبَٰٓئِثَ وَيَضَعُ عَنۡهُمۡ إِصۡرَهُمۡ وَٱلۡأَغۡلَٰلَ ٱلَّتِي كَانَتۡ
عَلَيۡهِمۡۚ فَٱلَّذِينَ ءَامَنُواْ بِهِۦ وَعَزَّرُوهُ وَنَصَرُوهُ وَٱتَّبَعُواْ
ٱلنُّورَ ٱلَّذِيٓ أُنزِلَ مَعَهُۥٓ أُوْلَٰٓئِكَ هُمُ ٱلۡمُفۡلِحُونَ ١٥٧ قُلۡ
يَٰٓأَيُّهَا ٱلنَّاسُ إِنِّي رَسُولُ ٱللَّهِ إِلَيۡكُمۡ جَمِيعًا ٱلَّذِي
لَهُۥ مُلۡكُ ٱلسَّمَٰوَٰتِ وَٱلۡأَرۡضِۖ لَآ إِلَٰهَ إِلَّا هُوَ يُحۡيِۦ وَيُمِيتُۖ
فَـَٔامِنُواْ بِٱللَّهِ وَرَسُولِهِ ٱلنَّبِيِّ ٱلۡأُمِّيِّ ٱلَّذِي يُؤۡمِنُ بِٱللَّهِ
وَكَلِمَٰتِهِۦ وَٱتَّبِعُوهُ لَعَلَّكُمۡ تَهۡتَدُونَ ١٥٨
وَمِن قَوۡمِ مُوسَىٰٓ أُمَّةٞ يَهۡدُونَ بِٱلۡحَقِّ وَبِهِۦ يَعۡدِلُونَ ١٥٩
وَقَطَّعۡنَٰهُمُ ٱثۡنَتَيۡ عَشۡرَةَ أَسۡبَاطًا أُمَمٗاۚ وَأَوۡحَيۡنَآ إِلَىٰ مُوسَىٰٓ
إِذِ ٱسۡتَسۡقَىٰهُ قَوۡمُهُۥٓ أَنِ ٱضۡرِب بِّعَصَاكَ ٱلۡحَجَرَۖ
فَٱنۢبَجَسَتۡ مِنۡهُ ٱثۡنَتَا عَشۡرَةَ عَيۡنٗاۖ قَدۡ عَلِمَ كُلُّ أُنَاسٖ
مَّشۡرَبَهُمۡۚ وَظَلَّلۡنَا عَلَيۡهِمُ ٱلۡغَمَٰمَ وَأَنزَلۡنَا عَلَيۡهِمُ ٱلۡمَنَّ
وَٱلسَّلۡوَىٰۖ كُلُواْ مِن طَيِّبَٰتِ مَا رَزَقۡنَٰكُمۡۚ وَمَا
ظَلَمُونَا وَلَٰكِن كَانُوٓاْ أَنفُسَهُمۡ يَظۡلِمُونَ ١٦٠ وَإِذۡ
قِيلَ لَهُمُ ٱسۡكُنُواْ هَٰذِهِ ٱلۡقَرۡيَةَ وَكُلُواْ مِنۡهَا حَيۡثُ
شِئۡتُمۡ وَقُولُواْ حِطَّةٞ وَٱدۡخُلُواْ ٱلۡبَابَ سُجَّدٗا نَّغۡفِرۡ
لَكُمۡ خَطِيٓـَٰٔتِكُمۡۚ سَنَزِيدُ ٱلۡمُحۡسِنِينَ ١٦١
فَبَدَّلَ ٱلَّذِينَ ظَلَمُواْ مِنۡهُمۡ قَوۡلًا غَيۡرَ ٱلَّذِي قِيلَ لَهُمۡ
فَأَرۡسَلۡنَا عَلَيۡهِمۡ رِجۡزٗا مِّنَ ٱلسَّمَآءِ بِمَا كَانُواْ
يَظۡلِمُونَ ١٦٢ وَسۡـَٔلۡهُمۡ عَنِ ٱلۡقَرۡيَةِ ٱلَّتِي كَانَتۡ

156. ***Prescribe good for us*** and make it mandatory for us ***in this world and*** good in ***the Next World. We have truly turned to You*** in repentance.***' He*** (Allah) ***said, 'As for My punishment, I strike with it anyone I will. My mercy extends to all things*** in this world, ***but I will prescribe it*** in the Next World ***for those who are godfearing and pay*** **zakāt*****, and those who believe in Our Signs:***

157. ***...those who follow the Messenger*** Muḥammad, may Allah bless him and grant him peace, ***the Unlettered Prophet, whom they find written down with them in the Torah and the Gospel*** – referring to the name and description of the Prophet – ***commanding them to do right and forbidding them to do wrong, making good things lawful for them*** – which were unlawful in their Sharī'a – ***and bad things,*** such as carrion and other things, ***unlawful for them, relieving them of their heavy loads and the chains which were around them***: a reference to the difficult penalties imposed upon them, such as having to kill themselves in repentance and cut out any trace of impurity. ***Those*** of them ***who believe in him and honour him and help him, and follow the Light*** (the Qur'an) ***that has been sent down with him, they are the ones who are successful.'***

158. ***Say*** (addressed to the Prophet, may Allah bless him and grant him peace)***: 'Mankind! I am the Messenger of Allah to you all, of Him to whom the kingdom of the heavens and earth belongs. There is no god but Him. He gives life and causes to die. So believe in Allah and His Messenger, the Unlettered Prophet, who believes in Allah and His words*** (the Qur'an), ***and follow him so that perhaps you will be guided.'***

159. ***Among the people of Mūsā there is a group who guide*** people ***by the truth and act justly*** in judgement ***in accordance with it.***

160. ***We divided them*** (the tribe of Israel) ***up into twelve tribes*** – communities. ***We revealed to Mūsā, when his people asked him for water*** in the desert***: 'Strike the rock with your staff.'*** And he struck it. ***Twelve fountains flowed out from it*** – a spring for each of the tribes – ***and all the people*** (each tribe) ***knew their drinking place. And We shaded them*** in the desert ***with clouds*** from the heat of the sun ***and sent down manna and quails to them*** and We said to them***: 'Eat of the good things We have provided you with.' They did not wrong Us; rather it was themselves they wronged.***

حَاضِرَةَ ٱلْبَحْرِ إِذْ يَعْدُونَ فِي ٱلسَّبْتِ إِذْ تَأْتِيهِمْ
حِيتَانُهُمْ يَوْمَ سَبْتِهِمْ شُرَّعًا وَيَوْمَ لَا يَسْبِتُونَ
لَا تَأْتِيهِمْ كَذَٰلِكَ نَبْلُوهُم بِمَا كَانُوا۟ يَفْسُقُونَ ١٦٣
وَإِذْ قَالَتْ أُمَّةٌ مِّنْهُمْ لِمَ تَعِظُونَ قَوْمًا ٱللَّهُ مُهْلِكُهُمْ أَوْ مُعَذِّبُهُمْ
عَذَابًا شَدِيدًا قَالُوا۟ مَعْذِرَةً إِلَىٰ رَبِّكُمْ وَلَعَلَّهُمْ يَتَّقُونَ ١٦٤
فَلَمَّا نَسُوا۟ مَا ذُكِّرُوا۟ بِهِۦٓ أَنجَيْنَا ٱلَّذِينَ يَنْهَوْنَ عَنِ ٱلسُّوٓءِ
وَأَخَذْنَا ٱلَّذِينَ ظَلَمُوا۟ بِعَذَابٍۭ بَـِٔيسٍۭ بِمَا كَانُوا۟ يَفْسُقُونَ
١٦٥ فَلَمَّا عَتَوْا۟ عَن مَّا نُهُوا۟ عَنْهُ قُلْنَا لَهُمْ كُونُوا۟ قِرَدَةً خَٰسِـِٔينَ
١٦٦ وَإِذْ تَأَذَّنَ رَبُّكَ لَيَبْعَثَنَّ عَلَيْهِمْ إِلَىٰ يَوْمِ ٱلْقِيَٰمَةِ مَن
يَسُومُهُمْ سُوٓءَ ٱلْعَذَابِ إِنَّ رَبَّكَ لَسَرِيعُ ٱلْعِقَابِ وَإِنَّهُۥ
لَغَفُورٌ رَّحِيمٌ ١٦٧ وَقَطَّعْنَٰهُمْ فِي ٱلْأَرْضِ أُمَمًا مِّنْهُمُ
ٱلصَّٰلِحُونَ وَمِنْهُمْ دُونَ ذَٰلِكَ وَبَلَوْنَٰهُم بِٱلْحَسَنَٰتِ
وَٱلسَّيِّـَٔاتِ لَعَلَّهُمْ يَرْجِعُونَ ١٦٨ فَخَلَفَ مِنۢ بَعْدِهِمْ خَلْفٌ
وَرِثُوا۟ ٱلْكِتَٰبَ يَأْخُذُونَ عَرَضَ هَٰذَا ٱلْأَدْنَىٰ وَيَقُولُونَ سَيُغْفَرُ لَنَا
وَإِن يَأْتِهِمْ عَرَضٌ مِّثْلُهُۥ يَأْخُذُوهُ أَلَمْ يُؤْخَذْ عَلَيْهِم مِّيثَٰقُ ٱلْكِتَٰبِ
أَن لَّا يَقُولُوا۟ عَلَى ٱللَّهِ إِلَّا ٱلْحَقَّ وَدَرَسُوا۟ مَا فِيهِ وَٱلدَّارُ ٱلْـَٔاخِرَةُ
خَيْرٌ لِّلَّذِينَ يَتَّقُونَ أَفَلَا تَعْقِلُونَ ١٦٩ وَٱلَّذِينَ يُمَسِّكُونَ
بِٱلْكِتَٰبِ وَأَقَامُوا۟ ٱلصَّلَوٰةَ إِنَّا لَا نُضِيعُ أَجْرَ ٱلْمُصْلِحِينَ ١٧٠
۞ وَإِذْ نَتَقْنَا ٱلْجَبَلَ فَوْقَهُمْ كَأَنَّهُۥ ظُلَّةٌ وَظَنُّوٓا۟ أَنَّهُۥ وَاقِعٌۢ بِهِمْ
خُذُوا۟ مَآ ءَاتَيْنَٰكُم بِقُوَّةٍ وَٱذْكُرُوا۟ مَا فِيهِ لَعَلَّكُمْ تَتَّقُونَ ١٧١

161. Remember ***when they were told: 'Live in this town*** (Jerusalem) ***and eat of it wherever you like and say, "Relieve us of our burdens!" and enter the gate*** of the city ***prostrating*** (bowing down). ***We will forgive*** (read as *naghfir* and also *tughfar*, in which case the meaning becomes, "Your mistakes will be forgiven you") ***your mistakes. We will grant increase*** (a reward) ***to good-doers*** (those who obey).***'***

162. ***But those of them who did wrong substituted words other than those they had been given***: they said, "A grain in a hair" and entered on their backsides. ***So We sent a plague*** (punishment) ***on them from heaven for their wrongdoing.***

163. ***Ask them***, Muḥammad, in rebuke, ***about the town which was by the sea*** – Ayla on the Red Sea – and about what happened to its inhabitants ***when they broke the Sabbath*** by fishing during it when they were commanded not to, ***when their fish came to them*** clearly ***near the surface on their Sabbath day, but did not come on the days which were not their Sabbath*** as a test from Allah. ***In this way We put them to the test because they were deviators.*** They showed that they had deviated by fishing on the Sabbath. At that point the people formed three groups: those who fished with them, those who forbade them to fish, and those who did not fish but did not forbid them.

164. This continues on from the previous *āyat*. ***When a group of them*** – those who did not fish and did not forbid others – ***said, 'Why do you rebuke a people whom Allah is going to destroy or severely punish?' they*** – those who had forbidden the others to fish – ***said, 'So that we have an excuse*** through our admonishment ***to present to your Lord,*** so that we will not be accused of failing to forbid them ***and so that perhaps they will become godfearing*** and fear fishing.***'***

165. ***Then when they forgot*** and abandoned ***what they had been reminded of*** and warned about and did not return, ***We rescued those who had forbidden the evil and seized those who did wrong*** by transgressing ***with a harsh punishment because they were deviators.***

166. ***When they were insolent*** and arrogant ***about what they had been forbidden to do, We said to them, 'Be apes, despised, cast***

out!' Their punishment is described. Ibn 'Abbās said, "I do not know what was done to the silent group." Ikrima said, "They were not utterly destroyed because their words (above), 'Why do you rebuke...?' showed that they disliked what the others were doing."

167. ***Then your Lord announced*** and informed them ***that He would send against them*** (the Jews) ***until the Day of Rising people who would inflict an evil punishment on them.*** People would abase them and take *jizya* from them. At first they paid it to the Magians and when our Prophet, may Allah bless him and grant him peace, was sent, he imposed it on them. ***Your Lord is Swift in Retribution*** for disobeying Him, ***and He is Ever-Forgiving*** to those who obey Him, ***Most Merciful*** to them.

168. ***And We divided them into nations in the earth. Some of them are righteous and some are other than that*** (unbelievers and deviators). ***We tried them with good*** (blessings) ***and evil*** (requital) ***so that perhaps they would return*** from their deviance.

169. ***An evil generation has succeeded them, inheriting the Book*** (the Torah) from their forebears, ***taking the goods of this lower world*** – rubbish which is the basest stuff whether lawful or unlawful – ***and saying, 'We will be forgiven*** for what we did.***' But if similar goods come to them again they still take them.*** They hope vainly for forgiveness when they revert to what they were doing and persist in it; but there is no promise in the Torah of forgiveness when people persist in wrongdoing. ***Has not a covenant been made with them in the Book, that they should only say the truth about Allah; and have they not studied*** and seen ***what is in it?*** Why do they deny it by ascribing to it the granting of forgiveness in spite of persistence in wrongdoing? ***The Final Abode is better for those who are godfearing*** in that they fear the *ḥarām.* ***Will you not use your intellect*** (read as *ta'qilūna* and also *ya'qiluna*, "Will they not use their intellect?") and realise that it is better, and therefore prefer the Next World to this world***?***

170. ***As for those*** of them ***who hold fast*** (read as *yumassikūna* and *yumsikūna)* ***to the Book and establish the prayer,*** such as 'Abdullah ibn Salām and his companions, ***We will not let the wage of the righteous be wasted.*** The second phrase contains a noun instead of a pro-

وَإِذْ أَخَذَ رَبُّكَ مِنۢ بَنِىٓ ءَادَمَ مِن ظُهُورِهِمْ ذُرِّيَّتَهُمْ وَأَشْهَدَهُمْ
عَلَىٰٓ أَنفُسِهِمْ أَلَسْتُ بِرَبِّكُمْ ۖ قَالُوا۟ بَلَىٰ ۛ شَهِدْنَآ ۛ أَن تَقُولُوا۟ يَوْمَ
ٱلْقِيَٰمَةِ إِنَّا كُنَّا عَنْ هَٰذَا غَٰفِلِينَ ١٧٢ أَوْ تَقُولُوٓا۟ إِنَّمَآ أَشْرَكَ
ءَابَآؤُنَا مِن قَبْلُ وَكُنَّا ذُرِّيَّةً مِّنۢ بَعْدِهِمْ ۖ أَفَتُهْلِكُنَا بِمَا فَعَلَ
ٱلْمُبْطِلُونَ ١٧٣ وَكَذَٰلِكَ نُفَصِّلُ ٱلْءَايَٰتِ وَلَعَلَّهُمْ يَرْجِعُونَ
١٧٤ وَٱتْلُ عَلَيْهِمْ نَبَأَ ٱلَّذِىٓ ءَاتَيْنَٰهُ ءَايَٰتِنَا فَٱنسَلَخَ مِنْهَا
فَأَتْبَعَهُ ٱلشَّيْطَٰنُ فَكَانَ مِنَ ٱلْغَاوِينَ ١٧٥ وَلَوْ شِئْنَا
لَرَفَعْنَٰهُ بِهَا وَلَٰكِنَّهُۥٓ أَخْلَدَ إِلَى ٱلْأَرْضِ وَٱتَّبَعَ هَوَىٰهُ ۚ فَمَثَلُهُۥ
كَمَثَلِ ٱلْكَلْبِ إِن تَحْمِلْ عَلَيْهِ يَلْهَثْ أَوْ تَتْرُكْهُ
يَلْهَث ۚ ذَّٰلِكَ مَثَلُ ٱلْقَوْمِ ٱلَّذِينَ كَذَّبُوا۟ بِـَٔايَٰتِنَا ۚ فَٱقْصُصِ
ٱلْقَصَصَ لَعَلَّهُمْ يَتَفَكَّرُونَ ١٧٦ سَآءَ مَثَلًا ٱلْقَوْمُ ٱلَّذِينَ
كَذَّبُوا۟ بِـَٔايَٰتِنَا وَأَنفُسَهُمْ كَانُوا۟ يَظْلِمُونَ ١٧٧ مَن يَهْدِ ٱللَّهُ
فَهُوَ ٱلْمُهْتَدِى ۖ وَمَن يُضْلِلْ فَأُو۟لَٰٓئِكَ هُمُ ٱلْخَٰسِرُونَ ١٧٨
وَلَقَدْ ذَرَأْنَا لِجَهَنَّمَ كَثِيرًا مِّنَ ٱلْجِنِّ وَٱلْإِنسِ ۖ لَهُمْ قُلُوبٌ
لَّا يَفْقَهُونَ بِهَا وَلَهُمْ أَعْيُنٌ لَّا يُبْصِرُونَ بِهَا وَلَهُمْ ءَاذَانٌ لَّا يَسْمَعُونَ
بِهَآ ۚ أُو۟لَٰٓئِكَ كَٱلْأَنْعَٰمِ بَلْ هُمْ أَضَلُّ ۚ أُو۟لَٰٓئِكَ هُمُ ٱلْغَٰفِلُونَ ١٧٩
وَلِلَّهِ ٱلْأَسْمَآءُ ٱلْحُسْنَىٰ فَٱدْعُوهُ بِهَا ۖ وَذَرُوا۟ ٱلَّذِينَ يُلْحِدُونَ فِىٓ
أَسْمَٰٓئِهِۦ ۚ سَيُجْزَوْنَ مَا كَانُوا۟ يَعْمَلُونَ ١٨٠ وَمِمَّنْ خَلَقْنَآ أُمَّةٌ
يَهْدُونَ بِٱلْحَقِّ وَبِهِۦ يَعْدِلُونَ ١٨١ وَٱلَّذِينَ كَذَّبُوا۟ بِـَٔايَٰتِنَا
سَنَسْتَدْرِجُهُم مِّنْ حَيْثُ لَا يَعْلَمُونَ ١٨٢ وَأُمْلِى لَهُمْ ۚ إِنَّ

noun, saying "the wage of the righteous" rather than "their wage", in order to stress the righteousness of those concerned.

171. Remember ***when We uprooted the mountain*** and raised it up, ***lifting it above them like a canopy, and they thought*** and were certain that ***it was about to fall on them***, because Allah had promised that it would happen if they did not accept the rulings of the Torah. They had refused to do so because it was difficult for them, but then they had to accept it. Then We said to them***: 'Seize hold vigorously*** – with gravity and striving – ***of what We have given you and remember what is in it*** by acting on it, ***so that perhaps you will be god-fearing.'***

172. Remember ***when your Lord took out all their descendants from the loins of the children of Adam*** by removing all of the descendants of Ādam from his loins, generation by generation, like atoms, at Nu'mān near 'Arafa, and set up for them evidence of His lordship and made them understand it***, and made them testify against themselves.*** He said, ***'Am I not your Lord?' they said,*** 'Indeed, You are our Lord. ***We testify that indeed You are!' Lest you say*** (read as *taqūlū* and *yaqūlū*, "lest they say", meaning the unbelievers) ***on the Day of Rising, 'We knew nothing of this** tawḥīd.'*

173. ***Or lest you say*** (again read as *taqūlū* and *yaqūlū*, "lest they say", meaning the unbelievers)***, 'Our forefathers associated others with Allah before our time, and we are merely descendants coming after them*** and imitating them. ***So are You going to destroy us*** and punish us ***for what those purveyors of falsehood*** among our forefathers ***did*** by establishing idolatry?' The meaning is that they shall have no defence when they say that, because they testified to Allah's Oneness before and were reminded of it by the Messenger who brought them the miracle which is a reminder to people.

174. ***That is how We make the Signs clear*** – in the same way that We made the covenant clear so that they would reflect – ***so that perhaps they will return*** from their unbelief.

175. ***Recite to them*** (the Jews), Muḥammad, ***the tale of him to whom We gave Our Signs, but who then cast them to one side*** because of his unbelief, as a snake casts off its skin. This was Balaam ibn Bā'ūrā', one of the scholars of the tribe of Israel. He was asked to curse Mūsā and was given a inducement. He made the supplication but then it turned back against him and his tongue lolled out onto his chest – ***and Shayṭān caught up with him*** and became his comrade. ***He was one of those lured into error.***

176. ***If We had wanted to, We would have raised him up*** to the high degrees of men of knowledge ***by them*** – by giving him success through his actions. ***But he gravitated towards the earth*** – to this world and inclining to it – ***and pursued his whims and base desires*** which called him to it, and so We left him there. ***His likeness is that of a dog: if you chase it away*** by driving it off and reprimanding it, ***it lolls out its tongue and pants, and if you leave it alone, it lolls out its tongue and pants.*** No other animal is like a dog. The metaphor indicates someone who is abased in every state. The intention is to make a metaphor of his lowliness and baseness as a consequence of his inclining to this world and following his desires. ***That is the likeness of those who deny Our Signs. So tell the story*** to the Jews ***so that perhaps they will reflect*** and believe.

177. ***How evil is the metaphor of those who deny Our Signs. It is themselves that they have badly wronged*** by their denial.

178. ***Whoever Allah guides is truly guided; but those He misguides are the lost.***

179. ***We created many of the jinn and mankind for Hell. They have hearts they do not understand*** the truth ***with. They have eyes they do not see*** the evidence of the power of Allah ***with*** and reflect. ***They have ears they do not hear*** the signs and warning ***with*** and take note. ***Such people are like cattle*** in their lack of understanding, seeing and hearing. ***No, they are even further astray*** than cattle because cattle seek benefit for themselves and flee from harm whereas these people deliberately advance towards the Fire! ***They are the unaware.***

180. ***To Allah belong the*** ninety-nine ***Most Beautiful Names,*** as reported in the *ḥadīth*, ***so call on Him*** and name Him ***by them and abandon those who desecrate His Names.*** "Desecrate" comes from the root *laḥada*, meaning "to incline away from the truth". They desecrate His Names by deriving the names of their idols from them, like *al-Lāt* from Allah, *al-'Uzzā* from *al-'Azīz*, and *Manā* from *al-*

كَيْدِى مَتِينٌ ﴿١٨٣﴾ أَوَلَمْ يَتَفَكَّرُوا۟ مَا بِصَاحِبِهِم مِّن جِنَّةٍ ۚ إِنْ
هُوَ إِلَّا نَذِيرٌ مُّبِينٌ ﴿١٨٤﴾ أَوَلَمْ يَنظُرُوا۟ فِى مَلَكُوتِ ٱلسَّمَٰوَٰتِ
وَٱلْأَرْضِ وَمَا خَلَقَ ٱللَّهُ مِن شَىْءٍ وَأَنْ عَسَىٰٓ أَن يَكُونَ قَدِ ٱقْتَرَبَ
أَجَلُهُمْ ۖ فَبِأَىِّ حَدِيثٍۭ بَعْدَهُۥ يُؤْمِنُونَ ﴿١٨٥﴾ مَن يُضْلِلِ ٱللَّهُ فَلَا
هَادِىَ لَهُۥ ۚ وَيَذَرُهُمْ فِى طُغْيَٰنِهِمْ يَعْمَهُونَ ﴿١٨٦﴾ يَسْـَٔلُونَكَ عَنِ ٱلسَّاعَةِ
أَيَّانَ مُرْسَىٰهَا ۖ قُلْ إِنَّمَا عِلْمُهَا عِندَ رَبِّى ۖ لَا يُجَلِّيهَا لِوَقْتِهَآ إِلَّا هُوَ ۚ ثَقُلَتْ
فِى ٱلسَّمَٰوَٰتِ وَٱلْأَرْضِ ۚ لَا تَأْتِيكُمْ إِلَّا بَغْتَةً ۗ يَسْـَٔلُونَكَ كَأَنَّكَ حَفِىٌّ
عَنْهَا ۖ قُلْ إِنَّمَا عِلْمُهَا عِندَ ٱللَّهِ وَلَٰكِنَّ أَكْثَرَ ٱلنَّاسِ لَا يَعْلَمُونَ ﴿١٨٧﴾
قُل لَّآ أَمْلِكُ لِنَفْسِى نَفْعًا وَلَا ضَرًّا إِلَّا مَا شَآءَ ٱللَّهُ ۚ وَلَوْ كُنتُ
أَعْلَمُ ٱلْغَيْبَ لَٱسْتَكْثَرْتُ مِنَ ٱلْخَيْرِ وَمَا مَسَّنِىَ ٱلسُّوٓءُ ۚ إِنْ
أَنَا۠ إِلَّا نَذِيرٌ وَبَشِيرٌ لِّقَوْمٍ يُؤْمِنُونَ ﴿١٨٨﴾ ۞ هُوَ ٱلَّذِى خَلَقَكُم
مِّن نَّفْسٍ وَٰحِدَةٍ وَجَعَلَ مِنْهَا زَوْجَهَا لِيَسْكُنَ إِلَيْهَا ۖ فَلَمَّا
تَغَشَّىٰهَا حَمَلَتْ حَمْلًا خَفِيفًا فَمَرَّتْ بِهِۦ ۖ فَلَمَّآ أَثْقَلَت دَّعَوَا
ٱللَّهَ رَبَّهُمَا لَئِنْ ءَاتَيْتَنَا صَٰلِحًا لَّنَكُونَنَّ مِنَ ٱلشَّٰكِرِينَ ﴿١٨٩﴾
فَلَمَّآ ءَاتَىٰهُمَا صَٰلِحًا جَعَلَا لَهُۥ شُرَكَآءَ فِيمَآ ءَاتَىٰهُمَا ۚ فَتَعَٰلَى
ٱللَّهُ عَمَّا يُشْرِكُونَ ﴿١٩٠﴾ أَيُشْرِكُونَ مَا لَا يَخْلُقُ شَيْـًٔا وَهُمْ يُخْلَقُونَ
﴿١٩١﴾ وَلَا يَسْتَطِيعُونَ لَهُمْ نَصْرًا وَلَآ أَنفُسَهُمْ يَنصُرُونَ ﴿١٩٢﴾
وَإِن تَدْعُوهُمْ إِلَى ٱلْهُدَىٰ لَا يَتَّبِعُوكُمْ ۚ سَوَآءٌ عَلَيْكُمْ أَدَعَوْتُمُوهُمْ
أَمْ أَنتُمْ صَٰمِتُونَ ﴿١٩٣﴾ إِنَّ ٱلَّذِينَ تَدْعُونَ مِن دُونِ ٱللَّهِ
عِبَادٌ أَمْثَالُكُمْ ۖ فَٱدْعُوهُمْ فَلْيَسْتَجِيبُوا۟ لَكُمْ إِن

Mannān. ***They will be repaid for what they did*** in the Next World. This Revelation came before the command to fight.

181. ***Among those We have created there is a community who guide by the Truth and act justly according to it.*** This is the community of Muḥammad, may Allah bless him and grant him peace, as stated in the *ḥadīth*.

182. ***But as for those*** among the people of Makka ***who deny Our Signs*** (the Qur'an), ***We will lead them, step by step, into destruction from where they do not know.***

183. ***I will give them more time. My strategy is sure*** – meaning strong and incapable of being bested.

184. ***Have they not reflected*** and therefore come to know***? Their companion*** Muḥammad, may Allah bless him and grant him peace, ***is not mad. He is only a clear warner.***

185. ***Have they not looked into the dominions of the heavens and the earth and what Allah has created*** and used this as evidence of the power of the Creator and His Oneness, ***and seen that it may well be that their appointed time is near*** and that they will die as unbelievers and go to the Fire*?* Therefore they should hasten to believe. ***In what discourse after this*** (the Qur'an) ***will they believe?***

186. ***If Allah misguides people, no one can guide them. He will abandon them*** (read as *yadharu* and *nadharu*, "We will abandon") ***to wander blindly in their excessive insolence.*** They waver in confusion.

187. ***They*** (the people of Makka) ***will ask you about the Hour*** (the Day of Resurrection)***: when is it due? Say*** to them***: 'Knowledge of it*** and when it will occur ***rests with my Lord alone. He alone will reveal it at its proper time. It hangs heavy*** for many people ***in the heavens and the earth*** because of the terror it inspires***. It will not come upon you except suddenly.' They will ask you*** insistently ***as if you had full knowledge of it. Say: 'Knowledge of it rests with Allah alone, but most people do not know that.'***

188. ***Say: 'I possess no power to*** bring ***help or*** avert ***harm*** from ***myself, except as Allah wills. If I had had knowledge of the Unseen,*** which is invisible to me, ***I would have sought to gain much good, and no evil*** such as poverty and other things ***would***

كُنتُمْ صَٰدِقِينَ ﴿١٩٤﴾ أَلَهُمْ أَرْجُلٌ يَمْشُونَ بِهَآ ۖ أَمْ لَهُمْ أَيْدٍ
يَبْطِشُونَ بِهَآ ۖ أَمْ لَهُمْ أَعْيُنٌ يُبْصِرُونَ بِهَآ ۖ أَمْ لَهُمْ ءَاذَانٌ
يَسْمَعُونَ بِهَا ۗ قُلِ ٱدْعُوا۟ شُرَكَآءَكُمْ ثُمَّ كِيدُونِ فَلَا تُنظِرُونِ ﴿١٩٥﴾
إِنَّ وَلِـِّۧىَ ٱللَّهُ ٱلَّذِى نَزَّلَ ٱلْكِتَٰبَ ۖ وَهُوَ يَتَوَلَّى ٱلصَّٰلِحِينَ ﴿١٩٦﴾
وَٱلَّذِينَ تَدْعُونَ مِن دُونِهِۦ لَا يَسْتَطِيعُونَ نَصْرَكُمْ وَلَآ
أَنفُسَهُمْ يَنصُرُونَ ﴿١٩٧﴾ وَإِن تَدْعُوهُمْ إِلَى ٱلْهُدَىٰ لَا يَسْمَعُوا۟ ۖ
وَتَرَىٰهُمْ يَنظُرُونَ إِلَيْكَ وَهُمْ لَا يُبْصِرُونَ ﴿١٩٨﴾ خُذِ ٱلْعَفْوَ وَأْمُرْ
بِٱلْعُرْفِ وَأَعْرِضْ عَنِ ٱلْجَٰهِلِينَ ﴿١٩٩﴾ وَإِمَّا يَنزَغَنَّكَ مِنَ
ٱلشَّيْطَٰنِ نَزْغٌ فَٱسْتَعِذْ بِٱللَّهِ ۚ إِنَّهُۥ سَمِيعٌ عَلِيمٌ ﴿٢٠٠﴾ إِنَّ
ٱلَّذِينَ ٱتَّقَوْا۟ إِذَا مَسَّهُمْ طَٰٓئِفٌ مِّنَ ٱلشَّيْطَٰنِ تَذَكَّرُوا۟
فَإِذَا هُم مُّبْصِرُونَ ﴿٢٠١﴾ وَإِخْوَٰنُهُمْ يَمُدُّونَهُمْ فِى ٱلْغَىِّ ثُمَّ
لَا يُقْصِرُونَ ﴿٢٠٢﴾ وَإِذَا لَمْ تَأْتِهِم بِـَٔايَةٍ قَالُوا۟ لَوْلَا ٱجْتَبَيْتَهَا ۚ
قُلْ إِنَّمَآ أَتَّبِعُ مَا يُوحَىٰٓ إِلَىَّ مِن رَّبِّى ۚ هَٰذَا بَصَآئِرُ مِن رَّبِّكُمْ
وَهُدًى وَرَحْمَةٌ لِّقَوْمٍ يُؤْمِنُونَ ﴿٢٠٣﴾ وَإِذَا قُرِئَ ٱلْقُرْءَانُ
فَٱسْتَمِعُوا۟ لَهُۥ وَأَنصِتُوا۟ لَعَلَّكُمْ تُرْحَمُونَ ﴿٢٠٤﴾ وَٱذْكُر رَّبَّكَ
فِى نَفْسِكَ تَضَرُّعًا وَخِيفَةً وَدُونَ ٱلْجَهْرِ مِنَ ٱلْقَوْلِ بِٱلْغُدُوِّ
وَٱلْـَٔاصَالِ وَلَا تَكُن مِّنَ ٱلْغَٰفِلِينَ ﴿٢٠٥﴾ إِنَّ ٱلَّذِينَ عِندَ رَبِّكَ
لَا يَسْتَكْبِرُونَ عَنْ عِبَادَتِهِۦ وَيُسَبِّحُونَهُۥ وَلَهُۥ يَسْجُدُونَ ۩ ﴿٢٠٦﴾

have touched me and I would have been careful to avoid harmful things. ***I am only a warner*** about the Fire for the unbelievers ***and a bringer of good news*** of the Garden ***to people who believe.'***

189. ***It is He*** (Allah) ***who created you from a single self*** (Ādam) ***and made from him his spouse*** (Ḥawwā') ***so that he might find repose in her*** and friendship with her. ***Then when he covered her*** and had sexual intercourse with her, ***she bore a light load*** (the foetus) ***and carried it around*** – moving around normally since it was light. ***Then when it became heavy*** – when the child grew in her womb and they feared that it might be an animal – ***they called on Allah, their Lord, 'If You grant us a healthy child, we will be among the thankful*** to You for it***!'***

190. ***Then when He granted them a healthy, upright child, they associated others*** (read as *shurakā'* and also *shirkan,* in which case the meaning becomes, "they associated what He had given them") ***with Him*** by naming him 'Abdu'l-Ḥārith. No one should be a slave to anyone other than Allah. This was not idolatry in respect of worship because Ādam was protected from that. Samura related that the Prophet, may Allah bless him and grant him peace, said, "Every time Ḥawwā' gave birth, Iblīs visited her and no child of hers lived. Iblīs told her, 'Name him 'Abdu'l-Ḥārith and he will live.' She named him that and he lived. That was from the inspiration and command of Shayṭān." Al-Ḥākim related this and described it as sound. At-Tirmidhī related it and said it is *ḥasan gharīb.* ***But Allah is far above what*** (the idols) ***they*** (the people of Makka) ***associate with Him.***

191. ***Do they make things into partner-gods*** in their worship ***which cannot create anything and are themselves created…***

192. ***…which are not capable of helping them*** (their worshippers) ***and cannot even help themselves*** – defend themselves if someone wishes to harm them by breaking them or in some other way***?*** The question is meant as a rebuke.

193. ***If you call them*** (the idols) ***to guidance they will not follow you*** (read as *yattabi'ūkum* and *yatba'ūkum*)***. It makes no difference if you call them*** to guidance ***or stay silent*** and do not call them, because they cannot hear you.

194. ***Those you call on*** and worship ***besides Allah are slaves just like yourselves. Call on them and let them respond to you*** – to your call – ***if you are telling the truth*** about them being gods. Then Allah explains the extent of their powerlessness and the fact that their worshippers are in fact superior to them, by saying:

195. ***Do they have legs they can walk with? Do they have hands they can grasp with? Do they have eyes they can see with? Do they have ears they can hear with?*** The answer to all of these questions will be negative. They have none of these things which you have. So how can you worship them when you are more complete than they are? ***Say*** to them, Muḥammad***: 'Call on your partner-gods*** to destroy me ***and try all your wiles against me and grant me no reprieve.*** I do not care what you do.

196. ***My Protector*** who is in charge of my affairs ***is Allah who sent down the Book*** (the Qur'an). ***He takes care of the righteous*** and protects them.***'***

197. ***Those you call on besides Him are not capable of helping you. They cannot even help themselves.*** So why should anyone care about them?

198. ***If you call them*** (the idols) ***to guidance, they do not hear. You see them*** (the idols) ***looking at you,*** Muḥammad, ***yet they do not see.***

199. ***Make allowances for people*** – be tolerant about people's behaviour and do not delve into it – ***command what is right, and turn away from the ignorant.*** Do not confront them on account of their foolishness.

200. ***If an evil impulse from Shayṭān provokes you*** – if he tries to divert you from what you are commanded to do – ***seek refuge in Allah.*** Allah will repel him from you. ***He is All-Hearing*** of words, ***All-Seeing*** of actions.

201. ***As for those who are godfearing, when they are bothered by visitors*** (read as *ṭā'if* and *ṭayf*, in which case the meaning becomes "something which pains them") ***from Shayṭān, they remember*** the punishment and the reward of Allah ***and immediately see*** the Truth ***clearly*** for what it really is, and so they return to right action.

202. ***But as for their brothers*** (the shayṭāns among the unbelievers) ***the visitors*** (shayṭāns) ***lead them further into error. And they do not***

stop at that! They continue in their error because they do not see what they are doing in the way that the godfearing do.

203. ***If you do not bring them*** (the people of Makka) ***a Sign*** which they demand, ***they say, 'Why have you not come up with one*** by yourself?' ***Say, 'I follow only what has been revealed to me from my Lord.*** I cannot bring anything from myself.' ***This*** (Qur'an) ***is clear insight from your Lord, and guidance and mercy, for people who believe.***

204. ***When the Qur'an is recited listen to it and be quiet*** and do not speak, ***so that perhaps you will gain mercy.*** This was revealed about not speaking during the *khuṭba*. It is referred to as the Qur'an since the *khuṭba* contains passages from the Qur'an. It is also said that it refers to recitation of the Qur'an in general.

205. ***Remember your Lord in yourself*** (silently) ***humbly and fearfully*** (at a whisper) ***without loudness of voice*** (at a medium volume) ***morning and evening*** – at the beginning and end of the day. ***Do not be one of the unaware*** who are neglectful of remembrance.

206. ***Those who are in the presence of your Lord*** (the angels) ***do not consider themselves too great*** or proud ***to worship Him. They glorify His praise*** – declaring Him above anything that is not appropriate for Him – ***and they prostrate to Him.*** They single Him out with their humility and worship, so be like them.

سُورَةُ الأَنفَال

بِسْمِ ٱللَّهِ ٱلرَّحْمَٰنِ ٱلرَّحِيمِ

يَسْـَٔلُونَكَ عَنِ ٱلْأَنفَالِ ۖ قُلِ ٱلْأَنفَالُ لِلَّهِ وَٱلرَّسُولِ ۖ فَٱتَّقُوا۟ ٱللَّهَ
وَأَصْلِحُوا۟ ذَاتَ بَيْنِكُمْ ۖ وَأَطِيعُوا۟ ٱللَّهَ وَرَسُولَهُۥٓ إِن كُنتُم
مُّؤْمِنِينَ ﴿١﴾ إِنَّمَا ٱلْمُؤْمِنُونَ ٱلَّذِينَ إِذَا ذُكِرَ ٱللَّهُ وَجِلَتْ
قُلُوبُهُمْ وَإِذَا تُلِيَتْ عَلَيْهِمْ ءَايَٰتُهُۥ زَادَتْهُمْ إِيمَٰنًا وَعَلَىٰ رَبِّهِمْ
يَتَوَكَّلُونَ ﴿٢﴾ ٱلَّذِينَ يُقِيمُونَ ٱلصَّلَوٰةَ وَمِمَّا رَزَقْنَٰهُمْ
يُنفِقُونَ ﴿٣﴾ أُو۟لَٰٓئِكَ هُمُ ٱلْمُؤْمِنُونَ حَقًّا ۚ لَّهُمْ دَرَجَٰتٌ عِندَ
رَبِّهِمْ وَمَغْفِرَةٌ وَرِزْقٌ كَرِيمٌ ﴿٤﴾ كَمَآ أَخْرَجَكَ رَبُّكَ
مِنۢ بَيْتِكَ بِٱلْحَقِّ وَإِنَّ فَرِيقًا مِّنَ ٱلْمُؤْمِنِينَ لَكَٰرِهُونَ ﴿٥﴾
يُجَٰدِلُونَكَ فِى ٱلْحَقِّ بَعْدَمَا تَبَيَّنَ كَأَنَّمَا يُسَاقُونَ إِلَى ٱلْمَوْتِ
وَهُمْ يَنظُرُونَ ﴿٦﴾ وَإِذْ يَعِدُكُمُ ٱللَّهُ إِحْدَى ٱلطَّآئِفَتَيْنِ أَنَّهَا
لَكُمْ وَتَوَدُّونَ أَنَّ غَيْرَ ذَاتِ ٱلشَّوْكَةِ تَكُونُ لَكُمْ
وَيُرِيدُ ٱللَّهُ أَن يُحِقَّ ٱلْحَقَّ بِكَلِمَٰتِهِۦ وَيَقْطَعَ دَابِرَ ٱلْكَٰفِرِينَ
﴿٧﴾ لِيُحِقَّ ٱلْحَقَّ وَيُبْطِلَ ٱلْبَٰطِلَ وَلَوْ كَرِهَ ٱلْمُجْرِمُونَ ﴿٨﴾
إِذْ تَسْتَغِيثُونَ رَبَّكُمْ فَٱسْتَجَابَ لَكُمْ أَنِّى مُمِدُّكُم بِأَلْفٍ
مِّنَ ٱلْمَلَٰٓئِكَةِ مُرْدِفِينَ ﴿٩﴾ وَمَا جَعَلَهُ ٱللَّهُ إِلَّا بُشْرَىٰ

Sūrat al-Anfāl
Booty

A Madinan *sūra*, except for *āyat*s 3 to 36 which are Makkan. It has 85, 86, or 87 *āyat*s, and it was revealed after *Sūrat al-Baqara.*

When the Muslims disagreed about the booty of Badr, the young men said, "It is for us because we directly participated in the fighting." The older men said, "We were a cloak for you under the banners. If we had been exposed, we would have joined you in the fighting and so you should not be preferred in respect of it." Then this was revealed.

1. ***They will ask you,*** Muḥammad, ***about booty. Say: 'Booty belongs to Allah*** who will assign it wherever He wills ***and the Messenger***, may Allah bless him and grant him peace, who will divide it equally between them, as is related by al-Ḥākim in *al-Mustadrak.* ***So be fearful of Allah and put things right between you*** by loving one another and abandoning conflict. ***Obey Allah and His Messenger if you are*** truly ***believers.'***

2. ***The believers*** who have complete faith ***are those whose hearts tremble*** with fear ***when Allah***'s threat ***is mentioned, whose belief is increased*** by affirming their truth ***when His Signs are recited to them, and who put their trust in their Lord*** alone, fearing no one else**...**

3. ***...those who establish the prayer*** with all the duties which it entails, ***and give of what We have provided for them*** in obedience to Allah.

4. ***They*** (the people of this description) ***are in truth the believers*** without any doubt. ***They have high ranks*** (degrees in the Garden) ***with their Lord and forgiveness and generous provision*** in the Garden.

5. ***Just as your Lord brought you out from your house with truth, even though a group of the believers disliked it*** – this phrase is adverbial describing how they went out and their state of disliking to do so. If they are brought out while disliking it, it is better for them. That is because Abū Sufyān brought a caravan from Syria and the

Prophet, may Allah bless him and grant him peace, and his Companions went out to loot it. The Quraysh learned about that and Abū Jahl and fighters from Makka set out to defend him in a group. Abū Sufyān took the caravan by the coastal road and escaped. Abu Jahl was told to return, but he refused.

6. ***...arguing with you about the Truth*** – the obligation to fight – ***after it had been made clear***, it appearing ***as though they were being driven to their death with open eyes*** in spite of their dislike for it.

7. Remember ***when Allah promised you that one of the two parties*** – either the caravan or the Makkan army – ***would be yours and you would have liked it to have been the unarmed one*** without force and weaponry – the caravan which had far fewer defenders – ***whereas Allah desired to verify the Truth by His words*** – His preordainment of the victory of Islam – ***and to cut off the last remnant of the unbelievers*** through His command to fight the army.

8. ***This was so that He might verify the Truth and nullify the false*** (unbelief) ***even though the evildoers*** (idolaters) ***hate that.***

9. ***Remember when you called on your Lord for help*** – asking Him to rescue you by giving you assistance against them – ***and He responded to you: 'I will reinforce you with a thousand angels riding rank after rank.'*** The angels came line after line as promised and first there were three thousand and then five thousand, as recorded in *Sūrat Āl 'Imrān.*

10. ***Allah only did this*** – informed you of these angelic reinforcements – ***to give you good news and that so your hearts would be at rest. Victory comes from no one but Allah. Allah is Almighty, All-Wise.***

11. ***And*** remember ***when He overcame you with sleep, making you feel secure*** from the fear you had been feeling, ***and sent you down water from heaven to purify you*** from minor and major impurities ***and remove the taint of Shayṭān from you*** – and his whispering to you when he whispered, "If you were in the right, you would not be thirsty and in a state of impurity when the idolaters have access to water." – ***and to fortify your hearts*** with certainty and steadfastness ***and make your feet firm,*** preventing them from slipping in the sand.

وَلِتَطْمَئِنَّ بِهِۦ قُلُوبُكُمْ ۚ وَمَا ٱلنَّصْرُ إِلَّا مِنْ عِندِ ٱللَّهِ ۚ إِنَّ ٱللَّهَ
عَزِيزٌ حَكِيمٌ ١٠ إِذْ يُغَشِّيكُمُ ٱلنُّعَاسَ أَمَنَةً مِّنْهُ وَيُنَزِّلُ
عَلَيْكُم مِّنَ ٱلسَّمَآءِ مَآءً لِّيُطَهِّرَكُم بِهِۦ وَيُذْهِبَ عَنكُمْ رِجْزَ
ٱلشَّيْطَٰنِ وَلِيَرْبِطَ عَلَىٰ قُلُوبِكُمْ وَيُثَبِّتَ بِهِ ٱلْأَقْدَامَ ١١
إِذْ يُوحِى رَبُّكَ إِلَى ٱلْمَلَٰٓئِكَةِ أَنِّى مَعَكُمْ فَثَبِّتُوا۟ ٱلَّذِينَ ءَامَنُوا۟ ۚ
سَأُلْقِى فِى قُلُوبِ ٱلَّذِينَ كَفَرُوا۟ ٱلرُّعْبَ فَٱضْرِبُوا۟ فَوْقَ
ٱلْأَعْنَاقِ وَٱضْرِبُوا۟ مِنْهُمْ كُلَّ بَنَانٍ ١٢ ذَٰلِكَ بِأَنَّهُمْ
شَآقُّوا۟ ٱللَّهَ وَرَسُولَهُۥ ۚ وَمَن يُشَاقِقِ ٱللَّهَ وَرَسُولَهُۥ فَإِنَّ ٱللَّهَ
شَدِيدُ ٱلْعِقَابِ ١٣ ذَٰلِكُمْ فَذُوقُوهُ وَأَنَّ لِلْكَٰفِرِينَ
عَذَابَ ٱلنَّارِ ١٤ يَٰٓأَيُّهَا ٱلَّذِينَ ءَامَنُوٓا۟ إِذَا لَقِيتُمُ ٱلَّذِينَ
كَفَرُوا۟ زَحْفًا فَلَا تُوَلُّوهُمُ ٱلْأَدْبَارَ ١٥ وَمَن يُوَلِّهِمْ يَوْمَئِذٍ
دُبُرَهُۥٓ إِلَّا مُتَحَرِّفًا لِّقِتَالٍ أَوْ مُتَحَيِّزًا إِلَىٰ فِئَةٍ فَقَدْ بَآءَ
بِغَضَبٍ مِّنَ ٱللَّهِ وَمَأْوَىٰهُ جَهَنَّمُ ۖ وَبِئْسَ ٱلْمَصِيرُ ١٦
فَلَمْ تَقْتُلُوهُمْ وَلَٰكِنَّ ٱللَّهَ قَتَلَهُمْ ۚ وَمَا رَمَيْتَ إِذْ رَمَيْتَ
وَلَٰكِنَّ ٱللَّهَ رَمَىٰ ۚ وَلِيُبْلِىَ ٱلْمُؤْمِنِينَ مِنْهُ بَلَآءً حَسَنًا ۚ
إِنَّ ٱللَّهَ سَمِيعٌ عَلِيمٌ ١٧ ذَٰلِكُمْ وَأَنَّ ٱللَّهَ مُوهِنُ كَيْدِ
ٱلْكَٰفِرِينَ ١٨ إِن تَسْتَفْتِحُوا۟ فَقَدْ جَآءَكُمُ ٱلْفَتْحُ ۖ
وَإِن تَنتَهُوا۟ فَهُوَ خَيْرٌ لَّكُمْ ۖ وَإِن تَعُودُوا۟ نَعُدْ وَلَن تُغْنِىَ عَنكُمْ
فِئَتُكُمْ شَيْـًٔا وَلَوْ كَثُرَتْ وَأَنَّ ٱللَّهَ مَعَ ٱلْمُؤْمِنِينَ ١٩ يَٰٓأَيُّهَا
ٱلَّذِينَ ءَامَنُوٓا۟ أَطِيعُوا۟ ٱللَّهَ وَرَسُولَهُۥ وَلَا تَوَلَّوْا۟ عَنْهُ وَأَنتُمْ

12. ***And when your Lord revealed to the angels*** who reinforced the Muslims, ***'I am with you*** with help and support ***so make those who believe firm*** through the help and good news you bring. ***I will cast terror*** (extreme fear) ***into the hearts of those who disbelieve, so strike their necks*** (behead them) ***and strike all their finger joints***, cutting off their fingers and toes*!'* It happened that a man would go to strike at the neck of an unbeliever and his head would fall off before his sword was able to get there. The Prophet, may Allah bless him and grant him peace, threw a handful of pebbles and there was not a single unbeliever whose eyes were not directly affected by it and they were completely routed.

13. ***This*** punishment ***was*** visited on them ***because they were hostile to*** and fought against ***Allah and His Messenger. If anyone is hostile to Allah and His Messenger, Allah is severe in retribution*** to him.

14. ***That*** punishment ***is your reward*** in this world, ***so taste it. The unbelievers will also have the punishment of the Fire*** in the Next World.

15. ***You who believe! When you encounter those who disbelieve advancing in massed ranks*** because of their great number ***into battle, do not turn your backs on them.***

16. ***Anyone who turns his back on them that day*** (a day of battle), ***unless he is withdrawing***, as a ruse with the appearance of flight but really intending ***to rejoin the fight or withdrawing to join another group*** of Muslims in order to reinforce them, ***brings Allah's anger down upon himself. His refuge is Hell. What an evil destination!***

17. ***You did not kill them*** at Badr through your own strength*:* ***it was Allah who killed them*** by His helping you. ***And you did not throw,*** Muḥammad, ***when you threw*** the pebbles into the eyes of the enemy because no handful of pebbles thrown by a human being would be able to reach the eyes of every soldier in a large army*:* ***it was Allah who threw*** by making that handful reach its target, causing the overthrow of the unbelievers*:* ***so He might test the believers with this excellent trial from Him*** (the gift of the booty). ***Allah is All-Hearing*** of what they say, ***All-Knowing*** of their states.

18. ***That is your reward. Allah always confounds the schemes of the unbelievers*** by making them ineffectual.

تَسۡمَعُونَ ٢٠ وَلَا تَكُونُواْ كَٱلَّذِينَ قَالُواْ سَمِعۡنَا وَهُمۡ
لَا يَسۡمَعُونَ ٢١ ۞إِنَّ شَرَّ ٱلدَّوَآبِّ عِندَ ٱللَّهِ ٱلصُّمُّ ٱلۡبُكۡمُ
ٱلَّذِينَ لَا يَعۡقِلُونَ ٢٢ وَلَوۡ عَلِمَ ٱللَّهُ فِيهِمۡ خَيۡرٗا لَّأَسۡمَعَهُمۡۖ
وَلَوۡ أَسۡمَعَهُمۡ لَتَوَلَّواْ وَّهُم مُّعۡرِضُونَ ٢٣ يَٰٓأَيُّهَا ٱلَّذِينَ
ءَامَنُواْ ٱسۡتَجِيبُواْ لِلَّهِ وَلِلرَّسُولِ إِذَا دَعَاكُمۡ لِمَا يُحۡيِيكُمۡۖ
وَٱعۡلَمُوٓاْ أَنَّ ٱللَّهَ يَحُولُ بَيۡنَ ٱلۡمَرۡءِ وَقَلۡبِهِۦ وَأَنَّهُۥٓ إِلَيۡهِ
تُحۡشَرُونَ ٢٤ وَٱتَّقُواْ فِتۡنَةٗ لَّا تُصِيبَنَّ ٱلَّذِينَ ظَلَمُواْ
مِنكُمۡ خَآصَّةٗۖ وَٱعۡلَمُوٓاْ أَنَّ ٱللَّهَ شَدِيدُ ٱلۡعِقَابِ ٢٥
وَٱذۡكُرُوٓاْ إِذۡ أَنتُمۡ قَلِيلٞ مُّسۡتَضۡعَفُونَ فِي ٱلۡأَرۡضِ تَخَافُونَ
أَن يَتَخَطَّفَكُمُ ٱلنَّاسُ فَـَٔاوَىٰكُمۡ وَأَيَّدَكُم بِنَصۡرِهِۦ وَرَزَقَكُم
مِّنَ ٱلطَّيِّبَٰتِ لَعَلَّكُمۡ تَشۡكُرُونَ ٢٦ يَٰٓأَيُّهَا ٱلَّذِينَ ءَامَنُواْ
لَا تَخُونُواْ ٱللَّهَ وَٱلرَّسُولَ وَتَخُونُوٓاْ أَمَٰنَٰتِكُمۡ وَأَنتُمۡ تَعۡلَمُونَ
٢٧ وَٱعۡلَمُوٓاْ أَنَّمَآ أَمۡوَٰلُكُمۡ وَأَوۡلَٰدُكُمۡ فِتۡنَةٞ وَأَنَّ ٱللَّهَ
عِندَهُۥٓ أَجۡرٌ عَظِيمٞ ٢٨ يَٰٓأَيُّهَا ٱلَّذِينَ ءَامَنُوٓاْ إِن تَتَّقُواْ
ٱللَّهَ يَجۡعَل لَّكُمۡ فُرۡقَانٗا وَيُكَفِّرۡ عَنكُمۡ سَيِّـَٔاتِكُمۡ وَيَغۡفِرۡ
لَكُمۡۗ وَٱللَّهُ ذُو ٱلۡفَضۡلِ ٱلۡعَظِيمِ ٢٩ وَإِذۡ يَمۡكُرُ بِكَ ٱلَّذِينَ
كَفَرُواْ لِيُثۡبِتُوكَ أَوۡ يَقۡتُلُوكَ أَوۡ يُخۡرِجُوكَۚ وَيَمۡكُرُونَ وَيَمۡكُرُ
ٱللَّهُۖ وَٱللَّهُ خَيۡرُ ٱلۡمَٰكِرِينَ ٣٠ وَإِذَا تُتۡلَىٰ عَلَيۡهِمۡ ءَايَٰتُنَا
قَالُواْ قَدۡ سَمِعۡنَا لَوۡ نَشَآءُ لَقُلۡنَا مِثۡلَ هَٰذَآۙ إِنۡ هَٰذَآ إِلَّآ
أَسَٰطِيرُ ٱلۡأَوَّلِينَ ٣١ وَإِذۡ قَالُواْ ٱللَّهُمَّ إِن كَانَ هَٰذَا

19. ***If it was a decisive victory you were looking for,*** unbelievers – when Abū Jahl said, "O Allah, destroy tomorrow the one of us who breaks ties of kinship more and brings us what we do not recognise!" – ***that victory has clearly been won*** – resulting in the destruction asked for by Abū Jahl, except that it was him and those with him who were killed rather than the Prophet, may Allah bless him and grant him peace, and the believers. ***If you desist*** from unbelief and war, ***it will better for you; but if you return*** to fighting the Prophet, may Allah bless him and grant him peace, ***We also will return*** by supporting him against you. ***Your troops will not help*** – be able to defend – ***you at all, however many they are. Allah is with the believers.***

20. ***You who believe! Obey Allah and His Messenger. And do not turn away from Him*** by opposing His commands ***when you are able to hear*** the Qur'an and its admonitions.

21. ***Do not be like those who say, 'We hear,' when they do not hear*** – because if they really heard it would result in their sincere reflection and their being admonished. This refers to the hypocrites or the idolaters.

22. ***The worst of beasts in Allah's sight are those who are deaf*** to the truth ***and dumb*** and so unable to give expression to it ***who have no intellect.***

23. ***If Allah knew of any good in them*** – meaning openness to hearing the truth – ***He would have made them able to hear*** – enabling them to understand it. ***But even if He had made them able to hear*** – a mere hypothesis since He knew there was no good in them – ***they would still have turned away*** from the truth out of their obstinacy and denial.

24. ***You who believe! Respond to Allah and to the Messenger*** by obeying them ***when He calls you to what will bring you to life*** – meaning the *dīn* of Islam since it is the means to eternal life***! Know that Allah intervenes between a man and his heart*** – so that he cannot believe or disbelieve except by the will of Allah – ***and that you will be gathered to Him*** so that He may repay you for your actions.

25. ***Be fearful of trials which***, if they happen to you, ***will not afflict solely those among you who do wrong*** – rather they will envelop them and others than them, so you should keep clear of them by objecting to those objectionable things which will bring them about. ***Know that Allah is severe in retribution*** to those who oppose Him.

26. ***When you were few and oppressed in the land*** (in Makka), ***afraid that the people*** (the unbelievers) ***would snatch you away*** – suddenly seizing you – ***He gave you refuge*** in Madina ***and supported you with His help*** – the angels at Badr – ***and provided you with good things*** (booty) ***so that perhaps you would be thankful*** for His blessings.

27. ***You who believe! Do not betray Allah and His Messenger*** – this was revealed about Abū Lubāba Marwān ibn 'Abdu'l-Mundhir. The Prophet, may Allah bless him and grant him peace, sent him to the Banu Qurayẓa to persuade them to agree to submit to the Prophet's judgement. They consulted him but he indicated to them, because he had family and wealth among them, that they were going to be executed – ***and do not knowingly betray your trusts*** – referring to both the *dīn* and other things you have been entrusted with.

28. ***Know that your wealth and children are a trial*** – a potential obstacle to you in your progress to the Next World, so do not be tempted by concern for your property and children into acting treacherously on their account – ***and that there is an immense reward with Allah.*** This was revealed about Abū Lubāba's repentance.

29. ***You who believe! If you are fearful of Allah*** by showing regret and in other ways ***He will give you discrimination*** – enabling you to thereby avoid what you fear so that you will be saved – ***and erase your bad actions from you and forgive you*** your wrong actions. ***Allah's favour is indeed immense.***

30. Remember, Muhammad, ***when those who disbelieve were plotting against you*** – consulting one another in the Dār an-Nadwa in Makka about what to do about you – ***to*** bind and ***imprison you or kill you*** – acting all together as a single man – ***or expel you*** from Makka: ***they were plotting and Allah was plotting*** – to take care of your interests by revealing to you what they had plotted and commanding you to leave – ***but Allah is the Best of Plotters*** – having more knowledge than they have.

هُوَ ٱلۡحَقَّ مِنۡ عِندِكَ فَأَمۡطِرۡ عَلَيۡنَا حِجَارَةٗ مِّنَ ٱلسَّمَآءِ
أَوِ ٱئۡتِنَا بِعَذَابٍ أَلِيمٖ ﴿٣٢﴾ وَمَا كَانَ ٱللَّهُ لِيُعَذِّبَهُمۡ
وَأَنتَ فِيهِمۡۚ وَمَا كَانَ ٱللَّهُ مُعَذِّبَهُمۡ وَهُمۡ يَسۡتَغۡفِرُونَ ﴿٣٣﴾
وَمَا لَهُمۡ أَلَّا يُعَذِّبَهُمُ ٱللَّهُ وَهُمۡ يَصُدُّونَ عَنِ ٱلۡمَسۡجِدِ
ٱلۡحَرَامِ وَمَا كَانُوٓاْ أَوۡلِيَآءَهُۥٓۚ إِنۡ أَوۡلِيَآؤُهُۥٓ إِلَّا ٱلۡمُتَّقُونَ
وَلَٰكِنَّ أَكۡثَرَهُمۡ لَا يَعۡلَمُونَ ﴿٣٤﴾ وَمَا كَانَ صَلَاتُهُمۡ
عِندَ ٱلۡبَيۡتِ إِلَّا مُكَآءٗ وَتَصۡدِيَةٗۚ فَذُوقُواْ ٱلۡعَذَابَ
بِمَا كُنتُمۡ تَكۡفُرُونَ ﴿٣٥﴾ إِنَّ ٱلَّذِينَ كَفَرُواْ يُنفِقُونَ
أَمۡوَٰلَهُمۡ لِيَصُدُّواْ عَن سَبِيلِ ٱللَّهِۚ فَسَيُنفِقُونَهَا ثُمَّ تَكُونُ
عَلَيۡهِمۡ حَسۡرَةٗ ثُمَّ يُغۡلَبُونَۗ وَٱلَّذِينَ كَفَرُوٓاْ إِلَىٰ جَهَنَّمَ
يُحۡشَرُونَ ﴿٣٦﴾ لِيَمِيزَ ٱللَّهُ ٱلۡخَبِيثَ مِنَ ٱلطَّيِّبِ وَيَجۡعَلَ
ٱلۡخَبِيثَ بَعۡضَهُۥ عَلَىٰ بَعۡضٖ فَيَرۡكُمَهُۥ جَمِيعٗا فَيَجۡعَلَهُۥ
فِي جَهَنَّمَۚ أُوْلَٰٓئِكَ هُمُ ٱلۡخَٰسِرُونَ ﴿٣٧﴾ قُل لِّلَّذِينَ
كَفَرُوٓاْ إِن يَنتَهُواْ يُغۡفَرۡ لَهُم مَّا قَدۡ سَلَفَ وَإِن يَعُودُواْ
فَقَدۡ مَضَتۡ سُنَّتُ ٱلۡأَوَّلِينَ ﴿٣٨﴾ وَقَٰتِلُوهُمۡ حَتَّىٰ
لَا تَكُونَ فِتۡنَةٞ وَيَكُونَ ٱلدِّينُ كُلُّهُۥ لِلَّهِۚ فَإِنِ
ٱنتَهَوۡاْ فَإِنَّ ٱللَّهَ بِمَا يَعۡمَلُونَ بَصِيرٞ ﴿٣٩﴾ وَإِن تَوَلَّوۡاْ
فَٱعۡلَمُوٓاْ أَنَّ ٱللَّهَ مَوۡلَىٰكُمۡۚ نِعۡمَ ٱلۡمَوۡلَىٰ وَنِعۡمَ ٱلنَّصِيرُ ﴿٤٠﴾
۞ وَٱعۡلَمُوٓاْ أَنَّمَا غَنِمۡتُم مِّن شَيۡءٖ فَأَنَّ لِلَّهِ خُمُسَهُۥ وَلِلرَّسُولِ
وَلِذِي ٱلۡقُرۡبَىٰ وَٱلۡيَتَٰمَىٰ وَٱلۡمَسَٰكِينِ وَٱبۡنِ ٱلسَّبِيلِ إِن

31. ***When Our Signs*** (the Qur'an) ***are recited to them, they say, 'We have already heard all this. If we wanted, we could say the same thing. This*** (the Qur'an) ***is nothing but the myths*** (fabrications) ***of previous peoples.'*** This was said by an-Naḍr ibn al-Ḥārith because he went to Hira to trade and purchased some books of the history of the Persians and recounted them to the people of Makka.

32. ***And they say, 'O Allah, if this*** – which Muḥammad has recited to us – ***is really the truth*** revealed ***from You, rain down stones on us out of heaven or send a painful punishment down on us*** for denying it.*'* An-Naḍr and others said this in mockery, pretending to have the necessary insight to be able to declare definitively that it was false.

33. ***Allah would not punish them*** in the way they were asking for ***while you were among them*** because when the punishment descends, it is all-inclusive, so a nation is only punished when their Prophet and the believers leave it. ***Allah would not punish them as long as they sought forgiveness*** – which the idolaters used to do when they said in their *ṭawāf,* "Your forgiveness! Your forgiveness!". It is also said that this *āyat* refers to the oppressed believers among them, as Allah says: *"and had those who disbelieved among them been clearly distinguishable, We would have punished them with a painful punishment."* (48:25)

34. ***But why should Allah not punish them*** with the sword ***now*** that you and the oppressed Muslims have left – it is said that this *āyat* abrogates the previous one, for Allah did punish them at Badr and elsewhere – ***when they bar access to*** the Prophet, may Allah bless him and grant him peace, and the Muslims, preventing them from doing *ṭawāf* at **al-Masjid al-Ḥarām*? They are not its guardians. Only people who are godfearing can be its guardians. But most of them do not know that*** they are not its proper guardians.

35. ***Their prayer at the House is nothing but whistling and clapping*** in place of the prayer of Islam which they have been commanded to do. ***So taste the punishment*** at Badr ***because you have disbelieved!***

36. ***Those who disbelieve spend their wealth*** in support of the war against the Prophet, may Allah bless him and grant him peace, ***bar -***

ring access to the Way of Allah. They will spend it; then – after they see what happens – ***they will regret it*** because they will have both lost what they spent and and also failed to achieve their aim in doing it; ***then they will be overthrown*** in this world. ***Those who disbelieve will be gathered*** (driven) ***into Hell*** in the Next World**...**

37. *...so that Allah can sift out* (read as *li-yumayyiza* and *li-yamiza*) ***the bad*** (the unbelievers) ***from the good*** (the believers) ***and pile the bad on top of one another, heaping them all together, and tip them into Hell. They are the lost.***

38. *Say to those who disbelieve* – such as Abū Sufyān and his companions – ***that if they stop*** their unbelief and fighting the Prophet, may Allah bless him and grant him peace, ***they will be forgiven what is past*** of their actions; ***but if they return to it*** (fighting), ***they have the pattern of previous peoples in the past*** – referring to their destruction, which is what will happen to them as well.

39. *Fight them until there is no more* fitna (*shirk*) ***and the* dīn *is Allah's alone*** – meaning that only He is worshipped. ***If they stop*** their unbelief, ***Allah sees what they do*** and will reward them for it**...**

40. *...but if they turn away* from belief, ***know that Allah is your Master*:** your Supporter who is in charge of your affairs – ***the Best of Masters, and the Best of Helpers!***

41. *Know that when you take any booty* from the unbelievers by military force ***a fifth of it belongs to Allah, and to the Messenger, and to close relatives*** of the Prophet, may Allah bless him and grant him peace, from the Banū Hāshim and the Banū'l-Muṭṭalib, ***orphans***, children of Muslims whose fathers have died and were poor – ***the very poor***, those in need among the Muslims, ***and travellers***, Muslims on journeys. Thus one fifth goes to the Prophet, may Allah bless him and grant him peace, and to the other four categories mentioned, so that each of five categories has a fifth of the fifth, and the remaining four-fifths go to those who took the booty – ***if you believe in Allah and in what We have sent down to Our slave*** Muḥammad, may Allah bless him and grant him peace – referring both to the angels and other Signs – ***on the Day of Discrimination***: the Day of Badr, when the truth was distinguished from the false, ***the day the two groups*** (the Muslims and the unbelievers) ***met – Allah***

كُنتُمْ ءَامَنتُم بِٱللَّهِ وَمَآ أَنزَلْنَا عَلَىٰ عَبْدِنَا يَوْمَ ٱلْفُرْقَانِ
يَوْمَ ٱلْتَقَى ٱلْجَمْعَانِ ۗ وَٱللَّهُ عَلَىٰ كُلِّ شَىْءٍ قَدِيرٌ ﴿٤١﴾ إِذْ
أَنتُم بِٱلْعُدْوَةِ ٱلدُّنْيَا وَهُم بِٱلْعُدْوَةِ ٱلْقُصْوَىٰ وَٱلرَّكْبُ
أَسْفَلَ مِنكُمْ ۚ وَلَوْ تَوَاعَدتُّمْ لَٱخْتَلَفْتُمْ فِى ٱلْمِيعَـٰدِ ۙ
وَلَـٰكِن لِّيَقْضِىَ ٱللَّهُ أَمْرًا كَانَ مَفْعُولًا لِّيَهْلِكَ مَنْ
هَلَكَ عَنۢ بَيِّنَةٍ وَيَحْيَىٰ مَنْ حَىَّ عَنۢ بَيِّنَةٍ ۗ وَإِنَّ ٱللَّهَ
لَسَمِيعٌ عَلِيمٌ ﴿٤٢﴾ إِذْ يُرِيكَهُمُ ٱللَّهُ فِى مَنَامِكَ قَلِيلًا ۖ
وَلَوْ أَرَىٰكَهُمْ كَثِيرًا لَّفَشِلْتُمْ وَلَتَنَـٰزَعْتُمْ فِى ٱلْأَمْرِ
وَلَـٰكِنَّ ٱللَّهَ سَلَّمَ ۗ إِنَّهُۥ عَلِيمٌۢ بِذَاتِ ٱلصُّدُورِ ﴿٤٣﴾ وَإِذْ
يُرِيكُمُوهُمْ إِذِ ٱلْتَقَيْتُمْ فِىٓ أَعْيُنِكُمْ قَلِيلًا وَيُقَلِّلُكُمْ
فِىٓ أَعْيُنِهِمْ لِيَقْضِىَ ٱللَّهُ أَمْرًا كَانَ مَفْعُولًا ۗ وَإِلَى ٱللَّهِ
تُرْجَعُ ٱلْأُمُورُ ﴿٤٤﴾ يَـٰٓأَيُّهَا ٱلَّذِينَ ءَامَنُوٓا۟ إِذَا لَقِيتُمْ فِئَةً
فَٱثْبُتُوا۟ وَٱذْكُرُوا۟ ٱللَّهَ كَثِيرًا لَّعَلَّكُمْ تُفْلِحُونَ ﴿٤٥﴾
وَأَطِيعُوا۟ ٱللَّهَ وَرَسُولَهُۥ وَلَا تَنَـٰزَعُوا۟ فَتَفْشَلُوا۟ وَتَذْهَبَ رِيحُكُمْ ۖ
وَٱصْبِرُوٓا۟ ۚ إِنَّ ٱللَّهَ مَعَ ٱلصَّـٰبِرِينَ ﴿٤٦﴾ وَلَا تَكُونُوا۟ كَٱلَّذِينَ
خَرَجُوا۟ مِن دِيَـٰرِهِم بَطَرًا وَرِئَآءَ ٱلنَّاسِ وَيَصُدُّونَ
عَن سَبِيلِ ٱللَّهِ ۚ وَٱللَّهُ بِمَا يَعْمَلُونَ مُحِيطٌ ﴿٤٧﴾ وَإِذْ زَيَّنَ لَهُمُ
ٱلشَّيْطَـٰنُ أَعْمَـٰلَهُمْ وَقَالَ لَا غَالِبَ لَكُمُ ٱلْيَوْمَ مِنَ
ٱلنَّاسِ وَإِنِّى جَارٌ لَّكُمْ ۖ فَلَمَّا تَرَآءَتِ ٱلْفِئَتَانِ نَكَصَ
عَلَىٰ عَقِبَيْهِ وَقَالَ إِنِّى بَرِىٓءٌ مِّنكُمْ إِنِّىٓ أَرَىٰ مَا لَا تَرَوْنَ

has power over all things – being able to give them victory in spite of their small number and the large number of the enemy –

42. ***...when you were on the nearer slope*** – nearer to Madina – ***and they were on the further slope, and the caravan was lower down than you*** – closer to the sea. ***If you had made an appointment with them*** to fight, ***you would have broken the appointment. However, it happened*** with no appointment ***so that Allah could settle a matter whose result was preordained*** in the foreknowledge of Allah – referring to the victory of Islam and the rout of unbelief***: so that those*** unbelievers ***who died would die with clear proof*** established against them, ***and those*** believers ***who lived would live with clear proof*** of the victory of the believers despite their small numbers in the face of the vastly greater numbers of the enemy army. ***Allah is All-Hearing, All-Knowing.***

43. ***Remember when Allah showed them to you in your dream as only a few*** – and you told your Companions about your dream and they were happy. ***If He had shown you them as many, you would have lost heart*** (become cowardly) ***and quarrelled*** (argued with one another) ***about the matter*** (the order to fight)***; but Allah saved you*** from losing heart and quarrelling. ***He knows what your hearts contain.***

44. ***Remember***, believers, ***when Allah made you see them as few*** – about seventy or a hundred when they were in fact a thousand – ***when you met them, and also made you seem few in their eyes*** so that they would not withdraw from fighting. This was before battle was actually joined, because when battle was joined Allah made them seem twice their actual number as we find in *Sūra Āl 'Imrān* 3:13. ***This was so that Allah could settle a matter whose result was preordained. All matters return to Allah.***

45. ***You who believe! When you meet a troop*** of unbelievers, ***stand firm*** when you fight ***and remember Allah repeatedly*** – asking for His help – ***so that perhaps you will be successful*** – gain victory.

46. ***Obey Allah and His Messenger and do not quarrel among yourselves lest you lose heart*** and fail ***and your momentum*** (strength and power) ***disappear. And be steadfast. Allah is with the steadfast***, giving them His help and victory.

إِنِّيٓ أَخَافُ ٱللَّهَۚ وَٱللَّهُ شَدِيدُ ٱلۡعِقَابِ ﴿٤٨﴾ إِذۡ يَقُولُ
ٱلۡمُنَٰفِقُونَ وَٱلَّذِينَ فِي قُلُوبِهِم مَّرَضٌ غَرَّ هَٰٓؤُلَآءِ دِينُهُمۗ
وَمَن يَتَوَكَّلۡ عَلَى ٱللَّهِ فَإِنَّ ٱللَّهَ عَزِيزٌ حَكِيمٞ ﴿٤٩﴾
وَلَوۡ تَرَىٰٓ إِذۡ يَتَوَفَّى ٱلَّذِينَ كَفَرُواْ ٱلۡمَلَٰٓئِكَةُ يَضۡرِبُونَ
وُجُوهَهُمۡ وَأَدۡبَٰرَهُمۡ وَذُوقُواْ عَذَابَ ٱلۡحَرِيقِ ﴿٥٠﴾ ذَٰلِكَ
بِمَا قَدَّمَتۡ أَيۡدِيكُمۡ وَأَنَّ ٱللَّهَ لَيۡسَ بِظَلَّٰمٖ لِّلۡعَبِيدِ ﴿٥١﴾
كَدَأۡبِ ءَالِ فِرۡعَوۡنَ وَٱلَّذِينَ مِن قَبۡلِهِمۡۚ كَفَرُواْ بِـَٔايَٰتِ ٱللَّهِ
فَأَخَذَهُمُ ٱللَّهُ بِذُنُوبِهِمۡۗ إِنَّ ٱللَّهَ قَوِيّٞ شَدِيدُ ٱلۡعِقَابِ ﴿٥٢﴾
ذَٰلِكَ بِأَنَّ ٱللَّهَ لَمۡ يَكُ مُغَيِّرٗا نِّعۡمَةً أَنۡعَمَهَا عَلَىٰ قَوۡمٍ حَتَّىٰ يُغَيِّرُواْ
مَا بِأَنفُسِهِمۡ وَأَنَّ ٱللَّهَ سَمِيعٌ عَلِيمٞ ﴿٥٣﴾ كَدَأۡبِ ءَالِ
فِرۡعَوۡنَ وَٱلَّذِينَ مِن قَبۡلِهِمۡۚ كَذَّبُواْ بِـَٔايَٰتِ رَبِّهِمۡ فَأَهۡلَكۡنَٰهُم
بِذُنُوبِهِمۡ وَأَغۡرَقۡنَآ ءَالَ فِرۡعَوۡنَۚ وَكُلّٞ كَانُواْ ظَٰلِمِينَ ﴿٥٤﴾
إِنَّ شَرَّ ٱلدَّوَآبِّ عِندَ ٱللَّهِ ٱلَّذِينَ كَفَرُواْ فَهُمۡ لَا يُؤۡمِنُونَ ﴿٥٥﴾
ٱلَّذِينَ عَٰهَدتَّ مِنۡهُمۡ ثُمَّ يَنقُضُونَ عَهۡدَهُمۡ فِي كُلِّ مَرَّةٖ
وَهُمۡ لَا يَتَّقُونَ ﴿٥٦﴾ فَإِمَّا تَثۡقَفَنَّهُمۡ فِي ٱلۡحَرۡبِ فَشَرِّدۡ بِهِم
مَّنۡ خَلۡفَهُمۡ لَعَلَّهُمۡ يَذَّكَّرُونَ ﴿٥٧﴾ وَإِمَّا تَخَافَنَّ مِن
قَوۡمٍ خِيَانَةٗ فَٱنۢبِذۡ إِلَيۡهِمۡ عَلَىٰ سَوَآءٍۚ إِنَّ ٱللَّهَ لَا يُحِبُّ ٱلۡخَآئِنِينَ
﴿٥٨﴾ وَلَا يَحۡسَبَنَّ ٱلَّذِينَ كَفَرُواْ سَبَقُوٓاْۚ إِنَّهُمۡ لَا يُعۡجِزُونَ ﴿٥٩﴾
وَأَعِدُّواْ لَهُم مَّا ٱسۡتَطَعۡتُم مِّن قُوَّةٖ وَمِن رِّبَاطِ ٱلۡخَيۡلِ
تُرۡهِبُونَ بِهِۦ عَدُوَّ ٱللَّهِ وَعَدُوَّكُمۡ وَءَاخَرِينَ مِن دُونِهِمۡ

47. ***Do not be like those who left their homes in arrogance*** to prevent the Muslims from seizing their caravan and then did not turn back when they knew the caravan was safe, ***showing off to people*** – saying, "We will not return until we drink wine, slaughter camels and have tents set up for us at Badr," making sure their words were heard – ***and*** thereby ***barring them from the way of Allah. Allah encompasses*** – has full knowledge of – ***what they do*** (read as *ya'malūna* and also *ta'malūna*, "you do") and He will repay them for it…

48. ***…when Shayṭān*** (Iblīs) ***made their actions appear good to them*** by encouraging them to meet the Muslims when they feared that their enemies, the Banū Bakr, would come out, ***saying*** to them, ***'No one will overcome you today for I am at your side*** in Kināna.*'* He came to them in the form of Surāqa ibn Mālik, the chief of that region. ***But when the two parties*** (the Muslims and the unbelievers) ***came in sight of one another*** – and Shayṭān saw the angels while he was holding the hand of al-Ḥārith ibn Hishām – ***he turned right round on his heels*** and fled ***saying, 'I wash my hands of you. I see what you do not see*** – meaning the angels. ***I fear*** that ***Allah*** will destroy me. ***Allah is severe in retribution.'***

49. ***And when the hypocrites and those with sickness*** (weakness of belief) ***in their hearts said, 'These people*** (the Muslims) ***have been deluded by their* dīn.*'*** The hypocrites said this when the Muslims went out to fight a large army, expecting to be victorious despite the smallness of their numbers. Allah Almighty answered them with the words: ***But those who put their trust in Allah*** will be victorious and ***will find Allah to be Almighty,*** in command of His affair, ***All-Wise*** in what He does.

50. ***If only you***, Muḥammad, ***could see when the angels take back*** (read as *yatawaffā* and *tatawaffā*) ***those who disbelieved at their death, beating their faces and their backs*** with iron bars and they will be told***: 'Taste the punishment of the Burning*** in the Fire!

51. ***That*** punishment ***is for what you did. Allah does not wrong His slaves.'*** He does not punish them if they have committed no wrong.

52. ***Such was the case with Pharaoh's people and those before them. They disbelieved in Allah's Signs, so Allah seized them*** with punishment *for their wrong actions. Allah is Strong,* enabling Him to do whatever He wills, ***Severe in Retribution.***

53. ***That is because Allah would never change a blessing He has conferred on a people*** – replacing it with its opposite – ***until they had changed what was in themselves*** out of unbelief – as the unbelievers of Makka exchanged their security from hunger and fear and the sending to them of the Prophet, may Allah bless him and grant him peace, for unbelief, barring people from the Way of Allah and fighting the believers. ***Allah is All-Hearing, All-Knowing.***

54. ***Such was the case with Pharaoh's people and those before them. They denied their Lord's Signs, so We destroyed them for their wrong actions. We drowned Pharaoh's people*** together with him. ***All of them*** (those sinful nations) ***were wrongdoers.***

55. ***The worst of animals in the sight of Allah are those who disbelieve and so do not believe,*** (this was revealed about the Banū Qurayẓa)

56. ***those with whom you make a treaty*** that they should not give support to the idolaters ***and who then break it every time. They show no fearfulness of Allah*** in their treachery.

57. ***So if you come upon such people in war, make a harsh example of them*** to mark them out by punishment in order ***to deter*** and admonish ***those coming after them so that perha[s they will pay heed.***

58. ***If you fear treachery on the part of a people*** with whom you have made a treaty and their deception becomes clear to you, ***revoke your treaty with them mutually*** in a way in which both you and they will know that the treaty is revoked, so that they will not accuse you of treachery. ***Allah does not love treacherous people.***

59. ***Do not imagine***, Muhammad, ***that those who disbelieve have got ahead*** of Allah. ***They are quite powerless*** to escape Him.

60. ***Arm yourselves*** to fight ***against them with all the firepower*** – literally "strength" which, as related by Muslim, the Messenger of Allah, may Allah bless him and grant him peace, said here meant shooting – ***and cavalry*** – horses devoted to fighting in the Way of Allah – ***you can muster, to terrify the enemies of Allah and your enemies*** (the unbelievers of Makka) ***and others besides them whom***

لَا تَعۡلَمُونَهُمُ ٱللَّهُ يَعۡلَمُهُمۡۚ وَمَا تُنفِقُواْ مِن شَيۡءٖ فِي سَبِيلِ
ٱللَّهِ يُوَفَّ إِلَيۡكُمۡ وَأَنتُمۡ لَا تُظۡلَمُونَ ٦٠ ۞ وَإِن جَنَحُواْ
لِلسَّلۡمِ فَٱجۡنَحۡ لَهَا وَتَوَكَّلۡ عَلَى ٱللَّهِۚ إِنَّهُۥ هُوَ ٱلسَّمِيعُ ٱلۡعَلِيمُ ٦١
وَإِن يُرِيدُوٓاْ أَن يَخۡدَعُوكَ فَإِنَّ حَسۡبَكَ ٱللَّهُۚ هُوَ ٱلَّذِيٓ أَيَّدَكَ
بِنَصۡرِهِۦ وَبِٱلۡمُؤۡمِنِينَ ٦٢ وَأَلَّفَ بَيۡنَ قُلُوبِهِمۡۚ لَوۡ أَنفَقۡتَ
مَا فِي ٱلۡأَرۡضِ جَمِيعٗا مَّآ أَلَّفۡتَ بَيۡنَ قُلُوبِهِمۡ وَلَٰكِنَّ
ٱللَّهَ أَلَّفَ بَيۡنَهُمۡۚ إِنَّهُۥ عَزِيزٌ حَكِيمٞ ٦٣ يَٰٓأَيُّهَا ٱلنَّبِيُّ حَسۡبُكَ
ٱللَّهُ وَمَنِ ٱتَّبَعَكَ مِنَ ٱلۡمُؤۡمِنِينَ ٦٤ يَٰٓأَيُّهَا ٱلنَّبِيُّ حَرِّضِ
ٱلۡمُؤۡمِنِينَ عَلَى ٱلۡقِتَالِۚ إِن يَكُن مِّنكُمۡ عِشۡرُونَ صَٰبِرُونَ
يَغۡلِبُواْ مِاْئَتَيۡنِۚ وَإِن يَكُن مِّنكُم مِّاْئَةٞ يَغۡلِبُوٓاْ أَلۡفٗا مِّنَ
ٱلَّذِينَ كَفَرُواْ بِأَنَّهُمۡ قَوۡمٞ لَّا يَفۡقَهُونَ ٦٥ ٱلۡـَٰٔنَ خَفَّفَ
ٱللَّهُ عَنكُمۡ وَعَلِمَ أَنَّ فِيكُمۡ ضَعۡفٗاۚ فَإِن يَكُن مِّنكُم مِّاْئَةٞ
صَابِرَةٞ يَغۡلِبُواْ مِاْئَتَيۡنِۚ وَإِن يَكُن مِّنكُمۡ أَلۡفٞ يَغۡلِبُوٓاْ أَلۡفَيۡنِ
بِإِذۡنِ ٱللَّهِۗ وَٱللَّهُ مَعَ ٱلصَّٰبِرِينَ ٦٦ مَا كَانَ لِنَبِيٍّ أَن يَكُونَ
لَهُۥٓ أَسۡرَىٰ حَتَّىٰ يُثۡخِنَ فِي ٱلۡأَرۡضِۚ تُرِيدُونَ عَرَضَ ٱلدُّنۡيَا
وَٱللَّهُ يُرِيدُ ٱلۡأٓخِرَةَۗ وَٱللَّهُ عَزِيزٌ حَكِيمٞ ٦٧ لَّوۡلَا كِتَٰبٞ مِّنَ
ٱللَّهِ سَبَقَ لَمَسَّكُمۡ فِيمَآ أَخَذۡتُمۡ عَذَابٌ عَظِيمٞ ٦٨ فَكُلُواْ مِمَّا
غَنِمۡتُمۡ حَلَٰلٗا طَيِّبٗاۚ وَٱتَّقُواْ ٱللَّهَۚ إِنَّ ٱللَّهَ غَفُورٞ رَّحِيمٞ ٦٩
يَٰٓأَيُّهَا ٱلنَّبِيُّ قُل لِّمَن فِيٓ أَيۡدِيكُم مِّنَ ٱلۡأَسۡرَىٰٓ إِن يَعۡلَمِ ٱللَّهُ
فِي قُلُوبِكُمۡ خَيۡرٗا يُؤۡتِكُمۡ خَيۡرٗا مِّمَّآ أُخِذَ مِنكُمۡ وَيَغۡفِرۡ لَكُمۡۚ

you do not know (the hypocrites or the Jews). ***Allah knows them. Anything you spend in the Way of Allah will be repaid to you in full. You will not be wronged*** – you will not lose out in any way at all.

61. ***If they incline to peace*** (read as both *silm* and *salm*), ***you too incline to it*** and make a treaty with them – Ibn 'Abbās said that this was abrogated by the "*Āyat* of the Sword". Mujāhid said that it is particular to the People of the Book since it was revealed about the Banū Qurayẓa – ***and put your trust in Allah. He is the All-Hearing*** of your words, ***the All-Knowing*** of your actions.

62. ***If they intend to deceive you*** by pretending to want peace when their true intention is to prepare their forces to fight you, ***Allah is enough for you. It is He who supported you with His help and with the believers…***

63. ***…and unified their hearts*** which had been divided by old feuds. ***Even if you had spent everything on the earth, you could not have unified their hearts. But Allah has unified them*** by His power. ***He is Almighty,*** in control of His affair, ***All-Wise***: nothing is neglected by His wisdom.

64. ***Prophet! Allah is enough for you, and*** enough ***for the believers who follow you.***

65. ***Prophet! Spur on the believers to fight*** the unbelievers. ***If there are twenty of you who are steadfast, they will overcome two hundred; and if there are*** (read as *yakūn* and *takūn*) ***a hundred of you, they will overcome a thousand of those who disbelieve, because they are people who do not understand.*** This is a command in the form of a report ordering twenty to fight two hundred and a hundred to fight a thousand and ordering them to stand firm in spite of the odds. It was later abrogated by the next *āyat* when the number of Muslims grew.

66. ***Now Allah has made it lighter on you*** by removing the obligation of fighting when the odds are ten to one, ***knowing there is weakness*** (read as *ḍa'f* and *ḍu'f*) ***in you. If there are*** (read as *yakūn* and *takūn*) ***a hundred of you who are steadfast, they will overcome two hundred; and if there are a thousand of you, they will overcome two thousand with Allah's permission*** (by Allah's will). This is another command in the form of a report ordering the believers to now fight and stand firm when the odds are two to one. ***Allah is with the steadfast*** by means of His help to them.

67. This *āyat* was revealed when ransom was accepted for the captives of Badr. ***It is*** (read as *yakūn* and *takūn*) ***not fitting for a Prophet to take captives until he has let much blood in the land*** – meaning slaughtered many unbelievers. ***You*** (believers) ***desire the goods of this world*** – the money you accepted as ransom – ***whereas Allah desires*** the reward of ***the Next World*** for you through fighting the unbelievers. ***Allah is Almighty, All-Wise.*** This *āyat* was abrogated by Allah's words: *"set them free or ransom them."* (47:4)

68. ***Were it not for a prior decree*** making booty and captives lawful for you, ***which had already proceeded from Allah, a terrible punishment would have afflicted you on account of what*** (the ransom) ***you took.***

69. ***So make full use of any booty you have taken which is lawful and good; and be fearful of Allah. Allah is Ever-Forgiving, Most Merciful.***

70. ***Prophet! Say to those you are holding prisoner*** (read as *al-asrā* and *al-usāra*), ***'If Allah knows of any good*** (belief and sincerity) ***in your hearts, He will give you something better than what has been taken from you*** – referring to the ransom money, which Allah will return doubled and also give you a firm place in the Next World – ***and forgive you*** your wrong actions.***' Allah is Ever-Forgiving, Most Merciful.***

71. ***But if they*** (the captives) ***mean to betray you*** by the words they come out with, ***they have already previously betrayed Allah*** by their unbelief before Badr, ***so He has given you power over them*** by your killing them and taking them prisoner at Badr, and they can expect the same result if they try again. ***Allah is All-Knowing*** of His creation, ***All-Wise*** in what He does.

72. ***Those who have believed and have emigrated and done* jihād *with their wealth and themselves in the Way of Allah*** (the Muhājirūn), ***and those who have given refuge*** to the Prophet, may Allah bless him and grant him peace, ***and help*** (the Anṣār), ***they are the friends and protectors of one another*** with respect to support

وَٱللَّهُ غَفُورٞ رَّحِيمٞ ٧٠ وَإِن يُرِيدُواْ خِيَانَتَكَ فَقَدۡ خَانُواْ
ٱللَّهَ مِن قَبۡلُ فَأَمۡكَنَ مِنۡهُمۡۗ وَٱللَّهُ عَلِيمٌ حَكِيمٌ ٧١ إِنَّ ٱلَّذِينَ
ءَامَنُواْ وَهَاجَرُواْ وَجَٰهَدُواْ بِأَمۡوَٰلِهِمۡ وَأَنفُسِهِمۡ فِي سَبِيلِ
ٱللَّهِ وَٱلَّذِينَ ءَاوَواْ وَّنَصَرُوٓاْ أُوْلَٰٓئِكَ بَعۡضُهُمۡ أَوۡلِيَآءُ بَعۡضٖۚ وَٱلَّذِينَ
ءَامَنُواْ وَلَمۡ يُهَاجِرُواْ مَا لَكُم مِّن وَلَٰيَتِهِم مِّن شَيۡءٍ حَتَّىٰ يُهَاجِرُواْۚ
وَإِنِ ٱسۡتَنصَرُوكُمۡ فِي ٱلدِّينِ فَعَلَيۡكُمُ ٱلنَّصۡرُ إِلَّا عَلَىٰ قَوۡمِۢ
بَيۡنَكُمۡ وَبَيۡنَهُم مِّيثَٰقٞۗ وَٱللَّهُ بِمَا تَعۡمَلُونَ بَصِيرٞ ٧٢ وَٱلَّذِينَ
كَفَرُواْ بَعۡضُهُمۡ أَوۡلِيَآءُ بَعۡضٍۚ إِلَّا تَفۡعَلُوهُ تَكُن فِتۡنَةٞ فِي
ٱلۡأَرۡضِ وَفَسَادٞ كَبِيرٞ ٧٣ وَٱلَّذِينَ ءَامَنُواْ وَهَاجَرُواْ
وَجَٰهَدُواْ فِي سَبِيلِ ٱللَّهِ وَٱلَّذِينَ ءَاوَواْ وَّنَصَرُوٓاْ أُوْلَٰٓئِكَ هُمُ
ٱلۡمُؤۡمِنُونَ حَقّٗاۚ لَّهُم مَّغۡفِرَةٞ وَرِزۡقٞ كَرِيمٞ ٧٤ وَٱلَّذِينَ ءَامَنُواْ مِنۢ
بَعۡدُ وَهَاجَرُواْ وَجَٰهَدُواْ مَعَكُمۡ فَأُوْلَٰٓئِكَ مِنكُمۡۚ وَأُوْلُواْ ٱلۡأَرۡحَامِ
بَعۡضُهُمۡ أَوۡلَىٰ بِبَعۡضٖ فِي كِتَٰبِ ٱللَّهِۚ إِنَّ ٱللَّهَ بِكُلِّ شَيۡءٍ عَلِيمُۢ ٧٥

and inheritance. ***But as for those who believe but have not emigrated, you are not in any way responsible for their protection*** (read as *wilāya* and *walāya*) – in other words there is no inheritance between you and them and they have no share in any booty you take – ***until they emigrate.*** This was abrogated by the end of the *sūra*. ***But if they ask you for help in respect of the* dīn, *it is your duty to help them*** against the unbelievers, ***except against people you have a treaty with*** – in which case you should not break it by helping them. ***Allah sees what you do.***

73. ***Those who disbelieve are the friends and protectors of one another*** with respect to support and inheritance. ***If you do not act in this way*** – in other words, if the Muslims do not take control and curb the idolaters – ***there will be turmoil in the land and great corruption*** because of the strength of unbelief and weakness of Islam.

74. ***Those who believe and have emigrated and done* jihād *in the Way of Allah, and those who have given refuge and help, they are the true believers. They will have forgiveness and generous provision*** in the Garden.

75. ***Those who believe and emigrate later on*** after the first wave of believers and Muhājirūn ***and accompany you in* jihād, *they also are of your number***, together with the Muhājirūn and Anṣār. ***But blood relations are closer to one another*** – more entitled to inherit from one another than the believers who are only connected by the belief and emigration mentioned in the previous *āyat* – ***in the Book of Allah*** – meaning the Preserved Tablet. ***Allah has knowledge of all things*** – among which is the wisdom of inheritance.

سُورَةُ التَّوْبَةِ

بَرَآءَةٌ مِّنَ ٱللَّهِ وَرَسُولِهِۦٓ إِلَى ٱلَّذِينَ عَٰهَدتُّم مِّنَ ٱلْمُشْرِكِينَ ﴿١﴾
فَسِيحُوا۟ فِى ٱلْأَرْضِ أَرْبَعَةَ أَشْهُرٍ وَٱعْلَمُوٓا۟ أَنَّكُمْ غَيْرُ مُعْجِزِى
ٱللَّهِ ۙ وَأَنَّ ٱللَّهَ مُخْزِى ٱلْكَٰفِرِينَ ﴿٢﴾ وَأَذَٰنٌ مِّنَ ٱللَّهِ وَرَسُولِهِۦٓ
إِلَى ٱلنَّاسِ يَوْمَ ٱلْحَجِّ ٱلْأَكْبَرِ أَنَّ ٱللَّهَ بَرِىٓءٌ مِّنَ ٱلْمُشْرِكِينَ ۙ
وَرَسُولُهُۥ ۚ فَإِن تُبْتُمْ فَهُوَ خَيْرٌ لَّكُمْ ۖ وَإِن تَوَلَّيْتُمْ فَٱعْلَمُوٓا۟
أَنَّكُمْ غَيْرُ مُعْجِزِى ٱللَّهِ ۗ وَبَشِّرِ ٱلَّذِينَ كَفَرُوا۟ بِعَذَابٍ أَلِيمٍ
﴿٣﴾ إِلَّا ٱلَّذِينَ عَٰهَدتُّم مِّنَ ٱلْمُشْرِكِينَ ثُمَّ لَمْ يَنقُصُوكُمْ
شَيْـًٔا وَلَمْ يُظَٰهِرُوا۟ عَلَيْكُمْ أَحَدًا فَأَتِمُّوٓا۟ إِلَيْهِمْ عَهْدَهُمْ إِلَىٰ
مُدَّتِهِمْ ۚ إِنَّ ٱللَّهَ يُحِبُّ ٱلْمُتَّقِينَ ﴿٤﴾ فَإِذَا ٱنسَلَخَ ٱلْأَشْهُرُ ٱلْحُرُمُ
فَٱقْتُلُوا۟ ٱلْمُشْرِكِينَ حَيْثُ وَجَدتُّمُوهُمْ وَخُذُوهُمْ وَٱحْصُرُوهُمْ
وَٱقْعُدُوا۟ لَهُمْ كُلَّ مَرْصَدٍ ۚ فَإِن تَابُوا۟ وَأَقَامُوا۟ ٱلصَّلَوٰةَ
وَءَاتَوُا۟ ٱلزَّكَوٰةَ فَخَلُّوا۟ سَبِيلَهُمْ ۚ إِنَّ ٱللَّهَ غَفُورٌ رَّحِيمٌ ﴿٥﴾
وَإِنْ أَحَدٌ مِّنَ ٱلْمُشْرِكِينَ ٱسْتَجَارَكَ فَأَجِرْهُ حَتَّىٰ يَسْمَعَ
كَلَٰمَ ٱللَّهِ ثُمَّ أَبْلِغْهُ مَأْمَنَهُۥ ۚ ذَٰلِكَ بِأَنَّهُمْ قَوْمٌ لَّا يَعْلَمُونَ ﴿٦﴾
كَيْفَ يَكُونُ لِلْمُشْرِكِينَ عَهْدٌ عِندَ ٱللَّهِ وَعِندَ
رَسُولِهِۦٓ إِلَّا ٱلَّذِينَ عَٰهَدتُّمْ عِندَ ٱلْمَسْجِدِ ٱلْحَرَامِ ۖ فَمَا

9. *Sūrat at-Tawba*
Repentance

This *sūra* is Madinan except for the last two *āyats* which are Makkan. It has 120 *āyat*s and was revealed after *Sūrat al-Mā'ida.*

The *basmala* ("In the Name of Allah All-Merciful, Most Merciful") does not introduce it because, according to a *ḥadīth* reported by al-Ḥākim, the Prophet, may Allah bless him and grant him peace, did not command that it should be. Something similar is reported from 'Alī, namely that the *basmala* is security and this *sūra* was revealed to remove security by the sword. Ḥudhayfa said, "You call it *Surat at-Tawba* while it is in fact *Surat al-'Adhāb* (The *Sūra* of Punishment)." Al-Bukhārī related from al-Barā' that it was the last *sūra* to be revealed.

1. ***An announcement to those idolaters you have a general treaty with*** for four months, more or less, ***that Allah and His Messenger are free of them:*** the treaty is cancelled by this statement.

2. ***'You may travel about*** safely ***in the land for four months,*** idolaters – the first month was Shawwāl, as will be shown later – after that you will have no security, ***and know that you cannot thwart Allah –*** escape His punishment – ***and that Allah will humiliate the unbelievers*** in this world by killing and in the Next by the Fire.*'*

3. ***A proclamation*** and announcement ***from Allah and His Messenger to mankind on the day of the greater pilgrimage*** (the Day of Sacrifice)***: 'Allah is free of the idolaters*** and their treaties***, as is His Messenger*** also free**.** The Prophet, may Allah bless him and grant him peace, sent 'Alī that year, which was 9 AH, and he proclaimed these *āyat*s at Mina on the Day of Sacrifice, adding that no unbeliever should make *ḥajj* after that year or do *ṭawāf* around the House naked. Al-Bukhārī related that. ***If you repent*** of unbelief, ***it will be better for you. But if you turn your backs*** on belief, ***know that you cannot thwart Allah.' Give the unbelievers the news of a painful punishment*** – referring to killing and capture in this world and the Fire in the Next World –

4. ***…except those among the idolaters you have treaties with, who have not then broken*** any of the terms of ***their treaties with you in any way, or granted assistance to anyone*** among the unbelievers ***against you. Honour their treaties until their time runs out. Allah loves those who are godfearing*** by completing their agreements.

5. ***Then, when the sacred months are over*** – in other words, at the end of the period of delay granted – ***kill the idolaters wherever you find them*** – whether they be in the *Ḥaram* or outside it – ***and seize them*** by capture ***and besiege them*** in citadels and fortresses until they either fight or become Muslim ***and lie in wait for them on every road*** on which they travel. ***If they repent*** of their unbelief ***and establish the prayer and pay* zakāt*, let them go on their way*** and do not interfere with them. ***Allah is Ever-Forgiving, Most Merciful*** to those who repent.

6. ***If any of the idolaters ask you for protection*** from being killed, ***give them protection*** and security ***until they have heard the words of Allah*** (the Qur'an). ***Then convey them to a place where they are safe*** (the land of their people) if they do not believe. Then grant them a delay while they consider their circumstances. ***That is because they are a people who do not know*** the *dīn* of Allah. They must listen to the Qur'an so that they know.

7. ***How could any of the idolaters possibly have a treaty with Allah and with His Messenger*** – when they are those who reject Allah and His Messenger treacherously – ***except for those you made a treaty with at* al-Masjid al-Ḥarām** (at al-Ḥudaybiyya)***?*** So it is the Quraysh who are excepted. ***As long as they are straight with you*** – as long as they do not break their treaty – ***be straight with them*** and keep the treaty. ***Allah loves those who are godfearing.*** The Prophet, may Allah bless him and grant him peace, kept the treaty he had made with them (the Quraysh) until they broke it by helping the Banū Bakr against Khuzā'a.

8. ***How indeed*** can they have a treaty***? For if they get the upper hand over you*** by defeating you, ***they will respect neither kinship nor treaty.*** Instead they will harm you as much as they can. ***They please you with their mouths*** by fair words ***but their hearts belie their words*** and they do not abide by what they say. ***Most of them are deviators*** and break their word.

ٱسۡتَقَٰمُواْ لَكُمۡ فَٱسۡتَقِيمُواْ لَهُمۡۚ إِنَّ ٱللَّهَ يُحِبُّ ٱلۡمُتَّقِينَ
﴿٧﴾ كَيۡفَ وَإِن يَظۡهَرُواْ عَلَيۡكُمۡ لَا يَرۡقُبُواْ فِيكُمۡ إِلّٗا
وَلَا ذِمَّةٗۚ يُرۡضُونَكُم بِأَفۡوَٰهِهِمۡ وَتَأۡبَىٰ قُلُوبُهُمۡ وَأَكۡثَرُهُمۡ
فَٰسِقُونَ ﴿٨﴾ ٱشۡتَرَوۡاْ بِـَٔايَٰتِ ٱللَّهِ ثَمَنٗا قَلِيلٗا فَصَدُّواْ
عَن سَبِيلِهِۦٓۚ إِنَّهُمۡ سَآءَ مَا كَانُواْ يَعۡمَلُونَ ﴿٩﴾ لَا يَرۡقُبُونَ
فِي مُؤۡمِنٍ إِلّٗا وَلَا ذِمَّةٗۚ وَأُوْلَٰٓئِكَ هُمُ ٱلۡمُعۡتَدُونَ ﴿١٠﴾
فَإِن تَابُواْ وَأَقَامُواْ ٱلصَّلَوٰةَ وَءَاتَوُاْ ٱلزَّكَوٰةَ فَإِخۡوَٰنُكُمۡ
فِي ٱلدِّينِۗ وَنُفَصِّلُ ٱلۡأٓيَٰتِ لِقَوۡمٖ يَعۡلَمُونَ ﴿١١﴾ وَإِن نَّكَثُوٓاْ
أَيۡمَٰنَهُم مِّنۢ بَعۡدِ عَهۡدِهِمۡ وَطَعَنُواْ فِي دِينِكُمۡ فَقَٰتِلُوٓاْ
أَئِمَّةَ ٱلۡكُفۡرِ إِنَّهُمۡ لَآ أَيۡمَٰنَ لَهُمۡ لَعَلَّهُمۡ يَنتَهُونَ
﴿١٢﴾ أَلَا تُقَٰتِلُونَ قَوۡمٗا نَّكَثُوٓاْ أَيۡمَٰنَهُمۡ وَهَمُّواْ
بِإِخۡرَاجِ ٱلرَّسُولِ وَهُم بَدَءُوكُمۡ أَوَّلَ مَرَّةٍۚ
أَتَخۡشَوۡنَهُمۡۚ فَٱللَّهُ أَحَقُّ أَن تَخۡشَوۡهُ إِن كُنتُم مُّؤۡمِنِينَ ﴿١٣﴾
قَٰتِلُوهُمۡ يُعَذِّبۡهُمُ ٱللَّهُ بِأَيۡدِيكُمۡ وَيُخۡزِهِمۡ وَيَنصُرۡكُمۡ
عَلَيۡهِمۡ وَيَشۡفِ صُدُورَ قَوۡمٖ مُّؤۡمِنِينَ ﴿١٤﴾ وَيُذۡهِبۡ
غَيۡظَ قُلُوبِهِمۡۗ وَيَتُوبُ ٱللَّهُ عَلَىٰ مَن يَشَآءُۗ وَٱللَّهُ عَلِيمٌ حَكِيمٌ
﴿١٥﴾ أَمۡ حَسِبۡتُمۡ أَن تُتۡرَكُواْ وَلَمَّا يَعۡلَمِ ٱللَّهُ ٱلَّذِينَ جَٰهَدُواْ
مِنكُمۡ وَلَمۡ يَتَّخِذُواْ مِن دُونِ ٱللَّهِ وَلَا رَسُولِهِۦ وَلَا ٱلۡمُؤۡمِنِينَ
وَلِيجَةٗۚ وَٱللَّهُ خَبِيرُۢ بِمَا تَعۡمَلُونَ ﴿١٦﴾ مَا كَانَ لِلۡمُشۡرِكِينَ
أَن يَعۡمُرُواْ مَسَٰجِدَ ٱللَّهِ شَٰهِدِينَ عَلَىٰٓ أَنفُسِهِم بِٱلۡكُفۡرِۚ

9. ***They have sold Allah's Signs*** (the Qur'an) ***for a paltry price*** (this world) – they did not follow the Qur'an but instead followed their appetites and desires – ***and they have barred access to His Way*** (His *dīn*)**.** ***What they have done*** in this regard ***is truly evil.***

10. ***They respect neither kinship nor treaty where a believer is concerned. They are the people who overstep the limits.***

11. ***But if they repent and establish the prayer and pay* zakāt*, they are your brothers in the* dīn*. We make the Signs clear for people who have knowledge*** and reflect.

12. ***If they break their oaths*** and agreements ***after making their treaty and defame*** and criticise ***your* dīn*, then fight the leaders of unbelief – their oaths*** and treaties ***mean nothing – so that hopefully they will stop*** their unbelief.

13. The following is for encouragement. ***Will you not fight a people who have broken their oaths*** (their treaties) ***and resolved to expel the Messenger*** from Makka when they plotted against him in the Dār an-Nadwa, ***and who initiated hostilities against you in the first place?*** They initiated the fighting when they fought Khuzā'a, your allies, with the Banū Bakr. Why, then, should you not fight them? ***Is it them you fear? Allah has more right to your fear*** if you do not fight them ***if you are believers.***

14. ***Fight them! Allah will punish them*** by killing them ***at your hands, and disgrace them*** by capture and defeat ***and help you against them, and heal the hearts of those who believe*** for what the Banū Khuzā'a did to them.

15 ***He will remove the rage*** and grief ***from their hearts. Allah turns to anyone He wills*** by making them turn to Islam – like Abū Sufyān. ***Allah is All-Knowing, All-Wise.***

16. ***Or did you suppose that you would be left without Allah knowing*** by outward knowledge ***those of you who performed* jihād** with sincerity ***and who have not taken anyone as their intimate friends besides Allah and His Messenger and the believers?*** This refers to those who are sincere, who can be described by what Allah mentions here. ***Allah is aware of what you do.***

17. ***It is not for the idolaters to frequent the mosques*** (read as *masājid* – plural – and *masjid* – singular) ***of Allah*** by entering and

أُوْلَٰٓئِكَ حَبِطَتْ أَعْمَٰلُهُمْ وَفِى ٱلنَّارِ هُمْ خَٰلِدُونَ ﴿١٧﴾
إِنَّمَا يَعْمُرُ مَسَٰجِدَ ٱللَّهِ مَنْ ءَامَنَ بِٱللَّهِ وَٱلْيَوْمِ ٱلْءَاخِرِ
وَأَقَامَ ٱلصَّلَوٰةَ وَءَاتَى ٱلزَّكَوٰةَ وَلَمْ يَخْشَ إِلَّا ٱللَّهَ ۖ فَعَسَىٰٓ
أُوْلَٰٓئِكَ أَن يَكُونُواْ مِنَ ٱلْمُهْتَدِينَ ﴿١٨﴾ ۞ أَجَعَلْتُمْ سِقَايَةَ
ٱلْحَآجِّ وَعِمَارَةَ ٱلْمَسْجِدِ ٱلْحَرَامِ كَمَنْ ءَامَنَ بِٱللَّهِ وَٱلْيَوْمِ ٱلْءَاخِرِ
وَجَٰهَدَ فِى سَبِيلِ ٱللَّهِ ۚ لَا يَسْتَوُۥنَ عِندَ ٱللَّهِ ۗ وَٱللَّهُ لَا يَهْدِى ٱلْقَوْمَ
ٱلظَّٰلِمِينَ ﴿١٩﴾ ٱلَّذِينَ ءَامَنُواْ وَهَاجَرُواْ وَجَٰهَدُواْ فِى سَبِيلِ ٱللَّهِ
بِأَمْوَٰلِهِمْ وَأَنفُسِهِمْ أَعْظَمُ دَرَجَةً عِندَ ٱللَّهِ ۚ وَأُوْلَٰٓئِكَ هُمُ ٱلْفَآئِزُونَ ﴿٢٠﴾
يُبَشِّرُهُمْ رَبُّهُم بِرَحْمَةٍ مِّنْهُ وَرِضْوَٰنٍ وَجَنَّٰتٍ لَّهُمْ فِيهَا
نَعِيمٌ مُّقِيمٌ ﴿٢١﴾ خَٰلِدِينَ فِيهَآ أَبَدًا ۚ إِنَّ ٱللَّهَ عِندَهُۥٓ أَجْرٌ
عَظِيمٌ ﴿٢٢﴾ يَٰٓأَيُّهَا ٱلَّذِينَ ءَامَنُواْ لَا تَتَّخِذُوٓاْ ءَابَآءَكُمْ
وَإِخْوَٰنَكُمْ أَوْلِيَآءَ إِنِ ٱسْتَحَبُّواْ ٱلْكُفْرَ عَلَى ٱلْإِيمَٰنِ ۚ
وَمَن يَتَوَلَّهُم مِّنكُمْ فَأُوْلَٰٓئِكَ هُمُ ٱلظَّٰلِمُونَ ﴿٢٣﴾ قُلْ إِن
كَانَ ءَابَآؤُكُمْ وَأَبْنَآؤُكُمْ وَإِخْوَٰنُكُمْ وَأَزْوَٰجُكُمْ وَعَشِيرَتُكُمْ
وَأَمْوَٰلٌ ٱقْتَرَفْتُمُوهَا وَتِجَٰرَةٌ تَخْشَوْنَ كَسَادَهَا وَمَسَٰكِنُ
تَرْضَوْنَهَآ أَحَبَّ إِلَيْكُم مِّنَ ٱللَّهِ وَرَسُولِهِۦ وَجِهَادٍ
فِى سَبِيلِهِۦ فَتَرَبَّصُواْ حَتَّىٰ يَأْتِىَ ٱللَّهُ بِأَمْرِهِۦ ۗ وَٱللَّهُ لَا يَهْدِى
ٱلْقَوْمَ ٱلْفَٰسِقِينَ ﴿٢٤﴾ لَقَدْ نَصَرَكُمُ ٱللَّهُ فِى مَوَاطِنَ
كَثِيرَةٍ ۙ وَيَوْمَ حُنَيْنٍ ۙ إِذْ أَعْجَبَتْكُمْ كَثْرَتُكُمْ فَلَمْ
تُغْنِ عَنكُمْ شَيْـًٔا وَضَاقَتْ عَلَيْكُمُ ٱلْأَرْضُ

sitting in them, ***bearing witness against themselves of their unbelief. They are the ones whose actions will come to nothing. They will be in the Fire timelessly, for ever.***

18. ***The mosques of Allah should only be frequented by those who believe in Allah and the Last Day and establish the prayer and pay* zakāt, *and fear no one but Allah. They are the ones most likely to be guided.***

19. ***Do you make the giving of water to the pilgrims and looking after the*** people of the ***Masjid al-Ḥarām the same as believing in Allah and the Last Day and doing* jihād *in the Way of Allah? They are not equal in the sight of Allah*** in respect of their excellence? ***Allah does not guide wrongdoing people*** (unbelievers). This was revealed to refute those who said they were equal, namely al-'Abbās and others.

20. ***Those who believe and emigrate and do* jihād *in the Way of Allah with their wealth and themselves have a higher rank with Allah*** than those who do not. ***They are the ones who are victorious*** and who win good.

21. ***Their Lord gives them the good news of His mercy and good pleasure and Gardens where they will enjoy everlasting delight…***

22. ***…remaining in them timelessly, for ever and ever. Truly there is an immense reward with Allah.***

23. This was revealed about those who did not emigrate because of their families and businesses. ***You who believe! Do not befriend your fathers and brothers if they prefer unbelief to belief. Those among you who do befriend them are wrongdoers.***

24. ***Say: 'If your fathers or your sons or your brothers or your wives or your tribe*** (your clan, read as *'ashīratukum* and *'ashīrātukum*), ***or any wealth you have acquired, or any business you fear may slump*** and not be carried out, ***or any house which pleases you, are dearer to you than Allah and His Messenger and doing* jihād *in His Way*** – and so you remain behind instead of emigrating and performing *jihād* – ***then wait until Allah brings about His command.*** This is a threat to them. ***Allah does not guide people who are deviators.'***

بِمَا رَحُبَتْ ثُمَّ وَلَّيْتُم مُّدْبِرِينَ ﴿٢٥﴾ ثُمَّ أَنزَلَ ٱللَّهُ سَكِينَتَهُۥ
عَلَىٰ رَسُولِهِۦ وَعَلَى ٱلْمُؤْمِنِينَ وَأَنزَلَ جُنُودًا لَّمْ تَرَوْهَا
وَعَذَّبَ ٱلَّذِينَ كَفَرُوا۟ ۚ وَذَٰلِكَ جَزَآءُ ٱلْكَٰفِرِينَ ﴿٢٦﴾
ثُمَّ يَتُوبُ ٱللَّهُ مِنۢ بَعْدِ ذَٰلِكَ عَلَىٰ مَن يَشَآءُ ۗ وَٱللَّهُ غَفُورٌ
رَّحِيمٌ ﴿٢٧﴾ يَٰٓأَيُّهَا ٱلَّذِينَ ءَامَنُوٓا۟ إِنَّمَا ٱلْمُشْرِكُونَ
نَجَسٌ فَلَا يَقْرَبُوا۟ ٱلْمَسْجِدَ ٱلْحَرَامَ بَعْدَ عَامِهِمْ هَٰذَا ۚ
وَإِنْ خِفْتُمْ عَيْلَةً فَسَوْفَ يُغْنِيكُمُ ٱللَّهُ مِن فَضْلِهِۦٓ إِن
شَآءَ ۚ إِنَّ ٱللَّهَ عَلِيمٌ حَكِيمٌ ﴿٢٨﴾ قَٰتِلُوا۟ ٱلَّذِينَ
لَا يُؤْمِنُونَ بِٱللَّهِ وَلَا بِٱلْيَوْمِ ٱلْءَاخِرِ وَلَا يُحَرِّمُونَ مَا حَرَّمَ
ٱللَّهُ وَرَسُولُهُۥ وَلَا يَدِينُونَ دِينَ ٱلْحَقِّ مِنَ ٱلَّذِينَ أُوتُوا۟
ٱلْكِتَٰبَ حَتَّىٰ يُعْطُوا۟ ٱلْجِزْيَةَ عَن يَدٍ وَهُمْ صَٰغِرُونَ
﴿٢٩﴾ وَقَالَتِ ٱلْيَهُودُ عُزَيْرٌ ٱبْنُ ٱللَّهِ وَقَالَتِ ٱلنَّصَٰرَى
ٱلْمَسِيحُ ٱبْنُ ٱللَّهِ ۖ ذَٰلِكَ قَوْلُهُم بِأَفْوَٰهِهِمْ ۖ
يُضَٰهِـُٔونَ قَوْلَ ٱلَّذِينَ كَفَرُوا۟ مِن قَبْلُ ۚ قَٰتَلَهُمُ
ٱللَّهُ ۚ أَنَّىٰ يُؤْفَكُونَ ﴿٣٠﴾ ٱتَّخَذُوٓا۟ أَحْبَارَهُمْ
وَرُهْبَٰنَهُمْ أَرْبَابًا مِّن دُونِ ٱللَّهِ وَٱلْمَسِيحَ ٱبْنَ
مَرْيَمَ وَمَآ أُمِرُوٓا۟ إِلَّا لِيَعْبُدُوٓا۟ إِلَٰهًا وَٰحِدًا ۖ
لَّآ إِلَٰهَ إِلَّا هُوَ ۚ سُبْحَٰنَهُۥ عَمَّا يُشْرِكُونَ ﴿٣١﴾
يُرِيدُونَ أَن يُطْفِـُٔوا۟ نُورَ ٱللَّهِ بِأَفْوَٰهِهِمْ وَيَأْبَى ٱللَّهُ إِلَّآ
أَن يُتِمَّ نُورَهُۥ وَلَوْ كَرِهَ ٱلْكَٰفِرُونَ ﴿٣٢﴾ هُوَ ٱلَّذِىٓ

25. ***Allah has helped you on many occasions*** in war – such as at Badr and the fight against Qurayẓa and an-Naḍīr – ***including the Day of Hunayn*** – a valley between Makka and Ṭā'if, referring to the day when the Muslims fought Hawāzin in Shawwāl, 8 AH – ***when your great numbers delighted you*** – you said, "We will not be defeated today due to lack of manpower." The Muslims numbered 12,000 and the unbelievers 4000 – ***but did not help you in any way, and the earth seemed narrow to you for all its great breadth*** – the *mā* in *bimā* is adverbial, meaning that in spite of its extent you could not find a place in which you felt safe due to the intensity of fear which you experienced – ***and you turned your backs*** in defeat while the Prophet, may Allah bless him and grant him peace, remained firm on his white mule and no one remained with him except al-'Abbās and Abū Sufyān, who was holding his stirrup.

26. ***Then Allah sent down His serenity*** (peace of mind) ***on His Messenger and on the believers*** – the believers returned to the Prophet, may Allah bless him and grant him peace, when, at his command, al-'Abbās called them back and they fought – ***and sent down troops you could not see*** (the angels) ***and punished those who were unbelievers*** by killing and capture. ***That is how the unbelievers are repaid.***

27. ***Then after that Allah will turn to anyone He wills*** with Islam. ***Allah is Ever-Forgiving, Most Merciful.***

28. ***You who believe! The idolaters are unclean*** through the foulness of their inward, ***so after this year*** (9 AH) ***they should not come near*** **al-Masjid al-Ḥarām.** ***If you fear impoverishment*** (poverty) through your by trade with them being cut off, ***Allah will enrich you*** through conquest and *jizya* ***from His bounty if He wills. Allah is All-Knowing, All-Wise.***

29. ***Fight those of the people who were given the Book who do not believe in Allah and the Last Day*** – shown by the fact that they did not accept the Prophet, may Allah bless him and grant him peace – ***and who do not make unlawful what Allah and His Messenger have made unlawful*** – such as things like wine – ***and do not take as their*** **dīn** ***the*** **dīn** ***of Truth,*** which confirms and abrogates other *dīns*, ***until they pay the*** **jizya** ***with their own hands*** – meaning the Jews and the Christians who must pay it in submission or directly with

أَرْسَلَ رَسُولَهُۥ بِٱلْهُدَىٰ وَدِينِ ٱلْحَقِّ لِيُظْهِرَهُۥ عَلَى ٱلدِّينِ
كُلِّهِۦ وَلَوْ كَرِهَ ٱلْمُشْرِكُونَ ﴿٣٣﴾ ۞ يَٰٓأَيُّهَا ٱلَّذِينَ
ءَامَنُوٓا۟ إِنَّ كَثِيرًا مِّنَ ٱلْأَحْبَارِ وَٱلرُّهْبَانِ لَيَأْكُلُونَ
أَمْوَٰلَ ٱلنَّاسِ بِٱلْبَٰطِلِ وَيَصُدُّونَ عَن سَبِيلِ ٱللَّهِ ۗ
وَٱلَّذِينَ يَكْنِزُونَ ٱلذَّهَبَ وَٱلْفِضَّةَ وَلَا يُنفِقُونَهَا
فِى سَبِيلِ ٱللَّهِ فَبَشِّرْهُم بِعَذَابٍ أَلِيمٍ ﴿٣٤﴾ يَوْمَ يُحْمَىٰ
عَلَيْهَا فِى نَارِ جَهَنَّمَ فَتُكْوَىٰ بِهَا جِبَاهُهُمْ وَجُنُوبُهُمْ
وَظُهُورُهُمْ ۖ هَٰذَا مَا كَنَزْتُمْ لِأَنفُسِكُمْ فَذُوقُوا۟ مَا كُنتُمْ
تَكْنِزُونَ ﴿٣٥﴾ إِنَّ عِدَّةَ ٱلشُّهُورِ عِندَ ٱللَّهِ ٱثْنَا عَشَرَ
شَهْرًا فِى كِتَٰبِ ٱللَّهِ يَوْمَ خَلَقَ ٱلسَّمَٰوَٰتِ وَٱلْأَرْضَ
مِنْهَآ أَرْبَعَةٌ حُرُمٌ ۚ ذَٰلِكَ ٱلدِّينُ ٱلْقَيِّمُ ۚ فَلَا تَظْلِمُوا۟ فِيهِنَّ
أَنفُسَكُمْ ۚ وَقَٰتِلُوا۟ ٱلْمُشْرِكِينَ كَآفَّةً كَمَا
يُقَٰتِلُونَكُمْ كَآفَّةً ۚ وَٱعْلَمُوٓا۟ أَنَّ ٱللَّهَ مَعَ ٱلْمُتَّقِينَ ﴿٣٦﴾
إِنَّمَا ٱلنَّسِىٓءُ زِيَادَةٌ فِى ٱلْكُفْرِ ۖ يُضَلُّ بِهِ ٱلَّذِينَ كَفَرُوا۟
يُحِلُّونَهُۥ عَامًا وَيُحَرِّمُونَهُۥ عَامًا لِّيُوَاطِـُٔوا۟ عِدَّةَ مَا حَرَّمَ ٱللَّهُ
فَيُحِلُّوا۟ مَا حَرَّمَ ٱللَّهُ ۚ زُيِّنَ لَهُمْ سُوٓءُ أَعْمَٰلِهِمْ ۗ وَٱللَّهُ
لَا يَهْدِى ٱلْقَوْمَ ٱلْكَٰفِرِينَ ﴿٣٧﴾ يَٰٓأَيُّهَا ٱلَّذِينَ
ءَامَنُوا۟ مَا لَكُمْ إِذَا قِيلَ لَكُمُ ٱنفِرُوا۟ فِى سَبِيلِ ٱللَّهِ ٱثَّاقَلْتُمْ
إِلَى ٱلْأَرْضِ ۚ أَرَضِيتُم بِٱلْحَيَوٰةِ ٱلدُّنْيَا مِنَ ٱلْءَاخِرَةِ ۚ
فَمَا مَتَٰعُ ٱلْحَيَوٰةِ ٱلدُّنْيَا فِى ٱلْءَاخِرَةِ إِلَّا قَلِيلٌ ﴿٣٨﴾

their actual hands – ***in a state of complete abasement*** – humble and subject to the judgements of Islam. The *jizya* is a poll tax that they are required to pay every year.

30. ***The Jews say, ''Uzayr is the son of Allah,' and the Christians say, 'The Messiah*** ('Īsā) ***is the son of Allah.' That is what they say with their mouths,*** having nothing on which to base it, ***copying the words of those who disbelieved before,*** thereby imitating their forefathers. ***Allah fight them!*** This is a type of curse. ***How perverted they are!*** How they have turned aside from the truth when the proof has been established!

31. ***They have taken their rabbis*** (Jewish scholars) ***and monks*** (Christian worshippers) ***as lords besides Allah*** — since they follow them rather than Allah in making lawful what Allah has made unlawful and making unlawful what Allah has made lawful — ***and also the Messiah, son of Maryam. Yet they were commanded*** in the Torah and Gospel ***to worship only one God. There is no god but Him! Glory be to Him*** who is far ***above anything they associate with Him!***

32. ***They desire to extinguish Allah's Light*** (His Sharī'a and His proofs) ***with*** the words of ***their mouths. But Allah refuses to do other than perfect*** and manifest ***His Light, even though the unbelievers detest it.***

33. ***It is He who sent His Messenger*** Muḥammad, may Allah bless him and grant him peace, ***with guidance and the* Dīn *of Truth to exalt it over every other* dīn** – any *dīn* opposed to His – ***even though the idolaters detest it.***

34. ***You who believe! Many of the rabbis and monks devour people's property under false pretences*** – such as by taking bribes for making favourable judgements – ***and bar people from access to the Way of Allah*** (His *dīn*). ***As for those who hoard up gold and silver and do not spend it*** (what has been hoarded) ***in the Way of Allah,*** not, for instance, paying what is due on it in the form of *zakāt* and charity – ***give them the news of a painful punishment...***

35. ***...on the Day it is heated up in the fire of Hell and their foreheads, sides and backs are branded*** and burned ***with it.*** Their skin will become large enough to take all of it. They will be told: ***'This is***

what you hoarded for yourselves, so taste the repayment for ***what you were hoarding!'***

36. ***There have been twelve months*** in the calculation of the year ***with Allah in the Book of Allah*** (the Preserved Tablet) ***from the day He first created the heavens and earth. Four of them*** (the months) ***are sacred*** – namely, Dhū'l-Qa'da, Dhū'l-Ḥijja, Muḥarram and Rajab. ***That*** making sacred ***is the True*** (Upright) **Dīn,** ***so do not wrong one another during them*** (the Sacred Months) by acts of disobedience, because in those months they constitute a greater sin than at other times. It is said that this means in all months. ***But fight the idolaters totally*** (at all times) ***just as they fight you totally, and know that Allah is with those who are godfearing*** by His help and victory.

37. ***Deferring a sacred month*** – deferring the inviolability of one month to another month, as they used to do in the Jāhiliyya when they were engaged in fighting – ***is an increase in disbelief*** – because they deny the judgement of Allah in it – ***by which the unbelievers lead many people astray*** (read as *yuḍillu* and *yuḍallu*). ***One year they make it profane and another sacred to tally with the number Allah has made sacred.*** They make this exchange to keep the right number of sacred months. So the number remains exactly the same but the specific months concerned are varied. ***In that way they profane what Allah has made sacred*** and think that what they do is good. ***Their bad actions are made to seem good to them. Allah does not guide disbelieving people.***

38. The following was revealed when the Prophet, may Allah bless him and grant him peace, called people to go on the Tabūk expedition. They were in difficulty and it was a time of great heat and so it was hard for them. ***You who believe! What is the matter with you that when you are told, 'Go out and fight in the way of Allah,' you sink down heavily to the earth*** – you incline away from *jihād* and sit on the ground? The question is meant to be a rebuke. ***Are you happier with this world than the Next World*** and its pleasures? ***Yet the enjoyment of this world is very small*** and insignificant ***compared to that of the Next World.***

39. ***If you do not go out to fight*** with the Prophet, may Allah bless him and grant him peace, for *jihād*, ***He*** (Allah) ***will punish you with***

إِلَّا تَنفِرُوا۟ يُعَذِّبْكُمْ عَذَابًا أَلِيمًا وَيَسْتَبْدِلْ قَوْمًا
غَيْرَكُمْ وَلَا تَضُرُّوهُ شَيْـًٔا ۗ وَٱللَّهُ عَلَىٰ كُلِّ شَىْءٍ
قَدِيرٌ ﴿٣٩﴾ إِلَّا تَنصُرُوهُ فَقَدْ نَصَرَهُ ٱللَّهُ إِذْ أَخْرَجَهُ
ٱلَّذِينَ كَفَرُوا۟ ثَانِىَ ٱثْنَيْنِ إِذْ هُمَا فِى ٱلْغَارِ إِذْ
يَقُولُ لِصَـٰحِبِهِۦ لَا تَحْزَنْ إِنَّ ٱللَّهَ مَعَنَا ۖ فَأَنزَلَ
ٱللَّهُ سَكِينَتَهُۥ عَلَيْهِ وَأَيَّدَهُۥ بِجُنُودٍ لَّمْ تَرَوْهَا
وَجَعَلَ كَلِمَةَ ٱلَّذِينَ كَفَرُوا۟ ٱلسُّفْلَىٰ ۗ
وَكَلِمَةُ ٱللَّهِ هِىَ ٱلْعُلْيَا ۗ وَٱللَّهُ عَزِيزٌ حَكِيمٌ ﴿٤٠﴾
ٱنفِرُوا۟ خِفَافًا وَثِقَالًا وَجَـٰهِدُوا۟ بِأَمْوَٰلِكُمْ وَأَنفُسِكُمْ
فِى سَبِيلِ ٱللَّهِ ۚ ذَٰلِكُمْ خَيْرٌ لَّكُمْ إِن كُنتُمْ تَعْلَمُونَ ﴿٤١﴾
لَوْ كَانَ عَرَضًا قَرِيبًا وَسَفَرًا قَاصِدًا لَّٱتَّبَعُوكَ وَلَـٰكِنۢ بَعُدَتْ
عَلَيْهِمُ ٱلشُّقَّةُ ۚ وَسَيَحْلِفُونَ بِٱللَّهِ لَوِ ٱسْتَطَعْنَا لَخَرَجْنَا
مَعَكُمْ يُهْلِكُونَ أَنفُسَهُمْ وَٱللَّهُ يَعْلَمُ إِنَّهُمْ لَكَـٰذِبُونَ ﴿٤٢﴾
عَفَا ٱللَّهُ عَنكَ لِمَ أَذِنتَ لَهُمْ حَتَّىٰ يَتَبَيَّنَ لَكَ ٱلَّذِينَ
صَدَقُوا۟ وَتَعْلَمَ ٱلْكَـٰذِبِينَ ﴿٤٣﴾ لَا يَسْتَـْٔذِنُكَ ٱلَّذِينَ
يُؤْمِنُونَ بِٱللَّهِ وَٱلْيَوْمِ ٱلْـَٔاخِرِ أَن يُجَـٰهِدُوا۟ بِأَمْوَٰلِهِمْ
وَأَنفُسِهِمْ ۗ وَٱللَّهُ عَلِيمٌۢ بِٱلْمُتَّقِينَ ﴿٤٤﴾ إِنَّمَا يَسْتَـْٔذِنُكَ ٱلَّذِينَ
لَا يُؤْمِنُونَ بِٱللَّهِ وَٱلْيَوْمِ ٱلْـَٔاخِرِ وَٱرْتَابَتْ قُلُوبُهُمْ فَهُمْ
فِى رَيْبِهِمْ يَتَرَدَّدُونَ ﴿٤٥﴾ ۞ وَلَوْ أَرَادُوا۟ ٱلْخُرُوجَ
لَأَعَدُّوا۟ لَهُۥ عُدَّةً وَلَـٰكِن كَرِهَ ٱللَّهُ ٱنۢبِعَاثَهُمْ فَثَبَّطَهُمْ

a painful punishment and substitute another people in your place. You will not harm Him in any way by not helping Him. This can refer to either Allah or to the Prophet, may Allah bless him and grant him peace. ***Allah has power over all things.*** Allah is the One who helps His *dīn*. He has the power to help His *dīn* and His Prophet.

40. ***If you do not help him*** (the Prophet, may Allah bless him and grant him peace) ***Allah did help him when the unbelievers drove him out*** of Makka – and he was forced to seek refuge outside when they intended to kill him or imprison him or to exile him after their meeting in the Dār an-Nadwa – ***and there were two of them in the Cave*** in Mount Thawr. The two of them in the Cave were the Prophet, may Allah bless him and grant him peace, and Abū Bakr. The implication is that just as Allah helped him in that situation He will not disappoint him in other similar situations. ***He said to his companion,*** Abū Bakr, who, upon seeing the feet of the idolaters at the mouth of the cave said, "If one of them looks under his feet, they will see us," ***'Do not be despondent, Allah is with us*** with His help.***' Then Allah sent down His serenity*** (peace of mind) ***upon him*** – this may refer either to the Prophet, may Allah bless him and grant him peace, or to Abū Bakr – ***and reinforced him*** (the Prophet, may Allah bless him and grant him peace) ***with troops you could not see*** – a reference to the angels in the Cave and in other places where they fought. ***He made the word of the unbelievers*** (the call to *shirk*) ***undermost*** (defeated). ***It is the word of Allah*** (the *shahāda*) ***that is uppermost*** (victorious), ***Allah is Almighty*** in His kingdom, ***All-Wise*** in what He does.

41. ***Go out to fight, whatever your circumstances or desires*** – literally "light and heavy" meaning both active and not active, or both strong and weak, or both rich and poor. It is abrogated by the *āyat*, *"Nothing is held against the weak..."* (9:91) – ***and do* jihād *with your wealth and yourselves in the Way of Allah. That is better for you if you only knew***, so do not sit down heavily. This was revealed about the hypocrites who stayed behind.

42. ***If it*** (what you have called them to) ***had been a case of easy gains*** of the goods of this world ***and a short journey*** to somewhere close-at-hand, ***they would have followed you*** for the sake of the booty, ***but the distance was too great for them*** and so they stayed behind. ***They will swear by Allah*** when you return to them: ***'Had we been able to*** go out, ***we would have gone out with you.' They are destroying their own selves*** by swearing false oaths. ***Allah knows that they are lying*** in what they say to you.

43. The Prophet, may Allah bless him and grant him peace, gave permission to a group to stay behind on his own initiative and the following was revealed to censure him. The pardon came before the censure, to calm his heart. ***Allah pardon you! Why did you excuse them*** for staying behind, rather than just leaving them ***until it was clear to you which of them were telling the truth*** in their excuse ***and until you knew the liars*** in that respect?

44. ***Those who believe in Allah and the Last Day do not ask you to excuse them from doing* jihād *with their wealth and themselves*** by requesting you to allow them to stay behind. ***Allah knows the people who are godfearing.***

45. ***Only those who do not believe in Allah and the Last Day ask you to excuse them*** for staying behind. ***Their hearts are full of doubt*** about the *dīn* ***and in their doubt they waver to and fro*** in confusion.

46. ***If they had really desired to go out*** with you, ***they would have made proper preparations*** in terms of equipment and provision ***for it, but Allah was averse to their setting out*** and did not will that they should do so, ***so He held them back*** and made them lazy ***and they were told: 'Stay behind with those who stay behind,'*** meaning with the sick, women and children. This means that Allah decreed that.

47. ***If they had gone out among you, they would have added nothing to you but confusion*** – "confusion" (*khabāl*) means corruption and consequent weakening of the Muslims. ***They would have scurried about amongst you*** – hurried back and forth among you spreading slander and rumour – ***seeking to cause conflict*** (enmity) ***between you; and among you there are some who would have listened to them*** and accepted what they said. ***Allah knows the wrongdoers.***

48. ***They have already tried to cause conflict*** among you ***before,*** when you first came to Madina, ***and turned things completely upside down for you*** – in an attempt to trick you and to invalidate

وَقِيلَ ٱقْعُدُوا۟ مَعَ ٱلْقَٰعِدِينَ ﴿٤٦﴾ لَوْ خَرَجُوا۟ فِيكُم
مَّا زَادُوكُمْ إِلَّا خَبَالًا وَلَأَوْضَعُوا۟ خِلَٰلَكُمْ يَبْغُونَكُمُ
ٱلْفِتْنَةَ وَفِيكُمْ سَمَّٰعُونَ لَهُمْ ۗ وَٱللَّهُ عَلِيمٌۢ بِٱلظَّٰلِمِينَ ﴿٤٧﴾
لَقَدِ ٱبْتَغَوُا۟ ٱلْفِتْنَةَ مِن قَبْلُ وَقَلَّبُوا۟ لَكَ ٱلْأُمُورَ حَتَّىٰ
جَآءَ ٱلْحَقُّ وَظَهَرَ أَمْرُ ٱللَّهِ وَهُمْ كَٰرِهُونَ ﴿٤٨﴾
وَمِنْهُم مَّن يَقُولُ ٱئْذَن لِّى وَلَا تَفْتِنِّىٓ ۚ أَلَا فِى ٱلْفِتْنَةِ
سَقَطُوا۟ ۗ وَإِنَّ جَهَنَّمَ لَمُحِيطَةٌۢ بِٱلْكَٰفِرِينَ
﴿٤٩﴾ إِن تُصِبْكَ حَسَنَةٌ تَسُؤْهُمْ ۖ وَإِن تُصِبْكَ
مُصِيبَةٌ يَقُولُوا۟ قَدْ أَخَذْنَآ أَمْرَنَا مِن قَبْلُ وَيَتَوَلَّوا۟
وَّهُمْ فَرِحُونَ ﴿٥٠﴾ قُل لَّن يُصِيبَنَآ إِلَّا مَا كَتَبَ
ٱللَّهُ لَنَا هُوَ مَوْلَىٰنَا ۚ وَعَلَى ٱللَّهِ فَلْيَتَوَكَّلِ ٱلْمُؤْمِنُونَ
﴿٥١﴾ قُلْ هَلْ تَرَبَّصُونَ بِنَآ إِلَّآ إِحْدَى ٱلْحُسْنَيَيْنِ ۖ وَنَحْنُ
نَتَرَبَّصُ بِكُمْ أَن يُصِيبَكُمُ ٱللَّهُ بِعَذَابٍ مِّنْ عِندِهِۦٓ
أَوْ بِأَيْدِينَا ۖ فَتَرَبَّصُوٓا۟ إِنَّا مَعَكُم مُّتَرَبِّصُونَ ﴿٥٢﴾ قُلْ
أَنفِقُوا۟ طَوْعًا أَوْ كَرْهًا لَّن يُتَقَبَّلَ مِنكُمْ ۖ إِنَّكُمْ كُنتُمْ
قَوْمًا فَٰسِقِينَ ﴿٥٣﴾ وَمَا مَنَعَهُمْ أَن تُقْبَلَ مِنْهُمْ نَفَقَٰتُهُمْ
إِلَّآ أَنَّهُمْ كَفَرُوا۟ بِٱللَّهِ وَبِرَسُولِهِۦ وَلَا يَأْتُونَ ٱلصَّلَوٰةَ
إِلَّا وَهُمْ كُسَالَىٰ وَلَا يُنفِقُونَ إِلَّا وَهُمْ كَٰرِهُونَ ﴿٥٤﴾
فَلَا تُعْجِبْكَ أَمْوَٰلُهُمْ وَلَآ أَوْلَٰدُهُمْ ۚ إِنَّمَا يُرِيدُ ٱللَّهُ لِيُعَذِّبَهُم
بِهَا فِى ٱلْحَيَوٰةِ ٱلدُّنْيَا وَتَزْهَقَ أَنفُسُهُمْ وَهُمْ كَٰفِرُونَ ﴿٥٥﴾

your *dīn* – ***until the truth*** (victory) ***came and Allah's command*** (His dīn) ***prevailed even though they detested it*** and they reluctantly entered the *dīn* outwardly.

49. ***Among them are there some who say, 'Give me permission to stay*** behind. ***Do not put temptation in my way.'*** The man who said this was al-Jadd ibn Qays. The Prophet, may Allah bless him and grant him peace, asked him, "Can you fight the strong men of the Greeks?" He replied, "I am desirous of women and I fear that if I see the Greek women, I will not be able to refrain from them and so I will be tempted." Allah said: ***Have they not fallen into that very temptation*** by staying behind? ***Hell hems in the unbelievers*** and they cannot escape.

50. ***If good*** (victory and booty) ***happens to you, it galls them. If a mishap*** (hardship) ***occurs to you they say, 'We made our preparations in advance*** by resolving to stay behind,***' and they turn away rejoicing*** at your misfortune.

51. ***Say*** to them: ***'Nothing can happen to us except what Allah has ordained for us. He is Our Master*** – Our Helper and the One who has charge of our affairs. ***It is in Allah that the believers should put their trust.'***

52. ***Say: 'What do you await for us except for one of the two best things*** (victory or martyrdom)? ***But what we await for you is for Allah to inflict a punishment on you either directly from Himself*** by a bolt from heaven ***or at our hands*** by giving us permission to fight you. ***So wait; we are waiting with you*** for the outcomes which have been described!'

53. ***Say: 'Whether you give*** in obedience to Allah ***readily or reluctantly, it*** (what you spend) ***will not be accepted from you. You are people who are deviators.'*** The imperative here has the meaning of a report.

54. ***Nothing prevents what they give from being accepted*** (read as *tuqbala* and *yuqbala*) ***from them but the fact that they have rejected Allah and His Messenger, and that they only come to the prayer lethargically*** – reluctantly, as if it were a burden – ***and that they only give reluctantly*** because they consider what they spend to be tantamount to a tax and imposition.

وَيَحۡلِفُونَ بِٱللَّهِ إِنَّهُمۡ لَمِنكُمۡ وَمَا هُم مِّنكُمۡ وَلَٰكِنَّهُمۡ
قَوۡمٞ يَفۡرَقُونَ ﴿٥٦﴾ لَوۡ يَجِدُونَ مَلۡجَـًٔا أَوۡ مَغَٰرَٰتٍ
أَوۡ مُدَّخَلٗا لَّوَلَّوۡاْ إِلَيۡهِ وَهُمۡ يَجۡمَحُونَ ﴿٥٧﴾ وَمِنۡهُم مَّن يَلۡمِزُكَ
فِي ٱلصَّدَقَٰتِ فَإِنۡ أُعۡطُواْ مِنۡهَا رَضُواْ وَإِن لَّمۡ يُعۡطَوۡاْ مِنۡهَآ إِذَا
هُمۡ يَسۡخَطُونَ ﴿٥٨﴾ وَلَوۡ أَنَّهُمۡ رَضُواْ مَآ ءَاتَىٰهُمُ ٱللَّهُ
وَرَسُولُهُۥ وَقَالُواْ حَسۡبُنَا ٱللَّهُ سَيُؤۡتِينَا ٱللَّهُ مِن فَضۡلِهِۦ
وَرَسُولُهُۥٓ إِنَّآ إِلَى ٱللَّهِ رَٰغِبُونَ ﴿٥٩﴾ ۞ إِنَّمَا ٱلصَّدَقَٰتُ
لِلۡفُقَرَآءِ وَٱلۡمَسَٰكِينِ وَٱلۡعَٰمِلِينَ عَلَيۡهَا وَٱلۡمُؤَلَّفَةِ قُلُوبُهُمۡ
وَفِي ٱلرِّقَابِ وَٱلۡغَٰرِمِينَ وَفِي سَبِيلِ ٱللَّهِ وَٱبۡنِ ٱلسَّبِيلِۖ
فَرِيضَةٗ مِّنَ ٱللَّهِۗ وَٱللَّهُ عَلِيمٌ حَكِيمٞ ﴿٦٠﴾ وَمِنۡهُمُ
ٱلَّذِينَ يُؤۡذُونَ ٱلنَّبِيَّ وَيَقُولُونَ هُوَ أُذُنٞۚ قُلۡ أُذُنُ خَيۡرٖ
لَّكُمۡ يُؤۡمِنُ بِٱللَّهِ وَيُؤۡمِنُ لِلۡمُؤۡمِنِينَ وَرَحۡمَةٞ لِّلَّذِينَ
ءَامَنُواْ مِنكُمۡۚ وَٱلَّذِينَ يُؤۡذُونَ رَسُولَ ٱللَّهِ لَهُمۡ عَذَابٌ أَلِيمٞ ﴿٦١﴾
يَحۡلِفُونَ بِٱللَّهِ لَكُمۡ لِيُرۡضُوكُمۡ وَٱللَّهُ وَرَسُولُهُۥٓ أَحَقُّ
أَن يُرۡضُوهُ إِن كَانُواْ مُؤۡمِنِينَ ﴿٦٢﴾ أَلَمۡ يَعۡلَمُوٓاْ أَنَّهُۥ
مَن يُحَادِدِ ٱللَّهَ وَرَسُولَهُۥ فَأَنَّ لَهُۥ نَارَ جَهَنَّمَ خَٰلِدٗا فِيهَاۚ
ذَٰلِكَ ٱلۡخِزۡيُ ٱلۡعَظِيمُ ﴿٦٣﴾ يَحۡذَرُ ٱلۡمُنَٰفِقُونَ
أَن تُنَزَّلَ عَلَيۡهِمۡ سُورَةٞ تُنَبِّئُهُم بِمَا فِي قُلُوبِهِمۡۚ قُلِ ٱسۡتَهۡزِءُوٓاْ
إِنَّ ٱللَّهَ مُخۡرِجٞ مَّا تَحۡذَرُونَ ﴿٦٤﴾ وَلَئِن سَأَلۡتَهُمۡ
لَيَقُولُنَّ إِنَّمَا كُنَّا نَخُوضُ وَنَلۡعَبُۚ قُلۡ أَبِٱللَّهِ وَءَايَٰتِهِۦ

55. ***Do not let their wealth and children impress you.*** Do not think that their blessings are good for them, letting that lead you into thinking they are all right. ***Allah merely wants to punish them by them*** through the difficulties involved in amassing their wealth and the misfortunes which occur to their children ***during their life in this world and for them to expire while they are unbelievers*** so that they will be punished in the worst way in the Next World.

56. ***They swear by Allah that they are of your number*** – that they are believers – ***but they are not of your number. Rather, they are people who are scared*** – afraid that you will deal with them like idolaters; and therefore they swear that out of dissimulation.

57. ***If they could find a bolt-hole, cave or burrow*** in which to take refuge, ***they would turn and scurry away into it*** – they would hurry into it and leave you without turning to anything, like a bolting horse.

58. ***Among them there are some who find fault with you concerning*** the distribution of ***the*** **zakāt.** ***If they are given some of it, they are pleased; but if they are not given any, they are angry.***

59. ***If only they had been pleased with what Allah and His Messenger had given them*** in terms of booty and other things ***and had said, 'Allah is enough for us. Allah will give us of His bounty,*** booty which will be enough for us, ***as will His Messenger. It is to Allah that we make our plea*** to enrich us.' That would be better for them.

60. The word used here, *ṣadaqāt*, means *zakāt* so: **Zakāt** ***is for*** and must be distributed to: ***the poor***, – those who do not have enough to cover their normal needs, ***the destitute*** – those without anything at all; ***those who collect it*** – those who collect the *zakāt* and distribute it, and the scribes who record it; ***reconciling people's hearts*** – to encourage them become Muslim or to make their Islam firm or so that those like them become Muslim or to turn groups from the Muslims, although the first and last categories are not given today, according to ash-Shāfi'ī, because of the strength of Islam, as opposed to the others which can be given in the soundest view; ***freeing slaves*** – those with a *kitāba* contract to fulfil in order to become free; ***those in debt*** – people who ask for help to pay debts which have not been incurred in disobedience to Allah, or only after they have repented, and who do not have enough to settle them, or to repair disputes, even if the people concerned are rich; ***spending in the Way of Allah*** – to enable those who do not have booty to undertake *jihād*, even if they are rich; ***and travellers*** – those who are prevented from finishing their journey. ***It is a legal obligation from Allah. Allah is All-Knowing*** of His creation, ***All-Wise*** in what He does. It is not permitted to give *zakāt* to people outside these categories or to deny it to any of them if the need exists. So the ruler should divide it among them equally. He can give more to some categories. It is not an obligation to give *zakāt* to someone with wealth when it is distributed if there is not very much of it. It is enough to give *zakāt* to three people in each category, but not less than that as the plural is used. The *sunna* makes it clear that the recipient must be a Muslim who is not a descendant of Hāshim or 'Abdu'l-Muṭṭalib.

61. ***Among them*** (the hypocrites) ***are some who insult the Prophet*** by criticising him and reporting what he says, ***saying*** – when they were forbidden to do that so that it would not reach him – ***he is only an ear*** who listens to everything said and accepts it. If we were to swear that we had not said anything, he would believe us." ***Say,*** '***He is an ear of good for you*** – hearing what is good about you but not what is evil – ***believing in Allah and believing in the believers*** – believing what the believers tell him and not others. The *lām* attached to 'believers' is to make a distinction between the faith of submission and other belief – ***and a mercy for those among you who believe.' As for those who insult the Messenger of Allah, they will have a painful punishment.***

62. ***They swear to you by Allah,*** believers, about what has reached you about their insulting of the Messenger, that they did not do it, ***in order to please you, but it would be more fitting for them to please Allah and His Messenger*** by obedience, ***if they*** really ***are believers.***

63. ***Do they not know that whoever opposes*** and splits from ***Allah and His Messenger, will have the*** repayment of the ***Fire of Hell, remaining in it timelessly, for ever? That is the great disgrace.***

64. ***The hypocrites are afraid that a*** **sūra** ***may be sent down*** to the believers ***about them, informing them of what is in their hearts*** – meaning hypocrisy. But in spite of this, they continued their mock-

وَرَسُولِهِۦ كُنتُمْ تَسْتَهْزِءُونَ ﴿٦٥﴾ لَا تَعْتَذِرُوا۟ قَدْ كَفَرْتُم
بَعْدَ إِيمَـٰنِكُمْ ۚ إِن نَّعْفُ عَن طَآئِفَةٍ مِّنكُمْ نُعَذِّبْ طَآئِفَةًۢ
بِأَنَّهُمْ كَانُوا۟ مُجْرِمِينَ ﴿٦٦﴾ ٱلْمُنَـٰفِقُونَ وَٱلْمُنَـٰفِقَـٰتُ
بَعْضُهُم مِّنۢ بَعْضٍ ۚ يَأْمُرُونَ بِٱلْمُنكَرِ وَيَنْهَوْنَ
عَنِ ٱلْمَعْرُوفِ وَيَقْبِضُونَ أَيْدِيَهُمْ ۚ نَسُوا۟ ٱللَّهَ فَنَسِيَهُمْ ۗ
إِنَّ ٱلْمُنَـٰفِقِينَ هُمُ ٱلْفَـٰسِقُونَ ﴿٦٧﴾ وَعَدَ ٱللَّهُ
ٱلْمُنَـٰفِقِينَ وَٱلْمُنَـٰفِقَـٰتِ وَٱلْكُفَّارَ نَارَ جَهَنَّمَ خَـٰلِدِينَ
فِيهَا ۚ هِىَ حَسْبُهُمْ ۚ وَلَعَنَهُمُ ٱللَّهُ ۖ وَلَهُمْ عَذَابٌ مُّقِيمٌ ﴿٦٨﴾
كَٱلَّذِينَ مِن قَبْلِكُمْ كَانُوٓا۟ أَشَدَّ مِنكُمْ قُوَّةً وَأَكْثَرَ
أَمْوَٰلًا وَأَوْلَـٰدًا فَٱسْتَمْتَعُوا۟ بِخَلَـٰقِهِمْ فَٱسْتَمْتَعْتُم بِخَلَـٰقِكُمْ
كَمَا ٱسْتَمْتَعَ ٱلَّذِينَ مِن قَبْلِكُم بِخَلَـٰقِهِمْ وَخُضْتُمْ
كَٱلَّذِى خَاضُوٓا۟ ۚ أُو۟لَـٰٓئِكَ حَبِطَتْ أَعْمَـٰلُهُمْ فِى ٱلدُّنْيَا
وَٱلْـَٔاخِرَةِ ۖ وَأُو۟لَـٰٓئِكَ هُمُ ٱلْخَـٰسِرُونَ ﴿٦٩﴾ أَلَمْ يَأْتِهِمْ
نَبَأُ ٱلَّذِينَ مِن قَبْلِهِمْ قَوْمِ نُوحٍ وَعَادٍ وَثَمُودَ وَقَوْمِ
إِبْرَٰهِيمَ وَأَصْحَـٰبِ مَدْيَنَ وَٱلْمُؤْتَفِكَـٰتِ ۚ أَتَتْهُمْ
رُسُلُهُم بِٱلْبَيِّنَـٰتِ ۖ فَمَا كَانَ ٱللَّهُ لِيَظْلِمَهُمْ وَلَـٰكِن
كَانُوٓا۟ أَنفُسَهُمْ يَظْلِمُونَ ﴿٧٠﴾ وَٱلْمُؤْمِنُونَ وَٱلْمُؤْمِنَـٰتُ بَعْضُهُمْ
أَوْلِيَآءُ بَعْضٍ ۚ يَأْمُرُونَ بِٱلْمَعْرُوفِ وَيَنْهَوْنَ عَنِ ٱلْمُنكَرِ
وَيُقِيمُونَ ٱلصَّلَوٰةَ وَيُؤْتُونَ ٱلزَّكَوٰةَ وَيُطِيعُونَ ٱللَّهَ
وَرَسُولَهُۥٓ ۚ أُو۟لَـٰٓئِكَ سَيَرْحَمُهُمُ ٱللَّهُ ۗ إِنَّ ٱللَّهَ عَزِيزٌ حَكِيمٌ ﴿٧١﴾

ery. ***Say*** as a threat to them: ***'Go on mocking! Allah will expose everything you are afraid of*** regarding your hypocrisy being brought to light.'

65. ***If you ask them*** about their mockery of you and the Qur'an while they are travelling with you to Tabūk, ***they will say*** to excuse themselves, ***'We were only joking and playing around*** in conversation to pass the time on the way and did not mean anything.' ***Say*** to them: ***'Would you make a mockery of Allah, and of His Signs and of His Messenger?***

66. ***Do not try to excuse yourselves*** for that. ***You have disbelieved after having believed*** – your unbelief has become clear after you made a display of faith. ***If We pardon*** (read as *na'fu* and also *ya'fu*, in which case the meaning is: "If one group of you is pardoned") ***one group of you*** due to their sincerity and repentance – those like Jaḥsh ibn Ḥimyar – ***We will punish another group*** (read as *nu'adhdhib* and also *yu'adhdhibu*: "another group will be punished") ***for being evildoers.'*** They will be punished for persisting in hypocrisy and mockery.

67. ***The men and women of the hypocrites are as bad as one another.*** They resemble one another in respect of the *dīn* like parts of a single thing. ***They command what is wrong*** (unbelief and acts of disobedience) ***and forbid what is right*** (faith and obedience) ***and keep their fists tightly closed*** – not spending in obedience to Allah. ***They have forgotten Allah, so He has forgotten them*** and excluded them from His kindness. ***The hypocrites are deviators.***

68. ***Allah has promised the men and women of the hypocrites and unbelievers the Fire of Hell, remaining in it timelessly for ever. It will suffice them*** as a repayment and penalty. ***Allah has cursed them*** and put them far from His mercyī ***They shall have everlasting punishment...***

69. ***...Like those*** hypocrites ***before you who had greater strength than you and more wealth and children. They enjoyed their portion*** of this world; ***so enjoy your portion,*** hypocrites, ***as those before you enjoyed theirs. You have plunged into defamation*** – into falsehood and attacking the Prophet, may Allah bless him and grant him

وَعَدَ ٱللَّهُ ٱلْمُؤْمِنِينَ وَٱلْمُؤْمِنَٰتِ جَنَّٰتٍ تَجْرِى مِن تَحْتِهَا
ٱلْأَنْهَٰرُ خَٰلِدِينَ فِيهَا وَمَسَٰكِنَ طَيِّبَةً فِى جَنَّٰتِ عَدْنٍ ۚ
وَرِضْوَٰنٌ مِّنَ ٱللَّهِ أَكْبَرُ ۚ ذَٰلِكَ هُوَ ٱلْفَوْزُ ٱلْعَظِيمُ ﴿٧٢﴾
يَٰٓأَيُّهَا ٱلنَّبِىُّ جَٰهِدِ ٱلْكُفَّارَ وَٱلْمُنَٰفِقِينَ وَٱغْلُظْ عَلَيْهِمْ ۚ
وَمَأْوَىٰهُمْ جَهَنَّمُ ۖ وَبِئْسَ ٱلْمَصِيرُ ﴿٧٣﴾ يَحْلِفُونَ بِٱللَّهِ
مَا قَالُوا۟ وَلَقَدْ قَالُوا۟ كَلِمَةَ ٱلْكُفْرِ وَكَفَرُوا۟ بَعْدَ إِسْلَٰمِهِمْ
وَهَمُّوا۟ بِمَا لَمْ يَنَالُوا۟ ۚ وَمَا نَقَمُوٓا۟ إِلَّآ أَنْ أَغْنَىٰهُمُ ٱللَّهُ وَرَسُولُهُۥ
مِن فَضْلِهِۦ ۚ فَإِن يَتُوبُوا۟ يَكُ خَيْرًا لَّهُمْ ۖ وَإِن يَتَوَلَّوْا۟ يُعَذِّبْهُمُ
ٱللَّهُ عَذَابًا أَلِيمًا فِى ٱلدُّنْيَا وَٱلْءَاخِرَةِ ۚ وَمَا لَهُمْ فِى ٱلْأَرْضِ
مِن وَلِىٍّ وَلَا نَصِيرٍ ﴿٧٤﴾ ۞ وَمِنْهُم مَّنْ عَٰهَدَ ٱللَّهَ لَئِنْ
ءَاتَىٰنَا مِن فَضْلِهِۦ لَنَصَّدَّقَنَّ وَلَنَكُونَنَّ مِنَ ٱلصَّٰلِحِينَ ﴿٧٥﴾
فَلَمَّآ ءَاتَىٰهُم مِّن فَضْلِهِۦ بَخِلُوا۟ بِهِۦ وَتَوَلَّوا۟ وَّهُم مُّعْرِضُونَ
﴿٧٦﴾ فَأَعْقَبَهُمْ نِفَاقًا فِى قُلُوبِهِمْ إِلَىٰ يَوْمِ يَلْقَوْنَهُۥ بِمَآ أَخْلَفُوا۟
ٱللَّهَ مَا وَعَدُوهُ وَبِمَا كَانُوا۟ يَكْذِبُونَ ﴿٧٧﴾ أَلَمْ يَعْلَمُوٓا۟
أَنَّ ٱللَّهَ يَعْلَمُ سِرَّهُمْ وَنَجْوَىٰهُمْ وَأَنَّ ٱللَّهَ عَلَّٰمُ
ٱلْغُيُوبِ ﴿٧٨﴾ ٱلَّذِينَ يَلْمِزُونَ ٱلْمُطَّوِّعِينَ مِنَ
ٱلْمُؤْمِنِينَ فِى ٱلصَّدَقَٰتِ وَٱلَّذِينَ لَا يَجِدُونَ إِلَّا
جُهْدَهُمْ فَيَسْخَرُونَ مِنْهُمْ ۙ سَخِرَ ٱللَّهُ مِنْهُمْ وَلَهُمْ عَذَابٌ أَلِيمٌ ﴿٧٩﴾
ٱسْتَغْفِرْ لَهُمْ أَوْ لَا تَسْتَغْفِرْ لَهُمْ إِن تَسْتَغْفِرْ لَهُمْ سَبْعِينَ مَرَّةً
فَلَن يَغْفِرَ ٱللَّهُ لَهُمْ ۚ ذَٰلِكَ بِأَنَّهُمْ كَفَرُوا۟ بِٱللَّهِ وَرَسُولِهِۦ ۗ

peace – ***as they plunged into it. The actions of such people come to nothing in this world or the Next World. They are the lost.***

70. ***Has the news of those who came before them not reached them: the people of Nūḥ and 'Ād*** (the people of Hūd) ***and Thamūd*** (the people of Ṣāliḥ) ***and the people of Ibrāhīm and the inhabitants of Madyan*** (the people of Shu'ayb) ***and the overturned cities*** (the people of Lūṭ)***? Their Messengers brought them the Clear Signs***, (miracles) but they denied them and so they were destroyed. ***Allah did not wrong them*** by punishing them for no reason***: rather they wronged themselves*** by committing sins.

71. ***The men and women of the believers are friends of one another. They command what is right and forbid what is wrong, and establish the prayer and pay* zakāt*, and obey Allah and His Messenger. They are the people on whom Allah will have mercy. Allah is Almighty***, having the power to do anything and carrying out His promise and His threat, ***All-Wise*** — only putting a thing in its proper place.

72. ***Allah has promised the men and women of the believers Gardens with rivers flowing under them, remaining in them timelessly, for ever, and fine dwellings in the Gardens of Eden. And Allah's good pleasure is even greater*** than all these things which have been mentioned. ***That is the great victory.***

73. ***O Prophet, do* jihād *against the unbelievers*** with the sword ***and*** against the ***hypocrites*** with the tongue and evidence ***and be harsh with them*** through rebuke and hatred. ***Their shelter will be Hell. What an evil destination!***

74. ***They*** (the hypocrites) ***swear by Allah that they said nothing*** of what was reported to you regarding their cursing, ***but they definitely spoke the word of unbelief and returned to unbelief after their Islam*** – demonstrating their disbelief after making a display of Islam. ***They planned something which they did not achieve*** when they wanted to assassinate the Prophet, may Allah bless him and grant him peace, on the night of his return from Tabūk. They were about ten men. 'Ammār ibn Yāsir struck the faces of the camels when they approached him and they went back – ***and they were vindictive for no other reason than that Allah and His Messenger had***

enriched them from His bounty – through booty after the poverty they had suffered. It means that this is all that happened to them and is the only reason for what they felt. It is certainly not something which should elicit bad feeling. ***If they were to repent*** from their hypocrisy and believe in you, ***it would be better for them. But if they turn away*** from belief, ***Allah will punish them with a painful punishment in this world*** by killing ***and*** by the Fire in ***the Next World, and they will not find any protector or helper*** to defend them and protect them ***on the earth.***

75. ***Among them there were some who made an agreement with Allah: 'If He gives us of His bounty we will definitely give*** **ṣadaqa** ***and be among the righteous.'*** This refers to Tha'laba ibn Ḥāṭib. He asked the Prophet, may Allah bless him and grant him peace, to pray to Allah to provide him with wealth so that he could pay every creditor what was owed to them. So he made supplication for him and his wealth expanded. Then Tha'laba cut himself off from the *Jumu'a* and the Community and refused to pay *zakāt*, as Allah recounts:

76. ***But when He does give them of His bounty they are tight-fisted with it and turn away*** from obeying Allah...

77. ***... so He has punished them by putting hypocrisy in their hearts*** and fixing it there ***until the day they meet Him*** (Allah) on the Day of Rising, ***because they failed Allah in what they promised Him and because they lied*** about it. After that, he came to the Prophet, may Allah bless him and grant him peace, with his *zakāt* but he said, "Allah has forbidden me to accept it from you." Tha'laba began to throw dust on his head. Then he brought it to Abū Bakr who would not accept it, and then to 'Umar who would not accept it. Then he brought it to 'Uthmān who did not accept it. He died during 'Uthmān's caliphate.

78. ***Do they*** (the hypocrites) ***not know that Allah knows their secrets*** which they conceal in themselves ***and their private*** (secret) ***talk*** between themselves, ***and that Allah is the Knower of all unseen things?*** He knows what cannot be seen. When the *āyat* concerning *ṣadaqa* was revealed, a man came and gave a lot and the hypocrites said, "He is showing off." A man came and gave a *ṣā'* measure and they said, "Allah has no need of this one's *ṣadaqa*." Then the next *āyat* was revealed:

وَٱللَّهُ لَا يَهْدِى ٱلْقَوْمَ ٱلْفَٰسِقِينَ ﴿٨٠﴾ فَرِحَ ٱلْمُخَلَّفُونَ
بِمَقْعَدِهِمْ خِلَٰفَ رَسُولِ ٱللَّهِ وَكَرِهُوٓا۟ أَن يُجَٰهِدُوا۟ بِأَمْوَٰلِهِمْ
وَأَنفُسِهِمْ فِى سَبِيلِ ٱللَّهِ وَقَالُوا۟ لَا تَنفِرُوا۟ فِى ٱلْحَرِّ ۗ قُلْ نَارُ جَهَنَّمَ
أَشَدُّ حَرًّا ۚ لَّوْ كَانُوا۟ يَفْقَهُونَ ﴿٨١﴾ فَلْيَضْحَكُوا۟ قَلِيلًا وَلْيَبْكُوا۟ كَثِيرًا
جَزَآءًۢ بِمَا كَانُوا۟ يَكْسِبُونَ ﴿٨٢﴾ فَإِن رَّجَعَكَ ٱللَّهُ إِلَىٰ طَآئِفَةٍ
مِّنْهُمْ فَٱسْتَـْٔذَنُوكَ لِلْخُرُوجِ فَقُل لَّن تَخْرُجُوا۟ مَعِىَ أَبَدًا وَلَن
تُقَٰتِلُوا۟ مَعِىَ عَدُوًّا ۖ إِنَّكُمْ رَضِيتُم بِٱلْقُعُودِ أَوَّلَ مَرَّةٍ فَٱقْعُدُوا۟
مَعَ ٱلْخَٰلِفِينَ ﴿٨٣﴾ وَلَا تُصَلِّ عَلَىٰٓ أَحَدٍ مِّنْهُم مَّاتَ أَبَدًا وَلَا تَقُمْ
عَلَىٰ قَبْرِهِۦٓ ۖ إِنَّهُمْ كَفَرُوا۟ بِٱللَّهِ وَرَسُولِهِۦ وَمَاتُوا۟ وَهُمْ فَٰسِقُونَ
﴿٨٤﴾ وَلَا تُعْجِبْكَ أَمْوَٰلُهُمْ وَأَوْلَٰدُهُمْ ۚ إِنَّمَا يُرِيدُ ٱللَّهُ أَن يُعَذِّبَهُم
بِهَا فِى ٱلدُّنْيَا وَتَزْهَقَ أَنفُسُهُمْ وَهُمْ كَٰفِرُونَ ﴿٨٥﴾ وَإِذَآ
أُنزِلَتْ سُورَةٌ أَنْ ءَامِنُوا۟ بِٱللَّهِ وَجَٰهِدُوا۟ مَعَ رَسُولِهِ ٱسْتَـْٔذَنَكَ
أُو۟لُوا۟ ٱلطَّوْلِ مِنْهُمْ وَقَالُوا۟ ذَرْنَا نَكُن مَّعَ ٱلْقَٰعِدِينَ ﴿٨٦﴾
رَضُوا۟ بِأَن يَكُونُوا۟ مَعَ ٱلْخَوَالِفِ وَطُبِعَ عَلَىٰ قُلُوبِهِمْ فَهُمْ
لَا يَفْقَهُونَ ﴿٨٧﴾ لَٰكِنِ ٱلرَّسُولُ وَٱلَّذِينَ ءَامَنُوا۟ مَعَهُۥ
جَٰهَدُوا۟ بِأَمْوَٰلِهِمْ وَأَنفُسِهِمْ ۚ وَأُو۟لَٰٓئِكَ لَهُمُ ٱلْخَيْرَٰتُ ۖ
وَأُو۟لَٰٓئِكَ هُمُ ٱلْمُفْلِحُونَ ﴿٨٨﴾ أَعَدَّ ٱللَّهُ لَهُمْ جَنَّٰتٍ تَجْرِى
مِن تَحْتِهَا ٱلْأَنْهَٰرُ خَٰلِدِينَ فِيهَا ۚ ذَٰلِكَ ٱلْفَوْزُ ٱلْعَظِيمُ ﴿٨٩﴾ وَجَآءَ
ٱلْمُعَذِّرُونَ مِنَ ٱلْأَعْرَابِ لِيُؤْذَنَ لَهُمْ وَقَعَدَ ٱلَّذِينَ كَذَبُوا۟
ٱللَّهَ وَرَسُولَهُۥ ۚ سَيُصِيبُ ٱلَّذِينَ كَفَرُوا۟ مِنْهُمْ عَذَابٌ أَلِيمٌ

79. ***As for the people who find fault with those believers who give*** voluntary **ṣadaqa** ***spontaneously, and with those who can find nothing to give but their own effort, and deride them, Allah derides them. They will have a painful punishment*** for their derision of the believers.

80. ***You***, Muḥammad, ***may ask forgiveness for them, or not ask forgiveness for them.*** He was given a choice of asking forgiveness or not asking it. The Prophet, may Allah bless him and grant him peace, said, "I was given a choice and I chose," meaning he chose to ask for forgiveness. Al-Bukhārī related this *ḥadīth*. ***Even if you asked forgiveness for them seventy times, Allah still would not forgive them.*** What is meant by "seventy" is a lot of asking forgiveness. In al-Bukhārī, "If I knew that by my doing it more than seventy times, someone would be forgiven, I would have done more." It is also said that what is meant is a specific number which is also based on the *ḥadīth*, "I would do more than seventy." It is clear to him that forgiveness is cut off by the *āyat*. ***That is because they have rejected Allah and His Messenger. Allah does not guide deviant people.***

81. ***Those who were left behind*** from Tabūk ***were glad to stay behind the Messenger of Allah. They did not want to do*** **jihād** ***with their wealth and themselves in the Way of Allah. They said*** to one another, ***'Do not go out to fight*** jihād ***in the heat.' Say: 'The Fire of Hell is much hotter*** than that of Tabūk – and so it is more appropriate to fear it and not stay behind – ***if they only understood.'*** If they had grasped the truth of that, they would not have stayed behind.

82. ***Let them laugh little*** in this world ***and weep much*** in the Next World, ***in repayment for what they have earned.*** This is a description of their state expressed in the verbal form of the imperative.

83. ***If Allah returns you*** from Tabūk ***to a group of them*** – a group of the hypocrites who stayed behind in Madina – ***and they ask you for permission to go out*** with you on another expedition, ***say*** to them, ***'You will never go out with me, nor will you ever fight an enemy with me. You were happy to stay behind the first time, so stay behind with those who are left behind*** the expedition, such as women, children, and others.'

84. The following was revealed when the Messenger of Allah, may Allah bless him and grant him peace, prayed over the grave of Ibn Ubayy. ***Never pray over any of them who die or stand at their graves*** for burial or to visit them. ***They rejected Allah and His Messenger and died as deviators.*** They are unbelievers.

85. ***Do not let their wealth and their children impress you. Allah merely wants to punish them by them in this world, and for them to expire*** and leave this world ***while they are unbelievers.***

86. ***When a* sūra *is sent down*** – a part of the Qur'an is revealed – ***saying: 'Believe in Allah and do* jihād *together with His Messenger,' those among them with wealth will ask you to excuse them, saying, 'Let us remain with those who stay behind.'***

87. ***They are pleased to be with those who stay behind*** – the women who stay behind in their houses. ***Their hearts have been stamped so they do not understand*** where the good lies.

88. ***But the Messenger and those who believe along with him have done* jihād *with their wealth and with themselves. They are the people who shall have the good things*** both in this world and the Next World. ***They are the ones who are successful.***

89. ***Allah has prepared Gardens for them with rivers flowing under them, remaining in them timelessly for ever. That is the great victory.***

90. ***The desert Arabs came*** to the Prophet, may Allah bless him and grant him peace, ***with their excuses*** (read as *mu'adhdhirūna* and *mu'dhirūna*), ***asking for permission to stay*** to stay behind; he excused them ***and those*** among the hypocritical desert Arabs ***who lied to Allah and His Messenger*** about their claim to believe ***stayed behind. A painful punishment will afflict those among them who disbelieve.***

91. ***Nothing is held against the weak***, such as old men, ***and the sick***, such as those who are blind and chronically ill – ***or against those who find nothing to spend*** in *jihād* – they incur no wrong action in staying behind – ***provided they are true to Allah and His Messenger*** – when they stay behind, and do not agitate or provoke, and they obey Allah: ***there is no way open against good-doers*** to punish

٩٠ لَّيۡسَ عَلَى ٱلضُّعَفَآءِ وَلَا عَلَى ٱلۡمَرۡضَىٰ وَلَا عَلَى ٱلَّذِينَ
لَا يَجِدُونَ مَا يُنفِقُونَ حَرَجٌ إِذَا نَصَحُواْ لِلَّهِ وَرَسُولِهِۦۚ
مَا عَلَى ٱلۡمُحۡسِنِينَ مِن سَبِيلٖۚ وَٱللَّهُ غَفُورٞ رَّحِيمٞ ٩١
وَلَا عَلَى ٱلَّذِينَ إِذَا مَآ أَتَوۡكَ لِتَحۡمِلَهُمۡ قُلۡتَ لَآ أَجِدُ
مَآ أَحۡمِلُكُمۡ عَلَيۡهِ تَوَلَّواْ وَّأَعۡيُنُهُمۡ تَفِيضُ مِنَ ٱلدَّمۡعِ
حَزَنًا أَلَّا يَجِدُواْ مَا يُنفِقُونَ ٩٢ ۞ إِنَّمَا ٱلسَّبِيلُ عَلَى
ٱلَّذِينَ يَسۡتَـٔۡذِنُونَكَ وَهُمۡ أَغۡنِيَآءُۚ رَضُواْ بِأَن يَكُونُواْ
مَعَ ٱلۡخَوَالِفِ وَطَبَعَ ٱللَّهُ عَلَىٰ قُلُوبِهِمۡ فَهُمۡ لَا يَعۡلَمُونَ ٩٣
يَعۡتَذِرُونَ إِلَيۡكُمۡ إِذَا رَجَعۡتُمۡ إِلَيۡهِمۡۚ قُل لَّا تَعۡتَذِرُواْ لَن
نُّؤۡمِنَ لَكُمۡ قَدۡ نَبَّأَنَا ٱللَّهُ مِنۡ أَخۡبَارِكُمۡۚ وَسَيَرَى
ٱللَّهُ عَمَلَكُمۡ وَرَسُولُهُۥ ثُمَّ تُرَدُّونَ إِلَىٰ عَٰلِمِ ٱلۡغَيۡبِ
وَٱلشَّهَٰدَةِ فَيُنَبِّئُكُم بِمَا كُنتُمۡ تَعۡمَلُونَ ٩٤ سَيَحۡلِفُونَ
بِٱللَّهِ لَكُمۡ إِذَا ٱنقَلَبۡتُمۡ إِلَيۡهِمۡ لِتُعۡرِضُواْ عَنۡهُمۡۖ فَأَعۡرِضُواْ
عَنۡهُمۡۖ إِنَّهُمۡ رِجۡسٞۖ وَمَأۡوَىٰهُمۡ جَهَنَّمُ جَزَآءَۢ بِمَا كَانُواْ
يَكۡسِبُونَ ٩٥ يَحۡلِفُونَ لَكُمۡ لِتَرۡضَوۡاْ عَنۡهُمۡۖ فَإِن
تَرۡضَوۡاْ عَنۡهُمۡ فَإِنَّ ٱللَّهَ لَا يَرۡضَىٰ عَنِ ٱلۡقَوۡمِ ٱلۡفَٰسِقِينَ
٩٦ ٱلۡأَعۡرَابُ أَشَدُّ كُفۡرٗا وَنِفَاقٗا وَأَجۡدَرُ أَلَّا يَعۡلَمُواْ
حُدُودَ مَآ أَنزَلَ ٱللَّهُ عَلَىٰ رَسُولِهِۦۗ وَٱللَّهُ عَلِيمٌ حَكِيمٞ ٩٧ وَمِنَ
ٱلۡأَعۡرَابِ مَن يَتَّخِذُ مَا يُنفِقُ مَغۡرَمٗا وَيَتَرَبَّصُ بِكُمُ ٱلدَّوَآئِرَۚ
عَلَيۡهِمۡ دَآئِرَةُ ٱلسَّوۡءِۗ وَٱللَّهُ سَمِيعٌ عَلِيمٞ ٩٨ وَمِنَ

them. ***Allah is Ever-Forgiving*** to them, ***Most Merciful*** to them in being expansive to them.

92. ***Nor is anything held against those who, when they came to you for you to provide them with mounts*** to go with you on the expedition – they were seven of the Anṣār or the Banū Muqarrin – ***and you said, 'I cannot find anything on which to mount you,' turned away with their eyes overflowing with tears, overcome by grief at having nothing to give*** in *jihād*.

93. ***There are only grounds against those who ask you for permission to stay*** behind ***when they are rich. They were pleased to be among those who were left behind. Allah has sealed up their hearts so they do not know.***

94. ***They will make excuses to you*** for having stayed behind ***when you return to them*** from the expedition. ***Say*** to them: ***'Do not make excuses; we will not believe you. Allah has already informed us about you*** – about the truth of your circumstances. ***Allah will see your actions, as will His Messenger. Then you will be returned*** by the Resurrection ***to the Knower of the Unseen and the Visible*** (Allah) ***and He will inform you regarding what you did***; and then He will repay you for it.'

95. ***They will swear to you by Allah when you return to them*** from Tabūk, and they will make their excuses about staying behind ***so that you leave them alone*** by not rebuking them. ***Leave them alone, then! They are filth*** because of their inward foulness. ***Their shelter will be Hell as repayment for what they did.***

96. ***They will swear to you to make you pleased with them, but even if you are pleased with them, Allah is certainly not pleased with deviant people.*** If Allah is angry with them, your being pleased with them will be of no benefit to them at all.

97. ***The desert Arabs are more obdurate in disbelief and hypocrisy*** than the people of cities, since they are coarse and have a rough nature and they are far from listening to the Qur'an ***and more likely not to know the limits which Allah has sent down to His Messenger.*** The limits referred to are the rulings and laws Allah has revealed. ***Allah is All-Knowing*** of His creation, ***All-Wise*** in what He does to them.

ٱلْأَعْرَابِ مَن يُؤْمِنُ بِٱللَّهِ وَٱلْيَوْمِ ٱلْءَاخِرِ وَيَتَّخِذُ
مَا يُنفِقُ قُرُبَٰتٍ عِندَ ٱللَّهِ وَصَلَوَٰتِ ٱلرَّسُولِ ۚ أَلَآ إِنَّهَا قُرْبَةٌ
لَّهُمْ ۚ سَيُدْخِلُهُمُ ٱللَّهُ فِى رَحْمَتِهِۦٓ ۗ إِنَّ ٱللَّهَ غَفُورٌ رَّحِيمٌ ﴿٩٩﴾
وَٱلسَّٰبِقُونَ ٱلْأَوَّلُونَ مِنَ ٱلْمُهَٰجِرِينَ وَٱلْأَنصَارِ وَٱلَّذِينَ
ٱتَّبَعُوهُم بِإِحْسَٰنٍ رَّضِىَ ٱللَّهُ عَنْهُمْ وَرَضُوا۟ عَنْهُ وَأَعَدَّ
لَهُمْ جَنَّٰتٍ تَجْرِى تَحْتَهَا ٱلْأَنْهَٰرُ خَٰلِدِينَ فِيهَآ أَبَدًا ۚ
ذَٰلِكَ ٱلْفَوْزُ ٱلْعَظِيمُ ﴿١٠٠﴾ وَمِمَّنْ حَوْلَكُم مِّنَ ٱلْأَعْرَابِ
مُنَٰفِقُونَ ۖ وَمِنْ أَهْلِ ٱلْمَدِينَةِ ۖ مَرَدُوا۟ عَلَى ٱلنِّفَاقِ لَا تَعْلَمُهُمْ ۖ
نَحْنُ نَعْلَمُهُمْ ۚ سَنُعَذِّبُهُم مَّرَّتَيْنِ ثُمَّ يُرَدُّونَ إِلَىٰ عَذَابٍ
عَظِيمٍ ﴿١٠١﴾ وَءَاخَرُونَ ٱعْتَرَفُوا۟ بِذُنُوبِهِمْ خَلَطُوا۟ عَمَلًا صَٰلِحًا
وَءَاخَرَ سَيِّئًا عَسَى ٱللَّهُ أَن يَتُوبَ عَلَيْهِمْ ۚ إِنَّ ٱللَّهَ غَفُورٌ رَّحِيمٌ ﴿١٠٢﴾
خُذْ مِنْ أَمْوَٰلِهِمْ صَدَقَةً تُطَهِّرُهُمْ وَتُزَكِّيهِم بِهَا وَصَلِّ عَلَيْهِمْ ۖ
إِنَّ صَلَوٰتَكَ سَكَنٌ لَّهُمْ ۗ وَٱللَّهُ سَمِيعٌ عَلِيمٌ ﴿١٠٣﴾ أَلَمْ يَعْلَمُوٓا۟
أَنَّ ٱللَّهَ هُوَ يَقْبَلُ ٱلتَّوْبَةَ عَنْ عِبَادِهِۦ وَيَأْخُذُ ٱلصَّدَقَٰتِ وَأَنَّ
ٱللَّهَ هُوَ ٱلتَّوَّابُ ٱلرَّحِيمُ ﴿١٠٤﴾ وَقُلِ ٱعْمَلُوا۟ فَسَيَرَى ٱللَّهُ عَمَلَكُمْ
وَرَسُولُهُۥ وَٱلْمُؤْمِنُونَ ۖ وَسَتُرَدُّونَ إِلَىٰ عَٰلِمِ ٱلْغَيْبِ وَٱلشَّهَٰدَةِ
فَيُنَبِّئُكُم بِمَا كُنتُمْ تَعْمَلُونَ ﴿١٠٥﴾ وَءَاخَرُونَ مُرْجَوْنَ لِأَمْرِ
ٱللَّهِ إِمَّا يُعَذِّبُهُمْ وَإِمَّا يَتُوبُ عَلَيْهِمْ ۗ وَٱللَّهُ عَلِيمٌ حَكِيمٌ ﴿١٠٦﴾
وَٱلَّذِينَ ٱتَّخَذُوا۟ مَسْجِدًا ضِرَارًا وَكُفْرًا وَتَفْرِيقًۢا بَيْنَ
ٱلْمُؤْمِنِينَ وَإِرْصَادًا لِّمَنْ حَارَبَ ٱللَّهَ وَرَسُولَهُۥ مِن قَبْلُ ۚ

98. ***Among the desert Arabs there are some who regard what they give*** in the Way of Allah ***as an imposition*** – a fine and loss because they do not hope for any reward from it, but give it out of fear. This is a reference to the tribes of Banū Asad and Ghaṭafān – ***and are waiting for your fortunes to change.*** They are waiting for time to turn against you so that they are delivered from you. ***The evil*** (read as *saw'* and *sū'*) ***turn of fortune will be theirs!*** It will be their punishment and destruction, not yours. ***Allah is All-Hearing*** of what His slaves say, ***All-Knowing*** of what they do.

99. ***And among the desert Arabs there are some who believe in Allah and the Last Day*** – such as Juhayna and Muzayna – ***and regard what they give*** in the Way of Allah ***as something*** (a means) ***which will bring them nearer to Allah and to the prayers*** (supplications) ***of the Messenger*** for them. ***It*** (their spending) ***does indeed bring them near*** (read as *qurba* and *quruba*). ***Allah will admit them into His mercy*** (His Garden)***: Allah is Ever-Forgiving*** to people who obey Him, ***Most Merciful*** to them.

100. ***The forerunners – the first of the Muhājirūn and the Anṣār*** – those who were present at Badr, or all of the Companions, ***and those who have followed them*** until the Day of Rising ***in doing good*** actions***: Allah is pleased with them*** for obeying Him ***and they are pleased with Him*** (with His reward)***. He has prepared Gardens for them with rivers flowing under them*** (read as *tajrī taḥtahā* and *tajrī min taḥtihā*). ***remaining in them timelessly, for ever and ever. That is the great victory.***

101. ***Some of the desert Arabs around you***, people of Madina, ***are hypocrites*** – a reference to the tribes of Aslam, Ashja' and Ghifār – ***and some of the people of Madina*** are also hypocrites and ***are obdurate in their hypocrisy*** – persisting and continuing in it. ***You*** – addressing the Prophet, may Allah bless him and grant him peace – ***do not know them but We know them. We will punish them twice over*** by disgrace or killing in this world and the punishment of the grave, ***and then they will be returned*** in the Next World ***to a terrible punishment*** (the Fire).

102. ***But others*** (other people) ***have acknowledged their wrong actions*** in staying behind ***and mixed a right action*** – their *jihād* before that, or their admission of their wrong actions, or something else – ***with another which is wrong*** – staying behind. ***It may well be that Allah will turn towards them. Allah is Ever-Forgiving, Most Merciful.*** This was revealed about Abū Lubāba and a group who tied themselves to the pillars of the mosque when they heard what had been revealed about those who stayed behind, and swore that they would not be released except by the Prophet, may Allah bless him and grant him peace, who released them when it was revealed.

103. ***Take* zakāt *from their wealth to purify and cleanse them*** of their wrong actions, ***and pray for them*** – make supplication for them. He took a third of their property and gave it as *ṣadaqa*. ***Your prayers bring relief*** – are a mercy – ***to them.*** This is also said to mean peace of mind, since their repentance has been accepted. ***Allah is All-Hearing, All-Knowing.***

104. ***Do they not know that Allah accepts repentance from His slaves and acknowledges*** and accepts ***their* zakāt*, and that Allah is the Ever-Returning*** to His slaves in acceptance of their repentance, ***the Most Merciful*** to them*?* The question implies an affirmative answer and it is an encouragement to repentance and *ṣadaqa*.

105. ***Say*** to them or to people in general***: 'Act*** as you will***, for Allah will see your actions, and so will His Messenger and the believers. You will be returned*** at the Resurrection ***to the Knower of the Unseen and the Visible*** (Allah)***, and He will inform you regarding what you did*** and repay you.***'***

106. ***And others*** (those who stayed behind) – whose repentance is deferred – ***are left awaiting*** (read as *murjawna* and *murja'una*) ***Allah's command*** to do what He wills with them, ***as to whether He will punish them*** by leaving them unrepentant ***or turn to them. Allah is All-Knowing*** of His creation, ***All-Wise*** in what He does to them. They were three men who will be mentioned shortly (see 9:118 below): Murāra ibn ar-Rabī', Ka'b ibn Mālik and Hilāl ibn Umayya. They stayed behind out of laziness and inclination to ease, not hypocrisy. They did not make their excuses to the Prophet, may Allah bless him and grant him peace, as others did. Their case remained suspended for fifty days and people shunned them until the time when Allah's acceptance of their repentance was revealed.

وَلَيَحْلِفُنَّ إِنْ أَرَدْنَآ إِلَّا ٱلْحُسْنَىٰ ۖ وَٱللَّهُ يَشْهَدُ إِنَّهُمْ لَكَـٰذِبُونَ
١٠٧ لَا تَقُمْ فِيهِ أَبَدًا ۚ لَّمَسْجِدٌ أُسِّسَ عَلَى ٱلتَّقْوَىٰ مِنْ أَوَّلِ
يَوْمٍ أَحَقُّ أَن تَقُومَ فِيهِ ۚ فِيهِ رِجَالٌ يُحِبُّونَ أَن يَتَطَهَّرُوا۟ ۚ
وَٱللَّهُ يُحِبُّ ٱلْمُطَّهِّرِينَ ١٠٨ أَفَمَنْ أَسَّسَ بُنْيَـٰنَهُۥ
عَلَىٰ تَقْوَىٰ مِنَ ٱللَّهِ وَرِضْوَٰنٍ خَيْرٌ أَم مَّنْ أَسَّسَ بُنْيَـٰنَهُۥ
عَلَىٰ شَفَا جُرُفٍ هَارٍ فَٱنْهَارَ بِهِۦ فِى نَارِ جَهَنَّمَ ۗ وَٱللَّهُ لَا يَهْدِى
ٱلْقَوْمَ ٱلظَّـٰلِمِينَ ١٠٩ لَا يَزَالُ بُنْيَـٰنُهُمُ ٱلَّذِى بَنَوْا۟ رِيبَةً
فِى قُلُوبِهِمْ إِلَّآ أَن تَقَطَّعَ قُلُوبُهُمْ ۗ وَٱللَّهُ عَلِيمٌ حَكِيمٌ ١١٠
۞ إِنَّ ٱللَّهَ ٱشْتَرَىٰ مِنَ ٱلْمُؤْمِنِينَ أَنفُسَهُمْ وَأَمْوَٰلَهُم
بِأَنَّ لَهُمُ ٱلْجَنَّةَ ۚ يُقَـٰتِلُونَ فِى سَبِيلِ ٱللَّهِ فَيَقْتُلُونَ
وَيُقْتَلُونَ ۖ وَعْدًا عَلَيْهِ حَقًّا فِى ٱلتَّوْرَىٰةِ وَٱلْإِنجِيلِ
وَٱلْقُرْءَانِ ۚ وَمَنْ أَوْفَىٰ بِعَهْدِهِۦ مِنَ ٱللَّهِ ۚ فَٱسْتَبْشِرُوا۟
بِبَيْعِكُمُ ٱلَّذِى بَايَعْتُم بِهِۦ ۚ وَذَٰلِكَ هُوَ ٱلْفَوْزُ ٱلْعَظِيمُ ١١١
ٱلتَّـٰٓئِبُونَ ٱلْعَـٰبِدُونَ ٱلْحَـٰمِدُونَ ٱلسَّـٰٓئِحُونَ
ٱلرَّٰكِعُونَ ٱلسَّـٰجِدُونَ ٱلْـَٔامِرُونَ بِٱلْمَعْرُوفِ
وَٱلنَّاهُونَ عَنِ ٱلْمُنكَرِ وَٱلْحَـٰفِظُونَ لِحُدُودِ ٱللَّهِ ۗ
وَبَشِّرِ ٱلْمُؤْمِنِينَ ١١٢ مَا كَانَ لِلنَّبِىِّ وَٱلَّذِينَ ءَامَنُوٓا۟ أَن
يَسْتَغْفِرُوا۟ لِلْمُشْرِكِينَ وَلَوْ كَانُوٓا۟ أُو۟لِى قُرْبَىٰ مِنۢ بَعْدِ
مَا تَبَيَّنَ لَهُمْ أَنَّهُمْ أَصْحَـٰبُ ٱلْجَحِيمِ ١١٣ وَمَا كَانَ
ٱسْتِغْفَارُ إِبْرَٰهِيمَ لِأَبِيهِ إِلَّا عَن مَّوْعِدَةٍ وَعَدَهَآ إِيَّاهُ

107. ***As for those*** among them ***who have set up a mosque*** – they were twelve of the hypocrites – ***causing harm*** to the people of the Mosque of Qubā' ***and out of unbelief*** – because they built it at the command of Abū 'Āmir ar-Rāhib to be a fortress for him where people could come and go from him. He wanted to bring the armies of the Byzantine emperor to fight the Prophet, may Allah bless him and grant him peace – ***to create division between the believers*** – to divide those who prayed in the Mosque of Qubā' by causing some of them to pray in their mosque – ***and in readiness for those*** (namely Abū 'Āmir) ***who previously*** – before it was built – ***made war on Allah and His Messenger they will swear, 'We only desired the best*** by building it. We have done it out of kindness to the poor to give shelter from the rain and heat and to expand the Muslims.***' But Allah bears witness that they are truly liars*** about that. They asked the Prophet, may Allah bless him and grant him peace, to pray in it and then the following *āyat* was revealed:

108. ***Do not ever stand*** and pray ***in it.*** The Prophet sent a group to it and they destroyed and burned it and turned it into a rubbish heap where carrion was thrown. ***A mosque founded on fear of Allah from the first day*** – built when the Prophet first arrived in the Abode of Hijra: a reference to the Mosque of Qubā', as is stated in al-Bukhārī – ***has a greater right*** than this one ***for you to stand*** and pray ***in it. In it there are men*** (the Anṣār) ***who love to purify themselves. Allah loves those who purify themselves.*** This means He will reward them. Ibn Khuzayma related a *hadīth* in his *Ṣahīh* from 'Uwaymir ibn Sā'ida says that the Prophet, may Allah bless him and grant him peace, came to the people in the Mosque of Qubā' and said, "Allah Almighty has praised you well for purity in His reference to your mosque. What is this purification which you practise?" They said, "By Allah, Messenger of Allah, we do not know anything but that we have Jewish neighbours who used to wash their anuses after defecating, and so we wash as they wash." In a *ḥadīth* which al-Bazzār related: "They said, 'We follow stones with water.' The Prophet, peace be upon him, said, 'That is it. You must do it too.'"

109. ***Who is better: someone who founds his building on fear of Allah and*** hope of ***His good pleasure, or someone who founds his***

building on the brink (read as *juruf* and *jurf*) ***of a crumbling*** (about to fall) ***precipice, so that it collapses with him into the Fire of Hell?*** This is an excellent metaphor for someone who builds with an intention opposite to fear of Allah. The question implies affirmation, meaning that clearly the former (the Mosque of Qubā') is better than the latter (the Mosque of Harm). ***Allah does not love wrongdoers.***

110. ***The buildings they have built will not cease to be a bone of contention*** and a source of doubt ***in their hearts, until their hearts are cut to shreds*** and they die. ***Allah is All-Knowing*** of His creation, ***All-Wise*** in what He does to them.

111. ***Allah has bought from the believers their selves and their wealth*** which they expend in obedience to Allah on things like *jihād* ***in return for the Garden. They fight in the Way of Allah and they kill*** (read as *yaqtulūna wa yuqtalūna* or as *yuqtalūna wa yaqtulūna* "are killed and kill") ***and are killed. It is a promise binding on Him in the Torah, the Gospel and the Qur'an; and who is truer to his contract than Allah?*** There is no one truer than Allah when He promises. ***Rejoice then*** – changing to the second person from the third – ***in the bargain you have made. That*** transaction ***is the great victory*** which obtains the Goal.

112. ***Those who repent*** of *shirk* and hypocrisy, ***those who worship*** Allah sincerely, ***those who praise*** Him every state, ***those who fast, those who bow, those who prostrate*** in prayer, ***those who command what is right, those who forbid the wrong, those who preserve the limits*** (the rulings) ***of Allah*** – by acting according to them: ***give good news*** of the Garden ***to the believers.***

113. The following was revealed about the Prophet, may Allah bless him and grant him peace, asking forgiveness for his uncle, Abū Ṭālib, and some of the Companions asking forgiveness for their idolatrous parents. ***It is not right for the Prophet and those who believe to ask forgiveness for the idolators – even if they are close relatives – after it has become clear to them that they are the Companions of the Blazing Fire*** by their dying as unbelievers.

114. ***Ibrāhīm would not have asked forgiveness for his father but for a promise he made to him*** when he promised him, "I will ask my Lord to forgive you", since he hoped that he would become Muslim,

فَلَمَّا تَبَيَّنَ لَهُۥٓ أَنَّهُۥ عَدُوٌّ لِّلَّهِ تَبَرَّأَ مِنۡهُۚ إِنَّ إِبۡرَٰهِيمَ لَأَوَّٰهٌ حَلِيمٌ
١١٤ وَمَا كَانَ ٱللَّهُ لِيُضِلَّ قَوۡمَۢا بَعۡدَ إِذۡ هَدَىٰهُمۡ حَتَّىٰ
يُبَيِّنَ لَهُم مَّا يَتَّقُونَۚ إِنَّ ٱللَّهَ بِكُلِّ شَيۡءٍ عَلِيمٌ ١١٥ إِنَّ ٱللَّهَ
لَهُۥ مُلۡكُ ٱلسَّمَٰوَٰتِ وَٱلۡأَرۡضِۖ يُحۡيِۦ وَيُمِيتُۚ وَمَا لَكُم مِّن
دُونِ ٱللَّهِ مِن وَلِيٍّ وَلَا نَصِيرٍ ١١٦ لَّقَد تَّابَ ٱللَّهُ عَلَى
ٱلنَّبِيِّ وَٱلۡمُهَٰجِرِينَ وَٱلۡأَنصَارِ ٱلَّذِينَ ٱتَّبَعُوهُ فِي
سَاعَةِ ٱلۡعُسۡرَةِ مِنۢ بَعۡدِ مَا كَادَ يَزِيغُ قُلُوبُ فَرِيقٍ
مِّنۡهُمۡ ثُمَّ تَابَ عَلَيۡهِمۡۚ إِنَّهُۥ بِهِمۡ رَءُوفٌ رَّحِيمٌ ١١٧
وَعَلَى ٱلثَّلَٰثَةِ ٱلَّذِينَ خُلِّفُواْ حَتَّىٰٓ إِذَا ضَاقَتۡ عَلَيۡهِمُ ٱلۡأَرۡضُ
بِمَا رَحُبَتۡ وَضَاقَتۡ عَلَيۡهِمۡ أَنفُسُهُمۡ وَظَنُّوٓاْ أَن لَّا مَلۡجَأَ
مِنَ ٱللَّهِ إِلَّآ إِلَيۡهِ ثُمَّ تَابَ عَلَيۡهِمۡ لِيَتُوبُوٓاْۚ إِنَّ ٱللَّهَ هُوَ ٱلتَّوَّابُ
ٱلرَّحِيمُ ١١٨ يَٰٓأَيُّهَا ٱلَّذِينَ ءَامَنُواْ ٱتَّقُواْ ٱللَّهَ وَكُونُواْ مَعَ
ٱلصَّٰدِقِينَ ١١٩ مَا كَانَ لِأَهۡلِ ٱلۡمَدِينَةِ وَمَنۡ حَوۡلَهُم
مِّنَ ٱلۡأَعۡرَابِ أَن يَتَخَلَّفُواْ عَن رَّسُولِ ٱللَّهِ وَلَا يَرۡغَبُواْ بِأَنفُسِهِمۡ
عَن نَّفۡسِهِۦۚ ذَٰلِكَ بِأَنَّهُمۡ لَا يُصِيبُهُمۡ ظَمَأٌ وَلَا نَصَبٌ
وَلَا مَخۡمَصَةٌ فِي سَبِيلِ ٱللَّهِ وَلَا يَطَـُٔونَ مَوۡطِئًا يَغِيظُ
ٱلۡكُفَّارَ وَلَا يَنَالُونَ مِنۡ عَدُوٍّ نَّيۡلًا إِلَّا كُتِبَ لَهُم
بِهِۦ عَمَلٌ صَٰلِحٌۚ إِنَّ ٱللَّهَ لَا يُضِيعُ أَجۡرَ ٱلۡمُحۡسِنِينَ ١٢٠
وَلَا يُنفِقُونَ نَفَقَةً صَغِيرَةً وَلَا كَبِيرَةً وَلَا يَقۡطَعُونَ
وَادِيًا إِلَّا كُتِبَ لَهُمۡ لِيَجۡزِيَهُمُ ٱللَّهُ أَحۡسَنَ مَا كَانُواْ

and when it became clear to him that he was an enemy of Allah – when he died an unbeliever – ***he renounced him*** and stopped asking forgiveness for him. ***Ibrāhīm was tender-hearted,*** making much supplication and entreaty, ***and forbearing*** in the face of harm.

115. ***Allah would never misguide a people after guiding them*** to Islam ***until He had made it clear to them how to fear Allah*** in action, which they fail to do, so they deserve to be misguided. ***Allah has knowledge of all things***, including those who deserve guidance and misguidance.

116. ***Allah is He to whom the kingdom of the heavens and earth belongs. He gives life and causes to die. You***, mankind, ***have no protector or helper besides Allah*** against Him.

117. ***Allah has turned*** constantly ***towards the Prophet, and the*** **Muhājirūn** ***and the*** **Anṣār,** ***those who followed him at the 'time of difficulty'*** – the time of the Tabūk expedition when two men would share one date and ten would take turns on one camel. The heat was so intense that they drank the contents of the camel's stomach – ***after the hearts of a group of them had almost deviated*** (read as *yazīghu* and *tazīghu*) – almost turned away from following him to staying behind because of the hardship. ***Then He*** (Allah) ***turned towards them*** by making them firm – ***He is All-Gentle, Most Merciful to them –***

118. ***…and*** He ***also*** turned ***towards the three who were left behind*** from His turning to them, ***so that when the earth became narrow for them, for all its great breadth,*** and they could not find any place where they were at peace, ***and their own selves became constricted for them*** – their hearts were full of sorrow and alienation at the delay of their acceptance and they felt no joy or friendliness – ***and they realised*** and were certain ***that there was no refuge from Allah except in Him, He turned to them*** and gave them success in repenting ***so that they might turn to Him. Allah is the Ever-Returning, the Most Merciful.***

119. ***You who believe. Be fearful of Allah*** by not disobeying Him ***and be with the truly sincere*** in respect of their faith and in respect of their contracts by their clinging to truthfulness.

120. ***It was not for people of Madina, and the desert Arabs around them, to remain behind the Messenger of Allah*** when he went on

يَعْمَلُونَ ﴿١٢١﴾ ۞ وَمَا كَانَ ٱلْمُؤْمِنُونَ لِيَنفِرُوا۟ كَآفَّةً ۚ

فَلَوْلَا نَفَرَ مِن كُلِّ فِرْقَةٍ مِّنْهُمْ طَآئِفَةٌ لِّيَتَفَقَّهُوا۟ فِى ٱلدِّينِ

وَلِيُنذِرُوا۟ قَوْمَهُمْ إِذَا رَجَعُوٓا۟ إِلَيْهِمْ لَعَلَّهُمْ يَحْذَرُونَ ﴿١٢٢﴾

يَـٰٓأَيُّهَا ٱلَّذِينَ ءَامَنُوا۟ قَـٰتِلُوا۟ ٱلَّذِينَ يَلُونَكُم مِّنَ ٱلْكُفَّارِ

وَلْيَجِدُوا۟ فِيكُمْ غِلْظَةً ۚ وَٱعْلَمُوٓا۟ أَنَّ ٱللَّهَ مَعَ ٱلْمُتَّقِينَ ﴿١٢٣﴾

وَإِذَا مَآ أُنزِلَتْ سُورَةٌ فَمِنْهُم مَّن يَقُولُ أَيُّكُمْ زَادَتْهُ هَـٰذِهِۦٓ

إِيمَـٰنًا ۚ فَأَمَّا ٱلَّذِينَ ءَامَنُوا۟ فَزَادَتْهُمْ إِيمَـٰنًا وَهُمْ يَسْتَبْشِرُونَ

﴿١٢٤﴾ وَأَمَّا ٱلَّذِينَ فِى قُلُوبِهِم مَّرَضٌ فَزَادَتْهُمْ رِجْسًا

إِلَىٰ رِجْسِهِمْ وَمَاتُوا۟ وَهُمْ كَـٰفِرُونَ ﴿١٢٥﴾ أَوَلَا يَرَوْنَ

أَنَّهُمْ يُفْتَنُونَ فِى كُلِّ عَامٍ مَّرَّةً أَوْ مَرَّتَيْنِ ثُمَّ

لَا يَتُوبُونَ وَلَا هُمْ يَذَّكَّرُونَ ﴿١٢٦﴾ وَإِذَا مَآ أُنزِلَتْ

سُورَةٌ نَّظَرَ بَعْضُهُمْ إِلَىٰ بَعْضٍ هَلْ يَرَىٰكُم مِّنْ أَحَدٍ

ثُمَّ ٱنصَرَفُوا۟ ۚ صَرَفَ ٱللَّهُ قُلُوبَهُم بِأَنَّهُمْ قَوْمٌ لَّا يَفْقَهُونَ

﴿١٢٧﴾ لَقَدْ جَآءَكُمْ رَسُولٌ مِّنْ أَنفُسِكُمْ عَزِيزٌ

عَلَيْهِ مَا عَنِتُّمْ حَرِيصٌ عَلَيْكُم بِٱلْمُؤْمِنِينَ

رَءُوفٌ رَّحِيمٌ ﴿١٢٨﴾ فَإِن تَوَلَّوْا۟ فَقُلْ حَسْبِىَ ٱللَّهُ لَآ إِلَـٰهَ

إِلَّا هُوَ ۖ عَلَيْهِ تَوَكَّلْتُ ۖ وَهُوَ رَبُّ ٱلْعَرْشِ ٱلْعَظِيمِ ﴿١٢٩﴾

an expedition, ***or to prefer themselves to him*** by protecting themselves from the hardships he was happy to undergo himself. This is a prohibition in the form of a report. ***That*** prohibition against staying behind ***is because no thirst or weariness or hunger will afflict them in the Way of Allah, nor will they take a single step to infuriate the unbelievers, nor secure any gain*** (killing, capture or booty) ***from the enemy*** of Allah, ***without a right action being written down for them because of it*** for which they will be rewarded. ***Allah does not let the wage of the good-doers go to waste.*** They will definitely receive their wages and will be rewarded.

121. ***Nor will they give away any amount*** in pursuance of that aim, ***whether large or small*** – even as little as a date, ***nor will they cross any valley, without it being written down for them*** as a righteous actions ***so that Allah can recompense them for the best of what they did.***

122. When they were rebuked for not going out and the Prophet, may Allah bless him and grant him peace, sent an expedition, they all went out without exception and then this was revealed. ***It is not necessary for the believers to go out all together*** on an expedition. ***If a party from each group*** (tribe) ***of them were to go out*** while the others remained behind ***so they could increase their knowledge of the* dīn*, they would be able to notify their people when they returned to them*** from the expedition, when they could teach them the rulings they had learned ***so that perhaps they would take warning*** of the punishment of Allah and obey His commands and avoid what he has prohibited. Ibn 'Abbās said, "This was specific to expeditions the Prophet, peace be upon him, sent out. The preceding passage concerned staying behind expeditions in which the Prophet, may Allah bless him and grant him peace, went out."

123. ***You who believe! Fight those of the unbelievers who are near to you*** – fight the nearest and then the next nearest – ***and let them find you implacable*** and severe towards them. ***Know that Allah is with those who are fearful of Him*** with help and victory.

124. ***Each time a* sūra** of the Qur'an ***is sent down there are some among them*** (the hypocrites) ***who say*** to their companions in mockery, ***'Which of you has this increased in faith*** and confirmation***?'***

Allah says: ***As for those who believe, it increases them in faith*** and confirmation of it ***and they rejoice at it.***

125. ***But as for those with sickness*** (weakness of belief) ***in their hearts, it adds defilement to their defilement*** – unbelief added to their existing unbelief – ***and they die unbelievers.***

126. ***Do they not see*** (read as *yarawna*, referring to the hypocrites, and *tarawna*, "you see", referring to the believers) ***that they are tried once or twice*** with drought and illnesses ***in every year? But still they do not turn back*** from their hypocrisy. ***They do not pay heed*** and are not warned.

127. ***Each time a* sūra *is sent down*** in which they are mentioned and which the Prophet, may Allah bless him and grant him peace, recites, ***they look at one another,*** wanting to run away, ***implying, 'Can anyone see you*** when you get up?' If no one saw them, they would get up. Otherwise they would remain where they were. ***Then they turn away*** to unbelief. ***Allah has turned their hearts away*** from guidance ***because they are people who do not understand*** the truth since they do not reflect.

128. ***A Messenger*** (Muḥammad, may Allah bless him and grant him peace) ***has come to you from among yourselves. Your suffering is*** very ***distressing to him*** when you encounter hardships and things you dislike; ***he is deeply concerned for you*** – for your guidance; ***he is gentle***, with great compassion, ***and merciful to the believers***, desiring good for them.

129. ***But if they turn away*** from believing in you, ***say, 'Allah is enough for me. There is no god but Him. I have put my trust in Him.*** I only trust in Him and no one else. ***He is the Lord of the Mighty Throne.'*** The Throne is mighty because it is the largest of created things. Al-Ḥākim related in *al-Mustadrak* from Ubayy ibn Ka'b that, "The last *āyat* to be revealed was "A Messenger has come…" to the end of the *āyat*.

سُورَةُ يُونُس

بِسْمِ ٱللَّهِ ٱلرَّحْمَٰنِ ٱلرَّحِيمِ

الٓر ۚ تِلْكَ ءَايَٰتُ ٱلْكِتَٰبِ ٱلْحَكِيمِ ﴿١﴾ أَكَانَ لِلنَّاسِ عَجَبًا
أَنْ أَوْحَيْنَآ إِلَىٰ رَجُلٍ مِّنْهُمْ أَنْ أَنذِرِ ٱلنَّاسَ وَبَشِّرِ ٱلَّذِينَ ءَامَنُوٓا۟
أَنَّ لَهُمْ قَدَمَ صِدْقٍ عِندَ رَبِّهِمْ ۗ قَالَ ٱلْكَٰفِرُونَ إِنَّ هَٰذَا
لَسَٰحِرٌ مُّبِينٌ ﴿٢﴾ إِنَّ رَبَّكُمُ ٱللَّهُ ٱلَّذِى خَلَقَ ٱلسَّمَٰوَٰتِ وَٱلْأَرْضَ
فِى سِتَّةِ أَيَّامٍ ثُمَّ ٱسْتَوَىٰ عَلَى ٱلْعَرْشِ ۖ يُدَبِّرُ ٱلْأَمْرَ ۖ مَا مِن شَفِيعٍ
إِلَّا مِنۢ بَعْدِ إِذْنِهِۦ ۚ ذَٰلِكُمُ ٱللَّهُ رَبُّكُمْ فَٱعْبُدُوهُ ۚ أَفَلَا
تَذَكَّرُونَ ﴿٣﴾ إِلَيْهِ مَرْجِعُكُمْ جَمِيعًا ۖ وَعْدَ ٱللَّهِ حَقًّا ۚ إِنَّهُۥ
يَبْدَؤُا۟ ٱلْخَلْقَ ثُمَّ يُعِيدُهُۥ لِيَجْزِىَ ٱلَّذِينَ ءَامَنُوا۟ وَعَمِلُوا۟ ٱلصَّٰلِحَٰتِ
بِٱلْقِسْطِ ۚ وَٱلَّذِينَ كَفَرُوا۟ لَهُمْ شَرَابٌ مِّنْ حَمِيمٍ وَعَذَابٌ
أَلِيمٌۢ بِمَا كَانُوا۟ يَكْفُرُونَ ﴿٤﴾ هُوَ ٱلَّذِى جَعَلَ ٱلشَّمْسَ
ضِيَآءً وَٱلْقَمَرَ نُورًا وَقَدَّرَهُۥ مَنَازِلَ لِتَعْلَمُوا۟ عَدَدَ ٱلسِّنِينَ
وَٱلْحِسَابَ ۚ مَا خَلَقَ ٱللَّهُ ذَٰلِكَ إِلَّا بِٱلْحَقِّ ۚ يُفَصِّلُ ٱلْءَايَٰتِ
لِقَوْمٍ يَعْلَمُونَ ﴿٥﴾ إِنَّ فِى ٱخْتِلَٰفِ ٱلَّيْلِ وَٱلنَّهَارِ وَمَا خَلَقَ
ٱللَّهُ فِى ٱلسَّمَٰوَٰتِ وَٱلْأَرْضِ لَءَايَٰتٍ لِّقَوْمٍ يَتَّقُونَ ﴿٦﴾
إِنَّ ٱلَّذِينَ لَا يَرْجُونَ لِقَآءَنَا وَرَضُوا۟ بِٱلْحَيَوٰةِ ٱلدُّنْيَا وَٱطْمَأَنُّوا۟
بِهَا وَٱلَّذِينَ هُمْ عَنْ ءَايَٰتِنَا غَٰفِلُونَ ﴿٧﴾ أُو۟لَٰٓئِكَ مَأْوَىٰهُمُ
ٱلنَّارُ بِمَا كَانُوا۟ يَكْسِبُونَ ﴿٨﴾ إِنَّ ٱلَّذِينَ ءَامَنُوا۟
وَعَمِلُوا۟ ٱلصَّٰلِحَٰتِ يَهْدِيهِمْ رَبُّهُم بِإِيمَٰنِهِمْ ۖ تَجْرِى مِن

10. *Sūrat Yūnus*
Jonah

This *sūra* is is Makkan except for *āyat*s 40, 94, 95, and 96 which are Madinan. It has 109 or 110 *āyat*s and was revealed after *Sūrat al-Isrā'*.

1. ***Alif Lam Ra.*** Allah knows best what these letters means. ***Those*** *āyat*s ***are the Signs of the Wise*** – here meaning masterly and perfect – ***Book*** (the Qur'an).

2. ***Do people*** (the people of Makka) – and this is a question demanding a negative response – ***find it surprising that We should reveal to a man among them*** – Muḥammad, may Allah bless him and grant him peace: ***'Warn mankind*** – make the unbelievers fear the punishment – ***and give good news to those who believe*** that they have an excellent reward for the actions which they have already done and ***that they are on a sure footing with their Lord'? The unbelievers say, 'This is clearly a magician!'*** (read as *sāḥir* and also *siḥr,* in which case the meaning is, "This is downright magic!" implying that the Qur'an contains that).***'***

3. ***Your Lord is Allah, Who created the heavens and the earth in six days:*** an indication of the time involved although it was before the creation of the sun or moon. If Allah had wished, He could have created them in an instant; but He did not do so, in order to teach His creation how to be firm – ***and then established Himself firmly on the Throne*** in a manner appropriate to Him. ***He directs the whole affair*** between His creatures. ***No one can intercede*** for someone else ***except with His permission.*** This refutes the idolaters' statement that idols intercede. ***That*** Managing Creator ***is Allah your Lord, so worship Him*** and proclaim His unity. ***Will you not pay heed?***

4. ***Each and every one of you will return to Him. Allah's promise is true. He*** (read as *innahu* and *annahu*) ***brings creation out of nothing*** and originates it ***and then regenerates it*** at the Resurrection ***so that He may repay with justice*** and reward ***those who believed and did right actions. Those who disbelieved will have scalding water to drink and a painful punishment because of their unbelief.***

تَحۡتِهِمُ ٱلۡأَنۡهَٰرُ فِي جَنَّٰتِ ٱلنَّعِيمِ ﴿٩﴾ دَعۡوَىٰهُمۡ فِيهَا سُبۡحَٰنَكَ
ٱللَّهُمَّ وَتَحِيَّتُهُمۡ فِيهَا سَلَٰمٞۚ وَءَاخِرُ دَعۡوَىٰهُمۡ أَنِ ٱلۡحَمۡدُ لِلَّهِ
رَبِّ ٱلۡعَٰلَمِينَ ﴿١٠﴾ ۞ وَلَوۡ يُعَجِّلُ ٱللَّهُ لِلنَّاسِ ٱلشَّرَّ
ٱسۡتِعۡجَالَهُم بِٱلۡخَيۡرِ لَقُضِيَ إِلَيۡهِمۡ أَجَلُهُمۡۖ فَنَذَرُ ٱلَّذِينَ
لَا يَرۡجُونَ لِقَآءَنَا فِي طُغۡيَٰنِهِمۡ يَعۡمَهُونَ ﴿١١﴾ وَإِذَا مَسَّ
ٱلۡإِنسَٰنَ ٱلضُّرُّ دَعَانَا لِجَنۢبِهِۦٓ أَوۡ قَاعِدًا أَوۡ قَآئِمٗا فَلَمَّا كَشَفۡنَا
عَنۡهُ ضُرَّهُۥ مَرَّ كَأَن لَّمۡ يَدۡعُنَآ إِلَىٰ ضُرّٖ مَّسَّهُۥۚ كَذَٰلِكَ زُيِّنَ
لِلۡمُسۡرِفِينَ مَا كَانُواْ يَعۡمَلُونَ ﴿١٢﴾ وَلَقَدۡ أَهۡلَكۡنَا ٱلۡقُرُونَ
مِن قَبۡلِكُمۡ لَمَّا ظَلَمُواْۖ وَجَآءَتۡهُمۡ رُسُلُهُم بِٱلۡبَيِّنَٰتِ وَمَا كَانُواْ
لِيُؤۡمِنُواْۚ كَذَٰلِكَ نَجۡزِي ٱلۡقَوۡمَ ٱلۡمُجۡرِمِينَ ﴿١٣﴾ ثُمَّ جَعَلۡنَٰكُمۡ
خَلَٰٓئِفَ فِي ٱلۡأَرۡضِ مِنۢ بَعۡدِهِمۡ لِنَنظُرَ كَيۡفَ تَعۡمَلُونَ ﴿١٤﴾
وَإِذَا تُتۡلَىٰ عَلَيۡهِمۡ ءَايَاتُنَا بَيِّنَٰتٖۖ قَالَ ٱلَّذِينَ لَا يَرۡجُونَ
لِقَآءَنَا ٱئۡتِ بِقُرۡءَانٍ غَيۡرِ هَٰذَآ أَوۡ بَدِّلۡهُۚ قُلۡ مَا يَكُونُ لِيٓ
أَنۡ أُبَدِّلَهُۥ مِن تِلۡقَآيِٕ نَفۡسِيٓۖ إِنۡ أَتَّبِعُ إِلَّا مَا يُوحَىٰٓ إِلَيَّۖ إِنِّيٓ
أَخَافُ إِنۡ عَصَيۡتُ رَبِّي عَذَابَ يَوۡمٍ عَظِيمٖ ﴿١٥﴾ قُل لَّوۡ شَآءَ
ٱللَّهُ مَا تَلَوۡتُهُۥ عَلَيۡكُمۡ وَلَآ أَدۡرَىٰكُم بِهِۦۖ فَقَدۡ لَبِثۡتُ
فِيكُمۡ عُمُرٗا مِّن قَبۡلِهِۦٓۚ أَفَلَا تَعۡقِلُونَ ﴿١٦﴾ فَمَنۡ أَظۡلَمُ
مِمَّنِ ٱفۡتَرَىٰ عَلَى ٱللَّهِ كَذِبًا أَوۡ كَذَّبَ بِـَٔايَٰتِهِۦٓۚ إِنَّهُۥ
لَا يُفۡلِحُ ٱلۡمُجۡرِمُونَ ﴿١٧﴾ وَيَعۡبُدُونَ مِن دُونِ ٱللَّهِ
مَا لَا يَضُرُّهُمۡ وَلَا يَنفَعُهُمۡ وَيَقُولُونَ هَٰٓؤُلَآءِ شُفَعَٰٓؤُنَا

5. ***It is He who appointed the sun to give radiance*** (light) ***and the moon to give light, assigning it phases***: – twenty-eight phases, one for every night of the month. It is concealed for two nights if the month is thirty days or for one night if it is twenty-nine days, ***so*** that by that ***you would know the number of years and the reckoning of time. Allah did not create these things except with truth.*** These things were not created without a purpose. ***He makes*** (read as *yufaṣṣilu* and *nufaṣṣilu*, "We make clear") ***the Signs clear for people who know*** and reflect.

6. ***In the alternation of night and day*** – the coming and going of night and day, and their shortening and lengthening – ***and what*** (angels, sun, moon, stars etc.) ***Allah has created in the heavens*** of ***and*** on ***the earth*** (animals, mountains, seas, rivers, trees etc.) ***there are Signs*** which indicate the power of Allah ***for people who are godfearing*** – who are fearful of Him and believe in Him. They are mentioned in particular because it is they who most benefit from these Signs.

7. ***As for those who do not expect to meet Us*** at the Resurrection ***and are content with the life of this world*** rather than the Next World – since they deny it – ***and at rest in it*** – relying on it – ***and those who are heedless of Our Signs*** which indicate Our Oneness, and fail to look at them,

8. ***their shelter will be the Fire because of what*** (the *shirk* and acts of disobedience they committed) ***they earned.***

9. ***But as for those who believe and do right actions, their Lord will guide them by their faith*** in Him: He will appoint a light for them by which they are guided on the Day of Rising. ***Rivers will flow under them in Gardens of Delight.***

10. ***Their call there is*** – all they want to do in the Garden is to say – ***'Glory be to You, O Allah!'*** When they seek Him, they will find Him in front of them. ***Their greeting there*** to one another ***is: 'Peace!' The end of their call is: 'Praise be to Allah, the Lord of all the worlds!'*** Then the desire of the idolaters to hasten the punishment is commented on:

11. ***If Allah were to hasten evil for people the way they try to hasten good, their term*** (read as *ajaluhum* and *ajalahum*) ***would***

already have been completed (read as *quḍiya* and *qaḍā*) ***for them*** and they would have been destroyed; but He grants them a delay. ***We abandon those who do not expect to meet Us to wander blindly*** in confusion ***in their excessive insolence.***

12. ***When harm*** (illness or poverty) ***touches*** (an unbelieving) ***man, he calls on Us, lying on his side or sitting down or standing up***: in other words, in every state. ***Then when We remove the harm from him he carries on*** with his unbelief ***as if he had never called on Us when the harm first touched him.*** So it seems good to him to make supplication to Allah when in difficulty and to turn away from Allah in times of ease. ***In that way We make what they have done appear good to the profligate*** (the idolaters).

13. ***We destroyed generations*** (nations) ***before you***, people of Makka, ***when they did wrong*** by committing *shirk*. ***Their Messengers brought them the Clear Signs*** – which demonstrate their truthfulness – ***but they were never going to believe. That*** – the way that We destroyed earlier generations – ***is how We repay evildoers.***

14. ***Then We appointed you,*** people of Makka, ***after them to be deputies on the earth so We might observe how you would act*** – to see if you would take note of the Signs and confirm Our Messengers.

15. ***When Our Clear*** (manifest) ***Signs*** (the Qur'an) ***are recited to them, those who do not expect to meet Us*** – and therefore do not fear the Resurrection – ***say, 'Bring a Qur'an other than this one*** which does not criticise our gods, ***or change it*** yourself.***'*** ***Say*** to them***: 'It is not*** appropriate ***for me to change it of my own accord. I follow nothing except what is revealed to me. I fear, were I to disobey my Lord*** by changing it, ***the punishment of a Dreadful Day*** (the Day of Rising).'

16. ***Say: 'Had Allah so wished, I would not have recited it*** (the Qur'an) ***to you nor would He have made it known to you*** (read as *la-adrākum* and *lā adrākum*) – He would have informed you of it on the tongue of someone other than me. ***I lived among you for many*** (forty) ***years before it came*** without telling you anything. ***Will you not use your intellect*** and understand that it does not come from me?'

عِندَ ٱللَّهِۚ قُلۡ أَتُنَبِّـُٔونَ ٱللَّهَ بِمَا لَا يَعۡلَمُ فِي ٱلسَّمَٰوَٰتِ وَلَا
فِي ٱلۡأَرۡضِۚ سُبۡحَٰنَهُۥ وَتَعَٰلَىٰ عَمَّا يُشۡرِكُونَ ١٨ وَمَا كَانَ
ٱلنَّاسُ إِلَّآ أُمَّةٗ وَٰحِدَةٗ فَٱخۡتَلَفُواْۚ وَلَوۡلَا كَلِمَةٞ
سَبَقَتۡ مِن رَّبِّكَ لَقُضِيَ بَيۡنَهُمۡ فِيمَا فِيهِ يَخۡتَلِفُونَ
١٩ وَيَقُولُونَ لَوۡلَآ أُنزِلَ عَلَيۡهِ ءَايَةٞ مِّن رَّبِّهِۦۖ فَقُلۡ إِنَّمَا
ٱلۡغَيۡبُ لِلَّهِ فَٱنتَظِرُوٓاْ إِنِّي مَعَكُم مِّنَ ٱلۡمُنتَظِرِينَ ٢٠
وَإِذَآ أَذَقۡنَا ٱلنَّاسَ رَحۡمَةٗ مِّنۢ بَعۡدِ ضَرَّآءَ مَسَّتۡهُمۡ إِذَا لَهُم مَّكۡرٞ فِيٓ
ءَايَاتِنَاۚ قُلِ ٱللَّهُ أَسۡرَعُ مَكۡرًاۚ إِنَّ رُسُلَنَا يَكۡتُبُونَ مَا تَمۡكُرُونَ
٢١ هُوَ ٱلَّذِي يُسَيِّرُكُمۡ فِي ٱلۡبَرِّ وَٱلۡبَحۡرِۖ حَتَّىٰٓ إِذَا كُنتُمۡ فِي ٱلۡفُلۡكِ
وَجَرَيۡنَ بِهِم بِرِيحٖ طَيِّبَةٖ وَفَرِحُواْ بِهَا جَآءَتۡهَا رِيحٌ عَاصِفٞ
وَجَآءَهُمُ ٱلۡمَوۡجُ مِن كُلِّ مَكَانٖ وَظَنُّوٓاْ أَنَّهُمۡ أُحِيطَ بِهِمۡ دَعَوُاْ
ٱللَّهَ مُخۡلِصِينَ لَهُ ٱلدِّينَ لَئِنۡ أَنجَيۡتَنَا مِنۡ هَٰذِهِۦ لَنَكُونَنَّ مِنَ
ٱلشَّٰكِرِينَ ٢٢ فَلَمَّآ أَنجَىٰهُمۡ إِذَا هُمۡ يَبۡغُونَ فِي ٱلۡأَرۡضِ بِغَيۡرِ
ٱلۡحَقِّۗ يَٰٓأَيُّهَا ٱلنَّاسُ إِنَّمَا بَغۡيُكُمۡ عَلَىٰٓ أَنفُسِكُمۖ مَّتَٰعَ ٱلۡحَيَوٰةِ
ٱلدُّنۡيَاۖ ثُمَّ إِلَيۡنَا مَرۡجِعُكُمۡ فَنُنَبِّئُكُم بِمَا كُنتُمۡ تَعۡمَلُونَ ٢٣
إِنَّمَا مَثَلُ ٱلۡحَيَوٰةِ ٱلدُّنۡيَا كَمَآءٍ أَنزَلۡنَٰهُ مِنَ ٱلسَّمَآءِ فَٱخۡتَلَطَ بِهِۦ
نَبَاتُ ٱلۡأَرۡضِ مِمَّا يَأۡكُلُ ٱلنَّاسُ وَٱلۡأَنۡعَٰمُ حَتَّىٰٓ إِذَآ أَخَذَتِ ٱلۡأَرۡضُ
زُخۡرُفَهَا وَٱزَّيَّنَتۡ وَظَنَّ أَهۡلُهَآ أَنَّهُمۡ قَٰدِرُونَ عَلَيۡهَآ
أَتَىٰهَآ أَمۡرُنَا لَيۡلًا أَوۡ نَهَارٗا فَجَعَلۡنَٰهَا حَصِيدٗا كَأَن لَّمۡ تَغۡنَ
بِٱلۡأَمۡسِۚ كَذَٰلِكَ نُفَصِّلُ ٱلۡأٓيَٰتِ لِقَوۡمٖ يَتَفَكَّرُونَ ٢٤ وَٱللَّهُ
يَدۡعُوٓاْ إِلَىٰ دَارِ ٱلسَّلَٰمِ وَيَهۡدِي مَن يَشَآءُ إِلَىٰ صِرَٰطٖ مُّسۡتَقِيمٖ ٢٥

17. ***Who could do greater wrong*** – no one could – ***than someone who invents lies against Allah*** by attributing a partner to Allah ***or denies His Signs*** (the Qur'an)***? Evildoers*** (idolaters) ***are certainly not successful.***

18. ***They worship, instead of Allah, what can neither harm them*** if they do not worship them ***nor help them*** if they do worship them – ***saying*** about them, ***'These are our intercessors with Allah.' Say*** to them***: 'Would you inform Allah of something about which He does not know either in the heavens or on the earth?'*** The question asked is one demanding a negative response. If Allah had had a partner, He would have known it since nothing is concealed from Him. ***May He be glorified and exalted above what they associate with Him!***

19. ***Mankind was only one community*** with a single *dīn*, which was Islam, from Ādam until Nūḥ, or from Ibrāhīm to 'Amr ibn Luḥayy, ***but then they differed*** when some remained firm and some disbelieved, ***and had it not been for a prior Word from your Lord*** to defer repayment for their actions until the Day of Rising ***they would already have been judged*** in this world ***in respect of the differences between them*** in the *dīn* by the punishment of the unbelievers.

20. ***They*** (the people of Makka) ***say, 'Why has a Sign not been sent down to him*** (Muḥammad, may Allah bless him and grant him peace) ***from his Lord*** – like past Prophets, who had signs such as the She-camel and the Staff and the White Hand***?' Say*** to them***: 'The Unseen*** – the business of the Unseen which is invisible to human beings – ***belongs to Allah alone.*** This includes the Signs, and only He can bring them. My task is only to convey the Message. ***So wait*** for the punishment if you do not believe. ***I am waiting with you.'***

21. ***When We let people*** (the unbelievers of Makka) ***taste mercy*** (rain and fertility) ***after hardship*** (difficulty and drought) ***has afflicted them, immediately they plot against Our Signs*** by mockery and denial. ***Say*** to them***: 'Allah is swifter at plotting*** as a repayment.***' Your plotting*** (read as *tamkarūna* and *yamkarūna*, "their plotting") ***is recorded by Our Messengers*** (the recording angels).

22. ***It is He who conveys you*** (read as *yusayyirukum*, but in one reading as *yanshurukum* "distributes you") ***on both land and sea so that***

when some of you are on a boat, running before a fair (gentle) ***wind, rejoicing at it,*** (there is a change of person midway in this verse from second to third person) ***and then a violent*** (the word means so fiercely strong that it smashes everything) ***squall comes upon them and the waves come at them from every side and they realise there is no way of escape*** and that they are about to be destroyed ***they call on Allah, making their*** **dīn** (supplication) ***sincerely His: 'If You rescue us from this*** terror ***we will truly be among the thankful*** who affirm the Divine Unity.'

23. ***But then, when He does rescue them, they become rebellious*** and commit *shirk* ***in the earth without any right to do so. Mankind, your rebelliousness is only against yourselves***, because its sin will rebound on you. ***There is the enjoyment*** (read as *matā'a* and *matā'u*) ***of the life of this world***, – which you will enjoy for a short time only, ***and then you will return to Us*** after death ***and We will inform you about what you did*** and repay you for it.

24. ***The likeness of the life of this world is that of water*** (rain) ***which We send down from the sky, and which then mingles with the plants of the earth*** and they combine ***to provide food for both people and animals***, such as wheat, barley and other crops for human consumption and fodder for animals. ***Then, when the earth is at its loveliest and takes on its fairest guise*** – when the plants are abundant on it – ***and its people think they have it under their control***, and will be able to harvest its fruits, ***Our command*** (Our decree or punishment) ***comes upon it by night or day and We reduce it*** (the plant-life) ***to dried-out stubble*** – as if it had been mown down with scythes – ***as though it had not been flourishing just the day before! In this way We make Our Signs clear for people who reflect.***

25. ***Allah calls to the Abode of Peace*** (the Garden) by calling people to faith, ***and He guides whom He wills to a straight path*** – the *dīn* of Islam.

26. ***Those who do good*** by believing ***will have the best*** (the Garden) ***and more*** – such as the vision of the Almighty, as mentoned in the *ḥadīth* of Muslim. ***Neither dust nor debasement will darken their faces. They shall be the Companions of the Garden, remaining in it timelessly, for ever.***

۞ لِّلَّذِينَ أَحۡسَنُواْ ٱلۡحُسۡنَىٰ وَزِيَادَةٞۖ وَلَا يَرۡهَقُ وُجُوهَهُمۡ قَتَرٞ
وَلَا ذِلَّةٌۚ أُوْلَٰٓئِكَ أَصۡحَٰبُ ٱلۡجَنَّةِۖ هُمۡ فِيهَا خَٰلِدُونَ ٢٦ وَٱلَّذِينَ
كَسَبُواْ ٱلسَّيِّـَٔاتِ جَزَآءُ سَيِّئَةِۭ بِمِثۡلِهَا وَتَرۡهَقُهُمۡ ذِلَّةٞۖ مَّا لَهُم مِّنَ
ٱللَّهِ مِنۡ عَاصِمٖۖ كَأَنَّمَآ أُغۡشِيَتۡ وُجُوهُهُمۡ قِطَعٗا مِّنَ ٱلَّيۡلِ مُظۡلِمًاۚ
أُوْلَٰٓئِكَ أَصۡحَٰبُ ٱلنَّارِۖ هُمۡ فِيهَا خَٰلِدُونَ ٢٧ وَيَوۡمَ نَحۡشُرُهُمۡ
جَمِيعٗا ثُمَّ نَقُولُ لِلَّذِينَ أَشۡرَكُواْ مَكَانَكُمۡ أَنتُمۡ وَشُرَكَآؤُكُمۡۚ فَزَيَّلۡنَا
بَيۡنَهُمۡۖ وَقَالَ شُرَكَآؤُهُم مَّا كُنتُمۡ إِيَّانَا تَعۡبُدُونَ ٢٨ فَكَفَىٰ بِٱللَّهِ
شَهِيدَۢا بَيۡنَنَا وَبَيۡنَكُمۡ إِن كُنَّا عَنۡ عِبَادَتِكُمۡ لَغَٰفِلِينَ ٢٩
هُنَالِكَ تَبۡلُواْ كُلُّ نَفۡسٖ مَّآ أَسۡلَفَتۡۚ وَرُدُّوٓاْ إِلَى ٱللَّهِ مَوۡلَىٰهُمُ
ٱلۡحَقِّۖ وَضَلَّ عَنۡهُم مَّا كَانُواْ يَفۡتَرُونَ ٣٠ قُلۡ مَن يَرۡزُقُكُم
مِّنَ ٱلسَّمَآءِ وَٱلۡأَرۡضِ أَمَّن يَمۡلِكُ ٱلسَّمۡعَ وَٱلۡأَبۡصَٰرَ وَمَن يُخۡرِجُ
ٱلۡحَيَّ مِنَ ٱلۡمَيِّتِ وَيُخۡرِجُ ٱلۡمَيِّتَ مِنَ ٱلۡحَيِّ وَمَن يُدَبِّرُ ٱلۡأَمۡرَۚ
فَسَيَقُولُونَ ٱللَّهُۚ فَقُلۡ أَفَلَا تَتَّقُونَ ٣١ فَذَٰلِكُمُ ٱللَّهُ رَبُّكُمُ ٱلۡحَقُّۖ
فَمَاذَا بَعۡدَ ٱلۡحَقِّ إِلَّا ٱلضَّلَٰلُۖ فَأَنَّىٰ تُصۡرَفُونَ ٣٢ كَذَٰلِكَ
حَقَّتۡ كَلِمَتُ رَبِّكَ عَلَى ٱلَّذِينَ فَسَقُوٓاْ أَنَّهُمۡ لَا يُؤۡمِنُونَ ٣٣
قُلۡ هَلۡ مِن شُرَكَآئِكُم مَّن يَبۡدَؤُاْ ٱلۡخَلۡقَ ثُمَّ يُعِيدُهُۥۚ قُلِ ٱللَّهُ يَبۡدَؤُاْ
ٱلۡخَلۡقَ ثُمَّ يُعِيدُهُۥۖ فَأَنَّىٰ تُؤۡفَكُونَ ٣٤ قُلۡ هَلۡ مِن شُرَكَآئِكُم مَّن يَهۡدِيٓ
إِلَى ٱلۡحَقِّۚ قُلِ ٱللَّهُ يَهۡدِي لِلۡحَقِّۗ أَفَمَن يَهۡدِيٓ إِلَى ٱلۡحَقِّ أَحَقُّ أَن
يُتَّبَعَ أَمَّن لَّا يَهِدِّيٓ إِلَّآ أَن يُهۡدَىٰۖ فَمَا لَكُمۡ كَيۡفَ تَحۡكُمُونَ ٣٥
وَمَا يَتَّبِعُ أَكۡثَرُهُمۡ إِلَّا ظَنًّاۚ إِنَّ ٱلظَّنَّ لَا يُغۡنِي مِنَ ٱلۡحَقِّ شَيۡـًٔاۚ إِنَّ ٱللَّهَ

27. ***But as for those who have earned bad actions, a bad action*** such as *shirk* ***will be repaid with one the like of it. Debasement will darken them. They will have no one to protect them from Allah. It is as if their faces were covered by dark patches*** (pieces) (read as *qiṭa'an* and *qiṭ'ān*) ***of the night. Those shall be the Companions of the Fire, remaining in it timelessly, for ever.***

28. ***On*** (remember) ***the Day We gather them*** (the whole of creation) ***all together, We will say then to those who associated others with Allah, 'To your place, you*** – the repetition of the pronoun "you" is to stress the pronoun built in to the *verb* – ***and your partner-gods*** (the idols)***!' Then We will sift them out*** – We will separate them from the believers, as in the *āyat*, *"'Keep yourselves apart today, you evildoers!"* (36:59) – ***and their partner-gods will say*** to those who worshipped them, ***'It was not us you worshipped.***

29. ***Allah is a sufficient witness between us and you. We were unaware of your worship.'***

30. ***Then and there*** (on that Day) ***every self will be tried*** (read as *tablū* and *tatlū*) ***for what it did before*** – the actions it did in this world. ***They will be returned to Allah, their Master, the Real and what*** (the partner-gods) ***they invented will abandon them.***

31. ***Say*** to them***: 'Who provides for you out of heaven*** – a reference to rain – ***and earth*** – a reference to plants***? Who controls hearing and sight?*** This means that He created them. ***Who brings forth the living from the dead and the dead from the living? Who directs the whole affair*** between creatures***?' They will say, 'Allah.' Say*** to them, ***'So will you not be godfearing*** and believe***?'***

32. ***That is Allah, your Lord, the*** firm ***Truth, and what is there after truth except misguidance?*** The expected answer is affirmative: there is nothing after it. Whoever fails to grasp the truth, which involves worshipping Allah, falls into misguidance. ***So how have you been distracted*** from believing, when the truth is clearly established***?***

33. ***In that way*** – in the way that those people are distracted from faith – ***the Word of your Lord is realised against those who are deviators*** (unbelievers) – a reference to Allah's words: *"I will fill Hellfire..."* (11:11) – ***in that they do not believe.***

عَلِيمُۢ بِمَا يَفْعَلُونَ ﴿٣٦﴾ وَمَا كَانَ هَٰذَا ٱلْقُرْءَانُ أَن يُفْتَرَىٰ مِن دُونِ
ٱللَّهِ وَلَٰكِن تَصْدِيقَ ٱلَّذِى بَيْنَ يَدَيْهِ وَتَفْصِيلَ ٱلْكِتَٰبِ لَا رَيْبَ
فِيهِ مِن رَّبِّ ٱلْعَٰلَمِينَ ﴿٣٧﴾ أَمْ يَقُولُونَ ٱفْتَرَىٰهُ ۖ قُلْ فَأْتُوا۟ بِسُورَةٍ
مِّثْلِهِۦ وَٱدْعُوا۟ مَنِ ٱسْتَطَعْتُم مِّن دُونِ ٱللَّهِ إِن كُنتُمْ صَٰدِقِينَ ﴿٣٨﴾
بَلْ كَذَّبُوا۟ بِمَا لَمْ يُحِيطُوا۟ بِعِلْمِهِۦ وَلَمَّا يَأْتِهِمْ تَأْوِيلُهُۥ ۚ كَذَٰلِكَ كَذَّبَ
ٱلَّذِينَ مِن قَبْلِهِمْ ۖ فَٱنظُرْ كَيْفَ كَانَ عَٰقِبَةُ ٱلظَّٰلِمِينَ ﴿٣٩﴾
وَمِنْهُم مَّن يُؤْمِنُ بِهِۦ وَمِنْهُم مَّن لَّا يُؤْمِنُ بِهِۦ ۚ وَرَبُّكَ أَعْلَمُ
بِٱلْمُفْسِدِينَ ﴿٤٠﴾ وَإِن كَذَّبُوكَ فَقُل لِّى عَمَلِى وَلَكُمْ عَمَلُكُمْ ۖ
أَنتُم بَرِيٓـُٔونَ مِمَّآ أَعْمَلُ وَأَنَا۠ بَرِىٓءٌ مِّمَّا تَعْمَلُونَ ﴿٤١﴾ وَمِنْهُم مَّن
يَسْتَمِعُونَ إِلَيْكَ ۚ أَفَأَنتَ تُسْمِعُ ٱلصُّمَّ وَلَوْ كَانُوا۟ لَا يَعْقِلُونَ ﴿٤٢﴾
وَمِنْهُم مَّن يَنظُرُ إِلَيْكَ ۚ أَفَأَنتَ تَهْدِى ٱلْعُمْىَ وَلَوْ كَانُوا۟
لَا يُبْصِرُونَ ﴿٤٣﴾ إِنَّ ٱللَّهَ لَا يَظْلِمُ ٱلنَّاسَ شَيْـًٔا وَلَٰكِنَّ
ٱلنَّاسَ أَنفُسَهُمْ يَظْلِمُونَ ﴿٤٤﴾ وَيَوْمَ يَحْشُرُهُمْ كَأَن لَّمْ يَلْبَثُوٓا۟ إِلَّا
سَاعَةً مِّنَ ٱلنَّهَارِ يَتَعَارَفُونَ بَيْنَهُمْ ۚ قَدْ خَسِرَ ٱلَّذِينَ كَذَّبُوا۟ بِلِقَآءِ ٱللَّهِ
وَمَا كَانُوا۟ مُهْتَدِينَ ﴿٤٥﴾ وَإِمَّا نُرِيَنَّكَ بَعْضَ ٱلَّذِى نَعِدُهُمْ أَوْ نَتَوَفَّيَنَّكَ
فَإِلَيْنَا مَرْجِعُهُمْ ثُمَّ ٱللَّهُ شَهِيدٌ عَلَىٰ مَا يَفْعَلُونَ ﴿٤٦﴾ وَلِكُلِّ
أُمَّةٍ رَّسُولٌ ۖ فَإِذَا جَآءَ رَسُولُهُمْ قُضِىَ بَيْنَهُم بِٱلْقِسْطِ وَهُمْ
لَا يُظْلَمُونَ ﴿٤٧﴾ وَيَقُولُونَ مَتَىٰ هَٰذَا ٱلْوَعْدُ إِن كُنتُمْ صَٰدِقِينَ
﴿٤٨﴾ قُل لَّآ أَمْلِكُ لِنَفْسِى ضَرًّا وَلَا نَفْعًا إِلَّا مَا شَآءَ ٱللَّهُ ۗ لِكُلِّ أُمَّةٍ
أَجَلٌ ۚ إِذَا جَآءَ أَجَلُهُمْ فَلَا يَسْتَـْٔخِرُونَ سَاعَةً ۖ وَلَا يَسْتَقْدِمُونَ ﴿٤٩﴾

34. ***Say: 'Can any of your partner-gods bring creation out of nothing and then regenerate it?' Say: 'Allah brings creation out of nothing and then regenerates it. So how have you been perverted?'*** How have you been perverted against worshipping Allah when the proof has been established?

35. ***Say: 'Can any of your partner-gods guide to the truth*** by establishing proofs and creating guidance***?' Say: 'Allah guides to the truth. Who has more right to be followed: He who guides to the truth*** – in other words Allah – ***or he who cannot guide unless he is guided?*** Whom is it better to follow? This question, which implies an affirmative response, is a rebuke, for it is clearly better to follow the former. ***What is the matter with you? How do you reach your judgement?'*** Your judgement to follow what should not be followed is clearly fallacious.

36. ***Most of them follow nothing but conjecture.*** By worshipping idols, they are only imitating their fathers. ***Conjecture is of no use whatsoever against the truth.*** Conjecture is not real knowledge. ***Allah most certainly knows what they are doing*** and will repay them for what they did.

37. ***This Qur'an could never have been devised by any besides Allah.*** It could not have been forged. ***Rather it is confirmation of what came before it*** (the Divinely Revealed Books) ***and an elucidation of the Book*** – making clear what Allah has prescribed in terms of rulings and other matters – ***which contains no doubt, from the Lord of all the worlds.***

38. ***Do they say, 'He*** (Muḥammad) ***has invented it'? Say: 'Then produce a* sūra *like it*** – one with the same eloquence and purity of Arabic which is forged since you are eloquent Arabs – ***and call*** for help ***on anyone you can besides Allah if you are telling the truth*** about him having forged it. You will not be able to do so.' Allah says:

39. ***No, the fact is that they have denied something*** (the Qur'an) which they do not reflect on and ***which their knowledge does not embrace and the meaning of which*** – the results of the threat in it – ***has not yet reached them. In the same way*** – referring to their denial – ***those before them also denied the truth*** – denied their

Messengers. ***See the final fate of the wrongdoers!*** Their fate was destruction and that is what will befall to these people as well.

40. ***Among them*** (the people of Makka) ***there are some who believe in it*** – and Allah knows this about them – ***and some who do not*** and never will. ***Your Lord best knows the corrupters.*** This is a threat.

41. ***If they deny you, say*** to them, ***'I have my actions and you have your actions.*** Each will have the repayment of their actions. ***You are not responsible for what I do and I am not responsible for what you do.'*** This *āyat* was abrogated by the *Āyat* of the Sword.

42. ***Among them there are some who listen to you*** when you recite the Qur'an; ***but can you make the deaf hear even though they cannot understand?*** They are likened to the deaf inasmuch as they do not benefit from what is recited to them, so it is as if they were deaf.

43. ***Among them there are some who look at you; but can you guide the blind, even though they cannot see?*** They are likened to the blind since they are not guided. In fact it is even worse for them because *"It is not the eyes that are blind but the hearts in the breasts that are blind."* (22:46)

44. ***Allah does not wrong people in any way; rather it is people who wrong themselves.***

45. ***On the day We gather them together – when it will seem as if they had tarried*** in this world or in their graves ***no more than an hour of a single day*** – owning to their terror at what they see – ***they will recognise one another.*** They recognise each other when they are resurrected and then they will cease to do so because of the intensity of the situation. ***Those who denied the meeting with Allah*** (the Resurrection) ***will have lost. They were not guided.***

46. ***Whether We show you something of what*** (the punishment) ***We have promised them*** during your lifetime ***or take you back to Us*** before punishing them, ***they will still return to Us. Then Allah*** sees and ***will be witness against what they are doing*** (their denial and disbelief) and will inflict the most terrible punishment on them.

47. ***Every nation has a Messenger, and when their Messenger comes*** to them and they deny him ***everything is decided between them justly.*** They will be punished, whereas the Messenger and

قُلْ أَرَءَيْتُمْ إِنْ أَتَىٰكُمْ عَذَابُهُۥ بَيَٰتًا أَوْ نَهَارًا مَّاذَا يَسْتَعْجِلُ مِنْهُ
ٱلْمُجْرِمُونَ ﴿٥٠﴾ أَثُمَّ إِذَا مَا وَقَعَ ءَامَنتُم بِهِۦٓ ءَآلْـَٰٔنَ وَقَدْ كُنتُم بِهِۦ
تَسْتَعْجِلُونَ ﴿٥١﴾ ثُمَّ قِيلَ لِلَّذِينَ ظَلَمُوا۟ ذُوقُوا۟ عَذَابَ ٱلْخُلْدِ
هَلْ تُجْزَوْنَ إِلَّا بِمَا كُنتُمْ تَكْسِبُونَ ﴿٥٢﴾ ۞ وَيَسْتَنۢبِـُٔونَكَ
أَحَقٌّ هُوَ ۖ قُلْ إِى وَرَبِّىٓ إِنَّهُۥ لَحَقٌّ ۖ وَمَآ أَنتُم بِمُعْجِزِينَ ﴿٥٣﴾
وَلَوْ أَنَّ لِكُلِّ نَفْسٍ ظَلَمَتْ مَا فِى ٱلْأَرْضِ لَٱفْتَدَتْ بِهِۦ ۗ وَأَسَرُّوا۟
ٱلنَّدَامَةَ لَمَّا رَأَوُا۟ ٱلْعَذَابَ ۖ وَقُضِىَ بَيْنَهُم بِٱلْقِسْطِ ۚ وَهُمْ
لَا يُظْلَمُونَ ﴿٥٤﴾ أَلَآ إِنَّ لِلَّهِ مَا فِى ٱلسَّمَٰوَٰتِ وَٱلْأَرْضِ ۗ أَلَآ إِنَّ
وَعْدَ ٱللَّهِ حَقٌّ وَلَٰكِنَّ أَكْثَرَهُمْ لَا يَعْلَمُونَ ﴿٥٥﴾ هُوَ يُحْىِۦ وَيُمِيتُ
وَإِلَيْهِ تُرْجَعُونَ ﴿٥٦﴾ يَٰٓأَيُّهَا ٱلنَّاسُ قَدْ جَآءَتْكُم مَّوْعِظَةٌ
مِّن رَّبِّكُمْ وَشِفَآءٌ لِّمَا فِى ٱلصُّدُورِ وَهُدًى وَرَحْمَةٌ لِّلْمُؤْمِنِينَ
﴿٥٧﴾ قُلْ بِفَضْلِ ٱللَّهِ وَبِرَحْمَتِهِۦ فَبِذَٰلِكَ فَلْيَفْرَحُوا۟ هُوَ خَيْرٌ مِّمَّا
يَجْمَعُونَ ﴿٥٨﴾ قُلْ أَرَءَيْتُم مَّآ أَنزَلَ ٱللَّهُ لَكُم مِّن رِّزْقٍ
فَجَعَلْتُم مِّنْهُ حَرَامًا وَحَلَٰلًا قُلْ ءَآللَّهُ أَذِنَ لَكُمْ ۖ أَمْ عَلَى ٱللَّهِ
تَفْتَرُونَ ﴿٥٩﴾ وَمَا ظَنُّ ٱلَّذِينَ يَفْتَرُونَ عَلَى ٱللَّهِ ٱلْكَذِبَ
يَوْمَ ٱلْقِيَٰمَةِ ۗ إِنَّ ٱللَّهَ لَذُو فَضْلٍ عَلَى ٱلنَّاسِ وَلَٰكِنَّ أَكْثَرَهُمْ
لَا يَشْكُرُونَ ﴿٦٠﴾ وَمَا تَكُونُ فِى شَأْنٍ وَمَا تَتْلُوا۟ مِنْهُ مِن قُرْءَانٍ
وَلَا تَعْمَلُونَ مِنْ عَمَلٍ إِلَّا كُنَّا عَلَيْكُمْ شُهُودًا إِذْ تُفِيضُونَ
فِيهِ ۚ وَمَا يَعْزُبُ عَن رَّبِّكَ مِن مِّثْقَالِ ذَرَّةٍ فِى ٱلْأَرْضِ وَلَا فِى
ٱلسَّمَآءِ وَلَآ أَصْغَرَ مِن ذَٰلِكَ وَلَآ أَكْبَرَ إِلَّا فِى كِتَٰبٍ مُّبِينٍ ﴿٦١﴾

those who believed him will be saved. ***They are not wronged*** by their punishment – punished for no crime. That is how Allah will treat them.

48. ***They say, 'When will this promise*** of punishment ***be kept if you are telling the truth*** about it?'

49. ***Say: 'I possess no power to harm*** – to inflict harm on – ***or help*** – bring benefit to – ***myself except as Allah wills*** – according to what He decrees. So how could I possibly control the descent of the punishment on you? ***Every nation has an appointed time*** – a known moment for its destruction. ***When their appointed time comes, they cannot delay it a single hour or bring it forward.'***

50. ***Say: 'What do you think?*** Tell me. ***If His*** (Allah's) ***punishment came upon you by night or day, what part of it*** (the punishment) ***would the evildoers*** (idolaters) ***then try to hasten?'*** What is intended by the question is to terrify them by stressing how terrible the fate is that they are trying to hasten!

51. ***And then, when it actually comes about*** and happens to you, it will be said: ***'Now do you believe in it?*** Will you believe in Allah or the punishment when it occurs? At that time your belief will not be accepted from you and this will be said to you. ***It was this that you were trying to hasten*** by your mockery!'

52. ***Then it will be said to those who did wrong, 'Taste the punishment of eternity*** in which you will remain for ever. ***Have you been repaid for anything other than what you earned?'***

53. ***They will ask you to tell them*** – asking you for information – ***if this is true*** – referring to what you have promised them by way of punishment and the Resurrection. ***Say: 'Yes indeed, by my Lord, it certainly is true and you can do nothing to prevent it*** and so escape the punishment.'

54. ***If every self that did wrong*** through disbelieving ***possessed everything on earth*** – all the wealth it contains – ***it would offer it as a ransom*** from the punishment on the Day of Rising. ***They will conceal*** their ***remorse*** for not believing ***when they see the punishment.*** Their leaders concealed it from the weak, whom they misled, for fear of being blamed by them. ***Everything will be decided between them*** (creatures) ***justly. They will not be wronged*** in any way.

55. ***Yes, everything in the heavens and earth belongs to Allah. Yes, Allah's promise*** of Resurrection and repayment ***is true*** and firm ***but most of them*** (most people) ***do not know it.***

56. ***He gives life and causes to die, and you will be returned to Him*** and He will repay you for your actions.

57. ***Mankind*** (people of Makka), ***admonition*** – a record which contains what you have and what you owe – ***has come to you from your Lord*** – referring to the Qur'an – ***and also healing for what is in the breasts*** – referring to false beliefs and doubts – ***and guidance*** from misguidance ***and mercy for the believers.***

58. ***Say: 'It is the favour of Allah*** (Islam) ***and His mercy*** (the Qur'an) ***that should be the cause of their rejoicing. That is better than anything they accumulate*** (read as *yajma'ūna* and *tajma'ūna* "you accumulate") of this world.*'*

59. ***Say:*** 'Tell me. ***What do you think about the things Allah has*** created and ***sent down to you as provision which you have then designated as lawful and unlawful*** – such as animals designated as *baḥira* and *sā'iba*[1] and carrion?' ***Say: 'Has Allah given you authority to do this*** – to declare things unlawful and lawful – ***or are you inventing lies against Allah*** – disbelieving by attributing that to Him?'

60. ***What will those who invent lies against Allah think*** after reckoning that they will not be punished ***on the Day of Rising?*** No! ***Allah shows favour to mankind*** by deferring their punishment and granting them blessings, ***but most of them are not thankful.***

61. ***You*** (Muḥammad) ***do not engage in any matter or recite any of the Qur'an*** which has been sent down to you ***or do*** – addressed now to him and his community – ***any action without Our witnessing you*** – there are watchers observing you – ***while you are occupied with it. Not even the smallest speck eludes your Lord, either on earth or in heaven. Nor is there anything smaller than that, or larger, which is not in a Clear Book*** which also makes things clear, meaning the Preserved Tablet.

62. ***Yes, the friends of Allah will feel no fear and will know no sorrow*** in the Next World:

1. See glossary.

أَلَآ إِنَّ أَوۡلِيَآءَ ٱللَّهِ لَا خَوۡفٌ عَلَيۡهِمۡ وَلَا هُمۡ يَحۡزَنُونَ
٦٢ ٱلَّذِينَ ءَامَنُواْ وَكَانُواْ يَتَّقُونَ ٦٣ لَهُمُ ٱلۡبُشۡرَىٰ
فِي ٱلۡحَيَوٰةِ ٱلدُّنۡيَا وَفِي ٱلۡأٓخِرَةِۚ لَا تَبۡدِيلَ لِكَلِمَٰتِ ٱللَّهِۚ
ذَٰلِكَ هُوَ ٱلۡفَوۡزُ ٱلۡعَظِيمُ ٦٤ وَلَا يَحۡزُنكَ قَوۡلُهُمۡۘ إِنَّ
ٱلۡعِزَّةَ لِلَّهِ جَمِيعًاۚ هُوَ ٱلسَّمِيعُ ٱلۡعَلِيمُ ٦٥ أَلَآ إِنَّ لِلَّهِ
مَن فِي ٱلسَّمَٰوَٰتِ وَمَن فِي ٱلۡأَرۡضِۗ وَمَا يَتَّبِعُ ٱلَّذِينَ
يَدۡعُونَ مِن دُونِ ٱللَّهِ شُرَكَآءَۚ إِن يَتَّبِعُونَ إِلَّا
ٱلظَّنَّ وَإِنۡ هُمۡ إِلَّا يَخۡرُصُونَ ٦٦ هُوَ ٱلَّذِي جَعَلَ لَكُمُ
ٱلَّيۡلَ لِتَسۡكُنُواْ فِيهِ وَٱلنَّهَارَ مُبۡصِرًاۚ إِنَّ فِي ذَٰلِكَ
لَأٓيَٰتٖ لِّقَوۡمٖ يَسۡمَعُونَ ٦٧ قَالُواْ ٱتَّخَذَ ٱللَّهُ وَلَدٗاۗ
سُبۡحَٰنَهُۥۖ هُوَ ٱلۡغَنِيُّۖ لَهُۥ مَا فِي ٱلسَّمَٰوَٰتِ وَمَا فِي ٱلۡأَرۡضِۚ
إِنۡ عِندَكُم مِّن سُلۡطَٰنِۭ بِهَٰذَآۚ أَتَقُولُونَ عَلَى ٱللَّهِ مَا
لَا تَعۡلَمُونَ ٦٨ قُلۡ إِنَّ ٱلَّذِينَ يَفۡتَرُونَ عَلَى ٱللَّهِ ٱلۡكَذِبَ
لَا يُفۡلِحُونَ ٦٩ مَتَٰعٞ فِي ٱلدُّنۡيَا ثُمَّ إِلَيۡنَا مَرۡجِعُهُمۡ ثُمَّ
نُذِيقُهُمُ ٱلۡعَذَابَ ٱلشَّدِيدَ بِمَا كَانُواْ يَكۡفُرُونَ ٧٠
۞ وَٱتۡلُ عَلَيۡهِمۡ نَبَأَ نُوحٍ إِذۡ قَالَ لِقَوۡمِهِۦ يَٰقَوۡمِ إِن كَانَ كَبُرَ عَلَيۡكُم
مَّقَامِي وَتَذۡكِيرِي بِـَٔايَٰتِ ٱللَّهِ فَعَلَى ٱللَّهِ تَوَكَّلۡتُ فَأَجۡمِعُوٓاْ
أَمۡرَكُمۡ وَشُرَكَآءَكُمۡ ثُمَّ لَا يَكُنۡ أَمۡرُكُمۡ عَلَيۡكُمۡ غُمَّةٗ ثُمَّ ٱقۡضُوٓاْ
إِلَيَّ وَلَا تُنظِرُونِ ٧١ فَإِن تَوَلَّيۡتُمۡ فَمَا سَأَلۡتُكُم مِّنۡ أَجۡرٍۖ إِنۡ
أَجۡرِيَ إِلَّا عَلَى ٱللَّهِۖ وَأُمِرۡتُ أَنۡ أَكُونَ مِنَ ٱلۡمُسۡلِمِينَ ٧٢

63. ***those who believe and are godfearing,*** obeying Allah's commands and prohibitions…

64. ***… there is good news for them in the life of this world*** – explained in a *ḥadīth,* which al-Ḥākim considers to be sound, as referring to true dreams which a person sees or is shown – ***and in Next World*** – referring to the Garden and the reward. ***There is no changing the words of Allah.*** Allah does not break His promises. ***That is the great victory!***

65. ***Do not be grieved by what they say***, saying things like "You are not a Messenger." ***All might belongs to Allah. He is the All-Hearing*** of words, ***the All-Knowing*** of actions, and He will repay you for them and help you.

66. ***Yes, indeed! Everyone in the heavens and everyone on the earth belongs to Allah*** as slaves, property and creatures of Allah. ***Those who call on*** and worship ***anything other than Allah*** – meaning idols – ***are not really following their partner-gods.*** They are not following partners in reality, because Allah is exalted above all of that. ***They are only following conjecture.*** It is only in their deluded opinion that these idols are gods which will intercede for them. ***They are only guessing*** and lying in that.

67. ***It is He who appointed the night for you, so that you could rest in it, and the day for seeing.*** "Seeing" is attributed to daytime since things become visible in it. ***There are certainly Signs in that*** – evidence of Allah's Unity – ***for people who listen*** – who hear, reflect and pay heed to them.

68. ***They*** – the Jews and Christians and those who claim that the angels are the daughters of Allah – ***say, 'Allah has a son.'*** Allah says to them: ***Glory be to Him!*** – to free Himself of having any child attributed to Him. ***He is the Rich Beyond Need*** of anyone. Only someone in need of a child seeks one. ***Everything in the heavens and everything on the earth belongs to Him*** – as His domain, creation and slaves. ***Have you authority*** or conclusive proof ***to say this*** which they say, ***or are you saying about Allah what you do not know?*** The question at the end is meant as a rebuke.

69. ***Say: 'People who invent lies against Allah*** by attributing a child to Him ***will not be successful.'***

فَكَذَّبُوهُ فَنَجَّيْنَٰهُ وَمَن مَّعَهُۥ فِى ٱلْفُلْكِ وَجَعَلْنَٰهُمْ خَلَٰٓئِفَ
وَأَغْرَقْنَا ٱلَّذِينَ كَذَّبُوا۟ بِـَٔايَٰتِنَا ۖ فَٱنظُرْ كَيْفَ كَانَ عَٰقِبَةُ ٱلْمُنذَرِينَ
﴿٧٣﴾ ثُمَّ بَعَثْنَا مِنۢ بَعْدِهِۦ رُسُلًا إِلَىٰ قَوْمِهِمْ فَجَآءُوهُم بِٱلْبَيِّنَٰتِ
فَمَا كَانُوا۟ لِيُؤْمِنُوا۟ بِمَا كَذَّبُوا۟ بِهِۦ مِن قَبْلُ ۚ كَذَٰلِكَ نَطْبَعُ عَلَىٰ قُلُوبِ
ٱلْمُعْتَدِينَ ﴿٧٤﴾ ثُمَّ بَعَثْنَا مِنۢ بَعْدِهِم مُّوسَىٰ وَهَٰرُونَ إِلَىٰ
فِرْعَوْنَ وَمَلَإِي۟هِۦ بِـَٔايَٰتِنَا فَٱسْتَكْبَرُوا۟ وَكَانُوا۟ قَوْمًا مُّجْرِمِينَ ﴿٧٥﴾
فَلَمَّا جَآءَهُمُ ٱلْحَقُّ مِنْ عِندِنَا قَالُوٓا۟ إِنَّ هَٰذَا لَسِحْرٌ مُّبِينٌ ﴿٧٦﴾
قَالَ مُوسَىٰٓ أَتَقُولُونَ لِلْحَقِّ لَمَّا جَآءَكُمْ ۖ أَسِحْرٌ هَٰذَا وَلَا يُفْلِحُ
ٱلسَّٰحِرُونَ ﴿٧٧﴾ قَالُوٓا۟ أَجِئْتَنَا لِتَلْفِتَنَا عَمَّا وَجَدْنَا عَلَيْهِ ءَابَآءَنَا
وَتَكُونَ لَكُمَا ٱلْكِبْرِيَآءُ فِى ٱلْأَرْضِ وَمَا نَحْنُ لَكُمَا بِمُؤْمِنِينَ ﴿٧٨﴾
وَقَالَ فِرْعَوْنُ ٱئْتُونِى بِكُلِّ سَٰحِرٍ عَلِيمٍ ﴿٧٩﴾ فَلَمَّا جَآءَ ٱلسَّحَرَةُ
قَالَ لَهُم مُّوسَىٰٓ أَلْقُوا۟ مَآ أَنتُم مُّلْقُونَ ﴿٨٠﴾ فَلَمَّآ أَلْقَوْا۟ قَالَ
مُوسَىٰ مَا جِئْتُم بِهِ ٱلسِّحْرُ ۖ إِنَّ ٱللَّهَ سَيُبْطِلُهُۥٓ ۖ إِنَّ ٱللَّهَ لَا يُصْلِحُ
عَمَلَ ٱلْمُفْسِدِينَ ﴿٨١﴾ وَيُحِقُّ ٱللَّهُ ٱلْحَقَّ بِكَلِمَٰتِهِۦ وَلَوْ كَرِهَ
ٱلْمُجْرِمُونَ ﴿٨٢﴾ فَمَآ ءَامَنَ لِمُوسَىٰٓ إِلَّا ذُرِّيَّةٌ مِّن قَوْمِهِۦ عَلَىٰ
خَوْفٍ مِّن فِرْعَوْنَ وَمَلَإِي۟هِمْ أَن يَفْتِنَهُمْ ۚ وَإِنَّ فِرْعَوْنَ لَعَالٍ
فِى ٱلْأَرْضِ وَإِنَّهُۥ لَمِنَ ٱلْمُسْرِفِينَ ﴿٨٣﴾ وَقَالَ مُوسَىٰ يَٰقَوْمِ إِن كُنتُمْ
ءَامَنتُم بِٱللَّهِ فَعَلَيْهِ تَوَكَّلُوٓا۟ إِن كُنتُم مُّسْلِمِينَ ﴿٨٤﴾ فَقَالُوا۟ عَلَى ٱللَّهِ
تَوَكَّلْنَا رَبَّنَا لَا تَجْعَلْنَا فِتْنَةً لِّلْقَوْمِ ٱلظَّٰلِمِينَ ﴿٨٥﴾ وَنَجِّنَا
بِرَحْمَتِكَ مِنَ ٱلْقَوْمِ ٱلْكَٰفِرِينَ ﴿٨٦﴾ وَأَوْحَيْنَآ إِلَىٰ مُوسَىٰ وَأَخِيهِ

70. ***There is the*** brief ***enjoyment of this world;*** which people can only enjoy during their lives in it. ***Then they will return to Us*** at death. ***Then We will make them taste the terrible punishment*** after death ***because they disbelieved.***

71. ***Recite,*** Muḥammad, ***to them*** (the unbelievers of Makka) ***the story of Nūḥ when he said to his people, 'My people, if my standing here*** – remaining among you – ***and*** admonishing you and ***reminding you of Allah's Signs has become too much*** and too difficult ***for you to bear, know that I have put my trust in Allah. So decide, you and your gods,*** and resolve ***on what you want to do*** to me ***and be open about it.*** Do not conceal what you want to do, but make it known. ***Do with me whatever you decide and do not keep me waiting.*** I do not care what you do.

72. ***If you turn your backs*** on my reminder, ***I have not asked you for any wage*** or reward for it. ***My wage*** and reward ***is the responsibility of Allah alone. I am commanded to be one of the Muslims.'***

73. ***But they denied him and so We rescued him, and all those with him, in the Ark and We made them*** – him and his companions – ***the successors*** – the khalifs in the earth – ***and We drowned*** in the Flood ***the people who denied Our Signs. See the final fate of those who were warned*** about their destruction! That is how We will treat those who deny the truth.

74. ***Then after him*** (Nūḥ) ***We sent Messengers to their people*** – such as Ibrāhīm, Hūd and Ṣāliḥ – ***and they brought them the Clear Signs*** (miracles) ***but they were never going to believe in something which they had previously denied*** when the Messengers were sent to them. ***That is how We seal up the hearts of those who overstep the limits*** and do not believe.

75. ***Then after them We sent Mūsā and Hārūn with Our*** nine ***Signs to Pharaoh and his ruling circle; but they were*** too ***arrogant*** to believe in them ***and were a people of evildoers.***

76. ***When the truth came to them from Us, they said, 'This is downright*** (clear) ***magic!'***

77. ***Mūsā said, 'Do you say to the truth when it comes to you, "This is magic"?*** Do you say this when those who bring the truth

أَن تَبَوَّءَا لِقَوْمِكُمَا بِمِصْرَ بُيُوتًا وَٱجْعَلُوا۟ بُيُوتَكُمْ قِبْلَةً
وَأَقِيمُوا۟ ٱلصَّلَوٰةَ ۗ وَبَشِّرِ ٱلْمُؤْمِنِينَ ﴿٨٧﴾ وَقَالَ مُوسَىٰ
رَبَّنَآ إِنَّكَ ءَاتَيْتَ فِرْعَوْنَ وَمَلَأَهُۥ زِينَةً وَأَمْوَٰلًا فِى ٱلْحَيَوٰةِ
ٱلدُّنْيَا رَبَّنَا لِيُضِلُّوا۟ عَن سَبِيلِكَ ۖ رَبَّنَا ٱطْمِسْ عَلَىٰٓ أَمْوَٰلِهِمْ
وَٱشْدُدْ عَلَىٰ قُلُوبِهِمْ فَلَا يُؤْمِنُوا۟ حَتَّىٰ يَرَوُا۟ ٱلْعَذَابَ ٱلْأَلِيمَ ﴿٨٨﴾
قَالَ قَدْ أُجِيبَت دَّعْوَتُكُمَا فَٱسْتَقِيمَا وَلَا تَتَّبِعَآنِّ سَبِيلَ
ٱلَّذِينَ لَا يَعْلَمُونَ ﴿٨٩﴾ ۞ وَجَٰوَزْنَا بِبَنِىٓ إِسْرَٰٓءِيلَ ٱلْبَحْرَ
فَأَتْبَعَهُمْ فِرْعَوْنُ وَجُنُودُهُۥ بَغْيًا وَعَدْوًا ۖ حَتَّىٰٓ إِذَآ أَدْرَكَهُ
ٱلْغَرَقُ قَالَ ءَامَنتُ أَنَّهُۥ لَآ إِلَٰهَ إِلَّا ٱلَّذِىٓ ءَامَنَتْ بِهِۦ بَنُوٓا۟ إِسْرَٰٓءِيلَ
وَأَنَا۠ مِنَ ٱلْمُسْلِمِينَ ﴿٩٠﴾ ءَآلْـَٔـٰنَ وَقَدْ عَصَيْتَ قَبْلُ وَكُنتَ
مِنَ ٱلْمُفْسِدِينَ ﴿٩١﴾ فَٱلْيَوْمَ نُنَجِّيكَ بِبَدَنِكَ لِتَكُونَ لِمَنْ
خَلْفَكَ ءَايَةً ۚ وَإِنَّ كَثِيرًا مِّنَ ٱلنَّاسِ عَنْ ءَايَٰتِنَا لَغَٰفِلُونَ ﴿٩٢﴾
وَلَقَدْ بَوَّأْنَا بَنِىٓ إِسْرَٰٓءِيلَ مُبَوَّأَ صِدْقٍ وَرَزَقْنَٰهُم مِّنَ ٱلطَّيِّبَٰتِ
فَمَا ٱخْتَلَفُوا۟ حَتَّىٰ جَآءَهُمُ ٱلْعِلْمُ ۚ إِنَّ رَبَّكَ يَقْضِى بَيْنَهُمْ يَوْمَ ٱلْقِيَٰمَةِ
فِيمَا كَانُوا۟ فِيهِ يَخْتَلِفُونَ ﴿٩٣﴾ فَإِن كُنتَ فِى شَكٍّ مِّمَّآ أَنزَلْنَآ إِلَيْكَ
فَسْـَٔلِ ٱلَّذِينَ يَقْرَءُونَ ٱلْكِتَٰبَ مِن قَبْلِكَ ۚ لَقَدْ جَآءَكَ
ٱلْحَقُّ مِن رَّبِّكَ فَلَا تَكُونَنَّ مِنَ ٱلْمُمْتَرِينَ ﴿٩٤﴾ وَلَا تَكُونَنَّ
مِنَ ٱلَّذِينَ كَذَّبُوا۟ بِـَٔايَٰتِ ٱللَّهِ فَتَكُونَ مِنَ ٱلْخَٰسِرِينَ
﴿٩٥﴾ إِنَّ ٱلَّذِينَ حَقَّتْ عَلَيْهِمْ كَلِمَتُ رَبِّكَ لَا يُؤْمِنُونَ
﴿٩٦﴾ وَلَوْ جَآءَتْهُمْ كُلُّ ءَايَةٍ حَتَّىٰ يَرَوُا۟ ٱلْعَذَابَ ٱلْأَلِيمَ ﴿٩٧﴾
فَلَوْلَا كَانَتْ قَرْيَةٌ ءَامَنَتْ فَنَفَعَهَآ إِيمَٰنُهَآ إِلَّا قَوْمَ يُونُسَ لَمَّآ

prosper and the magic of the magicians comes to nothing? ***Magicians are not successful.'*** Both questions demand a negative response.

78. ***They said, 'Have you come to us to turn us from what we found our fathers doing, and to gain greatness*** (dominion) ***in the land*** of Egypt? ***We do not believe you.'***

79. ***Pharaoh said, 'Bring me every knowledgeable magician:*** those with great skill in magic.'

80. ***When the magicians came, Mūsā said to them,*** after they had asked him, "Will you throw or shall we throw?" ***'Throw whatever you have to throw!'***

81. ***When they had thrown*** their staves and ropes, ***Mūsā said, 'What you have brought is magic. Allah will certainly prove it false*** and obliterate it: ***Allah does not uphold the actions of corrupters.'***

82. ***Allah confirms the Truth*** and makes it victorious ***by His words*** (His promises) ***even though the evildoers hate it.***

83. ***No one believed in Mūsā except for a few*** (a small group) ***of his*** (Pharaoh's) ***people out of fear that Pharaoh, and the elders, would persecute them*** and turn them from the *dīn* by torturing them. ***Pharaoh was high*** (arrogant) ***and mighty in the land*** of Egypt; ***He was one of the profligate*** – who exceeded the limits by laying claim to divinity.

84. ***Mūsā said, 'My people! if you believe in Allah, then put your trust in Him, if you are Muslims.'***

85. ***They said, 'We have put our trust in Allah. Our Lord, do not make us a target for this wrongdoing people:*** do not let them conquer us so that they suppose that they have the truth and are tempted through us to believe that…

86. ***…but rescue us, by Your mercy, from this unbelieving people!'***

87. ***We revealed to Mūsā and his brother: 'Settle your people in houses in Egypt and make your houses places of worship,*** places in which to pray so that you will be safe from fear. Pharaoh had forbidden them to pray, ***and establish the prayer*** and perform it ***and give good news to the believers*** of victory and the Garden.'

88. ***Mūsā said, 'Our Lord, You have given Pharaoh and his ruling circle finery and wealth in the life of this world, Our Lord, so that***

they may be misguided from Your Way (Your *dīn*) in the end. ***Our Lord, obliterate their wealth*** – transform it into worthless stones – ***and harden*** (seal up) ***their hearts so that they do not believe until they see the painful punishment.'*** This is a supplication against them. Hārūn said *"Āmīn"* to his supplication.

89. ***He*** (Allah) ***said, 'Your request is answered,"*** so their wealth turned to stones and Pharaoh did not believe until he was on the point of drowning – ***so go straight*** by following the Message and supplicating until the punishment comes to them – ***and do not follow the way of those who have no knowledge*** demonstrated by the fact that they try to hasten My decree.' It is related that Pharaoh remained for forty years after this.

90. ***We brought the tribe of Israel across the sea, and Pharaoh and his troops pursued them out of tyranny and enmity. Then, when he was on the point of drowning, he said, 'I believe that there is*** (read as *annahu* and *innahu*) ***no god but Him in whom the tribe of Israel believe. I am one of the Muslims.'*** He added his statement, "I am one of the Muslims", in the hope of ensuring that it would be accepted from him; but it was not accepted. Jibrīl put the mud of the sea in his mouth out of the fear that mercy would reach him. Then Allah continues:

91. ***'What, now*** believe*!* ***When previously you rebelled and were one of the corrupters:*** when you are misguided and have misguided others from believing*?*

92. ***Today We will preserve your body*** – We will bring your lifeless body out of the sea – ***so you can be a Sign*** (a lesson) ***for people who come after you*** in that they will recognise that you are merely a slave and will not dare to do the same as you did. Ibn 'Abbās said that some of the Banū Isrā'īl were unsure about his death, and so he was produced for them so that they could see him. ***Surely many people are heedless of Our Signs*** and do not learn from themī'

93. ***We settled the tribe of Israel in a noble place*** – a reference to Syria and Egypt – ***and gave them good things as provision. They did not differ*** – by some believing and some disbelieving – ***until knowledge came to them. Your Lord will decide between them on***

ءَامَنُوا۟ كَشَفْنَا عَنْهُمْ عَذَابَ ٱلْخِزْىِ فِى ٱلْحَيَوٰةِ ٱلدُّنْيَا وَمَتَّعْنَٰهُمْ
إِلَىٰ حِينٍ ﴿٩٨﴾ وَلَوْ شَآءَ رَبُّكَ لَءَامَنَ مَن فِى ٱلْأَرْضِ كُلُّهُمْ
جَمِيعًا ۚ أَفَأَنتَ تُكْرِهُ ٱلنَّاسَ حَتَّىٰ يَكُونُوا۟ مُؤْمِنِينَ ﴿٩٩﴾ وَمَا
كَانَ لِنَفْسٍ أَن تُؤْمِنَ إِلَّا بِإِذْنِ ٱللَّهِ ۚ وَيَجْعَلُ ٱلرِّجْسَ
عَلَى ٱلَّذِينَ لَا يَعْقِلُونَ ﴿١٠٠﴾ قُلِ ٱنظُرُوا۟ مَاذَا فِى ٱلسَّمَٰوَٰتِ
وَٱلْأَرْضِ ۚ وَمَا تُغْنِى ٱلْءَايَٰتُ وَٱلنُّذُرُ عَن قَوْمٍ لَّا يُؤْمِنُونَ ﴿١٠١﴾
فَهَلْ يَنتَظِرُونَ إِلَّا مِثْلَ أَيَّامِ ٱلَّذِينَ خَلَوْا۟ مِن قَبْلِهِمْ ۚ
قُلْ فَٱنتَظِرُوٓا۟ إِنِّى مَعَكُم مِّنَ ٱلْمُنتَظِرِينَ ﴿١٠٢﴾ ثُمَّ نُنَجِّى
رُسُلَنَا وَٱلَّذِينَ ءَامَنُوا۟ ۚ كَذَٰلِكَ حَقًّا عَلَيْنَا نُنجِ ٱلْمُؤْمِنِينَ
﴿١٠٣﴾ قُلْ يَٰٓأَيُّهَا ٱلنَّاسُ إِن كُنتُمْ فِى شَكٍّ مِّن دِينِى فَلَآ أَعْبُدُ ٱلَّذِينَ
تَعْبُدُونَ مِن دُونِ ٱللَّهِ وَلَٰكِنْ أَعْبُدُ ٱللَّهَ ٱلَّذِى يَتَوَفَّىٰكُمْ ۖ وَأُمِرْتُ
أَنْ أَكُونَ مِنَ ٱلْمُؤْمِنِينَ ﴿١٠٤﴾ وَأَنْ أَقِمْ وَجْهَكَ لِلدِّينِ حَنِيفًا
وَلَا تَكُونَنَّ مِنَ ٱلْمُشْرِكِينَ ﴿١٠٥﴾ وَلَا تَدْعُ مِن دُونِ ٱللَّهِ
مَا لَا يَنفَعُكَ وَلَا يَضُرُّكَ ۖ فَإِن فَعَلْتَ فَإِنَّكَ إِذًا مِّنَ ٱلظَّٰلِمِينَ ﴿١٠٦﴾
وَإِن يَمْسَسْكَ ٱللَّهُ بِضُرٍّ فَلَا كَاشِفَ لَهُۥٓ إِلَّا هُوَ ۖ وَإِن
يُرِدْكَ بِخَيْرٍ فَلَا رَآدَّ لِفَضْلِهِۦ ۚ يُصِيبُ بِهِۦ مَن يَشَآءُ مِنْ عِبَادِهِۦ ۚ
وَهُوَ ٱلْغَفُورُ ٱلرَّحِيمُ ﴿١٠٧﴾ قُلْ يَٰٓأَيُّهَا ٱلنَّاسُ قَدْ جَآءَكُمُ
ٱلْحَقُّ مِن رَّبِّكُمْ ۖ فَمَنِ ٱهْتَدَىٰ فَإِنَّمَا يَهْتَدِى لِنَفْسِهِۦ ۖ وَمَن
ضَلَّ فَإِنَّمَا يَضِلُّ عَلَيْهَا ۖ وَمَآ أَنَا۠ عَلَيْكُم بِوَكِيلٍ ﴿١٠٨﴾ وَٱتَّبِعْ
مَا يُوحَىٰٓ إِلَيْكَ وَٱصْبِرْ حَتَّىٰ يَحْكُمَ ٱللَّهُ ۚ وَهُوَ خَيْرُ ٱلْحَٰكِمِينَ ﴿١٠٩﴾

the Day of Rising regarding the things about which they differed in the *dīn*, by saving the believers and punishing the unbelievers.

94. ***If you***, Muḥammad, ***are in any doubt about what We have sent down to you*** – regarding some stories, for instance – ***then ask those who were reciting the Book*** (the Torah) ***before you*** – and they will tell you about its truthfulness. The Prophet, may Allah bless him and grant him peace, said, "I do not doubt and will not ask." ***The truth has come to you from your Lord, so on no account be one of the doubters*** who have doubts about it.

95. ***And on no account be among those who deny Allah's Signs and so become one of the lost.***

96. ***Those against whom the words of your Lord*** (His punishment) ***are justly carried out*** – and for whom they are mandatory – ***will never believe –***

97. ***...not even if every Sign were to come to them – until they see the painful punishment.*** Belief will not help them at that time.

98. ***How is it that there has never been a city*** – meaning its inhabitants – ***that believed*** before the punishment alighted on it, ***whose belief then brought it benefit*** when they saw the first signs of punishment and who did not put off believing until it was too late, ***except the people of Yūnus? When they had believed We removed from them the punishment of disgrace in the life of this world and We let them have enjoyment for a time*** until the end of their allotted term.

99. ***If your Lord had willed, all the people on the earth would have believed. Do you think you can force people to be believers*** if Allah has not willed that they shall be***?***

100. ***No self can believe except with Allah's permission*** (by His will). ***He places a blight*** (punishment) ***on those who do not use their intellect*** – who do not ponder the Signs of Allah.

101. ***Say*** to the unbelievers of Makka***: 'Look at what there is in the heavens and on the earth*** – the signs in the heaven and the earth which indicate the oneness of Allah Almighty.***' But Signs and warnings are of no avail to people who do not believe:*** without knowledge of Allah they will be of no benefit to them.

102. ***What are they waiting for*** in their denial ***but the same fate as those*** nations ***who passed away before them*** – meaning a punishment like theirs? ***Say: 'Wait*** for that, ***I will be among the people waiting with you.'***

103. ***Then We will rescue Our Messengers and those who believe as well*** from the punishment. ***It is incumbent upon Us to rescue the believers*** – meaning the Prophet, may Allah bless him and grant him peace, and his Companions – when We punish the idolaters.

104. ***Say: 'Mankind*** (people of Makka), ***if you are in any doubt about my* dīn** being true, ***I do not worship those you worship besides Allah*** (the idols) since you doubt in Him. ***Rather I worship Allah who will take you back to Him*** – in death, when He takes your souls – ***and I am commanded to be one of the believers:***

105. It was said to him: ***Turn your face towards the* dīn *in pure natural faith,*** – inclining spontaneously towards it – ***and on no account be among the idolaters.***

106. ***Do not call on*** and worship ***something besides Allah which can neither help*** – if you worship it – ***nor harm you*** – if you do not worship it. ***If you do*** – hypothetically – ***you will then be wrongdoers.'***

107. ***If Allah afflicts you with harm,*** such as poverty and illness, ***no one can remove it except Him. If He desires good for you, no one can avert*** or prevent ***His favour*** if He wants you to have it. ***He bestows it*** (good) ***on whichever of His slaves He wills. He is Ever-Forgiving, Most Merciful.***

108. ***Say: 'Mankind*** (people of Makka), ***the truth has come to you from your Lord. Whoever is guided is only guided for his own good*** – because he will have the reward of his guidance. ***Whoever is misguided is only misguided to his detriment*** because the evil effects of his misguidance will come back on him. ***I have not been set over you as a guardian*** – enabling me to compel you to guidance.'

109. ***Follow what has been revealed to you*** from your Lord ***and be steadfast*** in calling people to Allah and enduring harm from them ***until Allah's judgement*** about them ***comes. He is the Best of Judges.*** The Prophet was steadfast in the face of the idolaters by fighting, and with the People of the Book by taking *jizya* from them.

سُورَةُ هُودٍ

بِسۡمِ ٱللَّهِ ٱلرَّحۡمَٰنِ ٱلرَّحِيمِ

الٓرۚ كِتَٰبٌ أُحۡكِمَتۡ ءَايَٰتُهُۥ ثُمَّ فُصِّلَتۡ مِن لَّدُنۡ حَكِيمٍ خَبِيرٍ ١
أَلَّا تَعۡبُدُوٓاْ إِلَّا ٱللَّهَۚ إِنَّنِي لَكُم مِّنۡهُ نَذِيرٞ وَبَشِيرٞ ٢ وَأَنِ ٱسۡتَغۡفِرُواْ
رَبَّكُمۡ ثُمَّ تُوبُوٓاْ إِلَيۡهِ يُمَتِّعۡكُم مَّتَٰعًا حَسَنًا إِلَىٰٓ أَجَلٖ مُّسَمّٗى وَيُؤۡتِ
كُلَّ ذِي فَضۡلٖ فَضۡلَهُۥۖ وَإِن تَوَلَّوۡاْ فَإِنِّيٓ أَخَافُ عَلَيۡكُمۡ عَذَابَ يَوۡمٖ
كَبِيرٍ ٣ إِلَى ٱللَّهِ مَرۡجِعُكُمۡۖ وَهُوَ عَلَىٰ كُلِّ شَيۡءٖ قَدِيرٌ ٤ أَلَآ إِنَّهُمۡ
يَثۡنُونَ صُدُورَهُمۡ لِيَسۡتَخۡفُواْ مِنۡهُۚ أَلَا حِينَ يَسۡتَغۡشُونَ ثِيَابَهُمۡ
يَعۡلَمُ مَا يُسِرُّونَ وَمَا يُعۡلِنُونَۚ إِنَّهُۥ عَلِيمُۢ بِذَاتِ ٱلصُّدُورِ ٥
۞ وَمَا مِن دَآبَّةٖ فِي ٱلۡأَرۡضِ إِلَّا عَلَى ٱللَّهِ رِزۡقُهَا وَيَعۡلَمُ مُسۡتَقَرَّهَا
وَمُسۡتَوۡدَعَهَاۚ كُلّٞ فِي كِتَٰبٖ مُّبِينٖ ٦ وَهُوَ ٱلَّذِي خَلَقَ
ٱلسَّمَٰوَٰتِ وَٱلۡأَرۡضَ فِي سِتَّةِ أَيَّامٖ وَكَانَ عَرۡشُهُۥ
عَلَى ٱلۡمَآءِ لِيَبۡلُوَكُمۡ أَيُّكُمۡ أَحۡسَنُ عَمَلٗاۗ وَلَئِن قُلۡتَ
إِنَّكُم مَّبۡعُوثُونَ مِنۢ بَعۡدِ ٱلۡمَوۡتِ لَيَقُولَنَّ ٱلَّذِينَ كَفَرُوٓاْ
إِنۡ هَٰذَآ إِلَّا سِحۡرٞ مُّبِينٞ ٧ وَلَئِنۡ أَخَّرۡنَا عَنۡهُمُ ٱلۡعَذَابَ إِلَىٰٓ
أُمَّةٖ مَّعۡدُودَةٖ لَّيَقُولُنَّ مَا يَحۡبِسُهُۥٓۗ أَلَا يَوۡمَ يَأۡتِيهِمۡ لَيۡسَ
مَصۡرُوفًا عَنۡهُمۡ وَحَاقَ بِهِم مَّا كَانُواْ بِهِۦ يَسۡتَهۡزِءُونَ ٨

11. *Sūrat Hūd*
Hud

It is Makkan except for *āyat*s 12, 17, and 114, which are Madinan. It has 123 *āyat*s and was revealed after *Sūrat Yūnus*.

1. ***Alif Lam Ra.*** Allah knows best what is meant by the letters. ***A Book whose* āyats *are perfectly constructed*** with a wondrous order and amazing meanings ***and then demarcated*** – distinguishing rulings, stories and admonitions from Allah – ***coming directly from One who is All-Wise, All-Aware*** (Allah).

2. ***'Do not worship anyone but Allah! I am a warner*** – of the punishment if you disbelieve – ***and bringer of good news*** – of the reward if you believe – ***to you from Him.***

3. ***Ask your Lord for forgiveness*** for *shirk* ***and then repent to Him:*** turn to Him by obeying Him. ***He will let you enjoy a good life*** – give you a pleasant life and ample provision in this world – ***until a specified time*** (your death), ***and will give His favour to all who merit it*** by their actions in the Next World as repayment. ***But if you turn your backs, I fear for you the punishment of a Mighty Day*** (the Day of Rising).

4. ***You will return to Allah. He has power over all things***, including reward and punishment.'

5. This *āyat* was revealed, as al-Bukhārī related from Ibn 'Abbās, about people who were ashamed to go to the lavatory or to have sexual intercourse in the open air. It is also said that it is about the hypocrites. ***See how they wrap themselves round trying to conceal their feelings from Him*** (Allah)***! No, indeed! When they wrap their garments round themselves*** to cover themselves, ***He*** (Allah) ***knows what they keep secret and what they make public,*** so their concealment is of no effect. ***He knows what their hearts contain.***

6. ***There is no creature*** that crawls ***on the earth which is not dependent upon Allah for its provision*** – Allah is responsible for providing for it as a favour from Him. ***He knows where it lives*** – a reference to either this world or the loins – ***and where it dies*** – a reference to where it will be lodged after death or to the womb. ***They are all*** mentioned ***in a Clear Book*** (the Preserved Tablet).

وَلَئِنْ أَذَقْنَا ٱلْإِنسَٰنَ مِنَّا رَحْمَةً ثُمَّ نَزَعْنَٰهَا مِنْهُ إِنَّهُۥ
لَيَـُٔوسٌ كَفُورٌ ٩ وَلَئِنْ أَذَقْنَٰهُ نَعْمَآءَ بَعْدَ ضَرَّآءَ
مَسَّتْهُ لَيَقُولَنَّ ذَهَبَ ٱلسَّيِّـَٔاتُ عَنِّىٓ ۚ إِنَّهُۥ لَفَرِحٌ فَخُورٌ ١٠
إِلَّا ٱلَّذِينَ صَبَرُوا۟ وَعَمِلُوا۟ ٱلصَّٰلِحَٰتِ أُو۟لَٰٓئِكَ لَهُم مَّغْفِرَةٌ
وَأَجْرٌ كَبِيرٌ ١١ فَلَعَلَّكَ تَارِكٌۢ بَعْضَ مَا يُوحَىٰٓ إِلَيْكَ
وَضَآئِقٌۢ بِهِۦ صَدْرُكَ أَن يَقُولُوا۟ لَوْلَآ أُنزِلَ عَلَيْهِ كَنزٌ أَوْ جَآءَ
مَعَهُۥ مَلَكٌ ۚ إِنَّمَآ أَنتَ نَذِيرٌ ۚ وَٱللَّهُ عَلَىٰ كُلِّ شَىْءٍ وَكِيلٌ ١٢
أَمْ يَقُولُونَ ٱفْتَرَىٰهُ ۖ قُلْ فَأْتُوا۟ بِعَشْرِ سُوَرٍ مِّثْلِهِۦ مُفْتَرَيَٰتٍ
وَٱدْعُوا۟ مَنِ ٱسْتَطَعْتُم مِّن دُونِ ٱللَّهِ إِن كُنتُمْ صَٰدِقِينَ ١٣
فَإِلَّمْ يَسْتَجِيبُوا۟ لَكُمْ فَٱعْلَمُوٓا۟ أَنَّمَآ أُنزِلَ بِعِلْمِ ٱللَّهِ وَأَن لَّآ إِلَٰهَ
إِلَّا هُوَ ۖ فَهَلْ أَنتُم مُّسْلِمُونَ ١٤ مَن كَانَ يُرِيدُ ٱلْحَيَوٰةَ
ٱلدُّنْيَا وَزِينَتَهَا نُوَفِّ إِلَيْهِمْ أَعْمَٰلَهُمْ فِيهَا وَهُمْ فِيهَا لَا يُبْخَسُونَ
١٥ أُو۟لَٰٓئِكَ ٱلَّذِينَ لَيْسَ لَهُمْ فِى ٱلْءَاخِرَةِ إِلَّا ٱلنَّارُ ۖ وَحَبِطَ
مَا صَنَعُوا۟ فِيهَا وَبَٰطِلٌ مَّا كَانُوا۟ يَعْمَلُونَ ١٦ أَفَمَن كَانَ
عَلَىٰ بَيِّنَةٍ مِّن رَّبِّهِۦ وَيَتْلُوهُ شَاهِدٌ مِّنْهُ وَمِن قَبْلِهِۦ كِتَٰبُ
مُوسَىٰٓ إِمَامًا وَرَحْمَةً ۚ أُو۟لَٰٓئِكَ يُؤْمِنُونَ بِهِۦ ۚ وَمَن يَكْفُرْ بِهِۦ
مِنَ ٱلْأَحْزَابِ فَٱلنَّارُ مَوْعِدُهُۥ ۚ فَلَا تَكُ فِى مِرْيَةٍ مِّنْهُ ۚ إِنَّهُ ٱلْحَقُّ
مِن رَّبِّكَ وَلَٰكِنَّ أَكْثَرَ ٱلنَّاسِ لَا يُؤْمِنُونَ ١٧ وَمَنْ
أَظْلَمُ مِمَّنِ ٱفْتَرَىٰ عَلَى ٱللَّهِ كَذِبًا ۚ أُو۟لَٰٓئِكَ يُعْرَضُونَ
عَلَىٰ رَبِّهِمْ وَيَقُولُ ٱلْأَشْهَٰدُ هَٰٓؤُلَآءِ ٱلَّذِينَ كَذَبُوا۟ عَلَىٰ

7. ***It is He who created the heavens and the earth in six days*** – the first day was Sunday and the sixth Friday – ***when His Throne*** – before He created the heaven and the earth – ***was on the water*** – which was on the back of the wind – ***in order to test which of you has the best actions.*** In other words: Allah created the heavens and earth and everything they contain for the use and benefit of humanity in order to test them and see which of them are most obedient to Allah. ***If you***, Muḥammad, ***say, 'You will be raised up after death,' those who disbelieved will say, 'This*** Qur'an – which speaks of the Resurrection and what you say – ***is nothing but downright*** (clear) ***magic*** (read as *siḥr,* as here, and also *sāḥir* which means "magician", referring to the Prophet, may Allah bless him and grant him peace)***.'***

8. ***If We postpone the punishment for them for a limited time*** (*umma* here means "time"), ***they will say*** in mockery, ***'What is holding it back*** – stopping it from happening***?'*** Allah says: ***No, indeed! The day it reaches them it will not be averted from*** happening to ***them and the things they mocked at*** (the punishment) ***will encompass them.***

9. ***If We let*** an unbelieving ***man taste mercy*** (wealth and health) ***from Us, and then take it away from him, he is despairing*** of Allah's mercy, ***ungrateful*** – vehement in disbelieving in Allah…

10. ***…but if We let him taste blessings after hardship*** (poverty and difficulty) ***has afflicted him, he says, 'My troubles*** (afflictions) ***have gone away,'*** – when he did not expect them to depart and is not grateful for it – ***and he is overjoyed, boastful*** – he is arrogant and boasts to people about what he has been given –

11. ***… except for those who are steadfast*** in hardship ***and do right actions*** in times of blessing***. They will receive forgiveness and a great reward*** (the Garden)***.***

12. ***Perhaps you***, Muḥammad, ***are leaving aside part of what has been revealed to you*** – not conveying part of what has been revealed to you because they may despise it – ***and your breast is constricted by this*** when you recite it to them ***because they say, 'Why has treasure not been sent down to him or an angel not accompanied him*** to support him as we have demanded***?' You are only a warner:*** you only have to convey the Message to them, not to bring about what they have demanded – ***and Allah is Guardian over all things*** and He will repay them.

13. ***Or do they say, 'He has invented it*** (the Qur'an)***?' Say, 'Then produce ten invented*** **sūras** ***like this*** in eloquence and quality of Arabic, as you are Arabic speakers with eloquence like me. So Allah challenged them with this first and then with producing even one *sūra* – ***and call on anyone you can besides Allah*** for help in doing so, ***if you are telling the truth*** about it being forged.'

14. ***If they do not respond to you*** – to your invitation to them to help one another to come up with ten *sūra*s – ***then know***, idolaters, ***that it has been sent down with Allah's*** direct ***knowledge*** and is not a forgery ***and that there is no god but Him. So will you not become Muslims*** after this definitive proof?

15. ***As for those who desire the life of this world and its finery*** – a reference to those who persist in *shirk* and also said to be about those who show off – ***We will give them full payment in it*** (this world) ***for their actions.*** They will be repaid in this world for whatever good they did, such as their gifts of *ṣadaqa* and maintenance of ties of kinship, meaning that their provision will be expanded for them. ***They will not be deprived here of their due*** or short-changed for any good they have done.

16. ***But such people will have nothing in the Next World but the Fire. What they achieved here will come to nothing*** – will be nullified. ***What they did will prove to be null and void*** in the Next World and they will have no reward.

17. ***But as for those who have clear evidence from their Lord*** – a reference to the Prophet, may Allah bless him and grant him peace, or the believers, the evidence mentioned being the Qur'an – ***followed up by a witness*** to his truthfulness ***from Him*** (Allah), meaning Jibrīl – ***and before it*** (the Qur'an) ***the Book of Mūsā*** (the Torah) ***came*** which attests to him ***as a model and a mercy – such people*** – those who have clear evidence – ***believe in it*** (the Qur'an) and so they shall have the Garden. ***Any faction*** of the unbelievers ***which rejects it is promised the Fire. Be in no doubt about it*** (the Qur'an); ***it is the Truth from your Lord. But most people*** – including the people of Makka – ***do not believe.***

رَبِّهِمۡۚ أَلَا لَعۡنَةُ ٱللَّهِ عَلَى ٱلظَّٰلِمِينَ ١٨ ٱلَّذِينَ يَصُدُّونَ
عَن سَبِيلِ ٱللَّهِ وَيَبۡغُونَهَا عِوَجٗا وَهُم بِٱلۡأٓخِرَةِ هُمۡ كَٰفِرُونَ ١٩
أُوْلَٰٓئِكَ لَمۡ يَكُونُواْ مُعۡجِزِينَ فِي ٱلۡأَرۡضِ وَمَا كَانَ لَهُم مِّن
دُونِ ٱللَّهِ مِنۡ أَوۡلِيَآءَۘ يُضَٰعَفُ لَهُمُ ٱلۡعَذَابُۚ مَا كَانُواْ يَسۡتَطِيعُونَ
ٱلسَّمۡعَ وَمَا كَانُواْ يُبۡصِرُونَ ٢٠ أُوْلَٰٓئِكَ ٱلَّذِينَ خَسِرُوٓاْ
أَنفُسَهُمۡ وَضَلَّ عَنۡهُم مَّا كَانُواْ يَفۡتَرُونَ ٢١ لَا جَرَمَ أَنَّهُمۡ
فِي ٱلۡأٓخِرَةِ هُمُ ٱلۡأَخۡسَرُونَ ٢٢ إِنَّ ٱلَّذِينَ ءَامَنُواْ وَعَمِلُواْ
ٱلصَّٰلِحَٰتِ وَأَخۡبَتُوٓاْ إِلَىٰ رَبِّهِمۡ أُوْلَٰٓئِكَ أَصۡحَٰبُ ٱلۡجَنَّةِۖ
هُمۡ فِيهَا خَٰلِدُونَ ٢٣ ۞ مَثَلُ ٱلۡفَرِيقَيۡنِ كَٱلۡأَعۡمَىٰ
وَٱلۡأَصَمِّ وَٱلۡبَصِيرِ وَٱلسَّمِيعِۚ هَلۡ يَسۡتَوِيَانِ مَثَلًاۚ أَفَلَا تَذَكَّرُونَ
٢٤ وَلَقَدۡ أَرۡسَلۡنَا نُوحًا إِلَىٰ قَوۡمِهِۦٓ إِنِّي لَكُمۡ نَذِيرٞ مُّبِينٌ ٢٥
أَن لَّا تَعۡبُدُوٓاْ إِلَّا ٱللَّهَۖ إِنِّيٓ أَخَافُ عَلَيۡكُمۡ عَذَابَ يَوۡمٍ أَلِيمٖ
٢٦ فَقَالَ ٱلۡمَلَأُ ٱلَّذِينَ كَفَرُواْ مِن قَوۡمِهِۦ مَا نَرَىٰكَ إِلَّا بَشَرٗا
مِّثۡلَنَا وَمَا نَرَىٰكَ ٱتَّبَعَكَ إِلَّا ٱلَّذِينَ هُمۡ أَرَاذِلُنَا بَادِيَ
ٱلرَّأۡيِ وَمَا نَرَىٰ لَكُمۡ عَلَيۡنَا مِن فَضۡلِۭ بَلۡ نَظُنُّكُمۡ كَٰذِبِينَ
٢٧ قَالَ يَٰقَوۡمِ أَرَءَيۡتُمۡ إِن كُنتُ عَلَىٰ بَيِّنَةٖ مِّن رَّبِّي وَءَاتَىٰنِي رَحۡمَةٗ
مِّنۡ عِندِهِۦ فَعُمِّيَتۡ عَلَيۡكُمۡ أَنُلۡزِمُكُمُوهَا وَأَنتُمۡ لَهَا كَٰرِهُونَ ٢٨
وَيَٰقَوۡمِ لَآ أَسۡـَٔلُكُمۡ عَلَيۡهِ مَالًاۖ إِنۡ أَجۡرِيَ إِلَّا عَلَى ٱللَّهِۚ وَمَآ
أَنَا۠ بِطَارِدِ ٱلَّذِينَ ءَامَنُوٓاْۚ إِنَّهُم مُّلَٰقُواْ رَبِّهِمۡ وَلَٰكِنِّيٓ أَرَىٰكُمۡ
قَوۡمٗا تَجۡهَلُونَ ٢٩ وَيَٰقَوۡمِ مَن يَنصُرُنِي مِنَ ٱللَّهِ إِن طَرَدتُّهُمۡۚ

18. ***Who*** (no one) ***could do greater wrong than those who invent lies against Allah*** by ascribing a partner and child to him? ***Such people will be arrayed before their Lord*** on the Day of Rising with all creatures, ***and the witnesses*** – the angels who testify that the Messengers conveyed the Message and that the unbelievers denied it – ***will say, 'Those are the ones who lied against their Lord.' Yes indeed! Allah's curse is on the wrongdoers*** (idolaters),

19. ***...those who bar access to the Way of Allah*** (Islam), ***desiring to make it*** (the Way) ***crooked and reject the Next World.***

20. ***They were not able to thwart Allah on earth, and had no protectors*** to defend them against His punishment ***besides Allah. The punishment will be doubled for them*** because they misled others. ***They were unable to hear*** the truth ***and could not see*** it because of their excessive hatred, which made them like those physically unable to do that.

21. ***Those are the people who have lost their own selves*** because they go to the eternal Fire. ***What they invented*** against Allah – a reference to the partners they ascribed to Him – ***has abandoned them.***

22. ***Without question*** (truly) ***they will be the greatest losers in the Next World.***

23. ***As for those who believe and do right actions and humble themselves before their Lord, they are the Companions of the Garden, remaining in it timelessly, for ever.***

24. ***The likeness of the two groups*** (the unbelievers and the believers) ***is that of the blind and deaf*** – a simile for the unbelievers – ***and the seeing and hearing*** – a simile for the believers. ***Are they the same as one another? So will you not pay heed*** and be admonished?

25. ***We sent Nūḥ to his people: 'I am*** (read as *innī* and *annī*) ***a clear warner to you,*** someone who makes the warning clear to you.

26. ***Worship none but Allah.*** If you worship anything else, ***I fear for you the punishment of a painful Day*** in this world and the Next.'

27. ***The ruling circle*** (the nobles) ***of those of his people who disbelieved said, 'We do not see you as anything but a human being like ourselves.*** We do not see that you have any superiority over us. ***We do not see anyone following you but the lowest of us*** – such as

أَفَلَا تَذَكَّرُونَ ﴿٣٠﴾ وَلَآ أَقُولُ لَكُمْ عِندِى خَزَآئِنُ ٱللَّهِ وَلَآ
أَعْلَمُ ٱلْغَيْبَ وَلَآ أَقُولُ إِنِّى مَلَكٌ وَلَآ أَقُولُ لِلَّذِينَ تَزْدَرِىٓ
أَعْيُنُكُمْ لَن يُؤْتِيَهُمُ ٱللَّهُ خَيْرًا ۖ ٱللَّهُ أَعْلَمُ بِمَا فِىٓ أَنفُسِهِمْ ۖ إِنِّىٓ إِذًا
لَّمِنَ ٱلظَّٰلِمِينَ ﴿٣١﴾ قَالُوا۟ يَٰنُوحُ قَدْ جَٰدَلْتَنَا فَأَكْثَرْتَ
جِدَٰلَنَا فَأْتِنَا بِمَا تَعِدُنَآ إِن كُنتَ مِنَ ٱلصَّٰدِقِينَ ﴿٣٢﴾ قَالَ
إِنَّمَا يَأْتِيكُم بِهِ ٱللَّهُ إِن شَآءَ وَمَآ أَنتُم بِمُعْجِزِينَ ﴿٣٣﴾ وَلَا يَنفَعُكُمْ
نُصْحِىٓ إِنْ أَرَدتُّ أَنْ أَنصَحَ لَكُمْ إِن كَانَ ٱللَّهُ يُرِيدُ أَن يُغْوِيَكُمْ ۚ
هُوَ رَبُّكُمْ وَإِلَيْهِ تُرْجَعُونَ ﴿٣٤﴾ أَمْ يَقُولُونَ ٱفْتَرَىٰهُ ۖ
قُلْ إِنِ ٱفْتَرَيْتُهُۥ فَعَلَىَّ إِجْرَامِى وَأَنَا۠ بَرِىٓءٌ مِّمَّا تُجْرِمُونَ ﴿٣٥﴾
وَأُوحِىَ إِلَىٰ نُوحٍ أَنَّهُۥ لَن يُؤْمِنَ مِن قَوْمِكَ إِلَّا مَن قَدْ ءَامَنَ
فَلَا تَبْتَئِسْ بِمَا كَانُوا۟ يَفْعَلُونَ ﴿٣٦﴾ وَٱصْنَعِ ٱلْفُلْكَ بِأَعْيُنِنَا
وَوَحْيِنَا وَلَا تُخَٰطِبْنِى فِى ٱلَّذِينَ ظَلَمُوٓا۟ ۚ إِنَّهُم مُّغْرَقُونَ ﴿٣٧﴾
وَيَصْنَعُ ٱلْفُلْكَ وَكُلَّمَا مَرَّ عَلَيْهِ مَلَأٌ مِّن قَوْمِهِۦ سَخِرُوا۟
مِنْهُ ۚ قَالَ إِن تَسْخَرُوا۟ مِنَّا فَإِنَّا نَسْخَرُ مِنكُمْ كَمَا تَسْخَرُونَ ﴿٣٨﴾
فَسَوْفَ تَعْلَمُونَ مَن يَأْتِيهِ عَذَابٌ يُخْزِيهِ وَيَحِلُّ عَلَيْهِ عَذَابٌ
مُّقِيمٌ ﴿٣٩﴾ حَتَّىٰٓ إِذَا جَآءَ أَمْرُنَا وَفَارَ ٱلتَّنُّورُ قُلْنَا ٱحْمِلْ فِيهَا
مِن كُلٍّ زَوْجَيْنِ ٱثْنَيْنِ وَأَهْلَكَ إِلَّا مَن سَبَقَ عَلَيْهِ ٱلْقَوْلُ
وَمَنْ ءَامَنَ ۚ وَمَآ ءَامَنَ مَعَهُۥٓ إِلَّا قَلِيلٌ ﴿٤٠﴾ ۞ وَقَالَ ٱرْكَبُوا۟
فِيهَا بِسْمِ ٱللَّهِ مَجْر۪ىٰهَا وَمُرْسَىٰهَآ ۚ إِنَّ رَبِّى لَغَفُورٌ رَّحِيمٌ ﴿٤١﴾ وَهِىَ
تَجْرِى بِهِمْ فِى مَوْجٍ كَٱلْجِبَالِ وَنَادَىٰ نُوحٌ ٱبْنَهُۥ وَكَانَ

weavers and shoemakers – ***unthinkingly*** (read as *bādī'r-ra'y* and *badi'a'r-ra'y*, an expression implying acting without reflection, doing the first thing that comes to mind). ***We do not see you as superior to us.*** We do not think that you deserve to be followed by us. ***On the contrary, we consider you to be liars*** in claiming to have a Message.' They included his people with him when they addressed him, which is why the second person plural is used here.

28. ***He said, 'My people, what do you think?*** Tell me. ***If I were to have clear evidence from my Lord and He had given me a mercy*** (Prophethood) ***direct from Him, but it was hidden*** (read as *'ummiyat* and also *'amiyat,* in which case the meaning becomes "you were blind to it") ***from you, could we force it on you*** and compel you to accept it ***if you were unwilling*** to do so? We cannot do that.

29. ***My people, I do not ask you for any wealth for it*** – conveying the Message. ***My wage*** (reward) ***is the responsibility of Allah alone. I will not chase away those who believe*** as you command me. ***They are surely going to meet their Lord*** at the Resurrection – and He will repay them and take what is owed to them from those who wronged them and drove them away. ***But I see you as ignorant people***, ignorant of what your final outcome will be.

30. ***My people, who would help me*** and defend me ***against*** the punishment of ***Allah if I did drive them away?*** I would have no helper. ***So will you not pay heed*** and be admonished?

31. ***I do not say to you that I possess the treasuries of Allah; nor do I know the Unseen; nor do I say that I am an angel;*** I am merely a mortal like you; ***nor do I say to those who are vile in your eyes*** and whom you disdain ***that Allah will not give them any good. Allah knows best what is in their hearts. If I did*** say that, ***I would certainly be one of the wrongdoers.'***

32. ***They said, 'Nūḥ, you have argued with us*** and disputed with us ***and argued much; so bring us what you have promised us*** (the punishment) ***if you are telling the truth*** about it.'

33. ***He said, 'Allah will bring it to you if He wills*** to hasten it for you – and that is up to Him, not up to me – ***and you will not be able to prevent it*** and escape Allah.

34. ***My counsel will not benefit you, for all my desire to counsel you, if Allah desires to lead you into error. He is your Lord and you will return to Him.'***

35. Then Allah makes the following interpolation: ***Or do they*** (the unbelievers of Makka) ***say, 'He*** (Muḥammad) ***has invented it*** (the Qur'an)***'? Say: 'If I have invented it, the crime*** (the sin and its penalty) ***will be laid at my door; but I am innocent of the crimes which you commit*** in ascribing forgery to me.'

36. ***It was revealed to Nūḥ: 'None of your people are going to believe except for those who already believe, so do not be distressed*** and sad ***at what*** (the *shirk*) ***they do.*** So Nūḥ prayed against them, saying, *"My Lord, do not leave any of them on the earth..."* (71:28) and Allah answered his supplication and then said the following:

37. ***Build the Ark under Our supervision*** – We will oversee and protect it – ***and as We reveal*** and command. ***But do not address Me concerning the wrongdoers*** who disbelieve. Do not ask Me not to destroy them. ***They shall be drowned.'***

38. The present tense is used in this narrative even though it is a story about the past. ***He began to build the Ark and every time some nobles of his people passed him by, they ridiculed*** and mocked ***him. He said, 'Though you ridicule us now, we will certainly ridicule you as you do us.*** We will be saved and you will be drowned.

39. ***You will soon know who will receive a punishment which disgraces him and find unleashed against himself an everlasting punishment*** which will befall him.'

40. ***So when*** he finished constructing it ***Our command*** to destroy them ***came and water bubbled up from the earth*** (lit. oven) and that was a sign for Nūḥ. ***We said, 'Load into it*** (the Ark) ***a pair of every species*** – a male and female of every species. In one version of the story Allah gathered before Nūḥ the beasts and birds and other creatures. He began to place his hands on every species, his right hand on the male and his left on the female, and directed them into the Ark – ***and your family*** – his wife and children – ***except for those against whom the Word was preordained*** – that they would be destroyed. They were his son Kin'ān and his wife, but not Sām, Hām and Yāfith

فِي مَعۡزِلٖ يَٰبُنَيَّ ٱرۡكَب مَّعَنَا وَلَا تَكُن مَّعَ ٱلۡكَٰفِرِينَ ٤٢
قَالَ سَـَٔاوِيٓ إِلَىٰ جَبَلٖ يَعۡصِمُنِي مِنَ ٱلۡمَآءِۚ قَالَ لَا عَاصِمَ
ٱلۡيَوۡمَ مِنۡ أَمۡرِ ٱللَّهِ إِلَّا مَن رَّحِمَۚ وَحَالَ بَيۡنَهُمَا ٱلۡمَوۡجُ فَكَانَ
مِنَ ٱلۡمُغۡرَقِينَ ٤٣ وَقِيلَ يَٰٓأَرۡضُ ٱبۡلَعِي مَآءَكِ وَيَٰسَمَآءُ
أَقۡلِعِي وَغِيضَ ٱلۡمَآءُ وَقُضِيَ ٱلۡأَمۡرُ وَٱسۡتَوَتۡ عَلَى ٱلۡجُودِيِّۖ وَقِيلَ
بُعۡدٗا لِّلۡقَوۡمِ ٱلظَّٰلِمِينَ ٤٤ وَنَادَىٰ نُوحٞ رَّبَّهُۥ فَقَالَ رَبِّ إِنَّ
ٱبۡنِي مِنۡ أَهۡلِي وَإِنَّ وَعۡدَكَ ٱلۡحَقُّ وَأَنتَ أَحۡكَمُ ٱلۡحَٰكِمِينَ ٤٥
قَالَ يَٰنُوحُ إِنَّهُۥ لَيۡسَ مِنۡ أَهۡلِكَۖ إِنَّهُۥ عَمَلٌ غَيۡرُ صَٰلِحٖۖ فَلَا تَسۡـَٔلۡنِ
مَا لَيۡسَ لَكَ بِهِۦ عِلۡمٌۖ إِنِّيٓ أَعِظُكَ أَن تَكُونَ مِنَ ٱلۡجَٰهِلِينَ ٤٦
قَالَ رَبِّ إِنِّيٓ أَعُوذُ بِكَ أَنۡ أَسۡـَٔلَكَ مَا لَيۡسَ لِي بِهِۦ عِلۡمٞۖ وَإِلَّا
تَغۡفِرۡ لِي وَتَرۡحَمۡنِيٓ أَكُن مِّنَ ٱلۡخَٰسِرِينَ ٤٧ قِيلَ يَٰنُوحُ
ٱهۡبِطۡ بِسَلَٰمٖ مِّنَّا وَبَرَكَٰتٍ عَلَيۡكَ وَعَلَىٰٓ أُمَمٖ مِّمَّن مَّعَكَۚ
وَأُمَمٞ سَنُمَتِّعُهُمۡ ثُمَّ يَمَسُّهُم مِّنَّا عَذَابٌ أَلِيمٞ ٤٨ تِلۡكَ
مِنۡ أَنۢبَآءِ ٱلۡغَيۡبِ نُوحِيهَآ إِلَيۡكَۖ مَا كُنتَ تَعۡلَمُهَآ أَنتَ وَلَا قَوۡمُكَ
مِن قَبۡلِ هَٰذَاۖ فَٱصۡبِرۡۖ إِنَّ ٱلۡعَٰقِبَةَ لِلۡمُتَّقِينَ ٤٩ وَإِلَىٰ عَادٍ
أَخَاهُمۡ هُودٗاۚ قَالَ يَٰقَوۡمِ ٱعۡبُدُواْ ٱللَّهَ مَا لَكُم مِّنۡ إِلَٰهٍ
غَيۡرُهُۥٓۖ إِنۡ أَنتُمۡ إِلَّا مُفۡتَرُونَ ٥٠ يَٰقَوۡمِ لَآ أَسۡـَٔلُكُمۡ عَلَيۡهِ
أَجۡرًاۖ إِنۡ أَجۡرِيَ إِلَّا عَلَى ٱلَّذِي فَطَرَنِيٓۚ أَفَلَا تَعۡقِلُونَ ٥١
وَيَٰقَوۡمِ ٱسۡتَغۡفِرُواْ رَبَّكُمۡ ثُمَّ تُوبُوٓاْ إِلَيۡهِ يُرۡسِلِ ٱلسَّمَآءَ
عَلَيۡكُم مِّدۡرَارٗا وَيَزِدۡكُمۡ قُوَّةً إِلَىٰ قُوَّتِكُمۡ وَلَا تَتَوَلَّوۡاْ

whom he embarked with their three wives – ***and all who believe.' But those who believed with him were only few.*** It is said that there were six men and their wives, and it is also said that the total number of people in the Ark was about eighty, half of whom were men and half women.

41. ***He*** (Nūḥ) ***said, 'Embark in it. In the name of Allah be its voyage*** (read as *majrāhā* and *mujrāha*) ***and its landing*** (read as *marsāhā* and *mursāhā*) – meaning the journey and its ending***! Truly my Lord is Ever-Forgiving, Most Merciful*** since He did not destroy us.*'*

42. ***It sailed with them through mountainous waves*** – they were like mountains in their height and magnitude – ***and Nūḥ called out to his son*** Kin'ān ***who had kept himself apart*** from the Ark, ***'My son! Come on board with us. Do not stay with the unbelievers!'***

43. ***He said, 'I will take refuge on a mountain; it will protect me*** and defend me ***from the flood.' Nūḥ said, 'There is no protection from Allah's command*** and punishment ***today except for those He*** (Allah) ***has mercy on.'*** They are the ones who are protected. Allah said: ***The waves surged in between them and he*** (Kin'an) ***was among the drowned.***

44. ***It was said, 'Earth, swallow up your water*** which issued from you!' – and the earth drank it all up except what descended from the sky which became rivers and oceans – ***and, 'Heaven, hold back your rain!*** Stop raining,' and it stopped. ***And the water subsided and the affair*** of the destruction of the people of Nūḥ ***was concluded and the Ark came to land on al-Jūdī***, a mountain in Mesopotamia near to Mosul. ***And it was said, 'Away with*** (destruction to) ***the people of the wrongdoers*** (the unbelievers)***!'***

45. ***Nūḥ called out to his Lord and said, 'My Lord, my son*** Kin'an ***is one of my family,*** and You promised to save them ***and Your promise is surely the truth*** and will not be broken ***and You are the Justest*** (most knowledgeable and fair) ***of Judges.'***

46. ***He*** (Allah) ***said, 'Nūḥ, he is definitely not of your family*** – those of them who were destined to be saved – or one of the people of your *dīn*. ***He is someone whose action*** (read as *'amalun ghayru* and *'amala ghayra*) ***was not righteous.*** Your asking for him to be saved was not correct because he was an unbeliever and the unbelievers will not be saved. ***Do not, therefore, ask Me*** (read as *tas'alni* and *tas'alanna*) ***for something about which you have no knowledge*** – meaning the deliverance of his son. ***I admonish you lest you should be among the ignorant*** by asking for something you have no knowledge of.'

47. ***He said, 'My Lord, I seek refuge with You from asking You for anything about which I have no knowledge. If You do not forgive me*** for my neglect ***and have mercy on me, I will be among the lost.'***

48. ***It was said, 'Nūḥ, descend*** from the Ark ***with peace*** – or with the greeting – ***from Us and with blessings*** (good things) ***on you and on the nations which will issue from those who are with you*** in the Ark: in other words, from his children and descendants who were believers. ***But there are nations*** which come from among those who were with you ***to whom We will give enjoyment*** in this world ***and then a painful punishment from Us will afflict them*** in the Next World.' They are the unbelievers.

49. ***That*** (the story of Nūḥ) ***is some of the news of the Unseen*** which was concealed from you ***which We reveal to you***, Muḥammad. ***Neither you nor your people knew it*** (the Qur'an) ***before this time. So be steadfast*** in conveying the Message and in the face of injury as Nūḥ was. ***The best*** (most praiseworthy) ***end result is for those who are godfearing.***

50. ***And to 'Ād*** We sent ***their brother Hūd*** from their tribe. ***He said, 'My people, worship Allah*** and affirm His oneness. ***You have no god apart from Him. You are merely fabricators***, in that you worship idols and deny Allah.

51. ***My people, I do not ask you for any wage for it*** (conveying the Message). ***My wage is the responsibility of Him who brought me into being*** (created me); ***so will you not use your intellect?***

52. ***My people, ask forgiveness of your Lord*** for committing *shirk* ***and then repent to Him*** – turn to Him by obeying Him. ***He will send heaven down to you in abundant rain*** – and it was at a time of drought when rain was scarce – ***and increase you with strength*** (wealth) ***upon strength*** (children). ***Do not turn away as evildoers*** (idolaters).'

مُجۡرِمِينَ ٥٢ قَالُواْ يَٰهُودُ مَا جِئۡتَنَا بِبَيِّنَةٖ وَمَا نَحۡنُ
بِتَارِكِيٓ ءَالِهَتِنَا عَن قَوۡلِكَ وَمَا نَحۡنُ لَكَ بِمُؤۡمِنِينَ ٥٣
إِن نَّقُولُ إِلَّا ٱعۡتَرَىٰكَ بَعۡضُ ءَالِهَتِنَا بِسُوٓءٖۗ قَالَ إِنِّيٓ أُشۡهِدُ ٱللَّهَ
وَٱشۡهَدُوٓاْ أَنِّي بَرِيٓءٞ مِّمَّا تُشۡرِكُونَ ٥٤ مِن دُونِهِۦۖ فَكِيدُونِي
جَمِيعٗا ثُمَّ لَا تُنظِرُونِ ٥٥ إِنِّي تَوَكَّلۡتُ عَلَى ٱللَّهِ رَبِّي وَرَبِّكُمۚ مَّا
مِن دَآبَّةٍ إِلَّا هُوَ ءَاخِذُۢ بِنَاصِيَتِهَآۚ إِنَّ رَبِّي عَلَىٰ صِرَٰطٖ مُّسۡتَقِيمٖ
٥٦ فَإِن تَوَلَّوۡاْ فَقَدۡ أَبۡلَغۡتُكُم مَّآ أُرۡسِلۡتُ بِهِۦٓ إِلَيۡكُمۡۚ وَيَسۡتَخۡلِفُ
رَبِّي قَوۡمًا غَيۡرَكُمۡ وَلَا تَضُرُّونَهُۥ شَيۡـًٔاۚ إِنَّ رَبِّي عَلَىٰ كُلِّ شَيۡءٍ حَفِيظٞ
٥٧ وَلَمَّا جَآءَ أَمۡرُنَا نَجَّيۡنَا هُودٗا وَٱلَّذِينَ ءَامَنُواْ مَعَهُۥ بِرَحۡمَةٖ
مِّنَّا وَنَجَّيۡنَٰهُم مِّنۡ عَذَابٍ غَلِيظٖ ٥٨ وَتِلۡكَ عَادٞۖ جَحَدُواْ بِـَٔايَٰتِ
رَبِّهِمۡ وَعَصَوۡاْ رُسُلَهُۥ وَٱتَّبَعُوٓاْ أَمۡرَ كُلِّ جَبَّارٍ عَنِيدٖ ٥٩ وَأُتۡبِعُواْ
فِي هَٰذِهِ ٱلدُّنۡيَا لَعۡنَةٗ وَيَوۡمَ ٱلۡقِيَٰمَةِۗ أَلَآ إِنَّ عَادٗا كَفَرُواْ رَبَّهُمۡۗ أَلَا
بُعۡدٗا لِّعَادٖ قَوۡمِ هُودٖ ٦٠ ۞ وَإِلَىٰ ثَمُودَ أَخَاهُمۡ صَٰلِحٗاۚ قَالَ
يَٰقَوۡمِ ٱعۡبُدُواْ ٱللَّهَ مَا لَكُم مِّنۡ إِلَٰهٍ غَيۡرُهُۥۖ هُوَ أَنشَأَكُم مِّنَ ٱلۡأَرۡضِ
وَٱسۡتَعۡمَرَكُمۡ فِيهَا فَٱسۡتَغۡفِرُوهُ ثُمَّ تُوبُوٓاْ إِلَيۡهِۚ إِنَّ رَبِّي قَرِيبٞ مُّجِيبٞ
٦١ قَالُواْ يَٰصَٰلِحُ قَدۡ كُنتَ فِينَا مَرۡجُوّٗا قَبۡلَ هَٰذَآۖ أَتَنۡهَىٰنَآ أَن
نَّعۡبُدَ مَا يَعۡبُدُ ءَابَآؤُنَا وَإِنَّنَا لَفِي شَكّٖ مِّمَّا تَدۡعُونَآ إِلَيۡهِ مُرِيبٖ ٦٢
قَالَ يَٰقَوۡمِ أَرَءَيۡتُمۡ إِن كُنتُ عَلَىٰ بَيِّنَةٖ مِّن رَّبِّي وَءَاتَىٰنِي
مِنۡهُ رَحۡمَةٗ فَمَن يَنصُرُنِي مِنَ ٱللَّهِ إِنۡ عَصَيۡتُهُۥۖ فَمَا تَزِيدُونَنِي
غَيۡرَ تَخۡسِيرٖ ٦٣ وَيَٰقَوۡمِ هَٰذِهِۦ نَاقَةُ ٱللَّهِ لَكُمۡ ءَايَةٗ

53. ***They said, 'Hūd, you have not brought us any clear sign*** – proof of what you say. ***We will not forsake our gods for what you say. We do not believe you.***

54. ***We only say*** about you ***that one of our gods has driven you mad.'*** They said that one of their gods had made him mad and befuddled him because he had spoken badly of the idols. ***He said, 'I call on Allah to be my witness, and you also bear witness, that I am free of all the gods you have apart from Him.***

55. ***So scheme against me*** – plot my destruction – ***all of you together***, you and your idols, ***and then grant me no respite*** or reprieve.

56. ***I have put my trust in Allah, my Lord and your Lord. There is no creature*** – no living creature that crawls on the earth – ***He does not hold by the forelock*** – an expression meaning to have control over something and control it. There is no benefit or harm except by Allah's permission. The forelock is mentioned because if someone has his forelock seized, it means he is in a state of extreme humiliation. ***My Lord is on a Straight Path***: the Path of Truth and Justice.

57. ***If you turn your backs, I have transmitted to you what I was sent to you with, and my Lord will replace you with another people, and you will not harm Him at all*** by your *shirk*. ***My Lord is the*** Guardian and ***Preserver of everything.'***

58. ***When Our command*** (punishment) ***came, We rescued Hūd and those who had believed along with him by a mercy*** (guidance) ***from Us. We rescued them from a harsh punishment.***

59. ***That was 'Ād*** – a reference to their artefacts and remains. In other words, "Travel in the land and look at them." Then Allah describes their states and what they did. ***They denied the Signs of their Lord and disobeyed*** all ***His Messengers*** – in the plural because whoever disobeys one Messenger disobeys all the Messengers, since they share in the fundamental principle of what they brought, which is affirmation of Allah's unity – ***and*** (the lowly people) ***followed the command of every obdurate tyrant*** – their leaders who were obdurate against the Truth.

60. ***They were pursued by a curse*** from people ***in this world and on the Day of Rising*** they will be cursed in front of all creatures. ***Yes***

فَذَرُوهَا تَأْكُلْ فِىٓ أَرْضِ ٱللَّهِ وَلَا تَمَسُّوهَا بِسُوٓءٍ فَيَأْخُذَكُمْ
عَذَابٌ قَرِيبٌ ﴿٦٤﴾ فَعَقَرُوهَا فَقَالَ تَمَتَّعُوا۟ فِى دَارِكُمْ
ثَلَٰثَةَ أَيَّامٍ ذَٰلِكَ وَعْدٌ غَيْرُ مَكْذُوبٍ ﴿٦٥﴾ فَلَمَّا جَآءَ
أَمْرُنَا نَجَّيْنَا صَٰلِحًا وَٱلَّذِينَ ءَامَنُوا۟ مَعَهُۥ بِرَحْمَةٍ مِّنَّا
وَمِنْ خِزْىِ يَوْمِئِذٍ إِنَّ رَبَّكَ هُوَ ٱلْقَوِىُّ ٱلْعَزِيزُ ﴿٦٦﴾ وَأَخَذَ
ٱلَّذِينَ ظَلَمُوا۟ ٱلصَّيْحَةُ فَأَصْبَحُوا۟ فِى دِيَٰرِهِمْ جَٰثِمِينَ
﴿٦٧﴾ كَأَن لَّمْ يَغْنَوْا۟ فِيهَآ أَلَآ إِنَّ ثَمُودَا۟ كَفَرُوا۟ رَبَّهُمْ أَلَا بُعْدًا
لِّثَمُودَ ﴿٦٨﴾ وَلَقَدْ جَآءَتْ رُسُلُنَآ إِبْرَٰهِيمَ بِٱلْبُشْرَىٰ قَالُوا۟
سَلَٰمًا قَالَ سَلَٰمٌ فَمَا لَبِثَ أَن جَآءَ بِعِجْلٍ حَنِيذٍ ﴿٦٩﴾ فَلَمَّا
رَءَآ أَيْدِيَهُمْ لَا تَصِلُ إِلَيْهِ نَكِرَهُمْ وَأَوْجَسَ مِنْهُمْ خِيفَةً
قَالُوا۟ لَا تَخَفْ إِنَّآ أُرْسِلْنَآ إِلَىٰ قَوْمِ لُوطٍ ﴿٧٠﴾ وَٱمْرَأَتُهُۥ قَآئِمَةٌ
فَضَحِكَتْ فَبَشَّرْنَٰهَا بِإِسْحَٰقَ وَمِن وَرَآءِ إِسْحَٰقَ يَعْقُوبَ ﴿٧١﴾
قَالَتْ يَٰوَيْلَتَىٰٓ ءَأَلِدُ وَأَنَا۠ عَجُوزٌ وَهَٰذَا بَعْلِى شَيْخًا إِنَّ هَٰذَا
لَشَىْءٌ عَجِيبٌ ﴿٧٢﴾ قَالُوٓا۟ أَتَعْجَبِينَ مِنْ أَمْرِ ٱللَّهِ رَحْمَتُ ٱللَّهِ
وَبَرَكَٰتُهُۥ عَلَيْكُمْ أَهْلَ ٱلْبَيْتِ إِنَّهُۥ حَمِيدٌ مَّجِيدٌ ﴿٧٣﴾ فَلَمَّا ذَهَبَ
عَنْ إِبْرَٰهِيمَ ٱلرَّوْعُ وَجَآءَتْهُ ٱلْبُشْرَىٰ يُجَٰدِلُنَا فِى قَوْمِ لُوطٍ ﴿٧٤﴾
إِنَّ إِبْرَٰهِيمَ لَحَلِيمٌ أَوَّٰهٌ مُّنِيبٌ ﴿٧٥﴾ يَٰٓإِبْرَٰهِيمُ أَعْرِضْ عَنْ هَٰذَآ إِنَّهُۥ
قَدْ جَآءَ أَمْرُ رَبِّكَ وَإِنَّهُمْ ءَاتِيهِمْ عَذَابٌ غَيْرُ مَرْدُودٍ ﴿٧٦﴾ وَلَمَّا
جَآءَتْ رُسُلُنَا لُوطًا سِىٓءَ بِهِمْ وَضَاقَ بِهِمْ ذَرْعًا وَقَالَ هَٰذَا
يَوْمٌ عَصِيبٌ ﴿٧٧﴾ وَجَآءَهُۥ قَوْمُهُۥ يُهْرَعُونَ إِلَيْهِ وَمِن قَبْلُ كَانُوا۟

indeed! 'Ād rejected and denied ***their Lord, so away with 'Ād, the people of Hūd!*** They were placed far from the mercy of Allah.

61. ***To Thamūd*** We sent ***their brother Ṣāliḥ*** from their tribe. ***He said, 'My people, worship Allah*** and affirm His unity. ***You have no god apart from Him. He brought you into being*** (created you) ***from the earth*** by creating your ancestor Ādam from it ***and made you its inhabitants*** and gave you dwellings in which you live, ***so ask His forgiveness*** for committing *shirk* ***and then repent to Him***: turn to Him by obeying Him. ***My Lord is Close*** to His creation by His knowledge ***and Quick to Respond*** to those who ask of Him.'

62. ***They said, 'Ṣāliḥ, we had great hopes in you*** that you would be a notable man ***before this happened***: before you did this. ***Do you forbid us to worship what*** (the idols) ***our fathers worshipped? We have grave doubts about what*** (the message of Divine unity) ***you are calling us to.'***

63. ***He said, 'My people, what do you think? If I were to possess a Clear Sign from my Lord and He had given me mercy*** (Prophethood) ***from Him, who would help me*** and defend ***against*** the punishment of ***Allah if I disobeyed Him? You would not increase me*** – by commanding me to do that – ***in anything but loss*** (misguidance).

64. ***My people, here is the she-camel of Allah as a Sign for you. So leave her alone to eat on Allah's earth and do not inflict any harm on her*** by hamstringing her ***or you will be overcome by an imminent punishment*** if you do so.'

65. ***But they hamstrung her*** – a man named Quddūr did the action on their instructions – ***so he*** (Ṣāliḥ) ***said, 'Enjoy yourselves*** and live ***in your land for three more days.*** Then you will be destroyed. ***That is a promise which will not be belied.'***

66. ***Then when Our command came*** to destroy them, ***We rescued Ṣāliḥ and those who believed along with him*** – who numbered four thousand – ***by a mercy from Us*** and We saved them ***from the disgrace of that day*** (read as *yawmi'idhin* and *yawma'idhin*). ***Your Lord is the All-Strong, the Almighty.***

67. ***The Great Blast seized hold of those who did wrong and morning found them lying flattened in their homes***, dead bodies on the ground.

68. ***It was as if they had never lived there at all*** – as if they had never been in their homes. ***Yes indeed! Thamūd rejected their Lord. So away with Thamūd!*** This means both the area and the tribe.

69. ***Our messengers brought the good news*** of Isḥāq and Ya'qūb after him ***to Ibrāhīm. They said, 'Peace!' and he too said, 'Peace*** be upon you***!' and brought in a roasted calf without delay.***

70. ***When he saw that their hands were not reaching for it, he suspected them and felt afraid of them*** inside himself. ***They said, 'Have no fear! We have been sent to the people of Lūṭ*** to destroy them.***'***

71. ***His wife*** – whose name was Sāra – ***was standing there*** serving them ***and she laughed out loud*** at the news of their destruction. ***So We gave her the good news of Isḥāq, and beyond Isḥāq,*** his son ***Ya'qūb.*** The good news meant that she would live long enough to see Ya'qūb.

72. ***She said, 'Woe is me!*** This expression is used when something extraordinary happens. ***How can I give birth when I am an old woman*** of ninety-nine years ***and my husband here is an aged man*** of a hundred or a hundred and twenty***? This is indeed an astonishing thing*** – that a child should be born to two old people.

73. ***They said, 'Are you astonished at Allah's command*** (His power)***? May Allah's mercy and His blessings be upon you, People of the House*** of Ibrāhīm***! He is Praiseworthy, All-Glorious*** and Generous.***'***

74. ***When the feeling of fear left Ibrāhīm, and the good news*** of a child ***reached him, he disputed with Us*** (with Our messengers) ***about the people of Lūṭ.***

75. ***Ibrāhīm was forbearing*** – meaning that he had great patience – ***compassionate, penitent*** – continually repentant. He asked them, "Would you destroy a town which contains three hundred believers?" They said, "No." He asked, "Would you destroy a town with two hundred believers in it?' They replied, "No." He said, "Would you destroy a town with forty believers in it?" and they said, "No." He said, "Would you destroy a town with fourteen believers in it?" and they replied, "No." He said, "What if there was one believer in

يَعْمَلُونَ ٱلسَّيِّـَٔاتِ ۚ قَالَ يَٰقَوْمِ هَٰٓؤُلَآءِ بَنَاتِى هُنَّ أَطْهَرُ لَكُمْ ۖ
فَٱتَّقُوا۟ ٱللَّهَ وَلَا تُخْزُونِ فِى ضَيْفِىٓ ۖ أَلَيْسَ مِنكُمْ رَجُلٌ رَّشِيدٌ
﴿٧٨﴾ قَالُوا۟ لَقَدْ عَلِمْتَ مَا لَنَا فِى بَنَاتِكَ مِنْ حَقٍّ وَإِنَّكَ لَتَعْلَمُ مَا نُرِيدُ
﴿٧٩﴾ قَالَ لَوْ أَنَّ لِى بِكُمْ قُوَّةً أَوْ ءَاوِىٓ إِلَىٰ رُكْنٍ شَدِيدٍ ﴿٨٠﴾ قَالُوا۟
يَٰلُوطُ إِنَّا رُسُلُ رَبِّكَ لَن يَصِلُوٓا۟ إِلَيْكَ ۖ فَأَسْرِ بِأَهْلِكَ بِقِطْعٍ
مِّنَ ٱلَّيْلِ وَلَا يَلْتَفِتْ مِنكُمْ أَحَدٌ إِلَّا ٱمْرَأَتَكَ ۖ إِنَّهُۥ مُصِيبُهَا
مَآ أَصَابَهُمْ ۚ إِنَّ مَوْعِدَهُمُ ٱلصُّبْحُ ۚ أَلَيْسَ ٱلصُّبْحُ بِقَرِيبٍ ﴿٨١﴾
فَلَمَّا جَآءَ أَمْرُنَا جَعَلْنَا عَٰلِيَهَا سَافِلَهَا وَأَمْطَرْنَا عَلَيْهَا
حِجَارَةً مِّن سِجِّيلٍ مَّنضُودٍ ﴿٨٢﴾ مُّسَوَّمَةً عِندَ رَبِّكَ ۖ
وَمَا هِىَ مِنَ ٱلظَّٰلِمِينَ بِبَعِيدٍ ﴿٨٣﴾ ۞ وَإِلَىٰ مَدْيَنَ أَخَاهُمْ
شُعَيْبًا ۚ قَالَ يَٰقَوْمِ ٱعْبُدُوا۟ ٱللَّهَ مَا لَكُم مِّنْ إِلَٰهٍ غَيْرُهُۥ ۖ
وَلَا تَنقُصُوا۟ ٱلْمِكْيَالَ وَٱلْمِيزَانَ ۚ إِنِّىٓ أَرَىٰكُم بِخَيْرٍ
وَإِنِّىٓ أَخَافُ عَلَيْكُمْ عَذَابَ يَوْمٍ مُّحِيطٍ ﴿٨٤﴾ وَيَٰقَوْمِ
أَوْفُوا۟ ٱلْمِكْيَالَ وَٱلْمِيزَانَ بِٱلْقِسْطِ ۖ وَلَا تَبْخَسُوا۟
ٱلنَّاسَ أَشْيَآءَهُمْ وَلَا تَعْثَوْا۟ فِى ٱلْأَرْضِ مُفْسِدِينَ ﴿٨٥﴾
بَقِيَّتُ ٱللَّهِ خَيْرٌ لَّكُمْ إِن كُنتُم مُّؤْمِنِينَ ۚ وَمَآ أَنَا۠ عَلَيْكُم
بِحَفِيظٍ ﴿٨٦﴾ قَالُوا۟ يَٰشُعَيْبُ أَصَلَوٰتُكَ تَأْمُرُكَ أَن
نَّتْرُكَ مَا يَعْبُدُ ءَابَآؤُنَآ أَوْ أَن نَّفْعَلَ فِىٓ أَمْوَٰلِنَا مَا نَشَٰٓؤُا۟ ۖ
إِنَّكَ لَأَنتَ ٱلْحَلِيمُ ٱلرَّشِيدُ ﴿٨٧﴾ قَالَ يَٰقَوْمِ أَرَءَيْتُمْ إِن
كُنتُ عَلَىٰ بَيِّنَةٍ مِّن رَّبِّى وَرَزَقَنِى مِنْهُ رِزْقًا حَسَنًا ۚ وَمَآ أُرِيدُ أَنْ

it?" "No," they answered. He said, "Lūṭ is in it." They said, "We know better who is in it"...

76. When he went on for a long time arguing with them, they said, ***'Ibrāhīm, turn away from this*** arguing***! Your Lord's command*** to destroy them ***has come. A punishment is coming to them which cannot be repelled.'***

77. When Our messengers came to Lūṭ, he was distressed for them – sad on their behalf – ***and very concerned for them*** – because they were angels who had taken the form of handsome young men and he feared what his people might do to them – ***and said, 'This is a dreadful day.'***

78. ***His people came running to him excitedly*** when they learned of them – ***they were long used to committing evil acts*** – for a considerable period before their arrival the people had been committing sodomy with men. ***He*** (Lūṭ) ***said, 'My people, here are my daughters.*** Marry them. ***They are purer for you. So be fearful of Allah and do not shame me with my guests*** (although the word for "guest", *ḍayf,* is in the singular here it has a plural meaning). ***Is there not one rightly-guided man among you*** who will command the right and forbid the wrong***?'***

79. ***They said, 'You know we have no claim on*** (need of) ***your daughters. You know very well what it is we want*** – to commit sodomy.***'***

80. ***He said, 'If only I had the strength to combat you or could take refuge in some powerful support*** – such as a clan to help me fight you***!'***

81. When the angels saw this, ***they said, 'Lūṭ, we are messengers from your Lord. They will not be able to get at you*** with evil. ***Set out with your family – except for your wife*** (read as *imra'ataka* and *imra'atuka*), so do not travel with her – ***in the middle of the night and none of you should look back*** to see the terrible fate that will befall them. ***What strikes them will strike her as well.*** It is said that he did not set out with her; it is also said that she set out but then turned around and exclaimed, "O my people!" and a stone hit and killed her. Lūṭ asked the angels about the time of their destruction and they declared: ***Their promised appointment is the morning.*** He said, "I want it to be sooner than that," and they said: ***Is the morning not close at hand?'***

82. ***When Our command came*** to destroy them, ***We turned their cities upside down*** – Jibrīl lifted them up into the sky and slammed them upside down onto the earth – ***and rained down on them stones of hard baked clay, piled on top of one another in layers…***

83. ***…each one earmarked by your Lord*** – each stone bore the name of the person for whom it was intended. ***And they*** (the stones or their land) ***are never far from the wrongdoers*** such as the people of Makka.

84. ***And to Madyan*** We sent ***their brother Shu'ayb. He said, 'My people, worship Allah*** and affirm His unity***! You have no god apart from Him. Do not give short measure and short weight. I see you prospering*** – in possession of a blessing which makes you wealthy – ***and I fear for you*** – if you do not believe – ***the punishment of an all-encompassing Day*** which will destroy you.

85. ***My people, give full measure and full weight with justice; do not diminish people's goods*** – do not curtail what is due to them in any way***; and do not go about the earth, corrupting it***, by killing or any other type of wicked behaviour.

86. ***What endures with Allah*** – Allah's eternal provision for you, gained by your giving full weight and measure – ***is better for you*** – than what you might gain by cheating people – ***if you are believers. I am not set over you as your keeper*** – a guardian over you responsible for repaying you for what you do. I was sent to warn you.'

87. ***They said*** in mockery, ***'Shu'ayb, do your prayers instruct you*** to tell us ***that we should abandon what*** (the idols) ***our fathers worshipped or stop doing whatever we want to with our wealth?*** The meaning is that in their opinion this was clearly something fallacious to which someone who really meant good would never call them. ***You are clearly the forbearing, the rightly-guided!'*** They said that in mockery.

88. ***He said, 'My people, what do you think? If I do possess a Clear Sign from my Lord and He has given me His good*** (lawful) ***provision*** – why then should I want to mix it with the unlawful by miserliness and stinting? – ***I would clearly not want to go behind your***

أُخَالِفَكُمْ إِلَىٰ مَآ أَنْهَىٰكُمْ عَنْهُ ۚ إِنْ أُرِيدُ إِلَّا ٱلْإِصْلَـٰحَ
مَا ٱسْتَطَعْتُ ۚ وَمَا تَوْفِيقِىٓ إِلَّا بِٱللَّهِ ۚ عَلَيْهِ تَوَكَّلْتُ وَإِلَيْهِ أُنِيبُ ﴿٨٨﴾
وَيَـٰقَوْمِ لَا يَجْرِمَنَّكُمْ شِقَاقِىٓ أَن يُصِيبَكُم مِّثْلُ مَآ أَصَابَ
قَوْمَ نُوحٍ أَوْ قَوْمَ هُودٍ أَوْ قَوْمَ صَـٰلِحٍ ۚ وَمَا قَوْمُ لُوطٍ مِّنكُم
بِبَعِيدٍ ﴿٨٩﴾ وَٱسْتَغْفِرُوا۟ رَبَّكُمْ ثُمَّ تُوبُوٓا۟ إِلَيْهِ ۚ إِنَّ رَبِّى
رَحِيمٌ وَدُودٌ ﴿٩٠﴾ قَالُوا۟ يَـٰشُعَيْبُ مَا نَفْقَهُ كَثِيرًا مِّمَّا تَقُولُ
وَإِنَّا لَنَرَىٰكَ فِينَا ضَعِيفًا ۖ وَلَوْلَا رَهْطُكَ لَرَجَمْنَـٰكَ ۖ وَمَآ أَنتَ
عَلَيْنَا بِعَزِيزٍ ﴿٩١﴾ قَالَ يَـٰقَوْمِ أَرَهْطِىٓ أَعَزُّ عَلَيْكُم مِّنَ
ٱللَّهِ وَٱتَّخَذْتُمُوهُ وَرَآءَكُمْ ظِهْرِيًّا ۖ إِنَّ رَبِّى بِمَا تَعْمَلُونَ
مُحِيطٌ ﴿٩٢﴾ وَيَـٰقَوْمِ ٱعْمَلُوا۟ عَلَىٰ مَكَانَتِكُمْ إِنِّى عَـٰمِلٌ ۖ
سَوْفَ تَعْلَمُونَ مَن يَأْتِيهِ عَذَابٌ يُخْزِيهِ وَمَنْ هُوَ
كَـٰذِبٌ ۖ وَٱرْتَقِبُوٓا۟ إِنِّى مَعَكُمْ رَقِيبٌ ﴿٩٣﴾ وَلَمَّا جَآءَ
أَمْرُنَا نَجَّيْنَا شُعَيْبًا وَٱلَّذِينَ ءَامَنُوا۟ مَعَهُۥ بِرَحْمَةٍ مِّنَّا وَأَخَذَتِ
ٱلَّذِينَ ظَلَمُوا۟ ٱلصَّيْحَةُ فَأَصْبَحُوا۟ فِى دِيَـٰرِهِمْ جَـٰثِمِينَ ﴿٩٤﴾
كَأَن لَّمْ يَغْنَوْا۟ فِيهَآ ۗ أَلَا بُعْدًا لِّمَدْيَنَ كَمَا بَعِدَتْ ثَمُودُ ﴿٩٥﴾ وَلَقَدْ
أَرْسَلْنَا مُوسَىٰ بِـَٔايَـٰتِنَا وَسُلْطَـٰنٍ مُّبِينٍ ﴿٩٦﴾ إِلَىٰ فِرْعَوْنَ
وَمَلَإِي۟هِۦ فَٱتَّبَعُوٓا۟ أَمْرَ فِرْعَوْنَ ۖ وَمَآ أَمْرُ فِرْعَوْنَ بِرَشِيدٍ ﴿٩٧﴾
يَقْدُمُ قَوْمَهُۥ يَوْمَ ٱلْقِيَـٰمَةِ فَأَوْرَدَهُمُ ٱلنَّارَ ۖ وَبِئْسَ ٱلْوِرْدُ
ٱلْمَوْرُودُ ﴿٩٨﴾ وَأُتْبِعُوا۟ فِى هَـٰذِهِۦ لَعْنَةً وَيَوْمَ ٱلْقِيَـٰمَةِ ۚ بِئْسَ
ٱلرِّفْدُ ٱلْمَرْفُودُ ﴿٩٩﴾ ذَٰلِكَ مِنْ أَنۢبَآءِ ٱلْقُرَىٰ نَقُصُّهُۥ عَلَيْكَ ۖ

backs and do something I have forbidden you to do. I only want to put things right as far as I can by being just. ***My success is with Allah alone;*** I can only do this within the constraints my limited capability and that is also true of all acts of obedience. ***I have put my trust in Him and I turn to Him.***

89. ***My people, do not let your breach*** (disagreement) ***with me provoke you into doing wrong so that the same thing happens to you*** (the punishment) ***as happened to the people of Nūḥ and the people of Hūd and the people of Ṣāliḥ; and the people of Lūṭ are not far distant from you***, a reference either to the ruined houses of the people of Lūṭ which were quite near at hand or to the time of their destruction which was not so long before.

90. ***Ask your Lord for forgiveness and then repent to Him. My Lord is Most Merciful*** to the believers, ***Most Loving*** to them.'

91. ***They said***, proclaiming their lack of concern, ***'Shu'ayb, We do not understand much of what you say and we see you are weak*** and humble ***among us. Were it not for your clan, we would have stoned you. We do not hold you in high esteem!'*** In other words, they did not think that he was too noble to stone. It was his clan who were powerful.

92. ***He said, 'My people, do you esteem my clan more than you do Allah*** – so that you do not kill me because of them, not for the sake of Allah? ***You have made Him*** (Allah) ***into something to cast disdainfully behind your backs!*** You abandon Him and pay no attention to Him. ***But my Lord encompasses everything that you do*** in knowledge, and will repay you for it!

93. ***My people, do as you think best. That is what I am doing. You will certainly come to know who will receive a punishment to disgrace him, and who is a liar. So look out;*** Wait for the result of the business. ***I will be on the lookout with you.'***

94. ***When Our command came*** ordering their destruction, ***We rescued Shu'ayb and those who had believed along with him by a mercy from Us. The Great Blast*** (a shout from Jibrīl) ***seized hold of those who did wrong and morning found them lying flattened*** corpses ***in their homes***

95 ...as if they had never lived there at all. Yes indeed! Away with Madyan as with Thamūd!

96. *We sent Mūsā with Our Signs and clear* (manifest) ***authority...***

97. *...to Pharaoh and his ruling circle. They followed Pharaoh's command but Pharaoh's command was not rightly guided* (correct).

98. *He will go ahead of his people on the Day of Rising* – they will follow him then as they followed him in this world – ***and lead them down*** so that they enter ***into the Fire. What an evil watering-hole to be led to!***

99. *They are pursued by a curse in this world and* a curse ***on the Day of Rising. What an evil gift to be given!***

100. *That* which has been mentioned ***is some of the news of the cities which We relate to you***, Muḥammad. ***Some of them*** (the cities) ***are still standing***– although their people have been destroyed ***while others are now just stubble*** where the people have been destroyed and there is no trace of buildings either except for the equivalent of stubble after a field has been harvested.

101. *We did not wrong them* destroying them for no sin; ***rather they wronged themselves*** by committing *shirk*. ***The gods they called upon*** and worshipped ***besides Allah did not help them at all*** or defend them ***when Allah's command*** (punishment) ***came upon them: they did nothing but increase their ruin.*** Their worship of idols only increased them in loss.

102. *Such* a seizing ***is the iron grip of your Lord when He seizes the*** people of the ***cities which do wrong*** by perpetrating wrong actions: nothing will avail them when He seizes them. ***His grip is painful, violent.*** Al-Bukhārī and Muslim related from Abū Mūsā al-Ash'arī that the Messenger of Allah, may Allah bless him and grant him peace, said, "Allah gives respite to the wrongdoer but then, when He seizes him, he does not escape Him." Then the Messenger of Allah, may Allah bless him and grant him peace, recited this *āyat, "Such is the iron grip of your Lord..."*

103. *There is certainly a Sign* (lesson) ***in that*** (the stories mentioned) ***for anyone who fears the punishment of the Next World*** on the Day of Rising. ***That is a Day to which mankind will all be gath -***

مِنۡهَا قَآئِمٞ وَحَصِيدٞ ١٠٠ وَمَا ظَلَمۡنَٰهُمۡ وَلَٰكِن ظَلَمُوٓاْ
أَنفُسَهُمۡۖ فَمَآ أَغۡنَتۡ عَنۡهُمۡ ءَالِهَتُهُمُ ٱلَّتِي يَدۡعُونَ مِن دُونِ
ٱللَّهِ مِن شَيۡءٖ لَّمَّا جَآءَ أَمۡرُ رَبِّكَۖ وَمَا زَادُوهُمۡ غَيۡرَ تَتۡبِيبٖ ١٠١
وَكَذَٰلِكَ أَخۡذُ رَبِّكَ إِذَآ أَخَذَ ٱلۡقُرَىٰ وَهِيَ ظَٰلِمَةٌۚ إِنَّ أَخۡذَهُۥٓ
أَلِيمٞ شَدِيدٌ ١٠٢ إِنَّ فِي ذَٰلِكَ لَأٓيَةٗ لِّمَنۡ خَافَ عَذَابَ ٱلۡأٓخِرَةِۚ
ذَٰلِكَ يَوۡمٞ مَّجۡمُوعٞ لَّهُ ٱلنَّاسُ وَذَٰلِكَ يَوۡمٞ مَّشۡهُودٞ ١٠٣ وَمَا
نُؤَخِّرُهُۥٓ إِلَّا لِأَجَلٖ مَّعۡدُودٖ ١٠٤ يَوۡمَ يَأۡتِ لَا تَكَلَّمُ نَفۡسٌ
إِلَّا بِإِذۡنِهِۦۚ فَمِنۡهُمۡ شَقِيّٞ وَسَعِيدٞ ١٠٥ فَأَمَّا ٱلَّذِينَ شَقُواْ فَفِي
ٱلنَّارِ لَهُمۡ فِيهَا زَفِيرٞ وَشَهِيقٌ ١٠٦ خَٰلِدِينَ فِيهَا مَا دَامَتِ
ٱلسَّمَٰوَٰتُ وَٱلۡأَرۡضُ إِلَّا مَا شَآءَ رَبُّكَۚ إِنَّ رَبَّكَ فَعَّالٞ لِّمَا يُرِيدُ
١٠٧ ۞ وَأَمَّا ٱلَّذِينَ سُعِدُواْ فَفِي ٱلۡجَنَّةِ خَٰلِدِينَ فِيهَا مَا دَامَتِ
ٱلسَّمَٰوَٰتُ وَٱلۡأَرۡضُ إِلَّا مَا شَآءَ رَبُّكَۖ عَطَآءً غَيۡرَ مَجۡذُوذٖ ١٠٨
فَلَا تَكُ فِي مِرۡيَةٖ مِّمَّا يَعۡبُدُ هَٰٓؤُلَآءِۚ مَا يَعۡبُدُونَ إِلَّا كَمَا يَعۡبُدُ
ءَابَآؤُهُم مِّن قَبۡلُۚ وَإِنَّا لَمُوَفُّوهُمۡ نَصِيبَهُمۡ غَيۡرَ مَنقُوصٖ ١٠٩
وَلَقَدۡ ءَاتَيۡنَا مُوسَى ٱلۡكِتَٰبَ فَٱخۡتُلِفَ فِيهِۚ وَلَوۡلَا كَلِمَةٞ
سَبَقَتۡ مِن رَّبِّكَ لَقُضِيَ بَيۡنَهُمۡۚ وَإِنَّهُمۡ لَفِي شَكّٖ مِّنۡهُ مُرِيبٖ
١١٠ وَإِنَّ كُلّٗا لَّمَّا لَيُوَفِّيَنَّهُمۡ رَبُّكَ أَعۡمَٰلَهُمۡۚ إِنَّهُۥ بِمَا يَعۡمَلُونَ
خَبِيرٞ ١١١ فَٱسۡتَقِمۡ كَمَآ أُمِرۡتَ وَمَن تَابَ مَعَكَ وَلَا تَطۡغَوۡاْۚ
إِنَّهُۥ بِمَا تَعۡمَلُونَ بَصِيرٞ ١١٢ وَلَا تَرۡكَنُوٓاْ إِلَى ٱلَّذِينَ ظَلَمُواْ
فَتَمَسَّكُمُ ٱلنَّارُ وَمَا لَكُم مِّن دُونِ ٱللَّهِ مِنۡ أَوۡلِيَآءَ ثُمَّ

ered. That is a Day which will be witnessed by everyone – by all sentient creatures.

104. ***We will only postpone it until a predetermined time***, a time already known by Allah.

105. ***On the Day it comes, no self will speak except by His*** (Allah's) ***permission. Some of them will be wretched and others glad*** – and that was predestined before the beginning of time.

106. ***As for those who are wretched*** in Allah's foreknowledge, ***they will be in the Fire, where they will sigh and gasp,***

107. ***...remaining in it timelessly, for ever, as long as the heavens and earth endure, except as your Lord wills*** – to make it longer, which has no limit. The meaning is that they will be in it for ever. ***Your Lord is the Doer of what He wills.***

108. ***As for those who are glad*** (read as *su'idū* and *sa'idū*), ***they will be in the Garden, remaining in it timelessly, for ever, as long as the heavens and earth endure, except as your Lord wills*** – as mentioned above: and He indicates it for them – ***an uninterrupted gift.*** The gift is free of obligation, but Allah knows best what He means.

109. ***So be in no doubt***, Muḥammad, ***about what*** (the idols) ***these people worship*** – Allah will punish them as He punished those before them. This is solace for the Prophet, may Allah bless him and grant him peace. ***They only worship as their forebears worshipped previously*** and We punished them. ***We will pay them their portion*** of the punishment ***in full, with no rebate!***

110. ***We gave Mūsā the Book*** (the Torah) ***and people differed concerning it*** – there was both affirmation and denial, as was the case with the Qur'an – ***and had it not been for a prior Word from your Lord*** – that the Reckoning and repayment of creatures would be deferred until the Day of Rising – ***it*** – what they disagreed about – ***would already have been decided between them*** in this world. ***They*** (the deniers) ***are indeed in grave doubt about it.***

111. ***Your Lord will pay each one of them*** (each creature) ***in full*** repayment ***for their actions. He is aware of what they do.*** Allah knows their inward and their outward.

112. ***Go straight*** in terms of action, ***as you have been commanded*** by your Lord, and call people to Him ***and also those who turn with***

لَا تُنصَرُونَ ﴿١١٣﴾ وَأَقِمِ ٱلصَّلَوٰةَ طَرَفَيِ ٱلنَّهَارِ وَزُلَفٗا مِّنَ
ٱلَّيۡلِۚ إِنَّ ٱلۡحَسَنَٰتِ يُذۡهِبۡنَ ٱلسَّيِّـَٔاتِۚ ذَٰلِكَ ذِكۡرَىٰ لِلذَّٰكِرِينَ
﴿١١٤﴾ وَٱصۡبِرۡ فَإِنَّ ٱللَّهَ لَا يُضِيعُ أَجۡرَ ٱلۡمُحۡسِنِينَ ﴿١١٥﴾ فَلَوۡلَا
كَانَ مِنَ ٱلۡقُرُونِ مِن قَبۡلِكُمۡ أُوْلُواْ بَقِيَّةٖ يَنۡهَوۡنَ عَنِ ٱلۡفَسَادِ
فِي ٱلۡأَرۡضِ إِلَّا قَلِيلٗا مِّمَّنۡ أَنجَيۡنَا مِنۡهُمۡۗ وَٱتَّبَعَ ٱلَّذِينَ
ظَلَمُواْ مَآ أُتۡرِفُواْ فِيهِ وَكَانُواْ مُجۡرِمِينَ ﴿١١٦﴾ وَمَا كَانَ
رَبُّكَ لِيُهۡلِكَ ٱلۡقُرَىٰ بِظُلۡمٖ وَأَهۡلُهَا مُصۡلِحُونَ ﴿١١٧﴾
وَلَوۡ شَآءَ رَبُّكَ لَجَعَلَ ٱلنَّاسَ أُمَّةٗ وَٰحِدَةٗۖ وَلَا يَزَالُونَ مُخۡتَلِفِينَ
﴿١١٨﴾ إِلَّا مَن رَّحِمَ رَبُّكَۚ وَلِذَٰلِكَ خَلَقَهُمۡۗ وَتَمَّتۡ كَلِمَةُ رَبِّكَ
لَأَمۡلَأَنَّ جَهَنَّمَ مِنَ ٱلۡجِنَّةِ وَٱلنَّاسِ أَجۡمَعِينَ ﴿١١٩﴾ وَكُلّٗا نَّقُصُّ
عَلَيۡكَ مِنۡ أَنۢبَآءِ ٱلرُّسُلِ مَا نُثَبِّتُ بِهِۦ فُؤَادَكَۚ وَجَآءَكَ فِي هَٰذِهِ
ٱلۡحَقُّ وَمَوۡعِظَةٞ وَذِكۡرَىٰ لِلۡمُؤۡمِنِينَ ﴿١٢٠﴾ وَقُل لِّلَّذِينَ لَا يُؤۡمِنُونَ
ٱعۡمَلُواْ عَلَىٰ مَكَانَتِكُمۡ إِنَّا عَٰمِلُونَ ﴿١٢١﴾ وَٱنتَظِرُوٓاْ إِنَّا مُنتَظِرُونَ
﴿١٢٢﴾ وَلِلَّهِ غَيۡبُ ٱلسَّمَٰوَٰتِ وَٱلۡأَرۡضِ وَإِلَيۡهِ يُرۡجَعُ ٱلۡأَمۡرُ كُلُّهُۥ
فَٱعۡبُدۡهُ وَتَوَكَّلۡ عَلَيۡهِۚ وَمَا رَبُّكَ بِغَٰفِلٍ عَمَّا تَعۡمَلُونَ ﴿١٢٣﴾

you to Allah and believe should go straight; ***and do not exceed the bounds*** – the limits set by Allah. ***He sees what you do*** and will repay you.

113. ***Do not rely on*** – and incline with love and flattery to – ***those who do wrong*** – or be content with what they do, ***thus causing the Fire to afflict you, for you have no protector*** to protect you from it ***besides Allah; then you will not be helped*** against Allah's punishment.

114. ***Establish the prayer at each end of the day*** – morning and evening, referring to the *Ṣubḥ*, *Ẓuhr* and *'Aṣr* prayers – ***and in the first part of the night*** – referring to the *Maghrib* and *'Ishā'* prayers. ***Good actions*** – such as the five prayers – ***eradicate bad actions*** (minor wrong actions). This was revealed about someone who kissed a woman who was not a relative of his, and told the Prophet, may Allah bless him and grant him peace. He asked, "Is this for me?" The Prophet answered, "It is for all of my Community." (al-Bukhārī and Muslim) ***This is a reminder for people who pay heed*** and are warned.

115. ***And be steadfast***, Muḥammad, meaning "endure the harm your people do you" – or it may mean "be steadfast in the prayer. – ***Allah does not let the wage*** – for steadfastness in obedience – ***of good-doers go to waste.***

116. ***Would that there had been more people with a vestige of good*** – people who have *dīn* and excellence – ***among the generations*** (past nations) ***of those who came before you, who forbade corruption in the earth*** – in other words, they did not do that – ***other than the few among them whom We saved:*** they did forbid it, and so We saved them. ***Those who did wrong*** by perpetrating corruption and not forbidding it ***gladly pursued the life of luxury that they were given and were evildoers.***

117. ***Your Lord would never have destroyed the cities wrongfully while as their inhabitants (***the believers) ***were putting things right.***

118. ***If your Lord had wanted to, He would have made mankind into one community*** with one *dīn*, ***but they persist in their differences*** in respect of the *dīn*.

119. ***...except for those whom your Lord has mercy on*** and for whom He desires good so that they do not disagree. ***That is what He created them for*** – He created the people who disagree for this and the people on whom He has mercy for that – ***so that the Word of your Lord would be fulfilled: 'I will fill up Hell with the jinn and mankind all together.'***

120. ***We have given you all*** that is needed of ***this news about the Messengers so that We may make your heart firm*** and tranquil ***by means of it. The truth has come to you in this, and an admonishment and reminder to the believers.*** The believers are singled out for mention since they benefit by it through their belief in it as opposed to the unbelievers who do not.

121. ***Say to those who do not believe: 'Do*** (act) ***as you think best. That is what we are doing.*** This is a threat to them.

122. ***And wait*** for the outcome of your business. ***We too are waiting*** for that.'

123. ***The Unseen of the heavens and the earth belongs to Allah*** – He has knowledge of what is unseen in both heavens and the earth – ***and the whole affair will be returned to Him***: He will take revenge on those who disobeyed. ***So worship Him*** by affirming His unity ***and put your trust in Him.*** He will be enough for you. ***Your Lord is not unaware of what you do*** (read as *ta'malūna* and *ya'malūna*, "they do"). He defers them to their pre-determined time.

سُورَةُ يُوسُفَ

بِسۡمِ ٱللَّهِ ٱلرَّحۡمَٰنِ ٱلرَّحِيمِ

الٓرۚ تِلۡكَ ءَايَٰتُ ٱلۡكِتَٰبِ ٱلۡمُبِينِ ﴿١﴾ إِنَّآ أَنزَلۡنَٰهُ قُرۡءَٰنًا عَرَبِيّٗا
لَّعَلَّكُمۡ تَعۡقِلُونَ ﴿٢﴾ نَحۡنُ نَقُصُّ عَلَيۡكَ أَحۡسَنَ ٱلۡقَصَصِ
بِمَآ أَوۡحَيۡنَآ إِلَيۡكَ هَٰذَا ٱلۡقُرۡءَانَ وَإِن كُنتَ مِن قَبۡلِهِۦ
لَمِنَ ٱلۡغَٰفِلِينَ ﴿٣﴾ إِذۡ قَالَ يُوسُفُ لِأَبِيهِ يَٰٓأَبَتِ إِنِّي رَأَيۡتُ
أَحَدَ عَشَرَ كَوۡكَبٗا وَٱلشَّمۡسَ وَٱلۡقَمَرَ رَأَيۡتُهُمۡ لِي سَٰجِدِينَ ﴿٤﴾
قَالَ يَٰبُنَيَّ لَا تَقۡصُصۡ رُءۡيَاكَ عَلَىٰٓ إِخۡوَتِكَ فَيَكِيدُواْ لَكَ كَيۡدًاۖ
إِنَّ ٱلشَّيۡطَٰنَ لِلۡإِنسَٰنِ عَدُوّٞ مُّبِينٞ ﴿٥﴾ وَكَذَٰلِكَ يَجۡتَبِيكَ
رَبُّكَ وَيُعَلِّمُكَ مِن تَأۡوِيلِ ٱلۡأَحَادِيثِ وَيُتِمُّ نِعۡمَتَهُۥ عَلَيۡكَ
وَعَلَىٰٓ ءَالِ يَعۡقُوبَ كَمَآ أَتَمَّهَا عَلَىٰٓ أَبَوَيۡكَ مِن قَبۡلُ إِبۡرَٰهِيمَ وَإِسۡحَٰقَۚ
إِنَّ رَبَّكَ عَلِيمٌ حَكِيمٞ ﴿٦﴾ ۞ لَّقَدۡ كَانَ فِي يُوسُفَ وَإِخۡوَتِهِۦٓ
ءَايَٰتٞ لِّلسَّآئِلِينَ ﴿٧﴾ إِذۡ قَالُواْ لَيُوسُفُ وَأَخُوهُ أَحَبُّ إِلَىٰٓ
أَبِينَا مِنَّا وَنَحۡنُ عُصۡبَةٌ إِنَّ أَبَانَا لَفِي ضَلَٰلٖ مُّبِينٍ ﴿٨﴾ ٱقۡتُلُواْ
يُوسُفَ أَوِ ٱطۡرَحُوهُ أَرۡضٗا يَخۡلُ لَكُمۡ وَجۡهُ أَبِيكُمۡ وَتَكُونُواْ مِنۢ
بَعۡدِهِۦ قَوۡمٗا صَٰلِحِينَ ﴿٩﴾ قَالَ قَآئِلٞ مِّنۡهُمۡ لَا تَقۡتُلُواْ يُوسُفَ
وَأَلۡقُوهُ فِي غَيَٰبَتِ ٱلۡجُبِّ يَلۡتَقِطۡهُ بَعۡضُ ٱلسَّيَّارَةِ إِن كُنتُمۡ
فَٰعِلِينَ ﴿١٠﴾ قَالُواْ يَٰٓأَبَانَا مَا لَكَ لَا تَأۡمَ۫نَّا عَلَىٰ يُوسُفَ وَإِنَّا لَهُۥ
لَنَٰصِحُونَ ﴿١١﴾ أَرۡسِلۡهُ مَعَنَا غَدٗا يَرۡتَعۡ وَيَلۡعَبۡ وَإِنَّا لَهُۥ
لَحَٰفِظُونَ ﴿١٢﴾ قَالَ إِنِّي لَيَحۡزُنُنِيٓ أَن تَذۡهَبُواْ بِهِۦ وَأَخَافُ

12. *Sūrat Yūsuf*
Joseph

This *sūra* is Makkan except for *āyat*s 1, 2, 3, and 7 which are Madinan. It has 111 *āyat*s and was revealed after *Sūrat Hūd*.

1. ***Alif Lam Ra.*** Allah knows best what these letters mean. ***Those are the Signs of the Clear Book*** (*āyat*s of the Qur'an). It is clear in that it makes the truth clear from falsehood.

2. ***We have sent it down as an Arabic Qur'an*** – in the Arabic language – ***so that perhaps you will use your intellect*** and understand its meanings.

3. ***We tell you the best of stories in revealing this Qur'an to you, even though you were unaware of it before it came.***

4. Remember ***when Yūsuf told his father*** (Ya'qūb), ***'Father, I saw*** in a dream ***eleven bright stars, and the sun and moon as well. I saw them all prostrate in front of me.'*** The masculine plural *sājidīn* is used in "prostrate", even though it is usually only used for people, not other things.

5. ***He said, 'My son, do not tell your brothers your dream lest they devise some scheme to injure you.*** They might devise some way to destroy you out of envy because they might interpret the dream as the stars representing them, the sun your mother, and the moon your father. ***Shayṭān is a clear-cut enemy to man*** with clear enmity.

6. ***Accordingly*** – as shown by your dream – ***your Lord will pick you out*** (choose you) ***and teach you the true meaning of events*** (the interpretation of dreams) ***and perfectly fulfil His blessing*** (Prophethood) ***on you as well as on the family of Ya'qūb, as He fulfilled it perfectly before*** by bestowing Prophethood ***upon your forebears, Ibrāhīm and Isḥāq. Most certainly your Lord is Knowing*** of His creation, ***Wise*** in what He does to them.'

7. ***In Yūsuf and his*** twelve ***brothers there are Signs for every one of those who wants to ask*** and reflect.

8. Remember ***when they declared*** (the brothers said to one another), ***'Why! Yūsuf and his*** full ***brother*** Binyāmīn ***are dearer to our father than we are although we constitute a powerful group. Our***

أَن يَأْكُلَهُ ٱلذِّئْبُ وَأَنتُمْ عَنْهُ غَٰفِلُونَ ﴿١٣﴾ قَالُوا۟ لَئِنْ
أَكَلَهُ ٱلذِّئْبُ وَنَحْنُ عُصْبَةٌ إِنَّآ إِذًا لَّخَٰسِرُونَ ﴿١٤﴾
فَلَمَّا ذَهَبُوا۟ بِهِۦ وَأَجْمَعُوٓا۟ أَن يَجْعَلُوهُ فِى غَيَٰبَتِ ٱلْجُبِّ ۚ وَأَوْحَيْنَآ
إِلَيْهِ لَتُنَبِّئَنَّهُم بِأَمْرِهِمْ هَٰذَا وَهُمْ لَا يَشْعُرُونَ ﴿١٥﴾ وَجَآءُوٓ
أَبَاهُمْ عِشَآءً يَبْكُونَ ﴿١٦﴾ قَالُوا۟ يَٰٓأَبَانَآ إِنَّا ذَهَبْنَا نَسْتَبِقُ
وَتَرَكْنَا يُوسُفَ عِندَ مَتَٰعِنَا فَأَكَلَهُ ٱلذِّئْبُ ۖ وَمَآ أَنتَ
بِمُؤْمِنٍ لَّنَا وَلَوْ كُنَّا صَٰدِقِينَ ﴿١٧﴾ وَجَآءُو عَلَىٰ قَمِيصِهِۦ
بِدَمٍ كَذِبٍ ۚ قَالَ بَلْ سَوَّلَتْ لَكُمْ أَنفُسُكُمْ أَمْرًا ۖ فَصَبْرٌ جَمِيلٌ ۖ
وَٱللَّهُ ٱلْمُسْتَعَانُ عَلَىٰ مَا تَصِفُونَ ﴿١٨﴾ وَجَآءَتْ سَيَّارَةٌ فَأَرْسَلُوا۟
وَارِدَهُمْ فَأَدْلَىٰ دَلْوَهُۥ ۖ قَالَ يَٰبُشْرَىٰ هَٰذَا غُلَٰمٌ ۚ وَأَسَرُّوهُ بِضَٰعَةً ۚ
وَٱللَّهُ عَلِيمٌۢ بِمَا يَعْمَلُونَ ﴿١٩﴾ وَشَرَوْهُ بِثَمَنٍۭ بَخْسٍ
دَرَٰهِمَ مَعْدُودَةٍ وَكَانُوا۟ فِيهِ مِنَ ٱلزَّٰهِدِينَ ﴿٢٠﴾ وَقَالَ
ٱلَّذِى ٱشْتَرَىٰهُ مِن مِّصْرَ لِٱمْرَأَتِهِۦٓ أَكْرِمِى مَثْوَىٰهُ عَسَىٰٓ
أَن يَنفَعَنَآ أَوْ نَتَّخِذَهُۥ وَلَدًا ۚ وَكَذَٰلِكَ مَكَّنَّا لِيُوسُفَ فِى
ٱلْأَرْضِ وَلِنُعَلِّمَهُۥ مِن تَأْوِيلِ ٱلْأَحَادِيثِ ۚ وَٱللَّهُ غَالِبٌ عَلَىٰٓ
أَمْرِهِۦ وَلَٰكِنَّ أَكْثَرَ ٱلنَّاسِ لَا يَعْلَمُونَ ﴿٢١﴾ وَلَمَّا بَلَغَ
أَشُدَّهُۥٓ ءَاتَيْنَٰهُ حُكْمًا وَعِلْمًا ۚ وَكَذَٰلِكَ نَجْزِى ٱلْمُحْسِنِينَ ﴿٢٢﴾
وَرَٰوَدَتْهُ ٱلَّتِى هُوَ فِى بَيْتِهَا عَن نَّفْسِهِۦ وَغَلَّقَتِ ٱلْأَبْوَٰبَ
وَقَالَتْ هَيْتَ لَكَ ۚ قَالَ مَعَاذَ ٱللَّهِ ۖ إِنَّهُۥ رَبِّىٓ أَحْسَنَ مَثْوَاىَ ۖ
إِنَّهُۥ لَا يُفْلِحُ ٱلظَّٰلِمُونَ ﴿٢٣﴾ وَلَقَدْ هَمَّتْ بِهِۦ ۖ وَهَمَّ بِهَا

father is clearly making a mistake by preferring him and his brother to us.

9. ***Kill Yūsuf or expel him to some*** faraway ***land so that your father will look to you alone*** – turn to you and not pay attention to other than you after your killing or banishing Yūsuf – ***and then you can be people who do right*** by repenting.'

10. ***One of them*** (Yahudhā) ***said, 'Do not take Yūsuf's life, but throw him to the bottom of the*** dark ***well*** (read as *ghayāba* and *ghayābāt*), ***so that some travellers may discover him, if this is something that you have to do.*** If you want to get rid of him, then confine yourselves to this.'

11. ***They said, 'Our father, what is wrong with you that you refuse to trust us with Yūsuf when in truth we only wish him well*** and will take care of him?

12. ***Why don't you send him out with us tomorrow*** to the desert ***so he can enjoy himself and play about*** (read as *yarta' wa yal'ab* and also *narta' wa nal'ab,* "We can enjoy ourselves and play about.")? ***All of us will make sure that he is safe.'***

13. ***He said, 'It grieves me to let him go with you*** and to part with him. ***I fear a wolf might come and eat him up*** – there were many wolves in their land – ***while you are heedless, not attending him.'***

14. ***They said, 'If a wolf does come and eat him up when together we make up a powerful group in that case we would truly be in loss*** – if a group of us could not defend him!'

15. ***But when, in fact, they did go out with him and gathered all together and agreed to put him at the bottom of the well*** – which they did after removing his shirt, hitting him, humiliating him and almost killing him. When he had been lowered half way down the well, they dropped him the rest of the way so that he would die and he fell into the water. He saved himself by clambering onto a stone. They called to him and he answered them, thinking that they would have mercy on him. They then wanted to crack his head with a stone, but Yahūdhā stopped them doing that – ***We then revealed to him*** in the well – this was true revelation, even though he was only a young boy at the time, in order to set his heart at rest – ***that: 'You will***

inform them of this deed they perpetrate at a time in the future ***when they are totally unaware*** that it is you.'

16. ***That night they came back to their father in tears...***

17. ***... saying, 'Father, we went out to run a race and left Yūsuf together with our things*** (our clothes) ***and then a wolf appeared and ate him up; but you are never going to believe us now*** – believe that we are telling the truth – ***not even though we really tell the truth*** – because you suspect us regarding this story because of your love for Yūsuf and think badly of us.'

18. ***They then produced his shirt with false blood on it.*** There was blood on it because they had killed a lamb and splashed it with the blood but they neglected to rip it. They said that it was his blood. When Ya'qub saw that it was undamaged, he knew that they were lying. ***He said, 'It is merely that your lower selves have suggested something to you*** – and made it seem attractive – ***which you did; but beauty lies in showing steadfastness.*** There is no anxiety when steadfastness is displayed. ***It is Allah alone who is my Help*** and whom I ask for help ***in face of the event that you describe*** – what you have mentioned about what happened to Yūsuf.'

19. ***Some travellers*** from Madyan (Midian) on their way to Egypt ***came that way*** and camped close to the well where Yūsuf was ***and then dispatched their water-drawer*** to fetch them water, ***who let his bucket down*** into the well and Yūsuf held on to it and was brought out of the well. When he saw him, ***he said, 'Good news*** (read as *bushrā* or *bushrāya*) – the expression is metaphorical and means something like, "Look at this, my ship has come in!" – ***for me, I've found this boy!'*** That informed his fellows and they took him and concealed what had happened. ***They then hid him away among their goods.*** They said, "This is a runaway slave." Yūsuf remained silent out of fear that they would kill him. ***Allah knew very well what they were doing.***

20. ***They sold him for a pittance, a few small coins*** – a cheap price, reckoned to be between twenty and twenty-two dirhams – ***considering him to be of little worth.*** When the caravan reached Egypt, the one who had bought him then sold him for twenty dinars, a pair of sandals and two garments.

لَوۡلَآ أَن رَّءَا بُرۡهَٰنَ رَبِّهِۦۚ كَذَٰلِكَ لِنَصۡرِفَ عَنۡهُ ٱلسُّوٓءَ
وَٱلۡفَحۡشَآءَۚ إِنَّهُۥ مِنۡ عِبَادِنَا ٱلۡمُخۡلَصِينَ ٢٤ وَٱسۡتَبَقَا
ٱلۡبَابَ وَقَدَّتۡ قَمِيصَهُۥ مِن دُبُرٖ وَأَلۡفَيَا سَيِّدَهَا لَدَا ٱلۡبَابِۚ
قَالَتۡ مَا جَزَآءُ مَنۡ أَرَادَ بِأَهۡلِكَ سُوٓءًا إِلَّآ أَن يُسۡجَنَ أَوۡ عَذَابٌ
أَلِيمٞ ٢٥ قَالَ هِيَ رَٰوَدَتۡنِي عَن نَّفۡسِيۚ وَشَهِدَ شَاهِدٞ مِّنۡ
أَهۡلِهَآ إِن كَانَ قَمِيصُهُۥ قُدَّ مِن قُبُلٖ فَصَدَقَتۡ وَهُوَ مِنَ
ٱلۡكَٰذِبِينَ ٢٦ وَإِن كَانَ قَمِيصُهُۥ قُدَّ مِن دُبُرٖ فَكَذَبَتۡ وَهُوَ
مِنَ ٱلصَّٰدِقِينَ ٢٧ فَلَمَّا رَءَا قَمِيصَهُۥ قُدَّ مِن دُبُرٖ قَالَ إِنَّهُۥ
مِن كَيۡدِكُنَّۖ إِنَّ كَيۡدَكُنَّ عَظِيمٞ ٢٨ يُوسُفُ أَعۡرِضۡ عَنۡ
هَٰذَاۚ وَٱسۡتَغۡفِرِي لِذَنۢبِكِۖ إِنَّكِ كُنتِ مِنَ ٱلۡخَاطِـِٔينَ
٢٩ ۞ وَقَالَ نِسۡوَةٞ فِي ٱلۡمَدِينَةِ ٱمۡرَأَتُ ٱلۡعَزِيزِ تُرَٰوِدُ فَتَىٰهَا
عَن نَّفۡسِهِۦۖ قَدۡ شَغَفَهَا حُبًّاۖ إِنَّا لَنَرَىٰهَا فِي ضَلَٰلٖ مُّبِينٖ ٣٠
فَلَمَّا سَمِعَتۡ بِمَكۡرِهِنَّ أَرۡسَلَتۡ إِلَيۡهِنَّ وَأَعۡتَدَتۡ لَهُنَّ مُتَّكَـٔٗا وَءَاتَتۡ
كُلَّ وَٰحِدَةٖ مِّنۡهُنَّ سِكِّينٗا وَقَالَتِ ٱخۡرُجۡ عَلَيۡهِنَّۖ فَلَمَّا رَأَيۡنَهُۥٓ أَكۡبَرۡنَهُۥ
وَقَطَّعۡنَ أَيۡدِيَهُنَّ وَقُلۡنَ حَٰشَ لِلَّهِ مَا هَٰذَا بَشَرًا إِنۡ هَٰذَآ إِلَّا مَلَكٞ
كَرِيمٞ ٣١ قَالَتۡ فَذَٰلِكُنَّ ٱلَّذِي لُمۡتُنَّنِي فِيهِۖ وَلَقَدۡ رَٰوَدتُّهُۥ عَن
نَّفۡسِهِۦ فَٱسۡتَعۡصَمَۖ وَلَئِن لَّمۡ يَفۡعَلۡ مَآ ءَامُرُهُۥ لَيُسۡجَنَنَّ وَلَيَكُونٗا
مِّنَ ٱلصَّٰغِرِينَ ٣٢ قَالَ رَبِّ ٱلسِّجۡنُ أَحَبُّ إِلَيَّ مِمَّا يَدۡعُونَنِيٓ
إِلَيۡهِۖ وَإِلَّا تَصۡرِفۡ عَنِّي كَيۡدَهُنَّ أَصۡبُ إِلَيۡهِنَّ وَأَكُن مِّنَ ٱلۡجَٰهِلِينَ
٣٣ فَٱسۡتَجَابَ لَهُۥ رَبُّهُۥ فَصَرَفَ عَنۡهُ كَيۡدَهُنَّۚ إِنَّهُۥ هُوَ ٱلسَّمِيعُ

21. ***The Egyptian*** (Qaṭfīr, the 'Azīz) ***who had bought him told his wife*** (Zulaykhā), ***'Look after him with honour and respect*** among our family. ***It is possible he will be of use to us or perhaps we might adopt him as a son.'*** He was celibate. ***And thus*** – by saving Yūsuf from being killed and rescuing him from the well and making the heart of the 'Azīz incline towards him – ***We established Yūsuf in the land*** of Egypt so that he could convey what he conveyed and ***to teach him the true meaning of events*** (dream interpretation). ***Allah is in control of His affair*** and has the power to do anything He wishes, ***but most of mankind*** (the unbelievers) ***do not know*** that.

22. ***And then when he became a full-grown man***, of thirty or thirty-three years of age, ***We gave him knowledge*** – knowledge of the *dīn* before endowing him with Prophethood – ***and right judgement*** (wisdom) ***too. That is how We reward all doers of good.***

23. ***The woman whose house it was*** (Zulaykha) ***solicited him*** to have sexual intercourse with her. ***She barred the doors*** of the room ***and said, 'Come over here*** (read as *hi'ta lak, hīta lak,* and *haytu lak*)***!' He said, 'Allah is my refuge!*** I seek refuge in Allah from doing that! ***He*** – the one who bought me – ***is my lord and has been good to me with where I live***, and I will not betray him with his wife. ***Those who do wrong*** by committing adultery ***will surely not succeed.'***

24. ***She wanted*** to have sexual intercourse with ***him and he would have wanted*** to with ***her, had he not seen the Clear Proof of his Lord.*** Ibn 'Abbās said that the form of Ya'qūb appeared to him and struck him in the chest and the desire left him through his fingertips. ***That*** – demonstration to him of the Clear Proof – ***happened so We might avert from him all evil*** (treachery) ***and lust*** (fornication). ***He was one of Our sincere slaves*** (read as *mukhlaṣīn* and also *mukhliṣīn*, meaning "one of Our chosen slaves") with respect to obedience.

25. ***They raced to the door.*** Yūsuf hurried to it to escape and she tried to hold on to him. She grabbed his garment and pulled him to her and so ***she tore his shirt at the back. They met her husband by the door.*** She said that she was innocent. ***She*** then ***said, 'How should a man whose intention was to harm your family*** by committing adultery ***be punished for what he did except with prison or painful punishment*** by being beaten?'

26. Yūsuf said that he was innocent. ***He said, 'It was she who tried to seduce me.' A witness from her people*** – her cousin and it is reported that he was still in the cradle when he said this – ***then declared, 'If his shirt is torn in front, she speaks the truth and he has clearly told a shameless lie.***

27. ***If his shirt is torn at the back, then she has lied and he has clearly told the simple truth.'***

28. ***He*** (her husband) ***saw the shirt torn at the back and said, 'The source of this*** – what she said about punishing Yūsuf – ***is women's deviousness. Without a doubt your guile is very great.'***

29. Then he continued, ***'Yūsuf, ignore all this*** business – and do not mention it so that it does not spread – ***and you,*** Zulaykhā, ***should ask forgiveness for your evil act. There is no doubt that you are in the wrong*** – sinful in respect of what you have done.'

30. ***Some city women*** in the city of Egypt ***said, 'The governor's wife solicited her slave. He hass fired her heart with love.*** The word used here *shaghafa* means to cause to love violently and is derived from *shaghaf*, the pericardium or covering of the heart. ***We see that she is the one to blame*** – we see that she is the one who is in error and it is clear that she is in love with him.'

31. ***But when she heard of their malicious talk*** and slander of her, ***she sent for them and made a sumptuous meal*** – prepared a meal which had citrus fruit in it which require knives – ***and then she gave a knife to each of them. She said*** to Yūsuf, ***'Go out to them.' When they saw him, they were amazed by him and cut their hands*** with the knives but were unconscious of the pain because they were so distracted by the sight of Yūsuf. ***They said, 'Allah preserve us! This is no man*** – because of his beauty, which was far greater than is normally seen in a human being. A *ḥadīth* says, "He was given half of all beauty." ***What can this be but a noble angel here!'***

32. ***She*** (Zulaykhā) ***said*** – when she saw what they had done – ***'You see! It is him you blamed me for*** loving. ***I tried seducing him but he refused. If he does not do what I order him, he will be put in***

ٱلْعَلِيمُ ﴿٣٤﴾ ثُمَّ بَدَا لَهُم مِّنۢ بَعْدِ مَا رَأَوُا۟ ٱلْـَٔايَـٰتِ لَيَسْجُنُنَّهُۥ
حَتَّىٰ حِينٍ ﴿٣٥﴾ وَدَخَلَ مَعَهُ ٱلسِّجْنَ فَتَيَانِ ۖ قَالَ أَحَدُهُمَآ
إِنِّىٓ أَرَىٰنِىٓ أَعْصِرُ خَمْرًا ۖ وَقَالَ ٱلْـَٔاخَرُ إِنِّىٓ أَرَىٰنِىٓ أَحْمِلُ فَوْقَ
رَأْسِى خُبْزًا تَأْكُلُ ٱلطَّيْرُ مِنْهُ ۖ نَبِّئْنَا بِتَأْوِيلِهِۦٓ ۖ إِنَّا نَرَىٰكَ مِنَ
ٱلْمُحْسِنِينَ ﴿٣٦﴾ قَالَ لَا يَأْتِيكُمَا طَعَامٌ تُرْزَقَانِهِۦٓ إِلَّا نَبَّأْتُكُمَا
بِتَأْوِيلِهِۦ قَبْلَ أَن يَأْتِيَكُمَا ۚ ذَٰلِكُمَا مِمَّا عَلَّمَنِى رَبِّىٓ ۚ إِنِّى تَرَكْتُ
مِلَّةَ قَوْمٍ لَّا يُؤْمِنُونَ بِٱللَّهِ وَهُم بِٱلْـَٔاخِرَةِ هُمْ كَـٰفِرُونَ ﴿٣٧﴾
وَٱتَّبَعْتُ مِلَّةَ ءَابَآءِىٓ إِبْرَٰهِيمَ وَإِسْحَـٰقَ وَيَعْقُوبَ ۚ مَا كَانَ
لَنَآ أَن نُّشْرِكَ بِٱللَّهِ مِن شَىْءٍ ۚ ذَٰلِكَ مِن فَضْلِ ٱللَّهِ عَلَيْنَا وَعَلَى
ٱلنَّاسِ وَلَـٰكِنَّ أَكْثَرَ ٱلنَّاسِ لَا يَشْكُرُونَ ﴿٣٨﴾ يَـٰصَـٰحِبَىِ
ٱلسِّجْنِ ءَأَرْبَابٌ مُّتَفَرِّقُونَ خَيْرٌ أَمِ ٱللَّهُ ٱلْوَٰحِدُ ٱلْقَهَّارُ
﴿٣٩﴾ مَا تَعْبُدُونَ مِن دُونِهِۦٓ إِلَّآ أَسْمَآءً سَمَّيْتُمُوهَآ أَنتُمْ
وَءَابَآؤُكُم مَّآ أَنزَلَ ٱللَّهُ بِهَا مِن سُلْطَـٰنٍ ۚ إِنِ ٱلْحُكْمُ إِلَّا لِلَّهِ ۚ
أَمَرَ أَلَّا تَعْبُدُوٓا۟ إِلَّآ إِيَّاهُ ۚ ذَٰلِكَ ٱلدِّينُ ٱلْقَيِّمُ وَلَـٰكِنَّ أَكْثَرَ
ٱلنَّاسِ لَا يَعْلَمُونَ ﴿٤٠﴾ يَـٰصَـٰحِبَىِ ٱلسِّجْنِ أَمَّآ أَحَدُكُمَا
فَيَسْقِى رَبَّهُۥ خَمْرًا ۖ وَأَمَّا ٱلْـَٔاخَرُ فَيُصْلَبُ فَتَأْكُلُ ٱلطَّيْرُ
مِن رَّأْسِهِۦ ۚ قُضِىَ ٱلْأَمْرُ ٱلَّذِى فِيهِ تَسْتَفْتِيَانِ ﴿٤١﴾ وَقَالَ لِلَّذِى
ظَنَّ أَنَّهُۥ نَاجٍ مِّنْهُمَا ٱذْكُرْنِى عِندَ رَبِّكَ فَأَنسَىٰهُ
ٱلشَّيْطَـٰنُ ذِكْرَ رَبِّهِۦ فَلَبِثَ فِى ٱلسِّجْنِ بِضْعَ سِنِينَ
﴿٤٢﴾ وَقَالَ ٱلْمَلِكُ إِنِّىٓ أَرَىٰ سَبْعَ بَقَرَٰتٍ سِمَانٍ يَأْكُلُهُنَّ

prison and brought low and abased.***'*** They said to him, "Obey your mistress."

33. ***He said, 'My Lord, prison is preferable to me rather than what they call on me to do. Unless You turn their guile away from me, it may well be that I will fall for them*** and incline towards them ***and so become a man of ignorance*** (a sinner).***'*** This is a supplication to Allah. Allah then says:

34. ***His Lord replied to him*** – to his supplication – ***and turned away from him their female guile and deviousness. He is the One Who Hears*** all words***, the One Who Knows*** all actions.

35. ***Then, after they had seen the Signs*** which made it clear to them that Yūsuf was innocent ***they thought that they should still imprison him for a time*** to stop people talking; and they did so.

36. ***Two servants*** of the King ***entered prison along with him.*** One was a cupbearer and the other in charge of the royal food. They said, "We will test him." ***One*** (the cupbearer) ***said, 'I dreamt that I was pressing grapes.' The other*** (the one in charge of food) ***said, 'I dreamt I carried bread upon my head and birds were eating it. Tell us the true meaning of these dreams*** and interpret them. ***We see that you are one of the righteous.'***

37. ***He said*** to them – to inform them that he knew the interpretation of dreams – ***'No meal to feed you will arrive before I have informed you what they mean. That is part of what my Lord taught me*** – he said this to encourage them to believe***, for I have left the religion of a people who clearly do not believe in Allah and who disbelieve in the world to come.***

38. ***I hold fast to the creed of my forebears Ibrāhīm and Isḥāq and Ya'qūb. We do not associate anything with Allah*** because we are protected from doing so. ***And that*** understanding of Allah's unity ***is how Allah has favoured us and all mankind, yet most*** (the unbelievers) ***do not give thanks*** but commit *shirk*. Then he clearly calls on them to believe:

39. ***My fellow-prisoners, are many lords better, or Allah, the only One, the Conqueror?*** This is a question which demands an affirmative response.

سَبۡعٌ عِجَافٞ وَسَبۡعَ سُنۢبُلَٰتٍ خُضۡرٖ وَأُخَرَ يَابِسَٰتٖۖ
يَٰٓأَيُّهَا ٱلۡمَلَأُ أَفۡتُونِي فِي رُءۡيَٰيَ إِن كُنتُمۡ لِلرُّءۡيَا تَعۡبُرُونَ ٤٣
قَالُوٓاْ أَضۡغَٰثُ أَحۡلَٰمٖۖ وَمَا نَحۡنُ بِتَأۡوِيلِ ٱلۡأَحۡلَٰمِ بِعَٰلِمِينَ ٤٤
وَقَالَ ٱلَّذِي نَجَا مِنۡهُمَا وَٱدَّكَرَ بَعۡدَ أُمَّةٍ أَنَا۠ أُنَبِّئُكُم بِتَأۡوِيلِهِۦ
فَأَرۡسِلُونِ ٤٥ يُوسُفُ أَيُّهَا ٱلصِّدِّيقُ أَفۡتِنَا فِي سَبۡعِ بَقَرَٰتٖ
سِمَانٖ يَأۡكُلُهُنَّ سَبۡعٌ عِجَافٞ وَسَبۡعِ سُنۢبُلَٰتٍ خُضۡرٖ
وَأُخَرَ يَابِسَٰتٖ لَّعَلِّيٓ أَرۡجِعُ إِلَى ٱلنَّاسِ لَعَلَّهُمۡ يَعۡلَمُونَ ٤٦ قَالَ
تَزۡرَعُونَ سَبۡعَ سِنِينَ دَأَبٗا فَمَا حَصَدتُّمۡ فَذَرُوهُ فِي سُنۢبُلِهِۦٓ إِلَّا
قَلِيلٗا مِّمَّا تَأۡكُلُونَ ٤٧ ثُمَّ يَأۡتِي مِنۢ بَعۡدِ ذَٰلِكَ سَبۡعٞ شِدَادٞ يَأۡكُلۡنَ
مَا قَدَّمۡتُمۡ لَهُنَّ إِلَّا قَلِيلٗا مِّمَّا تُحۡصِنُونَ ٤٨ ثُمَّ يَأۡتِي مِنۢ بَعۡدِ ذَٰلِكَ
عَامٞ فِيهِ يُغَاثُ ٱلنَّاسُ وَفِيهِ يَعۡصِرُونَ ٤٩ وَقَالَ ٱلۡمَلِكُ ٱئۡتُونِي
بِهِۦۖ فَلَمَّا جَآءَهُ ٱلرَّسُولُ قَالَ ٱرۡجِعۡ إِلَىٰ رَبِّكَ فَسۡـَٔلۡهُ مَا بَالُ
ٱلنِّسۡوَةِ ٱلَّٰتِي قَطَّعۡنَ أَيۡدِيَهُنَّۚ إِنَّ رَبِّي بِكَيۡدِهِنَّ عَلِيمٞ ٥٠ قَالَ
مَا خَطۡبُكُنَّ إِذۡ رَٰوَدتُّنَّ يُوسُفَ عَن نَّفۡسِهِۦۚ قُلۡنَ حَٰشَ لِلَّهِ
مَا عَلِمۡنَا عَلَيۡهِ مِن سُوٓءٖۚ قَالَتِ ٱمۡرَأَتُ ٱلۡعَزِيزِ ٱلۡـَٰٔنَ حَصۡحَصَ
ٱلۡحَقُّ أَنَا۠ رَٰوَدتُّهُۥ عَن نَّفۡسِهِۦ وَإِنَّهُۥ لَمِنَ ٱلصَّٰدِقِينَ ٥١ ذَٰلِكَ
لِيَعۡلَمَ أَنِّي لَمۡ أَخُنۡهُ بِٱلۡغَيۡبِ وَأَنَّ ٱللَّهَ لَا يَهۡدِي كَيۡدَ ٱلۡخَآئِنِينَ ٥٢
۞ وَمَآ أُبَرِّئُ نَفۡسِيٓۚ إِنَّ ٱلنَّفۡسَ لَأَمَّارَةُۢ بِٱلسُّوٓءِ إِلَّا مَا رَحِمَ
رَبِّيٓۚ إِنَّ رَبِّي غَفُورٞ رَّحِيمٞ ٥٣ وَقَالَ ٱلۡمَلِكُ ٱئۡتُونِي بِهِۦٓ أَسۡتَخۡلِصۡهُ
لِنَفۡسِيۖ فَلَمَّا كَلَّمَهُۥ قَالَ إِنَّكَ ٱلۡيَوۡمَ لَدَيۡنَا مَكِينٌ أَمِينٞ ٥٤ قَالَ

40. ***What*** (the idols) ***you serve apart from Him are only names which you and your forefathers have made up. There is no man - date*** (evidence or proof) ***from Allah for*** worshipping ***them. Allah alone is qualified to judge. His order is to worship none but Him. That*** understanding of the Divine Unity ***is in truth the straight and upright*** **dīn,** ***but most of mankind*** (the unbelievers) ***do not know*** the punishment which awaits them and so they continue to worship others besides Allah.

41. ***My fellow-captives, one of you*** (the cupbearer) ***will serve his lord with wine*** – as was his custom, and he was indeed released three days later; ***the other of you will be crucified and birds will eat his head.'*** This was the interpretation of their dreams. They said, 'We have not really seen anything in a dream.' He said: ***'The thing you asked about is foreordained*** whether you were telling the truth or lying.***'***

42. ***He said to the one of them he knew*** (the word for "he knew" here, *ẓanna,* which normally implies uncertainty here implies certainty) ***was saved*** (the cupbearer), ***'Please mention me when you are with your lord*** and tell him that there is someone wrongfully imprisoned,***' but Shaytan made him forget to remind his lord*** about Yūsuf, ***and so he*** (Yūsuf) ***stayed in prison for several years*** – between seven and twelve years.

43. ***The King*** of Egypt – whose name was ar-Rayyān ibn al-Walīd – ***declared, 'I dreamt of seven fat cows which seven thin ones ate and seven green ears of wheat and seven others which were dry. O counsellors, explain my dream to me*** and make it clear ***if you are those who can interpret visions,*** Interpret it for me.***'***

44. ***They said,*** 'This is ***a jumbled mass of mixed-up dreams! We do not know the meaning of such dreams.'***

45. ***The one of them*** (the cupbearer) ***who had been saved then said, remembering*** Yūsuf ***after a period, 'I will tell you what it signifies, so send me out.'*** They sent him and he went to Yūsuf.

46. ***'O truthful Yūsuf, tell us of seven fat cows which seven thin ones ate and seven green ears of wheat and seven others which were dry, so that I may return to them*** (the King and his companions) ***and let them know*** what the dream meant.***'***

47. ***He said, 'Sow for seven years in the normal way*** – cultivate your crops for seven years in a row; that is what is meant by the seven fat cows – ***and leave that which you harvest in the ear*** so that it does not rot, ***except for a small amount from which you eat*** – which you should thresh.

48. ***Then after that*** (the seven fertile years), ***seven hard years*** of drought – signified by the seven thin cows – ***will come, in which you can eat from what you set aside for them*** – referring to the grain stored during the fertile years – ***except for a little which you store.***

49. ***Then after that*** (the seven years of drought) ***another year will come in which the people will be helped by rain in plenty and when they once more will press*** grapes in a time of fertility.***'***

50. ***The King said*** – when the messenger came and told him this interpretation of his dream – ***'Bring him*** who has interpreted it – meaning Yūsuf – ***to me straight away!' But when the envoy came to him*** to ask him to come out ***he said,*** desiring to prove his innocence: ***'Go back to your master and enquire of him what happened about the women who cut their hands. My Lord has knowledge of their cunning guile.'*** So the messenger went back and told the King and he summoned the women.

51. ***He said, 'What was this past affair of yours when you solicited Yūsuf?*** Did you find that he inclined to you at all?***' They then replied 'Allah forbid! We know no bad of him.' The governor's wife then said, 'The truth has now emerged*** and become clear. ***Indeed I tried to seduce him then and he has simply told the honest truth.'*** She admitted that he had spoken the truth. Yūsuf was informed of it and then said the following:

52. ***'In this way*** – by making his innocence known – ***he*** (the 'Azīz) ***may know at last that I did not dishonour him behind his back*** – and did not betray him with his wife – ***and that Allah most surely does not guide the deviousness of the dishonourable.*** Then he was humble and said:

53. ***I do not say my self was free from blame*** (faults). ***The self*** – here used generically meaning human selves in general – ***indeed***

ٱجۡعَلۡنِي عَلَىٰ خَزَآئِنِ ٱلۡأَرۡضِۖ إِنِّي حَفِيظٌ عَلِيمٞ ﴿٥٥﴾ وَكَذَٰلِكَ
مَكَّنَّا لِيُوسُفَ فِي ٱلۡأَرۡضِ يَتَبَوَّأُ مِنۡهَا حَيۡثُ يَشَآءُۚ نُصِيبُ
بِرَحۡمَتِنَا مَن نَّشَآءُۖ وَلَا نُضِيعُ أَجۡرَ ٱلۡمُحۡسِنِينَ ﴿٥٦﴾ وَلَأَجۡرُ
ٱلۡأٓخِرَةِ خَيۡرٞ لِّلَّذِينَ ءَامَنُواْ وَكَانُواْ يَتَّقُونَ ﴿٥٧﴾ وَجَآءَ إِخۡوَةُ
يُوسُفَ فَدَخَلُواْ عَلَيۡهِ فَعَرَفَهُمۡ وَهُمۡ لَهُۥ مُنكِرُونَ ﴿٥٨﴾ وَلَمَّا
جَهَّزَهُم بِجَهَازِهِمۡ قَالَ ٱئۡتُونِي بِأَخٖ لَّكُم مِّنۡ أَبِيكُمۡۚ أَلَا تَرَوۡنَ
أَنِّيٓ أُوفِي ٱلۡكَيۡلَ وَأَنَا۠ خَيۡرُ ٱلۡمُنزِلِينَ ﴿٥٩﴾ فَإِن لَّمۡ تَأۡتُونِي بِهِۦ فَلَا
كَيۡلَ لَكُمۡ عِندِي وَلَا تَقۡرَبُونِ ﴿٦٠﴾ قَالُواْ سَنُرَٰوِدُ عَنۡهُ أَبَاهُ
وَإِنَّا لَفَٰعِلُونَ ﴿٦١﴾ وَقَالَ لِفِتۡيَٰنِهِ ٱجۡعَلُواْ بِضَٰعَتَهُمۡ فِي رِحَالِهِمۡ
لَعَلَّهُمۡ يَعۡرِفُونَهَآ إِذَا ٱنقَلَبُوٓاْ إِلَىٰٓ أَهۡلِهِمۡ لَعَلَّهُمۡ يَرۡجِعُونَ
﴿٦٢﴾ فَلَمَّا رَجَعُوٓاْ إِلَىٰٓ أَبِيهِمۡ قَالُواْ يَٰٓأَبَانَا مُنِعَ مِنَّا ٱلۡكَيۡلُ
فَأَرۡسِلۡ مَعَنَآ أَخَانَا نَكۡتَلۡ وَإِنَّا لَهُۥ لَحَٰفِظُونَ ﴿٦٣﴾
قَالَ هَلۡ ءَامَنُكُمۡ عَلَيۡهِ إِلَّا كَمَآ أَمِنتُكُمۡ عَلَىٰٓ أَخِيهِ مِن
قَبۡلُۖ فَٱللَّهُ خَيۡرٌ حَٰفِظٗاۖ وَهُوَ أَرۡحَمُ ٱلرَّٰحِمِينَ ﴿٦٤﴾ وَلَمَّا فَتَحُواْ
مَتَٰعَهُمۡ وَجَدُواْ بِضَٰعَتَهُمۡ رُدَّتۡ إِلَيۡهِمۡۖ قَالُواْ يَٰٓأَبَانَا
مَا نَبۡغِيۖ هَٰذِهِۦ بِضَٰعَتُنَا رُدَّتۡ إِلَيۡنَاۖ وَنَمِيرُ أَهۡلَنَا وَنَحۡفَظُ
أَخَانَا وَنَزۡدَادُ كَيۡلَ بَعِيرٖۖ ذَٰلِكَ كَيۡلٞ يَسِيرٞ ﴿٦٥﴾ قَالَ لَنۡ
أُرۡسِلَهُۥ مَعَكُمۡ حَتَّىٰ تُؤۡتُونِ مَوۡثِقٗا مِّنَ ٱللَّهِ لَتَأۡتُنَّنِي بِهِۦٓ إِلَّآ
أَن يُحَاطَ بِكُمۡۖ فَلَمَّآ ءَاتَوۡهُ مَوۡثِقَهُمۡ قَالَ ٱللَّهُ عَلَىٰ مَا نَقُولُ وَكِيلٞ
﴿٦٦﴾ وَقَالَ يَٰبَنِيَّ لَا تَدۡخُلُواْ مِنۢ بَابٖ وَٰحِدٖ وَٱدۡخُلُواْ مِنۡ أَبۡوَٰبٖ

often ***commands to evil acts, except for those my Lord has mercy on*** and protects. ***My Lord is Forgiving, Merciful.'***

54. ***The king said, 'Bring him to me straight away so I may draw him very close to me*** – I can make him a special confidant for myself without any intermediary.' The messenger came to Yūsuf and said, "Respond to the king." He rose and said goodbye to the people in the prison and made supplication for them. Then he washed himself and put on good clothes and went to the king. ***When he*** (the king) ***had spoken with him, he declared, 'Today you are trusted, established in our sight.*** What do you think we should do?' He said, "Collect the food and sow many crops in the fertile years and store up food in the ear. Then many people will come to you to get provision from you." The king asked, "Who should be in charge of that?"

55. ***He*** (Yūsuf) ***said, 'Entrust the country's stores*** (the stores of Egypt) ***to me. In truth I am a knowing guardian.*** I know how to protect,' or, possibly, 'I am a writer with knowledge of calculation.'

56. ***And thus*** by delivering him from prison ***We established Yūsuf in the land*** (Egypt) ***so he could live in any place he pleased*** – after his constriction and imprisonment. It is said that the king met with him face to face and gave him the seal and appointed him to the position of governor, having dismissed the previous incumbent. After that the king died. Then Yūsuf married his widow and found her to be a virgin and she bore him two children. He established justice in Egypt and people were subject to him. ***We grant Our grace to anyone We will, and We do not allow to go to waste the wage of any who do good.***

57. ***But the wages of the Next World are the best*** – better than the wages of this world – ***for people who believe and fear their Lord.*** Then the years of drought came and it affected the lands of Canaan and Syria.

58. ***The brothers of Yūsuf*** – without Binyamīn – ***came into his presence*** to buy food, since they had heard that the governor of Egypt sold food for a price; ***and he knew them*** – Yūsuf recognised his brothers – ***but they did not know him*** because it had been a long time since they had seen him and they thought that he was dead. They spoke to him in Hebrew and he asked, as if he disapproved of them, "What has brought you from your land?" "Need for food," they answered. "Perhaps you are spies," he said. "We seek refuge with Allah!" they responded. "Where are you from?" he asked. "From Canaan," they replied. "Our father is Ya'qūb, the Prophet of Allah." He asked, "Does he have any children other than you?" he asked. They said, "Yes, we are twelve. The youngest of us went and was lost in the desert. Of all of us he was the one our father loved most. He kept his full brother with him to console himself for his loss." Yūsuf commanded that they be given hospitality and honoured.

59. ***Then, having supplied their needs*** and given them the measure of grain they came to procure ***he said to them, 'Bring me your brother,*** Binyāmīn, ***your father's youngest son***, so that I may know that you are speaking the truth. ***Do you not see that I dispense full measure*** without stinting ***and am the most hospitable of hosts?***

60. ***But if you do not bring him here to me, your measure from me then will be denied*** – you will not be able to buy any grain – ***and you will not come near to me at all.'***

61. ***They said, 'We will ask our father for him*** – we will try to ask him to send him with us. ***That is something we will surely do.'***

62. ***He told his serving men*** (read as *fityānihi* and *fityatihi*), ***'Put back their goods*** (dirhams) which they have brought to pay for their measure ***into their saddlebags for them to find when they arrive back to their families*** and open their bags, ***so that perhaps they will return again*** – because they will not think it proper to keep them.'

63. ***Then when they got back to their father's house, they said, 'Father, our measure will be denied*** if you do not send our brother to him. ***Please send our brother with us so we may obtain our measure*** (read as *naktal* and *yaktal*, in which case the meaning becomes "the measure may be obtained"). ***We will take care of him.'***

64. ***He said, 'How will my trusting him to your care be different from entrusting his brother*** Yūsuf ***before*** – when you did what you did? ***The Best of Guardians*** (read as *ḥāfiẓan* and *ḥifẓan*), ***however, is Allah. He is the Most Merciful of the merciful*** – and I hope that He will protect me.

مُّتَفَرِّقَةٖۖ وَمَآ أُغۡنِي عَنكُم مِّنَ ٱللَّهِ مِن شَيۡءٍۖ إِنِ ٱلۡحُكۡمُ إِلَّا
لِلَّهِۖ عَلَيۡهِ تَوَكَّلۡتُۖ وَعَلَيۡهِ فَلۡيَتَوَكَّلِ ٱلۡمُتَوَكِّلُونَ ٦٧ وَلَمَّا
دَخَلُواْ مِنۡ حَيۡثُ أَمَرَهُمۡ أَبُوهُم مَّا كَانَ يُغۡنِي عَنۡهُم
مِّنَ ٱللَّهِ مِن شَيۡءٍ إِلَّا حَاجَةٗ فِي نَفۡسِ يَعۡقُوبَ قَضَىٰهَاۚ وَإِنَّهُۥ
لَذُو عِلۡمٖ لِّمَا عَلَّمۡنَٰهُ وَلَٰكِنَّ أَكۡثَرَ ٱلنَّاسِ لَا يَعۡلَمُونَ
٦٨ وَلَمَّا دَخَلُواْ عَلَىٰ يُوسُفَ ءَاوَىٰٓ إِلَيۡهِ أَخَاهُۖ قَالَ
إِنِّيٓ أَنَا۠ أَخُوكَ فَلَا تَبۡتَئِسۡ بِمَا كَانُواْ يَعۡمَلُونَ ٦٩
فَلَمَّا جَهَّزَهُم بِجَهَازِهِمۡ جَعَلَ ٱلسِّقَايَةَ فِي رَحۡلِ أَخِيهِ ثُمَّ
أَذَّنَ مُؤَذِّنٌ أَيَّتُهَا ٱلۡعِيرُ إِنَّكُمۡ لَسَٰرِقُونَ ٧٠ قَالُواْ وَأَقۡبَلُواْ
عَلَيۡهِم مَّاذَا تَفۡقِدُونَ ٧١ قَالُواْ نَفۡقِدُ صُوَاعَ ٱلۡمَلِكِ
وَلِمَن جَآءَ بِهِۦ حِمۡلُ بَعِيرٖ وَأَنَا۠ بِهِۦ زَعِيمٞ ٧٢ قَالُواْ تَٱللَّهِ
لَقَدۡ عَلِمۡتُم مَّا جِئۡنَا لِنُفۡسِدَ فِي ٱلۡأَرۡضِ وَمَا كُنَّا سَٰرِقِينَ
٧٣ قَالُواْ فَمَا جَزَٰٓؤُهُۥٓ إِن كُنتُمۡ كَٰذِبِينَ ٧٤ قَالُواْ جَزَٰٓؤُهُۥ
مَن وُجِدَ فِي رَحۡلِهِۦ فَهُوَ جَزَٰٓؤُهُۥۚ كَذَٰلِكَ نَجۡزِي ٱلظَّٰلِمِينَ
٧٥ فَبَدَأَ بِأَوۡعِيَتِهِمۡ قَبۡلَ وِعَآءِ أَخِيهِ ثُمَّ ٱسۡتَخۡرَجَهَا مِن
وِعَآءِ أَخِيهِۚ كَذَٰلِكَ كِدۡنَا لِيُوسُفَۖ مَا كَانَ لِيَأۡخُذَ أَخَاهُ
فِي دِينِ ٱلۡمَلِكِ إِلَّآ أَن يَشَآءَ ٱللَّهُۚ نَرۡفَعُ دَرَجَٰتٖ مَّن نَّشَآءُۗ
وَفَوۡقَ كُلِّ ذِي عِلۡمٍ عَلِيمٞ ٧٦ ۞ قَالُوٓاْ إِن يَسۡرِقۡ
فَقَدۡ سَرَقَ أَخٞ لَّهُۥ مِن قَبۡلُۚ فَأَسَرَّهَا يُوسُفُ فِي نَفۡسِهِۦ
وَلَمۡ يُبۡدِهَا لَهُمۡۚ قَالَ أَنتُمۡ شَرّٞ مَّكَانٗاۖ وَٱللَّهُ أَعۡلَمُ بِمَا

65. ***Then when they opened up their saddlebags and found their merchandise returned to them, they said, 'Our father, what more could we ask*** – what greater generosity from the king could we ask for than this? They addressed this to Ya'qūb, to point out how the king had honoured them. ***Here is our merchandise returned to us. We can provide our families with food, and guard our brother and get an extra load*** for him. ***That is an easy measure to obtain.*** It is easy for the king because he is generous.'

66. ***He said, 'I will not send him out with you until you make a covenant with Allah*** (swear an oath) ***to bring him home unless you are overwhelmed*** by being killed or defeated so that you cannot bring him.' They did as he asked. ***When they had made their covenant*** concerning that, ***he said, 'Allah is Guardian over what we say.'*** So he sent him with them.

67. ***He said, 'My sons, you must not enter*** Egypt ***through a single gate. Go in through different gates*** – so that no one sentry sees you all. ***But I cannot save you from Allah at all*** in respect of what He has decreed for you by saying that, ***for judgement comes from no one but Allah.*** It is just because of the great compassion I feel for you. ***In Him I put my trust, and let all those who put their trust, put it in Him alone.'***

68. Allah continues: ***But when they entered*** by different gates ***as their father said, it did not save them from*** the decree of ***Allah at all, yet a need in Ya'qūb's soul was satisfied.*** His compassion made him want to avert the attention of the sentries from them. ***He had knowledge which We had taught him, but most of mankind*** (the unbelievers) ***simply do not know*** about Allah's inspiration to His friends.

69. ***Then when they entered into Yūsuf's presence, he drew his brother close to him*** – embracing him – ***and said, 'I am your brother. Do not be distressed concerning all the things they used to do*** out of envy towards us.' He ordered him not to tell them and to remain with him, and that he would contrive a way for him to stay with him.

70. ***Then when he had supplied them with their needs, he put the goblet*** – a gold vessel encrusted with gems – ***in his brother's***

(Binyāmīn's) ***bag. A herald called out,*** when they had left the assembly of Yūsuf, ***'Caravan! You are thieves!'***

71. ***They turned to them and asked, 'What are you missing?'***

72. ***They said, 'We are missing the goblet of the king. The man who brings it will get a camel's load*** of food. ***Of that I stand as guarantor.'***

73. ***They said, 'By Allah, you know we did not come to corrupt the land and that we are not thieves.*** We have never stolen."' This is an oath which implies amazement and surprise.

74. ***They*** (the herald and his fellows) ***said, 'What is the reparation for it*** – what should be done with the thief – ***if it in fact transpires that you are liars*** about being thieves and the goblet is found in your possession***?'***

75. ***They said, 'Its reparation shall be him in the saddlebags of whom it is discovered*** (the thief)***. Among us that is how wrongdoers are repaid.'*** The thief would be enslaved on account of his theft: that was the custom of the family of Ya'qūb in case of theft. They told Yūsuf that he should search their bags.

76. ***He started with their bags before his brother's*** and searched them so that they would not suspect anything – ***and then produced it*** (the goblet) ***from his brother's bag.*** Allah continues: ***In that way We devised a cunning scheme for Yūsuf*** – We taught him a means of taking his brother. ***He could not have held his brother*** – as a slave for theft ***according to the statutes of the King*** in the law of the king of Egypt, because the penalty for theft was beating and being liable for the equivalent of the object stolen, not enslavement: ***only because Allah had willed it so.*** Allah willed that he take him by the judgement of his own tribe. This means that the only way he could take him was by Allah inspiring him to question his brothers, who answered according to their custom. ***We raise the rank of anyone We will*** – such as Yūsuf. ***Over everyone with knowledge*** in creation ***is a Knower*** (Allah) who knows better than them.

77. ***They said, 'If he steals now, his brother*** Yūsuf ***stole before.'*** He had stole a gold idol belonging to his mother's father and broken it so that he would not worship it. ***But Yūsuf kept it to himself and still did not disclose it to them, saying*** to himself, ***'The plight that***

تَصِفُونَ ﴿٧٧﴾ قَالُوا۟ يَٰٓأَيُّهَا ٱلْعَزِيزُ إِنَّ لَهُۥٓ أَبًا شَيْخًا كَبِيرًا
فَخُذْ أَحَدَنَا مَكَانَهُۥٓ ۖ إِنَّا نَرَىٰكَ مِنَ ٱلْمُحْسِنِينَ ﴿٧٨﴾
قَالَ مَعَاذَ ٱللَّهِ أَن نَّأْخُذَ إِلَّا مَن وَجَدْنَا مَتَٰعَنَا عِندَهُۥٓ إِنَّآ
إِذًا لَّظَٰلِمُونَ ﴿٧٩﴾ فَلَمَّا ٱسْتَيْـَٔسُوا۟ مِنْهُ خَلَصُوا۟ نَجِيًّا ۖ
قَالَ كَبِيرُهُمْ أَلَمْ تَعْلَمُوٓا۟ أَنَّ أَبَاكُمْ قَدْ أَخَذَ عَلَيْكُم
مَّوْثِقًا مِّنَ ٱللَّهِ وَمِن قَبْلُ مَا فَرَّطتُمْ فِى يُوسُفَ ۖ فَلَنْ أَبْرَحَ
ٱلْأَرْضَ حَتَّىٰ يَأْذَنَ لِىٓ أَبِىٓ أَوْ يَحْكُمَ ٱللَّهُ لِى ۖ وَهُوَ خَيْرُ ٱلْحَٰكِمِينَ
﴿٨٠﴾ ٱرْجِعُوٓا۟ إِلَىٰٓ أَبِيكُمْ فَقُولُوا۟ يَٰٓأَبَانَآ إِنَّ ٱبْنَكَ سَرَقَ
وَمَا شَهِدْنَآ إِلَّا بِمَا عَلِمْنَا وَمَا كُنَّا لِلْغَيْبِ حَٰفِظِينَ
﴿٨١﴾ وَسْـَٔلِ ٱلْقَرْيَةَ ٱلَّتِى كُنَّا فِيهَا وَٱلْعِيرَ ٱلَّتِىٓ أَقْبَلْنَا فِيهَا ۖ
وَإِنَّا لَصَٰدِقُونَ ﴿٨٢﴾ قَالَ بَلْ سَوَّلَتْ لَكُمْ أَنفُسُكُمْ أَمْرًا ۖ
فَصَبْرٌ جَمِيلٌ ۖ عَسَى ٱللَّهُ أَن يَأْتِيَنِى بِهِمْ جَمِيعًا ۚ إِنَّهُۥ هُوَ
ٱلْعَلِيمُ ٱلْحَكِيمُ ﴿٨٣﴾ وَتَوَلَّىٰ عَنْهُمْ وَقَالَ يَٰٓأَسَفَىٰ عَلَىٰ
يُوسُفَ وَٱبْيَضَّتْ عَيْنَاهُ مِنَ ٱلْحُزْنِ فَهُوَ كَظِيمٌ ﴿٨٤﴾
قَالُوا۟ تَٱللَّهِ تَفْتَؤُا۟ تَذْكُرُ يُوسُفَ حَتَّىٰ تَكُونَ حَرَضًا
أَوْ تَكُونَ مِنَ ٱلْهَٰلِكِينَ ﴿٨٥﴾ قَالَ إِنَّمَآ أَشْكُوا۟ بَثِّى
وَحُزْنِىٓ إِلَى ٱللَّهِ وَأَعْلَمُ مِنَ ٱللَّهِ مَا لَا تَعْلَمُونَ ﴿٨٦﴾
يَٰبَنِىَّ ٱذْهَبُوا۟ فَتَحَسَّسُوا۟ مِن يُوسُفَ وَأَخِيهِ وَلَا تَا۟يْـَٔسُوا۟
مِن رَّوْحِ ٱللَّهِ ۖ إِنَّهُۥ لَا يَا۟يْـَٔسُ مِن رَّوْحِ ٱللَّهِ إِلَّا ٱلْقَوْمُ ٱلْكَٰفِرُونَ
﴿٨٧﴾ فَلَمَّا دَخَلُوا۟ عَلَيْهِ قَالُوا۟ يَٰٓأَيُّهَا ٱلْعَزِيزُ مَسَّنَا وَأَهْلَنَا ٱلضُّرُّ
وَجِئْنَا بِبِضَٰعَةٍ مُّزْجَىٰةٍ فَأَوْفِ لَنَا ٱلْكَيْلَ وَتَصَدَّقْ عَلَيْنَآ ۖ

you are in is worse than that – worse than that of Yūsuf and his brother, since you stole your brother from his father and wronged him. ***Allah knows best the matter you describe.'***

78. ***They said, 'Your Eminence, he has an old and venerable father*** who loves him more than he loves us and is consoled by him for his lost son; and it would grieve him to be parted from him, ***so take one of us*** to enslave ***instead of him. We see without a doubt that you are of the people who do good.'***

79. ***He said, 'Allah forbid that we should take anyone but him with whom our goods were found*** – he did not say, "The one who stole" to avoid telling a lie. ***In that case*** – if we took someone else – ***we would clearly be wrongdoers.'***

80. ***When they despaired of him, they went apart to talk alone*** among themselves. ***The eldest of them*** (Rubīl or Yahūdhā) ***said, 'You know full well your father had you make a covenant with Allah concerning this*** (your brother) ***and how before you failed him with Yūsuf. I will not leave this land*** of Egypt ***until I have permission from my father*** to return to him ***or Allah decides about the case on my behalf*** by releasing my brother. ***Truly He is the justest Judge of all.***

81. ***Return now to your father and say to him, "Your son stole, father. We can do no more than testify to what we know*** – since we certainly witnessed the discovery of the goblet in his bag – ***and we are not the guardians of the Unseen.*** We do not know what had happened when we offered the security. If we had known that he was a thief, we would not have taken him with us."

82. ***Ask questions of the town in which we were*** in Egypt – in other words, send someone to its people and ask them – ***and of the*** people of the ***caravan in which we came*** – who were people of Canaan – ***for we are surely telling you the truth."'*** They went to their father and told him that.

83. ***He said, 'It is merely that your lower selves suggested*** – and made seem attractive to you – ***something to you which you did.*** He suspected them because of what had happened before with Yūsuf. ***But beauty lies in*** my ***having steadfastness. Perhaps Allah will***

bring them (Yūsuf and his brothers) ***all together. He is indeed All-Knowing*** of my state ***and All-Wise*** in what He does.'

84. ***He*** stopped speaking to them and ***turned himself away from them and said, 'What anguish is my sorrow for Yūsuf!' And then his eyes turned white from hidden grief*** due to the intensity of weeping because of his deep sorrow. The word used, *kaẓīm,* describes someone who is suffering intense sorrow and grief but does not show it.

85. ***They said, 'By Allah, you will not ever cease to mention Yūsuf, till you waste away*** – and are at the point of death owing to the length of your illness – ***or are among the people of the grave!'***

86. ***He said*** to them, ***'I make complaint about my grief*** (the word used *bathth* means an immense sorrow which cannot normally be borne without telling people about it) ***and sorrow to Allah alone*** and none other, ***because*** – He is the only One who can answer my complaint, and ***I know things from Allah you do not know*** about the dream of Yūsuf which was true; and so he had to be alive for it to be fulfilled. Then Ya'qūb said:

87. ***My sons, seek news of Yūsuf and his brother. Do not despair of solace*** (mercy) ***from Allah. No one despairs of solace from Allah except for people who are unbelievers.'*** So they went towards Egypt looking for news of Yūsuf.

88. ***So when they came into his presence, they said, 'Your Eminence, hardship*** (hunger) ***has hit us and our families. We bring scant merchandise*** – which would normally be refused by people who saw it: some debased dirhams and similar things – ***but fill the measure for us generously*** in spite of the poorness of our goods. ***Allah always rewards a generous giver.'*** Allah rewards the generous, singles them out, bestows His mercy on them and removes the veil between Himself and them.

89. ***He said,*** to rebuke them, ***'Are you aware of what you did to Yūsuf*** – their beating and selling of him – ***and his brother*** – their wronging of him after his brother had left – ***in ignorance?*** You were ignorant of what happened to Yūsuf.'

90. ***They said*** – after they recognised him and his qualities became clear to them, asking this to confirm it – ***'Are you Yūsuf?' He said,***

إِنَّ ٱللَّهَ يَجۡزِي ٱلۡمُتَصَدِّقِينَ ﴿٨٨﴾ قَالَ هَلۡ عَلِمۡتُم مَّا فَعَلۡتُم
بِيُوسُفَ وَأَخِيهِ إِذۡ أَنتُمۡ جَٰهِلُونَ ﴿٨٩﴾ قَالُوٓاْ أَءِنَّكَ
لَأَنتَ يُوسُفُۖ قَالَ أَنَا۠ يُوسُفُ وَهَٰذَآ أَخِيۖ قَدۡ مَنَّ ٱللَّهُ
عَلَيۡنَآۖ إِنَّهُۥ مَن يَتَّقِ وَيَصۡبِرۡ فَإِنَّ ٱللَّهَ لَا يُضِيعُ أَجۡرَ
ٱلۡمُحۡسِنِينَ ﴿٩٠﴾ قَالُواْ تَٱللَّهِ لَقَدۡ ءَاثَرَكَ ٱللَّهُ عَلَيۡنَا
وَإِن كُنَّا لَخَٰطِـِٔينَ ﴿٩١﴾ قَالَ لَا تَثۡرِيبَ عَلَيۡكُمُ
ٱلۡيَوۡمَۖ يَغۡفِرُ ٱللَّهُ لَكُمۡۖ وَهُوَ أَرۡحَمُ ٱلرَّٰحِمِينَ ﴿٩٢﴾
ٱذۡهَبُواْ بِقَمِيصِي هَٰذَا فَأَلۡقُوهُ عَلَىٰ وَجۡهِ أَبِي يَأۡتِ بَصِيرٗا
وَأۡتُونِي بِأَهۡلِكُمۡ أَجۡمَعِينَ ﴿٩٣﴾ وَلَمَّا فَصَلَتِ
ٱلۡعِيرُ قَالَ أَبُوهُمۡ إِنِّي لَأَجِدُ رِيحَ يُوسُفَۖ لَوۡلَآ أَن
تُفَنِّدُونِ ﴿٩٤﴾ قَالُواْ تَٱللَّهِ إِنَّكَ لَفِي ضَلَٰلِكَ ٱلۡقَدِيمِ ﴿٩٥﴾
فَلَمَّآ أَن جَآءَ ٱلۡبَشِيرُ أَلۡقَىٰهُ عَلَىٰ وَجۡهِهِۦ فَٱرۡتَدَّ بَصِيرٗاۖ قَالَ
أَلَمۡ أَقُل لَّكُمۡ إِنِّيٓ أَعۡلَمُ مِنَ ٱللَّهِ مَا لَا تَعۡلَمُونَ ﴿٩٦﴾ قَالُواْ
يَٰٓأَبَانَا ٱسۡتَغۡفِرۡ لَنَا ذُنُوبَنَآ إِنَّا كُنَّا خَٰطِـِٔينَ ﴿٩٧﴾ قَالَ سَوۡفَ
أَسۡتَغۡفِرُ لَكُمۡ رَبِّيٓۖ إِنَّهُۥ هُوَ ٱلۡغَفُورُ ٱلرَّحِيمُ ﴿٩٨﴾ فَلَمَّا
دَخَلُواْ عَلَىٰ يُوسُفَ ءَاوَىٰٓ إِلَيۡهِ أَبَوَيۡهِ وَقَالَ ٱدۡخُلُواْ مِصۡرَ
إِن شَآءَ ٱللَّهُ ءَامِنِينَ ﴿٩٩﴾ وَرَفَعَ أَبَوَيۡهِ عَلَى ٱلۡعَرۡشِ وَخَرُّواْ
لَهُۥ سُجَّدٗاۖ وَقَالَ يَٰٓأَبَتِ هَٰذَا تَأۡوِيلُ رُءۡيَٰيَ مِن قَبۡلُ قَدۡ جَعَلَهَا
رَبِّي حَقّٗاۖ وَقَدۡ أَحۡسَنَ بِيٓ إِذۡ أَخۡرَجَنِي مِنَ ٱلسِّجۡنِ وَجَآءَ بِكُم
مِّنَ ٱلۡبَدۡوِ مِنۢ بَعۡدِ أَن نَّزَغَ ٱلشَّيۡطَٰنُ بَيۡنِي وَبَيۡنَ إِخۡوَتِيٓۚ إِنَّ

'I am indeed Yūsuf, and this here is my brother. Allah has acted graciously to us and blessed us by re-uniting us. ***As for those who fear Allah and are steadfast*** in respect of what befalls them. ***Allah does not allow to go to waste the wage of any people who do good.'***

91. ***They said, 'By Allah, Allah has favoured you*** and preferred you ***above us*** with sovereignty and other things. ***Clearly we were in the wrong*** in what we did to you, and so we are now humbled before you.*'*

92. ***He said, 'No blame at all will fall on you***; he said this because it was likely that there would be blame. ***Today you have forgiveness from Allah. He is the Most Merciful of the merciful.'*** He asked them about his father and they said that he had lost his sight. Then he said to them:

93. ***'Go with this shirt of mine*** – the shirt of Ibrāhīm, which he had been wearing when he was thrown into the fire, and which was with Yusuf in the well. It came from Paradise. Jibrīl had been commanded to send it and said that it contained the scent of Paradise, and when it is thrown on anyone suffering from an illness, he is cured – ***and cast it on my father's face, and he will see again. Then come to me with all your families.'***

94. ***And when the caravan went on its way*** and they left Egypt ***their father*** Ya'qūb ***said*** to those of his sons and grandchildren who were present, ***'I can smell Yūsuf's scent!*** He had caught scent of him on the wind by Allah's permission at a distance of seven or eight days or more. ***You probably think I have become senile*** and foolish.*'*

95. ***They said*** to him, ***'By Allah! Your mind is still astray.*** You are misled, because of your excessive love for him, into hoping to find him after all this time.'

96. ***But when the bringer of the good news came*** – Yahūdhā, who had brought Yūsuf's shirt with false blood, and who wanted to make him happy as he had made him sad – ***he cast it*** (the shirt) ***on his face and sight returned. He said, 'Did I not say to you before that I know things from Allah you do not know?'***

97. ***They said, 'Our father, may we be forgiven for all the many wrongs that we have done. We were indeed greatly mistaken.'***

رَبِّي لَطِيفٞ لِّمَا يَشَآءُۚ إِنَّهُۥ هُوَ ٱلۡعَلِيمُ ٱلۡحَكِيمُ ١٠٠ ۞ رَبِّ
قَدۡ ءَاتَيۡتَنِي مِنَ ٱلۡمُلۡكِ وَعَلَّمۡتَنِي مِن تَأۡوِيلِ ٱلۡأَحَادِيثِۚ فَاطِرَ
ٱلسَّمَٰوَٰتِ وَٱلۡأَرۡضِ أَنتَ وَلِيِّۦ فِي ٱلدُّنۡيَا وَٱلۡأٓخِرَةِۖ تَوَفَّنِي
مُسۡلِمٗا وَأَلۡحِقۡنِي بِٱلصَّٰلِحِينَ ١٠١ ذَٰلِكَ مِنۡ أَنۢبَآءِ ٱلۡغَيۡبِ
نُوحِيهِ إِلَيۡكَۖ وَمَا كُنتَ لَدَيۡهِمۡ إِذۡ أَجۡمَعُوٓاْ أَمۡرَهُمۡ وَهُمۡ يَمۡكُرُونَ
١٠٢ وَمَآ أَكۡثَرُ ٱلنَّاسِ وَلَوۡ حَرَصۡتَ بِمُؤۡمِنِينَ ١٠٣
وَمَا تَسۡـَٔلُهُمۡ عَلَيۡهِ مِنۡ أَجۡرٍۚ إِنۡ هُوَ إِلَّا ذِكۡرٞ لِّلۡعَٰلَمِينَ ١٠٤
وَكَأَيِّن مِّنۡ ءَايَةٖ فِي ٱلسَّمَٰوَٰتِ وَٱلۡأَرۡضِ يَمُرُّونَ عَلَيۡهَا
وَهُمۡ عَنۡهَا مُعۡرِضُونَ ١٠٥ وَمَا يُؤۡمِنُ أَكۡثَرُهُم بِٱللَّهِ إِلَّا
وَهُم مُّشۡرِكُونَ ١٠٦ أَفَأَمِنُوٓاْ أَن تَأۡتِيَهُمۡ غَٰشِيَةٞ مِّنۡ عَذَابِ ٱللَّهِ
أَوۡ تَأۡتِيَهُمُ ٱلسَّاعَةُ بَغۡتَةٗ وَهُمۡ لَا يَشۡعُرُونَ ١٠٧ قُلۡ هَٰذِهِۦ
سَبِيلِيٓ أَدۡعُوٓاْ إِلَى ٱللَّهِۚ عَلَىٰ بَصِيرَةٍ أَنَا۠ وَمَنِ ٱتَّبَعَنِيۖ وَسُبۡحَٰنَ
ٱللَّهِ وَمَآ أَنَا۠ مِنَ ٱلۡمُشۡرِكِينَ ١٠٨ وَمَآ أَرۡسَلۡنَا مِن قَبۡلِكَ
إِلَّا رِجَالٗا نُّوحِيٓ إِلَيۡهِم مِّنۡ أَهۡلِ ٱلۡقُرَىٰٓۗ أَفَلَمۡ يَسِيرُواْ فِي
ٱلۡأَرۡضِ فَيَنظُرُواْ كَيۡفَ كَانَ عَٰقِبَةُ ٱلَّذِينَ مِن قَبۡلِهِمۡۗ
وَلَدَارُ ٱلۡأٓخِرَةِ خَيۡرٞ لِّلَّذِينَ ٱتَّقَوۡاْۚ أَفَلَا تَعۡقِلُونَ ١٠٩ حَتَّىٰٓ
إِذَا ٱسۡتَيۡـَٔسَ ٱلرُّسُلُ وَظَنُّوٓاْ أَنَّهُمۡ قَدۡ كُذِبُواْ جَآءَهُمۡ
نَصۡرُنَا فَنُجِّيَ مَن نَّشَآءُۖ وَلَا يُرَدُّ بَأۡسُنَا عَنِ ٱلۡقَوۡمِ ٱلۡمُجۡرِمِينَ
١١٠ لَقَدۡ كَانَ فِي قَصَصِهِمۡ عِبۡرَةٞ لِّأُوْلِي ٱلۡأَلۡبَٰبِۗ مَا كَانَ
حَدِيثٗا يُفۡتَرَىٰ وَلَٰكِن تَصۡدِيقَ ٱلَّذِي بَيۡنَ يَدَيۡهِ
وَتَفۡصِيلَ كُلِّ شَيۡءٖ وَهُدٗى وَرَحۡمَةٗ لِّقَوۡمٖ يُؤۡمِنُونَ ١١١

98. ***He said, 'I will ask my Lord to pardon you. He is Ever-Forgiving, Most Merciful.'*** He delayed that supplication until dawn so that it would be more likely to be answered, or until Friday night. Then they went to Egypt and Yūsuf and the great men came out to meet them.

99. ***Then when they entered into Yūsuf's presence*** (his pavilion) ***he drew his parents*** (his father and mother or aunt) ***close to him*** (embraced them) ***and said*** to them, ***'Enter Egypt safe and sound, if Allah wills.'*** They entered and Yūsuf was sitting on his throne.

100. ***He raised his parents up onto the throne and*** – sitting them with him – ***the others*** – as well as his parents – ***fell prostrate in front of him.*** They prostrated to him by bowing low, not by actual prostration with the forehead on the ground. It was their greeting at that time. ***He said, 'My father, truly this is now the interpretation of the dream I had. My Lord has made it all come true; and He was kind to me by letting me out of prison*** – he did not mention the well out of generosity, so that his brothers would not be embarrassed – ***and brought you from the desert when Shayṭān had caused dissent*** and unsettled things ***between me and my brothers. My Lord is kind to anyone He wills. He is indeed All-Knowing*** of His creation ***and All-Wise*** in what He does.' His parents stayed with him for a further twenty-four or twenty-seven years. He had been apart from them for eighteen or forty or eighty years. When Ya'qūb died, Yūsuf ordered that he should be taken and buried with his father, Isḥāq. He took him himself and buried him there with him. Then he returned to Egypt and stayed there twenty-three years more. When his time was over and he knew that he would not live longer, his soul yearned for the Eternal King and he said:

101. ***'My Lord, You have granted soverignty to me and taught me the true meaning of events*** – how to interpret dreams. ***Originator*** (Creator) ***of the heavens and earth, You are my Friend in this world and the Next*** – You attend to my best interests – ***so take me as a Muslim at my death and join me to the people who are righteous*** among my ancestors.' He lived a week or more after that and died at the age of one hundred and twenty. The Egyptians placed him in a coffin of marble and buried him on the bank of the upper Nile so that the blessing would spread on its sides. Glory be to the One whose kingdom does not end.

102. ***This*** – what has been narrated about Yūsuf – ***is news of the Unseen*** that was unknown to you, Muḥammad, before – ***which We reveal to you. You were not with them*** (the brothers of Yūsuf) ***when they decided what to do*** – and plotted and resolved on it – ***and devised their scheme*** about him. You were not with them to know his story and be aware of it. Your knowledge of it comes from Revelation.

103. ***But most people***, including the people of Makka, ***for all your eagerness*** – for them to believe –***are not believers.***

104. ***You do not ask them for any wage for it*** (the Qur'an). ***It*** (the Qur'an) ***is only a reminder*** (a warning and admonition) ***to all beings.***

105. ***How many Signs there are in the heavens and earth*** that indicate the oneness of Allah which they witness***! Yet they pass them by, turning away from them*** and not reflecting on them.

106. ***Most of them do not believe in Allah*** – since they do not affirm that He is the Creator and Provider – ***without associating others with Him*** by worshipping other idols with him. That is why they used to say in the *talbiya*, "At Your service. You have no partner except a partner who is Yours. You rule him and he does not rule."

107. ***Do they feel secure that the all-enveloping punishment of Allah*** (His revenge) ***will not come upon them*** suddenly, ***or that the Last Hour will not come upon them all of a sudden when they least expect it?***

108. ***Say*** to them***: 'This is my way.*** It is that ***I call to*** the *dīn* of ***Allah with inner sight*** (clear proof) ***I and all who follow me*** and believe in me. ***Glory be to Allah!*** He is free of partners. ***I am not one of the idolaters.'***

109. ***We sent none before you but men inspired with revelation*** (read as *yuḥā* and *nuḥā* "We inspire") – not angels – ***from among the people of the cities.*** Cities are mentioned because the people in them are more knowledgeable and sensible than the people of the deserts, who are coarse and ignorant. ***Have they*** (the people of Makka) ***not travelled in the land and seen the final fate of those***

before them: the end and outcome of other peoples who were destroyed for their denial of their Messengers***? The abode of the Next World*** (the Garden) ***is better for those who are godfearing*** and fearful of Allah. ***So will you not use your intellect*** (read as *ta'qilūna* and *ya'qilūna*, "will they not use their intellect?")***?***

110. ***Then when the Messengers despaired and thought themselves denied*** (read as *kudhibū* and *kudhdhibū)* – in other words they thought that no one would believe in them and the nations thought that their Messengers would not have their promised help – ***Our help came to them, and those We willed were saved*** (read as *nujjiya* and *nunjī*). ***Our violent force*** (punishment) ***cannot be averted from people who are evildoers*** (the idolaters).

111. ***There is instruction in their stories*** (the stories of the Messengers) ***for people of intelligence. This*** Qur'an ***is not a narration which has been invented but confirmation of all*** Divine Books ***that came before, a clarification of everything*** that is necessary in the *dīn*, ***and a guidance*** away from misguidance ***and a mercy for people who believe.*** Those who believe are singled out for mention because they are the ones who benefit from the Qur'an and its contents.

سُورَةُ الرَّعْدِ

بِسْمِ ٱللَّهِ ٱلرَّحْمَٰنِ ٱلرَّحِيمِ

الٓمٓر ۚ تِلْكَ ءَايَٰتُ ٱلْكِتَٰبِ ۗ وَٱلَّذِىٓ أُنزِلَ إِلَيْكَ مِن رَّبِّكَ ٱلْحَقُّ
وَلَٰكِنَّ أَكْثَرَ ٱلنَّاسِ لَا يُؤْمِنُونَ ﴿١﴾ ٱللَّهُ ٱلَّذِى رَفَعَ ٱلسَّمَٰوَٰتِ بِغَيْرِ
عَمَدٍ تَرَوْنَهَا ۖ ثُمَّ ٱسْتَوَىٰ عَلَى ٱلْعَرْشِ ۖ وَسَخَّرَ ٱلشَّمْسَ وَٱلْقَمَرَ ۖ كُلٌّ
يَجْرِى لِأَجَلٍ مُّسَمًّى ۚ يُدَبِّرُ ٱلْأَمْرَ يُفَصِّلُ ٱلْءَايَٰتِ لَعَلَّكُم بِلِقَآءِ
رَبِّكُمْ تُوقِنُونَ ﴿٢﴾ وَهُوَ ٱلَّذِى مَدَّ ٱلْأَرْضَ وَجَعَلَ فِيهَا رَوَٰسِىَ
وَأَنْهَٰرًا ۖ وَمِن كُلِّ ٱلثَّمَرَٰتِ جَعَلَ فِيهَا زَوْجَيْنِ ٱثْنَيْنِ ۖ يُغْشِى ٱلَّيْلَ
ٱلنَّهَارَ ۚ إِنَّ فِى ذَٰلِكَ لَءَايَٰتٍ لِّقَوْمٍ يَتَفَكَّرُونَ ﴿٣﴾ وَفِى ٱلْأَرْضِ
قِطَعٌ مُّتَجَٰوِرَٰتٌ وَجَنَّٰتٌ مِّنْ أَعْنَٰبٍ وَزَرْعٌ وَنَخِيلٌ صِنْوَانٌ
وَغَيْرُ صِنْوَانٍ يُسْقَىٰ بِمَآءٍ وَٰحِدٍ وَنُفَضِّلُ بَعْضَهَا عَلَىٰ بَعْضٍ
فِى ٱلْأُكُلِ ۚ إِنَّ فِى ذَٰلِكَ لَءَايَٰتٍ لِّقَوْمٍ يَعْقِلُونَ ﴿٤﴾
۞ وَإِن تَعْجَبْ فَعَجَبٌ قَوْلُهُمْ أَءِذَا كُنَّا تُرَٰبًا أَءِنَّا لَفِى خَلْقٍ
جَدِيدٍ ۗ أُو۟لَٰٓئِكَ ٱلَّذِينَ كَفَرُوا۟ بِرَبِّهِمْ ۖ وَأُو۟لَٰٓئِكَ ٱلْأَغْلَٰلُ
فِىٓ أَعْنَاقِهِمْ ۖ وَأُو۟لَٰٓئِكَ أَصْحَٰبُ ٱلنَّارِ ۖ هُمْ فِيهَا خَٰلِدُونَ ﴿٥﴾
وَيَسْتَعْجِلُونَكَ بِٱلسَّيِّئَةِ قَبْلَ ٱلْحَسَنَةِ وَقَدْ خَلَتْ مِن
قَبْلِهِمُ ٱلْمَثُلَٰتُ ۗ وَإِنَّ رَبَّكَ لَذُو مَغْفِرَةٍ لِّلنَّاسِ عَلَىٰ ظُلْمِهِمْ ۖ
وَإِنَّ رَبَّكَ لَشَدِيدُ ٱلْعِقَابِ ﴿٦﴾ وَيَقُولُ ٱلَّذِينَ كَفَرُوا۟ لَوْلَآ
أُنزِلَ عَلَيْهِ ءَايَةٌ مِّن رَّبِّهِۦٓ ۗ إِنَّمَآ أَنتَ مُنذِرٌ ۖ وَلِكُلِّ قَوْمٍ هَادٍ
﴿٧﴾ ٱللَّهُ يَعْلَمُ مَا تَحْمِلُ كُلُّ أُنثَىٰ وَمَا تَغِيضُ ٱلْأَرْحَامُ

13. *Sūrat ar-Ra‘d*
Thunder

This *sūra* is Makkan except for the *āyats, "Those who disbelieve will not cease..."* (32) and *"Those who disbelieve say, 'You are not a Messenger.'"* (43); or else it is Madinan except for the two *āyats, "Even if there were a Qur'an ..."* (32-33). It has 43, 45, or 46 *āyats.*

1. ***Alif Lam Mim Ra.*** Allah knows best what the letters mean. ***Those are the Signs of the Book*** (the Qur'an)**.** ***And what has been sent down to you from your Lord*** (the Qur'an) ***is the Truth*** and there is no room for doubt regarding it, ***but most people*** – including the people of Makka – ***do not believe*** that it is from Allah Almighty**.**

2. ***Allah is He who raised up the heavens without any support*** – He tells the truth about it having no support ***you can see – and then established Himself firmly on the Throne*** in a manner which befits Him**.** ***He made the sun and moon subservient, each running*** in its own orbit ***for a specified term*** – up until the Day of Rising**.** ***He directs the whole affair*** – decreeing what will happen in His kingdom. ***He makes the Signs*** of His power ***clear so that perhaps you,*** people of Makka**,** ***will be certain about the meeting with your Lord*** at the Resurrection**.**

3. ***It is He who stretched out the earth and placed*** (created) ***firmly embedded mountains and rivers in it and made two types of every kind of fruit. He covers over day with*** the darkness of ***night. There are Signs*** of Allah's Oneness ***in that for people who reflect*** on the handiwork of Allah**.**

4. ***In the earth there are diverse regions side by side*** – different areas which adjoin one another; some are good, some saline, with little wind or much wind, all of which are among the signs of Allah's power – ***and gardens of grapes and cultivated fields, and palm-trees sharing one root*** – palm-trees which have a single root from which they branch out – ***and others with individual roots, all watered*** (read as *yusqā* and *tusqā*) ***with the same water. And We make some things better*** (read as *nufaḍḍilu* and *yufaḍḍilu*, "He makes") ***to eat*** (read as *ukul* and *ukl*) ***than others.*** Some things are sweet and some are bitter. ***There are Signs in that for people who use their intellect*** and ponder the creation.

5. ***If you***, Muḥammad, ***are surprised at their blindness*** – at how the unbelievers deny you – ***what could be more surprising than their words*** – which deny the Resurrection – ***'What, when*** (read as *a idhā* and *idhā*, without the interrogative particle) ***we are turned to dust, shall we then be created all anew?'*** That is because the One who is able to originate creation without any prior example is able to bring it back again. ***These are the people who disbelieve in their Lord. Such people have iron collars round their necks. Such people are the Companions of the Fire, remaining in it timelessly, for ever.***

6. The following was revealed when the unbelievers asked for the punishment to be hastened, out of mockery. ***They want you to hasten the bad*** (the punishment) ***rather than the good*** (mercy), ***when examples of punishment are there before them in the past. Your Lord has forgiveness for people for their wrongdoing;*** and if your Lord was not characterised by forgiveness, He would not leave any animal on the surface of the earth – ***but your Lord is also severe in retribution*** against those who disobey Him.

7. ***Those who disbelieve say, 'If only a Sign*** – such as the Staff of Mūsā, his White Hand, or the She-camel of Ṣāliḥ – ***could be sent down to him*** (Muḥammad) ***from his Lord!' You are only a warner***: your task is to alarm the unbelievers, not to bring Signs. ***Every people has a guide*** – a Prophet to call them to Allah with the Signs He gives him, not the ones they demand.

8. ***Allah knows what every female bears*** – every foetus, male or female, one or more, and all other things – ***and every shrinking of the womb*** after pregnancy ***and every swelling*** in pregnancy. ***Everything has its measure with Him***, an amount and a limit which it does not exceed,

9 ***...the Knower of the Unseen and the Visible, the Most Great, the High-Exalted*** (read as *muta'āli* and *muta'ālī*) – exalted over His creation by His power.

10 ***It makes no difference*** to His knowledge ***whether you keep secret what you say or voice it out loud, whether you hide in the*** darkness of the ***night or go out in the day.***

وَمَا تَزْدَادُ ۖ وَكُلُّ شَىْءٍ عِندَهُۥ بِمِقْدَارٍ ﴿٨﴾ عَٰلِمُ ٱلْغَيْبِ
وَٱلشَّهَٰدَةِ ٱلْكَبِيرُ ٱلْمُتَعَالِ ﴿٩﴾ سَوَآءٌ مِّنكُم مَّنْ أَسَرَّ
ٱلْقَوْلَ وَمَن جَهَرَ بِهِۦ وَمَنْ هُوَ مُسْتَخْفٍۭ بِٱلَّيْلِ وَسَارِبٌۢ
بِٱلنَّهَارِ ﴿١٠﴾ لَهُۥ مُعَقِّبَٰتٌ مِّنۢ بَيْنِ يَدَيْهِ وَمِنْ خَلْفِهِۦ يَحْفَظُونَهُۥ
مِنْ أَمْرِ ٱللَّهِ ۗ إِنَّ ٱللَّهَ لَا يُغَيِّرُ مَا بِقَوْمٍ حَتَّىٰ يُغَيِّرُوا۟ مَا بِأَنفُسِهِمْ ۗ
وَإِذَآ أَرَادَ ٱللَّهُ بِقَوْمٍ سُوٓءًا فَلَا مَرَدَّ لَهُۥ ۚ وَمَا لَهُم مِّن دُونِهِۦ مِن
وَالٍ ﴿١١﴾ هُوَ ٱلَّذِى يُرِيكُمُ ٱلْبَرْقَ خَوْفًا وَطَمَعًا
وَيُنشِئُ ٱلسَّحَابَ ٱلثِّقَالَ ﴿١٢﴾ وَيُسَبِّحُ ٱلرَّعْدُ بِحَمْدِهِۦ
وَٱلْمَلَٰٓئِكَةُ مِنْ خِيفَتِهِۦ وَيُرْسِلُ ٱلصَّوَٰعِقَ فَيُصِيبُ بِهَا
مَن يَشَآءُ وَهُمْ يُجَٰدِلُونَ فِى ٱللَّهِ وَهُوَ شَدِيدُ ٱلْمِحَالِ ﴿١٣﴾
لَهُۥ دَعْوَةُ ٱلْحَقِّ ۖ وَٱلَّذِينَ يَدْعُونَ مِن دُونِهِۦ لَا يَسْتَجِيبُونَ لَهُم بِشَىْءٍ إِلَّا
كَبَٰسِطِ كَفَّيْهِ إِلَى ٱلْمَآءِ لِيَبْلُغَ فَاهُ وَمَا هُوَ بِبَٰلِغِهِۦ ۚ وَمَا دُعَآءُ ٱلْكَٰفِرِينَ
إِلَّا فِى ضَلَٰلٍ ﴿١٤﴾ وَلِلَّهِ يَسْجُدُ مَن فِى ٱلسَّمَٰوَٰتِ وَٱلْأَرْضِ طَوْعًا
وَكَرْهًا وَظِلَٰلُهُم بِٱلْغُدُوِّ وَٱلْءَاصَالِ ۩ ﴿١٥﴾ قُلْ مَن رَّبُّ ٱلسَّمَٰوَٰتِ
وَٱلْأَرْضِ قُلِ ٱللَّهُ ۚ قُلْ أَفَٱتَّخَذْتُم مِّن دُونِهِۦٓ أَوْلِيَآءَ لَا يَمْلِكُونَ لِأَنفُسِهِمْ
نَفْعًا وَلَا ضَرًّا ۚ قُلْ هَلْ يَسْتَوِى ٱلْأَعْمَىٰ وَٱلْبَصِيرُ أَمْ هَلْ تَسْتَوِى
ٱلظُّلُمَٰتُ وَٱلنُّورُ ۗ أَمْ جَعَلُوا۟ لِلَّهِ شُرَكَآءَ خَلَقُوا۟ كَخَلْقِهِۦ فَتَشَٰبَهَ ٱلْخَلْقُ
عَلَيْهِمْ ۚ قُلِ ٱللَّهُ خَٰلِقُ كُلِّ شَىْءٍ وَهُوَ ٱلْوَٰحِدُ ٱلْقَهَّٰرُ ﴿١٦﴾ أَنزَلَ مِنَ
ٱلسَّمَآءِ مَآءً فَسَالَتْ أَوْدِيَةٌۢ بِقَدَرِهَا فَٱحْتَمَلَ ٱلسَّيْلُ زَبَدًا رَّابِيًا ۚ
وَمِمَّا يُوقِدُونَ عَلَيْهِ فِى ٱلنَّارِ ٱبْتِغَآءَ حِلْيَةٍ أَوْ مَتَٰعٍ زَبَدٌ مِّثْلُهُۥ ۚ كَذَٰلِكَ

11. ***Everyone*** – every human being – ***has a succession of angels in front of him and behind him, guarding him by Allah's command*** – from jinn and other things. ***Allah never changes a people's state*** – and removes blessings from them – ***until they change what is in themselves*** – exchange their good state for disobedience. ***When Allah desires evil*** (disobedience) ***for a people, there is no averting it*** (His punishment or anything else). ***They have no protector apart from Him.*** If Allah desires evil for them, who can defend them from Him.

12. ***It is He Who shows you the lightning, striking fear*** into travellers because of the lightning bolts ***and bringing hope*** to those who are resident and desire rain***; it is He Who heaps up*** and creates ***the heavy clouds*** which bring the rain.

13. ***The thunder*** – which is an angel who is entrusted with the clouds and drives them along – ***glorifies His praise*** – saying, "Glory be to Allah and with His praise!" – ***as do the angels, out of fear of Him. He discharges the thunderbolts*** – flashes of fire which emerges from the clouds – ***striking with them anyone He wills*** and burning whomever Allah wishes. This was revealed about a man to whom the Prophet, may Allah bless him and grant him peace, sent someone to call him to Allah. He asked, "Who is the Messenger of Allah? What is Allah? Is He made of gold, silver or brass?" So Allah sent down a thunderbolt and it took the top of his head off. ***Yet still they*** (the unbelievers) ***argue about Allah*** – with the Prophet, may Allah bless him and grant him peace – ***when He is inexorable in His power!*** The unbelievers still argue although the power and seizing of Allah is unstoppable.

14. ***The call of truth*** – the words, "There is no god but Allah" – ***is made to Him alone. Those*** (the idols) ***they call upon*** (read as *yad'ūna* and *tad'ūna* "you call upon") ***apart from Him do not respond to them at all*** in respect of what they ask for. ***It is like someone stretching out his cupped hands towards water*** at the top of a well, hoping ***to*** thereby ***convey it*** (the water) ***to his mouth: it will never get there.*** Just as the water will never reach a person's mouth by that means, so the idols will never answer their prayers. ***The call of the unbelievers*** – a reference to their worship of idols or their actual supplication – ***only goes astray.***

يَضْرِبُ ٱللَّهُ ٱلْحَقَّ وَٱلْبَٰطِلَ ۚ فَأَمَّا ٱلزَّبَدُ فَيَذْهَبُ جُفَآءً ۖ وَأَمَّا مَا
يَنفَعُ ٱلنَّاسَ فَيَمْكُثُ فِى ٱلْأَرْضِ ۚ كَذَٰلِكَ يَضْرِبُ ٱللَّهُ ٱلْأَمْثَالَ ﴿١٧﴾
لِلَّذِينَ ٱسْتَجَابُوا۟ لِرَبِّهِمُ ٱلْحُسْنَىٰ ۚ وَٱلَّذِينَ لَمْ يَسْتَجِيبُوا۟ لَهُۥ
لَوْ أَنَّ لَهُم مَّا فِى ٱلْأَرْضِ جَمِيعًا وَمِثْلَهُۥ مَعَهُۥ لَٱفْتَدَوْا۟ بِهِۦٓ ۚ
أُو۟لَٰٓئِكَ لَهُمْ سُوٓءُ ٱلْحِسَابِ وَمَأْوَىٰهُمْ جَهَنَّمُ ۖ وَبِئْسَ ٱلْمِهَادُ ﴿١٨﴾
۞ أَفَمَن يَعْلَمُ أَنَّمَآ أُنزِلَ إِلَيْكَ مِن رَّبِّكَ ٱلْحَقُّ كَمَنْ هُوَ أَعْمَىٰٓ ۚ إِنَّمَا يَتَذَكَّرُ
أُو۟لُوا۟ ٱلْأَلْبَٰبِ ﴿١٩﴾ ٱلَّذِينَ يُوفُونَ بِعَهْدِ ٱللَّهِ وَلَا يَنقُضُونَ ٱلْمِيثَٰقَ
﴿٢٠﴾ وَٱلَّذِينَ يَصِلُونَ مَآ أَمَرَ ٱللَّهُ بِهِۦٓ أَن يُوصَلَ وَيَخْشَوْنَ رَبَّهُمْ
وَيَخَافُونَ سُوٓءَ ٱلْحِسَابِ ﴿٢١﴾ وَٱلَّذِينَ صَبَرُوا۟ ٱبْتِغَآءَ وَجْهِ رَبِّهِمْ
وَأَقَامُوا۟ ٱلصَّلَوٰةَ وَأَنفَقُوا۟ مِمَّا رَزَقْنَٰهُمْ سِرًّا وَعَلَانِيَةً وَيَدْرَءُونَ
بِٱلْحَسَنَةِ ٱلسَّيِّئَةَ أُو۟لَٰٓئِكَ لَهُمْ عُقْبَى ٱلدَّارِ ﴿٢٢﴾ جَنَّٰتُ عَدْنٍ يَدْخُلُونَهَا
وَمَن صَلَحَ مِنْ ءَابَآئِهِمْ وَأَزْوَٰجِهِمْ وَذُرِّيَّٰتِهِمْ ۖ وَٱلْمَلَٰٓئِكَةُ يَدْخُلُونَ
عَلَيْهِم مِّن كُلِّ بَابٍ ﴿٢٣﴾ سَلَٰمٌ عَلَيْكُم بِمَا صَبَرْتُمْ ۚ فَنِعْمَ عُقْبَى ٱلدَّارِ
﴿٢٤﴾ وَٱلَّذِينَ يَنقُضُونَ عَهْدَ ٱللَّهِ مِنۢ بَعْدِ مِيثَٰقِهِۦ وَيَقْطَعُونَ مَآ
أَمَرَ ٱللَّهُ بِهِۦٓ أَن يُوصَلَ وَيُفْسِدُونَ فِى ٱلْأَرْضِ ۙ أُو۟لَٰٓئِكَ لَهُمُ ٱللَّعْنَةُ
وَلَهُمْ سُوٓءُ ٱلدَّارِ ﴿٢٥﴾ ٱللَّهُ يَبْسُطُ ٱلرِّزْقَ لِمَن يَشَآءُ وَيَقْدِرُ ۚ وَفَرِحُوا۟
بِٱلْحَيَوٰةِ ٱلدُّنْيَا وَمَا ٱلْحَيَوٰةُ ٱلدُّنْيَا فِى ٱلْءَاخِرَةِ إِلَّا مَتَٰعٌ ﴿٢٦﴾ وَيَقُولُ
ٱلَّذِينَ كَفَرُوا۟ لَوْلَآ أُنزِلَ عَلَيْهِ ءَايَةٌ مِّن رَّبِّهِۦ ۗ قُلْ إِنَّ ٱللَّهَ يُضِلُّ
مَن يَشَآءُ وَيَهْدِىٓ إِلَيْهِ مَنْ أَنَابَ ﴿٢٧﴾ ٱلَّذِينَ ءَامَنُوا۟ وَتَطْمَئِنُّ

15. ***Everyone in heaven and earth prostrates to Allah, willingly*** – referring to the believers – ***or unwillingly*** – referring to the hypocrites and those who are compelled to do so by the sword, ***as do their shadows in the morning and the evening.***

16. ***Say***, Muḥammad, to your people: ***'Who is the Lord of the heavens and the earth?'*** If they do not answer, there is only one possible answer, so ***Say*** to them: ***'Allah.' Say: 'So why have you taken protectors apart from Him*** – a reference to the idols which they worship – ***who possess no power to help or harm themselves?'*** Do you worship them and abandon their Creator? This question is to rebuke them. ***Say: 'Are the blind*** (the unbelievers) ***and the seeing*** (the believers) ***equal? Or are darkness*** (unbelief) ***and light*** (belief) ***the same?*** They are not. ***Or have they assigned partners to Allah who create as He creates, so that all creating seems the same to them?'*** Have their idols created in the way that Allah creates, so that all of them seem to them to be worthy of worship? The question implies a negative response, meaning that things are not like that. Only the true Creator deserves to be worshipped. ***Say: 'Allah is the Creator of everything.*** Allah has no partner in His creation and so He has no partner in worship. ***He is the One, the All-Conquering*** over His slaves.'

17. Then Allah makes a metaphor of truth and falsehood. ***He*** (Allah) ***sends down water from the sky*** (rain) ***and river-beds fill up and flow according to their size, and the floodwater carries with it an increasing layer of scum*** on its surface. ***A similar kind of scum comes from what they heat up*** (read as *yuqidūna* and *tuqidūna*, "you heat up") ***in the fire*** – a reference to minerals such as gold, silver and copper – ***when you desire to make jewellery or other things*** – such as utensils like vessels cast from molten metal. The scum on the melted metal resembles the scum found on floodwater. ***That is how Allah depicts the true and the false*** and makes a metaphor of them. ***As for the scum*** on the floodwater and melting metals, ***it is quickly swept away*** just as falsehood is swept away and discarded. ***But as for that which is of use to people*** – a reference to good water and pure metal – ***it remains behind in the ground*** for a time. In the same way falsehood disappears and vanishes, even if it appears to cover the truth at certain times, whereas the truth is firm and remains behind. ***That is a metaphor which Allah has made*** to make things clear.

18. ***Those who respond to their Lord*** by obeying Him (the believers) ***will receive the best*** (the Garden). ***But as for those who do not respond to Him*** (the unbelievers), ***even if they owned everything on the earth and the same again with it, they would offer it as a ransom*** from the punishment. ***They will receive an evil Reckoning***, that of being taken to task for all that they did and not forgiven for any of it. ***Their shelter will be Hell. What an evil resting-place!***

19. The following was revealed about Abū Jahl. ***Is he who knows that what has been sent down to you from your Lord*** and believes that it ***is the truth like him who is blind?*** Abū Jahl did not know it and did not believe in it. ***It is only people of intelligence who pay*** **heed** and respond to admonishment*:*

20. ***...those who fulfil Allah's contract*** – the one which was made with them in the world of spirits; or it may mean any contract – ***and do not break their agreement*** by not believing or by abandoning the obligations*;*

21. ***...those who join what Allah has commanded to be joined*** – referring to belief, kinship and other things – ***and are afraid of*** the threat of ***their Lord, and fear an evil Reckoning;***

22. ***...those who are steadfast*** – in respect of obedience and in the face of affliction and in terms of avoiding disobedience – ***in seeking the face of their Lord*** and not merely the goods of this world, ***and establish the prayer and spend*** – in obedience to Allah – ***from the provision We have given them, secretly and openly, and stave off evil with good*** by facing ignorance with forbearance and harm with steadfastness. ***It is they who will have the Ultimate Abode*** – the praiseworthy outcome in the Next World*:*

23. ***Gardens of Eden which they will enter, and all of their parents, wives and children who were righteous*** and believed – even if they did not do the same action as they did, they will be in their ranks to honour them. ***Angels will enter in to welcome them from every gate*** of the Garden – or at the gates of their palaces in the Garden when they enter them – to congratulate them.

24. They will say, ***'Peace be upon you because of your steadfast - ness*** in the world***! How wonderful is the Ultimate Abode!'***

25. *But as for those who break Allah's contract after it has been agreed and sever what Allah has commanded to be joined, and cause corruption in the earth* by unbelief and committing acts of disobedience, ***the curse*** – distance from the mercy of Allah – ***will be upon them. They will have the Evil Abode*** in the Next World (Hellfire).

26. *Allah expands provision to anyone He wills and restricts it* for anyone He wills**. *They*** (the people of Makka) ***rejoice*** arrogantly ***in the life of this world*** and the worldly things they have acquired**. *Yet the life of this world, compared to the Next World, is only fleeting enjoyment*** which will soon disappear.

27. *Those who disbelieve* among the people of Makka ***say, 'Why has a Sign*** – such as the Staff of Mūsā, his White Hand or the She-camel of Ṣāliḥ – ***not been sent down to him*** *(Muḥammad)* ***from his Lord?' Say*** to them***: 'Allah misguides whomever He wills*** – and the Signs would not help them to guidance to His *dīn* at all – ***and guides to Himself*** – to His *dīn* – ***all who turn*** back **to *Him:***

28. *...those who believe and whose hearts find peace in the remembrance of Allah* (His promise)**. *Truly in the remembrance of Allah the hearts*** of the believer ***can find peace.'***

29. *Those who believe and do right actions, happiness* – the word used here, *ṭūbā,* is a verbal noun from *ṭayyib* (good). It is said to refer to a tree in the Garden, in whose shade a rider can ride for a hundred years – ***will be theirs and a wonderful Homecoming.***

30. *In the same way* as We sent Prophets before you, ***We have sent you among a nation before which other nations passed away, to recite to them what We have revealed to you*** (the Qur'an)**. *Yet they still disbelieve in the All-Merciful.*** When they are commanded to prostrate to the All-Merciful, they say, "What is the All-Merciful?" ***Say*** to them, Muḥammad***: 'He is my Lord; there is no god but Him. I put my trust in Him and I turn to Him.'***

31. This *āyat* was revealed when they said to him, "If you are a Prophet, then make the mountains of Makka move away from us and make rivers and springs flow in it so that we can plant and cultivate,

قُلُوبُهُم بِذِكۡرِ ٱللَّهِۗ أَلَا بِذِكۡرِ ٱللَّهِ تَطۡمَئِنُّ ٱلۡقُلُوبُ ٢٨
ٱلَّذِينَ ءَامَنُواْ وَعَمِلُواْ ٱلصَّٰلِحَٰتِ طُوبَىٰ لَهُمۡ وَحُسۡنُ
مَـَٔابٖ ٢٩ كَذَٰلِكَ أَرۡسَلۡنَٰكَ فِيٓ أُمَّةٖ قَدۡ خَلَتۡ مِن قَبۡلِهَآ أُمَمٞ
لِّتَتۡلُوَاْ عَلَيۡهِمُ ٱلَّذِيٓ أَوۡحَيۡنَآ إِلَيۡكَ وَهُمۡ يَكۡفُرُونَ بِٱلرَّحۡمَٰنِۚ
قُلۡ هُوَ رَبِّي لَآ إِلَٰهَ إِلَّا هُوَ عَلَيۡهِ تَوَكَّلۡتُ وَإِلَيۡهِ مَتَابِ ٣٠
وَلَوۡ أَنَّ قُرۡءَانٗا سُيِّرَتۡ بِهِ ٱلۡجِبَالُ أَوۡ قُطِّعَتۡ بِهِ ٱلۡأَرۡضُ أَوۡ كُلِّمَ
بِهِ ٱلۡمَوۡتَىٰۗ بَل لِّلَّهِ ٱلۡأَمۡرُ جَمِيعًاۗ أَفَلَمۡ يَاْيۡـَٔسِ ٱلَّذِينَ ءَامَنُوٓاْ
أَن لَّوۡ يَشَآءُ ٱللَّهُ لَهَدَى ٱلنَّاسَ جَمِيعٗاۗ وَلَا يَزَالُ ٱلَّذِينَ كَفَرُواْ
تُصِيبُهُم بِمَا صَنَعُواْ قَارِعَةٌ أَوۡ تَحُلُّ قَرِيبٗا مِّن دَارِهِمۡ حَتَّىٰ يَأۡتِيَ
وَعۡدُ ٱللَّهِۚ إِنَّ ٱللَّهَ لَا يُخۡلِفُ ٱلۡمِيعَادَ ٣١ وَلَقَدِ ٱسۡتُهۡزِئَ بِرُسُلٖ
مِّن قَبۡلِكَ فَأَمۡلَيۡتُ لِلَّذِينَ كَفَرُواْ ثُمَّ أَخَذۡتُهُمۡۖ فَكَيۡفَ كَانَ
عِقَابِ ٣٢ أَفَمَنۡ هُوَ قَآئِمٌ عَلَىٰ كُلِّ نَفۡسِۢ بِمَا كَسَبَتۡۗ وَجَعَلُواْ
لِلَّهِ شُرَكَآءَ قُلۡ سَمُّوهُمۡۚ أَمۡ تُنَبِّـُٔونَهُۥ بِمَا لَا يَعۡلَمُ فِي ٱلۡأَرۡضِ أَم
بِظَٰهِرٖ مِّنَ ٱلۡقَوۡلِۗ بَلۡ زُيِّنَ لِلَّذِينَ كَفَرُواْ مَكۡرُهُمۡ وَصُدُّواْ عَنِ
ٱلسَّبِيلِۗ وَمَن يُضۡلِلِ ٱللَّهُ فَمَا لَهُۥ مِنۡ هَادٖ ٣٣ لَّهُمۡ عَذَابٞ فِي ٱلۡحَيَوٰةِ
ٱلدُّنۡيَاۖ وَلَعَذَابُ ٱلۡأٓخِرَةِ أَشَقُّۖ وَمَا لَهُم مِّنَ ٱللَّهِ مِن وَاقٖ ٣٤
۞ مَّثَلُ ٱلۡجَنَّةِ ٱلَّتِي وُعِدَ ٱلۡمُتَّقُونَۖ تَجۡرِي مِن تَحۡتِهَا ٱلۡأَنۡهَٰرُۖ
أُكُلُهَا دَآئِمٞ وَظِلُّهَاۚ تِلۡكَ عُقۡبَى ٱلَّذِينَ ٱتَّقَواْۖ وَّعُقۡبَى
ٱلۡكَٰفِرِينَ ٱلنَّارُ ٣٥ وَٱلَّذِينَ ءَاتَيۡنَٰهُمُ ٱلۡكِتَٰبَ يَفۡرَحُونَ
بِمَآ أُنزِلَ إِلَيۡكَۖ وَمِنَ ٱلۡأَحۡزَابِ مَن يُنكِرُ بَعۡضَهُۥۚ قُلۡ إِنَّمَآ أُمِرۡتُ

and resurrect for us our dead fathers to tell us that you are a Prophet. ***Even if there were a Qur'an which moved mountains*** from their places, ***or split the earth open or spoke to the dead*** by bringing the dead back to life, to make the people of Makka believe...***! On the contrary! The affair is Allah's altogether*** and belongs to no one else. Only those will believe whom He wishes to believe and not anyone else, even if He gives you what you demand. This was revealed when the Companions wanted to produce what the unbelievers asked for, out of desire for them to become believers. ***Do those who believe not know that if Allah had wanted to He could have guided all mankind*** without any Signs whatsoever***? Those who disbelieve*** among the people of Makka ***will not cease to be struck by disaster for what they have done*** – for their unbelief. The word used here for "disaster", *qāri'a,* is applied to various types of affliction: killing, capture, war and drought, ***or a disaster*** – at the hands of your army, Muḥammad – ***will happen close to their homes*** (Makka) ***until Allah's promise*** that you will be victorious over them ***is fulfilled. Allah will not fail to keep His promise.*** This happened at al-Ḥudaybiyya and continued until Makka was conquered.

32. ***Messengers before you were mocked*** – as you are being mocked. This is to offer solace to the Prophet, may Allah bless him and grant him peace. ***I gave those who disbelieved a little more time and then I seized them*** with the penalty. ***How terrible was My retribution*** which was inflicted on them*!* That is what I will do to all those who mock you.

33. ***What then of Him who is standing*** watching ***over every self, seeing everything it does?*** He knows what it earns of good and evil. That is Allah. Is He like those who are not like that among the idols? He is not! ***Yet still they associate others with Allah. Say: 'Name them!*** Who are they? ***Or would you inform Him*** (Allah) ***of something*** (a partner) ***in the earth He does not know?*** The answer to this is negative. He has no partner. If He had had one, He would have known it. Allah is exalted above that! ***Or are they*** – those they name as partners – ***words that are simply guesswork on your part?'*** It is a false supposition with no inward reality. ***Yet the plotting*** (*kufr*) ***of those who disbelieved seems good to them and they bar the way***: the path of guidance. ***Anyone misguided by Allah has no guide.***

أَنْ أَعْبُدَ ٱللَّهَ وَلَآ أُشْرِكَ بِهِۦٓ ۚ إِلَيْهِ أَدْعُوا۟ وَإِلَيْهِ مَـَٔابِ ﴿٣٦﴾
وَكَذَٰلِكَ أَنزَلْنَٰهُ حُكْمًا عَرَبِيًّا ۚ وَلَئِنِ ٱتَّبَعْتَ أَهْوَآءَهُم بَعْدَمَا
جَآءَكَ مِنَ ٱلْعِلْمِ مَا لَكَ مِنَ ٱللَّهِ مِن وَلِىٍّ وَلَا وَاقٍ ﴿٣٧﴾ وَلَقَدْ
أَرْسَلْنَا رُسُلًا مِّن قَبْلِكَ وَجَعَلْنَا لَهُمْ أَزْوَٰجًا وَذُرِّيَّةً ۚ وَمَا كَانَ
لِرَسُولٍ أَن يَأْتِىَ بِـَٔايَةٍ إِلَّا بِإِذْنِ ٱللَّهِ ۗ لِكُلِّ أَجَلٍ كِتَابٌ ﴿٣٨﴾
يَمْحُوا۟ ٱللَّهُ مَا يَشَآءُ وَيُثْبِتُ ۖ وَعِندَهُۥٓ أُمُّ ٱلْكِتَٰبِ ﴿٣٩﴾
وَإِن مَّا نُرِيَنَّكَ بَعْضَ ٱلَّذِى نَعِدُهُمْ أَوْ نَتَوَفَّيَنَّكَ فَإِنَّمَا عَلَيْكَ
ٱلْبَلَٰغُ وَعَلَيْنَا ٱلْحِسَابُ ﴿٤٠﴾ أَوَلَمْ يَرَوْا۟ أَنَّا نَأْتِى ٱلْأَرْضَ نَنقُصُهَا
مِنْ أَطْرَافِهَا ۚ وَٱللَّهُ يَحْكُمُ لَا مُعَقِّبَ لِحُكْمِهِۦ ۚ وَهُوَ سَرِيعُ
ٱلْحِسَابِ ﴿٤١﴾ وَقَدْ مَكَرَ ٱلَّذِينَ مِن قَبْلِهِمْ فَلِلَّهِ ٱلْمَكْرُ جَمِيعًا ۖ
يَعْلَمُ مَا تَكْسِبُ كُلُّ نَفْسٍ ۗ وَسَيَعْلَمُ ٱلْكُفَّٰرُ لِمَنْ عُقْبَى ٱلدَّارِ ﴿٤٢﴾
وَيَقُولُ ٱلَّذِينَ كَفَرُوا۟ لَسْتَ مُرْسَلًا ۚ قُلْ كَفَىٰ بِٱللَّهِ
شَهِيدًۢا بَيْنِى وَبَيْنَكُمْ وَمَنْ عِندَهُۥ عِلْمُ ٱلْكِتَٰبِ ﴿٤٣﴾

34. ***They will receive punishment in the life of this world*** by being killed and captured – ***and the punishment of the Next World is harsher still. They have no defender against*** the punishment of ***Allah.***

35. ***What is the Garden promised to those who are godfearing like?*** What can We say to you about the description of the Garden? ***It has rivers flowing under it and its foodstuffs and cool shade never fail. That*** Garden ***is the final fate of those who are godfearing*** and avoid *shirk*. ***But the final fate of the unbelievers is the Fire.***

36. ***Those to whom We gave the Book*** – such as 'Abdullah ibn Salām and others of the Jews who believed – ***rejoice at what has been sent down to you*** because it agreed with the Divine revelation which they had; ***but some of the parties*** – those idolaters and Jews who attacked you out of enmity – ***refuse to acknowledge part of it*** – and deny things like the mention of the All-Merciful and suchlike. ***Say: 'I have only been ordered*** – in what has been revealed to me – ***to worship Allah and not to associate anything with Him. I summon to Him and to Him I will return.'***

37. ***Accordingly We have sent it*** (the Qur'an) ***down as a judgement in Arabic*** – by which judgement between people can be given. ***If you followed their whims and desires*** – a reference to what the unbelievers invite to regarding their religion – ***after the knowledge*** of Allah's oneness ***that has come to you, you would have no protector or defender against*** the punishment of ***Allah.***

38. When they criticised him for the number of his wives, this *āyat* was revealed. ***We sent Messengers before you and gave them wives and children.*** You are like them. ***Nor was any Messenger*** among them ***able to bring a Sign except by Allah's permission.*** They were all human beings who were subject to the Lord. ***There is a prescribed limit to every term.***

39. ***Allah erases whatever*** ruling or anything else ***He wills or endorses it*** (read as *yuthbitu* and *yuthabbitu*). ***The Master Copy of the Book*** (*Umm al-Kitāb*) ***is in His Hands.*** *Umm al-Kitāb* is the source of Revelation in which nothing is changed and it was what was written before time.

40. ***Whether We show you something of what We have promised them*** – of the punishment while you are alive – ***or We take you back to Us*** before they are punished, ***your responsibility is*** nothing but ***transmission and the Reckoning is Ours.*** We will call them to account when they return to Us.

41. ***Do they*** (the people of Makka) ***not see how We come to the land*** (their homeland) ***eroding it at its extremities*** by conquest at the hands of the Prophet, may Allah bless him and grant him peace? ***Allah judges*** in whatever way He wishes in His creation – ***and there is no reversing His judgement. He is swift at reckoning.***

42. ***Those*** in nations ***before them plotted*** against their Prophets as they have plotted against you, ***but all plotting belongs to Allah.*** Their plotting is not like the plotting of Allah. ***He knows what each self earns*** and will calculate its repayment for it – this is all plotting because it comes from where they are not aware – ***and the unbeliever*** (*kāfir* here in the singular is generic for all unbelievers; one reading has the plural *kuffār*) ***will soon know who has the Ultimate Abode.*** The Ultimate Abode is the praiseworthy end in the Next World. He will know whether he will have it or whether the Prophet and his Companions will.

43. ***Those who disbelieve*** in you ***say, 'You are not a Messenger.' Say*** to them: ***'Allah is a sufficient witness between you and me*** – to my truthfulness – ***and anyone else who has knowledge of the Book*** – the believers among the Jews and Christians.'

سُورَةُ إِبۡرَاهِيمَ

بِسۡمِ ٱللَّهِ ٱلرَّحۡمَٰنِ ٱلرَّحِيمِ

الٓرۚ كِتَٰبٌ أَنزَلۡنَٰهُ إِلَيۡكَ لِتُخۡرِجَ ٱلنَّاسَ مِنَ ٱلظُّلُمَٰتِ
إِلَى ٱلنُّورِ بِإِذۡنِ رَبِّهِمۡ إِلَىٰ صِرَٰطِ ٱلۡعَزِيزِ ٱلۡحَمِيدِ ١
ٱللَّهِ ٱلَّذِي لَهُۥ مَا فِي ٱلسَّمَٰوَٰتِ وَمَا فِي ٱلۡأَرۡضِۗ وَوَيۡلٞ
لِّلۡكَٰفِرِينَ مِنۡ عَذَابٖ شَدِيدٍ ٢ ٱلَّذِينَ يَسۡتَحِبُّونَ
ٱلۡحَيَوٰةَ ٱلدُّنۡيَا عَلَى ٱلۡأٓخِرَةِ وَيَصُدُّونَ عَن سَبِيلِ ٱللَّهِ
وَيَبۡغُونَهَا عِوَجًاۚ أُوْلَٰٓئِكَ فِي ضَلَٰلِۭ بَعِيدٖ ٣ وَمَآ أَرۡسَلۡنَا
مِن رَّسُولٍ إِلَّا بِلِسَانِ قَوۡمِهِۦ لِيُبَيِّنَ لَهُمۡۖ فَيُضِلُّ ٱللَّهُ
مَن يَشَآءُ وَيَهۡدِي مَن يَشَآءُۚ وَهُوَ ٱلۡعَزِيزُ ٱلۡحَكِيمُ
٤ وَلَقَدۡ أَرۡسَلۡنَا مُوسَىٰ بِـَٔايَٰتِنَآ أَنۡ أَخۡرِجۡ
قَوۡمَكَ مِنَ ٱلظُّلُمَٰتِ إِلَى ٱلنُّورِ وَذَكِّرۡهُم بِأَيَّىٰمِ
ٱللَّهِۚ إِنَّ فِي ذَٰلِكَ لَأٓيَٰتٖ لِّكُلِّ صَبَّارٖ شَكُورٖ ٥
وَإِذۡ قَالَ مُوسَىٰ لِقَوۡمِهِ ٱذۡكُرُواْ نِعۡمَةَ ٱللَّهِ عَلَيۡكُمۡ
إِذۡ أَنجَىٰكُم مِّنۡ ءَالِ فِرۡعَوۡنَ يَسُومُونَكُمۡ سُوٓءَ ٱلۡعَذَابِ
وَيُذَبِّحُونَ أَبۡنَآءَكُمۡ وَيَسۡتَحۡيُونَ نِسَآءَكُمۡۚ وَفِي
ذَٰلِكُم بَلَآءٞ مِّن رَّبِّكُمۡ عَظِيمٞ ٦ وَإِذۡ تَأَذَّنَ
رَبُّكُمۡ لَئِن شَكَرۡتُمۡ لَأَزِيدَنَّكُمۡۖ وَلَئِن كَفَرۡتُمۡ إِنَّ
عَذَابِي لَشَدِيدٞ ٧ وَقَالَ مُوسَىٰٓ إِن تَكۡفُرُوٓاْ أَنتُمۡ وَمَن فِي ٱلۡأَرۡضِ
جَمِيعٗا فَإِنَّ ٱللَّهَ لَغَنِيٌّ حَمِيدٌ ٨ أَلَمۡ يَأۡتِكُمۡ نَبَؤُاْ ٱلَّذِينَ

14. *Sūrat Ibrāhīm*
Abraham

This *sūra* is Makkan except for *āyat*s 28 and 29 which are Madinan. It has 52, 54 or 55 *āyat*s.

1. ***Alif Lam Ra.*** Allah knows best what the letters mean. ***This*** Qur'an ***is a Book We have sent down to you,*** Muḥammad, ***so that you may bring mankind from the darkness*** of unbelief ***to the light*** of faith ***by the permission*** (command) ***of their Lord, to the Path of the Almighty, the Praiseworthy.***

2. ***Allah is He to Whom everything in the heavens and everything in the earth belongs.*** Everything in the world is His kingdom: creatures and people. ***Woe to the unbelievers because of a terrible punishment –***

3 ***…those who prefer*** and choose ***the life of this world to the Next World, and bar*** people ***access to the Way of Allah*** – the *dīn* of Islam – ***wanting to make it*** (the Way) ***crooked; they are greatly misguided*** from the Truth.

4. ***We have not sent any Messenger except with the language of his people so that he might make things clear to them*** – bring them to understanding of what he has brought. ***Allah misguides anyone He wills and guides anyone He wills. He is the Almighty*** in His kingdom, ***the All-Wise*** in what He does.

5 ***We sent Mūsā with Our*** nine ***Signs*** and We said to him: ***'Bring your people*** (the tribe of Israel) ***from the darkness*** of unbelief ***to the light*** of faith ***and remind them of the Days*** (blessings) ***of Allah.' There are certainly Signs in that*** reminder ***for everyone who is steadfast*** in obedience, ***thankful*** for blessings received.

6. Remember ***when Mūsā said to his people, 'Remember Allah's blessing upon you when He rescued you from the people of Pharaoh. They were inflicting an evil punishment on you, slaughtering your sons and letting your women live.*** This was a result of one of the soothsayers saying that a child would be born among the tribe of Israel who would bring about the loss of the kingdom of

مِن قَبۡلِكُمۡ قَوۡمِ نُوحٖ وَعَادٖ وَثَمُودَ ۛ وَٱلَّذِينَ مِنۢ
بَعۡدِهِمۡ ۛ لَا يَعۡلَمُهُمۡ إِلَّا ٱللَّهُ ۚ جَآءَتۡهُمۡ رُسُلُهُم بِٱلۡبَيِّنَٰتِ
فَرَدُّوٓاْ أَيۡدِيَهُمۡ فِيٓ أَفۡوَٰهِهِمۡ وَقَالُوٓاْ إِنَّا كَفَرۡنَا بِمَآ أُرۡسِلۡتُم
بِهِۦ وَإِنَّا لَفِي شَكّٖ مِّمَّا تَدۡعُونَنَآ إِلَيۡهِ مُرِيبٖ ﴿٩﴾ ۞ قَالَتۡ
رُسُلُهُمۡ أَفِي ٱللَّهِ شَكّٞ فَاطِرِ ٱلسَّمَٰوَٰتِ وَٱلۡأَرۡضِ ۖ يَدۡعُوكُمۡ
لِيَغۡفِرَ لَكُم مِّن ذُنُوبِكُمۡ وَيُؤَخِّرَكُمۡ إِلَىٰٓ أَجَلٖ
مُّسَمّٗى ۚ قَالُوٓاْ إِنۡ أَنتُمۡ إِلَّا بَشَرٞ مِّثۡلُنَا تُرِيدُونَ أَن تَصُدُّونَا
عَمَّا كَانَ يَعۡبُدُ ءَابَآؤُنَا فَأۡتُونَا بِسُلۡطَٰنٖ مُّبِينٖ ﴿١٠﴾
قَالَتۡ لَهُمۡ رُسُلُهُمۡ إِن نَّحۡنُ إِلَّا بَشَرٞ مِّثۡلُكُمۡ وَلَٰكِنَّ ٱللَّهَ
يَمُنُّ عَلَىٰ مَن يَشَآءُ مِنۡ عِبَادِهِۦ ۖ وَمَا كَانَ لَنَآ أَن نَّأۡتِيَكُم
بِسُلۡطَٰنٍ إِلَّا بِإِذۡنِ ٱللَّهِ ۚ وَعَلَى ٱللَّهِ فَلۡيَتَوَكَّلِ ٱلۡمُؤۡمِنُونَ
﴿١١﴾ وَمَا لَنَآ أَلَّا نَتَوَكَّلَ عَلَى ٱللَّهِ وَقَدۡ هَدَىٰنَا سُبُلَنَا ۚ
وَلَنَصۡبِرَنَّ عَلَىٰ مَآ ءَاذَيۡتُمُونَا ۚ وَعَلَى ٱللَّهِ فَلۡيَتَوَكَّلِ ٱلۡمُتَوَكِّلُونَ
﴿١٢﴾ وَقَالَ ٱلَّذِينَ كَفَرُواْ لِرُسُلِهِمۡ لَنُخۡرِجَنَّكُم مِّنۡ
أَرۡضِنَآ أَوۡ لَتَعُودُنَّ فِي مِلَّتِنَا ۖ فَأَوۡحَىٰٓ إِلَيۡهِمۡ رَبُّهُمۡ لَنُهۡلِكَنَّ
ٱلظَّٰلِمِينَ ﴿١٣﴾ وَلَنُسۡكِنَنَّكُمُ ٱلۡأَرۡضَ مِنۢ بَعۡدِهِمۡ ۚ
ذَٰلِكَ لِمَنۡ خَافَ مَقَامِي وَخَافَ وَعِيدِ ﴿١٤﴾ وَٱسۡتَفۡتَحُواْ
وَخَابَ كُلُّ جَبَّارٍ عَنِيدٖ ﴿١٥﴾ مِّن وَرَآئِهِۦ جَهَنَّمُ وَيُسۡقَىٰ
مِن مَّآءٖ صَدِيدٖ ﴿١٦﴾ يَتَجَرَّعُهُۥ وَلَا يَكَادُ يُسِيغُهُۥ
وَيَأۡتِيهِ ٱلۡمَوۡتُ مِن كُلِّ مَكَانٖ وَمَا هُوَ بِمَيِّتٖ ۖ وَمِن
وَرَآئِهِۦ عَذَابٌ غَلِيظٞ ﴿١٧﴾ مَّثَلُ ٱلَّذِينَ كَفَرُواْ بِرَبِّهِمۡ ۖ

Pharaoh. ***In that*** deliverance or punishment ***there was a tremendous trial*** – of either blessing or affliction – ***from your Lord.***

7. ***And when your Lord announced: 'If you show gratitude*** for My blessing by affirming My oneness and being obedient to Me ***I will certainly give you increase, but if you show ingratitude*** for My blessing by unbelief and disobedience, I will punish you for it. ***My punishment is severe.'***

8. ***Mūsā said*** to his people, ***'If you were to be ungrateful, you and everyone on the earth, Allah is Rich Beyond Need*** of His creation, ***Praiseworthy*** in what He does to them.'

9. ***Has news not reached you of those who came before you, the peoples of Nūḥ and 'Ād*** (the people of Hūd) ***and Thamūd*** (the people of Ṣāliḥ) ***and those who came after them who are known to no one but Allah*** – because there are so many of them? This is a question demanding an affirmative response. ***Their Messengers came to them with Clear Signs*** – clear evidence that they were speaking the truth – ***but they*** (these nations) ***put their hands to their mouths*** to bite on them because of their intense frustration, ***saying, 'We reject what you*** claim you ***have been sent with. We have grave doubts about what you are calling us to.'***

10. ***Their Messengers said, 'Is there any doubt about Allah, the Bringer into Being of the heavens and the earth?*** This question demands a negative response. In other words, there is no doubt about Allah's unitary existence because of the evident proofs of it. ***He summons you*** to obedience in order ***to forgive you for your wrong actions*** – as becoming a Muslim results in forgiveness for anything that happened before it. The words "*min*" is used before "wrong actions" to make it selective because responsibility for rights owed to other human beings is not removed – ***and to defer*** punishment from ***you until a specified time*** (your death).' ***They said, 'You are nothing but human beings like ourselves who want to debar us from what*** (the idols) ***our fathers worshipped; so bring us a clear authority*** – clear evidence that you are speaking the truth.'

11. ***Their Messengers told them, 'We are nothing but human beings like yourselves*** as you have said. ***But Allah shows favour*** – by granting Prophethood – ***to any of His slaves He wills. It is not***

proper *for us to bring you an authority except by Allah's permission* (command) because we are slaves subject to Him. ***So let the believers put their trust in Allah.***

12. ***And why indeed should we not put our trust in Allah when He has guided us to our ways?*** There is nothing to stop us from trusting in Him. ***We will be steadfast however much you harm us. Those who trust put their trust in Allah.'***

13. ***Those who disbelieved said to their Messengers, 'We will drive you from our land unless you return to our religion.' Their Lord revealed to them, 'We will destroy those who do wrong*** (the unbelievers).

14. ***We will leave you the land*** (their homeland) ***to live in after them*** after they have been destroyed. ***That*** – victory and inheritance of the land – ***is the reward of those who fear My station*** – standing before Me – ***and fear My threat*** of punishment.'

15. ***They asked for Allah's victory*** – they asked their Messengers for Allah to give them victory over the unbelievers of their people – ***and every obdurate tyrant*** who rejected the truth and refused to obey Allah ***failed.***

16. ***And beyond him is Hell,*** which he will enter, ***where he will be given pus*** – which will exude from the bellies of the people of the Fire as a mixture of pus and blood – ***to drink.***

17. ***He gulps at it*** – tries to swallow it down again and again, unable to because of its bitterness – ***but can hardly swallow it down*** because of its foulness and disgusting taste. ***Death*** – forms of punishment which would normally result in death – ***comes at him from every side but he does not die. And beyond him*** after that punishment ***is relentless*** – severe and continuous – ***punishment.***

18. ***The metaphor of those who disbelieve in their Lord is that their*** righteous ***actions*** such as maintaining ties of kinship and almsgiving ***are like ashes*** – and therefore of no use to them whatsoever – ***scattered by strong winds on a stormy day*** which disperse the dust, and about which nothing can be done. ***They*** (the unbelievers) ***have no power at all over anything they have earned*** in this world. They will have no reward because the necessary condition for it, that of true faith, is lacking. ***That is extreme misguidance.***

أَعْمَٰلُهُمْ كَرَمَادٍ ٱشْتَدَّتْ بِهِ ٱلرِّيحُ فِى يَوْمٍ عَاصِفٍ ۖ لَّا يَقْدِرُونَ
مِمَّا كَسَبُوا۟ عَلَىٰ شَىْءٍ ۚ ذَٰلِكَ هُوَ ٱلضَّلَٰلُ ٱلْبَعِيدُ ١٨
أَلَمْ تَرَ أَنَّ ٱللَّهَ خَلَقَ ٱلسَّمَٰوَٰتِ وَٱلْأَرْضَ بِٱلْحَقِّ ۚ إِن يَشَأْ
يُذْهِبْكُمْ وَيَأْتِ بِخَلْقٍ جَدِيدٍ ١٩ وَمَا ذَٰلِكَ عَلَى ٱللَّهِ بِعَزِيزٍ
٢٠ وَبَرَزُوا۟ لِلَّهِ جَمِيعًا فَقَالَ ٱلضُّعَفَٰٓؤُا۟ لِلَّذِينَ ٱسْتَكْبَرُوٓا۟
إِنَّا كُنَّا لَكُمْ تَبَعًا فَهَلْ أَنتُم مُّغْنُونَ عَنَّا مِنْ عَذَابِ ٱللَّهِ
مِن شَىْءٍ ۚ قَالُوا۟ لَوْ هَدَىٰنَا ٱللَّهُ لَهَدَيْنَٰكُمْ ۖ سَوَآءٌ عَلَيْنَآ
أَجَزِعْنَآ أَمْ صَبَرْنَا مَا لَنَا مِن مَّحِيصٍ ٢١ وَقَالَ ٱلشَّيْطَٰنُ
لَمَّا قُضِىَ ٱلْأَمْرُ إِنَّ ٱللَّهَ وَعَدَكُمْ وَعْدَ ٱلْحَقِّ وَوَعَدتُّكُمْ
فَأَخْلَفْتُكُمْ ۖ وَمَا كَانَ لِىَ عَلَيْكُم مِّن سُلْطَٰنٍ إِلَّآ أَن دَعَوْتُكُمْ
فَٱسْتَجَبْتُمْ لِى ۖ فَلَا تَلُومُونِى وَلُومُوٓا۟ أَنفُسَكُم ۖ مَّآ أَنَا۠
بِمُصْرِخِكُمْ وَمَآ أَنتُم بِمُصْرِخِىَّ ۖ إِنِّى كَفَرْتُ بِمَآ
أَشْرَكْتُمُونِ مِن قَبْلُ ۗ إِنَّ ٱلظَّٰلِمِينَ لَهُمْ عَذَابٌ أَلِيمٌ
٢٢ وَأُدْخِلَ ٱلَّذِينَ ءَامَنُوا۟ وَعَمِلُوا۟ ٱلصَّٰلِحَٰتِ جَنَّٰتٍ
تَجْرِى مِن تَحْتِهَا ٱلْأَنْهَٰرُ خَٰلِدِينَ فِيهَا بِإِذْنِ رَبِّهِمْ ۖ تَحِيَّتُهُمْ
فِيهَا سَلَٰمٌ ٢٣ أَلَمْ تَرَ كَيْفَ ضَرَبَ ٱللَّهُ مَثَلًا كَلِمَةً طَيِّبَةً
كَشَجَرَةٍ طَيِّبَةٍ أَصْلُهَا ثَابِتٌ وَفَرْعُهَا فِى ٱلسَّمَآءِ ٢٤
تُؤْتِىٓ أُكُلَهَا كُلَّ حِينٍۭ بِإِذْنِ رَبِّهَا ۗ وَيَضْرِبُ ٱللَّهُ ٱلْأَمْثَالَ
لِلنَّاسِ لَعَلَّهُمْ يَتَذَكَّرُونَ ٢٥ وَمَثَلُ كَلِمَةٍ خَبِيثَةٍ
كَشَجَرَةٍ خَبِيثَةٍ ٱجْتُثَّتْ مِن فَوْقِ ٱلْأَرْضِ مَا لَهَا مِن قَرَارٍ
٢٦ يُثَبِّتُ ٱللَّهُ ٱلَّذِينَ ءَامَنُوا۟ بِٱلْقَوْلِ ٱلثَّابِتِ فِى ٱلْحَيَوٰةِ

19. ***Do you not see that Allah has created the heavens and the earth with truth? If He wished He could eliminate you,*** mankind, ***and bring about a new creation.***

20. ***That is not difficult for Allah.***

21. ***They will all parade before Allah.*** All creatures will be made to appear. The past tense is used because its occurrence is a matter of certainty – ***and the weak*** followers ***will say to those who were arrogant*** – those who they followed – ***'We followed you, so can you help us at all against the punishment of Allah?' They will say, 'If Allah had guided us, we would have guided you*** – we would have called you to guidance. ***It makes no difference whether we cannot stand it or bear it patiently: we have no way of escape.'*** There is no refuge for us now.

22. ***When the affair is decided*** – and the people of the Garden enter the Garden and the people of the Fire enter the Fire and they gather in it – ***Shaytan*** (Iblīs) ***will say, 'Allah made you a promise*** – of resurrection and repayment and spoke the truth to you – ***a promise of truth, and I made you a promise but broke my promise. I had no authority over you*** to compel you to follow me ***except that I called you and you responded to me. Do not, therefore, blame me but blame yourselves*** for responding to me. ***I cannot come to your aid nor you to mine*** (read as *muṣrikhiyya* and *muṣrikhyī*). ***I reject the way you associated me*** and made me a partner ***with Allah before*** (in the world).' Then Allah will say that ***the wrongdoers*** (unbelievers) ***will have a painful punishment.***

23. ***Those who believed and did right actions will be admitted into Gardens with rivers flowing under them, remaining in them timelessly, for ever by the permission of their Lord. Their greeting there*** from the angels and between themselves ***is 'Peace!'***

24. ***Do you do not*** reflect and ***see how Allah makes a metaphor of a good word*** – said to be the statement: "There is no god but Allah"***: a good tree*** – such as a palm tree – ***whose roots are firm*** in the earth ***and whose branches are in heaven?***

25. ***It bears fruit regularly by its Lord's permission*** (by the will of Allah). In the same way the word of faith is fixed firmly in the heart of the believer, his actions rise to heaven, and he obtains their bless-

ٱلدُّنْيَا وَفِى ٱلْـَٔاخِرَةِ ۖ وَيُضِلُّ ٱللَّهُ ٱلظَّٰلِمِينَ ۚ وَيَفْعَلُ
ٱللَّهُ مَا يَشَآءُ ﴿٢٧﴾ ۞ أَلَمْ تَرَ إِلَى ٱلَّذِينَ بَدَّلُوا۟ نِعْمَتَ ٱللَّهِ كُفْرًا
وَأَحَلُّوا۟ قَوْمَهُمْ دَارَ ٱلْبَوَارِ ﴿٢٨﴾ جَهَنَّمَ يَصْلَوْنَهَا ۖ وَبِئْسَ
ٱلْقَرَارُ ﴿٢٩﴾ وَجَعَلُوا۟ لِلَّهِ أَندَادًا لِّيُضِلُّوا۟ عَن سَبِيلِهِۦ ۗ قُلْ
تَمَتَّعُوا۟ فَإِنَّ مَصِيرَكُمْ إِلَى ٱلنَّارِ ﴿٣٠﴾ قُل لِّعِبَادِىَ ٱلَّذِينَ
ءَامَنُوا۟ يُقِيمُوا۟ ٱلصَّلَوٰةَ وَيُنفِقُوا۟ مِمَّا رَزَقْنَٰهُمْ سِرًّا وَعَلَانِيَةً
مِّن قَبْلِ أَن يَأْتِىَ يَوْمٌ لَّا بَيْعٌ فِيهِ وَلَا خِلَٰلٌ ﴿٣١﴾ ٱللَّهُ ٱلَّذِى خَلَقَ
ٱلسَّمَٰوَٰتِ وَٱلْأَرْضَ وَأَنزَلَ مِنَ ٱلسَّمَآءِ مَآءً فَأَخْرَجَ
بِهِۦ مِنَ ٱلثَّمَرَٰتِ رِزْقًا لَّكُمْ ۖ وَسَخَّرَ لَكُمُ ٱلْفُلْكَ لِتَجْرِىَ
فِى ٱلْبَحْرِ بِأَمْرِهِۦ ۖ وَسَخَّرَ لَكُمُ ٱلْأَنْهَٰرَ ﴿٣٢﴾ وَسَخَّرَ لَكُمُ
ٱلشَّمْسَ وَٱلْقَمَرَ دَآئِبَيْنِ ۖ وَسَخَّرَ لَكُمُ ٱلَّيْلَ وَٱلنَّهَارَ ﴿٣٣﴾
وَءَاتَىٰكُم مِّن كُلِّ مَا سَأَلْتُمُوهُ ۚ وَإِن تَعُدُّوا۟ نِعْمَتَ ٱللَّهِ
لَا تُحْصُوهَآ ۗ إِنَّ ٱلْإِنسَٰنَ لَظَلُومٌ كَفَّارٌ ﴿٣٤﴾ وَإِذْ
قَالَ إِبْرَٰهِيمُ رَبِّ ٱجْعَلْ هَٰذَا ٱلْبَلَدَ ءَامِنًا وَٱجْنُبْنِى وَبَنِىَّ
أَن نَّعْبُدَ ٱلْأَصْنَامَ ﴿٣٥﴾ رَبِّ إِنَّهُنَّ أَضْلَلْنَ كَثِيرًا مِّنَ ٱلنَّاسِ ۖ
فَمَن تَبِعَنِى فَإِنَّهُۥ مِنِّى ۖ وَمَنْ عَصَانِى فَإِنَّكَ غَفُورٌ رَّحِيمٌ ﴿٣٦﴾
رَّبَّنَآ إِنِّىٓ أَسْكَنتُ مِن ذُرِّيَّتِى بِوَادٍ غَيْرِ ذِى زَرْعٍ عِندَ بَيْتِكَ
ٱلْمُحَرَّمِ رَبَّنَا لِيُقِيمُوا۟ ٱلصَّلَوٰةَ فَٱجْعَلْ أَفْـِٔدَةً مِّنَ ٱلنَّاسِ
تَهْوِىٓ إِلَيْهِمْ وَٱرْزُقْهُم مِّنَ ٱلثَّمَرَٰتِ لَعَلَّهُمْ يَشْكُرُونَ ﴿٣٧﴾
رَبَّنَآ إِنَّكَ تَعْلَمُ مَا نُخْفِى وَمَا نُعْلِنُ ۗ وَمَا يَخْفَىٰ عَلَى ٱللَّهِ مِن شَىْءٍ
فِى ٱلْأَرْضِ وَلَا فِى ٱلسَّمَآءِ ﴿٣٨﴾ ٱلْحَمْدُ لِلَّهِ ٱلَّذِى وَهَبَ لِى

ing and reward every moment. ***Allah makes metaphors for people*** – to make things clear – ***so that perhaps they will pay heed*** – be warned and believe.

26. ***The metaphor of a corrupt word*** – the expression of unbelief – ***is that of a rotten tree*** – such as a colocynth – ***uprooted on the surface of the earth. It has no staying-power.*** Since its roots are on the surface, it has no firmness or stability. Similarly the word of unbelief has no firmness or branches or blessing.

27. ***Allah makes those who believed firm with the Firm Word*** – the statement: "There is no god but Allah" – ***in the life of this world and the Next World.*** This takes place in the grave when the two angels question them about their Lord, their *dīn* and their Prophet and they answer correctly, as in the *ḥadīth* recorded by both al-Bukhārī and Muslim. ***But Allah misguides the wrongdoers*** (unbelievers) so that they are not guided to what is correct and instead have to say, "I do not know," as in the *ḥadīth.* ***Allah does whatever He wills.***

28. ***Do you not see those*** (the unbelievers of Quraysh) ***who have exchanged*** thankfulness for ***Allah's blessing for unbelief, and moved their people to the abode of ruin*** – brought their people to destruction by misguiding them:

29. ***Hell, where they will roast?*** They will enter the Fire. ***What an evil place to stay!***

30. ***They have made others*** (idols) ***equal to Allah to misguide*** (read as *yuḍillū* and *yaḍillū*) ***people from His Way*** (Islam). ***Say*** to them: ***'Enjoy yourselves*** in this world for a short time! ***Your destination is the Fire!'***

31. ***Tell My slaves who believe that they should establish the prayer and give from what We have provided for them, secretly and openly, before a Day arrives on which there will be no trading*** – to enable them to ransom themselves – ***and no friendship*** that will be of benefit to them. This is a reference to the Day of Rising.

32. ***Allah is He who created the heavens and the earth and sends down water from the sky and by it brings forth fruits as provision for you. He has made the ships subservient to you to run upon the***

sea to transport you and your cargo ***by His command*** – with His permission – ***and He has made the rivers subservient to you;***

33. ***...and He has made the sun and moon subservient to you, holding steady to their courses*** – revolving unfailingly in their orbits – ***and He has made the night*** – for you to rest in – ***and day*** – for you to strive for His bounty – ***subservient to you.***

34. ***He has given you everything you have asked Him for*** in accordance with your best interests. ***If you tried to number Allah's blessings, you could never count them. Man*** – when he is an unbeliever – ***is indeed wrongdoing, ungrateful*** – doing great wrong to himself by disobeying Allah and being ungrateful for the blessings of his Lord.

35. Remember ***when Ibrāhīm said, "My Lord, make this land*** (Makka) ***a place of safety*** and security – and Allah answered his prayer and made it a *Ḥaram* in which no human blood may be shed and no one may be wronged, no game may hunted and no plants uprooted, ***and keep me and my sons from worshipping idols.***

36. ***My Lord, they*** (the idols) ***have misguided many of mankind*** through their worship of them. ***If anyone follows me*** in affirming the unity of Allah ***he is with me*** – one of the people of my *dīn* – ***but if anyone disobeys me, You are Ever-Forgiving, Most Merciful.*** This was said before he knew that Allah does not forgive *shirk*.

37. ***Our Lord, I have settled some of my offspring*** – Isḥāq and his mother Hajar – ***by Your Sacred House*** – which was there before the Flood – ***in an uncultivated valley*** (Makka). ***Our Lord, let them establish the prayer! Make the hearts of mankind incline towards them*** – Ibn 'Abbās said that if Allah had said, *'af'idata'n-nās'* rather than *'af'idatan min an-nās'*, then Persia, Rome and all mankind would have inclined to it – ***and provide them with fruits, so that perhaps they will be thankful.*** People brought fruits there when they came to visit.

38. ***Our Lord, You know what we keep hidden and what we divulge. Nothing is hidden from Allah either on the earth or in heaven.*** It is possible that the words "Nothing is hidden from Allah..." are direct words of Allah rather than words attributed to Ibrāhīm.

عَلَى ٱلْكِبَرِ إِسْمَٰعِيلَ وَإِسْحَٰقَ ۚ إِنَّ رَبِّى لَسَمِيعُ ٱلدُّعَآءِ ﴿٣٩﴾
رَبِّ ٱجْعَلْنِى مُقِيمَ ٱلصَّلَوٰةِ وَمِن ذُرِّيَّتِى ۚ رَبَّنَا وَتَقَبَّلْ
دُعَآءِ ﴿٤٠﴾ رَبَّنَا ٱغْفِرْ لِى وَلِوَٰلِدَىَّ وَلِلْمُؤْمِنِينَ يَوْمَ يَقُومُ
ٱلْحِسَابُ ﴿٤١﴾ وَلَا تَحْسَبَنَّ ٱللَّهَ غَٰفِلًا عَمَّا يَعْمَلُ
ٱلظَّٰلِمُونَ ۚ إِنَّمَا يُؤَخِّرُهُمْ لِيَوْمٍ تَشْخَصُ فِيهِ ٱلْأَبْصَٰرُ ﴿٤٢﴾
مُهْطِعِينَ مُقْنِعِى رُءُوسِهِمْ لَا يَرْتَدُّ إِلَيْهِمْ طَرْفُهُمْ ۖ وَأَفْـِٔدَتُهُمْ
هَوَآءٌ ﴿٤٣﴾ وَأَنذِرِ ٱلنَّاسَ يَوْمَ يَأْتِيهِمُ ٱلْعَذَابُ فَيَقُولُ ٱلَّذِينَ
ظَلَمُوا۟ رَبَّنَآ أَخِّرْنَآ إِلَىٰٓ أَجَلٍ قَرِيبٍ نُّجِبْ دَعْوَتَكَ وَنَتَّبِعِ
ٱلرُّسُلَ ۗ أَوَلَمْ تَكُونُوٓا۟ أَقْسَمْتُم مِّن قَبْلُ مَا لَكُم
مِّن زَوَالٍ ﴿٤٤﴾ وَسَكَنتُمْ فِى مَسَٰكِنِ ٱلَّذِينَ ظَلَمُوٓا۟
أَنفُسَهُمْ وَتَبَيَّنَ لَكُمْ كَيْفَ فَعَلْنَا بِهِمْ وَضَرَبْنَا
لَكُمُ ٱلْأَمْثَالَ ﴿٤٥﴾ وَقَدْ مَكَرُوا۟ مَكْرَهُمْ وَعِندَ ٱللَّهِ
مَكْرُهُمْ وَإِن كَانَ مَكْرُهُمْ لِتَزُولَ مِنْهُ ٱلْجِبَالُ
﴿٤٦﴾ فَلَا تَحْسَبَنَّ ٱللَّهَ مُخْلِفَ وَعْدِهِۦ رُسُلَهُۥٓ ۗ إِنَّ ٱللَّهَ عَزِيزٌ
ذُو ٱنتِقَامٍ ﴿٤٧﴾ يَوْمَ تُبَدَّلُ ٱلْأَرْضُ غَيْرَ ٱلْأَرْضِ وَٱلسَّمَٰوَٰتُ ۖ
وَبَرَزُوا۟ لِلَّهِ ٱلْوَٰحِدِ ٱلْقَهَّارِ ﴿٤٨﴾ وَتَرَى ٱلْمُجْرِمِينَ يَوْمَئِذٍ
مُّقَرَّنِينَ فِى ٱلْأَصْفَادِ ﴿٤٩﴾ سَرَابِيلُهُم مِّن قَطِرَانٍ وَتَغْشَىٰ
وُجُوهَهُمُ ٱلنَّارُ ﴿٥٠﴾ لِيَجْزِىَ ٱللَّهُ كُلَّ نَفْسٍ مَّا كَسَبَتْ ۚ
إِنَّ ٱللَّهَ سَرِيعُ ٱلْحِسَابِ ﴿٥١﴾ هَٰذَا بَلَٰغٌ لِّلنَّاسِ وَلِيُنذَرُوا۟
بِهِۦ وَلِيَعْلَمُوٓا۟ أَنَّمَا هُوَ إِلَٰهٌ وَٰحِدٌ وَلِيَذَّكَّرَ أُو۟لُوا۟ ٱلْأَلْبَٰبِ ﴿٥٢﴾

39. ***Praise be to Allah Who, despite my old age, has given me Ismā'īl*** – he was ninety-nine years old at the time of his birth – **and** ***Isḥāq*** – when he was one hundred and twelve years old. ***My Lord is the Hearer of Prayer.***

40. ***My Lord, make me and my descendants people who establish the prayer*** – he uses the partitive particle *min* before "descendants" because he knows that some of them will be unbelievers. ***My Lord, accept my prayer.***

41. ***Our Lord, forgive me and my parents*** (read as *wālidayya* and also *walidī*, in the singular). This was before the enmity of his parents to Allah was made clear to him. It is said that his mother became Muslim – ***and the believers on the Day the Reckoning takes place.'***

42. Allah continues: ***Do not consider Allah to be unaware of what the wrongdoers*** – the unbelievers of the people of Makka – ***perpetrate. He is merely deferring them*** – delaying their punishment – ***to a Day on which their sight will be transfixed*** by the terror of what they see. This term is used when a person's eyes are fixed open without being closed.

43. ***... rushing headlong, heads back*** – their heads facing upwards to the sky, ***eyes vacant, hearts hollow*** – empty of understanding, due to their terror.

44. ***Warn,*** Muḥammad, ***mankind*** – the unbelievers among them – ***of the Day*** (the Day of Rising) ***when the punishment will reach them. Those who did wrong*** and disbelieved ***will say, 'Our Lord, reprieve us for a short time*** – and return us to the world. ***We will respond to Your call*** to affirm Allah's unity ***and follow the Messengers.'*** They will be rebuked: ***'But did you not swear to Me before*** in the world ***that you would never meet your downfall*** – removed from this world to the Next World –

45. ***...even though you inhabited the houses of those*** of past nations ***who had wronged themselves*** by unbelief ***and it was made clear to you how We had dealt with them*** – that We punished them, so will you not be restrained? – ***and We gave you many*** clear ***examples*** in the Qur'an?' Will you not reflect?

46. ***They concocted their plots*** against the Prophet, may Allah bless him and grant him peace, when they wanted to kill, imprison, or expel him; ***but their plots were with Allah*** – a reference to His knowledge or His repayment – ***even if they were such*** – and so immense – ***as to make the mountains vanish*** (read as *li-tazūla* and *la-tazūla*). This means that Allah pays no attention to them and they only harm themselves. By "mountains" here, it is said that actual mountains are meant; but it is also said that religions are meant, which can be said to resemble mountains with respect to stability and firmness. Some say that what is meant is to exalt their plotting and some say that it means their unbelief. The second meaning is appropriate according to a second *āyat*, *"The heavens are all but rent apart and the earth split open and the mountains brought crashing down."* (19:90)

47. ***Do not imagine that Allah will break His promise*** of help ***to His Messengers. Allah is Almighty,*** having the power to do anything He wants, ***Exactor of Revenge*** against those who disobey.

48. ***On the Day the earth is changed to other than the earth, and the heavens likewise,*** a reference to the Day of Rising when people will be gathered on a white empty earth as in the *ḥadīth* recorded in the two *Ṣaḥīḥ* Collections. Muslim also related the *ḥadīth*: "The Prophet, may Allah bless him and grant him peace, was asked, 'Where will people be on that day?' He replied, 'On the Narrow Bridge.'" – ***and they parade*** – they will be brought out of their graves – ***before Allah, the One, the All-Conquering;***

49. ***...that Day,*** Muḥammad, ***you will see the evildoers*** (the unbelievers) ***yoked together*** to their Shayṭāns ***in chains*** and shackles,

50. ***...wearing shirts of tar*** to increase the burning of the Fire, ***their faces enveloped in the Fire –***

51. ***so that Allah may repay every self for what it earned*** – of good and evil. ***Allah is swift at reckoning.*** The Reckoning of all creation will take place in the space of time of about half a day by the calculation of this world, as the *ḥadīth* states.

52. ***This*** Qur'an ***is a communication to be transmitted to mankind so that they may be warned by it and so that they may know*** by clear evidence ***that He is One God, and so that people of intelligence will pay heed.***

سُورَةُ الحِجۡرِ

بِسۡمِ ٱللَّهِ ٱلرَّحۡمَٰنِ ٱلرَّحِيمِ

الٓرۚ تِلۡكَ ءَايَٰتُ ٱلۡكِتَٰبِ وَقُرۡءَانٖ مُّبِينٖ ١ رُّبَمَا يَوَدُّ
ٱلَّذِينَ كَفَرُواْ لَوۡ كَانُواْ مُسۡلِمِينَ ٢ ذَرۡهُمۡ يَأۡكُلُواْ
وَيَتَمَتَّعُواْ وَيُلۡهِهِمُ ٱلۡأَمَلُۖ فَسَوۡفَ يَعۡلَمُونَ ٣ وَمَآ أَهۡلَكۡنَا
مِن قَرۡيَةٍ إِلَّا وَلَهَا كِتَابٞ مَّعۡلُومٞ ٤ مَّا تَسۡبِقُ مِنۡ أُمَّةٍ
أَجَلَهَا وَمَا يَسۡتَـٔۡخِرُونَ ٥ وَقَالُواْ يَٰٓأَيُّهَا ٱلَّذِي نُزِّلَ عَلَيۡهِ
ٱلذِّكۡرُ إِنَّكَ لَمَجۡنُونٞ ٦ لَّوۡ مَا تَأۡتِينَا بِٱلۡمَلَٰٓئِكَةِ إِن كُنتَ
مِنَ ٱلصَّٰدِقِينَ ٧ مَا نُنَزِّلُ ٱلۡمَلَٰٓئِكَةَ إِلَّا بِٱلۡحَقِّ وَمَا كَانُوٓاْ
إِذٗا مُّنظَرِينَ ٨ إِنَّا نَحۡنُ نَزَّلۡنَا ٱلذِّكۡرَ وَإِنَّا لَهُۥ لَحَٰفِظُونَ ٩
وَلَقَدۡ أَرۡسَلۡنَا مِن قَبۡلِكَ فِي شِيَعِ ٱلۡأَوَّلِينَ ١٠ وَمَا يَأۡتِيهِم مِّن
رَّسُولٍ إِلَّا كَانُواْ بِهِۦ يَسۡتَهۡزِءُونَ ١١ كَذَٰلِكَ نَسۡلُكُهُۥ فِي
قُلُوبِ ٱلۡمُجۡرِمِينَ ١٢ لَا يُؤۡمِنُونَ بِهِۦۖ وَقَدۡ خَلَتۡ سُنَّةُ ٱلۡأَوَّلِينَ
١٣ وَلَوۡ فَتَحۡنَا عَلَيۡهِم بَابٗا مِّنَ ٱلسَّمَآءِ فَظَلُّواْ فِيهِ يَعۡرُجُونَ
١٤ لَقَالُوٓاْ إِنَّمَا سُكِّرَتۡ أَبۡصَٰرُنَا بَلۡ نَحۡنُ قَوۡمٞ مَّسۡحُورُونَ ١٥
وَلَقَدۡ جَعَلۡنَا فِي ٱلسَّمَآءِ بُرُوجٗا وَزَيَّنَّٰهَا لِلنَّٰظِرِينَ ١٦
وَحَفِظۡنَٰهَا مِن كُلِّ شَيۡطَٰنٖ رَّجِيمٍ ١٧ إِلَّا مَنِ ٱسۡتَرَقَ ٱلسَّمۡعَ
فَأَتۡبَعَهُۥ شِهَابٞ مُّبِينٞ ١٨ وَٱلۡأَرۡضَ مَدَدۡنَٰهَا وَأَلۡقَيۡنَا فِيهَا
رَوَٰسِيَ وَأَنۢبَتۡنَا فِيهَا مِن كُلِّ شَيۡءٖ مَّوۡزُونٖ ١٩ وَجَعَلۡنَا لَكُمۡ فِيهَا
مَعَٰيِشَ وَمَن لَّسۡتُمۡ لَهُۥ بِرَٰزِقِينَ ٢٠ وَإِن مِّن شَيۡءٍ إِلَّا عِندَنَا

15. *Sūrat al-Ḥijr*

This *sūra* is Makkan and has 99 *āyat*s.

1. ***Alif Lam Ra.*** Allah knows best what these letters mean. ***Those*** *āyat*s ***are the Signs of the Book*** (the Qur'an) – the genitive structure here gives the meaning of "from" – ***and a clear Qur'an*** – which distinguishes what is true from what is false.

2. ***It may be*** (read as *rubamā* and *rubbamā*) ***that those who disbelieve will wish that they had been Muslims*** on the Day of Rising, when they see the difference between their state and that of the Muslims. The terrors will stupefy them so that the occasions on which they are able to wish for that are limited to a few.

3. ***Leave them*** (the unbelievers), Muḥammad, ***to eat and enjoy themselves*** in this world. ***Let false hope*** of a long life and other things ***divert them*** from faith. ***They will soon know*** the end result of their affair. This was before the command to fight.

4. ***We did not destroy*** the inhabitants of ***any city without it having a set time*** for its destruction.

5. ***No nation can advance its appointed time, nor can they delay it.***

6. ***They*** (the unbelievers of Makka) ***say*** to the Prophet, may Allah bless him and grant him peace – ***'You, to whom the Reminder*** (the Qur'an) ***has been sent down,*** according to your claim, ***are clearly mad.***

7. ***Why do you not bring angels to us if you are telling the truth*** and if this Qur'an is truly from Allah***?'***

8 Allah says: ***The angels only descend*** (read as *mā tunazzalu* and *mā'ttanazzalu*) ***with the truth*** (the punishment)***, and then they would be granted no reprieve*** – when the angels bring it down.

9. ***It is We*** – in the words *innā naḥnu* the pronoun *naḥnu* ("we") is repeated for stress or for separation – ***Who have sent down the Reminder*** (the Qur'an) ***and We Who will preserve it*** from alteration, distortion, additions, or deletions.

10. ***We sent Messengers before you among the disparate groups of previous peoples.***

11. ***No Messenger came to them without their mocking him.*** 'Previous peoples mocked their Messengers in the same way that your people mock you.' This is to give solace to the Prophet, may Allah bless him and grant him peace.

12. ***In that way We insert it*** (denial) ***into the evildoers' hearts*** – referring to the unbelievers of the people of Makka.

13. ***They do not believe in him*** – meaning the Prophet, may Allah bless him and grant him peace, or possibly "it", referring to the Qur'an – ***even though the example of the previous peoples has gone before***: a reference to their punishment for denying their Prophets. These people are like them.

14. ***Even if We opened up to them a door into heaven, and they spent the day ascending through it*** (the door),

15. ***...they would only say, 'Our eyesight is befuddled*** (blocked), ***or rather we have been put under a spell!*** This is just an illusion.'

16. ***We have placed constellations in heaven and made them beautiful for those who look.*** They are twelve: Aries, Taurus, Gemini, Cancer, Leo, Virgo, Libra, Scorpio, Sagittarius, Capricorn, Aquarius and Pisces. They are the stations of the seven moving planets: Mercury, which has Aries and Scorpio; Venus, which has Taurus and Libra; Saturn, which has Gemini and Virgo; the moon, which has Cancer; the sun, which has Leo; Jupiter, which has Sagittarius and Pisces; and Saturn, which has Capricorn and Aquarius.

17. ***We have guarded them*** with meteors ***from every cursed Shayṭān*** –

18. ***...except for the one who listens stealthily*** by eavesdropping, ***and he is followed by an open flame*** – a shooting star which burns him or pierces him or confuses him.

19. ***As for the earth, We stretched it out and cast firmly embedded mountains in it*** – so that it does not move under its inhabitants – ***and made everything grow in due proportion on it*** – by a known amount.

20. ***And We put livelihoods*** – fruits and grains – ***in it both for you and for those you do not provide for*** – referring to slaves and animals and livestock: Allah provides for them.

خَزَآئِنُهُۥ وَمَا نُنَزِّلُهُۥٓ إِلَّا بِقَدَرٍ مَّعْلُومٍ ﴿٢١﴾ وَأَرْسَلْنَا ٱلرِّيَٰحَ
لَوَٰقِحَ فَأَنزَلْنَا مِنَ ٱلسَّمَآءِ مَآءً فَأَسْقَيْنَٰكُمُوهُ وَمَآ أَنتُمْ لَهُۥ
بِخَٰزِنِينَ ﴿٢٢﴾ وَإِنَّا لَنَحْنُ نُحْيِۦ وَنُمِيتُ وَنَحْنُ ٱلْوَٰرِثُونَ ﴿٢٣﴾
وَلَقَدْ عَلِمْنَا ٱلْمُسْتَقْدِمِينَ مِنكُمْ وَلَقَدْ عَلِمْنَا ٱلْمُسْتَـْٔخِرِينَ ﴿٢٤﴾
وَإِنَّ رَبَّكَ هُوَ يَحْشُرُهُمْ إِنَّهُۥ حَكِيمٌ عَلِيمٌ ﴿٢٥﴾ وَلَقَدْ خَلَقْنَا ٱلْإِنسَٰنَ
مِن صَلْصَٰلٍ مِّنْ حَمَإٍ مَّسْنُونٍ ﴿٢٦﴾ وَٱلْجَآنَّ خَلَقْنَٰهُ مِن قَبْلُ مِن نَّارِ
ٱلسَّمُومِ ﴿٢٧﴾ وَإِذْ قَالَ رَبُّكَ لِلْمَلَٰٓئِكَةِ إِنِّى خَٰلِقٌۢ بَشَرًا مِّن
صَلْصَٰلٍ مِّنْ حَمَإٍ مَّسْنُونٍ ﴿٢٨﴾ فَإِذَا سَوَّيْتُهُۥ وَنَفَخْتُ فِيهِ مِن
رُّوحِى فَقَعُوا۟ لَهُۥ سَٰجِدِينَ ﴿٢٩﴾ فَسَجَدَ ٱلْمَلَٰٓئِكَةُ كُلُّهُمْ
أَجْمَعُونَ ﴿٣٠﴾ إِلَّآ إِبْلِيسَ أَبَىٰٓ أَن يَكُونَ مَعَ ٱلسَّٰجِدِينَ ﴿٣١﴾
قَالَ يَٰٓإِبْلِيسُ مَا لَكَ أَلَّا تَكُونَ مَعَ ٱلسَّٰجِدِينَ ﴿٣٢﴾ قَالَ لَمْ أَكُن
لِّأَسْجُدَ لِبَشَرٍ خَلَقْتَهُۥ مِن صَلْصَٰلٍ مِّنْ حَمَإٍ مَّسْنُونٍ ﴿٣٣﴾ قَالَ
فَٱخْرُجْ مِنْهَا فَإِنَّكَ رَجِيمٌ ﴿٣٤﴾ وَإِنَّ عَلَيْكَ ٱللَّعْنَةَ إِلَىٰ يَوْمِ
ٱلدِّينِ ﴿٣٥﴾ قَالَ رَبِّ فَأَنظِرْنِىٓ إِلَىٰ يَوْمِ يُبْعَثُونَ ﴿٣٦﴾ قَالَ فَإِنَّكَ
مِنَ ٱلْمُنظَرِينَ ﴿٣٧﴾ إِلَىٰ يَوْمِ ٱلْوَقْتِ ٱلْمَعْلُومِ ﴿٣٨﴾ قَالَ رَبِّ بِمَآ
أَغْوَيْتَنِى لَأُزَيِّنَنَّ لَهُمْ فِى ٱلْأَرْضِ وَلَأُغْوِيَنَّهُمْ أَجْمَعِينَ ﴿٣٩﴾
إِلَّا عِبَادَكَ مِنْهُمُ ٱلْمُخْلَصِينَ ﴿٤٠﴾ قَالَ هَٰذَا صِرَٰطٌ عَلَىَّ
مُسْتَقِيمٌ ﴿٤١﴾ إِنَّ عِبَادِى لَيْسَ لَكَ عَلَيْهِمْ سُلْطَٰنٌ إِلَّا مَنِ
ٱتَّبَعَكَ مِنَ ٱلْغَاوِينَ ﴿٤٢﴾ وَإِنَّ جَهَنَّمَ لَمَوْعِدُهُمْ أَجْمَعِينَ ﴿٤٣﴾
لَهَا سَبْعَةُ أَبْوَٰبٍ لِّكُلِّ بَابٍ مِّنْهُمْ جُزْءٌ مَّقْسُومٌ ﴿٤٤﴾ إِنَّ

21. ***There is nothing that does not have*** the keys to ***its stores with Us, and We only send it down in a known measure.*** It is all distributed according to the best interests of its recipients.

22. ***We send forth the pollinating winds*** – and they also make the clouds fill up with water – ***and send down water from the sky*** from the clouds ***and give it to you to drink. And it is not you who keep its stores*** – and you are not in control of them.

23. ***It is We who give life and cause to die, and We are the Inheritor*** – We will remain and all creation will return to Us.

24. ***We know those of you who have gone ahead*** – meaning all the creatures who have already appeared from the time of Ādam – ***and those who are still to come*** up until the Day of Rising.

25. ***It is your Lord Who will gather them. He is All-Wise*** in what He does, ***All-Knowing*** of His creation.

26. ***We created mankind*** – meaning Ādam – ***out of dried clay*** – from which a rattling sound could be heard when it was hollowed out – ***formed from fetid black mud.***

27. ***We created the jinn before*** the creation of Ādam ***out of the fire of a searing wind*** – a fire which has no smoke which that through the pores.

28 Remember ***when your Lord said to the angels, 'I am creating a human being out of dried clay formed from fetid black mud.***

29. ***When I have formed him*** and perfected him ***and breathed My*** **Rūḥ** ***into him*** – caused some of My *Rūḥ* (Spirit) to flow into him so that he becomes alive – ***fall down in prostration in front of him*** to honour him*!'* The prostration was a greeting which took the form of bowing.

30. ***Then the angels prostrated all together, every one of them –***

31. ***… except Iblīs.*** Iblīs was the father of the jinn. He was with the angels. ***He disdained to be one of the prostrators.***

32. ***He*** (Allah) ***said, 'Iblīs, what is it that prevents you being among the prostrators?'***

33. ***He said, 'I will not prostrate to a human being*** – it is not appropriate for me to do such a thing – ***whom You have created out of dried clay formed from fetid black mud.'***

34. ***He said, 'Get out from here*** – out of the Garden or the heavens. ***You are accursed*** (ousted).

35. ***The curse will be on you till the Day of Reckoning*** (Repayment).***'***

36. ***He said, 'My Lord, grant me a reprieve until the Day they*** (mankind) ***are raised again.'***

37. ***He said, 'You are among the reprieved…***

38 ***…until the Day whose time is known.'*** That is the time of the First Blast on the Trumpet.

39. ***He said, 'My Lord, because You misled me, I will make things on the earth*** (acts of disobedience) ***seem good to them and I will mislead them all, every one of them,***

40. ***…except Your slaves among them who are sincere*** (the believers).***'***

41. ***He*** (Allah) ***said, 'This is a Straight Path to Me.***

42. ***You have no authority over any of My slaves*** (the believers) ***except for the misled*** (the unbelievers) ***who follow you.'***

43. Allah says: ***Hell is the promised meeting-place for all of them.***

44. ***It has seven gates*** (layers) ***and each gate has its allotted share.***

45. ***Those who are godfearing will be amid Gardens and*** running ***Springs:***

46. It will be said to them: ***'Enter them in peace*** – safe from every fearful thing – ***in complete security,*** safe from every anxiety***!'***

47. ***We will strip away any rancour in their hearts – brothers, resting on couches face to face.*** No one looks at anyone else's back, because the couches are arranged in a circle.

48. ***They will not be affected by any tiredness there and they will never be made to leave.***

49. ***Tell My slaves***, Muḥammad, ***that I am the Ever-Forgiving*** to the believers, ***the Most Merciful*** to them,

50. ***…but also that My punishment*** *of the disobedient* ***is the Painful Punishment.***

51. ***And tell them about the guests of Ibrāhīm*** – angels, who were twelve, ten or three in number, one of whom was Jibrīl.

ٱلْمُتَّقِينَ فِي جَنَّٰتٍ وَعُيُونٍ ﴿٤٥﴾ ٱدْخُلُوهَا بِسَلَٰمٍ ءَامِنِينَ ﴿٤٦﴾
وَنَزَعْنَا مَا فِي صُدُورِهِم مِّنْ غِلٍّ إِخْوَٰنًا عَلَىٰ سُرُرٍ مُّتَقَٰبِلِينَ
﴿٤٧﴾ لَا يَمَسُّهُمْ فِيهَا نَصَبٌ وَمَا هُم مِّنْهَا بِمُخْرَجِينَ ﴿٤٨﴾
۞ نَبِّئْ عِبَادِيٓ أَنِّيٓ أَنَا ٱلْغَفُورُ ٱلرَّحِيمُ ﴿٤٩﴾ وَأَنَّ عَذَابِي
هُوَ ٱلْعَذَابُ ٱلْأَلِيمُ ﴿٥٠﴾ وَنَبِّئْهُمْ عَن ضَيْفِ إِبْرَٰهِيمَ ﴿٥١﴾
إِذْ دَخَلُوا۟ عَلَيْهِ فَقَالُوا۟ سَلَٰمًا قَالَ إِنَّا مِنكُمْ وَجِلُونَ ﴿٥٢﴾ قَالُوا۟
لَا تَوْجَلْ إِنَّا نُبَشِّرُكَ بِغُلَٰمٍ عَلِيمٍ ﴿٥٣﴾ قَالَ أَبَشَّرْتُمُونِي عَلَىٰٓ أَن
مَّسَّنِيَ ٱلْكِبَرُ فَبِمَ تُبَشِّرُونَ ﴿٥٤﴾ قَالُوا۟ بَشَّرْنَٰكَ بِٱلْحَقِّ
فَلَا تَكُن مِّنَ ٱلْقَٰنِطِينَ ﴿٥٥﴾ قَالَ وَمَن يَقْنَطُ مِن رَّحْمَةِ
رَبِّهِۦٓ إِلَّا ٱلضَّآلُّونَ ﴿٥٦﴾ قَالَ فَمَا خَطْبُكُمْ أَيُّهَا ٱلْمُرْسَلُونَ
﴿٥٧﴾ قَالُوٓا۟ إِنَّآ أُرْسِلْنَآ إِلَىٰ قَوْمٍ مُّجْرِمِينَ ﴿٥٨﴾ إِلَّآ ءَالَ لُوطٍ
إِنَّا لَمُنَجُّوهُمْ أَجْمَعِينَ ﴿٥٩﴾ إِلَّا ٱمْرَأَتَهُۥ قَدَّرْنَآ ۙ إِنَّهَا لَمِنَ
ٱلْغَٰبِرِينَ ﴿٦٠﴾ فَلَمَّا جَآءَ ءَالَ لُوطٍ ٱلْمُرْسَلُونَ ﴿٦١﴾ قَالَ
إِنَّكُمْ قَوْمٌ مُّنكَرُونَ ﴿٦٢﴾ قَالُوا۟ بَلْ جِئْنَٰكَ بِمَا كَانُوا۟ فِيهِ
يَمْتَرُونَ ﴿٦٣﴾ وَأَتَيْنَٰكَ بِٱلْحَقِّ وَإِنَّا لَصَٰدِقُونَ ﴿٦٤﴾ فَأَسْرِ
بِأَهْلِكَ بِقِطْعٍ مِّنَ ٱلَّيْلِ وَٱتَّبِعْ أَدْبَٰرَهُمْ وَلَا يَلْتَفِتْ مِنكُمْ أَحَدٌ
وَٱمْضُوا۟ حَيْثُ تُؤْمَرُونَ ﴿٦٥﴾ وَقَضَيْنَآ إِلَيْهِ ذَٰلِكَ ٱلْأَمْرَ أَنَّ
دَابِرَ هَٰٓؤُلَآءِ مَقْطُوعٌ مُّصْبِحِينَ ﴿٦٦﴾ وَجَآءَ أَهْلُ ٱلْمَدِينَةِ
يَسْتَبْشِرُونَ ﴿٦٧﴾ قَالَ إِنَّ هَٰٓؤُلَآءِ ضَيْفِي فَلَا تَفْضَحُونِ ﴿٦٨﴾ وَٱتَّقُوا۟
ٱللَّهَ وَلَا تُخْزُونِ ﴿٦٩﴾ قَالُوٓا۟ أَوَلَمْ نَنْهَكَ عَنِ ٱلْعَٰلَمِينَ ﴿٧٠﴾
قَالَ هَٰٓؤُلَآءِ بَنَاتِيٓ إِن كُنتُمْ فَٰعِلِينَ ﴿٧١﴾ لَعَمْرُكَ إِنَّهُمْ لَفِي سَكْرَتِهِمْ

52. ***When they came in to him, they said, 'Peace!' He*** (Ibrāhīm) ***said*** – when he offered them food, but they did not eat it, which caused him to be alarmed – ***'Truly we are afraid of you.'***

53. ***They said, 'Do not be afraid.*** We are the messengers of your Lord. ***We bring you the good news of a boy with great knowledge.'*** This was Isḥāq, as mentioned in *Sūrat Hūd*.

54. ***He asked, 'Do you bring me this good news*** of a child ***despite old age having reached me? What kind of good news are you bringing me?'*** The question is one of wonder.

55. ***They said, 'We bring you good news of the truth, so do not be among those who despair.'***

56. ***He said, 'Who despairs*** (read as *yaqnaṭu* and *yaqniṭu*) ***of the mercy of his Lord except for misguided people*** (unbelievers)***?'***

57. ***He added, 'What is your business, messengers?'***

58. ***They said, 'We have been sent to a people who are evildoers*** (unbelievers) – referring to the people of Lūṭ – in order to destroy them,

59. ***...except the family of Lūṭ, all of whom We will save*** because of their belief

60. ***... except for his wife. We have decreed her to be one of those who stay behind*** – to suffer the punishment because of her disbelief.*'*

61. ***When the Messengers came to the family of Lūṭ,***

62. ***he said*** to them, ***'You are people we do not know.'***

63. ***They said, 'We have come to you with what they*** (your people) ***had doubts about*** – a reference to the punishment.

64. ***We have brought you the truth and we are certainly truthful men*** in what we say.

65. ***Travel with your family in the dead of night, following behind*** – walking behind them – ***with them in front of you. None of you must look back*** – in order not to see the terrible fate which will befall them. ***Go where you are ordered to.'*** They were ordered to go to Syria.

66. ***We revealed to him the command We had decreed: that on the following morning the last remnant of those people would be cut off*** and eradicated.
67. ***The inhabitants of the city*** of Sodom (the people of Lūṭ) ***came, exulting at the news*** – when they heard that Lūṭ had handsome, beardless young men in his house. They were angels. The people desired to engage in disgusting actions with them.
68. ***He*** (Lūṭ) ***said, 'These are my guests, so do not put me to shame.***
69. ***Be fearful of Allah and do not dishonour me*** – by perpetrating the disgusting actions you intend to do with them.'
70. ***They said, 'Did we not forbid you to play host to anyone at all?'***
71. ***He said, 'Here are my daughters if you are determined to do something.*** If you desire to satisfy your lust, then marry them.' Then Allah says:
72. ***By your life!*** This is addressed to the Prophet, may Allah bless him and grant him peace. ***They were wandering*** back and forth ***blindly in their drunkenness.***
73. ***So the Great Blast*** – the Shout of Jibrīl – ***seized hold of them at the break of day*** (sunrise).
74. ***We turned the place*** (their cities) ***completely upside down*** – Jibrīl lifted them to heaven and turned them over and dropped them back to the earth – ***and rained down on them stones of hard-baked clay.***
75. ***There are certainly Signs in that*** which has been mentioned regarding the oneness of Allah, ***for the discerning*** – those who look and reflect.
76. ***They*** – the cities of the people of Lūṭ – ***were beside a road which still exists*** – the road that Quraysh took to Syria. The ruins still existed; 'so why do you not consider them?'
77. ***There is certainly a Sign*** (a lesson) ***in that for the believers.***
78. ***The people of the Thicket*** – a reference to a thicket of trees close to Madyan; they were the people of Shu'ayb – ***were also wrongdoers*** in denying the prophethood of Shu'ayb.

يَعۡمَهُونَ ٧٢ فَأَخَذَتۡهُمُ ٱلصَّيۡحَةُ مُشۡرِقِينَ ٧٣ فَجَعَلۡنَا عَٰلِيَهَا
سَافِلَهَا وَأَمۡطَرۡنَا عَلَيۡهِمۡ حِجَارَةٗ مِّن سِجِّيلٍ ٧٤ إِنَّ فِي ذَٰلِكَ
لَأٓيَٰتٖ لِّلۡمُتَوَسِّمِينَ ٧٥ وَإِنَّهَا لَبِسَبِيلٖ مُّقِيمٍ ٧٦ إِنَّ فِي ذَٰلِكَ
لَأٓيَةٗ لِّلۡمُؤۡمِنِينَ ٧٧ وَإِن كَانَ أَصۡحَٰبُ ٱلۡأَيۡكَةِ لَظَٰلِمِينَ ٧٨
فَٱنتَقَمۡنَا مِنۡهُمۡ وَإِنَّهُمَا لَبِإِمَامٖ مُّبِينٖ ٧٩ وَلَقَدۡ كَذَّبَ أَصۡحَٰبُ
ٱلۡحِجۡرِ ٱلۡمُرۡسَلِينَ ٨٠ وَءَاتَيۡنَٰهُمۡ ءَايَٰتِنَا فَكَانُواْ عَنۡهَا مُعۡرِضِينَ
٨١ وَكَانُواْ يَنۡحِتُونَ مِنَ ٱلۡجِبَالِ بُيُوتًا ءَامِنِينَ ٨٢ فَأَخَذَتۡهُمُ
ٱلصَّيۡحَةُ مُصۡبِحِينَ ٨٣ فَمَآ أَغۡنَىٰ عَنۡهُم مَّا كَانُواْ يَكۡسِبُونَ ٨٤
وَمَا خَلَقۡنَا ٱلسَّمَٰوَٰتِ وَٱلۡأَرۡضَ وَمَا بَيۡنَهُمَآ إِلَّا بِٱلۡحَقِّۗ وَإِنَّ
ٱلسَّاعَةَ لَأٓتِيَةٞۖ فَٱصۡفَحِ ٱلصَّفۡحَ ٱلۡجَمِيلَ ٨٥ إِنَّ رَبَّكَ هُوَ
ٱلۡخَلَّٰقُ ٱلۡعَلِيمُ ٨٦ وَلَقَدۡ ءَاتَيۡنَٰكَ سَبۡعٗا مِّنَ ٱلۡمَثَانِي وَٱلۡقُرۡءَانَ
ٱلۡعَظِيمَ ٨٧ لَا تَمُدَّنَّ عَيۡنَيۡكَ إِلَىٰ مَا مَتَّعۡنَا بِهِۦٓ أَزۡوَٰجٗا مِّنۡهُمۡ
وَلَا تَحۡزَنۡ عَلَيۡهِمۡ وَٱخۡفِضۡ جَنَاحَكَ لِلۡمُؤۡمِنِينَ ٨٨ وَقُلۡ إِنِّيٓ
أَنَا ٱلنَّذِيرُ ٱلۡمُبِينُ ٨٩ كَمَآ أَنزَلۡنَا عَلَى ٱلۡمُقۡتَسِمِينَ ٩٠
ٱلَّذِينَ جَعَلُواْ ٱلۡقُرۡءَانَ عِضِينَ ٩١ فَوَرَبِّكَ لَنَسۡـَٔلَنَّهُمۡ
أَجۡمَعِينَ ٩٢ عَمَّا كَانُواْ يَعۡمَلُونَ ٩٣ فَٱصۡدَعۡ بِمَا تُؤۡمَرُ وَأَعۡرِضۡ
عَنِ ٱلۡمُشۡرِكِينَ ٩٤ إِنَّا كَفَيۡنَٰكَ ٱلۡمُسۡتَهۡزِءِينَ ٩٥ ٱلَّذِينَ
يَجۡعَلُونَ مَعَ ٱللَّهِ إِلَٰهًا ءَاخَرَۚ فَسَوۡفَ يَعۡلَمُونَ ٩٦ وَلَقَدۡ نَعۡلَمُ
أَنَّكَ يَضِيقُ صَدۡرُكَ بِمَا يَقُولُونَ ٩٧ فَسَبِّحۡ بِحَمۡدِ رَبِّكَ وَكُن
مِّنَ ٱلسَّٰجِدِينَ ٩٨ وَٱعۡبُدۡ رَبَّكَ حَتَّىٰ يَأۡتِيَكَ ٱلۡيَقِينُ ٩٩

79. ***We took revenge on them as well***, by destroying them with intense heat. ***They are both beside a well-worn track.*** 'The cities of these people are on well-known routes, so will you not reflect on them, people of Makka?"

80. ***The people of al-Ḥijr denied the Messengers.*** Al-Ḥijr is a river valley between Madina and Syria and is another name for the tribe of Thamūd. They denied Ṣāliḥ and by doing so denied the rest of Allah's Messengers, because they all bring the Message of Allah's oneness.

81. ***We brought them Our Signs*** – specifically the She-camel – ***but they turned away from them*** and did not reflect.

82. ***They carved out houses from the mountains, feeling safe,***

83. ***but the Great Blast seized hold of them in the morning,***

84. ***...so all that they earned was of no use to them*** – incapable of defending them from the punishment: neither their fortresses nor all their wealth.

85. ***We did not create the heavens and earth and everything between them, except with truth. The Hour is certainly coming*** – the time when everyone will be repaid for their actions cannot be avoided. ***So,*** Muḥammad, ***turn away*** from your people ***graciously*** and do not be grieved by them. This was abrogated by the *Āyat* of the Sword.

86. ***Your Lord is the Creator*** of everything, ***the All-Knowing*** of everything.

87. ***We have given you the Seven Oft-repeated*** – the Prophet, may Allah bless him and grant him peace, said that this refers to the *Fātiḥa* (al-Bukhārī and Muslim related this.), so-called because it is recited twice in every pair of *rak'ats* – ***and the Magnificent Qur'an.***

88. ***Do not direct your eyes longingly to what We have given certain*** categories ***of them to enjoy. Do not feel sad concerning them*** if they do not believe; ***but take the believers under your wing*** (protection).

89. ***Say: 'I am indeed a clear warner*** of the punishment of Allah which will befall you, and I make the warning clear.'

90. ***Just as We sent down punishment on the dissectors*** (the Jews and Christians);

91. ***...those who divide the Qur'an into little pieces***: those who split the books revealed to them into parts, by believing in some of it and rejecting some of it. It is also said that what is meant by this are those who form groups on the roads of Makka to prevent people from becoming Muslims. Some of them said that the Qur'an was magic, some that it was soothsaying and some that it was poetry.

92. ***By your Lord, We will question them all,*** to rebuke them, ***every one of them,***

93. ***...about what they did!***

94. ***Proclaim***, Muḥammad, ***what you have been ordered to*** – out loud and broadcast it – ***and turn away from the idolaters.*** This was before the command to fight *jihād*.

95. ***We are enough for you against the mockers*** – We will prevent them from harming you by destroying them. Those referred to were al-Walīd ibn al-Mughīra, al-'Āṣī ibn Wā'il, 'Adī ibn Qays, al-Aswad ibn 'Abd al-Muṭṭalib and al-Aswad ibn 'Abdu Yaghūth.

96. ***...those who set up another god beside Allah. They will soon know*** the end of the affair*!*

97. ***We know that your breast is constricted by what they say,*** their mockery and denial,

98. ***So glorify your Lord with praise*** – say, *"Subḥāna'llāhi wa bi-ḥamdihi"* – ***and be one of the prostrators*** in prayer.

99. ***And worship your Lord until what is certain*** *(death)* ***comes to you.***

سُورَةُ النَّحْلِ

بِسْمِ ٱللَّهِ ٱلرَّحْمَٰنِ ٱلرَّحِيمِ

أَتَىٰٓ أَمْرُ ٱللَّهِ فَلَا تَسْتَعْجِلُوهُ ۚ سُبْحَٰنَهُۥ وَتَعَٰلَىٰ عَمَّا يُشْرِكُونَ
١ يُنَزِّلُ ٱلْمَلَٰٓئِكَةَ بِٱلرُّوحِ مِنْ أَمْرِهِۦ عَلَىٰ مَن يَشَآءُ مِنْ عِبَادِهِۦٓ
أَنْ أَنذِرُوٓا۟ أَنَّهُۥ لَآ إِلَٰهَ إِلَّآ أَنَا۠ فَٱتَّقُونِ ٢ خَلَقَ ٱلسَّمَٰوَٰتِ
وَٱلْأَرْضَ بِٱلْحَقِّ ۚ تَعَٰلَىٰ عَمَّا يُشْرِكُونَ ٣ خَلَقَ
ٱلْإِنسَٰنَ مِن نُّطْفَةٍ فَإِذَا هُوَ خَصِيمٌ مُّبِينٌ ٤ وَٱلْأَنْعَٰمَ
خَلَقَهَا ۗ لَكُمْ فِيهَا دِفْءٌ وَمَنَٰفِعُ وَمِنْهَا تَأْكُلُونَ
٥ وَلَكُمْ فِيهَا جَمَالٌ حِينَ تُرِيحُونَ وَحِينَ تَسْرَحُونَ ٦
وَتَحْمِلُ أَثْقَالَكُمْ إِلَىٰ بَلَدٍ لَّمْ تَكُونُوا۟ بَٰلِغِيهِ إِلَّا بِشِقِّ
ٱلْأَنفُسِ ۚ إِنَّ رَبَّكُمْ لَرَءُوفٌ رَّحِيمٌ ٧ وَٱلْخَيْلَ وَٱلْبِغَالَ
وَٱلْحَمِيرَ لِتَرْكَبُوهَا وَزِينَةً ۚ وَيَخْلُقُ مَا لَا تَعْلَمُونَ ٨
وَعَلَى ٱللَّهِ قَصْدُ ٱلسَّبِيلِ وَمِنْهَا جَآئِرٌ ۚ وَلَوْ شَآءَ لَهَدَىٰكُمْ
أَجْمَعِينَ ٩ هُوَ ٱلَّذِىٓ أَنزَلَ مِنَ ٱلسَّمَآءِ مَآءً ۖ لَّكُم مِّنْهُ
شَرَابٌ وَمِنْهُ شَجَرٌ فِيهِ تُسِيمُونَ ١٠ يُنۢبِتُ لَكُم
بِهِ ٱلزَّرْعَ وَٱلزَّيْتُونَ وَٱلنَّخِيلَ وَٱلْأَعْنَٰبَ وَمِن كُلِّ
ٱلثَّمَرَٰتِ ۗ إِنَّ فِى ذَٰلِكَ لَءَايَةً لِّقَوْمٍ يَتَفَكَّرُونَ ١١
وَسَخَّرَ لَكُمُ ٱلَّيْلَ وَٱلنَّهَارَ وَٱلشَّمْسَ وَٱلْقَمَرَ ۖ وَٱلنُّجُومُ
مُسَخَّرَٰتٌۢ بِأَمْرِهِۦٓ ۗ إِنَّ فِى ذَٰلِكَ لَءَايَٰتٍ لِّقَوْمٍ يَعْقِلُونَ
١٢ وَمَا ذَرَأَ لَكُمْ فِى ٱلْأَرْضِ مُخْتَلِفًا أَلْوَٰنُهُۥٓ ۗ إِنَّ

16. *Sūrat an-Naḥl*
The Bee

This *sūra* is Makkan except for the last three *āyat*s, which are Madinan. It has 128 *āyat*s and was revealed after *Sūrat al-Kahf*.

1. When the idolaters thought that the punishment was taking a long time to come, Allah revealed this. ***Allah's command*** (the Last Hour) ***is coming, so do not try to hasten it.*** The past tense is used because it is definite that it will occur, so that in effect it has already happened. 'Do not seek it before its time. It will occur and that is inevitable.' ***Glory be to Him! He is Exalted above anything they associate with Him.***

2. *He sends down angels* – including Jibrīl – ***with the* Rūḥ** (Revelation) ***of His command*** (by His will) ***to any of His slaves He wills*** – meaning the Prophets***: 'Give warning that there is no god but Me*** – alarm the unbelievers with news of the punishment and inform them of it, ***so be fearful of Me!'***

3. *He created the heavens and the earth with truth. He is exalted above anything* in terms of idols ***they associate with Him.***

4. *He created man from a drop of sperm* – and then he becomes strong – ***and yet he is an open challenger*** and strong opponent, as is made clear when he denies the resurrection, saying, "Who will bring the bones to life when they are decayed?"

5. *And He created livestock:* camels, cattle, sheep and goats**. *There is warmth for you***, all mankind, ***in them*** – in the garments and cloaks you make from their hair and wool, which you use to keep yourselves warm – ***and various uses*** – such as increase of wealth through their offspring, and for their milk, and for riding and haulage – ***and some you eat.***

6. *And there is beauty in them for you in the evening when you bring them home* to their night shelters ***and in the morning when you drive them out*** to their pastures ***to graze.***

7. *They carry your loads to lands you would never reach* without beasts of burden such as camels ***except with great difficulty. Your***

Lord is All-Gentle, Most Merciful – to you since He created them for you.

8. *And* He has created ***horses, mules and donkeys; both to ride and for adornment.*** This is to define the main blessings in their creation and does not preclude other blessings, such as eating horses as stated in the *ḥadīth* in the two *Ṣaḥīḥ* Collections. ***And He creates other*** wondrous and strange ***things you do not know.***

9. *The* clear, straight ***Way should lead to Allah, but there are those who deviate from it*** – from going straight on the Way. ***If He had wished He could have guided every one of you*** to go straight, so that all of you would choose to do it.

10. *It is He who sends down water from the sky. From it you drink and from it come the shrubs* – which grow because of it – ***among which you graze your herds.***

11. *And by it He makes crops grow for you, and olives and dates and grapes, and fruit of every kind. There is certainly a Sign in* all ***that*** which has been mentioned, which indicates the Oneness of Allah ***for people who reflect*** and believe.

12. *He has made night and day subservient to you, and the sun and moon and stars, all subject to His command* (His Will). ***There are certainly Signs in that for people who use their intellect*** and reflect.

13. *And also the things* – animals, plants and other natural phenomena – ***of varying colours*** – red, yellow, green and all other hues – ***He has created for you in the earth. There is certainly a Sign in that for people who pay heed.***

14. *It is He who made the sea subservient to you* – enabling you to sail on it and dive into it – ***so that you may eat fresh flesh*** (fish) ***from it and bring out from it ornaments*** (pearls and coral) ***to wear. And you see the ships cleaving through it*** – forwards and backwards on the same wind – ***so that you can seek His bounty*** through trade ***and so that perhaps you may show thanks*** to Allah for that.

15. *He cast firmly embedded mountains on the earth so it would not move under you, and rivers* – such as the Nile – ***and pathways so that perhaps you would be guided*** to reach your desired destinations.

فِي ذَٰلِكَ لَآيَةً لِّقَوْمٍ يَذَّكَّرُونَ ﴿١٣﴾ وَهُوَ الَّذِي
سَخَّرَ الْبَحْرَ لِتَأْكُلُوا مِنْهُ لَحْمًا طَرِيًّا وَتَسْتَخْرِجُوا
مِنْهُ حِلْيَةً تَلْبَسُونَهَا وَتَرَى الْفُلْكَ مَوَاخِرَ فِيهِ
وَلِتَبْتَغُوا مِن فَضْلِهِ وَلَعَلَّكُمْ تَشْكُرُونَ ﴿١٤﴾
وَأَلْقَىٰ فِي الْأَرْضِ رَوَاسِيَ أَن تَمِيدَ بِكُمْ وَأَنْهَارًا وَسُبُلًا
لَّعَلَّكُمْ تَهْتَدُونَ ﴿١٥﴾ وَعَلَامَاتٍ ۚ وَبِالنَّجْمِ هُمْ يَهْتَدُونَ
﴿١٦﴾ أَفَمَن يَخْلُقُ كَمَن لَّا يَخْلُقُ ۗ أَفَلَا تَذَكَّرُونَ ﴿١٧﴾ وَإِن
تَعُدُّوا نِعْمَةَ اللَّهِ لَا تُحْصُوهَا ۗ إِنَّ اللَّهَ لَغَفُورٌ رَّحِيمٌ ﴿١٨﴾
وَاللَّهُ يَعْلَمُ مَا تُسِرُّونَ وَمَا تُعْلِنُونَ ﴿١٩﴾ وَالَّذِينَ يَدْعُونَ
مِن دُونِ اللَّهِ لَا يَخْلُقُونَ شَيْئًا وَهُمْ يُخْلَقُونَ ﴿٢٠﴾ أَمْوَاتٌ غَيْرُ
أَحْيَاءٍ ۖ وَمَا يَشْعُرُونَ أَيَّانَ يُبْعَثُونَ ﴿٢١﴾ إِلَٰهُكُمْ إِلَٰهٌ وَاحِدٌ ۚ
فَالَّذِينَ لَا يُؤْمِنُونَ بِالْآخِرَةِ قُلُوبُهُم مُّنكِرَةٌ وَهُم مُّسْتَكْبِرُونَ
﴿٢٢﴾ لَا جَرَمَ أَنَّ اللَّهَ يَعْلَمُ مَا يُسِرُّونَ وَمَا يُعْلِنُونَ ۚ إِنَّهُ
لَا يُحِبُّ الْمُسْتَكْبِرِينَ ﴿٢٣﴾ وَإِذَا قِيلَ لَهُم مَّاذَا أَنزَلَ رَبُّكُمْ ۙ
قَالُوا أَسَاطِيرُ الْأَوَّلِينَ ﴿٢٤﴾ لِيَحْمِلُوا أَوْزَارَهُمْ كَامِلَةً
يَوْمَ الْقِيَامَةِ ۙ وَمِنْ أَوْزَارِ الَّذِينَ يُضِلُّونَهُم بِغَيْرِ عِلْمٍ ۗ أَلَا
سَاءَ مَا يَزِرُونَ ﴿٢٥﴾ قَدْ مَكَرَ الَّذِينَ مِن قَبْلِهِمْ
فَأَتَى اللَّهُ بُنْيَانَهُم مِّنَ الْقَوَاعِدِ فَخَرَّ عَلَيْهِمُ السَّقْفُ
مِن فَوْقِهِمْ وَأَتَاهُمُ الْعَذَابُ مِنْ حَيْثُ لَا يَشْعُرُونَ ﴿٢٦﴾
ثُمَّ يَوْمَ الْقِيَامَةِ يُخْزِيهِمْ وَيَقُولُ أَيْنَ شُرَكَائِيَ الَّذِينَ

16. ***...and landmarks*** which keep you on the paths, such as mountains by rivers. ***And they are guided by the stars*** to the direction of the *qibla* at night.

17. ***Is He who creates*** – in other words, Allah – ***like him who does not create*** – referring to the idols – since you worship them as well***?*** No. ***So will you not pay heed*** to this and believe in Him alone***?***

18. ***If you tried to number Allah's blessings, you could never count them.*** You could not even enumerate them, let alone be grateful for them. ***Allah is Ever-Forgiving, Most Merciful*** in spite of your falling short and your disobedience.

19. ***Allah knows what you keep secret and what you make public.***

20. ***Those they call on*** (read as *yad'ūna* and *tad'ūna*, "you call upon") and worship ***besides Allah*** (the idols) ***do not create anything. They are themselves created*** – made out of stones and other things.

21. ***They are dead*** – with no spirit in them, ***not alive, and they*** (the idols) ***are not aware of when they will be raised.*** They were not aware of creation, so how can they be worshipped sincerely since there is no god except the Living Creator, who knows the Unseen?

22. ***Your God*** – who alone is entitled to Your worship – ***is One God.*** There is no one like Him in respect of His Essence or His Attributes. He is Allah Almighty. ***As for those who do not believe in the Next World, their hearts are in denial*** of His oneness ***and they are puffed up with pride***: too arrogant to believe in it.

23. ***There is no doubt that Allah knows what they keep secret and what they make public*** and will repay them for that. ***He does not love people puffed up with pride*** and will punish them.

24. The following was revealed about an-Naḍr ibn al-Ḥārith. ***When they are asked, 'What has your Lord sent down*** to Muḥammad***?' they say, 'Myths and legends*** (fabrications) ***of previous peoples*** to misguide people.***'***

25. ***So on the Day of Rising*** the result of their affair is that ***they will carry the full weight of their own burdens*** (sins) – without any of them being expiated – ***and some of the burdens of those they misguided without knowledge*** so that they followed them, and for that

كُنتُمْ تُشَـٰٓقُّونَ فِيهِمْ ۚ قَالَ ٱلَّذِينَ أُوتُوا۟ ٱلْعِلْمَ إِنَّ ٱلْخِزْىَ
ٱلْيَوْمَ وَٱلسُّوٓءَ عَلَى ٱلْكَـٰفِرِينَ ﴿٢٧﴾ ٱلَّذِينَ تَتَوَفَّىٰهُمُ ٱلْمَلَـٰٓئِكَةُ
ظَالِمِىٓ أَنفُسِهِمْ ۖ فَأَلْقَوُا۟ ٱلسَّلَمَ مَا كُنَّا نَعْمَلُ مِن سُوٓءٍۭ ۚ بَلَىٰٓ
إِنَّ ٱللَّهَ عَلِيمٌۢ بِمَا كُنتُمْ تَعْمَلُونَ ﴿٢٨﴾ فَٱدْخُلُوٓا۟ أَبْوَٰبَ جَهَنَّمَ
خَـٰلِدِينَ فِيهَا ۖ فَلَبِئْسَ مَثْوَى ٱلْمُتَكَبِّرِينَ ﴿٢٩﴾ ۞ وَقِيلَ
لِلَّذِينَ ٱتَّقَوْا۟ مَاذَآ أَنزَلَ رَبُّكُمْ ۚ قَالُوا۟ خَيْرًا ۗ لِّلَّذِينَ أَحْسَنُوا۟ فِى
هَـٰذِهِ ٱلدُّنْيَا حَسَنَةٌ ۚ وَلَدَارُ ٱلْـَٔاخِرَةِ خَيْرٌ ۚ وَلَنِعْمَ دَارُ ٱلْمُتَّقِينَ
﴿٣٠﴾ جَنَّـٰتُ عَدْنٍ يَدْخُلُونَهَا تَجْرِى مِن تَحْتِهَا ٱلْأَنْهَـٰرُ ۖ لَهُمْ فِيهَا
مَا يَشَآءُونَ ۚ كَذَٰلِكَ يَجْزِى ٱللَّهُ ٱلْمُتَّقِينَ ﴿٣١﴾ ٱلَّذِينَ تَتَوَفَّىٰهُمُ
ٱلْمَلَـٰٓئِكَةُ طَيِّبِينَ ۙ يَقُولُونَ سَلَـٰمٌ عَلَيْكُمُ ٱدْخُلُوا۟ ٱلْجَنَّةَ بِمَا
كُنتُمْ تَعْمَلُونَ ﴿٣٢﴾ هَلْ يَنظُرُونَ إِلَّآ أَن تَأْتِيَهُمُ ٱلْمَلَـٰٓئِكَةُ
أَوْ يَأْتِىَ أَمْرُ رَبِّكَ ۚ كَذَٰلِكَ فَعَلَ ٱلَّذِينَ مِن قَبْلِهِمْ ۚ وَمَا ظَلَمَهُمُ
ٱللَّهُ وَلَـٰكِن كَانُوٓا۟ أَنفُسَهُمْ يَظْلِمُونَ ﴿٣٣﴾ فَأَصَابَهُمْ
سَيِّـَٔاتُ مَا عَمِلُوا۟ وَحَاقَ بِهِم مَّا كَانُوا۟ بِهِۦ يَسْتَهْزِءُونَ ﴿٣٤﴾
وَقَالَ ٱلَّذِينَ أَشْرَكُوا۟ لَوْ شَآءَ ٱللَّهُ مَا عَبَدْنَا مِن دُونِهِۦ مِن
شَىْءٍ نَّحْنُ وَلَآ ءَابَآؤُنَا وَلَا حَرَّمْنَا مِن دُونِهِۦ مِن شَىْءٍ ۚ كَذَٰلِكَ
فَعَلَ ٱلَّذِينَ مِن قَبْلِهِمْ ۚ فَهَلْ عَلَى ٱلرُّسُلِ إِلَّا ٱلْبَلَـٰغُ ٱلْمُبِينُ
﴿٣٥﴾ وَلَقَدْ بَعَثْنَا فِى كُلِّ أُمَّةٍ رَّسُولًا أَنِ ٱعْبُدُوا۟ ٱللَّهَ
وَٱجْتَنِبُوا۟ ٱلطَّـٰغُوتَ ۖ فَمِنْهُم مَّنْ هَدَى ٱللَّهُ وَمِنْهُم مَّنْ
حَقَّتْ عَلَيْهِ ٱلضَّلَـٰلَةُ ۚ فَسِيرُوا۟ فِى ٱلْأَرْضِ فَٱنظُرُوا۟ كَيْفَ

reason they share in the wrong action. ***What an evil load they bear*** because of this*!*

26. ***Those before them also plotted*** – said to be a reference to Nimrod, who built a tall tower by which to ascend to heaven so that he could fight its inhabitants, ***and Allah came at their building from the foundations*** – sending wind and an earthquake against it which destroyed it – ***and the roof caved in on top of them. The punishment came at them from where they did not expect*** and in a way which had not occurred to them. It is also said that this is a metaphor for the ruin of all the plotting of the unbelievers against their Messengers.

27. ***Then on the Day of Rising He*** (Allah) ***will disgrace them, and say*** to them on the tongues of the angels, to rebuke them, ***'Where are My partner gods*** you claimed ***for whose sake you became so hostile*** and opposed the believers*?'* ***Those given knowledge*** among the Prophets and believers ***will say, 'Today there is disgrace and evil for the unbelievers.'***

28. ***As for those the angels take in death*** (read as *tatawaffāhum* and *yatawaffāhum*) ***while they are wronging themselves*** through unbelief, ***they will offer their submission*** – they will obey and submit at death – saying*:* ***'We did not do any evil*** – meaning commit *shirk*.' The angels will say: ***'Oh yes you did! Allah knows what you were doing*** and will repay you for it.'

29. They will be told: ***'Enter the gates of Hell, remaining in it timelessly, for ever. How evil is the abode of the arrogant!'***

30. ***When those who are fearful of Allah*** and afraid of committing *shirk* ***are asked, 'What has your Lord sent down?' their reply is, 'Good!' There is good in*** the life of ***this world for those who do good*** accompanied by faith ***and the abode of the Next World*** (the Garden) ***is even better*** than this world and what it contains. Allah says about it*;* ***How wonderful is the abode of those who are godfearing!***

31. ***Gardens of Eden which they enter, with rivers flowing under them, where they have whatever they desire. That is how Allah repays those who are godfearing:***

32. ***...those the angels take in a virtuous state*** – free from unbelief. ***They say*** to them when they die***, 'Peace be upon you!'*** and they will be told in the Next World: ***'Enter the Garden for what you did.'***

33. ***What are they*** (the unbelievers) ***waiting for but the angels to come to them*** (read as *ta'tiyahum* and *ya'tiyahum*) to take their souls ***or for your Lord's command*** of the punishment or the Day of Rising ***to come? That*** which they did ***is like what those before them*** from earlier communities ***did*** when they denied their Messengers and so were destroyed. ***Allah did not wrong them*** by destroying them without their committing wrong***; rather they wronged themselves*** through their unbelief.

34. ***The*** repayment for the ***evil actions*** which ***they did assailed them. They were engulfed by what they mocked*** – meaning the punishment.

35. ***The idolaters*** among the people of Makka ***say, 'If Allah had willed we would not have worshipped anything apart from Him, neither we nor our fathers, nor would we have forbidden anything without His say*** – the result of superstitions such as *baḥīra* and *sā'iba* and other manifestations of their *shirk.'* They said that making such things *ḥarām* was by Allah's will and He was pleased with it. Allah says: ***Those before them said the same*** when they denied the Messengers regarding what they brought. ***Are the Mes-sengers responsible for anything but clear transmission?*** They are not held responsible for whether people follow their guidance.

36. ***We sent a Messenger among every people*** – as We sent Messengers to those peoples mentioned – ***saying: 'Worship Allah*** and affirm His unity ***and keep clear of*** worshipping ***all false gods.' Among them were some whom Allah guided*** – and who, therefore, believed – ***but others received the misguidance they deserved*** in Allah's foreknowledge, and so they did not believe. ***Travel***, unbelievers of Makka, ***about the earth and see the final fate of the deniers*** who belied the Messengers and were destroyed.

37. ***However eager you are***, Muḥammad, ***for them to be guided*** – if Allah has misguided them you will not be able to do so: ***Allah will not guide those whom He misguides. They will have no helpers*** to defend them against the punishment of Allah.

كَانَ عَـٰقِبَةُ ٱلْمُكَذِّبِينَ ﴿٣٦﴾ إِن تَحْرِصْ عَلَىٰ هُدَىٰهُمْ
فَإِنَّ ٱللَّهَ لَا يَهْدِى مَن يُضِلُّ ۖ وَمَا لَهُم مِّن نَّـٰصِرِينَ ﴿٣٧﴾
وَأَقْسَمُوا۟ بِٱللَّهِ جَهْدَ أَيْمَـٰنِهِمْ ۙ لَا يَبْعَثُ ٱللَّهُ مَن يَمُوتُ ۚ بَلَىٰ
وَعْدًا عَلَيْهِ حَقًّا وَلَـٰكِنَّ أَكْثَرَ ٱلنَّاسِ لَا يَعْلَمُونَ ﴿٣٨﴾
لِيُبَيِّنَ لَهُمُ ٱلَّذِى يَخْتَلِفُونَ فِيهِ وَلِيَعْلَمَ ٱلَّذِينَ كَفَرُوٓا۟ أَنَّهُمْ
كَانُوا۟ كَـٰذِبِينَ ﴿٣٩﴾ إِنَّمَا قَوْلُنَا لِشَىْءٍ إِذَآ أَرَدْنَـٰهُ أَن نَّقُولَ
لَهُۥ كُن فَيَكُونُ ﴿٤٠﴾ وَٱلَّذِينَ هَاجَرُوا۟ فِى ٱللَّهِ مِنۢ بَعْدِ مَا ظُلِمُوا۟
لَنُبَوِّئَنَّهُمْ فِى ٱلدُّنْيَا حَسَنَةً ۖ وَلَأَجْرُ ٱلْـَٔاخِرَةِ أَكْبَرُ ۚ لَوْ كَانُوا۟
يَعْلَمُونَ ﴿٤١﴾ ٱلَّذِينَ صَبَرُوا۟ وَعَلَىٰ رَبِّهِمْ يَتَوَكَّلُونَ ﴿٤٢﴾
وَمَآ أَرْسَلْنَا مِن قَبْلِكَ إِلَّا رِجَالًا نُّوحِىٓ إِلَيْهِمْ ۚ فَسْـَٔلُوٓا۟ أَهْلَ
ٱلذِّكْرِ إِن كُنتُمْ لَا تَعْلَمُونَ ﴿٤٣﴾ بِٱلْبَيِّنَـٰتِ وَٱلزُّبُرِ ۗ وَأَنزَلْنَآ إِلَيْكَ
ٱلذِّكْرَ لِتُبَيِّنَ لِلنَّاسِ مَا نُزِّلَ إِلَيْهِمْ وَلَعَلَّهُمْ يَتَفَكَّرُونَ
﴿٤٤﴾ أَفَأَمِنَ ٱلَّذِينَ مَكَرُوا۟ ٱلسَّيِّـَٔاتِ أَن يَخْسِفَ ٱللَّهُ بِهِمُ ٱلْأَرْضَ
أَوْ يَأْتِيَهُمُ ٱلْعَذَابُ مِنْ حَيْثُ لَا يَشْعُرُونَ ﴿٤٥﴾ أَوْ يَأْخُذَهُمْ
فِى تَقَلُّبِهِمْ فَمَا هُم بِمُعْجِزِينَ ﴿٤٦﴾ أَوْ يَأْخُذَهُمْ عَلَىٰ تَخَوُّفٍ فَإِنَّ
رَبَّكُمْ لَرَءُوفٌ رَّحِيمٌ ﴿٤٧﴾ أَوَلَمْ يَرَوْا۟ إِلَىٰ مَا خَلَقَ ٱللَّهُ مِن شَىْءٍ
يَتَفَيَّؤُا۟ ظِلَـٰلُهُۥ عَنِ ٱلْيَمِينِ وَٱلشَّمَآئِلِ سُجَّدًا لِّلَّهِ وَهُمْ دَٰخِرُونَ
﴿٤٨﴾ وَلِلَّهِ يَسْجُدُ مَا فِى ٱلسَّمَـٰوَٰتِ وَمَا فِى ٱلْأَرْضِ مِن دَآبَّةٍ
وَٱلْمَلَـٰٓئِكَةُ وَهُمْ لَا يَسْتَكْبِرُونَ ﴿٤٩﴾ يَخَافُونَ رَبَّهُم مِّن فَوْقِهِمْ
وَيَفْعَلُونَ مَا يُؤْمَرُونَ ۩ ﴿٥٠﴾ ۞ وَقَالَ ٱللَّهُ لَا تَتَّخِذُوٓا۟ إِلَـٰهَيْنِ

38. ***They swear by Allah with their most earnest oaths that Allah will not raise up those who die, when, on the contrary, it is a*** true and ***binding promise on Him*** to resurrect them***; but most*** of the ***people*** of Makka ***do not know it.***

39. ***It*** (resurrecting them) ***is so that He may make clear to them the things they differed about*** with the believers regarding their own punishment and the reward of the believers ***and so that those who disbelieved will know that they were liars*** when they denied the Resurrection.

40. ***Our Command to a thing when We desire*** to bring ***it*** into existence ***is just to say to it 'Be!' and it is*** (read as *fa-yakūnu* and *fa-yakūna*). This *āyat* is an indication of Allah's power to bring about the Re-surrection.

41. ***As for those who emigrate for Allah's sake*** – in order to establish His *dīn* – ***after being wronged*** through the harm done to them by the people of Makka, meaning the Prophet, may Allah bless him and grant him peace, and His Companions***: We shall give them good lodging in this world*** in Madina***, and the reward of the Next World*** in the Garden ***is greater still if they*** – the unbelievers, or those who did not emigrate – ***only knew*** about the honour which those who emigrate are given, in which case they would have done so too:

42. ***...those who are steadfast*** – in the face of the harm done to them by the idolaters and emigrate to make the *dīn* victorious – ***and put their trust in their Lord***, – Allah will provide for them from where they do not expect.

43. ***We have only ever sent before you men*** – not angels – ***who were given Revelation. Ask the People of the Reminder*** – those who know the Torah and the Gospel – ***if you do not know*** that. They do know it – and you are more likely to believe them than to believe those who believe in Muḥammad, may Allah bless him and grant him peace.

44 ***. ...who brought Clear Signs and Revealed Books. And We have sent down the Reminder*** (the Qur'an) ***to you so that you may make clear to mankind what has been sent down to them*** regarding the lawful and unlawful – ***so that perhaps they will reflect*** on that and take note.

45. ***Do those who plot evil actions*** against the Prophet, may Allah bless him and grant him peace, in the Dār an-Nadwa to imprison him, kill him, or expel him, as stated in *Sūrat al-Anfāl*, ***feel secure that Allah will not cause the earth to swallow them up*** in the way that Qārūn was swallowed up – ***or that a punishment will not come upon them from where they least expect?*** Such an event can occur from a direction which they have not thought about. They were destroyed at Badr and were not expecting that.

46. ***Or that He will not seize them on their travels*** for trade, ***some - thing they are powerless to prevent?*** They have no power to evade Allah's punishment.

47. ***Or that He will not seize them little by little?*** (The word here for "seize", *takhawwuf,* means to take them one by one until all are destroyed.) ***For your Lord is All-Compassionate, Most Merciful,*** since He does not hasten the punishment.

48. ***Do they not see the things Allah has created*** – such as trees and mountains – ***casting their shadows to the right and to the left*** – in other words, they stretch first to one side at the beginning of the day and then to the other later on – ***prostrating themselves*** – referring to the shadows – ***before Allah in complete humility?*** Shadows are here referred to as if they were beings with intelligence.

49. ***Everything in the heavens and every creature on the earth prostrates to Allah*** – is subject to Him and does what He wants it to and this includes things with no intelligence which are extremely numerous, ***as do the angels.*** The angels are specifically mentioned because of their excellence. ***They are not puffed up with pride*** – preventing them from worshipping Him.

50. ***They*** (the angels) ***fear their Lord above them*** – knowing His power over them – ***and do what they are ordered to do.***

51. ***Allah says, 'Do not take two gods.*** The word "two", *ithnayn*, is added despite being present in the dual form of the noun for reasons of stress. ***He is only One God*** – affirming both His divinity and unity, ***so dread Me alone*** and no one else.' This is an example of a change of person from the third person singular to the first person singular.

ٱثْنَيْنِ إِنَّمَا هُوَ إِلَٰهٌ وَٰحِدٌ فَإِيَّٰىَ فَٱرْهَبُونِ ﴿٥١﴾ وَلَهُۥ مَا فِى ٱلسَّمَٰوَٰتِ
وَٱلْأَرْضِ وَلَهُ ٱلدِّينُ وَاصِبًا أَفَغَيْرَ ٱللَّهِ تَتَّقُونَ ﴿٥٢﴾ وَمَا بِكُم مِّن
نِّعْمَةٍ فَمِنَ ٱللَّهِ ثُمَّ إِذَا مَسَّكُمُ ٱلضُّرُّ فَإِلَيْهِ تَجْـَٔرُونَ ﴿٥٣﴾ ثُمَّ
إِذَا كَشَفَ ٱلضُّرَّ عَنكُمْ إِذَا فَرِيقٌ مِّنكُم بِرَبِّهِمْ يُشْرِكُونَ ﴿٥٤﴾
لِيَكْفُرُوا۟ بِمَآ ءَاتَيْنَٰهُمْ فَتَمَتَّعُوا۟ فَسَوْفَ تَعْلَمُونَ ﴿٥٥﴾ وَيَجْعَلُونَ
لِمَا لَا يَعْلَمُونَ نَصِيبًا مِّمَّا رَزَقْنَٰهُمْ تَٱللَّهِ لَتُسْـَٔلُنَّ عَمَّا كُنتُمْ
تَفْتَرُونَ ﴿٥٦﴾ وَيَجْعَلُونَ لِلَّهِ ٱلْبَنَٰتِ سُبْحَٰنَهُۥ وَلَهُم مَّا يَشْتَهُونَ
﴿٥٧﴾ وَإِذَا بُشِّرَ أَحَدُهُم بِٱلْأُنثَىٰ ظَلَّ وَجْهُهُۥ مُسْوَدًّا وَهُوَ كَظِيمٌ
﴿٥٨﴾ يَتَوَٰرَىٰ مِنَ ٱلْقَوْمِ مِن سُوٓءِ مَا بُشِّرَ بِهِۦٓ أَيُمْسِكُهُۥ عَلَىٰ هُونٍ
أَمْ يَدُسُّهُۥ فِى ٱلتُّرَابِ أَلَا سَآءَ مَا يَحْكُمُونَ ﴿٥٩﴾ لِلَّذِينَ لَا يُؤْمِنُونَ
بِٱلْـَٔاخِرَةِ مَثَلُ ٱلسَّوْءِ وَلِلَّهِ ٱلْمَثَلُ ٱلْأَعْلَىٰ وَهُوَ ٱلْعَزِيزُ ٱلْحَكِيمُ
﴿٦٠﴾ وَلَوْ يُؤَاخِذُ ٱللَّهُ ٱلنَّاسَ بِظُلْمِهِم مَّا تَرَكَ عَلَيْهَا مِن دَآبَّةٍ وَلَٰكِن
يُؤَخِّرُهُمْ إِلَىٰٓ أَجَلٍ مُّسَمًّى فَإِذَا جَآءَ أَجَلُهُمْ لَا يَسْتَـْٔخِرُونَ
سَاعَةً وَلَا يَسْتَقْدِمُونَ ﴿٦١﴾ وَيَجْعَلُونَ لِلَّهِ مَا يَكْرَهُونَ
وَتَصِفُ أَلْسِنَتُهُمُ ٱلْكَذِبَ أَنَّ لَهُمُ ٱلْحُسْنَىٰ لَا جَرَمَ أَنَّ
لَهُمُ ٱلنَّارَ وَأَنَّهُم مُّفْرَطُونَ ﴿٦٢﴾ تَٱللَّهِ لَقَدْ أَرْسَلْنَآ إِلَىٰٓ أُمَمٍ مِّن
قَبْلِكَ فَزَيَّنَ لَهُمُ ٱلشَّيْطَٰنُ أَعْمَٰلَهُمْ فَهُوَ وَلِيُّهُمُ ٱلْيَوْمَ وَلَهُمْ
عَذَابٌ أَلِيمٌ ﴿٦٣﴾ وَمَآ أَنزَلْنَا عَلَيْكَ ٱلْكِتَٰبَ إِلَّا لِتُبَيِّنَ لَهُمُ
ٱلَّذِى ٱخْتَلَفُوا۟ فِيهِ وَهُدًى وَرَحْمَةً لِّقَوْمٍ يُؤْمِنُونَ ﴿٦٤﴾
وَٱللَّهُ أَنزَلَ مِنَ ٱلسَّمَآءِ مَآءً فَأَحْيَا بِهِ ٱلْأَرْضَ بَعْدَ مَوْتِهَآ إِنَّ فِى ذَٰلِكَ

52. ***Everything in the heavens and earth belongs to Him*** – as His kingdom, creation and slaves – ***and the* dīn *belongs to Him*** – obedience is due to Him – ***firmly and for ever. So why do you fear anyone other than Allah?*** He is the True God and there is no god but Him. This is a question implying rebuke and expecting a negative response.

53. ***Any blessing you have is from Allah*** – only Allah brings it about. ***Then when harm*** – such as poverty and illness – ***touches you, it is to Him you cry for help***, raising your voices in asking for help and in supplication and calling on Him alone.

54. ***But when He removes the harm from you, a group of you associate others with their Lord,***

55. ***...ungrateful for what*** (the blessings) ***We have given them. Enjoy yourselves*** in worshipping your idols. This is a threat to them. ***You will soon know*** the result of doing that*!*

56. ***They*** (the idolaters) ***allot a portion of the provision We have given them to things they have no knowledge of at all*** – they allot a portion of their crops and livestock to their idols when they do not know whether they harm or benefit them. They said, "This is for Allah and this is for our partner-gods." ***By Allah, you will be asked about what you invented*** by saying that Allah commanded you to do that*!* This is a rebuke.

57. ***They allot daughters to Allah*** by saying that the angels are His daughters – ***glory be to Him!*** – this interjection is to disconnect Him from their claims – ***while they have what*** (the sons) ***they want.*** In other words, they allot Him daughters, which they dislike, when He is far exalted above having any children; and they allot themselves the sons, which they prefer, so that they have what is more glorious than what they attribute to Him. This is also referred to in His words: *"Ask them their true opinion: Does your Lord have daughters while they themselves have sons?"* (37:149)

58. ***When one of them is given the good news of*** the birth of ***a baby girl, his face darkens*** with sorrow ***and he is furious.*** 'So how can you ascribe daughters to Allah?'

59. ***He hides away from*** his ***people because of the evil of the good news he has been given*** – out of fear of censure; but he hesitates about what he should do about it. ***Should he keep her*** alive ***igno - miniously or bury her*** alive ***in the earth? What an evil judgement they make*** in ascribing daughters to their Creator when they themselves take this position about it*!*

60. ***Those*** (the unbelievers) ***who do not believe in the Next World have an evil*** (ugly) ***likeness.*** That is a reference to their burying their daughters alive although they need them for marriage. ***Allah's is the Highest Likeness*** – embodied in the expression "there is no god but Allah". ***He is the Almighty*** in His kingdom, ***the All-Wise*** in His creation.

61. ***If Allah were to punish people for their wrong actions*** (acts of disobedience) ***not a single*** living ***creature would be left upon the earth, but He defers them till a predetermined time. When their specified time arrives, they cannot delay it for a single hour nor can they bring it forward.***

62. ***They allot to Allah what they themselves dislike*** – in respect of daughters, a share of power, and humiliation of the Messengers – ***and their tongues frame the lie that they will receive the Best*** (the Garden) with Allah – when they say, *"If I am returned to my Lord, I will definitely find the best reward with Him."* 41:50 Allah says: ***There is no doubt at all that they will receive the Fire and that they are people who go to excess*** (read as *mufraṭūn* and *mufriṭūn*).

63. ***By Allah, We sent Messengers to communities before your time, but Shayṭān made their*** evil ***actions seem good to them*** – so they denied the Messengers. ***Therefore today he is their protector.*** He is the one who manages their affairs today in this world. ***They will have a painful punishment*** in the Next World. It is also said that the word "today" here refers to the Day of Rising and it reports about a future state. In other words, they will then have no protector except him; but he will have no power to protect himself even, so how will he be able to help them?

64. ***We have only sent down the Book*** (the Qur'an) ***to you***, Muḥammad, ***so that you may make clear to them the things about which they differ*** regarding the *dīn*, ***and as a guidance and a mercy to people who believe.***

65. ***Allah sends down water from the sky and by it brings the dead earth back to life*** – with plants after it has been arid and lifeless.

لَأٓيَةً لِّقَوۡمٍ يَسۡمَعُونَ ﴿٦٥﴾ وَإِنَّ لَكُمۡ فِي ٱلۡأَنۡعَٰمِ لَعِبۡرَةًۖ نُّسۡقِيكُم مِّمَّا
فِي بُطُونِهِۦ مِنۢ بَيۡنِ فَرۡثٍ وَدَمٍ لَّبَنًا خَالِصًا سَآئِغًا لِّلشَّٰرِبِينَ ﴿٦٦﴾
وَمِن ثَمَرَٰتِ ٱلنَّخِيلِ وَٱلۡأَعۡنَٰبِ تَتَّخِذُونَ مِنۡهُ سَكَرًا وَرِزۡقًا
حَسَنًاۚ إِنَّ فِي ذَٰلِكَ لَأٓيَةً لِّقَوۡمٍ يَعۡقِلُونَ ﴿٦٧﴾ وَأَوۡحَىٰ رَبُّكَ إِلَى ٱلنَّحۡلِ
أَنِ ٱتَّخِذِي مِنَ ٱلۡجِبَالِ بُيُوتًا وَمِنَ ٱلشَّجَرِ وَمِمَّا يَعۡرِشُونَ ﴿٦٨﴾ ثُمَّ كُلِي
مِن كُلِّ ٱلثَّمَرَٰتِ فَٱسۡلُكِي سُبُلَ رَبِّكِ ذُلُلٗاۚ يَخۡرُجُ مِنۢ بُطُونِهَا
شَرَابٌ مُّخۡتَلِفٌ أَلۡوَٰنُهُۥ فِيهِ شِفَآءٌ لِّلنَّاسِۚ إِنَّ فِي ذَٰلِكَ لَأٓيَةً لِّقَوۡمٍ
يَتَفَكَّرُونَ ﴿٦٩﴾ وَٱللَّهُ خَلَقَكُمۡ ثُمَّ يَتَوَفَّىٰكُمۡۚ وَمِنكُم مَّن يُرَدُّ إِلَىٰٓ أَرۡذَلِ
ٱلۡعُمُرِ لِكَيۡ لَا يَعۡلَمَ بَعۡدَ عِلۡمٖ شَيۡـًٔاۚ إِنَّ ٱللَّهَ عَلِيمٞ قَدِيرٞ ﴿٧٠﴾ وَٱللَّهُ
فَضَّلَ بَعۡضَكُمۡ عَلَىٰ بَعۡضٖ فِي ٱلرِّزۡقِۚ فَمَا ٱلَّذِينَ فُضِّلُواْ بِرَآدِّي
رِزۡقِهِمۡ عَلَىٰ مَا مَلَكَتۡ أَيۡمَٰنُهُمۡ فَهُمۡ فِيهِ سَوَآءٌۚ أَفَبِنِعۡمَةِ
ٱللَّهِ يَجۡحَدُونَ ﴿٧١﴾ وَٱللَّهُ جَعَلَ لَكُم مِّنۡ أَنفُسِكُمۡ أَزۡوَٰجٗا
وَجَعَلَ لَكُم مِّنۡ أَزۡوَٰجِكُم بَنِينَ وَحَفَدَةٗ وَرَزَقَكُم مِّنَ
ٱلطَّيِّبَٰتِۚ أَفَبِٱلۡبَٰطِلِ يُؤۡمِنُونَ وَبِنِعۡمَتِ ٱللَّهِ هُمۡ يَكۡفُرُونَ ﴿٧٢﴾
وَيَعۡبُدُونَ مِن دُونِ ٱللَّهِ مَا لَا يَمۡلِكُ لَهُمۡ رِزۡقٗا مِّنَ ٱلسَّمَٰوَٰتِ
وَٱلۡأَرۡضِ شَيۡـٔٗا وَلَا يَسۡتَطِيعُونَ ﴿٧٣﴾ فَلَا تَضۡرِبُواْ لِلَّهِ ٱلۡأَمۡثَالَۚ
إِنَّ ٱللَّهَ يَعۡلَمُ وَأَنتُمۡ لَا تَعۡلَمُونَ ﴿٧٤﴾ ۞ ضَرَبَ ٱللَّهُ مَثَلًا عَبۡدٗا
مَّمۡلُوكٗا لَّا يَقۡدِرُ عَلَىٰ شَيۡءٖ وَمَن رَّزَقۡنَٰهُ مِنَّا رِزۡقًا حَسَنٗا
فَهُوَ يُنفِقُ مِنۡهُ سِرّٗا وَجَهۡرًاۖ هَلۡ يَسۡتَوُۥنَۚ ٱلۡحَمۡدُ لِلَّهِۚ
بَلۡ أَكۡثَرُهُمۡ لَا يَعۡلَمُونَ ﴿٧٥﴾ وَضَرَبَ ٱللَّهُ مَثَلٗا رَّجُلَيۡنِ

There is certainly a Sign of the Resurrection ***in that*** which has been mentioned ***for people who hear*** and reflect.

66. ***There is instruction for you in cattle: from the contents of their bellies, from between the dung and blood, We give you pure milk to drink*** – not sullied by either dung or blood in respect of its taste, smell, or colour, ***easy for drinkers to swallow.***

67. ***And from the fruit of the date-palm and the grape-vine you derive both intoxicants*** – this was revealed before wine was made unlawful – ***and wholesome provision*** such as dates, raisins, vinegar and grape syrup. ***There is certainly a Sign in that of*** the power of Allah ***for people who use their intellect*** and reflect.

68. ***Your Lord revealed*** by inspiration ***to the bees: 'Build dwellings*** for shelter ***in the mountains and the trees, and also in the structures which men erect*** – a reference to hives which people build for them. Without this Divine instruction, they would not resort to them.

69. ***Then eat from every kind of fruit and travel the paths of your Lord*** – in search of nectar – ***which have been made easy for you to follow.'*** These things have been placed at the service of bees and so they are not difficult for them to reach, even if the surroundings are rough, and bees do not normally get lost, even if they travel great distances. ***From inside them comes a drink of varying colours*** (honey) ***containing healing for mankind*** for illnesses. It is said this means "for some illnesses", indicated by the fact that the word "healing" is indefinite; or it may mean "all illnesses" since it is grammatically connected to mankind as a whole; or it may be that the healing is dependent on the intention with which it is administered. The Prophet, may Allah bless him and grant him peace, prescribed it for someone who had a stomach complaint, as related by al-Bukhārī and Muslim. ***There is certainly a Sign in that*** (Allah's handiwork) ***for people who reflect.***

70. ***Allah created you*** – when you were nothing – ***and then will take you back again*** at the end of your life-spans. ***And some of you revert to the lowest form of life*** – a reference to senility and dotage – ***so that after having knowledge, you know nothing at all.*** 'Ikrima said that this only applies to people who used to read (and act by) the

Qur'an and then cease to do so. ***Allah is All-Knowing*** of how to manage His creation, ***All-Powerful*** – able to do whatever He wills.

71. ***Allah has favoured some of you over others in provision*** – so some are rich and some poor, some are masters and some slaves – ***but those who have been favoured*** (the masters) ***do not give their provision to their slaves*** – by dividing their wealth, and other things with which Allah has provided them, between themselves and their slaves so that masters and slaves become partners in the masters' property – ***so they become the same in respect of it.*** The implication here is: Since people do not make their slaves partners in their property, how can they make some of Allah's slaves partners with Him? ***So why do they renounce the blessings of Allah*** and disbelieve by ascribing partners to Him?

72. ***Allah has given you wives from among yourselves*** – by creating Ḥawwā' from a rib of Ādam, and all others through sexual intercourse between men and women – ***and given you children and grandchildren from your wives, and provided good things for you*** – types of fruits, grains and animals. ***So why do they believe in falsehood*** (idols) ***and reject the blessings of Allah*** by associating others with Him –

73. ***...and worship, instead of Allah, things that have no control over their provision from the heavens*** (rain) ***or earth*** (plants) ***in any way, and are themselves completely impotent?*** The idols are impotent and cannot do anything.

74. ***Do not try to make metaphors for Allah.*** Do not make other things like Allah by associating them with Him. ***Allah knows*** that there is nothing like Him ***and you do not know*** that.

75. ***Allah does make a metaphor: an owned slave possessing no power over anything,*** who is clearly quite different from a free man, ***and someone We have given plentiful provision, who gives out from it secretly and openly.*** He disposes of it however He wishes. The first example (the owned slave) represents the idols and the second (the master) Allah Almighty. ***Are they the same?*** Are a powerless slave and a capable master equal? ***Praise be to Allah*** alone! ***They are not: but most people do not know it*** – do not know the

أَحَدُهُمَآ أَبۡكَمُ لَا يَقۡدِرُ عَلَىٰ شَيۡءٖ وَهُوَ كَلٌّ عَلَىٰ
مَوۡلَىٰهُ أَيۡنَمَا يُوَجِّههُّ لَا يَأۡتِ بِخَيۡرٍ هَلۡ يَسۡتَوِي هُوَ وَمَن
يَأۡمُرُ بِٱلۡعَدۡلِ وَهُوَ عَلَىٰ صِرَٰطٖ مُّسۡتَقِيمٖ ٧٦ وَلِلَّهِ غَيۡبُ
ٱلسَّمَٰوَٰتِ وَٱلۡأَرۡضِۚ وَمَآ أَمۡرُ ٱلسَّاعَةِ إِلَّا كَلَمۡحِ ٱلۡبَصَرِ
أَوۡ هُوَ أَقۡرَبُۚ إِنَّ ٱللَّهَ عَلَىٰ كُلِّ شَيۡءٖ قَدِيرٞ ٧٧ وَٱللَّهُ
أَخۡرَجَكُم مِّنۢ بُطُونِ أُمَّهَٰتِكُمۡ لَا تَعۡلَمُونَ شَيۡـٔٗا وَجَعَلَ
لَكُمُ ٱلسَّمۡعَ وَٱلۡأَبۡصَٰرَ وَٱلۡأَفۡـِٔدَةَ لَعَلَّكُمۡ تَشۡكُرُونَ
٧٨ أَلَمۡ يَرَوۡاْ إِلَى ٱلطَّيۡرِ مُسَخَّرَٰتٖ فِي جَوِّ ٱلسَّمَآءِ
مَا يُمۡسِكُهُنَّ إِلَّا ٱللَّهُۚ إِنَّ فِي ذَٰلِكَ لَأٓيَٰتٖ لِّقَوۡمٖ يُؤۡمِنُونَ ٧٩
وَٱللَّهُ جَعَلَ لَكُم مِّنۢ بُيُوتِكُمۡ سَكَنٗا وَجَعَلَ لَكُم مِّن جُلُودِ
ٱلۡأَنۡعَٰمِ بُيُوتٗا تَسۡتَخِفُّونَهَا يَوۡمَ ظَعۡنِكُمۡ وَيَوۡمَ إِقَامَتِكُمۡ
وَمِنۡ أَصۡوَافِهَا وَأَوۡبَارِهَا وَأَشۡعَارِهَآ أَثَٰثٗا وَمَتَٰعًا إِلَىٰ حِينٖ
٨٠ وَٱللَّهُ جَعَلَ لَكُم مِّمَّا خَلَقَ ظِلَٰلٗا وَجَعَلَ لَكُم
مِّنَ ٱلۡجِبَالِ أَكۡنَٰنٗا وَجَعَلَ لَكُمۡ سَرَٰبِيلَ تَقِيكُمُ
ٱلۡحَرَّ وَسَرَٰبِيلَ تَقِيكُم بَأۡسَكُمۡۚ كَذَٰلِكَ يُتِمُّ نِعۡمَتَهُۥ
عَلَيۡكُمۡ لَعَلَّكُمۡ تُسۡلِمُونَ ٨١ فَإِن تَوَلَّوۡاْ فَإِنَّمَا عَلَيۡكَ
ٱلۡبَلَٰغُ ٱلۡمُبِينُ ٨٢ يَعۡرِفُونَ نِعۡمَتَ ٱللَّهِ ثُمَّ يُنكِرُونَهَا
وَأَكۡثَرُهُمُ ٱلۡكَٰفِرُونَ ٨٣ وَيَوۡمَ نَبۡعَثُ مِن كُلِّ أُمَّةٖ
شَهِيدٗا ثُمَّ لَا يُؤۡذَنُ لِلَّذِينَ كَفَرُواْ وَلَا هُمۡ يُسۡتَعۡتَبُونَ
٨٤ وَإِذَا رَءَا ٱلَّذِينَ ظَلَمُواْ ٱلۡعَذَابَ فَلَا يُخَفَّفُ عَنۡهُمۡ وَلَا هُمۡ

reality of the punishment which they will suffer – and so they associate others with Allah.

76. ***Allah makes another metaphor: two men, one of them deaf and dumb, unable to do anything*** – because he does not understand and is not understood – ***a burden on his master, no matter where he directs him he brings no good*** (success) – this is what an unbeliever is like; ***is he the same as someone who commands justice*** – one who speaks and helps people since he can command and encourage them – ***and is on a straight path?*** This is what a believer is like. It is also said that this is a metaphor in which the second man represents Allah and the first the idols, rather than being a representation of unbelievers and the believers.

77. ***The*** knowledge of the ***Unseen of the heavens and earth belongs to Allah. The matter of the Hour is only the blink of an eye away, or even nearer*** – because it is simply a matter of the expression: "Be!" and it is. ***Allah has power over all things.***

78. ***Allah brought you out of your mothers' wombs knowing nothing at all, and gave you hearing, sight and hearts so that perhaps you would show thanks*** for that and believe.

79. ***Do they not see the birds suspended in mid-air up in the sky*** – able to fly through the air between heaven and earth? ***Nothing holds them there except Allah.*** When they draw in or stretch out their wings, all that keeps them from falling is the power of Allah. ***There are certainly Signs in that for people who believe.*** Birds are His creation, and He gives them the power to fly and created the atmosphere in such a way that they are able to fly in the air and remain in it.

80. ***Allah has made your houses places of rest for you and made houses for you out of cattle hides*** – such as tents and domed tents – ***which are light for you to carry both when you are travelling and when you are staying in one place. And from their wool*** – in the case of sheep – ***and fur*** – in the case of camels – ***and hair*** – in the case of goats – ***you obtain clothing and carpets*** (household furnishings) ***and household utensils for a time*** – meaning "which you use until they wear out."

81. ***Allah has made shaded places for you in what He has created*** – houses, trees and clouds, to protect you from the heat of the sun –

and He has made shelters – the word for "shelters", *āknān,* is the plural of *kann*, which means a place where people go for shelter and concealment, such as caves and burrows – ***for you in the mountains and He has made shirts for you to protect you from the heat*** and cold ***and shirts*** of mail ***to protect you from each other's violence*** in war from stabbing and blows. ***In that way*** – by creating these things – ***He perfects His blessing on you*** in this world – since He has created all that you need – ***so that perhaps,*** people of Makka, ***you will become Muslims*** and affirm His unity.

82. ***But if they turn their backs*** on Islam, Muhammad, ***you are only responsible for clear transmission.*** This was before the command to fight came.

83. ***They acknowledge Allah's blessings*** – by admitting that they come from Him – ***and then deny them*** by committing *shirk*. ***Most of them are unbelievers.***

84. ***On*** (remember) ***the Day We raise up a witness from every nation*** – their Prophet, who will testify both for and against them, and that will happen on the Day of Rising – ***those who disbelieved will not be excused, nor will they be able to appease Allah.*** There will nothing they can resort to in order to please Allah.

85. ***When those who did wrong*** (disbelieved) ***see the punishment*** (the Fire), ***it*** (the punishment) ***will not be lightened for them. They will be granted no reprieve*** when they see it.

86. ***When those who associated others*** (*shayṭān*s and idols) ***with Allah see those they associated, they will say, 'Our Lord, these are our partner gods, the ones we called upon*** and worshipped ***apart from You.' But they will fling their words back in their faces*** and will say to them: ***'You are truly liars*** in saying that you worshipped us!' And in another *āyat*, *"It was not us they were worshipping!"* (28:63) They will reject their worship.

87. ***On that Day they will offer their submission to Allah*** – and submit to His judgement – ***and the things they invented*** (their gods) ***will abandon them.***

88. ***As for those who disbelieved and barred*** people ***access to the way of Allah*** (His *dīn*), ***We will heap punishment on top of their punishment*** – which they deserve because of their unbelief. Ibn

يُنظَرُونَ ﴿٨٥﴾ وَإِذَا رَءَا ٱلَّذِينَ أَشۡرَكُواْ شُرَكَآءَهُمۡ
قَالُواْ رَبَّنَا هَٰٓؤُلَآءِ شُرَكَآؤُنَا ٱلَّذِينَ كُنَّا نَدۡعُواْ مِن دُونِكَۖ
فَأَلۡقَوۡاْ إِلَيۡهِمُ ٱلۡقَوۡلَ إِنَّكُمۡ لَكَٰذِبُونَ ﴿٨٦﴾ وَأَلۡقَوۡاْ
إِلَى ٱللَّهِ يَوۡمَئِذٍ ٱلسَّلَمَۖ وَضَلَّ عَنۡهُم مَّا كَانُواْ يَفۡتَرُونَ ﴿٨٧﴾
ٱلَّذِينَ كَفَرُواْ وَصَدُّواْ عَن سَبِيلِ ٱللَّهِ زِدۡنَٰهُمۡ عَذَابٗا فَوۡقَ
ٱلۡعَذَابِ بِمَا كَانُواْ يُفۡسِدُونَ ﴿٨٨﴾ وَيَوۡمَ نَبۡعَثُ فِي كُلِّ
أُمَّةٖ شَهِيدًا عَلَيۡهِم مِّنۡ أَنفُسِهِمۡۖ وَجِئۡنَا بِكَ شَهِيدًا عَلَىٰ
هَٰٓؤُلَآءِۚ وَنَزَّلۡنَا عَلَيۡكَ ٱلۡكِتَٰبَ تِبۡيَٰنٗا لِّكُلِّ شَيۡءٖ وَهُدٗى
وَرَحۡمَةٗ وَبُشۡرَىٰ لِلۡمُسۡلِمِينَ ﴿٨٩﴾ ۞ إِنَّ ٱللَّهَ يَأۡمُرُ بِٱلۡعَدۡلِ
وَٱلۡإِحۡسَٰنِ وَإِيتَآيِٕ ذِي ٱلۡقُرۡبَىٰ وَيَنۡهَىٰ عَنِ ٱلۡفَحۡشَآءِ
وَٱلۡمُنكَرِ وَٱلۡبَغۡيِۚ يَعِظُكُمۡ لَعَلَّكُمۡ تَذَكَّرُونَ
﴿٩٠﴾ وَأَوۡفُواْ بِعَهۡدِ ٱللَّهِ إِذَا عَٰهَدتُّمۡ وَلَا تَنقُضُواْ ٱلۡأَيۡمَٰنَ
بَعۡدَ تَوۡكِيدِهَا وَقَدۡ جَعَلۡتُمُ ٱللَّهَ عَلَيۡكُمۡ كَفِيلًاۚ إِنَّ
ٱللَّهَ يَعۡلَمُ مَا تَفۡعَلُونَ ﴿٩١﴾ وَلَا تَكُونُواْ كَٱلَّتِي نَقَضَتۡ
غَزۡلَهَا مِنۢ بَعۡدِ قُوَّةٍ أَنكَٰثٗا تَتَّخِذُونَ أَيۡمَٰنَكُمۡ دَخَلَۢا
بَيۡنَكُمۡ أَن تَكُونَ أُمَّةٌ هِيَ أَرۡبَىٰ مِنۡ أُمَّةٍۚ إِنَّمَا يَبۡلُوكُمُ
ٱللَّهُ بِهِۦۚ وَلَيُبَيِّنَنَّ لَكُمۡ يَوۡمَ ٱلۡقِيَٰمَةِ مَا كُنتُمۡ فِيهِ تَخۡتَلِفُونَ ﴿٩٢﴾
وَلَوۡ شَآءَ ٱللَّهُ لَجَعَلَكُمۡ أُمَّةٗ وَٰحِدَةٗ وَلَٰكِن يُضِلُّ مَن
يَشَآءُ وَيَهۡدِي مَن يَشَآءُۚ وَلَتُسۡـَٔلُنَّ عَمَّا كُنتُمۡ تَعۡمَلُونَ ﴿٩٣﴾
وَلَا تَتَّخِذُوٓاْ أَيۡمَٰنَكُمۡ دَخَلَۢا بَيۡنَكُمۡ فَتَزِلَّ قَدَمُۢ بَعۡدَ ثُبُوتِهَا

Mas'ūd spoke of "Scorpions with pincers the size of tall palm trees" – ***because of the corruption they brought about*** by barring people from belief.

89. On that Day We will raise up among every community a witness against them from amongst themselves (their Prophet) ***and bring you***, Muḥammad, ***as a witness against them*** (your people). ***We have sent down the Book*** (the Qur'an) ***to you making all things*** which people need in matters of the Sharī'a – ***clear and as guidance*** away from misguidance ***and mercy and good news*** of the Garden ***for the Muslims*** who affirm Allah's oneness.

90. ***Allah commands justice*** – meaning affirmation of His unity or fairness – ***and doing good*** – performing the obligations imposed by Allah or worshipping Allah as if you were seeing Him as in the *ḥadīth* – ***and giving to relatives.*** Giving to relatives is particularly singled out as important. ***And He forbids indecency*** (fornication) ***and doing*** what is ***wrong*** in legal terms – meaning unbelief and acts of disobedience – ***and tyranny*** – doing injustice to people, which is singled out for mention since it is important. ***He warns you*** – by His command and prohibition – ***so that perhaps you will pay heed*** and be warned. It is reported in *al-Mustadrak* that Ibn Mas'ūd said, "This is the most comprehensive *āyat* in the Book of Allah regarding good and evil."

91. ***Be true to Allah's contract*** – in respect of your sales and oaths and other things – ***when you have agreed to it*** – and they have become binding – ***and do not break your oaths once they are confirmed and you have made Allah your guarantee*** – you have sworn by Allah. ***Allah knows what you do.*** This is a threat.

92. ***Do not be like a woman who spoils the thread she has spun by unravelling it after it is strong*** – a foolish woman in Makka used to spin for the entire day and then unravel her yarn, so do not be like her in respect of your oaths – ***by making your oaths a means of deceiving one another*** – the word *dakhalan* used here, which literally means "ingredient", means what is put into something when it should not be there, to corrupt it or to deceive people – ***merely because one community is bigger than another.*** Do not break an oath you have made just because your nation has greater numbers than another nation. The Arabs used to swear an oath of allegiance to

وَتَذُوقُوا۟ ٱلسُّوٓءَ بِمَا صَدَدتُّمْ عَن سَبِيلِ ٱللَّهِ ۖ وَلَكُمْ عَذَابٌ
عَظِيمٌ ﴿٩٤﴾ وَلَا تَشْتَرُوا۟ بِعَهْدِ ٱللَّهِ ثَمَنًا قَلِيلًا ۚ إِنَّمَا عِندَ ٱللَّهِ
هُوَ خَيْرٌ لَّكُمْ إِن كُنتُمْ تَعْلَمُونَ ﴿٩٥﴾ مَا عِندَكُمْ يَنفَدُ ۖ
وَمَا عِندَ ٱللَّهِ بَاقٍ ۗ وَلَنَجْزِيَنَّ ٱلَّذِينَ صَبَرُوٓا۟ أَجْرَهُم بِأَحْسَنِ
مَا كَانُوا۟ يَعْمَلُونَ ﴿٩٦﴾ مَنْ عَمِلَ صَٰلِحًا مِّن ذَكَرٍ
أَوْ أُنثَىٰ وَهُوَ مُؤْمِنٌ فَلَنُحْيِيَنَّهُۥ حَيَوٰةً طَيِّبَةً ۖ وَلَنَجْزِيَنَّهُمْ
أَجْرَهُم بِأَحْسَنِ مَا كَانُوا۟ يَعْمَلُونَ ﴿٩٧﴾ فَإِذَا قَرَأْتَ ٱلْقُرْءَانَ
فَٱسْتَعِذْ بِٱللَّهِ مِنَ ٱلشَّيْطَٰنِ ٱلرَّجِيمِ ﴿٩٨﴾ إِنَّهُۥ لَيْسَ لَهُۥ سُلْطَٰنٌ
عَلَى ٱلَّذِينَ ءَامَنُوا۟ وَعَلَىٰ رَبِّهِمْ يَتَوَكَّلُونَ ﴿٩٩﴾ إِنَّمَا
سُلْطَٰنُهُۥ عَلَى ٱلَّذِينَ يَتَوَلَّوْنَهُۥ وَٱلَّذِينَ هُم بِهِۦ مُشْرِكُونَ
﴿١٠٠﴾ وَإِذَا بَدَّلْنَآ ءَايَةً مَّكَانَ ءَايَةٍ ۙ وَٱللَّهُ أَعْلَمُ
بِمَا يُنَزِّلُ قَالُوٓا۟ إِنَّمَآ أَنتَ مُفْتَرٍۭ ۚ بَلْ أَكْثَرُهُمْ لَا يَعْلَمُونَ
﴿١٠١﴾ قُلْ نَزَّلَهُۥ رُوحُ ٱلْقُدُسِ مِن رَّبِّكَ بِٱلْحَقِّ لِيُثَبِّتَ
ٱلَّذِينَ ءَامَنُوا۟ وَهُدًى وَبُشْرَىٰ لِلْمُسْلِمِينَ ﴿١٠٢﴾
وَلَقَدْ نَعْلَمُ أَنَّهُمْ يَقُولُونَ إِنَّمَا يُعَلِّمُهُۥ بَشَرٌ ۗ لِّسَانُ
ٱلَّذِى يُلْحِدُونَ إِلَيْهِ أَعْجَمِىٌّ وَهَٰذَا لِسَانٌ عَرَبِىٌّ
مُّبِينٌ ﴿١٠٣﴾ إِنَّ ٱلَّذِينَ لَا يُؤْمِنُونَ بِـَٔايَٰتِ ٱللَّهِ لَا يَهْدِيهِمُ
ٱللَّهُ وَلَهُمْ عَذَابٌ أَلِيمٌ ﴿١٠٤﴾ إِنَّمَا يَفْتَرِى ٱلْكَذِبَ ٱلَّذِينَ
لَا يُؤْمِنُونَ بِـَٔايَٰتِ ٱللَّهِ ۖ وَأُو۟لَٰٓئِكَ هُمُ ٱلْكَٰذِبُونَ
﴿١٠٥﴾ مَن كَفَرَ بِٱللَّهِ مِنۢ بَعْدِ إِيمَٰنِهِۦٓ إِلَّا مَنْ أُكْرِهَ

an ally and when they found one more numberous than them and more powerful, they would break their oath to the first one and swear allegiance to the other. ***Allah is only testing you by this*** command to keep to your oaths – in order to see who will obey and who will disobey, or it may mean that one nation will be larger than another to see whether they are godfearing or not; ***He will make clear to you on the Day of Rising the things about which you differed***, in terms of treaties and other things, by punishing those who broke their oaths and rewarding those who kept them.

93. ***If Allah had willed He would have made you one community*** having a single *dīn;* ***but He misguides anyone He wills and guides anyone He wills. You will be questioned*** on the Day of Rising ***about what you did*** and then you will be repaid for it.

94. This is repeated in order to stress it: ***Do not make your oaths a means of deceiving one another or your feet will slip*** from the Path of Islam ***after being firmly placed*** – when you were going straight on it – ***and you will taste evil*** (punishment) ***for barring access to the Way of Allah*** by not keeping to your oaths or for barring other people from the Path when it has been established by you – ***and you will have a terrible punishment*** in the Next World.

95. ***Do not sell Allah's contract for a paltry price*** (this world) – so that you break it for the sake of this world. ***What is with Allah*** (His reward) ***is better for you*** than what is in this world ***if you only knew.*** If you knew this, you would not break your contract with Him.

96. ***What is with you*** in this world ***runs out*** and vanishes, ***but what is with Allah goes on for ever. We will recompense*** (read as *najziyanna* and *yajziyanna*, in which case the meaning becomes "Those who were steadfast will be recompensed") ***those who were steadfast*** in fulfilling their contract ***according to the best of what they did.***

97. ***Anyone who acts rightly, male or female, being a believer, We will give them a good life*** – it is said that "a good life" refers to the Next World in the Garden, and it is also said that it refers to this world and means a life of contentment and plentiful lawful provision – ***and We will recompense them according to the best of what they did.***

98. ***Whenever you*** want to ***recite the Qur'an, seek refuge with Allah from the accursed Shaytan***: in other words, before you start reciting say, "I seek refuge with Allah from the Accursed Shayṭān."

99. ***He*** (Shayṭān) ***has no authority*** or power ***over those who believe and put their trust in their Lord.***

100. ***He only has authority over those who take him as a friend*** by obeying him ***and associate others with Allah.***

101. ***If We replace one* āyat *with another one*** by abrogating it and replacing it with another, in mankind's best interests – ***and Allah knows best what He is sending down – they*** (the unbelievers) ***say*** to the Prophet, may Allah bless him and grant him peace, ***'You are just inventing this*** and are lying, making it up*!'* ***No indeed! Most of them have no knowledge*** of the reality of the Qur'an and the benefit of abrogation.

102. ***Say*** to them*:* ***'The Purest* Rūḥ** (Jibrīl) ***has brought it down from your Lord with truth, to make those who believe firm*** in their belief***, and as guidance and good news for the Muslims.'***

103. ***We know that they say, 'It is only a human being who is teaching him*** the Qur'an*.'* The unbelievers said that he was being taught by a Christian slave, whom The Prophet, may Allah bless him and grant him peace, used to visit. ***The language of him they allude to is a foreign one, whereas this*** Qur'an ***is in clear and lucid Arabic.***

104. ***As for those who do not believe in Allah's Signs, Allah will not guide them and they will have a painful punishment.***

105. ***Those who do not believe in Allah's Signs*** (the Qur'an), saying that it is just the words of a human being, ***are merely inventing lies. It is they who are the liars.*** This is repeated for stress. The *āyat* refutes their words, "You are just inventing this!"

106. ***Those who disbelieve in Allah after having believed – except for someone forced to do it*** – forced to articulate words of unbelief – ***whose heart remains at rest in its faith*** are excused ***– but as for those whose breasts become dilated with unbelief, anger from Allah will come down on them.*** This is a severe threat for those who are content and happy about disbelieving. ***They will have a terrible punishment.***

وَقَلۡبُهُۥ مُطۡمَئِنُّۢ بِٱلۡإِيمَٰنِ وَلَٰكِن مَّن شَرَحَ بِٱلۡكُفۡرِ صَدۡرٗا
فَعَلَيۡهِمۡ غَضَبٞ مِّنَ ٱللَّهِ وَلَهُمۡ عَذَابٌ عَظِيمٞ ١٠٦
ذَٰلِكَ بِأَنَّهُمُ ٱسۡتَحَبُّواْ ٱلۡحَيَوٰةَ ٱلدُّنۡيَا عَلَى ٱلۡأٓخِرَةِ
وَأَنَّ ٱللَّهَ لَا يَهۡدِي ٱلۡقَوۡمَ ٱلۡكَٰفِرِينَ ١٠٧ أُوْلَٰٓئِكَ
ٱلَّذِينَ طَبَعَ ٱللَّهُ عَلَىٰ قُلُوبِهِمۡ وَسَمۡعِهِمۡ وَأَبۡصَٰرِهِمۡۖ
وَأُوْلَٰٓئِكَ هُمُ ٱلۡغَٰفِلُونَ ١٠٨ لَا جَرَمَ أَنَّهُمۡ فِي
ٱلۡأٓخِرَةِ هُمُ ٱلۡخَٰسِرُونَ ١٠٩ ثُمَّ إِنَّ رَبَّكَ
لِلَّذِينَ هَاجَرُواْ مِنۢ بَعۡدِ مَا فُتِنُواْ ثُمَّ جَٰهَدُواْ
وَصَبَرُوٓاْ إِنَّ رَبَّكَ مِنۢ بَعۡدِهَا لَغَفُورٞ رَّحِيمٞ ١١٠
۞ يَوۡمَ تَأۡتِي كُلُّ نَفۡسٖ تُجَٰدِلُ عَن نَّفۡسِهَا وَتُوَفَّىٰ كُلُّ
نَفۡسٖ مَّا عَمِلَتۡ وَهُمۡ لَا يُظۡلَمُونَ ١١١ وَضَرَبَ ٱللَّهُ مَثَلٗا
قَرۡيَةٗ كَانَتۡ ءَامِنَةٗ مُّطۡمَئِنَّةٗ يَأۡتِيهَا رِزۡقُهَا رَغَدٗا
مِّن كُلِّ مَكَانٖ فَكَفَرَتۡ بِأَنۡعُمِ ٱللَّهِ فَأَذَٰقَهَا ٱللَّهُ لِبَاسَ
ٱلۡجُوعِ وَٱلۡخَوۡفِ بِمَا كَانُواْ يَصۡنَعُونَ ١١٢ وَلَقَدۡ
جَآءَهُمۡ رَسُولٞ مِّنۡهُمۡ فَكَذَّبُوهُ فَأَخَذَهُمُ ٱلۡعَذَابُ وَهُمۡ
ظَٰلِمُونَ ١١٣ فَكُلُواْ مِمَّا رَزَقَكُمُ ٱللَّهُ حَلَٰلٗا طَيِّبٗا
وَٱشۡكُرُواْ نِعۡمَتَ ٱللَّهِ إِن كُنتُمۡ إِيَّاهُ تَعۡبُدُونَ ١١٤
إِنَّمَا حَرَّمَ عَلَيۡكُمُ ٱلۡمَيۡتَةَ وَٱلدَّمَ وَلَحۡمَ ٱلۡخِنزِيرِ وَمَآ
أُهِلَّ لِغَيۡرِ ٱللَّهِ بِهِۦۖ فَمَنِ ٱضۡطُرَّ غَيۡرَ بَاغٖ وَلَا عَادٖ فَإِنَّ
ٱللَّهَ غَفُورٞ رَّحِيمٞ ١١٥ وَلَا تَقُولُواْ لِمَا تَصِفُ أَلۡسِنَتُكُمُ

107. ***That*** threat ***is because they prefer the life of this world to the Next World and because Allah does not guide unbelieving people.***

108. ***Those are the people whose hearts, hearing and sight Allah has sealed up. They are the unaware***, heedless of what is desired of them.

109. ***There is no doubt that in the Next World they will be the losers*** because they will go to the Fire in which they will remain forever.

110. ***But to those who emigrated*** to Madina ***after they were persecuted*** (read as *futunū* and as *fatanū*) – after they were tortured and made to articulate words of unbelief – ***and then did* jihād *and remained steadfast*** in obedience after the persecution they had suffered, ***to them your Lord is Ever-Forgiving, Most Merciful.***

111. ***On that Day*** (the Day of Rising) ***every self will come to argue for itself*** – and will not be concerned with anyone else – ***and every self will be paid in full for what it did. They will not be wronged*** in any way.

112. ***Allah makes an example of a city*** (Makka) ***which was safe*** from attacks ***and at peace*** so that there was no need to move from it due to constriction or fear, ***its provision coming to it plentifully from every side. Then it showed ingratitude for Allah's blessings*** by denying the Prophet, may Allah bless him and grant him peace, ***so Allah made it wear the robes of hunger*** – by causing it to suffer drought for seven years – ***and fear*** – of expeditions made by the Prophet, may Allah bless him and grant him peace – ***for what it did.***

113. ***A Messenger from among them*** – Muḥammad, may Allah bless him and grant him peace – ***came to them but they denied him. So the punishment*** (hunger and fear) ***seized them and they were wrongdoers.***

114. ***So***, believers, ***eat from what Allah has provided for you, lawful and good, and be thankful for the blessing of Allah if it is Him you worship.***

115. ***He has forbidden you carrion, blood, pork, and anything consecrated to other than Allah. But if someone is forced to eat it, without desiring to or going to excess in it, your Lord is Ever-Forgiving, Most Merciful.***

ٱلۡكَذِبَ هَٰذَا حَلَٰلٞ وَهَٰذَا حَرَامٞ لِّتَفۡتَرُواْ عَلَى ٱللَّهِ ٱلۡكَذِبَۚ
إِنَّ ٱلَّذِينَ يَفۡتَرُونَ عَلَى ٱللَّهِ ٱلۡكَذِبَ لَا يُفۡلِحُونَ ١١٦ مَتَٰعٞ قَلِيلٞ
وَلَهُمۡ عَذَابٌ أَلِيمٞ ١١٧ وَعَلَى ٱلَّذِينَ هَادُواْ حَرَّمۡنَا مَا قَصَصۡنَا عَلَيۡكَ
مِن قَبۡلُۖ وَمَا ظَلَمۡنَٰهُمۡ وَلَٰكِن كَانُوٓاْ أَنفُسَهُمۡ يَظۡلِمُونَ ١١٨
ثُمَّ إِنَّ رَبَّكَ لِلَّذِينَ عَمِلُواْ ٱلسُّوٓءَ بِجَهَٰلَةٖ ثُمَّ تَابُواْ مِنۢ
بَعۡدِ ذَٰلِكَ وَأَصۡلَحُوٓاْ إِنَّ رَبَّكَ مِنۢ بَعۡدِهَا لَغَفُورٞ رَّحِيمٌ ١١٩
إِنَّ إِبۡرَٰهِيمَ كَانَ أُمَّةٗ قَانِتٗا لِّلَّهِ حَنِيفٗا وَلَمۡ يَكُ مِنَ ٱلۡمُشۡرِكِينَ
١٢٠ شَاكِرٗا لِّأَنۡعُمِهِۚ ٱجۡتَبَىٰهُ وَهَدَىٰهُ إِلَىٰ صِرَٰطٖ مُّسۡتَقِيمٖ
١٢١ وَءَاتَيۡنَٰهُ فِي ٱلدُّنۡيَا حَسَنَةٗۖ وَإِنَّهُۥ فِي ٱلۡأٓخِرَةِ لَمِنَ ٱلصَّٰلِحِينَ
١٢٢ ثُمَّ أَوۡحَيۡنَآ إِلَيۡكَ أَنِ ٱتَّبِعۡ مِلَّةَ إِبۡرَٰهِيمَ حَنِيفٗاۖ وَمَا كَانَ
مِنَ ٱلۡمُشۡرِكِينَ ١٢٣ إِنَّمَا جُعِلَ ٱلسَّبۡتُ عَلَى ٱلَّذِينَ
ٱخۡتَلَفُواْ فِيهِۚ وَإِنَّ رَبَّكَ لَيَحۡكُمُ بَيۡنَهُمۡ يَوۡمَ ٱلۡقِيَٰمَةِ فِيمَا
كَانُواْ فِيهِ يَخۡتَلِفُونَ ١٢٤ ٱدۡعُ إِلَىٰ سَبِيلِ رَبِّكَ بِٱلۡحِكۡمَةِ
وَٱلۡمَوۡعِظَةِ ٱلۡحَسَنَةِۖ وَجَٰدِلۡهُم بِٱلَّتِي هِيَ أَحۡسَنُۚ إِنَّ رَبَّكَ
هُوَ أَعۡلَمُ بِمَن ضَلَّ عَن سَبِيلِهِۦۖ وَهُوَ أَعۡلَمُ بِٱلۡمُهۡتَدِينَ ١٢٥
وَإِنۡ عَاقَبۡتُمۡ فَعَاقِبُواْ بِمِثۡلِ مَا عُوقِبۡتُم بِهِۦۖ وَلَئِن صَبَرۡتُمۡ
لَهُوَ خَيۡرٞ لِّلصَّٰبِرِينَ ١٢٦ وَٱصۡبِرۡ وَمَا صَبۡرُكَ إِلَّا بِٱللَّهِۚ
وَلَا تَحۡزَنۡ عَلَيۡهِمۡ وَلَا تَكُ فِي ضَيۡقٖ مِّمَّا يَمۡكُرُونَ
١٢٧ إِنَّ ٱللَّهَ مَعَ ٱلَّذِينَ ٱتَّقَواْ وَّٱلَّذِينَ هُم مُّحۡسِنُونَ ١٢٨

116. ***Do not say about what your lying tongues describe: 'This is lawful and this is unlawful,'*** – lying about what Allah has made unlawful and lawful – ***inventing lies against Allah*** – ascribing that to Him. ***Those who invent lies against Allah are not successful –***

117. ... they will have ***a brief enjoyment, then they will have a painful punishment*** in the Next World.

118. ***We forbade the Jews those things We told you about before*** in the *āyat*: *"We made unlawful for the Jews every animal with an undivided hoof..."*. (6:147) ***We did not wrong them*** by forbidding these things; ***rather they wronged themselves*** by committing acts of disobedience which make punishment mandatory for them.

119. ***But to those who do evil*** (*shirk*) ***in ignorance and then after that*** ignorance ***repent and put things right*** and act rightly, ***to them your Lord is Ever-Forgiving, Most Merciful.***

120. ***Ibrāhīm was a community in himself*** – an *imām* and a model, manifesting every good quality – ***exemplary, obedient to Allah, a man of pure natural belief*** – the Arabic word *ḥanīf* means someone who inclines naturally to the Straight *Dīn*. ***He was not one of the idolaters.***

121. ***He was thankful for His blessings. Allah chose him and guided him to a straight path.***

122. This is an example of a change of person from the third person singular to the first person plural. ***We gave him good*** – praise among the people of all religions – ***in this world, and in the Next World he will be one of the righteous*** who have the high degrees.

123. ***Then We revealed to you***, Muḥammad: ***'Follow the religion of Ibrāhīm, a man of pure natural belief. He was not one of the idolaters.'*** This is repeated to refute the claim of the Jews and Christians that they are following the *dīn* of Ibrāhīm.

124. ***The Sabbath was only enjoined on those who differed about it.*** It was made obligatory for the Jews to respect the Sabbath. The Jews differed from their Prophet. They were commanded to devote themselves to worship on Friday but said, "We do not want it," they chose Saturday, and it was made hard for them. ***Your Lord will judge between them on the Day of Rising regarding the things about***

which they differed – the obedient being rewarded and the disobedient being punished for violating the sanctity of the Sabbath.

125. ***Call*** people, Muḥammad, ***to the way*** (the *dīn*) ***of your Lord with wisdom*** (the Qur'an) ***and fair admonition*** (warning or gentle words) ***and argue with them in the kindest way*** – with what is better, like calling them to Allah by His Signs and citing the proofs of His existence. ***Your Lord knows best who is misguided from His way, and He knows best who are guided***, and He will repay them. This was revealed before the command to fight. When Ḥamza was killed and mutilated and the Prophet, may Allah bless him and grant him peace, saw him, he said, "I will mutilate seventy of them in retaliation for you." So the following was revealed.

126. ***If you want to retaliate, retaliate to the same degree as the injury done to you. But if you are patient*** and do not take revenge, ***it is better to be patient.*** Therefore the Prophet, may Allah bless him and grant him peace, refrained and expiated his oath. Al-Bazzār related it.

127. ***Be patient. But your patience is only by Allah*** – who gives success in exercising it. ***Do not be grieved by them*** (the unbelievers) – do not be grieved by the fact that they do not believe despite your eagerness for them to do so – ***and do not be constricted*** and worried ***by the plots they hatch.*** We will help you against them.

128. ***Allah is with those who are fearful of Him*** – and on their guard against unbelief and acts of disobedience – ***and with those who are good-doers*** by observing obedience and patience, and He gives them help and victory.

سُورَةُ الإِسۡرَاءِ

بِسۡمِ ٱللَّهِ ٱلرَّحۡمَٰنِ ٱلرَّحِيمِ

سُبۡحَٰنَ ٱلَّذِيٓ أَسۡرَىٰ بِعَبۡدِهِۦ لَيۡلٗا مِّنَ ٱلۡمَسۡجِدِ ٱلۡحَرَامِ
إِلَى ٱلۡمَسۡجِدِ ٱلۡأَقۡصَا ٱلَّذِي بَٰرَكۡنَا حَوۡلَهُۥ لِنُرِيَهُۥ مِنۡ ءَايَٰتِنَآۚ إِنَّهُۥ
هُوَ ٱلسَّمِيعُ ٱلۡبَصِيرُ ١ وَءَاتَيۡنَا مُوسَى ٱلۡكِتَٰبَ وَجَعَلۡنَٰهُ
هُدٗى لِّبَنِيٓ إِسۡرَٰٓءِيلَ أَلَّا تَتَّخِذُواْ مِن دُونِي وَكِيلٗا ٢
ذُرِّيَّةَ مَنۡ حَمَلۡنَا مَعَ نُوحٍۚ إِنَّهُۥ كَانَ عَبۡدٗا شَكُورٗا ٣
وَقَضَيۡنَآ إِلَىٰ بَنِيٓ إِسۡرَٰٓءِيلَ فِي ٱلۡكِتَٰبِ لَتُفۡسِدُنَّ فِي ٱلۡأَرۡضِ
مَرَّتَيۡنِ وَلَتَعۡلُنَّ عُلُوّٗا كَبِيرٗا ٤ فَإِذَا جَآءَ وَعۡدُ أُولَىٰهُمَا بَعَثۡنَا
عَلَيۡكُمۡ عِبَادٗا لَّنَآ أُوْلِي بَأۡسٖ شَدِيدٖ فَجَاسُواْ خِلَٰلَ ٱلدِّيَارِۚ
وَكَانَ وَعۡدٗا مَّفۡعُولٗا ٥ ثُمَّ رَدَدۡنَا لَكُمُ ٱلۡكَرَّةَ عَلَيۡهِمۡ
وَأَمۡدَدۡنَٰكُم بِأَمۡوَٰلٖ وَبَنِينَ وَجَعَلۡنَٰكُمۡ أَكۡثَرَ نَفِيرًا ٦
إِنۡ أَحۡسَنتُمۡ أَحۡسَنتُمۡ لِأَنفُسِكُمۡۖ وَإِنۡ أَسَأۡتُمۡ فَلَهَاۚ فَإِذَا جَآءَ
وَعۡدُ ٱلۡأٓخِرَةِ لِيَسُـُٔواْ وُجُوهَكُمۡ وَلِيَدۡخُلُواْ ٱلۡمَسۡجِدَ
كَمَا دَخَلُوهُ أَوَّلَ مَرَّةٖ وَلِيُتَبِّرُواْ مَا عَلَوۡاْ تَتۡبِيرًا ٧
عَسَىٰ رَبُّكُمۡ أَن يَرۡحَمَكُمۡۚ وَإِنۡ عُدتُّمۡ عُدۡنَاۘ وَجَعَلۡنَا جَهَنَّمَ لِلۡكَٰفِرِينَ
حَصِيرًا ٨ إِنَّ هَٰذَا ٱلۡقُرۡءَانَ يَهۡدِي لِلَّتِي هِيَ أَقۡوَمُ وَيُبَشِّرُ

17. *Sūrat al-Isrā'*
The Night Journey

This *sūra* is Makkan except for *āyat*s 26, 32, 57, and from 73 to the end of 80, which are Madinan. It has 111 *āyat*s and was revealed after *Al-Qaṣaṣ*.

1. *Glory be to Him who took His slave* – Muḥammad, may Allah bless him and grant him peace – ***on a journey by night*** – the word *sarā* means, by itself, to travel at night and the additional use of "by night", *laylan,* adverbially with it indicates that it is a short journey – ***from al-Masjid al-Ḥaram to al-Masjid al-Aqṣā*** (Jerusalem) ***whose surroundings We have blessed*** with fruits and rivers, ***in order to show him some of Our Signs*** – marvels of Our power. ***He is the All-Hearing, the All-Seeing.*** Allah hears the words of the Prophet, may Allah bless him and grant him peace, and sees his actions, and so He blessed him with the Night Journey in which he met the Prophets and ascended to heaven, saw the wonders of the *Malakūt*[1] and spoke intimately with Allah.

The Prophet, may Allah bless him and grant him peace, said, "The Burāq was brought to me. It was a white animal somewhat taller than a donkey, but smaller than a mule. Its step covered a distance equal to the range of its vision. I mounted it and rode until I was brought to Jerusalem. Then I tied it to the ring which the Prophets use. Then I entered the mosque and prayed two *rak'at*s there. I came out and Jibrīl brought me a vessel of milk and a vessel of wine. I chose the milk and Jibrīl said, 'You have chosen the *fitra*.

"Then he went up with me to the first heaven. Jibrīl asked for it to be opened and a voice said, 'Who is it?' He replied, 'Jibrīl.' The voice said, 'Who is with you?' He replied, 'Muḥammad.' It said, 'Was he sent for?' He replied, 'He was sent for,' and the door opened for us. I found Ādam who welcomed me and prayed for me. Then we went up to the second heaven and Jibrīl asked for it to be opened. A voice said, 'Who is it?' He replied, "Jibrīl." It said, "Who is with you?" He replied, "Muḥammad." It said, 'Was he sent for?'

1. The angelic world.

He replied, 'He was,' and the door was opened for us. There I found my cousins, 'Īsā ibn Maryam and Yaḥyā ibn Zakariyyā. They welcomed me and prayed for me. Then we went up to the third heaven and the same thing happened. It was opened for me and there was Yūsuf. He had been given half of all beauty. He welcomed me and prayed for me. Then we went up to the fourth heaven and the same thing happened. I found Idrīs, and he welcomed me and prayed for me. Allah has said, *'We raised him up to a high place.'* (19:56) Then we went up to the fifth heaven and the same thing happened. There was Hārūn, who welcomed me and prayed for me. Then we went up to the sixth heaven and the same thing happened. There I found Mūsā, who welcomed me and prayed for me. Then we went up to the seventh heaven and the same thing happened. There I found Ibrāhīm leaning against the Frequented House (*Al-Bayt al-Ma'mūr*). Every day, seventy thousand angels enter into it and do not emerge.

"Then he took me to the Lote-tree of the Furthest Limit ,whose leaves are the size of the ears of elephants and whose fruits are the size of earthenware vessels. When a command from Allah covers it, what is covered undergoes a change which no creature is capable of describing due to its sublime beauty. Then Allah revealed to me what He revealed and He made fifty prayers every day and night obligatory for me. I came down to Mūsā and he asked, 'What did your Lord make obligatory for your people?' I replied, 'Fifty prayers.' He said, 'Go back to your Lord and ask Him to lighten it. Your community will never be able to do that. I have tested the tribe of Isrā'īl and know by experience.' So I went back to my Lord and said, 'My Lord, lighten it for my community!' so He deducted five prayers. I went back to Mūsā and said, 'He deducted five for me.' He said, 'Your community will not be able to do that, so go back and ask Him to lighten it.'

"I kept going back and forth between my Lord and Mūsā until Allah said, 'Muḥammad, there are five prayers every day and night. Each prayer counts as ten, so that makes fifty prayers. Whoever intends to do something good, but then does not do it, a good action will be written for him. If he does it, then ten will be written for him. Whoever intends to do something bad but does not do it, nothing will be written against him. If he does it, then one bad action will be recorded.' Then I went down to Mūsā and told him about that. He said, 'Go back to your Lord and ask Him to lighten it.' The Messenger of Allah, may Allah bless him and grant him peace, replied, 'I have gone back to my Lord so often that I am ashamed before Him.'" It is related by al-Bukhārī and Muslim, and the version quoted here is that of Muslim. Al-Ḥākim also transmitted it in the *Mustadrak* from Ibn 'Abbās. He stated that the Messenger of Allah, may Allah bless him and grant him peace, said, "I saw my Almighty Lord."

2. Allah says: ***We gave Mūsā the Book*** (the Torah) ***and made it guidance for the tribe of Israel: 'Do not take*** (read as *tattakhidhū* or as *yattakhidhū*, when it means: "They should not take...") ***anyone besides Me as a guardian.'***

3. ***Descendants of those We carried with Nūḥ*** in the Ark; ***hhe was a grateful slave.*** He showed much gratitude to Us and praised us in all states.

4. ***We decreed*** and revealed ***in the Book*** (the Torah) ***for the tribe of Israel: 'You will twice cause corruption on the earth*** – firstly in Greater Syria by acts of disobedience – ***and you will rise to a great height*** and be very unjust.

5. ***When the promised first time*** of corruption ***came, We sent against you slaves of Ours possessing great force*** – in terms of fighting ability and general might – ***and they ransacked your houses, rampaging right through them*** – seeking to kill and capture you. ***It was a promise which was fulfilled.*** Their first act of corruption was killing Zakariyyā, and so Jālūt (Goliath) and his armies were sent against them and they killed them, captured their children, and laid waste to Jerusalem.

6. ***Then once again We gave you the upper hand over them*** – in state and dominance, after a hundred years, by Dā'ūd killing Jālūt – ***and provided you with more wealth and children, and made you the most numerous group.***

7. We said: ***If you do good*** by performing acts of obedience, ***you do it to yourselves*** because of the reward you receive for it. ***If you do evil*** by causing corruption, ***you do it to your detriment. When the next promised time arrived,*** We sent them and ***it was so that they***

ٱلْمُؤْمِنِينَ ٱلَّذِينَ يَعْمَلُونَ ٱلصَّٰلِحَٰتِ أَنَّ لَهُمْ أَجْرًا كَبِيرًا ﴿٩﴾
وَأَنَّ ٱلَّذِينَ لَا يُؤْمِنُونَ بِٱلْءَاخِرَةِ أَعْتَدْنَا لَهُمْ عَذَابًا أَلِيمًا ﴿١٠﴾
وَيَدْعُ ٱلْإِنسَٰنُ بِٱلشَّرِّ دُعَآءَهُۥ بِٱلْخَيْرِ ۖ وَكَانَ ٱلْإِنسَٰنُ عَجُولًا ﴿١١﴾
وَجَعَلْنَا ٱلَّيْلَ وَٱلنَّهَارَ ءَايَتَيْنِ ۖ فَمَحَوْنَآ ءَايَةَ ٱلَّيْلِ وَجَعَلْنَآ ءَايَةَ
ٱلنَّهَارِ مُبْصِرَةً لِّتَبْتَغُوا۟ فَضْلًا مِّن رَّبِّكُمْ وَلِتَعْلَمُوا۟ عَدَدَ
ٱلسِّنِينَ وَٱلْحِسَابَ ۚ وَكُلَّ شَىْءٍ فَصَّلْنَٰهُ تَفْصِيلًا ﴿١٢﴾ وَكُلَّ
إِنسَٰنٍ أَلْزَمْنَٰهُ طَٰٓئِرَهُۥ فِى عُنُقِهِۦ ۖ وَنُخْرِجُ لَهُۥ يَوْمَ ٱلْقِيَٰمَةِ كِتَٰبًا
يَلْقَىٰهُ مَنشُورًا ﴿١٣﴾ ٱقْرَأْ كِتَٰبَكَ كَفَىٰ بِنَفْسِكَ ٱلْيَوْمَ عَلَيْكَ حَسِيبًا
﴿١٤﴾ مَّنِ ٱهْتَدَىٰ فَإِنَّمَا يَهْتَدِى لِنَفْسِهِۦ ۖ وَمَن ضَلَّ فَإِنَّمَا يَضِلُّ
عَلَيْهَا ۚ وَلَا تَزِرُ وَازِرَةٌ وِزْرَ أُخْرَىٰ ۗ وَمَا كُنَّا مُعَذِّبِينَ حَتَّىٰ نَبْعَثَ
رَسُولًا ﴿١٥﴾ وَإِذَآ أَرَدْنَآ أَن نُّهْلِكَ قَرْيَةً أَمَرْنَا مُتْرَفِيهَا فَفَسَقُوا۟ فِيهَا
فَحَقَّ عَلَيْهَا ٱلْقَوْلُ فَدَمَّرْنَٰهَا تَدْمِيرًا ﴿١٦﴾ وَكَمْ أَهْلَكْنَا مِنَ
ٱلْقُرُونِ مِنۢ بَعْدِ نُوحٍ ۗ وَكَفَىٰ بِرَبِّكَ بِذُنُوبِ عِبَادِهِۦ خَبِيرًۢا بَصِيرًا ﴿١٧﴾
مَّن كَانَ يُرِيدُ ٱلْعَاجِلَةَ عَجَّلْنَا لَهُۥ فِيهَا مَا نَشَآءُ لِمَن نُّرِيدُ ثُمَّ
جَعَلْنَا لَهُۥ جَهَنَّمَ يَصْلَىٰهَا مَذْمُومًا مَّدْحُورًا ﴿١٨﴾ وَمَنْ أَرَادَ
ٱلْءَاخِرَةَ وَسَعَىٰ لَهَا سَعْيَهَا وَهُوَ مُؤْمِنٌ فَأُو۟لَٰٓئِكَ كَانَ
سَعْيُهُم مَّشْكُورًا ﴿١٩﴾ كُلًّا نُّمِدُّ هَٰٓؤُلَآءِ وَهَٰٓؤُلَآءِ مِنْ عَطَآءِ
رَبِّكَ ۚ وَمَا كَانَ عَطَآءُ رَبِّكَ مَحْظُورًا ﴿٢٠﴾ ٱنظُرْ كَيْفَ فَضَّلْنَا
بَعْضَهُمْ عَلَىٰ بَعْضٍ ۚ وَلَلْءَاخِرَةُ أَكْبَرُ دَرَجَٰتٍ وَأَكْبَرُ تَفْضِيلًا
﴿٢١﴾ لَّا تَجْعَلْ مَعَ ٱللَّهِ إِلَٰهًا ءَاخَرَ فَتَقْعُدَ مَذْمُومًا مَّخْذُولًا ﴿٢٢﴾

could injure you by killing and capture, your faces showed, ***and enter the Temple*** of Jerusalem to destroy it ***as they had entered it the first time*** and destroyed it, ***and in order to completely destroy what they had conquered.*** Their second act of corruption was killing ,ā and so Yaktinsar was sent against them. He killed thousands of them, took their children prisoner, and destroyed Jerusalem.

8. We said this in the Book. ***It may well be that your Lord will have mercy on you*** after the second time, if you repent. ***But if you revert to what you did*** in terms of corruption, ***We also will revert*** to punishing you. They reverted by denying Muhammad, may Allah bless him and grant him peace, and power over them was demonstrated by the killing of Qurayẓa and the Banū'n-Naḍīr and the imposition of *jizya* on them. ***We have made Hell a prison for the unbelievers.'***

9. *This Qur'an guides to the most upright Way* – the fairest and most correct – ***and gives good news to the believers who do right actions that they will have a large reward.***

10. *But as for those who do not believe in the Next World, We have prepared for them a painful punishment* in the Fire.

11. *Man prays for evil* – to come on himself and his family when he is annoyed – ***just as he prays for good. Man*** (which is generic here) ***is prone to be impetuous*** in invoking against himself without considering the consequences.

12. *We made the night and day two Signs* indicating Our power. ***We blotted out the Sign of the night*** – by darkness, so that you might rest in it – ***and made the Sign of the day a time for seeing*** – it allows vision by its light – ***so that you may seek favour from your Lord*** by earning ***and know the number of years and the reckoning of time. We have made all things*** that need to be made clear ***very clear.***

13. *We have fastened the destiny* of the actions ***of every man about his neck*** – the neck is singled out because anything attached to it is very difficult to dislodge. According to Mujāhid, "There is no one born without having a page on his neck on which is written whether he will be unfortunate or wretched. On the Day of Rising he will see the book in which his actions are recorded." – ***and on the Day of***

Rising We will bring out a Book for him which he will find spread open in front of him – which records all his actions.

14. He will be told, ***'Read your Book! Today your own self is reckoner enough against you!'***

15. ***Whoever is guided is only guided to his own good*** – because of the reward he receives for it. ***Whoever is misguided is only misguided to his detriment*** – because of the wrong action inherent in it. ***No burden-bearer can bear another's burden*** of wrong actions. ***We never punish*** anyone ***until We have sent a Messenger*** to make clear to him what is mandatory for him.

16. ***When We desire to destroy a city, We send a command to the affluent in it*** – meaning its leaders, who are commanded by the Messengers to obey – ***and they become deviant in it*** and disobey Our commands, ***and the Word*** (the punishment) ***is justly carried out against it and We annihilate it completely*** by destroying its inhabitants and laying ruin to it.

17. ***How many generations*** of different nations ***We destroyed after Nūḥ! Your Lord is well able to be aware of and see the wrong actions of His slaves.*** He knows their inward and outward and the wrong actions connected to them.

18. ***As for anyone who desires this fleeting existence*** by his actions, ***We hasten in it whatever We will to whoever We want. Then*** in the Next World ***We will consign him to Hell*** – which He will enter – ***where he will roast, reviled and driven out*** from mercy.

19. ***But as for anyone who desires the Next World, and strives for it with the striving it deserves*** – by doing the actions appropriate to it – ***being a believer, the striving of such people will be gratefully acknowledged.*** Allah will accept their actions and reward them for them.

20. ***We sustain each one*** each group, ***the former and the latter, through the generous giving of your Lord*** in this world***; and the giving of your Lord is not restricted*** to anyone in it.

21. ***Look how We favour some of them over others*** in position and rank. ***But the Next World has higher ranks and greater favours*** than this world – so people should be concerned with that rather than this world.

۞ وَقَضَىٰ رَبُّكَ أَلَّا تَعْبُدُوٓا۟ إِلَّآ إِيَّاهُ وَبِٱلْوَٰلِدَيْنِ إِحْسَـٰنًا ۚ إِمَّا
يَبْلُغَنَّ عِندَكَ ٱلْكِبَرَ أَحَدُهُمَآ أَوْ كِلَاهُمَا فَلَا تَقُل لَّهُمَآ
أُفٍّ وَلَا تَنْهَرْهُمَا وَقُل لَّهُمَا قَوْلًا كَرِيمًا ﴿٢٣﴾ وَٱخْفِضْ
لَهُمَا جَنَاحَ ٱلذُّلِّ مِنَ ٱلرَّحْمَةِ وَقُل رَّبِّ ٱرْحَمْهُمَا كَمَا رَبَّيَانِى
صَغِيرًا ﴿٢٤﴾ رَّبُّكُمْ أَعْلَمُ بِمَا فِى نُفُوسِكُمْ ۚ إِن تَكُونُوا۟ صَـٰلِحِينَ
فَإِنَّهُۥ كَانَ لِلْأَوَّٰبِينَ غَفُورًا ﴿٢٥﴾ وَءَاتِ ذَا ٱلْقُرْبَىٰ حَقَّهُۥ
وَٱلْمِسْكِينَ وَٱبْنَ ٱلسَّبِيلِ وَلَا تُبَذِّرْ تَبْذِيرًا ﴿٢٦﴾ إِنَّ ٱلْمُبَذِّرِينَ
كَانُوٓا۟ إِخْوَٰنَ ٱلشَّيَـٰطِينِ ۖ وَكَانَ ٱلشَّيْطَـٰنُ لِرَبِّهِۦ كَفُورًا ﴿٢٧﴾
وَإِمَّا تُعْرِضَنَّ عَنْهُمُ ٱبْتِغَآءَ رَحْمَةٍ مِّن رَّبِّكَ تَرْجُوهَا فَقُل لَّهُمْ قَوْلًا
مَّيْسُورًا ﴿٢٨﴾ وَلَا تَجْعَلْ يَدَكَ مَغْلُولَةً إِلَىٰ عُنُقِكَ وَلَا تَبْسُطْهَا
كُلَّ ٱلْبَسْطِ فَتَقْعُدَ مَلُومًا مَّحْسُورًا ﴿٢٩﴾ إِنَّ رَبَّكَ يَبْسُطُ ٱلرِّزْقَ
لِمَن يَشَآءُ وَيَقْدِرُ ۚ إِنَّهُۥ كَانَ بِعِبَادِهِۦ خَبِيرًۢا بَصِيرًا ﴿٣٠﴾ وَلَا تَقْتُلُوٓا۟
أَوْلَـٰدَكُمْ خَشْيَةَ إِمْلَـٰقٍ ۖ نَّحْنُ نَرْزُقُهُمْ وَإِيَّاكُمْ ۚ إِنَّ قَتْلَهُمْ كَانَ
خِطْـًٔا كَبِيرًا ﴿٣١﴾ وَلَا تَقْرَبُوا۟ ٱلزِّنَىٰٓ ۖ إِنَّهُۥ كَانَ فَـٰحِشَةً وَسَآءَ
سَبِيلًا ﴿٣٢﴾ وَلَا تَقْتُلُوا۟ ٱلنَّفْسَ ٱلَّتِى حَرَّمَ ٱللَّهُ إِلَّا بِٱلْحَقِّ ۗ وَمَن
قُتِلَ مَظْلُومًا فَقَدْ جَعَلْنَا لِوَلِيِّهِۦ سُلْطَـٰنًا فَلَا يُسْرِف فِّى
ٱلْقَتْلِ ۖ إِنَّهُۥ كَانَ مَنصُورًا ﴿٣٣﴾ وَلَا تَقْرَبُوا۟ مَالَ ٱلْيَتِيمِ إِلَّا بِٱلَّتِى
هِىَ أَحْسَنُ حَتَّىٰ يَبْلُغَ أَشُدَّهُۥ ۚ وَأَوْفُوا۟ بِٱلْعَهْدِ ۖ إِنَّ ٱلْعَهْدَ كَانَ
مَسْـُٔولًا ﴿٣٤﴾ وَأَوْفُوا۟ ٱلْكَيْلَ إِذَا كِلْتُمْ وَزِنُوا۟ بِٱلْقِسْطَاسِ ٱلْمُسْتَقِيمِ ۚ
ذَٰلِكَ خَيْرٌ وَأَحْسَنُ تَأْوِيلًا ﴿٣٥﴾ وَلَا تَقْفُ مَا لَيْسَ لَكَ بِهِۦ عِلْمٌ ۚ

22. ***Do not set up any other god together with Allah and so sit there reviled and forsaken*** without any helper.

23. ***Your Lord has decreed*** and commanded ***that you should worship none but Him, and that you should show kindness to your parents*** by being dutiful to them. ***Whether one or both of them reach*** (read as *yablughanna* and *yablughānna*) ***old age with you, do not say 'Ugh!*** (read as *uffin*, *uffa* and *uffi* meaning "Ugly!"),***' to them out of irritation, and do not*** rebuke or ***be harsh with them but speak to them with gentleness and generosity.***

24. ***Take them under your wing*** with kindness, ***out of mercy, with due humility and say: 'Lord, show mercy to them as they did in looking after me when I was small.'***

25. ***Your Lord knows best what is in your selves*** – in terms of dutifulness or lack of it. ***If you are righteous*** and obey Allah, ***He is Ever-Forgiving to the remorseful*** – forgiving those who return to His obedience and forgiving people for any impulsive mistakes they make in their behaviour towards their parents, provided they do not conceal a real lack of filiality.

26. ***Give your relatives their due*** – by way of kindness and gifts to maintain ties – ***and the very poor and travellers; but do not squander what you have*** by spending that is not obedience to Allah.

27. ***Squanderers are brothers to the shayṭāns*** – on the same path as them – ***and Shayṭān was ungrateful to his Lord.*** The word for "ungrateful", *kafūr* is an intensive form from *kufr*, meaning both ingratitude for Allah's blessings and also unbelief. So he is the brother of the squanderer.

28. ***But if you do turn away from them*** – from those relatives mentioned and the others mentioned after them – and do not give to them, ***seeking the mercy you hope for from your Lord*** – if you expect more provision to come to you from your Lord so that you can give them some of it – ***then speak to them with words that bring them ease*** – promising to give them something when more provision comes.

29. ***Do not keep your hand chained to your neck*** by refraining from spending completely, ***but do not extend it either to its full extent –***

by giving everything you have – ***so that you sit there blamed*** in the first case ***and destitute*** in the second.

30. ***Your Lord expands the provision of anyone He wills and restricts it*** as He wishes; ***He is aware of and sees His slaves.*** Allah knows the inward of His slaves and their outward and so He provides for them according to their best interests.

31. ***Do not kill your children*** by burying them alive ***out of fear of being poor. We will provide for them and you. Killing them is a terrible mistake*** and grave sin.

32. ***And do not go near*** (using this verb is more intensive than simply using to the verb *atā,* "to go to") ***to fornication. It is an indecent act, an evil way.***

33. ***Do not kill any person Allah has made inviolate, except with the right to do so. If someone is wrongly killed, We have given authority to his next of kin*** (his heir). He is given the authority over the killer. ***But he should not be excessive in taking life*** – by exceeding the limits in killing by killing: other than the killer or by killing in a manner other than the manner he which he killed. ***He will be helped.***

34. ***Do not go near the property of orphans before they reach maturity, except in a good way. Fulfil your contracts***, whether with Allah or with people: ***contracts will be asked about.***

35. ***Give full measure when you measure and weigh with a level balance. That is better and gives the best result.***

36. ***Do not pursue what you have no knowledge of. Hearing, sight and hearts will all be questioned*** about what their possessor did.

37. ***Do not strut arrogantly*** – with overweening pride – ***about the earth. You will certainly never split the earth apart*** – to reach the other side by your proud will – ***nor will you ever rival the mountains in height.*** So how can you be arrogant?

38. ***All of that*** – the things mentioned above – ***is evil action and hateful in the sight of your Lord.***

39. ***That is part of the wisdom*** (admonition) ***your Lord has revealed to you***, Muḥammad. ***Do not set up another god together with Allah and so be thrown into Hell, blamed, and driven out*** from Allah's mercy.

إِنَّ ٱلسَّمْعَ وَٱلْبَصَرَ وَٱلْفُؤَادَ كُلُّ أُو۟لَٰٓئِكَ كَانَ عَنْهُ مَسْـُٔولًا ﴿٣٦﴾
وَلَا تَمْشِ فِى ٱلْأَرْضِ مَرَحًا ۖ إِنَّكَ لَن تَخْرِقَ ٱلْأَرْضَ وَلَن تَبْلُغَ
ٱلْجِبَالَ طُولًا ﴿٣٧﴾ كُلُّ ذَٰلِكَ كَانَ سَيِّئُهُۥ عِندَ رَبِّكَ مَكْرُوهًا ﴿٣٨﴾
ذَٰلِكَ مِمَّآ أَوْحَىٰٓ إِلَيْكَ رَبُّكَ مِنَ ٱلْحِكْمَةِ ۗ وَلَا تَجْعَلْ مَعَ ٱللَّهِ إِلَٰهًا
ءَاخَرَ فَتُلْقَىٰ فِى جَهَنَّمَ مَلُومًا مَّدْحُورًا ﴿٣٩﴾ أَفَأَصْفَىٰكُمْ رَبُّكُم
بِٱلْبَنِينَ وَٱتَّخَذَ مِنَ ٱلْمَلَٰٓئِكَةِ إِنَٰثًا ۚ إِنَّكُمْ لَتَقُولُونَ قَوْلًا عَظِيمًا ﴿٤٠﴾
وَلَقَدْ صَرَّفْنَا فِى هَٰذَا ٱلْقُرْءَانِ لِيَذَّكَّرُوا۟ وَمَا يَزِيدُهُمْ إِلَّا نُفُورًا ﴿٤١﴾
قُل لَّوْ كَانَ مَعَهُۥٓ ءَالِهَةٌ كَمَا يَقُولُونَ إِذًا لَّٱبْتَغَوْا۟ إِلَىٰ ذِى ٱلْعَرْشِ سَبِيلًا
﴿٤٢﴾ سُبْحَٰنَهُۥ وَتَعَٰلَىٰ عَمَّا يَقُولُونَ عُلُوًّا كَبِيرًا ﴿٤٣﴾ تُسَبِّحُ لَهُ ٱلسَّمَٰوَٰتُ
ٱلسَّبْعُ وَٱلْأَرْضُ وَمَن فِيهِنَّ ۚ وَإِن مِّن شَىْءٍ إِلَّا يُسَبِّحُ بِحَمْدِهِۦ وَلَٰكِن
لَّا تَفْقَهُونَ تَسْبِيحَهُمْ ۗ إِنَّهُۥ كَانَ حَلِيمًا غَفُورًا ﴿٤٤﴾ وَإِذَا قَرَأْتَ
ٱلْقُرْءَانَ جَعَلْنَا بَيْنَكَ وَبَيْنَ ٱلَّذِينَ لَا يُؤْمِنُونَ بِٱلْءَاخِرَةِ حِجَابًا
مَّسْتُورًا ﴿٤٥﴾ وَجَعَلْنَا عَلَىٰ قُلُوبِهِمْ أَكِنَّةً أَن يَفْقَهُوهُ وَفِىٓ ءَاذَانِهِمْ
وَقْرًا ۚ وَإِذَا ذَكَرْتَ رَبَّكَ فِى ٱلْقُرْءَانِ وَحْدَهُۥ وَلَّوْا۟ عَلَىٰٓ أَدْبَٰرِهِمْ نُفُورًا
﴿٤٦﴾ نَّحْنُ أَعْلَمُ بِمَا يَسْتَمِعُونَ بِهِۦٓ إِذْ يَسْتَمِعُونَ إِلَيْكَ وَإِذْ هُمْ نَجْوَىٰٓ
إِذْ يَقُولُ ٱلظَّٰلِمُونَ إِن تَتَّبِعُونَ إِلَّا رَجُلًا مَّسْحُورًا ﴿٤٧﴾ ٱنظُرْ
كَيْفَ ضَرَبُوا۟ لَكَ ٱلْأَمْثَالَ فَضَلُّوا۟ فَلَا يَسْتَطِيعُونَ سَبِيلًا ﴿٤٨﴾
وَقَالُوٓا۟ أَءِذَا كُنَّا عِظَٰمًا وَرُفَٰتًا أَءِنَّا لَمَبْعُوثُونَ خَلْقًا جَدِيدًا ﴿٤٩﴾
۞ قُلْ كُونُوا۟ حِجَارَةً أَوْ حَدِيدًا ﴿٥٠﴾ أَوْ خَلْقًا مِّمَّا يَكْبُرُ فِى
صُدُورِكُمْ ۚ فَسَيَقُولُونَ مَن يُعِيدُنَا ۖ قُلِ ٱلَّذِى فَطَرَكُمْ أَوَّلَ مَرَّةٍ ۚ

40. ***Has your Lord honoured you*** – singled you out, people of Makka – ***with sons and Himself taken the angels as daughters? It is truly something terrible that you say!***

41. ***We have made things clear in this Qur'an*** – by means of parables, warnings and promises – ***so that they might pay heed*** and take note, ***but it only makes them run away*** from the truth ***the more!***

42. ***Say*** to them: ***'If there had, as you say, been other gods together with Him, they would have sought a way to the Master of the Throne*** and contended with Him.'

43. ***Glory be to Him! He is exalted above what they say*** about any partners ***in Greatness and Sublimity.***

44. ***The seven heavens and the earth and everyone in them glorify Him. There is nothing*** – no creature whatsoever – ***that does not glorify Him with praise*** – saying, 'Glory be to Allah and by His praise,' ***but you do not understand their glorification*** because it is not in your language. ***He is All-Forbearing, Ever-Forgiving*** – in that He does not immediately punish you.

45. ***When you recite the Qur'an, We place an obscuring veil between you*** – which veils you from them so that they do not see you – ***and those who do not believe in the Next World.*** This was revealed about those who wanted to assassinate the Prophet, may Allah bless him and grant him peace.

46. ***We have placed covers on their hearts, preventing them from understanding it*** – from understanding the Qur'an, so they do not understand it – ***and heaviness in their ears*** – so that they cannot listen to it properly. ***When you mention your Lord alone in the Qur'an, they turn their backs and run away.***

47. ***We know how they listen*** in a mocking way ***when they listen to you*** reciting, ***and when they confer together secretly, and when the wrongdoers say*** privately to one another, ***'You are only following a man who is bewitched*** – whose intellect is overwrought!' Allah says:

48. ***Look how they make likenesses of you*** – comparing you with someone bewitched, a soothsayer and poet – ***and go astray*** from guidance. ***They are unable to find their way.***

فَسَيُنْغِضُونَ إِلَيْكَ رُءُوسَهُمْ وَيَقُولُونَ مَتَىٰ هُوَ ۖ قُلْ عَسَىٰٓ أَن
يَكُونَ قَرِيبًا ﴿٥١﴾ يَوْمَ يَدْعُوكُمْ فَتَسْتَجِيبُونَ بِحَمْدِهِۦ
وَتَظُنُّونَ إِن لَّبِثْتُمْ إِلَّا قَلِيلًا ﴿٥٢﴾ وَقُل لِّعِبَادِى يَقُولُوا۟ ٱلَّتِى هِىَ
أَحْسَنُ ۚ إِنَّ ٱلشَّيْطَٰنَ يَنزَغُ بَيْنَهُمْ ۚ إِنَّ ٱلشَّيْطَٰنَ كَانَ لِلْإِنسَٰنِ
عَدُوًّا مُّبِينًا ﴿٥٣﴾ رَّبُّكُمْ أَعْلَمُ بِكُمْ ۖ إِن يَشَأْ يَرْحَمْكُمْ أَوْ إِن يَشَأْ
يُعَذِّبْكُمْ ۚ وَمَآ أَرْسَلْنَٰكَ عَلَيْهِمْ وَكِيلًا ﴿٥٤﴾ وَرَبُّكَ أَعْلَمُ
بِمَن فِى ٱلسَّمَٰوَٰتِ وَٱلْأَرْضِ ۗ وَلَقَدْ فَضَّلْنَا بَعْضَ ٱلنَّبِيِّۦنَ عَلَىٰ بَعْضٍ ۖ
وَءَاتَيْنَا دَاوُۥدَ زَبُورًا ﴿٥٥﴾ قُلِ ٱدْعُوا۟ ٱلَّذِينَ زَعَمْتُم مِّن دُونِهِۦ فَلَا
يَمْلِكُونَ كَشْفَ ٱلضُّرِّ عَنكُمْ وَلَا تَحْوِيلًا ﴿٥٦﴾ أُو۟لَٰٓئِكَ ٱلَّذِينَ
يَدْعُونَ يَبْتَغُونَ إِلَىٰ رَبِّهِمُ ٱلْوَسِيلَةَ أَيُّهُمْ أَقْرَبُ وَيَرْجُونَ
رَحْمَتَهُۥ وَيَخَافُونَ عَذَابَهُۥٓ ۚ إِنَّ عَذَابَ رَبِّكَ كَانَ مَحْذُورًا ﴿٥٧﴾
وَإِن مِّن قَرْيَةٍ إِلَّا نَحْنُ مُهْلِكُوهَا قَبْلَ يَوْمِ ٱلْقِيَٰمَةِ
أَوْ مُعَذِّبُوهَا عَذَابًا شَدِيدًا ۚ كَانَ ذَٰلِكَ فِى ٱلْكِتَٰبِ مَسْطُورًا ﴿٥٨﴾
وَمَا مَنَعَنَآ أَن نُّرْسِلَ بِٱلْـَٔايَٰتِ إِلَّآ أَن كَذَّبَ بِهَا ٱلْأَوَّلُونَ ۚ
وَءَاتَيْنَا ثَمُودَ ٱلنَّاقَةَ مُبْصِرَةً فَظَلَمُوا۟ بِهَا ۚ وَمَا نُرْسِلُ بِٱلْـَٔايَٰتِ
إِلَّا تَخْوِيفًا ﴿٥٩﴾ وَإِذْ قُلْنَا لَكَ إِنَّ رَبَّكَ أَحَاطَ بِٱلنَّاسِ ۚ وَمَا
جَعَلْنَا ٱلرُّءْيَا ٱلَّتِىٓ أَرَيْنَٰكَ إِلَّا فِتْنَةً لِّلنَّاسِ وَٱلشَّجَرَةَ ٱلْمَلْعُونَةَ
فِى ٱلْقُرْءَانِ ۚ وَنُخَوِّفُهُمْ فَمَا يَزِيدُهُمْ إِلَّا طُغْيَٰنًا كَبِيرًا ﴿٦٠﴾
وَإِذْ قُلْنَا لِلْمَلَٰٓئِكَةِ ٱسْجُدُوا۟ لِءَادَمَ فَسَجَدُوٓا۟ إِلَّآ إِبْلِيسَ
قَالَ ءَأَسْجُدُ لِمَنْ خَلَقْتَ طِينًا ﴿٦١﴾ قَالَ أَرَءَيْتَكَ هَٰذَا ٱلَّذِى

49. ***They say*** in denial of the resurrection, ***'What! When we are bones and crumbled dust, will we then be raised up as a new creation?'***

50. ***Say*** to them: ***'It would not matter if you were rock or iron…***

51. ***…or indeed any created thing that you think is harder still*** to bring to life than decayed bones.' Even if you were made of rock or iron, Allah would still be able to breathe the spirit into you. ***They will say, 'Who will bring us back*** to life ***again?' Say: 'He who brought you into being in the first place'*** when before that you were nothing. For the One who is able to originate something is able to bring it back again, because that is easier. ***They will shake their heads at you*** in wonder ***and ask*** in mockery, ***'When will it happen?' Say: 'It may well be that it*** (the Resurrection) ***is very near.'***

52. ***On the Day He calls you*** from the grave by the trumpet of Isrāfīl ***you will respond*** to the call to emerge from the grave ***by praising Him*** – at His command or with His praise – ***and think that you have only tarried a very short time*** in this world, because of the terror aroused by what you will see.

53. ***Say to My*** believing ***slaves that they should only say*** to the unbelievers ***the best. Shayṭān wants to stir up trouble between them; Shayṭān is an outright enemy to man.*** The best thing to say is:

54. ***Your Lord knows you best. If He wills, He will have mercy on you*** – by granting you repentance and faith – ***and, if He wills, He will punish you*** by making you die in unbelief. ***We did not send you to be their guardian.*** In other words: We did not send you to compel them to believe. This was revealed before the command to fight.

55. ***My Lord knows best everyone in the heavens and earth*** – and singles out for them what He wishes according to their states. ***We favoured some of the Prophets over others,*** and singled out each of them for a particular quality, such as direct speech for Mūsā, friendship for Ibrāhīm, and the Night Journey for Muḥammad, ***and We gave Dāwūd the* Zabūr.**

56. ***Say*** to them: ***'Call on those you make claims*** of divinity ***for apart from Him*** – such as the angels and the Prophets 'Īsā and

'Uzayr. ***They possess no power to remove any harm from you or to change anything.'***

57. ***Those they call on*** as gods ***are themselves seeking the means by which they might approach their Lord*** through obedience ***– even those who are the closest to Him – and are hoping for His mercy and fearing his punishment.*** So how can you call them gods? ***The punishment of your Lord is truly something to be feared.***

58. ***There is no city We will not destroy*** – meaning its inhabitants – ***before the Day of Rising, or punish with a terrible punishment*** – by killing or in other ways. ***That is inscribed in the Book*** (the Preserved Tablet).

59. ***Nothing has prevented Us sending you*** (people of Makka) ***Signs*** – which you asked for – ***except the fact that the previous peoples denied them*** when they were sent, so Allah destroyed them. If Allah had sent the Signs to the people of Makka, they would have denied them and merited destruction. However, Allah judged that they should be granted a deferment until the mission of Muḥammad, may Allah bless him and grant him peace, had been completed. ***We gave Thamūd the She-camel as a visible Sign, and then they mistreated her.*** They did wrong and disbelieved and so they were destroyed. ***We do not send Signs*** (miracles) ***except to frighten people*** so that they believe in Allah.

60. Remember ***when We said to you, 'Surely your Lord encompasses the people with His knowledge*** and power, so that they are within His grasp.' Therefore convey the Message to them and do not fear anyone. Allah will protect you from them. ***We only appointed the vision We showed you*** during the Night Journey ***and the Accursed Tree in the Qur'an*** – Zaqqūm, which grows in the bottom of Hell. We made it a trial for them when they said, "Fire burns trees, so how can it grow there?" – ***as a trial and temptation for the people*** – meaning the people of Makka, since they denied it and some of them apostatised when they were told about it. ***We frighten them*** by it, ***but it only increases them in their excessive insolence.***

61. Remember ***when We said to the angels, 'Prostrate yourselves to Ādam.'*** The prostration referred to is a kind of greeting by bowing.

كَرَّمۡتَ عَلَيَّ لَئِنۡ أَخَّرۡتَنِ إِلَىٰ يَوۡمِ ٱلۡقِيَٰمَةِ لَأَحۡتَنِكَنَّ
ذُرِّيَّتَهُۥٓ إِلَّا قَلِيلٗا ٦٢ قَالَ ٱذۡهَبۡ فَمَن تَبِعَكَ مِنۡهُمۡ فَإِنَّ
جَهَنَّمَ جَزَآؤُكُمۡ جَزَآءٗ مَّوۡفُورٗا ٦٣ وَٱسۡتَفۡزِزۡ مَنِ ٱسۡتَطَعۡتَ
مِنۡهُم بِصَوۡتِكَ وَأَجۡلِبۡ عَلَيۡهِم بِخَيۡلِكَ وَرَجِلِكَ وَشَارِكۡهُمۡ
فِي ٱلۡأَمۡوَٰلِ وَٱلۡأَوۡلَٰدِ وَعِدۡهُمۡۚ وَمَا يَعِدُهُمُ ٱلشَّيۡطَٰنُ إِلَّا
غُرُورًا ٦٤ إِنَّ عِبَادِي لَيۡسَ لَكَ عَلَيۡهِمۡ سُلۡطَٰنٞۚ وَكَفَىٰ
بِرَبِّكَ وَكِيلٗا ٦٥ رَّبُّكُمُ ٱلَّذِي يُزۡجِي لَكُمُ ٱلۡفُلۡكَ
فِي ٱلۡبَحۡرِ لِتَبۡتَغُواْ مِن فَضۡلِهِۦٓۚ إِنَّهُۥ كَانَ بِكُمۡ رَحِيمٗا ٦٦
وَإِذَا مَسَّكُمُ ٱلضُّرُّ فِي ٱلۡبَحۡرِ ضَلَّ مَن تَدۡعُونَ إِلَّآ إِيَّاهُۖ فَلَمَّا نَجَّىٰكُمۡ
إِلَى ٱلۡبَرِّ أَعۡرَضۡتُمۡۚ وَكَانَ ٱلۡإِنسَٰنُ كَفُورًا ٦٧ أَفَأَمِنتُمۡ أَن يَخۡسِفَ
بِكُمۡ جَانِبَ ٱلۡبَرِّ أَوۡ يُرۡسِلَ عَلَيۡكُمۡ حَاصِبٗا ثُمَّ لَا تَجِدُواْ لَكُمۡ
وَكِيلًا ٦٨ أَمۡ أَمِنتُمۡ أَن يُعِيدَكُمۡ فِيهِ تَارَةً أُخۡرَىٰ فَيُرۡسِلَ
عَلَيۡكُمۡ قَاصِفٗا مِّنَ ٱلرِّيحِ فَيُغۡرِقَكُم بِمَا كَفَرۡتُمۡ ثُمَّ لَا تَجِدُواْ
لَكُمۡ عَلَيۡنَا بِهِۦ تَبِيعٗا ٦٩ ۞ وَلَقَدۡ كَرَّمۡنَا بَنِيٓ ءَادَمَ وَحَمَلۡنَٰهُمۡ
فِي ٱلۡبَرِّ وَٱلۡبَحۡرِ وَرَزَقۡنَٰهُم مِّنَ ٱلطَّيِّبَٰتِ وَفَضَّلۡنَٰهُمۡ عَلَىٰ
كَثِيرٖ مِّمَّنۡ خَلَقۡنَا تَفۡضِيلٗا ٧٠ يَوۡمَ نَدۡعُواْ كُلَّ أُنَاسِۭ
بِإِمَٰمِهِمۡۖ فَمَنۡ أُوتِيَ كِتَٰبَهُۥ بِيَمِينِهِۦ فَأُوْلَٰٓئِكَ يَقۡرَءُونَ
كِتَٰبَهُمۡ وَلَا يُظۡلَمُونَ فَتِيلٗا ٧١ وَمَن كَانَ فِي هَٰذِهِۦٓ
أَعۡمَىٰ فَهُوَ فِي ٱلۡأٓخِرَةِ أَعۡمَىٰ وَأَضَلُّ سَبِيلٗا ٧٢ وَإِن كَادُواْ
لَيَفۡتِنُونَكَ عَنِ ٱلَّذِيٓ أَوۡحَيۡنَآ إِلَيۡكَ لِتَفۡتَرِيَ عَلَيۡنَا غَيۡرَهُۥۖ

They prostrated, except for Iblīs. He said 'What! Am I to prostrate to one You have created out of clay?'

62. ***He said,*** 'Tell me, ***do You see this creature You have honoured over me*** by commanding that he be prostrated to, when I am better than him because You created me from fire? ***If You reprieve me till the Day of Rising, I will be the master of his descendants*** – by making them go astray – ***except for a very few*** of them whom You protect.'

63. ***He*** (Allah) ***said, 'Go*** – you are reprieved until the time of the first Blast! ***And as for any who follow you, your repayment is Hell, repayment in full*** – for you and those who follow you.

64. ***Stir up*** and provoke ***any of them you can with your voice*** – and with your incitement of them through singing, musical instruments, and everything else which invites people to disobey Allah – ***and rally against them your cavalry and your infantry*** to abet them in acts of disobedience, ***and share with them in their children and their wealth*** – meaning unlawful wealth, such as that gained by means of usury and usurpation, and children resulting from fornication – ***and make them promises*** that there will be no resurrection or repayment. ***The promise of Shayṭān*** about that ***is nothing but delusion*** and falsehood.

65. ***But as for My*** believing ***slaves, you will not have any authority over them.' Your Lord suffices as a guardian*** – for them against you."

66. ***Your Lord is He who propels the ships on the sea for you so that you may seek His bounty*** through trade. ***He is indeed Most Merciful to you*** in subjecting them to you.

67. ***When harm*** – a violent storm – ***occurs to you at sea*** and you feel in danger of drowning, ***those you call on*** – the false gods you worship – ***vanish*** – forsaking you so you do not call on them – ***except for Him alone.*** You call on Allah Almighty alone because you are in a strait from which only He can deliver you. ***But when He delivers you*** – by saving you from drowning and bringing you to shore – ***to dry land, you turn away*** from affirmation of His unity. ***Man truly is ungrateful*** for the blessings he receives.

68. ***Do you feel secure against Him causing the shore to swallow you up*** – as happened to Qārūn – ***or sending against you a sudden squall of stones*** – as happened to the people of Lūṭ***? Then you will find no one to be your guardian*** and protect you.

69. Or do you feel secure against Him taking you back into it (the sea) ***another time and sending a violent storm against you*** – a strong wind against you, which flattens everything in its path and so causes your ship to be wrecked – ***and drowning you for your ingratitude?*** The root of the word for "ingratitude", *k-f-r*, also means "unbelief". ***Then you will find no one to defend you against Us.*** The word *tabī'* used here means a helper and partisan to pursue Us for what We have done to you.

70. ***We have honoured*** and prefered ***the sons of Ādam*** – by the gift of knowledge, speech, balanced physique and the like, and the fact that he is pure after death – ***and conveyed them on land*** – on animals – ***and sea*** – on ships – ***and provided them with good things, and favoured them greatly over many*** other animals and wild beasts ***We have created.***

71. ***On the Day*** (the Day of Rising) ***We summon every people with their records.*** The word *imām* used here is said to mean either the Book of their actions, when it will be said "O you who have done evil!", or it may mean their Prophet, in which case the words used will be, "O nation of so-and-so!" ***Those*** of them ***who are given their Book in their right hand*** – the fortunate, those whose inner eyes were open in this world – ***will read their Book and they will not be wronged by even the smallest speck.*** Their actions will not be diminished in any way. The Arabic word for "smallest speck", *fatīl*, means the tiny membrane found on the side of a date-stone.

72. ***Those who are blind*** to the truth ***in this world will be blind*** to the Path of salvation and the recitation of the Qur'an ***in the Next World and even further off the Path.*** This was revealed about the tribe of Thaqīf, who asked the Prophet, may Allah bless him and grant him peace, to turn their valley into a sanctuary and pressed him to do so.

وَإِذًا لَّٱتَّخَذُوكَ خَلِيلًا ﴿٧٣﴾ وَلَوْلَآ أَن ثَبَّتْنَٰكَ لَقَدْ كِدتَّ
تَرْكَنُ إِلَيْهِمْ شَيْـًٔا قَلِيلًا ﴿٧٤﴾ إِذًا لَّأَذَقْنَٰكَ ضِعْفَ
ٱلْحَيَوٰةِ وَضِعْفَ ٱلْمَمَاتِ ثُمَّ لَا تَجِدُ لَكَ عَلَيْنَا نَصِيرًا ﴿٧٥﴾
وَإِن كَادُوا۟ لَيَسْتَفِزُّونَكَ مِنَ ٱلْأَرْضِ لِيُخْرِجُوكَ مِنْهَا ۖ
وَإِذًا لَّا يَلْبَثُونَ خِلَٰفَكَ إِلَّا قَلِيلًا ﴿٧٦﴾ سُنَّةَ مَن قَدْ
أَرْسَلْنَا قَبْلَكَ مِن رُّسُلِنَا ۖ وَلَا تَجِدُ لِسُنَّتِنَا تَحْوِيلًا ﴿٧٧﴾ أَقِمِ
ٱلصَّلَوٰةَ لِدُلُوكِ ٱلشَّمْسِ إِلَىٰ غَسَقِ ٱلَّيْلِ وَقُرْءَانَ ٱلْفَجْرِ ۖ إِنَّ
قُرْءَانَ ٱلْفَجْرِ كَانَ مَشْهُودًا ﴿٧٨﴾ وَمِنَ ٱلَّيْلِ فَتَهَجَّدْ بِهِۦ
نَافِلَةً لَّكَ عَسَىٰٓ أَن يَبْعَثَكَ رَبُّكَ مَقَامًا مَّحْمُودًا ﴿٧٩﴾ وَقُل رَّبِّ
أَدْخِلْنِى مُدْخَلَ صِدْقٍ وَأَخْرِجْنِى مُخْرَجَ صِدْقٍ وَٱجْعَل لِّى مِن
لَّدُنكَ سُلْطَٰنًا نَّصِيرًا ﴿٨٠﴾ وَقُلْ جَآءَ ٱلْحَقُّ وَزَهَقَ ٱلْبَٰطِلُ ۚ
إِنَّ ٱلْبَٰطِلَ كَانَ زَهُوقًا ﴿٨١﴾ وَنُنَزِّلُ مِنَ ٱلْقُرْءَانِ مَا هُوَ شِفَآءٌ
وَرَحْمَةٌ لِّلْمُؤْمِنِينَ ۙ وَلَا يَزِيدُ ٱلظَّٰلِمِينَ إِلَّا خَسَارًا ﴿٨٢﴾ وَإِذَآ
أَنْعَمْنَا عَلَى ٱلْإِنسَٰنِ أَعْرَضَ وَنَـَٔا بِجَانِبِهِۦ ۖ وَإِذَا مَسَّهُ ٱلشَّرُّ كَانَ يَـُٔوسًا
﴿٨٣﴾ قُلْ كُلٌّ يَعْمَلُ عَلَىٰ شَاكِلَتِهِۦ فَرَبُّكُمْ أَعْلَمُ بِمَنْ هُوَ أَهْدَىٰ
سَبِيلًا ﴿٨٤﴾ وَيَسْـَٔلُونَكَ عَنِ ٱلرُّوحِ ۖ قُلِ ٱلرُّوحُ مِنْ أَمْرِ رَبِّى
وَمَآ أُوتِيتُم مِّنَ ٱلْعِلْمِ إِلَّا قَلِيلًا ﴿٨٥﴾ وَلَئِن شِئْنَا لَنَذْهَبَنَّ
بِٱلَّذِىٓ أَوْحَيْنَآ إِلَيْكَ ثُمَّ لَا تَجِدُ لَكَ بِهِۦ عَلَيْنَا وَكِيلًا ﴿٨٦﴾
إِلَّا رَحْمَةً مِّن رَّبِّكَ ۚ إِنَّ فَضْلَهُۥ كَانَ عَلَيْكَ كَبِيرًا ﴿٨٧﴾ قُل
لَّئِنِ ٱجْتَمَعَتِ ٱلْإِنسُ وَٱلْجِنُّ عَلَىٰٓ أَن يَأْتُوا۟ بِمِثْلِ هَٰذَا ٱلْقُرْءَانِ

73. ***They were very near to enticing you away from some of what We have revealed to you, hoping that you would invent something against Us. Then*** – if you had done that – ***they would have taken you as their intimate.***

74. ***If We had not made you firm*** in the truth – by protecting you from going wrong – ***you would have leaned towards them a little*** – owing to their endless devices and insistence. That is a clear statement that the Prophet, may Allah bless him and grant him peace, did not incline to them or approach them.

75. ***Then*** – if you had inclined – ***We would have let you taste a double punishment in life and a double punishment in death*** – double the punishment of others in this world and the Next. ***You would not have found any helper against Us*** to defend you.

76. The following was revealed when the Jews said to him, "If you are a Prophet, then you should go to Syria. It is the land of the Prophets." ***They were very near to scaring you from the land*** (Madīna) ***with the object of expelling you from it. But had they done so they would only have remained there a short time after you*** – and then they would have been destroyed.

77. ***That was the pattern with those We sent before you as Our Messengers.*** Allah's pattern was to bring about the destruction of those who expelled the Messengers sent to them. ***You will not find any changing of Our pattern.***

78. ***Establish the prayer from the time the sun declines until the darkening of the night*** – a reference to the prayers of *Ẓuhr, 'Aṣr, Maghrib* and *'Ishā'* – ***and also the recitation at dawn*** – a reference to the prayer of *Ṣubḥ*ī ***The dawn recitation is certainly witnessed*** by both the angels of the night and the angels of the day.

79. ***And stay awake for prayer***, reciting the Qur'an, ***during part of the night as a supererogatory action for yourself*** – as an extra obligation for you, but not for the rest of your community or as a supplementary prayer in addition to the obligatory prayers. ***It may well be that your Lord will raise you to a Praiseworthy Station*** in the Next World – a station in which you will be praised by the first and the last. That refers to the station of intercession once judgement has been rendered.

80. Then, when the Prophet, may Allah bless him and grant him peace, was commanded to emigrate, the following *āyat* was revealed: ***Say: 'My Lord, make my entry*** into Madina ***sincere*** and pleasing in such a way as to ensure that I do not find anything which I dislike – ***and make my leaving*** Makka ***sincere*** in such a way as to ensure that my heart does not turn back to it – ***and grant me supporting authority direct from Your Presence***, by which you help me against Your enemies.*'*

81. ***Say*** when you enter Makka: ***'Truth*** (Islam) ***has come and falsehood*** (unbelief) ***has vanished. Falsehood is always bound to vanish.'*** It vanishes and disappears. "When the Prophet, may Allah bless him and grant him peace, entered Makka, there were three hundred and sixty idols around the Ka'ba. He began to poke them with a stick he had in his hand while reciting this *āyat,* saying it until they fell." (Related by al-Bukhārī and Muslim)

82. ***We send down in the Qur'an that which is a healing*** for the sickness of misguidance ***and a mercy to the believers, but it only increases the wrongdoers*** (the unbelievers) ***in loss*** – because of their unbelief.

83. ***When We bless*** an unbelieving ***man, he turns away*** from thankfulness ***and draws aside*** arrogantly. ***When evil*** (poverty and hardship) ***touches him, he despairs*** of Allah's mercy.

84. ***Say: 'Each man*** – both us and you – ***acts according to his nature*** – in his own way – ***but your Lord knows best who is best guided on the Path*** and will reward him.*'*

85. ***They*** (the Jews) ***will ask you about the* Rūḥ** which gives life to the body. ***Say*** to them: ***'The* Rūḥ *is my Lord's concern.*** Allah knows it and you do not know it. ***You have only been given a little knowledge*** in relation to Allah's knowledge.*'*

86. ***If We wished, We could take away what We have revealed to you*** (the Qur'an) by erasing it from people's hearts and eliminating the physical copies of the Qur'an – ***and then you would not find any to guard you from Us –***

87. ***...but for a mercy from your Lord.*** Allah has ensured its continuance. ***His favour to you is indeed immense*** – in revealing it to you and giving you the Praiseworthy Station and other favours.

لَا يَأْتُونَ بِمِثْلِهِۦ وَلَوْ كَانَ بَعْضُهُمْ لِبَعْضٍ ظَهِيرًا ﴿٨٨﴾ وَلَقَدْ
صَرَّفْنَا لِلنَّاسِ فِي هَٰذَا ٱلْقُرْءَانِ مِن كُلِّ مَثَلٍ فَأَبَىٰٓ أَكْثَرُ ٱلنَّاسِ
إِلَّا كُفُورًا ﴿٨٩﴾ وَقَالُواْ لَن نُّؤْمِنَ لَكَ حَتَّىٰ تَفْجُرَ لَنَا مِنَ
ٱلْأَرْضِ يَنۢبُوعًا ﴿٩٠﴾ أَوْ تَكُونَ لَكَ جَنَّةٌ مِّن نَّخِيلٍ وَعِنَبٍ
فَتُفَجِّرَ ٱلْأَنْهَٰرَ خِلَٰلَهَا تَفْجِيرًا ﴿٩١﴾ أَوْ تُسْقِطَ ٱلسَّمَآءَ كَمَا
زَعَمْتَ عَلَيْنَا كِسَفًا أَوْ تَأْتِيَ بِٱللَّهِ وَٱلْمَلَٰٓئِكَةِ قَبِيلًا ﴿٩٢﴾
أَوْ يَكُونَ لَكَ بَيْتٌ مِّن زُخْرُفٍ أَوْ تَرْقَىٰ فِي ٱلسَّمَآءِ وَلَن نُّؤْمِنَ
لِرُقِيِّكَ حَتَّىٰ تُنَزِّلَ عَلَيْنَا كِتَٰبًا نَّقْرَؤُهُۥ ۗ قُلْ سُبْحَانَ رَبِّي هَلْ
كُنتُ إِلَّا بَشَرًا رَّسُولًا ﴿٩٣﴾ وَمَا مَنَعَ ٱلنَّاسَ أَن يُؤْمِنُوٓاْ إِذْ جَآءَهُمُ
ٱلْهُدَىٰٓ إِلَّآ أَن قَالُوٓاْ أَبَعَثَ ٱللَّهُ بَشَرًا رَّسُولًا ﴿٩٤﴾ قُل لَّوْ كَانَ
فِي ٱلْأَرْضِ مَلَٰٓئِكَةٌ يَمْشُونَ مُطْمَئِنِّينَ لَنَزَّلْنَا عَلَيْهِم
مِّنَ ٱلسَّمَآءِ مَلَكًا رَّسُولًا ﴿٩٥﴾ قُلْ كَفَىٰ بِٱللَّهِ
شَهِيدًۢا بَيْنِي وَبَيْنَكُمْ ۚ إِنَّهُۥ كَانَ بِعِبَادِهِۦ خَبِيرًۢا بَصِيرًا ﴿٩٦﴾
وَمَن يَهْدِ ٱللَّهُ فَهُوَ ٱلْمُهْتَدِ ۖ وَمَن يُضْلِلْ فَلَن تَجِدَ لَهُمْ أَوْلِيَآءَ
مِن دُونِهِۦ ۖ وَنَحْشُرُهُمْ يَوْمَ ٱلْقِيَٰمَةِ عَلَىٰ وُجُوهِهِمْ عُمْيًا وَبُكْمًا
وَصُمًّا ۖ مَّأْوَىٰهُمْ جَهَنَّمُ ۖ كُلَّمَا خَبَتْ زِدْنَٰهُمْ سَعِيرًا ﴿٩٧﴾
ذَٰلِكَ جَزَآؤُهُم بِأَنَّهُمْ كَفَرُواْ بِـَٔايَٰتِنَا وَقَالُوٓاْ أَءِذَا كُنَّا عِظَٰمًا
وَرُفَٰتًا أَءِنَّا لَمَبْعُوثُونَ خَلْقًا جَدِيدًا ﴿٩٨﴾ ۞ أَوَلَمْ يَرَوْاْ أَنَّ ٱللَّهَ
ٱلَّذِي خَلَقَ ٱلسَّمَٰوَٰتِ وَٱلْأَرْضَ قَادِرٌ عَلَىٰٓ أَن يَخْلُقَ مِثْلَهُمْ
وَجَعَلَ لَهُمْ أَجَلًا لَّا رَيْبَ فِيهِ فَأَبَى ٱلظَّٰلِمُونَ إِلَّا كُفُورًا ﴿٩٩﴾

88. ***Say: 'If both men and jinn banded together to produce the like of this Qur'an, they could never produce anything like it*** – in respect of eloquence and fluency – ***even if they backed each other up.'*** This was to refute their words, *"If we wanted, we could say the same thing."* (8:31)

89. ***We have variegated throughout this Qur'an*** and made clear ***all kinds of examples for people*** – so that they may be admonished ***but most people*** – the people of Makka and others – ***spurn anything but unbelief*** and denial of the Truth.

90. ***They say, 'We will not believe you until you make a spring*** of water ***gush out from the earth for us;***

91. ***...or have a garden of dates and grapes which you make rivers come pouring through*** the middle of;

92. ***...or make the sky, as you claim, fall down on us in lumps; or bring Allah and the angels here*** – openly in front of us so that we can see them – ***as a guarantee;***

93. ***... or possess a house built out of gleaming gold; or ascend up into heaven*** by means of a ladder – ***and even then we will not believe in your ascent*** if you do ascend ***unless you bring us down a book to read.' Say*** to them: ***'Glory be to my Lord! Am I anything but a human messenger*** like other Messengers?' They only brought a Sign with Allah's permission.

94. ***Nothing prevents people from believing when guidance comes to them but the fact that they say*** in denial, ***'Has Allah sent a human being as Messenger*** and not an angel?'

95. ***Say*** to them: ***'If there had been angels on the earth*** – instead of human beings – ***going about in peace, We would have sent down to them an angel from heaven as Messenger.'*** This is because a Messenger who is sent to a people is only ever sent from their own species, in order that he will be able to speak to them and they will be able to understand him.

96. ***Say: 'Allah is a sufficient witness*** – to my truthfulness – ***between me and you. He is certainly aware of and sees His slaves.'*** He knows their inward and outward.

97. ***Whoever Allah guides is truly guided. But as for those He leads astray, you will not find any protectors for them*** to guide them

قُل لَّوْ أَنتُمْ تَمْلِكُونَ خَزَآئِنَ رَحْمَةِ رَبِّيٓ إِذًا لَّأَمْسَكْتُمْ خَشْيَةَ
ٱلْإِنفَاقِ ۚ وَكَانَ ٱلْإِنسَٰنُ قَتُورًا ١٠٠ وَلَقَدْ ءَاتَيْنَا مُوسَىٰ تِسْعَ
ءَايَٰتٍۭ بَيِّنَٰتٍ ۖ فَسْـَٔلْ بَنِيٓ إِسْرَٰٓءِيلَ إِذْ جَآءَهُمْ فَقَالَ لَهُۥ فِرْعَوْنُ
إِنِّي لَأَظُنُّكَ يَٰمُوسَىٰ مَسْحُورًا ١٠١ قَالَ لَقَدْ عَلِمْتَ مَآ أَنزَلَ
هَٰٓؤُلَآءِ إِلَّا رَبُّ ٱلسَّمَٰوَٰتِ وَٱلْأَرْضِ بَصَآئِرَ وَإِنِّي لَأَظُنُّكَ
يَٰفِرْعَوْنُ مَثْبُورًا ١٠٢ فَأَرَادَ أَن يَسْتَفِزَّهُم مِّنَ ٱلْأَرْضِ
فَأَغْرَقْنَٰهُ وَمَن مَّعَهُۥ جَمِيعًا ١٠٣ وَقُلْنَا مِنۢ بَعْدِهِۦ لِبَنِيٓ إِسْرَٰٓءِيلَ
ٱسْكُنُوا۟ ٱلْأَرْضَ فَإِذَا جَآءَ وَعْدُ ٱلْـَٔاخِرَةِ جِئْنَا بِكُمْ لَفِيفًا ١٠٤
وَبِٱلْحَقِّ أَنزَلْنَٰهُ وَبِٱلْحَقِّ نَزَلَ ۗ وَمَآ أَرْسَلْنَٰكَ إِلَّا مُبَشِّرًا وَنَذِيرًا ١٠٥
وَقُرْءَانًا فَرَقْنَٰهُ لِتَقْرَأَهُۥ عَلَى ٱلنَّاسِ عَلَىٰ مُكْثٍ وَنَزَّلْنَٰهُ تَنزِيلًا ١٠٦
قُلْ ءَامِنُوا۟ بِهِۦٓ أَوْ لَا تُؤْمِنُوٓا۟ ۚ إِنَّ ٱلَّذِينَ أُوتُوا۟ ٱلْعِلْمَ مِن قَبْلِهِۦٓ إِذَا يُتْلَىٰ
عَلَيْهِمْ يَخِرُّونَ لِلْأَذْقَانِ سُجَّدًا ١٠٧ وَيَقُولُونَ سُبْحَٰنَ رَبِّنَآ إِن كَانَ
وَعْدُ رَبِّنَا لَمَفْعُولًا ١٠٨ وَيَخِرُّونَ لِلْأَذْقَانِ يَبْكُونَ وَيَزِيدُهُمْ
خُشُوعًا ۩ ١٠٩ قُلِ ٱدْعُوا۟ ٱللَّهَ أَوِ ٱدْعُوا۟ ٱلرَّحْمَٰنَ ۖ أَيًّا مَّا تَدْعُوا۟ فَلَهُ
ٱلْأَسْمَآءُ ٱلْحُسْنَىٰ ۚ وَلَا تَجْهَرْ بِصَلَاتِكَ وَلَا تُخَافِتْ بِهَا وَٱبْتَغِ
بَيْنَ ذَٰلِكَ سَبِيلًا ١١٠ وَقُلِ ٱلْحَمْدُ لِلَّهِ ٱلَّذِي لَمْ يَتَّخِذْ وَلَدًا وَلَمْ يَكُن
لَّهُۥ شَرِيكٌ فِي ٱلْمُلْكِ وَلَمْ يَكُن لَّهُۥ وَلِيٌّ مِّنَ ٱلذُّلِّ ۖ وَكَبِّرْهُ تَكْبِيرًا ١١١

apart from Him. We will gather them on the Day of Rising, flat on their faces, blind, dumb and deaf. Their shelter will be Hell. Whenever the Blaze dies down, We will re-kindle it and ***increase it for them.***

98. ***That is their repayment for rejecting Our Signs*** and denying the Resurrection ***and saying, 'What, when we are bones and crumbled dust, will we then be raised up as a new creation?'***

99. ***Do they not see*** and know ***that Allah, Who created the heavens and earth*** – which are vast – ***has the power to create the like of them*** – in respect of human beings, who are tiny in comparison – ***and has appointed fixed terms for them*** – for their death and resurrection – ***of which there is no doubt? But the wrongdoers still spurn anything but unbelief.***

100. ***Say*** to them: ***'Even if you possessed the vast storehouses*** – referring particularly to provision and rain – ***of my Lord's mercy, you would still hold back*** and be miserly, ***fearing they would run out*** through being spent, and that you would therefore become poor.'

101. ***We gave Mūsā nine Clear Signs***: his White Hand, his Staff, the Flood, the locusts, the fleas, the frogs, the blood or obliteration, the drought and decrease of fruits. ***Ask***, Muḥammad, ***the tribe of Israel*** – in order to confirm your truthfulness to the idolaters; or it may mean: "We said to him, 'Ask.'" (One reading has it in the past tense.) – ***about when he came to them and Pharaoh said to him, 'Mūsā, I think you are bewitched*** (deluded and muddled).''

102. ***He said, 'You know*** (read as *'alimta* and also *'alimtu*, in which case the meaning becomes "I know") ***that no one sent these*** Signs ***down but the Lord of the heavens and earth to be clear proofs*** (lessons) – but you are stubborn. ***Pharaoh, I think you are destroyed*** – or turned aside from good.'

103. ***He*** (Pharaoh) ***wanted to scare them*** (Mūsā and his people) ***from the land*** of Egypt, ***but We drowned him and every one of those with him.***

104. ***We said to the tribe of Israel after that, 'Inhabit the land and, when the promise of*** the Final Hour in ***the Next World comes, We will produce you as a motley crowd*** – both you and them.'

105. ***We have sent it*** (the Qur'an) ***down with*** the ***truth*** that it contains ***and with truth it has come down*** – as it was revealed without any change. ***We sent you***, Muḥammad, ***only to bring good news*** of the Garden to those who believe ***and to give warning*** of the Fire to those who disbelieve.

106. ***We have divided up the Qur'an*** – meaning "We have sent it down in parts over the course of twenty or twenty-three years" – ***so you may recite it to mankind at intervals*** – slowly and deliberately over time so that they may understand it – ***and We have sent it down little by little*** – in to their best interests.

107. ***Say*** to the unbelievers of Makka: ***'Believe in it or do not believe in it.'*** This is a threat to them. ***Certainly, when it is recited to them, those who were given knowledge before it*** – before the Qur'an was revealed: a reference to the believers of the People of the Book – ***fall on their faces in prostration,***

108. ***...saying, 'Glory be to our Lord!*** This is to absolve Allah from any accusation of breaking His promise. ***The promise of our Lord is truly fulfilled!*** His promise was that He would send a Messenger; and He did indeed send the Prophet, may Allah bless him and grant him peace.

109. ***Weeping, they fall to the ground in prostration, and it*** (the Qur'an) ***increases them in humility*** towards Allah.

110. The Prophet, may Allah bless him and grant him peace, used to say, "O Allah, O All-Merciful." The unbelievers said, "He forbids us to worship two gods, when he himself does so," and this was revealed. ***Say*** to them: ***'Call on Allah or call on the All-Merciful, whichever you call upon*** – or name Him with either of them, saying: "O Allah" or "O All-Merciful," both of these Names being excellent – ***the Most Beautiful Names are His.'*** This includes these two names, as in the *ḥadīth*: "Allah is He other than whom there is no other god: *ar-Raḥmān* (All-Merciful), *ar-Raḥīm* (Most Merciful), *al-Malik* (the King), *al-Quddūs* (Utterly Pure), *as-Salām* (Perfect Peace), *al-Mu'min* (Granter of Security), *al-Muhaymin* (Safeguarder), *al-'Azīz* (Almighty), *al-Jabbār* (the Compeller), *al-Mutakabbir* (Supremely Great), *al-Khāliq* (Creator), *al-Bāri'* (Maker), *al-Muṣawwir* (Giver of Form), *al-Ghaffār,* (Ever-Forgiving) *al-Qahhār* (All-Conquering), *al-Wahhāb* (Ever-Giving), *ar-Razzāq* (Provider), *al-Fattāḥ* (Just Decider), *al-'Alīm* (All-Knowing), *al-Qābiḍ* (Contracter), *al-Bāsiṭ* (Expander), *al-Khāfiḍ* (Abaser), *ar-Rāfi'* (Exalter), *al-Mu'izz* (Honourer), *al-Mudhill* (Dishonourer), *as-Samī'* (All-Hearing), *al-Baṣīr* (All-Seeing), *al-Ḥakam* (Judge), *al-'Adl* (Just), *al-Laṭīf* (All-Subtle), *al-Khabīr* (All-Aware), *al-Ḥalīm* (Forbearing), *al-'Aẓīm* (Magnificent), *al-Ghafūr* (Forgiving), *ash-Shakūr* (Ever-Thankful), *al-'Alī* (All-High), *al-Kabīr* (Incomparably Great), *al-Ḥafīẓ* (Preserver), *al-Muqīt* (Maintainer), *al-Ḥasīb* (Reckoner), *al-Jalīl* (Majestic), *al-Karīm* (Generous), *ar-Raqīb* (Watchful), *al-Mujīb* (Quick to Respond), *al-Wāsi'* (All-Encompassing), *al-Ḥakīm* (All-Wise), *al-Wadūd* (Loving), al-Majīd (Glorious), *al-Bā'ith* (the Raiser), *ash-Shahīd* (Witness), *al-Ḥaqq* (the Truly Real), *al-Wakīl* (Guardian), *al-Qawī* (All-Strong), *al-Matīn* (Sure), *al-Walī* (Protector), *al-Ḥamīd* (Praiseworthy), *al-Muḥṣī* (Appraiser), *al-Mubdi'* (Originator), *al-Mu'īd* (Restorer), *al-Muḥyī* (the One who gives life), *al-Mumīt* (the One who causes to die), *al-Ḥayy* (Living), *al-Qayyūm* (the Self-Sustaining), *al-Wājid* (Rich), *al-Mājid* (the Noble), *al-Wāḥid* (One), *al-Aḥad* (Absolute Oneness), *aṣ-Ṣamad* (Everlasting Sustainer of all), *al-Qādir* (All-Powerful), *al-Muqtadir* (Most Powerful), *al-Muqaddim* (Advancer), *al-Mu'akhkhir* (Delayer), *al-Awwal* (the First), *al-Ākhir* (the Last), *aẓ-Ẓāhir* (Outward), *al-Bāṭin* (Inward), *al-Walī* (the Friend), *al-Muta'āli* (High Exalted), *al-Barr* (All-Good), *at-Tawwāb* (Ever-Turning), *al-Muntaqim* (Exactor of Revenge), *al-'Afuww* (Pardoner), *ar-Ra'ūf* (All-Gentle), *Mālik al-Mulk* (Master of the Kingdom), *Dhū al-Jalāl wa'l-Ikrām* (Lord of Majesty and Generosity), *al-Muqsiṭ* (Equitable), *al-Jāmi'* (Gatherer), *al-Ghanī* (Rich Beyond Need), *al-Mughnī* (Enricher), *al-Māni'* (Unapproachable), *aḍ-Ḍārr* (Afflictor), *an-Nāfi'* (Benefiter), *an-Nūr* (Light), *al-Hādī* (Guide), *al-Badī'* (Originator), *al-Bāqī* (the Abiding), *al-Wārith* (the Inheritor), *ar-Rashīd* (Right Guide), *aṣ-Ṣabūr* (Most Patient)." At-Tirmidhī related it. ***Do not be too loud in your prayer*** in your recitation, or the idolaters may hear you and abuse you and abuse the Qur'an and the One Who sent it down – ***or too quiet in it*** – which would prevent your companions from benefiting from it; ***but try to find a*** middle ***way between the two.***

111. ***And say: 'Praise be to Allah Who has had no son, Who has no partner in His Kingdom, and Who needs no one to protect Him from abasement.'*** He is not abased, so He needs no helper; nor does he need anyone to absolve Him from taking a child or partner or from anything that does not befit Him. ***And proclaim His Greatness repeatedly.'*** This *āyat* is evidence that Allah deserves every form of praise because of the perfection of His Essence and because He is unique in His Attributes. In his *Musnad*, Imām Aḥmad related from Mu'ādh al-Juhanī that the Messenger of Allah, may Allah bless him and grant him peace, used to say, "The *Āyat* of Might is: 'Praise be to Allah Who has had no son and Who has no partner in His Kingdom …', and Allah knows best.

The author (Jalālu'd-Dīn as-Suyūṭī) said, "This is the end of my continuation and completion of the commentary of the Noble Qur'an that was written by the shaykh and *imām*, the precise scholar, Jalālu'd-Dīn al-Maḥallī ash-Shāfi'ī, may Allah be pleased with him. I applied myself to completing it and directed my attention to important points which will prove beneficial, Allah willing. I wrote it within the amount of time appointed for the one spoken to (Mūsā) [i.e. forty nights] and made it a means to obtain the Gardens of Bliss. In fact, it is derived from the book which it is intended to complete and on which I relied in dealing with the ambiguous *āyat*s. May Allah have mercy on a man who looks with a fair eye at it and finds an error in it and then informs me of it. I have said:

"I praise Allah, my Lord,
if He guides me when I bring something
to light in spite of my powerlessness and weakness.
Whatever errors I have made, I will reject.
Whatever is accepted is for me, even if it is only a letter."

If I did not turn my attention to any errors attributed to my predecessor, it was because I know that I am unable to delve into these matters. In any case I pray that Allah will grant benefit from this work and use it to open closed hearts, blind eyes, and deaf ears. Whoever is blind in this world, is blind in the Next World. May Allah provide him with guidance to the Path of the Truth, success, and awareness and realisation of the fine points of Allah's words, and by it may He make us *"among those whom Allah has blessed: the Prophets, the men of truth, the martyrs and the righteous. What excellent company such people are!"* (4:68)

He finished writing it on Sunday 10 Shawwāl 370, having started it at the beginning of Ramaḍān in the same year. He finished a fair copy of it on Wednesday 6 Ṣafar 371. Shaykh Shamsu'd-Dīn Muḥammad ibn Abī Bakr al-Khaṭīb aṭ-Ṭūkhī said, "My friend, the scholar Shaykh Kamālu'd-Dīn al-Maḥallī, the brother of our shaykh Jalālu'd-Dīn al-Maḥallī, may Allah have mercy on them both, reported to me that he saw his brother, Shaykh Jalālu'd-Dīn, in a dream. In front of him was our friend, the scholar, Shaykh Jalālu'd-Dīn as-Suyūṭī, the author of this continuation of his work. The shaykh took this continuation in his hands and looked through it and said to its author, 'Which of them is better: my composition or yours?' He added, 'Look,' and pointed out certain places in it. It was as if he was indicating places in it to which he objected with gentleness. Whenever the author of this continuation was shown something, he answered it while the shaykh was smiling and laughing.'"

Our shaykh Jalālu'd-Dīn 'Abdu'r-Raḥmān ibn Abī Bakr as-Suyūṭī, the author of this continuation, said, "What I believe and am certain of is that what Shaykh Jalālu'd-Dīn al-Maḥalli, may Allah have mercy on him, wrote in his portion is better than my writing on several levels. How could that not be the case when what I wrote here is clearly derived from his work? As for that which was in the dream above, perhaps by it the Shaykh was indicating the few places in which I differed from him regarding a few very slight points. I do not think that there can be more than ten instances of that.

"One example is that the Shaykh said concerning *Sūrat Ṣād*: 'The *rūḥ* is a subtle body by which the human being is given life when it penetrates it.' I followed him at first and mentioned this definition in *Sūrat al-Ḥijr*. Then I turned from it by the words of the Almighty, *"They will ask you about the* Rūḥ. *Say: "The* Rūḥ *is my Lord's concern. You have only been given a little knowledge."* (17:85) It is explicit, or close to being explicit, in saying that the *Rūḥ* (the Spirit) is part of Allah's knowledge which we do not know, and therefore it is more appropriate to refrain from defining it. This is why Shaykh

Tāju'd-Dīn ibn as-Subkī said in *Jam' al-Jawāmi'*: 'Muḥammad, may Allah bless him and grant him peace, did not speak about the *Rūḥ* and therefore we refrain from doing so.'

"Another point is that the Shaykh said in *Sūrat al-Ḥajj*, 'The Sabaeans are a sect of the Jews. I mentioned that in *Sūrat al-Baqara*, and added, 'or Christians' to set out a second view. That is something that is known, especially among our colleagues, the *fuqahā'*. In *al-Minhaj* we find: 'The Samaritans among the Jews and the Sabaeans among the Christians disagree about the basis of their *dīn*.' In the commentary on *al-Minhaj*, ash-Shāfi'ī, may Allah be pleased with him, stated that the Sabaeans are a sect of the Christians.

"I do not recall a third position. It is as though the Shaykh, may Allah have mercy on him, was indicating the like of this point [in my dream]. Allah knows best which is correct, and all returns to Him."

سُورَةُ الكَهْفِ

بِسْمِ ٱللَّهِ ٱلرَّحْمَٰنِ ٱلرَّحِيمِ

ٱلْحَمْدُ لِلَّهِ ٱلَّذِىٓ أَنزَلَ عَلَىٰ عَبْدِهِ ٱلْكِتَٰبَ وَلَمْ يَجْعَل لَّهُۥ عِوَجَا ۜ ﴿١﴾
قَيِّمًا لِّيُنذِرَ بَأْسًا شَدِيدًا مِّن لَّدُنْهُ وَيُبَشِّرَ ٱلْمُؤْمِنِينَ ٱلَّذِينَ
يَعْمَلُونَ ٱلصَّٰلِحَٰتِ أَنَّ لَهُمْ أَجْرًا حَسَنًا ﴿٢﴾ مَّٰكِثِينَ
فِيهِ أَبَدًا ﴿٣﴾ وَيُنذِرَ ٱلَّذِينَ قَالُوا۟ ٱتَّخَذَ ٱللَّهُ وَلَدًا ﴿٤﴾
مَّا لَهُم بِهِۦ مِنْ عِلْمٍ وَلَا لِءَابَآئِهِمْ ۚ كَبُرَتْ كَلِمَةً تَخْرُجُ مِنْ
أَفْوَٰهِهِمْ ۚ إِن يَقُولُونَ إِلَّا كَذِبًا ﴿٥﴾ فَلَعَلَّكَ بَٰخِعٌ نَّفْسَكَ
عَلَىٰٓ ءَاثَٰرِهِمْ إِن لَّمْ يُؤْمِنُوا۟ بِهَٰذَا ٱلْحَدِيثِ أَسَفًا ﴿٦﴾ إِنَّا
جَعَلْنَا مَا عَلَى ٱلْأَرْضِ زِينَةً لَّهَا لِنَبْلُوَهُمْ أَيُّهُمْ أَحْسَنُ عَمَلًا
﴿٧﴾ وَإِنَّا لَجَٰعِلُونَ مَا عَلَيْهَا صَعِيدًا جُرُزًا ﴿٨﴾ أَمْ حَسِبْتَ
أَنَّ أَصْحَٰبَ ٱلْكَهْفِ وَٱلرَّقِيمِ كَانُوا۟ مِنْ ءَايَٰتِنَا عَجَبًا ﴿٩﴾
إِذْ أَوَى ٱلْفِتْيَةُ إِلَى ٱلْكَهْفِ فَقَالُوا۟ رَبَّنَآ ءَاتِنَا مِن لَّدُنكَ رَحْمَةً
وَهَيِّئْ لَنَا مِنْ أَمْرِنَا رَشَدًا ﴿١٠﴾ فَضَرَبْنَا عَلَىٰٓ ءَاذَانِهِمْ فِى
ٱلْكَهْفِ سِنِينَ عَدَدًا ﴿١١﴾ ثُمَّ بَعَثْنَٰهُمْ لِنَعْلَمَ أَىُّ ٱلْحِزْبَيْنِ
أَحْصَىٰ لِمَا لَبِثُوٓا۟ أَمَدًا ﴿١٢﴾ نَّحْنُ نَقُصُّ عَلَيْكَ نَبَأَهُم بِٱلْحَقِّ ۚ
إِنَّهُمْ فِتْيَةٌ ءَامَنُوا۟ بِرَبِّهِمْ وَزِدْنَٰهُمْ هُدًى ﴿١٣﴾ وَرَبَطْنَا
عَلَىٰ قُلُوبِهِمْ إِذْ قَامُوا۟ فَقَالُوا۟ رَبُّنَا رَبُّ ٱلسَّمَٰوَٰتِ وَٱلْأَرْضِ

18. *Sūrat al-Kahf* The Cave

This *sūra* is Makkan except for *āyats* 28 and 82 to the end of 101, which are Madinan. It has 110 *āyats* and was sent down after *al-Ghāshiya*.

1. ***Praise belongs to Allah*** – this is ascribing all good and beauty to Him, as is confirmed for Allah. As to whether this is a pronouncement of faith, praise, or both, the most useful view is that it is the third – ***Who has sent down the Book*** (the Qur'an) ***to His slave*** (Muḥammad) ***and has put no crookedness*** – no disagreement or contradiction – ***in it.***

2. ***It is straight, to warn*** – the unbelievers through it – ***of violent force*** (punishment) ***direct from Him, and to give the good news to the believers, those who do right actions, that for them there is an excellent reward:***

3. ***…a place*** (the Garden) ***in which they will remain for ever,***

4. ***… and to warn those*** unbelievers ***who say 'Allah has a son.'***

5. ***They have no knowledge of this*** claim, ***neither they nor their fathers*** – nor was it stated by their ancestors before them. ***It is a monstrous utterance which has issued from their mouths.*** These words are terrible. ***What they say is nothing but a lie.***

6. ***Perhaps you may destroy yourself with grief, chasing after them*** – after they turn away from you – ***if they do not believe in these words*** (the Qur'ān). The adverbial phrase "with grief", *asafan*, expresses the exasperation and sorrow which the Prophet experienced on account of his eagerness for his people to believe.

7. ***We made everything*** – animals, plants, trees, rivers and other things – ***on the earth*** to be ***adornment for it so that We could test them to see whose actions are the best*** – which of them are least greedy with respect to the adornment of this world.

8. ***We will certainly make everything on it a barren wasteland*** – infertile, dry land with no plants in it.

9. ***Do you consider*** (think) ***that the Companions of the Cave and ar-Raqīm*** – the tablet on which their names and lineages were writ-

ten. The Prophet, may Allah bless him and grant him peace, was asked about their story – ***were one of the most remarkable of Our Signs?*** Do you think that their story was a greater marvel among the Signs of Allah than other Signs, or indeed that it was the most extraordinary? That is not, in fact, the case.

10. Remember ***when the noble young men*** – the word used here, *fitya*, is the plural of *fatā*, meaning a perfect young man – ***took refuge in the cave*** – fearing for their faith on account of their unbelieving people – ***and said, 'Our Lord, give us mercy directly from You and open the way for us to right guidance in our situation.'***

11. ***So We sealed their ears with sleep*** – making them sleep – ***in the cave for a number of years.***

12. ***Then We woke them up again so that We might*** openly ***see which of the two groups*** – who would disagree about how long they had remained there – ***would better calculate the time they had stayed there.***

13. ***We will relate their story to you with truth. They were young men who believed in their Lord and We increased them in guidance.***

14. ***We fortified their hearts when they stood up*** – thereby making their hearts strong enough to speak the truth when they stood before their king, who had commanded them to bow to idols – ***and said, 'Our Lord is the Lord of the heavens and the earth and We will not call on any god apart from Him. We would in that case have uttered an abomination.*** We would have made an utterance involving transgression and excessive unbelief if we were to claim that there is another god besides Allah.

15. ***These people of ours have taken gods apart from Him. Why do they not produce a clear authority concerning them*** – for worshipping them***? Who could do greater wrong than someone who invents a lie against Allah*** and ascribes a partner to Him***?***

16. The youths said to one another: ***'When you have separated yourselves from them and everything they worship except Allah, take refuge in the cave and your Lord will unfold His mercy to you and open the way to the best*** (read as *marfiqan* and *mirfaqan*) – lit-

لَن نَّدْعُوَا۟ مِن دُونِهِۦٓ إِلَـٰهًا ۖ لَّقَدْ قُلْنَآ إِذًا شَطَطًا ﴿١٤﴾ هَـٰٓؤُلَآءِ
قَوْمُنَا ٱتَّخَذُوا۟ مِن دُونِهِۦٓ ءَالِهَةً ۖ لَّوْلَا يَأْتُونَ عَلَيْهِم
بِسُلْطَـٰنٍۭ بَيِّنٍ ۖ فَمَنْ أَظْلَمُ مِمَّنِ ٱفْتَرَىٰ عَلَى ٱللَّهِ كَذِبًا ﴿١٥﴾
وَإِذِ ٱعْتَزَلْتُمُوهُمْ وَمَا يَعْبُدُونَ إِلَّا ٱللَّهَ فَأْوُۥٓا۟ إِلَى ٱلْكَهْفِ
يَنشُرْ لَكُمْ رَبُّكُم مِّن رَّحْمَتِهِۦ وَيُهَيِّئْ لَكُم مِّنْ أَمْرِكُم مِّرْفَقًا
﴿١٦﴾ ۞ وَتَرَى ٱلشَّمْسَ إِذَا طَلَعَت تَّزَٰوَرُ عَن كَهْفِهِمْ ذَاتَ
ٱلْيَمِينِ وَإِذَا غَرَبَت تَّقْرِضُهُمْ ذَاتَ ٱلشِّمَالِ وَهُمْ فِى فَجْوَةٍ
مِّنْهُ ۚ ذَٰلِكَ مِنْ ءَايَـٰتِ ٱللَّهِ ۗ مَن يَهْدِ ٱللَّهُ فَهُوَ ٱلْمُهْتَدِ ۖ وَمَن
يُضْلِلْ فَلَن تَجِدَ لَهُۥ وَلِيًّا مُّرْشِدًا ﴿١٧﴾ وَتَحْسَبُهُمْ أَيْقَاظًا
وَهُمْ رُقُودٌ ۚ وَنُقَلِّبُهُمْ ذَاتَ ٱلْيَمِينِ وَذَاتَ ٱلشِّمَالِ ۖ وَكَلْبُهُم
بَـٰسِطٌ ذِرَاعَيْهِ بِٱلْوَصِيدِ ۚ لَوِ ٱطَّلَعْتَ عَلَيْهِمْ لَوَلَّيْتَ مِنْهُمْ
فِرَارًا وَلَمُلِئْتَ مِنْهُمْ رُعْبًا ﴿١٨﴾ وَكَذَٰلِكَ بَعَثْنَـٰهُمْ
لِيَتَسَآءَلُوا۟ بَيْنَهُمْ ۚ قَالَ قَآئِلٌ مِّنْهُمْ كَمْ لَبِثْتُمْ ۖ قَالُوا۟ لَبِثْنَا
يَوْمًا أَوْ بَعْضَ يَوْمٍ ۚ قَالُوا۟ رَبُّكُمْ أَعْلَمُ بِمَا لَبِثْتُمْ فَٱبْعَثُوٓا۟
أَحَدَكُم بِوَرِقِكُمْ هَـٰذِهِۦٓ إِلَى ٱلْمَدِينَةِ فَلْيَنظُرْ أَيُّهَآ أَزْكَىٰ
طَعَامًا فَلْيَأْتِكُم بِرِزْقٍ مِّنْهُ وَلْيَتَلَطَّفْ وَلَا يُشْعِرَنَّ
بِكُمْ أَحَدًا ﴿١٩﴾ إِنَّهُمْ إِن يَظْهَرُوا۟ عَلَيْكُمْ يَرْجُمُوكُمْ
أَوْ يُعِيدُوكُمْ فِى مِلَّتِهِمْ وَلَن تُفْلِحُوٓا۟ إِذًا أَبَدًا ﴿٢٠﴾
وَكَذَٰلِكَ أَعْثَرْنَا عَلَيْهِمْ لِيَعْلَمُوٓا۟ أَنَّ وَعْدَ ٱللَّهِ حَقٌّ وَأَنَّ
ٱلسَّاعَةَ لَا رَيْبَ فِيهَآ إِذْ يَتَنَـٰزَعُونَ بَيْنَهُمْ أَمْرَهُمْ ۖ فَقَالُوا۟

erally this refers to the midday and evening meal but implies here complete maintenance – ***for you in your situation.'***

17. ***You would have seen the sun, when it rose, inclining away*** (read as *tazāwaru* and *tazzāwaru*) ***from their cave towards the right, and, when it set, leaving them behind on the left, while they were lying in an open part of it.*** The meaning is that direct sunlight did not touch them from sunrise to sunset. They were in a north-facing opening of the cave, where the coolness and breeze of the wind reached them. ***That was one of Allah's Signs*** – of His power. ***Whoever Allah guides is truly guided, but if He misguides some - one, you will find no protector for them to guide them rightly.***

18. If you had seen them ***you would have supposed them to be awake*** – because their eyes were open – ***whereas in fact they were asleep. We moved them to the right and to the left*** so that the earth would not consume their flesh, ***and at the entrance*** of the cave ***their dog stretched out its paws.*** Whenever they moved, it moved just as they did. ***If you had looked down and seen them, you would have turned from them and run and have been filled*** (read as *muli'ta* and *mulli'ta*) ***with terror*** (read as *ru'b* and *ru'ub*) ***at the sight of them.*** By this means Allah prevented anyone entering where they were.

19. ***That*** which We have described ***was the situation when we woke them up so they could question one another. One of them asked, 'How long have you been here?' They replied, 'We have been here for a day or part of a day'*** – because they had entered the cave at sunrise and were awakened at sunset and so they thought that it was sunset of the day that they entered it. ***They said*** – in a more judicious response – ***'Your Lord knows best how long you have been here. Send one of your number into the city*** – said to be the one known today as Tarsus – ***with this silver*** (read as *wariq* and *warq*) ***you have, so he can see which food is purest*** – the most lawful (*ḥalāl*) food available – ***and bring you some of it to eat. But he should go about with caution so that no one is aware of you,***

20. ***...for if they find out about you they will stone you*** – kill you with stones – ***or make you revert to their religion, and then you will never have success*** – if you do that.'

21. ***Accordingly*** – having made them wake up in this way – ***We made them*** (their people and the believers) ***chance upon them***

ٱبۡنُواْ عَلَيۡهِم بُنۡيَٰنٗاۖ رَّبُّهُمۡ أَعۡلَمُ بِهِمۡۚ قَالَ ٱلَّذِينَ غَلَبُواْ عَلَىٰٓ
أَمۡرِهِمۡ لَنَتَّخِذَنَّ عَلَيۡهِم مَّسۡجِدٗا ﴿٢١﴾ سَيَقُولُونَ ثَلَٰثَةٞ
رَّابِعُهُمۡ كَلۡبُهُمۡ وَيَقُولُونَ خَمۡسَةٞ سَادِسُهُمۡ كَلۡبُهُمۡ رَجۡمَۢا
بِٱلۡغَيۡبِۖ وَيَقُولُونَ سَبۡعَةٞ وَثَامِنُهُمۡ كَلۡبُهُمۡۚ قُل رَّبِّيٓ أَعۡلَمُ
بِعِدَّتِهِم مَّا يَعۡلَمُهُمۡ إِلَّا قَلِيلٞۗ فَلَا تُمَارِ فِيهِمۡ إِلَّا مِرَآءٗ ظَٰهِرٗا
وَلَا تَسۡتَفۡتِ فِيهِم مِّنۡهُمۡ أَحَدٗا ﴿٢٢﴾ وَلَا تَقُولَنَّ لِشَاْيۡءٍ
إِنِّي فَاعِلٞ ذَٰلِكَ غَدًا ﴿٢٣﴾ إِلَّآ أَن يَشَآءَ ٱللَّهُۚ وَٱذۡكُر رَّبَّكَ
إِذَا نَسِيتَ وَقُلۡ عَسَىٰٓ أَن يَهۡدِيَنِ رَبِّي لِأَقۡرَبَ مِنۡ هَٰذَا رَشَدٗا
﴿٢٤﴾ وَلَبِثُواْ فِي كَهۡفِهِمۡ ثَلَٰثَ مِاْئَةٖ سِنِينَ وَٱزۡدَادُواْ تِسۡعٗا
﴿٢٥﴾ قُلِ ٱللَّهُ أَعۡلَمُ بِمَا لَبِثُواْۖ لَهُۥ غَيۡبُ ٱلسَّمَٰوَٰتِ وَٱلۡأَرۡضِۖ
أَبۡصِرۡ بِهِۦ وَأَسۡمِعۡۚ مَا لَهُم مِّن دُونِهِۦ مِن وَلِيّٖ وَلَا يُشۡرِكُ
فِي حُكۡمِهِۦٓ أَحَدٗا ﴿٢٦﴾ وَٱتۡلُ مَآ أُوحِيَ إِلَيۡكَ مِن كِتَابِ
رَبِّكَۖ لَا مُبَدِّلَ لِكَلِمَٰتِهِۦ وَلَن تَجِدَ مِن دُونِهِۦ مُلۡتَحَدٗا ﴿٢٧﴾
وَٱصۡبِرۡ نَفۡسَكَ مَعَ ٱلَّذِينَ يَدۡعُونَ رَبَّهُم بِٱلۡغَدَوٰةِ وَٱلۡعَشِيِّ
يُرِيدُونَ وَجۡهَهُۥۖ وَلَا تَعۡدُ عَيۡنَاكَ عَنۡهُمۡ تُرِيدُ زِينَةَ ٱلۡحَيَوٰةِ
ٱلدُّنۡيَاۖ وَلَا تُطِعۡ مَنۡ أَغۡفَلۡنَا قَلۡبَهُۥ عَن ذِكۡرِنَا وَٱتَّبَعَ هَوَىٰهُ وَكَانَ
أَمۡرُهُۥ فُرُطٗا ﴿٢٨﴾ وَقُلِ ٱلۡحَقُّ مِن رَّبِّكُمۡۖ فَمَن شَآءَ فَلۡيُؤۡمِن وَمَن
شَآءَ فَلۡيَكۡفُرۡۚ إِنَّآ أَعۡتَدۡنَا لِلظَّٰلِمِينَ نَارًا أَحَاطَ بِهِمۡ سُرَادِقُهَاۚ
وَإِن يَسۡتَغِيثُواْ يُغَاثُواْ بِمَآءٖ كَٱلۡمُهۡلِ يَشۡوِي ٱلۡوُجُوهَۚ بِئۡسَ
ٱلشَّرَابُ وَسَآءَتۡ مُرۡتَفَقًا ﴿٢٩﴾ إِنَّ ٱلَّذِينَ ءَامَنُواْ وَعَمِلُواْ

unexpectedly so they (their people) ***might know that Allah's promise*** of the Resurrection ***is true*** since the One who has the power to make these young men die for a such long period and maintain them as they were without food must also be able to bring the dead to life – ***and that there is no doubt about the Hour. When they*** (the believers and unbelievers) ***were arguing among themselves about the matter*** – about what to build around the young men – ***they*** (the unbelievers) ***said, 'Wall up their cave*** around them to conceal them. ***Their Lord knows best about them.' But those who got the better of the argument concerning them*** – that is, the believers – ***said, 'We will build a place of worship over them.'*** That was at the mouth of the cave.

22. ***They*** – here referring to those who disputed about the number of the young men in the time of the Prophet, may Allah bless him and grant him peace – ***will say, 'There were three of them, their dog being the fourth.' They will say, 'There were five of them, their dog being the sixth,' guessing at the Unseen*** – conjecturing about something they had no real knowledge of, referring to both the preceding statements, which were made by the Christians of Najrān. ***And they*** (the believers) ***will say, 'There were seven of them, their dog being the eighth.'*** The first two views are described as being guesswork whereas the third is not, which indicates that it is pleasing and sound. ***Say: 'My Lord knows best their number. Those who know about them are very few.'*** Ibn 'Abbās said, "I am one of the few," and he mentioned that they were seven. ***So do not enter into any argument concerning them, except in relation to what is clearly known*** – what has been revealed to you. ***And do not seek the opinion*** (verdict) ***of any of them*** (the Christians and Jews) ***regarding them.*** The people of Makka asked the Prophet about the people of the Cave and he said, "I will tell them tomorrow," but did not say, "Allah willing."

23. Never say about anything, 'I will do that tomorrow,'

24. ***…without adding 'If Allah wills.'*** The matter is recognised as being subject to the will of Allah by one's saying, "If Allah wills." ***Remember*** the will of ***your Lord when you forget*** – by mentioning it in the way you have been instructed to, and al-Ḥasan and others said, "While you are still in the gathering" – ***and say, 'It may be that***

my Lord will guide me to something closer to right guidance than this about the details of the people of the Cave which will provide clearer evidence of my Prophethood.*'* Allah responded to him by saying:

25. ***They stayed in their Cave for three hundred years and added nine.*** The meaning of this is that counting in solar years the number was three hundred, whereas in the lunar years which the Arabs use for calculation it was three hundred and nine.

26. ***Say: 'Allah knows best how long they stayed*** – that being the subject of their disagreement. ***The*** – knowledge of the – ***Unseen of the heavens and the earth belongs to Him. How perfectly He sees, how well He hears!*** The meaning of this is that there is nothing whatsoever that is not perceived by His sight and heard by His hearing. ***They*** – the inhabitants of heaven and earth – ***have no protector apart from Him. Nor does He share His rule with anyone.'*** He has no need of any partner.

27. ***Recite what has been revealed to you of your Lord's Book. No one can change His Words. You will never find any safe haven apart from Him.***

28. ***Restrain yourself patiently with those who call on their Lord*** in worship in the ***morning and evening, desiring His face*** – without any ulterior motive in the form of desire for things of this world. This refers to the poor. ***Do not turn your eyes from them*** – this being addressed to the person looking – ***desiring the attractions of this world. And do not obey someone whose heart We have made neglectful of Our remembrance*** (the Qur'an) – the persons referred to are 'Uyayna ibn Ḥisn and his fellows – ***and who follows his own whims and desires*** by worshipping idols, ***and whose life has transgressed all bounds.***

29. ***Say*** to him and his companions: ***'It*** (the Qur'an) ***is the truth from your Lord; so let whoever wishes believe and whoever wishes disbelieve.'*** This is a threat to them. ***We have prepared for the wrongdoers*** (the unbelievers) ***a Fire whose billowing walls of smoke will hem them in. If they call for help, they will be helped with water like seething molten brass*** – like boiling oil – ***frying their faces*** with its heat when it is close to them. ***What a noxious***

ٱلصَّٰلِحَٰتِ إِنَّا لَا نُضِيعُ أَجْرَ مَنْ أَحْسَنَ عَمَلًا ﴿٣٠﴾ أُوْلَٰٓئِكَ
لَهُمْ جَنَّٰتُ عَدْنٍ تَجْرِى مِن تَحْتِهِمُ ٱلْأَنْهَٰرُ يُحَلَّوْنَ فِيهَا مِنْ أَسَاوِرَ
مِن ذَهَبٍ وَيَلْبَسُونَ ثِيَابًا خُضْرًا مِّن سُندُسٍ وَإِسْتَبْرَقٍ مُّتَّكِـِٔينَ
فِيهَا عَلَى ٱلْأَرَآئِكِ ۚ نِعْمَ ٱلثَّوَابُ وَحَسُنَتْ مُرْتَفَقًا ﴿٣١﴾ ۞ وَٱضْرِبْ
لَهُم مَّثَلًا رَّجُلَيْنِ جَعَلْنَا لِأَحَدِهِمَا جَنَّتَيْنِ مِنْ أَعْنَٰبٍ وَحَفَفْنَٰهُمَا
بِنَخْلٍ وَجَعَلْنَا بَيْنَهُمَا زَرْعًا ﴿٣٢﴾ كِلْتَا ٱلْجَنَّتَيْنِ ءَاتَتْ أُكُلَهَا وَلَمْ
تَظْلِم مِّنْهُ شَيْـًٔا ۚ وَفَجَّرْنَا خِلَٰلَهُمَا نَهَرًا ﴿٣٣﴾ وَكَانَ لَهُۥ ثَمَرٌ فَقَالَ
لِصَٰحِبِهِۦ وَهُوَ يُحَاوِرُهُۥٓ أَنَا۠ أَكْثَرُ مِنكَ مَالًا وَأَعَزُّ نَفَرًا ﴿٣٤﴾
وَدَخَلَ جَنَّتَهُۥ وَهُوَ ظَالِمٌ لِّنَفْسِهِۦ قَالَ مَآ أَظُنُّ أَن تَبِيدَ هَٰذِهِۦٓ
أَبَدًا ﴿٣٥﴾ وَمَآ أَظُنُّ ٱلسَّاعَةَ قَآئِمَةً وَلَئِن رُّدِدتُّ إِلَىٰ رَبِّى
لَأَجِدَنَّ خَيْرًا مِّنْهَا مُنقَلَبًا ﴿٣٦﴾ قَالَ لَهُۥ صَاحِبُهُۥ وَهُوَ يُحَاوِرُهُۥٓ
أَكَفَرْتَ بِٱلَّذِى خَلَقَكَ مِن تُرَابٍ ثُمَّ مِن نُّطْفَةٍ ثُمَّ سَوَّىٰكَ رَجُلًا
﴿٣٧﴾ لَّٰكِنَّا۠ هُوَ ٱللَّهُ رَبِّى وَلَآ أُشْرِكُ بِرَبِّىٓ أَحَدًا ﴿٣٨﴾ وَلَوْلَآ إِذْ
دَخَلْتَ جَنَّتَكَ قُلْتَ مَا شَآءَ ٱللَّهُ لَا قُوَّةَ إِلَّا بِٱللَّهِ ۚ إِن تَرَنِ أَنَا۠
أَقَلَّ مِنكَ مَالًا وَوَلَدًا ﴿٣٩﴾ فَعَسَىٰ رَبِّىٓ أَن يُؤْتِيَنِ خَيْرًا مِّن
جَنَّتِكَ وَيُرْسِلَ عَلَيْهَا حُسْبَانًا مِّنَ ٱلسَّمَآءِ فَتُصْبِحَ صَعِيدًا
زَلَقًا ﴿٤٠﴾ أَوْ يُصْبِحَ مَآؤُهَا غَوْرًا فَلَن تَسْتَطِيعَ لَهُۥ طَلَبًا ﴿٤١﴾
وَأُحِيطَ بِثَمَرِهِۦ فَأَصْبَحَ يُقَلِّبُ كَفَّيْهِ عَلَىٰ مَآ أَنفَقَ فِيهَا وَهِىَ خَاوِيَةٌ
عَلَىٰ عُرُوشِهَا وَيَقُولُ يَٰلَيْتَنِى لَمْ أُشْرِكْ بِرَبِّىٓ أَحَدًا ﴿٤٢﴾ وَلَمْ تَكُن لَّهُۥ
فِئَةٌ يَنصُرُونَهُۥ مِن دُونِ ٱللَّهِ وَمَا كَانَ مُنتَصِرًا ﴿٤٣﴾ هُنَالِكَ ٱلْوَلَٰيَةُ

drink! What an evil repose! This is in contrast with the image of the people in the Garden: "What a wonderful repose!" There is no repose in the Fire.

30. ***But as for those who believe and do right actions, We will not let the wage of good-doers go to waste.***

31. ***They will have Gardens of Eden with rivers flowing under them. They will be adorned in them with bracelets made of gold and wear green garments made of the finest silk*** – the word used here for "silk", *sundus*, is a kind of fine brocade – ***and rich brocade*** – the word for "brocade", *istabraq,* is a coarser variety of brocade and is also mentioned in *Sūrat ar-Raḥmān, "on couches lined with rich brocade."* (55:54) – ***reclining there on couches*** – the word *arā'ik* is the plural of *arīka,* which means a couch in an alcove, which is a room adorned with canopies and curtains ready for a bride – ***under canopies. What an excellent reward*** (the Garden)***! What a wonderful repose!***

32. ***Make an example for them*** – of the unbelievers and the believers – ***of two men. To one of them*** (the unbeliever) ***We gave two gardens of grape-vines and surrounded them with date-palms, putting between them some cultivated land*** from which he harvested crops.

33. ***Both gardens yielded their crops and did not suffer any loss, and We made a river flow right through the middle of them*** – between the two gardens.

34. ***He*** – the man with the two gardens – ***was a man of wealth*** (read as *thamar, thumur* and *thumr*, all of which are plurals of *thamra*) ***and property and he said to his companion*** (the believer), ***debating with him, 'I have more wealth than you and more people*** of my clan ***under me.'***

35. ***He entered his garden*** with his companion and walked around in it and showed him its fruits; Allah did not say "both gardens" but means by "garden" here the whole expanse of land. It is also said that it is sufficient to mention one – ***and wronged himself*** with unbelief ***by saying, 'I do not think that this will ever end.***

36. ***I do not think the Hour will ever come. But if I should be sent back to my Lord*** – in the Next World as you claim I will be – ***I will definitely get something better in return.'***

37. ***His companion, with whom he was debating, said to him, 'Do you then disbelieve in Him who created you from dust,*** because Ādam was created from dust, ***then from a drop of sperm, and then formed you*** – balanced – ***as a man?***

38. ***But He is Allah, my Lord, and I will not associate anyone with my Lord.***

39. ***Why, when you entered your garden*** and admired it ***did you not say, "It is as Allah wills; there is no strength but in Allah"?*** In a *ḥadīth* we find: "If someone is given good in the form of family or wealth, he should say about that, 'It is as Allah wills; there is no strength but in Allah,' and then he will not find anything disliked in it." ***Though you see me with less wealth and children than you possess,***

40. ***...it may well be that my Lord will give me something better than your garden and send down on it a fireball from the sky so that morning finds it a shifting heap of dust*** – smooth earth on which no foot can remain firm –

41. ***...or morning finds its water drained into the earth*** – a separate calamity, since water draining away into the earth is not the result of a fireball – ***so that you cannot get at it.'*** There is no way it can be drawn out.

42. ***The fruits of his labour were completely destroyed and he woke up wringing his hands in grief, rueing everything that he had spent on it.*** This is a comprehensive description of the destruction of his garden, which left him full of regret and grief over all the money and effort he had put into cultivating it. ***It was a ruin with all its trellises fallen in. He said, 'Oh, if only I had not associated anyone with my Lord!'***

43. ***There was*** (read as *takun* and *yakun*) ***no group to come to his aid, besides Allah*** – when the destruction took place – ***and he was not given any help.***

44. ***In that situation*** (on the Day of Rising) ***the only protection*** (read as *walāya*, as here, and also *wilāya*, meaning "dominion") ***is with Allah, the Real*** (read as *al-Ḥaqqi,* making it an attribute of Allah, as here, and also in two instances as *al-ḥaqqu,* in which case it is an adjective describing the nominative noun meaning, "the only

لِلَّهِ ٱلۡحَقِّۚ هُوَ خَيۡرٞ ثَوَابٗا وَخَيۡرٌ عُقۡبٗا ﴿٤٤﴾ وَٱضۡرِبۡ لَهُم مَّثَلَ ٱلۡحَيَوٰةِ
ٱلدُّنۡيَا كَمَآءٍ أَنزَلۡنَٰهُ مِنَ ٱلسَّمَآءِ فَٱخۡتَلَطَ بِهِۦ نَبَاتُ ٱلۡأَرۡضِ
فَأَصۡبَحَ هَشِيمٗا تَذۡرُوهُ ٱلرِّيَٰحُۗ وَكَانَ ٱللَّهُ عَلَىٰ كُلِّ شَيۡءٖ مُّقۡتَدِرًا ﴿٤٥﴾
ٱلۡمَالُ وَٱلۡبَنُونَ زِينَةُ ٱلۡحَيَوٰةِ ٱلدُّنۡيَاۖ وَٱلۡبَٰقِيَٰتُ ٱلصَّٰلِحَٰتُ
خَيۡرٌ عِندَ رَبِّكَ ثَوَابٗا وَخَيۡرٌ أَمَلٗا ﴿٤٦﴾ وَيَوۡمَ نُسَيِّرُ ٱلۡجِبَالَ وَتَرَى
ٱلۡأَرۡضَ بَارِزَةٗ وَحَشَرۡنَٰهُمۡ فَلَمۡ نُغَادِرۡ مِنۡهُمۡ أَحَدٗا ﴿٤٧﴾ وَعُرِضُواْ
عَلَىٰ رَبِّكَ صَفّٗا لَّقَدۡ جِئۡتُمُونَا كَمَا خَلَقۡنَٰكُمۡ أَوَّلَ مَرَّةِۭۚ بَلۡ زَعَمۡتُمۡ
أَلَّن نَّجۡعَلَ لَكُم مَّوۡعِدٗا ﴿٤٨﴾ وَوُضِعَ ٱلۡكِتَٰبُ فَتَرَى ٱلۡمُجۡرِمِينَ
مُشۡفِقِينَ مِمَّا فِيهِ وَيَقُولُونَ يَٰوَيۡلَتَنَا مَالِ هَٰذَا ٱلۡكِتَٰبِ
لَا يُغَادِرُ صَغِيرَةٗ وَلَا كَبِيرَةً إِلَّآ أَحۡصَىٰهَاۚ وَوَجَدُواْ مَا عَمِلُواْ
حَاضِرٗاۗ وَلَا يَظۡلِمُ رَبُّكَ أَحَدٗا ﴿٤٩﴾ وَإِذۡ قُلۡنَا لِلۡمَلَٰٓئِكَةِ ٱسۡجُدُواْ
لِأٓدَمَ فَسَجَدُوٓاْ إِلَّآ إِبۡلِيسَ كَانَ مِنَ ٱلۡجِنِّ فَفَسَقَ عَنۡ أَمۡرِ رَبِّهِۦٓۗ
أَفَتَتَّخِذُونَهُۥ وَذُرِّيَّتَهُۥٓ أَوۡلِيَآءَ مِن دُونِي وَهُمۡ لَكُمۡ عَدُوُّۢۚ
بِئۡسَ لِلظَّٰلِمِينَ بَدَلٗا ﴿٥٠﴾ ۞ مَّآ أَشۡهَدتُّهُمۡ خَلۡقَ ٱلسَّمَٰوَٰتِ
وَٱلۡأَرۡضِ وَلَا خَلۡقَ أَنفُسِهِمۡ وَمَا كُنتُ مُتَّخِذَ ٱلۡمُضِلِّينَ عَضُدٗا
﴿٥١﴾ وَيَوۡمَ يَقُولُ نَادُواْ شُرَكَآءِيَ ٱلَّذِينَ زَعَمۡتُمۡ فَدَعَوۡهُمۡ
فَلَمۡ يَسۡتَجِيبُواْ لَهُمۡ وَجَعَلۡنَا بَيۡنَهُم مَّوۡبِقٗا ﴿٥٢﴾ وَرَءَا ٱلۡمُجۡرِمُونَ
ٱلنَّارَ فَظَنُّوٓاْ أَنَّهُم مُّوَاقِعُوهَا وَلَمۡ يَجِدُواْ عَنۡهَا مَصۡرِفٗا ﴿٥٣﴾
وَلَقَدۡ صَرَّفۡنَا فِي هَٰذَا ٱلۡقُرۡءَانِ لِلنَّاسِ مِن كُلِّ مَثَلٖۚ وَكَانَ
ٱلۡإِنسَٰنُ أَكۡثَرَ شَيۡءٖ جَدَلٗا ﴿٥٤﴾ وَمَا مَنَعَ ٱلنَّاسَ أَن يُؤۡمِنُوٓاْ

true protection"). ***He gives the best reward*** – better than anyone else could possibly do even if they were to give the most magnificent reward – ***and the best outcome*** – meaning the outcome experienced by the believers.

45. ***Make a metaphor for them*** (mankind) ***of the life of this world. It is like water which We send down from the sky and the plants of the earth combine with it*** – and fill out because of the water being sent down; or the water mixes with the plants and so they are fresh and beautiful – ***but then they*** (the plants) ***become dry chaff scattered by the winds*** and so they disappear completely. Thus this world is like beautiful plants which then become dry and broken and are then dissipated by the wind. ***Allah has absolute power over everything.***

46. ***Wealth and sons are the embellishment of the life of this world. But in your Lord's sight, right actions which are lasting*** – said to be the statements: 'Glory be to Allah'; 'Praise be to Allah'; 'There is no god but Allah,' and 'Allah is greater'; and some add: 'There is no power nor strength except by Allah' – ***bring a better reward and are a better basis for hope*** for what people desire from Allah Almighty.

47. ***On the Day We make the mountains move*** (read as *nusayyiru'l-jibāla,* as here, and also as *tusayyiri'l-jibālu,* when the meaning becomes "On the Day the mountains move") – meaning that they are removed from the face of the earth and become dust – ***and you see the earth laid bare*** – with nothing on it: mountains or anything else – ***and We gather them together*** – believers and unbelievers – ***not leaving out a single one of them,***

48. ***...they will be paraded before your Lord in ranks*** – each nation in a row, and this will be said to them – ***'You have come to Us just as We created you at first*** – naked, barefoot and uncircumcised. It will be said to those who denied the resurrection – ***Yes indeed! Even though you claimed that We would not fix a time with you*** for the Resurrection.*'*

49. ***The Book*** – a generic term referring to the books recording the actions of every human being, those of believers being placed in their right hands and those of unbelievers in their left hands – ***will be set in place and you will see the evildoers*** (unbelievers) ***fearful of***

what is in it. They will say – when they see the evil deeds which are in it – ***'Alas for us!*** We are destroyed! ***What is this Book which does not pass over any*** wrong ***action, small or great, without recording it?'*** They will express amazement at that. ***They will find there everything they did*** recorded in detail, ***and your Lord will not wrong anyone at all.*** He does not punish anyone who has committed no crime, and does not diminish the reward of any believer.

50. ***When We said to the angels, 'Prostrate yourselves to Ādam,'*** and they were told to bow, not to prostrate on the ground, as a greeting to him, ***they prostrated with the exception of Iblīs. He was one of the jinn*** – it said that the *jinn* were a type of angel and so the exception is one of connection. It is also said that the exception marks a distinction of species between the angels and *jinn*, particularly since Iblīs is known to be the father of the *jinn* and has descendants who are mentioned with him afterwards, whereas the angels have no descendants – ***and wantonly deviated from his Lord's command*** by not bowing. ***Do you take him and his offspring as protectors*** – in other words, obey them – ***apart from Me when they are your enemy?*** This is addressed to Ādam and his offspring. ***How evil is the exchange the wrongdoers make!*** They are your enemies and it is very evil to obey Iblīs and his offspring instead of obeying Allah.

51. ***I did not make them*** (Iblīs and his offspring) ***witnesses of the creation of the heavens and the earth or of their own creation. I would not take as assistants those*** (the *shayāṭīn*) ***who lead astray!*** So how can you obey them?

52. ***On the Day He says*** (read as *yaqūlu* and *naqūlu,* meaning "We say"), ***'Call My partner-gods*** (idols), ***those for whom you made such claims'*** – that they would intercede for you – ***they will call on them but they will not respond to them. We will place between them*** – between the idols and those who worshipped them – ***an unbridgeable gulf.*** This refers to a particular chasm, one of the valleys of *Jahannam*, in which they will all be destroyed.

53. ***The evildoers will see the Fire and realise*** with certainty ***they are going to fall into it and find no way of escaping from it.***

إِذۡ جَآءَهُمُ ٱلۡهُدَىٰ وَيَسۡتَغۡفِرُواْ رَبَّهُمۡ إِلَّآ أَن تَأۡتِيَهُمۡ سُنَّةُ
ٱلۡأَوَّلِينَ أَوۡ يَأۡتِيَهُمُ ٱلۡعَذَابُ قُبُلٗا ٥٥ وَمَا نُرۡسِلُ ٱلۡمُرۡسَلِينَ
إِلَّا مُبَشِّرِينَ وَمُنذِرِينَۚ وَيُجَٰدِلُ ٱلَّذِينَ كَفَرُواْ بِٱلۡبَٰطِلِ
لِيُدۡحِضُواْ بِهِ ٱلۡحَقَّۖ وَٱتَّخَذُوٓاْ ءَايَٰتِي وَمَآ أُنذِرُواْ هُزُوٗا ٥٦ وَمَنۡ
أَظۡلَمُ مِمَّن ذُكِّرَ بِـَٔايَٰتِ رَبِّهِۦ فَأَعۡرَضَ عَنۡهَا وَنَسِيَ مَا قَدَّمَتۡ يَدَاهُۚ
إِنَّا جَعَلۡنَا عَلَىٰ قُلُوبِهِمۡ أَكِنَّةً أَن يَفۡقَهُوهُ وَفِيٓ ءَاذَانِهِمۡ وَقۡرٗاۖ
وَإِن تَدۡعُهُمۡ إِلَى ٱلۡهُدَىٰ فَلَن يَهۡتَدُوٓاْ إِذًا أَبَدٗا ٥٧ وَرَبُّكَ
ٱلۡغَفُورُ ذُو ٱلرَّحۡمَةِۖ لَوۡ يُؤَاخِذُهُم بِمَا كَسَبُواْ لَعَجَّلَ لَهُمُ
ٱلۡعَذَابَۚ بَل لَّهُم مَّوۡعِدٞ لَّن يَجِدُواْ مِن دُونِهِۦ مَوۡئِلٗا ٥٨
وَتِلۡكَ ٱلۡقُرَىٰٓ أَهۡلَكۡنَٰهُمۡ لَمَّا ظَلَمُواْ وَجَعَلۡنَا لِمَهۡلِكِهِم
مَّوۡعِدٗا ٥٩ وَإِذۡ قَالَ مُوسَىٰ لِفَتَىٰهُ لَآ أَبۡرَحُ حَتَّىٰٓ
أَبۡلُغَ مَجۡمَعَ ٱلۡبَحۡرَيۡنِ أَوۡ أَمۡضِيَ حُقُبٗا ٦٠ فَلَمَّا بَلَغَا
مَجۡمَعَ بَيۡنِهِمَا نَسِيَا حُوتَهُمَا فَٱتَّخَذَ سَبِيلَهُۥ فِي ٱلۡبَحۡرِ سَرَبٗا ٦١
فَلَمَّا جَاوَزَا قَالَ لِفَتَىٰهُ ءَاتِنَا غَدَآءَنَا لَقَدۡ لَقِينَا مِن سَفَرِنَا
هَٰذَا نَصَبٗا ٦٢ قَالَ أَرَءَيۡتَ إِذۡ أَوَيۡنَآ إِلَى ٱلصَّخۡرَةِ فَإِنِّي نَسِيتُ
ٱلۡحُوتَ وَمَآ أَنسَىٰنِيهُ إِلَّا ٱلشَّيۡطَٰنُ أَنۡ أَذۡكُرَهُۥۚ وَٱتَّخَذَ سَبِيلَهُۥ
فِي ٱلۡبَحۡرِ عَجَبٗا ٦٣ قَالَ ذَٰلِكَ مَا كُنَّا نَبۡغِۚ فَٱرۡتَدَّا عَلَىٰٓ ءَاثَارِهِمَا
قَصَصٗا ٦٤ فَوَجَدَا عَبۡدٗا مِّنۡ عِبَادِنَآ ءَاتَيۡنَٰهُ رَحۡمَةٗ مِّنۡ
عِندِنَا وَعَلَّمۡنَٰهُ مِن لَّدُنَّا عِلۡمٗا ٦٥ قَالَ لَهُۥ مُوسَىٰ هَلۡ أَتَّبِعُكَ
عَلَىٰٓ أَن تُعَلِّمَنِ مِمَّا عُلِّمۡتَ رُشۡدٗا ٦٦ قَالَ إِنَّكَ لَن تَسۡتَطِيعَ

54. ***We have variegated*** and made clear ***throughout this Qur'an all kinds of examples for people*** – so that they may be admonished – ***but, more than anything else*** – unbelieving – ***man is argumentative*** inwardly! The argumentativeness of man is the thing which is the most dominant in him.

55. ***When guidance*** (the Qur'an) ***came to the people*** (the unbelievers of Makka), ***nothing prevented them from believing and asking for forgiveness from their Lord but the fact that the pattern of previous peoples did not happen to them*** – a reference to Allah's custom with unbelieving nations, which was the destruction decreed for them – ***or that the punishment did not appear*** physically ***before their eyes.*** That changed at the Battle of Badr when punishment took the form of killing and they saw it directly.

56. ***We only send the Messengers to bring good news*** to the believers ***and to give warning*** to the unbelievers. ***Those who disbelieve use fallacious arguments to deny the truth*** (the Qur'an) – by saying, "Would Allah send a mortal as a messenger?" and other such things. ***They make a mockery of My Signs*** (the Qur'an) ***and also of the warning*** of the Fire ***they were given.***

57. ***Who could do greater wrong than someone who is reminded of the Signs of his Lord and then turns away from them, forgetting all*** the acts of unbelief and disobedience ***that he has done before? We have placed covers on their hearts, preventing them from understanding it*** (the Qur'an) ***and heaviness in their ears*** – so that they cannot hear it. ***Though you call them to guidance, they will still never be guided.***

58. ***Your Lord is the Ever-Forgiving, the Possessor of Mercy. If He had taken them to task*** in this world ***for what they have earned, He would have hastened their punishment*** in it. ***Instead, they have a promised appointment*** – on the Day of Rising – ***and they will not find any refuge from it.***

59. ***Those cities*** – referring to their inhabitants, such as 'Ād, Thamūd and others – ***We destroyed when they did wrong*** and disbelieved – ***and fixed a promised time for their destruction*** (read as *mahlakihim* and *muhlakihim*).

60. Remember ***when Mūsā*** ibn 'Imrān ***said to his servant*** – Yūsha' ibn Nūn, who followed him and served him and learned from him – ***'I will not give up*** – but will continue to travel – ***until I reach the meeting-place of the two seas*** – this is said by some to be where the Adriatic meets the Black Sea, which is towards the east, and by others where the Mediterranean meets the Atlantic in the West – ***even if I must press on for many years*** – if it takes a very long time to reach it.'

61. *But when they reached their meeting-place* – the place where the two seas come together – ***they forgot their fish*** – Yūsha' left behind his bundle during the journey and Mūsā forgot to remind him about it – ***which quickly burrowed its way into the sea.*** Allah made the fish travel back to the sea along something like a chute, which was a kind of long trench with only one entrance.

62. *When they had gone a distance further on* beyond that place and travelled until the time of the main meal on the second day ***he*** (Mūsā) ***said to his servant, 'Bring us our morning meal. Truly this journey of ours has made us tired.'*** He became tired after passing the place.

63. *He said, 'Do you see what has happened? When we went to find shelter at the rock, I forgot the fish. No one made me forget to remember it except Shayṭān. It* (the fish) ***found its way into the sea in an amazing way.'*** Mūsā and his servant were astonished by what happened.

64. *He* (Mūsā) ***said, 'That is the very thing that we were looking for!'*** Losing the fish was a sign of the existence of what they had been seeking. ***So, following their footsteps, they retraced their route*** to the rock.

65. *They found a slave of Ours* (al-Khiḍr) ***whom We had granted mercy from Us*** – said to be Prophethood in one view, and sainthood (*wilāya*) in another view, which is that of the majority of scholars – ***and whom We had also given knowledge*** of unseen matters ***direct from Us.*** Al-Bukhārī related the *ḥadīth*: "Mūsā was speaking among the tribe of Israel when he was asked, 'Who is the person who has the most knowledge?' He answered, 'I am.' Allah rebuked him because he did not ascribe knowledge to Him. He revealed to him,

مَعِيَ صَبۡرٗا ٦٧ وَكَيۡفَ تَصۡبِرُ عَلَىٰ مَا لَمۡ تُحِطۡ بِهِۦ خُبۡرٗا ٦٨ قَالَ
سَتَجِدُنِيٓ إِن شَآءَ ٱللَّهُ صَابِرٗا وَلَآ أَعۡصِي لَكَ أَمۡرٗا ٦٩ قَالَ
فَإِنِ ٱتَّبَعۡتَنِي فَلَا تَسۡـَٔلۡنِي عَن شَيۡءٍ حَتَّىٰٓ أُحۡدِثَ لَكَ مِنۡهُ ذِكۡرٗا
٧٠ فَٱنطَلَقَا حَتَّىٰٓ إِذَا رَكِبَا فِي ٱلسَّفِينَةِ خَرَقَهَاۖ قَالَ أَخَرَقۡتَهَا
لِتُغۡرِقَ أَهۡلَهَا لَقَدۡ جِئۡتَ شَيۡـًٔا إِمۡرٗا ٧١ قَالَ أَلَمۡ أَقُلۡ إِنَّكَ
لَن تَسۡتَطِيعَ مَعِيَ صَبۡرٗا ٧٢ قَالَ لَا تُؤَاخِذۡنِي بِمَا نَسِيتُ وَلَا
تُرۡهِقۡنِي مِنۡ أَمۡرِي عُسۡرٗا ٧٣ فَٱنطَلَقَا حَتَّىٰٓ إِذَا لَقِيَا غُلَٰمٗا فَقَتَلَهُۥ
قَالَ أَقَتَلۡتَ نَفۡسٗا زَكِيَّةَۢ بِغَيۡرِ نَفۡسٖ لَّقَدۡ جِئۡتَ شَيۡـٔٗا نُّكۡرٗا ٧٤
۞ قَالَ أَلَمۡ أَقُل لَّكَ إِنَّكَ لَن تَسۡتَطِيعَ مَعِيَ صَبۡرٗا ٧٥ قَالَ إِن
سَأَلۡتُكَ عَن شَيۡءِۭ بَعۡدَهَا فَلَا تُصَٰحِبۡنِيۖ قَدۡ بَلَغۡتَ مِن لَّدُنِّي عُذۡرٗا
٧٦ فَٱنطَلَقَا حَتَّىٰٓ إِذَآ أَتَيَآ أَهۡلَ قَرۡيَةٍ ٱسۡتَطۡعَمَآ أَهۡلَهَا فَأَبَوۡاْ
أَن يُضَيِّفُوهُمَا فَوَجَدَا فِيهَا جِدَارٗا يُرِيدُ أَن يَنقَضَّ فَأَقَامَهُۥۖ
قَالَ لَوۡ شِئۡتَ لَتَّخَذۡتَ عَلَيۡهِ أَجۡرٗا ٧٧ قَالَ هَٰذَا فِرَاقُ بَيۡنِي
وَبَيۡنِكَۚ سَأُنَبِّئُكَ بِتَأۡوِيلِ مَا لَمۡ تَسۡتَطِع عَّلَيۡهِ صَبۡرًا ٧٨ أَمَّا
ٱلسَّفِينَةُ فَكَانَتۡ لِمَسَٰكِينَ يَعۡمَلُونَ فِي ٱلۡبَحۡرِ فَأَرَدتُّ أَنۡ أَعِيبَهَا
وَكَانَ وَرَآءَهُم مَّلِكٞ يَأۡخُذُ كُلَّ سَفِينَةٍ غَصۡبٗا ٧٩ وَأَمَّا ٱلۡغُلَٰمُ
فَكَانَ أَبَوَاهُ مُؤۡمِنَيۡنِ فَخَشِينَآ أَن يُرۡهِقَهُمَا طُغۡيَٰنٗا وَكُفۡرٗا
٨٠ فَأَرَدۡنَآ أَن يُبۡدِلَهُمَا رَبُّهُمَا خَيۡرٗا مِّنۡهُ زَكَوٰةٗ وَأَقۡرَبَ رُحۡمٗا
٨١ وَأَمَّا ٱلۡجِدَارُ فَكَانَ لِغُلَٰمَيۡنِ يَتِيمَيۡنِ فِي ٱلۡمَدِينَةِ وَكَانَ
تَحۡتَهُۥ كَنزٞ لَّهُمَا وَكَانَ أَبُوهُمَا صَٰلِحٗا فَأَرَادَ رَبُّكَ أَن يَبۡلُغَآ

'There is a slave of Mine at the meeting of the two seas who knows more than you.' Mūsā said, 'O Lord, how can I meet him?' He said, 'Take a fish and put it in a basket. When you lose the fish, he will be there. So he took a fish and put it in a basket and then went with his servant, Yūsha' ibn Nūn, until they came to a rock and laid down their heads and went to sleep. The fish moved in the basket and jumped out and dived into the sea, *'and found its way into the sea in an amazing way.'* Allah kept the water from flowing over the fish and it became like an arch. When they woke up, his companion forgot to inform him about the fish. They continued to walk for the rest of the day and night until in the morning Mūsā said to his boy, *'Bring us our morning meal...'* to His words *'and found its way into the sea in an amazing way.'"* Its making its way into the sea was the miraculous event. Allah means, "The fish making a tunnel astonished Mūsā and his servant..."

66. *Mūsā said to him, 'May I follow you on condition that you teach me some of the right guidance* (read as *rashad* and *rushd*) ***you have been taught?'*** That is because it is desirable to seek more knowledge.

67. *He said, 'You will not be able to bear with me.*

68. *How indeed could you bear with patience something you have not encompassed in your knowledge?'* The *ḥadīth* says about this *āyat,* quoting al-Khiḍr: "O Mūsā, I have knowledge from Allah which He has taught me and you do not know, and you have knowledge from Allah which He has taught you and I do not know."

69. *Mūsā said, 'You will find me patient, if Allah wills, and I will not disobey you in any matter* you command me to do.*'* He limited his statement by the expression "if Allah wills" because he did not rely on his own resolve. This is the custom of the Prophets and *awliyā'*. They do not put any reliance on themselves even for the blink of an eye.

70. *He said, 'Then if you follow me, do not question me* (read as *tas'alnī* and *tas'alannī*) ***about anything*** which you do not know by your knowledge. Be patient ***until I myself make mention of*** the reason for ***it to you.'*** Mūsā accepted the condition to observe the proper behaviour of a student towards his teacher.

71. ***They continued*** walking along the shore ***until they boarded a boat*** which passed by them ***and he*** (al-Khiḍr) ***scuppered it*** – by ripping up a plank or two from the hull with an axe when they reached open water. ***Then Mūsā said*** to him: ***'Did you scupper it so that you might drown its people*** (read as *li-tughriqa ahlahā* and also *li-taghraqa ahluhā,* in which case the meaning becomes "so that its people would be drowned")***? This is truly a dreadful thing that you have done!'*** It is related that the water did not enter it.

72. ***He said, 'Did I not say that you would not be able to bear with me?'***

73. ***Mūsā said, 'Do not take me to task because I forgot*** to submit to you and not to object to what you do. ***Do not demand of me something*** (a task) ***which is too difficult.'*** In other words: Act towards me with pardon and leniency.

74. ***So they went on*** on foot after leaving the ship ***until they met a youngster*** who had not yet reached puberty, playing with some other children – and he was the most beautiful of them – ***whom he killed.*** Al-Khiḍr killed him with a knife while he was prone, or strangled him with his hands, or hit his head against a wall. ***Mūsā said, 'Have you killed a boy who has done no wrong*** (read as *zakiyya* and *zākiyya*) – who has not yet reached the age of responsibility and who has not killed anyone – ***without it being in retaliation for someone else? This is truly an appalling thing*** (read as *nukran* and *nukuran*) ***that you have done!'***

75. ***He said, 'Did I not tell you that you would not be able to bear with me?'***

76. ***Mūsā said, 'If I ask you about anything after this*** time ***then you should no longer keep me company*** – allow me to follow you no further. ***I will have given*** (read as *ladunī* and *ladnī*) ***you excuse enough.'***

77. ***So they went on until they reached the inhabitants of a town*** (Antioch). ***They asked them for food but they refused them hospitality. They found there a wall*** a hundred cubits high ***about to fall down*** – its closeness to collapse could be seen by the fact that it was leaning – ***and he built it up.*** Al-Khiḍr repaired it with his own hand. ***Mūsā said*** to him: ***'If you had wanted, you could have taken*** (read as *lattakhidhta* and *la-takhidhta*) ***a wage for doing that'*** – since they did not give them hospitality and they were in need of food.

78. ***He*** (al-Khiḍr) ***said*** to Mūsā: ***'This is*** the moment ***where you and I part company.*** But before we part ***I will let you know the explanation of those things about which you were not able to restrain yourself.***

79. ***As for the boat, it belonged to some poor people*** – there were ten of them – ***who worked on the sea*** – chartering it out for a living. ***I wanted to damage it because*** an unbelieving ***king was coming behind them, commandeering every*** sound ***boat.***

80. ***As for the boy, his parents were believers and we feared that he would darken their days with excessive insolence and unbelief.*** As we know from the *ḥadīth* related by Muslim, his nature was that of an unbeliever and if he had lived he might have imposed that on his parents who, because of their love for him, might have followed him in unbelief.

81. ***We wanted their Lord to give them in exchange*** (read as *yubdila* and *yubaddila*) ***a purer*** – more righteous and godfearing – ***child than him, one more compassionate*** (read as *ruḥman* and *ruḥuman*) – meaning one more dutiful towards its parents. In exchange, Allah gave them a daughter who married a Prophet and bore him a Prophet by whom Allah guided a nation.

82. ***As for the wall, it belonged to two young orphans in the town and there was a*** buried ***treasure*** of gold or silver ***underneath it, belonging to them. Their father was one of the righteous*** – and they were protected in their persons and property by the righteousness of their father – ***and your Lord wanted them to come of age and then to unearth their treasure as a mercy from your Lord. I did not do it*** – scuppering the boat, killing the child and repairing the wall – ***of my own volition*** and choice. It was by command and divine inspiration from Allah. ***That is the explanation of the things about which you were not able to restrain yourself.'***

83. ***They*** (the Jews) ***will ask you about Dhū'l-Qarnayn*** (Iskandar/Alexander). He was not a Prophet. ***Say: 'I will tell you something about him.'***

أَشُدَّهُمَا وَيَسْتَخْرِجَا كَنزَهُمَا رَحْمَةً مِّن رَّبِّكَ ۚ وَمَا فَعَلْتُهُۥ
عَنْ أَمْرِى ۚ ذَٰلِكَ تَأْوِيلُ مَا لَمْ تَسْطِع عَّلَيْهِ صَبْرًا ﴿٨٢﴾ وَيَسْـَٔلُونَكَ
عَن ذِى ٱلْقَرْنَيْنِ ۖ قُلْ سَأَتْلُوا۟ عَلَيْكُم مِّنْهُ ذِكْرًا ﴿٨٣﴾
إِنَّا مَكَّنَّا لَهُۥ فِى ٱلْأَرْضِ وَءَاتَيْنَٰهُ مِن كُلِّ شَىْءٍ سَبَبًا ﴿٨٤﴾ فَأَتْبَعَ سَبَبًا
﴿٨٥﴾ حَتَّىٰٓ إِذَا بَلَغَ مَغْرِبَ ٱلشَّمْسِ وَجَدَهَا تَغْرُبُ فِى عَيْنٍ حَمِئَةٍ
وَوَجَدَ عِندَهَا قَوْمًا ۗ قُلْنَا يَٰذَا ٱلْقَرْنَيْنِ إِمَّآ أَن تُعَذِّبَ وَإِمَّآ أَن تَتَّخِذَ
فِيهِمْ حُسْنًا ﴿٨٦﴾ قَالَ أَمَّا مَن ظَلَمَ فَسَوْفَ نُعَذِّبُهُۥ ثُمَّ يُرَدُّ إِلَىٰ رَبِّهِۦ
فَيُعَذِّبُهُۥ عَذَابًا نُّكْرًا ﴿٨٧﴾ وَأَمَّا مَنْ ءَامَنَ وَعَمِلَ صَٰلِحًا فَلَهُۥ جَزَآءً
ٱلْحُسْنَىٰ ۖ وَسَنَقُولُ لَهُۥ مِنْ أَمْرِنَا يُسْرًا ﴿٨٨﴾ ثُمَّ أَتْبَعَ سَبَبًا ﴿٨٩﴾ حَتَّىٰٓ
إِذَا بَلَغَ مَطْلِعَ ٱلشَّمْسِ وَجَدَهَا تَطْلُعُ عَلَىٰ قَوْمٍ لَّمْ نَجْعَل لَّهُم مِّن
دُونِهَا سِتْرًا ﴿٩٠﴾ كَذَٰلِكَ وَقَدْ أَحَطْنَا بِمَا لَدَيْهِ خُبْرًا ﴿٩١﴾ ثُمَّ أَتْبَعَ
سَبَبًا ﴿٩٢﴾ حَتَّىٰٓ إِذَا بَلَغَ بَيْنَ ٱلسَّدَّيْنِ وَجَدَ مِن دُونِهِمَا قَوْمًا
لَّا يَكَادُونَ يَفْقَهُونَ قَوْلًا ﴿٩٣﴾ قَالُوا۟ يَٰذَا ٱلْقَرْنَيْنِ إِنَّ يَأْجُوجَ وَمَأْجُوجَ
مُفْسِدُونَ فِى ٱلْأَرْضِ فَهَلْ نَجْعَلُ لَكَ خَرْجًا عَلَىٰٓ أَن تَجْعَلَ بَيْنَنَا وَبَيْنَهُمْ
سَدًّا ﴿٩٤﴾ قَالَ مَا مَكَّنِّى فِيهِ رَبِّى خَيْرٌ فَأَعِينُونِى بِقُوَّةٍ أَجْعَلْ بَيْنَكُمْ
وَبَيْنَهُمْ رَدْمًا ﴿٩٥﴾ ءَاتُونِى زُبَرَ ٱلْحَدِيدِ ۖ حَتَّىٰٓ إِذَا سَاوَىٰ بَيْنَ ٱلصَّدَفَيْنِ
قَالَ ٱنفُخُوا۟ ۖ حَتَّىٰٓ إِذَا جَعَلَهُۥ نَارًا قَالَ ءَاتُونِىٓ أُفْرِغْ عَلَيْهِ قِطْرًا
﴿٩٦﴾ فَمَا ٱسْطَٰعُوٓا۟ أَن يَظْهَرُوهُ وَمَا ٱسْتَطَٰعُوا۟ لَهُۥ نَقْبًا ﴿٩٧﴾
قَالَ هَٰذَا رَحْمَةٌ مِّن رَّبِّى ۖ فَإِذَا جَآءَ وَعْدُ رَبِّى جَعَلَهُۥ دَكَّآءَ ۖ وَكَانَ وَعْدُ رَبِّى
حَقًّا ﴿٩٨﴾ ۞ وَتَرَكْنَا بَعْضَهُمْ يَوْمَئِذٍ يَمُوجُ فِى بَعْضٍ ۖ وَنُفِخَ فِى ٱلصُّورِ

84. ***We gave him power and authority on the earth*** – making it easy for him to travel about the world – ***and granted him a way to every - thing*** – to obtain whatever he wanted.

85. ***So he followed a way*** towards the west

86. ***...until he reached the setting of the sun*** – the place where it set – ***and found it setting in a muddy spring*** – a spring with *ḥamā'* in it, which is a kind of black mud – ***and found a people by it.*** It appeared to the eye that the sun set in the spring. He found some unbelievers there. ***We said*** – through inspiration to him – ***'Dhū'l-Qarnayn, you can either punish them*** by killing them ***or else you can treat them with gentleness*** by taking them captive.'

87. ***He said, 'As for those who do wrong*** – by committing *shirk* – ***we will punish them*** by killing them ***and then they will be returned to their Lord; and He will punish them with a dreadful punish - ment*** (read as *nukran* or *nukuran*) – which will be in the Fire.

88. ***But as for him who believes and acts rightly, he will receive the best of rewards*** (the Garden) (read as *jazā'u'l-ḥusnā* and as *jazā'an al-ḥusnā*, which makes it descriptive) ***and we will issue a command, making things easy for him.'***

89. ***Then he followed a way*** towards the east –

90. ***...until he reached the rising of the sun*** the place where it rises – ***and found it rising on a people*** – the Zanj, who are a black race – ***to whom We had not given any shelter from it.*** They had no shelter from the sun in the form of either clothing or a roof because their land would not support structures. They had tunnels into which they disappeared when the sun rose and would reappear when the sun was high.

91. ***Our knowledge encompasses all that happened to him*** (Dhū'l-Qarnayn) – in terms of signs, his army and other matters.

92. ***Then he followed a path...***

93. ***...until he arrived between the two mountains*** (read as *saddayn* and *suddayn*) – a remote place in the land of the Turks; Iskandar blocked up the valley between them, as will be mentioned – ***where he found a people scarcely able to understand speech*** (read as *yafqahūna* and *yufqihūna*): they could only understand what was said with difficulty.

94. ***They said, 'Dhū'l-Qarnayn, Yājūj and Mājūj*** (read as Yājūj and Mājūj and as Ya'jūj and Ma'jūj) – names for two tribes which are not Arabic words and so are not declined – ***are causing corruption in the land*** by looting and attacking us whenever they appear. ***Can we, therefore, pay tribute*** (read as *kharaj* and *kharāj*) ***to you in return for your constructing a barrier between us and them*** so that they cannot reach us***?'***

95. ***He said, 'The power my Lord has granted me*** (read as *makkannī* and *makkananī*) – in the form of wealth and in other ways – ***is better than that*** – tribute which you offer me. I have no need of it and I will build the barrier wall for you without payment. ***Just give me a strong helping hand*** – by doing what I ask you to do – ***and I will build a*** fortified ***solid barrier between you and them.***

96. ***Bring me ingots of iron.'*** These are pieces of iron the size of stones with which to build. So he built it and put wood and charcoal between them. ***Then, when he had made it level between the two high mountain-sides*** (read as *ṣadafayn*, *ṣudufayn*, and *ṣudfayn*) – bellows and fire were placed around it and – ***he said, 'Blow!'*** They blew – ***and when he had made it*** (the iron) ***a red hot fire, he said, 'Bring me molten brass to pour over it.'*** Then molten brass was brought and poured over the hot iron and it poured into the gaps between the ingots and became one solid structure.

97. ***They*** (Yājūj and Mājūj) ***were therefore unable to climb over it*** – because of its height and smoothness – ***nor were they able to make a breach in it*** – because it was hard and thick.

98. ***He*** (Dhū'l-Qarnayn) ***said, 'This*** – ability to build the wall – ***is a mercy*** (blessing) ***from my Lord*** – because it was a barrier against them coming out. ***But when my Lord's promise comes about*** – to bring them out close to the Resurrection – ***He will crush it flat. The promise of my Lord*** about their emergence and other things ***is surely true.'***

99. ***We will abandon them, that Day*** when they emerge ***to pound against each other in surging waves*** – mixing together because of their great . ***And the Trumpet will be blown*** for the Resurrection ***and We will gather them all together*** – all creatures together in the same place on the Day of Rising.

فَجَمَعْنَٰهُمْ جَمْعًا ﴿٩٩﴾ وَعَرَضْنَا جَهَنَّمَ يَوْمَئِذٍ لِّلْكَٰفِرِينَ عَرْضًا ﴿١٠٠﴾
ٱلَّذِينَ كَانَتْ أَعْيُنُهُمْ فِى غِطَآءٍ عَن ذِكْرِى وَكَانُوا۟ لَا يَسْتَطِيعُونَ
سَمْعًا ﴿١٠١﴾ أَفَحَسِبَ ٱلَّذِينَ كَفَرُوٓا۟ أَن يَتَّخِذُوا۟ عِبَادِى مِن دُونِىٓ
أَوْلِيَآءَ ۚ إِنَّآ أَعْتَدْنَا جَهَنَّمَ لِلْكَٰفِرِينَ نُزُلًا ﴿١٠٢﴾ قُلْ هَلْ نُنَبِّئُكُم بِٱلْأَخْسَرِينَ
أَعْمَٰلًا ﴿١٠٣﴾ ٱلَّذِينَ ضَلَّ سَعْيُهُمْ فِى ٱلْحَيَوٰةِ ٱلدُّنْيَا وَهُمْ يَحْسَبُونَ أَنَّهُمْ
يُحْسِنُونَ صُنْعًا ﴿١٠٤﴾ أُو۟لَٰٓئِكَ ٱلَّذِينَ كَفَرُوا۟ بِـَٔايَٰتِ رَبِّهِمْ وَلِقَآئِهِۦ
فَحَبِطَتْ أَعْمَٰلُهُمْ فَلَا نُقِيمُ لَهُمْ يَوْمَ ٱلْقِيَٰمَةِ وَزْنًا ﴿١٠٥﴾ ذَٰلِكَ جَزَآؤُهُمْ
جَهَنَّمُ بِمَا كَفَرُوا۟ وَٱتَّخَذُوٓا۟ ءَايَٰتِى وَرُسُلِى هُزُوًا ﴿١٠٦﴾ إِنَّ ٱلَّذِينَ ءَامَنُوا۟
وَعَمِلُوا۟ ٱلصَّٰلِحَٰتِ كَانَتْ لَهُمْ جَنَّٰتُ ٱلْفِرْدَوْسِ نُزُلًا ﴿١٠٧﴾ خَٰلِدِينَ
فِيهَا لَا يَبْغُونَ عَنْهَا حِوَلًا ﴿١٠٨﴾ قُل لَّوْ كَانَ ٱلْبَحْرُ مِدَادًا لِّكَلِمَٰتِ رَبِّى
لَنَفِدَ ٱلْبَحْرُ قَبْلَ أَن تَنفَدَ كَلِمَٰتُ رَبِّى وَلَوْ جِئْنَا بِمِثْلِهِۦ مَدَدًا ﴿١٠٩﴾ قُلْ
إِنَّمَآ أَنَا۠ بَشَرٌ مِّثْلُكُمْ يُوحَىٰٓ إِلَىَّ أَنَّمَآ إِلَٰهُكُمْ إِلَٰهٌ وَٰحِدٌ ۖ فَمَن كَانَ يَرْجُوا۟
لِقَآءَ رَبِّهِۦ فَلْيَعْمَلْ عَمَلًا صَٰلِحًا وَلَا يُشْرِكْ بِعِبَادَةِ رَبِّهِۦٓ أَحَدًۢا ﴿١١٠﴾

100. ***That Day We will display Hell in its totality to the unbelievers*** – bringing it near to them:

101. ***...those*** unbelievers ***whose eyes were blind to My remembrance*** (the Qur'an), – meaning not guided by it – ***and whose ears were unable to hear*** what the Prophet recited to them, because of their hatred for him which prevented them from believing.

102. ***Do those who disbelieve imagine that they can take My slaves*** – such as the angels and the Prophets 'Īsā and 'Uzayr – ***as protectors*** (lords) ***instead of Me?*** Do they suppose that taking them as lords will not anger Me and I that will not punish them for it? No! ***We have prepared Hell as hospitality*** – as one prepares a place for a guest – ***for the unbelievers*** – meaning those people and others.

103. ***Say: 'Shall I inform you of the greatest losers in their actions?***

104. ***People whose efforts in the life of this world are misguided*** – their actions are worthless – ***while they suppose that they are doing good*** – for which they will be rewarded.'

105. ***Those are the people who reject their Lord's Signs*** – the evidence of His oneness in the Qur'an and elsewhere – ***and the meeting with Him*** at the Resurrection, Reckoning and reward and penalty. ***Their actions will come to nothing*** – they are null and void – ***and on the Day of Rising We will not assign them any weight*** or importance.

106. ***That*** which We have mentioned about their actions being worthless and other things ***is their repayment – Hell – because they disbelieved and made a mockery of My Signs and of My Messengers.***

107. Allah knows what they have done. ***Those who believe and do right actions will have the Gardens of Paradise as hospitality*** – a place located right at the centre of the Gardens which is also the highest of them –

108. ***...remaining in them timelessly, for ever, with no desire to move away from them*** – from the Gardens to any other place.

109. ***Say: 'If all*** the water of ***the sea were ink*** used ***to write down the Words of my Lord*** – describing His wisdoms and wonders – ***it***

would run out long before the Words of my Lord ran out (read as *tanfada* and *yanfada*)***,'*** – there would not be enough water in the sea to write it down – ***even if We were to bring the same amount of ink again.*** This would be true even if another sea of the same size were to be added: it would still run out and would not be enough.

110. ***Say: 'I am only a human being like yourselves*** – a descendant of Ādam like you***. It is revealed to me that your god is One God. So let him who hopes to meet his Lord*** – at the Resurrection and Repayment – ***act rightly and not associate anyone in the worship of his Lord.'***

سُورَةُ مَرۡيَمَ

بِسۡمِ ٱللَّهِ ٱلرَّحۡمَٰنِ ٱلرَّحِيمِ

كٓهيعٓصٓ ﴿١﴾ ذِكۡرُ رَحۡمَتِ رَبِّكَ عَبۡدَهُۥ زَكَرِيَّآ ﴿٢﴾
إِذۡ نَادَىٰ رَبَّهُۥ نِدَآءً خَفِيّٗا ﴿٣﴾ قَالَ رَبِّ إِنِّي وَهَنَ ٱلۡعَظۡمُ
مِنِّي وَٱشۡتَعَلَ ٱلرَّأۡسُ شَيۡبٗا وَلَمۡ أَكُنۢ بِدُعَآئِكَ رَبِّ
شَقِيّٗا ﴿٤﴾ وَإِنِّي خِفۡتُ ٱلۡمَوَٰلِيَ مِن وَرَآءِي وَكَانَتِ
ٱمۡرَأَتِي عَاقِرٗا فَهَبۡ لِي مِن لَّدُنكَ وَلِيّٗا ﴿٥﴾ يَرِثُنِي وَيَرِثُ
مِنۡ ءَالِ يَعۡقُوبَۖ وَٱجۡعَلۡهُ رَبِّ رَضِيّٗا ﴿٦﴾ يَٰزَكَرِيَّآ
إِنَّا نُبَشِّرُكَ بِغُلَٰمٍ ٱسۡمُهُۥ يَحۡيَىٰ لَمۡ نَجۡعَل لَّهُۥ مِن قَبۡلُ سَمِيّٗا
﴿٧﴾ قَالَ رَبِّ أَنَّىٰ يَكُونُ لِي غُلَٰمٞ وَكَانَتِ ٱمۡرَأَتِي
عَاقِرٗا وَقَدۡ بَلَغۡتُ مِنَ ٱلۡكِبَرِ عِتِيّٗا ﴿٨﴾ قَالَ كَذَٰلِكَ
قَالَ رَبُّكَ هُوَ عَلَيَّ هَيِّنٞ وَقَدۡ خَلَقۡتُكَ مِن قَبۡلُ وَلَمۡ تَكُ
شَيۡـٔٗا ﴿٩﴾ قَالَ رَبِّ ٱجۡعَل لِّيٓ ءَايَةٗۚ قَالَ ءَايَتُكَ أَلَّا
تُكَلِّمَ ٱلنَّاسَ ثَلَٰثَ لَيَالٖ سَوِيّٗا ﴿١٠﴾ فَخَرَجَ عَلَىٰ قَوۡمِهِۦ
مِنَ ٱلۡمِحۡرَابِ فَأَوۡحَىٰٓ إِلَيۡهِمۡ أَن سَبِّحُواْ بُكۡرَةٗ وَعَشِيّٗا ﴿١١﴾
يَٰيَحۡيَىٰ خُذِ ٱلۡكِتَٰبَ بِقُوَّةٖۖ وَءَاتَيۡنَٰهُ ٱلۡحُكۡمَ صَبِيّٗا ﴿١٢﴾
وَحَنَانٗا مِّن لَّدُنَّا وَزَكَوٰةٗۖ وَكَانَ تَقِيّٗا ﴿١٣﴾ وَبَرَّۢا بِوَٰلِدَيۡهِ وَلَمۡ

19. *Sūrat Maryam*
Mary

This *sūra* is Makkan except for *āyat*s 58 and 71, which are Madinan. It has 98 or 99 *āyat*s and was sent down after *Fāṭir*.

1. ***Kaf Ha Ya 'Ayn Sad.*** Allah knows best what this means.

2. ***Remembering your Lord's mercy to His slave Zakariyyā***

3. ***...when he called on his Lord in secret*** – he did this secretly in the middle of the night because supplication at that time has the swiftest response –

4. ***...and said, 'My Lord, my bones have*** all ***lost their strength and my head is crowned with white*** – whiteness spread through his hair as fire spreads through wood. ***But in calling on You, My Lord, I have never been disappointed*** – so do not disappoint me now.

5. ***I fear my relatives when I am gone,*** meaning: "I fear that after I die those close to me in kinship, such as cousins, will cause the *dīn* to be lost, as I have seen happen among the tribe of Israel who altered the *dīn*" – ***and my wife is barren, so give me an heir*** (a son) ***from You***

6. ***...to be my inheritor and the inheritor of the family of Ya'qūb*** – inheriting knowledge and Prophethood – ***and make him, my Lord, pleasing to You.'*** Then Allah Almighty answered his request for a son as a mercy to him, and said:

7. ***'Zakariyyā, We give you the good news of a boy named Yaḥyā*** – to inherit from you as you have asked – ***a name We have given to no one else before.'***

8. ***He said, 'My Lord, how can I have a boy when my wife is barren and I have reached advanced old age?'*** *'Atā* means to become dry, in this case, at the end of one's life. Zakariyyā was one hundred and twenty and his wife was ninety-eight years old.

9. ***He said, 'It shall be so!*** That is how it will be: you will have a boy. ***Your Lord says, "That is easy for Me to do*** – it is not difficult to return to you the power of intercourse and to open the womb of your wife to fertilisation. ***I created you before, when you were not***

anything.'" This is how Allah demonstrates His immense power. He inspired Zakariyyā to ask so that He could grant something which demonstrates it. Then Zakariyyā yearned for a sign of the good news given to him.

10. ***He said, 'My Lord, give me a Sign*** to show that my wife will become pregnant.***' He said, 'Your Sign is not to speak to people for three nights*** – he was prevented from speaking to people, without having any impediment, but not from invoking Allah – ***although you are perfectly able to.'***

11. ***He came out to his people from the Upper Room (***the Temple) – they used to wait for him to open it so that they could pray in it when he ordered them to, as was the custom – ***and gestured to them to glorify Allah*** (pray) ***in the morning and the evening*** as was the custom. He knew by his inability to speak that his wife was pregnant with Yaḥyā. Two years after Yaḥyā's birth, Allah Almighty said to him:

12. ***'Yaḥyā, take hold of the Book*** (the Torah) ***with vigour*** and seriousness.***' We gave him judgement*** (Prophethood) ***while still a child,*** when he was three years old.

13. ***...and tenderness*** – compassion towards people – ***and purity*** – truthfulness to them – ***from Us – he was godfearing*** – it is reported that he did not commit a single wrong action or even intend one.

14. ***...and devotion*** (kindness) ***to his parents. He was not insolent or disobedient*** to his Lord.

15. ***Peace*** from Us ***be upon him the day he was born, and the day he dies, and the day he is raised up again alive*** – referring to the fearful last days, in which things will be seen that have never been seen before. He will be safe during them.

16. ***Mention*** the news of ***Maryam in the Book*** (the Qur'an): ***how she withdrew from her people to an eastern place*** – in a part of Zakariyyā's house which was towards the east.

17. ***...and veiled herself from them.*** She let down a curtain to conceal herself so that she could delouse her hair or her clothes or have a *ghusl* after menstruation. ***Then We sent Our* Rūḥ** (Jibrīl) ***to her*** – after she had dressed – ***and it took on for her the form of a handsome, well-built man.***

يَكُن جَبَّارًا عَصِيًّا ﴿١٤﴾ وَسَلَٰمٌ عَلَيۡهِ يَوۡمَ وُلِدَ وَيَوۡمَ يَمُوتُ
وَيَوۡمَ يُبۡعَثُ حَيًّا ﴿١٥﴾ وَٱذۡكُرۡ فِي ٱلۡكِتَٰبِ مَرۡيَمَ إِذِ ٱنتَبَذَتۡ
مِنۡ أَهۡلِهَا مَكَانًا شَرۡقِيًّا ﴿١٦﴾ فَٱتَّخَذَتۡ مِن دُونِهِمۡ حِجَابًا
فَأَرۡسَلۡنَآ إِلَيۡهَا رُوحَنَا فَتَمَثَّلَ لَهَا بَشَرًا سَوِيًّا ﴿١٧﴾ قَالَتۡ إِنِّيٓ
أَعُوذُ بِٱلرَّحۡمَٰنِ مِنكَ إِن كُنتَ تَقِيًّا ﴿١٨﴾ قَالَ إِنَّمَآ أَنَا۠ رَسُولُ
رَبِّكِ لِأَهَبَ لَكِ غُلَٰمًا زَكِيًّا ﴿١٩﴾ قَالَتۡ أَنَّىٰ يَكُونُ لِي
غُلَٰمٌ وَلَمۡ يَمۡسَسۡنِي بَشَرٌ وَلَمۡ أَكُ بَغِيًّا ﴿٢٠﴾ قَالَ كَذَٰلِكِ
قَالَ رَبُّكِ هُوَ عَلَيَّ هَيِّنٞۖ وَلِنَجۡعَلَهُۥٓ ءَايَةً لِّلنَّاسِ وَرَحۡمَةً
مِّنَّاۚ وَكَانَ أَمۡرًا مَّقۡضِيًّا ﴿٢١﴾ ۞ فَحَمَلَتۡهُ فَٱنتَبَذَتۡ
بِهِۦ مَكَانًا قَصِيًّا ﴿٢٢﴾ فَأَجَآءَهَا ٱلۡمَخَاضُ إِلَىٰ جِذۡعِ ٱلنَّخۡلَةِ
قَالَتۡ يَٰلَيۡتَنِي مِتُّ قَبۡلَ هَٰذَا وَكُنتُ نَسۡيًا مَّنسِيًّا ﴿٢٣﴾
فَنَادَىٰهَا مِن تَحۡتِهَآ أَلَّا تَحۡزَنِي قَدۡ جَعَلَ رَبُّكِ تَحۡتَكِ سَرِيًّا ﴿٢٤﴾
وَهُزِّيٓ إِلَيۡكِ بِجِذۡعِ ٱلنَّخۡلَةِ تُسَٰقِطۡ عَلَيۡكِ رُطَبًا جَنِيًّا ﴿٢٥﴾
فَكُلِي وَٱشۡرَبِي وَقَرِّي عَيۡنًاۖ فَإِمَّا تَرَيِنَّ مِنَ ٱلۡبَشَرِ أَحَدًا فَقُولِيٓ
إِنِّي نَذَرۡتُ لِلرَّحۡمَٰنِ صَوۡمًا فَلَنۡ أُكَلِّمَ ٱلۡيَوۡمَ إِنسِيًّا ﴿٢٦﴾
فَأَتَتۡ بِهِۦ قَوۡمَهَا تَحۡمِلُهُۥۖ قَالُواْ يَٰمَرۡيَمُ لَقَدۡ جِئۡتِ شَيۡـٔٗا
فَرِيًّا ﴿٢٧﴾ يَٰٓأُخۡتَ هَٰرُونَ مَا كَانَ أَبُوكِ ٱمۡرَأَ سَوۡءٖ وَمَا كَانَتۡ
أُمُّكِ بَغِيًّا ﴿٢٨﴾ فَأَشَارَتۡ إِلَيۡهِۖ قَالُواْ كَيۡفَ نُكَلِّمُ مَن كَانَ فِي
ٱلۡمَهۡدِ صَبِيًّا ﴿٢٩﴾ قَالَ إِنِّي عَبۡدُ ٱللَّهِ ءَاتَىٰنِيَ ٱلۡكِتَٰبَ وَجَعَلَنِي
نَبِيًّا ﴿٣٠﴾ وَجَعَلَنِي مُبَارَكًا أَيۡنَ مَا كُنتُ وَأَوۡصَٰنِي بِٱلصَّلَوٰةِ

18. ***She said, 'I seek refuge from you with the All-Merciful, if you are godfearing.'*** 'If you are godfearing, you will leave me alone because of my seeking refuge.'

19. ***He said, 'I am only your Lord's messenger, so that He may give you a pure boy*** who will be a Prophet.'

20. ***She said, 'How can I have a boy, when no man has touched me*** – through marriage – ***and I am not an unchaste woman*** (fornicatress)***?'***

21. ***He said, 'It will be so!*** 'That is what is going to happen. You will give birth to a boy without a father.' ***Your Lord says, "That is easy for Me.*** It is not difficult for Me to breathe into you so that you become pregnant. ***It is so that We can make him a Sign for mankind*** – of Our power – ***and a mercy from Us*** for those who believe in him." ***It is a matter already decreed*** – in My foreknowledge.' So Jibrīl blew into the pocket of her shift and she felt herself become pregnant.

22. ***So she conceived him and withdrew with him to a distant place*** far away from her people.

23. ***The pains of labour drove her to the trunk of a date-palm.*** She leaned against it and gave birth. Pregnancy, formation and birth all took one hour. ***She said, 'Oh, if only I had died before this time and were something discarded and forgotten!'***

24. ***A voice*** (Jibrīl) ***called out to her from under her*** – lower than her – ***'Do not grieve! Your Lord has placed a small stream*** – the word used here means a spring which is dammed up and becomes a small pool – ***at your feet.***

25. ***Shake the trunk of the palm towards you and fresh, ripe dates will drop down*** (read as *tusāqiṭ*, and *tassāqaṭ* and *yassāqaṭ*) ***onto you.***

26. ***Eat*** the dates ***and drink*** from the stream ***and delight your eyes*** with your child. Be content and do not look for anything else. ***If you should see anyone at all*** – who asks you about your child – ***just say, "I have made a vow of abstinence*** – a vow not to speak about him to other people – ***to the All-Merciful and today I will not speak to any human being."'***

وَٱلزَّكَوٰةِ مَا دُمۡتُ حَيّٗا ٣١ وَبَرَّۢا بِوَٰلِدَتِي وَلَمۡ يَجۡعَلۡنِي
جَبَّارٗا شَقِيّٗا ٣٢ وَٱلسَّلَٰمُ عَلَيَّ يَوۡمَ وُلِدتُّ وَيَوۡمَ أَمُوتُ
وَيَوۡمَ أُبۡعَثُ حَيّٗا ٣٣ ذَٰلِكَ عِيسَى ٱبۡنُ مَرۡيَمَۖ قَوۡلَ ٱلۡحَقِّ
ٱلَّذِي فِيهِ يَمۡتَرُونَ ٣٤ مَا كَانَ لِلَّهِ أَن يَتَّخِذَ مِن وَلَدٖۖ سُبۡحَٰنَهُۥٓۚ
إِذَا قَضَىٰٓ أَمۡرٗا فَإِنَّمَا يَقُولُ لَهُۥ كُن فَيَكُونُ ٣٥ وَإِنَّ ٱللَّهَ رَبِّي وَرَبُّكُمۡ
فَٱعۡبُدُوهُۚ هَٰذَا صِرَٰطٞ مُّسۡتَقِيمٞ ٣٦ فَٱخۡتَلَفَ ٱلۡأَحۡزَابُ مِنۢ
بَيۡنِهِمۡۖ فَوَيۡلٞ لِّلَّذِينَ كَفَرُواْ مِن مَّشۡهَدِ يَوۡمٍ عَظِيمٍ ٣٧ أَسۡمِعۡ بِهِمۡ
وَأَبۡصِرۡ يَوۡمَ يَأۡتُونَنَاۖ لَٰكِنِ ٱلظَّٰلِمُونَ ٱلۡيَوۡمَ فِي ضَلَٰلٖ مُّبِينٖ ٣٨
وَأَنذِرۡهُمۡ يَوۡمَ ٱلۡحَسۡرَةِ إِذۡ قُضِيَ ٱلۡأَمۡرُ وَهُمۡ فِي غَفۡلَةٖ وَهُمۡ لَا يُؤۡمِنُونَ
٣٩ إِنَّا نَحۡنُ نَرِثُ ٱلۡأَرۡضَ وَمَنۡ عَلَيۡهَا وَإِلَيۡنَا يُرۡجَعُونَ ٤٠ وَٱذۡكُرۡ
فِي ٱلۡكِتَٰبِ إِبۡرَٰهِيمَۚ إِنَّهُۥ كَانَ صِدِّيقٗا نَّبِيًّا ٤١ إِذۡ قَالَ لِأَبِيهِ يَٰٓأَبَتِ
لِمَ تَعۡبُدُ مَا لَا يَسۡمَعُ وَلَا يُبۡصِرُ وَلَا يُغۡنِي عَنكَ شَيۡـٔٗا ٤٢ يَٰٓأَبَتِ
إِنِّي قَدۡ جَآءَنِي مِنَ ٱلۡعِلۡمِ مَا لَمۡ يَأۡتِكَ فَٱتَّبِعۡنِيٓ أَهۡدِكَ صِرَٰطٗا
سَوِيّٗا ٤٣ يَٰٓأَبَتِ لَا تَعۡبُدِ ٱلشَّيۡطَٰنَۖ إِنَّ ٱلشَّيۡطَٰنَ كَانَ لِلرَّحۡمَٰنِ
عَصِيّٗا ٤٤ يَٰٓأَبَتِ إِنِّيٓ أَخَافُ أَن يَمَسَّكَ عَذَابٞ مِّنَ ٱلرَّحۡمَٰنِ
فَتَكُونَ لِلشَّيۡطَٰنِ وَلِيّٗا ٤٥ قَالَ أَرَاغِبٌ أَنتَ عَنۡ ءَالِهَتِي
يَٰٓإِبۡرَٰهِيمُۖ لَئِن لَّمۡ تَنتَهِ لَأَرۡجُمَنَّكَۖ وَٱهۡجُرۡنِي مَلِيّٗا ٤٦ قَالَ
سَلَٰمٌ عَلَيۡكَۖ سَأَسۡتَغۡفِرُ لَكَ رَبِّيٓۖ إِنَّهُۥ كَانَ بِي حَفِيّٗا ٤٧
وَأَعۡتَزِلُكُمۡ وَمَا تَدۡعُونَ مِن دُونِ ٱللَّهِ وَأَدۡعُواْ رَبِّي عَسَىٰٓ
أَلَّآ أَكُونَ بِدُعَآءِ رَبِّي شَقِيّٗا ٤٨ فَلَمَّا ٱعۡتَزَلَهُمۡ وَمَا يَعۡبُدُونَ

27. ***She brought him to her people, carrying him. They said*** – when they saw her – ***'Maryam, you have done an unthinkable thing*** – producing a baby with no father***!***

28. ***Sister of Hārūn*** – Hārūn was a righteous man, so the meaning of this form of address is: "You who have always been considered the same as Hārūn in respect of chastity" – ***your father was not an evil man*** (a fornicator), ***nor was your mother an unchaste woman*** (a fornicatress)***!*** So how can you have this child?'

29. ***She pointed towards him*** – indicating that they should speak to him. ***They said, 'How can a baby in the cradle speak?'***

30. ***He*** ('Īsā) ***said, 'I am the slave of Allah. He has given me the Book*** (the Gospel) ***and made me a Prophet.***

31. ***He has made me blessed wherever I am*** – a benefit to people, reporting about what was destined for him – ***and directed me to do the prayer and give* zakāt *as long as I live,***

32. ***...and to show devotion to my mother. He has not made me insolent or arrogant*** towards my Lord.

33. ***Peace*** from Allah ***be upon me the day I was born, and the day I die and the day I am raised up again alive.'*** This is similar to what was said about the Prophet Yaḥyā.

34. ***That is 'Īsā, son of Maryam, the word of truth about which they are in doubt.*** The "they" mentioned here are the Christians who lie when they say that 'Īsā is the son of Allah.

35. It is not fitting for Allah to have a son. Glory be to Him! He is pure and above that. ***When He decides on*** bringing ***something*** – into existence – ***He just says to it, 'Be!' and it is.*** Allah is well able to create 'Īsā without a father.

36. There are two readings for the first word of this *āyat*: *inna* and *anna*. If it begins with *anna*, it means "Remember that...". If it begins with *inna*, it means, "Say:" The evidence for this is: *"I told them nothing but what You ordered me to say: 'Worship Allah, my Lord and your Lord.'"* (5:117)) ***'Allah is my Lord and your Lord, so worship Him. This is a straight path*** which leads to the Garden.***'***

37. ***The parties differed among themselves.*** The Christians disagreed about 'Īsā and whether he was the son of Allah or a god, co-existent with Him, or one of three. ***Woe*** (intense punishment) ***to***

those who disbelieve – in what has been mentioned and other things – ***when they are present on a terrible Day*** – on the Day of Rising, and experience its terrors*!*

38. ***How clear will be their hearing, how perfect their sight*** – the grammatical form of these words indicates wonder and astonishment – ***on the Day they come to Us*** in the Next World***; whereas today*** – in this world – ***the wrongdoers are clearly misguided.*** It is clear that they are deaf to hearing the truth and blind to seeing it. They will be amazed at the clearness of their hearing and perfection of their sight in the Next World when they were blind and deaf to the truth in this world.

39. ***Warn them*** (the unbelievers of Makka), Muḥammad, ***of the Day of Bitter Regret*** – to make them fear the Day of Rising, on which the evildoers will regret abandoning the doing of good in this world – ***when the affair will be resolved*** and the punishment decreed for them**.** ***But they take no notice*** – in this world**.** ***They do not believe*** it**.**

40. ***It is We who shall inherit the earth and all those on it*** – meaning those with consciousness on the earth and others, by destroying them**.** ***They will be returned to Us*** to be repaid for what they did**.**

41. ***Mention*** to them ***Ibrāhīm in the Book. He was a true*** – the word *ṣiddīq* used here is an intensive form, indicating intensive truthfulness – ***man and a Prophet.***

42. ***Remember when he said to his father*** (Āzar)***, 'Father, why do you worship what can neither hear nor see and is not of any use to you at all*** – in other words idols, which could neither defend, benefit or harm him*?*

43. ***Father, knowledge which never reached you has come to me, so follow me and I will guide you to the right*** (straight) ***path.***

44. ***Father, do not worship Shayṭān*** – in other words, do not obey him by worshipping idols. ***Shayṭān was*** very ***disobedient to the All-Merciful.***

45. ***Father, I am afraid that a punishment from the All-Merciful will afflict you*** – if you do not repent – ***and turn you into a comrade of Shayṭān*** in the Fire*.'*

46. ***He said, 'Do you forsake my gods, Ibrāhīm?*** Are you tired of them? ***If you do not stop*** rejecting them ***I will stone you*** either with

مِن دُونِ ٱللَّهِ وَهَبۡنَا لَهُۥٓ إِسۡحَٰقَ وَيَعۡقُوبَۖ وَكُلّٗا جَعَلۡنَا نَبِيّٗا ﴿٤٩﴾
وَوَهَبۡنَا لَهُم مِّن رَّحۡمَتِنَا وَجَعَلۡنَا لَهُمۡ لِسَانَ صِدۡقٍ عَلِيّٗا ﴿٥٠﴾
وَٱذۡكُرۡ فِي ٱلۡكِتَٰبِ مُوسَىٰٓۚ إِنَّهُۥ كَانَ مُخۡلَصٗا وَكَانَ رَسُولٗا نَّبِيّٗا ﴿٥١﴾
وَنَٰدَيۡنَٰهُ مِن جَانِبِ ٱلطُّورِ ٱلۡأَيۡمَنِ وَقَرَّبۡنَٰهُ نَجِيّٗا ﴿٥٢﴾ وَوَهَبۡنَا لَهُۥ مِن
رَّحۡمَتِنَآ أَخَاهُ هَٰرُونَ نَبِيّٗا ﴿٥٣﴾ وَٱذۡكُرۡ فِي ٱلۡكِتَٰبِ إِسۡمَٰعِيلَۚ إِنَّهُۥ كَانَ
صَادِقَ ٱلۡوَعۡدِ وَكَانَ رَسُولٗا نَّبِيّٗا ﴿٥٤﴾ وَكَانَ يَأۡمُرُ أَهۡلَهُۥ بِٱلصَّلَوٰةِ
وَٱلزَّكَوٰةِ وَكَانَ عِندَ رَبِّهِۦ مَرۡضِيّٗا ﴿٥٥﴾ وَٱذۡكُرۡ فِي ٱلۡكِتَٰبِ إِدۡرِيسَۚ
إِنَّهُۥ كَانَ صِدِّيقٗا نَّبِيّٗا ﴿٥٦﴾ وَرَفَعۡنَٰهُ مَكَانًا عَلِيًّا ﴿٥٧﴾ أُوْلَٰٓئِكَ ٱلَّذِينَ
أَنۡعَمَ ٱللَّهُ عَلَيۡهِم مِّنَ ٱلنَّبِيِّـۧنَ مِن ذُرِّيَّةِ ءَادَمَ وَمِمَّنۡ حَمَلۡنَا مَعَ نُوحٖ
وَمِن ذُرِّيَّةِ إِبۡرَٰهِيمَ وَإِسۡرَٰٓءِيلَ وَمِمَّنۡ هَدَيۡنَا وَٱجۡتَبَيۡنَآۚ إِذَا تُتۡلَىٰ عَلَيۡهِمۡ
ءَايَٰتُ ٱلرَّحۡمَٰنِ خَرُّواْۤ سُجَّدٗا وَبُكِيّٗا ۩ ﴿٥٨﴾ ۞ فَخَلَفَ مِنۢ بَعۡدِهِمۡ
خَلۡفٌ أَضَاعُواْ ٱلصَّلَوٰةَ وَٱتَّبَعُواْ ٱلشَّهَوَٰتِۖ فَسَوۡفَ يَلۡقَوۡنَ غَيًّا
﴿٥٩﴾ إِلَّا مَن تَابَ وَءَامَنَ وَعَمِلَ صَٰلِحٗا فَأُوْلَٰٓئِكَ يَدۡخُلُونَ ٱلۡجَنَّةَ
وَلَا يُظۡلَمُونَ شَيۡـٔٗا ﴿٦٠﴾ جَنَّٰتِ عَدۡنٍ ٱلَّتِي وَعَدَ ٱلرَّحۡمَٰنُ عِبَادَهُۥ
بِٱلۡغَيۡبِۚ إِنَّهُۥ كَانَ وَعۡدُهُۥ مَأۡتِيّٗا ﴿٦١﴾ لَّا يَسۡمَعُونَ فِيهَا لَغۡوًا إِلَّا سَلَٰمٗاۖ
وَلَهُمۡ رِزۡقُهُمۡ فِيهَا بُكۡرَةٗ وَعَشِيّٗا ﴿٦٢﴾ تِلۡكَ ٱلۡجَنَّةُ ٱلَّتِي نُورِثُ مِنۡ
عِبَادِنَا مَن كَانَ تَقِيّٗا ﴿٦٣﴾ وَمَا نَتَنَزَّلُ إِلَّا بِأَمۡرِ رَبِّكَۖ لَهُۥ مَا بَيۡنَ
أَيۡدِينَا وَمَا خَلۡفَنَا وَمَا بَيۡنَ ذَٰلِكَۚ وَمَا كَانَ رَبُّكَ نَسِيّٗا ﴿٦٤﴾
رَّبُّ ٱلسَّمَٰوَٰتِ وَٱلۡأَرۡضِ وَمَا بَيۡنَهُمَا فَٱعۡبُدۡهُ وَٱصۡطَبِرۡ لِعِبَٰدَتِهِۦۚ
هَلۡ تَعۡلَمُ لَهُۥ سَمِيّٗا ﴿٦٥﴾ وَيَقُولُ ٱلۡإِنسَٰنُ أَءِذَا مَا مِتُّ لَسَوۡفَ

actual stones or with ugly words. ***Keep away from me for a good long time.'***

47. ***He*** (Ibrāhīm) ***said, 'Peace be upon you*** – meaning that he would not do anything hateful to his father. ***I will ask my Lord to forgive you. He has always honoured me*** by answering my prayers; we find the fulfilment of Ibrāhīm's promise to his father in *Sūrat ash-Shu'arā'* when he said, *"and forgive my father ..."* (26:86). This was before it was clear to him that his father was an enemy of Allah, as is mentioned in *Sūrat at-Tawba* (9:114).

48. ***I will separate myself from you and all you call upon*** and worship ***besides Allah; and I will call upon my Lord. It may well be that, in calling on my Lord*** and worshipping Him ***I will not be disappointed*** – in the way you will be made wretched by worshipping idols.'

49. ***When he had separated himself from them, and what they worshipped besides Allah*** – by going to the Holy Land – ***We gave him Isḥāq and Ya'qūb, making each of them a Prophet.***

50. ***We endowed*** the three of ***them with Our mercy*** – in the form of wealth and children – ***and made them highly honoured.*** They were praised highly by all of the people of religions.

51. ***Mention Mūsā in the Book. He was truly sincere*** (read as *mukhlaṣan* and *mukhliṣan*) in His worship – or this may mean that Allah purified him of all uncleanness – ***and was a Messenger and a Prophet.***

52. ***We called out to him*** saying, "O Mūsā, I am Allah" ***from the right hand side*** – the right of Mūsā when he faced it, coming from Madyan – ***of the Mount*** – Ṭūr was the name of the mountain – ***and We brought him near in close communication*** – as is shown by the fact that Allah Almighty made him hear His words.

53. ***We endowed him with Our mercy*** (blessing), ***making his brother Hārūn a Prophet.*** Hārūn was made a Prophet in answer to Mūsā's supplication to send his brother with him. His brother was older than him.

54. ***Mention Ismā'īl in the Book. He was true to his promise*** so that whenever he made a promise, he kept it. Once he promised to meet someone, and waited for him for three days or, it is said a year, until the man returned to him where he was – ***and was a Messenger and a Prophet.***

55. ***He used to command his people to do the prayer and give*** **zakāt,** ***and he was pleasing to his Lord.***

56. ***Mention Idrīs in the Book.*** He was the great-grandfather of Nūḥ. ***He was a true man and a Prophet.***

57. ***We raised him up to a high place.*** He is alive in the fourth, sixth or seventh heaven, or in the Garden which he entered after experiencing death and being brought to life. He will never leave it.

58. ***Those are some of the Prophets Allah has blessed, from the descendants of Ādam*** – namely Idrīs – ***and from those We carried with Nūḥ*** – in the Ark, meaning Ibrāhīm, the descendant of Nūḥ's son Sām – ***and from the descendants of Ibrāhīm*** – namely Ismā'il and Isḥāq – ***and Isrā'īl*** – another name for Ya'qūb, among whose descendants are Mūsā, Hārūn, Zakariyyā, Yaḥyā, and 'Īsā – ***and from those We guided and chose*** – from all of them. ***When the Signs of the All-Merciful were recited to them they fell on their faces, weeping, in prostration.***

59. ***An evil generation succeeded them who neglected the prayer*** – by abandoning it, referring to Jews and Christians – ***and followed their appetites*** by perpetrating acts of disobedience. ***They will plunge into the Valley of Evil*** – a valley in Hellfire.

60. ***...except for those who repent and believe and act rightly. They will enter the Garden and they will not be wronged in any way*** by having their reward decreased by the slightest amount:

61. ...residing in ***Gardens of Eden which the All-Merciful has promised to His slaves in the Unseen*** – something which is veiled from them. ***His promise is always kept.*** What He promises will inevitably come to pass. What is promised here is the Garden, to which those destined for it will certainly come.

62. ***They will not hear any prattling there;*** they will hear ***nothing but 'Peace'*** – from the angels to them or between themselves. ***They will receive their provision there morning and night*** just as they do in this world, although in the Garden there will be no night or day; they will be in perpetual light and illumination.

أُخۡرَجُ حَيًّا ٦٦ أَوَلَا يَذۡكُرُ ٱلۡإِنسَٰنُ أَنَّا خَلَقۡنَٰهُ مِن قَبۡلُ
وَلَمۡ يَكُ شَيۡـٔٗا ٦٧ فَوَرَبِّكَ لَنَحۡشُرَنَّهُمۡ وَٱلشَّيَٰطِينَ ثُمَّ
لَنُحۡضِرَنَّهُمۡ حَوۡلَ جَهَنَّمَ جِثِيّٗا ٦٨ ثُمَّ لَنَنزِعَنَّ مِن كُلِّ
شِيعَةٍ أَيُّهُمۡ أَشَدُّ عَلَى ٱلرَّحۡمَٰنِ عِتِيّٗا ٦٩ ثُمَّ لَنَحۡنُ أَعۡلَمُ بِٱلَّذِينَ
هُمۡ أَوۡلَىٰ بِهَا صِلِيّٗا ٧٠ وَإِن مِّنكُمۡ إِلَّا وَارِدُهَاۚ كَانَ عَلَىٰ رَبِّكَ
حَتۡمٗا مَّقۡضِيّٗا ٧١ ثُمَّ نُنَجِّي ٱلَّذِينَ ٱتَّقَواْ وَّنَذَرُ ٱلظَّٰلِمِينَ
فِيهَا جِثِيّٗا ٧٢ وَإِذَا تُتۡلَىٰ عَلَيۡهِمۡ ءَايَٰتُنَا بَيِّنَٰتٖ قَالَ ٱلَّذِينَ كَفَرُواْ
لِلَّذِينَ ءَامَنُوٓاْ أَيُّ ٱلۡفَرِيقَيۡنِ خَيۡرٞ مَّقَامٗا وَأَحۡسَنُ نَدِيّٗا ٧٣ وَكَمۡ
أَهۡلَكۡنَا قَبۡلَهُم مِّن قَرۡنٍ هُمۡ أَحۡسَنُ أَثَٰثٗا وَرِءۡيٗا ٧٤ قُلۡ مَن
كَانَ فِي ٱلضَّلَٰلَةِ فَلۡيَمۡدُدۡ لَهُ ٱلرَّحۡمَٰنُ مَدًّاۚ حَتَّىٰٓ إِذَا رَأَوۡاْ مَا يُوعَدُونَ
إِمَّا ٱلۡعَذَابَ وَإِمَّا ٱلسَّاعَةَ فَسَيَعۡلَمُونَ مَنۡ هُوَ شَرّٞ مَّكَانٗا
وَأَضۡعَفُ جُندٗا ٧٥ وَيَزِيدُ ٱللَّهُ ٱلَّذِينَ ٱهۡتَدَوۡاْ هُدٗىۗ
وَٱلۡبَٰقِيَٰتُ ٱلصَّٰلِحَٰتُ خَيۡرٌ عِندَ رَبِّكَ ثَوَابٗا وَخَيۡرٞ مَّرَدًّا ٧٦
أَفَرَءَيۡتَ ٱلَّذِي كَفَرَ بِـَٔايَٰتِنَا وَقَالَ لَأُوتَيَنَّ مَالٗا وَوَلَدًا
٧٧ أَطَّلَعَ ٱلۡغَيۡبَ أَمِ ٱتَّخَذَ عِندَ ٱلرَّحۡمَٰنِ عَهۡدٗا ٧٨ كَلَّاۚ
سَنَكۡتُبُ مَا يَقُولُ وَنَمُدُّ لَهُۥ مِنَ ٱلۡعَذَابِ مَدّٗا ٧٩ وَنَرِثُهُۥ
مَا يَقُولُ وَيَأۡتِينَا فَرۡدٗا ٨٠ وَٱتَّخَذُواْ مِن دُونِ ٱللَّهِ ءَالِهَةٗ
لِّيَكُونُواْ لَهُمۡ عِزّٗا ٨١ كَلَّاۚ سَيَكۡفُرُونَ بِعِبَادَتِهِمۡ وَيَكُونُونَ
عَلَيۡهِمۡ ضِدًّا ٨٢ أَلَمۡ تَرَ أَنَّآ أَرۡسَلۡنَا ٱلشَّيَٰطِينَ عَلَى ٱلۡكَٰفِرِينَ
تَؤُزُّهُمۡ أَزّٗا ٨٣ فَلَا تَعۡجَلۡ عَلَيۡهِمۡۖ إِنَّمَا نَعُدُّ لَهُمۡ عَدّٗا ٨٤

63. ***That is the Garden which We will bequeath*** and give ***to those of Our slaves who*** show they ***are godfearing*** by obeying Us.

64. This was revealed when the Revelation was delayed for some days. The Prophet, may Allah bless him and grant him peace, asked Jibrīl what had kept him from visiting, and the reply came: ***'We only descend at your Lord's command. Everything in front of us*** – referring to what is going to happen in the Next World – ***and everything behind us*** – referring to what happens in this world – ***and everything in between*** – from this moment until the Last Day – ***belongs to Him.*** He has knowledge of all of that. ***Your Lord does not forget'*** – meaning that Allah will not abandon you by delaying Revelation to you.

65. ***He is Lord of the heavens and the earth and everything in between them, so worship Him and persevere in His worship. Do you know of any other with His Name?*** Do you know of any other called Allah? No.

66. The man referred to here who denied the resurrection was either Ubayy ibn Khalaf or al-Walīd ibn al-Mughīra and the *āyat* was revealed about him. ***Man says, 'When I am dead, will I then be brought out again alive*** from the graves as Muḥammad says?' The question is one which implies a negative response: in other words, he does not think he will be brought to life after death.

67. ***Does not man recall*** (read as *yadhkuru* and *yadhdhakkaru*) ***that We created him before when he was not anything?*** The fact that Allah originated man from non-existence indicates that He can bring him back again.

68. ***By your Lord, We will collect them*** (those who deny the resurrection) ***and the shaytans together.*** We will gather each of them shackled to his shayṭān in chains. ***Then We will assemble them around*** the outside of ***Hell on their knees*** (read as *jiththiyyan* and *juththiyyan*).

69. ***Then We will drag out from every sect the one among them most insolent towards the All-Merciful.***

70. ***Then it is We who will know best those most deserving to roast in it*** – to suffer the most severe punishment in Hellfire.

71. ***There is not one of you who will not come to it.*** Everyone will go through Hellfire. ***That is the final decision of your Lord*** – and will not fail to happen.

72. ***Then We will rescue*** (read as *nunajjī* and *nunajji*) ***those who were godfearing*** – avoiding both *shirk* and unbelief – ***and We will leave the wrongdoers in it on their knees.***

73. ***When Our Clear Signs*** (the Qur'an) ***are recited to them*** (the believers and unbelievers), ***those who disbelieve say to those who believe, 'Which of the two parties*** – we or you – ***has the better position*** (read as *maqām* and *muqām*) – dwelling – ***and the more illustrious gathering*** (read as *nadī* or *nādi*) – meaning a place where the people gathered to talk*?'* The implication is: "We are better than you."

74. ***How many generations*** of past nations ***We have destroyed before them who had finer furnishings*** – the word used here, *athāth*, means both wealth and goods – ***and a better outward show!*** Just as Allah destroyed those before them for their unbelief, so He will also destroy these.

75. ***Say: 'As for those who are astray, let the All-Merciful prolong their term*** in this world to draw them on ***until they see what they were promised, whether it be the punishment*** – such as killing or imprisonment – ***or the Hour*** – which includes entering Hellfire. ***Then they will know who is in the worse position and has the weaker troops*** (helpers)*.'* – whether they or the believers are better off. Their troops are *shayṭāns* and the troops of the believers are the angels who watch over them.

76. ***Allah augments those who are guided*** – by belief – ***by giving them greater guidance*** in the form of the Signs which sent down to them. ***In your Lord's sight, right actions*** – obedience to Allah which will remain forever in the person's record – ***which are lasting are better both in reward and in end result.*** That is not the case with the actions of the unbelievers.

77. ***Have you seen him who rejects Our Signs*** (al-'Āṣī ibn Wā'il) ***and says, 'I will certainly be given wealth and children there'?*** He said this to Khabbāb ibn al-Aratt. When Khabbāb asked him for the money he was owed, he told him, "You will be resurrected after death." Al-'Āṣī replied, "If I am resurrected, I will be given wealth and children and will pay you then."

78. ***Has he surveyed the Unseen*** – has he been informed of the Unseen and that He will be given what he says – ***or has he a contract with the All-Merciful*** that he will be given that***?***

79. ***No indeed*** – he will not be given that***! We will*** give the command to ***write down what he says and prolong the punishment for him.*** He will have an increased punishment on account of that; another punishment in addition to the one he will receive for his unbelief.

80. ***We will inherit from him the things he is talking about*** (his wealth and children) ***and he will come to Us all alone*** on the Day of Rising, without either wealth or children.

81. ***They*** (the unbelievers of Makka) ***have taken other gods besides Allah*** – the idols which they worship – ***to be a source of power and strength for them*** – to act as their intercessors with Allah so that they will not be punished***!***

82. ***No indeed!*** Nothing can prevent their punishment. ***They will reject their worship and will be opposed to them*** – meaning either that they will join forces against them or that they will be enemies to them. The deities they worshipped will deny their worship, as in another *āyat*, *"It was not us they were worshipping."* (28:63)

83. ***Do you not see that We send the shayṭāns*** with authority ***against those who disbelieve to goad them on*** to commit acts of disobedience?

84. ***So do not try to hasten their punishment. We are simply counting out the number of their days*** – days and nights; or it may mean their breaths until the moment when they are punished.

85. ***On that Day We will gather those who were godfearing*** – because of their faith – ***to the All-Merciful with due ceremony.***

86. ***But We will drive the evildoers to Hell*** – because of their unbelief – ***like cattle to a watering hole*** – the word *wird* used here is the plural of *wārid*, which means someone who walks in extreme thirst.

87. ***They*** (mankind in general) ***have no right of intercession. None do but those who have a contract with the All-Merciful*** – unless they have made a contract based on the formula *Lā ilaha illā'llāh wa*

يَوْمَ نَحْشُرُ ٱلْمُتَّقِينَ إِلَى ٱلرَّحْمَٰنِ وَفْدًا ﴿٨٥﴾ وَنَسُوقُ ٱلْمُجْرِمِينَ
إِلَىٰ جَهَنَّمَ وِرْدًا ﴿٨٦﴾ لَّا يَمْلِكُونَ ٱلشَّفَٰعَةَ إِلَّا مَنِ ٱتَّخَذَ عِندَ
ٱلرَّحْمَٰنِ عَهْدًا ﴿٨٧﴾ وَقَالُوا۟ ٱتَّخَذَ ٱلرَّحْمَٰنُ وَلَدًا ﴿٨٨﴾ لَّقَدْ
جِئْتُمْ شَيْـًٔا إِدًّا ﴿٨٩﴾ تَكَادُ ٱلسَّمَٰوَٰتُ يَتَفَطَّرْنَ مِنْهُ
وَتَنشَقُّ ٱلْأَرْضُ وَتَخِرُّ ٱلْجِبَالُ هَدًّا ﴿٩٠﴾ أَن دَعَوْا۟ لِلرَّحْمَٰنِ وَلَدًا
﴿٩١﴾ وَمَا يَنۢبَغِى لِلرَّحْمَٰنِ أَن يَتَّخِذَ وَلَدًا ﴿٩٢﴾ إِن كُلُّ مَن فِى
ٱلسَّمَٰوَٰتِ وَٱلْأَرْضِ إِلَّآ ءَاتِى ٱلرَّحْمَٰنِ عَبْدًا ﴿٩٣﴾ لَّقَدْ أَحْصَىٰهُمْ
وَعَدَّهُمْ عَدًّا ﴿٩٤﴾ وَكُلُّهُمْ ءَاتِيهِ يَوْمَ ٱلْقِيَٰمَةِ فَرْدًا ﴿٩٥﴾
إِنَّ ٱلَّذِينَ ءَامَنُوا۟ وَعَمِلُوا۟ ٱلصَّٰلِحَٰتِ سَيَجْعَلُ لَهُمُ
ٱلرَّحْمَٰنُ وُدًّا ﴿٩٦﴾ فَإِنَّمَا يَسَّرْنَٰهُ بِلِسَانِكَ لِتُبَشِّرَ بِهِ
ٱلْمُتَّقِينَ وَتُنذِرَ بِهِۦ قَوْمًا لُّدًّا ﴿٩٧﴾ وَكَمْ أَهْلَكْنَا قَبْلَهُم
مِّن قَرْنٍ هَلْ تُحِسُّ مِنْهُم مِّنْ أَحَدٍ أَوْ تَسْمَعُ لَهُمْ رِكْزًۢا ﴿٩٨﴾

lā hawla walā quwwata illā billāh (There is no god but Allah and there is no power nor strength except by Allah).

88. ***They say, 'The All-Merciful has a child'*** – a reference to the Jews and the Christians and those who claim that the angels are the daughters of Allah. Then Allah said to them:

89. ***They have devised a*** very ***monstrous thing.***

90. ***The heavens are all but*** (read as *takādu* and *yakādu*) ***rent apart*** (read as *yatafaṭṭarna* and *yanfaṭirna*) ***and the earth split open and the mountains brought crashing down*** – on account of the horrendous nature of what they say –

91. ***…at their ascription of a son to the All-Merciful!*** Then Allah says:

92. ***It is not fitting*** or appropriate ***for the All-Merciful to have a child.***

93. ***There is no one in the heavens and earth who will not come to the All-Merciful as a slave*** – submissive and humble on the Day of Rising, including 'Uzayr and 'Īsā.

94. ***He has counted them and numbered them precisely.*** Nothing is hidden from Him, neither their total number nor each one of them individually.

95. ***Each of them will come to Him on the Day of Rising all alone*** – without property or any helper to defend him.

96. ***As for those who believe and do right actions, the All-Merciful will bestow His love on them*** – both between them, so that they love one another, and also His love for them directly.

97. ***We have made it*** (the Qur'an) ***easy on your*** Arabic ***tongue so that you may give good news to those who are godfearing*** – those who have won faith – ***and warn stubbornly hostile people by it*** – those who are stubborn in arguing by adducing falsehood. These are the unbelievers of Makka.

98. ***How many generations*** of previous nations ***We have destroyed before them*** for denying the Messengers***! Do you see a trace of any one of them, or hear even a whisper of them?*** No. Just as We destroyed them, so We will also destroy these.

سُورَةُ طه

بِسۡمِ ٱللَّهِ ٱلرَّحۡمَٰنِ ٱلرَّحِيمِ

طه ﴿١﴾ مَآ أَنزَلۡنَا عَلَيۡكَ ٱلۡقُرۡءَانَ لِتَشۡقَىٰٓ ﴿٢﴾ إِلَّا تَذۡكِرَةٗ
لِّمَن يَخۡشَىٰ ﴿٣﴾ تَنزِيلٗا مِّمَّنۡ خَلَقَ ٱلۡأَرۡضَ وَٱلسَّمَٰوَٰتِ ٱلۡعُلَى ﴿٤﴾
ٱلرَّحۡمَٰنُ عَلَى ٱلۡعَرۡشِ ٱسۡتَوَىٰ ﴿٥﴾ لَهُۥ مَا فِي ٱلسَّمَٰوَٰتِ وَمَا فِي
ٱلۡأَرۡضِ وَمَا بَيۡنَهُمَا وَمَا تَحۡتَ ٱلثَّرَىٰ ﴿٦﴾ وَإِن تَجۡهَرۡ بِٱلۡقَوۡلِ
فَإِنَّهُۥ يَعۡلَمُ ٱلسِّرَّ وَأَخۡفَى ﴿٧﴾ ٱللَّهُ لَآ إِلَٰهَ إِلَّا هُوَۖ لَهُ ٱلۡأَسۡمَآءُ
ٱلۡحُسۡنَىٰ ﴿٨﴾ وَهَلۡ أَتَىٰكَ حَدِيثُ مُوسَىٰٓ ﴿٩﴾ إِذۡ رَءَا نَارٗا
فَقَالَ لِأَهۡلِهِ ٱمۡكُثُوٓاْ إِنِّيٓ ءَانَسۡتُ نَارٗا لَّعَلِّيٓ ءَاتِيكُم مِّنۡهَا بِقَبَسٍ
أَوۡ أَجِدُ عَلَى ٱلنَّارِ هُدٗى ﴿١٠﴾ فَلَمَّآ أَتَىٰهَا نُودِيَ يَٰمُوسَىٰٓ ﴿١١﴾
إِنِّيٓ أَنَا۠ رَبُّكَ فَٱخۡلَعۡ نَعۡلَيۡكَۖ إِنَّكَ بِٱلۡوَادِ ٱلۡمُقَدَّسِ طُوٗى ﴿١٢﴾
وَأَنَا ٱخۡتَرۡتُكَ فَٱسۡتَمِعۡ لِمَا يُوحَىٰٓ ﴿١٣﴾ إِنَّنِيٓ أَنَا ٱللَّهُ لَآ إِلَٰهَ إِلَّآ أَنَا۠
فَٱعۡبُدۡنِي وَأَقِمِ ٱلصَّلَوٰةَ لِذِكۡرِيٓ ﴿١٤﴾ إِنَّ ٱلسَّاعَةَ ءَاتِيَةٌ
أَكَادُ أُخۡفِيهَا لِتُجۡزَىٰ كُلُّ نَفۡسِۭ بِمَا تَسۡعَىٰ ﴿١٥﴾ فَلَا يَصُدَّنَّكَ
عَنۡهَا مَن لَّا يُؤۡمِنُ بِهَا وَٱتَّبَعَ هَوَىٰهُ فَتَرۡدَىٰ ﴿١٦﴾ وَمَا تِلۡكَ
بِيَمِينِكَ يَٰمُوسَىٰ ﴿١٧﴾ قَالَ هِيَ عَصَايَ أَتَوَكَّؤُاْ عَلَيۡهَا
وَأَهُشُّ بِهَا عَلَىٰ غَنَمِي وَلِيَ فِيهَا مَـَٔارِبُ أُخۡرَىٰ ﴿١٨﴾ قَالَ أَلۡقِهَا

20. *Sūrat Ṭāhā*

This *sūra* is Makkan except for *āyats* 120 and 121, which are Madinan. It has 135 *ayats* and was sent down after *Maryam.*

1. ***Ṭā Hā.*** Allah knows best what is meant by that.

2. ***We did not send down the Qur'an to you,*** Muḥammad, ***to make you miserable*** – to cause him to tire himself out by what he does after it has been revealed, by the length of time he spends standing in prayer during the night. The implication is that he should be easier on himself –

3. ***...but*** We ***only*** sent it down ***as a reminder for those who are fearful*** of Allah...

4. ***...a Revelation from Him who created the earth and the high heavens,***

5. ***...the All-Merciful, established firmly upon the Throne.*** In the Arabic language the word *'arsh* (throne) signifies the seat of authority. The way that the "establishing" took place is in a way that is appropriate for Allah.

6. ***Everything in the heavens and everything on the earth and everything in between them and everything under the ground belongs to Him.*** The word for "ground", *tharā*, means the moist soil on the earth's surface, and the "everything" referred to here is the seven earths, because they are what is under it.

7. ***Though you speak out loud*** in *dhikr* or supplication to Allah, ***He knows your secrets*** – and has no need for audible vocalisation of your desires – ***and what is even more concealed.*** He knows what the self says and the thoughts which occur to it but are not spoken; so there is no need to make an effort to do it aloud.

8. ***Allah, there is no god but Him. The Most Beautiful Names are His.*** He has the ninety-nine Names reported in the *ḥadīth* mentioned above in the commentary on 17:110.

9. ***Has the story of Mūsā not reached you?***

10. ***When he saw a fire and said to his family*** (his wife) – while he was travelling from Madyan towards Egypt – ***'Wait here. I can make out a fire. Maybe I will bring you a brand from it*** – go and light the end of a branch or stick – ***or will find guidance there'*** to direct him on the path he wished to follow. He had become lost because he was travelling at night. He says "maybe" because he was not certain that he would be able to fulfil that promise.

11. ***Then when he reached it*** – the boxthorn bush from which the fire was coming – ***a voice called out, 'Mūsā!***

12. ***I am*** (read as *innī anā* and *innā anā*) – the use of the preposition *anā* ("I") here when it is also included in the previous word is to give greater stress to it – ***your Lord. Take off your sandals. You are in the holy*** (pure or blessed) ***valley of Ṭuwā.***

13. ***I have chosen you*** – from your people – ***so listen well to what is revealed*** by Me.

14. ***I am Allah. There is no god but Me, so worship Me and establish the prayer to remember Me.***

15. ***The Hour is coming but I have concealed it*** from people, even though its proximity will be indicated by certain signs, ***so that every self may be repaid for its efforts*** – both good and evil.

16. ***Do not let those who not believe in it and follow their whims and desires debar you from it*** – divert you from believing in it – ***or you will be destroyed.*** If you were to be turned from belief, then you would certainly be destroyed.

17. ***What is that in your right hand, Mūsā?'*** This question is one by which confirmation of it is intended, since the staff was miraculous.

18. ***He said, 'It is my staff. I lean on it*** when getting up and walking ***and*** I use it to ***beat down leaves*** from the trees ***for my sheep*** to eat ***with it; and I have other uses for it.'*** Other uses might be things like carrying provisions and water or driving away vermin.

19. ***He said, 'Throw it down, Mūsā.'***

20. ***He threw it down and suddenly it was a slithering snake.*** It became a huge snake which moved as swiftly on its belly as small snakes usually do.

21. ***He said, 'Take hold of it and have no fear. We will return it to its original form.*** Mūsā put his hand in its mouth and it reverted to being a staff. It is clear that the place where he placed his hand was the grip between the truncated forked branches at the end of the

يَٰمُوسَىٰ ﴿١٩﴾ فَأَلْقَىٰهَا فَإِذَا هِىَ حَيَّةٌ تَسْعَىٰ ﴿٢٠﴾ قَالَ خُذْهَا
وَلَا تَخَفْ ۖ سَنُعِيدُهَا سِيرَتَهَا ٱلْأُولَىٰ ﴿٢١﴾ وَٱضْمُمْ يَدَكَ
إِلَىٰ جَنَاحِكَ تَخْرُجْ بَيْضَآءَ مِنْ غَيْرِ سُوٓءٍ ءَايَةً أُخْرَىٰ ﴿٢٢﴾ لِنُرِيَكَ
مِنْ ءَايَٰتِنَا ٱلْكُبْرَى ﴿٢٣﴾ ٱذْهَبْ إِلَىٰ فِرْعَوْنَ إِنَّهُۥ طَغَىٰ ﴿٢٤﴾ قَالَ
رَبِّ ٱشْرَحْ لِى صَدْرِى ﴿٢٥﴾ وَيَسِّرْ لِىٓ أَمْرِى ﴿٢٦﴾ وَٱحْلُلْ عُقْدَةً مِّن
لِّسَانِى ﴿٢٧﴾ يَفْقَهُوا۟ قَوْلِى ﴿٢٨﴾ وَٱجْعَل لِّى وَزِيرًا مِّنْ أَهْلِى ﴿٢٩﴾ هَٰرُونَ
أَخِى ﴿٣٠﴾ ٱشْدُدْ بِهِۦٓ أَزْرِى ﴿٣١﴾ وَأَشْرِكْهُ فِىٓ أَمْرِى ﴿٣٢﴾ كَىْ نُسَبِّحَكَ
كَثِيرًا ﴿٣٣﴾ وَنَذْكُرَكَ كَثِيرًا ﴿٣٤﴾ إِنَّكَ كُنتَ بِنَا بَصِيرًا ﴿٣٥﴾ قَالَ قَدْ
أُوتِيتَ سُؤْلَكَ يَٰمُوسَىٰ ﴿٣٦﴾ وَلَقَدْ مَنَنَّا عَلَيْكَ مَرَّةً أُخْرَىٰٓ ﴿٣٧﴾
إِذْ أَوْحَيْنَآ إِلَىٰٓ أُمِّكَ مَا يُوحَىٰٓ ﴿٣٨﴾ أَنِ ٱقْذِفِيهِ فِى ٱلتَّابُوتِ فَٱقْذِفِيهِ
فِى ٱلْيَمِّ فَلْيُلْقِهِ ٱلْيَمُّ بِٱلسَّاحِلِ يَأْخُذْهُ عَدُوٌّ لِّى وَعَدُوٌّ لَّهُۥ ۚ وَأَلْقَيْتُ
عَلَيْكَ مَحَبَّةً مِّنِّى وَلِتُصْنَعَ عَلَىٰ عَيْنِىٓ ﴿٣٩﴾ إِذْ تَمْشِىٓ أُخْتُكَ
فَتَقُولُ هَلْ أَدُلُّكُمْ عَلَىٰ مَن يَكْفُلُهُۥ ۖ فَرَجَعْنَٰكَ إِلَىٰٓ أُمِّكَ كَىْ تَقَرَّ
عَيْنُهَا وَلَا تَحْزَنَ ۚ وَقَتَلْتَ نَفْسًا فَنَجَّيْنَٰكَ مِنَ ٱلْغَمِّ وَفَتَنَّٰكَ فُتُونًا ۚ
فَلَبِثْتَ سِنِينَ فِىٓ أَهْلِ مَدْيَنَ ثُمَّ جِئْتَ عَلَىٰ قَدَرٍ يَٰمُوسَىٰ ﴿٤٠﴾
وَٱصْطَنَعْتُكَ لِنَفْسِى ﴿٤١﴾ ٱذْهَبْ أَنتَ وَأَخُوكَ بِـَٔايَٰتِى وَلَا تَنِيَا
فِى ذِكْرِى ﴿٤٢﴾ ٱذْهَبَآ إِلَىٰ فِرْعَوْنَ إِنَّهُۥ طَغَىٰ ﴿٤٣﴾ فَقُولَا لَهُۥ قَوْلًا لَّيِّنًا
لَّعَلَّهُۥ يَتَذَكَّرُ أَوْ يَخْشَىٰ ﴿٤٤﴾ قَالَا رَبَّنَآ إِنَّنَا نَخَافُ أَن يَفْرُطَ عَلَيْنَآ
أَوْ أَن يَطْغَىٰ ﴿٤٥﴾ قَالَ لَا تَخَافَآ ۖ إِنَّنِى مَعَكُمَآ أَسْمَعُ وَأَرَىٰ
﴿٤٦﴾ فَأْتِيَاهُ فَقُولَآ إِنَّا رَسُولَا رَبِّكَ فَأَرْسِلْ مَعَنَا بَنِىٓ إِسْرَٰٓءِيلَ

staff. Mūsā was shown that so that he would not be alarmed when it turned into a snake in the presence of Pharaoh.

22. ***Put*** the palm of ***your*** right ***hand under your*** left ***arm*** – under the armpit – ***and press it to your side.*** Then bring it out. ***It will emerge pure white*** – not its normal dark colour – ***yet quite unharmed*** – the change to white was not due to leprosy and it shone like the rays of the sun, dazzling the eyes: ***another Sign.***

23. ***In this way We show you*** – when you do that – ***some of Our greatest Signs*** which reinforce Your Message. When he wanted it to revert to its original state, he put it under his arm again and then brought it out.

24. ***Go*** – as a Messenger – ***to Pharaoh*** and those with him. ***He has overstepped the bounds*** in his unbelief by claiming to be a god.'

25. ***He said, 'O Lord, expand my breast for me*** – and make it ample enough to bear the Message –

26. ***…and make my task*** in conveying your Message ***easy for me.***

27. ***Loosen the knot in my tongue*** – which he had acquired by burning it with a hot coal he had put in his mouth when he was a child.

28. ***…so that they will understand my words*** when I convey the Message.

29. ***Assign me a helper from my family*** to help me in my mission,

30. ***…my brother Hārūn.***

31. ***Strengthen my back by him***

32. ***…and let him share in my task*** – delivering the Message –

33. ***…so that we may glorify You much***

34. ***… and remember You much,***

35. ***…for You are watching us.'*** You know and see us and have blessed us with the Message.

36. ***He said, 'Your request has been granted, Mūsā.***

37. ***We were gracious to you another time***

38. ***…when We revealed to your mother*** – in a dream or by inspiration, when she bore him and feared that Pharaoh would kill him with the children he was killing:

39. ***"Place him in the box and throw it into the sea*** (the Nile) ***and the sea will wash it up on the shore, where an enemy of Mine and his*** (Pharaoh) ***will pick it up." I showered you with love from Me*** – so that people will love you and Pharaoh and everyone who sees you will love you – ***so that you would be brought up under My supervision*** – in My care and with My protection.

40. ***When your sister,*** Maryam, ***went*** to learn what had happened to you ***and*** wet-nurses had been summoned, but you would not accept the breast of any of them, she ***said, "Shall I direct you to someone who will take care of him?"*** His sister made her suggestion, which was accepted, and she brought his mother and he accepted her breast; and – ***that was how We returned you to your mother so that she might delight her eyes*** at finding you ***and not be grieved. You killed a man*** (the Copt in Egypt) – and you were upset at what might happen from Pharaoh – ***and We rescued you from trouble and tested you with many trials*** – other things from which We saved you. ***You stayed some*** ten ***years among the people of Madyan*** after you went there from Egypt and stayed with the Prophet Shu'ayb and married his daughter. ***Then you arrived at the pre-ordained time*** for the Message, which We knew would come – ***Mūsā.*** That was when he was forty years old.

41. ***I have chosen you for Myself*** for conveying My Message.

42. ***Go, you and your brother,*** to the people ***with My*** nine ***Signs and do not slacken in remembering Me*** – by glorification of Me and in other ways.

43. ***Go to Pharaoh; he has overstepped the bounds*** by claiming divinity.

44. ***But speak to him with gentle words*** in answering him ***so that perhaps he will pay heed or show some fear*** – and therefore revert.' Both hopes are mentioned although Allah knew, of course, that Pharaoh would not revert.

45. ***They said, 'Our Lord, we are afraid that he might persecute us*** and hasten to punish us – ***or overstep the bounds*** with arrogance towards us.'

46. ***He said, 'Have no fear. I will be with you*** – with My help – ***All-Hearing*** of what he says ***and All-Seeing*** of what he does.

وَلَا تُعَذِّبْهُمْ قَدْ جِئْنَٰكَ بِـَٔايَةٍ مِّن رَّبِّكَ وَٱلسَّلَٰمُ عَلَىٰ مَنِ ٱتَّبَعَ
ٱلْهُدَىٰٓ ﴿٤٧﴾ إِنَّا قَدْ أُوحِىَ إِلَيْنَآ أَنَّ ٱلْعَذَابَ عَلَىٰ مَن كَذَّبَ
وَتَوَلَّىٰ ﴿٤٨﴾ قَالَ فَمَن رَّبُّكُمَا يَٰمُوسَىٰ ﴿٤٩﴾ قَالَ رَبُّنَا ٱلَّذِىٓ أَعْطَىٰ
كُلَّ شَىْءٍ خَلْقَهُۥ ثُمَّ هَدَىٰ ﴿٥٠﴾ قَالَ فَمَا بَالُ ٱلْقُرُونِ ٱلْأُولَىٰ ﴿٥١﴾
قَالَ عِلْمُهَا عِندَ رَبِّى فِى كِتَٰبٍ لَّا يَضِلُّ رَبِّى وَلَا يَنسَى ﴿٥٢﴾
ٱلَّذِى جَعَلَ لَكُمُ ٱلْأَرْضَ مَهْدًا وَسَلَكَ لَكُمْ فِيهَا سُبُلًا وَأَنزَلَ
مِنَ ٱلسَّمَآءِ مَآءً فَأَخْرَجْنَا بِهِۦٓ أَزْوَٰجًا مِّن نَّبَاتٍ شَتَّىٰ ﴿٥٣﴾ كُلُوا۟
وَٱرْعَوْا۟ أَنْعَٰمَكُمْ إِنَّ فِى ذَٰلِكَ لَءَايَٰتٍ لِّأُو۟لِى ٱلنُّهَىٰ ﴿٥٤﴾ ۞ مِنْهَا
خَلَقْنَٰكُمْ وَفِيهَا نُعِيدُكُمْ وَمِنْهَا نُخْرِجُكُمْ تَارَةً أُخْرَىٰ ﴿٥٥﴾ وَلَقَدْ
أَرَيْنَٰهُ ءَايَٰتِنَا كُلَّهَا فَكَذَّبَ وَأَبَىٰ ﴿٥٦﴾ قَالَ أَجِئْتَنَا لِتُخْرِجَنَا
مِنْ أَرْضِنَا بِسِحْرِكَ يَٰمُوسَىٰ ﴿٥٧﴾ فَلَنَأْتِيَنَّكَ بِسِحْرٍ مِّثْلِهِۦ
فَٱجْعَلْ بَيْنَنَا وَبَيْنَكَ مَوْعِدًا لَّا نُخْلِفُهُۥ نَحْنُ وَلَآ أَنتَ مَكَانًا
سُوًى ﴿٥٨﴾ قَالَ مَوْعِدُكُمْ يَوْمُ ٱلزِّينَةِ وَأَن يُحْشَرَ ٱلنَّاسُ ضُحًى
﴿٥٩﴾ فَتَوَلَّىٰ فِرْعَوْنُ فَجَمَعَ كَيْدَهُۥ ثُمَّ أَتَىٰ ﴿٦٠﴾ قَالَ لَهُم
مُّوسَىٰ وَيْلَكُمْ لَا تَفْتَرُوا۟ عَلَى ٱللَّهِ كَذِبًا فَيُسْحِتَكُم بِعَذَابٍ
وَقَدْ خَابَ مَنِ ٱفْتَرَىٰ ﴿٦١﴾ فَتَنَٰزَعُوٓا۟ أَمْرَهُم بَيْنَهُمْ وَأَسَرُّوا۟
ٱلنَّجْوَىٰ ﴿٦٢﴾ قَالُوٓا۟ إِنْ هَٰذَٰنِ لَسَٰحِرَٰنِ يُرِيدَانِ أَن يُخْرِجَاكُم
مِّنْ أَرْضِكُم بِسِحْرِهِمَا وَيَذْهَبَا بِطَرِيقَتِكُمُ ٱلْمُثْلَىٰ ﴿٦٣﴾ فَأَجْمِعُوا۟
كَيْدَكُمْ ثُمَّ ٱئْتُوا۟ صَفًّا وَقَدْ أَفْلَحَ ٱلْيَوْمَ مَنِ ٱسْتَعْلَىٰ ﴿٦٤﴾
قَالُوا۟ يَٰمُوسَىٰٓ إِمَّآ أَن تُلْقِىَ وَإِمَّآ أَن نَّكُونَ أَوَّلَ مَنْ أَلْقَىٰ ﴿٦٥﴾ قَالَ

47. ***Go to him and say, "We are your Lord's Messengers, so send the tribe of Israel away with us*** to Syria ***and do not punish them*** – do not continue to force them to do your onerous tasks, like digging, building and carrying heavy loads. ***We have brought you a Sign*** (evidence) ***from your Lord*** that we are speaking the truth regarding the Message. ***Peace be upon those who follow the guidance.*** They alone will be safe from punishment.

48. ***It has been revealed to us that punishment is for him who denies the truth*** which we have brought ***and turns away.'"*** The two of them went to Pharaoh and said all of these things.

49. ***Pharaoh said, 'Who then is your Lord, Mūsā?'*** He confined himself to asking this because it is the main issue, and then he pointed out to him how he himself had brought him up.

50. ***He*** (Mūsā) ***said, 'Our Lord is He who gives each thing its created form*** – distinct from every other – ***and then guides it*** – guides the animals among them to their food, drink, procreation and other things.***'***

51. ***He*** (Pharaoh) ***said, 'What about the previous generations*** such as the people of Nūḥ, Hūd, Lūt, and Ṣāliḥ, with their worship of idols***?'***

52. ***He*** (Mūsā) ***said, 'Knowledge of them*** (their state) ***is*** kept ***with my Lord in a Book*** (the Preserved Tablet). He will repay them accordingly on the Day of Rising. ***My Lord does not misplace, nor does He forget.'*** Nothing is hidden from Him and He does not forget anything.

53. ***It is He who made the earth a cradle for you and threaded pathways for you through it*** to make it easy for you to travel ***and sent down water*** – as rain – ***from the sky by which We have brought forth various different types of plants.*** Allah says this to complete His description of Mūsā and also addresses the people of Makka, mentioning that the rain brings forth different types of plants which vary in colour, taste and other things.

54. ***Eat*** from these plants ***and pasture your livestock*** among them. The Arabic word for "livestock", *an'ām*, includes camels, cattle and sheep, and gives the sense of something being allowed. ***Certainly there are Signs in that for people of sound intellect.*** The word for "intellect", *nuhā*, is the plural of *nuhya*, so called because it prevents (*yanha*) a person from committing ugly actions.

55. ***From it*** (the earth) ***We created you*** – by the creation of your ancestor, Ādam; ***to it We will return you*** – by burial after death; ***and from it We will bring you forth a second time*** – by the Resurrection, just as We brought you forth the first time when We created you.

56. ***We showed him*** (Pharaoh) ***all of Our*** nine ***Signs, but he denied*** them ***and spurned them*** and claimed that it was all magic, and refused to declare that Allah is One.

57. ***He said, 'Have you come to us to expel us from our land*** (Egypt) and to be the king in it ***by means of your magic, Mūsā?***

58. ***We will bring you magic to match it. So fix a time between us and you which neither we nor you will fail to keep, at a place where we can meet halfway*** (read as *suwā* and *siwā*),' – meaning a place which is the same distance from each of the two parties.

59. ***He*** (Mūsā) ***said, 'Your time is the day of the Festival*** – the Day of their *'Īd*, during which they dressed up and gathered together. ***The people*** of Egypt ***should gather in the late morning'*** to see what would happen.

60. ***So Pharaoh went away and concocted his scheme*** together with the magicians, ***and then he arrived*** at the appointed time.

61. ***Mūsā said to them*** – there were seventy-two of them, each of whom had a rope and staff – ***'Woe to you!*** Allah will punish you. ***Do not fabricate lies against Allah*** – by associating anyone with Him – ***or He will annihilate*** (read as *yusḥitakum* and *yasḥātakum*) ***you with His punishment*** and destroy you. ***Fabricators of lies*** against Allah ***are bound to fail.'***

62. ***They argued among themselves about the matter*** – about Mūsā and his brother – ***and had a secret conference*** concerning them.

63. ***They said*** among themselves: ***'These*** (read as *hādhāni* and *hādhīni*) ***two magicians*** (Mūsā and his brother) ***desire by their magic to expel you from your land and abolish your most excellent way of life.***

64. ***So decide*** (read as *fa-jmi'ū* and *fa-jmā'ū*) ***on your scheme*** – to use magic – ***and then arrive together in force*** (in ranks). ***He who***

بَلْ أَلْقُوا۟ ۖ فَإِذَا حِبَالُهُمْ وَعِصِيُّهُمْ يُخَيَّلُ إِلَيْهِ مِن سِحْرِهِمْ أَنَّهَا تَسْعَىٰ
﴿٦٦﴾ فَأَوْجَسَ فِى نَفْسِهِۦ خِيفَةً مُّوسَىٰ ﴿٦٧﴾ قُلْنَا لَا تَخَفْ إِنَّكَ
أَنتَ ٱلْأَعْلَىٰ ﴿٦٨﴾ وَأَلْقِ مَا فِى يَمِينِكَ تَلْقَفْ مَا صَنَعُوٓا۟ ۖ إِنَّمَا صَنَعُوا۟
كَيْدُ سَٰحِرٍ ۖ وَلَا يُفْلِحُ ٱلسَّاحِرُ حَيْثُ أَتَىٰ ﴿٦٩﴾ فَأُلْقِىَ ٱلسَّحَرَةُ سُجَّدًا
قَالُوٓا۟ ءَامَنَّا بِرَبِّ هَٰرُونَ وَمُوسَىٰ ﴿٧٠﴾ قَالَ ءَامَنتُمْ لَهُۥ قَبْلَ أَنْ ءَاذَنَ
لَكُمْ ۖ إِنَّهُۥ لَكَبِيرُكُمُ ٱلَّذِى عَلَّمَكُمُ ٱلسِّحْرَ ۖ فَلَأُقَطِّعَنَّ أَيْدِيَكُمْ
وَأَرْجُلَكُم مِّنْ خِلَٰفٍ وَلَأُصَلِّبَنَّكُمْ فِى جُذُوعِ ٱلنَّخْلِ وَلَتَعْلَمُنَّ
أَيُّنَآ أَشَدُّ عَذَابًا وَأَبْقَىٰ ﴿٧١﴾ قَالُوا۟ لَن نُّؤْثِرَكَ عَلَىٰ مَا جَآءَنَا مِنَ
ٱلْبَيِّنَٰتِ وَٱلَّذِى فَطَرَنَا ۖ فَٱقْضِ مَآ أَنتَ قَاضٍ ۖ إِنَّمَا تَقْضِى هَٰذِهِ
ٱلْحَيَوٰةَ ٱلدُّنْيَآ ﴿٧٢﴾ إِنَّآ ءَامَنَّا بِرَبِّنَا لِيَغْفِرَ لَنَا خَطَٰيَٰنَا وَمَآ أَكْرَهْتَنَا
عَلَيْهِ مِنَ ٱلسِّحْرِ ۗ وَٱللَّهُ خَيْرٌ وَأَبْقَىٰٓ ﴿٧٣﴾ إِنَّهُۥ مَن يَأْتِ رَبَّهُۥ مُجْرِمًا
فَإِنَّ لَهُۥ جَهَنَّمَ لَا يَمُوتُ فِيهَا وَلَا يَحْيَىٰ ﴿٧٤﴾ وَمَن يَأْتِهِۦ مُؤْمِنًا قَدْ
عَمِلَ ٱلصَّٰلِحَٰتِ فَأُو۟لَٰٓئِكَ لَهُمُ ٱلدَّرَجَٰتُ ٱلْعُلَىٰ ﴿٧٥﴾ جَنَّٰتُ عَدْنٍ
تَجْرِى مِن تَحْتِهَا ٱلْأَنْهَٰرُ خَٰلِدِينَ فِيهَا ۚ وَذَٰلِكَ جَزَآءُ مَن تَزَكَّىٰ ﴿٧٦﴾
وَلَقَدْ أَوْحَيْنَآ إِلَىٰ مُوسَىٰٓ أَنْ أَسْرِ بِعِبَادِى فَٱضْرِبْ لَهُمْ طَرِيقًا
فِى ٱلْبَحْرِ يَبَسًا لَّا تَخَٰفُ دَرَكًا وَلَا تَخْشَىٰ ﴿٧٧﴾ فَأَتْبَعَهُمْ فِرْعَوْنُ
بِجُنُودِهِۦ فَغَشِيَهُم مِّنَ ٱلْيَمِّ مَا غَشِيَهُمْ ﴿٧٨﴾ وَأَضَلَّ فِرْعَوْنُ قَوْمَهُۥ
وَمَا هَدَىٰ ﴿٧٩﴾ يَٰبَنِىٓ إِسْرَٰٓءِيلَ قَدْ أَنجَيْنَٰكُم مِّنْ عَدُوِّكُمْ وَوَٰعَدْنَٰكُمْ
جَانِبَ ٱلطُّورِ ٱلْأَيْمَنَ وَنَزَّلْنَا عَلَيْكُمُ ٱلْمَنَّ وَٱلسَّلْوَىٰ ﴿٨٠﴾ كُلُوا۟
مِن طَيِّبَٰتِ مَا رَزَقْنَٰكُمْ وَلَا تَطْغَوْا۟ فِيهِ فَيَحِلَّ عَلَيْكُمْ غَضَبِى ۖ

gains the upper hand today and is victorious ***will definitely pros - per.'***

65. ***They said, 'Mūsā*** – choose – ***will you throw*** your staff first ***or shall we be the first to throw?'***

66. ***He said, 'No, you throw.'*** They threw. ***And suddenly their ropes and staffs appeared to him, by their magic, to be*** snakes ***slithering about.***

67. ***Mūsā experienced in himself a feeling of alarm*** because their magic appeared to be similar to his miracle, and so it might confuse people and they would not believe him.

68. ***We said*** to him: ***'Have no fear. You will have the upper hand.***

69. ***Throw down what is in your right hand*** (your staff). ***It will swallow up their handiwork. Their handiwork is just a magician's trick. Magicians do not prosper wherever they go.'*** Mūsā threw down his staff and it swallowed up what they had produced.

70. ***The magicians threw themselves down in prostration*** to Allah. ***They said, 'We believe in the Lord of Hārūn and Mūsā.'***

71. ***Pharaoh said, 'Do you believe in him before I have authorised you? He is your chief, the one who taught you magic. I will cut off your hands and feet alternately*** – your right hands and left feet – ***and have you crucified on palm trunks. Then you will know for certain which of us*** – him or the Lord of Mūsā – ***has the harsher and longer lasting punishment.'***

72. ***They said, 'We will never prefer you to*** – and choose you over – ***the Clear Signs which have come to us*** – which show the truthfulness of Mūsā – ***nor to Him who brought us into being. Decide on any judgement you like.*** Do what you said you would do. ***Your jurisdiction only covers the life of this world.***

73. ***We have put our faith in our Lord, so that He may forgive us for our mistakes*** in committing *shirk* and other things ***and for the magic which you forced us to perform*** – to learn and do to oppose Mūsā. ***Allah is better*** in terms of reward than you are ***and longer lasting*** in terms of punishment.'

74. Allah says: ***As for those who come to their Lord as evildoers*** – unbelievers, like Pharaoh – ***they will have Hell, where they will nei -***

ther die – so that they have a rest – ***nor stay alive*** – so they can benefit.

75. ***But as for those who come to Him as believers, having done right actions*** – both obligatory and supererogatory ones – ***they will have the highest ranks:***

76. ***Gardens of Eden*** where they will abide ***with rivers flowing under them, remaining in them timelessly, for ever. That is the reward of those who purify themselves*** of wrong actions.

77. ***We revealed to Mūsā, 'Travel*** (read as *an asri* and *an'sri*) ***with My slaves by night*** out of the land of Egypt. ***Strike a dry path for them*** with your staff ***through the sea.*** Mūsā obeyed the command and Allah made the land dry for him, and so they crossed on it. ***Have no fear of being overtaken*** by Pharaoh ***and do not be afraid*** of drowning.'

78. ***Pharaoh pursued them with his troops and the sea overwhelmed them utterly*** and drowned them.

79. ***Pharaoh misguided his people*** by calling on them to worship him. ***He was no guide*** but rather caused them to fall into destruction, which was the opposite of his words: *"I only guide you to the Path of Rectitude."* (40:29)

80. ***Tribe of Israel, We rescued you from your enemy*** (Pharaoh) by drowning him ***and made an appointment with you on the right hand side of the Mount*** – where Mūsā was given the Torah – so that it might serve as basis for action – ***and sent down manna and quails for you.*** This *āyat* was addressed to those Jews who were present at the time of the Prophet, may Allah bless him and grant him peace, and were being addressed regarding the blessings which were bestowed on their ancestors in the time of the Prophet Mūsā. This is a prelude to the following *āyat*:

81. ***Eat of the good things We have provided for you*** – as blessings – ***but do not go to excess in it*** by being ungrateful for your blessings ***or My anger will be unleashed*** (read as *yaḥullu* and *yaḥlulu*) ***on you. Anyone who has My anger unleashed*** (read as *yaḥillu* and *yaḥlil*) ***on him has plunged to his ruin*** – into the Fire.

82. ***But I am Ever-Forgiving to anyone who repents*** – of committing *shirk* – ***and believes*** – by affirming Allah's unity – ***and acts***

وَمَن يَحۡلِلۡ عَلَيۡهِ غَضَبِي فَقَدۡ هَوَىٰ ﴿٨١﴾ وَإِنِّي لَغَفَّارٞ لِّمَن تَابَ
وَءَامَنَ وَعَمِلَ صَٰلِحٗا ثُمَّ ٱهۡتَدَىٰ ﴿٨٢﴾ ۞ وَمَآ أَعۡجَلَكَ عَن
قَوۡمِكَ يَٰمُوسَىٰ ﴿٨٣﴾ قَالَ هُمۡ أُوْلَآءِ عَلَىٰٓ أَثَرِي وَعَجِلۡتُ إِلَيۡكَ
رَبِّ لِتَرۡضَىٰ ﴿٨٤﴾ قَالَ فَإِنَّا قَدۡ فَتَنَّا قَوۡمَكَ مِنۢ بَعۡدِكَ وَأَضَلَّهُمُ
ٱلسَّامِرِيُّ ﴿٨٥﴾ فَرَجَعَ مُوسَىٰٓ إِلَىٰ قَوۡمِهِۦ غَضۡبَٰنَ أَسِفٗاۚ قَالَ
يَٰقَوۡمِ أَلَمۡ يَعِدۡكُمۡ رَبُّكُمۡ وَعۡدًا حَسَنًاۚ أَفَطَالَ عَلَيۡكُمُ
ٱلۡعَهۡدُ أَمۡ أَرَدتُّمۡ أَن يَحِلَّ عَلَيۡكُمۡ غَضَبٞ مِّن رَّبِّكُمۡ فَأَخۡلَفۡتُم
مَّوۡعِدِي ﴿٨٦﴾ قَالُواْ مَآ أَخۡلَفۡنَا مَوۡعِدَكَ بِمَلۡكِنَا وَلَٰكِنَّا حُمِّلۡنَآ
أَوۡزَارٗا مِّن زِينَةِ ٱلۡقَوۡمِ فَقَذَفۡنَٰهَا فَكَذَٰلِكَ أَلۡقَى ٱلسَّامِرِيُّ ﴿٨٧﴾
فَأَخۡرَجَ لَهُمۡ عِجۡلٗا جَسَدٗا لَّهُۥ خُوَارٞ فَقَالُواْ هَٰذَآ إِلَٰهُكُمۡ
وَإِلَٰهُ مُوسَىٰ فَنَسِيَ ﴿٨٨﴾ أَفَلَا يَرَوۡنَ أَلَّا يَرۡجِعُ إِلَيۡهِمۡ قَوۡلٗا وَلَا
يَمۡلِكُ لَهُمۡ ضَرّٗا وَلَا نَفۡعٗا ﴿٨٩﴾ وَلَقَدۡ قَالَ لَهُمۡ هَٰرُونُ مِن قَبۡلُ
يَٰقَوۡمِ إِنَّمَا فُتِنتُم بِهِۦۖ وَإِنَّ رَبَّكُمُ ٱلرَّحۡمَٰنُ فَٱتَّبِعُونِي وَأَطِيعُوٓاْ
أَمۡرِي ﴿٩٠﴾ قَالُواْ لَن نَّبۡرَحَ عَلَيۡهِ عَٰكِفِينَ حَتَّىٰ يَرۡجِعَ إِلَيۡنَا مُوسَىٰ
﴿٩١﴾ قَالَ يَٰهَٰرُونُ مَا مَنَعَكَ إِذۡ رَأَيۡتَهُمۡ ضَلُّوٓاْ ﴿٩٢﴾ أَلَّا تَتَّبِعَنِۖ
أَفَعَصَيۡتَ أَمۡرِي ﴿٩٣﴾ قَالَ يَبۡنَؤُمَّ لَا تَأۡخُذۡ بِلِحۡيَتِي وَلَا بِرَأۡسِيٓۖ
إِنِّي خَشِيتُ أَن تَقُولَ فَرَّقۡتَ بَيۡنَ بَنِيٓ إِسۡرَٰٓءِيلَ وَلَمۡ تَرۡقُبۡ
قَوۡلِي ﴿٩٤﴾ قَالَ فَمَا خَطۡبُكَ يَٰسَٰمِرِيُّ ﴿٩٥﴾ قَالَ بَصُرۡتُ
بِمَا لَمۡ يَبۡصُرُواْ بِهِۦ فَقَبَضۡتُ قَبۡضَةٗ مِّنۡ أَثَرِ ٱلرَّسُولِ
فَنَبَذۡتُهَا وَكَذَٰلِكَ سَوَّلَتۡ لِي نَفۡسِي ﴿٩٦﴾ قَالَ

rightly – by being sincere in obligatory and supererogatory acts – ***and then is guided*** – by continuing to act in the way that has been mentioned until he dies.

83. ***'Why have you hurried on ahead of your people, Mūsā*** to come to the meeting to receive the Torah***?'***

84. ***He said, 'They are following in my tracks*** – coming along close behind me***. I have hurried on ahead to you, My Lord, to gain*** more of ***Your good pleasure.'*** The reply was accepted because the excuse showed his good opinion of Allah.

85. ***He*** (Allah) ***said, 'We tried your people after you left*** them ***and the Sāmirī has misguided them*** into worshipping the Calf.***'***

86. ***Mūsā returned to his people in anger and great sorrow. He said, 'My people, did not your Lord make you a handsome promise*** to give you the Torah***? Did the fulfilment of the contract seem too long to you*** – a reference to the time Mūsā was away from them – ***or did you want to unleash your Lord's anger upon yourselves*** – did you want Allah to be wrathful towards you for worshipping the Calf – ***so you broke your promise to me*** and did not follow me***?'***

87. ***They said, 'We did not break our promise to you of our own volition*** (read as *malk*, *milk* and *mulk*) – meaning that they did not do it by their own power or from themselves. ***But we were weighed down*** (read as *ḥummilnā* and *ḥamalnā*) ***with the heavy loads of the people's jewellery*** – the jewellery of the people of Pharaoh which the tribe of Israel had borrowed from them for a wedding and which was still in their possession – ***and we threw them in*** – into the fire, as the Sāmirī commanded – ***for that is what the Sāmirī did.'*** The Sāmirī told them to throw it in, just as he was throwing in the jewellery which he had, and also some of the earth he had taken from the footprints of Jibrīl's horse as will be explained.

88. ***Then he produced a calf for them*** – from the jewellery – ***a physical form*** of flesh and blood ***which made a lowing sound*** – a sound that could be heard. It was transformed because of the earth from the angel's footprints, which produces life in anything in which it is placed. After it was made, he put the dust in its mouth. ***So they*** (the Sāmirī and his followers) ***said, 'This is your god – and Musa's***

god as well, but he (Mūsā) ***forgot*** his Lord and went to look for it.***'*** Allah said:

89. ***Could they not see that it*** (the Calf) ***did not reply to them and that it possessed no power to either harm or benefit them?*** It had no power to do anything, so why did they take it as a god?

90. ***Hārūn had earlier said to them*** – before Mūsā returned – ***'My people, it is just a trial for you. Your Lord is the All-Merciful, so follow me*** in worshipping Allah ***and obey my command!'***

91. ***They said, 'We will not stop devoting ourselves to it*** and worshipping it ***until Mūsā returns to us.'***

92. ***He*** (Mūsā) ***said*** – when he returned – ***'What prevented you following me,*** Hārūn, ***when you saw that they had gone astray*** by worshipping the Calf***?***

93. ***Did you too, then, disobey my command*** by staying among those who worshipped something other than Allah***?'*** The *lā* in this sentence is redundant.

94. ***He*** (Hārūn) ***said, 'Son of my mother,*** (read as *yabna'ummi* and *yabna'umma*) – he mentioned this to soften Mūsā's heart, as he had grabbed his hair in his right hand in anger – ***do not seize me by the beard or by the hair. I was afraid that*** if I had followed you, then all who did not worship the Calf would have followed me as well, and ***you would say*** in anger at me: ***"You have caused division in the tribe of Israel and taken no notice of anything I said."'***

95. ***He said, 'What do you think you were doing, Sāmirī?'*** Why were calling people to this?

96. ***He said, 'I saw what they did not see*** (read as *yabṣurū* and *tabṣuru,* "you did not see"). I knew what they did not know. ***So I gathered up a handful*** of earth ***from the Messenger's footprints*** – from the tracks left by the hooves of Jibrīl's horse – ***and threw it in*** – into the manufactured Calf***. That is what my inner self urged me to do.'*** That was what his self made seem attractive to him: to take the handful of earth and throw it into something which had no spirit so that it would have a spirit. He said, "I saw your people ask you to make a god for them, and so my self told me to make the Calf as a god for them."

فَٱذۡهَبۡ فَإِنَّ لَكَ فِي ٱلۡحَيَوٰةِ أَن تَقُولَ لَا مِسَاسَۖ وَإِنَّ لَكَ
مَوۡعِدٗا لَّن تُخۡلَفَهُۥۖ وَٱنظُرۡ إِلَىٰٓ إِلَٰهِكَ ٱلَّذِي ظَلۡتَ عَلَيۡهِ
عَاكِفٗاۖ لَّنُحَرِّقَنَّهُۥ ثُمَّ لَنَنسِفَنَّهُۥ فِي ٱلۡيَمِّ نَسۡفًا ٩٧ إِنَّمَآ
إِلَٰهُكُمُ ٱللَّهُ ٱلَّذِي لَآ إِلَٰهَ إِلَّا هُوَۚ وَسِعَ كُلَّ شَيۡءٍ عِلۡمٗا ٩٨
كَذَٰلِكَ نَقُصُّ عَلَيۡكَ مِنۡ أَنۢبَآءِ مَا قَدۡ سَبَقَۚ وَقَدۡ ءَاتَيۡنَٰكَ مِن لَّدُنَّا
ذِكۡرٗا ٩٩ مَّنۡ أَعۡرَضَ عَنۡهُ فَإِنَّهُۥ يَحۡمِلُ يَوۡمَ ٱلۡقِيَٰمَةِ وِزۡرًا
١٠٠ خَٰلِدِينَ فِيهِۖ وَسَآءَ لَهُمۡ يَوۡمَ ٱلۡقِيَٰمَةِ حِمۡلٗا ١٠١ يَوۡمَ يُنفَخُ
فِي ٱلصُّورِۚ وَنَحۡشُرُ ٱلۡمُجۡرِمِينَ يَوۡمَئِذٖ زُرۡقٗا ١٠٢ يَتَخَٰفَتُونَ
بَيۡنَهُمۡ إِن لَّبِثۡتُمۡ إِلَّا عَشۡرٗا ١٠٣ نَّحۡنُ أَعۡلَمُ بِمَا يَقُولُونَ إِذۡ يَقُولُ
أَمۡثَلُهُمۡ طَرِيقَةً إِن لَّبِثۡتُمۡ إِلَّا يَوۡمٗا ١٠٤ وَيَسۡـَٔلُونَكَ عَنِ ٱلۡجِبَالِ
فَقُلۡ يَنسِفُهَا رَبِّي نَسۡفٗا ١٠٥ فَيَذَرُهَا قَاعٗا صَفۡصَفٗا ١٠٦
لَّا تَرَىٰ فِيهَا عِوَجٗا وَلَآ أَمۡتٗا ١٠٧ يَوۡمَئِذٖ يَتَّبِعُونَ ٱلدَّاعِيَ
لَا عِوَجَ لَهُۥۖ وَخَشَعَتِ ٱلۡأَصۡوَاتُ لِلرَّحۡمَٰنِ فَلَا تَسۡمَعُ إِلَّا هَمۡسٗا
١٠٨ يَوۡمَئِذٖ لَّا تَنفَعُ ٱلشَّفَٰعَةُ إِلَّا مَنۡ أَذِنَ لَهُ ٱلرَّحۡمَٰنُ وَرَضِيَ لَهُۥ
قَوۡلٗا ١٠٩ يَعۡلَمُ مَا بَيۡنَ أَيۡدِيهِمۡ وَمَا خَلۡفَهُمۡ وَلَا يُحِيطُونَ بِهِۦ
عِلۡمٗا ١١٠ ۞ وَعَنَتِ ٱلۡوُجُوهُ لِلۡحَيِّ ٱلۡقَيُّومِۖ وَقَدۡ خَابَ مَنۡ
حَمَلَ ظُلۡمٗا ١١١ وَمَن يَعۡمَلۡ مِنَ ٱلصَّٰلِحَٰتِ وَهُوَ مُؤۡمِنٞ فَلَا
يَخَافُ ظُلۡمٗا وَلَا هَضۡمٗا ١١٢ وَكَذَٰلِكَ أَنزَلۡنَٰهُ قُرۡءَانًا عَرَبِيّٗا
وَصَرَّفۡنَا فِيهِ مِنَ ٱلۡوَعِيدِ لَعَلَّهُمۡ يَتَّقُونَ أَوۡ يُحۡدِثُ لَهُمۡ ذِكۡرٗا ١١٣
فَتَعَٰلَى ٱللَّهُ ٱلۡمَلِكُ ٱلۡحَقُّۗ وَلَا تَعۡجَلۡ بِٱلۡقُرۡءَانِ مِن قَبۡلِ أَن

97. ***He*** (Mūsā) ***said*** to him***, 'Go*** – from us! ***In this world*** – for as long as you live – ***you will have to say*** to whomever you meet, ***"Untouchable!"*** – meaning: "Do not come near me." He wandered in the desert and if anyone touched him or he touched anyone, they came down with a fever. ***And you have an appointment*** with your punishment ***which you will not fail to keep*** (read as *tukhlafahu* and *tukhlifahu*)***. Look at your god to which you devoted so much time! We will burn it up*** with fire ***and then scatter it as dust into*** the air above ***the sea.*** Mūsā did that after he slaughtered it.

98. ***Your god is Allah alone, there is no god but Him. He encom - passes all things in His knowledge.'***

99. ***In this way We give you news*** – which We recount to you, Muḥammad – ***of what has gone before*** – in respect of this story and other reports of past communities – ***and We have given you a reminder*** (the Qur'an) ***direct from Us.***

100. ***Those who turn away from it*** and do not believe in it ***will bear a heavy burden*** of sin ***on the Day of Rising,***

101. ***...remaining in it*** – in the punishment, on account of the burden – ***timelessly, for ever. What an evil load they will bear on the Day of Rising!***

102. ***On the Day*** the second blast of ***the Trumpet is blown, and We gather the evildoers*** (the unbelievers) ***sightless*** – the word used here, *zurq*, which normally means blue, comes to mean blind because the eyes turn bluish when blind from cataracts ***– on that Day...***

103. ***...they will whisper secretly to one other, 'You only stayed*** in this world ***for ten*** days and nights.'

104. ***We know best what they will say*** about that, but the truth is different from what they say ***when the most correct of them will say, 'You only stayed one day.'*** This statement is the most correct because it reflects the shortness of their time in this world once they see the Next World with all its terrors.

105. ***They will ask you about the mountains*** and how they will be on the Day of Rising. ***Say*** to them***: 'My Lord will scatter them as dust,*** like sand blown by the wind.

106. ***He will leave them as a barren, level plain***

107. ***…on which you will see no dip or gradient.'*** It will be spread out flat.

108. ***On that Day*** – the Last Day when the mountains become dust – ***they*** (all people) ***will follow the Summoner*** after they rise from the graves, to the Gathering led by his voice. This refers to Isrāfīl, who will say, "Come to the presentation of the All-Merciful" – ***who has no crookedness in him at all*** – to his followers, meaning that they will not be able to not follow him. ***Voices will be humbled*** and silent ***before the All-Merciful and nothing but a whisper will be heard.*** The only thing which will be heard will be the sound of feet as they come to the Gathering, sounding like the tramp of camels when they walk.

109. ***On that Day intercession will not be of any use except for him whom the All-Merciful has authorised*** to intercede ***and with whose speech He is well-pleased.*** The speech with which He is pleased is the formula, "There is no god but Allah."

110. ***He knows what is in front of them*** – of the business of the Next World – ***and behind them*** – of this world, ***but their knowledge does not encompass Him.*** They do not know what He is like.

111. ***Faces will be humbled to*** Allah, ***the Living, the All-Sustaining, and anyone weighed down with wrongdoing*** (committing *shirk*) ***will have failed.***

112. ***But anyone who does right actions*** (acts of obedience)***, being a believer, need fear no wrong*** – through his evil deeds being exaggerated – ***or any belittlement*** – through his good actions being made less.

113. ***In this way*** – as We have recounted this to you – ***We have sent it down as an Arabic Qur'an and We have made*** and repeated ***various threats in it so that perhaps they may be godfearing*** – and fear committing *shirk* – ***or it*** (the Qur'an) ***may spur them into remembrance*** of the destruction of those nations before them and they will learn from that.

114. ***High exalted be Allah, the King, the Real*** above what the idolaters say***! Do not rush ahead with the Qur'an*** and recite it ***before its revelation to you is complete*** – before Jibrīl finishes conveying it. ***And say: 'My Lord, increase me in knowledge*** through the Qur'an.'

يُقْضَىٰٓ إِلَيْكَ وَحْيُهُۥ ۖ وَقُل رَّبِّ زِدْنِى عِلْمًا ﴿١١٤﴾ وَلَقَدْ عَهِدْنَآ
إِلَىٰٓ ءَادَمَ مِن قَبْلُ فَنَسِىَ وَلَمْ نَجِدْ لَهُۥ عَزْمًا ﴿١١٥﴾ وَإِذْ قُلْنَا
لِلْمَلَٰٓئِكَةِ ٱسْجُدُوا۟ لِءَادَمَ فَسَجَدُوٓا۟ إِلَّآ إِبْلِيسَ أَبَىٰ
﴿١١٦﴾ فَقُلْنَا يَٰٓـَٔادَمُ إِنَّ هَٰذَا عَدُوٌّ لَّكَ وَلِزَوْجِكَ فَلَا يُخْرِجَنَّكُمَا
مِنَ ٱلْجَنَّةِ فَتَشْقَىٰٓ ﴿١١٧﴾ إِنَّ لَكَ أَلَّا تَجُوعَ فِيهَا وَلَا تَعْرَىٰ ﴿١١٨﴾
وَأَنَّكَ لَا تَظْمَؤُا۟ فِيهَا وَلَا تَضْحَىٰ ﴿١١٩﴾ فَوَسْوَسَ إِلَيْهِ
ٱلشَّيْطَٰنُ قَالَ يَٰٓـَٔادَمُ هَلْ أَدُلُّكَ عَلَىٰ شَجَرَةِ ٱلْخُلْدِ وَمُلْكٍ
لَّا يَبْلَىٰ ﴿١٢٠﴾ فَأَكَلَا مِنْهَا فَبَدَتْ لَهُمَا سَوْءَٰتُهُمَا وَطَفِقَا
يَخْصِفَانِ عَلَيْهِمَا مِن وَرَقِ ٱلْجَنَّةِ ۚ وَعَصَىٰٓ ءَادَمُ رَبَّهُۥ فَغَوَىٰ ﴿١٢١﴾
ثُمَّ ٱجْتَبَٰهُ رَبُّهُۥ فَتَابَ عَلَيْهِ وَهَدَىٰ ﴿١٢٢﴾ قَالَ ٱهْبِطَا مِنْهَا
جَمِيعًۢا ۖ بَعْضُكُمْ لِبَعْضٍ عَدُوٌّ ۖ فَإِمَّا يَأْتِيَنَّكُم مِّنِّى هُدًى
فَمَنِ ٱتَّبَعَ هُدَاىَ فَلَا يَضِلُّ وَلَا يَشْقَىٰ ﴿١٢٣﴾ وَمَنْ أَعْرَضَ عَن
ذِكْرِى فَإِنَّ لَهُۥ مَعِيشَةً ضَنكًا وَنَحْشُرُهُۥ يَوْمَ ٱلْقِيَٰمَةِ
أَعْمَىٰ ﴿١٢٤﴾ قَالَ رَبِّ لِمَ حَشَرْتَنِىٓ أَعْمَىٰ وَقَدْ كُنتُ بَصِيرًا ﴿١٢٥﴾
قَالَ كَذَٰلِكَ أَتَتْكَ ءَايَٰتُنَا فَنَسِيتَهَا ۖ وَكَذَٰلِكَ ٱلْيَوْمَ تُنسَىٰ ﴿١٢٦﴾ وَكَذَٰلِكَ
نَجْزِى مَنْ أَسْرَفَ وَلَمْ يُؤْمِنۢ بِـَٔايَٰتِ رَبِّهِۦ ۚ وَلَعَذَابُ ٱلْءَاخِرَةِ أَشَدُّ
وَأَبْقَىٰٓ ﴿١٢٧﴾ أَفَلَمْ يَهْدِ لَهُمْ كَمْ أَهْلَكْنَا قَبْلَهُم مِّنَ ٱلْقُرُونِ يَمْشُونَ
فِى مَسَٰكِنِهِمْ ۗ إِنَّ فِى ذَٰلِكَ لَءَايَٰتٍ لِّأُو۟لِى ٱلنُّهَىٰ ﴿١٢٨﴾ وَلَوْلَا كَلِمَةٌ
سَبَقَتْ مِن رَّبِّكَ لَكَانَ لِزَامًا وَأَجَلٌ مُّسَمًّى ﴿١٢٩﴾ فَٱصْبِرْ عَلَىٰ
مَا يَقُولُونَ وَسَبِّحْ بِحَمْدِ رَبِّكَ قَبْلَ طُلُوعِ ٱلشَّمْسِ وَقَبْلَ غُرُوبِهَا ۖ

Whenever some of it was sent down on him, it increased his knowledge of it.

115. ***We made a contract with Ādam before*** – ordering him not to eat from the Tree before he did eat from it – ***but he forgot*** and abandoned Our contract with him. ***We did not find that he had a firm resolve*** and the necessary steadfastness to avoid what We had forbidden him.

116. Remember ***when We said to the angels, 'Prostrate yourselves to Ādam', they prostrated, with the exception of Iblīs,*** the forefather of the jinn. He used to keep the company of the angels and worshipped Allah with them – ***who disdained to do it*** – to prostrate to Ādam, and said, "I am better than him."

117. ***We said, 'Ādam, this is an enemy to you and your wife*** (Ḥawwā'), ***so do not let him expel you from the Garden and thus make you miserable*** – cause you to become tired by cultivation, harvesting, milling, and making bread and the like. Ādam's misery alone is mentioned because naming the man automatically includes his wife.

118. ***You will not go hungry in it or suffer from nakedness.***

119. ***You*** (read as *annaka* and *innaka*) ***will not go thirsty in it or burn in the sun.'*** This means that in the Garden he did not suffer from the heat of the morning sun, not that there is no sunlight in the Garden.

120. ***But Shayṭān whispered to him, saying, 'Ādam, shall I show you the way to the Tree of Everlasting Life*** – a Tree such that if someone eats from it, he will become immortal – ***and to a kingdom which will never fade away*** – but will last forever?'

121. ***So the two of them*** (Ādam and Ḥawwā') ***ate from it and their private parts were disclosed to them*** – each of them noticed the private parts of the other, and they are called private parts (*sawā'a*) because their disclosure is bad (*sū'*) for a person – ***and they started stitching together the leaves of the Garden to cover themselves. Ādam disobeyed his Lord*** – when he ate from the Tree – ***and became misled.***

122. ***But then his Lord chose him*** – brought him near – ***and turned to him*** – before his repentance – ***and guided him*** to be constant in repentance.

123. ***He*** (Allah) ***said*** to Ādam and Ḥawwā' – and that includes all of their offspring – ***'Go down from it*** (the Garden) ***all of you, as enemies to one another!*** Their offspring would become enemies to one another by wronging one another. ***But when guidance*** (the Qur'an) ***comes to you from Me, all those who follow My guidance will not go astray*** in this world ***and will not be miserable*** in the Next World.

124. ***But if anyone turns away from My reminder*** (the Qur'an) and does not believe in it ***his life will be a dark and narrow*** (constricted) ***one*** – and a *ḥadīth* explains this as referring to the punishment of the unbeliever in his grave – ***and on the Day of Rising We will gather him*** – the one who turns away from the Qur'an – ***blind.'***

125. ***He will say, 'My Lord, why have you gathered me blind when before I was able to see*** – in the world and at the Resurrection***?'***

126. ***He will say,*** 'What else could you expect? – ***just as Our Signs came to you and you forgot them*** – rejected them and did not believe in them – ***in the same way*** as you ignored Our signs ***you too are forgotten today*** in the Fire.'

127. As We repay those who turn away from the Qur'an, ***that is how We*** also ***repay anyone who is profligate*** – by committing *shirk* – ***and does not believe in the Signs of his Lord. And punishment in the Next World is much harsher and longer lasting*** than punishment in this world and punishment in the grave.

128. ***Are they*** (the unbelievers of Makka) ***not guided*** – has it not been made clear to them – ***by the many generations We have destroyed before them*** – because of their denial of the Messengers – ***among whose dwelling places they walk about*** when they travel to Syria and elsewhere, so that they reflect***? There are Signs*** and lessons ***in that for people of sound intellect.***

129. ***And were it not for a prior word from your Lord*** – of the postponement of punishment for them until the Next World – ***and a specified term, it*** (their destruction) ***would inevitably have already taken place*** in this world.

وَمِنْ ءَانَآئِ ٱلَّيْلِ فَسَبِّحْ وَأَطْرَافَ ٱلنَّهَارِ لَعَلَّكَ تَرْضَىٰ ١٣٠ وَلَا
تَمُدَّنَّ عَيْنَيْكَ إِلَىٰ مَا مَتَّعْنَا بِهِۦٓ أَزْوَٰجًا مِّنْهُمْ زَهْرَةَ ٱلْحَيَوٰةِ ٱلدُّنْيَا
لِنَفْتِنَهُمْ فِيهِ ۚ وَرِزْقُ رَبِّكَ خَيْرٌ وَأَبْقَىٰ ١٣١ وَأْمُرْ أَهْلَكَ بِٱلصَّلَوٰةِ
وَٱصْطَبِرْ عَلَيْهَا ۖ لَا نَسْـَٔلُكَ رِزْقًا ۖ نَّحْنُ نَرْزُقُكَ ۗ وَٱلْعَٰقِبَةُ لِلتَّقْوَىٰ
١٣٢ وَقَالُوا۟ لَوْلَا يَأْتِينَا بِـَٔايَةٍ مِّن رَّبِّهِۦٓ ۚ أَوَلَمْ تَأْتِهِم بَيِّنَةُ مَا فِى
ٱلصُّحُفِ ٱلْأُولَىٰ ١٣٣ وَلَوْ أَنَّآ أَهْلَكْنَٰهُم بِعَذَابٍ مِّن قَبْلِهِۦ
لَقَالُوا۟ رَبَّنَا لَوْلَآ أَرْسَلْتَ إِلَيْنَا رَسُولًا فَنَتَّبِعَ ءَايَٰتِكَ مِن
قَبْلِ أَن نَّذِلَّ وَنَخْزَىٰ ١٣٤ قُلْ كُلٌّ مُّتَرَبِّصٌ فَتَرَبَّصُوا۟ ۖ
فَسَتَعْلَمُونَ مَنْ أَصْحَٰبُ ٱلصِّرَٰطِ ٱلسَّوِىِّ وَمَنِ ٱهْتَدَىٰ ١٣٥

130. ***So be steadfast in the face of what they say*** – but this was abrogated by the *Āyat* of Fighting – ***and*** pray and ***glorify your Lord with praise before the rising of the sun*** – in the *Ṣubḥ* prayer – ***and before its setting*** – in the *'Aṣr* prayer. ***And glorify Him during part of the night*** – in the prayers of *Maghrib* and *'Ishā'* – ***and at both ends of the day*** – in the *Ẓuhr* prayer, which divides the day into two – ***so that perhaps you may be pleased*** (rewarded).

131. ***Do not direct your eyes longingly to what We have given certain of them*** – the word *azwāj* (literally pairs) here means different categories – ***to enjoy, the flower*** and adornment ***of the life of this world, so that We may test them by it*** to see whether they will transgress. ***Your Lord's provision*** in Paradise ***is better and longer lasting*** than what they receive in this world.

132. ***Instruct your family to prayer, and be constant*** (steadfast) ***in it. We do not ask you for provision:*** either for yourself or for anyone else. ***We provide for you. And the best end result*** (the Garden) ***is gained by fearfulness of Allah.***

133. ***They*** (the idolaters) ***say, 'If only he*** (Muḥammad) ***would bring us a Sign from his Lord*** as we demand***!' Have they not received*** (read as *ta'tihim* and *ya'tihim*) ***the Clear Sign of what is written in the earlier texts?*** The Qur'an contains reports of past nations and their destruction on account of their denial of their Messengers.

134. ***If We had destroyed them with a punishment before this*** – before Muḥammad came as a Messenger – ***they would have said*** – on the Day of Rising, ***'Our Lord, why did You not send us a Messenger, so we could follow Your Signs before we were humbled*** at the Resurrection ***and disgraced*** in Hellfire***?'***

135. ***Say*** to them***: 'Everyone*** – we and you – ***is waiting expectantly*** for the final outcome, ***so wait expectantly. You will soon know*** – at the Resurrection – ***who are the Companions of the Right*** (straight) ***Path and who is guided*** away from misguidance: us or you.*'*

سُورَةُ الأَنبِيَاءِ

بِسْمِ ٱللَّهِ ٱلرَّحْمَٰنِ ٱلرَّحِيمِ

ٱقْتَرَبَ لِلنَّاسِ حِسَابُهُمْ وَهُمْ فِى غَفْلَةٍ مُّعْرِضُونَ ١
مَا يَأْتِيهِم مِّن ذِكْرٍ مِّن رَّبِّهِم مُّحْدَثٍ إِلَّا ٱسْتَمَعُوهُ وَهُمْ
يَلْعَبُونَ ٢ لَاهِيَةً قُلُوبُهُمْ ۗ وَأَسَرُّوا۟ ٱلنَّجْوَى ٱلَّذِينَ ظَلَمُوا۟
هَلْ هَٰذَآ إِلَّا بَشَرٌ مِّثْلُكُمْ ۖ أَفَتَأْتُونَ ٱلسِّحْرَ وَأَنتُمْ
تُبْصِرُونَ ٣ قَالَ رَبِّى يَعْلَمُ ٱلْقَوْلَ فِى ٱلسَّمَآءِ وَٱلْأَرْضِ ۖ
وَهُوَ ٱلسَّمِيعُ ٱلْعَلِيمُ ٤ بَلْ قَالُوٓا۟ أَضْغَٰثُ أَحْلَٰمٍۭ بَلِ
ٱفْتَرَىٰهُ بَلْ هُوَ شَاعِرٌ فَلْيَأْتِنَا بِـَٔايَةٍ كَمَآ أُرْسِلَ ٱلْأَوَّلُونَ
٥ مَآ ءَامَنَتْ قَبْلَهُم مِّن قَرْيَةٍ أَهْلَكْنَٰهَآ ۖ أَفَهُمْ يُؤْمِنُونَ
٦ وَمَآ أَرْسَلْنَا قَبْلَكَ إِلَّا رِجَالًا نُّوحِىٓ إِلَيْهِمْ ۖ فَسْـَٔلُوٓا۟ أَهْلَ
ٱلذِّكْرِ إِن كُنتُمْ لَا تَعْلَمُونَ ٧ وَمَا جَعَلْنَٰهُمْ جَسَدًا
لَّا يَأْكُلُونَ ٱلطَّعَامَ وَمَا كَانُوا۟ خَٰلِدِينَ ٨ ثُمَّ صَدَقْنَٰهُمُ
ٱلْوَعْدَ فَأَنجَيْنَٰهُمْ وَمَن نَّشَآءُ وَأَهْلَكْنَا ٱلْمُسْرِفِينَ ٩
لَقَدْ أَنزَلْنَآ إِلَيْكُمْ كِتَٰبًا فِيهِ ذِكْرُكُمْ ۖ أَفَلَا تَعْقِلُونَ ١٠
وَكَمْ قَصَمْنَا مِن قَرْيَةٍ كَانَتْ ظَالِمَةً وَأَنشَأْنَا بَعْدَهَا قَوْمًا
ءَاخَرِينَ ١١ فَلَمَّآ أَحَسُّوا۟ بَأْسَنَآ إِذَا هُم مِّنْهَا يَرْكُضُونَ ١٢
لَا تَرْكُضُوا۟ وَٱرْجِعُوٓا۟ إِلَىٰ مَآ أُتْرِفْتُمْ فِيهِ وَمَسَٰكِنِكُمْ لَعَلَّكُمْ
تُسْـَٔلُونَ ١٣ قَالُوا۟ يَٰوَيْلَنَآ إِنَّا كُنَّا ظَٰلِمِينَ ١٤ فَمَا زَالَت تِّلْكَ
دَعْوَىٰهُمْ حَتَّىٰ جَعَلْنَٰهُمْ حَصِيدًا خَٰمِدِينَ ١٥ وَمَا خَلَقْنَا

21. *Sūrat al-Anbiyā'*
The Prophets

This *sūra* is Makkan. It has 112 *āyats* and was sent down after *Sūrat Ibrāhim.*

1. ***Mankind's*** – referring especially to the people of Makka who denied the resurrection – ***Reckoning has drawn very close to them*** – meaning the Day of Rising – ***yet they heedlessly turn away*** from preparing for it by believing.

2. ***No fresh reminder comes to them*** – of the Qur'an, as it arrives piece by piece – ***from their Lord without their listening to it as if it was a game*** – and they make a mockery of it.

3. ***Their hearts are distracted*** – heedless to what it means. ***Those who do wrong confer together secretly, saying, 'Is this man*** (Muḥammad) ***anything but a*** mortal ***human being like yourselves? Do you succumb to magic with your eyes wide open*** – knowing that it is magic***?'***

4. ***Say*** – to them***: 'My Lord knows what is said*** secretly ***in heaven and earth. He is the All-Hearing, the All-Knowing.'***

5. ***Furthermore*** – the conjunction used here, *bal*, is employed in Arabic to move to another subject – ***they say*** about what the Qur'an brings: ***'A muddled jumble of dreams!' and, 'He has invented it!' and, 'He is a poet!' and, 'Let him bring us a Sign like those sent to previous peoples*** – such as the She-camel, the Staff and the White Hand.***'*** When they demand a sign Allah says to them:

6. ***None of the*** inhabitants of the ***cities which We destroyed before them*** for denying the Signs which came to them ***believed. So will they*** believe***?*** No.

7. ***We have only ever sent before you men to whom We gave Revelation*** (read as *nūḥā*, as here, and also *yūḥā* meaning, "men who were given Revelation") – not angels. ***Ask the People of the Reminder*** – the scholars who know the Torah and the Gospel – ***if you do not know*** that, for they know it. You are more likely to believe them than to believe those who believe in Muḥammad.

8. ***We did not give them*** (the Messengers) ***bodies*** – the singular *jasad* used here is generic – ***which did not eat food, nor were they immortal*** in this world.

9. ***But We kept Our promise to them*** – by saving them – ***and rescued them and those We willed*** – who believed them – ***and destroyed the profligate*** – who denied them.

10. ***We have sent down to you,*** company of Quraysh, ***a Book containing your Reminder*** in your own language to remind you, ***so will you not use your intellect*** and believe in it?

11. ***How many cities*** – meaning their inhabitants – ***which did wrong*** by disbelieving ***have We utterly destroyed, raising up other people after them!***

12. ***When they perceived Our violent force*** – and were aware of their imminent destruction – ***they ran away from it.***

13. The angels then said to them in mockery: ***'Do not run away! Return to the life of luxury you enjoyed and to the places where you lived, so that you may be interrogated*** about what you enjoyed in this world!'

14. ***They said, 'Alas for us*** and our destruction! ***We were indeed wrongdoers*** by disbelieving!'

15. ***That cry of theirs went on*** – the words with which they were making supplication continued to be repeated – ***until We made them*** like the ***stubble*** of scythed crops as they had been killed by the sword – ***silent, stamped out*** – still, like a fire that had been extinguished.

16. ***We did not create heaven and earth and everything in between them as a game*** but rather to show the power of Allah and how Allah helps His slaves.

17. ***If We had desired to have some amusement*** – in the form of a wife or child – ***We would have derived it from Our Presence*** – from the houris or angels; ***but We did not do that.*** We neither did that nor desired to.

18. ***Rather We hurl the truth*** (faith) ***against falsehood*** (unbelief) ***and it cuts right through it*** – the word used here means to strike a fatal blow which exposes the brain and removes it – ***and it vanishes clean away! Woe*** – a terrible punishment – ***without end to you,***

ٱلسَّمَآءَ وَٱلْأَرْضَ وَمَا بَيْنَهُمَا لَٰعِبِينَ ﴿١٦﴾ لَوْ أَرَدْنَآ أَن نَّتَّخِذَ لَهْوًا
لَّٱتَّخَذْنَٰهُ مِن لَّدُنَّآ إِن كُنَّا فَٰعِلِينَ ﴿١٧﴾ بَلْ نَقْذِفُ بِٱلْحَقِّ
عَلَى ٱلْبَٰطِلِ فَيَدْمَغُهُۥ فَإِذَا هُوَ زَاهِقٌ ۚ وَلَكُمُ ٱلْوَيْلُ مِمَّا تَصِفُونَ
﴿١٨﴾ وَلَهُۥ مَن فِى ٱلسَّمَٰوَٰتِ وَٱلْأَرْضِ ۚ وَمَنْ عِندَهُۥ لَا يَسْتَكْبِرُونَ
عَنْ عِبَادَتِهِۦ وَلَا يَسْتَحْسِرُونَ ﴿١٩﴾ يُسَبِّحُونَ ٱلَّيْلَ وَٱلنَّهَارَ
لَا يَفْتُرُونَ ﴿٢٠﴾ أَمِ ٱتَّخَذُوٓا۟ ءَالِهَةً مِّنَ ٱلْأَرْضِ هُمْ يُنشِرُونَ
﴿٢١﴾ لَوْ كَانَ فِيهِمَآ ءَالِهَةٌ إِلَّا ٱللَّهُ لَفَسَدَتَا ۚ فَسُبْحَٰنَ ٱللَّهِ رَبِّ ٱلْعَرْشِ
عَمَّا يَصِفُونَ ﴿٢٢﴾ لَا يُسْـَٔلُ عَمَّا يَفْعَلُ وَهُمْ يُسْـَٔلُونَ ﴿٢٣﴾ أَمِ
ٱتَّخَذُوا۟ مِن دُونِهِۦٓ ءَالِهَةً ۖ قُلْ هَاتُوا۟ بُرْهَٰنَكُمْ ۖ هَٰذَا ذِكْرُ مَن مَّعِىَ
وَذِكْرُ مَن قَبْلِى ۗ بَلْ أَكْثَرُهُمْ لَا يَعْلَمُونَ ٱلْحَقَّ ۖ فَهُم مُّعْرِضُونَ ﴿٢٤﴾
وَمَآ أَرْسَلْنَا مِن قَبْلِكَ مِن رَّسُولٍ إِلَّا نُوحِىٓ إِلَيْهِ أَنَّهُۥ لَآ إِلَٰهَ
إِلَّآ أَنَا۠ فَٱعْبُدُونِ ﴿٢٥﴾ وَقَالُوا۟ ٱتَّخَذَ ٱلرَّحْمَٰنُ وَلَدًا ۗ سُبْحَٰنَهُۥ ۚ
بَلْ عِبَادٌ مُّكْرَمُونَ ﴿٢٦﴾ لَا يَسْبِقُونَهُۥ بِٱلْقَوْلِ وَهُم
بِأَمْرِهِۦ يَعْمَلُونَ ﴿٢٧﴾ يَعْلَمُ مَا بَيْنَ أَيْدِيهِمْ وَمَا خَلْفَهُمْ
وَلَا يَشْفَعُونَ إِلَّا لِمَنِ ٱرْتَضَىٰ وَهُم مِّنْ خَشْيَتِهِۦ مُشْفِقُونَ
﴿٢٨﴾ ۞ وَمَن يَقُلْ مِنْهُمْ إِنِّىٓ إِلَٰهٌ مِّن دُونِهِۦ فَذَٰلِكَ نَجْزِيهِ
جَهَنَّمَ ۚ كَذَٰلِكَ نَجْزِى ٱلظَّٰلِمِينَ ﴿٢٩﴾ أَوَلَمْ يَرَ ٱلَّذِينَ كَفَرُوٓا۟
أَنَّ ٱلسَّمَٰوَٰتِ وَٱلْأَرْضَ كَانَتَا رَتْقًا فَفَتَقْنَٰهُمَا ۖ وَجَعَلْنَا
مِنَ ٱلْمَآءِ كُلَّ شَىْءٍ حَىٍّ ۖ أَفَلَا يُؤْمِنُونَ ﴿٣٠﴾ وَجَعَلْنَا فِى ٱلْأَرْضِ
رَوَٰسِىَ أَن تَمِيدَ بِهِمْ وَجَعَلْنَا فِيهَا فِجَاجًا سُبُلًا لَّعَلَّهُمْ

unbelievers of Makka – ***for what you portray*** about Allah having a wife or child*!*

19. ***Everyone in the heavens and the earth belongs to Him*** as His property. ***Those in His presence*** – the angels, who never grow weary of worship – ***do not consider themselves too great to worship Him and do not grow tired of it.***

20. ***They glorify Him by night and day, without ever flagging*** as we do, and nothing distracts them from it.

21. ***Or have they taken gods out of the earth*** – like their idols made of stone, gold and silver – ***who can bring the dead to life?*** The question demands a negative response, so the implication is that they cannot, and no one can be considered to have divinity except the One who can bring the dead to life.

22. ***If there had been any gods besides Allah in heaven or on earth, they would both have been ruined.*** Heaven and earth would have lost their normal orderedness since there would have inevitably been internal discord, as is normal when there are several rulers: they oppose one another in things and do not agree with one another. ***Glory be to Allah, Lord*** and Creator ***of the Throne, beyond what they*** (the unbelievers) ***describe*** and attribute to Him by way of a partner or anything else!

23. ***He will not be questioned about what He does, but they will be questioned*** about their actions.

24. ***Or have they taken other gods besides Him?*** This is a rebuke. ***Say: 'Produce your proof*** for that! There is no way to do so. ***This is the message of those with me*** (my community) – that is, the Qur'an – ***and the message of those before me*** (past nations) – that is, the Torah, the Gospel, and other Books of Allah.' Not one of those Books says that there is another god with Allah as they say. He is Exalted above that. ***But most of them do not know the truth*** – Allah's Oneness – ***so they turn away*** – and fail to understand it.

25. ***We sent no Messenger before you without revealing*** (read as *nūḥā* and *yūḥā:* see 21:7 above) ***to him: 'There is no god but Me, so worship Me*** and affirm My Unity.'

يَهْتَدُونَ ﴿٣١﴾ وَجَعَلْنَا ٱلسَّمَآءَ سَقْفًا مَّحْفُوظًا ۖ وَهُمْ عَنْ
ءَايَـٰتِهَا مُعْرِضُونَ ﴿٣٢﴾ وَهُوَ ٱلَّذِى خَلَقَ ٱلَّيْلَ وَٱلنَّهَارَ وَٱلشَّمْسَ
وَٱلْقَمَرَ ۖ كُلٌّ فِى فَلَكٍ يَسْبَحُونَ ﴿٣٣﴾ وَمَا جَعَلْنَا لِبَشَرٍ مِّن قَبْلِكَ
ٱلْخُلْدَ ۖ أَفَإِي۟ن مِّتَّ فَهُمُ ٱلْخَـٰلِدُونَ ﴿٣٤﴾ كُلُّ نَفْسٍ ذَآئِقَةُ
ٱلْمَوْتِ ۗ وَنَبْلُوكُم بِٱلشَّرِّ وَٱلْخَيْرِ فِتْنَةً ۖ وَإِلَيْنَا تُرْجَعُونَ ﴿٣٥﴾
وَإِذَا رَءَاكَ ٱلَّذِينَ كَفَرُوٓا۟ إِن يَتَّخِذُونَكَ إِلَّا هُزُوًا
أَهَـٰذَا ٱلَّذِى يَذْكُرُ ءَالِهَتَكُمْ وَهُم بِذِكْرِ ٱلرَّحْمَـٰنِ
هُمْ كَـٰفِرُونَ ﴿٣٦﴾ خُلِقَ ٱلْإِنسَـٰنُ مِنْ عَجَلٍ ۚ سَأُو۟رِيكُمْ
ءَايَـٰتِى فَلَا تَسْتَعْجِلُونِ ﴿٣٧﴾ وَيَقُولُونَ مَتَىٰ هَـٰذَا ٱلْوَعْدُ
إِن كُنتُمْ صَـٰدِقِينَ ﴿٣٨﴾ لَوْ يَعْلَمُ ٱلَّذِينَ كَفَرُوا۟ حِينَ
لَا يَكُفُّونَ عَن وُجُوهِهِمُ ٱلنَّارَ وَلَا عَن ظُهُورِهِمْ وَلَا
هُمْ يُنصَرُونَ ﴿٣٩﴾ بَلْ تَأْتِيهِم بَغْتَةً فَتَبْهَتُهُمْ فَلَا
يَسْتَطِيعُونَ رَدَّهَا وَلَا هُمْ يُنظَرُونَ ﴿٤٠﴾ وَلَقَدِ ٱسْتُهْزِئَ
بِرُسُلٍ مِّن قَبْلِكَ فَحَاقَ بِٱلَّذِينَ سَخِرُوا۟ مِنْهُم مَّا كَانُوا۟ بِهِۦ
يَسْتَهْزِءُونَ ﴿٤١﴾ قُلْ مَن يَكْلَؤُكُم بِٱلَّيْلِ وَٱلنَّهَارِ مِنَ
ٱلرَّحْمَـٰنِ ۗ بَلْ هُمْ عَن ذِكْرِ رَبِّهِم مُّعْرِضُونَ ﴿٤٢﴾ أَمْ
لَهُمْ ءَالِهَةٌ تَمْنَعُهُم مِّن دُونِنَا ۚ لَا يَسْتَطِيعُونَ نَصْرَ
أَنفُسِهِمْ وَلَا هُم مِّنَّا يُصْحَبُونَ ﴿٤٣﴾ بَلْ مَتَّعْنَا هَـٰٓؤُلَآءِ
وَءَابَآءَهُمْ حَتَّىٰ طَالَ عَلَيْهِمُ ٱلْعُمُرُ ۗ أَفَلَا يَرَوْنَ أَنَّا نَأْتِى
ٱلْأَرْضَ نَنقُصُهَا مِنْ أَطْرَافِهَآ ۚ أَفَهُمُ ٱلْغَـٰلِبُونَ ﴿٤٤﴾

26. ***They say, 'The All-Merciful has a son*** – one of the angels.***' Glory be to Him! No, they are but honoured slaves!*** They are honoured by Him, but slavehood is not compatible with being a son.

27. ***They do not precede Him in speech*** – only saying what they say after He says it – ***and they act on His command*** – only acting once He has made a command.

28. ***He knows what is in front of them and what is behind them*** – what they are going to do and what they did in the past. ***They only intercede on behalf of those with whom He is pleased*** – that they should be interceded for – ***and even they are apprehensive out of fear of Him.***

29. ***Were any of them to say, 'I am a god apart from Him,'*** a reference to Iblīs, who called on people to worship him and ordered them to obey him, ***We would repay him with Hell. That is how We repay wrongdoers*** (idolaters).

30. ***Do those who disbelieve not see*** (read as *aw lam yara* and *a-lam yara*) – meaning "know" – ***that the heavens and the earth were sewn together*** and compacted together ***and then We unstitched them*** and made them seven heavens and seven earths. The word "unstitch" as applied to the heavens means that before that there was no rain and then there was rain; as applied to the earth it means that the earth did not previously produce plants but then allowed plants to grow – ***and that We made from water*** which descends from heaven and springs from the earth ***every living thing*** – plants and other things? Water is the source of their life. ***So will they not believe*** in My Oneness?

31. ***We placed firmly embedded mountains on the earth, so it would not move under them, and We put broad valleys as roadways in it, so that perhaps they might be guided*** – so that they could travel through it and reach their destinations.

32. ***We made the sky a preserved and protected roof*** for the earth, as a house has a roof which does not collapse into it – ***yet still they turn away from Our Signs*** – meaning the sun, moon and stars; they do not reflect on them and thereby come to know that the Creator has no partner.

33. ***It is He who created night and day and the sun and moon*** and the stars; each has its own orbit in which it travels, like a millwheel in the sky – ***each one swimming in a sphere.*** The word "swim" is used to describe their speedy moving, which is compared to the way a swimmer moves in water. Because of the metaphor, the third person masculine plural pronoun built into the verb, which is normally only used for intelligent beings, is used in this instance to describe the sun and the moon.

34. The following was revealed when the unbelievers said, "Muḥammad will die." ***We did not give any human being before you immortality*** in this world; ***and if you die, will they then be immortal?*** This question demands a negative response.

35. ***Every self will taste death*** in this world. ***We test you with both good and evil*** – meaning poverty and wealth, illness and health, and similar things – ***as a trial*** to see whether or not you will be steadfast and thankful. ***And you will be returned to Us*** – and then We will repay you for what you did.

36. ***When those who disbelieve see you, they only make a mockery out of you*** and say: ***'Is this the one who makes mention of your gods*** – in other words, criticises them?' ***Yet they are unbelievers about the mention of the All-Merciful.*** When the All-Merciful is mentioned, they say, "We do not recognise Him."

37. This was revealed about hastening the punishment. ***Man was created hasty*** – he behaves hastily in many situations, as if it were part of his basic nature to do that. ***I will show you My Signs*** – evidence of the promised punishment to come – ***so do not try to hasten Me*** – in respect of that. Then Allah showed them by their slaughter at the Battle of Badr.

38. ***They say, 'When will this promise*** of the Resurrection ***come about, if you are telling the truth*** about it?'

39. Allah says: ***If those who disbelieved only knew of the time when they will not be able to keep the Fire away from their faces or their backs! And they will receive no help*** in warding it off from themselves on the Last Day.

40. ***No, it*** (the Day of Rising) ***will come upon them suddenly, confounding them, taking them completely by surprise, and they will***

قُلْ إِنَّمَآ أُنذِرُكُم بِٱلْوَحْىِ ۚ وَلَا يَسْمَعُ ٱلصُّمُّ ٱلدُّعَآءَ إِذَا
مَا يُنذَرُونَ ﴿٤٥﴾ وَلَئِن مَّسَّتْهُمْ نَفْحَةٌ مِّنْ عَذَابِ رَبِّكَ
لَيَقُولُنَّ يَٰوَيْلَنَآ إِنَّا كُنَّا ظَٰلِمِينَ ﴿٤٦﴾ وَنَضَعُ ٱلْمَوَٰزِينَ
ٱلْقِسْطَ لِيَوْمِ ٱلْقِيَٰمَةِ فَلَا تُظْلَمُ نَفْسٌ شَيْـًٔا ۖ وَإِن كَانَ
مِثْقَالَ حَبَّةٍ مِّنْ خَرْدَلٍ أَتَيْنَا بِهَا ۗ وَكَفَىٰ بِنَا حَٰسِبِينَ
﴿٤٧﴾ وَلَقَدْ ءَاتَيْنَا مُوسَىٰ وَهَٰرُونَ ٱلْفُرْقَانَ وَضِيَآءً وَذِكْرًا
لِّلْمُتَّقِينَ ﴿٤٨﴾ ٱلَّذِينَ يَخْشَوْنَ رَبَّهُم بِٱلْغَيْبِ وَهُم مِّنَ
ٱلسَّاعَةِ مُشْفِقُونَ ﴿٤٩﴾ وَهَٰذَا ذِكْرٌ مُّبَارَكٌ أَنزَلْنَٰهُ ۚ أَفَأَنتُمْ لَهُۥ
مُنكِرُونَ ﴿٥٠﴾ ۞ وَلَقَدْ ءَاتَيْنَآ إِبْرَٰهِيمَ رُشْدَهُۥ مِن قَبْلُ وَكُنَّا
بِهِۦ عَٰلِمِينَ ﴿٥١﴾ إِذْ قَالَ لِأَبِيهِ وَقَوْمِهِۦ مَا هَٰذِهِ ٱلتَّمَاثِيلُ ٱلَّتِىٓ
أَنتُمْ لَهَا عَٰكِفُونَ ﴿٥٢﴾ قَالُوا۟ وَجَدْنَآ ءَابَآءَنَا لَهَا عَٰبِدِينَ ﴿٥٣﴾
قَالَ لَقَدْ كُنتُمْ أَنتُمْ وَءَابَآؤُكُمْ فِى ضَلَٰلٍ مُّبِينٍ ﴿٥٤﴾ قَالُوٓا۟
أَجِئْتَنَا بِٱلْحَقِّ أَمْ أَنتَ مِنَ ٱللَّٰعِبِينَ ﴿٥٥﴾ قَالَ بَل رَّبُّكُمْ رَبُّ ٱلسَّمَٰوَٰتِ
وَٱلْأَرْضِ ٱلَّذِى فَطَرَهُنَّ وَأَنَا۠ عَلَىٰ ذَٰلِكُم مِّنَ ٱلشَّٰهِدِينَ
﴿٥٦﴾ وَتَٱللَّهِ لَأَكِيدَنَّ أَصْنَٰمَكُم بَعْدَ أَن تُوَلُّوا۟ مُدْبِرِينَ ﴿٥٧﴾
فَجَعَلَهُمْ جُذَٰذًا إِلَّا كَبِيرًا لَّهُمْ لَعَلَّهُمْ إِلَيْهِ يَرْجِعُونَ
﴿٥٨﴾ قَالُوا۟ مَن فَعَلَ هَٰذَا بِـَٔالِهَتِنَآ إِنَّهُۥ لَمِنَ ٱلظَّٰلِمِينَ ﴿٥٩﴾
قَالُوا۟ سَمِعْنَا فَتًى يَذْكُرُهُمْ يُقَالُ لَهُۥٓ إِبْرَٰهِيمُ ﴿٦٠﴾ قَالُوا۟ فَأْتُوا۟ بِهِۦ
عَلَىٰٓ أَعْيُنِ ٱلنَّاسِ لَعَلَّهُمْ يَشْهَدُونَ ﴿٦١﴾ قَالُوٓا۟ ءَأَنتَ فَعَلْتَ
هَٰذَا بِـَٔالِهَتِنَا يَٰٓإِبْرَٰهِيمُ ﴿٦٢﴾ قَالَ بَلْ فَعَلَهُۥ كَبِيرُهُمْ

not be able to ward it off. They will be granted no reprieve – no delay for repentance or making excuses.

41. ***Messengers before you were also mocked*** – this was revealed to console the Prophet, may Allah bless him and grant him peace – ***but those who jeered were engulfed by what*** (the punishment) ***they mocked.*** So in the same way the punishment will envelop those who mock you.

42. ***Say*** to them*:* ***'Who will protect you night and day from*** the punishment of ***the All-Merciful*** if it alights on you*?'* No one can do so. Those who are addressed do not fear the punishment of Allah because they deny it. ***Yet they turn away from the remembrance of their Lord*** – the Qur'an, which they do not think about.

43. ***Or do they have gods besides Us who will protect them*** from harm? The response to the question is negative. ***They*** (those gods) ***cannot even help themselves! They*** (the unbelievers) ***will not be safe from Us*** – from Our punishment.

44. ***No indeed! We have given these people enjoyment*** of blessings ***as We did their fathers, until life seemed long and good to them*** and they were deluded by having a long life. ***Do they not see how We come to the*** (their) ***land, eroding it from its extremities*** – decreasing its size by conquests by the Prophet*?* ***Or are they the victors?*** Who are victorious? It is the Prophet and his Companions.

45. ***Say*** to them*:* ***'I can only warn you through the Revelation*** – from Allah, not from myself.*'* ***But the deaf cannot hear the call when they are warned.*** They fail to act on the admonition which they have heard, as if they were deaf.

46. ***If even a single waft*** – the slightest trace – ***of the punishment were to touch them, they would say, 'Alas for us*** on account of our destruction*!* ***We were indeed wrongdoers*** by committing *shirk* and rejecting Muḥammad, may Allah bless him and grant him peace.*'*

47. ***We will set up the Just Balance on the Day of Rising and no self will be wronged in any way***: no one will be given any additional wrong actions or lose a single one of their good actions. ***Even if it*** (the action) ***be no more than the weight of a grain of mustard-seed, We will produce it. We are sufficient as a Reckoner*** of every action.

48. ***We gave to Mūsā and Hārūn the Discrimination*** – the Torah, which distinguishes between the truth and the false, and the lawful and unlawful – ***and a Shining Light and a Reminder for those who are godfearing:***

49. ***…those who fear their Lord in the Unseen*** – when no one can see them and they are alone – ***and are apprehensive about the*** terrors of the Last ***Hour.***

50. ***This*** Qur'an ***is a blessed Reminder which We have sent down. So are you going to ignore it?*** The question is a rebuke.

51. ***We gave Ibrāhīm his right guidance early on*** – before he came of age – ***and We had complete knowledge of him*** – knowledge that he was worthy of the guidance he received.

52. ***When he said to his father and his people, 'What are these statues*** (idols) ***you are clinging to*** and worshipping***?'***

53. ***They said, 'We found our fathers worshipping them*** and we imitated them.***'***

54. ***He said*** to them ***'You and your fathers are clearly misguided*** in worshipping them.***'***

55. ***They said, 'Have you brought us the truth*** in what you say ***or are you playing games?'***

56. ***He said, 'Far from it! Your Lord is the Lord of the heavens and the earth*** – He is the One who should be worshipped***: He who brought them into being*** without any prior model. ***I am one of those who bear witness to that.***

57. ***By Allah, I will devise some scheme against your idols when your backs are turned.'***

58. ***He broke them in pieces*** (read as *judhādh* and *jidhādh*) – with his axe after his people went to their gathering on their festival day – ***except for the biggest one,*** from whose neck he hung the axe, ***so that they would have it to consult*** about what it had done to the others***!***

59. ***They said*** – after they returned and saw what he had done – ***'Who has done this to our gods? He is definitely one of the wrongdoers!'***

هَٰذَا فَسۡـَٔلُوهُمۡ إِن كَانُواْ يَنطِقُونَ ٦٣ فَرَجَعُوٓاْ إِلَىٰٓ
أَنفُسِهِمۡ فَقَالُوٓاْ إِنَّكُمۡ أَنتُمُ ٱلظَّٰلِمُونَ ٦٤ ثُمَّ نُكِسُواْ عَلَىٰ
رُءُوسِهِمۡ لَقَدۡ عَلِمۡتَ مَا هَٰٓؤُلَآءِ يَنطِقُونَ ٦٥ قَالَ
أَفَتَعۡبُدُونَ مِن دُونِ ٱللَّهِ مَا لَا يَنفَعُكُمۡ شَيۡـٔٗا وَلَا
يَضُرُّكُمۡ ٦٦ أُفّٖ لَّكُمۡ وَلِمَا تَعۡبُدُونَ مِن دُونِ ٱللَّهِۖ أَفَلَا
تَعۡقِلُونَ ٦٧ قَالُواْ حَرِّقُوهُ وَٱنصُرُوٓاْ ءَالِهَتَكُمۡ إِن كُنتُمۡ
فَٰعِلِينَ ٦٨ قُلۡنَا يَٰنَارُ كُونِي بَرۡدٗا وَسَلَٰمًا عَلَىٰٓ إِبۡرَٰهِيمَ ٦٩
وَأَرَادُواْ بِهِۦ كَيۡدٗا فَجَعَلۡنَٰهُمُ ٱلۡأَخۡسَرِينَ ٧٠ وَنَجَّيۡنَٰهُ
وَلُوطًا إِلَى ٱلۡأَرۡضِ ٱلَّتِي بَٰرَكۡنَا فِيهَا لِلۡعَٰلَمِينَ ٧١ وَوَهَبۡنَا
لَهُۥٓ إِسۡحَٰقَ وَيَعۡقُوبَ نَافِلَةٗۖ وَكُلًّا جَعَلۡنَا صَٰلِحِينَ ٧٢
وَجَعَلۡنَٰهُمۡ أَئِمَّةٗ يَهۡدُونَ بِأَمۡرِنَا وَأَوۡحَيۡنَآ إِلَيۡهِمۡ فِعۡلَ
ٱلۡخَيۡرَٰتِ وَإِقَامَ ٱلصَّلَوٰةِ وَإِيتَآءَ ٱلزَّكَوٰةِۖ وَكَانُواْ لَنَا
عَٰبِدِينَ ٧٣ وَلُوطًا ءَاتَيۡنَٰهُ حُكۡمٗا وَعِلۡمٗا وَنَجَّيۡنَٰهُ مِنَ
ٱلۡقَرۡيَةِ ٱلَّتِي كَانَت تَّعۡمَلُ ٱلۡخَبَٰٓئِثَۚ إِنَّهُمۡ كَانُواْ قَوۡمَ سَوۡءٖ
فَٰسِقِينَ ٧٤ وَأَدۡخَلۡنَٰهُ فِي رَحۡمَتِنَآۖ إِنَّهُۥ مِنَ ٱلصَّٰلِحِينَ
٧٥ وَنُوحًا إِذۡ نَادَىٰ مِن قَبۡلُ فَٱسۡتَجَبۡنَا لَهُۥ فَنَجَّيۡنَٰهُ
وَأَهۡلَهُۥ مِنَ ٱلۡكَرۡبِ ٱلۡعَظِيمِ ٧٦ وَنَصَرۡنَٰهُ مِنَ ٱلۡقَوۡمِ
ٱلَّذِينَ كَذَّبُواْ بِـَٔايَٰتِنَآۚ إِنَّهُمۡ كَانُواْ قَوۡمَ سَوۡءٖ فَأَغۡرَقۡنَٰهُمۡ
أَجۡمَعِينَ ٧٧ وَدَاوُۥدَ وَسُلَيۡمَٰنَ إِذۡ يَحۡكُمَانِ فِي ٱلۡحَرۡثِ إِذۡ
نَفَشَتۡ فِيهِ غَنَمُ ٱلۡقَوۡمِ وَكُنَّا لِحُكۡمِهِمۡ شَٰهِدِينَ ٧٨

60. ***They said*** to one another: ***'We heard a young man mentioning*** and criticising ***them. They call him Ibrāhīm.'***

61. ***They said, 'Bring him*** publicly ***before the people's eyes so they can be witnesses*** and testify that he did it.'

62. ***They asked*** him after he was brought***: 'Did you do this to our gods, Ibrāhīm?'***

63. He was silent about what he did, and ***he said, 'No, this one, the biggest of them, did it. Ask them*** who did it, ***if they are able to speak!'*** This is an allusion to the fact that the specific idol was unable to act and unable to speak and therefore could not be a god.

64. ***They consulted among themselves*** – reflecting on his words – ***and said*** to each other: ***'It is you yourselves who are wrongdoers*** by worshipping those who do not speak.'

65. ***But then they relapsed*** from this insight ***back into their unbelief*** and said***: 'You know full well these idols cannot talk,*** so how can you ask us to ask them***?'***

66. ***He said, 'Do you then worship, instead of Allah, what cannot help or harm you in any way*** – in respect of provision or anything else***?*** It will not harm you if you do not worship them.

67. ***Shame on you*** (read as *uffin, uffa* and *uffi*, an exclamation used for something ugly and foul) ***and what you worship besides Allah! Will you not use your intellect?'*** Will you not realise that these idols do not deserve worship and are not a proper subject for it? Allah alone is the One who is entitled to worship.

68. ***They said, 'Burn him*** (Ibrāhīm) ***and support your gods*** by burning him ***if you are resolved to do something*** to help them.' They gathered a great deal of firewood, set fire to all of it, tied Ibrāhīm up, put him in a catapult, and shot him into the Fire. Then Allah said:

69. ***We said, 'Fire, be coolness and peace for Ibrāhīm!'*** The fire only burned his bonds. Its heat departed and its light remained. By "peace" what is meant is safety from death by means of the fire being made cool.

70. ***They desired to trap him*** and burn him; ***but We made them the losers*** – by the fact that they failed to achieve what they wanted.

71. ***We delivered both him and Lūṭ*** – the son of his brother Hārūn – from Iraq ***to the land which We had blessed for all beings*** with many rivers and trees, which was Syria. Ibrāhīm settled in Palestine and Lūṭ in Sodom; there was a day's distance between them.

72. ***And in addition to that We gave him Isḥāq and Ya'qūb*** – because he had asked for a child, as we find in *Sūrat aṣ-Ṣāffāt* (37:100). Ya'qūb was added as the grandchild – ***and made both of them righteous*** Prophets.

73. ***We made them leaders, guiding*** people to good ***by Our command*** – to the *dīn* of Allah – ***and revealed to them how to do good actions and establish the prayer and pay* zakāt, *and they worshipped Us.***

74. ***We gave right judgement*** – of how to decide between litigants – ***and knowledge to Lūṭ and rescued him from the city*** the inhabitants of ***which committed disgusting acts***, such as sodomy, sniping at passers-by, looking at omens and other things. ***They were*** inwardly ***evil people who were deviators.***

75. ***We admitted him into Our mercy*** and saved him from his people. ***He was one of the righteous.***

76. ***And*** remember ***Nūḥ, when he called out before*** Ibrāhīm and Lūṭ, and prayed against his people, saying, "Lord, do not leave...!" (71:28-30), ***and We responded to him and rescued him and his family from the terrible plight*** of drowning in the Flood, and from the denial of his people.

77. ***We helped him against the people who rejected Our Signs*** which proved His Message, so that they could not do evil to him. ***They were an evil people and We drowned them, every one.***

78. ***And*** remember the story of ***Dāwūd and Sulaymān when they gave judgement about the field*** – either a wheatfield or vineyard, which sheep went into at night without a shepherd when they got loose – ***when the people's sheep strayed into it at night. We were Witness to their judgement.*** Dāwūd said that the owner of the field should take the sheep. Sulaymān said that he should have the use of their milk, offspring and wool until the field was restored to the state it had been in and then the sheep should be returned.

79. ***We gave Sulaymān understanding of it*** – arbitration and judgement by *ijtihād*; and Dāwūd preferred Sulaymān's judgement. It is said that it came about by Revelation. Sulaymān's judgement super-

فَفَهَّمۡنَٰهَا سُلَيۡمَٰنَۚ وَكُلًّا ءَاتَيۡنَا حُكۡمٗا وَعِلۡمٗاۚ وَسَخَّرۡنَا
مَعَ دَاوُۥدَ ٱلۡجِبَالَ يُسَبِّحۡنَ وَٱلطَّيۡرَۚ وَكُنَّا فَٰعِلِينَ ٧٩
وَعَلَّمۡنَٰهُ صَنۡعَةَ لَبُوسٖ لَّكُمۡ لِتُحۡصِنَكُم مِّنۢ بَأۡسِكُمۡۖ
فَهَلۡ أَنتُمۡ شَٰكِرُونَ ٨٠ وَلِسُلَيۡمَٰنَ ٱلرِّيحَ عَاصِفَةٗ تَجۡرِي بِأَمۡرِهِۦٓ
إِلَى ٱلۡأَرۡضِ ٱلَّتِي بَٰرَكۡنَا فِيهَاۚ وَكُنَّا بِكُلِّ شَيۡءٍ عَٰلِمِينَ ٨١
وَمِنَ ٱلشَّيَٰطِينِ مَن يَغُوصُونَ لَهُۥ وَيَعۡمَلُونَ عَمَلٗا
دُونَ ذَٰلِكَۖ وَكُنَّا لَهُمۡ حَٰفِظِينَ ٨٢ ۞ وَأَيُّوبَ إِذۡ
نَادَىٰ رَبَّهُۥٓ أَنِّي مَسَّنِيَ ٱلضُّرُّ وَأَنتَ أَرۡحَمُ ٱلرَّٰحِمِينَ ٨٣
فَٱسۡتَجَبۡنَا لَهُۥ فَكَشَفۡنَا مَا بِهِۦ مِن ضُرّٖۖ وَءَاتَيۡنَٰهُ أَهۡلَهُۥ
وَمِثۡلَهُم مَّعَهُمۡ رَحۡمَةٗ مِّنۡ عِندِنَا وَذِكۡرَىٰ لِلۡعَٰبِدِينَ ٨٤
وَإِسۡمَٰعِيلَ وَإِدۡرِيسَ وَذَا ٱلۡكِفۡلِۖ كُلّٞ مِّنَ ٱلصَّٰبِرِينَ
٨٥ وَأَدۡخَلۡنَٰهُمۡ فِي رَحۡمَتِنَآۖ إِنَّهُم مِّنَ ٱلصَّٰلِحِينَ
٨٦ وَذَا ٱلنُّونِ إِذ ذَّهَبَ مُغَٰضِبٗا فَظَنَّ أَن لَّن نَّقۡدِرَ عَلَيۡهِ
فَنَادَىٰ فِي ٱلظُّلُمَٰتِ أَن لَّآ إِلَٰهَ إِلَّآ أَنتَ سُبۡحَٰنَكَ إِنِّي
كُنتُ مِنَ ٱلظَّٰلِمِينَ ٨٧ فَٱسۡتَجَبۡنَا لَهُۥ وَنَجَّيۡنَٰهُ
مِنَ ٱلۡغَمِّۚ وَكَذَٰلِكَ نُـۨجِي ٱلۡمُؤۡمِنِينَ ٨٨ وَزَكَرِيَّآ
إِذۡ نَادَىٰ رَبَّهُۥ رَبِّ لَا تَذَرۡنِي فَرۡدٗا وَأَنتَ خَيۡرُ ٱلۡوَٰرِثِينَ
٨٩ فَٱسۡتَجَبۡنَا لَهُۥ وَوَهَبۡنَا لَهُۥ يَحۡيَىٰ وَأَصۡلَحۡنَا
لَهُۥ زَوۡجَهُۥٓۚ إِنَّهُمۡ كَانُواْ يُسَٰرِعُونَ فِي ٱلۡخَيۡرَٰتِ
وَيَدۡعُونَنَا رَغَبٗا وَرَهَبٗاۖ وَكَانُواْ لَنَا خَٰشِعِينَ ٩٠

seded Dāwūd's. ***We gave each of them judgement*** (Prophethood) ***and knowledge*** of matters of the *dīn*. ***We subjected the mountains to Dāwūd, glorifying, and the birds as well.*** The birds were subjected to glorification with him at his command whenever he became tired, to encourage him. ***This is something We are well able to do.*** We are able to subject the glorification of the birds and the mountains to Dāwūd, even though you might find that surprising.

80. ***We taught him the art of making garments for you*** – coats of chain mail for the first time; before that plated armour was used – ***to protect you*** (read as *tuḥṣinakum* as here and *nuḥṣinakum* meaning, "so that We might protect you") ***against each others' violence*** – referring to war with enemies. ***But do you***, people of Makka, ***show any thanks*** for My blessings by believing the Messenger?

81. ***And to Sulaymān We gave*** power over ***the fiercely blowing wind*** – here it is described as "fiercely blowing" whereas in another *āyat* (38:36) it is described as blowing "softly", which indicates that both strong and gentle winds were subject to him, ***speeding at his command*** and will ***towards the land which We had blessed*** (Syria). ***And We had full knowledge of everything.*** Allah knew that what He gave Sulaymān would make him humble to his Lord, and He acted accordingly.

82. ***And*** We subjected ***some of the shaytans*** to Sulaymān who ***dived for him*** into the sea and brought out gems from it for him, ***and did other things apart from that***, such as building. ***And We were watching over them*** so that they did not ruin what they did; because when the jinn finish work before night, they ruin it if they are distracted by something else.

83. ***And*** remember ***Ayyūb when he called out to his Lord*** – when he was tested by the loss of all his wealth and children and the lesions on his body, and everyone except his wife shunned him for three, seven or eighteen years, restricting his livelihood – ***'Great harm has afflicted me, but You are the Most Merciful of the merciful.'***

84. ***We responded to him*** and his supplication, ***removed from him the harm which was afflicting him, and restored his family to him*** – giving him male and female children by bringing them back to life; and he had three or seven of each – ***and the same again with them*** –

from his wife, since his youth was restored. He had one threshing floor for wheat and another for barley. Allah sent two clouds, one of which emptied gold onto the wheat floor and the other silver onto the barley floor until they overflowed – ***as a mercy direct from Us and a Reminder to all worshippers*** to be steadfast so that they may be rewarded.

85. ***And*** remember ***Ismā'īl and Idrīs and Dhū'l-Kifl. Each one was among the steadfast*** in obeying Allah and in not disobeying Him.

86. ***We admitted them into Our mercy*** (Prophethood). ***They were among the righteous*** – suitably prepared for it. The name of Dhū'l-Kifl comes from the fact that he obliged (*takaffal*) himself to fast everyday and pray every night and to render judgement between people and not to become angry; and he fulfilled all of that. According to another opinion, though, he was not a Prophet.

87. ***And*** remember ***Dhū'n-Nūn*** – "Possessor of the fish", another name for Yūnus ibn Mattā – ***when he left*** his people ***in anger*** – although he did not have permission to do so, because of the obduracy he experienced from them – ***and thought We would not punish him*** – that We would not decree for him what We decreed, in that he was confined inside the belly of the fish; or that We would not constrict him for doing so. ***He called out in the pitch darkness*** – the plural is used and refers to the three darknesses of the night, the sea and the belly of the fish: ***'There is no god but You! Glory be to You! Truly I have been one of the wrongdoers*** in leaving my people without permission.*'*

88. ***We responded to him*** on account of those words ***and rescued him from his grief. That is how We rescue the believers*** from grief when they call on Us for help.

89. ***And*** remember ***Zakariyyā when he called out to his Lord, 'My Lord, do not leave me on my own*** – without a child to inherit from me – ***though You are the Best of Inheritors.*** You are the One who will remain after the rest of Your creation disappears.*'*

90. ***We responded to him*** after his plea ***and gave him*** – a son – ***Yaḥyā, restoring for him his wife's fertility*** after she had become barren. ***They*** – those of the Prophets We have mentioned – ***outdid one another in good actions*** – hastening to acts of obedience to

وَٱلَّتِىٓ أَحْصَنَتْ فَرْجَهَا فَنَفَخْنَا فِيهَا مِن رُّوحِنَا
وَجَعَلْنَٰهَا وَٱبْنَهَآ ءَايَةً لِّلْعَٰلَمِينَ ﴿٩١﴾ إِنَّ هَٰذِهِۦٓ
أُمَّتُكُمْ أُمَّةً وَٰحِدَةً وَأَنَا۠ رَبُّكُمْ فَٱعْبُدُونِ ﴿٩٢﴾
وَتَقَطَّعُوٓا۟ أَمْرَهُم بَيْنَهُمْ ۖ كُلٌّ إِلَيْنَا رَٰجِعُونَ ﴿٩٣﴾
فَمَن يَعْمَلْ مِنَ ٱلصَّٰلِحَٰتِ وَهُوَ مُؤْمِنٌ فَلَا كُفْرَانَ
لِسَعْيِهِۦ وَإِنَّا لَهُۥ كَٰتِبُونَ ﴿٩٤﴾ وَحَرَٰمٌ عَلَىٰ قَرْيَةٍ
أَهْلَكْنَٰهَآ أَنَّهُمْ لَا يَرْجِعُونَ ﴿٩٥﴾ حَتَّىٰٓ إِذَا فُتِحَتْ
يَأْجُوجُ وَمَأْجُوجُ وَهُم مِّن كُلِّ حَدَبٍ يَنسِلُونَ ﴿٩٦﴾
وَٱقْتَرَبَ ٱلْوَعْدُ ٱلْحَقُّ فَإِذَا هِىَ شَٰخِصَةٌ أَبْصَٰرُ ٱلَّذِينَ
كَفَرُوا۟ يَٰوَيْلَنَا قَدْ كُنَّا فِى غَفْلَةٍ مِّنْ هَٰذَا بَلْ كُنَّا
ظَٰلِمِينَ ﴿٩٧﴾ إِنَّكُمْ وَمَا تَعْبُدُونَ مِن دُونِ
ٱللَّهِ حَصَبُ جَهَنَّمَ أَنتُمْ لَهَا وَٰرِدُونَ ﴿٩٨﴾ لَوْ كَانَ
هَٰٓؤُلَآءِ ءَالِهَةً مَّا وَرَدُوهَا ۖ وَكُلٌّ فِيهَا خَٰلِدُونَ ﴿٩٩﴾
لَهُمْ فِيهَا زَفِيرٌ وَهُمْ فِيهَا لَا يَسْمَعُونَ ﴿١٠٠﴾ إِنَّ ٱلَّذِينَ
سَبَقَتْ لَهُم مِّنَّا ٱلْحُسْنَىٰٓ أُو۟لَٰٓئِكَ عَنْهَا مُبْعَدُونَ ﴿١٠١﴾
لَا يَسْمَعُونَ حَسِيسَهَا ۖ وَهُمْ فِى مَا ٱشْتَهَتْ أَنفُسُهُمْ
خَٰلِدُونَ ﴿١٠٢﴾ لَا يَحْزُنُهُمُ ٱلْفَزَعُ ٱلْأَكْبَرُ وَتَتَلَقَّىٰهُمُ
ٱلْمَلَٰٓئِكَةُ هَٰذَا يَوْمُكُمُ ٱلَّذِى كُنتُمْ تُوعَدُونَ

Allah – ***calling out to Us in yearning*** for Our mercy ***and in awe*** of Our punishment, ***and humbling themselves to Us*** in their worship.

91. ***And*** remember Maryam ***she who protected her private parts*** and guarded her chastity. ***We breathed into her some of Our*** **Rūḥ** – Jibrīl breathed into the pocket of her shift and she became pregnant with 'Īsā – ***and made her and her son a Sign for all the worlds*** – for human beings, jinn and angels, since she gave birth to him without a father.

92. ***This nation of yours*** – the nation of Islam – ***is one nation*** and your *dīn* which you are obliged to follow – ***and I am your Lord, so worship Me*** and affirm My Unity.

93. ***But they*** – some of those who were told to do this – ***disagreed and split into different sects*** regarding their *dīn*; this refers to the many sects of the Jews and Christians. Allah continues – ***Each one will return to Us*** and We will repay them for what they did.

94. ***As for anyone who does right actions and is a believer, his striving certainly does not go unthanked*** (unacknowledged). ***We are writing it down on his behalf.*** Allah commands the recording angels to write it down and then He will repay him for what he did.

95. ***There is a ban on any city*** – meaning its inhabitants – ***We have destroyed; they will not return*** to this world.

96. The prohibition against returning continues until ***when Ya'jūj and Ma'jūj*** – these are two non-Arabic names which are the names of tribes – ***are let loose*** (read as *futiḥat* and *futtiḥat*) – lit. "are opened", which may refer to the breaching of the wall holding them in. When this happens, it will be close to the time of the Rising – ***and rush*** rapidly ***down from every slope,***

97. ***...and the True Promise*** of the Day of Rising ***is very close, the eyes of those who disbelieved will be transfixed*** because of the intensity of that day and they will say: ***'Alas for us!*** We are destroyed! ***We were unmindful of this*** day in this world! ***No, rather we were certainly wrongdoers*** in denying the Messengers.'

98. ***You***, people of Makka, ***and what*** (the idols) ***you worship*** – according to your claim – ***besides Allah are fuel for Hell. You will go down into it.***

99. ***If those*** idols ***had really been gods*** – as you claim – ***they would not have gone down into it*** – into the Fire. ***Each one*** – those who worshipped idols and the idols they worshipped – ***will be in it timelessly, for ever.***

100. ***There will be sighing for them*** (those who worshipped idols) ***in it and they will not be able to hear*** anything – on account of the intensity of its boiling. This was revealed when Ibn az-Zib'ari asked, "'Uzayr, the Messiah, and the angels were worshipped. Will they be in the Fire, then?"

101. ***Those for whom the Best from Us was pre-ordained will be far away from it.***

102. ***They will not hear the slightest hint of it*** at all ***and they will remain there*** in bliss ***timelessly, for ever, among everything their selves desire.***

103. ***The greatest terror will not upset them*** – a reference to the time when people are commanded to go to the Fire – ***and the angels will welcome them*** – when they emerge from the graves: ***'This is your Day, the one that you were promised*** in the world.'

104. ***That Day We will fold up heaven like folding up the pages of a book*** (read as *kitāb* and *kutub*). The word for "pages" here, *sijil*, is also said to be the name of an angel, in which case the meaning becomes: "like when (the angel) Sijil folds up the Book." The "book" referred to is the record of the son of Ādam when he dies. ***As We originated the first creation*** – from non-existence – ***so We will regenerate it*** – after it has been made non-existent again. ***It is a promise binding on Us*** because We have made it; ***that is what We will do*** – as We promised.

105. ***We wrote down in the Zabūr*** – the word *zabūr* is sometimes used in the Qur'an to refer specifically to the biblical Psalms, but literally means any written text and in this case refers to every Divinely Revealed Book – ***after the Reminder*** – the Mother of the Book which is with Allah – ***came: 'It is My slaves who are righteous who will inherit the earth*** – in Paradise.' All who are righteous will inherit it.

106. ***Certainly there is*** an adequate ***transmission in this*** Qur'an about entering the Garden – ***for people who worship*** and act according to it.

﴿١٠٣﴾ يَوْمَ نَطْوِى ٱلسَّمَآءَ كَطَىِّ ٱلسِّجِلِّ لِلْكُتُبِ ۚ كَمَا
بَدَأْنَآ أَوَّلَ خَلْقٍ نُّعِيدُهُۥ ۚ وَعْدًا عَلَيْنَآ ۚ إِنَّا كُنَّا فَٰعِلِينَ
﴿١٠٤﴾ وَلَقَدْ كَتَبْنَا فِى ٱلزَّبُورِ مِنۢ بَعْدِ ٱلذِّكْرِ أَنَّ ٱلْأَرْضَ
يَرِثُهَا عِبَادِىَ ٱلصَّٰلِحُونَ ﴿١٠٥﴾ إِنَّ فِى هَٰذَا لَبَلَٰغًا
لِّقَوْمٍ عَٰبِدِينَ ﴿١٠٦﴾ وَمَآ أَرْسَلْنَٰكَ إِلَّا رَحْمَةً لِّلْعَٰلَمِينَ
﴿١٠٧﴾ قُلْ إِنَّمَا يُوحَىٰٓ إِلَىَّ أَنَّمَآ إِلَٰهُكُمْ إِلَٰهٌ وَٰحِدٌ ۖ
فَهَلْ أَنتُم مُّسْلِمُونَ ﴿١٠٨﴾ فَإِن تَوَلَّوْا۟ فَقُلْ ءَاذَنتُكُمْ
عَلَىٰ سَوَآءٍ ۖ وَإِنْ أَدْرِىٓ أَقَرِيبٌ أَم بَعِيدٌ مَّا تُوعَدُونَ ﴿١٠٩﴾
إِنَّهُۥ يَعْلَمُ ٱلْجَهْرَ مِنَ ٱلْقَوْلِ وَيَعْلَمُ مَا تَكْتُمُونَ
﴿١١٠﴾ وَإِنْ أَدْرِى لَعَلَّهُۥ فِتْنَةٌ لَّكُمْ وَمَتَٰعٌ إِلَىٰ حِينٍ ﴿١١١﴾ قَٰلَ
رَبِّ ٱحْكُم بِٱلْحَقِّ ۗ وَرَبُّنَا ٱلرَّحْمَٰنُ ٱلْمُسْتَعَانُ عَلَىٰ مَا تَصِفُونَ ﴿١١٢﴾

107. ***We have sent you,*** Muḥammad, ***only as a mercy to all the worlds*** – to both human beings and the jinn.

108. ***Say: 'It is revealed to me that your god is One God. So are you Muslims?'*** Will you obey what has been revealed to me about the Oneness of God? The question is in reality a command to become Muslim.

109. ***If they turn their backs*** on that, ***then say: 'I have informed all of you equally*** – of a war which will be waged against you and so we are all equal in that respect; the warning is not directed to me alone but to you as well, and so you should prepare yourselves for what is to come – ***and I do not know if what you have been promised*** – regarding the punishment or the Rising which entails it – ***is near or far.*** Allah alone knows that.

110. ***He*** (Allah) ***knows what is said openly*** – and what you and others do – ***and He knows what you hide*** and do secretly.

111. ***For all I know, it*** – what I have told you about, whose destined time I do not know – ***might be a trial for you*** – to see what you will do – ***and you will have enjoyment for a time*** until the end of your lifespan.***'***

112. ***He said*** (read as *qāla* and *qul*, "Say") – ***'Lord, judge*** between me and those who deny me ***with truth*** – by punishing them or granting us victory against them. They were punished at Badr, Uḥud, Ḥunayn, al-Aḥzāb and the Ditch and were finally defeated completely. ***Our Lord is the All-Merciful, the One Whose help is sought in the face of what you describe.'*** This refers to their denial of Allah in their words, "He has taken a son," and of the Prophet, peace be upon him, when they called him a magician and said that the Qur'an was poetry.

سُورَةُ الحَجِّ

بِسۡمِ ٱللَّهِ ٱلرَّحۡمَٰنِ ٱلرَّحِيمِ

يَٰٓأَيُّهَا ٱلنَّاسُ ٱتَّقُواْ رَبَّكُمۡۚ إِنَّ زَلۡزَلَةَ ٱلسَّاعَةِ شَيۡءٌ
عَظِيمٞ ١ يَوۡمَ تَرَوۡنَهَا تَذۡهَلُ كُلُّ مُرۡضِعَةٍ عَمَّآ
أَرۡضَعَتۡ وَتَضَعُ كُلُّ ذَاتِ حَمۡلٍ حَمۡلَهَا وَتَرَى ٱلنَّاسَ
سُكَٰرَىٰ وَمَا هُم بِسُكَٰرَىٰ وَلَٰكِنَّ عَذَابَ ٱللَّهِ شَدِيدٞ
٢ وَمِنَ ٱلنَّاسِ مَن يُجَٰدِلُ فِي ٱللَّهِ بِغَيۡرِ عِلۡمٖ وَيَتَّبِعُ كُلَّ
شَيۡطَٰنٖ مَّرِيدٖ ٣ كُتِبَ عَلَيۡهِ أَنَّهُۥ مَن تَوَلَّاهُ فَأَنَّهُۥ يُضِلُّهُۥ
وَيَهۡدِيهِ إِلَىٰ عَذَابِ ٱلسَّعِيرِ ٤ يَٰٓأَيُّهَا ٱلنَّاسُ إِن كُنتُمۡ فِي
رَيۡبٖ مِّنَ ٱلۡبَعۡثِ فَإِنَّا خَلَقۡنَٰكُم مِّن تُرَابٖ ثُمَّ مِن نُّطۡفَةٖ ثُمَّ
مِنۡ عَلَقَةٖ ثُمَّ مِن مُّضۡغَةٖ مُّخَلَّقَةٖ وَغَيۡرِ مُخَلَّقَةٖ لِّنُبَيِّنَ لَكُمۡۚ
وَنُقِرُّ فِي ٱلۡأَرۡحَامِ مَا نَشَآءُ إِلَىٰٓ أَجَلٖ مُّسَمّٗى ثُمَّ نُخۡرِجُكُمۡ
طِفۡلٗا ثُمَّ لِتَبۡلُغُوٓاْ أَشُدَّكُمۡۖ وَمِنكُم مَّن يُتَوَفَّىٰ
وَمِنكُم مَّن يُرَدُّ إِلَىٰٓ أَرۡذَلِ ٱلۡعُمُرِ لِكَيۡلَا يَعۡلَمَ مِنۢ
بَعۡدِ عِلۡمٖ شَيۡـٔٗاۚ وَتَرَى ٱلۡأَرۡضَ هَامِدَةٗ فَإِذَآ أَنزَلۡنَا عَلَيۡهَا
ٱلۡمَآءَ ٱهۡتَزَّتۡ وَرَبَتۡ وَأَنۢبَتَتۡ مِن كُلِّ زَوۡجِۭ بَهِيجٖ ٥
ذَٰلِكَ بِأَنَّ ٱللَّهَ هُوَ ٱلۡحَقُّ وَأَنَّهُۥ يُحۡيِ ٱلۡمَوۡتَىٰ وَأَنَّهُۥ عَلَىٰ كُلِّ شَيۡءٖ قَدِيرٞ

22. *Sūrat al-Ḥajj*
The Pilgrimage

This *sūra* is Madinan except for *āyats* 52, 53, 54, and 55, which are Makkan. It has 78 *āyats* and was sent down after *an-Nūr.*

1. ***Mankind,*** meaning people of Makka and others, ***be fearful of your Lord*** – of His punishment by obeying Him*!* ***The quaking of the Hour*** – which will occur after the sun rises from the West, an indication that the Final Hour is very near – ***is a terrible thing.*** People will experience terrible anxiety which is a form of punishment.

2. ***On the day they see it*** – because of it – ***every nursing woman will be oblivious of the baby at her breast, and every pregnant woman will abort the contents of her womb, and you will think people drunk*** – because of the effects of fear – ***although they are not drunk*** – from intoxicating drink – ***it is just that the punishment of Allah is so severe.***

3. ***On the day they see it*** – because of it – ***every nursing woman will be oblivious of the baby at her breast, and every pregnant woman will abort the contents of her womb, and you will think people drunk*** because of the effects of it. This was revealed about an-Naḍr ibn al-Ḥārith and his group. ***Among people there is one*** (an-Naḍr ibn al-Ḥārith) ***who argues about Allah without knowledge*** – saying, "The angels are the daughters of Allah and the Qur'an is simply the myths of earlier peoples." He denied the Resurrection and being brought back to life again from dust – ***and follows every rebellious shayṭān*** – in his argument.

4. ***It is written of him*** – and decreed – ***that if anyone takes him*** (Shayṭān) ***as a friend*** and follows him, ***he will mislead him and guide him to the punishment of the Searing Blaze.***

5. ***Mankind, if you are in any doubt about the Rising, know that We created you*** – in the form of Ādam – ***from dust, then*** – his offspring – ***from a drop of sperm, then from a*** congealed ***clot of blood, then from a lump of flesh, formed yet unformed*** – a form, but one which is not yet complete – ***so We may make things clear to you*** by

﴿٦﴾ وَأَنَّ ٱلسَّاعَةَ ءَاتِيَةٌ لَّا رَيْبَ فِيهَا وَأَنَّ ٱللَّهَ يَبْعَثُ مَن فِي
ٱلْقُبُورِ ﴿٧﴾ وَمِنَ ٱلنَّاسِ مَن يُجَٰدِلُ فِي ٱللَّهِ بِغَيْرِ عِلْمٍ وَلَا هُدًى
وَلَا كِتَٰبٍ مُّنِيرٍ ﴿٨﴾ ثَانِيَ عِطْفِهِۦ لِيُضِلَّ عَن سَبِيلِ ٱللَّهِ لَهُۥ فِي
ٱلدُّنْيَا خِزْيٌ وَنُذِيقُهُۥ يَوْمَ ٱلْقِيَٰمَةِ عَذَابَ ٱلْحَرِيقِ ﴿٩﴾ ذَٰلِكَ
بِمَا قَدَّمَتْ يَدَاكَ وَأَنَّ ٱللَّهَ لَيْسَ بِظَلَّٰمٍ لِّلْعَبِيدِ ﴿١٠﴾ وَمِنَ ٱلنَّاسِ
مَن يَعْبُدُ ٱللَّهَ عَلَىٰ حَرْفٍ فَإِنْ أَصَابَهُۥ خَيْرٌ ٱطْمَأَنَّ بِهِۦ وَإِنْ أَصَابَتْهُ
فِتْنَةٌ ٱنقَلَبَ عَلَىٰ وَجْهِهِۦ خَسِرَ ٱلدُّنْيَا وَٱلْءَاخِرَةَ ذَٰلِكَ هُوَ
ٱلْخُسْرَانُ ٱلْمُبِينُ ﴿١١﴾ يَدْعُوا۟ مِن دُونِ ٱللَّهِ مَا لَا يَضُرُّهُۥ
وَمَا لَا يَنفَعُهُۥ ذَٰلِكَ هُوَ ٱلضَّلَٰلُ ٱلْبَعِيدُ ﴿١٢﴾ يَدْعُوا۟ لَمَن
ضَرُّهُۥٓ أَقْرَبُ مِن نَّفْعِهِۦ لَبِئْسَ ٱلْمَوْلَىٰ وَلَبِئْسَ ٱلْعَشِيرُ ﴿١٣﴾
إِنَّ ٱللَّهَ يُدْخِلُ ٱلَّذِينَ ءَامَنُوا۟ وَعَمِلُوا۟ ٱلصَّٰلِحَٰتِ جَنَّٰتٍ
تَجْرِي مِن تَحْتِهَا ٱلْأَنْهَٰرُ إِنَّ ٱللَّهَ يَفْعَلُ مَا يُرِيدُ ﴿١٤﴾ مَن كَانَ
يَظُنُّ أَن لَّن يَنصُرَهُ ٱللَّهُ فِي ٱلدُّنْيَا وَٱلْءَاخِرَةِ فَلْيَمْدُدْ بِسَبَبٍ إِلَى
ٱلسَّمَآءِ ثُمَّ لْيَقْطَعْ فَلْيَنظُرْ هَلْ يُذْهِبَنَّ كَيْدُهُۥ مَا يَغِيظُ ﴿١٥﴾
وَكَذَٰلِكَ أَنزَلْنَٰهُ ءَايَٰتٍۭ بَيِّنَٰتٍ وَأَنَّ ٱللَّهَ يَهْدِي مَن يُرِيدُ
﴿١٦﴾ إِنَّ ٱلَّذِينَ ءَامَنُوا۟ وَٱلَّذِينَ هَادُوا۟ وَٱلصَّٰبِـِٔينَ وَٱلنَّصَٰرَىٰ
وَٱلْمَجُوسَ وَٱلَّذِينَ أَشْرَكُوٓا۟ إِنَّ ٱللَّهَ يَفْصِلُ بَيْنَهُمْ
يَوْمَ ٱلْقِيَٰمَةِ إِنَّ ٱللَّهَ عَلَىٰ كُلِّ شَيْءٍ شَهِيدٌ ﴿١٧﴾ أَلَمْ تَرَ أَنَّ ٱللَّهَ
يَسْجُدُ لَهُۥ مَن فِي ٱلسَّمَٰوَٰتِ وَمَن فِي ٱلْأَرْضِ وَٱلشَّمْسُ وَٱلْقَمَرُ
وَٱلنُّجُومُ وَٱلْجِبَالُ وَٱلشَّجَرُ وَٱلدَّوَآبُّ وَكَثِيرٌ مِّنَ ٱلنَّاسِ

demonstrating Our complete power to you, so that you will see evidence of the possibility of restoration in the origination of creation. ***We make whatever We want stay in the womb until a specified time*** – its birth – ***and then We bring you out*** of the wombs of your mothers ***as children so that you may reach your full maturity*** and strength, which is reckoned to be between thirty and forty years of age. ***Some of you die*** before reaching adulthood ***and some of you revert to the lowest form of life*** and become senile ***so that, after having knowledge, they then know nothing at all.*** According to 'Ikrima, "Whoever reads the Qur'an does not persist in this state of "knowing nothing at all". ***And you see the earth*** – arid – ***dead and barren; then when We send down water onto it, it quivers and swells and sprouts with luxuriant plants of every kind.***

6. ***That*** – what has been mentioned about the creation of man and the giving of life to the earth – ***is because Allah is the*** Abiding ***Real and gives life to the dead and has power over all things;***

7. ***...and the Hour is coming without any doubt, and Allah will raise up all those in the graves.***

8. The following was revealed about Abū Jahl. ***Among people there is one who argues about Allah without knowledge or guidance or any light-giving Book,***

9. ***...turning away*** his head from belief ***arrogantly, to misguide*** (read as *yuḍilla* or *yaḍilla*) ***people from the Way*** (*dīn*) ***of Allah. He will be disgraced*** by punishment ***in this world*** and by being killed at the Battle of Badr – ***and on the Day of Rising We will make him taste the punishment of the Burning:***

10. It will be said: ***'That is for what you*** (literally your hands) ***did before.*** The hands are mentioned because they are the limbs by which most actions are done. ***Allah does not wrong His slaves.'*** Allah does not inflict wrong on people by punishing them when they have committed no wrong action.

11. ***Among the people there is one who worships Allah right on the edge*** – meaning that he has doubt about His worship. He is likened to someone on the edge of a mountain in that he is not firm. ***If good*** – health and safety in respect of his wealth and his person – ***befalls him, he is content with it, but if a trial*** – affliction and illness in respect of his wealth and person – ***befalls him, he reverts to his former ways*** – to unbelief, ***losing both*** what he hopes for in ***this world and*** losing ***the Next World*** through unbelief. ***That is indeed sheer loss.***

12. ***Instead of Allah, he calls on*** – and worships – ***something*** (an idol) ***which cannot harm him*** if he does not worship it ***or help him*** if he does. ***That*** (calling on idols) ***is extreme misguidance*** – far from the truth.

13. ***He calls on what is far more likely to harm than help.*** His worship of idols is far more likely to harm him than help him in the way he imagines it will. ***What an evil protector! What an evil associate!***

14. After mentioning the loss that doubters will suffer, Allah then mentions the reward which the believers will receive. ***Allah will admit those who believe and do right actions*** – both obligatory and supererogatory ones – ***into Gardens with rivers flowing under them. Allah does whatever He wishes*** by honouring those to whom He gives and abasing those who disobey Him.

15. ***Anyone who thinks that Allah will not help him*** (Muḥammad, His Prophet) ***in this world and the Next World, should stretch a rope up to the ceiling*** of his house and put it around his neck ***and then hang himself*** – throttle himself, as is stated in the *Ṣaḥīḥ* Collections explaining this usage. ***Let him see whether his stratagem*** – that of not helping the Prophet – ***gets rid of what enrages him!*** Let him choke himself to death out of rage.

16. ***In this way*** – as We revealed the previous *āyat* – ***We have sent it*** – the rest of the Qur'an – ***down as Clear Signs. Allah guides anyone He wills*** to understanding of what He has revealed.

17. ***As for those who believe, and those who are Jews, and the Sabaeans*** (a group of Jews) ***and the Christians, Magians and idolaters, Allah will distinguish between them on the Day of Rising*** – the believers entering the Garden and the rest entering the Fire. ***Allah is witness of all things*** and knows all of their actions directly.

18. ***Do you not see*** (know) ***that everyone in the heavens and everyone on the earth prostrates to Allah, and the sun and moon and stars and the mountains, trees and beasts*** – are subject to Him and do what He wants – ***and many of mankind?*** – a reference to the

وَكَثِيرٌ حَقَّ عَلَيْهِ ٱلْعَذَابُ ۗ وَمَن يُهِنِ ٱللَّهُ فَمَا لَهُۥ مِن مُّكْرِمٍ ۚ
إِنَّ ٱللَّهَ يَفْعَلُ مَا يَشَآءُ ۩ ﴿١٨﴾ ۞ هَٰذَانِ خَصْمَانِ ٱخْتَصَمُوا۟
فِى رَبِّهِمْ ۖ فَٱلَّذِينَ كَفَرُوا۟ قُطِّعَتْ لَهُمْ ثِيَابٌ مِّن نَّارٍ يُصَبُّ
مِن فَوْقِ رُءُوسِهِمُ ٱلْحَمِيمُ ﴿١٩﴾ يُصْهَرُ بِهِۦ مَا فِى بُطُونِهِمْ
وَٱلْجُلُودُ ﴿٢٠﴾ وَلَهُم مَّقَٰمِعُ مِنْ حَدِيدٍ ﴿٢١﴾ كُلَّمَآ أَرَادُوٓا۟
أَن يَخْرُجُوا۟ مِنْهَا مِنْ غَمٍّ أُعِيدُوا۟ فِيهَا وَذُوقُوا۟ عَذَابَ ٱلْحَرِيقِ
﴿٢٢﴾ إِنَّ ٱللَّهَ يُدْخِلُ ٱلَّذِينَ ءَامَنُوا۟ وَعَمِلُوا۟ ٱلصَّٰلِحَٰتِ
جَنَّٰتٍ تَجْرِى مِن تَحْتِهَا ٱلْأَنْهَٰرُ يُحَلَّوْنَ فِيهَا مِنْ
أَسَاوِرَ مِن ذَهَبٍ وَلُؤْلُؤًا ۖ وَلِبَاسُهُمْ فِيهَا حَرِيرٌ ﴿٢٣﴾
وَهُدُوٓا۟ إِلَى ٱلطَّيِّبِ مِنَ ٱلْقَوْلِ وَهُدُوٓا۟ إِلَىٰ صِرَٰطِ ٱلْحَمِيدِ
﴿٢٤﴾ إِنَّ ٱلَّذِينَ كَفَرُوا۟ وَيَصُدُّونَ عَن سَبِيلِ ٱللَّهِ وَٱلْمَسْجِدِ
ٱلْحَرَامِ ٱلَّذِى جَعَلْنَٰهُ لِلنَّاسِ سَوَآءً ٱلْعَٰكِفُ فِيهِ وَٱلْبَادِ ۚ
وَمَن يُرِدْ فِيهِ بِإِلْحَادٍۭ بِظُلْمٍ نُّذِقْهُ مِنْ عَذَابٍ أَلِيمٍ ﴿٢٥﴾
وَإِذْ بَوَّأْنَا لِإِبْرَٰهِيمَ مَكَانَ ٱلْبَيْتِ أَن لَّا تُشْرِكْ بِى
شَيْـًٔا وَطَهِّرْ بَيْتِىَ لِلطَّآئِفِينَ وَٱلْقَآئِمِينَ وَٱلرُّكَّعِ
ٱلسُّجُودِ ﴿٢٦﴾ وَأَذِّن فِى ٱلنَّاسِ بِٱلْحَجِّ يَأْتُوكَ رِجَالًا وَعَلَىٰ
كُلِّ ضَامِرٍ يَأْتِينَ مِن كُلِّ فَجٍّ عَمِيقٍ ﴿٢٧﴾ لِّيَشْهَدُوا۟
مَنَٰفِعَ لَهُمْ وَيَذْكُرُوا۟ ٱسْمَ ٱللَّهِ فِىٓ أَيَّامٍ مَّعْلُومَٰتٍ
عَلَىٰ مَا رَزَقَهُم مِّنۢ بَهِيمَةِ ٱلْأَنْعَٰمِ ۖ فَكُلُوا۟ مِنْهَا وَأَطْعِمُوا۟
ٱلْبَآئِسَ ٱلْفَقِيرَ ﴿٢٨﴾ ثُمَّ لْيَقْضُوا۟ تَفَثَهُمْ وَلْيُوفُوا۟

believers who are humble in their prostration in the prayer. ***But many of them inevitably merit punishment.*** This means the unbelievers, because they refuse to prostrate, prostration being a matter of faith. ***Those Allah humiliates will have no one to honour them.*** Those He makes miserable will have no one to make them happy. ***Allah does whatever He wills*** by either honouring or humiliating.

19. ***Here are two rival groups*** – the believers and the unbelievers, although the former constitute one group and the latter five; the word for group used here, *khaṣm*, can refer to both the singular and the plural – ***who disputed concerning*** the *dīn* of ***their Lord. Those who disbelieve will have garments of fire cut out for them*** – which they will wear and so they will be enveloped in fire – ***and boiling water poured over their heads,***

20. ***...which will melt the contents of their bellies*** – the fat and everything else ***as well as*** roasting – ***their skin,***

21. ***...and they will be beaten*** on the head ***with cudgels made of iron.***

22. ***Every time they want to come out of it*** (the Fire) ***because of their suffering, they will be driven back into it*** with cudgels***: 'Taste the punishment of the Burning!'*** they will be told, using the word *ḥarīq,* which is an intensive form.

23. ***But Allah will admit those who believe and do right actions into Gardens with rivers flowing under them, where they will be adorned with gold bracelets and pearls*** (read as *lu'lu'an* and also as *lu'lu'in* in which case it means "bracelets of gold and pearl") ***and where their clothing will be of silk*** – which is unlawful for men to wear in this world.

24. ***They have been guided*** in this world ***to speak good words*** – meaning the formula *lā ilaha illā'llāh*, "there is no god but Allah" – ***and guided to the praiseworthy Path*** of Allah and His *dīn***.**

25. ***Those who disbelieve and bar access to the Way of Allah*** – obedience to Him – ***and to the Sacred Mosque which We have appointed*** to be the place of the *ḥajj* rites and worship ***for all mankind – equally for those who live near it and those who come from far away – those who desire to profane it with wrongdoing*** – even if

نُذُورَهُمْ وَلْيَطَّوَّفُواْ بِٱلْبَيْتِ ٱلْعَتِيقِ ٢٩ ذَٰلِكَ وَمَن
يُعَظِّمْ حُرُمَٰتِ ٱللَّهِ فَهُوَ خَيْرٌ لَّهُۥ عِندَ رَبِّهِۦۗ وَأُحِلَّتْ
لَكُمُ ٱلْأَنْعَٰمُ إِلَّا مَا يُتْلَىٰ عَلَيْكُمْۖ فَٱجْتَنِبُواْ
ٱلرِّجْسَ مِنَ ٱلْأَوْثَٰنِ وَٱجْتَنِبُواْ قَوْلَ ٱلزُّورِ ٣٠
حُنَفَآءَ لِلَّهِ غَيْرَ مُشْرِكِينَ بِهِۦۚ وَمَن يُشْرِكْ بِٱللَّهِ فَكَأَنَّمَا خَرَّ مِنَ
ٱلسَّمَآءِ فَتَخْطَفُهُ ٱلطَّيْرُ أَوْ تَهْوِى بِهِ ٱلرِّيحُ فِى مَكَانٍ سَحِيقٍ
٣١ ذَٰلِكَ وَمَن يُعَظِّمْ شَعَٰٓئِرَ ٱللَّهِ فَإِنَّهَا مِن تَقْوَى ٱلْقُلُوبِ
٣٢ لَكُمْ فِيهَا مَنَٰفِعُ إِلَىٰٓ أَجَلٍ مُّسَمًّى ثُمَّ مَحِلُّهَآ إِلَى ٱلْبَيْتِ
ٱلْعَتِيقِ ٣٣ وَلِكُلِّ أُمَّةٍ جَعَلْنَا مَنسَكًا لِّيَذْكُرُواْ ٱسْمَ
ٱللَّهِ عَلَىٰ مَا رَزَقَهُم مِّنۢ بَهِيمَةِ ٱلْأَنْعَٰمِۗ فَإِلَٰهُكُمْ إِلَٰهٌ وَٰحِدٌ
فَلَهُۥٓ أَسْلِمُواْۗ وَبَشِّرِ ٱلْمُخْبِتِينَ ٣٤ ٱلَّذِينَ إِذَا ذُكِرَ ٱللَّهُ وَجِلَتْ
قُلُوبُهُمْ وَٱلصَّٰبِرِينَ عَلَىٰ مَآ أَصَابَهُمْ وَٱلْمُقِيمِى ٱلصَّلَوٰةِ وَمِمَّا
رَزَقْنَٰهُمْ يُنفِقُونَ ٣٥ وَٱلْبُدْنَ جَعَلْنَٰهَا لَكُم مِّن شَعَٰٓئِرِ
ٱللَّهِ لَكُمْ فِيهَا خَيْرٌۖ فَٱذْكُرُواْ ٱسْمَ ٱللَّهِ عَلَيْهَا صَوَآفَّۖ فَإِذَا وَجَبَتْ
جُنُوبُهَا فَكُلُواْ مِنْهَا وَأَطْعِمُواْ ٱلْقَانِعَ وَٱلْمُعْتَرَّۚ كَذَٰلِكَ سَخَّرْنَٰهَا
لَكُمْ لَعَلَّكُمْ تَشْكُرُونَ ٣٦ لَن يَنَالَ ٱللَّهَ لُحُومُهَا وَلَا دِمَآؤُهَا
وَلَٰكِن يَنَالُهُ ٱلتَّقْوَىٰ مِنكُمْۚ كَذَٰلِكَ سَخَّرَهَا لَكُمْ لِتُكَبِّرُواْ
ٱللَّهَ عَلَىٰ مَا هَدَىٰكُمْۗ وَبَشِّرِ ٱلْمُحْسِنِينَ ٣٧ ۩ إِنَّ ٱللَّهَ
يُدَٰفِعُ عَنِ ٱلَّذِينَ ءَامَنُوٓاْۗ إِنَّ ٱللَّهَ لَا يُحِبُّ كُلَّ خَوَّانٍ كَفُورٍ ٣٨
أُذِنَ لِلَّذِينَ يُقَٰتَلُونَ بِأَنَّهُمْ ظُلِمُواْۚ وَإِنَّ ٱللَّهَ عَلَىٰ نَصْرِهِمْ

that only entails insulting a servant – ***We will let them taste a painful punishment.***

26. Remember when ***We located the position of the House for Ibrāhīm*** – which had been swept away in the Flood, so that he could rebuild it. We commanded him: ***'Do not associate anything with Me, but purify My House*** – of idols – ***for those who circle it, and those who stand and bow and prostrate*** in prayer there.

27. ***Announce the Ḥajj to mankind.*** Ibrāhīm announced it from the top of the mountain Abū Qubays, saying, "O people! Allah has built a House and obliged you to make *ḥajj* to it, so respond to your Lord." He turned his face to the south and north, east and west; and all of those for whom the *ḥajj* was destined in the loins of men and wombs of women, answered him: "At Your service, O Allah, at Your service!" ***They will come to you on foot and on every sort of lean animal, coming by every distant road...***

28. ***...so that they may be present at what will profit them*** – in terms of commerce in this world or reward in the Next World, or both, as different commentators say – ***and invoke Allah's name on specific days*** – a reference to the first ten days of Dhū'l-Ḥijja or the Day of 'Arafa, or the Day of Sacrifice to the end of the days of *tashrīq,* according to various views – ***over livestock He has provided for them*** – camels, cattle, and sheep and goats, which are sacrificed on the Day of the *'Īd* and eaten then and in the days after it. ***Eat of them and feed those who are poor and in need.*** This is recommended rather than obligatory.

29. ***Then they should end their state of self-neglect*** – their dirtiness and dishevelment, by acts like cutting their nails – ***and fulfil*** (read as *yūfū* and *yuwaffū*) ***their vows*** – by sacrificing animals – ***and circle the Ancient House*** in the *Ṭawāf al-Ifāḍa*. It is called "ancient" because it was "the first house established for mankind".

30. ***That is it.*** This implies: the command or the matter mentioned is like that. ***If someone honours Allah's sacred things*** – which it is unlawful to violate, ***that*** – esteeming – ***is better for him in his Lord's sight*** in the Next World. ***All livestock are permitted to you*** to eat after proper slaughter ***except what has already been recited to you*** as being forbidden in such *āyat*s as: *"Forbidden for you are car-*

rion...". (5:3) ***Have done with the defilement of idols and have done with telling lies*** – in the form of *shirk* in your *talbiya* invocation or false testimony.

31. ***Be people of pure natural belief in Allah*** – the word *ḥunafā'* used here means those who submit to Allah and turn away from every *dīn* except His, ***not associating anything else with Him*** – stressing the first phrase. ***As for anyone who associates others with Allah, it is as though he had fallen from the sky and the birds had seized him and carried him away, or the wind had dropped him in a distant place*** where there is no hope of rescue.

32. ***That is it.*** The matter is like that. ***As for those who honour Allah's sacred emblems*** – a reference to the camels which are brought for sacrifice and have been are fattened up; they are called "emblems" because they are marked *(ish'ār)* so that it is known that they are sacrifices, in such ways as marking their humps, ***that comes from the fearfulness of Allah in their hearts.***

33. ***You may make use of the sacrificial animals*** by riding them and using them to carry loads, as long as that does not harm them – ***until a specified time*** – the moment when they are sacrificed – ***and then their place of sacrifice is by the Ancient House*** – in other words, in the *Ḥaram.*

34. ***We have appointed a rite of sacrifice*** (read as *mansik*, meaning the actual sacrifice, and *mansak*, meaning the place where it is done) ***for every*** believing ***nation*** before you ***so that they may invoke Allah's name over the livestock He has given them*** – when slaughtering them. ***Your God is One God; so submit to Him*** – and obey Him. ***Give good news to the humble-hearted*** – those who obey Allah and are humble towards Him,

35. ***...whose hearts quake*** in fear ***at the mention of Allah, and who are steadfast in the face of all that happens to them*** of afflictions and difficulty***; those who establish the prayer*** at its times ***and give of what We have provided for them*** as *ṣadaqa.*

36. ***We have appointed the sacrificial animals*** – the word *budn* used here is the plural of *badana* and refers to camels – ***for you as one of the sacred emblems of Allah*** – hallmarks of His *dīn*. ***There is good in them for you*** – benefit in this world, as already stated, and a

لَقَدِيرٌ ٣٩ ٱلَّذِينَ أُخْرِجُوا۟ مِن دِيَـٰرِهِم بِغَيْرِ حَقٍّ إِلَّآ أَن
يَقُولُوا۟ رَبُّنَا ٱللَّهُ ۗ وَلَوْلَا دَفْعُ ٱللَّهِ ٱلنَّاسَ بَعْضَهُم بِبَعْضٍ لَّهُدِّمَتْ
صَوَٰمِعُ وَبِيَعٌ وَصَلَوَٰتٌ وَمَسَـٰجِدُ يُذْكَرُ فِيهَا ٱسْمُ ٱللَّهِ
كَثِيرًا ۗ وَلَيَنصُرَنَّ ٱللَّهُ مَن يَنصُرُهُۥٓ ۗ إِنَّ ٱللَّهَ لَقَوِىٌّ
عَزِيزٌ ٤٠ ٱلَّذِينَ إِن مَّكَّنَّـٰهُمْ فِى ٱلْأَرْضِ أَقَامُوا۟ ٱلصَّلَوٰةَ
وَءَاتَوُا۟ ٱلزَّكَوٰةَ وَأَمَرُوا۟ بِٱلْمَعْرُوفِ وَنَهَوْا۟ عَنِ ٱلْمُنكَرِ ۗ
وَلِلَّهِ عَـٰقِبَةُ ٱلْأُمُورِ ٤١ وَإِن يُكَذِّبُوكَ فَقَدْ كَذَّبَتْ
قَبْلَهُمْ قَوْمُ نُوحٍ وَعَادٌ وَثَمُودُ ٤٢ وَقَوْمُ إِبْرَٰهِيمَ وَقَوْمُ لُوطٍ ٤٣
وَأَصْحَـٰبُ مَدْيَنَ ۖ وَكُذِّبَ مُوسَىٰ فَأَمْلَيْتُ لِلْكَـٰفِرِينَ ثُمَّ
أَخَذْتُهُمْ ۖ فَكَيْفَ كَانَ نَكِيرِ ٤٤ فَكَأَيِّن مِّن قَرْيَةٍ
أَهْلَكْنَـٰهَا وَهِىَ ظَالِمَةٌ فَهِىَ خَاوِيَةٌ عَلَىٰ عُرُوشِهَا
وَبِئْرٍ مُّعَطَّلَةٍ وَقَصْرٍ مَّشِيدٍ ٤٥ أَفَلَمْ يَسِيرُوا۟ فِى ٱلْأَرْضِ
فَتَكُونَ لَهُمْ قُلُوبٌ يَعْقِلُونَ بِهَآ أَوْ ءَاذَانٌ يَسْمَعُونَ بِهَا ۖ فَإِنَّهَا
لَا تَعْمَى ٱلْأَبْصَـٰرُ وَلَـٰكِن تَعْمَى ٱلْقُلُوبُ ٱلَّتِى فِى ٱلصُّدُورِ ٤٦
وَيَسْتَعْجِلُونَكَ بِٱلْعَذَابِ وَلَن يُخْلِفَ ٱللَّهُ وَعْدَهُۥ ۚ وَإِنَّ يَوْمًا
عِندَ رَبِّكَ كَأَلْفِ سَنَةٍ مِّمَّا تَعُدُّونَ ٤٧ وَكَأَيِّن مِّن
قَرْيَةٍ أَمْلَيْتُ لَهَا وَهِىَ ظَالِمَةٌ ثُمَّ أَخَذْتُهَا وَإِلَىَّ ٱلْمَصِيرُ
٤٨ قُلْ يَـٰٓأَيُّهَا ٱلنَّاسُ إِنَّمَآ أَنَا۠ لَكُمْ نَذِيرٌ مُّبِينٌ ٤٩ فَٱلَّذِينَ
ءَامَنُوا۟ وَعَمِلُوا۟ ٱلصَّـٰلِحَـٰتِ لَهُم مَّغْفِرَةٌ وَرِزْقٌ كَرِيمٌ ٥٠
وَٱلَّذِينَ سَعَوْا۟ فِىٓ ءَايَـٰتِنَا مُعَـٰجِزِينَ أُو۟لَـٰٓئِكَ أَصْحَـٰبُ ٱلْجَحِيمِ

reward in the Hereafter – ***so invoke Allah's name over them*** – when sacrificing them – ***as they stand in rows*** – standing on three legs with a left foreleg hobbled. ***And then when they collapse on their sides*** – fall to the ground after being sacrificed – ***eat of them*** if you wish ***and feed both those who ask*** – the word used here, *mu'tarr*, means someone who begs or alludes to his need – ***and those who are too shy to ask*** – the word used here, *qāni'*, means someone who is content with what he is given and does not ask or indicate his state. ***In this way We have subjected them to you*** so that they can be sacrificed and ridden; otherwise you would be unable to do so – ***so that perhaps you may be thankful*** for Allah's blessing given you.

37. ***Their flesh and blood does not reach Allah, but your fearfulness of Allah*** – shown by righteous actions done sincerely for Him and accompanied by faith – ***does reach Him. In this way He has subjected them to you so that you may proclaim Allah's greatness for the way that He has guided you*** to His *dīn* and the practices of the *ḥajj*. ***Give good news to the good-doers*** – who affirm Allah's unity.

38. ***Allah will defend those who believe*** against the plots of the idolators; ***Allah does not love any thankless traitor*** – anyone who is treacherous by betraying His trust and ungrateful for Allah's blessings. They are the idolators. This means that He will punish them.

39. ***Permission to fight is given to those who are fought against*** (the believers) – this is the first *āyat* revealed about *jihād* – ***because they have been wronged*** by the unbelievers – ***truly Allah has the power to come to their support*** –

40. ***...those who were expelled from their homes without any right*** or cause, ***merely for*** their ***saying, 'Our Lord is Allah*** alone.' This statement is true, and so expulsion on account of it is expulsion without right. ***If Allah had not driven some people back by means of others, monasteries,*** Christian – ***churches,*** Jewish ***synagogues and*** Muslim ***mosques, where Allah's name is mentioned much, would have been pulled down and destroyed*** (read as *huddimat* and *hudimat*) – and worship is stopped when they fall into ruin. ***Allah will certainly help those who help Him*** and His *dīn*. ***Allah is All-Strong*** in His creation, ***Almighty*** – so that nothing can resist His authority or power –

41. ***...those who, if We establish them firmly on the earth*** – by helping them against their enemy – ***will establish the prayer and pay* zakāt*, and command what is right and forbid what is wrong. The end result of all affairs is with Allah*** and will return to Him.

42. The following contains solace for the Prophet, may Allah bless him and grant him peace. ***If they deny you, the people of Nūḥ before them denied him, and those of 'Ād*** – the people of Hūd – ***and of Thamūd*** – the people of Ṣāliḥ***;***

43. ***...and the people of Ibrāhīm and the people of Lūṭ***

44. ***...and the companions of Madyan*** – the people of Shu'ayb – ***and Mūsā was denied as well*** – by the Copts, not the tribe of Israel. All these Prophets were denied and so you have an example in them. ***I allowed time to the unbelievers*** – by delaying their punishment – ***but then I seized them*** with the punishment. ***How terrible was My denial*** – by destroying them***!***

45. ***How many wrongdoing cities*** – meaning that their inhabitants were wrongdoing through their unbelief – ***We destroyed*** (read as *ahlaknāyhā*, and *ahlaktuhā,* "I destroyed") ***and now all their roofs and walls are fallen in; how many abandoned wells and stuccoed palaces*** are empty because their people are dead***!***

46. ***Have they*** (the unbelievers of Makka) ***not travelled about the earth; and do they not have hearts to understand with*** – to grasp what befell those before them who denied – ***or ears to hear with*** about their destruction and the ruin of their houses, and taken note***? It is not eyes that are blind but the hearts in breasts that are blind.***

47. ***They ask you to hasten the punishment. Allah will not break His promise*** to send down the punishmen;t and He sent it down at Badr. ***A day*** – in the Next World because of the punishment – ***with your Lord is equivalent to a thousand years in the way you count*** (read as *ta'uddūna* and *ya'uddūna*, "they count") in this world.

48. ***How many wrongdoing cities I allowed time to and then I seized them*** (the inhabitants of the cities) – ***I am their final destination.***

49. ***Say: 'Mankind,*** especially the people of Makka, ***I am only a clear warner to you*** – and the bearer of good news to the believers.***'***

﴿٥١﴾ وَمَآ أَرْسَلْنَا مِن قَبْلِكَ مِن رَّسُولٍ وَلَا نَبِيٍّ إِلَّآ إِذَا تَمَنَّىٰٓ
أَلْقَى ٱلشَّيْطَٰنُ فِىٓ أُمْنِيَّتِهِۦ فَيَنسَخُ ٱللَّهُ مَا يُلْقِى ٱلشَّيْطَٰنُ
ثُمَّ يُحْكِمُ ٱللَّهُ ءَايَٰتِهِۦ ۗ وَٱللَّهُ عَلِيمٌ حَكِيمٌ ﴿٥٢﴾ لِّيَجْعَلَ
مَا يُلْقِى ٱلشَّيْطَٰنُ فِتْنَةً لِّلَّذِينَ فِى قُلُوبِهِم مَّرَضٌ وَٱلْقَاسِيَةِ
قُلُوبُهُمْ ۗ وَإِنَّ ٱلظَّٰلِمِينَ لَفِى شِقَاقٍۭ بَعِيدٍ ﴿٥٣﴾ وَلِيَعْلَمَ
ٱلَّذِينَ أُوتُوا۟ ٱلْعِلْمَ أَنَّهُ ٱلْحَقُّ مِن رَّبِّكَ فَيُؤْمِنُوا۟ بِهِۦ
فَتُخْبِتَ لَهُۥ قُلُوبُهُمْ ۗ وَإِنَّ ٱللَّهَ لَهَادِ ٱلَّذِينَ ءَامَنُوٓا۟ إِلَىٰ صِرَٰطٍ
مُّسْتَقِيمٍ ﴿٥٤﴾ وَلَا يَزَالُ ٱلَّذِينَ كَفَرُوا۟ فِى مِرْيَةٍ مِّنْهُ حَتَّىٰ
تَأْتِيَهُمُ ٱلسَّاعَةُ بَغْتَةً أَوْ يَأْتِيَهُمْ عَذَابُ يَوْمٍ عَقِيمٍ ﴿٥٥﴾
ٱلْمُلْكُ يَوْمَئِذٍ لِّلَّهِ يَحْكُمُ بَيْنَهُمْ ۚ فَٱلَّذِينَ ءَامَنُوا۟
وَعَمِلُوا۟ ٱلصَّٰلِحَٰتِ فِى جَنَّٰتِ ٱلنَّعِيمِ ﴿٥٦﴾ وَٱلَّذِينَ كَفَرُوا۟
وَكَذَّبُوا۟ بِـَٔايَٰتِنَا فَأُو۟لَٰٓئِكَ لَهُمْ عَذَابٌ مُّهِينٌ ﴿٥٧﴾
وَٱلَّذِينَ هَاجَرُوا۟ فِى سَبِيلِ ٱللَّهِ ثُمَّ قُتِلُوٓا۟ أَوْ مَاتُوا۟
لَيَرْزُقَنَّهُمُ ٱللَّهُ رِزْقًا حَسَنًا ۚ وَإِنَّ ٱللَّهَ لَهُوَ خَيْرُ
ٱلرَّٰزِقِينَ ﴿٥٨﴾ لَيُدْخِلَنَّهُم مُّدْخَلًا يَرْضَوْنَهُۥ ۗ وَإِنَّ
ٱللَّهَ لَعَلِيمٌ حَلِيمٌ ﴿٥٩﴾ ۞ ذَٰلِكَ وَمَنْ عَاقَبَ بِمِثْلِ
مَا عُوقِبَ بِهِۦ ثُمَّ بُغِىَ عَلَيْهِ لَيَنصُرَنَّهُ ٱللَّهُ ۗ إِنَّ ٱللَّهَ
لَعَفُوٌّ غَفُورٌ ﴿٦٠﴾ ذَٰلِكَ بِأَنَّ ٱللَّهَ يُولِجُ ٱلَّيْلَ فِى
ٱلنَّهَارِ وَيُولِجُ ٱلنَّهَارَ فِى ٱلَّيْلِ وَأَنَّ ٱللَّهَ سَمِيعٌۢ بَصِيرٌ
﴿٦١﴾ ذَٰلِكَ بِأَنَّ ٱللَّهَ هُوَ ٱلْحَقُّ وَأَنَّ مَا يَدْعُونَ مِن

50. ***As for those who believe and do right actions, they will have forgiveness*** – for their wrong actions – ***and generous provision*** (the Garden).

51. ***But as for those who strive against My Signs*** (the Qur'an) ***and try to thwart them*** (read as *mu'ājizīna* and *mu'ajjizīna*) – they try to stop people from following the Prophet, by making them powerless, and to keep them from believing. This means that they think that they will get ahead by denying the Resurrection and punishment – ***they will be the Companions of the Blazing Fire.***

52. ***We did not send any Messenger*** – a Prophet who is commanded to convey the Message – ***or any Prophet*** – who has no new Message to convey – ***before you without Shayṭān insinuating something into his recitation while he was reciting*** – inserting something into the recitation that is not part of it but which makes the Messenger pleasing to him. The Prophet, may Allah bless him and grant him peace, was reciting *Sūrat an-Najm* in a gathering of Quraysh. When he reached the words, *"Have you really considered al-Lāt and al-'Uzzā, and Manāt the third, the other one,"* Shayṭān cast onto his tongue without the knowledge of the Prophet, may Allah bless him and grant him peace, "those are the high cranes whose intercession is hoped for." Quraysh were happy about that. Then Jibrīl informed him about what Shayṭān had cast on his tongue, and he was grieved: and so solace was given to him by this *āyat*. ***But Allah revokes*** and cancels out ***whatever Shaytan insinuates and then Allah confirms His Signs*** – and makes them firm. ***Allah is All-Knowing*** of what Shayṭān insinuates, ***All-Wise*** in making firm whatever He wishes of that,

53. ***... so that He may make what Shaytan insinuates a trial for those with sickness*** – a reference to schism and hypocrisy – ***in their hearts and for those whose hearts are hard*** (the idolaters) – to see whether they will accept the truth – ***the wrongdoers*** (the unbelievers) ***are entrenched in hostility*** – long-standing enmity against the Prophet, may Allah bless him and grant him peace, and the believers because of what he said about their gods which pleased them and then was abrogated –

54. ***...and so that those who have been given knowledge*** of Allah's unity and the Qur'an ***may know it*** (the Qur'an) ***is the truth from***

their Lord and believe in it and their hearts may be humbled to Him and at peace. ***Allah guides those who believe to a straight path*** – the *Dīn* of Islam.

55. ***But those who disbelieve will not cease to be in doubt of it*** – meaning the Qur'an, because of what Shayṭān cast on the tongue of the Prophet but was later invalidated – ***until the Hour comes on them suddenly*** – meaning the hour of their death or the Day of Rising – ***or the punishment of a desolate Day arrives*** – meaning the Day of Badr, on which there was no good for the unbelievers, like a barren wind which brings no good, or the Day of the Rising after which there is no night.

56. ***Sovereignty on that Day*** (the Day of Rising) ***will be Allah's*** alone. ***He will judge between them. Those who believe and do right actions will be in Gardens of Delight*** – as a bounteous gift from Allah,

57. ***...but those who disbelieve and deny Our Signs will have a humiliating punishment*** because of their unbelief.

58. ***Those who emigrate in the Way of Allah*** – obey Allah by emigrating from Makka to Madina – ***and then are killed or die, Allah will provide for them handsomely*** with Paradise. ***Truly Allah is the best Provider***.

59. ***He will admit them by an entrance*** (read as *mudhkal* and *mad-khal,* meaning either the act of entering or the entrance itself) ***which is pleasing to them*** – into the Garden. ***Allah is All-Knowing*** of their intention, ***All-Forbearing*** by not punishing them.

60. ***That is so.*** It is as We have recounted to you. ***And if anyone*** of the believers ***inflicts an injury*** in retaliation which is ***the same as the one done to him*** wrongly by the idolators – such as fighting them as they fought him during a sacred month – ***and then is again oppressed*** when they wrong him again by expelling him from his home, ***Allah will come to his aid. Allah is All-Pardoning*** to the believers, ***Ever-Forgiving*** to them for fighting in the sacred month.

61. ***That*** victory ***is because Allah merges night into day and merges day into night*** by extending each of them, and that is an effect of His power by which victory comes ***and because Allah is***

دُونِهِۦ هُوَ ٱلۡبَٰطِلُ وَأَنَّ ٱللَّهَ هُوَ ٱلۡعَلِيُّ ٱلۡكَبِيرُ ٦٢
أَلَمۡ تَرَ أَنَّ ٱللَّهَ أَنزَلَ مِنَ ٱلسَّمَآءِ مَآءٗ فَتُصۡبِحُ ٱلۡأَرۡضُ
مُخۡضَرَّةًۚ إِنَّ ٱللَّهَ لَطِيفٌ خَبِيرٞ ٦٣ لَّهُۥ مَا فِي ٱلسَّمَٰوَٰتِ
وَمَا فِي ٱلۡأَرۡضِۗ وَإِنَّ ٱللَّهَ لَهُوَ ٱلۡغَنِيُّ ٱلۡحَمِيدُ ٦٤
أَلَمۡ تَرَ أَنَّ ٱللَّهَ سَخَّرَ لَكُم مَّا فِي ٱلۡأَرۡضِ وَٱلۡفُلۡكَ تَجۡرِي فِي ٱلۡبَحۡرِ
بِأَمۡرِهِۦ وَيُمۡسِكُ ٱلسَّمَآءَ أَن تَقَعَ عَلَى ٱلۡأَرۡضِ إِلَّا بِإِذۡنِهِۦٓۚ إِنَّ
ٱللَّهَ بِٱلنَّاسِ لَرَءُوفٞ رَّحِيمٞ ٦٥ وَهُوَ ٱلَّذِيٓ أَحۡيَاكُمۡ
ثُمَّ يُمِيتُكُمۡ ثُمَّ يُحۡيِيكُمۡۗ إِنَّ ٱلۡإِنسَٰنَ لَكَفُورٞ ٦٦
لِّكُلِّ أُمَّةٖ جَعَلۡنَا مَنسَكًا هُمۡ نَاسِكُوهُۖ فَلَا يُنَٰزِعُنَّكَ
فِي ٱلۡأَمۡرِۚ وَٱدۡعُ إِلَىٰ رَبِّكَۖ إِنَّكَ لَعَلَىٰ هُدٗى مُّسۡتَقِيمٖ ٦٧
وَإِن جَٰدَلُوكَ فَقُلِ ٱللَّهُ أَعۡلَمُ بِمَا تَعۡمَلُونَ ٦٨ ٱللَّهُ يَحۡكُمُ
بَيۡنَكُمۡ يَوۡمَ ٱلۡقِيَٰمَةِ فِيمَا كُنتُمۡ فِيهِ تَخۡتَلِفُونَ ٦٩
أَلَمۡ تَعۡلَمۡ أَنَّ ٱللَّهَ يَعۡلَمُ مَا فِي ٱلسَّمَآءِ وَٱلۡأَرۡضِۗ إِنَّ ذَٰلِكَ
فِي كِتَٰبٍۚ إِنَّ ذَٰلِكَ عَلَى ٱللَّهِ يَسِيرٞ ٧٠ وَيَعۡبُدُونَ مِن دُونِ
ٱللَّهِ مَا لَمۡ يُنَزِّلۡ بِهِۦ سُلۡطَٰنٗا وَمَا لَيۡسَ لَهُم بِهِۦ عِلۡمٞۗ وَمَا لِلظَّٰلِمِينَ
مِن نَّصِيرٖ ٧١ وَإِذَا تُتۡلَىٰ عَلَيۡهِمۡ ءَايَٰتُنَا بَيِّنَٰتٖ تَعۡرِفُ فِي
وُجُوهِ ٱلَّذِينَ كَفَرُواْ ٱلۡمُنكَرَۖ يَكَادُونَ يَسۡطُونَ
بِٱلَّذِينَ يَتۡلُونَ عَلَيۡهِمۡ ءَايَٰتِنَاۗ قُلۡ أَفَأُنَبِّئُكُم بِشَرّٖ مِّن
ذَٰلِكُمُۗ ٱلنَّارُ وَعَدَهَا ٱللَّهُ ٱلَّذِينَ كَفَرُواْۖ وَبِئۡسَ ٱلۡمَصِيرُ ٧٢
يَٰٓأَيُّهَا ٱلنَّاسُ ضُرِبَ مَثَلٞ فَٱسۡتَمِعُواْ لَهُۥٓۚ إِنَّ ٱلَّذِينَ

All-Hearing of the supplication of the believers, ***All-Seeing*** of them when He imbues them with faith and so He answers their call.

62. ***That*** – victory – ***is because Allah is the Real*** – the Confirmed Truth – ***and what they call*** (read as *yad'ūna* and *tad'ūna* "what you call on" addressed to the idolaters) ***on*** and worship ***apart from Him*** – in other words, the idols – ***is false*** and will vanish. ***Allah is the All-High*** over all things by His power, ***the Most Great***, so that everything is small in relation to Him.

63. ***Do you not see*** (know) ***that Allah sends down water*** (rain) ***from the sky and then in the morning the earth is covered in green?*** It causes the plants to grow which is an effect of Allah's power. ***Allah is All-Subtle*** – kind to His slaves in bringing forth plants by means of water, ***All-Aware*** of what is in their hearts when rain is delayed.

64. ***Everything in the heavens and everything in the earth belongs to Him*** as His domain. ***Allah is the Rich Beyond Need*** of His slaves, ***the Praiseworthy.***

65. ***Do you not see*** (know) ***that Allah has made everything*** – all the beasts – ***on the earth subservient to you and the ships running upon the sea*** – for travelling in and carrying loads – ***by His command*** and permission? ***He holds back the heaven, preventing it from falling to the earth – except by His permission*** – so that you are not destroyed. ***Allah is All-Compassionate*** to mankind, ***Most Merciful*** in subjecting all that to you.

66. ***It is He who gave you life*** – by forming you – ***and then will cause you to die*** – at the end of your lifespan – ***and then will give you life again*** – at the Resurrection. ***Man*** – when an idolator – ***is truly ungrateful*** for the blessings of Allah by failing to affirm His unity.

67. ***We have appointed for every nation a rite*** (read as *mansak* and *mansik*) – meaning a sacred law (*sharī'a*) – ***that they observe*** and act by, ***so let them not dispute with you about the matter*** – about the slaughtering of animals when the unbelievers said, "It is more proper for you to consume what Allah has killed (i.e. carrion) than what you have killed." – ***Call the people to your Lord*** – to His *dīn;* ***you are guided straight*** – to His *dīn.*

68. ***If they do argue with you*** about the *dīn* ***say: 'Allah knows best what you are doing*** and will repay you for it.' This was revealed before the command to fight.

69. ***Allah will judge between you***, believers and unbelievers, ***on the Day of Rising regarding everything about which you differed*** – regarding all your disputes.

70. ***Do you not know that Allah knows everything in heaven and earth?*** This question is for confirmation, demanding an affirmative response. ***That is*** mentioned ***in a Book*** (the Preserved Tablet). ***That*** knowledge ***is easy for Allah.***

71. ***They*** (idolators) ***worship besides Allah something*** (idols) ***for which no authority has come down, something about which they have no knowledge*** that they are gods. ***There is no helper for the wrongdoers.*** Those who do wrong by committing *shirk* will have no one to defend them against Allah.

72. ***When Our Signs*** (the Qur'an) ***are recited to them – Clear Signs – you can detect denial in the faces of those who disbelieve*** as they show their dislike by frowning. ***They all but*** physically ***assault those who recite Our Signs to them! Say: 'Shall I inform you of something worse than that*** – something which will be more hateful to you than the Qur'an which is recited to you***? The Fire which Allah has promised those who disbelieve***, to which you will go. ***What an evil destination!'***

73. ***Mankind,*** in particular the people of Makka, ***an example has been made, so listen to it carefully. Those*** idols ***whom you call upon*** and worship ***besides Allah are not even able to create a single fly, even if they were to join together to do it. And if a fly steals something from them*** – taking, for example, some scent or saffron with which they are daubed – ***they cannot get it back*** and restore it since they lack the power to do so. So how can people worship partners of Allah? That is something extraordinary. ***How feeble are both the seeker*** (the worshipper) ***and the sought*** (the worshipped)***!***

74. ***They do not measure*** and esteem ***Allah with His true measure*** of esteem, since they associate with Him something which cannot even defend itself against flies and they do not give Him what is His right. ***Allah is All-Strong, Almighty.***

تَدْعُونَ مِن دُونِ ٱللَّهِ لَن يَخْلُقُوا۟ ذُبَابًا وَلَوِ ٱجْتَمَعُوا۟ لَهُۥ ۖ
وَإِن يَسْلُبْهُمُ ٱلذُّبَابُ شَيْـًٔا لَّا يَسْتَنقِذُوهُ مِنْهُ ۚ ضَعُفَ
ٱلطَّالِبُ وَٱلْمَطْلُوبُ ﴿٧٣﴾ مَا قَدَرُوا۟ ٱللَّهَ حَقَّ قَدْرِهِۦٓ ۗ إِنَّ
ٱللَّهَ لَقَوِىٌّ عَزِيزٌ ﴿٧٤﴾ ٱللَّهُ يَصْطَفِى مِنَ ٱلْمَلَٰٓئِكَةِ
رُسُلًا وَمِنَ ٱلنَّاسِ ۚ إِنَّ ٱللَّهَ سَمِيعٌۢ بَصِيرٌ ﴿٧٥﴾ يَعْلَمُ
مَا بَيْنَ أَيْدِيهِمْ وَمَا خَلْفَهُمْ ۗ وَإِلَى ٱللَّهِ تُرْجَعُ ٱلْأُمُورُ ﴿٧٦﴾
يَٰٓأَيُّهَا ٱلَّذِينَ ءَامَنُوا۟ ٱرْكَعُوا۟ وَٱسْجُدُوا۟ وَٱعْبُدُوا۟
رَبَّكُمْ وَٱفْعَلُوا۟ ٱلْخَيْرَ لَعَلَّكُمْ تُفْلِحُونَ ۩ ﴿٧٧﴾
وَجَٰهِدُوا۟ فِى ٱللَّهِ حَقَّ جِهَادِهِۦ ۚ هُوَ ٱجْتَبَىٰكُمْ وَمَا جَعَلَ
عَلَيْكُمْ فِى ٱلدِّينِ مِنْ حَرَجٍ ۚ مِّلَّةَ أَبِيكُمْ إِبْرَٰهِيمَ ۚ هُوَ سَمَّىٰكُمُ
ٱلْمُسْلِمِينَ مِن قَبْلُ وَفِى هَٰذَا لِيَكُونَ ٱلرَّسُولُ شَهِيدًا عَلَيْكُمْ
وَتَكُونُوا۟ شُهَدَآءَ عَلَى ٱلنَّاسِ ۚ فَأَقِيمُوا۟ ٱلصَّلَوٰةَ وَءَاتُوا۟ ٱلزَّكَوٰةَ
وَٱعْتَصِمُوا۟ بِٱللَّهِ هُوَ مَوْلَىٰكُمْ ۖ فَنِعْمَ ٱلْمَوْلَىٰ وَنِعْمَ ٱلنَّصِيرُ ﴿٧٨﴾

75. ***Allah chooses Messengers from the angels and from mankind.*** This was revealed when the idolators said, *"Has the Reminder been sent down to him out of all of us?"* (38:8) ***Allah is All-Hearing*** of what they say, ***All-Seeing*** of whom He should take as a Messenger, such as Jibrīl, Mīkā'il, Ibrāhīm, Muḥammad and others, may Allah bless them and grant them peace.

76. He knows what is before them and what is behind them: what they have done and what they will still do. ***All matters return to Allah.***

77. You who believe! bow and prostrate in prayer ***and worship your Lord*** – affirming His unity – ***and do good*** – in ways like maintaining ties of kinship and demonstrating good character – ***so that perhaps you may be successful*** and obtain Paradise.

78. Do* jihād *for Allah – to establish His *dīn* – ***with the* jihād *due to Him*** – with all your ability. ***He has selected you*** for His *dīn* ***and not placed any constraint upon you in the* dīn** – but has rather made it easy when that is necessary, by shortening the prayer, *tayammum*, allowing the eating of carrion in necessity and absolving travellers and sick people from fasting, ***the religion of your forefather Ibrāhīm. He*** (Allah) ***named you Muslims before*** this Book ***and also in this*** Qur'an ***so that the Messenger could be witness against you*** on the Day of Rising, that he conveyed the Message to you – ***and you could be witnesses against all mankind*** that their Messengers conveyed the Message to them. ***So establish the prayer*** – be constant in it – ***and pay* zakāt. *And hold fast to Allah,*** trusting in Him. ***He is your Protector*** and takes charge of your affairs. ***How excellent a Protector and Helper*** for you.

سُورَةُ المُؤۡمِنُونَ

بِسۡمِ ٱللَّهِ ٱلرَّحۡمَٰنِ ٱلرَّحِيمِ

قَدۡ أَفۡلَحَ ٱلۡمُؤۡمِنُونَ ١ ٱلَّذِينَ هُمۡ فِي صَلَاتِهِمۡ خَٰشِعُونَ ٢
وَٱلَّذِينَ هُمۡ عَنِ ٱللَّغۡوِ مُعۡرِضُونَ ٣ وَٱلَّذِينَ هُمۡ لِلزَّكَوٰةِ
فَٰعِلُونَ ٤ وَٱلَّذِينَ هُمۡ لِفُرُوجِهِمۡ حَٰفِظُونَ ٥ إِلَّا عَلَىٰٓ
أَزۡوَٰجِهِمۡ أَوۡ مَا مَلَكَتۡ أَيۡمَٰنُهُمۡ فَإِنَّهُمۡ غَيۡرُ مَلُومِينَ ٦
فَمَنِ ٱبۡتَغَىٰ وَرَآءَ ذَٰلِكَ فَأُوْلَٰٓئِكَ هُمُ ٱلۡعَادُونَ ٧ وَٱلَّذِينَ هُمۡ
لِأَمَٰنَٰتِهِمۡ وَعَهۡدِهِمۡ رَٰعُونَ ٨ وَٱلَّذِينَ هُمۡ عَلَىٰ صَلَوَٰتِهِمۡ
يُحَافِظُونَ ٩ أُوْلَٰٓئِكَ هُمُ ٱلۡوَٰرِثُونَ ١٠ ٱلَّذِينَ يَرِثُونَ
ٱلۡفِرۡدَوۡسَ هُمۡ فِيهَا خَٰلِدُونَ ١١ وَلَقَدۡ خَلَقۡنَا ٱلۡإِنسَٰنَ مِن
سُلَٰلَةٖ مِّن طِينٖ ١٢ ثُمَّ جَعَلۡنَٰهُ نُطۡفَةٗ فِي قَرَارٖ مَّكِينٖ ١٣ ثُمَّ
خَلَقۡنَا ٱلنُّطۡفَةَ عَلَقَةٗ فَخَلَقۡنَا ٱلۡعَلَقَةَ مُضۡغَةٗ فَخَلَقۡنَا
ٱلۡمُضۡغَةَ عِظَٰمٗا فَكَسَوۡنَا ٱلۡعِظَٰمَ لَحۡمٗا ثُمَّ أَنشَأۡنَٰهُ خَلۡقًا
ءَاخَرَۚ فَتَبَارَكَ ٱللَّهُ أَحۡسَنُ ٱلۡخَٰلِقِينَ ١٤ ثُمَّ إِنَّكُم بَعۡدَ ذَٰلِكَ
لَمَيِّتُونَ ١٥ ثُمَّ إِنَّكُمۡ يَوۡمَ ٱلۡقِيَٰمَةِ تُبۡعَثُونَ ١٦ وَلَقَدۡ
خَلَقۡنَا فَوۡقَكُمۡ سَبۡعَ طَرَآئِقَ وَمَا كُنَّا عَنِ ٱلۡخَلۡقِ غَٰفِلِينَ ١٧
وَأَنزَلۡنَا مِنَ ٱلسَّمَآءِ مَآءَۢ بِقَدَرٖ فَأَسۡكَنَّٰهُ فِي ٱلۡأَرۡضِۖ وَإِنَّا عَلَىٰ ذَهَابِۭ
بِهِۦ لَقَٰدِرُونَ ١٨ فَأَنشَأۡنَا لَكُم بِهِۦ جَنَّٰتٖ مِّن نَّخِيلٖ وَأَعۡنَٰبٖ
لَّكُمۡ فِيهَا فَوَٰكِهُ كَثِيرَةٞ وَمِنۡهَا تَأۡكُلُونَ ١٩ وَشَجَرَةٗ تَخۡرُجُ مِن
طُورِ سَيۡنَآءَ تَنۢبُتُ بِٱلدُّهۡنِ وَصِبۡغٖ لِّلۡأٓكِلِينَ ٢٠ وَإِنَّ لَكُمۡ فِي

23. *Sūrat al-Mu'minūn*
The Believers

This *sūra* is Makkan. It has 118 or 119 *āyat*s and was sent down after *al-Anbiyā'*.

1. ***It is the believers who are successful*** – this is a definite statement*:*

2. ***...those who are humble in their prayer;***

3. ***...those who turn away from worthless talk*** and other worthless activities*;*

4. ***...those who pay* zakāt*;***

5. ***...those who guard their private parts*** from doing what is unlawful –

6. ***...except from their wives or those they own as slaves, in which case they are not blameworthy*** in approaching them,

7. ***...but those who desire anything more than that*** – than wives and slaves, or masturbation – ***are people who have gone beyond the limits*** to what is not lawful for them*;*

8. ***...those who honour their trusts*** (read as *amānātihim* and *amānatihim*) ***and their contracts*** – contracts made one with another, and also the contract between themselves and Allah in respect of the prayer and other duties*;*

9. ***...those who safeguard their prayers*** (read as *ṣalāwātihim* and *ṣalātihim*) and perform them at their times.

10. ***Such people are the inheritors*** – and no others –

11. ***...who will inherit Firdaws,*** one of the gardens of Paradise, ***remaining in it timelessly, for ever*** in the Next World.

12. ***We created man*** (Ādam) ***from the purest kind of clay*** – the word for "purest kind," *sulāla,* is what is extracted from a thing, its quintessence,

13. ***...then made him*** (the progeny of Ādam) ***a drop in a secure receptacle*** (the womb)*;*

14. ***...then formed the drop into a clot*** of congealed blood ***and formed the clot into a lump*** of flesh, ***and formed the lump into***

bones (read as *'iẓām* and *'aẓm*), ***and clothed the bones*** (read again as *'iẓām* and *'aẓm*) ***in flesh; and then brought him into being as another creature*** by breathing the *rūḥ* into him. ***So blessed be Allah, the Best of Creators*** – the Best of Determiners in his knowledge*!*

15. ***Then subsequently you will certainly die.***

16. ***Then on the Day of Rising you will be raised again*** for the Reckoning and the Repayment.

17. ***We created above you seven levels*** (heavens) – the paths of the angels – ***and We were not unaware of the creation*** of what was under them, and would not allow them to come unravelled. Allah holds them in place, as is stated in the *āyat, "He holds back the heaven, preventing it from falling to the earth."* (22:65)

18. ***We sent down a measured amount of water from heaven*** – which will be enough for mankind – ***and lodged it firmly in the earth; and We are well able to remove it.*** In that case they and their animals would die of thirst.

19. ***By means of it We produce gardens of dates and grapes for you*** – the kinds which in the eyes of the Arabs contain the greatest amount of fruit – ***in which there are many fruits for you, and from which you eat*** in both summer and winter;

20. ***...and*** We created ***a tree springing forth from Mount Sinai*** (read as *saynā'* and *sīnā'*. It is not declined since it is a place) ***yielding oil and a seasoning to those who eat.*** This is the olive tree, whose oil is used as a condiment as well as being an oil for cooking and other things.

21. ***And there is certainly a lesson*** – a warning which should be heeded – ***for you in your livestock*** – camels, cattle, sheep and goats. ***We give you to drink*** (read as *tusqīkum* and *tasqīkum*) ***from what is in their bellies*** (milk) ***and there are many ways in which you benefit from them,*** making use of their wool, hair, fur, skin and other things, ***and some of them you eat;***

22. ***...and you are conveyed on them*** (camels) ***and on ships as well.***

23. ***We sent Nūḥ to his people and he said, 'My people, worship Allah:*** obey Allah and affirm His unity. ***You have no god other than Him. So will you not be godfearing?'*** Do you not fear His punishment when you worship other than Him?'

ٱلْأَنْعَـٰمِ لَعِبْرَةً ۖ نُّسْقِيكُم مِّمَّا فِى بُطُونِهَا وَلَكُمْ فِيهَا مَنَـٰفِعُ كَثِيرَةٌ
وَمِنْهَا تَأْكُلُونَ ﴿٢١﴾ وَعَلَيْهَا وَعَلَى ٱلْفُلْكِ تُحْمَلُونَ ﴿٢٢﴾ وَلَقَدْ
أَرْسَلْنَا نُوحًا إِلَىٰ قَوْمِهِۦ فَقَالَ يَـٰقَوْمِ ٱعْبُدُوا۟ ٱللَّهَ مَا لَكُم مِّنْ إِلَـٰهٍ
غَيْرُهُۥٓ ۖ أَفَلَا تَتَّقُونَ ﴿٢٣﴾ فَقَالَ ٱلْمَلَؤُا۟ ٱلَّذِينَ كَفَرُوا۟ مِن قَوْمِهِۦ مَا هَـٰذَآ
إِلَّا بَشَرٌ مِّثْلُكُمْ يُرِيدُ أَن يَتَفَضَّلَ عَلَيْكُمْ وَلَوْ شَآءَ ٱللَّهُ لَأَنزَلَ
مَلَـٰٓئِكَةً مَّا سَمِعْنَا بِهَـٰذَا فِىٓ ءَابَآئِنَا ٱلْأَوَّلِينَ ﴿٢٤﴾ إِنْ هُوَ إِلَّا
رَجُلٌۢ بِهِۦ جِنَّةٌ فَتَرَبَّصُوا۟ بِهِۦ حَتَّىٰ حِينٍ ﴿٢٥﴾ قَالَ رَبِّ ٱنصُرْنِى
بِمَا كَذَّبُونِ ﴿٢٦﴾ فَأَوْحَيْنَآ إِلَيْهِ أَنِ ٱصْنَعِ ٱلْفُلْكَ بِأَعْيُنِنَا
وَوَحْيِنَا فَإِذَا جَآءَ أَمْرُنَا وَفَارَ ٱلتَّنُّورُ ۙ فَٱسْلُكْ فِيهَا مِن
كُلٍّ زَوْجَيْنِ ٱثْنَيْنِ وَأَهْلَكَ إِلَّا مَن سَبَقَ عَلَيْهِ ٱلْقَوْلُ
مِنْهُمْ ۖ وَلَا تُخَـٰطِبْنِى فِى ٱلَّذِينَ ظَلَمُوٓا۟ ۖ إِنَّهُم مُّغْرَقُونَ ﴿٢٧﴾
فَإِذَا ٱسْتَوَيْتَ أَنتَ وَمَن مَّعَكَ عَلَى ٱلْفُلْكِ فَقُلِ ٱلْحَمْدُ لِلَّهِ ٱلَّذِى نَجَّىٰنَا
مِنَ ٱلْقَوْمِ ٱلظَّـٰلِمِينَ ﴿٢٨﴾ وَقُل رَّبِّ أَنزِلْنِى مُنزَلًا مُّبَارَكًا وَأَنتَ خَيْرُ
ٱلْمُنزِلِينَ ﴿٢٩﴾ إِنَّ فِى ذَٰلِكَ لَـَٔايَـٰتٍ وَإِن كُنَّا لَمُبْتَلِينَ ﴿٣٠﴾ ثُمَّ أَنشَأْنَا
مِنۢ بَعْدِهِمْ قَرْنًا ءَاخَرِينَ ﴿٣١﴾ فَأَرْسَلْنَا فِيهِمْ رَسُولًا مِّنْهُمْ أَنِ ٱعْبُدُوا۟
ٱللَّهَ مَا لَكُم مِّنْ إِلَـٰهٍ غَيْرُهُۥٓ ۖ أَفَلَا تَتَّقُونَ ﴿٣٢﴾ وَقَالَ ٱلْمَلَأُ مِن قَوْمِهِ
ٱلَّذِينَ كَفَرُوا۟ وَكَذَّبُوا۟ بِلِقَآءِ ٱلْـَٔاخِرَةِ وَأَتْرَفْنَـٰهُمْ فِى ٱلْحَيَوٰةِ ٱلدُّنْيَا
مَا هَـٰذَآ إِلَّا بَشَرٌ مِّثْلُكُمْ يَأْكُلُ مِمَّا تَأْكُلُونَ مِنْهُ وَيَشْرَبُ مِمَّا
تَشْرَبُونَ ﴿٣٣﴾ وَلَئِنْ أَطَعْتُم بَشَرًا مِّثْلَكُمْ إِنَّكُمْ إِذًا لَّخَـٰسِرُونَ
﴿٣٤﴾ أَيَعِدُكُمْ أَنَّكُمْ إِذَا مِتُّمْ وَكُنتُمْ تُرَابًا وَعِظَـٰمًا أَنَّكُم مُّخْرَجُونَ

24. ***The ruling circle of those of his people who disbelieved said*** to their followers*:* ***'This is nothing but a human being like yourselves who simply wants to gain ascendancy over you*** so that he is followed and you become his followers*.* ***If Allah had wished*** that no one but Himself be worshipped**,** ***He would have sent angels down*** for that, rather than human beings**.** ***We never heard of anything like this*** religion to which Nūḥ calls ***among our ancestors, the earlier peoples*** (past nations)**.**

25. ***He*** (Nūḥ) ***is nothing but a man possessed*** (mad)***, so wait a while and see what happens to him.'*** You will see that he will die.

26. ***He*** (Nūḥ) ***said, 'My Lord, help me*** against them ***because of their calling me a liar*** – their denial of Me and assertion that You will never destroy them*!'*

27. ***We revealed to him: 'Build the Ship under Our supervision*** and Our protection ***and as We reveal*** and commanded**.** ***When Our command*** to destroy the unbelievers ***comes and water bubbles up from the earth*** – or, in one interpretation, from a bread oven, and water emerging from it was a sign for Nūḥ***, load into it*** (the Ship) ***a pair*** (male and female) ***of every species*** (read as *min kulli zawjan* and *min kullin zawjan*) – the story is recounted that Allah gathered for Nūḥ the wild animals, birds and all other creatures and he patted each species with his hand, putting his right hand on the male and left on the female, and loaded them in the Ship – ***and your family*** (wife and children) **–** ***except for those among them against whom the word*** of destruction ***has already gone ahead.*** That is a reference to his wife and his son, Kan'ān but not his sons Sām, Ḥām, and Yāfith: those three and their wives were in the Ship. Allah says in *Sūrat Hūd*, "*... and all who believe. But those who believed with him were only a few.*" (11:40) It is also said that there were six men and their wives, and it is said that there were a total of seventy-eight people in the Ship, half of whom were men and half women. ***And do not address Me concerning those who do wrong***, asking for those who disbelieved not to be destroyed**.** ***They shall be drowned.***

28. ***When you and those with you are settled in the Ship, then say: "Praise be to Allah who has rescued us from the people of the wrongdoers*** (the unbelievers) and destroyed them*!"*

﴿٣٥﴾ ۞ هَيْهَاتَ هَيْهَاتَ لِمَا تُوعَدُونَ ﴿٣٦﴾ إِنْ هِيَ إِلَّا حَيَاتُنَا

الدُّنْيَا نَمُوتُ وَنَحْيَا وَمَا نَحْنُ بِمَبْعُوثِينَ ﴿٣٧﴾ إِنْ هُوَ إِلَّا رَجُلٌ

افْتَرَىٰ عَلَى اللَّهِ كَذِبًا وَمَا نَحْنُ لَهُ بِمُؤْمِنِينَ ﴿٣٨﴾ قَالَ رَبِّ

انصُرْنِي بِمَا كَذَّبُونِ ﴿٣٩﴾ قَالَ عَمَّا قَلِيلٍ لَّيُصْبِحُنَّ نَادِمِينَ ﴿٤٠﴾

فَأَخَذَتْهُمُ الصَّيْحَةُ بِالْحَقِّ فَجَعَلْنَاهُمْ غُثَاءً ۚ فَبُعْدًا لِّلْقَوْمِ

الظَّالِمِينَ ﴿٤١﴾ ثُمَّ أَنشَأْنَا مِن بَعْدِهِمْ قُرُونًا آخَرِينَ ﴿٤٢﴾

مَا تَسْبِقُ مِنْ أُمَّةٍ أَجَلَهَا وَمَا يَسْتَأْخِرُونَ ﴿٤٣﴾ ثُمَّ أَرْسَلْنَا رُسُلَنَا تَتْرَىٰ ۖ

كُلَّ مَا جَاءَ أُمَّةً رَّسُولُهَا كَذَّبُوهُ ۚ فَأَتْبَعْنَا بَعْضَهُم بَعْضًا وَجَعَلْنَاهُمْ

أَحَادِيثَ ۚ فَبُعْدًا لِّقَوْمٍ لَّا يُؤْمِنُونَ ﴿٤٤﴾ ثُمَّ أَرْسَلْنَا مُوسَىٰ وَأَخَاهُ

هَارُونَ بِآيَاتِنَا وَسُلْطَانٍ مُّبِينٍ ﴿٤٥﴾ إِلَىٰ فِرْعَوْنَ وَمَلَئِهِ

فَاسْتَكْبَرُوا وَكَانُوا قَوْمًا عَالِينَ ﴿٤٦﴾ فَقَالُوا أَنُؤْمِنُ لِبَشَرَيْنِ مِثْلِنَا

وَقَوْمُهُمَا لَنَا عَابِدُونَ ﴿٤٧﴾ فَكَذَّبُوهُمَا فَكَانُوا مِنَ الْمُهْلَكِينَ

﴿٤٨﴾ وَلَقَدْ آتَيْنَا مُوسَى الْكِتَابَ لَعَلَّهُمْ يَهْتَدُونَ ﴿٤٩﴾ وَجَعَلْنَا

ابْنَ مَرْيَمَ وَأُمَّهُ آيَةً وَآوَيْنَاهُمَا إِلَىٰ رَبْوَةٍ ذَاتِ قَرَارٍ وَمَعِينٍ

﴿٥٠﴾ يَا أَيُّهَا الرُّسُلُ كُلُوا مِنَ الطَّيِّبَاتِ وَاعْمَلُوا صَالِحًا ۖ إِنِّي بِمَا

تَعْمَلُونَ عَلِيمٌ ﴿٥١﴾ وَإِنَّ هَٰذِهِ أُمَّتُكُمْ أُمَّةً وَاحِدَةً وَأَنَا رَبُّكُمْ

فَاتَّقُونِ ﴿٥٢﴾ فَتَقَطَّعُوا أَمْرَهُم بَيْنَهُمْ زُبُرًا ۖ كُلُّ حِزْبٍ بِمَا لَدَيْهِمْ

فَرِحُونَ ﴿٥٣﴾ فَذَرْهُمْ فِي غَمْرَتِهِمْ حَتَّىٰ حِينٍ ﴿٥٤﴾ أَيَحْسَبُونَ أَنَّمَا

نُمِدُّهُم بِهِ مِن مَّالٍ وَبَنِينَ ﴿٥٥﴾ نُسَارِعُ لَهُمْ فِي الْخَيْرَاتِ ۚ بَل لَّا يَشْعُرُونَ

﴿٥٦﴾ إِنَّ الَّذِينَ هُم مِّنْ خَشْيَةِ رَبِّهِم مُّشْفِقُونَ ﴿٥٧﴾ وَالَّذِينَ هُم

29. ***And say*** – when you alight from the Ship – ***"My Lord, land me in a blessed landing-place*** (read as *munzal* and *manzil*). This may mean either that the landing itself or that the place where the landing took place is blessed. ***You are the best Bringer to Land."'***

30. ***There are Signs in that*** which has been mentioned about Nūḥ and the Ship and the destruction of the unbelievers, which indicate the power of Allah Almighty. ***We are always putting people to the test*** – in this case, testing them by sending Nūḥ to them and his warning them.

31. ***Then We raised up another generation after them*** – the people of 'Ād –

32. ***...and sent a Messenger*** (Hūd) ***to them from themselves: 'Worship Allah. You have no god other than Him! So will you not be godfearing?'*** Will you not fear His punishment and believe?

33. ***The ruling circle of his people – those who disbelieved and denied the encounter of the Next World*** – and the journey to it – ***and whom We had given opulence*** and blessings ***in this world – said, 'This is nothing but a human being like yourselves who eats what you eat and drinks what you drink.***

34. ***If you were to obey a human being like yourselves, you would, in that case definitely be the losers*** (deluded).

35. ***Does he promise you that when you have died and become dust and bones you will be brought forth again?*** This stresses their denial of what he has promised because of the length of time involved.

36. ***What you have been promised is sheer nonsense!***

37. ***What is there*** – any life – ***but our life in this world? We die and we live and we will not be raised again.*** We only live on through our children.'

38. ***What is he*** (the Messenger) ***but a man who has invented a lie against Allah? We do not believe in him*** – nor do we believe that we will resurrected after death.'

39. ***He said, 'My Lord, help me because of their calling me a liar!'***

40. ***He said, 'In a short while they will be full of regret*** – for their unbelief and denial.'

41. ***The Great Blast*** – involving their punishment and destruction – ***seized hold of them inexorably*** – so that they died – ***and We turned them into dirty scum***: the film formed from crumbled dried plants found on the surface of floodwater. ***Away with the people of the wrongdoers!*** The wrongdoers are far away from Allah's mercy.

42. ***Then We raised up other generations*** of people ***after them.***

43. ***No nation can advance its appointed time, nor can they delay it.*** They will not die before it or later than it.

44. ***Then We sent Our Messengers one after another*** (read as *tatrā* and *tatran*) ***at intervals***, with a long period between each. ***Each time its Messenger came to a community they called him a liar, so We made them follow one another too*** – with regard to their respective destructions – ***and turned them into myths and legends. Away with the people who do not believe!***

45. ***Then We sent Mūsā and his brother Hārūn with Our Signs and clear authority***, in the form of the White Hand and other signs,

46. ***...to Pharaoh and his ruling circle. But they were*** too ***proud*** to believe ***and were a haughty people.*** They overpowered the tribe of Israel through injustice.

47. ***They said, 'What! Should we believe in two human beings like ourselves when their people are our slaves*** – humble and subjected to us***?'***

48. ***They denied them*** (Mūsā and Hārūn) ***so they were destroyed.***

49. ***We gave Mūsā the Book*** (the Torah) ***so that perhaps they*** (his people, the tribe of Israel) ***would be guided*** from misguidance. They were given that after the destruction of Pharaoh and his people.

50. ***And We made*** 'Īsā ***the son of Maryam and his mother a Sign*** – the two of them are considered to be a single sign, in that she gave birth to him without a father – ***and gave them shelter on a mountainside*** – the word *rabwa* means an elevated place, and it was situated in Jerusalem, Damascus, or Palestine – ***where there was a meadow*** – the word *qarār* means a level area which stretches out to a sufficient extent for people to be able to settle on it – ***and a flowing spring***, one which people can see.

51. ***Messengers, eat of the good*** and lawful ***things and act rightly***, performing both obligatory and supererogatory actions. ***I most certainly know what you do*** and will repay you for it.

52. Know that ***this faith of yours*** – the religion of Islam – ***is a single faith*** – your *dīn*, you who are addressed, is the one which you must follow – ***and I am your Lord, so be fearful of Me.***

53. ***But they*** (the people of religion) ***disagreed*** about their *dīn* ***and split up, dividing into sects*** – different disputing parties, as happened with the Jews, Christians and others – ***each party exulting in what it had*** of the *dīn*.

54. ***So leave them*** (the unbelievers of Makka) ***in their glut of ignorance*** (misguidance) ***for a while*** until they die.

55. ***Do they imagine that in the wealth and children We extend to them*** – in this world –

56. ***We are hastening to them with good things? No indeed; but they have no awareness*** that Allah is drawing them on.

57. ***Those who are filled with the fear of*** the punishment of ***their Lord;***

58. ***...those who believe the Signs of their Lord*** (the Qur'an)...

59. ***...those who do not associate anything with their Lord*** in their worship*;*

60. ***...those who give what they have given*** both by way of *ṣadaqa* and righteous actions, ***their hearts fearful of their return to their Lord*** – fearing that they will not be acceptable, and knowing that they will be returned to Allah –

61. ***...such people are truly racing towards good things, and they are the first to reach them*** in the knowledge of Allah.

62. ***We do not impose on any self any more than it can stand*** – oblige it to do anything beyond its ability; so whoever cannot pray standing, prays sitting and whoever cannot fast, breaks the fast. ***With Us there is a Book that speaks the truth*** about what they have done. This is the Preserved Tablet on which all actions are written. ***They*** – the souls which act – ***will not be wronged*** in any way, so the reward for good actions will not be decreased and evil deeds will not be exaggerated.

بِـَٔايَٰتِ رَبِّهِمۡ يُؤۡمِنُونَ ٥٨ وَٱلَّذِينَ هُم بِرَبِّهِمۡ لَا يُشۡرِكُونَ ٥٩
وَٱلَّذِينَ يُؤۡتُونَ مَآ ءَاتَواْ وَّقُلُوبُهُمۡ وَجِلَةٌ أَنَّهُمۡ إِلَىٰ رَبِّهِمۡ رَٰجِعُونَ ٦٠
أُوْلَٰٓئِكَ يُسَٰرِعُونَ فِي ٱلۡخَيۡرَٰتِ وَهُمۡ لَهَا سَٰبِقُونَ ٦١ وَلَا نُكَلِّفُ
نَفۡسًا إِلَّا وُسۡعَهَاۖ وَلَدَيۡنَا كِتَٰبٞ يَنطِقُ بِٱلۡحَقِّۚ وَهُمۡ لَا يُظۡلَمُونَ ٦٢
بَلۡ قُلُوبُهُمۡ فِي غَمۡرَةٖ مِّنۡ هَٰذَا وَلَهُمۡ أَعۡمَٰلٞ مِّن دُونِ ذَٰلِكَ هُمۡ لَهَا
عَٰمِلُونَ ٦٣ حَتَّىٰٓ إِذَآ أَخَذۡنَا مُتۡرَفِيهِم بِٱلۡعَذَابِ إِذَا هُمۡ يَجۡـَٔرُونَ
٦٤ لَا تَجۡـَٔرُواْ ٱلۡيَوۡمَۖ إِنَّكُم مِّنَّا لَا تُنصَرُونَ ٦٥ قَدۡ كَانَتۡ ءَايَٰتِي
تُتۡلَىٰ عَلَيۡكُمۡ فَكُنتُمۡ عَلَىٰٓ أَعۡقَٰبِكُمۡ تَنكِصُونَ ٦٦ مُسۡتَكۡبِرِينَ
بِهِۦ سَٰمِرٗا تَهۡجُرُونَ ٦٧ أَفَلَمۡ يَدَّبَّرُواْ ٱلۡقَوۡلَ أَمۡ جَآءَهُم مَّا لَمۡ يَأۡتِ
ءَابَآءَهُمُ ٱلۡأَوَّلِينَ ٦٨ أَمۡ لَمۡ يَعۡرِفُواْ رَسُولَهُمۡ فَهُمۡ لَهُۥ مُنكِرُونَ
٦٩ أَمۡ يَقُولُونَ بِهِۦ جِنَّةُۢۚ بَلۡ جَآءَهُم بِٱلۡحَقِّ وَأَكۡثَرُهُمۡ لِلۡحَقِّ
كَٰرِهُونَ ٧٠ وَلَوِ ٱتَّبَعَ ٱلۡحَقُّ أَهۡوَآءَهُمۡ لَفَسَدَتِ ٱلسَّمَٰوَٰتُ
وَٱلۡأَرۡضُ وَمَن فِيهِنَّۚ بَلۡ أَتَيۡنَٰهُم بِذِكۡرِهِمۡ فَهُمۡ عَن
ذِكۡرِهِم مُّعۡرِضُونَ ٧١ أَمۡ تَسۡـَٔلُهُمۡ خَرۡجٗا فَخَرَاجُ رَبِّكَ خَيۡرٞۖ
وَهُوَ خَيۡرُ ٱلرَّٰزِقِينَ ٧٢ وَإِنَّكَ لَتَدۡعُوهُمۡ إِلَىٰ صِرَٰطٖ مُّسۡتَقِيمٖ ٧٣
وَإِنَّ ٱلَّذِينَ لَا يُؤۡمِنُونَ بِٱلۡأٓخِرَةِ عَنِ ٱلصِّرَٰطِ لَنَٰكِبُونَ ٧٤
۞ وَلَوۡ رَحِمۡنَٰهُمۡ وَكَشَفۡنَا مَا بِهِم مِّن ضُرّٖ لَّلَجُّواْ فِي طُغۡيَٰنِهِمۡ
يَعۡمَهُونَ ٧٥ وَلَقَدۡ أَخَذۡنَٰهُم بِٱلۡعَذَابِ فَمَا ٱسۡتَكَانُواْ لِرَبِّهِمۡ
وَمَا يَتَضَرَّعُونَ ٧٦ حَتَّىٰٓ إِذَا فَتَحۡنَا عَلَيۡهِم بَابٗا ذَا عَذَابٖ شَدِيدٍ
إِذَا هُمۡ فِيهِ مُبۡلِسُونَ ٧٧ وَهُوَ ٱلَّذِيٓ أَنشَأَ لَكُمُ ٱلسَّمۡعَ وَٱلۡأَبۡصَٰرَ

63. ***But their*** (the unbelievers') ***hearts are overwhelmed by ignorance about this matter*** (the Qur'an) ***and they do other things as well*** to the believers, for which they will be punished.

64. ***But then when We seize the affluent*** – the wealthy and leading people – ***among them, with the punishment*** – by means of the sword at the Battle of Badr – ***they will suddenly start praying fervently.***

65. They will be told: ***'Do not pray fervently today. You will not get any help from Us.*** Their praying then will not help them.

66. ***My Signs*** (the Qur'an) ***were recited to you and you turned round on your heels*** away from it –

67. ***...arrogant towards it*** – too proud to believe, full of arrogance because they are the inhabitants of the Ḥaram of Makka and for that reason have a degree of security far beyond what most other people experience in their homes, ***talking arrant nonsense all night long*** while they are around the Ka'ba, when they reject the Qur'an and say things that are not true about the Prophet and the Qur'an.'

68. So Allah says: ***Do they not ponder these words*** (the Qur'an) which demonstrate the truthfulness of the Prophet? ***Has anything come to them that did not come to their ancestors, the previous peoples?***

69. ***Or is it that they do not recognise their Messenger and therefore do not acknowledge him?***

70. ***Or do they say, 'He is a man possessed,' when he has brought the truth to them?*** He has brought the truth to those who believe in that which he has brought; and what the Messengers brought to past communities is the truth, and in that he is not mad. He brought the Qur'an which contains knowledge of Allah and the laws of Islam. ***But most of them hate the truth.***

71. ***If the truth*** (the Qur'an) ***were to follow their whims and desires*** – for instance their attribution to Allah of a partner and child, when He is greatly exalted above that – ***the heavens and the earth and everyone in them would have been brought to ruin.*** Their order would have been disrupted, in view of the conflict which inevitably occurs in situations when there is more than one ruler. ***No indeed! We have given them their Reminder*** (the Qur'an) – which contains

وَٱلۡأَفۡـِٔدَةَۚ قَلِيلٗا مَّا تَشۡكُرُونَ ٧٨ وَهُوَ ٱلَّذِي ذَرَأَكُمۡ فِي ٱلۡأَرۡضِ
وَإِلَيۡهِ تُحۡشَرُونَ ٧٩ وَهُوَ ٱلَّذِي يُحۡيِۦ وَيُمِيتُ وَلَهُ ٱخۡتِلَٰفُ
ٱلَّيۡلِ وَٱلنَّهَارِۚ أَفَلَا تَعۡقِلُونَ ٨٠ بَلۡ قَالُواْ مِثۡلَ مَا قَالَ
ٱلۡأَوَّلُونَ ٨١ قَالُوٓاْ أَءِذَا مِتۡنَا وَكُنَّا تُرَابٗا وَعِظَٰمًا أَءِنَّا
لَمَبۡعُوثُونَ ٨٢ لَقَدۡ وُعِدۡنَا نَحۡنُ وَءَابَآؤُنَا هَٰذَا مِن قَبۡلُ إِنۡ هَٰذَآ
إِلَّآ أَسَٰطِيرُ ٱلۡأَوَّلِينَ ٨٣ قُل لِّمَنِ ٱلۡأَرۡضُ وَمَن فِيهَآ إِن
كُنتُمۡ تَعۡلَمُونَ ٨٤ سَيَقُولُونَ لِلَّهِۚ قُلۡ أَفَلَا تَذَكَّرُونَ
٨٥ قُلۡ مَن رَّبُّ ٱلسَّمَٰوَٰتِ ٱلسَّبۡعِ وَرَبُّ ٱلۡعَرۡشِ ٱلۡعَظِيمِ
٨٦ سَيَقُولُونَ لِلَّهِۚ قُلۡ أَفَلَا تَتَّقُونَ ٨٧ قُلۡ مَنۢ بِيَدِهِۦ
مَلَكُوتُ كُلِّ شَيۡءٖ وَهُوَ يُجِيرُ وَلَا يُجَارُ عَلَيۡهِ إِن
كُنتُمۡ تَعۡلَمُونَ ٨٨ سَيَقُولُونَ لِلَّهِۚ قُلۡ فَأَنَّىٰ تُسۡحَرُونَ ٨٩
بَلۡ أَتَيۡنَٰهُم بِٱلۡحَقِّ وَإِنَّهُمۡ لَكَٰذِبُونَ ٩٠ مَا ٱتَّخَذَ ٱللَّهُ مِن وَلَدٖ
وَمَا كَانَ مَعَهُۥ مِنۡ إِلَٰهٍۚ إِذٗا لَّذَهَبَ كُلُّ إِلَٰهِۢ بِمَا خَلَقَ وَلَعَلَا
بَعۡضُهُمۡ عَلَىٰ بَعۡضٖۚ سُبۡحَٰنَ ٱللَّهِ عَمَّا يَصِفُونَ ٩١ عَٰلِمِ
ٱلۡغَيۡبِ وَٱلشَّهَٰدَةِ فَتَعَٰلَىٰ عَمَّا يُشۡرِكُونَ ٩٢ قُل رَّبِّ
إِمَّا تُرِيَنِّي مَا يُوعَدُونَ ٩٣ رَبِّ فَلَا تَجۡعَلۡنِي فِي ٱلۡقَوۡمِ
ٱلظَّٰلِمِينَ ٩٤ وَإِنَّا عَلَىٰٓ أَن نُّرِيَكَ مَا نَعِدُهُمۡ لَقَٰدِرُونَ ٩٥
ٱدۡفَعۡ بِٱلَّتِي هِيَ أَحۡسَنُ ٱلسَّيِّئَةَۚ نَحۡنُ أَعۡلَمُ بِمَا يَصِفُونَ ٩٦
وَقُل رَّبِّ أَعُوذُ بِكَ مِنۡ هَمَزَٰتِ ٱلشَّيَٰطِينِ ٩٧ وَأَعُوذُ بِكَ
رَبِّ أَن يَحۡضُرُونِ ٩٨ حَتَّىٰٓ إِذَا جَآءَ أَحَدَهُمُ ٱلۡمَوۡتُ قَالَ رَبِّ

mention of them and honours them – ***but they have turned away from it.***

72. ***Are you asking them for payment*** (read as both *kharjan* and *kharājan*) – a wage for guiding them to faith***? Your Lord's payment*** (read as *kharj* and *kharāj*) – the wage, reward and provision He gives – ***is better. He is the Best of Providers.***

73. ***You are calling them to a straight path*** (the *dīn* of Islam)**,**

74. ***...but those who do not believe in the Next World*** – meaning the Resurrection, and the reward and punishment which follow it – ***recoil from the path.***

75. ***If We did have mercy on them and removed the harm*** – a reference to the famine which afflicted them in Makka for seven years – ***afflicting them, they would still obstinately persist in wandering blindly in their excessive insolence*** – in misguidance.

76. ***We seized them with the punishment*** (famine)***; but they did not go low before their Lord*** in humility, and did not make supplication to Him***, nor will they humble themselves*** –

77. ***...until We open to them a gate to a harsh punishment*** – a reference to their slaughter at the Battle of Badr – ***in which they will at once be crushed by despair.***

78. ***It is He who has created hearing, sight and hearts for you. What little thanks you show!***

79. ***It is He who dispersed you about the earth and*** then you will be resurrected, and then ***you will be gathered to Him.***

80. ***It is He who gives life*** – by breathing spirit into an inert lump of flesh – ***and causes to die, and His is the alternation of night and day*** – in terms of darkness and light and increase and decrease***. So will you not use your intellect*** – understand His work and then reflect***?***

81. ***And yet they say the same as previous peoples said.***

82. ***They*** (the first ones) ***say, 'When we are dead and turned to dust and bones, shall we then be raised again?***

83. ***We and our forefathers were promised this*** Resurrection after death ***before. This is nothing but the myths*** – lies like the legends and fables – ***of previous peoples!'***

84. ***Say*** to them: ***'To whom does the earth belong, and everyone*** created ***in it, if you have any knowledge*** of its Creator and Master?'

85. ***They will say: 'To Allah.' Say*** to them ***'So will you not pay heed?'*** Will you not be warned and know that the One who has the power to originate has the power to bring back to life after death?

86. ***Say: 'Who is the Lord of the Seven Heavens and the Lord of the Mighty Throne?'***

87. ***They will say: 'Allah.' Say: 'So will you not be godfearing*** – and fear to worship any other than Allah?'

88. ***Say: 'In whose hand is the dominion over everything, He who gives protection and from whom no protection can be given, if you have any knowledge?'***

89. ***They will say: 'Allah's*** (read as *lillāhi* and *Allāhu*).' ***Say: 'So how have you been bewitched?'*** How have they been deceived and turned from the Truth, which is worshipping Allah alone; how can they imagine it to be false?

90. ***The fact is that We have given them the truth and they are liars*** in denying it.

91. ***Allah has no son and there is no other god accompanying Him, for then each god would have gone off with what he created and one of them would have been exalted above the other.*** If there had been another god, each would have taken control of what belonged to him alone and kept the other from gaining power over it, as kings of this world do. ***Glory be to Allah above what they describe*** and say,

92. ***...Knower of the Unseen and the Visible!*** Nothing is hidden from Him. ***He is exalted above all they associate with Him!***

93. ***Say: 'My Lord, if You let me see what*** (punishment) ***they have been promised*** – that of being killed at Badr –

94. ***...do not then, my Lord, put me among the wrongdoing people*** and destroy me when they are destroyed!'

95. ***We are certainly capable of letting you see what We have promised them.***

96. ***Ward off evil with what is better.*** What is better is the quality of forbearance and turning away from them when they injure you. This

ٱرْجِعُونِ ﴿٩٩﴾ لَعَلِّيٓ أَعْمَلُ صَٰلِحًا فِيمَا تَرَكْتُۚ كَلَّآۚ إِنَّهَا كَلِمَةٌ
هُوَ قَآئِلُهَاۖ وَمِن وَرَآئِهِم بَرْزَخٌ إِلَىٰ يَوْمِ يُبْعَثُونَ ﴿١٠٠﴾ فَإِذَا نُفِخَ
فِي ٱلصُّورِ فَلَآ أَنسَابَ بَيْنَهُمْ يَوْمَئِذٍ وَلَا يَتَسَآءَلُونَ ﴿١٠١﴾
فَمَن ثَقُلَتْ مَوَٰزِينُهُۥ فَأُوْلَٰٓئِكَ هُمُ ٱلْمُفْلِحُونَ ﴿١٠٢﴾ وَمَنْ
خَفَّتْ مَوَٰزِينُهُۥ فَأُوْلَٰٓئِكَ ٱلَّذِينَ خَسِرُوٓاْ أَنفُسَهُمْ فِي جَهَنَّمَ
خَٰلِدُونَ ﴿١٠٣﴾ تَلْفَحُ وُجُوهَهُمُ ٱلنَّارُ وَهُمْ فِيهَا كَٰلِحُونَ ﴿١٠٤﴾
أَلَمْ تَكُنْ ءَايَٰتِي تُتْلَىٰ عَلَيْكُمْ فَكُنتُم بِهَا تُكَذِّبُونَ ﴿١٠٥﴾ قَالُواْ
رَبَّنَا غَلَبَتْ عَلَيْنَا شِقْوَتُنَا وَكُنَّا قَوْمًا ضَآلِّينَ ﴿١٠٦﴾ رَبَّنَآ
أَخْرِجْنَا مِنْهَا فَإِنْ عُدْنَا فَإِنَّا ظَٰلِمُونَ ﴿١٠٧﴾ قَالَ ٱخْسَـُٔواْ فِيهَا
وَلَا تُكَلِّمُونِ ﴿١٠٨﴾ إِنَّهُۥ كَانَ فَرِيقٌ مِّنْ عِبَادِي يَقُولُونَ رَبَّنَآ
ءَامَنَّا فَٱغْفِرْ لَنَا وَٱرْحَمْنَا وَأَنتَ خَيْرُ ٱلرَّٰحِمِينَ ﴿١٠٩﴾ فَٱتَّخَذْتُمُوهُمْ
سِخْرِيًّا حَتَّىٰٓ أَنسَوْكُمْ ذِكْرِي وَكُنتُم مِّنْهُمْ تَضْحَكُونَ ﴿١١٠﴾
إِنِّي جَزَيْتُهُمُ ٱلْيَوْمَ بِمَا صَبَرُوٓاْ أَنَّهُمْ هُمُ ٱلْفَآئِزُونَ ﴿١١١﴾ قَٰلَ
كَمْ لَبِثْتُمْ فِي ٱلْأَرْضِ عَدَدَ سِنِينَ ﴿١١٢﴾ قَالُواْ لَبِثْنَا يَوْمًا أَوْ بَعْضَ
يَوْمٍ فَسْـَٔلِ ٱلْعَآدِّينَ ﴿١١٣﴾ قَٰلَ إِن لَّبِثْتُمْ إِلَّا قَلِيلًاۖ لَّوْ أَنَّكُمْ
كُنتُمْ تَعْلَمُونَ ﴿١١٤﴾ أَفَحَسِبْتُمْ أَنَّمَا خَلَقْنَٰكُمْ عَبَثًا وَأَنَّكُمْ
إِلَيْنَا لَا تُرْجَعُونَ ﴿١١٥﴾ فَتَعَٰلَى ٱللَّهُ ٱلْمَلِكُ ٱلْحَقُّۖ لَآ إِلَٰهَ إِلَّا
هُوَ رَبُّ ٱلْعَرْشِ ٱلْكَرِيمِ ﴿١١٦﴾ وَمَن يَدْعُ مَعَ ٱللَّهِ إِلَٰهًا
ءَاخَرَ لَا بُرْهَٰنَ لَهُۥ بِهِۦ فَإِنَّمَا حِسَابُهُۥ عِندَ رَبِّهِۦٓۚ إِنَّهُۥ لَا يُفْلِحُ
ٱلْكَٰفِرُونَ ﴿١١٧﴾ وَقُل رَّبِّ ٱغْفِرْ وَٱرْحَمْ وَأَنتَ خَيْرُ ٱلرَّٰحِمِينَ ﴿١١٨﴾

was revealed before the command to fight was revealed. ***We know very well what they express***, their denial and their other statements; and We will repay them for it.

97. ***Say: 'My Lord, I seek refuge with You from the goadings*** and whispering ***of the shayṭāns…***

98. ***…and I seek refuge with You, my Lord, from their presence*** – from their being present in my affairs, because they bring evil.*'*

99. ***When death comes to one of them*** and he sees his place in the Fire, or his place in the Garden, if he is a believer, ***he says, 'My Lord, send me back again*** – the imperative "send" is in the plural for reasons of respect –

100. ***…so that perhaps I may act rightly*** – by testifying that there is no god but Allah – ***regarding the things I failed to do*** in my lifetime*!'* Allah will say: ***No indeed! They are merely words he utters.*** There is no going back. These words he says are useless. ***Before them there is an interspace*** – a barrier which prevents them from going back – ***until the Day they are raised up.***

101. ***Then when the Trumpet is blown*** for the first or second time, ***that Day there will be no family ties between them*** about which they can boast; ***they will not be able to question one another*** about that. That is unlike from the situation in this world, because the terrifying nature of what is happening will distract them from doing so during some of the events of the Rising. During others they will recover their senses, since it says in one *āyat*: *"They will confront each another, questioning on another."* (37:27)

102. ***Those whose scales are heavy*** with good actions, ***they are the successful.***

103. ***Those whose scales are light*** owing to evil deeds, ***they are the losers of their selves, remaining in Hell timelessly, for ever.***

104. ***The Fire will sear their faces, making them grimace horribly in it, their lips drawn back from their teeth.***

105. It will be said to them: ***'Were My Signs*** (the Qur'an) ***not recited to you*** to make you fear, ***and did you not deny them?'***

106. ***They will say, 'Our Lord, our miserable destiny*** (read as *shiqwatunā* and *shaqāwatunā*) ***overpowered us. We were misguided people.***

107. ***Our Lord, remove us from it! Then if we revert*** to disagreement ***again, we will definitely be wrongdoers.'***

108. ***He will say*** to them, on the tongue of the angel Mālik***: 'Slink away into it*** – far into the Fire, abased – ***and do not speak to Me*** about removing the punishment. This is to put an end to any hope they have.

109. ***There was a group of My slaves*** (the Muhājirūn) ***who said, "Our Lord, we believe, so forgive us and have mercy on us. You are the Best of the Merciful."***

110. ***But you made a mockery*** (read as *sikhriyyan* and *sukhriyyan*) ***of them*** – those referred to here included Bilāl, Ṣuhayb, 'Ammār and Salmān – ***so that they made you forget to remember Me*** – in other words, they abandoned Allah because they were busy mocking those Muslims; and so they became the reason for their forgetfulness, which is therefore ascribed to them – ***while you were laughing at them.***

111. ***Today I have rewarded them*** with abiding bliss ***for being steadfast*** in the face of mockery and injury***. They*** (read as *annahum* and *innahum*) ***are the ones who are victorious*** and will obtain their desire.***'***

112. ***He*** (Allah) ***will say*** to them on the tongue of Mālik – a variant reading has the imperative *qul* "Say!" here***: 'How many years did you tarry on the earth*** in the world and in the grave***?'***

113. ***They will say, 'We tarried there for a day or part of a day.*** They will be uncertain about this and think that it was short because of the terrible nature of the punishment they are suffering. ***Ask those able to count*** – a reference to the angels who count all the deeds of every human being.***'***

114. ***He*** (Allah) ***will say*** on the tongue of Mālik. As above in 23:112, a variant reading has the imperative *qul* "Say!" here – ***'You only tarried there for a little while*** compared to the length of time you will remain in the Fire***, if you did but know!***

115. ***Did you suppose that We created you*** merely ***for amusement*** – without a real and wise purpose – ***and that you would not be returned to Us?'*** We made you worshippers by imposing on you obedience to Our commands and prohibitions; then you will be

ٱرۡجِعُونِ ﴿٩٩﴾ لَعَلِّيٓ أَعۡمَلُ صَٰلِحٗا فِيمَا تَرَكۡتُۚ كَلَّآۚ إِنَّهَا كَلِمَةٌ
هُوَ قَآئِلُهَاۖ وَمِن وَرَآئِهِم بَرۡزَخٌ إِلَىٰ يَوۡمِ يُبۡعَثُونَ ﴿١٠٠﴾ فَإِذَا نُفِخَ
فِي ٱلصُّورِ فَلَآ أَنسَابَ بَيۡنَهُمۡ يَوۡمَئِذٖ وَلَا يَتَسَآءَلُونَ ﴿١٠١﴾
فَمَن ثَقُلَتۡ مَوَٰزِينُهُۥ فَأُوْلَٰٓئِكَ هُمُ ٱلۡمُفۡلِحُونَ ﴿١٠٢﴾ وَمَنۡ
خَفَّتۡ مَوَٰزِينُهُۥ فَأُوْلَٰٓئِكَ ٱلَّذِينَ خَسِرُوٓاْ أَنفُسَهُمۡ فِي جَهَنَّمَ
خَٰلِدُونَ ﴿١٠٣﴾ تَلۡفَحُ وُجُوهَهُمُ ٱلنَّارُ وَهُمۡ فِيهَا كَٰلِحُونَ ﴿١٠٤﴾
أَلَمۡ تَكُنۡ ءَايَٰتِي تُتۡلَىٰ عَلَيۡكُمۡ فَكُنتُم بِهَا تُكَذِّبُونَ ﴿١٠٥﴾ قَالُواْ
رَبَّنَا غَلَبَتۡ عَلَيۡنَا شِقۡوَتُنَا وَكُنَّا قَوۡمٗا ضَآلِّينَ ﴿١٠٦﴾ رَبَّنَآ
أَخۡرِجۡنَا مِنۡهَا فَإِنۡ عُدۡنَا فَإِنَّا ظَٰلِمُونَ ﴿١٠٧﴾ قَالَ ٱخۡسَـُٔواْ فِيهَا
وَلَا تُكَلِّمُونِ ﴿١٠٨﴾ إِنَّهُۥ كَانَ فَرِيقٞ مِّنۡ عِبَادِي يَقُولُونَ رَبَّنَآ
ءَامَنَّا فَٱغۡفِرۡ لَنَا وَٱرۡحَمۡنَا وَأَنتَ خَيۡرُ ٱلرَّٰحِمِينَ ﴿١٠٩﴾ فَٱتَّخَذۡتُمُوهُمۡ
سِخۡرِيًّا حَتَّىٰٓ أَنسَوۡكُمۡ ذِكۡرِي وَكُنتُم مِّنۡهُمۡ تَضۡحَكُونَ ﴿١١٠﴾
إِنِّي جَزَيۡتُهُمُ ٱلۡيَوۡمَ بِمَا صَبَرُوٓاْ أَنَّهُمۡ هُمُ ٱلۡفَآئِزُونَ ﴿١١١﴾ قَٰلَ
كَمۡ لَبِثۡتُمۡ فِي ٱلۡأَرۡضِ عَدَدَ سِنِينَ ﴿١١٢﴾ قَالُواْ لَبِثۡنَا يَوۡمًا أَوۡ بَعۡضَ
يَوۡمٖ فَسۡـَٔلِ ٱلۡعَآدِّينَ ﴿١١٣﴾ قَٰلَ إِن لَّبِثۡتُمۡ إِلَّا قَلِيلٗاۖ لَّوۡ أَنَّكُمۡ
كُنتُمۡ تَعۡلَمُونَ ﴿١١٤﴾ أَفَحَسِبۡتُمۡ أَنَّمَا خَلَقۡنَٰكُمۡ عَبَثٗا وَأَنَّكُمۡ
إِلَيۡنَا لَا تُرۡجَعُونَ ﴿١١٥﴾ فَتَعَٰلَى ٱللَّهُ ٱلۡمَلِكُ ٱلۡحَقُّۖ لَآ إِلَٰهَ إِلَّا
هُوَ رَبُّ ٱلۡعَرۡشِ ٱلۡكَرِيمِ ﴿١١٦﴾ وَمَن يَدۡعُ مَعَ ٱللَّهِ إِلَٰهًا
ءَاخَرَ لَا بُرۡهَٰنَ لَهُۥ بِهِۦ فَإِنَّمَا حِسَابُهُۥ عِندَ رَبِّهِۦٓۚ إِنَّهُۥ لَا يُفۡلِحُ
ٱلۡكَٰفِرُونَ ﴿١١٧﴾ وَقُل رَّبِّ ٱغۡفِرۡ وَٱرۡحَمۡ وَأَنتَ خَيۡرُ ٱلرَّٰحِمِينَ ﴿١١٨﴾

returned to Us, and We will repay you accordingly. *"I only created jinn and men to worship Me."* (51:56)

116. ***Exalted be Allah*** above doing anything for the sake of amusement or any other things which are not appropriate for Him – ***the King, the Real. There is no god but Him, Lord of the Noble Throne.***

117. ***Whoever calls on another god together with Allah, has no grounds*** – meaning no proof for it or argument with any sense to it justifying it – ***for doing so at all and his reckoning*** and repayment ***is with his Lord. Truly the unbelievers have no success*** and will not achieve happiness.

118. ***Say: 'My Lord, forgive and be merciful*** to the believers, having mercy on them as well as forgiveness for them***! You are the Best of the Merciful.'***

سُورَةُ النُّورِ

بِسْمِ ٱللَّهِ ٱلرَّحْمَٰنِ ٱلرَّحِيمِ

سُورَةٌ أَنزَلْنَٰهَا وَفَرَضْنَٰهَا وَأَنزَلْنَا فِيهَآ ءَايَٰتٍۭ بَيِّنَٰتٍ لَّعَلَّكُمْ تَذَكَّرُونَ
(١) ٱلزَّانِيَةُ وَٱلزَّانِى فَٱجْلِدُوا۟ كُلَّ وَٰحِدٍ مِّنْهُمَا مِا۟ئَةَ جَلْدَةٍ ۖ وَلَا تَأْخُذْكُم
بِهِمَا رَأْفَةٌ فِى دِينِ ٱللَّهِ إِن كُنتُمْ تُؤْمِنُونَ بِٱللَّهِ وَٱلْيَوْمِ ٱلْءَاخِرِ ۖ وَلْيَشْهَدْ
عَذَابَهُمَا طَآئِفَةٌ مِّنَ ٱلْمُؤْمِنِينَ (٢) ٱلزَّانِى لَا يَنكِحُ إِلَّا زَانِيَةً أَوْ
مُشْرِكَةً وَٱلزَّانِيَةُ لَا يَنكِحُهَآ إِلَّا زَانٍ أَوْ مُشْرِكٌ ۚ وَحُرِّمَ ذَٰلِكَ عَلَى
ٱلْمُؤْمِنِينَ (٣) وَٱلَّذِينَ يَرْمُونَ ٱلْمُحْصَنَٰتِ ثُمَّ لَمْ يَأْتُوا۟ بِأَرْبَعَةِ شُهَدَآءَ
فَٱجْلِدُوهُمْ ثَمَٰنِينَ جَلْدَةً وَلَا تَقْبَلُوا۟ لَهُمْ شَهَٰدَةً أَبَدًا ۚ وَأُو۟لَٰٓئِكَ هُمُ
ٱلْفَٰسِقُونَ (٤) إِلَّا ٱلَّذِينَ تَابُوا۟ مِنۢ بَعْدِ ذَٰلِكَ وَأَصْلَحُوا۟ فَإِنَّ ٱللَّهَ غَفُورٌ
رَّحِيمٌ (٥) وَٱلَّذِينَ يَرْمُونَ أَزْوَٰجَهُمْ وَلَمْ يَكُن لَّهُمْ شُهَدَآءُ إِلَّآ أَنفُسُهُمْ
فَشَهَٰدَةُ أَحَدِهِمْ أَرْبَعُ شَهَٰدَٰتٍۭ بِٱللَّهِ ۙ إِنَّهُۥ لَمِنَ ٱلصَّٰدِقِينَ (٦)
وَٱلْخَٰمِسَةُ أَنَّ لَعْنَتَ ٱللَّهِ عَلَيْهِ إِن كَانَ مِنَ ٱلْكَٰذِبِينَ (٧) وَيَدْرَؤُا۟
عَنْهَا ٱلْعَذَابَ أَن تَشْهَدَ أَرْبَعَ شَهَٰدَٰتٍۭ بِٱللَّهِ ۙ إِنَّهُۥ لَمِنَ ٱلْكَٰذِبِينَ
(٨) وَٱلْخَٰمِسَةَ أَنَّ غَضَبَ ٱللَّهِ عَلَيْهَآ إِن كَانَ مِنَ ٱلصَّٰدِقِينَ (٩)
وَلَوْلَا فَضْلُ ٱللَّهِ عَلَيْكُمْ وَرَحْمَتُهُۥ وَأَنَّ ٱللَّهَ تَوَّابٌ حَكِيمٌ (١٠)
إِنَّ ٱلَّذِينَ جَآءُو بِٱلْإِفْكِ عُصْبَةٌ مِّنكُمْ ۚ لَا تَحْسَبُوهُ شَرًّا لَّكُم ۖ بَلْ هُوَ

24. *Sūrat an-Nūr*
Light

This *sūra* is Madinan. It has 62 or 64 *āyats* and was sent down after *al-Ḥashr.*

1. *A sūra We have sent down and imposed* (read as *faraḍnā* and *farraḍnā*)**. *We have sent down Clear Signs*** (clear evidence) ***in it so that perhaps you will pay heed*** and be admonished by it.

2. *A woman and a man who commit fornication* – a man and woman who are not married; if they were, they would be stoned according to the *Sunna* – ***flog both of them with one hundred lashes*** – and the *Sunna* adds to this penalty that the man should be exiled for a year; slaves incur half of that punishment – ***and do not let compassion for either of them possess you where Allah's* dīn *is concerned*** – the ruling is that you should not abandon any of the punishment prescribed for them – ***if you believe in Allah and the Last Day*** (the Day of Resurrection)**.** This is to encourage what was mentioned above. ***A number of believers should witness their punishment*** by flogging**.** It is said that there must be at least three, and it is said that the minimum is four, which is the number of the required witnesses to fornication.

3. *A man who has fornicated may only marry a woman who has fornicated or a woman of the idolators. A woman who has fornicated may only marry a man who has fornicated or a man of the idolators.* This is appropriate for them according to what has been mentioned. ***Doing such a thing is unlawful for the believers.*** It is unlawful for the good believers to marry those who fornicate. This was revealed when the poor *Muhājirūn* wanted to marry the prostitutes of the idolators who were wealthy so that they could support them. It is said that the prohibition was particular to them. It is also said that it is general and was then abrogated by the words of Allah Almighty, *"Marry off those among you who are unmarried...* " (24:32)

4. *But those who make accusations* of fornication ***against chaste women and then do not produce four witnesses*** who actually saw the act, ***flog*** each of ***them with eighty lashes and never again accept them as witnesses*** about anything. ***Such people are deviators*** – because they have committed a grave wrong action –

5. ***...except for those who after that repent and put things right*** by doing right actions. ***Allah is Ever-Forgiving*** for their slander, ***Most Merciful*** to them by inspiring them to a repentance which will prevent their deviance and allow the acceptance of their testimony.

6. ***Those who make an accusation*** of fornication ***against their wives and have no witnesses except themselves*** – and this happened with some of the Companions, ***such people should testify four times by Allah that they are telling the truth*** – in accusing their wives of adultery –

7. ***...and a fifth time that Allah's curse will be upon them if they are lying.*** If they do this, then the punishment for slander is averted from them.

8. ***And the punishment*** for adultery – which would be established by her husband's testimony – ***is removed from her if she testifies four times by Allah that he is lying*** in making his accusation.

9. ***...and a fifth time that Allah's anger will be upon her if he is telling the truth*** about it.

10. ***Were it not for Allah's favour to you and His mercy*** in veiling that, ***and that Allah is Ever-Relenting***, by accepting repentance in from that and other things, ***All-Wise*** in what He decrees about that and other things in order to make the truth clear. He can hasten the punishment of those who deserve it.

11. ***There is a group of you who propagated the lie.*** They did wrong by lying about 'Ā'isha, *Umm al-Mu'minīn*, may Allah be pleased with her, by slandering her. This was a group of the believers: Ḥassān ibn Thābit, 'Abdullāh ibn Ubayy, Misṭaḥ and Ḥamna bint Jaḥsh. ***Do not suppose it to be bad for you*** believers other than this group; ***rather it is good for you*** – Allah will reward you for it. The innocence of 'Ā'isha and the one who was with her, Ṣafwān, was made clear. She said, "I was with the Prophet, may Allah bless him and grant him peace, on an expedition after the command (to women) to veil was revealed. It came to an end and we were returning and were near Madina. The Prophet, peace be upon him, gave

خَيْرٌ لَّكُمْ ۚ لِكُلِّ ٱمْرِئٍ مِّنْهُم مَّا ٱكْتَسَبَ مِنَ ٱلْإِثْمِ ۚ وَٱلَّذِى تَوَلَّىٰ
كِبْرَهُۥ مِنْهُمْ لَهُۥ عَذَابٌ عَظِيمٌ ﴿١١﴾ لَّوْلَآ إِذْ سَمِعْتُمُوهُ ظَنَّ ٱلْمُؤْمِنُونَ
وَٱلْمُؤْمِنَٰتُ بِأَنفُسِهِمْ خَيْرًا وَقَالُوا۟ هَٰذَآ إِفْكٌ مُّبِينٌ ﴿١٢﴾ لَّوْلَا
جَآءُو عَلَيْهِ بِأَرْبَعَةِ شُهَدَآءَ ۚ فَإِذْ لَمْ يَأْتُوا۟ بِٱلشُّهَدَآءِ فَأُو۟لَٰٓئِكَ
عِندَ ٱللَّهِ هُمُ ٱلْكَٰذِبُونَ ﴿١٣﴾ وَلَوْلَا فَضْلُ ٱللَّهِ عَلَيْكُمْ وَرَحْمَتُهُۥ
فِى ٱلدُّنْيَا وَٱلْءَاخِرَةِ لَمَسَّكُمْ فِى مَآ أَفَضْتُمْ فِيهِ عَذَابٌ عَظِيمٌ ﴿١٤﴾
إِذْ تَلَقَّوْنَهُۥ بِأَلْسِنَتِكُمْ وَتَقُولُونَ بِأَفْوَاهِكُم مَّا لَيْسَ لَكُم بِهِۦ عِلْمٌ
وَتَحْسَبُونَهُۥ هَيِّنًا وَهُوَ عِندَ ٱللَّهِ عَظِيمٌ ﴿١٥﴾ وَلَوْلَآ إِذْ سَمِعْتُمُوهُ
قُلْتُم مَّا يَكُونُ لَنَآ أَن نَّتَكَلَّمَ بِهَٰذَا سُبْحَٰنَكَ هَٰذَا بُهْتَٰنٌ عَظِيمٌ
﴿١٦﴾ يَعِظُكُمُ ٱللَّهُ أَن تَعُودُوا۟ لِمِثْلِهِۦٓ أَبَدًا إِن كُنتُم مُّؤْمِنِينَ ﴿١٧﴾
وَيُبَيِّنُ ٱللَّهُ لَكُمُ ٱلْءَايَٰتِ ۚ وَٱللَّهُ عَلِيمٌ حَكِيمٌ ﴿١٨﴾ إِنَّ ٱلَّذِينَ
يُحِبُّونَ أَن تَشِيعَ ٱلْفَٰحِشَةُ فِى ٱلَّذِينَ ءَامَنُوا۟ لَهُمْ عَذَابٌ أَلِيمٌ
فِى ٱلدُّنْيَا وَٱلْءَاخِرَةِ ۚ وَٱللَّهُ يَعْلَمُ وَأَنتُمْ لَا تَعْلَمُونَ ﴿١٩﴾ وَلَوْلَا
فَضْلُ ٱللَّهِ عَلَيْكُمْ وَرَحْمَتُهُۥ وَأَنَّ ٱللَّهَ رَءُوفٌ رَّحِيمٌ ﴿٢٠﴾
۞ يَٰٓأَيُّهَا ٱلَّذِينَ ءَامَنُوا۟ لَا تَتَّبِعُوا۟ خُطُوَٰتِ ٱلشَّيْطَٰنِ ۚ وَمَن يَتَّبِعْ
خُطُوَٰتِ ٱلشَّيْطَٰنِ فَإِنَّهُۥ يَأْمُرُ بِٱلْفَحْشَآءِ وَٱلْمُنكَرِ ۚ وَلَوْلَا فَضْلُ
ٱللَّهِ عَلَيْكُمْ وَرَحْمَتُهُۥ مَا زَكَىٰ مِنكُم مِّنْ أَحَدٍ أَبَدًا وَلَٰكِنَّ ٱللَّهَ يُزَكِّى
مَن يَشَآءُ ۗ وَٱللَّهُ سَمِيعٌ عَلِيمٌ ﴿٢١﴾ وَلَا يَأْتَلِ أُو۟لُوا۟ ٱلْفَضْلِ مِنكُمْ
وَٱلسَّعَةِ أَن يُؤْتُوٓا۟ أُو۟لِى ٱلْقُرْبَىٰ وَٱلْمَسَٰكِينَ وَٱلْمُهَٰجِرِينَ فِى
سَبِيلِ ٱللَّهِ ۖ وَلْيَعْفُوا۟ وَلْيَصْفَحُوٓا۟ ۗ أَلَا تُحِبُّونَ أَن يَغْفِرَ ٱللَّهُ لَكُمْ ۗ

the order to camp for the night. I went for a call of nature and came back to the party. Then I saw that my necklace had broken and went back to look for it. They lifted my howdah onto the camel thinking that I was in it. Women at that time used to be very light since they did not have much to eat. I found my necklace and came back after they had left. I sat down in the place I had been, assuming that people would miss me and come back for me. My eyes became heavy and I fell asleep.

Ṣafwān, who had stopped to rest for the night behind the army, came to the camp in the morning and saw the dark shape of a sleeping person. When he saw me, he recognised me. He had seen me before the Veiling. I woke up when he said, 'We belong to Allah and to Him we return.' I covered my face with my cloak. By Allah, he did not speak a single word to me and I did not hear a word from him except for his exclamation. He made his camel kneel and I mounted it and he led the camel with me on it until we reached the army after they had camped to rest from the midday heat. Then those who were destroyed were destroyed. The worst of them was 'Abdullāh ibn Ubayy ibn Salūl." This *ḥadīth* is related by al-Bukhārī and Muslim.

Every one of them will incur the evil he has earned for doing that, ***and the one who took it on himself to amplify it*** – to make it worse and delve into it with his party, a reference to 'Abdullāh ibn Ubayy – ***will receive a terrible punishment***: the Fire in the Next World.

12. ***Why, when you heard it, did you not, as men and women of the believers, instinctively think good thoughts and say, 'This is obviously a*** clear ***lie'?*** In this there is a change in person from the second to the third person, but it still refers to the group.

13. ***Why did they*** (the group) ***not produce four witnesses to it? Since they did not bring four witnesses*** to what they claim, ***in Allah's sight they are liars*** regarding that.

14. ***Were it not for Allah's favour to you and His mercy, both in this world and the Next, a terrible punishment would have afflicted you*** slanderers in the Next World ***for your plunging headlong into it.***

15. ***You were bandying it about on your tongues,*** repeating it to one another, ***your mouths uttering something about which you had no***

knowledge. You considered it to be a trivial matter and no sin, ***but in Allah's sight it is*** an ***immense*** sin.

16. ***Why, when you heard it, did you not say, 'We have no business speaking about this.*** It is not proper for us to do so. ***Glory be to You!*** This is an expression of amazement. ***This is a terrible slander*** – and a lie*!'?*

17. ***Allah warns you never to repeat the like of it again, if you are believers*** and are admonished by this.

18. ***Allah makes the Signs clear to you*** with respect to His commands and prohibitions***; and Allah is All-Knowing*** of what He commands and prohibits, ***All-Wise*** in doing so.

19. ***People who love to see filth being spread about*** by the tongue ***concerning those who believe*** – by ascribing fornication to them, a reference to the party mentioned above and those like them, ***will have a painful punishment both in this world*** – the legal punishment for slander – ***and the Next*** – in the Fire by the right due to Allah. ***Allah knows*** that the slander is not true about them ***and you,*** slanderers, ***do not know*** the lie which you tell about them to be true.

20. ***Were it not for Allah's favour to you and His mercy, and that Allah is All-Gentle, Most Merciful*** by not hastening the punishment to you…

21. ***You who believe, do not follow in the footsteps of Shayṭān*** – the paths which he makes seem attractive to you. ***Anyone who follows in Shayṭān's footsteps should know that he commands*** ugly ***indecency and wrongdoing*** – what is against Allah's laws. ***Were it not for Allah's favour upon you and His mercy, not one of you would ever have been purified*** by repentance, because of the lie you told. ***But Allah purifies whomever He wills*** of wrong actions by accepting their repentance. ***Allah is All-Hearing*** of what you say, ***All-Knowing*** of what you intend.

22. ***Those of you possessing affluence and ample wealth should not make oaths that they will not give to their relatives, the very poor, and those who have emigrated in the way of Allah.*** This was revealed about Abū Bakr. who swore that he would not give any more to Misṭaḥ, who was his cousin and a poor *Muhājir* and had been present at the Battle of Badr, when he became involved in the

وَٱللَّهُ غَفُورٌ رَّحِيمٌ ﴿٢٢﴾ إِنَّ ٱلَّذِينَ يَرْمُونَ ٱلْمُحْصَنَٰتِ ٱلْغَٰفِلَٰتِ
ٱلْمُؤْمِنَٰتِ لُعِنُوا۟ فِى ٱلدُّنْيَا وَٱلْءَاخِرَةِ وَلَهُمْ عَذَابٌ عَظِيمٌ ﴿٢٣﴾
يَوْمَ تَشْهَدُ عَلَيْهِمْ أَلْسِنَتُهُمْ وَأَيْدِيهِمْ وَأَرْجُلُهُم بِمَا كَانُوا۟ يَعْمَلُونَ
﴿٢٤﴾ يَوْمَئِذٍ يُوَفِّيهِمُ ٱللَّهُ دِينَهُمُ ٱلْحَقَّ وَيَعْلَمُونَ أَنَّ ٱللَّهَ هُوَ ٱلْحَقُّ
ٱلْمُبِينُ ﴿٢٥﴾ ٱلْخَبِيثَٰتُ لِلْخَبِيثِينَ وَٱلْخَبِيثُونَ لِلْخَبِيثَٰتِ ۖ
وَٱلطَّيِّبَٰتُ لِلطَّيِّبِينَ وَٱلطَّيِّبُونَ لِلطَّيِّبَٰتِ ۚ أُو۟لَٰٓئِكَ مُبَرَّءُونَ
مِمَّا يَقُولُونَ ۖ لَهُم مَّغْفِرَةٌ وَرِزْقٌ كَرِيمٌ ﴿٢٦﴾ يَٰٓأَيُّهَا ٱلَّذِينَ
ءَامَنُوا۟ لَا تَدْخُلُوا۟ بُيُوتًا غَيْرَ بُيُوتِكُمْ حَتَّىٰ تَسْتَأْنِسُوا۟
وَتُسَلِّمُوا۟ عَلَىٰٓ أَهْلِهَا ۚ ذَٰلِكُمْ خَيْرٌ لَّكُمْ لَعَلَّكُمْ تَذَكَّرُونَ ﴿٢٧﴾
فَإِن لَّمْ تَجِدُوا۟ فِيهَآ أَحَدًا فَلَا تَدْخُلُوهَا حَتَّىٰ يُؤْذَنَ لَكُمْ ۖ وَإِن
قِيلَ لَكُمُ ٱرْجِعُوا۟ فَٱرْجِعُوا۟ ۖ هُوَ أَزْكَىٰ لَكُمْ ۚ وَٱللَّهُ بِمَا تَعْمَلُونَ
عَلِيمٌ ﴿٢٨﴾ لَّيْسَ عَلَيْكُمْ جُنَاحٌ أَن تَدْخُلُوا۟ بُيُوتًا غَيْرَ مَسْكُونَةٍ
فِيهَا مَتَٰعٌ لَّكُمْ ۚ وَٱللَّهُ يَعْلَمُ مَا تُبْدُونَ وَمَا تَكْتُمُونَ ﴿٢٩﴾
قُل لِّلْمُؤْمِنِينَ يَغُضُّوا۟ مِنْ أَبْصَٰرِهِمْ وَيَحْفَظُوا۟ فُرُوجَهُمْ ۚ
ذَٰلِكَ أَزْكَىٰ لَهُمْ ۗ إِنَّ ٱللَّهَ خَبِيرٌۢ بِمَا يَصْنَعُونَ ﴿٣٠﴾ وَقُل لِّلْمُؤْمِنَٰتِ
يَغْضُضْنَ مِنْ أَبْصَٰرِهِنَّ وَيَحْفَظْنَ فُرُوجَهُنَّ وَلَا يُبْدِينَ
زِينَتَهُنَّ إِلَّا مَا ظَهَرَ مِنْهَا ۖ وَلْيَضْرِبْنَ بِخُمُرِهِنَّ عَلَىٰ جُيُوبِهِنَّ ۖ
وَلَا يُبْدِينَ زِينَتَهُنَّ إِلَّا لِبُعُولَتِهِنَّ أَوْ ءَابَآئِهِنَّ أَوْ
ءَابَآءِ بُعُولَتِهِنَّ أَوْ أَبْنَآئِهِنَّ أَوْ أَبْنَآءِ بُعُولَتِهِنَّ
أَوْ إِخْوَٰنِهِنَّ أَوْ بَنِىٓ إِخْوَٰنِهِنَّ أَوْ بَنِىٓ أَخَوَٰتِهِنَّ أَوْ نِسَآئِهِنَّ

Lie after he had been giving to him. Some of the Companions swore that they would not give *ṣadaqa* to any of those who were in any way involved in the Lie. ***They should rather pardon and overlook*** what those people did in that respect. ***Would you not love Allah to forgive you? Allah is Ever-Forgiving, Most Merciful*** to the believers. Abū Bakr said, "I want Allah to forgive me," and he continued to spend on Misṭaḥ what he had been spending before.

23. ***Those who accuse women who are chaste*** as regards fornication ***but who are careless*** – ingenuous regarding foul actions, so that it does not occur to them to commit them – ***but believe*** in Allah and His Messenger ***are cursed in both this world and the Next, and they will have a terrible punishment...***

24. ***...on the Day*** of Rising ***when their tongues and hands and feet will testify*** (read as *tashhadu* and *yashhadu*) ***against them about what they were doing*** – in respect of both words and deeds.

25. ***On that Day Allah will pay them in full what is due to them*** – repay them with the repayment which they deserve – ***and they will know that Allah is the Clear Truth*** because He will give them the repayment which they doubted they would receive. These include 'Abdullāh ibn Ubayy. Here the chaste women referred to were the wives of the Prophet, may Allah bless him and grant him peace. There is no mention of repentance for slandering them being accepted, although repentance is possible where other women are concerned.

26. ***Corrupt women*** – or possibly "corrupt words" – ***are for corrupt men*** (people) ***and corrupt men*** (people) ***are for corrupt women*** – or possibly "use corrupt words". ***Good women*** – or possibly "good words" – ***are for good men*** (people) ***and good men*** (people) ***are for good women*** – or possibly "use good words". ***The latter are innocent of what they say.*** Those good men and good women, including 'Ā'isha and Ṣafwān, are exonerated from the accusations the corrupt men and women made. ***They*** (the good men and women) ***will have forgiveness and generous provision*** in the Garden. 'Ā'isha boasted of many things, one of which was that she was created good and was promised forgiveness and a generous provision.

27. ***You who believe, do not enter houses other than your own until you have asked permission and greeted their inhabitants.*** One should say, "Peace be upon you. May I come in?" as is reported in *ḥadīth*. ***That is better for you*** than entering without permission, ***so that perhaps you will pay heed*** and act accordingly.

28. ***And if you find no one at home do not go in until permission has been granted you. If you are told to go away then go away. That is purer*** and better ***for you*** – than to remain sitting at the door. ***Allah knows what you do*** with respect to entering with permission or without it, and will repay you for it.

29. ***There is nothing wrong in your entering houses where no one lives and where there is some service for you*** – such as staying there or the like, which is the case with rooms in hotels. ***Allah knows what you divulge and what you conceal*** – with respect to entering other houses than your own for the purpose of a gaining a benefit or something else. It will be mentioned that when people enter their own houses, they should greet their own households.

30. ***Say to the believers that they should lower their eyes*** – and not look at what it is not lawful for them to look at – ***and guard their private parts*** from what is not lawful for them. ***That is purer*** and better ***for them. Allah is aware of what they do*** with their eyes and private parts and will repay them for it.

31. ***Say to the believing women that they should lower their eyes*** – and not look at what it is not lawful for them to look at – ***and guard their private parts*** – from what is not lawful for them – ***and not display their adornments – except for what normally shows*** – which is the face and hands. It is permitted for a non-related male to look at them if he does not fear temptation from doing so. Another person may be forbidden that, because he may be tempted ***– and draw their head-coverings across their breasts*** – covering their heads, necks and bosoms with cloth. ***They should only display their*** hidden ***adornments*** – a reference to everything other than their faces and hands – ***to their husbands or their fathers or their husbands' fathers, or their sons or their husbands' sons or their brothers or their brothers' sons or their sisters' sons or other women or those they own as slaves*** – it is permitted for the categories mentioned to look at the rest of the body, except for what is between the navel and

أَوْ مَا مَلَكَتْ أَيْمَٰنُهُنَّ أَوِ ٱلتَّٰبِعِينَ غَيْرِ أُو۟لِى ٱلْإِرْبَةِ مِنَ
ٱلرِّجَالِ أَوِ ٱلطِّفْلِ ٱلَّذِينَ لَمْ يَظْهَرُوا۟ عَلَىٰ عَوْرَٰتِ ٱلنِّسَآءِ ۖ
وَلَا يَضْرِبْنَ بِأَرْجُلِهِنَّ لِيُعْلَمَ مَا يُخْفِينَ مِن زِينَتِهِنَّ ۚ وَتُوبُوٓا۟
إِلَى ٱللَّهِ جَمِيعًا أَيُّهَ ٱلْمُؤْمِنُونَ لَعَلَّكُمْ تُفْلِحُونَ ﴿٣١﴾
وَأَنكِحُوا۟ ٱلْأَيَٰمَىٰ مِنكُمْ وَٱلصَّٰلِحِينَ مِنْ عِبَادِكُمْ وَإِمَآئِكُمْ ۚ إِن
يَكُونُوا۟ فُقَرَآءَ يُغْنِهِمُ ٱللَّهُ مِن فَضْلِهِۦ ۗ وَٱللَّهُ وَٰسِعٌ عَلِيمٌ ﴿٣٢﴾
وَلْيَسْتَعْفِفِ ٱلَّذِينَ لَا يَجِدُونَ نِكَاحًا حَتَّىٰ يُغْنِيَهُمُ ٱللَّهُ مِن فَضْلِهِۦ ۗ
وَٱلَّذِينَ يَبْتَغُونَ ٱلْكِتَٰبَ مِمَّا مَلَكَتْ أَيْمَٰنُكُمْ فَكَاتِبُوهُمْ إِنْ
عَلِمْتُمْ فِيهِمْ خَيْرًا ۖ وَءَاتُوهُم مِّن مَّالِ ٱللَّهِ ٱلَّذِىٓ ءَاتَىٰكُمْ ۚ وَلَا
تُكْرِهُوا۟ فَتَيَٰتِكُمْ عَلَى ٱلْبِغَآءِ إِنْ أَرَدْنَ تَحَصُّنًا لِّتَبْتَغُوا۟ عَرَضَ ٱلْحَيَوٰةِ
ٱلدُّنْيَا ۚ وَمَن يُكْرِههُّنَّ فَإِنَّ ٱللَّهَ مِنۢ بَعْدِ إِكْرَٰهِهِنَّ غَفُورٌ رَّحِيمٌ
﴿٣٣﴾ وَلَقَدْ أَنزَلْنَآ إِلَيْكُمْ ءَايَٰتٍ مُّبَيِّنَٰتٍ وَمَثَلًا مِّنَ ٱلَّذِينَ خَلَوْا۟
مِن قَبْلِكُمْ وَمَوْعِظَةً لِّلْمُتَّقِينَ ﴿٣٤﴾ ۞ ٱللَّهُ نُورُ ٱلسَّمَٰوَٰتِ
وَٱلْأَرْضِ ۚ مَثَلُ نُورِهِۦ كَمِشْكَوٰةٍ فِيهَا مِصْبَاحٌ ۖ ٱلْمِصْبَاحُ فِى زُجَاجَةٍ ۖ
ٱلزُّجَاجَةُ كَأَنَّهَا كَوْكَبٌ دُرِّىٌّ يُوقَدُ مِن شَجَرَةٍ مُّبَٰرَكَةٍ زَيْتُونَةٍ
لَّا شَرْقِيَّةٍ وَلَا غَرْبِيَّةٍ يَكَادُ زَيْتُهَا يُضِىٓءُ وَلَوْ لَمْ تَمْسَسْهُ نَارٌ ۚ
نُّورٌ عَلَىٰ نُورٍ ۗ يَهْدِى ٱللَّهُ لِنُورِهِۦ مَن يَشَآءُ ۚ وَيَضْرِبُ ٱللَّهُ ٱلْأَمْثَٰلَ
لِلنَّاسِ ۗ وَٱللَّهُ بِكُلِّ شَىْءٍ عَلِيمٌ ﴿٣٥﴾ فِى بُيُوتٍ أَذِنَ ٱللَّهُ أَن تُرْفَعَ
وَيُذْكَرَ فِيهَا ٱسْمُهُۥ يُسَبِّحُ لَهُۥ فِيهَا بِٱلْغُدُوِّ وَٱلْءَاصَالِ ﴿٣٦﴾
رِجَالٌ لَّا تُلْهِيهِمْ تِجَٰرَةٌ وَلَا بَيْعٌ عَن ذِكْرِ ٱللَّهِ وَإِقَامِ ٱلصَّلَوٰةِ وَإِيتَآءِ

the knees, which is forbidden to everyone other than spouses. Unbelieving women are excluded from this: it is not permitted for Muslim women to uncover themselves before them. "Slaves" includes male slaves – ***or their male attendants who have no sexual desire*** – and no need of women as they are impotent – ***or children who still have no awareness of women's private parts*** and are not aware of sexual matters. Women may display to them other than what is between their navels and knees. ***Nor should they stamp their feet so that their hidden ornaments are known*** – referring to making the sound of their anklets heard. ***Turn to Allah every one of you, believers*** – in repentance for what has occurred in respect of looking at what is forbidden and for other things – ***so that perhaps you will have success*** by having your repentance accepted.

32. ***Marry off those among you who are unmarried*** – those free people who have no husbands or wives, whether virgin or previously married – ***and those of your slaves and slavegirls who are righteous*** believers. ***If they*** (the free) ***are poor, Allah will enrich them*** – by marriage – ***from His bounty. Allah is All-Encompassing*** of His creation, ***All-Knowing*** them.

33. ***Those who cannot find*** adequate ***means to marry*** – in other words, enough for a dowry and subsequent maintenance – ***should be abstinent*** – refraining from fornication – ***until Allah enriches them from His bounty*** – and then marry. ***If any slaves*** – male or female – ***you own want to make a*** – *kitāba* – ***contract to free themselves, write it for them if you know of good in them*** – meaning trustworthiness and the ability to earn the money to pay off the contract. The wording should be, for instance, "I give you a *kitāba* contract for two thousand dirhams to be paid over two months, with one thousand dirhams to be paid each month. If you pay it, then you are free." The slave then says, "I accept" – ***and give*** (addressed to the owners) ***them some of the wealth Allah has given you*** – to help them to pay what they are obliged to pay. So that is actually reducing what they have obliged them to pay. ***Do not force your slavegirls to prostitute themselves if they desire to be virtuous women*** – it is only possible to force them if they want to be chaste – ***out of your desire for the goods of this world.*** This was revealed about 'Abdullāh ibn Ubayy, who used to force his slavegirls to prostitute themselves. ***If anyone***

forces them, then after they have been forced, Allah is Ever-Forgiving, Most Merciful to them.

34. ***We have sent down Clear Signs*** (read as *mubayyināt* and *mubayyanāt*) ***to you and the*** extraordinary ***example*** – a reference to the incident involving 'Ā'isha, and that ***of those who passed away before you*** – such as the story of Yūsuf and that of Maryam – ***and an admonition for those who are godfearing*** – as in Allah's words: *"Do not let compassion for either of them possess you where Allah's* dīn *is concerned,"* (24:2), *"Why, when you heard it, did you not, as men and women of the believers, instinctively think good thoughts... ?"* (24:2), *"Why, when you heard it, did you not say... ?"* (24:16) and *"Allah warns you never to repeat the like of it again... "* (24:17) The godfearing are singled out because they are the ones who benefit from that.

35. ***Allah is the Light of the heavens and the earth.*** He is the One who illuminates them by means of the sun and the moon. ***The metaphor of His Light*** in the heart of the believer ***is that of a niche*** – an opening in a wall which is not a window, in which a lamp is placed – ***in which is a lamp, the lamp inside a glass, the glass*** and the light inside it – ***like a brilliant star*** (read as *durriyyun*, meaning that it drives away the darkness, or *durriyyan*, meaning like pearls) – the lamp – ***lit*** (read as *yūqadu* and *tawaqqada* in the past tense, and also *tūqadu*) ***from*** the oil of ***a blessed tree, an olive, neither of the east nor of the west*** but between them, so there is no harm of heat or cold from it, ***its oil all but giving off light even if no fire touches it*** because of its purity. ***Light*** – by it – ***upon*** the ***Light*** of the fire. The light of Allah means that His guidance of the believer is a light on top of the light of faith. ***Allah guides to His Light*** – the *dīn* of Islam – ***whomever He wills, and Allah makes*** explanatory ***metaphors for mankind*** – to make it easier for them to understand, so that they may reflect and then believe***; and Allah has knowledge of all things*** – including the making of metaphors.

36. ***In houses which Allah has permitted to be built and in which His name is remembered, there are men who proclaim His glory*** (read as *yusabbiḥu* and *yusabbaḥu*) and pray to Him ***morning and evening*** – "evening" here refers to any time after midday.

ٱلزَّكَوٰةِ ۙ يَخَافُونَ يَوْمًا تَتَقَلَّبُ فِيهِ ٱلْقُلُوبُ وَٱلْأَبْصَـٰرُ ﴿٣٧﴾
لِيَجْزِيَهُمُ ٱللَّهُ أَحْسَنَ مَا عَمِلُوا۟ وَيَزِيدَهُم مِّن فَضْلِهِۦ ۗ وَٱللَّهُ يَرْزُقُ
مَن يَشَآءُ بِغَيْرِ حِسَابٍ ﴿٣٨﴾ وَٱلَّذِينَ كَفَرُوٓا۟ أَعْمَـٰلُهُمْ كَسَرَابٍۭ
بِقِيعَةٍ يَحْسَبُهُ ٱلظَّمْـَٔانُ مَآءً حَتَّىٰٓ إِذَا جَآءَهُۥ لَمْ يَجِدْهُ شَيْـًٔا
وَوَجَدَ ٱللَّهَ عِندَهُۥ فَوَفَّىٰهُ حِسَابَهُۥ ۗ وَٱللَّهُ سَرِيعُ ٱلْحِسَابِ ﴿٣٩﴾
أَوْ كَظُلُمَـٰتٍ فِى بَحْرٍ لُّجِّىٍّ يَغْشَىٰهُ مَوْجٌ مِّن فَوْقِهِۦ مَوْجٌ مِّن
فَوْقِهِۦ سَحَابٌ ۚ ظُلُمَـٰتٌۢ بَعْضُهَا فَوْقَ بَعْضٍ إِذَآ أَخْرَجَ يَدَهُۥ لَمْ
يَكَدْ يَرَىٰهَا ۗ وَمَن لَّمْ يَجْعَلِ ٱللَّهُ لَهُۥ نُورًا فَمَا لَهُۥ مِن نُّورٍ ﴿٤٠﴾ أَلَمْ تَرَ أَنَّ
ٱللَّهَ يُسَبِّحُ لَهُۥ مَن فِى ٱلسَّمَـٰوَٰتِ وَٱلْأَرْضِ وَٱلطَّيْرُ صَـٰٓفَّـٰتٍ ۖ كُلٌّ قَدْ
عَلِمَ صَلَاتَهُۥ وَتَسْبِيحَهُۥ ۗ وَٱللَّهُ عَلِيمٌۢ بِمَا يَفْعَلُونَ ﴿٤١﴾ وَلِلَّهِ مُلْكُ
ٱلسَّمَـٰوَٰتِ وَٱلْأَرْضِ ۖ وَإِلَى ٱللَّهِ ٱلْمَصِيرُ ﴿٤٢﴾ أَلَمْ تَرَ أَنَّ ٱللَّهَ يُزْجِى
سَحَابًا ثُمَّ يُؤَلِّفُ بَيْنَهُۥ ثُمَّ يَجْعَلُهُۥ رُكَامًا فَتَرَى ٱلْوَدْقَ يَخْرُجُ مِنْ
خِلَـٰلِهِۦ وَيُنَزِّلُ مِنَ ٱلسَّمَآءِ مِن جِبَالٍ فِيهَا مِنۢ بَرَدٍ فَيُصِيبُ بِهِۦ مَن يَشَآءُ
وَيَصْرِفُهُۥ عَن مَّن يَشَآءُ ۖ يَكَادُ سَنَا بَرْقِهِۦ يَذْهَبُ بِٱلْأَبْصَـٰرِ ﴿٤٣﴾
يُقَلِّبُ ٱللَّهُ ٱلَّيْلَ وَٱلنَّهَارَ ۚ إِنَّ فِى ذَٰلِكَ لَعِبْرَةً لِّأُو۟لِى ٱلْأَبْصَـٰرِ ﴿٤٤﴾
وَٱللَّهُ خَلَقَ كُلَّ دَآبَّةٍ مِّن مَّآءٍ ۖ فَمِنْهُم مَّن يَمْشِى عَلَىٰ بَطْنِهِۦ وَمِنْهُم مَّن
يَمْشِى عَلَىٰ رِجْلَيْنِ وَمِنْهُم مَّن يَمْشِى عَلَىٰٓ أَرْبَعٍ ۚ يَخْلُقُ ٱللَّهُ مَا يَشَآءُ ۚ
إِنَّ ٱللَّهَ عَلَىٰ كُلِّ شَىْءٍ قَدِيرٌ ﴿٤٥﴾ لَّقَدْ أَنزَلْنَآ ءَايَـٰتٍ مُّبَيِّنَـٰتٍ ۚ
وَٱللَّهُ يَهْدِى مَن يَشَآءُ إِلَىٰ صِرَٰطٍ مُّسْتَقِيمٍ ﴿٤٦﴾ وَيَقُولُونَ
ءَامَنَّا بِٱللَّهِ وَبِٱلرَّسُولِ وَأَطَعْنَا ثُمَّ يَتَوَلَّىٰ فَرِيقٌ مِّنْهُم مِّنۢ بَعْدِ

37. ***...not distracted by trade or commerce from the remembrance of Allah and the establishment of the prayer and the payment of*** **zakāt.** ***They fear a day when all hearts and eyes will be in turmoil*** from fear, because people's hearts will be between salvation and destruction and their eyes will be darting to the right and the left. This is the Day of Rising –

38. ***...so that Allah may reward them for the best of what they did*** – their good actions – ***and give them more from His unbounded favour. Allah provides for anyone He wills without reckoning.*** When someone provides without reckoning it means that they are generous to the point of not accounting for what they spend.

39. ***But the actions of those who disbelieve are like a mirage in the desert.*** A mirage is an effect to be seen in a desert coming from the light of the sun during the second half of a day of intense heat, which appears as if it were water flowing over the land. ***A thirsty man thinks it is water, but when he reaches it he finds it to be nothing at all –*** not what he thought it was; it is the same with an unbeliever who supposes that his actions, like *ṣadaqa*, will benefit him and then, when he dies, finds that his actions are of no use at all – ***but he finds Allah there. He will pay him his account in full*** for what he did in this world. ***Allah is swift at reckoning*** and repayment.

40. ***Or they*** – the evil deeds of those who are unbelievers – ***are like the darkness of a fathomless sea which is covered by waves above which are waves above which are clouds –*** these being ***layers of darkness, one upon the other*** – the darkness of the sea, the darkness of the surface waves, and the darkness of the clouds. ***If he puts out his hand*** in this darkness, ***he can scarcely see it. Those Allah gives no light to have no light.*** Whoever is not guided by Allah is not guided.

41. ***Do you not see that everyone in the heavens and earth glorifies Allah*** – and the prayer is an aspect of glorification, ***as do the birds with their outspread wings*** – suspended between heaven and earth? ***Each one knows its prayer and glorification*** of Allah. ***Allah knows what they do.***

ذَٰلِكَۚ وَمَآ أُوْلَٰٓئِكَ بِٱلۡمُؤۡمِنِينَ ٤٧ وَإِذَا دُعُوٓاْ إِلَى ٱللَّهِ وَرَسُولِهِۦ
لِيَحۡكُمَ بَيۡنَهُمۡ إِذَا فَرِيقٞ مِّنۡهُم مُّعۡرِضُونَ ٤٨ وَإِن يَكُن لَّهُمُ ٱلۡحَقُّ
يَأۡتُوٓاْ إِلَيۡهِ مُذۡعِنِينَ ٤٩ أَفِي قُلُوبِهِم مَّرَضٌ أَمِ ٱرۡتَابُوٓاْ أَمۡ يَخَافُونَ
أَن يَحِيفَ ٱللَّهُ عَلَيۡهِمۡ وَرَسُولُهُۥۚ بَلۡ أُوْلَٰٓئِكَ هُمُ ٱلظَّٰلِمُونَ ٥٠
إِنَّمَا كَانَ قَوۡلَ ٱلۡمُؤۡمِنِينَ إِذَا دُعُوٓاْ إِلَى ٱللَّهِ وَرَسُولِهِۦ لِيَحۡكُمَ بَيۡنَهُمۡ
أَن يَقُولُواْ سَمِعۡنَا وَأَطَعۡنَاۚ وَأُوْلَٰٓئِكَ هُمُ ٱلۡمُفۡلِحُونَ ٥١ وَمَن
يُطِعِ ٱللَّهَ وَرَسُولَهُۥ وَيَخۡشَ ٱللَّهَ وَيَتَّقۡهِ فَأُوْلَٰٓئِكَ هُمُ ٱلۡفَآئِزُونَ
٥٢ ۞ وَأَقۡسَمُواْ بِٱللَّهِ جَهۡدَ أَيۡمَٰنِهِمۡ لَئِنۡ أَمَرۡتَهُمۡ لَيَخۡرُجُنَّۖ قُل
لَّا تُقۡسِمُواْۖ طَاعَةٞ مَّعۡرُوفَةٌۚ إِنَّ ٱللَّهَ خَبِيرُۢ بِمَا تَعۡمَلُونَ ٥٣
قُلۡ أَطِيعُواْ ٱللَّهَ وَأَطِيعُواْ ٱلرَّسُولَۖ فَإِن تَوَلَّوۡاْ فَإِنَّمَا عَلَيۡهِ مَا حُمِّلَ
وَعَلَيۡكُم مَّا حُمِّلۡتُمۡۖ وَإِن تُطِيعُوهُ تَهۡتَدُواْۚ وَمَا عَلَى ٱلرَّسُولِ
إِلَّا ٱلۡبَلَٰغُ ٱلۡمُبِينُ ٥٤ وَعَدَ ٱللَّهُ ٱلَّذِينَ ءَامَنُواْ مِنكُمۡ وَعَمِلُواْ
ٱلصَّٰلِحَٰتِ لَيَسۡتَخۡلِفَنَّهُمۡ فِي ٱلۡأَرۡضِ كَمَا ٱسۡتَخۡلَفَ
ٱلَّذِينَ مِن قَبۡلِهِمۡ وَلَيُمَكِّنَنَّ لَهُمۡ دِينَهُمُ ٱلَّذِي ٱرۡتَضَىٰ لَهُمۡ
وَلَيُبَدِّلَنَّهُم مِّنۢ بَعۡدِ خَوۡفِهِمۡ أَمۡنٗاۚ يَعۡبُدُونَنِي لَا يُشۡرِكُونَ بِي
شَيۡـٔٗاۚ وَمَن كَفَرَ بَعۡدَ ذَٰلِكَ فَأُوْلَٰٓئِكَ هُمُ ٱلۡفَٰسِقُونَ ٥٥
وَأَقِيمُواْ ٱلصَّلَوٰةَ وَءَاتُواْ ٱلزَّكَوٰةَ وَأَطِيعُواْ ٱلرَّسُولَ لَعَلَّكُمۡ
تُرۡحَمُونَ ٥٦ لَا تَحۡسَبَنَّ ٱلَّذِينَ كَفَرُواْ مُعۡجِزِينَ فِي ٱلۡأَرۡضِۚ
وَمَأۡوَىٰهُمُ ٱلنَّارُۖ وَلَبِئۡسَ ٱلۡمَصِيرُ ٥٧ يَٰٓأَيُّهَا ٱلَّذِينَ ءَامَنُواْ
لِيَسۡتَـٔۡذِنكُمُ ٱلَّذِينَ مَلَكَتۡ أَيۡمَٰنُكُمۡ وَٱلَّذِينَ لَمۡ يَبۡلُغُواْ ٱلۡحُلُمَ مِنكُمۡ

42. ***The kingdom of the heavens and earth belongs to Allah*** – the treasures of the rain, provision and plants***; and Allah is the final destination.***

43. ***Do you not see that Allah propels the clouds*** – with gentleness – ***then makes them coalesce*** – making separate clumps into a single one – ***then heaps them up*** on top of one another***, and then you see the rain come pouring out of the middle of them? And He sends down mountains from the sky with hail inside them, striking with it anyone He wills and averting it from anyone He wills. The brightness of His lightning almost blinds the sight*** of anyone who looks at it.

44. ***Allah revolves night and day*** – making one of them come after the other. ***There is surely a lesson in that*** alternation ***for people with inner sight*** – indicating the power of Allah Almighty.

45. ***Allah created every animal from water (***sperm). ***Some of them go*** crawling ***on their bellies*** – like snakes and vermin***, some of them on two legs*** – like human beings and birds***, and some on four*** – like livestock and similar animals. ***Allah creates whatever He wills. Allah has power over all things.***

46. ***We have sent down Signs (***the Qur'an) ***making things clear. Allah guides whomever He wills to a straight path*** – the *dīn* of Islam.

47. ***They*** (the hypocrites) ***say, 'We believe in*** the unity of ***Allah and in the Messenger*** – Muḥammad – ***and we obey*** what Allah and His Messenger prescribe.***' Then after that a group of them turn away. Such people are not believers.*** Those who turn away are not believers: the latter are people whose hearts are in agreement with their tongues.

48. ***When they are summoned to Allah and His Messenger*** – who conveys the Message – ***so that he may judge between them, a group of them immediately turn away.***

49. ***But if right is on their side, they come to him most submissively*** – swiftly in obedience***!***

50. ***Is there a sickness*** of unbelief ***in their hearts, or do they have misgivings*** about his Prophethood***, or do they fear that Allah and***

His Messenger will be unjust to them regarding judgement? ***No, it is simply that they are wrongdoers*** – by turning away.

51. ***The reply of the believers, when they are summoned to Allah and His Messenger so that he can judge between them, is to say, 'We hear and we obey.' They are ones who are successful*** and are saved.

52. ***All who obey Allah and His Messenger and have awe of Allah and are fearful of Him*** and obey Him, ***they are the ones who are victorious*** – and attain Paradise.

53. ***They have sworn by Allah with their most earnest oaths that if you give them the command, they will go out*** to do *jihād*. ***Say*** to them: ***'Do not swear. Honourable obedience*** to the Prophet ***is enough.*** It is better to obey the prohibition than to swear an oath which is not credible. ***Allah is aware of what you do.'***

54. ***Say: 'Obey Allah and obey the Messenger. Then if they turn away*** from obedience to him ***he is only responsible for what he is charged with*** – in terms of transmission – ***and you are responsible for what you are charged with*** – in terms of obedience. ***If you obey him, you will be guided.' The Messenger is only responsible for clear transmission.***

55. ***Allah has promised those of you who believe and do right actions that He will make them successors in the land*** – to replace the unbelievers – ***as He made those before them*** (the tribe of Israel) ***successors*** (read as *istakhlafa* and *istukhlifa*) – to the tyrants – ***and will firmly establish for them their* dīn *with which He is pleased*** – this being Islam, which He will cause to dominate other religions; He will multiply them in the earth and give them dominance – ***and give them, in place*** (read as *yubaddilannanuhum* and as *yubdilannahum*) ***of their fear*** of the unbelievers, ***security.*** Allah kept His promise to them, as mentioned, and praised them saying: ***'They worship Me, not associating anything with Me.' Any who disbelieve after that*** blessing, ***such people are deviators.*** The first of those to disbelieve were those who murdered 'Uthmān, may Allah be pleased with him, and they started to fight one another after having been brothers.

56. ***Establish the prayer and pay* zakāt *and obey the Messenger so that perhaps mercy will be shown to you.***

ثَلَٰثُ مَرَّٰتٖۚ مِّن قَبۡلِ صَلَوٰةِ ٱلۡفَجۡرِ وَحِينَ تَضَعُونَ ثِيَابَكُم مِّنَ ٱلظَّهِيرَةِ
وَمِنۢ بَعۡدِ صَلَوٰةِ ٱلۡعِشَآءِۚ ثَلَٰثُ عَوۡرَٰتٖ لَّكُمۡۚ لَيۡسَ عَلَيۡكُمۡ
وَلَا عَلَيۡهِمۡ جُنَاحُۢ بَعۡدَهُنَّۚ طَوَّٰفُونَ عَلَيۡكُم بَعۡضُكُمۡ عَلَىٰ
بَعۡضٖۚ كَذَٰلِكَ يُبَيِّنُ ٱللَّهُ لَكُمُ ٱلۡأٓيَٰتِۗ وَٱللَّهُ عَلِيمٌ حَكِيمٞ ٥٨
وَإِذَا بَلَغَ ٱلۡأَطۡفَٰلُ مِنكُمُ ٱلۡحُلُمَ فَلۡيَسۡتَـٔۡذِنُواْ كَمَا ٱسۡتَـٔۡذَنَ
ٱلَّذِينَ مِن قَبۡلِهِمۡۚ كَذَٰلِكَ يُبَيِّنُ ٱللَّهُ لَكُمۡ ءَايَٰتِهِۦۗ وَٱللَّهُ
عَلِيمٌ حَكِيمٞ ٥٩ وَٱلۡقَوَٰعِدُ مِنَ ٱلنِّسَآءِ ٱلَّٰتِي لَا يَرۡجُونَ
نِكَاحٗا فَلَيۡسَ عَلَيۡهِنَّ جُنَاحٌ أَن يَضَعۡنَ ثِيَابَهُنَّ
غَيۡرَ مُتَبَرِّجَٰتِۭ بِزِينَةٖۖ وَأَن يَسۡتَعۡفِفۡنَ خَيۡرٞ لَّهُنَّۗ وَٱللَّهُ
سَمِيعٌ عَلِيمٞ ٦٠ لَّيۡسَ عَلَى ٱلۡأَعۡمَىٰ حَرَجٞ وَلَا عَلَى ٱلۡأَعۡرَجِ
حَرَجٞ وَلَا عَلَى ٱلۡمَرِيضِ حَرَجٞ وَلَا عَلَىٰٓ أَنفُسِكُمۡ أَن تَأۡكُلُواْ
مِنۢ بُيُوتِكُمۡ أَوۡ بُيُوتِ ءَابَآئِكُمۡ أَوۡ بُيُوتِ أُمَّهَٰتِكُمۡ
أَوۡ بُيُوتِ إِخۡوَٰنِكُمۡ أَوۡ بُيُوتِ أَخَوَٰتِكُمۡ أَوۡ بُيُوتِ
أَعۡمَٰمِكُمۡ أَوۡ بُيُوتِ عَمَّٰتِكُمۡ أَوۡ بُيُوتِ أَخۡوَٰلِكُمۡ
أَوۡ بُيُوتِ خَٰلَٰتِكُمۡ أَوۡ مَا مَلَكۡتُم مَّفَاتِحَهُۥٓ
أَوۡ صَدِيقِكُمۡۚ لَيۡسَ عَلَيۡكُمۡ جُنَاحٌ أَن تَأۡكُلُواْ
جَمِيعًا أَوۡ أَشۡتَاتٗاۚ فَإِذَا دَخَلۡتُم بُيُوتٗا فَسَلِّمُواْ عَلَىٰٓ أَنفُسِكُمۡ
تَحِيَّةٗ مِّنۡ عِندِ ٱللَّهِ مُبَٰرَكَةٗ طَيِّبَةٗۚ كَذَٰلِكَ
يُبَيِّنُ ٱللَّهُ لَكُمُ ٱلۡأٓيَٰتِ لَعَلَّكُمۡ تَعۡقِلُونَ ٦١
إِنَّمَا ٱلۡمُؤۡمِنُونَ ٱلَّذِينَ ءَامَنُواْ بِٱللَّهِ وَرَسُولِهِۦ وَإِذَا كَانُواْ مَعَهُۥ

57. ***Do not imagine*** (read as *taḥsabanna* and *yaḥsabanna*, meaning "they should not imagine...") ***that those who disbelieve are able to escape Allah on earth. Their shelter will be the Fire. What an evil destination!***

58. ***You who believe, those you own as slaves and those*** free people ***amongst you who have not yet reached puberty*** – referring to those who are not sexually aware of women – ***should ask your permission to enter at three times: before the Dawn Prayer, when you have undressed at noon, and after the 'Ishā' prayer – three times of nakedness for you*** – times when people remove their clothing. ***There is nothing wrong for you or them at other times in moving around among yourselves from one to another.*** At other times, slaves and children may enter without asking permission. ***In this way Allah makes the Signs clear to you*** – makes His rulings clear to His creatures. ***Allah is All-Knowing, All-Wise*** in managing it for them. It is said that the *āyat* of asking permission is abrogated; and it is said that it is not, but that there is leeway for people not to ask permission.

59. ***Once your children have reached puberty, they should ask your permission to enter*** – at all times – ***as those before them*** (adults) ***also asked permission. In this way Allah makes His Signs clear to you. Allah is All-Knowing, All-Wise.***

60. ***As for women who are past child-bearing age*** – past the age of menstruation – ***and no longer have any hope of getting married, there is nothing wrong in their removing their outer clothes*** – their outer covering, cloak and veil (*qinā'*) above the head covering – ***provided they do not flaunt their adornments*** – such as necklaces, bracelets and anklets; ***but to refrain from doing so*** – removing them – ***is better for them. Allah is All-Hearing*** of what you say, ***All-Knowing*** of what is in your hearts.

61. ***There is no objection to the blind, no objection to the lame, and no objection to the sick or to yourselves eating in your own houses*** – your children's houses – ***or your fathers' houses or your mothers' houses, or your brothers' houses or your sisters' houses, or the houses of your paternal uncles or paternal aunts, or the houses of your maternal uncles or maternal aunts, or places to which you own the keys*** – houses which belong to other people

عَلَىٰٓ أَمۡرٖ جَامِعٖ لَّمۡ يَذۡهَبُواْ حَتَّىٰ يَسۡتَـٔۡذِنُوهُۚ إِنَّ ٱلَّذِينَ يَسۡتَـٔۡذِنُونَكَ
أُوْلَـٰٓئِكَ ٱلَّذِينَ يُؤۡمِنُونَ بِٱللَّهِ وَرَسُولِهِۦۚ فَإِذَا ٱسۡتَـٔۡذَنُوكَ
لِبَعۡضِ شَأۡنِهِمۡ فَأۡذَن لِّمَن شِئۡتَ مِنۡهُمۡ وَٱسۡتَغۡفِرۡ لَهُمُ
ٱللَّهَۚ إِنَّ ٱللَّهَ غَفُورٞ رَّحِيمٞ ٦٢ لَّا تَجۡعَلُواْ دُعَآءَ ٱلرَّسُولِ
بَيۡنَكُمۡ كَدُعَآءِ بَعۡضِكُم بَعۡضٗاۚ قَدۡ يَعۡلَمُ ٱللَّهُ ٱلَّذِينَ
يَتَسَلَّلُونَ مِنكُمۡ لِوَاذٗاۚ فَلۡيَحۡذَرِ ٱلَّذِينَ يُخَالِفُونَ عَنۡ أَمۡرِهِۦٓ
أَن تُصِيبَهُمۡ فِتۡنَةٌ أَوۡ يُصِيبَهُمۡ عَذَابٌ أَلِيمٌ ٦٣ أَلَآ إِنَّ لِلَّهِ
مَا فِي ٱلسَّمَٰوَٰتِ وَٱلۡأَرۡضِۖ قَدۡ يَعۡلَمُ مَآ أَنتُمۡ عَلَيۡهِ وَيَوۡمَ
يُرۡجَعُونَ إِلَيۡهِ فَيُنَبِّئُهُم بِمَا عَمِلُواْۗ وَٱللَّهُ بِكُلِّ شَيۡءٍ عَلِيمُۢ ٦٤

whose keys are in your keeping, ***or those of your friends.*** It is permitted to eat in the houses of those who are mentioned, even if they are not present, provided that you know that they will accept it. ***There is nothing wrong in your eating together or eating separately*** – so that each one eats on his own; otherwise, if he did not find anyone to eat with, he might abandon eating altogether. ***And when you enter houses*** whose people are absent ***greet one another*** – say, "Peace be upon us and on the righteous slaves of Allah," and the angels will reply. If the inhabitants are there, then greet them – ***with a greeting from Allah, blessed and good*** – for which Allah will reward you. ***In this way Allah makes the Signs*** of His *dīn* ***clear to you so that perhaps you will use your intellect*** and understand.

62. ***The believers are those who believe in Allah and His Messenger and who, when they are with him*** (the Messenger) ***on a matter of common concern*** such as the *khuṭba* of *Jumu'a*, ***do not leave*** for any reason ***until they have asked him for permission. Those people who ask you for permission are the ones who truly believe in Allah and His Messenger. If they ask your permission to attend to their own affairs, give permission to any of them you please; and ask Allah's forgiveness for them. Allah is Ever-Forgiving, Most Merciful.***

63. ***Do not make your summoning of the Messenger the same as your summoning of one another*** by saying, "Muhammad!" You should rather say, "Prophet of Allah" or "Messenger of Allah" with gentleness, humbleness, and in a low voice. ***Allah knows those of you who sneak away*** – who leave the mosque during the *khutba* without asking permission softly. ***Those who oppose his command*** – that of Allah and His Messenger – ***should beware of a testing trial coming to them or a painful punishment striking them*** in the Next World.

64. ***Everything in the heavens and the earth belongs to Allah*** as His kingdom, domain and slaves. ***He knows what you are engaged upon*** in terms of your faith or hypocrisy, you who are responsible. ***On the Day when they are returned to Him*** – a change from the second to the third person plural – ***He will inform them of what they did*** – both good and evil. ***Allah has knowledge of all things*** – of what they do, and of everything else as well.

سُورَةُ الفُرقَانِ

بِسْمِ ٱللَّهِ ٱلرَّحْمَٰنِ ٱلرَّحِيمِ

تَبَارَكَ ٱلَّذِى نَزَّلَ ٱلْفُرْقَانَ عَلَىٰ عَبْدِهِۦ لِيَكُونَ لِلْعَٰلَمِينَ نَذِيرًا
١ ٱلَّذِى لَهُۥ مُلْكُ ٱلسَّمَٰوَٰتِ وَٱلْأَرْضِ وَلَمْ يَتَّخِذْ وَلَدًا وَلَمْ
يَكُن لَّهُۥ شَرِيكٌ فِى ٱلْمُلْكِ وَخَلَقَ كُلَّ شَىْءٍ فَقَدَّرَهُۥ تَقْدِيرًا ٢
وَٱتَّخَذُوا۟ مِن دُونِهِۦٓ ءَالِهَةً لَّا يَخْلُقُونَ شَيْـًٔا وَهُمْ يُخْلَقُونَ
وَلَا يَمْلِكُونَ لِأَنفُسِهِمْ ضَرًّا وَلَا نَفْعًا وَلَا يَمْلِكُونَ مَوْتًا
وَلَا حَيَوٰةً وَلَا نُشُورًا ٣ وَقَالَ ٱلَّذِينَ كَفَرُوٓا۟ إِنْ هَٰذَآ إِلَّآ إِفْكٌ
ٱفْتَرَىٰهُ وَأَعَانَهُۥ عَلَيْهِ قَوْمٌ ءَاخَرُونَ ۖ فَقَدْ جَآءُو ظُلْمًا وَزُورًا
٤ وَقَالُوٓا۟ أَسَٰطِيرُ ٱلْأَوَّلِينَ ٱكْتَتَبَهَا فَهِىَ تُمْلَىٰ
عَلَيْهِ بُكْرَةً وَأَصِيلًا ٥ قُلْ أَنزَلَهُ ٱلَّذِى يَعْلَمُ ٱلسِّرَّ
فِى ٱلسَّمَٰوَٰتِ وَٱلْأَرْضِ ۚ إِنَّهُۥ كَانَ غَفُورًا رَّحِيمًا ٦ وَقَالُوا۟
مَالِ هَٰذَا ٱلرَّسُولِ يَأْكُلُ ٱلطَّعَامَ وَيَمْشِى فِى ٱلْأَسْوَاقِ ۙ
لَوْلَآ أُنزِلَ إِلَيْهِ مَلَكٌ فَيَكُونَ مَعَهُۥ نَذِيرًا ٧ أَوْ يُلْقَىٰٓ
إِلَيْهِ كَنزٌ أَوْ تَكُونُ لَهُۥ جَنَّةٌ يَأْكُلُ مِنْهَا ۚ وَقَالَ
ٱلظَّٰلِمُونَ إِن تَتَّبِعُونَ إِلَّا رَجُلًا مَّسْحُورًا ٨ ٱنظُرْ
كَيْفَ ضَرَبُوا۟ لَكَ ٱلْأَمْثَٰلَ فَضَلُّوا۟ فَلَا يَسْتَطِيعُونَ
سَبِيلًا ٩ تَبَارَكَ ٱلَّذِىٓ إِن شَآءَ جَعَلَ لَكَ خَيْرًا مِّن ذَٰلِكَ
جَنَّٰتٍ تَجْرِى مِن تَحْتِهَا ٱلْأَنْهَٰرُ وَيَجْعَل لَّكَ قُصُورًا ١٠ بَلْ
كَذَّبُوا۟ بِٱلسَّاعَةِ ۖ وَأَعْتَدْنَا لِمَن كَذَّبَ بِٱلسَّاعَةِ سَعِيرًا ١١

25. *Sūrat al-Furqān*
Discrimination

This *sūra* is Makkan except for *āyats* 68, 69, and 70. It has 77 *āyats* and was sent down after *Ya Sin.*

1. ***Blessed is He*** (Allah) ***who has sent down the Discrimination*** (the Qur'an) – so called because it discriminates between the true and the false – ***to His slave*** (Muhammad, may Allah bless him and grant him peace) ***so that he can be a warner*** – about the punishment of Allah – ***to all beings*** – human beings and jinn, but not angels.

2. ***...He to whom the kingdom of the heavens and the earth belongs. He does not have a son and He has no partner in the Kingdom. He created everything and determined it most exactly*** in balance.

3. ***But they*** (the unbelievers) ***have adopted gods*** (idols) ***apart from Him*** (Allah) ***which do not create anything but are themselves created. They have no power to harm or help themselves. They have no power over death or life or resurrection.*** They cannot bring death or life to anyone, nor can they bring the dead back to life.

4. ***Those who disbelieve say, 'This*** Qur'an ***is nothing but a lie he*** (Muḥammad) ***has invented and other people*** – among the People of the Book – ***have helped him to do it.*** Allah says: ***They have brought injustice*** (unbelief) ***and falsehood*** (lies).'

5. ***They say, 'It is myths*** (fabrications) ***of previous peoples which he has had transcribed*** from those people ***and which are read out to him*** – and he memorises – ***in the morning and the evening.'*** Allah then refutes them:

6. ***Say: 'The One Who sent it down is He Who knows all hidden secrets*** of the Unseen ***in the heavens and earth. He is Ever-Forgiving, Most Merciful*** to the believers.'

7. ***They say, 'What is the matter with this Messenger, that he eats food and walks in the market-place? Why has an angel not been sent down to him*** – to confirm him – ***so that it can be a warner along with him?***

إِذَا رَأَتْهُم مِّن مَّكَانٍۭ بَعِيدٍ سَمِعُوا۟ لَهَا تَغَيُّظًا وَزَفِيرًا ﴿١٢﴾ وَإِذَآ
أُلْقُوا۟ مِنْهَا مَكَانًا ضَيِّقًا مُّقَرَّنِينَ دَعَوْا۟ هُنَالِكَ ثُبُورًا ﴿١٣﴾
لَّا تَدْعُوا۟ ٱلْيَوْمَ ثُبُورًا وَٰحِدًا وَٱدْعُوا۟ ثُبُورًا كَثِيرًا ﴿١٤﴾ قُلْ
أَذَٰلِكَ خَيْرٌ أَمْ جَنَّةُ ٱلْخُلْدِ ٱلَّتِى وُعِدَ ٱلْمُتَّقُونَ ۚ كَانَتْ
لَهُمْ جَزَآءً وَمَصِيرًا ﴿١٥﴾ لَّهُمْ فِيهَا مَا يَشَآءُونَ خَٰلِدِينَ ۚ
كَانَ عَلَىٰ رَبِّكَ وَعْدًا مَّسْـُٔولًا ﴿١٦﴾ وَيَوْمَ يَحْشُرُهُمْ وَمَا
يَعْبُدُونَ مِن دُونِ ٱللَّهِ فَيَقُولُ ءَأَنتُمْ أَضْلَلْتُمْ عِبَادِى
هَٰٓؤُلَآءِ أَمْ هُمْ ضَلُّوا۟ ٱلسَّبِيلَ ﴿١٧﴾ قَالُوا۟ سُبْحَٰنَكَ مَا كَانَ
يَنۢبَغِى لَنَآ أَن نَّتَّخِذَ مِن دُونِكَ مِنْ أَوْلِيَآءَ وَلَٰكِن مَّتَّعْتَهُمْ
وَءَابَآءَهُمْ حَتَّىٰ نَسُوا۟ ٱلذِّكْرَ وَكَانُوا۟ قَوْمًۢا بُورًا ﴿١٨﴾ فَقَدْ
كَذَّبُوكُم بِمَا تَقُولُونَ فَمَا تَسْتَطِيعُونَ صَرْفًا وَلَا
نَصْرًا ۚ وَمَن يَظْلِم مِّنكُمْ نُذِقْهُ عَذَابًا كَبِيرًا ﴿١٩﴾
وَمَآ أَرْسَلْنَا قَبْلَكَ مِنَ ٱلْمُرْسَلِينَ إِلَّآ إِنَّهُمْ لَيَأْكُلُونَ
ٱلطَّعَامَ وَيَمْشُونَ فِى ٱلْأَسْوَاقِ ۗ وَجَعَلْنَا بَعْضَكُمْ
لِبَعْضٍ فِتْنَةً أَتَصْبِرُونَ ۗ وَكَانَ رَبُّكَ بَصِيرًا ﴿٢٠﴾
۞ وَقَالَ ٱلَّذِينَ لَا يَرْجُونَ لِقَآءَنَا لَوْلَآ أُنزِلَ عَلَيْنَا ٱلْمَلَٰٓئِكَةُ
أَوْ نَرَىٰ رَبَّنَا ۗ لَقَدِ ٱسْتَكْبَرُوا۟ فِىٓ أَنفُسِهِمْ وَعَتَوْ عُتُوًّا كَبِيرًا
﴿٢١﴾ يَوْمَ يَرَوْنَ ٱلْمَلَٰٓئِكَةَ لَا بُشْرَىٰ يَوْمَئِذٍ لِّلْمُجْرِمِينَ وَيَقُولُونَ
حِجْرًا مَّحْجُورًا ﴿٢٢﴾ وَقَدِمْنَآ إِلَىٰ مَا عَمِلُوا۟ مِنْ عَمَلٍ فَجَعَلْنَٰهُ
هَبَآءً مَّنثُورًا ﴿٢٣﴾ أَصْحَٰبُ ٱلْجَنَّةِ يَوْمَئِذٍ خَيْرٌ مُّسْتَقَرًّا

8. ***Why has treasure not been showered down on him*** from heaven, which he could spend so that he would not need to walk in the markets seeking a livelihood***? Why does he not have a garden to give him food*** (read as *ya'kulu* and *na'kulu,* "to give us food") – a garden with produce he could eat so that he would have sufficient provision from it for his needs***?' The wrongdoers*** (unbelievers) ***say*** to the believers, ***'You are merely following a man who is bewitched*** – who is deluded and has lost his senses.*'*

9. Allah answers them: ***See how they make comparative judgements about you***, comparing you to someone who is bewitched, or who wants more provision, or wants a kingdom which he can rule**.** ***They are misguided*** – away from guidance by that – ***and cannot find the way*** to it**.**

10. ***Blessed is He who, if He wishes, will grant you better than that*** – He is full of blessings, and may give you better than the gardens and treasure***: Gardens with rivers flowing under them*** – in this world as well as the Next World***; and He will grant*** (read as *yaj'al* and *yaj'alu*) ***you Palaces.***

11. ***But instead, they deny the*** Last ***Hour; and We have prepared a Searing*** (fierce) ***Blaze for those who deny the Hour.***

12. ***When it sees them coming from a long way off, they will hear it seething*** – bubbling as in anger as when someone's breast seethes with rage – ***and rasping*** – a loud noise**.**

13. ***When they are flung into a narrow*** (read as *ḍayyiqan* and *ḍayqan*) ***place in it*** which bears in on them, describing a place which will constricts those in it***, shackled together in chains*** – their hands will be shackled to others' necks with many chains, ***they will cry out there for destruction.***

14. They will be told: ***'Do not cry out today for just one destruction; cry out for many destructions*** – like your punishment*!'*

15. ***Say: 'Is that better*** – the threat of the punishment and the Fire – ***or the Garden of Eternal Life which has been promised to those who are godfearing? That is their recompense and destination*** – in Allah's knowledge.*'*

16. ***They will have in it whatever they want timelessly, for ever. It is a binding promise of your Lord.*** They will ask Him about the promise He made: *"Our Lord, give us what You promised us through Your Messengers,"* (3:194) or the angels will ask for them, *"Our Lord, admit them into the gardens of 'Adn which you promised them."* (40:8)

17. ***On the Day He gathers*** (read as *yaḥshuru* and *naḥshuru*, "We gather") ***them together, and those they worship besides Allah*** – a reference to the angels, the Prophets 'Īsā, 'Uzayr, and also the jinn – ***and says*** (read as *yaqūlu* and *naqūlu*, "We say") to those worshippers, to establish the evidence against those who worshipped them, ***'Did you misguide these slaves of Mine*** – making them fall into misguidance by commanding them to worship you – ***or did they stray from the way*** of Truth ***of their own accord?'***

18. ***...they will say, 'Glory be to You!*** This proclaims Allah free of anything which does not befit Him. ***It would not have been fitting*** – or correct – ***for us to have taken any protectors apart from You.*** So how could we have commanded them to worship us? ***But You let them and their fathers enjoy themselves*** – by giving them a long life and ample provision – ***so that they forgot the Reminder*** – the admonition and belief in the Qur'an. ***They were people devoid of good.'*** The word *būr* (devoid of good) implies "ruined".

19. Allah says: ***So now they have disowned you*** – those who were worshipped will deny those who worshipped them – ***for what you said*** – in claiming that they were gods – ***and you cannot*** (read as *tastaṭi'yuna*, and *yastaṭi'yūna*, "they cannot") ***avert it*** (the punishment) ***or get any help*** to defend yourself. ***As for anyone among you who has done wrong*** by committing *shirk*. ***We will make him suffer great punishment*** in the Next World.

20. ***We never sent any Messengers before you who did not eat food and walk in the market-place.*** You are like the past Messengers in that respect. The same that is being said to you was also said to them. ***But We have made some of you a trial for others*** – by testing the poor through the rich, the sick through the healthy, and the lowly through the noble; in all the cases mentioned, the less well off tends to say, "Why am I not like the first?" – ***to see if you will be steadfast*** in the trial. This is actually an instruction which means, "Be steadfast." ***Your Lord sees everything*** – those who are steadfast and those who are anxious.

وَأَحۡسَنُ مَقِيلٗا ٢٤ وَيَوۡمَ تَشَقَّقُ ٱلسَّمَآءُ بِٱلۡغَمَٰمِ وَنُزِّلَ ٱلۡمَلَٰٓئِكَةُ
تَنزِيلًا ٢٥ ٱلۡمُلۡكُ يَوۡمَئِذٍ ٱلۡحَقُّ لِلرَّحۡمَٰنِۚ وَكَانَ يَوۡمًا عَلَى
ٱلۡكَٰفِرِينَ عَسِيرٗا ٢٦ وَيَوۡمَ يَعَضُّ ٱلظَّالِمُ عَلَىٰ يَدَيۡهِ يَقُولُ
يَٰلَيۡتَنِي ٱتَّخَذۡتُ مَعَ ٱلرَّسُولِ سَبِيلٗا ٢٧ يَٰوَيۡلَتَىٰ لَيۡتَنِي لَمۡ أَتَّخِذۡ
فُلَانًا خَلِيلٗا ٢٨ لَّقَدۡ أَضَلَّنِي عَنِ ٱلذِّكۡرِ بَعۡدَ إِذۡ جَآءَنِيۗ
وَكَانَ ٱلشَّيۡطَٰنُ لِلۡإِنسَٰنِ خَذُولٗا ٢٩ وَقَالَ ٱلرَّسُولُ
يَٰرَبِّ إِنَّ قَوۡمِي ٱتَّخَذُواْ هَٰذَا ٱلۡقُرۡءَانَ مَهۡجُورٗا ٣٠ وَكَذَٰلِكَ
جَعَلۡنَا لِكُلِّ نَبِيٍّ عَدُوّٗا مِّنَ ٱلۡمُجۡرِمِينَۗ وَكَفَىٰ بِرَبِّكَ هَادِيٗا
وَنَصِيرٗا ٣١ وَقَالَ ٱلَّذِينَ كَفَرُواْ لَوۡلَا نُزِّلَ عَلَيۡهِ ٱلۡقُرۡءَانُ جُمۡلَةٗ
وَٰحِدَةٗۚ كَذَٰلِكَ لِنُثَبِّتَ بِهِۦ فُؤَادَكَۖ وَرَتَّلۡنَٰهُ تَرۡتِيلٗا ٣٢
وَلَا يَأۡتُونَكَ بِمَثَلٍ إِلَّا جِئۡنَٰكَ بِٱلۡحَقِّ وَأَحۡسَنَ تَفۡسِيرًا ٣٣
ٱلَّذِينَ يُحۡشَرُونَ عَلَىٰ وُجُوهِهِمۡ إِلَىٰ جَهَنَّمَ أُوْلَٰٓئِكَ شَرّٞ
مَّكَانٗا وَأَضَلُّ سَبِيلٗا ٣٤ وَلَقَدۡ ءَاتَيۡنَا مُوسَى ٱلۡكِتَٰبَ
وَجَعَلۡنَا مَعَهُۥٓ أَخَاهُ هَٰرُونَ وَزِيرٗا ٣٥ فَقُلۡنَا ٱذۡهَبَآ إِلَى
ٱلۡقَوۡمِ ٱلَّذِينَ كَذَّبُواْ بِـَٔايَٰتِنَا فَدَمَّرۡنَٰهُمۡ تَدۡمِيرٗا ٣٦ وَقَوۡمَ
نُوحٖ لَّمَّا كَذَّبُواْ ٱلرُّسُلَ أَغۡرَقۡنَٰهُمۡ وَجَعَلۡنَٰهُمۡ لِلنَّاسِ
ءَايَةٗۖ وَأَعۡتَدۡنَا لِلظَّٰلِمِينَ عَذَابًا أَلِيمٗا ٣٧ وَعَادٗا وَثَمُودَاْ
وَأَصۡحَٰبَ ٱلرَّسِّ وَقُرُونَۢا بَيۡنَ ذَٰلِكَ كَثِيرٗا ٣٨ وَكُلّٗا ضَرَبۡنَا
لَهُ ٱلۡأَمۡثَٰلَۖ وَكُلّٗا تَبَّرۡنَا تَتۡبِيرٗا ٣٩ وَلَقَدۡ أَتَوۡاْ عَلَى ٱلۡقَرۡيَةِ
ٱلَّتِيٓ أُمۡطِرَتۡ مَطَرَ ٱلسَّوۡءِۚ أَفَلَمۡ يَكُونُواْ يَرَوۡنَهَاۚ بَلۡ

21. ***Those who do not expect to meet Us*** or fear the Resurrection ***say, 'Why have angels not been sent down to us*** – as Messengers to us***? Why do we not see our Lord*** – so that we can know from Him that Muḥammad is His Messenger***?'*** Allah says: ***They have become arrogant about themselves and are excessively insolent*** in seeking to see Allah Almighty in this world.

22. ***On the Day they see the angels*** among all the creatures gathered on the Day of Rising ***there will be no good news that Day for the evildoers*** (the unbelievers) – which is not the case with the believers, who receive the good news of the Garden. ***They will say, 'There is an absolute ban.'*** The custom in this world when a hardship afflicted people was to seek refuge with the angels.

23. Allah says: ***We will advance on the*** good ***actions they have done*** – such as gifts of *ṣadaqa*, maintaining ties of kinship, giving hospitality to the guest, and helping people in distress in this world – ***and make them scattered specks of dust*** – which only show in a sunbeam shining through a small aperture. That is a metaphor meaning that they will be of no use to them since there will be no reward for them because they lack the necessary precondition for the reward, which is sincere faith. They will be repaid for them in this world.

24. ***The Companions of the Garden on that Day*** (the Day of Rising) ***will have better lodging*** than the unbelievers had in this world ***and a better resting-place*** in which to rest at midday. It is deduced from that that the Reckoning will end in the middle of the day, as is reported in *ḥadīth* –

25. ***...on the Day when*** each ***Heaven is split apart*** (read as *tashaqqaqa* and *tashshaqqaqa*) ***in*** white ***clouds and the angels are sent down*** (read as *nunazzila* and *nunzilu*) from every heaven ***rank upon rank.*** This is the Day of Rising.

26. ***The Kingdom that Day will belong in truth to the All-Merciful*** – who does not share His kingdom with anyone. ***It will be a hard Day for the unbelievers*** – but not for the believers.

27. ***...the Day when a wrongdoer*** (idolator) – referring in particular to 'Uqba ibn Abī Mu'ayṭ, who said the *shahāda* and then retracted it to please Ubayy ibn Khalaf – ***will bite his hands*** out of regret on the Day of Rising ***and say, 'Alas for me! If only I had gone the way*** –

of guidance ***of the Messenger*** Muḥammad, may Allah bless him and grant him peace***!***

28. ***Alas for me!*** I am ruined. ***If only I had not taken so-and-so*** (Ubayy ibn Khalaf) ***for a friend!***

29. ***He led me astray from the Reminder*** (the Qur'an) ***after it came to me*** by making me revert from believing in it.***'*** Allah says: ***Shayṭān always leaves*** an unbelieving ***man in the lurch.*** He abandons unbelievers and declares himself free of them in their affliction.

30. ***The Messenger*** – Muḥammad – ***says, 'My Lord, my people*** (the tribe of Quraysh) ***treat this Qur'an as something to be ignored*** – and abandoned.***'***

31. Allah says: ***In this way*** – just as We have assigned you enemies among the idolators of Quraysh – ***We have assigned to every*** previous ***Prophet an enemy from among the evildoers*** (the idolators). Be steadfast as they were steadfast. ***But your Lord is a sufficient guide*** – for you – ***and helper*** – for you against your enemies.

32. ***Those who disbelieve say, 'Why was the Qur'an not sent down to him all in one go*** – like the Torah, the Gospel or the Psalms***?'*** Allah says: ***It is*** – We sent it down like that in parts – ***so that We may fortify your heart by it. We have recited it distinctly, little by little.*** 'We have revealed it piece by piece over time, slowly, in order to make it easy for you to understand it and remember it.'

33. ***Every time they come to you with a difficult point*** to try to discredit you, ***We bring you the*** – refuting – ***truth and the best of explanations*** to explain the matter to them.

34. ***Those who are herded headlong into Hell, such people are in the worst position. They are the most misguided from the way*** – further from the Path than others on account of their unbelief.

35. ***We gave Mūsā the Book*** (the Torah) ***and appointed his brother Hārūn with him as a helper.***

36. ***We said, 'Go to the people who have denied Our Signs,'*** (Pharaoh and his people) – they took the Message to them and they denied it – ***and*** so ***We annihilated them completely.***

37. ***And*** remember ***when the people of Nūḥ denied the Messengers*** – by denying Nūḥ, who had been among them for such a long time that it was as if he were several Messengers; or possibly their denial

كَانُوا۟ لَا يَرْجُونَ نُشُورًا ﴿٤٠﴾ وَإِذَا رَأَوْكَ إِن يَتَّخِذُونَكَ
إِلَّا هُزُوًا أَهَٰذَا ٱلَّذِى بَعَثَ ٱللَّهُ رَسُولًا ﴿٤١﴾ إِن كَادَ
لَيُضِلُّنَا عَنْ ءَالِهَتِنَا لَوْلَآ أَن صَبَرْنَا عَلَيْهَا ۚ وَسَوْفَ
يَعْلَمُونَ حِينَ يَرَوْنَ ٱلْعَذَابَ مَنْ أَضَلُّ سَبِيلًا ﴿٤٢﴾ أَرَءَيْتَ
مَنِ ٱتَّخَذَ إِلَٰهَهُۥ هَوَىٰهُ أَفَأَنتَ تَكُونُ عَلَيْهِ وَكِيلًا ﴿٤٣﴾
أَمْ تَحْسَبُ أَنَّ أَكْثَرَهُمْ يَسْمَعُونَ أَوْ يَعْقِلُونَ ۚ إِنْ هُمْ إِلَّا
كَٱلْأَنْعَٰمِ ۖ بَلْ هُمْ أَضَلُّ سَبِيلًا ﴿٤٤﴾ أَلَمْ تَرَ إِلَىٰ رَبِّكَ كَيْفَ مَدَّ
ٱلظِّلَّ وَلَوْ شَآءَ لَجَعَلَهُۥ سَاكِنًا ثُمَّ جَعَلْنَا ٱلشَّمْسَ عَلَيْهِ دَلِيلًا
﴿٤٥﴾ ثُمَّ قَبَضْنَٰهُ إِلَيْنَا قَبْضًا يَسِيرًا ﴿٤٦﴾ وَهُوَ ٱلَّذِى جَعَلَ
لَكُمُ ٱلَّيْلَ لِبَاسًا وَٱلنَّوْمَ سُبَاتًا وَجَعَلَ ٱلنَّهَارَ نُشُورًا ﴿٤٧﴾
وَهُوَ ٱلَّذِىٓ أَرْسَلَ ٱلرِّيَٰحَ بُشْرًۢا بَيْنَ يَدَىْ رَحْمَتِهِۦ ۚ وَأَنزَلْنَا
مِنَ ٱلسَّمَآءِ مَآءً طَهُورًا ﴿٤٨﴾ لِّنُحْـِۧىَ بِهِۦ بَلْدَةً مَّيْتًا وَنُسْقِيَهُۥ
مِمَّا خَلَقْنَآ أَنْعَٰمًا وَأَنَاسِىَّ كَثِيرًا ﴿٤٩﴾ وَلَقَدْ صَرَّفْنَٰهُ بَيْنَهُمْ
لِيَذَّكَّرُوا۟ فَأَبَىٰٓ أَكْثَرُ ٱلنَّاسِ إِلَّا كُفُورًا ﴿٥٠﴾ وَلَوْ شِئْنَا
لَبَعَثْنَا فِى كُلِّ قَرْيَةٍ نَّذِيرًا ﴿٥١﴾ فَلَا تُطِعِ ٱلْكَٰفِرِينَ
وَجَٰهِدْهُم بِهِۦ جِهَادًا كَبِيرًا ﴿٥٢﴾ ۞ وَهُوَ ٱلَّذِى مَرَجَ
ٱلْبَحْرَيْنِ هَٰذَا عَذْبٌ فُرَاتٌ وَهَٰذَا مِلْحٌ أُجَاجٌ وَجَعَلَ بَيْنَهُمَا بَرْزَخًا
وَحِجْرًا مَّحْجُورًا ﴿٥٣﴾ وَهُوَ ٱلَّذِى خَلَقَ مِنَ ٱلْمَآءِ بَشَرًا فَجَعَلَهُۥ
نَسَبًا وَصِهْرًا ۗ وَكَانَ رَبُّكَ قَدِيرًا ﴿٥٤﴾ وَيَعْبُدُونَ مِن دُونِ ٱللَّهِ
مَا لَا يَنفَعُهُمْ وَلَا يَضُرُّهُمْ ۗ وَكَانَ ٱلْكَافِرُ عَلَىٰ رَبِّهِۦ ظَهِيرًا ﴿٥٥﴾

of him was tantamount to denying the rest of the Messengers, since the basis of their Message is the same. ***We drowned them and made them a Sign*** (lesson) ***for all mankind. We have prepared*** in the Next World – ***a painful punishment for the wrongdoers*** (the unbelievers) – in addition to what they suffered in this world.

38. Remember 'Ād because – ***the same goes for 'Ād*** – the people of Hūd – ***and Thamūd*** – the people of Ṣāliḥ – ***and the Companions of the Well*** – the Prophet of the people of the Well is said to have been Shu'ayb, and it is also said to have been someone else; they lived around their well and it collapsed together with them and their dwellings – ***and many generations*** (peoples) ***in between*** – between 'Ād and the Companions of the Well.

39. ***We gave examples to each one of them*** which established the evidence against them. We only destroy them after warning them – ***and each one of them We utterly wiped out*** for denying the Prophets.

40. ***They themselves*** (the unbelievers of Makka) ***have come across the city which was rained on by an evil rain*** of stones which rained down, a reference to the largest of the towns of the people of Lūṭ; Allah destroyed its inhabitants for their indecent actions. ***Did they not then see it*** when they travelled to Syria, and take note? The question demands an affirmative response. ***But they do not expect to rise again.*** They do not think that they will be resurrected and so they do not have faith.

41. ***When they see you they only make a mockery of you*** and say: ***'Is this the one Allah has sent as a Messenger?*** This was to disparage his Message.

42. ***He might almost have misled*** (diverted) ***us from our gods, had we not stuck to them steadfastly!'*** Allah says: ***They will soon know, when they see the punishment*** with their own eyes in the Next World, ***whose way is the most misguided*** and incorrect: theirs or that of the believers.

43. Tell me: ***Have you seen him who has taken his whims and desires to be his god? Will you then be his guardian*** and thus prevent him from following his own desires?

44. ***Do you suppose that most of them hear or understand*** what you say to them? ***They are just like cattle. Indeed they are even more astray*** than cattle because cattle obey the person who cares for them, whereas these people do not obey their Master who bestows blessing on them.

45. ***Do you not see how your Lord stretches out shadows*** from the time of first light until sunrise? ***If He*** (your Lord) ***had wished He could have made them*** (the shadows) ***stationary*** – even after the sun has risen. ***Then We appoint the sun to be the pointer to them.*** The sun has been made an indicator of the shadow. If it were not for the sun, there would be no shadow.

46. ***Then We draw them back to Ourselves in gradual steps*** as the sun rises in the sky.

47. ***It is He who made the night a cloak*** (covering) ***for you and sleep a rest*** for bodies from their work, ***and He made the day a time for rising*** – to seek provision and other things.

48. ***It is He who sends out the winds*** (read as *riyāḥ* and *rīḥ*) ***bringing advance news*** (read as *bushran, nushran, nushuran* and *nashran*) ***of His mercy*** (rain). ***And We send down from heaven pure*** – and purifying – ***water…***

49. ***…so that by it We may bring a dead*** (read as *maytan* and *mayyitan*) ***land to life and give*** water to ***drink to many of the animals*** – such as camels, cattle and sheep – ***and people We created.***

50. ***We have variegated it*** – referring to water – ***for them so that they might pay heed*** (read as *yadhdhakkarū* and *yadhkurū*) – meaning, remember Allah's blessing by it – ***but most people spurn anything else but unbelief*** – they are ungrateful for Allah's blessing and deny it by falsely attributing rain to another cause, as when they say, "We have rain when such-and-such a star rises."

51. ***If We had wished We could have sent a warner to every town*** to alarm its people. We have sent you to warn the people of all the towns to make your reward greater.

52. ***So do not obey*** the whims of ***the unbelievers, but use this*** (the Qur'an) ***to battle against them with all your might.***

53. ***It is He who has unloosed both seas –*** adjacent to one another – ***one*** very ***sweet and refreshing, the other salty and bitter – and put***

وَمَآ أَرْسَلْنَٰكَ إِلَّا مُبَشِّرًا وَنَذِيرًا ﴿٥٦﴾ قُلْ مَآ أَسْـَٔلُكُمْ عَلَيْهِ
مِنْ أَجْرٍ إِلَّا مَن شَآءَ أَن يَتَّخِذَ إِلَىٰ رَبِّهِۦ سَبِيلًا ﴿٥٧﴾ وَتَوَكَّلْ
عَلَى ٱلْحَىِّ ٱلَّذِى لَا يَمُوتُ وَسَبِّحْ بِحَمْدِهِۦ ۚ وَكَفَىٰ بِهِۦ بِذُنُوبِ
عِبَادِهِۦ خَبِيرًا ﴿٥٨﴾ ٱلَّذِى خَلَقَ ٱلسَّمَٰوَٰتِ وَٱلْأَرْضَ وَمَا بَيْنَهُمَا
فِى سِتَّةِ أَيَّامٍ ثُمَّ ٱسْتَوَىٰ عَلَى ٱلْعَرْشِ ۚ ٱلرَّحْمَٰنُ فَسْـَٔلْ بِهِۦ
خَبِيرًا ﴿٥٩﴾ وَإِذَا قِيلَ لَهُمُ ٱسْجُدُوا۟ لِلرَّحْمَٰنِ قَالُوا۟ وَمَا ٱلرَّحْمَٰنُ
أَنَسْجُدُ لِمَا تَأْمُرُنَا وَزَادَهُمْ نُفُورًا ۩ ﴿٦٠﴾ تَبَارَكَ ٱلَّذِى جَعَلَ
فِى ٱلسَّمَآءِ بُرُوجًا وَجَعَلَ فِيهَا سِرَٰجًا وَقَمَرًا مُّنِيرًا ﴿٦١﴾ وَهُوَ
ٱلَّذِى جَعَلَ ٱلَّيْلَ وَٱلنَّهَارَ خِلْفَةً لِّمَنْ أَرَادَ أَن يَذَّكَّرَ أَوْ أَرَادَ
شُكُورًا ﴿٦٢﴾ وَعِبَادُ ٱلرَّحْمَٰنِ ٱلَّذِينَ يَمْشُونَ عَلَى ٱلْأَرْضِ
هَوْنًا وَإِذَا خَاطَبَهُمُ ٱلْجَٰهِلُونَ قَالُوا۟ سَلَٰمًا ﴿٦٣﴾ وَٱلَّذِينَ
يَبِيتُونَ لِرَبِّهِمْ سُجَّدًا وَقِيَٰمًا ﴿٦٤﴾ وَٱلَّذِينَ يَقُولُونَ
رَبَّنَا ٱصْرِفْ عَنَّا عَذَابَ جَهَنَّمَ ۖ إِنَّ عَذَابَهَا كَانَ غَرَامًا
﴿٦٥﴾ إِنَّهَا سَآءَتْ مُسْتَقَرًّا وَمُقَامًا ﴿٦٦﴾ وَٱلَّذِينَ إِذَآ أَنفَقُوا۟
لَمْ يُسْرِفُوا۟ وَلَمْ يَقْتُرُوا۟ وَكَانَ بَيْنَ ذَٰلِكَ قَوَامًا ﴿٦٧﴾
وَٱلَّذِينَ لَا يَدْعُونَ مَعَ ٱللَّهِ إِلَٰهًا ءَاخَرَ وَلَا يَقْتُلُونَ ٱلنَّفْسَ
ٱلَّتِى حَرَّمَ ٱللَّهُ إِلَّا بِٱلْحَقِّ وَلَا يَزْنُونَ ۚ وَمَن يَفْعَلْ ذَٰلِكَ يَلْقَ
أَثَامًا ﴿٦٨﴾ يُضَٰعَفْ لَهُ ٱلْعَذَابُ يَوْمَ ٱلْقِيَٰمَةِ وَيَخْلُدْ فِيهِۦ
مُهَانًا ﴿٦٩﴾ إِلَّا مَن تَابَ وَءَامَنَ وَعَمِلَ عَمَلًا صَٰلِحًا
فَأُو۟لَٰٓئِكَ يُبَدِّلُ ٱللَّهُ سَيِّـَٔاتِهِمْ حَسَنَٰتٍ ۗ وَكَانَ ٱللَّهُ غَفُورًا

a dividing line between them, an impassible barrier so that they do not mix with one another at all.

54. ***And it is He who created human beings from water*** (sperm) ***and then gave them relations by blood and marriage*** – because men and women marry to seek progeny. ***Your Lord is All-Powerful***, possessing the power to do whatever He wills.

55. ***Yet they*** (the unbelievers) ***worship instead of Allah what*** – something whose worship – ***can neither help nor harm them*** – in other words, idols. ***The unbelievers are always biased against their Lord*** and predisposed to obey Shayṭān.

56. ***We sent you only to bring good news*** of Paradise ***and to give warning*** about Hell.

57. ***Say: 'I do not ask you for any wage for it*** for conveying what I am sent with ***– only that anyone who wants to should make his way towards his Lord*** – by spending his wealth in a way pleasing to Allah.'

58. ***Put your trust in the Living who does not die and glorify Him with praise.*** Say, "Glory be to Allah and praise is His." ***He is well aware of the wrong actions of His slaves:***

59. ***He who created the heavens and the earth and everything in between them in six days*** – days of this world, meaning in an equivalent amount of time. since that was before the sun and time as such existed. If He had wished, He could have created them in the blink of an eye; but He did not do that, in order to teach His creation to be methodical – ***and then established Himself firmly on the Throne*** – which means linguistically the seat on which a king sits***: the All-Merciful. Ask***, human being, ***anyone who is informed about Him*** and His attributes.

60. ***When they*** (the unbelievers of Makka) ***are told to prostrate to the All-Merciful, they say, 'And what is the All-Merciful? Are we to prostrate to something you command us to*** (read as *ta'murunā* as here, referring to Muḥammad, may Allah bless him and grant him peace, and also *ya'murunā*, "He commands us to", in which case it refers to Allah, may He be exalted) – to worship something we do not recognise***?' And it*** – saying this to them – ***merely makes them run away all the more*** – makes them even more averse to belief.

61. Allah says to them: ***Blessed be He who placed constellations in the sky*** – the constellations are the twelve signs of the Zodiac: see 16:15 – ***and put a blazing lamp*** – the sun – ***and shining moon among them.***

62. ***It is He who made night and day succeed each other for those who want to pay heed*** (read as *yadhdhakkaru* and *yadhkuru*) – so that if someone misses something (like the prayer) in one, he can do it in the other – ***or to give thanks*** for the blessings of His Lord upon him in the day and night.

63. ***The slaves of the All-Merciful are those who walk lightly on the earth*** with tranquillity and humility ***and, who, when the ignorant speak to them*** – saying something they dislike – ***say, 'Peace'*** – by which they preserve themselves from wrong action;

64. ***...those who pass the night prostrating and standing before their Lord***, praying night prayers;

65. ***...those who say, 'Our Lord, avert from us the punishment of Hell. Its punishment is inescapable pain.***

66. ***It is indeed an evil lodging and abode*** in which to stay;

67. ***...those who, when they spend*** on their family ***are neither extravagant nor mean*** (read as *yaqturū* or *yuqtirū*), ***but take a stance midway between the two*** in terms of expenditure;

68. ***...those who do not call on any other god besides Allah and do not kill anyone Allah has made inviolate, except with the right to do so, and do not fornicate; anyone who does that*** – any of the three mentioned – ***will receive an evil punishment...***

69. ***...and on the Day of Rising his punishment will be doubled*** (read as *yuḍā'āfa* and *yuḍa''afa*) ***and he will be humiliated in it timelessly, forever,***

70. ***...except for those who repent and believe and act rightly: Allah will transform the wrong actions of such people into good*** – actions in the Next World – ***Allah is Ever-Forgiving, Most Merciful –***

71. ***... for certainly all who repent*** of wrong actions ***and act rightly have turned sincerely towards Allah*** – returned to Allah, and He will repay them;

رَحِيمًا ﴿٧٠﴾ وَمَن تَابَ وَعَمِلَ صَٰلِحًا فَإِنَّهُۥ يَتُوبُ إِلَى ٱللَّهِ
مَتَابًا ﴿٧١﴾ وَٱلَّذِينَ لَا يَشْهَدُونَ ٱلزُّورَ وَإِذَا مَرُّوا۟ بِٱللَّغْوِ
مَرُّوا۟ كِرَامًا ﴿٧٢﴾ وَٱلَّذِينَ إِذَا ذُكِّرُوا۟ بِـَٔايَٰتِ رَبِّهِمْ
لَمْ يَخِرُّوا۟ عَلَيْهَا صُمًّا وَعُمْيَانًا ﴿٧٣﴾ وَٱلَّذِينَ يَقُولُونَ رَبَّنَا
هَبْ لَنَا مِنْ أَزْوَٰجِنَا وَذُرِّيَّٰتِنَا قُرَّةَ أَعْيُنٍ وَٱجْعَلْنَا
لِلْمُتَّقِينَ إِمَامًا ﴿٧٤﴾ أُو۟لَٰٓئِكَ يُجْزَوْنَ ٱلْغُرْفَةَ بِمَا
صَبَرُوا۟ وَيُلَقَّوْنَ فِيهَا تَحِيَّةً وَسَلَٰمًا ﴿٧٥﴾ خَٰلِدِينَ
فِيهَا ۚ حَسُنَتْ مُسْتَقَرًّا وَمُقَامًا ﴿٧٦﴾ قُلْ مَا يَعْبَؤُا۟ بِكُمْ رَبِّى
لَوْلَا دُعَآؤُكُمْ ۖ فَقَدْ كَذَّبْتُمْ فَسَوْفَ يَكُونُ لِزَامًۢا ﴿٧٧﴾

72. ***...those who do not*** lie and ***bear false witness and who, when they pass by worthless talk*** – obscenities, backbiting, idle gossip and other such things – ***pass by with dignity;***

73. ***...those who, when they are*** admonished and ***reminded of the Signs of their Lord*** (the Qur'an), ***do not turn their backs, deaf and blind to them*** – but rather listen and look and benefit from them;

74. ***...those who say, 'Our Lord, give us joy in our wives and children*** (read as *dhurriyātinā* and *dhurriyatinā*) – when we see them obeying You – ***and make us a good example for those who are godfearing';***

75. ***...such people will be repaid for their steadfastness*** – in obeying Allah ***with the Highest Paradise*** – the highest degree in the Garden – ***where they will meet*** (read as *yulaqqayna* and *yalqayna*) ***with welcome and with 'Peace'*** – spoken by the angels.

76. ***They will remain in it timelessly, for ever. What an excellent lodging and abode!***

77. Say, Muḥammad, to the people of Makka: ***'What has My Lord to do with you if you do not call on Him***, when you are in difficulties, for Him to remove them? ***But you have denied the truth*** – the Messenger and the Qur'an – ***so punishment is bound to come*** in the Next World after whatever happens to them in this world.' Seventy of them were killed in the Battle of Badr.

سُورَةُ الشُّعَرَاءِ

بِسْمِ اللَّهِ الرَّحْمَٰنِ الرَّحِيمِ

طسٓمٓ ١ تِلْكَ ءَايَٰتُ ٱلْكِتَٰبِ ٱلْمُبِينِ ٢ لَعَلَّكَ بَٰخِعٌ نَّفْسَكَ
أَلَّا يَكُونُوا۟ مُؤْمِنِينَ ٣ إِن نَّشَأْ نُنَزِّلْ عَلَيْهِم مِّنَ ٱلسَّمَآءِ ءَايَةً فَظَلَّتْ
أَعْنَٰقُهُمْ لَهَا خَٰضِعِينَ ٤ وَمَا يَأْتِيهِم مِّن ذِكْرٍ مِّنَ ٱلرَّحْمَٰنِ مُحْدَثٍ
إِلَّا كَانُوا۟ عَنْهُ مُعْرِضِينَ ٥ فَقَدْ كَذَّبُوا۟ فَسَيَأْتِيهِمْ أَنۢبَٰٓؤُا۟ مَا كَانُوا۟
بِهِۦ يَسْتَهْزِءُونَ ٦ أَوَلَمْ يَرَوْا۟ إِلَى ٱلْأَرْضِ كَمْ أَنۢبَتْنَا فِيهَا مِن كُلِّ زَوْجٍ
كَرِيمٍ ٧ إِنَّ فِى ذَٰلِكَ لَءَايَةً ۖ وَمَا كَانَ أَكْثَرُهُم مُّؤْمِنِينَ ٨ وَإِنَّ
رَبَّكَ لَهُوَ ٱلْعَزِيزُ ٱلرَّحِيمُ ٩ وَإِذْ نَادَىٰ رَبُّكَ مُوسَىٰٓ أَنِ ٱئْتِ ٱلْقَوْمَ
ٱلظَّٰلِمِينَ ١٠ قَوْمَ فِرْعَوْنَ ۚ أَلَا يَتَّقُونَ ١١ قَالَ رَبِّ إِنِّىٓ أَخَافُ
أَن يُكَذِّبُونِ ١٢ وَيَضِيقُ صَدْرِى وَلَا يَنطَلِقُ لِسَانِى فَأَرْسِلْ
إِلَىٰ هَٰرُونَ ١٣ وَلَهُمْ عَلَىَّ ذَنۢبٌ فَأَخَافُ أَن يَقْتُلُونِ ١٤ قَالَ
كَلَّا ۖ فَٱذْهَبَا بِـَٔايَٰتِنَآ ۖ إِنَّا مَعَكُم مُّسْتَمِعُونَ ١٥ فَأْتِيَا فِرْعَوْنَ
فَقُولَآ إِنَّا رَسُولُ رَبِّ ٱلْعَٰلَمِينَ ١٦ أَنْ أَرْسِلْ مَعَنَا بَنِىٓ إِسْرَٰٓءِيلَ
١٧ قَالَ أَلَمْ نُرَبِّكَ فِينَا وَلِيدًا وَلَبِثْتَ فِينَا مِنْ عُمُرِكَ سِنِينَ ١٨
وَفَعَلْتَ فَعْلَتَكَ ٱلَّتِى فَعَلْتَ وَأَنتَ مِنَ ٱلْكَٰفِرِينَ ١٩
قَالَ فَعَلْتُهَآ إِذًا وَأَنَا۠ مِنَ ٱلضَّآلِّينَ ٢٠ فَفَرَرْتُ مِنكُمْ لَمَّا خِفْتُكُمْ
فَوَهَبَ لِى رَبِّى حُكْمًا وَجَعَلَنِى مِنَ ٱلْمُرْسَلِينَ ٢١ وَتِلْكَ نِعْمَةٌ تَمُنُّهَا
عَلَىَّ أَنْ عَبَّدتَّ بَنِىٓ إِسْرَٰٓءِيلَ ٢٢ قَالَ فِرْعَوْنُ وَمَا رَبُّ ٱلْعَٰلَمِينَ

26. *Sūrat ash-Shu'arā'*
The Poets

This *sūra* is Makkan except for *āyats* 197 and those from 224 to the end of the *sūra*, which are Madinan. It has 227 *āyats* and was sent down after *al-Wāq'ia.*

1. ***Ta Sin Mim.*** Allah knows best what is meant by this.

2. ***Those are the Signs of the Clear Book*** – the *āyats* of the Qur'an which make the truth clear from falsehood.

3. ***Perhaps you,*** Muḥammad, ***will destroy yourself with grief because they*** (the people of Makka) ***will not become believers.*** This is said out of compassion to him to instruct him so that his sorrow about that is diminished.

4. ***If We wished We could send down a Sign to them from heaven before which their heads would be bowed low in subjection*** – indicating that they would believe.

5. ***But no fresh reminder*** in the form of the Qur'an – ***from the All-Merciful reaches them without their turning away from it.***

6. ***They have denied the truth, but the news of what they mocked will certainly come to them.***

7. ***Have they not looked at the earth and seen how We have made every sort of*** its myriad and ***beneficial species grow in it?***

8. ***There is certainly a Sign in that,*** indicating the perfection of Allah's power, ***yet most of them are not believers*** – in Allah's knowledge.

9. ***Truly your Lord is the Almighty,*** possessing might with which He will take revenge on the unbelievers, ***the Most Merciful*** to the believers.

10. Mention to your people, Muḥammad, about ***when your Lord called out to Mūsā*** on the night when he saw the fire and the bush: ***'Go to the wrongdoing people*** as a Messenger,

11. ***...the people of Pharaoh*** who have wronged themselves by rejecting Allah and wronged the tribe of Israel by enslaving them.

Will they not be godfearing and show their fear of Allah by obeying Him and affirming His unity***?'*** The question is a rebuke to them.

12. ***He*** (Mūsā) ***said, 'My Lord, I fear they will deny me,***

13 . ***...and that my breast will be constricted*** by their denial of me, ***and that my tongue will not be free*** – will be unable to convey the Message because of my speech impediment. ***So send*** – my brother – ***Hārūn as a Messenger as well.***

14. ***They hold a wrong action against me*** – through my killing of the Copt – ***and I fear that they may kill me.'***

15. ***He*** (Allah) ***said, 'By no means!*** They will not kill you. ***Go, both of you, with Our Signs. We will certainly be together with you, listening.*** We will hear what you say and what is said to you.

16. ***Go to Pharaoh and say, "We are the Messenger of the Lord of all the worlds*** – to you –

17. ***...to tell you to send the tribe of Israel away*** to Syria ***with us."'*** They went to him and told him what they had been commanded to say.

18. ***He*** (Pharaoh) ***said*** to Mūsā, ***'Did we not bring you up among us as a child*** in our home ***and did you not spend many years of your life among us?*** He spent thirty years of his life wearing the garments of Pharaoh and riding in his entourage, and was called his son.

19. ***Yet you did the deed you did*** – a reference to Mūsā's killing of the Copt – ***and were ungrateful,*** refusing to acknowledge our beneficence towards you by bringing you up and not enslaving you.'

20. ***He*** (Mūsā) ***said, 'At the time I did it I was one of the misguided*** – unaware of the knowledge which Allah gave me later and of the Message,

21. ***...and so I fled from you when I was in fear of you. But my Lord has given me right judgement*** (knowledge) ***and made me one of the Messengers.***

22. ***And anyway you can only reproach me with this favour because you made the tribe of Israel into slaves!'*** You enslaved them but not me. Therefore that is not beneficence on your part, since you did wrong by enslaving them.

﴿٢٣﴾ قَالَ رَبُّ ٱلسَّمَٰوَٰتِ وَٱلْأَرْضِ وَمَا بَيْنَهُمَآ إِن كُنتُم مُّوقِنِينَ
﴿٢٤﴾ قَالَ لِمَنْ حَوْلَهُۥٓ أَلَا تَسْتَمِعُونَ ﴿٢٥﴾ قَالَ رَبُّكُمْ وَرَبُّ ءَابَآئِكُمُ
ٱلْأَوَّلِينَ ﴿٢٦﴾ قَالَ إِنَّ رَسُولَكُمُ ٱلَّذِىٓ أُرْسِلَ إِلَيْكُمْ لَمَجْنُونٌ ﴿٢٧﴾
قَالَ رَبُّ ٱلْمَشْرِقِ وَٱلْمَغْرِبِ وَمَا بَيْنَهُمَآ إِن كُنتُمْ تَعْقِلُونَ ﴿٢٨﴾ قَالَ
لَئِنِ ٱتَّخَذْتَ إِلَٰهًا غَيْرِى لَأَجْعَلَنَّكَ مِنَ ٱلْمَسْجُونِينَ ﴿٢٩﴾ قَالَ
أَوَلَوْ جِئْتُكَ بِشَىْءٍ مُّبِينٍ ﴿٣٠﴾ قَالَ فَأْتِ بِهِۦٓ إِن كُنتَ مِنَ
ٱلصَّٰدِقِينَ ﴿٣١﴾ فَأَلْقَىٰ عَصَاهُ فَإِذَا هِىَ ثُعْبَانٌ مُّبِينٌ ﴿٣٢﴾ وَنَزَعَ يَدَهُۥ
فَإِذَا هِىَ بَيْضَآءُ لِلنَّٰظِرِينَ ﴿٣٣﴾ قَالَ لِلْمَلَإِ حَوْلَهُۥٓ إِنَّ هَٰذَا لَسَٰحِرٌ
عَلِيمٌ ﴿٣٤﴾ يُرِيدُ أَن يُخْرِجَكُم مِّنْ أَرْضِكُم بِسِحْرِهِۦ فَمَاذَا
تَأْمُرُونَ ﴿٣٥﴾ قَالُوٓا۟ أَرْجِهْ وَأَخَاهُ وَٱبْعَثْ فِى ٱلْمَدَآئِنِ حَٰشِرِينَ
﴿٣٦﴾ يَأْتُوكَ بِكُلِّ سَحَّارٍ عَلِيمٍ ﴿٣٧﴾ فَجُمِعَ ٱلسَّحَرَةُ
لِمِيقَٰتِ يَوْمٍ مَّعْلُومٍ ﴿٣٨﴾ وَقِيلَ لِلنَّاسِ هَلْ أَنتُم مُّجْتَمِعُونَ ﴿٣٩﴾
لَعَلَّنَا نَتَّبِعُ ٱلسَّحَرَةَ إِن كَانُوا۟ هُمُ ٱلْغَٰلِبِينَ ﴿٤٠﴾ فَلَمَّا جَآءَ ٱلسَّحَرَةُ
قَالُوا۟ لِفِرْعَوْنَ أَئِنَّ لَنَا لَأَجْرًا إِن كُنَّا نَحْنُ ٱلْغَٰلِبِينَ ﴿٤١﴾ قَالَ نَعَمْ
وَإِنَّكُمْ إِذًا لَّمِنَ ٱلْمُقَرَّبِينَ ﴿٤٢﴾ قَالَ لَهُم مُّوسَىٰٓ أَلْقُوا۟ مَآ أَنتُم مُّلْقُونَ
﴿٤٣﴾ فَأَلْقَوْا۟ حِبَالَهُمْ وَعِصِيَّهُمْ وَقَالُوا۟ بِعِزَّةِ فِرْعَوْنَ إِنَّا لَنَحْنُ
ٱلْغَٰلِبُونَ ﴿٤٤﴾ فَأَلْقَىٰ مُوسَىٰ عَصَاهُ فَإِذَا هِىَ تَلْقَفُ مَا يَأْفِكُونَ
﴿٤٥﴾ فَأُلْقِىَ ٱلسَّحَرَةُ سَٰجِدِينَ ﴿٤٦﴾ قَالُوٓا۟ ءَامَنَّا بِرَبِّ ٱلْعَٰلَمِينَ ﴿٤٧﴾
رَبِّ مُوسَىٰ وَهَٰرُونَ ﴿٤٨﴾ قَالَ ءَامَنتُمْ لَهُۥ قَبْلَ أَنْ ءَاذَنَ لَكُمْ إِنَّهُۥ
لَكَبِيرُكُمُ ٱلَّذِى عَلَّمَكُمُ ٱلسِّحْرَ فَلَسَوْفَ تَعْلَمُونَ لَأُقَطِّعَنَّ أَيْدِيَكُمْ

23. ***Pharaoh said*** to Mūsā, ***'What is the Lord of all the worlds?'*** Who is this whose Messenger you say that you are?' There is no way for creation to know the reality of Allah; they only know Him through His attributes. Mūsā answered him by mentioning some of His attributes.

24. ***He replied, 'The Lord of the heavens and the earth and everything between them, if you knew for sure*** that He is your Creator; therefore believe in Him alone.*'*

25. ***He*** (Pharaoh) ***asked those*** nobles of his people ***around him, 'Are you listening?*** Do you not hear that his answer is not a proper answer to the question I asked?*'*

26. ***He*** (Mūsā) ***said, 'Your Lord and the Lord of your forefathers, the previous peoples.'*** This answer exasperated Pharaoh.

27. ***He said, 'This Messenger, who has been sent to you, is mad.'***

28. ***He*** (Mūsā) ***said, 'The Lord of the East and the West and everything between them, if you used your intellect.'*** So believe in Him and affirm His unity.

29. ***He*** (Pharaoh) ***said*** to Mūsā, ***'If you take any god other than me, I will certainly throw you into prison.'*** Prison was an extremely severe punishment in Pharaoh's Egypt. It was under the ground and the prisoners did not see or speak to anyone.

30. ***He*** (Mūsā) ***said, 'Even if I were to bring you something undeniable*** – clear evidence of my Prophethood***?'***

31. ***He*** (Pharaoh) ***said*** to him, ***'Produce it, then, if you are someone telling the truth.'***

32. ***So he threw down his staff and there it was, unmistakably a*** huge ***snake.***

33. ***And he drew out his hand*** from his pocket ***and there it was, pure white*** and shining, changed from its normal brown colour, ***to those who looked.***

34. ***He*** (Pharaoh) ***said to the High Council round about him, 'This certainly is a skilled magician*** – obviously well-versed in magic –

35. ***...who desires by his magic to expel you from your land; so what do you recommend?'***

36. ***They said, 'Detain him and his brother*** and delay them, ***and send out marshals to the cities*** – to gather the people –

37. ***...to bring you all the skilled magicians*** to demonstrate in public their superior knowledge of magic to that of Mūsā.*'*

38. ***So the magicians were assembled for a meeting on a specified day*** – midmorning on the Day of Adornment, which was their festival.

39. ***The people were asked, 'Are you all assembled,***

40. ***...so we can follow the magicians if they are the winners?'*** The question was to encourage the people to gather and anticipate victory so that they would continue in their religion and not follow Mūsā.

41. ***When the magicians came, they asked Pharaoh, 'Will we be rewarded if we are the winners?'***

42. ***He said, 'Yes, and in that case you will be among those brought near.'***

43. After the magicians said to him, "Will you throw or shall we be the first to throw?" ***Mūsā told them, 'Throw whatever it is you are going to throw!'*** The command implies giving them permission. Allowing them to throw first was a means to manifesting the truth.

44. ***They threw down their ropes and staffs and said, 'By the might of Pharaoh we are the winners.'***

45. ***But Mūsā threw down his staff and at once it swallowed up what they had fabricated*** – all their ropes and staffs which had appeared to be moving snakes.

46. ***The magicians threw themselves down, prostrating.***

47. ***They said, 'We believe in the Lord of all the worlds,***

48. ***...the Lord of Mūsā and Hārūn.'*** For they knew that what they had witnessed happening with Mūsā's staff was not the result of magic.

49. ***He*** (Pharaoh) ***said, 'Have you believed in him*** (Mūsā) ***before I authorised you? He is your chief who taught you magic.*** He taught you some magic, and defeated you with other magic which you did not learn from him. ***But you will soon know*** what I will do to you***! I will cut off your alternate hands and feet*** – the right hand and the left foot – ***and I will crucify every one of you.'***

وَأَرْجُلَكُم مِّنْ خِلَٰفٍ وَلَأُصَلِّبَنَّكُمْ أَجْمَعِينَ ﴿٤٩﴾ قَالُوا۟ لَا ضَيْرَ ۖ إِنَّآ
إِلَىٰ رَبِّنَا مُنقَلِبُونَ ﴿٥٠﴾ إِنَّا نَطْمَعُ أَن يَغْفِرَ لَنَا رَبُّنَا خَطَٰيَٰنَآ أَن كُنَّآ
أَوَّلَ ٱلْمُؤْمِنِينَ ﴿٥١﴾ ۞ وَأَوْحَيْنَآ إِلَىٰ مُوسَىٰٓ أَنْ أَسْرِ بِعِبَادِىٓ إِنَّكُم
مُّتَّبَعُونَ ﴿٥٢﴾ فَأَرْسَلَ فِرْعَوْنُ فِى ٱلْمَدَآئِنِ حَٰشِرِينَ ﴿٥٣﴾ إِنَّ هَٰٓؤُلَآءِ
لَشِرْذِمَةٌ قَلِيلُونَ ﴿٥٤﴾ وَإِنَّهُمْ لَنَا لَغَآئِظُونَ ﴿٥٥﴾ وَإِنَّا لَجَمِيعٌ حَٰذِرُونَ
﴿٥٦﴾ فَأَخْرَجْنَٰهُم مِّن جَنَّٰتٍ وَعُيُونٍ ﴿٥٧﴾ وَكُنُوزٍ وَمَقَامٍ كَرِيمٍ ﴿٥٨﴾
كَذَٰلِكَ وَأَوْرَثْنَٰهَا بَنِىٓ إِسْرَٰٓءِيلَ ﴿٥٩﴾ فَأَتْبَعُوهُم مُّشْرِقِينَ ﴿٦٠﴾
فَلَمَّا تَرَٰٓءَا ٱلْجَمْعَانِ قَالَ أَصْحَٰبُ مُوسَىٰٓ إِنَّا لَمُدْرَكُونَ ﴿٦١﴾ قَالَ
كَلَّآ ۖ إِنَّ مَعِىَ رَبِّى سَيَهْدِينِ ﴿٦٢﴾ فَأَوْحَيْنَآ إِلَىٰ مُوسَىٰٓ أَنِ ٱضْرِب
بِّعَصَاكَ ٱلْبَحْرَ ۖ فَٱنفَلَقَ فَكَانَ كُلُّ فِرْقٍ كَٱلطَّوْدِ ٱلْعَظِيمِ ﴿٦٣﴾
وَأَزْلَفْنَا ثَمَّ ٱلْءَاخَرِينَ ﴿٦٤﴾ وَأَنجَيْنَا مُوسَىٰ وَمَن مَّعَهُۥٓ أَجْمَعِينَ ﴿٦٥﴾
ثُمَّ أَغْرَقْنَا ٱلْءَاخَرِينَ ﴿٦٦﴾ إِنَّ فِى ذَٰلِكَ لَءَايَةً ۖ وَمَا كَانَ أَكْثَرُهُم
مُّؤْمِنِينَ ﴿٦٧﴾ وَإِنَّ رَبَّكَ لَهُوَ ٱلْعَزِيزُ ٱلرَّحِيمُ ﴿٦٨﴾ وَٱتْلُ عَلَيْهِمْ
نَبَأَ إِبْرَٰهِيمَ ﴿٦٩﴾ إِذْ قَالَ لِأَبِيهِ وَقَوْمِهِۦ مَا تَعْبُدُونَ ﴿٧٠﴾ قَالُوا۟
نَعْبُدُ أَصْنَامًا فَنَظَلُّ لَهَا عَٰكِفِينَ ﴿٧١﴾ قَالَ هَلْ يَسْمَعُونَكُمْ إِذْ
تَدْعُونَ ﴿٧٢﴾ أَوْ يَنفَعُونَكُمْ أَوْ يَضُرُّونَ ﴿٧٣﴾ قَالُوا۟ بَلْ وَجَدْنَآ ءَابَآءَنَا
كَذَٰلِكَ يَفْعَلُونَ ﴿٧٤﴾ قَالَ أَفَرَءَيْتُم مَّا كُنتُمْ تَعْبُدُونَ ﴿٧٥﴾ أَنتُمْ
وَءَابَآؤُكُمُ ٱلْأَقْدَمُونَ ﴿٧٦﴾ فَإِنَّهُمْ عَدُوٌّ لِّىٓ إِلَّا رَبَّ ٱلْعَٰلَمِينَ
﴿٧٧﴾ ٱلَّذِى خَلَقَنِى فَهُوَ يَهْدِينِ ﴿٧٨﴾ وَٱلَّذِى هُوَ يُطْعِمُنِى وَيَسْقِينِ
﴿٧٩﴾ وَإِذَا مَرِضْتُ فَهُوَ يَشْفِينِ ﴿٨٠﴾ وَٱلَّذِى يُمِيتُنِى ثُمَّ

50. ***They said, 'We do not care!*** That will not harm us. ***We are returning to our Lord*** in the Next World after we die, no matter how we die.

51. ***We remain hopeful that our Lord will forgive us our mistakes for being the first of the believers*** in our time.'

52. ***We revealed to Mūsā*** – after two years during which he stayed there, calling them to the Truth by the Signs of Allah, which only increased them in insolence – ***'Travel with Our slaves*** (the tribe of Israel) ***by night*** towards the sea. ***You will certainly be pursued.*** Pharaoh and his armies will follow you there and I will save you and drown them.'

53. When he heard that they had set out, ***Pharaoh sent marshals into the cities:*** It is said that there were one thousand cities and ten thousand towns. They were to marshal the people, saying:

54. ***'These people are a small group*** – and it is said that they were 670,000 whereas the vanguard of Pharaoh's army was 700,000, so they were few in comparison with Pharaoh's army –

55. ***...and we find them irritating*** in what they do,

56. ***...and we constitute a vigilant*** (read as *ḥādhirūna,* meaning ready and prepared, and also *ḥadhirūna* which means alert) ***majority.'***

57. Allah says: ***We expelled them*** (Pharaoh and his people) ***from gardens and springs*** – in their pursuit of Mūsā and his people. They had gardens beside the Nile, and streams from the Nile ran through their houses;

58. ***...from treasures*** – apparent wealth of gold and silver, which is called "treasure" because Allah's right on it had not been paid – ***and a splendid situation*** – a good assembly for commanders and ministers surrounded by their followers.

59. ***So it was*** – a reference to their expulsion from Egypt; ***and We bequeathed them to the tribe of Israel*** after Pharaoh and his people were drowned.

60. ***So they pursued them towards the east,*** catching them up just as the sun was rising,

61. ***...and when the two hosts came into sight of one another, Mūsā's companions said, 'We will surely be overtaken*** and do not have sufficient strength to resist them*!'*

62. ***He*** (Mūsā) ***said, 'Never!*** They will not catch us. ***My Lord is with me*** to help me ***and He will guide me*** on the path to safety.*'*

63. Allah says: ***So We revealed to Mūsā, 'Strike the sea with your staff;'*** he struck it – ***and it split in two*** – revealing twelve paths, ***each part like a towering cliff***: the two sides of the sea towered above them on either side, not wetting the saddle or garment of any rider.

64. ***And We brought the others*** (Pharaoh and his people) ***right up to it*** – so that they could start to follow the paths the tribe of Israel had taken.

65. ***We rescued Mūsā and all those who were with him*** and they emerged from the sea safely.

66. ***Then We drowned the rest*** (Pharaoh and his people) – because the sea came down on them when they had all entered it and the tribe of Israel had emerged from it.

67. ***There is certainly a Sign*** and lesson ***in that*** – the drowning of Pharaoh and his people, ***yet most of them are not believers*** in Allah. Exceptions were Āsiya, the wife of Pharaoh, Ḥizqīl, the believer of the family of Pharaoh, and Maryam bint Nāmūṣī who had directed people to the greatness of Yūsuf, peace be upon him.

68. ***Truly your Lord is the Almighty, the Most Merciful.*** His might was indicated in this instance by His taking revenge on the idolaters by drowning them and His mercy towards the believers by saving them from drowning.

69. ***Recite to them*** (the people of Makka) ***the story of Ibrāhīm...***

70. ***...when he said to his father and his people, 'What do you worship?'***

71. ***They said, 'We worship idols and will continue to cling to them.'*** They clearly stated what they did in the hope that they would look favourably on them. They added their determination to continue doing it as a boast.

72. ***He said, 'Do they hear you when you call...***

يُحۡيِينِ ٨١ وَٱلَّذِيٓ أَطۡمَعُ أَن يَغۡفِرَ لِي خَطِيٓـَٔتِي يَوۡمَ ٱلدِّينِ
٨٢ رَبِّ هَبۡ لِي حُكۡمٗا وَأَلۡحِقۡنِي بِٱلصَّٰلِحِينَ ٨٣
وَٱجۡعَل لِّي لِسَانَ صِدۡقٖ فِي ٱلۡأٓخِرِينَ ٨٤ وَٱجۡعَلۡنِي مِن وَرَثَةِ جَنَّةِ
ٱلنَّعِيمِ ٨٥ وَٱغۡفِرۡ لِأَبِيٓ إِنَّهُۥ كَانَ مِنَ ٱلضَّآلِّينَ ٨٦ وَلَا تُخۡزِنِي يَوۡمَ
يُبۡعَثُونَ ٨٧ يَوۡمَ لَا يَنفَعُ مَالٞ وَلَا بَنُونَ ٨٨ إِلَّا مَنۡ أَتَى ٱللَّهَ بِقَلۡبٖ
سَلِيمٖ ٨٩ وَأُزۡلِفَتِ ٱلۡجَنَّةُ لِلۡمُتَّقِينَ ٩٠ وَبُرِّزَتِ ٱلۡجَحِيمُ لِلۡغَاوِينَ
٩١ وَقِيلَ لَهُمۡ أَيۡنَ مَا كُنتُمۡ تَعۡبُدُونَ ٩٢ مِن دُونِ ٱللَّهِ هَلۡ يَنصُرُونَكُمۡ
أَوۡ يَنتَصِرُونَ ٩٣ فَكُبۡكِبُواْ فِيهَا هُمۡ وَٱلۡغَاوُۥنَ ٩٤ وَجُنُودُ إِبۡلِيسَ
أَجۡمَعُونَ ٩٥ قَالُواْ وَهُمۡ فِيهَا يَخۡتَصِمُونَ ٩٦ تَٱللَّهِ إِن كُنَّا لَفِي
ضَلَٰلٖ مُّبِينٍ ٩٧ إِذۡ نُسَوِّيكُم بِرَبِّ ٱلۡعَٰلَمِينَ ٩٨ وَمَآ أَضَلَّنَآ
إِلَّا ٱلۡمُجۡرِمُونَ ٩٩ فَمَا لَنَا مِن شَٰفِعِينَ ١٠٠ وَلَا صَدِيقٍ حَمِيمٖ ١٠١
فَلَوۡ أَنَّ لَنَا كَرَّةٗ فَنَكُونَ مِنَ ٱلۡمُؤۡمِنِينَ ١٠٢ إِنَّ فِي ذَٰلِكَ لَأٓيَةٗۖ وَمَا كَانَ
أَكۡثَرُهُم مُّؤۡمِنِينَ ١٠٣ وَإِنَّ رَبَّكَ لَهُوَ ٱلۡعَزِيزُ ٱلرَّحِيمُ ١٠٤ كَذَّبَتۡ
قَوۡمُ نُوحٍ ٱلۡمُرۡسَلِينَ ١٠٥ إِذۡ قَالَ لَهُمۡ أَخُوهُمۡ نُوحٌ أَلَا تَتَّقُونَ ١٠٦
إِنِّي لَكُمۡ رَسُولٌ أَمِينٞ ١٠٧ فَٱتَّقُواْ ٱللَّهَ وَأَطِيعُونِ ١٠٨ وَمَآ أَسۡـَٔلُكُمۡ
عَلَيۡهِ مِنۡ أَجۡرٍۖ إِنۡ أَجۡرِيَ إِلَّا عَلَىٰ رَبِّ ٱلۡعَٰلَمِينَ ١٠٩ فَٱتَّقُواْ ٱللَّهَ
وَأَطِيعُونِ ١١٠ ۞ قَالُوٓاْ أَنُؤۡمِنُ لَكَ وَٱتَّبَعَكَ ٱلۡأَرۡذَلُونَ ١١١
قَالَ وَمَا عِلۡمِي بِمَا كَانُواْ يَعۡمَلُونَ ١١٢ إِنۡ حِسَابُهُمۡ إِلَّا عَلَىٰ رَبِّيۖ
لَوۡ تَشۡعُرُونَ ١١٣ وَمَآ أَنَا۠ بِطَارِدِ ٱلۡمُؤۡمِنِينَ ١١٤ إِنۡ أَنَا۠ إِلَّا نَذِيرٞ مُّبِينٞ
١١٥ قَالُواْ لَئِن لَّمۡ تَنتَهِ يَٰنُوحُ لَتَكُونَنَّ مِنَ ٱلۡمَرۡجُومِينَ ١١٦ قَالَ

73. ***...or do they help you*** – when you worship them ***or do you harm*** when you do not worship them*?'*

74. ***They said, 'No, but this is*** the same as ***what we found our fathers doing.'***

75. ***He said, 'Have you really thought about what you worship...***

76. ***...you and your fathers who came before?***

77. ***They are all my enemies*** and I do not worship them; I worship nothing ***– except for the Lord of all the worlds:***

78. ***He who created me and guides me*** – to His *dīn;*

79. ***He who gives me food and gives me drink;***

80. ***and when I am ill, it is He who heals me;***

81. ***He who will cause my death, then give me life;***

82. ***He who I sincerely hope will forgive my mistakes on the Day of Reckoning*** and Repayment.

83. ***My Lord, give me right judgement*** (knowledge) ***and unite me with the righteous*** (the Prophets)*;*

84. ***...and make me highly esteemed among the later peoples,*** those who will come after me up until the Day of Rising –

85. ***...and make me one of the inheritors of the Garden of Delight*** – among those who are given it*;*

86. ***...and forgive my father*** by turning to him and pardoning him ***– he was one of the misguided.*** This was before it was clear that he was an enemy of Allah as mentioned in *Sūrat at-Tawba* (9:114).

87. ***And do not disgrace me on the Day they are raised up*** at the Resurrection,

88. Allah says of it: ***the Day when neither wealth nor sons will be of any use*** or help to anyone,

89. ***...except to those who come to Allah with sound and flawless hearts*** – free of hypocrisy and *shirk.'* That is the heart of the believer. That will benefit him.

90. ***The Garden will be brought near to those who are godfearing*** and they will see it.

91. ***The Blazing Fire will be displayed to the misled*** (the unbelievers).

92. ***They will be asked, 'Where are those...***

93. ... idols ***you used to worship besides Allah? Can they help you*** against the punishment ***or even help themselves*** against it?' They cannot.

94. ***They will be bundled into it head first, they and the misled,***

95. ***...and every one of Iblis's regiments*** – those who follow him among the men and jinn.

96. ***Arguing in it with one another, they*** (the misled) ***will say*** to those they worshipped:

97. ***'By Allah, we were plainly misguided...***

98. ***...when We equated you with the Lord of all the worlds*** – in terms of worship.

99. ***It was only the evildoers*** – referring either to the shayṭāns or to those who ruled them and whom they followed – ***who misled us*** away from guidance,

100. ***...and now we have no one to intercede for us*** – whereas the believers have the angels, Prophets and other believers;

101. ***...we do not have a single loyal friend*** who is concerned about us.

102. ***If only we could have another chance*** to return to the world – ***then we would be among the believers!'*** This is wishful thinking expressed by them.

103 ***There is certainly a Sign in that*** which has been mentioned about the story of Ibrāhīm and his people – ***yet most of them are not believers.***

104. ***Truly your Lord is the Almighty, the Most Merciful.***

105. The people of Nūḥ denied the Messengers by denying Nūḥ, who had been among them for such a long time that it was as if he were several messengers; or possibly their denial of him was tantamount to denying the rest of the Messengers by virtue of the fact that the basis of their Message is the same.

106. ***When their brother Nūḥ said to them, 'Will you not be godfearing*** and fear Allah?

107. ***I am a faithful Messenger to you*** in conveying to you what I was sent with,

108. ***...so be fearful of Allah and obey me*** by doing what I command you to do in terms of affirming Allah's unity and obeying Him.

109. ***I do not ask you for any wage for*** conveying ***it. My wage*** – and reward ***is the responsibility of no one but the Lord of all the worlds,***

110. ***...so be fearful of Allah and obey me,'*** This is repeated for stress.

111. ***...they said, 'Why should we believe you*** in what you say ***when the vilest people*** – the lowliest, like weavers and shoemakers – ***follow you*** (read as *wattaba'aka* as here and also as *wa atbā'uka,* meaning "your followers are the vilest people)***?'***

112. ***He said, 'What do I know about what they have been doing?***

113. ***Their reckoning is the concern of my Lord alone*** – and He will repay them – ***if you were but aware.*** If you knew that, you would not criticise them.

114. ***I am not going to chase away the believers.***

115. ***I am only a clear warner.'***

116. ***They said, 'Nūḥ, if you do not desist*** from what you are saying to us ***you will be stoned*** with rocks or abuse.***'***

117. ***He*** (Nūḥ) ***said, 'My Lord, my people have denied me...***

118. ***...so make a clear judgement between me and them and rescue me and the believers who are with me.'***

119. Allah said: ***So We rescued him and those with him in the loaded ship*** filled with people, animals, and birds.

120. ***Then afterwards We drowned the rest*** – after saving the believers from their people.

121. ***There is certainly a Sign in that, yet most of them are not believers.***

122. ***Truly your Lord is the Almighty, the Most Merciful.***

123. ***'Ād denied the Messengers...***

124. ***...when their brother Hūd said to them, 'Will you not be godfearing?***

125. ***I am a faithful Messenger to you...***

126. ***...so be fearful of Allah and obey me.***

رَبِّ إِنَّ قَوْمِى كَذَّبُونِ ﴿١١٧﴾ فَٱفْتَحْ بَيْنِى وَبَيْنَهُمْ فَتْحًا وَنَجِّنِى وَمَن
مَّعِىَ مِنَ ٱلْمُؤْمِنِينَ ﴿١١٨﴾ فَأَنجَيْنَٰهُ وَمَن مَّعَهُۥ فِى ٱلْفُلْكِ ٱلْمَشْحُونِ
﴿١١٩﴾ ثُمَّ أَغْرَقْنَا بَعْدُ ٱلْبَاقِينَ ﴿١٢٠﴾ إِنَّ فِى ذَٰلِكَ لَءَايَةً ۖ وَمَا كَانَ
أَكْثَرُهُم مُّؤْمِنِينَ ﴿١٢١﴾ وَإِنَّ رَبَّكَ لَهُوَ ٱلْعَزِيزُ ٱلرَّحِيمُ ﴿١٢٢﴾ كَذَّبَتْ
عَادٌ ٱلْمُرْسَلِينَ ﴿١٢٣﴾ إِذْ قَالَ لَهُمْ أَخُوهُمْ هُودٌ أَلَا تَتَّقُونَ ﴿١٢٤﴾ إِنِّى لَكُمْ
رَسُولٌ أَمِينٌ ﴿١٢٥﴾ فَٱتَّقُوا۟ ٱللَّهَ وَأَطِيعُونِ ﴿١٢٦﴾ وَمَآ أَسْـَٔلُكُمْ عَلَيْهِ
مِنْ أَجْرٍ ۖ إِنْ أَجْرِىَ إِلَّا عَلَىٰ رَبِّ ٱلْعَٰلَمِينَ ﴿١٢٧﴾ أَتَبْنُونَ بِكُلِّ رِيعٍ
ءَايَةً تَعْبَثُونَ ﴿١٢٨﴾ وَتَتَّخِذُونَ مَصَانِعَ لَعَلَّكُمْ تَخْلُدُونَ ﴿١٢٩﴾
وَإِذَا بَطَشْتُم بَطَشْتُمْ جَبَّارِينَ ﴿١٣٠﴾ فَٱتَّقُوا۟ ٱللَّهَ وَأَطِيعُونِ ﴿١٣١﴾
وَٱتَّقُوا۟ ٱلَّذِىٓ أَمَدَّكُم بِمَا تَعْلَمُونَ ﴿١٣٢﴾ أَمَدَّكُم بِأَنْعَٰمٍ وَبَنِينَ ﴿١٣٣﴾
وَجَنَّٰتٍ وَعُيُونٍ ﴿١٣٤﴾ إِنِّىٓ أَخَافُ عَلَيْكُمْ عَذَابَ يَوْمٍ عَظِيمٍ
﴿١٣٥﴾ قَالُوا۟ سَوَآءٌ عَلَيْنَآ أَوَعَظْتَ أَمْ لَمْ تَكُن مِّنَ ٱلْوَٰعِظِينَ ﴿١٣٦﴾
إِنْ هَٰذَآ إِلَّا خُلُقُ ٱلْأَوَّلِينَ ﴿١٣٧﴾ وَمَا نَحْنُ بِمُعَذَّبِينَ ﴿١٣٨﴾ فَكَذَّبُوهُ
فَأَهْلَكْنَٰهُمْ ۗ إِنَّ فِى ذَٰلِكَ لَءَايَةً ۖ وَمَا كَانَ أَكْثَرُهُم مُّؤْمِنِينَ ﴿١٣٩﴾ وَإِنَّ
رَبَّكَ لَهُوَ ٱلْعَزِيزُ ٱلرَّحِيمُ ﴿١٤٠﴾ كَذَّبَتْ ثَمُودُ ٱلْمُرْسَلِينَ ﴿١٤١﴾ إِذْ قَالَ
لَهُمْ أَخُوهُمْ صَٰلِحٌ أَلَا تَتَّقُونَ ﴿١٤٢﴾ إِنِّى لَكُمْ رَسُولٌ أَمِينٌ ﴿١٤٣﴾
فَٱتَّقُوا۟ ٱللَّهَ وَأَطِيعُونِ ﴿١٤٤﴾ وَمَآ أَسْـَٔلُكُمْ عَلَيْهِ مِنْ أَجْرٍ ۖ إِنْ أَجْرِىَ
إِلَّا عَلَىٰ رَبِّ ٱلْعَٰلَمِينَ ﴿١٤٥﴾ أَتُتْرَكُونَ فِى مَا هَٰهُنَآ ءَامِنِينَ ﴿١٤٦﴾
فِى جَنَّٰتٍ وَعُيُونٍ ﴿١٤٧﴾ وَزُرُوعٍ وَنَخْلٍ طَلْعُهَا هَضِيمٌ ﴿١٤٨﴾
وَتَنْحِتُونَ مِنَ ٱلْجِبَالِ بُيُوتًا فَٰرِهِينَ ﴿١٤٩﴾ فَٱتَّقُوا۟ ٱللَّهَ وَأَطِيعُونِ

127. ***I do not ask you for any wage for it. My wage is the responsibility of no one but the Lord of all the worlds.***

128. ***Do you build a tower on every hilltop, just to amuse yourselves*** at the expense of those who passed by, and to mock at them,

129. ***...and construct great fortresses*** – also said to mean aqueducts – ***hoping to live for ever;***

130. ***...and when you attack*** – by striking or killing people – ***attack as tyrants do*** – without compassion***?***

131. ***So be fearful of Allah*** alone ***and obey me*** in what I command you to do.

132. ***Be fearful of Him who has supplied you with what you know*** – bestowed His blessings on you***:***

133. ***...supplied you with livestock and children,***

134. ***...and gardens and clear springs.***

135. ***I fear for you the punishment of a terrible Day*** both in this world and the Next World, if you disobey me.***'***

136. ***They said, 'It makes no difference to us whether you preach or do not preach*** and admonish; we will not pay any attention to you.

137. ***This is only what the previous peoples*** (read as *khuluq* and *khalq*) ***did.*** What you are trying to frighten us with is only the legends and lies of earlier peoples.

138. ***We are not going to be punished.'***

139. ***So they denied him*** – or the punishment – ***and We destroyed them*** in this world, with a wind***. There is certainly a Sign in that, yet most of them are not believers.***

140. ***Truly your Lord is the Almighty, the Most Merciful.***

141. ***Thamūd denied the Messengers...***

142. ***...when their brother Ṣāliḥ said to them, 'Will you not be godfearing?***

143. ***I am a faithful Messenger to you...***

144. ***...so be fearful of Allah and obey me.***

145. ***I do not ask you for any wage for it. My wage is the responsibility of no one but the Lord of all the worlds.***

﴿١٥٠﴾ وَلَا تُطِيعُوٓا۟ أَمْرَ ٱلْمُسْرِفِينَ ﴿١٥١﴾ ٱلَّذِينَ يُفْسِدُونَ فِى ٱلْأَرْضِ
وَلَا يُصْلِحُونَ ﴿١٥٢﴾ قَالُوٓا۟ إِنَّمَآ أَنتَ مِنَ ٱلْمُسَحَّرِينَ ﴿١٥٣﴾ مَآ أَنتَ
إِلَّا بَشَرٌ مِّثْلُنَا فَأْتِ بِـَٔايَةٍ إِن كُنتَ مِنَ ٱلصَّـٰدِقِينَ ﴿١٥٤﴾ قَالَ
هَـٰذِهِۦ نَاقَةٌ لَّهَا شِرْبٌ وَلَكُمْ شِرْبُ يَوْمٍ مَّعْلُومٍ ﴿١٥٥﴾ وَلَا تَمَسُّوهَا
بِسُوٓءٍ فَيَأْخُذَكُمْ عَذَابُ يَوْمٍ عَظِيمٍ ﴿١٥٦﴾ فَعَقَرُوهَا فَأَصْبَحُوا۟
نَـٰدِمِينَ ﴿١٥٧﴾ فَأَخَذَهُمُ ٱلْعَذَابُ ۗ إِنَّ فِى ذَٰلِكَ لَـَٔايَةً ۖ وَمَا كَانَ
أَكْثَرُهُم مُّؤْمِنِينَ ﴿١٥٨﴾ وَإِنَّ رَبَّكَ لَهُوَ ٱلْعَزِيزُ ٱلرَّحِيمُ ﴿١٥٩﴾
كَذَّبَتْ قَوْمُ لُوطٍ ٱلْمُرْسَلِينَ ﴿١٦٠﴾ إِذْ قَالَ لَهُمْ أَخُوهُمْ لُوطٌ أَلَا تَتَّقُونَ
﴿١٦١﴾ إِنِّى لَكُمْ رَسُولٌ أَمِينٌ ﴿١٦٢﴾ فَٱتَّقُوا۟ ٱللَّهَ وَأَطِيعُونِ ﴿١٦٣﴾ وَمَآ
أَسْـَٔلُكُمْ عَلَيْهِ مِنْ أَجْرٍ ۖ إِنْ أَجْرِىَ إِلَّا عَلَىٰ رَبِّ ٱلْعَـٰلَمِينَ ﴿١٦٤﴾
أَتَأْتُونَ ٱلذُّكْرَانَ مِنَ ٱلْعَـٰلَمِينَ ﴿١٦٥﴾ وَتَذَرُونَ مَا خَلَقَ لَكُمْ رَبُّكُم
مِّنْ أَزْوَٰجِكُم ۚ بَلْ أَنتُمْ قَوْمٌ عَادُونَ ﴿١٦٦﴾ قَالُوا۟ لَئِن لَّمْ تَنتَهِ يَـٰلُوطُ
لَتَكُونَنَّ مِنَ ٱلْمُخْرَجِينَ ﴿١٦٧﴾ قَالَ إِنِّى لِعَمَلِكُم مِّنَ ٱلْقَالِينَ ﴿١٦٨﴾
رَبِّ نَجِّنِى وَأَهْلِى مِمَّا يَعْمَلُونَ ﴿١٦٩﴾ فَنَجَّيْنَـٰهُ وَأَهْلَهُۥٓ أَجْمَعِينَ ﴿١٧٠﴾
إِلَّا عَجُوزًا فِى ٱلْغَـٰبِرِينَ ﴿١٧١﴾ ثُمَّ دَمَّرْنَا ٱلْـَٔاخَرِينَ ﴿١٧٢﴾ وَأَمْطَرْنَا عَلَيْهِم
مَّطَرًا ۖ فَسَآءَ مَطَرُ ٱلْمُنذَرِينَ ﴿١٧٣﴾ إِنَّ فِى ذَٰلِكَ لَـَٔايَةً ۖ وَمَا كَانَ أَكْثَرُهُم
مُّؤْمِنِينَ ﴿١٧٤﴾ وَإِنَّ رَبَّكَ لَهُوَ ٱلْعَزِيزُ ٱلرَّحِيمُ ﴿١٧٥﴾ كَذَّبَ أَصْحَـٰبُ
لْـَٔيْكَةِ ٱلْمُرْسَلِينَ ﴿١٧٦﴾ إِذْ قَالَ لَهُمْ شُعَيْبٌ أَلَا تَتَّقُونَ ﴿١٧٧﴾ إِنِّى لَكُمْ
رَسُولٌ أَمِينٌ ﴿١٧٨﴾ فَٱتَّقُوا۟ ٱللَّهَ وَأَطِيعُونِ ﴿١٧٩﴾ وَمَآ أَسْـَٔلُكُمْ عَلَيْهِ
مِنْ أَجْرٍ ۖ إِنْ أَجْرِىَ إِلَّا عَلَىٰ رَبِّ ٱلْعَـٰلَمِينَ ﴿١٨٠﴾ ۞ أَوْفُوا۟ ٱلْكَيْلَ وَلَا

146. ***Are you going to be left secure amid what is here*** of blessings,

147. ***...amid gardens and clear springs...***

148. ***...and cultivated fields and palms with supple spathes?***

149. ***Will you continue hewing houses from the mountains with exultant skill*** (read as *fariḥīn* meaning "exultant" and *fāriḥīn* meaning "skilful")*?*

150. ***So be fearful of Allah and obey me.***

151. ***Do not obey the orders of the profligate,***

152. ***...those who corrupt the earth*** through acts of disobedience ***and do not put things right*** through acts of obedience.*'*

153. ***They said, 'You are merely someone bewitched*** – greatly, so that your intellect is totally overwhelmed by it.

154. ***You are nothing but a human being like ourselves, so produce a Sign if you are telling the truth*** about your Message.*'*

155. ***He said, 'Here is a she-camel. She has a time for drinking and you have a time for drinking*** – on specified days.

156. ***Do not do anything to harm her or the punishment of a terrible day will come down on you.'***

157. ***But they hamstrung her*** – with the consent of others – ***and woke up full of remorse,***

158. ***...for the*** promised ***punishment did come down on them*** – and so they were destroyed. ***There is certainly a Sign in that, yet most of them are not believers.***

159. ***Truly your Lord is the Almighty, the Most Merciful.***

160. ***The people of Lūṭ denied the Messengers...***

161. ***...when their brother Lūṭ said to them, 'Will you not be god-fearing?***

162. ***I am a faithful Messenger to you,***

163. ***...so be fearful of Allah and obey me.***

164. ***I do not ask you for any wage for it. My wage is the responsibility of no one but the Lord of all the worlds.***

165. ***Of all beings, do you lie with males,***

166. ***...leaving the wives*** – ceasing to have sexual intercourse with women – ***Allah has created for you? You are a people who have***

overstepped the limits.' You have left what is lawful for what is unlawful.

167. ***They said: 'Lūṭ, if you do not desist*** – and stop objecting to us – ***you will be expelled*** from our land.'

168. ***He*** (Lūṭ) ***said, 'I am someone who detests the deed you perpetrate.***

169. ***My Lord, rescue me and my family from*** the punishment for ***what they are doing.'***

170. ***Therefore We rescued him and all his family –***

171. ***...except for an old woman*** (his wife) ***who remained behind*** with those We destroyed.

172. ***Then We utterly destroyed the rest,***

173. ***...and made a Rain*** of stones ***come pouring down upon them. How evil is the rain of those who are warned!***

174. ***There is certainly a Sign in that, yet most of them are not believers.***

175. ***Truly your Lord is the Almighty, the Most Merciful.***

176. ***The Companions of the Thicket*** (read as *layka* and *al-ayka*) – referring to a thicket of trees close to Madyan – ***denied the Messengers...***

177. ***...when Shu'ayb said to them*** – it does not say "their brother" in this instance because he was not one of their tribe – ***'Will you not be godfearing?***

178. ***I am a faithful Messenger to you,***

179. ***...so be fearful of Allah and obey me.***

180. ***I do not ask you for any wage for it. My wage is the responsibility of no one but the Lord of all the worlds.***

181. ***Give full measure. Do not skimp*** by giving short measure*:*

182. ***...but weigh with a level balance.***

183. ***Do not diminish people's goods*** – by giving people less than their full due – ***and do not go about the earth, corrupting it*** by killing and other disruptive actions.

184. ***Be fearful of Him who created you and the earlier creatures.'***

185. ***They said, 'You are merely someone bewitched.***

تَكُونُواْ مِنَ ٱلۡمُخۡسِرِينَ ١٨١ وَزِنُواْ بِٱلۡقِسۡطَاسِ ٱلۡمُسۡتَقِيمِ ١٨٢
وَلَا تَبۡخَسُواْ ٱلنَّاسَ أَشۡيَآءَهُمۡ وَلَا تَعۡثَوۡاْ فِي ٱلۡأَرۡضِ مُفۡسِدِينَ ١٨٣
وَٱتَّقُواْ ٱلَّذِي خَلَقَكُمۡ وَٱلۡجِبِلَّةَ ٱلۡأَوَّلِينَ ١٨٤ قَالُوٓاْ إِنَّمَآ أَنتَ
مِنَ ٱلۡمُسَحَّرِينَ ١٨٥ وَمَآ أَنتَ إِلَّا بَشَرٞ مِّثۡلُنَا وَإِن نَّظُنُّكَ لَمِنَ
ٱلۡكَٰذِبِينَ ١٨٦ فَأَسۡقِطۡ عَلَيۡنَا كِسَفٗا مِّنَ ٱلسَّمَآءِ إِن كُنتَ
مِنَ ٱلصَّٰدِقِينَ ١٨٧ قَالَ رَبِّيٓ أَعۡلَمُ بِمَا تَعۡمَلُونَ ١٨٨ فَكَذَّبُوهُ
فَأَخَذَهُمۡ عَذَابُ يَوۡمِ ٱلظُّلَّةِۚ إِنَّهُۥ كَانَ عَذَابَ يَوۡمٍ عَظِيمٍ ١٨٩
إِنَّ فِي ذَٰلِكَ لَأٓيَةٗۖ وَمَا كَانَ أَكۡثَرُهُم مُّؤۡمِنِينَ ١٩٠ وَإِنَّ رَبَّكَ لَهُوَ
ٱلۡعَزِيزُ ٱلرَّحِيمُ ١٩١ وَإِنَّهُۥ لَتَنزِيلُ رَبِّ ٱلۡعَٰلَمِينَ ١٩٢ نَزَلَ بِهِ ٱلرُّوحُ
ٱلۡأَمِينُ ١٩٣ عَلَىٰ قَلۡبِكَ لِتَكُونَ مِنَ ٱلۡمُنذِرِينَ ١٩٤ بِلِسَانٍ عَرَبِيّٖ
مُّبِينٖ ١٩٥ وَإِنَّهُۥ لَفِي زُبُرِ ٱلۡأَوَّلِينَ ١٩٦ أَوَلَمۡ يَكُن لَّهُمۡ ءَايَةً أَن يَعۡلَمَهُۥ
عُلَمَٰٓؤُاْ بَنِيٓ إِسۡرَٰٓءِيلَ ١٩٧ وَلَوۡ نَزَّلۡنَٰهُ عَلَىٰ بَعۡضِ ٱلۡأَعۡجَمِينَ ١٩٨
فَقَرَأَهُۥ عَلَيۡهِم مَّا كَانُواْ بِهِۦ مُؤۡمِنِينَ ١٩٩ كَذَٰلِكَ سَلَكۡنَٰهُ
فِي قُلُوبِ ٱلۡمُجۡرِمِينَ ٢٠٠ لَا يُؤۡمِنُونَ بِهِۦ حَتَّىٰ يَرَوُاْ ٱلۡعَذَابَ
ٱلۡأَلِيمَ ٢٠١ فَيَأۡتِيَهُم بَغۡتَةٗ وَهُمۡ لَا يَشۡعُرُونَ ٢٠٢ فَيَقُولُواْ
هَلۡ نَحۡنُ مُنظَرُونَ ٢٠٣ أَفَبِعَذَابِنَا يَسۡتَعۡجِلُونَ ٢٠٤ أَفَرَءَيۡتَ
إِن مَّتَّعۡنَٰهُمۡ سِنِينَ ٢٠٥ ثُمَّ جَآءَهُم مَّا كَانُواْ يُوعَدُونَ ٢٠٦
مَآ أَغۡنَىٰ عَنۡهُم مَّا كَانُواْ يُمَتَّعُونَ ٢٠٧ وَمَآ أَهۡلَكۡنَا مِن قَرۡيَةٍ إِلَّا
لَهَا مُنذِرُونَ ٢٠٨ ذِكۡرَىٰ وَمَا كُنَّا ظَٰلِمِينَ ٢٠٩ وَمَا تَنَزَّلَتۡ بِهِ
ٱلشَّيَٰطِينُ ٢١٠ وَمَا يَنۢبَغِي لَهُمۡ وَمَا يَسۡتَطِيعُونَ ٢١١ إِنَّهُمۡ

186. ***You are nothing but a human being like ourselves. We think you are a liar.***

187. ***So make lumps*** (read as *kisaf* and *kisf*) ***from heaven fall down on us if you are telling the truth*** about your Message.'

188. ***He said, 'My Lord knows best what you are doing*** – and He will repay you.'

189. ***They denied him and the punishment of the Day of Shadow came down on them.*** This refers to a cloud which shaded them after a terrible heat had afflicted then and then rained down fire on them and they were burned up. ***It was indeed the punishment of a terrible Day.***

190. ***There is certainly a Sign in that, yet most of them are not believers.***

191. ***Truly your Lord is the Almighty, the Most Merciful.***

192. ***Truly it*** (the Qur'an) ***is Revelation sent down by the Lord of all the worlds.***

193. ***The Faithful* Rūḥ** (read as *ar-rūhū al-amīnu* and *ar-ruḥa al-amina*) – meaning Jibrīl – ***brought it down*** (read as *nazala* and also *nazzala,* in which case the meaning becomes: "He sent down the Faithful *Rūh* with it")…

194. ***…to your heart so you might be one of the Warners…***

195. ***… in a clear Arabic tongue.***

196. ***It*** – clearly referring to the Qur'an, which was revealed to Muḥammad – ***is certainly in the scriptures of the previous peoples*** – such as the Torah and the Gospel.

197. ***Is it*** (read as *yakun* and *takun*) ***not indeed a Sign for them*** (the unbelievers of Makka) ***that the scholars of the tribe of Israel*** – such as 'Abdullāh ibn Salām and his companions who believed (in Islam) – ***have knowledge of it?*** They told people about it.

198. ***If We had sent it down to a non-Arab…***

199. ***…who had then recited it to them*** (the unbelievers of Makka), ***they still would not believe in it.***

200. ***That is how We thread it*** – your claim that it comes from a non-Arab – ***into the hearts of the evildoers*** (the unbelievers of Makka).

This sort of thing entered their hearts when the Prophet, may Allah bless him and grant him peace, recited the Qur'an.

201. ***They will not believe in it until they see the painful punish - ment.***

202. ***It will come upon them suddenly when they are not expecting it.***

203. ***They will say, 'Can we be granted a reprieve*** to give us time to believe***?'*** The answer will be 'No.'

204. They say, "When is this punishment coming?" Allah says to them: ***Do they want to hasten Our punishment?***

205. Tell me: ***Do you think, if We let them enjoy themselves for years…***

206. ***…and then what they were promised*** by way of punishment ***comes to them,***

207. ***…that what they enjoyed will be of any use to them*** – in terms of repelling the punishment it or lightening it***?*** This means that nothing will be of any use.

208. ***We have never destroyed a city without giving it prior warning*** – sending a Messenger to warn its inhabitants **–**

209. ***…as a reminder*** and warning to them**.** ***We were never unjust*** – because We have only ever destroyed people after warning them first**.**

210. Then Allah reveals, in order to refute the idolators: ***The shayṭāns did not bring it*** (the Qur'an) ***down.***

211. ***It does not befit them and they are not capable of it.***

212. ***They are debarred from hearing it*** – prevented from hearing the words of the angels by meteors**.**

213. ***So do not call on any other god along with Allah, or you will be among those who will be punished*** – if you do what they invite you to do**.**

214. ***Warn your near relatives.*** This refers to the Banū Hāshim and Banū'l-Muṭṭalib. As is reported in al-Bukhārī and Muslim, "he called them openly [to Islam]."

215. ***…and take the believers who follow you under your wing.*** Be gentle to those who affirm Allah's unity.

عَنِ ٱلسَّمْعِ لَمَعْزُولُونَ ﴿٢١٢﴾ فَلَا تَدْعُ مَعَ ٱللَّهِ إِلَٰهًا ءَاخَرَ فَتَكُونَ
مِنَ ٱلْمُعَذَّبِينَ ﴿٢١٣﴾ وَأَنذِرْ عَشِيرَتَكَ ٱلْأَقْرَبِينَ ﴿٢١٤﴾ وَٱخْفِضْ
جَنَاحَكَ لِمَنِ ٱتَّبَعَكَ مِنَ ٱلْمُؤْمِنِينَ ﴿٢١٥﴾ فَإِنْ عَصَوْكَ فَقُلْ إِنِّى
بَرِىٓءٌ مِّمَّا تَعْمَلُونَ ﴿٢١٦﴾ وَتَوَكَّلْ عَلَى ٱلْعَزِيزِ ٱلرَّحِيمِ ﴿٢١٧﴾ ٱلَّذِى
يَرَىٰكَ حِينَ تَقُومُ ﴿٢١٨﴾ وَتَقَلُّبَكَ فِى ٱلسَّٰجِدِينَ ﴿٢١٩﴾ إِنَّهُۥ هُوَ ٱلسَّمِيعُ
ٱلْعَلِيمُ ﴿٢٢٠﴾ هَلْ أُنَبِّئُكُمْ عَلَىٰ مَن تَنَزَّلُ ٱلشَّيَٰطِينُ ﴿٢٢١﴾ تَنَزَّلُ عَلَىٰ
كُلِّ أَفَّاكٍ أَثِيمٍ ﴿٢٢٢﴾ يُلْقُونَ ٱلسَّمْعَ وَأَكْثَرُهُمْ كَٰذِبُونَ ﴿٢٢٣﴾
وَٱلشُّعَرَآءُ يَتَّبِعُهُمُ ٱلْغَاوُۥنَ ﴿٢٢٤﴾ أَلَمْ تَرَ أَنَّهُمْ فِى كُلِّ وَادٍ
يَهِيمُونَ ﴿٢٢٥﴾ وَأَنَّهُمْ يَقُولُونَ مَا لَا يَفْعَلُونَ ﴿٢٢٦﴾ إِلَّا ٱلَّذِينَ
ءَامَنُوا۟ وَعَمِلُوا۟ ٱلصَّٰلِحَٰتِ وَذَكَرُوا۟ ٱللَّهَ كَثِيرًا وَٱنتَصَرُوا۟ مِنۢ
بَعْدِ مَا ظُلِمُوا۟ ۗ وَسَيَعْلَمُ ٱلَّذِينَ ظَلَمُوٓا۟ أَىَّ مُنقَلَبٍ يَنقَلِبُونَ ﴿٢٢٧﴾

216. ***If they*** (your tribe) ***disobey you, say, 'I am free of what you do*** – from your worship of other than Allah.'

217. ***Put your trust*** (read as *fa-tawakkil* and *wa-tawakkil*) ***in the Almighty, the Most Merciful:*** entrust all your affairs to Him,

218. ***He who sees you when you stand up to pray,***

219. ***...and your movements with those who prostrate*** – meaning those who pray. This refers to the core elements of the prayer: standing, sitting, bowing and prostrating.

220. ***He is the All-Hearing, the All-Knowing.***

221. ***Shall I tell you,*** unbelievers of Makka, ***whom the shayṭāns descend upon?***

222. ***They descend on every evil liar***: every impious liar, such as Musaylima and other soothsayers.

223. ***They*** (the *shayṭāns*) ***give them*** (the soothsayers) ***a hearing*** – telling them what they heard from the angels – ***and most of them are liars*** – adding many lies to what they heard. This was before the *shayṭāns* were barred from the heavens.

224. ***And as for poets, it is the misled who follow them*** in their poetry, repeating it and relating it from them; and so they also are blameworthy.

225. ***Do you not see how they ramble on in every style*** – literally "in every valley," which here means every style and form of speech. They proceed and exceed the limits in their eulogies and satires –

226. ***...and say things which they do not do*** – such as: "We have done such-and-such," when they have not and so they are lying –

227. ***...except those*** poets ***who believe and do right actions and remember Allah repeatedly*** – so that their poetry does not distract them from remembering Allah – ***and defend themselves***, by using satire themselves, ***after they have been wronged*** by the unbelievers satirising them as believers? They are not blameworthy then. Allah says, *"Allah does not like evil words to be voiced out loud, except in the case of someone who has been wronged."* (4:148) He also says, *"So if anyone oversteps the limits against you, overstep against him the same as he did to you."* (2:194) ***Those*** poets and others ***who do wrong will soon know the kind of reversal they will receive*** – and where they will return to after they die.

سُورَةُ النَّمْلِ

بِسْمِ ٱللَّهِ ٱلرَّحْمَٰنِ ٱلرَّحِيمِ

طسٓۚ تِلْكَ ءَايَٰتُ ٱلْقُرْءَانِ وَكِتَابٍ مُّبِينٍ ١ هُدًى وَبُشْرَىٰ
لِلْمُؤْمِنِينَ ٢ ٱلَّذِينَ يُقِيمُونَ ٱلصَّلَوٰةَ وَيُؤْتُونَ ٱلزَّكَوٰةَ وَهُم
بِٱلْءَاخِرَةِ هُمْ يُوقِنُونَ ٣ إِنَّ ٱلَّذِينَ لَا يُؤْمِنُونَ بِٱلْءَاخِرَةِ زَيَّنَّا لَهُمْ
أَعْمَٰلَهُمْ فَهُمْ يَعْمَهُونَ ٤ أُوْلَٰٓئِكَ ٱلَّذِينَ لَهُمْ سُوٓءُ ٱلْعَذَابِ
وَهُمْ فِى ٱلْءَاخِرَةِ هُمُ ٱلْأَخْسَرُونَ ٥ وَإِنَّكَ لَتُلَقَّى ٱلْقُرْءَانَ مِن
لَّدُنْ حَكِيمٍ عَلِيمٍ ٦ إِذْ قَالَ مُوسَىٰ لِأَهْلِهِۦٓ إِنِّىٓ ءَانَسْتُ نَارًا سَـَٔاتِيكُم
مِّنْهَا بِخَبَرٍ أَوْ ءَاتِيكُم بِشِهَابٍ قَبَسٍ لَّعَلَّكُمْ تَصْطَلُونَ ٧ فَلَمَّا
جَآءَهَا نُودِىَ أَنۢ بُورِكَ مَن فِى ٱلنَّارِ وَمَنْ حَوْلَهَا وَسُبْحَٰنَ ٱللَّهِ رَبِّ
ٱلْعَٰلَمِينَ ٨ يَٰمُوسَىٰٓ إِنَّهُۥٓ أَنَا ٱللَّهُ ٱلْعَزِيزُ ٱلْحَكِيمُ ٩ وَأَلْقِ عَصَاكَۚ
فَلَمَّا رَءَاهَا تَهْتَزُّ كَأَنَّهَا جَآنٌّ وَلَّىٰ مُدْبِرًا وَلَمْ يُعَقِّبْۚ يَٰمُوسَىٰ لَا تَخَفْ
إِنِّى لَا يَخَافُ لَدَىَّ ٱلْمُرْسَلُونَ ١٠ إِلَّا مَن ظَلَمَ ثُمَّ بَدَّلَ حُسْنًۢا بَعْدَ
سُوٓءٍ فَإِنِّى غَفُورٌ رَّحِيمٌ ١١ وَأَدْخِلْ يَدَكَ فِى جَيْبِكَ تَخْرُجْ بَيْضَآءَ
مِنْ غَيْرِ سُوٓءٍۖ فِى تِسْعِ ءَايَٰتٍ إِلَىٰ فِرْعَوْنَ وَقَوْمِهِۦٓۚ إِنَّهُمْ كَانُوا۟ قَوْمًا فَٰسِقِينَ
١٢ فَلَمَّا جَآءَتْهُمْ ءَايَٰتُنَا مُبْصِرَةً قَالُوا۟ هَٰذَا سِحْرٌ مُّبِينٌ ١٣
وَجَحَدُوا۟ بِهَا وَٱسْتَيْقَنَتْهَآ أَنفُسُهُمْ ظُلْمًا وَعُلُوًّاۚ فَٱنظُرْ كَيْفَ
كَانَ عَٰقِبَةُ ٱلْمُفْسِدِينَ ١٤ وَلَقَدْ ءَاتَيْنَا دَاوُۥدَ وَسُلَيْمَٰنَ عِلْمًاۖ
وَقَالَا ٱلْحَمْدُ لِلَّهِ ٱلَّذِى فَضَّلَنَا عَلَىٰ كَثِيرٍ مِّنْ عِبَادِهِ ٱلْمُؤْمِنِينَ ١٥
وَوَرِثَ سُلَيْمَٰنُ دَاوُۥدَۖ وَقَالَ يَٰٓأَيُّهَا ٱلنَّاسُ عُلِّمْنَا مَنطِقَ ٱلطَّيْرِ

27. *Sūrat an-Naml*
The Ant

This *sūra* is Makkan. It has 93, 94 or 95 *āyat*s and was sent down after *Sūrat ash-Shu'arā'*.

1. ***Ta Sin.*** Allah knows best what the letters mean. ***Those** āyat*s ***are the Signs of the Qur'an and a Clear Book*** – which makes the truth clear from falsehood.

2. ***It is guidance*** from misguidance ***and good news*** of the Garden ***for the believers:***

3. ***...those who establish the prayer*** – as is obligatory – ***and pay zakāt*** – as is obligatory – ***and are certain about the Next World*** – and know by deduction that there is a Hereafter. The pronoun "they" is repeated to distinguish the reports.

4. ***As for those who do not believe in the Next World, We have made their*** ugly ***actions*** – instigated by their lower appetites – ***appear good to them, and they wander about blindly*** – confused about them, because they consider them good whereas Allah does not.

5. ***Such people will receive an evil punishment*** – and the worst of it in this world is killing and capture – ***and will be the greatest losers in the Next World*** – where they will be eternally in the Fire.

6. ***You receive the Qur'an directly*** – taking it firmly – ***from One who is All-Wise, All-Knowing.*** This is addressed to the Prophet, may Allah bless him and grant him peace.

7. Remember ***when Mūsā said to his household*** – to his wife, while he was travelling from Madyan to Egypt, ***'I can make out a fire*** in the distance. ***I will bring you news from it*** – about the route, because he was lost – ***or at least a burning brand*** (read as *shihābin qabasin* and *shihābi qabsin)* with which to light a fire ***so that perhaps you will be able to warm yourselves.'***

8. ***But when he reached it, a voice called out to him, 'Blessed be*** (may Allah bless) ***whoever*** – referring to Mūsā – ***is in the fire and whoever*** – referring to angels – ***is around it.*** Or else it means the angels who are in the fire and Mūsā who is beside it. ***Glory be to***

Allah, the Lord of all the worlds! These words are part of what was called out. It means that Allah is exalted above having any equal.

9. ***Mūsā, I am Allah, the Almighty, the All-Wise.***

10. ***Throw down your staff.' Then when he saw it*** moving and ***slithering like a snake, he turned and fled and did not turn back again.*** Allah said: ***'Have no fear, Mūsā. In My Presence the Messengers have no fear*** of snakes or anything else,

11. ***...except for one who did wrong and then*** repented and ***changed evil into good – for I am Ever-Forgiving, Most Merciful.*** I accept repentance and forgive wrong actions.

12. ***Put your hand inside your shirt front. It will emerge pure white*** rather than its normal brownish colour, pure white with a luminescence which dazzled the eyes, ***yet quite unharmed – one of nine Signs*** with which he was sent ***to Pharaoh and his people. They are a people of deviators.'***

13. ***When Our Signs came to them in all their*** luminous ***clarity, they said, 'This is*** only ***downright magic,'***

14. ***...and they repudiated*** and denied ***them wrongly and haughtily, in spite of their own certainty about them*** – that the Signs were from Allah; they were too proud to believe in what Mūsā had brought. ***See,*** Muḥammad, ***the final fate*** (destruction) ***of the corrupters!***

15. ***We gave knowledge to Dāwūd and Sulaymān*** son of Dāwūd – knowledge of judgement, of the speech of the birds and many other things – ***who said*** – to thank Allah – ***'Praise be to Allah who has favoured us*** – with Prophethood and mastery over the jinn, men and shayṭāns – ***over many of His slaves who are believers.'***

16. ***Sulaymān was Dāwūd's heir*** in respect of Prophethood and knowledge, to the exclusion of the rest of his children. ***He said, 'Mankind, we have been taught the speech of birds*** – and understanding of them – ***and we have been given everything*** that Prophets and kings are given. ***This is indeed a manifest blessing.'***

17. ***Sulaymān's troops, made up of jinn and men and birds, were assembled for him, paraded in tight ranks*** ready to march.

18. ***Then, when they reached the Valley of the Ants*** – a place either at Ta'if or in Syria, ***an ant*** – the queen of the ants, when she saw

وَأُوتِينَا مِن كُلِّ شَيْءٍ إِنَّ هَٰذَا لَهُوَ ٱلْفَضْلُ ٱلْمُبِينُ ﴿١٦﴾ وَحُشِرَ
لِسُلَيْمَٰنَ جُنُودُهُۥ مِنَ ٱلْجِنِّ وَٱلْإِنسِ وَٱلطَّيْرِ فَهُمْ يُوزَعُونَ ﴿١٧﴾
حَتَّىٰٓ إِذَآ أَتَوْا۟ عَلَىٰ وَادِ ٱلنَّمْلِ قَالَتْ نَمْلَةٌ يَٰٓأَيُّهَا ٱلنَّمْلُ ٱدْخُلُوا۟
مَسَٰكِنَكُمْ لَا يَحْطِمَنَّكُمْ سُلَيْمَٰنُ وَجُنُودُهُۥ وَهُمْ لَا يَشْعُرُونَ
﴿١٨﴾ فَتَبَسَّمَ ضَاحِكًا مِّن قَوْلِهَا وَقَالَ رَبِّ أَوْزِعْنِىٓ أَنْ أَشْكُرَ
نِعْمَتَكَ ٱلَّتِىٓ أَنْعَمْتَ عَلَىَّ وَعَلَىٰ وَٰلِدَىَّ وَأَنْ أَعْمَلَ صَٰلِحًا
تَرْضَىٰهُ وَأَدْخِلْنِى بِرَحْمَتِكَ فِى عِبَادِكَ ٱلصَّٰلِحِينَ ﴿١٩﴾
وَتَفَقَّدَ ٱلطَّيْرَ فَقَالَ مَا لِىَ لَآ أَرَى ٱلْهُدْهُدَ أَمْ كَانَ مِنَ
ٱلْغَآئِبِينَ ﴿٢٠﴾ لَأُعَذِّبَنَّهُۥ عَذَابًا شَدِيدًا أَوْ لَأَا۟ذْبَحَنَّهُۥٓ
أَوْ لَيَأْتِيَنِّى بِسُلْطَٰنٍ مُّبِينٍ ﴿٢١﴾ فَمَكَثَ غَيْرَ بَعِيدٍ فَقَالَ
أَحَطتُ بِمَا لَمْ تُحِطْ بِهِۦ وَجِئْتُكَ مِن سَبَإٍۭ بِنَبَإٍ يَقِينٍ ﴿٢٢﴾
إِنِّى وَجَدتُّ ٱمْرَأَةً تَمْلِكُهُمْ وَأُوتِيَتْ مِن كُلِّ شَيْءٍ وَلَهَا
عَرْشٌ عَظِيمٌ ﴿٢٣﴾ وَجَدتُّهَا وَقَوْمَهَا يَسْجُدُونَ لِلشَّمْسِ مِن
دُونِ ٱللَّهِ وَزَيَّنَ لَهُمُ ٱلشَّيْطَٰنُ أَعْمَٰلَهُمْ فَصَدَّهُمْ عَنِ ٱلسَّبِيلِ
فَهُمْ لَا يَهْتَدُونَ ﴿٢٤﴾ أَلَّا يَسْجُدُوا۟ لِلَّهِ ٱلَّذِى يُخْرِجُ ٱلْخَبْءَ
فِى ٱلسَّمَٰوَٰتِ وَٱلْأَرْضِ وَيَعْلَمُ مَا تُخْفُونَ وَمَا تُعْلِنُونَ ﴿٢٥﴾ ٱللَّهُ
لَآ إِلَٰهَ إِلَّا هُوَ رَبُّ ٱلْعَرْشِ ٱلْعَظِيمِ ۩ ﴿٢٦﴾ ۞ قَالَ سَنَنظُرُ
أَصَدَقْتَ أَمْ كُنتَ مِنَ ٱلْكَٰذِبِينَ ﴿٢٧﴾ ٱذْهَب بِّكِتَٰبِى هَٰذَا
فَأَلْقِهْ إِلَيْهِمْ ثُمَّ تَوَلَّ عَنْهُمْ فَٱنظُرْ مَاذَا يَرْجِعُونَ ﴿٢٨﴾ قَالَتْ يَٰٓأَيُّهَا
ٱلْمَلَؤُا۟ إِنِّىٓ أُلْقِىَ إِلَىَّ كِتَٰبٌ كَرِيمٌ ﴿٢٩﴾ إِنَّهُۥ مِن سُلَيْمَٰنَ وَإِنَّهُۥ بِسْمِ

Sulaymān's armies – ***said, 'Ants, enter your dwellings so that Sulaymān and his troops do not crush you unwittingly.'*** The form of direct speech used for intelligent beings is employed because the ant commanded them to do what those with sentience are commanded to do.

19. ***He*** (Sulaymān) ***smiled*** when he heard it at a distance of three miles because the wind had carried its voice, ***laughing at its words, and*** – halting his army, both cavalry and infantry – ***said, 'My Lord,*** inspire me and ***keep me thankful for the blessing You have bestowed on me and on my parents. Keep me acting rightly, pleasing You, and admit me, by Your mercy, among Your slaves who are righteous*** (the Prophets and *awliyā'*)***.'***

20. ***He inspected the birds and said, 'How is it that I do not see the hoopoe?*** The hoopoe can see water under the earth and directs people to it by pecking at the earth where it is. Then the *shayṭāns* could dig and bring it out when Sulaymān needed it for the prayer. When he could not see it, he said this. ***Or is it absent without leave?***

21. When he realised it actually was absent, he said: ***I will certainly punish it most severely*** – by plucking out its feathers and tail and then placing it in the sun so that it will not be able to defend itself against vermin – ***or slaughter it*** – by cutting its throat – ***if it does not bring me clear authority*** – evidence to support its excuse for being absent.***'***

22. ***However, it was not long delayed*** (read as *makatha* and *makutha*) – it was only a little late and came humbly to Sulaymān, raising its head and dropping its tail and wings. He excused it and asked about what had occurred while it was absent – ***and then it said, 'I have comprehended something which you have not, and bring you accurate intelligence from Sheba*** (Sabā') – the name of a tribe in Yemen named after their founding ancestor.

23. ***I found a woman ruling over them*** – a Queen named Bilqīs – ***who has been given everything*** that a sovereign needs in terms of accoutrements and other things. ***She possesses a mighty throne.*** Her throne was eighty cubits tall and forty cubits wide. It was raised up thirty cubits and made of gold and silver adorned with pearls, rubies, green topaz and emeralds. Its legs were made of red rubies, green topaz and emerald. There were seven anterooms leading up to it, each with a locked door.

24. ***I found both her and her people prostrating to the sun instead of Allah. Shayṭān has made their actions seem good to them and debarred them from the Way*** of Truth, ***so they are not guided…***

25. ***…and do not prostrate to Allah, Who brings out what is hidden*** – of the rain and plants – ***in the heavens and the earth, and knows what you conceal*** in your hearts ***and what you divulge*** on your tongue.

26. Allah – there is no god but Him – the Lord of the Mighty Throne.' The Throne of the All-Merciful is incomparably greater than the throne of Bilqīs.

27. ***He*** (Sulaymān) ***said*** to the hoopoe, ***'We shall soon see if you have told the truth or are a liar.'*** The hoopoe showed them where some water was and they drank and perfumed *wuḍū'* and prayed. Then Sulaymān wrote a letter which said: "From the slave of Allah, Sulaymān son of Dāwūd, to Bilqīs, the Queen of Sheba. In the Name of Allah, the All-Merciful, Most Merciful. Peace be upon whoever follows true guidance. Following on from that: Do not rise up against me, but come to me in submission."

28. Then he sealed the letter with musk and with his seal and said to the hoopoe: ***'Take this letter of mine and deliver it to them*** (Bilqīs and her people), ***and then withdraw from them a little*** – for a short time – ***and see how they respond.'*** It took the letter and brought it to her while her armies were around her, guarding her. It delivered the letter, casting it right into her room. When she saw it, she trembled and was overcome by fear. Then she read what it contained.

29. ***She said, 'Council*** of nobles, ***a noble letter*** – one which has been sealed – ***has been delivered to me.***

30. ***It is from Sulaymān and says: "In the name of Allah, All-Merciful, Most Merciful.***

31. ***Do not rise up against me, but come to me in submission."'***

32. ***She said, 'Council, give me your opinion about this matter*** and tell me what you think I should decide. ***It is not my habit to make a final decision until I have heard what you have to say.'***

ٱللَّهِ ٱلرَّحْمَٰنِ ٱلرَّحِيمِ ﴿٣٠﴾ أَلَّا تَعْلُواْ عَلَيَّ وَأْتُونِي مُسْلِمِينَ ﴿٣١﴾
قَالَتْ يَٰٓأَيُّهَا ٱلْمَلَؤُاْ أَفْتُونِي فِيٓ أَمْرِي مَا كُنتُ قَاطِعَةً أَمْرًا حَتَّىٰ
تَشْهَدُونِ ﴿٣٢﴾ قَالُواْ نَحْنُ أُوْلُواْ قُوَّةٍ وَأُوْلُواْ بَأْسٍ شَدِيدٍ وَٱلْأَمْرُ إِلَيْكِ
فَٱنظُرِي مَاذَا تَأْمُرِينَ ﴿٣٣﴾ قَالَتْ إِنَّ ٱلْمُلُوكَ إِذَا دَخَلُواْ قَرْيَةً
أَفْسَدُوهَا وَجَعَلُوٓاْ أَعِزَّةَ أَهْلِهَآ أَذِلَّةً ۖ وَكَذَٰلِكَ يَفْعَلُونَ ﴿٣٤﴾
وَإِنِّي مُرْسِلَةٌ إِلَيْهِم بِهَدِيَّةٍ فَنَاظِرَةُۢ بِمَ يَرْجِعُ ٱلْمُرْسَلُونَ ﴿٣٥﴾
فَلَمَّا جَآءَ سُلَيْمَٰنَ قَالَ أَتُمِدُّونَنِ بِمَالٍ فَمَآ ءَاتَىٰنِۦَ ٱللَّهُ خَيْرٌ مِّمَّآ
ءَاتَىٰكُم بَلْ أَنتُم بِهَدِيَّتِكُمْ تَفْرَحُونَ ﴿٣٦﴾ ٱرْجِعْ إِلَيْهِمْ فَلَنَأْتِيَنَّهُم
بِجُنُودٍ لَّا قِبَلَ لَهُم بِهَا وَلَنُخْرِجَنَّهُم مِّنْهَآ أَذِلَّةً وَهُمْ صَٰغِرُونَ ﴿٣٧﴾ قَالَ
يَٰٓأَيُّهَا ٱلْمَلَؤُاْ أَيُّكُمْ يَأْتِينِي بِعَرْشِهَا قَبْلَ أَن يَأْتُونِي مُسْلِمِينَ ﴿٣٨﴾
قَالَ عِفْرِيتٌ مِّنَ ٱلْجِنِّ أَنَا۠ ءَاتِيكَ بِهِۦ قَبْلَ أَن تَقُومَ مِن مَّقَامِكَ ۖ وَإِنِّي
عَلَيْهِ لَقَوِيٌّ أَمِينٌ ﴿٣٩﴾ قَالَ ٱلَّذِي عِندَهُۥ عِلْمٌ مِّنَ ٱلْكِتَٰبِ أَنَا۠ ءَاتِيكَ
بِهِۦ قَبْلَ أَن يَرْتَدَّ إِلَيْكَ طَرْفُكَ ۚ فَلَمَّا رَءَاهُ مُسْتَقِرًّا عِندَهُۥ قَالَ هَٰذَا
مِن فَضْلِ رَبِّي لِيَبْلُوَنِيٓ ءَأَشْكُرُ أَمْ أَكْفُرُ ۖ وَمَن شَكَرَ فَإِنَّمَا يَشْكُرُ
لِنَفْسِهِۦ ۖ وَمَن كَفَرَ فَإِنَّ رَبِّي غَنِيٌّ كَرِيمٌ ﴿٤٠﴾ قَالَ نَكِّرُواْ لَهَا عَرْشَهَا
نَنظُرْ أَتَهْتَدِيٓ أَمْ تَكُونُ مِنَ ٱلَّذِينَ لَا يَهْتَدُونَ ﴿٤١﴾ فَلَمَّا جَآءَتْ قِيلَ
أَهَٰكَذَا عَرْشُكِ ۖ قَالَتْ كَأَنَّهُۥ هُوَ ۚ وَأُوتِينَا ٱلْعِلْمَ مِن قَبْلِهَا وَكُنَّا مُسْلِمِينَ
﴿٤٢﴾ وَصَدَّهَا مَا كَانَت تَّعْبُدُ مِن دُونِ ٱللَّهِ ۖ إِنَّهَا كَانَتْ مِن قَوْمٍ كَٰفِرِينَ
﴿٤٣﴾ قِيلَ لَهَا ٱدْخُلِي ٱلصَّرْحَ ۖ فَلَمَّا رَأَتْهُ حَسِبَتْهُ لُجَّةً وَكَشَفَتْ عَن
سَاقَيْهَا ۚ قَالَ إِنَّهُۥ صَرْحٌ مُّمَرَّدٌ مِّن قَوَارِيرَ ۗ قَالَتْ رَبِّ إِنِّي

33. ***They said, 'We possess strength, and we possess great*** military ***force. But the matter is in your hands, so consider what you command*** – and we will obey you.'

34. ***She said, 'When kings enter a city, they lay waste to it and make its mightiest inhabitants the most abased. That is what they*** (the senders of this letter) ***too will do.***

35. ***I will send them a gift and then wait and see what the messengers bring back:*** see if they accept the gift or return it. If he is a king, he will accept it. If he is a Prophet, he will not accept it.' She sent a thousand male and female servants in equal numbers, five hundred gold ingots, crowns adorned with jewels, musk, amber, and other things, together with an envoy who carried a letter. The hoopoe went swiftly to Sulaymān to tell him the news. He ordered masses of gold and silver bricks to be made and that they should be laid round his palace to cover an area of several square miles and that a high wall of gold and silver should be built around it.

36. ***When it*** (the gift accompanied by the envoy and his entourage) ***reached Sulaymān he said, 'Would you give me wealth, when what Allah has given me*** – referring to Prophethood and his kingdom – ***is better than what He has given you*** of this world***? No, rather it is you who delight in your gift*** – which is merely the baubles of this world.

37. ***Return to them***, taking back the gift you brought. ***We will come to them with troops they cannot face and we will expel them from it*** – from their land of Sheba, which was named after the ancestor of their tribe ***abased and humiliated*** – if they do not come in submission.' When the messenger returned with the gift, she shut her throne up inside her castle behind seven guarded and locked doors and surrounded her castle with seven further fortifications. She prepared to travel to Sulaymān in order to see what he wanted from her. She travelled with twelve thousand chiefs. It is said that there were many thousand with each chief. He was aware of her when she was about five miles away.

38. ***He said, 'Council, who among you will bring me her throne before they come to me in submission?'***

39. ***An ifreet of the jinn*** – a very strong type of jinn – ***said, 'I will bring it*** (the throne) ***to you before you get up from your seat*** – where Sulaymān used to sit for judgement from early morning to midday. ***I am strong*** enough to carry it ***and trustworthy enough to do it*** and can be trusted with the jewels and other valuable materials it contains.*'* Sulaymān said, "I want it sooner than that."

40. ***He who possessed knowledge of the Book*** – a reference to Āṣaf ibn Barkhiyya, a true man who knew the Greatest Name of Allah; and when someone asks for something by it, the response is immediate – ***said, 'I will bring it to you before your glance returns to you.'*** He said, 'Look up to the sky,' and as Sulaymān did so, Āṣaf made supplication by the Greatest Name that Allah would bring the throne – and when Sulaymān looked back, it was there in front of him. It passed under the earth until it sprang up by the throne of Sulaymān. ***And when he saw it standing firmly in his presence, he said, 'This*** gift ***is part of my Lord's favour, to test me to see if I will give thanks or show ingratitude*** for Allah's blessings to me. ***Whoever gives thanks only does so to his own gain*** – being rewarded for his thankfulness to Allah. ***Whoever is ungrateful*** for blessings received, ***my Lord is Rich Beyond Need*** of thankfulness, ***Generous*** in continuing to give to those who are ungrateful to Him.*'*

41. ***He said, 'Disguise her throne.*** Change it so that she does not recognise it when she sees it. ***We shall see whether she is guided*** – to recognise it – ***or someone who is not guided*** – and does not recognise it because of the change.*'* By that he meant to test her intelligence because of what had been said, and they altered it.

42. ***Then when she came, she was asked, 'Is your throne like this?' She said, 'It is exactly like it.'*** She recognised it although it appeared to her as it appeared to them. He did not say, "Is this your throne?" If he had asked that, she would have answered, "Yes." When Sulaymān saw that she had recognition and knowledge, he said – ***'We were given knowledge before her and were already Muslims,***

43. ***...but what she worshipped besides Allah impeded her*** from worshipping Allah*:* ***she was from an unbelieving people.'***

44. ***She was told: 'Enter the courtyard,'*** which was paved with transparent crystal under which were flowing fresh water and fish;

ظَلَمْتُ نَفْسِى وَأَسْلَمْتُ مَعَ سُلَيْمَٰنَ لِلَّهِ رَبِّ ٱلْعَٰلَمِينَ ﴿٤٤﴾
وَلَقَدْ أَرْسَلْنَآ إِلَىٰ ثَمُودَ أَخَاهُمْ صَٰلِحًا أَنِ ٱعْبُدُوا۟ ٱللَّهَ فَإِذَا
هُمْ فَرِيقَانِ يَخْتَصِمُونَ ﴿٤٥﴾ قَالَ يَٰقَوْمِ لِمَ تَسْتَعْجِلُونَ
بِٱلسَّيِّئَةِ قَبْلَ ٱلْحَسَنَةِ ۖ لَوْلَا تَسْتَغْفِرُونَ ٱللَّهَ لَعَلَّكُمْ
تُرْحَمُونَ ﴿٤٦﴾ قَالُوا۟ ٱطَّيَّرْنَا بِكَ وَبِمَن مَّعَكَ ۚ قَالَ طَٰٓئِرُكُمْ
عِندَ ٱللَّهِ ۖ بَلْ أَنتُمْ قَوْمٌ تُفْتَنُونَ ﴿٤٧﴾ وَكَانَ فِى ٱلْمَدِينَةِ تِسْعَةُ
رَهْطٍ يُفْسِدُونَ فِى ٱلْأَرْضِ وَلَا يُصْلِحُونَ ﴿٤٨﴾ قَالُوا۟
تَقَاسَمُوا۟ بِٱللَّهِ لَنُبَيِّتَنَّهُۥ وَأَهْلَهُۥ ثُمَّ لَنَقُولَنَّ لِوَلِيِّهِۦ مَا شَهِدْنَا
مَهْلِكَ أَهْلِهِۦ وَإِنَّا لَصَٰدِقُونَ ﴿٤٩﴾ وَمَكَرُوا۟ مَكْرًا
وَمَكَرْنَا مَكْرًا وَهُمْ لَا يَشْعُرُونَ ﴿٥٠﴾ فَٱنظُرْ كَيْفَ
كَانَ عَٰقِبَةُ مَكْرِهِمْ أَنَّا دَمَّرْنَٰهُمْ وَقَوْمَهُمْ أَجْمَعِينَ
﴿٥١﴾ فَتِلْكَ بُيُوتُهُمْ خَاوِيَةًۢ بِمَا ظَلَمُوٓا۟ ۗ إِنَّ فِى ذَٰلِكَ
لَءَايَةً لِّقَوْمٍ يَعْلَمُونَ ﴿٥٢﴾ وَأَنجَيْنَا ٱلَّذِينَ ءَامَنُوا۟
وَكَانُوا۟ يَتَّقُونَ ﴿٥٣﴾ وَلُوطًا إِذْ قَالَ لِقَوْمِهِۦٓ
أَتَأْتُونَ ٱلْفَٰحِشَةَ وَأَنتُمْ تُبْصِرُونَ ﴿٥٤﴾ أَئِنَّكُمْ لَتَأْتُونَ
ٱلرِّجَالَ شَهْوَةً مِّن دُونِ ٱلنِّسَآءِ ۚ بَلْ أَنتُمْ قَوْمٌ تَجْهَلُونَ ﴿٥٥﴾
۞ فَمَا كَانَ جَوَابَ قَوْمِهِۦٓ إِلَّآ أَن قَالُوٓا۟ أَخْرِجُوٓا۟ ءَالَ
لُوطٍ مِّن قَرْيَتِكُمْ ۖ إِنَّهُمْ أُنَاسٌ يَتَطَهَّرُونَ ﴿٥٦﴾ فَأَنجَيْنَٰهُ
وَأَهْلَهُۥٓ إِلَّا ٱمْرَأَتَهُۥ قَدَّرْنَٰهَا مِنَ ٱلْغَٰبِرِينَ ﴿٥٧﴾ وَأَمْطَرْنَا
عَلَيْهِم مَّطَرًا ۖ فَسَآءَ مَطَرُ ٱلْمُنذَرِينَ ﴿٥٨﴾ قُلِ ٱلْحَمْدُ لِلَّهِ وَسَلَٰمٌ

Sulaymān had it constructed when he had been told that her legs and feet were those of a donkey – ***but when she saw it she supposed it to be a pool and bared her legs*** ready to enter it; Sulaymān was on his throne in the centre of the courtyard and he saw that her legs and feet were beautiful. ***He said*** to her***: 'It is a courtyard paved with glass,'*** and invited her to Islam. ***She said, 'My Lord, I have wronged myself*** by worshipping other than You, ***but I have submitted with Sulaymān to the Lord of all the worlds.'*** He wanted to marry her but disliked the hair on her legs and so the *shayṭāns* prepared a depilatory and she removed the hair with it. He married her and loved her and confirmed her as the ruler over her kingdom. He used to visit her once a month and would stay with her for three days. Her kingdom ended when the kingdom of Sulaymān ended. It is related that Sulaymān became king when he was thirteen years old and died when he was fifty-three. Glory be to the One whose kingdom has no end!

45. ***To Thamūd We sent their brother*** – from their tribe – ***Ṣāliḥ, telling them to worship Allah*** alone, ***but straightaway they divided in two*** parties ***arguing with one another*** about the *dīn*: one party being the believers who accepted he had been sent to them and the other party being unbelievers who denied him.

46. ***He said*** to those who denied, ***'My people, why are you so anxious to hasten the bad*** (Allah's punishment) ***before the good*** (Allah's mercy) – by saying the words: "If what you say is true, then bring us the punishment"***? If only you would ask for forgiveness from Allah*** for your *shirk* ***so that mercy might perhaps be shown to you*** – and you might not be punished.***'***

47. ***They said, 'We see you, and those with you, as an evil omen'*** since there was a drought and they were hungry. ***He said, 'No, your evil omen is with Allah*** – who will bring it to you; ***you are merely a people undergoing a trial*** – being tested by good and evil.***'***

48. ***There was a group of nine men in the city*** of Thamūd ***causing corruption in the land*** – by acts of disobedience like clipping dinars – ***and not putting things right*** by obeying Allah.

49. ***They said*** to one another, ***'Let us make an oath to one another by Allah that we will fall on him and his family in the night*** (read as *nubayyitannahu* and *tubayyitunnahu*, meaning "you will fall on him in the night") ***and then say*** (read as *naqūlanna* and *taqūlunna*, meaning "you will say") ***to his protector*** (relatives), ***"We did not witness*** – and were not present at – ***the destruction*** (read as *mahlik* and *muhlak*) ***of his family, and we are telling the truth.*** We do not know who killed him."'

50. ***They hatched a plot*** to do this ***and We hatched a plot*** – and repaid them by hastening their punishment – ***while they were not aware.***

51. ***So look at the end result of all their plotting; We utterly destroyed them and their whole people*** – by the Shout of Jibrīl, or by the angels casting down stones which they saw while not seeing the angels*!*

52. ***These are the*** empty ***ruins of their houses because of the wrong they did*** – because of their unbelief. ***There is certainly a Sign*** and lesson ***in that for people with knowledge*** of the power of Allah, so that they may be warned.

53. ***We rescued those who believed and who were godfearing*** – referring to Ṣāliḥ and those who believed, who numbered about four thousand. They feared committing *shirk.*

54. ***And*** remember ***when Lūṭ said to his people: 'Do you approach depravity*** (sodomy) ***with open eyes*** – knowing that it is disobeying Allah*?*

55. ***Do you come with lust to men instead of women? You are a people who are deeply ignorant*** of the consequences of what you are doing.*'* –

56. ***The only response of his people was to say: 'Drive the family of Lūṭ out of your city! They are people who keep themselves pure*** of this activity*!'*

57. ***So We rescued him and his family – except for his wife. We ordained her to be one of those who stayed behind*** in the punishment.

58. ***We rained down a rain*** – of stones of baked clay ***upon them*** – which destroyed them. ***How evil is the rain*** (the punishment) ***of those who are warned!***

عَلَىٰ عِبَادِهِ ٱلَّذِينَ ٱصۡطَفَىٰٓۗ ءَآللَّهُ خَيۡرٌ أَمَّا يُشۡرِكُونَ ﴿٥٩﴾
أَمَّنۡ خَلَقَ ٱلسَّمَٰوَٰتِ وَٱلۡأَرۡضَ وَأَنزَلَ لَكُم مِّنَ ٱلسَّمَآءِ
مَآءٗ فَأَنۢبَتۡنَا بِهِۦ حَدَآئِقَ ذَاتَ بَهۡجَةٖ مَّا كَانَ لَكُمۡ
أَن تُنۢبِتُواْ شَجَرَهَآۗ أَءِلَٰهٞ مَّعَ ٱللَّهِۚ بَلۡ هُمۡ قَوۡمٞ يَعۡدِلُونَ ﴿٦٠﴾
أَمَّن جَعَلَ ٱلۡأَرۡضَ قَرَارٗا وَجَعَلَ خِلَٰلَهَآ أَنۡهَٰرٗا وَجَعَلَ لَهَا
رَوَٰسِيَ وَجَعَلَ بَيۡنَ ٱلۡبَحۡرَيۡنِ حَاجِزًاۗ أَءِلَٰهٞ مَّعَ ٱللَّهِۚ بَلۡ
أَكۡثَرُهُمۡ لَا يَعۡلَمُونَ ﴿٦١﴾ أَمَّن يُجِيبُ ٱلۡمُضۡطَرَّ إِذَا دَعَاهُ
وَيَكۡشِفُ ٱلسُّوٓءَ وَيَجۡعَلُكُمۡ خُلَفَآءَ ٱلۡأَرۡضِۗ أَءِلَٰهٞ
مَّعَ ٱللَّهِۚ قَلِيلٗا مَّا تَذَكَّرُونَ ﴿٦٢﴾ أَمَّن يَهۡدِيكُمۡ فِي
ظُلُمَٰتِ ٱلۡبَرِّ وَٱلۡبَحۡرِ وَمَن يُرۡسِلُ ٱلرِّيَٰحَ بُشۡرَۢا بَيۡنَ يَدَيۡ
رَحۡمَتِهِۦٓۗ أَءِلَٰهٞ مَّعَ ٱللَّهِۚ تَعَٰلَى ٱللَّهُ عَمَّا يُشۡرِكُونَ ﴿٦٣﴾
أَمَّن يَبۡدَؤُاْ ٱلۡخَلۡقَ ثُمَّ يُعِيدُهُۥ وَمَن يَرۡزُقُكُم مِّنَ ٱلسَّمَآءِ وَٱلۡأَرۡضِۗ
أَءِلَٰهٞ مَّعَ ٱللَّهِۚ قُلۡ هَاتُواْ بُرۡهَٰنَكُمۡ إِن كُنتُمۡ صَٰدِقِينَ ﴿٦٤﴾
قُل لَّا يَعۡلَمُ مَن فِي ٱلسَّمَٰوَٰتِ وَٱلۡأَرۡضِ ٱلۡغَيۡبَ إِلَّا ٱللَّهُۚ وَمَا يَشۡعُرُونَ
أَيَّانَ يُبۡعَثُونَ ﴿٦٥﴾ بَلِ ٱدَّٰرَكَ عِلۡمُهُمۡ فِي ٱلۡأٓخِرَةِۚ بَلۡ هُمۡ
فِي شَكّٖ مِّنۡهَاۖ بَلۡ هُم مِّنۡهَا عَمُونَ ﴿٦٦﴾ وَقَالَ ٱلَّذِينَ كَفَرُوٓاْ
أَءِذَا كُنَّا تُرَٰبٗا وَءَابَآؤُنَآ أَئِنَّا لَمُخۡرَجُونَ ﴿٦٧﴾ لَقَدۡ وُعِدۡنَا
هَٰذَا نَحۡنُ وَءَابَآؤُنَا مِن قَبۡلُ إِنۡ هَٰذَآ إِلَّآ أَسَٰطِيرُ ٱلۡأَوَّلِينَ ﴿٦٨﴾
قُلۡ سِيرُواْ فِي ٱلۡأَرۡضِ فَٱنظُرُواْ كَيۡفَ كَانَ عَٰقِبَةُ ٱلۡمُجۡرِمِينَ
﴿٦٩﴾ وَلَا تَحۡزَنۡ عَلَيۡهِمۡ وَلَا تَكُن فِي ضَيۡقٖ مِّمَّا يَمۡكُرُونَ ﴿٧٠﴾

59. ***Say***, Muḥammad***: 'Praise be to Allah*** – for the destruction of the unbelievers of past nations – ***and peace be upon His slaves whom He has chosen.' Is Allah better, or what they associate*** (read as *yushrikūna* and *tushrikūna*, meaning "you associate") ***with Him?*** Who is most entitled to worship: Allah or the gods which the people of Makka worship?

60. ***He Who created the heavens and the earth and sends down water for you from the sky by which We make luxuriant gardens grow*** – a change of person from the third to the first. The word *hadā'iq* is the plural of *ḥadīqa*, which means a walled garden***; you could never make their trees grow*** – you lack the power to do so***. Is there another god besides Allah*** who could help in that***? No indeed***, there is no other god with Him***; but they are people who equate others with Him*** –

61. ***...He Who made the earth a stable dwelling place*** – so that it does not move under its inhabitants – ***and appointed rivers flowing through its midst and placed firmly embedded mountains on it*** – which make the earth firm – ***and set a barrier between the two seas*** – the sweet sea and the salt sea, so that they do not mix with one another. ***Is there another god besides Allah? No indeed, but most of them do not know it!*** –

62. ***...He Who responds to the oppressed*** – those in dire need – ***when they call on Him and removes their distress*** – and that of others – ***and has appointed you as khalif*****s *on the earth.*** The genitive grammatical usage here gives the meaning of "on". The word *khalif* (deputy) can also mean "successor" in the sense that each generation follows the generation before it. ***Is there another god besides Allah? How little you pay heed*** (read as *tadhakkarūna*, and *yadhakkarūna*, "they pay heed!") –

63. ***...He Who guides you*** to your destinations ***in the darkness of land and sea*** by means of the stars at night and by landmarks on the earth in the day, ***and sends out the winds bringing advance news of His mercy*** (rain). ***Is there another god besides Allah? Exalted is Allah above what they associate with Him!*** –

64. ***...He Who originates creation*** – in the wombs by means of sperm – ***and then regenerates it*** – after death, even if people do not acknowledge the evidence which indicates that it will happen, ***and provides for you from out of heaven*** – referring to rain – ***and earth*** – referring to plants. ***Is there another god besides Allah? Say***, Muḥammad***: 'Bring your proof if you are being truthful*** about there being a god who can do any of what has just been mentioned.*'*

65. Then they asked him about the time of the Last Hour, and the answer was: ***Say: 'No one in the heavens and the earth*** – whether angels or human beings – ***knows the Unseen*** – which they cannot see – ***except Allah.' They*** (the unbelievers of Makka and others) ***are not aware of*** the time ***when they will be raised.***

66. ***No, their knowledge stops short*** (read as *addāraka* and *adraka*) ***of the Next World.*** They lack knowledge and have to ask about the time of the coming of the Next World, while they do not really believe it will happen. ***In fact they have doubts about it; in fact they*** (their hearts) ***are blind to it.***

67. ***Those who disbelieve*** and deny the Resurrection ***say, 'When we and our fathers are turned to dust, will we then be brought forth again*** from the grave***?***

68. ***We have been promised this before, we and our fathers. This is nothing but myths and legends*** (fabrications) ***of previous peoples.'***

69. ***Say: 'Travel about the earth and see the final fate of the evildoers.'*** They were destroyed because of their denial.

70. The following is to give solace to the Prophet, may Allah bless him and grant him peace: ***Do not grieve over them and do not let the plots they make distress you.*** In other words: do not be concerned with their plotting against you. We will help you against them.

71. ***They say, 'When will this promise*** of the punishment ***be fulfilled, if you are telling the truth?'***

72. ***Say: 'It may well be that some of what you are anxious to hasten is right on your heels.'*** It is just behind you – and in fact came about when they were killed in the Battle of Badr. The rest of the punishment will come after death.

73. ***Allah shows favour to mankind*** by deferring the punishment from the unbelievers ***but most of them*** (the unbelievers) ***are not***

وَيَقُولُونَ مَتَىٰ هَٰذَا ٱلْوَعْدُ إِن كُنتُمْ صَٰدِقِينَ ٧١ قُلْ عَسَىٰٓ
أَن يَكُونَ رَدِفَ لَكُم بَعْضُ ٱلَّذِى تَسْتَعْجِلُونَ ٧٢ وَإِنَّ رَبَّكَ
لَذُو فَضْلٍ عَلَى ٱلنَّاسِ وَلَٰكِنَّ أَكْثَرَهُمْ لَا يَشْكُرُونَ ٧٣ وَإِنَّ
رَبَّكَ لَيَعْلَمُ مَا تُكِنُّ صُدُورُهُمْ وَمَا يُعْلِنُونَ ٧٤ وَمَا مِنْ غَآئِبَةٍ
فِى ٱلسَّمَآءِ وَٱلْأَرْضِ إِلَّا فِى كِتَٰبٍ مُّبِينٍ ٧٥ إِنَّ هَٰذَا ٱلْقُرْءَانَ
يَقُصُّ عَلَىٰ بَنِىٓ إِسْرَٰٓءِيلَ أَكْثَرَ ٱلَّذِى هُمْ فِيهِ يَخْتَلِفُونَ ٧٦
وَإِنَّهُۥ لَهُدًى وَرَحْمَةٌ لِّلْمُؤْمِنِينَ ٧٧ إِنَّ رَبَّكَ يَقْضِى بَيْنَهُم
بِحُكْمِهِۦ ۚ وَهُوَ ٱلْعَزِيزُ ٱلْعَلِيمُ ٧٨ فَتَوَكَّلْ عَلَى ٱللَّهِ ۖ إِنَّكَ عَلَى
ٱلْحَقِّ ٱلْمُبِينِ ٧٩ إِنَّكَ لَا تُسْمِعُ ٱلْمَوْتَىٰ وَلَا تُسْمِعُ ٱلصُّمَّ ٱلدُّعَآءَ
إِذَا وَلَّوْا۟ مُدْبِرِينَ ٨٠ وَمَآ أَنتَ بِهَٰدِى ٱلْعُمْىِ عَن ضَلَٰلَتِهِمْ ۖ إِن
تُسْمِعُ إِلَّا مَن يُؤْمِنُ بِـَٔايَٰتِنَا فَهُم مُّسْلِمُونَ ٨١ ۞ وَإِذَا
وَقَعَ ٱلْقَوْلُ عَلَيْهِمْ أَخْرَجْنَا لَهُمْ دَآبَّةً مِّنَ ٱلْأَرْضِ تُكَلِّمُهُمْ أَنَّ
ٱلنَّاسَ كَانُوا۟ بِـَٔايَٰتِنَا لَا يُوقِنُونَ ٨٢ وَيَوْمَ نَحْشُرُ مِن كُلِّ أُمَّةٍ
فَوْجًا مِّمَّن يُكَذِّبُ بِـَٔايَٰتِنَا فَهُمْ يُوزَعُونَ ٨٣ حَتَّىٰٓ إِذَا جَآءُو
قَالَ أَكَذَّبْتُم بِـَٔايَٰتِى وَلَمْ تُحِيطُوا۟ بِهَا عِلْمًا أَمَّاذَا كُنتُمْ تَعْمَلُونَ
٨٤ وَوَقَعَ ٱلْقَوْلُ عَلَيْهِم بِمَا ظَلَمُوا۟ فَهُمْ لَا يَنطِقُونَ ٨٥ أَلَمْ
يَرَوْا۟ أَنَّا جَعَلْنَا ٱلَّيْلَ لِيَسْكُنُوا۟ فِيهِ وَٱلنَّهَارَ مُبْصِرًا ۚ إِنَّ فِى
ذَٰلِكَ لَءَايَٰتٍ لِّقَوْمٍ يُؤْمِنُونَ ٨٦ وَيَوْمَ يُنفَخُ فِى ٱلصُّورِ فَفَزِعَ
مَن فِى ٱلسَّمَٰوَٰتِ وَمَن فِى ٱلْأَرْضِ إِلَّا مَن شَآءَ ٱللَّهُ ۚ وَكُلٌّ أَتَوْهُ
دَٰخِرِينَ ٨٧ وَتَرَى ٱلْجِبَالَ تَحْسَبُهَا جَامِدَةً وَهِىَ تَمُرُّ مَرَّ ٱلسَّحَابِ ۚ

thankful for the deferral of the punishment, because they deny that it will occur.

74. ***Certainly your Lord knows what their hearts keep hidden and what they divulge*** with their tongues.

75. ***Certainly there is no hidden thing in either heaven or earth*** – that is completely hidden from people ***which is not in a Clear Book*** – a reference to the Preserved Tablet and Allah's hidden knowledge. One aspect of that is the punishment of the unbelievers.

76. ***Certainly this Qur'an narrates to the tribe of Israel*** – those who were there in the time of our Prophet – ***most of the things about which they differ*** between themselves, whether they accept it and submit or not.

77. ***Certainly it is guidance*** from misguidance ***and a mercy*** – delivering them from the punishment – ***for the believers.***

78. ***Certainly your Lord will decide between them*** and others on the Day of Rising – ***with His just judgement. He is the Almighty, the All-Knowing***, knowing what judgement to give. No one can oppose Him, in the way that the unbelievers disagreed with their Prophets in this world.

79. ***So put your trust in Allah*** and rely on Him. ***You are clearly on a path of truth*** – the clear *dīn*. In the end you will have victory over the unbelievers.

80. Then Allah makes similes for them, comparing them to the dead, and to the deaf and blind, saying: ***You will not make dead men hear and you will not make deaf men hear the call when they turn their backs in flight.***

81. ***You will not guide blind men out of their error. You will not make anyone hear*** – meaning understand and accept – ***except for those who believe in Our Signs*** (the Qur'an) ***and so are Muslims***, sincere in their belief in the oneness of Allah.

82. ***When the Word is justly carried out against them*** – when the punishment befalls the unbelievers – ***We will produce a Beast from the earth which will speak to them*** in Arabic to those present when it emerges. ***Truly*** (read as *anna* and *inna*) ***mankind*** – particularly the unbelievers of Quraysh – ***had no certainty about Our Signs.*** They did not believe in the Qur'an which contains mention of the

Resurrection, the Reckoning, and the Punishment. When the Beast emerges, commanding people to do what is correct and forbidding them what is bad will stop. No unbeliever will believe after that: as Allah revealed to Nūḥ, *"None of your people are going to believe except those who have faith already."* (11:36)

83. ***On that Day We will collect from every community a crowd*** – the leaders who were followed – ***of those who denied Our Signs, paraded in tight ranks.*** They will be gathered from the first to the last and then driven.

84. ***Then when they arrive*** at the place of the Reckoning ***He will say*** to them***: 'Did you deny My Signs*** (My Prophets) ***even though you did not have proper knowledge of them*** – did not fully understand them***? What were you doing*** in the face of what you were commanded to do***?'***

85. ***The Word*** (the punishment) ***will be carried out against them for the wrong*** of *shirk* ***they did, and they will not speak*** since they have no proof.

86. ***Do they not see that We have made the night for them to rest in and the day for seeing*** – to pursue their business***? There are certainly Signs*** of Allah's power ***in that for people who believe.*** Those who believe are singled out for mention since they benefit from night and day, which is not the case with the unbelievers.

87. ***On the Day the Trumpet is blown*** – a reference to the first blast by Isrāfīl – ***and everyone in the heavens and everyone on the earth is terrified*** – and suffers a fear which leads to their death; another *āyat* says that they swoon. The past tense is used because it is absolutely certain that it will occur – ***except those Allah wills,*** – who are Jibrīl, Mīkā'il, Isrāfīl and the Angel of Death***;*** Ibn 'Abbās said that this refers to the martyrs since they are *"alive with their Lord, provided for."* Then, after they are brought to life on the Day of Rising, ***everyone will come to Him abject.***

88. ***You will see*** – at the moment of the blast of the Trumpet – ***the mountains you reckoned to be solid*** – and that they must stay firmly in place because of their great size – ***going past like*** rain ***clouds*** – moved by the wind like carded wool and then like scattered dust until they fall to the ground and are made level with it***: the handi-***

صُنْعَ ٱللَّهِ ٱلَّذِىٓ أَتْقَنَ كُلَّ شَىْءٍ ۚ إِنَّهُۥ خَبِيرٌۢ بِمَا تَفْعَلُونَ ﴿٨٨﴾
مَن جَآءَ بِٱلْحَسَنَةِ فَلَهُۥ خَيْرٌ مِّنْهَا وَهُم مِّن فَزَعٍ يَوْمَئِذٍ ءَامِنُونَ ﴿٨٩﴾
وَمَن جَآءَ بِٱلسَّيِّئَةِ فَكُبَّتْ وُجُوهُهُمْ فِى ٱلنَّارِ هَلْ تُجْزَوْنَ
إِلَّا مَا كُنتُمْ تَعْمَلُونَ ﴿٩٠﴾ إِنَّمَآ أُمِرْتُ أَنْ أَعْبُدَ رَبَّ هَٰذِهِ
ٱلْبَلْدَةِ ٱلَّذِى حَرَّمَهَا وَلَهُۥ كُلُّ شَىْءٍ ۖ وَأُمِرْتُ أَنْ أَكُونَ مِنَ
ٱلْمُسْلِمِينَ ﴿٩١﴾ وَأَنْ أَتْلُوَا۟ ٱلْقُرْءَانَ ۖ فَمَنِ ٱهْتَدَىٰ فَإِنَّمَا يَهْتَدِى
لِنَفْسِهِۦ ۖ وَمَن ضَلَّ فَقُلْ إِنَّمَآ أَنَا۠ مِنَ ٱلْمُنذِرِينَ ﴿٩٢﴾ وَقُلِ ٱلْحَمْدُ
لِلَّهِ سَيُرِيكُمْ ءَايَٰتِهِۦ فَتَعْرِفُونَهَا ۚ وَمَا رَبُّكَ بِغَٰفِلٍ عَمَّا تَعْمَلُونَ ﴿٩٣﴾

work of Allah – which is the most perfect, He ***who gives to every - thing its solidity. He is aware of what you do*** (read as *taf'alūna* and *yaf'alūna*, "what they do") – meaning that He knows the acts of disobedience done by His enemies and the acts of obedience by His friends.

89. ***Those who perform good actions*** – meaning the statement "There is no god but Allah" on the Day of Rising – ***will receive*** a ***better*** reward ***than them*** because of it; another *āyat* says that they will receive ten like it, ***and will be safe that Day*** (read as *faza'in yawma'idhin*, *faza'i yawma'idhin*, or *faza'i yawmi'idhin*) ***from ter - ror.***

90. ***Those who perform bad actions*** (*shirk*) ***will be flung head first into the Fire.*** The head is mentioned because it is the place of honour and so that is appropriate. Then they will be asked: ***'Are you being repaid for anything other than what you did*** in respect of the *shirk* and acts of disobedience you committed***?'***

91. ***'I have simply been ordered to worship the Lord of this land*** (Makka) ***which He has declared sacred*** – made a secure sanctuary in which no one may shed the blood of a human being, wrong anyone, hunt game, or cut down any plant, which was one of the blessings bestowed on Quraysh, the people of the Sanctuary (*Ḥaram*); another was that Allah removed from it the difficulties and seditions prevalent in all the other lands of the Arabs. ***Everything belongs to Him*** – to Allah who is its Lord, Creator and Master ***– and I have been ordered to be one of the Muslims,*** and to affirm His unity –

92. ***...and to recite the Qur'an*** – in order to you to call you to faith.***'***

Whoever is guided is only guided to his own good, since he will have the reward of being guided***; if anyone is misguided*** – from faith and is mistaken about the path of guidance***, just say*** to him***: 'I am only a warner.*** I am only responsible for conveying the Message.***'*** That was before the command to fight.

93. ***Say: 'Praise be to Allah. He will show you His Signs and you will recognise them.*** Allah showed them killing and capture at the Battle of Badr and the angels struck their faces and backs, and Allah hastened them to the Fire. ***Your Lord is not unaware of what you do*** (read as *ta'malūna* and *ya'malūna*, "what they do")***.'*** He grants them a respite until their time comes.

سُورَةُ القَصَصِ

بِسۡمِ ٱللَّهِ ٱلرَّحۡمَٰنِ ٱلرَّحِيمِ

طسٓمٓ ﴿١﴾ تِلۡكَ ءَايَٰتُ ٱلۡكِتَٰبِ ٱلۡمُبِينِ ﴿٢﴾ نَتۡلُواْ عَلَيۡكَ
مِن نَّبَإِ مُوسَىٰ وَفِرۡعَوۡنَ بِٱلۡحَقِّ لِقَوۡمٖ يُؤۡمِنُونَ ﴿٣﴾ إِنَّ
فِرۡعَوۡنَ عَلَا فِي ٱلۡأَرۡضِ وَجَعَلَ أَهۡلَهَا شِيَعٗا يَسۡتَضۡعِفُ
طَآئِفَةٗ مِّنۡهُمۡ يُذَبِّحُ أَبۡنَآءَهُمۡ وَيَسۡتَحۡيِۦ نِسَآءَهُمۡۚ إِنَّهُۥ كَانَ
مِنَ ٱلۡمُفۡسِدِينَ ﴿٤﴾ وَنُرِيدُ أَن نَّمُنَّ عَلَى ٱلَّذِينَ ٱسۡتُضۡعِفُواْ
فِي ٱلۡأَرۡضِ وَنَجۡعَلَهُمۡ أَئِمَّةٗ وَنَجۡعَلَهُمُ ٱلۡوَٰرِثِينَ ﴿٥﴾
وَنُمَكِّنَ لَهُمۡ فِي ٱلۡأَرۡضِ وَنُرِيَ فِرۡعَوۡنَ وَهَٰمَٰنَ وَجُنُودَهُمَا
مِنۡهُم مَّا كَانُواْ يَحۡذَرُونَ ﴿٦﴾ وَأَوۡحَيۡنَآ إِلَىٰٓ أُمِّ مُوسَىٰٓ
أَنۡ أَرۡضِعِيهِۖ فَإِذَا خِفۡتِ عَلَيۡهِ فَأَلۡقِيهِ فِي ٱلۡيَمِّ وَلَا تَخَافِي
وَلَا تَحۡزَنِيٓۖ إِنَّا رَآدُّوهُ إِلَيۡكِ وَجَاعِلُوهُ مِنَ ٱلۡمُرۡسَلِينَ ﴿٧﴾
فَٱلۡتَقَطَهُۥٓ ءَالُ فِرۡعَوۡنَ لِيَكُونَ لَهُمۡ عَدُوّٗا وَحَزَنًاۗ إِنَّ
فِرۡعَوۡنَ وَهَٰمَٰنَ وَجُنُودَهُمَا كَانُواْ خَٰطِـِٔينَ ﴿٨﴾
وَقَالَتِ ٱمۡرَأَتُ فِرۡعَوۡنَ قُرَّتُ عَيۡنٖ لِّي وَلَكَۖ لَا تَقۡتُلُوهُ عَسَىٰٓ
أَن يَنفَعَنَآ أَوۡ نَتَّخِذَهُۥ وَلَدٗا وَهُمۡ لَا يَشۡعُرُونَ ﴿٩﴾ وَأَصۡبَحَ
فُؤَادُ أُمِّ مُوسَىٰ فَٰرِغًاۖ إِن كَادَتۡ لَتُبۡدِي بِهِۦ لَوۡلَآ أَن
رَّبَطۡنَا عَلَىٰ قَلۡبِهَا لِتَكُونَ مِنَ ٱلۡمُؤۡمِنِينَ ﴿١٠﴾ وَقَالَتۡ
لِأُخۡتِهِۦ قُصِّيهِۖ فَبَصُرَتۡ بِهِۦ عَن جُنُبٖ وَهُمۡ لَا يَشۡعُرُونَ
﴿١١﴾ ۞ وَحَرَّمۡنَا عَلَيۡهِ ٱلۡمَرَاضِعَ مِن قَبۡلُ فَقَالَتۡ هَلۡ أَدُلُّكُمۡ
عَلَىٰٓ أَهۡلِ بَيۡتٖ يَكۡفُلُونَهُۥ لَكُمۡ وَهُمۡ لَهُۥ نَٰصِحُونَ ﴿١٢﴾

28. *Sūrat al-Qaṣaṣ* The Story

This *sūra* is Makkan except for *āyats* 52 to 55 which are Madinan, and *āyat* 85 which was revealed at al-Juḥfa during the *Hijra*. It has 88 *āyat*s and was sent down after *an-Naml*.

1. ***Ta Sin Mim.*** Allah knows best what the letters mean.

2. ***Those are the Signs of the Clear Book*** – *āyats* from the Book which distinguishes between truth and falsehood.

3. ***We recite to you with truth some news of Mūsā and Pharaoh for people who believe*** and so are able to benefit from it.

4. ***Pharaoh exalted himself arrogantly in the land*** of Egypt ***and divided its people into camps, oppressing one group of them*** (the tribe of Israel) ***by slaughtering their sons and letting their women live***, because one of their priests had told Pharaoh that a child would be born among the tribe of Israel who would be the reason for the loss of his kingdom. ***He was one of the corrupters*** – by killing and in other ways.

5. ***We desired to show kindness to those who were oppressed in the land and to make them leaders*** to be followed as good examples ***and make them inheritors*** of the kingdom of Pharaoh,

6. ***...and establish them firmly in the land*** of Egypt and Syria ***and to show*** (read as *narā* and also *yarā,* in which case the meaning becomes, "so that Pharaoh and Hāmān and their troops might see...") ***Pharaoh the very thing that they were fearing from them*** – in the form of a child who would remove their kingdom.

7. ***We revealed*** – either by inspiration or in a dream – ***to the mother of Mūsā*** – who was the child anticipated by the priest, and only his sister was aware that he had been born – ***'Suckle him and then when you fear for him cast him into the sea*** (the Nile). ***Do not fear*** that he will drown ***or grieve*** over parting from him; ***We will return him to you and make him one of the Messengers.'*** She nursed him for three months, during which time he did not cry and she did not fear for him. Then she placed him in a box covered with pitch on the inside and made comfortable for him. She closed it and put it into the Nile one night.

8. ***The household of Pharaoh*** (his servants) ***picked him up*** in the box, and it was placed in front of Pharaoh and he opened it and lifted out of it Mūsā, who was sucking milk from his thumb – ***so that he*** (Pharaoh) ***might be an enemy*** – by killing their men – ***and a source of grief*** (read as *ḥazn* and *ḥuzn*) ***to them*** – by enslaving their women. ***Certainly Pharaoh and Hāmān*** – the chief minister of Pharaoh – ***and their troops were in the wrong*** by disobeying Allah and would be punished at the hands of Mūsā.

9. ***The wife of Pharaoh,*** who was with the aides, ***said*** when Pharaoh wanted to kill him, ***'A source of delight for me and for you; do not kill him. It may well be that he will be of use to us or perhaps we could adopt him as a son.'*** They obeyed her. ***They were not aware*** of what the final outcome would be.

10. ***Mūsā's mother felt a great emptiness in her heart*** when she heard that he had been picked up, ***and she almost gave him away*** by admitting that he was her son; ***only We fortified her heart*** by making her steadfast and calm; ***so that she would be one of the believers*** who affirm the promise of Allah.

11. ***She said to his sister*** Maryam, ***'Go after him***: follow him in order to obtain news about him.***' And she kept an eye on him from afar, but they were not aware*** that she was his sister and that she was watching him.

12. ***We first made him refuse all wet-nurses*** – until he was returned to his mother – ***so she*** (his sister) ***said,*** when she saw that they were concerned for him, ***'Shall I show you to a household who will feed him for you and be good to him?'*** When Pharaoh agreed to her request, she brought her mother and Mūsā accepted her breast. When he asked her about that, she said that she had good milk with a good scent. He allowed her to nurse him in her house and she brought him back home with her. As Allah says:

13. ***That is how We returned him to his mother so that she might delight her eyes*** by having him returned to her ***and feel no grief; and so that she would know that Allah's promise*** to return him to her ***is true. But most of them*** (people) ***do not know this*** promise and

فَرَدَدْنَٰهُ إِلَىٰٓ أُمِّهِۦ كَىْ تَقَرَّ عَيْنُهَا وَلَا تَحْزَنَ وَلِتَعْلَمَ
أَنَّ وَعْدَ ٱللَّهِ حَقٌّ وَلَٰكِنَّ أَكْثَرَهُمْ لَا يَعْلَمُونَ ١٣
وَلَمَّا بَلَغَ أَشُدَّهُۥ وَٱسْتَوَىٰٓ ءَاتَيْنَٰهُ حُكْمًا وَعِلْمًا ۚ وَكَذَٰلِكَ نَجْزِى
ٱلْمُحْسِنِينَ ١٤ وَدَخَلَ ٱلْمَدِينَةَ عَلَىٰ حِينِ غَفْلَةٍ مِّنْ أَهْلِهَا
فَوَجَدَ فِيهَا رَجُلَيْنِ يَقْتَتِلَانِ هَٰذَا مِن شِيعَتِهِۦ وَهَٰذَا مِنْ عَدُوِّهِۦ ۖ
فَٱسْتَغَٰثَهُ ٱلَّذِى مِن شِيعَتِهِۦ عَلَى ٱلَّذِى مِنْ عَدُوِّهِۦ فَوَكَزَهُۥ مُوسَىٰ
فَقَضَىٰ عَلَيْهِ ۖ قَالَ هَٰذَا مِنْ عَمَلِ ٱلشَّيْطَٰنِ ۖ إِنَّهُۥ عَدُوٌّ مُّضِلٌّ مُّبِينٌ
١٥ قَالَ رَبِّ إِنِّى ظَلَمْتُ نَفْسِى فَٱغْفِرْ لِى فَغَفَرَ لَهُۥٓ ۚ إِنَّهُۥ هُوَ
ٱلْغَفُورُ ٱلرَّحِيمُ ١٦ قَالَ رَبِّ بِمَآ أَنْعَمْتَ عَلَىَّ فَلَنْ أَكُونَ
ظَهِيرًا لِّلْمُجْرِمِينَ ١٧ فَأَصْبَحَ فِى ٱلْمَدِينَةِ خَآئِفًا يَتَرَقَّبُ فَإِذَا
ٱلَّذِى ٱسْتَنصَرَهُۥ بِٱلْأَمْسِ يَسْتَصْرِخُهُۥ ۚ قَالَ لَهُۥ مُوسَىٰٓ إِنَّكَ لَغَوِىٌّ
مُّبِينٌ ١٨ فَلَمَّآ أَنْ أَرَادَ أَن يَبْطِشَ بِٱلَّذِى هُوَ عَدُوٌّ لَّهُمَا قَالَ
يَٰمُوسَىٰٓ أَتُرِيدُ أَن تَقْتُلَنِى كَمَا قَتَلْتَ نَفْسًۢا بِٱلْأَمْسِ ۖ إِن تُرِيدُ إِلَّآ
أَن تَكُونَ جَبَّارًا فِى ٱلْأَرْضِ وَمَا تُرِيدُ أَن تَكُونَ مِنَ ٱلْمُصْلِحِينَ ١٩
وَجَآءَ رَجُلٌ مِّنْ أَقْصَا ٱلْمَدِينَةِ يَسْعَىٰ قَالَ يَٰمُوسَىٰٓ إِنَّ ٱلْمَلَأَ
يَأْتَمِرُونَ بِكَ لِيَقْتُلُوكَ فَٱخْرُجْ إِنِّى لَكَ مِنَ ٱلنَّٰصِحِينَ ٢٠
فَخَرَجَ مِنْهَا خَآئِفًا يَتَرَقَّبُ ۖ قَالَ رَبِّ نَجِّنِى مِنَ ٱلْقَوْمِ ٱلظَّٰلِمِينَ ٢١
وَلَمَّا تَوَجَّهَ تِلْقَآءَ مَدْيَنَ قَالَ عَسَىٰ رَبِّىٓ أَن يَهْدِيَنِى سَوَآءَ
ٱلسَّبِيلِ ٢٢ وَلَمَّا وَرَدَ مَآءَ مَدْيَنَ وَجَدَ عَلَيْهِ أُمَّةً مِّنَ
ٱلنَّاسِ يَسْقُونَ وَوَجَدَ مِن دُونِهِمُ ٱمْرَأَتَيْنِ تَذُودَانِ ۖ
قَالَ مَا خَطْبُكُمَا ۖ قَالَتَا لَا نَسْقِى حَتَّىٰ يُصْدِرَ ٱلرِّعَآءُ ۖ وَأَبُونَا

that those involved were his sister and mother. He remained with her until she weaned him, and she was paid a dinar every day for that. She took it because it was the money of a *ḥarbī*, someone with whom they were at war. She brought him to Pharaoh and he grew up with him, as Allah Almighty reports in *Sūrat ash-Shu'arā'*: "*Did we not bring you up among us as a child and did you not spend many years of your life among us?"* (26:17)

14. ***And when he reached his full strength*** – at the age of thirty or thirty-three years old – ***and maturity*** – at the age of forty – ***We gave him judgement*** (wisdom) ***and knowledge***, in the form of understanding of the *dīn*, before sending him as a Prophet. ***That is how We recompense good-doers.***

15. ***He*** (Mūsā) ***entered the city*** of Pharaoh, which was Memphis, after he had been absent from it for a time – ***at a time when its inhabitants were unaware*** – at midday – ***and found two men,*** an Israelite and a Copt, ***fighting there – one from his party and the other from his enemy.*** The Copt was trying to force the Israelite to carry firewood to Pharaoh's kitchen. ***The one from his party*** (the Israelite) ***asked for his support against the other from his enemy.*** Mūsā said, "Let him go." It is said that he said to Mūsā, "You want me to attack you." ***So Mūsā hit him*** – with his open palm – ***dealing him a fatal blow.*** He was very strong and so killed him when it had not been his intention to kill him. He buried him in the sand. ***He said, 'This*** death ***is part of Shayṭān's handiwork*** who provoked my anger. ***He truly is an outright and misleading enemy*** to the sons of Ādam, and clearly misleads people.*'*

16. ***He said*** in regret for having killed him, ***'My Lord, I have wronged myself. Forgive me.' So He forgave him. He is the Ever-Forgiving, the Most Merciful*** both before and after time.

17. ***He said, 'My Lord, because of Your blessing upon me*** in forgiving me, You have protected me and ***I will never be a supporter of evildoers*** after this if You protect me.*'*

18. ***Morning found him in the city, fearful and on his guard*** – waiting to see what would happen to him on account of killing the Copt. ***Then suddenly the man who had sought his help the day before, shouted for help from him again*** against another Copt. ***Mūsā said***

شَيۡخٞ كَبِيرٞ ٢٣ فَسَقَىٰ لَهُمَا ثُمَّ تَوَلَّىٰٓ إِلَى ٱلظِّلِّ فَقَالَ
رَبِّ إِنِّي لِمَآ أَنزَلۡتَ إِلَيَّ مِنۡ خَيۡرٖ فَقِيرٞ ٢٤ فَجَآءَتۡهُ إِحۡدَىٰهُمَا
تَمۡشِي عَلَى ٱسۡتِحۡيَآءٖ قَالَتۡ إِنَّ أَبِي يَدۡعُوكَ لِيَجۡزِيَكَ
أَجۡرَ مَا سَقَيۡتَ لَنَاۚ فَلَمَّا جَآءَهُۥ وَقَصَّ عَلَيۡهِ ٱلۡقَصَصَ قَالَ
لَا تَخَفۡۖ نَجَوۡتَ مِنَ ٱلۡقَوۡمِ ٱلظَّٰلِمِينَ ٢٥ قَالَتۡ إِحۡدَىٰهُمَا
يَٰٓأَبَتِ ٱسۡتَـٔۡجِرۡهُۖ إِنَّ خَيۡرَ مَنِ ٱسۡتَـٔۡجَرۡتَ ٱلۡقَوِيُّ ٱلۡأَمِينُ
٢٦ قَالَ إِنِّيٓ أُرِيدُ أَنۡ أُنكِحَكَ إِحۡدَى ٱبۡنَتَيَّ هَٰتَيۡنِ عَلَىٰٓ أَن
تَأۡجُرَنِي ثَمَٰنِيَ حِجَجٖۖ فَإِنۡ أَتۡمَمۡتَ عَشۡرٗا فَمِنۡ عِندِكَۖ
وَمَآ أُرِيدُ أَنۡ أَشُقَّ عَلَيۡكَۚ سَتَجِدُنِيٓ إِن شَآءَ ٱللَّهُ مِنَ
ٱلصَّٰلِحِينَ ٢٧ قَالَ ذَٰلِكَ بَيۡنِي وَبَيۡنَكَۖ أَيَّمَا ٱلۡأَجَلَيۡنِ
قَضَيۡتُ فَلَا عُدۡوَٰنَ عَلَيَّۖ وَٱللَّهُ عَلَىٰ مَا نَقُولُ وَكِيلٞ ٢٨
۞ فَلَمَّا قَضَىٰ مُوسَى ٱلۡأَجَلَ وَسَارَ بِأَهۡلِهِۦٓ ءَانَسَ مِن جَانِبِ
ٱلطُّورِ نَارٗاۖ قَالَ لِأَهۡلِهِ ٱمۡكُثُوٓاْ إِنِّيٓ ءَانَسۡتُ نَارٗا لَّعَلِّيٓ ءَاتِيكُم
مِّنۡهَا بِخَبَرٍ أَوۡ جَذۡوَةٖ مِّنَ ٱلنَّارِ لَعَلَّكُمۡ تَصۡطَلُونَ
٢٩ فَلَمَّآ أَتَىٰهَا نُودِيَ مِن شَٰطِيِٕ ٱلۡوَادِ ٱلۡأَيۡمَنِ فِي ٱلۡبُقۡعَةِ
ٱلۡمُبَٰرَكَةِ مِنَ ٱلشَّجَرَةِ أَن يَٰمُوسَىٰٓ إِنِّيٓ أَنَا ٱللَّهُ رَبُّ
ٱلۡعَٰلَمِينَ ٣٠ وَأَنۡ أَلۡقِ عَصَاكَۖ فَلَمَّا رَءَاهَا تَهۡتَزُّ كَأَنَّهَا
جَآنّٞ وَلَّىٰ مُدۡبِرٗا وَلَمۡ يُعَقِّبۡۚ يَٰمُوسَىٰٓ أَقۡبِلۡ وَلَا تَخَفۡۖ إِنَّكَ
مِنَ ٱلۡأٓمِنِينَ ٣١ ٱسۡلُكۡ يَدَكَ فِي جَيۡبِكَ تَخۡرُجۡ بَيۡضَآءَ مِنۡ
غَيۡرِ سُوٓءٖ وَٱضۡمُمۡ إِلَيۡكَ جَنَاحَكَ مِنَ ٱلرَّهۡبِۖ فَذَٰنِكَ
بُرۡهَٰنَانِ مِن رَّبِّكَ إِلَىٰ فِرۡعَوۡنَ وَمَلَإِيْهِۦٓۚ إِنَّهُمۡ كَانُواْ

to him, 'You are clearly a misguided man because of what you did yesterday and today.*'*

19. ***But when he*** (Mūsā) ***was about to grab the man who was their common enemy, he*** (the one who asked for help) – thinking that he was going to hit him – ***said, 'Mūsā! do you want to kill me just as you killed a person yesterday? You only want to be a tyrant in the land; you do not want to be a reformer.'*** When the Copt heard him say that, he knew that it was Mūsā, he went to Pharaoh and told him that; and so Pharaoh commanded the executioners to kill Mūsā and they set out to arrest him.

20. ***A man*** – a believer of the family of Pharaoh – ***came running from the furthest part of the city*** by a shorter route than that Pharaoh's men were taking, ***saying, 'Mūsā, the Council*** of the people of Pharaoh ***are conspiring to kill you, so leave*** the city***! I am someone who brings you good advice*** by telling you to leave.*'*

21. ***So he left there fearful and on his guard*** – about those looking for him or looking for Allah to help him – ***saying, 'My Lord, rescue me from the people of the wrongdoers*** (the people of Pharaoh)***!'***

22. ***When turned his face in the direction of Madyan*** – the town of Shu'ayb, which was an eight day journey from Egypt. In Madyan, he was called 'the son of Ibrāhīm'. Mūsā did not know the route, and ***he said, 'Perhaps my Lord will guide me to the right way*** – the easiest way to it.*'* Allah sent an angel with a staff in his hand to direct him to it.

23. ***When he arrived at the water of*** the well of ***Madyan, he found a crowd of people drawing water there*** for their flocks. ***Standing apart from them, he found two women, holding back their sheep*** – from the water. ***He*** (Mūsā) ***said*** to them***: 'What are you two doing here?*** Why are you not drawing water?*'* ***They said, 'We cannot draw water until the shepherds have driven off*** (read as *yuṣdira* and *yaṣduru*) ***their sheep*** – out of fear of jostling with them. ***You see, our father is a very old man*** – too old to water the sheep.*'*

24. ***So he drew water for them*** – from another well close to them, removing from it a stone which it would normally have taken ten men to lift – ***and then withdrew into the shade*** of an acacia to escape the heat of the sun. He was hungry ***and said, 'My Lord, I am***

truly in need of any good (food) ***You have in store for me.'*** The two women returned to their father in less time than it usually took them. He asked them about it, and they told him about the man who had drawn water for them. He told one of them to invite him.

25. ***One of them came walking shyly up to him*** – and it is related that she veiled her face with the sleeve of her tunic out of modesty – ***and said, 'My father invites you so that he may pay you your wage for drawing water for us.'*** He responded to the invitation, even though he did not want to take a wage, since it appeared that she intended to offer recompense if he was the type of person who would want one. She walked in front of him and the wind began to blow aside her garment and expose her legs. He told her, "Walk behind me and direct me to the way." She did that until he came to her father, Shu'ayb, peace be upon him, who was having his evening meal. He said to him, "Sit and eat." He answered, "I fear that it is compensation for getting water for them, and I come from the people of a family who do not seek recompense for good deeds." He said, "No, but my custom and the custom of my fathers is to give hospitality to guests and to give them food." ***When he came to him and told him the whole story*** – about killing the Copt and of their intention to kill him and his fear of Pharaoh – ***he*** (Shu'ayb) ***said, 'Have no fear, you have escaped from wrongdoing people.'*** Pharaoh had no authority in Madyan.

26. ***One of them*** – the one who had been sent, which might have been either the younger or the elder – ***said, 'Hire him, father*** – take him on as an employee to tend to our sheep instead of us**.** ***The best person to hire is someone strong and trustworthy.'*** He should be hired on account of his strength and trustworthiness. Shu'ayb asked her about that, and she told him how he had lifted the stone from the well and had told her to walk behind him. When she went to him and he recognised her, he lowered his head and did not lift it. Shu'ayb wanted to marry one of his daughters to him.

27. ***He said, 'I would like to marry you to one of these two daughters of mine*** – either the elder or the younger – ***on condition that you work for me*** – tending my sheep – ***for eight full years. If you complete ten, that is up to you. I do not want to be hard on you*** by stipulating that you must stay for ten. ***You will find me, Allah willing, to be one of the righteous*** who fulfils his contracts.*'*

28. He (Mūsā) ***said, 'That*** which you said ***is agreed between me and you. Whichever of the two terms I fulfil*** – eight or ten years – ***there should be no bad feeling towards me*** – no hostility by way of seeking more than that. ***Allah is Guardian over what we say.'*** He completed that contract and Shu'ayb instructed his daughter to give Mūsā a staff with which to drive away wild animals from his flock. He had the staff of the Prophets with him. The staff of Ādam had come into his hand from the myrtle tree of Paradise, and Mūsā took it with Shu'ayb's knowledge.

29. ***When Mūsā had fulfilled the appointed term*** – possibly seven or eight years, although ten is more probable – ***and had set off with his family*** – his wife accompanied him, with the permission of her father, in the direction of Egypt – ***he noticed a fire from one side of the Mount.*** Ṭūr (Sinai) was the name of the mountain. ***He told his family, 'Stay here; I can see a fire. Perhaps I will bring you back some news from it*** of their route, since they had become lost, ***or a burning branch*** (read as *jadhwa* and *jidhwa*) ***from the fire*** to use to light a fire – ***so that you will be able to warm yourselves.'***

30. ***But when he reached it a voice called out to him*** (Mūsā) ***from the right hand side of the valley, in the part which was full of blessing*** for Mūsā, since he heard the words of Allah there – ***from out of the bush***, which was either jujube, bramble or boxthorn***: 'Mūsā, I am Allah, the Lord of all the worlds.***

31. ***Throw down your staff!'*** He threw it down. ***Then when he saw it slithering like a*** small quick ***snake, he turned and fled and did not turn back again. 'Mūsā, approach and have no fear!*** Come back! ***You are one of those who are secure.***

32. ***Put your*** right ***hand inside your shirt front. It will emerge pure white, yet quite unharmed.*** He brought it out it and it was pure white, changed from its normal brownish colour, and shone like the sun so that it dazzled the eyes. ***And hug your arms to your sides to still your fear*** (read as *rahb, rahab* and *ruhb*)**.** This refers to the fear he felt upon seeing the whiteness of his hand. He did as he was told

قَوْمًا فَٰسِقِينَ ﴿٣٢﴾ قَالَ رَبِّ إِنِّي قَتَلْتُ مِنْهُمْ نَفْسًا فَأَخَافُ
أَن يَقْتُلُونِ ﴿٣٣﴾ وَأَخِي هَٰرُونُ هُوَ أَفْصَحُ مِنِّي لِسَانًا
فَأَرْسِلْهُ مَعِيَ رِدْءًا يُصَدِّقُنِيٓۖ إِنِّيٓ أَخَافُ أَن يُكَذِّبُونِ ﴿٣٤﴾
قَالَ سَنَشُدُّ عَضُدَكَ بِأَخِيكَ وَنَجْعَلُ لَكُمَا سُلْطَٰنًا فَلَا
يَصِلُونَ إِلَيْكُمَاۚ بِـَٔايَٰتِنَآ أَنتُمَا وَمَنِ ٱتَّبَعَكُمَا ٱلْغَٰلِبُونَ ﴿٣٥﴾
فَلَمَّا جَآءَهُم مُّوسَىٰ بِـَٔايَٰتِنَا بَيِّنَٰتٍ قَالُوا۟ مَا هَٰذَآ إِلَّا سِحْرٌ
مُّفْتَرًى وَمَا سَمِعْنَا بِهَٰذَا فِيٓ ءَابَآئِنَا ٱلْأَوَّلِينَ ﴿٣٦﴾ وَقَالَ
مُوسَىٰ رَبِّيٓ أَعْلَمُ بِمَن جَآءَ بِٱلْهُدَىٰ مِنْ عِندِهِۦ وَمَن تَكُونُ
لَهُۥ عَٰقِبَةُ ٱلدَّارِۖ إِنَّهُۥ لَا يُفْلِحُ ٱلظَّٰلِمُونَ ﴿٣٧﴾ وَقَالَ فِرْعَوْنُ
يَٰٓأَيُّهَا ٱلْمَلَأُ مَا عَلِمْتُ لَكُم مِّنْ إِلَٰهٍ غَيْرِي فَأَوْقِدْ
لِي يَٰهَٰمَٰنُ عَلَى ٱلطِّينِ فَٱجْعَل لِّي صَرْحًا لَّعَلِّيٓ أَطَّلِعُ إِلَىٰٓ
إِلَٰهِ مُوسَىٰ وَإِنِّي لَأَظُنُّهُۥ مِنَ ٱلْكَٰذِبِينَ ﴿٣٨﴾ وَٱسْتَكْبَرَ
هُوَ وَجُنُودُهُۥ فِي ٱلْأَرْضِ بِغَيْرِ ٱلْحَقِّ وَظَنُّوٓا۟ أَنَّهُمْ إِلَيْنَا
لَا يُرْجَعُونَ ﴿٣٩﴾ فَأَخَذْنَٰهُ وَجُنُودَهُۥ فَنَبَذْنَٰهُمْ فِي
ٱلْيَمِّۖ فَٱنظُرْ كَيْفَ كَانَ عَٰقِبَةُ ٱلظَّٰلِمِينَ ﴿٤٠﴾
وَجَعَلْنَٰهُمْ أَئِمَّةً يَدْعُونَ إِلَى ٱلنَّارِۖ وَيَوْمَ ٱلْقِيَٰمَةِ
لَا يُنصَرُونَ ﴿٤١﴾ وَأَتْبَعْنَٰهُمْ فِي هَٰذِهِ ٱلدُّنْيَا لَعْنَةًۖ
وَيَوْمَ ٱلْقِيَٰمَةِ هُم مِّنَ ٱلْمَقْبُوحِينَ ﴿٤٢﴾ وَلَقَدْ ءَاتَيْنَا
مُوسَى ٱلْكِتَٰبَ مِنۢ بَعْدِ مَآ أَهْلَكْنَا ٱلْقُرُونَ ٱلْأُولَىٰ
بَصَآئِرَ لِلنَّاسِ وَهُدًى وَرَحْمَةً لَّعَلَّهُمْ يَتَذَكَّرُونَ ﴿٤٣﴾
وَمَا كُنتَ بِجَانِبِ ٱلْغَرْبِيِّ إِذْ قَضَيْنَآ إِلَىٰ مُوسَى ٱلْأَمْرَ وَمَا كُنتَ

and it returned to its normal state. The arm here is called *"janāḥ"* (lit. wing) since for a human being the arm is like what the wing is for a bird. ***These*** (read as *dhānika* and *dhānnika*) – referring to the staff and the hand – ***are two proofs from your Lord for Pharaoh and his ruling circle. They are a deviant people.'***

33. ***He said, 'My Lord, I killed one of them*** – meaning the Copt he had killed before – ***and I am afraid they will kill me…***

34. ***…and my brother Hārūn is more eloquent than me*** – with clearer speech – ***so send him with me*** as a helper ***to support me*** (read as *rid'an* and *ridan*) ***and back me up*** (read as *yuṣaddiqunī* and *yuṣaddiqnī*). ***I am afraid they will call me a liar.'***

35. ***He said, 'We will reinforce you with your brother and by Our Signs will give you both authority, so that they will not be able to lay a hand on you. You and those who follow you will be the victors*** over them.*'*

36. ***But when Mūsā brought them Our Clear Signs they said, 'This is nothing but trumped-up*** – invented – ***magic. We never heard anything like this among our earlier forefathers.'***

37. (The beginning of this āyat is read both with and without a *wāw*) ***Mūsā said, 'My Lord knows best who has come with guidance from Him and who will have*** (read as *takūna* and *yakūna*) ***the best Home in the end*** – a praiseworthy outcome in the Next World. ***The wrongdoers*** (the unbelievers) ***will certainly not be successful.'***

38. Pharaoh said, 'Council, I do not know of any other god for you apart from Me. Hāmān, kindle a fire for me over the clay and make bricks ***and build me a lofty tower so that perhaps I may be able to climb up to Mūsā's god*** and look at Him***! I consider him a blatant liar*** in saying that there is another god and that he is His Messenger.*'*

39. ***He and his troops were arrogant in the land*** of Egypt ***without any right. They thought that they would not return*** (read as *yurja'ūna* and *yarju'ūna*) ***to Us.***

40. ***So We seized him and his troops and flung them into the*** salt ***sea*** where they were drowned. ***See the final fate*** – the destruction – of ***the wrongdoers.***

مِنَ ٱلشَّٰهِدِينَ ﴿٤٤﴾ وَلَٰكِنَّآ أَنشَأۡنَا قُرُونٗا فَتَطَاوَلَ عَلَيۡهِمُ
ٱلۡعُمُرُۚ وَمَا كُنتَ ثَاوِيٗا فِيٓ أَهۡلِ مَدۡيَنَ تَتۡلُواْ عَلَيۡهِمۡ
ءَايَٰتِنَا وَلَٰكِنَّا كُنَّا مُرۡسِلِينَ ﴿٤٥﴾ وَمَا كُنتَ بِجَانِبِ
ٱلطُّورِ إِذۡ نَادَيۡنَا وَلَٰكِن رَّحۡمَةٗ مِّن رَّبِّكَ لِتُنذِرَ قَوۡمٗا
مَّآ أَتَىٰهُم مِّن نَّذِيرٖ مِّن قَبۡلِكَ لَعَلَّهُمۡ يَتَذَكَّرُونَ ﴿٤٦﴾
وَلَوۡلَآ أَن تُصِيبَهُم مُّصِيبَةُۢ بِمَا قَدَّمَتۡ أَيۡدِيهِمۡ فَيَقُولُواْ
رَبَّنَا لَوۡلَآ أَرۡسَلۡتَ إِلَيۡنَا رَسُولٗا فَنَتَّبِعَ ءَايَٰتِكَ وَنَكُونَ
مِنَ ٱلۡمُؤۡمِنِينَ ﴿٤٧﴾ فَلَمَّا جَآءَهُمُ ٱلۡحَقُّ مِنۡ عِندِنَا قَالُواْ
لَوۡلَآ أُوتِيَ مِثۡلَ مَآ أُوتِيَ مُوسَىٰٓۚ أَوَلَمۡ يَكۡفُرُواْ بِمَآ أُوتِيَ
مُوسَىٰ مِن قَبۡلُۖ قَالُواْ سِحۡرَانِ تَظَٰهَرَا وَقَالُوٓاْ إِنَّا بِكُلّٖ كَٰفِرُونَ
﴿٤٨﴾ قُلۡ فَأۡتُواْ بِكِتَٰبٖ مِّنۡ عِندِ ٱللَّهِ هُوَ أَهۡدَىٰ مِنۡهُمَآ أَتَّبِعۡهُ
إِن كُنتُمۡ صَٰدِقِينَ ﴿٤٩﴾ فَإِن لَّمۡ يَسۡتَجِيبُواْ لَكَ فَٱعۡلَمۡ
أَنَّمَا يَتَّبِعُونَ أَهۡوَآءَهُمۡۚ وَمَنۡ أَضَلُّ مِمَّنِ ٱتَّبَعَ هَوَىٰهُ بِغَيۡرِ
هُدٗى مِّنَ ٱللَّهِۚ إِنَّ ٱللَّهَ لَا يَهۡدِي ٱلۡقَوۡمَ ٱلظَّٰلِمِينَ ﴿٥٠﴾
۞ وَلَقَدۡ وَصَّلۡنَا لَهُمُ ٱلۡقَوۡلَ لَعَلَّهُمۡ يَتَذَكَّرُونَ ﴿٥١﴾ ٱلَّذِينَ
ءَاتَيۡنَٰهُمُ ٱلۡكِتَٰبَ مِن قَبۡلِهِۦ هُم بِهِۦ يُؤۡمِنُونَ ﴿٥٢﴾ وَإِذَا يُتۡلَىٰ عَلَيۡهِمۡ
قَالُوٓاْ ءَامَنَّا بِهِۦٓ إِنَّهُ ٱلۡحَقُّ مِن رَّبِّنَآ إِنَّا كُنَّا مِن قَبۡلِهِۦ مُسۡلِمِينَ ﴿٥٣﴾
أُوْلَٰٓئِكَ يُؤۡتَوۡنَ أَجۡرَهُم مَّرَّتَيۡنِ بِمَا صَبَرُواْ وَيَدۡرَءُونَ بِٱلۡحَسَنَةِ
ٱلسَّيِّئَةَ وَمِمَّا رَزَقۡنَٰهُمۡ يُنفِقُونَ ﴿٥٤﴾ وَإِذَا سَمِعُواْ ٱللَّغۡوَ
أَعۡرَضُواْ عَنۡهُ وَقَالُواْ لَنَآ أَعۡمَٰلُنَا وَلَكُمۡ أَعۡمَٰلُكُمۡ سَلَٰمٌ عَلَيۡكُمۡ

41. ***We made them leaders*** – in this world – ***summoning to the Fire*** – by their *shirk* – ***and on the Day of Rising they will not be helped*** against the punishment from Allah.

42. ***We pursued them with a curse*** and disgrace ***in this world; and on the Day of Rising they will be hideous and spurned.***

43. ***We gave Mūsā the Book*** (the Torah) ***after destroying the earlier nations*** – the peoples of Nūḥ, 'Ād, Thamūd and others – ***to awaken people's hearts and as a guidance*** away from misguidance, for those who act by it, ***and a mercy*** for those who believe in it, ***so that perhaps they might pay heed*** and be admonished by the warnings which it contains.

44. ***You,*** Muḥammad, ***were not on the western side*** of the mountain or the valley ***when We gave Mūsā the command***: the Message to Pharaoh and his people. ***You were not a witness*** so that you could know it.

45. ***Yet We produced further generations*** after Mūsā, ***and ages passed*** – so they forgot their contract with Allah, many knowledges disappeared, and Revelation ceased. Therefore We brought you as a Messenger and revealed to You the news of Mūsā and others. ***Nor did you live among the people of Madyan and recite Our Signs to them,*** enabling you to learn their story and report it, ***yet We have sent you news of them.*** We sent the Message to you with news of those who went before.

46. ***Nor were you on the side of the Mount when We called*** Mūsā to take hold of the Book with vigour***; yet it is a mercy from your Lord*** that He sent you ***so that you may warn a people*** (the people of Makka) ***to whom no warner came before, so that perhaps they will pay heed.***

47. ***If a disaster*** (punishment) ***had struck them because of what they*** (the unbelievers and others) ***had already done, they would have said, 'Our Lord, why did You not send us a Messenger so that we could have followed Your Signs and been believers?'***

48. ***But when the truth*** (Muḥammad) ***did come to them from Us they said, 'Why has he not been given the same*** signs ***as Mūsā was given*** – such as the white hand, staff and other things, or the Book all at once***?'*** Allah said: ***But did they not previously reject what Mūsā***

was given? They say about them, ***'Two magics*** – meaning the Qur'an and the Torah (also read as *sāḥirān*, meaning two magicians, referring to Muḥammad and Mūsā) – ***who back each other up.' And they say, 'We reject both*** – Books and Prophets – ***of them.'***

49. ***Say*** to them, ***'Bring a Book, then, from Allah which guides better than both of them*** – the Qur'an and the Torah – ***and follow it, if you are telling the truth.'***

50. ***If they do not respond to you*** – to your invitation to bring a Book – ***then know that they are merely following their whims and desires*** (unbelief). ***And who could be further astray than someone who follows his whims and desires without any guidance from Allah? Allah does not guide the people of the wrongdoers*** (unbelievers).

51. ***We have conveyed the Word to them*** – and made the Qur'an clear to them – ***so that perhaps they may pay heed*** – be warned and then believe.

52. ***Those We gave the Book before this*** – before the Qur'an was revealed – ***believe in it.*** This was revealed about a group of the Jews who became Muslims, such as 'Abdullāh ibn Salām and others, and Christians who came from Abyssinia and from Syria.

53. ***When it*** (the Qur'an) ***is recited to them they say, 'We believe in it; it is the truth from our Lord. We were already Muslims*** (believers in the Divine Unity) ***before it came.'***

54. ***They will be given their reward twice over*** – for believing in both Books – ***because they have been steadfast*** in acting by both of them ***and because they ward off the bad with the good and give*** *ṣadaqa* ***from what We have provided for them.***

55. ***When they hear worthless talk*** – abuse and criticism from the unbelievers – ***they turn away from it and say, 'We have our actions and you have your actions. Peace be upon you*** – a blessed peace in which you are safe from abuse and other things. ***We do not desire the company of the ignorant.'***

56. The following was revealed about the eagerness of the Prophet, may Allah bless him and grant him peace, for his uncle, Abū Ṭālib, to have faith. ***You cannot guide those you would like to but Allah guides those He wills. He has best knowledge of the guided.***

لَا نَبۡتَغِي ٱلۡجَٰهِلِينَ ﴿٥٥﴾ إِنَّكَ لَا تَهۡدِي مَنۡ أَحۡبَبۡتَ وَلَٰكِنَّ
ٱللَّهَ يَهۡدِي مَن يَشَآءُۚ وَهُوَ أَعۡلَمُ بِٱلۡمُهۡتَدِينَ ﴿٥٦﴾ وَقَالُوٓاْ إِن
نَّتَّبِعِ ٱلۡهُدَىٰ مَعَكَ نُتَخَطَّفۡ مِنۡ أَرۡضِنَآۚ أَوَلَمۡ نُمَكِّن لَّهُمۡ
حَرَمًا ءَامِنٗا يُجۡبَىٰٓ إِلَيۡهِ ثَمَرَٰتُ كُلِّ شَيۡءٖ رِّزۡقٗا مِّن لَّدُنَّا وَلَٰكِنَّ
أَكۡثَرَهُمۡ لَا يَعۡلَمُونَ ﴿٥٧﴾ وَكَمۡ أَهۡلَكۡنَا مِن قَرۡيَةِۭ
بَطِرَتۡ مَعِيشَتَهَاۖ فَتِلۡكَ مَسَٰكِنُهُمۡ لَمۡ تُسۡكَن مِّنۢ بَعۡدِهِمۡ
إِلَّا قَلِيلٗاۖ وَكُنَّا نَحۡنُ ٱلۡوَٰرِثِينَ ﴿٥٨﴾ وَمَا كَانَ رَبُّكَ مُهۡلِكَ
ٱلۡقُرَىٰ حَتَّىٰ يَبۡعَثَ فِيٓ أُمِّهَا رَسُولٗا يَتۡلُواْ عَلَيۡهِمۡ ءَايَٰتِنَاۚ وَمَا
كُنَّا مُهۡلِكِي ٱلۡقُرَىٰٓ إِلَّا وَأَهۡلُهَا ظَٰلِمُونَ ﴿٥٩﴾
وَمَآ أُوتِيتُم مِّن شَيۡءٖ فَمَتَٰعُ ٱلۡحَيَوٰةِ ٱلدُّنۡيَا وَزِينَتُهَاۚ وَمَا عِندَ
ٱللَّهِ خَيۡرٞ وَأَبۡقَىٰٓۚ أَفَلَا تَعۡقِلُونَ ﴿٦٠﴾ أَفَمَن وَعَدۡنَٰهُ وَعۡدًا حَسَنٗا
فَهُوَ لَٰقِيهِ كَمَن مَّتَّعۡنَٰهُ مَتَٰعَ ٱلۡحَيَوٰةِ ٱلدُّنۡيَا ثُمَّ هُوَ يَوۡمَ ٱلۡقِيَٰمَةِ
مِنَ ٱلۡمُحۡضَرِينَ ﴿٦١﴾ وَيَوۡمَ يُنَادِيهِمۡ فَيَقُولُ أَيۡنَ شُرَكَآءِيَ ٱلَّذِينَ
كُنتُمۡ تَزۡعُمُونَ ﴿٦٢﴾ قَالَ ٱلَّذِينَ حَقَّ عَلَيۡهِمُ ٱلۡقَوۡلُ رَبَّنَا هَٰٓؤُلَآءِ
ٱلَّذِينَ أَغۡوَيۡنَآ أَغۡوَيۡنَٰهُمۡ كَمَا غَوَيۡنَاۖ تَبَرَّأۡنَآ إِلَيۡكَۖ مَا كَانُوٓاْ إِيَّانَا
يَعۡبُدُونَ ﴿٦٣﴾ وَقِيلَ ٱدۡعُواْ شُرَكَآءَكُمۡ فَدَعَوۡهُمۡ فَلَمۡ يَسۡتَجِيبُواْ
لَهُمۡ وَرَأَوُاْ ٱلۡعَذَابَۚ لَوۡ أَنَّهُمۡ كَانُواْ يَهۡتَدُونَ ﴿٦٤﴾ وَيَوۡمَ يُنَادِيهِمۡ
فَيَقُولُ مَاذَآ أَجَبۡتُمُ ٱلۡمُرۡسَلِينَ ﴿٦٥﴾ فَعَمِيَتۡ عَلَيۡهِمُ ٱلۡأَنۢبَآءُ
يَوۡمَئِذٖ فَهُمۡ لَا يَتَسَآءَلُونَ ﴿٦٦﴾ فَأَمَّا مَن تَابَ وَءَامَنَ وَعَمِلَ
صَٰلِحٗا فَعَسَىٰٓ أَن يَكُونَ مِنَ ٱلۡمُفۡلِحِينَ ﴿٦٧﴾ وَرَبُّكَ

57. ***They*** (his people) ***say, 'If we follow the guidance with you, we shall*** quickly ***be forcibly uprooted from our land.'*** Allah said: ***Have We not established a safe haven for them*** – where they are safe from the attacks and killing which regularly occur among the Arabs – ***to which produce of every kind is brought*** (read as *yuḥbā* and *tuḥbā*), ***provision*** for them ***direct from Us? But most of them do not know it***: that what We say is the truth.

58. ***How many cities*** – referring to their inhabitants – ***We have destroyed which lived in insolent ingratitude*** – reflected in their lifestyle***! There are their houses, never again inhabited after them, except a little*** – referring to those who pass through them and rest there for a day or part of a day***. It was We who were their Heir.***

59. ***Your Lord would never destroy*** the inhabitants of ***any cities*** for wrong action ***without first sending to the chief of them a Messenger to recite Our Signs to them. We would never destroy any cities unless their inhabitants were wrongdoers*** in rejecting their Messengers.

60. ***Anything you have been given is only the enjoyment of the life of this world and its finery***, which you enjoy during your life and which will then vanish. ***What*** (reward) ***is with Allah is better and longer lasting; so will you not use your intellect*** (read as *ta'qilūna* and *ya'qilūna*) – and realise that that which lasts is better than that which vanishes***?***

61. ***Is someone whom We have promised good*** (the Garden) ***and who then obtains it the same as someone whom We have given enjoyment in the life of this world*** – which rapidly passes – ***and who then, on the Day of Rising, is one of those brought to punishment*** in the Fire***?*** – a reference to believers and unbelievers. They are not equal.

62. ***On the Day when He summons them He will say, 'Where are they, those you claimed were My associates?'***

63. ***Those*** (the leaders of misguidance) ***against whom the Word has been justly carried out*** – by their entering the Fire – ***will say, 'Our Lord, those people whom we misled we only misled as we too were misled.*** We did not force them into error. ***We disown responsibility to You*** for them. ***It was not us they were worshipping!'***

يَخْلُقُ مَا يَشَآءُ وَيَخْتَارُ مَا كَانَ لَهُمُ ٱلْخِيَرَةُ سُبْحَٰنَ
ٱللَّهِ وَتَعَٰلَىٰ عَمَّا يُشْرِكُونَ ٦٨ وَرَبُّكَ يَعْلَمُ مَا تُكِنُّ
صُدُورُهُمْ وَمَا يُعْلِنُونَ ٦٩ وَهُوَ ٱللَّهُ لَآ إِلَٰهَ إِلَّا هُوَ لَهُ
ٱلْحَمْدُ فِى ٱلْأُولَىٰ وَٱلْـَٔاخِرَةِ وَلَهُ ٱلْحُكْمُ وَإِلَيْهِ تُرْجَعُونَ ٧٠
قُلْ أَرَءَيْتُمْ إِن جَعَلَ ٱللَّهُ عَلَيْكُمُ ٱلَّيْلَ سَرْمَدًا إِلَىٰ يَوْمِ ٱلْقِيَٰمَةِ
مَنْ إِلَٰهٌ غَيْرُ ٱللَّهِ يَأْتِيكُم بِضِيَآءٍ أَفَلَا تَسْمَعُونَ ٧١
قُلْ أَرَءَيْتُمْ إِن جَعَلَ ٱللَّهُ عَلَيْكُمُ ٱلنَّهَارَ سَرْمَدًا إِلَىٰ
يَوْمِ ٱلْقِيَٰمَةِ مَنْ إِلَٰهٌ غَيْرُ ٱللَّهِ يَأْتِيكُم بِلَيْلٍ تَسْكُنُونَ
فِيهِ أَفَلَا تُبْصِرُونَ ٧٢ وَمِن رَّحْمَتِهِۦ جَعَلَ لَكُمُ ٱلَّيْلَ
وَٱلنَّهَارَ لِتَسْكُنُوا۟ فِيهِ وَلِتَبْتَغُوا۟ مِن فَضْلِهِۦ وَلَعَلَّكُمْ تَشْكُرُونَ
٧٣ وَيَوْمَ يُنَادِيهِمْ فَيَقُولُ أَيْنَ شُرَكَآءِىَ ٱلَّذِينَ كُنتُمْ
تَزْعُمُونَ ٧٤ وَنَزَعْنَا مِن كُلِّ أُمَّةٍ شَهِيدًا فَقُلْنَا
هَاتُوا۟ بُرْهَٰنَكُمْ فَعَلِمُوٓا۟ أَنَّ ٱلْحَقَّ لِلَّهِ وَضَلَّ عَنْهُم مَّا كَانُوا۟
يَفْتَرُونَ ٧٥ ۞ إِنَّ قَٰرُونَ كَانَ مِن قَوْمِ مُوسَىٰ فَبَغَىٰ
عَلَيْهِمْ وَءَاتَيْنَٰهُ مِنَ ٱلْكُنُوزِ مَآ إِنَّ مَفَاتِحَهُۥ لَتَنُوٓأُ بِٱلْعُصْبَةِ
أُو۟لِى ٱلْقُوَّةِ إِذْ قَالَ لَهُۥ قَوْمُهُۥ لَا تَفْرَحْ إِنَّ ٱللَّهَ لَا يُحِبُّ ٱلْفَرِحِينَ
٧٦ وَٱبْتَغِ فِيمَآ ءَاتَىٰكَ ٱللَّهُ ٱلدَّارَ ٱلْـَٔاخِرَةَ وَلَا تَنسَ
نَصِيبَكَ مِنَ ٱلدُّنْيَا وَأَحْسِن كَمَآ أَحْسَنَ ٱللَّهُ إِلَيْكَ
وَلَا تَبْغِ ٱلْفَسَادَ فِى ٱلْأَرْضِ إِنَّ ٱللَّهَ لَا يُحِبُّ ٱلْمُفْسِدِينَ ٧٧
قَالَ إِنَّمَآ أُوتِيتُهُۥ عَلَىٰ عِلْمٍ عِندِىٓ أَوَلَمْ يَعْلَمْ أَنَّ ٱللَّهَ قَدْ أَهْلَكَ
مِن قَبْلِهِۦ مِنَ ٱلْقُرُونِ مَنْ هُوَ أَشَدُّ مِنْهُ قُوَّةً وَأَكْثَرُ جَمْعًا

64. ***They will be told, 'Call on your partner-gods*** which you claimed were the partners of Allah*!'* ***They will call on them but they will not respond to them*** or their supplication. ***They will see the punishment. Oh, if only they had been guided*** in this world*!*

65. ***On the Day when He summons them He will say, 'How did you respond to the Messengers?'***

66. ***That Day the facts*** – the answer to that question – ***will be unclear to them*** and they will find no way to save themselves ***and they will not be able to question one another*** and will remain silent.

67. ***But as for those who repent*** of *shirk* ***and believe*** in the unity of Allah ***and act rightly*** – by performing the actions obligatory for them – ***they will perhaps be successful*** – and be saved by Allah's promise of mercy.

68. ***Your Lord creates and chooses whatever He wills. The choice is not theirs*** (the idolaters') in anything. ***Glory be to Allah! He is exalted above anything they associate with Him.***

69. ***Your Lord knows what their hearts conceal*** in terms of unbelief and other things, ***and what they divulge*** and say about that.

70. ***He is Allah. There is no god but Him. Praise be to Him in this world and the Next*** (Paradise). ***Judgement*** – which is carried out in respect of all things – ***belongs to Him. You will be returned to Him*** at the Resurrection.

71. ***Say*** to the people of Makka*:* 'Tell me, ***what do you think? If Allah made it permanently night for you till the Day of Rising, what god is there other than Allah*** – as you claim – ***to bring you light*** – referring to daytime when people seek their livelihood*?* ***Do you not then hear*** – in other words, understand and thereby turn away from *shirk?'*

72. ***Say*** to them*:* ***'What do you think? If Allah made it permanently day for you till the Day of Rising, what god is there other than Allah*** – as you claim – ***to bring you night to rest in*** from your labours*?* ***Do you not then see*** – the error you are in regarding *shirk* and turn away from it?'

73. ***But part of His mercy is that He has made both night and day for you so that you can have your rest*** in the night ***and seek His***

وَلَا يُسْـَٔلُ عَن ذُنُوبِهِمُ ٱلْمُجْرِمُونَ ﴿٧٨﴾ فَخَرَجَ عَلَىٰ قَوْمِهِۦ
فِى زِينَتِهِۦ ۖ قَالَ ٱلَّذِينَ يُرِيدُونَ ٱلْحَيَوٰةَ ٱلدُّنْيَا يَـٰلَيْتَ لَنَا
مِثْلَ مَآ أُوتِىَ قَـٰرُونُ إِنَّهُۥ لَذُو حَظٍّ عَظِيمٍ ﴿٧٩﴾ وَقَالَ
ٱلَّذِينَ أُوتُوا۟ ٱلْعِلْمَ وَيْلَكُمْ ثَوَابُ ٱللَّهِ خَيْرٌ لِّمَنْ ءَامَنَ
وَعَمِلَ صَـٰلِحًا وَلَا يُلَقَّىٰهَآ إِلَّا ٱلصَّـٰبِرُونَ ﴿٨٠﴾ فَخَسَفْنَا
بِهِۦ وَبِدَارِهِ ٱلْأَرْضَ فَمَا كَانَ لَهُۥ مِن فِئَةٍ يَنصُرُونَهُۥ مِن دُونِ
ٱللَّهِ وَمَا كَانَ مِنَ ٱلْمُنتَصِرِينَ ﴿٨١﴾ وَأَصْبَحَ ٱلَّذِينَ تَمَنَّوْا۟
مَكَانَهُۥ بِٱلْأَمْسِ يَقُولُونَ وَيْكَأَنَّ ٱللَّهَ يَبْسُطُ ٱلرِّزْقَ لِمَن
يَشَآءُ مِنْ عِبَادِهِۦ وَيَقْدِرُ ۖ لَوْلَآ أَن مَّنَّ ٱللَّهُ عَلَيْنَا لَخَسَفَ بِنَا ۖ
وَيْكَأَنَّهُۥ لَا يُفْلِحُ ٱلْكَـٰفِرُونَ ﴿٨٢﴾ تِلْكَ ٱلدَّارُ ٱلْـَٔاخِرَةُ نَجْعَلُهَا
لِلَّذِينَ لَا يُرِيدُونَ عُلُوًّا فِى ٱلْأَرْضِ وَلَا فَسَادًا ۚ وَٱلْعَـٰقِبَةُ لِلْمُتَّقِينَ
﴿٨٣﴾ مَن جَآءَ بِٱلْحَسَنَةِ فَلَهُۥ خَيْرٌ مِّنْهَا ۖ وَمَن جَآءَ بِٱلسَّيِّئَةِ فَلَا
يُجْزَى ٱلَّذِينَ عَمِلُوا۟ ٱلسَّيِّـَٔاتِ إِلَّا مَا كَانُوا۟ يَعْمَلُونَ ﴿٨٤﴾
إِنَّ ٱلَّذِى فَرَضَ عَلَيْكَ ٱلْقُرْءَانَ لَرَآدُّكَ إِلَىٰ مَعَادٍ ۚ قُل رَّبِّىٓ
أَعْلَمُ مَن جَآءَ بِٱلْهُدَىٰ وَمَنْ هُوَ فِى ضَلَـٰلٍ مُّبِينٍ ﴿٨٥﴾ وَمَا كُنتَ
تَرْجُوٓا۟ أَن يُلْقَىٰٓ إِلَيْكَ ٱلْكِتَـٰبُ إِلَّا رَحْمَةً مِّن رَّبِّكَ ۖ
فَلَا تَكُونَنَّ ظَهِيرًا لِّلْكَـٰفِرِينَ ﴿٨٦﴾ وَلَا يَصُدُّنَّكَ عَنْ ءَايَـٰتِ
ٱللَّهِ بَعْدَ إِذْ أُنزِلَتْ إِلَيْكَ ۖ وَٱدْعُ إِلَىٰ رَبِّكَ ۖ وَلَا تَكُونَنَّ مِنَ
ٱلْمُشْرِكِينَ ﴿٨٧﴾ وَلَا تَدْعُ مَعَ ٱللَّهِ إِلَـٰهًا ءَاخَرَ ۘ لَآ إِلَـٰهَ إِلَّا
هُوَ ۚ كُلُّ شَىْءٍ هَالِكٌ إِلَّا وَجْهَهُۥ ۚ لَهُ ٱلْحُكْمُ وَإِلَيْهِ تُرْجَعُونَ ﴿٨٨﴾

bounty in the day ***and so that perhaps you will be thankful*** for His blessings upon you.

74. ***On the Day when He summons them He will say, 'Where are they, those you claimed to be My associates?'***

75. ***We will drag out a witness from each nation*** – and that will be their Prophet who will testify against them regarding what they said – ***and*** We ***will say*** to them, ***'Produce your evidence*** for the *shirk* which you espouse*!'* ***They will know then that the truth*** regarding divinity ***is with Allah*** and that there is no partner with Him, ***and that what they invented*** in this world about Allah having a partner ***has forsaken them.***

76. ***Qārūn was one of the people of Mūsā*** – he was the cousin of Mūsā and believed in him – ***but he lorded it over them*** because of his pride, height and great wealth. ***We gave him treasures, the keys to which alone were a heavy weight for a party of strong men.*** It is said that the number of men who carried the keys was seventy, forty, ten, or some other number. So remember ***when his people*** – the believers of the tribe of Israel – ***said to him, 'Do not gloat*** about your wealth. ***Allah does not love people who gloat.***

77. ***Seek the abode of the Next World with what Allah has given you*** – by spending the wealth which Allah has given you in obedience to Allah – ***without forgetting your portion of this world.*** Do not forget to work in this world for the Next World. ***And do good*** – by giving *ṣadaqa* – ***as Allah has been good to you. And do not seek to cause corruption in the earth*** by doing acts of disobedience. ***Allah does not love corrupters*** and will punish them.*'*

78. ***He said, 'I have only been given it*** (wealth) ***because of knowledge I have.'*** He had the greatest knowledge of the Torah among the tribe of Israel, after Mūsā and Hārūn. Allah said: ***Did he not know that before him Allah had destroyed generations*** (nations) ***with far greater strength than his, and far more possessions?*** He knows that and knows that Allah destroyed them. ***The evildoers will not be questioned about their sins***; since He knows them, but they will enter the Fire without reckoning.

79. ***He*** (Qārūn) ***went out among his people in his finery***: with his many followers, who were mounted and adorned with clothing of gold and silk on decorated horses and mules. ***Those who desired the life of this world said, 'Oh! If only we had the same as Qārūn has been given*** in this world***! What immense good fortune he possesses.'***

80. ***But those who had been given knowledge*** of what Allah has promised in the Next World ***said*** to them***: 'Woe to you!*** This is a rebuke. ***Allah's reward*** of Paradise in the Next World ***is better*** than what Qārūn was given in this world ***for those who believe and act rightly. But only the steadfast*** – in respect of holding to obedience and avoiding disobedience – ***will obtain it.'***

81. ***We caused the earth to swallow up both him*** (Qārūn) ***and his house. There was no group to come to his aid*** and defend him from destruction ***besides Allah, and he was not someone who is helped.***

82. ***Those who had longed to take his place the day before woke up saying, 'Allah expands the provision of any of His slaves He wills, or restricts it. If Allah had not shown great kindness to us, we would have been swallowed up as well. Ah! Truly the unbelievers*** who are ungrateful for Allah's blessing ***are not successful.'***

83. ***That abode*** (the Garden) ***of the Next World – We grant it to those who do not seek to exalt themselves in the earth*** through insolence ***or to cause corruption in it*** by acts of disobedience. ***The successful outcome is for those who are godfearing*** – who fear the punishment of Allah and do righteous actions.

84. ***Anyone who does a good action will get something better*** – a reward for ten like it. ***As for anyone who does a bad action, those who have done bad actions will only be repaid for what they did.***

85. ***He who has imposed the Qur'an upon you*** – and sent it down – ***will most certainly bring you back home*** to Makka ***again.*** The Prophet yearned for that. ***Say: 'My Lord knows best who has brought true guidance and who is plainly misguided.'*** This was revealed to answer the unbelievers of Makka who said, "You are misguided." Allah knows who brings guidance, while they are in truth misguided.

86. ***You did not expect to be given the Book*** (the Qur'an). ***It is nothing but a mercy*** given to you ***from your Lord. So do not lend support to the unbelievers*** in their *dīn*, to which they invite you.

87. ***Do not let them debar you from Allah's Signs after they have been sent down to you.*** Do not revert to them in that respect. ***Call people to*** the unity of ***your Lord*** and His worship, ***and on no account be one of the idolators*** by helping them.

88. ***Do not call on*** – and worship – ***any other god along with Allah. There is no god but Him. All things are passing except His Face.*** Effective ***judgement belongs to Him. You will be returned to Him*** by being resurrected from your graves.

سُورَةُ العَنكَبُوتِ

بِسۡمِ ٱللَّهِ ٱلرَّحۡمَٰنِ ٱلرَّحِيمِ

الٓمٓ ﴿١﴾ أَحَسِبَ ٱلنَّاسُ أَن يُتۡرَكُوٓاْ أَن يَقُولُوٓاْ ءَامَنَّا وَهُمۡ لَا
يُفۡتَنُونَ ﴿٢﴾ وَلَقَدۡ فَتَنَّا ٱلَّذِينَ مِن قَبۡلِهِمۡۖ فَلَيَعۡلَمَنَّ ٱللَّهُ ٱلَّذِينَ
صَدَقُواْ وَلَيَعۡلَمَنَّ ٱلۡكَٰذِبِينَ ﴿٣﴾ أَمۡ حَسِبَ ٱلَّذِينَ يَعۡمَلُونَ
ٱلسَّيِّـَٔاتِ أَن يَسۡبِقُونَاۚ سَآءَ مَا يَحۡكُمُونَ ﴿٤﴾ مَن كَانَ يَرۡجُواْ
لِقَآءَ ٱللَّهِ فَإِنَّ أَجَلَ ٱللَّهِ لَأٓتٖۚ وَهُوَ ٱلسَّمِيعُ ٱلۡعَلِيمُ ﴿٥﴾ وَمَن
جَٰهَدَ فَإِنَّمَا يُجَٰهِدُ لِنَفۡسِهِۦٓۚ إِنَّ ٱللَّهَ لَغَنِيٌّ عَنِ ٱلۡعَٰلَمِينَ ﴿٦﴾
وَٱلَّذِينَ ءَامَنُواْ وَعَمِلُواْ ٱلصَّٰلِحَٰتِ لَنُكَفِّرَنَّ عَنۡهُمۡ سَيِّـَٔاتِهِمۡ
وَلَنَجۡزِيَنَّهُمۡ أَحۡسَنَ ٱلَّذِي كَانُواْ يَعۡمَلُونَ ﴿٧﴾ وَوَصَّيۡنَا ٱلۡإِنسَٰنَ
بِوَٰلِدَيۡهِ حُسۡنٗاۖ وَإِن جَٰهَدَاكَ لِتُشۡرِكَ بِي مَا لَيۡسَ لَكَ بِهِۦ عِلۡمٞ
فَلَا تُطِعۡهُمَآۚ إِلَيَّ مَرۡجِعُكُمۡ فَأُنَبِّئُكُم بِمَا كُنتُمۡ تَعۡمَلُونَ ﴿٨﴾
وَٱلَّذِينَ ءَامَنُواْ وَعَمِلُواْ ٱلصَّٰلِحَٰتِ لَنُدۡخِلَنَّهُمۡ فِي ٱلصَّٰلِحِينَ
﴿٩﴾ وَمِنَ ٱلنَّاسِ مَن يَقُولُ ءَامَنَّا بِٱللَّهِ فَإِذَآ أُوذِيَ فِي ٱللَّهِ جَعَلَ
فِتۡنَةَ ٱلنَّاسِ كَعَذَابِ ٱللَّهِ وَلَئِن جَآءَ نَصۡرٞ مِّن رَّبِّكَ لَيَقُولُنَّ
إِنَّا كُنَّا مَعَكُمۡۚ أَوَلَيۡسَ ٱللَّهُ بِأَعۡلَمَ بِمَا فِي صُدُورِ ٱلۡعَٰلَمِينَ
﴿١٠﴾ وَلَيَعۡلَمَنَّ ٱللَّهُ ٱلَّذِينَ ءَامَنُواْ وَلَيَعۡلَمَنَّ ٱلۡمُنَٰفِقِينَ
﴿١١﴾ وَقَالَ ٱلَّذِينَ كَفَرُواْ لِلَّذِينَ ءَامَنُواْ ٱتَّبِعُواْ سَبِيلَنَا
وَلۡنَحۡمِلۡ خَطَٰيَٰكُمۡ وَمَا هُم بِحَٰمِلِينَ مِنۡ خَطَٰيَٰهُم مِّن
شَيۡءٍۖ إِنَّهُمۡ لَكَٰذِبُونَ ﴿١٢﴾ وَلَيَحۡمِلُنَّ أَثۡقَالَهُمۡ وَأَثۡقَالٗا

29. *Sūrat al-'Ankabūt*
The Spider

This *sūra* is Makkan except from *āyat* 1 to the end of *āyat* 11, which is Madinan. It has 69 *āyats* and was sent down after *ar-Rūm.*

1. ***Alif Lam Mim.*** Allah knows best what is meant by that.

2. ***Do people imagine that they will be left to say 'We believe,' and will not be tested*** to make the reality of their faith clear? This was revealed about a group of people who believed and then were persecuted by the idolators.

3. ***We tested those before them so that Allah would know the truthful*** – in respect of their belief, by means of direct evidence – ***and would know the liars*** – concerning it.

4. ***Or do those who do bad actions*** – *shirk* and other acts of disobedience – ***imagine they can outstrip Us*** – escape Us, so that We will not take revenge on them? ***How bad their judgement is!***

5. ***As for those who look forward*** fearfully ***to meeting Allah, Allah's appointed time is certainly coming***, and so they should prepare for it. ***He is the All-Hearing*** of what they say, ***the All-Knowing*** of what they do.

6. ***Whoever does* jihād** – actual fighting or *jihād* against the self – ***does it entirely for himself.*** The benefit of the *jihād* goes to himself, not to Allah. ***Allah is Rich Beyond Need of any being*** – referring to men, *jinn* and angels, and their worship.

7. ***As for those who believe and do right actions, We will erase their bad actions from them*** because of their righteous actions ***and recompense them for the best of what they did*** – their righteous actions.

8. ***We have instructed man to honour his parents*** by being dutiful to them ***but if they endeavour to make you associate with Me something about which you have no knowledge, do not obey them*** in their *shirk*. ***It is to Me that you will return, and I will inform you about the things you did*** – and repay you for them.

مَعَ أَثْقَالِهِمْ ۖ وَلَيُسْأَلُنَّ يَوْمَ الْقِيَامَةِ عَمَّا كَانُوا يَفْتَرُونَ
﴿١٣﴾ وَلَقَدْ أَرْسَلْنَا نُوحًا إِلَىٰ قَوْمِهِ فَلَبِثَ فِيهِمْ أَلْفَ سَنَةٍ
إِلَّا خَمْسِينَ عَامًا فَأَخَذَهُمُ الطُّوفَانُ وَهُمْ ظَالِمُونَ ﴿١٤﴾
فَأَنْجَيْنَاهُ وَأَصْحَابَ السَّفِينَةِ وَجَعَلْنَاهَا آيَةً لِلْعَالَمِينَ
﴿١٥﴾ وَإِبْرَاهِيمَ إِذْ قَالَ لِقَوْمِهِ اعْبُدُوا اللَّهَ وَاتَّقُوهُ ۖ ذَٰلِكُمْ
خَيْرٌ لَكُمْ إِنْ كُنْتُمْ تَعْلَمُونَ ﴿١٦﴾ إِنَّمَا تَعْبُدُونَ مِنْ
دُونِ اللَّهِ أَوْثَانًا وَتَخْلُقُونَ إِفْكًا ۚ إِنَّ الَّذِينَ تَعْبُدُونَ مِنْ
دُونِ اللَّهِ لَا يَمْلِكُونَ لَكُمْ رِزْقًا فَابْتَغُوا عِنْدَ اللَّهِ الرِّزْقَ
وَاعْبُدُوهُ وَاشْكُرُوا لَهُ ۖ إِلَيْهِ تُرْجَعُونَ ﴿١٧﴾ وَإِنْ تُكَذِّبُوا
فَقَدْ كَذَّبَ أُمَمٌ مِنْ قَبْلِكُمْ ۖ وَمَا عَلَى الرَّسُولِ إِلَّا الْبَلَاغُ
الْمُبِينُ ﴿١٨﴾ أَوَلَمْ يَرَوْا كَيْفَ يُبْدِئُ اللَّهُ الْخَلْقَ ثُمَّ
يُعِيدُهُ ۚ إِنَّ ذَٰلِكَ عَلَى اللَّهِ يَسِيرٌ ﴿١٩﴾ قُلْ سِيرُوا فِي الْأَرْضِ
فَانْظُرُوا كَيْفَ بَدَأَ الْخَلْقَ ۚ ثُمَّ اللَّهُ يُنْشِئُ النَّشْأَةَ الْآخِرَةَ ۚ
إِنَّ اللَّهَ عَلَىٰ كُلِّ شَيْءٍ قَدِيرٌ ﴿٢٠﴾ يُعَذِّبُ مَنْ يَشَاءُ وَيَرْحَمُ
مَنْ يَشَاءُ ۖ وَإِلَيْهِ تُقْلَبُونَ ﴿٢١﴾ وَمَا أَنْتُمْ بِمُعْجِزِينَ فِي
الْأَرْضِ وَلَا فِي السَّمَاءِ ۖ وَمَا لَكُمْ مِنْ دُونِ اللَّهِ مِنْ وَلِيٍّ
وَلَا نَصِيرٍ ﴿٢٢﴾ وَالَّذِينَ كَفَرُوا بِآيَاتِ اللَّهِ وَلِقَائِهِ
أُولَٰئِكَ يَئِسُوا مِنْ رَحْمَتِي وَأُولَٰئِكَ لَهُمْ عَذَابٌ أَلِيمٌ ﴿٢٣﴾
فَمَا كَانَ جَوَابَ قَوْمِهِ إِلَّا أَنْ قَالُوا اقْتُلُوهُ أَوْ حَرِّقُوهُ
فَأَنْجَاهُ اللَّهُ مِنَ النَّارِ ۚ إِنَّ فِي ذَٰلِكَ لَآيَاتٍ لِقَوْمٍ يُؤْمِنُونَ
﴿٢٤﴾ وَقَالَ إِنَّمَا اتَّخَذْتُمْ مِنْ دُونِ اللَّهِ أَوْثَانًا مَوَدَّةَ بَيْنِكُمْ

9. ***As for those who believe and do right actions, We will admit them among the righteous*** – a reference to the Prophets and saints. They will be gathered in their company.

10. ***There are some people who say, 'We believe in Allah,' and then, when they suffer harm in Allah's cause*** – when people persecute them on account of their belief – ***they take people's persecution for Allah's punishment*** – fearing their persecution as they would fear Allah's punishment, so that they then obey them and become hypocrites; ***but if help comes from your Lord*** to the believers, so that they obtain booty, ***they say, 'We were with you*** in belief, through the ups and downs of fortune, and therefore we should share with you in the booty.*'* Allah says: ***Does Allah not know best what is in every person's heart*** – in terms of belief or hypocrisy***?***

11. ***Allah knows those who have belief*** in their hearts***, and He knows the hypocrites*** – and will repay both parties.

12. ***Those who disbelieve say to those who believe, 'Follow our way*** (dīn) ***and we will bear the weight of your mistakes*** for following us, if there is any.*'* Allah says: ***They will not bear the weight of a single one of their mistakes.*** The imperative tense used here has the sense of being a report. ***Truly they are liars*** about that.

13. ***They will bear their own burdens*** (sins) ***and other burdens together with their own*** for saying to the believers, "Follow our way", and for misguiding their followers. ***On the Day of Rising they will be questioned about what they invented*** – the lies they made up about Allah. This is to rebuke them.

14. ***We sent Nūḥ to his people*** – when he was 40 years old or older – ***and he remained among them for fifty short of a thousand years*** – calling them to recognise Allah's unity, but they denied him***; yet the Flood engulfed them while they were wrongdoers*** (idolators), and they were drowned.

15. ***We rescued him*** (Nūḥ) ***and the occupants of the Ark*** – who were with him – ***and made that into a Sign*** and a lesson ***for all the worlds*** – for those people who have come after him, if they disobey their Messengers. Nūḥ lived after the Flood for sixty years or longer until mankind had increased in number once again.

16. ***And*** remember ***Ibrāhīm, when he said to his people, 'Worship Allah and be fearful of Him*** and His punishment. ***That is better for you*** than worshipping idols ***if you only knew.***

17. ***Instead of Allah you worship only idols. You are inventing a lie*** by saying that the idols are partners with Allah. ***Those you worship besides Allah have no power to provide for you.*** They cannot provide for you. ***So seek your provision from Allah and worship Him and give thanks to Him. It is to Him you will be returned.'***

18. ***And if you deny it*** and me, people of Makka, ***nations before you*** and before me ***also denied the truth. The Messenger is only responsible for clear transmission.*** Both these examples are to provide solace for the Prophet, may Allah bless him and grant him peace. Allah then says about his people:

19. ***Have they not seen*** (read as *yaraw* and also *taraw*, "Have you not seen") ***how Allah brings creation out of nothing*** (read as *yubdi'u* and *yabdi'yu*), ***then reproduces it?*** He can bring it back as He originated it. ***That*** – both the first and second creation – ***is easy for Allah.*** How, then, can you deny the possibility of the second?

20. ***Say: 'Travel about the earth and see*** those before you and their nations and ***how He brought creation out of nothing. Then later Allah will bring about the next existence. Allah has power over all things*** – including origination and bringing back again.

21. ***He punishes anyone He wills and has mercy on anyone He wills. You will be returned to Him.***

22. ***There is no way out for you in earth or heaven.*** You cannot prevent your Lord from reaching you, no matter where you are, and cannot escape from Him. ***You have no protector*** from Allah ***or helper*** against His punishment ***besides Allah.'***

23. ***Those who reject Allah's Signs*** (the Qur'an) ***and the meeting with Him*** (the Resurrection) – ***such people can despair of My mercy*** (the Garden)***; such people will have a painful punishment.***

24. Continuing with the story of Ibrāhīm, peace be upon him, Allah says: ***The only answer of his people*** – when they flung him into the fire – ***was to say: 'Kill him or burn him!' But Allah rescued him from the fire*** and made it coolness and peace for him. ***There are certainly Signs in that*** – referring to his rescue from the fire and the

فِي ٱلۡحَيَوٰةِ ٱلدُّنۡيَاۖ ثُمَّ يَوۡمَ ٱلۡقِيَٰمَةِ يَكۡفُرُ بَعۡضُكُم
بِبَعۡضٖ وَيَلۡعَنُ بَعۡضُكُم بَعۡضٗا وَمَأۡوَىٰكُمُ ٱلنَّارُ
وَمَا لَكُم مِّن نَّٰصِرِينَ ٢٥ ۞ فَـَٔامَنَ لَهُۥ لُوطٞۘ وَقَالَ
إِنِّي مُهَاجِرٌ إِلَىٰ رَبِّيٓۖ إِنَّهُۥ هُوَ ٱلۡعَزِيزُ ٱلۡحَكِيمُ ٢٦ وَوَهَبۡنَا
لَهُۥٓ إِسۡحَٰقَ وَيَعۡقُوبَ وَجَعَلۡنَا فِي ذُرِّيَّتِهِ ٱلنُّبُوَّةَ وَٱلۡكِتَٰبَ
وَءَاتَيۡنَٰهُ أَجۡرَهُۥ فِي ٱلدُّنۡيَاۖ وَإِنَّهُۥ فِي ٱلۡأٓخِرَةِ لَمِنَ ٱلصَّٰلِحِينَ
٢٧ وَلُوطًا إِذۡ قَالَ لِقَوۡمِهِۦٓ إِنَّكُمۡ لَتَأۡتُونَ ٱلۡفَٰحِشَةَ
مَا سَبَقَكُم بِهَا مِنۡ أَحَدٖ مِّنَ ٱلۡعَٰلَمِينَ ٢٨
أَئِنَّكُمۡ لَتَأۡتُونَ ٱلرِّجَالَ وَتَقۡطَعُونَ ٱلسَّبِيلَ وَتَأۡتُونَ
فِي نَادِيكُمُ ٱلۡمُنكَرَۖ فَمَا كَانَ جَوَابَ قَوۡمِهِۦٓ إِلَّآ
أَن قَالُواْ ٱئۡتِنَا بِعَذَابِ ٱللَّهِ إِن كُنتَ مِنَ ٱلصَّٰدِقِينَ
٢٩ قَالَ رَبِّ ٱنصُرۡنِي عَلَى ٱلۡقَوۡمِ ٱلۡمُفۡسِدِينَ ٣٠
وَلَمَّا جَآءَتۡ رُسُلُنَآ إِبۡرَٰهِيمَ بِٱلۡبُشۡرَىٰ قَالُوٓاْ إِنَّا مُهۡلِكُوٓاْ
أَهۡلِ هَٰذِهِ ٱلۡقَرۡيَةِۖ إِنَّ أَهۡلَهَا كَانُواْ ظَٰلِمِينَ ٣١
قَالَ إِنَّ فِيهَا لُوطٗاۚ قَالُواْ نَحۡنُ أَعۡلَمُ بِمَن فِيهَاۖ لَنُنَجِّيَنَّهُۥ
وَأَهۡلَهُۥٓ إِلَّا ٱمۡرَأَتَهُۥ كَانَتۡ مِنَ ٱلۡغَٰبِرِينَ ٣٢ وَلَمَّآ
أَن جَآءَتۡ رُسُلُنَا لُوطٗا سِيٓءَ بِهِمۡ وَضَاقَ بِهِمۡ ذَرۡعٗا
وَقَالُواْ لَا تَخَفۡ وَلَا تَحۡزَنۡۖ إِنَّا مُنَجُّوكَ وَأَهۡلَكَ إِلَّا ٱمۡرَأَتَكَ
كَانَتۡ مِنَ ٱلۡغَٰبِرِينَ ٣٣ إِنَّا مُنزِلُونَ عَلَىٰٓ أَهۡلِ
هَٰذِهِ ٱلۡقَرۡيَةِ رِجۡزٗا مِّنَ ٱلسَّمَآءِ بِمَا كَانُواْ يَفۡسُقُونَ
٣٤ وَلَقَد تَّرَكۡنَا مِنۡهَآ ءَايَةَۢ بَيِّنَةٗ لِّقَوۡمٖ يَعۡقِلُونَ

fact that it had no effect on him in spite of its size and intensity and that it died down, and that there was a garden in its place in a short time – ***for people who are believers*** in the unity and power of Allah, because they benefit from that.

25. ***He*** (Ibrāhīm) ***said, 'You have adopted idols*** which you worship ***apart from Allah as tokens of mutual affection*** (read as *mawaddata baynikum*, *muwaddatan baynakum*, and *muwaddatu baynikum*) – loving one another in their worship – ***in this world. But then on the Day of Rising you will reject one another***, leaders declaring themselves free of their followers, ***and curse one another***, followers cursing their leaders. ***The Fire will be your shelter***, all of you. ***You will have no helpers*** to defend you against that.'

26. ***And Lūṭ believed in him*** (Ibrāhīm). Lūṭ was the son of his brother, Hārān. ***He*** (Ibrāhīm) ***said, 'I am leaving this place*** and my people ***to follow the pleasure of my Lord*** wherever my Lord has commanded me. He left his people and emigrated from the fertile land of Iraq to Syria. ***He is the Almighty*** in His kingdom, ***the All-Wise*** in what He does.'

27. ***We gave him*** – after Ismā'īl – ***Isḥāq and*** – after Isḥāq – ***Ya'qūb, and placed Prophethood and the Book*** – generic, in this instance, meaning all Revealed Books: the Torah, the Gospel, the Psalms and the *Furqān* – ***among his progeny.*** So all the Prophets after Ibrāhīm are from among his descendants. ***We gave him his reward in this world*** – meaning that he will be praised by the people of all religions – ***and in the Next World he will be among the righteous*** – who have high degrees in the Next World.

28. Remember ***when Lūṭ said to his people, 'You are committing an obscenity*** (sodomy) ***not perpetrated before you by anyone in all the world***, mankind or jinn.

29. ***Do you lie with men and waylay them on the road*** – as well as comitting sodomy, they also waylaid those who passed through with their vile actions, and so people stopped travelling through their land – ***and commit*** new ***depravities within your gatherings?' The only answer of his people was to say, 'Bring us Allah's punishment if you are telling the truth.'*** In other words, if he thought that what they were doing was disgusting and that they would suffer punishment for it, then he should make it happen straight away.

30. ***He said, 'My Lord, help me against the people of corruption*** who disobey Allah by having sexual intercourse with men, regarding what they say about the punishment*!'* Allah answered his supplication.

31. ***When Our messengers came with the good news*** of Isḥāq and Ya'qūb after him ***to Ibrāhīm, they said, 'We are going to destroy the people of this city*** – the city of Lūṭ. ***Truly its inhabitants are wrong - doers*** (unbelievers)*.'*

32. ***He*** (Ibrāhīm) ***said, 'Lūṭ is in it.' They*** (the messengers) ***said, 'We know very well who is in it. We are going to rescue*** (read as *nunajjiyannahu* and *nunjiyannahu*) ***him and his family – except for his wife. She will be one of those who stay behind*** – and suffer punishment*.'*

33. ***When Our Messengers came to Lūṭ, he was distressed on their account, feeling incapable of protecting them***, because they took the form of guests and had beautiful faces, and he feared what his people would do them. They then informed him that they were messengers from his Lord. ***They said, 'Do not fear and do not grieve. We are going to rescue you*** (read as *munajjūka* and *munjūka*) ***and your family – except for your wife; she will be one of those who stay behind.***

34. ***We will bring down*** (read as *munzilūna* and *munazzilūna*) ***on the inhabitants of this city a devastating punishment from heaven because of their deviance*** (wrongdoing)*.'*

35. ***We have left a Clear Sign of them behind*** – the ruins of their city – ***for people who use their intellect*** and reflect.

36. ***And to Madyan*** – "We sent" is implied – ***their brother Shu'ayb. He said, 'My people, worship Allah and look to the Last Day*** – fear the Day of Rising – ***and do not act unjustly on earth, corrupting it.'***

37. ***But they denied him; so the*** strong ***earthquake seized them and morning found them lying flattened*** – dead on their backs – ***in their homes.***

﴿٣٥﴾ وَإِلَىٰ مَدْيَنَ أَخَاهُمْ شُعَيْبًا فَقَالَ يَٰقَوْمِ ٱعْبُدُوا۟
ٱللَّهَ وَٱرْجُوا۟ ٱلْيَوْمَ ٱلْءَاخِرَ وَلَا تَعْثَوْا۟ فِى ٱلْأَرْضِ مُفْسِدِينَ
﴿٣٦﴾ فَكَذَّبُوهُ فَأَخَذَتْهُمُ ٱلرَّجْفَةُ فَأَصْبَحُوا۟ فِى
دَارِهِمْ جَٰثِمِينَ ﴿٣٧﴾ وَعَادًا وَثَمُودَا۟ وَقَد تَّبَيَّنَ
لَكُم مِّن مَّسَٰكِنِهِمْ ۖ وَزَيَّنَ لَهُمُ ٱلشَّيْطَٰنُ
أَعْمَٰلَهُمْ فَصَدَّهُمْ عَنِ ٱلسَّبِيلِ وَكَانُوا۟ مُسْتَبْصِرِينَ ﴿٣٨﴾
وَقَٰرُونَ وَفِرْعَوْنَ وَهَٰمَٰنَ ۖ وَلَقَدْ جَآءَهُم مُّوسَىٰ
بِٱلْبَيِّنَٰتِ فَٱسْتَكْبَرُوا۟ فِى ٱلْأَرْضِ وَمَا كَانُوا۟ سَٰبِقِينَ
﴿٣٩﴾ فَكُلًّا أَخَذْنَا بِذَنۢبِهِۦ ۖ فَمِنْهُم مَّنْ أَرْسَلْنَا عَلَيْهِ حَاصِبًا
وَمِنْهُم مَّنْ أَخَذَتْهُ ٱلصَّيْحَةُ وَمِنْهُم مَّنْ خَسَفْنَا بِهِ
ٱلْأَرْضَ وَمِنْهُم مَّنْ أَغْرَقْنَا ۚ وَمَا كَانَ ٱللَّهُ لِيَظْلِمَهُمْ
وَلَٰكِن كَانُوٓا۟ أَنفُسَهُمْ يَظْلِمُونَ ﴿٤٠﴾ مَثَلُ ٱلَّذِينَ
ٱتَّخَذُوا۟ مِن دُونِ ٱللَّهِ أَوْلِيَآءَ كَمَثَلِ ٱلْعَنكَبُوتِ
ٱتَّخَذَتْ بَيْتًا ۖ وَإِنَّ أَوْهَنَ ٱلْبُيُوتِ لَبَيْتُ ٱلْعَنكَبُوتِ ۖ
لَوْ كَانُوا۟ يَعْلَمُونَ ﴿٤١﴾ إِنَّ ٱللَّهَ يَعْلَمُ مَا يَدْعُونَ مِن
دُونِهِۦ مِن شَىْءٍ ۚ وَهُوَ ٱلْعَزِيزُ ٱلْحَكِيمُ ﴿٤٢﴾ وَتِلْكَ
ٱلْأَمْثَٰلُ نَضْرِبُهَا لِلنَّاسِ ۖ وَمَا يَعْقِلُهَآ إِلَّا ٱلْعَٰلِمُونَ
﴿٤٣﴾ خَلَقَ ٱللَّهُ ٱلسَّمَٰوَٰتِ وَٱلْأَرْضَ بِٱلْحَقِّ ۚ إِنَّ فِى ذَٰلِكَ
لَءَايَةً لِّلْمُؤْمِنِينَ ﴿٤٤﴾ ٱتْلُ مَآ أُوحِىَ إِلَيْكَ مِنَ ٱلْكِتَٰبِ
وَأَقِمِ ٱلصَّلَوٰةَ ۖ إِنَّ ٱلصَّلَوٰةَ تَنْهَىٰ عَنِ ٱلْفَحْشَآءِ

38. ***And*** We destroyed ***'Ād and Thamūd*** – meaning both the area and the tribe. ***It*** (their destruction) ***must be clear to you from their dwelling places*** – in Ḥijr and Yemen*!* ***Shayṭān made their actions*** of unbelief and of disobedience ***seem good to them and so debarred them from the Way*** of the Truth*,* ***even though they were intelligent people*** who possessed insight.

39. ***And*** We destroyed ***Qārūn and Pharaoh and Hāmān. Mūsā came*** before their destruction ***with the Clear Signs to them, but they were arrogant on the earth. They could not outstrip Us*** and thus escape Our punishment.

40. ***We seized each one of them*** (those mentioned) ***for their wrong actions. Against some We sent a sudden squall of stones*** – a fierce wind full of pebbles like that sent against the people of Lūṭ*;* ***some of them were seized by the Great Blast*** – such as Thamūd*;* ***some We caused the earth to swallow up*** – such as Qārūn*;* ***and some We drowned*** – such as the people of Nūḥ and Pharaoh and his people. ***Allah did not wrong them*** and punish them without their doing any wrong actions*;* ***rather they wronged themselves*** by committing wrong actions.

41. ***The metaphor of those who take protectors*** – idols which they hope will bring them benefit – ***besides Allah is that of a spider which builds itself a house*** where it takes refuge*;* ***but no house is flimsier than a spider's house*** which cannot defend it against heat or cold: a metaphor meaning that idols do not help those who worship them – ***if they only knew*** the truth about what they worshipped.

42. ***Allah knows what they call upon*** (read as *yad'ūna*, also *tad'ūna*, meaning "you call upon") and worship ***besides Himself. He is the Almighty*** in His kingdom*,* ***the All-Wise*** in what He does.

43. ***Such metaphors*** in the Qur'an ***We devise for mankind; but only those with knowledge*** – who reflect – ***understand them.***

44. ***Allah created the heavens and the earth with truth. There is certainly a Sign in that*** – indicating His power – ***for the believers*** – who are singled out for mention because they benefit from faith, as opposed to the unbelievers who do not.

45. ***Recite what has been revealed to you of the Book*** (the Qur'an) ***and establish the prayer. Prayer precludes indecency and wrong -***

وَٱلْمُنكَرِ ۗ وَلَذِكْرُ ٱللَّهِ أَكْبَرُ ۗ وَٱللَّهُ يَعْلَمُ مَا تَصْنَعُونَ ﴿٤٥﴾
۞ وَلَا تُجَٰدِلُوٓا۟ أَهْلَ ٱلْكِتَٰبِ إِلَّا بِٱلَّتِى هِىَ أَحْسَنُ إِلَّا
ٱلَّذِينَ ظَلَمُوا۟ مِنْهُمْ ۖ وَقُولُوٓا۟ ءَامَنَّا بِٱلَّذِىٓ أُنزِلَ إِلَيْنَا وَأُنزِلَ
إِلَيْكُمْ وَإِلَٰهُنَا وَإِلَٰهُكُمْ وَٰحِدٌ وَنَحْنُ لَهُۥ مُسْلِمُونَ ﴿٤٦﴾
وَكَذَٰلِكَ أَنزَلْنَآ إِلَيْكَ ٱلْكِتَٰبَ ۚ فَٱلَّذِينَ ءَاتَيْنَٰهُمُ ٱلْكِتَٰبَ
يُؤْمِنُونَ بِهِۦ ۖ وَمِنْ هَٰٓؤُلَآءِ مَن يُؤْمِنُ بِهِۦ ۚ وَمَا يَجْحَدُ بِـَٔايَٰتِنَآ
إِلَّا ٱلْكَٰفِرُونَ ﴿٤٧﴾ وَمَا كُنتَ تَتْلُوا۟ مِن قَبْلِهِۦ مِن كِتَٰبٍ
وَلَا تَخُطُّهُۥ بِيَمِينِكَ ۖ إِذًا لَّٱرْتَابَ ٱلْمُبْطِلُونَ ﴿٤٨﴾ بَلْ هُوَ
ءَايَٰتٌۢ بَيِّنَٰتٌ فِى صُدُورِ ٱلَّذِينَ أُوتُوا۟ ٱلْعِلْمَ ۚ وَمَا يَجْحَدُ
بِـَٔايَٰتِنَآ إِلَّا ٱلظَّٰلِمُونَ ﴿٤٩﴾ وَقَالُوا۟ لَوْلَآ أُنزِلَ عَلَيْهِ
ءَايَٰتٌ مِّن رَّبِّهِۦ ۖ قُلْ إِنَّمَا ٱلْءَايَٰتُ عِندَ ٱللَّهِ وَإِنَّمَآ أَنَا۠ نَذِيرٌ
مُّبِينٌ ﴿٥٠﴾ أَوَلَمْ يَكْفِهِمْ أَنَّآ أَنزَلْنَا عَلَيْكَ ٱلْكِتَٰبَ
يُتْلَىٰ عَلَيْهِمْ ۚ إِنَّ فِى ذَٰلِكَ لَرَحْمَةً وَذِكْرَىٰ لِقَوْمٍ
يُؤْمِنُونَ ﴿٥١﴾ قُلْ كَفَىٰ بِٱللَّهِ بَيْنِى وَبَيْنَكُمْ شَهِيدًا ۖ
يَعْلَمُ مَا فِى ٱلسَّمَٰوَٰتِ وَٱلْأَرْضِ ۗ وَٱلَّذِينَ ءَامَنُوا۟
بِٱلْبَٰطِلِ وَكَفَرُوا۟ بِٱللَّهِ أُو۟لَٰٓئِكَ هُمُ ٱلْخَٰسِرُونَ ﴿٥٢﴾
وَيَسْتَعْجِلُونَكَ بِٱلْعَذَابِ ۚ وَلَوْلَآ أَجَلٌ مُّسَمًّى لَّجَآءَهُمُ ٱلْعَذَابُ
وَلَيَأْتِيَنَّهُم بَغْتَةً وَهُمْ لَا يَشْعُرُونَ ﴿٥٣﴾ يَسْتَعْجِلُونَكَ بِٱلْعَذَابِ
وَإِنَّ جَهَنَّمَ لَمُحِيطَةٌۢ بِٱلْكَٰفِرِينَ ﴿٥٤﴾ يَوْمَ يَغْشَىٰهُمُ ٱلْعَذَابُ
مِن فَوْقِهِمْ وَمِن تَحْتِ أَرْجُلِهِمْ وَيَقُولُ ذُوقُوا۟ مَا كُنتُمْ تَعْمَلُونَ

doing while one is performing it, ***and remembrance of Allah is greater still*** – greater than other acts of obedience. ***Allah knows what you do*** and will repay you for it.

46. ***Only argue with the People of the Book in the kindest way*** – such as by calling people to Allah by His Signs and calling attention to His proofs – ***except in the case of those of them who do wrong*** by fighting you and refusing to pay the *jizya*, in which case argue with them by means of the sword until they become Muslim or pay the *jizya*, ***saying*** to those who agree to pay the *jizya* when they tell you about what is in their Books: ***'We believe in what has been sent down to us and what was sent down to you.*** In other words do not say that they are telling the truth or accuse them of lying. ***Our God and your God are One, and we submit to Him.'***

47. ***Accordingly We have sent down the Book*** (the Qur'an) – just as the Torah and other Books were sent down to them – ***to you, and those to whom We gave the Book*** (the Torah) – a reference to people like 'Abdullāh ibn Salām and others – ***believe in it*** (the Qur'an); ***and some of these people*** (the people of Makka) ***believe in it as well. Only the unbelievers deny Our Signs*** after they have become clear. This refers to the Jews who denied when it was clear to them that the Qur'an was the truth and the one who brought it was speaking the truth. They still denied it.

48. ***You never recited any Book before it*** (the Qur'an), ***nor did you write one down with your right hand*** – even if you had been able to read and write. ***If you had, the purveyors of falsehood*** (the Jews) ***would have voiced their doubts*** – about you by saying, "It is in the Torah that he will be illiterate, neither able to read or write."

49. ***No, it*** – the Qur'an which you have brought – ***is Clear Signs reposited in the hearts of those who have been given knowledge*** – those who believe in it and memorise it. ***Only wrongdoers deny Our Signs.*** The Jews deny them after they have become clear to them.

50. ***They*** (the unbelievers of Makka) ***say, 'Why have no Signs*** (read as *āyāt,* and *āyat,* sing.) – such as the She-camel of Ṣāliḥ, the staff of Mūsā and the table of 'Īsā – ***been sent down to him*** (Muḥammad) ***from his Lord?' Say*** to them: ***'The Signs are with Allah***, Who sends them down however He wishes. ***I am only a clear warner*** –

someone who makes the warning about the Fire clear to the people who are disobedient.'

51. ***Is it not enough for them*** – regarding what they ask for – ***that We have sent down to you the Book*** (the Qur'an) ***which is recited to them?*** It is a continuing Sign that will never end, which is not the case with the other Signs which have been mentioned. ***There is certainly a mercy and reminder in that*** Book ***for people who believe.***

52. ***Say: 'Allah is a sufficient witness between me and you*** – regarding my truthfulness.' ***He knows everything in the heavens and the earth,*** including my state and yours. ***Those who believe in falsehood*** – that which is worshipped instead of Allah – ***and reject Allah, they are the losers*** in their transaction, since they exchange belief for unbelief.

53. ***They ask you to hasten the punishment. If it were not for a stipulated term, the punishment would have come to them already. It*** (the punishment) ***will come upon them suddenly when they are not expecting it.***

54. ***They ask you to hasten the punishment*** in this world ***but Hell already encircles the unbelievers.***

55. ***On the Day the punishment envelops them from above them and from underneath their feet, He will say*** (read as *yaqūlu*, and *naqūlū*, "We will say..."), ***'Taste*** the punishment as a repayment for ***what you were doing!*** You will not escape it.'

56. ***My slaves, you who believe, My earth is wide, so worship Me alone.*** Worship Me in a place where it is easy to worship Me to which you should emigrate if you are living in a land in which it is not easy to worship Allah. This was revealed about the weak Muslims of Makka who were too constrained to be able to practise their Islam there.

57. ***Every self will taste death. Then you will be returned*** (read as *tarja'ūna*, and *yarja'ūna*, "they will be returned") ***to Us.***

58. ***As for those who believe and do right actions, We will lodge them*** (read as *nubawwi'annahum*, and also "*nathawwiyannahum*" from *thaw*?' which means to reside in a dwelling) ***in lofty chambers in Paradise, with rivers flowing under them, remaining in them timelessly, for ever. How excellent is the reward of those who act:***

﴿٥٥﴾ يَٰعِبَادِيَ ٱلَّذِينَ ءَامَنُوٓاْ إِنَّ أَرۡضِي وَٰسِعَةٞ فَإِيَّٰيَ فَٱعۡبُدُونِ
﴿٥٦﴾ كُلُّ نَفۡسٖ ذَآئِقَةُ ٱلۡمَوۡتِۖ ثُمَّ إِلَيۡنَا تُرۡجَعُونَ ﴿٥٧﴾ وَٱلَّذِينَ
ءَامَنُواْ وَعَمِلُواْ ٱلصَّٰلِحَٰتِ لَنُبَوِّئَنَّهُم مِّنَ ٱلۡجَنَّةِ غُرَفٗا تَجۡرِي
مِن تَحۡتِهَا ٱلۡأَنۡهَٰرُ خَٰلِدِينَ فِيهَاۚ نِعۡمَ أَجۡرُ ٱلۡعَٰمِلِينَ ﴿٥٨﴾ ٱلَّذِينَ
صَبَرُواْ وَعَلَىٰ رَبِّهِمۡ يَتَوَكَّلُونَ ﴿٥٩﴾ وَكَأَيِّن مِّن دَآبَّةٖ لَّا تَحۡمِلُ
رِزۡقَهَا ٱللَّهُ يَرۡزُقُهَا وَإِيَّاكُمۡۚ وَهُوَ ٱلسَّمِيعُ ٱلۡعَلِيمُ ﴿٦٠﴾ وَلَئِن
سَأَلۡتَهُم مَّنۡ خَلَقَ ٱلسَّمَٰوَٰتِ وَٱلۡأَرۡضَ وَسَخَّرَ ٱلشَّمۡسَ وَٱلۡقَمَرَ
لَيَقُولُنَّ ٱللَّهُۖ فَأَنَّىٰ يُؤۡفَكُونَ ﴿٦١﴾ ٱللَّهُ يَبۡسُطُ ٱلرِّزۡقَ لِمَن يَشَآءُ مِنۡ
عِبَادِهِۦ وَيَقۡدِرُ لَهُۥٓۚ إِنَّ ٱللَّهَ بِكُلِّ شَيۡءٍ عَلِيمٞ ﴿٦٢﴾ وَلَئِن سَأَلۡتَهُم
مَّن نَّزَّلَ مِنَ ٱلسَّمَآءِ مَآءٗ فَأَحۡيَا بِهِ ٱلۡأَرۡضَ مِنۢ بَعۡدِ مَوۡتِهَا
لَيَقُولُنَّ ٱللَّهُۚ قُلِ ٱلۡحَمۡدُ لِلَّهِۚ بَلۡ أَكۡثَرُهُمۡ لَا يَعۡقِلُونَ ﴿٦٣﴾
وَمَا هَٰذِهِ ٱلۡحَيَوٰةُ ٱلدُّنۡيَآ إِلَّا لَهۡوٞ وَلَعِبٞۚ وَإِنَّ ٱلدَّارَ ٱلۡأٓخِرَةَ
لَهِيَ ٱلۡحَيَوَانُۚ لَوۡ كَانُواْ يَعۡلَمُونَ ﴿٦٤﴾ فَإِذَا رَكِبُواْ فِي
ٱلۡفُلۡكِ دَعَوُاْ ٱللَّهَ مُخۡلِصِينَ لَهُ ٱلدِّينَ فَلَمَّا نَجَّىٰهُمۡ إِلَى ٱلۡبَرِّ إِذَا
هُمۡ يُشۡرِكُونَ ﴿٦٥﴾ لِيَكۡفُرُواْ بِمَآ ءَاتَيۡنَٰهُمۡ وَلِيَتَمَتَّعُواْۖ فَسَوۡفَ
يَعۡلَمُونَ ﴿٦٦﴾ أَوَلَمۡ يَرَوۡاْ أَنَّا جَعَلۡنَا حَرَمًا ءَامِنٗا وَيُتَخَطَّفُ
ٱلنَّاسُ مِنۡ حَوۡلِهِمۡۚ أَفَبِٱلۡبَٰطِلِ يُؤۡمِنُونَ وَبِنِعۡمَةِ ٱللَّهِ يَكۡفُرُونَ
﴿٦٧﴾ وَمَنۡ أَظۡلَمُ مِمَّنِ ٱفۡتَرَىٰ عَلَى ٱللَّهِ كَذِبًا أَوۡ كَذَّبَ بِٱلۡحَقِّ
لَمَّا جَآءَهُۥٓۚ أَلَيۡسَ فِي جَهَنَّمَ مَثۡوٗى لِّلۡكَٰفِرِينَ ﴿٦٨﴾ وَٱلَّذِينَ
جَٰهَدُواْ فِينَا لَنَهۡدِيَنَّهُمۡ سُبُلَنَاۚ وَإِنَّ ٱللَّهَ لَمَعَ ٱلۡمُحۡسِنِينَ ﴿٦٩﴾

59. ***...those who are steadfast*** – in the face of persecution by the idolators and in making *hijra* to give victory to the *dīn* – ***and put their trust in their Lord*** – that He will provide for them from where they do not expect.

60. ***How many creatures do not carry their provision with them*** because they are weak*!* ***Allah provides for them and He will for you***, Muhājirūn, even if you have no provision or maintenance with you. ***He is the All-Hearing*** of what you say, ***the All-Knowing*** of your inner thoughts.

61. ***If you ask them*** (the unbelievers), ***'Who created the heavens and the earth and made the sun and moon subservient?' they will say, 'Allah.' So how have they been perverted?*** How then have they been turned from believing in Allah's oneness after having affirmed it?

62. ***Allah expands the provision of any of His slaves He wills*** as a test, ***and restricts it*** to whomever He wishes, to test them. ***Allah has knowledge of all things*** – including where to expand provision and where to restrict it.

63. ***If you ask them, 'Who sends down water from the sky, bringing the earth back to life again after it was dead?' they will say, 'Allah.'*** So how can they associate other things with Him? ***Say*** to them, ***'Praise be to Allah*** for establishing the proof against them.' ***But most of them do not use their intellect*** and do not understand the contradiction in that.

64. ***The life of this world is nothing but a game and a diversion.*** Actions which bring about nearness to Allah are a matter of the Next World because they cause its fruits appear in this world. ***The abode of the Next World – that is truly Life if they only knew*** that, in which case they would not prefer this world to the Next World.

65. ***When they embark in ships, they call on Allah, making their* dīn *sincerely His*** – by sincere supplication, not calling on other than Him, out of the realization that He alone can rescue them from their predicament; ***but then when He delivers them safely to land, they associate others with Him.***

66. ***Let them be ungrateful for what*** (the blessings) ***We have given them! Let them enjoy*** (read as *wa li-yatamatta'ū* and *wal-yatamat-*

ta'ū) ***themselves*** in their worship of idols, **They will soon know** the result*!* This is a threat.

67. ***Do they not see*** (know) ***that We have established a safe haven*** – making their land of Makka a sanctuary – ***while people all round them are violently dispossessed*** by killing and capture outside of it*?* ***So why do they believe in falsehood*** (idols) ***and reject the blessing of Allah*** by associating others with Him*?*

68. ***Who could do greater wrong than someone who invents lies against Allah*** by associating others with Him, ***or denies the truth*** – the Prophet or the Book – ***when it comes to him?*** No one does greater wrong than such a person. ***Is there not shelter in Hell for the unbelievers?*** That is where they will end up.

69. ***As for those who do* jihād *in Our Way*** – for Our sake, ***We will guide them to Our Paths*** – which lead to Us. ***Truly Allah is with the good-doers*** (the believers) – by giving help and support.

سُورَةُ ٱلرُّومِ

بِسۡمِ ٱللَّهِ ٱلرَّحۡمَٰنِ ٱلرَّحِيمِ

الٓمٓ ١ غُلِبَتِ ٱلرُّومُ ٢ فِيٓ أَدۡنَى ٱلۡأَرۡضِ وَهُم مِّنۢ بَعۡدِ
غَلَبِهِمۡ سَيَغۡلِبُونَ ٣ فِي بِضۡعِ سِنِينَۗ لِلَّهِ ٱلۡأَمۡرُ
مِن قَبۡلُ وَمِنۢ بَعۡدُۚ وَيَوۡمَئِذٖ يَفۡرَحُ ٱلۡمُؤۡمِنُونَ ٤
بِنَصۡرِ ٱللَّهِۚ يَنصُرُ مَن يَشَآءُۖ وَهُوَ ٱلۡعَزِيزُ ٱلرَّحِيمُ ٥
وَعۡدَ ٱللَّهِۖ لَا يُخۡلِفُ ٱللَّهُ وَعۡدَهُۥ وَلَٰكِنَّ أَكۡثَرَ ٱلنَّاسِ لَا يَعۡلَمُونَ
٦ يَعۡلَمُونَ ظَٰهِرٗا مِّنَ ٱلۡحَيَوٰةِ ٱلدُّنۡيَا وَهُمۡ عَنِ ٱلۡأٓخِرَةِ هُمۡ غَٰفِلُونَ
٧ أَوَلَمۡ يَتَفَكَّرُواْ فِيٓ أَنفُسِهِمۗ مَّا خَلَقَ ٱللَّهُ ٱلسَّمَٰوَٰتِ وَٱلۡأَرۡضَ
وَمَا بَيۡنَهُمَآ إِلَّا بِٱلۡحَقِّ وَأَجَلٖ مُّسَمّٗىۗ وَإِنَّ كَثِيرٗا مِّنَ ٱلنَّاسِ
بِلِقَآيِٕ رَبِّهِمۡ لَكَٰفِرُونَ ٨ أَوَلَمۡ يَسِيرُواْ فِي ٱلۡأَرۡضِ فَيَنظُرُواْ
كَيۡفَ كَانَ عَٰقِبَةُ ٱلَّذِينَ مِن قَبۡلِهِمۡۚ كَانُوٓاْ أَشَدَّ مِنۡهُمۡ قُوَّةٗ
وَأَثَارُواْ ٱلۡأَرۡضَ وَعَمَرُوهَآ أَكۡثَرَ مِمَّا عَمَرُوهَا وَجَآءَتۡهُمۡ
رُسُلُهُم بِٱلۡبَيِّنَٰتِۖ فَمَا كَانَ ٱللَّهُ لِيَظۡلِمَهُمۡ وَلَٰكِن كَانُوٓاْ
أَنفُسَهُمۡ يَظۡلِمُونَ ٩ ثُمَّ كَانَ عَٰقِبَةَ ٱلَّذِينَ أَسَٰٓـُٔواْ ٱلسُّوٓأَىٰٓ
أَن كَذَّبُواْ بِـَٔايَٰتِ ٱللَّهِ وَكَانُواْ بِهَا يَسۡتَهۡزِءُونَ ١٠ ٱللَّهُ
يَبۡدَؤُاْ ٱلۡخَلۡقَ ثُمَّ يُعِيدُهُۥ ثُمَّ إِلَيۡهِ تُرۡجَعُونَ ١١ وَيَوۡمَ تَقُومُ

30. *Sūrat ar-Rūm*
The Romans

This *sūra* is Makkan except for *āyat* 17, which is Madinan. It has 60 *āyat*s and was sent down after *al-Inshiqāq*.

1. ***Alif Lam Mim.*** Allah knows best what is meant by that.

2. ***The Romans have been defeated*** – this means the People of the Book, whom the Persians, who were not People of the Book and who worshipped idols, defeated. The unbelievers of Makka were delighted by that event. They said to the Muslims, "We will defeat you as Persia defeated the Romans" –

3. ***...in the land nearby***: the land of the Romans which was closest to Persia was al-Jazīra (Mesopotamia) which was where the two armies met, the war beginning with a Persian attack – ***but after their defeat, they will themselves be victorious*** over the Persians,

4. ***...in a few years' time.*** The word used for "few" means a number between three and nine. The two armies in fact fought again seven years after this first meeting and the Romans defeated Persia. ***The affair is Allah's from beginning to end*** – both before the defeat of the Romans and after it. All of it is by the will of Allah. ***On that day, the believers will rejoice*** – the day when the Romans are victorious will be one on which the believers will rejoice –

5. ***...in Allah's help*** for them against the Persians. The news of the Persian defeat reached them during the Battle of Badr when Jibrīl revealed it and it added to their joy in defeating the idolators. ***He grants victory to whomever He wills. He is the Almighty, the Most Merciful*** to the believers.

6. ***That is Allah's promise***; He promised them victory. ***Allah does not break His promise, but most people*** (the unbelievers of Makka) ***do not know it*** – Allah's promise of victory to the believers.

7. ***They know an outward aspect of the life of this world*** – trade, agriculture, building, planting and other such things, ***but they*** – the pronoun "they" (*hum*) is repeated for emphasis – ***are heedless of the Next World.***

8. ***Have they not reflected within themselves*** and turned from their heedlessness***? Allah did not create the heavens and the earth and everything between them except with truth and for a fixed term.*** At the end of their term they will come to an end and after that the Resurrection will take place. ***Yet many people*** – like the unbelievers of Makka – ***reject the meeting with their Lord.*** They do not believe in the Resurrection after death.

9. ***Have they not travelled in the earth and seen the final fate of those before them*** – nations previous to them who were destroyed for denying their Messengers***? They had greater strength than them*** – like 'Ād and Thamūd***, and cultivated the land*** – using sophisticated agricultural techniques – ***and inhabited it in far greater numbers than they*** (the unbelievers of Makka) ***do. Their Messengers also came to them with the Clear Signs. Allah would never have wronged them*** by destroying them without any crime on their part, ***but they wronged themselves*** – by denying their Messengers.

10. ***Then the final fate of those who did evil will be the Worst*** – meaning Jahannam (Hellfire) and what will be done to them there – ***because they denied Allah's Signs*** (the Qur'an) ***and mocked at them.***

11. ***Allah originates creation*** – here meaning humankind – ***then will regenerate it*** – recreate them after their death***; then you will be returned to Him*** (read as *turja'ūna*, and also *yurja'ūna*, "they will be returned").

12. ***On the Day the Hour arrives the evildoers will be in despair*** – lost for words, because all their excuses will prove baseless.

13. ***None of their partner-gods*** – those they associated with Allah, who are their idols – ***will intercede for them. They will reject their partner-gods*** – and renounce them.

14. ***On the Day the Hour arrives, that Day they will be split up*** – separated out into believers and unbelievers.

15. ***As for those who believe and did right actions, they will be made joyful in a verdant meadow*** – in a Garden.

16. ***But as for those who disbelieved and denied Our Signs*** (the Qur'an) ***and the meeting of the Next World*** – the Resurrection and other associated things – ***they will be summoned to punishment.***

ٱلسَّاعَةُ يُبْلِسُ ٱلْمُجْرِمُونَ ﴿١٢﴾ وَلَمْ يَكُن لَّهُم مِّن شُرَكَآئِهِمْ
شُفَعَٰٓؤُاْ وَكَانُواْ بِشُرَكَآئِهِمْ كَٰفِرِينَ ﴿١٣﴾ وَيَوْمَ
تَقُومُ ٱلسَّاعَةُ يَوْمَئِذٍ يَتَفَرَّقُونَ ﴿١٤﴾ فَأَمَّا ٱلَّذِينَ ءَامَنُواْ
وَعَمِلُواْ ٱلصَّٰلِحَٰتِ فَهُمْ فِى رَوْضَةٍ يُحْبَرُونَ ﴿١٥﴾
وَأَمَّا ٱلَّذِينَ كَفَرُواْ وَكَذَّبُواْ بِـَٔايَٰتِنَا وَلِقَآءِ ٱلْأَخِرَةِ فَأُوْلَٰٓئِكَ
فِى ٱلْعَذَابِ مُحْضَرُونَ ﴿١٦﴾ فَسُبْحَٰنَ ٱللَّهِ حِينَ تُمْسُونَ
وَحِينَ تُصْبِحُونَ ﴿١٧﴾ وَلَهُ ٱلْحَمْدُ فِى ٱلسَّمَٰوَٰتِ وَٱلْأَرْضِ
وَعَشِيًّا وَحِينَ تُظْهِرُونَ ﴿١٨﴾ يُخْرِجُ ٱلْحَىَّ مِنَ ٱلْمَيِّتِ وَيُخْرِجُ
ٱلْمَيِّتَ مِنَ ٱلْحَىِّ وَيُحْىِ ٱلْأَرْضَ بَعْدَ مَوْتِهَا ۚ وَكَذَٰلِكَ تُخْرَجُونَ
﴿١٩﴾ وَمِنْ ءَايَٰتِهِۦٓ أَنْ خَلَقَكُم مِّن تُرَابٍ ثُمَّ إِذَآ أَنتُم بَشَرٌ
تَنتَشِرُونَ ﴿٢٠﴾ وَمِنْ ءَايَٰتِهِۦٓ أَنْ خَلَقَ لَكُم مِّنْ أَنفُسِكُمْ
أَزْوَٰجًا لِّتَسْكُنُوٓاْ إِلَيْهَا وَجَعَلَ بَيْنَكُم مَّوَدَّةً وَرَحْمَةً ۚ
إِنَّ فِى ذَٰلِكَ لَءَايَٰتٍ لِّقَوْمٍ يَتَفَكَّرُونَ ﴿٢١﴾ وَمِنْ ءَايَٰتِهِۦ خَلْقُ
ٱلسَّمَٰوَٰتِ وَٱلْأَرْضِ وَٱخْتِلَٰفُ أَلْسِنَتِكُمْ وَأَلْوَٰنِكُمْ ۚ إِنَّ
فِى ذَٰلِكَ لَءَايَٰتٍ لِّلْعَٰلِمِينَ ﴿٢٢﴾ وَمِنْ ءَايَٰتِهِۦ مَنَامُكُم بِٱلَّيْلِ
وَٱلنَّهَارِ وَٱبْتِغَآؤُكُم مِّن فَضْلِهِۦٓ ۚ إِنَّ فِى ذَٰلِكَ لَءَايَٰتٍ
لِّقَوْمٍ يَسْمَعُونَ ﴿٢٣﴾ وَمِنْ ءَايَٰتِهِۦ يُرِيكُمُ ٱلْبَرْقَ
خَوْفًا وَطَمَعًا وَيُنَزِّلُ مِنَ ٱلسَّمَآءِ مَآءً فَيُحْىِۦ بِهِ ٱلْأَرْضَ
بَعْدَ مَوْتِهَآ ۚ إِنَّ فِى ذَٰلِكَ لَءَايَٰتٍ لِّقَوْمٍ يَعْقِلُونَ ﴿٢٤﴾
وَمِنْ ءَايَٰتِهِۦٓ أَن تَقُومَ ٱلسَّمَآءُ وَٱلْأَرْضُ بِأَمْرِهِۦ ۚ ثُمَّ إِذَا دَعَاكُمْ

17. ***So glory be to Allah*** – you should glorify Him and pray to him – ***when you start the night*** – when darkness falls, encompassing the prayers of *Maghrib* and *'Ishā'* – ***and when you greet the day*** with the *Ṣubḥ* prayer.

18. ***Praise be to Him in the heavens and the earth*** – an interpolation meaning that the people of the heavens and the earth praise Him – ***in the afternoon*** – in the *'Aṣr* prayer – ***and when you reach midday*** – in the *Ẓuhr* prayer.

19. ***He brings forth the living from the dead*** – for example, by creating man from sperm and birds from eggs – ***and brings forth the dead*** – sperm and eggs – ***from the living, and brings the earth to life*** with plant-life ***after it was dead*** and barren. ***In the same way you too will be brought forth*** (read as *tukhrajūna* and *takhrujūna*) from the grave.

20. ***Among His Signs*** showing His power ***is that He created you from dust*** – referring to the fact that Ādam originated from dust – ***and here you are now, widespread human beings*** consisting of flesh and bone and spread throughout the earth***!***

21. ***Among His Signs is that He created spouses for you of your own kind*** – referring to the fact that Ḥawwā came from the rib of Ādam and all other people from the sperm of men and the ova of women – ***so that you might find tranquility*** and affection ***in them; and He has placed affection and compassion between you. There are certainly Signs in that for people who reflect*** on them.

22. ***Among His Signs is the creation of the heavens and earth and the variety of your languages*** – Arabic, Persian, and all other languages – ***and colours*** – white, black and other colours; and there is also the variety of skin shades in different children of the same man and woman. ***There are certainly Signs*** of the power of Allah ***in that for every being*** (read as *'ālamīn* and also as *'ālimīn,* meaning "all who know").

23. ***Among His Signs are your sleep by night*** – because He wills rest for you – ***and day and your seeking after His bounty*** – your livelihood, by His will. ***There are certainly Signs in that for people who hear*** – reflect and understand.

دَعْوَةً مِّنَ ٱلْأَرْضِ إِذَآ أَنتُمْ تَخْرُجُونَ ﴿٢٥﴾ وَلَهُۥ مَن فِى ٱلسَّمَٰوَٰتِ
وَٱلْأَرْضِ ۖ كُلٌّ لَّهُۥ قَٰنِتُونَ ﴿٢٦﴾ وَهُوَ ٱلَّذِى يَبْدَؤُا۟ ٱلْخَلْقَ
ثُمَّ يُعِيدُهُۥ وَهُوَ أَهْوَنُ عَلَيْهِ ۚ وَلَهُ ٱلْمَثَلُ ٱلْأَعْلَىٰ فِى ٱلسَّمَٰوَٰتِ
وَٱلْأَرْضِ ۚ وَهُوَ ٱلْعَزِيزُ ٱلْحَكِيمُ ﴿٢٧﴾ ضَرَبَ لَكُم مَّثَلًا مِّنْ
أَنفُسِكُمْ ۖ هَل لَّكُم مِّن مَّا مَلَكَتْ أَيْمَٰنُكُم مِّن شُرَكَآءَ فِى
مَا رَزَقْنَٰكُمْ فَأَنتُمْ فِيهِ سَوَآءٌ تَخَافُونَهُمْ كَخِيفَتِكُمْ
أَنفُسَكُمْ ۚ كَذَٰلِكَ نُفَصِّلُ ٱلْءَايَٰتِ لِقَوْمٍ يَعْقِلُونَ ﴿٢٨﴾
بَلِ ٱتَّبَعَ ٱلَّذِينَ ظَلَمُوٓا۟ أَهْوَآءَهُم بِغَيْرِ عِلْمٍ ۖ فَمَن يَهْدِى مَنْ
أَضَلَّ ٱللَّهُ ۖ وَمَا لَهُم مِّن نَّٰصِرِينَ ﴿٢٩﴾ فَأَقِمْ وَجْهَكَ لِلدِّينِ
حَنِيفًا ۚ فِطْرَتَ ٱللَّهِ ٱلَّتِى فَطَرَ ٱلنَّاسَ عَلَيْهَا ۚ لَا تَبْدِيلَ لِخَلْقِ
ٱللَّهِ ۚ ذَٰلِكَ ٱلدِّينُ ٱلْقَيِّمُ وَلَٰكِنَّ أَكْثَرَ ٱلنَّاسِ
لَا يَعْلَمُونَ ﴿٣٠﴾ ۞ مُنِيبِينَ إِلَيْهِ وَٱتَّقُوهُ وَأَقِيمُوا۟ ٱلصَّلَوٰةَ
وَلَا تَكُونُوا۟ مِنَ ٱلْمُشْرِكِينَ ﴿٣١﴾ مِنَ ٱلَّذِينَ فَرَّقُوا۟
دِينَهُمْ وَكَانُوا۟ شِيَعًا ۖ كُلُّ حِزْبٍۭ بِمَا لَدَيْهِمْ فَرِحُونَ ﴿٣٢﴾
وَإِذَا مَسَّ ٱلنَّاسَ ضُرٌّ دَعَوْا۟ رَبَّهُم مُّنِيبِينَ إِلَيْهِ ثُمَّ إِذَآ أَذَاقَهُم
مِّنْهُ رَحْمَةً إِذَا فَرِيقٌ مِّنْهُم بِرَبِّهِمْ يُشْرِكُونَ ﴿٣٣﴾ لِيَكْفُرُوا۟ بِمَآ
ءَاتَيْنَٰهُمْ ۚ فَتَمَتَّعُوا۟ فَسَوْفَ تَعْلَمُونَ ﴿٣٤﴾ أَمْ أَنزَلْنَا عَلَيْهِمْ
سُلْطَٰنًا فَهُوَ يَتَكَلَّمُ بِمَا كَانُوا۟ بِهِۦ يُشْرِكُونَ ﴿٣٥﴾ وَإِذَآ أَذَقْنَا
ٱلنَّاسَ رَحْمَةً فَرِحُوا۟ بِهَا ۖ وَإِن تُصِبْهُمْ سَيِّئَةٌۢ بِمَا قَدَّمَتْ أَيْدِيهِمْ
إِذَا هُمْ يَقْنَطُونَ ﴿٣٦﴾ أَوَلَمْ يَرَوْا۟ أَنَّ ٱللَّهَ يَبْسُطُ ٱلرِّزْقَ لِمَن يَشَآءُ

24. ***Among His Signs is that He shows you lightning, a source of fear*** – for those exposed to it by travel – ***and eager hope*** – for those safe at home, because of the rain that comes with it – ***and sends down water from the sky, bringing the dead earth back to life by it*** – making plants grow. ***There are certainly Signs in that for people who use their intellect*** and reflect.

25. ***Among His Signs is that heaven and earth hold firm*** – without visible support – ***by His command*** (will). ***Then, when He calls you forth from the earth*** – when Isrāfīl blows the trumpet for the Resurrection – ***you will emerge at once*** from your graves, alive. People's emergence at the summons is one of the Signs of Allah.

26. ***Everyone in the heavens and earth belongs to Him*** as His property, creation and slaves***: all are submissive to Him*** and obey Him.

27. ***It is He who originated the creation*** of mankind ***and then regenerates it*** after its destruction. ***That is very easy for Him.*** Bringing them back is easier than originating them since it is easier to repeat something than to do it for the first time. They are both equally easy for Allah. ***His is the most exalted designation in the heavens and the earth*** – a reference to the formula: "There is no god but Allah." ***He is the Almighty*** in His kingdom***, the All-Wise*** in His creation.

28. ***He has made an example for you*** – of the idolators – ***from among yourselves. Are any of the slaves you own partners with you in what We have provided for you*** in terms of property and other things – ***so that you*** and they ***are equal in respect of it, you fearing them the same as one another*** – making them your equals as free men***?*** The question implies a negative response: they are not equal partners with you. So how can you make some of Allah's property partners with Him? ***In that way We make Our Signs clear for people who use their intellect*** and reflect.

29. ***Yet those who do wrong*** by committing *shirk* ***pursue their whims and desires without any knowledge. Who can guide those whom Allah has led astray?*** They have no guide. ***They will have no helpers.*** No one will be able to defend them against the punishment of Allah.

30. ***So***, Muḥammad, ***set your face firmly towards the Dīn, as a pure natural believer –*** make your *dīn* sincere for Allah alone, both you and those who follow you – ***Allah's natural pattern on which He***

made mankind – His *dīn*, so hold fast to it. ***There is no changing Allah's creation*** – the *dīn* of Allah cannot be altered by attributing partners to Him. ***That is the true* Dīn** – the affirmation of Allah's unity – ***but most people***, including the unbelievers of Makka, ***do not know it …***

31. ***…turning towards Him*** in obedience to what He commands and forbids. ***Be fearful of Him and establish the prayer. Do not be among the idolators:***

32. ***…those who split up*** (read as *farraqū* and also *fāriqū,* in which case the meaning is that they abandon the *dīn* which they are commanded to adhere to) ***their* dīn, *and form into sects*** based on their disagreement about what to worship, ***each faction exulting*** and rejoicing ***in what they have.***

33. ***When harm*** or hardship ***touches people they call on their Lord, turning in repentance to Him*** rather than to others. ***But then, when He gives them a taste of mercy*** – such as abundant rainfall – ***from Him, a group of them immediately associate others with their Lord…***

34. ***…showing ingratitude for what We have given them. 'Enjoy yourselves; you will soon know*** the end of your enjoyment.*'* This is meant as a threat. This verse brings a change of person from third to second person plural.

35. ***Or have We sent down some authority*** – the word for authority (*sulṭān*) may mean either evidence or an actual Book – ***to them, which advocates associating others with Him?*** This implies a negative response. Does Scripture command them to associate with Him? It certainly does not.

36. ***When We give people*** – including the unbelievers of Makka and others – ***a taste of mercy*** (blessing), ***they rejoice in it*** exultantly***; but when something bad*** – such as a time of hardship – ***happens to them because of what they themselves have done, they immediately lose all hope*** of mercy. The believer should be thankful for blessings and always hope for good from his Lord in times of hardship.

37. ***Do they not see*** and know ***that Allah expands provision for whoever He wills*** as a test ***and also restricts it*** as He wills as a test***? There are certainly Signs in that for people who believe.***

وَيَقْدِرُ ۚ إِنَّ فِي ذَٰلِكَ لَآيَاتٍ لِّقَوْمٍ يُؤْمِنُونَ ﴿٣٧﴾ فَآتِ ذَا الْقُرْبَىٰ
حَقَّهُ وَالْمِسْكِينَ وَابْنَ السَّبِيلِ ۚ ذَٰلِكَ خَيْرٌ لِّلَّذِينَ يُرِيدُونَ
وَجْهَ اللَّهِ ۖ وَأُولَٰئِكَ هُمُ الْمُفْلِحُونَ ﴿٣٨﴾ وَمَا آتَيْتُم مِّن رِّبًا
لِّيَرْبُوا فِي أَمْوَالِ النَّاسِ فَلَا يَرْبُوا عِندَ اللَّهِ ۖ وَمَا آتَيْتُم مِّن زَكَاةٍ
تُرِيدُونَ وَجْهَ اللَّهِ فَأُولَٰئِكَ هُمُ الْمُضْعِفُونَ ﴿٣٩﴾ اللَّهُ الَّذِي
خَلَقَكُمْ ثُمَّ رَزَقَكُمْ ثُمَّ يُمِيتُكُمْ ثُمَّ يُحْيِيكُمْ ۖ هَلْ مِن
شُرَكَائِكُم مَّن يَفْعَلُ مِن ذَٰلِكُم مِّن شَيْءٍ ۚ سُبْحَانَهُ وَتَعَالَىٰ
عَمَّا يُشْرِكُونَ ﴿٤٠﴾ ظَهَرَ الْفَسَادُ فِي الْبَرِّ وَالْبَحْرِ بِمَا كَسَبَتْ
أَيْدِي النَّاسِ لِيُذِيقَهُم بَعْضَ الَّذِي عَمِلُوا لَعَلَّهُمْ يَرْجِعُونَ ﴿٤١﴾
قُلْ سِيرُوا فِي الْأَرْضِ فَانظُرُوا كَيْفَ كَانَ عَاقِبَةُ الَّذِينَ مِن قَبْلُ ۚ
كَانَ أَكْثَرُهُم مُّشْرِكِينَ ﴿٤٢﴾ فَأَقِمْ وَجْهَكَ لِلدِّينِ الْقَيِّمِ مِن
قَبْلِ أَن يَأْتِيَ يَوْمٌ لَّا مَرَدَّ لَهُ مِنَ اللَّهِ ۖ يَوْمَئِذٍ يَصَّدَّعُونَ ﴿٤٣﴾ مَن
كَفَرَ فَعَلَيْهِ كُفْرُهُ ۖ وَمَنْ عَمِلَ صَالِحًا فَلِأَنفُسِهِمْ يَمْهَدُونَ ﴿٤٤﴾
لِيَجْزِيَ الَّذِينَ آمَنُوا وَعَمِلُوا الصَّالِحَاتِ مِن فَضْلِهِ ۚ إِنَّهُ لَا يُحِبُّ
الْكَافِرِينَ ﴿٤٥﴾ وَمِنْ آيَاتِهِ أَن يُرْسِلَ الرِّيَاحَ مُبَشِّرَاتٍ وَلِيُذِيقَكُم
مِّن رَّحْمَتِهِ وَلِتَجْرِيَ الْفُلْكُ بِأَمْرِهِ وَلِتَبْتَغُوا مِن فَضْلِهِ وَلَعَلَّكُمْ
تَشْكُرُونَ ﴿٤٦﴾ وَلَقَدْ أَرْسَلْنَا مِن قَبْلِكَ رُسُلًا إِلَىٰ قَوْمِهِمْ فَجَاءُوهُم
بِالْبَيِّنَاتِ فَانتَقَمْنَا مِنَ الَّذِينَ أَجْرَمُوا ۖ وَكَانَ حَقًّا عَلَيْنَا نَصْرُ
الْمُؤْمِنِينَ ﴿٤٧﴾ اللَّهُ الَّذِي يُرْسِلُ الرِّيَاحَ فَتُثِيرُ سَحَابًا فَيَبْسُطُهُ
فِي السَّمَاءِ كَيْفَ يَشَاءُ وَيَجْعَلُهُ كِسَفًا فَتَرَى الْوَدْقَ يَخْرُجُ مِنْ

38. ***Give relatives their due*** – in terms of kindness and *ṣadaqa* – ***and the poor and travellers*** the *ṣadaqa* due to them. The community of the Prophet followed him in that. ***That is best for those who seek the pleasure of Allah*** – Allah's reward for what they do. ***They are the ones who are successful.***

39. ***What you give with usurious intent, aiming to get back a greater amount from people's wealth*** – when you give a gift in order to get something more in return for it, it is designated as usury because of the desired increase in the transaction and it ***does not become greater with Allah*** – the givers receive no reward. ***But anything you give as*** **zakāt** (*ṣadaqa*), ***seeking the Face of Allah – all who do that will get back twice as much***: a double reward. There is a change in person at the end of the *āyat* from second person to third person plural.

40. ***Allah is He who created you, then provides for you, then will cause you to die and then bring you back to life. Can any of your partner-gods*** – those you associate with Allah – ***do any of that? Glory be to Him and He is exalted above anything they associate with Him!***

41. ***Corruption has appeared in both land*** – wastelands have appeared through lack of rain and plant – ***and sea*** – rivers have dried up – ***because of what people's own hands have brought about*** – by their disobedience to Allah, ***so that they may taste*** (read as *yudhīqahum* and also *nudhīqahum*, "We may make them taste") the negative results of ***something of what they have done, so that perhaps they will turn back*** and repent.

42. ***Say*** to the unbelievers of Makka: ***'Travel about the earth and see the final fate of those before. Most of them were idolaters.'*** So they were destroyed for their *shirk*; and their houses and dwelling places are deserted.

43. ***So set your face firmly towards the True*** **Dīn** (Islam) ***before a Day*** (the Day of Rising) ***comes from Allah which cannot be turned back. On that Day they will be split up*** – separated after the Reckoning, going either to the Garden or the Fire.

44. ***Those who disbelieved will find that their unbelief was against themselves.*** The evil effects of their unbelief will come back on

خِلَٰلِهِۦۖ فَإِذَآ أَصَابَ بِهِۦ مَن يَشَآءُ مِنْ عِبَادِهِۦٓ إِذَا هُمْ يَسْتَبْشِرُونَ
﴿٤٨﴾ وَإِن كَانُوا۟ مِن قَبْلِ أَن يُنَزَّلَ عَلَيْهِم مِّن قَبْلِهِۦ لَمُبْلِسِينَ
﴿٤٩﴾ فَٱنظُرْ إِلَىٰٓ ءَاثَٰرِ رَحْمَتِ ٱللَّهِ كَيْفَ يُحْىِ ٱلْأَرْضَ بَعْدَ
مَوْتِهَآ ۚ إِنَّ ذَٰلِكَ لَمُحْىِ ٱلْمَوْتَىٰ ۖ وَهُوَ عَلَىٰ كُلِّ شَىْءٍ قَدِيرٌ ﴿٥٠﴾
وَلَئِنْ أَرْسَلْنَا رِيحًا فَرَأَوْهُ مُصْفَرًّا لَّظَلُّوا۟ مِنۢ بَعْدِهِۦ يَكْفُرُونَ
﴿٥١﴾ فَإِنَّكَ لَا تُسْمِعُ ٱلْمَوْتَىٰ وَلَا تُسْمِعُ ٱلصُّمَّ ٱلدُّعَآءَ إِذَا وَلَّوْا۟
مُدْبِرِينَ ﴿٥٢﴾ وَمَآ أَنتَ بِهَٰدِ ٱلْعُمْىِ عَن ضَلَٰلَتِهِمْ ۖ إِن تُسْمِعُ إِلَّا
مَن يُؤْمِنُ بِـَٔايَٰتِنَا فَهُم مُّسْلِمُونَ ﴿٥٣﴾ ۞ ٱللَّهُ ٱلَّذِى خَلَقَكُم
مِّن ضَعْفٍ ثُمَّ جَعَلَ مِنۢ بَعْدِ ضَعْفٍ قُوَّةً ثُمَّ جَعَلَ مِنۢ بَعْدِ
قُوَّةٍ ضَعْفًا وَشَيْبَةً ۚ يَخْلُقُ مَا يَشَآءُ ۖ وَهُوَ ٱلْعَلِيمُ ٱلْقَدِيرُ ﴿٥٤﴾
وَيَوْمَ تَقُومُ ٱلسَّاعَةُ يُقْسِمُ ٱلْمُجْرِمُونَ مَا لَبِثُوا۟ غَيْرَ سَاعَةٍ ۚ
كَذَٰلِكَ كَانُوا۟ يُؤْفَكُونَ ﴿٥٥﴾ وَقَالَ ٱلَّذِينَ أُوتُوا۟ ٱلْعِلْمَ وَٱلْإِيمَٰنَ
لَقَدْ لَبِثْتُمْ فِى كِتَٰبِ ٱللَّهِ إِلَىٰ يَوْمِ ٱلْبَعْثِ ۖ فَهَٰذَا يَوْمُ ٱلْبَعْثِ
وَلَٰكِنَّكُمْ كُنتُمْ لَا تَعْلَمُونَ ﴿٥٦﴾ فَيَوْمَئِذٍ لَّا يَنفَعُ ٱلَّذِينَ
ظَلَمُوا۟ مَعْذِرَتُهُمْ وَلَا هُمْ يُسْتَعْتَبُونَ ﴿٥٧﴾ وَلَقَدْ ضَرَبْنَا
لِلنَّاسِ فِى هَٰذَا ٱلْقُرْءَانِ مِن كُلِّ مَثَلٍ ۚ وَلَئِن جِئْتَهُم بِـَٔايَةٍ
لَّيَقُولَنَّ ٱلَّذِينَ كَفَرُوٓا۟ إِنْ أَنتُمْ إِلَّا مُبْطِلُونَ ﴿٥٨﴾ كَذَٰلِكَ
يَطْبَعُ ٱللَّهُ عَلَىٰ قُلُوبِ ٱلَّذِينَ لَا يَعْلَمُونَ ﴿٥٩﴾ فَٱصْبِرْ إِنَّ
وَعْدَ ٱللَّهِ حَقٌّ ۖ وَلَا يَسْتَخِفَّنَّكَ ٱلَّذِينَ لَا يُوقِنُونَ ﴿٦٠﴾

them. ***Those who did right were making the way*** towards their place in the Garden ***easy for themselves;***

45. ***...so that He might repay with His bounty those who believed and did right actions. He certainly does not love the unbelievers.*** The believers will be rewarded and the unbelievers punished.

46. ***Among His Signs is that He sends the winds bearing good news*** of rain ***to give you a taste of His mercy*** – rain and fertility – ***and to make the ships run by His command*** (will) ***and to enable you to seek His bounty*** – provision gained by trading across the seas – ***so that perhaps you may be thankful*** for these blessings and affirm Allah's unity.

47. ***Before you We sent other Messengers to their people, and they too brought them the Clear Signs*** – clear evidence of their truthfulness in respect of their Message to them***; but they denied them.*** Then Allah destroyed those who denied. ***We took revenge on those who did evil; and it is Our duty to help the believers*** against the unbelievers by destroying them and rescuing the believers.

48. ***It is Allah who sends the winds which stir up clouds*** – and make them move ***which He spreads about the sky however He wills*** – in greater or smaller quantity. ***He forms them into dark clumps*** (read as *kisafan* and *kasfan*) ***and you see the rain come pouring out from the middle of them. When He makes it fall on those of His slaves He wills, they rejoice*** in the rain,

49. ***...even though before He sent it down on them they were in despair*** – of rain coming.

50. ***So look at the effects*** (read as *āthāri*, and also in the singular form, *athari*) ***of the mercy of Allah*** in bringing rain, ***how He brings the dead earth back to life*** after it was dry and arid. ***Truly He is the One Who brings the dead to life. He has power over all things.***

51. ***But if We send a wind*** – which harms the plants – ***and they see it*** (the plant-life) ***turning yellow, still they persist after that*** yellowing ***in disbelieving*** – remaining ungrateful for Allah's blessing of rain.

52. ***You will not make dead men hear; you will not make deaf men hear the call, when they turn their backs in flight.***

53. ***You will not guide blind men away from their misguidance. You will not make anyone hear*** – understand and accept – ***except for those who believe in Our Signs*** (the Qur'an) ***and so are Muslims***, affirming Allah's unity.

54. ***It is Allah who created you from a weak beginning***, base liquid, ***then after weakness*** (read as *ḍa'f* and *ḍu'f*) – a reference to childhood – ***gave you strength*** – a reference to adulthood, ***then after strength ordained weakness*** (read as *ḍa'f* and *ḍu'f*) – a reference to old age – ***and grey hair. He creates whatever He wills*** in respect of weakness and strength, youth and old age. ***He is All-Knowing*** of how to manage His creation, ***All-Powerful*** in doing whatever He wishes.

55. ***On the Day the Last Hour arrives, the evildoers*** (unbelievers) ***will swear they have not even tarried for an hour*** in the grave. Allah says: ***That is the extent to which they are deceived.*** They fail to grasp the truth of Resurrection in the same way that they fail to grasp the truth about the length of time they remain in the grave.

56. ***Those*** – referring to the angels and others – ***who have been given knowledge and belief will say, 'You tarried in accordance with Allah's Decree until the Day of Rising***, which you denied. ***And this is the Day of Rising, but you did not know it.'***

57. ***On that Day the excuses of those who did wrong*** – their reasons for denying it – ***will not help*** (read as *yanfa'u* and *tanfa'ū*) ***them, nor will they be able to appease Allah.*** They will not be able to find anything with which to placate Allah.

58. ***We have made all kinds of examples for people in this Qur'an. If you*** – Muḥammad – ***bring them a Sign*** – such as the Staff and Hand which Mūsā was given, ***those who disbelieve will say, 'You*** and your Companions ***are just purveyors of falsehood!'***

59. ***In that way*** – the way their hearts are oblivious – ***Allah seals up the hearts of those who do not know*** about his Oneness.

60. ***So be steadfast. Allah's promise*** to help you against them ***is true. Do not let those who have no certainty*** about the Resurrection ***unsettle you.*** Do not let them move you to levity and cause you to abandon steadfastness.

سُورَةُ لُقْمَانَ

بِسْمِ ٱللَّهِ ٱلرَّحْمَٰنِ ٱلرَّحِيمِ

الٓمٓ ١ تِلْكَ ءَايَٰتُ ٱلْكِتَٰبِ ٱلْحَكِيمِ ٢ هُدًى وَرَحْمَةً
لِّلْمُحْسِنِينَ ٣ ٱلَّذِينَ يُقِيمُونَ ٱلصَّلَوٰةَ وَيُؤْتُونَ ٱلزَّكَوٰةَ وَهُم
بِٱلْـَٔاخِرَةِ هُمْ يُوقِنُونَ ٤ أُو۟لَٰٓئِكَ عَلَىٰ هُدًى مِّن رَّبِّهِمْ ۖ وَأُو۟لَٰٓئِكَ
هُمُ ٱلْمُفْلِحُونَ ٥ وَمِنَ ٱلنَّاسِ مَن يَشْتَرِى لَهْوَ ٱلْحَدِيثِ
لِيُضِلَّ عَن سَبِيلِ ٱللَّهِ بِغَيْرِ عِلْمٍ وَيَتَّخِذَهَا هُزُوًا ۚ أُو۟لَٰٓئِكَ لَهُمْ
عَذَابٌ مُّهِينٌ ٦ وَإِذَا تُتْلَىٰ عَلَيْهِ ءَايَٰتُنَا وَلَّىٰ مُسْتَكْبِرًا
كَأَن لَّمْ يَسْمَعْهَا كَأَنَّ فِىٓ أُذُنَيْهِ وَقْرًا ۖ فَبَشِّرْهُ بِعَذَابٍ أَلِيمٍ ٧
إِنَّ ٱلَّذِينَ ءَامَنُوا۟ وَعَمِلُوا۟ ٱلصَّٰلِحَٰتِ لَهُمْ جَنَّٰتُ ٱلنَّعِيمِ ٨
خَٰلِدِينَ فِيهَا ۖ وَعْدَ ٱللَّهِ حَقًّا ۚ وَهُوَ ٱلْعَزِيزُ ٱلْحَكِيمُ ٩ خَلَقَ
ٱلسَّمَٰوَٰتِ بِغَيْرِ عَمَدٍ تَرَوْنَهَا ۖ وَأَلْقَىٰ فِى ٱلْأَرْضِ رَوَٰسِىَ أَن تَمِيدَ
بِكُمْ وَبَثَّ فِيهَا مِن كُلِّ دَآبَّةٍ ۚ وَأَنزَلْنَا مِنَ ٱلسَّمَآءِ مَآءً فَأَنۢبَتْنَا فِيهَا
مِن كُلِّ زَوْجٍ كَرِيمٍ ١٠ هَٰذَا خَلْقُ ٱللَّهِ فَأَرُونِى مَاذَا
خَلَقَ ٱلَّذِينَ مِن دُونِهِۦ ۚ بَلِ ٱلظَّٰلِمُونَ فِى ضَلَٰلٍ مُّبِينٍ ١١
وَلَقَدْ ءَاتَيْنَا لُقْمَٰنَ ٱلْحِكْمَةَ أَنِ ٱشْكُرْ لِلَّهِ ۚ وَمَن يَشْكُرْ فَإِنَّمَا
يَشْكُرُ لِنَفْسِهِۦ ۖ وَمَن كَفَرَ فَإِنَّ ٱللَّهَ غَنِىٌّ حَمِيدٌ ١٢ وَإِذْ قَالَ
لُقْمَٰنُ لِٱبْنِهِۦ وَهُوَ يَعِظُهُۥ يَٰبُنَىَّ لَا تُشْرِكْ بِٱللَّهِ ۖ إِنَّ ٱلشِّرْكَ
لَظُلْمٌ عَظِيمٌ ١٣ وَوَصَّيْنَا ٱلْإِنسَٰنَ بِوَٰلِدَيْهِ حَمَلَتْهُ أُمُّهُۥ
وَهْنًا عَلَىٰ وَهْنٍ وَفِصَٰلُهُۥ فِى عَامَيْنِ أَنِ ٱشْكُرْ لِى وَلِوَٰلِدَيْكَ

31. *Sūrat Luqmān*
Luqman

This *sūra* is Makkan except for *āyats* 27, 28 and 29, which are Madinan. It has 34 *āyat*s and was sent down after *Sūrat aṣ-Ṣāffāt.*

1. ***Alif Lam Mim.*** Allah knows best what is meant by this.

2. ***Those*** *āyat*s ***are the Signs of the Wise Book*** (the Qur'an) –

3. ***...guidance and mercy*** (read as *raḥmatan* and *raḥmatun*) ***for the good-doers:***

4. ***...those who establish prayer and pay* zakāt, *and are certain of the Next World.***

5. ***Such people are following guidance from their Lord. They are the ones who are successful.***

6. ***But there are some people who trade in distracting tales*** – which divert others from what really should concern them – ***to misguide*** (read as *yuḍilla* and *yaḍilla*) ***people from Allah's Way*** – the Path of Islam, ***knowing nothing about it and to make*** (read as *yatattakhidhaha* and *yatattakhidhuha*) ***a mockery of it. Such people will have a humiliating punishment.***

7. ***When Our Signs*** (the Qur'an) ***are recited to such a person, he turns away arrogantly as if he had not heard, as if there were a great weight in his ears*** – as if he were deaf. ***So give him news of a painful punishment*** – and threaten him with it. This refers to an-Naḍr ibn al-Ḥārith. He used to go to Ḥīra to trade and he bought books of the history of the Persians and recounted them to the people of Makka. He said, "Muḥammad recounts to you the tales of 'Ād and Thamūd and I tell you the tales of Persia and the Romans." So they enjoyed his stories and stopped listening to the Qur'an.

8. ***For those who believe and do right actions there are Gardens of Delight,***

9. ***...to remain in them timelessly, for ever*** once they enter them. ***Allah's promise*** of that ***is true. He is the Almighty,*** so that nothing can overcome Him to prevent Him carrying out His promise and threat, ***the All-Wise*** who only ever puts anything in its right place.

10. ***It is Allah Who created the heavens with no support – you can see them*** without any supporting pillars ***– and cast firmly embedded*** high ***mountains on the earth so that it would not move under you, and scattered about in it creatures of every kind. And We send down water from the sky and make every generous*** (beautiful) ***species grow in it.*** The *āyat* contains a change of person from third person singular to first person plural.

11. ***This is Allah's creation. Show me*** (tell me) – people of Makka – ***then what those*** gods ***besides Him have created! The wrongdoers*** (unbelievers) ***are clearly misguided*** because of their *shirk* – and you, people of Makka, are among them.

12. ***We gave Luqmān wisdom*** – which includes knowledge, piety, correctness in speech, and many of his wise sayings have been transmitted. He used to give judgement (*fatwā*) before Dāwūd was sent and lived until the time he was sent, whereupon he learned from him and stopping giving judgement. He said about that, "Should I not be content when I have been given enough?" He was asked, "Which person is the worst?" He said, "The one who does not care if people think that he is an evildoer." We said to him***: 'Give thanks to Allah*** for the wisdom He has given you. ***Whoever gives thanks only does so for his own good*** because of the reward he receives for doing so. ***Whoever is ungrateful*** for blessings received, ***Allah is Rich Beyond Need*** of His creation, ***Praiseworthy*** in what He does.'

13. Remember ***when Luqmān said to his son, counselling him, 'My son*** – using the diminutive form of 'son' to show affection – ***do not associate anything with Allah. Associating others with Him is a terrible wrong***, so return to Allah and submit to Him.'

14. ***We have instructed man concerning his parents*** – commanded him to be good to his parents. ***Bearing him caused his mother great debility*** – during her pregnancy, in her labour, and also when she delivered him – ***and the period of his weaning was two years.*** We said to him***: 'Give thanks to Me and to your parents. I am your final destination.***

15. ***But if they try to make you associate something with Me about which you have no knowledge, do not obey them. Keep company with them correctly*** – through obedience and maintaining ties with

إِلَيَّ ٱلْمَصِيرُ ﴿١٤﴾ وَإِن جَٰهَدَاكَ عَلَىٰٓ أَن تُشْرِكَ بِي مَا لَيْسَ
لَكَ بِهِۦ عِلْمٌ فَلَا تُطِعْهُمَا ۖ وَصَاحِبْهُمَا فِي ٱلدُّنْيَا مَعْرُوفًا ۖ
وَٱتَّبِعْ سَبِيلَ مَنْ أَنَابَ إِلَيَّ ۚ ثُمَّ إِلَيَّ مَرْجِعُكُمْ فَأُنَبِّئُكُم
بِمَا كُنتُمْ تَعْمَلُونَ ﴿١٥﴾ يَٰبُنَيَّ إِنَّهَآ إِن تَكُ مِثْقَالَ حَبَّةٍ مِّنْ
خَرْدَلٍ فَتَكُن فِي صَخْرَةٍ أَوْ فِي ٱلسَّمَٰوَٰتِ أَوْ فِي ٱلْأَرْضِ يَأْتِ
بِهَا ٱللَّهُ ۚ إِنَّ ٱللَّهَ لَطِيفٌ خَبِيرٌ ﴿١٦﴾ يَٰبُنَيَّ أَقِمِ ٱلصَّلَوٰةَ وَأْمُرْ
بِٱلْمَعْرُوفِ وَٱنْهَ عَنِ ٱلْمُنكَرِ وَٱصْبِرْ عَلَىٰ مَآ أَصَابَكَ ۖ إِنَّ ذَٰلِكَ
مِنْ عَزْمِ ٱلْأُمُورِ ﴿١٧﴾ وَلَا تُصَعِّرْ خَدَّكَ لِلنَّاسِ وَلَا تَمْشِ فِي ٱلْأَرْضِ
مَرَحًا ۖ إِنَّ ٱللَّهَ لَا يُحِبُّ كُلَّ مُخْتَالٍ فَخُورٍ ﴿١٨﴾ وَٱقْصِدْ فِي مَشْيِكَ
وَٱغْضُضْ مِن صَوْتِكَ ۚ إِنَّ أَنكَرَ ٱلْأَصْوَٰتِ لَصَوْتُ ٱلْحَمِيرِ ﴿١٩﴾
أَلَمْ تَرَوْا۟ أَنَّ ٱللَّهَ سَخَّرَ لَكُم مَّا فِي ٱلسَّمَٰوَٰتِ وَمَا فِي ٱلْأَرْضِ وَأَسْبَغَ
عَلَيْكُمْ نِعَمَهُۥ ظَٰهِرَةً وَبَاطِنَةً ۗ وَمِنَ ٱلنَّاسِ مَن يُجَٰدِلُ فِي ٱللَّهِ
بِغَيْرِ عِلْمٍ وَلَا هُدًى وَلَا كِتَٰبٍ مُّنِيرٍ ﴿٢٠﴾ وَإِذَا قِيلَ لَهُمُ ٱتَّبِعُوا۟
مَآ أَنزَلَ ٱللَّهُ قَالُوا۟ بَلْ نَتَّبِعُ مَا وَجَدْنَا عَلَيْهِ ءَابَآءَنَآ ۚ أَوَلَوْ كَانَ
ٱلشَّيْطَٰنُ يَدْعُوهُمْ إِلَىٰ عَذَابِ ٱلسَّعِيرِ ﴿٢١﴾ ۞ وَمَن يُسْلِمْ
وَجْهَهُۥٓ إِلَى ٱللَّهِ وَهُوَ مُحْسِنٌ فَقَدِ ٱسْتَمْسَكَ بِٱلْعُرْوَةِ ٱلْوُثْقَىٰ ۗ
وَإِلَى ٱللَّهِ عَٰقِبَةُ ٱلْأُمُورِ ﴿٢٢﴾ وَمَن كَفَرَ فَلَا يَحْزُنكَ كُفْرُهُۥٓ ۚ
إِلَيْنَا مَرْجِعُهُمْ فَنُنَبِّئُهُم بِمَا عَمِلُوٓا۟ ۚ إِنَّ ٱللَّهَ عَلِيمٌۢ بِذَاتِ ٱلصُّدُورِ
﴿٢٣﴾ نُمَتِّعُهُمْ قَلِيلًا ثُمَّ نَضْطَرُّهُمْ إِلَىٰ عَذَابٍ غَلِيظٍ ﴿٢٤﴾
وَلَئِن سَأَلْتَهُم مَّنْ خَلَقَ ٱلسَّمَٰوَٰتِ وَٱلْأَرْضَ لَيَقُولُنَّ ٱللَّهُ ۚ قُلِ

gifts – ***and courteously in this world; but follow the Way of him who turns to Me*** in obedience. ***Then you will return to Me and I will inform you about the things you did*** and repay you for them.***'*** This is an interjection.

16. ***'My son, even if something*** – an evil deed – ***weighs as little as a mustard-seed and is inside a rock or anywhere else in the heavens or earth –*** or somewhere even more hidden, ***Allah will bring it out*** and reckon it. ***Allah is All-Pervading***, so that He is able to bring it out, ***All-Aware*** so that He knows where it is.

17. ***My son, establish the prayer and command what is right and forbid what is wrong, and be steadfast in the face of all that happens to you*** on account of commanding the right and forbidding the wrong. ***That*** – what has been mentioned – ***is certainly the most resolute course to follow*** – and that in which resolve is necessary.

18. ***Do not avert*** (read as *tuṣa''ir* and *tuṣā'ir*) ***your face from people out of haughtiness, and do not strut about arrogantly on the earth. Allah does not love anyone who is vain*** and arrogant in gait ***or boastful*** with people.

19. ***Be moderate in your tread*** – not walking either too quickly or too slowly, and being tranquil and dignified – ***and lower your voice. The most hateful of voices is the donkey's bray.'***

20. ***Do you not see*** and know, you who are addressed, ***that Allah has subjected to you everything in the heavens*** – the sun, the moon and the stars which are there for your benefit – ***and earth*** – along with the fruits, rivers and animals it contains – ***and has showered His*** ample ***blessings upon you, both outwardly*** – in the excellence of your form, the symmetry of your limbs, and other such things – ***and inwardly*** – in your ability to recognise and other such things***? Yet there are people*** – such as the the people of Makka – ***who argue about Allah without knowledge or guidance*** from any Messenger ***or any illuminating Book*** which Allah has revealed. They simply imitate.

21. ***When they are told: 'Follow what Allah has sent down,' they say, 'No, we will follow what we found our fathers doing.'*** Allah says: ***What!*** Would they follow him ***even if Shayṭān is calling them***

to what will make ***the punishment of the Blazing Fire*** mandatory for them***?***

22. ***Those who submit themselves completely to Allah*** – and agree to obey Allah – ***and do good*** while affirming Allah's unity ***have grasped the Firmest Handhold*** – which will never give way. ***The end result of all affairs is with Allah*** and goes back to Him.

23. ***And do not let the unbelief of those who disbelieve sadden you***, Muḥammad, and do not be worried about it. ***They will return to Us, and We will inform them about the things they did. Allah knows what the heart contains*** – and will certainly repay them.

24. ***We will let them enjoy themselves a little*** during their life in this world, ***and then*** – in the Next World – ***drive them to a harsh punishment*** of the Fire, from which there is no escape.

25. ***If you asked them, 'Who created the heavens and the earth?' they would say, 'Allah!' Say: 'Praise be to Allah*** for making the evidence of *tawḥīd* manifest to them***!' But most of them do not know*** that it is obligatory for them to obey Him.

26. ***Everything in the heavens and earth belongs to Allah*** as His property, creation and slaves. Only He is entitled to be worshipped in the heavens and earth. ***Allah is the Rich Beyond Need*** of His slaves, ***the Praiseworthy*** in what He does.

27. ***If all the trees on earth were pens and all the sea, with seven more seas besides, were ink, Allah's words still would not run dry*** – because what He knows is infinite. ***Allah is Almighty*** – so that nothing can withstand His power, ***All-Wise*** – and nothing is beyond His knowledge and wisdom.

28. ***Your creation and rising is only like that of a single self.*** He merely says, "Be!" and it happens. ***Allah is All-Hearing, All-Seeing*** – and nothing distracts Him from anything.

29. ***Do you not see*** (know) ***that Allah makes night merge into day and day merge into night*** – each of them increases as the other decreases – ***and that He has made the sun and moon subservient*** in their orbits, ***each one running for a specified time*** up until the Day of Rising***; and that Allah is aware of what you do?***

30. ***That*** which has been mentioned ***is because Allah, He is the*** firm ***Truth, and what they call upon*** (read as *yad'ūna*, and also *tad'ūna*,

ٱلۡحَمۡدُ لِلَّهِۚ بَلۡ أَكۡثَرُهُمۡ لَا يَعۡلَمُونَ ٢٥ لِلَّهِ مَا فِي ٱلسَّمَٰوَٰتِ
وَٱلۡأَرۡضِۚ إِنَّ ٱللَّهَ هُوَ ٱلۡغَنِيُّ ٱلۡحَمِيدُ ٢٦ وَلَوۡ أَنَّمَا فِي ٱلۡأَرۡضِ
مِن شَجَرَةٍ أَقۡلَٰمٞ وَٱلۡبَحۡرُ يَمُدُّهُۥ مِنۢ بَعۡدِهِۦ سَبۡعَةُ أَبۡحُرٖ
مَّا نَفِدَتۡ كَلِمَٰتُ ٱللَّهِۗ إِنَّ ٱللَّهَ عَزِيزٌ حَكِيمٞ ٢٧ مَّا خَلۡقُكُمۡ
وَلَا بَعۡثُكُمۡ إِلَّا كَنَفۡسٖ وَٰحِدَةٍۗ إِنَّ ٱللَّهَ سَمِيعُۢ بَصِيرٌ ٢٨
أَلَمۡ تَرَ أَنَّ ٱللَّهَ يُولِجُ ٱلَّيۡلَ فِي ٱلنَّهَارِ وَيُولِجُ ٱلنَّهَارَ فِي ٱلَّيۡلِ
وَسَخَّرَ ٱلشَّمۡسَ وَٱلۡقَمَرَۖ كُلّٞ يَجۡرِيٓ إِلَىٰٓ أَجَلٖ مُّسَمّٗى وَأَنَّ ٱللَّهَ
بِمَا تَعۡمَلُونَ خَبِيرٞ ٢٩ ذَٰلِكَ بِأَنَّ ٱللَّهَ هُوَ ٱلۡحَقُّ وَأَنَّ مَا يَدۡعُونَ
مِن دُونِهِ ٱلۡبَٰطِلُ وَأَنَّ ٱللَّهَ هُوَ ٱلۡعَلِيُّ ٱلۡكَبِيرُ ٣٠ أَلَمۡ تَرَ أَنَّ
ٱلۡفُلۡكَ تَجۡرِي فِي ٱلۡبَحۡرِ بِنِعۡمَتِ ٱللَّهِ لِيُرِيَكُم مِّنۡ ءَايَٰتِهِۦٓۚ إِنَّ
فِي ذَٰلِكَ لَأٓيَٰتٖ لِّكُلِّ صَبَّارٖ شَكُورٖ ٣١ وَإِذَا غَشِيَهُم مَّوۡجٞ
كَٱلظُّلَلِ دَعَوُاْ ٱللَّهَ مُخۡلِصِينَ لَهُ ٱلدِّينَ فَلَمَّا نَجَّىٰهُمۡ إِلَى ٱلۡبَرِّ
فَمِنۡهُم مُّقۡتَصِدٞۚ وَمَا يَجۡحَدُ بِـَٔايَٰتِنَآ إِلَّا كُلُّ خَتَّارٖ كَفُورٖ
٣٢ يَٰٓأَيُّهَا ٱلنَّاسُ ٱتَّقُواْ رَبَّكُمۡ وَٱخۡشَوۡاْ يَوۡمٗا لَّا يَجۡزِي وَالِدٌ
عَن وَلَدِهِۦ وَلَا مَوۡلُودٌ هُوَ جَازٍ عَن وَالِدِهِۦ شَيۡـًٔاۚ إِنَّ وَعۡدَ ٱللَّهِ
حَقّٞۖ فَلَا تَغُرَّنَّكُمُ ٱلۡحَيَوٰةُ ٱلدُّنۡيَا وَلَا يَغُرَّنَّكُم بِٱللَّهِ
ٱلۡغَرُورُ ٣٣ إِنَّ ٱللَّهَ عِندَهُۥ عِلۡمُ ٱلسَّاعَةِ وَيُنَزِّلُ ٱلۡغَيۡثَ
وَيَعۡلَمُ مَا فِي ٱلۡأَرۡحَامِۖ وَمَا تَدۡرِي نَفۡسٞ مَّاذَا تَكۡسِبُ غَدٗاۖ
وَمَا تَدۡرِي نَفۡسُۢ بِأَيِّ أَرۡضٖ تَمُوتُۚ إِنَّ ٱللَّهَ عَلِيمٌ خَبِيرُۢ ٣٤

"what you call upon") and worship ***besides Him is*** vanishing ***false-hood. Allah is the All-High*** with power over His creation, ***the Most Great.***

31. ***Do you not see that ships sail on the sea by Allah's blessing so that He may show you something of His Signs? There are certain-ly Signs*** and lessons ***in that for everyone who is steadfast*** – in not disobeying Allah – ***and thankful*** – for His blessing.

32. ***When the waves hang over them*** (unbelievers) ***like canopies*** – mountains under which they are shaded – ***they call on Allah, mak-ing their* dīn *sincerely His*** – making sincere supplication to Him to save them and not calling on anything else besides Him with Him. ***But then when He delivers them safely to the land, some of them are ambivalent*** – hesitating between unbelief and belief, some remaining unbelievers. ***None but a treacherous, thankless man*** – ungrateful for Allah's blessings – ***denies Our Signs*** – which include saving people from death by drowning.

33. ***Mankind,*** including the people of Makka, ***be fearful of your Lord and fear a day when no father will be able to atone for his son*** – or help his son in any way – ***or son for his father, in any way. Allah's promise*** of the Resurrection ***is true. So do not let the life of this world delude you*** about Islam ***and do not let the Deluder*** (Shaytan) ***delude you concerning Allah*** – by the fact that Allah has granted him a deferral.

34. ***Truly Allah has knowledge of the Hour*** – and when it will come – ***and sends down*** (read as *yunazzilu* and *yunzilu*) ***abundant rain*** – at a certain time which He knows – ***and knows what is in the womb***, whether male or female. ***And no self knows what*** good or evil ***it will earn tomorrow*** – only Allah knows these three things – ***and no self knows in what land it will die*** – whereas Allah does. ***Allah is All-Knowing, All-Aware*** of the inward as well as the outward of every-thing. Al-Bukhārī related the *ḥadīth* from Ibn 'Umar, "The keys of the unseen are given which are with Allah: the knowledge of the Final Hour…" to the end of the *ḥadīth*.

سُورَةُ السَّجۡدَةِ

بِسۡمِ ٱللَّهِ ٱلرَّحۡمَٰنِ ٱلرَّحِيمِ

الٓمٓ ١ تَنزِيلُ ٱلۡكِتَٰبِ لَا رَيۡبَ فِيهِ مِن رَّبِّ ٱلۡعَٰلَمِينَ
٢ أَمۡ يَقُولُونَ ٱفۡتَرَىٰهُۚ بَلۡ هُوَ ٱلۡحَقُّ مِن رَّبِّكَ لِتُنذِرَ قَوۡمٗا
مَّآ أَتَىٰهُم مِّن نَّذِيرٖ مِّن قَبۡلِكَ لَعَلَّهُمۡ يَهۡتَدُونَ ٣ ٱللَّهُ
ٱلَّذِي خَلَقَ ٱلسَّمَٰوَٰتِ وَٱلۡأَرۡضَ وَمَا بَيۡنَهُمَا فِي سِتَّةِ أَيَّامٖ
ثُمَّ ٱسۡتَوَىٰ عَلَى ٱلۡعَرۡشِۖ مَا لَكُم مِّن دُونِهِۦ مِن وَلِيّٖ وَلَا شَفِيعٍۚ أَفَلَا
تَتَذَكَّرُونَ ٤ يُدَبِّرُ ٱلۡأَمۡرَ مِنَ ٱلسَّمَآءِ إِلَى ٱلۡأَرۡضِ ثُمَّ يَعۡرُجُ
إِلَيۡهِ فِي يَوۡمٖ كَانَ مِقۡدَارُهُۥٓ أَلۡفَ سَنَةٖ مِّمَّا تَعُدُّونَ ٥ ذَٰلِكَ
عَٰلِمُ ٱلۡغَيۡبِ وَٱلشَّهَٰدَةِ ٱلۡعَزِيزُ ٱلرَّحِيمُ ٦ ٱلَّذِيٓ أَحۡسَنَ
كُلَّ شَيۡءٍ خَلَقَهُۥۖ وَبَدَأَ خَلۡقَ ٱلۡإِنسَٰنِ مِن طِينٖ ٧ ثُمَّ جَعَلَ
نَسۡلَهُۥ مِن سُلَٰلَةٖ مِّن مَّآءٖ مَّهِينٖ ٨ ثُمَّ سَوَّىٰهُ وَنَفَخَ فِيهِ
مِن رُّوحِهِۦۖ وَجَعَلَ لَكُمُ ٱلسَّمۡعَ وَٱلۡأَبۡصَٰرَ وَٱلۡأَفۡـِٔدَةَۚ قَلِيلٗا
مَّا تَشۡكُرُونَ ٩ وَقَالُوٓاْ أَءِذَا ضَلَلۡنَا فِي ٱلۡأَرۡضِ أَءِنَّا لَفِي
خَلۡقٖ جَدِيدِۭۚ بَلۡ هُم بِلِقَآءِ رَبِّهِمۡ كَٰفِرُونَ ١٠ ۞ قُلۡ يَتَوَفَّىٰكُم
مَّلَكُ ٱلۡمَوۡتِ ٱلَّذِي وُكِّلَ بِكُمۡ ثُمَّ إِلَىٰ رَبِّكُمۡ تُرۡجَعُونَ ١١
وَلَوۡ تَرَىٰٓ إِذِ ٱلۡمُجۡرِمُونَ نَاكِسُواْ رُءُوسِهِمۡ عِندَ رَبِّهِمۡ
رَبَّنَآ أَبۡصَرۡنَا وَسَمِعۡنَا فَٱرۡجِعۡنَا نَعۡمَلۡ صَٰلِحًا إِنَّا مُوقِنُونَ
١٢ وَلَوۡ شِئۡنَا لَأٓتَيۡنَا كُلَّ نَفۡسٍ هُدَىٰهَا وَلَٰكِنۡ حَقَّ ٱلۡقَوۡلُ

32. *Sūrat as-Sajda*
Prostration

This *sūra* is Makkan except for *āyat*s 16 to the end of 20, which are Madinan. It has 30 *āyat*s and was sent down after *Sūrat al-Mu'min.*

1. ***Alif Lam Mim.*** Allah knows best what is meant by this.

2. ***The revelation of the Book*** (the Qur'an), ***without any doubt of it, is from the Lord of the worlds.***

3. ***Or do they say, 'He*** (Muḥammad) ***has invented it'? No indeed! It is the truth from your Lord to warn*** – by it – ***a people to whom, before you, no warner came, so that perhaps they will be guided*** by your warning.

4. ***Allah is He who created the heavens and the earth and everything between them in six days*** – the first was Sunday and the last was Friday – ***and then established Himself firmly upon the Throne.*** The word "throne" linguistically refers to the seat of a king and for this reason is appropriate for Allah. ***You*** – unbelievers of Makka – ***have no protector or intercessor*** to protect you from His punishment ***apart from Him. So will you not pay heed*** to this and believe***?***

5. ***He directs the whole affair from heaven to earth*** for the period this world endures. ***Then it*** (the command and management) ***will again ascend to Him on a Day whose length is a thousand years by the way you measure*** in this world; and in another *sūra* mentions fifty thousand years. That means the Day of Rising which seems that long, owing to the intensity of its terrors for the unbelievers. For the believer, however, it will seem lighter than a prescribed prayer which he prayed in this world, as is related in a *ḥadīth*.

6. ***That*** Creator and Manager ***is the Knower of the Unseen and the Visible***, what is hidden from creatures and what is present and can be seen***, the Almighty*** who is unapproachable in His kingdom***, the Most Merciful*** to the people who obey Him***:***

7. ***He who has created all things*** (read as *khalaq* and *khalq*) ***in the best possible way. He commenced the creation of man*** (Ādam) ***from clay;***

8. ***...then produced his seed*** (progeny) ***from an extract of base fluid*** – a weak drop of sperm***;***

9. ***...then formed him*** (Ādam) ***and breathed His* Rūḥ *into him*** – gave him life and feeling after being an inanimate form – ***and gave you*** (his descendants) ***hearing, sight and hearts. What little thanks you show!***

10. ***They*** – those who deny the Resurrection – ***say, 'When we have been absorbed into the earth*** – turned to dust and mixed with the dust of the earth – ***are we then to be in a new creation?'*** Allah says: ***In fact they reject the meeting with their Lord*** – at the Resurrection.

11. ***Say*** to them***: 'The Angel of Death, who has been given charge of you, will take you back*** – taking your spirits – ***and then you will be sent back to your Lord*** alive so, that He may repay you for your actions.*'*

12. ***If only you could see the evildoers*** (the idolaters) ***hanging their heads in shame before their Lord.*** They will say***: 'Our Lord, we have seen*** the reality of the resurrection we denied ***and we have heard*** the truth in the words of the Messengers which we denied before***, so send us back again*** to the world ***and we will act rightly*** there***. Truly we now have certainty.'*** That plea will not benefit them and they will not be returned. Allah says:

13. ***'Had We so willed We could have given guidance to everyone*** – to obedience and faith – ***but now My Words are shown to be true: that I shall fill up Hell entirely with jinn and human beings*** and tell the guardians of the Fire to admit them into it.

14. ***So taste it*** (the punishment)***. Because you forgot the meeting on this Day*** and abandoned belief in it***. We have forgotten you*** and will abandon you in the punishment***. Taste the punishment of eternal timelessness for what you did*** in terms of unbelief and denial.*'*

15. ***The people who truly do believe in Our Signs*** (the Qur'an) ***are those who fall to the ground prostrating when they are reminded*** and warned ***of them and glorify their Lord with praise,*** saying,

مِنِّي لَأَمْلَأَنَّ جَهَنَّمَ مِنَ ٱلْجِنَّةِ وَٱلنَّاسِ أَجْمَعِينَ ﴿١٣﴾
فَذُوقُوا۟ بِمَا نَسِيتُمْ لِقَآءَ يَوْمِكُمْ هَٰذَآ إِنَّا نَسِينَٰكُمْ ۖ
وَذُوقُوا۟ عَذَابَ ٱلْخُلْدِ بِمَا كُنتُمْ تَعْمَلُونَ ﴿١٤﴾ إِنَّمَا يُؤْمِنُ
بِـَٔايَٰتِنَا ٱلَّذِينَ إِذَا ذُكِّرُوا۟ بِهَا خَرُّوا۟ سُجَّدًا وَسَبَّحُوا۟ بِحَمْدِ
رَبِّهِمْ وَهُمْ لَا يَسْتَكْبِرُونَ ۩ ﴿١٥﴾ تَتَجَافَىٰ جُنُوبُهُمْ
عَنِ ٱلْمَضَاجِعِ يَدْعُونَ رَبَّهُمْ خَوْفًا وَطَمَعًا وَمِمَّا رَزَقْنَٰهُمْ
يُنفِقُونَ ﴿١٦﴾ فَلَا تَعْلَمُ نَفْسٌ مَّآ أُخْفِىَ لَهُم مِّن قُرَّةِ أَعْيُنٍ جَزَآءًۢ
بِمَا كَانُوا۟ يَعْمَلُونَ ﴿١٧﴾ أَفَمَن كَانَ مُؤْمِنًا كَمَن كَانَ فَاسِقًا ۚ
لَّا يَسْتَوُۥنَ ﴿١٨﴾ أَمَّا ٱلَّذِينَ ءَامَنُوا۟ وَعَمِلُوا۟ ٱلصَّٰلِحَٰتِ فَلَهُمْ
جَنَّٰتُ ٱلْمَأْوَىٰ نُزُلًۢا بِمَا كَانُوا۟ يَعْمَلُونَ ﴿١٩﴾ وَأَمَّا ٱلَّذِينَ فَسَقُوا۟
فَمَأْوَىٰهُمُ ٱلنَّارُ ۖ كُلَّمَآ أَرَادُوٓا۟ أَن يَخْرُجُوا۟ مِنْهَآ أُعِيدُوا۟ فِيهَا وَقِيلَ
لَهُمْ ذُوقُوا۟ عَذَابَ ٱلنَّارِ ٱلَّذِى كُنتُم بِهِۦ تُكَذِّبُونَ ﴿٢٠﴾
وَلَنُذِيقَنَّهُم مِّنَ ٱلْعَذَابِ ٱلْأَدْنَىٰ دُونَ ٱلْعَذَابِ ٱلْأَكْبَرِ
لَعَلَّهُمْ يَرْجِعُونَ ﴿٢١﴾ وَمَنْ أَظْلَمُ مِمَّن ذُكِّرَ بِـَٔايَٰتِ رَبِّهِۦ ثُمَّ
أَعْرَضَ عَنْهَآ ۚ إِنَّا مِنَ ٱلْمُجْرِمِينَ مُنتَقِمُونَ ﴿٢٢﴾ وَلَقَدْ ءَاتَيْنَا
مُوسَى ٱلْكِتَٰبَ فَلَا تَكُن فِى مِرْيَةٍ مِّن لِّقَآئِهِۦ ۖ وَجَعَلْنَٰهُ
هُدًى لِّبَنِىٓ إِسْرَٰٓءِيلَ ﴿٢٣﴾ وَجَعَلْنَا مِنْهُمْ أَئِمَّةً يَهْدُونَ
بِأَمْرِنَا لَمَّا صَبَرُوا۟ ۖ وَكَانُوا۟ بِـَٔايَٰتِنَا يُوقِنُونَ ﴿٢٤﴾ إِنَّ رَبَّكَ
هُوَ يَفْصِلُ بَيْنَهُمْ يَوْمَ ٱلْقِيَٰمَةِ فِيمَا كَانُوا۟ فِيهِ يَخْتَلِفُونَ

"Glory be to Allah and by His praise" ***and are not*** too ***arrogant*** to believe and obey.

16. ***Their sides eschew their beds*** – rising from where they sleep to perform the *tahajjud* night prayers – ***as they call on their Lord in fear*** of Allah's punishment ***and ardent hope*** of His mercy. ***And they give*** *ṣadaqa* ***from what We have provided for them.***

17. ***No self knows the delight*** – for the eyes – ***that is hidden away*** (read as *ukhfīya* and *ukhfī*) ***for it in recompense for what it used to do.***

18. ***Is someone who believes like someone who is a deviator? They*** (the believers and deviants) ***are not the same!***

19. ***As for those who believe and do right actions, they will have the Gardens of Safe Refuge as hospitality for what they used to do.***

20. ***But as for those who are deviators*** through unbelief and denial, ***their refuge is the Fire. Every time that they want to get out, they are put straight back into it again and they are told, 'Taste the punishment of the Fire, which you denied.'***

21. ***We will give them a taste of lesser punishment*** in this world, by killing, capture, drought for years, and illnesses, ***before the greater punishment*** in the Next World, ***so that hopefully they will turn back*** to belief.

22. ***Who could do greater wrong than someone who is reminded of the Signs of his Lord*** (the Qur'an) ***and then turns away from them?*** No one does greater harm. ***We will take revenge on the evildoers*** (the idolaters).

23. ***We gave Mūsā the Book*** (the Torah) – ***be in no doubt about the meeting with him*** – a reference to when the Prophet, may Allah bless him and grant him peace, met Mūsā during the Night Journey – ***and made it*** – or him; a reference to either the Book or Mūsā – ***a guidance for the tribe of Israel.***

24. ***We appointed leaders from among them, guiding*** people ***by Our command when they were steadfast*** in their *dīn* and in the face of affliction from their enemy, ***and when*** (read as *lammā* and *limā*) ***they had certainty about Our Signs*** – things which indicate Allah's Power and Unity.

﴿٢٥﴾ أَوَلَمْ يَهْدِ لَهُمْ كَمْ أَهْلَكْنَا مِن قَبْلِهِم مِّنَ ٱلْقُرُونِ
يَمْشُونَ فِى مَسَٰكِنِهِمْ ۚ إِنَّ فِى ذَٰلِكَ لَءَايَٰتٍ ۖ أَفَلَا يَسْمَعُونَ
﴿٢٦﴾ أَوَلَمْ يَرَوْا۟ أَنَّا نَسُوقُ ٱلْمَآءَ إِلَى ٱلْأَرْضِ ٱلْجُرُزِ فَنُخْرِجُ
بِهِۦ زَرْعًا تَأْكُلُ مِنْهُ أَنْعَٰمُهُمْ وَأَنفُسُهُمْ ۖ أَفَلَا يُبْصِرُونَ ﴿٢٧﴾
وَيَقُولُونَ مَتَىٰ هَٰذَا ٱلْفَتْحُ إِن كُنتُمْ صَٰدِقِينَ ﴿٢٨﴾
قُلْ يَوْمَ ٱلْفَتْحِ لَا يَنفَعُ ٱلَّذِينَ كَفَرُوٓا۟ إِيمَٰنُهُمْ وَلَا هُمْ يُنظَرُونَ
﴿٢٩﴾ فَأَعْرِضْ عَنْهُمْ وَٱنتَظِرْ إِنَّهُم مُّنتَظِرُونَ ﴿٣٠﴾

25. ***On the Day of Rising your Lord will decide between them regarding everything about which they differed*** in matters of the *dīn.*

26. ***Are they not guided by the many generations We destroyed before them*** – a reminder to the unbelievers of Makka that Allah had destroyed many previous peoples on account of their unbelief – ***among whose ruined homes they walk around*** on their journeys to Syria and other places***? There are certainly Signs*** of Our power ***in that. So will they not listen*** – reflect and be warned***?***

27. ***Do they not see how We drive water to barren land*** – with no vegetation growing in it – ***and bring forth crops by it which their livestock and they themselves both eat? So will they not see*** – this and so understand that We have the power to bring them back to life again***?***

28. ***They say*** to the believers***: 'When will this victory*** of yours over us ***come, if you are telling the truth?'***

29. ***Say: 'On the Day of Victory*** – when the punishment descends on them – ***the belief of those who disbelieved will be of no use to them. They will be granted no reprieve.'*** They will not then be able to repent or offer any excuse.

30. ***So turn from them and wait*** for the punishment to befall them***. They too are waiting*** for you to die or be killed so that they may be relieved of you. This was before the command came to fight them.

سُورَةُ الأَحْزَابِ

بِسْمِ ٱللَّهِ ٱلرَّحْمَٰنِ ٱلرَّحِيمِ

يَٰٓأَيُّهَا ٱلنَّبِيُّ ٱتَّقِ ٱللَّهَ وَلَا تُطِعِ ٱلْكَٰفِرِينَ وَٱلْمُنَٰفِقِينَ ۗ إِنَّ ٱللَّهَ
كَانَ عَلِيمًا حَكِيمًا ﴿١﴾ وَٱتَّبِعْ مَا يُوحَىٰٓ إِلَيْكَ مِن
رَّبِّكَ ۚ إِنَّ ٱللَّهَ كَانَ بِمَا تَعْمَلُونَ خَبِيرًا ﴿٢﴾ وَتَوَكَّلْ عَلَى ٱللَّهِ ۚ
وَكَفَىٰ بِٱللَّهِ وَكِيلًا ﴿٣﴾ مَّا جَعَلَ ٱللَّهُ لِرَجُلٍ مِّن قَلْبَيْنِ فِى
جَوْفِهِۦ ۚ وَمَا جَعَلَ أَزْوَٰجَكُمُ ٱلَّٰٓـِٔى تُظَٰهِرُونَ مِنْهُنَّ أُمَّهَٰتِكُمْ ۚ
وَمَا جَعَلَ أَدْعِيَآءَكُمْ أَبْنَآءَكُمْ ۚ ذَٰلِكُمْ قَوْلُكُم بِأَفْوَٰهِكُمْ ۖ وَٱللَّهُ
يَقُولُ ٱلْحَقَّ وَهُوَ يَهْدِى ٱلسَّبِيلَ ﴿٤﴾ ٱدْعُوهُمْ لِءَابَآئِهِمْ
هُوَ أَقْسَطُ عِندَ ٱللَّهِ ۚ فَإِن لَّمْ تَعْلَمُوٓا۟ ءَابَآءَهُمْ فَإِخْوَٰنُكُمْ
فِى ٱلدِّينِ وَمَوَٰلِيكُمْ ۚ وَلَيْسَ عَلَيْكُمْ جُنَاحٌ فِيمَآ أَخْطَأْتُم
بِهِۦ وَلَٰكِن مَّا تَعَمَّدَتْ قُلُوبُكُمْ ۚ وَكَانَ ٱللَّهُ غَفُورًا رَّحِيمًا
﴿٥﴾ ٱلنَّبِىُّ أَوْلَىٰ بِٱلْمُؤْمِنِينَ مِنْ أَنفُسِهِمْ ۖ وَأَزْوَٰجُهُۥٓ أُمَّهَٰتُهُمْ ۗ
وَأُو۟لُوا۟ ٱلْأَرْحَامِ بَعْضُهُمْ أَوْلَىٰ بِبَعْضٍ فِى كِتَٰبِ ٱللَّهِ
مِنَ ٱلْمُؤْمِنِينَ وَٱلْمُهَٰجِرِينَ إِلَّآ أَن تَفْعَلُوٓا۟ إِلَىٰٓ أَوْلِيَآئِكُم
مَّعْرُوفًا ۚ كَانَ ذَٰلِكَ فِى ٱلْكِتَٰبِ مَسْطُورًا ﴿٦﴾
وَإِذْ أَخَذْنَا مِنَ ٱلنَّبِيِّۦنَ مِيثَٰقَهُمْ وَمِنكَ وَمِن نُّوحٍ وَإِبْرَٰهِيمَ
وَمُوسَىٰ وَعِيسَى ٱبْنِ مَرْيَمَ ۖ وَأَخَذْنَا مِنْهُم مِّيثَٰقًا غَلِيظًا ﴿٧﴾
لِّيَسْـَٔلَ ٱلصَّٰدِقِينَ عَن صِدْقِهِمْ ۚ وَأَعَدَّ لِلْكَٰفِرِينَ عَذَابًا أَلِيمًا
﴿٨﴾ يَٰٓأَيُّهَا ٱلَّذِينَ ءَامَنُوا۟ ٱذْكُرُوا۟ نِعْمَةَ ٱللَّهِ عَلَيْكُمْ إِذْ جَآءَتْكُمْ

33. *Sūrat al-Aḥzāb*
The Confederates

This *sūra* is Madinan. It has 73 *āyat*s and was sent down after *Āli 'Imrān.*

1. ***O Prophet,*** continue to ***be fearful of Allah and do not obey the unbelievers and hypocrites*** regarding anything which differs from your *Sharī'a*. ***Allah is All-Knowing*** of what will be before it exists, ***All-Wise*** with respect to what He creates.
2. ***Follow what has been revealed to you from your Lord*** – meaning the Qur'an. ***Allah is aware of what you do*** (read as *ta'lamūna*, and also *ya'lamūna*, "what they do").
3. ***And put your trust in*** the command of ***Allah. Allah suffices as a Guardian.*** Although this is all addressed to the Prophet his community should follow him in all of it.
4. ***Allah has not allotted to any man two hearts within his breast*** – refuting a claim by the unbelievers that someone had two hearts with which he understood so that his intellect was greater than that of Muḥammad – ***nor has He made those of your wives you equate with your mothers your actual mothers*** (read as *tuẓāhirūna*, *taẓāharūna* and *taẓẓāharūna*)***;*** this occurred when a man, by saying to his wife, "You are to me like the back of my mother," thereby made her unlawful for him. They used this in the Jāhiliyya as a form of divorce. Expiation is obliged for it with its preconditions, as is mentioned in *Sūrat al-Mudājala* – ***nor has He made your adopted sons your actual sons.*** The word for "adopted sons", *ad'iyā'*, is the plural of *da'ī* and refers to those whom people call their sons when they are not really their sons. ***These are just words coming out of your mouths*** – referring to the Jews and hypocrites. When the Prophet, may Allah bless him and grant him peace, married Zaynab bint Jaḥsh, who had been married to Zayd ibn Ḥāritha, whom the Prophet, may Allah bless him and grant him peace, had adopted, they said, "Muḥammad has married his son's wife." Those are things that Allah said that they lied about. ***But Allah speaks the truth*** about that ***and He guides to the Way*** of Truth.

5. ***Call them after their fathers. That is closer to justice in Allah's sight. And if you do not know who their fathers were, then they are your brothers in the* dīn *and people under your patronage. You are not to blame for any honest mistake you make, but only for what your hearts premeditate*** intentionally after the prohibition. ***Allah is Ever-Forgiving*** of what you did before it was prohibited, ***Most Merciful*** to you in that regard.

6. ***The Prophet has more right to the believers than their own selves*** with regard to what he invites them to when their own selves invite them to do something different, ***and his wives are their mothers*** in that it is forbidden for them to marry them. ***But blood-relations have more right*** – in respect of inheritance – ***to one another in the Book of Allah than the believers and* Muhājirūn** with regard to inheritance, which was the case at the beginning of Islam and then was abrogated. ***All the same, you should act correctly by your friends*** with regard to bequests which are permitted; ***that*** – the abrogation of inheritance by virtue of faith and emigration in favour of inheritance by virtue of kinship – ***is inscribed in the Book.*** "The Book" in both places refers to the Preserved Tablet.

7. Remember ***when We made a covenant with all the Prophets*** – when they emerged from the loins of Ādam like atoms – ***with you and with Nūḥ and Ibrāhīm and Mūsā and 'Īsā son of Maryam*** – to worship Allah and invite people to worship Him. The mention of five Prophets is a use of the particular to designate the general: in other words, all the Prophets are intended. ***We made a binding covenant with them*** to fulfil their task, involving them swearing an oath by Allah to do so –

8. ***...so that He might question the truthful about their sincerity*** in conveying the Message by which the unbelievers are rebuked; ***and He has prepared a painful punishment for the unbelievers.***

9. ***You who believe, remember Allah's blessing upon you when forces*** of unbelievers ***came against you*** in companies, during the time when the trench was dug; ***and We sent a wind against them and other forces*** – of angels – ***you could not see. Allah sees what you do*** (read as *ta'lamūna* and also *ya'lamūna*, "they do", referring to when the idolaters form into parties).

جُنُودٌ فَأَرْسَلْنَا عَلَيْهِمْ رِيحًا وَجُنُودًا لَّمْ تَرَوْهَا ۚ وَكَانَ ٱللَّهُ
بِمَا تَعْمَلُونَ بَصِيرًا ﴿٩﴾ إِذْ جَآءُوكُم مِّن فَوْقِكُمْ وَمِنْ أَسْفَلَ
مِنكُمْ وَإِذْ زَاغَتِ ٱلْأَبْصَٰرُ وَبَلَغَتِ ٱلْقُلُوبُ ٱلْحَنَاجِرَ
وَتَظُنُّونَ بِٱللَّهِ ٱلظُّنُونَا۠ ﴿١٠﴾ هُنَالِكَ ٱبْتُلِىَ ٱلْمُؤْمِنُونَ وَزُلْزِلُوا۟
زِلْزَالًا شَدِيدًا ﴿١١﴾ وَإِذْ يَقُولُ ٱلْمُنَٰفِقُونَ وَٱلَّذِينَ فِى قُلُوبِهِم
مَّرَضٌ مَّا وَعَدَنَا ٱللَّهُ وَرَسُولُهُۥٓ إِلَّا غُرُورًا ﴿١٢﴾ وَإِذْ قَالَت طَّآئِفَةٌ
مِّنْهُمْ يَٰٓأَهْلَ يَثْرِبَ لَا مُقَامَ لَكُمْ فَٱرْجِعُوا۟ ۚ وَيَسْتَـْٔذِنُ فَرِيقٌ
مِّنْهُمُ ٱلنَّبِىَّ يَقُولُونَ إِنَّ بُيُوتَنَا عَوْرَةٌ وَمَا هِىَ بِعَوْرَةٍ ۖ إِن يُرِيدُونَ إِلَّا
فِرَارًا ﴿١٣﴾ وَلَوْ دُخِلَتْ عَلَيْهِم مِّنْ أَقْطَارِهَا ثُمَّ سُئِلُوا۟ ٱلْفِتْنَةَ
لَءَاتَوْهَا وَمَا تَلَبَّثُوا۟ بِهَآ إِلَّا يَسِيرًا ﴿١٤﴾ وَلَقَدْ كَانُوا۟ عَٰهَدُوا۟
ٱللَّهَ مِن قَبْلُ لَا يُوَلُّونَ ٱلْأَدْبَٰرَ ۚ وَكَانَ عَهْدُ ٱللَّهِ مَسْـُٔولًا ﴿١٥﴾
قُل لَّن يَنفَعَكُمُ ٱلْفِرَارُ إِن فَرَرْتُم مِّنَ ٱلْمَوْتِ أَوِ ٱلْقَتْلِ وَإِذًا
لَّا تُمَتَّعُونَ إِلَّا قَلِيلًا ﴿١٦﴾ قُلْ مَن ذَا ٱلَّذِى يَعْصِمُكُم مِّنَ ٱللَّهِ إِنْ
أَرَادَ بِكُمْ سُوٓءًا أَوْ أَرَادَ بِكُمْ رَحْمَةً ۚ وَلَا يَجِدُونَ لَهُم مِّن دُونِ ٱللَّهِ
وَلِيًّا وَلَا نَصِيرًا ﴿١٧﴾ ۞ قَدْ يَعْلَمُ ٱللَّهُ ٱلْمُعَوِّقِينَ مِنكُمْ وَٱلْقَآئِلِينَ
لِإِخْوَٰنِهِمْ هَلُمَّ إِلَيْنَا ۖ وَلَا يَأْتُونَ ٱلْبَأْسَ إِلَّا قَلِيلًا ﴿١٨﴾ أَشِحَّةً
عَلَيْكُمْ ۖ فَإِذَا جَآءَ ٱلْخَوْفُ رَأَيْتَهُمْ يَنظُرُونَ إِلَيْكَ تَدُورُ أَعْيُنُهُمْ
كَٱلَّذِى يُغْشَىٰ عَلَيْهِ مِنَ ٱلْمَوْتِ ۖ فَإِذَا ذَهَبَ ٱلْخَوْفُ سَلَقُوكُم
بِأَلْسِنَةٍ حِدَادٍ أَشِحَّةً عَلَى ٱلْخَيْرِ ۚ أُو۟لَٰٓئِكَ لَمْ يُؤْمِنُوا۟ فَأَحْبَطَ
ٱللَّهُ أَعْمَٰلَهُمْ ۚ وَكَانَ ذَٰلِكَ عَلَى ٱللَّهِ يَسِيرًا ﴿١٩﴾ يَحْسَبُونَ ٱلْأَحْزَابَ

10. ***When they came at you from above you and below you*** – from the top and bottom of the wadi, from the east and the west – ***when your eyes rolled*** – seeing nothing but the enemy on every side – ***and your hearts rose to your throats*** – a metaphor designating intensity of fear, ***and you thought unworthy thoughts about Allah*** – going from expectation of victory to despair –

11. ***...at that point the believers were tested*** – to make it clear who were sincere – ***and severely shaken*** by the intensity of the alarm they experienced.

12. Remember ***when the hypocrites and people with sickness*** – meaning weakness of belief – ***in their hearts said, 'What Allah and His Messenger promised us*** regarding victory ***was mere delusion*** and false.*'*

13. ***And a group of them*** (the hypocrites) ***said, 'People of Yathrib*** – the old name of Madina – ***your position*** (read as *muqām* or *maqām*) ***is untenable*** – literally, you have no place – ***so return*** to your homes in Madina.*'* They had gone out with the Prophet, may Allah bless him and grant him peace, to Sal', a mountain outside of Madina, to fight. ***Some of them asked the Prophet*** for permission to go back and ***to excuse them, saying, 'Our houses are exposed,'*** meaning that they were not fortified and they feared for their safety – ***when they were not exposed.*** Allah said: ***It was merely that they wanted to run away*** from the battle.

14. ***If they had been overrun*** – in Madina – ***from every side, and had then been asked to revert to unbelief*** (idol worship) by the invaders, ***they would have done so and hesitated very little about it.***

15. ***Yet they had previously made a contract with Allah that they would never turn their backs. Contracts made with Allah will be asked about*** – and whether they were fulfilled or not.

16. ***Say: 'Flight will not benefit you if you try to run away from death or being killed,*** because after you flee ***then you will only enjoy a short respite***: you will have a short time of enjoyment in this world before you die.*'*

17. ***Say: 'Who is going to shield you*** and protect you ***from Allah if He desires evil*** – destruction and defeat – ***for you, or*** who is going to inflict evil on you if Allah ***desires mercy*** (good) ***for you?' They will***

لَمْ يَذْهَبُوا۟ ۖ وَإِن يَأْتِ ٱلْأَحْزَابُ يَوَدُّوا۟ لَوْ أَنَّهُم بَادُونَ
فِى ٱلْأَعْرَابِ يَسْـَٔلُونَ عَنْ أَنۢبَآئِكُمْ ۖ وَلَوْ كَانُوا۟ فِيكُم
مَّا قَٰتَلُوٓا۟ إِلَّا قَلِيلًا ﴿٢٠﴾ لَّقَدْ كَانَ لَكُمْ فِى رَسُولِ ٱللَّهِ أُسْوَةٌ
حَسَنَةٌ لِّمَن كَانَ يَرْجُوا۟ ٱللَّهَ وَٱلْيَوْمَ ٱلْءَاخِرَ وَذَكَرَ ٱللَّهَ كَثِيرًا ﴿٢١﴾
وَلَمَّا رَءَا ٱلْمُؤْمِنُونَ ٱلْأَحْزَابَ قَالُوا۟ هَٰذَا مَا وَعَدَنَا ٱللَّهُ وَرَسُولُهُۥ
وَصَدَقَ ٱللَّهُ وَرَسُولُهُۥ ۚ وَمَا زَادَهُمْ إِلَّآ إِيمَٰنًا وَتَسْلِيمًا ﴿٢٢﴾
مِّنَ ٱلْمُؤْمِنِينَ رِجَالٌ صَدَقُوا۟ مَا عَٰهَدُوا۟ ٱللَّهَ عَلَيْهِ ۖ فَمِنْهُم مَّن
قَضَىٰ نَحْبَهُۥ وَمِنْهُم مَّن يَنتَظِرُ ۖ وَمَا بَدَّلُوا۟ تَبْدِيلًا ﴿٢٣﴾ لِّيَجْزِىَ
ٱللَّهُ ٱلصَّٰدِقِينَ بِصِدْقِهِمْ وَيُعَذِّبَ ٱلْمُنَٰفِقِينَ إِن شَآءَ
أَوْ يَتُوبَ عَلَيْهِمْ ۚ إِنَّ ٱللَّهَ كَانَ غَفُورًا رَّحِيمًا ﴿٢٤﴾ وَرَدَّ ٱللَّهُ ٱلَّذِينَ
كَفَرُوا۟ بِغَيْظِهِمْ لَمْ يَنَالُوا۟ خَيْرًا ۚ وَكَفَى ٱللَّهُ ٱلْمُؤْمِنِينَ ٱلْقِتَالَ ۚ
وَكَانَ ٱللَّهُ قَوِيًّا عَزِيزًا ﴿٢٥﴾ وَأَنزَلَ ٱلَّذِينَ ظَٰهَرُوهُم مِّنْ
أَهْلِ ٱلْكِتَٰبِ مِن صَيَاصِيهِمْ وَقَذَفَ فِى قُلُوبِهِمُ ٱلرُّعْبَ
فَرِيقًا تَقْتُلُونَ وَتَأْسِرُونَ فَرِيقًا ﴿٢٦﴾ وَأَوْرَثَكُمْ أَرْضَهُمْ
وَدِيَٰرَهُمْ وَأَمْوَٰلَهُمْ وَأَرْضًا لَّمْ تَطَـُٔوهَا ۚ وَكَانَ ٱللَّهُ عَلَىٰ كُلِّ
شَىْءٍ قَدِيرًا ﴿٢٧﴾ يَٰٓأَيُّهَا ٱلنَّبِىُّ قُل لِّأَزْوَٰجِكَ إِن كُنتُنَّ تُرِدْنَ
ٱلْحَيَوٰةَ ٱلدُّنْيَا وَزِينَتَهَا فَتَعَالَيْنَ أُمَتِّعْكُنَّ وَأُسَرِّحْكُنَّ
سَرَاحًا جَمِيلًا ﴿٢٨﴾ وَإِن كُنتُنَّ تُرِدْنَ ٱللَّهَ وَرَسُولَهُۥ وَٱلدَّارَ
ٱلْءَاخِرَةَ فَإِنَّ ٱللَّهَ أَعَدَّ لِلْمُحْسِنَٰتِ مِنكُنَّ أَجْرًا عَظِيمًا ﴿٢٩﴾
يَٰنِسَآءَ ٱلنَّبِىِّ مَن يَأْتِ مِنكُنَّ بِفَٰحِشَةٍ مُّبَيِّنَةٍ يُضَٰعَفْ

find no one to protect or help them besides Allah. No one but Allah can benefit them or keep them from harm.

18. ***Allah knows the obstructers among you*** – who hinder others from fighting *jihād* – ***and those who say to their brothers, 'Come to us,' and who only come to fight a very little*** – merely for appearance's sake –

19. ***…and are begrudging as regards*** helping ***you. Then when fear comes, you see them looking at you, their eyes rolling like people scared to death*** – like someone in its throes. ***But when fear departs*** and booty is taken ***they flay you with sharp tongues,*** harming you with their words, ***grasping for wealth*** – greedy to have some of the booty. ***Such people do not*** truly ***believe and Allah will make their actions come to nothing. That is easy for Allah*** if He so wishes.

20. ***They think that the Confederates*** of the unbelievers ***have not departed*** for Makka, because they are so afraid of them***; and if the Confederates did appear*** again ***then they would wish they were out in the desert with the desert Arabs, asking for news of you*** with the unbelievers. ***If they were with you they would only fight a very little*** – for appearance's sake because of their fear.

21. You have an excellent model (read as *uswa* and *iswa*) ***in the Messenger of Allah*** – with regard to imitating him in fighting and in remaining firm in his position – ***for all*** of you ***who put their hope in Allah*** – and fear Him – ***and the Last Day and remember Allah much.***

22. ***When the believers saw the Confederates*** of the unbelievers ***they said: 'This is what Allah and His Messenger promised us*** – in terms of victory and testing. ***Allah and His Messenger told us the truth*** with respect to this promise.***' It only increased them in belief*** in Allah's promise ***and in submission*** to His command.

23. ***Among the believers there are men who have been true to the contract they made with Allah*** – a reference to their undertaking to remain firm with the Prophet, may Allah bless him and grant him peace. ***Some of them have fulfilled their pact by death*** – by dying or being killed in the Way of Allah – ***and some are still waiting to do so, not having changed*** their contract ***in any way at all*** – this is different from the state of the hypocrites.

24. ***So that Allah might recompense the truthful for their sincerity and punish the hypocrites, if He wills,*** by making them die in their unbelief, ***or turn towards them. Allah is Ever-Forgiving*** to those who repent, ***Most Merciful.***

25. ***Allah sent back those who disbelieved*** – meaning the Confederates – ***in their rage without their achieving any good at all*** with respect to their desire to defeat the believers. ***Allah saved the believers from having to fight*** by sending the angels and the wind. ***Allah is Most Strong,*** enabling Him to bring into being whatever He wishes, ***Almighty*** – controlling all things.

26. ***He brought down from their fortresses those of the People of the Book*** – meaning the Jewish clan of Qurayẓa – ***who supported them, and cast terror into their hearts. You killed some of them*** – those who were fighters – ***and some you took prisoner.***

27. ***He bequeathed their land, their houses and their wealth to you, and another land you had not yet trodden on.*** The first reference is to the expulsion of Qurayẓa from Madina, the second to Khaybar which was taken well after this was revealed. ***Allah has power over all things.***

28. ***O Prophet, tell your*** nine ***wives,*** when they asked him for the adornment of this world ,which he did not have: ***'If you desire the life of this world and its finery, come and I will give you all you need*** – in the form of a gift given to a divorced wife – ***and release you with kindness*** – a divorce without causing them any harm.

29. ***But if you desire Allah and His Messenger and the abode of the Next World*** – meaning the Garden – ***Allah has prepared an immense reward*** – in the Next World, which is Pardise – ***for those among you who are good-doers*** and choose the Next World rather than this world.

30. ***Wives of the Prophet, if any of you commits an obvious*** (read as *mubayyina* and *mubayyana*) ***act of indecency she will receive double*** (read as *yuḍā'if* and *yuḍa''if*) ***the punishment*** that other women would receive. ***That is an easy matter for Allah.***

31. ***But those of you who are obedient to Allah and His Messenger and act rightly*** (read as *ta'mal* and *ya'mal*), ***We will give*** (read as *nu'tihā*, and also *yu'tihā*, which then means, "they will be given")

ard twice over – double the reward received by other . – *and We have prepared generous provision for them* in ıse on top of that.

Wives of the Prophet, you are not like other women provided u are godfearing. If you fear Allah, you are greater than other women. *Do not be too soft-spoken in your speech* – when speaking to men – *lest someone with sickness* (hypocrisy) *in his heart become desirous. Speak correct and courteous words* without submissiveness.

33. ***Remain*** (read as *waqarna* and *waqirna*) ***in your houses and do not display your beauty as it was previously displayed in the Time of Ignorance.*** Before Islam, women used to display their beauty to men. Showing oneself after Islam came is mentioned in another *āyat*: *"and not display their adornments, except for what normally shows".* (24:31) ***Establish the prayer and pay* zakāt*; and obey Allah and His Messenger. Allah desires to remove all impurity from you, People of the House*** – meaning the wives of the Prophet, may Allah bless him and grant him peace – ***and to purify you completely.***

34. ***And remember the Signs of Allah*** (the Qur'an) ***and the wise words*** (the Sunna) ***which are recited in your rooms. Allah is All-Pervading*** – kind to His friends, ***All-Aware*** of the totality of His creation.

35. ***Men and women who are Muslims, men and women who are believers, men and women who are obedient, men and women who are sincere*** regarding their faith, ***men and women who are steadfast*** in acts of obedience, ***men and women who are humble, men and women who give ṣadaqa, men and women who fast, men and women who guard their private parts*** from anything unlawful, ***men and women who remember Allah much: Allah has prepared forgiveness for them*** – for any acts of disobedience they have committed – ***and an immense reward*** – for their obedience.

36. ***When Allah and His Messenger have decided something, it is*** (read as *yakūna* or *takūna*) ***not for any man or woman of the believers to have a choice about it*** – to want something different from what Allah and His Messenger have commanded. This was revealed

مِّنْهَا وَطَرًا زَوَّجْنَٰكَهَا لِكَىْ لَا يَكُونَ عَلَى ٱلْمُؤْمِنِينَ حَرَجٌ فِىٓ
أَزْوَٰجِ أَدْعِيَآئِهِمْ إِذَا قَضَوْا۟ مِنْهُنَّ وَطَرًا ۚ وَكَانَ أَمْرُ ٱللَّهِ مَفْعُولًا
﴿٣٧﴾ مَّا كَانَ عَلَى ٱلنَّبِىِّ مِنْ حَرَجٍ فِيمَا فَرَضَ ٱللَّهُ لَهُۥ ۖ سُنَّةَ ٱللَّهِ فِى
ٱلَّذِينَ خَلَوْا۟ مِن قَبْلُ ۚ وَكَانَ أَمْرُ ٱللَّهِ قَدَرًا مَّقْدُورًا ﴿٣٨﴾ ٱلَّذِينَ
يُبَلِّغُونَ رِسَٰلَٰتِ ٱللَّهِ وَيَخْشَوْنَهُۥ وَلَا يَخْشَوْنَ أَحَدًا إِلَّا ٱللَّهَ ۗ وَكَفَىٰ
بِٱللَّهِ حَسِيبًا ﴿٣٩﴾ مَّا كَانَ مُحَمَّدٌ أَبَآ أَحَدٍ مِّن رِّجَالِكُمْ وَلَٰكِن
رَّسُولَ ٱللَّهِ وَخَاتَمَ ٱلنَّبِيِّـۧنَ ۗ وَكَانَ ٱللَّهُ بِكُلِّ شَىْءٍ عَلِيمًا ﴿٤٠﴾
يَٰٓأَيُّهَا ٱلَّذِينَ ءَامَنُوا۟ ٱذْكُرُوا۟ ٱللَّهَ ذِكْرًا كَثِيرًا ﴿٤١﴾ وَسَبِّحُوهُ بُكْرَةً
وَأَصِيلًا ﴿٤٢﴾ هُوَ ٱلَّذِى يُصَلِّى عَلَيْكُمْ وَمَلَٰٓئِكَتُهُۥ لِيُخْرِجَكُم
مِّنَ ٱلظُّلُمَٰتِ إِلَى ٱلنُّورِ ۚ وَكَانَ بِٱلْمُؤْمِنِينَ رَحِيمًا ﴿٤٣﴾
تَحِيَّتُهُمْ يَوْمَ يَلْقَوْنَهُۥ سَلَٰمٌ ۚ وَأَعَدَّ لَهُمْ أَجْرًا كَرِيمًا ﴿٤٤﴾ يَٰٓأَيُّهَا
ٱلنَّبِىُّ إِنَّآ أَرْسَلْنَٰكَ شَٰهِدًا وَمُبَشِّرًا وَنَذِيرًا ﴿٤٥﴾ وَدَاعِيًا
إِلَى ٱللَّهِ بِإِذْنِهِۦ وَسِرَاجًا مُّنِيرًا ﴿٤٦﴾ وَبَشِّرِ ٱلْمُؤْمِنِينَ بِأَنَّ لَهُم
مِّنَ ٱللَّهِ فَضْلًا كَبِيرًا ﴿٤٧﴾ وَلَا تُطِعِ ٱلْكَٰفِرِينَ وَٱلْمُنَٰفِقِينَ
وَدَعْ أَذَىٰهُمْ وَتَوَكَّلْ عَلَى ٱللَّهِ ۚ وَكَفَىٰ بِٱللَّهِ وَكِيلًا ﴿٤٨﴾
يَٰٓأَيُّهَا ٱلَّذِينَ ءَامَنُوٓا۟ إِذَا نَكَحْتُمُ ٱلْمُؤْمِنَٰتِ ثُمَّ طَلَّقْتُمُوهُنَّ
مِن قَبْلِ أَن تَمَسُّوهُنَّ فَمَا لَكُمْ عَلَيْهِنَّ مِنْ عِدَّةٍ تَعْتَدُّونَهَا ۖ
فَمَتِّعُوهُنَّ وَسَرِّحُوهُنَّ سَرَاحًا جَمِيلًا ﴿٤٩﴾ يَٰٓأَيُّهَا ٱلنَّبِىُّ إِنَّآ
أَحْلَلْنَا لَكَ أَزْوَٰجَكَ ٱلَّٰتِىٓ ءَاتَيْتَ أُجُورَهُنَّ وَمَا مَلَكَتْ
يَمِينُكَ مِمَّآ أَفَآءَ ٱللَّهُ عَلَيْكَ وَبَنَاتِ عَمِّكَ وَبَنَاتِ عَمَّٰتِكَ

about 'Abdullāh ibn Jaḥsh and his sister, Zaynab. The Prophet proposed to her on behalf of Zayd ibn Ḥāritha. They disliked that when they learned about it because they had thought that the Prophet, may Allah bless him and grant him peace, himself would ask to marry her. Then they were content because of this *āyat*. ***Anyone who disobeys Allah and His Messenger is clearly misguided.*** The Prophet, may Allah bless him and grant him peace, gave her in marriage to Zayd. Then later he looked at her and felt love for her whereas Zayd disliked her. Then he told the Prophet, may Allah bless him and grant him peace, "I want to divorce her." He told him, *"Keep your wife to yourself,"* as Allah tells us in the following *āyat.*

37. Remember – ***when you said to him whom Allah has blessed*** – with Islam – ***and you yourself have greatly favoured*** – by setting him free: a reference to Zayd ibn Ḥāritha, who had been captured in the Jāhiliyya and whom the Messenger of Allah, may Allah bless him and grant him peace, bought before he was sent as a Messenger and then adopted – ***'Keep your wife to yourself and be fearful of Allah'*** with regard to divorcing her, ***while concealing something in yourself which Allah wished to bring to light*** – meaning his love for her and that if Zayd were to divorce her, he would marry her – ***you were fearing people*** – and that they would say, "He has married his son's wife," – ***when Allah has more right to your fear*** in every matter, so that you should not fear what people say. Then Zayd divorced her and her *'idda* passed and Allah said: ***Then when Zayd divorced her We married her to you*** – Allah married her to the Prophet and he celebrated the marriage by feeding people with bread and meat – ***so that there should be no restriction for the believers regarding the wives of their adopted sons when they have divorced them. Allah's command is always carried out.***

38. *There is no restriction on the Prophet regarding anything Allah allots to him* and makes lawful for him. ***This was Allah's pattern with those*** Prophets ***who passed away before*** – nothing can be held against them in respect of what Allah allowed them in marriage, ***and Allah's command is a pre-ordained decree –***

39. *...those who conveyed Allah's Message and were fearful of Him* – meaning the previous Prophets – ***fearing no one except Allah*** and not fearing what people say about what Allah has made lawful to them. ***Allah suffices as a Reckoner*** of the actions of His creatures.

40. ***Muḥammad is not the father of any of your men*** – not the father of Zayd, and so it is not unlawful for him to marry his ex-wife, Zaynab – ***but the Messenger of Allah and the Final Seal*** (read as *khātam* and *khātim*) – the instrument by which something is ended and sealed – ***of the Prophets.*** He was not the father of any man and no one after him would be a Prophet. ***Allah has knowledge of all things.*** He knows that there is no Prophet after him and that when 'Īsā descends, he will judge by his *Sharī'a.*

41. ***You who believe, remember Allah much,***

42. ***...and glorify Him in the morning and the evening*** – the beginning and end of the day.

43. ***It is He Who calls down blessing on you,*** showing mercy to you, ***as do His angels*** – asking for forgiveness for you – ***to bring you out of the darkness*** of unbelief ***into the light*** of faith. ***He is Most Merciful to the believers.***

44. ***Their greeting*** from Allah ***on the Day they meet Him*** – on the tongues of the angels – ***will be 'Peace!' and He has prepared a generous reward for them***: – Paradise.

45. ***O Prophet, We have sent you as a witness*** – against those to whom he was sent – ***and a bringer of good news*** of the Garden, to those who affirm him – ***and a warner*** about the Fire, for those who deny him,

46. ***...and a caller to*** obedience to ***Allah by His permission*** (command), ***and a light-giving*** (guiding) ***lamp.***

47. ***Give good news to the believers that they will receive immense favour from Allah*** – meaning Paradise.

48. ***Do not obey the unbelievers and hypocrites*** in their opposition to your *Sharī'a*, ***and disregard their abuse of you.*** Do not harm them and do not pay them back for it until you are ordered to do so. ***Put your trust in Allah.*** He is well able to take care of your affairs. ***Allah suffices as Protector.***

49. ***You who believe, when you marry believing women and then divorce them before you have touched them*** (read as *tamassūhunna* and as *tumāssūhunna*) – meaning, have sexual intercourse with them

وَبَنَاتِ خَالِكَ وَبَنَاتِ خَٰلَٰتِكَ ٱلَّٰتِي هَاجَرۡنَ مَعَكَ وَٱمۡرَأَةٗ
مُّؤۡمِنَةً إِن وَهَبَتۡ نَفۡسَهَا لِلنَّبِيِّ إِنۡ أَرَادَ ٱلنَّبِيُّ أَن يَسۡتَنكِحَهَا
خَالِصَةٗ لَّكَ مِن دُونِ ٱلۡمُؤۡمِنِينَۗ قَدۡ عَلِمۡنَا مَا فَرَضۡنَا
عَلَيۡهِمۡ فِيٓ أَزۡوَٰجِهِمۡ وَمَا مَلَكَتۡ أَيۡمَٰنُهُمۡ لِكَيۡلَا
يَكُونَ عَلَيۡكَ حَرَجٞۗ وَكَانَ ٱللَّهُ غَفُورٗا رَّحِيمٗا ٥٠
۞ تُرۡجِي مَن تَشَآءُ مِنۡهُنَّ وَتُـٔۡوِيٓ إِلَيۡكَ مَن تَشَآءُۖ وَمَنِ ٱبۡتَغَيۡتَ
مِمَّنۡ عَزَلۡتَ فَلَا جُنَاحَ عَلَيۡكَۚ ذَٰلِكَ أَدۡنَىٰٓ أَن تَقَرَّ أَعۡيُنُهُنَّ
وَلَا يَحۡزَنَّ وَيَرۡضَيۡنَ بِمَآ ءَاتَيۡتَهُنَّ كُلُّهُنَّۚ وَٱللَّهُ يَعۡلَمُ
مَا فِي قُلُوبِكُمۡۚ وَكَانَ ٱللَّهُ عَلِيمًا حَلِيمٗا ٥١ لَّا يَحِلُّ لَكَ
ٱلنِّسَآءُ مِنۢ بَعۡدُ وَلَآ أَن تَبَدَّلَ بِهِنَّ مِنۡ أَزۡوَٰجٖ وَلَوۡ أَعۡجَبَكَ
حُسۡنُهُنَّ إِلَّا مَا مَلَكَتۡ يَمِينُكَۗ وَكَانَ ٱللَّهُ عَلَىٰ كُلِّ شَيۡءٖ رَّقِيبٗا
٥٢ يَٰٓأَيُّهَا ٱلَّذِينَ ءَامَنُواْ لَا تَدۡخُلُواْ بُيُوتَ ٱلنَّبِيِّ إِلَّآ أَن
يُؤۡذَنَ لَكُمۡ إِلَىٰ طَعَامٍ غَيۡرَ نَٰظِرِينَ إِنَىٰهُ وَلَٰكِنۡ إِذَا دُعِيتُمۡ
فَٱدۡخُلُواْ فَإِذَا طَعِمۡتُمۡ فَٱنتَشِرُواْ وَلَا مُسۡتَـٔۡنِسِينَ لِحَدِيثٍۚ إِنَّ
ذَٰلِكُمۡ كَانَ يُؤۡذِي ٱلنَّبِيَّ فَيَسۡتَحۡيِۦ مِنكُمۡۖ وَٱللَّهُ لَا
يَسۡتَحۡيِۦ مِنَ ٱلۡحَقِّۚ وَإِذَا سَأَلۡتُمُوهُنَّ مَتَٰعٗا فَسۡـَٔلُوهُنَّ مِن
وَرَآءِ حِجَابٖۚ ذَٰلِكُمۡ أَطۡهَرُ لِقُلُوبِكُمۡ وَقُلُوبِهِنَّۚ وَمَا كَانَ
لَكُمۡ أَن تُؤۡذُواْ رَسُولَ ٱللَّهِ وَلَآ أَن تَنكِحُوٓاْ أَزۡوَٰجَهُۥ
مِنۢ بَعۡدِهِۦٓ أَبَدًاۚ إِنَّ ذَٰلِكُمۡ كَانَ عِندَ ٱللَّهِ عَظِيمًا ٥٣ إِن
تُبۡدُواْ شَيۡـًٔا أَوۡ تُخۡفُوهُ فَإِنَّ ٱللَّهَ كَانَ بِكُلِّ شَيۡءٍ عَلِيمٗا ٥٤

– ***there is no* 'idda *for you to calculate for them*** by menstrual cycles or other means***; so give them a gift*** – which they can enjoy if no dower has been stipulated for them. If a dower has been fixed, they should have half of the stipulated amount only. This is what Ibn 'Abbās said and is also the position of ash-Shāfi'ī – ***and let them go with kindness*** – without causing them harm.

50. ***O Prophet, We have made lawful for you: your wives to whom you have given dowries and any slavegirls you own from the booty Allah has allotted you*** – from among those unbelievers you have captured, such as Ṣafiyya and Juwayriyya – ***and the daughters of your paternal uncles and the daughters of your paternal aunts and the daughters of your maternal uncles and the daughters of your maternal aunts who have emigrated with you*** – but not of those who have not – ***and any believing woman who gives herself to the Prophet if the Prophet desires to marry her*** without any dowry – ***exclusively for you*** – meaning this option of marriage by gift without a dowry – ***as opposed to the rest of the believers – We know very well what We have prescribed for them*** (the believers) – in terms of rulings ***regarding their wives***, so they may not have more than four wives, and may only marry with a guardian, witnesses and dowry – ***and any slavegirls they possess*** by means of purchase or other means such as capture, on condition that she be a woman of the Book, not a Magian or pagan, and the period of *istibrā'* (the waiting period for slavegirls) has been observed – ***in order that there be no restriction on you*** regarding marriage. ***Allah is Ever-Forgiving*** of what is difficult to avoid, ***Most Merciful*** in respect of that.

51. ***You may refrain from any of them you will*** – defer the turn of any of your wives – ***and keep close to you*** (visit) ***any of them you will. And if you desire*** to visit ***any you have left alone*** – and missed their turn – ***there is nothing wrong in that.*** He was given a choice in that, whereas equal turns had previously been mandatory for him. ***This*** choice ***makes it more likely they will be comforted and not be grieved, and all of them will be content with what you give them. Allah knows what is in your hearts*** regarding women and inclination towards some of them rather than others. We have given you a choice about them to make it easier for you. ***Allah is All-Knowing*** about His creation, ***All-Forbearing*** with respect to His penalty.

52. ***After that*** – the nine wives about whom you have been given a choice – ***no other women are lawful*** (read as *yaḥillu* and *taḥillu*) ***for you; nor may you exchange them for other wives*** – in other words, you may not divorce them and marry other women instead – ***even though their beauty might be pleasing to you, except for any you own as slaves*** – who are still lawful for you. The Prophet, may Allah bless him and grant him peace, owned Māriya, who bore him Ibrāhīm, who died while the Prophet was still alive. ***Allah is watchful over all things*** and records them.

53. ***You who believe, do not go into the Prophet's rooms except when you are invited to come and eat. Do not wait there while the food is being cooked. However, when you are called, go in, and when you have eaten, disperse, not remaining there to chat with one another. Doing that causes annoyance to the Prophet though he is too reticent to tell you so*** and ask you to leave. ***But Allah is not reticent with the truth*** – making it clear that you should leave. ***When you ask his wives*** – meaning the wives of the Prophet – ***for something, ask them from behind a screen. That is purer for your hearts and their hearts*** – to avoid ambivalent thoughts. ***It is not right for you to cause annoyance to the Messenger of Allah*** – in any way ***or ever to marry his wives after him. To do that would be a dreadful thing in Allah's sight.***

54. ***Whether you divulge a thing*** – a reference to possible desire for marriage to them – ***or conceal it, Allah has knowledge of all things*** and will repay you for it.

55. ***They incur no blame in respect of their fathers or their sons or their brothers or their brothers' or sisters' sons, or their*** believing ***women or any slaves they own*** – male or female, if any of these people see them and speak to them without a screen. ***Be fearful of Allah*** with respect to what He commands. ***Allah is witness of all things.*** Nothing is hidden from Him.

56. ***Allah and His angels call down blessings on the Prophet*** Muḥammad, may Allah bless him and grant him peace. ***You who believe, call down blessings on him and ask for complete peace***

لَّا جُنَاحَ عَلَيْهِنَّ فِىٓ ءَابَآئِهِنَّ وَلَآ أَبْنَآئِهِنَّ وَلَآ إِخْوَٰنِهِنَّ وَلَآ أَبْنَآءِ
إِخْوَٰنِهِنَّ وَلَآ أَبْنَآءِ أَخَوَٰتِهِنَّ وَلَا نِسَآئِهِنَّ وَلَا مَا مَلَكَتْ
أَيْمَٰنُهُنَّ ۗ وَٱتَّقِينَ ٱللَّهَ ۚ إِنَّ ٱللَّهَ كَانَ عَلَىٰ كُلِّ شَىْءٍ شَهِيدًا
٥٥ إِنَّ ٱللَّهَ وَمَلَٰٓئِكَتَهُۥ يُصَلُّونَ عَلَى ٱلنَّبِىِّ ۚ يَٰٓأَيُّهَا ٱلَّذِينَ
ءَامَنُوا۟ صَلُّوا۟ عَلَيْهِ وَسَلِّمُوا۟ تَسْلِيمًا ٥٦ إِنَّ ٱلَّذِينَ يُؤْذُونَ
ٱللَّهَ وَرَسُولَهُۥ لَعَنَهُمُ ٱللَّهُ فِى ٱلدُّنْيَا وَٱلْءَاخِرَةِ وَأَعَدَّ لَهُمْ عَذَابًا
مُّهِينًا ٥٧ وَٱلَّذِينَ يُؤْذُونَ ٱلْمُؤْمِنِينَ وَٱلْمُؤْمِنَٰتِ
بِغَيْرِ مَا ٱكْتَسَبُوا۟ فَقَدِ ٱحْتَمَلُوا۟ بُهْتَٰنًا وَإِثْمًا مُّبِينًا ٥٨
يَٰٓأَيُّهَا ٱلنَّبِىُّ قُل لِّأَزْوَٰجِكَ وَبَنَاتِكَ وَنِسَآءِ ٱلْمُؤْمِنِينَ يُدْنِينَ
عَلَيْهِنَّ مِن جَلَٰبِيبِهِنَّ ۚ ذَٰلِكَ أَدْنَىٰٓ أَن يُعْرَفْنَ فَلَا يُؤْذَيْنَ ۗ وَكَانَ
ٱللَّهُ غَفُورًا رَّحِيمًا ٥٩ ۞ لَّئِن لَّمْ يَنتَهِ ٱلْمُنَٰفِقُونَ وَٱلَّذِينَ
فِى قُلُوبِهِم مَّرَضٌ وَٱلْمُرْجِفُونَ فِى ٱلْمَدِينَةِ لَنُغْرِيَنَّكَ
بِهِمْ ثُمَّ لَا يُجَاوِرُونَكَ فِيهَآ إِلَّا قَلِيلًا ٦٠ مَّلْعُونِينَ ۖ
أَيْنَمَا ثُقِفُوٓا۟ أُخِذُوا۟ وَقُتِّلُوا۟ تَقْتِيلًا ٦١ سُنَّةَ ٱللَّهِ فِى
ٱلَّذِينَ خَلَوْا۟ مِن قَبْلُ ۖ وَلَن تَجِدَ لِسُنَّةِ ٱللَّهِ تَبْدِيلًا ٦٢
يَسْـَٔلُكَ ٱلنَّاسُ عَنِ ٱلسَّاعَةِ ۖ قُلْ إِنَّمَا عِلْمُهَا عِندَ ٱللَّهِ ۚ وَمَا يُدْرِيكَ
لَعَلَّ ٱلسَّاعَةَ تَكُونُ قَرِيبًا ٦٣ إِنَّ ٱللَّهَ لَعَنَ ٱلْكَٰفِرِينَ وَأَعَدَّ
لَهُمْ سَعِيرًا ٦٤ خَٰلِدِينَ فِيهَآ أَبَدًا ۖ لَّا يَجِدُونَ وَلِيًّا وَلَا نَصِيرًا
٦٥ يَوْمَ تُقَلَّبُ وُجُوهُهُمْ فِى ٱلنَّارِ يَقُولُونَ يَٰلَيْتَنَآ أَطَعْنَا ٱللَّهَ
وَأَطَعْنَا ٱلرَّسُولَا۠ ٦٦ وَقَالُوا۟ رَبَّنَآ إِنَّآ أَطَعْنَا سَادَتَنَا وَكُبَرَآءَنَا

and safety for him. Say, "O Allah, bless our master Muḥammad and grant him peace."

57. ***As for those who abuse Allah and His Messenger*** – meaning unbelievers who describe Allah in a way which is inappropriate for Him, such as attributing a son or partner to Him, and who deny His Messenger – ***Allah's curse is on them in this world and the Next World. He has prepared a humiliating punishment for them*** – meaning the Fire.

58. ***And those who abuse men and women who are believers, when they have not merited it*** – accusing them of something they have not done – ***bear the weight of slander*** and lying ***and clear wrongdoing.***

59. ***O Prophet, tell your wives and daughters and the women of the believers to draw their outer garments*** (*jalābīb*) ***closely round themselves.*** *Jalābīb* is the plural of *jalbāb*, which is a covering cloth that a woman wraps round herself, part of which hangs over the head and face when they go out for their needs. ***This makes it more likely that they will be recognised*** – as free women and not slaves – ***and not be harmed*** by allusions, as happens with slavegirls who do not cover their faces. The hypocrites used to make overtures to them. ***Allah is Ever-Forgiving*** of what happened before owing to lack of covering, ***Most Merciful*** after covering has taken place.

60. ***If the hypocrites and those with sickness in their hearts*** – meaning those open to fornication – ***and the rumour-mongers in Madina do not desist*** from unsettling the believers by saying, "The enemy has come against you! Your forces have been slain! They have been defeated," ***We will set you onto them*** and give you power over them. ***Then they will only be your neighbours*** – living near you – ***there a very short time*** and then they will be expelled.

61. ***They are an accursed people*** – far from mercy. ***Wherever they are found they should be seized and mercilessly put to death.*** This is the judgement on them.

62. ***This is Allah's pattern*** and custom ***with those who passed away before*** – a reference to what happened in past nations to hypocrites who unsettled believers. ***You will not find any alteration in Allah's pattern.***

فَأَضَلُّونَا ٱلسَّبِيلَا۠ ﴿٦٧﴾ رَبَّنَآ ءَاتِهِمۡ ضِعۡفَيۡنِ مِنَ ٱلۡعَذَابِ
وَٱلۡعَنۡهُمۡ لَعۡنًا كَبِيرًا ﴿٦٨﴾ يَٰٓأَيُّهَا ٱلَّذِينَ ءَامَنُواْ لَا تَكُونُواْ كَٱلَّذِينَ
ءَاذَوۡاْ مُوسَىٰ فَبَرَّأَهُ ٱللَّهُ مِمَّا قَالُواْۚ وَكَانَ عِندَ ٱللَّهِ وَجِيهًا ﴿٦٩﴾
يَٰٓأَيُّهَا ٱلَّذِينَ ءَامَنُواْ ٱتَّقُواْ ٱللَّهَ وَقُولُواْ قَوۡلًا سَدِيدًا ﴿٧٠﴾ يُصۡلِحۡ
لَكُمۡ أَعۡمَٰلَكُمۡ وَيَغۡفِرۡ لَكُمۡ ذُنُوبَكُمۡۗ وَمَن يُطِعِ ٱللَّهَ وَرَسُولَهُۥ
فَقَدۡ فَازَ فَوۡزًا عَظِيمًا ﴿٧١﴾ إِنَّا عَرَضۡنَا ٱلۡأَمَانَةَ عَلَى ٱلسَّمَٰوَٰتِ
وَٱلۡأَرۡضِ وَٱلۡجِبَالِ فَأَبَيۡنَ أَن يَحۡمِلۡنَهَا وَأَشۡفَقۡنَ مِنۡهَا وَحَمَلَهَا
ٱلۡإِنسَٰنُۖ إِنَّهُۥ كَانَ ظَلُومًا جَهُولًا ﴿٧٢﴾ لِّيُعَذِّبَ ٱللَّهُ ٱلۡمُنَٰفِقِينَ
وَٱلۡمُنَٰفِقَٰتِ وَٱلۡمُشۡرِكِينَ وَٱلۡمُشۡرِكَٰتِ وَيَتُوبَ ٱللَّهُ
عَلَى ٱلۡمُؤۡمِنِينَ وَٱلۡمُؤۡمِنَٰتِۗ وَكَانَ ٱللَّهُ غَفُورًا رَّحِيمَۢا ﴿٧٣﴾

63. ***People will ask you about the Last Hour*** and when it will come. ***Say: 'Only Allah has knowledge of it. What will make you understand? It may be that the Last Hour is very near.'***

64. ***Allah has cursed the unbelievers and prepared a Searing Blaze for them***, which they will enter –

65. ***…where they will remain timelessly, for ever and ever, not finding any protector*** to guard them from it ***or any helper*** to defend them from it.

66. ***They will say on the Day their faces are rolled over in the Fire, 'If only we had obeyed Allah and obeyed the Messenger!'***

67. ***And they*** (the followers) ***will say, 'Our Lord, we obeyed our masters*** (read as *sādātanā* and *sādātinā*) ***and great men and they misguided us away from the Way*** of guidance.

68. ***Our Lord, give them double the punishment and curse them many times over!'*** One reading has *kabīran* instead of *kathīran* in which case the meaning becomes "curse them greatly".

69. ***You who believe, do not be*** – towards your Prophet – ***like those who abused Mūsā*** – as when they said, "All that keeps him from bathing with us is that he has a defect." ***Allah absolved him of what they said*** – when he placed his garment on a stone so that he could bathe and the rock ran away with it until it stopped with a group of the tribe of Israel. Mūsā caught up with it and took his garment and covered himself with it. They saw him and that he did not have the defect in his private parts imputed to him – ***and he was highly honoured in Allah's sight.*** They abused our Prophet, may Allah bless him and grant him peace, when he divided some booty and a man said, "This is a division which is not for the sake of Allah Almighty." The Prophet, may Allah bless him and grant him peace, became angry at that and said, "May Allah have mercy on Mūsā. He was abused with worse than this and remained steadfast." Al-Bukhārī related it.

70. ***You who believe, be fearful of Allah and speak words which hit the mark*** – meaning words which are correct and to the point.

71. ***He will put your actions right for you*** – and accept them – ***and forgive you your wrong deeds. All who obey Allah and His Messenger have won a mighty victory.***

72. ***We offered the Trust*** – the prayers and other things which there is a reward for doing and a penalty for omitting – ***to the heavens, the earth and the mountains*** – and He created consciousness and articulation in them – ***but they refused to take it on and shrank from it. But man*** (Ādam) ***took it on*** when it was offered to him. ***He is indeed wrongdoing and ignorant*** of it.

73. ***This was so that Allah might punish the men and women of the hypocrites, and the men and women of the idolators*** – who have squandered the trust – ***and turn towards the men and women of the believers*** – who have fulfilled the trust. ***Allah is Ever-Forgiving, Most Merciful*** to the believers.

سُورَةُ سَبَإٍ

بِسْمِ ٱللَّهِ ٱلرَّحْمَٰنِ ٱلرَّحِيمِ

ٱلْحَمْدُ لِلَّهِ ٱلَّذِى لَهُۥ مَا فِى ٱلسَّمَٰوَٰتِ وَمَا فِى ٱلْأَرْضِ وَلَهُ ٱلْحَمْدُ
فِى ٱلْءَاخِرَةِ ۚ وَهُوَ ٱلْحَكِيمُ ٱلْخَبِيرُ ﴿١﴾ يَعْلَمُ مَا يَلِجُ فِى ٱلْأَرْضِ
وَمَا يَخْرُجُ مِنْهَا وَمَا يَنزِلُ مِنَ ٱلسَّمَآءِ وَمَا يَعْرُجُ فِيهَا ۚ وَهُوَ
ٱلرَّحِيمُ ٱلْغَفُورُ ﴿٢﴾ وَقَالَ ٱلَّذِينَ كَفَرُوا۟ لَا تَأْتِينَا ٱلسَّاعَةُ ۖ
قُلْ بَلَىٰ وَرَبِّى لَتَأْتِيَنَّكُمْ عَٰلِمِ ٱلْغَيْبِ ۖ لَا يَعْزُبُ عَنْهُ مِثْقَالُ
ذَرَّةٍ فِى ٱلسَّمَٰوَٰتِ وَلَا فِى ٱلْأَرْضِ وَلَآ أَصْغَرُ مِن ذَٰلِكَ
وَلَآ أَكْبَرُ إِلَّا فِى كِتَٰبٍ مُّبِينٍ ﴿٣﴾ لِّيَجْزِىَ ٱلَّذِينَ
ءَامَنُوا۟ وَعَمِلُوا۟ ٱلصَّٰلِحَٰتِ ۚ أُو۟لَٰٓئِكَ لَهُم مَّغْفِرَةٌ وَرِزْقٌ
كَرِيمٌ ﴿٤﴾ وَٱلَّذِينَ سَعَوْ فِىٓ ءَايَٰتِنَا مُعَٰجِزِينَ أُو۟لَٰٓئِكَ
لَهُمْ عَذَابٌ مِّن رِّجْزٍ أَلِيمٌ ﴿٥﴾ وَيَرَى ٱلَّذِينَ أُوتُوا۟ ٱلْعِلْمَ
ٱلَّذِىٓ أُنزِلَ إِلَيْكَ مِن رَّبِّكَ هُوَ ٱلْحَقَّ وَيَهْدِىٓ إِلَىٰ صِرَٰطِ
ٱلْعَزِيزِ ٱلْحَمِيدِ ﴿٦﴾ وَقَالَ ٱلَّذِينَ كَفَرُوا۟ هَلْ نَدُلُّكُمْ عَلَىٰ رَجُلٍ
يُنَبِّئُكُمْ إِذَا مُزِّقْتُمْ كُلَّ مُمَزَّقٍ إِنَّكُمْ لَفِى خَلْقٍ جَدِيدٍ ﴿٧﴾
أَفْتَرَىٰ عَلَى ٱللَّهِ كَذِبًا أَم بِهِۦ جِنَّةٌ ۗ بَلِ ٱلَّذِينَ لَا يُؤْمِنُونَ بِٱلْءَاخِرَةِ
فِى ٱلْعَذَابِ وَٱلضَّلَٰلِ ٱلْبَعِيدِ ﴿٨﴾ أَفَلَمْ يَرَوْا۟ إِلَىٰ مَا بَيْنَ أَيْدِيهِمْ

34. *Sūrat Sabā'*
Sheba

This *sūra* is Makkan except for *āyat* 2, which is Madinan. It has 54 or 55 *āyat*s and was sent down after *Luqmān.*

1. ***Praise be to Allah*** – Allah is here praising Himself, and what is intended by it is confirmation of the praise which belongs to Him in every state and emphasises the beauty of Allah – ***to Whom every - thing in the heavens and everything in the earth belongs*** as His kingdom and creation, ***and praise be to Him in the Next World*** as well as in this world. His friends will praise Him when they enter the Garden. ***He is the All-Wise*** in what He does, ***the All-Aware*** of His creation.

2. ***He knows what goes into the earth*** – such as water and other things – ***and what comes out of it*** – such as plants and other things – ***and what comes down from heaven*** – such as rain and other things – ***and what goes up into it*** – such as actions and other things. ***And He is the Most Merciful*** to His friends, ***the Ever-Forgiving*** towards them.

3. ***Those who disbelieve say, 'The Hour*** of the Resurrection ***will never come.' Say*** to them, ***'Yes, by my Lord, it certainly will come!' He is the Knower of the Unseen, Whom not even the weight of the smallest particle eludes, either in the heavens or in the earth; nor is there anything smaller or larger than that which is not in a Clear Book*** – meaning the Preserved Tablet.

4. ***This is so that He may recompense those who believe and do right actions. They will have forgiveness and generous provision*** in Paradise.

5. ***But those who strive against Our Signs*** (the Qur'an), ***trying to nullify them*** (read as *mu'ājizīna* and *mu'ajjizīna*), they cannot escape Allah merely by thinking that there will be no Resurrection or punishment, ***will have a punishment of agonising pain.***

6. ***Those who have been given knowledge*** – referring here to the believers of the people of the Book such as 'Abdullāh ibn Salām and

وَمَا خَلْفَهُم مِّنَ ٱلسَّمَآءِ وَٱلْأَرْضِ ۚ إِن نَّشَأْ نَخْسِفْ بِهِمُ
ٱلْأَرْضَ أَوْ نُسْقِطْ عَلَيْهِمْ كِسَفًا مِّنَ ٱلسَّمَآءِ ۚ إِنَّ فِى ذَٰلِكَ
لَءَايَةً لِّكُلِّ عَبْدٍ مُّنِيبٍ ﴿٩﴾ ۞ وَلَقَدْ ءَاتَيْنَا دَاوُۥدَ مِنَّا فَضْلًا ۖ
يَٰجِبَالُ أَوِّبِى مَعَهُۥ وَٱلطَّيْرَ ۖ وَأَلَنَّا لَهُ ٱلْحَدِيدَ ﴿١٠﴾ أَنِ ٱعْمَلْ
سَٰبِغَٰتٍ وَقَدِّرْ فِى ٱلسَّرْدِ ۖ وَٱعْمَلُوا۟ صَٰلِحًا ۖ إِنِّى بِمَا تَعْمَلُونَ
بَصِيرٌ ﴿١١﴾ وَلِسُلَيْمَٰنَ ٱلرِّيحَ غُدُوُّهَا شَهْرٌ وَرَوَاحُهَا شَهْرٌ ۖ
وَأَسَلْنَا لَهُۥ عَيْنَ ٱلْقِطْرِ ۖ وَمِنَ ٱلْجِنِّ مَن يَعْمَلُ بَيْنَ يَدَيْهِ بِإِذْنِ
رَبِّهِۦ ۖ وَمَن يَزِغْ مِنْهُمْ عَنْ أَمْرِنَا نُذِقْهُ مِنْ عَذَابِ ٱلسَّعِيرِ ﴿١٢﴾
يَعْمَلُونَ لَهُۥ مَا يَشَآءُ مِن مَّحَٰرِيبَ وَتَمَٰثِيلَ وَجِفَانٍ كَٱلْجَوَابِ
وَقُدُورٍ رَّاسِيَٰتٍ ۚ ٱعْمَلُوٓا۟ ءَالَ دَاوُۥدَ شُكْرًا ۚ وَقَلِيلٌ مِّنْ عِبَادِىَ
ٱلشَّكُورُ ﴿١٣﴾ فَلَمَّا قَضَيْنَا عَلَيْهِ ٱلْمَوْتَ مَا دَلَّهُمْ عَلَىٰ مَوْتِهِۦٓ
إِلَّا دَآبَّةُ ٱلْأَرْضِ تَأْكُلُ مِنسَأَتَهُۥ ۖ فَلَمَّا خَرَّ تَبَيَّنَتِ ٱلْجِنُّ
أَن لَّوْ كَانُوا۟ يَعْلَمُونَ ٱلْغَيْبَ مَا لَبِثُوا۟ فِى ٱلْعَذَابِ ٱلْمُهِينِ ﴿١٤﴾
لَقَدْ كَانَ لِسَبَإٍ فِى مَسْكَنِهِمْ ءَايَةٌ ۖ جَنَّتَانِ عَن يَمِينٍ وَشِمَالٍ ۖ
كُلُوا۟ مِن رِّزْقِ رَبِّكُمْ وَٱشْكُرُوا۟ لَهُۥ ۚ بَلْدَةٌ طَيِّبَةٌ وَرَبٌّ غَفُورٌ
﴿١٥﴾ فَأَعْرَضُوا۟ فَأَرْسَلْنَا عَلَيْهِمْ سَيْلَ ٱلْعَرِمِ وَبَدَّلْنَٰهُم بِجَنَّتَيْهِمْ
جَنَّتَيْنِ ذَوَاتَىْ أُكُلٍ خَمْطٍ وَأَثْلٍ وَشَىْءٍ مِّن سِدْرٍ قَلِيلٍ
﴿١٦﴾ ذَٰلِكَ جَزَيْنَٰهُم بِمَا كَفَرُوا۟ ۖ وَهَلْ نُجَٰزِىٓ إِلَّا ٱلْكَفُورَ ﴿١٧﴾
وَجَعَلْنَا بَيْنَهُمْ وَبَيْنَ ٱلْقُرَى ٱلَّتِى بَٰرَكْنَا فِيهَا قُرًى ظَٰهِرَةً
وَقَدَّرْنَا فِيهَا ٱلسَّيْرَ ۖ سِيرُوا۟ فِيهَا لَيَالِىَ وَأَيَّامًا ءَامِنِينَ ﴿١٨﴾

his people – **see** (know) ***that what has been sent down to you*** – meaning the Qur'an – ***from your Lord is the truth and that it guides to the Path of the Almighty, the Praiseworthy.***

7. ***Those who disbelieve say*** – to one another in astonishment: ***'Shall we lead you to a man*** – Muḥammad – ***who will tell you that when you have completely disintegrated, you will then be recreated all anew?***

8. ***Has he invented a lie against Allah*** by saying that, ***or is he possessed*** – mad, so that he imagines it?' Allah says: ***No indeed! Those who do not believe in the Next World*** – which involves belief in the Resurrection and the Punishment – ***are in punishment and deeply misguided*** – away from the truth in this world.

9. ***Have they not looked at the sky and the earth in front of them and behind them*** – and above them and below them? ***If We willed*** (read as *nasha'*, and also *yasha'* "He willed") ***We would cause the earth to swallow*** (read as *nakhsif* and also *yakhsif*, "He") ***them up or make great lumps*** (read as *kisafan* and *kisfan*) ***fall down*** (read as *nasqiṭ* and also *yasqiṭ*, "He") ***on them from the sky. There is certainly a Sign*** – indicating the power of Allah to resurrect and to do whatever else He wishes – ***in that*** – which can be seen – ***for every remorseful slave.***

10. ***We gave Dāwūd great favour*** – meaning Prophethood and a Book – ***from Us: 'O mountains and birds, echo with him in his praise*** – and glorification of Allah!' ***And We made iron malleable*** – like putty in his hands – ***for him:***

11. ***'Make full-length coats of mail*** – the word *sābighāt* implies that they are so long so that the skirts drag on the ground – ***measuring the links*** – the word *sard* refers to the meshing of the chains of the armour – ***with care. And act rightly*** – family of Dāwūd – ***all of you, for I see what you do*** – and will repay you for it.'

12. ***And We gave Sulaymān power over the wind*** (read as *rīḥa* and *rīḥu*): ***a month's journey in the morning*** – during the time from dawn up until midday it travelled the distance it takes people a month to travel – ***and a month's in the afternoon*** – covering the distance it takes people a month to travel. ***And We made a fount of molten brass flow out for him*** – which flowed for three days and nights like water; and people still use today what Sulaymān was given. ***And some of the jinn worked in front of him by his Lord's permission*** (command)*.* ***And if a single one of them deviates at all from Our command*** – and does not obey – ***We make him taste the punishment of the Searing Blaze*** in the Next World. It is also said that the punishment referred to takes place in this world by being beaten by a angel with a whip that will burn them.

13. ***They made for him anything he wished: high arches*** – tall structures which could be climbed by means of ladders – ***and statues*** made of brass, glass and marble, as making images was not unlawful in their religion, ***huge dishes like cisterns*** big enough for a thousand people, ***great built-in cooking vats*** which could not be moved, built from stone taken from mountains in Yemen and which needed rope ladders to be reached. ***'Work, family of Dāwūd*** – to obey Allah – ***in thankfulness*** for what He has given you*!'* ***But very few of My slaves are thankful*** and obey Allah out of thankfulness for His blessings upon them.

14. ***Then when We decreed that he*** (Sulaymān) ***should die*** – he died and then remained upright leaning on his staff while dead for a year. The jinn continued to do those arduous tasks as normal. They were not aware that he had died until woodworms ate the staff and he fell down – ***nothing divulged his death to them except the worm which ate his staff*** – which he used to discipline them – ***so that when he fell down*** dead ***it was made clear to the jinn that if they had truly had knowledge of the Unseen*** they would have known that Sulaymān had died and ***they need not have stayed there suffering humiliating punishment*** – meaning their arduous tasks. They only did so because they thought that Sulaymān was still alive. It took some time, because the woodworms could not consume the staff in a day and a night.

15. ***There was also a sign*** – indicating the power of Allah Almighty – ***for Sabā'*** – the name of the tribe which was named after an Arab ancestor of theirs – ***in their dwelling place*** in Yemen*:* ***two gardens, one to the right and one to the left*** of their valley. They were told: ***'Eat of your Lord's provision and give thanks to Him*** for His blessing you with the land of Sabā' – ***a bountiful land*** of good fertile earth, with no salt in it or gnats, flies, fleas, scorpions or snakes so

فَقَالُواْ رَبَّنَا بَٰعِدۡ بَيۡنَ أَسۡفَارِنَا وَظَلَمُوٓاْ أَنفُسَهُمۡ فَجَعَلۡنَٰهُمۡ
أَحَادِيثَ وَمَزَّقۡنَٰهُمۡ كُلَّ مُمَزَّقٍۚ إِنَّ فِي ذَٰلِكَ لَأٓيَٰتٖ لِّكُلِّ صَبَّارٖ
شَكُورٖ ١٩ وَلَقَدۡ صَدَّقَ عَلَيۡهِمۡ إِبۡلِيسُ ظَنَّهُۥ فَٱتَّبَعُوهُ إِلَّا
فَرِيقٗا مِّنَ ٱلۡمُؤۡمِنِينَ ٢٠ وَمَا كَانَ لَهُۥ عَلَيۡهِم مِّن سُلۡطَٰنٍ
إِلَّا لِنَعۡلَمَ مَن يُؤۡمِنُ بِٱلۡأٓخِرَةِ مِمَّنۡ هُوَ مِنۡهَا فِي شَكّٖۗ وَرَبُّكَ
عَلَىٰ كُلِّ شَيۡءٍ حَفِيظٞ ٢١ قُلِ ٱدۡعُواْ ٱلَّذِينَ زَعَمۡتُم مِّن دُونِ
ٱللَّهِ لَا يَمۡلِكُونَ مِثۡقَالَ ذَرَّةٖ فِي ٱلسَّمَٰوَٰتِ وَلَا فِي
ٱلۡأَرۡضِ وَمَا لَهُمۡ فِيهِمَا مِن شِرۡكٖ وَمَا لَهُۥ مِنۡهُم مِّن ظَهِيرٖ ٢٢
وَلَا تَنفَعُ ٱلشَّفَٰعَةُ عِندَهُۥٓ إِلَّا لِمَنۡ أَذِنَ لَهُۥۚ حَتَّىٰٓ إِذَا فُزِّعَ عَن
قُلُوبِهِمۡ قَالُواْ مَاذَا قَالَ رَبُّكُمۡۖ قَالُواْ ٱلۡحَقَّۖ وَهُوَ ٱلۡعَلِيُّ ٱلۡكَبِيرُ
٢٣ ۞ قُلۡ مَن يَرۡزُقُكُم مِّنَ ٱلسَّمَٰوَٰتِ وَٱلۡأَرۡضِۖ قُلِ ٱللَّهُۖ
وَإِنَّآ أَوۡ إِيَّاكُمۡ لَعَلَىٰ هُدًى أَوۡ فِي ضَلَٰلٖ مُّبِينٖ ٢٤ قُل
لَّا تُسۡـَٔلُونَ عَمَّآ أَجۡرَمۡنَا وَلَا نُسۡـَٔلُ عَمَّا تَعۡمَلُونَ ٢٥ قُلۡ
يَجۡمَعُ بَيۡنَنَا رَبُّنَا ثُمَّ يَفۡتَحُ بَيۡنَنَا بِٱلۡحَقِّ وَهُوَ ٱلۡفَتَّاحُ ٱلۡعَلِيمُ
٢٦ قُلۡ أَرُونِيَ ٱلَّذِينَ أَلۡحَقۡتُم بِهِۦ شُرَكَآءَۖ كَلَّاۚ بَلۡ هُوَ ٱللَّهُ
ٱلۡعَزِيزُ ٱلۡحَكِيمُ ٢٧ وَمَآ أَرۡسَلۡنَٰكَ إِلَّا كَآفَّةٗ لِّلنَّاسِ
بَشِيرٗا وَنَذِيرٗا وَلَٰكِنَّ أَكۡثَرَ ٱلنَّاسِ لَا يَعۡلَمُونَ ٢٨
وَيَقُولُونَ مَتَىٰ هَٰذَا ٱلۡوَعۡدُ إِن كُنتُمۡ صَٰدِقِينَ ٢٩
قُل لَّكُم مِّيعَادُ يَوۡمٖ لَّا تَسۡتَـٔۡخِرُونَ عَنۡهُ سَاعَةٗ وَلَا تَسۡتَقۡدِمُونَ
٣٠ وَقَالَ ٱلَّذِينَ كَفَرُواْ لَن نُّؤۡمِنَ بِهَٰذَا ٱلۡقُرۡءَانِ وَلَا

that a stranger could travel through it without danger and the lice in his clothes would die due to the wholesomeness of its air – ***and a most forgiving Lord*** (Allah).'

16. ***But they turned away*** from thankfulness and were ungrateful, ***so We unleashed against them the flood from the great dam*** – the word for "dam", *'arim*, comes from *'urma*, and means a structure or something else which blocks the water until the time when it is needed; and it was released on their valley and flooded their gardens and property – ***and exchanged their two gardens for two others containing bitter-tasting plants and tamarisk and a few lote trees.***

17. ***That*** exchange ***is how We repaid them for their ingratitude. Do We repay any but the ungrateful*** (read as *nujāzi illa'l-kufūra*, and also *yujāza' illa'l-kufūru*, in which case the meaning becomes, "Are any but the ungrateful repaid") ***like this?***

18. ***We placed between them*** – Sabā in Yemen – ***and the cities We had blessed*** – with water and trees, meaning the towns of Syria to which they travelled for trade – ***other clearly conspicuous cities*** on a continuous route from Yemen to Syria, ***making them measured stages on the way***, in such a way that travellers could be in one town at midday and another at nightfall until the end of the journey, so that they did not need to carry provision or water. Allah said: ***'Travel between them in safety*** – without fear – ***by night and day.'***

19. ***They said, 'Our Lord, put more distance*** (read as *bā'id* and *ba''id*) ***between our staging posts*** – on the journey to Syria, so that there are deserts to make the journey too long for the poor people because of the need for riding animals and for carrying provision and water.' ***They wronged themselves*** – with unbelief – ***so We made legends of them*** for those after them ***and scattered them*** – into little groups throughout the land – ***without a trace. There are certainly Signs in that for everyone who is steadfast*** in avoiding acts of disobedience ***and thankful*** for blessings received.

20. ***Iblīs was correct*** (read as *ṣaddaqa* and *ṣadaqa*) ***in his assessment of them*** – meaning the unbelievers, including Sabā, in thinking that they would follow his misguidance – ***and they followed him*** – and proved him correct in what he said – ***except for a group of believers*** who did not follow him.

21. ***He had no authority over them except to enable Us to know*** – by outward signs – ***those who believe in the Next World from those who are in doubt about it***; and We will repay each group. ***Your Lord is the Preserver of all things.***

22. ***Say***, Muḥammad, to the unbelievers of Makka***: 'Call on those you make claims for*** – to be gods – ***besides Allah*** – to help you in the way you claim that they can. Allah says of them: ***They have no power over even the smallest particle*** of either good or evil ***either in the heavens or in the earth. They have no share in them. He*** (Allah) ***has no need of their*** (gods') ***support.'***

23. ***Intercession with Him will be of no benefit*** – this refutes what they say about their gods interceding for them – ***except from some - one who has His permission*** (read as *adhina* and *udhina*). ***So that when the terror has left*** (read as *fuzza'a* and *fazza'a*) ***their hearts*** – by Allah's permission – ***they will say*** to one another in joy: ***'What did your Lord say*** about it***?' They will say, 'The truth. He is the All-High*** above His creation***, the Most Great.'***

24. ***Say: 'Who provides for you from the heavens*** (rain) ***and earth*** (plants)***?' Say: 'Allah. It is certain that one or the other of us, either we or you, is following guidance or else clearly astray.'***

25. ***Say: 'You will not be asked about any evil we committed and we will not be asked about what you did*** – because we are innocent of what you did.***'***

26. ***Say: 'Our Lord will bring us all together*** on the Day of Rising ***and then will judge between us with the truth.*** Those who supported the truth will enter the Garden and those who followed falsehood will enter the Fire. ***He is the Just Decider, the All-Knowing*** of what to decree.

27. ***Say: 'Show me*** – and inform me about – ***those you have joined to Him as associates*** in your worship. ***No indeed! He is Allah, the Almighty*** in His command, ***the All-Wise*** in managing His creation and having no partner in His kingdom.***'***

28. ***We only sent you for the whole of mankind*** – the adjective is put before the noun in the Arabic to emphasise it – ***to bring good news*** of Paradise to the believers ***and to give warning*** to the unbelievers of

بِٱلَّذِى بَيْنَ يَدَيْهِ ۗ وَلَوْ تَرَىٰٓ إِذِ ٱلظَّٰلِمُونَ مَوْقُوفُونَ عِندَ
رَبِّهِمْ يَرْجِعُ بَعْضُهُمْ إِلَىٰ بَعْضٍ ٱلْقَوْلَ يَقُولُ ٱلَّذِينَ
ٱسْتُضْعِفُوا۟ لِلَّذِينَ ٱسْتَكْبَرُوا۟ لَوْلَآ أَنتُمْ لَكُنَّا مُؤْمِنِينَ ٣١
قَالَ ٱلَّذِينَ ٱسْتَكْبَرُوا۟ لِلَّذِينَ ٱسْتُضْعِفُوٓا۟ أَنَحْنُ صَدَدْنَٰكُمْ
عَنِ ٱلْهُدَىٰ بَعْدَ إِذْ جَآءَكُم ۖ بَلْ كُنتُم مُّجْرِمِينَ ٣٢ وَقَالَ ٱلَّذِينَ
ٱسْتُضْعِفُوا۟ لِلَّذِينَ ٱسْتَكْبَرُوا۟ بَلْ مَكْرُ ٱلَّيْلِ وَٱلنَّهَارِ إِذْ
تَأْمُرُونَنَآ أَن نَّكْفُرَ بِٱللَّهِ وَنَجْعَلَ لَهُۥٓ أَندَادًا ۚ وَأَسَرُّوا۟ ٱلنَّدَامَةَ
لَمَّا رَأَوُا۟ ٱلْعَذَابَ وَجَعَلْنَا ٱلْأَغْلَٰلَ فِىٓ أَعْنَاقِ ٱلَّذِينَ كَفَرُوا۟ ۚ
هَلْ يُجْزَوْنَ إِلَّا مَا كَانُوا۟ يَعْمَلُونَ ٣٣ وَمَآ أَرْسَلْنَا فِى قَرْيَةٍ
مِّن نَّذِيرٍ إِلَّا قَالَ مُتْرَفُوهَآ إِنَّا بِمَآ أُرْسِلْتُم بِهِۦ كَٰفِرُونَ ٣٤
وَقَالُوا۟ نَحْنُ أَكْثَرُ أَمْوَٰلًا وَأَوْلَٰدًا وَمَا نَحْنُ بِمُعَذَّبِينَ ٣٥
قُلْ إِنَّ رَبِّى يَبْسُطُ ٱلرِّزْقَ لِمَن يَشَآءُ وَيَقْدِرُ وَلَٰكِنَّ أَكْثَرَ ٱلنَّاسِ
لَا يَعْلَمُونَ ٣٦ وَمَآ أَمْوَٰلُكُمْ وَلَآ أَوْلَٰدُكُم بِٱلَّتِى تُقَرِّبُكُمْ عِندَنَا
زُلْفَىٰٓ إِلَّا مَنْ ءَامَنَ وَعَمِلَ صَٰلِحًا فَأُو۟لَٰٓئِكَ لَهُمْ جَزَآءُ ٱلضِّعْفِ
بِمَا عَمِلُوا۟ وَهُمْ فِى ٱلْغُرُفَٰتِ ءَامِنُونَ ٣٧ وَٱلَّذِينَ يَسْعَوْنَ فِىٓ
ءَايَٰتِنَا مُعَٰجِزِينَ أُو۟لَٰٓئِكَ فِى ٱلْعَذَابِ مُحْضَرُونَ ٣٨ قُلْ
إِنَّ رَبِّى يَبْسُطُ ٱلرِّزْقَ لِمَن يَشَآءُ مِنْ عِبَادِهِۦ وَيَقْدِرُ لَهُۥ ۚ وَمَآ
أَنفَقْتُم مِّن شَىْءٍ فَهُوَ يُخْلِفُهُۥ ۖ وَهُوَ خَيْرُ ٱلرَّٰزِقِينَ ٣٩
وَيَوْمَ يَحْشُرُهُمْ جَمِيعًا ثُمَّ يَقُولُ لِلْمَلَٰٓئِكَةِ أَهَٰٓؤُلَآءِ إِيَّاكُمْ كَانُوا۟
يَعْبُدُونَ ٤٠ قَالُوا۟ سُبْحَٰنَكَ أَنتَ وَلِيُّنَا مِن دُونِهِم ۖ بَلْ كَانُوا۟

the Punishment; ***but most of mankind*** – including the unbelievers of Makka – ***do not know it.***

29. ***They say, 'When will this promise*** of the Punishment ***come about if you are telling the truth?'***

30. ***Say: 'You have a promised appointment on a Day*** – meaning the Day of Resurrection – ***which you cannot delay or advance a single hour.'***

31. ***Those who disbelieve*** among the people of Makka ***say, 'We will never believe in this Qur'an, nor in what came before it*** – meaning the Torah and Gospel, which also speak of the Resurrection, because they deny it.' Allah says: ***If only you***, Muḥammad, ***could see when the wrongdoers*** (unbelievers) ***standing in the presence of their Lord, cast accusations back and forth at one another! Those deemed weak*** (the followers), ***will say to those deemed great*** (the leaders), ***'Were it not for you*** preventing us from believing – ***we would have been believers*** in the Prophet!'

32. ***Those deemed great will say to those deemed weak, 'Did we debar you from the guidance when it came to you? No, it is you who were evildoers*** to yourselves.'

33. ***Those deemed weak will say to those deemed great, 'No, it was your scheming night and day*** against us ***when you commanded us to reject Allah and assign equals*** (partners) ***to Him.' But they*** (both parties) ***will show their remorse*** for not believing in Allah ***when they see the punishment.*** The word for "show" here, *asarruu*, can also mean "conceal", in which case the meaning is that they will hide their remorse from their companions out of fear of being blamed. ***We will put iron collars round the necks of those who disbelieved*** in Hell. ***Will they be repaid for anything but what they did*** in this world?

34. ***We never sent a warner into any city without the affluent people*** (its leaders) ***in it saying, 'We reject what you have been sent with.'***

35. ***They also said, 'We have more wealth and children*** than those who believe. ***We are not going to be punished.'***

36. ***Say: 'My Lord expands the provision of anyone He wills or restricts it*** – as a test, ***but the majority of mankind*** – including the unbelievers of Makka – ***do not know it.'***

37. ***It is not your wealth or your children that will bring you near to Us, only in the case of people who believe and act rightly; such people will have a multiplied recompense for what they did*** – ten like it or more. ***They will be safe from all harm*** – death and all other harmful things – ***in the High Halls of Paradise.***

38. ***But people who strive against Our Signs*** (the Qur'an), ***trying to nullify them*** – declare them meaningless – ***such people will be summoned to the Punishment*** and will not escape it.

39. ***Say: 'My Lord expands the provision of any of His slaves He wills or restricts it*** – as a test of constriction after expansion, or simply as a test. ***But anything*** good ***you expend will be replaced by Him. He is the Best of Providers.'*** The provision anyone gives to his dependants is from the provision of Allah.

40. ***On the Day We gather them*** (the idolaters) ***all together and then say to the angels, 'Was it you whom these people were worshipping?',***

41. ***...they will say, 'Glory be to You!*** You are above having any partner. ***You are our Protector, not them.*** There is no friendship between us and them. ***No, they were worshipping the jinn*** – meaning *shayṭāns*, by obeying them. ***They mostly had faith in*** what they said to ***them.'***

42. Allah says: ***'Today you possess no power to help or harm one another.'*** Those who were worshipped will not help those who worshipped them; nor will they intercede for them or punish them. ***And We will say to those who did wrong*** and disbelieved***: 'Taste the punishment of the Fire which you denied.'***

43. ***When Our Clear Signs*** (the Qur'an) ***are recited to them*** – on the tongue of Our Prophet Muḥammad, may Allah bless him and grant him peace – ***they say, 'This is nothing but a man who wants to debar you from what*** (the idols) ***your fathers used to worship.' They say, 'This*** Qur'an ***is nothing but an invented lie*** against Allah.' ***Those who disbelieve say to the truth***, meaning the Qur'an, ***when it comes to them, 'This is nothing but downright magic.'***

يَعْبُدُونَ ٱلْجِنَّ ۖ أَكْثَرُهُم بِهِم مُّؤْمِنُونَ ﴿٤١﴾ فَٱلْيَوْمَ لَا يَمْلِكُ
بَعْضُكُمْ لِبَعْضٍ نَّفْعًا وَلَا ضَرًّا وَنَقُولُ لِلَّذِينَ ظَلَمُوا۟ ذُوقُوا۟ عَذَابَ
ٱلنَّارِ ٱلَّتِى كُنتُم بِهَا تُكَذِّبُونَ ﴿٤٢﴾ وَإِذَا تُتْلَىٰ عَلَيْهِمْ ءَايَٰتُنَا بَيِّنَٰتٍ
قَالُوا۟ مَا هَٰذَآ إِلَّا رَجُلٌ يُرِيدُ أَن يَصُدَّكُمْ عَمَّا كَانَ يَعْبُدُ ءَابَآؤُكُمْ
وَقَالُوا۟ مَا هَٰذَآ إِلَّآ إِفْكٌ مُّفْتَرًى ۚ وَقَالَ ٱلَّذِينَ كَفَرُوا۟ لِلْحَقِّ لَمَّا
جَآءَهُمْ إِنْ هَٰذَآ إِلَّا سِحْرٌ مُّبِينٌ ﴿٤٣﴾ وَمَآ ءَاتَيْنَٰهُم مِّن كُتُبٍ
يَدْرُسُونَهَا ۖ وَمَآ أَرْسَلْنَآ إِلَيْهِمْ قَبْلَكَ مِن نَّذِيرٍ ﴿٤٤﴾ وَكَذَّبَ
ٱلَّذِينَ مِن قَبْلِهِمْ وَمَا بَلَغُوا۟ مِعْشَارَ مَآ ءَاتَيْنَٰهُمْ فَكَذَّبُوا۟ رُسُلِى ۖ
فَكَيْفَ كَانَ نَكِيرِ ﴿٤٥﴾ ۞ قُلْ إِنَّمَآ أَعِظُكُم بِوَٰحِدَةٍ ۖ أَن
تَقُومُوا۟ لِلَّهِ مَثْنَىٰ وَفُرَٰدَىٰ ثُمَّ تَتَفَكَّرُوا۟ ۚ مَا بِصَاحِبِكُم
مِّن جِنَّةٍ ۚ إِنْ هُوَ إِلَّا نَذِيرٌ لَّكُم بَيْنَ يَدَىْ عَذَابٍ شَدِيدٍ ﴿٤٦﴾
قُلْ مَا سَأَلْتُكُم مِّنْ أَجْرٍ فَهُوَ لَكُمْ ۖ إِنْ أَجْرِىَ إِلَّا عَلَى ٱللَّهِ ۖ وَهُوَ عَلَىٰ
كُلِّ شَىْءٍ شَهِيدٌ ﴿٤٧﴾ قُلْ إِنَّ رَبِّى يَقْذِفُ بِٱلْحَقِّ عَلَّٰمُ ٱلْغُيُوبِ ﴿٤٨﴾
قُلْ جَآءَ ٱلْحَقُّ وَمَا يُبْدِئُ ٱلْبَٰطِلُ وَمَا يُعِيدُ ﴿٤٩﴾ قُلْ إِن ضَلَلْتُ
فَإِنَّمَآ أَضِلُّ عَلَىٰ نَفْسِى ۖ وَإِنِ ٱهْتَدَيْتُ فَبِمَا يُوحِىٓ إِلَىَّ رَبِّىٓ ۚ إِنَّهُۥ
سَمِيعٌ قَرِيبٌ ﴿٥٠﴾ وَلَوْ تَرَىٰٓ إِذْ فَزِعُوا۟ فَلَا فَوْتَ وَأُخِذُوا۟ مِن
مَّكَانٍ قَرِيبٍ ﴿٥١﴾ وَقَالُوٓا۟ ءَامَنَّا بِهِۦ وَأَنَّىٰ لَهُمُ ٱلتَّنَاوُشُ مِن
مَّكَانٍۭ بَعِيدٍ ﴿٥٢﴾ وَقَدْ كَفَرُوا۟ بِهِۦ مِن قَبْلُ ۖ وَيَقْذِفُونَ
بِٱلْغَيْبِ مِن مَّكَانٍۭ بَعِيدٍ ﴿٥٣﴾ وَحِيلَ بَيْنَهُمْ وَبَيْنَ مَا يَشْتَهُونَ
كَمَا فُعِلَ بِأَشْيَاعِهِم مِّن قَبْلُ ۚ إِنَّهُمْ كَانُوا۟ فِى شَكٍّ مُّرِيبٍۭ ﴿٥٤﴾

44. ***We have not given them any books which they are studying; nor did We send, before you, any warner to them.*** So how can they say that you are lying?

45. ***Those before them also denied the truth, but these people do not have even a tenth of what We gave to them*** in terms of strength, long life and great wealth. ***They denied My Messengers*** to them; ***and how complete was My denial!*** – meaning Allah's rejection of them with respect to punishment and destruction.

46. ***Say: 'I exhort you to do one thing alone: to stand before Allah in pairs and on your own and then reflect. Your companion*** (Muḥammad) ***is not possessed*** (mad). ***He is only a warner come to you ahead of a terrible punishment*** in the Next World if you disobey Him.*'*

47. ***Say*** to them: ***'I have not asked you for any wage*** for warning you and conveying the Message: ***it is all for you. My wage*** (reward) ***is the responsibility of Allah alone. He is witness of everything*** – and knows my truthfulness.*'*

48. ***Say: 'My Lord hurls forth the Truth*** to His Prophets, ***the Knower of all unseen things*** – everything hidden that He has created in the heavens and the earth.*'*

49. ***Say: 'The Truth*** (Islam) ***has come. Falsehood*** (unbelief) ***cannot originate or regenerate*** – and has no real effect.*'*

50. ***Say: 'If I am misguided*** – away from the truth – ***it is only to my detriment*** – meaning only he will suffer from the wrong action of his misguidance; ***but if I am guided, it is by what my Lord reveals to me*** – through both the Qur'an and other wisdom. ***He is All-Hearing*** of supplication, ***Close at hand.'***

51. ***If you***, Muḥammad, ***could only see when they are terrified*** by the Resurrection, then you would see something terrible – ***and there is no way out*** for them to escape from Us, ***and they are seized from a nearby place*** (their graves).

52. ***They will say, 'We believe in it'*** – a reference to either Muḥammad or the Qur'an – ***but how can they reach out for it*** (faith) ***from a distant place*** – meaning from the Next World, when the time for it was this world –

53. ***...when before they had rejected it*** in this world, ***shooting forth about the Unseen, from a distant place?*** – guessing at matters which are invisible to them and very far from their perception, as when they called the Prophet a magician or a poet or a soothsayer, all of which allegations are mentioned in the Qur'an.

54. ***A barrier will be set up between them and the thing that they desire,*** which is acceptance of faith, ***just as was done with their kind before*** – the unbelievers before them***: they too were in a state of crippling doubt.*** They doubted what they now believe, and did not recognise the evidence they were shown in this world.

سُورَةُ فَاطِرٍ

بِسْمِ ٱللَّهِ ٱلرَّحْمَٰنِ ٱلرَّحِيمِ

ٱلْحَمْدُ لِلَّهِ فَاطِرِ ٱلسَّمَٰوَٰتِ وَٱلْأَرْضِ جَاعِلِ ٱلْمَلَٰٓئِكَةِ رُسُلًا أُو۟لِىٓ
أَجْنِحَةٍ مَّثْنَىٰ وَثُلَٰثَ وَرُبَٰعَ ۚ يَزِيدُ فِى ٱلْخَلْقِ مَا يَشَآءُ ۚ إِنَّ ٱللَّهَ عَلَىٰ كُلِّ
شَىْءٍ قَدِيرٌ ﴿١﴾ مَّا يَفْتَحِ ٱللَّهُ لِلنَّاسِ مِن رَّحْمَةٍ فَلَا مُمْسِكَ لَهَا ۖ
وَمَا يُمْسِكْ فَلَا مُرْسِلَ لَهُۥ مِنۢ بَعْدِهِۦ ۚ وَهُوَ ٱلْعَزِيزُ ٱلْحَكِيمُ ﴿٢﴾ يَٰٓأَيُّهَا
ٱلنَّاسُ ٱذْكُرُوا۟ نِعْمَتَ ٱللَّهِ عَلَيْكُمْ ۚ هَلْ مِنْ خَٰلِقٍ غَيْرُ ٱللَّهِ يَرْزُقُكُم
مِّنَ ٱلسَّمَآءِ وَٱلْأَرْضِ ۚ لَآ إِلَٰهَ إِلَّا هُوَ ۖ فَأَنَّىٰ تُؤْفَكُونَ ﴿٣﴾
وَإِن يُكَذِّبُوكَ فَقَدْ كُذِّبَتْ رُسُلٌ مِّن قَبْلِكَ ۚ وَإِلَى ٱللَّهِ تُرْجَعُ ٱلْأُمُورُ
﴿٤﴾ يَٰٓأَيُّهَا ٱلنَّاسُ إِنَّ وَعْدَ ٱللَّهِ حَقٌّ ۖ فَلَا تَغُرَّنَّكُمُ ٱلْحَيَوٰةُ ٱلدُّنْيَا ۖ
وَلَا يَغُرَّنَّكُم بِٱللَّهِ ٱلْغَرُورُ ﴿٥﴾ إِنَّ ٱلشَّيْطَٰنَ لَكُمْ عَدُوٌّ فَٱتَّخِذُوهُ
عَدُوًّا ۚ إِنَّمَا يَدْعُوا۟ حِزْبَهُۥ لِيَكُونُوا۟ مِنْ أَصْحَٰبِ ٱلسَّعِيرِ ﴿٦﴾ ٱلَّذِينَ
كَفَرُوا۟ لَهُمْ عَذَابٌ شَدِيدٌ ۖ وَٱلَّذِينَ ءَامَنُوا۟ وَعَمِلُوا۟ ٱلصَّٰلِحَٰتِ لَهُم
مَّغْفِرَةٌ وَأَجْرٌ كَبِيرٌ ﴿٧﴾ أَفَمَن زُيِّنَ لَهُۥ سُوٓءُ عَمَلِهِۦ فَرَءَاهُ حَسَنًا ۖ
فَإِنَّ ٱللَّهَ يُضِلُّ مَن يَشَآءُ وَيَهْدِى مَن يَشَآءُ ۖ فَلَا تَذْهَبْ نَفْسُكَ
عَلَيْهِمْ حَسَرَٰتٍ ۚ إِنَّ ٱللَّهَ عَلِيمٌۢ بِمَا يَصْنَعُونَ ﴿٨﴾ وَٱللَّهُ ٱلَّذِىٓ أَرْسَلَ
ٱلرِّيَٰحَ فَتُثِيرُ سَحَابًا فَسُقْنَٰهُ إِلَىٰ بَلَدٍ مَّيِّتٍ فَأَحْيَيْنَا بِهِ ٱلْأَرْضَ بَعْدَ

35. *Sūrat Fāṭir*
The Bringer into Being

This *sūra* is Makkan and has 45 or 46 *āyat*s and was sent down after *al-Furqān.*

1. ***Praise be to Allah*** – Allah's praise of Himself in this way was explained at the beginning of *Sūrat Sabā'*, ***the Bringer into Being of the heavens and earth***; the name *Fāṭir* means the One who creates without any prior model. ***He who made the angels messengers*** to the Prophets ***with wings – two, three or four. He adds to creation in any way He wills. Allah has power over all things.***

2. ***Any mercy*** – such as provision and rain – ***Allah opens up to people, no one can withhold; and any He withholds, no one can afterwards release. He is the Almighty*** in His affair***; the All-Wise*** in what He does.

3. ***Mankind*** – particularly the people of Makka, ***remember Allah's blessing upon you*** – by letting you live in the *Ḥaram* and preventing attacks on you. ***Is there any creator other*** (read as *khāliqin ghayru* and *khāliqin ghayri*) ***than Allah providing for you*** with rain ***from heaven and*** with plants from the ***earth?*** The question demands the negative response that there is no Creator and Provider other than Him. ***There is no god but Him. So how have you been perverted?*** How have you turned away from affirming His unity while understanding that He is your Creator and Provider?

4. ***If they deny you,*** Muḥammad, and the Message you bring of Allah's unity, the Resurrection, the Reckoning and the Punishment, ***Messengers before you were also denied*** in the same way; so remain steadfast as they remained steadfast. ***All matters return to Allah*** in the Next World, and He will repay those who deny and those who help the Muslims.

5. ***Mankind, Allah's promise*** regarding the Resurrection and other things ***is true. Do not let the life of this world delude you*** and seduce you into not believing in Allah's promise, ***and do not let the Deluder*** (Shayṭān) ***delude you about Allah*** on account of His deferral of your punishment and His forbearance towards you.

مَوْتِهَا كَذَٰلِكَ ٱلنُّشُورُ ﴿٩﴾ مَن كَانَ يُرِيدُ ٱلْعِزَّةَ فَلِلَّهِ ٱلْعِزَّةُ جَمِيعًا
إِلَيْهِ يَصْعَدُ ٱلْكَلِمُ ٱلطَّيِّبُ وَٱلْعَمَلُ ٱلصَّٰلِحُ يَرْفَعُهُۥ وَٱلَّذِينَ
يَمْكُرُونَ ٱلسَّيِّـَٔاتِ لَهُمْ عَذَابٌ شَدِيدٌ وَمَكْرُ أُو۟لَٰٓئِكَ هُوَ يَبُورُ
﴿١٠﴾ وَٱللَّهُ خَلَقَكُم مِّن تُرَابٍ ثُمَّ مِن نُّطْفَةٍ ثُمَّ جَعَلَكُمْ أَزْوَٰجًا
وَمَا تَحْمِلُ مِنْ أُنثَىٰ وَلَا تَضَعُ إِلَّا بِعِلْمِهِۦ وَمَا يُعَمَّرُ مِن مُّعَمَّرٍ
وَلَا يُنقَصُ مِنْ عُمُرِهِۦٓ إِلَّا فِى كِتَٰبٍ إِنَّ ذَٰلِكَ عَلَى ٱللَّهِ يَسِيرٌ ﴿١١﴾
وَمَا يَسْتَوِى ٱلْبَحْرَانِ هَٰذَا عَذْبٌ فُرَاتٌ سَآئِغٌ شَرَابُهُۥ وَهَٰذَا
مِلْحٌ أُجَاجٌ وَمِن كُلٍّ تَأْكُلُونَ لَحْمًا طَرِيًّا وَتَسْتَخْرِجُونَ
حِلْيَةً تَلْبَسُونَهَا وَتَرَى ٱلْفُلْكَ فِيهِ مَوَاخِرَ لِتَبْتَغُوا۟ مِن فَضْلِهِۦ
وَلَعَلَّكُمْ تَشْكُرُونَ ﴿١٢﴾ يُولِجُ ٱلَّيْلَ فِى ٱلنَّهَارِ وَيُولِجُ
ٱلنَّهَارَ فِى ٱلَّيْلِ وَسَخَّرَ ٱلشَّمْسَ وَٱلْقَمَرَ كُلٌّ يَجْرِى
لِأَجَلٍ مُّسَمًّى ذَٰلِكُمُ ٱللَّهُ رَبُّكُمْ لَهُ ٱلْمُلْكُ وَٱلَّذِينَ
تَدْعُونَ مِن دُونِهِۦ مَا يَمْلِكُونَ مِن قِطْمِيرٍ ﴿١٣﴾ إِن
تَدْعُوهُمْ لَا يَسْمَعُوا۟ دُعَآءَكُمْ وَلَوْ سَمِعُوا۟ مَا ٱسْتَجَابُوا۟ لَكُمْ
وَيَوْمَ ٱلْقِيَٰمَةِ يَكْفُرُونَ بِشِرْكِكُمْ وَلَا يُنَبِّئُكَ مِثْلُ خَبِيرٍ
﴿١٤﴾ ۞ يَٰٓأَيُّهَا ٱلنَّاسُ أَنتُمُ ٱلْفُقَرَآءُ إِلَى ٱللَّهِ وَٱللَّهُ هُوَ ٱلْغَنِىُّ
ٱلْحَمِيدُ ﴿١٥﴾ إِن يَشَأْ يُذْهِبْكُمْ وَيَأْتِ بِخَلْقٍ جَدِيدٍ ﴿١٦﴾
وَمَا ذَٰلِكَ عَلَى ٱللَّهِ بِعَزِيزٍ ﴿١٧﴾ وَلَا تَزِرُ وَازِرَةٌ وِزْرَ أُخْرَىٰ وَإِن
تَدْعُ مُثْقَلَةٌ إِلَىٰ حِمْلِهَا لَا يُحْمَلْ مِنْهُ شَىْءٌ وَلَوْ كَانَ ذَا قُرْبَىٰٓ
إِنَّمَا تُنذِرُ ٱلَّذِينَ يَخْشَوْنَ رَبَّهُم بِٱلْغَيْبِ وَأَقَامُوا۟ ٱلصَّلَوٰةَ

6. ***Shaytan is your enemy, so treat him as an enemy*** by obeying Allah and not obeying him. ***He summons his party*** – those who follow him in unbelief – ***to be among the people of the Searing Blaze.***

7. ***Those who disbelieve will suffer a harsh punishment, but those who believe and do right actions will receive forgiveness and an immense reward.*** This explains what will happen to those who side with Shayṭān and to those who oppose him.

8. This was revealed about Abū Jahl and others. ***And what of him the evil of whose actions appears fine to him*** – through distortion – ***so that he sees them as good?*** Is such a person like someone Allah has guided? ***Allah misguides whomever He wills and guides whomever He wills. So do not let yourself waste away out of regret for them*** – about the fact that they do not believe. ***Allah knows what they do*** and will repay them for it.

9. ***It is Allah who sends the winds*** (read as *riyāḥ,* pl. and also *rīḥ,* sing.) ***which raise*** and stir up ***the clouds which We then drive to a dead*** (read as *mayyit* and *mayt*) ***land*** – with no plants in it – ***and by them bring the earth to life after it was*** dry and ***dead***, making crops and fodder grow in it. ***That is how the Resurrection*** and bringing back to life ***will be.***

10. ***If anyone wants power, all power belongs to Allah*** – in this world and the Next World. If anyone wants power, it is only obtained by obeying Allah, who then gives it to him if He wills. ***All good words rise to Him*** – and He knows them, and they are "There is no god but Allah" and things like that – ***and He raises up*** and accepts ***all virtuous deeds. But people who plot evil deeds*** against the Prophet in the Dār an-Nadwa, to imprison him, kill him or expel him, as mentioned in *Sūrat al-Anfāl* (8:30), ***will suffer a harsh punishment. The plotting of such people is profitless*** and they will be destroyed.

11. ***Allah created you from dust,*** by creating your forefather, Ādam, from it, ***and then from a drop of sperm,*** by creating all his descendants from that, ***and then made you into pairs***, male and female. ***No female becomes pregnant or gives birth except with His knowledge, and no living thing lives long or has its life cut short without that being in a Book*** – the Preserved Tablet. ***That is easy for Allah.***

12. ***The two seas are not the same: the one is*** *very* ***sweet, refresh-ing, delicious to drink; the other salty, bitter to the taste. Yet from both of them you eat fresh flesh*** – fish – ***and extract*** – from the salt sea or from both fresh and salt – ***ornaments for yourselves to wear*** such as pearls and coral. ***And you see ships on them, cleaving through the waves so that you may seek His bounty*** through trade ***and so that perhaps you will be thankful*** to Allah for that.

13. ***He makes night merge into day and day merge into night*** – making them increase – ***and He has made the sun and moon sub-servient, each one running until a specified time*** – until the Day of Rising. ***That is Allah, your Lord. All Sovereignty is His. Those*** (idols) ***you call on*** and worship ***besides Him have no power over even the smallest speck.***

14. ***If you call on them they will not hear your call, and were they to hear they would not respond to you. On the Day of Rising they will reject your making associates of them*** with Allah, meaning declare themselves free of you and your worship of them. ***No one can inform you*** about the states of this world and the Next ***like One who is All-aware*** – and that is Allah Almighty.

15. ***Mankind, you are the poor in need of Allah*** in every state, ***whereas Allah is the Rich Beyond Need*** of His creation, ***the Praiseworthy*** with respect to whatever He does with them.

16. ***If He wills He can dispense with you and bring about a new creation*** to replace you.

17. ***That is not difficult for Allah.***

18. ***No burden-bearer*** (soul) ***can bear another's burden*** of sin. ***If someone weighed down calls for help to bear his load, none of it will be borne for him, even by his next of kin*** – such as a father or son. This mutual inability is the decree of Allah. ***You can only warn those who fear their Lord in the Unseen*** without seeing Him, because they are the ones who benefit from the warning, ***and estab-lish the prayer*** regularly. ***Whoever is purified*** – of *shirk* and other things – ***is purified for himself alone*** – and alone reaps the benefit of it. ***Allah is your final destination***, and He will repay people in the Next World for their actions in this world.

وَمَن تَزَكَّىٰ فَإِنَّمَا يَتَزَكَّىٰ لِنَفْسِهِۦ ۚ وَإِلَى ٱللَّهِ ٱلْمَصِيرُ ﴿١٨﴾
وَمَا يَسْتَوِى ٱلْأَعْمَىٰ وَٱلْبَصِيرُ ﴿١٩﴾ وَلَا ٱلظُّلُمَٰتُ وَلَا ٱلنُّورُ
﴿٢٠﴾ وَلَا ٱلظِّلُّ وَلَا ٱلْحَرُورُ ﴿٢١﴾ وَمَا يَسْتَوِى ٱلْأَحْيَآءُ وَلَا ٱلْأَمْوَٰتُ ۚ
إِنَّ ٱللَّهَ يُسْمِعُ مَن يَشَآءُ ۖ وَمَآ أَنتَ بِمُسْمِعٍ مَّن فِى ٱلْقُبُورِ ﴿٢٢﴾ إِنْ
أَنتَ إِلَّا نَذِيرٌ ﴿٢٣﴾ إِنَّآ أَرْسَلْنَٰكَ بِٱلْحَقِّ بَشِيرًا وَنَذِيرًا ۚ وَإِن مِّنْ
أُمَّةٍ إِلَّا خَلَا فِيهَا نَذِيرٌ ﴿٢٤﴾ وَإِن يُكَذِّبُوكَ فَقَدْ كَذَّبَ ٱلَّذِينَ
مِن قَبْلِهِمْ جَآءَتْهُمْ رُسُلُهُم بِٱلْبَيِّنَٰتِ وَبِٱلزُّبُرِ وَبِٱلْكِتَٰبِ
ٱلْمُنِيرِ ﴿٢٥﴾ ثُمَّ أَخَذْتُ ٱلَّذِينَ كَفَرُوا۟ ۖ فَكَيْفَ كَانَ نَكِيرِ ﴿٢٦﴾
أَلَمْ تَرَ أَنَّ ٱللَّهَ أَنزَلَ مِنَ ٱلسَّمَآءِ مَآءً فَأَخْرَجْنَا بِهِۦ ثَمَرَٰتٍ مُّخْتَلِفًا
أَلْوَٰنُهَا ۚ وَمِنَ ٱلْجِبَالِ جُدَدٌۢ بِيضٌ وَحُمْرٌ مُّخْتَلِفٌ أَلْوَٰنُهَا
وَغَرَابِيبُ سُودٌ ﴿٢٧﴾ وَمِنَ ٱلنَّاسِ وَٱلدَّوَآبِّ وَٱلْأَنْعَٰمِ
مُخْتَلِفٌ أَلْوَٰنُهُۥ كَذَٰلِكَ ۗ إِنَّمَا يَخْشَى ٱللَّهَ مِنْ عِبَادِهِ ٱلْعُلَمَٰٓؤُا۟ ۗ
إِنَّ ٱللَّهَ عَزِيزٌ غَفُورٌ ﴿٢٨﴾ إِنَّ ٱلَّذِينَ يَتْلُونَ كِتَٰبَ ٱللَّهِ
وَأَقَامُوا۟ ٱلصَّلَوٰةَ وَأَنفَقُوا۟ مِمَّا رَزَقْنَٰهُمْ سِرًّا وَعَلَانِيَةً
يَرْجُونَ تِجَٰرَةً لَّن تَبُورَ ﴿٢٩﴾ لِيُوَفِّيَهُمْ أُجُورَهُمْ
وَيَزِيدَهُم مِّن فَضْلِهِۦٓ ۚ إِنَّهُۥ غَفُورٌ شَكُورٌ ﴿٣٠﴾
وَٱلَّذِىٓ أَوْحَيْنَآ إِلَيْكَ مِنَ ٱلْكِتَٰبِ هُوَ ٱلْحَقُّ مُصَدِّقًا لِّمَا بَيْنَ
يَدَيْهِ ۗ إِنَّ ٱللَّهَ بِعِبَادِهِۦ لَخَبِيرٌۢ بَصِيرٌ ﴿٣١﴾ ثُمَّ أَوْرَثْنَا ٱلْكِتَٰبَ
ٱلَّذِينَ ٱصْطَفَيْنَا مِنْ عِبَادِنَا ۖ فَمِنْهُمْ ظَالِمٌ لِّنَفْسِهِۦ وَمِنْهُم
مُّقْتَصِدٌ وَمِنْهُمْ سَابِقٌۢ بِٱلْخَيْرَٰتِ بِإِذْنِ ٱللَّهِ ۚ ذَٰلِكَ هُوَ

19. ***The blind*** (unbelievers) ***and seeing*** (believers) ***are not the same,***

20. ***...nor are darkness*** (unbelief) ***and light*** (faith),

21. ***...nor are cool shade*** (the Garden) ***and fierce heat*** (the Fire).

22. ***The living*** (believers) ***and dead*** (unbelievers) ***are not the same. Allah makes anyone He wills hear*** – and guides them so they respond by believing – ***but you cannot make those in the grave hear*** – meaning unbelievers, who are likened to those in graves who do not respond.

23. ***You are only a warner.***

24. ***We have sent you with the truth*** (guidance), ***bringing good news*** to those who respond to you ***and giving warning*** to those who do not respond. ***There is no community to which a warner*** (Prophet) ***has not come.***

25. ***If they*** (the people of Makka) ***deny you, those before them also denied the truth. Their Messengers came to them with Clear Signs*** (miracles) ***and Psalms*** – which include the Pages of Ibrāhīm – ***and the Illuminating Book*** – the Torah and the Gospel. Be steadfast as they were steadfast.

26. ***Then I seized hold of those who disbelieved,*** on account of their denial, ***and how absolute was My rejection*** of them demonstrated by their punishment and destruction***!***

27. ***Do you not see*** (know) ***that Allah sends down water from the sky and by it We bring forth fruits of varying colours*** – green, red, yellow and other colours? There is a change of person in this sentence from third person singular to first person plural. ***And in the mountains there are streaks of white and red*** – such as paths and other things which are white, red and yellow – ***of varying shades*** of intensity, ***and rocks of deep jet black.***

28. ***And mankind and beasts and livestock are likewise of varying colours*** – in the same way as fruits and mountains. ***Only those of His slaves with knowledge have fear of Allah*** – unlike the ignorant, such as the unbelievers of Makka. ***Allah is Almighty*** in His kingdom, ***Ever-Forgiving*** of the wrong actions of His believing slaves.

29. ***Those who recite the Book of Allah and establish the prayer*** regularly ***and give of what We have provided for them, secretly and***

openly – in other words, pay *zakāt* and give other charity ***hope for a transaction which will not prove profitless*** and come to nothing –

30. ***...that He may pay them their wages in full*** – their reward for those actions mentioned – ***and give them more from His unbounded favour. He is Ever-Forgiving, Ever-Thankful.*** He forgives their wrong actions on account of their obedience.

31. ***What We have revealed to you of the Book*** (the Qur'an) ***is the truth, confirming what*** (Books) ***came before it. Allah is aware of and sees His slaves*** – both their inward and outward.

32. ***Then We made Our chosen slaves inherit the Book*** (the Qur'an). This means the Muslims. ***But some of them wrong themselves*** – by falling short in acting by it; ***some are ambivalent*** – and act by it most of the time; ***and some outdo each other in good by Allah's permission*** (will) – combining teaching and guidance to action with knowledge by the will of Allah. ***That*** – inheritance of the Book – ***is the great favour.***

33. ***They will enter*** (read as *yadkhulūnahā* and *yudkhalūnahā*) – and abide in – ***Gardens of Eden, where they will be adorned with gold bracelets and pearls, and where their clothing will be of silk.***

34. ***They will say, 'Praise be to Allah Who has removed all sadness from us. Truly our Lord is Ever-Forgiving*** of wrong actions, ***Ever-Thankful*** for obedience:

35. ***He who has lodged us, out of His munificence, in the Abode of Permanence where no weariness or fatigue affects us*** – since there is no responsibility.' Both are mentioned, despite their similarity, to stress the absence of them.

36. ***But for those who disbelieve there will be the Fire of Hell. They will not be killed off so that they die, and its punishment will not be lightened for them*** – for even the blink of an eye. ***That is how We repay*** (read as *najzī,* and also *yuzjā*, in which case the meaning becomes "is repaid") ***every thankless man.***

37. ***They will shout out*** for help ***in it, 'Our Lord, take us out*** of it! ***We will act rightly, differently from the way we used to act!'*** They will be told: ***Did We not let you live long enough for anyone who was going to pay heed to pay heed? And did not the warner*** (Messenger) ***come to you*** – and yet you failed to respond? ***Taste it,***

ٱلۡفَضۡلُ ٱلۡكَبِيرُ ﴿٣٢﴾ جَنَّٰتُ عَدۡنٖ يَدۡخُلُونَهَا يُحَلَّوۡنَ
فِيهَا مِنۡ أَسَاوِرَ مِن ذَهَبٖ وَلُؤۡلُؤٗاۖ وَلِبَاسُهُمۡ فِيهَا حَرِيرٞ ﴿٣٣﴾
وَقَالُواْ ٱلۡحَمۡدُ لِلَّهِ ٱلَّذِيٓ أَذۡهَبَ عَنَّا ٱلۡحَزَنَۖ إِنَّ رَبَّنَا لَغَفُورٞ
شَكُورٌ ﴿٣٤﴾ ٱلَّذِيٓ أَحَلَّنَا دَارَ ٱلۡمُقَامَةِ مِن فَضۡلِهِۦ لَا يَمَسُّنَا
فِيهَا نَصَبٞ وَلَا يَمَسُّنَا فِيهَا لُغُوبٞ ﴿٣٥﴾ وَٱلَّذِينَ كَفَرُواْ لَهُمۡ
نَارُ جَهَنَّمَ لَا يُقۡضَىٰ عَلَيۡهِمۡ فَيَمُوتُواْ وَلَا يُخَفَّفُ عَنۡهُم مِّنۡ
عَذَابِهَاۚ كَذَٰلِكَ نَجۡزِي كُلَّ كَفُورٖ ﴿٣٦﴾ وَهُمۡ يَصۡطَرِخُونَ
فِيهَا رَبَّنَآ أَخۡرِجۡنَا نَعۡمَلۡ صَٰلِحًا غَيۡرَ ٱلَّذِي كُنَّا نَعۡمَلُۚ
أَوَلَمۡ نُعَمِّرۡكُم مَّا يَتَذَكَّرُ فِيهِ مَن تَذَكَّرَ وَجَآءَكُمُ ٱلنَّذِيرُۖ
فَذُوقُواْ فَمَا لِلظَّٰلِمِينَ مِن نَّصِيرٍ ﴿٣٧﴾ إِنَّ ٱللَّهَ عَٰلِمُ
غَيۡبِ ٱلسَّمَٰوَٰتِ وَٱلۡأَرۡضِۚ إِنَّهُۥ عَلِيمُۢ بِذَاتِ ٱلصُّدُورِ ﴿٣٨﴾
هُوَ ٱلَّذِي جَعَلَكُمۡ خَلَٰٓئِفَ فِي ٱلۡأَرۡضِۚ فَمَن كَفَرَ فَعَلَيۡهِ كُفۡرُهُۥۖ وَلَا
يَزِيدُ ٱلۡكَٰفِرِينَ كُفۡرُهُمۡ عِندَ رَبِّهِمۡ إِلَّا مَقۡتٗاۖ وَلَا يَزِيدُ ٱلۡكَٰفِرِينَ
كُفۡرُهُمۡ إِلَّا خَسَارٗا ﴿٣٩﴾ قُلۡ أَرَءَيۡتُمۡ شُرَكَآءَكُمُ ٱلَّذِينَ تَدۡعُونَ مِن
دُونِ ٱللَّهِ أَرُونِي مَاذَا خَلَقُواْ مِنَ ٱلۡأَرۡضِ أَمۡ لَهُمۡ شِرۡكٞ فِي ٱلسَّمَٰوَٰتِ
أَمۡ ءَاتَيۡنَٰهُمۡ كِتَٰبٗا فَهُمۡ عَلَىٰ بَيِّنَتٖ مِّنۡهُۚ بَلۡ إِن يَعِدُ ٱلظَّٰلِمُونَ
بَعۡضُهُم بَعۡضًا إِلَّا غُرُورًا ﴿٤٠﴾ ۞ إِنَّ ٱللَّهَ يُمۡسِكُ ٱلسَّمَٰوَٰتِ
وَٱلۡأَرۡضَ أَن تَزُولَاۚ وَلَئِن زَالَتَآ إِنۡ أَمۡسَكَهُمَا مِنۡ أَحَدٖ مِّنۢ بَعۡدِهِۦٓۚ
إِنَّهُۥ كَانَ حَلِيمًا غَفُورٗا ﴿٤١﴾ وَأَقۡسَمُواْ بِٱللَّهِ جَهۡدَ أَيۡمَٰنِهِمۡ لَئِن
جَآءَهُمۡ نَذِيرٞ لَّيَكُونُنَّ أَهۡدَىٰ مِنۡ إِحۡدَى ٱلۡأُمَمِۖ فَلَمَّا جَآءَهُمۡ نَذِيرٞ

then! There is no helper for the wrongdoers (unbelievers). They will have no helper to avert the punishment from them.

38. ***Allah knows the Unseen of the heavens and earth. Allah knows what the heart contains*** – and so it is more likely that He will know other things about people's situation.

39. ***It is He who made you khalifs on the earth*** – meaning that they succeed one another. ***So whoever disbelieves, his unbelief is against himself. In Allah's sight,*** the evil consequences of ***the unbelief of the unbelievers only increases their loathsomeness*** by incurring Allah's anger***; the unbelief of the unbelievers only increases their loss*** in the Next World.

40. ***Say: 'Have you thought about your partner gods, those you call upon*** and worship ***besides Allah*** – meaning the idols which you claim are the partners of Allah***? Show*** (inform) ***me what they have created of the earth; or do they have a partnership*** with Allah ***in the heavens?' Have We given them a Book whose Clear Signs they follow*** – stating that they have partnership***? No indeed! The wrong-doers*** (unbelievers) ***promise each other nothing but delusion*** – falsehood, when they say that the idols will intercede for them.

41. ***Allah keeps a firm hold on the heavens and earth, preventing them from vanishing away. And if they vanished no one could then keep hold of them*** except Him. ***Certainly He is Most Forbearing, Ever-Forgiving*** – and defers the punishment of the unbelievers.

42. ***They*** (the unbelievers of Makka) ***swore by Allah with their most earnest*** and strongest ***oaths that if a warner*** (Messenger) ***came to them they would be better guided than any other community*** – than the Jews, the Christians and others. This was when they saw that they denied one another, since the Jews said, "The Christians have no basis," and the Christians say, "The Jews have no basis." ***But then when a warner*** – Muḥammad, may Allah bless him and grant him peace – ***did come to them, it only increased their aversion*** to guidance –

43. ***...shown by their arrogance*** – regarding the faith – ***in the land and evil plotting*** – *shirk* and other things. ***But evil plotting envelops only those who do it.*** It encompasses the one who plots. Plotting was described as fundamentally evil. ***Do they expect anything but the***

مَّا زَادَهُمْ إِلَّا نُفُورًا ﴿٤٢﴾ ٱسْتِكْبَارًا فِى ٱلْأَرْضِ وَمَكْرَ ٱلسَّيِّئِ ۚ
وَلَا يَحِيقُ ٱلْمَكْرُ ٱلسَّيِّئُ إِلَّا بِأَهْلِهِۦ ۚ فَهَلْ يَنظُرُونَ إِلَّا سُنَّتَ
ٱلْأَوَّلِينَ ۚ فَلَن تَجِدَ لِسُنَّتِ ٱللَّهِ تَبْدِيلًا ۖ وَلَن تَجِدَ لِسُنَّتِ ٱللَّهِ تَحْوِيلًا
﴿٤٣﴾ أَوَلَمْ يَسِيرُوا۟ فِى ٱلْأَرْضِ فَيَنظُرُوا۟ كَيْفَ كَانَ عَـٰقِبَةُ ٱلَّذِينَ مِن
قَبْلِهِمْ وَكَانُوٓا۟ أَشَدَّ مِنْهُمْ قُوَّةً ۚ وَمَا كَانَ ٱللَّهُ لِيُعْجِزَهُۥ مِن شَىْءٍ
فِى ٱلسَّمَـٰوَٰتِ وَلَا فِى ٱلْأَرْضِ ۚ إِنَّهُۥ كَانَ عَلِيمًا قَدِيرًا ﴿٤٤﴾
وَلَوْ يُؤَاخِذُ ٱللَّهُ ٱلنَّاسَ بِمَا كَسَبُوا۟ مَا تَرَكَ عَلَىٰ
ظَهْرِهَا مِن دَآبَّةٍ وَلَـٰكِن يُؤَخِّرُهُمْ إِلَىٰٓ أَجَلٍ مُّسَمًّى ۖ
فَإِذَا جَآءَ أَجَلُهُمْ فَإِنَّ ٱللَّهَ كَانَ بِعِبَادِهِۦ بَصِيرًۢا ﴿٤٥﴾

pattern of previous peoples? The custom of Allah with them is to punish them for their denying their Messengers. ***You will not find any changing in the pattern of Allah. You will not find any alteration in the pattern of Allah.*** There is no alteration with regard to His punishing others nor with regard to letting it descend on other than those who merit it.

44. ***Have they not travelled in the land and seen the final fate of those before them?*** Allah destroyed these people for their denial of their Messengers. ***They were far greater than them in strength. Allah cannot be withstood in any way, either in the heavens or on earth.*** He cannot be escaped. ***He is All-Knowing, All-Powerful.***

45. ***If Allah were to take mankind to task for what*** – acts of disobedience – ***they have earned, He would not leave a single creature crawling on it*** (the earth)***; but He is deferring them until a specified time*** – the Day of Rising. ***Then, when their time comes, Allah sees His slaves*** – and will repay them for their actions by rewarding the believers and punishing the unbelievers.

سُورَةُ يسٓ

بِسْمِ ٱللَّهِ ٱلرَّحْمَٰنِ ٱلرَّحِيمِ

يسٓ ﴿١﴾ وَٱلْقُرْءَانِ ٱلْحَكِيمِ ﴿٢﴾ إِنَّكَ لَمِنَ ٱلْمُرْسَلِينَ ﴿٣﴾ عَلَىٰ
صِرَٰطٍ مُّسْتَقِيمٍ ﴿٤﴾ تَنزِيلَ ٱلْعَزِيزِ ٱلرَّحِيمِ ﴿٥﴾ لِتُنذِرَ قَوْمًا مَّآ
أُنذِرَ ءَابَآؤُهُمْ فَهُمْ غَٰفِلُونَ ﴿٦﴾ لَقَدْ حَقَّ ٱلْقَوْلُ عَلَىٰٓ أَكْثَرِهِمْ
فَهُمْ لَا يُؤْمِنُونَ ﴿٧﴾ إِنَّا جَعَلْنَا فِىٓ أَعْنَٰقِهِمْ أَغْلَٰلًا فَهِىَ إِلَى
ٱلْأَذْقَانِ فَهُم مُّقْمَحُونَ ﴿٨﴾ وَجَعَلْنَا مِنۢ بَيْنِ أَيْدِيهِمْ سَدًّا
وَمِنْ خَلْفِهِمْ سَدًّا فَأَغْشَيْنَٰهُمْ فَهُمْ لَا يُبْصِرُونَ ﴿٩﴾ وَسَوَآءٌ
عَلَيْهِمْ ءَأَنذَرْتَهُمْ أَمْ لَمْ تُنذِرْهُمْ لَا يُؤْمِنُونَ ﴿١٠﴾ إِنَّمَا تُنذِرُ
مَنِ ٱتَّبَعَ ٱلذِّكْرَ وَخَشِىَ ٱلرَّحْمَٰنَ بِٱلْغَيْبِ ۖ فَبَشِّرْهُ بِمَغْفِرَةٍ
وَأَجْرٍ كَرِيمٍ ﴿١١﴾ إِنَّا نَحْنُ نُحْىِ ٱلْمَوْتَىٰ وَنَكْتُبُ
مَا قَدَّمُوا۟ وَءَاثَٰرَهُمْ ۚ وَكُلَّ شَىْءٍ أَحْصَيْنَٰهُ فِىٓ إِمَامٍ مُّبِينٍ ﴿١٢﴾
وَٱضْرِبْ لَهُم مَّثَلًا أَصْحَٰبَ ٱلْقَرْيَةِ إِذْ جَآءَهَا ٱلْمُرْسَلُونَ ﴿١٣﴾
إِذْ أَرْسَلْنَآ إِلَيْهِمُ ٱثْنَيْنِ فَكَذَّبُوهُمَا فَعَزَّزْنَا بِثَالِثٍ فَقَالُوٓا۟ إِنَّآ
إِلَيْكُم مُّرْسَلُونَ ﴿١٤﴾ قَالُوا۟ مَآ أَنتُمْ إِلَّا بَشَرٌ مِّثْلُنَا وَمَآ أَنزَلَ
ٱلرَّحْمَٰنُ مِن شَىْءٍ إِنْ أَنتُمْ إِلَّا تَكْذِبُونَ ﴿١٥﴾ قَالُوا۟ رَبُّنَا يَعْلَمُ إِنَّآ
إِلَيْكُمْ لَمُرْسَلُونَ ﴿١٦﴾ وَمَا عَلَيْنَآ إِلَّا ٱلْبَلَٰغُ ٱلْمُبِينُ ﴿١٧﴾
قَالُوٓا۟ إِنَّا تَطَيَّرْنَا بِكُمْ ۖ لَئِن لَّمْ تَنتَهُوا۟ لَنَرْجُمَنَّكُمْ وَلَيَمَسَّنَّكُم
مِّنَّا عَذَابٌ أَلِيمٌ ﴿١٨﴾ قَالُوا۟ طَٰٓئِرُكُم مَّعَكُمْ ۚ أَئِن ذُكِّرْتُم ۚ
بَلْ أَنتُمْ قَوْمٌ مُّسْرِفُونَ ﴿١٩﴾ وَجَآءَ مِنْ أَقْصَا ٱلْمَدِينَةِ رَجُلٌ

36. *Sūrat Yasin*
Yasin

This *sūra* is Makkan except for *āyat* 45, which is Madinan. It has 83 *āyat*s and was sent down after *al-Jinn.*

1. ***Ya Sin.*** Allah knows best what is meant by that.

2. ***By the Wise Qur'an.*** The meaning of "Wise" here is connected to the wondrous order of the Qur'an as well as its profound meanings.

3. ***Truly you,*** Muḥammad, ***are one of the Messengers...***

4. ***...on a Straight Path*** – the Path of those before who had *tawḥīd* and guidance. It is stressed by the oath and other things to refute the unbelievers' statement to the Prophet that he was not one of the Messengers.

5. ***...the revelation of the Almighty*** in His kingdom, ***the Most Merciful*** to His creation. This refers to the Qur'an –

6. ***... so that you may warn a people whose fathers were not warned*** – during the gap between Prophets – ***and who are therefore unaware*** and have neglected faith and guidance.

7. ***The sentence*** that they would be punished ***has been justly carried out against most of them, so they do not believe.***

8. ***We have put iron collars round their necks, reaching up to the chin, so that their heads are forced back.*** Their hands are chained to their necks and pulled up to their necks, so their heads are forced back so that they cannot lower them. This is a metaphor. What is meant is that they do not submit to Islam and so their heads will be forced back.

9. ***We have placed a barrier*** (read as *saddan* and *suddan*) ***in front of them and a barrier behind them, blindfolding them so that they cannot see.*** This is another metaphor for how the path of faith is barred to them.

10. ***It makes no difference to them whether you warn them or do not warn them: they will not believe.***

11. ***You can only warn those who act on the Reminder*** (the Qur'an) – and benefit from your warning – ***and fear the All-Merciful in the***

Unseen. Give them the good news of forgiveness and a generous reward – the Garden.

12. ***We bring the dead to life*** at the Resurrection ***and We record*** in the Preserved Tablet ***what they send ahead*** – the good and evil they do in this world in order to repay them – ***and what they leave behind*** – the customs and traditions they institute which remain behind when they die. ***We have listed*** and explained ***everything*** precisely ***in a clear register*** a reference to the Preserved Tablet.

13. ***Make an example for them of the inhabitants of the city*** (Antioch) ***when the Messengers*** – from 'Īsā – ***came to it.***

14. ***When We sent them two and they denied them both, so We reinforced*** (read as *'azzaznā* and *'azaznā*) ***them with a third. They said, 'Truly We have been sent to you as Messengers.'***

15. ***They said, 'You are nothing but human beings like ourselves. The All-Merciful has not sent down anything. You are simply lying.'***

16. ***They said, 'Our Lord knows we have been sent as Messengers to you.*** This is like an oath and stresses what they say because of the denial they were facing.

17. ***We are only responsible for clear transmission.'*** This was done on the basis of clear evidence such as healing the blind, lepers and the sick and bringing the dead to life.

18. ***They said, 'We see an evil omen in you*** – we think that you are bad luck for us since rain has been withheld from us because of you. ***If you do not stop we will stone you and you will suffer a painful punishment at our hands.'***

19. ***They said, 'Your evil omen is in yourselves*** – on account of your unbelief. ***Is it not just that you have been reminded?*** This question implies rebuke. ***No, you are an unbridled people!'*** You have exceeded the limits through your attribution of partners to Allah.

20. ***A man*** – this was someone called Ḥabīb an-Najjār who believed in the Messengers and lived in the furthest part of the city – ***came running from the far side of the city*** – when he heard that the people had denied the Messengers – ***saying, 'My people, follow the Messengers!***

يَسْعَىٰ قَالَ يَـٰقَوْمِ ٱتَّبِعُوا۟ ٱلْمُرْسَلِينَ ﴿٢٠﴾ ٱتَّبِعُوا۟ مَن
لَّا يَسْـَٔلُكُمْ أَجْرًا وَهُم مُّهْتَدُونَ ﴿٢١﴾ وَمَا لِىَ لَآ أَعْبُدُ ٱلَّذِى
فَطَرَنِى وَإِلَيْهِ تُرْجَعُونَ ﴿٢٢﴾ ءَأَتَّخِذُ مِن دُونِهِۦٓ ءَالِهَةً إِن
يُرِدْنِ ٱلرَّحْمَـٰنُ بِضُرٍّ لَّا تُغْنِ عَنِّى شَفَـٰعَتُهُمْ شَيْـًٔا وَلَا
يُنقِذُونِ ﴿٢٣﴾ إِنِّىٓ إِذًا لَّفِى ضَلَـٰلٍ مُّبِينٍ ﴿٢٤﴾ إِنِّىٓ ءَامَنتُ
بِرَبِّكُمْ فَٱسْمَعُونِ ﴿٢٥﴾ قِيلَ ٱدْخُلِ ٱلْجَنَّةَ ۖ قَالَ يَـٰلَيْتَ قَوْمِى
يَعْلَمُونَ ﴿٢٦﴾ بِمَا غَفَرَ لِى رَبِّى وَجَعَلَنِى مِنَ ٱلْمُكْرَمِينَ ﴿٢٧﴾
۞ وَمَآ أَنزَلْنَا عَلَىٰ قَوْمِهِۦ مِنۢ بَعْدِهِۦ مِن جُندٍ مِّنَ ٱلسَّمَآءِ وَمَا
كُنَّا مُنزِلِينَ ﴿٢٨﴾ إِن كَانَتْ إِلَّا صَيْحَةً وَٰحِدَةً فَإِذَا هُمْ خَـٰمِدُونَ
﴿٢٩﴾ يَـٰحَسْرَةً عَلَى ٱلْعِبَادِ ۚ مَا يَأْتِيهِم مِّن رَّسُولٍ إِلَّا كَانُوا۟ بِهِۦ
يَسْتَهْزِءُونَ ﴿٣٠﴾ أَلَمْ يَرَوْا۟ كَمْ أَهْلَكْنَا قَبْلَهُم مِّنَ ٱلْقُرُونِ
أَنَّهُمْ إِلَيْهِمْ لَا يَرْجِعُونَ ﴿٣١﴾ وَإِن كُلٌّ لَّمَّا جَمِيعٌ لَّدَيْنَا مُحْضَرُونَ
﴿٣٢﴾ وَءَايَةٌ لَّهُمُ ٱلْأَرْضُ ٱلْمَيْتَةُ أَحْيَيْنَـٰهَا وَأَخْرَجْنَا مِنْهَا حَبًّا
فَمِنْهُ يَأْكُلُونَ ﴿٣٣﴾ وَجَعَلْنَا فِيهَا جَنَّـٰتٍ مِّن نَّخِيلٍ
وَأَعْنَـٰبٍ وَفَجَّرْنَا فِيهَا مِنَ ٱلْعُيُونِ ﴿٣٤﴾ لِيَأْكُلُوا۟ مِن ثَمَرِهِۦ
وَمَا عَمِلَتْهُ أَيْدِيهِمْ ۖ أَفَلَا يَشْكُرُونَ ﴿٣٥﴾ سُبْحَـٰنَ ٱلَّذِى
خَلَقَ ٱلْأَزْوَٰجَ كُلَّهَا مِمَّا تُنۢبِتُ ٱلْأَرْضُ وَمِنْ أَنفُسِهِمْ
وَمِمَّا لَا يَعْلَمُونَ ﴿٣٦﴾ وَءَايَةٌ لَّهُمُ ٱلَّيْلُ نَسْلَخُ مِنْهُ ٱلنَّهَارَ
فَإِذَا هُم مُّظْلِمُونَ ﴿٣٧﴾ وَٱلشَّمْسُ تَجْرِى لِمُسْتَقَرٍّ لَّهَا ۚ
ذَٰلِكَ تَقْدِيرُ ٱلْعَزِيزِ ٱلْعَلِيمِ ﴿٣٨﴾ وَٱلْقَمَرَ قَدَّرْنَـٰهُ مَنَازِلَ حَتَّىٰ

21. ***Follow*** – the word "follow" is repeated for emphasis – ***those who do not ask you for any wage*** for conveying the Message ***and who have received guidance.*** They said to him, "You follow their religion." He replied:

22. ***Why indeed should I not worship Him Who brought me into being***, meaning that there is nothing to keep him or them from worshipping Allah***: Him to Whom you will be returned*** after death and He Who will repay you for your unbelief***?***

23. ***Am I to take as gods*** (idols) ***instead of Him those whose intercession, if the All-Merciful desires harm for me, will not help me at all and cannot save me?*** This is a question which demands a negative response. That for which they claim divinity will not be able to help anyone against Allah.

24. ***In that case*** – if I were to worship other than Allah – ***I would clearly be misguided.***

25. ***I believe in your Lord, so listen to me!'*** But they stoned him to death.

26. ***He was told*** – when he died – ***'Enter the Garden!'*** It is said that he entered it when he was still alive. ***He said, 'If my people only knew…***

27. ***…how my Lord has forgiven me and placed me among the honoured ones!'***

28. ***We did not send down to his people*** – the people of Ḥabīb – ***any host from heaven*** – angels to destroy them – ***after him*** – after his death – ***nor would We send one down.***

29. ***It was but one Great Blast and they were extinct.*** Their punishment was one Shout from Jibrīl and they were dead.

30. ***Alas for My slaves*** – those and their like who denied the Messengers sent to them and were destroyed***!*** This is a vocal expression indicating very great pain. It is metaphorical, with the meaning: "This is your time, so attend!" – ***No Messenger comes to them without their mocking him*** – and this mockery is what leads to their destruction.

31. ***Do they*** – the people of Makka who say to the Prophet, "You are not a Messenger" – ***not see how many generations*** (past nations)

before them We have destroyed and that they will not return to them? So will they not reflect on what happened to them?

32. ***Each and every one*** (read as *inna kullun lammā* and *inna kullun lamā*) ***will be summoned to Our presence*** – in the Place of Standing after they are resurrected and are summoned for the Reckoning.

33. ***A Sign*** – evidence of the Resurrection – ***for them is the dead land*** (read as *mayta* and *mayyata*) ***which We bring to life and from which*** – after mixing it with water – ***We bring forth grain*** (wheat) ***of which they eat.***

34. ***We place in it gardens of dates and grapes, and cause springs to gush out in*** some of ***it,***

35. ***…so they may eat its fruits*** (read as *thamarihi* and *thumurihi*) – the fruits of the palm and other plants. ***They did not do it them - selves.*** They did not create the fruits themselves. ***So will they not be thankful*** for Allah's blessings***?***

36. ***Glory be to Him who created all the pairs*** (species) ***from what the earth produces*** – in terms of grains and other things, ***and from*** – males and females among ***themselves and from things unknown to them*** – strange and wondrous creatures about which they do not know.

37. ***A Sign*** – evidence of Allah's immense power – ***for them is the night: We peel the day away*** – separate it – ***from it and there they are, in darkness.***

38. ***And the sun runs to its resting place.*** The sun is a Sign for them on its own, or it is an aspect of the previous Sign. The moon is also a Sign. ***That is the decree of the Almighty*** in His kingdom, ***the All-Knowing*** of His creation.

39. ***And We have decreed*** twenty-eight ***set phases for the moon*** (read as *al-qamara* and *al-qamaru*) each month ***until it ends up looking like an old palm spathe.*** It is concealed for two nights if the month is thirty days and one night if it is twenty-nine, and then it appears to the eye like a curved, yellow old palm spathe.

40. ***It is not for the sun to overtake the moon*** in the night ***nor for the night to outstrip the day*** – and come before the end of the day***;*** ***each one*** – each luminous body: the sun, moon and stars – ***is swim -***

عَادَ كَٱلْعُرْجُونِ ٱلْقَدِيمِ ﴿٣٩﴾ لَا ٱلشَّمْسُ يَنۢبَغِي لَهَآ أَن تُدْرِكَ
ٱلْقَمَرَ وَلَا ٱلَّيْلُ سَابِقُ ٱلنَّهَارِ وَكُلٌّ فِي فَلَكٍ يَسْبَحُونَ ﴿٤٠﴾
وَءَايَةٌ لَّهُمْ أَنَّا حَمَلْنَا ذُرِّيَّتَهُمْ فِي ٱلْفُلْكِ ٱلْمَشْحُونِ ﴿٤١﴾ وَخَلَقْنَا
لَهُم مِّن مِّثْلِهِۦ مَا يَرْكَبُونَ ﴿٤٢﴾ وَإِن نَّشَأْ نُغْرِقْهُمْ فَلَا صَرِيخَ لَهُمْ
وَلَا هُمْ يُنقَذُونَ ﴿٤٣﴾ إِلَّا رَحْمَةً مِّنَّا وَمَتَٰعًا إِلَىٰ حِينٍ ﴿٤٤﴾ وَإِذَا
قِيلَ لَهُمُ ٱتَّقُوا۟ مَا بَيْنَ أَيْدِيكُمْ وَمَا خَلْفَكُمْ لَعَلَّكُمْ تُرْحَمُونَ ﴿٤٥﴾
وَمَا تَأْتِيهِم مِّنْ ءَايَةٍ مِّنْ ءَايَٰتِ رَبِّهِمْ إِلَّا كَانُوا۟ عَنْهَا مُعْرِضِينَ
﴿٤٦﴾ وَإِذَا قِيلَ لَهُمْ أَنفِقُوا۟ مِمَّا رَزَقَكُمُ ٱللَّهُ قَالَ ٱلَّذِينَ كَفَرُوا۟
لِلَّذِينَ ءَامَنُوٓا۟ أَنُطْعِمُ مَن لَّوْ يَشَآءُ ٱللَّهُ أَطْعَمَهُۥٓ إِنْ أَنتُمْ إِلَّا فِي
ضَلَٰلٍ مُّبِينٍ ﴿٤٧﴾ وَيَقُولُونَ مَتَىٰ هَٰذَا ٱلْوَعْدُ إِن كُنتُمْ صَٰدِقِينَ
﴿٤٨﴾ مَا يَنظُرُونَ إِلَّا صَيْحَةً وَٰحِدَةً تَأْخُذُهُمْ وَهُمْ يَخِصِّمُونَ
﴿٤٩﴾ فَلَا يَسْتَطِيعُونَ تَوْصِيَةً وَلَآ إِلَىٰٓ أَهْلِهِمْ يَرْجِعُونَ ﴿٥٠﴾
وَنُفِخَ فِي ٱلصُّورِ فَإِذَا هُم مِّنَ ٱلْأَجْدَاثِ إِلَىٰ رَبِّهِمْ يَنسِلُونَ
﴿٥١﴾ قَالُوا۟ يَٰوَيْلَنَا مَنۢ بَعَثَنَا مِن مَّرْقَدِنَا ۜ هَٰذَا مَا وَعَدَ ٱلرَّحْمَٰنُ
وَصَدَقَ ٱلْمُرْسَلُونَ ﴿٥٢﴾ إِن كَانَتْ إِلَّا صَيْحَةً
وَٰحِدَةً فَإِذَا هُمْ جَمِيعٌ لَّدَيْنَا مُحْضَرُونَ ﴿٥٣﴾ فَٱلْيَوْمَ لَا تُظْلَمُ
نَفْسٌ شَيْـًٔا وَلَا تُجْزَوْنَ إِلَّا مَا كُنتُمْ تَعْمَلُونَ ﴿٥٤﴾
إِنَّ أَصْحَٰبَ ٱلْجَنَّةِ ٱلْيَوْمَ فِي شُغُلٍ فَٰكِهُونَ ﴿٥٥﴾ هُمْ وَأَزْوَٰجُهُمْ
فِي ظِلَٰلٍ عَلَى ٱلْأَرَآئِكِ مُتَّكِـُٔونَ ﴿٥٦﴾ لَهُمْ فِيهَا فَٰكِهَةٌ وَلَهُم
مَّا يَدَّعُونَ ﴿٥٧﴾ سَلَٰمٌ قَوْلًا مِّن رَّبٍّ رَّحِيمٍ ﴿٥٨﴾ وَٱمْتَٰزُوا۟ ٱلْيَوْمَ

ming in a sphere – an orbit. The form of the verb used here is that usually reserved for sentient creatures.

41. ***A Sign for them*** – of the power of Allah – ***is that We carried their families*** (read as *dhuriyya*, singular, and *dhuriyyāt*, plural) – here meaning ancestors – ***in the laden ship*** – the Ark of Nūḥ.

42. ***And We have created for them the like of it*** (Nūḥ's Ark) – similar ships, large and small, which they make in the same form thanks to Allah's teaching them how to do so – ***in which they sail.***

43. ***If We wished, We could drown them*** – in spite of the existence of the ships – ***with no one to hear their cry*** for help, ***and then they would not be saved –***

44. ***...except as an act of mercy from Us, to give them enjoyment for a time.*** Nothing could save them except for Our mercy to them and then they would only enjoy the pleasures of life until the end of their decreed life-spans.

45. ***They are told, 'Be fearful of what is before you*** – punishment in this world like what happened to others before you – ***and behind you*** – meaning the punishment coming in the Next World – ***so that perhaps you may have mercy shown to you*** and your wrong actions may be overlooked.'

46. ***Not one of your Lord's Signs comes to them without their turning away from it.***

47. ***And when they are told*** by the poor among the Companions, ***'Spend*** on us ***from the provision*** of wealth ***Allah has given you,' those who disbelieve say*** in mockery ***to those who believe, 'Why should we feed someone whom*** – according to your belief – ***if He wished, Allah would feed Himself? You are clearly in error.'*** This is an explicit statement of their unbelief.

48. ***And they say, 'When will this promise*** – of the Resurrection – ***come about if you are telling the truth*** about it?'

49. Allah says: ***What are they waiting for but one Great Blast*** – the first blast of the Trumpet by Isrāfīl – ***to seize them while they are quibbling*** (read as *yakhaṣṣimūna* and *yakhṣimūna*)? This means that they are heedless of it because they are involved in quibbling, selling, eating, drinking and other things.

50. ***They will not be able to make a will or return to their families*** from their markets and business: they will die there.

51. ***The Trumpet will be blown*** – this refers to the second blast of the Trumpet for the Resurrection; there will be forty years between the two blasts – ***and at once they will be sliding*** swiftly ***from their graves towards their Lord.***

52. ***They*** – the unbelievers among them – ***will say, 'Alas for us!*** – "Alas on account of our destruction!" The word for "alas", *wayl,* is a verbal noun for which there is no actual verbal form. ***Who has raised us from our resting-place?*** They say this because, between the Two Blasts, they were unconscious and not being punished. ***This*** Resurrection ***is what the All-Merciful promised us. The Messengers were telling the truth.'*** They will affirm what the Messengers said at a time when that will be of no avail to them. It is also said that those words will be said to them.

53. ***It will be but one Great Blast, and they will all be summoned to Our presence.***

54. ***Today no self will be wronged in any way. You will only be repaid for what you did.***

55. ***The Companions of the Garden are busy*** (read as *shughulin* and *shughlin*) ***enjoying themselves today,*** made oblivious to what the People of the Fire are suffering by the delights they are enjoying such as consorting with virgins. There is no occupation in which they become tired, because there is no weariness in the Garden. They will be in absolute bliss –

56. ***...they and their wives reclining on couches*** – the word used refers to a couch or a bed in an alcove – ***in the shade*** – away from the direct impact of the sun.

57. ***They will have fruits there and*** enjoy ***whatever they request.***

58. ***'Peace!' A word from a Merciful Lord.*** This is what He says to them, meaning, "Peace be upon you."

59. ***'Keep yourselves apart today, you evildoers!*** "Separate yourselves from the believers!" This is when they are mixed together.

60. ***Did I not make a contract with you, tribe of Ādam,*** and command you on the tongues of My Messengers ***not to worship*** and obey ***Shayṭān, who truly is an outright*** clear ***enemy to you...***

أَيُّهَا ٱلْمُجْرِمُونَ ﴿٥٩﴾ ۞ أَلَمْ أَعْهَدْ إِلَيْكُمْ يَٰبَنِىٓ ءَادَمَ أَن لَّا
تَعْبُدُوا۟ ٱلشَّيْطَٰنَ ۖ إِنَّهُۥ لَكُمْ عَدُوٌّ مُّبِينٌ ﴿٦٠﴾ وَأَنِ ٱعْبُدُونِى ۚ
هَٰذَا صِرَٰطٌ مُّسْتَقِيمٌ ﴿٦١﴾ وَلَقَدْ أَضَلَّ مِنكُمْ جِبِلًّا كَثِيرًا ۖ
أَفَلَمْ تَكُونُوا۟ تَعْقِلُونَ ﴿٦٢﴾ هَٰذِهِۦ جَهَنَّمُ ٱلَّتِى كُنتُمْ تُوعَدُونَ
﴿٦٣﴾ ٱصْلَوْهَا ٱلْيَوْمَ بِمَا كُنتُمْ تَكْفُرُونَ ﴿٦٤﴾ ٱلْيَوْمَ نَخْتِمُ
عَلَىٰٓ أَفْوَٰهِهِمْ وَتُكَلِّمُنَآ أَيْدِيهِمْ وَتَشْهَدُ أَرْجُلُهُم بِمَا كَانُوا۟
يَكْسِبُونَ ﴿٦٥﴾ وَلَوْ نَشَآءُ لَطَمَسْنَا عَلَىٰٓ أَعْيُنِهِمْ فَٱسْتَبَقُوا۟
ٱلصِّرَٰطَ فَأَنَّىٰ يُبْصِرُونَ ﴿٦٦﴾ وَلَوْ نَشَآءُ لَمَسَخْنَٰهُمْ
عَلَىٰ مَكَانَتِهِمْ فَمَا ٱسْتَطَٰعُوا۟ مُضِيًّا وَلَا يَرْجِعُونَ
﴿٦٧﴾ وَمَن نُّعَمِّرْهُ نُنَكِّسْهُ فِى ٱلْخَلْقِ ۖ أَفَلَا يَعْقِلُونَ ﴿٦٨﴾
وَمَا عَلَّمْنَٰهُ ٱلشِّعْرَ وَمَا يَنۢبَغِى لَهُۥٓ ۚ إِنْ هُوَ إِلَّا ذِكْرٌ وَقُرْءَانٌ مُّبِينٌ
﴿٦٩﴾ لِّيُنذِرَ مَن كَانَ حَيًّا وَيَحِقَّ ٱلْقَوْلُ عَلَى ٱلْكَٰفِرِينَ ﴿٧٠﴾
أَوَلَمْ يَرَوْا۟ أَنَّا خَلَقْنَا لَهُم مِّمَّا عَمِلَتْ أَيْدِينَآ أَنْعَٰمًا فَهُمْ لَهَا
مَٰلِكُونَ ﴿٧١﴾ وَذَلَّلْنَٰهَا لَهُمْ فَمِنْهَا رَكُوبُهُمْ وَمِنْهَا يَأْكُلُونَ ﴿٧٢﴾
وَلَهُمْ فِيهَا مَنَٰفِعُ وَمَشَارِبُ ۖ أَفَلَا يَشْكُرُونَ ﴿٧٣﴾ وَٱتَّخَذُوا۟
مِن دُونِ ٱللَّهِ ءَالِهَةً لَّعَلَّهُمْ يُنصَرُونَ ﴿٧٤﴾ لَا يَسْتَطِيعُونَ
نَصْرَهُمْ وَهُمْ لَهُمْ جُندٌ مُّحْضَرُونَ ﴿٧٥﴾ فَلَا يَحْزُنكَ قَوْلُهُمْ
إِنَّا نَعْلَمُ مَا يُسِرُّونَ وَمَا يُعْلِنُونَ ﴿٧٦﴾ أَوَلَمْ يَرَ ٱلْإِنسَٰنُ أَنَّا
خَلَقْنَٰهُ مِن نُّطْفَةٍ فَإِذَا هُوَ خَصِيمٌ مُّبِينٌ ﴿٧٧﴾ وَضَرَبَ لَنَا
مَثَلًا وَنَسِىَ خَلْقَهُۥ ۖ قَالَ مَن يُحْىِ ٱلْعِظَٰمَ وَهِىَ رَمِيمٌ ﴿٧٨﴾

61. ***...but to worship*** and obey ***Me***, affirming My unity***? That is a straight path.***

62. ***He has led huge numbers*** (read as *jibillan* and *jubulan*) ***of you into error. Why did you not use your intellect*** – and see his enmity and misguidance, or the punishment which befell your predecessors and so believe*?* This will be said to them in the Next World.

63. ***This is the Hell that you were promised.***

64. ***Roast in it today because you were unbelievers.'***

65. ***Today We seal up their*** (the unbelievers') ***mouths*** – when they say, "*By Allah, our Lord, We were not idolaters*" (6:23) – ***and their hands speak to us, and their feet bear witness to what they have earned.*** Each of their limbs will speak and say what it did.

66. ***If We wished, We could put out their eyes*** and blind them. ***Then, though they might race for the path*** – as it was their custom to do – ***how would they see*** it then*?* They would not be able to.

67. ***If We wished, We could transform them*** into monkeys and pigs, or into stones ***where they stand*** (read as *makānatihim*, sing. and *makānātihim* pl.) – meaning in their homes – ***so they would neither be able to go out nor return.***

68. ***When We grant long life*** (read as *nunakkis'hu* and *nankus'hu*) ***to people, We return them to their primal state*** – so that after strength and youth come weakness and senility**.** ***So will they not use their intellect*** (read as *ya'qilūna* and *ta'qilūna*, "will you not use")***?*** "Will you not understand that it is known that the One who has the power to do that has the power to resurrect you? Then you should believe."

69. ***We did not teach him*** (the Prophet) ***poetry nor would it be right for him.*** This refutes their claim that the Qur'an is poetry. Poetry is not easy for him. ***It is simply a reminder and a clear Qur'an*** – a recitation which makes clear Divine judgements and other things –

70. ***...so that they may warn*** (read as *yundhiru* and *tundhiru*, "you may warn") ***those who are truly alive*** – and understand what is said to them, in other words the believers, ***and so that the Word*** – decreeing punishment for them – ***may be carried out against the unbelievers*** – who are like the dead who do not understand what is said to them.

71. ***Have they not seen*** and grasped ***how We created for them*** (mankind) ***by Our own handiwork*** – without any partner or helper – ***livestock*** – camels, cattle and sheep and goats – ***which are under their control?*** The question demands a positive response.

72. ***We have made them tame for them*** – and subjected them to them – ***and some they ride and some they eat.***

73. ***And they have other uses*** – for example in their wool, fur and hair – ***for them, and milk to drink. So will they not be thankful*** to the One who has blessed them with these things, and therefore believe*?* In other words, they have not done so.

74. ***They have taken gods besides Allah*** – the idols which they worship – ***so that perhaps they may be helped*** – defended from the punishment of Allah Almighty by the alleged intercession of their gods.

75. ***They*** (their gods) ***cannot help them even though they are an army mobilised in their support*** – as they allege. The plural of sentient things is used for them. They will be present with them in the Fire.

76. ***So do not let their words distress you*** – their saying, "You are not a Messenger" and other such things. ***We know what they keep secret and what they divulge*** – and We will repay them for that.

77. ***Does not man*** – said to refer specifically to al-'Āṣi ibn Wā'il – ***see*** and know ***that We created him from a drop*** of sperm and nurtured him until he was strong, ***yet there he is, an open antagonist*** – strongly opposing Allah and clearly denying the Resurrection*!*

78. ***He makes likenesses of Us*** – attributing divine powers to other things – ***and forgets his own creation*** – from sperm, which is more extraordinary than the likenesses he makes – ***saying, 'Who will give life to bones when they are decayed?'*** It is related that Allah will take the decayed bones and knit them together. Al-'Āṣi ibn Wā'il asked the Prophet, may Allah bless him and grant him peace, "Do you think that Allah will bring this (body of mine) to life after it is decayed and crushed?" The Prophet, may Allah bless him and grant him peace, answered, "Yes, and He will make you enter the Fire."

79. ***Say 'He who made them in the first place will bring them back to life. He has total knowledge of each created thing*** – He knows all things in detail and in whole before and after their creation.

قُلۡ يُحۡيِيهَا ٱلَّذِيٓ أَنشَأَهَآ أَوَّلَ مَرَّةٖۖ وَهُوَ بِكُلِّ خَلۡقٍ عَلِيمٌ
٧٩ ٱلَّذِي جَعَلَ لَكُم مِّنَ ٱلشَّجَرِ ٱلۡأَخۡضَرِ نَارٗا فَإِذَآ أَنتُم
مِّنۡهُ تُوقِدُونَ ٨٠ أَوَلَيۡسَ ٱلَّذِي خَلَقَ ٱلسَّمَٰوَٰتِ وَٱلۡأَرۡضَ
بِقَٰدِرٍ عَلَىٰٓ أَن يَخۡلُقَ مِثۡلَهُمۚ بَلَىٰ وَهُوَ ٱلۡخَلَّٰقُ ٱلۡعَلِيمُ ٨١
إِنَّمَآ أَمۡرُهُۥٓ إِذَآ أَرَادَ شَيۡـًٔا أَن يَقُولَ لَهُۥ كُن فَيَكُونُ ٨٢
فَسُبۡحَٰنَ ٱلَّذِي بِيَدِهِۦ مَلَكُوتُ كُلِّ شَيۡءٖ وَإِلَيۡهِ تُرۡجَعُونَ ٨٣

80. ***He Who produces fire for you*** and all mankind ***from*** the wood of ***green trees*** – the stick of the fire-drill of the Arabs which comes from the Markh tree and the 'Afār tree, or any tree except the vine – ***so that you use them to light your fires.'*** You ignite fires with them. This is further evidence of Allah's power to resurrect. There is both water, fire and wood in it. The water does not extinguish the fire and the fire does not burn up the wood.

81. ***Does He who created the heavens and earth*** – in all their immensity – ***not have the power to create the same again*** – meaning human beings, who are far less of a challenge***? Yes indeed!*** He indeed has the power to do that. ***He is the Creator*** – using the intensive form, a*l-Khallāq,* implying that He creates a a great deal***, the All-Knowing*** of everything He creates**.**

82. ***His command when He desires*** to create ***a thing is just to say to it, 'Be!' and it is*** (read as *yakūnu* and *yakūna).*

83. ***Glory be to Him Who has the Dominion of all things in His Hand. To Him you will be returned*** in the Next World**.**

سُورَةُ الصَّافَّاتِ

بِسۡمِ ٱللَّهِ ٱلرَّحۡمَٰنِ ٱلرَّحِيمِ

وَٱلصَّٰٓفَّٰتِ صَفّٗا ١ فَٱلزَّٰجِرَٰتِ زَجۡرٗا ٢ فَٱلتَّٰلِيَٰتِ ذِكۡرًا ٣
إِنَّ إِلَٰهَكُمۡ لَوَٰحِدٞ ٤ رَّبُّ ٱلسَّمَٰوَٰتِ وَٱلۡأَرۡضِ وَمَا بَيۡنَهُمَا وَرَبُّ
ٱلۡمَشَٰرِقِ ٥ إِنَّا زَيَّنَّا ٱلسَّمَآءَ ٱلدُّنۡيَا بِزِينَةٍ ٱلۡكَوَاكِبِ ٦ وَحِفۡظٗا
مِّن كُلِّ شَيۡطَٰنٖ مَّارِدٖ ٧ لَّا يَسَّمَّعُونَ إِلَى ٱلۡمَلَإِ ٱلۡأَعۡلَىٰ وَيُقۡذَفُونَ
مِن كُلِّ جَانِبٖ ٨ دُحُورٗاۖ وَلَهُمۡ عَذَابٞ وَاصِبٌ ٩ إِلَّا مَنۡ خَطِفَ
ٱلۡخَطۡفَةَ فَأَتۡبَعَهُۥ شِهَابٞ ثَاقِبٞ ١٠ فَٱسۡتَفۡتِهِمۡ أَهُمۡ أَشَدُّ خَلۡقًا
أَم مَّنۡ خَلَقۡنَآۚ إِنَّا خَلَقۡنَٰهُم مِّن طِينٖ لَّازِبِۭ ١١ بَلۡ عَجِبۡتَ
وَيَسۡخَرُونَ ١٢ وَإِذَا ذُكِّرُواْ لَا يَذۡكُرُونَ ١٣ وَإِذَا رَأَوۡاْ ءَايَةٗ يَسۡتَسۡخِرُونَ
١٤ وَقَالُوٓاْ إِنۡ هَٰذَآ إِلَّا سِحۡرٞ مُّبِينٌ ١٥ أَءِذَا مِتۡنَا وَكُنَّا تُرَابٗا وَعِظَٰمًا
أَءِنَّا لَمَبۡعُوثُونَ ١٦ أَوَءَابَآؤُنَا ٱلۡأَوَّلُونَ ١٧ قُلۡ نَعَمۡ وَأَنتُمۡ دَٰخِرُونَ
١٨ فَإِنَّمَا هِيَ زَجۡرَةٞ وَٰحِدَةٞ فَإِذَا هُمۡ يَنظُرُونَ ١٩ وَقَالُواْ يَٰوَيۡلَنَا هَٰذَا
يَوۡمُ ٱلدِّينِ ٢٠ هَٰذَا يَوۡمُ ٱلۡفَصۡلِ ٱلَّذِي كُنتُم بِهِۦ تُكَذِّبُونَ ٢١
۞ ٱحۡشُرُواْ ٱلَّذِينَ ظَلَمُواْ وَأَزۡوَٰجَهُمۡ وَمَا كَانُواْ يَعۡبُدُونَ ٢٢ مِن دُونِ
ٱللَّهِ فَٱهۡدُوهُمۡ إِلَىٰ صِرَٰطِ ٱلۡجَحِيمِ ٢٣ وَقِفُوهُمۡۖ إِنَّهُم مَّسۡـُٔولُونَ ٢٤
مَا لَكُمۡ لَا تَنَاصَرُونَ ٢٥ بَلۡ هُمُ ٱلۡيَوۡمَ مُسۡتَسۡلِمُونَ ٢٦ وَأَقۡبَلَ بَعۡضُهُمۡ
عَلَىٰ بَعۡضٖ يَتَسَآءَلُونَ ٢٧ قَالُوٓاْ إِنَّكُمۡ كُنتُمۡ تَأۡتُونَنَا عَنِ ٱلۡيَمِينِ ٢٨
قَالُواْ بَل لَّمۡ تَكُونُواْ مُؤۡمِنِينَ ٢٩ وَمَا كَانَ لَنَا عَلَيۡكُم مِّن سُلۡطَٰنِۭۖ
بَلۡ كُنتُمۡ قَوۡمٗا طَٰغِينَ ٣٠ فَحَقَّ عَلَيۡنَا قَوۡلُ رَبِّنَآۖ إِنَّا لَذَآئِقُونَ ٣١

37. *Sūrat aṣ-Ṣāffāt*
Those in Ranks

This *sūra* is Makkan. It has 182 *āyat*s and was sent down after *al-An'ām.*

1. ***By those*** angels ***drawn up in ranks*** – in prayer lines or on their wings in the air, waiting to see what they will be commanded to do –

2. ***...and by the warners crying warning*** – the angels who drive along the clouds –

3. ***...and by the reciters of the Reminder*** (the Qur'an)*:*

4. ***...your God is One,***

5. ***Lord of the heavens and the earth and everything between them; Lord of the Easts*** and the Wests, which is a reference to the rising and setting of the sun every day.

6. ***We have adorned the lowest heaven with the beauty of the stars*** – or the light given by them –

7. ***...and guarded it*** with meteors ***against every defiant*** – the word for "defiant", *mārid* means refusing any obedience – ***shayṭān.***

8. They (the *shayāṭīn*) ***cannot eavesdrop*** (read as *yassamma'ūna* and *yasma'ūna*) ***on the Highest Assembly*** – a gathering of angels in heaven which is guarded in the way described***; and they are stoned*** – by meteors ***from every side*** of heaven –

9. ***...repelled*** – driven far away and expelled – ***with harshness. They will suffer eternal punishment*** in the Next World –

10. ***...except for him who*** passes by and ***snatches a snippet and then is pursued by a piercing flame.*** The only one able to eavesdrop is one *shayṭān* who hears a word from the angels and takes it swiftly but is then pursued by a luminous star to pierce him, burn him, or confuse him.

11. ***Ask them*** (the people of Makka) ***for a* fatwā** (decision) – this is for affirmation or for rebuke***: is it they who are stronger in structure or other things*** – such as the angels, the heavens and the earths and what is in them – ***We have created? We created them*** in the primary form of Ādam ***from sticky clay*** – which sticks to the hand, the implication being that having been created weak people should not be arrogant by denying the Prophet and the Qur'an. That will lead to their quick destruction.

12. ***No wonder you are surprised*** (read as *'ajabta* and *'ajabtu* meaning "I am surprised") ***as they laugh with scorn!*** This is addressed to the Prophet, may Allah bless him and grant him peace, and refers to their denial of him.

13. ***When they are reminded*** – by means of the Qur'an – ***they do not pay heed.***

14. ***When they see a Sign*** – like the splitting of the moon – ***they only laugh with scorn*** and make a mockery of it.

15. ***They say*** about it, ***'This is just downright magic.*** They deny the resurrection:

16. ***When*** (read as *annā* and, *a'innā*) ***we are dead and turned to dust and bones, will we then be raised up again alive?***

17. ***And our early forefathers*** (read as *awa abā'un* and *aw abā'un*) ***as well?'*** The question is: will they be among those who are resurrected as well?

18. ***Say*** to them: ***'Yes***, you will be raised up ***– and you will be in a despicable state*** of abasement.'

19. ***There will be but one Great Blast*** – after which all creatures will be brought back to life – ***and then their eyes will open,*** waiting to see what will be done to them.

20. ***They*** (the unbelievers) ***will say, 'Alas for us!*** – referring to the reality they are now facing. ***This is the Day of Reckoning*** and Repayment!'

21. ***This is the Day of Decision*** between creatures which ***you used to deny.*** Then the angels will be instructed:

22. ***Assemble those who did wrong*** to themselves by committing *shirk*, ***together with their associates*** among the jinn ***and what*** (idols) ***they worshipped...***

23. ***...besides Allah, and guide*** and drive ***them to the Path of the Blazing Fire!***

24. ***And call them to a halt*** at the *Ṣirāṭ*. ***They will be asked*** about all of their words and deeds. Then they will be rebuked as follows:

25. ***'Why are you not helping one another*** – as you did in your worldly lives***?'*** It will be said of them:

26. ***No, today they come*** – humbled – ***in absolute submission.***

27. ***They will confront each other, questioning one another*** – blaming and arguing with one another.

28. ***One group*** (the followers) ***will say*** to those they followed***, 'You used to come at us from a position of power.'*** Literally: "Come at us from the right," meaning from a direction which they completely trusted since they swore that they had the truth. That is why they believed them and followed them. But they misled them.

29. ***The others*** (those who were followed) ***will say*** to their followers***: 'The truth is that you were not believers.*** You were happy to be misguided. If you had been believers, you would not have believed in us.

30. ***We had no authority over you*** to compel you to follow us***; rather you were unbridled people*** – misguided like us.

31. ***Our Lord's Word*** decreeing punishment ***has been carried out against us*** – and is mandatory for all of us, an example of which is Allah's words: *"I will fill up Hell with the jinn and mankind all together."* (11:119) – ***that we would taste it*** (the punishment).

32. ***We misled you and*** (because) ***we were ourselves misled.'***

33. Allah says: ***On that Day*** – the Day of Rising – ***they will be partners in the punishment*** – just as they were partners in the error.

34. ***That is how We deal with evildoers.*** We will deal with them as we dealt with those people in the past by punishing both followers and followed.

35. ***When they were told, 'There is no god but Allah,' they were arrogant.***

36. ***They said, 'Are we to forsake our gods for a mad poet*** – meaning Muḥammad***?'***

37. Allah says: ***Rather he has brought the truth and confirmed the Messengers*** – who brought it. It is: "There is no god but Allah."

38. ***You will definitely taste the painful punishment…***

39. ***…and you will only be repaid for what you did –***

40. ***except for Allah's chosen slaves.***

فَأَغْوَيْنَٰكُمْ إِنَّا كُنَّا غَٰوِينَ ﴿٣٢﴾ فَإِنَّهُمْ يَوْمَئِذٍ فِى ٱلْعَذَابِ مُشْتَرِكُونَ
﴿٣٣﴾ إِنَّا كَذَٰلِكَ نَفْعَلُ بِٱلْمُجْرِمِينَ ﴿٣٤﴾ إِنَّهُمْ كَانُوٓا۟ إِذَا قِيلَ لَهُمْ
لَآ إِلَٰهَ إِلَّا ٱللَّهُ يَسْتَكْبِرُونَ ﴿٣٥﴾ وَيَقُولُونَ أَئِنَّا لَتَارِكُوٓا۟ ءَالِهَتِنَا
لِشَاعِرٍ مَّجْنُونٍۭ ﴿٣٦﴾ بَلْ جَآءَ بِٱلْحَقِّ وَصَدَّقَ ٱلْمُرْسَلِينَ ﴿٣٧﴾ إِنَّكُمْ
لَذَآئِقُوا۟ ٱلْعَذَابِ ٱلْأَلِيمِ ﴿٣٨﴾ وَمَا تُجْزَوْنَ إِلَّا مَا كُنتُمْ تَعْمَلُونَ
﴿٣٩﴾ إِلَّا عِبَادَ ٱللَّهِ ٱلْمُخْلَصِينَ ﴿٤٠﴾ أُو۟لَٰٓئِكَ لَهُمْ رِزْقٌ مَّعْلُومٌ ﴿٤١﴾
فَوَٰكِهُ ۖ وَهُم مُّكْرَمُونَ ﴿٤٢﴾ فِى جَنَّٰتِ ٱلنَّعِيمِ ﴿٤٣﴾ عَلَىٰ سُرُرٍ مُّتَقَٰبِلِينَ
﴿٤٤﴾ يُطَافُ عَلَيْهِم بِكَأْسٍ مِّن مَّعِينٍۭ ﴿٤٥﴾ بَيْضَآءَ لَذَّةٍ لِّلشَّٰرِبِينَ
﴿٤٦﴾ لَا فِيهَا غَوْلٌ وَلَا هُمْ عَنْهَا يُنزَفُونَ ﴿٤٧﴾ وَعِندَهُمْ قَٰصِرَٰتُ
ٱلطَّرْفِ عِينٌ ﴿٤٨﴾ كَأَنَّهُنَّ بَيْضٌ مَّكْنُونٌ ﴿٤٩﴾ فَأَقْبَلَ بَعْضُهُمْ عَلَىٰ
بَعْضٍ يَتَسَآءَلُونَ ﴿٥٠﴾ قَالَ قَآئِلٌ مِّنْهُمْ إِنِّى كَانَ لِى قَرِينٌ ﴿٥١﴾
يَقُولُ أَءِنَّكَ لَمِنَ ٱلْمُصَدِّقِينَ ﴿٥٢﴾ أَءِذَا مِتْنَا وَكُنَّا تُرَابًا وَعِظَٰمًا أَءِنَّا
لَمَدِينُونَ ﴿٥٣﴾ قَالَ هَلْ أَنتُم مُّطَّلِعُونَ ﴿٥٤﴾ فَٱطَّلَعَ فَرَءَاهُ فِى سَوَآءِ
ٱلْجَحِيمِ ﴿٥٥﴾ قَالَ تَٱللَّهِ إِن كِدتَّ لَتُرْدِينِ ﴿٥٦﴾ وَلَوْلَا نِعْمَةُ رَبِّى
لَكُنتُ مِنَ ٱلْمُحْضَرِينَ ﴿٥٧﴾ أَفَمَا نَحْنُ بِمَيِّتِينَ ﴿٥٨﴾ إِلَّا مَوْتَتَنَا
ٱلْأُولَىٰ وَمَا نَحْنُ بِمُعَذَّبِينَ ﴿٥٩﴾ إِنَّ هَٰذَا لَهُوَ ٱلْفَوْزُ ٱلْعَظِيمُ ﴿٦٠﴾
لِمِثْلِ هَٰذَا فَلْيَعْمَلِ ٱلْعَٰمِلُونَ ﴿٦١﴾ أَذَٰلِكَ خَيْرٌ نُّزُلًا أَمْ شَجَرَةُ
ٱلزَّقُّومِ ﴿٦٢﴾ إِنَّا جَعَلْنَٰهَا فِتْنَةً لِّلظَّٰلِمِينَ ﴿٦٣﴾ إِنَّهَا شَجَرَةٌ
تَخْرُجُ فِىٓ أَصْلِ ٱلْجَحِيمِ ﴿٦٤﴾ طَلْعُهَا كَأَنَّهُۥ رُءُوسُ ٱلشَّيَٰطِينِ
﴿٦٥﴾ فَإِنَّهُمْ لَءَاكِلُونَ مِنْهَا فَمَالِـُٔونَ مِنْهَا ٱلْبُطُونَ ﴿٦٦﴾ ثُمَّ إِنَّ لَهُمْ

41. ***They will have preordained provision*** – in Paradise, morning and evening –

42. ***...sweet fruits*** – this refers to things that are eaten for pleasure, not for the preservation of health, because the people of the Garden have no need to preserve their bodies which are everlasting there, ***and high honour*** – indicated by the reward from Allah –

43. ***...in Gardens of Delight...***

44. ***...on couches face to face*** – so they do not see one another's backs.

45. ***A cup from a flowing spring will pass round among them,*** so that each of them drink from it. The spring is one of wine which flows on the surface of the earth like rivers of water in this world –

46. ***... as white as driven snow*** – whiter than milk, ***delicious to those who drink*** – unlike the wine of this world, which is unpleasant,

47. ***...which has no headache in it*** – and does not befuddle their intellects – ***and does not leave them stupefied*** (read as *yunzafūna* and *yunzifūna*) – meaning make them insensible. It is therefore different from the wine of this world.

48. ***There will be dark-eyed maidens with them, with eyes reserved for them alone*** – meaning that they confine their eyes to their husbands and do not look at anyone other than them –

49. ***...just like closely guarded pearls.*** This refers to their colour; they are like the white of ostriches, covered with their feathers so that dust does not reach them. This whitish yellow is the best complexion for women.

50. They (the people of the Garden) ***will confront each other, questioning one another*** about what happened to them in this world.

51. ***One of them will say, 'I used to have a friend*** – who denied the Resurrection –

52. ***...who would say to me*** – to rebuke him for believing in the Resurrection – ***"Are you one of those who say that it is true:***

53. ***...that when we have died and are turned to dust and bones, we will face a Reckoning*** – and be paid back?"'

54. ***He will say*** to his brothers**,** ***'Are you looking down*** with me at Hell to see what his state is***?'*** They will answer, "No."

55. ***So he*** – the speaker, who is one of the people of Paradise – ***will look down and see him*** (his comrade) ***in the midst of the Blazing Fire…***

56. ***…and say*** to him in rebuke***: 'By Allah, you almost ruined me*** by your error***!***

57. ***If it were not for the blessing of my Lord*** – the faith He gave me – ***I would have been among those arraigned*** with you in the Fire***.'*** Then the people of the Garden say:

58. ***Are we not going to die,***

59. ***…except for our first death*** in the world***? Are we not going to be punished?*** This question is prompted by their joy at the blessing of Allah by granting them eternal life and not punishing them.

60. ***Truly this*** – what has been mentioned regarding the reward of the people of the Garden – ***is the Great Victory!***

61. ***It is for the like of this that all workers should work!'*** It is possible that these words are said to them; it is also said that they are the ones who say them.

62. ***Is that*** – the things which have been mentioned – ***better by way of hospitality*** – and other things prepared for the one who alights there – ***or the tree of Zaqqūm***, which is prepared for the people of the Fire***?*** Zaqqūm is the foulest of bitter trees in Tihāma which Allah will make grow in Hellfire, as will be discussed later –

63. ***…which We have made to be an ordeal for the wrongdoers?*** It was a test for the unbelievers among the people of Makka when they said, "Fire burns trees, so how can it grow there?"

64. ***It is a tree that emerges in the depths of the Blazing Fire*** – the base of Hellfire, and its branches rise through its levels**.**

65. ***Its fruits are just like the heads of*** **shayṭāns** – resembling ugly snakes.

66. ***They*** (the unbelievers) ***will eat from it and fill their bellies with it*** in spite of its ugliness, because of the severity of their hunger**.**

عَلَيْهَا لَشَوْبًا مِّنْ حَمِيمٍ ﴿٦٧﴾ ثُمَّ إِنَّ مَرْجِعَهُمْ لَإِلَى ٱلْجَحِيمِ ﴿٦٨﴾
إِنَّهُمْ أَلْفَوْا۟ ءَابَآءَهُمْ ضَآلِّينَ ﴿٦٩﴾ فَهُمْ عَلَىٰٓ ءَاثَٰرِهِمْ يُهْرَعُونَ ﴿٧٠﴾
وَلَقَدْ ضَلَّ قَبْلَهُمْ أَكْثَرُ ٱلْأَوَّلِينَ ﴿٧١﴾ وَلَقَدْ أَرْسَلْنَا فِيهِم
مُّنذِرِينَ ﴿٧٢﴾ فَٱنظُرْ كَيْفَ كَانَ عَٰقِبَةُ ٱلْمُنذَرِينَ ﴿٧٣﴾
إِلَّا عِبَادَ ٱللَّهِ ٱلْمُخْلَصِينَ ﴿٧٤﴾ وَلَقَدْ نَادَىٰنَا نُوحٌ فَلَنِعْمَ
ٱلْمُجِيبُونَ ﴿٧٥﴾ وَنَجَّيْنَٰهُ وَأَهْلَهُۥ مِنَ ٱلْكَرْبِ ٱلْعَظِيمِ ﴿٧٦﴾
وَجَعَلْنَا ذُرِّيَّتَهُۥ هُمُ ٱلْبَاقِينَ ﴿٧٧﴾ وَتَرَكْنَا عَلَيْهِ فِى ٱلْـَٔاخِرِينَ ﴿٧٨﴾ سَلَٰمٌ
عَلَىٰ نُوحٍ فِى ٱلْعَٰلَمِينَ ﴿٧٩﴾ إِنَّا كَذَٰلِكَ نَجْزِى ٱلْمُحْسِنِينَ ﴿٨٠﴾ إِنَّهُۥ مِنْ
عِبَادِنَا ٱلْمُؤْمِنِينَ ﴿٨١﴾ ثُمَّ أَغْرَقْنَا ٱلْـَٔاخَرِينَ ﴿٨٢﴾ ۞ وَإِنَّ مِن
شِيعَتِهِۦ لَإِبْرَٰهِيمَ ﴿٨٣﴾ إِذْ جَآءَ رَبَّهُۥ بِقَلْبٍ سَلِيمٍ ﴿٨٤﴾ إِذْ قَالَ
لِأَبِيهِ وَقَوْمِهِۦ مَاذَا تَعْبُدُونَ ﴿٨٥﴾ أَئِفْكًا ءَالِهَةً دُونَ ٱللَّهِ تُرِيدُونَ
﴿٨٦﴾ فَمَا ظَنُّكُم بِرَبِّ ٱلْعَٰلَمِينَ ﴿٨٧﴾ فَنَظَرَ نَظْرَةً فِى ٱلنُّجُومِ ﴿٨٨﴾
فَقَالَ إِنِّى سَقِيمٌ ﴿٨٩﴾ فَتَوَلَّوْا۟ عَنْهُ مُدْبِرِينَ ﴿٩٠﴾ فَرَاغَ إِلَىٰٓ ءَالِهَتِهِمْ
فَقَالَ أَلَا تَأْكُلُونَ ﴿٩١﴾ مَا لَكُمْ لَا تَنطِقُونَ ﴿٩٢﴾ فَرَاغَ عَلَيْهِمْ ضَرْبًۢا
بِٱلْيَمِينِ ﴿٩٣﴾ فَأَقْبَلُوٓا۟ إِلَيْهِ يَزِفُّونَ ﴿٩٤﴾ قَالَ أَتَعْبُدُونَ مَا تَنْحِتُونَ
﴿٩٥﴾ وَٱللَّهُ خَلَقَكُمْ وَمَا تَعْمَلُونَ ﴿٩٦﴾ قَالُوا۟ ٱبْنُوا۟ لَهُۥ بُنْيَٰنًا فَأَلْقُوهُ
فِى ٱلْجَحِيمِ ﴿٩٧﴾ فَأَرَادُوا۟ بِهِۦ كَيْدًا فَجَعَلْنَٰهُمُ ٱلْأَسْفَلِينَ ﴿٩٨﴾
وَقَالَ إِنِّى ذَاهِبٌ إِلَىٰ رَبِّى سَيَهْدِينِ ﴿٩٩﴾ رَبِّ هَبْ لِى مِنَ ٱلصَّٰلِحِينَ
﴿١٠٠﴾ فَبَشَّرْنَٰهُ بِغُلَٰمٍ حَلِيمٍ ﴿١٠١﴾ فَلَمَّا بَلَغَ مَعَهُ ٱلسَّعْىَ قَالَ
يَٰبُنَىَّ إِنِّىٓ أَرَىٰ فِى ٱلْمَنَامِ أَنِّىٓ أَذْبَحُكَ فَٱنظُرْ مَاذَا تَرَىٰ ۚ قَالَ
يَٰٓأَبَتِ ٱفْعَلْ مَا تُؤْمَرُ ۖ سَتَجِدُنِىٓ إِن شَآءَ ٱللَّهُ مِنَ ٱلصَّٰبِرِينَ ﴿١٠٢﴾

67. ***Then they will have a boiling brew*** – scalding water which they drink – ***to drink on top of it*** – and it mixes with what they have eaten and makes the pain worse.

68. ***Then their destination will be the Blazing Fire.*** This implies that they emerge from it to drink the boiling water.

69. ***They found their fathers misguided...***

70. ***...and they are following hard upon their heels.*** They are moved to follow them and hasten to do so.

71. ***Most of the earlier peoples*** (past nations) ***went astray before them,***

72. ***...though We sent warners to them*** – Messengers who tried to make them fear.

73. ***See the final fate of those who were warned;*** the unbelievers whose final end is the Fire –

74. ***...except for Allah's chosen slaves*** (the believers). They will be saved from the punishment because of their sincerity in worship or because Allah will deliver them.

75. ***Nūḥ called out to Us*** with the words: *"I am overwhelmed, so help me!"* (54:10), ***and what an excellent Responder We are!*** He asked us to help him against his people and so We destroyed them with the Flood.

76. ***We rescued him and his family from the terrible plight*** of drowning –

77. ***...and made his descendants the survivors,*** so all human beings are the descendants of Nūḥ, peace be upon him. He had three sons: Sām, who is the father of the Arabs, Persians and Greeks; Ḥām, who is the father of the blacks; and Yāfith, who is the father of the Turks the Khazars, and Ya'jūj and Ma'jūj and the rest –

78. ***...and We left the later people*** – both Prophets and their nations – ***to say of him*** – in praise until the Day of Rising:

79. ***'Peace*** – from us – ***be upon Nūḥ among all beings!'***

80. ***That*** – repayment – ***is how we recompense the good-doers.***

81. ***He truly was one of Our slaves who are believers.***

82. ***Then We drowned the rest***: the unbelievers of his people.

83. ***One of his followers*** – the word used here, *shī'a*, means party or followers on the basis of their *dīn* – ***in faith was Ibrāhīm*** – there was a long time between them, said to be 2640 years, during which the Prophets Hūd and Ṣāliḥ were sent –

84. ***...when he came to his Lord with an unblemished heart*** – free from doubt and any other flaws –

85. ***...and said to his father and his people*** – to rebuke them – ***'What are you worshipping?***

86. ***Is it falsehood*** – the word used here, *ifk,* denotes the worst form of lying, ***gods besides Allah, that you desire?*** This means: Why do you worship something other than Allah?"

87. ***So what are your thoughts about the Lord of all the worlds?'*** Did they think that Allah would leave them to worship something other than Him without punishing them? They were astrologers. They went out to their festival and left their food with their idols, claiming that they would receive blessing for doing so. Then when they returned, they ate the food. They told Ibrāhīm, "Come out with us."

88. ***He took a look at the stars,*** suggesting to them that he relied on them so that they would trust him,

89. ***...and said, 'I am sick.'*** He pretended to see there that he would become ill.

90. ***So they turned their backs on him*** and went off to their festival.

91. ***He turned surreptitiously to their gods*** – the idols they worshipped, where the food had been left – ***and said, 'Do you not eat?*** –

92. ... and continued: ***What is the matter with you that you do not speak?'*** They did not answer him.

93. ***He turned on them, striking out*** forcefully ***with his right hand*** and broke them. Those who saw him told his people.

94. ***They came rushing back to him*** and said to him, "We worship them and you have broken them!"

95. ***He said*** – to rebuke them – ***'Do you worship something you have carved*** – idols you have created from stone and other things –

96. ***...when Allah created both you and what you do*** – your carving and what you carve? So worship Him and affirm His unity***?'***

فَلَمَّآ أَسۡلَمَا وَتَلَّهُۥ لِلۡجَبِينِ ﴿١٠٣﴾ وَنَٰدَيۡنَٰهُ أَن يَٰٓإِبۡرَٰهِيمُ ﴿١٠٤﴾ قَدۡ
صَدَّقۡتَ ٱلرُّءۡيَآۚ إِنَّا كَذَٰلِكَ نَجۡزِي ٱلۡمُحۡسِنِينَ ﴿١٠٥﴾ إِنَّ هَٰذَا لَهُوَ
ٱلۡبَلَٰٓؤُاْ ٱلۡمُبِينُ ﴿١٠٦﴾ وَفَدَيۡنَٰهُ بِذِبۡحٍ عَظِيمٖ ﴿١٠٧﴾ وَتَرَكۡنَا عَلَيۡهِ فِي
ٱلۡأٓخِرِينَ ﴿١٠٨﴾ سَلَٰمٌ عَلَىٰٓ إِبۡرَٰهِيمَ ﴿١٠٩﴾ كَذَٰلِكَ نَجۡزِي ٱلۡمُحۡسِنِينَ
﴿١١٠﴾ إِنَّهُۥ مِنۡ عِبَادِنَا ٱلۡمُؤۡمِنِينَ ﴿١١١﴾ وَبَشَّرۡنَٰهُ بِإِسۡحَٰقَ نَبِيّٗا مِّنَ
ٱلصَّٰلِحِينَ ﴿١١٢﴾ وَبَٰرَكۡنَا عَلَيۡهِ وَعَلَىٰٓ إِسۡحَٰقَۚ وَمِن ذُرِّيَّتِهِمَا
مُحۡسِنٞ وَظَالِمٞ لِّنَفۡسِهِۦ مُبِينٞ ﴿١١٣﴾ وَلَقَدۡ مَنَنَّا عَلَىٰ مُوسَىٰ
وَهَٰرُونَ ﴿١١٤﴾ وَنَجَّيۡنَٰهُمَا وَقَوۡمَهُمَا مِنَ ٱلۡكَرۡبِ ٱلۡعَظِيمِ
﴿١١٥﴾ وَنَصَرۡنَٰهُمۡ فَكَانُواْ هُمُ ٱلۡغَٰلِبِينَ ﴿١١٦﴾ وَءَاتَيۡنَٰهُمَا ٱلۡكِتَٰبَ
ٱلۡمُسۡتَبِينَ ﴿١١٧﴾ وَهَدَيۡنَٰهُمَا ٱلصِّرَٰطَ ٱلۡمُسۡتَقِيمَ ﴿١١٨﴾ وَتَرَكۡنَا
عَلَيۡهِمَا فِي ٱلۡأٓخِرِينَ ﴿١١٩﴾ سَلَٰمٌ عَلَىٰ مُوسَىٰ وَهَٰرُونَ
﴿١٢٠﴾ إِنَّا كَذَٰلِكَ نَجۡزِي ٱلۡمُحۡسِنِينَ ﴿١٢١﴾ إِنَّهُمَا مِنۡ
عِبَادِنَا ٱلۡمُؤۡمِنِينَ ﴿١٢٢﴾ وَإِنَّ إِلۡيَاسَ لَمِنَ ٱلۡمُرۡسَلِينَ ﴿١٢٣﴾
إِذۡ قَالَ لِقَوۡمِهِۦٓ أَلَا تَتَّقُونَ ﴿١٢٤﴾ أَتَدۡعُونَ بَعۡلٗا وَتَذَرُونَ أَحۡسَنَ
ٱلۡخَٰلِقِينَ ﴿١٢٥﴾ ٱللَّهَ رَبَّكُمۡ وَرَبَّ ءَابَآئِكُمُ ٱلۡأَوَّلِينَ ﴿١٢٦﴾
فَكَذَّبُوهُ فَإِنَّهُمۡ لَمُحۡضَرُونَ ﴿١٢٧﴾ إِلَّا عِبَادَ ٱللَّهِ ٱلۡمُخۡلَصِينَ ﴿١٢٨﴾
وَتَرَكۡنَا عَلَيۡهِ فِي ٱلۡأٓخِرِينَ ﴿١٢٩﴾ سَلَٰمٌ عَلَىٰٓ إِلۡ يَاسِينَ ﴿١٣٠﴾ إِنَّا كَذَٰلِكَ
نَجۡزِي ٱلۡمُحۡسِنِينَ ﴿١٣١﴾ إِنَّهُۥ مِنۡ عِبَادِنَا ٱلۡمُؤۡمِنِينَ ﴿١٣٢﴾ وَإِنَّ لُوطٗا
لَّمِنَ ٱلۡمُرۡسَلِينَ ﴿١٣٣﴾ إِذۡ نَجَّيۡنَٰهُ وَأَهۡلَهُۥٓ أَجۡمَعِينَ ﴿١٣٤﴾ إِلَّا عَجُوزٗا
فِي ٱلۡغَٰبِرِينَ ﴿١٣٥﴾ ثُمَّ دَمَّرۡنَا ٱلۡأٓخَرِينَ ﴿١٣٦﴾ وَإِنَّكُمۡ لَتَمُرُّونَ عَلَيۡهِم
مُّصۡبِحِينَ ﴿١٣٧﴾ وَبِٱلَّيۡلِۚ أَفَلَا تَعۡقِلُونَ ﴿١٣٨﴾ وَإِنَّ يُونُسَ لَمِنَ
ٱلۡمُرۡسَلِينَ ﴿١٣٩﴾ إِذۡ أَبَقَ إِلَى ٱلۡفُلۡكِ ٱلۡمَشۡحُونِ ﴿١٤٠﴾ فَسَاهَمَ فَكَانَ

97. ***They said*** to one another ***'Build a pyre*** of wood ***for him*** – and set it alight so that it burns fiercely – ***and fling him into the blaze!'***

98. ***They tried to outwit him*** by throwing him into the Fire to kill him ***but We made them the lowest.*** They were overcome and he emerged unharmed from the fire.

99. ***He said, 'I am going towards my Lord*** – I will emigrate for Allah's sake alone from the Abode of unbelief. ***He will be my guide*** to wherever He commands me to go – which was greater Syria. When he reached the Holy Land, he said:

100. ***My Lord, bestow on me a right-acting child!'*** The word "child" is not actually mentioned, but is clearly implied.

101. ***And We gave him the good news of a*** very ***forbearing boy.***

102. ***When he was of an age to work with him*** and help him, which is variously reckoned to be at either seven or thirteen years old – ***he said, 'My son, I have seen in a dream that I must sacrifice you.*** The dreams of Prophets are true and their actions are commanded by Allah. ***What do you think about this?'*** He consulted him so that he would be aware of what was going on and submit to what he was commanded to do to him. ***He said, 'Do as you are ordered, father. Allah willing, you will find me resolute*** with regard to it.'

103. ***Then when they had both submitted*** to the command of Allah ***and he had laid him face down on the ground,*** and put the knife to his throat, but did not do anything because he was prevented by the power of Allah –

104. ***We called out to him, 'Ibrāhīm,***

105. ***You have fulfilled your vision.'*** You have done as much as you could to sacrifice your son. That is enough for you. ***That is how We recompense good-doers*** – those who obey Allah's command: by removing hardship from them.

106. ***This*** commanded sacrifice – ***as indeed a most manifest trial*** – a clear test.

107. ***We ransomed him*** – this pronoun refers to the son he was commanded to sacrifice, who was either Ismā'īl or Isḥāq, as there are two views about it – ***with a mighty sacrifice*** – a large ram from Paradise. It was the one which Hābīl, the son of Ādam, had sacrificed, and Jibrīl, peace be upon him, brought it, and Ibrāhīm sacrificed it, pronouncing the *takbīr* as he did so.

108. ***and left the later people saying of him*** in praise*:*

109. ***'Peace*** from us ***be upon Ibrāhīm.'***

110. ***That is how We recompense good-doers.***

111. ***He truly was one of Our believing slaves.***

112. ***We gave him the good news of Isḥāq, a Prophet, one of the righteous.*** This is an indication that the one who was offered for sacrifice was Ismā'īl rather than Ishāq.

113. ***We showered blessings upon him and upon Isḥāq*** – by giving them many descendants, and among the offspring of his son, Isḥāq, there were many Prophets. ***Among their descendants are good-doers*** (believers) ***and also people who clearly wrong themselves*** (unbelievers).

114. ***We showed great kindness*** – in the form of Prophethood – ***to Mūsā and Hārūn.***

115. ***We rescued them and their people*** (the tribe of Israel) ***from their terrible plight*** – which was that of being enslaved by Pharaoh.

116. ***We supported them*** against the Copts ***and so they were the victors.***

117. ***We gave them the clarifying Book*** – one which is extremely clear with respect to the limits, laws and other things it conveys, meaning the Torah,

118. ***...and guided them on the Straight Path,***

119. ***...and left the later people saying*** – in praise – ***of them,***

120. ***'Peace*** from us ***be upon Mūsā and Hārūn!'***

121. ***That is how We recompense good-doers.***

122. ***They truly were among Our slaves who are believers.***

123. ***Ilyās was one of the Messengers.*** It is said that he was the nephew of Hārūn, Mūsā's brother. There are also different reports on the subject. He was sent to the people of Baalbek and the surrounding area.

124. Remember ***when he said to his people, 'Will you not be godfearing*** and fear Allah*?*

125. ***Do you call on Baal and abandon the Best of Creators?*** Baal was the name of a golden idol of theirs, from which the name of the town is derived.

126. ***Allah is your Lord*** (read as *rabba* and *rabbu*) ***and Lord of your forefathers, the previous peoples.'***

127. ***They denied him and so they will be among those arraigned*** in the Fire,

128. ***...except for Allah's chosen slaves*** – the believers who will be saved from it.

129. ***We left the later people saying*** in praise ***of him,***

130. ***'Peace*** from us ***be upon the family of Yāsīn!'*** Yāsīn is Ilyās. This is wishing peace upon him and those who believed with him, based on the reading *il yāsīn*. If it is read as *āl yāsīn*, it means his family.

131. ***That is how We recompense good-doers.***

132. ***He truly was one of Our slaves who are believers.***

133. ***And Lūṭ was one of the Messengers.***

134. Remember ***when We rescued him and all his family –***

135. ***...except an old woman among those who stayed behind*** and suffered the punishment.

136. ***Then We utterly destroyed the rest*** – the unbelievers of his people.

137. ***And you pass by them*** – the ruins of their houses, when you travel ***in the daytime...***

138. ***...and at night. So will you*** people of Makka ***not use your intellect?***

139. ***Yūnus too was one of the Messengers,***

140. ***... when he ran away to the fully laden ship*** – he did this when he was angry with his people and the punishment which he had promised them did not befall them. He embarked on a ship and then it stopped in an ocean gulf. The sailors said, "There is a slave on board who has run away from his master." He was exposed when they drew lots.

141. ***...and*** the people of the ship ***cast lots and he lost*** – and so they threw him into the sea.

مِنَ ٱلۡمُدۡحَضِينَ ﴿١٤١﴾ فَٱلۡتَقَمَهُ ٱلۡحُوتُ وَهُوَ مُلِيمٞ ﴿١٤٢﴾ فَلَوۡلَآ أَنَّهُۥ
كَانَ مِنَ ٱلۡمُسَبِّحِينَ ﴿١٤٣﴾ لَلَبِثَ فِي بَطۡنِهِۦٓ إِلَىٰ يَوۡمِ يُبۡعَثُونَ ﴿١٤٤﴾
۞ فَنَبَذۡنَٰهُ بِٱلۡعَرَآءِ وَهُوَ سَقِيمٞ ﴿١٤٥﴾ وَأَنۢبَتۡنَا عَلَيۡهِ شَجَرَةٗ
مِّن يَقۡطِينٖ ﴿١٤٦﴾ وَأَرۡسَلۡنَٰهُ إِلَىٰ مِاْئَةِ أَلۡفٍ أَوۡ يَزِيدُونَ ﴿١٤٧﴾
فَـَٔامَنُواْ فَمَتَّعۡنَٰهُمۡ إِلَىٰ حِينٖ ﴿١٤٨﴾ فَٱسۡتَفۡتِهِمۡ أَلِرَبِّكَ ٱلۡبَنَاتُ
وَلَهُمُ ٱلۡبَنُونَ ﴿١٤٩﴾ أَمۡ خَلَقۡنَا ٱلۡمَلَٰٓئِكَةَ إِنَٰثٗا وَهُمۡ
شَٰهِدُونَ ﴿١٥٠﴾ أَلَآ إِنَّهُم مِّنۡ إِفۡكِهِمۡ لَيَقُولُونَ ﴿١٥١﴾ وَلَدَ
ٱللَّهُ وَإِنَّهُمۡ لَكَٰذِبُونَ ﴿١٥٢﴾ أَصۡطَفَى ٱلۡبَنَاتِ عَلَى ٱلۡبَنِينَ ﴿١٥٣﴾
مَا لَكُمۡ كَيۡفَ تَحۡكُمُونَ ﴿١٥٤﴾ أَفَلَا تَذَكَّرُونَ ﴿١٥٥﴾ أَمۡ لَكُمۡ سُلۡطَٰنٞ مُّبِينٞ
﴿١٥٦﴾ فَأۡتُواْ بِكِتَٰبِكُمۡ إِن كُنتُمۡ صَٰدِقِينَ ﴿١٥٧﴾ وَجَعَلُواْ بَيۡنَهُۥ وَبَيۡنَ ٱلۡجِنَّةِ
نَسَبٗاۚ وَلَقَدۡ عَلِمَتِ ٱلۡجِنَّةُ إِنَّهُمۡ لَمُحۡضَرُونَ ﴿١٥٨﴾ سُبۡحَٰنَ ٱللَّهِ عَمَّا
يَصِفُونَ ﴿١٥٩﴾ إِلَّا عِبَادَ ٱللَّهِ ٱلۡمُخۡلَصِينَ ﴿١٦٠﴾ فَإِنَّكُمۡ وَمَا تَعۡبُدُونَ ﴿١٦١﴾
مَآ أَنتُمۡ عَلَيۡهِ بِفَٰتِنِينَ ﴿١٦٢﴾ إِلَّا مَنۡ هُوَ صَالِ ٱلۡجَحِيمِ ﴿١٦٣﴾ وَمَا مِنَّآ إِلَّا
لَهُۥ مَقَامٞ مَّعۡلُومٞ ﴿١٦٤﴾ وَإِنَّا لَنَحۡنُ ٱلصَّآفُّونَ ﴿١٦٥﴾ وَإِنَّا لَنَحۡنُ ٱلۡمُسَبِّحُونَ
﴿١٦٦﴾ وَإِن كَانُواْ لَيَقُولُونَ ﴿١٦٧﴾ لَوۡ أَنَّ عِندَنَا ذِكۡرٗا مِّنَ ٱلۡأَوَّلِينَ ﴿١٦٨﴾ لَكُنَّا
عِبَادَ ٱللَّهِ ٱلۡمُخۡلَصِينَ ﴿١٦٩﴾ فَكَفَرُواْ بِهِۦۖ فَسَوۡفَ يَعۡلَمُونَ ﴿١٧٠﴾ وَلَقَدۡ
سَبَقَتۡ كَلِمَتُنَا لِعِبَادِنَا ٱلۡمُرۡسَلِينَ ﴿١٧١﴾ إِنَّهُمۡ لَهُمُ ٱلۡمَنصُورُونَ ﴿١٧٢﴾ وَإِنَّ
جُندَنَا لَهُمُ ٱلۡغَٰلِبُونَ ﴿١٧٣﴾ فَتَوَلَّ عَنۡهُمۡ حَتَّىٰ حِينٖ ﴿١٧٤﴾ وَأَبۡصِرۡهُمۡ فَسَوۡفَ
يُبۡصِرُونَ ﴿١٧٥﴾ أَفَبِعَذَابِنَا يَسۡتَعۡجِلُونَ ﴿١٧٦﴾ فَإِذَا نَزَلَ بِسَاحَتِهِمۡ فَسَآءَ
صَبَاحُ ٱلۡمُنذَرِينَ ﴿١٧٧﴾ وَتَوَلَّ عَنۡهُمۡ حَتَّىٰ حِينٖ ﴿١٧٨﴾ وَأَبۡصِرۡ فَسَوۡفَ
يُبۡصِرُونَ ﴿١٧٩﴾ سُبۡحَٰنَ رَبِّكَ رَبِّ ٱلۡعِزَّةِ عَمَّا يَصِفُونَ ﴿١٨٠﴾
وَسَلَٰمٌ عَلَى ٱلۡمُرۡسَلِينَ ﴿١٨١﴾ وَٱلۡحَمۡدُ لِلَّهِ رَبِّ ٱلۡعَٰلَمِينَ ﴿١٨٢﴾

142. ***Then the fish devoured him and he was to blame.*** He had gone to the coast in a blameworthy way and embarked on the ship without permission from his Lord.

143. ***Had it not been that he was a man who glorified Allah,*** remembering Allah frequently, even in the belly of the fish. He said, *"There is no god but You. Glory be to You. I have been one of the wrongdoers,"* as Allah relates about him in *Sūrat al-Anbiyā'* (21:86) –

144. ***...he would have remained inside its belly*** – and it would have been his grave – ***until the Day*** (the Day of Rising) ***they are raised again.***

145. ***So We cast him up*** out of the belly of the fish ***onto the beach*** – either on the same day, after three days, after seven days, after twenty days, or after forty days – ***and he was sick*** like a featherless fledgling*;*

146. ***and We caused a gourd tree to grow over him*** on a trunk to shade him, which is different from the normal growth of the gourd, as a miracle for him. He drank from its juice until he became strong.

147. ***We sent him to a hundred thousand or even more*** – as before, to the people of Nineveh in the land of Mosul. The number exceeded a hundred thousand by twenty, thirty or seventy thousand.

148. ***They had believed,*** when they saw the punishment they had been promised, ***and so We gave them enjoyment for a time*** and allowed them to remain enjoying their property until the end of their life spans.

149. ***Ask them*** (the unbelievers of Makka) ***for a*** **fatwā** (a statement) – as a rebuke*:* ***does your Lord have daughters*** – after their claim about the angels being the daughters of Allah – ***while they themselves have sons?*** So they consider themselves better.

150. ***Or did We create the angels female, with them as witnesses*** to their creation so that they can say this*?*

151. ***No indeed! It is one of their blatant lies to say,***

152. ***'Allah has given birth'*** – when they say that the angels are the daughters of Allah. ***They are truly liars*** in what they say.

153. ***Has He chosen daughters over sons?***

154. ***What is the matter with you? How do you reach your judge - ment?*** Your judgement is a false one.

155. ***Will you not pay heed*** and remember that Allah is glorious and exalted above having a child***?***

156. ***Or do you have some clear authority*** – clear evidence that Allah has a child***?***

157. ***Bring your Book, then*** – meaning the Torah, and show me where that is in it – ***if you are telling the truth*** in what you say***!***

158. ***They*** (the idolaters) ***claim there is a blood-tie between Him and the jinn*** through the angels, since they are hidden from the eyes according to their statement that they are His daughters***; but the jinn know very well that they will be arraigned*** – they know that those who say that will be punished in the Fire.

159. ***Glory be to Allah above what they describe*** – Allah is too exalted to have a child –

160. ***…except for Allah's chosen slaves*** (the believers)**.** They exalt Allah above what the other people describe Him as.

161. ***You and those you worship*** (the idols)***:***

162. ***…you will entice no one to them*** – to what you worship,

163. ***…except for him who is to roast in the Blazing Fire*** – in the foreknowledge of Allah.

164. Jibrīl said the following to the Prophet, may Allah bless him and grant him peace. ***'There is not one of us*** (the angels) ***who does not have a known station*** in the heavens, in which he worships Allah and which he does not exceed.

165. ***We are those drawn up in ranks*** – standing in rows in the prayer.

166. ***We are those who glorify.'*** We proclaim Allah free of everything which is not fitting for Him.

167. ***They*** (the unbelievers of Makka) ***used to say,***

168. ***'If we had only had a Reminder*** (a Book) ***from*** the Books of ***the previous peoples*** (past nations)***,***

169. ***…we would certainly have been sincere slaves of Allah*** in worshipping Him!'

170. Allah says: ***But they have rejected it*** – the Book which has come to them, meaning the Noble Qur'an – ***and they will soon know*** the result of their unbelief.

171. ***Our Word*** – meaning victory in this instance – ***was given before to Our slaves, the Messengers,*** a reference to Allah's words: *"I will be victorious, I and My Messengers."* (58:21)

172. ***...that they would certainly be helped.***

173. ***It is Our army*** (the believers) ***which will be victorious*** over the unbelievers by the proof and victory over them in this world. If some of them are not victorious in this world, they will be in the Next World.

174. ***Therefore turn from them*** (the unbelievers of Makka) ***for a time,*** until the time when you are commanded to fight them,

175. ***... and watch them*** when the punishment befalls them, ***for they will soon see*** the consequences of their unbelief.

176. They said in mockery, "When will this punishment occur?" Allah then threatens them: ***Are they trying to hasten Our punishment?***

177. ***When it descends in their courtyard*** – the word used here, *sāḥa*, means the courtyard around a house. According to al-Farrā', when the Arabs mention the courtyard, it really means the people there – ***how evil will be the morning of those who were warned!***

178. ***So turn from them for a time.***

179. ***And watch, for they will soon see!*** This is repeated to stress the threat against them and to give solace to the Prophet, may Allah bless him and grant him peace.

180. ***Glory be to your Lord, the Lord of Might, beyond anything they describe*** about Him having a child.

181. ***And peace be upon the Messengers*** who conveyed the Message of Allah's unity and laws.

182. ***And praise be to Allah*** – for helping them and destroying the unbelievers – ***the Lord of all the worlds!***

سُورَةُ صٓ

بِسۡمِ ٱللَّهِ ٱلرَّحۡمَٰنِ ٱلرَّحِيمِ

صٓۚ وَٱلۡقُرۡءَانِ ذِي ٱلذِّكۡرِ ١ بَلِ ٱلَّذِينَ كَفَرُواْ فِي عِزَّةٖ وَشِقَاقٖ ٢
كَمۡ أَهۡلَكۡنَا مِن قَبۡلِهِم مِّن قَرۡنٖ فَنَادَواْ وَّلَاتَ حِينَ مَنَاصٖ ٣ وَعَجِبُوٓاْ
أَن جَآءَهُم مُّنذِرٞ مِّنۡهُمۡۖ وَقَالَ ٱلۡكَٰفِرُونَ هَٰذَا سَٰحِرٞ كَذَّابٌ ٤
أَجَعَلَ ٱلۡأٓلِهَةَ إِلَٰهٗا وَٰحِدًاۖ إِنَّ هَٰذَا لَشَيۡءٌ عُجَابٞ ٥ وَٱنطَلَقَ ٱلۡمَلَأُ
مِنۡهُمۡ أَنِ ٱمۡشُواْ وَٱصۡبِرُواْ عَلَىٰٓ ءَالِهَتِكُمۡۖ إِنَّ هَٰذَا لَشَيۡءٞ يُرَادُ ٦
مَا سَمِعۡنَا بِهَٰذَا فِي ٱلۡمِلَّةِ ٱلۡأٓخِرَةِ إِنۡ هَٰذَآ إِلَّا ٱخۡتِلَٰقٌ ٧ أَءُنزِلَ
عَلَيۡهِ ٱلذِّكۡرُ مِنۢ بَيۡنِنَاۚ بَلۡ هُمۡ فِي شَكّٖ مِّن ذِكۡرِيۖ بَل لَّمَّا يَذُوقُواْ عَذَابِ
٨ أَمۡ عِندَهُمۡ خَزَآئِنُ رَحۡمَةِ رَبِّكَ ٱلۡعَزِيزِ ٱلۡوَهَّابِ ٩ أَمۡ لَهُم
مُّلۡكُ ٱلسَّمَٰوَٰتِ وَٱلۡأَرۡضِ وَمَا بَيۡنَهُمَاۖ فَلۡيَرۡتَقُواْ فِي ٱلۡأَسۡبَٰبِ ١٠
جُندٞ مَّا هُنَالِكَ مَهۡزُومٞ مِّنَ ٱلۡأَحۡزَابِ ١١ كَذَّبَتۡ قَبۡلَهُمۡ قَوۡمُ
نُوحٖ وَعَادٞ وَفِرۡعَوۡنُ ذُو ٱلۡأَوۡتَادِ ١٢ وَثَمُودُ وَقَوۡمُ لُوطٖ وَأَصۡحَٰبُ
لۡـَٔيۡكَةِۚ أُوْلَٰٓئِكَ ٱلۡأَحۡزَابُ ١٣ إِن كُلٌّ إِلَّا كَذَّبَ ٱلرُّسُلَ
فَحَقَّ عِقَابِ ١٤ وَمَا يَنظُرُ هَٰٓؤُلَآءِ إِلَّا صَيۡحَةٗ وَٰحِدَةٗ مَّا لَهَا
مِن فَوَاقٖ ١٥ وَقَالُواْ رَبَّنَا عَجِّل لَّنَا قِطَّنَا قَبۡلَ يَوۡمِ ٱلۡحِسَابِ ١٦
ٱصۡبِرۡ عَلَىٰ مَا يَقُولُونَ وَٱذۡكُرۡ عَبۡدَنَا دَاوُۥدَ ذَا ٱلۡأَيۡدِۖ إِنَّهُۥٓ أَوَّابٌ ١٧
إِنَّا سَخَّرۡنَا ٱلۡجِبَالَ مَعَهُۥ يُسَبِّحۡنَ بِٱلۡعَشِيِّ وَٱلۡإِشۡرَاقِ ١٨ وَٱلطَّيۡرَ
مَحۡشُورَةٗۖ كُلّٞ لَّهُۥٓ أَوَّابٞ ١٩ وَشَدَدۡنَا مُلۡكَهُۥ وَءَاتَيۡنَٰهُ ٱلۡحِكۡمَةَ
وَفَصۡلَ ٱلۡخِطَابِ ٢٠ ۞ وَهَلۡ أَتَىٰكَ نَبَؤُاْ ٱلۡخَصۡمِ إِذۡ تَسَوَّرُواْ

38. *Sūrat Ṣād*
Ṣād

This *sūra* is Makkan. It has 86 or 88 *āyat*s and was sent down after *al-Qamar.*

1. *Ṣād.* Allah knows best what is meant by this. ***By the Qur'an holding the Remembrance!*** This is an oath whose apodosis is elided: in other words, the truth of the matter is as not as the unbelievers of Makka say about there being many gods.

2. *But those who disbelieve* – including the the people of Makka – ***are full of vainglory*** – in other words, they are too proud to believe – ***and entrenched in hostility*** – in enmity towards the Prophet, may Allah bless him and grant him peace.

3. *How many generations* (nations) ***We have destroyed before them! And they cried out*** when the punishment fell on them and ***when it was too late to escape*** and they had nowhere to run. So the unbelievers of Makka should take note.

4. *They are surprised that a warner* – a Messenger from among themselves – ***should come to them from among themselves*** and alert them to the Fire after the Resurrection. That is the Prophet, may Allah bless him and grant him peace. ***The unbelievers say, 'This is a lying magician.***

5. *Has he turned all the gods into One God?* They said this when he said to them, "Say, 'There is no god except Allah." They said, "How can one god be enough for all creation? ***That is truly astonishing*"*!'***

6. *Their leaders went off* from the meeting they had with Abū Ṭālib in which they listened to the Prophet, may Allah bless him and grant him peace, when he told them to say, "There is no god but Allah" – ***saying*** to one another***: 'Carry on as you are!*** Continue! ***Hold fast to your gods*** and to worshipping them. ***This*** doctrine of unity ***is clearly something planned.***

7. *We have not heard of this in the old religion* the religion of 'Īsā. ***This is merely something contrived*** – a lie.

8. ***Has the Reminder*** (the Qur'an) ***been sent down to him*** (Muḥammad) ***out of all of us*** – when he is not the oldest of us or the noblest of us? Why was it sent down on him?' Allah says, ***They are in doubt about My Reminder*** – the Revelation of the Qur'an – since they denied the one who brought it. ***They have yet to taste My punishment.*** If they had tasted the punishment, they would have believed the Prophet, may Allah bless him and grant him peace, regarding what he brought, but their affirmation would not then benefited them.

9. ***Or do they possess the treasuries of your Lord's mercy, the Almighty, the Ever-Giving?*** He is the One who gives Prophethood and other things to whomever He wishes.

10. ***Or does the kingdom of the heavens and earth and everything between them belong to them?*** If they claim that – ***let them, in that case, climb the ropes to heaven*** and bring the Revelation and choose whomever they wish!

11. ***Even a whole army of Confederates*** who deny you, such as the armies of those who formed parties against the Prophets before you, ***will be routed there!*** Previous armies were overwhelmed and destroyed. That is how We will destroy these as well.

12. ***Before them the people of Nūḥ denied the truth, as did 'Ād and Pharaoh of the Stakes*** – he is called by this name because when he was angry with someone, he would tie their feet and hands to four stakes and then torture them –

13. ***...and Thamūd and the people of Lūṭ and the Companions of the Thicket*** – the people of Shu'ayb, peace be upon him. ***Those too were Confederates.***

14. ***Each one of them*** (the Confederates) ***denied the Messengers*** – because if people deny one, they deny all of them since they all call people to the same thing, which is affirmation of Allah's unity – ***and so My punishment was*** inevitable and ***justly carried out.***

15. ***These people*** (the unbelievers of Makka) ***too are only awaiting a single Blast*** – the blast of the Rising and then the punishment will alight on them – ***and it will not be repeated*** (read as *fawāq* or *fuwāq*).

ٱلۡمِحۡرَابَ ٢١ إِذۡ دَخَلُواْ عَلَىٰ دَاوُۥدَ فَفَزِعَ مِنۡهُمۡۖ قَالُواْ لَا تَخَفۡۖ
خَصۡمَانِ بَغَىٰ بَعۡضُنَا عَلَىٰ بَعۡضٖ فَٱحۡكُم بَيۡنَنَا بِٱلۡحَقِّ وَلَا تُشۡطِطۡ
وَٱهۡدِنَآ إِلَىٰ سَوَآءِ ٱلصِّرَٰطِ ٢٢ إِنَّ هَٰذَآ أَخِي لَهُۥ تِسۡعٞ وَتِسۡعُونَ نَعۡجَةٗ
وَلِيَ نَعۡجَةٞ وَٰحِدَةٞ فَقَالَ أَكۡفِلۡنِيهَا وَعَزَّنِي فِي ٱلۡخِطَابِ ٢٣ قَالَ
لَقَدۡ ظَلَمَكَ بِسُؤَالِ نَعۡجَتِكَ إِلَىٰ نِعَاجِهِۦۖ وَإِنَّ كَثِيرٗا مِّنَ ٱلۡخُلَطَآءِ لَيَبۡغِي
بَعۡضُهُمۡ عَلَىٰ بَعۡضٍ إِلَّا ٱلَّذِينَ ءَامَنُواْ وَعَمِلُواْ ٱلصَّٰلِحَٰتِ وَقَلِيلٞ
مَّا هُمۡۗ وَظَنَّ دَاوُۥدُ أَنَّمَا فَتَنَّٰهُ فَٱسۡتَغۡفَرَ رَبَّهُۥ وَخَرَّۤ رَاكِعٗاۤ وَأَنَابَ
۩ ٢٤ فَغَفَرۡنَا لَهُۥ ذَٰلِكَۖ وَإِنَّ لَهُۥ عِندَنَا لَزُلۡفَىٰ وَحُسۡنَ مَـَٔابٖ
٢٥ يَٰدَاوُۥدُ إِنَّا جَعَلۡنَٰكَ خَلِيفَةٗ فِي ٱلۡأَرۡضِ فَٱحۡكُم بَيۡنَ ٱلنَّاسِ
بِٱلۡحَقِّ وَلَا تَتَّبِعِ ٱلۡهَوَىٰ فَيُضِلَّكَ عَن سَبِيلِ ٱللَّهِۚ إِنَّ ٱلَّذِينَ يَضِلُّونَ
عَن سَبِيلِ ٱللَّهِ لَهُمۡ عَذَابٞ شَدِيدُۢ بِمَا نَسُواْ يَوۡمَ ٱلۡحِسَابِ ٢٦
وَمَا خَلَقۡنَا ٱلسَّمَآءَ وَٱلۡأَرۡضَ وَمَا بَيۡنَهُمَا بَٰطِلٗاۚ ذَٰلِكَ ظَنُّ ٱلَّذِينَ كَفَرُواْۚ
فَوَيۡلٞ لِّلَّذِينَ كَفَرُواْ مِنَ ٱلنَّارِ ٢٧ أَمۡ نَجۡعَلُ ٱلَّذِينَ ءَامَنُواْ وَعَمِلُواْ
ٱلصَّٰلِحَٰتِ كَٱلۡمُفۡسِدِينَ فِي ٱلۡأَرۡضِ أَمۡ نَجۡعَلُ ٱلۡمُتَّقِينَ كَٱلۡفُجَّارِ
٢٨ كِتَٰبٌ أَنزَلۡنَٰهُ إِلَيۡكَ مُبَٰرَكٞ لِّيَدَّبَّرُوٓاْ ءَايَٰتِهِۦ وَلِيَتَذَكَّرَ أُوْلُواْ
ٱلۡأَلۡبَٰبِ ٢٩ وَوَهَبۡنَا لِدَاوُۥدَ سُلَيۡمَٰنَۚ نِعۡمَ ٱلۡعَبۡدُۖ إِنَّهُۥٓ أَوَّابٌ
٣٠ إِذۡ عُرِضَ عَلَيۡهِ بِٱلۡعَشِيِّ ٱلصَّٰفِنَٰتُ ٱلۡجِيَادُ ٣١ فَقَالَ إِنِّيٓ
أَحۡبَبۡتُ حُبَّ ٱلۡخَيۡرِ عَن ذِكۡرِ رَبِّي حَتَّىٰ تَوَارَتۡ بِٱلۡحِجَابِ ٣٢
رُدُّوهَا عَلَيَّۖ فَطَفِقَ مَسۡحَۢا بِٱلسُّوقِ وَٱلۡأَعۡنَاقِ ٣٣ وَلَقَدۡ فَتَنَّا
سُلَيۡمَٰنَ وَأَلۡقَيۡنَا عَلَىٰ كُرۡسِيِّهِۦ جَسَدٗا ثُمَّ أَنَابَ ٣٤ قَالَ رَبِّ ٱغۡفِرۡ

16. ***They say*** – in mockery when the *āyat* was revealed: *"As for him who is given his Book in his right hand..."* (84:7) – ***'Our Lord, advance our share*** – the Book of our actions – ***to us before the Day of Reckoning.'***

17. Allah says: ***Be steadfast in the face of what they say and remember Our slave Dāwūd, who possessed true strength*** in worship. He used to fast every other day. He would pray half of the night and then sleep for a third and then pray for a sixth. ***He truly turned to*** the pleasure of ***his Lord.***

18. ***We subjected the mountains to glorify with him in the evening*** – at the time of *'Ishā'* – ***and at sunrise*** – at the time of *Ḍuḥā*, so both at the time when the sun shines and when its light disappears;

19. ***... and also*** We subjected ***the birds, flocking together*** to glorify with him – ***all of them*** – mountains and birds – ***turned to Him*** to obey Him by glorifying Him.

20. ***We made his kingdom strong*** – by means of guards and armies. Thirty thousand men used to guard his small room every night – ***and gave him wisdom*** – meaning Prophethood and correct judgement about things in general – ***and decisive speech*** – clear speech which achieves the desired result.

21. ***Has the story of the litigants reached you?*** This question implies wonder and encourages one to listen to what follows. O Muḥammad, have you heard? ***How they climbed up to the Upper Room*** – which was his place of prayer. They did this when they were prevented from entering by the door since he was busy worshipping. Tell them this story –

22. ***...and came in on Dāwūd who was alarmed by them. They said, 'Do not be afraid. We are two litigants*** – it is said that there were two groups of litigants because of the use of the plural; but the usual opinion is that there were only two men. They were two angels who came in the form of two litigants in order to point out to him what he had done. He had ninety-nine wives and wanted the wife of someone who had no other wife but her. He married her and consummated the marriage with her – ***one of whom has acted unjustly towards the other, so judge between us with truth*** – and guide us to what is correct – ***and do not be unjust and guide us to the Right Path.***

23. ***This brother of mine*** in the *dīn* ***has ninety-nine ewes*** – sheep, here representing wives – ***and I have only one. He said, "Let me have charge of it," and got the better of me with his words.'*** He won the argument and the other man put the sheep in his care.

24. ***He said, 'He has wronged you by asking for your ewe to add to his ewes. Truly many partners are unjust to one another – except those who believe and do right actions, and how few they are!'*** The angels who reverted to their proper form and returned to heaven said, "The man has judged against himself." Dāwūd understood. Allah says: ***Dāwūd realised*** with certainty ***that We had put him to the test*** – meaning that he had fallen into affliction because of his love for that woman. ***He begged forgiveness from his Lord and fell down prone, prostrating, and repented.***

25. ***So We forgave him for that; and he has nearness to Us*** – in addition to the good of this world he received and his high position there – ***and a good Homecoming*** in the Next World.

26. ***'Dāwūd, We have made you a*** **khalif** ***on the earth*** – giving you the management of people's affairs – ***so judge between people with truth, and do not follow your own desires*** – the whims of your lower self – ***letting them misguide you from the Way of Allah*** – from the evidence which indicates the unity of Allah. ***Those who are misguided from the Way of Allah*** – from belief in Allah – ***will receive a harsh punishment because they forgot the Day of Reckoning*** and therefore failed to believe. If they had had certainty about the Day of Rising, they would have believed when they were in this world.'

27. ***We did not create heaven and earth and everything between them to no purpose. That*** there is no purpose to creation ***is the opinion of those who disbelieve. Woe*** – *wayl*, which is the name of a valley in the Fire – ***to those who disbelieve, because of the Fire!***

28. ***Would We make those who believe and do right actions the same as those who cause corruption on the earth? Would We make those who are godfearing the same as the dissolute?*** This was revealed when the unbelievers of Makka said to the believers, "In the Next World we will be given the same as you are given."

29. ***It is a Book We have sent down to you, full of blessing, so let people of intelligence ponder its Signs*** – reflect on its meanings – ***and take heed*** – and therefore believe. Those who possess intelligence will be warned by it.

30. ***We gave Dāwūd Sulaymān***, – his son. ***What an excellent slave! He truly turned to his Lord.*** He frequently remembered Allah at all times.

31. ***When swift horses*** – the word used here, *ṣāfināt* which is the plural of *ṣāfina*, is a kind of horse that lifts up one of its feet, pointing the hoof down, and stands on the others. It comes from the verb, *ṣafana*, to stand with one foot slightly raised. *Jiyād* is the plural of *jawād*, meaning a swift runner. When they stand, they are still, and when they run, they win – ***champing at the bit, were displayed before him in the afternoon*** – a thousand horses were presented to him after he had prayed *Ẓuhr*, since he wished to do *jihād* on them against the enemy. When he had only inspected nine hundred, the sun set and he had not yet prayed *'Aṣr*, so he was unhappy –

32. ***...he said, 'I have put the love of good things*** – these horses – ***above the remembrance of my Lord*** – by failing to perform the *'Aṣr* prayer in its time – ***until the sun disappeared behind its veil*** – disappeared from sight.

33. ***Return them*** (the horses) ***to me!'*** They were brought back. He took up a sword – ***and he set about slashing through their shanks and necks*** – slaughtering them out of desire to draw near to Allah since they had distracted him from the prayer. He gave the meat away as *ṣadaqa* and Allah gave him in their place something better and swifter: the wind which went at his command wherever he wished.

34. ***We tested Sulaymān*** – by removing his kingdom – ***and placed a lifeless body on his throne.*** That came about because he married a woman he was passionately in love with and she used to worship an idol in his house without his knowledge. The power over his kingdom resided in his signet ring. He removed it once when he went to the lavatory and left it with his wife, Umayna, as was his custom. A

لِي وَهَبۡ لِي مُلۡكٗا لَّا يَنۢبَغِي لِأَحَدٖ مِّنۢ بَعۡدِيٓۖ إِنَّكَ أَنتَ ٱلۡوَهَّابُ ٣٥
فَسَخَّرۡنَا لَهُ ٱلرِّيحَ تَجۡرِي بِأَمۡرِهِۦ رُخَآءً حَيۡثُ أَصَابَ ٣٦ وَٱلشَّيَٰطِينَ
كُلَّ بَنَّآءٖ وَغَوَّاصٖ ٣٧ وَءَاخَرِينَ مُقَرَّنِينَ فِي ٱلۡأَصۡفَادِ ٣٨ هَٰذَا
عَطَآؤُنَا فَٱمۡنُنۡ أَوۡ أَمۡسِكۡ بِغَيۡرِ حِسَابٖ ٣٩ وَإِنَّ لَهُۥ عِندَنَا لَزُلۡفَىٰ وَحُسۡنَ
مَـَٔابٖ ٤٠ وَٱذۡكُرۡ عَبۡدَنَآ أَيُّوبَ إِذۡ نَادَىٰ رَبَّهُۥٓ أَنِّي مَسَّنِيَ ٱلشَّيۡطَٰنُ
بِنُصۡبٖ وَعَذَابٍ ٤١ ٱرۡكُضۡ بِرِجۡلِكَۖ هَٰذَا مُغۡتَسَلُۢ بَارِدٞ وَشَرَابٞ ٤٢
وَوَهَبۡنَا لَهُۥٓ أَهۡلَهُۥ وَمِثۡلَهُم مَّعَهُمۡ رَحۡمَةٗ مِّنَّا وَذِكۡرَىٰ لِأُوْلِي ٱلۡأَلۡبَٰبِ
٤٣ وَخُذۡ بِيَدِكَ ضِغۡثٗا فَٱضۡرِب بِّهِۦ وَلَا تَحۡنَثۡۗ إِنَّا وَجَدۡنَٰهُ صَابِرٗاۚ
نِّعۡمَ ٱلۡعَبۡدُ إِنَّهُۥٓ أَوَّابٞ ٤٤ وَٱذۡكُرۡ عِبَٰدَنَآ إِبۡرَٰهِيمَ وَإِسۡحَٰقَ وَيَعۡقُوبَ
أُوْلِي ٱلۡأَيۡدِي وَٱلۡأَبۡصَٰرِ ٤٥ إِنَّآ أَخۡلَصۡنَٰهُم بِخَالِصَةٖ ذِكۡرَى
ٱلدَّارِ ٤٦ وَإِنَّهُمۡ عِندَنَا لَمِنَ ٱلۡمُصۡطَفَيۡنَ ٱلۡأَخۡيَارِ ٤٧ وَٱذۡكُرۡ
إِسۡمَٰعِيلَ وَٱلۡيَسَعَ وَذَا ٱلۡكِفۡلِۖ وَكُلّٞ مِّنَ ٱلۡأَخۡيَارِ ٤٨ هَٰذَا ذِكۡرٞۚ
وَإِنَّ لِلۡمُتَّقِينَ لَحُسۡنَ مَـَٔابٖ ٤٩ جَنَّٰتِ عَدۡنٖ مُّفَتَّحَةٗ لَّهُمُ ٱلۡأَبۡوَٰبُ
٥٠ مُتَّكِـِٔينَ فِيهَا يَدۡعُونَ فِيهَا بِفَٰكِهَةٖ كَثِيرَةٖ وَشَرَابٖ ٥١
۞ وَعِندَهُمۡ قَٰصِرَٰتُ ٱلطَّرۡفِ أَتۡرَابٌ ٥٢ هَٰذَا مَا تُوعَدُونَ لِيَوۡمِ
ٱلۡحِسَابِ ٥٣ إِنَّ هَٰذَا لَرِزۡقُنَا مَا لَهُۥ مِن نَّفَادٍ ٥٤ هَٰذَاۚ وَإِنَّ
لِلطَّٰغِينَ لَشَرَّ مَـَٔابٖ ٥٥ جَهَنَّمَ يَصۡلَوۡنَهَا فَبِئۡسَ ٱلۡمِهَادُ ٥٦ هَٰذَا
فَلۡيَذُوقُوهُ حَمِيمٞ وَغَسَّاقٞ ٥٧ وَءَاخَرُ مِن شَكۡلِهِۦٓ أَزۡوَٰجٌ ٥٨
هَٰذَا فَوۡجٞ مُّقۡتَحِمٞ مَّعَكُمۡ لَا مَرۡحَبَۢا بِهِمۡۚ إِنَّهُمۡ صَالُواْ ٱلنَّارِ ٥٩
قَالُواْ بَلۡ أَنتُمۡ لَا مَرۡحَبَۢا بِكُمۡۖ أَنتُمۡ قَدَّمۡتُمُوهُ لَنَاۖ فَبِئۡسَ ٱلۡقَرَارُ ٦٠

jinn came in the form of Sulaymān and took it from her. The name of the jinn was Ṣakhr, or possibly something else. He sat on the throne of Sulaymān and the birds and other creatures devoted themselves to him. Sulaymān came out looking different from his normal appearance and saw him on his throne. He said to the people, "I am Sulaymān," but they did not recognise him. ***Then he repented.*** Then after some days Sulaymān was restored to his kingdom because he regained his ring and put it on and sat on his throne.

35. ***He said, 'My Lord, forgive me and give me a kingdom the like of which will never be granted to anyone after me. Truly You are the Ever-Giving.'***

36. ***So We subjected the wind to him to blow at his command, softly, wherever he directed*** and wished –

37. ***... and the*** **shayṭāns*****, every builder*** of wondrous buildings ***and diver*** into the sea to bring out pearls –

38. ***...and others of them, yoked together in chains*** – jinn with shackles which fastened their hands to their necks.

39. We said to him: ***'This is Our gift: so bestow it*** on anyone you want ***or withhold it*** from anyone you want ***without reckoning.'***

40. ***He will have nearness to Us and a good Homecoming.***

41. ***Remember Our slave Ayyūb; when he called on his Lord: 'Shayṭān has afflicted me with exhaustion and suffering.'*** He ascribed his difficulties to Shayṭān, even if all things come from Allah, out of courtesy towards Allah.

42. He was told: ***'Stamp*** on the ground with ***your foot!*** When he did so, a spring of water gushed forth. He was told: ***Here is a cool bath*** – water with which you can wash yourself – ***and water to drink.'*** He washed and drank and all his illness left him, inside and out.

43. ***We gave him back his family and the same again with them*** – Allah brought back to life those of his children who had died and Allah gave him the same number again – ***as a mercy*** (blessing) ***from Us and a reminder*** and warning ***for people of intellect.***

44. ***'Take a bundle of rushes*** (grass or canes) ***in your hand and strike*** your wife ***with that,*** since he had sworn an oath that he would strike her a hundred times because she was slow in coming to him one day***; but do not break your oath*** by not striking her.*'* So he took a hundred sticks of *idhkhir* herb or something else and hit her with them once. ***We found him*** (Ayyūb) ***steadfast. What an excellent slave! He truly*** often ***turned to his Lord.***

45. *And remember Our slaves Ibrāhīm, Isḥāq and Ya'qūb, men of true strength* in worship ***and insight*** into the *dīn.*

46. *We purified their sincerity through sincere remembrance of the Abode* of the Next World, meaning by remembering it and acting for it.

47. *In Our eyes they are among the best of chosen men.*

48. *Remember Our slaves Ismā'īl, Al-Yasa' and Dhū'l-Kifl; each of them was among the best of men.* There is disagreement about whether Dhū'l-Kifl was a Prophet or not. It is said that he supported a hundred Prophets who fled to him to avoid being killed.

49. *This is a Reminder* praising them. ***Those who are godfearing will have a good Homecoming*** in the Next World:

50. *Gardens of Eden* – they will be the good Homecoming – ***whose gates will be open to them,***

51. *...where they will recline* on couches, ***calling for plentiful fruit and drink;***

52. *...and there will be dark-eyed maidens with them, with eyes reserved for them* (their husbands) ***alone.*** They will have the same age: thirty-three years.

53. *This* – what has been mentioned – ***is what you are promised*** – in the Unseen – ***on the Day of Reckoning.***

54. *This is Our provision which will never run out* – it will never come to an end, but is constant and will abide.

55. *This* is what the believers will receive! ***Whereas for the profligate there is an evil Homecoming:***

56. *Hell, where they will* enter and ***roast. What an evil resting-place!***

57. *This* punishment is what they will receive! ***So let them taste it: boiling water and scalding pus*** (read as *ghassāq* and *ghasāq*) – which is discharged from the people of the Fire –

قَالُوا رَبَّنَا مَن قَدَّمَ لَنَا هَٰذَا فَزِدْهُ عَذَابًا ضِعْفًا فِي النَّارِ ٦١
وَقَالُوا مَا لَنَا لَا نَرَىٰ رِجَالًا كُنَّا نَعُدُّهُم مِّنَ الْأَشْرَارِ ٦٢ أَتَّخَذْنَاهُمْ
سِخْرِيًّا أَمْ زَاغَتْ عَنْهُمُ الْأَبْصَارُ ٦٣ إِنَّ ذَٰلِكَ لَحَقٌّ تَخَاصُمُ أَهْلِ
النَّارِ ٦٤ قُلْ إِنَّمَا أَنَا مُنذِرٌ ۖ وَمَا مِنْ إِلَٰهٍ إِلَّا اللَّهُ الْوَاحِدُ الْقَهَّارُ ٦٥
رَبُّ السَّمَاوَاتِ وَالْأَرْضِ وَمَا بَيْنَهُمَا الْعَزِيزُ الْغَفَّارُ ٦٦ قُلْ هُوَ نَبَأٌ
عَظِيمٌ ٦٧ أَنتُمْ عَنْهُ مُعْرِضُونَ ٦٨ مَا كَانَ لِيَ مِنْ عِلْمٍ بِالْمَلَإِ الْأَعْلَىٰ
إِذْ يَخْتَصِمُونَ ٦٩ إِن يُوحَىٰ إِلَيَّ إِلَّا أَنَّمَا أَنَا نَذِيرٌ مُّبِينٌ ٧٠ إِذْ قَالَ رَبُّكَ
لِلْمَلَائِكَةِ إِنِّي خَالِقٌ بَشَرًا مِّن طِينٍ ٧١ فَإِذَا سَوَّيْتُهُ وَنَفَخْتُ فِيهِ
مِن رُّوحِي فَقَعُوا لَهُ سَاجِدِينَ ٧٢ فَسَجَدَ الْمَلَائِكَةُ كُلُّهُمْ
أَجْمَعُونَ ٧٣ إِلَّا إِبْلِيسَ اسْتَكْبَرَ وَكَانَ مِنَ الْكَافِرِينَ ٧٤ قَالَ
يَا إِبْلِيسُ مَا مَنَعَكَ أَن تَسْجُدَ لِمَا خَلَقْتُ بِيَدَيَّ ۖ أَسْتَكْبَرْتَ أَمْ كُنتَ
مِنَ الْعَالِينَ ٧٥ قَالَ أَنَا خَيْرٌ مِّنْهُ ۖ خَلَقْتَنِي مِن نَّارٍ وَخَلَقْتَهُ مِن طِينٍ
٧٦ قَالَ فَاخْرُجْ مِنْهَا فَإِنَّكَ رَجِيمٌ ٧٧ وَإِنَّ عَلَيْكَ لَعْنَتِي إِلَىٰ يَوْمِ
الدِّينِ ٧٨ قَالَ رَبِّ فَأَنظِرْنِي إِلَىٰ يَوْمِ يُبْعَثُونَ ٧٩ قَالَ فَإِنَّكَ مِنَ
الْمُنظَرِينَ ٨٠ إِلَىٰ يَوْمِ الْوَقْتِ الْمَعْلُومِ ٨١ قَالَ فَبِعِزَّتِكَ
لَأُغْوِيَنَّهُمْ أَجْمَعِينَ ٨٢ إِلَّا عِبَادَكَ مِنْهُمُ الْمُخْلَصِينَ ٨٣
قَالَ فَالْحَقُّ وَالْحَقَّ أَقُولُ ٨٤ لَأَمْلَأَنَّ جَهَنَّمَ مِنكَ وَمِمَّن تَبِعَكَ
مِنْهُمْ أَجْمَعِينَ ٨٥ قُلْ مَا أَسْأَلُكُمْ عَلَيْهِ مِنْ أَجْرٍ وَمَا أَنَا مِنَ الْمُتَكَلِّفِينَ
٨٦ إِنْ هُوَ إِلَّا ذِكْرٌ لِّلْعَالَمِينَ ٨٧ وَلَتَعْلَمُنَّ نَبَأَهُ بَعْدَ حِينٍ ٨٨

58. ***...and other*** (read as *ākhar* and *akhar,* pl. and sing.) ***such torments*** – like boiling water and pus and many different punishments.

59. The following is what will be said to them when they enter the Fire with their followers: ***This! A crowd hurtling in with you*** – entering with harshness. Then those who were followed will say: ***There is no welcome for them*** – meaning they will have no comfort. ***They will certainly roast in the Fire.***

60. ***They*** (the followers) ***will say, 'No, it is you who have no welcome. It is you who brought it*** (unbelief) ***upon us. What an evil place to settle*** is the Fire for us and you*!'*

61. ***They will say, 'Our Lord, give him who brought this on us double the punishment*** – for his unbelief – ***in the Fire!'***

62. ***They*** (the unbelievers) ***will say*** – in the Fire – ***'How is it that we do not see some men whom we used to count*** in the world ***among the worst of people?***

63. ***Did we turn them into figures of fun*** (read as *sukhriyya* and *sikhriyya*)***?*** They will notice their absence. ***Did our eyes disdain to look at them*** so that they cannot see them now***?'*** This refers to the poor Muslims like 'Ammār, Bilāl, Ṣuhayb and Salmān.

64. ***All this is certainly true*** and must occur***: the bickering of the people of Hell.***

65. ***Say***, Muḥammad, to the unbelievers of Makka***: 'I am only a warner*** about the Fire***. There is no god except Allah, the One, the All-Conquering…***

66. ***...Lord of the heavens and the earth and everything between them, the Almighty*** over all things, ***the Endlessly Forgiving*** towards His creation.*'*

67. ***Say*** to them***: 'This is momentous news...***

68. ***...yet you ignore it!*** You turn away from the Qur'an, which informs you and brings you news of that which is only known by Revelation.

69. ***I knew nothing of the Highest Assembly*** of the angels ***when they debated*** about Ādam when Allah said, *"I am putting a regent on the earth."* (2:30)

70. ***It is only revealed to me that I am a clear warner*** – making the warning clear to you.*'*

71. Remember when ***your Lord said to the angels, 'I am going to create a human being out of clay*** – meaning Ādam.

72. ***When I have*** completely ***formed him and breathed*** some of ***My Spirit into him*** – so that he has life: the spirit is ascribed to Allah to honour Ādam. Spirit is a subtle substance which gives life to the human being when it enters it – ***fall down in prostration to him*** – to greet him by bowing before him*!'*

73. ***So the angels prostrated, all of them together …***

74. ***…except for Iblīs*** – the father of the jinn, who was with the angels – ***who was arrogant and was one of the unbelievers*** – in the knowledge of Allah.

75. ***He said, 'Iblīs, what prevented you prostrating to what I created with My own Hands?*** This allusion of direct contact is to show honour to Ādam, as Allah created all things. ***Were you*** now ***overcome by arrogance*** – said to rebuke him – ***or are you one of the exalted*** – too proud to prostrate because you are one of them*?'*

76. ***He said, 'I am better than him. You created me from fire but You created him from clay.'***

77. ***He said, 'Get out*** of the Garden*!* It is said that this means "out of the heavens". ***You are accursed*** and expelled*!*

78. ***My curse is upon you until the Day of Reckoning*** and repayment.*'*

79. ***He said, 'My Lord, grant me a reprieve until the Day they*** (mankind) ***are raised again.'***

80. ***He said, 'You are among the reprieved…***

81. ***…until the Day whose time is known.'*** This is the time of the first Blast.

82. ***He said, 'By Your might, I will mislead all of them…***

83. ***…except for Your chosen slaves*** (the believers) ***among them.'***

84. ***He said, 'By the truth*** (read as *fa'l-ḥaqqu* and *fa'l-ḥaqqi*) ***– and I speak the truth –***

85. ***I will fill up Hell with you*** (your descendants) ***and every one of them who follows you.'***

86. ***Say: 'I do not ask you for any wage for it*** – for conveying the Message, ***nor am I a man of false pretensions.*** He does not lay claim to what he does not merit, meaning that the Qur'an is not from him.

87. ***It*** (the Qur'an) ***is simply a reminder to all the worlds*** – in other words, to men and jinn and all creatures with understanding except for the angels.

88. ***You will come to know,*** people of Makka, the truth of ***what it is talking about after a while*** (after the Day of Resurrection).' This implies an oath that that will be fulfilled.

سُورَةُ الزُّمَرِ

بِسۡمِ ٱللَّهِ ٱلرَّحۡمَٰنِ ٱلرَّحِيمِ

تَنزِيلُ ٱلۡكِتَٰبِ مِنَ ٱللَّهِ ٱلۡعَزِيزِ ٱلۡحَكِيمِ ١ إِنَّآ أَنزَلۡنَآ إِلَيۡكَ
ٱلۡكِتَٰبَ بِٱلۡحَقِّ فَٱعۡبُدِ ٱللَّهَ مُخۡلِصٗا لَّهُ ٱلدِّينَ ٢ أَلَا
لِلَّهِ ٱلدِّينُ ٱلۡخَالِصُۚ وَٱلَّذِينَ ٱتَّخَذُواْ مِن دُونِهِۦٓ أَوۡلِيَآءَ
مَا نَعۡبُدُهُمۡ إِلَّا لِيُقَرِّبُونَآ إِلَى ٱللَّهِ زُلۡفَىٰٓ إِنَّ ٱللَّهَ يَحۡكُمُ بَيۡنَهُمۡ
فِي مَا هُمۡ فِيهِ يَخۡتَلِفُونَۗ إِنَّ ٱللَّهَ لَا يَهۡدِي مَنۡ هُوَ كَٰذِبٞ
كَفَّارٞ ٣ لَّوۡ أَرَادَ ٱللَّهُ أَن يَتَّخِذَ وَلَدٗا لَّٱصۡطَفَىٰ مِمَّا
يَخۡلُقُ مَا يَشَآءُۚ سُبۡحَٰنَهُۥۖ هُوَ ٱللَّهُ ٱلۡوَٰحِدُ ٱلۡقَهَّارُ ٤
خَلَقَ ٱلسَّمَٰوَٰتِ وَٱلۡأَرۡضَ بِٱلۡحَقِّۖ يُكَوِّرُ ٱلَّيۡلَ عَلَى ٱلنَّهَارِ
وَيُكَوِّرُ ٱلنَّهَارَ عَلَى ٱلَّيۡلِۖ وَسَخَّرَ ٱلشَّمۡسَ وَٱلۡقَمَرَۖ
كُلّٞ يَجۡرِي لِأَجَلٖ مُّسَمًّىۗ أَلَا هُوَ ٱلۡعَزِيزُ ٱلۡغَفَّٰرُ ٥
خَلَقَكُم مِّن نَّفۡسٖ وَٰحِدَةٖ ثُمَّ جَعَلَ مِنۡهَا زَوۡجَهَا وَأَنزَلَ لَكُم
مِّنَ ٱلۡأَنۡعَٰمِ ثَمَٰنِيَةَ أَزۡوَٰجٖۚ يَخۡلُقُكُمۡ فِي بُطُونِ أُمَّهَٰتِكُمۡ
خَلۡقٗا مِّنۢ بَعۡدِ خَلۡقٖ فِي ظُلُمَٰتٖ ثَلَٰثٖۚ ذَٰلِكُمُ ٱللَّهُ رَبُّكُمۡ لَهُ
ٱلۡمُلۡكُۖ لَآ إِلَٰهَ إِلَّا هُوَۖ فَأَنَّىٰ تُصۡرَفُونَ ٦ إِن تَكۡفُرُواْ فَإِنَّ
ٱللَّهَ غَنِيٌّ عَنكُمۡۖ وَلَا يَرۡضَىٰ لِعِبَادِهِ ٱلۡكُفۡرَۖ وَإِن تَشۡكُرُواْ يَرۡضَهُ
لَكُمۡۗ وَلَا تَزِرُ وَازِرَةٞ وِزۡرَ أُخۡرَىٰۗ ثُمَّ إِلَىٰ رَبِّكُم مَّرۡجِعُكُمۡ
فَيُنَبِّئُكُم بِمَا كُنتُمۡ تَعۡمَلُونَۚ إِنَّهُۥ عَلِيمُۢ بِذَاتِ ٱلصُّدُورِ ٧
۞ وَإِذَا مَسَّ ٱلۡإِنسَٰنَ ضُرّٞ دَعَا رَبَّهُۥ مُنِيبًا إِلَيۡهِ ثُمَّ إِذَا خَوَّلَهُۥ

39. *Sūrat az-Zumar*
The Companies

This *sūra* is Makkan except for *āyat*s 52, 53, and 54, which are Madinan. It has 75 *āyat*s and was sent down after *Sabā'*.

1. ***The revelation of the Book*** (the Qur'an) ***is from Allah, the Almighty*** in His kingdom***, the All-Wise*** in what He does.

2. ***We have sent down the Book to you***, Muḥammad, ***with truth. So worship Allah, making your dīn sincerely His*** – free from *shirk*; so proclaim His Unity.

3. ***Indeed is the sincere* dīn *not Allah's alone?*** None but Him deserve it. ***If people take protectors*** (idols) ***besides Him***, saying: ***'We only worship them so that they may bring us nearer to Allah', Allah will judge between them*** and the Muslims ***regarding the things about which they differed*** concerning the *dīn*; and the believers will enter Paradise and the unbelievers Hell. ***Allah does not guide anyone who is an ungrateful liar*** – lying by ascribing a son to Him, and ungrateful by worshipping gods other than Allah.

4. ***If Allah had desired to have a son*** – as they maintain in saying, *"The All-Merciful has a son"* (19:88) – ***He would have chosen whatever He wished from what He has created*** – and would have had a son rather than what they say about the angels being the daughters of Allah, 'Uzayr being the son of Allah or the Messiah being the son of Allah. ***Glory be to Him!*** He is far exalted above having a child. ***He is Allah, the One, the All-Conquering.***

5. ***He created the heavens and the earth with truth. He wraps the night around the day*** – and it increases – ***and wraps the day around the night*** – and it increases, ***and has made the sun and moon subservient, each one running*** in their orbit ***for a specified term*** – until the Day of Resurrection. ***Is He not indeed the Almighty,*** with absolute power who takes revenge on His enemies, ***the Endlessly Forgiving*** to His friends***?***

6. ***He created you from a single self*** (Ādam), ***then produced its mate*** (Ḥawwā') ***from it, and sent down livestock*** – comprising

نِعْمَةً مِّنْهُ نَسِيَ مَا كَانَ يَدْعُوٓاْ إِلَيْهِ مِن قَبْلُ وَجَعَلَ لِلَّهِ أَندَادًا
لِّيُضِلَّ عَن سَبِيلِهِۦۚ قُلْ تَمَتَّعْ بِكُفْرِكَ قَلِيلًاۖ إِنَّكَ مِنْ أَصْحَٰبِ
ٱلنَّارِ ﴿٨﴾ أَمَّنْ هُوَ قَٰنِتٌ ءَانَآءَ ٱلَّيْلِ سَاجِدًا وَقَآئِمًا يَحْذَرُ
ٱلْأَاخِرَةَ وَيَرْجُواْ رَحْمَةَ رَبِّهِۦۗ قُلْ هَلْ يَسْتَوِى ٱلَّذِينَ يَعْلَمُونَ وَٱلَّذِينَ
لَا يَعْلَمُونَۗ إِنَّمَا يَتَذَكَّرُ أُوْلُواْ ٱلْأَلْبَٰبِ ﴿٩﴾ قُلْ يَٰعِبَادِ ٱلَّذِينَ
ءَامَنُواْ ٱتَّقُواْ رَبَّكُمْۚ لِلَّذِينَ أَحْسَنُواْ فِى هَٰذِهِ ٱلدُّنْيَا حَسَنَةٌۗ
وَأَرْضُ ٱللَّهِ وَٰسِعَةٌۗ إِنَّمَا يُوَفَّى ٱلصَّٰبِرُونَ أَجْرَهُم بِغَيْرِ حِسَابٍ ﴿١٠﴾
قُلْ إِنِّىٓ أُمِرْتُ أَنْ أَعْبُدَ ٱللَّهَ مُخْلِصًا لَّهُ ٱلدِّينَ ﴿١١﴾ وَأُمِرْتُ لِأَنْ أَكُونَ
أَوَّلَ ٱلْمُسْلِمِينَ ﴿١٢﴾ قُلْ إِنِّىٓ أَخَافُ إِنْ عَصَيْتُ رَبِّى عَذَابَ يَوْمٍ عَظِيمٍ
﴿١٣﴾ قُلِ ٱللَّهَ أَعْبُدُ مُخْلِصًا لَّهُۥ دِينِى ﴿١٤﴾ فَٱعْبُدُواْ مَا شِئْتُم مِّن دُونِهِۦۗ
قُلْ إِنَّ ٱلْخَٰسِرِينَ ٱلَّذِينَ خَسِرُوٓاْ أَنفُسَهُمْ وَأَهْلِيهِمْ يَوْمَ ٱلْقِيَٰمَةِۗ أَلَا
ذَٰلِكَ هُوَ ٱلْخُسْرَانُ ٱلْمُبِينُ ﴿١٥﴾ لَهُم مِّن فَوْقِهِمْ ظُلَلٌ مِّنَ ٱلنَّارِ
وَمِن تَحْتِهِمْ ظُلَلٌۚ ذَٰلِكَ يُخَوِّفُ ٱللَّهُ بِهِۦ عِبَادَهُۥۚ يَٰعِبَادِ فَٱتَّقُونِ ﴿١٦﴾
وَٱلَّذِينَ ٱجْتَنَبُواْ ٱلطَّٰغُوتَ أَن يَعْبُدُوهَا وَأَنَابُوٓاْ إِلَى ٱللَّهِ لَهُمُ ٱلْبُشْرَىٰۚ
فَبَشِّرْ عِبَادِ ﴿١٧﴾ ٱلَّذِينَ يَسْتَمِعُونَ ٱلْقَوْلَ فَيَتَّبِعُونَ أَحْسَنَهُۥٓۚ
أُوْلَٰٓئِكَ ٱلَّذِينَ هَدَىٰهُمُ ٱللَّهُۖ وَأُوْلَٰٓئِكَ هُمْ أُوْلُواْ ٱلْأَلْبَٰبِ ﴿١٨﴾
أَفَمَنْ حَقَّ عَلَيْهِ كَلِمَةُ ٱلْعَذَابِ أَفَأَنتَ تُنقِذُ مَن فِى ٱلنَّارِ ﴿١٩﴾
لَٰكِنِ ٱلَّذِينَ ٱتَّقَوْاْ رَبَّهُمْ لَهُمْ غُرَفٌ مِّن فَوْقِهَا غُرَفٌ مَّبْنِيَّةٌ تَجْرِى
مِن تَحْتِهَا ٱلْأَنْهَٰرُۖ وَعْدَ ٱللَّهِۖ لَا يُخْلِفُ ٱللَّهُ ٱلْمِيعَادَ ﴿٢٠﴾ أَلَمْ تَرَ
أَنَّ ٱللَّهَ أَنزَلَ مِنَ ٱلسَّمَآءِ مَآءً فَسَلَكَهُۥ يَنَٰبِيعَ فِى ٱلْأَرْضِ ثُمَّ

camels, cattle, sheep and goats, a male and female of each, as is explained in *Sūrat al-An'ām* – ***to you – eight kinds in pairs. He creates you stage by stage in your mothers' wombs*** – first as a drop, then a clot, then a piece of flesh – ***in a threefold darkness*** – the darkness of the belly, the darkness of the womb and the darkness of the placenta. ***That is Allah, your Lord. Sovereignty is His. There is no god but Him. So what has made you deviate*** from worshipping Him to the worship of something else?

7. ***If you are ungrateful, Allah is rich beyond need of any of you and He is not pleased with ingratitude in His slaves.*** Even if He has willed that some people worship other than Him, He is nevertheless not pleased with that. ***But if you are grateful*** to Allah and believe – ***He is pleased with you for that*** gratitude. ***No burden-bearer*** (soul) ***can bear another's burden. Then you will return to your Lord and He will inform you of what you did. He knows what the heart contains.***

8. ***When harm touches*** an unbelieving ***man he calls upon his Lord,*** entreating and turning to him – ***repenting to Him. Then when He grants him a blessing from Him, he forgets what he was calling for before*** from Allah and, stops doing that – ***and ascribes rivals*** (partners) ***to Allah, so as to misguide*** (read as *yuḍilla* and *yaḍilla*) ***others from His Way*** – Islam. ***Say: 'Enjoy your unbelief for a little while*** – the rest of your lifespan. ***You are among the Companions of the Fire.'***

9. ***What of him who spends the night hours in prayer prostrating and standing up, mindful of the Next World*** – fearing the punishment of the Next World, ***hoping for the mercy of his Lord*** in Paradise? ***Say: 'Are they the same, those who know and those who do not know?'*** Is such a person like someone who disobeys as an unbeliever? They are not equal, in the same way that a person with knowledge and an ignorant person are not equal. ***It is only people of intelligence who pay heed*** and are warned.

10. ***Say: 'Slaves of Mine who believe, be fearful of your Lord*** – and demonstrate your fear of His punishment by obeying Him. ***For those who do good in this world*** by obeying Allah ***there is good*** – the Garden; ***and Allah's earth is spacious*** – so that it is possible to emigrate, leaving the unbelievers and the sight of objectionable things.

The steadfast – in obedience and in the face of the tests they undergo – ***will be paid their wages in full without any reckoning*** by measure or weight.*'*

11. ***Say: 'I am commanded to worship Allah, making my* dīn *sincerely His*** – free of any *shirk*,

12. ***...and I am commanded to be the first of the Muslims*** of this community.*'*

13. ***Say: 'I fear, were I to disobey my Lord, the punishment of a Terrible Day.'***

14. ***Say: 'It is Allah I worship, making my* dīn *sincerely His*** – free of any *shirk* –

15. ***… so worship anything you will apart from Him!'*** This is a threat to them and an announcement that they do not worship Allah Almighty. Allah says: ***Say: 'The real losers are those who lose themselves and their families on the Day of Rising.'*** This is because their souls will be in the Fire for ever and will not reach the houris that would have been made ready for them in the Garden if they had believed. ***Is not that a clear loss?***

16. ***They will have awnings*** made ***of Fire above them and awnings below them. By that Allah strikes fear into His slaves*** – the believers who fear Him – ***'So be fearful, My slaves, of Me!'***

17. ***Those who shun the worship of false gods*** (idols) ***and turn towards Allah will have good news*** of Paradise, ***so give good news to My slaves.***

18. ***Those who listen well to what is said and follow the best of it,*** that in which their best interest lies, ***they are the ones whom Allah has guided; they are the people of intelligence.***

19. ***But as for those against whom the decree of Punishment*** – which is found in the words: *"I will fill Hellfire…"* (7:18) – ***is justly carried out, can you rescue*** and bring out ***those who are in the Fire?*** You cannot guide such people and save them from the Fire.

20. ***But those who are fearful of their Lord*** and obey Him ***will have high-ceilinged Halls, and more such Halls built one above the other, and rivers flowing under them. That is Allah's promise. Allah does not break His promise.***

يُخْرِجُ بِهِۦ زَرْعًا مُّخْتَلِفًا أَلْوَٰنُهُۥ ثُمَّ يَهِيجُ فَتَرَىٰهُ مُصْفَرًّا ثُمَّ
يَجْعَلُهُۥ حُطَٰمًا ۚ إِنَّ فِى ذَٰلِكَ لَذِكْرَىٰ لِأُو۟لِى ٱلْأَلْبَٰبِ ٢١
أَفَمَن شَرَحَ ٱللَّهُ صَدْرَهُۥ لِلْإِسْلَٰمِ فَهُوَ عَلَىٰ نُورٍ مِّن رَّبِّهِۦ ۚ فَوَيْلٌ
لِّلْقَٰسِيَةِ قُلُوبُهُم مِّن ذِكْرِ ٱللَّهِ ۚ أُو۟لَٰٓئِكَ فِى ضَلَٰلٍ مُّبِينٍ ٢٢
ٱللَّهُ نَزَّلَ أَحْسَنَ ٱلْحَدِيثِ كِتَٰبًا مُّتَشَٰبِهًا مَّثَانِىَ تَقْشَعِرُّ مِنْهُ
جُلُودُ ٱلَّذِينَ يَخْشَوْنَ رَبَّهُمْ ثُمَّ تَلِينُ جُلُودُهُمْ وَقُلُوبُهُمْ
إِلَىٰ ذِكْرِ ٱللَّهِ ۚ ذَٰلِكَ هُدَى ٱللَّهِ يَهْدِى بِهِۦ مَن يَشَآءُ ۚ وَمَن
يُضْلِلِ ٱللَّهُ فَمَا لَهُۥ مِنْ هَادٍ ٢٣ أَفَمَن يَتَّقِى بِوَجْهِهِۦ سُوٓءَ
ٱلْعَذَابِ يَوْمَ ٱلْقِيَٰمَةِ ۚ وَقِيلَ لِلظَّٰلِمِينَ ذُوقُوا۟ مَا كُنتُمْ تَكْسِبُونَ
٢٤ كَذَّبَ ٱلَّذِينَ مِن قَبْلِهِمْ فَأَتَىٰهُمُ ٱلْعَذَابُ مِنْ حَيْثُ
لَا يَشْعُرُونَ ٢٥ فَأَذَاقَهُمُ ٱللَّهُ ٱلْخِزْىَ فِى ٱلْحَيَوٰةِ ٱلدُّنْيَا ۖ وَلَعَذَابُ
ٱلْـَٔاخِرَةِ أَكْبَرُ ۚ لَوْ كَانُوا۟ يَعْلَمُونَ ٢٦ وَلَقَدْ ضَرَبْنَا لِلنَّاسِ فِى
هَٰذَا ٱلْقُرْءَانِ مِن كُلِّ مَثَلٍ لَّعَلَّهُمْ يَتَذَكَّرُونَ ٢٧ قُرْءَانًا عَرَبِيًّا
غَيْرَ ذِى عِوَجٍ لَّعَلَّهُمْ يَتَّقُونَ ٢٨ ضَرَبَ ٱللَّهُ مَثَلًا رَّجُلًا فِيهِ
شُرَكَآءُ مُتَشَٰكِسُونَ وَرَجُلًا سَلَمًا لِّرَجُلٍ هَلْ يَسْتَوِيَانِ مَثَلًا ۚ
ٱلْحَمْدُ لِلَّهِ ۚ بَلْ أَكْثَرُهُمْ لَا يَعْلَمُونَ ٢٩ إِنَّكَ مَيِّتٌ وَإِنَّهُم مَّيِّتُونَ
٣٠ ثُمَّ إِنَّكُمْ يَوْمَ ٱلْقِيَٰمَةِ عِندَ رَبِّكُمْ تَخْتَصِمُونَ ٣١
۞ فَمَنْ أَظْلَمُ مِمَّن كَذَبَ عَلَى ٱللَّهِ وَكَذَّبَ بِٱلصِّدْقِ
إِذْ جَآءَهُۥٓ ۚ أَلَيْسَ فِى جَهَنَّمَ مَثْوًى لِّلْكَٰفِرِينَ ٣٢ وَٱلَّذِى
جَآءَ بِٱلصِّدْقِ وَصَدَّقَ بِهِۦٓ ۙ أُو۟لَٰٓئِكَ هُمُ ٱلْمُتَّقُونَ ٣٣

21. ***Do you not see*** and know ***that Allah sends down water from the sky*** which penetrates the earth, ***and threads it through the earth to emerge as springs and then by it brings forth crops of varying colours, which then*** dry and ***wither; and you see them turning yellow*** after having been green, ***and then He makes them into broken stubble? There is a reminder in that for people of intelligence*** – who are reminded by that of the evidence it provides of the oneness and power of Allah Almighty.

22. ***Is he whose breast is opened to Islam*** – and thus is guided – ***and who is therefore illuminated by his Lord*** like one whose heart is sealed ***…? Woe*** – in other words they will be punished – ***to those whose hearts are hardened against the remembrance of Allah***, preventing them from accepting the Qur'an***! Such people are clearly misguided.***

23. ***Allah has sent down the Supreme Discourse*** (the Qur'an) ***a Book consistent*** – the word used means that its parts resemble one another in organisation – ***in its frequent repetitions*** – the word used means that threats, promises, and other things are repeated in it. ***The skins of those who fear their Lord tremble at it*** – when they hear His threat mentioned – ***and then their skins and hearts yield softly to the remembrance of Allah*** when His promise is mentioned. ***That is Allah's guidance by which He guides whoever He wills. And no one can guide those whom Allah misguides.***

24. ***Is someone who tries to shield himself with his face from the worst of the torment on the Day of Rising…?*** He tries to protect his face from the intensity of the heat when he is cast into the Fire with his hands chained to his neck. Is he like the one who is made safe from that by entering Paradise? ***The wrongdoers will be told, 'Taste what you have earned.'***

25. ***Those before them also denied the truth*** – by denying their Messenger's warnings about Divine punishment – ***and the punishment came upon them from where they did not expect*** – in a manner which had not occurred to them.

26. ***So Allah made them taste disgrace*** – humiliation and abasement – ***in the life of this world*** – in the form of transmogrification, being killed and other things – ***and the punishment of the Next World is far worse if they*** (the deniers) ***only knew*** it.

27. ***We have given all kinds of examples to people in this Qur'an, so that perhaps they will may heed –***

28. ***...an Arabic Qur'an with no distortion in it*** – no confusion or disagreement – ***so that perhaps they will be godfearing*** and beware of unbelief.

29. ***Allah has made a comparison for them*** of idolaters and those who affirm Allah's unity***: of a man owned by several partners in dispute with one another –*** whose evil qualities contend with one another – ***and another man wholly owned by a single man*** – who is wholehearted. ***Are they the same?*** A slave with several owners is not the same as a slave with one master. If the owners of the first all demand his service at the same time, he is bewildered about which of them to serve. This is like the idolater. The second is like the true believer. ***Praise be to Allah*** alone***! The fact is that most of them*** (the people of Makka) ***do not know*** the punishment which will befall them, and so they attribute partners to Allah.

30. This *āyat* is addressed to the Prophet, may Allah bless him and grant him peace. ***You will die and they too will die.*** You will die just as they will die, and so the fact of dying cannot be a source of insult. This was revealed because they thought he was taking a long time to die, may Allah bless him and grant him peace.

31. ***Then on the Day of Rising you*** – mankind – ***will argue*** about the differences between you ***in the presence of your Lord.***

32. ***Who could do greater wrong than those who lie about Allah*** – and ascribe a partner and a child to Him – ***and deny the truth*** (the Qur'an) ***when it comes to them?*** No one could do a greater wrong than this. ***Do the unbelievers not have a dwelling place in Hell?*** Indeed they do.

33. ***He who brings the truth*** – meaning the Prophet, may Allah bless him and grant him peace – ***and those who confirm it*** – meaning the believers – ***those*** (although the singular form, *alladhī,* is used here, the meaning is the plural *alladhīna*) ***are the people who are god-fearing*** and wary of *shirk*.

لَهُم مَّا يَشَآءُونَ عِندَ رَبِّهِمْۚ ذَٰلِكَ جَزَآءُ ٱلْمُحْسِنِينَ ﴿٣٤﴾
لِيُكَفِّرَ ٱللَّهُ عَنْهُمْ أَسْوَأَ ٱلَّذِى عَمِلُوا۟ وَيَجْزِيَهُمْ أَجْرَهُم
بِأَحْسَنِ ٱلَّذِى كَانُوا۟ يَعْمَلُونَ ﴿٣٥﴾ أَلَيْسَ ٱللَّهُ بِكَافٍ
عَبْدَهُۥۖ وَيُخَوِّفُونَكَ بِٱلَّذِينَ مِن دُونِهِۦۚ وَمَن يُضْلِلِ
ٱللَّهُ فَمَا لَهُۥ مِنْ هَادٍ ﴿٣٦﴾ وَمَن يَهْدِ ٱللَّهُ فَمَا لَهُۥ مِن مُّضِلٍّۗ
أَلَيْسَ ٱللَّهُ بِعَزِيزٍ ذِى ٱنتِقَامٍ ﴿٣٧﴾ وَلَئِن سَأَلْتَهُم مَّنْ خَلَقَ
ٱلسَّمَٰوَٰتِ وَٱلْأَرْضَ لَيَقُولُنَّ ٱللَّهُۚ قُلْ أَفَرَءَيْتُم مَّا تَدْعُونَ
مِن دُونِ ٱللَّهِ إِنْ أَرَادَنِىَ ٱللَّهُ بِضُرٍّ هَلْ هُنَّ كَٰشِفَٰتُ ضُرِّهِۦٓ
أَوْ أَرَادَنِى بِرَحْمَةٍ هَلْ هُنَّ مُمْسِكَٰتُ رَحْمَتِهِۦۚ قُلْ حَسْبِىَ
ٱللَّهُۖ عَلَيْهِ يَتَوَكَّلُ ٱلْمُتَوَكِّلُونَ ﴿٣٨﴾ قُلْ يَٰقَوْمِ ٱعْمَلُوا۟
عَلَىٰ مَكَانَتِكُمْ إِنِّى عَٰمِلٌۖ فَسَوْفَ تَعْلَمُونَ ﴿٣٩﴾
مَن يَأْتِيهِ عَذَابٌ يُخْزِيهِ وَيَحِلُّ عَلَيْهِ عَذَابٌ مُّقِيمٌ ﴿٤٠﴾
إِنَّآ أَنزَلْنَا عَلَيْكَ ٱلْكِتَٰبَ لِلنَّاسِ بِٱلْحَقِّۖ فَمَنِ ٱهْتَدَىٰ
فَلِنَفْسِهِۦۖ وَمَن ضَلَّ فَإِنَّمَا يَضِلُّ عَلَيْهَاۖ وَمَآ أَنتَ عَلَيْهِم
بِوَكِيلٍ ﴿٤١﴾ ٱللَّهُ يَتَوَفَّى ٱلْأَنفُسَ حِينَ مَوْتِهَا وَٱلَّتِى
لَمْ تَمُتْ فِى مَنَامِهَاۖ فَيُمْسِكُ ٱلَّتِى قَضَىٰ عَلَيْهَا ٱلْمَوْتَ
وَيُرْسِلُ ٱلْأُخْرَىٰٓ إِلَىٰٓ أَجَلٍ مُّسَمًّىۚ إِنَّ فِى ذَٰلِكَ لَءَايَٰتٍ
لِّقَوْمٍ يَتَفَكَّرُونَ ﴿٤٢﴾ أَمِ ٱتَّخَذُوا۟ مِن دُونِ ٱللَّهِ شُفَعَآءَۚ
قُلْ أَوَلَوْ كَانُوا۟ لَا يَمْلِكُونَ شَيْـًٔا وَلَا يَعْقِلُونَ ﴿٤٣﴾
قُل لِّلَّهِ ٱلشَّفَٰعَةُ جَمِيعًاۖ لَّهُۥ مُلْكُ ٱلسَّمَٰوَٰتِ وَٱلْأَرْضِۖ ثُمَّ

34. ***They shall have anything they wish for from their Lord. That is the recompense of the good-doers*** for their faith –

35. ***… so that Allah may erase from their records the worst of what they did and pay them their wages for the best of what they did.*** This means their good and bad actions.

36. ***Is Allah not enough for His slave*** (the Prophet)***? Yet they try to scare you*** (addressed to him) ***with others*** (idols) ***apart from Him.*** They tried to scare him with idols, saying that they would kill him.

37. ***If Allah misguides anyone, he has no guide; and if Allah guides anyone, he cannot be misguided. Is Allah not Almighty, Exactor of Revenge*** against His enemies?

38. ***If you ask them, 'Who created the heavens and the earth?' they will say, 'Allah.' Say: 'So what do you think? If Allah desires harm for me, can those*** (the idols) ***you call upon*** and worship ***besides Allah remove His harm*** (read as *ḍurrihi* and *ḍurrahu*)***? Or if He desires mercy for me, can they withhold His mercy*** (read as *raḥmatihi* and *raḥmatahu*)***?'*** They cannot. ***Say: 'Allah is enough for me. All those who truly trust put their trust in Him.'***

39. ***Say: 'My people, do as you think best; that is what I am doing.*** This is my state and your state. ***You will soon know…***

40. ***…who will receive a punishment which disgraces him and will unleash against himself an everlasting punishment'*** – the punishment of the Fire. Allah disgraced the idolaters at the Battle of Badr.

41. ***We have sent down to you the Book for mankind with truth. So whoever is guided is guided to his own good and whoever is misguided, it is to his detriment. You are not set over them as a guardian*** – to compel them to follow guidance.

42. ***Allah takes back people's souls when their death arrives; and those who have not yet died,*** He takes their souls ***while they are asleep. He keeps hold of those whose death has been decreed and sends the others back for a specified term*** – until the time of their death. Releasing the soul means that the body remains alive, which is not the case when Allah keeps hold of the soul. ***There are certainly Signs in that for people who reflect*** and therefore know that the One who has the power to do that has the power to resurrect. Quraysh did not deny that.

إِلَيْهِ تُرْجَعُونَ ﴿٤٤﴾ وَإِذَا ذُكِرَ ٱللَّهُ وَحْدَهُ ٱشْمَأَزَّتْ
قُلُوبُ ٱلَّذِينَ لَا يُؤْمِنُونَ بِٱلْـَٔاخِرَةِ ۖ وَإِذَا ذُكِرَ ٱلَّذِينَ مِن
دُونِهِۦٓ إِذَا هُمْ يَسْتَبْشِرُونَ ﴿٤٥﴾ قُلِ ٱللَّهُمَّ فَاطِرَ ٱلسَّمَٰوَٰتِ
وَٱلْأَرْضِ عَٰلِمَ ٱلْغَيْبِ وَٱلشَّهَٰدَةِ أَنتَ تَحْكُمُ بَيْنَ عِبَادِكَ
فِى مَا كَانُوا۟ فِيهِ يَخْتَلِفُونَ ﴿٤٦﴾ وَلَوْ أَنَّ لِلَّذِينَ ظَلَمُوا۟
مَا فِى ٱلْأَرْضِ جَمِيعًا وَمِثْلَهُۥ مَعَهُۥ لَٱفْتَدَوْا۟ بِهِۦ مِن سُوٓءِ ٱلْعَذَابِ
يَوْمَ ٱلْقِيَٰمَةِ ۚ وَبَدَا لَهُم مِّنَ ٱللَّهِ مَا لَمْ يَكُونُوا۟ يَحْتَسِبُونَ ﴿٤٧﴾
وَبَدَا لَهُمْ سَيِّـَٔاتُ مَا كَسَبُوا۟ وَحَاقَ بِهِم مَّا كَانُوا۟ بِهِۦ
يَسْتَهْزِءُونَ ﴿٤٨﴾ فَإِذَا مَسَّ ٱلْإِنسَٰنَ ضُرٌّ دَعَانَا ثُمَّ إِذَا خَوَّلْنَٰهُ
نِعْمَةً مِّنَّا قَالَ إِنَّمَآ أُوتِيتُهُۥ عَلَىٰ عِلْمٍۭ ۚ بَلْ هِىَ فِتْنَةٌ وَلَٰكِنَّ
أَكْثَرَهُمْ لَا يَعْلَمُونَ ﴿٤٩﴾ قَدْ قَالَهَا ٱلَّذِينَ مِن قَبْلِهِمْ فَمَآ أَغْنَىٰ
عَنْهُم مَّا كَانُوا۟ يَكْسِبُونَ ﴿٥٠﴾ فَأَصَابَهُمْ سَيِّـَٔاتُ مَا كَسَبُوا۟ ۚ
وَٱلَّذِينَ ظَلَمُوا۟ مِنْ هَٰٓؤُلَآءِ سَيُصِيبُهُمْ سَيِّـَٔاتُ مَا كَسَبُوا۟
وَمَا هُم بِمُعْجِزِينَ ﴿٥١﴾ أَوَلَمْ يَعْلَمُوٓا۟ أَنَّ ٱللَّهَ يَبْسُطُ ٱلرِّزْقَ
لِمَن يَشَآءُ وَيَقْدِرُ ۚ إِنَّ فِى ذَٰلِكَ لَـَٔايَٰتٍ لِّقَوْمٍ يُؤْمِنُونَ ﴿٥٢﴾
۞ قُلْ يَٰعِبَادِىَ ٱلَّذِينَ أَسْرَفُوا۟ عَلَىٰٓ أَنفُسِهِمْ لَا تَقْنَطُوا۟ مِن
رَّحْمَةِ ٱللَّهِ ۚ إِنَّ ٱللَّهَ يَغْفِرُ ٱلذُّنُوبَ جَمِيعًا ۚ إِنَّهُۥ هُوَ ٱلْغَفُورُ ٱلرَّحِيمُ
﴿٥٣﴾ وَأَنِيبُوٓا۟ إِلَىٰ رَبِّكُمْ وَأَسْلِمُوا۟ لَهُۥ مِن قَبْلِ أَن يَأْتِيَكُمُ
ٱلْعَذَابُ ثُمَّ لَا تُنصَرُونَ ﴿٥٤﴾ وَٱتَّبِعُوٓا۟ أَحْسَنَ مَآ أُنزِلَ
إِلَيْكُم مِّن رَّبِّكُم مِّن قَبْلِ أَن يَأْتِيَكُمُ ٱلْعَذَابُ

43. ***Or have they adopted intercessors besides Allah*** – idols as gods, claiming that they will intercede for them with Allah*?* ***Say*** to them*:* 'Will they intercede ***even though they do not control a thing*** by way of intercession or anything else*,* ***and have no awareness*** that they worship them or any anything else*?* They will not.

44. ***Say: 'Intercession is entirely Allah's affair.*** He alone has power of intercession and no one is allowed to intercede except with His permission. ***The kingdom of the heavens and earth is His. Then you will be returned to Him.'***

45. ***When Allah is mentioned on His own*** – rather than with their other gods – ***the hearts of those who do not believe in the Next World shrink back shuddering*** – exhibiting great aversion and contraction – ***but when others*** (idols) ***apart from Him are mentioned, they jump for joy.***

46. ***Say: 'O Allah, Originator of the heavens and the earth, Knower of the Unseen and the Visible, You will judge between Your slaves regarding what they differed about*** in respect of the *dīn*, so guide me to the truth in that on which there is disagreement.*'*

47. ***If those who did wrong owned everything on earth, and the same again with it, they would offer it as a ransom to save themselves from the evil of the punishment on the Day of Rising. What confronts them from Allah will be something they did not reckon with*** – which they did not think would happen.

48. ***What confronts them will be the evil actions which they earned, and what they used to mock at will engulf them*** – in other words, the punishment they had been warned about.

49. ***When harm touches man*** – mankind in general – ***he calls on Us. Then when We grant him a blessing from Us he says, 'I have only been given this because of my knowledge*** – which I have been given by Allah; so I am entitled to it and deserve it.*'* ***In fact it*** – referring to the statement or the blessing – ***is a trial*** – a test to which the slave is subjected – ***but most of them do not know it*** – how they are tried and led on.

50. ***Those who came before them*** – referring to past nations like Qārūn and his people who thought like that – ***also said that, but what they earned did not avail them.***

بَغْتَةً وَأَنتُمْ لَا تَشْعُرُونَ ﴿٥٥﴾ أَن تَقُولَ نَفْسٌ يَٰحَسْرَتَىٰ
عَلَىٰ مَا فَرَّطتُ فِي جَنۢبِ ٱللَّهِ وَإِن كُنتُ لَمِنَ ٱلسَّٰخِرِينَ ﴿٥٦﴾
أَوْ تَقُولَ لَوْ أَنَّ ٱللَّهَ هَدَىٰنِي لَكُنتُ مِنَ ٱلْمُتَّقِينَ ﴿٥٧﴾
أَوْ تَقُولَ حِينَ تَرَى ٱلْعَذَابَ لَوْ أَنَّ لِي كَرَّةً فَأَكُونَ
مِنَ ٱلْمُحْسِنِينَ ﴿٥٨﴾ بَلَىٰ قَدْ جَآءَتْكَ ءَايَٰتِي فَكَذَّبْتَ بِهَا
وَٱسْتَكْبَرْتَ وَكُنتَ مِنَ ٱلْكَٰفِرِينَ ﴿٥٩﴾ وَيَوْمَ ٱلْقِيَٰمَةِ
تَرَى ٱلَّذِينَ كَذَبُوا۟ عَلَى ٱللَّهِ وُجُوهُهُم مُّسْوَدَّةٌ ۚ أَلَيْسَ فِي
جَهَنَّمَ مَثْوًى لِّلْمُتَكَبِّرِينَ ﴿٦٠﴾ وَيُنَجِّي ٱللَّهُ ٱلَّذِينَ ٱتَّقَوْا۟
بِمَفَازَتِهِمْ لَا يَمَسُّهُمُ ٱلسُّوٓءُ وَلَا هُمْ يَحْزَنُونَ ﴿٦١﴾ ٱللَّهُ
خَٰلِقُ كُلِّ شَيْءٍ ۖ وَهُوَ عَلَىٰ كُلِّ شَيْءٍ وَكِيلٌ ﴿٦٢﴾ لَّهُۥ مَقَالِيدُ
ٱلسَّمَٰوَٰتِ وَٱلْأَرْضِ ۗ وَٱلَّذِينَ كَفَرُوا۟ بِـَٔايَٰتِ ٱللَّهِ أُو۟لَٰٓئِكَ
هُمُ ٱلْخَٰسِرُونَ ﴿٦٣﴾ قُلْ أَفَغَيْرَ ٱللَّهِ تَأْمُرُوٓنِّيٓ أَعْبُدُ أَيُّهَا
ٱلْجَٰهِلُونَ ﴿٦٤﴾ وَلَقَدْ أُوحِيَ إِلَيْكَ وَإِلَى ٱلَّذِينَ مِن قَبْلِكَ لَئِنْ
أَشْرَكْتَ لَيَحْبَطَنَّ عَمَلُكَ وَلَتَكُونَنَّ مِنَ ٱلْخَٰسِرِينَ ﴿٦٥﴾ بَلِ ٱللَّهَ
فَٱعْبُدْ وَكُن مِّنَ ٱلشَّٰكِرِينَ ﴿٦٦﴾ وَمَا قَدَرُوا۟ ٱللَّهَ حَقَّ قَدْرِهِۦ
وَٱلْأَرْضُ جَمِيعًا قَبْضَتُهُۥ يَوْمَ ٱلْقِيَٰمَةِ وَٱلسَّمَٰوَٰتُ
مَطْوِيَّٰتٌۢ بِيَمِينِهِۦ ۚ سُبْحَٰنَهُۥ وَتَعَٰلَىٰ عَمَّا يُشْرِكُونَ ﴿٦٧﴾
وَنُفِخَ فِي ٱلصُّورِ فَصَعِقَ مَن فِي ٱلسَّمَٰوَٰتِ وَمَن فِي ٱلْأَرْضِ
إِلَّا مَن شَآءَ ٱللَّهُ ۖ ثُمَّ نُفِخَ فِيهِ أُخْرَىٰ فَإِذَا هُمْ قِيَامٌ يَنظُرُونَ
﴿٦٨﴾ وَأَشْرَقَتِ ٱلْأَرْضُ بِنُورِ رَبِّهَا وَوُضِعَ ٱلْكِتَٰبُ وَجِا۟يٓءَ

51. ***The*** repayment for the ***evil deeds they earned caught up with them. And the evil deeds which the wrongdoers among these people*** (Quraysh) ***earn will also catch up with them, and they can do nothing to prevent it.*** They suffered a drought for seven years and then they were given relief.

52. ***Do they not know that Allah expands the provision of anyone He wills and restricts it*** – as a test? ***There are certainly Signs in that for people who believe*** in it.

53. ***Say: 'My slaves, you who have transgressed against yourselves, do not despair*** (read as *taqnaṭū* and *taqniṭū*) ***of the mercy of Allah. Truly Allah forgives all wrong actions*** – provided there is repentance of any *shirk*. ***He is the Ever-Forgiving, the Most Merciful.'***

54. ***Turn in repentance to your Lord and submit to Him*** – acting sincerely for Him alone – ***before punishment comes upon you, for then you cannot be helped.*** You cannot prevent the punishment if you have not repented.

55. ***Follow the best that has been sent down to you from your Lord*** (the Qur'an) ***before the punishment comes upon you suddenly when you are not expecting it*** – and unaware of its time of arrival;

56. Make haste ***lest anyone should say, 'Alas for me*** and what regret I feel ***for neglecting what Allah was due*** – failing to obey Him – ***and being one of the scoffers*** who scoffed at His *dīn* and His Book' –

57. ***...or lest they should say, 'If only Allah had guided me*** – to obedience, I would have been guided and ***I would have been god-fearing***, and had fear of His punishment'

58. ***...or lest he should say, when he sees the punishment, 'If only I could have another chance*** to return to the world ***so that I could be a good-doer*** – one of the believers.'

59. Allah then tells them: ***'No, the fact is that My Signs*** (the Qur'an) – which are the means to guidance – ***came to you, but you denied them and were*** too ***arrogant*** – to believe in it, ***and were one of the unbelievers.'***

60. ***On the Day of Resurrection you will see those who lied against Allah*** – by saying that He has a partner and a child – ***with their faces***

blackened. Do not the arrogant – who were too arrogant to believe – ***have a dwelling place in Hell?***

61. ***Allah will give security*** from Hellfire ***to those who were god-fearing*** and wary of *shirk* – ***in their victorious Safe Haven*** – the place where they achieve success in Paradise. ***No evil will touch them and they will know no sorrow.***

62. ***Allah is the Creator of everything and He is Guardian over everything*** – and does whatever He wishes with all things.

63. ***The keys of the heavens and earth*** – the keys of their treasures in the form of of rain, plants and other things – ***belong to Him. It is those who reject Allah's Signs*** (the Qur'an) ***who are the losers.*** *"It is those who reject Allah's Signs who are the losers"* continues on from "Allah will give security to those who were godfearing…" and what is in between is an interpolation.

64. ***Say: 'Do you order me to worship something other than Allah, you ignorant people?'***

65. ***It has been revealed to you and those before you: 'If you associate others with Allah, your actions will come to nothing and you will be among the losers.'***

66. ***No! Worship Allah*** only ***and be among the thankful*** – who thank Him for the blessings He has given them.

67. ***They do not measure Allah with His true measure.*** They do not recognise Allah as He should be recognised or respect Him as He should be respected, because they associate another with Him. ***The whole earth will be a mere handful for Him*** – under His dominion and at His disposal – ***on the Day of Rising, the heavens folded up in His right hand. Glory be to Him! He is exalted above the partners they ascribe!***

68. ***The Trumpet will be blown*** – with the first Blast – ***and those in the heavens and those in the earth will all lose consciousness*** – and die – ***except those Allah wills*** – of the houris, youths and other things. ***Then it will be blown a second time, and at once they*** – all the dead creatures – ***will be standing upright, looking on*** – waiting to see what will be done to them.

69. ***And the earth will shine with the Pure Light of its Lord*** when Allah manifests Himself in order to carry out the Final Judgement.

بِٱلنَّبِيِّـۧنَ وَٱلشُّهَدَآءِ وَقُضِيَ بَيۡنَهُم بِٱلۡحَقِّ وَهُمۡ لَا يُظۡلَمُونَ
٦٩ وَوُفِّيَتۡ كُلُّ نَفۡسٖ مَّا عَمِلَتۡ وَهُوَ أَعۡلَمُ بِمَا يَفۡعَلُونَ ٧٠
وَسِيقَ ٱلَّذِينَ كَفَرُوٓاْ إِلَىٰ جَهَنَّمَ زُمَرًاۖ حَتَّىٰٓ إِذَا جَآءُوهَا
فُتِحَتۡ أَبۡوَٰبُهَا وَقَالَ لَهُمۡ خَزَنَتُهَآ أَلَمۡ يَأۡتِكُمۡ رُسُلٞ مِّنكُمۡ
يَتۡلُونَ عَلَيۡكُمۡ ءَايَٰتِ رَبِّكُمۡ وَيُنذِرُونَكُمۡ لِقَآءَ يَوۡمِكُمۡ
هَٰذَاۚ قَالُواْ بَلَىٰ وَلَٰكِنۡ حَقَّتۡ كَلِمَةُ ٱلۡعَذَابِ عَلَى ٱلۡكَٰفِرِينَ
٧١ قِيلَ ٱدۡخُلُوٓاْ أَبۡوَٰبَ جَهَنَّمَ خَٰلِدِينَ فِيهَاۖ فَبِئۡسَ مَثۡوَى
ٱلۡمُتَكَبِّرِينَ ٧٢ وَسِيقَ ٱلَّذِينَ ٱتَّقَوۡاْ رَبَّهُمۡ إِلَى
ٱلۡجَنَّةِ زُمَرًاۖ حَتَّىٰٓ إِذَا جَآءُوهَا وَفُتِحَتۡ أَبۡوَٰبُهَا وَقَالَ لَهُمۡ
خَزَنَتُهَا سَلَٰمٌ عَلَيۡكُمۡ طِبۡتُمۡ فَٱدۡخُلُوهَا خَٰلِدِينَ ٧٣
وَقَالُواْ ٱلۡحَمۡدُ لِلَّهِ ٱلَّذِي صَدَقَنَا وَعۡدَهُۥ وَأَوۡرَثَنَا ٱلۡأَرۡضَ
نَتَبَوَّأُ مِنَ ٱلۡجَنَّةِ حَيۡثُ نَشَآءُۖ فَنِعۡمَ أَجۡرُ ٱلۡعَٰمِلِينَ ٧٤
وَتَرَى ٱلۡمَلَٰٓئِكَةَ حَآفِّينَ مِنۡ حَوۡلِ ٱلۡعَرۡشِ يُسَبِّحُونَ بِحَمۡدِ
رَبِّهِمۡۖ وَقُضِيَ بَيۡنَهُم بِٱلۡحَقِّ وَقِيلَ ٱلۡحَمۡدُ لِلَّهِ رَبِّ ٱلۡعَٰلَمِينَ ٧٥

The Book of actions will be set up for the reckoning and ***will be put in place; the Prophets and witnesses will be brought*** – Muhammad, may Allah bless him and grant him peace, and his community will be brought to testify on behalf of the Messengers, saying that they conveyed the Message. ***It will be decided between them with the truth*** and justice ***and they will not be wronged*** to the slightest extent.

70. ***Every self will be repaid in full for what it did. He knows best what they are doing*** – and has no need of witnesses to know that.

71. ***Those who disbelieve will be driven to Hell*** harshly ***in companies; and when they arrive there and its gates are opened its custodians will say to them, 'Did Messengers from yourselves not come to you, reciting your Lord's Signs*** – including the Qur'an and other things – ***to you and warning you of the meeting on this Day of yours?' They will say, 'Indeed they did, but the decree of punishment is justly carried out against the unbelievers.'***

72. ***They will be told, 'Enter the gates of Hell and stay there timelessly, for ever. How evil is*** Jahannam, ***the abode of the arrogant!'***

73. ***And those who are fearful of their Lord will be driven*** gently ***to Pardise in companies; and when they arrive there, finding its gates open, its custodians will say to them, 'Peace be upon you! You have done well so enter it timelessly, forever.'*** The greeting they are given is to honour them. When the unbelievers are driven to Hell, the gates will be opened when they reach it so that its heat is kept for them to humiliate them.

74. ***They will say, 'Praise be to Allah Who has fulfilled His promise*** (Paradise) ***to us and made us the inheritors of this land***, in Paradise, ***letting us settle in Paradise wherever we want.*** No part rather than another is chosen in it. ***How excellent is the wage of those who work*** – which is the Garden*!'*

75. ***You will see the angels circling round the Throne*** on all sides, – ***glorifying their Lord with praise*** – saying, "Glory be to Allah and with His praise". ***It will be decided between them*** (all creatures) ***with truth*** and justice, and the believers will enter the Garden and the unbelievers will enter the Fire. ***And it will be said: 'Praise be to Allah, the Lord of all the worlds.'*** Both groups end with the affirmation of praise spoken by the angels.

سُورَةُ غَافِرٍ

بِسۡمِ ٱللَّهِ ٱلرَّحۡمَٰنِ ٱلرَّحِيمِ

حمٓ ١ تَنزِيلُ ٱلۡكِتَٰبِ مِنَ ٱللَّهِ ٱلۡعَزِيزِ ٱلۡعَلِيمِ ٢ غَافِرِ
ٱلذَّنۢبِ وَقَابِلِ ٱلتَّوۡبِ شَدِيدِ ٱلۡعِقَابِ ذِي ٱلطَّوۡلِۖ لَآ إِلَٰهَ إِلَّا هُوَۖ
إِلَيۡهِ ٱلۡمَصِيرُ ٣ مَا يُجَٰدِلُ فِيٓ ءَايَٰتِ ٱللَّهِ إِلَّا ٱلَّذِينَ كَفَرُواْ
فَلَا يَغۡرُرۡكَ تَقَلُّبُهُمۡ فِي ٱلۡبِلَٰدِ ٤ كَذَّبَتۡ قَبۡلَهُمۡ قَوۡمُ
نُوحٖ وَٱلۡأَحۡزَابُ مِنۢ بَعۡدِهِمۡۖ وَهَمَّتۡ كُلُّ أُمَّةِۭ بِرَسُولِهِمۡ
لِيَأۡخُذُوهُۖ وَجَٰدَلُواْ بِٱلۡبَٰطِلِ لِيُدۡحِضُواْ بِهِ ٱلۡحَقَّ فَأَخَذۡتُهُمۡۖ
فَكَيۡفَ كَانَ عِقَابِ ٥ وَكَذَٰلِكَ حَقَّتۡ كَلِمَتُ رَبِّكَ عَلَى
ٱلَّذِينَ كَفَرُوٓاْ أَنَّهُمۡ أَصۡحَٰبُ ٱلنَّارِ ٦ ٱلَّذِينَ يَحۡمِلُونَ ٱلۡعَرۡشَ
وَمَنۡ حَوۡلَهُۥ يُسَبِّحُونَ بِحَمۡدِ رَبِّهِمۡ وَيُؤۡمِنُونَ بِهِۦ وَيَسۡتَغۡفِرُونَ
لِلَّذِينَ ءَامَنُواْ رَبَّنَا وَسِعۡتَ كُلَّ شَيۡءٖ رَّحۡمَةٗ وَعِلۡمٗا
فَٱغۡفِرۡ لِلَّذِينَ تَابُواْ وَٱتَّبَعُواْ سَبِيلَكَ وَقِهِمۡ عَذَابَ ٱلۡجَحِيمِ ٧
رَبَّنَا وَأَدۡخِلۡهُمۡ جَنَّٰتِ عَدۡنٍ ٱلَّتِي وَعَدتَّهُمۡ وَمَن صَلَحَ
مِنۡ ءَابَآئِهِمۡ وَأَزۡوَٰجِهِمۡ وَذُرِّيَّٰتِهِمۡۚ إِنَّكَ أَنتَ ٱلۡعَزِيزُ
ٱلۡحَكِيمُ ٨ وَقِهِمُ ٱلسَّيِّـَٔاتِۚ وَمَن تَقِ ٱلسَّيِّـَٔاتِ
يَوۡمَئِذٖ فَقَدۡ رَحِمۡتَهُۥۚ وَذَٰلِكَ هُوَ ٱلۡفَوۡزُ ٱلۡعَظِيمُ ٩ إِنَّ
ٱلَّذِينَ كَفَرُواْ يُنَادَوۡنَ لَمَقۡتُ ٱللَّهِ أَكۡبَرُ مِن مَّقۡتِكُمۡ
أَنفُسَكُمۡ إِذۡ تُدۡعَوۡنَ إِلَى ٱلۡإِيمَٰنِ فَتَكۡفُرُونَ ١٠
قَالُواْ رَبَّنَآ أَمَتَّنَا ٱثۡنَتَيۡنِ وَأَحۡيَيۡتَنَا ٱثۡنَتَيۡنِ فَٱعۡتَرَفۡنَا بِذُنُوبِنَا
فَهَلۡ إِلَىٰ خُرُوجٖ مِّن سَبِيلٖ ١١ ذَٰلِكُم بِأَنَّهُۥٓ إِذَا دُعِيَ

40. *Sūrat Ghāfir* or *al-Mu'min* - Forgiving or The Believer

This *sūra* is Makkan except for *āyats* 56 and 57, which are Madinan. It has 85 *āyats* and was sent down after *az-Zumar.*

1. ***Ḥa Mim.*** Allah knows best what is meant by this.

2. ***The revelation of the Book*** (the Qur'an) ***is from Allah, the Almighty, the All-Knowing,***

3. ***... the Forgiver of wrong action*** committed by believers, ***the Accepter of*** their ***repentance, the Severe in retribution*** for the unbelievers, ***the Possessor of abundance*** – in other words, ample blessings. He is always described by these attributes. ***There is no god but Him. He is the final destination*** and place of return.

4. ***No one disputes Allah's Signs*** (the Qur'an) ***except those who disbelieve. Do not let their free movement about the earth deceive you.*** Do not let the fact that they have ample livelihood and are healthy deceive you. Their final end will be the Fire.

5. ***The people of Nūḥ denied the truth before them, and the Confederates after them*** – peoples such as 'Ād, Thamūd and others. ***Every nation planned to seize its Messenger*** – and kill him – ***and used false arguments to rebut the truth*** and deny it. ***So I seized them*** with the Punishment ***and how was My retribution*** against them***!***

6. ***So your Lord's Words about those who disbelieved proved true*** – *"I will fill Hellfire..."* (7:18) – ***that they are indeed the Companions of the Fire.***

7. ***Those who bear the Throne, and all those around it glorify their Lord with praise*** – by saying, "Glory be to Allah and with His praise" – ***and believe in Him*** with their inner sight; in other words, they affirm His unity, ***and ask forgiveness for those who believe.*** They say: ***'Our Lord, You encompass everything in*** Your ***mercy and knowledge! Forgive those who turn to You*** – repenting of their *shirk* – ***and who follow Your Way*** of Islam***; and safeguard them from the punishment of the Blazing Fire.***

8. ***Our Lord, admit them to the Gardens of Eden You have promised them, and all of their parents, wives and children who acted rightly. Truly You are the Almighty, the All-Wise*** in what You do.

9. ***And safeguard them from*** Punishment for their ***evil acts*** on the Day of Rising. ***Those You safeguard from evil acts are truly the recipients of Your mercy on that Day. That is the Mighty Victory.'***

10. ***Those who disbelieved will be addressed*** by the angels. They will hate themselves when they enter the Fire, but ***'Allah's hatred of you, when you were called to belief but then chose unbelief*** – in the world – ***is even greater than your hatred of yourselves.'***

11. ***They will say, 'Our Lord, twice You caused us to die and twice You gave us life.*** They were dead sperm and then were brought to life. Then they were made to die and then brought to life for the Resurrection. ***We admit our wrong actions*** in denying the Resurrection. ***Is there no way out*** of the Fire and no way to return to the world so that we may obey our Lord? The answer is: "No".

12. ***That*** punishment which you are suffering ***is because when Allah alone is called upon*** in the world ***you disbelieve*** in His unity, ***but if others are associated with Him*** as partners ***you believe*** in idolatry. ***Judgement*** in punishing you ***belongs to Allah, the All-High*** over His creation, ***the All-Great.***

13. ***It is He who shows you His Signs*** – evidence of His unity – ***and sends down provision*** (rain) ***to you out of heaven. But none pay heed*** – and are warned – ***save those who repent*** and turn from *shirk*.

14. ***So call upon Allah*** and worship Him, ***making your* dīn *sincerely His*** – free of any *shirk* – ***even though the unbelievers detest it*** – hate your sincere devotion to the *dīn*.

15. ***He is the Raiser of ranks*** – this may mean that Allah has immense attributes or that He is the One who elevates the ranks of the believers in the Garden, ***the Possessor of the Throne*** – in other words, its Creator. ***He sends the Spirit*** (Revelation) ***by His command to whichever of His slaves He wills so that he may warn mankind about the Day of Meeting*** (read as *at-talāqi* and *at-talāqī*) – that is the Day when the people of heaven and people of earth meet

ٱللَّهُ وَحۡدَهُۥ كَفَرۡتُمۡ ۖ وَإِن يُشۡرَكۡ بِهِۦ تُؤۡمِنُوا۟ ۚ فَٱلۡحُكۡمُ لِلَّهِ
ٱلۡعَلِيِّ ٱلۡكَبِيرِ ﴿١٢﴾ هُوَ ٱلَّذِى يُرِيكُمۡ ءَايَٰتِهِۦ وَيُنَزِّلُ
لَكُم مِّنَ ٱلسَّمَآءِ رِزۡقًا ۚ وَمَا يَتَذَكَّرُ إِلَّا مَن يُنِيبُ ﴿١٣﴾
فَٱدۡعُوا۟ ٱللَّهَ مُخۡلِصِينَ لَهُ ٱلدِّينَ وَلَوۡ كَرِهَ ٱلۡكَٰفِرُونَ ﴿١٤﴾
رَفِيعُ ٱلدَّرَجَٰتِ ذُو ٱلۡعَرۡشِ يُلۡقِى ٱلرُّوحَ مِنۡ أَمۡرِهِۦ عَلَىٰ مَن
يَشَآءُ مِنۡ عِبَادِهِۦ لِيُنذِرَ يَوۡمَ ٱلتَّلَاقِ ﴿١٥﴾ يَوۡمَ هُم بَٰرِزُونَ ۖ لَا يَخۡفَىٰ
عَلَى ٱللَّهِ مِنۡهُمۡ شَىۡءٌ ۚ لِّمَنِ ٱلۡمُلۡكُ ٱلۡيَوۡمَ ۖ لِلَّهِ ٱلۡوَٰحِدِ ٱلۡقَهَّارِ ﴿١٦﴾
ٱلۡيَوۡمَ تُجۡزَىٰ كُلُّ نَفۡسٍۭ بِمَا كَسَبَتۡ ۚ لَا ظُلۡمَ ٱلۡيَوۡمَ ۚ إِنَّ
ٱللَّهَ سَرِيعُ ٱلۡحِسَابِ ﴿١٧﴾ وَأَنذِرۡهُمۡ يَوۡمَ ٱلۡأَزِفَةِ إِذِ ٱلۡقُلُوبُ
لَدَى ٱلۡحَنَاجِرِ كَٰظِمِينَ ۚ مَا لِلظَّٰلِمِينَ مِنۡ حَمِيمٍ وَلَا شَفِيعٍ
يُطَاعُ ﴿١٨﴾ يَعۡلَمُ خَآئِنَةَ ٱلۡأَعۡيُنِ وَمَا تُخۡفِى ٱلصُّدُورُ ﴿١٩﴾
وَٱللَّهُ يَقۡضِى بِٱلۡحَقِّ ۖ وَٱلَّذِينَ يَدۡعُونَ مِن دُونِهِۦ لَا يَقۡضُونَ
بِشَىۡءٍ ۗ إِنَّ ٱللَّهَ هُوَ ٱلسَّمِيعُ ٱلۡبَصِيرُ ﴿٢٠﴾ ۞ أَوَلَمۡ يَسِيرُوا۟ فِى
ٱلۡأَرۡضِ فَيَنظُرُوا۟ كَيۡفَ كَانَ عَٰقِبَةُ ٱلَّذِينَ كَانُوا۟ مِن قَبۡلِهِمۡ ۚ
كَانُوا۟ هُمۡ أَشَدَّ مِنۡهُمۡ قُوَّةً وَءَاثَارًا فِى ٱلۡأَرۡضِ فَأَخَذَهُمُ ٱللَّهُ
بِذُنُوبِهِمۡ وَمَا كَانَ لَهُم مِّنَ ٱللَّهِ مِن وَاقٍ ﴿٢١﴾ ذَٰلِكَ بِأَنَّهُمۡ
كَانَت تَّأۡتِيهِمۡ رُسُلُهُم بِٱلۡبَيِّنَٰتِ فَكَفَرُوا۟ فَأَخَذَهُمُ ٱللَّهُ ۚ إِنَّهُۥ
قَوِىٌّ شَدِيدُ ٱلۡعِقَابِ ﴿٢٢﴾ وَلَقَدۡ أَرۡسَلۡنَا مُوسَىٰ بِـَٔايَٰتِنَا
وَسُلۡطَٰنٍ مُّبِينٍ ﴿٢٣﴾ إِلَىٰ فِرۡعَوۡنَ وَهَٰمَٰنَ وَقَٰرُونَ
فَقَالُوا۟ سَٰحِرٌ كَذَّابٌ ﴿٢٤﴾ فَلَمَّا جَآءَهُم بِٱلۡحَقِّ مِنۡ

as well as the worshipper and the Worshipped, the wronger and the wronged –

16. ***...the Day when they will issue forth*** from their graves ***and when not one thing about them will be hidden from Allah. 'To whom does the kingdom belong today?*** Allah answers His own question. ***To Allah, the One, the Conqueror!***

17. ***Every self will be repaid today for what it earned. Today there will be no injustice. Allah is swift at reckoning.'*** He will reckon all creation in half a day measuring by the days of this world, as stated in *ḥadīth*.

18. ***And warn them of the Day of Immediacy*** – another name for the Day of Rising. The word for "Immediacy", *āzifa*, is taken from the verb *azifa*, used for when a traveller approaches his destination – ***when hearts rise*** – because of fear – ***choking to the throat*** – filling the throats out of anxiety. ***The wrongdoers will have no close friend nor any intercessor who might be heard.*** They will have no intercessor whose intercession will be accepted. There is sense in the description since they have no intercessors at all, as Allah says, *"Now we have no one to intercede for us."* (26:100) So this is based on their claim to have intercessors, meaning that even if someone were to intercede, it would not be accepted.

19. ***He*** (Allah) ***knows the eyes' deceit*** – stolen glances at the unlawful – ***and what people's breasts conceal*** – what is hidden inside their hearts.

20. ***Allah will judge with truth; and those they*** (the unbelievers of Makka) ***call upon*** (read as *yad'ūna* and *tad'ūna*, "you call upon") and worship ***apart from Him*** – meaning the idols – ***will not judge with anything at all.*** So how can they attribute partners to Allah? ***It is Allah who is the All-Hearing*** – of their words, ***the All-Seeing*** – of what they do.

21. ***Have they not travelled in the earth and seen the final fate of those before them? They were greater than them*** (read as *minhum* and also as *minkum*, "greater than you") ***in strength and left far deeper traces on the earth*** – a reference to buildings and castles; ***yet Allah seized them*** and destroyed them ***for their wrong actions and they had no one to protect them from*** the Punishment of ***Allah.***

22. ***That was because their Messengers brought them the Clear Signs*** (miracles) ***but they remained unbelievers. So Allah seized them. He is Most Strong, Severe in Retribution.***

23. ***We sent Mūsā with Our Signs and clear authority*** – manifest proof –

24. ***...to Pharaoh, Hāmān and Qārūn. But they said, 'A lying magician.'***

25. ***When he brought them the truth from Us they said, 'Slaughter the sons of those who believe with him but let their women live.' The stratagems of the unbelievers are nothing but errors*** – and come to nothing.

26. ***Pharaoh said, 'Let me kill Mūsā*** – indicating that his people were trying to restrain him from doing so – ***and let him call upon his Lord*** to defend him from me***! I am afraid that he may change your* dīn** and stop you from worshipping me if you follow him***, and bring about*** (read as *yuẓhira* and *yaẓhara*) ***corruption in the land*** – such as killing and other things.'

27. ***Mūsā said, 'I seek refuge in my Lord and your Lord from every proud man who does not believe in the Day of Reckoning.'***

28. ***A man among Pharaoh's people who had faith*** – said to be his cousin – ***but kept his faith concealed, said, 'Are you going to kill a man for saying "My Lord is Allah" when he has brought you Clear Signs*** (miracles) ***from your Lord? If he is telling a lie, be it on his own head*** – the harm of his lie will come back on him***. But if he is telling the truth, then some of what he is promising you*** – in terms of punishment – ***will certainly happen to you. Allah does not guide any unbridled inveterate*** (idolatrous) ***liar.***

29. ***My people, the kingdom is yours today, as masters in the land*** – you have control of the land of Egypt – ***but who will help us against Allah's violent force*** – and inevitable punishment if we kill His friends – ***if it comes upon us?*** We will have no helper.' ***Pharaoh said, 'I only show you what I see myself*** – I only direct you to that to which I direct myself: in other words, the killing of Mūsā – ***and I only guide you to the path of rectitude*** – the correct way.'

30. ***The man who had faith said, 'My people, I fear for you a day like that of the Confederates...***

عِندِنَا قَالُوا۟ ٱقْتُلُوٓا۟ أَبْنَآءَ ٱلَّذِينَ ءَامَنُوا۟ مَعَهُۥ وَٱسْتَحْيُوا۟
نِسَآءَهُمْ ۚ وَمَا كَيْدُ ٱلْكَـٰفِرِينَ إِلَّا فِى ضَلَـٰلٍ ﴿٢٥﴾
وَقَالَ فِرْعَوْنُ ذَرُونِىٓ أَقْتُلْ مُوسَىٰ وَلْيَدْعُ رَبَّهُۥٓ ۖ إِنِّىٓ أَخَافُ
أَن يُبَدِّلَ دِينَكُمْ أَوْ أَن يُظْهِرَ فِى ٱلْأَرْضِ ٱلْفَسَادَ ﴿٢٦﴾
وَقَالَ مُوسَىٰٓ إِنِّى عُذْتُ بِرَبِّى وَرَبِّكُم مِّن كُلِّ مُتَكَبِّرٍ
لَّا يُؤْمِنُ بِيَوْمِ ٱلْحِسَابِ ﴿٢٧﴾ وَقَالَ رَجُلٌ مُّؤْمِنٌ مِّنْ ءَالِ
فِرْعَوْنَ يَكْتُمُ إِيمَـٰنَهُۥٓ أَتَقْتُلُونَ رَجُلًا أَن يَقُولَ رَبِّىَ
ٱللَّهُ وَقَدْ جَآءَكُم بِٱلْبَيِّنَـٰتِ مِن رَّبِّكُمْ ۖ وَإِن يَكُ كَـٰذِبًا
فَعَلَيْهِ كَذِبُهُۥ ۖ وَإِن يَكُ صَادِقًا يُصِبْكُم بَعْضُ ٱلَّذِى
يَعِدُكُمْ ۖ إِنَّ ٱللَّهَ لَا يَهْدِى مَنْ هُوَ مُسْرِفٌ كَذَّابٌ ﴿٢٨﴾ يَـٰقَوْمِ
لَكُمُ ٱلْمُلْكُ ٱلْيَوْمَ ظَـٰهِرِينَ فِى ٱلْأَرْضِ فَمَن يَنصُرُنَا مِنۢ
بَأْسِ ٱللَّهِ إِن جَآءَنَا ۚ قَالَ فِرْعَوْنُ مَآ أُرِيكُمْ إِلَّا مَآ أَرَىٰ وَمَآ
أَهْدِيكُمْ إِلَّا سَبِيلَ ٱلرَّشَادِ ﴿٢٩﴾ وَقَالَ ٱلَّذِىٓ ءَامَنَ يَـٰقَوْمِ إِنِّىٓ
أَخَافُ عَلَيْكُم مِّثْلَ يَوْمِ ٱلْأَحْزَابِ ﴿٣٠﴾ مِثْلَ دَأْبِ قَوْمِ نُوحٍ
وَعَادٍ وَثَمُودَ وَٱلَّذِينَ مِنۢ بَعْدِهِمْ ۚ وَمَا ٱللَّهُ يُرِيدُ ظُلْمًا لِّلْعِبَادِ ﴿٣١﴾
وَيَـٰقَوْمِ إِنِّىٓ أَخَافُ عَلَيْكُمْ يَوْمَ ٱلتَّنَادِ ﴿٣٢﴾ يَوْمَ تُوَلُّونَ مُدْبِرِينَ
مَا لَكُم مِّنَ ٱللَّهِ مِنْ عَاصِمٍ ۗ وَمَن يُضْلِلِ ٱللَّهُ فَمَا لَهُۥ مِنْ هَادٍ ﴿٣٣﴾
وَلَقَدْ جَآءَكُمْ يُوسُفُ مِن قَبْلُ بِٱلْبَيِّنَـٰتِ فَمَا زِلْتُمْ فِى شَكٍّ
مِّمَّا جَآءَكُم بِهِۦ ۖ حَتَّىٰٓ إِذَا هَلَكَ قُلْتُمْ لَن يَبْعَثَ ٱللَّهُ
مِنۢ بَعْدِهِۦ رَسُولًا ۚ كَذَٰلِكَ يُضِلُّ ٱللَّهُ مَنْ هُوَ مُسْرِفٌ

31. ***...the same as happened to the people of Nūḥ and 'Ād and Thamūd and those who followed after them*** – in other words, the same repayment and punishment as that meted out to those who disbelieved before you in this world. ***Allah does not want any injustice for His slaves.***

32. ***My people, I fear for you the Day of Calling Out*** (read as *tanādi* and *tanādī*) – another name used for the Day of Rising, because the people of the Garden will call to the people of the Fire and vice versa. The people of the Garden will call out about their happiness and the people of the Fire about their wretchedness and other things –

33. ***...the Day when you will turn your backs in flight*** from the place of reckoning towards the Fire, ***having no one to protect you from*** the punishment of ***Allah. Whoever Allah misguides will have no guide.***

34. ***Yūsuf brought you the Clear Signs*** (miracles) ***before*** – a reference to Yūsuf, the son of Ya'qūb because, according to one view, he lived until the time of Mūsā; or to Yūsuf son of Ibrāhīm son of Yūsuf son of Ya'qūb according to another view – ***but you never stopped doubting what he brought to you, to the extent that when he died, you said*** – without any proof – ***"Allah will never send another Messenger after him."*** So they continued to reject Yūsuf and others. ***That is how Allah misguides those who are unbridled*** – and idolaters ***and full of doubt*** – about the Signs which you had witnessed.'

35. ***Those who argue about the Signs of Allah*** (miracles) ***without any authority*** or proof ***coming to them do something hateful in the sight of Allah and in the sight of the people who believe. That*** – misguidance – ***is how Allah seals up the heart of every arrogant oppressor*** – through their misguidance. When the heart of a person is arrogant, then the person himself is arrogant. Misguidance permeates the entire heart.

36. ***Pharaoh said, 'Hāmān, build me a*** high ***tower so that perhaps I may gain means of access,***

37. ***...access to the heavens, so that I can*** reach the heavens and ***look on Mūsā's God. Truly I think he*** (Mūsā) ***is a liar*** in saying that he has a god other than me.*'* Pharaoh said that out of a distortion of what had been said. ***That is how Pharaoh's evil actions were made attractive to him and he was debarred*** (read as *ṣudda* and also *ṣadda,* meaning "he debarred others") ***from the Path*** of guidance. ***Pharaoh's scheming led to nothing but ruin*** and loss.

38. ***The man who believed said, 'My people, follow me and I will guide you to the path of rectitude.***

39. ***My people, the life of this world is only fleeting enjoyment*** – which will soon pass. ***It is the Next World which is the abode of permanence.***

40. ***Whoever does an evil act will only be repaid with its equivalent. But whoever acts rightly, male or female, being a believer, such a person will enter*** (read as *yadkhulūna* and *yudkhilūna*) ***the Garden, provided for in it without any reckoning.***

41. ***My people, how is it that I call you to salvation while you call me to the Fire?***

42. ***You call me to reject Allah and to associate something with Him about which I have no knowledge, while I call you to the Almighty,*** Who has power over all things, ***the Endlessly Forgiving*** of those who repent.

43. ***There is no question that what you call me to*** worship ***has no foundation*** and cannot respond to prayer ***either in this world or the Next World, that our return is to Allah, and that the profligate*** (the unbelievers) ***will be Companions in the Fire.***

44. ***You will remember what I am telling you*** when you see the Punishment. ***I consign my destiny completely to Allah. Truly Allah sees His slaves.'*** He said that when they threatened him for opposing their religion.

45. ***So Allah safeguarded him from the evil things they plotted*** – when they plotted to kill him – ***and a most evil torment engulfed*** Pharaoh and ***Pharaoh's people*** – in other words, drowning and then –

46. ***...the Fire, morning and night, to which they are exposed*** – and in which they are burned – ***and on the Day the Hour takes place*** – Resurrection Day when they hear the words*: **'Admit*** (read as *adkhilū* and *adkhulū*) ***Pharaoh's people to the harshest punishment*** of Hell*!'* This is a command to the angels.

مُّرْتَابٌ ﴿٣٤﴾ ٱلَّذِينَ يُجَٰدِلُونَ فِىٓ ءَايَٰتِ ٱللَّهِ بِغَيْرِ سُلْطَٰنٍ
أَتَىٰهُمْ ۖ كَبُرَ مَقْتًا عِندَ ٱللَّهِ وَعِندَ ٱلَّذِينَ ءَامَنُوا۟ ۚ كَذَٰلِكَ
يَطْبَعُ ٱللَّهُ عَلَىٰ كُلِّ قَلْبِ مُتَكَبِّرٍ جَبَّارٍ ﴿٣٥﴾ وَقَالَ فِرْعَوْنُ
يَٰهَٰمَٰنُ ٱبْنِ لِى صَرْحًا لَّعَلِّىٓ أَبْلُغُ ٱلْأَسْبَٰبَ ﴿٣٦﴾ أَسْبَٰبَ
ٱلسَّمَٰوَٰتِ فَأَطَّلِعَ إِلَىٰٓ إِلَٰهِ مُوسَىٰ وَإِنِّى لَأَظُنُّهُۥ كَٰذِبًا ۚ
وَكَذَٰلِكَ زُيِّنَ لِفِرْعَوْنَ سُوٓءُ عَمَلِهِۦ وَصُدَّ عَنِ ٱلسَّبِيلِ ۚ
وَمَا كَيْدُ فِرْعَوْنَ إِلَّا فِى تَبَابٍ ﴿٣٧﴾ وَقَالَ ٱلَّذِىٓ
ءَامَنَ يَٰقَوْمِ ٱتَّبِعُونِ أَهْدِكُمْ سَبِيلَ ٱلرَّشَادِ ﴿٣٨﴾
يَٰقَوْمِ إِنَّمَا هَٰذِهِ ٱلْحَيَوٰةُ ٱلدُّنْيَا مَتَٰعٌ وَإِنَّ ٱلْءَاخِرَةَ هِىَ
دَارُ ٱلْقَرَارِ ﴿٣٩﴾ مَنْ عَمِلَ سَيِّئَةً فَلَا يُجْزَىٰٓ إِلَّا مِثْلَهَا ۖ
وَمَنْ عَمِلَ صَٰلِحًا مِّن ذَكَرٍ أَوْ أُنثَىٰ وَهُوَ مُؤْمِنٌ
فَأُو۟لَٰٓئِكَ يَدْخُلُونَ ٱلْجَنَّةَ يُرْزَقُونَ فِيهَا بِغَيْرِ حِسَابٍ ﴿٤٠﴾
۞ وَيَٰقَوْمِ مَا لِىٓ أَدْعُوكُمْ إِلَى ٱلنَّجَوٰةِ وَتَدْعُونَنِىٓ إِلَى
ٱلنَّارِ ﴿٤١﴾ تَدْعُونَنِى لِأَكْفُرَ بِٱللَّهِ وَأُشْرِكَ بِهِۦ مَا لَيْسَ
لِى بِهِۦ عِلْمٌ وَأَنَا۠ أَدْعُوكُمْ إِلَى ٱلْعَزِيزِ ٱلْغَفَّٰرِ ﴿٤٢﴾ لَا جَرَمَ
أَنَّمَا تَدْعُونَنِىٓ إِلَيْهِ لَيْسَ لَهُۥ دَعْوَةٌ فِى ٱلدُّنْيَا وَلَا فِى ٱلْءَاخِرَةِ
وَأَنَّ مَرَدَّنَآ إِلَى ٱللَّهِ وَأَنَّ ٱلْمُسْرِفِينَ هُمْ أَصْحَٰبُ ٱلنَّارِ
﴿٤٣﴾ فَسَتَذْكُرُونَ مَآ أَقُولُ لَكُمْ ۚ وَأُفَوِّضُ أَمْرِىٓ إِلَى
ٱللَّهِ ۚ إِنَّ ٱللَّهَ بَصِيرٌۢ بِٱلْعِبَادِ ﴿٤٤﴾ فَوَقَىٰهُ ٱللَّهُ سَيِّـَٔاتِ
مَا مَكَرُوا۟ ۖ وَحَاقَ بِـَٔالِ فِرْعَوْنَ سُوٓءُ ٱلْعَذَابِ ﴿٤٥﴾ ٱلنَّارُ

47. Remember ***when they*** (the unbelievers) ***are squabbling with one another in the Fire, the weak will say to those deemed great, 'We were your followers, so why do you not relieve us of a portion of the Fire?'***

48. ***Those deemed great will say, 'All of us are in it. Allah has clearly judged between His slaves.'*** Then the believers will enter the Garden and the unbelievers will enter the Fire.

49. ***Those in the Fire will say to the custodians of Hell, 'Call on your Lord to make the punishment less for us for just*** the length of ***one day.'***

50. ***They*** (the custodians) ***will ask*** – in mockery: ***'Did your Messengers not bring you the Clear Signs*** (miracles)***?' They will answer, 'Yes.'*** But they rejected them. ***They will say, 'Then you call!*** We will not intercede for the unbelievers.' Allah says – ***But the calling of the unbelievers only goes astray.*** It is useless.

51. ***We will certainly help Our Messengers and those who believe both in the life of this world and on the Day the witnesses appear*** – these are angels who testify that the Messengers conveyed the Message and the unbelievers rejected it –

52. ***...the Day when the excuses of the wrongdoers will not help*** (read as *yanfa'u* and *tanfa'u*) ***them*** – if they make excuses. ***The curse*** – meaning a great gulf between them and mercy – ***will be on them and they will have the most evil Home*** – the worst possible punishment in the Next World.

53. ***We gave Mūsā the guidance*** – in the form of the Torah and miracles – ***and bequeathed the Book*** (the Torah) ***to the tribe of Israel*** after him –

54. ***...as guidance and a reminder for people of intelligence.***

55. ***So***, Muḥammad, ***remain steadfast. Allah's promise*** to help His friends ***is true*** and it applies to you and those who follow you. ***Ask forgiveness for your wrong action and glorify your Lord with praise in the evening and the early morning.*** This refers to doing the prayer at these times.

56. ***Certainly those who argue about the Signs of Allah*** (the Qur'an) ***without any authority*** (evidence) ***having come to them have nothing in their breasts except for pride*** – taking the form of

يُعۡرَضُونَ عَلَيۡهَا غُدُوّٗا وَعَشِيّٗاۚ وَيَوۡمَ تَقُومُ ٱلسَّاعَةُ أَدۡخِلُوٓاْ
ءَالَ فِرۡعَوۡنَ أَشَدَّ ٱلۡعَذَابِ ٤٦ وَإِذۡ يَتَحَآجُّونَ فِي
ٱلنَّارِ فَيَقُولُ ٱلضُّعَفَٰٓؤُاْ لِلَّذِينَ ٱسۡتَكۡبَرُوٓاْ إِنَّا كُنَّا
لَكُمۡ تَبَعٗا فَهَلۡ أَنتُم مُّغۡنُونَ عَنَّا نَصِيبٗا مِّنَ ٱلنَّارِ
٤٧ قَالَ ٱلَّذِينَ ٱسۡتَكۡبَرُوٓاْ إِنَّا كُلّٞ فِيهَآ إِنَّ ٱللَّهَ
قَدۡ حَكَمَ بَيۡنَ ٱلۡعِبَادِ ٤٨ وَقَالَ ٱلَّذِينَ فِي ٱلنَّارِ لِخَزَنَةِ
جَهَنَّمَ ٱدۡعُواْ رَبَّكُمۡ يُخَفِّفۡ عَنَّا يَوۡمٗا مِّنَ ٱلۡعَذَابِ ٤٩
قَالُوٓاْ أَوَلَمۡ تَكُ تَأۡتِيكُمۡ رُسُلُكُم بِٱلۡبَيِّنَٰتِۖ قَالُواْ
بَلَىٰۚ قَالُواْ فَٱدۡعُواْۗ وَمَا دُعَٰٓؤُاْ ٱلۡكَٰفِرِينَ إِلَّا فِي ضَلَٰلٍ
٥٠ إِنَّا لَنَنصُرُ رُسُلَنَا وَٱلَّذِينَ ءَامَنُواْ فِي ٱلۡحَيَوٰةِ ٱلدُّنۡيَا
وَيَوۡمَ يَقُومُ ٱلۡأَشۡهَٰدُ ٥١ يَوۡمَ لَا يَنفَعُ ٱلظَّٰلِمِينَ مَعۡذِرَتُهُمۡۖ
وَلَهُمُ ٱللَّعۡنَةُ وَلَهُمۡ سُوٓءُ ٱلدَّارِ ٥٢ وَلَقَدۡ ءَاتَيۡنَا مُوسَى
ٱلۡهُدَىٰ وَأَوۡرَثۡنَا بَنِيٓ إِسۡرَٰٓءِيلَ ٱلۡكِتَٰبَ ٥٣ هُدٗى
وَذِكۡرَىٰ لِأُوْلِي ٱلۡأَلۡبَٰبِ ٥٤ فَٱصۡبِرۡ إِنَّ وَعۡدَ ٱللَّهِ
حَقّٞ وَٱسۡتَغۡفِرۡ لِذَنۢبِكَ وَسَبِّحۡ بِحَمۡدِ رَبِّكَ بِٱلۡعَشِيِّ
وَٱلۡإِبۡكَٰرِ ٥٥ إِنَّ ٱلَّذِينَ يُجَٰدِلُونَ فِيٓ ءَايَٰتِ
ٱللَّهِ بِغَيۡرِ سُلۡطَٰنٍ أَتَىٰهُمۡ إِن فِي صُدُورِهِمۡ إِلَّا كِبۡرٞ
مَّا هُم بِبَٰلِغِيهِۚ فَٱسۡتَعِذۡ بِٱللَّهِۖ إِنَّهُۥ هُوَ ٱلسَّمِيعُ
ٱلۡبَصِيرُ ٥٦ لَخَلۡقُ ٱلسَّمَٰوَٰتِ وَٱلۡأَرۡضِ أَكۡبَرُ مِنۡ
خَلۡقِ ٱلنَّاسِ وَلَٰكِنَّ أَكۡثَرَ ٱلنَّاسِ لَا يَعۡلَمُونَ ٥٧

arrogance and desire to be above you – ***which they will never be able to vindicate. Therefore seek refuge with Allah*** from their evil; ***He is the All-Hearing*** of what they say, ***the All-Seeing*** of their states. Then the following *āyat* was revealed about people who deny the Resurrection.

57. ***The*** original ***creation of the heavens and earth is far greater than the*** later ***creation of mankind. But most of mankind do not know it*** – and so they are like the blind. Those who do know it are like the seeing.

58. ***The blind and the seeing are not the same. Nor are those who believe and do right actions the same as evildoers. What little heed you pay*** (read as *tatadhakkarūna*, and also *yatadhakkarūna*, meaning, "What little heed they pay")***!***

59. ***The Hour is coming – there is no doubt about it. But most of mankind do not believe*** in it.

60. ***Your Lord says, 'Call on Me and*** worship Me, and ***I will answer you. Those who are too proud to worship Me will enter*** (read as *sa-yadkhulūna* and *sa-yadhkalūna*) ***Hell abject.'***

61. ***Allah is He who appointed the night for you so that you might rest in it, and the day for seeing. Allah pours out His favour on mankind but most people do not show thanks*** – and so they do not believe.

62. ***That is Allah, your Lord, the Creator of all things. There is no god but Him; so how have you been perverted*** and turned from faith when the proof has been established***?***

63. ***That is how those who deny Allah's Signs*** (miracles) ***have been perverted.***

64. ***It is Allah who made the earth a stable home for you and the sky a dome*** – like a ceiling – ***and formed you, giving you the best of forms, and provided you with good and wholesome things. That is Allah, your Lord. Blessed be Allah, the Lord of all the worlds!***

65. ***He is the Living – there is no god but Him; so call on Him*** and worship Him, ***making your* dīn *sincerely His*** – free of any *shirk*. ***Praise be to Allah, the Lord of all the worlds.***

66. ***Say: 'I have been forbidden to worship those you call upon besides Allah when the Clear Signs*** – evidence of His unity – ***came***

وَمَا يَسْتَوِي ٱلْأَعْمَىٰ وَٱلْبَصِيرُ وَٱلَّذِينَ ءَامَنُوا۟ وَعَمِلُوا۟
ٱلصَّٰلِحَٰتِ وَلَا ٱلْمُسِىٓءُ ۚ قَلِيلًا مَّا تَتَذَكَّرُونَ ﴿٥٨﴾
إِنَّ ٱلسَّاعَةَ لَءَاتِيَةٌ لَّا رَيْبَ فِيهَا وَلَٰكِنَّ أَكْثَرَ ٱلنَّاسِ
لَا يُؤْمِنُونَ ﴿٥٩﴾ وَقَالَ رَبُّكُمُ ٱدْعُونِىٓ أَسْتَجِبْ لَكُمْ ۚ
إِنَّ ٱلَّذِينَ يَسْتَكْبِرُونَ عَنْ عِبَادَتِى سَيَدْخُلُونَ جَهَنَّمَ
دَاخِرِينَ ﴿٦٠﴾ ٱللَّهُ ٱلَّذِى جَعَلَ لَكُمُ ٱلَّيْلَ لِتَسْكُنُوا۟
فِيهِ وَٱلنَّهَارَ مُبْصِرًا ۚ إِنَّ ٱللَّهَ لَذُو فَضْلٍ عَلَى ٱلنَّاسِ
وَلَٰكِنَّ أَكْثَرَ ٱلنَّاسِ لَا يَشْكُرُونَ ﴿٦١﴾ ذَٰلِكُمُ
ٱللَّهُ رَبُّكُمْ خَٰلِقُ كُلِّ شَىْءٍ لَّآ إِلَٰهَ إِلَّا هُوَ ۖ فَأَنَّىٰ تُؤْفَكُونَ
﴿٦٢﴾ كَذَٰلِكَ يُؤْفَكُ ٱلَّذِينَ كَانُوا۟ بِـَٔايَٰتِ ٱللَّهِ يَجْحَدُونَ
﴿٦٣﴾ ٱللَّهُ ٱلَّذِى جَعَلَ لَكُمُ ٱلْأَرْضَ قَرَارًا وَٱلسَّمَآءَ
بِنَآءً وَصَوَّرَكُمْ فَأَحْسَنَ صُوَرَكُمْ وَرَزَقَكُم مِّنَ
ٱلطَّيِّبَٰتِ ۚ ذَٰلِكُمُ ٱللَّهُ رَبُّكُمْ ۖ فَتَبَارَكَ ٱللَّهُ رَبُّ
ٱلْعَٰلَمِينَ ﴿٦٤﴾ هُوَ ٱلْحَىُّ لَآ إِلَٰهَ إِلَّا هُوَ فَٱدْعُوهُ
مُخْلِصِينَ لَهُ ٱلدِّينَ ۗ ٱلْحَمْدُ لِلَّهِ رَبِّ ٱلْعَٰلَمِينَ ﴿٦٥﴾ ۞ قُلْ
إِنِّى نُهِيتُ أَنْ أَعْبُدَ ٱلَّذِينَ تَدْعُونَ مِن دُونِ ٱللَّهِ لَمَّا جَآءَنِىَ
ٱلْبَيِّنَٰتُ مِن رَّبِّى وَأُمِرْتُ أَنْ أُسْلِمَ لِرَبِّ ٱلْعَٰلَمِينَ ﴿٦٦﴾
هُوَ ٱلَّذِى خَلَقَكُم مِّن تُرَابٍ ثُمَّ مِن نُّطْفَةٍ ثُمَّ مِنْ عَلَقَةٍ ثُمَّ
يُخْرِجُكُمْ طِفْلًا ثُمَّ لِتَبْلُغُوٓا۟ أَشُدَّكُمْ ثُمَّ لِتَكُونُوا۟
شُيُوخًا ۚ وَمِنكُم مَّن يُتَوَفَّىٰ مِن قَبْلُ ۖ وَلِتَبْلُغُوٓا۟ أَجَلًا مُّسَمًّى

to me from my Lord and I have been commanded to submit to the Lord of all the worlds.'

67. ***It is He who created you from earth*** in the form of your father Ādam, ***then from a drop of sperm, then from a clot of blood, then He brings you out as infants, then*** makes you continue ***so you may achieve full strength*** – which is the period from thirty to forty years old***; then so you may become old men*** (read as *shuyūkhan* and *shiyūkhan*) ***– though some of you may die before that time*** – before reaching maturity or old age, and He does that ***so that*** even if you live for a limited period of time ***you may reach a predetermined age and so that perhaps you may use your intellect*** and grasp the evidence of Allah's unity and therefore believe.

68. ***It is He who gives life and causes to die. When He decides on something*** – decides to bring it into existence – it happens immediately and ***He just says to it, 'Be!' and it is*** (read as *yakūnu* and *yakūna*). It comes into existence after He wills it.

69. ***Do you not see those who argue about Allah's Signs*** (the Qur'an)***? How have they been turned around*** from faith to unbelief***?***

70. ***Those who deny the Book*** (the Qur'an) ***and that with which We sent Our Messengers*** – regarding *tawḥīd* and the Resurrection – ***will certainly come to know*** the outcome of their denial –

71. ***...when they have shackles and chains around their necks and are dragged along the ground*** – the fact that there are fetters on their feet as well is also implied here –

72. ***...into the boiling water and then are thrown into the Fire*** – and roasted in Jahannam***!***

73. ***Then they will be asked*** – in rebuke – ***'Where are those*** idols ***besides Allah you associated with Him?'***

74. ***...and they will reply, 'They have forsaken us*** – disappeared and left us, so we cannot see them ***– or rather we were not calling to anything at all before.'*** They will deny their worship of the idols. Then the idols will be brought and Allah will say, *"You and what you worship besides Allah are fuel for Hell."* (21:98) ***That is how Allah misguides the unbelievers*** who deny.

وَلَعَلَّكُمْ تَعْقِلُونَ ﴿٦٧﴾ هُوَ ٱلَّذِى يُحْىِۦ وَيُمِيتُ ۖ فَإِذَا
قَضَىٰٓ أَمْرًا فَإِنَّمَا يَقُولُ لَهُۥ كُن فَيَكُونُ ﴿٦٨﴾ أَلَمْ تَرَ إِلَى ٱلَّذِينَ
يُجَٰدِلُونَ فِىٓ ءَايَٰتِ ٱللَّهِ أَنَّىٰ يُصْرَفُونَ ﴿٦٩﴾ ٱلَّذِينَ كَذَّبُوا۟
بِٱلْكِتَٰبِ وَبِمَآ أَرْسَلْنَا بِهِۦ رُسُلَنَا ۖ فَسَوْفَ يَعْلَمُونَ
﴿٧٠﴾ إِذِ ٱلْأَغْلَٰلُ فِىٓ أَعْنَٰقِهِمْ وَٱلسَّلَٰسِلُ يُسْحَبُونَ ﴿٧١﴾
فِى ٱلْحَمِيمِ ثُمَّ فِى ٱلنَّارِ يُسْجَرُونَ ﴿٧٢﴾ ثُمَّ قِيلَ لَهُمْ أَيْنَ
مَا كُنتُمْ تُشْرِكُونَ ﴿٧٣﴾ مِن دُونِ ٱللَّهِ ۖ قَالُوا۟ ضَلُّوا۟ عَنَّا بَل لَّمْ
نَكُن نَّدْعُوا۟ مِن قَبْلُ شَيْـًٔا ۚ كَذَٰلِكَ يُضِلُّ ٱللَّهُ ٱلْكَٰفِرِينَ ﴿٧٤﴾
ذَٰلِكُم بِمَا كُنتُمْ تَفْرَحُونَ فِى ٱلْأَرْضِ بِغَيْرِ ٱلْحَقِّ وَبِمَا كُنتُمْ
تَمْرَحُونَ ﴿٧٥﴾ ٱدْخُلُوٓا۟ أَبْوَٰبَ جَهَنَّمَ خَٰلِدِينَ فِيهَا ۖ فَبِئْسَ
مَثْوَى ٱلْمُتَكَبِّرِينَ ﴿٧٦﴾ فَٱصْبِرْ إِنَّ وَعْدَ ٱللَّهِ حَقٌّ ۚ فَإِمَّا
نُرِيَنَّكَ بَعْضَ ٱلَّذِى نَعِدُهُمْ أَوْ نَتَوَفَّيَنَّكَ فَإِلَيْنَا يُرْجَعُونَ ﴿٧٧﴾
وَلَقَدْ أَرْسَلْنَا رُسُلًا مِّن قَبْلِكَ مِنْهُم مَّن قَصَصْنَا عَلَيْكَ
وَمِنْهُم مَّن لَّمْ نَقْصُصْ عَلَيْكَ ۗ وَمَا كَانَ لِرَسُولٍ أَن يَأْتِىَ
بِـَٔايَةٍ إِلَّا بِإِذْنِ ٱللَّهِ ۚ فَإِذَا جَآءَ أَمْرُ ٱللَّهِ قُضِىَ بِٱلْحَقِّ وَخَسِرَ
هُنَالِكَ ٱلْمُبْطِلُونَ ﴿٧٨﴾ ٱللَّهُ ٱلَّذِى جَعَلَ لَكُمُ ٱلْأَنْعَٰمَ
لِتَرْكَبُوا۟ مِنْهَا وَمِنْهَا تَأْكُلُونَ ﴿٧٩﴾ وَلَكُمْ فِيهَا
مَنَٰفِعُ وَلِتَبْلُغُوا۟ عَلَيْهَا حَاجَةً فِى صُدُورِكُمْ وَعَلَيْهَا وَعَلَى
ٱلْفُلْكِ تُحْمَلُونَ ﴿٨٠﴾ وَيُرِيكُمْ ءَايَٰتِهِۦ فَأَىَّ ءَايَٰتِ

75. This will be said to them: ***'That*** punishment ***is because you exulted on the earth, without any right to do so*** – associating others with Allah and denying of the Resurrection – ***and strutted about*** with excessive joy in what you were doing.

76. ***Enter the gates of Hell, remaining in it timelessly, for ever. How evil is the abode of the arrogant!'***

77. ***So be steadfast, Allah's promise*** of punishment ***is true. Whether We show you some of what We have promised them*** – in terms of punishment during your lifetime – ***or take you back to Us*** before We punish them, ***they will in any case be returned to Us*** and We will inflict the most severe punishment on them.

78. ***We sent Messengers before you. Some of them We have told you about and others We have not told you about.*** It is related that Allah sent eight thousand Prophets: four thousand from the tribe of Israel and four thousand from others. ***No Messenger*** among them ***can bring a Sign except with Allah's permission*** – because they are slaves with a Master. ***But when Allah's command*** – meaning the punishment which befalls the unbelievers – ***comes, the matter*** between the Messengers and those who denied them ***will be decided with truth and then and there the liars will be lost.*** Then the judgement will appear and the liars will be in loss.

79. ***It is Allah who has given you livestock*** – it is said that this refers only to camels here, but it is evident that the word includes cattle and sheep as well – ***some for you to ride and some to eat.***

80. ***You gain various benefits from them*** – such as milk, their offspring, wool and fur – ***and on them you can obtain what your hearts desire*** by using them for transport; ***and on them*** – on land – ***and on ships you are transported*** on the sea.

81. ***He shows you His Signs*** of His unity, ***so which of Allah's Signs do you deny?*** This is to rebuke people.

82. ***Have they not travelled in the land and seen the final fate of those before them? They were more numerous than them and greater in strength, and left more and deeper traces on earth*** – such as buildings and castles; ***but what they earned was of no use to them.***

ٱللَّهِ تُنكِرُونَ ٨١ أَفَلَمْ يَسِيرُوا۟ فِى ٱلْأَرْضِ فَيَنظُرُوا۟ كَيْفَ
كَانَ عَـٰقِبَةُ ٱلَّذِينَ مِن قَبْلِهِمْ ۚ كَانُوٓا۟ أَكْثَرَ مِنْهُمْ وَأَشَدَّ
قُوَّةً وَءَاثَارًا فِى ٱلْأَرْضِ فَمَآ أَغْنَىٰ عَنْهُم مَّا كَانُوا۟ يَكْسِبُونَ
٨٢ فَلَمَّا جَآءَتْهُمْ رُسُلُهُم بِٱلْبَيِّنَـٰتِ فَرِحُوا۟ بِمَا عِندَهُم
مِّنَ ٱلْعِلْمِ وَحَاقَ بِهِم مَّا كَانُوا۟ بِهِۦ يَسْتَهْزِءُونَ ٨٣ فَلَمَّا
رَأَوْا۟ بَأْسَنَا قَالُوٓا۟ ءَامَنَّا بِٱللَّهِ وَحْدَهُۥ وَكَفَرْنَا بِمَا كُنَّا بِهِۦ
مُشْرِكِينَ ٨٤ فَلَمْ يَكُ يَنفَعُهُمْ إِيمَـٰنُهُمْ لَمَّا رَأَوْا۟ بَأْسَنَا ۖ سُنَّتَ
ٱللَّهِ ٱلَّتِى قَدْ خَلَتْ فِى عِبَادِهِۦ ۖ وَخَسِرَ هُنَالِكَ ٱلْكَـٰفِرُونَ ٨٥

83. ***When their Messengers brought them the Clear Signs*** (miracles) ***they*** (the unbelievers) mockingly ***exulted in the knowledge they*** (the Messengers) ***had*** – and laughed at it in denial – ***and then were engulfed by the very things they mocked*** – meaning the punishment.

84. ***When they saw Our violent force*** (severe punishment) ***they said, 'We believe in Allah alone and reject what we associated with Him.'***

85. ***But when they saw Our violent force their belief was of no use to them. That is the pattern Allah has always followed with His slaves*** – in past communities, whose faith did not help them when the punishment arrived. ***Then and there the unbelievers were lost.*** Their loss will be clear to everyone. They were already lost in every moment before that.

سُورَةُ فُصِّلَتۡ

بِسۡمِ ٱللَّهِ ٱلرَّحۡمَٰنِ ٱلرَّحِيمِ

حمٓ ﴿١﴾ تَنزِيلٞ مِّنَ ٱلرَّحۡمَٰنِ ٱلرَّحِيمِ ﴿٢﴾ كِتَٰبٞ فُصِّلَتۡ
ءَايَٰتُهُۥ قُرۡءَانًا عَرَبِيّٗا لِّقَوۡمٖ يَعۡلَمُونَ ﴿٣﴾ بَشِيرٗا وَنَذِيرٗا فَأَعۡرَضَ
أَكۡثَرُهُمۡ فَهُمۡ لَا يَسۡمَعُونَ ﴿٤﴾ وَقَالُواْ قُلُوبُنَا فِيٓ أَكِنَّةٖ
مِّمَّا تَدۡعُونَآ إِلَيۡهِ وَفِيٓ ءَاذَانِنَا وَقۡرٞ وَمِنۢ بَيۡنِنَا وَبَيۡنِكَ حِجَابٞ
فَٱعۡمَلۡ إِنَّنَا عَٰمِلُونَ ﴿٥﴾ قُلۡ إِنَّمَآ أَنَا۠ بَشَرٞ مِّثۡلُكُمۡ يُوحَىٰٓ إِلَيَّ
أَنَّمَآ إِلَٰهُكُمۡ إِلَٰهٞ وَٰحِدٞ فَٱسۡتَقِيمُوٓاْ إِلَيۡهِ وَٱسۡتَغۡفِرُوهُۗ وَوَيۡلٞ
لِّلۡمُشۡرِكِينَ ﴿٦﴾ ٱلَّذِينَ لَا يُؤۡتُونَ ٱلزَّكَوٰةَ وَهُم بِٱلۡأٓخِرَةِ
هُمۡ كَٰفِرُونَ ﴿٧﴾ إِنَّ ٱلَّذِينَ ءَامَنُواْ وَعَمِلُواْ ٱلصَّٰلِحَٰتِ لَهُمۡ
أَجۡرٌ غَيۡرُ مَمۡنُونٖ ﴿٨﴾ ۞ قُلۡ أَئِنَّكُمۡ لَتَكۡفُرُونَ بِٱلَّذِي خَلَقَ
ٱلۡأَرۡضَ فِي يَوۡمَيۡنِ وَتَجۡعَلُونَ لَهُۥٓ أَندَادٗاۚ ذَٰلِكَ رَبُّ ٱلۡعَٰلَمِينَ ﴿٩﴾
وَجَعَلَ فِيهَا رَوَٰسِيَ مِن فَوۡقِهَا وَبَٰرَكَ فِيهَا وَقَدَّرَ فِيهَآ أَقۡوَٰتَهَا فِيٓ
أَرۡبَعَةِ أَيَّامٖ سَوَآءٗ لِّلسَّآئِلِينَ ﴿١٠﴾ ثُمَّ ٱسۡتَوَىٰٓ إِلَى ٱلسَّمَآءِ وَهِيَ دُخَانٞ
فَقَالَ لَهَا وَلِلۡأَرۡضِ ٱئۡتِيَا طَوۡعًا أَوۡ كَرۡهٗا قَالَتَآ أَتَيۡنَا طَآئِعِينَ ﴿١١﴾
فَقَضَىٰهُنَّ سَبۡعَ سَمَٰوَاتٖ فِي يَوۡمَيۡنِ وَأَوۡحَىٰ فِي كُلِّ سَمَآءٍ أَمۡرَهَاۚ
وَزَيَّنَّا ٱلسَّمَآءَ ٱلدُّنۡيَا بِمَصَٰبِيحَ وَحِفۡظٗاۚ ذَٰلِكَ تَقۡدِيرُ ٱلۡعَزِيزِ

41. *Fuṣṣilat* or *Sūrat as-Sajda* Prostration, or Made Plain

This *sūra* is Makkan. It has 53 or 4 *āyat*s and was sent down after *Ghāfir.*

1. ***Ha Mim.*** Allah knows best what this means.

2. ***A revelation from the All-Merciful, the Most Merciful.***

3. ***A Book whose verses have been demarcated*** – and makes clear judgements, stories and warnings – ***for people who know*** and understand it, meaning the Arabs – ***as an Arabic Qur'an...***

4. ***...bringing good news and giving warning; but most of them have turned away and do not hear*** or accept.

5. ***They say*** to the Prophet, may Allah bless him and grant him peace, ***'Our hearts are covered up against what you call us to and there is a heaviness in our ears. There is a screen*** – of disagreement about the *dīn* – ***between us and you. So act*** – by your *dīn* – ***we are certainly acting*** – by our *dīn.*'

6. ***Say: 'I am only a human being like yourselves. It is revealed to me that your god is One God. So be straight with Him*** – by acting with faith and obedience – ***and ask His forgiveness.' Woe*** (punishment) ***to those who associate others with Him:***

7. ***...those who do not pay* zakāt *and who deny the Next World.***

8. ***Those who believe and do right actions will have a wage which never fails*** or ceases.

9. ***Say: 'Do you reject Him who created the earth in two days*** – said to be Sunday and Monday – ***and make others*** (partners) ***equal to Him? That is the Lord of all the worlds.'*** He is the Master of all the worlds, which means all that is other than Allah. It is plural because of the many varieties in it.

10. ***He placed firmly embedded mountains on it, towering over it, and blessed it*** – with plentiful water, crops and livestock – ***and measured out its nourishment in it*** – for mankind and animals, over four days – ***laid out for those who seek it – all in four days*** – adding

ٱلْعَلِيمِ ﴿١٢﴾ فَإِنْ أَعْرَضُوا۟ فَقُلْ أَنذَرْتُكُمْ صَـٰعِقَةً مِّثْلَ صَـٰعِقَةِ
عَادٍ وَثَمُودَ ﴿١٣﴾ إِذْ جَآءَتْهُمُ ٱلرُّسُلُ مِنۢ بَيْنِ أَيْدِيهِمْ وَمِنْ
خَلْفِهِمْ أَلَّا تَعْبُدُوٓا۟ إِلَّا ٱللَّهَ ۖ قَالُوا۟ لَوْ شَآءَ رَبُّنَا لَأَنزَلَ مَلَـٰٓئِكَةً
فَإِنَّا بِمَآ أُرْسِلْتُم بِهِۦ كَـٰفِرُونَ ﴿١٤﴾ فَأَمَّا عَادٌ فَٱسْتَكْبَرُوا۟ فِى
ٱلْأَرْضِ بِغَيْرِ ٱلْحَقِّ وَقَالُوا۟ مَنْ أَشَدُّ مِنَّا قُوَّةً ۖ أَوَلَمْ يَرَوْا۟ أَنَّ ٱللَّهَ
ٱلَّذِى خَلَقَهُمْ هُوَ أَشَدُّ مِنْهُمْ قُوَّةً ۖ وَكَانُوا۟ بِـَٔايَـٰتِنَا يَجْحَدُونَ
﴿١٥﴾ فَأَرْسَلْنَا عَلَيْهِمْ رِيحًا صَرْصَرًا فِىٓ أَيَّامٍ نَّحِسَاتٍ لِّنُذِيقَهُمْ
عَذَابَ ٱلْخِزْىِ فِى ٱلْحَيَوٰةِ ٱلدُّنْيَا ۖ وَلَعَذَابُ ٱلْـَٔاخِرَةِ أَخْزَىٰ ۖ وَهُمْ
لَا يُنصَرُونَ ﴿١٦﴾ وَأَمَّا ثَمُودُ فَهَدَيْنَـٰهُمْ فَٱسْتَحَبُّوا۟ ٱلْعَمَىٰ عَلَى
ٱلْهُدَىٰ فَأَخَذَتْهُمْ صَـٰعِقَةُ ٱلْعَذَابِ ٱلْهُونِ بِمَا كَانُوا۟ يَكْسِبُونَ
﴿١٧﴾ وَنَجَّيْنَا ٱلَّذِينَ ءَامَنُوا۟ وَكَانُوا۟ يَتَّقُونَ ﴿١٨﴾ وَيَوْمَ يُحْشَرُ
أَعْدَآءُ ٱللَّهِ إِلَى ٱلنَّارِ فَهُمْ يُوزَعُونَ ﴿١٩﴾ حَتَّىٰٓ إِذَا مَا جَآءُوهَا شَهِدَ
عَلَيْهِمْ سَمْعُهُمْ وَأَبْصَـٰرُهُمْ وَجُلُودُهُم بِمَا كَانُوا۟ يَعْمَلُونَ ﴿٢٠﴾
وَقَالُوا۟ لِجُلُودِهِمْ لِمَ شَهِدتُّمْ عَلَيْنَا ۖ قَالُوٓا۟ أَنطَقَنَا ٱللَّهُ ٱلَّذِىٓ
أَنطَقَ كُلَّ شَىْءٍ وَهُوَ خَلَقَكُمْ أَوَّلَ مَرَّةٍ وَإِلَيْهِ تُرْجَعُونَ ﴿٢١﴾
وَمَا كُنتُمْ تَسْتَتِرُونَ أَن يَشْهَدَ عَلَيْكُمْ سَمْعُكُمْ وَلَآ أَبْصَـٰرُكُمْ
وَلَا جُلُودُكُمْ وَلَـٰكِن ظَنَنتُمْ أَنَّ ٱللَّهَ لَا يَعْلَمُ كَثِيرًا مِّمَّا تَعْمَلُونَ
﴿٢٢﴾ وَذَٰلِكُمْ ظَنُّكُمُ ٱلَّذِى ظَنَنتُم بِرَبِّكُمْ أَرْدَىٰكُمْ فَأَصْبَحْتُم
مِّنَ ٱلْخَـٰسِرِينَ ﴿٢٣﴾ فَإِن يَصْبِرُوا۟ فَٱلنَّارُ مَثْوًى لَّهُمْ ۖ وَإِن
يَسْتَعْتِبُوا۟ فَمَا هُم مِّنَ ٱلْمُعْتَبِينَ ﴿٢٤﴾ ۞ وَقَيَّضْنَا لَهُمْ

Tuesday and Wednesday to the first two days. This is the answer for those who ask about the creation of the earth and what is in it.

11. ***Then He turned*** His attention ***to heaven when it was smoke*** – a rising mist – ***and said to it and to the earth, 'Come willingly or unwillingly***, obediently or reluctantly, to what I desire of you.***' They both said, 'We come*** – together with those within us – ***willingly.'***

12. ***In two days*** – Thursday and Friday – ***He determined them as seven heavens*** – and completed that in the last hour of Friday during which He created Ādam, and so He created all existent things in six days – ***and revealed, in every heaven, its own mandate*** – inspired every heaven with what it was commanded to do by way of obedience and worship. ***We adorned the lowest heaven with lamps*** (stars) ***and guarded it*** against the eavesdropping of the shaytans with meteors. ***That is the decree of the Almighty*** in His kingdom, ***the All-Knowing*** of His creation.

13. ***If they*** – the unbelievers of Makka – ***turn away*** from faith after things have been made clear, ***then say***, to frighten them: ***'I warn you of a lightning-bolt*** – which will destroy you – ***like the lightning-bolt of 'Ād and of Thamūd*** – which destroyed them.'

14. ***When the Messengers came to them from in front and from behind*** – and they rejected their message, as will be mentioned – ***saying, 'Do not worship anyone but Allah.' they said, 'If our Lord had willed, He could have sent angels down*** to us; ***so we reject the message you have been sent with.'***

15. ***'Ād were arrogant in the land, without any right, saying*** – when they were threatened with the punishment – ***'Who has greater strength than us?'*** No one, they thought! One of them could wrench out an immense stone from a mountain and put it wherever He wished. ***Did they not see*** and know ***that Allah, who created them, had greater strength than them? But they renounced Our Signs*** (miracles).

16. ***So We sent a howling wind*** – the word used here means a bitterly cold wind with no rain in it – ***against them on disastrous ill-fated*** (read as *naḥisāt* and *naḥsāt*) ***days to make them taste the punishment of degradation in this world. But the punishment of the Next***

World is even more degrading, and they will not be helped. No one will defend them.

17. ***As for Thamūd, We guided them*** – making the Path of guidance clear to them – ***but they preferred blindness to guidance*** by choosing unbelief. ***So the lightning-bolt of the humiliating punishment seized them on account of what they earned.***

18. ***And We rescued those*** among them ***who believed and were god - fearing.***

19. ***On the Day the enemies of Allah are crowded*** (read as *yuḥsharu*, and also *naḥshuru*, in which case the meaning is "We crowd") ***into the Fire and they are driven in close-packed ranks,***

20. ***...when they reach it, their hearing, sight and skin will testify against them concerning what they did.***

21. ***They will ask their skins, 'Why did you testify against us?' and they will reply, 'Allah gave us speech as He has given speech to everything*** by His will. ***He created you in the first place and you will be returned to Him.*** This is said to be spoken by their skins and is also said to be the words of Allah, as is what follows. The One who had the power to originate them the first time and can restore them to life has the power to make their skins and limbs speak.

22. ***You did not think to shield yourselves*** – by not committing foul actions – ***from your hearing, sight and skin testifying against you,*** because you did not think you would be resurrected; ***and you thought that Allah would never know much of what you did.***

23. ***It is that thought you had about your Lord that has destroyed you so now you find yourselves among the lost.'***

24. ***Even if they are steadfast*** in face of the the punishment ***the Fire will still be their residence! If they ask for favour; no favour will be given*** to them by anyone.

25. ***We have assigned to them close comrades*** from among the *shayṭān*s, ***who have made what is before them*** – love of this world and the pursuit of gross appetites – ***and behind them*** – meaning the reality of the Next World, by telling them that there is no Resurrection and no Reckoning – ***seem good to them. And the statement*** – the decree of punishment when Allah says, *"I will fill Hellfire..."* (7:18) – ***about the nations, both of jinn and men, who passed away***

قُرَنَآءَ فَزَيَّنُواْ لَهُم مَّا بَيْنَ أَيْدِيهِمْ وَمَا خَلْفَهُمْ وَحَقَّ عَلَيْهِمُ
ٱلْقَوْلُ فِىٓ أُمَمٍ قَدْ خَلَتْ مِن قَبْلِهِم مِّنَ ٱلْجِنِّ وَٱلْإِنسِ ۖ إِنَّهُمْ
كَانُواْ خَٰسِرِينَ ﴿٢٥﴾ وَقَالَ ٱلَّذِينَ كَفَرُواْ لَا تَسْمَعُواْ لِهَٰذَا ٱلْقُرْءَانِ
وَٱلْغَوْاْ فِيهِ لَعَلَّكُمْ تَغْلِبُونَ ﴿٢٦﴾ فَلَنُذِيقَنَّ ٱلَّذِينَ كَفَرُواْ عَذَابًا
شَدِيدًا وَلَنَجْزِيَنَّهُمْ أَسْوَأَ ٱلَّذِى كَانُواْ يَعْمَلُونَ ﴿٢٧﴾ ذَٰلِكَ جَزَآءُ
أَعْدَآءِ ٱللَّهِ ٱلنَّارُ ۖ لَهُمْ فِيهَا دَارُ ٱلْخُلْدِ ۖ جَزَآءًۢ بِمَا كَانُواْ بِـَٔايَٰتِنَا يَجْحَدُونَ
﴿٢٨﴾ وَقَالَ ٱلَّذِينَ كَفَرُواْ رَبَّنَآ أَرِنَا ٱلَّذَيْنِ أَضَلَّانَا مِنَ ٱلْجِنِّ
وَٱلْإِنسِ نَجْعَلْهُمَا تَحْتَ أَقْدَامِنَا لِيَكُونَا مِنَ ٱلْأَسْفَلِينَ ﴿٢٩﴾
إِنَّ ٱلَّذِينَ قَالُواْ رَبُّنَا ٱللَّهُ ثُمَّ ٱسْتَقَٰمُواْ تَتَنَزَّلُ عَلَيْهِمُ
ٱلْمَلَٰٓئِكَةُ أَلَّا تَخَافُواْ وَلَا تَحْزَنُواْ وَأَبْشِرُواْ بِٱلْجَنَّةِ
ٱلَّتِى كُنتُمْ تُوعَدُونَ ﴿٣٠﴾ نَحْنُ أَوْلِيَآؤُكُمْ فِى ٱلْحَيَوٰةِ
ٱلدُّنْيَا وَفِى ٱلْءَاخِرَةِ ۖ وَلَكُمْ فِيهَا مَا تَشْتَهِىٓ أَنفُسُكُمْ
وَلَكُمْ فِيهَا مَا تَدَّعُونَ ﴿٣١﴾ نُزُلًا مِّنْ غَفُورٍ رَّحِيمٍ ﴿٣٢﴾
وَمَنْ أَحْسَنُ قَوْلًا مِّمَّن دَعَآ إِلَى ٱللَّهِ وَعَمِلَ صَٰلِحًا وَقَالَ
إِنَّنِى مِنَ ٱلْمُسْلِمِينَ ﴿٣٣﴾ وَلَا تَسْتَوِى ٱلْحَسَنَةُ وَلَا ٱلسَّيِّئَةُ ۚ
ٱدْفَعْ بِٱلَّتِى هِىَ أَحْسَنُ فَإِذَا ٱلَّذِى بَيْنَكَ وَبَيْنَهُۥ عَدَٰوَةٌ كَأَنَّهُۥ
وَلِىٌّ حَمِيمٌ ﴿٣٤﴾ وَمَا يُلَقَّىٰهَآ إِلَّا ٱلَّذِينَ صَبَرُواْ وَمَا يُلَقَّىٰهَآ
إِلَّا ذُو حَظٍّ عَظِيمٍ ﴿٣٥﴾ وَإِمَّا يَنزَغَنَّكَ مِنَ ٱلشَّيْطَٰنِ نَزْغٌ
فَٱسْتَعِذْ بِٱللَّهِ ۖ إِنَّهُۥ هُوَ ٱلسَّمِيعُ ٱلْعَلِيمُ ﴿٣٦﴾ وَمِنْ ءَايَٰتِهِ
ٱلَّيْلُ وَٱلنَّهَارُ وَٱلشَّمْسُ وَٱلْقَمَرُ ۚ لَا تَسْجُدُواْ لِلشَّمْسِ

before them has proved true of them as well. Certainly they were lost and destroyed.

26. ***Those who disbelieved say*** – when the Prophet, may Allah bless him and grant him peace, is reciting the Qur'an – ***'Do not listen to this Qur'an. Drown it out*** – in other words, make a noise and shout while he is reciting – ***so that perhaps you may gain the upper hand*** and he will stop reciting.'

27. Allah says about them: ***We will make those who disbelieved suffer a severe punishment and repay them for the worst of what they did***: make them suffer most horrendous requital for their actions.

28. ***That*** terrible punishment and repayment ***is the requital of the enemies of Allah – the Fire. They will have it for their Eternal Home*** – and abide in it for ever and never leave it – ***as repayment for their renunciation of Our Signs*** (the Qur'an).

29. ***Those who disbelieve say***, in the Fire: ***'Our Lord, show us those jinn and men who misguided us*** – a reference to Iblīs and Qābīl who made unbelief and murder a custom among men – ***and we will place them beneath our feet*** in the Fire ***so that they will be among the lowest of the low*** – receive a worse punishment than us.'

30. ***The angels descend on those who say, 'Our Lord is Allah,' and then go straight*** – in other words, affirm Allah's unity and do all the things which are mandatory for them – ***'Do not fear*** death and what lies after it ***and do not grieve*** about any family and children you have left behind ***– but rejoice in the Garden you have been promised.***

31. ***We are your protectors*** – guarding you – ***in the life of this world and the Next World*** and we will be with you until you enter the Garden. ***You will have there all that your selves could wish for. You will have there everything you demand,***

32. *... as hospitality* – welcome and provision – ***from One who is Ever-Forgiving, Most Merciful*** (Allah).'

33. ***Who could say anything better than someone who summons to*** the unity of ***Allah, acts rightly and says, 'I am one of the Muslims'?*** No one can say anything better than this.

34. ***A good action and a bad action are not the same*** – this may also mean that good and bad actions vary according to the extent of their

وَلَا لِلْقَمَرِ وَاسْجُدُوا لِلَّهِ الَّذِي خَلَقَهُنَّ إِن كُنتُمْ
إِيَّاهُ تَعْبُدُونَ ﴿٣٧﴾ فَإِنِ اسْتَكْبَرُوا فَالَّذِينَ عِندَ
رَبِّكَ يُسَبِّحُونَ لَهُ بِاللَّيْلِ وَالنَّهَارِ وَهُمْ لَا يَسْأَمُونَ ۩ ﴿٣٨﴾
وَمِنْ آيَاتِهِ أَنَّكَ تَرَى الْأَرْضَ خَاشِعَةً فَإِذَا أَنزَلْنَا عَلَيْهَا الْمَاءَ
اهْتَزَّتْ وَرَبَتْ ۚ إِنَّ الَّذِي أَحْيَاهَا لَمُحْيِي الْمَوْتَىٰ ۚ إِنَّهُ عَلَىٰ كُلِّ شَيْءٍ
قَدِيرٌ ﴿٣٩﴾ إِنَّ الَّذِينَ يُلْحِدُونَ فِي آيَاتِنَا لَا يَخْفَوْنَ عَلَيْنَا ۗ أَفَمَن
يُلْقَىٰ فِي النَّارِ خَيْرٌ أَم مَّن يَأْتِي آمِنًا يَوْمَ الْقِيَامَةِ ۚ اعْمَلُوا مَا شِئْتُمْ ۖ
إِنَّهُ بِمَا تَعْمَلُونَ بَصِيرٌ ﴿٤٠﴾ إِنَّ الَّذِينَ كَفَرُوا بِالذِّكْرِ لَمَّا جَاءَهُمْ ۖ
وَإِنَّهُ لَكِتَابٌ عَزِيزٌ ﴿٤١﴾ لَّا يَأْتِيهِ الْبَاطِلُ مِن بَيْنِ يَدَيْهِ وَلَا مِنْ
خَلْفِهِ ۖ تَنزِيلٌ مِّنْ حَكِيمٍ حَمِيدٍ ﴿٤٢﴾ مَّا يُقَالُ لَكَ إِلَّا مَا قَدْ قِيلَ
لِلرُّسُلِ مِن قَبْلِكَ ۚ إِنَّ رَبَّكَ لَذُو مَغْفِرَةٍ وَذُو عِقَابٍ أَلِيمٍ ﴿٤٣﴾
وَلَوْ جَعَلْنَاهُ قُرْآنًا أَعْجَمِيًّا لَّقَالُوا لَوْلَا فُصِّلَتْ آيَاتُهُ ۖ أَأَعْجَمِيٌّ
وَعَرَبِيٌّ ۗ قُلْ هُوَ لِلَّذِينَ آمَنُوا هُدًى وَشِفَاءٌ ۖ وَالَّذِينَ
لَا يُؤْمِنُونَ فِي آذَانِهِمْ وَقْرٌ وَهُوَ عَلَيْهِمْ عَمًى ۚ أُولَٰئِكَ
يُنَادَوْنَ مِن مَّكَانٍ بَعِيدٍ ﴿٤٤﴾ وَلَقَدْ آتَيْنَا مُوسَى الْكِتَابَ
فَاخْتُلِفَ فِيهِ ۗ وَلَوْلَا كَلِمَةٌ سَبَقَتْ مِن رَّبِّكَ لَقُضِيَ
بَيْنَهُمْ ۚ وَإِنَّهُمْ لَفِي شَكٍّ مِّنْهُ مُرِيبٍ ﴿٤٥﴾ مَّنْ عَمِلَ صَالِحًا
فَلِنَفْسِهِ ۖ وَمَنْ أَسَاءَ فَعَلَيْهَا ۗ وَمَا رَبُّكَ بِظَلَّامٍ لِّلْعَبِيدِ ﴿٤٦﴾
۞ إِلَيْهِ يُرَدُّ عِلْمُ السَّاعَةِ ۚ وَمَا تَخْرُجُ مِن ثَمَرَاتٍ مِّنْ أَكْمَامِهَا
وَمَا تَحْمِلُ مِنْ أُنثَىٰ وَلَا تَضَعُ إِلَّا بِعِلْمِهِ ۚ وَيَوْمَ يُنَادِيهِمْ أَيْنَ

respective goodness or badness. ***Repel*** the bad action ***with some-thing better*** – a quality that is better than it: for instance you may repel anger with steadfastness, rashness with forbearance and harm with forgiveness, ***and if there is enmity between you and someone else, he will be like a bosom friend.*** Then your enemy will become like a close friend in his love for you if you do that.

35. ***None will obtain it but those who are truly steadfast. None will obtain it*** (the better quality) ***but those who have great good fortune*** (reward).

36. ***If an evil urge from Shayṭān eggs you on*** – and he turns you aside from that quality and other good attributes – ***seek refuge in Allah. He is the All-Hearing*** of what is said, ***the All-Knowing*** of what is done.

37. ***Among His Signs are the night and day and the sun and moon. Do not prostrate to the sun nor to the moon. Prostrate to Allah who created them*** (these signs) ***if you worship Him.***

38. ***If they grow*** too ***arrogant*** to prostrate to Allah alone, ***those who are with your Lord*** – meaning the angels – ***glorify Him night and day*** in prayer ***and never grow tired.***

39. ***Among His Signs is that you see the earth laid bare*** and arid, with no plants on it, ***and then, when We send down water on it, it quivers and swells. He who gives it life is He who gives life to the dead. Certainly He has power over all things.***

40. ***Those who adulterate*** (read as *yulḥidūna* and *yalḥadūna*) ***Our Signs*** (the Qur'an) which they deny ***are not concealed from Us*** – and We will repay them. ***Who is better: someone who will be thrown into the fire or someone who will arrive in safety on the Day of Rising? Do what you like. He sees whatever you do.*** This is a threat.

41. ***Those who reject the Remembrance*** (the Qur'an) ***when it comes to them***, We will repay them. ***Truly it is a Mighty Book;***

42. ***…falsehood cannot reach it from before it or behind it.*** Nothing can invalidate it before it or after it. ***It is a revelation from One who is All-Wise, Praiseworthy*** in what He does.

43. ***Nothing has been said to you*** by way of denial ***that was not said to the Messengers before you. Your Lord is the Possessor of***

forgiveness for believers – ***but also of painful retribution*** for unbelievers.

44. ***If We had made it*** (the Reminder) ***a Qur'an in a foreign tongue they would have said, 'Why have its Signs not been made plain*** – so that we may understand it***? What! A foreign language for an Arab?'*** Is the Qur'an in a foreign tongue, when the Prophet is an Arab? This implies a negative answer. ***Say: 'It is guidance*** away from error ***and healing*** for ignorance ***for people who believe. Those who do not believe have heaviness in their ears*** – preventing them from hearing – ***and for them it is blindness*** – meaning that they do not understand it. ***Such people are being called from a very distant place.'*** They are like someone who is being called from a distance and so they do not hear or understand what is being said.

45. ***We gave Mūsā the Book*** (the Torah) ***but there was disagreement about it*** – some people denying it and some affirming it, which is also the case with the Qur'an. ***And had it not been for a prior Word from your Lord*** – that the reckoning and repayment of creatures would be deferred until the Day of Rising – ***the judgement between them would already have been made*** in this world about their disagreement. ***They are indeed in grave doubt about it.***

46. ***Whoever acts rightly, it is for his own good*** and benefit. ***Whoever does evil, it is to his detriment*** – and his evil comes back on himself. ***Your Lord does not wrong His slaves.*** Allah never wrongs anyone in any way: as He says, *"Allah does not wrong anyone by so much as the smallest mote."* (4:40)

47. ***Knowledge of the Hour is referred to Him.*** Allah knows when it will occur, and no one but Him knows that. ***And no fruit*** (read as *thamarāt* or *thamara*, plural and singular) ***emerges from its husk*** except by His knowledge, ***nor does any female get pregnant or give birth, without His knowledge. On the Day He calls out to them: 'Where are My associates?' they will say, 'We declare to you*** that we now know ***that none of us is a witness*** that You have a partner.'

48. ***What*** (the idols) ***they called upon*** and worshipped ***before*** – in this world – ***will have forsaken them and they will realise*** with certainty that ***they have no way of escape*** from the punishment.

شُرَكَآءِي قَالُوٓاْ ءَاذَنَّٰكَ مَا مِنَّا مِن شَهِيدٖ ﴿٤٧﴾ وَضَلَّ
عَنۡهُم مَّا كَانُواْ يَدۡعُونَ مِن قَبۡلُۖ وَظَنُّواْ مَا لَهُم مِّن مَّحِيصٖ ﴿٤٨﴾
لَّا يَسۡـَٔمُ ٱلۡإِنسَٰنُ مِن دُعَآءِ ٱلۡخَيۡرِ وَإِن مَّسَّهُ ٱلشَّرُّ فَيَـُٔوسٞ
قَنُوطٞ ﴿٤٩﴾ وَلَئِنۡ أَذَقۡنَٰهُ رَحۡمَةٗ مِّنَّا مِنۢ بَعۡدِ ضَرَّآءَ مَسَّتۡهُ
لَيَقُولَنَّ هَٰذَا لِي وَمَآ أَظُنُّ ٱلسَّاعَةَ قَآئِمَةٗ وَلَئِن رُّجِعۡتُ إِلَىٰ
رَبِّيٓ إِنَّ لِي عِندَهُۥ لَلۡحُسۡنَىٰۚ فَلَنُنَبِّئَنَّ ٱلَّذِينَ كَفَرُواْ بِمَا عَمِلُواْ
وَلَنُذِيقَنَّهُم مِّنۡ عَذَابٍ غَلِيظٖ ﴿٥٠﴾ وَإِذَآ أَنۡعَمۡنَا عَلَى ٱلۡإِنسَٰنِ
أَعۡرَضَ وَنَـَٔا بِجَانِبِهِۦ وَإِذَا مَسَّهُ ٱلشَّرُّ فَذُو دُعَآءٍ عَرِيضٖ
﴿٥١﴾ قُلۡ أَرَءَيۡتُمۡ إِن كَانَ مِنۡ عِندِ ٱللَّهِ ثُمَّ كَفَرۡتُم
بِهِۦ مَنۡ أَضَلُّ مِمَّنۡ هُوَ فِي شِقَاقِۭ بَعِيدٖ ﴿٥٢﴾ سَنُرِيهِمۡ
ءَايَٰتِنَا فِي ٱلۡأٓفَاقِ وَفِيٓ أَنفُسِهِمۡ حَتَّىٰ يَتَبَيَّنَ لَهُمۡ أَنَّهُ ٱلۡحَقُّۗ
أَوَلَمۡ يَكۡفِ بِرَبِّكَ أَنَّهُۥ عَلَىٰ كُلِّ شَيۡءٖ شَهِيدٌ ﴿٥٣﴾ أَلَآ إِنَّهُمۡ
فِي مِرۡيَةٖ مِّن لِّقَآءِ رَبِّهِمۡۗ أَلَآ إِنَّهُۥ بِكُلِّ شَيۡءٖ مُّحِيطُۢ ﴿٥٤﴾

49. ***Man never tires of praying for what is good*** and continues to ask his Lord for wealth and health and other things***; and if evil touches him*** – poverty and hardship – ***he despairs*** of Allah's mercy ***and loses hope.***

50. This and what follows is about the unbelievers. ***But if We let him taste mercy*** as a gift, such as wealth and health, ***from Us after he has suffered hardship*** – harm and affliction – ***then he says: 'This is my due*** because of my actions**.** ***I do not think that the Hour is going to come, and if am returned to my Lord, I will definitely find the best reward*** (the Garden) ***with Him.' But We will inform those who disbelieved of what they did, and make them suffer an implca - ble punishment.***

51. ***When We grant blessing to a man*** – meaning people in general – ***he turns away***– from thankfulness ***and draws aside, but when any evil touches him, he is full of*** many ***endless prayers!***

52. ***Say: 'What do you think? If it*** (the Qur'an) ***is from Allah*** – as the Prophet says – ***and you reject it, who could be more misguided*** (further from the truth) ***than someone entrenched in hostility to it?'*** This explains their state.

53. ***We will show them Our Signs on the horizon*** – in the heavens and the earth there are signs in the form of lights, plants and trees – ***and within themselves*** – in the subtle workmanship and marvelous wisdom of their physical makeup – ***until it is clear to them that it*** (the Qur'an) ***is the truth*** sent down from Allah regarding the Resurrection, Reckoning and Punishment**.** They will then be punished for their unbelief. ***Is it not enough for your Lord that He is Witness of everything*** and nothing is hidden from Him***?***

54. ***What! Are they in doubt about the meeting with their Lord*** and do they deny the Resurrection***? What! Does He not encompass all things?*** Allah has total knowledge and power and will repay the unbelievers for their unbelief.

سُورَةُ الشُّورَىٰ

بِسۡمِ ٱللَّهِ ٱلرَّحۡمَٰنِ ٱلرَّحِيمِ

حمٓ ﴿١﴾ عٓسٓقٓ ﴿٢﴾ كَذَٰلِكَ يُوحِيٓ إِلَيۡكَ وَإِلَى ٱلَّذِينَ مِن قَبۡلِكَ
ٱللَّهُ ٱلۡعَزِيزُ ٱلۡحَكِيمُ ﴿٣﴾ لَهُۥ مَا فِي ٱلسَّمَٰوَٰتِ وَمَا فِي ٱلۡأَرۡضِۖ وَهُوَ
ٱلۡعَلِيُّ ٱلۡعَظِيمُ ﴿٤﴾ تَكَادُ ٱلسَّمَٰوَٰتُ يَتَفَطَّرۡنَ مِن فَوۡقِهِنَّۚ
وَٱلۡمَلَٰٓئِكَةُ يُسَبِّحُونَ بِحَمۡدِ رَبِّهِمۡ وَيَسۡتَغۡفِرُونَ لِمَن فِي
ٱلۡأَرۡضِۗ أَلَآ إِنَّ ٱللَّهَ هُوَ ٱلۡغَفُورُ ٱلرَّحِيمُ ﴿٥﴾ وَٱلَّذِينَ ٱتَّخَذُواْ
مِن دُونِهِۦٓ أَوۡلِيَآءَ ٱللَّهُ حَفِيظٌ عَلَيۡهِمۡ وَمَآ أَنتَ عَلَيۡهِم بِوَكِيلٖ
﴿٦﴾ وَكَذَٰلِكَ أَوۡحَيۡنَآ إِلَيۡكَ قُرۡءَانًا عَرَبِيّٗا لِّتُنذِرَ أُمَّ ٱلۡقُرَىٰ وَمَنۡ
حَوۡلَهَا وَتُنذِرَ يَوۡمَ ٱلۡجَمۡعِ لَا رَيۡبَ فِيهِۚ فَرِيقٞ فِي ٱلۡجَنَّةِ وَفَرِيقٞ فِي
ٱلسَّعِيرِ ﴿٧﴾ وَلَوۡ شَآءَ ٱللَّهُ لَجَعَلَهُمۡ أُمَّةٗ وَٰحِدَةٗ وَلَٰكِن يُدۡخِلُ
مَن يَشَآءُ فِي رَحۡمَتِهِۦۚ وَٱلظَّٰلِمُونَ مَا لَهُم مِّن وَلِيّٖ وَلَا نَصِيرٍ ﴿٨﴾
أَمِ ٱتَّخَذُواْ مِن دُونِهِۦٓ أَوۡلِيَآءَۖ فَٱللَّهُ هُوَ ٱلۡوَلِيُّ وَهُوَ يُحۡيِ ٱلۡمَوۡتَىٰ وَهُوَ
عَلَىٰ كُلِّ شَيۡءٖ قَدِيرٞ ﴿٩﴾ وَمَا ٱخۡتَلَفۡتُمۡ فِيهِ مِن شَيۡءٖ فَحُكۡمُهُۥٓ
إِلَى ٱللَّهِۚ ذَٰلِكُمُ ٱللَّهُ رَبِّي عَلَيۡهِ تَوَكَّلۡتُ وَإِلَيۡهِ أُنِيبُ ﴿١٠﴾
فَاطِرُ ٱلسَّمَٰوَٰتِ وَٱلۡأَرۡضِۚ جَعَلَ لَكُم مِّنۡ أَنفُسِكُمۡ أَزۡوَٰجٗا
وَمِنَ ٱلۡأَنۡعَٰمِ أَزۡوَٰجٗاۖ يَذۡرَؤُكُمۡ فِيهِۚ لَيۡسَ كَمِثۡلِهِۦ شَيۡءٞۖ

42. *Sūrat ash-Shūrā*
Counsel

This *sūra* is Makkan except for *āyat*s 23, 24, 25, and 26 which are Madinan. It has 53 *āyat*s and was sent down after *Fuṣṣilat.*

1. ***Ḥā Mīm***

2. ***'Ayn Sīn Qāf.*** Allah knows best what this means.

3. ***That*** Revelation ***is how He sends Revelation to you and those before you. Allah is Almighty*** in His kingdom, ***the All-Wise*** in what He does.

4. ***Everything in the heavens and everything in the earth belongs to Him*** as His property, creation and slaves. ***He is the Most High, the Magnificent.***

5. ***The heavens are all but*** (read as *takādu* and *yakādu*) ***rent asunder*** (read as *yatafaṭṭarna* and *yanfaṭirna*) ***from above*** – each almost split above the one next to it because of the immense power of Allah – ***when the angels glorify their Lord with praise and ask forgiveness for those*** believers ***who are on the earth. Allah is the Ever-Forgiving*** to His friends, ***the Most Merciful*** to them.

6. ***As for those who take others*** (idols) ***besides Him as protectors, Allah will take care of them*** and will repay them. ***You are not set over them as a guardian.*** You are only asked to convey the Message.

7. ***Accordingly We have revealed to you an Arabic Qur'an so that you may warn the Mother of Cities*** – the people of Makka – ***and those around it*** – all other human beings, ***and give warning*** to humankind ***of the Day of Gathering*** – another name for the Day of Resurrection, because it is the day on which all creatures will be gathered together – ***about which there is no doubt: one group in the Garden, the other in the Blazing Fire.***

8. ***If Allah had willed, He would have made them a single nation*** following the same *dīn*, namely Islam. ***But He admits whomever He wills into His mercy and the wrongdoers*** (unbelievers) ***have no protector and no helper*** to defend them from the Punishment.

﴿١٩﴾ مَن كَانَ يُرِيدُ حَرْثَ ٱلْـَٔاخِرَةِ نَزِدْ لَهُۥ فِى حَرْثِهِۦ ۖ وَمَن
كَانَ يُرِيدُ حَرْثَ ٱلدُّنْيَا نُؤْتِهِۦ مِنْهَا وَمَا لَهُۥ فِى ٱلْـَٔاخِرَةِ مِن
نَّصِيبٍ ﴿٢٠﴾ أَمْ لَهُمْ شُرَكَٰٓؤُا۟ شَرَعُوا۟ لَهُم مِّنَ ٱلدِّينِ
مَا لَمْ يَأْذَنۢ بِهِ ٱللَّهُ ۚ وَلَوْلَا كَلِمَةُ ٱلْفَصْلِ لَقُضِىَ بَيْنَهُمْ ۗ
وَإِنَّ ٱلظَّٰلِمِينَ لَهُمْ عَذَابٌ أَلِيمٌ ﴿٢١﴾ تَرَى ٱلظَّٰلِمِينَ
مُشْفِقِينَ مِمَّا كَسَبُوا۟ وَهُوَ وَاقِعٌۢ بِهِمْ ۗ وَٱلَّذِينَ
ءَامَنُوا۟ وَعَمِلُوا۟ ٱلصَّٰلِحَٰتِ فِى رَوْضَاتِ ٱلْجَنَّاتِ ۖ
لَهُم مَّا يَشَآءُونَ عِندَ رَبِّهِمْ ۚ ذَٰلِكَ هُوَ ٱلْفَضْلُ ٱلْكَبِيرُ ﴿٢٢﴾
ذَٰلِكَ ٱلَّذِى يُبَشِّرُ ٱللَّهُ عِبَادَهُ ٱلَّذِينَ ءَامَنُوا۟ وَعَمِلُوا۟ ٱلصَّٰلِحَٰتِ ۗ قُل لَّآ
أَسْـَٔلُكُمْ عَلَيْهِ أَجْرًا إِلَّا ٱلْمَوَدَّةَ فِى ٱلْقُرْبَىٰ ۗ وَمَن يَقْتَرِفْ حَسَنَةً نَّزِدْ
لَهُۥ فِيهَا حُسْنًا ۚ إِنَّ ٱللَّهَ غَفُورٌ شَكُورٌ ﴿٢٣﴾ أَمْ يَقُولُونَ ٱفْتَرَىٰ عَلَى ٱللَّهِ
كَذِبًا ۖ فَإِن يَشَإِ ٱللَّهُ يَخْتِمْ عَلَىٰ قَلْبِكَ ۗ وَيَمْحُ ٱللَّهُ ٱلْبَٰطِلَ وَيُحِقُّ ٱلْحَقَّ
بِكَلِمَٰتِهِۦٓ ۚ إِنَّهُۥ عَلِيمٌۢ بِذَاتِ ٱلصُّدُورِ ﴿٢٤﴾ وَهُوَ ٱلَّذِى يَقْبَلُ ٱلتَّوْبَةَ
عَنْ عِبَادِهِۦ وَيَعْفُوا۟ عَنِ ٱلسَّيِّـَٔاتِ وَيَعْلَمُ مَا تَفْعَلُونَ ﴿٢٥﴾
وَيَسْتَجِيبُ ٱلَّذِينَ ءَامَنُوا۟ وَعَمِلُوا۟ ٱلصَّٰلِحَٰتِ وَيَزِيدُهُم مِّن فَضْلِهِۦ ۚ
وَٱلْكَٰفِرُونَ لَهُمْ عَذَابٌ شَدِيدٌ ﴿٢٦﴾ ۞ وَلَوْ بَسَطَ ٱللَّهُ ٱلرِّزْقَ
لِعِبَادِهِۦ لَبَغَوْا۟ فِى ٱلْأَرْضِ وَلَٰكِن يُنَزِّلُ بِقَدَرٍ مَّا يَشَآءُ ۚ إِنَّهُۥ بِعِبَادِهِۦ
خَبِيرٌۢ بَصِيرٌ ﴿٢٧﴾ وَهُوَ ٱلَّذِى يُنَزِّلُ ٱلْغَيْثَ مِنۢ بَعْدِ مَا قَنَطُوا۟
وَيَنشُرُ رَحْمَتَهُۥ ۚ وَهُوَ ٱلْوَلِىُّ ٱلْحَمِيدُ ﴿٢٨﴾ وَمِنْ ءَايَٰتِهِۦ خَلْقُ
ٱلسَّمَٰوَٰتِ وَٱلْأَرْضِ وَمَا بَثَّ فِيهِمَا مِن دَآبَّةٍ ۚ وَهُوَ عَلَىٰ جَمْعِهِمْ

9. ***Have they then taken others*** (idols) ***besides Him as protectors? But Allah is the Protector.*** It is Allah who helps the believers. ***He gives life to the dead. He has power over all things.***

10. ***The judgement concerning anything you differ about*** with the unbelievers regarding matters of the *dīn* and other things ***is Allah's concern*** on the Day of Rising. He will decide between you. Say to them: ***That is Allah, my Lord – I have put my trust in Him and to Him I turn –***

11. ***...the Bringer into Being of the heavens and the earth: He has given you mates from among yourselves*** – a reference to the creation of Ḥawwā' from the rib of Ādam – ***and given mates*** – male and female – ***to the livestock, in that way multiplying you*** through procreation. ***Nothing is like Him. He is the All-Hearing*** of what is said, ***the All-Seeing*** of what is done.

12. ***The Keys of the heavens and earth*** – the keys to the treasuries of rain, plants and other things – ***belong to Him. He expands the provision of anyone He wills or restricts it*** as a test and a trial. ***He has knowledge of all things.***

13. ***He has laid down the same* dīn *for you as He enjoined on Nūḥ*** – the first of the Prophets of *Sharī'a* – ***that which We have revealed to you and which We enjoined on Ibrāhīm, Mūsā and 'Īsā: 'Establish the* dīn *and do not make divisions in it.'*** This is the Law which is commanded and revealed to Muḥammad, may Allah bless him and grant him peace. ***What you call the idolators*** – who refuse to acknowledge Allah's unity – ***to follow is very hard for them. Allah chooses for Himself anyone He wills*** – those who affirm His unity – ***and guides to Himself those who turn to Him*** and agree to obey Him.

14. ***They*** (the people of the different religions) ***only split up*** – and disagreed about their religion, so that some affirmed Allah's unity and some rejected it – ***after knowledge*** of the truth ***came to them*** – the unbelievers – ***tyrannising one another. And were it not for a prior decree from your Lord*** – that the repayment would be delayed ***for a specified term*** until the Day of Rising – ***the judgement between them would already have been made*** and the unbelievers would have been punished in this world. ***Those who inherited the***

Book after them – after the Jews and Christians – ***are indeed in grave doubt about it*** – or about him, meaning Muḥammad, may Allah bless him and grant him peace.

15. ***So call*** – people to Allah's unity, Muḥammad – ***and go straight*** in His *dīn* ***as you have been ordered to. Do not follow their whims and desires*** by abandoning it ***but say, 'I believe in a Book sent down by Allah and I am ordered to be just between you*** in rendering judgement. ***Allah is our Lord and your Lord. We have our actions and you have your actions.*** Allah will repay everyone for what they do. ***There is no debate between us and you.*** This was before *jihād* was ordered. ***Allah will gather us all together*** and decide between all of us in the Final Judgement***: He is our final destination.'***

16. ***The argument of those who argue about*** the *dīn* of ***Allah*** – with His Prophet – ***once He*** (or he) ***has been acknowledged*** – by faith because his miracles have appeared. This is a reference to the Jews – ***has no basis whatsoever with their Lord.*** Their argument is false and invalid. ***There is anger upon them and they will have a harsh punishment.***

17. ***It is Allah who has sent down the Book*** (the Qur'an) ***with truth and with the Just Balance*** (justice). ***What will make you realise*** – and inform you***? Perhaps the*** Last ***Hour is close.***

18. ***Those who do not believe in it try to hasten it.*** They say, "When will it come?" thinking that it will not come. ***But those who believe in it are afraid of it. They know it is the truth. Those who doubt the Hour*** and argue about it ***are greatly misguided.***

19. ***Allah is very gentle with His slaves*** – both the pious and the impious among them, and does not make them perish from hunger because of their disobedience***. He provides for anyone He wills*** – all of them, in whatever way He wishes. ***He is the Most Strong, the Almighty.***

20. ***If anyone desires to cultivate the Next World*** – by performing actions whose fruit is the reward of the Next World – ***We will increase him in his cultivation*** – his good actions being multiplied up to ten times and more. ***If anyone desires to cultivate this world,***

We will give him some of it – without any multiplication taking place – ***but he will have no share in the Next World.***

21. ***Or do they*** (the unbelievers of Makka) ***have partners*** (shayṭāns) ***who have laid down a*** false **dīn** – involving partners – ***for them*** (the unbelievers) ***for which Allah has not given any authority*** (permission) – for attributing partners to Him and denying the Resurrection***? Were it not for the prior Word of Decision*** that repayment for our actions will come on the Day of Rising ***the judgement between them*** and the believers about punishment in this world ***would already have been made. The wrongdoers*** (unbelievers) ***will have a painful punishment.***

22. ***You will see the wrongdoers*** – on the Day of Rising – ***afraid of what they have earned*** – in this world, for which they will be repaid – ***when it is about to land right on top of them, whereas those who believe and do right actions will be in the lush Meadows of the Gardens*** – which only they will enjoy. ***They will have whatever they wish for with their Lord. That is the great favour.***

23. ***That is the good news*** (read as *yubashshiru* and *yabshuru*) ***which Allah gives to His slaves who believe and do right actions. Say: 'I do not ask you for any wage for this*** – for conveying the Message – ***except for you to love your near of kin.*** I only ask you to love my kin, who are also your kin. There was no sub-tribe among Quraysh which did not have kinship with the Prophet, may Allah bless him and grant him peace. ***If anyone does a good action*** in obedience to Allah ***We will increase the good of it for him*** and multiply it. ***Allah is Ever-Forgiving*** of wrong actions, ***Ever-Thankful*** for a few right actions which He multiplies.***'***

24. ***Or do they ask, 'Has he invented a lie about Allah*** – by ascribing the Qur'an to Allah***?' If Allah willed, He could shore up your heart*** by making you steadfast in the face of their harming you by saying that and other things. He did indeed do so. ***By His Words Allah wipes out the false*** things which they say ***and confirms the truth*** – by the words which He sent down to His Prophet. ***He knows what the heart contains.***

25. ***It is He who accepts repentance from His slaves and pardons evil acts, and He knows what you do*** (read as *taf'alūna* and also *yaf'alūna*, "what they do").

إِذَا يَشَآءُ قَدِيرٞ (٢٩) وَمَآ أَصَٰبَكُم مِّن مُّصِيبَةٖ فَبِمَا
كَسَبَتۡ أَيۡدِيكُمۡ وَيَعۡفُواْ عَن كَثِيرٖ (٣٠) وَمَآ أَنتُم بِمُعۡجِزِينَ
فِي ٱلۡأَرۡضِۖ وَمَا لَكُم مِّن دُونِ ٱللَّهِ مِن وَلِيّٖ وَلَا نَصِيرٖ (٣١)
وَمِنۡ ءَايَٰتِهِ ٱلۡجَوَارِ فِي ٱلۡبَحۡرِ كَٱلۡأَعۡلَٰمِ (٣٢) إِن يَشَأۡ يُسۡكِنِ ٱلرِّيحَ
فَيَظۡلَلۡنَ رَوَاكِدَ عَلَىٰ ظَهۡرِهِۦٓۚ إِنَّ فِي ذَٰلِكَ لَأٓيَٰتٖ لِّكُلِّ صَبَّارٖ شَكُورٍ
(٣٣) أَوۡ يُوبِقۡهُنَّ بِمَا كَسَبُواْ وَيَعۡفُ عَن كَثِيرٖ (٣٤) وَيَعۡلَمَ ٱلَّذِينَ
يُجَٰدِلُونَ فِيٓ ءَايَٰتِنَا مَا لَهُم مِّن مَّحِيصٖ (٣٥) فَمَآ أُوتِيتُم مِّن شَيۡءٖ فَمَتَٰعُ
ٱلۡحَيَوٰةِ ٱلدُّنۡيَاۖ وَمَا عِندَ ٱللَّهِ خَيۡرٞ وَأَبۡقَىٰ لِلَّذِينَ ءَامَنُواْ وَعَلَىٰ رَبِّهِمۡ
يَتَوَكَّلُونَ (٣٦) وَٱلَّذِينَ يَجۡتَنِبُونَ كَبَٰٓئِرَ ٱلۡإِثۡمِ وَٱلۡفَوَٰحِشَ وَإِذَا مَا
غَضِبُواْ هُمۡ يَغۡفِرُونَ (٣٧) وَٱلَّذِينَ ٱسۡتَجَابُواْ لِرَبِّهِمۡ وَأَقَامُواْ ٱلصَّلَوٰةَ
وَأَمۡرُهُمۡ شُورَىٰ بَيۡنَهُمۡ وَمِمَّا رَزَقۡنَٰهُمۡ يُنفِقُونَ (٣٨) وَٱلَّذِينَ إِذَآ أَصَابَهُمُ
ٱلۡبَغۡيُ هُمۡ يَنتَصِرُونَ (٣٩) وَجَزَٰٓؤُاْ سَيِّئَةٖ سَيِّئَةٞ مِّثۡلُهَاۖ فَمَنۡ عَفَا
وَأَصۡلَحَ فَأَجۡرُهُۥ عَلَى ٱللَّهِۚ إِنَّهُۥ لَا يُحِبُّ ٱلظَّٰلِمِينَ (٤٠) وَلَمَنِ ٱنتَصَرَ
بَعۡدَ ظُلۡمِهِۦ فَأُوْلَٰٓئِكَ مَا عَلَيۡهِم مِّن سَبِيلٍ (٤١) إِنَّمَا ٱلسَّبِيلُ عَلَى ٱلَّذِينَ
يَظۡلِمُونَ ٱلنَّاسَ وَيَبۡغُونَ فِي ٱلۡأَرۡضِ بِغَيۡرِ ٱلۡحَقِّۚ أُوْلَٰٓئِكَ لَهُمۡ
عَذَابٌ أَلِيمٞ (٤٢) وَلَمَن صَبَرَ وَغَفَرَ إِنَّ ذَٰلِكَ لَمِنۡ عَزۡمِ ٱلۡأُمُورِ
(٤٣) وَمَن يُضۡلِلِ ٱللَّهُ فَمَا لَهُۥ مِن وَلِيّٖ مِّنۢ بَعۡدِهِۦۗ وَتَرَى ٱلظَّٰلِمِينَ
لَمَّا رَأَوُاْ ٱلۡعَذَابَ يَقُولُونَ هَلۡ إِلَىٰ مَرَدّٖ مِّن سَبِيلٖ (٤٤)
وَتَرَىٰهُمۡ يُعۡرَضُونَ عَلَيۡهَا خَٰشِعِينَ مِنَ ٱلذُّلِّ يَنظُرُونَ
مِن طَرۡفٍ خَفِيّٖۗ وَقَالَ ٱلَّذِينَ ءَامَنُوٓاْ إِنَّ ٱلۡخَٰسِرِينَ ٱلَّذِينَ

26. ***He responds to those who believe and do right actions*** – and grants them what they ask for – ***and gives them increase from His favour. But the unbelievers will have a harsh punishment.***

27. ***Were Allah to expand the provision of*** all ***His slaves, they would*** all ***act as tyrants on the earth. But He sends down*** (read as *yunazzilu* and *yunzal*) ***whatever*** provision ***He wills in a measured way.*** He sends it down and gives more to some and less to others. Tyranny results from excessive provision. ***He is aware of and He sees His slaves.***

28. ***It is He who sends down abundant rain, after they have lost all hope*** of it, ***and unfolds His mercy*** in the form of rain. ***He is the Protector*** who is good to the believers, ***the Praiseworthy*** – praised by them.

29. ***Among His Signs is the creation of the heavens and earth and all the creatures He has spread about in them***: all the animals and people that move about the earth. ***And He has the power to gather them together whenever He wills.***

30. This is addressed to the believers. ***Any disaster*** – affliction or hardship – ***that strikes you is through what*** – the wrong actions – ***your own hands have earned*** – "hands" are mentioned because most actions are done using them – ***and He pardons much.*** He pardons many of them and does not exact repayment for them. As for those who do not do wrong, the afflictions which befall them in this world come in order to raise their degrees in the Next World.

31. ***You,*** idolaters, ***will not be able to thwart Him on the earth*** – flee from Allah or escape Him – ***and you have no protector or helper besides Allah*** to avert the punishment from you.

32. ***Among His Signs are the tall ships sailing like*** tall ***mountains through the sea.***

33. ***If He wills He makes the wind stop blowing*** – and then ships stop moving – ***and then they lie motionless on its back. There are certainly Signs in that for everyone who is steadfast and thankful*** – meaning believers who are steadfast in affliction and thankful in ease.

34. ***Or*** the wind can destroy the ship and then ***He wrecks*** it and drowns ***them for what*** (the wrong actions) ***they have earned, though He pardons much*** of that and does not drown people.

35. ***Those who argue about Our Signs should know that they have no way of escape*** – and that He may drown them in order to take revenge on them and they will have no way to run away.

36. This is addressed to the believers and others. ***Whatever you have been given is only the enjoyment of*** goods in ***the life of this world*** – and it will soon vanish. ***What is with Allah*** by way of reward ***is better and longer lasting for those who believe and trust in their Lord:***

37. ***...those who avoid major wrong actions and indecencies*** – which necessitate the *ḥudūd* punishments – ***and who, when they are angered, then*** overlook and ***forgive;***

38. ***...those who respond to their Lord*** – and act on what He calls them to in terms of *tawḥīd* and worship – ***and establish*** regular ***prayer, and manage their affairs*** in the way which seems right to them ***by mutual consultation*** – about them and are not hasty, ***and give*** (spend) ***of what We have provided for them*** in obedience to Allah***;***

39. ***...those who, when they are wronged, defend themselves.*** The word for "wronged", *baghī*, means "suffer injustice". They may revenge themselves on those who have wronged them with the like of the wrong done to them, as Allah says in the next *āyat*.

40. ***The repayment of a bad action is one equivalent to it.*** The second action is called a bad action because its form resembles the first. This is clear when retaliation for wounds is taken. It is said that when someone says, "May Allah disgrace you," he answers him with "May Allah disgrace you too." ***But if someone pardons*** the person who wrongs him ***and puts things right*** – restores the love between him and the one he pardons – ***his reward*** for doing that ***is with Allah. Certainly He does not love wrongdoers*** who initiate wrongdoing, and so He will punish them.

41. ***But if people do defend themselves when they are wronged*** – and wrong those who have wronged them – ***nothing can be held against them for doing that***, and there is no punishment.

خَسِرُوٓا۟ أَنفُسَهُمْ وَأَهْلِيهِمْ يَوْمَ ٱلْقِيَـٰمَةِ ۗ أَلَآ إِنَّ ٱلظَّـٰلِمِينَ
فِى عَذَابٍ مُّقِيمٍ ﴿٤٥﴾ وَمَا كَانَ لَهُم مِّنْ أَوْلِيَآءَ يَنصُرُونَهُم
مِّن دُونِ ٱللَّهِ ۗ وَمَن يُضْلِلِ ٱللَّهُ فَمَا لَهُۥ مِن سَبِيلٍ ﴿٤٦﴾ ٱسْتَجِيبُوا۟
لِرَبِّكُم مِّن قَبْلِ أَن يَأْتِىَ يَوْمٌ لَّا مَرَدَّ لَهُۥ مِنَ ٱللَّهِ ۚ مَا لَكُم
مِّن مَّلْجَإٍ يَوْمَئِذٍ وَمَا لَكُم مِّن نَّكِيرٍ ﴿٤٧﴾ فَإِنْ أَعْرَضُوا۟
فَمَآ أَرْسَلْنَـٰكَ عَلَيْهِمْ حَفِيظًا ۖ إِنْ عَلَيْكَ إِلَّا ٱلْبَلَـٰغُ ۗ وَإِنَّآ إِذَآ
أَذَقْنَا ٱلْإِنسَـٰنَ مِنَّا رَحْمَةً فَرِحَ بِهَا ۖ وَإِن تُصِبْهُمْ سَيِّئَةٌۢ
بِمَا قَدَّمَتْ أَيْدِيهِمْ فَإِنَّ ٱلْإِنسَـٰنَ كَفُورٌ ﴿٤٨﴾ لِّلَّهِ مُلْكُ
ٱلسَّمَـٰوَٰتِ وَٱلْأَرْضِ ۚ يَخْلُقُ مَا يَشَآءُ ۚ يَهَبُ لِمَن يَشَآءُ إِنَـٰثًا
وَيَهَبُ لِمَن يَشَآءُ ٱلذُّكُورَ ﴿٤٩﴾ أَوْ يُزَوِّجُهُمْ ذُكْرَانًا وَإِنَـٰثًا ۖ
وَيَجْعَلُ مَن يَشَآءُ عَقِيمًا ۚ إِنَّهُۥ عَلِيمٌ قَدِيرٌ ﴿٥٠﴾ ۞ وَمَا كَانَ
لِبَشَرٍ أَن يُكَلِّمَهُ ٱللَّهُ إِلَّا وَحْيًا أَوْ مِن وَرَآئِ حِجَابٍ أَوْ يُرْسِلَ
رَسُولًا فَيُوحِىَ بِإِذْنِهِۦ مَا يَشَآءُ ۚ إِنَّهُۥ عَلِىٌّ حَكِيمٌ ﴿٥١﴾
وَكَذَٰلِكَ أَوْحَيْنَآ إِلَيْكَ رُوحًا مِّنْ أَمْرِنَا ۚ مَا كُنتَ تَدْرِى مَا ٱلْكِتَـٰبُ
وَلَا ٱلْإِيمَـٰنُ وَلَـٰكِن جَعَلْنَـٰهُ نُورًا نَّهْدِى بِهِۦ مَن نَّشَآءُ مِنْ عِبَادِنَا ۚ
وَإِنَّكَ لَتَهْدِىٓ إِلَىٰ صِرَٰطٍ مُّسْتَقِيمٍ ﴿٥٢﴾ صِرَٰطِ ٱللَّهِ ٱلَّذِى لَهُۥ
مَا فِى ٱلسَّمَـٰوَٰتِ وَمَا فِى ٱلْأَرْضِ ۗ أَلَآ إِلَى ٱللَّهِ تَصِيرُ ٱلْأُمُورُ ﴿٥٣﴾

42. ***There are only grounds against those who wrong people and act as tyrants*** – and commit acts of disobedience – ***in the earth without any right to do so. Such people will have a painful punishment.***

43. ***But if someone is steadfast*** – and does not defend himself – ***and forgives*** – and overlooks ***that*** steadfastness and overlooking ***is the most resolute course to follow*** – qualities which are desired in the *Sharī'a.*

44. ***Whoever Allah misguides has no one to protect them after that.*** No one can undertake the guidance of someone after Allah has misguided him. ***You will see the wrongdoers saying, when they see the punishment, 'Is there no way back*** to the world?'

45. ***You will see them as they are exposed to it*** (the Fire), ***abject in their abasement*** – humble and fearful, ***glancing around them furtively*** – stealing glances. ***Those who believe will say, 'Truly the losers are those who lose themselves and their families on the Day of Rising.'*** They will be for ever in the Fire and will not obtain the houris prepared for them in the Garden which they would have had if they had believed. ***The wrongdoers*** (unbelievers) ***are in an everlasting*** – continuous – ***punishment.***

46. ***They have no one to protect or help them apart from Allah*** – there is no one who can avert the punishment of Allah. ***There is no way out for anyone Allah misguides*** – no path to the truth in this world or to the Garden in the Next World.

47. ***Respond to your Lord*** by affirming His unity and worshipping Him, ***before a Day*** – the Day of Resurrection – ***comes from Allah which cannot be turned back.*** No one can turn it aside. ***On that Day you will have no hiding-place*** – nowhere to seek refuge – ***and no means of denial*** of your wrong actions.

48. ***But if they turn away*** – and fail to respond – ***We have not sent you to be their guardian*** to ensure that their actions conform to what is desired: ***you are only responsible for transmission.*** This was before the command to fight *jihād.* ***When We let a man*** – used generically to mean all human beings – ***taste mercy*** – meaning here a blessing like wealth or health – ***from Us he exults in it. But if something bad*** (an affliction) ***strikes him for what he has done*** – literally "what his hands have advanced", because hands are the limbs by which most actions are carried out – ***he is ungrateful*** for the blessings he has received.

49. ***The kingdom of the heavens and earth belongs to Allah. He creates whatever He wills. He gives daughters to whoever He wishes; and He gives sons to whoever He wishes;***

50. ***...or He gives them both sons and daughters; and He makes whoever He wishes barren*** – without children. ***Truly He is All-Knowing, All-Powerful*** – and therefore able to do whatever He wishes.

51. ***It does not befit Allah to address any human being except by inspiration*** – while they are asleep or actual inspiration while awake – ***or from behind a veil*** – so that he hears His words but does not see Him, as was the case with Mūsā, peace be upon him***; or He sends a messenger*** – an angel like Jibrīl – ***who then reveals*** – to the Messenger to whom He is sent by speaking to him – ***by His*** (Allah's) ***permission whatever He wills. He is indeed Most High*** above the attributes of temporal beings, ***All-Wise*** – in whatever He does.

52. ***Accordingly We have revealed to you***, Muḥammad, ***a*** **Rūḥ** – meaning the Qur'an, which gives life to the hearts, as We revealed to other Messengers – ***by Our command.*** Before the revelation came ***you had no idea of what the Book*** (the Qur'an) ***was, or faith*** – meaning the laws and practices of Islam. ***Yet We have made it*** (the *Rūḥ* or the Book) ***a Light by which We guide those of Our slaves We will. Truly you are guiding*** – by the revelation given to you – ***to a Straight Path*** – the *dīn* of Islam:

53. ***...the Path of Allah to Whom everything in the heavens and everything on the earth belongs. Indeed all matters return eventually to Allah.***

سُورَةُ الزُّخۡرُفِ

بِسۡمِ ٱللَّهِ ٱلرَّحۡمَٰنِ ٱلرَّحِيمِ

حمٓ ١ وَٱلۡكِتَٰبِ ٱلۡمُبِينِ ٢ إِنَّا جَعَلۡنَٰهُ قُرۡءَٰنًا عَرَبِيّٗا
لَّعَلَّكُمۡ تَعۡقِلُونَ ٣ وَإِنَّهُۥ فِيٓ أُمِّ ٱلۡكِتَٰبِ لَدَيۡنَا
لَعَلِيٌّ حَكِيمٌ ٤ أَفَنَضۡرِبُ عَنكُمُ ٱلذِّكۡرَ صَفۡحًا
أَن كُنتُمۡ قَوۡمٗا مُّسۡرِفِينَ ٥ وَكَمۡ أَرۡسَلۡنَا مِن نَّبِيّٖ فِي
ٱلۡأَوَّلِينَ ٦ وَمَا يَأۡتِيهِم مِّن نَّبِيٍّ إِلَّا كَانُواْ بِهِۦ يَسۡتَهۡزِءُونَ
٧ فَأَهۡلَكۡنَآ أَشَدَّ مِنۡهُم بَطۡشٗا وَمَضَىٰ مَثَلُ ٱلۡأَوَّلِينَ
٨ وَلَئِن سَأَلۡتَهُم مَّنۡ خَلَقَ ٱلسَّمَٰوَٰتِ وَٱلۡأَرۡضَ لَيَقُولُنَّ
خَلَقَهُنَّ ٱلۡعَزِيزُ ٱلۡعَلِيمُ ٩ ٱلَّذِي جَعَلَ لَكُمُ ٱلۡأَرۡضَ
مَهۡدٗا وَجَعَلَ لَكُمۡ فِيهَا سُبُلٗا لَّعَلَّكُمۡ تَهۡتَدُونَ ١٠
وَٱلَّذِي نَزَّلَ مِنَ ٱلسَّمَآءِ مَآءَۢ بِقَدَرٖ فَأَنشَرۡنَا بِهِۦ بَلۡدَةٗ مَّيۡتٗاۚ
كَذَٰلِكَ تُخۡرَجُونَ ١١ وَٱلَّذِي خَلَقَ ٱلۡأَزۡوَٰجَ كُلَّهَا وَجَعَلَ
لَكُم مِّنَ ٱلۡفُلۡكِ وَٱلۡأَنۡعَٰمِ مَا تَرۡكَبُونَ ١٢ لِتَسۡتَوُۥاْ عَلَىٰ ظُهُورِهِۦ
ثُمَّ تَذۡكُرُواْ نِعۡمَةَ رَبِّكُمۡ إِذَا ٱسۡتَوَيۡتُمۡ عَلَيۡهِ وَتَقُولُواْ سُبۡحَٰنَ
ٱلَّذِي سَخَّرَ لَنَا هَٰذَا وَمَا كُنَّا لَهُۥ مُقۡرِنِينَ ١٣ وَإِنَّآ إِلَىٰ رَبِّنَا
لَمُنقَلِبُونَ ١٤ وَجَعَلُواْ لَهُۥ مِنۡ عِبَادِهِۦ جُزۡءًاۚ إِنَّ ٱلۡإِنسَٰنَ
لَكَفُورٞ مُّبِينٌ ١٥ أَمِ ٱتَّخَذَ مِمَّا يَخۡلُقُ بَنَاتٖ وَأَصۡفَىٰكُم

43. *Sūrat az-Zukhruf*
The Gold Ornaments

This *sūra* is Makkan except for *āyat* 45, which is Madinan. It has 89 *āyat*s and was sent down after *ash-Shūra.*

1. ***Ḥā Mīm.*** Allah knows best what is meant by this.

2. ***By the Book*** (the Qur'an) ***which makes things clear*** – makes clear the path of guidance and the *Sharī'a* rulings needed for it.

3. ***We have made it an Arabic Qur'an so that perhaps you***, people of Makka, ***may use your intellect*** and understand its meanings.

4. ***It is in the Source Book with Us*** – the source of all divinely revealed Books, the Preserved Tablet; ***high-exalted*** over the Books before it, ***full of*** vast ***wisdom.***

5. ***Shall We then deprive you of the Reminder*** – keep the Qur'an back from you so that you cannot command or prohibit by means of it – ***for being a profligate people*** (idolaters)***?*** No!

6. ***How many Prophets We sent to the previous peoples!***

7. ***But no Prophet came to them without their mocking him*** – previous Prophets were mocked as your people mock you. This is solace for the Prophet, may Allah bless him and grant him peace –

8. ***...and so We destroyed people with greater power than they have*** – who were more powerful than your people – ***and the pattern of the previous peoples has gone before.*** There are signs in the earlier peoples and how they were destroyed, and the end of your people will be like that.

9. ***If you were to ask them, 'Who created the heavens and the earth?' they would reply, 'The Almighty, the All-Knowing created them.'*** It is only Allah, who possesses the necessary might and knowledge. Allah adds:

10. ***It is He who made the earth a cradle for you*** – a comfortable berth for you as a cradle is for an infant – ***and made pathways for you in it so that perhaps you might be guided*** to your destinations when you travel.

11. ***It is He who sends down water in due measure from the sky*** – according to your need for it; He does not make it an overwhelming flood – ***by which We bring a dead land back to life. That is how you too*** will be brought back to life and ***will be brought forth*** from your graves alive.

12. ***It is He who created all species, and gave you ships and livestock*** – such as camels – ***for you to ride…***

13. ***…so that you might sit firmly on their backs and remember your Lord's blessing while you are seated on them, saying, 'Glory be to Him who has subjected this to us*** and made it obey us. ***We could never have accomplished it by ourselves.***

14. ***Indeed we are returning to our Lord!'***

15. ***They have assigned to Him a portion of His creatures!*** This was done in saying, "The angels are the daughters of Allah" because the child is a portion of the father. The angels are the slaves of Allah. ***Truly man is openly ungrateful*** and clearly demonstrating unbelief.

16. ***Has He then taken daughters from what He has created and chosen sons for you?*** Do you say this? This is a sentence which negates what they have said.

17. ***When any of them is given the good news of the very thing which he himself has ascribed to the All-Merciful*** – in other words, when he is given the good news of a girl, which is like the daughters they ascribe to Him – ***his face darkens*** with sorrow ***and he is furious*** – filled with rage. Then how can he ascribe daughters to Allah?

18. ***'What!*** Do you attribute to Allah ***someone brought up among pretty trinkets*** and jewellery and ***who cannot produce a cogent argument*** – in her weakness***!'***

19. ***They have designated the angels as female, those who are in the presence of the All-Merciful! Were they present to witness their creation? Their testimony*** that the angels are female ***will be recorded and they will be asked about it*** in the Next World and will endure punishment on that account.

20. ***They say, 'If the All-Merciful had so willed, we would not have worshipped them.'*** If Allah had willed, they would not have worshipped the angels. They claim that they worship them by His will, which shows that He must be pleased with it. Allah responds: ***They***

بِٱلۡبَنِينَ ﴿١٦﴾ وَإِذَا بُشِّرَ أَحَدُهُم بِمَا ضَرَبَ لِلرَّحۡمَٰنِ مَثَلٗا
ظَلَّ وَجۡهُهُۥ مُسۡوَدّٗا وَهُوَ كَظِيمٌ ﴿١٧﴾ أَوَمَن يُنَشَّؤُاْ فِي
ٱلۡحِلۡيَةِ وَهُوَ فِي ٱلۡخِصَامِ غَيۡرُ مُبِينٖ ﴿١٨﴾ وَجَعَلُواْ ٱلۡمَلَٰٓئِكَةَ
ٱلَّذِينَ هُمۡ عِبَٰدُ ٱلرَّحۡمَٰنِ إِنَٰثًاۚ أَشَهِدُواْ خَلۡقَهُمۡۚ سَتُكۡتَبُ
شَهَٰدَتُهُمۡ وَيُسۡـَٔلُونَ ﴿١٩﴾ وَقَالُواْ لَوۡ شَآءَ ٱلرَّحۡمَٰنُ مَا عَبَدۡنَٰهُمۗ
مَّا لَهُم بِذَٰلِكَ مِنۡ عِلۡمٍۖ إِنۡ هُمۡ إِلَّا يَخۡرُصُونَ ﴿٢٠﴾ أَمۡ ءَاتَيۡنَٰهُمۡ
كِتَٰبٗا مِّن قَبۡلِهِۦ فَهُم بِهِۦ مُسۡتَمۡسِكُونَ ﴿٢١﴾ بَلۡ قَالُوٓاْ
إِنَّا وَجَدۡنَآ ءَابَآءَنَا عَلَىٰٓ أُمَّةٖ وَإِنَّا عَلَىٰٓ ءَاثَٰرِهِم مُّهۡتَدُونَ ﴿٢٢﴾
وَكَذَٰلِكَ مَآ أَرۡسَلۡنَا مِن قَبۡلِكَ فِي قَرۡيَةٖ مِّن نَّذِيرٍ إِلَّا قَالَ مُتۡرَفُوهَآ
إِنَّا وَجَدۡنَآ ءَابَآءَنَا عَلَىٰٓ أُمَّةٖ وَإِنَّا عَلَىٰٓ ءَاثَٰرِهِم مُّقۡتَدُونَ ﴿٢٣﴾
۞ قَٰلَ أَوَلَوۡ جِئۡتُكُم بِأَهۡدَىٰ مِمَّا وَجَدتُّمۡ عَلَيۡهِ ءَابَآءَكُمۡۖ قَالُوٓاْ
إِنَّا بِمَآ أُرۡسِلۡتُم بِهِۦ كَٰفِرُونَ ﴿٢٤﴾ فَٱنتَقَمۡنَا مِنۡهُمۡۖ فَٱنظُرۡ كَيۡفَ
كَانَ عَٰقِبَةُ ٱلۡمُكَذِّبِينَ ﴿٢٥﴾ وَإِذۡ قَالَ إِبۡرَٰهِيمُ لِأَبِيهِ وَقَوۡمِهِۦٓ
إِنَّنِي بَرَآءٞ مِّمَّا تَعۡبُدُونَ ﴿٢٦﴾ إِلَّا ٱلَّذِي فَطَرَنِي فَإِنَّهُۥ سَيَهۡدِينِ
﴿٢٧﴾ وَجَعَلَهَا كَلِمَةَۢ بَاقِيَةٗ فِي عَقِبِهِۦ لَعَلَّهُمۡ يَرۡجِعُونَ ﴿٢٨﴾ بَلۡ
مَتَّعۡتُ هَٰٓؤُلَآءِ وَءَابَآءَهُمۡ حَتَّىٰ جَآءَهُمُ ٱلۡحَقُّ وَرَسُولٞ مُّبِينٞ ﴿٢٩﴾
وَلَمَّا جَآءَهُمُ ٱلۡحَقُّ قَالُواْ هَٰذَا سِحۡرٞ وَإِنَّا بِهِۦ كَٰفِرُونَ ﴿٣٠﴾ وَقَالُواْ
لَوۡلَا نُزِّلَ هَٰذَا ٱلۡقُرۡءَانُ عَلَىٰ رَجُلٖ مِّنَ ٱلۡقَرۡيَتَيۡنِ عَظِيمٍ ﴿٣١﴾ أَهُمۡ
يَقۡسِمُونَ رَحۡمَتَ رَبِّكَۚ نَحۡنُ قَسَمۡنَا بَيۡنَهُم مَّعِيشَتَهُمۡ فِي ٱلۡحَيَوٰةِ
ٱلدُّنۡيَاۚ وَرَفَعۡنَا بَعۡضَهُمۡ فَوۡقَ بَعۡضٖ دَرَجَٰتٖ لِّيَتَّخِذَ بَعۡضُهُم

have no knowledge of that – about His being pleased with the worship of those idols***; they are only conjecturing.*** They lie and will suffer punishment on account of that.

21. ***Or did We give them a Book before*** (the Qur'an) which contains instructions to worship other than Allah and ***which they are holding to?*** No, that has not occurred.

22. ***No; in fact they say, 'We found our fathers following a religion*** – the word *umma*, which normally means "community", here means "religion" – ***and we are simply guided in their footsteps.*** They used to worship other than Allah and so we do too.'

23. ***Similarly We never sent any warner before you to any city without the affluent among them*** – those who were given blessings similar to those your people enjoy – ***saying, 'We found our fathers following a religion and we are simply following in their footsteps.'***

24. ***Say*** to them: 'Do you follow that? ***What if I have come with better guidance than what you found your fathers following?' They say, 'We reject what you*** – and the Prophets before you ***have been sent with.'***

25. Then Allah threatens them by saying: ***So We took revenge on them*** – meaning those who denied the Messengers before you. ***And see the final fate of the deniers!***

26. Remember ***when Ibrāhīm said to his father and his people, 'I am free of everything you worship...***

27. ***...except for Him Who*** created me and ***brought me into being, Who will certainly guide me*** to His *dīn,'*

28. ***...he made it*** – the formula of *tawḥīḍ*, which is understood from his words, *"I am going towards my Lord; He will be my guide"* (37:99) – ***an ongoing word among his descendants*** – and there are those who will continue to affirm the unity of Allah among them – ***so that perhaps they might turn back*** – so that the people of Makka may return from what they are doing to the *dīn* of Ibrāhīm, their ancestor.

29. ***I let those people*** (the idolaters) ***and their forefathers enjoy themselves*** – and did not bring on their punishment – ***until the truth*** (the Qur'an) ***came to them and a Messenger to make it clear*** – to

بَعْضًا سُخْرِيًّا ۗ وَرَحْمَتُ رَبِّكَ خَيْرٌ مِّمَّا يَجْمَعُونَ ﴿٣٢﴾ وَلَوْلَآ
أَن يَكُونَ ٱلنَّاسُ أُمَّةً وَٰحِدَةً لَّجَعَلْنَا لِمَن يَكْفُرُ بِٱلرَّحْمَٰنِ
لِبُيُوتِهِمْ سُقُفًا مِّن فِضَّةٍ وَمَعَارِجَ عَلَيْهَا يَظْهَرُونَ ﴿٣٣﴾
وَلِبُيُوتِهِمْ أَبْوَٰبًا وَسُرُرًا عَلَيْهَا يَتَّكِـُٔونَ ﴿٣٤﴾ وَزُخْرُفًا ۚ وَإِن
كُلُّ ذَٰلِكَ لَمَّا مَتَٰعُ ٱلْحَيَوٰةِ ٱلدُّنْيَا ۚ وَٱلْـَٔاخِرَةُ عِندَ رَبِّكَ
لِلْمُتَّقِينَ ﴿٣٥﴾ وَمَن يَعْشُ عَن ذِكْرِ ٱلرَّحْمَٰنِ نُقَيِّضْ لَهُۥ شَيْطَٰنًا
فَهُوَ لَهُۥ قَرِينٌ ﴿٣٦﴾ وَإِنَّهُمْ لَيَصُدُّونَهُمْ عَنِ ٱلسَّبِيلِ وَيَحْسَبُونَ
أَنَّهُم مُّهْتَدُونَ ﴿٣٧﴾ حَتَّىٰٓ إِذَا جَآءَنَا قَالَ يَٰلَيْتَ بَيْنِى وَبَيْنَكَ
بُعْدَ ٱلْمَشْرِقَيْنِ فَبِئْسَ ٱلْقَرِينُ ﴿٣٨﴾ وَلَن يَنفَعَكُمُ ٱلْيَوْمَ
إِذ ظَّلَمْتُمْ أَنَّكُمْ فِى ٱلْعَذَابِ مُشْتَرِكُونَ ﴿٣٩﴾ أَفَأَنتَ تُسْمِعُ
ٱلصُّمَّ أَوْ تَهْدِى ٱلْعُمْىَ وَمَن كَانَ فِى ضَلَٰلٍ مُّبِينٍ ﴿٤٠﴾
فَإِمَّا نَذْهَبَنَّ بِكَ فَإِنَّا مِنْهُم مُّنتَقِمُونَ ﴿٤١﴾ أَوْ نُرِيَنَّكَ ٱلَّذِى
وَعَدْنَٰهُمْ فَإِنَّا عَلَيْهِم مُّقْتَدِرُونَ ﴿٤٢﴾ فَٱسْتَمْسِكْ بِٱلَّذِىٓ أُوحِىَ
إِلَيْكَ ۖ إِنَّكَ عَلَىٰ صِرَٰطٍ مُّسْتَقِيمٍ ﴿٤٣﴾ وَإِنَّهُۥ لَذِكْرٌ لَّكَ وَلِقَوْمِكَ ۖ
وَسَوْفَ تُسْـَٔلُونَ ﴿٤٤﴾ وَسْـَٔلْ مَنْ أَرْسَلْنَا مِن قَبْلِكَ مِن رُّسُلِنَآ
أَجَعَلْنَا مِن دُونِ ٱلرَّحْمَٰنِ ءَالِهَةً يُعْبَدُونَ ﴿٤٥﴾ وَلَقَدْ أَرْسَلْنَا
مُوسَىٰ بِـَٔايَٰتِنَآ إِلَىٰ فِرْعَوْنَ وَمَلَإِي۟هِۦ فَقَالَ إِنِّى رَسُولُ
رَبِّ ٱلْعَٰلَمِينَ ﴿٤٦﴾ فَلَمَّا جَآءَهُم بِـَٔايَٰتِنَآ إِذَا هُم مِّنْهَا يَضْحَكُونَ ﴿٤٧﴾
وَمَا نُرِيهِم مِّنْ ءَايَةٍ إِلَّا هِىَ أَكْبَرُ مِنْ أُخْتِهَا ۖ وَأَخَذْنَٰهُم
بِٱلْعَذَابِ لَعَلَّهُمْ يَرْجِعُونَ ﴿٤٨﴾ وَقَالُوا۟ يَٰٓأَيُّهَ ٱلسَّاحِرُ ٱدْعُ لَنَا
رَبَّكَ بِمَا عَهِدَ عِندَكَ إِنَّنَا لَمُهْتَدُونَ ﴿٤٩﴾ فَلَمَّا كَشَفْنَا عَنْهُمُ

show them the rulings of the *Sharī'a*. That was Muḥammad, may Allah bless him and grant him peace.

30. ***But when the truth*** (the Qur'an) ***came to them they said, 'This is magic and we reject it.'***

31. ***They say, 'Why was this Qur'an not sent down to one of the great men of the two cities*** (Makka and Taif)***?'*** The men referred to were al-Walīd ibn al-Mughīra in Makka and 'Urwa ibn Mas'ūd ath-Thaqafī in Taif.

32. ***Is it they, then who allocate the mercy*** – meaning Prophethood in this instance – ***of your Lord? We have allocated their livelihood among them in the life of this world*** – and made some of them wealthy and some of them poor – ***and raised some of them above others in rank*** by means of their wealth ***so that some of them are subservient to others*** by having to work for a wage because of their poverty. ***But the mercy of your Lord*** (the Garden) ***is better than anything they amass*** in this world.

33. ***Were it not that mankind might all become one community*** in unbelief ***We would have given those who reject the All-Merciful silver roofs*** (read as *suqufan* and *saqfan*) ***to their houses and silver stairways to ascend*** to the roof –

34. ***...and silver doors to their houses, and silver couches on which to recline,***

35. ***...and gold ornaments.*** If it were not for the fear of unbelief mentioned, Allah would have given mankind those things because of the lack of importance of this world in His sight. ***All that is merely the trappings of the life of this world. But the Next World*** (the Garden) ***with your Lord is for those who are godfearing.***

36. ***If someone shuts his eyes to the remembrance of the All-Merciful*** – turns away from the Qur'an – ***We assign him a*** **shayṭān** ***who becomes his bosom friend*** and never leaves him –

37. ***...they*** (the *shayṭāns*) ***debar them*** (those who shut their eyes) ***from the path*** of guidance; ***yet they still think they are guided –***

38. ***...until, when he*** (the one who shut his eyes) ***reaches Us*** – together with his companion, on the Day of Rising – ***he says, 'If only there were the distance of the two Easts between you and me!' What an evil companion!***

39. Allah says to such people: ***It*** (their wish and regret) ***will not benefit you*** (those who shut their eyes) ***today, since you did wrong*** – and their wrongdoing by associating others with Allah in this world will become clear to them, ***that you*** and your fellows ***share equally in the punishment*** – since nothing will help them.

40. ***Can you make the dead hear, or guide the blind and those who are patently misguided?*** This means that they will not believe.

41. ***Either We will extricate you and take revenge on them*** – Allah will make the Prophet die before He punishes them in this world, and they will then be punished in the Next World as well –

42. ***...or let you see what*** punishment ***We have promised them*** while you are still alive. ***They are completely in Our power.***

43. ***So hold fast to what has been revealed to you*** (the Qur'an). ***You are on a straight path.***

44. ***It is certainly a reminder*** – meaning "honour" in this instance – ***to you and to your people*** – since it was revealed in their language – ***and you will be questioned*** about fulfilling what it demands of you.

45. ***Ask those We sent before you as Our Messengers: have We ever designated any gods to be worshipped besides the All-Merciful?*** It is said that this is to be taken literally since the Messengers were gathered together with him on his Night Journey. It is also said that what is meant are their communities, the People of the two previous Scriptures. He did not actually ask anyone according to either view. What is meant by the command to ask is to tell the idolaters of Quraysh that no Messenger from Allah and no Book has brought the worship of anything other than Allah.

46. ***We sent Mūsā with Our Signs to Pharaoh and his nobles*** (the Copts). ***He said, 'I am the Messenger of the Lord of the worlds.'***

47. ***But when he came to them with Our Signs*** – which proved that He was a Messenger – ***they merely laughed at them.***

48. ***We showed them no Sign*** of punishment, such as the flood which entered their houses, submerging those who were sitting down up to their necks for seven days, and the locusts, ***that was not greater than the one before it. We seized them with punishment so that perhaps they would turn back*** from unbelief.

ٱلْعَذَابَ إِذَا هُمْ يَنكُثُونَ ﴿٥٠﴾ وَنَادَىٰ فِرْعَوْنُ فِى قَوْمِهِۦ
قَالَ يَٰقَوْمِ أَلَيْسَ لِى مُلْكُ مِصْرَ وَهَٰذِهِ ٱلْأَنْهَٰرُ تَجْرِى مِن
تَحْتِىٓ ۖ أَفَلَا تُبْصِرُونَ ﴿٥١﴾ أَمْ أَنَا۠ خَيْرٌ مِّنْ هَٰذَا ٱلَّذِى هُوَ مَهِينٌ
وَلَا يَكَادُ يُبِينُ ﴿٥٢﴾ فَلَوْلَآ أُلْقِىَ عَلَيْهِ أَسْوِرَةٌ مِّن ذَهَبٍ أَوْ جَآءَ
مَعَهُ ٱلْمَلَٰٓئِكَةُ مُقْتَرِنِينَ ﴿٥٣﴾ فَٱسْتَخَفَّ قَوْمَهُۥ
فَأَطَاعُوهُ ۚ إِنَّهُمْ كَانُوا۟ قَوْمًا فَٰسِقِينَ ﴿٥٤﴾ فَلَمَّآ ءَاسَفُونَا
ٱنتَقَمْنَا مِنْهُمْ فَأَغْرَقْنَٰهُمْ أَجْمَعِينَ ﴿٥٥﴾ فَجَعَلْنَٰهُمْ
سَلَفًا وَمَثَلًا لِّلْءَاخِرِينَ ﴿٥٦﴾ ۞ وَلَمَّا ضُرِبَ ٱبْنُ مَرْيَمَ
مَثَلًا إِذَا قَوْمُكَ مِنْهُ يَصِدُّونَ ﴿٥٧﴾ وَقَالُوٓا۟ ءَأَٰلِهَتُنَا
خَيْرٌ أَمْ هُوَ ۚ مَا ضَرَبُوهُ لَكَ إِلَّا جَدَلًۢا ۚ بَلْ هُمْ قَوْمٌ خَصِمُونَ ﴿٥٨﴾
إِنْ هُوَ إِلَّا عَبْدٌ أَنْعَمْنَا عَلَيْهِ وَجَعَلْنَٰهُ مَثَلًا لِّبَنِىٓ إِسْرَٰٓءِيلَ
وَإِنَّهُۥ لَعِلْمٌ لِّلسَّاعَةِ فَلَا تَمْتَرُنَّ بِهَا وَٱتَّبِعُونِ ۚ هَٰذَا صِرَٰطٌ
مُّسْتَقِيمٌ ﴿٦١﴾ وَلَا يَصُدَّنَّكُمُ ٱلشَّيْطَٰنُ ۖ إِنَّهُۥ لَكُمْ عَدُوٌّ مُّبِينٌ
﴿٦٢﴾ وَلَمَّا جَآءَ عِيسَىٰ بِٱلْبَيِّنَٰتِ قَالَ قَدْ جِئْتُكُم بِٱلْحِكْمَةِ
وَلِأُبَيِّنَ لَكُم بَعْضَ ٱلَّذِى تَخْتَلِفُونَ فِيهِ ۖ فَٱتَّقُوا۟ ٱللَّهَ وَأَطِيعُونِ
﴿٦٣﴾ إِنَّ ٱللَّهَ هُوَ رَبِّى وَرَبُّكُمْ فَٱعْبُدُوهُ ۚ هَٰذَا صِرَٰطٌ مُّسْتَقِيمٌ
﴿٦٤﴾ فَٱخْتَلَفَ ٱلْأَحْزَابُ مِنۢ بَيْنِهِمْ ۖ فَوَيْلٌ لِّلَّذِينَ ظَلَمُوا۟
مِنْ عَذَابِ يَوْمٍ أَلِيمٍ ﴿٦٥﴾ هَلْ يَنظُرُونَ إِلَّا ٱلسَّاعَةَ أَن
تَأْتِيَهُم بَغْتَةً وَهُمْ لَا يَشْعُرُونَ ﴿٦٦﴾ ٱلْأَخِلَّآءُ يَوْمَئِذٍۭ
بَعْضُهُمْ لِبَعْضٍ عَدُوٌّ إِلَّا ٱلْمُتَّقِينَ ﴿٦٧﴾ يَٰعِبَادِ لَا خَوْفٌ

49. ***They said*** to Mūsā, when they saw the punishment: ***'Magician*** – the word for "magician" means "one with complete knowledge", because they considered magic to be a great knowledge – ***invoke your Lord for us by the contract He has made with you*** – to remove the punishment from us if we believe – ***and we shall certainly follow the guidance*** and believe.'

50. ***But when We removed the punishment from them*** through the supplication of Mūsā ***they immediately broke their word*** – broke their agreement and persisted in their unbelief.

51. ***Pharaoh called to his people*** – in arrogant boastfulness – ***saying, 'My people, does the kingdom of Egypt not belong to me? Do not all these rivers*** – referring to branches of the Nile – ***flow*** – under my palaces – ***under my control? Do you not then see*** my might?

52. Do you not see? ***Am I not better than this man*** (Mūsā) ***who is contemptible*** (weak and servile) ***and can scarcely make anything clear*** – in other words, cannot speak clearly because of the injury which occurred to his tongue, caused by a hot ember when he was a child?

53. ***Why have gold bracelets not been put upon his arms,*** if he is speaking the truth, since it was the custom of men at the time to wear gold bracelets and necklaces – ***and why is there not a train of angels accompanying him*** – successive ranks of angels which attest to his truthfulness?'

54. ***In that way he*** (Pharaoh) ***swayed his people and they succumbed to him*** – and they did what he wanted and denied Mūsā. ***They were a people of deviators.***

55. ***Then when they had provoked Our wrath We took revenge on them and drowned every one of them.***

56. ***We made them a thing of the past, an example for later peoples.*** They were a lesson for those after them so that they should not do the same as those before them did.

57. ***When an example is made of the son of Maryam, your people*** (the idolators) ***laugh uproariously*** at what they hear. When Allah revealed, *"You and what you worship apart from Allah are fuel for Jahannam,"* (21:98) the idolaters said, "We are content that our gods should be with 'Īsā, because he was worshipped instead of Allah."

58. ***They retort, 'Who is better, then: our gods or him*** ('Īsā)***?'*** We are content that our gods should be compared to him.' ***They only say this to you for argument's sake.*** They are arguing knowingly using false premises since they know that their idols have no intelligence and so are nothing like 'Īsā, peace be upon him. ***They are indeed a*** strongly ***disputatious people.***

59. ***He*** ('Īsā) ***is only a slave on whom We bestowed Our blessing*** – the gift of Prophethood – ***and whom We made an example*** – by his coming into existence without a father – ***for the tribe of Israel*** – because the unusual nature of his birth is evidence of Allah's power to do whatever He wills.

60. ***If We wished We could appoint angels in exchange for you*** and replace you – ***to succeed you on the earth*** – by destroying you.

61. ***He*** ('Īsā) ***is a Sign of the*** Last ***Hour*** because he will descend then***; have no doubt about it*** (the Hour). Tell them: ***But follow me*** in affirming the unity of Allah. ***This*** – which I command you to do – ***is a straight path.***

62. ***Do not let Shayṭān bar your way*** – turn you from the *dīn* of Allah. ***He truly is an outright*** – clear – ***enemy to you.***

63. ***And when 'Īsā came with the Clear Signs*** – here meaning miracles and laws – ***he said, 'I have come to you with Wisdom*** – meaning Prophethood and the laws of the Gospel – ***and to clarify for you some of the things about which you have differed*** regarding some of the rulings of the Torah about the *dīn* and other matters. ***Therefore be fearful of Allah and obey me.***

64. ***Allah is my Lord and your Lord, so worship Him. This is a straight path.'***

65. ***The various factions among them differed*** about 'Īsā and whether he was God, the son of God, or part of a trinity. ***Woe*** (punishment), ***then, to those who did wrong*** by disbelieving as is shown by what they said about 'Īsā – ***on account of the punishment of a painful Day!***

66. ***What are they*** (the unbelievers of Makka) ***waiting for, but the*** Last ***Hour to come upon them suddenly when they are not expecting it*** to arrive***?***

عَلَيْكُمُ ٱلْيَوْمَ وَلَآ أَنتُمْ تَحْزَنُونَ ﴿٦٨﴾ ٱلَّذِينَ ءَامَنُوا۟ بِـَٔايَـٰتِنَا
وَكَانُوا۟ مُسْلِمِينَ ﴿٦٩﴾ ٱدْخُلُوا۟ ٱلْجَنَّةَ أَنتُمْ وَأَزْوَٰجُكُمْ
تُحْبَرُونَ ﴿٧٠﴾ يُطَافُ عَلَيْهِم بِصِحَافٍ مِّن ذَهَبٍ وَأَكْوَابٍ ۖ
وَفِيهَا مَا تَشْتَهِيهِ ٱلْأَنفُسُ وَتَلَذُّ ٱلْأَعْيُنُ ۖ وَأَنتُمْ فِيهَا
خَـٰلِدُونَ ﴿٧١﴾ وَتِلْكَ ٱلْجَنَّةُ ٱلَّتِىٓ أُورِثْتُمُوهَا بِمَا كُنتُمْ
تَعْمَلُونَ ﴿٧٢﴾ لَكُمْ فِيهَا فَـٰكِهَةٌ كَثِيرَةٌ مِّنْهَا تَأْكُلُونَ ﴿٧٣﴾
إِنَّ ٱلْمُجْرِمِينَ فِى عَذَابِ جَهَنَّمَ خَـٰلِدُونَ ﴿٧٤﴾ لَا يُفَتَّرُ عَنْهُمْ وَهُمْ
فِيهِ مُبْلِسُونَ ﴿٧٥﴾ وَمَا ظَلَمْنَـٰهُمْ وَلَـٰكِن كَانُوا۟ هُمُ ٱلظَّـٰلِمِينَ ﴿٧٦﴾
وَنَادَوْا۟ يَـٰمَـٰلِكُ لِيَقْضِ عَلَيْنَا رَبُّكَ ۖ قَالَ إِنَّكُم مَّـٰكِثُونَ ﴿٧٧﴾ لَقَدْ
جِئْنَـٰكُم بِٱلْحَقِّ وَلَـٰكِنَّ أَكْثَرَكُمْ لِلْحَقِّ كَـٰرِهُونَ ﴿٧٨﴾ أَمْ أَبْرَمُوٓا۟ أَمْرًا
فَإِنَّا مُبْرِمُونَ ﴿٧٩﴾ أَمْ يَحْسَبُونَ أَنَّا لَا نَسْمَعُ سِرَّهُمْ وَنَجْوَىٰهُم ۚ بَلَىٰ
وَرُسُلُنَا لَدَيْهِمْ يَكْتُبُونَ ﴿٨٠﴾ قُلْ إِن كَانَ لِلرَّحْمَـٰنِ وَلَدٌ فَأَنَا۠ أَوَّلُ
ٱلْعَـٰبِدِينَ ﴿٨١﴾ سُبْحَـٰنَ رَبِّ ٱلسَّمَـٰوَٰتِ وَٱلْأَرْضِ رَبِّ ٱلْعَرْشِ
عَمَّا يَصِفُونَ ﴿٨٢﴾ فَذَرْهُمْ يَخُوضُوا۟ وَيَلْعَبُوا۟ حَتَّىٰ يُلَـٰقُوا۟ يَوْمَهُمُ
ٱلَّذِى يُوعَدُونَ ﴿٨٣﴾ وَهُوَ ٱلَّذِى فِى ٱلسَّمَآءِ إِلَـٰهٌ وَفِى ٱلْأَرْضِ
إِلَـٰهٌ ۚ وَهُوَ ٱلْحَكِيمُ ٱلْعَلِيمُ ﴿٨٤﴾ وَتَبَارَكَ ٱلَّذِى لَهُۥ مُلْكُ ٱلسَّمَـٰوَٰتِ
وَٱلْأَرْضِ وَمَا بَيْنَهُمَا وَعِندَهُۥ عِلْمُ ٱلسَّاعَةِ وَإِلَيْهِ تُرْجَعُونَ
﴿٨٥﴾ وَلَا يَمْلِكُ ٱلَّذِينَ يَدْعُونَ مِن دُونِهِ ٱلشَّفَـٰعَةَ إِلَّا مَن
شَهِدَ بِٱلْحَقِّ وَهُمْ يَعْلَمُونَ ﴿٨٦﴾ وَلَئِن سَأَلْتَهُم مَّنْ خَلَقَهُمْ
لَيَقُولُنَّ ٱللَّهُ ۖ فَأَنَّىٰ يُؤْفَكُونَ ﴿٨٧﴾ وَقِيلِهِۦ يَـٰرَبِّ إِنَّ هَـٰٓؤُلَآءِ قَوْمٌ
لَّا يُؤْمِنُونَ ﴿٨٨﴾ فَٱصْفَحْ عَنْهُمْ وَقُلْ سَلَـٰمٌ ۚ فَسَوْفَ يَعْلَمُونَ ﴿٨٩﴾

67. ***On that Day the closest friends*** – people who were friends in disobedience to Allah in this world – ***will be enemies to one another*** on the Day of Resurrection, ***except for those who are godfearing*** – those who loved one another in Allah and in obedience to Him. They will be friends and the following will be said to them:

68. ***'My slaves, you will feel no fear today; you will know no sor - row.'***

69. ***As for those who believed in Our Signs*** (the Qur'an) ***and became Muslims:***

70. ***'Enter the Garden, you and your wives, delighting in your joy.'***

71. ***Platters and cups*** – the word for "cups", *akwāb,* means drinking vessels without handles such that those who drink from them may do so from any side they wish – ***of gold will passed around among them; and they will have there all that their hearts desire and their eyes find delight in. 'You will remain in it timelessly, for ever.***

72. ***That is the Garden you will inherit for what you did.***

73. ***There will be many*** varieties of ***fruits in it for you to eat.'***

74. ***The evildoers will remain timelessly, for ever, in the punish - ment of Hell.***

75. ***It will not be eased for them. They will be crushed there by despair.*** They will be dumb with despair.

76. ***We have not wronged them; it was they who were wrongdoers.***

77. ***They will call out, 'Mālik,*** the angel in charge of the Fire, ***let your Lord put an end to us*** and allow us to die*!'* ***He*** (Mālik) ***will say*** – after a thousand years have passed – ***'You will stay the way you are*** – forever in the punishment*.'*

78. Allah says: ***We brought you the truth***, people of Makka, on the tongue of the Messenger, ***but most of you hated the truth.***

79. ***Or have they*** (the unbelievers of Makka) ***hatched a plot*** against the Prophet Muḥammad*?* ***It is We who are the Plotter*** and will contrive their destruction.

80. ***Or do they imagine that We do not hear their secrets and their private talk?*** Their secrets are what they confide to others. and their private talk is what they say among themselves. ***On the contrary:***

Our messengers – meaning the angels who record the actions – ***are right there with them writing it down!***

81. ***Say: 'If the All-Merciful had a son I would be the first to worship him.'*** It is not true, and it is confirmed that He has no child and hence no one else is worthy of worship.

82. ***Glory be to the Lord of the heavens and the earth, the Lord of the Throne, beyond what they describe*** – the lies they tell when they ascribe a child to Him.

83. ***So leave them to plunge*** – in their falsehoods – ***and play around*** – in this world – ***until they meet their Day*** (the Day of Rising) ***which they are promised,*** when the punishment will take place.

84. ***It is He who is God*** – the One who is worshipped – ***in heaven and God on earth. He is the All-Wise*** in managing His creation, ***the All-Knowing*** of the best interests of His creatures.

85. ***Blessed be Him to Whom belongs the sovereignty of the heavens and the earth and everything in between them. The knowledge of*** when ***the Hour*** will come ***is with Him. You will be returned*** (read as *turja'ūna* and also *yurja'ūna,* "They will be returned") ***to Him.***

86. ***Those you call upon*** and worship ***apart from Him*** – referring to the unbelievers – ***possess no power of intercession*** for anyone – ***only those who bore witness to the truth*** by saying, "There is no god but Allah" ***and have full knowledge*** in their hearts of what their tongues attest to. This means 'Īsā, 'Uzayr and the angels. They will intercede for the believers.

87. ***If you asked them who created them, they would say, 'Allah!' So how have they been perverted:*** turned away from worshipping Allah***?***

88. ***And as for your words*** – the words of Muḥammad, the Prophet, – ***'My Lord, these are people who do not believe!'***

89. Allah says: ***Turn from them and say, 'Peace*** – from us. This was before the command to fight them. ***They will soon come to know*** (read as *ya'lamūna* and also *ta'lamūna*, "you will come to know").***'***

سُورَةُ الدُّخَانِ

بِسۡمِ ٱللَّهِ ٱلرَّحۡمَٰنِ ٱلرَّحِيمِ

حمٓ ﴿١﴾ وَٱلۡكِتَٰبِ ٱلۡمُبِينِ ﴿٢﴾ إِنَّآ أَنزَلۡنَٰهُ فِي لَيۡلَةٖ
مُّبَٰرَكَةٍۚ إِنَّا كُنَّا مُنذِرِينَ ﴿٣﴾ فِيهَا يُفۡرَقُ كُلُّ أَمۡرٍ حَكِيمٍ ﴿٤﴾
أَمۡرٗا مِّنۡ عِندِنَآۚ إِنَّا كُنَّا مُرۡسِلِينَ ﴿٥﴾ رَحۡمَةٗ مِّن رَّبِّكَۚ إِنَّهُۥ هُوَ
ٱلسَّمِيعُ ٱلۡعَلِيمُ ﴿٦﴾ رَبِّ ٱلسَّمَٰوَٰتِ وَٱلۡأَرۡضِ وَمَا بَيۡنَهُمَآۖ
إِن كُنتُم مُّوقِنِينَ ﴿٧﴾ لَآ إِلَٰهَ إِلَّا هُوَ يُحۡيِۦ وَيُمِيتُۖ رَبُّكُمۡ
وَرَبُّ ءَابَآئِكُمُ ٱلۡأَوَّلِينَ ﴿٨﴾ بَلۡ هُمۡ فِي شَكّٖ يَلۡعَبُونَ
﴿٩﴾ فَٱرۡتَقِبۡ يَوۡمَ تَأۡتِي ٱلسَّمَآءُ بِدُخَانٖ مُّبِينٖ ﴿١٠﴾ يَغۡشَى
ٱلنَّاسَۖ هَٰذَا عَذَابٌ أَلِيمٞ ﴿١١﴾ رَّبَّنَا ٱكۡشِفۡ عَنَّا ٱلۡعَذَابَ
إِنَّا مُؤۡمِنُونَ ﴿١٢﴾ أَنَّىٰ لَهُمُ ٱلذِّكۡرَىٰ وَقَدۡ جَآءَهُمۡ رَسُولٞ مُّبِينٞ ﴿١٣﴾
ثُمَّ تَوَلَّوۡاْ عَنۡهُ وَقَالُواْ مُعَلَّمٞ مَّجۡنُونٌ ﴿١٤﴾ إِنَّا كَاشِفُواْ ٱلۡعَذَابِ قَلِيلًاۚ
إِنَّكُمۡ عَآئِدُونَ ﴿١٥﴾ يَوۡمَ نَبۡطِشُ ٱلۡبَطۡشَةَ ٱلۡكُبۡرَىٰٓ إِنَّا مُنتَقِمُونَ
﴿١٦﴾ ۞ وَلَقَدۡ فَتَنَّا قَبۡلَهُمۡ قَوۡمَ فِرۡعَوۡنَ وَجَآءَهُمۡ رَسُولٞ
كَرِيمٌ ﴿١٧﴾ أَنۡ أَدُّوٓاْ إِلَيَّ عِبَادَ ٱللَّهِۖ إِنِّي لَكُمۡ رَسُولٌ أَمِينٞ ﴿١٨﴾
وَأَن لَّا تَعۡلُواْ عَلَى ٱللَّهِۖ إِنِّيٓ ءَاتِيكُم بِسُلۡطَٰنٖ مُّبِينٖ ﴿١٩﴾ وَإِنِّي عُذۡتُ
بِرَبِّي وَرَبِّكُمۡ أَن تَرۡجُمُونِ ﴿٢٠﴾ وَإِن لَّمۡ تُؤۡمِنُواْ لِي فَٱعۡتَزِلُونِ ﴿٢١﴾ فَدَعَا

44. *Sūrat ad-Dukhān*
Smoke

This *sūra* is Makkan except for *āyat* 15. It has 56, 57 or 59 *āyat*s.

1. ***Ḥā Mīm.*** Allah knows best what is meant by this.

2. ***By the Book*** (the Qur'an) ***which makes things clear*** – makes clear what is lawful and unlawful.

3. ... ***We sent it down on a blessed night*** – a reference to the Night of Power or the Night of the Middle of Sha'bān, during which the Mother of the Book descended from the seventh heaven to the lowest heaven. ***We are constantly giving warning*** by it.

4. ***During it*** – the night referred to above – ***every wise decree is specified*** – it specifies everything that is determined with respect to provision, length of life and other similar things for the coming year.

5. ***...by a*** specifying ***command from Our presence. We are constantly sending out*** Messengers, meaning Muḥammad and those before him.

6. ***...as a mercy from your Lord. He is the All-Hearing*** of their words, ***the All-Knowing*** of their actions:

7. ***...the Lord of the heavens and the earth and everything in between them, if you***, people of Makka, ***are people with certainty*** that Allah is the Lord of the heavens and the earth and that Muḥammad is His Messenger.

8. ***There is no god but Him – He gives life and causes to die – your Lord and the Lord of your forefathers, the previous peoples.***

9. ***Yet they play around in doubt*** about the Resurrection, mocking you, Muḥammad. He said, "O Allah, help me against them with seven like the seven of Yūsuf."

10. Allah says: ***So be on the watch for a day when heaven brings forth a distinctive smoke*** – when there is a drought in the land and they are so hungry that they see something like smoke between the heaven and the earth,

11. ***...which enshrouds mankind.*** They said: ***'This is a painful punishment!***

12. ***Our Lord, remove the punishment from us. We are really believers*** in Your Prophet.'

13. Allah says: ***How can they expect a Reminder when a clear Messenger has already come to them?*** Belief will not help them after the punishment descends when a Messenger who made things clear has come to them.

14. ***But then they turned away from him and said, 'He is an instructed madman!'*** They said that another human being had taught him the Qur'an.

15. ***We remove the punishment*** (hunger) ***a little*** – for a short period – ***and you revert*** to unbelief.

16. Remember that ***on the day We launch the Great Assault*** – a reference to the coming Battle of Badr – ***We will certainly take Our revenge*** in the form of force and punishment.

17. ***Before them We put Pharaoh's people to the test when a noble Messenger*** – Mūsā, peace be upon him – ***came to them, saying,***

18. ***'Hand over to me the slaves of Allah.*** It is also said that this means: Give me the faith to which I summon you – in other words, show your faith in me. ***I am a trustworthy Messenger to you.'***

19. ***And: 'Do not exalt yourselves above Allah.*** Do not show arrogance by not obeying Allah. ***I come to you with clear authority*** – clear evidence of my Message. Then they threatened to stone him.

20. He said: ***I have sought refuge with my Lord and your Lord against your stoning me.***

21. ***If you do not believe in me, then at least leave me alone*** and stop harming me.' But they did not leave him alone.

22. ***He called out to his Lord, 'These are evildoing people*** (idolaters).'

23. Allah said: ***'Then set out with My slaves*** (the tribe of Israel) ***by night. You will certainly be pursued*** by Pharaoh and his people.

24. ***Leave the sea divided as it is*** – still and open, when you and your companions passed through it, so that the Copts will enter it. ***They are an army who will be drowned.'*** Be assured of that. They were indeed drowned.

25. ***How many gardens and fountains they left behind,***

رَبَّهُۥٓ أَنَّ هَٰٓؤُلَآءِ قَوْمٌ مُّجْرِمُونَ ﴿٢٢﴾ فَأَسْرِ بِعِبَادِى لَيْلًا إِنَّكُم
مُّتَّبَعُونَ ﴿٢٣﴾ وَٱتْرُكِ ٱلْبَحْرَ رَهْوًا ۖ إِنَّهُمْ جُندٌ مُّغْرَقُونَ ﴿٢٤﴾ كَمْ
تَرَكُوا۟ مِن جَنَّٰتٍ وَعُيُونٍ ﴿٢٥﴾ وَزُرُوعٍ وَمَقَامٍ كَرِيمٍ ﴿٢٦﴾ وَنَعْمَةٍ
كَانُوا۟ فِيهَا فَٰكِهِينَ ﴿٢٧﴾ كَذَٰلِكَ ۖ وَأَوْرَثْنَٰهَا قَوْمًا ءَاخَرِينَ ﴿٢٨﴾
فَمَا بَكَتْ عَلَيْهِمُ ٱلسَّمَآءُ وَٱلْأَرْضُ وَمَا كَانُوا۟ مُنظَرِينَ ﴿٢٩﴾ وَلَقَدْ
نَجَّيْنَا بَنِىٓ إِسْرَٰٓءِيلَ مِنَ ٱلْعَذَابِ ٱلْمُهِينِ ﴿٣٠﴾ مِن فِرْعَوْنَ ۚ إِنَّهُۥ
كَانَ عَالِيًا مِّنَ ٱلْمُسْرِفِينَ ﴿٣١﴾ وَلَقَدِ ٱخْتَرْنَٰهُمْ عَلَىٰ عِلْمٍ عَلَى
ٱلْعَٰلَمِينَ ﴿٣٢﴾ وَءَاتَيْنَٰهُم مِّنَ ٱلْءَايَٰتِ مَا فِيهِ بَلَٰٓؤٌا۟ مُّبِينٌ
﴿٣٣﴾ إِنَّ هَٰٓؤُلَآءِ لَيَقُولُونَ ﴿٣٤﴾ إِنْ هِىَ إِلَّا مَوْتَتُنَا ٱلْأُولَىٰ وَمَا
نَحْنُ بِمُنشَرِينَ ﴿٣٥﴾ فَأْتُوا۟ بِـَٔابَآئِنَآ إِن كُنتُمْ صَٰدِقِينَ ﴿٣٦﴾ أَهُمْ
خَيْرٌ أَمْ قَوْمُ تُبَّعٍ وَٱلَّذِينَ مِن قَبْلِهِمْ ۚ أَهْلَكْنَٰهُمْ ۖ إِنَّهُمْ كَانُوا۟ مُجْرِمِينَ
﴿٣٧﴾ وَمَا خَلَقْنَا ٱلسَّمَٰوَٰتِ وَٱلْأَرْضَ وَمَا بَيْنَهُمَا لَٰعِبِينَ ﴿٣٨﴾
مَا خَلَقْنَٰهُمَآ إِلَّا بِٱلْحَقِّ وَلَٰكِنَّ أَكْثَرَهُمْ لَا يَعْلَمُونَ ﴿٣٩﴾
إِنَّ يَوْمَ ٱلْفَصْلِ مِيقَٰتُهُمْ أَجْمَعِينَ ﴿٤٠﴾ يَوْمَ لَا يُغْنِى مَوْلًى
عَن مَّوْلًى شَيْـًٔا وَلَا هُمْ يُنصَرُونَ ﴿٤١﴾ إِلَّا مَن رَّحِمَ ٱللَّهُ ۚ
إِنَّهُۥ هُوَ ٱلْعَزِيزُ ٱلرَّحِيمُ ﴿٤٢﴾ إِنَّ شَجَرَتَ ٱلزَّقُّومِ ﴿٤٣﴾
طَعَامُ ٱلْأَثِيمِ ﴿٤٤﴾ كَٱلْمُهْلِ يَغْلِى فِى ٱلْبُطُونِ ﴿٤٥﴾ كَغَلْىِ
ٱلْحَمِيمِ ﴿٤٦﴾ خُذُوهُ فَٱعْتِلُوهُ إِلَىٰ سَوَآءِ ٱلْجَحِيمِ ﴿٤٧﴾ ثُمَّ
صُبُّوا۟ فَوْقَ رَأْسِهِۦ مِنْ عَذَابِ ٱلْحَمِيمِ ﴿٤٨﴾ ذُقْ إِنَّكَ
أَنتَ ٱلْعَزِيزُ ٱلْكَرِيمُ ﴿٤٩﴾ إِنَّ هَٰذَا مَا كُنتُم بِهِۦ تَمْتَرُونَ

26. ***...and ripe crops and noble residences.***

27. ***What comfort and ease they had delighted in!*** They enjoyed many blessings.

28. ***So it was. Yet We bequeathed these things*** – their forms of wealth – ***to another people***, the tribe of Israel.

29. ***Neither heaven nor earth shed any tears for them*** – This is not the case with the believers. When they die, they are wept for by the place where they prayed on earth and by the place where their actions rose in heaven – ***and they were granted no reprieve*** – a delay to enable them to repent.

30. ***We rescued the tribe of Israel from the humiliating punishment*** – which took the form of killing their sons and letting their women live.

31. ***...from*** punishment by ***Pharaoh. He was haughty, one of the profligate.***

32. ***We chose them*** (the tribe of Israel) ***knowingly*** – with full knowledge of their circumstances – ***above all other people*** of their time;

33. ***...and We gave them Signs containing a clear trial*** – clear blessings in the parting of the sea, the manna and quail and other things.

34. ***These people*** (the unbelievers of Makka) ***say:***

35. ***'There is nothing more than our first death.*** There is no life after death except for being alive after being sperm. ***We will not be raised up a second time*** after dying.

36. ***Bring us our fathers*** – alive – ***if you are telling the truth*** – about being resurrected after death.'

37. Allah says: ***Are they better or the people of Tubba'*** – who was either a Prophet or a righteous man – ***and those*** nations ***before them whom We destroyed*** – on account of their unbelief? They are not stronger than their predecessors who were destroyed. ***They were certainly evildoers.***

38. ***We did not create the heavens and the earth and everything between them as a game.***

39. ***We did not create them*** and what is between them ***except with truth*** – and We were true in accomplishing that, so that it provides evidence of Our power and oneness and other things*; but most of them* – including the unbelievers of Makka – *do not know it.*

40. ***The Day of Decision*** – another name for the Day of Rising on which Allah will render judgement between His slaves – ***will be their appointment all together***, for everlasting punishment –

41. ***...the Day when friends will be of no use at all to one another*** – and no kinship or friendship will be of any use against the punishment – ***and they will not be helped*** against it,

42. ***... except for those Allah has mercy on*** – meaning believers who may intercede for one another by Allah's permission. ***He is the Almighty*** – and so able to take His revenge on the unbelievers, ***the Most Merciful*** to the believers.

43. ***The Tree of az-Zaqqūm*** – the foulest tree which Allah makes grow in Hellfire –

44. ***... is the food of the wicked*** – among whom are Abū Jahl and his companions, who are full of immense wrong actions –

45. ***...seething*** (read as *yaghlī* and *taghlī)* ***in the belly like molten brass*** – looking like the dregs of black oil –

46. ***... as boiling water bubbles and seethes.***

47. The Zabāniya will be told: ***'Seize*** (read as *fa'tilūhu* and *fa'tulūhu*) ***him and drag him bodily*** – roughly and harshly – ***into the middle of the Blazing Fire.***

48. ***Then pour the punishment of boiling water on his head.'***

49. He will be told: ***'Taste that*** punishment***! You are the mighty one, the noble one!*** You claimed that you were mighty and noble, and you said, "There is no one between the two mountains more mighty and noble than I am."

50. He will be told: ***This*** punishment which you see ***is the very thing you used to doubt.'***

51. ***The people who are godfearing will be in a secure place*** – where they are safe from fear –

52. ***...amid gardens and fountains,***

53. ***... wearing fine silk and rich brocade, face to face with one another.*** They will not look at one another's backs, because their couches are arranged in a circle.

﴿٥٠﴾ إِنَّ ٱلۡمُتَّقِينَ فِي مَقَامٍ أَمِينٖ ﴿٥١﴾ فِي جَنَّٰتٖ وَعُيُونٖ
﴿٥٢﴾ يَلۡبَسُونَ مِن سُندُسٖ وَإِسۡتَبۡرَقٖ مُّتَقَٰبِلِينَ ﴿٥٣﴾
كَذَٰلِكَ وَزَوَّجۡنَٰهُم بِحُورٍ عِينٖ ﴿٥٤﴾ يَدۡعُونَ فِيهَا بِكُلِّ
فَٰكِهَةٍ ءَامِنِينَ ﴿٥٥﴾ لَا يَذُوقُونَ فِيهَا ٱلۡمَوۡتَ
إِلَّا ٱلۡمَوۡتَةَ ٱلۡأُولَىٰۖ وَوَقَىٰهُمۡ عَذَابَ ٱلۡجَحِيمِ ﴿٥٦﴾ فَضۡلٗا
مِّن رَّبِّكَۚ ذَٰلِكَ هُوَ ٱلۡفَوۡزُ ٱلۡعَظِيمُ ﴿٥٧﴾ فَإِنَّمَا يَسَّرۡنَٰهُ بِلِسَانِكَ
لَعَلَّهُمۡ يَتَذَكَّرُونَ ﴿٥٨﴾ فَٱرۡتَقِبۡ إِنَّهُم مُّرۡتَقِبُونَ ﴿٥٩﴾

54. ***So it will be.*** That is how the matter will be. ***We will marry them to dark-eyed maidens*** – beautiful women with large, lustrous eyes.

55. ***They will call there*** (in the Garden) – asking their servants ***for fruit of every kind*** – from it – ***in complete security.*** They are safe from their provision ever being cut off and from any harm coming to them and from anything alarming.

56. ***They will not taste any death there – other than the first one.*** They will not die again after their death in this world. Some say that "except", *illā,* here means *ba'd*, "after". ***He will safeguard them from the punishment of the Blazing Fire:***

57. ***a*** fore-ordained ***favour from your Lord. That is the Great Victory.***

58. ***We have made it*** (the Qur'an) ***easy in your own tongue*** – in your own language, so that the Arabs will understand it from you – ***so that perhaps they may pay heed*** and believe in you. Those Arabs did not, however, believe.

59. ***So watch and wait*** for their destruction. ***They too are waiting*** for your destruction. This was before the revelation of the command to fight them.

سُورَةُ الجَاثِيَةِ

بِسۡمِ ٱللَّهِ ٱلرَّحۡمَٰنِ ٱلرَّحِيمِ

حمٓ ﴿١﴾ تَنزِيلُ ٱلۡكِتَٰبِ مِنَ ٱللَّهِ ٱلۡعَزِيزِ ٱلۡحَكِيمِ ﴿٢﴾ إِنَّ فِي ٱلسَّمَٰوَٰتِ
وَٱلۡأَرۡضِ لَأٓيَٰتٖ لِّلۡمُؤۡمِنِينَ ﴿٣﴾ وَفِي خَلۡقِكُمۡ وَمَا يَبُثُّ مِن دَآبَّةٍ ءَايَٰتٞ
لِّقَوۡمٖ يُوقِنُونَ ﴿٤﴾ وَٱخۡتِلَٰفِ ٱلَّيۡلِ وَٱلنَّهَارِ وَمَآ أَنزَلَ ٱللَّهُ مِنَ ٱلسَّمَآءِ
مِن رِّزۡقٖ فَأَحۡيَا بِهِ ٱلۡأَرۡضَ بَعۡدَ مَوۡتِهَا وَتَصۡرِيفِ ٱلرِّيَٰحِ ءَايَٰتٞ لِّقَوۡمٖ
يَعۡقِلُونَ ﴿٥﴾ تِلۡكَ ءَايَٰتُ ٱللَّهِ نَتۡلُوهَا عَلَيۡكَ بِٱلۡحَقِّۖ فَبِأَيِّ حَدِيثِۭ بَعۡدَ
ٱللَّهِ وَءَايَٰتِهِۦ يُؤۡمِنُونَ ﴿٦﴾ وَيۡلٞ لِّكُلِّ أَفَّاكٍ أَثِيمٖ ﴿٧﴾ يَسۡمَعُ ءَايَٰتِ
ٱللَّهِ تُتۡلَىٰ عَلَيۡهِ ثُمَّ يُصِرُّ مُسۡتَكۡبِرٗا كَأَن لَّمۡ يَسۡمَعۡهَاۖ فَبَشِّرۡهُ بِعَذَابٍ أَلِيمٖ
﴿٨﴾ وَإِذَا عَلِمَ مِنۡ ءَايَٰتِنَا شَيۡـًٔا ٱتَّخَذَهَا هُزُوًاۚ أُوْلَٰٓئِكَ لَهُمۡ عَذَابٞ
مُّهِينٞ ﴿٩﴾ مِّن وَرَآئِهِمۡ جَهَنَّمُۖ وَلَا يُغۡنِي عَنۡهُم مَّا كَسَبُواْ شَيۡـٔٗا
وَلَا مَا ٱتَّخَذُواْ مِن دُونِ ٱللَّهِ أَوۡلِيَآءَۖ وَلَهُمۡ عَذَابٌ عَظِيمٌ ﴿١٠﴾ هَٰذَا
هُدٗىۖ وَٱلَّذِينَ كَفَرُواْ بِـَٔايَٰتِ رَبِّهِمۡ لَهُمۡ عَذَابٞ مِّن رِّجۡزٍ أَلِيمٌ ﴿١١﴾
۞ ٱللَّهُ ٱلَّذِي سَخَّرَ لَكُمُ ٱلۡبَحۡرَ لِتَجۡرِيَ ٱلۡفُلۡكُ فِيهِ بِأَمۡرِهِۦ وَلِتَبۡتَغُواْ مِن
فَضۡلِهِۦ وَلَعَلَّكُمۡ تَشۡكُرُونَ ﴿١٢﴾ وَسَخَّرَ لَكُم مَّا فِي ٱلسَّمَٰوَٰتِ وَمَا فِي
ٱلۡأَرۡضِ جَمِيعٗا مِّنۡهُۚ إِنَّ فِي ذَٰلِكَ لَأٓيَٰتٖ لِّقَوۡمٖ يَتَفَكَّرُونَ ﴿١٣﴾
قُل لِّلَّذِينَ ءَامَنُواْ يَغۡفِرُواْ لِلَّذِينَ لَا يَرۡجُونَ أَيَّامَ ٱللَّهِ لِيَجۡزِيَ

45. *Sūrat al-Jāthiyya*
Kneeling

This *sūra* is Makkan except for *āyat* 13, which is Madinan. It has 36 or 37 *āyat*s.

1. ***Ḥā Mīm.*** Allah knows best what is meant by this.

2. ***The revelation of the Book*** (the Qur'an) ***is from Allah, the Almighty*** in His kingdom***, the All-Wise*** in what He does.

3. ***In the*** creation of the ***heavens and earth there are certainly Signs for the believers*** which indicate the power and unity of Allah.

4. ***And in your creation*** – the creation of each of you from a sperm drop, then a clot, then a piece of flesh, until you emerge as a human being – ***and all the creatures*** – animals and people – ***He has spread about*** on the surface of the earth ***there are Signs for people with certainty*** about the Resurrection.

5. ***And in the alternation of night and day*** – their coming and going – ***and the provision*** – meaning here rain, which is a means by which provision comes to people – ***Allah sends down from the sky, bringing the earth to life by it after it has died, and the varying direction of the winds*** – sometimes south, sometimes north, sometimes cold and sometimes dry – ***there are Signs for people who use their intellect*** – who understand the evidence and come to believe.

6. ***Those*** Signs mentioned ***are Allah's Signs*** that indicate His unity – ***which We recite to you with truth. In what discourse, then, after*** the speech of ***Allah*** – meaning the Qur'an – ***and His Signs*** – evidence of His unity – ***will they believe*** (read as *yu'minūna* and also *tu'minūna*, "will you believe") in***?*** This means that they do not believe.

7. ***Woe*** (punishment) ***to every wicked*** (full of wrong actions) ***liar …***

8. ***…who hears the Signs of Allah*** (the Qur'an) ***recited to him and then persists in his arrogance*** – in his unbelief, too proud to believe – ***as if he had never heard them. Give him the news of a painful punishment.***

9. ***When he does learn something of Our Signs*** (the Qur'an) ***he makes a mockery of them. Such people*** (those liars) ***will have a humiliating punishment.***

10. ***Hell is right at their heels*** – right in front of them, because they are in this world. ***Nothing they have earned*** – in terms of wealth and actions – ***will be of any use to them, nor will those*** idols ***they took as protectors besides Allah. They will have a terrible punishment.***

11. ***This*** Qur'an ***is guidance*** away from misguidance***; and those who reject the Signs of their Lord will have a punishment of agonising pain.***

12. ***It is Allah who has made the sea subservient to you so that the ships sail on it at His command*** (permission) ***enabling you to seek His bounty*** by trading ***so that perhaps you may be thankful.***

13. ***And He has made everything in the heavens*** – the sun and moon and stars and water and other things – ***and everything on the earth*** – animals, trees, plants, rivers and other things – ***subservient to you*** – He created all of that for your benefit***; it is all from Him.*** The word "all" is used for emphasis. ***There are certainly Signs in that for people who reflect*** and believe.

14. ***Tell those who believe that they should forgive those who feel no fear*** – the word *yarjūna*, which normally means "hope", here means "fear" – ***about the Days of Allah*** – the momentous events He causes to occur, the meaning being: Forgive the unbelievers for the harm they have done to you. This was before the command to fight them in *jihād* – ***when He will repay*** (read as *yajzā* and also *najzā*, "We will repay") ***people according to what they earned*** – in other words, will reward them for forgiving the harm done to them by the unbelievers.

15. ***Whoever acts rightly, it is to his own good. Whoever does evil, it is to his detriment. Then you will be returned to your Lord*** – and He will repay both the good-doer and the evildoer.

16. ***We gave the Book*** (the Torah) ***and Judgement*** – by it between people – ***and Prophethood to the tribe of Israel*** – Mūsā, Hārūn, and others, ***and provided them with good things*** – lawful things like manna and quail – ***and favoured them over all other people*** of their time.

قَوۡمَۢا بِمَا كَانُواْ يَكۡسِبُونَ ﴿١٤﴾ مَنۡ عَمِلَ صَٰلِحٗا فَلِنَفۡسِهِۦۖ
وَمَنۡ أَسَآءَ فَعَلَيۡهَاۖ ثُمَّ إِلَىٰ رَبِّكُمۡ تُرۡجَعُونَ ﴿١٥﴾ وَلَقَدۡ ءَاتَيۡنَا
بَنِيٓ إِسۡرَٰٓءِيلَ ٱلۡكِتَٰبَ وَٱلۡحُكۡمَ وَٱلنُّبُوَّةَ وَرَزَقۡنَٰهُم مِّنَ ٱلطَّيِّبَٰتِ
وَفَضَّلۡنَٰهُمۡ عَلَى ٱلۡعَٰلَمِينَ ﴿١٦﴾ وَءَاتَيۡنَٰهُم بَيِّنَٰتٖ مِّنَ ٱلۡأَمۡرِۖ
فَمَا ٱخۡتَلَفُوٓاْ إِلَّا مِنۢ بَعۡدِ مَا جَآءَهُمُ ٱلۡعِلۡمُ بَغۡيَۢا بَيۡنَهُمۡۚ إِنَّ
رَبَّكَ يَقۡضِي بَيۡنَهُمۡ يَوۡمَ ٱلۡقِيَٰمَةِ فِيمَا كَانُواْ فِيهِ يَخۡتَلِفُونَ
﴿١٧﴾ ثُمَّ جَعَلۡنَٰكَ عَلَىٰ شَرِيعَةٖ مِّنَ ٱلۡأَمۡرِ فَٱتَّبِعۡهَا وَلَا تَتَّبِعۡ
أَهۡوَآءَ ٱلَّذِينَ لَا يَعۡلَمُونَ ﴿١٨﴾ إِنَّهُمۡ لَن يُغۡنُواْ عَنكَ مِنَ ٱللَّهِ
شَيۡـٔٗاۚ وَإِنَّ ٱلظَّٰلِمِينَ بَعۡضُهُمۡ أَوۡلِيَآءُ بَعۡضٖۖ وَٱللَّهُ وَلِيُّ ٱلۡمُتَّقِينَ
﴿١٩﴾ هَٰذَا بَصَٰٓئِرُ لِلنَّاسِ وَهُدٗى وَرَحۡمَةٞ لِّقَوۡمٖ يُوقِنُونَ
﴿٢٠﴾ أَمۡ حَسِبَ ٱلَّذِينَ ٱجۡتَرَحُواْ ٱلسَّيِّـَٔاتِ أَن نَّجۡعَلَهُمۡ كَٱلَّذِينَ
ءَامَنُواْ وَعَمِلُواْ ٱلصَّٰلِحَٰتِ سَوَآءٗ مَّحۡيَاهُمۡ وَمَمَاتُهُمۡۚ سَآءَ
مَا يَحۡكُمُونَ ﴿٢١﴾ وَخَلَقَ ٱللَّهُ ٱلسَّمَٰوَٰتِ وَٱلۡأَرۡضَ بِٱلۡحَقِّ
وَلِتُجۡزَىٰ كُلُّ نَفۡسِۭ بِمَا كَسَبَتۡ وَهُمۡ لَا يُظۡلَمُونَ ﴿٢٢﴾
أَفَرَءَيۡتَ مَنِ ٱتَّخَذَ إِلَٰهَهُۥ هَوَىٰهُ وَأَضَلَّهُ ٱللَّهُ عَلَىٰ عِلۡمٖ وَخَتَمَ عَلَىٰ سَمۡعِهِۦ
وَقَلۡبِهِۦ وَجَعَلَ عَلَىٰ بَصَرِهِۦ غِشَٰوَةٗ فَمَن يَهۡدِيهِ مِنۢ بَعۡدِ ٱللَّهِۚ أَفَلَا
تَذَكَّرُونَ ﴿٢٣﴾ وَقَالُواْ مَا هِيَ إِلَّا حَيَاتُنَا ٱلدُّنۡيَا نَمُوتُ وَنَحۡيَا وَمَا يُهۡلِكُنَآ
إِلَّا ٱلدَّهۡرُۚ وَمَا لَهُم بِذَٰلِكَ مِنۡ عِلۡمٍۖ إِنۡ هُمۡ إِلَّا يَظُنُّونَ ﴿٢٤﴾ وَإِذَا تُتۡلَىٰ
عَلَيۡهِمۡ ءَايَٰتُنَا بَيِّنَٰتٖ مَّا كَانَ حُجَّتَهُمۡ إِلَّآ أَن قَالُواْ ٱئۡتُواْ بِـَٔابَآئِنَآ إِن
كُنتُمۡ صَٰدِقِينَ ﴿٢٥﴾ قُلِ ٱللَّهُ يُحۡيِيكُمۡ ثُمَّ يُمِيتُكُمۡ ثُمَّ يَجۡمَعُكُمۡ إِلَىٰ يَوۡمِ

17. ***We made the Commandments very clear to them*** – the commandments of the *dīn* defining the lawful and unlawful, and the sending of Muḥammad, may the best prayer and blessing be upon him – ***and they only differed*** about his mission ***after knowledge came to them, tyrannising one other*** out of envy about him. ***Your Lord will decide between them on the Day of Rising regarding the things they differed about.***

18. ***Then We placed you***, Muḥammad, ***on the right road of Our Command*** (the *dīn* of Islam)***, so follow it. Do not follow the whims and desires of those who do not know.*** In other words, do not worship anything other than Allah.

19. ***They will not help*** or defend ***you in any way against*** the punishment of ***Allah. The wrongdoers*** (the unbelievers) ***are protectors of one another; but Allah is the Protector of those who are godfearing.***

20. ***This*** Qur'an ***is clear insight for mankind*** – a medium by which one can discern the rulings and limits – ***and guidance and mercy for people with certainty*** about the Resurrection.

21. ***Or do those who perpetrate evil deeds*** of unbelief and disobedience ***suppose that We will make them like those who believe and do right actions, so that their lives and deaths will be the same?*** They imagine that We will give them good in the Next World as We will the believers, in the form of a life comparable to the one they had in this world, as when they told the believers, "If we are resurrected, we will be given the same good things which we have been given in this world." Allah denies this by saying, ***How bad their judgement is!*** That is not how it will be in the Next World. In the Next World they will suffer punishment contrary to their experience during their life in this world, while the believers will have a reward in the Next World for doing righteous actions in this world in the form of prayer, *zakāt*, fasting, and other things.

22. ***Allah created the heavens and earth with truth*** – to provide evidence of His power and unity – ***so that every self might be repaid for what it earned*** for its acts of disobedience and obedience, showing that unbelievers and believers are not the same, ***and they will not be wronged.***

ٱلْقِيَٰمَةِ لَا رَيْبَ فِيهِ وَلَٰكِنَّ أَكْثَرَ ٱلنَّاسِ لَا يَعْلَمُونَ ﴿٢٦﴾ وَلِلَّهِ مُلْكُ
ٱلسَّمَٰوَٰتِ وَٱلْأَرْضِ ۚ وَيَوْمَ تَقُومُ ٱلسَّاعَةُ يَوْمَئِذٍ يَخْسَرُ ٱلْمُبْطِلُونَ
﴿٢٧﴾ وَتَرَىٰ كُلَّ أُمَّةٍ جَاثِيَةً ۚ كُلُّ أُمَّةٍ تُدْعَىٰٓ إِلَىٰ كِتَٰبِهَا ٱلْيَوْمَ تُجْزَوْنَ مَا كُنتُمْ
تَعْمَلُونَ ﴿٢٨﴾ هَٰذَا كِتَٰبُنَا يَنطِقُ عَلَيْكُم بِٱلْحَقِّ ۚ إِنَّا كُنَّا نَسْتَنسِخُ
مَا كُنتُمْ تَعْمَلُونَ ﴿٢٩﴾ فَأَمَّا ٱلَّذِينَ ءَامَنُوا۟ وَعَمِلُوا۟ ٱلصَّٰلِحَٰتِ
فَيُدْخِلُهُمْ رَبُّهُمْ فِى رَحْمَتِهِۦ ۚ ذَٰلِكَ هُوَ ٱلْفَوْزُ ٱلْمُبِينُ ﴿٣٠﴾ وَأَمَّا
ٱلَّذِينَ كَفَرُوٓا۟ أَفَلَمْ تَكُنْ ءَايَٰتِى تُتْلَىٰ عَلَيْكُمْ فَٱسْتَكْبَرْتُمْ وَكُنتُمْ قَوْمًا
مُّجْرِمِينَ ﴿٣١﴾ وَإِذَا قِيلَ إِنَّ وَعْدَ ٱللَّهِ حَقٌّ وَٱلسَّاعَةُ لَا رَيْبَ فِيهَا قُلْتُم
مَّا نَدْرِى مَا ٱلسَّاعَةُ إِن نَّظُنُّ إِلَّا ظَنًّا وَمَا نَحْنُ بِمُسْتَيْقِنِينَ ﴿٣٢﴾
وَبَدَا لَهُمْ سَيِّـَٔاتُ مَا عَمِلُوا۟ وَحَاقَ بِهِم مَّا كَانُوا۟ بِهِۦ يَسْتَهْزِءُونَ ﴿٣٣﴾
وَقِيلَ ٱلْيَوْمَ نَنسَىٰكُمْ كَمَا نَسِيتُمْ لِقَآءَ يَوْمِكُمْ هَٰذَا وَمَأْوَىٰكُمُ ٱلنَّارُ وَمَا
لَكُم مِّن نَّٰصِرِينَ ﴿٣٤﴾ ذَٰلِكُم بِأَنَّكُمُ ٱتَّخَذْتُمْ ءَايَٰتِ ٱللَّهِ هُزُوًا وَغَرَّتْكُمُ
ٱلْحَيَوٰةُ ٱلدُّنْيَا ۚ فَٱلْيَوْمَ لَا يُخْرَجُونَ مِنْهَا وَلَا هُمْ يُسْتَعْتَبُونَ ﴿٣٥﴾
فَلِلَّهِ ٱلْحَمْدُ رَبِّ ٱلسَّمَٰوَٰتِ وَرَبِّ ٱلْأَرْضِ رَبِّ ٱلْعَٰلَمِينَ ﴿٣٦﴾ وَلَهُ
ٱلْكِبْرِيَآءُ فِى ٱلسَّمَٰوَٰتِ وَٱلْأَرْضِ ۖ وَهُوَ ٱلْعَزِيزُ ٱلْحَكِيمُ ﴿٣٧﴾

23. Tell me, ***have you seen him who takes his whims and desires to be his god, and whom Allah has misguided knowingly*** – knowing that he would be one of the misguided before He created him, ***sealing up his hearing and his heart*** – so that he is unable to hear guidance and does not understand it – ***and placing a blindfold over his eyes*** so that he is unable to recognise guidance? Here there is an elision which implies: "Do you think he will be guided? ***Who then will guide him after Allah*** has misguided him? He will not be guided. ***So will you not pay heed*** and be warned?

24. ***They*** (those who deny the Resurrection) ***say, 'There is nothing but our existence in this world. We die and we live*** – and continue by producing children – ***and nothing destroys us except*** the passage of ***time.'*** Allah says: ***They have no knowledge of that. They are only conjecturing.***

25. ***When Our Clear Signs*** – verses of the Qur'an which indicate Our power to Resurrect – ***are recited to them, their only argument is to say, 'Bring us our fathers*** alive ***if you are telling the truth*** about us being resurrected.'

26. ***Say: 'Allah gives you life***, when you have been sperm, ***then causes you to die, and then will gather you together*** alive ***for the Day of Rising, about which there is no doubt. But most people do not know it.'***

27. ***The kingdom of the heavens and earth belongs to Allah – and, on the Day that the Hour arrives, that Day the liars*** (unbelievers) ***will be lost.*** Their loss will be clear because they will go to the Fire.

28. ***You will see every nation*** – the people of every religion – ***on its knees***, herded together, ***every nation summoned to its Book*** – the book of their actions. They will be told: ***'Today you will be repaid for what you did.***

29. ***This is Our Book*** – the register kept by the guardian angels – ***speaking against you with the truth. We have been recording*** and preserving ***everything you did.'***

30. ***As for those who believed and did right actions, their Lord will admit them into His mercy*** (His Garden). ***That is the Clear Victory.***

31. ***But as for those who disbelieved***, they will be told***: 'Were My Signs*** (the Qur'an) ***not recited to you? And yet you proved arro - gant; you were a people of evildoers*** (unbelievers).

32. ***When you***, unbelievers, ***were told, "Allah's promise*** of the Resurrection ***is true and so is the Hour*** (read as *as-sā'atu* and *as-sā'ata*), ***of which there is no doubt," you said, "We have no idea what the Hour is. We have only been conjecturing; we are by no means certain*** that it will come."

33. ***The*** recompense for the ***evil deeds they did*** in this world ***will appear before them*** in the Next World ***and*** the punishment for ***the things they mocked at will engulf them.***

34. ***They will be told, 'Today We have forgotten you*** – and will leave you in the Fire – ***as you forgot the meeting of this your Day*** and failed to act for it. ***Your refuge is the Fire and you have no helpers*** to defend you from the Fire.

35. ***That is because you made a mockery of Allah's Signs*** (the Qur'an) ***and the life of this world deluded you*** – so that you said that there was no Resurrection and no Reckoning.' ***Therefore, today they will not get out*** (read as *yukhrajūna* and *yakhrujūna*) ***of it*** (the Fire). ***They will not be able to appease Allah*** – to please their Lord by repentance and obedience, because that will be of no benefit on that day.

36. ***All praise belongs to Allah*** – because He will fulfil His promise about the deniers, ***the Lord of the heavens and the Lord of the earth, Lord of all the worlds.*** He created the heavens and the earth and all the worlds. *'Ālām* (world) is all that is other than Allah. It is in the plural because of the variety of species in existence.

37. ***All greatness belongs to Him in the heavens and earth. He is the Almighty, the All-Wise.***

سُورَةُ الأَحْقَافِ

بِسْمِ ٱللَّهِ ٱلرَّحْمَٰنِ ٱلرَّحِيمِ

حمٓ ﴿١﴾ تَنزِيلُ ٱلْكِتَٰبِ مِنَ ٱللَّهِ ٱلْعَزِيزِ ٱلْحَكِيمِ ﴿٢﴾ مَا خَلَقْنَا
ٱلسَّمَٰوَٰتِ وَٱلْأَرْضَ وَمَا بَيْنَهُمَآ إِلَّا بِٱلْحَقِّ وَأَجَلٍ مُّسَمًّى ۚ وَٱلَّذِينَ
كَفَرُوا۟ عَمَّآ أُنذِرُوا۟ مُعْرِضُونَ ﴿٣﴾ قُلْ أَرَءَيْتُم مَّا تَدْعُونَ مِن
دُونِ ٱللَّهِ أَرُونِى مَاذَا خَلَقُوا۟ مِنَ ٱلْأَرْضِ أَمْ لَهُمْ شِرْكٌ فِى ٱلسَّمَٰوَٰتِ ۖ
ٱئْتُونِى بِكِتَٰبٍ مِّن قَبْلِ هَٰذَآ أَوْ أَثَٰرَةٍ مِّنْ عِلْمٍ إِن كُنتُمْ
صَٰدِقِينَ ﴿٤﴾ وَمَنْ أَضَلُّ مِمَّن يَدْعُوا۟ مِن دُونِ ٱللَّهِ مَن
لَّا يَسْتَجِيبُ لَهُۥٓ إِلَىٰ يَوْمِ ٱلْقِيَٰمَةِ وَهُمْ عَن دُعَآئِهِمْ غَٰفِلُونَ ﴿٥﴾
وَإِذَا حُشِرَ ٱلنَّاسُ كَانُوا۟ لَهُمْ أَعْدَآءً وَكَانُوا۟ بِعِبَادَتِهِمْ كَٰفِرِينَ ﴿٦﴾ وَإِذَا
تُتْلَىٰ عَلَيْهِمْ ءَايَٰتُنَا بَيِّنَٰتٍ قَالَ ٱلَّذِينَ كَفَرُوا۟ لِلْحَقِّ لَمَّا جَآءَهُمْ هَٰذَا
سِحْرٌ مُّبِينٌ ﴿٧﴾ أَمْ يَقُولُونَ ٱفْتَرَىٰهُ ۖ قُلْ إِنِ ٱفْتَرَيْتُهُۥ فَلَا تَمْلِكُونَ
لِى مِنَ ٱللَّهِ شَيْـًٔا ۖ هُوَ أَعْلَمُ بِمَا تُفِيضُونَ فِيهِ ۖ كَفَىٰ بِهِۦ شَهِيدًۢا بَيْنِى
وَبَيْنَكُمْ ۖ وَهُوَ ٱلْغَفُورُ ٱلرَّحِيمُ ﴿٨﴾ قُلْ مَا كُنتُ بِدْعًا مِّنَ ٱلرُّسُلِ
وَمَآ أَدْرِى مَا يُفْعَلُ بِى وَلَا بِكُمْ ۖ إِنْ أَتَّبِعُ إِلَّا مَا يُوحَىٰٓ إِلَىَّ وَمَآ أَنَا۠
إِلَّا نَذِيرٌ مُّبِينٌ ﴿٩﴾ قُلْ أَرَءَيْتُمْ إِن كَانَ مِنْ عِندِ ٱللَّهِ وَكَفَرْتُم بِهِۦ
وَشَهِدَ شَاهِدٌ مِّنۢ بَنِىٓ إِسْرَٰٓءِيلَ عَلَىٰ مِثْلِهِۦ فَـَٔامَنَ وَٱسْتَكْبَرْتُمْ ۖ

46. *Sūrat al-Aḥqāf*
The Sand-Dunes

This *sūra* is Makkan except for *āyat*s 10, 15, and 35 which are Madinan. It has 34 or 35 *āyat*s.

1. ***Hā Mīm*** Allah knows best what is meant by this.

2. ***The revelation of the Book*** (the Qur'an) ***is from Allah, the Almighty*** in His kingdom, **the All-Wise** in what He does.

3. ***We have not created the heavens and earth and everything between them except with truth*** – so as to indicate Our power and unity – ***and for a set term*** – until the set time when they will vanish on the Last Day of Rising. ***But those who disbelieve turn away from what they have been warned*** regarding the punishment.

4. ***Say:*** 'Tell me: ***have you thought about those*** idols ***you call upon*** and worship ***apart from Allah? Show me what they have created on the earth. Or do they have a partnership in*** the creation of ***the heavens?*** This demands a negative response. ***Produce a*** revealed ***Book for me before this one*** (the Qur'an) ***or a shred of*** ancient ***knowledge*** which validates your claim in respect of your worship of idols: the claim that worshipping them brings you near to Allah – ***if you are telling the truth*** in respect of your claim.'

5. ***Who could be further astray than those who call on*** and worship ***other things besides Allah, which will not*** ever ***respond to them*** – to their worshippers in respect of anything that they ask them – ***until the Day of Rising and which are unaware of their prayers?*** They are unaware of their worship because they are inanimate and do not understand.

6. ***When mankind is gathered together, they*** (the idols) ***will be their enemies*** – hostile to those who worshipped them – ***and will reject their worship.***

7. ***When Our Clear Signs*** (the Qur'an) ***are recited to them*** (the people of Makka), ***those who reject say to the truth*** (the Qur'an) ***when it comes to them, 'This is*** clear and ***downright magic.'***

إِنَّ ٱللَّهَ لَا يَهْدِى ٱلْقَوْمَ ٱلظَّٰلِمِينَ ﴿١٠﴾ وَقَالَ ٱلَّذِينَ كَفَرُوا۟
لِلَّذِينَ ءَامَنُوا۟ لَوْ كَانَ خَيْرًا مَّا سَبَقُونَآ إِلَيْهِ ۚ وَإِذْ لَمْ يَهْتَدُوا۟ بِهِۦ
فَسَيَقُولُونَ هَٰذَآ إِفْكٌ قَدِيمٌ ﴿١١﴾ وَمِن قَبْلِهِۦ كِتَٰبُ مُوسَىٰٓ
إِمَامًا وَرَحْمَةً ۚ وَهَٰذَا كِتَٰبٌ مُّصَدِّقٌ لِّسَانًا عَرَبِيًّا لِّيُنذِرَ
ٱلَّذِينَ ظَلَمُوا۟ وَبُشْرَىٰ لِلْمُحْسِنِينَ ﴿١٢﴾ إِنَّ ٱلَّذِينَ قَالُوا۟ رَبُّنَا
ٱللَّهُ ثُمَّ ٱسْتَقَٰمُوا۟ فَلَا خَوْفٌ عَلَيْهِمْ وَلَا هُمْ يَحْزَنُونَ ﴿١٣﴾
أُو۟لَٰٓئِكَ أَصْحَٰبُ ٱلْجَنَّةِ خَٰلِدِينَ فِيهَا جَزَآءًۢ بِمَا كَانُوا۟ يَعْمَلُونَ ﴿١٤﴾
وَوَصَّيْنَا ٱلْإِنسَٰنَ بِوَٰلِدَيْهِ إِحْسَٰنًا ۖ حَمَلَتْهُ أُمُّهُۥ كُرْهًا وَوَضَعَتْهُ
كُرْهًا ۖ وَحَمْلُهُۥ وَفِصَٰلُهُۥ ثَلَٰثُونَ شَهْرًا ۚ حَتَّىٰٓ إِذَا بَلَغَ أَشُدَّهُۥ وَبَلَغَ
أَرْبَعِينَ سَنَةً قَالَ رَبِّ أَوْزِعْنِىٓ أَنْ أَشْكُرَ نِعْمَتَكَ ٱلَّتِىٓ أَنْعَمْتَ
عَلَىَّ وَعَلَىٰ وَٰلِدَىَّ وَأَنْ أَعْمَلَ صَٰلِحًا تَرْضَىٰهُ وَأَصْلِحْ لِى فِى
ذُرِّيَّتِىٓ ۖ إِنِّى تُبْتُ إِلَيْكَ وَإِنِّى مِنَ ٱلْمُسْلِمِينَ ﴿١٥﴾ أُو۟لَٰٓئِكَ ٱلَّذِينَ
نَتَقَبَّلُ عَنْهُمْ أَحْسَنَ مَا عَمِلُوا۟ وَنَتَجَاوَزُ عَن سَيِّـَٔاتِهِمْ فِىٓ أَصْحَٰبِ
ٱلْجَنَّةِ ۖ وَعْدَ ٱلصِّدْقِ ٱلَّذِى كَانُوا۟ يُوعَدُونَ ﴿١٦﴾ وَٱلَّذِى قَالَ
لِوَٰلِدَيْهِ أُفٍّ لَّكُمَآ أَتَعِدَانِنِىٓ أَنْ أُخْرَجَ وَقَدْ خَلَتِ ٱلْقُرُونُ مِن
قَبْلِى وَهُمَا يَسْتَغِيثَانِ ٱللَّهَ وَيْلَكَ ءَامِنْ إِنَّ وَعْدَ ٱللَّهِ حَقٌّ فَيَقُولُ
مَا هَٰذَآ إِلَّآ أَسَٰطِيرُ ٱلْأَوَّلِينَ ﴿١٧﴾ أُو۟لَٰٓئِكَ ٱلَّذِينَ حَقَّ عَلَيْهِمُ
ٱلْقَوْلُ فِىٓ أُمَمٍ قَدْ خَلَتْ مِن قَبْلِهِم مِّنَ ٱلْجِنِّ وَٱلْإِنسِ ۖ إِنَّهُمْ كَانُوا۟
خَٰسِرِينَ ﴿١٨﴾ وَلِكُلٍّ دَرَجَٰتٌ مِّمَّا عَمِلُوا۟ ۖ وَلِيُوَفِّيَهُمْ أَعْمَٰلَهُمْ وَهُمْ
لَا يُظْلَمُونَ ﴿١٩﴾ وَيَوْمَ يُعْرَضُ ٱلَّذِينَ كَفَرُوا۟ عَلَى ٱلنَّارِ أَذْهَبْتُمْ طَيِّبَٰتِكُمْ

8. ***Or do they say, 'He has invented it*** (the Qur'an)'***?*** There is a negative answer to the question. ***Say*** – hypothetically – ***'If I have invented it, then you possess no power to help me against*** punishment by ***Allah in any way.*** You cannot defend me against Allah if He inflicts punishment on me. ***He knows best what you hold forth about*** and say about the Qur'an. ***He*** (Allah) ***is Witness enough between me and you. He is the Ever-Forgiving*** of those who repent, ***the Most Merciful***, and does not hasten the penalty.***'***

9. ***Say: 'I am nothing new*** – no innovation – ***among the Messengers*** – not the first Messenger. There were many before me, so how can you deny me? ***I have no idea what will be done with me or you*** in this world: whether I will be expelled from my land or killed as happened to Prophets before me, or whether you will throw stones at me or whether the earth will swallow you up as happened with others before you. ***I only follow what has been revealed to me*** – in other words, the Qur'an, and I do not innovate anything from myself. ***I am only a clear warner.'***

10. ***Say: 'What do you think?*** Tell me what your state will be. ***If it*** (the Qur'an) ***is from Allah and you reject it, when a witness from the tribe of Israel*** ('Abdullāh ibn Salām) ***testifies to its similarity*** to previous Revelations, affirming that it is from Allah, ***and*** so the witness ***believes while you are*** too ***arrogant*** to believe ***… !*** You are wrongdoers and ***Allah certainly does not guide wrongdoing people.'***

11. ***Those who disbelieve say of those who believe, 'If there were any good in it*** (belief), ***they would not have beaten us to it.' And since they have not been guided by it*** (the Qur'an), ***they are bound to say, 'This*** Qur'an ***is an antiquated falsehood.'***

12. ***But before it*** (the Qur'an) ***there was the Book of Mūsā*** (the Torah) ***as a model and a mercy*** to the believers***; and this is a corroborating Book*** – confirming the Books before it – ***in the Arabic tongue so that you may warn those who do wrong*** – including the idolaters of Makka – ***and as good news for the good-doers*** – the believers.

13. ***Those who say, 'Our Lord is Allah,' and then go straight*** in obedience to Allah ***will feel no fear and will know no sorrow.***

14. ***Such people are the Companions of the Garden, remaining in it timelessly, for ever, as repayment for what they did.***

15. ***We have instructed man to be good*** (read as *ḥusnan* and *iḥsānan*) ***to his parents. His mother bore him with difficulty and with difficulty gave birth to him; and his bearing and weaning take thirty months.*** Thirty months refers to the period of pregnancy, whose minimum is six months, and the rest of it is suckling. If it be said that if she is pregnant for six or nine months, then the period of suckling is that which makes up the total. If the child survives, the age of maturity with respect to strength, intelligence and discernment is thirty-three, or between thirty and forty. ***Then when he achieves his full strength and reaches forty, he says, 'My Lord, keep me thankful for the blessing***, and inspire me to be grateful for the blessing of *tawḥīḍ*. ***You bestowed on me and on my parents, and keep me acting rightly, pleasing You.*** It is said that this was revealed about Abū Bakr aṣ-Ṣiddīq. He reached the age of forty two years after the Prophet, may Allah bless him and grant him peace, was sent, and became a believer. Then his parents became believers and then his son, 'Abdu'r-Raḥmān, and then the son of 'Abdu'r-Raḥmān, 'Atīq. He set free nine believers who were being tortured on account of their belief in Allah. ***And make my descendants righteous*** – and all of his offspring were believers. ***I have turned in repentance to You and I am truly one of the Muslims.'***

16. ***Those*** – such as Abū Bakr and others like him – ***are people whose best deeds will be accepted and whose wrong deeds will be overlooked. They are among the Companions of the Garden, in fulfilment of the true promise made to them*** which is found in Allah's words: *"Allah has promised the believers, men and women, the Gardens of Paradise."* (9:72)

17. ***But what of him who says to his parents, 'Fie*** (read as *uffin*, *uffa* and *uff*) ***on you!*** This is a word indicating foulness and ugliness, used to express annoyance with someone. ***Do you promise me that I will be resurrected*** from the grave ***when generations*** of nations ***before me have passed away*** and have not emerged from their graves***?' They both call on Allah for help: 'Woe to you!*** You will be destroyed! ***Believe*** in the Resurrection***! Allah's promise is true.'***

فِي حَيَاتِكُمُ ٱلدُّنْيَا وَٱسْتَمْتَعْتُم بِهَا فَٱلْيَوْمَ تُجْزَوْنَ عَذَابَ ٱلْهُونِ
بِمَا كُنتُمْ تَسْتَكْبِرُونَ فِي ٱلْأَرْضِ بِغَيْرِ ٱلْحَقِّ وَبِمَا كُنتُمْ تَفْسُقُونَ ﴿٢٠﴾
۞ وَٱذْكُرْ أَخَا عَادٍ إِذْ أَنذَرَ قَوْمَهُۥ بِٱلْأَحْقَافِ وَقَدْ خَلَتِ ٱلنُّذُرُ
مِنۢ بَيْنِ يَدَيْهِ وَمِنْ خَلْفِهِۦٓ أَلَّا تَعْبُدُوٓا۟ إِلَّا ٱللَّهَ إِنِّيٓ أَخَافُ عَلَيْكُمْ
عَذَابَ يَوْمٍ عَظِيمٍ ﴿٢١﴾ قَالُوٓا۟ أَجِئْتَنَا لِتَأْفِكَنَا عَنْ ءَالِهَتِنَا فَأْتِنَا
بِمَا تَعِدُنَآ إِن كُنتَ مِنَ ٱلصَّٰدِقِينَ ﴿٢٢﴾ قَالَ إِنَّمَا ٱلْعِلْمُ عِندَ ٱللَّهِ
وَأُبَلِّغُكُم مَّآ أُرْسِلْتُ بِهِۦ وَلَٰكِنِّيٓ أَرَىٰكُمْ قَوْمًا تَجْهَلُونَ ﴿٢٣﴾
فَلَمَّا رَأَوْهُ عَارِضًا مُّسْتَقْبِلَ أَوْدِيَتِهِمْ قَالُوا۟ هَٰذَا عَارِضٌ مُّمْطِرُنَا ۚ
بَلْ هُوَ مَا ٱسْتَعْجَلْتُم بِهِۦ ۖ رِيحٌ فِيهَا عَذَابٌ أَلِيمٌ ﴿٢٤﴾ تُدَمِّرُ كُلَّ
شَيْءٍۭ بِأَمْرِ رَبِّهَا فَأَصْبَحُوا۟ لَا يُرَىٰٓ إِلَّا مَسَٰكِنُهُمْ ۚ كَذَٰلِكَ نَجْزِي
ٱلْقَوْمَ ٱلْمُجْرِمِينَ ﴿٢٥﴾ وَلَقَدْ مَكَّنَّٰهُمْ فِيمَآ إِن مَّكَّنَّٰكُمْ فِيهِ
وَجَعَلْنَا لَهُمْ سَمْعًا وَأَبْصَٰرًا وَأَفْـِٔدَةً فَمَآ أَغْنَىٰ عَنْهُمْ سَمْعُهُمْ
وَلَآ أَبْصَٰرُهُمْ وَلَآ أَفْـِٔدَتُهُم مِّن شَيْءٍ إِذْ كَانُوا۟ يَجْحَدُونَ
بِـَٔايَٰتِ ٱللَّهِ وَحَاقَ بِهِم مَّا كَانُوا۟ بِهِۦ يَسْتَهْزِءُونَ ﴿٢٦﴾ وَلَقَدْ
أَهْلَكْنَا مَا حَوْلَكُم مِّنَ ٱلْقُرَىٰ وَصَرَّفْنَا ٱلْـَٔايَٰتِ لَعَلَّهُمْ يَرْجِعُونَ
﴿٢٧﴾ فَلَوْلَا نَصَرَهُمُ ٱلَّذِينَ ٱتَّخَذُوا۟ مِن دُونِ ٱللَّهِ قُرْبَانًا ءَالِهَةًۢ ۖ
بَلْ ضَلُّوا۟ عَنْهُمْ ۚ وَذَٰلِكَ إِفْكُهُمْ وَمَا كَانُوا۟ يَفْتَرُونَ ﴿٢٨﴾
وَإِذْ صَرَفْنَآ إِلَيْكَ نَفَرًا مِّنَ ٱلْجِنِّ يَسْتَمِعُونَ ٱلْقُرْءَانَ فَلَمَّا
حَضَرُوهُ قَالُوٓا۟ أَنصِتُوا۟ ۖ فَلَمَّا قُضِيَ وَلَّوْا۟ إِلَىٰ قَوْمِهِم مُّنذِرِينَ
﴿٢٩﴾ قَالُوا۟ يَٰقَوْمَنَآ إِنَّا سَمِعْنَا كِتَٰبًا أُنزِلَ مِنۢ بَعْدِ مُوسَىٰ

But he says, 'This claim of resurrection ***is nothing but the myths*** and lies ***of previous peoples.'***

18. ***Those are people of whom the statement about the nations*** – that they will be punished – ***both of jinn and men, who passed away before them, has also proved true; truly they were the lost.***

19. ***Everyone*** – believer and unbeliever – ***will be ranked according to what they did.*** The believers will have high ranks in the Garden and the unbelievers will have low ranks in the Fire. ***He will pay them*** (read as *yuwaffiyahum* and *nuwaffiyahum*, "We will pay") ***in full for their actions*** – the believers being repaid for their acts of obedience and the unbelievers for their acts of disobedience – ***and they will not be wronged*** in the slightest, either by decrease for the believers or by increase for the unbelievers.

20. ***On the Day when those who disbelieved are exposed to the Fire*** they will be told: ***'You dissipated the good things you had in your worldly life*** – by being occupied with its pleasures – ***and enjoyed yourself in it. So today you are being repaid with the punishment of humiliation for being arrogant in the earth without any right and for being deviators*** – and you are receiving the punishment for it now.*'*

21. ***Remember the brother of 'Ād*** – Hūd, peace be upon him – ***when he warned his people by the sand-dunes*** – this place, named al-Aḥqāf, is a wadi in Yemen where their houses where located – ***and warners*** – Messengers – ***passed away before and after him*** (Hūd) who were sent to their people, saying to them: ***'Worship no one but Allah. I fear for you the punishment of a terrible Day*** if you worship gods other than Allah.*'*

22. ***They said, 'Have you come to us to divert us from our gods*** – to stop us from worshipping our gods? ***Bring us what you have promised us*** in terms of punishment for worshipping them, ***if you are telling the truth*** about it coming to us.*'*

23. ***He*** (Hūd) ***said, 'All knowledge is with Allah***, and it is He Who knows when the punishment will come to you. ***I only transmit to you what I have been sent*** to you ***with. But I see that you are a people who are ignorant***, as is shown by your seeking to hasten the punishment.*'*

24. ***When they saw it*** (the punishment) ***as a stormcloud*** which appeared on the horizon ***advancing on their valleys, they said, 'This is a storm cloud which will give us rain.'*** Allah says: ***No, rather it is what*** (the punishment) ***you desired to hasten: a wind containing painful punishment,***

25. ***...destroying everything at its Lord's command.*** In other words, it destroyed everything that Allah wished to be destroyed and so it destroyed their men, women, children and property by throwing all of everything into the air and ripping it apart. Hūd and those who were believers remained unharmed. ***When morning came you could see nothing but their dwellings. That is how We repay the people of the evildoers.*** And that is how other evildoers will also be repaid.

26. ***We established them far more firmly*** in strength and wealth ***than We have established you***, people of Makka, ***and gave them hearing, sight and hearts. But their hearing, sight and hearts were of no use to them at all when they renounced Allah's*** clear ***Signs and what they mocked at*** (the punishment) ***engulfed them.***

27. ***We destroyed the cities round about you*** – the people of those cities, such as Thamūd, 'Ād and the people of Lūṭ – ***and have variegated the*** clear ***Signs so that perhaps they may back.***

28. ***Why have those*** idols ***they took as gods besides Allah, to bring them near to Him, not come to their aid*** to avert the punishment from them***? No, in fact they have forsaken them!*** They were absent when the punishment descended ***That was a fiction, something they invented*** – a lie they told.

29. ***And We diverted a group of jinn*** – these were *jinn* from Nisibiyyin in Yemen or *jinn* from Nineveh and were seven or nine in number – ***towards you*** – this occurred when the Prophet, may Allah bless him and grant him peace, was in a wadi containing some palm trees leading his Companions in the *Fajr* prayer, as is reported in al-Bukhārī and Muslim – ***to listen to the Qur'an. When they were in earshot of it they said*** to one another ***'Be quiet and listen*** to it.' ***When it*** (his recitation) ***was over they went back to their people, warning them*** – of punishment if they did not believe. They had been Jews and became Muslim.

مُصَدِّقًا لِّمَا بَيْنَ يَدَيْهِ يَهْدِىٓ إِلَى ٱلْحَقِّ وَإِلَىٰ طَرِيقٍ مُّسْتَقِيمٍ
٣٠ يَـٰقَوْمَنَآ أَجِيبُوا۟ دَاعِىَ ٱللَّهِ وَءَامِنُوا۟ بِهِۦ يَغْفِرْ لَكُم مِّن
ذُنُوبِكُمْ وَيُجِرْكُم مِّنْ عَذَابٍ أَلِيمٍ ٣١ وَمَن لَّا يُجِبْ دَاعِىَ ٱللَّهِ
فَلَيْسَ بِمُعْجِزٍ فِى ٱلْأَرْضِ وَلَيْسَ لَهُۥ مِن دُونِهِۦٓ أَوْلِيَآءُ ۚ أُو۟لَـٰٓئِكَ
فِى ضَلَـٰلٍ مُّبِينٍ ٣٢ أَوَلَمْ يَرَوْا۟ أَنَّ ٱللَّهَ ٱلَّذِى خَلَقَ ٱلسَّمَـٰوَٰتِ
وَٱلْأَرْضَ وَلَمْ يَعْىَ بِخَلْقِهِنَّ بِقَـٰدِرٍ عَلَىٰٓ أَن يُحْـِۧىَ ٱلْمَوْتَىٰ ۚ بَلَىٰٓ
إِنَّهُۥ عَلَىٰ كُلِّ شَىْءٍ قَدِيرٌ ٣٣ وَيَوْمَ يُعْرَضُ ٱلَّذِينَ كَفَرُوا۟ عَلَى ٱلنَّارِ
أَلَيْسَ هَـٰذَا بِٱلْحَقِّ ۖ قَالُوا۟ بَلَىٰ وَرَبِّنَا ۚ قَالَ فَذُوقُوا۟ ٱلْعَذَابَ بِمَا
كُنتُمْ تَكْفُرُونَ ٣٤ فَٱصْبِرْ كَمَا صَبَرَ أُو۟لُوا۟ ٱلْعَزْمِ مِنَ ٱلرُّسُلِ
وَلَا تَسْتَعْجِل لَّهُمْ ۚ كَأَنَّهُمْ يَوْمَ يَرَوْنَ مَا يُوعَدُونَ لَمْ يَلْبَثُوٓا۟ إِلَّا
سَاعَةً مِّن نَّهَارٍ ۚ بَلَـٰغٌ ۚ فَهَلْ يُهْلَكُ إِلَّا ٱلْقَوْمُ ٱلْفَـٰسِقُونَ ٣٥

30. ***They said, 'Our people, we have heard a Book*** (the Qur'an) ***which was sent down after Mūsā, confirming what came before it,*** such as the Torah, ***guiding to the truth*** (Islam) ***and to a straight path.***

31. Our people, respond to Allah's caller to faith, meaning Muḥammad, may Allah bless him and grant him peace, ***and believe in Him. He*** (Allah) ***will forgive you some of your wrong actions*** – this is qualified by the word "some" because some wrongs can only be forgiven with the consent of those who were wronged – ***and save you from a painful punishment.***

32. ***Those who do not respond to Allah's caller cannot thwart Allah on earth*** – they cannot escape Allah by flight – ***and have no protectors apart from Him*** to protect them from His punishment. ***Such people*** who do not respond ***are clearly misguided.'***

33. ***Do they*** (those who deny the resurrection) ***not see*** and know ***that Allah – He who created the heavens and the earth and was not wearied by creating them – has the power to bring the dead to life? Yes indeed! He has power over all things.***

34. ***On the Day when those who disbelieved are exposed to the Fire*** when they are being punished, ***they will be asked, 'Is this*** punishment ***not true?' They will say, 'Yes, by our Lord.' He will say, 'Then taste the punishment for having disbelieved.'***

35. ***So be steadfast*** in the face of persecution from your people ***as the Messengers*** before you ***with firm resolve were also steadfast.*** They showed steadfastness and fortitude in the face of hardships and had firm resolve. It (the noun "Messengers") is also said to be partitive as Ādam was not one of them, for Allah says, *"We did not find that he had a firm resolve"* (20:115); nor was Yūnus, since He says, *"Do not be like the Companion of the Fish."* (68:48) ***And do not seek to hasten it*** (the punishment) ***for them*** (your people). It is said that it was as if the Prophet, peace and blessings be upon him, was annoyed at them and wanted the punishment to befall them, and so he was commanded to be steadfast and not seek to hasten the punishment which will inevitably befall them at the due time. ***On the Day they see what they were promised*** – meaning the punishment in the Next World, because of its length – ***it will be as if they had only***

tarried in this world ***for just one hour of a single day. It*** (the Qur'an) ***has been transmitted*** from Allah to you***. Will any be destroyed*** when they see the punishment ***except for deviant people*** (the unbelievers)***?***

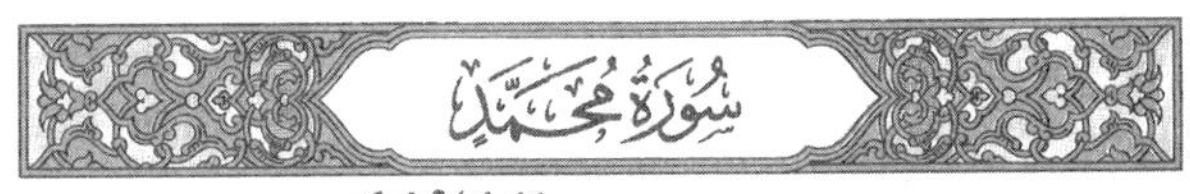

بِسْمِ ٱللَّهِ ٱلرَّحْمَٰنِ ٱلرَّحِيمِ

ٱلَّذِينَ كَفَرُوا۟ وَصَدُّوا۟ عَن سَبِيلِ ٱللَّهِ أَضَلَّ أَعْمَٰلَهُمْ ﴿١﴾ وَٱلَّذِينَ
ءَامَنُوا۟ وَعَمِلُوا۟ ٱلصَّٰلِحَٰتِ وَءَامَنُوا۟ بِمَا نُزِّلَ عَلَىٰ مُحَمَّدٍ وَهُوَ ٱلْحَقُّ مِن
رَّبِّهِمْ ۙ كَفَّرَ عَنْهُمْ سَيِّـَٔاتِهِمْ وَأَصْلَحَ بَالَهُمْ ﴿٢﴾ ذَٰلِكَ بِأَنَّ ٱلَّذِينَ كَفَرُوا۟
ٱتَّبَعُوا۟ ٱلْبَٰطِلَ وَأَنَّ ٱلَّذِينَ ءَامَنُوا۟ ٱتَّبَعُوا۟ ٱلْحَقَّ مِن رَّبِّهِمْ ۚ كَذَٰلِكَ يَضْرِبُ
ٱللَّهُ لِلنَّاسِ أَمْثَٰلَهُمْ ﴿٣﴾ فَإِذَا لَقِيتُمُ ٱلَّذِينَ كَفَرُوا۟ فَضَرْبَ ٱلرِّقَابِ حَتَّىٰٓ
إِذَآ أَثْخَنتُمُوهُمْ فَشُدُّوا۟ ٱلْوَثَاقَ فَإِمَّا مَنًّۢا بَعْدُ وَإِمَّا فِدَآءً حَتَّىٰ تَضَعَ ٱلْحَرْبُ
أَوْزَارَهَا ۚ ذَٰلِكَ وَلَوْ يَشَآءُ ٱللَّهُ لَٱنتَصَرَ مِنْهُمْ وَلَٰكِن لِّيَبْلُوَا۟ بَعْضَكُم
بِبَعْضٍ ۗ وَٱلَّذِينَ قُتِلُوا۟ فِى سَبِيلِ ٱللَّهِ فَلَن يُضِلَّ أَعْمَٰلَهُمْ ﴿٤﴾ سَيَهْدِيهِمْ
وَيُصْلِحُ بَالَهُمْ ﴿٥﴾ وَيُدْخِلُهُمُ ٱلْجَنَّةَ عَرَّفَهَا لَهُمْ ﴿٦﴾ يَٰٓأَيُّهَا ٱلَّذِينَ
ءَامَنُوٓا۟ إِن تَنصُرُوا۟ ٱللَّهَ يَنصُرْكُمْ وَيُثَبِّتْ أَقْدَامَكُمْ ﴿٧﴾ وَٱلَّذِينَ كَفَرُوا۟
فَتَعْسًا لَّهُمْ وَأَضَلَّ أَعْمَٰلَهُمْ ﴿٨﴾ ذَٰلِكَ بِأَنَّهُمْ كَرِهُوا۟ مَآ أَنزَلَ ٱللَّهُ
فَأَحْبَطَ أَعْمَٰلَهُمْ ﴿٩﴾ ۞ أَفَلَمْ يَسِيرُوا۟ فِى ٱلْأَرْضِ فَيَنظُرُوا۟ كَيْفَ
كَانَ عَٰقِبَةُ ٱلَّذِينَ مِن قَبْلِهِمْ ۚ دَمَّرَ ٱللَّهُ عَلَيْهِمْ ۖ وَلِلْكَٰفِرِينَ أَمْثَٰلُهَا ﴿١٠﴾
ذَٰلِكَ بِأَنَّ ٱللَّهَ مَوْلَى ٱلَّذِينَ ءَامَنُوا۟ وَأَنَّ ٱلْكَٰفِرِينَ لَا مَوْلَىٰ لَهُمْ ﴿١١﴾
إِنَّ ٱللَّهَ يُدْخِلُ ٱلَّذِينَ ءَامَنُوا۟ وَعَمِلُوا۟ ٱلصَّٰلِحَٰتِ جَنَّٰتٍ تَجْرِى مِن
تَحْتِهَا ٱلْأَنْهَٰرُ ۖ وَٱلَّذِينَ كَفَرُوا۟ يَتَمَتَّعُونَ وَيَأْكُلُونَ كَمَا تَأْكُلُ ٱلْأَنْعَٰمُ
وَٱلنَّارُ مَثْوًى لَّهُمْ ﴿١٢﴾ وَكَأَيِّن مِّن قَرْيَةٍ هِىَ أَشَدُّ قُوَّةً مِّن قَرْيَتِكَ
ٱلَّتِىٓ أَخْرَجَتْكَ أَهْلَكْنَٰهُمْ فَلَا نَاصِرَ لَهُمْ ﴿١٣﴾ أَفَمَن كَانَ عَلَىٰ بَيِّنَةٍ

47. *Sūrat Muḥammad*

This *sūra* is Madinan except for *āyat* 13, which is Makkan. It has 38 or 39 *āyats*.

1. ***For those who disbelieve*** – among the people of Makka and others – ***and bar others from the Way of Allah*** (faith), ***Allah will make their*** good ***actions*** – such as feeding people and maintaining ties of kinship – ***go astray*** and come to nothing. They will find no reward for them in the Next World. They are repaid in this world by the bounty of Allah.

2. ***But as for those who believe and do right actions*** – such as the Anṣār and others – ***and believe in what has been sent down to Muḥammad*** (the Qur'an) – ***and it is the truth from their Lord – He will erase their bad actions from them*** and forgive them ***and better their condition*** so that they do not disobey Him.

3. ***That*** – the loss of the actions of the unbelievers and the erasure of the bad actions of the believers – ***is because those who disbelieve follow falsehood*** in the form of Shayṭān ***whereas those who believe follow the truth from their Lord*** (the Qur'an). ***In that way Allah makes comparisons for mankind*** – makes it clear to people that the actions of unbelievers come to nothing and that the errors of believers will be forgiven.

4. ***Therefore when you meet those who disbelieve, strike their necks*** – meaning "kill them". Striking people's necks generally results in their death. ***Then when you have slaughtered them*** – killed many of them – ***tie their bonds tightly*** – hold them as prisoners and bind them firmly, ***and set them free*** – show grace to them by releasing them without them having to pay anything – ***or ransom them*** for money or in exchange for Muslim captives ***until the war is finally over.*** The literal translation of this is "war lays down its burdens", which comes from the combatants laying down their weapons, although it may be brought about by other things such as unbelievers becoming Muslim or entering into a treaty. It marks the end of killing and capture. ***That*** command regarding them ***is how it is to be. If Allah willed, He could avenge Himself on them*** without any need for fighting, ***but it*** (that command) ***is so that He may test***

some of you by means of others by their having to fight. Those of you who are killed will go to the Garden and those of them who are killed will go the Fire. ***As for those who are killed*** (read as *qutilū* and also *qātalū*, in which case the meaning is "those who fight") ***in the Way of Allah, He will not let their actions go astray.*** This *āyat* was revealed on the day of the Battle of Uḥud when a lot of killing and wounds was inflicted on the Muslims.

5. ***He will guide them*** in this world and in the Next to what will benefit them ***and better their condition*** in both worlds. This is world for those who are not killed, and there will be high degrees in Paradise for those who are …

6. ***…and He will admit them into the Garden which He has made known*** and clear ***to them.*** They will be guided to their places in it, and to their wives and servants there, without needing to be directed.

7. ***You who believe, if you help Allah*** by supporting the *dīn* of Allah and His Messenger, ***He will help you*** against your enemies ***and make your feet firm*** in battle.

8. ***But those who disbelieve will have utter ruin*** – destruction and loss from Allah – ***and He will make their actions go astray*** and come to nothing.

9. ***That*** ruin and misguidance ***is because they hate what Allah has sent down*** of the Qur'an which contains obligations, ***so He has made their actions come to nothing.***

10. ***Have they not travelled about the earth and seen the final fate of those before them? Allah destroyed them utterly.*** Have you not seen how He destroyed them, their children and their wealth? ***And those who disbelieved will suffer the same fate.***

11. ***That*** support of the believers and defeat of the unbelievers ***is because Allah is the Protector*** and Helper ***of those who believe and because those who disbelieve have no protector.***

12. Allah will admit those who believe to Gardens with rivers flowing under them. Those who disbelieve have their enjoyment in this world, ***eating as cattle eat*** – having no concern other than the filling their bellies and the indulging of their sexual appetites, so that they do not show any concern for the Next World – ***but the Fire will be their final residence.***

مِّن رَّبِّهِۦ كَمَن زُيِّنَ لَهُۥ سُوٓءُ عَمَلِهِۦ وَٱتَّبَعُوٓاْ أَهْوَآءَهُم ﴿١٤﴾ مَّثَلُ ٱلْجَنَّةِ
ٱلَّتِى وُعِدَ ٱلْمُتَّقُونَ ۖ فِيهَآ أَنْهَـٰرٌ مِّن مَّآءٍ غَيْرِ ءَاسِنٍ وَأَنْهَـٰرٌ مِّن لَّبَنٍ لَّمْ
يَتَغَيَّرْ طَعْمُهُۥ وَأَنْهَـٰرٌ مِّنْ خَمْرٍ لَّذَّةٍ لِّلشَّـٰرِبِينَ وَأَنْهَـٰرٌ مِّنْ عَسَلٍ مُّصَفًّى ۖ
وَلَهُمْ فِيهَا مِن كُلِّ ٱلثَّمَرَٰتِ وَمَغْفِرَةٌ مِّن رَّبِّهِمْ ۖ كَمَنْ هُوَ خَـٰلِدٌ فِى ٱلنَّارِ
وَسُقُواْ مَآءً حَمِيمًا فَقَطَّعَ أَمْعَآءَهُمْ ﴿١٥﴾ وَمِنْهُم مَّن يَسْتَمِعُ إِلَيْكَ
حَتَّىٰٓ إِذَا خَرَجُواْ مِنْ عِندِكَ قَالُواْ لِلَّذِينَ أُوتُواْ ٱلْعِلْمَ مَاذَا قَالَ ءَانِفًا ۚ
أُوْلَـٰٓئِكَ ٱلَّذِينَ طَبَعَ ٱللَّهُ عَلَىٰ قُلُوبِهِمْ وَٱتَّبَعُوٓاْ أَهْوَآءَهُمْ ﴿١٦﴾ وَٱلَّذِينَ
ٱهْتَدَوْاْ زَادَهُمْ هُدًى وَءَاتَىٰهُمْ تَقْوَىٰهُمْ ﴿١٧﴾ فَهَلْ يَنظُرُونَ إِلَّا
ٱلسَّاعَةَ أَن تَأْتِيَهُم بَغْتَةً ۖ فَقَدْ جَآءَ أَشْرَاطُهَا ۚ فَأَنَّىٰ لَهُمْ إِذَا جَآءَتْهُمْ
ذِكْرَىٰهُمْ ﴿١٨﴾ فَٱعْلَمْ أَنَّهُۥ لَآ إِلَـٰهَ إِلَّا ٱللَّهُ وَٱسْتَغْفِرْ لِذَنۢبِكَ
وَلِلْمُؤْمِنِينَ وَٱلْمُؤْمِنَـٰتِ ۗ وَٱللَّهُ يَعْلَمُ مُتَقَلَّبَكُمْ وَمَثْوَىٰكُمْ ﴿١٩﴾
وَيَقُولُ ٱلَّذِينَ ءَامَنُواْ لَوْلَا نُزِّلَتْ سُورَةٌ ۖ فَإِذَآ أُنزِلَتْ سُورَةٌ
مُّحْكَمَةٌ وَذُكِرَ فِيهَا ٱلْقِتَالُ ۙ رَأَيْتَ ٱلَّذِينَ فِى قُلُوبِهِم مَّرَضٌ
يَنظُرُونَ إِلَيْكَ نَظَرَ ٱلْمَغْشِىِّ عَلَيْهِ مِنَ ٱلْمَوْتِ ۖ فَأَوْلَىٰ لَهُمْ
﴿٢٠﴾ طَاعَةٌ وَقَوْلٌ مَّعْرُوفٌ ۚ فَإِذَا عَزَمَ ٱلْأَمْرُ فَلَوْ صَدَقُواْ ٱللَّهَ
لَكَانَ خَيْرًا لَّهُمْ ﴿٢١﴾ فَهَلْ عَسَيْتُمْ إِن تَوَلَّيْتُمْ أَن تُفْسِدُواْ
فِى ٱلْأَرْضِ وَتُقَطِّعُوٓاْ أَرْحَامَكُمْ ﴿٢٢﴾ أُوْلَـٰٓئِكَ ٱلَّذِينَ لَعَنَهُمُ ٱللَّهُ
فَأَصَمَّهُمْ وَأَعْمَىٰٓ أَبْصَـٰرَهُمْ ﴿٢٣﴾ أَفَلَا يَتَدَبَّرُونَ ٱلْقُرْءَانَ
أَمْ عَلَىٰ قُلُوبٍ أَقْفَالُهَآ ﴿٢٤﴾ إِنَّ ٱلَّذِينَ ٱرْتَدُّواْ عَلَىٰٓ أَدْبَـٰرِهِم
مِّنۢ بَعْدِ مَا تَبَيَّنَ لَهُمُ ٱلْهُدَى ۙ ٱلشَّيْطَـٰنُ سَوَّلَ لَهُمْ وَأَمْلَىٰ

13. ***How many cities We have destroyed*** – meaning their inhabitants – ***greater in strength than your city*** – the population of Makka – ***which has driven you out, and there was no one to help them*** against Our destructive power*!*

14. ***Is someone on a clear path from his Lord*** – with clear evidence and proof: in other words, the believers – ***like those whose bad actions have been made to seem good to them*** – meaning the unbelievers – ***and who follow their own desires*** in respect of worshipping idols*?* There is no comparison between them.

15. ***An image of the Garden which is promised to those who are godfearing*** who will enter it: ***in it there are rivers of water which will never spoil*** (read as *āsin* and *asin*) – unlike water in this world, which changes when something comes into contact with it – ***and rivers of milk whose taste will never change*** – unlike milk in this world, which goes sour after a time – ***and rivers of wine, delightful to all who drink it*** – unlike wine in this world, which is unpleasant to drink – ***and rivers of honey of undiluted purity*** – unlike honey in this world, which emerges from the bellies of bees mixed with wax and other things. ***In it they will have fruit of every kind and forgiveness from their Lord. Is that*** – people in this bliss – ***like those who will be in the Fire timelessly, for ever, with boiling water to drink which lacerates their bowels?***

16. ***Among them*** (the unbelievers) ***are those who listen to you*** in the Friday *khuṭba* – meaning that they are hypocrites – ***and then, when they leave your presence, say to those who have been given knowledge*** – such as Ibn Mas'ūd and Ibn 'Abbās, out of mockery and derision – ***'What was that he just said*** about the Last Hour*?'* ***They are those whose hearts Allah has sealed up*** with unbelief ***and who follow their own desires*** in their hypocrisy.

17. ***He*** (Allah) ***increases in guidance those who are already guided*** (the believers) ***and makes them godfearing*** – He inspires them to safeguard themselves against the Fire.

18. ***What are they*** (the unbelievers of Makka) ***awaiting but for the Hour to come upon them suddenly? Its Signs have already come.*** Some of its Signs have already come, like the sending of the Prophet, may Allah bless him and grant him peace, the splitting of the moon, and the Smoke. ***What good will their Reminder be to***

them when it (the Last Hour) ***does arrive?*** Then the Reminder will be of no benefit to them.

19. ***Know, then, that there is no god except Allah*** – in other words, persist, Muḥammad, in your knowledge of that which will be of benefit on the Day of Rising – ***and ask forgiveness for your wrongdoing*** – because he was told that, in spite of his immunity and protection from wrong action, it became the *sunna* for his community. The Prophet, may Allah bless him and grant him peace, himself did that. He said, "I ask forgiveness of Allah a hundred times every day" – ***and for the men and women who believe.*** The believers are honoured by Allah's command to their Prophet to ask forgiveness for them. ***Allah knows both your activity and your repose.*** Allah knows what you do when you are going about in your business in the day and when you retire to your beds in the night. This means that He knows all of your states and none of them are hidden from Him, so fear Allah and show caution. This is addressed both to the believers and others.

20. ***Those who believe say***, when *jihād* is mentioned, ***'If only a*** **sūra** ***could be sent down*** which speaks of *jihād*.***' But when a straightforward*** **sūra** – meaning that none of it is abrogated – ***is sent down and fighting is mentioned in it*** as you asked, ***you see those with sickness in their hearts*** (the hypocrites) ***looking at you with the look of someone about to faint from fear of death*** and dislike of it. This means that they fear and dislike fighting. ***More fitting for them…***

21. ***…would be obedience and honourable words.*** They should speak well to you. ***Once the matter is resolved upon*** – when it is necessary for them to fight – ***being true to Allah*** with respect to faith and obedience ***would be better for them.***

22. ***Is it not likely*** (read as *'asaytum* and *'asītum*) ***that, if you did turn away*** from faith ***you would cause corruption in the earth*** – revert to the behaviour of the *Jāhiliyya* in terms of injustice and fighting – ***and sever your ties of kinship?***

23. ***Such*** (those who corrupt) ***are the people Allah has cursed, making them deaf*** to the truth ***and blinding their eyes*** to the Path of guidance.

لَهُمْ ﴿٢٥﴾ ذَٰلِكَ بِأَنَّهُمْ قَالُوا۟ لِلَّذِينَ كَرِهُوا۟ مَا نَزَّلَ
ٱللَّهُ سَنُطِيعُكُمْ فِى بَعْضِ ٱلْأَمْرِ ۖ وَٱللَّهُ يَعْلَمُ إِسْرَارَهُمْ
﴿٢٦﴾ فَكَيْفَ إِذَا تَوَفَّتْهُمُ ٱلْمَلَٰٓئِكَةُ يَضْرِبُونَ وُجُوهَهُمْ
وَأَدْبَٰرَهُمْ ﴿٢٧﴾ ذَٰلِكَ بِأَنَّهُمُ ٱتَّبَعُوا۟ مَآ أَسْخَطَ ٱللَّهَ
وَكَرِهُوا۟ رِضْوَٰنَهُۥ فَأَحْبَطَ أَعْمَٰلَهُمْ ﴿٢٨﴾ أَمْ حَسِبَ
ٱلَّذِينَ فِى قُلُوبِهِم مَّرَضٌ أَن لَّن يُخْرِجَ ٱللَّهُ أَضْغَٰنَهُمْ ﴿٢٩﴾
وَلَوْ نَشَآءُ لَأَرَيْنَٰكَهُمْ فَلَعَرَفْتَهُم بِسِيمَٰهُمْ ۚ وَلَتَعْرِفَنَّهُمْ فِى
لَحْنِ ٱلْقَوْلِ ۚ وَٱللَّهُ يَعْلَمُ أَعْمَٰلَكُمْ ﴿٣٠﴾ وَلَنَبْلُوَنَّكُمْ حَتَّىٰ نَعْلَمَ
ٱلْمُجَٰهِدِينَ مِنكُمْ وَٱلصَّٰبِرِينَ وَنَبْلُوَا۟ أَخْبَارَكُمْ ﴿٣١﴾ إِنَّ ٱلَّذِينَ
كَفَرُوا۟ وَصَدُّوا۟ عَن سَبِيلِ ٱللَّهِ وَشَآقُّوا۟ ٱلرَّسُولَ مِنۢ بَعْدِ مَا تَبَيَّنَ
لَهُمُ ٱلْهُدَىٰ لَن يَضُرُّوا۟ ٱللَّهَ شَيْـًٔا وَسَيُحْبِطُ أَعْمَٰلَهُمْ ﴿٣٢﴾
۞ يَٰٓأَيُّهَا ٱلَّذِينَ ءَامَنُوٓا۟ أَطِيعُوا۟ ٱللَّهَ وَأَطِيعُوا۟ ٱلرَّسُولَ وَلَا تُبْطِلُوٓا۟
أَعْمَٰلَكُمْ ﴿٣٣﴾ إِنَّ ٱلَّذِينَ كَفَرُوا۟ وَصَدُّوا۟ عَن سَبِيلِ ٱللَّهِ ثُمَّ مَاتُوا۟
وَهُمْ كُفَّارٌ فَلَن يَغْفِرَ ٱللَّهُ لَهُمْ ﴿٣٤﴾ فَلَا تَهِنُوا۟ وَتَدْعُوٓا۟ إِلَى ٱلسَّلْمِ
وَأَنتُمُ ٱلْأَعْلَوْنَ وَٱللَّهُ مَعَكُمْ وَلَن يَتِرَكُمْ أَعْمَٰلَكُمْ ﴿٣٥﴾ إِنَّمَا
ٱلْحَيَوٰةُ ٱلدُّنْيَا لَعِبٌ وَلَهْوٌ ۚ وَإِن تُؤْمِنُوا۟ وَتَتَّقُوا۟ يُؤْتِكُمْ أُجُورَكُمْ
وَلَا يَسْـَٔلْكُمْ أَمْوَٰلَكُمْ ﴿٣٦﴾ إِن يَسْـَٔلْكُمُوهَا فَيُحْفِكُمْ
تَبْخَلُوا۟ وَيُخْرِجْ أَضْغَٰنَكُمْ ﴿٣٧﴾ هَٰٓأَنتُمْ هَٰٓؤُلَآءِ تُدْعَوْنَ
لِتُنفِقُوا۟ فِى سَبِيلِ ٱللَّهِ فَمِنكُم مَّن يَبْخَلُ ۖ وَمَن يَبْخَلْ
فَإِنَّمَا يَبْخَلُ عَن نَّفْسِهِۦ ۚ وَٱللَّهُ ٱلْغَنِىُّ وَأَنتُمُ ٱلْفُقَرَآءُ ۚ وَإِن
تَتَوَلَّوْا۟ يَسْتَبْدِلْ قَوْمًا غَيْرَكُمْ ثُمَّ لَا يَكُونُوٓا۟ أَمْثَٰلَكُم ﴿٣٨﴾

24. ***Will they not then ponder the Qur'an*** and recognise the truth, ***or are there locks upon their hearts*** so that they do not understand?

25. ***Those who have turned back on their tracks*** through hypocrisy ***after the guidance became clear to them, it was Shayṭān who talked them into it*** – made that seem good to them – ***and filled*** (read as *amlā* and *umli*) ***them with false hopes.*** Shayṭān does this by Allah's will and so he misleads them.

26. ***That*** misguidance ***is because they said to those*** idolaters ***who hate what Allah has sent down, 'We will obey you in part of the affair.'*** In other words, they would help them in their opposition to the Prophet, may Allah bless him and grant him peace, and try to keep people from doing *jihād* with him. They said that in secret, but Allah made it public. ***But Allah knows their secrets*** (read as *asrārahum* and *isrārahum*, the first being a plural and the second a verbal noun).

27. ***How will it*** (their state) ***be when the angels take them in death, beating their faces and their backs*** with iron hammers?

28. ***That*** – dying in that state – ***is because they followed what angers Allah and hated what*** action ***is pleasing to Him; so He made their actions come to nothing.***

29. ***Or did those with sickness in their hearts imagine that Allah would not expose their malevolence?*** They showed their rancour and malice towards the Prophet, may Allah bless him and grant him peace, and the believers.

30. ***If We wished, We would show them to you*** – acquaint you with them – ***and you would know them by their mark and know them by their ambivalent speech*** – the way which they twist words from their proper meanings in order to satirise the Muslims. ***Allah knows your actions.***

31. ***We will test*** (read as *nabluwanna* and *yabluwanna*, "He will test") ***you*** by means of *jihād* and other things ***until We know*** (read as *na'lama* and *ya'lama*, "He knows") with clear knowledge ***the true fighters among you and those who are steadfast*** in *jihād* and other things, ***and test*** (read as *nablū* and *yablū*, "He tests") ***what is reported of you*** regarding your obedience and disobedience in *jihād* and other things.

32. ***Those who disbelieve obstruct the Way of Allah*** – the way of the truth – ***and are entrenched in hostility towards the Messenger*** and opposition to him ***after the guidance*** (the Way of Allah) ***has become clear to them, do not harm Allah in any way; and He will make their actions come to nothing.*** Their actions, such as the *ṣadaqa* they have given, will come to nothing and so they will not see any reward for them in the Next World. This was revealed about those who brought food to the enemy in the Battle of Badr or about the tribes of Qurayẓa and an-Naḍīr.

33. ***You who believe, obey Allah and obey the Messenger. Do not make your actions of no worth*** through disobedience.

34. ***Those who disbelieve and obstruct the Way of Allah and then die as unbelievers, Allah will not forgive them.*** This was revealed about the people in the well into which the unbelievers killed in the Battle of Badr were thrown.

35. ***Do not become faint-hearted and call for peace*** (read as *salm* and *silm*) – meaning conclude a peace treaty with the unbelievers when you meet them – ***when you are uppermost and*** winning. ***Allah is with you*** helping you. ***He would never cheat you of*** the reward for ***your deeds.***

36. Occupation with ***the life of this world is merely a game and a diversion. If you believe and are godfearing*** – if you have fear of Allah in regard to the events of the Next World – ***He will pay you your wages and not ask you for all your wealth***, but only for the obligatory *zakāt* due on it.

37. ***If He did ask you for it and put you under pressure*** – and He asked you for a large amount – ***you would be tight-fisted and it would bring out your malevolence*** towards the *dīn* of Islam.

38. ***Here you are then: people who are called upon to spend*** what is obligatory for you ***in the Way of Allah, and then some of you are tight-fisted! But whoever is tight-fisted is only tight-fisted towards himself. Allah is Rich*** and has no need of your spending, ***and you are poor*** and in need of Him. ***If you turn away*** from obedience to Him ***He will replace you with a people other than yourselves*** who will not turn away from obedience; ***and they will not be like you*** but will obey Him.

سُورَةُ الفَتْحِ

بِسْمِ ٱللَّهِ ٱلرَّحْمَٰنِ ٱلرَّحِيمِ

إِنَّا فَتَحْنَا لَكَ فَتْحًا مُّبِينًا ﴿١﴾ لِّيَغْفِرَ لَكَ ٱللَّهُ مَا تَقَدَّمَ مِن ذَنۢبِكَ
وَمَا تَأَخَّرَ وَيُتِمَّ نِعْمَتَهُۥ عَلَيْكَ وَيَهْدِيَكَ صِرَٰطًا مُّسْتَقِيمًا ﴿٢﴾
وَيَنصُرَكَ ٱللَّهُ نَصْرًا عَزِيزًا ﴿٣﴾ هُوَ ٱلَّذِىٓ أَنزَلَ ٱلسَّكِينَةَ فِى قُلُوبِ
ٱلْمُؤْمِنِينَ لِيَزْدَادُوٓا۟ إِيمَٰنًا مَّعَ إِيمَٰنِهِمْ ۗ وَلِلَّهِ جُنُودُ ٱلسَّمَٰوَٰتِ
وَٱلْأَرْضِ ۚ وَكَانَ ٱللَّهُ عَلِيمًا حَكِيمًا ﴿٤﴾ لِّيُدْخِلَ ٱلْمُؤْمِنِينَ وَٱلْمُؤْمِنَٰتِ
جَنَّٰتٍ تَجْرِى مِن تَحْتِهَا ٱلْأَنْهَٰرُ خَٰلِدِينَ فِيهَا وَيُكَفِّرَ عَنْهُمْ
سَيِّـَٔاتِهِمْ ۚ وَكَانَ ذَٰلِكَ عِندَ ٱللَّهِ فَوْزًا عَظِيمًا ﴿٥﴾ وَيُعَذِّبَ
ٱلْمُنَٰفِقِينَ وَٱلْمُنَٰفِقَٰتِ وَٱلْمُشْرِكِينَ وَٱلْمُشْرِكَٰتِ ٱلظَّآنِّينَ
بِٱللَّهِ ظَنَّ ٱلسَّوْءِ ۚ عَلَيْهِمْ دَآئِرَةُ ٱلسَّوْءِ ۖ وَغَضِبَ ٱللَّهُ عَلَيْهِمْ
وَلَعَنَهُمْ وَأَعَدَّ لَهُمْ جَهَنَّمَ ۖ وَسَآءَتْ مَصِيرًا ﴿٦﴾ وَلِلَّهِ جُنُودُ
ٱلسَّمَٰوَٰتِ وَٱلْأَرْضِ ۚ وَكَانَ ٱللَّهُ عَزِيزًا حَكِيمًا ﴿٧﴾ إِنَّآ أَرْسَلْنَٰكَ
شَٰهِدًا وَمُبَشِّرًا وَنَذِيرًا ﴿٨﴾ لِّتُؤْمِنُوا۟ بِٱللَّهِ وَرَسُولِهِۦ
وَتُعَزِّرُوهُ وَتُوَقِّرُوهُ وَتُسَبِّحُوهُ بُكْرَةً وَأَصِيلًا ﴿٩﴾
إِنَّ ٱلَّذِينَ يُبَايِعُونَكَ إِنَّمَا يُبَايِعُونَ ٱللَّهَ يَدُ ٱللَّهِ فَوْقَ أَيْدِيهِمْ ۚ
فَمَن نَّكَثَ فَإِنَّمَا يَنكُثُ عَلَىٰ نَفْسِهِۦ ۖ وَمَنْ أَوْفَىٰ بِمَا عَٰهَدَ عَلَيْهُ
ٱللَّهَ فَسَيُؤْتِيهِ أَجْرًا عَظِيمًا ﴿١٠﴾ سَيَقُولُ لَكَ ٱلْمُخَلَّفُونَ
مِنَ ٱلْأَعْرَابِ شَغَلَتْنَآ أَمْوَٰلُنَا وَأَهْلُونَا فَٱسْتَغْفِرْ لَنَا ۚ يَقُولُونَ

48. *Sūrat al-Fatḥ* Victory

This *sūra* is Madinan, and was sent down on the road coming from al-Ḥudaybiyya. It contains 29 *āyat*s.

1. ***Truly We have granted you a clear victory***: the conquest of Makka and other places in the future by *jihād*.

2. ***...so that Allah may forgive you*** – because of your *jihād* – ***your earlier errors and any later ones*** – this was in order to encourage the Muslims and to make them desire to fight *jihād*, and is also interpreted as referring to the immunity of the Prophets, peace and blessings be upon them, from wrong actions, ***and complete His blessing upon you*** by the conquest, ***and guide you on a Straight Path*** – to establish you firmly on the path of Allah, which is the *dīn* of Islam.

3. ***...and so that Allah may help you with a mighty help*** in which there is no abasement.

4. ***It is He who sent down serenity into the hearts of the believers, thereby increasing their belief with more belief*** in the laws of the *dīn*. Whenever one of the laws was revealed, they believed in it. One such law was the command to fight *jihād*. ***The legions of the heavens and the earth belong to Allah.*** If Allah had wished to help His *dīn*, He could have done so without any need for your support. ***Allah is All-Knowing*** of His creation, ***All-Wise*** in what He does, and that will always be the case –

5. ***...so that*** through *jihād* ***He may admit the men and women of the believers into Gardens with rivers flowing under them, to remain in them timelessly, for ever, and erase their bad actions from them; and in Allah's sight that is a mighty victory;***

6. ***...and so that He may punish the men and women of the hypocrites and the men and women of the idolators – those who think bad*** (read as *saw'* and *su'*) ***thoughts about Allah.*** They think that Allah will not help Muḥammad, may Allah bless him and grant him peace, and the believers. ***They will suffer an evil turn of fate*** – by abasement and punishment. ***Allah is angry with them, and has***

بِأَلْسِنَتِهِم مَّا لَيْسَ فِي قُلُوبِهِمْ قُلْ فَمَن يَمْلِكُ لَكُم مِّنَ اللَّهِ
شَيْئًا إِنْ أَرَادَ بِكُمْ ضَرًّا أَوْ أَرَادَ بِكُمْ نَفْعًا بَلْ كَانَ اللَّهُ بِمَا تَعْمَلُونَ
خَبِيرًا ١١ بَلْ ظَنَنتُمْ أَن لَّن يَنقَلِبَ الرَّسُولُ وَالْمُؤْمِنُونَ إِلَىٰ
أَهْلِيهِمْ أَبَدًا وَزُيِّنَ ذَٰلِكَ فِي قُلُوبِكُمْ وَظَنَنتُمْ ظَنَّ السَّوْءِ
وَكُنتُمْ قَوْمًا بُورًا ١٢ وَمَن لَّمْ يُؤْمِن بِاللَّهِ وَرَسُولِهِ فَإِنَّا
أَعْتَدْنَا لِلْكَافِرِينَ سَعِيرًا ١٣ وَلِلَّهِ مُلْكُ السَّمَاوَاتِ وَالْأَرْضِ
يَغْفِرُ لِمَن يَشَاءُ وَيُعَذِّبُ مَن يَشَاءُ وَكَانَ اللَّهُ غَفُورًا
رَّحِيمًا ١٤ سَيَقُولُ الْمُخَلَّفُونَ إِذَا انطَلَقْتُمْ إِلَىٰ
مَغَانِمَ لِتَأْخُذُوهَا ذَرُونَا نَتَّبِعْكُمْ يُرِيدُونَ أَن يُبَدِّلُوا
كَلَامَ اللَّهِ قُل لَّن تَتَّبِعُونَا كَذَٰلِكُمْ قَالَ اللَّهُ مِن قَبْلُ
فَسَيَقُولُونَ بَلْ تَحْسُدُونَنَا بَلْ كَانُوا لَا يَفْقَهُونَ إِلَّا قَلِيلًا ١٥
قُل لِّلْمُخَلَّفِينَ مِنَ الْأَعْرَابِ سَتُدْعَوْنَ إِلَىٰ قَوْمٍ أُولِي بَأْسٍ شَدِيدٍ
تُقَاتِلُونَهُمْ أَوْ يُسْلِمُونَ فَإِن تُطِيعُوا يُؤْتِكُمُ اللَّهُ أَجْرًا حَسَنًا
وَإِن تَتَوَلَّوْا كَمَا تَوَلَّيْتُم مِّن قَبْلُ يُعَذِّبْكُمْ عَذَابًا أَلِيمًا ١٦ لَّيْسَ
عَلَى الْأَعْمَىٰ حَرَجٌ وَلَا عَلَى الْأَعْرَجِ حَرَجٌ وَلَا عَلَى الْمَرِيضِ حَرَجٌ
وَمَن يُطِعِ اللَّهَ وَرَسُولَهُ يُدْخِلْهُ جَنَّاتٍ تَجْرِي مِن تَحْتِهَا الْأَنْهَارُ
وَمَن يَتَوَلَّ يُعَذِّبْهُ عَذَابًا أَلِيمًا ١٧ ۞ لَّقَدْ رَضِيَ اللَّهُ عَنِ
الْمُؤْمِنِينَ إِذْ يُبَايِعُونَكَ تَحْتَ الشَّجَرَةِ فَعَلِمَ مَا فِي قُلُوبِهِمْ
فَأَنزَلَ السَّكِينَةَ عَلَيْهِمْ وَأَثَابَهُمْ فَتْحًا قَرِيبًا ١٨ وَمَغَانِمَ
كَثِيرَةً يَأْخُذُونَهَا وَكَانَ اللَّهُ عَزِيزًا حَكِيمًا ١٩ وَعَدَكُمُ اللَّهُ

cursed them by distancing them from His mercy ***and prepared Hell for them. What an evil destination!***

7. *The legions of the heavens and the earth belong to Allah. Allah is Almighty* in His kingdom, ***All-Wise*** in what He does.

8. *We have sent you bearing witness* against your community at the Resurrection, ***bringing good news*** to them in this world, ***and giving warning*** to them about the Fire on account of their evil deeds **…**

9. *…so that you may all believe* (read as *tu'minū* and also *yu'minū*, "they might believe") ***in Allah and His Messenger and honour*** (read as *tu'azzirūhu* and *yu'azzirūhu*) ***Him, and respect*** (read as *tuwaqqirūhu* and *yuwaqqirūhu*) ***Him, and glorify Him in the morning and the evening.***

10. *Those who pledge you their allegiance* in the Homage of *Riḍwān* at Ḥudaybiyya ***pledge allegiance to Allah Himself.*** This *āyat* is similar to *"Whoever obeys the Messenger has obeyed Allah."* (4:80) ***Allah's hand is over their hands*** – the hands with which they gave allegiance to the Prophet. This means that Allah Almighty is looking at their allegiance and will reward them for it. ***He who breaks his pledge*** of allegiance ***only breaks it against himself*** and will experience the evil effects of that. ***But to him who fulfils the contract he has made with Allah, He*** (read as *yu'tīhi,* also read *nu'tīhi*, "We will pay him") ***will pay an immense reward.***

11. *Those* desert ***Arabs*** around Madina ***who remained behind*** – those whom Allah kept from accompanying the Prophet when he asked them to go out with him, to Makka but they were afraid that Quraysh would confront him in the Year of al-Ḥudaybiyya – ***will say to you*** when he returns from there***: 'Our wealth and families kept us occupied*** so that they did not go out with him***, so ask forgiveness*** of Allah ***for us*** for their not going out with him***.'*** Allah says, to refute what they say: ***They say with their tongues***, in asking for forgiveness and the rest, ***what is not in their hearts.*** They are lying in their excuses. ***Say: 'Who can control Allah for you in any way, whether He wants harm*** (read as *ḍarr* and *ḍurr*) ***for you or wants benefit for you?' Allah is aware of what you do.***

12. *No!* The preposition *bal* used here and many other places is employed to show a contrast with what has preceded. ***You thought***

that the Messenger and the believers were not going to return to their families, and that seemed pleasing to your hearts – they wanted the Messenger and the believers to be eliminated by being killed, so that they would not return. ***and You thought evil thoughts*** – this and other things – ***and you were a blighted people*** – destroyed in the sight of Allah for thinking this.

13. ***Whoever does not believe in Allah and His Messenger, We have prepared a*** fiercely ***Blazing Fire for the unbelievers.***

14. ***The kingdom of the heavens and the earth belongs to Allah. He forgives those He wills and punishes those He wills. Allah is Ever-Forgiving, Most Merciful.*** He is always described in this way.

15. ***When you go out to get the booty*** of Khaybar, ***those who remained behind will say, 'Allow us to follow you*** so that we may get some of the booty,' ***desiring to alter Allah's words*** (read as *kalām* and *kalim*) – the promise of Allah about the booty of Khaybar being especially for the people who had been at Ḥudaybiyya. ***Say: 'You may not follow us. That is what Allah said before*** our return.' ***They will say, 'It is only because you envy us***, causing you not to want to give us anything from the portions which you have of the booty.' ***No indeed! How little they have understood*** about the *dīn!*

16. ***Say to the Arabs*** – mentioned above – ***who remained behind: 'You will be called up against a people who possess great force*** – this is said to be a reference to the Banū Ḥanīfa, the people of Yamāma, or Persia and the Romans – ***whom you must fight unless they submit.*** Then you do not fight them. ***If you obey*** and fight, ***Allah will give you an excellent reward. But if you turn your backs as you did before, He will punish you with a painful punishment.'***

17. ***There is no constraint on the blind, nor on the lame, nor on the sick*** – nothing held against these categories for not doing *jihād*. ***He will admit*** (read as *yudkhilhu* and *nudkhilhu*, "We will admit") ***all who obey Allah and His Messenger into Gardens with rivers flowing under them. But He will punish*** (read as *yu'adhdhibu* and *nu'adhdhibu*, "We will punish") ***with a painful punishment anyone who turns his back.***

18. ***Allah was pleased with the believers when they pledged allegiance to you under the tree*** at Ḥudaybiyya. It was an acacia tree. They numbered 1300 or more. They gave allegiance on the basis that

مَغَانِمَ كَثِيرَةً تَأْخُذُونَهَا فَعَجَّلَ لَكُمْ هَٰذِهِۦ وَكَفَّ أَيْدِيَ
ٱلنَّاسِ عَنكُمْ وَلِتَكُونَ ءَايَةً لِّلْمُؤْمِنِينَ وَيَهْدِيَكُمْ صِرَٰطًا
مُّسْتَقِيمًا ﴿٢٠﴾ وَأُخْرَىٰ لَمْ تَقْدِرُوا۟ عَلَيْهَا قَدْ أَحَاطَ ٱللَّهُ بِهَا ۚ
وَكَانَ ٱللَّهُ عَلَىٰ كُلِّ شَىْءٍ قَدِيرًا ﴿٢١﴾ وَلَوْ قَٰتَلَكُمُ ٱلَّذِينَ كَفَرُوا۟
لَوَلَّوُا۟ ٱلْأَدْبَٰرَ ثُمَّ لَا يَجِدُونَ وَلِيًّا وَلَا نَصِيرًا ﴿٢٢﴾ سُنَّةَ
ٱللَّهِ ٱلَّتِى قَدْ خَلَتْ مِن قَبْلُ ۖ وَلَن تَجِدَ لِسُنَّةِ ٱللَّهِ تَبْدِيلًا ﴿٢٣﴾
وَهُوَ ٱلَّذِى كَفَّ أَيْدِيَهُمْ عَنكُمْ وَأَيْدِيَكُمْ عَنْهُم بِبَطْنِ مَكَّةَ مِنۢ
بَعْدِ أَنْ أَظْفَرَكُمْ عَلَيْهِمْ ۚ وَكَانَ ٱللَّهُ بِمَا تَعْمَلُونَ بَصِيرًا ﴿٢٤﴾ هُمُ
ٱلَّذِينَ كَفَرُوا۟ وَصَدُّوكُمْ عَنِ ٱلْمَسْجِدِ ٱلْحَرَامِ وَٱلْهَدْىَ
مَعْكُوفًا أَن يَبْلُغَ مَحِلَّهُۥ ۚ وَلَوْلَا رِجَالٌ مُّؤْمِنُونَ وَنِسَآءٌ مُّؤْمِنَٰتٌ
لَّمْ تَعْلَمُوهُمْ أَن تَطَـُٔوهُمْ فَتُصِيبَكُم مِّنْهُم مَّعَرَّةٌۢ بِغَيْرِ عِلْمٍ ۖ
لِّيُدْخِلَ ٱللَّهُ فِى رَحْمَتِهِۦ مَن يَشَآءُ ۚ لَوْ تَزَيَّلُوا۟ لَعَذَّبْنَا ٱلَّذِينَ
كَفَرُوا۟ مِنْهُمْ عَذَابًا أَلِيمًا ﴿٢٥﴾ إِذْ جَعَلَ ٱلَّذِينَ كَفَرُوا۟
فِى قُلُوبِهِمُ ٱلْحَمِيَّةَ حَمِيَّةَ ٱلْجَٰهِلِيَّةِ فَأَنزَلَ ٱللَّهُ سَكِينَتَهُۥ
عَلَىٰ رَسُولِهِۦ وَعَلَى ٱلْمُؤْمِنِينَ وَأَلْزَمَهُمْ كَلِمَةَ ٱلتَّقْوَىٰ
وَكَانُوٓا۟ أَحَقَّ بِهَا وَأَهْلَهَا ۚ وَكَانَ ٱللَّهُ بِكُلِّ شَىْءٍ عَلِيمًا ﴿٢٦﴾
لَّقَدْ صَدَقَ ٱللَّهُ رَسُولَهُ ٱلرُّءْيَا بِٱلْحَقِّ ۖ لَتَدْخُلُنَّ ٱلْمَسْجِدَ
ٱلْحَرَامَ إِن شَآءَ ٱللَّهُ ءَامِنِينَ مُحَلِّقِينَ رُءُوسَكُمْ وَمُقَصِّرِينَ
لَا تَخَافُونَ ۖ فَعَلِمَ مَا لَمْ تَعْلَمُوا۟ فَجَعَلَ مِن دُونِ ذَٰلِكَ
فَتْحًا قَرِيبًا ﴿٢٧﴾ هُوَ ٱلَّذِىٓ أَرْسَلَ رَسُولَهُۥ بِٱلْهُدَىٰ وَدِينِ

they would fight Quraysh and would not flee from death. ***He*** (Allah) ***knew what was in their hearts*** by way of truthfulness and fidelity ***and sent down serenity to them, and has rewarded them with an imminent victory*** – and the imminent victory was at Khaybar after they had left Ḥudaybiyya –

19. ***… and with much booty which they will take*** at Khaybar. ***Allah is Almighty, All-Wise.***

20. ***Allah has promised you much booty which you will take*** in conquests, ***and has hastened this*** booty at Khaybar ***for you and held people's hands back from you*** – from harming your families, when you set out after the Jews plotted against you; but Allah cast fear into their hearts – ***so that it*** (its imminence) ***might be a Sign to the believers*** – so they could be thankful for victory – ***and so that He might guide you*** in victory ***to a straight path*** – the path of reliance on Him and entrusting your affairs to Him.

21. ***And other booty*** – meaning the wealth of the Persians and Byzantines – ***which you do not yet have the power to take – Allah has already encompassed it*** in knowledge and knows that you will take it. ***Allah has power over all things.***

22. ***If those who disbelieved*** at Ḥudaybiyya ***should fight you, they would turn their backs and then find no one to protect or help them.***

23. ***That is Allah's pattern which has passed away before*** – meaning defeat for the unbelievers and victory for the believers; ***you will not find any changing in the pattern of Allah.***

24. ***It is He who held their hands back from you, and your hands from them in the valley of Makka*** – at Ḥudaybiyya – ***after giving you the upper hand over them.*** Eight of them went around your army to get at you and they were captured and brought to the Messenger of Allah, may Allah bless him and grant him peace, who pardoned them and let them go. That was the reason for the truce. ***Allah sees what you do*** (read as *ta'malūna*, and *ya'malūna*, "what they do").

25. ***They are those who disbelieved and debarred you from al-Masjid al-Ḥarām*** – and prevented you from reaching it – ***and prevented the sacrifice*** – the sacrificial camels – ***from reaching its***

proper place where they are normally sacrificed within the confines of the *Ḥaram*. ***Had it not been for some men and women who are believers*** – who were still in Makka with the unbelievers – ***whom you did not know*** – of whose belief you are unaware – ***and might trample underfoot*** – you might slay them together with the unbelievers if you were given permission to conquer it – ***and so unknowingly incur blame on their account*** for the sin of killing them – ***so that Allah might admit into His mercy those He wills*** – such as those believers – ***and had those among them*** (the people of Makka) ***who disbelieve been clearly distinguishable*** from the believers ***We would have punished them with a painful punishment*** by allowing you to conquer it.

26. ***Those who disbelieve filled their hearts with fanatical rage*** (stubborn unbelief) – ***the fanatical rage of the Time of Ignorance*** – which was demonstrated by their barring the Prophet, may Allah bless him and grant him peace, and his Companions from *al-Masjid al-Ḥarām*, and by other things; ***and Allah sent down serenity upon His Messenger and to the believers*** – and they made peace with them on the basis that they could return the following year, and rage did not affect them as it did the unbelievers, causing the latter to fight them – ***and bound them*** (the believers) ***to the expression of godfearing*** – the statement: 'There is no god but Allah; Muḥammad is the Messenger of Allah', which is connected to being godfearing because it is the reason for it – ***which they had most right to and were most entitled to.*** They were more entitled to make that statement than the unbelievers. ***Allah has knowledge of all things.*** Allah always has knowledge of all things, and part of Allah's knowledge is that they were the most entitled to it.

27. ***Allah has confirmed His Messenger's vision with truth.*** In the year of al-Ḥudaybiyya, before he set out, the Messenger of Allah, may Allah bless him and grant him peace, had a dream that he and his Companions would enter Makka in safety, shaving their heads and cutting their hair short. He told his Companions about it, and they were filled with joy. When the unbelievers blocked them at al-Ḥudaybiyya and they had to turn back, that was hard for them and some of the hypocrites expressed their doubts. Then this was revealed – ***'You will enter al-Masjid al-Ḥarām in safety, Allah will -***

ٱلْحَقِّ لِيُظْهِرَهُۥ عَلَى ٱلدِّينِ كُلِّهِۦ ۚ وَكَفَىٰ بِٱللَّهِ شَهِيدًا ﴿٢٨﴾
مُّحَمَّدٌ رَّسُولُ ٱللَّهِ ۚ وَٱلَّذِينَ مَعَهُۥٓ أَشِدَّآءُ عَلَى ٱلْكُفَّارِ رُحَمَآءُ بَيْنَهُمْ ۖ
تَرَىٰهُمْ رُكَّعًا سُجَّدًا يَبْتَغُونَ فَضْلًا مِّنَ ٱللَّهِ وَرِضْوَٰنًا ۖ سِيمَاهُمْ
فِى وُجُوهِهِم مِّنْ أَثَرِ ٱلسُّجُودِ ۚ ذَٰلِكَ مَثَلُهُمْ فِى ٱلتَّوْرَىٰةِ ۚ وَمَثَلُهُمْ
فِى ٱلْإِنجِيلِ كَزَرْعٍ أَخْرَجَ شَطْـَٔهُۥ فَـَٔازَرَهُۥ فَٱسْتَغْلَظَ فَٱسْتَوَىٰ
عَلَىٰ سُوقِهِۦ يُعْجِبُ ٱلزُّرَّاعَ لِيَغِيظَ بِهِمُ ٱلْكُفَّارَ ۗ وَعَدَ ٱللَّهُ ٱلَّذِينَ
ءَامَنُوا۟ وَعَمِلُوا۟ ٱلصَّـٰلِحَـٰتِ مِنْهُم مَّغْفِرَةً وَأَجْرًا عَظِيمًۢا ﴿٢٩﴾

ing – mentioned for the blessing of it and confirming Allah's hand in it, ***shaving*** some of ***your heads*** completely ***and*** some of you merely ***cutting your hair, without any fear.' He knew what you did not know*** about the benefits of this truce ***and ordained, in place of this*** thwarted entry into Makka, ***an imminent victory*** – the conquest of Khaybar and the realisation of the Prophet's vision in the following year.

28. ***It is He who sent His Messenger with the Guidance and the*** **Dīn** ***of Truth to exalt it over every other*** **dīn*****; and Allah suffices as a witness*** that you have been sent with what has been mentioned.

29. ***Muḥammad is the Messenger of Allah, and those who are with him*** – his Companions among the believers – ***are fierce to the unbelievers***, and do not show mercy to them, ***merciful to one another*** – gentle with one another, and showing mutual love as between parents and their children. ***You see them bowing and prostrating, seeking Allah's good favour and His pleasure. Their mark is on their faces*** – light and brightness by which they will be recognised in the Next World since they prostrated themselves in this world – ***the traces of prostration. That is their likeness*** and description ***in the Torah. And their likeness in the Gospel is that of a seed which puts up a shoot*** (read as *shaṭ'a* and *shaṭa'a*) ***and makes it strong*** (read as *fa-āzzarahu* and *fa-azzarahu*) ***so that it thickens and grows up straight upon its stalk, filling the sowers with delight***: when farmers see their crops like this, they are delighted by them because of their beauty. The Companions, may Allah be pleased with them, are likened to that because they began as a few and then became many, and were strong in the best human qualities – ***so that by them He may infuriate the unbelievers.*** The unbelievers are enraged that the believers are like that. ***Allah has promised those of them who believe and do right actions*** – the Companions who are like that – ***forgiveness and an immense reward.*** Those who are like that after them will also receive the same.

سُورَةُ الحُجُرَاتِ

بِسْمِ ٱللَّهِ ٱلرَّحْمَٰنِ ٱلرَّحِيمِ

يَٰٓأَيُّهَا ٱلَّذِينَ ءَامَنُوا۟ لَا تُقَدِّمُوا۟ بَيْنَ يَدَىِ ٱللَّهِ وَرَسُولِهِۦ ۖ وَٱتَّقُوا۟ ٱللَّهَ ۚ
إِنَّ ٱللَّهَ سَمِيعٌ عَلِيمٌ ﴿١﴾ يَٰٓأَيُّهَا ٱلَّذِينَ ءَامَنُوا۟ لَا تَرْفَعُوٓا۟ أَصْوَٰتَكُمْ
فَوْقَ صَوْتِ ٱلنَّبِىِّ وَلَا تَجْهَرُوا۟ لَهُۥ بِٱلْقَوْلِ كَجَهْرِ بَعْضِكُمْ
لِبَعْضٍ أَن تَحْبَطَ أَعْمَٰلُكُمْ وَأَنتُمْ لَا تَشْعُرُونَ ﴿٢﴾ إِنَّ ٱلَّذِينَ
يَغُضُّونَ أَصْوَٰتَهُمْ عِندَ رَسُولِ ٱللَّهِ أُو۟لَٰٓئِكَ ٱلَّذِينَ ٱمْتَحَنَ ٱللَّهُ
قُلُوبَهُمْ لِلتَّقْوَىٰ ۚ لَهُم مَّغْفِرَةٌ وَأَجْرٌ عَظِيمٌ ﴿٣﴾ إِنَّ ٱلَّذِينَ
يُنَادُونَكَ مِن وَرَآءِ ٱلْحُجُرَٰتِ أَكْثَرُهُمْ لَا يَعْقِلُونَ ﴿٤﴾
وَلَوْ أَنَّهُمْ صَبَرُوا۟ حَتَّىٰ تَخْرُجَ إِلَيْهِمْ لَكَانَ خَيْرًا لَّهُمْ ۚ وَٱللَّهُ غَفُورٌ
رَّحِيمٌ ﴿٥﴾ يَٰٓأَيُّهَا ٱلَّذِينَ ءَامَنُوٓا۟ إِن جَآءَكُمْ فَاسِقٌۢ بِنَبَإٍ فَتَبَيَّنُوٓا۟
أَن تُصِيبُوا۟ قَوْمًۢا بِجَهَٰلَةٍ فَتُصْبِحُوا۟ عَلَىٰ مَا فَعَلْتُمْ نَٰدِمِينَ ﴿٦﴾
وَٱعْلَمُوٓا۟ أَنَّ فِيكُمْ رَسُولَ ٱللَّهِ ۚ لَوْ يُطِيعُكُمْ فِى كَثِيرٍ مِّنَ ٱلْأَمْرِ لَعَنِتُّمْ
وَلَٰكِنَّ ٱللَّهَ حَبَّبَ إِلَيْكُمُ ٱلْإِيمَٰنَ وَزَيَّنَهُۥ فِى قُلُوبِكُمْ وَكَرَّهَ إِلَيْكُمُ
ٱلْكُفْرَ وَٱلْفُسُوقَ وَٱلْعِصْيَانَ ۚ أُو۟لَٰٓئِكَ هُمُ ٱلرَّٰشِدُونَ ﴿٧﴾
فَضْلًا مِّنَ ٱللَّهِ وَنِعْمَةً ۚ وَٱللَّهُ عَلِيمٌ حَكِيمٌ ﴿٨﴾ وَإِن طَآئِفَتَانِ
مِنَ ٱلْمُؤْمِنِينَ ٱقْتَتَلُوا۟ فَأَصْلِحُوا۟ بَيْنَهُمَا ۖ فَإِنۢ بَغَتْ إِحْدَىٰهُمَا
عَلَى ٱلْأُخْرَىٰ فَقَٰتِلُوا۟ ٱلَّتِى تَبْغِى حَتَّىٰ تَفِىٓءَ إِلَىٰٓ أَمْرِ ٱللَّهِ ۚ فَإِن فَآءَتْ
فَأَصْلِحُوا۟ بَيْنَهُمَا بِٱلْعَدْلِ وَأَقْسِطُوٓا۟ ۖ إِنَّ ٱللَّهَ يُحِبُّ ٱلْمُقْسِطِينَ
﴿٩﴾ إِنَّمَا ٱلْمُؤْمِنُونَ إِخْوَةٌ فَأَصْلِحُوا۟ بَيْنَ أَخَوَيْكُمْ ۚ وَٱتَّقُوا۟ ٱللَّهَ

49. *Sūrat al-Ḥujurāt*
The Private Quarters

This *sūra* is Madinan and it has 18 *āyat*s.

1. ***You who believe, do not put yourselves forward in front of Allah and of His Messenger*** – do not act or speak before Allah and His Messenger who conveys His Message: in other words, without their permission***; and be fearful of Allah. Allah is All-Hearing*** of your words***, All-Knowing*** of your actions. This was revealed about a disagreement between Abū Bakr and 'Umar, may Allah be pleased with both of them, which took place in the presence of the Prophet, may Allah bless him and grant him peace, about whether to put al-Aqra' ibn Ḥābis or al-Qa'qā' ibn Ma'bad in command.

2. Then this was revealed about anyone who raises his voice in the presence of the Prophet, may Allah bless him and grant him peace: ***You who believe, do not raise your voices***, when you speak, ***above the voice of the Prophet*** when he speaks***; and do not be as loud when speaking*** privately ***to him as you are when speaking to one another*** – to show respect to him – ***lest your actions should come to nothing*** by your doing so ***without your realising it.*** This was revealed about those who used to lower their voices in the presence of the Prophet, may Allah bless him and grant him peace, such as Abū Bakr, 'Umar and others, may Allah be pleased with them.

3. ***Those who lower their voices when they are with the Messenger of Allah are people whose hearts Allah has tested for fearfulness of Him*** – so that their fearfulness of Him becomes evident. ***They will have forgiveness and an immense reward*** (Paradise).

4. Then this was revealed about some people who came at midday while the Prophet, may Allah bless him and grant him peace, was in his house and called out to him. ***As for those who call out to you from outside your private quarters,*** meaning the rooms of the wives of the Prophet, may Allah bless him and grant him peace. They used to call to him from behind the wall because they did not know which room he was in. The desert Arabs did this out of their coarseness and rudeness – ***most of them do not use their intellect*** and understand that what they do is incompatible with respect for him.

5. ***If they had only been patient until you came out to them, it would have been better for them. But Allah is Ever-Forgiving, Most Merciful*** to those of them who repented. This was revealed about al-Walīd ibn 'Uqba. The Prophet, may Allah bless him and grant him peace, sent him to the Banū'l-Muṣṭaliq to take their *zakāt*. He feared them because of a vendetta from the time of the Jāhiliyya. He returned and said that they had refused to pay the *zakāt* and had tried to kill him. The Prophet, may Allah bless him and grant him peace, intended to attack them, but they came and denied what al-Walid had said about them.

6. ***You who believe, if a deviator brings you a report, scrutinize it carefully*** (read as *tabayyanū* and also *tathabbatū,* from the root, "to make firm") – to ascertain whether it is true or a lie – ***in case you attack people in ignorance*** – out of fear that you might assault a people wrongly – ***and so come to greatly regret what you have done*** – your mistaken attack. The Prophet, may Allah bless him and grant him peace, sent Khālid to them after they had returned to their land; he only experienced obedience and good from them and reported that to the Prophet, may Allah bless him and grant him peace.

7. ***Know that the Messenger of Allah is among you.*** Do not give false reports, because Allah will inform him of the matter. ***If he were to obey you in many things*** which you tell him which are different from the truth of the matter, ***you would suffer for it*** by incurring the sin of its consequences. ***But Allah has given you love of belief and made it pleasing to your hearts, and has made unbelief, deviance and disobedience hateful to you. People such as these are rightly guided*** and are firm in their *dīn*.

8. ***It is a great favour from Allah and a blessing. Allah is All-Knowing*** of them, ***All-Wise*** in bestowing blessing on them.

9. ***If two parties of the believers fight*** – the plural rather than the dual is used for the verb "fight" because a "party" includes a number of people and so is considered to have a plural rather than singular meaning – ***make peace between them.*** This *āyat* was revealed about a case in which the Prophet, may Allah bless him and grant him

لَعَلَّكُمْ تُرْحَمُونَ ﴿١٠﴾ يَٰٓأَيُّهَا ٱلَّذِينَ ءَامَنُوا۟ لَا يَسْخَرْ قَوْمٌ مِّن قَوْمٍ
عَسَىٰٓ أَن يَكُونُوا۟ خَيْرًا مِّنْهُمْ وَلَا نِسَآءٌ مِّن نِّسَآءٍ عَسَىٰٓ أَن يَكُنَّ خَيْرًا
مِّنْهُنَّ ۖ وَلَا تَلْمِزُوٓا۟ أَنفُسَكُمْ وَلَا تَنَابَزُوا۟ بِٱلْأَلْقَٰبِ ۖ بِئْسَ ٱلِٱسْمُ
ٱلْفُسُوقُ بَعْدَ ٱلْإِيمَٰنِ ۚ وَمَن لَّمْ يَتُبْ فَأُو۟لَٰٓئِكَ هُمُ ٱلظَّٰلِمُونَ ﴿١١﴾
يَٰٓأَيُّهَا ٱلَّذِينَ ءَامَنُوا۟ ٱجْتَنِبُوا۟ كَثِيرًا مِّنَ ٱلظَّنِّ إِنَّ بَعْضَ ٱلظَّنِّ إِثْمٌ ۖ
وَلَا تَجَسَّسُوا۟ وَلَا يَغْتَب بَّعْضُكُم بَعْضًا ۚ أَيُحِبُّ أَحَدُكُمْ أَن
يَأْكُلَ لَحْمَ أَخِيهِ مَيْتًا فَكَرِهْتُمُوهُ ۚ وَٱتَّقُوا۟ ٱللَّهَ ۚ إِنَّ ٱللَّهَ تَوَّابٌ
رَّحِيمٌ ﴿١٢﴾ يَٰٓأَيُّهَا ٱلنَّاسُ إِنَّا خَلَقْنَٰكُم مِّن ذَكَرٍ وَأُنثَىٰ وَجَعَلْنَٰكُمْ
شُعُوبًا وَقَبَآئِلَ لِتَعَارَفُوٓا۟ ۚ إِنَّ أَكْرَمَكُمْ عِندَ ٱللَّهِ أَتْقَىٰكُمْ ۚ إِنَّ ٱللَّهَ
عَلِيمٌ خَبِيرٌ ﴿١٣﴾ ۞ قَالَتِ ٱلْأَعْرَابُ ءَامَنَّا ۖ قُل لَّمْ تُؤْمِنُوا۟ وَلَٰكِن
قُولُوٓا۟ أَسْلَمْنَا وَلَمَّا يَدْخُلِ ٱلْإِيمَٰنُ فِى قُلُوبِكُمْ ۖ وَإِن تُطِيعُوا۟ ٱللَّهَ
وَرَسُولَهُۥ لَا يَلِتْكُم مِّنْ أَعْمَٰلِكُمْ شَيْـًٔا ۚ إِنَّ ٱللَّهَ غَفُورٌ رَّحِيمٌ ﴿١٤﴾
إِنَّمَا ٱلْمُؤْمِنُونَ ٱلَّذِينَ ءَامَنُوا۟ بِٱللَّهِ وَرَسُولِهِۦ ثُمَّ لَمْ يَرْتَابُوا۟
وَجَٰهَدُوا۟ بِأَمْوَٰلِهِمْ وَأَنفُسِهِمْ فِى سَبِيلِ ٱللَّهِ ۚ أُو۟لَٰٓئِكَ هُمُ
ٱلصَّٰدِقُونَ ﴿١٥﴾ قُلْ أَتُعَلِّمُونَ ٱللَّهَ بِدِينِكُمْ وَٱللَّهُ
يَعْلَمُ مَا فِى ٱلسَّمَٰوَٰتِ وَمَا فِى ٱلْأَرْضِ ۚ وَٱللَّهُ بِكُلِّ شَىْءٍ عَلِيمٌ
﴿١٦﴾ يَمُنُّونَ عَلَيْكَ أَنْ أَسْلَمُوا۟ ۖ قُل لَّا تَمُنُّوا۟ عَلَىَّ إِسْلَٰمَكُم ۖ بَلِ ٱللَّهُ
يَمُنُّ عَلَيْكُمْ أَنْ هَدَىٰكُمْ لِلْإِيمَٰنِ إِن كُنتُمْ صَٰدِقِينَ ﴿١٧﴾ إِنَّ ٱللَّهَ
يَعْلَمُ غَيْبَ ٱلسَّمَٰوَٰتِ وَٱلْأَرْضِ ۚ وَٱللَّهُ بَصِيرٌۢ بِمَا تَعْمَلُونَ ﴿١٨﴾

peace, rode a donkey and passed by Ibn Ubayy. The donkey urinated and Ibn Ubayy held his nose. Ibn Rawāḥa said, "By Allah, the urine of his donkey is more fragrant than your musk!" Words were exchanged between the two groups of people and they began to hit one another with their hands, sandals and palm branches. ***But if one of them attacks the other unjustly, fight the attackers until they revert to Allah's command*** (the truth). ***If they revert, make peace between them with justice, and be even-handed. Allah loves those who are even-handed.***

10. ***The believers are brothers*** in the *dīn*, ***so make peace between your brothers*** (read as *akhawaykum* and *ikhwatikum*) in any disputes they have***; and be fearful of Allah so that perhaps you may gain mercy.***

11. This *āyat* was revealed about the delegation of Tamīm when they mocked the poor Muslims such as 'Ammār and Ṣuhayb. ***You who believe, people should not ridicule*** – treat with mockery and derision – ***others who may be better than themselves*** in the sight of Allah, ***nor should any women ridicule other women who may be better than themselves. And do not find fault with one another or insult each other with derogatory nicknames*** – names which the person dislikes, such as "O deviant" and "O unbeliever"***. How evil it is to have a name for evil conduct*** – because of ridicule, fault-finding and insult – ***after coming to belief!*** This sort of mockery and insinuation are very evil. ***Those people who do not turn from it are wrongdoers.***

12. ***You who believe, avoid most suspicion. Indeed some suspicion is a crime.*** In fact much of it is, as for instance having a bad opinion of the people of good among the believers who are the majority of them, whereas the deviants among them are few. There is no sin in mentioning what the deviants do publicly. ***And do not spy*** – which means seeking out the faults and shortcomings of Muslims by investigating them – ***and do not backbite one another*** by mentioning anything about someone which he would dislike, even if it is true. ***Would any of you like to eat his brother's dead flesh*** (read as *maytan* and *mayyitan*)***? No, you would hate it.*** Backbiting him while he is alive is like eating his flesh after he is dead. As you detest the idea of the latter, you should also detest the former. ***And be fearful of***

Allah. Fear the punishment of Allah and avoid slander by repenting of it. ***Allah is Ever-Relenting*** – accepting the repentance of those who repent, ***Most Merciful*** to them.

13. ***Mankind, We created you from a male and female*** – Ādam and Ḥawwā' – ***and made you into peoples*** – the word *shu'ūb* (peoples), the plural of *sha'b*, represents the broadest type of affiliation between people – ***and tribes*** – the word *qabā'il* (tribes), the plural of *qabīla*, is the next level down, then come subtribes (*'amā'ir*), then *buṭūn*, then *afkhād*, and then *faṣā'il*. An example of this is that Khuzayma is a people; Kināna is a tribe; Quraysh is an *'imāra;* Quṣayy is a *baṭn;* Hāshim is a *fakhdh*, and al-'Abbās is a *faṣīla* – ***so that you might come to know each other*** – and not boast about high lineage when it is only by being more godfearing that one person can be considered better than another, because: ***the noblest among you in Allah's sight is the one who is most godfearing. Allah is All-Knowing, All-Aware*** of your inward.

14. ***The desert Arabs*** – specifically a group of the Banū Asad – ***say, 'We believe*** in our hearts.' ***Say*** to them: ***'You do not believe. Say rather, "We have become Muslim*** outwardly," ***for belief has not yet entered into your hearts. If you obey Allah and His Messenger*** by faith and in other ways, ***He will not undervalue*** (read as *yalitkum* and *ya'litkum*) the reward for ***your actions in any way. Allah is Ever-Forgiving*** to the believers, ***Most Merciful*** to them.'

15. ***The*** true ***believers are only those who believe in Allah and His Messenger and then have had no doubt*** regarding their faith ***and have done* jihād *with their wealth and themselves in the Way of Allah.*** Their *jihād* displays the sincerity of their faith. ***They are the ones who are true to their word*** in their faith, not those who say "We believe," but in whom nothing more than Islam exists in.

16. ***Say*** to them: ***'Do you presume to teach Allah your* dīn *when Allah knows everything in the heavens and everything in the earth? Allah has knowledge of all things.'***

17. ***They think they have done you a favour by becoming Muslims*** without fighting, as opposed to others who became Muslim after fighting him! ***Say: 'Do not consider your Islam a favour to me. No***

لَعَلَّكُمۡ تُرۡحَمُونَ ١٠ يَٰٓأَيُّهَا ٱلَّذِينَ ءَامَنُواْ لَا يَسۡخَرۡ قَوۡمٞ مِّن قَوۡمٍ
عَسَىٰٓ أَن يَكُونُواْ خَيۡرٗا مِّنۡهُمۡ وَلَا نِسَآءٞ مِّن نِّسَآءٍ عَسَىٰٓ أَن يَكُنَّ خَيۡرٗا
مِّنۡهُنَّۖ وَلَا تَلۡمِزُوٓاْ أَنفُسَكُمۡ وَلَا تَنَابَزُواْ بِٱلۡأَلۡقَٰبِۖ بِئۡسَ ٱلِٱسۡمُ
ٱلۡفُسُوقُ بَعۡدَ ٱلۡإِيمَٰنِۚ وَمَن لَّمۡ يَتُبۡ فَأُوْلَٰٓئِكَ هُمُ ٱلظَّٰلِمُونَ ١١
يَٰٓأَيُّهَا ٱلَّذِينَ ءَامَنُواْ ٱجۡتَنِبُواْ كَثِيرٗا مِّنَ ٱلظَّنِّ إِنَّ بَعۡضَ ٱلظَّنِّ إِثۡمٞۖ
وَلَا تَجَسَّسُواْ وَلَا يَغۡتَب بَّعۡضُكُم بَعۡضًاۚ أَيُحِبُّ أَحَدُكُمۡ أَن
يَأۡكُلَ لَحۡمَ أَخِيهِ مَيۡتٗا فَكَرِهۡتُمُوهُۚ وَٱتَّقُواْ ٱللَّهَۚ إِنَّ ٱللَّهَ تَوَّابٞ
رَّحِيمٞ ١٢ يَٰٓأَيُّهَا ٱلنَّاسُ إِنَّا خَلَقۡنَٰكُم مِّن ذَكَرٖ وَأُنثَىٰ وَجَعَلۡنَٰكُمۡ
شُعُوبٗا وَقَبَآئِلَ لِتَعَارَفُوٓاْۚ إِنَّ أَكۡرَمَكُمۡ عِندَ ٱللَّهِ أَتۡقَىٰكُمۡۚ إِنَّ ٱللَّهَ
عَلِيمٌ خَبِيرٞ ١٣ ۞ قَالَتِ ٱلۡأَعۡرَابُ ءَامَنَّاۖ قُل لَّمۡ تُؤۡمِنُواْ وَلَٰكِن
قُولُوٓاْ أَسۡلَمۡنَا وَلَمَّا يَدۡخُلِ ٱلۡإِيمَٰنُ فِي قُلُوبِكُمۡۖ وَإِن تُطِيعُواْ ٱللَّهَ
وَرَسُولَهُۥ لَا يَلِتۡكُم مِّنۡ أَعۡمَٰلِكُمۡ شَيۡـًٔاۚ إِنَّ ٱللَّهَ غَفُورٞ رَّحِيمٌ ١٤
إِنَّمَا ٱلۡمُؤۡمِنُونَ ٱلَّذِينَ ءَامَنُواْ بِٱللَّهِ وَرَسُولِهِۦ ثُمَّ لَمۡ يَرۡتَابُواْ
وَجَٰهَدُواْ بِأَمۡوَٰلِهِمۡ وَأَنفُسِهِمۡ فِي سَبِيلِ ٱللَّهِۚ أُوْلَٰٓئِكَ هُمُ
ٱلصَّٰدِقُونَ ١٥ قُلۡ أَتُعَلِّمُونَ ٱللَّهَ بِدِينِكُمۡ وَٱللَّهُ
يَعۡلَمُ مَا فِي ٱلسَّمَٰوَٰتِ وَمَا فِي ٱلۡأَرۡضِۚ وَٱللَّهُ بِكُلِّ شَيۡءٍ عَلِيمٞ
١٦ يَمُنُّونَ عَلَيۡكَ أَنۡ أَسۡلَمُواْۖ قُل لَّا تَمُنُّواْ عَلَيَّ إِسۡلَٰمَكُمۖ بَلِ ٱللَّهُ
يَمُنُّ عَلَيۡكُمۡ أَنۡ هَدَىٰكُمۡ لِلۡإِيمَٰنِ إِن كُنتُمۡ صَٰدِقِينَ ١٧ إِنَّ ٱللَّهَ
يَعۡلَمُ غَيۡبَ ٱلسَّمَٰوَٰتِ وَٱلۡأَرۡضِۚ وَٱللَّهُ بَصِيرُۢ بِمَا تَعۡمَلُونَ ١٨

indeed! It is Allah who has favoured you by guiding you to belief if you are telling the truth in by saying that you believe.*'*

18. ***Allah knows the unseen things of the heavens and the earth. Allah sees what you do*** (read as *ta'malūna* and *ya'malūna*, "what they do"). Nothing is hidden from Him.

سُورَةُ قٓ

بِسۡمِ ٱللَّهِ ٱلرَّحۡمَٰنِ ٱلرَّحِيمِ

قٓۚ وَٱلۡقُرۡءَانِ ٱلۡمَجِيدِ ١ بَلۡ عَجِبُوٓاْ أَن جَآءَهُم مُّنذِرٞ مِّنۡهُمۡ
فَقَالَ ٱلۡكَٰفِرُونَ هَٰذَا شَيۡءٌ عَجِيبٌ ٢ أَءِذَا مِتۡنَا وَكُنَّا تُرَابٗاۖ ذَٰلِكَ
رَجۡعُۢ بَعِيدٞ ٣ قَدۡ عَلِمۡنَا مَا تَنقُصُ ٱلۡأَرۡضُ مِنۡهُمۡۖ وَعِندَنَا كِتَٰبٌ
حَفِيظُۢ ٤ بَلۡ كَذَّبُواْ بِٱلۡحَقِّ لَمَّا جَآءَهُمۡ فَهُمۡ فِيٓ أَمۡرٖ مَّرِيجٍ
٥ أَفَلَمۡ يَنظُرُوٓاْ إِلَى ٱلسَّمَآءِ فَوۡقَهُمۡ كَيۡفَ بَنَيۡنَٰهَا وَزَيَّنَّٰهَا
وَمَا لَهَا مِن فُرُوجٖ ٦ وَٱلۡأَرۡضَ مَدَدۡنَٰهَا وَأَلۡقَيۡنَا فِيهَا رَوَٰسِيَ
وَأَنۢبَتۡنَا فِيهَا مِن كُلِّ زَوۡجِۭ بَهِيجٖ ٧ تَبۡصِرَةٗ وَذِكۡرَىٰ لِكُلِّ عَبۡدٖ
مُّنِيبٖ ٨ وَنَزَّلۡنَا مِنَ ٱلسَّمَآءِ مَآءٗ مُّبَٰرَكٗا فَأَنۢبَتۡنَا بِهِۦ جَنَّٰتٖ
وَحَبَّ ٱلۡحَصِيدِ ٩ وَٱلنَّخۡلَ بَاسِقَٰتٖ لَّهَا طَلۡعٞ نَّضِيدٞ ١٠
رِّزۡقٗا لِّلۡعِبَادِۖ وَأَحۡيَيۡنَا بِهِۦ بَلۡدَةٗ مَّيۡتٗاۚ كَذَٰلِكَ ٱلۡخُرُوجُ ١١ كَذَّبَتۡ
قَبۡلَهُمۡ قَوۡمُ نُوحٖ وَأَصۡحَٰبُ ٱلرَّسِّ وَثَمُودُ ١٢ وَعَادٞ وَفِرۡعَوۡنُ وَإِخۡوَٰنُ
لُوطٖ ١٣ وَأَصۡحَٰبُ ٱلۡأَيۡكَةِ وَقَوۡمُ تُبَّعٖۚ كُلّٞ كَذَّبَ ٱلرُّسُلَ فَحَقَّ وَعِيدِ
١٤ أَفَعَيِينَا بِٱلۡخَلۡقِ ٱلۡأَوَّلِۚ بَلۡ هُمۡ فِي لَبۡسٖ مِّنۡ خَلۡقٖ جَدِيدٖ ١٥
وَلَقَدۡ خَلَقۡنَا ٱلۡإِنسَٰنَ وَنَعۡلَمُ مَا تُوَسۡوِسُ بِهِۦ نَفۡسُهُۥۖ وَنَحۡنُ أَقۡرَبُ إِلَيۡهِ
مِنۡ حَبۡلِ ٱلۡوَرِيدِ ١٦ إِذۡ يَتَلَقَّى ٱلۡمُتَلَقِّيَانِ عَنِ ٱلۡيَمِينِ وَعَنِ ٱلشِّمَالِ قَعِيدٞ
١٧ مَّا يَلۡفِظُ مِن قَوۡلٍ إِلَّا لَدَيۡهِ رَقِيبٌ عَتِيدٞ ١٨ وَجَآءَتۡ سَكۡرَةُ
ٱلۡمَوۡتِ بِٱلۡحَقِّۖ ذَٰلِكَ مَا كُنتَ مِنۡهُ تَحِيدُ ١٩ وَنُفِخَ فِي ٱلصُّورِۚ ذَٰلِكَ
يَوۡمُ ٱلۡوَعِيدِ ٢٠ وَجَآءَتۡ كُلُّ نَفۡسٖ مَّعَهَا سَآئِقٞ وَشَهِيدٞ ٢١ لَّقَدۡ

50. *Sūrat Qāf*
Qaf

This *sūra* is Makkan except *āyat* 38, which is Madinan. It has 45 *āyat*s.

1. ***Qaf.*** Allah knows best what the letter means. ***By the Glorious Qur'an!*** The Qur'an is noble even though the unbelievers of Makka did not believe in Muḥammad, may Allah bless him and grant him peace.

2. ***Nonetheless they are amazed that a warner*** – a Messenger, who frightens them about the Fire after the Resurrection – ***should have come to them from among themselves; and those who disbelieve say, 'What an extraordinary thing*** this warning is***!***

3. ***When we are dead and turned to dust . . . ? That would be a most unlikely return!'***

4. ***We know exactly how the earth eats them away. We possess an all-preserving Book*** – the Preserved Tablet which contains all decreed things**.**

5. ***But they denied the truth*** about the Prophet, may Allah bless him and grant him peace, and the Qur'an ***when it came to them. They are, therefore, in a very muddled state.*** Sometimes they said that he was a magician and the Qur'an magic, sometimes that he was a poet and the Qur'an poetry, and sometimes that he was a soothsayer and the Qur'an soothsaying.

6. ***Have they not looked at the sky above them*** with their eyes while reflecting with their intellects when they denied the Resurrection***: how We structured it*** without support ***and made it beautiful*** with stars ***and how there are no fissures in it*** to mar it***?***

7. ***And the earth: how We stretched it out*** on the surface of the water ***and cast firmly embedded mountains onto it*** to make it firm ***and caused luxuriant*** beautiful ***plants of every kind to grow in it…***

8. ***…an instruction and a reminder for every penitent human being.*** Allah did that so that people would see and to remind people to return to obedience to Him.

9. ***And We sent down blessed*** – meaning that great blessing results from it – ***water from the sky and made gardens grow by it and grain for harvesting…***

10. ***… and soaring*** – very tall – ***date-palms with layered spathes*** – their spathes are joined one to another…

11. ***…as provision for Our slaves. By it We brought a dead land to life; that*** bringing to life ***is how the Emergence*** from the graves ***will take place.*** How then can you deny it? When people look at these things and reflect on them, they should be able to understand what happens on the Last Day.

12. ***Before them the people of Nūḥ also denied the truth, and the Companions of Rass and Thamūd*** – Rass was a well around which they stayed with their flocks, worshipping idols. It is said that their Prophet was Ḥanẓala ibn Ṣafwān, but it is also said that it is someone else. Thamūd were the people of Ṣāliḥ.

13. ***…and 'Ād*** – the people of Hūd – ***and Pharaoh and the brothers of Lūṭ…***

14. ***…and the Companions of the Thicket*** – the people of Shu'ayb – ***and the people of Tubba'.*** Tubba' was a king in Yemen who became Muslim and called his people to Islam, but they rejected him. ***Each one*** of those mentioned ***denied the Messengers*** as Quraysh have done, ***and My threat proved true.*** "The descent of the punishment was mandatory for all of them, so do not be grieved by the fact that Quraysh reject you."

15. ***Were We exhausted by the first creation?*** Allah was not tired by it, so He would certainly not be tired by regenerating it. ***Yet they are dubious about new creation*** on the Day of Resurrection.

16. ***We created man and We know what his own self whispers to him. We are nearer to him*** in Our knowledge ***than his jugular vein.***

17. ***And*** – it is said that "remember" is implied here – ***the two recording angels***, the two angels entrusted to man who register and confirm what he does, ***are recording, sitting on the right and on the left.***

18. ***He does not utter a single word without a watcher being by him, pen in hand!*** There is a guardian angel always present.

كُنتَ فِي غَفۡلَةٖ مِّنۡ هَٰذَا فَكَشَفۡنَا عَنكَ غِطَآءَكَ فَبَصَرُكَ ٱلۡيَوۡمَ حَدِيدٞ
٢٢ وَقَالَ قَرِينُهُۥ هَٰذَا مَا لَدَيَّ عَتِيدٌ ٢٣ أَلۡقِيَا فِي جَهَنَّمَ كُلَّ كَفَّارٍ
عَنِيدٖ ٢٤ مَّنَّاعٖ لِّلۡخَيۡرِ مُعۡتَدٖ مُّرِيبٍ ٢٥ ٱلَّذِي جَعَلَ مَعَ ٱللَّهِ إِلَٰهًا
ءَاخَرَ فَأَلۡقِيَاهُ فِي ٱلۡعَذَابِ ٱلشَّدِيدِ ٢٦ ۞ قَالَ قَرِينُهُۥ رَبَّنَا مَآ أَطۡغَيۡتُهُۥ
وَلَٰكِن كَانَ فِي ضَلَٰلِۭ بَعِيدٖ ٢٧ قَالَ لَا تَخۡتَصِمُواْ لَدَيَّ وَقَدۡ قَدَّمۡتُ
إِلَيۡكُم بِٱلۡوَعِيدِ ٢٨ مَا يُبَدَّلُ ٱلۡقَوۡلُ لَدَيَّ وَمَآ أَنَا۠ بِظَلَّٰمٖ لِّلۡعَبِيدِ ٢٩
يَوۡمَ نَقُولُ لِجَهَنَّمَ هَلِ ٱمۡتَلَأۡتِ وَتَقُولُ هَلۡ مِن مَّزِيدٖ ٣٠ وَأُزۡلِفَتِ
ٱلۡجَنَّةُ لِلۡمُتَّقِينَ غَيۡرَ بَعِيدٍ ٣١ هَٰذَا مَا تُوعَدُونَ لِكُلِّ أَوَّابٍ حَفِيظٖ
٣٢ مَّنۡ خَشِيَ ٱلرَّحۡمَٰنَ بِٱلۡغَيۡبِ وَجَآءَ بِقَلۡبٖ مُّنِيبٍ ٣٣ ٱدۡخُلُوهَا
بِسَلَٰمٖۖ ذَٰلِكَ يَوۡمُ ٱلۡخُلُودِ ٣٤ لَهُم مَّا يَشَآءُونَ فِيهَا وَلَدَيۡنَا مَزِيدٞ ٣٥
وَكَمۡ أَهۡلَكۡنَا قَبۡلَهُم مِّن قَرۡنٍ هُمۡ أَشَدُّ مِنۡهُم بَطۡشٗا فَنَقَّبُواْ فِي
ٱلۡبِلَٰدِ هَلۡ مِن مَّحِيصٍ ٣٦ إِنَّ فِي ذَٰلِكَ لَذِكۡرَىٰ لِمَن كَانَ
لَهُۥ قَلۡبٌ أَوۡ أَلۡقَى ٱلسَّمۡعَ وَهُوَ شَهِيدٞ ٣٧ وَلَقَدۡ خَلَقۡنَا
ٱلسَّمَٰوَٰتِ وَٱلۡأَرۡضَ وَمَا بَيۡنَهُمَا فِي سِتَّةِ أَيَّامٖ وَمَا مَسَّنَا
مِن لُّغُوبٖ ٣٨ فَٱصۡبِرۡ عَلَىٰ مَا يَقُولُونَ وَسَبِّحۡ بِحَمۡدِ رَبِّكَ
قَبۡلَ طُلُوعِ ٱلشَّمۡسِ وَقَبۡلَ ٱلۡغُرُوبِ ٣٩ وَمِنَ ٱلَّيۡلِ فَسَبِّحۡهُ
وَأَدۡبَٰرَ ٱلسُّجُودِ ٤٠ وَٱسۡتَمِعۡ يَوۡمَ يُنَادِ ٱلۡمُنَادِ مِن مَّكَانٖ قَرِيبٖ
٤١ يَوۡمَ يَسۡمَعُونَ ٱلصَّيۡحَةَ بِٱلۡحَقِّۚ ذَٰلِكَ يَوۡمُ ٱلۡخُرُوجِ ٤٢ إِنَّا
نَحۡنُ نُحۡيِۦ وَنُمِيتُ وَإِلَيۡنَا ٱلۡمَصِيرُ ٤٣ يَوۡمَ تَشَقَّقُ ٱلۡأَرۡضُ
عَنۡهُمۡ سِرَاعٗاۚ ذَٰلِكَ حَشۡرٌ عَلَيۡنَا يَسِيرٞ ٤٤ نَّحۡنُ أَعۡلَمُ بِمَا يَقُولُونَۖ
وَمَآ أَنتَ عَلَيۡهِم بِجَبَّارٖۖ فَذَكِّرۡ بِٱلۡقُرۡءَانِ مَن يَخَافُ وَعِيدِ ٤٥

19. ***The*** agony and ***throes of death come, revealing the truth*** of the Next World so that the one who previously denied it now sees it right before his eyes. That is the source of his agony. ***That is what*** you feared and ***you were trying to evade!***

20. ***The Trumpet*** blown for the Resurrection ***will be blown. That is the Day of the Threat*** when the punishment the unbelievers were threatened with will take place.

21. ***Every self will come*** when they are driven to the place of gathering ***together with a driver*** – an angel who drives him to it – ***and a witness*** who testifies against him regarding his actions. That witness consists of the person's own hands, feet and other limbs. Then the unbeliever will be told:

22. 'In the world ***you were heedless of this*** – what is happening to you today – ***so We have stripped you of your covering*** – your heedlessness, by what you witness today – ***and today your sight is sharp.'*** "Today your sight perceives what you used to deny in the world."

23. ***His inseparable comrade*** – his guardian angel – ***will say, 'This is what I have ready for you.'***

24. Mālik, the angel in charge of Hellfire will be told: ***'Hurl into Hell every obdurate unbeliever*** who denied the truth,

25. ***impeder of good*** – meaning here someone who refuses to pay *zakāt*, ***doubt-causing aggressor*** – someone who does wrong and has doubts about the *dīn* –

26. ***...who set up another god together with Allah. Hurl him into the terrible punishment.'***

27. ***His inseparable comrade*** – this time referring to Shayṭān – ***will say, 'Our Lord, I did not*** mislead him and ***make him overstep the limits. He was in any case far astray.'*** "I merely called him and he responded to me." He will say, "He made me overstep by calling to me."

28. ***He*** (Allah) ***will say, 'Do not argue in My presence*** – arguing will be of no benefit here – ***when I gave you advance warning*** in the world ***of the Threat*** – meaning of punishment in the Next World. "If you did not believe, then you must inevitably experience the punishment."

29. ***My Word, once given, is not subject to change; and I do not wrong My slaves.'*** "I will not punish them without them having done wrong." Allah says, *"Today there will be no injustice."* (40:17)

30. ***On the Day We say*** (read as *naqūlu*, also *yaqūlu*, "He says") ***to Hell, 'Are you full?'*** – this question demonstrates the realisation of Allah's promise to fill it – ***it will ask, 'Are there no more to come?'*** The second question is asked by Hell and it means, "I can only encompass what fills me up," which means that it is full.

31. ***And the Garden will be brought up close to those who are god - fearing, not far away*** – close to them so that they see it.

32. Then they will be told: ***'This*** – which is visible – ***is what you were promised*** (read as *tū'adūna*, also *yū'adūna*, "What they were promised") in the first world. ***It is for every careful penitent:***

33. ***...those who fear the All-Merciful in the Unseen*** – without having seen Him – ***and come with a contrite heart***, obeying Him. The godfearing will be told:

34. ***Enter it in peace*** – secure from any alarming thing, or with every kind of peace. ***This is the Day of Timeless Eternity*** – the Day on which people will be admitted to everlasting life in the Garden.*'*

35. ***They will have there everything they want, and with Us there is still more*** for what they did, more than they asked for.

36. ***How many generations*** of unbelievers ***before them*** (Quraysh) ***We destroyed who had greater force than them and scoured*** and spread through ***many lands! Did they*** or others ***find any way of escape*** from death*?* They did not.

37. ***There is a reminder in that*** which has been mentioned ***for anyone who has a heart*** (intelligence) ***or who listens well*** to the admonition, ***having seen the evidence*** with an attentive heart.

38. ***We created the heavens and the earth, and everything between them, in six days,*** the first day being Sunday and the last Friday, ***and We were not affected by fatigue.*** This was revealed to refute the Jews, who said that Allah rested on the Sabbath, and to negate the idea that He could be subject to fatigue. For Allah is exalted above the attributes of creatures and there is no contiguity between Him and others. *"His command when He desires a thing is simply to say to it, 'Be!' and it is."* (36:82)

39. This is addressed to the Prophet, may Allah bless him and grant him peace. ***So be patient in the face of what they*** (the Jews and others) ***say*** – in terms of anthropomorphism and denial – ***and glorify your Lord with praise before the rising of the sun*** – in the *Ṣubḥ* prayer – ***and before it sets*** – in the *Ẓuhr* and *'Aṣr* prayers.

40. ***And glorify Him during the night*** – in the *Maghrib* and *'Ishā'* prayers – ***and after*** (read as *adbār* and *idbā*) ***you have prostrated*** – meaning, "Pray the *nāfila* prayers which are *sunna* after the obligatory prayers." It is also said that what is meant is actual glorification at those times.

41. ***Listen out for the Day when the Summoner*** (Isrāfīl) ***shall call out from a nearby place*** – when he is at the Rock in Jerusalem, the closest place on earth to heaven. He will say, "O decayed bones, separated joints, shredded flesh and scattered hair! Allah commands you to come together for the rendering of Judgement."

42. ***The Day they*** (all creatures) ***hear the Blast in truth*** – the second Blast by Isrāfīl which is for the Resurrection, or it is possible that it is before and after his call ***that*** Day of the call and hearing it***: is the Day of Emergence*** from the graves. They will know the outcome of their denial.

43. ***It is We who give life and cause to die, and We are their final destination.***

44. ***The Day the earth splits open*** (read as *tashaqqaqu* and *tashshaqqaqu*) ***all around them as they come rushing forth: that is a gathering, easy for Us to accomplish.*** It is easy for Allah to bring things back to life after their annihilation and to gather people for the presentation and Reckoning.

45. ***We know best what they*** (the unbelievers of Quraysh) ***say. You are not a dictator over them.*** You cannot compel them to believe. This was before the command to fight in *jihād*. ***So remind with the Qur'an whoever fears My Threat*** – meaning the believers.

سُورَةُ الذَّارِيَاتِ

بِسْمِ اللَّهِ الرَّحْمَٰنِ الرَّحِيمِ

وَالذَّارِيَاتِ ذَرْوًا ﴿١﴾ فَالْحَامِلَاتِ وِقْرًا ﴿٢﴾ فَالْجَارِيَاتِ يُسْرًا ﴿٣﴾
فَالْمُقَسِّمَاتِ أَمْرًا ﴿٤﴾ إِنَّمَا تُوعَدُونَ لَصَادِقٌ ﴿٥﴾ وَإِنَّ الدِّينَ لَوَاقِعٌ ﴿٦﴾
وَالسَّمَاءِ ذَاتِ الْحُبُكِ ﴿٧﴾ إِنَّكُمْ لَفِي قَوْلٍ مُخْتَلِفٍ ﴿٨﴾ يُؤْفَكُ عَنْهُ مَنْ
أُفِكَ ﴿٩﴾ قُتِلَ الْخَرَّاصُونَ ﴿١٠﴾ الَّذِينَ هُمْ فِي غَمْرَةٍ سَاهُونَ ﴿١١﴾
يَسْأَلُونَ أَيَّانَ يَوْمُ الدِّينِ ﴿١٢﴾ يَوْمَ هُمْ عَلَى النَّارِ يُفْتَنُونَ ﴿١٣﴾ ذُوقُوا
فِتْنَتَكُمْ هَٰذَا الَّذِي كُنْتُمْ بِهِ تَسْتَعْجِلُونَ ﴿١٤﴾ إِنَّ الْمُتَّقِينَ فِي جَنَّاتٍ
وَعُيُونٍ ﴿١٥﴾ آخِذِينَ مَا آتَاهُمْ رَبُّهُمْ ۚ إِنَّهُمْ كَانُوا قَبْلَ ذَٰلِكَ مُحْسِنِينَ
﴿١٦﴾ كَانُوا قَلِيلًا مِنَ اللَّيْلِ مَا يَهْجَعُونَ ﴿١٧﴾ وَبِالْأَسْحَارِ هُمْ يَسْتَغْفِرُونَ
﴿١٨﴾ وَفِي أَمْوَالِهِمْ حَقٌّ لِلسَّائِلِ وَالْمَحْرُومِ ﴿١٩﴾ وَفِي الْأَرْضِ آيَاتٌ
لِلْمُوقِنِينَ ﴿٢٠﴾ وَفِي أَنْفُسِكُمْ ۚ أَفَلَا تُبْصِرُونَ ﴿٢١﴾ وَفِي السَّمَاءِ رِزْقُكُمْ
وَمَا تُوعَدُونَ ﴿٢٢﴾ فَوَرَبِّ السَّمَاءِ وَالْأَرْضِ إِنَّهُ لَحَقٌّ مِثْلَ مَا أَنَّكُمْ
تَنْطِقُونَ ﴿٢٣﴾ هَلْ أَتَاكَ حَدِيثُ ضَيْفِ إِبْرَاهِيمَ الْمُكْرَمِينَ ﴿٢٤﴾
إِذْ دَخَلُوا عَلَيْهِ فَقَالُوا سَلَامًا ۖ قَالَ سَلَامٌ قَوْمٌ مُنْكَرُونَ ﴿٢٥﴾ فَرَاغَ إِلَىٰ
أَهْلِهِ فَجَاءَ بِعِجْلٍ سَمِينٍ ﴿٢٦﴾ فَقَرَّبَهُ إِلَيْهِمْ قَالَ أَلَا تَأْكُلُونَ
﴿٢٧﴾ فَأَوْجَسَ مِنْهُمْ خِيفَةً ۖ قَالُوا لَا تَخَفْ ۖ وَبَشَّرُوهُ بِغُلَامٍ عَلِيمٍ
﴿٢٨﴾ فَأَقْبَلَتِ امْرَأَتُهُ فِي صَرَّةٍ فَصَكَّتْ وَجْهَهَا وَقَالَتْ عَجُوزٌ عَقِيمٌ
﴿٢٩﴾ قَالُوا كَذَٰلِكِ قَالَ رَبُّكِ ۖ إِنَّهُ هُوَ الْحَكِيمُ الْعَلِيمُ ﴿٣٠﴾
۞ قَالَ فَمَا خَطْبُكُمْ أَيُّهَا الْمُرْسَلُونَ ﴿٣١﴾ قَالُوا إِنَّا أُرْسِلْنَا إِلَىٰ قَوْمٍ

51. *Sūrat adh-Dhāriyāt* The Scatterers

This *sūra* is Makkan and has 60 *āyat*s.

1. ***By the scatterers scattering*** – the winds which scatter the dust and other things·

2. ***...and those bearing weighty loads*** – the clouds which bear water,

3. ***...and those speeding along with ease*** – ships which sail with the winds across the surface of the seas,

4. ***...and those apportioning the command*** – the angels who distribute provision, rain and other things between different lands and people with ease*!*

5. ***What you are promised*** regarding the Resurrection and other things ***is certainly true –***

6. ***...the Judgement*** – the Repayment after the Reckoning – ***will certainly take place!***

7. ***By Heaven with its oscillating orbits*** – there are paths through it in the same way as there are paths through the desert sand,

8. ***...you,*** people of Makka, ***certainly have differing beliefs*** – you say different things about the Prophet, may Allah bless him and grant him peace, and the Qur'an. It was said that he was a poet, magician or soothsayer, and that the Qur'an was poetry, magic or soothsaying.

9. ***Averted from it*** – or him, meaning from belief in the Prophet, may Allah bless him and grant him peace, or the Qur'an – ***is he who is averted*** – turned aside from guidance, in the foreknowledge of Allah.

10. ***Death to the conjecturers*** – may the liars be cursed*!* They are the ones with differing beliefs –

11. ***...those who flounder in a glut of ignorance*** – and are unmindful of the business of the Next World,

12. ***...asking, 'When is the Day of Judgement?'*** They ask the Prophet, may Allah bless him and grant him peace, this out of mockery.

13. ***On the Day they are tormented by the Fire***, they are punished in it, and the following will be said to them while they are being punished:

14. ***'Taste your torment! This is what you were trying to hasten:*** in this world out of mockery*!'*

15. ***The people who are godfearing will be among Gardens and Fountains,***

16. ***...receiving what their Lord has given them*** – meaning "obtaining in the Garden the good things and the reward their Lord had promised them." ***Certainly before that*** – before they entered the Garden – ***they were good-doers*** in this world**.**

17. ***The part of the night they spent asleep was small*** – they slept for a short portion of the night and prayed for the majority of it,

18. ***...and they would seek forgiveness before the dawn,*** with the words: "O Allah, forgive us!"**...**

19. ***...and beggars and the destitute*** – referring to people who do not beg because of their diffidence – ***received a due share of their wealth.***

20. ***There are certainly Signs in the earth for people with certainty*** – such as mountains, soil, seas, trees, fruits, plants and other things –

21. ***...and in yourselves*** there are signs ***as well*** – from the beginning of your gestation to its end, and in the wonders which the human body contains**.** ***Do you not then see?*** "Do you not see that and take it as evidence of your Maker and His power?"

22. ***Your provision is in heaven*** – a reference to the rain which sustains plant life from which much of our provision comes – ***and what you are promised***, which is the Resurrection and the reward or penalty that follow it, meaning that it is written in heaven.

23. ***By the Lord of heaven and earth, it*** (what you are promised) ***is certainly the truth, just as you have speech.*** "As you speak in reality, neaning you have knowledge of that *a priori* as it issues from you."

24. This is addressed to the Prophet, may Allah bless him and grant him peace. ***Has the story reached you of the honoured guests of Ibrāhīm?*** The honoured guests were angels. There were twelve, ten or three of them. Jibrīl was one of them.

25. ***When they entered his dwelling and said, 'Peace!' he said, 'Peace, to people we do not know.'*** He said to himself, "We do not recognise them."

26. ***So he slipped off*** secretly ***to his household and brought a fattened calf.*** The Qur'an says in *Sūrat Hūd* that it was roasted.

27. ***He offered it to them*** to eat, but they would not eat, ***and then exclaimed, 'Do you not then eat?'***

28. ***He felt afraid of them*** – and concealed this in himself – ***but they said, 'Do not be afraid!*** We are the messengers of your Lord', ***and gave him the good news of a son imbued with*** much ***knowledge.*** That was Isḥāq, as mentioned in *Sūrat Hūd.*

29. ***His wife*** – Sāra – ***came up with a shriek and struck her face and said, 'What, and me a barren old woman?*** Those like me do not give birth!' She was 99 and Ibrāhīm was 100, or he was 120 and she was 90.

30. ***They said, 'That is what your Lord says.*** That is our good news. ***He is the All-Wise*** in what He does, ***the All-Knowing*** of His creation.'

31. ***He inquired, 'What, then, is your business, O messengers?'***

32. ***They said, 'We have been sent to a people of evildoers*** (unbelievers) – the people of Lūṭ –

33. ***…to unleash upon them lumps of clay*** baked with fire …

34. ***…earmarked*** with the name of the person they are intended for ***by your Lord for the profligate*** on account of their unbelief.'

35. ***We brought out all the believers who were there,*** so that the unbelievers could be destroyed,

36. ***…but found in it only one house of Muslims***: Lūṭ and his sons, who were true in their hearts and performed acts of obedience with their limbs.

37. ***And We left a Sign*** of their destruction ***in it*** – after the unbelievers were destroyed there – ***for those who fear painful punishment*** and hence do not do the same as they did.

38. ***And also*** We left a Sign ***in*** the story of ***Mūsā, when We sent him to Pharaoh with clear authority*** – clear evidence.

مُّجْرِمِينَ ﴿٣٢﴾ لِنُرْسِلَ عَلَيْهِمْ حِجَارَةً مِّن طِينٍ ﴿٣٣﴾ مُّسَوَّمَةً عِندَ رَبِّكَ
لِلْمُسْرِفِينَ ﴿٣٤﴾ فَأَخْرَجْنَا مَن كَانَ فِيهَا مِنَ الْمُؤْمِنِينَ ﴿٣٥﴾ فَمَا وَجَدْنَا
فِيهَا غَيْرَ بَيْتٍ مِّنَ الْمُسْلِمِينَ ﴿٣٦﴾ وَتَرَكْنَا فِيهَا آيَةً لِّلَّذِينَ يَخَافُونَ
الْعَذَابَ الْأَلِيمَ ﴿٣٧﴾ وَفِي مُوسَىٰ إِذْ أَرْسَلْنَاهُ إِلَىٰ فِرْعَوْنَ بِسُلْطَانٍ
مُّبِينٍ ﴿٣٨﴾ فَتَوَلَّىٰ بِرُكْنِهِ وَقَالَ سَاحِرٌ أَوْ مَجْنُونٌ ﴿٣٩﴾ فَأَخَذْنَاهُ وَجُنُودَهُ
فَنَبَذْنَاهُمْ فِي الْيَمِّ وَهُوَ مُلِيمٌ ﴿٤٠﴾ وَفِي عَادٍ إِذْ أَرْسَلْنَا عَلَيْهِمُ الرِّيحَ
الْعَقِيمَ ﴿٤١﴾ مَا تَذَرُ مِن شَيْءٍ أَتَتْ عَلَيْهِ إِلَّا جَعَلَتْهُ كَالرَّمِيمِ ﴿٤٢﴾
وَفِي ثَمُودَ إِذْ قِيلَ لَهُمْ تَمَتَّعُوا حَتَّىٰ حِينٍ ﴿٤٣﴾ فَعَتَوْا عَنْ أَمْرِ رَبِّهِمْ
فَأَخَذَتْهُمُ الصَّاعِقَةُ وَهُمْ يَنظُرُونَ ﴿٤٤﴾ فَمَا اسْتَطَاعُوا مِن قِيَامٍ
وَمَا كَانُوا مُنتَصِرِينَ ﴿٤٥﴾ وَقَوْمَ نُوحٍ مِّن قَبْلُ إِنَّهُمْ كَانُوا قَوْمًا
فَاسِقِينَ ﴿٤٦﴾ وَالسَّمَاءَ بَنَيْنَاهَا بِأَيْدٍ وَإِنَّا لَمُوسِعُونَ ﴿٤٧﴾ وَالْأَرْضَ
فَرَشْنَاهَا فَنِعْمَ الْمَاهِدُونَ ﴿٤٨﴾ وَمِن كُلِّ شَيْءٍ خَلَقْنَا زَوْجَيْنِ
لَعَلَّكُمْ تَذَكَّرُونَ ﴿٤٩﴾ فَفِرُّوا إِلَى اللَّهِ إِنِّي لَكُم مِّنْهُ نَذِيرٌ مُّبِينٌ ﴿٥٠﴾
وَلَا تَجْعَلُوا مَعَ اللَّهِ إِلَٰهًا آخَرَ إِنِّي لَكُم مِّنْهُ نَذِيرٌ مُّبِينٌ ﴿٥١﴾
كَذَٰلِكَ مَا أَتَى الَّذِينَ مِن قَبْلِهِم مِّن رَّسُولٍ إِلَّا قَالُوا سَاحِرٌ أَوْ مَجْنُونٌ
﴿٥٢﴾ أَتَوَاصَوْا بِهِ بَلْ هُمْ قَوْمٌ طَاغُونَ ﴿٥٣﴾ فَتَوَلَّ عَنْهُمْ فَمَا أَنتَ
بِمَلُومٍ ﴿٥٤﴾ وَذَكِّرْ فَإِنَّ الذِّكْرَىٰ تَنفَعُ الْمُؤْمِنِينَ ﴿٥٥﴾ وَمَا
خَلَقْتُ الْجِنَّ وَالْإِنسَ إِلَّا لِيَعْبُدُونِ ﴿٥٦﴾ مَا أُرِيدُ مِنْهُم مِّن رِّزْقٍ
وَمَا أُرِيدُ أَن يُطْعِمُونِ ﴿٥٧﴾ إِنَّ اللَّهَ هُوَ الرَّزَّاقُ ذُو الْقُوَّةِ الْمَتِينُ
﴿٥٨﴾ فَإِنَّ لِلَّذِينَ ظَلَمُوا ذَنُوبًا مِّثْلَ ذَنُوبِ أَصْحَابِهِمْ فَلَا يَسْتَعْجِلُونِ
﴿٥٩﴾ فَوَيْلٌ لِّلَّذِينَ كَفَرُوا مِن يَوْمِهِمُ الَّذِي يُوعَدُونَ ﴿٦٠﴾

39. ***But he turned away*** from faith ***with his forces,*** because they supported him, ***saying*** 'Mūsā is ***a magician or a madman!'***

40. ***So We seized him and his armies and hurled them into the sea*** and they were drowned***; and he was to blame.*** Pharoah did what was reprehensible by denying the Messengers and claiming to be divine.

41. ***And also in*** the destruction of ***'Ād*** there is a sign – ***when We unleashed against them the barren wind*** in which there was no good because it did not bring rain and did not fertilise the trees. It was a west wind –

42. ***...which left nothing*** – neither living person nor property – ***it touched without turning it to dust.***

43. ***And also in*** the destruction of ***Thamūd*** there is a Sign – ***when they were told*** after they had hamstrung the Camel, ***'Enjoy yourselves a while*** until the end of your set term,' as in the *āyat*: *"Enjoy yourselves in your land for three more days."* (11:65)

44. ***But they spurned their Lord's command*** out of arrogance, and did not obey their Messenger, ***so the Blast seized them*** three days later ***as they watched.***

45. ***They could not stand upright*** – being unable to rise when the punishment descended – ***and they were not helped*** against what destroyed them.

46. ***And*** there is a Sign in the destruction of ***the people of Nūḥ before*** who were destroyed by Allah before these others were destroyed – ***they were a people of deviators.***

47. ***As for heaven, We built it with great power and gave it its vast expanse.*** "We had the power to do so and made it contain vastness and strength."

48. ***And the earth – We spread it like a carpet*** and stretched it out – ***and how well We smoothed it out!***

49. ***And We created all things in pairs*** of opposites, such as male and female, earth and heaven, sun and moon, plains and mountains, summer and winter, sweet and sour, light and darkness, ***so that perhaps you would pay heed***, know that the Creator of the pairs is unique, and worship Him.

50. ***So flee to Allah*** – to His reward from the punishment from Him that awaits you if you do not obey Him. Do not disobey Him. ***Truly I bring you a clear warning from Him.***

51. ***Do not set up another god together with Allah. Truly I bring you a clear warning from Him.*** This is repeating the command to flee to Him.

52. ***Equally, no Messenger came to those before them without their saying, 'A magician or a madman!'*** Their denial of Muḥammad by saying that he was a magician or madman mirrors how earlier nations also denied their Messengers by saying that.

53. ***Did they*** all ***bequeathe this to one another?*** The answer is "No". ***Indeed they are an unbridled people.*** All who called him that were a people who transgressed.

54. ***So turn away from them, for you are not to blame*** – because you have conveyed the Message;

55. ***…and remind them*** – admonish them by the Qur'an, ***for truly the believers benefit from being reminded*** – those who Allah knows will believe.

56. ***I created jinn and man only to worship Me.*** This is not incompatible with the unbelievers' failure to worship Allah because the statement does not demand that it actually happen, as is the case when you say, "I have sharpened this pen so that I can write with it," and then you do not write with it.

57. ***I do not require any provision from them*** for Myself or themselves or for anyone else ***and I do not require them to nourish Me.***

58. ***Truly Allah is the Provider, the Possessor of Strength, the Sure.***

59. ***Those who do wrong*** to themselves by disbelief among the people of Makka and others ***will have their due*** portion of the punishment, ***the same as that of their friends*** – those who were destroyed before them — ***so they should not hurry Me***: hasten the punishment if it is delayed for them until the Day of Rising.

60. ***Woe*** (a great punishment), ***then, to those who disbelieve, on account of the Day they have been promised*** – the Day of Rising.

سُورَةُ الطُّورِ

بِسْمِ ٱللَّهِ ٱلرَّحْمَٰنِ ٱلرَّحِيمِ

وَٱلطُّورِ ﴿١﴾ وَكِتَٰبٍ مَّسْطُورٍ ﴿٢﴾ فِى رَقٍّ مَّنشُورٍ ﴿٣﴾ وَٱلْبَيْتِ
ٱلْمَعْمُورِ ﴿٤﴾ وَٱلسَّقْفِ ٱلْمَرْفُوعِ ﴿٥﴾ وَٱلْبَحْرِ ٱلْمَسْجُورِ ﴿٦﴾ إِنَّ
عَذَابَ رَبِّكَ لَوَٰقِعٌ ﴿٧﴾ مَّا لَهُۥ مِن دَافِعٍ ﴿٨﴾ يَوْمَ تَمُورُ ٱلسَّمَآءُ
مَوْرًا ﴿٩﴾ وَتَسِيرُ ٱلْجِبَالُ سَيْرًا ﴿١٠﴾ فَوَيْلٌ يَوْمَئِذٍ لِّلْمُكَذِّبِينَ
﴿١١﴾ ٱلَّذِينَ هُمْ فِى خَوْضٍ يَلْعَبُونَ ﴿١٢﴾ يَوْمَ يُدَعُّونَ إِلَىٰ نَارِ
جَهَنَّمَ دَعًّا ﴿١٣﴾ هَٰذِهِ ٱلنَّارُ ٱلَّتِى كُنتُم بِهَا تُكَذِّبُونَ ﴿١٤﴾
أَفَسِحْرٌ هَٰذَآ أَمْ أَنتُمْ لَا تُبْصِرُونَ ﴿١٥﴾ ٱصْلَوْهَا فَٱصْبِرُوٓا۟
أَوْ لَا تَصْبِرُوا۟ سَوَآءٌ عَلَيْكُمْ ۖ إِنَّمَا تُجْزَوْنَ مَا كُنتُمْ تَعْمَلُونَ ﴿١٦﴾
إِنَّ ٱلْمُتَّقِينَ فِى جَنَّٰتٍ وَنَعِيمٍ ﴿١٧﴾ فَٰكِهِينَ بِمَآ ءَاتَىٰهُمْ رَبُّهُمْ
وَوَقَىٰهُمْ رَبُّهُمْ عَذَابَ ٱلْجَحِيمِ ﴿١٨﴾ كُلُوا۟ وَٱشْرَبُوا۟ هَنِيٓـًٔۢا بِمَا
كُنتُمْ تَعْمَلُونَ ﴿١٩﴾ مُتَّكِـِٔينَ عَلَىٰ سُرُرٍ مَّصْفُوفَةٍ ۖ وَزَوَّجْنَٰهُم
بِحُورٍ عِينٍ ﴿٢٠﴾ وَٱلَّذِينَ ءَامَنُوا۟ وَٱتَّبَعَتْهُمْ ذُرِّيَّتُهُم بِإِيمَٰنٍ أَلْحَقْنَا
بِهِمْ ذُرِّيَّتَهُمْ وَمَآ أَلَتْنَٰهُم مِّنْ عَمَلِهِم مِّن شَىْءٍ ۚ كُلُّ ٱمْرِئٍۭ بِمَا كَسَبَ
رَهِينٌ ﴿٢١﴾ وَأَمْدَدْنَٰهُم بِفَٰكِهَةٍ وَلَحْمٍ مِّمَّا يَشْتَهُونَ ﴿٢٢﴾ يَتَنَٰزَعُونَ
فِيهَا كَأْسًا لَّا لَغْوٌ فِيهَا وَلَا تَأْثِيمٌ ﴿٢٣﴾ ۞ وَيَطُوفُ عَلَيْهِمْ غِلْمَانٌ
لَّهُمْ كَأَنَّهُمْ لُؤْلُؤٌ مَّكْنُونٌ ﴿٢٤﴾ وَأَقْبَلَ بَعْضُهُمْ عَلَىٰ بَعْضٍ يَتَسَآءَلُونَ
﴿٢٥﴾ قَالُوٓا۟ إِنَّا كُنَّا قَبْلُ فِىٓ أَهْلِنَا مُشْفِقِينَ ﴿٢٦﴾ فَمَنَّ ٱللَّهُ
عَلَيْنَا وَوَقَىٰنَا عَذَابَ ٱلسَّمُومِ ﴿٢٧﴾ إِنَّا كُنَّا مِن قَبْلُ

52. *Sūrat at-Ṭūr*
The Mount

This *sūra* is Makkan and has 49 *āyat*s.

1. ***By the Mount*** – this is the mountain on which Allah spoke to Mūsā –

2. ***...and an Inscribed Book***

3. ***...on an Unfurled Scroll*** – the Torah or the Qur'an –

4. ***...by the Visited House*** – in the third, sixth or seventh heaven above the Ka'ba. Seventy thousand angels visit it every day, perform *ṭawāf* and pray, and never return to it again***;***

5. ***...by the Raised Canopy*** – meaning the sky***;***

6. ***...by the Overflowing Ocean:***

7. ***...your Lord's punishment*** of those who deserve it ***will certainly take place.***

8. ***No one can ward it off.***

9. ***On the Day when heaven*** shakes and ***sways to and fro...***

10. ***...and the mountains shift about*** and become scattered dust. That will occur on the Day of Rising***:***

11. ***... woe that Day to the deniers*** – a great punishment for those who deny the Messengers –

12. ***...who play at frivolous games*** – occupied and diverted with false things because of their unbelief,

13. ***...the Day they are shoved roughly into the Fire of Hell*** and are told as a rebuke to them***:***

14. ***'This is the Fire which you denied!***

15. ***So is this*** punishment ***magic***, as you used to say about the Revelation, ***or is it that you do not see?***

16. ***Roast in it, and bear it patiently or do not bear it patiently; it makes no difference either way.*** "Your patience and fear are the same because your patience will not help you." ***You are simply being repaid for what you did.'***

17. ***The godfearing will be in Gardens of Delight,***

18. ***...savouring what their Lord has given them. Their Lord will safeguard them from the punishment of the Blazing Fire.*** They will be told*:*

19. ***'Eat and drink with relish for what you did.'***

20. They will recline in the Garden ***on couches ranged in rows*** – side by side – ***and We will marry them to*** beautiful ***dark-eyed maidens*** (houris).

21. ***And We will unite those who believed with their offspring*** (read as *dhurriyyatuhum* and *dhurriyyātuhum*, singular and plural) ***who followed them*** (read as *attaba'athum* and *atba'nāhum*) ***in belief*** – in the Garden and they will be in different ranks, even if they did not act worthily of them*;* to honour their fathers by joining their children to them – ***and We will not undervalue*** (read as *alitnā* and *alatnā*) ***their own actions in any way. Every man*** (human being) ***is in pledge for what he earned*** by his actions, good or bad. Evil will be punished and good will be rewarded.

22. ***We will supply them*** time after time ***with any kind of fruit and meat that they desire*** – and they do not have to look for it.

23. ***They will pass round there*** – in Paradise – ***a drinking cup*** of wine ***to one another with no foolish talk*** between them as a result of drinking it ***and no wrong action in it*** – which is not the case with wine in this world.

24. ***Circulating among them there will be youths*** – as servants – ***like hidden pearls*** as regards their beauty and fineness. A pearl when it is protected in its shell is more beautiful there than it is elsewhere.

25. ***Some of them will come up to others and they will question one another*** about what they had before in the world and the delight they are now experiencing, and they will acknowledge the blessing they have received.

26. ***They will say*** – indicating the reason for their arrival – ***'Beforehand we used live in fear among our families.*** "In this world, we used to fear Allah's punishment."

27. ***But Allah was gracious to us*** by forgiving us ***and safeguarded us from the punishment of the searing wind*** – heated by having entered the Fire.

نَدْعُوهُ إِنَّهُۥ هُوَ ٱلْبَرُّ ٱلرَّحِيمُ ﴿٢٨﴾ فَذَكِّرْ فَمَآ أَنتَ بِنِعْمَتِ
رَبِّكَ بِكَاهِنٍ وَلَا مَجْنُونٍ ﴿٢٩﴾ أَمْ يَقُولُونَ شَاعِرٌ نَّتَرَبَّصُ بِهِۦ رَيْبَ
ٱلْمَنُونِ ﴿٣٠﴾ قُلْ تَرَبَّصُوا۟ فَإِنِّى مَعَكُم مِّنَ ٱلْمُتَرَبِّصِينَ ﴿٣١﴾
أَمْ تَأْمُرُهُمْ أَحْلَٰمُهُم بِهَٰذَآ ۚ أَمْ هُمْ قَوْمٌ طَاغُونَ ﴿٣٢﴾ أَمْ يَقُولُونَ تَقَوَّلَهُۥ ۚ
بَل لَّا يُؤْمِنُونَ ﴿٣٣﴾ فَلْيَأْتُوا۟ بِحَدِيثٍ مِّثْلِهِۦٓ إِن كَانُوا۟ صَٰدِقِينَ
﴿٣٤﴾ أَمْ خُلِقُوا۟ مِنْ غَيْرِ شَىْءٍ أَمْ هُمُ ٱلْخَٰلِقُونَ ﴿٣٥﴾ أَمْ خَلَقُوا۟
ٱلسَّمَٰوَٰتِ وَٱلْأَرْضَ ۚ بَل لَّا يُوقِنُونَ ﴿٣٦﴾ أَمْ عِندَهُمْ خَزَآئِنُ
رَبِّكَ أَمْ هُمُ ٱلْمُصَۣيْطِرُونَ ﴿٣٧﴾ أَمْ لَهُمْ سُلَّمٌ يَسْتَمِعُونَ فِيهِ ۖ فَلْيَأْتِ
مُسْتَمِعُهُم بِسُلْطَٰنٍ مُّبِينٍ ﴿٣٨﴾ أَمْ لَهُ ٱلْبَنَٰتُ وَلَكُمُ ٱلْبَنُونَ ﴿٣٩﴾
أَمْ تَسْـَٔلُهُمْ أَجْرًا فَهُم مِّن مَّغْرَمٍ مُّثْقَلُونَ ﴿٤٠﴾ أَمْ عِندَهُمُ ٱلْغَيْبُ فَهُمْ
يَكْتُبُونَ ﴿٤١﴾ أَمْ يُرِيدُونَ كَيْدًا ۖ فَٱلَّذِينَ كَفَرُوا۟ هُمُ ٱلْمَكِيدُونَ ﴿٤٢﴾
أَمْ لَهُمْ إِلَٰهٌ غَيْرُ ٱللَّهِ ۚ سُبْحَٰنَ ٱللَّهِ عَمَّا يُشْرِكُونَ ﴿٤٣﴾ وَإِن يَرَوْا۟ كِسْفًا
مِّنَ ٱلسَّمَآءِ سَاقِطًا يَقُولُوا۟ سَحَابٌ مَّرْكُومٌ ﴿٤٤﴾ فَذَرْهُمْ حَتَّىٰ يُلَٰقُوا۟
يَوْمَهُمُ ٱلَّذِى فِيهِ يُصْعَقُونَ ﴿٤٥﴾ يَوْمَ لَا يُغْنِى عَنْهُمْ كَيْدُهُمْ شَيْـًٔا
وَلَا هُمْ يُنصَرُونَ ﴿٤٦﴾ وَإِنَّ لِلَّذِينَ ظَلَمُوا۟ عَذَابًا دُونَ ذَٰلِكَ وَلَٰكِنَّ
أَكْثَرَهُمْ لَا يَعْلَمُونَ ﴿٤٧﴾ وَٱصْبِرْ لِحُكْمِ رَبِّكَ فَإِنَّكَ بِأَعْيُنِنَا ۖ وَسَبِّحْ
بِحَمْدِ رَبِّكَ حِينَ تَقُومُ ﴿٤٨﴾ وَمِنَ ٱلَّيْلِ فَسَبِّحْهُ وَإِدْبَٰرَ ٱلنُّجُومِ ﴿٤٩﴾

28. ***Beforehand we certainly used to call on*** and worship ***Him*** alone in this world ***because He is the All-Good*** – the Divine Name used here, *al-Barr,* is the one who is good and truthful in His promise***, the Most Merciful.'***

29. ***Remind them, then!*** "Continue to remind the idolaters and do not cease doing that in spite of what they say about you being a soothsayer or a madman!" ***For, by the blessing of your Lord*** on you ***you are neither a soothsayer nor a madman.***

30. ***Or do they say, 'He is a poet and We are waiting for something bad to happen to him'?*** "We are waiting for the events of time to destroy him like other poets."

31. ***Say: 'Wait then*** for my destruction***! I am waiting with you*** for your destruction***.'*** They were punished by the sword in the Battle of Badr.

32. ***Is it their intellects that direct them to say this*** – that he is a magician, soothsayer or madman, meaning that their intelligence did not make them say this***, or is it that they are an unbridled people*** in their obduracy***?***

33. ***Or do they say, 'He has simply made it up'?*** "Do they say that he has forged the Qur'an?" He did not. ***No, the truth is that they do not believe*** out of arrogance.

34. If they do say that he has forged it, then: ***Let them produce a*** forged ***discourse like it if they are telling the truth.***

35. ***Or were they created out of nothing*** without a Creator***, or are they the creators?*** Did they create themselves? It is not logical that there should be a creature without a Creator or that something non-existent should create. So they must have a Creator, namely the One God. Yet they do not proclaim His unity nor believe in His Messenger and His Book.

36. ***Or did they create the heavens and the earth?*** Only Allah, the Creator, is capable of creating the heavens and the earth, so why do they not worship Him? ***No, in truth they have no certainty*** about Him. If they had had, they would have believed in His Prophet.

37. ***Or do they possess the treasuries of your Lord*** – referring to Prophethood, provision and other things, so that they can give whomever they wish whatever they wish – ***or do they have control of them*** and manage them*?*

38. ***Or do they have a ladder on which*** they can ascend to heaven and from which ***they listen*** to the words of the angels, so that they can argue with the Prophet to validate the allegations which they make*?* ***Then let their listener*** – the one who claims to listen – ***bring clear evidence*** for their claim that the angels are the daughters of Allah; so Allah says:

39. ***Or does He have daughters whereas they have sons?*** This is their baseless claim.

40. ***Or do you ask them for a wage*** for bringing them the *dīn* ***so that they are weighed down with debt*** by that and for that reason do not become Muslim*?*

41. ***Or is*** knowledge of ***the Unseen in their hands so they can write out what is to happen*** – so that they can argue with the Prophet, may Allah bless him and grant him peace, about the Resurrection and the matters of the Next World*?*

42. ***Or do they desire to dupe you?*** "Do they desire to outwit you so that they can murder you by plotting in the Dār an-Nadwa?" ***But the duped ones are those who disbelieve*** – who are defeated in their devising**.** For Allah protected him from them and then destroyed them at the Battle of Badr.

43. ***Or do they have some god other than Allah? Glory be to Allah above any idol they propose!*** He is exalted above any of their deities! Such questions convey rebuke and finding something to be ugly.

44. ***If they saw a lump of heaven falling down*** on them, as they had said, "Let parts of the heaven fall on us," which would happen in order to punish them, ***they would just say,*** 'It is ***banked-up clouds!'*** and would not believe.

45. ***Leave them, then, until they meet their Day when they will be struck down by the Blast*** and then die,

46. ***...the Day their ploys will not profit them at all and they will not be helped*** and defended from punishment on the Last Day**.**

47. ***And those who do wrong*** by their unbelief ***will have a punishment besides that*** in this world before their death*;* and they were punished by hunger and drought for seven years and by being killed on the Day of Badr – ***but most of them do not know it*** – that the punishment will befall them.

48. ***So wait steadfastly for the judgement of your Lord*** when He delays their punishment***; you are certainly before Our eyes.*** "We see you and We will preserve you." ***And glorify and praise your Lord*** by saying, "Glory be to Allah and with His praise" ***when you get up*** from sleep or rise from your gathering.

49. ***...and glorify Him in the night and when the stars fade out***: this may mean praying the night prayers (*Maghrib* and *'Ishā'*) and "when the stars fade" is praying *Fajr* and *Ṣubḥ*.

سُورَةُ ٱلنَّجْمِ

بِسْمِ ٱللَّهِ ٱلرَّحْمَٰنِ ٱلرَّحِيمِ

وَٱلنَّجْمِ إِذَا هَوَىٰ ﴿١﴾ مَا ضَلَّ صَاحِبُكُمْ وَمَا غَوَىٰ ﴿٢﴾ وَمَا يَنطِقُ
عَنِ ٱلْهَوَىٰٓ ﴿٣﴾ إِنْ هُوَ إِلَّا وَحْىٌ يُوحَىٰ ﴿٤﴾ عَلَّمَهُۥ شَدِيدُ ٱلْقُوَىٰ ﴿٥﴾
ذُو مِرَّةٍ فَٱسْتَوَىٰ ﴿٦﴾ وَهُوَ بِٱلْأُفُقِ ٱلْأَعْلَىٰ ﴿٧﴾ ثُمَّ دَنَا فَتَدَلَّىٰ ﴿٨﴾
فَكَانَ قَابَ قَوْسَيْنِ أَوْ أَدْنَىٰ ﴿٩﴾ فَأَوْحَىٰٓ إِلَىٰ عَبْدِهِۦ مَآ أَوْحَىٰ ﴿١٠﴾
مَا كَذَبَ ٱلْفُؤَادُ مَا رَأَىٰٓ ﴿١١﴾ أَفَتُمَٰرُونَهُۥ عَلَىٰ مَا يَرَىٰ ﴿١٢﴾ وَلَقَدْ رَءَاهُ
نَزْلَةً أُخْرَىٰ ﴿١٣﴾ عِندَ سِدْرَةِ ٱلْمُنتَهَىٰ ﴿١٤﴾ عِندَهَا جَنَّةُ ٱلْمَأْوَىٰٓ ﴿١٥﴾
إِذْ يَغْشَى ٱلسِّدْرَةَ مَا يَغْشَىٰ ﴿١٦﴾ مَا زَاغَ ٱلْبَصَرُ وَمَا طَغَىٰ ﴿١٧﴾ لَقَدْ رَأَىٰ
مِنْ ءَايَٰتِ رَبِّهِ ٱلْكُبْرَىٰٓ ﴿١٨﴾ أَفَرَءَيْتُمُ ٱللَّٰتَ وَٱلْعُزَّىٰ ﴿١٩﴾ وَمَنَوٰةَ
ٱلثَّالِثَةَ ٱلْأُخْرَىٰٓ ﴿٢٠﴾ أَلَكُمُ ٱلذَّكَرُ وَلَهُ ٱلْأُنثَىٰ ﴿٢١﴾ تِلْكَ إِذًا قِسْمَةٌ
ضِيزَىٰٓ ﴿٢٢﴾ إِنْ هِىَ إِلَّآ أَسْمَآءٌ سَمَّيْتُمُوهَآ أَنتُمْ وَءَابَآؤُكُم مَّآ أَنزَلَ
ٱللَّهُ بِهَا مِن سُلْطَٰنٍ ۚ إِن يَتَّبِعُونَ إِلَّا ٱلظَّنَّ وَمَا تَهْوَى ٱلْأَنفُسُ ۖ
وَلَقَدْ جَآءَهُم مِّن رَّبِّهِمُ ٱلْهُدَىٰٓ ﴿٢٣﴾ أَمْ لِلْإِنسَٰنِ مَا تَمَنَّىٰ ﴿٢٤﴾ فَلِلَّهِ
ٱلْءَاخِرَةُ وَٱلْأُولَىٰ ﴿٢٥﴾ ۞ وَكَم مِّن مَّلَكٍ فِى ٱلسَّمَٰوَٰتِ لَا تُغْنِى
شَفَٰعَتُهُمْ شَيْـًٔا إِلَّا مِنۢ بَعْدِ أَن يَأْذَنَ ٱللَّهُ لِمَن يَشَآءُ وَيَرْضَىٰٓ ﴿٢٦﴾
إِنَّ ٱلَّذِينَ لَا يُؤْمِنُونَ بِٱلْءَاخِرَةِ لَيُسَمُّونَ ٱلْمَلَٰٓئِكَةَ تَسْمِيَةَ ٱلْأُنثَىٰ ﴿٢٧﴾
وَمَا لَهُم بِهِۦ مِنْ عِلْمٍ ۖ إِن يَتَّبِعُونَ إِلَّا ٱلظَّنَّ ۖ وَإِنَّ ٱلظَّنَّ لَا يُغْنِى مِنَ
ٱلْحَقِّ شَيْـًٔا ﴿٢٨﴾ فَأَعْرِضْ عَن مَّن تَوَلَّىٰ عَن ذِكْرِنَا وَلَمْ يُرِدْ إِلَّا ٱلْحَيَوٰةَ
ٱلدُّنْيَا ﴿٢٩﴾ ذَٰلِكَ مَبْلَغُهُم مِّنَ ٱلْعِلْمِ ۚ إِنَّ رَبَّكَ هُوَ أَعْلَمُ بِمَن ضَلَّ عَن

53. *Sūrat an-Najm*
The Star

This *sūra* is Makkan except for *āyat* 32, which is Madinan. It has 62 *āyat*s.

1. ***By the star*** (the Pleiades) ***when it descends*** and sets…

2. …***your companion is not misguided or misled,*** referring to Muḥammad, peace and blessing be upon him. He is guided on the Path of right guidance and is untouched by error, which is ignorance in the form of false belief –

3. **…**in what he brings, ***nor does he speak from whim*** – from his own desires.

4. ***It is nothing but Revelation revealed*** to him,

5. ***… taught him by one immensely strong,*** an angel,

6. ***…possessing power and splendour*** – meaning Jibrīl. ***He stood, stationary –***

7. ***…there on the highest horizon.*** The horizon is that of the sun, in other words where it rises. He appeared in the form in which he was created. The Prophet, may Allah bless him and grant him peace, saw him. This happened at Ḥirā' and the angel filled the entire horizon. He fainted. He had asked Jibrīl to show himself to him in the form in which he had been created. Jibrīl told him that it would happen at Ḥirā', where he had previously descended in a human form.

8. ***Then he drew near*** to him ***and hung suspended***, coming nearer still.

9. ***He was two bow-lengths away or even closer*** when he recovered consciousness and his terror was stilled.

10. ***Then He revealed to His slave*** – Jibrīl – ***what he*** – Jibrīl – ***revealed*** to the Prophet, may Allah bless him and grant him peace. The Name of the Revealer is not mentioned because of His incomparable greatness.

11. ***His*** (the Prophet's) ***heart did not lie about*** (read as *kadhaba* and *kadhdhaba* which means "deny") ***what he saw*** with respect to the form of Jibrīl.

12. ***What! Do you dispute with him*** – argue with him and try to overcome him – ***about what he saw?*** This is addressed to the idolaters who denied that the Prophet, may Allah bless him and grant him peace, saw Jibrīl.

13. ***He saw him*** in his true form ***again another time...***

14. ***...by the Lote-tree of the Final Limit*** – this was when he travelled by night through the heavens. It is a lote tree to the right of the Throne which none of the angels or anyone else can go beyond –

15. ***...beside which is the Garden of Refuge*** – a garden in which the angels and spirits of the martyrs and godfearing seek refuge –

16. ***...when that which covered the Lote-tree covered it***: birds and other things.

17. ***His eye*** – that of the Prophet, may Allah bless him and grant him peace – ***did not waver, nor did he look away*** from what he was meant to see or exceed it on that night.

18. ***He saw*** in that ***some of the Greatest Signs of his Lord.*** He saw some of the wonders of the Malakūt: green meadows which filled the horizon of heaven, and Jibrīl with six hundred wings.

19. ***Have you really considered al-Lāt and al-'Uzzā...***

20. ***...and Manāt, the third, the other one?*** These were stone idols which the idolaters used to worship, claiming that they would bring them near to Allah. The implied meaning is: "Tell me: Are these idols capable of anything, that you should worship them instead of Allah who truly does have the power which has already been mentioned?" When they claimed that the angels were the daughters of Allah in spite of their dislike of daughters, Allah revealed:

21. ***Do you have males and He females?***

22. ***That is a most unfair division!*** The word "unfair", *ḍīzā* , comes from the verb *ḍāza, yaḍīzu*, to do wrong.

23. ***They*** (the idols) ***are nothing but names which you yourselves have given*** to the idols which you worship, ***you and your forefathers. Allah has sent down no authority for them*** – for worshipping them. ***They are following nothing but conjecture and what their own selves desire.*** Worshipping idols is only something which Shayṭān has made seem attractive to them, claiming that they will intercede with Allah on their behalf. ***And that when guidance has***

reached them on the tongue of the Prophet, may Allah bless him and grant him peace, with absolute evidence ***from their Lord!*** Yet they still do not revert from what they are doing.

24. ***Shall man then have whatever he covets?*** Shall every human being have whatever he wishes where the intercession of idols is concerned? That is not how existence works.

25. ***The last*** – meaning the Next World – ***and the first*** – meaning this world – ***belong to Allah.*** Nothing occurs in them except what He wishes.

26. ***And how many angels there are in the heavens whose intercession*** – in spite of their high place with Allah – ***is of no benefit at all until Allah has authorised those*** of His slaves ***He wills and is pleased with them!*** Allah says: *"They do not intercede except on behalf of those with whom He is pleased."* (21:28) It is known that intercession can only be given by any creature after Allah has granted permission: *"Who can intercede with Him except by His permission?"* (2:255)

27. ***Those who do not believe in the Next World give the angels female names.*** That is because they say that they are the daughters of Allah.

28. ***They have no knowledge of this*** statement; ***they are only following conjecture.*** It is only something that they imagine. ***Conjecture is of no avail whatever against the truth*** – no help in acquiring the knowledge which is desired.

29. ***So turn away from him who turns away from Our remembrance*** (the Qur'ān) ***and desires nothing but the life of this world.*** This was before the command to engage in *jihād*.

30. ***That*** (seeking this world) ***is as far as their knowledge extends.*** That is the goal of their knowledge since they prefer this world. ***Your Lord knows best those who are misguided from His Way and He knows best those who are guided***, and will repay them.

31. ***Everything in the heavens and everything in the earth belongs to Allah*** – He is the Master of all that. This includes the misguided and the guided. He misleads whomever He wishes and guides whomever He wishes – ***so that He may repay those who do evil for what they did*** – in terms of *shirk* and other things – ***and repay those***

سَبِيلِهِۦ وَهُوَ أَعْلَمُ بِمَنِ ٱهْتَدَىٰ ﴿٣٠﴾ وَلِلَّهِ مَا فِى ٱلسَّمَٰوَٰتِ وَمَا
فِى ٱلْأَرْضِ لِيَجْزِىَ ٱلَّذِينَ أَسَٰٓـُٔوا۟ بِمَا عَمِلُوا۟ وَيَجْزِىَ ٱلَّذِينَ أَحْسَنُوا۟
بِٱلْحُسْنَى ﴿٣١﴾ ٱلَّذِينَ يَجْتَنِبُونَ كَبَٰٓئِرَ ٱلْإِثْمِ وَٱلْفَوَٰحِشَ إِلَّا ٱللَّمَمَ
إِنَّ رَبَّكَ وَٰسِعُ ٱلْمَغْفِرَةِ هُوَ أَعْلَمُ بِكُمْ إِذْ أَنشَأَكُم مِّنَ ٱلْأَرْضِ
وَإِذْ أَنتُمْ أَجِنَّةٌ فِى بُطُونِ أُمَّهَٰتِكُمْ فَلَا تُزَكُّوٓا۟ أَنفُسَكُمْ هُوَ أَعْلَمُ
بِمَنِ ٱتَّقَىٰٓ ﴿٣٢﴾ أَفَرَءَيْتَ ٱلَّذِى تَوَلَّىٰ ﴿٣٣﴾ وَأَعْطَىٰ قَلِيلًا وَأَكْدَىٰٓ
﴿٣٤﴾ أَعِندَهُۥ عِلْمُ ٱلْغَيْبِ فَهُوَ يَرَىٰٓ ﴿٣٥﴾ أَمْ لَمْ يُنَبَّأْ بِمَا فِى صُحُفِ
مُوسَىٰ ﴿٣٦﴾ وَإِبْرَٰهِيمَ ٱلَّذِى وَفَّىٰٓ ﴿٣٧﴾ أَلَّا تَزِرُ وَازِرَةٌ وِزْرَ أُخْرَىٰ
﴿٣٨﴾ وَأَن لَّيْسَ لِلْإِنسَٰنِ إِلَّا مَا سَعَىٰ ﴿٣٩﴾ وَأَنَّ سَعْيَهُۥ سَوْفَ
يُرَىٰ ﴿٤٠﴾ ثُمَّ يُجْزَىٰهُ ٱلْجَزَآءَ ٱلْأَوْفَىٰ ﴿٤١﴾ وَأَنَّ إِلَىٰ رَبِّكَ ٱلْمُنتَهَىٰ
﴿٤٢﴾ وَأَنَّهُۥ هُوَ أَضْحَكَ وَأَبْكَىٰ ﴿٤٣﴾ وَأَنَّهُۥ هُوَ أَمَاتَ وَأَحْيَا ﴿٤٤﴾
وَأَنَّهُۥ خَلَقَ ٱلزَّوْجَيْنِ ٱلذَّكَرَ وَٱلْأُنثَىٰ ﴿٤٥﴾ مِن نُّطْفَةٍ إِذَا تُمْنَىٰ ﴿٤٦﴾ وَأَنَّ
عَلَيْهِ ٱلنَّشْأَةَ ٱلْأُخْرَىٰ ﴿٤٧﴾ وَأَنَّهُۥ هُوَ أَغْنَىٰ وَأَقْنَىٰ ﴿٤٨﴾ وَأَنَّهُۥ هُوَ رَبُّ
ٱلشِّعْرَىٰ ﴿٤٩﴾ وَأَنَّهُۥٓ أَهْلَكَ عَادًا ٱلْأُولَىٰ ﴿٥٠﴾ وَثَمُودَا۟ فَمَآ أَبْقَىٰ ﴿٥١﴾
وَقَوْمَ نُوحٍ مِّن قَبْلُ إِنَّهُمْ كَانُوا۟ هُمْ أَظْلَمَ وَأَطْغَىٰ ﴿٥٢﴾ وَٱلْمُؤْتَفِكَةَ
أَهْوَىٰ ﴿٥٣﴾ فَغَشَّىٰهَا مَا غَشَّىٰ ﴿٥٤﴾ فَبِأَىِّ ءَالَآءِ رَبِّكَ تَتَمَارَىٰ ﴿٥٥﴾
هَٰذَا نَذِيرٌ مِّنَ ٱلنُّذُرِ ٱلْأُولَىٰٓ ﴿٥٦﴾ أَزِفَتِ ٱلْءَازِفَةُ ﴿٥٧﴾ لَيْسَ لَهَا مِن
دُونِ ٱللَّهِ كَاشِفَةٌ ﴿٥٨﴾ أَفَمِنْ هَٰذَا ٱلْحَدِيثِ تَعْجَبُونَ ﴿٥٩﴾ وَتَضْحَكُونَ
وَلَا تَبْكُونَ ﴿٦٠﴾ وَأَنتُمْ سَٰمِدُونَ ﴿٦١﴾ فَٱسْجُدُوا۟ لِلَّهِ وَٱعْبُدُوا۟ ۩ ﴿٦٢﴾

who do good through their affirmation of Allah's unity and other acts of obedience ***with the Very Best*** (the Garden).

32. He makes the good-doers clear – ***to whoever avoids the major wrong actions and indecencies – except for minor lapses*** – things such as illicit glances, kisses or touches, indicating that minor wrong actions are forgiven if major ones are avoided. ***Truly your Lord is vast in forgiveness*** and accepts repentance. ***He has most knowledge of you when He first produced you from the earth*** – creating your father Ādam from dust – ***and when you were embryos in your mothers' wombs. So do not claim purity for yourselves.*** Do not praise yourselves out self-admiration. If it is done purely by way of acknowledgement of blessing, it is good. ***He knows best those who are godfearing.***

33. ***Have you seen him who turns away,*** turns away from faith and apostasises after being criticised for having faith. He said, "I feared the penalty of Allah," The critic guaranteed that he would bear the punishment of Allah for that man if he would revert to *shirk*, and also gave him money; and so he recanted.

34. ***…and gives little*** of his wealth ***and that grudgingly?*** The word "grudgingly", *akda,* is derived from *kudya*, which means stony earth that impedes someone who is digging a well when he reaches it.

35. ***Does he have knowledge of the Unseen, enabling him to see?*** Does he know of anyone else who is able to remove the punishment of the Next World from him? This is a reference to al-Walīd ibn al-Mughīra or someone else.

36. ***Or has he not been informed what is in the texts of Mūsā*** – the scrolls of the Torah, or the scrolls revealed before his time –

37. ***…and*** the scrolls ***of Ibrāhīm, who paid his dues in full:*** in other words, did what he was commanded to do – as Allah confirms in His words: *"Remember when Ibrāhīm was tested by his Lord with certain words, which he accomplished completely."* (2:124) –

38. ***…that no burden-bearer*** (soul) ***can bear another's burden*** – in other words, another's sins;

39. ***…that man will have nothing but what he strives for*** – not what someone else strives for;

40. *...that his striving will most certainly be seen* in the Next World*;*

41. *...that he will then receive repayment of the fullest kind* for his striving*;*

42. *...that the ultimate end is with your Lord* – all will return to Him after death and He will repay them*;*

43. *...that it is He Who brings about both laughter and tears* – Allah makes whomever He wishes laugh with joy, and causes sorrow to whomever He wishes*;*

44. *...that it is He Who brings about both death* – in this world – ***and life*** at the Resurrection*;*

45. *...that He created the two sexes, male and female,*

46. *...out of a sperm-drop when it spurted forth* and lodged in the womb*;*

47. *...that He is responsible for the second existence* (read as *nasha'a* and *nashā'a*) – the second creation for the Resurrection, which is after the first creation*;*

48. *...that it is He Who enriches* with wealth ***and Who satisfies*** by giving it*;*

49. *...that it is He Who is the Lord of Sirius* – a star behind Gemini which used to be worshipped in the Jāhiliyya*;*

50. *...that He destroyed 'Ād, the earlier people,*

51. *...and Thamūd* – the people of Ṣāliḥ – ***as well, sparing none of them*** – so that not one of them remained*;*

52. *...and* We destroyed ***the people of Nūḥ before*** 'Ād and Thamūd; ***they were most unjust and exorbitant*** – more unjust than 'Ād and Thamūd, because of the long time that Nūḥ was among them: *"He remained among them for fifty short of a thousand years."* (29:14) After all that time, they still did not believe him and harmed him, but hit him*;*

53. *...and the Overturned City which He turned upside down* – the city of the people of Lūt. Allah made it crash down after raising it up into the sky and then turning it upside down when He commanded Jibrīl to do so*;*

54. ***...so that what*** (stones) ***enveloped it enveloped it*** and they were stupefied with terror. We read in *Sūra Hūd*: *"We turned their cities upside down and rained down on them stones of hard baked clay."* (11:81)

55. ***Which one of your Lord's blessings do you then dispute?*** The blessings of Allah indicate His oneness and power. So, O human being, do you doubt or deny?

56. ***This*** – from Muḥammad – ***is a warning like the warnings of old***: in other words, he is a Messenger like the Messengers before him. He has been sent to you as they were sent to their people.

57. ***The Imminent is imminent!*** The Resurrection is near.

58. ***No one besides Allah can unveil it.*** None can reveal it and make it appear except Him. This is like Allah's words: *"He alone will reveal it at its proper time."* (7:187)

59. ***Are you then amazed at this discourse*** (the Qur'an)***?*** Do you deny it –

60. ***...and laugh; and do you not cry*** – do you mock and not weep at the His promise and threat,

61. ***...treating life as a game*** – playing about and heedless about what He asks of you*?*

62. ***Prostrate before Allah*** Who created you ***and worship Him!*** Do not prostrate to idols and do not worship them.

سُورَةُ القَمَرِ

بِسْمِ اللَّهِ الرَّحْمَٰنِ الرَّحِيمِ

اقْتَرَبَتِ السَّاعَةُ وَانشَقَّ الْقَمَرُ ﴿١﴾ وَإِن يَرَوْا آيَةً يُعْرِضُوا
وَيَقُولُوا سِحْرٌ مُّسْتَمِرٌّ ﴿٢﴾ وَكَذَّبُوا وَاتَّبَعُوا أَهْوَاءَهُمْ
وَكُلُّ أَمْرٍ مُّسْتَقِرٌّ ﴿٣﴾ وَلَقَدْ جَاءَهُم مِّنَ الْأَنبَاءِ
مَا فِيهِ مُزْدَجَرٌ ﴿٤﴾ حِكْمَةٌ بَالِغَةٌ فَمَا تُغْنِ النُّذُرُ
﴿٥﴾ فَتَوَلَّ عَنْهُمْ يَوْمَ يَدْعُ الدَّاعِ إِلَىٰ شَيْءٍ نُّكُرٍ ﴿٦﴾
خُشَّعًا أَبْصَارُهُمْ يَخْرُجُونَ مِنَ الْأَجْدَاثِ كَأَنَّهُمْ جَرَادٌ مُّنتَشِرٌ ﴿٧﴾
مُّهْطِعِينَ إِلَى الدَّاعِ يَقُولُ الْكَافِرُونَ هَٰذَا يَوْمٌ عَسِرٌ ﴿٨﴾ ۞ كَذَّبَتْ
قَبْلَهُمْ قَوْمُ نُوحٍ فَكَذَّبُوا عَبْدَنَا وَقَالُوا مَجْنُونٌ وَازْدُجِرَ ﴿٩﴾ فَدَعَا
رَبَّهُ أَنِّي مَغْلُوبٌ فَانتَصِرْ ﴿١٠﴾ فَفَتَحْنَا أَبْوَابَ السَّمَاءِ بِمَاءٍ مُّنْهَمِرٍ
﴿١١﴾ وَفَجَّرْنَا الْأَرْضَ عُيُونًا فَالْتَقَى الْمَاءُ عَلَىٰ أَمْرٍ قَدْ قُدِرَ ﴿١٢﴾
وَحَمَلْنَاهُ عَلَىٰ ذَاتِ أَلْوَاحٍ وَدُسُرٍ ﴿١٣﴾ تَجْرِي بِأَعْيُنِنَا جَزَاءً لِّمَن كَانَ
كُفِرَ ﴿١٤﴾ وَلَقَد تَّرَكْنَاهَا آيَةً فَهَلْ مِن مُّدَّكِرٍ ﴿١٥﴾ فَكَيْفَ كَانَ
عَذَابِي وَنُذُرِ ﴿١٦﴾ وَلَقَدْ يَسَّرْنَا الْقُرْآنَ لِلذِّكْرِ فَهَلْ مِن مُّدَّكِرٍ
﴿١٧﴾ كَذَّبَتْ عَادٌ فَكَيْفَ كَانَ عَذَابِي وَنُذُرِ ﴿١٨﴾ إِنَّا أَرْسَلْنَا عَلَيْهِمْ
رِيحًا صَرْصَرًا فِي يَوْمِ نَحْسٍ مُّسْتَمِرٍّ ﴿١٩﴾ تَنزِعُ النَّاسَ كَأَنَّهُمْ أَعْجَازُ
نَخْلٍ مُّنقَعِرٍ ﴿٢٠﴾ فَكَيْفَ كَانَ عَذَابِي وَنُذُرِ ﴿٢١﴾ وَلَقَدْ يَسَّرْنَا الْقُرْآنَ
لِلذِّكْرِ فَهَلْ مِن مُّدَّكِرٍ ﴿٢٢﴾ كَذَّبَتْ ثَمُودُ بِالنُّذُرِ ﴿٢٣﴾ فَقَالُوا أَبَشَرًا
مِّنَّا وَاحِدًا نَّتَّبِعُهُ إِنَّا إِذًا لَّفِي ضَلَالٍ وَسُعُرٍ ﴿٢٤﴾ أَأُلْقِيَ الذِّكْرُ عَلَيْهِ

54. *Sūrat al-Qamar*
The Moon

This *sūra* is Makkan except for *āyat* 45, which is Madinan. It has 55 *āyat*s.

1. ***The Hour*** of the Rising ***has drawn near and the moon has split*** – into two halves over the hill Abū Qubays as a sign for him, may Allah bless him and grant him peace. He was asked for it and he said, "Bear witness!" Al-Bukhārī and Muslim related this.

2. ***If they*** (the unbelievers of Quraysh) ***see a Sign*** – a miracle of the Prophet, may Allah bless him and grant him peace – ***they turn away, saying 'There is no end to this witchcraft!'*** 'It is prolonged, strong sorcery.'

3. ***They have denied the truth*** – here meaning the Prophet, may Allah bless him and grant him peace – ***and followed their*** false ***whims and desires, but everything*** good and evil ***has its time*** – and is fixed and their adherents will be in the Garden and the Fire respectively.

4. ***News has come to them which contains a threat*** – information about the destruction of the nations who denied their Messengers. It contains a harsh deterrent,

5. ***...consummate*** – total – ***wisdom; but warnings are profitless.***

6. ***So turn away from them. On the Day the Summoner*** (Isrāfīl) ***summons them to something unspeakably terrible*** (read as *nukur* or *nukr*), something which souls find atrocious and horrible. That is the Reckoning –

7. ***...they will emerge from their graves with downcast*** (read as *khushsha'an* and *khāsi'an*) ***eyes*** – humble – ***like swarming locusts*** – not knowing where to go out of fear and confusion –

8. ***...necks outstretched, eyes transfixed, rushing headlong to the Summoner. The unbelievers will say, 'This is a pitiless day*** – for the unbelievers***!'*** – as in *Sūrat al-Muddaththir*: *"That Day will be a difficult day, not easy for the unbelievers."* (74:9-10)

9. ***Before them*** (Quraysh) ***the people of Nūḥ denied the truth. They denied Our slave*** – Nūḥ – ***saying, 'He is a madman,' and he was driven away with jeers*** – insults and other things.

10. ***He called upon his Lord: 'I am overwhelmed, so help me!'***

11. ***So We opened*** (read as *fataḥnā* and *fattaḥnā*) ***the gates of heaven with torrential water,***

12. ***...and made the earth burst forth with gushing springs. And the waters*** of heaven and earth ***met together in a way which was decreed*** before time. That was the decree that Nūḥ's people would be destroyed by drowning.

13. ***We bore him*** (Nūḥ) ***on a planked and well-caulked*** – the word used here, *dusur,* is palm-fibre cord or other things used to bind ships' planks together – ***ship***, the Ark,

14. ***...which ran before Our eyes*** – with Our knowledge, meaning it was preserved and protected – ***a reward for him who had been rejected*** – help for Nūḥ by drowning them. That was their punishment.

15. ***We left it*** (this action) ***as a Sign*** for anyone who reflects, because knowledge of it is widespread and will continue to spread. ***But is there any rememberer there?*** Is there anyone who will reflect and be warned by it?

16. ***How terrible were My punishment and warnings!*** This is confirmation in the form of a rhetorical question, intended to make those addressed affirm the fact that Allah's punishment descended on those who denied Nūḥ.

17. ***We have made the Qur'an easy to remember.*** We made it easy to memorise and an immediate reminder to people. ***But is there any rememberer there?*** Is there any who is admonished by it and memorises it? The question here is an instruction with the object of encouraging people to memorise it and be admonished by it. No other Book is memorised by heart in the same way.

18. ***'Ād denied the truth.*** Their Prophet was Hūd and they were punished. ***How terrible were My punishment and warnings!*** – My warning to them before the punishment descended on them. Then Allah explains what that punishment was.

19. ***We unleashed a howling wind against them on a day of unremitting horror.*** That was on the last Wednesday of the month.

20. ***It plucked up men like uprooted stumps.*** It sucked people up from pits in the earth in which they had taken refuge. It threw them on their heads and tore their necks so that their heads were ripped off their bodies. They looked like the stumps of palm trees cut down and fallen on the earth. They are likened to palm trees because of their height.

21. ***How terrible were My punishment and warnings!***

22. ***We have made the Qur'an easy to remember. But is there any rememberer there?***

23. ***Thamūd denied the warnings.*** These were the warnings brought by their Prophet Ṣāliḥ who warned them what would happen if they did not believe him and follow him.

24. ***They said, 'Are we to follow a human being, one of us?*** "How can we follow a human being when we are a large group and he is only one of us and is not an angel?", meaning that they would not follow him. ***Then we would truly be misguided*** from what is correct, and ***quite insane!***

25. ***Has the Reminder*** (the Revelation) ***been given to him, of all of us?*** They are saying that he has not been given Revelation. ***No indeed! He is an impudent liar*** in what he says about being given Revelation. He is arrogant and proud.'

26. Allah answers them: ***'They will know tomorrow*** – in the Next World – ***who the impudent liar is.*** They will be punished for denying their Prophet Ṣāliḥ.

27. ***We will send the she-camel as a trial for them.*** It was brought out from a mountain of stone, as they had requested, as a test. ***Just keep a watchful eye on them,*** Ṣāliḥ, ***and be steadfast*** – meaning wait and see what they do and what will be done to them. "Be patient in the face of their persecution."

28. ***Inform them that the water is to be shared out between them*** and the she-camel, ***each drinking by turn.'*** They would have it one day and the she-camel the next day, each having a share of the water. They continued for some time like this but then they became dissatisfied with it and decided to kill the camel.

مِنۢ بَيْنِنَا بَلْ هُوَ كَذَّابٌ أَشِرٌ ﴿٢٥﴾ سَيَعْلَمُونَ غَدًا مَّنِ ٱلْكَذَّابُ
ٱلْأَشِرُ ﴿٢٦﴾ إِنَّا مُرْسِلُوا۟ ٱلنَّاقَةِ فِتْنَةً لَّهُمْ فَٱرْتَقِبْهُمْ وَٱصْطَبِرْ ﴿٢٧﴾
وَنَبِّئْهُمْ أَنَّ ٱلْمَآءَ قِسْمَةٌۢ بَيْنَهُمْ ۖ كُلُّ شِرْبٍ مُّحْتَضَرٌ ﴿٢٨﴾ فَنَادَوْا۟ صَاحِبَهُمْ
فَتَعَاطَىٰ فَعَقَرَ ﴿٢٩﴾ فَكَيْفَ كَانَ عَذَابِى وَنُذُرِ ﴿٣٠﴾ إِنَّآ أَرْسَلْنَا عَلَيْهِمْ
صَيْحَةً وَٰحِدَةً فَكَانُوا۟ كَهَشِيمِ ٱلْمُحْتَظِرِ ﴿٣١﴾ وَلَقَدْ يَسَّرْنَا ٱلْقُرْءَانَ
لِلذِّكْرِ فَهَلْ مِن مُّدَّكِرٍ ﴿٣٢﴾ كَذَّبَتْ قَوْمُ لُوطٍۭ بِٱلنُّذُرِ ﴿٣٣﴾ إِنَّآ أَرْسَلْنَا
عَلَيْهِمْ حَاصِبًا إِلَّآ ءَالَ لُوطٍ ۖ نَّجَّيْنَٰهُم بِسَحَرٍ ﴿٣٤﴾ نِّعْمَةً مِّنْ عِندِنَا ۚ
كَذَٰلِكَ نَجْزِى مَن شَكَرَ ﴿٣٥﴾ وَلَقَدْ أَنذَرَهُم بَطْشَتَنَا فَتَمَارَوْا۟
بِٱلنُّذُرِ ﴿٣٦﴾ وَلَقَدْ رَٰوَدُوهُ عَن ضَيْفِهِۦ فَطَمَسْنَآ أَعْيُنَهُمْ فَذُوقُوا۟
عَذَابِى وَنُذُرِ ﴿٣٧﴾ وَلَقَدْ صَبَّحَهُم بُكْرَةً عَذَابٌ مُّسْتَقِرٌّ ﴿٣٨﴾
فَذُوقُوا۟ عَذَابِى وَنُذُرِ ﴿٣٩﴾ وَلَقَدْ يَسَّرْنَا ٱلْقُرْءَانَ لِلذِّكْرِ فَهَلْ مِن مُّدَّكِرٍ
﴿٤٠﴾ وَلَقَدْ جَآءَ ءَالَ فِرْعَوْنَ ٱلنُّذُرُ ﴿٤١﴾ كَذَّبُوا۟ بِـَٔايَٰتِنَا كُلِّهَا فَأَخَذْنَٰهُمْ
أَخْذَ عَزِيزٍ مُّقْتَدِرٍ ﴿٤٢﴾ أَكُفَّارُكُمْ خَيْرٌ مِّنْ أُو۟لَٰٓئِكُمْ أَمْ لَكُم بَرَآءَةٌ
فِى ٱلزُّبُرِ ﴿٤٣﴾ أَمْ يَقُولُونَ نَحْنُ جَمِيعٌ مُّنتَصِرٌ ﴿٤٤﴾ سَيُهْزَمُ ٱلْجَمْعُ
وَيُوَلُّونَ ٱلدُّبُرَ ﴿٤٥﴾ بَلِ ٱلسَّاعَةُ مَوْعِدُهُمْ وَٱلسَّاعَةُ أَدْهَىٰ وَأَمَرُّ
﴿٤٦﴾ إِنَّ ٱلْمُجْرِمِينَ فِى ضَلَٰلٍ وَسُعُرٍ ﴿٤٧﴾ يَوْمَ يُسْحَبُونَ فِى ٱلنَّارِ
عَلَىٰ وُجُوهِهِمْ ذُوقُوا۟ مَسَّ سَقَرَ ﴿٤٨﴾ إِنَّا كُلَّ شَىْءٍ خَلَقْنَٰهُ بِقَدَرٍ ﴿٤٩﴾

وَمَآ أَمْرُنَآ إِلَّا وَٰحِدَةٌ كَلَمْحٍۭ بِٱلْبَصَرِ ﴿٥٠﴾ وَلَقَدْ أَهْلَكْنَآ
أَشْيَاعَكُمْ فَهَلْ مِن مُّدَّكِرٍ ﴿٥١﴾ وَكُلُّ شَىْءٍ فَعَلُوهُ
فِى ٱلزُّبُرِ ﴿٥٢﴾ وَكُلُّ صَغِيرٍ وَكَبِيرٍ مُّسْتَطَرٌ ﴿٥٣﴾ إِنَّ ٱلْمُتَّقِينَ
فِى جَنَّٰتٍ وَنَهَرٍ ﴿٥٤﴾ فِى مَقْعَدِ صِدْقٍ عِندَ مَلِيكٍ مُّقْتَدِرٍۭ ﴿٥٥﴾

29. ***They called on their companion,*** Quddār, to kill the camel ***and*** he took his sword and ***he set to it and hamstrung her*** and killed her as they had told him to.

30. ***How terrible were My punishment and warnings*** to them about the punishment before it occurred*!*

31. ***We sent a single Blast against them and they were just like a fencer's reeds.*** A fencer is someone who makes an enclosure for his flock from dried branches and thorns to protect them from wolves and wild animals.

32. ***We have made the Qur'an easy to remember. But is there any rememberer there?***

33. ***The people of Lūṭ denied the warnings*** that he gave them.

34. ***We unleashed a sudden squall of stones*** – these were pebbles, small stones less in size than a fist – ***against all of them*** and they were destroyed ***except the family of Lūṭ*** and his sons, ***whom We rescued before dawn.*** The day is unspecified.

35. ***It was a blessing direct from Our presence. That is how We recompense those who give thanks*** – a reference to the believers, or those who believe in Allah and His Messenger and obey them.

36. ***He*** (Lūṭ) ***warned them of Our onslaught*** – to make them fear the punishment, but they argued – ***but they dismissed the warnings.***

37. ***They even wanted to seduce his guests!*** They wanted him to let them have the people who came to him in the form of guests so that they could copulate with them. The guests were angels. ***So We put out their eyes*** – Allah blinded them and made the place where their eyes had been skin like the rest of their faces when Jibrīl slapped them with his wing. We said to them: ***'Taste*** (experience) ***My punishment and warnings!'***

38. Early morning brought them enduring punishment, which is connected to punishment in the Next World.

39. ***'Taste My punishment and warnings!'***

40. ***We have made the Qur'an easy to remember. But is there any rememberer there?***

41. ***Warnings came to Pharaoh's people*** on the tongue of Mūsā and Hārūn, but they did not believe.

42. ***They dismissed every one of Our*** nine ***Signs*** that Mūsā was given, ***and so We seized them*** with the punishment – ***with the seizing of One who is Almighty, All-Powerful***, against whom none can stand.

43. ***Are your unbelievers***, Quraysh, ***better than those peoples*** mentioned, from the people of Nūḥ to those of Pharaoh***?*** They were not excused. ***Or have you***, unbelievers of Quraysh, ***been given exemption*** from the punishment ***in the Books?*** Both questions demand a negative response: that is not the case.

44. ***Or do they*** (the unbelievers of Quraysh) ***say, 'We are an assembly who will win*** against Muḥammad***'?*** When Abū Jahl said on the Day of Badr, "We are an assembly who will win," the following *āyat* was revealed:

45. ***The assembly will be routed and will turn their backs in flight.*** They were defeated at Badr and the Messenger of Allah, may Allah bless him and grant him peace, was victorious against them.

46. ***In fact the Hour is their promised appointment*** for their punishment, ***and the Hour is more disastrous and bitter*** than their punishment in this world.

47. ***The evildoers are indeed misguided and insane*** – destroyed by killing in this world and punished by an intense Fire in the Next World –

48. ***...on the Day that they are dragged face-first into the Fire*** in the Next World, they will be told: ***'Taste the scorching touch of Saqar!'*** This is what they will be told when the heat of Jahannam hits them.

49. ***We have created all things in due measure*** – in a predetermined amount.

50. ***Our command***, when We desire something to come into existence, ***is only one word like the blinking of an eye*** in quickness. It is His word "Be!", upon which it comes into existence. *"His command when He desires a thing is simply to say to it, 'Be!' and it is."* (36:81)

51. ***We destroyed those of your kind*** – like you in respect of unbelief – ***in the past*** nations. ***But is there any rememberer there?*** This is a command, meaning, "Remember and be warned!"

52. *Everything they did is in the Books.* Everything Allah's slaves have done is in the books recorded by their guardian angels.

53. *Everything* – wrong or right actions – ***is recorded*** in the Preserved Tablet, ***great or small.***

54. *The people who are godfearing will be amid Gardens and Rivers* – although the singular of river here is used it is generic and means "rivers". They will drink from its rivers of water, milk, honey and wine.

55. *...on seats* (read as *maq'ad* and *maqā'id*) ***of honour***: seats of truth with no prattle or wrongdoing in them. They will be in gatherings in the Gardens, free of prattle and wrongdoing which is not the case with gatherings of this world which are rarely free from that – ***in the presence of an All-Powerful King***, One with a mighty kingdom who is Vast for whom there is nothing which is beyond His power. That is Allah. This indicates that high rank and nearness are part of His bounty.

سُورَةُ الرَّحۡمَٰن

بِسۡمِ ٱللَّهِ ٱلرَّحۡمَٰنِ ٱلرَّحِيمِ

ٱلرَّحۡمَٰنُ ١ عَلَّمَ ٱلۡقُرۡءَانَ ٢ خَلَقَ ٱلۡإِنسَٰنَ ٣
عَلَّمَهُ ٱلۡبَيَانَ ٤ ٱلشَّمۡسُ وَٱلۡقَمَرُ بِحُسۡبَانٖ ٥ وَٱلنَّجۡمُ
وَٱلشَّجَرُ يَسۡجُدَانِ ٦ وَٱلسَّمَآءَ رَفَعَهَا وَوَضَعَ ٱلۡمِيزَانَ
٧ أَلَّا تَطۡغَوۡاْ فِي ٱلۡمِيزَانِ ٨ وَأَقِيمُواْ ٱلۡوَزۡنَ بِٱلۡقِسۡطِ
وَلَا تُخۡسِرُواْ ٱلۡمِيزَانَ ٩ وَٱلۡأَرۡضَ وَضَعَهَا لِلۡأَنَامِ ١٠
فِيهَا فَٰكِهَةٞ وَٱلنَّخۡلُ ذَاتُ ٱلۡأَكۡمَامِ ١١ وَٱلۡحَبُّ ذُو ٱلۡعَصۡفِ
وَٱلرَّيۡحَانُ ١٢ فَبِأَيِّ ءَالَآءِ رَبِّكُمَا تُكَذِّبَانِ ١٣ خَلَقَ
ٱلۡإِنسَٰنَ مِن صَلۡصَٰلٖ كَٱلۡفَخَّارِ ١٤ وَخَلَقَ ٱلۡجَآنَّ
مِن مَّارِجٖ مِّن نَّارٖ ١٥ فَبِأَيِّ ءَالَآءِ رَبِّكُمَا تُكَذِّبَانِ ١٦
رَبُّ ٱلۡمَشۡرِقَيۡنِ وَرَبُّ ٱلۡمَغۡرِبَيۡنِ ١٧ فَبِأَيِّ ءَالَآءِ رَبِّكُمَا تُكَذِّبَانِ ١٨
مَرَجَ ٱلۡبَحۡرَيۡنِ يَلۡتَقِيَانِ ١٩ بَيۡنَهُمَا بَرۡزَخٞ لَّا يَبۡغِيَانِ ٢٠ فَبِأَيِّ ءَالَآءِ
رَبِّكُمَا تُكَذِّبَانِ ٢١ يَخۡرُجُ مِنۡهُمَا ٱللُّؤۡلُؤُ وَٱلۡمَرۡجَانُ ٢٢ فَبِأَيِّ
ءَالَآءِ رَبِّكُمَا تُكَذِّبَانِ ٢٣ وَلَهُ ٱلۡجَوَارِ ٱلۡمُنشَـَٔاتُ فِي ٱلۡبَحۡرِ كَٱلۡأَعۡلَٰمِ
٢٤ فَبِأَيِّ ءَالَآءِ رَبِّكُمَا تُكَذِّبَانِ ٢٥ كُلُّ مَنۡ عَلَيۡهَا فَانٖ ٢٦ وَيَبۡقَىٰ
وَجۡهُ رَبِّكَ ذُو ٱلۡجَلَٰلِ وَٱلۡإِكۡرَامِ ٢٧ فَبِأَيِّ ءَالَآءِ رَبِّكُمَا تُكَذِّبَانِ
٢٨ يَسۡـَٔلُهُۥ مَن فِي ٱلسَّمَٰوَٰتِ وَٱلۡأَرۡضِۚ كُلَّ يَوۡمٍ هُوَ فِي شَأۡنٖ ٢٩ فَبِأَيِّ
ءَالَآءِ رَبِّكُمَا تُكَذِّبَانِ ٣٠ سَنَفۡرُغُ لَكُمۡ أَيُّهَ ٱلثَّقَلَانِ ٣١ فَبِأَيِّ
ءَالَآءِ رَبِّكُمَا تُكَذِّبَانِ ٣٢ يَٰمَعۡشَرَ ٱلۡجِنِّ وَٱلۡإِنسِ إِنِ ٱسۡتَطَعۡتُمۡ

55. *Sūrat ar-Raḥmān* The All-Merciful

This *sūra* is Madinan except for *āyat* 29. It has 76 or 78 *āyats*.

1. ***The All-Merciful*** (Allah)

2. ***...taught the Qur'an*** to whomever He wished.

3. ***He created man*** (generically meant)

4. ***...and taught him clear expression.***

5. ***The sun and the moon both run with precision.***

6. ***The stars and the trees all bow down in prostration.*** It is said that "stars" can also mean plants without stalks or trunks. They all submit to whatever Allah desires.

7. ***He erected heaven and established the balance*** of justice ...

8. ***...so that you would not transgress the balance*** and not be unjust in respect of what you weigh out.

9. ***Give just weight – do not skimp in the balance***, giving short weight.

10. ***He laid out the earth for all living creatures*** and made it firm for men, jinn and others.

11. ***In it are fruits and date-palms with covered spathes,***

12. ***...and grains on leafy stems, and fragrant herbs.*** Grains are crops like wheat and barley, but this is also said to include things like figs. The herbs are either basil or all sweet-smelling herbs.

13. ***So which of your Lord's blessings do you both,*** mankind and jinn, ***then deny?*** The question is for confirmation, according to what al-Ḥākim related that Jābir said: "The Messenger of Allah, may Allah bless him and grant him peace, recited *Sūrat ar-Raḥmān* to us right to the end and then said, 'Why do I see you silent? The jinn had a better reply than you. Once I recited to them this *āyat*, '*So which of your Lord's blessings do you both then deny?'* They said, 'We do not deny any of Your blessings, our Lord. All praise is Yours.'"

14. ***He created man*** (Ādam) ***from dry earth like baked clay*** – dry clay which makes a sound when it is hollow –

15. ***...and He created*** the father of ***the jinn,*** Iblīs, ***from a fusion of fire*** – flames free of smoke.

16. ***So which of your Lord's blessings do you both then deny?***

17. ***The Lord of the two Easts and the Lord of the two Wests***, meaning the east and west of the summer and the east and west of the winter.

18. ***So which of your Lord's blessings do you both then deny?***

19. ***He has let loose the two seas*** – the sweet and the salty, which the eye sees as ***converging together...***

20. ***...with a barrier*** of the power of Allah Almighty ***between them they do not break through.*** Neither of them encroaches on the other and mixes with it.

21. ***So which of your Lord's blessings do you both then deny?***

22. ***From out of them come glistening pearls and coral*** – actually from one of the them, the salt sea.

23. ***So which of your Lord's blessings do you both then deny?***

24. ***His, too, are the ships sailing like mountain peaks on the sea*** – like mountains because of their size and height.

25. ***So which of your Lord's blessings do you both then deny?***

26. ***Everyone on it will pass away*** – all living creatures on the earth will die. The use of the pronoun for intelligent beings predominates,

27. ***...but the Face of your Lord*** (His Immense Essence) ***will remain, Master of Majesty and Generosity.*** He is generous to the believers by blessing them.

28. ***So which of your Lord's blessings do you both then deny?***

29. ***Everyone in the heavens and earth requests His aid.*** The asking is by words or state for the strength they need to worship Allah, provision, forgiveness and other things. ***Every day He is engaged in some affair.*** At every moment Allah manifests something according to what He has decreed before time, in terms of giving life, taking life, exalting, abasing, enriching, impoverishing, answering the supplication, giving to the one who asks, and other similar things.

30. ***So which of your Lord's blessings do you both then deny?***

أَن تَنفُذُوا۟ مِنْ أَقْطَارِ ٱلسَّمَٰوَٰتِ وَٱلْأَرْضِ فَٱنفُذُوا۟ ۚ لَا تَنفُذُونَ
إِلَّا بِسُلْطَٰنٍ ٣٣ فَبِأَىِّ ءَالَآءِ رَبِّكُمَا تُكَذِّبَانِ ٣٤ يُرْسَلُ عَلَيْكُمَا
شُوَاظٌ مِّن نَّارٍ وَنُحَاسٌ فَلَا تَنتَصِرَانِ ٣٥ فَبِأَىِّ ءَالَآءِ رَبِّكُمَا
تُكَذِّبَانِ ٣٦ فَإِذَا ٱنشَقَّتِ ٱلسَّمَآءُ فَكَانَتْ وَرْدَةً كَٱلدِّهَانِ
٣٧ فَبِأَىِّ ءَالَآءِ رَبِّكُمَا تُكَذِّبَانِ ٣٨ فَيَوْمَئِذٍ لَّا يُسْـَٔلُ عَن ذَنۢبِهِۦٓ
إِنسٌ وَلَا جَآنٌّ ٣٩ فَبِأَىِّ ءَالَآءِ رَبِّكُمَا تُكَذِّبَانِ ٤٠
يُعْرَفُ ٱلْمُجْرِمُونَ بِسِيمَٰهُمْ فَيُؤْخَذُ بِٱلنَّوَٰصِى وَٱلْأَقْدَامِ ٤١ فَبِأَىِّ
ءَالَآءِ رَبِّكُمَا تُكَذِّبَانِ ٤٢ هَٰذِهِۦ جَهَنَّمُ ٱلَّتِى يُكَذِّبُ بِهَا ٱلْمُجْرِمُونَ
٤٣ يَطُوفُونَ بَيْنَهَا وَبَيْنَ حَمِيمٍ ءَانٍ ٤٤ فَبِأَىِّ ءَالَآءِ رَبِّكُمَا تُكَذِّبَانِ
٤٥ وَلِمَنْ خَافَ مَقَامَ رَبِّهِۦ جَنَّتَانِ ٤٦ فَبِأَىِّ ءَالَآءِ رَبِّكُمَا تُكَذِّبَانِ
٤٧ ذَوَاتَآ أَفْنَانٍ ٤٨ فَبِأَىِّ ءَالَآءِ رَبِّكُمَا تُكَذِّبَانِ ٤٩ فِيهِمَا عَيْنَانِ
تَجْرِيَانِ ٥٠ فَبِأَىِّ ءَالَآءِ رَبِّكُمَا تُكَذِّبَانِ ٥١ فِيهِمَا مِن كُلِّ فَٰكِهَةٍ
زَوْجَانِ ٥٢ فَبِأَىِّ ءَالَآءِ رَبِّكُمَا تُكَذِّبَانِ ٥٣ مُتَّكِـِٔينَ عَلَىٰ فُرُشٍۭ
بَطَآئِنُهَا مِنْ إِسْتَبْرَقٍ ۚ وَجَنَى ٱلْجَنَّتَيْنِ دَانٍ ٥٤ فَبِأَىِّ ءَالَآءِ رَبِّكُمَا
تُكَذِّبَانِ ٥٥ فِيهِنَّ قَٰصِرَٰتُ ٱلطَّرْفِ لَمْ يَطْمِثْهُنَّ إِنسٌ قَبْلَهُمْ
وَلَا جَآنٌّ ٥٦ فَبِأَىِّ ءَالَآءِ رَبِّكُمَا تُكَذِّبَانِ ٥٧ كَأَنَّهُنَّ ٱلْيَاقُوتُ
وَٱلْمَرْجَانُ ٥٨ فَبِأَىِّ ءَالَآءِ رَبِّكُمَا تُكَذِّبَانِ ٥٩ هَلْ جَزَآءُ
ٱلْإِحْسَٰنِ إِلَّا ٱلْإِحْسَٰنُ ٦٠ فَبِأَىِّ ءَالَآءِ رَبِّكُمَا تُكَذِّبَانِ
٦١ وَمِن دُونِهِمَا جَنَّتَانِ ٦٢ فَبِأَىِّ ءَالَآءِ رَبِّكُمَا تُكَذِّبَانِ
٦٣ مُدْهَآمَّتَانِ ٦٤ فَبِأَىِّ ءَالَآءِ رَبِّكُمَا تُكَذِّبَانِ ٦٥ فِيهِمَا

31. ***Soon We will settle your affairs, you two weighty throngs.*** We will deal with Your Reckoning, mankind and jinn!

32. ***So which of your Lord's blessings do you both then deny?***

33. ***Company of jinn and men, if you are able to pierce through the confines of the heavens and earth, pierce through them.*** Can you go beyond the confines of heaven and earth? ***You will not pierce through except with a clear authority.*** That is impossible except with a strength which you do not possess.

34. ***So which of your Lord's blessings do you both then deny?***

35. ***He will pursue you with a piercing flame*** – a smokeless flame – ***and fiery smoke*** – hot flameless smoke – ***and you will not be helped*** against that. They will be driven to the Gathering.

36. ***So which of your Lord's blessings do you both then deny?***

37. ***When heaven is split apart*** – the gates of heaven are opened and the angels descend – ***and goes red like dregs of oil.*** It will be a chestnut red like red leather which is not its normal colour. There will be a great terror.

38. ***So which of your Lord's blessings do you both then deny?***

39. ***That Day no man or jinn will be asked about his sin.*** They will be asked about it at another time. *"By your Lord, We will question them all, every one of them."* (15:92) Here the word for "jinn", *al-jānn,* is generic term for all the jinn as the word, *ins,* is generic for all mankind.

40. ***So which of your Lord's blessings do you both then deny?***

41. ***The evildoers will be recognised by their mark*** – the darkness of their faces and blueness of their eyes – ***and seized by their forelocks and their feet.***

42. ***So which of your Lord's blessings do you both then deny?*** They will be told, when the evildoers are seized by their forelocks and feet and flung into Hell:

43. ***This is Hell which the evildoers deny.***

44. ***They will go back and forth between fire and scalding water.*** They will drink scalding water when they seek help from the heat of the Fire.

45. ***So which of your Lord's blessings do you both then deny?***

46. ***For those who fear the Station of their Lord*** – the time when they will stand before Him for the Reckoning and so do not disobey Him – ***there are two Gardens.***

47. ***So which of your Lord's blessings do you both then deny?***

48. ***Shaded by spreading branches.***

49. ***So which of your Lord's blessings do you both then deny?***

50. ***In them are two clear flowing springs.***

51. ***So which of your Lord's blessings do you both then deny?***

52. ***In them are two kinds of every fruit*** of this world, or simply two kinds of any sort of fruit. There are fresh and dry, and the kind which is bitter in this world, like colocynth, will be sweet there.

53. ***So which of your Lord's blessings do you both then deny?***

54. ***They will be reclining on couches lined with rich brocade,*** experiencing delight, ***the fruits of the Gardens hanging close to hand*** – they are brought right up to everyone there, whether they are standing, sitting or lying down.

55. ***So which of your Lord's blessings do you both then deny?***

56. ***In them*** (both Gardens) – as well as in the high buildings and palaces which are there – ***are maidens with eyes for them alone*** – only looking at their reclining husbands, whether human or jinn – ***untouched before them by either man or jinn.*** These are some of the houris and some women from this world.

57. ***So which of your Lord's blessings do you both then deny?***

58. ***Like precious gems of*** pure ***ruby and*** white ***pearl.***

59. ***So which of your Lord's blessings do you both then deny?***

60. ***Will the reward for doing good*** and acts of obedience ***be anything other than good*** – meaning the bliss of the Garden***?***

61. ***So which of your Lord's blessings do you both then deny?***

62. ***As well as those two*** Gardens ***there will be two other Gardens*** for those who fear the time when they will stand before their Lord.

63. ***So which of your Lord's blessings do you both then deny?***

64. ***Of deep viridian green.*** They appear black from the intensity of their greenness.

65. ***So which of your Lord's blessings do you both then deny?***

عَيْنَانِ نَضَّاخَتَانِ ٦٦ فَبِأَيِّ ءَالَآءِ رَبِّكُمَا تُكَذِّبَانِ ٦٧
فِيهِمَا فَٰكِهَةٌ وَنَخْلٌ وَرُمَّانٌ ٦٨ فَبِأَيِّ ءَالَآءِ رَبِّكُمَا تُكَذِّبَانِ ٦٩
فِيهِنَّ خَيْرَٰتٌ حِسَانٌ ٧٠ فَبِأَيِّ ءَالَآءِ رَبِّكُمَا تُكَذِّبَانِ ٧١ حُورٌ
مَّقْصُورَٰتٌ فِى ٱلْخِيَامِ ٧٢ فَبِأَيِّ ءَالَآءِ رَبِّكُمَا تُكَذِّبَانِ ٧٣
لَمْ يَطْمِثْهُنَّ إِنسٌ قَبْلَهُمْ وَلَا جَآنٌّ ٧٤ فَبِأَيِّ ءَالَآءِ رَبِّكُمَا تُكَذِّبَانِ
٧٥ مُتَّكِـِٔينَ عَلَىٰ رَفْرَفٍ خُضْرٍ وَعَبْقَرِىٍّ حِسَانٍ ٧٦ فَبِأَيِّ
ءَالَآءِ رَبِّكُمَا تُكَذِّبَانِ ٧٧ تَبَٰرَكَ ٱسْمُ رَبِّكَ ذِى ٱلْجَلَٰلِ وَٱلْإِكْرَامِ ٧٨

66. ***In them are two gushing springs.***

67. ***So which of your Lord's blessings do you both then deny?***

68. ***In them are fruits and date-palms and pomegranates.*** These are said to be the same as those in this world, but are also said to be quite different.

69. ***So which of your Lord's blessings do you both then deny?***

70. ***In them are sweet, lovely maidens*** of good character and with beautiful faces.

71. ***So which of your Lord's blessings do you both then deny?***

72. ***Dark-eyed, secluded in cool pavilions.*** The black and white of their eyes is very intense and they are veiled in pavilions made of hollowed-out pearls beside the palaces.

73. ***So which of your Lord's blessings do you both then deny?***

74. ***Untouched before them by either man or jinn.***

75. ***So which of your Lord's blessings do you both then deny?***

76. Their wives and their companions are – ***reclining on green quilts*** – the word used here, *rafraf,* can mean carpets or cushions – ***and exquisite rugs.***

77. ***So which of your Lord's blessings do you both then deny?***

78. ***Blessed be the name of your Lord, Master of Majesty and Generosity!*** This is a repetition of an *āyat* in *Sūrat al-Furqān.*

سُورَةُ الوَاقِعَةِ

بِسْمِ ٱللَّهِ ٱلرَّحْمَٰنِ ٱلرَّحِيمِ

إِذَا وَقَعَتِ ٱلْوَاقِعَةُ ﴿١﴾ لَيْسَ لِوَقْعَتِهَا كَاذِبَةٌ ﴿٢﴾ خَافِضَةٌ رَّافِعَةٌ
﴿٣﴾ إِذَا رُجَّتِ ٱلْأَرْضُ رَجًّا ﴿٤﴾ وَبُسَّتِ ٱلْجِبَالُ بَسًّا ﴿٥﴾
فَكَانَتْ هَبَآءً مُّنۢبَثًّا ﴿٦﴾ وَكُنتُمْ أَزْوَٰجًا ثَلَٰثَةً ﴿٧﴾ فَأَصْحَٰبُ
ٱلْمَيْمَنَةِ مَآ أَصْحَٰبُ ٱلْمَيْمَنَةِ ﴿٨﴾ وَأَصْحَٰبُ ٱلْمَشْـَٔمَةِ مَآ أَصْحَٰبُ
ٱلْمَشْـَٔمَةِ ﴿٩﴾ وَٱلسَّٰبِقُونَ ٱلسَّٰبِقُونَ ﴿١٠﴾ أُو۟لَٰٓئِكَ ٱلْمُقَرَّبُونَ ﴿١١﴾
فِى جَنَّٰتِ ٱلنَّعِيمِ ﴿١٢﴾ ثُلَّةٌ مِّنَ ٱلْأَوَّلِينَ ﴿١٣﴾ وَقَلِيلٌ مِّنَ ٱلْءَاخِرِينَ
﴿١٤﴾ عَلَىٰ سُرُرٍ مَّوْضُونَةٍ ﴿١٥﴾ مُّتَّكِـِٔينَ عَلَيْهَا مُتَقَٰبِلِينَ ﴿١٦﴾
يَطُوفُ عَلَيْهِمْ وِلْدَٰنٌ مُّخَلَّدُونَ ﴿١٧﴾ بِأَكْوَابٍ وَأَبَارِيقَ وَكَأْسٍ مِّن مَّعِينٍ
﴿١٨﴾ لَّا يُصَدَّعُونَ عَنْهَا وَلَا يُنزِفُونَ ﴿١٩﴾ وَفَٰكِهَةٍ مِّمَّا يَتَخَيَّرُونَ
﴿٢٠﴾ وَلَحْمِ طَيْرٍ مِّمَّا يَشْتَهُونَ ﴿٢١﴾ وَحُورٌ عِينٌ ﴿٢٢﴾ كَأَمْثَٰلِ ٱللُّؤْلُؤِ
ٱلْمَكْنُونِ ﴿٢٣﴾ جَزَآءًۢ بِمَا كَانُوا۟ يَعْمَلُونَ ﴿٢٤﴾ لَا يَسْمَعُونَ فِيهَا لَغْوًا وَلَا
تَأْثِيمًا ﴿٢٥﴾ إِلَّا قِيلًا سَلَٰمًا سَلَٰمًا ﴿٢٦﴾ وَأَصْحَٰبُ ٱلْيَمِينِ مَآ أَصْحَٰبُ
ٱلْيَمِينِ ﴿٢٧﴾ فِى سِدْرٍ مَّخْضُودٍ ﴿٢٨﴾ وَطَلْحٍ مَّنضُودٍ ﴿٢٩﴾ وَظِلٍّ مَّمْدُودٍ
﴿٣٠﴾ وَمَآءٍ مَّسْكُوبٍ ﴿٣١﴾ وَفَٰكِهَةٍ كَثِيرَةٍ ﴿٣٢﴾ لَّا مَقْطُوعَةٍ وَلَا
مَمْنُوعَةٍ ﴿٣٣﴾ وَفُرُشٍ مَّرْفُوعَةٍ ﴿٣٤﴾ إِنَّآ أَنشَأْنَٰهُنَّ إِنشَآءً ﴿٣٥﴾ فَجَعَلْنَٰهُنَّ
أَبْكَارًا ﴿٣٦﴾ عُرُبًا أَتْرَابًا ﴿٣٧﴾ لِّأَصْحَٰبِ ٱلْيَمِينِ ﴿٣٨﴾ ثُلَّةٌ مِّنَ
ٱلْأَوَّلِينَ ﴿٣٩﴾ وَثُلَّةٌ مِّنَ ٱلْءَاخِرِينَ ﴿٤٠﴾ وَأَصْحَٰبُ ٱلشِّمَالِ مَآ أَصْحَٰبُ
ٱلشِّمَالِ ﴿٤١﴾ فِى سَمُومٍ وَحَمِيمٍ ﴿٤٢﴾ وَظِلٍّ مِّن يَحْمُومٍ ﴿٤٣﴾ لَّا بَارِدٍ

56. *Sūrat al-Wāqi'a*
The Occurrence

This *sūra* is Makkan, except for *āyat*s 81 and 82, which are Madinan. It has 96, 97 or 99 *āyat*s.

1. ***When the Great Event*** – the Resurrection – ***occurs –***

2. ***...none will deny its occurrence*** – no soul will deny it then as they denied it in this world –

3. ***...bringing low, raising high.*** Some people will be brought low by being driven into the Fire while others will be raised high by being admitted into the Garden.

4. ***When the earth is convulsed*** violently,

5. ***...and the mountains are crushed*** to powder,

6. ***...and become scattered*** flecks of ***dust in the air.***

7. ***And you will be classed into three*** on the Day of Rising.

8. ***The Companions of the Right: what of the Companions of the Right?*** They are the people who are given their books in their right hands. This exalts their position because they will enter the Paradise.

9. ***The Companions of the Left: what of the Companions of the Left?*** These are given their books in their left hands and they will be debased because they will enter the Fire.

10. ***And the Forerunners, the Forerunners.*** Those who race first to good. They are the Prophets. Repetition is used to stress their importance.

11. ***Those are the ones brought near,***

12. ***...in Gardens of Delight.***

13. ***A large group of the earlier people*** of past nations,

14. ***...but few of the later ones*** – few of the community of Muḥammad, may Allah bless him and grant him peace. They are the forerunners of past nations and this nation.

15. ***On sumptuous woven couches*** inlaid with gold and gems,

16. ***...reclining on them face to face.***

17. ***Ageless youths will circulate among them*** – young servants who do not age –

18. ***...carrying goblets and decanters*** – the former are vessels with no handle and the latter vessels with a nose or spout and handles to hold them by – ***and a cup from a flowing spring*** which never stops.

19. ***It does not give them any headache, nor does it leave them stu - pefied*** (read as *yunzafūna* and *yunzifūna*). They do not get a headache from it nor does their intellect become disturbed as is the case with wine in this world.

20. ***And any fruit they specify,***

21. ***...and any bird-meat they desire,***

22. ***...and dark-eyed maidens*** (read as *ḥūrun 'īnun* and *ḥūrin 'īnin*) – girls with very large dark eyes –

23. ***...like hidden pearls,***

24. ***...as recompense for what they did.***

25. ***They will hear no prattling in it*** (the Garden) ***nor any word of wrong*** – coarse language which is sinful.

26. ***All that is said is, 'Peace! Peace!'*** That is all that they will hear there.

27. ***And the Companions of the Right: what of the Companions of the Right?***

28. ***Amid thornless lote-trees*** – lote-trees in this world have thorns –

29. ***...and fruit-laden acacias,*** also said to be banana trees which will be full of fruit from top to bottom,

30. ***...and wide-spreading*** constant ***shade,***

31. ***...and*** constantly ***outpouring water,***

32. ***...and fruits in abundance,***

33. ***...never failing*** at any time ***unrestricted*** – not costing anything –

34. ***...and on elevated couches.***

35. ***We have brought maidens into being*** – houris who were created without being born –

36. ***...and made them purest virgins*** – whenever their husbands come to them, they find them virgins;

وَلَا كَرِيمٍ ﴿٤٤﴾ إِنَّهُمْ كَانُوا۟ قَبْلَ ذَٰلِكَ مُتْرَفِينَ ﴿٤٥﴾ وَكَانُوا۟ يُصِرُّونَ
عَلَى ٱلْحِنثِ ٱلْعَظِيمِ ﴿٤٦﴾ وَكَانُوا۟ يَقُولُونَ أَئِذَا مِتْنَا وَكُنَّا تُرَابًا
وَعِظَٰمًا أَءِنَّا لَمَبْعُوثُونَ ﴿٤٧﴾ أَوَءَابَآؤُنَا ٱلْأَوَّلُونَ ﴿٤٨﴾ قُلْ إِنَّ
ٱلْأَوَّلِينَ وَٱلْـَٔاخِرِينَ ﴿٤٩﴾ لَمَجْمُوعُونَ إِلَىٰ مِيقَٰتِ يَوْمٍ مَّعْلُومٍ ﴿٥٠﴾
ثُمَّ إِنَّكُمْ أَيُّهَا ٱلضَّآلُّونَ ٱلْمُكَذِّبُونَ ﴿٥١﴾ لَءَاكِلُونَ مِن شَجَرٍ مِّن زَقُّومٍ ﴿٥٢﴾
فَمَالِـُٔونَ مِنْهَا ٱلْبُطُونَ ﴿٥٣﴾ فَشَٰرِبُونَ عَلَيْهِ مِنَ ٱلْحَمِيمِ ﴿٥٤﴾ فَشَٰرِبُونَ
شُرْبَ ٱلْهِيمِ ﴿٥٥﴾ هَٰذَا نُزُلُهُمْ يَوْمَ ٱلدِّينِ ﴿٥٦﴾ نَحْنُ خَلَقْنَٰكُمْ فَلَوْلَا
تُصَدِّقُونَ ﴿٥٧﴾ أَفَرَءَيْتُم مَّا تُمْنُونَ ﴿٥٨﴾ ءَأَنتُمْ تَخْلُقُونَهُۥٓ أَمْ نَحْنُ
ٱلْخَٰلِقُونَ ﴿٥٩﴾ نَحْنُ قَدَّرْنَا بَيْنَكُمُ ٱلْمَوْتَ وَمَا نَحْنُ بِمَسْبُوقِينَ ﴿٦٠﴾
عَلَىٰٓ أَن نُّبَدِّلَ أَمْثَٰلَكُمْ وَنُنشِئَكُمْ فِى مَا لَا تَعْلَمُونَ ﴿٦١﴾ وَلَقَدْ
عَلِمْتُمُ ٱلنَّشْأَةَ ٱلْأُولَىٰ فَلَوْلَا تَذَكَّرُونَ ﴿٦٢﴾ أَفَرَءَيْتُم مَّا تَحْرُثُونَ
﴿٦٣﴾ ءَأَنتُمْ تَزْرَعُونَهُۥٓ أَمْ نَحْنُ ٱلزَّٰرِعُونَ ﴿٦٤﴾ لَوْ نَشَآءُ لَجَعَلْنَٰهُ
حُطَٰمًا فَظَلْتُمْ تَفَكَّهُونَ ﴿٦٥﴾ إِنَّا لَمُغْرَمُونَ ﴿٦٦﴾ بَلْ نَحْنُ مَحْرُومُونَ
﴿٦٧﴾ أَفَرَءَيْتُمُ ٱلْمَآءَ ٱلَّذِى تَشْرَبُونَ ﴿٦٨﴾ ءَأَنتُمْ أَنزَلْتُمُوهُ مِنَ ٱلْمُزْنِ
أَمْ نَحْنُ ٱلْمُنزِلُونَ ﴿٦٩﴾ لَوْ نَشَآءُ جَعَلْنَٰهُ أُجَاجًا فَلَوْلَا تَشْكُرُونَ
﴿٧٠﴾ أَفَرَءَيْتُمُ ٱلنَّارَ ٱلَّتِى تُورُونَ ﴿٧١﴾ ءَأَنتُمْ أَنشَأْتُمْ شَجَرَتَهَآ أَمْ
نَحْنُ ٱلْمُنشِـُٔونَ ﴿٧٢﴾ نَحْنُ جَعَلْنَٰهَا تَذْكِرَةً وَمَتَٰعًا لِّلْمُقْوِينَ
﴿٧٣﴾ فَسَبِّحْ بِٱسْمِ رَبِّكَ ٱلْعَظِيمِ ﴿٧٤﴾ ۞ فَلَآ أُقْسِمُ
بِمَوَٰقِعِ ٱلنُّجُومِ ﴿٧٥﴾ وَإِنَّهُۥ لَقَسَمٌ لَّوْ تَعْلَمُونَ عَظِيمٌ ﴿٧٦﴾
إِنَّهُۥ لَقُرْءَانٌ كَرِيمٌ ﴿٧٧﴾ فِى كِتَٰبٍ مَّكْنُونٍ ﴿٧٨﴾ لَّا يَمَسُّهُۥٓ إِلَّا

37. ***...devoted, passionate*** (read as *'urub* and *'urb*) towards their spouses, ***of like age,***

38. ... appointed ***for the Companions of the Right:***

39. ***...a large group of the earlier people...***

40. ***...and a large group of the later ones.***

41. ***And the Companions of the Left: what of the Companions of the Left?***

42. ***Amid searing blasts*** – the word used here, *samūm,* is a wind of intense heat – ***and scalding water...***

43. ***...and the murk of thick black smoke,***

44. ***...providing no coolness*** – which other kinds of shade do – ***and no pleasure*** when you see it.

45. ***Before that***, in this world, ***they were living in luxury*** – in great affluence, but did not bother themselves with obeying Allah,

46. ***... persisting in immense wrongdoing***: wrong actions and *shirk,...*

47. ***...and saying, 'When we are dead and turned to dust and bones, shall we then be raised again?***

48. ***And our forefathers, the earlier peoples?'*** Their question means that they think that it is unlikely.

49. ***Say: 'The earlier and the later peoples...***

50. ***...will certainly all be gathered to the appointment of a specified Day*** – the Day of Rising.

51. ***Then you, you misguided, you deniers,***

52. ***...will eat from the tree of Zaqqūm,***

53. ***...filling your stomachs with it,***

54. ***...and drink scalding water on top of it*** – those who eat from Zaqqūm will also drink boiling water,

55. ***...slurping*** (read as *shurb* and *sharb*) ***like thirst-crazed camels.*** The word for "thirst-crazed camels", *hīm,* is the plural of *hayām,* which means a camel suffering from a disease that makes it madly thirsty.

56. ***This will be their hospitality*** prepared for them ***on the Day of Judgment!'***

57. ***We created you, so why do you not confirm the truth?*** We brought you into existence from non-existence. Why then do you not believe in the Resurrection since the One who is able to originate is certainly able to regenerate?

58. ***Have you thought about the sperm that you ejaculate*** – which settles into the wombs of women***?***

59. ***Is it you who create it*** (sperm) ***or are We the Creator?***

60. ***We have decreed*** (read as *qaddarnā* and *qadarnā*) ***death for you and We will not be forestalled*** – and no one can escape Us –

61. ***...in replacing you with others the same as you and re-forming you in a way you know nothing about***: in other forms, like monkeys and pigs.

62. ***You have known the first formation*** (read as *nash'a* and *nasha'a*) ***so will you not pay heed?***

63. ***Have you thought about what you cultivate?*** – the land you plough and put your seeds into.

64. ***Is it you who make it germinate*** and grow ***or are We the Germinator?***

65. ***If We wished We could have made it broken stubble*** – dry broken chaff with no grain in it. ***You would then be left devoid of crops, distraught*** – stunned and distressed by that – and say***:***

66. ***'We are ruined*** – in debt for what we spent on our crops –

67. ***...in fact we are destitute!'*** "We have no provision at all."

68. ***Have you thought about the water that you drink?***

69. ***Is it you who sent it down from the clouds or are We the Sender?***

70. ***If We wished We could have made it bitter*** – so salty that it cannot be drunk – ***so will you not give thanks?***

71. ***Have you thought about the fire that you light?*** The fire which comes from the green trees whose wood is used as a fire lighter.

72. ***Is it you who make the trees that fuel it grow or are We the Grower?***

73. ***We have made it to be a reminder*** of Hellfire ***and a comfort for travellers in the wild*** – a means of warmth and light for those travelling in places where there are neither plants nor water.

ٱلۡمُطَهَّرُونَ ﴿٧٩﴾ تَنزِيلٞ مِّن رَّبِّ ٱلۡعَٰلَمِينَ ﴿٨٠﴾ أَفَبِهَٰذَا ٱلۡحَدِيثِ
أَنتُم مُّدۡهِنُونَ ﴿٨١﴾ وَتَجۡعَلُونَ رِزۡقَكُمۡ أَنَّكُمۡ تُكَذِّبُونَ ﴿٨٢﴾ فَلَوۡلَآ
إِذَا بَلَغَتِ ٱلۡحُلۡقُومَ ﴿٨٣﴾ وَأَنتُمۡ حِينَئِذٖ تَنظُرُونَ ﴿٨٤﴾ وَنَحۡنُ أَقۡرَبُ
إِلَيۡهِ مِنكُمۡ وَلَٰكِن لَّا تُبۡصِرُونَ ﴿٨٥﴾ فَلَوۡلَآ إِن كُنتُمۡ غَيۡرَ مَدِينِينَ
﴿٨٦﴾ تَرۡجِعُونَهَآ إِن كُنتُمۡ صَٰدِقِينَ ﴿٨٧﴾ فَأَمَّآ إِن كَانَ مِنَ ٱلۡمُقَرَّبِينَ
﴿٨٨﴾ فَرَوۡحٞ وَرَيۡحَانٞ وَجَنَّتُ نَعِيمٖ ﴿٨٩﴾ وَأَمَّآ إِن كَانَ مِنۡ أَصۡحَٰبِ
ٱلۡيَمِينِ ﴿٩٠﴾ فَسَلَٰمٞ لَّكَ مِنۡ أَصۡحَٰبِ ٱلۡيَمِينِ ﴿٩١﴾ وَأَمَّآ إِن كَانَ مِنَ
ٱلۡمُكَذِّبِينَ ٱلضَّآلِّينَ ﴿٩٢﴾ فَنُزُلٞ مِّنۡ حَمِيمٖ ﴿٩٣﴾ وَتَصۡلِيَةُ جَحِيمٍ
﴿٩٤﴾ إِنَّ هَٰذَا لَهُوَ حَقُّ ٱلۡيَقِينِ ﴿٩٥﴾ فَسَبِّحۡ بِٱسۡمِ رَبِّكَ ٱلۡعَظِيمِ ﴿٩٦﴾

74. ***So glorify the name of your Lord, the Magnificent!*** Proclaim Allah to be pure from any association.

75. ***No! I swear by the falling*** (setting) ***of the stars –***

76. ***...and that is a mighty oath if you only knew –*** swearing by that is an immense oath. If you were someone with knowledge, you would have known that –

77. ***...it*** (what is recited to you) ***truly is a Noble Qur'an...***

78. ***...in a well protected Book*** – written and safeguarded, referring to bound copies of the Qur'an.

79. ***No one may touch it except the purified –*** this is a prohibition. Those who have purified themselves of minor impurities are the only ones who should touch copies of the Qur'an.

80. ***...revelation sent down from the Lord of all the worlds*** – Allah.

81. ***Do you nonetheless regard this discourse*** (the Qur'an) ***with scorn*** – disdaining and denying it –

82. ***...and think your provision depends on your denial of the truth?*** Do you make your gratitude for rain a denial of Allah by saying that the rain occurs through the setting of a certain star?

83. ***Why then, when death reaches his throat*** – when a person's soul arrives at the moment of being wrenched from the body,

84. ***...and you are at that moment looking on*** – present with the dying person,

85. ***...and We are nearer him*** – through Our knowledge – ***than you, but you cannot see –***

86. ***...why then, if you are not subject to Our command*** – not subject to account when you are resurrected, as you claim –

87. ***...do you not send it back*** – return the spirit to the body after it reaches the throat – ***if you are telling the truth?*** You will not bring it back, in spite of the fact that you deny the Resurrection and claim not to be subject to Allah's command.

88. ***But the truth is that if he*** (the dead person) ***is one of those brought near...***

89. ***...there is solace*** (rest) ***and sweetness*** (good provision) ***and a Garden of Delight.***

90. ***And if he is one of the Companions of the Right,***

91. ***'Peace be upon you!' from the Companions of the Right***:
"Safety from the punishment" is what they say to him.
92. ***And if he is one of the misguided deniers,***
93. ***...there is hospitality of scalding water***
94. ***...and roasting in the Blazing Fire.***
95. ***This is indeed the Truth of Certainty.***
96. ***So glorify the Name of your Lord, the Magnificent!***

سُورَةُ الحَدِيدِ

بِسۡمِ ٱللَّهِ ٱلرَّحۡمَٰنِ ٱلرَّحِيمِ

سَبَّحَ لِلَّهِ مَا فِي ٱلسَّمَٰوَٰتِ وَٱلۡأَرۡضِۖ وَهُوَ ٱلۡعَزِيزُ ٱلۡحَكِيمُ ١ لَهُۥ مُلۡكُ
ٱلسَّمَٰوَٰتِ وَٱلۡأَرۡضِۖ يُحۡيِۦ وَيُمِيتُۖ وَهُوَ عَلَىٰ كُلِّ شَيۡءٖ قَدِيرٌ ٢
هُوَ ٱلۡأَوَّلُ وَٱلۡأٓخِرُ وَٱلظَّٰهِرُ وَٱلۡبَاطِنُۖ وَهُوَ بِكُلِّ شَيۡءٍ عَلِيمٌ ٣
هُوَ ٱلَّذِي خَلَقَ ٱلسَّمَٰوَٰتِ وَٱلۡأَرۡضَ فِي سِتَّةِ أَيَّامٖ ثُمَّ ٱسۡتَوَىٰ
عَلَى ٱلۡعَرۡشِۚ يَعۡلَمُ مَا يَلِجُ فِي ٱلۡأَرۡضِ وَمَا يَخۡرُجُ مِنۡهَا وَمَا يَنزِلُ مِنَ
ٱلسَّمَآءِ وَمَا يَعۡرُجُ فِيهَاۖ وَهُوَ مَعَكُمۡ أَيۡنَ مَا كُنتُمۡۚ وَٱللَّهُ بِمَا تَعۡمَلُونَ
بَصِيرٞ ٤ لَّهُۥ مُلۡكُ ٱلسَّمَٰوَٰتِ وَٱلۡأَرۡضِۚ وَإِلَى ٱللَّهِ تُرۡجَعُ ٱلۡأُمُورُ
٥ يُولِجُ ٱلَّيۡلَ فِي ٱلنَّهَارِ وَيُولِجُ ٱلنَّهَارَ فِي ٱلَّيۡلِۚ وَهُوَ عَلِيمُۢ بِذَاتِ
ٱلصُّدُورِ ٦ ءَامِنُواْ بِٱللَّهِ وَرَسُولِهِۦ وَأَنفِقُواْ مِمَّا جَعَلَكُم
مُّسۡتَخۡلَفِينَ فِيهِۖ فَٱلَّذِينَ ءَامَنُواْ مِنكُمۡ وَأَنفَقُواْ لَهُمۡ أَجۡرٞ كَبِيرٞ ٧
وَمَا لَكُمۡ لَا تُؤۡمِنُونَ بِٱللَّهِ وَٱلرَّسُولُ يَدۡعُوكُمۡ لِتُؤۡمِنُواْ بِرَبِّكُمۡ وَقَدۡ
أَخَذَ مِيثَٰقَكُمۡ إِن كُنتُم مُّؤۡمِنِينَ ٨ هُوَ ٱلَّذِي يُنَزِّلُ عَلَىٰ عَبۡدِهِۦٓ
ءَايَٰتِۭ بَيِّنَٰتٖ لِّيُخۡرِجَكُم مِّنَ ٱلظُّلُمَٰتِ إِلَى ٱلنُّورِۚ وَإِنَّ ٱللَّهَ بِكُمۡ
لَرَءُوفٞ رَّحِيمٞ ٩ وَمَا لَكُمۡ أَلَّا تُنفِقُواْ فِي سَبِيلِ ٱللَّهِ وَلِلَّهِ مِيرَٰثُ
ٱلسَّمَٰوَٰتِ وَٱلۡأَرۡضِۚ لَا يَسۡتَوِي مِنكُم مَّنۡ أَنفَقَ مِن قَبۡلِ ٱلۡفَتۡحِ
وَقَٰتَلَۚ أُوْلَٰٓئِكَ أَعۡظَمُ دَرَجَةٗ مِّنَ ٱلَّذِينَ أَنفَقُواْ مِنۢ بَعۡدُ وَقَٰتَلُواْۚ
وَكُلّٗا وَعَدَ ٱللَّهُ ٱلۡحُسۡنَىٰۚ وَٱللَّهُ بِمَا تَعۡمَلُونَ خَبِيرٞ ١٠ مَّن ذَا
ٱلَّذِي يُقۡرِضُ ٱللَّهَ قَرۡضًا حَسَنٗا فَيُضَٰعِفَهُۥ لَهُۥ وَلَهُۥٓ أَجۡرٞ كَرِيمٞ ١١

57. *Sūrat al-Ḥadīd*
Iron

This *sūra* is Madinan and has 29 *āyat*s.

1. *Everything in the heavens and the earth glorifies Allah.* He is exalted beyond association with anything. ***He is the Almighty*** in His kingdom, ***the All-Wise*** in everything He does.

2. *The kingdom of the heavens and the earth belongs to Him. He gives life* by originating it ***and causes to die*** after that. ***He has power over all things.***

3. *He is the First* – before everything without beginning – ***and the Last*** – after everything without end, ***the Outward*** – manifest through evidence which indicates Him – ***and the Inward*** – hidden from the perception of the senses. ***He has knowledge of all things.***

4. *It is He Who created the heavens and the earth in six days* – the days of this world, the first of which is Sunday and the last Friday – ***then established Himself firmly on the Throne*** – in a manner appropriate to Him. ***He knows what goes into the earth*** – such as rain and the dead – ***and what comes out of it*** – such as plants and minerals, ***what comes down from heaven*** – such as mercy and punishment – ***and what goes up into it*** – such as righteous actions and evil actions. ***He is with you wherever you are*** by His knowledge. ***Allah sees what you do.***

5. *The kingdom of the heavens and the earth belongs to Him. All* existent ***things return to Allah.***

6. *He makes night merge into day* – and it becomes longer and shorter – ***and day merge into night*** – and it also becomes longer and shorter. ***He knows what the heart contains*** by way of secrets and creeds.

7. *Believe in Allah and His Messenger* – meaning "persist in your belief" – ***and give*** – spend in the Way of Allah – ***of that*** wealth ***to which He has made you successors*** after those before you. This was revealed about the Expedition of Hardship, which was the Tabūk expedition. ***Those of you who believe and give will have an***

immense reward. The one who spent most was 'Uthmān, may Allah be pleased with him.

8. ***And what is the matter with you with you*** – addressed to the unbelievers – ***that you do not believe in Allah*** – what prevents you from believing, ***when the Messenger calls you to believe in your Lord and He has made*** (read as *akhadha* and *ukhidha*) ***a covenant with you*** – in the world of atoms when He made them (i.e. all of humanity) witness against themselves "Am I not your Lord?" – ***if you are believers?*** If you desire to believe in Him, then make haste to do so.

9. ***It is He who sends down Clear Signs*** of the Qur'an ***to His slave to bring you out of the darkness*** of unbelief ***to the light*** of faith. ***Allah is All-Gentle with you, Most Merciful*** in doing that for you.

10. ***And how is it with you that*** after believing ***you do not give in the Way of Allah, when the inheritance of the heavens and the earth*** – everything in them – ***belongs to Allah?*** Everything in the heavens and the earth will go back to Him, and so your property will reach Him without you having any reward for spending it. There is a reward for what you do spend. ***Those of you who gave and fought before the Victory*** – the Conquest of Makka – ***are not the same as those who gave and fought afterwards: they are higher in rank. But to each of them*** (the two groups) ***Allah has promised the Best*** (the Garden). ***Allah is aware of what you do*** and will repay you for your actions.

11. ***Who will make a good loan to Allah*** by spending their property in the Way of Allah ***so that He may multiply*** (read as *yuḍā'ifahu* and *yuḍa''ifahu*) ***it for him*** from ten times to more than seven hundred times, as is mentioned in *Sūrat al-Baqara?* ***He will*** also ***have a generous reward*** which is coupled with Allah's pleasure and acceptance by Him,

12. ***...on the Day you see the men and women of the believers, with their light streaming out in front of them, and to their right.*** They will be told: ***'Good news for you today of Gardens*** – meaning admission into them – ***with rivers flowing under them, remaining in them timelessly, for ever. That is the Great Victory.'***

يَوْمَ تَرَى ٱلْمُؤْمِنِينَ وَٱلْمُؤْمِنَٰتِ يَسْعَىٰ نُورُهُم بَيْنَ أَيْدِيهِمْ وَبِأَيْمَٰنِهِم
بُشْرَىٰكُمُ ٱلْيَوْمَ جَنَّٰتٌ تَجْرِى مِن تَحْتِهَا ٱلْأَنْهَٰرُ خَٰلِدِينَ فِيهَا ۚ ذَٰلِكَ
هُوَ ٱلْفَوْزُ ٱلْعَظِيمُ ﴿١٢﴾ يَوْمَ يَقُولُ ٱلْمُنَٰفِقُونَ وَٱلْمُنَٰفِقَٰتُ لِلَّذِينَ
ءَامَنُوا۟ ٱنظُرُونَا نَقْتَبِسْ مِن نُّورِكُمْ قِيلَ ٱرْجِعُوا۟ وَرَآءَكُمْ فَٱلْتَمِسُوا۟ نُورًا
فَضُرِبَ بَيْنَهُم بِسُورٍ لَّهُۥ بَابٌۢ بَاطِنُهُۥ فِيهِ ٱلرَّحْمَةُ وَظَٰهِرُهُۥ مِن قِبَلِهِ
ٱلْعَذَابُ ﴿١٣﴾ يُنَادُونَهُمْ أَلَمْ نَكُن مَّعَكُمْ ۖ قَالُوا۟ بَلَىٰ وَلَٰكِنَّكُمْ فَتَنتُمْ
أَنفُسَكُمْ وَتَرَبَّصْتُمْ وَٱرْتَبْتُمْ وَغَرَّتْكُمُ ٱلْأَمَانِىُّ حَتَّىٰ جَآءَ أَمْرُ
ٱللَّهِ وَغَرَّكُم بِٱللَّهِ ٱلْغَرُورُ ﴿١٤﴾ فَٱلْيَوْمَ لَا يُؤْخَذُ مِنكُمْ فِدْيَةٌ وَلَا
مِنَ ٱلَّذِينَ كَفَرُوا۟ ۚ مَأْوَىٰكُمُ ٱلنَّارُ ۖ هِىَ مَوْلَىٰكُمْ ۖ وَبِئْسَ ٱلْمَصِيرُ
﴿١٥﴾ ۞ أَلَمْ يَأْنِ لِلَّذِينَ ءَامَنُوٓا۟ أَن تَخْشَعَ قُلُوبُهُمْ لِذِكْرِ ٱللَّهِ
وَمَا نَزَلَ مِنَ ٱلْحَقِّ وَلَا يَكُونُوا۟ كَٱلَّذِينَ أُوتُوا۟ ٱلْكِتَٰبَ مِن قَبْلُ
فَطَالَ عَلَيْهِمُ ٱلْأَمَدُ فَقَسَتْ قُلُوبُهُمْ ۖ وَكَثِيرٌ مِّنْهُمْ فَٰسِقُونَ ﴿١٦﴾
ٱعْلَمُوٓا۟ أَنَّ ٱللَّهَ يُحْىِ ٱلْأَرْضَ بَعْدَ مَوْتِهَا ۚ قَدْ بَيَّنَّا لَكُمُ ٱلْءَايَٰتِ
لَعَلَّكُمْ تَعْقِلُونَ ﴿١٧﴾ إِنَّ ٱلْمُصَّدِّقِينَ وَٱلْمُصَّدِّقَٰتِ وَأَقْرَضُوا۟
ٱللَّهَ قَرْضًا حَسَنًا يُضَٰعَفُ لَهُمْ وَلَهُمْ أَجْرٌ كَرِيمٌ ﴿١٨﴾
وَٱلَّذِينَ ءَامَنُوا۟ بِٱللَّهِ وَرُسُلِهِۦٓ أُو۟لَٰٓئِكَ هُمُ ٱلصِّدِّيقُونَ ۖ وَٱلشُّهَدَآءُ
عِندَ رَبِّهِمْ لَهُمْ أَجْرُهُمْ وَنُورُهُمْ ۖ وَٱلَّذِينَ كَفَرُوا۟ وَكَذَّبُوا۟
بِـَٔايَٰتِنَآ أُو۟لَٰٓئِكَ أَصْحَٰبُ ٱلْجَحِيمِ ﴿١٩﴾ ٱعْلَمُوٓا۟ أَنَّمَا ٱلْحَيَوٰةُ
ٱلدُّنْيَا لَعِبٌ وَلَهْوٌ وَزِينَةٌ وَتَفَاخُرٌۢ بَيْنَكُمْ وَتَكَاثُرٌ فِى ٱلْأَمْوَٰلِ
وَٱلْأَوْلَٰدِ ۖ كَمَثَلِ غَيْثٍ أَعْجَبَ ٱلْكُفَّارَ نَبَاتُهُۥ ثُمَّ يَهِيجُ فَتَرَىٰهُ

13. ***That Day the men and women of the hypocrites will say to those who believe, 'Wait*** (read as *anẓurūnā* and *anẓirūnā*) ***for us so that we may borrow some of your light.'*** "Let us have a brand from your light." ***They will be told*** in mockery***: 'Go back and look for light!'*** Then they will go back ***and a wall*** – said to be the wall of the Ramparts[1] – ***will be erected between them*** and the believers ***with a gate in it, on the inside of which*** – facing the believers – ***there will be mercy, but before whose exterior*** – facing the hypocrites – ***lies the punishment.***

14. ***They will call out to them, 'Were we not with you*** in obedience***?' They will reply, 'Indeed you were. But you made trouble for yourselves*** by your hypocrisy***, and hung back*** to wait for disasters to befall the believers ***and doubted*** the *dīn* of Islam***; and false hopes deluded you until Allah's command*** (death) ***arrived. The Deluder*** (Shayṭān) ***deluded you about Allah.***

15. ***So today no ransom will be accepted*** (read as *yu'khadhu* and *ta'khadhu*) ***from you or from those who disbelieved. Your refuge is the Fire: it is your master. What an evil destination!'***

16. This was revealed about the Companions when they joked a lot. ***Has the time not arrived for the hearts of those who believe to yield to the remembrance of Allah and to the truth*** (the Qur'an) ***He has sent down*** (read as *nazzala* and *nazala*)***, so that they will not be like those who were given the Book before*** – the Jews and Christians – ***for whom the time seemed over long*** between them and their Prophets ***so that their hearts became hard*** and did not yield to the remembrance of Allah***? Many of them are deviators.***

17. This is addressed to the believers already mentioned. ***Know that Allah brings the earth to life after it has been dead*** – through the growth of plant-life, and so He can also do that with your hearts and make them return to humility***. We have made the Signs clear to you*** – indicating Our power to do this and other things – ***so that hopefully you will use your intellect.***

18. ***The men and women who give ṣadaqa*** (read as *muṣṣaddiqīna* and *muṣaddiqīna*, with the same differences in the feminine form) ***and make a good loan to Allah shall have it increased*** (read as

1. See *Sūrat al-A'rāf* (7:46).

مُصْفَرًّا ثُمَّ يَكُونُ حُطَٰمًا ۖ وَفِى ٱلْءَاخِرَةِ عَذَابٌ شَدِيدٌ وَمَغْفِرَةٌ
مِّنَ ٱللَّهِ وَرِضْوَٰنٌ ۚ وَمَا ٱلْحَيَوٰةُ ٱلدُّنْيَآ إِلَّا مَتَٰعُ ٱلْغُرُورِ ﴿٢٠﴾
سَابِقُوٓا۟ إِلَىٰ مَغْفِرَةٍ مِّن رَّبِّكُمْ وَجَنَّةٍ عَرْضُهَا كَعَرْضِ ٱلسَّمَآءِ
وَٱلْأَرْضِ أُعِدَّتْ لِلَّذِينَ ءَامَنُوا۟ بِٱللَّهِ وَرُسُلِهِۦ ۚ ذَٰلِكَ فَضْلُ
ٱللَّهِ يُؤْتِيهِ مَن يَشَآءُ ۚ وَٱللَّهُ ذُو ٱلْفَضْلِ ٱلْعَظِيمِ ﴿٢١﴾ مَآ أَصَابَ
مِن مُّصِيبَةٍ فِى ٱلْأَرْضِ وَلَا فِىٓ أَنفُسِكُمْ إِلَّا فِى كِتَٰبٍ
مِّن قَبْلِ أَن نَّبْرَأَهَآ ۚ إِنَّ ذَٰلِكَ عَلَى ٱللَّهِ يَسِيرٌ ﴿٢٢﴾ لِّكَيْلَا
تَأْسَوْا۟ عَلَىٰ مَا فَاتَكُمْ وَلَا تَفْرَحُوا۟ بِمَآ ءَاتَىٰكُمْ ۗ وَٱللَّهُ
لَا يُحِبُّ كُلَّ مُخْتَالٍ فَخُورٍ ﴿٢٣﴾ ٱلَّذِينَ يَبْخَلُونَ وَيَأْمُرُونَ
ٱلنَّاسَ بِٱلْبُخْلِ ۗ وَمَن يَتَوَلَّ فَإِنَّ ٱللَّهَ هُوَ ٱلْغَنِىُّ ٱلْحَمِيدُ ﴿٢٤﴾
لَقَدْ أَرْسَلْنَا رُسُلَنَا بِٱلْبَيِّنَٰتِ وَأَنزَلْنَا مَعَهُمُ ٱلْكِتَٰبَ
وَٱلْمِيزَانَ لِيَقُومَ ٱلنَّاسُ بِٱلْقِسْطِ ۖ وَأَنزَلْنَا ٱلْحَدِيدَ فِيهِ
بَأْسٌ شَدِيدٌ وَمَنَٰفِعُ لِلنَّاسِ وَلِيَعْلَمَ ٱللَّهُ مَن يَنصُرُهُۥ وَرُسُلَهُۥ
بِٱلْغَيْبِ ۚ إِنَّ ٱللَّهَ قَوِىٌّ عَزِيزٌ ﴿٢٥﴾ وَلَقَدْ أَرْسَلْنَا نُوحًا وَإِبْرَٰهِيمَ
وَجَعَلْنَا فِى ذُرِّيَّتِهِمَا ٱلنُّبُوَّةَ وَٱلْكِتَٰبَ ۖ فَمِنْهُم مُّهْتَدٍ ۖ
وَكَثِيرٌ مِّنْهُمْ فَٰسِقُونَ ﴿٢٦﴾ ثُمَّ قَفَّيْنَا عَلَىٰٓ ءَاثَٰرِهِم
بِرُسُلِنَا وَقَفَّيْنَا بِعِيسَى ٱبْنِ مَرْيَمَ وَءَاتَيْنَٰهُ ٱلْإِنجِيلَ
وَجَعَلْنَا فِى قُلُوبِ ٱلَّذِينَ ٱتَّبَعُوهُ رَأْفَةً وَرَحْمَةً وَرَهْبَانِيَّةً
ٱبْتَدَعُوهَا مَا كَتَبْنَٰهَا عَلَيْهِمْ إِلَّا ٱبْتِغَآءَ رِضْوَٰنِ ٱللَّهِ فَمَا
رَعَوْهَا حَقَّ رِعَايَتِهَا ۖ فَـَٔاتَيْنَا ٱلَّذِينَ ءَامَنُوا۟ مِنْهُمْ أَجْرَهُمْ ۖ

yuḍā'afu and *yuḍa''afu*) ***for them and they shall have a generous reward.***

19. ***Those who believe in Allah and His Messengers – such people are the truly sincere – and the martyrs*** – the word for martyrs, *shuhadā'*, can also mean witnesses, meaning that they will bear witness against those nations who disbelieved – ***who are with their Lord will receive their wages and their light. But those who disbelieve and deny Our Signs*** indicating Our unity ***will be Companions of the Blazing Fire.***

20. ***Know that the life of this world is merely a game and a diversion and ostentation and a cause of boasting among yourselves and*** being preoccupied with ***trying to outdo one another in wealth and children,*** while acts of obedience and whatever helps them are matters of the Next World; an example of the extraordinary nature of this world is ***like the plant-growth after rain which delights the cultivators, but then it withers and you see it turning yellow, and then it becomes broken stubble*** – chaff which is blown on the wind. ***In the Next World there is terrible punishment*** for the person who prefers this world to it, ***but also forgiveness from Allah and His good pleasure*** for those who did not prefer this world to the Next. ***The*** enjoyment of the ***life of this world is nothing but the enjoyment of*** passing ***delusion.***

21. ***Race each other to forgiveness from your Lord and to a Garden whose breadth is like that of heaven*** – meaning all seven heavens – ***and earth combined, made ready for those who believe in Allah and His Messengers. That is Allah's favour which He gives to those He wills. Allah's favour is indeed immense.***

22. ***Nothing occurs, either in the earth*** – such as drought – ***or in yourselves*** – such as illness and loss of children, ***without its being in a Book*** – the Preserved Tablet – ***before We*** create it and ***make it happen.*** The same is true of blessings. ***That is something easy for Allah.***

23. ***That is so that you may not be grieved*** and troubled ***about the things that pass you by or exult*** arrogantly ***about the things*** (blessings) ***that come to you.*** Rather you should be joyful and thankful for any blessing you have received. ***Allah does not love any vain or***

boastful man who exults in what he has been given and boasts to people about it –

24. ***...those who are tight-fisted*** – reluctant to give what it is mandatory for them to give – ***and tell others to be tight-fisted.*** This is a strong threat. ***If anyone turns away*** from what is obligatory for him, ***Allah is the Rich Beyond Need*** of others, ***the Praiseworthy.***

25. ***We sent Our Messengers*** (the angels to the Prophets) ***with the Clear Signs*** (definitive proofs) ***and sent down the Book*** – meaning Divinely Revealed Books in general – ***and the Balance*** (justice) ***with them so that mankind might establish justice. And We sent down iron*** from mines ***in which there lies great force*** with which you fight ***and which has many uses for mankind, so that Allah might know*** by direct witnessing ***those who help Him*** – His *dīn* with iron weapons of war and other things – ***and His Messengers in the Unseen.*** He sees them although they do not see Him in this world. Ibn 'Abbās said, "They help Him but do not see Him." ***Allah is All-Strong, Almighty.*** He has no need of help, but it benefits the one who gives it.

26. ***We sent Nūḥ and Ibrāhīm and placed Prophethood and the Book*** – in the form of the Torah, the Gospel, the Psalms and the Furqān – ***among their descendants. Some of them are guided but many of them are deviators.***

27. ***Then We sent Our Messengers following in their footsteps and sent 'Īsā son of Maryam after them, giving him the Gospel. We put compassion and mercy in the hearts of those who followed him. They invented monasticism*** themselves, rejecting women and moving into hermitages – ***We did not prescribe it for them*** – they did it ***purely out of desire to gain the pleasure of Allah, but even so they did not observe it as it should have been observed.*** Many of them left it, rejected the *dīn* of 'Īsā, and joined the *dīn* of their king, while many did remain in the *dīn* of 'Īsā and believed in our Prophet. ***To those of them who believed We gave their reward; but many of them are deviators.***

28. ***You who believe*** in 'Īsā, ***be fearful of Allah and believe in His Messenger*** – Muḥammad, may Allah bless him and grant him peace, and 'Īsā. ***He will give you a double portion of His mercy*** – because

وَكَثِيرٌ مِّنْهُمْ فَٰسِقُونَ ٢٧ يَٰٓأَيُّهَا ٱلَّذِينَ ءَامَنُوا۟ ٱتَّقُوا۟ ٱللَّهَ
وَءَامِنُوا۟ بِرَسُولِهِۦ يُؤْتِكُمْ كِفْلَيْنِ مِن رَّحْمَتِهِۦ وَيَجْعَل لَّكُمْ
نُورًا تَمْشُونَ بِهِۦ وَيَغْفِرْ لَكُمْ ۚ وَٱللَّهُ غَفُورٌ رَّحِيمٌ ٢٨ لِّئَلَّا يَعْلَمَ
أَهْلُ ٱلْكِتَٰبِ أَلَّا يَقْدِرُونَ عَلَىٰ شَىْءٍ مِّن فَضْلِ ٱللَّهِ ۙ وَأَنَّ
ٱلْفَضْلَ بِيَدِ ٱللَّهِ يُؤْتِيهِ مَن يَشَآءُ ۚ وَٱللَّهُ ذُو ٱلْفَضْلِ ٱلْعَظِيمِ ٢٩

you believed in both Prophets – ***and grant you a Light by which to walk*** on the Path, ***and forgive you. Allah is Ever-Forgiving, Most Merciful;***

29. I inform you of that ***so that the People of the Book*** (the Torah) – who do not believe in Muḥammad, may Allah bless him and grant him peace – ***may know that they have no power at all over any of Allah's favour*** – and it is not true, as they had claimed, that they were the ones whom Allah loved and those with whom He was pleased – ***and that all favour is in the Hand of Allah. He gives it to anyone He wills.*** So the believers among them are given their reward twice over. ***Allah's favour is indeed immense.***

سُورَةُ المُجَادَلَةِ

بِسْمِ ٱللَّهِ ٱلرَّحْمَٰنِ ٱلرَّحِيمِ

قَدْ سَمِعَ ٱللَّهُ قَوْلَ ٱلَّتِى تُجَٰدِلُكَ فِى زَوْجِهَا وَتَشْتَكِىٓ إِلَى ٱللَّهِ
وَٱللَّهُ يَسْمَعُ تَحَاوُرَكُمَآ ۚ إِنَّ ٱللَّهَ سَمِيعٌۢ بَصِيرٌ ﴿١﴾ ٱلَّذِينَ يُظَٰهِرُونَ
مِنكُم مِّن نِّسَآئِهِم مَّا هُنَّ أُمَّهَٰتِهِمْ ۖ إِنْ أُمَّهَٰتُهُمْ إِلَّا ٱلَّٰٓـِٔى
وَلَدْنَهُمْ ۚ وَإِنَّهُمْ لَيَقُولُونَ مُنكَرًا مِّنَ ٱلْقَوْلِ وَزُورًا ۚ وَإِنَّ
ٱللَّهَ لَعَفُوٌّ غَفُورٌ ﴿٢﴾ وَٱلَّذِينَ يُظَٰهِرُونَ مِن نِّسَآئِهِمْ ثُمَّ يَعُودُونَ
لِمَا قَالُوا۟ فَتَحْرِيرُ رَقَبَةٍ مِّن قَبْلِ أَن يَتَمَآسَّا ۚ ذَٰلِكُمْ تُوعَظُونَ
بِهِۦ ۚ وَٱللَّهُ بِمَا تَعْمَلُونَ خَبِيرٌ ﴿٣﴾ فَمَن لَّمْ يَجِدْ فَصِيَامُ شَهْرَيْنِ
مُتَتَابِعَيْنِ مِن قَبْلِ أَن يَتَمَآسَّا ۖ فَمَن لَّمْ يَسْتَطِعْ فَإِطْعَامُ سِتِّينَ
مِسْكِينًا ۚ ذَٰلِكَ لِتُؤْمِنُوا۟ بِٱللَّهِ وَرَسُولِهِۦ ۚ وَتِلْكَ حُدُودُ ٱللَّهِ ۗ
وَلِلْكَٰفِرِينَ عَذَابٌ أَلِيمٌ ﴿٤﴾ إِنَّ ٱلَّذِينَ يُحَآدُّونَ ٱللَّهَ وَرَسُولَهُۥ كُبِتُوا۟
كَمَا كُبِتَ ٱلَّذِينَ مِن قَبْلِهِمْ ۚ وَقَدْ أَنزَلْنَآ ءَايَٰتٍۭ بَيِّنَٰتٍ ۚ وَلِلْكَٰفِرِينَ
عَذَابٌ مُّهِينٌ ﴿٥﴾ يَوْمَ يَبْعَثُهُمُ ٱللَّهُ جَمِيعًا فَيُنَبِّئُهُم بِمَا
عَمِلُوٓا۟ ۚ أَحْصَىٰهُ ٱللَّهُ وَنَسُوهُ ۚ وَٱللَّهُ عَلَىٰ كُلِّ شَىْءٍ شَهِيدٌ ﴿٦﴾
أَلَمْ تَرَ أَنَّ ٱللَّهَ يَعْلَمُ مَا فِى ٱلسَّمَٰوَٰتِ وَمَا فِى ٱلْأَرْضِ ۖ مَا يَكُونُ
مِن نَّجْوَىٰ ثَلَٰثَةٍ إِلَّا هُوَ رَابِعُهُمْ وَلَا خَمْسَةٍ إِلَّا هُوَ سَادِسُهُمْ
وَلَآ أَدْنَىٰ مِن ذَٰلِكَ وَلَآ أَكْثَرَ إِلَّا هُوَ مَعَهُمْ أَيْنَ مَا كَانُوا۟ ۖ ثُمَّ يُنَبِّئُهُم
بِمَا عَمِلُوا۟ يَوْمَ ٱلْقِيَٰمَةِ ۚ إِنَّ ٱللَّهَ بِكُلِّ شَىْءٍ عَلِيمٌ ﴿٧﴾ أَلَمْ تَرَ إِلَى ٱلَّذِينَ
نُهُوا۟ عَنِ ٱلنَّجْوَىٰ ثُمَّ يَعُودُونَ لِمَا نُهُوا۟ عَنْهُ وَيَتَنَٰجَوْنَ بِٱلْإِثْمِ

58. *Sūrat al-Mujādila*
The Disputer

This *sūra* is Madinan and has 22 *āyats*.

1. ***Allah has heard the words of the woman who disputes with you about her husband*** – consults you, Muḥammad, about her husband who pronounced a *ẓihār* divorce on her. This occurs when a man says to his wife, "You are to me like my mother's back." She asked the Messenger of Allah, may Allah bless him and grant him peace, about it; and he told her that she was now unlawful to her husband as it was the custom among them that the *ẓihār* divorce necessitated a perpetual separation. The woman was Khawla bint Tha'laba and the man was Aws ibn aṣ-Ṣāmit – ***and lays her complaint*** – about her isolation, poverty and small children – ***before Allah*** – saying, "I have small children by him. If I keep them, they will be hungry, and if I hand them over to him, they will be lost." ***Allah hears the two of you talking together. Allah is All-Hearing, All-Seeing*** – and All-Knowing.

2. ***For those of you who divorce your wives by equating them with your mothers*** (read as *yuẓāhirūna*, *yuẓẓahharūna* and *yuẓāharūna*), pronouncing the *ẓihār* divorce mentioned in the previous *āyat*, ***they are not your mothers.*** The *ziḥār* pronouncement equates them with your mothers. ***Your mothers are only those who gave birth to you. What you are saying is wrong and a slanderous lie*** – and anyone who does this must do a *kaffāra* to expiate that. ***But Allah is Ever-Pardoning, Ever-Forgiving.***

3. ***Those who divorce their wives by equating them with their mothers, and then wish to go back on what they said*** – and want to keep their wives, in spite of the *ẓihār* pronouncement which has made them unlawful to them – ***must set free a slave before the two of them may touch one another*** – meaning, have sexual intercourse. ***This is what you are enjoined to do. Allah is aware of what you do.***

4. ***Anyone who cannot find the means*** (to free a slave) ***must fast for two consecutive months before the two of them may touch one another again. And anyone who is unable to do that*** (fast) ***must***

feed sixty poor people before the couple may have sexual intercourse. Each poor person should be fed the staple food of the land where they live. ***That*** alleviation through *kaffāra* ***is to affirm your belief in Allah and His Messenger. These*** rulings ***are Allah's limits. The unbelievers will have a painful punishment.***

5. ***Those who*** disagree and ***oppose Allah and His Messenger will be subdued and overcome as those before them were also subdued and overcome*** when they opposed their Messengers before. ***We have sent down Clear Signs*** which indicate that the Messengers speak the truth. ***The unbelievers will have a humiliating punishment.***

6. ***On the Day Allah raises up all of them together, He will inform them of what they did. Allah has recorded it although they have forgotten it. Allah is Witness of all things.***

7. ***Do you not see*** and know ***that Allah knows what is in the heavens and on the earth? Three men cannot confer together secretly without Him being the fourth of them*** – through His knowledge – ***or five without Him being the sixth of them, or fewer than that or more, without Him being with them wherever they are. Then He will inform them on the Day of Rising of what they did. Allah has knowledge of all things.***

8. ***Do you not see those who were forbidden to confer together secretly returning to the very thing they were forbidden to do, and conferring together secretly in wrongdoing and enmity and disobedience to the Messenger?*** This is a reference to the Jews. The Prophet, may Allah bless him and grant him peace, forbade them the secret conferring which they were doing, whispering together so that doubt would fall into their hearts. ***And when they come to you they greet you***, Prophet, ***with words Allah has never used in greeting you*** – by saying, *"as-sāmu 'alayka"*, which means "poison be upon you", showing that they wished him dead – ***and say to themselves 'Why does Allah not punish us for what we say*** in the greeting we gave? If he had been a Prophet, then Allah would have punished us. So he is not a Prophet.***' Hell will be enough for them! They will roast in it. What an evil destination!***

9. ***You who believe, when you confer together secretly, do not do so in wrongdoing and enmity and disobedience to the Messenger;***

وَٱلْعُدْوَٰنِ وَمَعْصِيَتِ ٱلرَّسُولِ وَإِذَا جَآءُوكَ حَيَّوْكَ بِمَا لَمْ يُحَيِّكَ
بِهِ ٱللَّهُ وَيَقُولُونَ فِىٓ أَنفُسِهِمْ لَوْلَا يُعَذِّبُنَا ٱللَّهُ بِمَا نَقُولُ ۚ حَسْبُهُمْ
جَهَنَّمُ يَصْلَوْنَهَا ۖ فَبِئْسَ ٱلْمَصِيرُ ﴿٨﴾ يَٰٓأَيُّهَا ٱلَّذِينَ ءَامَنُوٓا۟ إِذَا
تَنَٰجَيْتُمْ فَلَا تَتَنَٰجَوْا۟ بِٱلْإِثْمِ وَٱلْعُدْوَٰنِ وَمَعْصِيَتِ ٱلرَّسُولِ وَتَنَٰجَوْا۟
بِٱلْبِرِّ وَٱلتَّقْوَىٰ ۖ وَٱتَّقُوا۟ ٱللَّهَ ٱلَّذِىٓ إِلَيْهِ تُحْشَرُونَ ﴿٩﴾ إِنَّمَا ٱلنَّجْوَىٰ
مِنَ ٱلشَّيْطَٰنِ لِيَحْزُنَ ٱلَّذِينَ ءَامَنُوا۟ وَلَيْسَ بِضَآرِّهِمْ شَيْـًٔا
إِلَّا بِإِذْنِ ٱللَّهِ ۚ وَعَلَى ٱللَّهِ فَلْيَتَوَكَّلِ ٱلْمُؤْمِنُونَ ﴿١٠﴾ يَٰٓأَيُّهَا ٱلَّذِينَ
ءَامَنُوٓا۟ إِذَا قِيلَ لَكُمْ تَفَسَّحُوا۟ فِى ٱلْمَجَٰلِسِ فَٱفْسَحُوا۟ يَفْسَحِ
ٱللَّهُ لَكُمْ ۖ وَإِذَا قِيلَ ٱنشُزُوا۟ فَٱنشُزُوا۟ يَرْفَعِ ٱللَّهُ ٱلَّذِينَ ءَامَنُوا۟
مِنكُمْ وَٱلَّذِينَ أُوتُوا۟ ٱلْعِلْمَ دَرَجَٰتٍ ۚ وَٱللَّهُ بِمَا تَعْمَلُونَ خَبِيرٌ ﴿١١﴾
يَٰٓأَيُّهَا ٱلَّذِينَ ءَامَنُوٓا۟ إِذَا نَٰجَيْتُمُ ٱلرَّسُولَ فَقَدِّمُوا۟ بَيْنَ يَدَىْ نَجْوَىٰكُمْ
صَدَقَةً ۚ ذَٰلِكَ خَيْرٌ لَّكُمْ وَأَطْهَرُ ۚ فَإِن لَّمْ تَجِدُوا۟ فَإِنَّ ٱللَّهَ غَفُورٌ رَّحِيمٌ
﴿١٢﴾ ءَأَشْفَقْتُمْ أَن تُقَدِّمُوا۟ بَيْنَ يَدَىْ نَجْوَىٰكُمْ صَدَقَٰتٍ ۚ فَإِذْ لَمْ تَفْعَلُوا۟
وَتَابَ ٱللَّهُ عَلَيْكُمْ فَأَقِيمُوا۟ ٱلصَّلَوٰةَ وَءَاتُوا۟ ٱلزَّكَوٰةَ وَأَطِيعُوا۟ ٱللَّهَ
وَرَسُولَهُۥ ۚ وَٱللَّهُ خَبِيرٌۢ بِمَا تَعْمَلُونَ ﴿١٣﴾ ۞ أَلَمْ تَرَ إِلَى ٱلَّذِينَ تَوَلَّوْا۟ قَوْمًا
غَضِبَ ٱللَّهُ عَلَيْهِم مَّا هُم مِّنكُمْ وَلَا مِنْهُمْ وَيَحْلِفُونَ عَلَى ٱلْكَذِبِ
وَهُمْ يَعْلَمُونَ ﴿١٤﴾ أَعَدَّ ٱللَّهُ لَهُمْ عَذَابًا شَدِيدًا ۖ إِنَّهُمْ سَآءَ مَا كَانُوا۟
يَعْمَلُونَ ﴿١٥﴾ ٱتَّخَذُوٓا۟ أَيْمَٰنَهُمْ جُنَّةً فَصَدُّوا۟ عَن سَبِيلِ ٱللَّهِ فَلَهُمْ
عَذَابٌ مُّهِينٌ ﴿١٦﴾ لَّن تُغْنِىَ عَنْهُمْ أَمْوَٰلُهُمْ وَلَآ أَوْلَٰدُهُم مِّنَ ٱللَّهِ
شَيْـًٔا ۚ أُو۟لَٰٓئِكَ أَصْحَٰبُ ٱلنَّارِ ۖ هُمْ فِيهَا خَٰلِدُونَ ﴿١٧﴾ يَوْمَ يَبْعَثُهُمُ

rather confer together in goodness and fearfulness of Allah. Be fearful of Allah – Him to Whom you will be gathered.

10. ***Conferring in secret*** about sin and other bad things ***is from*** the delusion of ***Shayṭān, to cause grief to those who believe; but it cannot harm them at all, unless by Allah's permission*** – by His will. ***So let the believers put their trust in Allah.***

11. ***You who believe, when you are told: 'Make room in the gathering*** (read as *majlis* and as *majālis* in the plural)***,'*** – a reference to the gathering of the Prophet, may Allah bless him and grant him peace, and to *dhikr*, remembrance of Allah, so that those who come to join you can sit down – ***then make room and Allah will make room for you*** in the Garden***! And when you are told, 'Get up'*** – for the prayer and other good actions – ***get up*** (read as *inshuzū* and *inshizū*)***. Allah will raise in rank*** – in the Paradise – ***those of you who believe*** – and obey by doing so – ***and those who have been given knowledge. Allah is aware of what you do.***

12. ***You who believe, when you*** want to ***consult the Messenger privately precede your private consultation by giving* ṣadaqa *– that is better for you and purer***: more likely to purify you of your wrong actions***. But if you cannot find the means*** to give any *ṣadaqa*, ***Allah is Ever-Forgiving, Most Merciful.*** The implication was that they should not engage in private consultation with the Prophet, may Allah bless him and grant him peace, until they had given *ṣadaqa*. Then this was abrogated by the next *āyat*.

13. ***Are you afraid to give gifts of* ṣadaqa *before your private consultation?*** Does poverty make you fear giving *ṣadaqa*? ***If you do not*** give *ṣadaqa* ***but Allah turns to you*** and excuses you, ***at least establish the prayer and pay* zakāt*, and obey Allah and His Messenger. Allah is aware of what you do.***

14. ***Do you not see those*** hypocrites ***who have turned to people*** – meaning here the Jews – ***with whom Allah is angry? They*** (the hypocrites) ***belong neither to you*** (the believers) ***nor to them*** (the Jews). They waver between the two. ***And they swear to falsehood*** – saying that they are believers – ***and do so knowingly*** – knowing that they are lying in what they say.

15. ***Allah has prepared a terrible punishment for them. How evil is what*** (the acts of disobedience) ***they have been doing!***

ٱللَّهُ جَمِيعًا فَيَحْلِفُونَ لَهُۥ كَمَا يَحْلِفُونَ لَكُمْ ۖ وَيَحْسَبُونَ أَنَّهُمْ عَلَىٰ شَىْءٍ ۚ أَلَآ
إِنَّهُمْ هُمُ ٱلْكَٰذِبُونَ ﴿١٨﴾ ٱسْتَحْوَذَ عَلَيْهِمُ ٱلشَّيْطَٰنُ فَأَنسَىٰهُمْ ذِكْرَ
ٱللَّهِ ۚ أُو۟لَٰٓئِكَ حِزْبُ ٱلشَّيْطَٰنِ ۚ أَلَآ إِنَّ حِزْبَ ٱلشَّيْطَٰنِ هُمُ ٱلْخَٰسِرُونَ
﴿١٩﴾ إِنَّ ٱلَّذِينَ يُحَآدُّونَ ٱللَّهَ وَرَسُولَهُۥٓ أُو۟لَٰٓئِكَ فِى ٱلْأَذَلِّينَ ﴿٢٠﴾
كَتَبَ ٱللَّهُ لَأَغْلِبَنَّ أَنَا۠ وَرُسُلِىٓ ۚ إِنَّ ٱللَّهَ قَوِىٌّ عَزِيزٌ ﴿٢١﴾
لَّا تَجِدُ قَوْمًا يُؤْمِنُونَ بِٱللَّهِ وَٱلْيَوْمِ ٱلْءَاخِرِ يُوَآدُّونَ مَنْ
حَآدَّ ٱللَّهَ وَرَسُولَهُۥ وَلَوْ كَانُوٓا۟ ءَابَآءَهُمْ أَوْ أَبْنَآءَهُمْ
أَوْ إِخْوَٰنَهُمْ أَوْ عَشِيرَتَهُمْ ۚ أُو۟لَٰٓئِكَ كَتَبَ فِى قُلُوبِهِمُ
ٱلْإِيمَٰنَ وَأَيَّدَهُم بِرُوحٍ مِّنْهُ ۖ وَيُدْخِلُهُمْ جَنَّٰتٍ تَجْرِى
مِن تَحْتِهَا ٱلْأَنْهَٰرُ خَٰلِدِينَ فِيهَا ۚ رَضِىَ ٱللَّهُ عَنْهُمْ وَرَضُوا۟
عَنْهُ ۚ أُو۟لَٰٓئِكَ حِزْبُ ٱللَّهِ ۚ أَلَآ إِنَّ حِزْبَ ٱللَّهِ هُمُ ٱلْمُفْلِحُونَ ﴿٢٢﴾

16. ***They made their oaths into a cloak*** – a covering to protect themselves and their property – ***and barred*** the believers from doing *jihād* in ***the Way of Allah*** by killing them and taking their property***; so they will have a humiliating punishment.***

17. ***Neither their wealth nor their children will help them at all against*** the punishment of ***Allah. Such people are the Companions of the Fire, remaining in it timelessly, for ever.***

18. ***On the Day Allah raises up all of them them together they will swear to Him*** that they are believers ***just as they have sworn to you, and imagine they have something to stand upon*** – that their oaths will help them in the Next World as they helped them in this world. ***No indeed! It is they who are the liars.***

19. ***Shayṭān has gained mastery over them*** because they obey him ***and made them forget the remembrance of Allah. Such people are the party*** and followers ***of Shayṭān. No indeed! It is the party of Shaytan who are the losers.***

20. ***Those who oppose Allah and His Messenger, such people will be among the most abased*** and defeated.

21. ***Allah has written*** on the Preserved Tablet or, alternatively has decreed***: 'I will be victorious*** – both by means of evidence and with the sword – ***I and and My Messengers.' Allah is Most Strong, Almighty.***

22. ***You will not find people who believe in Allah and the Last Day having love for anyone who opposes Allah and His Messenger, though they be their fathers, their sons, their brothers or their clan.*** If they oppose Allah and His Messenger, the believers should oppose them and fight them. This happened with a group of Companions, may Allah be pleased with him. ***Allah has inscribed belief upon such people's hearts*** and fixed it there ***and will reinforce them with a* Rūḥ** (light) ***from Him and admit them into Gardens with rivers flowing under them, to remain in them timelessly, for ever. Allah is pleased with them*** for obeying Him ***and they are pleased with Him***: content with the reward that He gives them. ***Such people are the party of Allah***: they follow His command and avoid what He has prohibited. ***Truly it is the party of Allah who are successful.***

سُورَةُ الحَشۡرِ

بِسۡمِ ٱللَّهِ ٱلرَّحۡمَٰنِ ٱلرَّحِيمِ

سَبَّحَ لِلَّهِ مَا فِي ٱلسَّمَٰوَٰتِ وَمَا فِي ٱلۡأَرۡضِۖ وَهُوَ ٱلۡعَزِيزُ ٱلۡحَكِيمُ
١ هُوَ ٱلَّذِيٓ أَخۡرَجَ ٱلَّذِينَ كَفَرُواْ مِنۡ أَهۡلِ ٱلۡكِتَٰبِ مِن دِيَٰرِهِمۡ
لِأَوَّلِ ٱلۡحَشۡرِۚ مَا ظَنَنتُمۡ أَن يَخۡرُجُواْۖ وَظَنُّوٓاْ أَنَّهُم مَّانِعَتُهُمۡ
حُصُونُهُم مِّنَ ٱللَّهِ فَأَتَىٰهُمُ ٱللَّهُ مِنۡ حَيۡثُ لَمۡ يَحۡتَسِبُواْۖ وَقَذَفَ
فِي قُلُوبِهِمُ ٱلرُّعۡبَۚ يُخۡرِبُونَ بُيُوتَهُم بِأَيۡدِيهِمۡ وَأَيۡدِي ٱلۡمُؤۡمِنِينَ
فَٱعۡتَبِرُواْ يَٰٓأُوْلِي ٱلۡأَبۡصَٰرِ ٢ وَلَوۡلَآ أَن كَتَبَ ٱللَّهُ عَلَيۡهِمُ
ٱلۡجَلَآءَ لَعَذَّبَهُمۡ فِي ٱلدُّنۡيَاۖ وَلَهُمۡ فِي ٱلۡأٓخِرَةِ عَذَابُ ٱلنَّارِ ٣
ذَٰلِكَ بِأَنَّهُمۡ شَآقُّواْ ٱللَّهَ وَرَسُولَهُۥۖ وَمَن يُشَآقِّ ٱللَّهَ فَإِنَّ ٱللَّهَ شَدِيدُ
ٱلۡعِقَابِ ٤ مَا قَطَعۡتُم مِّن لِّينَةٍ أَوۡ تَرَكۡتُمُوهَا قَآئِمَةً
عَلَىٰٓ أُصُولِهَا فَبِإِذۡنِ ٱللَّهِ وَلِيُخۡزِيَ ٱلۡفَٰسِقِينَ ٥ وَمَآ أَفَآءَ ٱللَّهُ
عَلَىٰ رَسُولِهِۦ مِنۡهُمۡ فَمَآ أَوۡجَفۡتُمۡ عَلَيۡهِ مِنۡ خَيۡلٍ وَلَا رِكَابٍ
وَلَٰكِنَّ ٱللَّهَ يُسَلِّطُ رُسُلَهُۥ عَلَىٰ مَن يَشَآءُۚ وَٱللَّهُ عَلَىٰ كُلِّ شَيۡءٍ
قَدِيرٌ ٦ مَّآ أَفَآءَ ٱللَّهُ عَلَىٰ رَسُولِهِۦ مِنۡ أَهۡلِ ٱلۡقُرَىٰ فَلِلَّهِ وَلِلرَّسُولِ
وَلِذِي ٱلۡقُرۡبَىٰ وَٱلۡيَتَٰمَىٰ وَٱلۡمَسَٰكِينِ وَٱبۡنِ ٱلسَّبِيلِ كَيۡ لَا يَكُونَ
دُولَةَۢ بَيۡنَ ٱلۡأَغۡنِيَآءِ مِنكُمۡۚ وَمَآ ءَاتَىٰكُمُ ٱلرَّسُولُ فَخُذُوهُ وَمَا
نَهَىٰكُمۡ عَنۡهُ فَٱنتَهُواْۚ وَٱتَّقُواْ ٱللَّهَۖ إِنَّ ٱللَّهَ شَدِيدُ ٱلۡعِقَابِ ٧

59. *Sūrat al-Ḥashr* The Gathering

This *sūra* is Madinan and has 24 *āyat*s.

1. ***Everything in the heavens and everything in the earth glorifies Allah*** – proclaims Him free of and above all other things. ***He is the Almighty, the All-Wise.***

2. ***It is He who expelled those who disbelieved among the People of the Book*** – meaning here the Jewish clan of the Banū'n-Naḍīr – ***from their homes*** in Madina ***to the first gathering-place*** on the way to Syria; the final step was when 'Umar exiled them from Khaybar when he was *khalīfa*. ***You*** believers ***did not think that they would leave; and they thought that their fortresses would protect them from*** the punishment of ***Allah. Then*** the command and punishment of ***Allah came upon them from where they least expected it*** – from the believers, which possibility had not occurred to them – ***and cast terror*** (read as *ru'b* and *ru'ub*) ***into their hearts*** by the killing of their leader, Ka'b ibn al-Ashraf. ***Their houses were pulled down*** (read as *yukhribūna* and *yukharribūna*) ***by their own hands and by the hands of the believers. People of insight, take note!***

3. ***If Allah had not prescribed*** and decreed ***banishment for them, He would have punished them in this world*** by killing and capture, as was done to the Jewish clan of Qurayẓa. ***But in the Next World they will have the punishment of the Fire.***

4. ***That is because they were entrenched in hostility towards Allah and His Messenger. If anyone is hostile towards Allah, Allah is Severe in Retribution.***

5. ***Whatever palm-trees you*** Muslims ***cut down, or left standing upright on their roots, it was done by Allah's permission*** – and Allah gave you a choice about it – ***in order to disgrace the deviators*** (the Jews) – in the face of their objection that cutting down the fruit trees was a corrupt deed.

6. ***Whatever booty from them Allah has given to His Messenger – and you*** Muslims ***spurred on neither horse nor camel in its acquisition***, a reference to spoils taken without fighting. ***But Allah gives***

power to His Messengers over anyone He wills; Allah has power over all things. You (believers) have no right to such spoils, which are exclusively for the Prophet, may Allah bless him and grant him peace, and the four categories (of recipients) mentioned in the following *āyat*. He used to divide them by giving each category one fifth, and the Prophet, may Allah bless him and grant him peace, had the remaining fifth to do what he wished with. He gave it to the *Muhājirūn* and three of the *Anṣār* because they were poor.

7. *Whatever booty Allah gives to His Messenger from city dwellers* – such as Ṣufrā' (the land of Qurayẓa and an-Naḍīr), Wādī'l-Qura and Yanbū' – ***belongs to Allah and to the Messenger*** – and Allah gives whatever instructions He wishes about it, ***and to near relatives*** of the Prophet, may Allah bless him and grant him peace, from the Banū Hāshim and Banū'l-Muṭṭalib, ***orphans*** – children of the Muslims whose fathers have died, ***the very poor, and travellers*** – Muslims who are unable to continue their journey for financial reasons – ***so that it does not become something which merely circulates between the rich among you.*** This means that those entitled to it are the Prophet, may Allah bless him and grant him peace, and the four categories, so that each of the four receive one-fifth and the Prophet, may Allah bless him and grant him peace, received the rest. This is done so that the spoils may not be enjoyed by the rich rather than the poor. ***Whatever the Messenger gives you*** by way of booty or anything else ***you should accept; and whatever he forbids you, you should forgo. Be fearful of Allah: Allah is severe in retribution.***

8. *It is for the poor of the* Muhājirūn *who were driven from their homes and wealth desiring the favour and the pleasure of Allah and supporting Allah and His Messenger. Such people are the truly sincere* in their faith.

9. *Those who were already settled in the abode* (Madina) ***and in belief*** – meaning the *Anṣār* – ***before they came, love those who have emigrated to them and do not find in their hearts any need*** or envy ***for what they have been given*** – a reference to the property of the Banū'n-Naḍīr which the Prophet, may Allah bless him and grant him peace, gave the *Muhājirūn;* ***and they prefer them to themselves***

لِلْفُقَرَآءِ ٱلْمُهَٰجِرِينَ ٱلَّذِينَ أُخْرِجُوا۟ مِن دِيَٰرِهِمْ وَأَمْوَٰلِهِمْ
يَبْتَغُونَ فَضْلًا مِّنَ ٱللَّهِ وَرِضْوَٰنًا وَيَنصُرُونَ ٱللَّهَ وَرَسُولَهُۥٓ ۚ أُو۟لَٰٓئِكَ
هُمُ ٱلصَّٰدِقُونَ ﴿٨﴾ وَٱلَّذِينَ تَبَوَّءُو ٱلدَّارَ وَٱلْإِيمَٰنَ مِن قَبْلِهِمْ
يُحِبُّونَ مَنْ هَاجَرَ إِلَيْهِمْ وَلَا يَجِدُونَ فِى صُدُورِهِمْ حَاجَةً
مِّمَّآ أُوتُوا۟ وَيُؤْثِرُونَ عَلَىٰٓ أَنفُسِهِمْ وَلَوْ كَانَ بِهِمْ خَصَاصَةٌ ۚ
وَمَن يُوقَ شُحَّ نَفْسِهِۦ فَأُو۟لَٰٓئِكَ هُمُ ٱلْمُفْلِحُونَ ﴿٩﴾
وَٱلَّذِينَ جَآءُو مِنۢ بَعْدِهِمْ يَقُولُونَ رَبَّنَا ٱغْفِرْ لَنَا
وَلِإِخْوَٰنِنَا ٱلَّذِينَ سَبَقُونَا بِٱلْإِيمَٰنِ وَلَا تَجْعَلْ فِى قُلُوبِنَا
غِلًّا لِّلَّذِينَ ءَامَنُوا۟ رَبَّنَآ إِنَّكَ رَءُوفٌ رَّحِيمٌ ﴿١٠﴾ ۞ أَلَمْ تَرَ إِلَى
ٱلَّذِينَ نَافَقُوا۟ يَقُولُونَ لِإِخْوَٰنِهِمُ ٱلَّذِينَ كَفَرُوا۟ مِنْ أَهْلِ
ٱلْكِتَٰبِ لَئِنْ أُخْرِجْتُمْ لَنَخْرُجَنَّ مَعَكُمْ وَلَا نُطِيعُ فِيكُمْ
أَحَدًا أَبَدًا وَإِن قُوتِلْتُمْ لَنَنصُرَنَّكُمْ وَٱللَّهُ يَشْهَدُ إِنَّهُمْ لَكَٰذِبُونَ
﴿١١﴾ لَئِنْ أُخْرِجُوا۟ لَا يَخْرُجُونَ مَعَهُمْ وَلَئِن قُوتِلُوا۟ لَا يَنصُرُونَهُمْ
وَلَئِن نَّصَرُوهُمْ لَيُوَلُّنَّ ٱلْأَدْبَٰرَ ثُمَّ لَا يُنصَرُونَ ﴿١٢﴾
لَأَنتُمْ أَشَدُّ رَهْبَةً فِى صُدُورِهِم مِّنَ ٱللَّهِ ۚ ذَٰلِكَ بِأَنَّهُمْ قَوْمٌ
لَّا يَفْقَهُونَ ﴿١٣﴾ لَا يُقَٰتِلُونَكُمْ جَمِيعًا إِلَّا فِى قُرًى
مُّحَصَّنَةٍ أَوْ مِن وَرَآءِ جُدُرٍۭ ۚ بَأْسُهُم بَيْنَهُمْ شَدِيدٌ ۚ تَحْسَبُهُمْ
جَمِيعًا وَقُلُوبُهُمْ شَتَّىٰ ۚ ذَٰلِكَ بِأَنَّهُمْ قَوْمٌ لَّا يَعْقِلُونَ ﴿١٤﴾
كَمَثَلِ ٱلَّذِينَ مِن قَبْلِهِمْ قَرِيبًا ۖ ذَاقُوا۟ وَبَالَ أَمْرِهِمْ وَلَهُمْ عَذَابٌ
أَلِيمٌ ﴿١٥﴾ كَمَثَلِ ٱلشَّيْطَٰنِ إِذْ قَالَ لِلْإِنسَٰنِ ٱكْفُرْ فَلَمَّا كَفَرَ

even if they themselves are needy. It is those who are safeguarded from the avarice of their own selves for wealth ***who are successful.***

10. ***Those who have come after them*** – after the *Muhājirūn* and *Anṣār* until the Day of Resurrection – ***say, 'Our Lord, forgive us and our brothers who preceded us in belief, and do not put rancour in our hearts towards those who believe. Our Lord, You are All-Gentle, Most Merciful.'***

11. ***Did you not see the hypocrites saying to their brothers, those among the People of the Book who disbelieve*** – meaning the Banū'n-Naḍīr and their brothers in unbelief – ***'If you are driven out*** of Madina, ***we will leave with you; we will never obey anyone to your detriment*** and forsake you. ***And if you are fought against we will help you'? Allah bears witness that they are truly liars.***

12. ***If they are driven out they will not leave with them. If they are fought against*** and their help is sought ***they will not help them. Even if they did help them they would turn their backs, and then they*** (the Jews) ***would not be helped.***

13. ***You are a greater cause of terror in their*** (the hypocrites') ***breasts than Allah***, because Allah's punishment is deferred! ***That is because they are people who do not understand.***

14. ***They*** (the Jews) ***will not fight against you all together as a group except in fortified towns or behind*** fortified ***high walls*** (read as *judur* and *jidār*). ***Their hostility*** and belligerence ***towards each other is intense. They are full of bravado in each other's company. You consider them united but their hearts are scattered wide*** owing to their dissension. ***That is because they are people who do not use their intellects.***

15. ***They are the same*** – in respect of abandoning their faith – ***as those a short time before them*** – namely the idolaters at the Battle of Badr – ***who tasted the evil consequences of what they did*** by being killed and in other ways. ***They will*** also ***have a painful punishment*** in the Next World.

16. In their listening to the hypocrites and staying behind them, ***they are like Shayṭān when he says to a human being, 'Disbelieve,' and then when he disbelieves, says, 'I wash my hands of you. Truly I fear Allah, the Lord of all the worlds.'***

قَالَ إِنِّي بَرِيٓءٞ مِّنكَ إِنِّيٓ أَخَافُ ٱللَّهَ رَبَّ ٱلۡعَٰلَمِينَ ﴿١٦﴾
فَكَانَ عَٰقِبَتَهُمَآ أَنَّهُمَا فِي ٱلنَّارِ خَٰلِدَيۡنِ فِيهَاۚ وَذَٰلِكَ جَزَٰٓؤُاْ
ٱلظَّٰلِمِينَ ﴿١٧﴾ يَٰٓأَيُّهَا ٱلَّذِينَ ءَامَنُواْ ٱتَّقُواْ ٱللَّهَ وَلۡتَنظُرۡ
نَفۡسٞ مَّا قَدَّمَتۡ لِغَدٖۖ وَٱتَّقُواْ ٱللَّهَۚ إِنَّ ٱللَّهَ خَبِيرُۢ بِمَا تَعۡمَلُونَ
﴿١٨﴾ وَلَا تَكُونُواْ كَٱلَّذِينَ نَسُواْ ٱللَّهَ فَأَنسَىٰهُمۡ أَنفُسَهُمۡۚ أُوْلَٰٓئِكَ
هُمُ ٱلۡفَٰسِقُونَ ﴿١٩﴾ لَا يَسۡتَوِيٓ أَصۡحَٰبُ ٱلنَّارِ وَأَصۡحَٰبُ
ٱلۡجَنَّةِۚ أَصۡحَٰبُ ٱلۡجَنَّةِ هُمُ ٱلۡفَآئِزُونَ ﴿٢٠﴾ لَوۡ أَنزَلۡنَا هَٰذَا
ٱلۡقُرۡءَانَ عَلَىٰ جَبَلٖ لَّرَأَيۡتَهُۥ خَٰشِعٗا مُّتَصَدِّعٗا مِّنۡ خَشۡيَةِ
ٱللَّهِۚ وَتِلۡكَ ٱلۡأَمۡثَٰلُ نَضۡرِبُهَا لِلنَّاسِ لَعَلَّهُمۡ يَتَفَكَّرُونَ
﴿٢١﴾ هُوَ ٱللَّهُ ٱلَّذِي لَآ إِلَٰهَ إِلَّا هُوَۖ عَٰلِمُ ٱلۡغَيۡبِ وَٱلشَّهَٰدَةِۖ
هُوَ ٱلرَّحۡمَٰنُ ٱلرَّحِيمُ ﴿٢٢﴾ هُوَ ٱللَّهُ ٱلَّذِي لَآ إِلَٰهَ إِلَّا هُوَ
ٱلۡمَلِكُ ٱلۡقُدُّوسُ ٱلسَّلَٰمُ ٱلۡمُؤۡمِنُ ٱلۡمُهَيۡمِنُ ٱلۡعَزِيزُ
ٱلۡجَبَّارُ ٱلۡمُتَكَبِّرُۚ سُبۡحَٰنَ ٱللَّهِ عَمَّا يُشۡرِكُونَ
﴿٢٣﴾ هُوَ ٱللَّهُ ٱلۡخَٰلِقُ ٱلۡبَارِئُ ٱلۡمُصَوِّرُۖ لَهُ ٱلۡأَسۡمَآءُ ٱلۡحُسۡنَىٰۚ
يُسَبِّحُ لَهُۥ مَا فِي ٱلسَّمَٰوَٰتِ وَٱلۡأَرۡضِۖ وَهُوَ ٱلۡعَزِيزُ ٱلۡحَكِيمُ ﴿٢٤﴾

17. ***The final fate of both of them*** – the one who errs and the one who makes others err – ***is that they will be timelessly, for ever, in the Fire. That is the repayment of the wrongdoers*** (the unbelievers).

18. ***You who believe, be fearful of Allah and let each self look to what it has sent forward for Tomorrow*** (the Day of Rising). ***Be fearful of Allah: Allah is aware of what you do.***

19. ***Do not be like those who forgot Allah*** and abandoned obedience to Allah, ***so He made them forget*** to advance good for ***themselves. Such people are the deviators.***

20. ***The Companions of the Fire and the Companions of the Garden are not the same. It is the Companions of the Garden who are the victors.***

21. ***If We had sent down this Qur'an onto a mountain*** – and given the mountain consciousness like a human being's – ***you would have seen it humbled, crushed to pieces from awe of Allah. We make such examples for people so that hopefully they will reflect*** and then believe.

22. ***He is Allah – there is no god but Him, the Knower of the Unseen and the Visible. He is the All-Merciful, the Most Merciful.***

23. ***He is Allah – there is no god but Him, the King, the Most Pure*** of anything not befitting Him, ***the Perfect Peace*** preserved from any imperfection, ***the Trustworthy*** who confirms His Messengers by creating miracles for them, ***the Safeguarder*** Who is watcher over and witness of His slaves and their actions, ***the Almighty, the Compeller*** who compels His creation to do whatever He wills, ***the Supremely Great*** – greater than anything else in existence. ***Glory be to Allah*** – to proclaim Him transcendent ***above all they associate with Him!***

24. ***He is Allah – the Creator, the Maker*** Who brings everything into existence from non-existence, ***the Giver of Form. To Him belong the*** ninety-nine ***Most Beautiful Names. Everything in the heavens and earth glorifies Him. He is the Almighty, the All-Wise.***

سُورَةُ المُمۡتَحَنَةِ

بِسۡمِ ٱللَّهِ ٱلرَّحۡمَٰنِ ٱلرَّحِيمِ

يَٰٓأَيُّهَا ٱلَّذِينَ ءَامَنُواْ لَا تَتَّخِذُواْ عَدُوِّي وَعَدُوَّكُمۡ أَوۡلِيَآءَ تُلۡقُونَ
إِلَيۡهِم بِٱلۡمَوَدَّةِ وَقَدۡ كَفَرُواْ بِمَا جَآءَكُم مِّنَ ٱلۡحَقِّ يُخۡرِجُونَ ٱلرَّسُولَ
وَإِيَّاكُمۡ أَن تُؤۡمِنُواْ بِٱللَّهِ رَبِّكُمۡ إِن كُنتُمۡ خَرَجۡتُمۡ جِهَٰدٗا فِي سَبِيلِي
وَٱبۡتِغَآءَ مَرۡضَاتِيۚ تُسِرُّونَ إِلَيۡهِم بِٱلۡمَوَدَّةِ وَأَنَا۠ أَعۡلَمُ بِمَآ أَخۡفَيۡتُمۡ
وَمَآ أَعۡلَنتُمۡۚ وَمَن يَفۡعَلۡهُ مِنكُمۡ فَقَدۡ ضَلَّ سَوَآءَ ٱلسَّبِيلِ ﴿١﴾ إِن
يَثۡقَفُوكُمۡ يَكُونُواْ لَكُمۡ أَعۡدَآءٗ وَيَبۡسُطُوٓاْ إِلَيۡكُمۡ أَيۡدِيَهُمۡ وَأَلۡسِنَتَهُم
بِٱلسُّوٓءِ وَوَدُّواْ لَوۡ تَكۡفُرُونَ ﴿٢﴾ لَن تَنفَعَكُمۡ أَرۡحَامُكُمۡ وَلَآ أَوۡلَٰدُكُمۡۚ
يَوۡمَ ٱلۡقِيَٰمَةِ يَفۡصِلُ بَيۡنَكُمۡۚ وَٱللَّهُ بِمَا تَعۡمَلُونَ بَصِيرٞ ﴿٣﴾ قَدۡ
كَانَتۡ لَكُمۡ أُسۡوَةٌ حَسَنَةٞ فِيٓ إِبۡرَٰهِيمَ وَٱلَّذِينَ مَعَهُۥٓ إِذۡ قَالُواْ لِقَوۡمِهِمۡ
إِنَّا بُرَءَٰٓؤُاْ مِنكُمۡ وَمِمَّا تَعۡبُدُونَ مِن دُونِ ٱللَّهِ كَفَرۡنَا بِكُمۡ وَبَدَا بَيۡنَنَا
وَبَيۡنَكُمُ ٱلۡعَدَٰوَةُ وَٱلۡبَغۡضَآءُ أَبَدًا حَتَّىٰ تُؤۡمِنُواْ بِٱللَّهِ وَحۡدَهُۥٓ إِلَّا
قَوۡلَ إِبۡرَٰهِيمَ لِأَبِيهِ لَأَسۡتَغۡفِرَنَّ لَكَ وَمَآ أَمۡلِكُ لَكَ مِنَ ٱللَّهِ مِن شَيۡءٖۖ
رَّبَّنَا عَلَيۡكَ تَوَكَّلۡنَا وَإِلَيۡكَ أَنَبۡنَا وَإِلَيۡكَ ٱلۡمَصِيرُ ﴿٤﴾ رَبَّنَا لَا تَجۡعَلۡنَا
فِتۡنَةٗ لِّلَّذِينَ كَفَرُواْ وَٱغۡفِرۡ لَنَا رَبَّنَآۖ إِنَّكَ أَنتَ ٱلۡعَزِيزُ ٱلۡحَكِيمُ ﴿٥﴾
لَقَدۡ كَانَ لَكُمۡ فِيهِمۡ أُسۡوَةٌ حَسَنَةٞ لِّمَن كَانَ يَرۡجُواْ ٱللَّهَ وَٱلۡيَوۡمَ ٱلۡأٓخِرَۚ

60. *Sūrat al-Mumtaḥana*
The Woman Tested

This *sūra* is Madinan and has 13 *āyat*s.

1. ***You who believe, do not take My enemy and your enemy*** – meaning the unbelievers of Makka – ***as friends, showing love for them*** – and maintaining affectionate connections with them – ***when they have rejected the truth*** – the *dīn* of Islam and the Qur'an – ***that has come to you*** – this was revealed when the Prophet, may Allah bless him and grant him peace, intended to raid them and kept that a secret. Ḥāṭib ibn Abī Bala'ta wrote a letter to them telling them about it since he had children and family among the idolaters. The Prophet, may Allah bless him and grant him peace, sought to bring back the messenger he had sent his letter with, Allah having informed him of the matter. He accepted Ḥāṭib's apology, ***driving out the Messenger and yourselves*** – from Makka by making your life difficult for you – ***simply because you believe in Allah your Lord. If you go out to fight*** **jihād** ***in My Way and seeking My pleasure, keeping secret the love you have for them, I know best what you conceal and what you make known. Any of you who do that have strayed from the right way*** – have left the Path of guidance and straightness.

2. ***If they come upon you*** and defeat you ***they will be your enemies and stretch out their hands*** against you to kill and strike you, ***and tongues against you with evil intent***, abusing and cursing you; ***and they would dearly love you to disbelieve*** and revert to unbelief.

3. ***Neither your blood relations nor your children*** who are idolaters and for whose sake you concealed the news ***will be of any avail to you*** – or help you against punishment in the Next World. ***On the Day of Rising He will differentiate*** (read as *yafṣilu* and *yufaṣṣilu*) ***between you*** and them, as you will be in the Garden and they will be with the rest of the unbelievers in the Fire. ***Allah sees what you do.***

4. ***You have an excellent example*** (read as *iswa* and *uswa*) ***in Ibrāhīm*** – in his words and deeds – ***and those*** believers ***with him, when they said to their people, 'We wash our hands of you and all***

that you worship apart from Allah, and we reject you. Between us and you there will be enmity and hatred forever, unless and until you believe in Allah alone.' Except for Ibrāhīm's words to his father: 'I will ask forgiveness for you – which is an exception where the excellent example is concerned, meaning that you should not imitate him in that by asking forgiveness for unbelievers – ***but I have no power to help you in any way against Allah*** with respect to His punishment and His reward. All I can do is ask forgiveness.' He asked forgiveness for him before it was clear to him that he was the enemy of Allah, as is mentioned in *Sūrat at-Tawba* (9:115). ***'Our Lord, we have put our trust in You and have repented to You. You are our final destination.*** These are the words of Ibrāhīm.

5. ***Our Lord, do not make us a target for those who disbelieve and forgive us.*** Do not let them defeat us so that they think that they have the truth and are in the right. ***Our Lord, You are the Almighty, the All-Wise*** in Your kingdom and in what You do.

6. ***There is an excellent example in them for you***, community of Muhammad, ***to follow, for those whose hope is in Allah and the Last Day*** – who fear Allah and the Last Day and think that there will be reward and punishment. ***But if anyone turns away*** and takes the unbelievers as friends, ***Allah is the Rich Beyond Need*** of His creation, ***the Praiseworthy***, praised by those who obey Him.

7. ***It may well be that Allah will restore the love between you and those of them who are now your enemies***, meaning the unbelievers of Makka, and bring them to obedience to Allah Almighty by guiding them to faith and so they may become your friends again. ***Allah is All-Powerful*** and has the power to do that and indeed did so after the conquest of Makka. ***Allah is Ever-Forgiving*** of what happened in the past, ***Most Merciful.***

8. ***Allah does not forbid you from being good to those*** unbelievers ***who have not fought you in the* dīn *or driven you from your homes, or from being just towards them.*** This was before the command to fight them in *jihād*. ***Allah loves those who are just.***

9. ***Allah merely forbids you from taking as friends*** – helpers and protectors – ***those who have fought you over the* dīn *and driven***

وَمَن يَتَوَلَّ فَإِنَّ ٱللَّهَ هُوَ ٱلْغَنِيُّ ٱلْحَمِيدُ ﴿٦﴾ ۞ عَسَى ٱللَّهُ أَن يَجْعَلَ
بَيْنَكُمْ وَبَيْنَ ٱلَّذِينَ عَادَيْتُم مِّنْهُم مَّوَدَّةً ۚ وَٱللَّهُ قَدِيرٌ ۚ وَٱللَّهُ غَفُورٌ رَّحِيمٌ
﴿٧﴾ لَّا يَنْهَىٰكُمُ ٱللَّهُ عَنِ ٱلَّذِينَ لَمْ يُقَٰتِلُوكُمْ فِى ٱلدِّينِ وَلَمْ يُخْرِجُوكُم
مِّن دِيَٰرِكُمْ أَن تَبَرُّوهُمْ وَتُقْسِطُوٓا۟ إِلَيْهِمْ ۚ إِنَّ ٱللَّهَ يُحِبُّ ٱلْمُقْسِطِينَ
﴿٨﴾ إِنَّمَا يَنْهَىٰكُمُ ٱللَّهُ عَنِ ٱلَّذِينَ قَٰتَلُوكُمْ فِى ٱلدِّينِ وَأَخْرَجُوكُم
مِّن دِيَٰرِكُمْ وَظَٰهَرُوا۟ عَلَىٰٓ إِخْرَاجِكُمْ أَن تَوَلَّوْهُمْ ۚ وَمَن يَتَوَلَّهُمْ فَأُو۟لَٰٓئِكَ
هُمُ ٱلظَّٰلِمُونَ ﴿٩﴾ يَٰٓأَيُّهَا ٱلَّذِينَ ءَامَنُوٓا۟ إِذَا جَآءَكُمُ ٱلْمُؤْمِنَٰتُ
مُهَٰجِرَٰتٍ فَٱمْتَحِنُوهُنَّ ۖ ٱللَّهُ أَعْلَمُ بِإِيمَٰنِهِنَّ ۖ فَإِنْ عَلِمْتُمُوهُنَّ مُؤْمِنَٰتٍ
فَلَا تَرْجِعُوهُنَّ إِلَى ٱلْكُفَّارِ ۖ لَا هُنَّ حِلٌّ لَّهُمْ وَلَا هُمْ يَحِلُّونَ لَهُنَّ ۖ وَءَاتُوهُم
مَّآ أَنفَقُوا۟ ۚ وَلَا جُنَاحَ عَلَيْكُمْ أَن تَنكِحُوهُنَّ إِذَآ ءَاتَيْتُمُوهُنَّ أُجُورَهُنَّ ۚ
وَلَا تُمْسِكُوا۟ بِعِصَمِ ٱلْكَوَافِرِ وَسْـَٔلُوا۟ مَآ أَنفَقْتُمْ وَلْيَسْـَٔلُوا۟ مَآ أَنفَقُوا۟ ۚ
ذَٰلِكُمْ حُكْمُ ٱللَّهِ ۖ يَحْكُمُ بَيْنَكُمْ ۚ وَٱللَّهُ عَلِيمٌ حَكِيمٌ ﴿١٠﴾ وَإِن فَاتَكُمْ
شَىْءٌ مِّنْ أَزْوَٰجِكُمْ إِلَى ٱلْكُفَّارِ فَعَاقَبْتُمْ فَـَٔاتُوا۟ ٱلَّذِينَ ذَهَبَتْ
أَزْوَٰجُهُم مِّثْلَ مَآ أَنفَقُوا۟ ۚ وَٱتَّقُوا۟ ٱللَّهَ ٱلَّذِىٓ أَنتُم بِهِۦ مُؤْمِنُونَ ﴿١١﴾
يَٰٓأَيُّهَا ٱلنَّبِىُّ إِذَا جَآءَكَ ٱلْمُؤْمِنَٰتُ يُبَايِعْنَكَ عَلَىٰٓ أَن لَّا يُشْرِكْنَ
بِٱللَّهِ شَيْـًٔا وَلَا يَسْرِقْنَ وَلَا يَزْنِينَ وَلَا يَقْتُلْنَ أَوْلَٰدَهُنَّ وَلَا يَأْتِينَ
بِبُهْتَٰنٍ يَفْتَرِينَهُۥ بَيْنَ أَيْدِيهِنَّ وَأَرْجُلِهِنَّ وَلَا يَعْصِينَكَ
فِى مَعْرُوفٍ ۙ فَبَايِعْهُنَّ وَٱسْتَغْفِرْ لَهُنَّ ٱللَّهَ ۖ إِنَّ ٱللَّهَ غَفُورٌ رَّحِيمٌ
﴿١٢﴾ يَٰٓأَيُّهَا ٱلَّذِينَ ءَامَنُوا۟ لَا تَتَوَلَّوْا۟ قَوْمًا غَضِبَ ٱللَّهُ عَلَيْهِمْ
قَدْ يَئِسُوا۟ مِنَ ٱلْءَاخِرَةِ كَمَا يَئِسَ ٱلْكُفَّارُ مِنْ أَصْحَٰبِ ٱلْقُبُورِ ﴿١٣﴾

you from your homes, and who supported your expulsion. Any who take them as friends are wrongdoers.

10. ***You who believe, when women who believe*** – professing faith on their tongues – ***come to you as emigrants*** – from the unbelievers, after the treaty made with them at al-Ḥudaybiyya, which stated that if any believers came to them they would be returned – ***submit them to a test*** – asking them to take an oath that they have only emigrated for Islam, not out of hatred for their idolatrous husbands or out of passion for Muslim men. Therefore the Prophet, may Allah bless him and grant him peace, made them swear an oath. ***Allah has best knowledge of their belief. If you know they are believers*** – from their oaths – ***do not return them to the unbelievers. They are not lawful for the unbelievers, nor are the unbelievers lawful for them. Give the unbelievers*** – meaning here their husbands – ***whatever dowry they paid*** them. ***There is nothing wrong in your marrying them provided, you pay them their due*** – dowry. ***Do not hold on*** (read as *tumsikū* and *tumassikū*) ***to any marriage ties with women who disbelieve.*** Your becoming Muslim annuls your marriage to unbelieving women or those who stay with the idolaters, having reverted to unbelief since their apostasy severs the tie of marriage. ***Ask for what you paid*** them from the unbelievers whom they marry, ***and let them ask for what they paid*** for the dowries of the women emigrants. ***That is Allah's judgement. Allah will judge between them. Allah is All-Knowing, All-Wise.***

11. ***If any of your wives rejoin the unbelievers*** – so that you lose their dowries – ***you should have compensation.*** When you raid and take booty, pay them back from the booty the same as they paid. ***So repay to those whose wives have gone the dowry they paid out. Be fearful of Allah, Him in Whom you believe.*** The believers gave what they were commanded to give to the unbelievers and believers. Then this ruling was removed.

12. ***O Prophet, when women who believe come to you pledging allegiance to you on the basis that they will not associate anything with Allah, steal, fornicate, kill their children*** – as was done in the time of the *Jāhiliyya* by burying them alive out of fear of shame and poverty – ***or give a false ascription of paternity*** – ascribing a child to her husband when it is not his, ***making up lies about their bodies***

– the Arabic literally means "forging between their hands and their feet" because when the child is born, it is born between the hands and feet, ***or disobey you in respect of anything right*** – anything that is in accord with obedience to Allah, such as refraining from wailing, rending the clothes, cutting off the hair, ripping the shirt and scratching the face, ***then accept their pledge and ask forgiveness for them.*** The Prophet, may Allah bless him and grant him peace, accepted their allegiance in words but did not shake hands with any of them. ***Allah is Ever-Forgiving, Most Merciful.***

13. ***You who believe, do not make friends of people with whom Allah is angry*** – meaning the Jews – ***who have despaired of*** reward ***in the Next World*** – although they are certain about it, because of their stubborn opposition to the Prophet, may Allah bless him and grant him peace, even though they knew that he was telling the truth – ***as the unbelievers have despaired of the inhabitants of the graves.*** In the same way, the unbelievers who are in their graves despair having good in the Next World when they are shown the places that they would have had in Paradise if they had believed; and they are also shown where they will go in Hell.

سُورَةُ الصَّفِّ

بِسْمِ اللَّهِ الرَّحْمَٰنِ الرَّحِيمِ

سَبَّحَ لِلَّهِ مَا فِي السَّمَاوَاتِ وَمَا فِي الْأَرْضِ ۖ وَهُوَ الْعَزِيزُ الْحَكِيمُ
﴿١﴾ يَا أَيُّهَا الَّذِينَ آمَنُوا لِمَ تَقُولُونَ مَا لَا تَفْعَلُونَ ﴿٢﴾
كَبُرَ مَقْتًا عِنْدَ اللَّهِ أَنْ تَقُولُوا مَا لَا تَفْعَلُونَ ﴿٣﴾ إِنَّ
اللَّهَ يُحِبُّ الَّذِينَ يُقَاتِلُونَ فِي سَبِيلِهِ صَفًّا كَأَنَّهُمْ
بُنْيَانٌ مَرْصُوصٌ ﴿٤﴾ وَإِذْ قَالَ مُوسَىٰ لِقَوْمِهِ يَا قَوْمِ لِمَ
تُؤْذُونَنِي وَقَدْ تَعْلَمُونَ أَنِّي رَسُولُ اللَّهِ إِلَيْكُمْ ۖ فَلَمَّا
زَاغُوا أَزَاغَ اللَّهُ قُلُوبَهُمْ ۚ وَاللَّهُ لَا يَهْدِي الْقَوْمَ الْفَاسِقِينَ ﴿٥﴾
وَإِذْ قَالَ عِيسَى ابْنُ مَرْيَمَ يَا بَنِي إِسْرَائِيلَ إِنِّي رَسُولُ اللَّهِ إِلَيْكُمْ مُصَدِّقًا
لِمَا بَيْنَ يَدَيَّ مِنَ التَّوْرَاةِ وَمُبَشِّرًا بِرَسُولٍ يَأْتِي مِنْ بَعْدِي اسْمُهُ أَحْمَدُ ۖ فَلَمَّا
جَاءَهُمْ بِالْبَيِّنَاتِ قَالُوا هَٰذَا سِحْرٌ مُبِينٌ ﴿٦﴾ وَمَنْ أَظْلَمُ مِمَّنِ افْتَرَىٰ
عَلَى اللَّهِ الْكَذِبَ وَهُوَ يُدْعَىٰ إِلَى الْإِسْلَامِ ۚ وَاللَّهُ لَا يَهْدِي الْقَوْمَ الظَّالِمِينَ
﴿٧﴾ يُرِيدُونَ لِيُطْفِئُوا نُورَ اللَّهِ بِأَفْوَاهِهِمْ وَاللَّهُ مُتِمُّ نُورِهِ وَلَوْ كَرِهَ
الْكَافِرُونَ ﴿٨﴾ هُوَ الَّذِي أَرْسَلَ رَسُولَهُ بِالْهُدَىٰ وَدِينِ الْحَقِّ لِيُظْهِرَهُ
عَلَى الدِّينِ كُلِّهِ وَلَوْ كَرِهَ الْمُشْرِكُونَ ﴿٩﴾ يَا أَيُّهَا الَّذِينَ آمَنُوا هَلْ أَدُلُّكُمْ
عَلَىٰ تِجَارَةٍ تُنْجِيكُمْ مِنْ عَذَابٍ أَلِيمٍ ﴿١٠﴾ تُؤْمِنُونَ بِاللَّهِ وَرَسُولِهِ وَتُجَاهِدُونَ
فِي سَبِيلِ اللَّهِ بِأَمْوَالِكُمْ وَأَنْفُسِكُمْ ۚ ذَٰلِكُمْ خَيْرٌ لَكُمْ إِنْ كُنْتُمْ تَعْلَمُونَ ﴿١١﴾
يَغْفِرْ لَكُمْ ذُنُوبَكُمْ وَيُدْخِلْكُمْ جَنَّاتٍ تَجْرِي مِنْ تَحْتِهَا الْأَنْهَارُ وَمَسَاكِنَ

61. *Sūrat aṣ-Ṣaff*
The Ranks

This *sūra* is Madinan and has 14 *āyat*s.

1. ***Everything in the heavens and everything in the earth glorifies Allah***: proclaims His purity and transcendence of created things. ***He is the Almighty*** in His kingdom, ***the All-Wise*** in what He does.

2. You who believe, why do you say what you do not do when you are asked to perform *jihād?* This was after the Muslims' defeat in the Battle of Uḥud.

3. ***It is deeply abhorrent to Allah that you should say what you do not do.***

4. ***Allah loves*** helps and honours ***those who fight in His Way in ranks*** close to one another ***like well-built walls*** – making them solid and firm.

5. ***Remember when Mūsā said to his people, 'My people, why do you mistreat me when you know that I am the Messenger of Allah to you?'*** They said that his testicles were swollen, which was not true, and they disbelieved him. He reminded them that any Messenger of Allah is entitled to respect. ***So when they deviated*** from the truth by abusing him ***Allah made their hearts deviate*** away from guidance, as had been decreed from before time. ***Allah does not guide people who are deviators*** – those whom Allah knew to be unbelievers.

6. ***And*** remember ***when 'Īsā son of Maryam said, 'Tribe of Israel I am the Messenger of Allah to you, confirming the Torah which came before me and giving you the good news of a Messenger after me whose name shall be Aḥmad.'*** Allah says: ***When he*** (Aḥmad) ***brought them*** (the unbelievers) ***the Clear Signs, they said, 'This*** – which you have brought – ***is downright magic*** (read as *siḥr* and also *sāḥir,* "magician").***' Who could do greater wrong than someone who invents a lie against Allah*** – ascribes a partner or a child to Allah and describes His Signs as magic – ***when he has been called to Islam?*** No one could. ***Allah does not guide wrongdoing people*** (unbelievers).

طَيِّبَةً فِي جَنَّٰتِ عَدۡنٍۚ ذَٰلِكَ ٱلۡفَوۡزُ ٱلۡعَظِيمُ ١٢ وَأُخۡرَىٰ تُحِبُّونَهَاۖ نَصۡرٞ
مِّنَ ٱللَّهِ وَفَتۡحٞ قَرِيبٞۗ وَبَشِّرِ ٱلۡمُؤۡمِنِينَ ١٣ يَٰٓأَيُّهَا ٱلَّذِينَ ءَامَنُواْ كُونُوٓاْ
أَنصَارَ ٱللَّهِ كَمَا قَالَ عِيسَى ٱبۡنُ مَرۡيَمَ لِلۡحَوَارِيِّـۧنَ مَنۡ أَنصَارِيٓ إِلَى ٱللَّهِۖ
قَالَ ٱلۡحَوَارِيُّونَ نَحۡنُ أَنصَارُ ٱللَّهِۖ فَـَٔامَنَت طَّآئِفَةٞ مِّنۢ بَنِيٓ إِسۡرَٰٓءِيلَ
وَكَفَرَت طَّآئِفَةٞۖ فَأَيَّدۡنَا ٱلَّذِينَ ءَامَنُواْ عَلَىٰ عَدُوِّهِمۡ فَأَصۡبَحُواْ ظَٰهِرِينَ ١٤

8. ***They desire to extinguish Allah's Light*** – the Law and proofs of Allah – ***with their mouths*** – by saying it is magic, poetry and soothsaying ***– but Allah will perfect His Light*** (read as *mutimmu nūrihi* and *mutimmun nūrahu*) and make it manifest ***though the unbelievers hate it.***

9. ***It is He who sent His Messenger with guidance and the* Dīn *of Truth to exalt it over every other* dīn** – opposed to it, ***though the idolators hate it.***

10. ***You who believe, shall I direct you to a transaction which will save*** (read as *tunjīkum* and *tunajjīkum*) ***you from a painful punishment?***

11. ***It is to*** continue to ***believe in Allah and His Messenger and to do* jihād *in the Way of Allah with your wealth and your selves. That is better for you if you only knew***, and so you should do it.

12. If you do so, ***He will forgive you your wrong actions and admit you into Gardens with rivers flowing under them, and fine dwellings in the Gardens of Eden. That is the Great Victory.***

13. ***And*** He will give you other blessings in ***other things you love: support from Allah and imminent victory. Give good news to the believers*** – of victory and conquest.

14. ***You who believe, be helpers of*** the *Dīn* of ***Allah*** (read as *anṣāra'llāhi* and as *anṣāran lillāhi*) – as the Disciples were – ***as 'Īsā son of Maryam said to the Disciples, 'Who will be my helpers for Allah?'*** "Who will be among the Helpers who will go with me to help Allah?" ***The Disciples said, 'We will be the helpers of Allah.'*** The Disciples were the sincere friends of 'Īsā and they were the first to believe in him. They were twelve men. The word *ḥawārī* (disciple) comes from *ḥawar*, which means pure white. It is said that they were fullers who dyed garments white. ***One faction of the tribe of Israel believed*** in 'Īsā, and declared that he was the slave of Allah and had been taken up to heaven – ***and the other disbelieved*** by saying that he was the son of Allah, Who had raised him up. The two groups fought. ***So We supported those who believed against their enemy*** – the group who had disbelieved – ***and they became victorious.***

سُورَةُ الجُمُعَةِ

بِسۡمِ ٱللَّهِ ٱلرَّحۡمَٰنِ ٱلرَّحِيمِ

يُسَبِّحُ لِلَّهِ مَا فِى ٱلسَّمَٰوَٰتِ وَمَا فِى ٱلۡأَرۡضِ ٱلۡمَلِكِ ٱلۡقُدُّوسِ ٱلۡعَزِيزِ
ٱلۡحَكِيمِ ١ هُوَ ٱلَّذِى بَعَثَ فِى ٱلۡأُمِّيِّـۧنَ رَسُولٗا مِّنۡهُمۡ يَتۡلُواْ
عَلَيۡهِمۡ ءَايَٰتِهِۦ وَيُزَكِّيهِمۡ وَيُعَلِّمُهُمُ ٱلۡكِتَٰبَ وَٱلۡحِكۡمَةَ وَإِن كَانُواْ
مِن قَبۡلُ لَفِى ضَلَٰلٖ مُّبِينٖ ٢ وَءَاخَرِينَ مِنۡهُمۡ لَمَّا يَلۡحَقُواْ بِهِمۡۚ
وَهُوَ ٱلۡعَزِيزُ ٱلۡحَكِيمُ ٣ ذَٰلِكَ فَضۡلُ ٱللَّهِ يُؤۡتِيهِ مَن يَشَآءُۚ وَٱللَّهُ
ذُو ٱلۡفَضۡلِ ٱلۡعَظِيمِ ٤ مَثَلُ ٱلَّذِينَ حُمِّلُواْ ٱلتَّوۡرَىٰةَ ثُمَّ لَمۡ
يَحۡمِلُوهَا كَمَثَلِ ٱلۡحِمَارِ يَحۡمِلُ أَسۡفَارَۢاۚ بِئۡسَ مَثَلُ ٱلۡقَوۡمِ
ٱلَّذِينَ كَذَّبُواْ بِـَٔايَٰتِ ٱللَّهِۚ وَٱللَّهُ لَا يَهۡدِى ٱلۡقَوۡمَ ٱلظَّٰلِمِينَ ٥
قُلۡ يَٰٓأَيُّهَا ٱلَّذِينَ هَادُوٓاْ إِن زَعَمۡتُمۡ أَنَّكُمۡ أَوۡلِيَآءُ لِلَّهِ مِن
دُونِ ٱلنَّاسِ فَتَمَنَّوُاْ ٱلۡمَوۡتَ إِن كُنتُمۡ صَٰدِقِينَ ٦ وَلَا يَتَمَنَّوۡنَهُۥٓ
أَبَدَۢا بِمَا قَدَّمَتۡ أَيۡدِيهِمۡۚ وَٱللَّهُ عَلِيمُۢ بِٱلظَّٰلِمِينَ ٧ قُلۡ إِنَّ
ٱلۡمَوۡتَ ٱلَّذِى تَفِرُّونَ مِنۡهُ فَإِنَّهُۥ مُلَٰقِيكُمۡۖ ثُمَّ تُرَدُّونَ
إِلَىٰ عَٰلِمِ ٱلۡغَيۡبِ وَٱلشَّهَٰدَةِ فَيُنَبِّئُكُم بِمَا كُنتُمۡ تَعۡمَلُونَ ٨
يَٰٓأَيُّهَا ٱلَّذِينَ ءَامَنُوٓاْ إِذَا نُودِىَ لِلصَّلَوٰةِ مِن يَوۡمِ ٱلۡجُمُعَةِ
فَٱسۡعَوۡاْ إِلَىٰ ذِكۡرِ ٱللَّهِ وَذَرُواْ ٱلۡبَيۡعَۚ ذَٰلِكُمۡ خَيۡرٞ لَّكُمۡ إِن كُنتُمۡ
تَعۡلَمُونَ ٩ فَإِذَا قُضِيَتِ ٱلصَّلَوٰةُ فَٱنتَشِرُواْ فِى ٱلۡأَرۡضِ
وَٱبۡتَغُواْ مِن فَضۡلِ ٱللَّهِ وَٱذۡكُرُواْ ٱللَّهَ كَثِيرٗا لَّعَلَّكُمۡ تُفۡلِحُونَ
١٠ وَإِذَا رَأَوۡاْ تِجَٰرَةً أَوۡ لَهۡوًا ٱنفَضُّوٓاْ إِلَيۡهَا وَتَرَكُوكَ قَآئِمٗاۚ قُلۡ
مَا عِندَ ٱللَّهِ خَيۡرٞ مِّنَ ٱللَّهۡوِ وَمِنَ ٱلتِّجَٰرَةِۚ وَٱللَّهُ خَيۡرُ ٱلرَّٰزِقِينَ ١١

62. *Sūrat al-Jumu'a*
The Friday Prayer

This *sūra* is Madinan and has 11 *āyat*s.

1. Everything in the heavens and everything in the earth glorifies Allah, the King, the All-Pure – transcending all that is not appropriate to Him – ***the Almighty, the All-Wise*** in His kingdom and everything He does.

2. *It is He who raised up among the unlettered people* – meaning the Arabs who for the most part did not read or write – ***a Messenger*** – Muḥammad, may Allah bless him and grant him peace – ***from them to recite His Signs*** (the Qur'an) ***to them, purify them*** of *shirk*, ***and teach them the Book*** (the Qur'an) ***and Wisdom*** (the rulings in it), ***even though before that they were clearly misguided.***

3. *And others of them* – meaning others who will join them after them in precedence and excellence – ***who have not yet joined them. He is the Almighty, the All-Wise.*** He is Mighty and Wise in His kingdom and work. This is a reference to the *Tābi'ūn* (the generationa after the Companions). Singling them out for mention is enough to show clearly the excellence of the Companions among whom the Prophet, may Allah bless him and grant him peace, was sent. It puts them above all others to whom he has been sent and who have believed in him, among all of human beings and jinn until the Day of Rising; for each generation is better than the one after it.

4. *That is Allah's favour which He gives to whoever He wills* – meaning Prophets or those mentioned together with them; ***Allah's favour is indeed immense.***

5. *The likeness of those who were charged with the Torah* – those who were obliged to act by it – ***but then have not upheld it*** – they have not acted by it, particularly regarding the description it contains of the Prophet, may Allah bless him and grant him peace, by not believing in him – ***is that of a donkey loaded with weighty tomes*** – because they are simply a burden to it and do not benefit it in any way. ***How evil is the likeness of those who deny Allah's Signs*** which confirm the Prophet, may Allah bless him and grant him peace*!* They are singled out for criticism. ***Allah does not guide wrongdoing people*** (unbelievers).

6. ***Say: 'You Jews, if you claim to be the friends of Allah to the exclusion of all other people then wish for death, if you are telling the truth.'***

7. ***But they will never ever wish for it – because of what they have done*** – meaning their rejection of the Prophet, may Allah bless him and grant him peace. ***Allah knows the wrongdoers*** (the unbelievers).

8. ***Say: 'Death, from which you are fleeing, will certainly catch up with you. Then you will be returned to the Knower of the Unseen and the Visible and He will inform you about what you did*** – and repay you for it.*'*

9. ***You who believe, when you are called to the prayer on the Day of Jumu'a, hasten to the remembrance of Allah*** – meaning the prayer – ***and abandon trade***: stop all business transactions. ***That is better for you if you only knew*** – so do it.

10. ***Then when the prayer is finished, spread through the earth*** – this command is in fact a dispensation – ***and seek Allah's bounty*** (provision) ***and remember Allah much so that perhaps you may be successful.*** The Prophet, may Allah bless him and grant him peace, was giving *a khuṭba* one Friday when a caravan arrived and drums were beaten to announce it, as was the custom. The people left the mosque and went out to the caravan, except for twelve men; and then this was revealed.

11. ***But when they see a chance of trade or entertainment they scatter off to it*** (trade) – because that is what they were seeking, not entertainment – ***and leave you standing there*** giving the *khuṭba*. ***Say: 'What*** (reward) ***is with Allah is better*** for those who believe ***than trade or entertainment. Allah is the Best of Providers.'*** "Providers" is in the plural because it is said, "A man provides for his dependants," i.e. from Allah's provision.

سُورَةُ المُنَافِقُونَ

بِسْمِ ٱللَّهِ ٱلرَّحْمَٰنِ ٱلرَّحِيمِ

إِذَا جَآءَكَ ٱلْمُنَٰفِقُونَ قَالُوا۟ نَشْهَدُ إِنَّكَ لَرَسُولُ ٱللَّهِ ۗ وَٱللَّهُ يَعْلَمُ
إِنَّكَ لَرَسُولُهُۥ وَٱللَّهُ يَشْهَدُ إِنَّ ٱلْمُنَٰفِقِينَ لَكَٰذِبُونَ ﴿١﴾
ٱتَّخَذُوٓا۟ أَيْمَٰنَهُمْ جُنَّةً فَصَدُّوا۟ عَن سَبِيلِ ٱللَّهِ ۚ إِنَّهُمْ سَآءَ مَا كَانُوا۟
يَعْمَلُونَ ﴿٢﴾ ذَٰلِكَ بِأَنَّهُمْ ءَامَنُوا۟ ثُمَّ كَفَرُوا۟ فَطُبِعَ عَلَىٰ قُلُوبِهِمْ
فَهُمْ لَا يَفْقَهُونَ ﴿٣﴾ ۞ وَإِذَا رَأَيْتَهُمْ تُعْجِبُكَ أَجْسَامُهُمْ ۖ
وَإِن يَقُولُوا۟ تَسْمَعْ لِقَوْلِهِمْ ۖ كَأَنَّهُمْ خُشُبٌ مُّسَنَّدَةٌ ۖ يَحْسَبُونَ كُلَّ
صَيْحَةٍ عَلَيْهِمْ ۚ هُمُ ٱلْعَدُوُّ فَٱحْذَرْهُمْ ۚ قَٰتَلَهُمُ ٱللَّهُ ۖ أَنَّىٰ يُؤْفَكُونَ ﴿٤﴾
وَإِذَا قِيلَ لَهُمْ تَعَالَوْا۟ يَسْتَغْفِرْ لَكُمْ رَسُولُ ٱللَّهِ لَوَّوْا۟ رُءُوسَهُمْ
وَرَأَيْتَهُمْ يَصُدُّونَ وَهُم مُّسْتَكْبِرُونَ ﴿٥﴾ سَوَآءٌ عَلَيْهِمْ
أَسْتَغْفَرْتَ لَهُمْ أَمْ لَمْ تَسْتَغْفِرْ لَهُمْ لَن يَغْفِرَ ٱللَّهُ لَهُمْ ۚ إِنَّ
ٱللَّهَ لَا يَهْدِى ٱلْقَوْمَ ٱلْفَٰسِقِينَ ﴿٦﴾ هُمُ ٱلَّذِينَ يَقُولُونَ
لَا تُنفِقُوا۟ عَلَىٰ مَنْ عِندَ رَسُولِ ٱللَّهِ حَتَّىٰ يَنفَضُّوا۟ ۗ وَلِلَّهِ
خَزَآئِنُ ٱلسَّمَٰوَٰتِ وَٱلْأَرْضِ وَلَٰكِنَّ ٱلْمُنَٰفِقِينَ لَا يَفْقَهُونَ
﴿٧﴾ يَقُولُونَ لَئِن رَّجَعْنَآ إِلَى ٱلْمَدِينَةِ لَيُخْرِجَنَّ ٱلْأَعَزُّ

63. *Sūrat al-Munāfiqūn*
The Hypocrites

This *sūra* is Madinan and has 11 *āyats*.

1. *When the hypocrites come to you they say* with their tongues what is not in their hearts*:* ***'We bear witness that you are indeed the Messenger of Allah.' Allah knows that you are indeed His Messenger and Allah bears witness that the hypocrites are certainly liars*** – and that they conceal the opposite of what they say.

2. *They have made their oaths into a cloak* to protect their property and lives ***and barred the Way of Allah*** to prevent people from doing *jihād* against them. ***What they have done is truly evil.***

3. *That* evil-doing ***is because they have believed*** with their tongues ***and then returned to unbelief*** in their hearts, by persisting in their rejection of him. ***So their hearts have been sealed up*** with unbelief ***and they cannot understand*** faith.

4. *When you see them, their* beautiful ***outward form appeals to you, and if they speak you listen to what they say*** because of their eloquent speech. ***But they are like propped-up planks of wood*** (read as *khushub* and *khushb*) against a wall in their lack of understanding. ***They imagine every cry to be against them*** – like a call in the military camp or announcement of a lost camel. Their hearts are filled with terror because they think that it will be revealed that to shed their blood is lawful. ***They are the enemy, so beware of them*** – because they may divulge your secrets to the enemy. ***Allah fight them!*** "May Allah destroy them!" ***How they are perverted!*** How can they turn away from faith after the proof has been established?

5. *When they are told, 'Come* and apologise, ***and the Messenger of Allah will ask forgiveness for you,' they turn*** (read as *lawwaw* and *lawaw*) ***their heads*** in aversion to that ***and you see them turn away in haughty arrogance.***

6. *In their case it makes no difference whether you ask forgiveness for them or do not ask forgiveness for them. Allah will never forgive them. Allah does not guide deviant people.*

مِنْهَا ٱلْأَذَلَّ ۚ وَلِلَّهِ ٱلْعِزَّةُ وَلِرَسُولِهِۦ وَلِلْمُؤْمِنِينَ وَلَٰكِنَّ
ٱلْمُنَٰفِقِينَ لَا يَعْلَمُونَ ﴿٨﴾ يَٰٓأَيُّهَا ٱلَّذِينَ ءَامَنُوا۟ لَا تُلْهِكُمْ
أَمْوَٰلُكُمْ وَلَآ أَوْلَٰدُكُمْ عَن ذِكْرِ ٱللَّهِ ۚ وَمَن يَفْعَلْ
ذَٰلِكَ فَأُو۟لَٰٓئِكَ هُمُ ٱلْخَٰسِرُونَ ﴿٩﴾ وَأَنفِقُوا۟ مِمَّا رَزَقْنَٰكُم
مِّن قَبْلِ أَن يَأْتِىَ أَحَدَكُمُ ٱلْمَوْتُ فَيَقُولَ رَبِّ لَوْلَآ أَخَّرْتَنِىٓ
إِلَىٰٓ أَجَلٍ قَرِيبٍ فَأَصَّدَّقَ وَأَكُن مِّنَ ٱلصَّٰلِحِينَ ﴿١٠﴾ وَلَن
يُؤَخِّرَ ٱللَّهُ نَفْسًا إِذَا جَآءَ أَجَلُهَا ۚ وَٱللَّهُ خَبِيرٌۢ بِمَا تَعْمَلُونَ ﴿١١﴾

7. ***They are the people who say*** to their Companions among the *Anṣār:* ***'Do not spend on those*** *Muhājirūn* ***who are with the Messenger of Allah, so that they may go away*** and leave him.***' The treasuries of the heavens and earth belong to Allah*** – and so He is the One who provides for the *Muhājirūn* and for everyone else. ***But the hypocrites do not understand this.***

8. ***They say, 'If we return to Madina*** after the expedition to the Banū'l-Muṣṭaliq ***the mightier*** – meaning they themselves – ***will drive out the inferior*** – meaning the believers.***' But all might*** (victory) ***belongs to Allah and to His Messenger and the believers, though the hypocrites do not know this.***

9. ***You who believe, do not let your wealth or children divert you from the remembrance of Allah*** – meaning in particular the five prayers. ***Whoever does that is lost.***

10. ***Give from what We have provided for you*** – and pay the *zakāt* on it – ***before death comes to one of you and he says, 'My Lord, if only you would give me a little more time so that I can give ṣadaqa*** – and pay *zakāt* – ***and be one of the righteous*** and perform *ḥajj!'* Ibn 'Abbās, may Allah be pleased with him, said, "No one falls short in respect of *zakāt* and the *ḥajj* but that he will ask to go back when he dies."

11. ***Allah will not give anyone more time, once their time has come. Allah is aware of what you do*** (read as *ta'lamūna* and *ya'lamūna*, "what they do").

سُورَةُ التَّغَابُنِ

بِسْمِ اللَّهِ الرَّحْمَٰنِ الرَّحِيمِ

يُسَبِّحُ لِلَّهِ مَا فِي السَّمَاوَاتِ وَمَا فِي الْأَرْضِ ۖ لَهُ الْمُلْكُ وَلَهُ الْحَمْدُ ۖ
وَهُوَ عَلَىٰ كُلِّ شَيْءٍ قَدِيرٌ ﴿١﴾ هُوَ الَّذِي خَلَقَكُمْ فَمِنْكُمْ كَافِرٌ
وَمِنْكُمْ مُؤْمِنٌ ۚ وَاللَّهُ بِمَا تَعْمَلُونَ بَصِيرٌ ﴿٢﴾ خَلَقَ السَّمَاوَاتِ
وَالْأَرْضَ بِالْحَقِّ وَصَوَّرَكُمْ فَأَحْسَنَ صُوَرَكُمْ ۖ وَإِلَيْهِ الْمَصِيرُ ﴿٣﴾
يَعْلَمُ مَا فِي السَّمَاوَاتِ وَالْأَرْضِ وَيَعْلَمُ مَا تُسِرُّونَ وَمَا تُعْلِنُونَ ۚ وَاللَّهُ
عَلِيمٌ بِذَاتِ الصُّدُورِ ﴿٤﴾ أَلَمْ يَأْتِكُمْ نَبَأُ الَّذِينَ كَفَرُوا مِنْ قَبْلُ
فَذَاقُوا وَبَالَ أَمْرِهِمْ وَلَهُمْ عَذَابٌ أَلِيمٌ ﴿٥﴾ ذَٰلِكَ بِأَنَّهُ كَانَتْ تَأْتِيهِمْ
رُسُلُهُمْ بِالْبَيِّنَاتِ فَقَالُوا أَبَشَرٌ يَهْدُونَنَا فَكَفَرُوا وَتَوَلَّوْا ۚ وَاسْتَغْنَى
اللَّهُ ۚ وَاللَّهُ غَنِيٌّ حَمِيدٌ ﴿٦﴾ زَعَمَ الَّذِينَ كَفَرُوا أَنْ لَنْ يُبْعَثُوا ۚ قُلْ بَلَىٰ وَرَبِّي
لَتُبْعَثُنَّ ثُمَّ لَتُنَبَّؤُنَّ بِمَا عَمِلْتُمْ ۚ وَذَٰلِكَ عَلَى اللَّهِ يَسِيرٌ ﴿٧﴾ فَآمِنُوا بِاللَّهِ
وَرَسُولِهِ وَالنُّورِ الَّذِي أَنْزَلْنَا ۚ وَاللَّهُ بِمَا تَعْمَلُونَ خَبِيرٌ ﴿٨﴾ يَوْمَ
يَجْمَعُكُمْ لِيَوْمِ الْجَمْعِ ۖ ذَٰلِكَ يَوْمُ التَّغَابُنِ ۗ وَمَنْ يُؤْمِنْ بِاللَّهِ وَيَعْمَلْ
صَالِحًا يُكَفِّرْ عَنْهُ سَيِّئَاتِهِ وَيُدْخِلْهُ جَنَّاتٍ تَجْرِي مِنْ تَحْتِهَا
الْأَنْهَارُ خَالِدِينَ فِيهَا أَبَدًا ۚ ذَٰلِكَ الْفَوْزُ الْعَظِيمُ ﴿٩﴾

64. *Sūrat at-Taghābun*
Profit and Loss

This *sūra* is Madinan and has 18 *āyat*s.

1. ***Everything in the heavens and everything on earth glorifies Allah. Sovereignty and praise belong to Him. He has power over all things.***

2. ***It is He who created you, yet among you are disbelievers as well as believers. Allah sees what you do.***

3. ***He created the heavens and the earth with truth and formed you, giving you the best of forms.*** The form of Ādam is the best of forms. ***And He is your final destination.***

4. ***He knows everything in the heavens and earth. He knows what you keep secret and what you divulge. Allah knows what*** secrets and beliefs ***the heart contains.***

5. ***Has the news not reached you***, unbelievers of Makka, ***of those who disbelieved before and tasted the evil consequences of what they did*** in their unbelief in this world? ***They will have a painful punishment*** in the Next World.

6. ***That*** punishment ***is because their Messengers brought them the Clear Signs*** – clear proofs in favour of faith – ***but they said, 'Are human beings going to guide us?' So they disbelieved and turned away*** from faith. ***But Allah is completely independent of them*** and whether they have faith. ***Allah is Rich Beyond Need*** of His creation, ***Praisewor-thy*** in what He does.

7. ***Those who disbelieve claim that they will never be raised again. Say: 'Oh yes, by my Lord, you certainly will be raised again, and then you will be informed about what you did! That is easy for Allah.'***

8. ***So believe in Allah and His Messenger and in the Light*** (the Qur'an) ***We have sent down. Allah is aware of what you do.***

9. ***On the Day He gathers you for the Day of Gathering*** – the Day of Rising – ***that is the Day of Profit and Loss.*** "Profit and loss" refers to the fact that the believers will cause loss to the unbelievers

وَٱلَّذِينَ كَفَرُوا۟ وَكَذَّبُوا۟ بِـَٔايَـٰتِنَآ أُو۟لَـٰٓئِكَ أَصْحَـٰبُ
ٱلنَّارِ خَـٰلِدِينَ فِيهَا ۖ وَبِئْسَ ٱلْمَصِيرُ ﴿١٠﴾ مَآ أَصَابَ مِن
مُّصِيبَةٍ إِلَّا بِإِذْنِ ٱللَّهِ ۗ وَمَن يُؤْمِنۢ بِٱللَّهِ يَهْدِ قَلْبَهُۥ ۚ وَٱللَّهُ بِكُلِّ
شَىْءٍ عَلِيمٌ ﴿١١﴾ وَأَطِيعُوا۟ ٱللَّهَ وَأَطِيعُوا۟ ٱلرَّسُولَ ۚ فَإِن
تَوَلَّيْتُمْ فَإِنَّمَا عَلَىٰ رَسُولِنَا ٱلْبَلَـٰغُ ٱلْمُبِينُ ﴿١٢﴾ ٱللَّهُ لَآ إِلَـٰهَ
إِلَّا هُوَ ۚ وَعَلَى ٱللَّهِ فَلْيَتَوَكَّلِ ٱلْمُؤْمِنُونَ ﴿١٣﴾ يَـٰٓأَيُّهَا
ٱلَّذِينَ ءَامَنُوٓا۟ إِنَّ مِنْ أَزْوَٰجِكُمْ وَأَوْلَـٰدِكُمْ عَدُوًّا
لَّكُمْ فَٱحْذَرُوهُمْ ۚ وَإِن تَعْفُوا۟ وَتَصْفَحُوا۟ وَتَغْفِرُوا۟
فَإِنَّ ٱللَّهَ غَفُورٌ رَّحِيمٌ ﴿١٤﴾ إِنَّمَآ أَمْوَٰلُكُمْ وَأَوْلَـٰدُكُمْ
فِتْنَةٌ ۚ وَٱللَّهُ عِندَهُۥٓ أَجْرٌ عَظِيمٌ ﴿١٥﴾ فَٱتَّقُوا۟ ٱللَّهَ مَا ٱسْتَطَعْتُمْ
وَٱسْمَعُوا۟ وَأَطِيعُوا۟ وَأَنفِقُوا۟ خَيْرًا لِّأَنفُسِكُمْ ۗ وَمَن
يُوقَ شُحَّ نَفْسِهِۦ فَأُو۟لَـٰٓئِكَ هُمُ ٱلْمُفْلِحُونَ ﴿١٦﴾ إِن تُقْرِضُوا۟
ٱللَّهَ قَرْضًا حَسَنًا يُضَـٰعِفْهُ لَكُمْ وَيَغْفِرْ لَكُمْ ۚ وَٱللَّهُ شَكُورٌ
حَلِيمٌ ﴿١٧﴾ عَـٰلِمُ ٱلْغَيْبِ وَٱلشَّهَـٰدَةِ ٱلْعَزِيزُ ٱلْحَكِيمُ ﴿١٨﴾

by taking the places and family in the Garden which they would have had if they had believed. ***As for those who believe in Allah and act rightly, He will erase*** (read as *yukaffir* and *nukaffir*, "We will erase") ***their bad actions from their record and admit*** (read as *yudkhil* and *nudkhil*, "We will admit") ***them to Gardens with rivers flowing under them, remaining in them timelessly, for ever and ever. That is the Great Victory!***

10. ***But as for those who disbelieve and deny Our Signs*** (the Qur'an)***, they are the Companions of the Fire, remaining in it timelessly, forever. What an evil destination!***

11. ***No misfortune occurs except by Allah's permission*** – in other words, His decree**.** ***Whoever believes in Allah,*** and that everything happens by the decree of Allah, ***He will guide his heart*** to be steadfast in accepting it**.** ***Allah has knowledge of all things.***

12. ***Obey Allah and obey the Messenger. But if you turn your backs, the Messenger is only responsible for clear transmission.***

13. ***Allah – there is no god but Him, so let the believers put their trust in Allah.***

14. ***You who believe, some of your wives and children are an enemy to you, so be wary of them.*** Beware of obeying them and staying behind instead of doing good actions, such as *jihād* and *hijra*. The reason for the revelation of the *āyat* was that some people obeyed their families in that respect. ***But if you pardon and exonerate and forgive*** those people for staying behind you and not doing what is good, because separation from you would be hard on them, ***Allah is Ever-Forgiving, Most Merciful.***

15. ***Your wealth and children are a trial*** because they distract you from matters of the Next World***, but with Allah there is an immense reward***, so do not forfeit it by being distracted by property and children**.**

16. ***So be fearful of Allah, as much as you are able to*** – abrogating His words, *"Be fearful of Allah with the fear that is His due"* (3:102) – ***and listen*** to what you are commanded to do ***and obey*** Allah ***and spend for your own benefit*** in obedience to Allah**.** ***It is the people who are safeguarded from the avarice of their own selves who are successful.***

17. ***If you make a generous loan to Allah*** by giving *ṣadaqa* cheerfully ***He will multiply*** (read as *yuḍā'ifhu* and as *yuḍa''ifhu*) ***it for you*** from ten times over to seven hundred or more ***and forgive you*** as He wills. ***Allah is All-Thankful*** for your obedience, ***Most Forbearing*** in not punishing you for your disobedience –

18. ***The Knower of the Unseen and the Visible, the Almighty*** in His kingdom, ***the All-Wise*** in what He does.

سُورَةُ الطَّلَاقِ

بِسْمِ ٱللَّهِ ٱلرَّحْمَٰنِ ٱلرَّحِيمِ

يَٰٓأَيُّهَا ٱلنَّبِىُّ إِذَا طَلَّقْتُمُ ٱلنِّسَآءَ فَطَلِّقُوهُنَّ لِعِدَّتِهِنَّ وَأَحْصُوا۟
ٱلْعِدَّةَ ۖ وَٱتَّقُوا۟ ٱللَّهَ رَبَّكُمْ ۖ لَا تُخْرِجُوهُنَّ مِنۢ بُيُوتِهِنَّ
وَلَا يَخْرُجْنَ إِلَّآ أَن يَأْتِينَ بِفَٰحِشَةٍ مُّبَيِّنَةٍ ۚ وَتِلْكَ حُدُودُ
ٱللَّهِ ۚ وَمَن يَتَعَدَّ حُدُودَ ٱللَّهِ فَقَدْ ظَلَمَ نَفْسَهُۥ ۚ لَا تَدْرِى لَعَلَّ
ٱللَّهَ يُحْدِثُ بَعْدَ ذَٰلِكَ أَمْرًا ﴿١﴾ فَإِذَا بَلَغْنَ أَجَلَهُنَّ فَأَمْسِكُوهُنَّ
بِمَعْرُوفٍ أَوْ فَارِقُوهُنَّ بِمَعْرُوفٍ وَأَشْهِدُوا۟ ذَوَىْ عَدْلٍ مِّنكُمْ
وَأَقِيمُوا۟ ٱلشَّهَٰدَةَ لِلَّهِ ۚ ذَٰلِكُمْ يُوعَظُ بِهِۦ مَن كَانَ يُؤْمِنُ
بِٱللَّهِ وَٱلْيَوْمِ ٱلْءَاخِرِ ۚ وَمَن يَتَّقِ ٱللَّهَ يَجْعَل لَّهُۥ مَخْرَجًا ﴿٢﴾ وَيَرْزُقْهُ
مِنْ حَيْثُ لَا يَحْتَسِبُ ۚ وَمَن يَتَوَكَّلْ عَلَى ٱللَّهِ فَهُوَ حَسْبُهُۥٓ ۚ إِنَّ ٱللَّهَ
بَٰلِغُ أَمْرِهِۦ ۚ قَدْ جَعَلَ ٱللَّهُ لِكُلِّ شَىْءٍ قَدْرًا ﴿٣﴾ وَٱلَّٰٓـِٔى يَئِسْنَ
مِنَ ٱلْمَحِيضِ مِن نِّسَآئِكُمْ إِنِ ٱرْتَبْتُمْ فَعِدَّتُهُنَّ ثَلَٰثَةُ أَشْهُرٍ
وَٱلَّٰٓـِٔى لَمْ يَحِضْنَ ۚ وَأُو۟لَٰتُ ٱلْأَحْمَالِ أَجَلُهُنَّ أَن يَضَعْنَ حَمْلَهُنَّ ۚ
وَمَن يَتَّقِ ٱللَّهَ يَجْعَل لَّهُۥ مِنْ أَمْرِهِۦ يُسْرًا ﴿٤﴾ ذَٰلِكَ أَمْرُ ٱللَّهِ أَنزَلَهُۥٓ
إِلَيْكُمْ ۚ وَمَن يَتَّقِ ٱللَّهَ يُكَفِّرْ عَنْهُ سَيِّـَٔاتِهِۦ وَيُعْظِمْ لَهُۥٓ أَجْرًا ﴿٥﴾

65. *Sūrat aṭ-Ṭalāq*
Divorce

This *sūra* is Madinan and has 12 *āyats*.

1. *O Prophet,* meaning here his community in relation to what follows; or it may be that "Say" is elided – ***when any of you*** – want to – ***divorce women, divorce them during their period of purity and calculate their* 'idda *carefully.*** Divorce should be pronounced when the woman is pure and not menstruating and the husband has not had intercourse with her since she became pure, as the Prophet, may Allah bless him and grant him peace, explained and as is related by both al-Bukhārī and Muslim. Count the *'idda* carefully since a wife can be taken back before it ends. ***And have* taqwā *of Allah, your Lord***, and obey Him in respect of His commands and prohibitions. ***Do not evict them from their homes, nor should they leave*** their homes until they have finished their *'idda*, ***unless they commit an outright*** (read as *mubayyina* and *mubayyana*) ***indecency*** – meaning here illicit sexual intercourse, in which case they are brought out to receive the *ḥadd* punishment. ***Those are Allah's limits, and anyone who oversteps Allah's limits has wronged himself. You never know, it may well be that after that*** divorce ***Allah will cause a new situation to develop*** – meaning possible reconciliation if there has only been a single or double pronouncement of divorce.

2. *Then when they have reached the end of their* 'idda – or are close to the end of it – ***either retain them*** and take them back ***with correctness and courtesy*** – without harming them – ***or part from them*** and leave them to finish their *'idda* ***with correctness and courtesy***; and do not harm them by taking them back. ***Call two upright men from among yourselves as witnesses*** when you take back your wives or divorce them; ***and they*** (the witnesses) ***should carry out the witnessing for*** the sake of ***Allah*** – not for the sake of the person against or for whom he testifies. ***This is an admonishment for all who believe in Allah and the Last Day. Whoever is fearful of Allah, He will give him a way out*** of the grief of this world and the Next –

3. ***...and provide for him from where he does not expect. Whoever puts his trust in Allah*** regarding his affairs, ***He will be enough for him. Allah always achieves His aim*** (read as *bālighu amrihi* and *bālighun amrahu*). ***Allah has appointed a measure for all things*** – an allotted time for ease and an allotted time for hardship.

4. ***In the case of those of your wives who are past the age of men - struation, if you have any doubt*** about their *'idda*, ***their* 'idda *should be three months, and that also applies to those who have not yet menstruated*** because of their youth. The two cases here refer to divorce, not to when a woman is widowed. The *'idda* of a widowed woman is always as in the *āyat*: *"Those of you who die leaving wives: they should wait by themselves for four months and ten nights."* (2:234). ***The time for women who are pregnant is when they give birth.*** The *'idda* of a pregnant woman who is divorced or widowed, however, lasts until she gives birth. ***Whoever is fearful of Allah, He will make matters easy for him*** in this world and the Next World.

5. ***That is Allah's command*** about the *'idda* ***which He has sent down to you. Whoever is fearful of Allah, He will erase his bad actions from his record and greatly increase his reward.***

6. ***Let them*** (divorced women) ***live where you live*** – in one of your houses – ***according to your*** financial ***means. Do not put pressure on them*** – do not constrict their living circumstances so that they need to go out, or their maintenance so that they are forced to ransom themselves from you – ***in order to harass them. If they are pregnant, maintain them until they give birth. If they are suckling for you, give them their wages*** for breast-feeding ***and consult together with correctness and courtesy*** about the children so that they agree to a stated wage for breast-feeding. ***But if you make things difficult for one another*** – cause difficulties for one another in that, and the father refuses to pay and the mother refuses to do it – ***another woman should do the suckling for you***: then the father should find another woman and not force the mother to breast-feed the child.

7. ***He who has plenty should spend*** – on his divorced wife and women who are breastfeeding for him – ***from his plenty; but he***

أَسْكِنُوهُنَّ مِنْ حَيْثُ سَكَنتُم مِّن وُجْدِكُمْ وَلَا تُضَآرُّوهُنَّ لِتُضَيِّقُوا۟
عَلَيْهِنَّ ۚ وَإِن كُنَّ أُو۟لَٰتِ حَمْلٍ فَأَنفِقُوا۟ عَلَيْهِنَّ حَتَّىٰ يَضَعْنَ حَمْلَهُنَّ ۚ
فَإِنْ أَرْضَعْنَ لَكُمْ فَـَٔاتُوهُنَّ أُجُورَهُنَّ ۖ وَأْتَمِرُوا۟ بَيْنَكُم بِمَعْرُوفٍ ۖ وَإِن
تَعَاسَرْتُمْ فَسَتُرْضِعُ لَهُۥٓ أُخْرَىٰ ﴿٦﴾ لِيُنفِقْ ذُو سَعَةٍ مِّن سَعَتِهِۦ ۖ
وَمَن قُدِرَ عَلَيْهِ رِزْقُهُۥ فَلْيُنفِقْ مِمَّآ ءَاتَىٰهُ ٱللَّهُ ۚ لَا يُكَلِّفُ ٱللَّهُ نَفْسًا
إِلَّا مَآ ءَاتَىٰهَا ۚ سَيَجْعَلُ ٱللَّهُ بَعْدَ عُسْرٍ يُسْرًا ﴿٧﴾ وَكَأَيِّن مِّن قَرْيَةٍ
عَتَتْ عَنْ أَمْرِ رَبِّهَا وَرُسُلِهِۦ فَحَاسَبْنَٰهَا حِسَابًا شَدِيدًا وَعَذَّبْنَٰهَا
عَذَابًا نُّكْرًا ﴿٨﴾ فَذَاقَتْ وَبَالَ أَمْرِهَا وَكَانَ عَٰقِبَةُ أَمْرِهَا خُسْرًا ﴿٩﴾
أَعَدَّ ٱللَّهُ لَهُمْ عَذَابًا شَدِيدًا ۖ فَٱتَّقُوا۟ ٱللَّهَ يَٰٓأُو۟لِى ٱلْأَلْبَٰبِ ٱلَّذِينَ ءَامَنُوا۟ ۚ
قَدْ أَنزَلَ ٱللَّهُ إِلَيْكُمْ ذِكْرًا ﴿١٠﴾ رَّسُولًا يَتْلُوا۟ عَلَيْكُمْ ءَايَٰتِ ٱللَّهِ مُبَيِّنَٰتٍ
لِّيُخْرِجَ ٱلَّذِينَ ءَامَنُوا۟ وَعَمِلُوا۟ ٱلصَّٰلِحَٰتِ مِنَ ٱلظُّلُمَٰتِ إِلَى ٱلنُّورِ ۚ
وَمَن يُؤْمِنۢ بِٱللَّهِ وَيَعْمَلْ صَٰلِحًا يُدْخِلْهُ جَنَّٰتٍ تَجْرِى مِن تَحْتِهَا
ٱلْأَنْهَٰرُ خَٰلِدِينَ فِيهَآ أَبَدًا ۖ قَدْ أَحْسَنَ ٱللَّهُ لَهُۥ رِزْقًا ﴿١١﴾ ٱللَّهُ ٱلَّذِى خَلَقَ
سَبْعَ سَمَٰوَٰتٍ وَمِنَ ٱلْأَرْضِ مِثْلَهُنَّ يَتَنَزَّلُ ٱلْأَمْرُ بَيْنَهُنَّ لِتَعْلَمُوٓا۟ أَنَّ
ٱللَّهَ عَلَىٰ كُلِّ شَىْءٍ قَدِيرٌ وَأَنَّ ٱللَّهَ قَدْ أَحَاطَ بِكُلِّ شَىْءٍ عِلْمًۢا ﴿١٢﴾

whose provision is restricted should spend from what Allah has given him. Allah does not demand from any self more than He has given it. Allah will appoint after difficulty, ease – by conquest.

8. ***How many*** of the inhabitants of ***cities spurned their Lord's command and His Messengers*** and disobeyed them! ***And so We called them harshly to account*** in the Next World ***and punished them with a terrible*** (read as *nukran* and *nukuran*) ***punishment*** (the Fire).

9. ***They tasted the evil consequences of*** – meaning the penalty for – ***what they did and the end of their affair was total loss*** and destruction.

10. ***Allah has prepared a terrible punishment for them.*** The mention of the punishment is repeated to intensify the threat. ***So be fearful of Allah, people of intelligence*** – those who believe: ***Allah has sent down a reminder*** (the Qur'an) ***to you,***

11. … and sent ***a Messenger,*** Muḥammad, may Allah bless him and grant him peace, ***reciting Allah's Clear Signs*** (read as *mubayyināt* and *mubayyanāt*) ***to you to bring those who believe and do right actions*** – after the Reminder and the Messenger has come – ***out of the darkness*** of unbelief which they were in ***into the Light*** of faith which they have after having been unbelievers. ***Whoever believes in Allah and acts rightly, He will admit*** (read as *yudkhil* and *nudkhil*, "We will admit") ***him into Gardens with rivers flowing under them. to remain in them timelessly, for ever and ever. Allah has provided for him excellently*** by giving him Paradise whose bliss will never be cut off.

12. ***It is Allah who created the seven heavens, and of the earth the same number*** – seven, ***the Command*** (Revelation) ***descending down through all of them*** – between the heavens and the earth, as Jibrīl brings it down from the seventh heaven to the seventh earth – ***so that*** by that creation and descent ***you might know that Allah has power over all things and that Allah encompasses all things in His knowledge.*** Allah informs you that He has power and knowledge of all things.

سُورَةُ التَّحْرِيمِ

بِسۡمِ ٱللَّهِ ٱلرَّحۡمَٰنِ ٱلرَّحِيمِ

يَٰٓأَيُّهَا ٱلنَّبِيُّ لِمَ تُحَرِّمُ مَآ أَحَلَّ ٱللَّهُ لَكَۖ تَبۡتَغِي مَرۡضَاتَ أَزۡوَٰجِكَۚ وَٱللَّهُ
غَفُورٞ رَّحِيمٞ ﴿١﴾ قَدۡ فَرَضَ ٱللَّهُ لَكُمۡ تَحِلَّةَ أَيۡمَٰنِكُمۡۚ وَٱللَّهُ مَوۡلَىٰكُمۡۖ
وَهُوَ ٱلۡعَلِيمُ ٱلۡحَكِيمُ ﴿٢﴾ وَإِذۡ أَسَرَّ ٱلنَّبِيُّ إِلَىٰ بَعۡضِ أَزۡوَٰجِهِۦ حَدِيثٗا
فَلَمَّا نَبَّأَتۡ بِهِۦ وَأَظۡهَرَهُ ٱللَّهُ عَلَيۡهِ عَرَّفَ بَعۡضَهُۥ وَأَعۡرَضَ عَنۢ بَعۡضٖۖ
فَلَمَّا نَبَّأَهَا بِهِۦ قَالَتۡ مَنۡ أَنۢبَأَكَ هَٰذَاۖ قَالَ نَبَّأَنِيَ ٱلۡعَلِيمُ ٱلۡخَبِيرُ
﴿٣﴾ إِن تَتُوبَآ إِلَى ٱللَّهِ فَقَدۡ صَغَتۡ قُلُوبُكُمَاۖ وَإِن تَظَٰهَرَا عَلَيۡهِ
فَإِنَّ ٱللَّهَ هُوَ مَوۡلَىٰهُ وَجِبۡرِيلُ وَصَٰلِحُ ٱلۡمُؤۡمِنِينَۖ وَٱلۡمَلَٰٓئِكَةُ
بَعۡدَ ذَٰلِكَ ظَهِيرٌ ﴿٤﴾ عَسَىٰ رَبُّهُۥٓ إِن طَلَّقَكُنَّ أَن يُبۡدِلَهُۥٓ أَزۡوَٰجًا
خَيۡرٗا مِّنكُنَّ مُسۡلِمَٰتٖ مُّؤۡمِنَٰتٖ قَٰنِتَٰتٖ تَٰٓئِبَٰتٍ عَٰبِدَٰتٖ سَٰٓئِحَٰتٖ
ثَيِّبَٰتٖ وَأَبۡكَارٗا ﴿٥﴾ يَٰٓأَيُّهَا ٱلَّذِينَ ءَامَنُواْ قُوٓاْ أَنفُسَكُمۡ وَأَهۡلِيكُمۡ
نَارٗا وَقُودُهَا ٱلنَّاسُ وَٱلۡحِجَارَةُ عَلَيۡهَا مَلَٰٓئِكَةٌ غِلَاظٞ شِدَادٞ
لَّا يَعۡصُونَ ٱللَّهَ مَآ أَمَرَهُمۡ وَيَفۡعَلُونَ مَا يُؤۡمَرُونَ ﴿٦﴾ يَٰٓأَيُّهَا
ٱلَّذِينَ كَفَرُواْ لَا تَعۡتَذِرُواْ ٱلۡيَوۡمَۖ إِنَّمَا تُجۡزَوۡنَ مَا كُنتُمۡ تَعۡمَلُونَ ﴿٧﴾

66. *Sūraṭ at-Taḥrīm* The Prohibition

This *sūra* is Madinan and has 12 *āyat*s.

1. ***O Prophet, why do you make unlawful what Allah has made lawful for you*** – this has to do with his slavegirl, Māriya the Copt, when he slept with her in the house of Ḥafṣa, who was absent. When Ḥafṣa came back unexpectedly, it was hard for her that this had happened in her house and on her bed. The Prophet then said, "She is *ḥarām* for me," – ***seeking*** by doing this ***to please your wives? Allah is Ever-Forgiving*** – and forgives you making this unlawful for yourself, ***Most Merciful.***

2. ***Allah has made the expiation of your oaths obligatory for you*** and shown you how to release oaths by expiation, as is mentioned in *Sūrat al-Mā'ida*. One such oath was to make the slavegirl unlawful. Did the Prophet, may Allah bless him and grant him peace, perform the *kaffāra*? Muqātil said, "He freed a slave on account of making Māriya unlawful." Al-Ḥasan said that he, may Allah bless him and grant him peace, did not perform an expiation, as Allah forgave him. ***Allah is your Master; He is the All-Knowing, the All-Wise.***

3. Remember when ***the Prophet confided a certain matter*** – meaning the making unlawful of Māriya – ***to one of his wives*** – Ḥafṣa, and he told her not to divulge it. ***Then when she divulged it*** to 'Ā'isha, thinking that there was no harm in doing so, ***Allah disclosed that to him, and he communicated part of it*** to Ḥafṣa ***and withheld part of it*** – out of generosity on his part. ***When he told her of it, she said, 'Who told you of this?' He said, 'The All-Knowing and All-Aware informed me of it.'***

4. ***If the two of you*** ('Ā'isha and Ḥafṣa) ***would only turn to Allah, for your hearts clearly deviated!*** – because they wanted to make Māriya unlawful and were happy about that although the Prophet, may Allah bless him and grant him peace, disliked it. That was a wrong action. The plural "hearts" is used instead of "two hearts" because the plural has greater weight. ***But if you support one another*** (read as *taẓāharā* and *taẓẓahārā*) ***against him*** – the Prophet, may

Allah bless him and grant him peace, in what he dislikes – ***Allah is his Protector; and so are Jibril and every right-acting man of the believers*** – particularly 'Āisha's and Ḥafṣa's fathers, Abū Bakr and 'Umar, may Allah be pleased with them – ***and, furthermore, the angels too will come to his support*** against the two wives referred to.

5. ***It may be that if he does divorce you*** – referring to the Prophet divorcing his wives – ***his Lord will give him in exchange*** (read as *yubdilahu* and *yubaddilahu*) ***better wives than you*** – the exchange did not happen, because he did not divorce them – ***Muslim women, believing women, obedient women, penitent women, women who worship, women who fast much*** (or emigrants) – ***previously married women as well as virgins.***

6. ***You who believe, safeguard yourselves and your families*** – by obeying Allah – ***from a Fire whose fuel is people*** (unbelievers) ***and stones*** – particularly idols made of stone. It will burn extremely fiercely, not like the fire of this world which only burns wood and similar fuels. ***Harsh*** (hard-hearted), ***terrible*** (very strong) ***angels are in charge of it*** – who are nineteen in number, as mentioned in *Sūrat al-Muddaththir* (74:30) – ***who do not disobey Allah in respect of any order He gives them and who carry out what they are ordered to do.*** This *āyat* is intended to alarm and frighten the believers, so that they never revert to unbelief, and to frighten the hypocrites who express belief on their tongues, but not in their hearts.

7. ***'You who disbelieve, do not try to excuse yourselves today.*** This will be said to them when they enter the Fire: their excuses will be of no use to them. ***You are merely being repaid for what you did.'***

8. ***You who believe, repent sincerely to Allah*** (read as *naṣūḥan* and *nuṣūḥan*). This means having a sincere intention not to revert to wrong actions or repeat them. ***It may*** (perhaps) ***be that your Lord will erase your bad actions from you and admit you into Gardens with rivers flowing under them, on the Day when Allah will not disgrace the Prophet and those who believed along with him*** by making them enter the Fire. ***Their light will stream out ahead of them and on their right. They will say, 'Our Lord, perfect our light for us and forgive us!*** The light of the hypocrites will be put out,

يَٰٓأَيُّهَا ٱلَّذِينَ ءَامَنُواْ تُوبُوٓاْ إِلَى ٱللَّهِ تَوۡبَةٗ نَّصُوحًا عَسَىٰ رَبُّكُمۡ
أَن يُكَفِّرَ عَنكُمۡ سَيِّـَٔاتِكُمۡ وَيُدۡخِلَكُمۡ جَنَّٰتٖ تَجۡرِي
مِن تَحۡتِهَا ٱلۡأَنۡهَٰرُ يَوۡمَ لَا يُخۡزِي ٱللَّهُ ٱلنَّبِيَّ وَٱلَّذِينَ ءَامَنُواْ
مَعَهُۥۖ نُورُهُمۡ يَسۡعَىٰ بَيۡنَ أَيۡدِيهِمۡ وَبِأَيۡمَٰنِهِمۡ يَقُولُونَ رَبَّنَآ
أَتۡمِمۡ لَنَا نُورَنَا وَٱغۡفِرۡ لَنَآۖ إِنَّكَ عَلَىٰ كُلِّ شَيۡءٖ قَدِيرٞ ٨
يَٰٓأَيُّهَا ٱلنَّبِيُّ جَٰهِدِ ٱلۡكُفَّارَ وَٱلۡمُنَٰفِقِينَ وَٱغۡلُظۡ عَلَيۡهِمۡۚ
وَمَأۡوَىٰهُمۡ جَهَنَّمُۖ وَبِئۡسَ ٱلۡمَصِيرُ ٩ ضَرَبَ ٱللَّهُ مَثَلٗا
لِّلَّذِينَ كَفَرُواْ ٱمۡرَأَتَ نُوحٖ وَٱمۡرَأَتَ لُوطٖۖ كَانَتَا تَحۡتَ
عَبۡدَيۡنِ مِنۡ عِبَادِنَا صَٰلِحَيۡنِ فَخَانَتَاهُمَا فَلَمۡ يُغۡنِيَا عَنۡهُمَا
مِنَ ٱللَّهِ شَيۡـٔٗا وَقِيلَ ٱدۡخُلَا ٱلنَّارَ مَعَ ٱلدَّٰخِلِينَ ١٠
وَضَرَبَ ٱللَّهُ مَثَلٗا لِّلَّذِينَ ءَامَنُواْ ٱمۡرَأَتَ فِرۡعَوۡنَ إِذۡ
قَالَتۡ رَبِّ ٱبۡنِ لِي عِندَكَ بَيۡتٗا فِي ٱلۡجَنَّةِ وَنَجِّنِي مِن فِرۡعَوۡنَ
وَعَمَلِهِۦ وَنَجِّنِي مِنَ ٱلۡقَوۡمِ ٱلظَّٰلِمِينَ ١١ وَمَرۡيَمَ ٱبۡنَتَ
عِمۡرَٰنَ ٱلَّتِيٓ أَحۡصَنَتۡ فَرۡجَهَا فَنَفَخۡنَا فِيهِ مِن رُّوحِنَا
وَصَدَّقَتۡ بِكَلِمَٰتِ رَبِّهَا وَكُتُبِهِۦ وَكَانَتۡ مِنَ ٱلۡقَٰنِتِينَ ١٢

while the light of the believers will run ahead of them to the Garden. ***You have power over all things.'***

9. ***O Prophet, do*** **jihād** with the sword ***against the unbelievers and*** with the tongue and proof against ***the hypocrites, and be harsh with them*** – with rebuke and hatred. ***Their refuge is Hell. What an evil destination!***

10. ***Allah has made an example for those who disbelieve: the wife of Nūḥ and the wife of Lūṭ. They were married to two of Our slaves who were righteous but they betrayed them*** – in respect of the *dīn* since they disbelieved. The wife of Nūḥ, who was named Wāhila, used to tell her people that he was insane. The wife of Lūṭ, whose name was Wā'ila, directed his people to his guests when they stayed with him in the night by lighting a fire and in the day by making smoke – ***and were not helped at all against Allah.*** Neither Nūḥ nor Lūṭ could help them against Allah's punishment. ***They were told, 'Enter the Fire along with all who enter it*** – meaning the unbelievers of the people of Nūḥ and the people of Lūṭ.***'***

11. ***Allah has made an example for those who believe: the wife of Pharaoh*** – Āsiya, who believed in Mūsā, and whom Pharaoh tortured by staking her out by the hands and feet with pegs, placing a large millstone on her chest, and leaving her in the sun. When he left her, the angels who were entrusted with her shaded her and ***when*** she was being tortured ***she said, 'My Lord, build a house in the Garden for me in Your presence*** – and her place in the Garden was shown to her, and so the torture was made easy for her to bear – ***and rescue me from Pharaoh and his deeds*** – specifically his torture – ***and rescue me from this wrongdoing people*** – the people of his religion.***'*** Allah took her soul. According to Ibn Kaysān, she was raised alive to the Garden, where she is now, eating and drinking.

12. ***And Maryam, the daughter of 'Imrān, who guarded her chastity: We breathed Our*** **Rūḥ** ***into her*** – Jibrīl breathed a breath of Allah's creating into the front of her shift, so that it reached her womb and she became pregnant with 'Īsā – ***and she confirmed the Words of her Lord*** (His laws) ***and His*** Revealed ***Books, and was one of the obedient*** to Allah.

سُورَةُ المُلْكِ

بِسْمِ ٱللَّهِ ٱلرَّحْمَٰنِ ٱلرَّحِيمِ

تَبَٰرَكَ ٱلَّذِى بِيَدِهِ ٱلْمُلْكُ وَهُوَ عَلَىٰ كُلِّ شَىْءٍ قَدِيرٌ ١ ٱلَّذِى خَلَقَ
ٱلْمَوْتَ وَٱلْحَيَوٰةَ لِيَبْلُوَكُمْ أَيُّكُمْ أَحْسَنُ عَمَلًا وَهُوَ ٱلْعَزِيزُ ٱلْغَفُورُ ٢
ٱلَّذِى خَلَقَ سَبْعَ سَمَٰوَٰتٍ طِبَاقًا مَّا تَرَىٰ فِى خَلْقِ ٱلرَّحْمَٰنِ مِن
تَفَٰوُتٍ فَٱرْجِعِ ٱلْبَصَرَ هَلْ تَرَىٰ مِن فُطُورٍ ٣ ثُمَّ ٱرْجِعِ ٱلْبَصَرَ كَرَّتَيْنِ
يَنقَلِبْ إِلَيْكَ ٱلْبَصَرُ خَاسِئًا وَهُوَ حَسِيرٌ ٤ وَلَقَدْ زَيَّنَّا ٱلسَّمَآءَ
ٱلدُّنْيَا بِمَصَٰبِيحَ وَجَعَلْنَٰهَا رُجُومًا لِّلشَّيَٰطِينِ وَأَعْتَدْنَا لَهُمْ عَذَابَ
ٱلسَّعِيرِ ٥ وَلِلَّذِينَ كَفَرُوا۟ بِرَبِّهِمْ عَذَابُ جَهَنَّمَ وَبِئْسَ ٱلْمَصِيرُ
٦ إِذَآ أُلْقُوا۟ فِيهَا سَمِعُوا۟ لَهَا شَهِيقًا وَهِىَ تَفُورُ ٧ تَكَادُ تَمَيَّزُ
مِنَ ٱلْغَيْظِ كُلَّمَآ أُلْقِىَ فِيهَا فَوْجٌ سَأَلَهُمْ خَزَنَتُهَآ أَلَمْ يَأْتِكُمْ نَذِيرٌ ٨
قَالُوا۟ بَلَىٰ قَدْ جَآءَنَا نَذِيرٌ فَكَذَّبْنَا وَقُلْنَا مَا نَزَّلَ ٱللَّهُ مِن شَىْءٍ إِنْ أَنتُمْ
إِلَّا فِى ضَلَٰلٍ كَبِيرٍ ٩ وَقَالُوا۟ لَوْ كُنَّا نَسْمَعُ أَوْ نَعْقِلُ مَا كُنَّا فِىٓ أَصْحَٰبِ
ٱلسَّعِيرِ ١٠ فَٱعْتَرَفُوا۟ بِذَنۢبِهِمْ فَسُحْقًا لِّأَصْحَٰبِ ٱلسَّعِيرِ ١١
إِنَّ ٱلَّذِينَ يَخْشَوْنَ رَبَّهُم بِٱلْغَيْبِ لَهُم مَّغْفِرَةٌ وَأَجْرٌ كَبِيرٌ ١٢
وَأَسِرُّوا۟ قَوْلَكُمْ أَوِ ٱجْهَرُوا۟ بِهِۦٓ إِنَّهُۥ عَلِيمٌۢ بِذَاتِ ٱلصُّدُورِ ١٣ أَلَا
يَعْلَمُ مَنْ خَلَقَ وَهُوَ ٱللَّطِيفُ ٱلْخَبِيرُ ١٤ هُوَ ٱلَّذِى جَعَلَ لَكُمُ

67. *Sūrat al-Mulk*
The Kingdom

This *sūra* is Makkan and has 30 *āyat*s.

1. ***Blessed is He who has the Kingdom in His Hand!*** He is disconnected and above the attributes of all temporal things. ***He has power*** – dominion and authority – ***over all things;***

2. ***He who created death*** in this world ***and life*** in the Next World; or both of them in this world. The drop of sperm is given life and it is by its life that it gains sensation. Death is the opposite or the absence of life. There are two views about that. According to the second view, creation means to decree it – ***to test which of you is best in action*** and who is most obedient to Allah while you are alive. ***He is the Almighty*** with the power to take revenge on those who disobey Him, ***the Ever-Forgiving*** of those who turn to Him in repentance.

3. ***He who created the seven heavens in layers*** – one on top of the other without their being in direct contact. ***You will not find any flaw in the creation*** of the heavens or anything else ***of the All-Merciful.*** There is no lack of proportion or discordance in the creation of Allah. ***Look again*** at the sky***; do you see any gaps*** – in other words, fissures or breaks in it***?***

4. ***Then look again and again. Your sight will return to you dazzled and exhausted!*** Your sight will be exhausted without finding any gaps.

5. ***We have adorned the lowest heaven*** – the one which is closest to earth – ***with lamps*** – meaning the stars – ***and made some of them stones for the* shayṭāns** when they eavesdrop, so that meteors are detached from stars as a brand is taken from a fire, and kill the listening jinn or confuse them. It does not mean that the star moves from its position – ***for whom We have prepared the punishment of the Blaze*** (the Fire).

6. ***Those who reject their Lord will have the punishment of Hell. What an evil destination!***

7. ***When they are flung into it they will hear it gasping harshly as it seethes.*** This is an unpleasant sound like the braying of a donkey. It will be boiling.

8. ***It all but bursts*** (read as *tamayyazu* and *ittamayyazu*) ***with rage*** – with anger at unbelievers. ***Each time a group is flung into it its custodians will question them*** in rebuke: ***'Did no warner come to you?'*** "Did no Messenger come to you to warn you about Allah's punishment?"

9. ***They will say, 'Yes indeed: a warner did come to us, but we denied him and said, "Allah has sent nothing down. You are just greatly misguided."'*** This latter sentence might be something said by angels to the unbelievers when they report their denial, or it might be something said by the unbelievers to the warner.

10. ***They will say, 'If only we had really listened*** – and understood – ***and used our intellect*** – and reflected – ***we would not have been Companions of the Blaze.'***

11. ***Then they will acknowledge their wrong actions*** – now that acknowledgement will be of no use to them. Their wrong action is their denial of the warners. ***Away*** (read as *suḥqan* and *suḥuqan*) ***with the Companions of the Blaze!*** They are far from the mercy of Allah!

12. ***Those who fear their Lord in the Unseen*** – when they are not seen by people, so they obey Him in secret as well as publicly – ***will have forgiveness and an immense reward*** (the Garden).

13. ***Whether you***, mankind, ***keep your words secret or say them out loud He knows what the heart contains*** – let alone what you say. The reason behind this was that the idolaters said to one another, "Conceal your words and the God of Muḥammad will not hear you."

14. ***Does He who created not know*** what they conceal? ***He is the All-Pervading*** in His knowledge, ***the All-Aware.***

15. ***It is He who made the earth submissive to you*** – it submits to being walked on, ***so walk its broad trails and eat what it provides*** – created on your behalf. ***The Resurrection is to Him.*** When you arise from the graves you will go to Him for repayment.

16. ***Do you feel secure against*** – the power and authority of Allah – ***Him Who is in heaven causing the earth to swallow you up when suddenly it rocks from side to side*** and rises above you?

ٱلۡأَرۡضَ ذَلُولٗا فَٱمۡشُواْ فِي مَنَاكِبِهَا وَكُلُواْ مِن رِّزۡقِهِۦۖ وَإِلَيۡهِ ٱلنُّشُورُ
﴿١٥﴾ ءَأَمِنتُم مَّن فِي ٱلسَّمَآءِ أَن يَخۡسِفَ بِكُمُ ٱلۡأَرۡضَ فَإِذَا هِيَ
تَمُورُ ﴿١٦﴾ أَمۡ أَمِنتُم مَّن فِي ٱلسَّمَآءِ أَن يُرۡسِلَ عَلَيۡكُمۡ حَاصِبٗاۖ
فَسَتَعۡلَمُونَ كَيۡفَ نَذِيرِ ﴿١٧﴾ وَلَقَدۡ كَذَّبَ ٱلَّذِينَ مِن قَبۡلِهِمۡ فَكَيۡفَ
كَانَ نَكِيرِ ﴿١٨﴾ أَوَلَمۡ يَرَوۡاْ إِلَى ٱلطَّيۡرِ فَوۡقَهُمۡ صَٰٓفَّٰتٖ وَيَقۡبِضۡنَۚ مَا
يُمۡسِكُهُنَّ إِلَّا ٱلرَّحۡمَٰنُۚ إِنَّهُۥ بِكُلِّ شَيۡءِۭ بَصِيرٌ ﴿١٩﴾ أَمَّنۡ هَٰذَا ٱلَّذِي
هُوَ جُندٞ لَّكُمۡ يَنصُرُكُم مِّن دُونِ ٱلرَّحۡمَٰنِۚ إِنِ ٱلۡكَٰفِرُونَ إِلَّا فِي غُرُورٍ
﴿٢٠﴾ أَمَّنۡ هَٰذَا ٱلَّذِي يَرۡزُقُكُمۡ إِنۡ أَمۡسَكَ رِزۡقَهُۥۚ بَل لَّجُّواْ فِي عُتُوّٖ
وَنُفُورٍ ﴿٢١﴾ أَفَمَن يَمۡشِي مُكِبًّا عَلَىٰ وَجۡهِهِۦٓ أَهۡدَىٰٓ أَمَّن يَمۡشِي سَوِيًّا
عَلَىٰ صِرَٰطٖ مُّسۡتَقِيمٖ ﴿٢٢﴾ قُلۡ هُوَ ٱلَّذِيٓ أَنشَأَكُمۡ وَجَعَلَ لَكُمُ ٱلسَّمۡعَ
وَٱلۡأَبۡصَٰرَ وَٱلۡأَفۡـِٔدَةَۖ قَلِيلٗا مَّا تَشۡكُرُونَ ﴿٢٣﴾ قُلۡ هُوَ ٱلَّذِي ذَرَأَكُمۡ
فِي ٱلۡأَرۡضِ وَإِلَيۡهِ تُحۡشَرُونَ ﴿٢٤﴾ وَيَقُولُونَ مَتَىٰ هَٰذَا ٱلۡوَعۡدُ إِن كُنتُمۡ
صَٰدِقِينَ ﴿٢٥﴾ قُلۡ إِنَّمَا ٱلۡعِلۡمُ عِندَ ٱللَّهِ وَإِنَّمَآ أَنَا۠ نَذِيرٞ مُّبِينٞ ﴿٢٦﴾
فَلَمَّا رَأَوۡهُ زُلۡفَةٗ سِيٓـَٔتۡ وُجُوهُ ٱلَّذِينَ كَفَرُواْ وَقِيلَ هَٰذَا ٱلَّذِي
كُنتُم بِهِۦ تَدَّعُونَ ﴿٢٧﴾ قُلۡ أَرَءَيۡتُمۡ إِنۡ أَهۡلَكَنِيَ ٱللَّهُ وَمَن مَّعِيَ
أَوۡ رَحِمَنَا فَمَن يُجِيرُ ٱلۡكَٰفِرِينَ مِنۡ عَذَابٍ أَلِيمٖ ﴿٢٨﴾ قُلۡ هُوَ
ٱلرَّحۡمَٰنُ ءَامَنَّا بِهِۦ وَعَلَيۡهِ تَوَكَّلۡنَاۖ فَسَتَعۡلَمُونَ مَنۡ هُوَ فِي ضَلَٰلٖ مُّبِينٖ
﴿٢٩﴾ قُلۡ أَرَءَيۡتُمۡ إِنۡ أَصۡبَحَ مَآؤُكُمۡ غَوۡرٗا فَمَن يَأۡتِيكُم بِمَآءٖ مَّعِينِۭ ﴿٣٠﴾

17. ***Or do you feel secure against Him Who is in heaven releasing against you a sudden squall of stones*** – which will hit you – ***so that you will know how true My warning was?*** When you see the punishment with your own eyes, then you will know that My warning of coming punishment was true.

18. ***Those*** nations ***before them also denied, but then how great was My denial*** of them when they were destroyed*!* This means that it was true.

19. ***Have they not looked at the birds above them*** in the air ***with wings outspread and folded back?*** Allah keeps them from falling while they open and close their wings, by His power. ***Nothing holds them up but the All-Merciful. He sees all things.*** Why do they not see the stability of the birds in the air as evidence of Our power to punish them in the way that was mentioned?

20. ***Who is there who could be a force for you, to come to your support, apart from the All-Merciful?*** None can defend you against His punishment, so you have no helper. ***The unbelievers are only living in delusion.*** Shayṭān has deluded them into believing that they will not be punished.

21. ***Who is there who could provide for you if He withholds His provision?*** If Allah withholds rain from you. who can bring it? None provides for you except Him. ***Yet still they obstinately persist in insolence and evasion***, and are far from the truth**.**

22. ***Who is better guided: he who goes grovelling on his face or he who walks upright on a straight path?*** Who is better guided: the unbeliever or the believer?

23. Say: 'It is He who created you and ***brought you into being and gave you hearing, sight and hearts. What little thanks you show!'*** This conveys the unbelievers' lack of gratitude for those blessings.

24. ***Say: 'It is He who*** created and ***scattered you about the earth and you will be gathered to Him*** for the final reckoning***.'***

25. ***They*** will ***say*** to the believers***: 'When will this promise*** – meaning the gathering – ***come about if you are telling the truth?'***

26. ***Say: 'The knowledge*** of its coming ***is with Allah alone and I am only a clear warner.'***

27. ***When they see it*** (the punishment after the gathering) ***right up close, the faces of those who disbelieve will be appalled*** and will become black, ***and they will be told*** by the Guardians of the Fire: ***'This*** punishment about which you were warned ***is what you were calling for*** when you claimed that you would not be resurrected.*'* The verb is in the perfect tense because its occurrence is definite.

28. ***Say: 'What do you think? If Allah destroys me and those with me*** – of the believers with His punishment, as you intend – ***or if He has mercy on us*** and does not punish us, ***who can shelter the unbelievers from a painful punishment?'*** If He punishes us none can avert that from them.

29. ***Say: 'He is the All-Merciful. We believe in Him and trust in Him. You will soon know*** (read as *sa-ta'lamūna* and *sa-ya'lamūna*, "they will soon know") – when they see the punishment with their own eyes – ***who is clearly misguided.'*** It will become clear who is is in clear misguidance: you or them.

30. ***Say: 'What do you think? If one morning your water disappears into the earth, who will bring you running water?'*** Who will bring it in buckets if it disappears? This means that no one but Allah can bring it, so how can you deny that He will resurrect you?

It is recommended that when the reciter says *"ma'īn"* (running water), he should say, "Allah, the Lord of the worlds," as is reported in *ḥadīth*. This *āyat* was recited in the presence of someone who espoused fatalism, and he said, "Axes and picks would bring it." Then the water of his spring disappeared and he went blind. We seek refuge with Allah from being insolent towards Allah or towards His Signs.

سُورَةُ القَلَمِ

بِسۡمِ ٱللَّهِ ٱلرَّحۡمَٰنِ ٱلرَّحِيمِ

نٓۚ وَٱلۡقَلَمِ وَمَا يَسۡطُرُونَ ١ مَآ أَنتَ بِنِعۡمَةِ رَبِّكَ بِمَجۡنُونٖ ٢
وَإِنَّ لَكَ لَأَجۡرًا غَيۡرَ مَمۡنُونٖ ٣ وَإِنَّكَ لَعَلَىٰ خُلُقٍ عَظِيمٖ ٤
فَسَتُبۡصِرُ وَيُبۡصِرُونَ ٥ بِأَييِّكُمُ ٱلۡمَفۡتُونُ ٦ إِنَّ رَبَّكَ هُوَ
أَعۡلَمُ بِمَن ضَلَّ عَن سَبِيلِهِۦ وَهُوَ أَعۡلَمُ بِٱلۡمُهۡتَدِينَ ٧ فَلَا تُطِعِ
ٱلۡمُكَذِّبِينَ ٨ وَدُّواْ لَوۡ تُدۡهِنُ فَيُدۡهِنُونَ ٩ وَلَا تُطِعۡ كُلَّ
حَلَّافٖ مَّهِينٍ ١٠ هَمَّازٖ مَّشَّآءِۭ بِنَمِيمٖ ١١ مَّنَّاعٖ لِّلۡخَيۡرِ مُعۡتَدٍ
أَثِيمٍ ١٢ عُتُلِّۭ بَعۡدَ ذَٰلِكَ زَنِيمٍ ١٣ أَن كَانَ ذَا مَالٖ وَبَنِينَ
١٤ إِذَا تُتۡلَىٰ عَلَيۡهِ ءَايَٰتُنَا قَالَ أَسَٰطِيرُ ٱلۡأَوَّلِينَ ١٥
سَنَسِمُهُۥ عَلَى ٱلۡخُرۡطُومِ ١٦ إِنَّا بَلَوۡنَٰهُمۡ كَمَا بَلَوۡنَآ أَصۡحَٰبَ ٱلۡجَنَّةِ إِذۡ أَقۡسَمُواْ
لَيَصۡرِمُنَّهَا مُصۡبِحِينَ ١٧ وَلَا يَسۡتَثۡنُونَ ١٨ فَطَافَ عَلَيۡهَا طَآئِفٞ مِّن رَّبِّكَ
وَهُمۡ نَآئِمُونَ ١٩ فَأَصۡبَحَتۡ كَٱلصَّرِيمِ ٢٠ فَتَنَادَوۡاْ مُصۡبِحِينَ ٢١ أَنِ
ٱغۡدُواْ عَلَىٰ حَرۡثِكُمۡ إِن كُنتُمۡ صَٰرِمِينَ ٢٢ فَٱنطَلَقُواْ وَهُمۡ يَتَخَٰفَتُونَ ٢٣
أَن لَّا يَدۡخُلَنَّهَا ٱلۡيَوۡمَ عَلَيۡكُم مِّسۡكِينٞ ٢٤ وَغَدَوۡاْ عَلَىٰ حَرۡدٖ قَٰدِرِينَ ٢٥ فَلَمَّا
رَأَوۡهَا قَالُوٓاْ إِنَّا لَضَآلُّونَ ٢٦ بَلۡ نَحۡنُ مَحۡرُومُونَ ٢٧ قَالَ أَوۡسَطُهُمۡ أَلَمۡ أَقُل
لَّكُمۡ لَوۡلَا تُسَبِّحُونَ ٢٨ قَالُواْ سُبۡحَٰنَ رَبِّنَآ إِنَّا كُنَّا ظَٰلِمِينَ ٢٩ فَأَقۡبَلَ

68. *Sūrat al-Qalam*
The Pen

This *sūra* is Makkan and has 52 *āyat*s.

1. ***Nūn*** – one of the letters whose meaning Allah has the best knowledge of. ***By the Pen*** – which is that which inscribed all created things on the Preserved Tablet – ***and what they*** (the angels) ***write down*** in terms of good and righteousness*!*

2. ***By the blessing of your Lord, you*** – Muḥammad – ***are not mad.*** Allah has blessed you with Prophethood and other things. This refutes the assertion of the idolaters that he was insane.

3. ***You shall have a wage which never fails.***

4. ***Indeed you are truly vast in character*** – meaning, in *dīn*.

5. ***So you will see and they will see…***

6. ***…which of you is mad.***

7. ***Your Lord knows best who is misguided away from His Way, and He knows best those who are guided.***

8. ***So do not obey those who deny the truth.***

9. ***They wish that you would conciliate them*** and be easy with them ***– then they too would be conciliating.***

10. ***But do not obey any vile swearer of oaths*** who swears many false oaths*;*

11. ***…any backbiter, slandermonger*** – a backbiter is someone who criticises people and a slandermonger is one who listens to what people say in order to spread corruption among them*;*

12. ***…impeder of good*** – one who is miserly with wealth and does not pay the due on it, ***evil aggressor;***

13. ***…gross, coarse*** (rough and rude) ***and furthermore, despicable –*** all of this is a reference to al-Walīd ibn al-Mughīra. Ibn 'Abbās said, "We do not know that Allah described anyone with the faults with which He described him. A shame was attached to him which will never leave him."

14. ***…simply because he possesses wealth and sons.***

15. ***When Our Signs*** (the Qur'an) ***are recited to him, he says, 'Just myths*** (lies) ***of previous peoples!'***

16. ***We will brand him on the snout!*** We will put a mark on his nose by which he will be marked as long as he lives. His nose was cut by a sword during the Battle of Badr.

17. ***We have tried them*** (the people of Makka) with drought and hunger ***as We tried the owners of the garden when they swore that they would harvest in the morning*** – so that the poor would not be aware of it and they would not have to give them any of what their father used to give the poor as charity –

18. ***... but did not say the redeeming words, 'If Allah wills'*** when they swore their oath.

19. ***So a visitation from your Lord came upon it while they slept*** – a fire which burned it up during the night –

20. ***...and in the morning it was like burnt land stripped bare*** – like night, because it was dark and blackened.

21. ***In the morning they called out to one another,***

22. ***'Leave early for your land if you want to pick the fruit.'***

23. ***So they set off, quietly saying to one another*** – whispering –

24. ***'Do not let any poor man into it today while you are there.'*** This explains the preceding sentences.

25. ***They left early, intent on carrying out their scheme*** to deprive the poor, and thought that they could achieve that.

26. ***But when they saw it*** black and burned ***they said, 'We must have lost our way.***

27. ***No, the truth is we are destitute!'*** They were deprived of its fruits because of their denying the poor some of it.

28. ***The best of them said, 'Did I not say to you, "Why do you not glorify Allah*** and repent and turn to Him?"'

29. ***They said, 'Glory be to our Lord! Truly we have been wrongdoers*** in denying the poor their due.'

30. ***They turned to face each other in mutual accusation.***

31. ***They said, 'Woe to us! We were indeed inordinate.***

32. ***Maybe our Lord will give us something better than it in exchange*** (read as *yubdilanā* and *yubaddilanā*). ***We entreat our***

بَعۡضُهُمۡ عَلَىٰ بَعۡضٖ يَتَلَٰوَمُونَ ٣٠ قَالُواْ يَٰوَيۡلَنَآ إِنَّا كُنَّا طَٰغِينَ ٣١ عَسَىٰ
رَبُّنَآ أَن يُبۡدِلَنَا خَيۡرٗا مِّنۡهَآ إِنَّآ إِلَىٰ رَبِّنَا رَٰغِبُونَ ٣٢ كَذَٰلِكَ ٱلۡعَذَابُۖ وَلَعَذَابُ
ٱلۡأٓخِرَةِ أَكۡبَرُۚ لَوۡ كَانُواْ يَعۡلَمُونَ ٣٣ إِنَّ لِلۡمُتَّقِينَ عِندَ رَبِّهِمۡ جَنَّٰتِ ٱلنَّعِيمِ
٣٤ أَفَنَجۡعَلُ ٱلۡمُسۡلِمِينَ كَٱلۡمُجۡرِمِينَ ٣٥ مَا لَكُمۡ كَيۡفَ تَحۡكُمُونَ ٣٦ أَمۡ
لَكُمۡ كِتَٰبٞ فِيهِ تَدۡرُسُونَ ٣٧ إِنَّ لَكُمۡ فِيهِ لَمَا تَخَيَّرُونَ ٣٨ أَمۡ لَكُمۡ أَيۡمَٰنٌ
عَلَيۡنَا بَٰلِغَةٌ إِلَىٰ يَوۡمِ ٱلۡقِيَٰمَةِ إِنَّ لَكُمۡ لَمَا تَحۡكُمُونَ ٣٩ سَلۡهُمۡ أَيُّهُم
بِذَٰلِكَ زَعِيمٌ ٤٠ أَمۡ لَهُمۡ شُرَكَآءُ فَلۡيَأۡتُواْ بِشُرَكَآئِهِمۡ إِن كَانُواْ صَٰدِقِينَ ٤١
خَٰشِعَةً أَبۡصَٰرُهُمۡ تَرۡهَقُهُمۡ ذِلَّةٞۖ وَقَدۡ كَانُواْ يُدۡعَوۡنَ إِلَى ٱلسُّجُودِ وَهُمۡ سَٰلِمُونَ
٤٣ فَذَرۡنِي وَمَن يُكَذِّبُ بِهَٰذَا ٱلۡحَدِيثِۖ سَنَسۡتَدۡرِجُهُم مِّنۡ حَيۡثُ
لَا يَعۡلَمُونَ ٤٤ وَأُمۡلِي لَهُمۡۚ إِنَّ كَيۡدِي مَتِينٌ ٤٥ أَمۡ تَسۡـَٔلُهُمۡ أَجۡرٗا فَهُم
مِّن مَّغۡرَمٖ مُّثۡقَلُونَ ٤٦ أَمۡ عِندَهُمُ ٱلۡغَيۡبُ فَهُمۡ يَكۡتُبُونَ ٤٧ فَٱصۡبِرۡ
لِحُكۡمِ رَبِّكَ وَلَا تَكُن كَصَاحِبِ ٱلۡحُوتِ إِذۡ نَادَىٰ وَهُوَ مَكۡظُومٞ ٤٨ لَّوۡلَآ
أَن تَدَٰرَكَهُۥ نِعۡمَةٞ مِّن رَّبِّهِۦ لَنُبِذَ بِٱلۡعَرَآءِ وَهُوَ مَذۡمُومٞ ٤٩ فَٱجۡتَبَٰهُ رَبُّهُۥ
فَجَعَلَهُۥ مِنَ ٱلصَّٰلِحِينَ ٥٠ وَإِن يَكَادُ ٱلَّذِينَ كَفَرُواْ لَيُزۡلِقُونَكَ بِأَبۡصَٰرِهِمۡ
لَمَّا سَمِعُواْ ٱلذِّكۡرَ وَيَقُولُونَ إِنَّهُۥ لَمَجۡنُونٞ ٥١ وَمَا هُوَ إِلَّا ذِكۡرٞ لِّلۡعَٰلَمِينَ ٥٢

Lord to accept our repentance and to give us something better than our garden.*'* It is reported that they did receive something better than it.

33. *Such* – the punishment of these people – ***is the punishment*** that will alight on those unbelievers of Makka and others who oppose Allah's command***; and the punishment of the Next World is much greater*** than the punishment of this world if they oppose Our command, ***if they only knew.*** This was revealed when they said, "If we are resurrected, we will be given better than you."

34. *The people who are godfearing will have Gardens of Delight with their Lord.*

35. *Would We make the Muslims the same as the evildoers?* Would they be given the same?

36. *What is the matter with you? On what basis do you judge?* That is an unsound decision.

37. *Or have you a* revealed ***Book which you study*** and read,

38. *...so that you may have anything in it you choose?*

39. *Or have you* firm ***oaths that bind Us, extending*** (lasting) ***to the Day of Rising, that you will have whatever you decide*** for yourselves***?***

40. *Ask them which of them stands as guarantor* – the word *zā'im* means one who guarantees a business he undertakes – ***for that*** – the judgement which they make for themselves that they will be given better than the believers in the Next World.

41. *Or do they have Divine partners* who agree with them about this claim and will act as guarantors for them***? Then let them produce their partners if they are telling the truth!***

42. Remember that – ***on the Day when legs are bared*** – a metaphor for the hardship of the trials of the Day of Rising with respect to the Reckoning and Repayment. Metaphorically, one says, "War has bared its leg" when the fighting is very hard – ***and they are called on to prostrate*** – as a test of their faith – ***they will not be able to do so.*** When they attempt to do so, they will not be able to because their backs will become rigid.

43. ***Their eyes will be downcast, darkened by debasement; for they were called on to prostrate*** – in this world but did not do so – ***when they were in full possession of their faculties.*** But they did not pray.

44. ***So leave anyone who denies this discourse*** (the Qur'an) ***to Me! We will lead them, step by step*** – little by little – ***into destruction from where they do not know.***

45. ***I will allow them more time. My subterfuge*** and devising ***is sure.***

46. ***Or do you ask them for a wage*** for conveying the Message ***so they are weighed down with debt*** by what they have to pay you so that they do not believe it***?***

47. ***Or is the Unseen in their hands*** – the Preserved Tablet which contains the Unseen – ***so they can write out what is to happen*** from it***?***

48. ***So wait steadfastly for the judgement of your Lord*** to do what He wills with them. ***Do not be like the Companion of the Fish*** – Yūnus, peace be upon him – ***when he called out in absolute despair*** – annoyance and haste, when he called on his Lord and was filled with sorrow in the belly of the Fish.

49. ***Had a blessing*** (mercy) ***from his Lord not overtaken him, he would have been thrown up on the naked shore*** – on barren land, ***for he was at fault;*** but Allah had mercy and saved him without rendering him blameworthy.

50. ***Instead, his Lord chose him*** for Prophethood ***and made him one of the righteous*** Prophets.

51. ***Those who disbelieve all but strike you down*** (read as *la-yuzliqūnaka* and *la-yazliqūnaka*) ***with their evil looks*** – looking at you harshly with a look which nearly fells you – ***when they hear the Reminder*** (the Qur'an) ***and say*** – out of envy that he is mad, because of the Qur'an which he brought – ***'He is quite mad.'***

52. ***But it*** (the Qur'an) ***is nothing less than a Reminder to all the worlds***: the worlds of jinn and men. It is not the result of madness.

سُورَةُ الحَاقَّةِ

بِسْمِ ٱللَّهِ ٱلرَّحْمَـٰنِ ٱلرَّحِيمِ

ٱلْحَآقَّةُ ﴿١﴾ مَا ٱلْحَآقَّةُ ﴿٢﴾ وَمَآ أَدْرَىٰكَ مَا ٱلْحَآقَّةُ ﴿٣﴾ كَذَّبَتْ ثَمُودُ
وَعَادٌۢ بِٱلْقَارِعَةِ ﴿٤﴾ فَأَمَّا ثَمُودُ فَأُهْلِكُوا۟ بِٱلطَّاغِيَةِ ﴿٥﴾ وَأَمَّا
عَادٌ فَأُهْلِكُوا۟ بِرِيحٍ صَرْصَرٍ عَاتِيَةٍ ﴿٦﴾ سَخَّرَهَا عَلَيْهِمْ
سَبْعَ لَيَالٍ وَثَمَـٰنِيَةَ أَيَّامٍ حُسُومًا فَتَرَى ٱلْقَوْمَ فِيهَا صَرْعَىٰ
كَأَنَّهُمْ أَعْجَازُ نَخْلٍ خَاوِيَةٍ ﴿٧﴾ فَهَلْ تَرَىٰ لَهُم مِّنۢ بَاقِيَةٍ ﴿٨﴾
وَجَآءَ فِرْعَوْنُ وَمَن قَبْلَهُۥ وَٱلْمُؤْتَفِكَـٰتُ بِٱلْخَاطِئَةِ ﴿٩﴾ فَعَصَوْا۟ رَسُولَ
رَبِّهِمْ فَأَخَذَهُمْ أَخْذَةً رَّابِيَةً ﴿١٠﴾ إِنَّا لَمَّا طَغَا ٱلْمَآءُ حَمَلْنَـٰكُمْ فِى ٱلْجَارِيَةِ
﴿١١﴾ لِنَجْعَلَهَا لَكُمْ تَذْكِرَةً وَتَعِيَهَآ أُذُنٌ وَٰعِيَةٌ ﴿١٢﴾ فَإِذَا نُفِخَ فِى ٱلصُّورِ
نَفْخَةٌ وَٰحِدَةٌ ﴿١٣﴾ وَحُمِلَتِ ٱلْأَرْضُ وَٱلْجِبَالُ فَدُكَّتَا دَكَّةً وَٰحِدَةً ﴿١٤﴾
فَيَوْمَئِذٍ وَقَعَتِ ٱلْوَاقِعَةُ ﴿١٥﴾ وَٱنشَقَّتِ ٱلسَّمَآءُ فَهِىَ يَوْمَئِذٍ وَاهِيَةٌ
﴿١٦﴾ وَٱلْمَلَكُ عَلَىٰٓ أَرْجَآئِهَا ۚ وَيَحْمِلُ عَرْشَ رَبِّكَ فَوْقَهُمْ يَوْمَئِذٍ ثَمَـٰنِيَةٌ
﴿١٧﴾ يَوْمَئِذٍ تُعْرَضُونَ لَا تَخْفَىٰ مِنكُمْ خَافِيَةٌ ﴿١٨﴾ فَأَمَّا مَنْ أُوتِىَ
كِتَـٰبَهُۥ بِيَمِينِهِۦ فَيَقُولُ هَآؤُمُ ٱقْرَءُوا۟ كِتَـٰبِيَهْ ﴿١٩﴾ إِنِّى ظَنَنتُ أَنِّى مُلَـٰقٍ
حِسَابِيَهْ ﴿٢٠﴾ فَهُوَ فِى عِيشَةٍ رَّاضِيَةٍ ﴿٢١﴾ فِى جَنَّةٍ عَالِيَةٍ ﴿٢٢﴾
قُطُوفُهَا دَانِيَةٌ ﴿٢٣﴾ كُلُوا۟ وَٱشْرَبُوا۟ هَنِيٓـًٔۢا بِمَآ أَسْلَفْتُمْ فِى ٱلْأَيَّامِ

69. *Sūrat al-Ḥāqqa*
The Undeniable

This *sūra* is Makkan and has 51 or 52 *āyats*.

1. ***The Undeniable!*** It is the Rising, which has been denied but will prove to be true: the Resurrection, the Reckoning and the Repayment, will undoubtedly come to pass.

2. ***What is the Undeniable?***

3. ***What will convey to you what the Undeniable is?*** – because it is so great.

4. ***Thamūd and 'Ād denied the Crushing Blow*** (the Rising). It is called that because it crushes people's hearts with its terrors.

5. ***Thamūd were destroyed by the Deafening Blast*** – a Shout which was beyond measure in its intensity.

6. ***'Ād were destroyed by a savage howling wind.*** It made a loud noise and had immense strength with which it struck 'Ād, who considered themselves strong.

7. ***Allah subjected them to it*** – sent it against them with force – ***for seven whole nights and eight whole days without a break.*** The first day was the morning of Wednesday 22nd Shawwāl at the end of winter. It blew non-stop. It is said that the word used here, *ḥusūm,* is the plural of *ḥāsim*, from *ḥasm*, which means cutting, as one cuts for cauterisation for an illness again and again until it is finished (*taḥassama*). ***You could see the people flattened in their homes*** – dead and prone – ***just like the hollow stumps of uprooted palms.***

8. ***Can you see any remnant of them left?***

9. ***Pharaoh and those before him*** (read as *man qablahu* as here, meaning previous unbelieving nations, and also as *man qibalahu*, meaning "those who follow him) ***and*** the people of ***the Overturned Cities*** of Lūṭ ***made a great mistake.***

10. ***They disobeyed the Messenger of their Lord***, meaning Lūṭ and others, ***so He seized them in an ever-tightening grip.***

11. ***When the waters rose*** – above everything, mountains and everything else in the Flood – ***We carried you*** – meaning your ancestors, since you were in their loins – ***in the ship*** – the Ark which Nūḥ had made, in which he and those with him were saved while the rest were drowned –

12. *...to make it a reminder for you* – by enabling the believers to survive and destroying the unbelievers – ***and something to be retained by retentive ears***: remembered when heard.

13. *So when the Trumpet is blown with a single blast* – the Blast for the Divine Judgement between all creatures, which is the second blast –

14. *...and the earth and the mountains are lifted and crushed with a single blow,*

15. *...on that Day* (the Day of Rising) ***the Occurrence will occur...***

16. *...and Heaven will be split apart, for that Day it will be very frail* and insubstantial.

17. *The angels* – the singular *malak* used here is the generic name for angels as a whole – ***will be gathered round its edge*** – referring to the sky above them. ***On that Day, eight*** angels ***will bear the Throne of their Lord above their heads***, or they will be part of their ranks.

18. *On that Day you will be exposed* to the Reckoning and ***no concealed act you did will stay concealed*** (read as *takhfā* and *yakhfā*).

19. *As for him who is given his Book in his right hand* – addressed to the group who will be delighted with what they receive, ***he will say, 'Here, come and read my Book!***

20 *I counted on meeting my Reckoning* and was certain of it.'

21. *He will have a very pleasant life...*

22. *...in an elevated Garden,*

23. *...its ripe fruit* – the word used here, *quṭūf,* are fruits which are plucked and gathered – ***hanging close to hand***, so that they can be plucked by someone standing, sitting or lying down.

24. They will be told: ***'Eat and drink with relish for what you did before in days gone by*** in the world!'

25. *But as for him who is given his Book in his left hand, he will say, 'If only I had not been given my Book...*

26. *...and had not known about my Reckoning!*

ٱلْخَالِيَةِ ﴿٢٤﴾ وَأَمَّا مَنْ أُوتِىَ كِتَٰبَهُۥ بِشِمَالِهِۦ فَيَقُولُ يَٰلَيْتَنِى لَمْ أُوتَ كِتَٰبِيَهْ
﴿٢٥﴾ وَلَمْ أَدْرِ مَا حِسَابِيَهْ ﴿٢٦﴾ يَٰلَيْتَهَا كَانَتِ ٱلْقَاضِيَةَ ﴿٢٧﴾ مَآ أَغْنَىٰ
عَنِّى مَالِيَهْ ۜ ﴿٢٨﴾ هَلَكَ عَنِّى سُلْطَٰنِيَهْ ﴿٢٩﴾ خُذُوهُ فَغُلُّوهُ ﴿٣٠﴾ ثُمَّ ٱلْجَحِيمَ
صَلُّوهُ ﴿٣١﴾ ثُمَّ فِى سِلْسِلَةٍ ذَرْعُهَا سَبْعُونَ ذِرَاعًا فَٱسْلُكُوهُ ﴿٣٢﴾ إِنَّهُۥ
كَانَ لَا يُؤْمِنُ بِٱللَّهِ ٱلْعَظِيمِ ﴿٣٣﴾ وَلَا يَحُضُّ عَلَىٰ طَعَامِ ٱلْمِسْكِينِ ﴿٣٤﴾
فَلَيْسَ لَهُ ٱلْيَوْمَ هَٰهُنَا حَمِيمٌ ﴿٣٥﴾ وَلَا طَعَامٌ إِلَّا مِنْ غِسْلِينٍ ﴿٣٦﴾ لَّا يَأْكُلُهُۥٓ
إِلَّا ٱلْخَٰطِـُٔونَ ﴿٣٧﴾ فَلَآ أُقْسِمُ بِمَا تُبْصِرُونَ ﴿٣٨﴾ وَمَا لَا تُبْصِرُونَ ﴿٣٩﴾
إِنَّهُۥ لَقَوْلُ رَسُولٍ كَرِيمٍ ﴿٤٠﴾ وَمَا هُوَ بِقَوْلِ شَاعِرٍ ۚ قَلِيلًا مَّا تُؤْمِنُونَ ﴿٤١﴾
وَلَا بِقَوْلِ كَاهِنٍ ۚ قَلِيلًا مَّا تَذَكَّرُونَ ﴿٤٢﴾ تَنزِيلٌ مِّن رَّبِّ ٱلْعَٰلَمِينَ ﴿٤٣﴾ وَلَوْ
تَقَوَّلَ عَلَيْنَا بَعْضَ ٱلْأَقَاوِيلِ ﴿٤٤﴾ لَأَخَذْنَا مِنْهُ بِٱلْيَمِينِ ﴿٤٥﴾ ثُمَّ لَقَطَعْنَا
مِنْهُ ٱلْوَتِينَ ﴿٤٦﴾ فَمَا مِنكُم مِّنْ أَحَدٍ عَنْهُ حَٰجِزِينَ ﴿٤٧﴾ وَإِنَّهُۥ لَتَذْكِرَةٌ
لِّلْمُتَّقِينَ ﴿٤٨﴾ وَإِنَّا لَنَعْلَمُ أَنَّ مِنكُم مُّكَذِّبِينَ ﴿٤٩﴾ وَإِنَّهُۥ لَحَسْرَةٌ عَلَى
ٱلْكَٰفِرِينَ ﴿٥٠﴾ وَإِنَّهُۥ لَحَقُّ ٱلْيَقِينِ ﴿٥١﴾ فَسَبِّحْ بِٱسْمِ رَبِّكَ ٱلْعَظِيمِ ﴿٥٢﴾

27. ***If only death had really been the end!*** "Would that there had only been death in this world, and its end had been the end of my existence and I had not been raised!"

28. ***My wealth has been of no use to me.***

29. ***My power*** – strength and evidence – ***has vanished.'***

30. ***'Seize him and truss him up.*** This is addressed to the Guardians of Hellfire. Bind his hands to his neck with fetters.

31. ***Then roast him in the Blazing Fire.***

32. ***Then bind him with a chain which is seventy cubits long.*** A cubit is measured by the forearm of the king. Put him in the chains after he is admitted into the Fire.

33. ***He used not to believe in Allah the Magnificent,***

34. ***...nor did he urge that the poor be fed.***

35. ***Therefore here today he has no friend*** to help him,

36. ***...nor any food but exuding pus*** – the word *ghislīn* may be either the pus of the people of the Fire or a tree in the Fire,

37. ***...which no one will eat except those who were in error*** – meaning the unbelievers.

38. ***I swear both by what you see*** – meaning the creatures you come into contact with –

39. ***...and what you do not see*** – meaning all creatures –

40. ***...that this*** Qur'an ***is the word of a noble Messenger*** – a Message from Allah Almighty.

41. ***It is not the word of a poet – how little faith you have*** (read as *tu'minūna* and *yu'minūna*, "they have")***! –***

42. ***...nor the word of a fortune-teller – how little heed you pay*** (read as *tadhakkarūna* and *yadhakkarūna*, "they pay")***!*** The meaning is that they believe in and remember few of the things which the Prophet, may Allah bless him and grant him peace, brought them about goodness, maintaining ties of kinship and chastity, and so it will not help them at all.

43. ***It is a revelation from the Lord of all the worlds.***

44. ***If he*** (the Prophet) ***had made up any sayings and ascribed them to Us*** by saying that We said something We did not say,

45. ***We would have seized him by force*** – inflicted on him a punishment with strength and power –

46. ***...and then We would have cut off his life-blood*** **–** the vein to the heart. When it is cut, a person dies –

47. ***...and not one of you could have protected him.*** The linguistic form used here stresses the fact. "No one could have protected the Prophet, may Allah bless him and grant him peace, from Our punishment."

48. ***It*** (the Qur'an) ***is a reminder to the people who are godfearing.***

49. ***We know that some of you*** – mankind – ***will deny it*** (the Qur'an) and some affirm it.

50. ***It*** (the Qur'an) ***is a cause of great distress to the unbelievers*** – when they see the reward of those who affirmed it and the punishment of those who denied it,

51. ***...and it*** (the Qur'an) ***is undeniably the*** absolute ***Truth of Certainty.***

52. ***Glorify, then, the name of your Lord, the Magnificent.*** Disassociate Him from creation.

سُورَةُ الْمَعَارِجِ

بِسۡمِ ٱللَّهِ ٱلرَّحۡمَٰنِ ٱلرَّحِيمِ

سَأَلَ سَآئِلُۢ بِعَذَابٖ وَاقِعٖ ١ لِّلۡكَٰفِرِينَ لَيۡسَ لَهُۥ دَافِعٞ ٢ مِّنَ
ٱللَّهِ ذِي ٱلۡمَعَارِجِ ٣ تَعۡرُجُ ٱلۡمَلَٰٓئِكَةُ وَٱلرُّوحُ إِلَيۡهِ فِي
يَوۡمٖ كَانَ مِقۡدَارُهُۥ خَمۡسِينَ أَلۡفَ سَنَةٖ ٤ فَٱصۡبِرۡ صَبۡرٗا جَمِيلًا ٥
إِنَّهُمۡ يَرَوۡنَهُۥ بَعِيدٗا ٦ وَنَرَىٰهُ قَرِيبٗا ٧ يَوۡمَ تَكُونُ ٱلسَّمَآءُ كَٱلۡمُهۡلِ
٨ وَتَكُونُ ٱلۡجِبَالُ كَٱلۡعِهۡنِ ٩ وَلَا يَسۡـَٔلُ حَمِيمٌ حَمِيمٗا ١٠
يُبَصَّرُونَهُمۡۚ يَوَدُّ ٱلۡمُجۡرِمُ لَوۡ يَفۡتَدِي مِنۡ عَذَابِ يَوۡمِئِذِۭ بِبَنِيهِ ١١
وَصَٰحِبَتِهِۦ وَأَخِيهِ ١٢ وَفَصِيلَتِهِ ٱلَّتِي تُـٔۡوِيهِ ١٣ وَمَن فِي ٱلۡأَرۡضِ
جَمِيعٗا ثُمَّ يُنجِيهِ ١٤ كَلَّآۖ إِنَّهَا لَظَىٰ ١٥ نَزَّاعَةٗ لِّلشَّوَىٰ ١٦ تَدۡعُواْ
مَنۡ أَدۡبَرَ وَتَوَلَّىٰ ١٧ وَجَمَعَ فَأَوۡعَىٰٓ ١٨ ۞ إِنَّ ٱلۡإِنسَٰنَ خُلِقَ هَلُوعًا
١٩ إِذَا مَسَّهُ ٱلشَّرُّ جَزُوعٗا ٢٠ وَإِذَا مَسَّهُ ٱلۡخَيۡرُ مَنُوعًا ٢١ إِلَّا
ٱلۡمُصَلِّينَ ٢٢ ٱلَّذِينَ هُمۡ عَلَىٰ صَلَاتِهِمۡ دَآئِمُونَ ٢٣ وَٱلَّذِينَ فِيٓ
أَمۡوَٰلِهِمۡ حَقّٞ مَّعۡلُومٞ ٢٤ لِّلسَّآئِلِ وَٱلۡمَحۡرُومِ ٢٥ وَٱلَّذِينَ يُصَدِّقُونَ
بِيَوۡمِ ٱلدِّينِ ٢٦ وَٱلَّذِينَ هُم مِّنۡ عَذَابِ رَبِّهِم مُّشۡفِقُونَ ٢٧ إِنَّ عَذَابَ
رَبِّهِمۡ غَيۡرُ مَأۡمُونٖ ٢٨ وَٱلَّذِينَ هُمۡ لِفُرُوجِهِمۡ حَٰفِظُونَ ٢٩ إِلَّا عَلَىٰٓ
أَزۡوَٰجِهِمۡ أَوۡ مَا مَلَكَتۡ أَيۡمَٰنُهُمۡ فَإِنَّهُمۡ غَيۡرُ مَلُومِينَ ٣٠ فَمَنِ ٱبۡتَغَىٰ وَرَآءَ
ذَٰلِكَ فَأُوْلَٰٓئِكَ هُمُ ٱلۡعَادُونَ ٣١ وَٱلَّذِينَ هُمۡ لِأَمَٰنَٰتِهِمۡ وَعَهۡدِهِمۡ رَٰعُونَ

70. *Sūrat al-Ma'ārij*
The Ascending Steps

This *sūra* is Makkan and has 44 *āyat*s.

1. *An inquirer asked* – a caller called out – ***about an impending punishment.***

2. *It is for the unbelievers and cannot be averted* – the one who asked was an-Naḍr ibn al-Ḥārith. He said, "O Allah, if this is the truth…" (8:32) –

3. *…from Allah, the Lord of the Ascending Steps* by which the angels go up, meaning the heavens.

4. *The angels and the Spirit* (Jibrīl) ***ascend*** (read as *ta'ruju* and *ya'ruju*) ***to Him*** – when His command descends from heaven – ***in a day whose length is fifty thousand years.*** This is the Day when the punishment occurs: in other words, the Day of Resurrection. For an unbeliever it will seem like that because of the hardships he will encounter on it. For a believer, it will seem less than the time it takes to pray a prescribed prayer, as has been reported in *ḥadīth.*

5. *Therefore be patient with a patience that is beautiful.* This was before the command to fight. This is patience without anxiety.

6. *They see it as something distant* – they think that the punishment will not occur –

7. *…but We see it as very close* – and that it must come to pass.

8. *On the Day the sky is like molten brass…*

9. *…and the mountains are like tufts of coloured wool* because of their lightness and being blown about by the wind,

10. *…no good friend will ask about his friend* – because he will be too busy with his own state,

11. *…even though they* (close friends) ***can see each other*** – they will recognise but not speak to one another, ***an evildoer*** (unbeliever) ***will wish he could ransom himself from the punishment of that Day*** (*yawmi'idhin* and *yawma'idhin*) ***by means of his sons,***

12. *…or his wife or his brother,*

13. ***...or his family who sheltered him,***

14. ***...or everyone else on earth, if that only meant that he could save himself.*** He would offer all that as a ransom.

15. ***But no! It is a Raging Blaze,*** which burns the unbelievers –

16. ***...stripping away the limbs and scalp,***

17. ***...which calls for all who drew back and turned away*** – from faith. It will call, "To me! To me!" –

18. ***...and amassed*** wealth ***and hoarded up*** – kept it without paying what was due to Allah on it.

19. ***Truly man was created headstrong –***

20. ***...desperate when bad things happen,***

21. ***...begrudging when good things come*** – when Allah gives him wealth, he does not give it to people*;*

22. ***...except for those who pray*** – the believers –

23. ***...and are constant in it;***

24. ***...those in whose wealth there is a known share*** – meaning *zakāt* –

25. ***...for beggars and the destitute*** – those who refrain from asking and so are deprived of their needs*;*

26. ***...those who affirm the Day of Judgement*** and Repayment*;*

27. ***...those who are fearful of the punishment of their Lord –***

28. ***...no one is safe from the punishment of his Lord;***

29. ***...those who guard their private parts,***

30. ***...except from their wives and any slaves they own, in which case they incur no blame,***

31. ***...but if anyone desires any more than that, they have overstepped the limits*** of the *ḥalāl* and *ḥarām*;

32. ***...those who honour their trusts*** (read as *āmānāt* and *āmāna*) – with respect to the *dīn* and this world – ***and contracts*** which they made*;*

33. ***...those who stand by their testimony*** (read as *shahādāt* and *shahāda*) – and do not conceal it*;*

34. ***...those who safeguard their prayer*** – perform their prayers at their proper times.

٣٢ وَٱلَّذِينَ هُم بِشَهَٰدَٰتِهِمْ قَآئِمُونَ ٣٣ وَٱلَّذِينَ هُمْ عَلَىٰ صَلَاتِهِمْ يُحَافِظُونَ
٣٤ أُوْلَٰٓئِكَ فِي جَنَّٰتٍ مُّكْرَمُونَ ٣٥ فَمَالِ ٱلَّذِينَ كَفَرُواْ قِبَلَكَ مُهْطِعِينَ
٣٦ عَنِ ٱلْيَمِينِ وَعَنِ ٱلشِّمَالِ عِزِينَ ٣٧ أَيَطْمَعُ كُلُّ ٱمْرِيٍٕ مِّنْهُمْ
أَن يُدْخَلَ جَنَّةَ نَعِيمٍ ٣٨ كَلَّآ إِنَّا خَلَقْنَٰهُم مِّمَّا يَعْلَمُونَ ٣٩
فَلَآ أُقْسِمُ بِرَبِّ ٱلْمَشَٰرِقِ وَٱلْمَغَٰرِبِ إِنَّا لَقَٰدِرُونَ ٤٠ عَلَىٰٓ أَن نُّبَدِّلَ خَيْرًا مِّنْهُمْ
وَمَا نَحْنُ بِمَسْبُوقِينَ ٤١ فَذَرْهُمْ يَخُوضُواْ وَيَلْعَبُواْ حَتَّىٰ يُلَٰقُواْ يَوْمَهُمُ ٱلَّذِي
يُوعَدُونَ ٤٢ يَوْمَ يَخْرُجُونَ مِنَ ٱلْأَجْدَاثِ سِرَاعًا كَأَنَّهُمْ إِلَىٰ نُصُبٍ يُوفِضُونَ
٤٣ خَٰشِعَةً أَبْصَٰرُهُمْ تَرْهَقُهُمْ ذِلَّةٌ ذَٰلِكَ ٱلْيَوْمُ ٱلَّذِي كَانُواْ يُوعَدُونَ ٤٤

35. ***Such people will be in Gardens, highly honoured.***

36. ***What is the matter with those who disbelieve? They run about in front of you*** – towards you – ***with outstretched necks and staring eyes,***

37. ***...on the right and on the left in scattered groups!*** They used to say in mockery to the believers, "If those people enter the Garden, we will enter it before them!"

38. ***Does each one of them aspire to be admitted into a Garden of Delight?*** This is in answer to what they used to say in mockery.

39. ***Certainly not!*** – refuting their desire to enter the Garden. ***We created them*** and others ***from what they know full well*** – from sperm. One cannot aspire to the Garden through that – only through being godfearing.

40. ***No! I swear by the Lord of the Easts and Wests*** – this is an oath by the sun, moon and all the stars – ***that We have the power...***

41. ***...to replace them with something better than them*** – put others in their place. ***We will not be outstripped.*** We do not lack the power to do that.

42. ***So leave them to plunge and play around*** – in their falsehood and vanity in this world – ***until they meet their Day*** and their punishment ***which they are promised:***

43. ***the Day they will emerge swiftly from their graves*** for the Gathering ***as if rushing to rally to the flag*** (read as *nuṣub* and *naṣb*) – something set up as a marker or a banner –

44. ***...eyes downcast*** (abased), ***darkened by debasement; that will be the Day which they were promised.*** This is what happens on the Day of Rising.

سُورَةُ نُوحٍ

بِسْمِ ٱللَّهِ ٱلرَّحْمَٰنِ ٱلرَّحِيمِ

إِنَّآ أَرْسَلْنَا نُوحًا إِلَىٰ قَوْمِهِۦٓ أَنْ أَنذِرْ قَوْمَكَ مِن قَبْلِ أَن يَأْتِيَهُمْ
عَذَابٌ أَلِيمٌ ﴿١﴾ قَالَ يَٰقَوْمِ إِنِّى لَكُمْ نَذِيرٌ مُّبِينٌ ﴿٢﴾ أَنِ ٱعْبُدُوا۟
ٱللَّهَ وَٱتَّقُوهُ وَأَطِيعُونِ ﴿٣﴾ يَغْفِرْ لَكُم مِّن ذُنُوبِكُمْ وَيُؤَخِّرْكُمْ
إِلَىٰٓ أَجَلٍ مُّسَمًّى ۚ إِنَّ أَجَلَ ٱللَّهِ إِذَا جَآءَ لَا يُؤَخَّرُ ۖ لَوْ كُنتُمْ تَعْلَمُونَ
﴿٤﴾ قَالَ رَبِّ إِنِّى دَعَوْتُ قَوْمِى لَيْلًا وَنَهَارًا ﴿٥﴾ فَلَمْ يَزِدْهُمْ دُعَآءِىٓ إِلَّا
فِرَارًا ﴿٦﴾ وَإِنِّى كُلَّمَا دَعَوْتُهُمْ لِتَغْفِرَ لَهُمْ جَعَلُوٓا۟ أَصَٰبِعَهُمْ
فِىٓ ءَاذَانِهِمْ وَٱسْتَغْشَوْا۟ ثِيَابَهُمْ وَأَصَرُّوا۟ وَٱسْتَكْبَرُوا۟ ٱسْتِكْبَارًا
﴿٧﴾ ثُمَّ إِنِّى دَعَوْتُهُمْ جِهَارًا ﴿٨﴾ ثُمَّ إِنِّىٓ أَعْلَنتُ لَهُمْ وَأَسْرَرْتُ
لَهُمْ إِسْرَارًا ﴿٩﴾ فَقُلْتُ ٱسْتَغْفِرُوا۟ رَبَّكُمْ إِنَّهُۥ كَانَ غَفَّارًا ﴿١٠﴾
يُرْسِلِ ٱلسَّمَآءَ عَلَيْكُم مِّدْرَارًا ﴿١١﴾ وَيُمْدِدْكُم بِأَمْوَٰلٍ وَبَنِينَ وَيَجْعَل
لَّكُمْ جَنَّٰتٍ وَيَجْعَل لَّكُمْ أَنْهَٰرًا ﴿١٢﴾ مَّا لَكُمْ لَا تَرْجُونَ لِلَّهِ وَقَارًا ﴿١٣﴾
وَقَدْ خَلَقَكُمْ أَطْوَارًا ﴿١٤﴾ أَلَمْ تَرَوْا۟ كَيْفَ خَلَقَ ٱللَّهُ سَبْعَ سَمَٰوَٰتٍ
طِبَاقًا ﴿١٥﴾ وَجَعَلَ ٱلْقَمَرَ فِيهِنَّ نُورًا وَجَعَلَ ٱلشَّمْسَ سِرَاجًا ﴿١٦﴾
وَٱللَّهُ أَنۢبَتَكُم مِّنَ ٱلْأَرْضِ نَبَاتًا ﴿١٧﴾ ثُمَّ يُعِيدُكُمْ فِيهَا وَيُخْرِجُكُمْ
إِخْرَاجًا ﴿١٨﴾ وَٱللَّهُ جَعَلَ لَكُمُ ٱلْأَرْضَ بِسَاطًا ﴿١٩﴾ لِّتَسْلُكُوا۟ مِنْهَا

71. *Sūrat Nūḥ*
Noah

This *sūra* is Makkan and has 28 or 29 *āyat*s.

1. ***We sent Nūḥ to his people: 'Warn your people*** to believe ***before a painful punishment comes to them*** in this world and Next.'

2. ***He said, 'My people, I am a clear warner to you*** making the warning clear to you.

3. I tell you to ***worship Allah, be fearful of Him and obey me.***

4. ***He will forgive you your wrong actions*** – because Islam forgives what is before it, or it is a partial forgiving, because the rights of people are excluded from this forgiveness – ***and defer you*** without punishment ***until a specified time*** – the time of your death. ***When Allah's time comes*** to punish you for not believing ***it cannot be deferred, if you only knew*** it; so believe.'

5. ***He said, 'My Lord, I have called my people night and day*** constantly without stopping –

6. ***...but my calling has only made them more evasive*** of faith.

7. ***Indeed, every time I called them to Your forgiveness, they put their fingers in their ears*** so that they would not hear my words, ***wrapped themselves up in their clothes*** – wrapped their clothes round their heads so that they would not see me – ***and were overweeningly arrogant.*** They persisted in their unbelief and were too arrogant to believe.

8. ***Then I called them openly*** in my loudest voice.

9. ***Then I addressed them publicly and addressed them privately.***

10. ***I said, "Ask forgiveness of your Lord*** for *shirk*. ***Truly He is Endlessly Forgiving.***

11. ***He will send heaven down on you in abundant rain*** – they had not had rain for some time, and he told them that it would come down in quantity –

12. ***...and reinforce you with more wealth and sons, and grant you gardens and grant you waterways.***

13. ***What is the matter with you that you do not hope for honour from Allah*** – "why do you not expect that Allah will give you esteem if you believe" –

14. ***...when He created you by successive stages?*** He created you as a drop of sperm, then a blood clot, and then completed the creation of the human being. Examining the creative process of the human being obliges a person to believe in his Creator.

15. ***Do you not see how He created seven heavens in layers*** – one on top of the other –

16. ***...and placed the moon as a light in*** all of ***them*** – or possibly only in the nearest heaven – ***and made the sun a blazing lamp*** – whose light is stronger than the moon***?***

17. ***Allah caused you to grow from the earth*** when He created your father Ādam from it,

18. ***...then will return you to it*** – to graves in it – ***and bring you out again*** at the Resurrection.

19. ***Allah has spread the earth out as a carpet for you...***

20. ***...so that you may use its wide valleys as roadways.'"***

21. ***Nūḥ said, 'My Lord, they have disobeyed me and*** the foolish and poor have ***followed those whose wealth and children*** (read as *walad* and *wuld*) ***have only increased them in loss*** – in other words, trangression and unbelief.

22. ***They*** (the leaders) ***have hatched a mighty plot*** by denying Nūḥ and inflicting harm on him and those who followed him,

23. ***...saying*** to the foolish, ***"Do not abandon your gods. Do not abandon Wadd*** (also read as *Wudd*) ***or Suwā' or Yaghūth or Ya'ūq or Nasr."*** These are names of idols they had.

24. ***They have misguided many people*** by commanding them to worship their idols. ***Do not increase the wrongdoers in anything but misguidance!'*** This was added to his supplication against them when it was revealed to him, *"None of your people are going to believe except for those who have believed already."* (11:36)

25. ***Because of their errors*** (read as *khāṭāyātihim* and *khaṭī'ātihim*) ***they were drowned*** in the Flood ***and put into the Fire*** – punished

سُبُلًا فِجَاجًا ﴿٢٠﴾ قَالَ نُوحٌ رَّبِّ إِنَّهُمْ عَصَوْنِي وَاتَّبَعُوا مَن لَّمْ يَزِدْهُ
مَالُهُ وَوَلَدُهُ إِلَّا خَسَارًا ﴿٢١﴾ وَمَكَرُوا مَكْرًا كُبَّارًا ﴿٢٢﴾ وَقَالُوا
لَا تَذَرُنَّ آلِهَتَكُمْ وَلَا تَذَرُنَّ وَدًّا وَلَا سُوَاعًا وَلَا يَغُوثَ وَيَعُوقَ
وَنَسْرًا ﴿٢٣﴾ وَقَدْ أَضَلُّوا كَثِيرًا وَلَا تَزِدِ الظَّالِمِينَ إِلَّا ضَلَالًا ﴿٢٤﴾
مِّمَّا خَطِيئَاتِهِمْ أُغْرِقُوا فَأُدْخِلُوا نَارًا فَلَمْ يَجِدُوا لَهُم مِّن دُونِ
اللَّهِ أَنصَارًا ﴿٢٥﴾ وَقَالَ نُوحٌ رَّبِّ لَا تَذَرْ عَلَى الْأَرْضِ مِنَ الْكَافِرِينَ
دَيَّارًا ﴿٢٦﴾ إِنَّكَ إِن تَذَرْهُمْ يُضِلُّوا عِبَادَكَ وَلَا يَلِدُوا إِلَّا فَاجِرًا
كَفَّارًا ﴿٢٧﴾ رَّبِّ اغْفِرْ لِي وَلِوَالِدَيَّ وَلِمَن دَخَلَ بَيْتِيَ
مُؤْمِنًا وَلِلْمُؤْمِنِينَ وَالْمُؤْمِنَاتِ وَلَا تَزِدِ الظَّالِمِينَ إِلَّا تَبَارًا ﴿٢٨﴾

with the Fire after being drowned under the water. ***They found no one to help them*** against the punishment ***besides Allah.***

27. ***Nūḥ said, 'My Lord, do not leave a single one of the unbeliev - ers on earth! If You leave any they will misguide Your slaves and spawn nothing but more dissolute unbelievers.*** They will only beget dissolute people who disbelieve. This was in accordance with the Revelation with which Allah had inspired him.

28. ***My Lord, forgive me and my parents*** – who were believers – ***and all who enter my house*** – or place of worship – ***as believers, and all the men and women of the believers*** until the Day of Rising. ***But do not increase the wrongdoers except in ruin!'*** "Only destroy the unbelievers!"

سُورَةُ الجِنّ

بِسْمِ ٱللَّهِ ٱلرَّحْمَٰنِ ٱلرَّحِيمِ

قُلْ أُوحِيَ إِلَيَّ أَنَّهُ ٱسْتَمَعَ نَفَرٌ مِّنَ ٱلْجِنِّ فَقَالُوٓا۟ إِنَّا سَمِعْنَا قُرْءَانًا
عَجَبًا ١ يَهْدِىٓ إِلَى ٱلرُّشْدِ فَـَٔامَنَّا بِهِۦ ۖ وَلَن نُّشْرِكَ بِرَبِّنَآ أَحَدًا ٢
وَأَنَّهُۥ تَعَٰلَىٰ جَدُّ رَبِّنَا مَا ٱتَّخَذَ صَٰحِبَةً وَلَا وَلَدًا ٣ وَأَنَّهُۥ كَانَ
يَقُولُ سَفِيهُنَا عَلَى ٱللَّهِ شَطَطًا ٤ وَأَنَّا ظَنَنَّآ أَن لَّن تَقُولَ ٱلْإِنسُ
وَٱلْجِنُّ عَلَى ٱللَّهِ كَذِبًا ٥ وَأَنَّهُۥ كَانَ رِجَالٌ مِّنَ ٱلْإِنسِ يَعُوذُونَ بِرِجَالٍ
مِّنَ ٱلْجِنِّ فَزَادُوهُمْ رَهَقًا ٦ وَأَنَّهُمْ ظَنُّوا۟ كَمَا ظَنَنتُمْ أَن لَّن يَبْعَثَ
ٱللَّهُ أَحَدًا ٧ وَأَنَّا لَمَسْنَا ٱلسَّمَآءَ فَوَجَدْنَٰهَا مُلِئَتْ حَرَسًا
شَدِيدًا وَشُهُبًا ٨ وَأَنَّا كُنَّا نَقْعُدُ مِنْهَا مَقَٰعِدَ لِلسَّمْعِ ۖ فَمَن
يَسْتَمِعِ ٱلْـَٔانَ يَجِدْ لَهُۥ شِهَابًا رَّصَدًا ٩ وَأَنَّا لَا نَدْرِىٓ أَشَرٌّ أُرِيدَ
بِمَن فِى ٱلْأَرْضِ أَمْ أَرَادَ بِهِمْ رَبُّهُمْ رَشَدًا ١٠ وَأَنَّا مِنَّا ٱلصَّٰلِحُونَ
وَمِنَّا دُونَ ذَٰلِكَ ۖ كُنَّا طَرَآئِقَ قِدَدًا ١١ وَأَنَّا ظَنَنَّآ أَن لَّن نُّعْجِزَ
ٱللَّهَ فِى ٱلْأَرْضِ وَلَن نُّعْجِزَهُۥ هَرَبًا ١٢ وَأَنَّا لَمَّا سَمِعْنَا ٱلْهُدَىٰٓ
ءَامَنَّا بِهِۦ ۖ فَمَن يُؤْمِنۢ بِرَبِّهِۦ فَلَا يَخَافُ بَخْسًا وَلَا رَهَقًا ١٣
وَأَنَّا مِنَّا ٱلْمُسْلِمُونَ وَمِنَّا ٱلْقَٰسِطُونَ ۖ فَمَنْ أَسْلَمَ فَأُو۟لَٰٓئِكَ
تَحَرَّوْا۟ رَشَدًا ١٤ وَأَمَّا ٱلْقَٰسِطُونَ فَكَانُوا۟ لِجَهَنَّمَ حَطَبًا ١٥
وَأَلَّوِ ٱسْتَقَٰمُوا۟ عَلَى ٱلطَّرِيقَةِ لَأَسْقَيْنَٰهُم مَّآءً غَدَقًا ١٦ لِّنَفْتِنَهُمْ
فِيهِ ۚ وَمَن يُعْرِضْ عَن ذِكْرِ رَبِّهِۦ يَسْلُكْهُ عَذَابًا صَعَدًا ١٧ وَأَنَّ
ٱلْمَسَٰجِدَ لِلَّهِ فَلَا تَدْعُوا۟ مَعَ ٱللَّهِ أَحَدًا ١٨ وَأَنَّهُۥ لَمَّا قَامَ عَبْدُ ٱللَّهِ

72. *Sūrat al-Jinn*
The Jinn

This *sūra* is Makkan and has 28 *āyat*s.

1. ***Say***, Muḥammad, to people***: 'It has been revealed to me*** from Allah ***that a band of the* jinn** of Nisibis ***listened*** to my recitation in the *Ṣubḥ* prayer at Baṭn Nakhl, a place between Makka and Ṭā'if. They are the ones who are mentioned in the words of Allah, *"And We diverted a group of* jinn *towards you to listen to the Qur'an..."* (46:29), ***and said*** when they returned to their people***: "We have heard a most amazing Recitation*** – in respect of its eloquence and its abundant meanings, and in other ways**.**

2. ***It leads to right guidance*** – faith and correct action***, so we believe in it and will not associate anyone with our Lord*** after today**.**

3. ***He – exalted be the Majesty of our Lord! – has neither wife nor son.*** His Majesty is far above such assertions.

4. ***The*** ignorant ***fools among us have uttered a vile slander against Allah*** in describing Allah has having a wife and child**.**

5. ***We did not think it possible for either man or jinn*** to say something like that and ***to tell a lie against Allah.***

6. ***Certain men from among mankind used to seek refuge with certain men from among the* jinn** when they camped on their journeys in dangerous places. Each man would say, "I seek refuge with the master of this place from the evil of its foolish ones*;*" ***but they increased them*** by this seeking refuge ***in wickedness*** so that they said, "We are the masters of jinn and human beings**.**"

7. ***They*** (the jinn) ***thought – as you*** human beings ***also think – that Allah would never raise up anyone*** after death.

8. The jinn said: ***We tried, as usual, to travel to heaven*** to eavesdrop ***in search of news but found it filled with fierce guards*** from the angels ***and*** burning ***meteors.*** That happened when the Prophet, may Allah bless him and grant him peace, began his mission.

9. ***We used to sit there on special seats to listen in*** before he was sent***, but anyone listening now finds a fiery meteor in wait for him*** – which is thrown at him**.**

10. ***We have no idea*** – after eavesdropping – ***whether evil is intended for those on the earth, or whether their Lord intends them to be rightly guided.***

11. ***Among us there are some who*** after listening to the Qur'an ***are righteous and some who are other than that. We follow many different paths.*** "We are in different groups: Muslims and unbelievers."

12. ***We realised we would never thwart Allah on earth and would never thwart Him by flight*** – we cannot escape Him, whether we remain on earth or flee from it to the heavens –

13. ***...and when we heard the guidance*** (the Qur'an), ***we believed in it. Anyone who believes in his Lord need fear neither belittlement*** – reduction of his good deeds – ***nor tyranny*** – injustice by having his evil deeds increased.

14. ***Some of us are Muslims and some are deviators*** – by disbelieving. ***Those who have become Muslim are those who sought right guidance;***

15. ***...the deviators will be firewood*** and fuel ***for Hellfire.'"***

16. Allah says about the unbelievers of Makka – ***If only they were to go straight on the Path*** of Islam ***We would give them abundant water to drink*** – rain from heaven. That was after rain was withheld for seven years –

17. ***...so that We could test them by it*** to see how thankful they would be publicly. ***Whoever turns aside from the remembrance of his Lord*** (the Qur'an), ***He will introduce*** (read as *yu'riḍ,* and also *nu'riḍ,* "We will introduce") ***him to an arduous punishment.***

18. ***All mosques belong to Allah so do not call on anyone else besides Allah.*** When in them do not associate anyone else with Him as the Jews and the Christians do when they enter their synagogues and churches.

19. ***When the slave of Allah*** – Muḥammad, may Allah bless him and grant him peace – ***stands calling on Him*** – worshipping Him in Baṭn Nakhl – ***they*** (the jinn listening to his recitation) ***almost swarm*** (read as *libad* and *lubad*) ***all over him*** – pressed together against one another almost like matted felt, in their eagerness to hear the Qur'an.

يَدۡعُوهُ كَادُواْ يَكُونُونَ عَلَيۡهِ لِبَدٗا ١٩ قُلۡ إِنَّمَآ أَدۡعُواْ رَبِّي وَلَآ أُشۡرِكُ
بِهِۦٓ أَحَدٗا ٢٠ قُلۡ إِنِّي لَآ أَمۡلِكُ لَكُمۡ ضَرّٗا وَلَا رَشَدٗا ٢١ قُلۡ إِنِّي
لَن يُجِيرَنِي مِنَ ٱللَّهِ أَحَدٞ وَلَنۡ أَجِدَ مِن دُونِهِۦ مُلۡتَحَدًا ٢٢ إِلَّا بَلَٰغٗا
مِّنَ ٱللَّهِ وَرِسَٰلَٰتِهِۦۚ وَمَن يَعۡصِ ٱللَّهَ وَرَسُولَهُۥ فَإِنَّ لَهُۥ نَارَ جَهَنَّمَ
خَٰلِدِينَ فِيهَآ أَبَدًا ٢٣ حَتَّىٰٓ إِذَا رَأَوۡاْ مَا يُوعَدُونَ فَسَيَعۡلَمُونَ
مَنۡ أَضۡعَفُ نَاصِرٗا وَأَقَلُّ عَدَدٗا ٢٤ قُلۡ إِنۡ أَدۡرِيٓ أَقَرِيبٞ
مَّا تُوعَدُونَ أَمۡ يَجۡعَلُ لَهُۥ رَبِّيٓ أَمَدًا ٢٥ عَٰلِمُ ٱلۡغَيۡبِ فَلَا
يُظۡهِرُ عَلَىٰ غَيۡبِهِۦٓ أَحَدًا ٢٦ إِلَّا مَنِ ٱرۡتَضَىٰ مِن رَّسُولٖ فَإِنَّهُۥ
يَسۡلُكُ مِنۢ بَيۡنِ يَدَيۡهِ وَمِنۡ خَلۡفِهِۦ رَصَدٗا ٢٧ لِّيَعۡلَمَ أَن قَدۡ أَبۡلَغُواْ
رِسَٰلَٰتِ رَبِّهِمۡ وَأَحَاطَ بِمَا لَدَيۡهِمۡ وَأَحۡصَىٰ كُلَّ شَيۡءٍ عَدَدَۢا ٢٨

20. ***He said*** – also read as "Say", to answer the unbelievers when they said, "Retract what you are saying," – ***'I call only upon my Lord and do not associate anyone else*** as another god ***with Him.'***

21. ***Say: 'I possess no power to do you harm*** – make you err – ***or to guide you right*** and so do you good.***'***

22. ***Say: 'No one can protect me from*** the punishment of ***Allah and I will never find any refuge apart from Him*** except in Him **–**

23. ***...only in transmitting from Allah and His Messages.*** "I can only convey the Message of Allah to you from Him." This stresses his inability to do more. ***As for him who disobeys Allah and His Messenger*** – disbelieves in His unity and does not believe – ***he will have the Fire of Hell, remaining in it timelessly, for ever and ever.'***

24. ***So that*** if they continue in their unbelief until ***when they see what they were promised*** of the punishment ***they will know who has less support*** (fewer helpers) ***and smaller numbers***: they or the believers, according to one view, or "I or them" according to another. This refers to when that happened at the Battle of Badr, or to what will happen on the Day of Rising. One of them asked, "When will this promise come to pass?" and the next *āyat* was then revealed.

25. ***Say: 'I do not know whether what you are promised*** by way of punishment ***is close or whether my Lord will appoint a longer time before it.'*** Only Allah knows its time.

26. ***He is the Knower of the Unseen*** – He knows what His creatures do not see – ***and does not divulge His Unseen to anyone.*** The exception to this follows in the next *āyat* –

27. ***...except a Messenger with whom He is well pleased*** – Allah acquaints His Messenger with any of the Unseen He wishes as a miracle for him. ***Then He posts sentinels*** (angels) ***before him and behind him*** – to protect him until the revelation is conveyed –

28. ***...so that He may know*** – with outward knowledge – ***that they*** (the Messengers) ***have indeed transmitted the Messages of their Lord. He*** knows and ***encompasses what is in their hands and has counted*** accurately ***the exact number of*** each and ***every thing.***

سُورَةُ المُزَّمِّلِ

بِسْمِ ٱللَّهِ ٱلرَّحْمَـٰنِ ٱلرَّحِيمِ

يَـٰٓأَيُّهَا ٱلْمُزَّمِّلُ ١ قُمِ ٱلَّيْلَ إِلَّا قَلِيلًا ٢ نِّصْفَهُۥٓ أَوِ ٱنقُصْ مِنْهُ قَلِيلًا
٣ أَوْ زِدْ عَلَيْهِ وَرَتِّلِ ٱلْقُرْءَانَ تَرْتِيلًا ٤ إِنَّا سَنُلْقِى عَلَيْكَ قَوْلًا
ثَقِيلًا ٥ إِنَّ نَاشِئَةَ ٱلَّيْلِ هِىَ أَشَدُّ وَطْـًٔا وَأَقْوَمُ قِيلًا ٦ إِنَّ لَكَ فِى
ٱلنَّهَارِ سَبْحًا طَوِيلًا ٧ وَٱذْكُرِ ٱسْمَ رَبِّكَ وَتَبَتَّلْ إِلَيْهِ تَبْتِيلًا ٨
رَّبُّ ٱلْمَشْرِقِ وَٱلْمَغْرِبِ لَآ إِلَـٰهَ إِلَّا هُوَ فَٱتَّخِذْهُ وَكِيلًا ٩ وَٱصْبِرْ
عَلَىٰ مَا يَقُولُونَ وَٱهْجُرْهُمْ هَجْرًا جَمِيلًا ١٠ وَذَرْنِى وَٱلْمُكَذِّبِينَ
أُو۟لِى ٱلنَّعْمَةِ وَمَهِّلْهُمْ قَلِيلًا ١١ إِنَّ لَدَيْنَآ أَنكَالًا وَجَحِيمًا ١٢
وَطَعَامًا ذَا غُصَّةٍ وَعَذَابًا أَلِيمًا ١٣ يَوْمَ تَرْجُفُ ٱلْأَرْضُ وَٱلْجِبَالُ
وَكَانَتِ ٱلْجِبَالُ كَثِيبًا مَّهِيلًا ١٤ إِنَّآ أَرْسَلْنَآ إِلَيْكُمْ رَسُولًا شَـٰهِدًا
عَلَيْكُمْ كَمَآ أَرْسَلْنَآ إِلَىٰ فِرْعَوْنَ رَسُولًا ١٥ فَعَصَىٰ فِرْعَوْنُ ٱلرَّسُولَ
فَأَخَذْنَـٰهُ أَخْذًا وَبِيلًا ١٦ فَكَيْفَ تَتَّقُونَ إِن كَفَرْتُمْ يَوْمًا يَجْعَلُ
ٱلْوِلْدَٰنَ شِيبًا ١٧ ٱلسَّمَآءُ مُنفَطِرٌۢ بِهِۦ ۚ كَانَ وَعْدُهُۥ مَفْعُولًا ١٨
إِنَّ هَـٰذِهِۦ تَذْكِرَةٌ ۖ فَمَن شَآءَ ٱتَّخَذَ إِلَىٰ رَبِّهِۦ سَبِيلًا ١٩
۞ إِنَّ رَبَّكَ يَعْلَمُ أَنَّكَ تَقُومُ أَدْنَىٰ مِن ثُلُثَىِ ٱلَّيْلِ وَنِصْفَهُۥ وَثُلُثَهُۥ وَطَآئِفَةٌ
مِّنَ ٱلَّذِينَ مَعَكَ ۚ وَٱللَّهُ يُقَدِّرُ ٱلَّيْلَ وَٱلنَّهَارَ ۚ عَلِمَ أَن لَّن تُحْصُوهُ فَتَابَ
عَلَيْكُمْ ۖ فَٱقْرَءُوا۟ مَا تَيَسَّرَ مِنَ ٱلْقُرْءَانِ ۚ عَلِمَ أَن سَيَكُونُ مِنكُم مَّرْضَىٰ ۙ
وَءَاخَرُونَ يَضْرِبُونَ فِى ٱلْأَرْضِ يَبْتَغُونَ مِن فَضْلِ ٱللَّهِ ۙ وَءَاخَرُونَ

73. *Sūrat al-Muzzammil*
The Enwrapped

This *sūra* is Makkan and has 20 *āyats*.

1. ***You who are enwrapped in your clothing!*** This is a reference to the Prophet, may Allah bless him and grant him peace, meaning the one wrapped up in his garment when Revelation came to him, out of fear of it because of his great awe for it.

2. ***Stay up*** to pray ***at night, except a little,***

3. ***...half of it, or a little less*** – this is in relation to the whole night. "A little less" is from a half to a third,

4. ***...or a little more*** – up to two-thirds, or there is a choice – ***and recite the Qur'an distinctly*** – firmly and deliberately.

5. ***We will impose a weighty Word*** (the Qur'an) ***upon you.*** "Weighty" means that it is awesome, or possibly severe, because of the obligations which it contains.

6. ***Certainly rising at night*** to pray ***has a stronger effect and is more conducive to concentration*** for the heart to listen and understand the Qur'an, and pronunciation is more distinct.

7. ***In the daytime much of your time is taken up by business matters*** and so you do not have time to recite the Qur'an.

8. ***Remember the Name of your Lord*** – say, "In the name of Allah, the Merciful, the Compassionate" when you begin to recite – ***and devote yourself to Him completely*** with worship and reliance on Him alone.

9. ***Lord of the East and West – there is no god but Him; so take Him as your Guardian*** and entrust all your affairs to Him.

10. ***Be steadfast in the face of what they*** (the unbelievers of Makka) ***say*** to harm you, ***and cut yourself off from them – but courteously.*** "Avoid them in a way which is without anxiety." This was before the command came to fight them.

11. ***Leave the deniers, who live a life of ease, to Me, and tolerate them a little longer.*** "I will deal with them for you." This refers to the leaders of Quraysh.

12. ***With Us there are*** heavy iron ***shackles, a Blazing Fire,***

13. ***...and food that chokes*** – sticks in the throat, which is Zaqqūm, or pus or suppuration, or thorns from the Fire which do not go down the throat or come up ***– and a painful punishment*** – in addition to the painful punishment which awaits those who denied the Prophet, may Allah bless him and grant him peace –

14. ***...on the Day*** of Rising when ***the earth and mountains shake and the mountains become like shifting dunes*** of sand.

15. ***We have sent you***, people of Makka, ***a Messenger*** – Muḥammad, may Allah bless him and grant him peace – ***to bear witness against you*** on the Day of Rising about the disobedience which appeared in you ***just as We sent Pharaoh a Messenger*** – Mūsā, peace and blessings be upon him.

16. ***But Pharaoh disobeyed the Messenger, so We seized him with terrible severity.***

17. ***How will you safeguard yourselves*** and what fortresses will you have ***if you disbelieve*** in this world ***against*** the punishment of ***a Day which will turn children grey*** – their hair will turn grey because of the hardship of that day. One says about a difficult day that the forelocks of children turn grey. It is a metaphor. It is also possible that what is meant is a real sign –

18. ***...by which heaven will be split apart?*** That is the Day when the sky will split in two because of its severity. ***His promise will be fulfilled*** and will inevitably come to pass.

19. ***This*** (these frightening signs) ***truly is a reminder*** for creatures, ***so let anyone who wills take the Way towards his Lord*** by faith and obedience.

20. ***Your Lord knows that you stay up nearly two-thirds of the night – or half of it, or a third of it and a group of those with you*** – some of your Companions. That is how one emulates him. Some of them did not know how much of the night to pray and how much of it to leave, and so they would pray the entire night out of caution. They stood in prayer until their feet were swollen for a year or more. Then Allah lightened it for them, saying: ***Allah determines the night and day. He knows you will not keep count of it*** – and that you will not be able to calculate the prayer in it except by praying all

يُقَٰتِلُونَ فِي سَبِيلِ ٱللَّهِۖ فَٱقۡرَءُواْ مَا تَيَسَّرَ مِنۡهُۚ وَأَقِيمُواْ ٱلصَّلَوٰةَ وَءَاتُواْ
ٱلزَّكَوٰةَ وَأَقۡرِضُواْ ٱللَّهَ قَرۡضًا حَسَنٗاۚ وَمَا تُقَدِّمُواْ لِأَنفُسِكُم مِّنۡ خَيۡرٖ تَجِدُوهُ
عِندَ ٱللَّهِ هُوَ خَيۡرٗا وَأَعۡظَمَ أَجۡرٗاۚ وَٱسۡتَغۡفِرُواْ ٱللَّهَۖ إِنَّ ٱللَّهَ غَفُورٞ رَّحِيمُۢ ٢٠

of it, and that that is hard for you, ***so He has turned towards you*** by making that lighter for you. ***Recite as much of the Qur'an as is easy for you*** by praying as much as is feasible. ***He knows that some of you are ill, and that others are travelling in the land seeking Allah's bounty*** through trade and other work, ***and that others are fighting in the Way of Allah*** in *jihād*. It was hard for these three groups to pray at night in the way that has been mentioned, and therefore that was lightened for them so that they should pray as much as was feasible for them. Then that was abrogated by the five obligatory prayers. ***So recite as much of it as is easy for you. And establish the*** obligatory ***prayer, pay*** **zakāt** ***and lend a generous loan to Allah*** by spending more than the obligatory amount of wealth in the cause of good with cheerfulness. ***Whatever good you send ahead for yourselves, you will find it with Allah as something better*** than what you leave behind ***and as a greater reward. And seek forgiveness from Allah; Allah is Ever-Forgiving, Most Merciful*** to believers.

سُورَةُ المُدَّثِّرِ

بِسْمِ ٱللَّهِ ٱلرَّحْمَٰنِ ٱلرَّحِيمِ

يَٰٓأَيُّهَا ٱلْمُدَّثِّرُ ﴿١﴾ قُمْ فَأَنذِرْ ﴿٢﴾ وَرَبَّكَ فَكَبِّرْ ﴿٣﴾ وَثِيَابَكَ فَطَهِّرْ ﴿٤﴾
وَٱلرُّجْزَ فَٱهْجُرْ ﴿٥﴾ وَلَا تَمْنُن تَسْتَكْثِرُ ﴿٦﴾ وَلِرَبِّكَ فَٱصْبِرْ ﴿٧﴾
فَإِذَا نُقِرَ فِى ٱلنَّاقُورِ ﴿٨﴾ فَذَٰلِكَ يَوْمَئِذٍ يَوْمٌ عَسِيرٌ ﴿٩﴾ عَلَى ٱلْكَٰفِرِينَ
غَيْرُ يَسِيرٍ ﴿١٠﴾ ذَرْنِى وَمَنْ خَلَقْتُ وَحِيدًا ﴿١١﴾ وَجَعَلْتُ لَهُۥ مَالًا
مَّمْدُودًا ﴿١٢﴾ وَبَنِينَ شُهُودًا ﴿١٣﴾ وَمَهَّدتُّ لَهُۥ تَمْهِيدًا ﴿١٤﴾ ثُمَّ يَطْمَعُ
أَنْ أَزِيدَ ﴿١٥﴾ كَلَّآ ۖ إِنَّهُۥ كَانَ لِءَايَٰتِنَا عَنِيدًا ﴿١٦﴾ سَأُرْهِقُهُۥ صَعُودًا ﴿١٧﴾
إِنَّهُۥ فَكَّرَ وَقَدَّرَ ﴿١٨﴾ فَقُتِلَ كَيْفَ قَدَّرَ ﴿١٩﴾ ثُمَّ قُتِلَ كَيْفَ قَدَّرَ ﴿٢٠﴾ ثُمَّ نَظَرَ
﴿٢١﴾ ثُمَّ عَبَسَ وَبَسَرَ ﴿٢٢﴾ ثُمَّ أَدْبَرَ وَٱسْتَكْبَرَ ﴿٢٣﴾ فَقَالَ إِنْ هَٰذَآ إِلَّا سِحْرٌ
يُؤْثَرُ ﴿٢٤﴾ إِنْ هَٰذَآ إِلَّا قَوْلُ ٱلْبَشَرِ ﴿٢٥﴾ سَأُصْلِيهِ سَقَرَ ﴿٢٦﴾ وَمَآ أَدْرَىٰكَ
مَا سَقَرُ ﴿٢٧﴾ لَا تُبْقِى وَلَا تَذَرُ ﴿٢٨﴾ لَوَّاحَةٌ لِّلْبَشَرِ ﴿٢٩﴾ عَلَيْهَا تِسْعَةَ عَشَرَ
﴿٣٠﴾ وَمَا جَعَلْنَآ أَصْحَٰبَ ٱلنَّارِ إِلَّا مَلَٰٓئِكَةً ۙ وَمَا جَعَلْنَا عِدَّتَهُمْ إِلَّا فِتْنَةً
لِّلَّذِينَ كَفَرُوا۟ لِيَسْتَيْقِنَ ٱلَّذِينَ أُوتُوا۟ ٱلْكِتَٰبَ وَيَزْدَادَ ٱلَّذِينَ ءَامَنُوٓا۟ إِيمَٰنًا ۙ
وَلَا يَرْتَابَ ٱلَّذِينَ أُوتُوا۟ ٱلْكِتَٰبَ وَٱلْمُؤْمِنُونَ ۙ وَلِيَقُولَ ٱلَّذِينَ فِى قُلُوبِهِم مَّرَضٌ
وَٱلْكَٰفِرُونَ مَاذَآ أَرَادَ ٱللَّهُ بِهَٰذَا مَثَلًا ۚ كَذَٰلِكَ يُضِلُّ ٱللَّهُ مَن يَشَآءُ وَيَهْدِى
مَن يَشَآءُ ۚ وَمَا يَعْلَمُ جُنُودَ رَبِّكَ إِلَّا هُوَ ۚ وَمَا هِىَ إِلَّا ذِكْرَىٰ لِلْبَشَرِ ﴿٣١﴾ كَلَّا

74. *Sūrat al-Muddaththir*
The Enveloped

This *sūra* is Makkan and has 56 *āyat*s.

1. ***You who are enveloped in your cloak!*** This is addressed to the Prophet, may Allah bless him and grant him peace. He was enveloped in his garment when the Revelation was sent down on him.

2. ***Arise and warn*** the people of Makka about what will happen if they do not believe.

3. ***Magnify your Lord***, exalting Him above the *shirk* of the idolaters.

4. ***Purify your clothes*** of impurity; or, shorten your garments to avoid the custom of the Arabs of dragging their garments on the ground out of pride, and to avoid impurity getting on them.

5. ***Shun all filth.*** The Prophet, may Allah bless him and grant him peace, explained "filth" as meaning idols. Continue to avoid them.

6. ***Do not give*** anything ***out of a desire for gain*** – in order to seek a greater gift in return. This is peculiar to the Prophet, may Allah bless him and grant him peace, because he was commanded to have the most beautiful character and noblest manners.

7. ***Be steadfast for your Lord*** in observing His commands and prohibitions.

8. ***For when the*** second blast of the ***Trumpet is blown,***

9. ***...that Day*** when the Trumpet is blown ***will be a difficult day,***

10. ***...not easy for the unbelievers.*** This indicates that it will be easy for the believers.

11. ***Leave the person I created on his own to Me alone*** without his family or wealth, meaning al-Walīd ibn al-Mughīra –

12. ***...him to whom I have given great wealth*** – vast fields and flocks and trade –

13. ***...and sons who stay with him*** – al-Walīd had ten or more sons present in assemblies, whose testimony was accepted –

14. ***...and whose way I have smoothed*** with respect to his livelihood, life and children.

15. ***Then he wants Me to add yet more!***

16. ***No indeed!*** I will not give him more. ***He is obdurate about Our Signs*** – meaning that he opposes the Qur'an.

17. ***I will force him to climb a fiery slope*** – endure a difficult punishment; or it may refer to a mountain of fire which he will constantly climb up and then slip down and then do it again.

18. ***He reflected*** on what the Qur'an says, which he heard from the Prophet, may Allah bless him and grant him peace, ***and considered*** it further.

19. ***Curse him, how he considered!*** The word *qutila* is an invocation against someone.

20. ***Again curse him, how he considered!***

21. ***Then he looked*** at the faces of his people, or thought of how he would be rebuked if he accepted it.

22. ***Then he frowned and glowered.*** Glowering is a stronger form of frowning.

23. ***Then he drew back*** from faith ***and was*** too ***proud*** to follow the Prophet, may Allah bless him and grant him peace.

24. ***He said, 'This is nothing but*** a transmitted ***magic from the past.***

25. ***This is nothing but the words of a human being*** – another human being taught him this.'

26. ***I will*** make him enter Hellfire and ***roast him in* Saqar.**

27. ***What will convey to you what* Saqar *is?*** Because it is so immense and terrifying.

28. ***It does not spare*** anything of flesh or sinew, but destroys it all ***and does not ease up,*** and then it is restored to what it was before –

29. ***...ceaselessly scorching*** the outside of ***the flesh.***

30. ***There are nineteen*** angels ***in charge of it.*** One of the unbelievers who was very strong said, "I can deal with seventeen and you can deal with two for me." Then Allah revealed:

31. ***We have only appointed angels as masters of the Fire*** – and they are not as they imagine – ***and We have only specified their***

وَٱلْقَمَرِ ﴿٣٢﴾ وَٱلَّيْلِ إِذْ أَدْبَرَ ﴿٣٣﴾ وَٱلصُّبْحِ إِذَآ أَسْفَرَ ﴿٣٤﴾ إِنَّهَا لَإِحْدَى
ٱلْكُبَرِ ﴿٣٥﴾ نَذِيرًا لِّلْبَشَرِ ﴿٣٦﴾ لِمَن شَآءَ مِنكُمْ أَن يَتَقَدَّمَ أَوْ يَتَأَخَّرَ ﴿٣٧﴾ كُلُّ
نَفْسٍۭ بِمَا كَسَبَتْ رَهِينَةٌ ﴿٣٨﴾ إِلَّآ أَصْحَٰبَ ٱلْيَمِينِ ﴿٣٩﴾ فِى جَنَّٰتٍ يَتَسَآءَلُونَ
﴿٤٠﴾ عَنِ ٱلْمُجْرِمِينَ ﴿٤١﴾ مَا سَلَكَكُمْ فِى سَقَرَ ﴿٤٢﴾ قَالُوا۟ لَمْ نَكُ مِنَ
ٱلْمُصَلِّينَ ﴿٤٣﴾ وَلَمْ نَكُ نُطْعِمُ ٱلْمِسْكِينَ ﴿٤٤﴾ وَكُنَّا نَخُوضُ مَعَ
ٱلْخَآئِضِينَ ﴿٤٥﴾ وَكُنَّا نُكَذِّبُ بِيَوْمِ ٱلدِّينِ ﴿٤٦﴾ حَتَّىٰٓ أَتَىٰنَا ٱلْيَقِينُ ﴿٤٧﴾
فَمَا تَنفَعُهُمْ شَفَٰعَةُ ٱلشَّٰفِعِينَ ﴿٤٨﴾ فَمَا لَهُمْ عَنِ ٱلتَّذْكِرَةِ مُعْرِضِينَ
﴿٤٩﴾ كَأَنَّهُمْ حُمُرٌ مُّسْتَنفِرَةٌ ﴿٥٠﴾ فَرَّتْ مِن قَسْوَرَةٍۭ ﴿٥١﴾ بَلْ يُرِيدُ
كُلُّ ٱمْرِئٍ مِّنْهُمْ أَن يُؤْتَىٰ صُحُفًا مُّنَشَّرَةً ﴿٥٢﴾ كَلَّا ۖ بَل لَّا يَخَافُونَ
ٱلْءَاخِرَةَ ﴿٥٣﴾ كَلَّآ إِنَّهُۥ تَذْكِرَةٌ ﴿٥٤﴾ فَمَن شَآءَ ذَكَرَهُۥ ﴿٥٥﴾
وَمَا يَذْكُرُونَ إِلَّآ أَن يَشَآءَ ٱللَّهُ ۚ هُوَ أَهْلُ ٱلتَّقْوَىٰ وَأَهْلُ ٱلْمَغْفِرَةِ ﴿٥٦﴾

number as a trial for those who disbelieve – to misguide them so that they would say what they did say – ***so that those who were given the Book*** – meaning the Jews who believed in the Prophet, may Allah bless him and grant him peace – ***might gain in certainty*** – might confirm their number as being nineteen, that since was in their Book as well***; and that those who believe*** among the People of the Book ***might increase in their belief*** by realising that what the Prophet, may Allah bless him and grant him peace, brought was in harmony with the previous Books, ***and that both those who were given the Book and the believers might have no doubt*** about the number of the angels***; and so that those with sickness in their hearts*** in Madina ***and the unbelievers*** in Makka ***might say, 'What did Allah intend by this example*** involving their number***?'*** because of the strangeness of it. ***In this way*** – as He misguides the one who denies this number and the guides the one who affirms it – ***Allah misguides those He wills and guides those He wills. No one knows the legions of your Lord*** – meaning here the angels with their power and their helpers – ***but Him. This*** (*Saqar*) ***is nothing but a reminder to all human beings.***

32. ***No indeed! By the moon…***

33. ***…and the night when it withdraws*** (read as *adbara* and *dabara*) – and the day comes after it –

34. ***…and the dawn when it grows*** clear and ***bright,***

35. ***…it*** (*Saqar*) ***truly is one of the greatest of all things*** – trials…

36. ***…a warning to human beings,***

37. ***…for any of you who want to go forward*** to good or to the Garden by means of faith ***or hang back*** and go to evil or to the Fire because of unbelief.

38. ***Every self is held in pledge against what it earned*** – it will be seized in the Fire on account of its actions –

39. ***…except for the companions of the Right*** – the believers. They will be saved from the Fire.

40. ***In Gardens they will ask…***

41. ***…the evildoers,***

42. ***'What caused you to enter*** **Saqar*****?'***

43. ***They will say, 'We were not among those who performed the prayer…***

44. ***…and we did not feed the poor.***

45. ***We plunged*** into falsehood and vanity ***with those who plunged…***

46. ***…and denied the Day of Judgement*** – meaning the Resurrection and Repayment –

47. ***…until the Certain*** (death) ***came to us.'***

48. ***The intercession of the interceders will not help them.*** The interceders are the angels, the Prophets, and righteous. This means that there will be no intercession for them.

49. ***What is the matter with them that they run from the Reminder*** – and turn away from the Warning –

50. ***…like panicked*** wild ***donkeys…***

51. ***…fleeing from a lion***, as fast as one can flee***?***

52. ***In fact each one of them wants to be given an unfurled scroll*** from Allah before they follow the Prophet, for they said, "We will not believe until a book is sent down on us which we can read."

53. ***No indeed!*** This is to reject what they wanted ***The truth is that they do not fear*** the punishment of ***the Next World.***

54. ***No indeed! It is truly a reminder*** (Qur'an)…

55. ***…to which anyone who wills may pay heed.*** Anyone who wishes may recite it and be admonished.

56. ***But they will only pay heed*** (read as *yadhkurūna* and *tadhkurū - na*, "you will only pay heed") ***if Allah wills. He is entitled to be feared, and entitled to forgive.*** Allah should be feared and He will forgive those who fear Him.

سُورَةُ القِيَامَةِ

بِسۡمِ ٱللَّهِ ٱلرَّحۡمَٰنِ ٱلرَّحِيمِ

لَآ أُقۡسِمُ بِيَوۡمِ ٱلۡقِيَٰمَةِ ١ وَلَآ أُقۡسِمُ بِٱلنَّفۡسِ ٱللَّوَّامَةِ ٢ أَيَحۡسَبُ
ٱلۡإِنسَٰنُ أَلَّن نَّجۡمَعَ عِظَامَهُۥ ٣ بَلَىٰ قَٰدِرِينَ عَلَىٰٓ أَن نُّسَوِّيَ بَنَانَهُۥ ٤ بَلۡ
يُرِيدُ ٱلۡإِنسَٰنُ لِيَفۡجُرَ أَمَامَهُۥ ٥ يَسۡـَٔلُ أَيَّانَ يَوۡمُ ٱلۡقِيَٰمَةِ ٦ فَإِذَا بَرِقَ ٱلۡبَصَرُ
٧ وَخَسَفَ ٱلۡقَمَرُ ٨ وَجُمِعَ ٱلشَّمۡسُ وَٱلۡقَمَرُ ٩ يَقُولُ ٱلۡإِنسَٰنُ يَوۡمَئِذٍ
أَيۡنَ ٱلۡمَفَرُّ ١٠ كَلَّا لَا وَزَرَ ١١ إِلَىٰ رَبِّكَ يَوۡمَئِذٍ ٱلۡمُسۡتَقَرُّ ١٢ يُنَبَّؤُاْ ٱلۡإِنسَٰنُ
يَوۡمَئِذِۭ بِمَا قَدَّمَ وَأَخَّرَ ١٣ بَلِ ٱلۡإِنسَٰنُ عَلَىٰ نَفۡسِهِۦ بَصِيرَةٞ ١٤ وَلَوۡ أَلۡقَىٰ
مَعَاذِيرَهُۥ ١٥ لَا تُحَرِّكۡ بِهِۦ لِسَانَكَ لِتَعۡجَلَ بِهِۦٓ ١٦ إِنَّ عَلَيۡنَا جَمۡعَهُۥ
وَقُرۡءَانَهُۥ ١٧ فَإِذَا قَرَأۡنَٰهُ فَٱتَّبِعۡ قُرۡءَانَهُۥ ١٨ ثُمَّ إِنَّ عَلَيۡنَا بَيَانَهُۥ ١٩
كَلَّا بَلۡ تُحِبُّونَ ٱلۡعَاجِلَةَ ٢٠ وَتَذَرُونَ ٱلۡأٓخِرَةَ ٢١ وُجُوهٞ يَوۡمَئِذٖ نَّاضِرَةٌ ٢٢
إِلَىٰ رَبِّهَا نَاظِرَةٞ ٢٣ وَوُجُوهٞ يَوۡمَئِذِۭ بَاسِرَةٞ ٢٤ تَظُنُّ أَن يُفۡعَلَ بِهَا فَاقِرَةٞ ٢٥
كَلَّآ إِذَا بَلَغَتِ ٱلتَّرَاقِيَ ٢٦ وَقِيلَ مَنۡۜ رَاقٖ ٢٧ وَظَنَّ أَنَّهُ ٱلۡفِرَاقُ ٢٨ وَٱلۡتَفَّتِ
ٱلسَّاقُ بِٱلسَّاقِ ٢٩ إِلَىٰ رَبِّكَ يَوۡمَئِذٍ ٱلۡمَسَاقُ ٣٠ فَلَا صَدَّقَ وَلَا صَلَّىٰ
٣١ وَلَٰكِن كَذَّبَ وَتَوَلَّىٰ ٣٢ ثُمَّ ذَهَبَ إِلَىٰٓ أَهۡلِهِۦ يَتَمَطَّىٰٓ ٣٣ أَوۡلَىٰ لَكَ
فَأَوۡلَىٰ ٣٤ ثُمَّ أَوۡلَىٰ لَكَ فَأَوۡلَىٰٓ ٣٥ أَيَحۡسَبُ ٱلۡإِنسَٰنُ أَن يُتۡرَكَ سُدًى ٣٦
أَلَمۡ يَكُ نُطۡفَةٗ مِّن مَّنِيّٖ يُمۡنَىٰ ٣٧ ثُمَّ كَانَ عَلَقَةٗ فَخَلَقَ فَسَوَّىٰ ٣٨ فَجَعَلَ مِنۡهُ
ٱلزَّوۡجَيۡنِ ٱلذَّكَرَ وَٱلۡأُنثَىٰٓ ٣٩ أَلَيۡسَ ذَٰلِكَ بِقَٰدِرٍ عَلَىٰٓ أَن يُحۡـِۧيَ ٱلۡمَوۡتَىٰ ٤٠

75. *Sūrat al-Qiyāma*
The Rising

This *sūra* is Makkan and has 40 *āyat*s.

1. ***No! I swear by the Day of Rising.*** The *lā* is emphatic in this *āyat* and the next.

2. ***No! I swear by the self-reproaching self***, which is critical of itself, even if it strives to do good.

3. ***Does man*** (the unbeliever) ***imagine We will not reassemble his bones*** for the Resurrection and being brought back to life***?***

4. ***On the contrary! We are well able to reshape his fingers*** as they were, in spite of their small size. So how can that not be the case with what is larger?

5. ***Yet man still wants to deny what is ahead of him*** – the Day of Rising –

6. ***...asking, 'So when is the Day of Rising?'*** They ask this question out of mockery and denial.

7. ***But when the eyesight is dazzled*** (read as *bariqa* and *baraqa*) when it sees what it used to deny –

8. ***...and the moon is eclipsed*** – it goes dark and its light departs –

9. ***...and the sun and moon are fused together*** when they both rise from the West or when the light of both of them disappears: that is, the Day of Rising,

10. ***...on that Day man will say, 'Where can I flee to?'***

11. ***No indeed! There will be no safe place*** where they can escape to and no refuge in which they can protect themselves.

12. ***That Day the only resting place will be your Lord*** – where creatures stop for their Reckoning and Repayment.

13. ***That Day man will be told what he did and failed to do***: his actions, first to last.

14. ***In fact, man will be clear proof against himself.*** His limbs will bear witness against him, testifying about what he did. Repayment for one's actions is inevitable –

15. ***...in spite of any excuses he might offer.*** No excuse that anyone brings will be accepted. Allah said to His Prophet:

16. ***Do not move your tongue trying to hasten it*** – to hasten the Qur'an before Jibrīl finishes conveying it, out of fear that you may lose some of it.

17. ***Its collection and recitation are Our concern.*** "We collect it in your breast and make you recite it on your tongue."

18. ***So when We recite it, follow its recitation.*** "When Jibrīl recites it to you, then listen to its recitation." The Prophet, may Allah bless him and grant him peace, would listen to it and then recite it.

19. ***Then its explanation is Our concern.*** Then We make you understand it.

20. ***No indeed! But you love*** (read as *tuḥibbūna* and *yuḥibbūna*, "they love") ***this fleeting world,***

21. ***...and you disregard the Next World*** and do not work for it.

22. ***Faces that Day*** – the Day of Rising – ***will be*** beautiful and ***radiant,***

23. ***...gazing at their Lord.*** They will see Allah – Glorified and Exalted is He! – in the Next World.

24. ***And faces that Day will be glowering*** in intense displeasure,

25. ***...realising that a back-breaking blow has fallen.*** They are certain that a disaster has occurred which breaks the back due to its severity.

26. ***No indeed! When it*** (the breath) ***reaches the gullet*** (the throat)

27. ***...and he hears the words*** from those around him***: 'Who can heal him now?'***

28. ***...and he knows it is indeed the final parting***: he is certain that his spirit has reached the moment of departing from this world,

29. ***...and one leg is entwined with the other*** in death, or it is a metaphor for the intensity of the experience of leaving this world and going to the Next World,

30. ***...that Day he will be driven to your Lord.*** The meaning is: when the breath reaches the gullet, he will be driven to the judgement of his Lord.

31. ***He neither affirmed the truth nor did he do the prayer...***

32. ***...but rather denied the truth*** (the Qur'an) ***and turned away*** from faith,

33. ***...and then went off to his family, swaggering*** – arrogant in his gait.

34. ***Closer to you and closer!*** **–** There is a change to the second person. What you dislike is coming nearer and it is nearer to you than anything else.

35. ***Then closer to you and closer still!*** – This is for emphasis.

36. ***Does man reckon he will be left to go on unchecked*** – left ignored, and not subject to laws or taken to account for thatīĪ

37. ***Was he not a drop of ejaculated*** (read as *yumnā* and *tumnā*) ***sperm,***

38. ***...then a blood-clot which He created and shaped*** when the drop of sperm became a blood-clot, from which Allah created the human being and made his limbs balanced,

39. ***...making from it both sexes, male and female?*** Allah makes a clot of blood from the sperm and then a piece of flesh from that, and then male and female, sometimes both together, and sometimes each one separately.

40. ***Is He who does that not able to bring the dead to life?*** In answer to this question, the Prophet, may Allah bless him and grant him peace, said, "Yes indeed, He is!"

سُورَةُ الإِنسَانِ

بِسْمِ ٱللَّهِ ٱلرَّحْمَٰنِ ٱلرَّحِيمِ

هَلْ أَتَىٰ عَلَى ٱلْإِنسَٰنِ حِينٌ مِّنَ ٱلدَّهْرِ لَمْ يَكُن شَيْـًٔا مَّذْكُورًا ﴿١﴾
إِنَّا خَلَقْنَا ٱلْإِنسَٰنَ مِن نُّطْفَةٍ أَمْشَاجٍ نَّبْتَلِيهِ فَجَعَلْنَٰهُ سَمِيعًۢا
بَصِيرًا ﴿٢﴾ إِنَّا هَدَيْنَٰهُ ٱلسَّبِيلَ إِمَّا شَاكِرًا وَإِمَّا كَفُورًا ﴿٣﴾
إِنَّآ أَعْتَدْنَا لِلْكَٰفِرِينَ سَلَٰسِلَا۟ وَأَغْلَٰلًا وَسَعِيرًا ﴿٤﴾ إِنَّ
ٱلْأَبْرَارَ يَشْرَبُونَ مِن كَأْسٍ كَانَ مِزَاجُهَا كَافُورًا ﴿٥﴾
عَيْنًا يَشْرَبُ بِهَا عِبَادُ ٱللَّهِ يُفَجِّرُونَهَا تَفْجِيرًا ﴿٦﴾ يُوفُونَ بِٱلنَّذْرِ وَيَخَافُونَ
يَوْمًا كَانَ شَرُّهُۥ مُسْتَطِيرًا ﴿٧﴾ وَيُطْعِمُونَ ٱلطَّعَامَ عَلَىٰ حُبِّهِۦ مِسْكِينًا
وَيَتِيمًا وَأَسِيرًا ﴿٨﴾ إِنَّمَا نُطْعِمُكُمْ لِوَجْهِ ٱللَّهِ لَا نُرِيدُ مِنكُمْ جَزَآءً وَلَا شُكُورًا
﴿٩﴾ إِنَّا نَخَافُ مِن رَّبِّنَا يَوْمًا عَبُوسًا قَمْطَرِيرًا ﴿١٠﴾ فَوَقَىٰهُمُ ٱللَّهُ شَرَّ ذَٰلِكَ
ٱلْيَوْمِ وَلَقَّىٰهُمْ نَضْرَةً وَسُرُورًا ﴿١١﴾ وَجَزَىٰهُم بِمَا صَبَرُوا۟ جَنَّةً وَحَرِيرًا
﴿١٢﴾ مُّتَّكِـِٔينَ فِيهَا عَلَى ٱلْأَرَآئِكِ لَا يَرَوْنَ فِيهَا شَمْسًا وَلَا زَمْهَرِيرًا ﴿١٣﴾
وَدَانِيَةً عَلَيْهِمْ ظِلَٰلُهَا وَذُلِّلَتْ قُطُوفُهَا تَذْلِيلًا ﴿١٤﴾ وَيُطَافُ عَلَيْهِم بِـَٔانِيَةٍ
مِّن فِضَّةٍ وَأَكْوَابٍ كَانَتْ قَوَارِيرَا۠ ﴿١٥﴾ قَوَارِيرَا۟ مِن فِضَّةٍ قَدَّرُوهَا تَقْدِيرًا ﴿١٦﴾
وَيُسْقَوْنَ فِيهَا كَأْسًا كَانَ مِزَاجُهَا زَنجَبِيلًا ﴿١٧﴾ عَيْنًا فِيهَا تُسَمَّىٰ سَلْسَبِيلًا
﴿١٨﴾ ۞ وَيَطُوفُ عَلَيْهِمْ وِلْدَٰنٌ مُّخَلَّدُونَ إِذَا رَأَيْتَهُمْ حَسِبْتَهُمْ لُؤْلُؤًا مَّنثُورًا

76. *Sūrat al-Insān*
Man

This *sūra* is Makkan or Madinan, and has 31 *āyat*s.

1. ***Has man*** (Ādam) ***ever known a point of time*** – said to be forty years, during which he was being formed from mud – ***when he was not something remembered?*** Or it may be that the word "man" is being used here as a generic term and the "time" referred to is the period in the womb.

2. ***We created man from a mingled drop*** – referring to the liquid coming from the man mixing with that of the woman – ***to test him*** by making him responsible for his actions once he reaches puberty, ***and We made him hearing and seeing.***

3. ***We guided him on the Way*** – the Path of guidance, by sending the Messengers – ***whether he is thankful*** – by being a believer – ***or unthankful*** – by being an ungrateful unbeliever, the two states being clear and distinct from one another.

4. ***We have made ready for the unbelievers shackles*** with which they will be chained in the Fire ***and*** collars on their necks which are attached to ***chains and*** they will be punished in ***a Searing Blaze.***

5. ***The truly good*** – they are those who obey Allah – ***will drink from a cup*** of wine ***mixed with the coolness of camphor*** in its sweetness***:***

6. ***…a spring*** – a fountain of camphor in which is a cool fragrance – ***from which Allah's slaves*** (the *awliyā'*) ***will drink, making it gush forth at will abundantly.*** They will be guided to it from their homes in the Garden.

7. ***They fulfil their vows*** to obey Allah ***and fear a Day whose evil will spread far and wide.***

8. ***They give food, despite their love for it, to the poor and orphans and captives*** (those rightly imprisoned)***:***

9. ***'We feed you only out of desire for the Face of Allah*** – for His reward. ***We do not want any repayment from you or any thanks*** for feeding you. There are two views about this *āyat*: either they may be saying that or Allah knows it about them and praises them for it.

10. ***Truly We fear from our Lord a glowering, calamitous Day'*** on the Day when faces look gloomy because of the hardship which they experience.

11. ***So Allah has safeguarded them from the evil of that Day and has made them meet with radiance and pure joy*** – Allah has given their faces beauty and light,

12. ***...and will reward them for their steadfastness*** – in avoiding disobedience ***with a Garden and with silk*** – to wear.

13. This is their state when they enter it – ***reclining in it on couches, they will experience there neither burning sun nor bitter cold.*** The word for "sun", *zamharīr,* is also said to mean the moon, indicating that there will be neither sun nor moon there.

14. ***Its shading branches*** – those of its trees – ***will droop down over them*** close at hand from a place which they cannot see, ***its ripe fruit hanging ready to be picked*** – so that anyone standing, sitting down or lying down can pluck them.

15. ***Vessels*** – cups without handles – ***of silver and goblets of pure crystal will be passed round among them –***

16. ***...crystalline silver*** – made of silver so fine that it is like glass in its transparency; ***they have measured them very exactly.*** Those who pass them around have measured the amount very exactly so that they contain the amount which they want to drink, no more and no less; and it is the most delicious drink.

17. ***They will be given there a cup*** of wine ***to drink mixed with the warmth of ginger.***

18. ***In it there is a flowing spring called Salsabīl*** – a spring whose water is like *zanjabīl* (ginger) which the Arabs enjoy and which is easy to drink.

19. ***Ageless youths*** – who never grow old – ***will circulate among them, serving them. Seeing them*** – because of their beauty and how they are dispersed – ***you would think them scattered pearls*** – detached from a necklace or from a shell, or more beautiful still.

20. ***Seeing them*** in the Garden, ***you see delight and a great king - dom*** – indescribable bliss and a vast, limitless realm.

21. ***They will wear*** (read as *'āliyahum* and *'ālīhim*) ***green garments of fine silk and rich*** silk ***brocade*** which has the thick silk on the out-

﴿١٩﴾ وَإِذَا رَأَيْتَ ثَمَّ رَأَيْتَ نَعِيمًا وَمُلْكًا كَبِيرًا ﴿٢٠﴾ عَٰلِيَهُمْ ثِيَابُ سُندُسٍ
خُضْرٌ وَإِسْتَبْرَقٌ ۖ وَحُلُّوٓا۟ أَسَاوِرَ مِن فِضَّةٍ وَسَقَىٰهُمْ رَبُّهُمْ شَرَابًا
طَهُورًا ﴿٢١﴾ إِنَّ هَٰذَا كَانَ لَكُمْ جَزَآءً وَكَانَ سَعْيُكُم مَّشْكُورًا ﴿٢٢﴾ إِنَّا
نَحْنُ نَزَّلْنَا عَلَيْكَ ٱلْقُرْءَانَ تَنزِيلًا ﴿٢٣﴾ فَٱصْبِرْ لِحُكْمِ رَبِّكَ وَلَا تُطِعْ
مِنْهُمْ ءَاثِمًا أَوْ كَفُورًا ﴿٢٤﴾ وَٱذْكُرِ ٱسْمَ رَبِّكَ بُكْرَةً وَأَصِيلًا ﴿٢٥﴾
وَمِنَ ٱلَّيْلِ فَٱسْجُدْ لَهُۥ وَسَبِّحْهُ لَيْلًا طَوِيلًا ﴿٢٦﴾ إِنَّ
هَٰٓؤُلَآءِ يُحِبُّونَ ٱلْعَاجِلَةَ وَيَذَرُونَ وَرَآءَهُمْ يَوْمًا ثَقِيلًا ﴿٢٧﴾ نَّحْنُ
خَلَقْنَٰهُمْ وَشَدَدْنَآ أَسْرَهُمْ ۖ وَإِذَا شِئْنَا بَدَّلْنَآ أَمْثَٰلَهُمْ تَبْدِيلًا
﴿٢٨﴾ إِنَّ هَٰذِهِۦ تَذْكِرَةٌ ۖ فَمَن شَآءَ ٱتَّخَذَ إِلَىٰ رَبِّهِۦ سَبِيلًا ﴿٢٩﴾
وَمَا تَشَآءُونَ إِلَّآ أَن يَشَآءَ ٱللَّهُ ۚ إِنَّ ٱللَّهَ كَانَ عَلِيمًا حَكِيمًا ﴿٣٠﴾
يُدْخِلُ مَن يَشَآءُ فِى رَحْمَتِهِۦ ۚ وَٱلظَّٰلِمِينَ أَعَدَّ لَهُمْ عَذَابًا أَلِيمًا ﴿٣١﴾

side and the fine on the inside, or the reverse. ***They will be adorned with silver bracelets.*** Silver bracelets are mentioned here, whereas gold bracelets are mentioned elsewhere (in *Sūrat al-Kahf)*. They wear both together or separately. ***And their Lord will give them a pure draught to drink***: extremely pure and clean, which is not the case with the wine of this world.

22. ***'This*** bliss ***is your reward. Your striving is fully acknowledged.'***

23. ***It is We*** – the word "We" is stressed – ***who have sent the Qur'an down to you little by little***: in parts, not all at once.

24. ***Therefore wait patiently for the judgement of your Lord*** as to how He decides to convey His Message. ***Do not obey any*** unbelieving ***evildoer or thankless man among them.*** This refers to 'Utba ibn Rabī'a and al-Walīd ibn al-Mughīra, who said to the Prophet, may Allah bless him and grant him peace, "Desist from this business." It can also refer to every evildoer or unbeliever, meaning "Do not obey any of them, whoever they are, in respect of any act of evildoing or unbelief they invite you to do."

25. ***Remember the Name of your Lord in the morning and the evening*** – in the prayers of *Fajr*, *Ẓuhr* and *'Aṣr*.

26. ***Prostrate to Him during the night*** – in the prayers of *Maghrib* and *'Ishā'* – ***and glorify Him throughout the long night*** – in the voluntary night prayers of *tahajjud*, for two-thirds, a half or a third of it.

27. ***Those people love this fleeting world and have put the thought of a Momentous Day*** (the Day of Rising) ***behind their backs*** – for which they did not work.

28. ***We created them and made*** their limbs and ***their joints strong, and if We wish We can replace them with others like them.*** We can destroy them and put others in their place.

29. ***This*** *sūra* ***truly is a Reminder*** for all creation; ***so whoever wills should take the Way towards his Lord*** through obedience to Him.

30. ***But you will not will*** (read as *tashā'ūna*, and *yashā'ūna*, "they will not will") ***unless Allah wills.*** This refers to taking the path of obedience. "You will not do this unless Allah wills it." ***Allah is All-Knowing*** of His creation, ***All-Wise*** in what He does.

31. ***He admits whomever He wills into His mercy*** – His Garden. That means are the believers. ***But He has prepared a painful punishment for the wrongdoers*** – the unbelievers.

سُورَةُ المُرْسَلَاتِ

بِسْمِ ٱللَّهِ ٱلرَّحْمَٰنِ ٱلرَّحِيمِ

وَٱلْمُرْسَلَٰتِ عُرْفًا ﴿١﴾ فَٱلْعَٰصِفَٰتِ عَصْفًا ﴿٢﴾ وَٱلنَّٰشِرَٰتِ نَشْرًا ﴿٣﴾
فَٱلْفَٰرِقَٰتِ فَرْقًا ﴿٤﴾ فَٱلْمُلْقِيَٰتِ ذِكْرًا ﴿٥﴾ عُذْرًا أَوْ نُذْرًا ﴿٦﴾ إِنَّمَا
تُوعَدُونَ لَوَٰقِعٌ ﴿٧﴾ فَإِذَا ٱلنُّجُومُ طُمِسَتْ ﴿٨﴾ وَإِذَا ٱلسَّمَآءُ فُرِجَتْ
﴿٩﴾ وَإِذَا ٱلْجِبَالُ نُسِفَتْ ﴿١٠﴾ وَإِذَا ٱلرُّسُلُ أُقِّتَتْ ﴿١١﴾ لِأَىِّ يَوْمٍ أُجِّلَتْ
﴿١٢﴾ لِيَوْمِ ٱلْفَصْلِ ﴿١٣﴾ وَمَآ أَدْرَىٰكَ مَا يَوْمُ ٱلْفَصْلِ ﴿١٤﴾ وَيْلٌ يَوْمَئِذٍ
لِّلْمُكَذِّبِينَ ﴿١٥﴾ أَلَمْ نُهْلِكِ ٱلْأَوَّلِينَ ﴿١٦﴾ ثُمَّ نُتْبِعُهُمُ ٱلْءَاخِرِينَ
﴿١٧﴾ كَذَٰلِكَ نَفْعَلُ بِٱلْمُجْرِمِينَ ﴿١٨﴾ وَيْلٌ يَوْمَئِذٍ لِّلْمُكَذِّبِينَ ﴿١٩﴾
أَلَمْ نَخْلُقكُّم مِّن مَّآءٍ مَّهِينٍ ﴿٢٠﴾ فَجَعَلْنَٰهُ فِى قَرَارٍ مَّكِينٍ ﴿٢١﴾ إِلَىٰ قَدَرٍ
مَّعْلُومٍ ﴿٢٢﴾ فَقَدَرْنَا فَنِعْمَ ٱلْقَٰدِرُونَ ﴿٢٣﴾ وَيْلٌ يَوْمَئِذٍ لِّلْمُكَذِّبِينَ ﴿٢٤﴾
أَلَمْ نَجْعَلِ ٱلْأَرْضَ كِفَاتًا ﴿٢٥﴾ أَحْيَآءً وَأَمْوَٰتًا ﴿٢٦﴾ وَجَعَلْنَا فِيهَا رَوَٰسِىَ
شَٰمِخَٰتٍ وَأَسْقَيْنَٰكُم مَّآءً فُرَاتًا ﴿٢٧﴾ وَيْلٌ يَوْمَئِذٍ لِّلْمُكَذِّبِينَ ﴿٢٨﴾
ٱنطَلِقُوٓا۟ إِلَىٰ مَا كُنتُم بِهِۦ تُكَذِّبُونَ ﴿٢٩﴾ ٱنطَلِقُوٓا۟ إِلَىٰ ظِلٍّ ذِى ثَلَٰثِ
شُعَبٍ ﴿٣٠﴾ لَّا ظَلِيلٍ وَلَا يُغْنِى مِنَ ٱللَّهَبِ ﴿٣١﴾ إِنَّهَا تَرْمِى بِشَرَرٍ
كَٱلْقَصْرِ ﴿٣٢﴾ كَأَنَّهُۥ جِمَٰلَتٌ صُفْرٌ ﴿٣٣﴾ وَيْلٌ يَوْمَئِذٍ لِّلْمُكَذِّبِينَ ﴿٣٤﴾
هَٰذَا يَوْمُ لَا يَنطِقُونَ ﴿٣٥﴾ وَلَا يُؤْذَنُ لَهُمْ فَيَعْتَذِرُونَ ﴿٣٦﴾ وَيْلٌ يَوْمَئِذٍ

77. *Sūrat al-Mursalāt*
Those Sent Forth

This *sūra* is Makkan except and it has 50 *āyat*s.

1. ***By those*** winds ***sent forth in succession***, which follow one another like horses following one another –

2. ***...by the violently gusting blasts*** – fierce winds;

3. ***...by the scatterers scattering*** – winds which spread the rain;

4. ***...by the winnowers winnowing*** – *āyat*s of the Qur'an which distinguish the truth from the false and the lawful from the unlawful;

5. ***...by those hurling a reminder*** – angels who descend with Revelation to the Prophets and Messengers, who give it to their nations;

6. ***...excusing*** (read as *'udhr* and *'udhur*) ***or warning*** (read as *nudhr* or *nudhur*) from Allah Almighty –

7. ***...what you***, unbelievers of Makka, ***are promised*** in terms of Resurrection and Punishment ***will certainly happen!***

8. ***When the stars are extinguished*** and their light disappears;

9. ***...when heaven is split open;***

10. ***...when the mountains are pulverised*** and become powder, and shift;

11. ***...when the Messengers' time is appointed*** (read as *uqqitat* and *wuqqitat*);

12. ***...until what day is that deferred?*** That is a terrible day when it is time for nations to testify that the Message was conveyed to them.

13. ***Until the Day of Decision*** between creatures, when accounting will take place between them.

14. ***And what will teach you what the*** terrifying ***Day of Decision is?***

15. ***On that*** promised ***Day, woe to the deniers!***

16. ***Did We not destroy the earlier peoples*** for their denial? This means that Allah destroyed them,

17. ***...then succeed them with later ones*** who denied and were destroyed? A threat to the unbelievers of Makka.

18. ***That is how We deal with evildoers*** who deny and will continue to deal with those who deny in the future: they too will be destroyed.

19. ***On that Day, woe to the deniers!***

20. ***Did We not create you from a base fluid,*** sperm,

21. ***...then place it in a secure repository,*** the womb,

22. ***...for a recognised term*** – until the day of your birth***?***

23. ***It is We who determine. What an excellent Determiner*** We are***!***

24. ***On that Day, woe to the deniers!***

25. ***Did We not make the earth a receptacle*** – using the word *kifāt*, from *kafata* which means to collect together and gather –

26. ***...for the living*** on the surface of the earth ***and the dead*** inside the earth***?***

27. ***Did We not place firmly embedded mountains in it, soaring high into the air, and give you sweet fresh water to drink?***

28. ***On that Day, woe to the deniers!*** Then this will be said to the deniers on the Day of Rising.

29. ***Proceed to that which you denied!***

30. ***Proceed to a shadow*** – the smoke of Hellfire when it rises – ***which forks into three*** because of its immensity,

31. ***...but gives no shade or protection from the flames:*** nothing shades people from the heat of that day or defends them from the Fire –

32. ... the Fire ***shooting up great sparks the size of castles*** – in their size and height –

33. ***...like a herd of yellow camels*** (read as *jimālāt* and *jimālat*). They are "yellow" (*ṣufr*) in appearance and colour. In a *ḥadīth* we find: "The worst of people will be black like pitch." The Arabs call black camels "yellow" because their blackness is tinged with yellow. It is said that *ṣufr* in the *āyat* means black, for the reason just mentioned; but it is also said that that is not the case.

34. ***On that Day, woe to the deniers!***

35. ***This is the Day*** of Resurrection, on which ***they will not say a single word,***

36. ***...nor will they be allowed to offer any excuses.*** There is no permission and so there is no offering of excuses.

لِّلْمُكَذِّبِينَ ﴿٣٧﴾ هَٰذَا يَوْمُ ٱلْفَصْلِ جَمَعْنَٰكُمْ وَٱلْأَوَّلِينَ ﴿٣٨﴾ فَإِن كَانَ
لَكُمْ كَيْدٌ فَكِيدُونِ ﴿٣٩﴾ وَيْلٌ يَوْمَئِذٍ لِّلْمُكَذِّبِينَ ﴿٤٠﴾ إِنَّ ٱلْمُتَّقِينَ فِى
ظِلَٰلٍ وَعُيُونٍ ﴿٤١﴾ وَفَوَٰكِهَ مِمَّا يَشْتَهُونَ ﴿٤٢﴾ كُلُوا۟ وَٱشْرَبُوا۟ هَنِيٓـًٔۢا
بِمَا كُنتُمْ تَعْمَلُونَ ﴿٤٣﴾ إِنَّا كَذَٰلِكَ نَجْزِى ٱلْمُحْسِنِينَ ﴿٤٤﴾ وَيْلٌ يَوْمَئِذٍ
لِّلْمُكَذِّبِينَ ﴿٤٥﴾ كُلُوا۟ وَتَمَتَّعُوا۟ قَلِيلًا إِنَّكُم مُّجْرِمُونَ ﴿٤٦﴾ وَيْلٌ يَوْمَئِذٍ
لِّلْمُكَذِّبِينَ ﴿٤٧﴾ وَإِذَا قِيلَ لَهُمُ ٱرْكَعُوا۟ لَا يَرْكَعُونَ ﴿٤٨﴾ وَيْلٌ
يَوْمَئِذٍ لِّلْمُكَذِّبِينَ ﴿٤٩﴾ فَبِأَىِّ حَدِيثٍۭ بَعْدَهُۥ يُؤْمِنُونَ ﴿٥٠﴾

37. ***On that Day, woe to the deniers!***

38. ***'This is the Day of Decision. We have gathered you***, deniers in this community, ***and the earlier peoples*** – the deniers before you. All of you will receive your reckoning and be punished.

39. ***So if you have a ploy, use it against Me now!'*** If you have any stratagem by which to evade the punishment, then use it.

40. ***On that Day, woe to the deniers!***

41. ***The godfearing will be amid shade*** of dense trees ***and fountains*** flowing with water;

42. ***...and have any fruits that they desire.*** This tells us that food and drink in the Garden will appear according to people's desires – which is not the case in this world, where it is generally according to what people find. They will be told:

43. ***'Eat and drink with relish for what you did*** by way of obedience.

44. ***This is the way We reward good-doers*** – the godfearing.'

45. ***On that Day, woe to the deniers!***

46. This is addressed to the unbelievers in this world: ***'Eat and enjoy yourselves for a little while*** – while you are in this world, until death. This is a threat to them. ***You are evildoers.'***

47. ***On that Day, woe to the deniers!***

48. ***When they are told to bow, they do not bow.*** When they are told to pray, they do not pray.

49. ***On that Day, woe to the deniers!***

50. ***In what discourse after this*** Qur'an, ***then, will they believe?*** They cannot truly believe in other Books of Allah if they deny it, because it has the quality of inimitability which the others do not.

سُورَةُ النَّبَإِ

بِسْمِ ٱللَّهِ ٱلرَّحْمَٰنِ ٱلرَّحِيمِ

عَمَّ يَتَسَآءَلُونَ ﴿١﴾ عَنِ ٱلنَّبَإِ ٱلْعَظِيمِ ﴿٢﴾ ٱلَّذِى هُمْ فِيهِ مُخْتَلِفُونَ ﴿٣﴾
كَلَّا سَيَعْلَمُونَ ﴿٤﴾ ثُمَّ كَلَّا سَيَعْلَمُونَ ﴿٥﴾ أَلَمْ نَجْعَلِ ٱلْأَرْضَ مِهَٰدًا ﴿٦﴾
وَٱلْجِبَالَ أَوْتَادًا ﴿٧﴾ وَخَلَقْنَٰكُمْ أَزْوَٰجًا ﴿٨﴾ وَجَعَلْنَا نَوْمَكُمْ سُبَاتًا
﴿٩﴾ وَجَعَلْنَا ٱلَّيْلَ لِبَاسًا ﴿١٠﴾ وَجَعَلْنَا ٱلنَّهَارَ مَعَاشًا ﴿١١﴾ وَبَنَيْنَا
فَوْقَكُمْ سَبْعًا شِدَادًا ﴿١٢﴾ وَجَعَلْنَا سِرَاجًا وَهَّاجًا ﴿١٣﴾ وَأَنزَلْنَا
مِنَ ٱلْمُعْصِرَٰتِ مَآءً ثَجَّاجًا ﴿١٤﴾ لِّنُخْرِجَ بِهِۦ حَبًّا وَنَبَاتًا ﴿١٥﴾ وَجَنَّٰتٍ
أَلْفَافًا ﴿١٦﴾ إِنَّ يَوْمَ ٱلْفَصْلِ كَانَ مِيقَٰتًا ﴿١٧﴾ يَوْمَ يُنفَخُ فِى ٱلصُّورِ
فَتَأْتُونَ أَفْوَاجًا ﴿١٨﴾ وَفُتِحَتِ ٱلسَّمَآءُ فَكَانَتْ أَبْوَٰبًا ﴿١٩﴾ وَسُيِّرَتِ
ٱلْجِبَالُ فَكَانَتْ سَرَابًا ﴿٢٠﴾ إِنَّ جَهَنَّمَ كَانَتْ مِرْصَادًا ﴿٢١﴾ لِّلطَّٰغِينَ
مَـَٔابًا ﴿٢٢﴾ لَّٰبِثِينَ فِيهَآ أَحْقَابًا ﴿٢٣﴾ لَّا يَذُوقُونَ فِيهَا بَرْدًا وَلَا شَرَابًا
﴿٢٤﴾ إِلَّا حَمِيمًا وَغَسَّاقًا ﴿٢٥﴾ جَزَآءً وِفَاقًا ﴿٢٦﴾ إِنَّهُمْ كَانُوا۟
لَا يَرْجُونَ حِسَابًا ﴿٢٧﴾ وَكَذَّبُوا۟ بِـَٔايَٰتِنَا كِذَّابًا ﴿٢٨﴾ وَكُلَّ شَىْءٍ
أَحْصَيْنَٰهُ كِتَٰبًا ﴿٢٩﴾ فَذُوقُوا۟ فَلَن نَّزِيدَكُمْ إِلَّا عَذَابًا ﴿٣٠﴾
إِنَّ لِلْمُتَّقِينَ مَفَازًا ﴿٣١﴾ حَدَآئِقَ وَأَعْنَٰبًا ﴿٣٢﴾ وَكَوَاعِبَ أَتْرَابًا ﴿٣٣﴾ وَكَأْسًا
دِهَاقًا ﴿٣٤﴾ لَّا يَسْمَعُونَ فِيهَا لَغْوًا وَلَا كِذَّٰبًا ﴿٣٥﴾ جَزَآءً مِّن رَّبِّكَ عَطَآءً
حِسَابًا ﴿٣٦﴾ رَّبِّ ٱلسَّمَٰوَٰتِ وَٱلْأَرْضِ وَمَا بَيْنَهُمَا ٱلرَّحْمَٰنِ لَا يَمْلِكُونَ

78. *Sūrat an-Nabā'*
The News

This *sūra* is Makkan and has 40 or 41 *āyat*s.

1. ***About what are they*** (Quraysh) ***asking one another?***

2. ***About the momentous news*** – clarifying what it is that they are asking about, meaning the parts of the Qur'an that the Prophet, may Allah bless him and grant him peace, had brought, containing information about the Resurrection and other things:

3. ***…the thing about which they differ.*** The believers affirm it and the unbelievers deny it.

4. ***No indeed! They will soon know!*** They will know, when the things they denied happen to them.

5. ***Again, no indeed! They will soon know*!** The repetition is for emphasis. The announcement of a second threat is stronger than the first. Then Allah indicates His power to resurrect them.

6. ***Have We not made the earth a flat carpet,*** spread out like a bed,

7. ***…and the mountains its pegs?*** They make the earth stable, as a tent is made stable by pegs. The question demands a positive response.

8. ***We have created you in pairs*** – male and female.

9. ***We made your sleep a break*** – rest for your bodies.

10. ***We made the night a cloak*** which veils things with its darkness.

11. ***We made the day*** a time ***for earning a living.***

12. ***We built seven firm layers above you*** – referring to the seven heavens, which are strong and firm and not affected by the passage of time.

13. ***We installed a blazing lamp*** – referring to the sun. The word for "blazing", *wahhāj*, refers to a kind of burning that gives out strong light.

14. ***We sent down cascading water*** (rain) ***from the clouds*** – when it is the time for rain. *Mu'ṣir a*re rain clouds which are on the point of having the rain pressed out of them. The word is also used for a girl who is about to menstruate, but has not done so yet –

15. ***...so that by it We might bring forth grains*** such as wheat ***and plants*** such as figs,

16. ***...and luxuriant gardens.***

17. ***The Day of Decision is a fixed appointment:*** the Day when decision is rendered between creatures. It is the time appointed for the delivery of reward and punishment,

18. ***...the Day the Trumpet is blown*** by Isrāfīl ***and you come in droves*** – different groups, from your graves for the Gathering;

19. ***...and heaven is opened*** (read as *futiḥat* and *futtiḥat*) – for the descent of the angels – ***and becomes doorways,***

20. ***...and the mountains are shifted*** from their places, turning into dust, ***and become a mirage.*** They are like a mirage in that they are so insubstantial.

21. ***Hell lies in wait –***

22. ***...a homecoming for the profligate*** (the unbelievers) – they will not go beyond it. It is where they will return to and enter,

23. ***...to remain in it for countless aeons*** – ages without end,

24. ***...not tasting any coolness there or any drink*** – they have no sleep in it, no escape from the heat and nothing pleasant to drink –

25. ***...except for boiling water*** – as hot as it is possible to be – ***and scalding pus*** (read as *ghassāq* and *ghasāq*) – which oozes from the people of the Fire, and which they drink –

26. ***...a fitting recompense*** for what they did. There is no wrong action worse than unbelief and no punishment more terrible than the Fire.

27. ***They did not expect to have a reckoning*** – they did not fear that there would be a reckoning, because they denied the Resurrection,

28. ***...and utterly denied Our Signs*** (the Qur'an).

29. ***We have recorded all things in writing.*** "We have written down all actions exactly. Every single thing is recorded on the Preserved Tablet so that We may repay people for their actions." One of those actions is their disbelief in the Qur'an.

30. This will be said to them in the Next World when the punishment is inflicted on them: ***So taste*** your repayment***! We will increase you only in punishment*** – a punishment on top of your punishment.

مِنْهُ خِطَابًا ﴿٣٧﴾ يَوْمَ يَقُومُ ٱلرُّوحُ وَٱلْمَلَٰٓئِكَةُ صَفًّا ۖ لَّا يَتَكَلَّمُونَ
إِلَّا مَنْ أَذِنَ لَهُ ٱلرَّحْمَٰنُ وَقَالَ صَوَابًا ﴿٣٨﴾ ذَٰلِكَ ٱلْيَوْمُ ٱلْحَقُّ ۖ فَمَن
شَآءَ ٱتَّخَذَ إِلَىٰ رَبِّهِۦ مَـَٔابًا ﴿٣٩﴾ إِنَّآ أَنذَرْنَٰكُمْ عَذَابًا قَرِيبًا يَوْمَ
يَنظُرُ ٱلْمَرْءُ مَا قَدَّمَتْ يَدَاهُ وَيَقُولُ ٱلْكَافِرُ يَٰلَيْتَنِى كُنتُ تُرَٰبًۢا ﴿٤٠﴾

31. ***For the godfearing there is triumph:*** the Garden.

32. ***...gardens and grapevines*** – describing the form their triumph takes –

33. ***...and nubile maidens*** – with swelling breasts – ***of similar age,***

34. ***...and an overflowing cup*** of wine which is filled to the brim. *Sūrat Muḥammad* mentions "rivers of wine" (47:15).

35. ***In it they will hear no prattle and no denial*** (read as *kidhdhāb* and *kidhāb*) – in the Garden when they drink the wine and in other states, they will hear no useless words, lies or denial, which is differen from what happens in this world when someone drinks wine –

36. ***...a recompense from your Lord, a commensurate gift*** – which is so abundant that you would say, "It is enough for me".

37. ***Lord*** (read as *Rabbi* and *Rabbu*) ***of the heavens and earth and everything between them, the All-Merciful*** (read as *ar-Raḥmāni* and *ar-Raḥmānu*). ***They*** (creatures) ***will not have the power to speak to Him*** – out of fear of Him.

38. ***On the Day when the Spirit*** (Jibrīl or the army of Allah) ***and the angels stand in ranks, no one will speak, except for him who is authorised by the All-Merciful*** to speak ***and says what is right*** – among the believers and the angels who will intercede for those whom He is pleased with.

39. ***That will be the True Day.*** The occurrence of this Day is confirmed: it is the Day of Rising. ***So whoever wills should take the way back to his Lord.*** He should return to Allah by obeying Him so that he may be safe from the Punishment on that day.

40. ***We have warned you***, unbelievers of Makka, ***of an imminent punishment*** which is coming ***on the Day*** of Resurrection ***when a man will see what his hands have produced*** – everyone will see what they have done, be it good or evil – ***and the unbeliever will say, 'Oh, if only I were dust!'*** He will wish that he were dust so that he could not be punished. He will say that when Allah Almighty says to the animals, after they have exacted retaliation from one another: "Be dust".

سُورَةُ النَّازِعَاتِ

بِسْمِ ٱللَّهِ ٱلرَّحْمَٰنِ ٱلرَّحِيمِ

وَٱلنَّٰزِعَٰتِ غَرْقًا ١ وَٱلنَّٰشِطَٰتِ نَشْطًا ٢ وَٱلسَّٰبِحَٰتِ سَبْحًا
٣ فَٱلسَّٰبِقَٰتِ سَبْقًا ٤ فَٱلْمُدَبِّرَٰتِ أَمْرًا ٥ يَوْمَ تَرْجُفُ ٱلرَّاجِفَةُ
٦ تَتْبَعُهَا ٱلرَّادِفَةُ ٧ قُلُوبٌ يَوْمَئِذٍ وَاجِفَةٌ ٨ أَبْصَٰرُهَا
خَٰشِعَةٌ ٩ يَقُولُونَ أَءِنَّا لَمَرْدُودُونَ فِى ٱلْحَافِرَةِ ١٠ أَءِذَا كُنَّا
عِظَٰمًا نَّخِرَةً ١١ قَالُوا۟ تِلْكَ إِذًا كَرَّةٌ خَاسِرَةٌ ١٢ فَإِنَّمَا هِىَ زَجْرَةٌ
وَٰحِدَةٌ ١٣ فَإِذَا هُم بِٱلسَّاهِرَةِ ١٤ هَلْ أَتَىٰكَ حَدِيثُ مُوسَىٰٓ ١٥
إِذْ نَادَىٰهُ رَبُّهُۥ بِٱلْوَادِ ٱلْمُقَدَّسِ طُوًى ١٦ ٱذْهَبْ إِلَىٰ فِرْعَوْنَ إِنَّهُۥ طَغَىٰ ١٧
فَقُلْ هَل لَّكَ إِلَىٰٓ أَن تَزَكَّىٰ ١٨ وَأَهْدِيَكَ إِلَىٰ رَبِّكَ فَتَخْشَىٰ ١٩ فَأَرَىٰهُ
ٱلْءَايَةَ ٱلْكُبْرَىٰ ٢٠ فَكَذَّبَ وَعَصَىٰ ٢١ ثُمَّ أَدْبَرَ يَسْعَىٰ ٢٢ فَحَشَرَ
فَنَادَىٰ ٢٣ فَقَالَ أَنَا۠ رَبُّكُمُ ٱلْأَعْلَىٰ ٢٤ فَأَخَذَهُ ٱللَّهُ نَكَالَ ٱلْءَاخِرَةِ وَٱلْأُولَىٰٓ
٢٥ إِنَّ فِى ذَٰلِكَ لَعِبْرَةً لِّمَن يَخْشَىٰٓ ٢٦ ءَأَنتُمْ أَشَدُّ خَلْقًا أَمِ ٱلسَّمَآءُ بَنَىٰهَا
٢٧ رَفَعَ سَمْكَهَا فَسَوَّىٰهَا ٢٨ وَأَغْطَشَ لَيْلَهَا وَأَخْرَجَ ضُحَىٰهَا ٢٩
وَٱلْأَرْضَ بَعْدَ ذَٰلِكَ دَحَىٰهَآ ٣٠ أَخْرَجَ مِنْهَا مَآءَهَا وَمَرْعَىٰهَا ٣١
وَٱلْجِبَالَ أَرْسَىٰهَا ٣٢ مَتَٰعًا لَّكُمْ وَلِأَنْعَٰمِكُمْ ٣٣ فَإِذَا جَآءَتِ ٱلطَّآمَّةُ
ٱلْكُبْرَىٰ ٣٤ يَوْمَ يَتَذَكَّرُ ٱلْإِنسَٰنُ مَا سَعَىٰ ٣٥ وَبُرِّزَتِ ٱلْجَحِيمُ

79. *Sūrat an-Nāzi'āt*
The Pluckers

This *sūra* is Makkan and has 46 *āyat*s.

1. ***By those who pluck out harshly*** – the angels who pluck out the souls of the unbelievers with violent force,

2. ***...and those who draw out gently*** – the angels who draw out the souls of the believers with gentleness and kindness,

3. ***...and those who glide serenely*** – the angels who glide down from heaven with the command of Allah,

4. ***...and those who outrun easily*** – the angels who race with the souls of the believers to the Garden,

5. ***...and those who direct affairs!*** – the angels who manage the business of this world. The subject of these oaths which is elided is: "O unbelievers of Makka, you will be resurrected."

6. ***On the Day the first Blast shudders*** – the first Blast shakes everything and so is described by what happens in it –

7. ***...and the second Blast follows it*** – there are forty years between the two. The Last Day is long enough for both blasts and other things as well,

8. ***...hearts that Day will be pounding*** – anxious and full of fear –

9. ***...and eyes will be cast down*** – abject because of the terrifying sights they see.

10. ***They*** (those with hearts and eyes) ***will say*** – in mockery, to deny the Resurrection: ***'Are we to be restored to how we were*** – after death? The word used here *al-ḥāfira* is a noun meaning the beginning of something. One says that someone returns to his *"ḥāfira"* when he goes back to where he came from –

11. ***...when we have become perished*** (read as *nākhira* and *nakhir*, meaning old and crumbling), ***worm-eaten bones?'***

12. ***They say, 'That will clearly be a losing restoration!'*** Being restored to life, if it is true, will entail loss.

13. ***There will be but one Great Blast*** – a reference to the second Blast that is followed by the Resurrection. It will only be blown once.

14. ***...and at once they will be on the surface, wide awake!*** All creatures will be alive on the surface of the earth after having been dead inside it.

15. ***Has the story of Mūsā reached you*** – addressed to Muḥammad, may Allah bless him and grant him peace –

16. ***...when his Lord called out to him in the holy valley of Ṭuwā*** (read as *Ṭuwā* and *Ṭuwan*)***?***

17. ***'Go to Pharaoh – he has overstepped the limits*** in unbelief –

18. ***...and say: "Do you resolve to purify yourself*** (read as *tazzakka* and *tazakkā*)***?*** – I call on you to purify yourselves from *shirk* by testifying that there is no god but Allah.

19. ***I will guide you to*** recognition of ***your Lord*** – by evidence – ***so that you may fear Him."'***

20. ***Then he showed him the Great Sign*** – one of the seven signs, referring to the hand or the staff,

21. ***... but he denied it and disobeyed*** – Pharaoh denied Mūsā and disobeyed Allah –

22. ***...and then he hastily backed away*** from faith and strove to bring about corruption in the earth.

23. ***But then he rallied*** the magicians and his army ***and called out...***

24. ***...saying, 'I am your Lord Most High!'*** "There is no Lord above me!"

25. ***So Allah made an example of him*** and drowned him ***seizing him with punishment in the Next World and this world.*** It is also said that what is referred to here are not the Next World and this world, but rather that the punishment is because of an earlier and later statement made by Pharaoh; the later being the one mentioned here, *"I am your Lord Most High!"*, and the earlier, *"I do not know of any other god for you apart from me."* (28:38) Forty years passed between the two statements.

26. ***There is certainly instruction in that*** which has been mentioned ***for those who fear*** Allah.

27. ***Are you*** who deny the Resurrection ***stronger in structure or is heaven? He built it.***

28. ***He raised its vault high and made it level.*** This describes how He built it. He made its elevation high. It is also said that this refers to its ceiling. He made it level without any fault in it.

29. ***He darkened its night and brought forth its morning light.*** He made the light of the sun appear. He ascribed night to the sky because it makes it dark and the sun to it because it is the lamp of the sky.

30. ***After that He smoothed out the earth*** and spread it out. The earth was created before the sky, but was not spread out –

31. ***...and brought forth from it its water*** as springs ***and its pasture - land*** to be grazed by animals: in other words, grass, trees and bushes and foodstuffs and fruits that are edible for mankind,

32. ***...and made the mountains firm*** on the surface of the earth so that it would be stable –

33. ***...for you and for your livestock to enjoy.*** That is enjoyment and goods for you and for your flocks of camels, cattle and sheep and goats.

34. ***When the Great Calamity*** – the Second Blast of the Trumpet – ***comes,***

35. ***...that Day man will remember*** the good and evil of ***what he has striven for*** in this world...

36. ***...and the Blazing Fire will be displayed for all who can see*** – meaning everyone.

37. ***As for him who overstepped the bounds*** and disbelieved ...

38. ***...and preferred*** to follow his appetites in ***the life of this world,***

39. ***...the Blazing Fire will be his refuge.***

40. ***But as for him who feared the Station of his Lord*** – the time when he will stand before Allah – ***and forbade the lower self*** – which commands to evil the ruinous passions displayed by following ***its appetites,***

41. ***...the Garden will be his refuge.*** The disobedient will go to the Fire and the obedient to the Garden.

لِمَن يَرَىٰ ﴿٣٦﴾ فَأَمَّا مَن طَغَىٰ ﴿٣٧﴾ وَءَاثَرَ ٱلْحَيَوٰةَ ٱلدُّنْيَا ﴿٣٨﴾ فَإِنَّ ٱلْجَحِيمَ
هِىَ ٱلْمَأْوَىٰ ﴿٣٩﴾ وَأَمَّا مَنْ خَافَ مَقَامَ رَبِّهِۦ وَنَهَى ٱلنَّفْسَ عَنِ ٱلْهَوَىٰ
﴿٤٠﴾ فَإِنَّ ٱلْجَنَّةَ هِىَ ٱلْمَأْوَىٰ ﴿٤١﴾ يَسْـَٔلُونَكَ عَنِ ٱلسَّاعَةِ أَيَّانَ مُرْسَىٰهَا
﴿٤٢﴾ فِيمَ أَنتَ مِن ذِكْرَىٰهَآ ﴿٤٣﴾ إِلَىٰ رَبِّكَ مُنتَهَىٰهَآ ﴿٤٤﴾ إِنَّمَآ أَنتَ مُنذِرُ
مَن يَخْشَىٰهَا ﴿٤٥﴾ كَأَنَّهُمْ يَوْمَ يَرَوْنَهَا لَمْ يَلْبَثُوٓا۟ إِلَّا عَشِيَّةً أَوْ ضُحَىٰهَا ﴿٤٦﴾

42. ***They*** (the unbelievers of Makka) ***ask you about the*** Last ***Hour: 'When will it arrive?'***

43. ***What are you doing mentioning it*** – anything about it***?*** "You have insufficient knowledge even to mention it."

44. ***Its coming is your Lord's affair.*** The knowledge of its time is with Allah, and only He knows it.

45. ***You are only the warner of those who fear it.*** Your warning only benefits those who fear it.

46. ***On the Day they see it, it will be as if they had only lingered*** in their graves ***for the evening or the morning of a single day.***

سُورَةُ عَبَسَ

بِسۡمِ ٱللَّهِ ٱلرَّحۡمَٰنِ ٱلرَّحِيمِ

عَبَسَ وَتَوَلَّىٰٓ ١ أَن جَآءَهُ ٱلۡأَعۡمَىٰ ٢ وَمَا يُدۡرِيكَ لَعَلَّهُۥ يَزَّكَّىٰٓ ٣ أَوۡ
يَذَّكَّرُ فَتَنفَعَهُ ٱلذِّكۡرَىٰٓ ٤ أَمَّا مَنِ ٱسۡتَغۡنَىٰ ٥ فَأَنتَ لَهُۥ تَصَدَّىٰ ٦
وَمَا عَلَيۡكَ أَلَّا يَزَّكَّىٰ ٧ وَأَمَّا مَن جَآءَكَ يَسۡعَىٰ ٨ وَهُوَ يَخۡشَىٰ ٩ فَأَنتَ
عَنۡهُ تَلَهَّىٰ ١٠ كَلَّآ إِنَّهَا تَذۡكِرَةٞ ١١ فَمَن شَآءَ ذَكَرَهُۥ ١٢ فِي صُحُفٖ مُّكَرَّمَةٖ
١٣ مَّرۡفُوعَةٖ مُّطَهَّرَةِۭ ١٤ بِأَيۡدِي سَفَرَةٖ ١٥ كِرَامِۭ بَرَرَةٖ ١٦ قُتِلَ ٱلۡإِنسَٰنُ
مَآ أَكۡفَرَهُۥ ١٧ مِنۡ أَيِّ شَيۡءٍ خَلَقَهُۥ ١٨ مِن نُّطۡفَةٍ خَلَقَهُۥ فَقَدَّرَهُۥ ١٩ ثُمَّ
ٱلسَّبِيلَ يَسَّرَهُۥ ٢٠ ثُمَّ أَمَاتَهُۥ فَأَقۡبَرَهُۥ ٢١ ثُمَّ إِذَا شَآءَ أَنشَرَهُۥ ٢٢ كَلَّا لَمَّا
يَقۡضِ مَآ أَمَرَهُۥ ٢٣ فَلۡيَنظُرِ ٱلۡإِنسَٰنُ إِلَىٰ طَعَامِهِۦٓ ٢٤ أَنَّا صَبَبۡنَا ٱلۡمَآءَ صَبّٗا
٢٥ ثُمَّ شَقَقۡنَا ٱلۡأَرۡضَ شَقّٗا ٢٦ فَأَنۢبَتۡنَا فِيهَا حَبّٗا ٢٧ وَعِنَبٗا وَقَضۡبٗا ٢٨
وَزَيۡتُونٗا وَنَخۡلٗا ٢٩ وَحَدَآئِقَ غُلۡبٗا ٣٠ وَفَٰكِهَةٗ وَأَبّٗا ٣١ مَّتَٰعٗا لَّكُمۡ
وَلِأَنۡعَٰمِكُمۡ ٣٢ فَإِذَا جَآءَتِ ٱلصَّآخَّةُ ٣٣ يَوۡمَ يَفِرُّ ٱلۡمَرۡءُ مِنۡ أَخِيهِ ٣٤
وَأُمِّهِۦ وَأَبِيهِ ٣٥ وَصَٰحِبَتِهِۦ وَبَنِيهِ ٣٦ لِكُلِّ ٱمۡرِيٕٖ مِّنۡهُمۡ يَوۡمَئِذٖ شَأۡنٞ
يُغۡنِيهِ ٣٧ وُجُوهٞ يَوۡمَئِذٖ مُّسۡفِرَةٞ ٣٨ ضَاحِكَةٞ مُّسۡتَبۡشِرَةٞ ٣٩ وَوُجُوهٞ
يَوۡمَئِذٍ عَلَيۡهَا غَبَرَةٞ ٤٠ تَرۡهَقُهَا قَتَرَةٌ ٤١ أُوْلَٰٓئِكَ هُمُ ٱلۡكَفَرَةُ ٱلۡفَجَرَةُ ٤٢

80. *Sūrat ‘Abasa*
He Frowned

This *sūra* is Makkan and has 42 *āyat*s.

1. ***He*** (the Prophet, may Allah bless him and grant him peace) ***frowned and turned away…***

2. ***…because the blind man came to him.*** The blind man was named ‘Abdullāh ibn Umm Maktūm. The Prophet stopped him doing what he was doing because he hoped that some of the nobles of Quraysh would become Muslim and was eager for that to happen. The blind man, not knowing that he was preoccupied with that, called out to him, "Teach me some of what Allah has taught you!" The Prophet, may Allah bless him and grant him peace, went to his house. He was rebuked for his reaction by what was revealed in this *sūra*. After that, whenever ‘Abdullāh ibn Umm Maktūm came, he used to say, "Welcome to the one for whose sake He censured me," and he would spread out his cloak for him.

3. ***But how do you know?*** What will tell you? ***Perhaps he would be purified*** of wrong actions by what he hears from you –

4. ***…or reminded, and the reminder benefit him.*** What he hears from you will benefit him.

5. ***As for him who thinks himself self-sufficient*** because of his wealth,

6. ***…you give*** (read as *taṣaddā* and *taṣṣaddā*) ***him your complete attention –***

7. ***…but it is not up to you whether or not he is purified***: whether or not he believes.

8. ***But as for him who comes to you eagerly,***

9. ***…showing fearfulness***, meaning the blind man,

10. ***…from him you are distracted*** (read as *‘anhu talahhā* and *‘anhu’ttalahhā*).

11. ***No indeed!*** Do not act like that. ***Truly it*** (the *sūra* or the *āyats*) ***is a reminder*** to all mankind –

12. ***...and whoever wills pays heed to it*** – remembers and is warned by it;

13. ***...inscribed on Honoured Pages*** – honoured in the sight of Allah;

14. ***...exalted*** in the heavens, ***purified*** of the touch of the *shayṭāns* –

15. ***...by the hands of scribes*** – who copy it out from the Preserved Tablet –

16. ***...noble, virtuous*** – obeying Allah Almighty: meaning the angels.

17. ***Curse man for his ingratitude!*** "Curse the unbelievers." Allah rebukes them for the unbelief they display.

18. ***From what thing did He create him?*** This is a rhetorical question which Allah then elucidates.

19. ***From a drop of sperm He created him and proportioned him***, as a clot and then a lump of flesh, until he was fully formed.

20. ***Then He eases the way for him*** – to emerge from the womb of his mother.

21. ***Then He causes him to die and has him buried*** in his grave, where He covers him with earth.

22. ***Then, when He wills, He raises him from the dead*** at the Resurrection.

23. ***No indeed! He has not done what He*** (his Lord) ***ordered him.***

24. ***Man has only to look at his food.*** "Look" here means to reflect on and consider. "Has he not considered how his food is decreed and managed for him?"

25. ***We pour down plentiful water*** from the clouds,

26. ***...then split the earth*** – by means of plants – ***into furrows.***

27. ***Then We make grain*** – such as wheat and barley – ***grow in it,***

28. ***...and grapes and herbs,***

29. ***...and olives and dates,***

30. ***...and luxuriant gardens*** with many trees in them,

31. ***...and orchards and meadows*** – it is said that the word *abb* is where animals graze, and it is also said to mean figs –

32. ***...for you and your livestock to enjoy*** – or use, as was stated in the previous *sūra.*

33. ***When the Deafening Blast*** – the Second Blast – ***comes –***

34. ***...the Day a man will flee from his brother,***

35. ***...and his mother and his father,***

36. ***...and his wife and his children:***

37. ***...on that Day every man among them will have concerns enough of his own.*** His own situation will distract him from everything else.

38. ***That Day some faces will be radiant*** with joy,

39. ***...laughing, rejoicing***: full of joy. These are the believers.

40. ***That Day some faces will be dust-covered,***

41. ***...overcast with gloom***: dark.

42. ***Those are the dissolute unbelievers.*** They are subject to both unbelief and deviance.

سُورَةُ التَّكْوِيرِ

بِسْمِ ٱللَّهِ ٱلرَّحْمَٰنِ ٱلرَّحِيمِ

إِذَا ٱلشَّمْسُ كُوِّرَتْ ﴿١﴾ وَإِذَا ٱلنُّجُومُ ٱنكَدَرَتْ ﴿٢﴾ وَإِذَا ٱلْجِبَالُ
سُيِّرَتْ ﴿٣﴾ وَإِذَا ٱلْعِشَارُ عُطِّلَتْ ﴿٤﴾ وَإِذَا ٱلْوُحُوشُ حُشِرَتْ
﴿٥﴾ وَإِذَا ٱلْبِحَارُ سُجِّرَتْ ﴿٦﴾ وَإِذَا ٱلنُّفُوسُ زُوِّجَتْ ﴿٧﴾ وَإِذَا
ٱلْمَوْءُۥدَةُ سُئِلَتْ ﴿٨﴾ بِأَىِّ ذَنۢبٍ قُتِلَتْ ﴿٩﴾ وَإِذَا ٱلصُّحُفُ نُشِرَتْ
﴿١٠﴾ وَإِذَا ٱلسَّمَآءُ كُشِطَتْ ﴿١١﴾ وَإِذَا ٱلْجَحِيمُ سُعِّرَتْ ﴿١٢﴾ وَإِذَا ٱلْجَنَّةُ
أُزْلِفَتْ ﴿١٣﴾ عَلِمَتْ نَفْسٌ مَّآ أَحْضَرَتْ ﴿١٤﴾ فَلَآ أُقْسِمُ بِٱلْخُنَّسِ ﴿١٥﴾
ٱلْجَوَارِ ٱلْكُنَّسِ ﴿١٦﴾ وَٱلَّيْلِ إِذَا عَسْعَسَ ﴿١٧﴾ وَٱلصُّبْحِ إِذَا تَنَفَّسَ ﴿١٨﴾
إِنَّهُۥ لَقَوْلُ رَسُولٍ كَرِيمٍ ﴿١٩﴾ ذِى قُوَّةٍ عِندَ ذِى ٱلْعَرْشِ مَكِينٍ ﴿٢٠﴾ مُّطَاعٍ
ثَمَّ أَمِينٍ ﴿٢١﴾ وَمَا صَاحِبُكُم بِمَجْنُونٍ ﴿٢٢﴾ وَلَقَدْ رَءَاهُ بِٱلْأُفُقِ ٱلْمُبِينِ
﴿٢٣﴾ وَمَا هُوَ عَلَى ٱلْغَيْبِ بِضَنِينٍ ﴿٢٤﴾ وَمَا هُوَ بِقَوْلِ شَيْطَٰنٍ رَّجِيمٍ ﴿٢٥﴾
فَأَيْنَ تَذْهَبُونَ ﴿٢٦﴾ إِنْ هُوَ إِلَّا ذِكْرٌ لِّلْعَٰلَمِينَ ﴿٢٧﴾ لِمَن شَآءَ مِنكُمْ أَن
يَسْتَقِيمَ ﴿٢٨﴾ وَمَا تَشَآءُونَ إِلَّآ أَن يَشَآءَ ٱللَّهُ رَبُّ ٱلْعَٰلَمِينَ ﴿٢٩﴾

81. *Sūrat at-Takwīr* The Compacting

This *sūra* is Makkan and has 29 *āyat*s.

1. ***When the sun is compacted in blackness*** – it is wound up and its light disappears***;***

2. ***...when the stars*** go out and ***fall*** to the earth ***in rapid succession;***

3. ***...when the mountains are set in motion*** and become dust, and vanish from the face of the earth***;***

4. ***...when the camels in foal are neglected*** – when pregnant camels are left without a shepherd or milk camels are left unmilked, when people are in shock because of what is happening. There is no type of property dearer to the Arabs than these***;***

5. ***...when the wild beasts are all herded together*** after the Resurrection so that they can take retaliation from one another before turning to dust***;***

6. ***...when the oceans surge*** (read as *sujjirat* and *sujirat*) ***into each other*** – when they are mixed and set on fire***;***

7. ***...when the souls are arranged into classes*** – one meaning of this is that it is when they are rejoined to their bodies***;***

8. ***...when the baby girl buried alive*** out of fear of shame and poverty ***is asked*** – to rebuke her killer –

9. ***...for what crime she was killed*** (read as *qutilat* and *quttilat*) – she will say, "I was not killed for any crime"***;***

10. ***...when the Pages*** of actions ***are opened up*** (read as *nushirat* and *nushirrat*)***;***

11. ***...when the Heaven is peeled away*** from its place***;***

12. ***...when the Fire is set ablaze*** (read as *su''irat* and *su'irat*)***;***

13. ***...when the Garden is brought up close*** to those destined for it so that they may enter it***;***

14. ***...then each soul will know what it has done.*** At the time when these things happen, which is the Day of Rising, every self will know whatever good or evil it has done.

15. ***No! I swear by the planets with their retrograde motion,***

16. ***...swiftly moving, self-concealing*** – these are the five planets: Saturn, Jupiter, Mars, Venus and Mercury. "Retrograde" means that they appear to move backwards, in that sometimes you will see a planet at the end of a constellation and then it will go back to the beginning of it. They hide themselves when they go into occultation in various places, at which time they are no longer visible,

17. ***...and by the night when it draws in*** – comes with its darkness, or when it withdraws,

18. ***...and by the dawn when it exhales*** – expands until it becomes clear daylight*!*

19. ***Truly it*** (the Qur'an) ***is the speech of a noble Messenger*** from Allah Almighty. This is a reference to Jibrīl and is ascribed to him because he is the one who brought it down,

20. ***...possessing great strength, securely placed with the Lord of the Throne*** – he has a high position before Allah Almighty,

21. ***...obeyed there, trustworthy.*** The angels in the heavens obey Jibrīl and He is entrusted with the Revelation.

22. ***Your companion is not mad.*** This is the subject of the earlier oath. Muḥammad, may Allah bless him and grant him peace, is not mad as you claim.

23. ***He*** (Muḥammad, may Allah bless him and grant him peace) ***saw him*** (Jibrīl) in the form in which he was created, ***on the clear horizon*** – the highest horizon towards the east.

24. ***Nor is he*** (Muḥammad, may Allah bless him and grant him peace) ***miserly with the Unseen.*** He does not conceal the Revelation. There are two readings in this *āyat*: One is *ḍanīn*, meaning he is not miserly in conveying what has been conveyed to him by concealing it. The second is *ẓanīn*, meaning that he does not doubt it.

25. ***Nor is it*** (the Qur'an) ***the word of an accursed* Shayṭān** which he overheard.

26. ***Where, then, are you going?*** What path are you travelling in your denial of the Qur'an and turning away from it?

27. ***It is nothing but a Reminder to all the worlds*** – to jinn and mankind –

28. ***...to whoever among you*** – whether from the jinn or from mankind – ***wishes to go straight*** and follow the Truth.

29. ***But you will not wish*** to go straight ***unless Allah wills*** you to go straight, ***the Lord of all the Worlds*** – all creatures.

سُورَةُ الانفِطَار

بِسۡمِ ٱللَّهِ ٱلرَّحۡمَٰنِ ٱلرَّحِيمِ

إِذَا ٱلسَّمَآءُ ٱنفَطَرَتۡ ١ وَإِذَا ٱلۡكَوَاكِبُ ٱنتَثَرَتۡ ٢ وَإِذَا ٱلۡبِحَارُ
فُجِّرَتۡ ٣ وَإِذَا ٱلۡقُبُورُ بُعۡثِرَتۡ ٤ عَلِمَتۡ نَفۡسٞ مَّا قَدَّمَتۡ
وَأَخَّرَتۡ ٥ يَٰٓأَيُّهَا ٱلۡإِنسَٰنُ مَا غَرَّكَ بِرَبِّكَ ٱلۡكَرِيمِ ٦ ٱلَّذِي
خَلَقَكَ فَسَوَّىٰكَ فَعَدَلَكَ ٧ فِيٓ أَيِّ صُورَةٖ مَّا شَآءَ رَكَّبَكَ ٨
كَلَّا بَلۡ تُكَذِّبُونَ بِٱلدِّينِ ٩ وَإِنَّ عَلَيۡكُمۡ لَحَٰفِظِينَ ١٠ كِرَامٗا
كَٰتِبِينَ ١١ يَعۡلَمُونَ مَا تَفۡعَلُونَ ١٢ إِنَّ ٱلۡأَبۡرَارَ لَفِي نَعِيمٖ ١٣ وَإِنَّ
ٱلۡفُجَّارَ لَفِي جَحِيمٖ ١٤ يَصۡلَوۡنَهَا يَوۡمَ ٱلدِّينِ ١٥ وَمَا هُمۡ عَنۡهَا بِغَآئِبِينَ
١٦ وَمَآ أَدۡرَىٰكَ مَا يَوۡمُ ٱلدِّينِ ١٧ ثُمَّ مَآ أَدۡرَىٰكَ مَا يَوۡمُ ٱلدِّينِ
١٨ يَوۡمَ لَا تَمۡلِكُ نَفۡسٞ لِّنَفۡسٖ شَيۡـٔٗاۖ وَٱلۡأَمۡرُ يَوۡمَئِذٖ لِّلَّهِ ١٩

82. *Sūrat al-Infiṭār*
The Splitting

This *sūra* is Makkan and has 19 *āyat*s.

1. ***When the sky is split apart;***

2. ***...when the stars*** fall from their places and ***are strewn about;***

3. ***...when the seas flood and overflow*** – run into one another and become one body of water, and the salt and sweet water mix***;***

4. ***...when the graves are emptied out*** and their dead are resurrected***;***

5. ***...each self will know*** at that moment ***what it has sent ahead and left behind*** by way of actions it did and did not do. That means the Day of Resurrection.

6. ***O*** unbelieving ***man! What has deluded you in respect of your Noble Lord*** so that you disobeyed Him***?*** –

7. ***He Who created you*** when you were nothing, ***and formed you, and proportioned*** (read as *'adalaka* and *'addalalaka*) ***you*** as a balanced creation with symmetrical limbs, so that a hand is not in the place of a foot or vice versa, or one foot larger than the other,

8. ***...and assembled you in whatever way He willed.***

9. ***Yes indeed! But still you***, unbelievers of Makka, ***deny the Judgement*** – the repayment for actions. This denial stems from their being deluded by the generosity of Allah.

10. ***Standing over you are guardians*** – angels who record actions,

11. ***...noble*** in Allah's sight, ***recorders*** of actions –

12. ***...who know what you do.***

13. ***The truly good*** – the believers who are true in their faith – ***will be in perfect Bliss*** in Paradise.

14. ***The dissolute*** (unbelievers) ***will be in a Blazing Fire.***

15. ***They will*** enter it and ***roast in it on the Day of Judgement,***

16. ***...and will never get away from it.***

17. ***What will convey to you what the Day of Judgement is?***

18. ***Again, what will convey to you what the Day of Judgement is?*** The repetition is to emphasise its immensity.

19. ***It is the Day when no soul will have no power to help any other soul in any way.*** You will not be able to benefit anyone then. ***The command that Day will be Allah's alone*** – and there will be no middle ground, which is not the case in this world.

سُورَةُ المُطَفِّفِين

بِسْمِ ٱللَّهِ ٱلرَّحْمَٰنِ ٱلرَّحِيمِ

وَيْلٌ لِّلْمُطَفِّفِينَ ١ ٱلَّذِينَ إِذَا ٱكْتَالُوا۟ عَلَى ٱلنَّاسِ يَسْتَوْفُونَ ٢
وَإِذَا كَالُوهُمْ أَو وَّزَنُوهُمْ يُخْسِرُونَ ٣ أَلَا يَظُنُّ أُو۟لَٰٓئِكَ أَنَّهُم
مَّبْعُوثُونَ ٤ لِيَوْمٍ عَظِيمٍ ٥ يَوْمَ يَقُومُ ٱلنَّاسُ لِرَبِّ ٱلْعَٰلَمِينَ ٦
كَلَّآ إِنَّ كِتَٰبَ ٱلْفُجَّارِ لَفِى سِجِّينٍ ٧ وَمَآ أَدْرَىٰكَ مَا سِجِّينٌ ٨ كِتَٰبٌ
مَّرْقُومٌ ٩ وَيْلٌ يَوْمَئِذٍ لِّلْمُكَذِّبِينَ ١٠ ٱلَّذِينَ يُكَذِّبُونَ بِيَوْمِ ٱلدِّينِ ١١
وَمَا يُكَذِّبُ بِهِۦٓ إِلَّا كُلُّ مُعْتَدٍ أَثِيمٍ ١٢ إِذَا تُتْلَىٰ عَلَيْهِ ءَايَٰتُنَا قَالَ أَسَٰطِيرُ
ٱلْأَوَّلِينَ ١٣ كَلَّا ۖ بَلْ ۜ رَانَ عَلَىٰ قُلُوبِهِم مَّا كَانُوا۟ يَكْسِبُونَ ١٤ كَلَّآ إِنَّهُمْ
عَن رَّبِّهِمْ يَوْمَئِذٍ لَّمَحْجُوبُونَ ١٥ ثُمَّ إِنَّهُمْ لَصَالُوا۟ ٱلْجَحِيمِ ١٦ ثُمَّ يُقَالُ
هَٰذَا ٱلَّذِى كُنتُم بِهِۦ تُكَذِّبُونَ ١٧ كَلَّآ إِنَّ كِتَٰبَ ٱلْأَبْرَارِ لَفِى عِلِّيِّينَ
١٨ وَمَآ أَدْرَىٰكَ مَا عِلِّيُّونَ ١٩ كِتَٰبٌ مَّرْقُومٌ ٢٠ يَشْهَدُهُ ٱلْمُقَرَّبُونَ
٢١ إِنَّ ٱلْأَبْرَارَ لَفِى نَعِيمٍ ٢٢ عَلَى ٱلْأَرَآئِكِ يَنظُرُونَ ٢٣ تَعْرِفُ فِى
وُجُوهِهِمْ نَضْرَةَ ٱلنَّعِيمِ ٢٤ يُسْقَوْنَ مِن رَّحِيقٍ مَّخْتُومٍ ٢٥
خِتَٰمُهُۥ مِسْكٌ ۚ وَفِى ذَٰلِكَ فَلْيَتَنَافَسِ ٱلْمُتَنَٰفِسُونَ ٢٦ وَمِزَاجُهُۥ
مِن تَسْنِيمٍ ٢٧ عَيْنًا يَشْرَبُ بِهَا ٱلْمُقَرَّبُونَ ٢٨ إِنَّ ٱلَّذِينَ
أَجْرَمُوا۟ كَانُوا۟ مِنَ ٱلَّذِينَ ءَامَنُوا۟ يَضْحَكُونَ ٢٩ وَإِذَا مَرُّوا۟ بِهِمْ
يَتَغَامَزُونَ ٣٠ وَإِذَا ٱنقَلَبُوٓا۟ إِلَىٰٓ أَهْلِهِمُ ٱنقَلَبُوا۟ فَكِهِينَ ٣١
وَإِذَا رَأَوْهُمْ قَالُوٓا۟ إِنَّ هَٰٓؤُلَآءِ لَضَآلُّونَ ٣٢ وَمَآ أُرْسِلُوا۟ عَلَيْهِمْ
حَٰفِظِينَ ٣٣ فَٱلْيَوْمَ ٱلَّذِينَ ءَامَنُوا۟ مِنَ ٱلْكُفَّارِ يَضْحَكُونَ ٣٤
عَلَى ٱلْأَرَآئِكِ يَنظُرُونَ ٣٥ هَلْ ثُوِّبَ ٱلْكُفَّارُ مَا كَانُوا۟ يَفْعَلُونَ ٣٦

83. *Sūrat al-Muṭaffifīn* The Stinters

This *sūra* is Makkan or Madinan. It has 36 *āyats*.

1. ***Woe to the stinters!*** The word "Woe", *wayl*, means punishment or a valley in the Fire. –

2. ***Those who, when they take a measure from people, exact full measure,***

3. ***...but when they give them a measure or weight, hand over less than is due.*** They exact their due and then give short measure or weight to others.

4. ***Do such people not realise that they will be raised up*** – this question is a rebuke –

5. ***...on a Terrible Day*** – the Day of Rising –

6. ***...the Day mankind will stand before the Lord of all the worlds?*** – when they will be raised up from their graves in front of the Lord of all creatures for His command, reckoning and repayment.

7. ***No indeed! The Book of the dissolute is in Sijjīn*** – the Book of the actions of the unbelievers. It is said that Sijjīn is the book of all the actions of the *shayṭāns* and the unbelievers. It is also said to be the place of the lowest of the seven earths, and is the place of Iblīs and his armies.

8. ***And what will convey to you what*** the Book of ***Sijjin is?***

9. ***A clearly written*** sealed ***Book.***

10. ***Woe that Day to the deniers!***

11. ***Those who deny the Day of Reckoning*** and Repayment.

12. ***No one denies it except for every evil aggressor*** who exceeds the limits.

13. ***When Our Signs*** (the Qur'an) ***are recited to him, he says, 'Mere myths and legends of the previous peoples*** – stories which they wrote down in the past*!'*

14. ***No indeed!*** This is a rebuke and reprimand for what they said. ***But what they have earned*** by way of acts of disobedience ***has rusted up*** and covered ***their hearts.***

15. ***No indeed! Rather that Day*** – the Day of Rising – ***they will be veiled from their Lord*** and will not see Him.

16. ***Then they will*** enter and ***roast in the Blazing Fire.***

17. ***Then they will be told, 'This is what*** (the punishment) ***you denied.'***

18. ***No indeed! The Book of the truly good*** – the Book of the deeds of the believers who are sincere in their faith – ***is in 'Illiyūn.*** It is said to be the Book of all the good actions of the angels, and of the believers among the jinn and mankind. It is a place in the seventh heaven under the Throne.

19. ***And what will convey to you what*** the Book of ***'Illiyūn is?***

20. ***A clearly written***, sealed ***book.***

21. ***Those*** angels ***brought near will witness it.***

22. ***The truly good will be in perfect Bliss*** in the Garden,

23. ***...on couches*** in alcoves, ***gazing in wonder*** – contemplating the gifts that they have been given.

24. ***You will recognise in their faces the radiance of delight.***

25. ***They shall be given the choicest sealed wine to drink*** – this is a wine that is free from any impurity; its container is sealed and only opened by the person who drinks it –

26. ***...whose seal is musk*** – the dregs of his drink give off the fragrance of musk – ***let people with aspiration aspire to that*** – and race one another to obey Allah –

27. ***...mixed with Tasnīm,*** explained as

28. ***...a fountain at which Those Brought Near will drink*** and which they will enjoy.

29. ***Those who did evil*** – such as Abū Jahl and others like him – ***used to laugh at those who believed*** – such as 'Ammār, Bilāl and others like them.

30. ***When they passed by them*** (the believers), ***they*** (the wrongdoers) ***would wink at one another*** – they would indicate the believers with winks to mock them.

31. ***When they returned to their families, they would make a joke*** (read as *fakihīn* and *fākihīn*) ***of them*** (the believers).

32. ***When they saw them*** (the believers), ***they would say, 'Those people are misguided'*** because they believe in Muhammad, may Allah bless him and grant him peace.

33. Allah says: ***But they were not sent as guardians over them*** – of the believers or their actions, that they could turn them to their best interests.

34. ***So today*** (the Day of Rising) ***those who believe are laughing at the unbelievers,***

35. ***...on couches, gazing in wonder*** in Paradise. The believers will look from their houses at the unbelievers who are being punished. They will laugh at them as the unbelievers laughed at them in this world.

36. ***Have the unbelievers been rewarded*** and repaid ***for what they did?***

سُورَةُ الانشِقَاقِ

بِسۡمِ ٱللَّهِ ٱلرَّحۡمَٰنِ ٱلرَّحِيمِ

إِذَا ٱلسَّمَآءُ ٱنشَقَّتۡ ١ وَأَذِنَتۡ لِرَبِّهَا وَحُقَّتۡ ٢ وَإِذَا ٱلۡأَرۡضُ مُدَّتۡ
٣ وَأَلۡقَتۡ مَا فِيهَا وَتَخَلَّتۡ ٤ وَأَذِنَتۡ لِرَبِّهَا وَحُقَّتۡ ٥ يَٰٓأَيُّهَا
ٱلۡإِنسَٰنُ إِنَّكَ كَادِحٌ إِلَىٰ رَبِّكَ كَدۡحٗا فَمُلَٰقِيهِ ٦ فَأَمَّا مَنۡ أُوتِيَ
كِتَٰبَهُۥ بِيَمِينِهِۦ ٧ فَسَوۡفَ يُحَاسَبُ حِسَابٗا يَسِيرٗا ٨ وَيَنقَلِبُ
إِلَىٰٓ أَهۡلِهِۦ مَسۡرُورٗا ٩ وَأَمَّا مَنۡ أُوتِيَ كِتَٰبَهُۥ وَرَآءَ ظَهۡرِهِۦ ١٠ فَسَوۡفَ
يَدۡعُواْ ثُبُورٗا ١١ وَيَصۡلَىٰ سَعِيرًا ١٢ إِنَّهُۥ كَانَ فِيٓ أَهۡلِهِۦ مَسۡرُورًا ١٣
إِنَّهُۥ ظَنَّ أَن لَّن يَحُورَ ١٤ بَلَىٰٓۚ إِنَّ رَبَّهُۥ كَانَ بِهِۦ بَصِيرٗا ١٥ فَلَآ أُقۡسِمُ
بِٱلشَّفَقِ ١٦ وَٱلَّيۡلِ وَمَا وَسَقَ ١٧ وَٱلۡقَمَرِ إِذَا ٱتَّسَقَ ١٨
لَتَرۡكَبُنَّ طَبَقًا عَن طَبَقٖ ١٩ فَمَا لَهُمۡ لَا يُؤۡمِنُونَ ٢٠ وَإِذَا قُرِئَ
عَلَيۡهِمُ ٱلۡقُرۡءَانُ لَا يَسۡجُدُونَ ۩ ٢١ بَلِ ٱلَّذِينَ كَفَرُواْ يُكَذِّبُونَ
٢٢ وَٱللَّهُ أَعۡلَمُ بِمَا يُوعُونَ ٢٣ فَبَشِّرۡهُم بِعَذَابٍ أَلِيمٍ ٢٤
إِلَّا ٱلَّذِينَ ءَامَنُواْ وَعَمِلُواْ ٱلصَّٰلِحَٰتِ لَهُمۡ أَجۡرٌ غَيۡرُ مَمۡنُونِۭ ٢٥

84. *Sūrat al-Inshiqāq*
The Bursting

This *sūra* is Makkan and has 23 or 25 *āyat*s.

1. ***When the sky bursts open,***

2. ***...hearkening to its Lord as it is bound to do!*** When it hears and obeys and splits open as it must.

3. ***When the earth is flattened out***, its expanse is increased as a skin is stretched, and there no longer remains on it any building or mountain –

4. ***...and disgorges what is inside it*** – of the dead – ***and empties out*** – casts them onto the surface,

5. ***...hearkening to its Lord as it is bound to do*** – when it hears and obeys what is required of it. All of that will take place on the Day of Rising. After that, human beings will be shown their actions.

6. ***... Man, you are toiling laboriously*** – striving by means of your actions – ***towards*** the meeting with ***your Lord*** which happens at death, ***but meet Him you will!*** Man will be faced with his actions of good or evil on the Day of Rising.

7. ***As for him who is given his Book*** – the Book of his actions – ***in his right hand*** – in other words, the believer,

8. ***...he will be given an easy reckoning*** – this is in the presentation of his actions, as is reported in the *ḥadīth* in the two *Ṣaḥīḥ* Collections which states, "Whoever has his reckoning examined will be punished." After the presentation, he will be pardoned –

9. ***...and return to his family*** in Paradise ***joyfully.***

10. ***But as for him who is given his Book behind his back*** – this is the unbeliever who has his right hand chained to his neck; his left hand is put behind his back and he is given his book in it,

11. ***...he will cry out for destruction*** – when he sees the situation he is in, he will pray to be destroyed –

12. ***...but will*** enter and ***be roasted*** (read as *yaṣlā* and *yuṣallā*) ***in a Searing Blaze.***

13. ***He used to be exultant in his family*** – his clan in this world. He used to exult in his followers because of his clan*;*

14. ***...he thought that he was never going to return*** to his Lord.

15. Indeed, he certainly will return to Him. ***But in fact his Lord was always watching him!*** Allah knows that he will return to Him.

16. *No!*– (The word "No" is redundant) – ***I swear by the evening glow*** – the redness on the horizon after the setting of the sun,

17. ***...and the night and all it enshrouds*** – the animals and other things,

18. ***...and the moon when it is full*** of light and its light is at its greatest which is on the "white night" , the 14th of the lunar month,

19. ***...you will certainly mount up*** (read as *tarkabunna* and *tarka - banna*) ***stage by stage.*** "O people, you will proceed state after state, first death, then resurrected life, and after that the states of the Rising."

20. ***What is the matter with them*** (the unbelievers) ***that they do not believe*** – what prevents them from believing? What evidence do they have for abandoning faith when the proofs exist? –

21. ***...and, when the Qur'an is recited to them, do not prostrate?*** Why do they not humble themselves when it is recited and believe because of its inimitability?

22. ***In fact those who disbelieve say that it*** (the Resurrection and other things) ***is lies.***

23. ***But Allah knows best what they are storing in their hearts.*** He knows what is being collected in the pages of their actions in terms of unbelief, denial and evil deeds.

24. ***Give them the news of a painful punishment,***

25. ***...except those who believe and do right actions: they will have a wage that never fails.*** Their reward is not cut off nor decreased and they are not indebted for it.

سُورَةُ البُرُوجِ

بِسۡمِ ٱللَّهِ ٱلرَّحۡمَٰنِ ٱلرَّحِيمِ

وَٱلسَّمَآءِ ذَاتِ ٱلۡبُرُوجِ ﴿١﴾ وَٱلۡيَوۡمِ ٱلۡمَوۡعُودِ ﴿٢﴾ وَشَاهِدٖ وَمَشۡهُودٖ
﴿٣﴾ قُتِلَ أَصۡحَٰبُ ٱلۡأُخۡدُودِ ﴿٤﴾ ٱلنَّارِ ذَاتِ ٱلۡوَقُودِ ﴿٥﴾ إِذۡ هُمۡ عَلَيۡهَا
قُعُودٞ ﴿٦﴾ وَهُمۡ عَلَىٰ مَا يَفۡعَلُونَ بِٱلۡمُؤۡمِنِينَ شُهُودٞ ﴿٧﴾ وَمَا نَقَمُواْ
مِنۡهُمۡ إِلَّآ أَن يُؤۡمِنُواْ بِٱللَّهِ ٱلۡعَزِيزِ ٱلۡحَمِيدِ ﴿٨﴾ ٱلَّذِي لَهُۥ مُلۡكُ
ٱلسَّمَٰوَٰتِ وَٱلۡأَرۡضِۚ وَٱللَّهُ عَلَىٰ كُلِّ شَيۡءٖ شَهِيدٌ ﴿٩﴾ إِنَّ ٱلَّذِينَ
فَتَنُواْ ٱلۡمُؤۡمِنِينَ وَٱلۡمُؤۡمِنَٰتِ ثُمَّ لَمۡ يَتُوبُواْ فَلَهُمۡ عَذَابُ جَهَنَّمَ وَلَهُمۡ
عَذَابُ ٱلۡحَرِيقِ ﴿١٠﴾ إِنَّ ٱلَّذِينَ ءَامَنُواْ وَعَمِلُواْ ٱلصَّٰلِحَٰتِ لَهُمۡ
جَنَّٰتٞ تَجۡرِي مِن تَحۡتِهَا ٱلۡأَنۡهَٰرُۚ ذَٰلِكَ ٱلۡفَوۡزُ ٱلۡكَبِيرُ ﴿١١﴾ إِنَّ بَطۡشَ
رَبِّكَ لَشَدِيدٌ ﴿١٢﴾ إِنَّهُۥ هُوَ يُبۡدِئُ وَيُعِيدُ ﴿١٣﴾ وَهُوَ ٱلۡغَفُورُ ٱلۡوَدُودُ ﴿١٤﴾
ذُو ٱلۡعَرۡشِ ٱلۡمَجِيدُ ﴿١٥﴾ فَعَّالٞ لِّمَا يُرِيدُ ﴿١٦﴾ هَلۡ أَتَىٰكَ حَدِيثُ ٱلۡجُنُودِ
﴿١٧﴾ فِرۡعَوۡنَ وَثَمُودَ ﴿١٨﴾ بَلِ ٱلَّذِينَ كَفَرُواْ فِي تَكۡذِيبٖ ﴿١٩﴾ وَٱللَّهُ مِن
وَرَآئِهِم مُّحِيطُۢ ﴿٢٠﴾ بَلۡ هُوَ قُرۡءَانٞ مَّجِيدٞ ﴿٢١﴾ فِي لَوۡحٖ مَّحۡفُوظِۭ ﴿٢٢﴾

85. *Sūrat al-Burūj*
The Houses of the Zodiac

This *sūra* is Makkan and has 22 *āyat*s.

1. ***By Heaven, with its Houses of the Zodiac*** – the twelve constellations mentioned in *Sūrat al-Furqān,*

2. ***...and the Promised Day*** – the Day of Rising,

3. ***...and the witness and the witnessed!*** This may mean that the "witness" is Friday and the "witnessed" is the Day of 'Arafa, an interpretation made by three people in a *ḥadīth*. The first is an agreed time and the second has actions witnessed in it. The third is that the people and the angels visit it. The object of the oath is elided.

4. ***Cursed*** – the word *qutila*, which literally means "killed", is used as a curse – ***be the Companions of the Pit,***

5. ***...the fire well stocked with fuel,***

6. ***...when they were seated right beside it*** on chairs at the side of the pit,

7. ***...witnessing what they did to the believers***: how they tortured those who believed in Allah by throwing them into the fire when they would not recant their faith. The witnesses were present. It is related that Allah saved the believers cast into the fire by taking their souls before they actually fell into it – and that the fire rose up and burned the others who were present.

8. ***The only reason they punished them was because they believed in Allah, the Almighty*** in His kingdom, ***the All-Praiseworthy*** in what He does;

9. ***...Him to whom the Kingdom of the heavens and the earth belongs. Allah is Witness of all things*** – to all the objections made by the unbelievers against the believers simply because they believe.

10. ***Those who persecute believing men and women*** by burning them ***and then do not repent will have the punishment of Hell*** for their unbelief; and they ***shall have the punishment of the Burning*** of Hellfire. They will be punished in the Next World for burning the believers. It is said that that came about in this world when the fire burst out of the pit and burned them.

11. ***But those who believe and do right actions will have Gardens with rivers flowing under them. That is the Great Victory.***

12. ***Your Lord's assault*** on the unbelievers ***is very fierce.***

13. ***He originates*** creation ***and regenerates*** it***;*** and so He does not lack the power to do whatever He wishes.

14. ***He is the Ever-Forgiving*** of believers who do wrong actions***, the All-Loving*** towards His friends by honouring them***;***

15. ***...the Possessor of the Throne*** – its Creator and Owner***, the All-Glorious;***

16. ***... always the Doer of whatever He desires.*** Nothing is beyond His power.

17. ***Has the story reached you***, Muḥammad, ***of the legions...***

18. ***...of Pharaoh and Thamūd?*** It is their legions that are mentioned: they were destroyed because of their unbelief. This is directed to those who rejected the Prophet, may Allah bless him and grant him peace, and the Qur'an, so that they might be admonished.

19. ***Yet those who disbelieve insist on their denial*** of what was mentioned above –

20. ***...while Allah is encircling them from behind.*** No one and nothing can defend them from Him.

21. ***It is indeed a Glorious Qur'an...***

22. ***...preserved on a Tablet.*** It is above the seventh heaven. It is preserved from *shayṭān*s and from anything being altered in it. Its height extends between heaven and the earth and its width is from the east to the west. It is made of white pearl. All that was stated by Ibn 'Abbās, may Allah be pleased with him.

سُورَةُ الطَّارِق

بِسْمِ ٱللَّهِ ٱلرَّحْمَٰنِ ٱلرَّحِيمِ

وَٱلسَّمَآءِ وَٱلطَّارِقِ ١ وَمَآ أَدْرَىٰكَ مَا ٱلطَّارِقُ ٢ ٱلنَّجْمُ ٱلثَّاقِبُ ٣ إِن كُلُّ
نَفْسٍ لَّمَّا عَلَيْهَا حَافِظٌ ٤ فَلْيَنظُرِ ٱلْإِنسَٰنُ مِمَّ خُلِقَ ٥ خُلِقَ مِن مَّآءٍ
دَافِقٍ ٦ يَخْرُجُ مِنۢ بَيْنِ ٱلصُّلْبِ وَٱلتَّرَآئِبِ ٧ إِنَّهُۥ عَلَىٰ رَجْعِهِۦ لَقَادِرٌ ٨
يَوْمَ تُبْلَى ٱلسَّرَآئِرُ ٩ فَمَا لَهُۥ مِن قُوَّةٍ وَلَا نَاصِرٍ ١٠ وَٱلسَّمَآءِ ذَاتِ ٱلرَّجْعِ ١١
وَٱلْأَرْضِ ذَاتِ ٱلصَّدْعِ ١٢ إِنَّهُۥ لَقَوْلٌ فَصْلٌ ١٣ وَمَا هُوَ بِٱلْهَزْلِ ١٤ إِنَّهُمْ
يَكِيدُونَ كَيْدًا ١٥ وَأَكِيدُ كَيْدًا ١٦ فَمَهِّلِ ٱلْكَٰفِرِينَ أَمْهِلْهُمْ رُوَيْدًۢا ١٧

86. *Sūrat aṭ-Ṭāriq* The Night-Comer

This *sūra* is Makkan and has 17 *āyats*.

1. ***By Heaven and the Night-Comer!*** The word *ṭāriq* is said to mean anything that comes at night. This includes the stars, because they rise at night.

2. ***And what will convey to you what the Night-Comer is?*** What will teach you what it is? This repetition stresses its importance.

3. ***The Piercing Star!*** Possibly the Pleiades, or any star which emits light that pierces through the darkness.

4. ***There is no self that*** (read as *lammā* and *lamā*) ***has no guardian over it.*** This refers to the guardian angels who record all our good and evil actions.

5. ***Man has only to look at*** – reflect on and consider – ***what he was created from.***

6. ***He was created from a spurting fluid*** – the liquid proceeding from the sexual union of the man and the woman within the womb –

7. … a liquid ***emerging from between the back-bone*** of a man ***and the breast-bone*** of a woman.

8. ***He*** (Allah) ***certainly has the power to return him to life*** – to resurrect human beings after death. If a human being reflects on his origin, he will know that the One who is able to bring him into being must also have the power to resurrect him –

9. ***…on the Day when the secrets are sought out*** – tested and then exposed. "Secrets" means the innermost beliefs of the heart with respect to its faith and its intentions –

10. ***…and man*** – anyone who denies the Resurrection – ***will have no strength or helper*** – no power to defend himself against the Punishment or to avert it from himself.

11. ***By Heaven with its cyclical systems*** – the word used here, *raj'*, can also mean rain, because it recurs again and again –

12. ***…and the earth with its splitting seeds*** – plants which split open the earth,

13. *...it is truly a Decisive Word.* The Qur'an is a Word which distinguishes truth from falsehood.

14. *It is no joke.* It is neither a game nor vain falsehood.

15. *They* (the unbelievers) ***are hatching a plot*** – scheming against the Prophet, may Allah bless him and grant him peace.

16. *I too am hatching a plot.* I am leading them on from where they do not know.

17. *So bear with the unbelievers – bear with them for a while.* This is addressed to Muḥammad. The repetition is for emphasis. He is instructed to go easy with them. Then Allah seized them in the Battle of Badr. Bearing with them was abrogated by the *Āyat* of the Sword, when the command to fight and engage in *jihād* was given.

سُورَةُ الأَعْلَىٰ

بِسْمِ ٱللَّهِ ٱلرَّحْمَٰنِ ٱلرَّحِيمِ

سَبِّحِ ٱسْمَ رَبِّكَ ٱلْأَعْلَى ١ ٱلَّذِى خَلَقَ فَسَوَّىٰ ٢ وَٱلَّذِى قَدَّرَ فَهَدَىٰ
٣ وَٱلَّذِىٓ أَخْرَجَ ٱلْمَرْعَىٰ ٤ فَجَعَلَهُۥ غُثَآءً أَحْوَىٰ ٥ سَنُقْرِئُكَ
فَلَا تَنسَىٰٓ ٦ إِلَّا مَا شَآءَ ٱللَّهُ إِنَّهُۥ يَعْلَمُ ٱلْجَهْرَ وَمَا يَخْفَىٰ ٧ وَنُيَسِّرُكَ
لِلْيُسْرَىٰ ٨ فَذَكِّرْ إِن نَّفَعَتِ ٱلذِّكْرَىٰ ٩ سَيَذَّكَّرُ مَن يَخْشَىٰ ١٠
وَيَتَجَنَّبُهَا ٱلْأَشْقَى ١١ ٱلَّذِى يَصْلَى ٱلنَّارَ ٱلْكُبْرَىٰ ١٢ ثُمَّ لَا يَمُوتُ
فِيهَا وَلَا يَحْيَىٰ ١٣ قَدْ أَفْلَحَ مَن تَزَكَّىٰ ١٤ وَذَكَرَ ٱسْمَ رَبِّهِۦ فَصَلَّىٰ ١٥
بَلْ تُؤْثِرُونَ ٱلْحَيَوٰةَ ٱلدُّنْيَا ١٦ وَٱلْءَاخِرَةُ خَيْرٌ وَأَبْقَىٰٓ ١٧ إِنَّ
هَٰذَا لَفِى ٱلصُّحُفِ ٱلْأُولَىٰ ١٨ صُحُفِ إِبْرَٰهِيمَ وَمُوسَىٰ ١٩

87. *Sūrat al-A'lā*
The Most High

This *sūra* is Makkan and has 19 *āyat*s.

1. ***Glorify the Name of your Lord, the Most High:*** dissociate your Lord from anything that is not appropriate to Him.

2. ***...He who created and moulded*** – who gave His creation form and made its parts harmonious and balanced***;***

3. ***...He who determined*** whatever He wished ***and guided*** to whatever good or evil He has decreed***;***

4. ***...He who brings forth green pasture***: causes plantlife to grow***,***

5. ***...then makes it blackened stubble.*** After it has been green, He makes it dried out stubble, black and brittle.

6. ***We will cause you to recite*** the Qur'an – ***so that you do not forget*** – what you recite***,***

7. ***...except what Allah wills.*** You will only forget what Allah wills that you forget if He wishes to abrogate its recitation and judgement. The Prophet, may Allah bless him and grant him peace, used to recite the Qur'an aloud along with Jibrīl, fearing that he would forget. It is as if he was told, "Do not hasten it. You will not forget, so do not tire yourself by reciting it aloud." ***He*** (Allah) ***knows what is voiced out loud*** – in words and actions – ***and what is hidden.***

8. ***We will ease you to the Easy Way*** (Islam).

9. ***Remind, then,*** by means of the Qur'an, ***if the reminder benefits.*** Warn them, even if it does not benefit: it will benefit some and not benefit others.

10. ***He who has fear*** of Allah ***will be reminded*** by it echoing the *āyat*, *"So remind, with the Qur'an, whoever fears My Threat."* (50:45) –

11. ***...but the most miserable*** – meaning the unbelievers – ***will shun it*** and not pay any attention to it***:***

12. ***...those who will roast in the Greater Fire*** – the Fire in the Next World, the lesser fire being fire in this world –

13. ***...and then neither die nor live in it.*** They will not die and so have rest, nor will they have any kind of life.

14. ***He who has purified himself*** through faith ***will have success:***

15. ***...he who invokes the Name of his Lord and prays.*** He says the *takbīr* and prays the five prayers. That is something which concerns the Next World. The unbelievers of Makka turn away from it.

16. ***Yet still you prefer*** (read as *tu'thirūna*, and *yu'thirūna,* "they prefer") ***the life of this world*** to the Next World,

17. ***...though the Next World*** – which contains Paradise – ***is better and longer lasting.***

18. ***This is certainly in the earlier scriptures*** – the success of those who purify themselves and the Next World being better is in the earlier Books revealed before the Qur'an –

19. ***...the scri[tures*** – the ten scrolls ***of Ibrāhīm and*** the Torah of – ***Mūsā.***

سُورَةُ الغَاشِيَةِ

بِسۡمِ ٱللَّهِ ٱلرَّحۡمَٰنِ ٱلرَّحِيمِ

هَلۡ أَتَىٰكَ حَدِيثُ ٱلۡغَٰشِيَةِ ١ وُجُوهٞ يَوۡمَئِذٍ خَٰشِعَةٌ ٢
عَامِلَةٞ نَّاصِبَةٞ ٣ تَصۡلَىٰ نَارًا حَامِيَةٗ ٤ تُسۡقَىٰ مِنۡ عَيۡنٍ ءَانِيَةٖ ٥
لَّيۡسَ لَهُمۡ طَعَامٌ إِلَّا مِن ضَرِيعٖ ٦ لَّا يُسۡمِنُ وَلَا يُغۡنِي مِن جُوعٖ ٧
وُجُوهٞ يَوۡمَئِذٖ نَّاعِمَةٞ ٨ لِّسَعۡيِهَا رَاضِيَةٞ ٩ فِي جَنَّةٍ عَالِيَةٖ ١٠
لَّا تَسۡمَعُ فِيهَا لَٰغِيَةٗ ١١ فِيهَا عَيۡنٞ جَارِيَةٞ ١٢ فِيهَا سُرُرٞ مَّرۡفُوعَةٞ ١٣
وَأَكۡوَابٞ مَّوۡضُوعَةٞ ١٤ وَنَمَارِقُ مَصۡفُوفَةٞ ١٥ وَزَرَابِيُّ مَبۡثُوثَةٌ ١٦
أَفَلَا يَنظُرُونَ إِلَى ٱلۡإِبِلِ كَيۡفَ خُلِقَتۡ ١٧ وَإِلَى ٱلسَّمَآءِ كَيۡفَ
رُفِعَتۡ ١٨ وَإِلَى ٱلۡجِبَالِ كَيۡفَ نُصِبَتۡ ١٩ وَإِلَى ٱلۡأَرۡضِ كَيۡفَ
سُطِحَتۡ ٢٠ فَذَكِّرۡ إِنَّمَآ أَنتَ مُذَكِّرٞ ٢١ لَّسۡتَ عَلَيۡهِم
بِمُصَيۡطِرٍ ٢٢ إِلَّا مَن تَوَلَّىٰ وَكَفَرَ ٢٣ فَيُعَذِّبُهُ ٱللَّهُ ٱلۡعَذَابَ
ٱلۡأَكۡبَرَ ٢٤ إِنَّ إِلَيۡنَآ إِيَابَهُمۡ ٢٥ ثُمَّ إِنَّ عَلَيۡنَا حِسَابَهُم ٢٦

88. *Sūrat al-Ghāshiya* The Overwhelmer

This *sūra* is Makkan and has 26 *āyat*s.

1. ***Has news of the Overwhelmer*** – the Day of Rising, which is so called because it will overwhelm creatures with its terrors – ***reached you?***

2. ***Some faces on that Day will be downcast;***

3. ***...labouring, toiling endlessly*** – burdened down with chains and fetters;

4. ***...roasting*** (read as *taṣlā* and *tuṣlā*) ***in a red-hot Fire;***

5. ***...drinking from a boiling spring.***

6. ***They will have no food but a bitter, thorny bush*** – a sort of thorn bush which animals do not eat because of its disgusting taste –

7. ***...which neither nourishes nor satisfies.***

8. ***Some faces on that Day will be radiant*** and beautiful,

9. In the Next World, they will be ***well-pleased with their efforts*** and obedience in this world because of the reward that they have received for it –

10. ***...in an elevated Garden*** – elevated both physically and spiritually –

11. ***...where no prattle is ever heard*** (read as *tasma'u, tusma'u* and *yusma'u*).

12. ***In it are a gushing spring*** – a generic, here meaning "springs",

13. ***...and raised-up couches*** – elevated in essence, worth and actuality,

14. ***...and goblets set out*** – which are drinking vessels without handles. They are placed at the edge of springs, ready to be drunk,

15. ***...and lined-up cushions*** piled by their sides for them to lean on;

16. ***...and outspread*** velvet ***rugs.***

17. ***Have they*** (the unbelievers of Makka) ***not looked at*** and considered ***the camel, how it was created?*** –

18. *...and at the sky, how it was raised up? –*

19. *...and at the mountains, how they were embedded? –*

20. *...and at the earth, – how it was smoothed out?* All these things are cited as evidence of the power and oneness of Allah. Camels are mentioned first because the Arabs had closer contact with them than any other animals. "Smoothed out" is used of the earth because it has the appearance of being level.

21. *So remind them* of the blessings of Allah and the evidence of His oneness***: You are only a reminder.***

22. *You are not in control* (read as *muṣayṭir* and *musayṭir*) ***of them.*** You are not their overseer. This was before the command came to engage in *jihād.*

23. *But as for anyone who turns away* from faith ***and disbelieves*** in the Qur'an,

24. *Allah will punish him with the Greater Punishment* – punishment in the Next World, the lesser being punishment in this world by killing and capture.

25. *Certainly it is to Us they will return* after death.

26. *Then their Reckoning is Our concern.* We will repay them with an eternal repayment.

سُورَةُ الفَجْرِ

بِسْمِ اللَّهِ الرَّحْمَٰنِ الرَّحِيمِ

وَالْفَجْرِ ﴿١﴾ وَلَيَالٍ عَشْرٍ ﴿٢﴾ وَالشَّفْعِ وَالْوَتْرِ ﴿٣﴾ وَاللَّيْلِ إِذَا يَسْرِ
﴿٤﴾ هَلْ فِي ذَٰلِكَ قَسَمٌ لِّذِي حِجْرٍ ﴿٥﴾ أَلَمْ تَرَ كَيْفَ فَعَلَ رَبُّكَ بِعَادٍ
﴿٦﴾ إِرَمَ ذَاتِ الْعِمَادِ ﴿٧﴾ الَّتِي لَمْ يُخْلَقْ مِثْلُهَا فِي الْبِلَادِ ﴿٨﴾
وَثَمُودَ الَّذِينَ جَابُوا الصَّخْرَ بِالْوَادِ ﴿٩﴾ وَفِرْعَوْنَ ذِي الْأَوْتَادِ ﴿١٠﴾
الَّذِينَ طَغَوْا فِي الْبِلَادِ ﴿١١﴾ فَأَكْثَرُوا فِيهَا الْفَسَادَ ﴿١٢﴾ فَصَبَّ
عَلَيْهِمْ رَبُّكَ سَوْطَ عَذَابٍ ﴿١٣﴾ إِنَّ رَبَّكَ لَبِالْمِرْصَادِ ﴿١٤﴾ فَأَمَّا
الْإِنسَانُ إِذَا مَا ابْتَلَاهُ رَبُّهُ فَأَكْرَمَهُ وَنَعَّمَهُ فَيَقُولُ رَبِّي أَكْرَمَنِ
﴿١٥﴾ وَأَمَّا إِذَا مَا ابْتَلَاهُ فَقَدَرَ عَلَيْهِ رِزْقَهُ فَيَقُولُ رَبِّي أَهَانَنِ ﴿١٦﴾
كَلَّا بَل لَّا تُكْرِمُونَ الْيَتِيمَ ﴿١٧﴾ وَلَا تَحَاضُّونَ عَلَىٰ طَعَامِ
الْمِسْكِينِ ﴿١٨﴾ وَتَأْكُلُونَ التُّرَاثَ أَكْلًا لَّمًّا ﴿١٩﴾
وَتُحِبُّونَ الْمَالَ حُبًّا جَمًّا ﴿٢٠﴾ كَلَّا إِذَا دُكَّتِ الْأَرْضُ دَكًّا
دَكًّا ﴿٢١﴾ وَجَاءَ رَبُّكَ وَالْمَلَكُ صَفًّا صَفًّا ﴿٢٢﴾ وَجِيءَ يَوْمَئِذٍ
بِجَهَنَّمَ يَوْمَئِذٍ يَتَذَكَّرُ الْإِنسَانُ وَأَنَّىٰ لَهُ الذِّكْرَىٰ ﴿٢٣﴾
يَقُولُ يَا لَيْتَنِي قَدَّمْتُ لِحَيَاتِي ﴿٢٤﴾ فَيَوْمَئِذٍ لَّا يُعَذِّبُ عَذَابَهُ أَحَدٌ ﴿٢٥﴾
وَلَا يُوثِقُ وَثَاقَهُ أَحَدٌ ﴿٢٦﴾ يَا أَيَّتُهَا النَّفْسُ الْمُطْمَئِنَّةُ ﴿٢٧﴾ ارْجِعِي
إِلَىٰ رَبِّكِ رَاضِيَةً مَّرْضِيَّةً ﴿٢٨﴾ فَادْخُلِي فِي عِبَادِي ﴿٢٩﴾ وَادْخُلِي جَنَّتِي ﴿٣٠﴾

89. *Sūrat al-Fajr*
The Dawn

This *sūra* is Makkan. It has 30 *āyats*.

1. ***By the dawn*** of every day

2. ***...and ten nights*** of Dhū'l-Ḥijja,

3. ***...and the even and odd,***

4. ***...and the night when it travels on*** – comes and goes***!***

5. ***Is there not in that an oath for the intelligent?*** The word *ḥijr* means intellect here. "Is that not an oath by which you will be punished, o unbelievers of Makka?"

6. ***Do you,*** Muḥammad, ***not see what your Lord did with 'Ād –***

7. ***Iram of the*** tall ***Columns*** – that was the first nation of 'Ād. Some of the columns were forty cubits tall –

8. ***...whose like was not created in any land*** – no one was like them in their power and strength***,***

9. ***...and Thamūd who carved out*** huge ***rocks in the valley-side*** – and made them into dwellings, the valley referred to being Wadī'l-Qurā***,***

10. ***...and Pharaoh of the Stakes*** – he used to drive four pegs into the ground, to which he would tie the hands and feet of those he was going to torture **–**

11. ***...all of whom were*** insolent and unjust ***tyrants in their lands...***

12. ***...and caused much corruption in them*** by killing and other things***?***

13. ***So your Lord unleashed on them a scourging punishment?***

14. ***Your Lord is always lying in wait*** – observing the actions of His slaves; He does not miss any of them, so that He can repay them for them**.**

15. ***As for*** unbelieving ***man, when his Lord tests him by honouring him*** with wealth and other things ***and favouring him, he says, 'My Lord has honoured me!'***

16. ***But then when He tests him by restricting his provision, he says, 'My Lord has humiliated me!'***

17. ***No indeed! You*** (the unbelievers of Makka) ***do not honour*** (read as *tukrimūna* or as *yukrimūna*, "they do not honour") ***orphans*** – you are not good to orphans in spite of their wealth, or they do not give them their rightful inheritance…

18. ***…nor do you urge*** (*taḥāḍḍūna, taḥuḍḍūna* also *yaḥāḍḍūna*, "they do not urge") ***the feeding of the poor*** – on yourselves or others…

19. ***…you devour*** (read as *ta'kulūna*, also *ya'kulūna*, "they devour") ***inheritance with voracious appetites*** – taking the portions of inheritance which should go to women and children as well as your own shares or added to your property –

20. ***…and you have*** (read as *tuḥibbūna*, also *yuḥībbūna*, "they have") ***an insatiable love of wealth*** and so do not spend it.

21. ***No indeed!*** The "No" here indicates the introduction of a new subject. ***When the earth is crushed and ground to dust*** and everything on it is destroyed and brought to nothing,

22. ***…and*** the command of ***your Lord arrives with the angels*** – the word "*malak,*" which is singular, is here used generically, meaning the angels in general – ***rank upon rank*** – row on row or in many rows –

23. ***…and that Day Hell is produced*** – Hell will be brought on that day, drawn by seven thousand thongs, and each thong will be pulled by seventy thousand angels. It will be seething and hissing – ***that Day*** unbelieving ***man will remember*** what he neglected then***; but how will the remembrance help him?*** It will be of no use to him at that time.

24. ***He will say*** – when he remembers – ***'Oh! If only I had prepared in advance for this life of mine!'*** "Would that I had advanced good deeds and faith for a pleasing life in the Next World or for my time in the life of this world."

25. ***That Day no one will punish*** (read as *yu'adhdhibu* and *yu'adhdhabu*) ***as He punishes,***

26. ***…and no one will shackle*** (read as *yūthiqu* and *yūthaqu*) ***as He shackles.*** The pronoun refers to Allah Almighty: He will not leave it to anyone else. Those punished and shackled are the unbelievers.

27. ***'O self at rest and at peace*** – this is the soul which has certainty: it means the true believer,

28. ***…return to your Lord, well-pleasing and well-pleased!*** This will be said to him when he dies. In other words: "Return to Allah's command and will, pleased with His reward and pleasing to Allah because of His actions." He will have both qualities. At the Resurrection, the soul will be told:

29. ***Enter among My*** righteous ***slaves.***

30. ***Enter My Garden*** with them.*'*

سُورَةُ ٱلۡبَلَدِ

بِسۡمِ ٱللَّهِ ٱلرَّحۡمَٰنِ ٱلرَّحِيمِ

لَآ أُقۡسِمُ بِهَٰذَا ٱلۡبَلَدِ ١ وَأَنتَ حِلُّۢ بِهَٰذَا ٱلۡبَلَدِ ٢ وَوَالِدٖ وَمَا وَلَدَ
٣ لَقَدۡ خَلَقۡنَا ٱلۡإِنسَٰنَ فِي كَبَدٍ ٤ أَيَحۡسَبُ أَن لَّن يَقۡدِرَ عَلَيۡهِ
أَحَدٞ ٥ يَقُولُ أَهۡلَكۡتُ مَالٗا لُّبَدًا ٦ أَيَحۡسَبُ أَن لَّمۡ يَرَهُۥٓ أَحَدٌ
٧ أَلَمۡ نَجۡعَل لَّهُۥ عَيۡنَيۡنِ ٨ وَلِسَانٗا وَشَفَتَيۡنِ ٩ وَهَدَيۡنَٰهُ
ٱلنَّجۡدَيۡنِ ١٠ فَلَا ٱقۡتَحَمَ ٱلۡعَقَبَةَ ١١ وَمَآ أَدۡرَىٰكَ مَا ٱلۡعَقَبَةُ ١٢
فَكُّ رَقَبَةٍ ١٣ أَوۡ إِطۡعَٰمٞ فِي يَوۡمٖ ذِي مَسۡغَبَةٖ ١٤ يَتِيمٗا ذَا مَقۡرَبَةٍ
١٥ أَوۡ مِسۡكِينٗا ذَا مَتۡرَبَةٖ ١٦ ثُمَّ كَانَ مِنَ ٱلَّذِينَ ءَامَنُواْ وَتَوَاصَوۡاْ
بِٱلصَّبۡرِ وَتَوَاصَوۡاْ بِٱلۡمَرۡحَمَةِ ١٧ أُوْلَٰٓئِكَ أَصۡحَٰبُ ٱلۡمَيۡمَنَةِ ١٨ وَٱلَّذِينَ
كَفَرُواْ بِـَٔايَٰتِنَا هُمۡ أَصۡحَٰبُ ٱلۡمَشۡـَٔمَةِ ١٩ عَلَيۡهِمۡ نَارٞ مُّؤۡصَدَةُۢ ٢٠

90. *Sūrat al-Balad*
The City

This *sūra* is Makkan. It has 20 *āyats*.

1. ***I swear by this city*** (Makka) –

2. ***...and you***, Muḥammad, ***are resident in this city*** – this is one meaning of the word *ḥill;* another is "This land is lawful to you and so you may fight in it." Allah carried out this promise on the day of the Conquest of Makka. This sentence is interposed in the middle of the oath.

3. ***...and by a father and what he fathered*** – meaning Ādam and his descendants.

4. ***We created man*** – meant generically – ***in trouble.*** He was created in toil and difficulty in the disasters of this world and in the hardships of the Next World.

5. ***Does he suppose that no one has power over him?*** Does the strongman of Quraysh suppose this? It is said that he was Abū'l-Ashadd ibn Kalda.

6. ***He says, 'I have consumed*** (spent) ***vast quantities of wealth*** in opposition to Muḥammad.*'*

7. ***Does he imagine that no one has seen him?*** Does he think that no one saw what he spent, and so knows how much it was? Allah knows the amount and will repay him for his evil deeds.

8. ***Have We not given him two eyes,***

9. ***...and a tongue and two lips,***

10. ***...and shown him the two highways*** – made clear to him the path of good and the path of evil*?*

11. ***But he has not braved the steep ascent.***

12. ***What will convey to you what the steep ascent is?*** This is repeated because of its great importance.

13. ***It is to free a slave,***

14. ***...or to feed on a day of hunger***

15. ***...an orphaned relative...***

16. ***...or a poor man in the dust*** because of his poverty;

17. ***...then*** at the same time ***to be one of those who believe and urge each other to be steadfast*** – in performing acts of obedience and in refraining from acts of disobedience – ***and urge each other to be compassionate*** – to have mercy on creatures.

18. ***Those*** who have these qualities ***are the Companions of the Right.***

19. ***Those who reject Our signs, they are the Companions of the Left.***

20. ***Above them is a sealed*** (read as *mu'ṣada* and *muṣada*) – covering – ***vault of Fire.***

سُورَةُ الشَّمْسِ

بِسْمِ ٱللَّهِ ٱلرَّحْمَٰنِ ٱلرَّحِيمِ

وَٱلشَّمْسِ وَضُحَىٰهَا ﴿١﴾ وَٱلْقَمَرِ إِذَا تَلَىٰهَا ﴿٢﴾ وَٱلنَّهَارِ إِذَا جَلَّىٰهَا ﴿٣﴾
وَٱلَّيْلِ إِذَا يَغْشَىٰهَا ﴿٤﴾ وَٱلسَّمَآءِ وَمَا بَنَىٰهَا ﴿٥﴾ وَٱلْأَرْضِ وَمَا طَحَىٰهَا
﴿٦﴾ وَنَفْسٍ وَمَا سَوَّىٰهَا ﴿٧﴾ فَأَلْهَمَهَا فُجُورَهَا وَتَقْوَىٰهَا ﴿٨﴾ قَدْ
أَفْلَحَ مَن زَكَّىٰهَا ﴿٩﴾ وَقَدْ خَابَ مَن دَسَّىٰهَا ﴿١٠﴾ كَذَّبَتْ ثَمُودُ
بِطَغْوَىٰهَآ ﴿١١﴾ إِذِ ٱنۢبَعَثَ أَشْقَىٰهَا ﴿١٢﴾ فَقَالَ لَهُمْ رَسُولُ ٱللَّهِ
نَاقَةَ ٱللَّهِ وَسُقْيَٰهَا ﴿١٣﴾ فَكَذَّبُوهُ فَعَقَرُوهَا فَدَمْدَمَ
عَلَيْهِمْ رَبُّهُم بِذَنۢبِهِمْ فَسَوَّىٰهَا ﴿١٤﴾ وَلَا يَخَافُ عُقْبَٰهَا ﴿١٥﴾

91. *Sūrat ash-Shams*
The Sun

This *sūra* is Makkan and has 15 *āyat*s.

1. ***By the sun and its morning brightness,***

2. ***...and the moon when it follows it*** by rising when the sun set,

3. ***...and the day when it displays it*** – when it is high in the sky,

4. ***...and the night when it conceals it*** and envelops it with its darkness,

5. ***...and the sky and what erected it,***

6. ***...and the earth and what extended it,***

7. ***...and the self*** – meant generically – ***and what proportioned it,***

8. ***...and inspired it with depravity or fear of Allah*** – made clear to it the path of good and evil*!*

9. ***He who purifies it*** of wrong actions ***has succeeded;***

10. ***...he who covers it up*** by acts of disobedience ***has failed.***

11. ***Thamūd denied in their excessive tyranny*** and insolence; the Messenger to Thamūd was Ṣāliḥ,

12. ***...when the worst of them rushed ahead*** – this was a man named Quddār who rushed to hamstring the camel with their approval –

13. ***...and the Messenger of Allah*** – Ṣāliḥ – ***had said to them, 'This is the she-camel of Allah, so let her drink*** on her day*!'* They alternated at the water source – one day for the She-camel and the next day for them.

14. ***But they denied him*** when he said that that the instruction was from Allah; and as a consequence of their disobeying the punishment of Allah descended on them – ***and they hamstrung her*** – and killed the She-camel so that they could have the water that she drank. ***So their Lord crushed them*** with the punishment ***for their sin and flattened them***: in other words, He totally enveloped them in it so that none of them escaped.

15. ***And*** (read as *walā* and *falā*) ***He does not fear the consequences.***

سُورَةُ اللَّيۡلِ

بِسۡمِ ٱللَّهِ ٱلرَّحۡمَٰنِ ٱلرَّحِيمِ

وَٱلَّيۡلِ إِذَا يَغۡشَىٰ ١ وَٱلنَّهَارِ إِذَا تَجَلَّىٰ ٢ وَمَا خَلَقَ ٱلذَّكَرَ وَٱلۡأُنثَىٰٓ ٣
إِنَّ سَعۡيَكُمۡ لَشَتَّىٰ ٤ فَأَمَّا مَنۡ أَعۡطَىٰ وَٱتَّقَىٰ ٥ وَصَدَّقَ بِٱلۡحُسۡنَىٰ ٦
فَسَنُيَسِّرُهُۥ لِلۡيُسۡرَىٰ ٧ وَأَمَّا مَنۢ بَخِلَ وَٱسۡتَغۡنَىٰ ٨ وَكَذَّبَ بِٱلۡحُسۡنَىٰ
٩ فَسَنُيَسِّرُهُۥ لِلۡعُسۡرَىٰ ١٠ وَمَا يُغۡنِي عَنۡهُ مَالُهُۥٓ إِذَا تَرَدَّىٰٓ ١١ إِنَّ عَلَيۡنَا
لَلۡهُدَىٰ ١٢ وَإِنَّ لَنَا لَلۡأٓخِرَةَ وَٱلۡأُولَىٰ ١٣ فَأَنذَرۡتُكُمۡ نَارٗا تَلَظَّىٰ ١٤
لَا يَصۡلَىٰهَآ إِلَّا ٱلۡأَشۡقَى ١٥ ٱلَّذِي كَذَّبَ وَتَوَلَّىٰ ١٦ وَسَيُجَنَّبُهَا
ٱلۡأَتۡقَى ١٧ ٱلَّذِي يُؤۡتِي مَالَهُۥ يَتَزَكَّىٰ ١٨ وَمَا لِأَحَدٍ عِندَهُۥ مِن
نِّعۡمَةٖ تُجۡزَىٰٓ ١٩ إِلَّا ٱبۡتِغَآءَ وَجۡهِ رَبِّهِ ٱلۡأَعۡلَىٰ ٢٠ وَلَسَوۡفَ يَرۡضَىٰ ٢١

92. *Sūrat al-Layl*
The Night

This *sūra* is Makkan and has 21 *āyat*s.

1. ***By the night when it conceals*** what is between heaven and earth with its darkness,

2. ***...and the day when it reveals*** things and manifests them,

3. ***...and the creation of male and female*** **–** Ādam and Ḥawwā', and every male and female since. Anyone whom we consider a hermaphrodite is either male or female in the sight of Allah. If someone swears that he will not speak to a male or female and then speaks to a hermaphrodite, he has broken his oath –

4. ***...truly there is a vast difference in your striving*** in your actions*!* Some act in ways that lead to the Garden by obedience and some act in ways that lead to the Fire by disobedience.

5. ***As for him who gives*** what is due to Allah ***and is godfearing,***

6. ***...and confirms the Good,*** meaning the statement: "There is no god but Allah,"

7. ***We will pave his way to Ease*** (the Garden).

8. ***But as for him who is stingy*** about what is due to Allah ***and self-satisfied,*** feeling he has no need of Allah's reward,

9. ***...and denies the Good*** – see *āyat* 6 above,

10. ***We will ease his way to Difficulty*** (the Fire).

11. ***His wealth will not help him when he plummets to the depths*** of the Fire.

12. ***Assuredly guidance is up to Us*** – Allah makes the Path of Guidance clear from the Path of Misguidance, so that He is obeyed when the former is followed; and He forbids people to engage in the latter,

13. ***...and both the Last and First belong to Us.*** The First is this world. "Whoever seeks them from anyone other than Us errs."

14. ***I have warned you***, people of Makka, ***of a Fire that rages*** and burns,

15. ***...in which only the most wretched will*** enter and ***roast:***

16. ***...those who denied*** the Prophet ***and turned away*** from faith. This extenuation is the explanation of His words, *"He forgives whomever He wills for anything apart from that."* (4:48) What is meant here is eternal roasting.

17. ***Those who are the most godfearing will be far removed from it:***

18. ***...those who give their wealth to purify themselves*** – they purify their wealth in the sight of Allah Almighty by giving Allah the due on it without showing off or seeking a good reputation in return. Then it becomes pure in the sight of Allah. This was revealed about Abū Bakr aṣ-Ṣiddīq, may Allah be pleased with him. when he bought Bilāl, who was being tortured for his faith, and set him free. The unbelievers said, "He did that for a favour he owed him," and then this was revealed,

19. ***...not to repay someone else for a favour done –***

20. ***...desiring only the Face of their Lord Most High*** – in other words, seeking the reward of Allah.

21. ***They will certainly be satisfied*** with the reward that they are given in Paradise. The *āyat* includes all those who perform actions which please Allah and who will therefore be far from the Fire and rewarded.

سُورَةُ الضُّحَىٰ

بِسْمِ اللَّهِ الرَّحْمَٰنِ الرَّحِيمِ

وَالضُّحَىٰ ١ وَاللَّيْلِ إِذَا سَجَىٰ ٢ مَا وَدَّعَكَ رَبُّكَ وَمَا قَلَىٰ ٣
وَلَلْآخِرَةُ خَيْرٌ لَّكَ مِنَ الْأُولَىٰ ٤ وَلَسَوْفَ يُعْطِيكَ رَبُّكَ
فَتَرْضَىٰ ٥ أَلَمْ يَجِدْكَ يَتِيمًا فَآوَىٰ ٦ وَوَجَدَكَ ضَالًّا
فَهَدَىٰ ٧ وَوَجَدَكَ عَائِلًا فَأَغْنَىٰ ٨ فَأَمَّا الْيَتِيمَ فَلَا تَقْهَرْ
٩ وَأَمَّا السَّائِلَ فَلَا تَنْهَرْ ١٠ وَأَمَّا بِنِعْمَةِ رَبِّكَ فَحَدِّثْ ١١

93. *Sūrat aḍ-Ḍuḥā*
The Morning Brightness

This *sūra* is Makkan. It has 11 *āyats*. When it was revealed, the Prophet, may Allah bless him and grant him peace, said the *takbīr* at the end of it, and so it is *sunna* to say the *takbīr* at the end of it. It should be said at the end of this *sūra* and at the end of every *sūra* after it. The formula to be used is either *"Allāhu akbar"* or *"Lā ilaha illā'llāhu wa'llāhu akbar"*.

1. ***By the morning brightness*** – the beginning of the day, or all of the morning –

2. ***...and the night when it is still!*** – covers everything with its darkness, or is still –

3. ***...your Lord has not abandoned you,*** Muḥammad, ***nor does He hate you.*** This was revealed at a time when nothing had been revealed for fifteen days and the unbelievers said, "Your Lord has abandoned you and hates you."

4. ***And the Last will indeed be better for you than the First.*** Because of the honours for you in the Next World, which will be better than anything in this world.

5. ***Your Lord will soon give to you*** ample good things in the Next World ***and you will be satisfied*** with that. The Prophet, may Allah bless him and grant him peace, said, "I will not be pleased if any of my Community remains in the Fire." This is the end of the oath.

6. ***Did He not find you orphaned and shelter you?*** "He found you without a father before you were born or else after that, and gave you shelter with your uncle, Abū Ṭālib."

7. ***Did He not find you wandering*** without the Sharī'a ***and guide you*** to it***?***

8. ***Did He not find you impoverished and enrich you?*** He enriched you with what was enough for you, from booty and other things. We read in a *ḥadīth*, "Wealth does not come from an abundance of goods. True wealth is contentment."

9. ***So as for orphans, do not oppress them*** – do not take their property or inflict any other form of oppression*;*

10. ***…and as for beggars, do not berate them*** for being poor.

11. ***And as for the blessing of your Lord*** – those of Prophethood and other things – ***speak out!***

سُورَةُ الشَّرْحِ

بِسْمِ ٱللَّهِ ٱلرَّحْمَٰنِ ٱلرَّحِيمِ

أَلَمْ نَشْرَحْ لَكَ صَدْرَكَ ﴿١﴾ وَوَضَعْنَا عَنكَ وِزْرَكَ ﴿٢﴾ ٱلَّذِىٓ
أَنقَضَ ظَهْرَكَ ﴿٣﴾ وَرَفَعْنَا لَكَ ذِكْرَكَ ﴿٤﴾ فَإِنَّ مَعَ ٱلْعُسْرِ يُسْرًا ﴿٥﴾ إِنَّ
مَعَ ٱلْعُسْرِ يُسْرًا ﴿٦﴾ فَإِذَا فَرَغْتَ فَٱنصَبْ ﴿٧﴾ وَإِلَىٰ رَبِّكَ فَٱرْغَب ﴿٨﴾

سُورَةُ التِّينِ

بِسْمِ ٱللَّهِ ٱلرَّحْمَٰنِ ٱلرَّحِيمِ

وَٱلتِّينِ وَٱلزَّيْتُونِ ﴿١﴾ وَطُورِ سِينِينَ ﴿٢﴾ وَهَٰذَا ٱلْبَلَدِ ٱلْأَمِينِ ﴿٣﴾
لَقَدْ خَلَقْنَا ٱلْإِنسَٰنَ فِىٓ أَحْسَنِ تَقْوِيمٍ ﴿٤﴾ ثُمَّ رَدَدْنَٰهُ أَسْفَلَ سَٰفِلِينَ
﴿٥﴾ إِلَّا ٱلَّذِينَ ءَامَنُوا۟ وَعَمِلُوا۟ ٱلصَّٰلِحَٰتِ فَلَهُمْ أَجْرٌ غَيْرُ مَمْنُونٍ ﴿٦﴾
فَمَا يُكَذِّبُكَ بَعْدُ بِٱلدِّينِ ﴿٧﴾ أَلَيْسَ ٱللَّهُ بِأَحْكَمِ ٱلْحَٰكِمِينَ ﴿٨﴾

94. *Sūrat al-Inshirāḥ*
The Expanding

This *sūra* is Makkan and has 8 *ayat*s.

1. ***Did We not expand your breast for you*** – Muḥammad, with Prophethood and other things –

2. ***...and remove from you your load***

3. ***...which weighed down your back?*** An aspect of that is the words of Allah Almighty, *"So that Allah may forgive you your earlier errors and any later ones."* (48:2)

4. ***Did We not raise your renown high*** – so that you are mentioned together with Allah in the *adhān, iqāma, tashahhud*, *khuṭba*, and other things***?***

5. ***For truly with hardship comes ease;***

6. ***...truly with hardship comes ease.*** The Prophet, may Allah bless him and grant him peace, experienced harshness from the unbelievers but then had ease when he was given victory over them.

7. ***So when you have finished*** the prayer ***work on*** – strive in making supplication –

8. ***...and make your Lord your goal*** – and entreat Him.

95. *Sūrat at-Tīn*
The Fig

This *sūra* is Makkan and has 8 *āyat*s.

1. ***By the fig and the olive*** – this is either the fruit which is eaten or possibly refers to two mountains in greater Syria where both trees grow,

2. ***...and Mount Sinai*** – the mountain where Allah Almighty spoke to Mūsā. *"Sīnīn"* means either blessed or beautified with fruit trees,

3. ***...and this safe land!*** – meaning Makka, because people are safe in it, both in the Jāhiliyya and in Islam.

4. ***We created man*** – meant generically – ***in the finest mould***: the most balanced and harmonious form.

5. ***Then We reduced him to the lowest of the low*** – as occurs with some individuals, indicating senility and weakness. So the actions of the believer are less than they were when he was young, and yet he will still have the reward for them. Allah says,

6. ***...except for those who believe and do right actions: they will have a*** perpetual ***wage that never fails.*** In a *ḥadīth* we find: "When a believer reaches old age, whatever actions he is unable to do are recorded for him."

7. ***What could make you***, unbelievers, ***deny the Reckoning after this?*** – after what has been mentioned about the creation of the human being in the best form and then his return to the lowest of the low, which proves that Allah has the power to resurrect, how can you deny the coming repayment which is preceded by resurrection and reckoning?

8. ***Is Allah not the Justest of Judges?*** He gives the best decree, and His decree is that there be repayment. We read in a *ḥadīth*: "Whoever recites *Sūrat at-Tīn* in full should then say, 'Yes indeed, and I am one of those who bear witness to that.'"

96. *Sūrat al-'Alaq*
The Blood-clot

This *sūra* is Makkan and has 19 *āyat*s. The beginning of the *sūra* up to "what he did not know" was the first passage of the Qur'an to be revealed. That happened in the Cave of Ḥirā'. Al-Bukhārī related it.

1. ***Recite: In the Name of your Lord who created*** all creatures*:*

2. ***...created man*** – meant generically – ***from clots of blood.***

سُورَةُ العَلَقِ

بِسۡمِ ٱللَّهِ ٱلرَّحۡمَٰنِ ٱلرَّحِيمِ

ٱقۡرَأۡ بِٱسۡمِ رَبِّكَ ٱلَّذِي خَلَقَ ١ خَلَقَ ٱلۡإِنسَٰنَ مِنۡ عَلَقٍ ٢ ٱقۡرَأۡ وَرَبُّكَ
ٱلۡأَكۡرَمُ ٣ ٱلَّذِي عَلَّمَ بِٱلۡقَلَمِ ٤ عَلَّمَ ٱلۡإِنسَٰنَ مَا لَمۡ يَعۡلَمۡ ٥ كَلَّآ إِنَّ
ٱلۡإِنسَٰنَ لَيَطۡغَىٰٓ ٦ أَن رَّءَاهُ ٱسۡتَغۡنَىٰٓ ٧ إِنَّ إِلَىٰ رَبِّكَ ٱلرُّجۡعَىٰٓ ٨ أَرَءَيۡتَ
ٱلَّذِي يَنۡهَىٰ ٩ عَبۡدًا إِذَا صَلَّىٰٓ ١٠ أَرَءَيۡتَ إِن كَانَ عَلَى ٱلۡهُدَىٰٓ ١١ أَوۡ أَمَرَ
بِٱلتَّقۡوَىٰٓ ١٢ أَرَءَيۡتَ إِن كَذَّبَ وَتَوَلَّىٰٓ ١٣ أَلَمۡ يَعۡلَم بِأَنَّ ٱللَّهَ يَرَىٰ ١٤ كَلَّا لَئِن
لَّمۡ يَنتَهِ لَنَسۡفَعَۢا بِٱلنَّاصِيَةِ ١٥ نَاصِيَةٖ كَٰذِبَةٍ خَاطِئَةٖ ١٦ فَلۡيَدۡعُ نَادِيَهُۥ
١٧ سَنَدۡعُ ٱلزَّبَانِيَةَ ١٨ كَلَّا لَا تُطِعۡهُ وَٱسۡجُدۡۤ وَٱقۡتَرِب ۩ ١٩

3. ***Recite: And your Lord is the Most Generous*** **–** the repetition of the word "recite" is for emphasis. No one is equal to Him in His generosity –

4. ***...He who taught*** writing ***by the pen*** – the first to write with it was Idrīs, peace be upon him,

5. ***...taught man what he did not know.*** Allah taught him guidance, writing, crafts and other things.

6. ***No indeed! Truly man is unbridled,***

7. ***...seeing himself as self-sufficient*** because of his wealth. This was revealed about Abū Jahl. "Seeing" means "knowing" rather than physically seeing.

8. ***Truly***, human being, ***it is to your Lord that you shall return.*** The transgressor will be given the retribution he deserves.

9. ***Have you seen him who prevents*** – the person being described is Abū Jahl –

10. ***...a slave*** – meaning the Prophet, may Allah bless him and grant him peace – ***when he goes to pray?***

11. ***Do you think he*** (the person who prevents someone from praying) ***is rightly guided...***

12. ***...or commands to be godfearing?***

13. ***Or do you see how he has denied and turned away?***

14. ***Does he not know that Allah sees?*** It is a wonder that such a person forbids the prayer, when the one he forbids has guidance and commands to do what is right while the one who forbids denies and turns away from the truth.

15. ***No indeed! If he does not desist*** from the unbelief he is involved in ***We will grab him by the forelock*** and drag him to the Fire **–**

16. ***...a lying, sinful forelock!*** This is a metaphor that means the person himself.

17. ***Let him call his attendants*** – meaning the people of his circle who meet to consult him and talk together. When the Prophet, may Allah bless him and grant him peace, rebuked Abū Jahl for forbidding him to pray, he said, "You know that there is no man with a greater assembly than mine! I can fill this valley with them against you if I wish, with men on foot and mounted."

18. ***We will call the Guards of Hell!*** The *Zabāniyya* are the harsh, strong angels who will destroy him, as is found in the *ḥadīth*: "If he calls on his assembly, the *Zabāniyya* will seize him before their eyes."

19. ***No indeed! Do not obey him,*** Muḥammad – by abandoning the prayer – ***but prostrate*** – and pray to Allah – ***and draw near*** to Him by acts of obedience.

97. *Sūrat al-Qadr*
Power

This *sūra* is Makkan or Madinan and has 5 or 6 *āyats*.

1. ***Truly We sent it*** (the Qur'an) ***down*** all at once from the Preserved Tablet to the lowest heaven ***on the Night of Power*** so called because of its immense honour.

2. ***And what will convey to you,*** Muḥammad, ***what the Night of Power is*** – and its immensity and wonder***?***

3. ***The Night of Power is better than a thousand months*** that do not contain the Night of Power. Righteous actions done during it are better than those done in a thousand months that do not contain it.

4. ***In it the angels and the*** **Rūḥ** (Jibrīl) ***descend*** in the night ***by their Lord's authority*** and command ***with every ordinance*** – the decrees of Allah for that coming year.

5. ***It is Peace until the coming*** (read as *maṭla'* and *maṭli'*) ***of the dawn.*** It is called "Peace", *salām,* because it contains many greetings, *salām,* from the angels during it. They do not pass by any believer, man or woman, without greeting them.

98. *Sūrat al-Bayyina*
The Clear Sign

This *sūra* is Makkan or Madinan and has 8 *āyats*.

سُورَةُ القَدْرِ

بِسْمِ ٱللَّهِ ٱلرَّحْمَٰنِ ٱلرَّحِيمِ

إِنَّآ أَنزَلْنَٰهُ فِى لَيْلَةِ ٱلْقَدْرِ ١ وَمَآ أَدْرَىٰكَ مَا لَيْلَةُ ٱلْقَدْرِ ٢
لَيْلَةُ ٱلْقَدْرِ خَيْرٌ مِّنْ أَلْفِ شَهْرٍ ٣ تَنَزَّلُ ٱلْمَلَٰٓئِكَةُ وَٱلرُّوحُ
فِيهَا بِإِذْنِ رَبِّهِم مِّن كُلِّ أَمْرٍ ٤ سَلَٰمٌ هِىَ حَتَّىٰ مَطْلَعِ ٱلْفَجْرِ ٥

سُورَةُ البَيِّنَةِ

بِسْمِ ٱللَّهِ ٱلرَّحْمَٰنِ ٱلرَّحِيمِ

لَمْ يَكُنِ ٱلَّذِينَ كَفَرُوا۟ مِنْ أَهْلِ ٱلْكِتَٰبِ وَٱلْمُشْرِكِينَ مُنفَكِّينَ
حَتَّىٰ تَأْتِيَهُمُ ٱلْبَيِّنَةُ ١ رَسُولٌ مِّنَ ٱللَّهِ يَتْلُوا۟ صُحُفًا مُّطَهَّرَةً ٢
فِيهَا كُتُبٌ قَيِّمَةٌ ٣ وَمَا تَفَرَّقَ ٱلَّذِينَ أُوتُوا۟ ٱلْكِتَٰبَ إِلَّا مِنۢ
بَعْدِ مَا جَآءَتْهُمُ ٱلْبَيِّنَةُ ٤ وَمَآ أُمِرُوٓا۟ إِلَّا لِيَعْبُدُوا۟ ٱللَّهَ مُخْلِصِينَ
لَهُ ٱلدِّينَ حُنَفَآءَ وَيُقِيمُوا۟ ٱلصَّلَوٰةَ وَيُؤْتُوا۟ ٱلزَّكَوٰةَ ۚ وَذَٰلِكَ دِينُ
ٱلْقَيِّمَةِ ٥ إِنَّ ٱلَّذِينَ كَفَرُوا۟ مِنْ أَهْلِ ٱلْكِتَٰبِ وَٱلْمُشْرِكِينَ
فِى نَارِ جَهَنَّمَ خَٰلِدِينَ فِيهَآ ۚ أُو۟لَٰٓئِكَ هُمْ شَرُّ ٱلْبَرِيَّةِ ٦ إِنَّ
ٱلَّذِينَ ءَامَنُوا۟ وَعَمِلُوا۟ ٱلصَّٰلِحَٰتِ أُو۟لَٰٓئِكَ هُمْ خَيْرُ ٱلْبَرِيَّةِ ٧
جَزَآؤُهُمْ عِندَ رَبِّهِمْ جَنَّٰتُ عَدْنٍ تَجْرِى مِن تَحْتِهَا ٱلْأَنْهَٰرُ خَٰلِدِينَ
فِيهَآ أَبَدًا ۖ رَّضِىَ ٱللَّهُ عَنْهُمْ وَرَضُوا۟ عَنْهُ ۚ ذَٰلِكَ لِمَنْ خَشِىَ رَبَّهُۥ ٨

1. ***The People of the Book who disbelieve and the idolators would not be cut off*** from what they have ***until the Clear Sign***, Muḥammad, may Allah bless him and grant him peace, ***came to them:***

2. ***...a Messenger*** (the Prophet Muḥammad, may Allah bless him and grant him peace) ***from Allah reciting purified texts*** – pages which are free of any falsehood –

3. ***...containing upright precepts*** – written judgements when it is recited, meaning the Qur'an. Some believed in it and some rejected it.

4. ***Those who were given the Book*** which mentions belief in the Prophet, may Allah bless him and grant him peace, ***did not divide into sects until after the Clear Sign*** – referring to the Prophet Muḥammad, may Allah bless him and grant him peace, or the Qur'an which he brought as a miracle – ***came to them.*** Before that, they used to agree that they would believe in him when he came. Those of them who rejected him envied him.

5. ***They were only ordered*** – in their Books, the Torah and the Gospel – ***to worship Allah*** without committing *shirk*, ***making their* dīn *sincerely His, as people of pure natural belief*** – the word *ḥunafā'*, the plural of *ḥanīf,* means being upright by following the *dīn* of Ibrāhīm and the *dīn* of Muḥammad – ***and to establish the prayer and pay* zakāt. *That is the correct* dīn.** So how can they reject that?

6. ***The People of the Book who disbelieve and the idolators will be in the Fire of Hell, remaining in it timelessly, for ever.*** This is from Allah Almighty. ***They are the worst of creatures.***

7. ***But those who believe and do right actions are the best of creatures.***

8. ***Their reward is with their Lord:*** they will stay in ***Gardens of Eden with rivers flowing under them, remaining in them timelessly, for ever and ever. Allah is pleased with them*** for their obedience – ***and they are pleased with Him*** for the rewards He gives. ***That is for those who fear*** the Punishment of ***their Lord*** and do not disobey Him.

سُورَةُ الزَّلْزَلَةِ

بِسْمِ ٱللَّهِ ٱلرَّحْمَٰنِ ٱلرَّحِيمِ

إِذَا زُلْزِلَتِ ٱلْأَرْضُ زِلْزَالَهَا ١ وَأَخْرَجَتِ ٱلْأَرْضُ أَثْقَالَهَا
٢ وَقَالَ ٱلْإِنسَٰنُ مَا لَهَا ٣ يَوْمَئِذٍ تُحَدِّثُ أَخْبَارَهَا ٤
بِأَنَّ رَبَّكَ أَوْحَىٰ لَهَا ٥ يَوْمَئِذٍ يَصْدُرُ ٱلنَّاسُ أَشْتَاتًا
لِّيُرَوْا۟ أَعْمَٰلَهُمْ ٦ فَمَن يَعْمَلْ مِثْقَالَ ذَرَّةٍ خَيْرًا
يَرَهُۥ ٧ وَمَن يَعْمَلْ مِثْقَالَ ذَرَّةٍ شَرًّا يَرَهُۥ ٨

سُورَةُ العَادِيَاتِ

بِسْمِ ٱللَّهِ ٱلرَّحْمَٰنِ ٱلرَّحِيمِ

وَٱلْعَٰدِيَٰتِ ضَبْحًا ١ فَٱلْمُورِيَٰتِ قَدْحًا ٢ فَٱلْمُغِيرَٰتِ صُبْحًا
٣ فَأَثَرْنَ بِهِۦ نَقْعًا ٤ فَوَسَطْنَ بِهِۦ جَمْعًا ٥ إِنَّ ٱلْإِنسَٰنَ
لِرَبِّهِۦ لَكَنُودٌ ٦ وَإِنَّهُۥ عَلَىٰ ذَٰلِكَ لَشَهِيدٌ ٧ وَإِنَّهُۥ لِحُبِّ
ٱلْخَيْرِ لَشَدِيدٌ ٨ ۞ أَفَلَا يَعْلَمُ إِذَا بُعْثِرَ مَا فِى ٱلْقُبُورِ ٩
وَحُصِّلَ مَا فِى ٱلصُّدُورِ ١٠ إِنَّ رَبَّهُم بِهِمْ يَوْمَئِذٍ لَّخَبِيرٌۢ ١١

99. *Sūrat az-Zilzala* The Earthquake

This *sūra* is either Makkan or Madinan and has 8 *ayat*s.

1. *When the earth is convulsed with its quaking* when the Last Hour comes, as is proper owing to its immensity,

2. *...and the earth then disgorges its charges* – casts up its treasures and dead onto its surface,

3. *...and man* – meaning those who deny the Resurrection – ***asks, 'What is wrong with it?'*** – such a person will not recognise its state,

4. *on that Day it will impart all its news* – all the good and evil that was done on it –

5. *...because your Lord has inspired it.* The reason that it will do this is that Allah has commanded it to. In a *ḥadīth* we find: "It will testify against every slave, male and female, to all that they did while on its surface."

6. *That Day people will emerge segregated* from the place of Standing ***to see the results of their actions.*** Some will go to the right to the Garden and some to the left to the Fire, so that they may see the repayment of their actions in the Garden or the Fire.

7. *Whoever does an atom's weight of good will see it.*

8. *Whoever does an atom's weight of evil will see it.* The word "*dharra*" means a tiny ant. Everyone will see the repayment for their actions.

100. *Sūrat al-'Ādiyāt* The Chargers

This *sūra* is either Makkan or Madinan, and has 11 *āyat*s.

1. *By the charging horses panting hard* – which attack in a raid, making a loud noise as they attack,

2. *...striking sparks from their flashing hooves* when their hooves strike the stones in the ground at night,

3. *...raiding at full gallop in the early dawn* – horsemen attacking the enemy at first light,

4. *...leaving a trailing dust-cloud in their wake* – raising dust because the speed of their movement,

5. *...cleaving through the middle of the foe!* – penetrating to the heart of the enemy settlement –

6. *Truly* unbelieving ***man is ungrateful to his Lord*** denying the blessings of Allah –

7. *...and indeed he bears witness to that* – to his ingratitude against himself by his actions.

8. *Truly he is fierce in his love of wealth* and is miserly with it.

9. *Does he not know that when the graves are emptied out* – and the dead emerge from them at the Resurrection –

10. *...and the heart's contents* – whether unbelief and faith – ***are brought into the open*** and made clear and public,

11. *...on that Day their Lord will certainly be aware of them.* He has knowledge and He will repay them for their unbelief. The pronoun here moves to the plural, indicating that "man" is generic and includes all human beings. Here the statement is particular to this moment, which is the Day of Repayment, although of course Allah is always aware of them.

101. *Sūrat al-Qāri'a*
The Crashing Blow

This *sūra* is Makkan and has 11 *āyat*s.

1. *The Crashing Blow!*

2. *What is the Crashing Blow?* This is the Day of Rising, which will crush the hearts with its terrors. It is repeated to emphasise its dreadfulness.

3. *What will convey to you what the Crashing Blow is?* This question is to emphasize further the terrible nature of that Day.

سُورَةُ القَارِعَةِ

بِسۡمِ ٱللَّهِ ٱلرَّحۡمَٰنِ ٱلرَّحِيمِ

ٱلۡقَارِعَةُ ١ مَا ٱلۡقَارِعَةُ ٢ وَمَآ أَدۡرَىٰكَ مَا ٱلۡقَارِعَةُ
٣ يَوۡمَ يَكُونُ ٱلنَّاسُ كَٱلۡفَرَاشِ ٱلۡمَبۡثُوثِ ٤
وَتَكُونُ ٱلۡجِبَالُ كَٱلۡعِهۡنِ ٱلۡمَنفُوشِ ٥ فَأَمَّا
مَن ثَقُلَتۡ مَوَٰزِينُهُۥ ٦ فَهُوَ فِي عِيشَةٖ رَّاضِيَةٖ
٧ وَأَمَّا مَنۡ خَفَّتۡ مَوَٰزِينُهُۥ ٨ فَأُمُّهُۥ هَاوِيَةٞ
٩ وَمَآ أَدۡرَىٰكَ مَا هِيَهۡ ١٠ نَارٌ حَامِيَةُۢ ١١

سُورَةُ التَّكَاثُرِ

بِسۡمِ ٱللَّهِ ٱلرَّحۡمَٰنِ ٱلرَّحِيمِ

أَلۡهَىٰكُمُ ٱلتَّكَاثُرُ ١ حَتَّىٰ زُرۡتُمُ ٱلۡمَقَابِرَ ٢ كَلَّا سَوۡفَ
تَعۡلَمُونَ ٣ ثُمَّ كَلَّا سَوۡفَ تَعۡلَمُونَ ٤ كَلَّا لَوۡ تَعۡلَمُونَ
عِلۡمَ ٱلۡيَقِينِ ٥ لَتَرَوُنَّ ٱلۡجَحِيمَ ٦ ثُمَّ لَتَرَوُنَّهَا
عَيۡنَ ٱلۡيَقِينِ ٧ ثُمَّ لَتُسۡـَٔلُنَّ يَوۡمَئِذٍ عَنِ ٱلنَّعِيمِ ٨

سُورَةُ العَصۡرِ

بِسۡمِ ٱللَّهِ ٱلرَّحۡمَٰنِ ٱلرَّحِيمِ

وَٱلۡعَصۡرِ ١ إِنَّ ٱلۡإِنسَٰنَ لَفِي خُسۡرٍ ٢ إِلَّا ٱلَّذِينَ ءَامَنُواْ
وَعَمِلُواْ ٱلصَّٰلِحَٰتِ وَتَوَاصَوۡاْ بِٱلۡحَقِّ وَتَوَاصَوۡاْ بِٱلصَّبۡرِ ٣

4. ***It is the Day when mankind will be*** crushed and dispersed ***like scattered moths*** – confused locusts, surging into one another out of bewilderment at being summoned for the Reckoning –

5. ***...and the mountains like*** insubstantial ***tufts of coloured wool.***

6. ***As for him whose balance is heavy*** – him whose good actions outweigh his evil actions,

7. ***...he will have a most pleasant life*** in the Garden. He will be delighted with it.

8. ***But as for him whose balance is light*** – him whose evil deeds outweigh his good deeds,

9. ***...his motherland*** (dwelling-place) ***is Hāwiya.***

10. ***And what will convey to you what that is?***

11. ***A raging Fire!***

102. *Sūrat at-Takāthur* Competition for Gain

This *sūra* is Makkan and has 8 *āyat*s.

1. ***Fierce competition for this world distracted you*** from obeying Allah. This means boasting to one another about wealth, children and followers –

2. ***...until you went down to the graves*** – when you die and are buried in them, or you count the dead in boasting to one another.

3. ***No indeed, you will soon know!***

4. ***Again no indeed, you will soon know*** the evil end of your mutual boasting, when you die and then are in the grave!

5. ***No indeed, if you only knew with the Knowledge of Certainty*** what the result of the competition which distracted you would be –

6. ***...you will certainly see the Blazing Fire!***

7. ***Then you will certainly see it with the Eye of Certainty.*** This repetition is for emphasis.

8. ***Then you will be asked that Day*** – when you see this – ***about the pleasures you enjoyed*** in this world, in terms of good health, free time, security, food and drink, and other things.

103. *Sūrat al-'Aṣr* The Late Afternoon

This *sūra* is either Makkan or Madinan, and has 3 *āyat*s.

1. ***By the Late Afternoon*** – the word *'aṣr* means either time, or between midday and sunset, or the *'Aṣr* prayer*!*

2. ***Truly man*** – meant generically – ***is in loss*** in his life-transaction,

3. ***...except for those who believe and do right actions*** – who are not in loss, ***and urge each other to the truth*** – which means faith, ***and urge each other to steadfastness*** – to obey and not to disobey.

104. *Sūrat al-Humaza* The Backbiter

This *sūra* is either Makkan or Madina, and has 9 *āyat*s.

1. ***Woe to every faultfinding backbiter*** – the word *wayl* is a word meaning punishment or a valley in Hell. This was revealed about those who used to slander the Prophet, may Allah bless him and grant him peace, and the believers: men such as Umayya ibn Khalaf, al-Walīd ibn al-Mughīra and others –

2. ***...who has amassed*** (read as *jama'a* and *jamma'a*) ***wealth and hoarded it*** – counted it and stored it against the vicissitudes of time.

3. ***He thinks his wealth will make him live for ever*** – because of his ignorance.

4. ***No indeed! He will be flung into the Shatterer.*** The word *ḥuṭama* is something which crushes everything that is thrown into it.

5. ***And what will convey to you what the Shatterer is?***

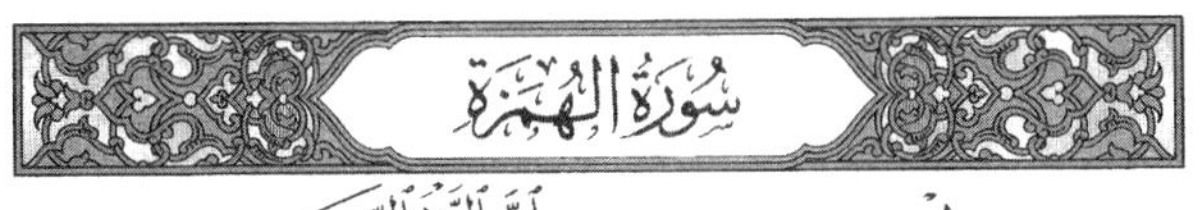

بِسْمِ ٱللَّهِ ٱلرَّحْمَٰنِ ٱلرَّحِيمِ

وَيْلٌ لِّكُلِّ هُمَزَةٍ لُّمَزَةٍ ﴿١﴾ ٱلَّذِى جَمَعَ مَالًا وَعَدَّدَهُۥ ﴿٢﴾
يَحْسَبُ أَنَّ مَالَهُۥٓ أَخْلَدَهُۥ ﴿٣﴾ كَلَّا ۖ لَيُنۢبَذَنَّ فِى ٱلْحُطَمَةِ ﴿٤﴾
وَمَآ أَدْرَىٰكَ مَا ٱلْحُطَمَةُ ﴿٥﴾ نَارُ ٱللَّهِ ٱلْمُوقَدَةُ ﴿٦﴾ ٱلَّتِى تَطَّلِعُ
عَلَى ٱلْأَفْـِٔدَةِ ﴿٧﴾ إِنَّهَا عَلَيْهِم مُّؤْصَدَةٌ ﴿٨﴾ فِى عَمَدٍ مُّمَدَّدَةٍۭ ﴿٩﴾

سُورَةُ الفِيلِ

بِسْمِ ٱللَّهِ ٱلرَّحْمَٰنِ ٱلرَّحِيمِ

أَلَمْ تَرَ كَيْفَ فَعَلَ رَبُّكَ بِأَصْحَٰبِ ٱلْفِيلِ ﴿١﴾ أَلَمْ يَجْعَلْ كَيْدَهُمْ
فِى تَضْلِيلٍ ﴿٢﴾ وَأَرْسَلَ عَلَيْهِمْ طَيْرًا أَبَابِيلَ ﴿٣﴾ تَرْمِيهِم
بِحِجَارَةٍ مِّن سِجِّيلٍ ﴿٤﴾ فَجَعَلَهُمْ كَعَصْفٍ مَّأْكُولٍۭ ﴿٥﴾

6. ***The kindled Fire of Allah,***

7. ***...reaching right into the heart.*** The fire rises above the hearts and burns them, and that involves a far greater pain than any other pain.

8. ***It is sealed in above them*** – covering each of them,

9. ***...in towering columns*** (read as *'amad* and *'umud*). The fire is inside the columns.

105. *Sūrat al-Fīl* The Elephant

This *sūra* is Makkan and has 5 *āyat*s.

1. ***Do you not see what your Lord did with the Companions of the Elephant?*** This is a question which implies wonder. The Companions of the Elephant, Maḥmūd, and his owner, Abraha, the King of Yemen and his army. He built a temple in Ṣan'a in order to divert people from making pilgrimage to Makka. A man of the tribe of Kināna went and defiled it and soiled the *qibla* of the temple with faeces to desecrate it. Abraha swore that he would destroy the Ka'ba. He came to Makka with his army on the elephant of Yemen, with Maḥmūd in the vanguard. When they set out to destroy the Ka'ba, Allah sent against them what is mentioned in the following verses.

2. ***Did He not bring all their schemes to nothing*** – Allah thwarted their plan to destroy the Ka'ba,

3. ***...unleashing upon them flock after flock of birds;*** most commentators say that *abābīl* has no singular, although some say that its plural is *abūl*, *ibāl*, or *ibīl;*

4. ***...bombarding them with stones of hard-baked clay***;

5. ***...then making them like stripped wheat-stalks eaten bare?*** like leaves of crops eaten by animals, crushed and crumbled. Allah destroyed each of them with a stone on which was written the name of the person it hit. These stones were larger than lentils and smaller than chickpeas. They pierced the skulls of men and camels before

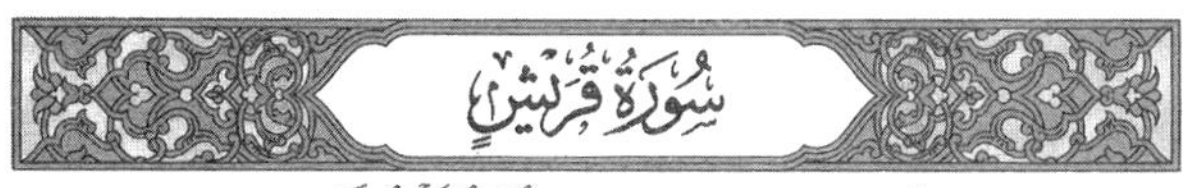

بِسْمِ ٱللَّهِ ٱلرَّحْمَٰنِ ٱلرَّحِيمِ

لِإِيلَٰفِ قُرَيْشٍ ﴿١﴾ إِۦلَٰفِهِمْ رِحْلَةَ ٱلشِّتَآءِ وَٱلصَّيْفِ
﴿٢﴾ فَلْيَعْبُدُوا۟ رَبَّ هَٰذَا ٱلْبَيْتِ ﴿٣﴾ ٱلَّذِىٓ أَطْعَمَهُم
مِّن جُوعٍ وَءَامَنَهُم مِّنْ خَوْفٍۭ ﴿٤﴾

سُورَةُ الْمَاعُونِ

بِسْمِ ٱللَّهِ ٱلرَّحْمَٰنِ ٱلرَّحِيمِ

أَرَءَيْتَ ٱلَّذِى يُكَذِّبُ بِٱلدِّينِ ﴿١﴾ فَذَٰلِكَ ٱلَّذِى
يَدُعُّ ٱلْيَتِيمَ ﴿٢﴾ وَلَا يَحُضُّ عَلَىٰ طَعَامِ ٱلْمِسْكِينِ ﴿٣﴾
فَوَيْلٌ لِّلْمُصَلِّينَ ﴿٤﴾ ٱلَّذِينَ هُمْ عَن صَلَاتِهِمْ سَاهُونَ
﴿٥﴾ ٱلَّذِينَ هُمْ يُرَآءُونَ ﴿٦﴾ وَيَمْنَعُونَ ٱلْمَاعُونَ ﴿٧﴾

سُورَةُ الْكَوْثَرِ

بِسْمِ ٱللَّهِ ٱلرَّحْمَٰنِ ٱلرَّحِيمِ

إِنَّآ أَعْطَيْنَٰكَ ٱلْكَوْثَرَ ﴿١﴾ فَصَلِّ لِرَبِّكَ وَٱنْحَرْ ﴿٢﴾
إِنَّ شَانِئَكَ هُوَ ٱلْأَبْتَرُ ﴿٣﴾

reaching the ground. These events took place the year that the Prophet, may Allah bless him and grant him peace, was born.

106. *Sūrat Quraysh*
Quraysh

This *sūra* is either Makkan or Madinan, and has 4 *āyat*s.

1. ***In acknowledgment of the established tradition of Quraysh,***

2. ***...their tradition of the winter and summer caravans*** – the repetition is for emphasis. The winter caravan went to Yemen and the summer caravan to Syria. This happened every year. They used the proceeds of the trade of the two caravans to serve the House which was their pride. They were the descendants of an-Naḍr ibn Kināna,

3. ***...so let them worship the Lord of this House,***

4. ***...who has preserved them from hunger and secured them from fear.*** "He has fed them and given them security." They experienced hunger because of the lack of crops in Makka and they feared the Army of the Elephant.

107. *Sūrat al-Mā‘ūn*
Helping Others

This *sūra* is either Makkan or Madinan or half and half, and has 6 or 7 *āyat*s.

1. ***Have you seen him who denies the* dīn** – denies the Repayment and the Reckoning*?* "Do you recognise him, even if he does not acknowledge it?"

2. ***He is the one who harshly rebuffs the orphan*** – and fails to give him his rights –

3. ***...and does not urge*** on himself or anyone else ***the feeding of the poor.*** This was revealed about al-‘Āṣ ibn Wā’il or al-Walīd ibn al-Mughīra.

4. ***So woe to those who do the prayer,***

5. ***... but are forgetful of their prayer*** – neglect their prayer and delay it past its time –

6. ***...those who show off*** in the prayer and other actions –

7. ***...and deny help to others.*** They refuse to lend even things like needles, axes, pots and plates.

108. *Sūrat al-Kawthar* The Great Abundance

This *sūra* either is Makkan or Madinan and has 3 *āyat*s.

1. ***Truly We have given you the Great Abundance.*** This is addressed to Muḥammad, may Allah bless him and grant him peace. *Kawthar* is a river in the Garden from which the Basin of his Community is watered. *Kawthar* means immense good, in the form of Prophethood, Qur'an, intercession and other things.

2. ***So pray to your Lord and sacrifice.*** This refers to the prayer of the *'Īd* of Sacrifice. "Sacrifice your sacrificial animals."

3. ***It is the one who hates you who is cut off without posterity***: cut off from all good, or cut off from having descendants. This was revealed about al-Āṣ ibn Wā'il, who called the Prophet *abtar* (cut off) when his son al-Qāsim died.

109. *Sūrat al-Kāfirūn* The Rejectors

This *sūra* is either Makkan or Madinan and has 6 *āyat*s. This was revealed when a group of unbelievers said to the Messenger of Allah, may Allah bless him and grant him peace, "Worship our gods for a year and we will worship your God for a year."

1. ***Say: 'O Unbelievers!***

2. ***I do not worship what you worship*** – "I do not worship idols" –

سُورَةُ الكَافِرُونَ

بِسْمِ ٱللَّهِ ٱلرَّحْمَٰنِ ٱلرَّحِيمِ

قُلْ يَٰٓأَيُّهَا ٱلْكَٰفِرُونَ ﴿١﴾ لَآ أَعْبُدُ مَا تَعْبُدُونَ ﴿٢﴾
وَلَآ أَنتُمْ عَٰبِدُونَ مَآ أَعْبُدُ ﴿٣﴾ وَلَآ أَنَا۠ عَابِدٌ مَّا عَبَدتُّمْ ﴿٤﴾
وَلَآ أَنتُمْ عَٰبِدُونَ مَآ أَعْبُدُ ﴿٥﴾ لَكُمْ دِينُكُمْ وَلِىَ دِينِ ﴿٦﴾

سُورَةُ النَّصرِ

بِسْمِ ٱللَّهِ ٱلرَّحْمَٰنِ ٱلرَّحِيمِ

إِذَا جَآءَ نَصْرُ ٱللَّهِ وَٱلْفَتْحُ ﴿١﴾ وَرَأَيْتَ ٱلنَّاسَ
يَدْخُلُونَ فِى دِينِ ٱللَّهِ أَفْوَاجًا ﴿٢﴾ فَسَبِّحْ بِحَمْدِ رَبِّكَ
وَٱسْتَغْفِرْهُ ۚ إِنَّهُۥ كَانَ تَوَّابًۢا ﴿٣﴾

سُورَةُ المَسَدِ

بِسْمِ ٱللَّهِ ٱلرَّحْمَٰنِ ٱلرَّحِيمِ

تَبَّتْ يَدَآ أَبِى لَهَبٍ وَتَبَّ ﴿١﴾ مَآ أَغْنَىٰ عَنْهُ مَالُهُۥ وَمَا
كَسَبَ ﴿٢﴾ سَيَصْلَىٰ نَارًا ذَاتَ لَهَبٍ ﴿٣﴾ وَٱمْرَأَتُهُۥ
حَمَّالَةَ ٱلْحَطَبِ ﴿٤﴾ فِى جِيدِهَا حَبْلٌ مِّن مَّسَدٍۭ ﴿٥﴾

3. ***...and you do not worship what I worship.*** "You do not worship Allah Almighty alone."

4. ***Nor will I worship what you worship*** in the future,

5. ***...nor will you worship what I worship*** in the future. Allah knows that they will not believe.

6. ***You have your* dīn *and I have my* dīn*'*** "You have *shirk* and I have Islam." This was revealed before the command to fight came.

110. *Sūrat an-Naṣr*
Victory

It was revealed at Minā during the Farewell *Ḥajj* and so it is counted as Madinan even though it was revealed in Makka. It was the last *sūra* to be revealed, and has 3 *āyats.*

1. ***When Allah's help*** – given to His Prophet, may Allah bless him and grant him peace, against his enemies – ***and victory*** – the Conquest of Makka – ***have arrived,***

2. ***...and you have seen people entering Allah's* dīn** (Islam) ***in droves*** – whereas before they used to enter it one by one. That happened after the Conquest of Makka when the Arabs began to come from all areas of the land to offer their submission*;*

3. ***...then glorify your Lord's praise and ask His forgiveness. He is the Ever-Relenting.*** After this *sūra* was revealed, the Prophet, may Allah bless him and grant him peace, often said, "Glory be to Allah and by His praise. I ask forgiveness of Allah and I turn in repentance to Him." From this Revelation, he realised that his death was near. Makka was conquered in Ramaḍān 8 AH and the Prophet, may Allah bless him and grant him peace, died in Rabīʿ al-Awwal 10 AH.

111. *Sūrat al-Lahab* or *al-Masad*
The Flame or Palm Fibre

This *sūra* is Makkan and has 5 *āyats.*

1. ***Ruin to the hands of Abū Lahab and ruin to him!*** When the Prophet, may Allah bless him and grant him peace, called his people, saying, "I am a warner to you of a terrible punishment," his uncle, Abū Lahab, said, "Ruin to you! Did you gather us for this?" Then this was revealed. "The hands" means "all of him": it is used metaphorically to denote the entire person because most actions are done using the hands. This sentence is an imprecation. When the Prophet warned him about the punishment, he said, "If what my nephew says is true, then I will ransom myself from it with my wealth and children," so the next *āyat* was revealed.

2. ***His wealth has not helped him*** – nor have his children – ***nor has anything he has earned.***

3. ***He will burn in a Flaming Fire*** – *"dhāt lahab"* means a fire with flames. This alludes to his nickname, Abū Lahab, lit. "Father of Flame," by which he was called due to the redness of his face*;*

4. ***...and so will his wife, the firewood-carrier,*** burn. She was named Umm Jamīl. She carried wood and thorns and threw them in the path of the Prophet, may Allah bless him and grant him peace.

5. ***...with a rope of twisted fibre round her neck.*** This describes her appearance at the time.

112. *Sūrat al-Ikhlāṣ*
Sincerity

This *sūra* is Makkan or Madinan and has 4 or 5 *āyat*s.

1. ***Say: 'He is Allah, Absolute Oneness.*** The Prophet, may Allah bless him and grant him peace, was asked about his Lord and then this was revealed.

2. ***Allah, the Everlasting Sustainer of all.*** He is the One to whom people always turn for their needs.

3. ***He has not given birth, and was not born.*** This is a negation of any one else having the same nature as Him, because He is not subject to temporality.

4. ***And no one is comparable to Him.'***

بِسْمِ ٱللَّهِ ٱلرَّحْمَٰنِ ٱلرَّحِيمِ

قُلْ هُوَ ٱللَّهُ أَحَدٌ ﴿١﴾ ٱللَّهُ ٱلصَّمَدُ ﴿٢﴾ لَمْ يَلِدْ
وَلَمْ يُولَدْ ﴿٣﴾ وَلَمْ يَكُن لَّهُۥ كُفُوًا أَحَدٌۢ ﴿٤﴾

سُورَةُ الفَلَق

بِسْمِ ٱللَّهِ ٱلرَّحْمَٰنِ ٱلرَّحِيمِ

قُلْ أَعُوذُ بِرَبِّ ٱلْفَلَقِ ﴿١﴾ مِن شَرِّ مَا خَلَقَ ﴿٢﴾ وَمِن
شَرِّ غَاسِقٍ إِذَا وَقَبَ ﴿٣﴾ وَمِن شَرِّ ٱلنَّفَّٰثَٰتِ فِى
ٱلْعُقَدِ ﴿٤﴾ وَمِن شَرِّ حَاسِدٍ إِذَا حَسَدَ ﴿٥﴾

سُورَةُ النَّاس

بِسْمِ ٱللَّهِ ٱلرَّحْمَٰنِ ٱلرَّحِيمِ

قُلْ أَعُوذُ بِرَبِّ ٱلنَّاسِ ﴿١﴾ مَلِكِ ٱلنَّاسِ ﴿٢﴾ إِلَٰهِ
ٱلنَّاسِ ﴿٣﴾ مِن شَرِّ ٱلْوَسْوَاسِ ٱلْخَنَّاسِ ﴿٤﴾ ٱلَّذِى
يُوَسْوِسُ فِى صُدُورِ ٱلنَّاسِ ﴿٥﴾
مِنَ ٱلْجِنَّةِ وَٱلنَّاسِ ﴿٦﴾

113. *Sūrat al-Falaq* Daybreak

This *sūra* is either Makkan or Madinan and has 5 *āyat*s. Both it and the one after it were revealed when Labīd the Jew bewitched the Prophet, may Allah bless him and grant him peace, using a string with twelve knots in it. Allah informed him of that and of where it was. Someone appeared before him, may Allah bless him and grant him peace, and commanded him to recite the two *sūra*s. Each time he recited an *āyat* of them, a knot was released and he experienced relief, until all the knots were undone, when he rose as if released from a hobble.

1. ***Say: 'I seek refuge with the Lord of Daybreak,***

2. ***...from the evil of what He has created*** – both domesticated animals and wild animals and inanimate things like poison and suchlike,

3. ***...and from the evil of the darkness when it gathers*** – the night when it gets dark and the moon when it is invisible,

4. ***...and from the evil of women who blow on knots*** – witches who blow on their knots tied in pieces of string. It is a kind of blowing like spitting without actual spittle. According to az-Zamakhsharī, it means people like the daughters of Labīd,

5. ***...and from the evil of an envier when he envies.'*** – One who shows his envy and acts on it as Labīd did for the Jews who envied the Prophet, may Allah bless him and grant him peace.

114. *Sūrat an-Nās* Mankind

This *sūra* is either Makkan or Madinan and has 6 *āyat*s.

1. ***Say: 'I seek refuge with the Lord of mankind,*** their Creator and Master. "Mankind" are singled out for mention to honour them and because it is appropriate since they are seeking refuge from the evil of the Whisperer inside their breasts –

2. …*the King of mankind,*

3. …*the God of mankind,*

4. …*from the evil of the insidious whisperer* (Shayṭān). He is so-called because that is what he often does. He is called *khannās* (insidious), or slinking, because he slinks and retreats from the heart whenever Allah is remembered,

5. …*who whispers in people's breasts* – in their hearts, when they neglect to remember Allah –

6. …*and comes from the jinn and from mankind.'* The Shayṭān who whispers can be a jinn or human, as Allah Almighty says in another place "*Shayṭāns of men and jinn.*" (6:112) It can mean that that the whispering comes from jinn and men, and include those who are evil like Labīd and his daughters. Human beings do not whisper in the breasts of people: jinn whisper in their breasts while men whisper in the breasts of jinn. Men, however, also "whisper" by means of what they do outwardly, which then reaches the heart and becomes fixed in it. Allah knows best.

Glossary

Abū Jahl: One of the important men of the tribe of Quraysh who was violently opposed to Islam.

Abū Lahab: One of the Prophet Muhammad's uncles, who was a great enemy of Islam.

Abū Qubays: a mountain in Makka.

'Ād: an ancient people in southern Arabia to whom the Prophet Hūd was sent.

adhān: the call to prayer.

Anṣār: the "Helpers", the people of Madina who welcomed and aided the Prophet.

'āqila: the paternal kinsmen of an offender who are liable for the payment of blood money.

'Arafa: a plain fifteen miles to the east of Makka on which stands the Jabal ar-Raḥma, the Mount of Mercy. One of the essential rites of the *Ḥajj* is to stand at 'Arafa on the 9th of Dhū'l-Ḥijja.

'aṣaba: male relatives on the father's side who take the remaining estate, if any, after the heirs with fixed shares have received their shares. Sometimes translated as "universal heir".

'Aṣr: the afternoon prayer.

awliyā': plural of *walī.*

āyat: a verse of the Qur'an.

Badr: a place near the Red Sea coast, about 95 miles to the south of Madina where in 2 AH, in the first battle fought by the newly established Muslim community, 300 Muslims led by the Messenger of Allah overwhelmingly defeated more than 1000 Makkan idolaters.

basmala: the Arabic expression meaning "In the name of Allah, the All-Merciful, the All-Compassionate".

baḥīra: an animal whose milk was set aside for idols and which was not allowed to be milked

Banū Muqarrin: six brothers who were Companions of the Prophet.

Dajjāl: the false Messiah, whose appearance marks the imminent ends of the world.

Dār an-Nadwa: the assembly of chiefs of Quraysh in Makka.

dhikr: lit. remembrance, mention. As commonly used, it means invocation of Allah by repetition of His names or particular formulae.

dhimma: obligation or contract, in particular a treaty of protection for non-Muslims living in Muslim territory.

dīn: the life-transaction, lit. the debt between two parties, in this usage between the Creator and created.

Ḍuḥā: forenoon, in particular the voluntary morning prayer.

fatwā: an authoritative statement on a point of law.

fidya: a ransom, or compensation paid for rites or acts of worship missed or wrongly performed because of ignorance or ill health.

fiqh: the science of the theoretical basis and application of the *Sharī'a*. A practitioner or expert in *fiqh* is called a *faqīh*.

Firdaws: Paradise, one of the highest parts of the Garden.

fisq: deviant behaviour, leaving the correct way or abandoning the truth, disobeying Allah, immoral behaviour. The testimony of someone who is *fāsiq*, who behaves in a manner which can be described as *fisq*, is not accepted as evidence in court.

fitna: civil strife, sedition, schism, trial, temptation. When used in the Qur'an, it often refers to *shirk*, associating others with Allah.

fiṭra: the first nature, the natural, primal condition of mankind in harmony with nature.

ghusl: major ablution of the whole body with water, required to regain ritual purity after menstruation, lochia and sexual intercourse.

ḥadd: Allah's limits between the lawful and unlawful. The *ḥadd* punishments are fixed penalties laid down by Allah for specified crimes.

ḥadīth: reported speech of the Prophet.

ḥadīth qudsī: those words of Allah that were spoken by the tongue of His Messenger which are not part of the Revelation of the Qur'an.

Ḥajj: the annual pilgrimage to Makka which is one of the five pillars of Islam.

ḥalāl: lawful in the *Sharī'a*.

Ḥanafiyya: the religion of Ibrāhīm, the primordial religion of *tawḥīd* and sincerity to Allah.

ḥanīf: one who possesses the true religion innately.

Ḥaram: Sacred Precinct, a protected area in which certain behaviour is forbidden and other behaviour necessary. The area around the Ka'ba in Makka is a *Ḥaram*, and the area around the Prophet's Mosque in Madina is a *Ḥaram*. They are referred to together as *al-Ḥaramayn*, 'the two *Ḥarams*'.

ḥarām: unlawful in the *Sharī'a*.

ḥasan: good, excellent, often used to describe a *ḥadīth* which is reliable, but which is not as strictly authenticated as one which is *ṣaḥīḥ*.

ḥarbī: a belligerent.

Ḥijāz: the region along the western seaboard of Arabia in which Makka, Madina, Jeddah and Ṭā'if are situated.

hijra: emigration for the Cause of Allah. Islamic dates begin with the *Hijra* of the Prophet Muhammad from Makka to Madina in 622 AD.

ḥudūd: plural of *ḥadd*.

Iblīs: the personal name of the Devil. He is also called Shayṭān or the "enemy of Allah".

'Īd: a festival, the festival either at the end of Ramaḍān or at the time of the sacrifice during *Hajj*.

'idda: a period after divorce or the death of her husband for which a woman must wait before re-marrying.

iḥrām: the conditions of clothing and behaviour adopted by someone performing *ḥajj* or *'umra*.

ijtihād: to exercise personal judgement in legal matters.

imām: leader of Muslim congregational worship.

'Ishā': the night prayer.

istibrā': the waiting period for slavegirls, equivalent to *'idda* for free women.

i'tikāf: seclusion, while fasting, in a mosque, particularly in the last ten days of Ramaḍān.

Jahannam: Hellfire.

Jāhiliyya: the Time of Ignorance before the coming of Islam.

jamra: lit. a small walled place, but in this usage a stone-built pillar. There are three *jamarāt* at Minā. One of the rites of *ḥajj* is to stone them.

Jamrat al-'Aqaba: the largest of the three *jamra*s at Minā.

janāba: major ritual impurity which requires *ghusl*.

jihād: struggle, particularly fighting for the Cause of Allah to establish Islam.

jinn: inhabitants of the heavens and the earth, made of smokeless fire, who are usually invisible to mankind.

jizya: a protection tax payable by non-Muslims living under Muslim rule as tribute to the Muslim ruler.

Jumadā al-Ākhira: the sixth month of the Muslim lunar calendar.

Jumu'a: Friday, the day of gathering in mosques, and particularly the *Jumu'a* prayer which is performed instead of *Ẓuhr* for worship by those who attend it.

Ka'ba: the cube-shaped building at the centre of the *Ḥaram* in Makka, originally built by the Prophet Ibrāhīm, also known as the House of Allah. It is towards the Ka'ba that Muslims face when praying.

kaffāra: atonement, prescribed way of making amends for wrong actions, especially missed obligatory actions.

Khaybar: a Jewish colony to the north of Madina which was besieged and captured by the Muslims in the seventh year after the Hijra because of the Jews' continual treachery.

khul': a form of divorce initiated by the wife.

khuṭba: a speech, and in particular a standing speech given by the imām before the *Jumu'a* prayer and after the two *'Īd* prayers.

kitāba: a contract by which a slave acquires his freedom against a future payment, or payment by instalments, to his master.

Kitābī: Jew or Christian, one of the People of the Book.

lā ilaha illā'llāh: The Arabic expression, "There is no god but Allah".

Maghrib: the sunset prayer.

mahr: dowry given by a husband to his bride.

Malakūt: the angelic world.

Minā: a valley five miles from Makka on the road to 'Arafa where the three *jamra*s stand. It is part of *Ḥajj* to spend three or possibly four nights in Minā during the days of *tashrīq*.

mudd: a measure of volume, approximately equivalent to a double-handed scoop.

Muhājirūn: Companions of the Messenger of Allah who accepted Islam in Makka and made *hijra* to Madina.

Muzdalifa: a place between 'Arafa and Minā where the pilgrims returning from 'Arafa spend a night in the open between the ninth and tenth day of Dhū'l-Ḥijja after performing *Maghrib* and *'Ishā'* there.

People of the Book: people who possess a Revealed Scripture.

qunūt: a supplication said in the prayer, in the standing position in the *Ṣubḥ* or the *Witr* prayer.

qibla: the direction faced in the prayer, which is towards the Ka'ba in Makka.

qirān: combining *ḥajj* and *'umra* simultaneously.

Quraysh: one of the great tribes of Arabia who lived in Makka. The Prophet Muḥammad belonged to this tribe, which had great power spiritually and financially both before and after Islam came. Someone from this tribe is called a Qurayshī.

Rajab: the seventh month of the Muslim lunar calendar.

rak'at: a unit of the prayer consisting of a series of standings, bowings, prostrations and sittings.

Ramaḍān: the month of obligatory fasting, the ninth in the Muslim lunar calendar.

rukhṣa: concession or concessionary law, a law is modified due to the presence of mitigating factors.

rukū': bowing, particularly the bowing position in the prayer.

rūḥ: the soul, vital spirit.

ṣā': a measure of volume equal to four *mudd*s, a *mudd* being a double-handed scoop.

ṣadaqa: charitable giving for the Cause of Allah.

ṣaḥīḥ: sound and without defects, used to describe an authentic *ḥadīth*.

sā'iba: a she-camel which used to be let loose in free pastures in the name of idols, gods, and false deities.

Saqar: Scorching Fire, a name for Hell.

sa'y: the main rite of *'umra* and part of *ḥajj*. It consists of going between the hills of Ṣafā and Marwa seven times.

shahāda: bearing witness, witnessing that there is no god but Allah and that Muḥammad is the Messenger of Allah. It is one of the pillars of Islam. The same word is also used to mean either legal testimony in a court of law or martyrdom.

Sharī'a: The legal modality of a people, based on the Revelation of their Prophet. The final *Sharī'a* is that of Islam.

shayṭān: a devil, particularly Iblīs, one of the jinn.

shirk: the unforgiveable wrong action of worshipping something or someone other than Allah or associating something or someone as a partner with Him.

Sijjīn: the register where the actions of the evil are recorded, or the place where the register is kept.

Ṣirāṭ: the narrow bridge which spans the Fire and must be crossed to enter the Garden. It is described as sharper than a sword and thinner than a hair.

Ṣubḥ: the Dawn prayer.

Ṣuffa: a verandah attached to the Prophet's Mosque where the poor Muslims used to study and sleep.

Sunna: the customary practice of a person or group of people. It has come to refer almost exclusively to the practice of the Messenger of Allah.

sūra: a chapter of the Qur'an.

Tābi'ūn: the second generation of the early Muslims, who did not meet the Prophet Muḥammad, may Allah bless him and grant him peace, but learned the *dīn* of Islam from his Companions.

Tabūk: a town in northern Arabia close to Jordan. In the ninth year after the *Hijra*, the Messenger of Allah, hearing that the Byzantines were gathering a large army to march against the Muslims, led a large expedition to Tabūk in difficult conditions in his last campaign.

tafsīr: commentary of explanation of the meanings of the Qur'an.

tahajjud: voluntary prayers performed at night between *'Ishā'* and *Fajr*.

takbīr: saying *"Allāhu Akbar"*, "Allah is greater".

talbiya: saying *"Labbayk"* ("At Your service") during the *ḥajj*.

tamattu': a form of *ḥajj* in which *'umra* is done first, and then the *ḥājjī* comes out of *iḥrām* before going back into *iḥrām* for the *ḥajj* itself.

taqwā: awe or fear of Allah, which inspires a person to be on guard against wrong action and eager for actions which please Him.

tashrīq: "drying meat in the sun", the 10th, 11th, 12th and 13th days of Dhū'l-Ḥijja, when the pilgrims sacrifice their animals and stone the *jamras* at Minā.

ṭawāf: circumambulation of the Ka'ba, done in sets of seven circuits.

ṭawāf al-ifāḍa: the *ṭawāf* of the Ka'ba that the pilgrims must perform after coming from Mina to Makka on the 10th of Dhū'l-Ḥijja. It is one of the essential rites of *ḥajj*.

tawḥīd: the doctrine of Divine Unity.

tayammum: purification for the prayer with clean dust, earth, or stone, when water for *ghusl* or *wuḍū'* is unavailable or its use would be detrimental to health.

Thamūd: a people to whom the Prophet Ṣāliḥ was sent, possibly a group of Nabateans. Madā'in Ṣāliḥ is located at al-Ḥijr in Najd, about 180 miles north of Madina.

Tihāma: the coastal plain adjoining the Red Sea.

Uḥud: a mountain just outside Madina where, five years after the Hijra, the Muslims lost a battle against the Makkan idolaters. Many great Companions, and in particular Ḥamza, the uncle of the Prophet, were killed in this battle.

'umra: the lesser pilgrimage to the Ka'ba in Makka, which may performed at any time of the year.

wuḍū': ritual washing to be pure for the prayer.

Zabāniyya: "the violent thrusters", the angels who thrust people into Hellfire, who are nineteen in number.

zakāt: a wealth tax, one of the five pillars of Islam.

az-Zaqqūm: a tree with bitter fruit which grows at the bottom of the Fire. Its fruit resembles the heads of devils.

ẓihār: an oath by the husband that his wife is like his mother's back, meaning she is unlawful for him. It was a form of divorce in the *Jāhiliyya*, not permitted in Islam after the Qur'anic revelation fobidding it.

Ẓuhr: the Midday prayer.

Index